RANDOM HOUSE
WORD
MENU™

RANDOM HOUSE®
WORD
MENU™

by Stephen Glazier

RANDOM HOUSE
New York

This is a revised, updated, and completely retypeset edition of the *Random House Word Menu* published in 1992.

Word Menu is a trademark of the Estate of Stephen Glazier.

LIBRARY OF CONGRESS CATALOGING-IN-PUBLICATION DATA

Glazier, Stephen.
    Random House word menu / by Stephen Glazier. — [Newly rev. and updated]
        p.   cm.
    Includes index.
    Other title: Word menu.
    ISBN 0-679-44963-9
    1. English language—Glossaries, vocabularies, etc.   2. English language—Synonyms and antonyms.   3. English language—Terms and phrases. 4. Vocabulary.   I. Title.
PE1680.G58   1997
423'.1—dc20   92-27251
                                                         CIP

Random House Web address http://www.randomhouse.com/

Typeset and Printed in the United States of America

9 8 7 6 5 4 3 2 1

Revised Edition

New York   Toronto   London   Sydney   Auckland

In memory of my father, Bill Glazier,
and for Anna, *sine qua nihil*.

BRIEF TABLE OF CONTENTS

ACKNOWLEDGMENTS

Hundreds of people have contributed in many different ways to the creation of the *Random House Word Menu*. Without three in particular, the book might never have been completed. These three are Karen Pedersen, Heide Lange, and Bob Costello.

Karen Pedersen served as my right hand, associate, and collaborator in the early stages of creating the structure and gathering the list of words. She did her conscientious and professional best for deferred payments at well under her regular fee and well below the value of her work.

Heide Lange, my agent at Sanford J. Greenburger, was the finest and most devoted agent an author could hope to have and never lost faith in me. She orchestrated the business aspects brilliantly from beginning to end and stood beside me as an agent and as a friend, providing me the moral and emotional support that I needed.

Bob Costello, as Editor-in-Chief of the Random House Dictionaries, was the first professional lexicographer to recognize my work as valuable and unique. He had the foresight and the courage to place his authority behind it.

For the past twenty years, two very special friends have worked with me in all areas of my writing, providing invaluable encouragement at all times. They are my closest friend and brother, Jeff Spurrier, who listened to all my complaints and ravings and always responded with generosity out of the goodness of his spirit; and Angus Cameron, my mentor in publishing, who worked with me through not one but two ten-year projects and instilled in me the belief that, no matter how audacious, I could do anything I set out to do.

I am grateful to B.J. Markel, my colleague at the Disney Channel magazine, who suggested that the list of words I had been keeping for many years might be useful to other writers and students. For the first time, I realized that these lists, which had always been a private writer's tool for me, might be compiled in a systematic way and made available commercially.

My dear friend Jack Siler (the Colossus of Bouzigues) helped me create the original proposal and develop the initial list of categories. Don Erik Franzen, my attorney in Los Angeles, devised a mechanism through which investors could acquire a portion of the book and other spinoff products. These investors included Dr. Jack Zoldan; Alex Carlin; my mother, Harriet Glazier; Florence Nixon; Mort Olshan; and Mark Wallner.

In the late summer of 1986, Karen and I were deep at work, creating a structure by studying old classification systems and arranging 3 x 5 cards in a fluid and contemporary hierarchy while also developing individual lists. I also hired outside research assistants to take over certain special categories. First and foremost of these contributors was Michael Rich, generator of the original lists for Chemistry, Biology, and Medicine. Several others who deserve special mention are Barry Koffler, Georg Zappler, Terence Mulry, and Roger Packard.

My thanks also go to Phil Friedman, who introduced me to the distinguished lexicographer Walter Glanze. Walter lent his considerable reputation and intellectual support to this project. Peter Skolnik, my first agent at Sanford J. Greenburger, was another early supporter, as was Jim Landis.

I must also thank Mike Weiner and his staff: Karen Atkinson, Jonathan Sacks, Paul Wetehnall, Mark Momuth, Mike Reidlinger, Fran Knight, Kathy Schaeffer, and Caroline Hodgkins. They encouraged me greatly in the development of the hierarchical system.

The entire staff of the Reference and Electronic Publishing Division at Random House deserve my gratitude, particularly my editors, Sol Steinmetz and Enid Pearsons. I feel privileged to have worked with them. Charles Levine and Jack Hornor gave unstintingly of their time and efforts, as did the rest of the staff, especially Catherine Fowler, Charlotte Mayerson, Pat Ehresmann, Joyce O'Connor, Naomi Osnos, Alice Kovac Somoroff, Chris Mohr, Lani Mysak, Barbara Burke, Terry Chisholm, Gus Panagakis, and Maria Padilla.

I would also like to thank my friend and publisher, Michael Mellin, whose enthusiasm and creativity were a constant inspiration. It was he who guided the *Random House Word Menu* through its final year of publication.

In the summer of 1991, I deposited the final version of the 3000-page manuscript at Random House. I then left for a vacation in Mexico, where I became ill. My friends Clifford Irving and Maureen Earl literally saved my life and sent me back to New York, where Dr. Richard Bergland, Chief of Neurosurgery at Beth Israel Medical Center, diagnosed and treated me with skill and compassion. I wish to thank the Higher Power, who enabled me to recognize the need for a book such as this in the world, provided the inspiration to see how to fill that need, and sustained my will over the years it took to bring the conception of the book to its fully realized form.

And finally, I come to my beloved Anna—my muse, editor, co-conspirator, gadfly, and, ultimately, wife—who stood by me every difficult step of the way, offering support, feedback, editorial guidance, and love—*sine qua nihil.*

Stephen Glazier
New York
1991

STAFF AND CONSULTANTS

Conceived and Created by Stephen Glazier in Association with Karen Pedersen

Editors: Sol Steinmetz, Enid Pearsons

Managing Editor: Jennifer L. Dowling

General Editors: Carol Braham, Robert B. Costello, Joyce O'Connor

Contributing Editors: Barry Koffler (Life Sciences), Penny Marienthal, Terence Mulry (Religion), Roger Packard (Chemistry), Michael Rich (Medicine), Roberta Rubin-Dorsky, Georg Zappler (Life Sciences)

Copy Editors: James Gullickson, Judy Johnson, Felice Levy, Linda Massie, Jesse T Sheidlower, Alice Kovac Somoroff

Production Director: Patricia W. Ehresmann

Designer: Steve Kennedy

Publisher: Charles M. Levine

Revision and Updates: Frank R. Abate, Elizabeth J. Jewell

Consultants

Lisa Andreini (Photography)
Karen Atkinson (Computers)
Harriet Balkind (Advertising)
Paula Biran (Classical Music)
David Black (Publishing)
Christopher Blunden (Law)
Michael Bunyaner (Securities)
Angus Cameron (Fishing/Hunting/Firearms)
Carl P. Carrigan (Theater)
Dan Del Col (Advertising)
Stephen Donaldson (Prison/Eastern Religions)
Wayne Dynes (Homosexuality)
Peter R. Feuche (Theater)
Andrew Field (Real Estate)
Gary Fleisher (Medicine)
Carl Giordano (Sports)
Donald Goldstein (Economics)
Sharon Goldstein (Linguistics/Grammar/Phonetics)
Jeff Grambs (Weapons/Military)
Lee Greathouse (Telecommunications)
Elizabeth Greenberg (Theater)
Ruth Gross (Psychology)
Joan Keener (Ballet)
Verly Klinkenborg (Literature)
Denise Marika (Sculpture)
Bob Merlis (Rock Era Dances)
Joyce O'Connor (Fashion)

Joan Pancoe (New Age)
Ian Paradise (Medicine)
Enid Pearsons (Computers)
David Peters (Graphic Design)
Alison Postman (Hair Styles)
Bruce Postman (Cinema)
Charles Pye (Taxation/Accounting)
James Rader (Birds/Prefixes and Suffixes)
Anna Raviv (Theater)
Jon Resier (Anatomy)
Kurt Richards (Aircraft)
Deane Rink (Physics)
Jon Rubin (Popular Music)
Carol Sacks (Geology)
Roger Scorcio (Building Materials/Structural Components)
Simon Sheridan (Tools and Hardware)
Martin Smith (Television)
Zachary Smith (Basketball)
Alice Kovac Somoroff (Geography)
Jeff Spurrier (Journalism)
Ann Summa (Photography)
Emanuel Thorne (Mathematics)
Richard Van Dorn (Electricity and Electronics)
William Van Dorn (Ships and Boats)
Antoinette White (Ballet)
Wendell Williams (Automobiles)

PREFACE

The explosion of knowledge and information in the second half of the twentieth century has been the catalyst of enormous social and technological changes. Since language is an ever-evolving reflection of these changes, lexicons too should reflect them. Yet the most recent classification system for language is Roget's thesaurus, published in 1852.

Not only has the English language evolved to keep pace with new technology and cultural growth, but the way we think has changed as well. Our approach to work and learning in the high-speed age of the computer cannot always accommodate the more patient, intellectual approach of the past. There are times when we want our information quickly, in bite-size chunks, and times when we cannot afford the luxury of searching through disparate sources to find the information we need. The average person today is forced to be a narrow specialist, with only a smattering of knowledge about other subjects, which are often difficult and unfamiliar. Making sense of our complex existence is a daunting task.

In keeping with this task, the *Random House Word Menu*™, conceived and created by the late Stephen Glazier (see Biography of the Author) and produced over a period of eight years, presents an entirely new classification system for language and information. Its goal is to help bring the expanding, multilayered world of the late twentieth century into clearer focus by creating a framework for ordering the mass of information that is constantly bombarding us. This framework is in the form of a structure that allows users to find information with ease in any of hundreds of different subjects and areas of interest.

A hierarchical structure is familiar to most users of the standard thesaurus: it goes from the general to the specific, from the idea or subject to particular words, from the whole to the parts. But whereas the structure of the standard thesaurus is based on philosophical categories such as "Abstract Relations," "Space," "Matter," and "Volition," the structure of this book (outlined in the Table of Contents) is built on natural, contemporary categories and logical relations among not just concepts, but things. Thus the seven major classes in our structure are everyday subjects: Nature, Science and Technology, Domestic Life, Institutions, Arts and Leisure, Language, and The Human Condition. Nature as a class is further divided into three subclasses: The Human

Body, Living Things, and The Earth. The Earth, in turn, is broken down into five categories: Geology; Geography; Minerals, Metals, and Rocks; Landscapes and Seascapes; and Weather and Natural Phenomena. Each of these categories is then divided into subcategories, such as (under Landscapes and Seascapes) Hills, Hollows, and Valleys; Plains and Marshes; Woods and Brush; Inland Waterways and Lakes; and Coastal Land, Islands, and the Sea.

Another important difference between this book and the standard thesaurus is that while the latter deals with common synonyms and antonyms, this book is concerned with *words related by subject*, i.e., with the vocabulary or terminology of hundreds of different areas of knowledge or activity. While we include under certain categories (as Character and Behavior or Common Expressions) numerous synonyms and antonyms, these are subordinate to the purpose of this book, which is to provide information about words in a manner that is not found in any standard thesaurus or dictionary.

Thus, for example, this book contains much information that is usually found in encyclopedias and almanacs, such as the Nations of the World, each with its capital, area in square miles, population number, language, major religion, and currency; the names and descriptions of all the Christian denominations and sects; major world cities; States of the United States; annual national and religious holidays; military ranks; names and functions of government departments; list of common abbreviations; and so on.

Finally, this work differs from the standard thesaurus because it discriminates among its entries with far greater precision, offering definitions of the words it identifies.

The author did not intend this work to replace the usual thesaurus or dictionary. Like a dictionary, it includes thousands of definitions, but it is not a general dictionary. The *Random House Word Menu* is quite different from either a dictionary or a thesaurus, and it is precisely this unique quality that makes it so useful as a companion to these standard references.

The book is designed to be a language tool as well as a creativity tool. As a language tool, it serves the functions of: a reverse dictionary, for finding a word when one knows only the meaning or definition; a thesaurus of related terms, organized by category or subject matter and with entries defined as in a dictionary; a collection of diverse glossaries, for learning the terminology of an unfamiliar field or for learning to use technical terms correctly.

As a creativity tool, the book's logical structure and word associations can assist in brainstorming, aid in preliminary research, help overcome creative blocks or memory lapses, and provide a source of words for enlivening everything one writes. We hope that users will also browse through the pages to expand their knowledge and vocabulary as well as for entertainment.

Stephen Glazier created this book as a reference tool for busy writers like himself. All the organizing and defining of terms is done for them. The internal logic and easy associations of the classification system allow them to know instantly where to look for an unknown word in one of the nearly 800 categories and subcategories. The range of subjects, the concise, telegraphic definitions, and the contemporary format offer not only a resource for serious writers but a natural way to build vocabulary, help to solve crossword puzzles or to win at word games, or add vigor and variety to any piece of writing.

The author chose the title carefully, to reflect the idea of a detailed list of items, or minutiae, married to the computer-age concept of a menu: a list of options available to the user. The *Random House Word Menu*'s lists provide a schematic that opens up the English language in a way never before realized. Its single and overriding purpose is to help the writer or speaker find the *mot juste*—the indispensable word that the occasion calls for, no matter how arcane or specialized its references.

All difficult or technical terms, as well as most slang and informal terms, are defined in this book. In order to in-sure the accuracy and clarity of the definitions, the author availed himself of consultants in many fields, with whom he reviewed not only the pertinent definitions but also the selection of entries for each subject or category. Definitions were thus updated and sharpened, relationships between entries clarified, and obsolete terms replaced with current ones.

In every field, close attention was paid to the most recent advances and developments, especially as reflected in changes and innovations in terminology. The category Biology, for example, includes the Five Kingdoms now used to classify organisms, and the subcategory Viruses is further divided into Bacteriophages, Plant Viruses, and Animal Viruses. The user is urged to examine the classification system in the Table of Contents, for an understanding of the various divisions and subdivisions will make the book's contents more familiar and accessible.

This book extends a lexicographic tradition for which Stephen Glazier had profound respect. He hoped to create a work that would become part of that tradition, that would complement its predecessors by providing a new tool for improving the accuracy and clarity with which we can explore and exploit the incredible range of the English language. He wanted to give us new ways of discovering language and new ways to increase our expressive powers. We who worked closely with Stephen, and came to admire and respect him for his intense dedication, regard this book as a fitting memorial to his indomitable spirit. We believe it is an important contribution to English lexicography, deserving far-reaching recognition and widespread use.

The Editors

BIOGRAPHY OF THE AUTHOR

Stephen Glazier was born in 1947 in Washington, D.C. A gifted child, he learned to read and write at an early age, encouraged by parents who read to him from the English classics. When he was five years old, the family moved to California. Inspired by family trips to the Shakespeare festival in Ashland, Oregon, Stephen began writing plays at the age of seven on such subjects as the Trojan War, the Three Musketeers, and English royal history. He skipped several grades in elementary school and later attended high school in Exeter, New Hampshire, and La Jolla, California. During his senior year in La Jolla, he was both managing editor of the school paper and a reporter for a local weekly, *La Jolla Journal*. After graduation in 1965 he was admitted to Harvard University, his father's alma mater.

Although he did well at Harvard, after a year he decided to follow his La Jolla classmates, most of whom had enrolled at the University of California at Berkeley. This was then the center of the Free Speech movement and a mecca for the radical young. At Berkeley, Stephen majored in theater, wrote plays, marched in the streets, and became involved with the music scene in the Bay area. He graduated from Berkeley in 1969 and the following year toured Great Britain and the Continent. While in London, he began writing a novel, a sprawling saga of three different families, which he called *Patches*. It was while working on this novel, part of which was set in the 1800s, that he started going through a recently acquired unabridged dictionary, making lists of words, mostly clothing and housing terms, to use in the historical sections of the novel.

The word list expanded as did the novel, which by 1977 had grown to 1400 pages. To make ends meet while writing, Glazier taught English as a second language and spent three months every winter doing income tax work for various accounting firms. In 1978 he found a literary agent and began working at once on the first draft of a new historical novel, *The Lost Provinces*. This book was published in 1981 to excellent reviews, and a year later was optioned for a movie. The producer who optioned it invited Glazier to write the screenplay, which resulted in a new career in Los Angeles as a screenwriter, copywriter, and editor.

In 1982 Glazier became associate editor of the Disney Channel magazine, where he wrote descriptions of shows and on-air programming material. Meanwhile his lists of words continued to grow. One day in 1984 he showed the lists of colors and of verbs of motion to a fellow copywriter at the Disney Channel. His colleague asked to see more of the lists and suggested to Glazier that his personal writer's tool might benefit other writers.

This prospect led Glazier to develop a more systematic and comprehensive approach to his word collection. Recognizing that he was dissatisfied with the existing methods of classifying words and information, he made a study of the classification systems used by Melvil Dewey (of the Dewey catalog system), the Library of Congress, and Peter Mark Roget, back to Francis Bacon and the trivium and quadrivium of the Middle Ages. The system he finally developed combined a traditional approach to the division of knowledge with a contemporary hierarchical structure influenced by the computer age. Glazier believed this to be a compelling marriage of classic and modern intellectual elements.

During the next two years he divided his time between synopsizing science fiction stories for the story department of Steven Spielberg's *Amazing Stories*, working on the draft of a new historical novel, *The Caliph's Cup*, and organizing his lists of words on a 64K CPM computer.

By 1985 the basic format and nucleus of what was to become the present book had been worked out, and Glazier's agent had begun submitting proposals for the book to publishing houses. After several rounds of submissions, one publisher accepted it and Glazier set out to create the large book of words he envisioned. He hired a staff of research assistants and solicited investors for the project. Within a year he was able to raise the funds he needed. Much of the money went to pay for consultants in the many fields covered in the book. Glazier himself consulted over four hundred books for glossary words and verification of usages.

Two years of work produced a 2000-page manuscript, which was too long for the publisher. A new round of submissions began while Glazier continued working on the book. Finally, in 1989, a 2500-page manuscript was submitted to Random House, and a year later this firm bought the book rights to what is now the *Random House Word Menu*. Glazier was jubilant, for this was the house he had always hoped would publish his book.

During the following two years Glazier became almost a fixture in the Random House Reference Department. He was a charming, personable man, filled with energy and creativity. No amount of work seemed to faze him. He was indefatigable. He could spend hours researching a single fact, for nothing but the truth would satisfy him. He was welcomed at Random House as a colleague and friend, having earned the affection and esteem of the Reference Department staff.

In the fall of 1991, after putting the finishing touches on the now 3000-page manuscript, Glazier set out for a well-deserved vacation in Mexico. Some weeks later friends and relatives received alarming news that he was seriously ill and was returning to New York City for hospital tests and treatment. The tests showed that he had a malignant brain tumor. After surgery and extensive radiation therapy, Stephen seemed to be doing better. Though physically debilitated, his mind was alert and his personality as warm and outgoing as always. His will to live and work was evident. He had lengthy discussions with his editors and publisher over plans for this book. Always by his side was his beloved wife, the actress Anna Raviv, whom he had met in 1985. He seemed happy and at peace. Early in 1992, his condition suddenly worsened. Stephen died on January 20, 1992. He was forty-four years old.

USER'S GUIDE

The *Random House Word Menu*™ organizes the English language by subject matter. Subject categories are listed in the Table of Contents. The categories are arranged in a logical structure that runs from the general—Nature, or Arts and Leisure—to the specific—the Reproductive System, or Stringed Instruments. The lowest level of the structure contains nearly 800 individual lists, each with 50 to 200 defined terms.

The logical structure and its word associations are designed to make it easy to find the group of words one is seeking. In technical and institutional areas this logic is virtually absolute—*Parts of Ships, Sails, and Equipment* must lie within *Ships and Boats*, which must lie within *Transportation*, which must lie within *Science and Technology*. In nonconcrete areas like *Language, Cognition,* or *Faith*, users will quickly become familiar with the structure so that they can locate *Judgment and Criticism,* or *Magic and the Occult,* or *Exclamations,* or *Verbs of Motion.*

Thus, to find a verb that describes disagreement or opposition, turn first to the category *Judgment and Criticism,* where you will find the subcategory *Opposition, Disagreement, and Attack.* There you can compare definitions and choose from among such terms as "niggle," "nitpick," "quibble," "repudiate," and "take issue with." If these do not seem strong enough, move on to the next subcategory: *Blame, Censure, Ridicule, and Contempt.*

Or to find the difference between a davenport, a divan, an ottoman, and a settee (perhaps you need the word to describe a room in a story, or you plan to talk to a furniture salesperson), turn to the subcategory *Chairs and Sofas* in the list of *Furnishings* under *The Home* in the general class *Domestic Life.*

If you want to know the names of the moons of Jupiter, go to *Celestial Bodies* (in *Astronomy and Space Science*) to find the Galilean moons Callisto, Europa, Ganymede, and Io.

Or, if you can't remember the word for "a close-fitting academic cap with flat, square top and tassel," look under *Hats* (in the category *Hats, Headgear, and Hairpieces*) to find the word "mortarboard."

The reverse-dictionary function can also be useful in solving crossword puzzles, where the clue is a definition and leads to the appropriate subject. For example, a five-letter word beginning with *k* for "a short, curved sword with a broad blade used in India" would lead you to the list of *Blades, Clubs, and Projectiles* under the category *Weapons and Armaments,* where you would find the word "kukri."

Conversely, if you know the word and wish to learn its spelling, definition, or part of speech, look up the word in the Index at the back of the book. Or, if you don't know the word but do know a synonym or related word, look up the latter in the Index. Parts, chapters, and categories are also listed in the Index, in boldface. The Index leads you directly to the page where the word you are looking for is listed.

Another quick way to find information in the book is by checking the Guide Words above the black line at the top of each page. The Guide Words indicate the chapter number, chapter name, and subclass.

Most words listed under a category have concise definitions, except where they form a long list defined by its heading, as the list of *Pet Names* under the category *Terms of Endearment and Respect* or the list under *Meats and Cuts of Meat.*

Many entry words are followed by italicized labels that describe the level of usage of a word. The commonest of these restrictive labels are *Slang* and *Informal.* These labels are often very specific, as, for example, *Vulgar Slang, Yiddish Derogatory Slang.* Labels serve to warn you that using the labeled word in formal contexts may be inappropriate. Trademarks are indicated by the italicized label *Trademark* before the definition.

Though this book includes definitions, it is clearly not intended to replace a standard dictionary. Pronunciations of words, etymologies, and usage notes are not included in this book, and users should consult a standard college-level dictionary, such as the *Random House Webster's College Dictionary,* to obtain this and other more detailed lexical information.

Again, unlike a standard dictionary, this book does not provide all the meanings of a word in one place. Instead, each meaning or usage of a word appears as a separate entry in the appropriate place in the structure. For example, the word "mole" appears in eight places: *Animals; Chemistry; Medical Problems; Machinery; Ships and Boats; Foods; International Relations;* and *Strategy, Intrigue, and Deception.*

Definitions of the same word appearing under different categories (for example, *Trinity,* appearing under two categories) may differ in wording in order to focus on the distinctive use of the word in each category.

All listed words, defined and undefined, are arranged

in alphabetical order. Example: *solar, solar corona, solar eclipse, solar flare, solar nebula, solar wind, solstice.*

With few exceptions, nouns and noun phrases are listed without a part-of-speech label. Verbs, adjectives, and adverbs are given an abbreviated part-of-speech label after the entry word. The labels appear in italics within parentheses, thus: (*vb*) for verbs, (*adj*) for adjectives, (*adv*) for adverbs. Defined entries whose headings indicate exclusive verbal use (e.g., *Eating Verbs*) do not show the (*vb*) part-of-speech label.

Derivatives of words, as those ending in *-ed, -ing, -ly, -ness,* and *-ation,* are usually not listed separately from the base word. We thus enter "abjure" but not abjuration, "indict" but not indictment, "relative" but not relatively, "paradox" but not paradoxical or paradoxically.

To show the network of relationships among subject categories, a list of "See also" cross references to related subjects is given at the beginning of each category. Thus, below the heading of the category *Kinship and Family Relations,* you will find cross references to the categories *Marriage and Divorce, Parents and Children, Anthropology,* and *Sociology.*

The following abbreviations occur in the book:

adj	=	adjective
adv	=	adverb
arch.	=	archaic
Brit.	=	British
c.	=	century
etc.	=	et cetera

esp.	=	especially
lit.	=	literally
n	=	noun
opp.	=	opposite
orig.	=	originally
pl.	=	plural
sing.	=	singular
usu.	=	usually
vb	=	verb

The best way to become familiar with this book is to use it, especially as a quick reference for certain types of information: a list of the world's currencies (Chapter 12 - THE ECONOMY, *Finance, World Currencies*); or a list of medical prefixes and suffixes (Chapter 4 - THE SCIENCES, *Medicine, Prefixes and Suffixes*); or a list of cyclical events (Chapter 3 - THE EARTH, *Weather and Natural Phenomena, Forecasting and Meteorology/ Cyclical Events*).

Or you might use the book to find a Latin, French, or other synonym for an English word (Chapter 21 -FOREIGN EXPRESSIONS); or to find a particular job title (Chapter 12 - THE ECONOMY, *Occupations and Job Titles*) or a list of titles and ranks (Chapter 11 - SOCIAL ORDER, *Titles of Rank*); or to find the correct name of a particular tool (Chapter 5 - TECHNOLOGY, *Tools and Hardware, Common Tools and Tool Types*).

You can find all of these and many other types of information by any of the three routes described above: the Table of Contents, the Guide Words, or the Index. Before long you will find this volume to be a useful and indispensable reference book.

TABLE OF CONTENTS

RANDOM HOUSE
WORD
MENU™

PART ONE
NATURE

CHAPTER ONE
THE HUMAN BODY

Head and Neck

Adam's apple projection of thyroid cartilage in front of throat; thyroid cartilage

adenoids growths of lymphoid tissue in upper pharynx at rear of throat

beak *Slang.* nose

bean *Slang.* head

bridge bony portion of nose where it joins brow

brow forehead

buccal cavity hollow formed by mouth containing tongue, teeth, and salivary glands

cheek side of face below eye, between nose and ear

cheekbone outer portion of eye's bony orbit, reaching across upper cheek

chin portion of face below lower lip at projection of lower jaw

coconut *Slang.* head, skull

cranial cavity hollow formed by skull, containing brain

cranium bone enclosing brain; skull excluding lower jaw

epiglottis flap of cartilage covering windpipe to prevent swallowed food from entering lungs

esophagus tube through which food passes from pharynx to stomach

face front of head beneath hairline, including eyes, nose, mouth, and chin

forehead flat front of face between eyebrows and hairline

gourd *Slang.* head

hair fine, threadlike growth, esp. covering top of skull

head bony topmost portion of body, containing brain and sense organs

jaw hinged bones that frame mouth, open and close it, and hold teeth

kisser *Slang.* face

larynx muscles and cartilage at upper end of trachea holding vocal cords

lip either of two fleshy folds that form opening of mouth, used in speech

mandible bone of lower jaw

mastoid process projection of skull behind ear

maxilla bone of upper jaw

mouth opening framed by lips through which food enters body; speech organ

mug *Slang.* face

muzzle *Slang.* projecting portion of face, esp. nose

nape back of neck

nares nostrils, nasal openings

nasal cavity hollow containing sinuses and interior of nose

neck top of spinal column between skull and shoulders, connecting head to trunk

noggin *Slang.* head

noodle *Slang.* head

nose narrow, projecting part of face between mouth and eyes with two openings for passage of air into body; organ of smell

nostril one of two external openings of nose; one of the nares

occiput back portion of skull

orbital cavity bony hollow containing eyeball

pate top of head

pharynx top of alimentary canal leading from mouth and nose to larynx and esophagus

philtrum vertical groove on surface of upper lip, below septum of nose

proboscis snoutlike nose

puss *Slang.* face

scalp skin across top and rear of skull, usu. covered with hair

schnozz *Slang.* nose

scruff back of neck

sebum oily secretion of sebaceous glands that keeps hair and scalp soft and waterproof

septum dividing wall or membrane, esp. between nostrils of nose

sinus hollow air cavity beneath skull connected to nostrils

skull bones that cover brain and frame face

snoot *Slang.* nose

snout *Slang.* nose

temple flattened surface on either side of forehead in front of ear

throat interior passageway through neck from chin to collarbone

thyroid cartilage Adam's apple

tongue movable muscular part of floor of mouth, used in talking, tasting, and eating

tonsil either of two masses of lymphoid tissue lying on each side of throat at rear of mouth

trachea main tube carrying air from larynx to two bronchi entering lungs

vocal cords the lower of two pairs of mucous membrane folds in laryngeal cavity that vibrate to produce speech sounds

voice box larynx

windpipe trachea

Eyes

aqueous humor jellylike fluid that fills eye chamber in front of lens

baby blues *Slang.* eyes

blind spot point where optic nerve joins retina that is insensitive to light

blinkers *Slang.* eyes

bony orbit framework of bones surrounding eye socket

choroid coat pigmented membrane that is continuous with iris and that nourishes retina and absorbs scattered light

ciliary body smooth muscle and its connection to suspensory ligament of lens

conjunctiva protective layer of mucous membrane lining inner surface of eyelid over cornea

cornea transparent covering over iris that produces refraction needed to focus image on retina

epicanthic fold epicanthus

epicanthus long fold of skin on upper eyelid; epicanthic fold

eye receptor of light and organ of sight

eyeball globe of the eye containing nervous tissue stimulated by light

eyebrow ridge over eye socket with hair growing on it

eyelash fringe of hair growing on edge of eyelid

eyelid protective lid of skin and muscle that closes over eye

eye socket hollow of bone in face holding eyeball; orbital cavity

fovea centralis small depression at back of retina that is point of sharpest vision

iris colored circular muscle in front of eye that controls amount of light entering eye

lens transparent, biconvex element between iris and vitreous humor that focuses light rays on retina

optic nerve nerve that sends sight impulses from eye to brain

orbital cavity bony hollow containing eyeball

peepers *Slang.* eyes

pupil round contractile aperture in iris of eye

retina inner layer of eye wall composed of nervous tissue stimulated by light to send impulses to brain

sclera tough, white, fibrous membrane forming protective outer wall of eyeball except area of cornea

twenty-twenty (*adj*) having normal visual acuity

vitreous humor jellylike material that fills eyeball and forms its shape

Ears

auditory nerve either of pair of cranial nerves, consisting of sensory fibers that conduct impulses from ear to brain

auricle pinna

cerumen ear wax; yellow, waxlike secretion of external ear

cochlea spiral tube in inner ear filled with liquid that senses loudness and pitch and sends nerve impulses to brain

concha shell-like structure of external ear

ear organ of hearing and equilibrium consisting of outer, middle, and inner ears

ear canal bony cavity from eardrum to opening of external ear

eardrum thin, vibrating membrane over middle ear; tympanic membrane

ear wax cerumen

Eustachian tube canal from middle ear to pharynx

helix curved fold along rim of external ear

incus anvil-shaped ossicle of middle ear

inner ear receptor for sound and sense organ of balance

labyrinth system of tubes and hollows in inner ear

lobe fleshy lower tip of outer ear

malleus hammerlike outermost ossicle of middle ear

middle ear part of ear with eardrum and bony adjacent cavity; tympanum

organ of Corti part of ear in cochlea that hears sounds

ossicle small bone in middle ear that passes vibrations from eardrum to oval window: incus, malleus, or stapes

outer ear short, protective tube leading to eardrum

oval window thin membrane that passes vibrations from middle ear to labyrinth of inner ear

pinna structure of skin and cartilage fixed to head forming visible portion of outer ear; auricle

saccule smaller of two saclike cavities in labyrinth

semicircular canal one of three curved tubular canals in labyrinth of ear, serving to maintain equilibrium

stapes stirrup-shaped innermost ossicle of middle ear

tragus nublike prominence at front of external opening of ear

tympanic membrane eardrum

tympanum middle ear

utricle larger of two saclike cavities in labyrinth

vestibule hollow forming approach to inner ear

Mouth and Teeth

alveolus socket within jawbone in which roots of teeth are set

bicuspid premolar tooth with two-pointed crown

buccal cavity hollow formed by mouth containing tongue, teeth, and salivary glands

canine sharp, pointed tooth behind incisor

cementum thin bony tissue covering roots of tooth

choppers *Slang.* teeth

crown enameled portion of tooth above gum line

cusp pointed projection on crown of tooth

cuspid canine tooth with single-pointed crown

dentine hard, bonelike substance forming main part of tooth

enamel hard substance forming outer cover of tooth

fangs *Slang.* teeth, esp. cuspids

gingiva gum

grinders *Slang.* teeth, esp. molars

gum soft tissue portion of jaw enveloping bases of teeth; gingiva

incisor tooth with cutting edge at front of mouth

ivories *Slang.* teeth

lips two fleshy folds that form opening of mouth

molar flat-surfaced grinding tooth at rear of mouth

mouth opening through which food enters body, also used in forming speech sounds

neck narrowed portion of tooth between crown and root

occlusion fitting together of teeth of lower jaw with teeth of upper jaw

overbite occlusion in which upper incisor teeth overlap lower ones

palate roof of mouth, separating it from nasal cavity

pearly whites *Slang.* teeth

periodontal membrane fibrous connective tissue between cementum of tooth and alveolus

premolar bicuspid tooth in front of molar

pulp soft tissue at center of tooth containing nerves and blood vessels

rictus opening of the mouth

root part of tooth embedded in and attached to gum

saliva mucus-containing liquid secreted by glands in mouth to lubricate passage of food through alimentary canal

soft palate posterior, muscular portion of palate; velum

taste bud receptor of taste on surface of tongue that responds to bitter, sweet, sour, or salt

tongue movable fleshy part of floor of mouth with sense receptors and small glands that assists in talking and eating

tooth hard, usu. sharp, bony structure in mouth for biting food

trap *Slang.* mouth

underbite occlusion in which lower incisor teeth overlap upper ones

uvula pendent fleshy lobe in middle posterior of palate

velum soft palate

wisdom tooth third molar at rear of mouth

yap *Slang.* mouth

Trunk

abdomen part of body lying between thorax and pelvis and containing digestive organs; belly

abdominal cavity hollow within abdomen containing digestive organs

appendix narrow, blind tube three inches long in lower right part of abdomen; vermiform appendix

back rear part of body from neck to base of spine

backbone spinal column

belly midriff; abdomen

bellybutton *Informal.* navel

bosom breast, esp. female

breadbasket *Slang.* stomach

breast front upper portion of chest; either of two milk-secreting glands in upper chest of female; corresponding undeveloped gland in male

breastbone sternum

buttocks rear of hip forming fleshy seat for body, *Slang.* arse, ass, backside, behind, bippy, booty, bottom, bum, buns, butt, can, cheeks, derrière, duff, fanny, gluteus maximus, heinie, hind end, keister, patootie, posterior, prat, rear, rear end, rump, seat, stern, tail, tokus, tush

chest part of body enclosed by ribs and sternum

clavicle bone linking sternum and scapula; collarbone

coccyx end of spinal column beyond sacrum that represents vestigial tail

collarbone clavicle

crotch point where legs fork from base of trunk

dorsal (*adj*) on or near the backside

groin juncture of lower abdomen and inner thigh

hipbone either of two bones forming sides of pelvis

ilium broad upper portion of hipbone

ischium lower portion of hipbone

loin region on either side of spinal column between hip and ribs

love handles *Slang.* rolls of fat around midriff

midriff front of torso between abdomen and chest

navel small scar, usu. depression, in middle of abdomen where umbilical cord was attached to fetus

nipple small protuberance of breast where milk duct discharges in female; teat

paunch flabby midriff

pectoral girdle arch formed by scapulae and clavicles

pelvic cavity bony hollow formed by pelvic girdle

pelvic girdle arch formed by ilium, ischium, and pubis

pelvis basin-shaped skeletal structure formed by pelvic girdle and adjoining bones of spine

pericardial cavity thin, membranous sac enclosing heart

perineum area between anus and male scrotum or edge of vulva in female

pleural cavity thin, membranous lining of chest cavity that encloses lungs

potbelly flabby midriff

pubis part of hipbone forming front of pelvis

rib paired curved bones protecting entire viscera, ten fixed and two floating

sacrum compound bone forming back of pelvis

scapula large triangular bone lying in each dorsal lateral part of thorax; shoulder blade

shoulder blade scapula

solar plexus nerve complex at pit of stomach

spare tire *Informal.* roll of fat around midriff

spinal column series of joined vertebrae forming axial support for skeleton and carrying nerves; backbone; spine

spine spinal column

sternum flat bone of upper chest connecting ribs to shoulder girdle; breastbone

teat nipple

thoracic cavity hollow in trunk containing heart and lungs

thorax part of body between neck and abdomen, containing thoracic cavity

torso trunk containing organs

trunk central portion of body apart from head, arms, and legs

tummy *Informal.* stomach

umbilicus navel

ventral (*adj*) abdominal; located on lower front surface of trunk, opposite back

vermiform appendix appendix

viscera organs in thoracic and abdominal cavities, including heart, lungs, stomach, liver, and kidneys

Limbs and Extremities

ankle joint between foot and leg

annulary ring finger, esp. on left hand

arm upper limb between shoulder and wrist

armpit axilla

axilla hollow under shoulder where arm joins trunk; armpit; underarm

ball rounded portion at front of bottom of foot, behind the toes

biceps lateral muscle along inside of upper arm

big toe largest toe, on inner edge of foot

calf fleshy hind part of leg below knee

carpus wrist, esp. bones of wrist

crazy bone *Slang.* elbow

crook inside bend of elbow or knee

cuticle hardened epidermis that accumulates at base of fingernail

digit finger or toe

dogs *Slang.* feet

dukes *Slang.* hands, fists

elbow hinge joint at mid-arm

extremity limb, esp. hand or foot

femur proximal bone of upper leg; thighbone

fibula outer, smaller bone between knee and ankle

fin *Slang.* arm

finger any of five terminating digits of upper forelimb: thumb, index finger, middle finger, ring finger, little finger

fist hand clenched with fingers curled inward

flapper *Slang.* arm

foot terminal part of leg upon which person stands

footsies *Slang.* feet

forearm half of arm between elbow and wrist; forelimb

funny bone *Slang.* elbow

gams *Slang.* legs

hamstring long muscle down back of thigh

hand grasping extremity, with fingers, at end of arm

haunch hip, hindquarter

heel rear portion of foot below ankle

hip region on each side of lower part of trunk, formed by pelvis and upper femur

hollow pit beneath shoulder

hoof *Slang.* foot

index finger finger closest to thumb

instep arched middle portion of foot

knee joint where upper and lower leg meet

knuckle protuberance at joint of finger, esp. large joint at middle of finger

leg lower limb used to walk and support body

limb arm or leg

little finger smallest finger, farthest from thumb; pinkie

middle finger second finger from thumb, usu. longest finger

mitt *Slang.* hand

paw *Slang.* hand

pinkie *Informal.* little finger

pins *Slang.* legs

pups *Slang.* feet

ring finger third finger from thumb, next to little finger, traditionally finger on which engagement ring or wedding band is worn

shank part of leg between knee and ankle

shinbone tibia

shoulder joint that connects arm to upper trunk

soupbone *Slang.* arm

sticks *Slang.* legs, esp. thin ones

stumps *Slang.* legs, esp. thick ones

tarsus ankle, esp. bones of ankle

thigh segment of lower limb from hip to knee

thighbone femur

thumb short, thick digit of hand nearest wrist, in opposition to other fingers

tibia long, inner bone of leg between knee and ankle; shinbone

toe one of five terminal digits of foot

tootsies *Slang.* feet

triceps lateral muscle along back of upper arm

ulna bone on little finger side of forearm

underarm axilla

upper arm portion of arm between elbow and shoulder

wheels *Slang.* legs

wing *Slang.* arm

wrist ball-and-socket joint between hand and lower arm

Brain and Central Nervous System

alpha wave long, slow brain wave of relaxation

axon long, threadlike part of neuron that conducts impulses away from cell body

beta wave short, fast brain wave of activity

brain seat of nervous system controlling neural coordination and thought

central nervous system CNS; portion of nervous system comprising brain and spinal cord

cerebellum part of brain that regulates coordination of voluntary muscle movement

cerebral cortex gray matter covering forebrain

cerebral hemisphere either of the rounded halves of the cerebrum

cerebrospinal fluid liquid that fills space in middle of spine and cavities in brain

cerebrum left and right hemispheres at front of brain that send and receive stimuli to and from voluntary muscles, perceive sensory input, and control memory and thought

CNS central nervous system

corpus callosum mass of nerve fibers connecting two hemispheres of cerebrum

cortex outer layer of gray matter covering most of brain; pallium

dendrite short, branching, threadlike part of neuron that carries impulses to cell body

frontal lobe anterior portion of each cerebral hemisphere

ganglion solid mass of neural cell bodies that serves as relay center for impulses

gray matter nervous tissue forming inner part of spinal cord and outer part of brain

hypothalamus basal part of third ventricle beneath thalamus that regulates pituitary gland, body temperature, and sleep

impulse traveling wave of excitation that sends message through neuron

limbic system ringlike section in midline of brain, concerned with emotions and memory

medulla part of brain joined to spinal cord that controls sense organs, respiration, and cardiac muscle

meninges *sing.* meninx; three membranes covering spinal cord and brain

meninx one of three meninges

motor (*adj*) designating nerve that stimulates muscle or organ to move or act

myelin protective sheath around peripheral nerve fibers

neocortex outer layer of brain, center of intellect and imagination

nerve bundle of neurons supported by connective tissue, conveying impulses of sensation or motion

nervous system nerve tissue that coordinates all activities and receives all sensory stimuli, consisting of brain, spinal cord, axons, dendrites, and synapses, and composed of the following major nerves:

brachial nerve nerve in upper arm
cervical nerve nerve in neck and shoulder
coccygeal nerve nerve at base of spine
digital nerve nerve in fingers
femoral nerve nerve in thigh
intercostal nerve nerve between ribs
lumbar nerve nerve in groin
mandibular nerve nerve in lower jaw

maxillary nerve nerve in jaw
median nerve nerve in middle of arm
ophthalmic nerve nerve in eye
peroneal nerve nerve in lower leg near fibula
radial nerve nerve around lower arm
sacral nerve nerve from spinal cord in sacrum
sciatic nerve nerve running down spinal cord and back of each thigh
thoracic nerve nerve in thorax
tibial nerve nerve in lower leg near tibia
ulnar nerve nerve in forearm and elbow

neuron single cell consisting of axon and dendrites in system of nerves that conducts impulses
node of Ranvier recurring gap at intervals in myelin sheath along nerve axon
occipital lobe most posterior portion of each cerebral hemisphere
olfactory lobe anterior portion of each cerebral hemisphere, responsible for sense of smell
pallium cortex
parietal lobe middle portion of each cerebral hemisphere
pons band of nerve fibers through which impulses pass between various parts of brain
sciatic nerve largest nerve in body, running down spinal cord and back of each thigh
sense organs eyes, ears, nose, and taste buds, the organs containing nervous tissue that responds to particular external stimuli
sensory receptors sense organs and other tissue that respond to external stimuli, recording temperature and sensations such as pain and heat
spinal column series of jointed vertebrae forming axial support for skeleton and carrying nerves
spinal cord cylindrical mass of nervous tissue running through spinal column
synapse meeting place of axons and dendrites along which impulse travels from neuron to neuron
temporal lobe lateral portion of each cerebral hemisphere, in front of occipital lobe
thalamus lower anterior portion of brain above pituitary gland that acts as main relay center for impulses to cerebrum
ventricle any of four cavities within brain filled with cerebrospinal fluid

Heart and Circulatory and Lymphatic Systems

agglutination sticking together of red blood cells
aorta main artery leaving heart
arteriole small artery with walls of smooth muscle that controls blood supply to capillaries
artery blood vessel conducting blood from heart to tissue
atrium auricle
auricle upper chamber in heart that receives blood from veins; atrium
blood liquid of circulatory system containing dissolved digestive products and conveying

oxygen to tissue: plasma, red and white blood cells, and platelets
bloodstream flow of blood through circulatory system
blood vessel artery, vein, or capillary
capillary very small blood vessel with thin, permeable walls
capillary network arrangement of branching capillaries in tissue
cardiac muscle muscle in walls of heart with action that is automatic, regular, and faster than that of involuntary muscle
carotid artery one of two principal arteries on either side of neck that conveys blood from aorta to head
circulatory system network of vessels through which blood is pumped by heart
clot network of fibrin fibers that trap red blood cells and platelets to form solid mass
coronary artery either of two arteries that originate in aorta and supply heart with blood
corpuscle free-floating blood or lymph cell
diastole stage of relaxation in action of heart muscle
erythrocyte red blood cell
fibrin insoluble protein that forms fibers in blood clotting
heart hollow organ with muscular walls that pumps blood through circulatory system
heartbeat pulsation of heart, including one complete systole and diastole
hematic (adj) of, pertaining to, or contained in blood
hemoglobin oxygen-carrying substance in red blood cells which gives them red color
homeostasis state of maintaining constant blood composition
leukocyte white blood cell
lymph colorless fluid that bathes body cells and contains lymphocytes
lymphatic system system of small vessels by which lymph is circulated through body
lymph node small organ that produces lymphocytes to filter foreign bodies and bacteria from lymph
lymphocyte white blood cell of the immune system that attacks foreign substances directly or by producing antibodies
pericardial cavity thin, membranous sac enclosing heart
phagocyte white blood cell that defends against bacterial attack and digests tissue debris
plasma clear, colorless liquid left after blood cells are taken out of blood
platelet minute disk of cytoplasm formed in bone marrow that assists in blood clotting; thrombocyte
portal system veins that conduct blood from one capillary network to another
pulmonary artery artery that conveys blood from right ventricle of heart to lungs
pulmonary vein vein that conveys blood from lungs to left auricle of heart
pump Slang. heart

red blood cell elastic blood cell formed in bone marrow and containing hemoglobin; erythrocyte
Rhesus factor antigen present on surface of red blood cells of most people; Rh positive blood
serum liquid obtained from clotted blood; form of plasma
spleen organ that produces lymphocytes and stores red blood cells
systole stage of contraction in action of heart muscle
thrombin enzyme in blood serum that promotes production of fibrin
thrombocyte platelet
ticker Slang. heart
vascular system circulatory and lymphatic systems of vessels for conducting blood and lymph through body
vein blood vessel conducting blood from tissue back to heart
vena cava main vein entering auricle of heart with blood from upper and lower parts of body
ventricle lower chamber in heart that receives blood from auricle and pumps it back through circulatory system
white blood cell phagocyte or lymphocyte blood cell without coloring material that fights bacteria in body; leukocyte

Digestive and Excretory System

alimentary canal long tube, running from mouth to anus, for digestion and absorption of food
anus excretory opening at end of alimentary canal
ascending colon portion of colon rising from cecum
bladder urinary bladder
bowel any of divisions of intestine; gut
cecum small bag at start of large intestine
colon main absorptive part of large intestine, running from cecum to rectum
defecation act of passing feces from rectum out through anus
descending colon portion of colon leading to rectum
digestive system organs causing chemical decomposition of food into substances that body can absorb or excrete
duodenum part of small intestine joined to stomach, with ducts leading to liver and pancreas
enzyme complex protein substance produced by cells to catalyze metabolic processes such as digestion
esophagus long muscular tube from pharynx down neck to stomach
excrement waste products discharged from body
excretion discharge of waste products from body
feces remains of undigested food excreted from bowels through anus

gastric juice liquid secretion produced by walls of stomach to aid digestion

gastrointestinal tract portion of alimentary canal from esophagus to rectum

gullet esophagus; throat

gut portion of alimentary canal between pylorus and anus; bowel; intestine

ileum last division of small intestine, opening into large intestine

intestine part of alimentary canal between stomach and anus for absorption of food into body

jejunum middle portion of small intestine between ileum and duodenum

kishkes *Slang.* intestines

large intestine broad tube with muscular walls, consisting of colon and rectum, that absorbs water, leaving feces

peristalsis wavelike muscle movement in alimentary canal that pushes contents along

pylorus opening between stomach and duodenum

rectum storage area for feces in last part of large intestine, ending with anus

sigmoid flexure curving final portion of colon that ends in rectum

small intestine long tube between stomach and large intestine where absorption and digestion of food occur

sphincter annular muscle that closes and opens rectum

stomach baglike part of alimentary canal below esophagus with muscular walls that mix food with gastric juice

transverse colon portion of colon running from ascending colon to descending colon

ureter tube leading from kidney to urinary bladder

urethra tube from urinary bladder to outside of body for discharge of urine; in males, also used to discharge sperm through penis

urinary bladder baglike structure for storing urine prior to its discharge from body; bladder

urinary tract system of tubes that conducts urine from kidney through ureter, urinary bladder, and urethra

urine liquid containing dissolved urea and salts, discharged by kidney to bladder and through urethra out of body

villus small, fingerlike structure growing out of mucous membrane of small intestine that absorbs and carries off food material

Respiratory System

alveolus tiny, blind-ended cavity in lung that receives carbon dioxide from blood and gives back oxygen

bronchiole small air passageway in lung; division of bronchus

bronchus tube leading from trachea to each lung

cilium hairlike fringe on walls of trachea and bronchus that flaps to drive dust from lungs back up to mouth

diaphragm cup-shaped muscle between thorax and abdomen that flattens when air is drawn into lungs

exhalation process of pushing air out of lungs; expiration

expiration exhalation

inhalation process of taking air into lungs; inspiration

inspiration inhalation

intercostal muscle muscle between two ribs that contracts when air is inhaled

lung either of two organs for breathing that takes carbon dioxide from blood and returns oxygen to it

pleura membranous, baglike outer covering of lung

pleural cavity thin, membranous sac that lines chest cavity and contains lungs

respiration process by which oxygen is conveyed to tissues and carbon dioxide is given off in exchange

respiratory system organs involved in exchange of carbon dioxide and oxygen between body and environment: nose and mouth, pharynx, larynx, trachea, bronchi, and lungs

sputum saliva ejected from respiratory passages

trachea tube leading from mouth and nose down throat to lungs for in-and-out passage of air

Endocrine System and Glands

adrenal gland either of two endocrine glands lying above the kidney; suprarenal gland

adrenalin epinephrine

apocrine (*adj*) designating glands in which part of secreting cell goes into secretion, as in mammary gland

bile green, alkaline liquid produced by liver that forms emulsion with fat to assist enzyme action

bile duct tube that conducts bile from liver to duodenum

duct short pipe through which secretions leave gland

eccrine (*adj*) designating glands that secrete externally, as certain sweat glands

endocrine gland any gland that secretes a hormone into the bloodstream

epinephrine hormone secreted by adrenal glands that increases heartbeat, sends blood to brain and muscles, increases perspiration, and enlarges eye pupil; adrenalin

exocrine gland any gland that discharges a secretion through an opening on epithelial surface

follicle small cavity or gland

gallbladder small vessel near liver for bile storage

gland organ that selectively removes materials from blood, chemically alters them, and secretes them for further use in body or discharges them from body

glandular system system of organs that produce secretions

holocrine (*adj*) designating glands in which cells disintegrate entirely to form secretion, as in sebaceous glands

hormone organic substance, such as insulin, prolactin, adrenalin, estrogen, or testosterone, produced by endocrine glands and carried by bloodstream to produce a metabolic effect

islets of Langerhans insulin-producing cells in pancreas

kidney either of a pair of bean-shaped glands in upper abdominal cavity that control amount of water in blood, maintain homeostasis, and excrete waste water as urine

lacrimal gland either of two tear-secreting glands located at top of eye

lactation production of milk in mammary glands

liver large gland that secretes bile and stores glycogen

mammary gland either of two milk-producing glands on female upper chest

melatonin hormone secreted by pineal gland, important in regulating biological rhythms

merocrine (*adj*) designating glands in which secreting cells remain intact, as in sweat glands

ovary female reproductive gland that produces ova

pancreas gland that produces digestive juice and insulin

pancreatic juice digestive juice secreted by pancreas and passed to duodenum

parathyroid gland one of four small glands on or near thyroid

parotid gland largest salivary gland, located below each ear

pineal body small endocrine gland in brain that secretes melatonin

pituitary gland endocrine gland beneath floor of brain that controls action of all other endocrine glands

prostate gland muscular gland surrounding male urethra at base of bladder

renal (*adj*) designating artery supplying blood to kidneys

salivary glands three pairs of glands in mouth that secrete saliva: parotid, sublingual, submaxillary

sebaceous gland gland in dermis, opening onto hair root, that produces oily sebum

sublingual gland one of a pair of salivary glands located below the tongue

submaxillary gland one of a pair of salivary glands located on each side of and below the lower jaw

suprarenal gland adrenal gland

sweat gland small, coiled, tubular gland in subcutaneous tissue that regulates body temperature by secretion of perspiration through duct and out pores in skin

testis male reproductive gland that produces sperm

thymus gland in neck that produces lymphocytes and becomes vestigial after puberty

thyroid gland endocrine gland that controls rate of metabolism and growth and production of body heat

urea soluble organic compound formed from ammonia in liver

Reproductive System

afterbirth placenta and fetal membranes

cervix short, narrow tube leading from uterus to vagina

clitoris small, sensitive organ at anterior part of vulva

embryo developing human in womb during first eight weeks after conception

epididymis long tube that receives and stores sperm

fallopian tube tube that conducts ovum from ovary to uterus

fetus embryo that has appearance of fully developed offspring; also, *esp. Brit.* foetus

gamete reproductive cell with chromosomes in nucleus: male spermatozoon, female ovum

genitals external reproductive organs, male or female

glans head of penis or clitoris

gonad reproductive gland that produces gametes: male testis, female ovary

labia folds at margin of vulva, majora and minora

menstruation periodic discharge of blood, secretions, and tissue due to shedding of uterine lining when ovum is not fertilized

mons veneris rounded eminence of fatty tissue on female pubic region

ovary female reproductive gland that produces ova

ovum female gamete or unfertilized egg cell

penis erectile male organ with many blood vessels, through which sperm passes for internal fertilization of ova, also used for urination

placenta vascular organ that surrounds fetus and unites it with uterus for nutrition

reproductive system organs and structures concerned with production of gametes and conception of new individuals of a given species

scrotum external pouch containing male testes

seminal vesicle either of two glands on each side of male bladder that add nutrients to sperm passing through vas deferens

smegma cheesy secretion by sebaceous glands at genitalia

spermatozoon male gamete with flagellum that allows it to swim toward female gamete; sperm

testicle male gonad; baglike structure that produces sperm

testis male reproductive gland that produces sperm; testicle

umbilical cord cord connecting fetus with placenta

urethra tube in males used to discharge sperm through penis

uterus muscular hollow organ in female in which embryo and fetus develop; womb

vagina canal leading from cervix to outside of body in female that receives sperm and acts as birth passage

vas deferens long tube that passes sperm from testes to urethra

vulva external portion of female genital organs

womb uterus

Skeleton

backbone spinal column

ball-and-socket joint round end of one bone that fits into hollow of another, allowing movement in any direction

bone hard, largely calcareous substance of skeleton

boss round, knoblike protuberance on bone

cartilage tough, elastic, whitish tissue that forms skeleton of embryo, most of which later turns to bone

flex (*vb*) bend joint so angle between two bones becomes smaller

gliding joint joint where surface of one bone moves over surface of another

Haversian canal small tube in bones containing nerves and blood vessels

hinge joint joint such as knee or elbow, in which round end of one bone turns on flat surface of another in one direction only

joint structure that joins two bones so they can move

ligament strong band of fiber that holds bones of joint together

marrow soft, fatty material that forms inside of bone

ossification hardening of cartilage into bone

process bony outgrowth on larger structure

skeleton hard internal structure that supports organs and tissue, composed of the following major bones:

> **acetabulum** hip socket
> **calcaneus** heel bone
> **carpus** wrist bones
> **clavicle** collarbone
> **coccyx** base of spine
> **coxa** hip joint
> **cranium** skull bone
> **femur** upper leg bone
> **fibula** lower leg bone
> **frontal** front of cranium
> **gladiolus** sternum, breastbone
> **humerus** upper arm bone
> **ilium** upper portion of hipbone
> **ischium** lower portion of hipbone
> **lacrimal** forehead
> **lumbar vertebrae** five vertebrae of middle back
> **mandible** lower jawbone
> **manubrium** upper breastbone
> **mastoid** bone behind ear
> **maxilla** upper jawbone
> **metacarpus** bone in fingers
> **metatarsus** bone in toes
> **nasal** nose bone
> **occipital** back of cranium
> **orbit** eye socket
> **parietal** top of cranium
> **patella** knee bone
> **pelvis** bone forming pelvic cavity
> **phalanges** bones at ends of toes and fingers
> **pubis** groin bone

radius lower arm bone

ribs twenty-four curved bones around chest cavity

sacral vertebrae five vertebrae of lower back

sacroiliac joint between sacrum and ilium

sacrum bone forming back of pelvis

scapula shoulder blade

skull bones covering brain

sphenoid base of skull

sternum breastbone

tarsus foot bone

temporal side of cranium

thoracic vertebrae twelve vertebrae of upper back

tibia shinbone

ulna bone in forearm

vertebrae thirty-three bony segments of spinal column

xiphoid process point of lower breastbone

zygomatic cheek bone

spinal column series of joined vertebrae forming axial support for skeleton and carrying nerves; backbone; spine; vertebral column

spine spinal column

tailbone coccyx

torus rounded projection on bone

vertebra hollow bone with large central mass and fingerlike pieces of bone standing out from core

vertebral column spinal column

Muscles

abductor muscle that moves from median axis of body

adductor muscle that pulls toward median axis of body

constrictor muscle that contracts cavity of opening or compresses organ

coordination muscles acting together to produce same effect

erector muscle that erects body or body parts

involuntary muscle muscle tissue in sheets around hollow organs that contracts slowly without conscious control

muscle tissue consisting of long cells with power to contract, causing all movements of body parts

muscular system system of muscles that cause all bodily movements, composed of the following major muscles:

> **abdominal** stomach muscle
> **biceps** muscle at front of upper arm
> **deltoid** shoulder muscle
> **erector** lower back muscle
> **extensor** forearm muscle
> **fascia lata** hip muscle
> **flexor** forearm muscle
> **gastrocnemius** calf muscle
> **gluteus** buttocks muscle
> **hamstring** muscle at back of thigh
> **latissimus dorsi** back muscle
> **oblique** muscle at side of torso
> **pectoral** upper chest muscle
> **quadriceps** muscle at front of thigh
> **rectus abdominis** long muscle in abdomen
> **rectus femoris** long muscle in front of thigh

rotator cuff muscle in shoulder under deltoid
sartorius muscle across front of thigh
soleus muscle down back of lower leg to foot
sternocleidomastoid neck muscle
trapezius upper back muscle
triceps muscle at back of upper arm

reflex simple behavior in which nerve stimulus causes set response in muscle
tendon band of connective tissue that attaches muscle to bone
tensor muscle that stretches a body part, making it tight
voluntary muscle long muscle able to contract rapidly that moves bones of joints in locomotion by conscious control

Tissue, Fiber, and Integumentary System

adipose (*adj*) designating fat in connective tissue
cartilage tough, elastic, whitish tissue around bones or through muscles; embryonic skeleton that turns to bone
connective tissue fibrous tissue that provides support for other tissue or organs
cuticle epidermis, esp. hardened outer layer of skin
dermis inside layer of skin cells, providing elastic strength
epidermis outside layer of cells
epithelium tissue that forms surface or outside of organism, such as skin, or covers inside of tubes and cavities
fascia thin layer of connective tissue around and between muscles or organs
fat ester of glycerol and fatty acid; tissue of cells expanded with greasy or oily matter
fiber strong, threadlike structure of protein
hair fine, threadlike growth from skin, concentrated on head, in armpits, and above genitals
hair follicle small cavity in epidermis from which hair develops
horny layer tough, protective outer layer of epidermis
integumentary system any of various kinds of tissue covering body or enclosing organs
irritability ability to respond to stimuli, characteristic of all living tissue
ligament strong band of fiber holding bones of joint together
lobe portion of an organ separated by fissures
marrow soft, fatty material that forms inside of bone
matrix solid material made by cells and secreted around them
melanin insoluble pigment that gives dark color to skin and hair
melanocyte cell that produces melanin in skin and hair
membrane thin, pliable sheet of tissue that forms covering or lining
mucous membrane lubricating membrane lining organ or internal surface such as alimentary or respiratory canal

mucus sticky, lubricating liquid secreted by some membranes
nail thin, horny plate covering end of top of finger or toe
organ body part with definite structure and particular function
skin outer covering, containing dermis and epidermis
soft tissue muscle, fat, or tissue not part of skeleton or organ
subcutaneous (*adj*) designating tissue situated just beneath epithelium
synovial capsule baglike membrane in joint filled with sticky lubricating liquid
system all organs and tissues concerned with particular function of organism
tendon band of connective tissue that attaches muscle to bone
tissue mass of cells and intercellular material which performs specific function in organism
vessel tube for conducting fluids within organism

MEDICAL PROBLEMS
Diseases and Infestations
Afflictions and Conditions
Defects and Disabilities
Injuries and Accidents
Signs and Symptoms
Diagnostic Terminology

See also: Chap. 1: Anatomy; Health, Fitness, and Enhancement; Chap. 2: Biology; Chap. 4: Medicine

---

Diseases and Infestations

acquired immune deficiency syndrome AIDS
Addison's disease condition marked by weakness, low blood pressure, and dark pigmentation due to inadequate hormone secretion by adrenal glands
adenitis regional inflammation of gland or lymph node
adenocarcinoma malignant epithelial tumor in glandular pattern
agranulocytosis acute illness caused by chemicals or drug reaction in which certain white blood cells disappear, causing rapid, massive infection
ague malaria; general malaise marked by fever
AIDS **a**cquired **i**mmune**d**eficiency **s**yndrome; severe weakening or destruction of body's immune system by human immunodeficiency virus, allowing opportunistic diseases and infections to attack, spread by direct contact of body fluids such as blood or semen; SIDA
AIDS-related complex ARC; chronic enlargement of lymph nodes and persistent fever caused by AIDS virus
ailment physical disorder or chronic disease
Alzheimer's disease progressive, untreatable dementia and brain degeneration in elderly

amebiasis infection with or disease caused by amebas
amebic dysentery severe dysentery caused by protozoan amebas
amyotrophic lateral sclerosis progressive loss of muscle bulk and control due to nerve disease; Lou Gehrig's disease
anthrax acute infectious livestock disease, transmitted to humans by contact, causing pneumonia or skin ulcerations
aplastic anemia anemia due to failure of bone marrow to produce sufficient leukocytes and blood platelets
apoplexy stroke
appendicitis acute inflammation of vermiform appendix that requires surgical removal
ARC AIDS-related complex
arteriosclerosis deposit of cholesterol on artery walls; hardening of the arteries
arthritis inflammation of joints
asbestosis lung disease caused by inhalation of asbestos fibers, sometimes leading to lung cancer
atheroma degeneration of artery walls due to fatty plaques and scar tissue; common form of arteriosclerosis; atherosclerosis
atherosclerosis atheroma
autoimmune disease disorder that permits destruction of tissue by body's own antibodies
bacterial endocarditis inflammation of lining of heart cavity and valves due to bacterial infection
basal cell carcinoma common, usu. curable, slow-growing malignant tumor on skin
beriberi often fatal nutritional disorder due to vitamin B_1 deficiency
bilirubinemia excess bile pigment in blood that causes jaundice
Black Death bubonic plague
black lung slow-developing respiratory disease due to regular inhalation of coal dust or asbestos; miner's lung; pneumoconiosis
blackwater fever rare complication of malaria, with massive destruction of red blood cells, that causes hemoglobin in urine
blastomycosis infectious, potentially fatal lung disease that can spread to skin, caused by fungus
blepharitis inflammation, scaling, and crusting of eyelids
botulism serious toxin-produced bacterial food poisoning
Bright's disease nephritis
bronchitis inflammation of walls of bronchi in lungs due to virus or bacteria, causing coughing and production of sputum
brown lung occupational disease due to inhalation of cotton dust; byssinosis
brucellosis bacterial infection causing remittent fever
bubonic plague often fatal bacterial epidemic disease transmitted to humans by rat fleas, with painful swelling of lymph nodes; Black Death
byssinosis brown lung

cancer malignant tumor anywhere in body due to uncontrolled cell division, causing disruption of metabolism and invasion and destruction of neighboring tissue

candidiasis yeastlike fungus infection in mouth and moist areas of body; thrush

carbuncle staphylococcus infection of skin that causes boils with multiple drainage channels

carcinoma cancer in epithelium lining skin or internal organs

cardiac arrest cessation of heart pumping, due esp. to fibrillation, that results in rapid brain damage or death

cardiac stenosis abnormal narrowing of heart valve

cardiomyopathy chronic viral, congenital, or other disorder that affects heart muscle and causes heart failure, arrhythmias, or embolisms

carditis inflammation of heart

caries decay and crumbling of tooth or bone; dental cavity

cat-scratch disease viral infection causing fever and swelling of lymph glands, due to scratch of cat

cellulitis inflammation of connective tissue due to bacterial infection

cerebrospinal fever bacterial meningitis; spotted fever

cerebrovascular accident sudden and severe attack of cerebrovascular disease; stroke

cerebrovascular disease disorder of blood vessels in brain due to atheroma or hypertension, causing cerebral hemorrhage or thrombosis and cerebrovascular accident

cervicitis inflammation of cervix

chickenpox mild, highly infectious viral disease primarily in children with itchy rash of red pimples, blisters, and pustules; varicella

childbed fever puerperal fever

chlamydia sexually transmitted, viruslike microorganism causing conjunctivitis, urethritis, and cervicitis

cholera acute bacterial infection of small intestine causing massive diarrhea, often leading to dehydration

chorea neurological disease of the basal ganglia that causes jerky, involuntary movements and distorted posture of shoulders, hips, and face; St. Vitus's dance

chronic fatigue syndrome persistent, extreme exhaustion and weakness due to unknown causes

cirrhosis progressive liver condition from various causes, esp. alcoholism or hepatitis, in which cells die and the liver turns tawny and knobby

clap *Vulgar slang.* gonorrhea

coccidioidomycosis fungal infection characterized by cough, fever, and abscesses under the skin, often disappearing spontaneously but can be fatal

cold contagious respiratory infection that causes inflammation of mucous membrane and nasal discharge; common cold

colitis any inflammation of colon, causing diarrhea and lower abdominal pain

collagen diseases various diseases characterized by changes in makeup of connective tissue: lupus, rheumatic fever, rheumatoid arthritis, and scleroderma

common cold cold

congestive heart failure inability of heart to adequately supply blood to body tissue, often due to weakening of cardiac muscle, causing body swelling and shortness of breath

conjunctivitis inflammation of mucous membrane covering front of eye, often with discharge of pus; pinkeye

consumption any disease that causes wasting of tissues, esp. pulmonary tuberculosis

contact dermatitis skin inflammation produced by contact with some substance that causes redness, swelling, and often itching

coronary coronary heart disease; heart attack

coronary heart disease serious condition affecting coronary artery

coronary infarction myocardial infarction

coronary occlusion coronary thrombosis

coronary thrombosis formation of a blood clot in coronary artery that obstructs blood flow to heart and causes coronary infarction, usu. due to atherosclerosis; coronary occlusion

coryza catarrhal inflammation of mucous membrane in nose

cowpox viral infection of cow's udder, transmitted to humans by direct contact, causing mild version of symptoms similar to smallpox

crab louse crablike louse that infests pubic regions, transmitted by sexual contact

crib death sudden infant death syndrome

Crohn's disease condition marked by chronic inflammation and thickening of alimentary tract

croup inflammation and obstruction of larynx in young children due to viral respiratory infections, characterized by harsh cough

cryptococcosis severe fungal infection, usu. in men of middle age, that affects central nervous system and brain membranes

Cushing's disease syndrome due to excess corticosteroid hormone, causing weight gain, excess body hair, and high blood pressure

cystic fibrosis hereditary disease of exocrine glands that produces respiratory infections, malabsorption, and sweat with high salt content

cystitis often infectious inflammation of urinary bladder that causes frequent painful passage of urine

deficiency disease any disease, such as beriberi, caused by nutritional deficiency

dengue viral disease transmitted by mosquitoes in the tropics, causing fever, severe pain in back and joints, rash, and sore throat

dermatitis skin inflammation

diabetes diabetes mellitus

diabetes insipidus rare deficiency of pituitary hormone that causes constant thirst and excessive urination

diabetes mellitus common deficiency, possibly inherited, of the pancreatic hormone insulin, causing disorder in carbohydrate metabolism and inability to properly utilize sugars; diabetes

diphtheria acute, highly contagious bacterial infection of the throat that can cause death from respiratory obstruction or carditis

disease physical disorder with specific physiological cause and recognizable signs and symptoms

diverticulitis colonic diverticulosis with inflammation

diverticulosis condition characterized by existence of diverticular sacs at weak points in walls of alimentary tract, esp. intestine

dracontiasis infestation from contaminated drinking water of tropical parasitic guinea worm beneath skin, causing large blisters on extremities

droplet infection disease spread by droplets expelled by sneezing or coughing

duodenal ulcer ulcer in lining of duodenum caused by excess stomach acid

dysentery infection of intestinal tract that causes severe diarrhea mixed with blood and mucus

dystrophy organ or muscle disorder caused by insufficient nourishment or hereditary disorder

elephantiasis gross enlargement of legs or other body parts due to obstructed lymph drainage, caused by parasitic worm transmitted by mosquitoes

emphysema air in tissues; pulmonary disorder, characterized by increase in size of air sacs due to destruction of their walls, causing shortness of breath

encephalitis viral or bacterial inflammation of brain, also caused by infection or allergic reaction; sleeping sickness

endocarditis inflammation and damage to heart cavity lining due to bacterial infection or rheumatic fever

enteritis viral or bacterial inflammation of small intestine, causing diarrhea

epilepsy one of various brain disorders that cause recurrent, sudden convulsive attacks

Epstein-Barr syndrome infectious mononucleosis caused by herpeslike virus; glandular fever

erysipelas skin infection from streptococcus bacteria that causes inflammation, swelling, and fever

fibroma usu. benign tumor composed mainly of fibrous or connective tissue

fibrosarcoma malignant tumor of connective tissue, esp. in legs

filariasis disorder that affects lymphatic system, caused by parasite

flu influenza

food poisoning digestive system disorder, usu. from the consumption of bacteria or bacterial toxins in food, causing vomiting, diarrhea, nausea, and fever

frambesia yaws

functional disorder condition for which no physical cause can be found

fungus simple parasitic organism that can infect humans and cause disease

gastric ulcer stomach ulcer caused by action of acid on stomach lining

gastritis inflammation of stomach lining from an ingested substance, infection, or chronic irritation

gastroenteritis inflammation of stomach and intestine, due to virus, bacteria, or food poisoning, that causes vomiting

genital herpes infection of genital area by herpes simplex virus

German measles rubella

gingivitis inflammation of gums, sometimes with bleeding

glandular fever Epstein-Barr syndrome; mononucleosis

glaucoma abnormally high fluid pressure in the eye, often leading to loss of vision

glioma cancer of nerve tissue

glomerulonephritis potentially fatal streptococcal infection of kidney

gonorrhea sexually transmitted bacterial disease that affects mucous membranes in genital tract, pharynx, or rectum

gout accumulation of excess uric acid in bloodstream and joints that causes joint destruction, kidney stones, and arthritis

grand mal generalized epileptic seizure with flexion and extension of extremities and loss of consciousness

Graves' disease disease characterized by enlarged thyroid and increased basal metabolism, due to excessive thyroid secretion

grippe influenza

Hansen's disease leprosy, caused by aerobic bacteria Hansen's bacilli

heart attack myocardial infarction

heart failure inadequate pumping of heart ventricle due to coronary thrombosis, hypertension, or arrhythmia; congestive heart failure

hepatitis inflammation of liver, due to virus transmitted by food or drink (infectious hepatitis) or blood on needle or in transfusion (serum hepatitis), causing fever and jaundice

herpes herpes simplex; small viral blisters on skin

herpes simplex virus in herpes family; nonvenereal blisters on mucous membrane that can cause conjunctivitis, vaginal inflammation, or cold sores; herpes

herpes zoster virus in herpes family characterized by vesicles, often with severe pain along distribution of nerve; shingles

histoplasmosis fungal infection of lymph nodes, usu. caused by inhalation

HIV human immunodeficiency virus

Hodgkin's disease condition marked by malignancy in lymphatic tissue that causes enlarged lymph nodes, fever, and profuse sweating

hookworm infestation of small intestine by parasitic hookworm that penetrates skin and causes diarrhea, debility, and sometimes anemia

human immunodeficiency virus HIV; virus that causes AIDS

Huntington's chorea hereditary chorea with progressive dementia due to widespread degeneration of neurons throughout brain

hydrophobia rabies

hypernephroma malignant tumor in kidney cells

hyperthyroidism overactivity of thyroid gland that causes rapid heartbeat, sweating, tremors, weight loss, and anxiety

hypoglycemia glucose deficiency in bloodstream that causes weakness, confusion, and sweating, often in patients with diabetes mellitus who take an insulin overdose

hypothyroidism subnormal thyroid gland activity that can lead to cretinism if present at birth

icthyosis hereditary skin disease causing flaking of skin in large scales

ileitis inflammation of ileum in small intestine

illness disease or condition that causes poor health

impetigo contagious skin infection from streptococcal or staphylococcal bacteria, esp. in children, causing crusty yellow blisters

infantile paralysis poliomyelitis

infectious disease disease caused by a microorganism or parasite and usu. passed by direct human contact; communicable or contagious disease

infestation invasion of body by animal parasites

influenza highly contagious viral infection of respiratory system, transmitted by coughing or sneezing, that causes headache, fever, general aches and pains; flu; grippe

kala-azar chronic, often fatal disease transmitted by sandfly in which liver and spleen become enlarged

Kaposi's sarcoma KS; cancer of skin characterized by multiple purplish lesions on face and extremities, often associated with AIDS and usu. fatal

keratitis inflammation of cornea of eye due to infection or outside agent

KS Kaposi's sarcoma

kwashiorkor malnutrition due to protein deficiency in diet, esp. in children ages one to three

laryngitis inflammation of larynx and vocal cords, due to bacterial or viral infection, causing coughing, husky voice, or complete voice loss

Lassa fever highly contagious viral disease that produces wide range of symptoms affecting most parts of body and leading to death

legionnaires' disease bacterial lung infection that causes malaise, fever, chest pain, and coughing

leprosy chronic contagious tropical disease caused by Hansen's bacilli that results in lumps and patches on skin, thickening of nerves and skin, numbness, and paralysis; Hansen's disease

leptospirosis bacterial infection passed by contact with infected rats, causing fever, muscle pain, and jaundice

leukemia overproduction of abnormal white blood cells by bone marrow and other blood-forming organs, usu. causing fatal systemic malignancy

lockjaw tetanus

Lou Gehrig's disease amyotrophic lateral sclerosis

louse small, wingless insect that is an external parasite

lung cancer malignancy in epithelium of air passages or lung, esp. due to smoke or other outside agents

lupus any of several chronic skin diseases, esp. lupus erythematosus

lupus erythematosus chronic inflammation of connective tissue that causes red scaly rash on face, arthritis, and organ damage

lupus vulgaris rare tuberculous skin infection

Lyme disease spirochetal infection transmitted by a tiny tick that causes skin rash, headache, fever, and sometimes arthritis and heart damage

lymphoma malignant tumor of lymph nodes that is not Hodgkin's disease

malady disease or illness

malaria infection caused by parasitic protozoa in red blood cells, transmitted by mosquito in tropics and subtropics, causing fever, sweating, and anemia

mastitis inflammation of breasts due to bacterial infection, often through damaged nipples

measles highly infectious viral epidemic disease, mainly in children, that causes high fever and elevated pink rash; rubeola

melanoma malignant tumor of melanin-forming cells, esp. in skin

Ménière's syndrome disease of labyrinth of inner ear, causing deafness and vertigo

meningitis inflammation of membranes lining skull and vertebral canal, due to viral or bacterial infection, causing fever, intense headache, muscular rigidity, and sometimes convulsion, delirium, or death; spinal meningitis

mesothelioma tumor of pleural epithelium, often due to exposure to asbestos dust

miliaria inflammatory skin disease characterized by formation of vesicles or papules about sweat glands; prickly heat

Minamata disease form of mercury poisoning found in Japan that causes numbness, impaired speech and hearing, and lack of coordination

miner's lung black lung

mononucleosis infectious disease that manifests a high number of monocytes in blood, enlarged lymph nodes, prolonged fever, appetite loss, and malaise, esp. in young adults; glandular disease caused by Epstein-Barr virus; glandular fever

MS multiple sclerosis

multiple sclerosis MS; chronic nervous system disease with recurrent symptoms of unsteady gait, shaky limb movements, rapid involuntary eye movements, and speech defects

mumps viral infection that causes fever and swelling of parotid salivary glands, esp. among children

muscular dystrophy inherited muscle disease marked by degeneration of muscle fiber

myasthenia gravis muscular weakness that has its onset with repetitive activity and leads to paralysis

mycosis fungus infection

myeloma malignancy of bone marrow

myocardial infarction death of portion of heart muscle due to interrupted blood supply; heart attack; coronary infarction

myocarditis acute or chronic inflammation of heart muscle

nephritis inflammation of kidney; Bright's disease

neuritis inflammation of nerves; neuropathy

neurodermatitis localized skin disease with itching and thickening of skin

neurofibromatosis congenital disease that causes growth on fibrous nerve coverings of benign tumors that may become malignant

neuropathy neuritis

orchitis inflammation of testis that causes pain, redness, and swelling of scrotum, usu. due to infection such as mumps

organic disorder disorder associated with physiological changes in structure of organ or tissue

osteoarthritis joint cartilage disease that causes pain and impaired joint function and occurs in later life, due to overuse of joint or as a complication of rheumatoid arthritis

osteomyelitis inflammation of bone marrow and adjacent bone, mostly from infection, esp. after compound fractures where marrow is exposed

osteoporosis loss of bony matrix that causes brittle bones, due to injury, infection, or old age

otitis inflammation of ear, due to viral or bacterial infection, causing severe pain and high fever

otosclerosis disease of bone surrounding inner ear, causing impaired hearing

pancreatitis inflammation of pancreas with sudden, severe pain

paratyphoid fever bacterial infectious disease, caused by nontyphoidal salmonella and spread by poor sanitation, marked by diarrhea, fever, and pink rash on chest

parkinsonism Parkinson's disease

Parkinson's disease neurological disorder of late middle age characterized by tremor, rigidity, and little spontaneous movement; parkinsonism

pediculosis infestation of body and/or scalp by lice, causing itching and sometimes bacterial infection with weeping lesions

pellagra B-vitamin nutritional deficiency that causes scaly dermatitis, diarrhea, and depression

peptic ulcer breach in lining of digestive tract due to excess acid, occurring in esophagus, stomach, or duodenum

pericarditis acute or chronic inflammation of sac surrounding heart, due to viral infection, uremia, or cancer, often causing fever, chest pain, and fluid accumulation

periodontal disease disease of gums, mouth lining, and bony structures supporting teeth, caused by plaque; pyorrhea

peritonitis inflammation of abdominal cavity membrane, often due to bacteria spread in bloodstream or perforation or rupture of abdominal organ, causing pain, swelling, fever, and shock

pernicious anemia autoimmune disease, due to vitamin B_{12} deficiency, that can affect nervous system

pertussis whooping cough

pestilence severe contagious or infectious epidemic disease

petit mal lesser epileptic seizure characterized by brief spells of sleepiness or unconsciousness

pharyngitis inflammation of pharynx that causes sore throat or tonsillitis

phlebitis inflammation of vein wall, esp. in legs as complication of varicose veins, causing extreme tenderness

pinkeye conjunctivitis

plague acute epidemic bacterial disease of rats, transmitted to humans by rat fleas, causing severe headache, fever, enlarged lymph nodes, and delirium, usu. fatal

pleurisy inflammation of pleura that cover lungs, usu. due to pneumonia or other lung disease, causing painful breathing

pneumoconiosis black lung

pneumonia inflammation or infection of lungs in which air sacs fill with pus, causing coughing and chest pain

pneumonic plague plague bacterium in lungs, usu. fatal

podagra gout of foot, esp. big toe

polio poliomyelitis

poliomyelitis infectious viral disease of central nervous system, formerly epidemic, causing stiffness and sometimes paralysis of muscles, esp. respiratory system muscles; infantile paralysis; polio

prickly heat miliaria

prostatitis inflammation of prostate gland, due to bacterial infection, sometimes causing urinary obstruction

psychosomatic illness disease caused at least in part by emotional state

puerperal fever blood poisoning in mother shortly after childbirth due to infection of womb lining or vagina; childbed fever

pyorrhea periodontal disease

Q fever typhuslike, systemic disease caused by microorganism, transmitted to humans from ruminants through raw milk

quinsy pus-discharging inflammation of tonsils

rabies acute viral infection of central nervous system, transmitted by bite of infected mammal, causing fever, excitation, painful spasms of throat muscles, paralysis, and death; hydrophobia

radiation sickness acute disease caused by exposure to radioactive emissions, causing nausea, vomiting, diarrhea, bleeding, hair loss, and death

relapsing fever infectious bacterial disease transmitted by tick and lice bites, causing fever, headache, and muscle pain that lapse and then recur

reticulosis abnormal malignant overgrowth of cells of lymphatic glands or immune system

Reye's syndrome acute disorder primarily in children after viral infections such as chickenpox or influenza, associated with aspirin use, causing brain swelling and affecting organs

rheumatic fever delayed complication of upper respiratory streptococcus infection, esp. in young, characterized by fever, arthritis of joints, chorea, carditis, and erythematosus rash

rheumatic heart disease scarring and chronic heart inflammation from progressive state of rheumatic fever

rheumatism any disorder causing aches and pains in muscles or joints

rheumatoid arthritis common form of arthritis that affects extremities, digits, and hips

rickets malformation of unhardened bones in children due to vitamin D deficiency

Rocky Mountain spotted fever disease caused by rickettsial microorganism, transmitted to humans by dogs and wood ticks, characterized by fever, muscle pain, and profuse red rash

roseola rubella

rubella highly contagious viral infection, primarily in children, causing enlarged lymph nodes in neck and pink rash, German measles, roseola

rubeola measles

salmonella poisoning food poisoning caused by aerobic intestinal bacteria

sandfly fever influenzalike viral fever transmitted by bite of sandfly in Mediterranean area

sarcoma tumor of connective tissue

scabies skin infection from infestation of mites that causes severe itching, esp. around groin, nipples, and between fingers

scarlatina scarlet fever

scarlet fever highly contagious childhood disease caused by streptococcus bacteria, characterized by sore throat and widespread rash; scarlatina

schistosomiasis intestinal disease in tropics, due to infestation of blood flukes, that causes anemia, diarrhea, dysentery, and cirrhosis; snail fever

scleroderma thickening and hardening of tissues beneath skin, causing rigidity of skin

scrofula tuberculosis of lymph nodes in neck

scurvy vitamin C deficiency from absence of fresh fruit and vegetables in diet that causes swollen, bleeding gums, subcutaneous bleeding, and death when prolonged

seborrheic dermatitis skin eruption due to

excess secretion of sebum, common on face at puberty

serum hepatitis liver inflammation that causes fever and jaundice, transmitted by infected hypodermic needle or blood transfusion

sexually transmitted disease STD; modern term for venereal disease

shingles herpes zoster

sickle cell anemia hereditary blood disease that mainly affects blacks, in which abnormal hemoglobin distorts blood cells and causes anemia

sickness disease, illness; condition of poor health caused by disease

SIDA common name for AIDS outside United States, based on Spanish **s**índrome**i**nmuno-**d**eficiencia **a**dquirido or French **s**yndrome **i**mmuno-**d**éficitaire**a**cquis

SIDS **s**udden **i**nfant **d**eath **s**yndrome

silicosis chronic lung disease caused by prolonged exposure to silica dust

sinusitis inflammation or infection of sinus sacs behind and around nose, causing headache and discharge through nose

sleeping sickness condition characterized by presence in blood of parasite from bite of African tsetse fly, causing lethargy, drowsiness, and pain in limbs and joints; encephalitis

smallpox acute viral infection that causes high fever and a scarring rash of blisters, usu. fatal, now eradicated by vaccine; variola

snail fever schistosomiasis

social disease *Informal.* venereal disease

somatogenic psychosomatic disorder disease caused by lowering of immunity to pathogens, due to stress

spinal meningitis meningitis

spotted fever type of bacterial meningitis; cerebrospinal fever

STD **s**exually **t**ransmitted **d**isease

strep throat infection of throat by streptococcus bacteria

stroke sudden weakness or paralysis, often on one side of body, due to interruption of blood flow to brain caused by thrombosis, embolus, or hemorrhage; apoplexy; cerebrovascular accident

St. Vitus's dance chorea

sty acute bacterial infection of gland at base of eyelash

sudden infant death syndrome SIDS; death of baby in its bed due to undetermined cause; crib death

Sydenham's chorea chorea that affects children, associated with rheumatic fever

syphilis bacterial sexually transmitted disease that causes a chancre in acute stage and may lead to blindness or paralysis in chronic stage and insanity in advanced stage

tabes dorsalis syphilis of spinal cord and its appendages, sometimes leading to paralysis

tapeworm parasitic flatworm that lives in human intestine

TB tuberculosis

teratoma tumor composed of tissues not normally found at site, esp. in testis or ovary

tetanus acute bacterial infection of contaminated wound with release of toxin that affects central nervous system and causes muscle spasms and rigidity, convulsions, and extreme pain; lockjaw

thrombophlebitis inflammation of a vein and formation of blood clot that adheres to its wall

thrush whitish spots and ulcers on mouth due to parasite, esp. in children; candidiasis

tonsillitis inflammation of tonsils, due to bacterial or viral infection, causing sore throat and fever

Tourette's syndrome neurological disorder characterized by excessive, sudden, violent movements and convulsive noises and thoughts

toxicosis any disease caused by toxic effect of a substance

toxoplasmosis infection of lymph nodes caused by protozoan that can cause blindness and mental retardation in newborn when transmitted to fetus, often acquired from cats

trachoma chronic, contagious, rickettsial conjunctivitis, often causing blindness

trench mouth respiratory infection caused by bacteria, producing ulcers on mucous membrane of mouth and throat

trichinosis intestinal infestation by worm larvae from undercooked meat that causes diarrhea, nausea, and pain in limbs

trypanosomiasis any of various debilitating, parasitic diseases transmitted by flies, including sleeping sickness

tuberculosis TB; infectious bacterial disease characterized by formation of nodular lesions in tissue, esp. lungs and lymph nodes, causing coughing, fever, night sweats, and spitting of blood

tularemia disease transmitted to humans from rabbits by deer flies or direct contamination, characterized by infection with ulcers, fever, aches, and enlarged lymph nodes

typhoid fever bacterial infection of digestive system, transmitted through contaminated food or water, that causes high fever, red rash on stomach, chills, sweating, and sometimes intestinal hemorrhage

typhus one of various infections caused by parasitic rickettsiae that results in high fever, severe headache, widespread rash, and delirium

ulcerative colitis inflammation and ulceration of colon and rectum

urethritis inflammation of urethra, esp. among males, due to bacterial or viral infection or obstruction

vaginitis irritation of vagina, due to inflammation or infection, causing burning pain and discharge

varicella chickenpox

variola smallpox

VD **v**enereal **d**isease

venereal disease VD; any infectious disease

transmitted by sexual contact, now usu. called sexually transmitted disease; social disease

whooping cough acute contagious bacterial infection of mucous membrane lining air passages, esp. in children, causing fever and paroxysmal cough with bleeding from mouth and nose; pertussis

xanthoma skin condition characterized by raised patches on eyelids, neck, or back, related to liver disease

yaws tropical infectious disease caused by spirochete in skin, marked by fever, pain, small crusty tumors, and lesions; frambesia

yellow fever infectious viral disease of tropics, transmitted by mosquitoes, causing liver and kidney degeneration with reduced urine flow, jaundice, and death

Afflictions and Conditions

acidosis excess acidity in blood, due to kidney malfunction or diabetes

acne inflammation of sebaceous glands in skin, esp. on face during adolescence

addiction state of physical or psychological dependence due to habitual consumption of habit-forming substance; dependence

aeroembolism compressed air sickness

affliction painful or debilitating condition, esp. a chronic one

airsickness motion sickness during air flight

alcoholism addiction to alcoholic liquor

alkalosis condition in which blood becomes too alkaline, due to acid loss from vomiting, kidney malfunction, or ingestion of alkalis

allergy hypersensitivity to particular substance or antigen, such as pollens, furs, feathers, mold, dust, drugs, dyes, cosmetics, or foods, causing characteristic symptoms when encountered, ingested, or inhaled

alopecia absence of hair from area where it normally grows, esp. progressive hair loss in men; baldness

altitude sickness respiratory illness from lack of oxygen and reduced atmospheric pressure at high altitudes that causes nausea and exhaustion

amaurosis partial or complete blindness

amblyopia poor sight not caused by intrinsic eye disease

amenorrhea absence or cessation of menstruation due to congenital defect, hormonal deficiency, hypothalamus disorder, or emotional problem

amnesia total or partial memory loss due to disease, injury, or trauma

anaphylaxis acute, allergic reaction to substance to which person has been previously sensitized, resulting in faintness, palpitations, loss of color, difficulty in breathing, and shock

anemia reduced hemoglobin in blood, causing fatigue, breathlessness, and pallor

anorexia nervosa extreme loss of appetite, esp. in adolescent females, causing severe weight loss and starvation

anoxia condition in which body tissues receive inadequate oxygen

anxiety disorder physiological symptoms caused by anxiety neurosis

asthma paroxysmal attacks of bronchial spasms that cause difficulty in breathing, often hereditary; bronchial asthma

astigmatism distortion of visual images due to failure of retina to focus light

athlete's foot contagious fungal infection of skin between toes; tinea

atopy allergic reaction, esp. one separate from point of contact with antigen, such as eczema on skin due to swallowed substance

autism severe psychiatric disorder of childhood that causes inability to speak or form abstract concepts and withdrawal from reality

backache chronic and persistent or recurrent pain in lower back or shoulders, usu. due to tension or injury

bacteremia blood poisoning

baldness alopecia

Barlow's syndrome congenital heart murmur due to defective mitral valve, causing susceptibility to bacterial infection

bedwetting enuresis

Bell's palsy paralysis of muscles on one side of face and inability to close eye, sometimes with loss of taste and excess sensitivity to noise

bends compressed air sickness

binge-purge syndrome bulimia

blood poisoning prolonged invasion of bloodstream by pathogenic bacteria due to infectious disease or skin lesions; bacteremia; septicemia, toxemia

boil tender, inflamed, pustulant area of skin, usu. due to staphylococcus infection; furuncle

bronchial asthma asthma

bulimia usu. psychogenic syndrome of overeating followed by vomiting, also caused by hypothalamus lesion; binge-purge syndrome

bunion swelling of joint between big toe and first metatarsal

bursitis inflammation of small fibrous sacs lined with synovial membrane, due to injury or infection, characterized by pain and stiffness in joints

caisson disease compressed air sickness

calcinosis abnormal deposit of calcium salts in tissue

cancrum ulceration of lip or mouth; canker

canker cancrum

carpal tunnel syndrome compression of median nerve entering palm of hand that causes pain and numbing in middle and index fingers

carsickness motion sickness in automobile

catalepsy maintenance of abnormal postures or physical attitudes, esp. in catatonia

cataplexy recurrent, sudden collapses without loss of consciousness

cataract opacity of eye lens that causes blurred vision, esp. in elderly

catatonia syndrome of motor abnormalities, usu. stupor and catalepsy, due to mental condition

celiac disease hereditary intestinal disorder involving intolerance to wheat and rye

chapping sore roughening or cracking of skin from overexposure to elements

cholelithiasis presence of gallstones

claudication cramping pain from inadequate blood supply to muscle

compressed air sickness formation of nitrogen bubbles in bloodstream after experiencing high pressure at great ocean depths or high altitudes, characterized by pain and blockage of circulation; aeroembolism; bends; caisson disease; decompression sickness

condition state of ill health, esp. recurrent or chronic, caused by illness, injury, or heredity

convergence insufficiency difficulty in focusing eyes upon a nearby point or object

corn area of hard or thickened skin on or between toes

cyst any of various abnormal, liquid-filled sacs lined with epithelium, due to blocked duct, tumor, or congenital problem

dandruff small flakes of dead skin on scalp; scurf

decompression sickness compressed air sickness

dehydration deficiency or loss of water in body tissues marked by thirst, nausea, and exhaustion

delirium acute mental disorder due to organic brain disease, causing hallucinations, disorientation, and extreme excitation

delirium tremens dt's; psychosis due to alcoholic withdrawal, causing tremors, anxiety, sweating, and vivid hallucinations

dependence physical or psychological compulsion to consume certain drugs; addiction

diaper rash painful, reddened, raw area of skin around anus, buttocks, and genitals due to irritant stools, urine-soaked diapers, or candidiasis infection

diplegia paralysis involving both sides of body, esp. legs

disorder malfunction of normal metabolic or physiological process or part

dropsy former term for edema

dysmenorrhea painful, difficult menstruation

ectopic pregnancy state in which fertilized egg implants at site other than uterus

eczema superficial inflammation of skin characterized by itching, red rash, and scaling, due to various causes

edema excessive accumulation of fluid in tissues; dropsy

enuresis involuntary urination, esp. at night, usu. functional in nature; bedwetting

fibrosis thickening and scarring of connective tissue due to injury or inflammation

furuncle boil

gallstone hard mass of bile pigments, cholesterol, and calcium salts in gallbladder that causes pain or passes into and obstructs bile duct

gangrene decay and death of body tissue due to insufficient or absent blood supply, caused by disease or injury

goiter swollen neck due to enlarged thyroid gland

hangnail sliver of cuticle separated along edge of fingernail

hay fever common, usu. seasonal allergy to plant pollen that causes sneezing, runny nose, and watery eyes

heat exhaustion heat prostration

heat prostration fatigue and collapse from low blood pressure due to loss of body fluids after prolonged exposure to heat; heat exhaustion

heatstroke increased body temperature and eventual loss of consciousness without sweating, due to failure of body's heat regulating mechanism after prolonged exposure to heat; sunstroke

hemophilia hereditary deficiency of one blood coagulant that causes slowness in clotting and prolonged or spontaneous bleeding

hemorrhoids enlarged veins in anus walls, esp. due to prolonged constipation or diarrhea, characterized by fissure, painful swelling, and bleeding, piles

hives round, red itching wheals up to several inches across on skin, caused by acute or chronic allergic reaction; urticaria

housemaid's knee fluid filled swelling of bursa in front of kneecap, often caused by prolonged kneeling

hydrocephalus excess of cerebrospinal fluid in brain ventricles that causes enlargement of head in children and pressure and drowsiness in adults

hyperinsulinism overproduction of insulin, due to glandular disturbances or poor nutrition, producing symptoms of hypoglycemia

incontinence involuntary passage or leakage of urine

ingrown toenail condition in which toenail grows into surrounding tissue

intestinal obstruction blockage that prevents passage of feces through intestine, due to hernia, tumor, or inflammation, causing pain and sometimes vomiting

irritable bowel syndrome recurrent chronic abdominal pain with constipation and/or diarrhea caused by abnormal contractions of colon muscles; spastic colon

jet lag disruption of biological and psychological rhythms by lengthy jet travel, causing mood alterations, sleep disturbance, and stress

kidney stone hard, pebblelike mass in kidney that causes pain and blood in urine; nephrolithiasis; renal calculus

lentigo liver spot

liver spot brown, roundish flat spot on skin that results from excess melanin, usu. in elderly; lentigo

malnutrition insufficient food consumption to satisfy bodily needs over prolonged period

menorrhagia excessive or prolonged menstrual bleeding

migraine recurrent, intense headache, often accompanied by blurred vision and vomiting, caused by contraction and dilation of arteries in brain

mole flat or raised area of brown pigment in skin

motion sickness nausea, vomiting, dizziness, and headache caused by motion

myxedema dry, firm, waxy swelling of skin and subcutaneous tissue, also characterized by labored speech and blunted senses

narcolepsy extreme tendency to fall asleep in quiet circumstances or during monotonous activities

nephrolithiasis presence of kidney stones

nephrosis syndrome characterized by edema, excess albumin in urine, and cholesterol in blood

obesity accumulation of excess fat, esp. in subcutaneous tissues, usu. due to overeating or nutritional imbalance

pica abnormal craving for unnatural foods due to nutritional deficiencies

piles hemorrhoids

plantar wart deep wart on sole of foot

pneumonitis inflammation of walls of air sacs in lungs due to virus or unknown causes

premature birth birth of baby before full term of pregnancy

priapism persistent erection of penis due to blood clottage

psilosis falling out of hair; sprue

psoriasis condition characterized by chronic, itchy, scaly silvery patches of skin, esp. on elbows, forearms, knees, and scalp, of unknown cause but sometimes due to anxiety

pulmonary embolism obstruction by blood clot of artery that conveys blood from heart to lungs

Raynaud's disease disorder, esp. in women, in which spasms of arteries to extremities cause fingertips and toes to turn pale, blue, and numb

renal calculus kidney stone

retinitis pigmentosa hereditary condition that causes progressive degeneration of retina of eye

ringworm highly contagious fungal infection of skin, esp. scalp and feet or under beard

rosacea chronic acne characterized by red, pustular lesions about nose, cheeks, and forehead

sciatica condition marked by pain down back of thigh, due to disintegration of intervertebral disk, accompanied by numbness and stiff back

sclerosis hardening of tissue after inflammation due to scarring, esp. in spinal cord or brain, causing progressive paralysis

scurf dandruff

seasickness motion sickness on ship or boat

sebaceous cyst cyst in oil-secreting gland of skin, filled with sebum; wen

seborrhea excessive secretion by sebaceous glands in face, esp. at puberty

septicemia tissue destruction by disease-causing bacteria or toxins absorbed from bloodstream; blood poisoning

spastic colon irritable bowel syndrome

spondylosis degeneration of intervertebral disks in backbone, causing pain and restricting movement

sprue deficient absorption of food due to intestinal disease that causes diarrhea, anemia, and inflamed tongue; psilosis

stretch marks whitish streaks, usu. on abdomen or thighs, due to short-term stretching of skin, as during pregnancy

sunstroke heatstroke

surfer's knot fluid-filled swelling of bursa in front of kneecap due to prolonged kneeling on surfboard

tendonitis inflammation of bands of connective tissue that join muscle to bones and joints, due to physical trauma or hereditary disease

tennis elbow painful inflammation of tendon on outer side of elbow due to overuse

thalassemia genetic, anemic condition characterized by deficiency of hemoglobin in blood

thrombocytosis condition marked by increase in number of platelets in blood

thromboembolism condition in which blood clot forms at one point in circulation, dislodges, and moves to another point

thrombosis formation of clots in blood, potentially causing obstruction of blood vessels

tinea athlete's foot

tolerance lessening of normal response to drug or other substance taken over a prolonged period, requiring increased dosages for normal reaction

toxemia blood poisoning caused by toxins formed by bacteria at site of infection

tubal pregnancy pregnancy in which fertilized egg implants in fallopian tube

ulcer open, inflamed, nonhealing sore in skin or mucous membrane, esp. in lining of alimentary canal

urticaria hives

varicose veins bulging, distended, sometimes painful veins in legs, rectum, or scrotum due to obstruction of blood flow

vegetative state severe brain damage and deep, persistent coma that cannot be reversed, necessitating maintenance of life functions by machines

verruca wart

vertigo feeling that one's surroundings are in motion, esp. spinning or tilting, due to disease of inner ear or vestibular nerve

wart small, hard, benign growth in skin, caused by virus; verucca

wen sebaceous cyst

withdrawal syndrome of sweating, vomiting, and tremors at cessation of consumption of substance to which one is addicted

Defects and Disabilities

abnormality physical malformation or dysfunction

achondroplasia hereditary defect in bone and cartilage of limbs, which fail to grow to normal size; form of dwarfism

acromegaly abnormal growth of face, hands, and feet due to excessive pituitary production of growth hormone

agnosia associational brain disorder that prevents correct interpretation of sensations despite functioning sense organs

albinism inherited deficiency of pigment in skin, hair, and eyes

alexia acquired inability to read due to brain disease

amaurosis partial or complete blindness

amputation loss or removal of a limb or part of a limb

anencephaly partial or complete absence of bones of skull and large portions of brain, causing death in infants

aphasia speech and language comprehension disorder due to disease in left half of brain

birth defect disability or physical deformity present at birth, either inherited or acquired, that stems from problems during fetal period; congenital defect

birthmark skin blemish present at birth, often diminishing in size over time; nevus

blindness inability or marked reduction in ability to see, due to disease, injury, or birth defect

blue baby infant with congenital malformation of heart in which deoxygenated blood is pumped through body, producing bluish color in skin and lips

bowleg abnormal outcurving of legs that creates gap between knees

bucktooth extreme overbite of teeth of upper jaw over lower jaw

cauliflower ear enlarged and permanently deformed ear due to injury or repeated blows

central hearing loss hearing loss due to damage to auditory nerve between inner ear and brain or to brain's hearing center

cerebral palsy abnormal development of brain, usu. due to birth defect, that causes weakness and lack of limb coordination

clawfoot foot with excessively high arch and instep, usu. due to neuromuscular disease

clawhand extension of fingers at joint to hand, giving clawlike appearance, due to injury or leprosy

cleft palate fissure in midline of palate that did not properly fuse in embryonic stage

clubfoot birth defect in which foot is twisted downward and inward so sole cannot be placed flat on ground; talipes

color blindness any of various inherited conditions causing confusion of one or more colors; daltonism

conductive hearing loss hearing loss caused by block to passage of sound vibrations through outer or middle ear

congenital defect birth defect

cretinism congenital dwarfism, mental

retardation, and coarseness of skin due to lack of thyroid hormone

crippling birth defect, disease, or injury that severely inhibits movement of limbs, esp. ability to walk

crossed eyes strabismus in which eyes turn inward toward nose

curvature of the spine abnormal deviation in position of spine: scoliosis, lordosis, or kyphosis

daltonism color blindness, esp. difficulty in distinguishing red and green

deaf muteness inability to hear or speak

deafness partial or total inability to hear in one or both ears due to birth defect, disease, injury, or lesion

debility physical weakness or feebleness

defect abnormal functioning, physical flaw, or blemish

deformity abnormal or disfigured body part

dementia chronic mental disorder or incapacity due to organic brain disease

deviated septum abnormal position of wall or partition in anatomical part, esp. nose

diplopia double vision

disability condition that makes one unfit, incapacitated, or crippled

double vision vision disorder due to various diseases or drug reaction, causing doubling of perceived images

Down's syndrome chromosomal abnormality that causes oblique slant to eyes, round head, flat nose, small ears, short stature, and reduced mental capacity; mongolism

dwarfism abnormally short stature from pituitary deficiency, genetic defect, or cretinism

dyslalia speech disorder due to aphasia in which patient uses peculiar vocabulary or sounds

dyslexia developmental disorder that hinders the ability to learn to read and write

elephant man's disease neurofibromatosis

Erb's palsy partial paralysis of baby's arm due to injury during birth

erectile dysfunction inability to attain or maintain erection

eunuchoidism deficiency of testicular function that retards development of genitals and secondary sex characteristics

farsightedness hyperopia

fetal alcohol syndrome FAS; fetal abnormalities due to consumption of alcohol by mother during pregnancy, leading to retardation and severe behavioral disorders in later life

galactosemia genetic inability to convert galactose in milk into usable glucose, causing feeding difficulties and vomiting in newborn infants

gigantism abnormal growth to excessive height due to oversecretion of growth hormone by pituitary gland

hammertoe clawlike deformity of toe with permanent flexion of second and third joints

handicap physical malfunction that causes partial or total inability to perform an activity

harelip congenital cleft in upper lip due to failure of embryonic tissue of lip to fuse properly

heart defects congenital anomalies in circulatory system during embryonic development, causing murmurs and hypertension

hemiplegia paralysis of one side of body only

hereditary defect congenital defect inherited from one's parents through genes

heterotropia strabismus

humpback enlarged, rounded deformation of upper back; hunchback; kyphosis

hunchback humpback

hyperopia condition in which parallel light rays focus behind retina, causing blurred appearance of objects closer than 20 feet (6 m); farsightedness

hypospadias congenital abnormality in which opening of urethra is on underside of penis

idiocy severe mental subnormality with IQ under 20, due to physical brain damage

knock-knee abnormal incurving of legs that causes gap between feet when knees touch and leads to degenerative arthritis

kyphosis humpback

lameness condition of having a limb disabled enough to impair normal movement, esp. walking

learning disabilities various conditions, esp. nervous system disorders such as dyslexia, that interfere with the ability to learn to read and write

lordosis accentuation of inward curvature of lower back or neck, causing swaybacked appearance; swayback

malformation physical deformity or abnormality

malocclusion irregularity between teeth of upper and lower jaw that causes overbite or underbite

mental retardation deficiency from birth in some mental functions, often from congenital condition such as Down's syndrome

microcephalic (*adj*) having a smaller-than-normal head

mongolism Down's syndrome

mutation altered inherited characteristic due to genetic change

muteness inability to speak due to congenital condition, disease, or injury

myopia condition in which parallel light rays focus in front of retina, causing blurred appearance of objects farther than 20 feet (6 m); nearsightedness

nearsightedness myopia

neural tube defect any congenital abnormality caused by failure of closure of embryonic neural tube from which brain and spinal cord develop

neurofibromatosis inherited genetic disorder characterized by bumps and patches on skin and sometimes skeletal deformity; elephant man's disease

nevus birthmark

night blindness inability to see in dim light or at night, due to disorder of cells in retina, caused esp. by vitamin A deficiency

nystagmus congenital or acquired, persistent, rapid, involuntary movement of eyeball, usu. from side to side

otosclerosis deafness commencing in adulthood due to disorder of bones in middle ear

palsy rare term for paralysis

paralysis muscle weakness of varying severity due to injury or disease, total paralysis resulting in motor inability

paraparesis weakness of both legs due to central nervous system disease

paraplegia paralysis of both legs due to disease or spinal injury

paresis muscular weakness and mental deterioration, less severe than paralysis, due to neurological disease, esp. syphilitic infection

phenylketonuria PKU; birth defect in protein metabolism that causes damage to nervous system and severe mental retardation

pigeon toes toes with abnormal inward turning, associated with knock-knee

PKU phenylketonuria

presbyopia farsightedness in which lens of eye is unable to focus properly

quadriplegia paralysis of both legs and both arms due to disease or spinal injury

scoliosis S-shaped lateral curvature of spine due to congenital or acquired abnormalities of vertebrae or muscles

senile dementia progressive, irreversible impairment of cognitive function in old age

Siamese twins identical twins joined at birth

speech disorders language defects due to organic or sensory deficiency, poor speech mechanisms, or psychological disorders

spina bifida congenital cleft of vertebral column

squint strabismus

strabismus any abnormal alignment of eyes due to muscle imbalance; heterotropia; squint

stuttering speech disorder characterized by blocks or spasms that interrupt normal speech rhythm

subnormality state of arrested or incomplete mental development due to congenital defect, injury, or gross environmental deprivation

swayback lordosis

talipes clubfoot

tardive dyskinesia nervous system disorder characterized by facial tics and involuntary motor movements, often caused by antipsychotic drugs

Tay-Sachs disease inherited disorder of lipid metabolism that causes blindness, mental retardation, and death in infancy

walleye strabismus in which eye turns outward, showing more white than normal

Injuries and Accidents

abarticulation dislocation of joint

abrasion wearing away of surface of skin or mucous membrane by rubbing or scraping; scrape

accident unexpected or unintended occurrence that causes physical harm or injury

acute abdomen emergency condition caused by damage to one or more abdominal organs that results in intense pain and shock

aneurysm balloonlike swelling of arterial wall

avulsion tearing or separation of part or tissue

black eye bruising of eyelid and area around eye's orbit

blood blister swelling just beneath skin filled with blood, caused by unaccustomed friction

blow sudden, hard stroke against body surface with hard object

break simple or compound fracture of bone

bruise skin discoloration caused by escape of blood under skin following injury; contusion

bump bruising blow to body without breaking of skin

burn first, second, or third degree injury and damage to skin and subcutaneous tissue caused by heat, fire, wind, radiation, or caustic substance

cerebral hemorrhage bleeding from cerebral artery into brain tissue

charley horse injury to arm or leg in which muscles, blood vessels, nerves, and other soft tissues are damaged and cramp up

chilblain red, round, itchy swelling of skin on fingers or toes due to exposure to cold

chip small, thin piece broken loose from bone

collapsed lung folding together and contracting of lung due to air in surrounding chest cavity; pneumothorax

compound fracture breakage of bone into multiple fragments, sometimes with bone end piercing overlying skin

concussion injury to brain from violent, jarring blow to head, often with limited period of unconsciousness and impaired brain function

contrecoup injury to body part due to blow on opposite side away from injury

contusion surface injury in which skin is not broken; bruise

crack minor fracture that causes fissure in bone but not separation of bone parts

cut pierced or broken skin

detached retina separation of retina from layer of eyeball, causing loss of vision

dislocation displacement of bone from proper position in joint

embolism obstruction of artery by lodged blood clot, fat, air, or foreign body carried by circulating blood

first-degree burn reddening of outer layer of skin

fissure crack in bone or thin cleft in tissue

flash burn destruction of body tissue by exposure to radiant heat, esp. from nuclear explosion

fracture simple or compound breakage of bone

frostbite tissue damage from exposure to intense cold, esp. freezing of tissue and cessation of blood circulation

gash deep, ragged cut through skin

hernia protrusion of tissue or organ outside cavity it normally occupies, esp. in lower abdomen, due to physical strain or coughing

herniated disk slipped disk

injury physical damage to body part by action of external force

laceration tear in flesh, esp. with irregular edges

maiming injury that causes loss or crippling of body part

miscarriage spontaneous abortion and expulsion of fetus, usu. between 12th and 28th weeks of pregnancy

mutilation removal of or severe damage to essential body part

perforation piercing of skin and underlying tissue, or of any hollow viscus, by sharp object; puncture

pneumothorax collapsed lung

poisoning condition produced by introduction of natural or synthetic toxic substance into body or sometimes by toxin produced by organism itself

pull strain of muscle or ligament

puncture wound made by sharp object, with small entry hole and little or no bleeding

rupture forcible tearing apart or bursting of organ; hernia

scald burn inflicted by hot liquid or steam

scrape abrasion

scratch superficial lengthwise abrasion

second-degree burn blistering of surface skin and damage to underlying dermis

separation disarticulation of bone from normal joint position

simple fracture clean breakage of bone at one site without piercing of skin

slash long, sweeping deep cut made with blade

slice thin cut through skin and underlying tissue

slipped disk abnormal protrusion of disk between abutting vertebrae, esp. in lumbar region, causing painful pressure against spinal cord; herniated disk

soft tissue damage generalized injury to tissue without damage to bones or organs

spontaneous abortion birth or expulsion of fetus before it has developed enough for independent survival

sprain excessive overstretching of ligament

strain excessive stretching of muscle

stress fracture hairline break, often in bone of lower leg, due to intense physical activity

stub bumping of foot or toe against immovable object

suffocation cutting off of supply of air, esp. by strangling of throat or smothering of mouth and nose

sunburn burn due to overexposure to sunlight, usu. first degree

tear ripping or pulling apart of muscle; ragged cut in skin

third-degree burn total destruction of skin and damage to tissue beneath

trauma physical wound or injury, esp. one causing shock

whiplash damage to ligaments, vertebrae, and spinal cord in neck caused by sudden jerking back of head, esp. in auto accident

wound external injury in which skin is broken, torn, or pierced

Signs and Symptoms

abscess localized accumulation of pus surrounded by inflamed tissue

adenoma benign tumor of glandular origin or structure

adhesion union by fibrous connective tissue of two normally separate parts

albuminuria presence of protein albumin in urine

anesthesia loss of sensation in part or all of body

angina feeling of suffocation; chest pain

angina pectoris pain in center of chest that spreads to jaws and arms, due to insufficient blood supply to heart

ankylosis fusion of bones across joint

anxiety fear neurosis that dominates personality

apnea temporary cessation of breathing

arrhythmia irregularity or deviation from normal rhythm or force of heartbeat

asphyxiation suffocation; failure of oxygen to reach tissues due to respiratory obstruction

asthma difficulty in breathing due to recurrent bronchospasm

ataxia shaky movements and unsteady gait when brain fails to regulate posture or direction of limb movements

atony lack of normal elastic muscle tone

atrophy wasting away of normally developed organ or tissue due to degeneration of cells

attrition normal wearing away of surface of teeth

bacteremia presence of bacteria in blood, indicating infection

bad breath halitosis

bedsore skin ulceration due to continuous pressure and rubbing on body part

belch audible expulsion of intestinal gas through mouth

bellyache *Informal.* pain in stomach

black-and-blue mark ecchymosis

blackhead black clump of fatty sebum and keratin in outlet of sebaceous gland; comedo

blackout temporary loss of consciousness, vision, or memory

blennorrhagia heavy discharge of mucus, esp. from urethra

blister external swelling that contains watery fluid and blood or pus, caused by friction

bradycardia slowing of heart rate to under fifty beats per minute

brain damage congenital or acquired injury to tissues of brain, due esp. to inadequate oxygen supply, trauma, incomplete brain development, or disease, manifested by range of symptoms from impaired speech to retardation to vegetative state

break wind audibly expel intestinal gas through anus

breathlessness dyspnea

bronchospasm muscular contraction that narrows bronchi and causes difficulty esp. in exhalation

bruit any abnormal sound or murmur heard esp. with a stethoscope

bubo swollen and inflamed lymph node in armpit or groin

burp *Informal.* audible expulsion of intestinal gas through mouth

cachexia weight loss, weakness, and debility associated with chronic disease

calculus pebblelike mass, such as gallstone or kidney stone, formed within body; hard tartar layer formed on teeth by plaque

callus hard thickening of area of skin undergoing rubbing, esp. on hands or feet; mass of tissue forming around fractured bone ends

cardiac arrest abrupt cessation of heartbeat, causing loss of pulse, consciousness, and breathing

caries decay of bone tissue, esp. tooth; cavity

catarrh excessive secretion of thick phlegm or mucus by mucous membrane of nose

cavity hollow in tooth produced by carious decay

cephalalgia headache

chancre painless ulcer on lips, genitals, urethra, or eyelid

Cheyne-Stokes respiration cyclical slowing of breathing to cessation, then speeding up to peak

chills coldness and shivering esp. during fever

choking obstruction of windpipe, causing partial or complete stoppage of breathing

cicatrix scar

clubbing thickening of tissue at base of fingernail or toenail, esp. enlargement of fingertip

cold sore small swelling or eruption of skin around lips that dries to leave crusty patch; fever blister

colic severe abdominal pain, usu. in waves, due to gas or intestinal obstruction; inexplicable crying in infancy

collapse sudden, severe failure of health; falling down from upright position

collywobbles *Informal.* bellyache

coma prolonged state of deep unconsciousness from which patient cannot be roused

comedo blackhead

concretion stony mass coated with calcium deposits in internal organ; calculus

confusion mental disorder, distraction, or inability to distinguish things clearly

congestion accumulation of blood within an organ; clogging of upper respiratory system with mucus

constipation infrequent, difficult, often painful bowel movements with hard feces; irregularity

convulsion involuntary muscle contraction that causes contorted movements of body and limbs

cough violent exhalation of irritant particles or congestive mucus from respiratory system; tussis

cramp prolonged painful contraction or spasm of muscle

crepitation soft crackling sound heard in lungs through stethoscope; rale

crepitus crackling sound made by grating of bone on bone or cartilage, esp. in arthritic joint

crick painful muscle spasm or cramp in neck or upper back

cyanosis bluish discoloration of skin and mucous membrane due to inadequate oxygenation of blood

cyst abnormal sac or cavity lined with epithelium and filled with liquid or semisolid substance

decrepit (*adj*) wasted away or weakened by, or as if by, old age

dehiscence splitting open of a wound

detumescence reduction or subsidence of swelling

deviation abnormal position, esp. of one or both eyes

diaphoresis excessive sweating, esp. when artificially induced

diarrhea frequent bowel evacuation, esp. of soft or liquid feces; Montezuma's revenge; runs

dizziness feeling off balance, unstable, confused, as though whirling in place

dumping syndrome faintness, sweating, and paleness due to rapid emptying of stomach, esp. in one who has had gastrectomy

dyspepsia digestive disorder with abdominal pain and gas after eating, sometimes with nausea and vomiting; indigestion

dyspnea labored or difficult breathing; breathlessness

earache pain in inner ear; otalgia

ecchymosis bluish black mark on skin from release of blood into tissues, usu. due to injury; black-and-blue mark

eclampsia convulsions, esp. due to toxemia during pregnancy

efflorescence skin eruption, rash, or other lesion

emaciation severe weight loss and wasting of body from malnutrition, cancer, tuberculosis, or parasites

emesis vomiting; vomited matter

empyema accumulation of pus in body cavity, esp. pleural cavity

enervation weakness, lack of energy

epistaxis attack of bleeding from the nose

eruption skin irritation, esp. rash

excitation state of uncontrollable mental activity

exhaustion extreme fatigue

exophthalmic goiter enlargement of thyroid gland accompanied by protrusion of eyeball from orbit

fainting temporary loss of consciousness due to insufficient flow of blood to brain; syncope

fart *Vulgar.* audible expulsion of intestinal gas through anus

fatigue intense, prolonged tiredness

febrile (*adj*) affected with fever

fever rise in body temperature above normal 98.6 degrees F, often accompanied by delirium when over 104 degrees F; pyrexia

fever blister swelling or eruption of skin around lips with high or prolonged fever; cold sore

fibrillation rapid, uncontrolled irregular twitching of heart muscle

fissure crack in membrane lining

flatulence expulsion of intestinal gas through mouth by belching or through anus by passing flatus

flatus intestinal gas

flush reddening of face and/or neck

flux abnormally copious flow from organ or body cavity

gas mixture of swallowed air and fermented contents of stomach; flatus; intestinal gas

glycosuria excretion of excess sugar in urine, as in diabetes

goose bumps goose flesh

goose flesh tiny puckers of skin with hair standing on end due to contraction of blood vessels and small muscle attached to base of each hair follicle; goose bumps; horripilation

granuloma nodule of connective tissue and capillaries associated with tuberculosis, syphilis, or nonorganic foreign bodies

growth abnormal formation on or in body; tumor

halitosis offensive breath, esp. from diseases of gums, teeth, throat, or lungs; bad breath

hallucination false perception of something not there, esp. visual image

headache pain within skull, commonly due to stress or fatigue; cephalalgia

heartburn pain rising from abdomen to throat, often accompanied by bitter fluid in mouth; pyrosis

heart murmur blowing or swishing noise produced by blood passing through defective heart valve

hematoma clotted accumulation of blood in tissue forming solid swelling

hemolysis abnormally high level of red blood cell destruction, usu. due to toxins or hereditary defects

hemorrhage outflow of blood from ruptured blood vessel, esp. internal bleeding

hiccup characteristic sound made by abrupt involuntary lowering of diaphragm and closing of upper end of trachea

high blood pressure elevation of pressure of blood in main arteries above normal range for age group; hypertension

horripilation goose flesh

hydrocele accumulation of watery fluid, esp. about testis

hyperglycemia excess of sugar in bloodstream, esp. due to diabetes mellitus

hyperplasia increase in number of fat cells, causing obesity

hypersensitivity uncommonly strong reaction to stimulus such as sunlight or a chemical, including most allergies

hypertension high blood pressure

hyperthermia exceptionally high body temperature of 105 degrees F or above; fever induced as treatment

hypertrophy increase in size of tissue or organ due to enlargement of cells

hyperventilation abnormally rapid breathing that lowers carbon dioxide concentration in blood

hypopraxia listlessness, enfeeblement, or lack of interest in activity

hypotension low blood pressure

hypothermia dropping of body temperature below normal range

hysteria extreme emotional excitation, sensory and motor disturbances, and outbursts of uncontrolled feeling

illusion false perception due to misinterpreted stimuli; belief in existence of that which does not exist

incapacity inability to perform some action

incoherence inability to produce intelligible, logical speech or thought

incontinence inability to control passage of urine

indigestion dyspepsia

infirmity feebleness, frailty

inflammation immediate defense reaction of tissue to injury or attack, involving pain, heat, redness, and swelling

insomnia inability to fall asleep or remain asleep

intestinal gas gas; flatus

irregularity constipation

ischemia insufficient blood flow to body part due to constriction or blockage of blood vessels

itching minor local skin irritation relieved by scratching; pruritus

jaundice yellowing of skin and whites of eyes from excess bilirubin in blood, often due to obstructed ducts or liver disease

labored breathing difficulty in inhaling air

lesion any localized, abnormal structural change in tissue or body part resulting in impaired function, including abscess, ulcer, or tumor

leukocytosis abnormal level in number of white blood cells, usu. due to infection

leukopenia reduction in number of white blood cells to below normal level

lightheadedness dizziness, mental confusion

lividity bluish coloration of skin

low blood pressure dropping of pressure of blood in main arteries below normal range for age

low-grade fever slight rise in body temperature above normal 98.6 degrees F

lumbago lower backache due to injury or sciatica

macule discoloration or thickening of skin in contrast to surrounding area

malaise general sense of being unwell, often accompanied by physical discomfort and weakness

mania excessive activity and euphoria

Montezuma's revenge *Slang.* diarrhea, usu.

caused by eating contaminated food in foreign country

mottling blotches, streaks, or spots on skin

mucus viscous fluid secreted by mucous membrane, esp. in upper respiratory tract

nasal discharge drainage of mucus through nose

nausea feeling that one is about to vomit

necrosis death of cells in organ or tissue

neoplasm new tumor caused by uncontrolled reproduction of abnormal cells

nephralgia pain in kidney and loin area

neuralgia severe burning or stabbing pain along course of nerve

neurasthenia outdated or nontechnical term for fatigue, irritability, headache, dizziness, anxiety, and intolerance to noise due to head injury or mental illness

night sweats copious perspiration while sleeping

nit louse egg that attaches to body

obesity distinct, intense accumulation of excess fat in body

otalgia earache

pain sensation of strong discomfort in bodily part

palpitation abnormally rapid or violent heartbeat, esp. due to fear, exertion, neurosis, or arrhythmia

papule small, superficial bump or spot on skin, often part of rash

paroxysm sudden, violent spasm or convulsion; abrupt worsening of symptom

perspiration sweating

phlegm sputum

pimple small, pustulant, inflamed swelling on skin, often from bacterial infection

plaque sticky, colorless mixture of saliva, bacteria, and carbohydrates on surface of teeth that causes tartar and caries

pock small pus-filled eruption of skin

poliosis premature graying of hair

polyp benign growth on mucous membrane, esp. in nose, ear, or stomach

postnasal drip draining of mucus from nose onto pharynx

proptosis forward displacement of an organ, esp. eyeball

prostration total exhaustion

pruritus itching

purpura skin rash due to bleeding into skin from defective capillaries or blood platelet deficiency

pus thick yellow or green liquid containing blood cells and dead cells, formed at site of infection or inflammation

pustule small, pus-containing skin blister

putrescence foul smell caused by decomposition of tissue

pyrexia fever

pyrosis heartburn

rale crepitation

rash temporary skin eruption characterized by reddening and itching, esp. in form of pimples, hives, or wheals

regurgitation vomiting

renal colic severe pain in kidney

respiratory arrest cessation of breathing

rheum watery discharge from mucous membrane of mouth, eyes, or nose

runny nose discharge of mucus from nose

runs *Informal.* diarrhea

scab hard crust of blood, serum, or pus over healing wound

scar mark left on skin by healing wound where connective tissues replace damaged tissues; cicatrix

seizure sudden attack of disease or condition

senescence bodily degeneration after maturity

senility loss of intellectual faculties in old age

shin splint pain in front of shin, usu. caused by running on hard surface

shivers uncontrollable trembling

shock acute, progressive circulatory collapse, with blood pressure too low to maintain adequate blood supply to tissues, causing cold sweat, paleness, weak but rapid pulse, dilated pupils, irregular breathing, dry mouth, and reduced urine flow

side effect incidental or secondary manifestation, esp. of medication

sign physical, psychological, or behavioral manifestation of a disease, injury, condition, or disability

skin eruption swelling, discoloration, or roughening of skin

sneeze involuntary violent reflex expulsion of air caused by irritation of mucous membrane lining nasal cavity

sore ulcer or open wound on skin or mucous membrane from injury or infection

spasm sustained involuntary muscular contraction

spasticity resistance to passive movement of limb; lack of motor coordination

sputum mucus coughed up from respiratory tract; phlegm

stitch sudden, sharp pain, usu. in muscle between ribs

stomachache generalized intestinal pain, often accompanied by diarrhea, nausea, and vomiting

strangury painful urination in which the urine is emitted in droplets due to muscle spasms

stridor loud, harsh breathing noise due to partial obstruction of trachea or larynx

suppuration formation and discharge of pus

sweating secretion of salty, watery fluid by glands lying in dermis of skin; perspiration

swelling growth of body part, curving outward from surface, esp. due to pressure from within; tumescence

sycosis inflammation and itching of hair follicles

symptom indication of disease or disorder, esp. one recognizable by patient

syncope fainting

syndrome combination of signs and symptoms

tachycardia rapid heart rate

tachypnea rapid breathing

tartar calcareous deposit and encrustation on teeth

tetany spasm and twitching of muscles of face, hands, and feet

throw up (*vb*) vomit

tic uncontrolled muscle twitch, esp. in face

tic douloureux neuralgia of facial nerves

tinnitus ringing in the ears

toothache pain associated with teeth, gums, and surrounding tissue, usu. due to tooth decay or caries

torpor sluggishness, unresponsiveness to stimuli

toxemia accumulation of toxins in blood

toxicosis reaction to toxin in body; poisoning

toxic shock shock syndrome caused by toxin in body, often associated with tampon use

tremor uncontrollable, rhythmical alternating movement of body part, esp. hands

tubercle nodular lesion of lung due to tuberculosis

tumescence swelling, esp. due to accumulation of blood or other fluid in tissue

tumor abnormal growth of tissue in or on body part

tussis cough

unconsciousness lack of awareness of one's surroundings and unresponsiveness to stimuli; state of being asleep

underweight state of insufficient or subnormal accumulation of body fat

uremia toxic condition due to presence in blood of excess urea and other nitrogenous wastes excreted by kidney

vesicle very small skin blister containing clear serum

vital signs pulse rate, blood pressure, respiration, and body temperature, forming index of essential body functions

vomiting reflex ejection of contents of stomach through mouth; emesis; regurgitation

watery eyes eyes that discharge rheum or tears

welt raised ridge on skin caused by slash or blow

wheal temporary, itching, red or pale raised area of skin due to abrasion or allergy

wheezing high-pitched breathing sounds due to bronchospasm

withdrawal symptoms sweating, anxiety, nausea, vomiting, cramps, and tremors at cessation of addictive substance abuse

withering drying out or shriveling of patch of skin

xerostomia diminished secretion of saliva that causes abnormally dry mouth, esp. as drug reaction

zit *Slang.* pimple

Diagnostic Terminology

abnormality malformed part or dysfunctional process

abruptio separation

acquired (*adj*) designating condition or disorder contracted after birth, not hereditary

active immunity production of antibodies by body's cells following attack of disease or immunization

acute (*adj*) designating disease with rapid onset, severe symptoms, and brief duration, opposite of chronic

affliction condition that causes pain and suffering

agonal (*adj*) describing phenomena associated with death, such as cessation of breathing or heartbeat

allergen antigen that causes allergy in sensitive person

ambulatory (*adj*) designating patient who is able to leave bed and walk

ameba single-celled, microscopic organism that may cause disease

anodynia absence of pain

antibiotic substance derived from a microorganism or fungus that destroys or inhibits growth of other microorganisms

antibody special blood protein synthesized in lymphoid tissue in response to antigen, which it attacks and neutralizes

antigen foreign substance, usu. protein, against which body produces an antibody

arbovirus RNA-containing virus that can cause disease when transmitted from animals to humans by insects

asepsis complete absence of disease-causing bacteria, viruses, fungi, or microorganisms

asymptomatic (*adj*) showing no evidence of a disease

atresia congenital absence or abnormal narrowing of body opening

autoimmune (*adj*) designating disorder of body's defense mechanism in which antibodies are produced against body's own tissues, treating them as foreign substances

autologous (*adj*) derived from same individual or organism

autonomic (*adj*) occurring involuntarily, controlled by autonomic nervous system

bacillus rod-shaped bacterium

bacteria *pl., sing.* **bacterium**; primitive microorganisms, usu. unicellular with unique cell wall composition, that reproduce by simple division and often cause disease

bacterial (*adj*) designating disease, condition, or infection caused by bacteria

bedridden (*adj*) descriptive of patient unable to leave bed

benign (*adj*) consisting of localized mass of nonmalignant specialized cells within connective tissue that do not invade and destroy tissue or spread throughout body

blood alcohol content measure of alcohol concentration in blood; blood alcohol level

blood pressure pressure of blood in main arteries

breech presentation abnormal position of baby in womb, causing it to be delivered buttocks first

carcinogen substance that may produce cancer in living tissue

carrier individual that harbors pathogen without displaying symptoms

cast mass of dead, cellular, fatty material within body cavity that takes the shape of the cavity and can be released to appear elsewhere

cerebral (*adj*) of the brain

chronic (*adj*) designating disease of long duration with very slow changes and often gradual onset of recurrent symptoms, opposite of acute

clot soft, thickened lump formed in liquid, esp. blood

coccus spherical bacterium

communicable (*adj*) designating disease that can be transmitted from one person to another by physical contact, a carrier, or droplets exhaled into air

condition something causing state of poor health; official status of hospitalized patient, such as grave, critical, serious, poor, guarded, stable, fair, satisfactory, or good

congenital (*adj*) designating condition present at birth, often inherited

contagious (*adj*) designating any communicable disease, esp. one transmitted by physical contact

contract (*vb*) acquire a disease

coronary (*adj*) of or pertaining to arteries of heart

cortical (*adj*) involving external layers of brain

cryptogenic (*adj*) of unknown origin

cytomegalovirus DNA virus in herpes family that causes enlargement of epithelial cells and mononucleosislike disease

defect abnormal functioning, physical flaw or blemish

deformity abnormal or disfigured body part

degenerative (*adj*) designating disease or condition growing progressively worse due to deterioration in cell structure or function

deterioration worsening of condition

diagnosis process of determining by examination the nature of a disease or condition

disability condition that makes one unfit, incapacitated, or crippled

discharge liquid or semisolid substance emitted from body

disease particular disorder of organism with specific cause and recognizable symptoms

disorder any bodily abnormality or failure to function

DOA dead on arrival: describing patient's condition on reaching hospital

dose-response phenomenon condition in which there is increased risk with greater exposure to toxic substance

dysfunction abnormality, impairment, or cessation of bodily function

dystrophy faulty nutrition; disorder characterized by abnormal development of muscle

embolus blood clot, fat, air, amniotic fluid, or foreign body circulated by blood and lodged at some point in cardiovascular system

endemic disease that is constantly present in particular region but generally under control

epidemic contagious disease that spreads rapidly through population of a specific region

etiology cause of specific disease

failure total cessation of bodily function

fastigium point at which symptoms of disease are most pronounced

fatal (*adj*) causing death

fistula abnormal passage that leads from abscess or cavity to skin or to another abscess or cavity, caused by disease or injury

genetic (*adj*) designating condition inherited through chromosomes from one's parents

germ any disease-causing microorganism

gusher *Informal.* cut artery

hereditary (*adj*) designating condition transmitted from parents to offspring

hypochondria obsession with real and imagined physical ailments

iatrogenic (*adj*) resulting from treatment, esp. of a condition or disease

idiopathic (*adj*) describing condition of unknown cause or one that develops spontaneously

immunity ability of body to recognize and neutralize foreign matter, either natural or acquired

impairment damage to or weakening of body part or function

inborn immunity congenital resistance to specific disease

incubation period time between entry of disease organisms into body and onset of disease symptoms

infarction death of tissue due to oxygen deprivation

infection invasion of body by harmful pathogen

infectious (*adj*) designating a communicable disease, esp. one caused by invasion of harmful organisms such as bacterium, fungus, protozoan, or virus into body

infestation attack on body by parasitic microorganism

injury physical damage to body part by action of external force

intervention treatment or procedure designed to prevent disease from running its course

intramuscular (*adj*) situated in or administered by entering a muscle, used esp. of injections

irreversible (*adj*) impossible to halt or reverse by treatment

languishing (*adj*) failing in health, weakening, losing vigor

life-threatening (*adj*) designating a potentially fatal condition or procedure

malabsorption failure to digest certain nutrients or disruption of process by which digestive by-products are passed through intestinal wall into bloodstream

malignant (*adj*) consisting of a tumor that invades and destroys tissue in which it originates and can spread to other sites in body through vascular system

metastasis spread of malignant tumor far from site of origin, usu. through vascular system

microbe microorganism

microorganism any organism not visible to naked eye, such as bacterium, protozoan, fungus, and virus; microbe

mold multicellular filamentous fungus

morbidity state of being diseased

morbific (*adj*) causing disease

moribund (*adj*) dying

mortify (*vb*) cause body tissue to decay

motor (*adj*) designating muscular activity stimulated by impulses from central nervous system

mutagen external agent that increases mutation rate in cells

mycosis infection due to yeast or mold

natural immunity inborn lack of susceptibility to specific disease

necrosis death of discrete region of tissue

nosocomial (*adj*) hospital-induced, used esp. of a disease

occlusion closing or obstruction of hollow organ or body part

opportunistic (*adj*) designating disease or infection occurring only under certain conditions, as when immune system is impaired

pandemic (*adj*) designating epidemic disease that spreads to different countries over large region

parasite organism that lives in or on another living organism while contributing nothing to host's welfare, often causing irritation or interfering with function

passive immunity short-term resistance to disease from injection of another's antibodies

pathogen microorganism that produces a communicable disease

pathogenic (*adj*) disease-causing

pathology study of disease processes; course of a disease

perfusion passage of fluid through tissue, esp. blood through lungs

plasma liquid in which blood cells are suspended

prognosis assessment of future course and outcome of patient's disease

progressive (*adj*) growing steadily worse, often fatal

psychomotor (*adj*) relating to disorders of muscular activity affected by cerebral disturbances

psychosomatic (*adj*) designating a disease caused by interaction of physical and mental factors

purulent (*adj*) pustulant

pustulant (*adj*) containing and/or discharging pus; purulent

referred pain pain felt in unexpected part of body separate from its source

reflex automatic, involuntary activity caused by simple nervous circuits

rejection immune reaction to transplanted organ or foreign substance

relapse recurrence of disease symptoms after apparent recovery

remission lessening of severity of symptoms, esp. temporary disappearance during course of chronic or terminal illness

resistance measure of body's immunity to disease; degree to which disease is unaffected by antibiotics or drugs

rickettsiae group of parasitic organisms similar to bacteria that infest body through ticks or mites

saprophyte free-living organism that lives on dead or putrefying tissues

scabbing formation of hard crust of blood, serum, and pus over healing wound

scourge wasting disease that affects large region

septic (*adj*) affected with putrefactive destruction by disease-carrying bacteria or their toxins

serum fluid that separates from clotted blood or standing blood plasma

spirillum spiral bacterium

spirochete corkscrew-shaped bacterium

spore small reproductive body produced by microorganisms

staphylococcus any of several spherical, pathogenic bacteria in irregular clusters, both saprophytes and parasites

stenosis abnormal narrowing of blood vessel or heart valve

streptobacillus any of various rodlike bacteria that tend to form filaments

streptococcus any of several spherical, chain-forming pathogenic bacteria, mostly saprophytes

stress effect on human body of physical and mental demands and pressures

subclinical (*adj*) designating suspected disease or injury that is not developed enough to produce definite signs and symptoms

symptom characteristic indication of disease or disorder

syndrome set of signs and symptoms indicative of particular disease or condition

systemic (*adj*) affecting entire body, not just one part

teratogen substance or process that causes developmental abnormalities in fetus

terminal (*adj*) fatal; in or of final stage of fatal disease

touch *Informal.* mild onset of illness

toxic (*adj*) poisonous

toxin poisonous substance

vector any agent, such as insect or tick, that transmits parasitic microorganisms and infectious diseases from host to host

viral (*adj*) produced by a virus

viral infection infection caused by virus

virulent (*adj*) disease-producing

virus ultramicroscopic, metabolically inert agent composed of DNA or RNA core and protein coating, capable of replication only within living host cells; *Informal.* disease caused by a virus

wasting (*adj*) severely destructive to health

yeast unicellular fungus that usu. reproduces asexually by budding

zoonosis any infectious disease of animals, such as rabies, that can be transmitted to humans

HEALTH, FITNESS, AND ENHANCEMENT
Activities and Treatments
Equipment and Resources
Martial Arts
Nutrition for Fitness

See also: *Chap. 1: Hair and Grooming; Chap. 2: Biology; Chap. 4: Medicine; Chap. 9: Cooking and Cuisine; Chap. 17: Games, Activities, and Toys; Chap. 25: Truth, Wisdom, and Spiritual Attainment*

Activities and Treatments

acupressure massage therapy technique that uses acupuncture points to release tension and promote relaxation and healing; shiatsu

acupuncture Chinese practice of puncturing body with needles at specific points along meridians to relieve pain and cure disease

aerobic dance vigorous cardiovascular exercise that incorporates dance movements

aerobics vigorous exercise that induces accelerated heartbeat to improve cardiovascular health

aikido Japanese martial art form

Alexander technique *Trademark.* body alignment and coordination through efficient movement and stress release

Ayurveda ancient Indian medical system of classifying and treating somatic types for optimal health and functioning

biofeedback technique that involves instrument stress readings and training of bodily systems to increase awareness and control of pain and tension

bodybuilding development of muscle layer through program of weightlifting and nutritional supplements

body contouring cosmetic surgery to reshape body outline

body mechanics science and study of bodily motion, esp. for optimal benefits of exercise

body work physical therapy, healing, or relaxation treatments based on a particular system, such as polarity, yoga, Alexander, Reiki, acupressure, Rolfing, shiatsu, or massage therapy

body wrap herbal, steam, or heat weight-loss treatment

breast augmentation surgical silicone implantation in breast for cosmetic enhancement

breast reduction surgical removal of excess breast tissue

breathing exercises practice of deep, regular breathing to increase lung capacity, improve overall health, and relieve tension

buddy system pairing of two individuals for mutual safety in dangerous activity

bulking increasing size of muscles by weight work

calisthenics individual gymnastic exercises

cap artificial coating of teeth to enhance size, shape, and whiteness

cardiopulmonary resuscitation CPR; procedure to restore normal breathing and heart activity after cardiac arrest, by heart massage and often electrical and mechanical equipment

cardiorespiratory endurance stamina of heart and lungs during exercise

cellulite reduction treatment to diminish irregular fatty tissue deposits, esp. on thighs and buttocks

chemical peel cosmetic chemical burning of facial skin to promote new, smooth skin growth

chiropractic adjustment manipulation of spine to relieve tension, pressure, and imbalances in bones, muscles, and nerves

circuit training system that uses series of weight machines to work all muscle areas

collagen injection implantation of collagen into wrinkles and folds to improve appearance of skin

colonic irrigation treatment involving cleansing of colon with water to flush toxic impurities

cooldown period of gentle, reduced activity after vigorous exercise

cosmetic surgery surgical alteration of face or body for aesthetic enhancement; plastic surgery

CPR cardiopulmonary resuscitation

crunch sit-up in which one reaches out with arms toward bent knees

dancercise system of vigorous dance movements done to music for fitness

dermabrasion process of stripping top layer of facial skin to promote new, smooth skin growth

detoxification program of exercise, nutrition, and cleansing of system to remove pollutants from body, esp. narcotics or alcohol

diet specific program of food preparation and eating to enhance health and appearance

endurance stamina, capacity for prolonged exercise

ergonomics study or practice of adapting working environment to needs of body

exercise physical activity performed to enhance health and appearance

eye tuck cosmetic surgery to remove excess skin folds around eyes

face-lift cosmetic surgery to remove excess facial skin folds and wrinkles

fast period of abstention from food; (*vb*) abstain from eating for prolonged period

Feldenkrais method *Trademark.* system of exploration and adjustment of movement patterns for flexibility, coordination, and dynamic posture

first aid simple medical procedures for health and safety

fitness maintenance and improvement of health through exercise and proper diet; condition of being in good health

flexibility degree of movement, rotation possible in body and joints

hamstring stretch bending exercise for back of thigh

Heimlich maneuver procedure that involves clearing windpipe of choking victim by sudden upward pressure on abdomen

herbalism use of herbs for healing

holistic health approach that stresses complete system rather than treatment of specific parts and symptoms, based on theory that entity is more than sum of its parts

isometric exercise system that uses muscle groups acting in opposition or against a fixed object

isotonic exercise system that uses normal contraction of muscles

jazzercise vigorous aerobic exercises done to fast-paced music

jogging gentle, medium-slow running gait, esp. as regular program of exercise

jujitsu Japanese martial art based on use of opponent's weight against him or her through leverage and understanding of anatomy

jumping jack calisthenic exercise that involves jumping and reaching up simultaneously

karate Japanese martial art form usu. used for defense by striking sensitive areas of attacker's body with hands, elbows, legs, or feet

kinesiology principles of anatomy and mechanics in human movement

kung fu Chinese martial art form usu. used for defense by striking vulnerable parts of attacker's body with hands and legs

lifesaving training in activities connected with saving of human life, esp. from drowning

liposuction surgical removal of excess body fat by suctioning it away through a tube

low-impact aerobics gentle form of aerobic exercise, with reduced stress to feet and joints

marathon running long-distance running, traditionally over twenty-six mile course

martial arts Asian forms of exercise and self-defense that emphasize balance and harmony of passive and active motions

massage system of relaxation using hands to knead, rub, stroke, and press body parts

mouth-to-mouth resuscitation method of blowing air directly into victim's mouth for artificial respiration

nose job *Informal.* rhinoplasty

overstretching excessively intense or abrupt stretching that results in torn or bruised muscle tissue

passive exercise machine electronic device that electrically stimulates muscles

physiotherapy massage, heat treatments, and other physical manipulations

plastic surgery cosmetic surgery

polarity therapy body work to balance magnetic polarization by manipulation, exercise, and diet

power lifting lifting substantial amounts of weight to increase muscle bulk

pulse rate heartbeats per minute; measure of exercise intensity and cardiovascular benefits

push-up exercise done by pushing upper body away from floor with arms to build upper body strength

race walking competitive speedwalking

reflexology massage of specific areas of foot, or sometimes hand, to treat ailments or relieve stress elsewhere in body

regime program or system of exercise and nutrition for better health; regimen

regimen regime

Reiki method of activating and balancing life force energy, used esp. by chiropractors and in massage

resistance training strengthening exercise incorporating muscle resistance to a sprung lever or similar device

rhinoplasty cosmetic surgery on the nose; nose job

Rolfing *Trademark.* physical therapy system that emphasizes realignment of body's internal dynamics through intense deep massage and stretching of connective tissue

rope jumping cardiovascular exercise done by jumping over rope held by jumper and rotated around body

rubdown vigorous massage

running physical fitness regime of running either long distances or short intense distances for maximum speed

shiatsu Japanese massage system that involves bodily points and meridians responsive to pressure; acupressure

silicone implant cosmetic surgery that involves buildup of bodily proportions by addition of silicone, esp. in breasts

sit-up abdominal exercise in which one bends upper body from supine position with legs flat

slimnastics gymnastic exercises specifically for weight reduction

speedwalking vigorous, quick walking exercise with arms swinging

stamina power to sustain effort or activity

step aerobics aerobic exercise using a stepping block

steroid any of various hormonal compounds that accelerate increase in muscle bulk from exercise, often with harmful side effects

strength ability to apply muscular force

stress management system of coping with stress and tension using biofeedback, relaxation techniques, and exercise

sunbathing exposing most or all of one's body to sun's rays, usu. for suntan

suntan darkened pigmentation of skin from exposure to sun

Swedish massage systematic massage that uses manipulation and gradual soothing of muscles and nervous system

swimnastics calisthenic exercises done while immersed in water

tae kwon do Korean martial art form that resembles karate

ta'i chi chu'an Chinese Taoist martial art form that emphasizes balance, graceful meditative movements, and coordinated breathing

taking the waters visiting a spa for beneficial effects of mineral spring water

tanning developing deeper skin tone from intentional exposure to sun's rays or sunlamp

toning firming muscles by moderate weight work without building bulk

tooth bonding cosmetic dental procedure of coating front surface of tooth for improved appearance

tooth capping cosmetic dental procedure of covering entire tooth with white enamel-like cap, for improved appearance

training regular pursuit of athletic activities to build strength and endurance or improve performance

triathletics exercise system that involves swimming, running, and bicycling over significant distances

walking least strenuous, most natural aerobic exercise

warmup brief period of stretching and loosening activity prior to vigorous exercise

weightlifting practice of lifting substantial amounts of weight to tone and strengthen muscles; weight work

weight work weightlifting

work out (*vb*) engage in period of strenuous exercise

workout strenuous exercise, esp. aerobic

wushu Chinese philosophical teachings that form the basis of certain martial arts

yoga system of physical postures and meditative breathing to tone muscles and organs, improve balance, flexibility, and strength, and create integration of mind and body

Equipment and Resources

aerobic trainer any of various devices used to facilitate an aerobic workout

ankle weights weighted straps worn on ankles while one exercises

barbell rod with weighted disks at both ends

bike pants tight-fitting elastic pants or shorts as worn by cylists

compression shorts tight-fitting elastic shorts designed to support thigh muscles

dojo karate or martial arts gymnasium

dumbbell hand-held weight; barbell

earplug piece of soft material inserted in outer ear to keep out noise or water

exercise machine mechanical device that aids weightlifting and muscle-toning exercises

exercycle stationary bicycle

fat farm *Informal.* weight-loss clinic at sanitarium or resort

free weights dumbbells or barbells; weights lifted without weight machines

gravity boots sturdy boots that hold wearer upside down

gymnasium enclosed area for physical activity, training, and contests

health club gymnasium, usu. for members only, with exercise and spa facilities

heating pad electric or water-heated pad for soothing sore muscles or injuries

hot tub whirlpool

hot water bag rubber container filled with hot water, used to soothe injured muscles

ice pack cold compress for sore or injured muscles or ligaments and pain reduction

isolation tank enclosed, sensory-deprivation container in which one floats, without stimuli, for deep relaxation

Jacuzzi *Trademark.* whirlpool spa with turbulent hot water

jump rope length of rope with handles, swung over head and under uplifted feet in jumping exercise

leg warmers knitted socklike garments that cover and warm lower legs during exercise

leotard tight, lightweight, knitted exercise garment for torso

Lifecycle *Trademark.* stationary exercise bicycle that measures rider's pulse and calories burned

life jacket buoyant, sleeveless jacket to prevent drowning; life vest

life net strong net used to catch people jumping from burning building

life preserver buoyant vest, jacket, or ring used to remain afloat in water

life vest life jacket

Mae West inflatable life jacket, esp. for aviator downed at sea

masseur male practitioner of massage

masseuse female practitioner of massage

medicine ball large, heavy ball for exercise and recreation

mineral bath immersion in mineral-rich waters, esp. at spa

mud bath immersion in mud formed by interaction of clay and hot spring water

Nautilus machines *Trademark.* system of weight training machines

Nordic Track *Trademark.* aerobic exercise machine that simulates the action of cross-country skiing

oxygen mask covering for mouth and nose connected to oxygen tank

parcourse outdoor running and exercise course, esp. in urban areas

prosthetic device artificial replacement for body part

punching bag inflated leather bag suspended at eye level for punching

rider aerobic exercise used in a seated position

rowing machine device that simulates exercise of rowing a boat with oars

running shoes rubber-soled shoes with good support for running or jogging

sauna Scandinavian steam bath that uses dry heat

Soloflex *Trademark.* strength-training machine with resistance provided by thick rubber bands

spa mineral spring resort; area of health club with sauna, steam room, and whirlpool

sports bra bra designed to give support and comfort during exercise or when playing sports

Stairmaster *Trademark.* stationary, adjustable electronic stairs for aerobic climbing exercise

stall bar series of horizontal wooden rungs between uprights, used for climbing or stretching exercises

stationary bicycle exercise bicycle for cardiovascular and muscular toning

steam room tiled room heated with abundant steam, for bathing, refreshment, sweating, and relaxation

sudatorium dry heat room, sauna

sunlamp electric light that produces ultraviolet tanning rays

sweatband headband worn to keep perspiration from dripping onto face during exercise

tanning salon establishment that uses sunlamps to cultivate artificial suntan

Thighmaster *Trademark.* exercise machine designed to strengthen the thighs using resistance training

track path for runners, usu. oval

treadmill rotary track for running or walking in place

Turkish bath steam bath

Universal machines *Trademark.* system of weight training machines

weight belt weighted strap worn around waist while exercising; wide leather belt worn as back support when lifting weights

weight loss clinic salon, spa, or gymnasium for weight reduction through diet and exercise

weight machine apparatus with weights suspended over pulleys and connected to handgrips, often with seat or bench

whirlpool tub in which jets or agitator propel current of hot water in soothing, swirling motion; hot tub

Martial Arts

aikido Japanese method of self-defense using various holds to throw one's opponent

ashi waza foot techniques

atemi the body, especially vital points considered as targets in karate

bo long staff

budo martial ways

bushi Japanese warrior class

bushido way of the warrior

chagi kick in tae kwan do

chudan torso

chui penalty in judo or jiu jitsu contests

chusoku ball of the foot

dachi stance

dan black-belt ranking in karate

do way of (life, art, etc.), used in combination (karate-do, the way of karate); protective breastplate worn by kendo fighters

dojo training or practice facility

empi elbow

encho-sen extension of a karate match to break a tie

fumikomi stamping kick in karate

gedan area below the belt or waist

geri (or keri) kick in karate

gi uniform for martial arts, consisting of trousers, jacket, and a colored belt indicating the wearer's level of competence in the sport

gohon five-finger strike

gyaku reverse

hachimaki headcloth worn by kendo fighters

hadake choke hold

hadan makki low block in tae kwan do

hai yes (Japanese)

haishu back of the hand

haisoku instep

hajime call made by the referee to begin a contest

hakama ankle-length divided skirt worn in kendo

hansoko-make disqualification penalty in judo contests

hansoku-chui penalty in karate contests

hantei referee's call at the end of an undecided contest

hara belly; lower abdomen

hidari left side

hiji elbow strike

hikiwake draw in a kendo match

hikkiwake draw in a aikido or jiu jitsu contest

hittsui knee

hiza knee

liun fingers

hosinsul concept of self-defense in tae kwan do

hyong form exercises in tae kwan do

ippon score of one point in a martial arts contest

jigo-tai defensive posture

jimi (*vb*) choke; strangle

jiu jitsu Japanese method of self-defense that emphasizes causing one's opponent to lose his or her balance (also jujitsu, jiu jutsu)

jo short staff

jodan head area; area above shoulders

judo East Asian method of self-defense without weapons that emphasizes throwing techniques

judoka practitioner of judo

kakato heel

kama sickle

kamae posture

kansetsu joint; joint lock

kareta-ka individual training in karate

karate Japanese method of self-defense without weapons that emphasizes striking the opponent

kata formal competition in aikido; stylized, pre-arranged forms or formal exercises in karate

katame grappling

katamewaza holding technique used in judo

katana long sword

keikogi shirt worn by kendo fighters

keikoku penalty in judo or karate contests

kekomi thrust

kendo traditional Japanese martial art using bamboo swords

kentsui hammer fist

keri (or geri) kick

keri waza kicking techniques

ki vital energy

kiai loud cry or shout given by fighters (also kihap, kiap)

kick boxing form of boxing that incorporates martial-art style kicking

kihon basic techniques in karate

kime focus

kio tsuke call for attention in karate

koshi ball of foot; hip

kote protective gauntlets worn by kendo fighters

kumikata methods of holding

kumite sparring; competition

kun motto; oath

kung fu Chinese martial art form

kusho kyu-sho

kyek pa breaking test (as of boards) in tae kwan do

kyu color belt ranking in karate for ranks under black belt

kyu-sho (or kusho) vital point, such as the temple, windpipe, sternum, solar plexus, groin, shin, back of knee, instep, etc.

mae front

makiwara punching board used in karate

matae stop

matte judge's request in jiu jitsu that action stop but with positions held

men protective mask worn by kendo fighters

migi right side

mokuso meditation; contemplation

nage throwing

nagewaza throwing technique used in judo

ne-waza techniques of fighting in judo when both contestants are on the ground

nikomme official's call to restart a kendo match after one point has been scored

ninja member of a Japanese society of mercenary warriors skilled in martial arts and stealth

nukite spear finger or spear hand

nunchaku weapon of two rods joined by rope or chain

obi belt tied over the jacket worn by martial arts practitioners

osaekomi pinning or holding down an opponent in a jiu jitsu contest

ouse acknowledgment; greeting

randori practice; sparring

rei bow

ryu traditional system or style of a martial arts school

sai three-pronged metal weapon

sanbon winning score in a karate contest

seiza kneeling or sitting position for meditation

sempai senior or advanced student

sensei teacher

shiai contest in martial arts

shiaijo contest area in judo

shido penalty in a judo contest

shihan master instructor

shikkaku penalty in a karate contest that results in disqualification shime choke

shin heart-mind

shinai bamboo sword used in kendo

shiro white

shuto knife-edge hand

sogi stances or body position in tae kwan do

soremade end of a round or a fight in aikido

sumo Japanese style of wrestling in which two usu. heavy-set contestants vie to force the opponent out of the ring or off his feet

tae kwan do Korean martial art based on karate, literally, "foot-fist-way," or a way of fighting using the feet and fists

t'ai chi (ch'uan) Chinese martial art form emphasizing balance and graceful, controlled movements

tanden point just below the navel

tanto short sword or knife

tare protective apron worn by kendo fighters

taeryon sparring in tae kwan do

tameshiware breaking (boards, etc.) in karate

te hand

tettsui hammer fist, a blow with the side of a closed fist

tobi jumping

toketa breaking a hold in jiu jitsu

tonfa weapon of a wooden rod with a handle at a right angle, used in pairs

tori defending position in aikido or jiu jitsu

tsuki punch

uchi strike

uchi waza striking techniques

ude arm or forearm

uke attacking position in aikido or jiu jitsu; block in karate

ukemi falling and rolling exercises

ura opposite, reverse, or back

waza techniques

waza-ari score of half a point in a judo, jiu jitsu, aikido, or karate contest

yame official's call for an interruption in a kendo, jiu jitsu, or aikido match

yari spear

yoi call used to signal readiness for the competition to begin

yoko side

yoshi official's call to continue a jiu jitsu match

yudansha holder of a black belt in karate

zanshin alertness of mind as demonstrated in karate movements

Nutrition For Fitness

additive often chemical substance added to processed food to retard spoilage and improve appearance or taste of food

alimentotherapy treatment of disease through diet and nutrition

banting diet without sweets or carbohydrates

basal metabolism basic rate at which body expends energy to maintain itself in resting state

betacarotene isomer of carotene converted by the body to Vitamin A

calorie measurement of energy provided by food

carbohydrate essential nutrient substance in sugars and starches

carboloading Informal. ingestion of large amounts of complex carbohydrates to produce extra energy reserves, esp. prior to exercise

cholesterol fatty substance found in foodstuffs, or formed by body itself, that coats and constricts arteries

complementary proteins proteins found in vegetables that, when combined, form nutritionally complete proteins otherwise normally found only in meats and milk

complex carbohydrate carbohydrate such as sucrose or starch in foods

diet pattern of eating; range of foodstuffs ingested; programmed course of eating to gain or lose weight or improve health

electrolytes dietary components (sodium, potassium, and chloride) essential to fluid retention, nerve impulse transmission, and digestion

empty calories highly caloric foods without significant nutritional value

fad diet eating regimen designed to appeal more to short-term weight loss goals than to sound nutritional principles

fats saturated, monounsaturated, polyunsaturated, and unsaturated essential nutrient material rich in calories

fiber dietary substance, usu. cellulose, found in plants, that promotes gastrointestinal fitness

folic acid nutrient that facilitates protein synthesis and cell division

food combining system of combining certain food groups in meals for health or weight control

food group basic category of nutritional foodstuffs, including milk, meat, vegetable and fruit, and bread and cereal groups

food guide pyramid chart indicating proportions of food groups for a healthy diet, issued by the U.S. Department of Agriculture

health food any food considered healthful, esp. natural, unprocessed, or organic food

junk food processed food rich in fats and sugars but low in nutrition

lipids class of organic compounds that include fats and fatty acids

macrobiotics restricted diet program, primarily of whole grains, beans, and vegetables, based on balance of yin and yang natural cycles

macronutrients proteins, carbohydrates, and fats

malnutrition chronic lack of essential and beneficial nutritional foodstuffs

megavitamin therapy use of massive amounts of vitamins to treat illness and promote vitality

micronutrients vitamins and minerals

minerals chemical elements and compounds necessary in small amounts for health

multivitamin dietary supplement containing several essential nutrients

nutrient dietary substance that provides chemical compounds necessary for growth and replenishment of body

nutrition process by which animals consume and process food; study of dietary requirements

obesity condition of having excess body fat

olestra patented synthetic fat substitute made from fatty acids and sugar

omega-3 fatty acid fatty acid, found esp. in fish oil, that reduces cholesterol levels in blood

organic food foodstuffs grown and prepared without chemical additives, pesticides, or fertilizers

polyunsaturated fat dietary fat, usu. vegetable fat

protein essential nutrient material composed of amino acids

protein supplement concentrated nutritional powder or liquid

RDA recommendeddietary allowance of nutritional elements

reducing pills prescription drugs that cause appetite loss and promote weight reduction

roughage foodstuffs rich in fiber

saturated fat dietary fat, usu. animal fat, that increases cholesterol level in blood

Simplesse Trademark. synthetic fat substitute made from egg and milk proteins

sitology science of diet and nutrition

sorbital naturally occurring organic compound used as a sugar substitute

starch foodstuff rich in complex carbohydrates

supplement vitamin, mineral, or protein preparation that boosts intake of nutrients

trace minerals chemical elements necessary in minute amounts for health

triglycerides principal fat component of foods

vegetarianism practice of eating vegetables, fruits, and grains, and of eliminating animal products from diet

vitamin one of various organic nutrient elements and compounds necessary in very small quantities for health

vitamin pills nutritional supplements containing vitamins in condensed tablet or capsule form

weight loss reduction in body fat and weight, esp. by consumption of fewer calories relative to calories burned

yo-yo dieting repeated weight loss followed by weight gain

HAIR AND GROOMING
Hair Styles
Beards and Mustaches
Grooming Aids and Processes

See also: *Chap. 1: Health, Fitness, and Enhancement; Chap. 4: Medicine; Chap. 10: Hats, Headgear, and Hairpieces*

Hair Styles

Afro tight, bushy, natural curls, worn esp. by African-Americans

artichoke full, teased hair cut tight at nape of neck

auburn (*adj*) having reddish brown hair, natural or dyed

back combed having hair teased or ratted

bald (*adj*) having no hair, minimal or thinning hair, or a shaved head

bangs fringe of hair above forehead cut straight across

beckoning curl single curl of hair hanging on forehead

beehive dome of teased hair piled high atop head

blaze streak of contrasting color through hair

bleached blond person with artificially lightened hair

blond person with gold or yellow-toned hair, natural or bleached

bob hair cut all one length, to shoulders or shorter

bouffant hair puffed to large volume, piled high

braid hair plaited singly or in pairs

brunette person with brown or black hair, natural or dyed

brush cut short, bristly haircut

bun long hair pulled into knot or roll at back of head

burr cut *Slang*. extremely short, bristly haircut; crew cut

butch extremely short haircut for men

buzz cut usu. short haircut done with electric clippers

chignon knot or roll of long hair at back of head

clean-cut (*adj*) having short, neat hair style

close-cropped (*adj*) having hair cut close to scalp

coiffure hair style

coil long hair pulled into roll at back of head

coloring adding streaks or highlights or totally changing one's hair color

conk naturally curly hair chemically processed to be straight, esp. among African-Americans

coquette bob short, pixie bob haircut

cornrows small, tightly braided rows of hair along scalp, esp. for African-Americans, sometimes with beads braided into rows

cowlick natural whorl or lock of hair standing straight up

crest plumelike tuft of hair

crew cut close-cropped hair, usu. on men; burr cut

crimp tight wave in hair made with crimping iron

curls tight coils or loose waves of hair

DA duck's ass; hair oiled and combed back over ears, dovetailing at rear; ducktail

do *Slang*. hair style, hairdo

dreadlocks long, unbrushed, woolly braids, worn esp. by Rastafarians

ducktail DA

fade *Slang*. modified raised or slanted flattop, sometimes with thin, close-shaven trails through it, worn usu. by African-American men;

variations include gumby, slope, high-top, high-low, and tribal

feathercut hair cut to resemble layered feathers

finger wave curl set by pressing fingers into damp hair

fishtail braid strand braid of hair

flattop short crew cut with flat, brushlike surface at crown

fluff hair puffed up and teased out from head

forelock lock of hair hanging down forehead

French braid braid with three strands pulled back from hairline

French knot long hair rolled into spiral at back of head; French twist; twist

French twist French knot

fringe bangs of hair on forehead

frisette frizz hair style (19th c.)

frizz very tightly curled hair that forms a wiry mass

frosting bleached hair ends prelightened to white

fuzz cut very short crew cut

haircut style of cutting and shaping hair

hairdo style in which hair is worn

hair style fashion in which hair is worn, cut, arranged, or combed

henna plant extract used to dye hair red

jarhead *Slang*. person with totally shaved head

knot hair rolled or twisted into tight mass

layered cut hair cut in many different layers

locks strands of hair

lovelock long curl of hair hanging alone over shoulder (17th-18th c.)

mane abundant or long, thick hair

marcel deeply waved hair style consisting of tight waves set close to head

mohawk narrow band of bristled, erect hair from forehead to nape of neck, surrounded by shaved scalp

moptop shaggy hair style that partially covers brow or face

natural very curly hair grown long and bushy, esp. by African-Americans

pageboy straight, chin-length hair turned gently under at ends

part separation of hair falling along head, usu. at side of crown

perm *Informal*. permanent wave in hair

permanent wave chemical treatment that curls hair; perm

peroxide blond person with very pale, bleached blond hair

peyes long, uncut side curls worn by Hasidic Jewish men

pigtails hair worn in several braids

pixie short, layered haircut

plait braid of hair

platinum (*adj*) having very pale, esp. bleached blond, hair

pleach (*vb*) braid hair

pompadour hair fluffed and elevated at forehead

ponytail long hair drawn into single tassel at back of head

pouf hair piled high in rolled puffs

Prince Valiant thick, straight bangs and chin-length, cropped hair around back of head

process chemically straightened curly hair; conk

psyche knot hair brushed and twisted into conical coil ending above nape of neck

queue very long braid of hair down back

quiff elaborate pompadour of hair

ratted (*adj*) having hair teased or back combed

razor cut hair cut for layering with razor instead of scissors

receding hairline balding at top of brow, causing hairline to move back on crown

redhead person with reddish orange-toned hair, natural or dyed

ringlets long, spiraling curls of hair

roach roll of hair brushed straight back from forehead, sometimes to one side

roll hair bunched and held together

set hair styled by curling or waving on rollers

shag usu. long, bushy, layered hair

shingle hair bobbed and cut close in point at nape of neck, gradually longer up back of head, just covering ears

shingling cutting hair with scissors over comb to create tapering effect

shock bushy or tangled mass of hair

shorn (*adj*) having hair cut short, close to skull

skinhead *Slang*. person with shaved head

spikes hair formed into pointed projections with setting lotion or fixative

spit curl precise curl of hair pressed against face, formed by saliva, water, or fixative

split ends condition in which ends of hair split or fray from abuse or over time

strawberry blond person with light reddish gold blond hair, natural or dyed

streaking contrasting colors in strips through hair

styling cutting, coloring, shaping, and manipulating hair into a specific, distinguishing form

swirl long hair coiled into a circular shape

tail few locks of nape hairs left long with the rest cut short

teased (*adj*) having hair ratted or back combed

thatch thick growth of hair

thinning early stage of baldness with loss of some hair

tint chemical coloration of hair

tint back (*vb*) return tinted hair to natural color

tone (*vb*) subtly alter degree of light and dark shades in hair color

tonsure ring of fringed hair around bald crown

topknot tuft, roll, or fluff of hair at crown

tortoiseshell warm, golden brown shade created by toning medium dark hair

tousled (*adj*) windblown, uncombed, or natural in hair style

towhead person with extremely pale, whitish blond hair, esp. a young child

tresses hair, esp. long and luxuriant; plait or braid of hair

tuft projecting lock of hair

twist French knot
updo upsweep
upsweep hairdo in which hair is combed or brushed upward to top of head; updo; upswept hairdo
upswept hairdo upsweep
wave hair formed into loose curls
widow's peak point formed by hair on forehead
wig artificial hairpiece
windblown bob affectedly tousled hair style

Beards and Mustaches

Abe Lincoln thin beard along jaw with mustache shaved
beard man's facial hair, esp. when trimmed into shape, sometimes excluding mustache
burnsides sideburns
bushy (*adj*) describing full, untrimmed beard
chin whiskers short, thin beard at bottom of face only
down soft, boyish growth of beard
dundrearies long, flowing side whiskers
facial hair beard and mustache
five o'clock shadow growth of heavy beard several hours after shaving, giving unshaven appearance
full beard untrimmed, abundant beard
Fu Manchu thin, delicately trimmed beard and drooping mustache
goatee close-trimmed, pointed beard on chin
grizzled (*adj*) having unkempt, unshaven appearance, esp. from several days' growth of facial hair
handlebar mustache long, full mustache turning up at ends
hirsute (*adj*) having facial hair, esp. rough or coarse
imperial beard single tuft of hair on chin and tufted mustache
mustache facial hair between upper lip and nose; usu. worn by men
mustaches former term for thick, long, or elaborately shaped mustache
mustachioed (*adj*) wearing a mustache
muttonchops sideburns extending nearly to jaw line
peach fuzz *Slang.* very soft down of facial hair
sideboards *Chiefly Brit.* sideburns
sideburns beard growth along sides of face below ears; burnsides
sidelocks long sideburns, often extending off face
side whiskers sideburns, esp. untrimmed
stubble growth of beard or mustache shortly after shaving
three day's growth dense stubble of facial hair that gives ungroomed, scruffy appearance
tuft tassel-like beard
unshaven (*adj*) having some growth of beard on one's face, giving unkempt appearance
Van Dyke close-trimmed, pointed beard
walrus mustache extremely long, bushy, drooping mustache covering upper lip

weepers *Slang.* long, flowing side whiskers
whiskers facial hair, esp. a beard

Grooming Aids and Processes

aftershave scented liquid tonic applied to face after shaving beard
antiperspirant chemical solution used to suppress perspiration, esp. under arms
astringent tonic lotion that tightens pores
atomizer small bottle for spraying cologne or water
baliage method of combing highlighting into hair
balm ointment, lotion, or cream for soothing skin
balsam soothing oil; balm
bath immersion of body in hot water for cleanliness and relaxation
bath oil scented skin oil placed in bath water
bath salts scented chemicals dissolved in bath water
bay rum popular, traditional aftershave lotion
beautician manager or employee of beauty parlor; hairdresser
beauty parlor business providing cosmetic treatments and hairstyling
bikini waxing removal of stray pubic hairs by coating with hot paraffin and stripping off wax when cooled
blow-dry (*vb*) dry and style hair with electric drying appliance that shoots hot air across hair
blusher rouge
bobby pin small, curved, metal or plastic hair fastener
bracer stimulating liquid tonic applied to face after shaving
brush bristles or hairs gathered into handle, used to apply cosmetics or groom hair
bubble bath sudsing, oily powder placed in bath water
cachou pastille for sweetening breath
castile soap fine, hard, bland soap containing olive oil
clipper small cutting implement for hair and nails
coconut oil oil from coconut used to smooth and lubricate skin
cold cream mineral oil compound used to remove cosmetics and soothe skin
cologne fragrant liquid for scenting body
coloring dyes or tints for altering hair color
colorist hairdresser who alters color of all or some of one's hair with dyes or tints
comb stiff-toothed implement for grooming hair
compact small case holding face powder, puff, and mirror, sometimes also with rouge
conditioner creamy softening lotion applied to hair after shampoo; creme rinse
cosmetician professional trained in application of cosmetics
cosmetics paints, powders, ointments, and lotions used to beautify face and body; makeup; maquillage; war paint

cosmetology art, techniques, or profession of applying cosmetics
cotton swab cotton-tipped stick used to apply or remove cosmetics
creme rinse conditioner
croquignole method of waving hair by winding it on rollers from ends of hair toward scalp
curler small, usu. tubular framework used to set curl in wet hair
curling iron heated metal rod used to curl hair
curl relaxing chemical process that straightens naturally curly hair
dental floss waxed string used to clean between teeth
dentifrice tooth cleaning paste or powder
deodorant chemical solution that neutralizes perspiration odors
depilatory cream that removes facial or body hair
diffuser attachment to blow drier used to dry hair
eau de Cologne dilute solution of cologne
eau de parfum dilute solution of perfume
electric razor electrically powered shaving device, often with many small blades on movable head
emery board abrasive surface used to smooth and shape fingernails
eyebrow pencil colorant stick used to darken and define eyebrows
eyelash curler small, clamping tool for curling eyelashes
eyeliner paint in liquid or pencil form used to outline eyes
eyeliner tattoo permanent dying of eyelash line around eyes
eye shadow colored powder or cream applied to eyelid
eyewash soothing chemical solution used to refresh eyes
face powder cosmetic powder, often talc or cornstarch, applied to face to reduce shine and give matte finish
facial deep cleaning of pores of face
false eyelashes long lashes attached to eyelid
false nails long fingernails attached at natural cuticle
falsies artificial cosmetic aid, esp. breast pads
fragrance perfume or cologne for scenting body
friseur *French.* hairdresser
grooming methods, practices, and techniques of creating and maintaining a neat, presentable appearance
hairdresser person trained in cutting, setting, and styling hair; hair stylist
hairdressing grooming of hair; shampoo or conditioner
hair drier appliance that blows hot air to dry hair
hair net fine mesh that holds hair in place
hair spray sticky aerosol used to hold hair in place
hair stylist hairdresser, esp. in cinema and advertising

highlighter cosmetic used to emphasize some feature or portion of face

highlights streaks of hair of different color or shade than rest of head of hair

ice bag small bag that holds ice, for applying to face or eyes

jojoba oil soothing oil made from wax of North American tree

Kleenex *Trademark.* paper tissue

kohl black eyelining pencil

lanolin rich oil used to lubricate skin

lip gloss creamy cosmetic used to give shine to lips, often tinted

lipstick colorant cream for lips

makeover extensive series of beauty and cosmetic treatments

makeup cosmetics

manicure grooming of fingernails

maquillage cosmetics

mascara darkening cream for eyelashes

moisturizer cosmetic cream or lotion used to restore softness and moisture to skin

mousse foam or gel that keeps groomed hair in place

mouthwash chemical solution used to rinse and refresh mouth

mudpack facial treatment that uses drying mud

nail polish colored enamel for fingernails and toenails

orange stick small, pointed wooden stick used to groom fingernails

pancake thick cover up cream for skin, esp. face

pastille breath-sweetening drop

podioure grooming of toenails

perfume volatile scented oil extracted from flowers or prepared synthetically, applied as fragrance

polish remover solvent for removing old nail polish

pomade fragrant, sometimes medicated ointment for hair and scalp

pomander small ball or box of perfume

powder fine grains of soothing colorant applied to skin, often made from talc

powder puff soft applicator for powder

razor small, sharp blade used to remove body or facial hair

rinse temporary hair coloring

rollers plastic or metal tubes for curling hair

rosewater rose-scented water used to refresh skin

rouge reddening colorant for cheeks; blusher

roundbrush tubular brush with bristles extending in all directions, used to style hair

safety razor handle with protective sheath for razor blade

sandalwood oil perfume oil

set (*vb*) style hair while wet so as to retain shape when dry; (*n*) hair thus shaped

shampoo soap for hair, often scented and with various additives for health of hair

shaver razor unit

snood net for holding hair at back of head

sunscreen chemical lotion for preventing or retarding sunburn

swab small, flexible stick tipped in cotton for cleaning ears and applying makeup

talc talcum powder

talcum powder absorbent white powder used to refresh skin; talc

tattoo art and practice of marking the skin with indelible designs and legends by puncturing the skin and inserting pigments; any design or legend so produced

tinting altering natural hair color with dye or tint

tissue thin, soft paper sheet used to clean skin and apply or remove cosmetics

toilet general term for grooming aids and their use

toilet paper tissue paper, usu. in roll, used esp. to wipe anus after defecating

toilet powder absorbent, scented white powder for skin

toiletries grooming aids

toilet water scented liquid

toothbrush small brush with handle, used to clean teeth

toothpaste dentifrice in soft, moist form

toothpick small, pointed stick used to clean between teeth

tooth powder dentifrice in dry, granular, gently abrasive form

tweezers small pincer tool used to grasp or remove hairs and other small particles

unguent soothing ointment

Vaseline *Trademark.* petroleum jelly ointment for soothing skin

vent brush brush with air vents used in styling hair

war paint colored ointments applied to face and body before going to war (Native Americans); *Informal.* cosmetics

wash lotion

waxing stripping away of body hair with hot wax

witch hazel astringent lotion

zinc oxide ointment creamy white paste for sun protection or soothing burns and rashes

grouped into three pairs of opposites, such as Healthy/Sickly. Each pair is broken down into two undefined lists of virtual synonyms and words with casually related meanings. The parameters for these lists are defined by the three or four adjectives forming the section title. While the meanings of the terms in each list vary, this category is intended to serve as a reminder of similar but slightly different and familiar words. The subcategory Physical Attributes includes adjectives describing a wide variety of physical states.

Aspects and Components of Appearance

air manifestation of some personal quality or emotion in one's appearance and bearing

appearance outward, physical look

aspect particular appearance or mien

attitude arrangement or position of body parts

aura impression given off of one's spiritual or emotional nature

bearing manner in which one stands, moves, and acts

body physical substance of a person; trunk as distinguished from limbs

body language gestures and mannerisms, both intended and subconscious, that communicate one's feelings

brow expression or mien, esp. on forehead

build muscular development and posture; form of one's body

bulk primary mass of one's body

bust torso between neck and waist, esp. woman's breasts

carriage posture and manner of carrying one's body

cleavage area between a woman's breasts

coloring complexion, natural skin tone

complexion color and texture of skin, esp. on face

comportment bearing, demeanor

condition state of physical health and fitness

conduct manner in which one behaves and carries oneself

constitution one's physical makeup, both inherited traits and acquired characteristics

corpus body, esp. when dead

countenance demeanor and expression, esp. on face as indication of feelings

demeanor outward manner, behavior toward others

deportment manner of carrying and conducting oneself; bearing

disposition prevailing mood and emotional makeup as revealed through expressions and actions

expression arrangement of facial features, body posture, and use of vocal intonation to manifest a particular feeling

extremities limbs, hands, and feet

facade expression or image presented to others

face front of head including chin, mouth, nose, cheeks, eyes, ears, and forehead

Adjectives describing human physical appearance or physiological states have been

features elements of face, esp. mouth, nose, and eyes

fettle condition of body and mind

figure shape, musculature, and posture of body

form external appearance of body as distinct from face; figure

frame physique or figure, esp. underlying skeletal structure

gait manner of walking

gestures movements of hands and limbs and expressions revealed through these movements

girth size or measure around middle of torso

grin open, wide smile

grooming manner of caring for hygiene, hair, and body hair

hairline point on forehead above which hair growth occurs

hand terminal part of forelimb with five fingers used for manual operations and expressive gestures

height distance from bottom of feet to top of head when standing erect

image impression given off by facial expressions, bearing, posture, deportment, gestures, and voice

impression outward physical appearance

limbs arms and legs, ending in hands and feet; extremities

looks physical appearance and countenance, esp. attractiveness

manner distinct or characteristic air and bearing

mannerism characteristic gesture or peculiarity of conduct

mien expression of mood revealed through demeanor and bearing

nature essential character as shown through physical traits

pate crown or top of head, normally covered with hair

person general image or impression given off by physical appearance and manner

physique form and musculature of body; figure

port *Archaic.* manner in which one bears oneself

posture position and bearing of body, esp. when standing erect

presence aura, impression, or sense of personality given off by physical appearance and manner

profile side view of face

proportions relation of parts of body to one another

puss *Slang.* face, esp. mouth

shape form and proportions of bodily parts; figure; physical condition

skin smooth outer covering of body, forming complexion on face

smile facial expression, usu. upward curl of corners of mouth and brightening of eyes

stance posture, way of standing, esp. as expression of feeling

stature natural height in upright position

tic habitual spasmodic movement of facial muscles

tone tautness of musculature

torso trunk

traits form and expression of body parts and facial features

trunk central part of body to which limbs and head are attached; torso

visage face and its expressions

walk posture and manner of moderate forward movement in upright position

weight relative measurement of one's mass

Physical Attributes

almond-eyed, androgynous, aquiline
bald, barefoot, blank, blind, blond, bowlegged, brachycephalic, bristling, brunette, buxom
chip-toothed, clubfooted, cross-legged, curled lip, curvaceous
dark, deadpan, deaf, dewy-eyed, doe-eyed, dolichocephalic, domed, downy
eagle-eyed, erect, exophthalmic
feline, flatfooted, flattened, flossy, fluffy, flushed, freckled, freckle-faced, full-mouthed, goggle-eyed
grimacing, grinning, gummy
hairy, hewn, hirsute, horny, horrent
irregular
jowly
knock-kneed
lambent, lanky, large, leathery, left-handed, life-size, limping, long-faced, loose-jointed, loose-limbed
microcephalic, mongoloid, mute
naked
oblong, open-eyed
pigeon-toed, pinched, poker-faced, popeyed, pouty, puckered, pug-nosed, pursed, pursy
rawboned, red-headed, retroussé, right-handed, roundheaded, round-shouldered, rubicund
saurian, scowling, setaceous, sharp-nosed, shorn, shovel-nosed, sinewy, sinuous, skinhead, slanted, slant-eyed, sloe-eyed, slow-footed, smirking, sneering, snub-nosed, speckled, spindle-legged, splayfooted, squinty, straight-faced, stubbly, sulky, swarthy, swivel-hipped
taliped, throaty, toothy
vacuous, varicose veined
wavy, wide-eyed, widemouthed

Small/Large

SMALL, SHORT, OR THIN

bantam, bareboned, bony
compact
dainty, diminutive, dinky, dwarfish
elfin
flat-chested
gangling, gawky
half pint
infinitesimal, insubstantial, itsy-bitsy, itty-bitty
lanky, lean, Lilliputian, little
meager, measly, micro, microscopic, midget, miniature, minimal, minute
narrow, negligible, nipped
peewee, petite, puny, pygmy

reedlike, reedy, runty
sawed-off, scant, scanty, scarce, scraggy, scrawny, scrubby, short, shrimpy, shriveled, shrunken, sinewy, skinny, slender, slight, slim, slinky, small, spindly, spiny, squat, stringbean, stringy, stubby, stumpy, stunted
teensy-weensy, teeny, teeny-weeny, thin, tiny
undersized, underweight
wasp-waisted, wee, weedy, weeny, willowy, wiry, wispy

LARGE, TALL, OR FAT

adipose, amazon, ample, Antaean
barrel-chested, beefy, behemoth, big, big-bellied, boundless, bovine, brawny, broad, broad of beam, Brobdingnagian, brutish, bulky, bull-necked, burly, buxom
capacious, chubby, chunky, clumpish, colossal, considerable, corpulent, cumbersome, Cyclopean
distended, dumpy
elephantine, elongated, embonpoint, endomorphic, enormous
fat, fleshy, fubsy, full, full-grown
gargantuan, generous, giant, gigantic, goliath, gross
heavy, hefty, herculean, huge, hulking, hunky, husky
immeasurable, immense, imposing
jumbo, Junoesque
large, leggy, leviathan, limitless, long, long-legged, long-limbed, lumbering, lumpish
mammoth, massive, mastodonic, meaty, mesomorphic, mighty, monumental, musclebound
obese, overblown, overdeveloped, overgrown, oversized, overstuffed, overweight
paunchy, plump, podgy, ponderous, porcine, portly, potbellied, prodigious, pudgy, pursy
rangy, roly-poly, rotund
sizable, squat, squdgy, stacked, stocky, stout, strapping, substantial, swollen
tall, thick, thickset, titanic, top-heavy, towering, tremendous, tubby
unwieldy
voluminous, voluptuous
wide
zaftig

Healthy/Sickly

HEALTHY, FIT, BRIGHT, OR STRONG

able-bodied, agile
beaming, blooming, blushing, bouncing, bright, bright-eyed, bursting, bushy-tailed
chipper, clean, clear-eyed
dexterous
elastic, exercised
fit, fit as a fiddle, florid, flush
glossy, glowing
hale, hardy, healthful, healthy, hearty
in fine fettle, in shape, in the pink
light-footed, limber, lissome, lithe, lively, lusty
mighty, muscular
peppy, perky, pink-cheeked, pliable
radiant, red, ripe, robust, rosy, rosy-cheeked, rubicund, ruddy, rugged

scrubbed, shapely, shining, shiny, shipshape, sinuous, sleek, sound, spare, sparkling, spry, square-shouldered, stalwart, staunch, steady, stout, strapping, streamlined, strong, sturdy, sunny, supple, svelte
toned, trim, twenty-twenty, twinkling
vigorous, vital
well-fed, wholesome
youthful

SICKLY, OUT OF SHAPE, DULL, OR WEAK

aged, ailing, amputee, anemic, attenuated
bedridden, bent, blanched, bleary-eyed, blind, bloated, bloodshot
cadaverous, chalky, corpselike, crippled
debilitated, decrepit, delicate, disabled, doddering, droopy, dull
emaciated, enfeebled, etiolated
faint, farsighted, feeble, feverish, flabby, flaccid, flimsy, flushed, fossilized, fragile, frail
gaunt, glabrous, glassy-eyed
haggard, hollow-eyed, humpbacked
ill, incontinent, infirm
lame, limp, lumpish, lurid
mute, myopic
nearsighted
obese, off-color, out of shape, out of whack, overweight
pale, pallid, palsied, paltry, peaked, peglegged, phthisic, pigeon-toed, pinched, pursy
ravaged, rheumy, rickety, rugose, run-down
scorbutic, shaky, shriveled, shrunken, sick, sickly, skeletal, skinny, slack, soft, sparse, spindle-legged, starved, stone-blind, stone-deaf, strabismic, sunken, swollen
tabetic, tottering, tubercular
underfed, undernourished, underweight
walleyed, wan, washed-out, wasted, waxen, waxy, weak, web-footed, wispy, withered, wizened, wraithlike, wrinkled

Beautiful/Ugly

BEAUTIFUL, ATTRACTIVE, OR WELL-FORMED

adorable, agreeable, alluring, angelic, appealing, appetizing, attractive
beaming, beauteous, beautiful, becoming, beguiling, bewitching, bonny, breathtaking, bright, built
callipygian, captivating, catching, charismatic, charming, classic, clear, clear-eyed, come-hither, comely, coquettish, curvaceous, cute
dainty, dashing, delectable, delicate, delicious, delightful, desirable, devastating, dimpled, divine, doll-like
enchanting, engaging, enticing, entrancing, enviable, exotic, exquisite, eye-catching
fair, fancy, fascinating, fetching, fine, flawless
glamorous, glorious, glossy, good-looking, gorgeous, graceful, great-looking
handsome, hot, hunky, hypnotic
immaculate, intoxicating, intriguing, inviting, irresistible
killer
light, lovable, lovely, luscious, lustrous
magnetic, magnificent, mignon, moon-eyed, mouth-watering
nifty
ornamental
perfect, photogenic, picturesque, pleasing, precious, prepossessing, pretty, provocative
redolent, regular, resplendent
scrumptious, sculptured, seductive, sensuous, sexy, shapely, showy, sightly, silky, slick, smiling, spellbinding, spotless, stacked, statuesque, streamlined, striking, stunning, sublime, sumptuous, symmetrical
taking, tantalizing, tasty, tempting, titillating, toylike
voluptuous
well-built, well-conditioned, well-favored, well-formed, well-groomed, well-made, well-proportioned, well-set, winning, winsome

UGLY, UNATTRACTIVE, OR MALFORMED

angular, askew, awful, awkward
bandy-legged, beetle-browed, bent, blemished, blimpish, bloated, blowzy, blubbery, bovine, bucktoothed, bug-eyed
cadaverous, chalky, clammy, cleft, clumsy, crippled, crooked, cross-eyed, cumbersome
defaced, deformed, disfigured, disgusting, disheveled, droopy, dumpy
elephantine, emaciated
farinaceous, fat, foul, frightful, frowzy, fubsy
gap-toothed, gawky, geeky, ghastly, gnarled, goggle-eyed, graceless, grim-faced, grimy, grisly, grizzled, grotesque, grubby, gruesome, grungy
halt, harelipped, hatchet-faced, heavy-footed, hideous, homely, horrent, horrible, hulking, hunched
ill-formed, ill-made, irregular
jagged
leprous, loathsome, lopsided, lumpish
macabre, malformed, malodorous, mangy, marred, mealy, misshapen, moldering, monstrous, musty
offensive, oleaginous
pasty, pendulous, pitted, plain, pocked, ponderous, porcine, putrescent, putrid
ragged, repellent, repugnant, repulsive, revolting, rickety, rumpled, rumply, runty
sallow, scabby, scabrous, scaly, sclerotic, scorbutic, scraggy, scrawny, scrofulous, scruffy, shabby, shaggy, shapeless, sickening, simian, skew-eyed, sneering, splotchy, spoiled, spongy, squat, squinched, stooped, straggly, stumpy, stunted, sunken, swaybacked, swollen
tabescent, terrible, tubercular
ugly, unappealing, unattractive, ungainly, unprepossessing, unsavory, unsightly, unwieldy
walleyed, washed-out, wasted, waxen, withered

CHAPTER TWO
LIVING THINGS

BIOLOGY

Branches and Disciplines
Genetics, Heredity, and Evolution
Cell Structure and Function
Physiology
Environment, Ecology, and Animal Behavior
Reproduction and Development
Tools and Techniques
Taxonomy
    Five Kingdoms
    Major Taxonomic Subgroups

See also: *Chap. 1: Anatomy; Medical Problems; Chap. 2: Animals; Plants; Simpler Life Forms; Chap. 3: Geology; Geography; Chap. 4: Chemistry; Chap. 8: Parents and Children; Chap. 12: Agriculture; Chap. 17: Gardening; Chap. 22: Sex, Love, and Romance*

Branches and Disciplines

algology study of algae

anatomy study of structures of organisms

bacteriology study of bacteria

behaviorism study of interaction between organism and organism or organism and environment

biochemistry study of chemical processes necessary to sustain life

biology science that deals with the morphology, physiology, origin, and distribution of living organisms

biometry use of statistical techniques in biology

bionics design of systems that duplicate living organisms

bionomics ecology

biophysics use of principles and techniques of physics to study biological phenomena

biotechnology recombinant DNA, genetic engineering, cloning, and related applications of genetic research

botany science of organisms of Kingdom Plantae, dealing with life, structure, growth, and classification of plants

bryology branch of botany dealing with mosses and other bryophytes

cell biology study of cell organelles, their functions and interactions

cell physiology study of structure and functioning of cells

comparative anatomy study of similar structures among organisms

comparative biochemistry study of chemical similarities among organisms

comparative embryology study of similar development among organisms

conchology study of shells

cytology study of structure and functions of cells

dendrology study of trees and woody plants, esp. their taxonomy

developmental biology embryology

ecology study of relationships and balance between organisms and their environment; bionomics

embryology study of development of organism from meiosis to birth; developmental biology

endocrinology study of endocrine glands and hormonal control

entomology study of insects

environmental physiology study of adaptations of living things to environmental conditions

enzymology study of structure and catalytic properties of enzymes

epidemiology study of prevalence and spread of disease in a population

ethology study of animal behavior

evolution study of origin of species as process of development from earlier forms

exobiology study of life beyond Earth's atmosphere

genetics study of heredity

helminthology study of parasitic worms

hematology study of blood

herpetology study of reptiles and amphibians

histology study of tissues

ichthyology study of fish

immunology study of how body protects itself from invading organisms and chemicals

life science any of a group of sciences dealing with living creatures and their life processes, esp. biology, zoology, and botany

limnology study of freshwater lakes, ponds, and streams as discrete ecosystems

malacology study of mollusks

mammalogy study of mammals

microbiology study of microscopic organisms and agents, such as bacteria, protists, and viruses

molecular biology study of complex chemistry of biological macromolecules, esp. those involved in genetics

morphology study of physical forms of living things

mycology study of fungi

natural history biology, physiology, origin, and distribution of living things as seen through perspective of time

neurobiology study of nervous systems of animals

nutrition study of foods and how they are used by body

ornithology study of birds

paleontology study of fossil record of living things

parasitology study of animal parasites

phycology study of algae

physiology study of functions and vital processes of living organisms and their parts

phytology former term for botany

phytosociology ecology concerned with origin, composition, classification, and distribution of plant communities

protozoology study of microscopic, usu. single-celled, protozoans

systematics study of kinds, diversity, and relationships of living things

taxonomy classification of living things

zoology science of organisms of Kingdom Animalia, dealing with life, structure, growth, and classification of animals

Genetics, Heredity, and Evolution

abiogenesis discredited theory that living organisms can develop by spontaneous generation from inanimate material

adaptation any feature that increases fitness of organism to its environment; process of developing or altering these features by natural selection

adenine one of four nitrogenous bases used to carry genetic information in nucleotides of DNA and RNA

albino organism lacking normal coloration, usu. due to genetic factors

allele form that gene may take at one locus

allopatry populations, esp. species, with geographic ranges that show no overlap, often affecting speciation

ameba unicellular, microscopic protist that reproduces by fission

analogy resemblance in structure or function due to evolutionary adaptation rather than common ancestry

anaphase stage in meiosis or mitosis in which chromatids separate and move to opposite poles

anticodon set of three bases at end of tRNA that fits only with specific codon of mRNA

autosome any chromosome not carrying sex information

bacterial transformation form of genetic recombination in which one bacterium breaks open and part of its DNA enters another bacterium

bacteriophage virus that attacks bacteria only, used extensively in genetic research

biogenesis principle that living organisms originate from other living organisms similar to themselves

book of man projected mapping and sequencing of entire human genome

capsid protein coat surrounding nucleic acid core of virus

cenogenesis development of adaptive structures in embryonic or larval stage that are not part of evolutionary history of taxonomic group

centromere round body made of chromatin that holds two strands of chromosome together

character displacement state in which two related species become increasingly different in areas where both occur

chromatid individual strand of double-stranded chromosome in mitosis

chromatin stainable mass of material in nucleus that realigns into chromosomes during cell division

chromosome distinct body in nucleus that appears during cell division, composed of DNA and protein and containing genes

chromosome map diagram showing linear order of genes on chromosome

cline pattern of gradual change in character across species' geographic range

clone strain of genetically identical cells

codon sequence of three nitrogenous bases representing specific amino acid

conjugation transfer of nuclear material between two bacteria

continuous variation existence of varying degrees of a characteristic, controlled by more than one pair of genes

convergence two related species becoming increasingly similar over time

cosmid vector of DNA segment flanked by bacteriophage lambda, used in recombinant DNA technology

crossing over exchange of segments of chromosomal material between two strands of a tetrad during prophase of meiosis

cytosine one of four nitrogenous bases used to carry genetic information in nucleotides of DNA and RNA

Darwinism Charles Darwin's theory of evolution by variation and natural selection

deoxyribonucleic acid DNA

diploid number chromosome number equal to twice that found in gametes; found in somatic cells

divergence two related species becoming increasingly different over time

DNA deoxyribonucleic acid; nucleic acid that carries encoded message of gene, comprised of double helix ladder of paired nitrogenous bases bonded to phosphate group and deoxyribose sugar

dominant trait allele whose phenotypic trait dominates or prevents expression of recessive traits

double helix intertwining chains of nucleic acid linked by hydrogen bonds that constitutes basic structure of DNA

ecotype locally adapted variant of a species, genetically different from other ecotypes of that species

endemic species found only in limited geographic area

evolution development of species or organism from primitive state to present or specialized state

exon section of DNA that contains information that codes for protein product of gene

extinction dying out of species or population

first filial generation first offspring produced from parental cross

fitness measure of evolutionary success in terms of contribution to next generation

fossil remains of an organism long dead or direct evidence of it, such as its tracks, usu. preserved in rock

fossil record succession of fossilized living forms, usu. growing more complex, serving as evidence of macroevolution

gene segment of DNA responsible for transmitting hereditary traits

gene pool all genetic variability within a population

genetic code nucleotide triplet sequences in DNA and RNA that encode for protein synthesis

genetic counseling advising people of the probability of their having children with hereditary abnormalities

genetic drift changes in gene distribution due to random effects only

genetic engineering incorporation of new genes into an organism to alter it

genetic isolation absence of genetic exchange between populations due to geographical separation or mechanisms of behavior, anatomy, or physiology that prevent reproduction

genetic map diagram of gene locations on chromosome

genetic recombination change in gene combinations of offspring from that of parents

genetics study of heredity and similarities or differences between related organisms

genome one complete haploid set of chromosomes and their genes for an organism, containing all its inheritable traits

genomic DNA fragment or fragments of DNA produced by restriction enzymes acting on the DNA of a cell or organism

genotype genetic makeup of organism or cell

geographic range area inhabited by population

guanine one of four nitrogenous bases used to carry genetic information in nucleotides of DNA and RNA

haploid (*adj*) possessing only one set of chromosomes, in gametes

Hardy-Weinberg principle theory that frequencies of alleles and genotypes in population will remain constant in absence of evolutionary forces

heredity transmission of genetic information from generation to generation

heterosis hybrid vigor

heterozygote organism carrying different alleles for the same trait

histones positively charged proteins in chromatin

homologs members of chromosome pair carrying corresponding genes

homology similarity based on common descent that may or may not reflect functional similarity

homozygote organism carrying identical alleles for the same trait

hybrid offspring from parents of two different species

hybrid vigor condition in which heterozygotes are more fit than either homozygote

inbreeding mating of kin

incomplete dominance state in which one allele only partially inhibits the expression of its alternate

independent assortment tendency of unlinked genes to segregate independently

intron nucleotide sequence that does not code for a protein

isolation prevention of interbreeding between populations due to factors such as geography or behavior

karyotype form, size, and number of chromosomes of an organism: in humans, forty-six chromosomes, including twenty-two pairs of autosomes and two sex chromosomes

Klinefelter syndrome abnormal development toward female traits in males with XXY genotype

Lamarckism inheritance of acquired characteristics, esp. theory that environmental change causes structural changes in organisms that are inherited by offspring

law of dominance Gregor Mendel's rule that in certain traits, one allele in a heterozygote can be phenotypically expressed in preference to its alternate

law of independent assortment principle that unlinked genes segregate independently

law of segregation principle that alleles for a trait segregate independently during meiosis

lethal gene mutation that causes early death when expressed

life distinguishing characteristics of organisms, esp. growth capacity, metabolism, reproduction, and adaptation to environment

linkage tendency of genes located near each other on chromosomes to be inherited together

living things organisms distinguished from dead inorganic objects by basic characteristics of life: growth, metabolism, reproduction, and adaptability to environment

locus position of allele on chromosome

macroevolution long-term evolutionary phenomena occurring above level of species

meiosis cell division in which the diploid chromosome number is reduced to the haploid as part of process of gamete formation

Mendel's laws first law: alleles segregate in meiosis; second law: unlinked genes assort independently

messenger RNA mRNA; single strand of RNA that carries genetic information from DNA to ribosome

microevolution small-scale, rapidly occurring evolutionary phenomena in a single species

modern synthesis merging of Darwinism and Mendelian genetics

mRNA messenger RNA

multiple alleles set of genes potentially occurring at one locus

mutagen substance or condition that increases mutation rate

mutation sudden inheritable change to new allelic form of gene

natural selection process that results in survival of those organisms best suited to their environment, based on inherited favorable variations that increase from generation to generation; selection

neo-Darwinism modern synthesis of Darwinism and Mendelian genetics

nucleic acids main component of DNA and RNA, whose arrangement carries genetic code

nucleoprotein protein associated with nucleic acids in nucleus of living cells

nucleotide structural segment of nucleic acid chain, composed of phosphate group, five-carbon sugar, and purine or pyrimidine base

operator gene segment of DNA to which repressor protein bonds, serving to regulate transcription activity

operon set of structural genes related to single process and subject to the same repressor

organism any discrete life form belonging to one of the five kingdoms

palingenesis phase in development of individual that seems to repeat evolutionary history of its taxonomic group; recapitulation

parental cross first cross in experiment to study genotypic and phenotypic characteristics of trait or traits

phage bacteriophage

phenotype observable characteristics of an organism

phyletic group species related to each other through common descent

phylogeny evolutionary history of taxonomic group

plasmid small DNA molecule outside chromosome in prokaryotic organism that reproduces independently

pleiotropy capacity of gene to assume several different phenotypic characteristics

polymorphism occurrence in population of two or more distinct forms with no intermediate forms

population interbreeding group of organisms

population genetics study of gene movement and variation among interbreeding organisms

prophase early stage in nuclear division during which chromosomes move toward equator of spindle

protein synthesis transfer of encoded genetic information in DNA from nucleotides to amino acid sequence through initiation, elongation, and termination

Punnett square graphic method for observing phenotypic and genotypic ratios

purine either adenine or guanine

pyrimidine cytosine, thymine, or uracil

recapitulation palingenesis

recessive trait allele whose phenotype is not expressed in heterozygous organism

recombinant DNA DNA in which half of DNA double helix has been spliced from each of two different organisms to form new genetic code

recombination change of gene groupings from generation to generation due to independent assortment and crossing over

regulator gene controller of transcription rate of other genes

replication method by which nucleic acids duplicate themselves

repressor functional protein of regulator genes

restriction enzyme enzyme that splits DNA double helix at specific nucleotide sequences

ribonucleic acid RNA; usu. single-stranded nucleic acid, characterized by nitrogenous bases bonded to phosphate group and ribose sugar, that acts as genetic material in viruses and as transcriber of genetic information in other cells

RNA ribonucleic acid

second filial generation offspring of first filial cross

segregation assortment of paired alleles into separate gametes

selection natural selection

selection pressure any environmental feature that results in natural selection

sex chromosomes pair of chromosomes that determines sex and sex-linked characteristics of organism

sex-linked characteristic any trait whose alleles are found on sex chromosomes

sexual dimorphism distinct differences between male and female in addition to primary sex characteristics

sexual selection differential abilities of individuals to acquire mates

speciation process of genetic diversification through which new species arise by natural selection

spindle fibers structural components of centromere

splicing separating two halves of DNA double helix and recombining each with strip from another organism

structural gene gene that produces a protein distinct from those of the operator and regulator genes of the same operon

survival of the fittest process of Darwinian natural selection

sympatry populations, esp. species, with geographic ranges that overlap at least in part

telophase final stage of mitosis and meiosis, in which chromosomes form two new nuclei

tetrad four chromatids of pair of replicated homologous chromosomes in prophase of meiosis

thymine one of four nitrogenous bases used to carry genetic information in nucleotides of DNA and RNA

transcription formation of RNA chain complementary to a DNA chain

transduction process in which genetic information in cellular DNA is transferred from one host cell to another by viruses or other filterable agents

transfer RNA tRNA; RNA that carries specific amino acids to messenger RNA

transformation genetic change induced by incorporation of DNA from one bacterial cell into another

translation construction of polypeptide through mRNA activity

transposition movement of gene or set of genes from one DNA site to another

transposon DNA segment that can insert copies of itself into other DNA sites within the same cell

tRNA transfer RNA

Turner's syndrome abnormality due to lack of one X chromosome in female, creating an XO genotype and retarding growth of gonads

uracil one of four nitrogenous bases used to carry genetic information in nucleotides of DNA and RNA

variation chance differences among individual organisms, some of them inheritable, that interact with environment to determine which individuals will survive and reproduce

Watson-Crick model double helix structure of DNA, first posited in 1953

X chromosome sex chromosome carrying female traits in mammals

Y chromosome sex chromosome carrying male traits in mammals

Cell Structure and Function

A cells glucagon-secreting cells in islets of Langerhans of pancreas; alpha cells

active transport energy-requiring, carrier-mediated transport system in which molecules can be moved across cell membrane against electrochemical gradient

adenosine diphosphate ADP; compound formed by hydrolysis of ATP

adenosine triphosphate ATP; major molecule that accepts energy from nutrients and donates this energy to cell functions

adipocyte fat cell specialized for synthesis and storage of triacylglycerol

ADP adenosine diphosphate

aerobic (*adj*) living, growing, or occurring in the presence of oxygen

agonist agent that produces a response that enhances the response of another agent

agranular endoplasmic reticulum smooth endoplasmic reticulum without ribosomes that modifies proteins and metabolizes barbiturates

alpha cells A cells

anabolism synthesizing of small molecules to form larger molecules

anaerobic (*adj*) living, growing, or occurring in the absence of oxygen

angry macrophage macrophage whose activity has been facilitated by chemicals released from T cells

antagonist molecule that competes for binding site with chemical messenger but does not trigger cell's response

ATP adenosine triphosphate

axon transport movement of materials along axons by means of intracellular filamentous structures

basement membrane thin layer of extracellular material associated with plasma membrane of epithelial cells

basophil granulocytic leukocyte whose granules stain with basic dyes

B cell lymphocyte in immune system that proliferates and differentiates into antibody-secreting plasma cells; insulin-secreting cell in pancreas

beta cells endocrine system B cells

B lymphocyte B cell

calmodulin intracellular protein that binds calcium and mediates many of calcium's second messenger functions

cAMP cyclic AMP

carrier integral membrane protein that combines with specific molecules, enabling them to pass through membrane

catabolism fragmentation of molecule into smaller parts

cell basic structural and functional unit of living organisms; smallest unit into which living thing can be divided and retain characteristics associated with life

cell division process by which cellular material is divided between two new cells, either by meiosis or mitosis

centrioles two small bodies composed of nine fused sets of microtubules, located in cell cytoplasm, which participate in nuclear and cell division

cGMP cyclic GMP

channel passage formed by integral membrane proteins through which certain small-diameter molecules and ions diffuse across membrane

chemosynthesis synthesis of organic material within an organism in which chemical reactions serve as energy source

chief cells gastric gland cells that secrete pepsinogen

chloroplast chlorophyll-containing plastid surrounded by two membranes and having complex internal membrane system in which photosynthesis takes place

cilia hairlike projections from surface of specialized epithelial cells that sweep back and forth to propel material along cell surface

citric acid cycle Krebs cycle

connective tissue cells cells specialized for the formation and secretion of extracellular elements that connect, anchor, and support body structures

cotransport form of secondary active transport in which energy-producing substance and transported substance move in same direction

countertransport form of secondary active transport in which energy-producing substance and transported substance move in opposite directions

creatine phosphate molecule used to store energy in muscle cells, quickly converted to ATP for energy

creatinine waste derived from muscle creatine

cyclic AMP cAMP; cylic form of adenosine monophosphate that serves as second messenger for many nonsteroid hormones and neurotransmitters

cyclic GMP cGMP; cyclic form of guanosine

monophosphate that acts as second messenger in some cells, possibly in opposition to cyclic AMP

cytochrome carrier molecule in mitochondria that participates in transfer of electrons in oxidation reactions

cytokinesis stage of cell division following mitosis, in which cytoplasm divides to form two new cells

cytoplasm entire contents of cell excluding nucleus

cytoskeleton rodlike filaments of various sizes in cytoplasm of most cells, associated with cell shape and movement

cytotoxic T cells class of T cells that upon activation by specific antigen, directly attack cells bearing that type of antigen

depolarization change in value of membrane potential toward zero to make inside of cell less negative

desmosome cell junction consisting of fibers extending between plasma membranes of slightly separated cells, binding them together with flexible strength

diffusion movement of molecules by random motion from region of higher to one of lower concentration

diffusion equilibrium equality of diffusion fluxes in opposite directions

ECF extracellular fluid

endocytosis process in which plasma membrane invaginates, engulfing extracellular material and pinching off to form a vesicle around it

endoplasmic reticulum ER; organelle in cytoplasm made up of interconnected network of branched tubules and flattened sacs that assembles or modifies proteins; agranular or granular endoplasmic reticulum

eosinophil leukocyte involved with allergic responses and destruction of parasitic worms

epithelial cells cells forming tissue that covers body surfaces, lines body cavities, and comprises most glands

ER endoplasmic reticulum

erythrocyte enucleated cell that contains hemoglobin for transport of gases by blood; red blood cell

eukaryote any cell with membrane-bound nucleus containing genetic material in chromosomes and dividing by mitosis or meiosis, including all life forms except bacteria, blue-green algae, and some primitive organisms

exocytosis process in which membrane of intracellular vesicle fuses with plasma membrane, vesicle opens, and its contents are released into extracellular fluid

extracellular fluid ECF; fluid outside cells that forms environment in which cells live; interstitial fluid and plasma

facilitated diffusion transport system that moves molecules from high to low concentration across membrane until concentrations on both sides of membrane are equal

flagella threadlike organelles used for locomotion and feeding by some eukaryotic organisms

gap junction cell junction that allows ions and small molecules to move between cytoplasms of adjacent cells via small channels or tubes

glial cell cell that supports and nourishes neurons

glycolysis metabolic pathway of cellular reactions that break down glucose to form pyruvic acid, in presence of oxygen, or lactic acid, in absence of oxygen, plus ATP

Golgi apparatus cell organelle of membranes and vesicles near nucleus that processes and packages newly synthesized proteins for other organelles or secretion

granular endoplasmic reticulum endoplasmic reticulum with ribosome-studded membrane that assembles proteins

granulocyte white blood cell containing granules in cytoplasm

ground substance thin gel in intercellular substance of connective tissue

helper T cell one of class of T cells that enhances antibody production and cytotoxic T cell function

histocompatibility antigens antigenic protein molecules on surface of nucleated cells

hypertonic solution fluid whose osmolarity exceeds that of plasma

hypotonic solution fluid whose osmolarity is less than that of plasma

intercellular fluid liquid between cells

interphase stage between two meiotic or mitotic cycles

interstitial fluid cells between germinal cells in reproductive organs

isotonic solution fluid with same osmolarity as plasma

Krebs cycle stage of cellular respiration and energy metabolism that occurs in mitochondria; citric acid cycle; tricarboxylic acid cycle

leukocyte cell involved with immune response; white blood cell

lymphocyte agranular white blood cell

lysosome membrane-enclosed organelle in which digestive enzymes are confined

macrophage large white blood cell that engulfs invaders such as bacteria

mast cell connective tissue cell containing heparin and histamine

matrix connective tissue ground substance

mediated transport movement of substances with assistance of cell membrane components

megakaryocyte large bone marrow cell that produces platelets

meiosis cell division in which diploid chromosome number is reduced to haploid and received by gametes

membrane plasma membrane

memory cell agent of lasting immunity; long-lived lymphocyte that rapidly initiates immune response to previously encountered antigen

microfilament fibrous structure in eukaryotic cytoplasm that may be involved in cytoplasmic motion

microphage neutrophil, esp. one containing granulocytes

microtubule hollow tube in cytoplasm that provides structural support for cell

mitochondria organelles involved in cellular respiration and breakdown of energy into small units convenient for most cellular processes

mitosis cell division that forms two identical cells with original number of chromosomes

monocyte agranulocytic white blood cell that matures into macrophage

mucopolysaccharide gummy carbohydrate macromolecule

myofibrils contractile elements of muscle fiber

NAD nicotinamide adenine dinucleotide

neutrophil most common white blood cell, which protects body against infection

nicotinamide adenine dinucleotide NAD; coenzyme that accepts hydrogen and transfers it to cytochrome B

nuclear envelope double membrane surrounding nucleus of eukaryotic cell

nucleolus dense body in eukaryotic nucleus that is site of ribosomal RNA production

nucleus control center for all cellular activities

organelles membrane-bound compartments, nonmembranous particles, and filamentous structures that perform specialized functions and constitute internal structure of cells

osmolarity capacity for osmosis

osmosis diffusion of water across semipermeable membrane

osmotic pressure difference of solute concentrations on either side of semipermeable membrane

osteoblast bone-forming cell

oxidative phosphorylation use of electron energy released during cell respiration that yields energy-rich ATP

oxyntic cells parietal cells

parietal cells acid-secreting cells of stomach lining; oxyntic cells

pathway sequence of enzyme-catalyzed reactions by which energy-yielding substance is catabolized by protoplasm

peroxisome vesicle in which purines are broken down by cell

phagocytosis intake of solid particle by cell

photosynthesis process by which chlorophyll in green plant produces organic compounds from radiant light energy

pili rigid, cylindrical rods, comparable to flagella, that attach some prokaryotic bacteria to food sources

plasma cell antibody-producing cell cloned from B cell

plasma membrane outer layer of cell that separates it from environment; membrane

plastid any of various membrane-bound organelles in plants and algae that store starch, contain pigment, or are chlorophyll-containing site of photosynthesis

platelet protoplasmic blood cell fragment involved in clotting

polymorphonuclear granulocytes white blood cells with variable nuclei

prokaryote any cell that lacks distinct membrane-bound nucleus and organelles in its cytoplasm, including bacteria and blue-green algae

red blood cell erythrocyte

RER rough endoplasmic reticulum

respiration process that releases energy by breakdown of complex organic compound

Rhesus factor Rh factor

Rh factor group of antigens that may (Rh+) or may not (Rh-) be present on plasma membranes of erythrocytes; Rhesus factor

ribosome small cytoplasmic organelle and site of protein synthesis

rough endoplasmic reticulum RER; granular endoplasmic reticulum

sarcoplasmic reticulum network in muscle cell that transmits excitation to contractile proteins

Schwann cells cells forming neurilemma sheath around peripheral nerves

secretory vesicles membranous sac formed by Golgi apparatus, involved in exocytosis

semipermeable membrane membrane that allows only certain substances to pass through

SER smooth endoplasmic reticulum

smooth endoplasmic reticulum SER; agranular endoplasmic reticulum

spindle assembly of microtubules responsible for separating sister chromatids during mitosis

suppressor T cell T cell capable of inhibiting activity of B cells and other T cells

T cell lymphocyte originating in thymus gland, involved in cellular immunity; T lymphocyte

tight junction relatively impermeable discrete intercellular union

T lymphocyte T cell

transport molecule protein molecule involved in active transport and facilitated diffusion

tricarboxylic acid cycle Krebs cycle

vacuole membranous cavity within protoplasm, usu. containing watery fluid

vesicle intracellular membrane-bound sac that is much smaller than a vacuole

white blood cell leukocyte

zymogen granule particle that stores active enzymes

Physiology

abscess microbes, leukocytes, and liquefied tissue debris walled off by fibroblasts and collagen

absorption passage of water or dissolved substance, esp. nutrient materials, into cell, blood, tissue, or organism

absorptive state period during which nutrients are entering bloodstream from gastrointestinal tract

accommodation adjustment of eye for viewing at various distances by changing shape of lens

acetylcholine ACh; a neurotransmitter

acidosis abnormal state of reduced alkalinity of blood and tissues

ACTH adrenocorticotropic hormone

actin protein located in thin filaments of muscle that, in conjunction with myosin, contracts muscle

action potential electrical signal propagated over long distance by nerve and muscle cells

active hyperemia increased blood flow through tissue as a result of increase in metabolic activity

active site area on enzyme to which substrate binds

adaptation decrease in frequency of action potentials fired by neuron despite stimulus of constant magnitude

ADH antidiuretic hormone

adipose fat in connective tissue

adrenaline epinephrine

adrenergic compound that acts like epinephrine or norepinephrine

adrenocorticotropic hormone ACTH; polypeptide secreted by anterior pituitary that stimulates adrenal cortex to secrete cortisol

afferent neuron neuron that transmits impulses to central nervous system and brain

afferent pathway component of reflex arc that transmits information from receptor to integrating center

albumin most abundant protein found in blood plasma

aldosterone steroid hormone secreted by adrenal cortex that regulates electrolyte balance in blood

alkalosis abnormal state of increased alkalinity of blood and tissues

all-or-none response event that occurs either maximally or not at all, usu. contraction of muscle fiber or firing of neuron

allosteric enzyme enzyme whose activity can be altered by modulator molecules binding to areas other than binding site

alpha rhythm prominent 8-13 Hz oscillation in EEG of awake, relaxed adult with closed eyes

alveolar pressure air pressure within alveoli of lungs

alveolar ventilation volume of air entering alveoli per minute

amino acid any of twenty-five organic acids containing an amino group that link together into polypeptide chains to form the proteins required for life, ten of which cannot be synthesized by the body and must be consumed

amylase enzyme that breaks down starch into disaccharides

anabolism constructive metabolism in which food is changed into living tissue

androgen male sex hormone

antibody protein secreted by plasma cells capable of combining with specific antigen that stimulated its production

antidiuretic hormone ADH; peptide hormone

synthesized in hypothalamus and released from posterior pituitary, causing retention of more water in body

antihistamine chemical that blocks action of histamine

antivenin antidote to venom produced by venomous animal

aortic-body chemoreceptor sensor of oxygen and carbon dioxide pressure and acidity of blood, located in aorta

apocrine secretion release of substance by breaking away of entire top of gland cell

arterial baroreceptors nerve endings in arterial walls that sense changes in blood pressure

arteriolar resistance resistance to blood flow of arterioles

atrophy wasting away of muscle or organ, esp. from disuse

automaticity capacity for self-excitation

autoregulation independent ability of individual organs to self-regulate blood flow to the organ

bacteria *pl., sing.* **bacterium**; ubiquitous, unicellular organisms appearing singly or in chains in spherical, spiral, or rod-shaped form

baroreceptor neural receptor sensitive to pressure and rate of change in pressure; stretch receptor

basal (*adj*) at resting level

basal metabolic rate BMR; metabolic rate when subject is awake but at mental and physical rest, at a comfortable temperature, and without food for at least twelve hours

beta rhythm low, fast oscillations in EEG pattern of alert, awake adult who is actively paying attention or thinking

bile greenish liver secretion that is stored in gallbladder until released to emulsify fats in small intestine

bile salts steroid molecules in bile that promote solubilization and digestion of fats

bilirubin yellow substance that results from breakdown of red blood cells, excreted as component of bile

binding site area on protein with chemical groups that react with a specific substrate, binding it to surface of protein

biological clock internal factors that control innate body rhythms without external stimulation

bioluminescence emission of light produced by living organism

biosynthesis formation of organic compounds from elements or simple compounds by living organisms

blocking antibody antibody whose production is induced by cancer cells or tissue transplants and that blocks the killing of those cells by cytotoxic T cells

blood liquid that serves as an exchange medium between external environment and cells of organism

blood-brain barrier group of anatomical barriers and transport systems that tightly controls types of substances entering extracellular space of brain

blood clot network of fibers and other blood parts that covers wound and prevents additional blood loss

blood pressure pressure exerted by blood on walls of vessels

blood sugar glucose

blood types classification of blood by presence of A, B, O, or AB antigens on plasma membranes of erythrocytes, or presence of anti-A or anti-B antibodies in plasma

BMR basal metabolic rate

bradykinin peptide vasodilator that increases capillary permeability and probably stimulates pain receptors

breathing movement of air in and out of lungs

bulk flow movement of fluids or gases from region of higher pressure to one of lower pressure

calcitonin peptide hormone secreted by thyroid that reduces excess of calcium in blood by depositing it in bone

carbohydrate any of various organic saccharide sugars, starches, and celluloses that supply energy to body when consumed

carbonic anhydrase enzyme that catalyzes reaction combining water and carbon dioxide into carbonic acid, essential to effective respiration and production of stomach acid

cardiac output volume of blood pumped by either ventricle per minute

carotid-body chemoreceptor sensor of oxygen and carbon dioxide pressure and acidity in blood, located near origin of carotid artery

catabolism destructive metabolism in which living tissue is changed into energy and waste products

catecholamines chemically similar neurotransmitters dopamine, epinephrine, and norepinephrine

CCK cholecystokinin

cell-mediated immunity specific immune response mediated by cytotoxic T lymphocytes

central thermoreceptors temperature sensors located in hypothalamus, spinal cord, and internal organs

chemical specificity property of protein binding site such that only one or a few substrates can bind with it

chemoreceptors afferent nerve endings or associated sensory cells that respond to concentrations of certain chemicals

chemotaxis orientation and movement of cells in specific direction in response to chemical stimulus

chitin tough, horny substance that forms most of outer covering of insects and crustaceans

cholecystokinin CCK; peptide hormone secreted by small intestine that regulates motility and secretions of stomach, gallbladder contraction, and pancreatic enzyme secretion; pancreozymin

cholesterol steroid molecule that is precursor of steroid hormones and bile salts, component of plasma membranes, and present in fat and blood

cholinergic (*adj*) pertaining to or acting like acetylcholine

chyme solution of partially digested food in lumen of stomach and intestines

clearance volume per minute of plasma from which a specific substance has been completely removed

climacteric physical and emotional changes as sexual maturity gives way to cessation of reproductive function in female and testosterone decrease in male

closed circulatory system system in which blood is enclosed in vessels and does not directly bathe organs

coenzyme nonprotein organic molecule that temporarily joins with enzyme during reaction, serves as a carrier molecule, is not consumed in reaction, and can be reused until degraded; cofactor

cofactor coenzyme

collagen extremely strong fibrous protein that functions as structural element in connective tissue, tendons, and ligaments

colloid large molecule, such as plasma protein, to which capillaries are relatively impermeable

command neuron neuron whose activity initiates a series of neural events that result in a voluntary action

compensatory growth type of regeneration present in many organs after tissue damage

complement set of enzymes in bloodstream that work with antibodies to attack foreign cells and bacteria

complex carbohydrate polysaccharide

compliance distensibility of chest and lungs

conducting portion air passages whose walls are too thick to allow gas exchange between air and blood

conducting system network of cardiac muscle fibers specialized to conduct electrical activity to different areas of heart

cone one of two major photoreceptor types in retina that give rise to color vision

contractility force of contraction that is independent of fiber length

contraction tension-generating process of a muscle

contraction time interval between muscle action potential and development of peak twitch tension or shortening by muscle

control system interconnected components that function to keep physical or chemical value within predetermined range

convergence synapses from many presynaptic neurons acting on a single postsynaptic neuron

core temperature temperature inside of body

corneal reflex closure of eyelid in response to irritation of cornea

corticotropin releasing hormone CRH; hormone produced in hypothalamus that stimulates ACTH secretion by anterior pituitary

cortisol steroid hormone secreted by adrenal cortex that regulates organic metabolism by converting fats and proteins to glucose

cortisone steroid hormone secreted by adrenal cortex that counteracts pain and swelling

countercurrent multiplier system mechanism that creates high osmolarity in medulla of kidney, allowing higher urine concentration

CRH corticotropin releasing hormone

cross bridge projection of myosin molecule from thick filament of muscle that is capable of exerting force on thin filament, causing it to slide past thick filament

crossed-extensor reflex increased activation of extensor muscle on side of body opposite a limb flexion

current movement of electrical charge caused by movement of ions

dark adaptation improvement in sensitivity of vision after one is in darkness for some time

dead space area of respiratory system in which very little or no respiration occurs

defecation expulsion of feces from rectum

deoxyhemoglobin hemoglobin not combined with oxygen; reduced hemoglobin

diastole period of cardiac cycle in which ventricles are not contracting

diastolic pressure minimum blood pressure during cardiac cycle

digestion process of breaking down large particles and high-molecular weight substances into small molecules

disaccharide carbohydrate molecule consisting of two covalently bonded monosaccharides

disinhibition removal of inhibition from a neuron, allowing its activity to increase

diuretic substance that inhibits fluid reabsorption in kidney, causing increase in excreted urine

divergence single presynaptic neuron synapsing with and influencing activity of multiple postsynaptic neurons

dominant hemisphere cerebral hemisphere that controls hand used most frequently for intricate tasks

dopamine catecholamine neurotransmitter, precursor of epinephrine and norepinephrine

dual innervation innervation of organ or gland by both sympathetic and parasympathetic nerves

ectopic focus region of heart other than sinoatrial node that assumes role of cardiac pacemaker

edema accumulation of fluid in interstitial space

EDV end-diastolic volume

EEG arousal transformation of electroencephalogram pattern from alpha rhythm to beta rhythm, associated with increased level of attention

effector cell or tissue whose change in activity constitutes response to stimulus

efferent neuron neuron that carries information away from central nervous system to postganglionic neurons, muscles, or gland cells

electrolyte substance that ionizes in solution and conducts electric current

embolus mass of matter that obstructs blood flow

emulsification maintenance of lipid droplets in solution

end-diastolic volume EDV; amount of blood in heart just prior to systole

endocrine gland ductless organ that synthesizes hormones and releases them directly into bloodstream

endocrine system all ductless glands in body

endorphin neurotransmitter that exhibits painkilling activity

endoskeleton internal bony or cartilaginous supporting structure of vertebrates

end-plate potential EPP; excitatory change in voltage across motor end plate of muscle cell membrane

end-systolic volume ESV; amount of blood remaining in ventricle after ejection

enzyme organic catalyst for physiological activity not used up in reaction

enzyme induction process in which cell is induced to form enzyme in response to substance entering cell

epinephrine hormone released by adrenal medulla that elevates blood sugar and initiates fight-or-flight response; adrenaline

EPP end-plate potential

equilibrium potential millivolts required to oppose movement caused by concentration gradient of specific ion

erythropoiesis formation of erythrocytes

erythropoietin hormone secreted mainly by kidney that stimulates erythrocyte production

essential amino acids ten amino acids that cannot be synthesized in body and must be derived from diet

essential nutrients substances necessary for normal body function that cannot be synthesized by body

ESV end-systolic volume

excitability ability to produce action potentials

excitatory synapse synapse that, when activated, either increases likelihood of postsynaptic neuron reaching threshold and firing or increases firing frequency of existing action potentials

excretion loss of substance through urine, feces, or other material expelled from body

exocrine gland gland that secretes products through duct

exoskeleton hard external supporting structure of invertebrates, such as shell of crustacean

expiration movement of air out of lungs

expiratory reserve volume supplemental air that can be forced out of lungs

extension straightening of flexed limb

extrinsic clotting pathway series of reactions by which clotting is initiated

facilitation rendering excitation of nerve cells easier

fat any of various mixtures of solid or semisolid triglycerides in adipose tissue, insoluble in water

fatty acid organic compound whose carbon chain ends in a carboxyl group

feces digestive waste products

feedback change in quantity of substance that initiates either release or suppression of release of that substance

fermentation conversion of complex carbohydrates or other organic substances into other chemicals by enzyme action

ferritin protein in liver, spleen, and bone marrow that stores iron for metabolic use

fever abnormal increase of body temperature

fibrillation lack of coordination in contraction of muscle fibers

fibrin insoluble protein formed during clotting

fibrinogen soluble protein that transforms to fibrin

fight-or-flight response adrenal-activated mobilization of body for extraordinary exertion

filtration passing of fluid through membrane under pressure

flexion bending of limb at joint

flexion reflex contraction of flexor muscle; withdrawal reflex

flexor muscle muscle that causes bending at joint by contraction

flux excessive fluid discharge from bowels

folic acid vitamin in B complex

GABA gamma-aminobutyric acid

gamma-aminobutyric acid GABA; inhibitory neurotransmitter of central nervous system

gamma globulin IgG; globular protein antibody in plasma; most abundant class of plasma antibodies

gastrin digestive system hormone that stimulates hydrochloric acid release by stomach and secretion of digestive enzyme by pancreas

GFR glomerular filtration rate

globulin protein insoluble in water; plasma protein complex comprised mainly of globulins

glomerular filtration rate GFR; milliliters of plasma per minute filtered through kidney

glucagon pancreatic hormone that increases blood glucose levels

glucocorticoid adrenal cortex hormone that effects salt and water metabolism and stimulates conversion of noncarbohydrates to carbohydrates

gluconeogenesis glucose formation from noncarbohydrates

glucose monosaccharide six-carbon sugar in blood; blood sugar

glutamic acid amino acid that may be brain neurotransmitter

glycerol three-carbon alcohol derived from fats

glycine simplest amino acid, present in most proteins

glycogen white polysaccharide sugar, derived from glucose, that is principal form in which carbohydrate is stored in tissue

glycogenolysis conversion of glycogen to glucose

glycolipid sugar lipid containing short, water-soluble carbohydrate chain

glycolytic fast fibers skeletal muscle fibers energized aerobically

glycoprotein carbohydrate-protein complex

Golgi tendon organs sensory nerve fibers that monitor tension between tendons and muscle cells

granuloma mass of chronically inflamed tissue

Hb hemoglobin

HDL high-density lipoprotein

hematocrit percentage of total blood volume made up of blood cells

heme iron-containing pigment

hemoglobin Hb; iron-containing protein that carries oxygen in red blood cells and gives them red color

hemostasis stoppage of bleeding

heparin anticoagulant secreted by liver

high-density lipoprotein HDL; lipid-protein aggregate with low proportion of lipid or cholesterol that removes cholesterol from arteries

histamine amine derived from amino acid histidine that is released in allergic reaction, causing dilation of blood vessels and lowering of blood pressure

histone protein that is integral to chromosome structure

holocrine secretion process by which exocrine glands shed whole cells and their contents

homeostasis maintenance of constant internal environment

hormone chemical agent usu. released by ductless gland that has regulatory effect on functions in other parts of body

humoral immunity defense against disease by antibodies in body fluids

hydrochloric acid acid secreted by stomach during digestion

hydrolysis splitting of molecules by addition of water

hydrostatic pressure pressure exerted by a fluid

hyperemia increased blood flow

hyperpolarization presence of larger than normal number of oppositely charged ions on opposite sides of membrane

hypersensitivity allergic reaction

hypertrophy increase in size of cells, tissues, or organ

hypoxia oxygen deficiency at tissue level

hypoxic hypoxia hypoxia due to decreased oxygen pressure in arterial blood

Ig immunoglobulin

IgG gamma globulin

immune responses body's defense reaction through dual modes of antibody and cellular response

immunity resistance to specific disease

immunoglobulin Ig; any of five classes of antibodies: IgG, IgM, IgA, IgD, and IgE

inspiration taking of air into lungs

inspiratory reserve volume amount of air that can be drawn into lungs in excess of tidal volume

insulin pancreatic hormone that regulates blood sugar level

interferon molecule that inhibits viral replication in cells

internal environment conditions within an organism

interneuron internuncial neuron

internuncial neuron nerve cell connecting sensory and motor neurons in brain and spinal cord; interneuron

intrinsic clotting pathway series of reactions that initiate clotting of blood

intrinsic factor glycoprotein secreted by stomach and required for absorption of vitamin B_{12}

ischemia reduced blood supply to organ or tissue

isometric contraction increase of force in muscle whose length does not change

isotonic contraction development of force that remains the same during shortening of muscle

ketone product of lipid metabolism characterized by CO group

kinesthesia sensation of position and movement of limbs

kinin vasodilatory polypeptide

lactase enzyme that cleaves lactose into glucose and galactose

lactic acid three-carbon breakdown product of glucose

latent period elapsed time between stimulus and response

lateral inhibition inhibitory interaction between adjacent neurons

LDL low-density lipoprotein

lecithin phospholipid in nerve tissue and blood

ligand any molecule or ion that binds to protein surface by noncovalent bonds

lipase fat-splitting enzyme

lipid fat or fatlike substance insoluble in water, typically serving as energy-storage molecule

lipoprotein molecule combining protein and lipid

low-density lipoprotein LDL; protein-lipid aggregate that is major cholesterol carrier in plasma

lumen cavity within tubular structure

lymph colorless fluid derived from blood and carried in small ducts of lymphatic vessels

lymphoid tissue connective tissue containing lymphocytes

lymphokine regulatory soluble protein secreted by T cells

mechanoreceptor sensory cell or organ that receives mechanical stimuli

metabolic acidosis abnormal decrease in blood pH not caused by respiratory phenomena

metabolic alkalosis abnormal increase in blood pH not caused by respiratory phenomena

metabolic rate level of energy expenditure

metabolism sum of all chemical reactions in living cell or organism

microorganism any living organism too small to be viewed by unaided eye, including bacteria, viruses, protists, and some algae and fungi

micturition excretion of urine

mineral naturally occurring inorganic substance required for growth or functioning of organism

mineralocorticoid steroid salt-retaining hormone of adrenal cortex

mononuclear phagocyte system monocytes and macrophages

monosaccharide carbohydrate, such as glucose or fructose, consisting of a single sugar molecule, generally made up of five or six carbon atoms

monosynaptic reflex pathway involving single junction between two neurons

motor (*adj*) having to do with muscles and movement

motor neuron efferent neuron that innervates skeletal muscle fibers

mucin protein that forms mucus when mixed with water

mucous membrane mucus-secreting membrane lining body cavities and canals connecting with external air

mucus viscid, watery lubricating solution secreted by mucous membranes

muscle fatigue depressed metabolic activity of muscle cells due to increased concentration of lactic acid

muscle spindle modified skeletal muscle cell with stretch receptors that regulate muscle tone

muscle tone condition in which muscles are always slightly contracted

myogenic (*adj*) originating within muscle

myoglobin protein in muscles that binds oxygen

myosin contractile protein that forms thick filaments of muscle

negative feedback condition in which increase in substance over certain level produces responses which inhibit synthesis of that substance

nerve growth factor protein secreted by cells that attracts neurons to grow toward them

neuron functional unit of a nerve, including cell body, axon, and dendrites

neurotransmitter substance that transmits or inhibits nerve impulses from nerve cell to another cell at synapse

neutrophil exudation release of white blood cells

night vision higher than normal concentration of rods in retina, causing increased ability to see in darkness

nociceptor pain receptor

norepinephrine hormone of adrenal medulla that elevates blood pressure and blood sugar levels

optimal length length at which muscle fiber develops maximal tension

organ collection of tissues joined in structural unit to serve a common function

organ system group of organs with integrated functions

osmoreceptor hypothalamic neuron that

responds to osmotic pressure changes in blood and influences sense of thirst

oxidative (*adj*) using oxygen

oxidative fast fibers skeletal muscle fibers energized aerobically

oxidative slow fibers slow-fatiguing skeletal muscle fibers energized aerobically

oxyhemoglobin globular protein with a molecule of oxygen bonded to iron

pacemaker area of vertebrate heart that initiates heartbeat; sinoatrial node

pacinian corpuscle deep-pressure sensory receptor

palpitation abnormally rapid heartbeat

pancreozymin cholecystokinin

paradoxical sleep sleep with rapid eye movement and intermittent muscular twitching, associated with dream state; REM sleep

parahormone chemical control agent that can be synthesized by more than one cell type

parathyroid hormone PTH; hormone that promotes vitamin D synthesis and elevates blood calcium

pepsin stomach enzyme that degrades proteins

peptide compound of two or more amino acids

peripheral resistance opposition to flow of blood in vessels

peristaltic waves successive contractions of tubular wall that move its contents forward

permissiveness potentiation

phasic (*adj*) intermittent, as opposed to tonic

phospholipid lipid compound containing water-soluble phosphate group

phosphorylation addition of phosphate to molecule

photopigment colored substance that absorbs light over narrow band of wavelengths

photoreceptor cell or organ capable of detecting light

physiology study of functions and vital processes of organisms and their parts or organs

plasma fluid portion of blood and lymph

plasmin enzyme involved in blood clotting

pneumothorax condition of having air in thoracic cavity outside of lungs

polypeptide protein, polymer of amino acid subunits

polysaccharide complex carbohydrate compound of chains of simple sugars, such as cellulose or starch

positive feedback stimulation by message to cell or organ of increased activity by original message sender

postsynaptic neuron neuron that conducts information away from synapse

potential voltage difference between two points

potentiation one event making possible the occurrence of another; permissiveness

presynaptic neuron neuron that conducts action potential toward synapse

prion infectious, viruslike particle composed solely of protein without a genetic component, found in animals

prohormone inactive substance converted to active hormone after release into bloodstream

proprioception awareness of position, balance, and movement

prostaglandin fatty, acid-derived parahormone

protease protein-splitting enzyme

protein any of a large class of organic nitrogenous substances containing amino acids that occur in all animal and vegetable matter and are essential to diet

prothrombin inactive precursor of clotting enzyme thrombin

PTH parathyroid hormone

pulmonary ventilation volume of air exchanged by lungs per minute

pulse pressure difference between systolic and diastolic arterial blood pressures

P wave deflection in electrocardiogram caused by depolarization of atria

QRS complex electrocardiogram pattern that occurs during ventricular depolarization

rapid eye movement sleep REM sleep

RDA recommended dietary allowance

reactive hyperemia increased blood flow that causes body temperature above normal range; fever

receptor sensory cell or organ

receptor potential potential transmitted from receptor to second neuron along way to central nervous system

recommended dietary allowance RDA; government estimate of minimal nutrient requirements of vitamins and minerals

recruitment involvement of excitable cells in process due to increase in stimulus strength

red muscle fibers tissues that bind and store myoglobin

reduced hemoglobin deoxyhemoglobin

reflex involuntary response to stimulus

reflex arc functional pathway of neuron system consisting of at least one afferent and one efferent neuron and usu. one interneuron

refractory period recovery time during which excitable neuron membrane is unresponsive to stimulus

relative refractory period recovery time during which excitable neuron membrane will respond only to stimulus that is stronger than initial stimulus

relaxation time period required for tension in muscle fiber to decrease from peak to zero

REM sleep rapid *eye movement* sleep; paradoxical sleep

renin enzyme secreted by kidneys

residual volume air left in lungs after forcible expiration

respiration exchange of gases between body tissues and surrounding environment, specifically intake of oxygen by tissues, which give off carbon dioxide and water

respiratory acidosis abnormal decrease in blood pH due to respiratory dysfunction

respiratory alkalosis abnormal increase in blood pH due to respiratory dysfunction

respiratory quotient RQ; ratio of carbon dioxide produced to oxygen consumed as food is metabolized

respiratory rate depth and frequency of exhalation and inhalation, related to carbon dioxide levels

respiratory system all organs involved in respiration

resting membrane potential all voltage measurable across membrane when it is not transmitting

rod visual cell of retina of eye sensitive to low levels of light

RQ respiratory quotient

saliva watery, slightly acidic secretion of salivary glands that moistens food and initiates its breakdown

sarcomere structural and functional unit of contraction in striated muscle

saturated fat fat in which carbon chains are bonded by single bonds while simultaneously bound to as much hydrogen as possible

SDA specific dynamic action

secretin duodenal hormone that promotes secretion of pancreatic juice

secretion synthesis and release of substance by cell or organ; such a released substance

segmentation division of body into more or less similar parts

sensor cell that receives signals

serotonin brain neurotransmitter that seems to have calming effect

serum liquid portion of coagulated blood

sinoatrial node pacemaker

sliding-filament mechanism contraction of muscle due to sliding past each other of thick and thin filaments

slow-wave sleep sleep pattern characterized by slow delta waves for four-fifths of total sleep time

somatic receptor neuron in voluntary nervous system connected directly to central nervous system

spatial summation increased response of nerve due to increased excitation

specific dynamic action SDA; increase of body temperature and basal metabolic rate after consumption of meal

specificity influence directed toward one response or body part

split brain division of brain into left and right hemispheres, which control different functions

starch complex molecule composed of many monosaccharides; main food storage substance in plants

steady state continuous exchange of substances in and out of cells with no apparent change in concentrations

steroid nonfat lipid characterized by four interconnected carbon rings

stimulus any change or phenomenon that causes response in organism or its component

stress stimulus that causes imbalance in homeostasis

stretch receptor baroreceptor

striated muscle voluntary muscle with cylindrical fibers that controls skeleton

stroke volume milliliters per heartbeat of blood pumped by either ventricle

substrate substance that is recipient of enzymic action

summation temporal or spatial addition of electrical effects of multiple stimuli

surfactant substance that reduces surface tension

synapse junction between two excitable cells, esp. point at which neurotransmitters send impulses in response to action potential in one neuron

synaptic cleft intercellular space between two excitable cells

synergistic muscle muscle with additive effects

synthetic reactions anabolic reactions in which food is synthesized into living tissue

systemic circulation movement of blood from heart to all tissues except lungs and back of heart

systole contraction of heart muscle

systolic pressure blood pressure produced when ventricles contract

temporal summation increase of nerve or muscle cell response due to increased frequency of excitation

tetanus continuous contraction of muscle due to fusion of twitches

TH thyroid hormone

thermogenesis production of heat within body

thermoreceptor sensory receptor that responds to temperature changes

thick filaments myosin molecules in muscle cells

thin filaments threads consisting of actin, troponin, and tropomyosin molecules in muscle cells

threshold minimal level at which stimulus excites a response

thrombin enzymatic molecule involved in blood coagulation

thyroid hormone TH; thyroxine

thyrotropin thyroid stimulating hormone

thyroxine active thyroid hormone

tidal volume quantity of air moved during normal, quiet breathing

tissue group of similar cells that performs particular function

tolerance diminished response due to repeated exposure

trace element mineral present in body in extremely small amounts

transferrin protein that aids blood in transporting iron

triacylglycerol neutral fat lipid molecule composed of glycerol and three fatty acids; triglyceride

triglyceride triacylglycerol

triiodothyronine form of thyroxine

tropomyosin cablelike muscle protein in thin filaments

troponin structural muscle protein involved with contraction

trypsin pancreatic protein-cleaving enzyme

T wave electrocardiographic representation of electrical activity just prior to ventricular relaxation in diastole

twitch single contraction of muscle fiber

ultrafiltrate material separated from blood during filtering through renal capillaries

unsaturated fat fat in which some carbons are linked by double bonds

urea nitrogenous waste product of kidneys

uric acid nitrogenous waste product secreted in urine

vasoconstriction narrowing of blood vessel

vasodilation widening of blood vessel

vasopressin antidiuretic hormone

ventilation movement of air in and out of lungs

vestibular system sensory labyrinth of air in body cavities that responds to balance and movement

vestigial organ body part, such as tonsils or appendix, that no longer functions usefully

viroid infectious agent found in plants, consisting of single strand of RNA with no protein coat

virus ultramicroscopic, metabolically inert agent that can reproduce only within a host cell, containing RNA or DNA within protein coat

vital capacity maximal amount of air that can be moved by lungs

vitamin any of various organic compounds necessary for normal metabolic functions

withdrawal reflex flexion reflex

Environment, Ecology, and Animal Behavior

abiotic factors nonliving components that interact with and affect organisms in an ecosystem

abyssal zone deepest part of ocean where light is absent

acclimatization adaptive change in physiological system induced by prolonged exposure to environmental stress or a new environment

acid rain rain with abnormally high acid level, esp. due to combustion of fossil fuels

agonistic (*adj*) displaying any type of fighting behavior

algal bloom rapid growth of algae

altitudinal succession continuous succession of community types from low to high altitudes

altricial (*adj*) displaying condition in which young are born helpless and remain so for some time

altruism self-destructive behavior performed to benefit or protect others, esp. kin

amphibious (*adj*) capable of living both on land and in water

anaerobe bacterium that lives and grows without oxygen

animal multicellular, heterotrophic, usu. mobile organism

aquatic (*adj*) water-dwelling

arboreal (*adj*) tree-dwelling

autotroph organism that can produce its own food by using inorganic materials as its source of nutrients and usu. photosynthesis as its source of energy

avifauna bird life of particular area

behavior organism's observable responses to environment and stimuli

biodegradable (*adj*) capable of being broken down and absorbed in a natural environment, esp. susceptible to being broken down by microorganisms into simple compounds such as water and carbon dioxide

biohazard life-endangering substance, phenomenon, or activity

biological magnification increased concentration of chemicals along food chain

biomass total mass of organisms per unit area

biome discrete community and region, such as desert or tropical rain forest, characterized by same major life forms and climactic conditions

bioremediation use of biological means to restore biosphere or solve ecological problems, such as oil-eating microbes on an oil spill

biosphere sphere of life on Earth from crust into lower troposphere

biota flora and fauna of an area

biotic factors relationships among living organisms in an ecosystem

biotic potential reproductive potential of a species

birthrate number of organisms born per unit of time

boreal forest biome of wooded regions with cold, dry climate, sandy soil, and coniferous trees

camouflage any means of blending appearance with environment

canopy top layer of forest, where most food is produced

carbon cycle circulation of carbon in biosphere by plant photosynthesis, animal metabolism, and decomposition

carnivore meat-eating organism; consumer that feeds on other consumers

carrying capacity number of individuals of any species that a particular environment can support

circadian rhythm pattern in which a behavior occurs regularly in twenty-four hour cycle

clear-cutting logging of all trees in an area

climax community final stage in evolution of community

cold-blooded (*adj*) having body temperature that varies with approximate surrounding environment, as in fish and reptiles; poikilothermal

colonial (*adj*) designating species that occupies its habitat in groups

commensalism relationship in which one organism benefits from a host organism without affecting it

communication behavior that influences behavior of another organism in adaptive manner

community naturally occurring group of organisms living in a certain area

competition struggle between organisms of same or different species for access to limited resources

competitive exclusion principle rule that two populations cannot occupy the same ecological niche

conservation protection and preservation of natural environment and resources

conspecific member of same species

consumer organism that consumes other organisms as food

courtship behavior patterns used to attract potential mate

cryptic coloration type of camouflage in which color of organism blends with environment

death rate number of organisms that die per unit of time

deciduous forest biome with trees that lose their leaves in winter, forming belt through temperate latitudes, including monsoon rain forests of Asia and Africa

decomposer organism, such as bacterium, that causes decay

desert biome of arid regions with sparse, widely spaced vegetation and rainfall under 10 inches (25 cm) per year

detritus substrate litter composed of decaying organic matter

dispersion way in which species uses its habitat, such as colonial or solitary

displacement behavior activity, often due to ambivalence, not directly related to immediate stimulus

display behavior or series of behaviors modified by evolution for communication

dominance ability of one member of community to exercise control over other members and their environment

dominant species characteristic species of a community

echolocation determination of size, shape, and location of an object by bouncing high-frequency sound waves off it, used by organisms such as bats and porpoises

ecological niche specific role organism plays in community, esp. behavior and position in food cycle

ecological succession replacement of one community by another

ecology relationship and balance between organisms and their environment

ecosystem all interactions of a community of organisms with its physical environment

ecotage extreme measures, such as destruction of tree-cutting machinery, used in opposition to humanly caused ecological damage

ecotone transition zone between communities

edge effect increase in variety and density of organisms in ecotone

effluent outflow, usu. offensive, of human works and waste

emigration aggregate of movement of animals out of an area

endangered species species of organism in imminent danger of extinction, due usu. to destruction of its habitat, loss of food supply, evolutionary deselection, or destruction by humans

endogenous (*adj*) originating or developing from within the organism

environment all external factors acting on an organism

environmental resistance environmental factors that check biotic potential of a population

estuary semienclosed body of water along coast, often brackish

ethogram detailed description of behavior of an organism

eusociality presence of nonreproductive castes, such as worker bees, within a species

eutrophication aging and death of lake, esp. due to upset in ecological balance

exogenous (*adj*) originating or derived from outside the organism

fauna animal life of an area

feeding level level of energy transfer in ecosystem

first-order consumer consumer that feeds directly on producer; herbivore

flora plant life of an area

food chain route of passage of energy and materials through community of organisms, with successively larger ones feeding on smaller ones

food web all possible feeding relationships in an ecosystem

forest floor bottommost stratum of a forest

geographic isolation populations separated by geographical features

global warming increase in Earth's average atmospheric temperature and corresponding changes in climate, esp. due to greenhouse effect

grassland biome of plains regions, characterized by grasses

greenhouse effect increase of carbon dioxide in Earth's atmosphere that prevents radiated heat from dissipating, thereby raising its temperature

grooming manipulative cleaning of body surface

growth basic capacity of all organisms to develop or increase, usu. by assimilation of nutriments

habitat natural environment of an organism

habituation depletion of response to often repeated stimulus

herbivore plant-eating organism, consumer of producers

heterotroph organism that cannot produce food and that requires living or dead organic materials as its principal source of nutrition

hibernation period of dormancy during time of low temperatures when metabolic processes slow to minimum

home range area to which organism habitually restricts its movement

homing ability of displaced organism to return to its home range or place of birth

homoiotherm warm-blooded organism that maintains relatively constant body temperature

host organism that harbors and provides benefits to another organism

imprinting bonding of newborn, esp. bird, to first organism that mothers it

insectivore animal that feeds on insects

insessorial (*adj*) adapted for perching, as bird's foot

instinct innate behavior genetically keyed for and not learned

interspecific competition competition between populations of different species

intraspecific competition competition between members of same species

jungle dense forest community that results from secondary succession of rain forest

K selection process that favors competitive ability within a population and few offspring with great investment in each

laterite hard, impermeable crust formed by water leaching exposed soils in areas cleared of tropical rain forest

latitudinal succession continuous succession of community types from equator to poles

learning process by which responses and behavior of an organism are modified due to experience, as through conditioning and associative learning, imprinting in early life, and imitation

lek area repeatedly used for communal courtship displays

limiting factor component of environment that prevents population increase at given time

littoral zone area of ocean close to shore and subject to action of tides

marine (*adj*) sea-dwelling

Mediterranean scrub biome with mild winters and long, dry summers, characterized by small trees and spiny, evergreen shrubs, primarily in California and around Mediterranean Sea

microenvironment small area in ecosystem that differs from rest of area

migration seasonal movement of populations of animals

mimicry evolution of one species to resemble another for some selective advantage

mobbing group assault to drive off predator

molting regular shedding of all or part of outer layer of skin, esp. in snakes and crabs; shedding of feathers in birds

mutualism relationship in which two animals live in mutually beneficial, often necessary, association

neritic zone area of ocean along continental shelf beyond littoral zone

niche ecological niche

nitrogen cycle circulation of nitrogen through plants and animals in biosphere

nitrogenous waste nitrogen-containing animal waste product

ocean aquatic community covering almost three fourths of Earth's surface

omnivore plant- and animal-eating organism, feeding on both producers and consumers

oxygen cycle circulation of oxygen through biosphere by its release from plants during photosynthesis and utilization by animals during respiration

pair-bonding long-lasting association between male and female for cooperative rearing of young

parasite organism that lives in or on host from which it obtains nourishment

parasitism relationship in which parasite organism is completely dependent on host organism for nourishment and host is usu. harmed

pecking order social hierarchy, dominance

pelagic (adj) dwelling in the open sea

pheromones chemicals produced by one organism that influence behavior of another

pioneering stage first stage in ecological succession, usu. consisting of hardy autotrophs

plankton aggregate of microscopic, passively floating or slightly motile organisms in body of water, being primarily algae and protozoans that serve as food for marine animals

poikilotherm cold-blooded organism having body temperature that varies with that of environment

pollutant any substance that makes air, water, or soil unclean

pollution introduction of impurities and contaminants into environment, esp. air and water pollution

population group of organisms that naturally interbreeds, living in same locality

population density number of individuals per unit area

population dynamics combination of various factors affecting the size of populations

population growth changes in size of population with time

precocial condition in which young are able to move about and forage for food shortly after birth

predation feeding of one organism on another

predator animal that feeds on other organisms

primary production energy accumulated and stored in plants through photosynthesis

primary succession ecological succession that begins with lifeless terrain, first succession in an ecosystem

producer organism that can make its own food, autotroph

pyramid of biomass relationship revealing decrease of biomass with each successive feeding level

pyramid of energy relationship revealing loss of energy as it is transferred along food chain

pyramid of numbers relationship revealing decrease in number of organisms at each higher feeding level

rain forest tropical rain forest

reciprocal altruism seemingly altruistic social behavior performed in expectation that favor will be returned

recycling reprocessing of used materials, esp. nonbiodegradable ones

red tide overabundance of dinoflagellate protozoans in usu. subtropical marine waters, turning them reddish-brown and producing a fish-killing toxin

renewable resource resource that can be replaced naturally

reproductive isolation any barrier to interbreeding

resource anything humans take from environment; anything an organism needs to live

resource partitioning division of resources among similar species coexisting in same ecological niche

ritualization evolutionary modification of behavior patterns to serve as communication

R selection process that favors rapid population increase, with many offspring and little investment in each

saprophyte organism that feeds on dead and decaying matter

savanna biome consisting of tropical grasslands with scattered clumps of trees, found esp. in Africa

scavenger animal that feeds on dead animals

secondary succession series of ecological changes that occur when species of a climax community are removed

second-order consumer animal that eats a first-order consumer

sedentary (adj) not migratory; living in one place

smog fog and mist made heavier, darker, and more toxic by absorption of chemical fumes and smoke, usu. in urban areas

social behavior interactions among animals of one species living in structured, mutually dependent groups

social hierarchy series of dominance-subordination relationships in group; pecking order

sociality conditions and processes of social existence and interaction among organisms of species and among species

solar collector device for collecting and converting radiant energy of sunlight into electric power

solar energy radiant energy of sunlight, an abundant and nonpolluting alternative to fossil fuels

solitary species whose members live separately

species diversity number of species in community

S-shaped curve normal population growth curve

stimulus substance or phenomenon that causes or changes activity of an organism

strip mining laying bare of mineral deposits in earth to extract them, causing erosion

substrate surface on which an organism lives or moves

succession ecological succession

symbiosis relationship in which two organisms live in close, mutually beneficial association

taiga subarctic biome characterized by coniferous forests

temperate deciduous forest biome characterized by even distribution of rain averaging 39 inches (100 cm) per year; region in which trees periodically shed leaves

temperate grassland biome with flat to rolling terrain, covered by sod-forming grasses and legumes, forming transitional area to deserts, including plains, steppes, veld, and pampas

terrestrial (adj) ground-dwelling

territory area defended from intruders, usu. of same species, by organism or organisms

tetrapod four-legged vertebrate such as mammal or reptile

third-order consumer animal that eats a second-order consumer

trophic levels series of steps on food chain

tropical rain forest equatorial biome characterized by constant warm temperature, heavy rainfall, dense, varied, evergreen plant growth, and enormous diversity of life forms

tropism involuntary response of organism to stimulus

tundra arctic biome characterized by low average temperature and rainfall, permafrost, and few large plants

vertical stratification layers of a forest from top to bottom

warm-blooded (adj) having relatively constant body temperature regardless of surrounding environment; homoiothermal

warning coloration display of bright colors to announce rather than conceal animal's presence

water cycle worldwide circulation of water molecules throughout atmosphere, powered by sun through evaporation and precipitation

weathering mechanical process of freezing, thawing, and erosion

zero population growth birthrate equal to death rate

Reproduction and Development

allantois membrane for respiratory exchange in embryonic birds and reptiles; part of placenta in mammals

amnion membrane enclosing fluid-filled cavity containing embryo

androgen male sex hormone

anisogamy condition in most animals in which gametes are of different sizes

baculum slim bone supporting rigidity of penis in many mammals

bilateral symmetry mirroring of right and left halves of body

blastula hollow ball of cells formed from developing egg in early stage of noneutherian embryo

budding direct growth of new individual from body of old one

CG chorionic gonadotropin

chorionic gonadotropin CG; protein hormone secreted by blastocyst and placenta during first trimester of pregnancy

cleavage progressive subdivision of zygote by mitotic cell division

clitoris female erectile organ homologous to penis

cloaca combined urogenital and rectal chamber in most nonmammalian vertebrates

coitus sexual intercourse

colostrum thin, milky fluid secreted by mammary glands for several days after birth prior to onset of milk production

copulation sexual intercourse, esp. mammalian

cytokinesis stage of cell division in which cytoplasm divides to form two new cells

deuterostome animal, such as any chordate, in which anus and mouth form separately in the developing embryo

development stages of growth from conception through birth to maturity and death

diapause period in some species between fertilization of egg and beginning of development

differentiation development of specialized tissue from nonspecialized tissue

ectoderm outermost germ layer in early embryo that forms nervous system and integument

egg female gamete; protective reproductive structure enclosing ovum and nutrient supply, esp. of birds, fish, reptiles, and insects

embryo organism in early stages of development before birth

endoderm innermost germ layer in early embryo that forms gut and glands

estradiol estrogen hormone secreted by ovaries

estriol estrogen hormone secreted by placenta

estrogen group of steroid hormones secreted by female reproductive system

estrous cycle repeated series of changes in reproductive physiology culminating in estrus

estrus period of maximum sexual receptivity in female mammals, usu. related to release of eggs; heat

eutherian (*adj*) designating placental mammals or condition in which mammalian embryo is nourished by placenta

fallopian tube one of a pair of tubes that carries eggs away from ovaries in humans

fertilization union of two gametes that activates development of egg

fetus human embryo after third month

follicle stimulating hormone FSH; anterior pituitary hormone that stimulates maturation of ova and sperm

FSH follicle stimulating hormone

fusion joining of two gametes to form zygote

gamete mature sex cell: egg or sperm

genitalia reproductive organs, esp. external organs

germ formative structure

germ cell gamete

gestation developmental period of young in uterus of mammal

GH growth hormone

gonad organ that produces gametes: female ovary or male testis

gonadotropic hormone anterior pituitary hormone that stimulates sexual functions

gonopodium appendage used in fertilization

Graafian follicle ovarian follicle

growth hormone GH; anterior pituitary hormone that stimulates growth; somatotropin

hatching emergence of embryo as newborn from egg

heat estrus

hermaphrodite organism with both male and female reproductive organs

implantation settling of early mammalian embryo into uterine wall

inbreeding mating of closely related individuals within the same species

incubation development of egg by means of body warmth

interstitial cells cells between germ cells in reproductive organs

in utero unborn and developing in uterus

in vitro conceived and developing in isolation from living organism, as in test tube

lactation production of milk by mother's mammary glands

larva immature organism, such as caterpillar, that undergoes metamorphosis to become adult

LH luteinizing hormone

lordosis mating posture of many female mammals with back arched, rump raised, and vulva exposed

luteinizing hormone LH; anterior pituitary hormone that stimulates testosterone secretion in male and maturation of ovarian follicles in female

maggot larval form of certain insects, esp. flies

maturity stage in development at which organism's secondary sex characteristics and reproductive capacity are functioning

menarche onset of female menstrual cycle at puberty

menopause termination of female menstrual cycle and reproductive capability

menses menstruation

menstrual cycle hormone-regulated changes in uterine lining of human and certain other primate females

menstruation cyclical shedding of lining of uterus with loss of blood and fluid; menses

mesoderm middle germ layer in early embryo that forms muscles and supporting tissue

metamorphosis structural change from larval into adult form

milk letdown hormonal response to suckling of baby that ejects milk from mammarian nipples

monogamy practice of mating with only one partner

morphogenesis origin of form

myoblast embryonic cell that develops into skeletal muscle

neonate newborn

neoteny attainment of sexual maturity while still in larval form

nest structure in which organisms, esp. birds, lay eggs

nidus nest in which insects or spiders deposit eggs

notocord supporting axis in vertebrate embryo and in lower chordates

nullipara female that has never produced young

ontogeny development and life cycle of single organism or individual

oocyte cell giving rise by meiosis to an ovum, as in humans

oogamy sexual reproduction involving one large nonmotile, female gamete and one small, motile, male gamete

oogenesis origin and development of the ovum

ovarian follicle vesicle in ovary that contains developing egg; Graafian follicle

ovary female gonad

oviduct tube carrying egg from ovary to uterus or outside of body; fallopian tube in humans

oviparous (*adj*) egg-laying

ovoviviparous (*adj*) having membrane-enclosed eggs that remain in female until hatching

ovum egg; female gamete

oxytocin posterior pituitary hormone that stimulates milk letdown

parthenogenesis production of organism from unfertilized egg

parturition birth process

penis male erectile organ for copulation, esp. in mammals

placenta organ for nourishing embryo and removing waste products in most mammals

planula swimming larva of certain invertebrates

polyandry practice of female having more than one mate

polygamy practice of mating with more than one partner

polygyny practice of male having more than one mate

postpartum (*adj*) designating period immediately following birth

progesterone ovarian hormone that promotes continuation of pregnancy

prolactin anterior pituitary hormone that stimulates milk secretion

pseudopregnancy false pregnancy

puberty stage of life at which organism reaches sexual maturity and is capable of reproduction

pupa immobile, nonfeeding stage in metamorphosis of insect from larva to adult

regeneration regrowth of lost parts of organ or organism, as in worms

reproduction sexual or asexual process by which organisms produce new individuals of their species

secondary sex characteristics characteristics that distinguish between male and female of species, such as facial hair and enlarged breasts, but do not produce or convey gametes

semen male reproductive fluid that carries sperm

Sertoli cell cell that assists development of immature sperm

sex hormone any hormone that effects secondary sex characteristics or reproduction

sexual reproduction reproduction by fertilization and meiosis

somatoplasm reproductive cells of organism; germ plasm

somatotropin growth hormone

sperm spermatozoon

spermatogenesis origin and development of spermatozoon

spermatophore capsule of sperm passed to female during mating of some species

spermatozoon male gamete; sperm

STH somatotropin hormone

syngamy point in fertilization at which nuclei of sex cells meet and fuse

testis male gonad

testosterone primary male sex hormone

umbilical cord connection between embryo and placenta

uterus enlarged area of female mammalian oviduct where implantation occurs

vagina canal leading from uterus to outside of body that receives erect penis during copulation and acts as birth passage

viviparous (*adj*) giving birth to live young rather than laying eggs

vulva external genitalia in female mammals

womb uterus

yolk complex nutrient storage material in egg

zygospore cell formed by fusion of two similar gametes, as in certain algae and fungi

zygote cell formed by union of two gametes

Tools and Techniques

agar culture medium for growing bacteria

aquarium glass-sided container for holding aquatic organisms

binomial standard scientific name for organism, including genus and species in Latin, such as *Canis familiaris* for dog

calipers jawed instrument for measuring thickness or distance

cast plaster reproduction

centrifuge machine that removes moisture or separates different densities of substance by force directed outward from center of rotation

chromatography separation of chemical compounds on adsorbent material

cladistics classification of organisms based on lines of descent from common ancestor

control unmanipulated sample used for comparison with experimental group

culture laboratory growth of bacteria, microorganisms, or plant or animal cells in special nourishing fluid or solid

dermestid beetle used to remove dried flesh from skeletons for study collections

dissection cutting apart of specimen for study

electron microscope powerful optical instrument that uses electron beam to enlarge image of minute object

electrophoresis use of electrical field to separate chemical compounds into components

ether volatile, flammable liquid used as solvent and, formerly, as anesthetic

field glass binoculars, device for observing distant objects

forceps tweezerlike instrument for grasping small objects

formalin aqueous solution used for wet preservation of study specimens

hydrophone device for detecting underwater sounds

hydroscope instrument for viewing objects that are deep underwater

life table statistical device for studying population growth

live trap device for capturing an animal without harming it

manometer device for measuring pressure of gas

medium material, such as agar, on which a culture is grown

metabolism chamber controlled environment for studying metabolic processes

microscope optical device for enlarging images

microtome instrument for cutting very thin slices of tissue for microscopic examination

model simulation of natural event used for prediction

oscilloscope device that shows electrical pulses as light flashes on screen, used for study of physiological processes

paper chromatography use of solvent to separate amino acids on filter paper

perfusion forcing of fluid into system of vessels

petri dish shallow glass vessel with loose cover, used for growing culture of microorganisms

photomicrograph photograph of enlarged image observed through microscope

preservation any method for permanently storing a scientific specimen

press device for drying and flattening botanical specimens

radiocarbon dating method of determining age of fossils by using disintegration rate of carbon-14 isotope

radio telemetry use of radio transmitter placed on organism to monitor its movement or physiological processes

remote sensing obtaining information on biosphere by noncontact method, esp. with satellites

respirometer instrument for measuring gas pressure

scalpel fine-bladed knife used for dissecting specimen

scanning scope electron microscope used to magnify image of surface structures

Secchi disc device for measuring light penetration into body of water

slide flat piece of glass used to hold object for observation through microscope

sonogram sound spectrograph

sound spectrograph visual representation of auditory communication; sonogram

specimen sample of organism for study and experimentation

staining use of various dyes to improve visibility of microscopic structures

study skins uniformly preserved dry specimens for systematic research

synonymy scientific names in different nomenclature systems used to designate same species or genus

syringe device for withdrawing or injecting fluids through needle

taxidermy preparing, stuffing, and mounting of animal skins

terrarium usu. glass-sided container enclosing garden of small plants

type specimen single specimen designated as one on which original taxonomic description and name are based

vivisection experiments conducted on living organisms

zoo parklike facility in which live animals are kept for public exhibition

zymoscope device that monitors fermentation by recording amount of carbon dioxide produced

Taxonomy

taxonomy system of classifying organisms into natural related groups based on shared features or traits, with categories in descending order from kingdom to species, as follows:

kingdom one of the five broadest, principal divisions of living things: Animalia (animals), Plantae (plants), Fungi, Protista (algae and protozoa), and Monera (bacteria)

subkingdom category of related phyla within a kingdom (as: Eumetazoa subkingdom of kingdom Animalia)

superphylum subkingdom (as: Schizomycetes superphylum of kingdom Monera)

phylum principal category within a kingdom, used in classification of animals, protists, and monerans (as: Chordata)

division principal category within a kingdom, used in classification of plants, algae, and fungi (as: Anthophyta, or vascular flowering plants)

subphylum intermediate category between phylum and class or superclass (as: Vertebrata)

superclass intermediate category between subphylum and class (as: Tetrapoda)

class category of organisms ranking below phylum and above order (as: Mammalia)

subclass intermediate category between class and order (as: Eutheria)

order category of organisms ranking below class and above family (as: Primates)

superfamily intermediate category between order and genus (as: Hominoidea)

family category of organisms ranking below order and above genus (as: Hominidae)

genus category of closely related species ranking below family and above species (as: Homo)

species basic unit of biological classification ranking below genus, including structurally similar organisms capable of interbreeding (as: Homo sapiens)

FIVE KINGDOMS

Animalia kingdom of multicellular, eukaryotic organisms, usu. motile with ingestion as principal mode of nutrition and primarily sexual reproduction, including all animals: divided into thirty-two phyla

Plantae kingdom of multicellular, photosynthetic, eukaryotic organisms primarily adapted to life on land, including all plants: divided into ten divisions

Fungi kingdom of unicellular or filamentous, multinucleate, eukaryotic organisms, including molds, mildews, and mushrooms, that live by decomposing and feed on dead or living organic matter in which they grow and decompose: divided into four divisions

Protista kingdom of eukaryotic algae, amebas, and protozoans, consisting of photosynthetic autotrophs and heterotrophs: divided into ten divisions and five phyla

Monera kingdom of prokaryotic organisms, or cells without a membrane-bound nucleus and membrane-bound organelles, that reproduce by asexual budding or fission, including bacteria

MAJOR TAXONOMIC SUBGROUPS

NOTE: Orders of mammals and lists of species appear under Animals, Plants, and Simpler Life Forms. Latin names are used for entries, with English equivalents given in the definition.

Agnatha class of cold-blooded, aquatic, jawless, boneless fish: about 60 species

Amphibia class of cold-blooded, scaleless amphibians born in water with gills but developing lungs and living on land, including the ancestors of reptiles: about 2500 species, including frogs, toads, and salamanders

Annelida animal phylum of segmented annelid worms with well-defined nervous systems: about 9000 species, including earthworms, leeches, and marine worms

Anthophyta division of flowering plants or angiosperms with ovules enclosed in carpels and mature seeds borne within fruits: about 235,000 species divided into two classes, Monocotyledones and Dicotyledones

Arachnida class of mostly terrestrial arachnid arthropods with four pairs of jointed legs: about 57,000 species, including spiders, mites, ticks, and scorpions

Arthropoda phylum of invertebrate arthropods with paired, jointed limbs, a segmented body,

and a hard exoskeleton: over one million species, including insects, arachnids, and crustaceans

Aves class of warm-blooded, egg-laying, two-legged birds covered by feathers, with forelimbs used as wings and an embryo enclosed in an eggshell: about 9000 species

Bryophyta division of multicellular plants with photosynthetic pigments and food reserves similar to those of green algae: about 16,000 species, including mosses, liverworts, and hornworts

Chondrichthyes class of cold-blooded, aquatic, cartilaginous fish such as sharks and rays: about 625 species

Chordata phylum of animal chordates having a notochord at some stage of development, a hollow nerve cord, and a tail, including vertebrates: about 43,000 species

Coniferophyta division of seed plants with needlelike leaves: about 550 species of conifers, including gymnosperms

Crustacea class of mostly aquatic crustacean arthropods with two pairs of antennae, appendages on the thoracic segment, and a hard exoskeleton: about 25,000 species, including lobsters, crabs, crayfish, and shrimps

Echinodermata animal phylum of radially symmetrical, marine echinoderms, having an endoskeleton of ossicles and spines: about 6000 species, including starfish and sea urchins

Eumetazoa animal subkingdom of multicellular organisms with a true digestive cavity, including almost all animals; Metazoa

Eutheria subclass of all mammals other than marsupials and monotremes, broken down into seventeen orders with nearly 4500 species

Insecta class of mostly terrestrial insect arthropods that breathe by means of tracheae and have a tripartite body, one pair of antennae, three pairs of legs, and usu. two pairs of wings: about one million species, including bees, ants, fleas, flies, beetles, butterflies, and lice

invertebrate nontaxonomic grouping of all animals without a backbone or spinal column, comprising all thirty-one phyla of animals other than chordates

Mammalia class of warm-blooded, four-limbed, usu. hairy mammals that nourish their young with milk secreted by female mammary glands: about 4500 species divided into three subclasses

Mesozoa animal subkingdom of fifty species of extremely simple, wormlike organisms that are parasites of marine invertebrates

Metatheria subclass of marsupial mammals whose young are born undeveloped and are carried in the female's pouch: about 260 species, including kangaroos and opossums

Metazoa former term equivalent to Eumetazoa

Mollusca animal phylum of mostly aquatic, unsegmented mollusks with a muscular foot, soft body, and usu. one or more hard shells: about 47,000 species, with major classes being Bivalvia (clams, oysters, mussels, and scallops),

Gastropoda (snails and slugs), and Cephalopoda (octopuses and squids)

Nematoda animal phylum of minute, free-living roundworms and plant and animal parasites: over 12,000 species

Osteichthyes class of cold-blooded, aquatic, usu. scaly, bony fish: about 19,000 species

Parazoa animal subkingdom of multicellular organisms without a true digestive cavity, primarily sponges of phylum Porifera

Prototheria subclass of mammals composed of egg-laying monotremes: only five living species

Protozoa nontaxonomic grouping, similar to superphylum, of animallike, eukaryotic organisms belonging to kingdom Protista that are primarily unicellular, colonial, and nonphotosynthetic, formerly categorized as animals

Pterophyta division of primarily homosporous plants: about 12,000 species of ferns

Reptilia class of cold-blooded reptiles with lungs, completely bony skeletons, and bodies covered with scales or horny plates: about 6000 living species, including snakes, turtles, lizards, and crocodiles, and also extinct species such as dinosaurs

Sarcodina phylum of kingdom Protista, including unicellular heterotrophs with pseudopods: about 11,500 species, including amebas

Vertebrata subphylum of chordates whose notochord is replaced by a backbone or spinal column after its embryonic stage, and having a cranium enclosing a well-developed brain: about 41,700 species of mammals, birds, fish, amphibians, and reptiles

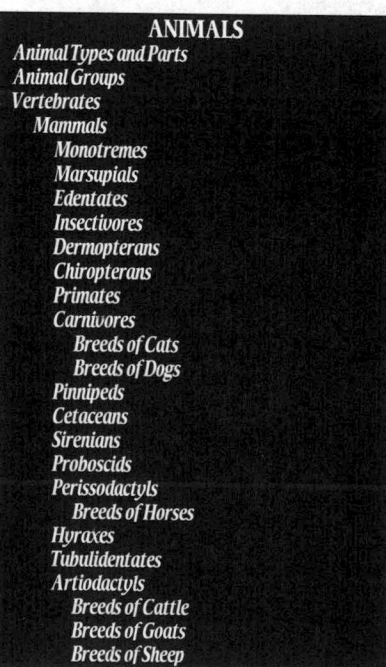

ANIMALS
Animal Types and Parts
Animal Groups
Vertebrates
  Mammals
    Monotremes
    Marsupials
    Edentates
    Insectivores
    Dermopterans
    Chiropterans
    Primates
    Carnivores
      Breeds of Cats
      Breeds of Dogs
    Pinnipeds
    Cetaceans
    Sirenians
    Proboscids
    Perissodactyls
      Breeds of Horses
    Hyraxes
    Tubulidentates
    Artiodactyls
      Breeds of Cattle
      Breeds of Goats
      Breeds of Sheep

See also: *Chap. 2: Biology; Simpler Life Forms*

Animals are categorized by shared characteristics provided in the definition for each descending level of the standard biological taxonomy. Thus, users can infer that a "kangaroo" has the characteristics of a marsupial, a mammal, a vertebrate, and an animal. This largely eliminates the necessity for thousands of definitions, which would be primarily descriptive or provide only a Latin species name and the locale for each species. Where more than one term is frequently used to designate a single species, all such names appear, as for "platypus" and "duckbill platypus." The list of breeds (of chickens, dogs, cats, cattle, etc.) refer only to domestic breeds, not species.

Animal Types and Parts

alley cat mixed-breed domestic cat, esp. living unowned in city

alter (*vb*) neuter a male animal

animal member of kingdom of living organisms distinguished from plants by their ability to move about independently and to respond quickly to stimuli

antler branched, bony growth on head of deer and some other mammals, usu. shed annually

ass domesticated donkey or similar wild species

avian (*adj*) of or like a bird

axilla area under wing of bird

baleen horny substance attached along upper jaw of certain whales; whalebone

bantam miniature breed of chicken

bay brown horse with black mane and tail

beak bird's bill, esp. sharp, horny bill of bird of prey

beast large quadruped, esp. domesticated

biddy female chicken

bilateral symmetry body form in which right and left halves of organism are mirror images

bill hard jaws of a bird, usu. projecting to point

billy goat male goat

biped animal that moves on two feet

bitch female dog

boar male pig

bovine (*adj*) of or like an ox

bronco wild horse that resists being ridden

brood offspring from one hatching of bird's eggs

broody hen sitting on eggs

broomtail wild horse

brumby wild horse (Australia)

buck male deer, goat, rabbit, or kangaroo

bull male of various large mammals, esp. cattle

bullock castrated bull or steer

bunny *Informal.* rabbit

calf young of various large mammals, esp. cattle

calico domestic cat marked with black, orange, red, and white, usu. female; horse with similar markings

canine member of family of carnivores including dogs, wolves, and foxes; (*adj*) of or like a dog

cannibal animal that feeds on its own species

capon neutered rooster

carnivore animal that feeds on other animals

caterpillar wormlike larva of certain insects, esp. butterflies or moths

cayuse range horse

chanticleer rooster

charger horse ridden in battle or on parade; destrier

chick young bird, esp. chicken

chordate member of phylum comprising all true vertebrates and animals having a notochord

claw sharp, usu. hooked, horny structure or nail on foot of birds and some reptiles and mammals

cloven-foot mammal with hoof comprising two major toes for support

clutch group of eggs laid at one time by bird

coat natural outer covering of wool or fur

cob male swan

cock male chicken over one year old

cockerel male chicken under one year old

colt male horse before maturity

comb fleshy protuberance on head of chicken

cony small rabbit; Biblical term for hyrax

corvine (*adj*) of or like a crow

covert one of small feathers that cover bases of large feathers on wings and tail of bird

cow female of various large mammals, esp. cattle

creature animal

crest comb or feathered tuft on head of animal, usu. bird

critter *Informal.* animal

cub young of various large carnivores, esp. bears

cud food regurgitated from ruminant's stomach to be rechewed

cur mixed-breed dog of little value

cursorial (*adj*) having limbs and feet adapted for running

cygnet young swan

destrier war-horse; charger

dock (*vb*) shorten tail or ears of animal

doe female deer, rabbit, goat, or kangaroo

dogie orphaned calf

domestic animal animal bred and raised in captivity as a pet, to perform work, or for food

draft animal animal used to pull wagon or plow

drake male duck

drone male bee or ant that serves only for reproduction and does no work

duck esp. female duck

duckling young duck

eclipse plumage dull plumage of birds, esp. adult males, that exhibit brilliant nuptial plumage when mating

equine (*adj*) of or like a horse

ewe female sheep

fang long, pointed canine tooth of carnivores, esp. used to tear flesh

fauna animals of a specific region or time

fawn young deer

feather one of horny shafts with soft branching barbs covering body of bird and comprising wing surface

feline member of the cat family of carnivores; (*adj*) of or like a cat

feral wild animal, esp. domestic animal gone wild

filly female horse under four years old

fin winglike membrane on body of fish, used for swimming

fledgling young bird just beginning to fly

flipper limb of pinniped or cetacean, broadened and flattened for swimming

foal young or newborn horse

fowl poultry

gander male goose

gelding neutered male horse

gill respiratory organ of fish and water animals

gilt young female pig

gobbler male turkey

goose esp. female goose

gosling young goose

grimalkin old female cat

hand unit of linear measure equal to four inches (10.2 cm), used to determine the height of horses

hart adult male red deer

heat estrus condition

heifer young cow

hen female chicken

hind adult female red deer

hinny offspring of a stallion and a jenny

hoof hard, horny foot of ungulate mammals

horn hard, hollow, bony, often pointed growth on head of certain hoofed animals; hard substance forming horns and other growths

hound any dog

incisor cutting tooth near front of mouth

invertebrate any animal without a backbone or spinal column

jack male donkey; jackass

jenny female donkey

joey baby kangaroo

jumbuck sheep (Australia)

keet guinea fowl chick

kid young goat

kine domestic cattle

kitten young cat

kitty kitten; pet name for cat

lamb young sheep

leonine (*adj*) of or like a lion

liger offspring of male lion and female tiger

litter several offspring from one birth, esp. in mammals

livestock domestic animals raised on a farm, esp. for profit

lupine (*adj*) of or like a wolf

mandibles upper and lower parts of bird's bill

mane long hair growing on animal's neck, esp. a horse or lion

manx tailless domestic cat

mare female horse

marmalade yellow cat

maverick unbranded range cow

maw stomach of ruminant, from which cud is regurgitated

melanism excess of dark pigmentation in skin, hair, or feathers

minnow any very small fish, usu. freshwater

mongrel mixed-breed dog; mutt

mule sterile hybrid between a horse and donkey, esp. between a mare and jack; any sterile hybrid

mustang wild horse

mutt *Slang.* mongrel

muzzle projecting portion of head of certain mammals, esp. dogs or horses, comprising mouth, nose, and jaws

nag broken-down old horse, esp. female; *Slang.* any horse

nanny goat female goat

nest structure made or place chosen for breeding or laying eggs, esp. by birds

nuptial plumage brilliant plumage exhibited by certain birds, usu. males, during mating season

omnivore animal that feeds on other animals and plants

palfrey saddle horse

passerine (*adj*) designating any small or medium-sized perching songbird with grasping feet

paw the foot of any quadruped with claws

peahen female peafowl

pelt skin of fur-bearing animal, esp. when stripped from carcass

pen female swan

piebald pinto

piglet young pig

pileum top of bird's head from base of bill back to nape

pinto horse with black and white patches; piebald

piscine (*adj*) of or like a fish

plumage feathers or cluster of feathers on head or body of bird

polled (*adj*) hornless

pony small breed of horse under 14.2 hands high

pooch *Informal.* dog, esp. one of mixed breed

porcine (*adj*) of or like a pig

pouch fold of skin on abdomen of female marsupial in which newborn young are carried

poulard spayed hen

poult young turkey

poultry domestic birds kept for meat or eggs; fowl

predator animal that lives by hunting and feeding on other animals

prehensile tail tail, as of certain monkeys, used for grasping or seizing

prey animal that is hunted and eaten by a predator

proboscis tubular organ, such as elephant's trunk, used for sucking, food-gathering, or sensing

pullet female chicken less than one year old

pup young dog; young seal

puppy young dog

puss any cat

pussycat any cat, esp. one of mixed breed

quadruped four-legged animal, usu. a mammal

queen female cat used for breeding; dominant mother bee in hive

quill stiff wing or tail feathers of bird; spine of porcupine or hedgehog

radial symmetry body form in which parts are arranged around central axis as mirror images to left and right of plane through that axis, as in coral and jellyfish

ram male sheep

roan horse of reddish-brown or black color with thick sprinkling of white

rooster male chicken; chanticleer

ruminant cud-chewing mammal with four-chambered stomach

runt smallest member of litter

saurian (*adj*) of or like a lizard

scales thin, overlapping, rigid plates forming protective covering of most fishes and reptiles and a few mammals

scavenger animal that feeds on refuse and decaying organic matter

seal point cat with pale body and dark brown face, ears, tail, and paws

serpentine (*adj*) of or like a snake

shoat pig under one year old

sire male parent of any quadruped, esp. a horse

snood fleshy appendage trailing from above the beak of a male turkey

snout projecting nose and jaws of various mammals

songbird any common passerine bird that makes musical vocal sounds

sow female pig

spay (*vb*) neuter female animal

spine sharp, stiff projection from body of a porcupine or from a fish's fin

squab fledgling pigeon

stag male deer

stallion male horse

steer neutered bull

stray lost or abandoned domestic animal

stud male horse used for breeding

sunfisher bucking horse, esp. one that falls on its rider

tabby cat with swirls of dark color on light background, esp. tigerlike stripes

tadpole larval, gilled stage of amphibious frog

tail flexible appendage at rear of animal's body; feathers extending from rump of bird

tetrapod any four-legged vertebrate, esp. mammals, birds, and reptiles

thoroughbred racing horse bred by crossing Arabian or Turkish stallion with English mare

tiger domestic cat with striped tabby markings

tom male cat or turkey

tortoise shell hard, mottled, yellow-and-brown shell of some turtles and tortoises; similar coloration of some female cats

trunk long, flexible snout or proboscis, as on elephant

tusk one of a pair of very long, large, pointed teeth projecting outside of the mouth of some mammals

ungulate hoofed mammal

ursine (*adj*) of or like a bear

vermin destructive, disease-carrying insects or small animals

vertebrate animal with backbone or spinal column, such as mammals, birds, fish, amphibians, and reptiles

vixen female fox

vulpine (*adj*) of or like a fox

wattle fleshy protuberance hanging below the head of chicken or turkey.

wether neutered ram

whalebone baleen

whelp young of a dog

wing either of the feathered forelimbs of a bird, used for flying; forelimb of a flying mammal, formed by membrane stretched between digits

worker sterile ant or bee that performs work for colony

Animal Groups

bale group of turtles

bed group of snakes

bevy group of quail

bouquet group of pheasants in flight

cete group of badgers

charm group of finches

clowder group of cats

colony group of ants, badgers, or frogs

confusion group of guinea fowls

covert group of coots

covey group of partridges, pheasants, or quail on the ground

drove group of animals moving together; group of oxen, sheep, or swine

exaltation group of larks

flight group of birds or insects

flock group of birds; group of sheep

gaggle group of geese on water or ground

gam group of whales

gang group of elk

herd group of animals grazing together, esp. cattle or sheep; group of elephants

hive group of bees

host group of sparrows

husk group of hares

kennel group of dogs

knot group of toads

labor group of moles

leap group of leopards

murmuration flock of starlings

muster group of peacocks

nest group of rabbits; group of wasps; group of vipers

pace group of asses

pack group of wild animals moving together, esp. dogs or wolves; group of grouse

parliament group of owls

plague group of locusts

pod group of seals or whales

pride group of lions; group of peacocks

sault group of lions

school group of fish

shoal group of fish, esp. bass

shrewdness group of apes

skein group of geese in flight

skulk group of foxes

sloth group of bears

swarm group of insects, esp. bees

team group of ducks in flight; group of oxen or horses

trace group of hares or rabbits

troop group of monkeys

watch group of nightingales

Vertebrates

vertebrate member of the subphylum of chordates whose notochord is replaced by a backbone or spinal column after its embryonic stage, having a cranium enclosing a well-developed brain, including mammals, birds, reptiles, amphibians, and fish

MAMMALS

mammal member of a class of warm-blooded, usu. hairy vertebrates that nourish their young with milk secreted by female mammary glands

Monotremes

monotreme member of the most primitive, egg-laying order of mammals, comprising the subclass Prototheria

    duckbill, duckbill platypus
    echidna
    platypus
    spiny anteater

Marsupials

marsupial member of mammalian order whose young are born undeveloped and carried in the female's pouch, comprising the subclass Metatheria

    banded anteater, bandicoot, bettong
    cuscus
    dasyure, dunnart
    euro
    flying phalanger
    glider
    kangaroo, koala
    marsupial mole, marsupial mouse
    native cat, numbat
    opossum
    pademelon, phalanger, possum, potoroo
    quokka, quoll
    rabbit-eared bandicoot, rat opossum, ringtail
    Tasmanian devil, Tasmanian wolf, thylacine, tree kangaroo
    wallaby, wombat
    yapok

Edentates

edentate member of mammalian order without teeth or with single-rooted molars only

    ant bear, anteater, armadillo
    giant ground sloth (extinct)
    peba, peludo
    sloth
    tamandua, tatou, tatouay, tatoupeba

Insectivores

insectivore member of small, primitive, nocturnal order of mammals with weak eyesight that feed on invertebrates, esp. insects

    desman
    elephant shrew
    golden mole, gymnure
    hedgehog
    mole, moon rat
    otter shrew
    shrew, solenodon, star-nosed mole
    tenrec
    water shrew

Dermopterans

dermopteran member of mammalian order of nocturnal, herbivorous gliders that do not actually fly

    colugo
    flying lemur

Chiropterans

chiropteran member of mammalian order with forelimbs ending in membranes stretched between elongated digits, used for flying

    barbastelle, bat, brown bat
    chauvesouris
    false vampire, fishing bat, flittermouse, flying fox, free-tailed bat, fruit bat
    horseshoe bat
    leaf-nosed bat, little brown bat
    myotis
    noctule
    pipistrelle
    serotine
    vampire bat

Primates

primate member of mammalian order with flexible, grasping hands and feet with five digits, usu. omnivorous and arboreal

    angwantibo, anthropoid ape, ape, aye-aye
    baboon, bandar, Barbary ape, bonnet monkey, bush baby
    capuchin, chacma, chimpanzee, colobus, cynomolgus
    drill, dwarf lemur
    entellus
    galago, gelada, gibbon, gorilla, grivet, guenon, guereza
    hamadryas baboon, hanuman, hominid, homo sapiens, howler, human being
    indri
    langur, lar gibbon, leaf monkey, lemur, lion-tailed monkey, loris
    macaque, man, mandrill, mangabey, marmoset, monkey, mountain gorilla
    night monkey
    orangutan
    patas monkey, potto, prosimian, proboscis monkey
    quenon
    rhesus monkey
    saki, siamang, simian, snow monkey, spider monkey, squirrel monkey
    tamarin, tarsier, titi, tree shrew
    uakari
    vervet
    wanderoo, white-handed gibbon, woolly monkey

Carnivores

carnivore member of mammalian order of flesh-eating predators with prominent canine fangs and shearing molars, having retractable or unretractable claws on toed feet

    aardwolf, American lion, Arctic fox
    badger, bassarisk, bat-eared fox, bear, binturong, black bear, bobcat, brown bear, brush wolf, buffalo wolf, bush dog
    cacomistle, canine, Cape fox, cape hunting dog, caracal, cat (Abyssinian, Angora, Archangel, Balinese, Birman, Burmese, color point, Cornish Rex, domestic shorthair, Egyptian, Havana brown, Himalayan, Korat, Maine coon, Maltese, Manx, Persian, Rex, Russian blue, Siamese, Somali, Turkish swimming, Turkish van), **catamount, cheetah, cinnamon bear, civet cat, clouded leopard, coati, coon, cougar, coyote, cusimanse**
    dhole, dingo, dog (affenpinscher, Afghan hound, Airedale terrier, Akita, Alaskan malamute, Alsatian, American foxhound, American pit bull terrier, American water spaniel, Australian cattle dog, Australian heeler, Australian kelpie, Australian shepherd, Australian terrier, badger dog, Basenji, basset hound, beagle, bearded collie, Bedlington terrier, Belgian Malinois, Belgian sheepdog, Belgian Tervuren, Bernese mountain dog, Bichon Frise, black and tan

coonhound, bloodhound, bluetick coonhound, boarhound, Border collie, Border terrier, borzoi, Boston bull terrier, Bouvier des Flandres, boxer, Boykin spaniel, Briard, Brittany spaniel, Brussels griffon, bulldog, bullmastiff, bull terrier, cairn terrier, cavalier King Charles spaniel, Chesapeake Bay retriever, Chihuahua, Chinese Shar-Pei, chow chow, clumber spaniel, Clydesdale terrier, cocker spaniel, collie, coonhound, corgi, Coton de Tulear, curly-coated retriever, dachshund, Dalmation, Dandie Dinmont terrier, deerhound, Doberman pinscher, elkhound, English bulldog, English cocker spaniel, English foxhound, English setter, English shepherd, English springer spaniel, English toy spaniel, Eskimo dog, field spaniel, flat-coated retriever, foxhound, fox terrier, French bulldog, gazelle hound, German shepherd, German shorthaired pointer, German wirehaired pointer, giant schnauzer, golden retriever, Gordon setter, Great Dane, Great Pyrenees, greyhound, griffon, Groenendael, harrier, hound, husky, Ibizan hound, Irish setter, Irish terrier, Irish water spaniel, Irish wolfhound, Italian greyhound, Jack Russell terrier, Japanese Chin, Japanese spaniel, keeshond, kelpie, Kerry blue terrier, King Charles spaniel, Komondor, kuvasz, Labrador retriever, Lakeland terrier, Lhasa apso, lurcher, malamute, Malinois, Maltese dog, Manchester terrier, mastiff, Mexican hairless, miniature dachshund, miniature poodle, miniature pinscher, miniature schnauzer, Neapolitan mastiff, Newfoundland, Norfolk terrier, Norwegian elkhound, Norwich terrier, Old English sheepdog, otterhound, papillon, pariah dog, Pekingese, pharaoh hound, Plott hound, pointer, Pomeranian, poodle, Portuguese water dog, pug, puli, rat terrier, redbone coonhound, red setter, retriever, Rhodesian ridgeback, Rottweiler, Russian owtchar, Russian wolfhound, Saluki, Samoyed, schipperke, schnauzer, Scotch collie, Scottish deerhound, Scottish terrier, Sealyham terrier, setter, shepherd dog, Shetland sheepdog, Shiba-Inu, Shih Tzu, Siberian Husky, silky terrier, Skye terrier, soft-coated wheaten terrier, spaniel, spitz, springer spaniel, Staffordshire bull terrier, staghound, standard schnauzer, St. Bernard, Sussex spaniel, terrier, Tibetan mastiff, Tibetan spaniel, Tibetan terrier, toy fox terrier, toy poodle, toy spaniel, toy terrier, Treeing Walker coonhound, turnspit, vizsla, water spaniel, Weimaraner, Welsh collie, Welsh corgi, Welsh springer spaniel, Welsh terrier, West Highland white terrier, whippet, wirehair, wirehaired pointing griffon, wirehaired terrier, wolfhound, Yorkshire terrier)
ermine, eyra
feline, fennec, ferret, fisher, fitch, fossa, fox
genet, giant panda, glutton, gray fox, gray wolf, grison, grizzly bear
hyena
ice bear
jackal, jaguar, jaguarundi
kinkajou, kit fox, Kodiak bear

laughing hyena, leopard, leopard cat, linsang, lion, lynx
maned wolf, manul, margay, marten, meerkat, mink, mongoose, mountain lion
ocelot, olingo, otter, ounce
painter, Pallas's cat, panda, panther, polar bear, polar fox, polecat, prairie wolf, puma
raccoon, raccoon dog, ratel, red dog, red fox, Reynard, ring-tailed cat
saber-toothed tiger (extinct), sable, sand cat, sea otter, serval, silver fox, simba, skunk, sloth bear, snow leopard, spectacled bear, stoat, sun bear, suricate, swift fox, Syrian bear
tayra, tiger, timber wolf
weasel, white fox, white wolf, wildcat, wolf, wolverine
zoril

Pinnipeds

pinniped member of mammalian order of aquatic carnivores that breed on land, with forelimbs adapted as flippers for swimming
eared seal, elephant seal
fur seal
hair seal, harbor seal
ross seal
sea cat, sea dog, sea elephant, seal, sea lion
walrus

Cetaceans

cetacean member of aquatic, nearly hairless order of mammals lacking hind limbs, with forelimbs adapted as flippers for swimming, a flat tail, and nasal blowholes on top of head, having either teeth or baleen
baleen whale, beaked whale, beluga, blackfish, blue whale, bottle-nosed dolphin, bouto, bowhead
cachalot, cowfish
dolphin
finback, fin whale
grampus, gray whale
humpback whale
killer whale
narwhal
orca
pilot whale, porpoise
right whale, rorqual
sea hog, sei whale, sperm whale, susu
toothed whale
whale, white whale

Sirenians

sirenian member of herbivorous aquatic order of mammals lacking hind limbs, with forelimbs modified as flippers for swimming and a flat tail
dugong
manatee
sea cow

Proboscids

proboscid member of mammalian order of large herbivores with long, flexible trunk, incisors modified as tusks, and huge, grinding molars

elephant
imperial mammoth (extinct)
jumbo
mammoth (extinct), mastodon (extinct)
pachyderm
tusker
woolly mammoth (extinct)

Perissodactyls

perissodactyl member of mammalian order of large herbivores with an odd number of toes on each hoof
ass
burro
donkey
horse (American quarter horse, American saddle horse, American trotter, Andalusian, Appaloosa, Arabian, Barbary, Belgian, Cleveland bay, Connemara, Clydesdale, French coach horse, German coach horse, hackney, Haflinger, hunter, jennet, Lippizaner, Morgan, palomino, Paso, Percheron, pinto, Plantation walking horse, polo pony, pony of the Americas, quarter horse, saddle horse, Shetland pony, Shire, Standardbred, Suffolk, Tennessee walking horse, thoroughbred, Trakehner, Turk, Waler, Welsh pony)
jackass
kiang, kulan
mule, mustang
onager
pony, Przewalski's horse
quagga (extinct)
rhinoceros
tapir, tarpan (extinct)
wild ass
zebra

Hyraxes

hyrax member of herbivorous, rodentlike, hoofed order of mammals related to proboscids
cony
dassie
hyrax
klippdach
rock hyrax

Tubulidentates

tubulidentate member of mammalian order of large, powerful diggers that eat ants and termites with a long, sticky tongue and have teeth only in cheeks
aardvark, ant bear
earth pig

Artiodactyls

artiodactyl member of mammalian order of large herbivores, often ruminants, with even number of toes on each hoof, often with antlers or horns
addax, alpaca, anoa, antelope, aoudad, argali, aurochs (extinct), axis deer
babirusa, Bactrian camel, banteng, barasingha,

Barbary sheep, beisa, bezoar goat, bharal, bighorn sheep, bison, blackbuck, blesbok, blue sheep, boar, bongo, buffalo, bull, bushbuck

camel, cameleopard, Cape buffalo, caribou, **cattle** (Aberdeen, Angus, Ayrshire, beefalo, Brahman, Brown Swiss, cattalo, Charbray, Charolais, Galloway, Guernsey, Hereford, Holstein, Jersey, Longhorn, Santa Gertrudis, Scotch Highland, Shorthorn, Texas Longhorn, West Highland, zebu), **chamois, chevrotain, chital, cow**

dama gazelle, deer, dik-dik, dromedary, duiker

eland, elk

fallow deer

gaur, gazelle, gemsbok, gerenuk, giraffe, gnu, **goat** (Angora, French Alpine, Kashmir, Nubian, Saanen, Toggenburg), **goat antelope, goral, guanaco**

harnessed antelope, hartebeest, hippopotamus, hog

ibex, impala, Indian buffalo

javelina

kaama, kob, kudu

llama

Marco Polo's sheep, markhor, mazama, moose, mouflon, mountain goat, mountain sheep, mouse deer, mule deer, muntjac, musk deer, musk hog, musk ox

nilgai, nyala

okapi, oribi, oryx, ox

peccary, Père David's deer, pig, pronghorn, pronghorn antelope, pudu

razorback, red deer, reindeer, river horse, Rocky Mountain goat, roe deer

sable antelope, saiga, sambar, serow, sheep (Cheviot, Corriedale, Dorset Horn, Hampshire, Karakul, Merino, Romney, Scotch Blackface, Suffolk), **sika, springbok, stag, steenbok, swine**

tahr, takin, topi

urial

vicuna, Virginia deer

wapiti, warthog, waterbuck, water buffalo, whitetail, white-tailed deer, wild boar, wildebeest, wild goat, wild ox, wild pig, wild sheep

yak

zebu

Pangolins

pangolin member of mammalian order Pholidota of toothless, digging insectivores, with whiplike tongue and hairs flattened into scales, that curls into a ball for defense
   anteater
   pangolin
   scaly anteater

Rodents

rodent member of mammalian order of small, gnawing herbivores with one pair of evergrowing, chisellike incisors
   agouti, antelope chipmunk, antelope squirrel
   bandicoot, beaver, black rat, blesmol, brown rat
   capybara, carpincho, cavy, chickaree, chinchilla, chipmunk, cloud rat, coendou, cotton mouse, cotton rat, coypu

deer mouse, degu, dormouse

edible dormouse

field mouse, flickertail, flying squirrel, fox squirrel

gerbil, gopher, grasshopper mouse, groundhog, ground squirrel, guinea pig

hamster, harvest mouse, house mouse, house rat, hutia

jerboa, jird, jumping mouse

kangaroo mouse, kangaroo rat

lemming

mara, marmot, meadow mouse, mole rat, mouse, muskrat

Norway rat, nutria

paca, pacarana, pack rat, Patagonian hare, pine mouse, pocket gopher, pocket mouse, pocket rat, porcupine, pouched rat, prairie dog

quill pig

rat, red squirrel, rice rat, rock squirrel, roof rat

sewellel, spiny rat, springhaas, squirrel, suslik

tree squirrel, tuco-tuco

viscacha, vole

wharf rat, whistle pig, whistler, woodchuck, wood mouse, wood rat

Lagomorphs

lagomorph member of mammalian order of terrestrial herbivores with two pairs of evergrowing incisors and long hind limbs that are used for jumping
   Arctic hare
   Belgian hare
   cony, cottontail
   hare
   jack rabbit
   lapin, leveret
   pika
   rabbit
   snowshoe hare, swamp rabbit

Birds

bird member of a class of warm-blooded, egg-laying, two-legged vertebrates covered by feathers, with forelimbs used as wings and an embryo enclosed in an eggshell, that live on land, shore, or sea

Passerine songbirds

passerine member of the order Passeriformes of land birds having feet adapted for perching, including all songbirds of Oscine and Suboscine suborders

songbird any passerine bird of Oscine suborder

Oscines

oscine member of suborder of passerine songbirds having highly developed vocal organs
   Audubon's warbler
   Baltimore oriole, bank swallow, barn swallow, blackbird, Blackburnian warbler, blackcap, bluebill, bluebird, blue jay, bobolink, bowerbird, brown thrasher, brown thrush, bulbul, bullfinch, bunting, bush tit, butcherbird
   canary, cardinal, catbird, cedar bird, cedar waxwing, chaffinch, chat, chewink,

chickadee, chiffchaff, chipping sparrow, cliff swallow, corbie, cotinga, cowbird, creeper, crossbill, crow

dipper, drongo

English sparrow

finch

gnatcatcher, goldfinch, grackle, grosbeak

hermit thrush, honeycreeper, house finch, house martin

indigo bunting

jackdaw, jay, junco

kingbird, kinglet

lark, linnet

magpie, martin, mavis, meadowlark, merle, mistle thrush, mockingbird, myna

nutcracker, nuthatch

oriole, ortolan, ouzel, oxpecker

pipit, purple finch, purple martin

quelea

raven, redbird, redpoll, redstart, redwing, red-winged blackbird, reedbird, reed bunting, ring ouzel, robin, rook

scarlet tanager, scissortail, shama, shrike, siskin, snowbird, solitaire, song sparrow, song thrush, sparrow, starling, sunbird, swallow

tanager, thrasher, thrush, tit, titlark, titmouse, towhee, tree swallow, troupial

veery, vesper sparrow, vireo

wagtail, warbler, water ouzel, water thrush, waxbill, waxwing, weaver, wheatear, white-eye, whydah, wood warbler, wren, wren-tit

yellowbird, yellow finch, yellowhammer, yellow-rumped warbler, yellowthroat

zebra finch

Suboscines

suboscine member of suborder of passerine songbirds having less well-developed vocal organs
   antbird
   bellbird, broadbill, bush wren
   cock-of-the-rock
   flycatcher
   lyrebird
   manakin
   ovenbird
   pewee, phoebe, pitta
   tyrant flycatcher
   woodcreeper

Other land birds

American eagle, ani

bald eagle, barbet, barn owl, bee-eater, bird of paradise, black grouse, bobwhite quail, brush turkey, budgerigar, bustard, button quail, buzzard

California condor, capercaillie, caracara, cassowary, cattle egret, chicken (Andalusian, Araucana, Australorp, Barnevelder, Barred Rock, Brahma, Campine, Cochin, Cornish, Dominiker, Dorking, Frizzle, Game, Golden Sebright bantam, Hamburg, Japanese bantam, Jersey Giant, Lakenvelder, Leghorn, Mille Fleur bantam, Minorca, New Hampshire, Old English Game, Orpington, Phoenix, Plymouth Rock, Polish, Rhode Island Red, Rhode Island White, Rock Cornish, Rosecomb bantam, Silkie, Sultan, Sumatra, Sussex, Turken, White Leghorn, Wyandotte), chicken hawk, chimney swift, cockatiel, cockatoo, condor, crane,

cuckoo, culver, curassow
dodo (extinct), dove
eagle, egret, emu, erne
falcon, flicker, francolin, frogmouth
goatsucker, golden eagle, goshawk, grouse, guacharo, guan, guinea fowl, gyrfalcon
harpy eagle, harrier, hawk, hawk owl, hemipode, hoatzin, hobby, honey guide, hoopoe, hoot owl, hornbill, horned owl, horned screamer, hummingbird
ivory-billed woodpecker
jacamar, jungle fowl
kea, kestrel, killdeer, kite, kiwi, kookaburra
lammergeier, lanner, lapwing, laughing jackass, lorikeet, lory, lovebird
macaw, mallee fowl, marabou, megapode, merlin, moa (extinct), motmot, moundbird, mound builder, mourning dove
nighthawk, nightingale, nightjar, notornis
oilbird, ostrich, owl
parakeet, parrot, partridge, passenger pigeon (extinct), peacock, peafowl, peregrine falcon, pheasant, pigeon (carrier, fantail, homer, homing pigeon, Jacobin, king, Modena, nun, pouter, roller, runt, trumpeter, tumbler), pigeon hawk, plover, poorwill, potoo, prairie chicken, ptarmigan
quail, quetzal
raptor, red grouse, red-headed woodpecker, rhea, ringdove, ring-necked pheasant, roadrunner, rock dove, roller, rosella, ruffed grouse
sage grouse, sage hen, sapsucker, screamer, screech owl, scrub fowl, secretary bird, seriema, snipe, snow bunting, sparrow hawk, stork, sun bittern, swift, swiftlet
tercel, tinamou, tody, toucan, touraco, tragopan, trogon, trumpeter, turkey, turkey buzzard, turkey vulture, turtledove
vulture
whippoorwill, whistler, woodcock, wood owl, woodpecker, wood pigeon, wryneck

Seabirds and waterfowl

seabird any bird living on the sea or along the coast and usu. able to swim, esp. gulls and terns
waterfowl swimming water birds, including ducks, geese, and swans

albatross, anhinga, auk, auklet
barnacle goose, belted kingfisher, bluebill, booby, brant, bufflehead
Canada goose, canvasback duck, coot, cormorant
dabbling duck, dabchick, darter, diver, dovekie, duck (Aylesbury, Blue Swedish, call, Cayuga, crested, Khaki Campbell, Muscovy, Pekin, Rouen, runner)
eider, erne
fish hawk, frigate bird, fulmar
gallinule, gannet, garganey, goldeneye, gooney bird, goose (African, Buff, Chinese, Embden, Pilgrim, Sebastopol, Toulouse), graylag goose, grebe, guillemot, gull
honker
jaeger
kingfisher, kittiwake
loon
mallard, mandarin duck, man-o-war bird, merganser, mew, moorhen, murre, mute swan
nene, notornis
osprey
pelican, penguin, petrel, pintail, pochard, puffin

razorbill, razor-billed, redhead, ring-necked duck, ruddy duck
scaup, scoter, sea duck, sea eagle, sea gull, sea raven, shearwater, sheldrake, shoveler, skua, snow goose, stormy petrel, swan, swan goose
takahe, teal, tern, tropic bird
waterfowl, water hen, whooper swan, widgeon, wood duck

Waders and shorebirds

wader any of various long-legged, long-necked, long-billed birds adapted for wading in shallow waters, including bitterns, cranes, flamingos, herons, rails, and storks
shorebird any bird that frequents seashores and estuaries, esp. members of order Charadriiformes, including sandpipers and plovers

avocet
bittern
corn crake, crake, crane, curlew
dunlin
egret
flamingo
godwit, greenshank, gull
hammerhead, heron
ibis
jacana
killdeer, knot
lily-trotter, limpkin
marabou
night heron
oystercatcher
pewit, phalarope, plover
rail, redshank, ring ouzel
sacred ibis, sanderling, sandpiper, shoebill, skimmer, snipe, spoonbill, stilt, stint, stone curlew, stork, surfbird
turnstone
whimbrel, willet
yellowlegs

Birds of prey

bird of prey any of various flesh-eating predator birds having a sharp, downwardly curved beak and talons, that live on land or sea

American eagle
bald eagle, barn owl, buzzard
California condor, caracara, chicken hawk, condor
eagle, erne
falcon, fish hawk
golden eagle, goshawk, gyrfalcon
harpy eagle, harrier, hawk, hawk owl, hobby, hoot owl, horned owl
jaeger
kestrel, kite
lammergeier, lanner
merlin
osprey, owl
peregrine falcon, pigeon hawk
raptor
screech owl, sea eagle, sparrow hawk
tercel, turkey buzzard, turkey vulture
vulture
wood owl

REPTILES

reptile member of a class of cold-blooded vertebrates with lungs, completely bony skeletons, and bodies covered with scales or horny plates, including snakes and dinosaurs

dinosaur extinct herbivorous or carnivorous member of the reptilian orders Saurischia and Ornithischia of the Mesozoic era, including the largest known land animals

snake member of limbless, scaly, elongate reptilian suborder Serpentes, many of which are venomous

agama, alligator, alligator lizard, alligator snapper, anole
basilisk, beaded lizard, blindworm, bog turtle, box turtle, butterfly agama
caiman, chameleon, chicken turtle, chuckwalla, cooter, crocodile
diamondback terrapin, dinosaurs (allosaur, ankylosaur, antrodemus, apatosaur, archaeopteryx, atlantosaur, brachiosaur, brontosaur, camarasaur, camptosaur, ceratopsian, coelophysis, diplodocus, elasmosaurus, hadrosaur, ichthyosaur, iguanodon, mixosaurus, oligokyphus, ornithiscian, ornithopod, peloneustes, plesiosaur, prosauropod, pterodactyl, quetzalcoatlus, saurischian, sauropod, scleromochlus, scolosaurus, stegosaur, steneosaurus, styracosaurus, tarbosaurus, theropod, titanophoneus, titanosaur, tylosaurus, tyrannosaur)
dragon
false map turtle, fence lizard, flying dragon
galliwasp, gavial, gecko, Gila monster, girdle-tailed lizard, glass snake, gopher tortoise, green turtle
hawksbill turtle, horned toad
iguana
Komodo dragon
leatherback turtle, lizard, loggerhead turtle
marine iguana, matamata, moloch, monitor, mugger
red-ear
sand lizard, sea turtle, side-necked turtle, skink, slider, slowworm, snake-necked turtle, snakes (adder, anaconda, asp, blacksnake, blind snake, boa, boa constrictor, boomslang, bullsnake, bushmaster, cobra, cobra de capello, constrictor, copperhead, coral snake, corn snake, cottonmouth, daboia, diamondback rattlesnake, egg-eating snake, fer-de-lance, garter snake, gopher snake, hamadryad, harlequin, hognose snake, horned rattlesnake, horned viper, indigo snake, king cobra, king snake, krait, mamba, massasauga, milk snake, moccasin, pine snake, puff adder, python, racer, rat snake, rattlesnake, rear-fanged snake, Russell's viper, scarlet snake, sea snake, sidewinder, spectacled cobra, spitting cobra, taipan, tic-polonga, tiger snake, timber rattlesnake, urutu, viper, water moccasin, water snake, worm snake)
snapping turtle, soft-shelled turtle, stinkpot, stump-tailed lizard, swift
tegu, terrapin, tokay gecko, tortoise, tuatara, turtle
wood turtle

AMPHIBIANS

amphibian member of a class of cold-blooded, scaleless vertebrates born in water with gills but developing lungs and living on land, including the ancestors of reptiles

anuran, axolotl
blindworm, bullfrog
caecilian, clawed frog, congo eel, congo snake, cricket frog
edible frog, eft
fire salamander, frog
grass frog, green frog
hellbender, hop toad, horned frog
leopard frog
marine toad, midwife toad, mudpuppy
narrow-mouthed toad, natterjack, newt
paradoxical frog, pickerel frog, poison arrow frog
red-eyed tree frog
salamander, siren, spadefoot toad, spring frog, spring peeper, Surinam toad
toad, tree frog
urodele
waterdog, wood frog

FISH

fish any of various cold-blooded, aquatic vertebrates with gills for breathing, fins, and usu. with scales, being a member of any of three classes: Agnatha (jawless, boneless fish), Chondrichthyes (cartilaginous fish such as sharks and rays), and Osteichthyes (bony fish)

albacore, alewife, alligator gar, amberjack, anchovy, angelfish, arapaima, arauana, archerfish, argusfish
balloonfish, barb, barbel, barn-door skate, barracuda, basking shark, bass, batfish, beluga, betta, black bass, blackfish, bleak, blenny, blindfish, blowfish, blueback salmon, blue catfish, bluefish, bluegill, blue shark, bonefish, bonito, bowfin, bream, brisling, brook trout, brown trout, buffalofish, bullhead, burbot, butterfish, butterflyfish
candlefish, capelin, carp, catfish, channel bass, channel catfish, char, characin, chimaera, Chinook salmon, chub, cichlid, cisco, clingfish, clown anemone, clown fish, cobia, cod, codfish, coelacanth, coney, conger eel, corydoras, cowfish, crappie, croaker, cutlassfish, cutthroat trout
dace, darter, devilfish, devil ray, discus, doctorfish, dogfish, dolphin, dorado, Dover sole, dragonfish, drumfish
eel, eelpout, electric eel, electric ray
filefish, flame tetra, flatfish, flounder, fluke, flying fish, flying gurnard, frogfish
gambusia, gar, garpike, giant bass, globefish, goatfish, goby, golden trout, goldfish, gourami, grayling, greenling, grouper, grunion, grunt, gudgeon, guitarfish, gunnel, guppy, gurnard
haddock, hagfish, hake, halfbeak, halibut, hammerhead shark, hatchetfish, headstander, herring, hogfish, horse mackerel, humuhumunukunukuapuaa
jack, jewfish
kelp bass, kelpfish, killifish, kingfish, koi
lake trout, lamprey, lanternfish, lingcod, loach, lumpfish, lungfish, lyretail
mackerel, mako shark, manta, marlin, menhaden, miller's-thumb, minnow, molly, Moorish idol, moray eel, mosquitofish, mudfish, mudskipper, mullet, muskellunge
needlefish, neon tetra, northern pike
oarfish, oscar
paddlefish, panchax, papagallo, paradise fish, parrotfish, pencilfish, perch, permit, pickerel, pike, pikeperch, pilchard, pilotfish, pipefish, piranha, plaice, platyfish, pollack, pollyfish, pompano, porbeagle shark, porgy, puffer, pupfish
rabbitfish, rainbow trout, rasbora, ray, redfin, redfish, red salmon, red snapper, remora, ribbonfish, roach, roosterfish, rudd
sailfish, salmon, salmon trout, sandfish, sardine, sawfish, scad, scat, scorpionfish, sculpin, scup, sea bass, sea bream, sea horse, seaperch, sea trout, sergeantfish, shark, shiner, shovelhead shark, shovelnose catfish, shovelnose sturgeon, Siamese fighting fish, silver salmon, skate, smelt, snapper, snook, sockeye salmon, sole, spadefish, Spanish mackerel, spearfish, speckled trout, sprat, squawfish, squirrelfish, steelhead, stickleback, stingray, stonefish, striped bass, sturgeon, sucker, Sunapee trout, sunfish, surffish, surfperch, surf smelt, surgeonfish, swordfish
tarpon, tautog, tench, tetra, thornback ray, thresher shark, tiger barb, tigerfish, tiger shark, tilapia, tilefish, toadfish, tope, torpedo fish, trevally, triggerfish, trout, tuna, tunny (*esp. Brit.*), turbot
veiltail goldfish
wahoo, walking catfish, walleyed pike, weakfish, whale shark, whitebait, white bass, whitefish, white shark, whiting, wolffish, wrasse
yellowtail, yellowtail flounder
zebrafish

Invertebrates

invertebrate any animal without a backbone or spinal column, including all thirty-one phyla of animals other than chordates

ARTHROPODS

arthropod invertebrate with paired, jointed limbs, a segmented body, and a hard exoskeleton that is molted from time to time, including arachnids, insects, and crustaceans

Insects and arachnids

arachnid any of a class of mostly terrestrial invertebrate arthropods, usu. with four pairs of jointed legs, no wings or antennae, and simple eyes, that have a liquid diet, including spiders, mites, ticks, and scorpions

insect any of a class of mostly terrestrial invertebrate arthropods with a segmented body consisting of a head, thorax, and abdomen, three pairs of jointed legs, usu. two pairs of wings, and one pair of antennae, including bees, ants, fleas, flies, beetles, butterflies, and lice

acarine, admiral butterfly, ant, ant lion, aphid, apple maggot, assassin bug
bark beetle, bedbug, bee, bee fly, beetle, billbeetle, billbug, blackbeetle, black fly, black widow, bloodworm, blow fly, bluebottle, boll weevil, bombardier beetle, bookworm, borer, botfly, bristletail, buffalo bug, buffalo carpet beetle, bumblebee, buprestid beetle, butterfly
cabbage butterfly, caddisfly, cadelle, carpet beetle, caterpillar, cattle grub, cattle tick, Cecropia moth, centipede, chafer, chigger, chigoe, chinch bug, cicada, cicala, click beetle, cockchafer, cockroach, codling moth, Colorado potato beetle, conenose, copper butterfly, crane fly, cricket, crotonbug, cucumber beetle, curculio
daddy-longlegs, damselfly, darkling beetle, deer fly, dermestid, dipteran, dobsonfly, dor, dragonfly, drosophila, dung beetle
earwig, elaterid, elm bark beetle, elm leaf beetle, emperor butterfly, ephemerid
firefly, flea, flea beetle, flesh fly, flour beetle, flour moth, flower fly, fly, frit fly, fritillary, fruit fly, fruit-tree bark beetle
gadfly, gallfly, gall midge, gall mite, girdler, glowworm, gnat, grain beetle, grasshopper, greenbottle fly, greenbug, greenfly, ground beetle, grub, gypsy moth
hairstreak butterfly, harlequin beetle, harlequin cabbage bug, hawk moth, Hessian fly, honeybee, hornet, horn fly, horntail, horse fly, housefly
ichneumon fly
Japanese beetle, jigger flea, June bug
katydid, khapra beetle, kissing bug
lacewing, ladybeetle, ladybug, lanternfly, leaf beetle, leaf-cutting bee, leaf-footed bug, leafhopper, Lepisma, locust, longhorn, long-horned beetle, long-horned grasshopper, louse
mayfly, mealworm, mealybug, medfly, Mediterranean fruit fly, Mexican bean beetle, Mexican fruit fly, midge, miller, mite, mole cricket, monarch butterfly, mosquito, mosquito hawk, moth, mourning cloak
oil beetle
painted lady, pill bug, podura, potatobug, praying mantis, punkie
railroad worm, red admiral butterfly, rhinoceros beetle, roach, robber fly, rose beetle, rose chafer, rove beetle
sawfly, sawyer, scarab, scorpion, scorpionfly, screwworm, shadfly, silkworm, silverfish, skipjack, skipper, snapping beetle, snout beetle, sow bug, spider, spider mite, spider wasp, springtail, squash bug, stag beetle, stink bug, St. Mark's fly, stonefly, swallowtail butterfly, syrphid fly
tabanid, tarantula, tenebrionid, tent caterpillar, tent fly, termite, tettigoniid, thrips, tick, tiger beetle, tiger moth, tiger swallowtail, tortoise beetle, tsetse fly, tumblebug, twig girdler
viceroy, vinegar fly
walking stick, warble fly, wasp, water beetle, water bug, water strider, weevil, whip scorpion, whirligig beetle, white ant, wood nymph, wood tick, wood wasp
yellow jacket

Crustaceans

crustacean member of a subphylum of mostly aquatic, invertebrate arthropods with gills, a hard outer shell, a jointed body, appendages on the thoracic segment, and two pairs of antennae

barnacle, beach flea
copepod, crab, crawdad, crayfish
Dungeness crab
fiddler crab
hermit crab, horseshoe crab
isopod
king crab, krill
lobster
prawn
sand hopper, shrimp, soft-shell crab, spider crab
water flea, wood louse

MOLLUSKS AND AQUATIC INVERTEBRATES

mollusk member of a phylum of mostly aquatic invertebrates with an unsegmented body enclosed in one or more hard shells, with a muscular foot for moving and usu. gills, including clams, mussels, octopuses, oysters, scallops, slugs, snails, and squid

aquatic invertebrates members of any of several phyla of cnidarians, echinoderms, and sponges

cnidarian formerly coelenterate; member of a phylum of invertebrates having a single, internal digestive cavity with tentacles on the oral end, a primitive nervous system, and special protective stinger cells, including jellyfish, sea anemones, and coral

echinoderm member of marine invertebrate phylum having a body wall stiffened by calcareous protruding spines, no head, and tubed feet, that lives on the seafloor, including starfish, sea urchins, sand dollars, and sea cucumbers

sponge member of the chiefly marine invertebrate phylum Porifera having a porous structure and usu. a horny skeleton formed from hard substances that become stuck in its body walls, that lives in large colonies attached to rocks

abalone, acorn worm, amphioxus, anemone, angel's wing
barnacle, bivalve, bloodworm, brain coral, brittle star
cannonball jellyfish, clam, cockle, comb jelly, conch, coquina, coral, cowrie, crown-of-thorns starfish, cuttlefish
dead man's fingers, devilfish
elkhorn coral
gastropod, giant squid
hydra, hydrozoan coral
jellyfish
limpet, lion's mane
mussel
nautilus, nudibranch
octocorallian, octopod, octopus, oyster
periwinkle, polyp, pompano, Portuguese man-of-war
quahog

razor clam
sand dollar, sand flea, sandworm, scallop, scleractinian coral, sea anenome, sea cucumber, sea fan, sea feather, sea hare, sea nettle, sea slug, seasnail, sea star, sea urchin, sea wasp, sea whip, shellfish, shipworm, slug, snail, sponge, squid, staghorn coral, star coral, starfish
tubeworm
whelk
zoanthid

WORMS

worm any slender, soft-bodied, legless, symmetrical invertebrate, often segmented, that lives underground, in water, or as a parasite, esp. an insect larva

acanthocephalan, angleworm, annelid, armyworm, arrowworm
bloodworm, bollworm, bookworm
cankerworm, clamworm, cottonworm, cutworm, cysticercus
earthworm, earworm, eelworm
filaria, fireworm, flatworm, fluke
hairworm, hellgrammite, helminth, hookworm, hornworm, horsehair worm
inchworm
larva, leech, looper, lugworm
measuringworm
nemathelminth, nematode, nemertean
pinworm, planarian, platyhelminth, polychaete
red worm, ribbon worm, rotifer, roundworm
sandworm, sea mouse, sea worm, silkworm
tapeworm, teredo, threadworm, tobacco hornworm, tomato hornworm, trematode, tubeworm, tubifex, tussah
vinegar eel, vinegar worm
webworm, wireworm, woodworm

PLANTS

Botany and Plant Parts
Trees
Shrubs
Flowering Plants
Grasses, Sedges, and Grasslike Plants
Herbaceous Plants
Ferns
Vines
Weeds

See also: *Chap. 2: Biology; Simpler Life Forms; Chap. 9: Foods; Chap. 12: Agriculture; Chap. 17: Gardening*

Plants are grouped under taxonomically distinctive subheadings with generic definitions, similar to the treatment accorded Animals.

Botany and Plant Parts

algae unicellular organism distinguished from plants by having no true root, stem, or leaf; see under Algae in Simpler Life Forms

alternation of generations life cycle in many plants, in which diploid and haploid generations alternate

angiosperm flowering plant, esp. one having its seeds enclosed in an ovary

annual plant with life cycle of one year or season

annulus veil remnant on stalk of mushroom

anther part of stamen that produces and releases pollen

articulation joint in stem or between branch and leaf

auxin plant growth hormone

axil upper angle formed by leaf or twig and the stem from which it grows

axillary bud bud formed at axil

bark outside covering of stems and roots of trees and woody plants

berry small, fleshy fruit or dry seed or kernel of various plants

biennial plant with two-year life cycle in which the vegetative first-year growth is followed by fruiting and dying during second year

blade broad, expanded part of leaf

botany branch of biology dealing with life, structure, growth, and classification of plants

bract leaflike structure growing below or encircling flower cluster or flower

bromeliad member of the pineapple family of plants, usu. epiphytic with stiff, leathery leaves and spikes of bright flowers

bryophyte any member of the division of nonvascular plants, including mosses and liverworts, that lack water-gathering roots and tissues to conduct water

bud small swelling on plant from which shoot, leaf cluster, or flower develops

bulb dormant underground bud stage of some plants

bush shrub

Calvin cycle sequence of reactions in second stage of photosynthesis by which carbon dioxide is reduced to carbohydrate

calyx outer whorl of protective leaves on a flower

cambium layer of formative cells beneath bark of tree

cap pileus of mushroom

carpel ovule-bearing leaf or leaflike structure that is primary segment of pistil

chlorophyll pigment in chloroplast, needed for photosynthesis

chloroplast membrane-bound organelle that is site of photosynthesis

club moss any of various small, non-seed-bearing vascular plants with conelike, spore-bearing structures on top of stems; lycopod

cohesion-tension theory theory that upward movement of water in plants results from negative pressure in leaf cells, inducing water from vascular tissue to pull cohering chain of water molecules up from root

coleoptile protective sheathing around young shoot in germinating grass seed

composite one of a large family of herbaceous plants with flower heads of dense clusters of small florets surrounded by ring of small leaves or bracts

cone reproductive structure of certain nonflowering plants with overlapping scales or bracts containing pollen, ovules, or spores

conifer cone-bearing gymnosperm, usu. with narrow, needlelike or small, scalelike leaves

corm underground stem base that acts as reproductive structure

cormel small corm

corolla flower petals

corymb flat-topped or convex cluster of flowers in which outer flowers open first

cotyledon first or second leaf of seedling

crustose (*adj*) having a thin thallus that clings to substratum of rock, bark, or soil

cuticle waxy layer on outer surface of plants

cycad any of the order of gymnosperms intermediate between ferns and palms, often with thick, columnar trunk crowned by large, tough, pinnate leaves

cyme inflorescence in which primary axis bears single central or terminal flower that blooms first

cyst sporelike cell with resistant, protective wall

cytokinin plant hormone that promotes cell division

deciduous (*adj*) designating any plant that sheds all its leaves once each year

dehiscence splitting open of pod or anther, esp. at maturity to discharge seeds

dicot dicotyledon

dicotyledon angiosperm having two seed leaves or cotyledons; dicot

dioecious (*adj*) having male and female flowers on different individuals

division major primary subdivision of plant kingdom, comparable to animal phylum

dormancy period of time in which growth ceases

double fertilization process in flowering plants in which one pollen sperm cell fertilizes egg cell and a second fuses with two polar nuclei

endophyte plant living within another plant, usu. as a parasite

epiphyte nonparasitic plant growing upon another plant for support

evergreen plant that maintains functional green foliage throughout year

fern nonflowering, vascular plant having roots, stems, and fronds and reproducing by spores instead of seeds

fertilization fusion of male and female sex cells, preceded by pollination in seed plants

filament stalklike portion of stamen, bearing the anther

flora plants of specific region or time

floret small flower; one of individual flowers comprising the head of a composite plant

flower seed-producing plant, usu. nonwoody, with shortened stem bearing leaflike sepals, colorful petals, and pollen-bearing stamens

clustered around pistils; blossom; plant cultivated for its blossoms; reproductive organ of some plants; (*vb*) produce blossoms

flowering plant any angiosperm that produces flowers, fruit, and seeds in an enclosed ovary

foliage leaves of plant or tree

foliose (*adj*) covered with leaves

frond fern or palm foliage

fructose yellowish to white, crystalline, water-soluble sugar found in many fruits

fruit mature ovary of flowering plant, sometimes edible; see list under Foods

fungus unicellular or filamentous organism that lives by decomposing, formerly classified with plants; see under kingdom Fungi in Simpler Life Forms

funicle stalk of ovule or seed

gametophyte gamete-bearing, haploid, multicelled stage of many plants, beginning with haploid spores and ending at fertilization

germinate (*vb*) sprout and start to grow from spore, seed, or bud

gill lamella

grass member of the family of flowering plants with long, narrow leaves, jointed stems, flowers in spikelets, and seedlike fruit

gravitropism growth or movement of plant in which force of gravity is determining factor

gymnosperm member of the division of seed plants having ovules on open scales, esp. cones

gynoecium pistil

herb nonwoody, seed-producing plant whose stem withers away to ground after one season's growth, often having medicinal or culinary uses

herbaceous (*adj*) designating nonwoody plant

holdfast portion of rootless plant that attaches to a surface

horsetail nonseed-bearing vascular plant with jointed stem, siliceous ribs, and a spore-bearing cone atop its stem; sphenopsid

hypha threadlike part forming mycelium of fungus

indehiscent (*adj*) not opening at maturity to discharge seeds

inflorescence production of blossoms; flower cluster on a common axis

kernel grain or seed, esp. inside fruit

lamella one of the radiating vertical plates on underside of cap of mushroom; gill

lateral bud bud growing on side of stem

leaf flat, thin structure growing from stem or twig of plant, used in photosynthesis and transpiration

legume any of the family of herbaceous plants, shrubs, and vines having compound leaves, clusters of flowers, and fruit in form of pod

lenticel spongy area of bark on woody plant that permits exchange of gases between stem and atmosphere

lichen fungus in symbiotic union with an alga, formerly classified with plants; see under kingdom Fungi in Simpler Life Forms

ligneous (*adj*) forming or having the nature of wood; woody

lignin organic substance that serves as binder for cellulose fibers in wood and certain plants

liverwort any of various small, flat bryophytes, usu. encrusting logs, rocks, or soil in moist areas

lycopod club moss

meristem undifferentiated tissue from which new tissue arises

midrib central vein of leaf

monocot monocotyledon

monocotyledon angiosperm having only one seed leaf or cotyledon; monocot

monoecious (*adj*) having male and female flowers on same individual

moss any of various small bryophytes without true stems, reproducing by spores, and growing in velvety clusters in moist areas on rocks, trees, and the ground

mycelium mass of threadlike tubes forming the vegetative part of a fungus

mycorrhiza close symbiosis between mycelia of certain fungi and root cells of some vascular plants

nectar sugary fluid in many flowers, which attracts animal pollinators

nectary organ of plant that secretes nectar

nonvascular plant bryophyte

nut dry, single-seeded fruit of various trees and shrubs, consisting of kernel enclosed in hard or tough shell

nutation spontaneous movement of plant parts during growth

olfactory (*adj*) affecting, emitting, or having to do with smell

ovary enlarged base of pistil in flowering plants that encloses ovules

ovule female germ cell or rudimentary seed prior to fertilization

palisade cell chloroplast-containing cell just below surface of a leaf

palynology study of pollen grains and spores

panicle loose, diversely branching flower clusters; compound raceme

parenchyma soft tissue forming chief substance of leaves and roots, fruit pulp, and center of stems

pectin white, colloidal carbohydrate, found in certain ripe fruits, that has thickening properties

pedicel stalk of single flower, fruit, or leaf

peduncle stalk supporting flower or flower cluster of an angiosperm or bearing the fruiting body of a fungus

perennial plant that lives more than two years, esp. herbaceous plant that produces flowers from the same root structure several years in a row

petal one of the circle of flower parts inside the sepals

petiole stem connecting a branch to a leaf blade

phloem nutrient-conducting tissue of vascular plants

photoperiodism capacity of plants to measure relative periods of daylight and darkness, thus anticipating and accommodating themselves to seasonal changes

photosynthesis production of organic substances from carbon dioxide and water in green plant cells which chemically transform radiant energy of sunlight

phototropism plant growth and movement toward light source

phytochrome light-detecting pigment involved in photoperiodism

phytoplankton aggregate of plants and other organisms in plankton

pileus horizontal part at top of mushroom stalk, bearing gills on its underside; cap

pinna one of the leaflets in featherlike arrangement along axis of a pinnate leaf

pistil central, seed-bearing part of flower, comprised of one or more carpels, each with style and stigma; gynoecium

plankton aggregate of passively floating or slightly motile organisms in a body of water, primarily algae and protozoa

plant member of the kingdom Plantae of multicelled organisms capable of carrying on photosynthesis in their cells, primarily adapted for terrestrial life

pod vessel enclosing one or more seeds, usu. splitting along two sutures at maturity

pollen fine, dustlike grains containing male sexual cells, produced in anthers or similar structures of seed plants

pollination transfer of pollen from stamen to upper tip of pistil

raceme diversely branching flowers lying along common axis

ray any of the flower stalks of an umbel

receptacle modified portion of stem or axis of flowering plant that bears the organs of a flower or flower head; torus

reticulate (*adj*) having veins arranged in netlike threads on leaves

rhizome creeping horizontal stem lying at or just beneath soil surface, which bears leaves at its tip and roots from its underside

root underground part of plant that functions in absorption, aeration, food storage, and as support system

runner long, slender stem growing from base of some perennials; stolon

saprophyte plant or fungus that feeds on dead and decaying organic matter

scale small leaf or bract covering and protecting the bud of a seed plant

sedge any of the family of rushlike or grasslike herbaceous plants growing in wet areas and having solid stems, slender leaves, and spikes of small flowers

seed fertilized plant ovule containing embryo, capable of germinating to produce new plant

self-pollination transfer of pollen from anther to stigma of same flower, another flower on same plant, or plant of same clone

sepal leaflike, usu. green outer circle of calyx

sessile (*adj*) attached at the base or without separate support structure

shrub woody perennial plant with several stems

branching off near its base rather than a single trunk like a tree; bush

sieve tube longitudinal tube in phloem of flowering plants that conducts organic food materials through plant

sorus cluster of spore containers, esp. under a fern frond

sphenopsid horsetail

spike inflorescence in which flowers bloom along entire length of single stalk

sporangium organ or single cell producing spores

spore haploid reproductive cell that on germination develops into the gametophyte

sporophyte spore-bearing, diploid, multicelled stage of many plants that begins with fertilized egg and ends with production of haploid spores

stalk stem or main axis of plant; any slender, supporting or connecting part of plant

stamen pollen-producing part of central flower, comprised of filament and anther

stem main upward-growing axis of plant

stigma free upper tip of a flower style on which pollen falls and develops

stipe stalk or slender support, such as petiole of a fern or stem of a mushroom

stolon stem that takes root at intervals along ground, forming new plants; runner

stoma microscopic opening in plant epidermis, esp. one through which gases are exchanged with the environment

style slender, stalklike part of carpel between stigma and ovary

succulent plant with thick, fleshy tissues that store water

taproot deep main root from which lateral roots develop

tendril threadlike, often spiral part of climbing plant which clings to or coils around objects

terminal bud bud growing at end of stem

thallus nonvascular plant body without clear differentiation into stems, leaves, or roots

torus receptacle of a flower

touch responses twining, coiling, and other rapid movements in plants sensitive to touch

translocation transport of products of photosynthesis from leaf to other parts of plant

transpiration loss of water vapor from plant body

tree tall, woody perennial with single stem or trunk and branches that usu. begin at some height above the ground

tropophilous (*adj*) adapted to climate having marked environmental changes

trunk main stem of tree

tuber fat underground stem from which some plants grow, similar to but shorter and thicker than a rhizome

umbel cluster of flowers with stalks of nearly equal length that spring from the same point

vascular bundle arrangement of xylem and phloem that forms conducting system of a vascular plant

vascular plant any plant, such as the angiosperms, gymnosperms, or ferns, in which the xylem and phloem conduct water and organic nutrients

vegetable any plant, or part of a plant, that is used as food; see list under Foods

vegetative (*adj*) of plants, esp. pertaining to plant growth and nutrition; capable of growing as a plant

veil membrane that covers immature mushroom and breaks open, leaving veillike remnants usu. on stalk; annulus; velum

velum veil

vessel water-conducting tube in xylem

vine plant that grows along the ground or clings to a vertical support by means of twining stems, tendrils, or rootlets

volva membranous enclosure on base of certain mushrooms, formed when veil breaks

weed vigorous plant of rank growth that tends to overcrowd more desirable neighboring plants; any plant that is unwanted

whorl circular growth of leaves or petals

woody (*adj*) designating a plant consisting of or forming wood; ligneous

xerophyte plant adapted for growth in arid conditions

xylem water- and mineral-conducting woody tissue of vascular plants, found in stems, roots, and leaves, that supports softer tissues of plant

zygophyte plant that reproduces by means of zygospores

zygospore cell formed by fusion of two similar gametes, as in certain algae and fungi

Trees

tree tall, woody perennial with single stem or trunk and branches that usu. begin at some height above the ground

acacia, ailanthus, alder, algarroba, allspice, almond, American elm, annatto, apple, apricot, araucaria, arborvitae, arbutus, ash, aspen, avocado

bald cypress, balsa, balsam fir, balsam poplar, banana, banksia, banyan, baobab, basswood, bay, bayberry, bean tree, beech, betel palm, bigleaf maple, birch, black acacia, black alder, black ash, black cherry, black locust, black maple, black oak, blackthorn, black walnut, bombax, bottlebrush, box elder, boxwood, Brazil nut, brazilwood, breadfruit, bristlecone pine, buckeye, buckthorn, bumelia, butternut, buttonwood

cacao, California laurel, camphor tree, candleberry, carnauba, carob, cashew, cassia, catalpa, cedar, cercis, cherimoya, cherry, cherry plum, chestnut, chestnut oak, chinaberry, China tree, Chinese date, chinquapin, cinnamon, citron, citrus, clove, coconut, coffee tree, cork oak, cornel, cottonwood, cycad, cypress

dahoon, date palm, dogwood, Douglas fir, dungon

eastern hemlock, ebony, elder, elm, encina, eucalyptus

fig, fir, frankincense, fringe tree
gardenia, giant sequoia, ginkgo, gleditsia,
   grapefruit, guava, gum, gumbo-limbo
hackberry, hawthorn, hazel, hemlock, henna,
   hickory, holly, honey locust, hoptree,
   hornbeam, horse chestnut
Indian mulberry, ironwood
jacaranda, jarrah, Joshua tree, Judas tree,
   juniper
kauri, Kentucky coffee tree, kumquat
laburnum, lancewood, larch, laurel, lehua,
   lemon, lime, linden, litchi, locust, logwood,
   longleaf pine
madrone, magnolia, mahogany, manchineel,
   mango, mangosteen, mangrove, maple,
   mastic, medlar, mescal bean, mesquite,
   mimosa, ming tree, monkeypod, mountain
   ash, mulberry
Norway maple, nutmeg, nux vomica
oak, ohia lehua, Ohio buckeye, olive, orange,
   Osage orange
palm, palmetto, papaw, papaya, paper
   mulberry, paulownia, pawpaw, peach, pear,
   pecan, persimmon, pine, pistachio, plane,
   plum, pomegranate, pomelo, pond-apple,
   poplar
quince
raffia palm, rain tree, rambutan, redbud, red
   cedar, redwood, rosewood, rowan, royal
   poinciana, rubber
sago palm, sandalwood, sandarac, sapodilla,
   sappanwood, sassafras, satinwood, senna,
   sequoia, serviceberry, silk oak, silver maple,
   slash pine, snowbell, soapberry, sorb, sorrel
   tree, sour gum, soursop, speedwell, spruce,
   star apple, St. John's-bread, sumac, sweet
   cherry, sweet gum, sweetsop, sycamore
tacamahac, tamarack, tamarind, tangerine, tan
   oak, teak, thorn apple, thorn tree, thuja, tolu,
   tonka bean, toon, torreya, Torrey pine, tree of
   heaven, tulip oak, tulip tree, tupelo
upas
walnut, Washingtonia, Washington thorn, water
   elm, wattle, weeping willow, white fir, white
   poplar, white spruce, willow, willow oak,
   witch hazel
yellow pine, yellow poplar, yew

Shrubs

shrub woody perennial plant with several stems
   branching off near its base rather than a single
   trunk like a tree
   alder, allspice, aloe, althea, arbutus, azalea
   barbasco, barberry, bayberry, bignonia, bilberry,
      blackberry, black currant, blackthorn,
      bladdernut, blueberry, box, bramble, broom,
      buddleia, buffalo berry, buttonbush
   caper, cascarilla, cassia, cayenne, chokeberry,
      cinchona, clematis, cleome, coca, coffee,
      coffeeberry, coralberry, cranberry, crowberry,
      cubeb, currant
   daphne, deerberry, divi-divi
   elder, elderberry, erica, euonymus
   farkleberry, firethorn, flowering maple,
      forsythia, frangipani, fuchsia, furze
   gardenia, genista, germander, gooseberry,
      gorse, grape, greasewood, greenbrier, guava,
      guayule, guelder rose
   haw, heath, heather, hemlock, hemp tree,

henna, hibiscus, holly, honeysuckle,
   huckleberry, hydrangea
Indian currant, Indian hawthorn, indigo, Italian
   jasmine
jojoba, Juneberry, jute
kalmia, kat, kumquat
laurel, lavender, leadwort, leatherleaf,
   lespedeza, lilac, ling
magnolia, manzanita, milkwort, mistletoe, mock
   orange, mountain cranberry, mountain
   currant, mountain fetterbush, mountain holly,
   mountain maple, myrtle
nandina, night jasmine, ninebark
oleander, Oregon grape
partridgeberry, pepper, Persian berry,
   philodendron, photinia, poison haw, poison
   ivy, poison oak, poison sumac, prickly ash,
   privet, pussy willow
quassia
raspberry, rhododendron, rose, rosebay,
   rosemary, rose of Sharon
sad tree, sage, sagebrush, sand myrtle, scarlet
   sage, serviceberry, sheepberry, shrimp plant,
   silverberry, sisal, sloe, smilax, snowberry,
   spicebush, spirea, staggerbush, strawberry
   guava, strawberry tree, sumac, syringa
tamarisk, tea tree, titi, toyon
veronica, viburnum
whin, wild hydrangea, winterberry, winter
   cherry, wintercreeper, wintergreen barberry,
   wisteria, witch hazel
yaupon, yellowroot
zenobia

Flowering Plants

flower seed-producing plant, usu. nonwoody,
   with a shortened stem bearing leaflike sepals,
   colorful petals, and pollen-bearing stamens
   clustered around pistils
flowering plant any angiosperm that produces
   flowers, fruit, and seeds in an enclosed ovary
   acacia, adder's-tongue, African violet, agave,
      ageratum, ailanthus, amaranth, amaryllis,
      American Beauty rose, anemone, arbutus,
      arethusa, arnica, arrowhead, artichoke,
      asphodel, aspidistra, aster, atamasco lily,
      azalea
   baby-blue-eyes, baby's-breath,
      bachelor's-button, begonia, berseem, betony,
      bird-of-paradise, bitterroot, black-eyed
      Susan, blazing star, bleeding heart,
      bloodroot, bluebell, bluebonnet, bluebottle,
      blue flag, bluet, boltonia, bridal wreath,
      broccoli, bromegrass, broom, brown-eyed
      Susan, buttercup, buttonbush
   cactus, calendula, calla lily, calypso, camass,
      camellia, campanula, Canada thistle,
      candytuft, carnation, catalpa, cat's-paw,
      cattail, century plant, chamomile, Cherokee
      rose, Chinese lantern plant, Christmas rose,
      chrysanthemum, cineraria, clematis, clethra,
      cockscomb, colicroot, columbine, comfrey,
      compass plant, cornel, cornflower, corydalis,
      cosmos, cowslip, crocus, cyclamen
   daffodil, dahlia, daisy, damask rose, dandelion,
      delphinium, dogwood, dragon's mouth,
      duckweed, Dutchman's-breeches,
      Dutchman's-pipe
   edelweiss, eglantine, erigeron
   fairy-slipper, figwort, fireweed, flax,

fleur-de-lis, forget-me-not, forsythia,
   foxglove, foxtail, frangipani, fuchsia
gardenia, gentian, geranium, gladiolus,
   goatsbeard, golden aster, goldenrod, ground
   ivy, groundsel
harebell, hawkweed, hawthorn, heather,
   hepatica, hibiscus, hogweed, hollyhock,
   honeysuckle, horehound, horsemint, hyacinth,
   hydrangea
impatiens, Indian cress, Indian fig, Indian hemp,
   Indian paintbrush, Indian pipe, Indian
   strawberry, Indian warrior, indigo, iris, Italian
   aster
jack-in-the-pulpit, japonica, jasmine,
   jessamine, jonquil
knotweed
ladies'-tobacco, lady's-slipper, larkspur,
   lavender, lehua, lilac, lily, lily of the valley,
   lobelia, lotus, love-lies-bleeding, lupine
magnolia, mallow, marguerite, marigold, marsh
   mallow, marsh marigold, mayflower,
   maypop, mayweed, mignonette, mimosa,
   moccasin flower, mock orange, monkshood,
   morning glory, moss rose, motherwort,
   mountain laurel, mullein, myrtle
narcissus, nasturtium
ohia lehua, oleander, opium poppy, orchid,
   Oregon grape, Oswego tea, oxalis
pansy, pasqueflower, passionflower,
   pennyroyal, peony, periwinkle, petunia,
   phlox, pilewort, pink, pinxter flower,
   poinsettia, poppy, portulaca, prickly pear,
   primrose, pussy-toes, pyrethrum
Queen Anne's lace
rafflesia, ragwort, ranunculus, red fescue,
   resurrection plant, Rhode Island bent, rose,
   rose of Jericho, rudbeckia
safflower, saffron, saguaro, sansevieria,
   santonica, scarlet sage, shooting star, smilax,
   snapdragon, snowball, snowberry, snowdrop,
   snow plant, spirea, stock, strawflower,
   sunflower, swamp pink, sweet alyssum, sweet
   pea, sweet william
tamarisk, teasel, thistle, tidytips, trefoil,
   trillium, trumpet flower, trumpet vine, tulip
umbrella plant
vanilla, Venus's flytrap, verbena, vetch,
   viburnum, viola, violet
wallflower, water lily, wild rose, wisteria,
   wolfbane, woundwort
yarrow, yucca
zinnia

Grasses, Sedges, and Grasslike Plants

grass member of the family of flowering plants
   with long, narrow leaves, jointed stems, flowers
   in spikelets, and seedlike fruit
sedge any of the family of rushlike or grasslike
   herbaceous plants growing in wet areas and
   having solid stems, slender leaves, and spikes of
   small flowers
   alfalfa, alfilaria, Australian rye grass
   Bahia grass, bamboo, barley, barn grass,
      barnyard grass, beach grass, beard grass,
      bengal grass, bent, bent grass, Bermuda
      grass, blue grama, bluegrass, bluejoint, bog
      grass, bristly foxtail grass, bromegrass,
      broomcorn, buckwheat, buffalo grass,
      bulrush, bunch grass

canary grass, cane, China grass, chufa, cock's-foot, corn, cotton grass, couch grass, crab grass

darnel, durra, durum wheat

eelgrass, English rye grass

feather grass, fescue, finger grass, flyaway grass, foxtail, frog's-bit

gama grass, grama, guinea grass

hair grass, hassock, hay, herd's grass, horsetail

Indian corn, Italian rye grass

Japanese lawn grass, Job's-tears

Kentucky bluegrass, khus-khus, Korean lawn grass

lawn grass, lemon grass, little quaking grass, lovegrass, lyme grass

maize, meadow fescue, meadow foxtail, meadow grass, mesquite grass, millet, myrtle grass

oat, oat grass, orchard grass

paddy, pampas grass, papyrus, peppergrass, pin grass, plume grass, pony grass

quitch

red fescue, redtop, reed grass, Rhode Island bent, ribbon grass, rice, rush, rye, ryegrass

scouring rush, scutch grass, sedge, sheep fescue, silk grass, slender foxtail, sorghum, spear grass, squirrel-tail grass, squitch, star grass, striped grass, sugarcane, switch grass, sword grass

tear grass, timothy, tule, twitch grass

umbrella plant

vetiver, viper's grass

wheat, wild oat, wild rye, windlestraw, wire grass, witch grass, wood meadow grass, woolly beard grass, worm grass

yellow-eyed grass

zebra grass, zoysia

Herbaceous Plants

herb nonwoody, seed-producing plant whose stem withers away to the ground after season's growth, often having medicinal or culinary uses

ajuga, aluminum plant, amaranth, angelica, anise

balm, basil, belladonna, bellwort, bergamot, betony, birthwort, bitterroot, bladderwort, blue-curls, boneset, borage, bugle, bugleweed, burning bush, butterwort, button snakeroot

calamint, calendula, caraway, cardamom, carrot, castor-oil plant, catmint, catnip, cauliflower, celery, chamomile, charlock, chervil, chicory, cilantro, clover, coleus, coriander, corydalis, cowbane, cow parsnip, Cretan dittany, crowfoot, cumin

datura, deadly nightshade, death camass, dill, dittany, dropwort

eryngo

fennel, fenugreek, feverroot, figwort, finochio, Florence fennel, fool's-parsley, fraxinella

gas plant, germander, ginger, glasswort, ground ivy, ground pine

heliotrope, hemlock, hemp, hemp nettle, henbane, henbit, honewort, horehound, horsemint, hound's-tongue, hyssop

leadwort, lespedeza, licorice, lovage, lupine

mandrake, marijuana, marjoram, May apple, mint, monarda, monkshood, mullein, mustard

nutmeg

oregano, Oswego tea

parsley, parsnip, patchouli, pennyroyal, peppermint, perilla, philodendron

rattlesnake weed, rosemary, rudbeckia, rue

safflower, sage, salvia, samphire, sanicle, savory, scarlet sage, sea holly, sesame, sorrel, spearmint, spiderwort, sweet cicely, sweet woodruff

tansy, tarragon, teasel, thyme, tobacco, trefoil, turmeric

water hemlock, wild bergamot, wild marjoram, wintergreen, woodruff, wormwood, wort, woundwort

yarrow

Ferns

fern nonflowering, vascular plant having roots, stems, and fronds and reproducing by spores instead of seeds

adder's-tongue

basket fern, bead fern, beech fern, bladder fern, Boston fern, boulder fern, bracken, bristle fern, brittle fern, buckler fern

chain fern, Christmas fern, cinnamon fern, cliff brake, climbing fern, crested fern, curly grass fern, fragile fern

grape fern

hart's-tongue, hay-scented fern, holly fern

interrupted fern

lady fern, limestone fern, lip fern

maidenhair, male fern, marsh fern, moonwort, mosquito fern

New York fern

oak fern, osmund, ostrich fern

parsley fern, polypody, pteridosperm

rattlesnake fern, resurrection fern, rock brake, royal fern

seed fern, sensitive fern, shield fern, snuffbox fern, spleenwort

walking fern, walking leaf, wall fern, water fern, wood fern, woodsia

Vines

vine plant that grows along the ground or clings to a vertical support by means of twining stems, tendrils, or rootlets

actinidia, Algerian ivy, ampelopsis, Amur grape, asparagus fern

balsam apple, balsam pear, bean, bittersweet, Boston ivy, bottle gourd, bougainvillea, boxthorn, bramble, bryony

cantaloupe, cape plumbago, casaba, catclaw vine, chayote, Chinese wisteria, clematis, convolvulus, coral greenbrier, creeping fig, cross-vine, cucumber, curly clematis

dewberry, dichondra

elephant's-foot, English ivy, everblooming honeysuckle

fleevine, fox grape

gloryvine, golden clematis, gourd, grape, grapevine, greenbrier

Hall's honeysuckle, honeysuckle, hop, horsebrier, Hottentot's bread

ipomoea, ivy

jackman clematis, Japanese creeper, Japanese wisteria, jasmine, jovin clematis

kudzu vine

liana, loofah

matrimony vine, melon, milkweed, monk's-hood vine, moonseed, morning glory, muscat

pea, peppervine, poison ivy, poison oak, pokeweed, porcelain ampelopsis, primrose jasmine, pumpkin

rag gourd, rambler rose, Regel's tripterygium, runner bean

scarlet clematis, scarlet kadsura, sevenleaf creeper, silvervine, similax, squash, star jasmine, stephanotis, string bean, summer squash, sweet honeysuckle

teasel gourd, traveler's-joy, trumpet creeper, trumpet honeysuckle, trumpet vine

vanilla, vegetable sponge, vetch, Virginia creeper, virgin's bower

wandering Jew, watermelon, wintercreeper, winter jasmine, winter squash, wire vine, wisteria, woodbine

yam

Weeds

weed vigorous plant of rank growth that usu. reproduces profusely, is difficult to eliminate, and tends to overcrowd more desirable neighboring plants; any plant that is unwanted and interferes with growth of other plants, including many grasses, herbs, and mosses

barren strawberry, bedstraw, beggar-ticks, Bermuda grass, bindweed, bird's-eye pearlwort, bitter nightshade, black bindweed, bluegrass, blueweed, bracken, brake, broad-leaved dock, buckthorn, buckhorn plantain, bugleweed, bull thistle, bur, burdock

Canada thistle, Carolina horse nettle, carpetweed, cat's-ear, cattail, charlock, chickweed, chicory, cinquefoil, clover, cocklebur, corn spurry, cottonweed, couch grass, crab grass, crane's-bill, crazyweed, creeping buttercup, creeping cinquefoil, creeping speedwell, creeping veronica, curled dock

dandelion, devil's paintbrush, dewberry, dock, duckweed

English lawn daisy, Eurasian water milfoil

field bindweed, field chickweed, field horsetail, figwort, fireweed, foxtail

galinsoga, goose grass, goutweed, ground ivy, groundsel

hawkweed, heal-all, hedge bindweed, hemlock, hemp nettle, henbit, hogweed, horehound, horseradish, horsetail, horseweed, hydrilla

ice plant

Japanese fleeceflower, Japanese knotweed, jimson weed, Johnson grass

knawel, knotweed

lace grass, lady's-thumb, lamb's-quarters, liverwort, locoweed

mallow, mayweed, milfoil, milkweed, motherwort, mouse-ear chickweed, mouse-ear hawkweed, mustard

nettle, nut sedge

Oldfield cinquefoil, oxalis, oxeye daisy

pearlwort, peppergrass, pepperweed, pigweed, pilewort, pineapple weed, plantain, poison ivy, poke, pokeberry, pokeweed, prickly lettuce, prostrate knotweed, purslane

quack grass, quitch

ragweed, redroot pigweed, red sorrel, Russian thistle

sandbur, scarlet pimpernel, Scotch broom,

self-heal, sheep sorrel, shepherd's-purse, skunk cabbage, smartweed, sorrel, sow thistle, spatterdock, speedwell, spotted lady's-thumb, spotted spurge, spurge, spurry, statice, stinging nettle, stinkweed, St.-John's-wort, strawflower, sulfur cinquefoil, swallowwort

tall buttercup, tansy, tarweed, tassel flower, thistle, thorn apple, tumbleweed

velvetleaf, Virginia pepperwood

water chestnut, water hyacinth, western sage, wheatgrass, white clover, wild carrot, wild garlic, wild lettuce, wild mustard, wild oat, wild onion, wild parsnip, wild radish, wild vetch, witch grass, witchweed

yarrow, yellow foxtail, yellow nut sedge, yellow wood sorrel

SIMPLER LIFE FORMS

Fungi
   Zygomycota
   Ascomycota
   Basidiomycota
   Deuteromycota
Algae
   Photosynthetic Autotrophs
   Heterotrophs
Bacteria
   Bacterial Form Groups
   Eubacteria
   Archaebacteria
Viruses
   Bacteriophages
   Plant Viruses
   Animal Viruses

See also: *Chap. 1: Medical Problems; Chap. 2: Biology; Animals; Plants*

Fungi, protists, monerans, and viruses are grouped under taxonomically distinctive subheadings with generic definitions, similar to the treatment accorded Animals and Plants.

Fungi

fungus member of the kingdom Fungi, consisting of unicellular or filamentous, multinucleate, eukaryotic organisms that live by decomposing and feed on dead or living organic matter in which they grow and decompose, formerly classified with plants, consisting of four divisions: Zygomycota, Ascomycota, Basidiomycota, and Deuteromycota
lichen fungus in symbiotic union with an alga

ZYGOMYCOTA

zygomycota free-living terrestrial fungi, as well as plant and animal parasites, that reproduce sexually by formation of zygospores
   black bread mold
   dung fungus
   zygomycetes

ASCOMYCOTA

ascomycota sac fungi, having sexual spores in a sac
   ascomycetes
   black mold, blue-green mold, bread mold
   cup fungus
   dead-man's fingers, downy mildew
   earth tongue
   false mildew, false morel
   lorchel
   mildew, mold, morel, mushroom pimple
   powdery mildew
   red bread mold
   sac fungus
   truffle
   yeast

BASIDIOMYCOTA

basidiomycota club fungi, bearing spores at tips of slender projections on a basidium, including most forms commonly called mushrooms
   basidiomycetes, bird's-nest fungus, boletus, bracket fungus, brittlegill
   chanterelle, coral fungus, crumblecap
   deathcap
   earthstar
   field mushroom
   gill fungus, groundwart
   inky cap
   jelly fungus
   meadow mushroom, milkcap, mottlegill, mushroom
   oyster cap
   parasol mushroom, pink gill, pore fungus, puffball
   ringstalk, roof mushroom, rust
   scalecap, sheath mushroom, shelf fungus, shiitake, slime mushroom, smoothcap, smut, stinkhorn
   toadstool, tooth fungus, tricholoma
   waxy cap, webcap, woodcrust

DEUTEROMYCOTA

deuteromycota imperfect fungi, mostly parasitic with no sexual stage
   aspergillus
   blue mold
   deuteromycetes
   Fungi Imperfecti
   green mold
   moniliales
   penicillium
   ringworm fungus
   thrush fungus
   verticillium

Algae

alga any unicellular, colonial, or filamentous eukaryotic organism belonging to kingdom Protista, with no root, stem, or leaf and having no nonreproductive cells in its reproductive structures, containing chlorophyll masked by red or brown pigment, and growing in water or damp places

Protista kingdom of algae, amebas, and protozoans, consisting of photosynthetic autotrophs and heterotrophs

PHOTOSYNTHETIC AUTOTROPHS

photosynthetic autotroph organism capable of self-nourishment by using inorganic materials as its source of nutrients and photosynthesis as its source of energy
   brown algae
   carrageen, chlorophytes, chrysophytes, conferva, cryptomonads
   diatoms, dinoflagellates, dulse
   euglenas, euglenophytes
   fucus
   golden-brown algae, green algae, gulfweed
   Irish moss
   kelp
   olive-brown seaweed
   phaeophytes, pond scum, pyrrophytes
   red algae, rhodophytes, rockweed
   sargasso, sargassum, sea lettuce, sea moss, seaweed, sea wrack, stonewort
   wrack
   yellow-green algae

HETEROTROPHS

heterotroph organism requiring living or dead organic materials as its principal source of nutrients
protozoans animallike, eukaryotic organisms of kingdom Protista, primarily unicellular, colonial, and nonphotosynthetic, categorized by means of motility as ciliates, flagellates, or pseudopods
   acrasiomycetes, amebas
   cellular slime molds, chytrids, ciliates
   flagellates
   myxomycetes
   oomycetes, opalinids
   plasmodial slime molds, protozoans, pseudopods
   slime molds, sporozoans
   water molds

Bacteria

bacteria *pl., sing.* **bacterium;** ubiquitous, unicellular organisms appearing singly or in chains in spherical, spiral, or rod-shaped form, forming major phylum of kingdom Monera
Monera kingdom of prokaryotic organisms, or cells without a membrane-bound nucleus and membrane-bound organelles, that reproduce by asexual budding or fission

BACTERIAL FORM GROUPS

bacilli *pl., sing.* **bacillus;** rod-shaped bacteria
cocci *pl., sing.* **coccus;** spherical bacteria
spirilla *pl., sing.* **spirillum;** long, spiral, rod-shaped bacteria
vibrios *pl., sing.* **vibrio;** short, curved, or S-shaped bacteria

EUBACTERIA

eubacteria true bacteria, including most free-living and parasitic bacteria with simple, undifferentiated cells having rigid walls
    actinomycetes
    blue-green algae
    cyanobacteria
    endospore-forming bacteria
    green nonsulfur bacteria, green sulfur bacteria
    lactic acid bacteria
    mycoplasmas
    purple nonsulfur bacteria, purple sulfur
      bacteria
    spirochetes

ARCHAEBACTERIA

archaebacteria surviving members of branch of prokaryotes adapted to earliest stages of biological evolution
    halobacteria, halophiles
    methanobacteria, methanogens
    thermoacidophiles

Viruses

virus ultramicroscopic, metabolically inert agent that can reproduce only within a host cell but is partially independent, consisting of nucleic acid enclosed in a protein coat, not fitting into any of the five kingdoms and classified by whether it infects bacteria, plants, or animals

BACTERIOPHAGES

bacteriophage any virus that infects specific bacteria; phage
    corticovirus, cystovirus
    inovirus
    levivirus
    microvirus, myovirus
    pedovirus, plasmavirus
    stylovirus
    tectivirus

PLANT VIRUSES

alfalfa mosaic virus
bromovirus
carlavirus, caulimovirus, closterovirus, comovirus, cucumovirus
hordeivirus
ilarvirus
luteovirus
nepovirus
potexvirus, potyvirus
tobacco mosaic virus, tobacco necrosis virus, tobamovirus, tobravirus, tomato spotted wilt virus, tombusvirus, tymovirus

ANIMAL VIRUSES

adenovirus, arbovirus, arenavirus
baculovirus, bunyavirus
coronavirus
enterovirus, Epstein-Barr virus
herpesvirus
influenza virus, iridovirus
orbivirus, orthomyxovirus
papovavirus, paramyxovirus, parvovirus, picornavirus, poliovirus, poxvirus
reovirus, retrovirus, rhabdovirus, rhinovirus, Rous sarcoma virus
togavirus

CHAPTER THREE
THE EARTH

GEOLOGY

Branches and Disciplines
Materials, Formations, and Substances
Processes, Phenomena, Events, and Techniques
Geological Time Scale
Mining

▶ *See also: Chap. 2: Biology; Chap. 3: Geography;*
Minerals, Metals, and Rocks; Landscapes and
Seascapes; Weather and Natural Phenomena;
Chap. 4: Chemistry; Chap. 12: Agriculture

Branches and Disciplines

astrogeology geology of celestial bodies in our solar system

chronostratigraphy system of dividing geologic time into eras, periods, epochs, and ages

crystallography study of form, structure, and properties of crystals

earth sciences various sciences dealing with Earth and its nonliving components

ecology study of the relationship between organisms and their environments

environmental geology study of the interaction between human beings and the Earth

geobotany study of the distribution of plant species; phytogeography

geochemistry study of chemical composition and activity in Earth's crust

geochronology study of the age of Earth and dating of evolutionary stages of development

geochronometry measurement of geologic time by radioactive decay

geodesy branch of mathematics concerned with determining size and shape of Earth and position of points on its surface

geodynamics study of activity and forces inside Earth

geognosy study of composition of Earth and distribution of strata and mineral deposits

geography descriptive science that deals with Earth's surface

geology science of Earth's origin, evolution, and structure as recorded in rocks, crust, interior, and fossils

geomorphology study of nature, origin, and development of Earth's landforms

geophysics physics of phenomena occurring on Earth

geopolitics interrelationship of politics and geography

historical geology study of the history of Earth

hydrology study of Earth's water, its distribution and cycles

lithology study of rocks based on megascopic examination of samples

magnetostratigraphy use of magnetized rocks to determine record of changes in Earth's magnetic field

marine geology study of ocean's origin and structure, esp. its floor

metallurgy science and technology of metals and their separation from ores

mineralogy scientific study of minerals

mining engineering applied mineralogy and metallurgy

oceanography science of ocean movement and life

orography physical geography of mountains

paleogeography study of geography of the past

paleontology study of fossils

pedology soil science

petrology study of rocks

physical geology study of material composing Earth

phytogeography geobotany

planetology study of the planetary system

seismology study of seismic waves generated by earthquakes or other Earth vibrations

soil science applied study of soil and earth

stratigraphy study of deposition of sediments

structural geology study of structural features of rocks and geographical distributions of these features

tectonics study of movements that shape Earth's crust

Materials, Formations, and Substances

abyssal plain flat plain on ocean floor

abyssal zone lightless depths of open sea, usu. deeper than 12,000 feet (3700m)

agglomerate mass of heat-fused fragments of volcanic rock

aggregate rock composed of mixture of mineral fragments, crystals, and other materials

alloy two or more metals, or a metal and nonmetal, fused together when molten

alluvial fan cone-shaped deposit of earth made by flowing water

alluvium clay, silt, sand, or gravel sediment deposited by running water

alpine glacier valley glacier

amalgam alloy of mercury with another metal or metals

anthracite hard coal that burns almost without flame

anticline configuration of folded, stratified rocks in which rocks dip in two directions away from a crest

aquifer permeable rock that holds groundwater

artesian well well under pressure from weight of water in aquifer column

ash finely powdered volcanic lava

asthenosphere layer of Earth's crust near melting point, almost fluid

atoll coral island remaining after reef sinks below sea level

axial plane plane that divides rock fold symmetrically

barrier beach narrow strip of sand and rock separated from coast by channel

batholith large mass of intrusive, igneous rock extending very deep into Earth's crust

bathyal zone ocean area extending beyond continental shelf to depth of about 12,000 feet (3700m)

beach strip of loose, grainy material where land and large body of water meet

bed thin layer of sedimentary rock separating different materials lying above and below it

bed load heavy matter rolling along river bottom but not carried by upper layer of water

bedrock solid rock underneath soil layer

berm low ridge built up by storm waves

bitumen naturally occurring asphalt; hard or semisolid tarlike residue of petroleum or coal tar distillation

bituminous coal soft coal

bole easily pulverized, reddish clay

boulder detached, rounded, and worn large mass of rock

breccia rock composed of angular fragments of older rocks

Bryozoa phylum of attached and incrusting marine invertebrates

caldera crater formed by explosion and collapse of volcano

calf mass of ice broken off from glacier or iceberg

caliche crusted calcium carbonate formed on certain soils by evaporation of rising solutions in dry regions

cannel coal oily, compact coal that burns easily and brightly

cast mineral or mud deposited and hardened where body of an organism decayed to form a fossil

catchment basin drainage basin (Britain)

cave hollow area in earth with opening at surface

cavern large, roofed-over cave or passageway in rock, often formed by groundwater passing through cracks in limestone

chatter mark small, curved abrasion on surface of glaciated rock caused by passage of glacier over it

cinder rough piece of solid volcanic lava; slag from reduction of metal ores; intermediate state of burned matter not yet reduced to ash

cinder cone accumulated debris around volcanic vent forming steep-sided hill

cirque hollow mountain basin that collects snow, caused by glaciation

clastic rock containing rock particles, minerals, and crushed shells

clay soil composed of fine particles of hydrous aluminum silicates, plastic when wet, and hard when exposed to high temperature and/or pressure

clod lump of earth, clay, or loam

coal black, combustible mineral solid that results from partial decomposition of organic matter under heat and pressure over millions of years

composite rock made up of several distinct parts

composite volcano strato-volcano

conchoidae fracture fracture that produces curved surfaces similar to those of interior of a shell

cone peak of volcano

conglomerate rock, such as hardened clay, composed of rounded fragments of varying sizes in cement; pudding stone

continent large landmass on surface of Earth

continental glacier large glacier covering major part of a landmass

continental shelf edge of continental landmass covered by ocean

continental slope edge of continental shelf that slopes steeply down to ocean floor

coral reef structure on continental shelf made of shells of colonial marine organisms

core innermost part of Earth

crag steep, rugged rock projecting above rock mass

crater round pit, esp. at summit of volcano

crevasse deep crack in glacial ice

crust thin outer layer of Earth's surface, composed of sial and sima layers

crystal body created by solidification of chemical element or compound into regular atomic arrangement with plane faces; quartz that is close to transparent

culm carboniferous formation of beds of impure anthracite containing shale or sandstone; waste from anthracite coal mines

delta sediment deposited at river mouth

deposit sediment laid down in new location; pocket of mineral or ore in earth

detritus rock fragments resulting from disintegration by weathering and erosion

diamond mineral of nearly pure crystalline carbon, hardest natural substance known

dike igneous rock formation that cuts across another rock formation

dip acute angle that rock surface makes with horizontal plane

dissected mountains range formed by erosion of plateaus or plains

divide ridge separating two drainage basins

dome volcano small, steep volcano of rhyolite lava

drainage basin area drained by river and its tributaries; catchment basin

drumlin oval mound of till formed by glacier

dune mound or ridge of sand accumulated by wind

earth soft, granular, crumbly part of land; soil; land surface of the world

eluvium rock debris produced by weathering or disintegration

erratic large stone or boulder carried by glacier to place where it rests on bedrock of different composition

esker deposit formed by water running under glacier

eugeosyncline part of geosyncline in which the products of volcanism are associated with clastic sedimentation

evaporite rock formed by water evaporating from a mineral mass

extrusive rock igneous rock formed on Earth's surface or seabed, not underground

facies sedimentological record of depositional environment

facies fossil fossil species adapted to limited environment

firn granular ice formed by recrystallization of snow

flint hard quartz that produces spark when struck by steel

fluvial (*adj*) produced by rivers

footwall block of rock underlying a fault plane

fossil living thing preserved from previous geologic era in petrified rock form

fossil fuel fuel source, such as coal or petroleum, deposited in earth from organic remains during earlier geologic age

freestone stone, such as limestone or sandstone, that may be cut freely without splitting

gemstone hard mineral, crystal, or petrified material used as jewelry when cut and faceted, designated precious or semiprecious

geode hollow stone nodule lined by mineral crystals growing inward

geosyncline very large, troughlike depression in Earth's surface containing masses of sedimentary and volcanic rock

geyser thermal spring that intermittently ejects water with considerable force

glacier massive, moving ice layer formed in previous geologic era by accumulation and recrystallization of snow

Gondwanaland hypothetical continent that broke apart in Mesozoic era

granite very hard crystalline igneous rock found in mountain cores

gravel loose, rounded fragments of rock; stratum of gravel

ground moraine debris remaining from melting of glacier and forming gently rolling surface

groundwater water trapped in underground pores or fissures in earth

guyot submerged, flat-topped seamount

hadal zone the deepest trenches of the ocean bottom, usu. deeper than 20,000 feet (6000m)

hanging wall block of rock overhanging a fault plane

hard pan bedrock or cemented, compacted clayey layer unable to be penetrated by roots; hard, unbroken ground

horn high, steep mountain peak formed by glaciers

humus portion of soil made up of decomposed organic matter

hydrocarbon compound of hydrogen and carbon, including fossil fuels

hydrosphere Earth's water environment, including glaciers, oceans, atmospheric vapor, lakes, streams, groundwater, snow, and ice

iceberg mass of ice detached from glacier and floating at sea

icecap localized ice sheet

ice pack expanse of floating ice formed over time due to compaction of ice by wind and currents

ice sheet broad, moundlike mass of glacial ice of considerable extent

igneous rock rock formed by cooling and hardening of magma

index fossil fossil from specific time range, used to date rock layer surrounding it

inner core innermost solid layer of Earth

inorganic material matter that is not animal or vegetable, esp. compounds not containing carbon and derived from mineral sources

inselberg monadnock

intrusive rock igneous rock formed by magma cooling and hardening underground, esp. in cracks or cavities in existing rock

joint break in rock mass with no movement of rock on opposite sides of break

kame detrital mound left by retreating ice sheet, usu. stratified sand and gravel

kettle lake body of water formed by melting glaciers moving over a basin

laccolith large body of intrusive igneous rock, domed horizontally over surrounding rock mass, forcing overlying strata to bulge upward

lava magma reaching surface of Earth, usu. through volcano

lignite low-grade brown coal

limestone calcium carbonate rock formed by accumulation of organic remains of sea animals

lithosphere Earth's crust and upper part of mantle

load soil particles and rock carried by running water, wind, or glaciers

loam rich soil of clay, sand, and organic matter

lodestone rock that possesses magnetic polarity

loess fine, windblown dust particles that are unconsolidated and unstratified

lopolith tabular igneous intrusion shaped like bowl with roof and floor sagging downward

macle spot or discoloration in mineral; rough prism that shows cross or checkered pattern in cross section

mafic magma readily flowing magma produced in mantle

magma hot, molten rock within Earth

mantle solid layer beneath Earth's crust to depth of 1800 miles (2900 km)

mantle rock loose material, residual or transported, resting on solid rock of Earth's crust

marl loose, crumbling earthy deposit of clay and limestone

massif block of Earth's crust bounded by faults and displaced as unchanged unit to form principal mountain mass

mélange heterogeneous mixture of rock materials

meltwater water melted from glacial ice

mesa hill with flattened top of hard sandstone or limestone

metal opaque, fusible, ductile, conductive, lustrous substance, often a chemical element or compound yielding oxides or hydroxides

metamorphic rock igneous or sedimentary rock that has been transformed by heat, pressure, or chemically active fluids

meteorite small particle of matter from space that reaches surface of Earth without being vaporized

mid-ocean ridge underwater volcanic mountain chain running parallel to edges of continents bounding ocean

mineral inorganic chemical solid naturally occurring in Earth's crust and having definite chemical composition and tendency to form crystals

miogeosyncline that portion of geosyncline in which volcanism is absent

monadnock resistant rock hill standing well above surrounding peneplain; inselberg

monolith single large block of stone

moraine rock ridge left after disappearance of glacier, composed of till

mountain natural landform or ridge in Earth's crust, elevated at least to 2000 feet (600 m)

mountain core granite rock at center of mountain, surrounded by metamorphic rock

native metal pure metal, usu. found in vein

natural gas combustible mixture of gaseous hydrocarbons, largely methane, that accumulates in porous sedimentary rocks, used as a fossil fuel

noble mineral precious, pure mineral, esp. corrosion-resistant metal such as gold

nodule mineral lump composed primarily of chert or flint

nonclastic rock sedimentary rock composed of interlocking rock that forms grains

nonfoliated rock nonbanded metamorphic rock

oolite spherical grain of sand size, usu. composed of calcium carbonate, originated by inorganic precipitation

organic material substance derived from living organism

outcropping emergence of rock formation from Earth to surface exposure

outer core liquid part of Earth's core

outwash material carried by glacier and laid down in stratified deposits

Pangaea hypothetical continent that broke apart to form continents as they now exist

peat partly carbonized decaying vegetable matter; first stage in formation of coal

pebble small stone worn smooth and round

peneplain flat area just slightly above sea level worn down by streams and mass wasting

permafrost permanently frozen subsoil in arctic regions

petroleum oily, flammable hydrocarbon found in rock strata, refined to produce gasoline

piedmont flat expanse of land lying at foot of mountain

piedmont glacier glacier formed at foot of mountain

placer alluvial deposit containing heavy minerals

plain flat, broad land area slightly above sea level

plate one of huge, movable segments into which Earth's crust is divided and which float over mantle

plateau flat, broad land area at least 2000 feet (600 m) above sea level

playa flat-floored center of undrained desert basin

playa lake temporary lake formed in playa

plutonic rock igneous rock formed by slow crystallization, usu. at great depth

porphyry rock with two or more grain sizes

precious metal rare and therefore valuable metal, such as gold or silver, used in jewelry

precious stone designation for most valuable gemstones, such as diamonds or emeralds

precipitate rock formed from discharge or evaporation of water

pudding stone *Chiefly Brit.* conglomerate

quartz common, colorless, usu. transparent mineral of hexagonal crystals or crystalline masses; silicon dioxide

range system of connected mountains

reef wave-resistant structure composed of sedentary, carbonate-secreting organisms

regolith mantle rock of loose material resting on solid bedrock

residual soil with composition similar to that of bedrock below it

rhyolite fine-grained volcanic rock produced by lava flow

rill miniature stream channel carrying sheet wash

rimrock top stratum of plateau that outcrops to form vertical face

rock large mass of stone, concreted mass of stony material, or broken piece of such a mass

rubble rough, irregular, loose fragments broken from larger mass of rock

sand loose granular material formed by disintegration of rocks into particles smaller than gravel but coarser than silt

sandstone sedimentary rock usu. of quartz sand cemented by silica or calcium carbonate

schist metamorphic rock that can be easily split due to effects of heat

scoria loose, cinderlike lava; slag left after smelting

scree loose rock debris; talus

seamount volcanic mountain at bottom of ocean

sediment material deposited by water, wind, or glaciers

sedimentary rock rock formed on Earth's surface from accumulation of material deposited by water, wind, or glaciers

semiprecious stone designation for gems less valuable than precious stones, such as garnets or turquoise

shale consolidation of clay, mud, or silt into finely stratified rock structure of unaltered minerals

sheet wash thin sheet of water accumulating on slope

shield large area of exposed Precambrian rock

shield volcano volcano built on shield material

shingle coarse, round detritus or alluvial material on seashore

sialic magma thick, stiff magma forming just below crust, composed primarily of silicon and aluminum

sial layer granitelike upper layer of Earth's crust

silica silicon dioxide that occurs as crystalline quartz, opal, or sand

silicon dioxide quartz

sill thin layer of igneous rock extruded between layers of sedimentary rocks or volcanic ejecta

silt loose sedimentary material with particles finer than sand and coarser than clay

sima layer shell of dark, heavy rock composed primarily of silicon and magnesium, found throughout world; layer under sial layer

slag refuse material separated from metal in smelting; lava resembling such refuse

sludge muddy, slushy mass or sediment, esp. on riverbed

slurry water mixture of insoluble mud or lime

soil fragments of weathered rock combined with organic matter

soil horizon layer of soil parallel to land surface

spatter cone low, steep-sided volcanic cone built up from erupted droplets or blobs of lava

stalactite columnar deposit of minerals hanging from cave ceiling

stalagmite columnar deposit of minerals on cavern floor, caused by accretion of dripping mineral-rich water from ceiling

stone concretion of earthy or mineral matter of indeterminate size and shape; one piece of such concretion

stratified rock rock made up of many different layers

strato-volcano steeply shaped volcano that emits fragmented material and viscous lava; composite volcano

stratum sheetlike mass of sedimentary or igneous rock, usu. lying between other strata beds

syncline fold in rock where strata dip inward from both sides

talus sloping mass formed by pile of loose rock fragments and weathered matter collected at foot of cliff or on slope below rock face

tarn lake formed at bottom of cirque after glacial ice has disappeared

tarpit flat area in which natural bitumens, such as tar or asphalt, collect and are exposed to air so that animals fall in and have their bones preserved

terminal moraine debris piled up at point of farthest glacial advance

terrace flat platform at base of eroded sea cliff

till mix of material dropped from melting glacier

topsoil fertile soil made up mainly of humus

trace fossil imprint left by animal track or burrow

transported soil soil moved from its place of origin

trench long, very deep trough in ocean floor bordering some continents

tufa limestone deposited by springs

tundra polar area soil, composed mainly of peat,

whose top layer thaws each spring while base remains frozen year-round

underground rock rock deposits not exposed at Earth's surface

valley glacier glacier formed at high elevation, covering river valley; alpine glacier

vent opening at Earth's surface from which volcanic material is emitted

vesicle small cavity in rock formed by gas bubble, occurring in rock in its molten state

volcanic rock igneous rock that solidified rapidly from molten lava at Earth's surface

volcano cone-shaped mountain that vents hot, molten lava, gases, and rock fragments from Earth's interior

Processes, Phenomena, Events, and Techniques

abrasion wearing away of rock by solid particles carried by wind, water, ice, or gravity

aftershock minor earthquake following greater one and originating at same place

age interval of geologic time shorter than an epoch

antipodes two places at opposite sides of Earth

avalanche expanding mass of loosened material sliding suddenly and swiftly down mountain

belt elongated area, smaller than a zone, characterized by particular features or occurrences

body wave earthquake that moves underground

Brinell hardness measure of hardness of metal or alloy

carat unit of weight for diamonds or gemstones, equal to 200 mg (.007 ounce)

carbon-14 dating radiocarbon dating

carboniferous (*adj*) designating coal making period of Paleozoic era

cataclysm great upheaval that causes sudden, violent changes in Earth

cementation binding of rock particles together

chemical weathering chemical transformation of original rock material into new chemical composition

cleavage pattern of breakage of rock or minerals along flat planes

cleavage plane smooth surface along which mineral breaks

coal gasification process by which coal is changed to gas

coalification process by which vegetable matter is transformed into coal

columnar jointing columns of rock formed by slowly cooling lava

comminution particle size reduction by physical processes

compaction reduction in pore space between individual grains due to pressure

compression stress force squeezing crustal rock together

concretion sedimentary rock with succeeding layers of minerals forming around a grain of sand or other nucleus

contact metamorphism metamorphism at contact between metamorphic and igneous rock

continental drift very slow motion of major landmasses around Earth's surface

convergent boundary area where two landmasses or plates move toward one another

Coriolis effect tendency of any moving body starting from surface of Earth to continue in direction propelled by Earth's rotation

creep gradual movement of soil particles downhill

crystallization process in which crystals separate from fluid, viscous, or dispersed structure

decomposition chemical formation of new compounds from elements within rock; chemical weathering

deep ocean current water motion caused by differences in temperature and density

deflation removal of loose particles from ground by action of wind

dendrite branching pattern made by one mineral crystallizing in another

diagenesis formation of sedimentary rock by compaction of sediment and chemical reactions

disintegration breakage of large rocks into smaller fragments; mechanical weathering

divergent boundary boundary between two landmasses pulling apart

earthquake sudden, violent shaking of Earth's crust

elasticity ability of material to recover from a deforming force

elevation height above sea level

emergent coast land exposed by lowering of sea level

eolian (*adj*) carried, deposited, or eroded by the wind

epicenter point on Earth's surface directly above focus of earthquake

epoch smallest major unit of geologic time; subdivision of period

era largest major unit of geologic time, divided into periods and epochs

erosion wearing down of natural landforms by wind, water, ice, or gravity

eruption sudden, often violent, outflow of lava from volcano

eustasy uniformly global change in sea level, due to change in quantity of water or shape of ocean basins

fault crack in Earth's crust from rock slippage up, down, or sideways

fault block large mass separated from surrounding material by faults on at least two sides

fault zone region of Earth's surface with high number of faults

flood plain river valley area flooded at high water

focus underground center of earthquake

fold bend or turn in crustal rock

folded mountains mountains formed by forces of flexing rock

foliation metamorphic rock banding

foreshock minor earthquake that precedes larger earthquake and originates at its focus

fracture characteristic manner of breakage of mineral

geodetic survey precise description of large land area corrected for Earth's curvature

geologic column layering of rock strata in order from oldest at bottom to youngest at top

geologic time scale convention of viewing geologic history in eras, epochs, and periods, based on fossil data

geomagnetic (*adj*) relating to magnetic properties of Earth

geomorphic (*adj*) pertaining to shape of Earth and its topography

geotectonic (*adj*) relating to structure, distribution, and shape of rock bodies in Earth's crust; pertaining to the conditions within Earth that resulted in movement of crust

geothermal gradient rate of increase of temperature downward into Earth

geothermal power energy from heat of Earth's interior

geothermic (*adj*) relating to heat of Earth's interior

glacial varve chronology determination of geologic age by reference to layers of silt and clay deposited by melting of retreating glaciers

hade angle between fault plane and vertical plane

hardness resistance of substance to scratching

horizon specific position in stratigraphic column that identifies stratum with a particular period; soil layer

hydrologic cycle movement of Earth's water from oceans to atmosphere to land and back to oceans

hysteresis retardation of recovery from elastic deformation after stress is removed

ice age any time of widespread glaciation, esp. Pleistocene glacial epoch

induration concretion of porous rocks and soils due to weather and chemical action

interglacial age historic period between ice ages

isostasy balancing of floating crustal rock on denser mantle

joint fracture plane in rocks, usu. arranged in parallel intersecting systems

karst topography irregular topography developed by action of surface and underground water in soluble rock such as limestone

landslide collapse of sloped or vertical face of earth or rock

law of superimposition rule that in layered beds of rock, oldest is deepest, youngest is closest to surface

leaching washing away of soluble minerals, esp. alkalines, from upper layers of soil by water

lithification hardening into rock

luster capacity of minerals to reflect light off their surfaces

meander curve formed in riverbed

microseism irregular wave caused by constant movement of Earth's surface

Moho Mohorovicic discontinuity

Mohorovicic discontinuity boundary between Earth's solid crust and soft mantle; Moho

mold fossil cavity left in rock after body of organism has decayed

nonconformity unconformity

normal fault fault formed when one side moves up, the other down

oasis fertile area in desert formed by erosion of surface down to water table

orogeny formation of mountains by folding of Earth's crust

outwash plain area with mineral and other deposits left by passing glacier

period second major unit of geologic time, subdivision of era, divided into epochs

permeability measure of the ease with which fluid can be passed through pore space of rock

petrified (*adj*) designating organic matter replaced by minerals over time

phase description of minerals present in a rock or soil sample

plate tectonics theory of formation and motion of Earth's crust and its moving plates

plucking erosion caused by glacier pulling rocks out of earth as it moves along surface

porosity percent of total volume of rock not occupied by solid mineral matter

primary waves seismic waves that move fastest through all forms of matter

profile of equilibrium shape of riverbank equally affected by erosion and deposition of material

radioactive decay breaking apart over time of atomic nucleus, with emission of radiant energy

radiocarbon dating dating of fossil remains by measuring ratio of remaining radioactive carbon 14 to total carbon; carbon-14 dating

recrystallization melting and recooling of rock, resulting in larger grain

regional metamorphism changes in rock over large area caused by increases in temperature and pressure deep in Earth

relief elevation differences among landforms

Richter scale logarithmic scale, ranging from 1 to 10, that indicates magnitude of an earthquake in terms of energy released

rift valley long, narrow valley formed between two faults

rift zone system of fractures in Earth's crust

ring of fire area of earthquake and volcanic activity around rim of Pacific Ocean

rock cycle change in form of Earth materials subjected to geological processes, esp. from magma to igneous, metamorphic, and sedimentary rock, and back to magma

seafloor spreading widening of ocean floor by addition of basaltic material at mid-ocean ridge

secondary waves seismic waves that pass through solids but not liquids or gases and that move slower than primary waves

seismic wave earthquake wave

seismograph instrument that records magnitude of earthquake as moving graph line

shearing force that changes shape of rocks but does not affect their volume

sheeting formation of joints parallel to ground surface by expansion of rock after removal of overlying material

slump downward movement of material caused by slippage of weak rock layer

soil layer horizon

soil profile cross section of soil horizons that shows different levels

solfatara volcanic fissure that emits vapors, steam, and sometimes hot mud, but not lava

spit curved sand deposit formed by current turning and slowing into a bay

stable platform area surrounding shield covered by relatively undisturbed sedimentary rock

stack vertical block of resistant rock cut off from mainland by wave action

strain change in dimensions of material due to stress

stratification formation into layers or beds

stress force applied to material that tends to change its dimensions

structural mountain mountain formed from uplift of crust

subduction act of one lithospheric block descending under another

surface wave earthquake moving on surface of Earth

survey detailed description of tract of land

suspended load sediment picked up from bed and carried off by water or air

tension stretching stress that tends to increase volume of a material

texture size, shape, and arrangement of particles that make up a rock

thrust fault fault in which hanging wall has moved upward relative to footwall

topography physical features of geographical area

traction process of carrying material along bottom of a stream

transform fault boundary where two plates slide past one another

tsunami huge ocean wave caused by underwater earthquake or volcanic eruption

unconformity break in continuity of geologic record; nonconformity

uniformitarianism concept that present is key to the past

upheaval powerful upward movement in Earth's crust

upthrust elevation of part of Earth's surface

valley train elongated formation of sand and gravel deposited in glacial channel

vein narrow water channel in rock or earth

vent volcano opening from which lava erupts

volcanism volcanic activity and phenomena

water table level of water saturation into soil and rock; upper surface of zone of saturation below ground

weathering changes in rock produced by heat, cold, wind, precipitation, and living matter

zone large region of Earth's surface with distinctive characteristics

zone of aeration area above water table where rock openings fill with air between rainstorms

zone of saturation area above impermeable rock layer where all openings are filled with water

Geological Time Scale

NOTE: *Entries for geological eras, periods, and epochs have been listed in chronological order, from the earliest to the most recent.*

Precambrian era 3800 million to 600 million years ago; Archeozoic and Proterozoic eras

Azoic era earliest Precambrian era, preceding appearance of life; former term for Archeozoic era

Archeozoic era early Precambrian era, beginning 3800 million years ago; Earth's crust solidifies; blue-green algae and earliest life forms appear

Proterozoic era later Precambrian era, ending 600 million years ago; bacteria, algae, and primitive multicellular life

Paleozoic era 600 to 225 million years ago; Cambrian, Ordovician, Silurian, Devonian, Carboniferous, and Permian periods

Cambrian period 600 to 500 million years ago; age of marine invertebrates, shellfish, and echinoderms

Ordovician period 500 to 425 million years ago; primitive fishes, seaweeds, and fungi

Silurian period 425 to 400 million years ago; abundant shellfish; first land plants and modern fungi

Devonian period 400 to 345 million years ago; age of fishes; first amphibians, insects, and land animals appear

Carboniferous period 345 to 280 million years ago; Mississippian and Pennsylvanian periods

Mississippian period 345 to 320 million years ago; age of amphibians; shallow seas, low lands, and fern forests

Pennsylvanian period 320 to 280 million years ago; first reptiles; warm climate with swamps and cool forests

Permian period 280 to 225 million years ago; conifer forests; extinction of many marine invertebrates

Mesozoic era 225 to 65 million years ago; Triassic, Jurassic, and Cretaceous periods

Triassic period 225 to 190 million years ago; age of reptiles; active volcanoes

Jurassic period 190 to 135 million years ago; age of dinosaurs and flying reptiles; first birds and mammals

Cretaceous period 135 to 65 million years ago; last dinosaurs; modern insects; flowering plants

Cenozoic era 65 million years ago to present; Tertiary and Quaternary periods

Tertiary period 65 to 1.7 million years ago;

Paleocene, Eocene, Oligocene, Miocene, and Pliocene epochs

Paleocene epoch 65 to 54 million years ago; age of mammals begins; mild to cool climate; first primates

Eocene epoch 54 to 38 million years ago; modern birds and mammals; warm climate; giant birds

Oligocene epoch 38 to 26 million years ago; browsing mammals and saber-toothed tigers

Miocene epoch 26 to 12 million years ago; widespread grasslands; grazing mammals; apes; whales

Pliocene epoch 12 to 1.7 million years ago; cool climate; mountain uplift; mammals increase in size and numbers

Quaternary period 1.7 million years ago to present; Pleistocene and Holocene epochs

Pleistocene epoch 1.7 million to 10,000 years ago; ice ages

Holocene epoch 10,000 years ago to present; modern humans

Mining

adit almost horizontal passageway into mine

afterdamp mixture of gases left in mine after explosion of fire

airway ventilating passage in mine

assay analysis of ore or alloy to determine proportion and purity of components; (vb) make such an analysis

bed layer, stratum, or substance in which minerals or ores are lodged

bench working elevation platform in mine

blackdamp chokedamp

black lung disease caused by inhalation of coal dust

bonanza rich vein of ore

bore (vb) make mine tunnel by drilling

borehole hole drilled in earth to extract core or release gas, oil, or water

borrow pit excavated area from which material has been removed to fill another spot

brattice air passage in mine formed of planks or cloth lining the tunnel

breast face or heading where work is occurring

cave-in collapse of mine shaft or tunnel

chokedamp mine atmosphere that is low in oxygen, causing choking; blackdamp

claim piece of land staked out by one person who has exclusive rights to mine it

clinker hard mass of stony matter fused in furnace from coal impurities

coal car open railroad car for transporting coal from mine

coal gas gas produced by destructive distillation of bituminous coal

collar topmost rim of vertical shaft in mine

collier coal miner; ship for transporting coal

colliery coal mine and its equipment

continuous cutter machine that takes coal from mine face and loads it onto cars or conveyors

core cylindrical sample of mineral or rock

extracted from ground by hollow drill that leaves strata intact

corf small cart for transporting coal or ore

cradle box on rockers for washing sand or gravel to separate gold; rocker

crosscut cut made across vein

culm coal dust

cupel small, shallow, porous cup used in assaying gold and silver

deposit minerals or ores laid down by nature; location where minerals are found

dig excavation

distillation purification by heating to separate more volatile parts of mixture, then cooling and condensing vapor to produce more refined substance

drift horizontal passageway in mine; gallery

drill (vb) bore deep hole into earth, esp. seeking oil

excavation hole or cavity dug into earth to find minerals

extraction removal or separation of mineral from ore

face front or end of excavation and location of mined substance

firedamp combustible gases in coal mine, esp. methane

footwall top of rock stratum beneath vein or bed of ore

gallery small tunnel for inspection or drainage; drift

gangue worthless mineral matter associated with valuable metallic mineral deposits; matrix

gangway primary, level passageway in mine

gold rush large, sudden influx of miners to area where large vein of gold has been discovered

gondola open railroad car with low sides used for carrying coal

gusher high-capacity, flowing oil well

heading road or level leading into coal deposit where mining occurs

horse mass of rock within lode or vein

jack-up rig floating offshore drill rig with retractable legs that lift hull above water level

jig device for separating ore by shaking in water

kerf deep cut a few inches high, used to undermine coal or mineral seam

ledge underground rock layer

lode ore deposit; vein; reef

longwall continuous face being mined, with roof supported by temporary supports

matrix gangue

mine large excavation in Earth from which to extract metallic ores, coal, precious stones, or salt

mine car small, open, low-sided vehicle for moving coal within mine, often on rails

miner person whose work is digging in a mine; mineworker

mineworker miner

mining process of removing ores, coal, and precious metals from Earth

mining engineer designer and builder of mines

mother lode main vein of ore in particular region

muck useless materials to be removed in order to get at desired mineral

offshore drilling sinking of oil wells into ocean bottom from floating platforms

oil well shaft into earth with pump for extracting crude petroleum

open cut designating mine in which excavation is performed from the surface

ore mineral embedded in the earth

orebody well-defined mass of ore-bearing rock

panning washing gravel in porous pan when searching for gold

pay dirt spot that can be mined successfully

pillar isolated mass of rock or ore that serves as roof support in early stages of mining operations

pinch (vb) diminish a vein to nothing

pit man-made cavity in ground for mining

pithead mine entrance and adjacent area

placer glacial deposit of gravel or sand that contains heavy ore minerals eroded from bedrock and that is concentrated as small particles that can be washed out

pocket usu. isolated body of ore in ground

portal entrance to mine tunnel

power shovel usu. diesel-powered excavating shovel

prospect place where mineral deposits are sought; (vb) search for ore

prospector person searching for valuable ores

pulp pulverized ore

quarry place where stone is excavated by cutting and blasting

reef lode or vein

refinery facility for purifying crude oil or raw metal

riddle coarse sieve for grading gravel

riffle grooved lining at bottom of sluice, used to collect particles of ore

road tunnel used for hauling excavated material

rocker cradle

safety lamp lamp designed so as to avoid ignition of mine gases

salt (vb) scatter minerals or ores in mine to deceive prospective buyers

scuttle deep bucket for carrying coal

seam relatively thin stratum or bed

shaft long, narrow, vertical or slanting passage sunk into earth

shoot small tunnel branching off from larger tunnel

shortwall mine with face one-third the length of a longwall, mined by continuous cutter

slack fine coal screenings

sluice sloping trough or flume through which water is run in washing gold ore

smelt (vb) melt or fuse ore to separate impurities and extract pure metal

spoil waste material from excavation

stannary Chiefly Brit. tin-mining region

stope steplike excavation formed by removal of ore from around shaft

strike discovery of rich deposit of ore, coal, or minerals

strip mining mining, esp. for coal, by laying bare deposits near surface rather than sinking shaft

stull timber prop between walls of stope

tailings residue of mining

tailrace channel for carrying off tailings

tipple apparatus for emptying coal from mine car

tram car on rails for conveying loads in mine

trepan heavy boring tool for opening shafts or quarrying

trommel revolving cylindrical sieve for screening ore

tunnel usu. horizontal passageway in mine

vein lengthy, regularly shaped bed of useful mineral matter that fills narrow water channel in rock and earth; lode; reef

vug cavity in rock or lode, often lined with crystals

wash (vb) separate ore or stones by passing water through gravel or earth

well shaft sunk into earth to tap underground supply of oil, gas, or water

wellhead machinery standing above opening of oil or gas well

wellhole shaft of oil or gas well

well log record of geological formations encountered while drilling a well

wildcat oil well drilled in area without known oil deposits

winze inclined shaft that connects levels in mine

workings active portion of mine or quarry

GEOGRAPHY

Branches and Disciplines
Maps and Cartography
Earth's Atmosphere and Topographic Features
Populations and Resources
Nations of the World
States of the United States
Major World Cities

See also: *Chap. 2: Biology; Chap. 3: Geology; Minerals, Metals, and Rocks; Landscapes and Seascapes; Weather and Natural Phenomena; Chap. 4: Astronomy and Space Science; Chap. 8: Kinship and Family Relations; Chap. 12: Business and Economics; Agriculture; Chap. 13: Sociology*

Branches and Disciplines

cartography art and practice of making maps and charts

chorography art of mapping and describing a region or district

cultural geography human geography

demography statistical study of distribution, density, and attributes of human populations

economic geography study of how people use Earth's resources and their distribution

geodesy mathematical determining of Earth's shape and location of points on surface

geographer one trained in or practicing geography

geography study of Earth's surface, physical features, climates, resources, products, and people

geophysics study of materials of which Earth is composed

geoscopy observational knowledge of earth and soil

human geography study of people and their ways of life in different parts of Earth; cultural geography

hydrography science of mapping and describing surface waters of Earth, esp. for navigation

hypsography branch of geography involved with measurement and mapping of Earth's topography above sea level

hypsometry measurement of elevations or altitudes

meteorology study of Earth's atmosphere, climate, and weather

orography branch of physical geography dealing with mountains

physical geography study of nature and history of Earth's surface and atmosphere; physiography

physiography physical geography

soil science applied study of soils

topography science of drawing maps and representing natural surface and man-made features of region

---

Maps and Cartography

aclinic line magnetic equator

acre unit of area measure equal to 43,560 square feet (4047 square meters)

Africa second largest continent, divided between Northern and Southern hemispheres, between Asia and South America, south of Europe, extending from Atlantic to Indian Ocean

altitude height above sea level; elevation

angle of declination angle between direction indicated by magnetic needle and true meridian

angle of depression angle that descending line makes with horizon

angle of elevation angle that ascending line makes with horizon

Antarctica land area surrounding South Pole, forming fifth largest continent

Antarctic Circle parallel of latitude 66 1/2 degrees south of equator, which is in perpetual daylight in midsummer

Arctic land area surrounding North Pole

Arctic Circle parallel of latitude 66 1/2 degrees north of equator, which is in perpetual daylight in midsummer

arrow symbols map signs indicating motion and direction

Asia world's largest continent, extending from Arctic to Singapore and from Bering Strait to Ural Mountains

atlas bound maps showing different parts of world

Australia island continent, smallest of seven

continents, in Southern Hemisphere, between Africa and South America, extending from Indian to Pacific Ocean

axis imaginary line through Earth's center from North to South Pole around which Earth rotates

azimuth angular measurement clockwise around horizon from north or south to location of object or intersection of object's vertical circle with horizon

azimuthal equidistant projection map projection in which great circles projected through a central point provide shortest distance from center to any point; zenithal equidistant projection

bipolar (adj) involving both North and South poles

border dividing line between countries or other geographical units

cardinal points four principal points of compass: north, south, east, and west

cartogram type of map in which size of nations is based on something other than area

celestial equator great circle of celestial sphere projected from plane of equator

celestial globe sphere on which is depicted map of the heavens

celestial horizon great circle on celestial sphere midway between zenith and nadir

chart outline map, such as weather or resource map, with special information plotted geographically

chorograph map or description of particular region

circumpolar (adj) surrounding or near either pole

coastline point at which land meets ocean or sea

compass directional device with magnetic needle pivoting freely and pointing north

conformal (adj) designating map or projection in which scale and angles are preserved

conic projection map in which Earth's surface is projected on conical surface which is unrolled to make plane surface

continent one of seven major landmasses of Earth

Continental Divide Rocky Mountain ridge forming North American watershed that separates rivers flowing east and west; Great Divide

contour interval vertical distance between contour lines on topographic map

contour line line on map that connects all points at same elevation or same ocean depth

coordinates location finders on map, marked by letters or numbers arranged horizontally and vertically along edges

country bounded territory of sovereign nation or state

cylindrical projection map projection of celestial sphere on cylinder that is then unrolled as plane

degree unit of measurement for latitude and longitude

distortion inaccuracies in size and shape of landmasses and oceans on flat map projections

Earth terrestrial globe on which all people live

Eastern Hemisphere half of Earth's surface, lying east of prime meridian

elevation altitude

equal-area projection map in which regions of Earth's surface that are of equal size are shown as equal in size

equator line of latitude halfway between North and South poles at zero degrees

Eurasia landmass made up of continents of Europe and Asia

Europe sixth and smallest continent except Australia, extending from Atlantic Ocean to Ural Mountains

gazetteer geographical dictionary that lists places in alphabetical order

geopolitical map map showing nonphysical as well as physical features

globe spherical model of Earth showing physical features

graticule network of parallels and meridians used as grid on map

great circle imaginary circle on Earth's surface formed by plane passing through its center, dividing Earth into two hemispheres; pair of opposing meridians

Great Divide watershed ridge forming continental divide, esp. Rocky Mountains of North America; Continental Divide

Greenwich English city through which prime meridian runs at zero degrees longitude

grid intersections of parallels of latitude and meridians of longitude around globe

hachure one of a series of short parallel lines used on map to represent sloping or elevated surface

hemisphere half of Earth, divided into northern and southern by equator, eastern and western by Atlantic and Pacific oceans

high latitudes areas more than sixty degrees north or south of equator

homolosine projection equal-area map projection in which ocean areas are distorted to reduce distortion of continents

International Date Line line based on 180-degree meridian that separates one calendar day from another, with west of line twenty-four hours later than east of it

interrupted projection map projection that breaks up oceans for accurate presentation and reduced distortion of continents

isobar map line that joins places having equal atmospheric pressure over or at a given time

isobath map line that joins places on seabed having equal depth below surface

isoclinic line map line that joins points at which magnetic needle has same inclination to plumb line

isogloss boundary on map between places with differing linguistic features or dialects

isogonic line map line that joins points at which magnetic declination is equal

isogram map line along which there is some constant value, such as that for temperature, pressure, or rainfall

isohel map line that joins points with equal duration of sunshine

isohyet map line that joins places having equal rainfall over a given period

isometric line map line that indicates true constant value for its extent

isopach isogram line that connects points of equal thickness of geological stratum formation

isopleth map line that connects points at which a given variable has specified constant value

isotherm map line that joins places having same temperature

key list of map's symbols and their meanings; legend

latitude north/south position of place, measured in degrees from zero to ninety in reference to equator by an imaginary arc passing through both poles

legend key

longitude east/west position of place, measured in degrees from zero to 180 along equator in reference to prime meridian

low latitudes areas less than thirty degrees north or south of equator

loxodromic (adj) noting or pertaining to a map projection in which rhumb lines appear straight

magnetic equator imaginary line around Earth near equator where lines of force of Earth's magnetic field are parallel with Earth's surface; aclinic line

map representation, usu. on flat surface, of physical characteristics of whole or part of some area

Melanesia portion of Oceania including Pacific Ocean islands south of equator

Mercator projection conformal map projection that shows meridians of longitude as parallel lines, thus distorting shapes of areas near poles

meridian line of longitude; imaginary line approximating semicircle around Earth through both poles at right angles to equator

Micronesia portion of Oceania including Pacific Ocean islands north of equator

midlatitudes areas between thirty and sixty degrees north and south of equator

minute one-sixtieth of one degree of latitude or longitude

Mollweide projection equal-area projection of Earth's surface as ellipse, with all parallels as straight lines more widely spaced at equator than at poles and all meridians equally spaced with central meridian half the length of equator

nadir point on celestial sphere opposite zenith and directly below observer

North America third largest continent, extending from Atlantic to Pacific oceans and from Arctic to Panama

Northern Hemisphere half of Earth's surface, lying north of equator

North Pole ninety degrees north latitude; point at northern end of Earth's axis

Oceania Pacific Ocean islands

parallel line of latitude; imaginary line on map or globe parallel to equator, connecting places on same latitude

physical feature land or water form on Earth's surface, esp. as depicted on map

polar projection map centered on one of poles

poles two points at northern and southern ends of Earth's axis; North Pole and South Pole

political feature national boundary or other feature showing how humans have divided Earth's surface

polyconic projection map projection in which the parallels are arcs of circles equally spaced along a central straight meridian and the other meridians are curves equally spaced along the parallels

Polynesia eastern portion of Oceania including Hawaiian Islands

prime meridian line of longitude at zero degrees from which other longitudes are measured, running through Greenwich, England

projection one of various ways in which Earth's curved surface is represented two-dimensionally: azimuthal equidistant, conformal, conic, cylindrical, equal-area, homolosine, interrupted, loxodromic, Mercator, Mollweide, polar, polyconic, sinusoidal, and zenithal equidistant

relief elevation differences in land

relief map map showing contour variations of land surface

rhumb line curve on Earth's surface that cuts all meridians at same angle, such as constant compass direction course

scale proportion between actual size of place and its representation on map

sea level mean level of sea surface between high and low tides, used as standard for measuring elevations and ocean depths

second one-sixtieth of one minute of one degree of latitude or longitude

sinusoidal projection equal-area map projection with evenly spaced, straight-line parallels, a straight-line central meridian one-half the length of equator, and other meridians shown as curves symmetrical to central meridian

South America fourth largest continent, largely in Southern Hemisphere, lying between Atlantic and Pacific oceans south of Panama

Southern Hemisphere half of Earth's surface, lying south of equator

South Pole ninety degrees south latitude; point at southern end of Earth's axis

special-purpose map map showing neither physical nor political features but features such as population, vegetation, or climate

state geographical and political division of nation

strip map narrow map showing immediate area to be covered

subantarctic (adj) bordering on the Antarctic

subarctic (adj) bordering on the Arctic

subcontinent major division of continent, often set off geographically

subtropical (*adj*) bordering on the tropics

surveying determining location, form, and boundaries of tract of land through application of geometry and trigonometry

time zone one of twenty-four longitudinal divisions of one hour each that divide Earth

topographic map detailed, large-scale map that shows physical and cultural features of one area

transcontinental (*adj*) reaching from one edge of a continent to the other

transoceanic (*adj*) reaching from one coast of an ocean to the other

triangulation process of determining distance between points on Earth's surface by use of series of connected triangles and angles made by lines to points

tropic of Cancer parallel at 23 1/2 degrees north

tropic of Capricorn parallel at 23 1/2 degrees south

tropics area of Earth closest to the equator, between tropic of Cancer and tropic of Capricorn

Western Hemisphere half of Earth's surface, lying west of prime meridian

zenith point directly overhead on celestial sphere

zenithal equidistant projection azimuthal equidistant projection

Earth's Atmosphere and Topographic Features

ab-polar current air current moving from either pole toward equator

abyssal (*adj*) pertaining to dark, cold, lifeless ocean depths

acclivity upward slope of ground

aggrade (*vb*) raise level of valley or riverbed by deposit of sediment and detritus

alluvial fan fan-shaped deposit of detrital material at place where swiftly flowing water enters plain or open valley

alluvial plain plain formed by deposits of detrital material

anthropomorphic soil soil altered from surrounding environment by human activity

area amount of surface covered by a physical feature or region

atmosphere air forming gaseous envelope that surrounds Earth, consisting of troposphere, stratosphere, mesosphere, thermosphere, ionosphere, and exosphere, which merges into outer space at altitude of several hundred miles

badlands arid area cut by large number of deep gullies and nearly bare of vegetation

catchment area area draining into river or reservoir

chernozem fertile soil, rich in humus, found in temperate zones

climate all weather conditions typical of a specific region

climatic graph combined bar and line graph showing precipitation and average temperature for each month at specific place

coast area where landmass meets body of water

coniferous forests forests comprised of evergreen cone-bearing trees, growing across northern North America and Eurasia

continental margin continent's edge

continental shelf relatively flat seabed lying beneath shallow waters bordering continents

continental slope sharp descent between continental shelf and ocean basin

cordillera mountain system consisting of several parallel ranges

Coriolis effect change in path of object or fluid moving above Earth's surface due to Earth's rotation

deciduous forests forests with trees that lose their leaves at some point during year, found primarily in midlatitudes

declivity downward slope of ground

deep zone cold ocean water below thermocline

deserts extremely dry regions with little or no vegetation

diastrophism process that causes movement and reshaping of Earth's surface

doldrums low-pressure region near equator

echo sounding determination of water depth by measuring time required for sound wave to be reflected from bottom

equinox date in spring and fall on which day and night are of equal length

estuary river basin affected by ocean tides, having mixture of fresh and salt water

exosphere outermost portion of Earth's atmosphere, with air density so low that an air molecule is more likely to escape atmosphere than hit other molecules, beginning at altitude of 300 miles (483 km), forming outer portion of ionosphere

fall line line indicating edge of plateau, marked by waterfalls and rapids

flood plain low-lying area subject to flooding by river

horizon point in distance where sky seems to meet curve of Earth; soil layer

horse latitudes areas of high pressure over oceans between trade winds and westerlies

hypolimnion cold layer of water below thermocline in some lakes

interfluve land area separating adjacent stream valleys

ionosphere region of Earth's atmosphere beyond mesosphere, containing ionized layers of thermosphere and exosphere, extending outward from 50 miles (80 km) altitude

island landmass smaller than a continent, surrounded by water

land solid part of Earth's surface, not covered by water

landmass very large area of land, esp. a continent

landscape tract or characteristic aspect of Earth's surface, esp. as viewed extensively from one point

littoral (*adj*) designating intertidal zone along shore, below high-water mark and above low-water mark

mainland principal landmass of continent or country as distinguished from island or peninsula

maritime (*adj*) proximate to and influenced by sea or ocean

massif mountain mass of uniform height broken into individual peaks

mesopause boundary of transition between mesosphere and ionosphere, around 50 miles (80 km) altitude

mesosphere coldest layer of Earth's atmosphere, from 30 to 50 miles (48 to 80 km) altitude

neritic zone ocean life zone from low tide line to end of continental shelf

oasis fertile place with water in middle of desert

ocean great body of water covering almost three-fourths of Earth's surface; one of its four geographic divisions: Atlantic, Pacific, Indian, Arctic

ocean basin vast, deep hollow in Earth's surface filled by ocean waters

ooze liquid mud, largely of plankton remains, covering deep-sea plains

ozone hole any part of ozone layer that has become depleted by atmospheric pollution, permitting excess ultraviolet radiation to pass through and warm the atmosphere

ozone layer type of oxygen concentrated in stratosphere that blocks much of sun's ultraviolet radiation

peneplain land surface worn nearly flat

peninsula narrow land area almost completely surrounded by water except at point where it connects to mainland

permafrost permanently frozen ground underlying surface soil

planetary winds polars, westerlies, and trade winds; major winds on Earth's surface

polar winds very cold winds blowing from high pressure areas around poles

pollutant harmful substance in atmosphere

pollution contamination of environment with waste

radial stream pattern flowing of streams from central source

rain forest tropical rain forest

range system of connected mountains

revolution circling of Earth around sun

ridge long, narrow crest of elevated portion of Earth's crust

rift valley depression formed by land subsiding between parallel faults

rotation spinning of Earth on its axis

runoff water flowing over Earth's surface after rainfall or spring thaw

salinity amount of dissolved salts in body of water

sea large body of salt water, mainly enclosed by land and usu. connected to ocean

snow line line along mountain slope that represents lower limit of permanent snow

soil layer distinctive layer in a vertical cross section of soil

solstice one of two days each year when period of daylight reaches limit; longest or shortest day of year, June 21 or December 21

stratopause boundary of transition between stratosphere and mesosphere, around 30 miles (48 km) altitude

stratosphere layer of atmosphere from tropopause to inner edge of mesosphere, characterized by little change in temperature with increased altitude, extending from 10 to 30 miles (16 to 48 km) above Earth's surface

subcontinent landmass almost as big as a continent; India or Greenland

taiga extensive, subarctic coniferous forest beginning south of the tundra

temperate (*adj*) without temperature extremes

temperate zone midlatitudes between equator and poles

thermocline zone in body of water exhibiting rapid temperature decrease with increasing depth

thermosphere layer of upper atmosphere above mesosphere with very thin air and temperature that increases continuously with altitude, extending from 50 to 300 miles (80 to 483 km) above Earth's surface; inner portion of ionosphere

tideland land at seashore alternately exposed and covered by normal ebb and flow of tide

timberline boundary marking highest altitude for natural growth of trees

topsoil fertile soil, largely humus, in top horizon layer

trade winds winds blowing from high pressure subtropics toward low pressure at equator

tributary branch stream feeding main river

tropical grassland area between tropical rain forest and desert

tropical rain forest dense evergreen forest of equatorial regions; rain forest

tropopause boundary of transition between troposphere and stratosphere, around 10 miles (16 km) altitude

troposphere layer of atmosphere nearest Earth's surface, extending to altitude of 6 miles (10 km) over poles and 10 miles (16 km) over equator

tundra vast, cold, nearly treeless region north of coniferous forests with permanently frozen subsoil

Van Allen radiation belt doughnut-shaped region of high-energy particles trapped in Earth's magnetic field, extending from 2000 to 12,000 miles (3218 to 19,312 km) altitude

wadi watercourse in arid region that contains water only after heavy rainfall

watershed ridge separating runoff to two different river basins

westerlies winds blowing from subtropical high pressure toward low-pressure midlatitudes

wind erosion removal of powdery topsoil by wind, esp. in areas of prolonged heavy cultivation

woodland forested region of Earth

Populations and Resources

aborigine original inhabitant of area or region

avulsion separation of one's land by flooding or change in course of stream that cuts off part of property

bioclimatic (*adj*) relating to effect of climate on living things

birthrate number of births per year per thousand of population for given region or population

caste one of social groups into which population is divided, esp. among Hindus

census official population count, often accompanied by collection of demographic information

civilization organized society with developing art and technology

clan group of families, often with common ancestor, who live and work together

conservation actions taken to protect, preserve, or replenish natural resources

conurbation group of towns or cities extended to form continuous urban area

cultivation plowing of earth and planting of crops

cultural region geographic area in which most people have common language and customs distinct from other peoples

diversify (*vb*) create and maintain variety of economic forms in one culture

drainage system designation for region from which and means by which water flows off

dynasty series of rulers over generations from single family line

endangered species species of animal or plant in danger of becoming extinct

environment surroundings as they affect living things

ethnic group large group of people with shared heritage and more in common with each other than with other peoples

extended family household or family unit including more than two generations and more than nuclear family

extinct (*adj*) no longer living

extinction fact of being a species no longer living on Earth or no longer capable of regenerating

fallow (*adj*) designating cultivated land left unsown for one season or more

fossil fuel fuel derived from organic material lying underground for millions of years

greenbelt area surrounding city reserved for parks or farms

heartland central or most important area of nation, esp. agricultural region

homeland region or nation of one's birth

homogeneous population people of one ethnic or cultural group

hydroelectric power power of falling water used to generate electricity

illiteracy inability to read and write

immigration movement of peoples from one area to another

independent nation self-governing, economically self-sufficient state

indigenous (*adj*) native to some place

infant mortality percentage of children who die shortly after birth

irrigation process of bringing water for cultivation to area with insufficient rain

landlocked (*adj*) having no border on or outlet to the sea

land reclamation process of making land suitable for cultivation or other use, esp. through irrigation

life expectancy statistical estimate of the number of years an individual is expected to live, based on such criteria as sex, race, health, and occupation

malnutrition chronic, pervasive lack of proper food

mestizo person of mixed Latin American Indian and Spanish descent

metropolitan area urban center and its suburbs

migration movement of peoples from their homeland

minority people people belonging to a different ethnic group than most of nation's population

mulatto person of mixed European and African descent

nation group of people sharing a political system, culture, and territory

natural harbor coastal area where land protects ships from open sea

natural resource material found on or in Earth and used by people

natural vegetation indigenous plant life

nomads people who move from place to place as a way of life, with no permanent home

nonrenewable resource useful and irreplaceable material coming from Earth's crust

people collection of persons belonging to certain region or ethnic group

plantation large farm specializing in one crop with many workers, often slaves

polder area reclaimed from sea or lake and protected from flooding by dikes

polygamy simultaneous marriage to more than one spouse

population total number of people in country or region; specific part of people in given region

population profile bar graph showing proportion of different age groups in total population

raw materials substances occurring in nature and used to manufacture goods

reforestation planting of new forests, esp. in areas where trees have been cut down or burned

renewable resource material that can be replaced by nature

resource any useful element of environment

self-sufficiency ability to produce all resources required to meet one's own needs

solar energy energy from sun used as fuel

subsistence farming raising just enough crops to feed one's own family

sudd floating mass of vegetable matter on White Nile River

territory large tract of land under jurisdiction of nation or government

Third World developing nations not allied with superpowers, primarily in Southern Hemisphere

threatened species a species likely to become an endangered species in the near future, within all or much of its range

tree chart chart showing people or things branching out from common source

vegetation plant life on Earth

zero population growth condition in which birthrate equals death rate and population remains constant

NOTE: The listings for Nations of the World provide the following information: country name — former name where appropriate; official name; location; capital; area in square miles; population; major language or languages; primary religion or religions; currency. The listings for States of the United States provide the following information: state name — postal code; order of admission, date admitted; location; capital; rank among states in area, population; nickname.

Nations of the World

Afghanistan Republic of; in central W Asia; capital Kabul; area 250,000 sq. mi., pop. 15,592,000; Pashtu; Sunni Muslim; afghani

Albania Republic of; in SE Europe; capital Tirana; area 11,100 sq. mi., pop. 3,268,000; Albanian; Muslim; lek

Algeria Democratic and Popular Republic of; in N Africa; capital Algiers; area 919,590 sq. mi., pop. 25,714,000; Arabic; Sunni Muslim; dinar

Andorra Republic of; in SW Europe; capital Andorra la Vella; area 191 sq. mi., pop. 51,000; Catalan; Catholic; franc and peseta

Angola People's Republic of; in W Africa; capital Luanda; area 481,352 sq. mi., pop. 8,802,000; Portuguese and Bantu; Catholic; kwanza

Antigua and Barbuda group of islands in Caribbean Sea; capital St. John's; area 170 sq. mi., pop. 64,000; English; Anglican; dollar

Argentina Republic of; in S South America; capital Buenos Aires; area 1,068,000 sq. mi., pop. 32,291,000; Spanish; Catholic; peso

Australia Commonwealth of; in S Pacific; capital Canberra; area 2,967,909 sq. mi., pop. 16,646,000; English; Christian; dollar

Austria Republic of; in central Europe; capital Vienna; area 32,375 sq. mi., pop. 7,595,000; German; Catholic; schilling

Bahamas Commonwealth of the; group of islands in W Atlantic; capital Nassau; area 5,380 sq. mi., pop. 251,000; English; Christian; dollar

Bahrain State of; in Persian Gulf; capital Manama; area 250 sq. mi., pop. 512,000; Arabic; Shi'a Muslim; dinar

Bangladesh People's Republic of; in S Asia; capital Dhaka; area 55,126 sq. mi., pop. 117,976,000; Bengali; Muslim; taka

Barbados island in West Indies; capital Bridgetown; area 166 sq. mi., pop. 260,000; English; Anglican; dollar

Basutoland Lesotho

Bechuanaland Botswana

Belgium Kingdom of; in W Europe; capital Brussels; area 11,781 sq. mi., pop. 9,895,000; Flemish and French; Catholic; franc

Belize formerly British Honduras; in Central America; capital Belmopan; area 8,866 sq. mi., pop. 180,400; English and Spanish; Catholic; dollar

Benin formerly Dahomey; Republic of; in W Africa; capital Porto-Novo; area 43,483 sq. mi., pop. 4,840,000; French and Fon; indigenous religions; franc

Bermuda Dependency of; British colony, island in W Atlantic; capital Hamilton; area 20 sq. mi., pop. 58,800; English; Christian; dollar

Bhutan Kingdom of; in E Asia; capital Thimbu; area 18,147 sq. mi., pop. 1,566,000; Dzongkha and Nepalese; Lamaistic Buddhist; ngultrum

Bolivia Republic of; in W central South America; capital Sucre and LaPaz; area 424,163 sq. mi., pop. 6,730,000; Spanish; Catholic; boliviano

Bosnia and Herzegovina formerly part of Yugoslavia; in SE Europe; capital Sarajevo; area 19,741 sq. mi., pop. 4,440,000; Serbian; Eastern Orthodox, Catholic and Muslim; dinar

Botswana formerly Bechuanaland; Republic of; in S Africa; capital Gaborone; area 231,804 sq. mi., pop. 1,218,000; English and Setswana; Christian and indigenous religions; pula

Brazil Federative Republic of; in E South America; capital Brasilia; area 3,286,478 sq. mi., pop. 153,771,000; Portuguese; Catholic; cruzeiro

British Honduras Belize

Brunei Brunei Darussalam; in SE Asia; capital Bandar Seri Begawan; area 2,226 sq. mi., pop. 372,000; Malay; Muslim; dollar

Bulgaria Republic of; in SE Europe; capital Sofia; area 44,365 sq. mi., pop. 8,978,000; Bulgarian; Bulgarian Orthodox; lev

Burkina Faso formerly Upper Volta; in W Africa; capital Ouagadougou; area 105,870 sq. mi., pop. 8,941,000; French; indigenous religions; franc

Burma Myanmar

Burundi Republic of; in E central Africa; capital Bujumbura; area 10,747 sq. mi., pop. 5,647,000; Kirundi and French; Catholic; franc

Cambodia formerly Kampuchea; State of; in SE Asia; capital Phnom Penh; area 69,898 sq. mi., pop. 6,993,000; Khmer and French; Buddhist; riel

Cameroon Republic of; in W Africa; capital Yaoundé; area 185,569 sq. mi., pop. 11,109,000; French and English; indigenous religions and Christian; franc

Canada confederation in N North America; capital Ottawa; area 3,558,096 sq. mi., pop. 26,527,000; English and French; Catholic and Protestant; dollar; provinces: Alberta, British Columbia, Manitoba, New Brunswick, Newfoundland, Nova Scotia, Ontario, Prince Edward Island, Quebec, Saskatchewan; territories: Northwest Territories, Yukon

Cape Verde Republic of; group of islands in E Atlantic; capital Praia; area 1,557 sq. mi., pop. 375,000; Portuguese; Catholic; escudo

Central African Republic in central Africa; capital Bangui; area 240,535 sq. mi., pop. 2,879,000; French; indigenous religions and Christian; franc

Ceylon Sri Lanka

Chad Republic of; in N central Africa; capital N'djamena; area 495,754 sq. mi., pop. 5,064,000; French and Arabic; Muslim and indigenous religions; franc

Chile Republic of; in SW South America; capital Santiago; area 292,250 sq. mi., pop. 13,000,000; Spanish; Catholic; peso

China People's Republic of; in E Asia; capital Beijing; area 3,705,000 sq. mi., pop. 1,130,065,000; Mandarin; Taoist and Confucian traditions but officially atheist; yuan

Colombia Republic of; in NW South America; capital Bogotá; area 439,700 sq. mi., pop. 32,598,000; Spanish; Catholic; peso

Commonwealth of Independent States formerly part of the Union of Soviet Socialist Republics; in E Europe and N Asia; capital Minsk; area 8,555,000 sq. mi., pop. 273,307,000; Russian, Ukrainian, and other indigenous languages; Russian Orthodox, Muslim, and others; ruble; republics: Armenia, Azerbaijan, Belarus, Kazakhstan, Kyrgyzstan, Moldova, Russia, Tajikistan, Turkmenistan, Ukraine, Uzbekistan

Comoros Republic of; group of islands in S Indian Ocean; capital Moroni; area 838 sq. mi., pop. 459,000; Comoran, French and Arabic; Sunni Muslim; franc

Congo People's Republic of; in W central Africa; capital Brazzaville; area 132,046 sq. mi., pop. 2,305,000; French; Christian and animist; franc

Costa Rica Republic of; in S Central America; capital San José; area 19,575 sq. mi., pop. 3,032,000; Spanish; Catholic; colon

Côte d'Ivoire Ivory Coast

Croatia formerly part of Yugoslavia; in SE Europe; capital Zagreb; area 21,829 sq. mi., pop. 4,680,000; Croatian; Catholic; dinar

Cuba Republic of; island in Caribbean Sea; capital Havana; area 44,218 sq. mi., pop. 10,582,000; Spanish; Catholic; peso

Cyprus Republic of; island in E Mediterranean Sea; capital Nicosia; area 3,572 sq. mi., pop. 708,000; Greek and Turkish; Greek Orthodox and Muslim; pound

Czechoslovakia Czech and Slovak Federative Republic; in central Europe; capital Prague; area 49,365 sq. mi., pop. 15,695,000; Czech and Slovak; Catholic; koruna

Dahomey Benin

Denmark Kingdom of; in N Europe; capital Copenhagen; area 16,629 sq. mi., pop. 5,134,000; Danish; Lutheran; krone

Djibouti Republic of; in E Africa; capital Djibouti; area 8,490 sq. mi., pop. 337,000; French and Arabic; Muslim; franc

Dominica Commonwealth of; island in West Indies; capital Roseau; area 290 sq. mi., pop. 85,000; English; Catholic; dollar

Dominican Republic part of an island in West Indies; capital Santo Domingo; area 18,703 sq. mi., pop. 7,253,000; Spanish; Catholic; peso

East Germany former German Democratic Republic, since 1990 part of united Germany

Ecuador Republic of; in NW South America; capital Quito; area 109,483 sq. mi., pop. 10,506,000; Spanish; Catholic; sucre

Egypt Arab Republic of; in NE Africa; capital Cairo; area 386,660 sq. mi., pop. 54,139,000; Arabic; Sunni Muslim; pound

El Salvador Republic of; in Central America; capital San Salvador; area 8,260 sq. mi., pop. 5,221,000; Spanish; Catholic; colon

England largest division of United Kingdom, part of Great Britain with Scotland and Wales

Equatorial Guinea Republic of; in W Africa; capital Malabo; area 10,831 sq. mi., pop. 360,000; Spanish; Christian and indigenous religions; franc

Estonia formerly part of the Union of Soviet Socialist Republics; Republic of, in N Europe; capital Tallinn; area 17,413 sq. mi., pop. 1,573,000; Estonian and Russian; Lutheran; ruble

Ethiopia People's Democratic Republic of; in E Africa; capital Addis Ababa; area 471,777 sq. mi., pop. 51,375,000; Amharic; Muslim and Ethiopian Orthodox; birr

Faeroe Islands Danish island province in the N Atlantic; capital Torshavn; area 541 sq. mi., pop. 46,000; Faeroese and Danish; Lutheran; krona

Fiji Republic of; group of islands in SW Pacific Ocean; capital Suva; area 7,053 sq. mi., pop. 772,000; English and Fijian; Christian and Hindu; dollar

Finland Republic of; in N Europe; capital Helsinki; area 130,120 sq. mi., pop. 4,977,000; Finnish; Lutheran; markka

France French Republic, in W Europe; capital Paris; area 220,668 sq. mi., pop. 56,184,000; French; Catholic; franc

French Polynesia Territory of; French island territory in S Pacific; capital Papeete; area 1,544 sq. mi., pop. 185,000; Polynesian and French; Christian; franc

Gabon Gabonese Republic; in W Africa; capital Libreville; area 103,346 sq. mi., pop. 1,069,000; French and Fang; Christian; franc

Gambia Republic of the; in W Africa; capital Banjul; area 4,361 sq. mi., pop. 820,000; English and Mandinka; Muslim; dalasi

Georgia formerly part of the Union of Soviet Socialist Republics; Georgian Republic; in SE Europe and SW Asia; capital Tbilisi; area 26,872 sq. mi., pop. 5,449,000; Georgian; Georgian Orthodox; ruble

Germany formerly East Germany and West Germany; Federal Republic of; in central Europe; capital Berlin; area 137,616 sq. mi., pop. 77,555,000; German; Protestant and Catholic; mark

Ghana Republic of; in W Africa; capital Accra; area 92,099 sq. mi., pop. 15,310,000; English and Akan; Christian, Muslim and indigenous religions; cedi

Gilbert Island Kiribati

Great Britain England, Scotland, and Wales, three divisions within United Kingdom

Greece Hellenic Republic; in SE Europe; capital Athens; area 51,146 sq. mi., pop. 10,066,000; Greek; Greek Orthodox; drachma

Greenland Kalaallit Nunaat; semiautonomous colony of Denmark in NW Atlantic; capital Nuuk; area 840,000 sq. mi., pop. 55,415; Greenlandic and Danish; Lutheran; krone

Grenada group of islands in SE Caribbean Sea; capital St. George's; area 131 sq. mi., pop. 84,000; English; Catholic; dollar

Guatemala Republic of; in Central America; capital Guatemala City; area 42,042 sq. mi., pop. 9,340,000; Spanish; Catholic; quetzal

Guinea Republic of, in W Africa; capital Conakry; area 94,964 sq. mi., pop. 7,269,000; French; Muslim; franc

Guinea-Bissau Republic of; in W Africa; capital Bissau; area 13,948 sq. mi., pop. 998,000; Portuguese; Muslim and indigenous religions; peso

Guyana Co-operative Republic of; in NE South America; capital Georgetown; area 83,000 sq. mi., pop. 765,000; English; Christian and Hindu; dollar

Haiti Republic of; part of an island in Caribbean Sea; capital Port-au-Prince; area 10,714 sq. mi., pop. 6,409,000; French; Catholic; gourde

Honduras Republic of; in Central America; capital Tegucigalpa; area 43,277 sq. mi., pop. 5,261,000; Spanish; Catholic; lempira

Hong Kong Dependency of; British crown colony in E Asia on South China Sea; capital Victoria; area 402 sq. mi., pop. 5,700,000; Cantonese; Taoist, Confucian, and Christian; dollar

Hungary Republic of; in central Europe; capital Budapest; area 35,919 sq. mi., pop. 10,546,000; Hungarian; Catholic; forint

Iceland Republic of; group of islands in N Atlantic; capital Reykjavik; area 39,768 sq. mi., pop. 251,000; Icelandic; Lutheran; krona

India Republic of; in S Asia; capital New Delhi; area 1,266,598 sq. mi., pop. 850,067,000; Hindi and English; Hindu and Muslim; rupee

Indonesia Republic of; in SE Asia; capital Jakarta; area 735,269 sq. mi., pop. 191,266,000; Indonesian; Muslim; rupiah

Iran Islamic Republic of; on Persian Gulf in Middle East; capital Teheran; area 636,294 sq. mi., pop. 55,647,000; Farsi; Shi'a Muslim; rial

Iraq Republic of; in Middle East; capital Baghdad; area 167,923 sq. mi., pop. 18,782,000; Arabic; Muslim; dinar

Ireland Republic of; part of an island in NW Europe; capital Dublin; area 27,136 sq. mi., pop. 3,557,000; English and Irish; Catholic; pound

Israel State of; in Middle East; capital Jerusalem; area 8,019 sq. mi., pop. 4,371,000; Hebrew; Jewish; shekel

Italy Italian Republic; in S Europe; capital Rome; area 116,303 sq. mi., pop. 57,657,000; Italian; Catholic; lira

Ivory Coast Republic of; Côte d'Ivoire; in W Africa; capital Abidjan; area 124,503 sq. mi., pop. 12,070,000; French; Christian, Muslim and indigenous religions; franc

Jamaica island in Caribbean Sea; capital Kingston; area 4,243 sq. mi., pop. 2,513,000; English; Protestant; dollar

Japan Nippon; in E Asia; capital Tokyo; area 145,882 sq. mi., pop. 123,778,000; Japanese; Shinto and Buddhist; yen

Jordan Hashemite Kingdom of; in Middle East; capital Amman; area 37,738 sq. mi., pop. 3,065,000; Arabic; Sunni Muslim; dinar

Kalaallit Nunaat Greenland

Kampuchea Cambodia

Kenya Republic of; in E Africa; capital Nairobi; area 224,960 sq. mi., pop. 25,393,000; English and Swahili; Christian; shilling

Kiribati formerly Gilbert Islands; Republic of; group of islands in S Pacific; capital Tarawa; area 277 sq. mi., pop. 65,000; English and Gilbertese; Christian; dollar

Korea, North Democratic People's Republic of Korea; in NE Asia; capital Pyong Yang; area 46,541, pop. 23,059,000; Korean; Buddhist and Confucian traditions but officially atheist; won

Korea, South Republic of Korea; in NE Asia; capital Seoul; area 38,023 sq. mi., pop. 43,919,000; Korean; Buddhist, Confucian, and Christian; won

Kuwait State of; in NE Arabian peninsula; capital Kuwait; area 6,880 sq. mi., pop. 2,080,000; Arabic; Sunni Muslim; dinar

Laos People's Democratic Republic of; in SE Asia; capital Vientiane; area 91,428 sq. mi., pop. 4,024,000; Lao and French; Buddhist; kip

Latvia formerly part of the Union of Soviet Socialist Republics; Republic of; in N Europe; capital Riga; area 25,395 sq. mi., pop. 2,681,000; Latvian and Russian; Lutheran; ruble

Lebanon Republic of; in Middle East; capital Beirut; area 4,015 sq. mi., pop. 3,340,000; Arabic; Muslim; pound

Lesotho formerly Basutoland; Kingdom of; within Republic of South Africa; capital Maseru; area 11,720 sq. mi., pop. 1,757,000; Sesotho and English; Christian; loti

Liberia Republic of; in W Africa; capital Monrovia; area 38,250 sq. mi., pop. 2,644,000; English; Christian and indigenous religions; dollar

Libya Socialist People's Libyan Arab Jamahiriya; in N Africa; capital Tripoli; area 679,216 sq. mi., pop. 4,280,000; Arabic; Sunni Muslim; dinar

Liechtenstein Principality of; in W central Europe; capital Vaduz; area 62 sq. mi., pop. 30,000; German; Catholic; franc

Lithuania formerly part of the Union of Soviet Socialist Republics; Republic of; in N Europe; capital Vilnius; area 25,174 sq. mi., pop. 3,690,000; Lithuanian; Roman Catholic; ruble

Luxembourg Grand Duchy of; in W Europe; capital Luxembourg; area 999 sq. mi., pop. 369,000; Luxembourgian, French and German; Catholic; franc

Macao Territory of; Portuguese dependency on South China Sea in E Asia; capital Macao; area 6 sq. mi., pop. 484,000; Cantonese and Portuguese; Buddhist; pataca

Macedonia formerly part of Yugoslavia; in SE Europe; capital Skopje; area 9928 sq. mi, pop. 2,090,000; Macedonian; Eastern Orthodox and Muslim; dinar

Madagascar Democratic Republic of; island in Indian Ocean east of Africa; capital Antananarivo; area 226,657 sq. mi., pop. 11,802,000; French and Malagasy; Christian and indigenous religions; franc

Malawi Republic of; in E central Africa; capital Lilongwe; area 45,747 sq. mi., pop. 9,080,000; English and Chichewa; Protestant; kwacha

Malaysia Federation of; in SE Asia; capital Kuala Lumpur; area 127,316 sq. mi., pop. 17,053,000; Malay; Muslim; ringgit

Maldives Republic of; group of islands in N Indian Ocean; capital Male; area 115 sq. mi., pop. 219,000; Divehi and English; Sunni Muslim; rufiyaa

Mali Republic of; in W Africa; capital Bamako; area 478,764 sq. mi., pop. 9,182,000; French and Bambara; Muslim; franc

Malta Republic of; island in Mediterranean Sea; capital Valletta; area 122 sq. mi., pop. 373,000; Maltese; Catholic; lira

Mariana Islands Commonwealth of the Northern Mariana Islands; group of islands in Pacific Ocean; capital Saipan; area 184 sq. mi., pop. 22,591; Chamorro and English; Christian and indigenous religions; dollar

Marshall Islands Republic of; group of islands in Pacific Ocean; capital Majuro; area 70 sq. mi., pop. 40,609; English and indigenous languages; Christian and indigenous religions; dollar

Martinique Territory of; French dependency, island in Caribbean Sea; capital Fort-de-France; area 425 sq. mi., pop. 336,000; French; Catholic; franc

Mauritania Islamic Republic of; in W Africa; capital Nouakchott; area 397,954 sq. mi., pop. 2,038,000; Arabic and French; Muslim; ouguiya

Mauritius island in Indian Ocean; capital Port Louis; area 790 sq. mi., pop. 1,141,900; English; Hindu; rupee

Mexico United States of; in S North America; capital Mexico City; area 761,604 sq. mi., pop. 88,335,000; Spanish; Catholic; peso

Micronesia Federated States of; group of islands in Pacific Ocean; capital Kolonia; area 271 sq. mi., pop. 86,094; English and indigenous languages; Christian and indigenous religions; dollar

Monaco Principality of; on Mediterranean Sea, surrounded on other sides by France; capital Monaco-Ville; area 0.6 sq. mi., pop. 29,000; French; Catholic; franc

Mongolia Mongolian People's Republic; in central Asia; capital Ulan Bator; area 604,247 sq. mi., pop. 2,185,000; Khalkha Mongol; Buddhist; tugrik

Morocco Kingdom of; in N Africa; capital Rabat; area 172,413 sq. mi., pop. 26,249,000; Arabic and French; Sunni Muslim; dirham

Mozambique People's Republic of; in E Africa; capital Maputo; area 303,769 sq. mi., pop. 14,718,000; Portuguese; indigenous religions; metical

Myanmar formerly Burma; Union of; in SE Asia; capital Yangon, formerly Rangoon; area 261,789 sq. mi., pop. 41,279,000; Burmese; Buddhist; kyat

Namibia formerly South-West Africa; Republic of; in SW Africa; capital Windhoek; area 317,818 sq. mi., pop. 1,372,000; English and Afrikaans; Christian; rand

Nauru Republic of; island in S Pacific; capital Yaren; area 8 sq. mi., pop. 8,100; Nauruan; Christian; dollar

Nepal Kingdom of; in central Asia; capital Katmandu; area 56,136 sq. mi., pop. 19,158,000; Nepali; Hindu; rupee

Netherlands Kingdom of the; in NW Europe; capital Amsterdam and the Hague; area 15,770 sq. mi., pop. 14,864,000; Dutch; Protestant and Catholic; guilder

Netherlands Antilles Territory of; Dutch island dependency in Caribbean Sea; capital Willemstad; area 385 sq. mi., pop. 187,000; Dutch; Catholic; guilder

New Zealand group of islands in S Pacific; capital Wellington; area 103,736 sq. mi., pop. 3,397,000; English and Maori; Christian; dollar

Nicaragua Republic of; in Central America; capital Managua; area 50,193 sq. mi., pop. 3,606,000; Spanish; Catholic; cordoba

Niger Republic of; in W Africa; capital Niamey; area 489,189 sq. mi., pop. 7,691,000; French and Hausa; Muslim; franc

Nigeria Federal Republic of; in W Africa; capital Abuja; area 356,669 sq. mi., pop. 118,865,000; English and Hausa; Muslim; naira

Northern Ireland a division of the United Kingdom

North Korea Korea, North

North Yemen former Yemen Arab Republic, since 1990 part of Yemen

Norway Kingdom of; in N Europe; capital Oslo; area 125,181 sq. mi., pop. 4,214,000; Norwegian; Lutheran; krone

Oman Sultanate of; on SE Arabian peninsula; capital Muscat; area 82,030 sq. mi., pop. 1,305,000; Arabic; Muslim; rial

Pakistan Islamic Republic of; in S Asia; capital Islamabad; area 310,402 sq. mi., pop. 113,163,000; Urdu; Sunni Muslim; rupee

Palau Republic of; group of islands in Pacific Ocean; capital Koror; area 192 sq. mi., pop. 14,106; English and Palauan; Christian and indigenous religions; dollar

Panama Republic of; in Central America; capital Panama City; area 29,208 sq. mi., pop. 2,423,000; Spanish; Catholic; balboa

Papua New Guinea group of islands in SW Pacific; capital Port Moresby; area 178,221 sq. mi., pop. 3,613,000; Pidgin English; Christian; kina

Paraguay Republic of; in central South America; capital Asuncion; area 157,047 sq. mi., pop. 4,660,000; Spanish; Catholic; guarani

Peru Republic of; in W South America; capital Lima; area 496,223 sq. mi., pop. 21,904,000; Spanish; Catholic; inti

Philippines Republic of the; in SE Asia; capital Quezon City (official), Manila (de facto); area 115,830 sq. mi., pop. 66,647,000; Tagalog; Catholic; peso

Poland Republic of; in N central Europe; capital Warsaw; area 120,724 sq. mi., pop. 38,363,000; Polish; Catholic; zloty

Portugal Republic of; in SW Europe; capital Lisbon; area 36,390 sq. mi., pop. 10,528,000; Portuguese; Catholic; escudo

Qatar State of; on Persian Gulf; capital Doha; area 4,247 sq. mi., pop. 498,000; Arabic; Muslim; riyal

Rhodesia Zimbabwe

Romania in SE Europe; capital Bucharest; area 91,700 sq. mi., pop. 23,269,000; Romanian; Romanian Orthodox; leu

Russia largest republic within Commonwealth of Independent States

Rwanda Republic of; in E central Africa; capital Kigali; area 10,169 sq. mi., pop. 7,603,000; Kinyarwanda and French; Catholic; franc

San Marino Most Serene Republic of; in Apennines, surrounded by Italy; capital San Marino; area 24 sq. mi., pop. 23,000; Italian; Catholic; lira

São Tomé and Principe Republic of; two islands in E Atlantic off W coast of Africa; capital São Tomé; area 372 sq. mi., pop. 125,000; Portuguese; Catholic; dobra

Saudi Arabia Kingdom of; on Arabian peninsula; capital Riyadh; area 839,996 sq. mi., pop. 16,758,000; Arabic; Muslim; riyal

Scotland a division of United Kingdom; part of Great Britain with England and Wales

Senegal Republic of; in W Africa; capital Dakar; area 75,750 sq. mi., pop. 7,740,000; French and Wolof; Muslim; franc

Seychelles Republic of; group of islands in Indian Ocean; capital Victoria; area 176 sq. mi., pop. 71,000; English; Catholic; rupee

Sierra Leone Republic of; in W Africa; capital Freetown; area 27,925 sq. mi., pop. 4,168,000; English; Muslim and indigenous religions; leone

Singapore Republic of; in SE Asia; capital Singapore; area 225 sq. mi., pop. 2,703,000; Malay and Mandarin; Buddhist; dollar

Slovenia formerly part of Yugoslavia; in SE Europe; capital Ljubljana; area 7819 sq. mi., pop. 1,940,000; Slovene; Catholic; dinar

Solomon Islands group of islands in W Pacific; capital Honiara; area 10,640 sq. mi., pop. 314,000; English and Melanesian; Christian; dollar

Somalia Somali Democratic Republic; in NE Africa; capital Mogadishu; area 246,300 sq. mi., pop. 8,415,000; Somali; Sunni Muslim; shilling

South Africa Republic of; in S Africa; capital Pretoria (administrative), Capetown (legislative), Bloemfontein (judicial); area 472,359 sq. mi., pop. 39,550,000; Afrikaans, English, and Zulu; Christian; rand

South Korea Korea, South

South-West Africa Namibia

South Yemen former People's Democratic Republic of Yemen, since 1990 part of Yemen

Soviet Union Union of Soviet Socialist Republics

Spain Kingdom of; in SW Europe; capital Madrid; area 194,897 sq. mi., pop. 39,623,000; Spanish; Catholic; peseta

Sri Lanka formerly Ceylon; Democratic Socialist Republic of; island in S Asia in Indian Ocean, capital Colombo; area 25,332 sq. mi., pop. 17,135,000; Sinhala; Buddhist; rupee

St. Kitts and Nevis Federation of; twin-island state in Caribbean Sea; capital Basseterre; area 101 sq. mi., pop. 40,000; English; Anglican; dollar

St. Lucia island in W Atlantic; capital Castries; area 239 sq. mi., pop. 153,000; English; Catholic; dollar

St. Vincent and the Grenadines group of islands in W Atlantic; capital Kingstown; area 150 sq. mi., pop. 106,000; English; Anglican; dollar

Sudan Democratic Republic of; in N Africa; capital Khartoum; area 966,757 sq. mi., pop. 25,164,000; Arabic; Sunni Muslim; pound

Suriname Republic of; in NE South America; capital Paramaribo; area 63,037 sq. mi., pop. 408,000; Dutch; Hindu and Christian; guilder

Swaziland Kingdom of; in S Africa; capital Mbabane; area 6,704 sq. mi., pop. 779,000; English and Siswati; Christian and indigenous religions; lilangeni

Sweden Kingdom of; in N Europe; capital Stockholm; area 173,731 sq. mi., pop. 8,407,000; Swedish; Lutheran; krona

Switzerland Swiss Confederation; in W Europe; capital Bern; area 15,941 sq. mi., pop. 6,628,000; French, German, and Italian; Catholic and Protestant; franc

Syria Syrian Arab Republic; in Middle East; capital Damascus; area 71,498 sq. mi., pop. 12,471,000; Arabic; Sunni Muslim; pound

Taiwan Republic of China; island in SE Asia in South China Sea; capital Taipei; area 13,885 sq. mi., pop. 20,454,000; Mandarin; Buddhist and Taoist; dollar

Tanzania United Republic of; in E Africa; capital Dar es Salaam; area 364,882 sq. mi., pop. 26,070,000; Swahili; Muslim and Christian; shilling

Thailand Kingdom of; in SE Asia; capital Bangkok; area 198,456 sq. mi., pop. 54,890,000; Thai; Buddhist; baht

Togo Togolese Republic; in W Africa; capital Lomé; area 21,617 sq. mi., pop. 3,566,000; French and Ewe; indigenous religions; franc

Tonga Kingdom of; group of islands in SW Pacific; capital Nuku'alofa; area 270 sq. mi., pop. 108,000; Tongan; Catholic and Hindu; pa'anga

Trinidad and Tobago Republic of; two islands in West Indies; capital Port of Spain; area 1,980 sq. mi., pop. 1,270,000; English; Catholic and Hindu; dollar

Tunisia Republic of; in N Africa; capital Tunis; area 63,170 sq. mi., pop. 8,094,000; Arabic; Muslim; dinar

Turkey Republic of; in SW Asia and SE Europe; capital Ankara; area 301,381 sq. mi., pop. 56,549,000; Turkish; Muslim; lira

Tuvalu group of islands in S Pacific; capital Funafuti; area 10 sq. mi., pop. 9,000; Tuvaluan; Christian; dollar

Uganda Republic of; in E central Africa; capital Kampala; area 93,354 sq. mi., pop. 17,593,000; English and Swahili; Christian and Muslim; shilling

Union of Soviet Socialist Republics former country, now divided into Commonwealth of Independent States, Estonia, Georgia, Latvia, Lithuania

United Arab Emirates on Persian Gulf on N Arabian Peninsula; capital Abu Dhabi; area 32,278 sq. mi., pop. 2,250,000; Arabic; Muslim; dirham

United Kingdom United Kingdom of Great Britain and Northern Ireland; two islands in NW Europe; capital London; area 94,226, pop. 57,121,000; English; Anglican; pound; comprised of: England, Scotland, Wales, and Northern Ireland

United States United States of America; in central North America; capital Washington, D.C.; area 3,618,774 sq. mi., pop. 250,372,000; English; Christian; dollar

Upper Volta Burkina Faso

Uruguay Republic of; in SE South America; capital Montevideo; area 68,037 sq. mi., pop. 3,002,000; Spanish; Catholic; peso

Vanuatu Republic of; group of islands in W Pacific; capital Vila; area 5,700 sq. mi., pop. 150,000; Bislama and French; Christian; vatu

Vatican City Catholic state within Rome, Italy; area 109 acres, pop. 750; Italian and Latin; Catholic; lira

Venezuela Republic of; in N South America; capital Caracas; area 352,143 sq. mi., pop. 19,753,000; Spanish; Catholic; bolivar

Vietnam Democratic Republic of; in SE Asia; capital Hanoi; area 127,243 sq. mi., pop. 68,488,000; Vietnamese and French; Buddhist; dong

Wales division of United Kingdom, part of Great Britain with England and Scotland

Western Samoa Independent State of; part of an island in SW Pacific; capital Apia; area 1,133 sq. mi., pop. 169,000; Samoan; Christian; tala

West Germany former Federal Republic of Germany, since 1990 part of united Germany

Yemen formerly North Yemen and South Yemen; Republic of; on S Arabian peninsula; capital Sanaa; area 207,000 sq. mi., pop. 11,000,000; Arabic; Muslim; dinar

Yugoslavia Federal Republic of; in SE Europe; capital Belgrade; area 39,449 sq. mi., pop. 10,400,000; Serbian; Eastern Orthodox, Catholic and Muslim; dinar; comprised of: Serbia and Montenegro

Zaire Republic of; in W central Africa; capital Kinshasa; area 905,563 sq. mi., pop. 35,330,000; French; Catholic; zaire

Zambia Republic of; in S central Africa; capital Lusaka; area 290,585 sq. mi., pop. 8,119,000; English; Christian and indigenous religions; kwacha

Zimbabwe formerly Rhodesia; in S central Africa; capital Harare; area 150,803 sq. mi., pop. 10,205,000; English and Shona; indigenous religions; dollar

States of the United States

Alabama AL; 22nd state, admitted 1819; SE United States; capital Montgomery; ranks 29th in area, pop. 4,063,000; Camellia State

Alaska AK; 49th state, admitted 1959; NW of continental United States; capital Juneau; ranks 1st in area, pop. 552,000; The Last Frontier

Arizona AZ; 48th state, admitted 1912; SW United States; capital Phoenix; ranks 6th in area, pop. 3,678,000; Grand Canyon State

Arkansas AR; 25th state, admitted 1836; S central United States; capital Little Rock; ranks 27th in area, pop. 2,362,000; Land of Opportunity

California CA; 31st state, admitted 1850; W United States; capital Sacramento; ranks 3rd in area, pop. 29,840,000; Golden State

Colorado CO; 38th state, admitted 1876; W central United States; capital Denver; ranks 8th in area, pop. 3,308,000; Centennial State

Connecticut CT; 5th state, admitted 1788; NE United States; capital Hartford; ranks 48th in area, pop. 3,296,000; Constitution State

Delaware DE; 1st state, admitted 1787; E United States; capital Dover; ranks 49th in area, pop. 669,000; First State

Florida FL; 27th state, admitted 1845; SE United States; capital Tallahassee; ranks 22nd in area, pop. 13,003,000; Sunshine State

Georgia GA; 4th state, admitted 1788; SE United States; capital Atlanta; ranks 21st in area, pop. 6,508,000; Peach State

Hawaii HI; 50th state, admitted 1959; WSW of continental United States; capital Honolulu; ranks 47th in area, pop. 1,115,000; Aloha State

Idaho ID; 43rd state, admitted 1890; NW United States; capital Boise; ranks 13th in area, pop. 1,012,000; Gem State

Illinois IL; 21st state, admitted 1818; N central United States; capital Springfield; ranks 24th in area, pop. 11,467,000; Prairie State

Indiana IN; 19th state, admitted 1816; N central United States; capital Indianapolis; ranks 38th in area, pop. 5,564,000; Hoosier State

Iowa IA; 29th state, admitted 1846; N central United States; capital Des Moines; ranks 25th in area, pop. 2,787,000; Hawkeye State

Kansas KS; 34th state, admitted 1861; NW central United States; capital Topeka; ranks 14th in area, pop. 2,486,000; Sunflower State

Kentucky KY; 15th state, admitted 1792; SE central United States; capital Frankfort; ranks 37th in area, pop. 3,699,000; Bluegrass State

Louisiana LA; 18th state, admitted 1812; S central United States; capital Baton Rouge; ranks 31st in area, pop. 4,238,000; Pelican State

Maine ME; 23rd state, admitted 1820; NE United States; capital Augusta; ranks 39th in area, pop. 1,233,000; Pine Tree State

Maryland MD; 7th state, admitted 1788; E United States; capital Annapolis; ranks 42nd in area, pop. 4,799,000; Old Line State

Massachusetts MA; 6th state, admitted 1788; NE United States; capital Boston; ranks 45th in area, pop. 6,029,000; Bay State

Michigan MI; 26th state, admitted 1837; N central United States; capital Lansing; ranks 23rd in area, pop. 9,329,000; Wolverine State

Minnesota MN; 32nd state, admitted 1858; N central United States; capital St. Paul; ranks 12th in area, pop. 4,387,000; North Star State

Mississippi MS; 20th state, admitted 1817; S central United States; capital Jackson; ranks 32nd in area, pop. 2,586,000; Magnolia State

Missouri MO; 24th state, admitted 1821; NW central United States; capital Jefferson City; ranks 19th in area, pop. 5,138,000; Show-Me State

Montana MT; 41st state, admitted 1889; NW United States; capital Helena; ranks 4th in area, pop. 804,000; Treasure State

Nebraska NE; 37th state, admitted 1867; NW central United States; capital Lincoln; ranks 15th in area, pop. 1,585,000; Cornhusker State

Nevada NV; 36th state, admitted 1864; W United States; capital Carson City; ranks 7th in area, pop. 1,206,000; Sagebrush State

New Hampshire NH; 9th state, admitted 1788; NE United States; capital Concord; ranks 44th in area, pop. 1,114,000; Granite State

New Jersey NJ; 3rd state, admitted 1787; E United States; capital Trenton; ranks 46th in area, pop. 7,749,000; Garden State

New Mexico NM; 47th state, admitted 1912; SW United States; capital Santa Fe; ranks 5th in area, pop. 1,522,000; Land of Enchantment

New York NY; 11th state, admitted 1788; NE United States; capital Albany; ranks 30th in area, pop. 18,044,000; Empire State

North Carolina NC; 12th state, admitted 1789; SE United States; capital Raleigh; ranks 28th in area, pop. 6,658,000; Tar Heel State

North Dakota ND; 39th state, admitted 1889; NW central United States; capital Bismarck; ranks 17th in area, pop. 641,000; Peace Garden State

Ohio OH; 17th state, admitted 1803; NE central United States; capital Columbus; ranks 35th in area, pop. 10,888,000; Buckeye State

Oklahoma OK; 46th state, admitted 1907; SW central United States; capital Oklahoma City; ranks 18th in area, pop. 3,158,000; Sooner State

Oregon OR; 33rd state, admitted 1859; NW United States; capital Salem; ranks 10th in area, pop. 2,854,000; Beaver State

Pennsylvania PA; 2nd state, admitted 1787; E United States; capital Harrisburg; ranks 33rd in area, pop. 12,000,000; Keystone State

Rhode Island RI; 13th state, admitted 1790; NE United States; capital Providence; ranks 50th in area, pop. 1,006,000; Ocean State

South Carolina SC; 8th state, admitted 1788; SE United States; capital Columbia; ranks 40th in area, pop. 3,506,000; Palmetto State

South Dakota SD; 40th state, admitted 1889; NW central United States; capital Pierre; ranks 16th in area, pop. 700,000; Coyote State

Tennessee TN; 16th state, admitted 1796; SE central United States; capital Nashville; ranks 34th in area, pop. 4,896,000; Volunteer State

Texas TX; 28th state, admitted 1845; SW central United States; capital Austin; ranks 2nd in area, pop. 17,060,000; Lone Star State

Utah UT; 45th state, admitted 1896; W central United States; capital Salt Lake City; ranks 11th in area, pop. 1,680,000; Beehive State

Vermont VT; 14th state, admitted 1791; NE United States; capital Montpelier; ranks 43rd in area, pop. 565,000; Green Mountain State

Virginia VA; 10th state, admitted 1788; SE United States; capital Richmond; ranks 36th in area, pop. 6,217,000; Old Dominion

Washington WA; 42nd state, admitted 1889; NW United States; capital Olympia; ranks 20th in area, pop. 4,888,000; Evergreen State

West Virginia WV; 35th state, admitted 1863; E central United States; capital Charleston; ranks 41st in area, pop. 1,802,000; Mountain State

Wisconsin WI; 30th state, admitted 1848; N central United States; capital Madison; ranks 26th in area, pop. 4,906,000; Badger State

Wyoming WY; 44th state, admitted 1890; W central United States; capital Cheyenne; ranks 9th in area, pop. 456,000; Equality State

Major World Cities

Accra seaport capital of Ghana, on Gulf of Guinea in W Africa, pop. 949,000

Addis Ababa capital of Ethiopia in E Africa, pop. 1,412,000

Ahmedabad city in W India in central Asia, pop. 2,300,000

Alexandria ancient seaport in Egypt, in Nile delta on N coast of Africa, pop. 2,893,000

Algiers seaport capital of Algeria, on Mediterranean Sea in N Africa, pop. 1,483,000

Amman capital of Jordan, in Near East, pop. 900,000

Amsterdam capital of the Netherlands, in W Europe, pop. 691,000

Ankara capital of Turkey and ancient capital of Galatia, in Near East, pop. 1,700,000

Athens ancient city and capital of Greece, in SE Europe, pop. 3,027,000

Atlanta capital of Georgia in SE United States, pop. 425,000

Auckland original capital of New Zealand, in SW Pacific Ocean, pop. 324,400

Baghdad capital of Iraq and ancient center of Islamic culture, on Tigris River in Near East, pop. 3,400,000

Bandung city on Java in Indonesia in SE Asia, pop. 1,400,000

Bangalore city in India in central Asia, pop. 3,900,000

Bangkok seaport capital of Thailand, in SE Asia, pop. 4,700,000

Barcelona ancient seaport in NE Spain, on Mediterranean Sea in SW Europe, pop. 2,000,000

Beijing formerly Peking or Peiping; capital of People's Republic of China, in NE Asia, pop. 9,330,000

Beirut seaport capital of Lebanon and ancient Phoenician city, on Mediterranean Sea in Near East, pop. 500,000

Belgrade capital of Yugoslavia, on Danube River in SE Europe, pop. 1,250,000

Belo Horizonte city in Brazil in E South America, pop. 1,122,000

Berlin capital of united Germany in E Europe, pop. 3,050,000

Birmingham industrial city in central England in W Europe, pop. 1,008,000

Bogota capital of Colombia, in N South America, pop. 3,968,000

Bombay seaport in W India, on Arabian Sea in central Asia, pop. 8,700,000

Brazzaville river port capital of People's Republic of Congo, on Congo River in central Africa, pop. 595,000

Brussels capital of Belgium, in W Europe, pop. 970,000

Bucharest capital of Romania, in SE Europe, pop. 1,900,000

Budapest capital of Hungary, on Danube River in E Europe, pop. 2,115,000

Buenos Aires seaport capital of Argentina, in SE

South America on Atlantic Ocean, pop. 3,000,000

Cairo capital of Egypt, on Nile River in N Africa, pop. 6,305,000

Calcutta seaport and former capital of British India, in central Asia, pop. 9,900,000

Canberra seaport capital of Australia, on E coast on Pacific Ocean, pop. 297,300

Canton Guangzhou

Capetown seaport and legislative capital of South Africa, in SW Africa on Atlantic Ocean, pop. 1,900,000

Caracas capital of Venezuela, in N South America, pop. 1,275,000

Casablanca seaport in Morocco, in NW Africa on Atlantic Ocean, pop. 2,600,000

Chengdu provincial capital in central China in E Asia, pop. 2,600,000

Chicago city in Illinois in central United States, on Lake Michigan, pop. 2,800,000

Chongqing formerly Chungking; city in S central China, in E Asia, pop. 3,890,000

Chungking Chongqing

Copenhagen seaport capital of Denmark, in N Europe on Baltic Sea, pop. 1,358,000

Dakar seaport capital of Senegal, in W Africa on Atlantic Ocean, pop. 1,300,000

Dallas city in Texas in SW United States, pop. 1,007,000

Damascus ancient capital of Syria in Near East, oldest continuously existing city in world, pop. 1,361,000

Dar es Salaam seaport capital of Tanzania in E Africa, on Indian Ocean, pop. 1,400,000

Delhi former capital of Mogul Empire adjacent to present capital of India (New Delhi), in central Asia, pop. 5,800,000

Detroit river port in Michigan in N central United States, on Detroit River and Lake Erie, pop. 1,028,000

Dhaka capital of Bangladesh, in central Asia, pop. 3,400,000

Dublin seaport capital of Ireland, in W Europe on Irish Sea, pop. 502,000

Essen industrial city in W Germany, in N Europe, pop. 622,000

Glasgow river port in Scotland in W Europe, on River Clyde, pop. 733,000

Guadalajara city in W Mexico in S North America, pop. 3,000,000

Guangzhou formerly Canton; seaport in SE China in E Asia, on Zhu Jiang River, pop. 3,300,000

Hamburg seaport in W Germany in N Europe, on Elbe River, pop. 1,600,000

Han Cities Wuhan

Hanoi capital of Vietnam, in SE Asia, pop. 3,100,000

Harbin provincial capital in NE China in E Asia, pop. 3,730,000

Havana seaport capital of Cuba, in Caribbean Sea, pop. 2,059,000

Helsinki seaport capital of Finland, in N Europe on Baltic Sea, pop. 487,000

Ho Chi Minh City formerly Saigon; seaport in Vietnam in SE Asia, pop. 3,900,000

Hong Kong seaport bordering SE China, in E Asia on South China Sea, pop. 5,700,000

Houston canal port in Texas in SW United States, on Gulf of Mexico, pop. 1,630,000

Hyderabad city in central India in central Asia, pop. 2,800,000

Istanbul port in Turkey in W Near East on Black Sea, at site of ancient Byzantium, pop. 5,800,000

Jakarta seaport capital of Indonesia on Java, in SE Asia on Java Sea, pop. 8,800,000

Jerusalem ancient holy city and capital of Israel, in Near East, pop. 457,000

Johannesburg city in South Africa in S Africa, pop. 1,600,000

Kabul capital of Afghanistan, in central Asia, pop. 1,200,000

Kanpur city in N India in central Asia, on Ganges River, pop. 1,688,000

Karachi seaport in Pakistan in central Asia, on Indus River delta and Arabian Sea, pop. 5,103,000

Khartoum capital of Sudan in N Africa, on Nile River, pop. 476,000

Kiev capital of Ukraine, in E Europe, pop. 2,400,000

Kinshasa formerly Leopoldville; river port capital of Zaire in central Africa, on Congo River, pop. 3,000,000

Kobe ancient seaport in Japan in E Asia, on Pacific Ocean, pop. 1,400,000

Kuala Lumpur seaport capital of Malaysia in SE Asia, on Strait of Malacca, pop. 1,000,000

Lagos seaport and former capital of Nigeria in W Africa, on Atlantic Ocean, pop. 1,243,000

Lahore Punjab capital in Pakistan, in central Asia, pop. 2,922,000

La Paz administrative capital of Bolivia in NW South America, pop. 955,000

Leningrad St. Petersburg

Leopoldville Kinshasa

Lima seaport capital of Peru in NW South America, on Pacific Ocean, pop. 5,493,000

Lisbon ancient Phoenician trading center and seaport capital of Portugal in SW Europe, on Atlantic Ocean, pop. 2,000,000

London ancient city and port capital of United Kingdom, in W Europe, on Thames River, pop. 6,700,000

Los Angeles seaport in California in SW United States, pop. 3,500,000

Madras seaport in India in central Asia, on Bay of Bengal, pop. 4,900,000

Madrid capital of Spain, in SW Europe, pop. 3,500,000

Managua capital of Nicaragua, in Central America, pop. 1,000,000

Manchester canal port in England in W Europe, on Irish Sea, pop. 451,000

Manila seaport capital of Philippines in E Asia, on South China Sea, pop. 1,700,000

Melbourne seaport in SE Australia, on S Pacific Ocean, pop. 3,000,000

Mexico City officially Mexico Distrito Federal; capital of Mexico in S North America, most populous city in world, pop. 18,000,000

Miami port city in Florida in SE United States, on Atlantic Ocean, pop. 347,000

Milan industrial city in N Italy, in S Europe, pop. 1,400,000

Monterrey industrial city in E Mexico in S North America, pop. 2,700,000

Montevideo seaport capital of Uruguay in S South America, on Atlantic Ocean, pop. 1,246,000

Montreal river port in E Canada, on St. Lawrence River, pop. 2,921,000

Moscow capital of Russia and former Soviet Union in E Europe, pop. 8,500,000

Mukden Shenyang

Munich Bavarian capital in SW Germany in central Europe, pop. 1,300,000

Nagoya industrial city in Japan in E Asia, pop. 2,100,000

Nairobi capital of Kenya, in E Africa, pop. 959,000

Nanjing formerly Nanking; river port and former capital of China, in E Asia, pop. 4,560,000

Nanking Nanjing

Naples ancient seaport in Italy in S Europe, pop. 1,200,000

New York City seaport in New York State in NE United States, on Atlantic Ocean, pop. 7,322,000

Osaka former capital of Japan, in E Asia, pop. 2,600,000

Oslo seaport capital of Norway in N Europe, on North Sea, pop. 449,000

Ottawa capital of Canada in N North America, pop. 819,000

Panama City canal port on Panama Canal and capital of Panama in Central America, pop. 1,200,000

Paris capital of France in W Europe, on Seine River, pop. 2,200,000

Peking Beijing

Philadelphia city in Pennsylvania in E United States, on Delaware River, pop. 1,600,000

Phnom Penh capital of Cambodia, in SE Asia, pop. 300,000

Pôrto Alegre seaport in Brazil in SE South America, on Atlantic Ocean, pop. 2,600,000

Prague capital of Czechoslovakia in E Europe, pop. 1,200,000

Pretoria administrative capital of South Africa in S Africa, pop. 822,000

Pusan seaport in South Korea in E Asia, on Korean Strait, pop. 3,700,000

Quezon City former capital of Philippines in E Asia, pop. 1,300,000

Quito capital of Ecuador in N South America, pop. 1,200,000

Rangoon Yangon

Recife seaport in N Brazil in E South America, on Atlantic Ocean, pop. 1,300,000

Rio de Janeiro seaport and former capital of Brazil, in E South America, on Atlantic Ocean, pop. 5,600,000

Riyadh capital of Saudi Arabia in Near East, pop. 1,380,000

Rome ancient city and capital of Italy in S Europe, on Tiber River, pop. 2,800,000

Saigon Ho Chi Minh City

San Diego seaport in California in SW United States, on Pacific Ocean, pop. 1,110,000

San Francisco seaport in California in W United States, on Pacific Ocean, pop. 724,000

Santiago capital of Chile in S South America, pop. 4,858,000

Santo Domingo seaport capital of Dominican Republic, in Caribbean Sea, pop. 1,700,000

São Paulo city in Brazil in SE South America, pop. 10,100,000

Seattle seaport in Washington in NW United States, on Puget Sound, off Pacific Ocean, pop. 516,000

Seoul capital of South Korea in NE Asia, pop. 10,200,000

Shanghai ancient seaport and municipality in China in E Asia, pop. 7,000,000

Shenyang formerly Mukden; one-time Manchurian capital in N China in E Asia, pop. 4,200,000

Singapore capital of Singapore, at tip of Malay peninsula, in SE Asia, on South China Sea, pop. 2,600,000

Sofia capital of Bulgaria in E Europe, pop. 1,119,000

St. Louis river port in Missouri in central United States, on Mississippi River, pop. 453,000

Stockholm seaport capital of Sweden, in N Europe, on Baltic Sea, pop. 663,000

St. Petersburg formerly Leningrad; seaport in NW Russia in Europe, on Baltic Sea, pop. 4,800,000

Surabaya seaport in Indonesia on Java, in SE Asia, on Java Sea, pop. 2,500,000

Sydney seaport in E Australia, on S Pacific Ocean, pop. 3,500,000

Taipei capital of Taiwan in E Asia, on South China Sea, pop. 2,637,000

Tashkent capital of Uzbekistan and ancient Caucasian city in Near East, pop. 2,100,000

Tbilisi formerly Tiflis; capital of Georgian Republic in SE Europe, on Kura River, pop. 1,174,000

Teheran capital of Iran in Near East, pop. 6,022,000

Tianjin formerly Tientsin; ancient trading center and seaport in N China in E Asia, on Yellow Sea, pop. 6,000,000

Tientsin Tianjin

Tiflis Tbilisi

Tokyo ancient seaport and capital of Japan in E Asia, on Tokyo Bay, off N Pacific Ocean, pop. 8,300,000

Toronto lake port in Canada in N North America, on Lake Ontario, pop. 3,427,000

Tripoli seaport capital of Libya, in N Africa, on Mediterranean Sea, pop. 591,000

Tunis ancient Carthaginian seaport and capital of

Tunisia, in N Africa, on Mediterranean Sea, pop. 1,000,000

Vancouver seaport in SW Canada in North America, on Pacific Ocean, pop. 1,380,000

Venice ancient seaport built on numerous small islands in N Italy, in S Europe, on Adriatic Sea, pop. 327,000

Vienna river port and capital of Austria, in central Europe, on Danube River, pop. 1,500,000

Vientiane capital of Laos, in SE Asia, on Mekong River, pop. 120,000

Warsaw capital of Poland, in E Europe, on Vistula River, pop. 1,600,000

Washington District of Columbia; capital of United States in North America, on Potomac River, pop. 607,000

Wellington seaport capital of New Zealand, on S Pacific Ocean, pop. 137,000

Wuhan conglomerate city and provincial capital in China in E Asia, pop. 3,400,00; also Han Cities

Yangon formerly Rangoon; ancient seaport capital of Myanmar in SE Asia, on Bay of Bengal, pop. 2,500,000

Yokohama ancient seaport in Japan in E Asia, on Tokyo Bay, pop. 3,100,000

MINERALS, METALS, AND ROCKS

Minerals
  Mineral Compounds
  Gemstones
Metals
  Pure Metals
  Alloys
Rocks
  Igneous Rocks
  Metamorphic Rocks
  Sedimentary Rocks

See also: *Chap. 3: Geology; Chap. 4: Chemistry; Chap. 10: Ornaments and Accessories*

Minerals

mineral inorganic chemical solid naturally occurring in Earth's crust and having definite chemical composition and tendency to form crystals

MINERAL COMPOUNDS

acanthite, acmite, actinolite, adamite, alabaster, allanite, alunite, amblygonite, amphibole, analcime, andalusite, anglesite, anhydrite, anthophyllite, apatite, apophyllite, aragonite, argentite, arsenopyrite, asbestos, asphaltum, augite, aurichalcite, austinite, autunite, aventurine, axinite, azurite

babingtonite, barite, bauxite, benitoite, beryl, biotite, bismuth, bismuthite, bixbyite, borax, bornite, boulangerite, bournonite, brochantite, brookite, brucite

calaverite, calcite, cancrinite, carnallite, carnotite, cassiterite, celestite, cerargyrite, cerussite, chabazite, chalcanthite, chalcedony, chalcocite, chalcopyrite, chloragyrite, chlorite, chromite,

chrondrodite, chrysoberyl, chrysocolla, cinnabar, clinozoisite, cobaltite, colemanite, columbite, conichalcite, copalite, cordierite, corundum, covellite, crocoite, cryolite, cuprite, cyanotrichite

danburite, datolite, dendrite, descloizite, diaspore, diopside, dioptase, dolomite, dumortierite

emery, enargite, enstatite, epidote, epsomite, erythrite

feldspar, fluorite, franklinite

gadolinite, galena, garnet, garnierite, gilsonite, glauberite, glauconite, glaucophane, goethite, graphite, gummite, gypsum

halite, hedenbergite, hematite, hemimorphite, heubnerite, heulandite, hornblende, howlite, hypersthene

idocrase, ilmenite, inesite

jadeite, jamesonite, jarosite

kaolinite, kernite, kyanite

laumontite, lawsonite, lazulite, lazurite, legrandite, lepidolite, leucite, limonite, linarite

magnesite, magnetite, malachite, manganite, marcasite, melanterite, mesolite, mica, millerite, mimetite, mineral coal, molybdenite, monazite, muscovite

natrolite, nepheline, neptunite, niccolite, nickeline

olivenite, olivine, orpiment, ozocerite

pargasite, pectolite, pentlandite, phenakite, phlogopite, plagioclase, polybasite, prehnite, proustite, psilomelane, pumpellyite, pyrargyrite, pyrite, pyrolusite, pyromorphite, pyrophyllite, pyroxene, pyrrhotite

quartz

realgar, rhodochrosite, rhodonite, riebeckite, rutile

scapolite, scheelite, scolecite, serpentine, shattuckite, siderite, sillimanite, skutterudite, smaltite, smithsonite, sodalite, soda niter, sperrylite, sphalerite, sphene, spinel, spodumene, stannite, staurolite, stephanite, stibnite, stilbite, strontianite, sulfur, sylvanite, sylvite

talc, tantalite, tephroite, tetrahedrite, thenardite, thomsonite, thorite, torbernite, tourmaline, tremolite, triphylite, trona

ulexite, uraninite, uranophane

vanadinite, variscite, vivianite

wavellite, willemite, witherite, wolframite, wollastonite, wulfenite

zincite, zoisite

GEMSTONES

gemstone hard mineral, crystal, or petrified material used as jewelry when cut and faceted, designated precious or semiprecious

agate, alexandrite, almandine, amber, amethyst, amorzonite, andradite, aquamarine, aventurine

beryl, bloodstone

cairngorm, carbuncle, carnelian, cat's eye, chalcedony, chrysoberyl, chrysolite, chrysoprase, citrine

demantoid, diamond

emerald

fire opal

garnet, girasol

harlequin opal, heliotrope, hyacinth

jacinth, jade, jasper, jet

kunzite

lapis lazuli, lazurite

malachite, melanite, milky quartz, moonstone,
    morganite
nephrite
olivine, onyx, opal
peridot, pyrope
red jasper, rose quartz, rubasse, ruby, rutile
sapphire, sard, sardonyx, smoky quartz, smoky
    topaz, sodalite, spinel, star sapphire,
    sunstone
tiger's-eye, topaz, tourmaline, turquoise
white sapphire
zircon

Metals

metal opaque, fusible, ductile, conductive,
lustrous substance, often a chemical element or
compound yielding oxides or hydroxides

PURE METALS

aluminum, americium, antimony, arsenic
barium, beryllium, bismuth
cadmium, calcium, cerium, cesium, chromium,
    cobalt, columbium, copper
dysprosium
erbium, europium
gadolinium, gallium, germanium, gold
hafnium, holmium
indium, iridium, iron
lanthanum, lead, lithium, lutetium
magnesium, manganese, mercury, molybdenum
neodymium, nickel, niobium
osmium
palladium, phosphorus, platinum, polonium,
    potassium, praseodymium, promethium,
    protactinium
radium, rhenium, rubidium, ruthenium
samarium, scandium, silver, sodium, strontium
tantalum, technetium, terbium, thallium, thorium,
    thulium, tin, titanium, tungsten
uranium
vanadium
ytterbium, yttrium
zinc, zirconium

ALLOYS

alloy two or more metals, or a metal and
nonmetal, fused together when molten
    alnico, amalgam
    Babbitt, brass, bronze
    Carboloy, carbon steel, cast iron, chrome, coin
        nickel, constantan
    Damascus steel, damask
    electrum, elinvar
    graphite steel
    invar
    permalloy, perminvar, pewter, pinchbeck, pink
        gold
    solder, spiegeleisen, stainless steel, steel,
        sterling silver
    tombac
    white gold, wrought iron

Rocks

rock concretion of earthly or mineral matter of
variable size, shape, and chemical composition

IGNEOUS ROCKS

igneous rock rock formed by cooling and
hardening of hot, molten rock within Earth
    andesite, anorthosite, aplite
    basalt
    carbonatite, clinkstone
    dacite, diabase, diorite, dolerite, dunite
    felsite
    gabbro, granite, granite pegmatite, granodiorite
    kimberlite
    lava
    monzonite
    nepheline syenite
    obsidian
    pegmatite, peridotite, phonolite, pitchstone,
        porphyry, pumice, pyroxenite
    rhyolite
    scoria, syenite
    trachyte, trap, traprock, tuff
    volcanic ash

METAMORPHIC ROCKS

metamorphic rock igneous or sedimentary rock
that has been transformed by heat, pressure, or
chemically active fluids
    amphibolite
    calc-silicate
    gneiss, granulite, greenstone
    halite, hornblende schist, hornfels
    ironstone
    marble, metaquartzite
    phyllite
    quartzite
    schist, serpentine, skarn, slate, soapstone,
        steatite

SEDIMENTARY ROCKS

sedimentary rock rock formed on Earth's
surface from accumulation of material deposited
by water, wind, or glaciers
    anhydrite
    breccia, brownstone, buhr, buhrstone
    chalk, chert, coal, conglomerate
    dolomite, dripstone
    flint
    grit, gypsum
    hematite
    limestone
    marl, mudstone
    oolite
    rock salt, rottenstone
    sandstone, shale, stalactite, stalagmite,
        stinkstone
    touchstone, travertine, tufa

LANDSCAPES AND SEASCAPES
Hills, Hollows, and Valleys
Plains and Marshes
Woods and Brush
Inland Waterways and Lakes
Coastal Land, Islands, and the Sea

See also: *Chap. 3: Geography; Weather and
Natural Phenomena*

Hills, Hollows, and Valleys

acclivity upward slope of hill
alp high mountain
arete ridge in craggy mountains with sharp crest
arroyo steep-sided gully in arid region, carved by
    heavy rains
badlands highly eroded area of hills in fantastic
    shapes
barranca deep, steep-sided gully or arroyo
barrow pile of earth or rocks at location of
    ancient grave
basin depression in earth's surface, often with
    lake or pond at bottom; drainage outlet for river
berm narrow shelf at bottom, top, or along side
    of slope
bluff high, steep, broad-faced bank or cliff
bowl large, round hollow
box canyon narrow valley with vertical walls
    terminating in wall at upstream end
brae *Scot.* hillside above river
bunker mound of earth
butte sheer-faced, isolated, flat-topped hill with
    smaller summit than mesa
caldera large basin formed by explosion and
    collapse of center of volcano
cañon canyon
canyon deep, narrow valley with steep sides
    carved by river; cañon
cave underground hollow that opens into a hill
cavern underground chamber, usu. large
cavity hollowed space in rocks, cliffs, or hills
cenote deep limestone sinkhole
chasm deep cleft in earth; gorge
chine ridge or crest of ravine or gorge
chink small cleft, fissure
chip deformity in earth's surface where piece has
    been displaced
cirque deep, natural bowl in mountains; corrie;
    cwm
cleft small fissure in earth
cliff tall, steep, vertical face of rock overlooking
    lower area
col depression in crest of ridge; mountain pass
combe *Chiefly Brit.* valley or depression on side
    of hill
cordillera series of parallel mountain ranges
corrie cirque
coulee dry streambed; shallow depression
couloir mountainous gorge, esp. in Alps
crag steep rocks or cliff with sharp outcroppings
crater bowl-shaped depression, esp. at mouth of
    volcano
crest highest ridge of mountain or hill
crevasse deep cleft in glacier or earth
crevice crack in earth
cuesta ridge or hill with steep face on one side
    and long gentle slope on other
cut slash in earth's surface; small, steep canyon
cwm cirque
dale valley, vale
declivity downward slope of hill
defile long, narrow passage between hills or
    cliffs

dell small, secluded, wooded valley

depression any hollow place or low point in earth's surface

dingle small, wooded valley or dell

divide mountain ridge from which streams drain in opposite directions

donga narrow, steep-sided ravine, dry except in rainy season

draw gully less deep than a ravine

drift glacial deposit of gravel or boulders

drumlin long, oval hill of glacial drift

dune hill of sand formed by wind

elevation height

escarpment steep cliff separating two level surfaces

esker elongated ridge of sand and boulders deposited by stream running beneath stagnant glacier

fissure crack or split in earth

foothills low-lying hills at base of mountain range

gap mountain pass; ravine

glacier large mass of moving ice

glacis gentle slope; mound of earth, esp. before fortification

glen secluded, narrow, grassy valley, usu. level at bottom

gorge narrow, steep ravine with rocky walls

grotto cave or cavern, usu. not deep

gulch deep, steep-walled ravine formed by swift stream

gully channel or small valley worn in earth by running water

headland promontory

height elevated tract of land, esp. mountain peak; elevation

highland rolling hills in elevated tract of land

hill usu. rounded elevation of land, smaller than a mountain

hillock small hill

hillside one slope of hill

hilltop peak, crest, or ridge of hill

hogback ridge with sharp crest and sides of steeply inclined strata

hollow depression, low sunken place

hummock low, rounded hillock

intervale low-lying tract of land along river

kloof deep gorge or ravine (South Africa)

knap summit, hill top

knoll small, rounded hill

kopje small hill on veld (southern Africa)

krantz steep cliff or precipice (southern Africa)

massif central, compact portion of mountain range

monticule secondary cone of volcano

mound pile of earth or stones; knoll

mountain landmass elevated far above surroundings, higher than a hill

nunatak hill or mountain totally encircled by glacial ice

overlook elevated land that affords view of surrounding flatlands

palisade line of steep cliffs, esp. above river

pass low point suitable for crossing mountain range

peak top of mountain with distinct, pointed summit

pike *Chiefly Brit.* mountain with pointed summit

pinnacle tall mountain peak

pit narrow, deep, steep-sided depression in earth

piton sharp peak of mountain

precipice vertical or near vertical face of hill or mountain; cliff

promontory point of high land projecting out over water; headland

puna treeless, wind-swept mesa or basin in high Andes (Peru)

range series of connected mountains

ravine narrow, steep-sided depression in earth's surface formed by running water, larger than a gully, smaller than a canyon

recess cleft in earth, often concealed from view

ridge range of hills or mountains; long, narrow elevation in earth's surface or ocean floor

rift crack, fissure

rincon small, secluded valley; sharp recess in cliff

rise slope, hillside

rut cut, furrow, or track in ground

saddle mountain ridge connecting two peaks; col

scarp line of cliffs formed by erosion or fracturing of earth

serac tall peak or mass of ice projecting upward from glacier

sierra mountain range, esp. with irregular contour of jagged peaks

sink depression in earth's surface without drainage, often saline lake

sinkhole limestone hollow connected to underground passage

slough depression in swamp full of soft, deep mud

spur ridge projecting from mountain or range; projection of elevated land

steptoe isolated hill or mountain surrounded by lava

strath *Scot.* steep-sided, wide, flat-bottomed valley

submontane land at foot of or lying under mountain

summit highest point of mountain or hill

tableland flat-topped, elevated tract of land

talus slope formed by pile of rock debris at foot of cliff

tor high, rugged hill

trench long, narrow furrow in ground or deep ocean floor

trough long, narrow, shallow depression between ridges or slopes

vale valley, esp. one hidden between hills

valley long depression in earth's surface lying between hills or mountains, usu. formed by river flowing through it

vista height affording view over large expanse of land

wadi rocky desert riverbed, dry except for rainy season

water gap gap across mountain ridge, cut by and giving passage to stream

watershed area on one side of divide drained by rivers all flowing in same direction; ridge dividing two drainage areas

Plains and Marshes

alluvial plain flat plain where river leaves gorge or joins larger waterway

barrens expanse of flat, treeless land

bog small marsh or swamp; wet, spongy ground

bottoms low-lying area at edge of waterway

campo grassy plain (South America)

champaign extensive area of level, open land

chott shallow, brackish, saline marsh, usu. dry in summer (North Africa)

clearing tract of land with trees and brush removed

coastal plain flat expanse of land from coast to first range of mountains

delta nearly flat alluvial plain at mouth of river, usu. triangular

desert arid, barren region that may support sparse vegetation

down rolling, open, upland region of grassy land

erg vast area covered with shifting sands, esp. in Sahara Desert

everglade swampy grassland, esp. in south Florida

fen low boggy land partly covered by water

field open land, usu. without many trees

fjeld rocky, barren plateau (Scandinavia)

flat expanse of level land

flatland tract of level land

glade open space in forest; marshy or grassy clearing

grassland plain covered with grasses

heath tract of open land with uncultivated vegetation such as heather and shrubs

kipuka tract of land surrounded by recent lava flow (Hawaii)

llano open grassy plain (southwestern United States or Latin America)

mainland primary part of continent, as distinguished from islands

marsh wet, boggy land; swamp

meadow expanse of grassland, often in mountains or along river

mesa small, high plateau; flat-topped, steep-sided, rocky land formation

mire muddy bog, swamp

moor tract of open wasteland often overgrown with low shrubs; heath

morass marsh, swamp

mud flat level area of muddy land, usu. at edge of body of water

paludal (*adj*) marshy, swampy

pampas broad, grass-covered plains in South America, esp. Argentina

peat bog marsh of partially carbonized decomposing vegetable matter

piedmont area lying at base of mountain range

plain expanse of flat or rolling, usu. treeless, land

plateau extensive tract of level land raised above adjoining land

playa sandy, salty, or mud-caked flat floor of desert basin, usu. occupied by shallow lake following heavy rain (western United States)

pocosin upland swamp of coastal plain

polder tract of lowland reclaimed from sea or lake and protected by dikes or dams

prairie large tract of rolling grassland

quag quagmire

quagmire marsh, bog; wet ground with difficult footing; quag

quicksand deep bed of loose sand saturated with water that yields underfoot

salina saline marsh or spring

salt flat level tract of dried salt land left by evaporation of lake or sea

salt marsh marshy tract in stage between saline lake and salt flat

salt pan undrained natural depression in which evaporation of water leaves deposit of salt

savanna grassy plain with scattered trees; treeless plain in tropics

scabland tract of high, rocky land with no topsoil and dry streambeds

solfatara level area surrounding volcano emitting vapors

steppe vast plain of eastern Europe having few trees

swale low, marshy depression or hollow

swamp wet, boggy land

sword grassy surface of land, turf, sod and soil with roots

tarpit flat area filled with natural tar or asphalt which is exposed to air

tickle land covered with grasses, esp. witch grass

tract any expanse of land

tundra level, treeless plain in arctic region with dark wet soil on base of permanently frozen subsoil

vega flat, barren plain (Spain)

veld field or plain (southern Africa)

wallow soft, muddy area

wash bog, marsh

wasteland barren land, desert

wetlands land with nonflowing surface water, such as marsh, swamp, or bog

Woods and Brush

backwoods remote, densely forested region

bosc boscage

boscage thicket or grove of shrubbery; bosc

bracken thicket of large coarse ferns

brake often marshy land overgrown with one plant, esp. ferns

broom shrubbery, esp. with yellow flowers

brush land covered with scrub vegetation

brushwood thicket of shrubs or small trees

bush dense growth of low shrubs; expanse of uncleared area

canebrake thicket of cane

chaparral dense thicket of stunted evergreen oaks

clump cluster of trees or shrubs

coppice thicket or wood of small trees; copse

copse coppice

covert thicket giving cover to game

deadfall tangled mass of fallen trees and branches

forest large tract of thickly wooded land

furze gorse

gorse growth of spiny, yellow-flowering shrub; furze

grove small wood or group of trees growing close together

heath shrubby evergreen plants covering tract of open land

hedge row of closely planted shrubs that forms a boundary

jungle wild land overgrown with dense mass of tropical vegetation

motte grove of trees on open prairie (southwestern United States)

oasis fertile area of vegetation in desert

orchard field of fruit or nut trees

park wooded tract of land, often cultivated

rain forest tropical woods covered by tall, dense canopy of branches in area of heavy rainfall

rush hollow-stemmed marsh grass

scrub growth of low trees and shrubs

scrubland dry tract of land covered with scrub

sedge tufted marsh plant

shinnery dense growth of small trees, esp. scrub oak

shrubbery growth of shrubs

shrubs short, multistemmed, woody plants

spinney *Chiefly Brit.* small wood with undergrowth

stand group of trees or shrubs growing together or in a line

sylvan (*adj*) covered with woods or groves of trees

thicket dense growth of shrubs and underbrush

timberland forested tract

tussock clump or tuft of sedge or marsh grass

underbrush shrubs, bushes, and small trees growing beneath taller trees; undergrowth

undergrowth underbrush

underwood small trees, shrubs

vineyard field of grapevines

weald forest, wilderness; rolling, upland region of woods; wold

wild wilderness

wilderness uncultivated, uninhabited region in natural state; wild

windbreak line or stand of trees affording protection from wind

wold weald

wood dense growth of trees, larger than a grove and smaller than a forest

woodland timberland, forest

woods region covered with trees and shrubs

Inland Waterways and Lakes

bank ground sloping upward from edge of lake, river, or sea

bayou creek or stream that is tributary of larger watercourse; marshy, stagnant body of water

bed bottom of body of water

bend curve in flowing waterway

bight bend in river; curved coast or bay

billabong dry streambed that fills in rainy season; stagnant pool in wilds (Australia)

boca *Spanish.* river mouth; harbor opening

branch small stream flowing into larger stream; one fork of divided waterway

brink riverbank

brook small stream of fresh water

canal artificial navigable waterway that connects bodies of water or is used for irrigation

cascade small waterfall, esp. one of a series

channel bed where natural stream runs; deeper part of river

creek small, usu. slow-moving stream

current swiftest part of stream

cutoff new channel in river, formed by water cutting across bend in its course

debouchement river mouth

distributary branch leading from main waterway and not rejoining it

eddy circular movement of water in pool in stream

euripus strait, esp. one with violent flow of water

falls waterfall; series of waterfalls

feeder tributary leading to larger watercourse

floating island mass of earth and decomposing vegetation held together by intertwined roots and floating on a lake

ford shallow part of stream that allows crossing by wading

fork point where river branches into two or more parts

fountainhead source of a stream, usu. a spring; wellspring

freshet stream springing from overflow of melting snow

geyser spring issuing intermittent jets of steam

headwaters small streams and freshets that converge to form source of river, often at high altitude

kill channel, creek

lagoon shallow body of water connected to larger body of water but cut off by atoll or sandbar

laguna small lake or pond

lake inland body of standing fresh water, usu. of considerable size

loch *Scot.* lake

lough *Irish.* lake, arm of the sea

meander curve or bend in river on level ground

mere small lake, pool

millpond pond created by damming of river

mouth point where stream enters lake or sea

narrows portion of stream decidedly less wide than other portions

nyanza lake in central or eastern Africa

outlet mouth of river

oxbow U-shaped bend in river

oxbow lake bow-shaped lake formed when river cuts across U-shaped neck of land
pond inland body of standing fresh water, smaller than a lake
pool deep, quiet place in stream; small body of water
puddle very small, shallow body of water
race strong current flowing through narrow channel
rapids shallow part of stream with strong current broken by obstacles such as rocks; white water
reach straight portion of river or stream
reservoir artificial, man-made lake, esp. for storing water supply
riffle shoal or reef in stream that causes choppy water or rapids
rill runnel
ripple shallow stretch of rough water in stream; rapids
river natural stream of significant length and volume that follows definite course
riverbank rising ground at edge of river; brink
riverhead source of river
riverside bank of river
rivulet small stream, brook
run creek
runnel very small brook; rill
runoff rainwater or melted snow flowing down mountain into streams
salt lake body of water in dry region, with no outlet, that has become saline through evaporation
sandbar ridge of sand accumulated by currents in stream
sault waterfall or rapids
shallows portion of stream with slight depth
shoal shallow place in river; sandbar
sike *Scot.* small stream, usu. dry in summer
sink saline lake with no outlet
spout waterspout
spring source of water issuing from ground
strait narrow waterway that passes between larger bodies of water
stream flowing body of water smaller than a river
swash narrow channel between sandbar and shore or within sandbar
torrent stream with strong, rapid current
tributary stream leading into larger stream, river, or lake
vortex whirlpool
watercourse any natural stream of flowing water; waterway
waterfall very steep or perpendicular stream of water, often over precipice; falls
water hole small hollow filled with standing water
waterspout geyser; spout
water system river with all its branches and tributaries
waterway watercourse
well pool filled by spring; flow of water from earth

wellspring source of a stream; fountainhead
whirlpool water spinning rapidly in a circle that produces downward sucking force at its center into which floating objects are pulled; vortex
white water rapids

Coastal Land, Islands, and the Sea

archipelago group of sea islands, esp. in curved row
arm narrow inland extension of sea
atoll ring-shaped coral reef enclosing lagoon
barrier reef coral reef separated from shore by lagoon
bay body of water forming indentation on shoreline of sea or large lake; wide inlet of sea smaller than a gulf
beach rocky or sandy area along edge of sea or ocean
cape point of land extending into water; peninsula
cay key
channel strait of sea between two landmasses
coast land along shore of ocean or sea
coastline boundary between land and sea
côte *French.* coast
cove small, sheltered recess in shoreline
current tidal movement of ocean waters
estuary point where river mouth meets sea's tide; arm of sea at river mouth
firth *Scot.* narrow arm of sea; mouth of river into sea
fjord long, narrow arm of sea with steep cliffs
floe large, flat mass of ice floating on sea
gulf section of ocean or sea that extends into land, larger than a bay
harbor coastal waters protected from open sea and deep enough for anchoring ships
headland high point of land projecting into sea; promontory
high seas open ocean several miles or more from shore
holm small inland or inshore island
hook curved spit of land
horizon distant point where sky seems to meet sea
iceberg large mass of ice broken off from glacier, floating in sea
inlet indent in shoreline, esp. narrow passage between points of land or islands, often forming entrance to lagoon
island land area completely surrounded by water, smaller than a continent
isle island
islet small island
isthmus narrow strip of land with water on both sides connecting two larger bodies of land
key low island or reef, esp. coral islet off south Florida; cay
lagoon shallow body of water connected to the sea
littoral (*adj*) of, on, or along the shore
marine (*adj*) of or at the sea or ocean

neck narrow strip of land, usu. between bodies of water
ocean any of vast, connected bodies of salt water that cover almost three-fourths of Earth's surface
oceanfront land directly along seashore
offshore (*adj*) designating area of sea lying a short way from beach
pelagic (*adj*) of or on the open sea
peninsula large land area almost completely surrounded by water, usu. connected to mainland by isthmus
plage *French.* beach
playa *Spanish.* beach
point land projecting into sea and narrowing at end
polynya area of open water enclosed by sea ice
promontory headland
reach narrow arm of sea that extends inland
reef ridge of rock or coral just under water surface
ria long, narrow inlet where sea has overflowed river valley
riviera coastal region of sea used as a resort area
sandbank large deposit of sand that forms a shoal
sand bar underwater ridge of sand formed in coastal waters
sand dune tall mound of sand on beach
sea large body of salt water, generally landlocked and smaller than the ocean; also used as synonym for ocean
seaboard seashore
sea cliff steep slope overlooking ocean
seacoast land situated along ocean
seascape view or scene of sea or ocean
seashore land at edge of sea, esp. beach; seaboard
sea strand long section of seashore
seaway deep inland waterway connecting with sea
shingle coarse alluvial material along seashore
shoal sandbar beneath shallow water, sometimes exposed at low tide
shore land bordering a sea or ocean; coast
shoreline edge of land where a large body of water meets land
skerry reef; rocky island
sound passage between bodies of water; long inlet or arm of sea; water separating island from mainland
spit narrow point of land extending into water; long, narrow reef
strait narrow waterway connecting larger bodies of water
strand land along body of water; beach; tidal land alternately covered and exposed by tides
surf waves breaking against rocks and beach at shore
tidal basin artificial body of water open to river and subject to tides
tidal land flatland at seashore exposed at low tide, covered at high tide; tideland
tide rise and fall of surface of ocean and

connected bodies of water due to gravitational pull of moon and sun

tideland tidal land

tide pool tiny lagoon left in rocks along shore by withdrawing tide

tidewater ocean water that overflows land at high tide

tideway channel through which tide rises and falls

tombolo sandbar extending from an island to the mainland or another island

waterfront strip of land at edge of ocean or other waterway

WEATHER AND NATURAL PHENOMENA

Storms
Winds
Clouds
Disasters and Phenomena
Weather Conditions
Forecasting and Meteorology
Cyclical Events

See also: *Chap. 3: Geology; Geography; Landscapes and Seascapes*

Storms

anticyclone wind system that rotates around high-pressure center in opposite direction from cyclone

blizzard severe snowstorm with large accumulations of snow

cloudburst sudden, intense rainstorm

cyclone advancing wind system with heavy rain that rotates around low-pressure pressure center clockwise in Southern Hemisphere, counterclockwise in Northern Hemisphere

deluge heavy rainstorm that causes flooding

downpour intense rainstorm

dust storm whirlwind of dust in dry region with hot, electrically charged air

electrical storm storm with atmospheric electrical discharge, thunder, and lightning

gale moderate windstorm, 32 to 63 mph, esp. at sea

graupel soft hail or granular snow pellets

haboob violent storm of dust or sand in North Africa, the Middle East, or India

hail shower of small lumps of snow or compacted ice pellets, graded by size: pea, marble, golf ball, hen's egg, tennis ball, grapefruit, football

hurricane tropical cyclone at sea with heavy rain and winds over 72 mph, sometimes moving into temperate latitudes; tropical cyclone

ice storm storm with rain that freezes on contact with air

line squall thunderstorm along cold front

maelstrom powerful, turbulent whirlpool or whirlwind

---

monsoon seasonal windstorm that brings heavy rains off Indian Ocean

neutercane subtropical cyclone less than 100 miles in diameter

rain water droplets formed by condensation of atmospheric vapor falling to earth

rainsquall rain with gusty winds

rainstorm steady, prolonged rainfall

shower mild, brief rainfall

sleet frozen or partly frozen rain

slush partly melted, watery snow

snow precipitation formed into white ice crystals from water vapor at temperatures below freezing

snow flurries occasional windblown bursts of snowfall

snowstorm precipitation of small, dry crystals of water vapor

squall sudden, violent windstorm, often with rain or snow

storm atmospheric disturbance marked by wind and/or precipitation

tempest extensive, violent windstorm with rain or snow

thundershower mild thunderstorm

thunderstorm rainstorm with thunder and lightning

tornado violent whirlwind, advancing over land with funnel-shaped cloud; twister

torrential rain very heavy rainstorm

tropical cyclone hurricane

tropical storm tropical cyclone with winds under 72 mph

twister *Informal.* tornado

typhoon tropical cyclone in China Sea

weather front advancing storm

willy-willy severe tropical cyclone (Australia)

Winds

anemometer wind-measuring instrument

arctic icy wind from north

austral wind southerly wind

Beaufort scale measure of wind force in miles per hour on scale from one (calm) to twelve (hurricane)

berg warm, dry wind blowing toward coast (South Africa)

bise cold, dry, northerly wind in Alps

bora cold, violent, northerly wind off Adriatic

boreal northerly wind

breath wind under 3 mph

breeze relatively gentle wind of 4-31 mph; any light wind

cat's paw light air that ruffles calm water surface

chinook warm, dry wind off eastern Rocky Mountains

downwind (*adv*) in direction toward which wind is blowing

dust devil small whirlwind of sand and dust

favonian wind west wind

foehn warm, dry wind blowing down mountainside

---

fresh breeze 19-24 mph wind

fresh gale 39-46 mph wind

gale 32-63 mph wind

gentle breeze 8-12 mph wind

ghibli hot desert wind of northern Africa

gust sudden, sharp burst of wind

harmattan dusty wind on Atlantic coast of Africa

headwind wind blowing against course of ship or aircraft

howling wind wild, loud gust of wind

hurricane storm with winds over 72 mph

katabatic wind wind blowing down mountain valley at night

khamsin hot southerly wind (Egypt)

knot measure of wind velocity equal to 1 nautical mile per hour

levanter strong easterly wind on Mediterranean

light breeze 4-7 mph wind

mistral cold, dry, strong northerly wind in southern France

moderate breeze 13-18 mph wind

moderate gale 32-38 mph wind

nor'easter wind from northeast

norther strong wind from north

northerly wind from north

nor'wester wind from northwest

offshore (*adj*) blowing from shore to sea

onshore (*adj*) blowing from sea to shore

pampero strong, cold westerly or southwesterly wind on pampas (Argentina)

prevailing wind general direction of swirling wind

puna cold mountain wind (Peru)

samiel hot, dry, violent, dusty desert wind (Africa)

Santa Ana hot, dry wind off desert in southern California

sea breeze moist wind off ocean

simoom hot, dry desert wind (Middle East and North Africa)

sirocco hot, oppressive wind from arid region, esp. on Mediterranean from Libyan desert

solano hot, easterly, Mediterranean wind that brings rain

southeaster wind from southeast

southerly wind from south

southwester wind from southwest

squall sudden, violent windstorm

strong breeze 25-31 mph wind

strong gale 47-54 mph wind

tailwind wind blowing in same direction as course of ship or aircraft

tourbillion whirlwind, esp. vortex of whirlwind

trade wind wind blowing almost continually toward equator

tramontane violent, polar wind from northwest (southern France)

updraft air pulling upward into atmosphere

upwind (*adv*) in direction from which wind is blowing

violent storm 64-72 mph wind

vortex whirlwind

waft light breath of moving air

westerlies winds from subtropical areas in west toward middle latitudes

whirlwind air current rotating violently upward around vertical axis and moving forward; vortex

whole gale 55 to 63 mph wind; windstorm

williwaw sudden, violent squall of cold wind, common on mountainous coasts at near-polar latitudes

wind natural movement of air at any velocity, esp. horizontal relative to Earth's surface

windstorm strong winds with no rain

zephyr gentle breeze from west

zonda warm, humid northerly wind (South America)

Clouds

altocumulus white, globular cloudlets that appear in broken patches at altitudes around 10,000 feet (3048 m), usu. producing rain showers

altostratus dark, drab, thin cloud streaks at middle altitudes

billowing (*adj*) describing bulging masses of high clouds

cirrocumulus irregular, small, white sheets of cloud segments at altitudes around 20,000 feet (6096 m)

cirrostratus even layer of translucent, fibrous cloud streaks at altitudes of 20,000 feet (6096 m) or more, indicating that rain is coming

cirrus wispy, white cloud tufts and filaments at high altitudes up to 40,000 feet (12,192 m)

cloud visible mass of water or ice particles suspended at considerable height

cumulocirrus small, delicate cumulus at high altitude

cumulonimbus thunderstorm cumulus that spreads from dark portions at 5000 feet (1524 m) to towers rising upward to 50,000 feet (15,240 m)

cumulostratus cumulus with flat stratus base

cumulus cloud with flat, dark base around 2000 feet (610 m) and rounded, white mountainous outlines to altitudes of 10,000 feet (3048 m), that appears in a broken mass

nimbostratus low, dark gray rain cloud a few hundred feet above ground with ragged tops upward to 3000 feet (914 m), producing continuous precipitation

nimbus rain cloud of uniform gray that covers entire sky

noctilucent cloud luminous, thin, colored cloud seen at night

nubilous (*adj*) relating to clouds

rack wind-driven mass of high, broken clouds

stratocumulus large, rounded mass of dark cloud covering the entire sky, esp. in winter, at altitudes from 1500 to 6500 feet (457 to 1981 m), not producing rain

stratus flattened streaks of cloud at altitudes of a few hundred feet, similar to ground fog and producing drizzle

thundercloud electrically charged cloud that produces thunder and lightning; esp. cumulonimbus

woolpack cumulus cloud of fleecy appearance with flat base

Disasters and Phenomena

acid rain precipitation with excess acidity due to industrial pollutants

aftershock smaller tremor following main shock of earthquake

air pollution condition in which toxic substances are in atmosphere, esp. as a result of industrial and automobile emissions

alpenglow reddish glow at sunset and sunrise on mountain summit

aurora australis antarctic version of aurora borealis

aurora borealis streamers and bands of electrically caused radiant emissions that light up arctic night sky

avalanche large mass of snow, ice, and mud moving rapidly down mountain

ball lightning rare, luminous floating ball of lightning

black ice thin sheet of ice, often caused by freezing mist on roadway; transparent coating of ice on the sea

bolt of lightning common, streaking flash of lightning, usu. with thunder

bore tidal flood caused by rapid rise in water in channel

corn snow pellets or grains of snow formed by alternate melting and freezing

corona discharge storm phenomenon caused by discharge of electricity shaped like flames at surface of conductor; corposant; Saint Elmo's fire

corposant corona discharge

dew moisture condensed at night on surfaces of cool objects

dewfall nightly accumulation of dew

dew point temperature at which vapor condenses

drizzle very light, misty rain

drought prolonged period without rain

earthquake volcanic or tectonic crustal movement of Earth resulting in trembling, shaking, and fracturing; quake; temblor

eclipse total or partial obscuring of one celestial body by another

ecocatastrophe destructive upset in balance of nature, esp. from people's activities or negligence

eddy air or water current running against main current; whirlpool

El Niño unusually warm Pacific Ocean current that occurs periodically and often causes catastrophic weather conditions

epicenter Earth's surface directly above true center of earthquake

erosion wearing away of topsoil by wind and water

eruption violent release of steam and lava from volcano

eye calm region at center of cyclone or hurricane

fault line fracture in Earth's crust with displacement indicating and causing earthquakes

flash flood sudden, localized, massive rush of water due to heavy rainfall

flood overflow of body of water onto normally dry land; inundation

flux continuous flow of water, resulting in flood

fog thick mist or vapor suspended in lower atmosphere near ground

freeze drop in temperature below 32° F, or 0° C

frost minute ice crystals that form on surfaces; hoar

frost heave uplift of ground caused by freezing of moist soil

frost hollow low-lying area in which dense, cold air accumulates

greenhouse effect warming of Earth's surface and lower atmosphere when solar radiation is converted to heat and trapped in atmosphere by cloud layers and gases

ground fog low, often dense fog, esp. one through which sky and clouds above can be seen; radiation fog

Gulf Stream warm Atlantic current flowing from Florida to New England and Newfoundland

haar *Chiefly Brit.* cold sea mist or fog

hailstone pellet of compressed ice and snow

hoar frost

hyperborean (*adj*) of or relating to the extreme north; frozen

hypocenter focus of earthquake; epicenter

ice floe flat, floating mass of ice at sea

ice fog frozen fog vapor

ignis fatuus eerie light at night over marshland due to combustion of gas from decomposing organic matter

Indian summer unseasonably hot weather in autumn

inundation flood

Jack Frost personification of frosty weather

jet stream long, narrow, westerly 250 mph air current at high altitude in tropopause

killing frost last frost of spring or first frost of fall, limiting growing season for all but hardiest plants

landslide mass of rock and earth moving rapidly down slope

lava molten rock that issues from volcano

lightning flash of light from discharge of atmospheric electricity between clouds or between clouds and Earth

lunar eclipse condition produced by Earth lying directly between sun and moon so that moon passes through Earth's shadow

meteor shower cluster of falling rocks, incandescent from passage through Earth's atmosphere, generally burned up before reaching ground

midnight sun midsummer phenomenon at arctic and antarctic latitudes, where sun does not sink below horizon during night

mist fine light rain or thick fog

mizzle rain in very fine droplets; drizzle

mudflow mass of soil moved by rain and melting snow

mud slide mass of mud, swelled by rain or flood, moving down slope

natural phenomenon distinct, observable event, fact, or circumstance not caused directly by humans

ozone depletion chemical breakup in stratosphere of ozone layer, which absorbs sun's ultraviolet radiation

pea soup *Informal.* extremely thick fog

pogonip dense ice fog found in mountain valleys of western United States

pollution man-made contamination of Earth and atmosphere

quake earthquake

radiation fog fog produced by nocturnal cooling of surface boundary layer so that its content of water vapor condenses; ground fog

rainbow arc of prismatic colors in sky, formed by reflection and refraction of sun's rays through water vapor drops

red snow snow colored red by airborne dust and algae

rime frost, esp. coating of tiny granular ice tufts, due to supercooling and exposure to wind

rip current undertow

riptide strong, narrow surface current that opposes another tide and disturbs sea

runoff water from rain or melted snow flowing over land surface and reaching streams

Saint Elmo's fire corona discharge

sea puss swirling shore undertow

seismic (*adj*) of or relating to earthquakes

sheet lightning lightning obscured and diffused by clouds so that it appears over a broad area

smaze mixture of smoke and haze

smog fog augmented by smoke, chemical fumes, and automobile exhausts

snowbank mound of snow

snowcap snow covering mountain peak

snowdrift tall bank of windblown snow

snowfield broad expanse of snow

snowflake small, tabular, columnar, or otherwise geometrically regular, white ice crystal

snowpack accumulation of winter snow at high altitudes

snowslide landslide of snow and ice; avalanche

solar eclipse condition in which moon passes directly between sun and Earth

spindrift spray swept by wind from waves during storm at sea; spoondrift

spoondrift spindrift

storm surge sudden high tide, 10 to 20 feet (3 to 6 m) above normal, accompanying hurricane

sunburst flash of sunlight through break in clouds

temblor earthquake

tephra dust and solid matter ejected in volcanic eruption

thunder sudden, loud, booming noise following lightning, due to expansion of air heated by electrical discharge

thunderbolt single flash of lightning with accompanying thunder

thunderclap booming crash of thunder

thunderhead rounded upper mass of cumulonimbus clouds, signaling thunderstorm

tidal wave unusually high sea wave, often following earthquake; unusually high tide due to high winds and storm; tsunami

total eclipse complete obscuring of one celestial body by another

tremor mild earthquake

tsunami tidal wave

undertow current beneath ocean surface moving forcefully out to sea; rip current

vapor diffuse fog or smoke floating in air

virga streaks of precipitation that fall from cloud but evaporate before reaching ground

volcano vent in Earth's crust from which steam and molten rock are expelled

waterspout funnel-shaped column of mist and spray reaching from surface of sea or lake to underside of cloud

whirlpool eddy

whiteout severe blizzard condition with low visibility, no shadows, and only dark objects distinguishable

zero-zero condition of zero visibility in vertical and horizontal directions

zodiacal light luminous tract in sky in west after twilight and in east before dawn

Weather Conditions

CLEAR WEATHER

azure
blue skies
clear, cloudless
fair
high visibility
shiny, sunny, sunshine

COLD WEATHER

arctic
biting, bitter, boreal, brisk
chilly, cold, cold snap, cold wave, cool
freezing, frigid, frosty
gelid, glacial
icy
nippy
subzero

HOT WEATHER

close
dog days
hot, humid
muggy
sultry, sweltering
torrid, tropical

MILD WEATHER

balmy
calm

dry
fair
mild
seasonable
temperate
warm

OVERCAST WEATHER

cloudy
dark
foggy, foul
half-light, hazy
lowering, low visibility
misty, murky
overcast
partly cloudy
shady, smoggy, soupy, sunless

WET WEATHER

deluge, downpour, drizzle
freezing rain
inclement
rainy
showers, sleet, slush, snowing, soaking, sprinkles
torrential rains

WINDY WEATHER

blast, blow, blustery, breath, breeze
draft
flurry
gale, gusty
swirling
turbulent
windy

Forecasting and Meteorology

air mass body of air hundreds of miles across and extending upward to the stratosphere, with uniform temperature and humidity

air pressure weight of air pushing down on Earth's surface

anemometer instrument for determining wind speed

aneroid barometer barometer in which atmospheric pressure moves pointer

Antarctic region surrounding South Pole, 66 1/2 degrees south of equator

Arctic region surrounding North Pole, 66 1/2 degrees north of equator

arctic air mass cold front moving from frigid to temperate zone in Northern Hemisphere

atmosphere entire mass of air enveloping Earth

atmospheric pressure pressure of air at any given point, equal to 14.7 pounds per square inch at sea level

backing counterclockwise change in wind direction at specific place

barometer instrument for measuring atmospheric pressure as indicator of weather change

barometric pressure pressure of atmosphere measured by height of column of mercury in which standard atmospheric pressure equals 29.92 inches (760 mm)

ceiling altitude of base of cloud layer obscuring at least half the sky

ceilometer photoelectric device for measuring and recording height of cloud ceiling above Earth

Celsius thermometric scale with zero degrees as freezing point of water and one hundred degrees as boiling point, designated C; Centigrade

Centigrade Celsius

chill factor windchill factor

climate prevailing temperature, wind velocity, humidity, cloudiness, and precipitation at given location over period of years

col area of intermediate pressure between two anticyclones or two depressions

cold front advancing edge of cold air mass

depression area in which atmospheric pressure is lower than surrounding areas, causing unsettled weather; low pressure

equator great circle of Earth, equidistant from two poles, dividing surface into northern and southern hemispheres

Fahrenheit thermometric scale of 180 degrees with freezing point of water at 32 degrees and boiling point at 212 degrees, designated F

fogbound (*adj*) surrounded by fog; unable to navigate because of fog

forecast prediction of weather based on meteorological data

front advancing edge of air mass

gale warning weather bureau prediction of gale force sea winds

Groundhog Day February 2, day on which legend has it that sunny skies mean six more weeks of winter, cloudy skies, an early spring

heavy rain significant rainfall

heavy snow significant snowfall

high high-pressure air mass

high-pressure (*adj*) designating air mass with barometric pressure exceeding atmospheric pressure

horse latitudes region thirty degrees north to thirty degrees south of equator, characterized by high pressure and relative calm

humidity measure of percentage of moisture in atmosphere

inversion increase of air temperature at higher altitude

isobar map line that connects locations of equal barometric pressure

isohyet map line that connects locations of equal rainfall

isotherm map line that connects locations of equal temperature

low low-pressure air mass

low-pressure (*adj*) designating air mass with barometric pressure less than atmospheric pressure

meteorology scientific study of atmospheric phenomena, used to forecast weather

occluded front air mass forced aloft when cold front overtakes warm front

occlusion cutting off of contact between air mass and Earth's surface

pluviometer gauge for measuring rainfall

polar front boundary between cold arctic air and warm air of lower latitudes

precipitation falling to earth of hail, rain, or snow

radiosonde instrument that transmits meteorological data from balloon at high altitude

rainfall measure of total precipitation over specified period in given location

rain gauge instrument used to measure rainfall over given period of time; pluviometer

relative humidity ratio of moisture present in air to maximum moisture possible at given temperature

ridge elongated high-pressure area between two depressions

saturated air air containing maximum water vapor possible at given temperature

seasonable (*adj*) normal for time of year

seeding producing rain by sprinkling dry ice or silver iodide crystals in stratus cloud layers

semitropical (*adj*) subtropical

sferics electronic storm detection and tracking

small craft warning advisory of gale force winds at sea

snowfall total inches of accumulated snow

stationary front air mass holding fixed position

storm warning weather bureau notice of impending high winds and heavy precipitation

subarctic (*adj*) adjacent to Arctic Circle

subtropical (*adj*) typical of regions bordering the tropics; semitropical

system interacting fronts and air masses that cause weather conditions

temperate zone latitudes between tropic of Cancer and Arctic Circle, or between tropic of Capricorn and Antarctic Circle

temperature degree of hotness or coldness as measured on standardized scale

temperature inversion layer of warm air that surmounts cooler air and traps pollutants near ground

thermal rising current of warm air

thermometer device used to measure temperature, esp. by height of column of mercury

torrid zone area surrounding equator, extending north to tropic of Cancer and south to tropic of Capricorn; tropics

tropic either of two parallels of celestial latitude bounding torrid zone and marking sun's southernmost and northernmost declinations

tropic of Cancer latitude 23 1/2 degrees north of equator

tropic of Capricorn latitude 23 1/2 degrees south of equator

tropics latitudes between tropics of Cancer and Capricorn, extending 23 1/2 degrees north and south of equator; torrid zone

troposphere layer of atmosphere nearest Earth, where weather conditions occur

trough elongated low-pressure area between two areas of higher pressure

unseasonable (*adj*) abnormal for time of year

veering clockwise change in wind direction at specific place

visibility degree of atmospheric clearness; measure of greatest distance at which object can be seen by naked eye

warm front advancing edge of warm air mass

wave period of intense, unseasonable heat or cold

weather state of Earth's atmosphere at specific time with regard to heat, humidity, visibility, pressure, wind speed, and disturbance

weather bureau office for collecting weather information, making predictions, and compiling statistics

weathercock mounted, rotating vane in form of cock that indicates wind direction

weather forecast scientific prediction of weather

weather front mass of air with specific pressure and temperature

weatherman male weatherperson, formerly used for either sex

weather map chart with meteorological elements shown at specific times and places

weatherperson individual who reports and predicts weather

weather station installation for recording meteorological measurements and observations

weather system interacting fronts and air masses generating specific weather conditions

weather vane mounted, rotating object that indicates wind direction

wedge high-pressure area between two depressions, narrower than a ridge

windchill factor temperature felt on exposed skin equal to combination of actual temperature and wind speed; chill factor

wind sleeve mounted cone open at both ends, used to indicate wind direction; windsock

windsock wind sleeve

zone one of five major latitudinal divisions of Earth's surface with respect to temperature: frigid (north and south), temperate (north and south), torrid (equatorial)

Cyclical Events

autumn September 22 to December 20; fall

autumnal (*adj*) occurring in autumn

autumnal equinox first day of autumn, usu. September 22 in Northern Hemisphere

blue moon occurrence of two full moons in one month, taking place approximately every thirty-two months

canicular (*adj*) of or relating to dog days

crepuscule twilight

crescent moon phase of moon between new

and first quarter or between last quarter and new

dawn hour during and after sunrise with first light

daylight hours between sunrise and sunset

dog days period of hot, sultry weather from July to late August in Northern Hemisphere

dusk hour during and after sunset with last light

ebb tide diminishing tide

equinox time of year when sun crosses equator, making day and night of equal length everywhere, usu. March 21 and September 22

fall September 22 to December 20; autumn

full moon phase in which entire visible disk of moon is illuminated by sun

gibbous moon phase between full and quarter moon, either waxing or waning

gloaming hour of darkness during and after sunset

harvest moon full moon nearest autumnal equinox

hibernal (*adj*) occurring in winter

high tide highest point reached by tide, usu. twice daily

low tide lowest point reached by tide, usu. twice daily

moonrise hour of moon's appearance in sky

moonset hour of moon's disappearance from sky

neap tide tide of minimum range at first and third lunar quarters

new moon phase in which dark side of moon faces Earth, with thin crescent moon seen a few days thereafter

quarter moon phase midway between full and new moon

seasonal (*adj*) occurring regularly during a specific season

slack tide period at turn of tide with little or no horizontal motion of tidal water

solstice time of year when sun is furthest north or south of celestial equator, June 21 or December 21

spring March 21 to June 20

summer June 21 to September 21

summer solstice June 21, being first day of summer and longest daylight period in Northern Hemisphere

sundown hour of sunset

sunrise hour of sun's appearance in east

sunset hour of sun's disappearance in west

thaw period in spring when snow and ice melt

tide twice daily alternate rising and falling of ocean waters due to unequal gravitational attraction of sun and moon

twilight hour after sunset; crepuscule

vernal (*adj*) occurring in spring

vernal equinox first day of spring, usu. March 21 in Northern Hemisphere

wane tide decreasing tide

wax tide increasing tide

winter December 21 to March 20

winter solstice December 21, being first day of winter and shortest daylight period in Northern Hemisphere

PART TWO
SCIENCE AND TECHNOLOGY

CHAPTER FOUR
THE SCIENCES

PHYSICS
Branches and Disciplines
Principles Of Mechanics, Waves, and Measurement
Electricity and Magnetism
Nuclear and Particle Physics
Cosmology
Heat
Optics
Acoustics

See also: *Chap. 3: Geology; Weather and Natural Phenomena; Chap. 4: Astronomy and Space Science; Chemistry; Chap. 5: Machinery and Fabrication; Electricity and Electronics*

Branches and Disciplines

acoustics study of production, control, transmission, reception, effects, and nature of sound waves

actinology study of the chemical effects produced by electromagnetic radiation

astrophysics study of physical and chemical constitution of the universe, esp. celestial matter

atomic physics study of the nature of the atom and subatomic particles

biophysics application of principles and methods of physics to biological problems

chaos study of hidden, ordered structures or regularities in seemingly chaotic phenomena

Copernican physics theories formulated by Nicolaus Copernicus that Earth revolves with other planets in orbits around sun

cosmology study of structure, origin, evolution, and probable fate of the universe

cryogenics study of production and application of effects of very low temperatures

crystallography study of form, structure, properties, and classification of crystals

dynamics branch of mechanics dealing with motion of material bodies under action of given forces

electricity study of phenomena and laws governing attraction and repulsion of electrons and other charged particles

electronics study of electron behavior

fluid mechanics hydraulics

geophysics branch of geology dealing with Earth physics: meteorology, oceanography, seismology, magnetism, radioactivity, geodesy

gravitation study of the force of acceleration toward each other of two material particles or bodies

heat study of production, properties, and effects of thermal energy

heliology study of sunlight

hydraulics study of mechanical properties of water and other liquids in motion and the engineering applications of these properties; fluid mechanics

hydrodynamics study of fluids in motion and their interaction with their boundaries

hydrostatics study of fluids at rest

kinetics branch of mechanics dealing with all aspects of motion

magnetism study of phenomena associated with magnets and electric currents

mechanics study of energy and forces and their effect on matter

Newtonian physics system based on laws of gravitation and motion developed by Sir Isaac Newton

nuclear physics study of structure, behavior, and radioactive properties of atomic nuclei

nucleonics study of nucleons and practical applications of nuclear phenomena

optics study of propagation, control, transmission, reception, effects, and phenomena of light waves

particle physics study of nature and interaction of subatomic particles

physics study of properties and interaction of matter and energy

pneumatics study of mechanical properties of air and other gases in closed systems

quantum mechanics modern theory of matter which supersedes classical physics and concentrates on atomic and subatomic phenomena in terms of observable quantities

relativity system of thought based on theories of Albert Einstein regarding universal character of propagation speed of light and consequent dependence of space, time, and other mechanical measurements on motion of observer performing measurements

statics branch of mechanics dealing with action of forces on bodies at rest

thermionics study of electron or ion emissions from heated surfaces

thermodynamics study of quantitative relationship and conversion between heat and other energy forms, esp. mechanical energy or work

wave mechanics form of quantum mechanics in which particle motion is described by wave motion

Principles of Mechanics, Waves, and Measurement

acceleration rate of change in velocity with respect to time

acceleration of gravity change in velocity due to gravitational attraction

accuracy proximity of measurement to true or absolute value

angular displacement amount of rotation of point, line, or body in specified direction about an axis

angular impulse product of a torque and the time interval during which it acts

angular momentum product of rotational inertia of a body and its angular velocity

angular velocity time rate of change of angular displacement

antinodal line line connecting points at which

two waves interfere constructively at their maximum amplitudes

Archimedes' principle object immersed in a fluid is buoyed up by a force equal to the weight of the fluid it displaces

beat oscillation in amplitude of complex wave and interference resulting from it

Bernoulli effect pressure exerted by a fluid decreases as its velocity increases

bond electrostatic attraction between atoms or groups of atoms

calculus system of calculation using symbolic notations, essential to modern physics

capillary attraction tendency of liquid to rise in narrow tube or move through absorbent material, due to greater adhesion of liquid to solid than internal adhesion of the liquid itself

center of gravity fixed point in body through which force of gravitational attraction acts

centrifugal force force that tends to move particles rotating about an axis outward from center of rotation

centripetal acceleration acceleration always at right angles to velocity of particle

centripetal force force directed toward the center of a circle that keeps particles in uniform circular motion, assumed to be equal and opposite to centrifugal force

cogeneration simultaneous generation of electrical energy and low grade heat from same fuel

components of a vector two or more perpendicular vectors that when added together produce the original vector

compression reduction in volume of substance due to pressure

concurrent forces forces acting on same point

coordinates numbers that specify position in space and time

correspondence principle laws of quantum mechanics and any other new theory reduce to laws of Newtonian mechanics when Planck's constant is negligible, wavelengths are relatively small, and dimensions are relatively large

crest region of upward displacement in transverse wave

damping reduction in wave amplitude due to energy dissipation

de Broglie principle material particles have wavelike characteristics which can give rise to interference effects and diffraction

deceleration negative acceleration; rate at which motion slows

density mass per unit of volume; distribution per unit of space

derived unit unit of measurement defined in terms of other units

dimensional quantities physical measurements expressed in defined mathematical units

direct variation increase or decrease in one variable causing proportional increase or decrease in another variable

displacement vector quantity representing change in position of an object

dissipative forces frictional forces for which law of conservation of mechanical energy does not hold true

distance spatial separation of two points measured by length of hypothetical straight line joining them

Doppler effect amount of decrease or increase in frequency of radiation as source and observer of waves move toward or away from each other

efficiency ratio of machine's useful power output to power input

elastic collision collision in which total kinetic energy of two colliding objects is the same before and after collision

elasticity ability of object to return to its original form after removal of deforming forces

endothermic (*adj*) referring to process that absorbs energy

energy capacity to do work

energy-matter relationship energy is equal to mass times the velocity of light squared, expressed as $e=mc^2$

entropy measure of disorder of a system; internal energy of a system that cannot be converted to mechanical work

equilibrant force equal in magnitude to resultant, but opposite in direction, producing an equilibrium

equilibrium condition in which net force on object is zero and there is no change in its motion

equivalence principle gravitational and inertial masses are equal

exothermic (*adj*) referring to process that releases energy

explosion violent, outward expansion of forces

extrapolation extending of graph beyond measured points to infer values outside known range

field region of space containing lines of force with direction and strength; force that acts through space and time, as opposed to particle existing at one fixed point in space and time

fluid material that flows, such as liquid or gas

force action that results in acceleration or deformation of an object; measure of momentum gained per second by accelerating object

frame of reference coordinate system used to assign positions and times to events in describing motion

friction force resisting motion between two objects that are in contact

fundamental forces four basic forces acting in nature: strong force, electromagnetic force, weak force, gravitational force

fundamental units units of measurement defined in terms of a physical standard, not other units; seven basic units of measurement; International System of Units

gas phase of matter in which substance expands readily to fill any containing vessel, characterized by relatively low density

general theory of relativity Einstein's theory of gravitation, expressed in terms of curved space-time, which stipulates that the laws of science are identical for all observers regardless of their motion

graph plot on rectangular coordinates showing relationship of two variables

gravitational field region in space in which particles experience gravitational force

gravitational force mutual attraction between particles due to their masses

gravitational potential energy potential energy acquired by object when moved against gravity

heat energy resulting from disordered motion of molecules

Hooke's law stress applied to a solid body is directly proportional to strain produced

ideal gas theoretical gas composed of infinitely small molecules that exert no force on each other

ideal mechanical advantage ratio of distance through which effort is exerted to distance over which resistance is encountered in a machine

imaginary time measurement of time in complex numbers based on square root of -1

implosion opposite of explosion, in which forces are directed inward

impulse product of a force and the time during which it acts

inclined plane flat surface at angle to some force or reference line

inelastic collision collision in which total kinetic energy of colliding particles is not the same after collision as before it

inertia tendency of a body to remain at rest or in motion unless acted upon by an outside force

instantaneous quantity value at any given instant of a quantity that is changing

International System of Units SI; system of measurement based on these fundamental units: mass (kilogram), length (meter), time (second), temperature (kelvin), amount of substance (mole), electric current (ampere), luminous intensity (candela)

inverse variation increase in one variable that causes proportional decrease in another variable

isolated system system not being acted upon by outside forces

joule SI unit of work or energy equal to one newton acting through one meter

kinetic energy energy of an object due to its motion

kinetic theory of matter concept that all matter is made of small particles in constant motion whose collisions are perfectly elastic

law verbal or mathematical statement of relationship between phenomena that is always the same under the same conditions

law of conservation of energy energy can be neither created nor destroyed and is constant in a closed system

law of conservation of mass-energy sum of matter and energy in the universe is constant

law of conservation of mechanical energy sum of potential and kinetic energies of ideal energy system is constant

law of conservation of momentum total vector momentum of an object is always constant in a system free of external forces

law of entropy all natural processes tend to increase the measure of disorder in the universe

law of universal gravitation gravitational force between two objects is constant G times the product of the masses of the two objects and the distance between them

length distance between two points

line of flux line whose tangent indicates direction of magnetic field

liquefaction condensation of a gas or solid to a liquid

liquid state of matter in which particles are in proximity greater than that of a gas but less than that of a solid, restricting their random motions to vibrations around moving points

longitudinal wave wave in which vibrations are parallel to the direction of its propagation

mass quantity of matter in an object, measured by its resistance to a change in its motion

mass density mass per unit volume of a substance

matter any substance with mass and inertia

mechanical advantage ratio of resistance force to effort force in a machine

mechanical impedance ratio of applied wave-producing force to resulting displacement velocity in any wave-transmitting medium

mechanical wave displacement of portion of elastic medium that causes oscillation about an equilibrium position

mechanics effect of energy and other forces on matter

meniscus crescent shaped surface of column of liquid

metric system internationally recognized system of weights and measures, based on decimal system

moment tendency to produce motion, esp. about an axis; product of physical quantity such as area or mass and its directed distance from axis

momentum product of the mass of a moving object and its velocity

newton SI unit of force required to accelerate a one kilogram mass at a rate of one meter per second per second

Newton's first law of motion object remains at rest or in motion with a constant velocity unless acted upon by an outside force

Newton's law of universal gravitation force of attraction between any two particles of matter is directly proportional to the product of their masses and inversely proportional to the square of the distance between their centers of mass

Newton's second law of motion the change in motion of an object acted upon by an outside force is directly proportional to the force and inversely proportional to the object's mass

Newton's third law of motion every action

force has a reaction force equal in magnitude and opposite in direction

nodal line line that connects nodes

node point in medium or field that remains undisturbed when acted upon simultaneously by more than one disturbance

normal force force perpendicular to a surface

orbital angular momentum component of angular momentum of electron in atom or nucleon in nucleus, arising from its orbital motion rather than its spin

parabolic relationship one quantity varying as the square of another quantity

parallax shift in relative position of objects due to change in angle of perspective

parity symmetry property that expresses difference between wave function and its negative mirror image, expressed as +1 or -1

pascal SI unit of pressure, equal to one newton per square meter

Pascal's law external pressure applied to fluid in a closed vessel is transmitted uniformly throughout the fluid

period time duration of phenomenon or event, esp. one complete cycle, vibration, revolution, or oscillation

periodic motion identical motions that recur at equal time intervals

phase number describing wave position within each oscillation or cycle at specific time

Planck's constant fundamental determinant of values in quantum mechanics, expressing ratio of energy of one quantum of radiation to its frequency, equal to 6.624×10^{-27} erg-seconds

plasma high temperature state of matter in which atoms, separated into electrons and positive ions or nuclei, produce conductive gas

potential energy energy based on position of object

power work done per unit of time

precession motion due to torque that displaces axis of rotation in spinning object

precision degree of exactitude and reproducibility in measured data; agreement between two or more measurements of same quantity made in same way

pressure force per unit area

principle of parity for every process in nature there exists an indistinguishable, mirror-image process

projectile motion motion of object moving in two dimensions under influence of gravity

propagation transmission of a wave through material or space

property any measurable aspect of matter

pulse single, nonrepeated disturbance in medium or field

quantum discrete, indivisible, and elemental unit of energy that emits or absorbs waves

quantum jump abrupt transition of system in quantum mechanics from one distinct energy level to another; quantum leap

quantum leap quantum jump

quantum number notation used to characterize

discrete value and magnitude that a quantized physical variable may assume

ray line drawn to represent path traveled by a wave front; single line of light from luminous point

relative deviation average deviation of set of measurements, expressed as percentages

resolution location of vector force components acting in given direction

rest mass mass of an object not in motion

resultant single force that has same effect as two or more concurrent vectors applied at same point

rotary motion motion of a body about an internal axis

rotational equilibrium state of body in which sum of clockwise torques in given plane equals sum of counterclockwise torques about pivot point

rotational inertia resistance to change in angular velocity of rotating object

scalar quantity, such as time or mass, that has magnitude only

scientific notation method in which numbers are expressed in the form of $M \times 10^n$, where M is a number between one and ten and n is an integral power of ten

second fundamental SI unit of time measurement, equivalent to 9,192,631,770 emission cycles of cesium-133

shear strain ratio of amount of deformation of the side of a body to length of the side

SI Système Internationale; internationally recognized metric system of measurement

simple harmonic motion motion in which particle repeats the same path periodically

simple machine lever, pulley, wheel and axle, inclined plane, wedge, or screw

solid state of matter in which particles are close together and in fixed positions relative to each other

special theory of relativity theory formulated by Albert Einstein that physical laws remain constant in inertial reference systems for all freely moving observers, regardless of their speed

standing wave wave in which nodes are stationary; resultant of two identical waves traveling in opposite directions through same medium

state physical condition of matter

stationary state condition not changing with time and therefore appearing identical at any instant

strain amount of distortion produced in body under stress

stress distorting force per unit area

sublimation change from solid to gaseous state without intermediate liquid phase

surface tension strong attraction of surface particles for each other due to unbalanced forces; tendency of liquid surface to contract

surface wave surface disturbance with

characteristics of both transverse and longitudinal waves

symmetry property that is unchanged by altered operations or reference frames; invariance

Système Internationale *French.* SI; International System of Units

tensile strength maximum stress any material subjected to a stretching load can withstand without tearing

terminal velocity velocity of falling object when flow of air resistance is equal to weight

torque force producing torsion or rotation in an object

torque arm perpendicular distance between force producing torque and axis of rotation

trajectory curve described by an object moving through space as it is affected by gravitational attraction of other objects

translational equilibrium state in which no unbalanced forces are acting on body

transverse wave wave in which disturbance is at right angles to direction of wave

trough region of downward displacement in transverse wave

uncertainty principle theory in quantum mechanics, formulated by Werner Heisenberg, that the more accurately the position of a particle is specified, the less accurately its momentum can be known, and that one can never be exactly sure of both

unified field theory principle that gravitational and electromagnetic forces can be expressed within single unified framework

uniform circular motion circular path described by particles that move at a constant angular velocity

uniform quantity quantity of constant value, such as acceleration or speed

universal gas constant constant of proportionality in ideal gas equation

universal gravitational constant constant of proportionality in Newton's law of universal gravitation

vacuum enclosed space out of which almost all matter has been removed

vapor gaseous phase of substance normally a solid or liquid

vaporization change of liquid or solid to gas or vapor by application of heat; volatilization

vector quantity that has both magnitude and direction

velocity rate of change of position in particular direction

viscosity resistance that a gas or liquid system offers to flow when it is subjected to shear stress

viscous fluid slow-flowing fluid

volatile fluid fluid that is easily evaporated

volatilization vaporization

wave traveling disturbance in a medium that does not create any permanent displacement in that medium

wave equation any of the fundamental equations of quantum mechanics whose solutions are possible wave functions of a particle

wave front real or imaginary surface at which phase of oscillation is identical for all adjacent points

wavelength distance between corresponding phase points, such as two adjacent troughs or crests, on two successive waves

weight measure of gravitational force of Earth or celestial body on an object, proportional but not equal to mass

work product of displacement and force in direction of displacement

work function energy needed to remove one electron from surface of material into field-free space

Young's modulus ratio of stress to strain in a solid

Electricity and Magnetism

AC alternating current

acceptor substance with three valence electrons added to semiconductor crystal to provide electron holes in lattice

adhesion attraction between unlike particles

alternating current AC; current that periodically changes direction at certain levels, measured in volts

ampere unit that measures rate of flow of charged particles, equal to one coulomb of charge per second

angstrom unit of linear measure used to express wavelengths of optical spectra, equal to 10^{-10} meter

anode positive terminal of electrolytic cell

armature coil of wire that produces current in generator and rotation in electric motor

back electromotive force potential difference created by motion of armature in operating motor; counter electromotive force

battery cell two dissimilar conductors that combine with an electrolyte to produce a potential difference

cathode negative electrode in electrolytic cell

conductor material that can transmit charged particles

coulomb SI unit of electric charge, equal to the charge found on 6.25×10^{18} electrons; amount of charge that crosses surface in one second when current of one ampere flows across it

Coulomb's law product of the charges on two objects divided by square of the distance between the charges times constant K equals the force between the charges

counter electromotive force back electromotive force

DC direct current

diamagnetism property by which an object is repelled by a powerful magnet

dielectric nonconducting medium; insulator

diode solid-state device or tube with anode and cathode which rectifies alternating current and

allows current to pass freely in one direction only

direct current DC; current that flows in one direction only and has virtually invariable magnitude

domain region of solid in which magnetic fields in atoms are aligned in common direction

donor substance with five valence electrons that provides free electrons in lattice structure of semiconductor crystal

dynamo generator

effective resistance resistance of a single resistor that could replace a combination of resistors

electric charge property of particle that attracts or repels other particles of opposite or like charge

electric circuit continuous path that can be followed by charged particles

electric current flow of charged particles

electric field space around charged object in which force acts on other charged objects

electric field intensity ratio of force exerted by electric field on charged particle per unit of positive charge

electric field lines lines representing direction of electric field

electric force force created between two objects due to their charges

electricity fundamental physical property caused by movement of electrons and other charged particles, manifested as attraction and repulsion

electrode grid

electrolyte conducting medium in which flow of current leads to movement of charged ions

electromagnet device in which magnetic field is generated by electric current

electromagnetic force fundamental force that exists between electrically charged particles

electromagnetic induction generation of electric current when magnetic flux lines cut through wire

electromagnetic interaction force that keeps electrons in orbit and forms bonds between atoms and molecules

electromagnetic wave wave composed of electric and magnetic fields that are perpendicular to each other and that move at speed of light in space

electromagnetism interrelationship of magnetic fields and electric currents

electromotive force EMF; potential difference generated by electromagnetic induction

electron subatomic particle of small mass and negative charge that orbits atomic nucleus

electron collision excitation collision between electron and atom that results in excited atom

electron gas free electrons moving through metallic conductor

electronics branch of physics dealing with behavior of electrons

electroscope device used to detect presence of electrostatic charges

electrostatic charge charge at rest, as on an object

EMF electromotive force

excited atom atom with one or more electrons at higher than normal energy level

farad unit of capacitance equal to one coulomb per volt

faraday quantity of electricity required to deposit one chemical equivalent of an element during electrolysis, equal to 96,500 coulombs

Faraday's law mass of an element deposited during electrolysis is proportional both to amount of charge passing through the electrolytic cell and to chemical equivalent of that element

frequency number of vibrations, oscillations, or cycles per unit of time

fresnel unit of frequency equal to 10^{12} cycles per second

galvanic cell battery cell

galvanometer instrument used to measure very small electric current

generator device that uses mechanical energy to produce electric energy; dynamo

grid element of electronic tube; electrode

grounding connection of charged object to Earth or other neutral site to remove object's charge

henry unit of inductance in closed circuit where electromotive force of one volt is produced by current variation of one ampere per second

hertz unit of frequency equal to one cycle per second

impedance total opposition to alternating current by circuit, expressed in ohms

inductance property of electric circuit by which varying current induces electromotive force in that circuit

inductive reactance opposition to alternating current due to self-induction

insulator material that greatly restricts the transmission of charged particles; dielectric

interference combination of two waves or disturbances that arrive at same point at same time

inverse photoelectric effect emission of photons from material bombarded by high speed electrons

ion charged atom or group of atoms resulting from loss or gain of one or more electrons

ionization energy energy required to remove an electron from an atom to an infinite distance

Joule's law amount of heat generated in watts when electricity flows through a substance, equal to the resistance of the substance in ohms times the square of the current in amperes

law of conservation of charge electric charge can be neither created nor destroyed

Lenz's law magnetic field generated by an induced current always opposes the field generating the current

line of force imaginary line in field of force positioned so that its tangent indicates direction of electric field

magnetic field region around a magnet in which magnetic forces can be detected

magnetic flux total of all magnetic flux lines through a region of a magnetic field

magnetic flux density number of magnet flux lines per unit area; magnetic induction

magnetic flux line line of force representing magnetic induction

magnetic force force between two objects due to magnetic flux of one or both objects

magnetic induction strength of a magnetic field; magnetic flux density

magnetic moment vector quantity that when multiplied by magnetic induction equals torque of given magnet or current acting on given object

magnetism fundamental phenomena in which magnets and electric currents exhibit force fields

microwave radio wave of a few centimeters' wavelength

ohm unit of electric resistance equal to one volt per ampere

Ohm's law current that flows in a circuit varies directly with the potential difference, or voltage, and inversely with the resistance

oscilloscope instrument with cathode-ray tube in which external voltages deflect electron beam simultaneously along vertical and horizontal axes to form image of wave

paramagnetism property exhibited by substances which, when placed in magnetic field, are magnetized in direct proportion to the field strength

phase angular relationship between current and AC voltage

photovoltaic cell device for converting light into electric energy

piezoelectricity production of electric current in certain crystals through deformation by mechanical stress

plate anode of electronic tube

potential difference difference in potential energy per unit charge between two points in electric field

potentiometer variable resistor

primary transformer winding that carries or induces current in one or more secondary windings

radio waves electromagnetic radiations produced by rapid current shifts in conductor

reactance opposition of inductance and capacitance to alternating current, expressed in ohms

receiver device used to detect electromagnetic waves and render them perceptible to the senses

rectifier device that changes AC to DC

resistance opposition to flow of electric current; ratio of potential difference across conductor to magnitude of current in it

schematic diagram map of electric circuit using symbols

secondary transformer output winding in which current is produced

self-induction production of voltage in a circuit, induced when the current is varied rapidly in that same circuit

series circuit circuit in which charged particles follow a single path through components

siemens SI unit of electrical conductance equal to reciprocal of the ohm

storage cell electrochemical cell that can be regenerated by external reverse currents

superconductivity state of some materials which exhibit zero resistance at very low temperatures; similar state exhibited by ceramic materials at higher temperatures

temporary magnet magnet produced by induction

tesla unit of magnetic induction equal to one weber per square meter

thermionic emission electron emission from surface of heated body

thermocouple electric circuit composed of two dissimilar metals joined at different temperatures

thermoelectric effect production of current in closed circuit composed of two dissimilar metals, in which the junctions are maintained at different temperatures

transformer device used to transfer energy from one circuit to another circuit by mutual inductance across two coils

transistor semiconductor device used as substitute for vacuum tube to control current flow in electronics

triode vacuum tube consisting of grid between anode and cathode

vacuum tube electron tube that contains grids and from which air has been evacuated to highest possible degree

Van de Graaff generator particle accelerator that transfers charge from electron source to insulated sphere on moving insulator belt

volt SI unit of potential difference between two points of conductor with constant one ampere current when one watt of power is dissipated between them

voltaic cell device that changes chemical into electric energy by immersion of two dissimilar metals in electrolyte

voltmeter device used to measure potential difference between two points in circuit

watt unit of power equal to one joule per second

weber SI unit of magnetic flux, equal to one volt x one second

Nuclear and Particle Physics

accelerator device that uses electromagnets to increase velocity and add energy to moving charged particles; atom smasher

albedo degree to which surface reflects subatomic particles that strike it

alpha particle helium nucleus that consists of two protons and two neutrons after it is emitted from radioactive atom's nucleus

amu atomic mass unit

antimatter substance composed of antiparticles

antiparticle particle that has the same mass and spin as its subatomic counterpart but opposite charge and magnetic moment

antiquark antiparticle of quark

atom basic unit of matter, composed of protons, neutrons, and electrons

atomic mass unit amu; unit of mass for atomic and subatomic particles, equal to 1/12 the mass of most common isotope of carbon, used to express atomic weight; dalton

atomic number number of protons in nucleus of an atom

atomic theory explanation of various phenomena by theory of properties and interactions of atoms and subatomic particles

atomic weight mass of atom expressed in atomic mass units

atom smasher accelerator

atom-splitting fission

backscatter reflection and reversal of direction of radiation by traversed medium

baryon subatomic particle with large rest mass undergoing strong interactions

beta particle high-speed electron or positron emitted from radioactive nucleus

binding energy energy required to separate nucleus into individual nucleons; separation energy

Bohr theory electrons revolve around nucleus in definite orbits and radiation is absorbed or emitted only when an electron moves from one orbit to another

boson subatomic particle, such as a photon or pi meson, that does not obey exclusion principle

breeder reactor nuclear reactor that produces more fissionable material than is consumed

bubble chamber container of superheated liquid in which paths of ionizing particles appear as strings of vapor bubbles

calutron early device for separating isotopes by atomic mass

carbon 14 radioactive isotope of carbon used in radiocarbon dating

cascade particle least massive of xi particles

chain reaction self-sustaining series of nuclear reactions, in which products of reaction sustain process

charm quantum number assigned the value +1 for one kind of quark, -1 for its antiquark, and zero for all other quarks

cloud chamber closed vessel in which paths of charged subatomic particles appear as trails of liquid droplets

cohesive force attraction between like particles

cold fusion hypothetical fusion of atomic nuclei at much lower temperature and pressure than now required

collider particle accelerator in which positively and negatively charged particles circulate in opposite directions and collide head-on

color hypothetical force or charge on each type of quark that controls how they combine to form hadrons

Compton effect increase in X-ray wavelength due to interaction of X-rays and electrons as X-rays traverse matter

control rods devices in nuclear reactor used to regulate rate of nuclear reaction

core central part of reactor containing fissile fuel and rods

critical mass amount of particular fissionable material required to make fission reaction self-sustaining

curie unit of radioactivity equal to 3.7×10^{10} disintegrations per second of any radioactive nuclide

cyclotron device that accelerates positively charged atomic particles by means of D-shaped electrodes, used to initiate nuclear transformations

dalton atomic mass unit

decay spontaneous radioactive disintegration in which nucleus undergoes transformation into one or more different nuclei and emits radiation, loses electrons, or undergoes fission

dee electrode of cyclotron

deuterium isotope which replaces hydrogen in heavy water

deuteron charged particle equivalent to nucleus of hydrogen isotope deuterium, consisting of one proton and one neutron

dose quantity of radiation absorbed by matter

drift tube tubular electrode placed in vacuum chamber of circular accelerator to accelerate charged subatomic particles

dynamics study of the motion of particles acted upon by forces

dyne unit of force that produces acceleration of one centimeter per second per second on mass of one gram

electron cloud region of high probability of finding an electron

elementary particle indivisible particle within atomic nucleus

enrichment process in which number of fissionable nuclei of an element such as uranium is increased

erg unit equal to work done by force of one dyne acting across one centimeter

excited particle atom or subatomic particle raised to higher energy state

exclusion principle no two identical particles in a system can carry the same quantum number

fast neutron neutron with kinetic energy greater than thermal energy

fermion subatomic particle, such as a lepton or baryon, that obeys exclusion principle

fission splitting of heavy nucleus into nuclei of intermediate mass; atom-splitting

fusion reaction in which nuclei of light atoms combine to form nuclei with larger mass numbers

gamma ray electromagnetic wave of extremely high frequency emitted by nucleus of radioactive atom; high-energy photon

gas centrifuge device used to separate enriched, fissionable isotopes of an element from nonfissionable isotopes by centrifugal action

Geiger counter Geiger-Müller tube

Geiger-Müller tube device that detects radiation of subatomic particles by use of ionizing property of radiation; Geiger counter

gluon massless quantum of energy believed to carry force that binds quarks together within subatomic particles

graviton theoretical subatomic particle, without charge or mass, believed to carry gravitational force between bodies

hadron any heavy elementary particle that takes part in the strong interaction

half-life length of time during which one half of a sample of radioactive nuclides decays

heavy hydrogen hydrogen isotope with mass number greater than one; deuterium or tritium

heavy water water in which hydrogen atoms are replaced by heavier deuterium isotopes

hodoscope instrument that traces the paths of high-energy particles

hypercharge property of some baryons and leptons conserved in strong electromagnetic interactions

hyperon any baryon which has nonzero strangeness quantum number and relatively long lifetime

inertial confinement method of producing fusion by laser implosion of deuterium or tritium pellets

interaction change in quantum numbers of particles in close proximity

isobar one of two atoms that have equal mass numbers but different atomic numbers

isomer any of two or more nuclei with same number of neutrons and protons but different energy states

isotone atom with same number of neutrons as another atom but different atomic number

isotope any of two or more forms of an atom of some element with nearly identical chemical properties, but containing different number of neutrons and same number of protons, therefore having different mass

isotopic spin quantum number related to number of different values of electric charge that given baryon or meson may have

kaon any of four mesons that are positive, negative, or neutral, with mass 970 times that of electron; k meson

k meson kaon

lambda particle neutral baryon with strangeness number -1 and isotopic spin zero

lepton subatomic particle with small rest mass

linear accelerator device that accelerates charged particles in a straight line through many stages of small potential difference

mass defect difference in mass between actual atomic nucleus and sum of particles from which nucleus is made

mass number sum of protons and neutrons in nucleus of atom, being integer nearest to its atomic weight

mass spectroscope device used to measure the mass of small, electrically charged particles

meltdown melting of nuclear reactor core due to inadequate cooling of fuel, possibly leading to escape of radiation

meson any hadron or subatomic particle with rest mass intermediate between lepton and baryon, consisting of a quark and antiquark

moderator material used to decrease speed of fast neutrons in nuclear reactor

Mössbauer effect phenomenon in which gamma rays do not lose energy from the recoil of certain radioactive isotope nuclei which are bound in a crystal lattice, resulting in sharply defined wavelength

mu meson muon

muon high-speed lepton, either positive or negative, with mass 207 times that of electron, that decays into electron and two neutrinos with very brief life; mu meson

neutrino chargeless, nearly massless elementary particle affected only by weak force; type of lepton emitted along with beta particles

neutron uncharged subatomic particle of approximate mass comparable to proton, making up half of the particles in all atomic nuclei except those of hydrogen

nuclear binding energy energy required to separate an atom into its constituent nucleons

nuclear equation equation representing a nuclear reaction; strong force equation

nuclear force very short-range force that holds protons and neutrons together in atomic nucleus; strong force

nuclear moderator substance used to slow neutrons in reactor

nuclear reactor device used to obtain energy from controlled fission reaction; reactor

nucleon proton or neutron in atomic nucleus

nucleus positively charged, dense core of an atom, containing protons and neutrons

nuclide any atom of a particular element

omega particle particle that decays into cascade particle after colliding with pi meson

pair production creation of electron-positron pair from energy

particle piece of matter of negligible size that has both charge and mass

photon massless quantum of electromagnetic radiation or light energy

pile early term for nuclear reactor

pi meson meson with mass 270 times that of electron and spin of zero

Planck's law light or other waves can be emitted or absorbed only in discrete quanta whose energy is proportional to their frequency

planetary model model of an atom in which the electrons orbit the nucleus as the planets orbit the sun

positron positively charged antiparticle of electron

protium most common hydrogen isotope, with mass number one

proton positively charged subatomic particle of

mass one atomic mass unit that is fundamental constituent of all atomic nuclei

quark any of basic, hypothetical particles that, along with antiquarks, constitute all elementary particles: designated up, down, strange, charm, beauty or bottom, and truth or top

rad measured dosage of absorbed ionizing radiation, equal to 100 ergs per gram

radiation energy emitted as electromagnetic waves, gamma or X-rays, or as energetic nuclear particles

radioactive materials substances that exhibit phenomenon of radioactivity

radioactivity spontaneous decay of unstable atomic nucleus with emission of particles and rays

radiocarbon dating determination of age of artifact based on known rate of decay of carbon-14 isotope

radioelement radioactive element occurring naturally or produced artificially

radioisotope radioactive isotope, usu. artificially produced

reactor nuclear reactor

rem measured dose of ionizing radiation whose biological effect is equal to that produced by one roentgen of X-rays

rod control rod in nuclear reactor

roentgen standard unit that measures ionizing radiation from X-rays or gamma rays

Rutherford atom atom in which negatively charged electrons revolve around a small, positively charged nucleus that constitutes nearly its entire atomic mass

scintillation flash of light or charged subatomic particle emitted when substance is struck by radiation

secondary emission emission of electrons due to bombardment of electrode by high-velocity electrons

separation energy binding energy

sigma particle unstable hyperon having strangeness number -1

slow neutron neutron with less kinetic energy than thermal energy

solid state detector device used to detect passage of charged subatomic particles by their ionizing or distorting effects on a non- or semi-conducting solid

spark chamber device used to detect passage of charged subatomic particles by light flashes they trigger

spin intrinsic angular momentum of each kind of elementary particle that exists even when particle is at rest, as distinguished from orbital angular momentum

strangeness number quantum number characteristic of a quark or a strongly interacting particle that is conserved in strong interactions with other fundamental particles, assigned a value of +1, -1, or zero

strange quark quark having strangeness -1 and a charge one-third that of an elementary charge, being more massive than up and down quarks

string hypothetical basic unit of matter, neither wave nor particle but thin, curved string with length dimension only

string theory theory of fundamental physics in which basic entity in four dimensions of space-time is one-dimensional object rather than zero-dimensional point of conventional elementary particle physics

strong force force that holds quarks together with protons and neutrons within atomic nucleus, independent of charge; strongest of four fundamental forces, but with shortest range

strong force equation nuclear equation

strong interaction interaction between gluons and between gluons and quarks that is responsible for strong force

strontium 90 deadly radioactive isotope of strontium present in fallout from nuclear explosions and other fission-produced waste

subatomic particle one of several constituent parts of atoms: protons, neutrons, electrons, their component particles, and quarks

supercollider massive, extremely high-speed particle accelerator

superstring theory fundamental theory of subatomic particles in which all matter and energy are derived from vibration modes of one-dimensional strings that control all forces and matter; combination of string theory and supersymmetry

supersymmetry hypothetical symmetry among groups of particles containing fermions and bosons, esp. in theory of gravity as single unified force encompassing strong force, weak force, and electromagnetism

synchrotron particle accelerator with variable oscillating frequency

thermonuclear reaction nuclear fusion reaction

tracer radioactive isotope used to follow chemical process or determine physical properties

transmutation nuclear change of one element into another

transuranic element any element that has an atomic number greater than 92

tritium radioactive isotope of hydrogen with atomic weight three, used in thermonuclear devices and as tracer

truth elusive sixth quark, also designated top, believed to have a mass 90 to 250 times that of proton

virtual particle particle that cannot be directly detected but whose existence has measurable effects

wave-particle duality quantum mechanics theory that waves and particles are indistinguishable and sometimes behave alike

weak force force involved in decay of atomic nuclei and nuclear particles; second weakest of four fundamental forces, with very short range and no effect on force-carrying particles

weak interaction interaction between elementary particles and the bosons that carry the weak force from particle to particle

weakly interactive massive particle WIMP; small gravitational mass particle, believed to form cold, dark matter comprising ninety percent of universe

WIMP weakly interactive massive particle

xi particle baryon having strangeness number -2 and isotopic spin 1/2

Z-zero particle short-lived, very heavy particle, identical to photon except for mass, that conveys part of weak force between neighboring hadrons and leptons

Cosmology

anthropic principle the universe appears as it does because if it were different we would not be here to observe it

antigravity hypothetical force by which one body would repel another; opposite of gravity, never detected experimentally

big bang model theory that universe originated in explosion of hot, dense core that rapidly expanded to cooler, more diffuse states

big crunch singularity at end of universe that reverses big bang effect

black dwarf cold remnant of white dwarf star after thermal energy is exhausted

black hole highly concentrated mass that has collapsed to such a degree that the escape velocity from its surface is greater than the speed of light, so that light and all other energy and matter is trapped in an intense gravitational field

blue shift shift of spectral lines toward shorter wavelengths, observed in celestial objects that are approaching observer

Chandrasekhar limit maximum possible mass of stable cold star, beyond which it will collapse to become a black hole

chaos phenomenon of unpredictability and randomness on all scales of physical structures, opp. of cosmos

chaotic dynamics time-dependent, nonperiodic regime in which individual histories corresponding to initially close states tend to diverge exponentially over time

cold dark matter fundamental particles with no force other than gravity that comprise ninety percent of universe

cosmic background radiation uniform radioactive hiss that fills space, measured at 3 degrees Kelvin

cosmogony study of possible origin and evolution of universe

cosmological principle assumption that universe would appear the same viewed from any point in it

cosmology study of structure of universe as a whole

cosmos orderly and harmonious universe that follows ascertainable laws, opp. of chaos

critical density mass density above which expansion of universe should slow down and reverse

curved space warping of space-time due to presence of massive bodies

determinism doctrine that every occurrence in universe is the result of a sequence of causes and effects

differential microwave radiometer device used to measure variations in brightness of cosmic background radiation

event specific point in space-time

event horizon boundary of black hole or other singularity

expanding universe model of universe based on big bang

grand unification energy energy above which electromagnetic, strong, and weak nuclear forces become indistinguishable

grand unification theory theory which unifies electromagnetic, strong, and weak forces

Hubble constant constant that represents rate of expansion of universe

light cone surface in space-time delineating possible directions for light rays that pass through given event

matter era period beginning 100,000 years after big bang, when universe had cooled so that electrons and protons could begin forming hydrogen atoms

microwave background radiation redshifted radiation from glow of early universe that does not appear as light but as microwaves of extremely high frequency

naked singularity space time singularity not surrounded by an event horizon, thus kept from our view

neutron star cold or collapsed star in which gravitational force has caused combination of electrons and protons to form neutrons

no boundary condition theory that universe is finite but has no boundary

primordial black hole black hole created very early in life of universe

pulsar rotating neutron star whose radio emissions reach Earth in pulses, usu. at regular intervals

pulsating universe theory variation on expanding universe theory, in which cycle of expansion and contraction to and from primeval nucleus is endlessly repeated

quasar *quasi*-stellar radio source; powerful source of light and radio energy at limits of known universe, probably a highly luminous galaxy that has violently exploded

radiation era early stage of universe prior to matter era, when simple nuclei could be formed

redshift shift, due to Doppler effect, in spectral lines of object toward red end of spectrum as it recedes from observer, with degree of shift proportional to object's speed

Schwarzschild radius radius at which gravitationally collapsing celestial body becomes a black hole

singularity point in space-time at which space-time curvature becomes infinite and at

which measurable quantities become exactly zero or infinitely large

singularity theory theory that universe started with a singularity

space-time continuum four-dimensional continuum with coordinates being three spatial dimensions and time; way of representing universe suggested by theory of relativity

space-time curvature conceptual form in which four-dimensional space-time is represented as a curve

spatial dimension any of three dimensions of space-time, other than time

steady state model theory of expanding universe stipulating continuous creation of matter, and stating that universe maintains uniform large-scale structure and constant average density at all times

supermassive black hole hypothetical singularity at center of some active galaxies or quasars

supernova explosion of massive star near end of its life, possibly due to gravitational collapse, causing greatly increased luminosity and loss of most of star's mass, sometimes leaving behind dense core; white dwarf star in close binary system producing explosions from mass taken from its companion star

unified field theory principle that all forces in universe are part of single concept

universe sum total of potentially knowable objects, matter, and energy, believed to be infinite in space and time

white dwarf very small, faint, cold star that has undergone gravitational collapse

white hole hypothetical time-reversed black hole

Heat

absolute zero temperature at which gas has zero volume and molecular kinetic energy is at minimum, equal to -459.7 degrees F, -273.2 degrees C, or zero degrees Kelvin

adiabatic process thermal process in which no heat is added to or removed from system

advection horizontal flow of atmospheric properties

aneroid barometer device that uses partially evacuated box to measure atmospheric pressure

bimetallic strip two dissimilar metals welded together so that thermal expansion causes strip to bend

Boyle's law volume of a fixed mass of gas kept at constant temperature varies inversely with pressure

British thermal unit BTU; quantity of heat equal to 252 calories

Brownian motion (or **movement**) random motion of colloidal particles due to bombardment of the particles by molecules of the surrounding medium.

BTU **B**ritish **t**hermal **u**nit

calorie quantity of heat equal to 4.187 joules

Celsius temperature scale with zero degrees equal to freezing point of water and 100 degrees equal to boiling point of water at standard atmospheric pressure; Centigrade

Centigrade Celsius

Charles' law volume of a fixed mass of gas at constant pressure varies directly with its absolute temperature

coefficient of expansion change in area, volume, or length per unit area, volume, or length of a solid per degree change in its temperature

condensation change of state from gas to liquid

convection transfer of heat in a fluid, either by absorption or by rejection once the fluid has moved

convection current current caused by motion of a fluid, caused by differences in density due to thermal expansion

critical constant density, pressure, or temperature associated with critical point of pure element or compound

critical point point at which pure element or compound in one phase, as liquid, has same density, pressure, and temperature as in another phase, as gaseous

cryogenics production and effects of very low temperatures

dew point temperature to which air must be cooled at given pressure to reach saturation

Edison effect emission of electrons from metal when heated in a vacuum

evaporation change of state from liquid to gas or vapor

Fahrenheit temperature scale with 32 degrees equal to freezing point of water and 212 degrees equal to boiling point of water at standard atmospheric pressure

first law of thermodynamics when heat is converted to another form of energy, or vice versa, there is no loss of energy

heat quantity of thermal energy being added to an object, or moved from one object to another, because of a temperature difference

heat capacity quantity of heat required to increase temperature of a body by one degree

heat engine device that converts heat energy into mechanical work

heat of fusion energy required per unit mass to change substance from solid to liquid at its melting point

heat of vaporization energy required per unit mass to change substance from liquid to gas at its boiling point

heat sink entity that absorbs heat without significant temperature increase

kelvin SI unit of heat measurement, equal to 1/273 of Kelvin temperature scale

Kelvin temperature scale with zero degrees equaling absolute zero, and 273.16 degrees equaling freezing point of water

kinetic theory of heat theory that particles in a gas move freely and rapidly in straight lines and often collide, causing changes in their velocity and direction

law of heat exchange in any heat transfer system, hot materials lose amount of heat equal to that gained by cold materials

mechanical equivalent of heat conversion factor relating heat units to work units, equal to 4.19 joules per calorie

melting point temperature at which solid changes to liquid

regelation phenomenon in which a substance kept at constant temperature melts under pressure and refreezes when pressure is eliminated

relative humidity ratio of water vapor pressure in atmosphere to equilibrium vapor pressure at given temperature

second law of thermodynamics heat flows from area of high temperature to area of lower temperature unless work is done to reverse this process

specific heat energy required to change temperature of one kilogram of a substance one degree Kelvin

standard pressure pressure exerted by 760 mm of mercury at zero degrees Celsius

supercooling cooling of substance below normal phase-change point without inducing change of phase

temperature physical quantity measured by the average kinetic energy of particles in matter

thermal energy sum of potential energy and kinetic energy in random motion of particles of a material

thermal excitation act of stimulating and altering an atom by heating it

thermal expansion moving apart of particles as their temperature rises

thermal unit any of various standard measures of heat

thermometer device used to measure temperature

third law of thermodynamics temperature of a system cannot be reduced to absolute zero in a finite number of operations

transition temperature temperature at which resistance of some materials to electric current suddenly drops to zero

Optics

absorption spectrum continuous spectrum of energy absorbed by gaseous atoms of element as white light passes through it

achromatic lens lens which forms images whose outline is free from prismatic colors

actinic rays light rays, esp. at ultraviolet end of spectrum, that produce chemical changes

actinology study of the chemical effects of light rays

albedo reflecting power of a body, expressed as ratio of reflected light to total light falling on surface

angle of incidence angle between light ray and line perpendicular to surface the ray is meeting

angle of reflection angle between reflected light ray and line perpendicular to the point of incidence

angle of refraction angle between refracted ray and line perpendicular to surface the ray is leaving

band spectrum emission spectrum consisting of fluted bands of color, characteristic of molecular gases and chemical compounds

beam parallel rays of light considered together

black light ultraviolet or infrared radiation used for fluorescent effects in the dark

candela SI unit of luminous intensity, equal to intensity of a source that emits monochromatic radiation of frequency 540×10^{12} hertz

candle former standard unit of luminous intensity, equal to five square millimeters of platinum at 1773.5 degrees C

candlepower measure of luminous intensity

center of curvature center of sphere from which a spherical mirror is cut

chromatic aberration failure of a lens to bring all wavelengths of light in focus at the same point

chromatics study of hue and saturation of colors

coherent light light in which all waves leaving the source are in phase and have identical wavelengths

color property of an object with respect to light reflected by it in particular wavelengths forming a spectrum from red to violet

complementary colors primary and secondary colors that combine to produce white light

concave lens lens that diverges parallel light rays

concave mirror mirror that converges parallel light rays on its surface

continuous spectrum spectrum without dark lines or bands or with uninterrupted changes between colors

converging lens lens, thick in the middle and thin at the edge, that bends parallel rays toward common point

converging mirror concave mirror that causes parallel rays to converge

convex lens lens that converges parallel rays

convex mirror mirror that diverges parallel light rays on its surface

critical angle minimum angle of incidence that produces total internal reflection

diffraction bending of light waves around an object in their path into region behind obstacle

diffraction angle angle that diffracted wave front forms with grating plane

diffraction grating optical surface ruled with thousands of parallel, equally spaced grooves, used to diffract light

diffuse reflection irregularly reflected light scattered in many directions

dispersion refraction of polychromatic light into spectrum of its component wavelengths

diverging lens lens, thin in the middle and thick at the edge, that causes incident parallel rays to diverge as though from a common point

diverging mirror convex mirror that causes parallel light rays to diverge

elementary colors seven color regions in spectrum observed by dispersion of sunlight: red, orange, yellow, green, blue, indigo, and violet

emission spectrum spectrum produced by dispersion of light from excited atoms of an element

fiber optics branch of optics dealing with transmission of data or communications in form of light pulses through transparent fibers

first law of photoelectric emission rate of photoelectron emission is proportional to intensity of incident light

fluorescence emission of light by atoms excited during absorption of radiation from outside source

focal length distance from focal point to vertex or optical center of mirror or lens

focal point point of convergence, real or apparent, of rays reflected by mirror or refracted by lens

focus point at which light rays meet, or from which light rays appear to diverge or converge

Fraunhofer spectrum absorption lines that appear in the solar spectrum, due to gases in solar atmosphere

hertz SI unit of frequency, equal to one cycle per second

illuminated body object on which light is falling

illumination rate at which light energy falls on a given area of a surface

image optical counterpart of object formed by lenses or mirrors

incandescence emission of light due to thermal excitation

incident light light rays that fall upon or strike something

index of refraction number expressing speed of light in given medium, as ratio of either speed of light in a vacuum or speed in some specified medium to that in the given medium

infrared light electromagnetic waves longer than visible light and shorter than microwaves

irregular reflection scattering of light in many different directions from an irregular surface

laser light amplification by stimulated emission of radiation; device used to produce coherent light of great intensity

law of reflection angle of incidence is equal to angle of reflection when a light ray is reflected from a smooth surface

light electromagnetic radiation, ranging in wavelength from 4×10^{-7} to 7×10^{-7} meter, that causes sensation of vision

line spectrum electromagnetic spectrum made up of discrete lines, usu. characteristic of excited atoms or molecules

lumen unit of luminous flux on surface, all

points of which are at unit distance from a point source of one candle

luminescence emission of light caused by absorption of radiant or corpuscular energy, not by incandescence

luminous body object visible due to emission of light from oscillating particles

luminous flux flow of light from a source

luminous intensity measure of light emitted by a source

magnification ratio of image distance or size to object distance or size

monochromatic light light of only one wavelength and color

Nicol prism one of a pair of prisms cemented together, used to produce and analyze light vibrating in a single plane as it passes through them

objective lens light-gathering and image-forming lens of microscope or telescope

opaque material material that does not transmit light

optical density property that determines the speed of light, and thus index of refraction, through a transparent medium

optical fiber very thin, flexible, transparent glass or plastic fiber that makes use of total internal reflection to transmit information in form of light pulses

optics study of propagation, control, transmission, reception, effects, and phenomena of light waves

penumbra partially illuminated portion of a shadow

phosphorescence emission of light from atoms excited by outside source that persists for a time after outside source is removed

photic (*adj*) of or relating to light

photoelastic (*adj*) of or pertaining to certain materials that are capable of double refraction when under stress

photoelectric effect ejection of electrons from surface, usu. of metal, exposed to light or electromagnetic radiation

photoelectron electron ejected by photoelectric effect

photometry quantitative measurement of visible radiation emitted from light sources

photon quantum of electromagnetic waves or light energy

photon collision excitation collision between photon and atom resulting in an excited atom

photovoltaic cell device used to convert light into electric energy

plane polarization polarization of light in which vibrations are confined to a single plane

polarized light light in which vibrations of all waves are in the same or parallel planes in optical region

polychromatic light light composed of several wavelengths and colors

primary color red, yellow, or blue light, from which all other colors may be described or evolved by mixture

primary pigment yellow, cyan, or magenta pigment; complement of primary colors

principal axis radius connecting center of curvature of curved mirror with its geometric vertex, or center of curvature of lens with its optical center

principal focus point at which rays parallel to principal axis either converge or diverge after reflection or refraction

pumping excitation of very large number of atoms by laser

quantum theory of light light is emitted and absorbed in small discrete packets called quanta; the energy in each quantum can be expressed as $E = hf$, where E is energy, h is Planck's constant, and f is frequency

ray single line of light that radiates from a luminous point

real image image formed by rays of light that actually recombine

reflection return of light wave from boundary of a medium

refraction bending of wave front as it passes obliquely from one medium to another

resolving power ability of optical device to produce separate images of two closely spaced objects

saturation degree of purity of a color, measured by absence of dilution by white

secondary color color, such as orange, green, or violet, produced by mixing two primary colors

secondary pigment red, green, or blue pigment; complement of secondary color

second law of photoelectric emission kinetic energy of photoelectrons is independent of intensity of incident light

Snell's law equation relating angle of incidence and index of refraction for ray incident on interface of two media

solar ray ray of sunlight

solar spectrum band of colors produced by dispersal of sunlight through a prism

spectroscope optical instrument used to study spectra

spectrum array of various wavelengths that compose light

speed of light 3.00×10^8 meters per second in a vacuum, or approximately 186,000 miles per second

spherical aberration failure of spherical mirror to focus all rays that are parallel to principal axis at the same point

spherical concave mirror converging mirror formed of spherical segment of one base

stopping potential potential difference needed to prevent photoelectric effect for specific metal and light of specific frequency

threshold frequency lowest frequency of light that will cause photoelectric effect for specific substance

total internal reflection reflection of a light ray at such a large angle that ray remains in its original medium

translucent material material that transmits light but distorts it during passage

transparent material material that transmits light undistorted

ultraviolet light electromagnetic radiations of shorter wavelength than visible light but longer than X-rays

umbra portion of a shadow from which all light rays are excluded

vertex center of curved mirror

virtual image image formed by light rays that appear to emanate from a point without actually doing so

white light light, such as sunlight, that is mixture of wavelengths from red to violet

X-ray invisible electromagnetic radiation that has a very short wavelength and great penetrating power

Acoustics

acoustics science of the production, effects, and transmission of sound

anechoic (*adj*) completely absorbing sound waves, therefore free from echoes

audio frequency band of audible sound frequencies between 15 hertz and 20,000 hertz

audiogram graph of hearing loss in ear as measured by audiometer

audiometer device used to measure sharpness and range of hearing

aural (*adj*) received through or relating to the sense of hearing

consonance complex sound wave perceived as harmonious chord

decibel unit of sound intensity level, one decibel being the smallest change of sound intensity perceptible to human ear

dissonance sound waves perceived as inharmonious noise

echo rebound of sound wave from impenetrable surface that results in repetition of sound

fundamental lowest frequency of sound produced by an instrument or other tone source

harmonics fundamental tone and tones whose frequencies are whole number multiples of the fundamental

octave interval between given tone and one with double or half its frequency

overtones sound waves of higher frequency than the fundamental, expressed in integral multiples only

pitch perceived tonal characteristic that is equivalent to frequency

resonance production of abnormally large vibration in response to external stimulus, occurring when stimulus frequency is at natural vibration frequency of system

sonic (*adj*) having to do with sound waves; equal to or being speed of sound in air

sonic boom shock wave associated with object moving through fluid or gas at speed greater than that of sound

sound wave longitudinal disturbance in matter

that is audible to human ear; similar disturbance that exists above and below audible range

sound intensity rate at which sound energy flows through given unit area

speed of sound approximately 741 miles per hour in air at sea level

subsonic (*adj*) less than speed of sound

supersonic (*adj*) greater than speed of sound

threshold frequency lowest sound intensity audible to average human ear

timbre quality of sound

ultrasound sound with frequency over 20,000 hertz, beyond upper limit of human hearing

white noise blend of all audible frequencies distributed equally over range of frequency band

ASTRONOMY AND SPACE SCIENCE

Celestial Bodies
Celestial Phenomena and Points
Branches, Laws, Theories, and Techniques
Signs of the Zodiac
Space Exploration and Rocketry

See also: *Chap. 3: Geology; Landscapes and Seascapes; Weather and Natural Phenomena; Chap. 4: Physics; Chap. 5: Weapons and Armaments; Chap. 6: Aircraft*

Celestial Bodies

Alpha Centauri trinary star containing Proxima Centauri

Andromeda Galaxy large, spiral galaxy relatively close to Milky Way, with similar size and shape

Ariel satellite of Uranus

asteroid one of thousands of minor planets that revolve around sun, usu. between orbital paths of Mars and Jupiter; minor planet; planetoid

asteroid belt any group of asteroids that revolve around sun in orbital path between Mars and Jupiter

barred spiral spiral galaxy with barlike structure across its center

binary star two stars in orbit around one another; double star

black dwarf cold remains of white dwarf after thermal energy is exhausted

brown dwarf lump of celestial matter larger than a planet but not massive enough to be a star or produce thermonuclear reactions at its core

Callisto one of four Galilean satellites of Jupiter

Canopus second brightest star in heavens, 650 light years distant

celestial body celestial object

celestial object any solid or gaseous entity moving through space; celestial body; heavenly body

Ceres first and largest minor planet to be discovered

Charon only known moon of Pluto

cluster star one of a group of stars that share a common origin and common motion through space

Coma cluster large collection of galaxies located visually in constellation Coma Berenices

comet diffuse cluster of gas, dust, and ice moving about sun in eccentric orbit, with dust tail trailing in its path and ion tail pointing away from sun

Crab Nebula supernova remnant in constellation Taurus

cynosure Polaris; northern constellation Ursa Minor

dark nebula nebula that obscures background starlight and does not reflect starlight toward Earth

Deimos smaller of two moons of Mars

diffuse nebula luminous formation or irregular cloud of interstellar matter within Milky Way

Dog Star Sirius

double star binary star

Dumbbell Nebula planetary nebula consisting of faint star surrounded by cloud of gas shaped like dumbbell

dwarf star with small size or mass and low luminosity

Earth fifth largest planet of solar system and third from sun: orbits sun in 365 days and rotates on its axis in twenty-four hours

eclipsing binary binary star system in which one star appears to pass in front of the other

elliptical galaxy galaxy having round or lenticular shape, without spiral arms as internal structure

equant celestial body having equal diameters in all directions

Europa one of four Galilean satellites of Jupiter

fireball brilliant meteor that often trails bright sparks

galaxy vast system of about 100 billion stars, such as Milky Way, held together by gravity in spiral, elliptical, or irregular region about 100,000 light years across

Galilean satellites four largest moons of Jupiter, first seen by Galileo Galilei: Callisto, Europa, Ganymede, and Io

Ganymede largest of four Galilean satellites of Jupiter

gas giant large planet of low density, esp. one of major planets of our solar system: Jupiter, Saturn, Uranus, or Neptune

globular cluster large collection of closely grouped old and dead stars containing little or no gas between them

Great Wall huge chain of galaxies and superclusters stretching 500 million light years across universe

Halley's Comet famous comet visible from Earth every 76 years

heavenly body celestial object

Horsehead Nebula dark nebula in constellation Orion, silhouetted against bright nebula in shape of horse's head

Io one of four Galilean satellites of Jupiter, having active volcanoes

irregular galaxy galaxy having neither spiral nor elliptical shape

Jovian satellites system of at least seventeen moons that orbit Jupiter

Jupiter largest planet of solar system and fifth from sun, famous for its Great Red Spot: orbits sun in 11.9 years and rotates on its axis in 9 hours and 50 minutes

Large Magellanic Cloud larger of two irregular galaxies interacting with Milky Way as a satellite

lenticular galaxy elliptical galaxy in elongated form with nearly pointed ends

Local Group Milky Way, Magellanic clouds, Andromeda Galaxy, and other nearby galaxies forming a local cluster in the universe two million light years across

local supercluster supercluster of galaxies relatively near Milky Way

Magellanic clouds two irregular galaxies near Milky Way, visible only from Earth's Southern Hemisphere

magnetic star star that emits strong magnetic field, detected by its effect on spectrum

major planets four largest planets of solar system: Jupiter, Saturn, Uranus, and Neptune; gas giants

Mars seventh largest planet of solar system and fourth from sun: orbits sun in 687 days and rotates on its axis in 24 hours and 24 minutes

Mercury eighth largest planet of solar system and nearest to sun: orbits sun in 88 days and rotates on its axis in 59 days

metagalaxy entire system of galaxies including the Milky Way

meteor very small particle of rock or metal orbiting sun, usu. in a swarm, that enters Earth's atmosphere and burns up; shooting star

meteorite portion of meteor that enters Earth's atmosphere and reaches ground without disintegrating

meteoroid small, solid chunk of iron, stone, or waxy material that flares to produce bright meteor

Milky Way twelve-billion-year-old spiral galaxy of which our sun is one of 150 billion stars

minor planet large asteroid in orbit around sun that is not large enough to be considered a planet

Miranda satellite of Uranus

Mira variable star whose overall brightness changes over period of about one year

moon natural satellite of a planet, esp. the celestial body that revolves around Earth from west to east every 29 1/2 days

nebula diffuse cloud of interstellar matter

Neptune fourth largest planet in solar system, usu. eighth from sun, sometimes farther from sun than Pluto: orbits sun in 165 years and rotates on its axis in 15 hours and 48 minutes

Nereid large satellite of Neptune

neutron star collapsed star of extremely high density, such as a pulsar, that is composed primarily of neutrons

North Star Polaris

nova star that increases in brilliance by several

magnitudes in a few hours due to explosive ejection of surface material

Oberon satellite of Uranus

open cluster large collection of young, massive stars, loosely grouped with abundant gas between them

Orion Nebula bright, diffuse nebula formed around stars comprising sword region of Orion constellation

Phobos larger of two moons of Mars

planet one of nine massive bodies in our solar system that revolve around sun and reflect its light; similar bodies that revolve around other stars

planetary nebula star in last stage of life, surrounded by expelled outer layers of gas, originally thought to be planets

planetoid asteroid; minor planet

Pluto smallest planet of solar system, usu. farthest from sun, with highly eccentric orbit that sometimes brings it closer to sun than Neptune: orbits sun in 248 years and rotates on its axis in 6 days and 7 hours

Polaris nearly stationary, bright, supergiant binary star located near north celestial pole; North Star; polestar

polestar conspicuous star that lies nearest to north celestial pole, Polaris

primary star or planet around which another celestial body revolves

protoplanet whirling, gaseous eddy within gas and dust cloud rotating around a sun that gives rise to a planet

protostar hypothetical, flat, circular, gaseous dust cloud in space that develops into a star

Proxima Centauri closest star to sun

pulsar rotating, collapsed neutron star of high density, composed primarily of neutrons, whose radio emissions or light reach Earth in pulses, usu. at regular intervals

quasar quasi-stellar radio source; highly luminous galaxy at limits of known universe, probably undergoing violent explosion, being a powerful source of light and energy

radio galaxy galaxy that emits stronger than normal radio waves

radio source cosmic object or phenomenon that emits radio waves; radio star

radio star radio source

red dwarf small star of low spectrum-luminosity and surface temperature

red giant large star of low surface temperature in late stage of stellar evolution, with absolute magnitude near zero

red supergiant exceptionally luminous red giant having diameter 100 times that of sun

reflection nebula nebula that reflects the light of nearby stars

Ring Nebula planetary nebula consisting of faint star surrounded by ring of gas

satellite one of many known moons of planets in solar system; artificial satellite set in orbit around planet

Saturn second largest planet of solar system and

sixth from sun, famous for its rings: orbits sun in 29.5 years and rotates on its axis in 10 hours and 39 minutes

Seyfert galaxy one of several spiral galaxies with intensely bright nuclei and strong, broad spectral lines

shepherd satellite satellite that keeps particles of a ring in their proper orbit around planet

shooting star meteor

Sirius brightest star in heavens, only nine light years distant in constellation Canis Major; Dog Star

Small Magellanic Cloud smaller of two irregular galaxies interacting with Milky Way as a satellite

solar system group of planets that orbit around common star or stars, esp. portion of Milky Way subject to gravity of our sun, including nine planets

spectroscopic binary binary star in which shifting of lines in system's spectrum indicates orbital revolution

spiral galaxy galaxy with central nucleus and concentrations of matter that extend in curved arms to create its spiral or pinwheel appearance

star massive, very hot, luminous ball of highly ionized gases that derives its energy from continuous nuclear reactions

starburst galaxy galaxy undergoing rapid wave of stellar birth

sun any star that is center of a planetary system, esp. central star of Earth's solar system

supercluster clusters of galaxies and local groups up to fifty million light years across

supergiant star exceptionally luminous star of first magnitude, having diameter more than 100 times that of sun

supernova explosion of massive star near the end of its life, possibly due to gravitational collapse, causing greatly increased luminosity and loss of most of star's mass, sometimes leaving behind dense core; white dwarf star in close binary system that produces explosions from mass taken from its companion star

supernova remnant portion of supernova blown outward to form nebula

terra Earth

terrestrial planets four inner planets of solar system: Mercury, Venus, Earth, and Mars

Titan largest satellite of Saturn and largest satellite in solar system

Titania satellite of Uranus

trinary star three stars bound to each other by gravitation

Triton largest satellite of Neptune and only body in solar system with active ice volcanism

Umbriel satellite of Uranus

Uranus third largest planet of solar system and seventh from sun: orbits sun in 84 years and rotates on its axis in 23 hours

variable star star that varies in intrinsic brightness

Venus sixth largest and brightest planet of solar

system and second from sun: orbits sun in 225 days and rotates on its axis in 244 days

Vesta one of first two minor planets discovered in solar system

Virgo cluster large collection of galaxies located visually in constellation Virgo

visual binary double star in which separate components may be distinguished through powerful telescope

whirlpool galaxy interacting spiral galaxy connected to its companion galaxy by bridge of stars

white dwarf small, faint, cold star that has undergone gravitational collapse

Celestial Phenomena and Points

aberration apparent displacement of star due to Earth's orbit and bending of star's light rays

absorption lines dark gaps in spectrum of sun or star due to layers of cooler gases in its atmosphere

accretion disk rapidly spinning disk of gas, usu. found around neutron star or black hole

altitude angular distance of celestial object located vertically above plane of celestial equator

annular eclipse solar eclipse in which the moon's angular diameter is smaller than the sun's

antapex point on celestial sphere from which sun appears to recede

anthelion bright white spot on parhelic circle opposite sun

apex point on celestial sphere toward which sun appears to move, relative to nearby stars

aphelion point in elliptical orbit of planet or comet that is farthest from sun

apocenter point on elliptical orbit that is farthest from body that is focus of orbit

apogee point in elliptical orbit of moon or artificial satellite that is farthest from Earth

arc apparent path of celestial body above and below horizon

arroyo channel formed by fluid erosion on Earth and sun

asterism pattern formed by stars on celestial sphere, esp. a constellation

atmosphere gaseous envelope surrounding star, planet, or other celestial body

atmospheric layers divisions of atmosphere that extend outward from surface of body: troposphere, stratosphere, mesosphere, thermosphere, and exosphere

aureole luminous area that surrounds sun as seen through thin cloud; corona

aurora display of changing colored light high in atmosphere at arctic and antarctic latitudes, caused by charged particles in Earth's magnetic field interacting with upper atmospheric gases

axis imaginary line through center of body about which it rotates

azimuth angle between celestial object and

southern point of horizon, measured clockwise from horizon

basin huge, multiringed lunar crater, produced by asteroidal impact, later filled with lava to form mare

Becklin-Neugebauer object strong infrared source near Orion nebula

Big Dipper asterism within constellation Ursa Major formed by seven stars in shape of dipper

biosphere ecosphere

black hole highly concentrated mass that has collapsed to such a degree that the escape velocity from its surface is greater than the speed of light, trapping light and all other energy and matter in an intense gravitational field

blue moon occurrence of two full moons within one month

blue shift shift of spectral lines toward shorter wavelengths at blue end of spectrum, observed in celestial objects approaching Earth

brightline spectrum emission spectrum that appears as bright lines against dark background

canals linear grooves on surface of Mars once believed to be artificial waterways

carbonaceous chondrites uncommon meteorite class believed to be most primitive form of matter in solar system

celestial equator projection of Earth's equator on celestial sphere

celestial sphere apparent sphere of sky on which celestial bodies appear to lie, centered on observer on Earth

chondrite member of most abundant class of stony meteorites

chromosphere layer in sun's atmosphere between corona and photosphere

collision sudden, violent impact of two or more celestial bodies and ensuing reactions

comet tail tail of dust that trails away from path of comet nucleus and points away from sun, appearing when comet is near sun

conjunction occasion when two or more celestial bodies line up at same longitude on celestial sphere

constellation pattern formed by stars on celestial sphere, used to describe positions of celestial objects; area of celestial sphere enclosing such stars

corona layer of ionized gases that surround and extend a great distance from sun, visible as halo in solar eclipse; aureole

cosmic noise radio frequency radiations that emanate from Milky Way; galactic noise

cosmic rays highly charged ions that move at enormous speed and strike Earth continuously from all sides

crater circular rocky formation located on surface of moon and some other celestial bodies, caused by meteoritic impact

crescent moon phase of moon halfway between quarter and new moon

declination angular distance of celestial object north or south of celestial equator

deferent orbit of celestial body in Ptolemaic system

dust cloud of powdery matter floating in space

eclipse celestial event in which light from one celestial object is obscured by another object interposed between it and observer, esp. sun's light by moon on Earth or by Earth on moon

ecliptic great circle that represents apparent path of sun on celestial sphere

ecosphere zone of Earth or other celestial body in which living organisms could be supported

electromagnetic spectrum range of radiation wavelengths: gamma rays, X-rays, ultraviolet rays, visible light, infrared rays, microwaves, and radio waves

emission lines bright lines in spectrum of light emitted by glowing gas

equinox one of two points in which great circle of ecliptic intersects great circle of celestial equator on celestial sphere: vernal on March 21, autumnal on September 22

exosphere outermost portion of planet's atmosphere

extragalactic (*adj*) outside the Milky Way system

first point of Aries position of celestial bodies on first day of zodiacal calendar

flash spectrum brightline spectrum that can be observed briefly before and after a total solar eclipse, produced by sun's reversing layer

flocculus one of the bright or dark patches on sun's surface, visible by spectroheliograph

force field space through which electric, gravitational, or magnetic force acts

Fraunhofer lines dark lines in solar spectrum

full moon phase of moon when it is on side of Earth away from sun, so that its entire face reflects sunlight to Earth

galactic equator great circle of celestial sphere halfway between galactic poles, parallel to and one degree north of centerline of Milky Way

galactic noise cosmic noise

galactic pole either of two opposite points of celestial sphere at greatest average distance from Milky Way

geomagnetic axis single diameter of Earth that is axis of Earth's magnetic field in conventionalized symmetrical approximation

gibbous moon phase of moon halfway between quarter and full moon

gravitation force by which celestial objects attract and are attracted by other celestial objects

gravitational collapse contraction of dying star that occurs when thermonuclear reactions cannot sustain force of self-gravitation

halo circle of definite size around sun or moon caused by ice particles in atmosphere

horizon great circle on celestial sphere perpendicular to hypothetical line that connects observer's zenith to nadir; distant line where sky seems to meet Earth

interacting galaxies two or more galaxies in

such close proximity that their shapes are distorted by gravitational forces

intercrater plain flat surface of celestial body between craters

intergalactic (*adj*) existing or occurring between or among galaxies

intergalactic medium gas found between galaxies

interplanetary (*adj*) being or occurring within solar system but outside atmosphere of any planet or sun

interplanetary medium gas dust found between planets

interstellar cloud dense region of gas and dust from which stars are formed that lies between stars in galaxy

ionosphere very high layer in atmosphere of planets in which gases are largely ionized

lines of force field lines in force field: magnetic, electric, or gravitational

Little Dipper constellation Ursa Minor that contains Polaris and resembles a dipper

luminosity intrinsic brightness of any star when compared with sun

lunar (*adj*) of or relating to the moon

lunar eclipse passage of Earth between sun and moon that causes moon to be in Earth's shadow

lunar occultation disappearance of celestial body behind moon

magnetic field field arising from electric charge in motion that produces a force on another electric charge

magnetosphere region surrounding planet in which planet's magnetic field is stronger than interplanetary field

mare large, flat plain on moon, formerly called sea

Mare Imbrium round basin on near side of moon that is largest lunar sea

meridian great circle on celestial sphere that passes through zenith, nadir, north, and south points on horizon

Messier object one of 109 objects numbered from M1 as cataloged by French astronomer Charles Messier to distinguish clusters, nebulae, and galaxies from comets

meteor shower apparent divergence from single point by luminous paths of members as meteor swarm encounters Earth's atmosphere

microwave background radiation redshifted radiation from glow of early universe that appears not as light but as microwaves

nadir point on celestial sphere opposite zenith and directly below observer

new moon first phase of moon when it is between Earth and sun with side toward Earth in shadow

nodes two points at which orbit of celestial body intersects a reference plane, usu. ecliptic or celestial equator

Northern Lights aurora display in Northern Hemisphere

nutation slight, periodic oscillation in precession of Earth's axis in space

occultation passage of one celestial object in front of another, as in an eclipse

Olympus Mons largest volcano on Mars, probably largest in solar system

optical double pair of stars that form apparent binary double when viewed from Earth but are actually widely separated in space

orbit elliptical path of one celestial sphere or satellite around another larger body, in accordance with Newton's laws of gravitation and motion

Orientale basin youngest lunar basin

outer space space outside Earth's solar system

outgassing extrusion of gases from body of planet after its formation

parhelic circle luminous circle or halo parallel to horizon at altitude of sun

penumbra partly lighted area that surrounds complete shadow of celestial body during eclipse

perigee point closest to Earth in orbit of moon or other object around Earth

perihelion point closest to sun in orbit of member of solar system

perturbation disturbance in regular motion of one celestial body around another, esp. due to gravitational presence of third body

phase particular appearance of celestial body due to recurrent cycle in its illumination; recurrent stage in illumination and apparent shape of moon: new, quarter, full, and gibbous

photosphere visible surface of sun

plasma low-density, ionized gas with complex magnetic field that moves through space

polar cap large region of ice covering north or south polar region of planet, esp. Earth and Mars

precession slow shifting of celestial equator due to motion of Earth's axis from gravitational pull of sun and moon on Earth's equatorial bulge

primordial black hole black hole created very early in life of universe

proper motion apparent angular motion of star across observer's line of sight

quarter moon phase of moon halfway between new and full

radiant point on celestial sphere from which a meteor stream appears to come

radio wave electromagnetic wave that exists at radio frequency

ray beam of light from bright source; stream of particles emitted by radioactive substance

redshift shift, due to Doppler effect, in spectral lines of object toward longer wavelengths at red end of spectrum as it recedes from Earth, with amount of shift proportional to object's speed

regolith blanket of rubble on moon's surface from lunar impacts

retrograde motion motion in direction opposite usual orbit of similar celestial bodies

rift valley elongated depression of planet's crust between two faults

ring plain lunar crater of exceptional diameter with relatively smooth interior

ring system flat, thin, reflective band of dust and ice crystals that orbit and encircle a planet, esp. Jupiter, Saturn, Uranus, and Neptune

Saturn's rings wide system of visible rings around planet Saturn

seeing blurring of telescopic images of celestial bodies due to turbulence in Earth's atmosphere

semimajor axis one half the major axis of elliptical orbit described by a celestial body

solar (adj) of or relating to the sun

solar corona outer atmosphere of sun

solar eclipse interposition of moon between Earth and sun

solar flare sudden, brief increase in intensity of sun's light, usu. near sunspots, accompanied by increase in radiations

solar nebula large cloud of hot gas and dust from which sun and planets formed

solar wind stream of radiation and ionized gas that spirals outward from sun at high speed

solstice date on which sun reaches position farthest north or south of celestial equator; northern on June 21, southern on December 21

space three-dimensional continuous expanse in all directions that contains all matter; distance between and area not filled by celestial bodies

space velocity velocity of star's motion relative to sun

spectrum light emitted by star or other source, dispersed according to wavelength

spicule gas jet located in sun's chromosphere

spiral arm curved concentration of matter that extends from nucleus of spiral galaxy

star cloud large luminous patch of Milky Way that can be resolved with optical aid into dense concentration of stars

sunspot temporarily cooler region that appears as dark spot on sun's surface, accompanied by geomagnetic disturbances

surface temperature measure of heat at outer face of celestial object

synodic month interval between two successive conjunctions of same celestial bodies

syzygy straight alignment of three celestial bodies, esp. point in orbit at which moon is in conjunction or opposition with sun

Tharsis ridge principal area of Martian volcanic activity

tidal friction frictional effect of tides that very slowly retards rotational velocity of Earth

tides rising and falling of surface of bodies of water on Earth due to attraction of moon and sun as Earth rotates

transit passage of smaller body in front of larger one as seen from Earth

umbra dark central cone of shadow that projects from celestial body on side opposite sun; shadow of body in eclipse

Van Allen radiation belts doughnut-shaped regions around Earth in which high-speed, charged particles oscillate in Earth's magnetic field

vertical circle great circle of celestial sphere with plane perpendicular to horizon

visible spectrum portion of electromagnetic spectrum detectable by human eye

waning moon moon proceeding from full to new

waxing moon moon proceeding from new to full

zenith point on celestial sphere lying vertically above observer

zodiacal light faint glow above horizon, esp. at tropical latitudes, on clear moonless night after sunset in west and before sunrise in east

zone portion of spherical surface lying between two parallel circles

zone of avoidance region of sky where no galaxies can be seen due to light-absorbing clouds of dust

Branches, Laws, Theories, and Techniques

absolute magnitude astronomical measure of brightness of a star as it would appear at distance of 10 parsecs

absolute zero zero kelvins; temperature at which all molecular motion ceases

albedo ratio of amount of light reflected and scattered by a surface to amount of light falling on that surface

apparent magnitude brightness of star as seen from Earth

armillary sphere ancient instrument consisting of a set of rings, used to show relative positions of celestial equator and other circles on the celestial sphere

astrobiology study of living organisms beyond the atmosphere of Earth

astrolabe medieval instrument consisting of a graduated, vertical circle with movable arm, formerly used to find altitude of star

astrology study attempting to interpret the influence of celestial bodies on human events and individual personality, esp. at moment of birth

astrometeorology study of the theoretical effects of astronomical bodies and forces on Earth's atmosphere

astrometric binary binary system in which the existence of an invisible companion is inferred by its effects on orbital motion of a visible star

astrometry branch of astronomy that deals with measurement of the positions of celestial objects

astronomer person trained in and expert at the practice of astronomy

astronomical unit AU; measurement based on mean distance of Earth from sun, approximately 93 million miles (149.6 million km)

astronomy observation and theoretical study of celestial bodies, space, and the universe

astrophotography photography of celestial objects

astrophysics branch of astronomy dealing with physical properties of celestial objects, space, and the universe

AU **a**stronomical **u**nit

big bang model theory that universe originated in explosion of hot, dense core that rapidly expanded to cooler, less dense states; expanding universe

big crunch singularity at end of universe in which universe contracts, opposite to big bang

binary accretion model theory of formation of Earth-moon system due to accretion from one cloud of gas and dust

Bode's law mathematical relationship which agrees with distances of planets from sun in astronomical units

Cassegrain reflector compact, portable reflecting telescope, orig. 17th c.

celestial mechanics branch of astronomy concerned with motions and gravitational interactions of celestial objects

Chandrasekhar limit maximum possible mass of stable cold star, beyond which it will become a supernova or collapse to become a black hole

chaos disorderly and unpredictable universe

coelostat clock-driven mirror system in telescope that follows path of observed celestial object across sky

Copernican system first heliocentric theory of solar system, published by Nicolaus Copernicus in 1543

coronagraph disk in telescope used to create artificial solar eclipse that permits photography of sun's corona

cosmogony study of possible origin and evolution of universe

cosmological principle assumption that universe would appear the same viewed from any galaxy in it

cosmology study of structure of universe as a whole

cosmos orderly and harmonious universe

coudé telescope telescope in which focus remains fixed while observed object moves, used esp. with spectrograph

dispersion separation between different wavelengths in spectrum

Doppler shift change in wave frequency due to approach or recession of source relative to observer

eccentricity scale that expresses degree of flattening of elliptical orbit, with zero being circular and one being perfectly elliptical

ephemeris table giving computed position of celestial body for each day in given period

epicycle planetary motion described in Ptolemaic system as circle whose center moves along circumference of another larger circle

epoch time at which positions of celestial bodies are observed

ether quintessence

expanding universe big bang model

Galilean telescope first refracting telescope with positive objective lens and negative eye lens, developed by Galileo Galilei in 17th c.

Geiger counter Geiger-Müller tube

Geiger-Müller tube radiation detector that counts cosmic rays and gamma rays; Geiger counter

geocentric (*adj*) viewing universe as though Earth were its center

gnomon vertical plate of sundial, set parallel to Earth's axis; shaft perpendicular to horizon, used to find sun's meridian altitude

gravitational lensing bending of light of celestial body around another body closer to observer along same line of sight, so that the more distant body appears as ring or arc around closer body

gravity anomaly theory that force of gravity would be constant at surface of uniform spherical mass

harmonic law Kepler's third law, which states that the squares of periods of any two planets are in same proportion as cubes of their average distances from sun

heliocentric (*adj*) viewing universe as though sun were its center

Hertzsprung-Russell diagram graph that shows luminosities of stars plotted against their temperatures

horizon system system of celestial coordinates, such as altitude and azimuth, that are based on observer's horizon

horoscope positions of planets and stars relative to one another at time of person's birth, regarded in astrology as factor that determines one's character and destiny

Hubble classification scheme sequence of different types of galaxies: elliptical, spiral, and irregular

image-intensifier tube instrument used to increase brightness of image from telescope

interferometer instrument that produces interference patterns of light that enable precise measurement of minute wavelengths

Kepler's laws Johann Kepler's three laws of planetary motion: *first law* orbit of each planet is ellipse with sun at one of its foci; *second law* each planet revolves so that imaginary line between it and sun sweeps over equal areas of space in equal intervals of time; *third law* harmonic law

light speed distance light travels in one second, equal to approximately 186,000 miles (299,792 km)

light year astronomical unit of measurement equal to distance light travels in one year, approximately 6 trillion miles (9.5 trillion km), used as measure of astronomical distances

magnitude brightness of star in sky measured on logarithmic scale from zero (brightest) to five (faintest), with fifth-magnitude stars being 100 times fainter than zero-magnitude stars

main sequence band on Hertzsprung-Russell diagram that contains stage of stellar life in which star consumes hydrogen in its core through nuclear reactions, descriptive of majority of stars

major axis maximum diameter across an ellipse

mascon *mas*s *con*centration; local concentration of very dense material beneath moon's surface

mass-luminosity law the greater the absolute magnitude of a star the greater its luminosity

mass spectrometry separation and measurement of molecules that have different masses by deflection of beam of ionized molecules

monochromator device with prism and slits, used to obtain desired narrow band of wavelengths from light source

New General Catalogue NGC; listing of galaxies, clusters, and nebulae that includes all Messier objects, numbered from NGC1

Newtonian reflector telescope with spherical or parabolic primary mirror and flat reflector set at 45 degree angle to optical axis to focus light at side of telescope tube

Newton's first law of motion an object remains at rest or in motion with a constant velocity unless acted upon by an outside force

Newton's law of universal gravitation force of attraction between any two particles of matter is directly proportional to the product of their masses and inversely proportional to the square of the distance between their centers of mass

Newton's second law of motion the change in motion of an object acted upon by an outside force is directly proportional to the force and inversely proportional to the object's mass

Newton's third law of motion every action force has a reaction force equal in magnitude and opposite in direction

NGC New General Catalogue

no boundary condition theory that universe is finite but has no boundary

objective lens in telescope nearest to object observed that focuses light to form image of object

observable universe portion of universe that can be viewed directly with telescopes or other optical aids

observatory building equipped with large telescope and other devices used for astronomical studies

orrery mechanical model that shows positions, motion, and phases of bodies in solar system, as in a planetarium

parallax apparent shift in position or direction of celestial body when viewed from Earth at changing points of its orbit around sun

parsec unit of astronomical measurement equal to 3.26 light years, distance required to produce parallax angle of one arc second

period time taken to complete cycle of events, esp. revolution of planet around sun

period-luminosity relation established relation between periods of certain stars and their intrinsic brightness

photometry process in which intensity of light or radiation emitted by celestial source is measured by electrical voltage or pulse counter

photomultiplier tube photometry device that amplifies electron current from photoelectric surface to permit accurate measurement of light from celestial source

planetarium complex revolving projector used to simulate motion and position of celestial objects inside a dome; building that houses projector and dome used for this purpose

planetesimal any of numerous small bodies that moved in orbits through space and may have formed planets

plate tectonics theory that planets and some other celestial bodies consist of crustal slabs that are in constant motion against each other

Ptolemaic system geocentric model of universe, postulated by Claudius Ptolemaeus in second century A.D., in which planets, moon, and sun revolve around Earth

pulsating universe theory variation on expanding universe theory, in which cycle of expansion and contracting to and from primeval nucleus is endlessly repeated

quintessence substance other than fire, air, water, or earth believed to compose celestial bodies in ancient and medieval philosophy; ether

radial velocity rate of linear motion of source toward or away from observer in line of sight, as in Doppler shift

radio astronomy study of radio energy sources in space by means of large, reflecting radio telescopes

radio beam steady stream of radio or radar signals sent from source location

radio telescope one or more radio antennas that receive and measure radio waves from celestial sources

reflector telescope with mirror as objective

refractor telescope with system of lenses as objective

right ascension angle in sky east of vernal equinox

Roche limit distance from planet's center below which a satellite cannot approach without suffering disruption

Schmidt telescope reflector telescope with spherical mirror as objective, used for wide-angle photography

Schwarzschild radius critical size that gravitationally collapsing mass must reach to be dense enough to trap light and become black hole

seismometer instrument that measures seismic waves on Earth or moon

SETI search for extraterrestrial intelligence

sextant instrument used, esp. by navigators, to measure angular distance of celestial object from horizon

sidereal (adj) expressed or measured in reference to stars

sidereal period time in which planet or satellite completes one revolution around its primary relative to a star seen from the primary

sidereal time time measured by rotation of Earth with respect to stars, not sun

signal-to-noise ratio error inherent in

measurement of brightness of faint star based on background light or noise

singularity point in space-time at which space-time curvature becomes infinite, such as black hole

space-time four-dimensional order of universe specified by three spatial coordinates and one temporal coordinate

space velocity velocity of star's motion relative to sun

spectral type classification of star based on analysis of certain spectral lines and stated as letter (O, B, A, F, G, K, or M) in order of decreasing temperature and number within letter group, such as the sun, a G2 star

spectrograph combination of spectroscope and photographic equipment used in studying spectra of celestial objects

spectroheliograph spectrograph modified to study sun's spectrum

spectroscopic parallax distance of star indicated by absolute magnitude deduced from relative intensities of selected spectrum lines

spectroscopy study of radiative output of celestial source

spectrum-luminosity diagram graph that plots spectral type of each star against absolute magnitude

stargazing astronomy or astrology

steady state model theory of expanding universe stipulating continuous creation of matter, and stating that universe maintains uniform large-scale structure and constant average density at all times

supermassive black hole black hole that may exist at center of some active galaxies or quasars

telescope instrument used to collect light from celestial objects and resolve images of these objects; reflector, refractor, and Schmidt

universe sum total of potentially knowable objects, matter, and energy, believed to be infinite in space and time

uranography branch of astronomy that describes and maps the position of the heavens, esp. fixed stars

uranology former term for astronomy

uranometry measurement of positions, magnitudes, and distances of celestial objects

Very Large Array VLA; large set of radio telescopes arranged in Y-shape in New Mexico

VLA Very Large Array

white hole hypothetical time-reversed black hole

Widmanstatten figures designs appearing on etched meteoric iron and exhibiting its crystalline structure

X-ray burster source of intense X-ray flashes in Milky Way

zodiac band of twelve constellations on celestial sphere with ecliptic as its middle line that includes paths of every planet except Pluto, divided into twelve zones and used in astrology

Signs of the Zodiac

Aquarius the Water Bearer, a constellation between Capricorn and Pisces and eleventh sign of the zodiac; the fixed air sign and birth sign of persons born between January 20th and February 18th

Aries the Ram, a constellation between Pisces and Taurus and first sign of the zodiac; the cardinal fire sign and birth sign of persons born between March 21st and April 19th

Cancer the Crab, a constellation between Gemini and Leo and fourth sign of the zodiac; the cardinal water sign and birth sign of persons born between June 21st and July 22nd

Capricorn the Goat, a constellation between Sagittarius and Aquarius and tenth sign of the zodiac; the cardinal earth sign and birth sign of persons born between December 22nd and January 19th

Gemini the Twins, a constellation between Taurus and Cancer and third sign of the zodiac; the mutable air sign and birth sign of persons born between May 21st and June 20th

Leo the Lion, a constellation between Cancer and Virgo and fifth sign of the zodiac; the fixed fire sign and birth sign of persons born between July 23rd and August 22nd

Libra the Balance, a constellation between Virgo and Scorpius and seventh sign of the zodiac; the cardinal air sign and birth sign of persons born between September 23rd and October 22nd

Pisces the Fishes, a constellation between Aquarius and Aries and twelfth sign of the zodiac; the mutable water sign and birth sign of persons born between February 19th and March 20th

Sagittarius the Archer, a constellation between Scorpius and Capricorn and ninth sign of the zodiac; the mutable fire sign and birth sign of persons born between November 22nd and December 21st

Scorpio the Scorpion, the constellation Scorpius between Libra and Sagittarius and eighth sign of the zodiac; the fixed water sign and birth sign of persons born between October 23rd and November 21st

Taurus the Bull, a constellation between Aries and Gemini and second sign of the zodiac; the fixed earth sign and birth sign of persons born between April 20th and May 20th

Virgo the Virgin, a constellation between Leo and Libra and sixth sign of the zodiac; the mutable earth sign and birth sign of persons born between August 23rd and September 22nd

Space Exploration and Rocketry

abort (vb) cancel or terminate mission or procedure prematurely, esp. due to equipment failure

aerodynamic heating surface heating of spacecraft produced by friction during reentry

aerospace science study and exploration of Earth's atmosphere and space beyond; rocket science; space science

airlock vacuum-tight door in cabin's pressure hull that can be opened to place equipment outside

anti-G suit totally enclosed uniform that equalizes G-force on astronaut

A-OK (*adj*) *Informal.* all systems go; okay to proceed as planned

Apollo series of manned NASA missions to moon

artificial satellite man-made object set in orbit around Earth

astronaut person sent on space mission

astronautics science of spacecrafts and outer space travel; cosmonautics

Atlantis space shuttle orbiter vehicle

Atlas family of launch vehicles; first-stage booster rocket

atmospheric drag frictional force that retards spacecraft or meteoroid moving through upper atmosphere

backout reversal of launch countdown due to poor weather or mechanical failure

ballistic missile unmanned military rocket with warhead; rocket bomb

bearing horizontal direction of object or point measured clockwise from reference line

bird *Informal.* rocket, spacecraft

bits radio transmission to and from spacecraft in binary code comprehensible to digital computers

blastoff launch; liftoff

blowoff separation of portion or stage of rocket by explosive force

booster rocket first stage of multistage rocket that provides thrust for liftoff

Brennschluss *German.* rocket's peak velocity

burn firing of rocket engine

burnout moment of final oxidation or combustion of fuel in a rocket engine

burn rate rate at which solid propellant is consumed

capsule small, pressurized compartment for astronauts

cargo bay unpressurized part of fuselage in which cargo is carried

ceiling altitude at which cloud cover limits vertical visibility

centrifuge apparatus with long arm in which individual is revolved to simulate effects of prolonged acceleration in space

Challenger NASA space shuttle which exploded in 1986

CM command module

Columbia first space shuttle orbiter, launched in 1981

command module CM; component of Apollo spacecraft attached to service module until reentry into Earth's atmosphere

communications satellite satellite designed to reflect or relay electromagnetic signals used in communications; comsat

Comsat *Trademark. com*munications *sat*ellite

cosmic particle cosmic ray

cosmic ray highly energized particle moving at near speed of light that strikes spacecraft; cosmic particle

cosmonaut Soviet astronaut

cosmonautics astronautics, esp. Soviet space program

Cosmos series of unmanned Soviet satellites

countdown backward counting off of seconds before launch; operations during such a count

counter radiation detection instrument or survey meter

crawlerway heavily reinforced roadway for transport of rockets

cutoff termination of propellant flow in rocket; stoppage of combustion

decompression sickness disorder associated with reduced atmospheric pressure that causes gas bubbles in body and pain in chest and extremities

deep space region beyond Earth's solar system

descent drop from Earth orbit, reentry into atmosphere, and touchdown

Discovery space shuttle orbiter vehicle

docking maneuver in which two or more spacecraft or orbiting objects are joined together

docking maneuver change in spacecraft path or trajectory to facilitate docking

downlink radio or television transmission from spacecraft to Earth station

drift lateral divergence from prescribed flight path

drogue recovery system of spacecraft recovery after reentry that uses small and large parachutes to slow descent, stabilize vehicle, and decrease landing impact

ESA **E**uropean **S**pace **A**gency

escape velocity speed required to place spacecraft in orbit or break free of Earth's gravitational field

European Space Agency ESA; cooperative organization of ten European nations for space exploration

EVMU **e**xtra**v**ehicular **m**obility **u**nit

exobiology study of extraterrestrial environments for living organisms

Explorer first series of NASA space probes

external tank liquid oxygen or hydrogen propellant tank on space shuttle

extraterrestrial (*adj*) not from Earth

extravehicular activity space walks and other experiments conducted outside confines of spacecraft

extravehicular mobility unit EVMU; space suit, including life support system and manned maneuvering unit; pressure suit; spacesuit

failsafe design that ensures ability to sustain malfunction yet successfully terminate or abort mission

flight movement of craft through space

flight deck area of orbiter module occupied by crew

flight path launch, orbit, and trajectory followed by spacecraft on mission

flyby mission in which spacecraft passes close to target planet but does not orbit or impact it

flying saucer unidentified flying object

footprint area taken up by spacecraft on ground

G acceleration due to gravity, equal to one G at sea level on Earth's surface

Gemini series of NASA Earth orbital missions manned by two astronauts

G-force force in excess of one G experienced by everything inside spacecraft during launch or reentry

go/no-go (*adj*) being the point at which decision to launch or not launch must be made

ground test procedure by which spacecraft, systems, or rockets are tested without launch

guidance system control system that selects flight path of spacecraft and directs its movements in space

gyro spinning wheel resistant to change of direction of its axis of rotation, used to steady orientation of spacecraft

hangfire faulty condition in rocket engine ignition system that causes delay in firing

hatch door in pressurized hull of spacecraft

heat shield structural overlay that protects reentry body of spacecraft from aerodynamic heating

heat sink material that absorbs heat, used for heat shield

Hubble Space Telescope powerful telescope operating outside Earth's atmosphere that has capability to see much deeper into universe than telescopes on Earth's surface

hydrogen gas used as fuel for space shuttle main engine when cryogenically cooled to liquid form

ice frost layer of ice on outside of surfaces supercooled by cryogenic propellants such as oxygen and hydrogen

impact rocket or spacecraft striking surface of planet or any other object

impact area projected location of impact

inclination angle between orbital plane of satellite and plane of ecliptic

interplanetary travel hypothetical manned flights to other planets in solar system

jacket shell around combustion chamber through which liquid propellant is circulated in regenerative cooling

Jet Propulsion Laboratory JPL; center for basic and applied research in space science, located in Pasadena, California

JPL **J**et **P**ropulsion **L**aboratory

Jupiter three-stage booster rocket used to place first U.S. satellite Explorer I in orbit in January, 1958

Kennedy Space Center KSC; primary launching base for U.S. spacecraft, located at Cape Canaveral, Florida

KREEP set of elements found in lunar rocks and soil: K, symbol for potassium; REE, rare Earth elements; P, phosphorus

KSC **K**ennedy **S**pace **C**enter

launch initiation of space flight with takeoff of rocket from Earth's surface; blastoff; liftoff

launch complex site and facilities at launching base

launch crew technicians and engineers who prepare spacecraft for launch and run launch operation

launcher structure with tubes and set of tracks from which rockets are launched

launching base NASA station used to launch spacecraft

launch pad area from which spacecraft and booster rockets are sent forth, either tower, tube, or platform

launch window interval of time during which spacecraft can be launched to accomplish specific task or mission

LEM lunar excursion module

life-support system environmental control system that provides comfortable, shirtsleeve conditions for crew by control of temperature, pressure, humidity, and oxygen and nitrogen supply

liftoff moment in which rocket leaves launch pad on Earth; blastoff; launch

liquid propellant cryogenically cooled oxygen or hydrogen used in external fuel tanks of space shuttle

LM lunar module

LOX liquid *oxygen*, used as liquid propellant

lunar excursion module LEM; lunar module

lunar module LM; detachable vehicle on Apollo spacecraft used in manned moon landings; lunar excursion module

lunar orbiter command service module that remained in lunar orbit while lunar module landed on surface of moon

lunar rock rocks and soil returned to Earth by Apollo astronauts; moon rock

Mach number expressing ratio of speed of a body with respect to surrounding air or fluid; Mach 1 is speed of sound, supersonic being above Mach 1, subsonic below

Magellan unmanned spacecraft launched from shuttle to orbit and examine Venus during 1991

manned flight space mission with one or more humans on board

Manned Space Center MSC; NASA headquarters located in Houston, Texas, that serves as mission control for U.S. space flights

manned station orbiting space lab with crew on board

Mariner series of NASA spacecraft used for planet flyby missions

Mercury first series of NASA orbital and suborbital manned space missions

microinstrumentation telemetry equipment

Mir small Soviet space station used primarily for scientific experiments

missile unmanned military rocket aimed at target, usu. with warhead

mission space flight with prescribed goals and operations

mission control ground center that provides manned space missions with total support and control over all phases of flight

module self-contained unit attached to launch vehicle or spacecraft; pressurized manned laboratory

moon rock lunar rock

MSC Manned Space Center

multistage rocket space vehicle that uses two or more firing stages to boost payload into orbit, each stage being jettisoned when fuel is exhausted

NASA National Aeronautics and Space Administration; U.S. government agency administering space program

NORAD North American Air Defense; U.S. defense radar network covering North America

nozzle throat opening through which fuel from tanks is fed into engine

orbit path followed by satellite or spacecraft around Earth or other celestial body

O-ring plastic sealing ring on propellant tanks

parking orbit orbit around Earth maintained for long duration

pass single orbit of Earth by spacecraft or satellite

payload passengers, cargo, instruments, equipment, supplies, and support hardware carried by rocket over and above what is necessary to operate vehicle in flight

photomosaic space photograph composed of many individual images of segments of photographed objects

Pioneer series of unmanned NASA probes that explore solar system as far as Jupiter and Saturn

plasma engine hypothetical rocket engine powered by expelling jet of highly ionized plasma gas

pod detachable compartment of spacecraft

pressure hull main body of spacecraft comparable to aircraft fuselage

pressure suit extravehicular mobility unit

probe unmanned space mission on trajectory from Earth orbit to study another celestial object

propellant solid or liquid fuel used to provide thrust and launch rocket, place it in orbit, break it out of orbit, or slow its descent

propulsion system vehicle system of engines, fuel tanks, and lines providing thrust

proving ground testing ground

radar tracking station tracking station that maintains only radar contact with spacecraft

Ranger early series of NASA space probes

reentry return of space capsule into Earth's atmosphere

retroengine small engine used to produce retarding thrust and reduce velocity, esp. on reentry

retrofire ignition of retroengine

retrograde orbit of satellite in westerly direction, opposite easterly motion of earthbound observer

retropack group of retroengines

retrorocket rocket fired to reduce spacecraft motion, so that it descends from orbit or slows down in free fall

rocket portion of spacecraft in which combustible materials provide thrust for launch and orbit

rocket bomb ballistic missile

rocketman *Informal.* astronaut

rocketry study and practice of aerospace science

rocket science aerospace science

Rover vehicle used on lunar surface by astronauts

satellite artificial object sent into Earth orbit

Saturn first-stage booster rocket on Apollo missions

scrub (*vb*) cancel flight or mission

sealing rings mechanical devices designed to prevent loss of cabin atmosphere

Sea of Tranquillity large lunar basin and landing point of Apollo 11, first manned lunar expedition

separation stage in which launch vehicle booster rockets are jettisoned once fuel is exhausted

service module section of spacecraft containing propulsion and electrical systems and supplies

shot space flight to specific celestial body, such as moonshot

shuttle reusable spacecraft that replaced expendable launch vehicles and can return payloads and land on Earth

silo large, underground facility for storage and launching of long-range ballistic missiles

Skylab large NASA space workshop operated in the 1970's

solid propellant chemical mixture or compound containing fuel and oxidizer that burn to produce very hot gases at high pressure

solid rocket boosters two solid fuel rockets that augment thrust of shuttle from launch through first two minutes of ascent and are then separated and retrieved for reuse

Soyuz series of Soviet manned spacecraft

Space Age era of space exploration that began with launch of first Sputnik on October 4, 1957

space colony hypothetical large, semipermanent community living on space station or on another planet

spacecraft manned or unmanned platform or object placed in Earth orbit or in trajectory to another celestial body

Spacelab laboratory payload on shuttle, product of joint effort between ESA and NASA

spaceman astronaut; extraterrestrial being

spaceport space station

space probe probe

space science aerospace science; astronomy

spaceship spacecraft or satellite

space station permanently orbiting, large spacecraft designed to accommodate long-term human habitation; spaceport

spacesuit extravehicular mobility unit

spacewalk extravehicular activity in which astronaut, often connected by support umbilical, leaves confines of spacecraft

spaghetti suit *Slang.* long underwear worn by astronauts, having tubes that carry cooling water

splashdown spacecraft landing in ocean

Sputnik first Soviet artificial satellite series that began with October 4, 1957 launch

staging separation of spent stages of launch vehicle from capsule

starship interstellar spacecraft

step rocket multistage rocket with boosters

suborbital flight one of early manned Mercury flights that did not enter Earth orbit

Surveyor class of unmanned NASA space probes undertaken in preparation for manned Apollo lunar flights

sustainer small rocket engine that maintains spacecraft's speed after booster is jettisoned

synodic period time between two consecutive orbital passes over one reference longitude on Earth

takeoff launch; liftoff

telemetry coding and measuring of data obtained on spacecraft in form comprehensible to digital computers and transmission to Earth stations for interpretation

terrestrial (*adj*) of the Earth

test flight flight for controlled observation of operations, rocket, and spacecraft

testing ground area and facilities designated for test flights; proving ground

test rocket rocket designed for test flight only

throttling varying thrust of rocket engine during flight by fuel line constriction or changes in nozzle expansion and thrust chamber pressure

thrust propulsive force developed by rocket engines during firing, used to launch spacecraft and place it in orbit or on trajectory out of Earth's atmosphere

thrust coefficient ratio of engine thrust to product of nozzle throat area times nozzle inlet pressure

Titan first-stage booster launch vehicle

touchdown landing of spacecraft on Earth or another celestial body

tracking station facility that observes, plots, and monitors path of spacecraft

trajectory nonorbital flight path from one point to another

t-time specific time, plus or minus, that refers to launch time or zero at end of countdown

UFO unidentified flying object; hypothetical spacecraft from another solar system; flying saucer

umbilical electrical or fluid servicing line between tower on launch pad and upright rocket prior to launch, or between spacecraft and astronaut on spacewalk

unidentified flying object UFO

unmanned flight space mission without humans on board

uplink transmission path for sending signals from earth station to communications satellite or airborne platform

upweight spacecraft weight at launch, including payloads, support items, and unburned fuel

Viking series of NASA spacecraft designed to land on Mars

visual tracking station facility from which visual sightings of spacecraft are possible

Vostok series of manned Soviet spacecraft, used to make world's first manned space flights in 1961

Voyager series of NASA probes that explored outer planets on flybys of Jupiter in 1979, Saturn in 1980, Uranus in 1986, and Neptune in 1989

V-2 German rocket bomb used in World War II

weather satellite unmanned spacecraft that returns meteorological data to Earth

weightlessness zero-G state

window gap in continuum; interval of time favorable to launch for specific mission

yaw angular motion of vehicle about vertical axis through center of gravity

zero-G condition of weightlessness and free fall experienced when no gravitational forces are acting on objects in spacecraft

---

MATHEMATICS
Branches and Computational Systems
Quantities, Relationships, and Operations
Geometric Shapes and Mathematically Defined
  Forms
Mathematical Tools

See also: *Chap. 23: Spatial Positions and Relations; Shapes*

Branches and Computational Systems

algebra theory and practice of arithmetic operations that uses symbols, esp. letters, to represent unknown variables in equations

algorithm set of rules for solving problems through finite repetitions of basic given procedure

analysis approach to functions and limits, esp. by use of differential and integral calculus

analytic geometry use of coordinate graphing system to demonstrate numerical relationships of algebraic equations; Cartesian geometry

applied mathematics study of physical phenomena using mathematical methods, as in mechanics, statistics, and physics

arithmetic study of usu. positive real numbers in addition, subtraction, multiplication, and division operations that yield sums, remainders, products, and quotients

Boolean algebra form of propositional calculus; algebra of elementary propositions in symbolic logic

calculus methods of calculation for continuously changing quantities, based on differentiation and integration of functions and related concepts

Cartesian geometry analytic geometry

descriptive geometry theory of geometry treated by means of projections on two planes at right angles to each other

differential calculus branch of mathematics

dealing with rate of change of functions with respect to variables on which they depend

elementary arithmetic simple arithmetic computations that involve one- and two-digit positive integers

Euclidean geometry study of geometry within limits of Euclidean space, i.e. ordinary one-, two-, and three-dimensional space

Fourier analysis expression of periodic function as sum of infinite series of trigonometric functions

game theory field of study concerned with decision-making problems in competitive situations governed by rules

geodesy measurement and theory of curvature, shape, and dimensions of Earth's surface

geometry branch of mathematics that deals with deduction of properties, measurement, and relationships of points, lines, angles, surfaces, and solid figures in space

group theory study of the properties and relationships of mathematical groups, with associated operations that obey specific set of rules

higher arithmetic general theory of integers

integral calculus branch of mathematics used to find indefinite integrals of functions, evaluate definite integrals, determine dimensions, and solve simple differential equations

linear algebra algebra of vectors and matrices as opposed to real numbers

math mathematics

mathematical biology application of mathematics to problems in theoretical biology, esp. by construction of mathematical models

mathematical physics application of mathematics to problems in physics, esp. by construction of mathematical models

mathematics science dealing through symbolic representation with the relationship of numbers, magnitudes, and forms, including quantitative operations and the solution of quantitative problems

matrix algebra generalized algebra that deals with operations and relationships among ordered sets of elements arranged in rows and columns

non-Euclidean geometry geometry not in accordance with all of the postulates of Euclidean space, esp. the single parallel postulate

number theory advanced arithmetic devoted to study of properties of integers

plane geometry elementary form of geometry that deals with two-dimensional figures

plane trigonometry form of trigonometry that deals with triangles in the Euclidean plane

political arithmetic science of economic and demographic statistics that describe political units

propositional calculus branch of symbolic logic dealing with analysis of relationships between statements that have been reduced into conjunctions, disjunctions, and negations of more elementary statements

quadratics form of algebra that treats quadratic polynomial equations

set theory branch of mathematics and symbolic logic dealing with nature and relations of aggregates or sets

solid geometry geometry that deals with solid, three-dimensional figures

statistics collection, analysis, interpretation, and presentation of masses of empirical, numerical data

symbolic logic science of developing and representing logical principles by means of symbols to provide rules of deduction for computations

systems analysis study of an activity by mathematical means to determine how most efficiently to attain desired ends

topology investigation of those properties of a geometric configuration that remain unaltered when subjected to one-to-one transformations that are continuous in both directions

trigonometry branch of mathematics that measures relations between sides and angles of triangles

vector analysis study of the properties of vectors

Quantities, Relationships, and Operations

abscissa horizontal coordinate of two-dimensional coordinate system in the Cartesian plane; x-axis

addend one of a group of numbers to be added together

addition arithmetic operation that combines numbers to generate sum

aggregate whole sum, total amount, set of mathematical elements with a common property

algebraic function sum, difference, product, quotient, or root of polynomial function

antilogarithm number of which a given number is the logarithm

Arabic numeral one of standard number symbols: 0,1,2,3,4,5,6,7,8,9; digit

area number of unit squares required to cover surface; measurement of surface

arithmetic mean average

arithmetic progression sequence in which each succeeding term is derived by adding common difference to preceding term

associative law result of multiple operations does not depend on how they are grouped

asymptote straight line in relation to curve such that as point moves along infinite branch of curve the distance from point to line approaches zero

average result that occurs when sum of two or more quantities is divided by the number of quantities; arithmetic mean

axiom proposition assumed to be true without proof in order to study its applied consequences; self-evident truth

axis straight line for reference in graph, such as Cartesian coordinate; straight line through

center of plane or solid around which it is symmetrically arranged

base number multiplied by itself in scientific notation; number that is raised to a power

billion one thousand million

binary (adj) designating system of numbers having two as its base

binomial expression that is a sum or difference of two unlike terms

binomial distribution probability function that indicates how often two outcomes with constant probability will occur in a succession of repetitive experiments

bisection division of angle or form into two equal parts

cancel (vb) remove either common divisor from numerator and denominator of fraction or equivalents from opposite sides of equation

cardinal number number used in simple counting to indicate an amount, such as how many of something are in a set

Cartesian coordinate either of two coordinates that locate point on Cartesian plane and measure its distance from x-axis or y-axis

chain rule rule for taking derivative of composite function in which second function is taken as independent variable in differentiating first function

chi-square distribution widely used probability density function that shows distribution of sum of squares of several independent random variables

circular function trigonometric function

circumference distance measured around outside of circle

coefficient number that multiplies another quantity; factor of a product

common denominator common multiple of denominators of two or more fractions

commutative law rule of combination in which an operation on two terms is independent of the order of the terms

complement angle or arc that when added to another angle or arc equals a right angle

complex number real or imaginary number expressed as a + bi where a and b are real numbers and i is the square root of -1

composite function function obtained from two given functions by applying one function to an independent variable and applying the second function to the result

composite number integer divisible by a whole number other than itself or 1

compound number number expressed in more than one denomination or unit, such as 6 feet, 2 inches

computation act or method of determining an amount, esp. by arithmetic

concentric (adj) designating two or more figures having a common center

congruence property of having exactly the same size and shape

conjugate (adj) having the same or similar

properties, such as two lines; (n) one of two adjacent angles that total 360°

constant quantity with fixed value, opposite of variable

continuous function function whose value at each point is nearly the same as its values at nearby points

conversion change in form but not value of quantity or unit

coordinates numbers associated with points on number line or graph

corollary theorem proved by application of a previously proved theorem

correlation coefficient any measure of concomitant variation in two or more variables

corresponding angles pair of nonadjacent angles on same side of line that crosses two other lines, one interior and one exterior

cosecant trigonometric ratio expressed as secant of the complement of an arc or angle

cosine trigonometric ratio expressed as sine of the complement of an arc or angle

cotangent trigonometric ratio expressed as tangent of the complement of an arc or angle

count (vb) recite numbers in standard order; add units in group one at a time

cross multiply determine two products by multiplying numerator of each of two fractions by denominator of other

cryptarithm arithmetic problem with letters substituted for numbers, solved by finding all possible pairings of digits and letters that produce numerically correct answer

cube third power of a number; number multiplied by itself two times

cube root number whose cube is given number

cubic equation polynomial equation with no variable exponent higher than three

data numerical information

decimal (adj) designating system of numbers having ten as its base

decimal point mark indicating division between integers and fractions in mixed number

degree unit of angular measure; measure around fixed point, with total of 360 degrees in circle

denominator lower number of fraction, indicating number of parts into which the whole has been divided

dependent variable element in second set of a function associated with independent variable selected from first

derivative rate of change of mathematical function with respect to change in independent variable

deviation amount by which any single value differs from the mean

diameter straight line extending from edge to edge through center point of sphere or circle

difference amount of inequality between two quantities; result obtained when one quantity is subtracted from another

differential product of the derivative of a function of one variable times the small increment of an independent variable

differential equation equation containing derivatives

digit one of Arabic numeral symbols: 0,1,2,3,4,5,6,7,8,9

distribution arrangement of statistical population when one or more specific criteria are applied

distributive law rule of combination in which specified operation applied to combination of terms equals combination of that operation applied individually to each term

dividend number that is divided by divisor

division arithmetic operation that finds how many times one number is contained in another, producing a quotient

divisor number that divides dividend

domain set of elements by which a function is limited or defined

eccentricity number used to define form of a conic section as an ellipse, circle, parabola, or hyperbola

equation mathematical statement containing the equals (=) sign between two different but equal algebraic formulations

even number number that is divisible by two, where result is an integer

expansion replacement of an expression by the sum of its individual terms or by an infinite series

exponent superscript symbol used to indicate how many times a number is to be used as factor or multiplied by itself

exponential function function with independent variable as an exponent

expression symbol or combination of symbols representing a value or relationship

extrapolation estimating value of a function beyond range of its known values

factor two or more numbers multiplied together, each number being a factor of the product

factor analysis statistical method that reduces large number of measures or tests to smaller number of factors that account for all results

factorial product of all positive integers from given positive integer down to 1

Fibonacci sequence unending sequence of numbers, each of which is the sum of its two predecessors

formula equation illustrating rule for mathematical relationship of quantities

fraction quantity expressed as the ratio of two integers that is not itself an integer

frequency distribution grouping of observations or outcomes into classes and tabulation of number of occurrences of each class in given period

function exact association of one element from one set with element from another set

geodesic (*adj*) describing shortest line between two points on surface, esp. curved surface

geometric mean square root of product of two numbers

geometric progression sequence in which ratio

of each succeeding term to preceding term is constant throughout

Gödel's incompleteness theorem theorem that within a given logical system there exists at least one mathematical formula that can be neither proved nor disproved

googol number that is equal to 1 followed by 100 zeros

googolplex number that is equal to 1 followed by a googol of zeros

hypotenuse side of right triangle opposite right angle

hypothesis provisionally true statement; supposition to be proved

imaginary number square root of negative number, esp. imaginary unit represented by square root of -1

independent variable element in function whose value is specified first and determines value of one or more other elements in expression of function

infinity boundlessly great number, amount, or geometric magnitude

integer any natural number, or positive or negative whole number, including zero; whole number

interpolation determination of the intermediate unknown values of a function between two known values

inverse function function that replaces another function when variables of first function are interchanged for set of values of independent variable

inverse proportion ratio of x to y when one unknown is multiplied by a number and its proportional unknown is divided by that number

irrational number any real number that cannot be expressed as the ratio of two integers

least common denominator smallest number that divides evenly into numerator of fraction; multiple of denominators of two or more specified fractions; lowest common denominator

limit value approached by function as its independent variable approaches some specific value

linear equation algebraic equation in which variables are in first power and whose graph is a straight line

linear function function with variables in first degree, multiplied only by constants, and combined by addition or subtraction

locus set of all points satisfying given conditions

logarithm exponent of that power of a fixed base number that equals another given number

logarithmic function inverse of exponential function

lowest common denominator least common denominator

magic square matrix in which each column, row, and both main diagonals produce same constant sum

mantissa decimal part of common logarithm

mapping examination of entities with no

meaning beyond themselves as they relate to a different set of entities, in order to generate conclusions

mathematical model set of formulae or equations that describe behavior of physical system in mathematical terms

matrix ordered set of elements arranged in rows and columns, esp. one that can be combined with similar arrays having comparable number of rows and columns

mean average

median middle item in array of data ranked from smallest to largest, used as statistical measure of primary tendency

million one thousand thousand

minuend number from which another number is subtracted

mixed number number consisting of whole number and fraction

mode statistical measure of primary tendency made by determining item that occurs most frequently in a data set

monomial expression in form of single term that is either a constant, variable, or product of numbers and variables

multiplicand number to be multiplied by another

multiplication arithmetic operation in which additions of a number are repeated a specified number of times to produce a product

multiplier number by which multiplicand is multiplied

natural number positive integer

number abstract unit in numeral series that represents an arbitrarily determined quantity; arithmetic total, sum of units involved

numeral word, letter, symbol, or figure expressing or representing a number

numerator upper number of fraction, indicating number of parts taken of denominator

odd number number that is not evenly divisible by two

one-to-one function function in which change in value in domain always gives different value for function

ordinal number number indicating position in a series, as *first* or *third*

ordinate vertical coordinate of two-dimensional coordinate system in Cartesian plane; y-axis

origin point of intersection in coordinate system, esp. x-axis and y-axis system

parameter arbitrary constant whose values describe some member of a system of curves, expressions, or functions; independent variable used to express coordinates of variable point and their functions

percent percentage

percentage ratio with denominator of 100; rate or proportion per hundred; percent

percentile percentage of sample rated equal to or higher than given level in statistical study

perigon round angle totaling 360 degrees

perimeter distance measured around outer boundary of any two-dimensional figure

periodic function function of a real or complex variable that has graph that repeats after fixed interval of the independent variable

permutation arrangement of given number of objects in a set into any of various possibilities

pi ratio of circumference of circle to its diameter, with a value equal to 22/7 or approximately 3.14159265, designated θ

polynomial expression containing sums or differences of monomials

polynomial function function composed of one or more polynomials

population entire group with which a given statistical study is concerned

postulate unproved assumption

power product resulting from repeated multiplication of a number by itself, square being second power, cube third

prime number any integer other than one evenly divisible only by one and itself

probability ratio of number of outcomes in a given series of events to total number of possible outcomes in that series

product result of multiplication

proof sequence of axioms, postulates, and theorems used to conclude that a statement is true

proportion equality between ratios, esp. quotients of two fractions; ratio of x to y when both unknowns are multiplied or divided by the same number

Pythagorean theorem in a right triangle the square of the hypotenuse is equal to the sum of the squares of the other two sides

quadratic equation equation in which highest exponent of variable is two

quadratic function function with elements expressed in at least first degree but no higher than second degree

quartile one of the values of a variable that divides a frequency distribution into four groups having equal frequencies

quotient result of dividing one number by another

radian unit of angular measure equal to 57.296 degrees, being angle subtended at center of circle by arc of length equal to radius of that circle

radical root of number or quantity, esp. square root symbol

radicand expression under radical symbol; number whose square root is to be determined

radius line segment from center of circle or sphere to point on circle or sphere

radix base number

range complete set of values a function may assume

ratio comparison of two numbers, expressed as fractional quotient

rational function quotient of two polynomials

rational number number that can be expressed as integer or ratio of two integers

real number part of complex number that is not imaginary, either rational or irrational

reciprocal multiplicative inverse; number which when multiplied by its reciprocal is one

recurring decimal decimal fraction ending in pattern of digits repeated indefinitely

remainder number left after subtraction; portion of the dividend, not evenly divisible, left after division

Roman numeral any of system of numerical notation based on values: I=1, V=5, X=10, L=50, C=100, D=500, M=1,000

root quantity that when multiplied by itself a certain number of times produces a given quantity; square root or cube root

scientific notation method of expressing number as product of number between 1 and 10, with integral power of ten as exponent

secant trigonometric ratio of hypotenuse of right triangle to leg adjacent to its acute angle

series expression obtained by adding sequence of terms, finite or infinite

set collection of elements of same kind or class

significant digits all nonzero digits in a number and zeros either between them or at end, where they signify accuracy to a number of places

simultaneous equations two or more equations having common solutions, when used in same problem

sine trigonometric ratio of side of right triangle opposite a given acute angle to hypotenuse

single parallel postulate essential postulate of Euclidean geometry which states that only one line may be drawn through a given point parallel to a given line

square product of number multiplied by itself

square root one of two equal factors of a number

standard deviation measure of variability in frequency distribution based on squares of deviations from mean

subtraction arithmetic operation in which one number is reduced by another to produce a difference

subtrahend number to be subtracted from minuend

sum number resulting from addition of two or more numbers

supplement angle or arc that when added to another angle or arc totals 180 degrees

tangent trigonometric ratio between leg opposite acute angle in right triangle and leg adjacent to it

ten base for decimal system of numbers

tens successive places in multidigit integer in decimal system: tens, hundreds, thousands, etc.

theorem statement that can be proved by mathematical deduction from given facts and justifiable assumptions

total sum of two or more numbers

transcendental function function that cannot be expressed by finite number of algebraic operations; exponential, logarithmic, or trigonometric function

transcendental number number that cannot be

root of algebraic equation with rational coefficients, such as pi

transfinite (*adj*) designating number larger than any finite positive integer

transpose (*vb*) transfer term from one side of algebraic equation to the other, reversing plus or minus sign in the process

trigonometric function function of arc or angle expressed as ratio of any pair of sides of right triangle; circular function

trillion one thousand billion; one million million

universe set of all objects that are admissible to that set based on its parameters

unknown variable whose value can be found by solving equation

variable unknown placeholder in algebraic expression, opposite of constant, usu. indicated by a letter; (*adj*) having no fixed value

variance in statistics, the square of the standard deviation

variation manner in which two or more quantities change in relation to each other

vector quantity possessing both magnitude and direction, represented by line segment of specific length and direction

volume cubic magnitude of three-dimensional figure

whole number zero or any positive or negative multiple of one; integer

x-axis abscissa

x-coordinate number associated with point on x-axis

y-axis ordinate

y-coordinate number associated with point on y-axis

zero numeral 0, being point from which positive and negative quantities are measured, symbolizing the absence of quantity

Geometric Shapes and Mathematically Defined Forms

acute angle angle of less than ninety degrees

angle open figure formed by two lines joined at common endpoint

arc portion of a curve

bi- prefix meaning two, as in *bisect*: divide into two parts

bilinear (*adj*) involving or formed by two lines; linear relative to each of two variables

circle two-dimensional area defined by curved set of points all equidistant from a single, central point

cissoid curve converging into pointed tip

complementary angle either of two angles that combine to form 90 degree angle

cone three-dimensional figure with circular base and single point as vertex

conic section curve formed by intersection of plane with right circular cone

correspondence property in which two figures have angles, lines, and points in similar relationships

cross two straight lines that intersect

cube three-dimensional figure with six congruent square faces

curve one-dimensional continuum of points in space of two or more dimensions

cusp tip of pointed curve

cycloid curve traced by point on radius of circle that rolls through one complete revolution in straight line

cylinder three-dimensional figure with two congruent, parallel, circular bases connected by a curved, lateral surface

deca- prefix meaning ten, as in *decagon*: ten-sided polygon

disk two-dimensional figure defined by all points enclosed by circle's circumference

dodeca- prefix meaning twelve, as in *dodecahedron*: twelve-faced figure

dome hemisphere

ellipse closed plane curve generated by point moving so that sum of point's distance from two fixed points is constant; plane section of right circular cone

ellipsoid solid figure, all plane sections of which are ellipses or circles

equi- prefix meaning equal, as in *equilateral* triangle: triangle with all sides of equal length and all angles equal to 60 degrees

equilateral triangle triangle with all sides congruent and all angles equal to 60 degrees

fractal geometrical structure having irregular or fragmented shape at all scales, such that certain phenomena behave as if the structure's dimensions are greater than they are in space

frustum conical solid with top cut off by plane parallel to base

gnomon shape that, when added to figure, preserves figure's original shape but increases its size

helix three-dimensional curve whose spiral arms maintain constant angle relative to base

hemisphere half of sphere, formed by plane through sphere's center

hepta- prefix meaning seven, as in *heptagon*: seven-sided polygon

hexa- prefix meaning six, as in *hexagon*: six-sided polygon

hyper- prefix meaning beyond, extra, above the norm, as in *hyperspace*: space with more than three dimensions

hyperbola set of points in a plane whose distances to two fixed points in the plane have a constant difference

icosa- prefix meaning twenty, as in *icosahedron*: twenty-sided figure

iso- prefix meaning equal, as in *isosceles* triangle: triangle with two equal sides

isosceles triangle three-sided, two-dimensional figure with two congruent sides and two equal angles

line straight, one-dimensional figure defined by all points along path connecting two points

oblique (*adj*) neither perpendicular nor parallel; without a right angle

oblong square, circle, or sphere that is elongated in one dimension, esp. rectangular figure with unequal adjacent sides

obtuse angle angle of more than 90 but less than 180 degrees

octa- prefix meaning eight, as in *octagon*: eight-sided polygon

oval body or plane that is ellipsoidal or elliptical in shape

para- prefix meaning equal or same, as in *parallelogram*: figure with both pairs of opposite sides equal

parabola plane curve generated by movement of point at equal distance from fixed point and fixed line

parallel (*adj*) constantly equidistant and in the same plane

parallelepiped prism with six faces, all parallelograms

parallelogram four-sided, two-dimensional figure with both pairs of opposite sides parallel

penta- prefix meaning five, as in *pentagon*: five-sided polygon

perpendicular (*adj*) at right angle to plane or line

plane flat, unbounded, two-dimensional surface

point single, specific location with no extension in space; geometric element determined by ordered set of coordinates

poly- prefix meaning many, usu. three or more, as in *polygon*: multisided figure

polygon closed plane figure of three or more line segments

polyhedron closed, three-dimensional figure composed of faces, or polygonal areas, connected along edges

prism three-dimensional figure with two parallel, congruent, polygon-shaped bases

pyramid three-dimensional figure with polygonal base and three or more triangular faces that converge in single point at vertex

quadrangle two-dimensional, four-sided, four-angled figure

quadrant quarter of a circle; any of four parts into which plane is divided by rectangular coordinate axes

quadratic (*adj*) relating to or resembling a square

quadri- prefix meaning four, as in *quadrilateral*: four-sided polygon

quadrilateral four-sided polygon

rectangle two-dimensional figure with four sides at right angles

reflex angle angle greater than 180 degrees and less than 360 degrees

rhomboid oblique-angled parallelogram with only its opposite sides equal

rhombus equilateral parallelogram with oblique angles

right angle angle of 90 degrees

right triangle two-dimensional figure with three sides, two of which form 90 degree angle

scalene triangle two-dimensional figure with three sides, no two of which are congruent

semicircle half of a circle, formed by arc from one end of diameter to the other

simplex any figure in Euclidean space having one more boundary point than its number of dimensions, such as a line segment, which has one dimension and two boundary points

solid figure having length, breadth, and thickness

sphere three-dimensional figure formed by set of all points in space equidistant from central fixed point

square two-dimensional figure with four equilateral, right-angled sides; right-angled rhombus

supplementary angle either of two angles that combine to form an angle of 180 degrees

tetra- prefix meaning four, as in *tetrahedron*: four-faced polyhedron

three-dimensional (*adj*) having length, breadth, and thickness

torus doughnut-shaped surface generated by rotation of a circle about an axis in its plane that does not intersect it

trapezium two-dimensional, irregular, four-sided figure with no two sides parallel

trapezoid two-dimensional, four-sided figure with two parallel sides

tri- prefix meaning three, as in *trisect*: divide into three parts

triangle three-sided, two-dimensional figure

truncated (*adj*) designating geometric figure, such as cone, having its apex or vertex end cut off by a plane

two-dimensional (*adj*) having height and width only

vector line segment of specific length and direction, used to represent quantity that has both direction and magnitude

vertex point at which two lines or planes meet to form angle

Mathematical Tools

abacus counting and computational device consisting of beads mounted in groups of tens on wires in frame, esp. used in Asia

calculator machine that performs arithmetic functions

compass instrument used to draw arcs and circles

computer programmable electronic device for storage and retrieval of data that performs very rapid calculations

graph diagrammatic representation of numerical values and relationships, esp. using Cartesian coordinates

graticule grid or network of lines projected onto flat surface; coordinate network

histogram vertical block graph

multiplication table graphlike arrangement used to memorize products of each number in series, usu. 1 through 12, multiplied by each number in same series

protractor instrument used to measure and lay down angles in drawing

quadrille (*adj*) marked or ruled with squares for making graphs

ruler straight-edged strip of hard material, used to measure distances and draw straight lines

slide rule instrument consisting of ruler and slide, each graduated with similar logarithmic scales used for calculations

trammel mechanical device used to generate curve from fixed point

Venn diagram diagram that uses overlapping circles to show relationship between sets

---

CHEMISTRY

Branches and Disciplines
Substances, Particles, and Atomic Architecture
Elements
Physical Properties and Changes
Chemical Properties and Reactions
Constants, Theories, and Values
Tools, Tests, Units, and Scales

See also: *Chap. 2: Biology; Chap. 3: Geology;*
Minerals, Metals, and Rocks; Chap. 4: Physics;
Chap. 5: Electricity and Electronics

Branches and Disciplines

alchemy medieval chemistry and speculative philosophy that attempted to transmute base metals into gold and to discover cures for disease

analytical chemistry branch of chemistry dealing with the qualitative and quantitative determination of the chemical composition of substances

astrochemistry study of chemical composition of universe beyond Earth

biochemistry study of chemical characteristics and processes occurring in living organisms or systems

chemical engineering industrial applications of chemistry

chemistry science dealing with the composition, structure, properties, and reactions of substances

chemosurgery chemical removal of diseased or unwanted tissue

chemotherapy use of chemical agents to treat and control disease, esp. cancer

chemurgy division of applied chemistry dealing with industrial utilization of organic materials, esp. farm products

crystallography study of crystal form and structure

cytochemistry study of the chemistry of cell constituents, esp. by staining

electrochemistry study of the interaction of electric current, ions, atoms, and molecules

geochemistry study of chemical composition of Earth's crust, interior, and atmosphere

inorganic chemistry branch of chemistry dealing with compounds not containing carbon and certain simple carbon compounds

kinetics study of the rates of chemical reactions

magnetochemistry study of magnetic properties of compounds

microchemistry branch of chemistry dealing with microscopic and submicroscopic quantities

neurochemistry study of chemical composition and behavior of the nervous system

nuclear chemistry branch of chemistry dealing with radioactive materials; radiochemistry

organic chemistry branch of chemistry dealing with carbon-containing compounds, excepting certain simple carbon compounds

petrochemistry division of applied chemistry dealing with petroleum and natural gas products

physical chemistry study of effect of chemical structure on physical properties

piezochemistry study of effects of high pressure on chemical reactions

polymer chemistry study of structure and synthesis of polymer molecules

radiochemistry nuclear chemistry

spectroscopy investigation of matter by generation and study of spectra of light or radiation

stereochemistry study of structure of molecules and effects of molecular structure on chemical properties

stoichiometry study of quantitative relationships of elements in combination

thermochemistry study of relationship of heat to chemical change

zymurgy branch of applied chemistry dealing with fermentation

Substances, Particles, and Atomic Architecture

acceptor atom that receives pair of electrons from another atom to form covalent bond

acid substance that produces hydrogen ions (H+) in water solution, acts as proton donor, or acts as electron-pair acceptor

alcohol organic compound containing hydroxyl group (-OH)

alkali base that dissolves in water to give hydroxyl ions; soluble substance with pH over 7.0 that can neutralize acids

alkane series series of saturated hydrocarbons, including methane and ethane

allotrope one of two or more different molecular forms of an element in same physical state, with differences in physical and chemical properties

alloy combination of two or more metals or metal and nonmetal

alpha particle helium nucleus: two protons and two neutrons

anion negatively charged ion

atom smallest subdivision of an element that displays properties of that element and remains undivided in chemical reactions except for limited loss or exchange of electrons

atomic orbital region around atomic nucleus in which an electron may be found

atomic shell grouping of electrons in one or more atomic orbitals, grouped by average distance from nucleus

azeotrope mixture of two liquids that maintains constant composition when boiled

base substance that produces hydroxide ions (OH-) in water solution, acts as proton acceptor, or acts as electron-pair donor

benzene ring structural unit in molecules of aromatic organic compounds, based on ring of six carbon atoms with one hydrogen atom attached to each

bond force holding atoms together in molecule or crystal

bond angle angle between two bond axes extending from same atom

bond axis line connecting nuclei of two bonded atoms

bond character relative ionic or covalent character of a bond

bond energy amount of energy associated with bond in a chemical compound

buffer substance that minimizes changes in pH of a solution by neutralizing added amounts of acid or base

carbon nonmetallic element found in all organic compounds; diamond and graphite are its two main allotropes

catalyst substance that changes reaction rate without being consumed or affected itself

cation positively charged ion

chelate compound in which the central atom, usu. a metal ion, is attached to its neighbors by two or more coordinate bonds forming a closed chain

chemical element or chemical compound obtained by a chemical process or producing a chemical effect

clathrate solid mixture in which molecules of one substance are entrapped in the crystal structure of another

colloid mixture of fine particles in a continuous medium that do not settle out rapidly and are not readily filtered, being smaller than particles of a suspension but larger than those of a solution

complex compound in which molecules form coordinate bonds with a metal atom or ion

compound substance composed of atoms from two or more elements chemically united in fixed proportions

conductor substance that conducts electricity or heat

conjugate acid substance created by addition of a proton to a base

conjugate acid-base pair acid proton donor and its conjugate base

conjugate base substance remaining after an acid has donated a proton

coordinate covalent bond covalent bond in which both shared electrons were donated by the same atom

covalent bond chemical bond formed by sharing, rather than by transfer, of one or more electrons between atoms

crystal solid in which atoms, ions, or molecules are arranged in a regular, repeating pattern

dehydrating agent substance that absorbs water from other substances; desiccant

desiccant dehydrating agent

dipole molecule with oppositely charged ends; polar molecule

dipole-dipole force electrical attraction between dipoles

dipole-induced dipole force electrical attraction between a dipole and a nonpolar molecule it has induced to become a dipole

dispersion force force between particles due to the instantaneous distribution of their electrical charges

donor atom that contributes a pair of electrons to another atom to form a coordinate covalent bond

electrolyte liquid that conducts electricity due to presence of ions

electron subatomic particle of very low mass carrying single, negative electrical charge

electron configuration distribution of electrons among atomic orbitals

electron-deficient compound compound in which the number of valence electrons around one or more atoms other than hydrogen is less than eight

electron spin rotation of electrons giving them magnetic properties that permit opposite spin electrons to occupy one orbital

element one of a class of substances composed of atoms having the same number of protons in each nucleus and incapable of being separated into simpler substances by chemical means; currently 107 such substances are listed on periodic table of elements

energy level definite, fixed energy that a molecule, atom, electron, or nucleus can possess

enzyme biological catalyst

ester compound produced by reaction between an acid and an alcohol with the elimination of a water molecule

excited state condition in which nucleus, electron, atom, or molecule has an energy level higher than its ground state

fluid material that flows; liquid or gas

free electron electron not bound to an atom or associated with a bond

free radical any neutral, usu. highly reactive fragment of a molecule with an unpaired valence electron

fuel any material used to produce energy, including combustible substances usu. derived from organic hydrocarbons or materials from which atomic energy can be liberated in a reactor

functional group group of atoms responsible for characteristic reactions of a compound

gamma ray electromagnetic radiation having short wavelength, emitted by excited atomic nuclei as they pass to lower energy level

gas state of matter characterized by the nearly unrestricted, random motion of molecules that are far apart in relation to their diameters

ground state lowest stable energy level of a system

gum any of numerous colloidal substances of plant origin that harden from gelatinous state when dried

halogen any of the electronegative elements fluorine, chlorine, iodine, bromine, and astatine, that form binary salts by direct union with metals and comprise the group next to noble gases in periodic table

heterogeneous mixture combination of substances in which components remain physically separate and retain their individual chemical properties

homogeneous mixture combination of substances in which composition and concentrations of components are uniform throughout, the atoms or molecules of each substance being interspersed

hydrate substance formed by combining a compound with water

hydrocarbon organic compound containing only hydrogen and carbon

hydrogen bond exceptionally strong dipole-dipole attraction between hydrogen and a highly electronegative element such as oxygen or nitrogen

hydroxide chemical compound containing hydroxyl group

hydroxyl (*adj*) containing the negatively charged OH group

ideal gas hypothetical gas in which molecules are viewed as occupying no space, exerting no remote forces on each other, and whose collisions are completely elastic

ideal solution mixture that obeys Raoult's law at all concentrations

indicator substance used to show the presence of a substance or ion by its color

induced dipole dipole created when an ion or polar molecule approaches a nonpolar molecule

inert gas noble gas

inhibitor catalyst used to slow or stop a reaction

insulator substance that is a poor conductor of heat or electricity

interface area of contact between physical states of a substance (solid/liquid, liquid/gas) or between different substances

intermolecular force force acting between molecules

intramolecular force force acting between atoms in the same molecule

ion charged particle formed by loss or addition of electrons in neutral atom or molecule

ionic bond strong electrostatic attraction holding ions of opposite charge together in molecule or crystal, often formed by transfer of electrons

ion pair cation and anion held together by ionic bond; smallest division of an ionic compound

isomer any of two or more compounds with the same molecular formulas but different structures

isomorph any of two or more substances that have the same crystal structure

isotope any of two or more forms of an element with same atomic number but different atomic mass

ligand ion or molecule that donates a pair of electrons during formation of a complex

limiting reactant reactant that is used up completely in a reaction, limiting further chemical change

liquid state of matter characterized by particles in proximity greater than that of a gas but less than that of a solid, restricting their random motions to vibrations around moving points

lone pair valence electron pair not involved in bond formation

matter anything that occupies space and possesses mass

metal any of a class of elements that typically lose electrons in chemical reactions, conduct heat and electricity well, and form cations or coordinate covalent bonds

metallic bond electrostatic attraction holding atoms together in metal or alloy, with their valence electrons able to move almost freely

metalloid element with properties of both metals and nonmetals

mineral any naturally occurring, homogeneous substance having definite chemical composition and usu. crystalline structure

mixture aggregate of two or more substances in which each substance retains its identity and can be separated by physical means such as distillation or crystallization

molecular orbital region of molecule in which an electron, under the influence of two or more nuclei, can be found

molecule two or more atoms held together in a definite arrangement by electrical forces; smallest subdivision of a compound

monobasic acid acid containing one replaceable hydrogen atom

monomer molecule that can join with others to form a polymer

monoprotic acid acid that is capable of donating only one hydrogen ion to a base

multiple bond covalent bond in which two atoms share two or three electron pairs

neighbor atom to which another atom is bonded

neutron particle that occurs in all atomic nuclei except normal hydrogen, with neutral electrical charge and mass of about 1 amu

noble gas any of the class of stable gases, such as helium and neon, that do not easily react chemically due to electron-full outer atomic shells; inert gas

nonbonding electrons lone pair

nonbonding orbitals atomic orbitals not involved in bond formation

nonelectrolyte substance that does not conduct electricity when dissolved in water or another polar solvent

nonmetal any of a class of elements that

typically gain electrons in chemical reactions, conduct heat and electricity poorly, and form anions or covalent bonds in compounds

nonorganic compound any compound not containing carbon

nucleus small, dense, positively charged central core of an atom, constituting a tiny fraction of the atom's volume but almost all of its mass, composed primarily of protons and neutrons

optical isomer one of a pair of asymmetrical molecules that are mirror images of each other, revealed by how they rotate polarized light

orbital atomic orbital, or molecular orbital

organic compound any compound containing carbon

oxide any compound in which oxygen is bonded to one or more electropositive atoms

oxidizing agent any substance that tends to gain electrons, oxidizing other substances while itself being reduced

particle any minute, distinguishable subdivision of matter

phase homogeneous part of a heterogeneous system that is separated by some distinguishable boundary, such as the solid, liquid, and gaseous phases of a system

phosphor substance that is capable of luminescence

physical state one of three states in which matter can exist: solid, liquid, and gas

plasma highly ionized gas, often at high temperature, in which free electrons and positive ions are present in approximately equal numbers

plastic any of various materials, generally made from synthetic resins, that can be shaped by applying heat or pressure and then hardened

polar molecule dipole

polymer large molecule made up of smaller monomers repeated many times

polyprotic acid acid with more than one ionizable hydrogen atom

precipitate solid produced by reaction occurring in a solution

product new substance formed by chemical reaction

promoter substance added to catalyst to increase its activity

proton particle that occurs in all atomic nuclei, with a single positive charge and mass of about 1 amu

quantum minimum amount by which certain properties of a system, such as energy or angular momentum, can change

radical group of atoms, either in a compound or existing alone

reactant any substance that undergoes chemical change in a reaction

reagent any substance used to detect, measure, or examine another substance, or to transform it by causing a reaction

reducing agent substance that tends to donate electrons, reducing other substances while itself being oxidized

resin any of various semisolid, organic polymers formed synthetically or occurring naturally in plant secretions

resonance phenomenon exhibited in certain bonds that can be accurately described only by a combination of alternative models, as when a covalent bond shows polarity and hence exhibits some ionic character

salt compound formed by the positive ion of a base and the negative ion of an acid

saturated compound compound consisting of molecules having only single rather than double or triple bonds

saturated solution solution containing as much solute as can be dissolved in solvent at given temperature, with dissolved and undissolved solute in dynamic equilibrium

saturated vapor vapor that is in dynamic equilibrium with its liquid or solid phase

solid state of matter characterized by particles in such close proximity that their random motions are restricted to vibration about fixed points

solute solid or gas dissolved in a liquid; substance present in lesser amount in a solution of two liquids; substance dissolved in a solvent

solution homogeneous mixture of two or more substances

solvent component of a solution that is present in the greatest amount or that undergoes no change of state; substance in which a solute is dissolved to form a solution

spectator ion ion present in a solution, but not taking part in a reaction

strong acid acid that dissociates completely in an aqueous solution

strong base base that dissociates completely in an aqueous solution

substance matter that has definite composition and distinct properties

superconductor substance that exhibits no measurable electrical resistance at low temperatures

suspension mixture in which relatively large particles are scattered throughout a continuous medium and can be filtered out or will settle out if left standing

synthetic (*adj*) man-made, not occurring in nature; (*n*) such a substance

valence electrons electrons in outermost atomic orbitals of an atom that take part in forming bonds with other atoms to form molecules

van der Waals' forces weak attractive forces between neutral atoms and molecules, including dipole-dipole, dipole-induced dipole, and dispersion forces; weak forces

water of hydration water present in definite proportions in crystalline compounds

weak acid acid that is only partially dissociated in an aqueous solution

weak base base that is only partially dissociated in an aqueous solution

weak forces van der Waals' forces

Elements

actinium Ac; atomic number 89, atomic weight 227

aluminum Al; atomic number 13, atomic weight 27

americium Am; atomic number 95, atomic weight 243

antimony Sb; atomic number 51, atomic weight 122

argon Ar or A; atomic number 18, atomic weight 40

arsenic As; atomic number 33, atomic weight 75

astatine At; atomic number 85, atomic weight 210

barium Ba; atomic number 56, atomic weight 137

berkelium Bk; atomic number 97, atomic weight 247

beryllium Be; atomic number 4, atomic weight 9

bismuth Bi; atomic number 83, atomic weight 209

boron B; atomic number 5, atomic weight 11

bromine Br; atomic number 35, atomic weight 80

cadmium Cd; atomic number 48, atomic weight 112

calcium Ca; atomic number 20, atomic weight 40

californium Cf; atomic number 98, atomic weight 210

carbon C; atomic number 6, atomic weight 12

cerium Ce; atomic number 58, atomic weight 140

cesium Cs; atomic number 55, atomic weight 133

chlorine Cl; atomic number 17, atomic weight 35

chromium Cr; atomic number 24, atomic weight 52

cobalt Co; atomic number 27, atomic weight 59

columbium niobium

copper Cu; atomic number 29, atomic weight 64

curium Cm; atomic number 96, atomic weight 247

dysprosium Dy; atomic number 66, atomic weight 163

einsteinium Es or E; atomic number 99, atomic weight 254

erbium Er; atomic number 68, atomic weight 167

europium Eu; atomic number 63, atomic weight 152

fermium Fm; atomic number 100, atomic weight 253

fluorine F; atomic number 9, atomic weight 19

francium Fr; atomic number 87, atomic weight 223

gadolinium Gd; atomic number 64, atomic weight 157

gallium Ga; atomic number 31, atomic weight 70

germanium Ge; atomic number 32, atomic weight 73

gold Au; atomic number 79, atomic weight 197

hafnium Hf; atomic number 72, atomic weight 178

hahnium Ha; atomic number 105, atomic weight 262; unnilpentium
helium He; atomic number 2, atomic weight 4
holmium Ho; atomic number 67, atomic weight 165
hydrogen H; atomic number 1, atomic weight 1
indium In; atomic number 49, atomic weight 115
iodine I; atomic number 53, atomic weight 127
iridium Ir; atomic number 77, atomic weight 192
iron Fe; atomic number 26, atomic weight 56
krypton Kr; atomic number 36, atomic weight 84
lanthanum La; atomic number 57, atomic weight 139
lawrencium Lw; atomic number 103, atomic weight 257
lead Pb; atomic number 82, atomic weight 207
lithium Li; atomic number 3, atomic weight 7
lutetium Lu; atomic number 71, atomic weight 175
magnesium Mg; atomic number 12, atomic weight 24
manganese Mn; atomic number 25, atomic weight 55
mendelevium Md or Mv; atomic number 101, atomic weight 256
mercury Hg; atomic number 80, atomic weight 201
molybdenum Mo; atomic number 42, atomic weight 96
neodymium Nd; atomic number 60, atomic weight 144
neon Ne; atomic number 10, atomic weight 20
neptunium Np; atomic number 93, atomic weight 237
nickel Ni; atomic number 28, atomic weight 59
niobium Nb; atomic number 41, atomic weight 93; formerly columbium
nitrogen N; atomic number 7, atomic weight 14
nobelium No; atomic number 102, atomic weight 254
osmium Os; atomic number 76, atomic weight 190
oxygen O; atomic number 8, atomic weight 16
palladium Pd; atomic number 46, atomic weight 106
phosphorus P; atomic number 15, atomic weight 31
platinum Pt; atomic number 78, atomic weight 195
plutonium Pu; atomic number 94, atomic weight 242
polonium Po; atomic number 84, atomic weight 210
potassium K; atomic number 19, atomic weight 39
praseodymium Pr; atomic number 59, atomic weight 141
promethium Pm; atomic number 61, atomic weight 147
protactinium Pa; atomic number 91, atomic weight 231
radium Ra; atomic number 88, atomic weight 226
radon Rn; atomic number 86, atomic weight 222
rhenium Re; atomic number 75, atomic weight 186

rhodium Rh; atomic number 45, atomic weight 103
rubidium Rb; atomic number 37, atomic weight 85
ruthenium Ru; atomic number 44, atomic weight 101
rutherfordium Rf; atomic number 104, atomic weight 261; unnilquadium
samarium Sm; atomic number 62, atomic weight 150
scandium Sc; atomic number 21, atomic weight 45
selenium Se; atomic number 34, atomic weight 79
silicon Si; atomic number 14, atomic weight 28
silver Ag; atomic number 47, atomic weight 108
sodium Na; atomic number 11, atomic weight 23
strontium Sr; atomic number 38, atomic weight 88
sulfur S; atomic number 16, atomic weight 32
tantalum Ta; atomic number 73, atomic weight 181
technetium Tc; atomic number 43, atomic weight 99
tellurium Te; atomic number 52, atomic weight 128
terbium Tb; atomic number 65, atomic weight 159
thallium Tl; atomic number 81, atomic weight 204
thorium Th; atomic number 90, atomic weight 232
thulium Tm; atomic number 69, atomic weight 169
tin Sn; atomic number 50, atomic weight 119
titanium Ti; atomic number 22, atomic weight 48
tungsten wolfram
unnilhexium provisional name for transuranic element with atomic number 106 and atomic weight 259
unnilpentium hahnium
unnilquadium rutherfordium
unnilseptium provisional name for transuranic element with atomic number 107 and atomic weight 262
uranium U; atomic number 92, atomic weight 238
vanadium V; atomic number 23, atomic weight 51
wolfram W; atomic number 74, atomic weight 184; formerly tungsten
xenon Xe; atomic number 54, atomic weight 131
ytterbium Yb; atomic number 70, atomic weight 173
yttrium Y; atomic number 39, atomic weight 89
zinc Zn; atomic number 30, atomic weight 65
zirconium Zr; atomic number 40, atomic weight 91

Physical Properties and Changes

absorbance measure of electromagnetic radiation absorbed by a substance, applied to total radiation or part of spectrum
absorption assimilation of one substance into another

adiabatic (*adj*) designating process in which no energy is transferred between a system and its surroundings
adsorption attachment of one substance to the surface of another
amorphous (*adj*) describing a solid without crystalline structure
Brownian motion random motion of colloidal particles due to bombardment of the particles by molecules of the surrounding medium
capillary attraction tendency of a liquid to rise in a narrow tube or move through absorbent material, due to greater adhesion of the liquid to the solid than the internal adhesion of the liquid itself
capillary repulsion tendency of a liquid to pull away from a solid surface, due to greater internal cohesion of the liquid than the adhesion of the liquid to a solid surface
cohesion physical force by which molecules of a substance are held together
colligative property property of a substance that depends on solution concentration rather than type of solute or nature of its molecules or atoms
concentration amount of solute per unit of solvent in a solution
condensation change from vapor phase to liquid phase
conductivity ability of a substance to transmit electricity or heat
crystallization formation of crystals or assumption of crystalline structure
density mass per unit of volume
diagonal relationship similarities observed among elements in the periodic table
diamagnetic (*adj*) describing substances containing only paired electrons in which a magnetic field is induced in the opposite direction to that of an applied field
diffusion mixture of one substance with another throughout a given volume as a result of random molecular motion
dipole moment vector quantity having magnitude equal to product of either of two equal electrical charges times the distance between them in a dipole
dissolution breaking up into separate parts
ductility ability of a substance to be drawn into a fine wire
effusion passage of gas molecules through a small opening
electron affinity attraction of an atom for an electron, expressed as the energy needed to restore neutrality by removing an electron from the atom's anion
electronegative (*adj*) having the ability to attract electrons in a molecule and form negative ions; nonmetallic
electropositive (*adj*) tending to migrate to the negative pole in electrolysis; basic, as an element or group
endothermic (*adj*) absorbing heat energy

energy capacity to do work, which diminishes in a system when work is done by an amount equal to work so done

enthalpy change measure of heat gained or lost by a system when it undergoes a chemical reaction or physical change at constant pressure

entropy thermodynamic quantity describing amount of disorder or randomness in system

equilibrium state in which forces acting on a system are balanced

evaporation change from liquid to gas at temperature below boiling point of liquid, occurring at surface of liquid as molecules with higher kinetic energies escape into their gas phase

excited state any of the energy levels of an atom, molecule, or other physical system that has higher energy than the lowest energy level

exothermic (*adj*) releasing heat energy

extensive properties additive properties such as mass or length that depend on the quantity of matter under consideration

ferromagnetic (*adj*) designating a metal strongly capable of modifying a magnetic field, and in which magnetization persists after removal of an applied field

fission nuclear reaction in which an atomic nucleus splits into fragments, usu. two nuclei of comparable size

fluorescence emission of light that does not persist significantly after the exciting cause is removed

fusion change from solid to liquid, nuclear reaction in which two or more smaller nuclei combine into one larger nucleus

heat energy associated with the motion of particles

hydration solution in which the solvent is water

immiscible (*adj*) designating two liquids that will not dissolve in each other

incandescence emission of light by a substance as a result of raising it to a high temperature

insoluble (*adj*) incapable of being dissolved in specific solvent

intensive properties nonadditive properties, such as temperature, that are independent of the quantity of matter present

internal energy total kinetic and potential energies of atoms and molecules in a system

ionization potential minimum energy required to remove an electron from the ground state in a specific atom

isobaric (*adj*) occurring at constant pressure

isoelectronic (*adj*) possessing same number of valence electrons

isolated system system in which no energy or mass is exchanged with its surroundings

isomerism existence of chemical compounds with the same molecular formulas but different structures

isomorphism existence of two or more substances having the same crystalline structure

isothermic (*adj*) occurring at constant temperature

kinetic energy energy associated with motion

liquefaction change from gas phase to liquid phase

luminescence emission of light by a substance for any reason other than an increase in its temperature

malleability ability of a substance to be shaped or hammered into thin sheets

mass quantity of matter in an object, measured by its resistance to a change in its motion

melting change from solid phase to liquid phase

miscible (*adj*) designating two liquids that are mutually soluble in all proportions

neutral (*adj*) having neither positive nor negative electric charge

nonpolar (*adj*) describing a covalent bond between two atoms with equal electron attraction, or a molecule with no charged ends

optical activity ability of certain substances to rotate the plane of polarized light passed through the substance or a solution containing it

osmosis net movement of solvent molecules through a semipermeable membrane separating two solutions, the direction of movement tending to equalize concentrations of the solutions

paramagnetic (*adj*) describing substances containing one or more unpaired electrons, in which a magnetic field is induced in the same direction as that of an applied field

partial pressure pressure that one gas in a mixture of gases would exert if it occupied the entire volume by itself

phosphorescence emission of light that persists significantly after the exciting cause is removed

physical property any trait that can be measured without changing the composition or identity of a substance, such as color, melting point, boiling point, density, or solubility

polar (*adj*) describing a covalent bond in which one atom has a stronger electron attraction than the other, or a molecule with oppositely charged ends

polarity asymmetrical charge distribution

polarization separation of positive and negative charges

potential difference difference in potential energy of electrons located at different points in an electric field

potential energy energy of an object due to its position in a force field

pressure force per unit area

radioactivity spontaneous disintegration of atomic nuclei accompanied by emission of alpha or beta particles or gamma radiation

solidification change from liquid phase to solid phase

solubility maximum amount of solute that will dissolve in a specific quantity of solvent at specific temperature

solution equilibrium state in which a solute is dissolving and crystallizing at the same rate

solvation interaction of solvent molecules with solute ions

specific heat capacity thermal energy needed to raise temperature of one gram of specific substance one degree Celsius

spontaneous (*adj*) occurring without outside influence

state function property of a system that is fixed by its present state; thermodynamic quantity determined solely by conditions, not by method of arriving at those conditions

sublimation process in which a substance changes state without becoming a liquid, usu. from solid to gas but also from gas to solid

superconductivity absence of electrical resistance in a substance at low temperature

supcrcooling cooling of a liquid below its freezing point without a change of state or solidification

supersaturated solution solution containing more solute than is present in its saturated state at the same temperature

surface tension property of a liquid that makes its surface behave like elastic skin due to unbalanced, molecular cohesive forces at or near surface

temperature property of a body or region of space that determines direction of net flow of heat with neighboring objects or regions

transmutation conversion of one element into another occurring by nuclear reaction, previously sought by alchemists using other means

vapor equilibrium state in which evaporation and condensation take place at same rate

vaporization change from liquid phase to gas phase

viscosity resistance of a fluid to flow

volatility tendency of a substance to evaporate at normal temperatures and pressures

weight force that gravity exerts on an object

Chemical Properties and Reactions

acid-base reaction acid and base mixed together yielding water and salt

acidic (*adj*) describing a solution with pH less than 7

activated complex midstage between reaction and products; unstable intermediate substance formed when reactants have acquired sufficient energy to meet activation energy requirements

activation energy energy required to start a chemical reaction

actual yield mass of product obtained from reaction

addition reaction reaction in which a small molecule is added to the multiple bonds of an organic compound

adiabatic (*adj*) designating a process in which no energy is transferred between a system and its surroundings

amphoteric (*adj*) capable of acting as an acid or base

anhydrous (*adj*) having no water of crystallization

aqueous (*adj*) describing a solution in water

atomization decomposition into composite atoms

basic (*adj*) describing a solution with pH greater than 7

bioluminescence emission of light produced by a living organism

breakdown decomposition into composite elements or molecules

buffer range pH range in which buffer is effective

catalysis modification of the rate of a reaction by addition of an agent that does not undergo chemical change

chain reaction self-sustaining series of chemical reactions, as the products of one step initiate a subsequent step

chemical property manner and quality of substance's interaction with another substance in a reaction substance

chemiluminescence emission of light resulting from chemical reaction

combination union of substances to form chemical compound

combustion rapid oxidation accompanied by production of heat and light

common ion effect shift in ionic equilibrium upon addition of ion that takes part in the equilibrium

condensation reaction combination of two molecules to form a larger molecule with the elimination of a small molecule, usu. water

corrosion chemical or electrochemical deterioration of metal

covalence number of electron pairs an atom can share with its neighboring atom

decomposition breakdown of a substance into two or more simpler substances

diagonal relationship similarities observed between certain elements in the periodic table and elements appearing diagonally below and to their right

dissociation breakdown of molecule or other group of atoms into smaller groups of atoms or ions

double decomposition metathesis

dynamic equilibrium equilibrium in which both a reaction and its reverse are occurring at rates that are exactly balanced

electrolysis redox reaction produced by passing electric current through an electrolyte

elimination reaction reaction in which a small molecule is removed from a larger molecule

endothermic (*adj*) absorbing heat energy

end point point at which an indicator changes color in a titration, showing that stoichiometric amounts of the reactants have been added; equivalence point

enthalpy change measure of heat gained or lost by system when it undergoes chemical reaction or physical change at constant pressure

equilibrium state in which forces acting on a system are balanced

equivalence point end point

equivalent (*adj*) having the same capacity to combine or react chemically

exothermic (*adj*) releasing heat energy

free energy chemical potential energy of a substance or system, used to indicate condition under which reaction will occur

half reaction oxidation or reduction reaction only

hydrated (*adj*) formed by combination of water and another substance in definite molecular ratio

hydrolysis solvolysis in which the solvent is water

hydrophilic (*adj*) attracted to and interacting with water

hydrophobic (*adj*) not attracted to or interacting with water

hygroscopic (*adj*) capable of absorbing water from air

intensive properties nonadditive properties, such as temperature, that are independent of the quantity of matter present

isobaric (*adj*) occurring at constant pressure

isothermic (*adj*) occurring at constant temperature

metathesis reaction involving an exchange of radicals; double decomposition

neutral (*adj*) describing a compound or solution that is neither acidic nor basic

neutralization reaction between an acid and a base that produces water and a salt

oxidation reaction involving the loss of electrons or an increase of the oxidation number in a compound

oxidation number number equal to valence of an element or radical

precipitation reaction in which small, solid particles form in a liquid

reactivity tendency of a substance to interact chemically with other substances

redox reaction reaction involving transfer of electrons from one substance to another; simultaneous reduction and oxidation reactions

reduction reaction involving the gain of electrons or a decrease of the oxidation number in a compound

reversible (*adj*) describing reactions in which products are changed back into original reactants under certain conditions

solvolysis reaction between a compound and its solvent

spontaneous (*adj*) occurring without outside influence

stability resistance of a substance to decomposition or disintegration

substitution reaction in which one atom or molecule is replaced by another atom or molecule

synthesis formation of a compound from two or more simpler compounds

theoretical yield amount of product stoichiometrically predicted to be present when a limiting reactant is used up

valence measure of capacity of an element or radical to combine with another element or radical to form molecules

Constants, Theories, and Values

absolute zero lowest temperature theoretically attainable, at which substances will have minimal atomic and molecular kinetic energy; base of 0 degrees on Kelvin scale, equal to -273.2 degrees C or -459.7 degrees F

atomic theory theory of the structure, properties, and behavior of atoms

Avogadro's law equal volumes of different gases at the same temperature and pressure contain equal numbers of molecules

Avogadro's number number of molecules in a mole, approximately 6.023×10^{23}

boiling point temperature at which the vapor pressure of a liquid equals the pressure of a gas above the liquid

Boyle's law at constant temperature, the volume of a gas is inversely proportional to its pressure

Charles' law at constant pressure, the volume of a gas varies directly with its absolute temperature; Gay-Lussac's law

critical pressure pressure needed to liquefy a gas at its critical temperature

critical temperature temperature above which no amount of pressure will liquefy a gas

Curie point temperature at which magnetic properties of a substance change from ferromagnetic to paramagnetic

Dalton's law total pressure of a mixture of gases is sum of the partial pressures of its component gases

de Broglie's hypothesis theory asserting that material particles have wavelike characteristics that can give rise to interference effects

equilibrium constant ratio of the equilibrium concentrations of products to reactants, each raised to the power of its stoichiometric coefficient, the value of this ratio being constant for any reaction

equivalent weight measure of the combining power of a substance; mass of a substance that can combine with or displace one gram of hydrogen in a chemical reaction

exclusion principle Pauli exclusion principle

first law of thermodynamics energy can be neither created nor destroyed, merely converted from one form to another; law of conservation of energy

freezing point temperature at which liquid changes to solid

Gay-Lussac's law Charles' law

Graham's law rates at which gases diffuse are inversely proportional to the square roots of their densities

heat capacity ratio of heat supplied to an object to its increase in temperature

heat of combustion energy liberated by the combustion of one mole of a substance in excess oxygen

heat of formation energy liberated or absorbed when one mole of a compound is formed from its elements

heat of fusion energy absorbed in changing one mole of a substance from its solid to liquid state at the substance's melting temperature

heat of reaction energy liberated or absorbed by the complete reaction of molar amounts of reactants

heat of solution energy liberated or absorbed in dissolving one mole of a substance in a large volume of solvent

heat of sublimation energy absorbed in changing one mole of a solid to a gas without intervening phase as a liquid

heat of vaporization energy absorbed in changing one mole of a substance from its liquid to gaseous state at the substance's boiling temperature

Henry's law amount of a gas that will dissolve in a specific amount of liquid varies directly with the partial pressure of the gas

Hess's law enthalpy change of a reaction is equal to the sum of the enthalpy changes of individual steps of the reaction

heterogeneous equilibrium equilibrium between reactants and products that are in different phases

homogeneous equilibrium equilibrium between reactants and products in the same phase

Hund's rule the most stable arrangement of electrons in orbitals is that with the greatest number of parallel spins

ideal gas equation product of a gas's pressure and volume equals the product of its number of moles, the universal gas constant, and Kelvin temperature

ionization constant equilibrium constant for ionization of a substance

Joule-Thomson effect cooling achieved when a gas expands through a small opening into a region of lower pressure

k rate constant, used in rate equation

kinetic theory theory explaining physical properties of matter in terms of the motion of its particles

law of conservation of energy first law of thermodynamics

law of conservation of mass and energy total amount of mass and energy in the universe is constant

law of conservation of matter in all changes, matter can be neither created nor destroyed; in a chemical reaction, the mass of the products equals the mass of the reactants

law of definite proportions elements composing a compound are always present in the same proportions by mass

law of multiple proportion for two elements that can combine to form more than one

compound, the ratio by mass of one element to a given mass of the second is a small whole number

Le Châtelier principle when stress is placed on a system in equilibrium, the system's equilibrium will shift to offset the effect of the stress

melting point temperature at which a solid changes to a liquid

molal (*adj*) denoting a property of weight expressed per mole of a substance

molal boiling point constant value characteristic of a solvent, equal to the rise in the boiling point of one kilogram of the solvent when one mole of solute is added

molal freezing point constant value characteristic of a solvent, equal to the drop in the freezing point of one kilogram of the solvent when one mole of solute is added

molar (*adj*) denoting a property of volume expressed per mole of a substance

molecular orbital theory model of molecular structure, based on the formation of molecular orbitals from corresponding atomic orbitals

octet rule bonded atoms tend to be surrounded by eight valence electrons, except hydrogen, which has two valence electrons

Pauli exclusion principle no two electrons in a system can carry the same four quantum numbers

pH value on a logarithmic scale from zero to fourteen, used to express the acidity or alkalinity of a solution, with pH of seven being neutral

photoelectric effect emission of electrons from a substance when energized by exposure to electromagnetic radiation

Planck's constant h; fundamental constant of quantum theory, equal to the ratio of the energy of a quantum of radiation to its frequency, or 6.63×10^{-34} joule-seconds

quantum minimum amount by which certain properties of a system can change

quantum number one of a set of four numbers used to describe energy levels of an electron in an atom, the numbers representing orbital size, shape, orientation, and electron spin

quantum theory theory according to which energy is emitted in quanta, each with an energy proportional to the frequency of the radiation

R universal gas constant, used in the ideal gas equation

Raoult's law for dilute solutions and certain others, the partial pressure of the solvent is proportional to its mole fraction

rate constant k; the constant in a reaction's rate equation

rate-determining step slowest step in a reaction involving more than one step

rate equation expression for the rate of a chemical reaction in terms of concentrations, the form of which depends on the reaction mechanism

rate law expression relating reaction rate to rate constant and concentrations of reactants raised to appropriate powers

reaction mechanism step-by-step description of the interaction of atoms, ions, and molecules in a reaction

reaction order sum of exponents to which concentrations of reactants are raised in the rate equation

reaction rate rate of disappearance of reactant or appearance of product

second law of thermodynamics entropy or disorder of a closed system increases spontaneously and never decreases; in a reversible reaction, entropy remains unchanged

solubility product equilibrium constant for a saturated solution of a slightly soluble salt

specific (*adj*) denoting a property of volume expressed per unit mass of a substance

standard atmospheric pressure average barometric pressure at sea level, equal to 760 mm of mercury or 101,325 pascal

standard state set of reference conditions for thermodynamic measurements, with temperature equal to 298.15 K, pressure equal to 101,325 pascal, and concentration equal to 1 mole

standard temperature and pressure STP; set of reference conditions for dealing with gases, with temperature equal to 273.15 K and pressure equal to 101,325 pascal

stoichiometric amounts exact molar amounts of reactants and products as they appear in a balanced chemical equation

STP standard temperature and pressure

third law of thermodynamics temperature of a system cannot be reduced to absolute zero in a finite number of operations

triple point temperature and pressure at which all three phases of a substance are in equilibrium

universal gas constant constant value in ideal gas equation, equal to 8.31 joules per Kevin-moles

vapor pressure pressure generated by vapor in equilibrium with its liquid or solid phase

wave-particle duality concept that waves and particles may at times behave alike

Tools, Tests, Units, and Scales

adsorption chromatography chromatographic technique in which molecules from a sample are differentially adsorbed on the stationary phase

alembic apparatus formerly used for distillation, often a retort

ampere A; SI unit of electrical current, equal to one coulomb of charge per second

amu atomic mass unit

analysis determination of components in chemical sample

anode positive electrode; electrode at which oxidation occurs in a cell

atmosphere unit of pressure equal to that exerted by a column of mercury 760 mm high, equal to 101,325 pascal, based on average atmospheric pressure at sea level

atomic mass mass of atom in atomic mass

units, usu. referring to weighted average mass of naturally-occurring mixture of isotopes; atomic weight

atomic mass unit amu; unit of mass, based on 12 as mass of most common isotope of carbon, used to express mass of atomic and subatomic particles

atomic number number of protons in nucleus of each atom of an element

atomic weight atomic mass

balance electronic or mechanical device for measuring weight

barometer manometer that measures atmospheric pressure

beaker wide-topped, cylindrical glass container used in a laboratory

bell jar bell-shaped covering used to protect delicate instruments or maintain controlled environment in experiments

Brix scale graduated scale, used on hydrometer, that measures percentage by weight of sugar in aqueous sugar solutions

Buchner funnel funnel used with filter paper and suction device to separate solids from a liquid

Bunsen burner small gas burner for heating substances

burette glass tube with graduated volume markings and stopcock, used to deliver specific volumes of liquid accurately

calorie amount of heat necessary to raise the temperature of one gram of water from 14.5 to 15.5 degrees C, equal to 4.187 joules

calorimeter device for measuring change of enthalpy

candela SI unit of luminous intensity, based on monochromatic radiation of frequency 540 x 10^{12} hertz

capillary tube thin tube in which liquid rises by capillary action

cathode negative electrode; electrode at which reduction occurs in a cell

cathode ray beam of electrons emitted by cathode in gas discharge tube

cell system in which two electrodes are in contact with an electrolyte

Celsius C; temperature scale based on 0 degrees as freezing point and 100 degrees as boiling point of water at 1 atmosphere of pressure; formerly Centigrade

Centigrade former name for 100 point Celsius scale

centrifuge device with spinning chamber, used to separate substances of different densities by forcing those substances outward from center of rotation

chemical equation symbolic, shorthand representation of a chemical reaction, describing the nature and proportions of its reactants and products

chemical formula molecular formula

chromatography any of various techniques used for analyzing or separating a sample mixture of gases, liquids, or dissolved substances, based on

the differential competition for molecules of the sample between a mobile phase sample and a stationary phase sample

coefficient number placed before a formula in a balanced chemical equation to indicate the relative amount of the substance involved in the reaction

colorimeter instrument used to determine the concentration of a solution by comparing it with the color of standard solutions

column chromatography chromatographic technique using vertical column packed with adsorbent through which sample is poured

coordination number number of groups, molecules, atoms, or ions surrounding an atom or ion in a complex or crystal

coulomb SI unit of electrical charge, equal to the charge transferred by a current of one ampere in one second

counting tube device that allows high-speed particles to cause ionization, creating current or voltage pulses that can be counted

crucible container in which materials may be heated to high temperatures

desiccator drying chamber, esp. one that uses chemicals to absorb water or vapor

distillation process of evaporation and condensation, used to separate liquid mixture and purify liquids

distillation column glass column used in distillation

dry cell cell in which electrolytes are in paste form

electrolytic cell cell in which electrolysis is carried out

electrophoresis technique for analysis and separation of colloids, based on differential migration of particles in an electric field

empirical formula expression showing simplest ratio between elements in compound

Erlenmeyer flask flat-bottomed, conical laboratory flask

evaporating dish flat dish, or watch glass, that allows liquids to evaporate

exponential notation scientific notation

Fahrenheit F; temperature scale based on 32 degrees as freezing point and 212 degrees as boiling point of water at one atmosphere of pressure

filtration process of separating solid particles from a liquid or gas by passing the mixture through a porous material

flask narrow-topped, wide-bottomed glass container used in laboratory

formula mass sum of atomic masses of atoms in a molecule, calculated from its molecular formula

fractional crystallization method of separating soluble solids, based on differences in the temperatures at which they crystallize out of solution

fractional distillation method of separating a mixture of liquids, based on differences in their boiling points

fractionating column long, vertical column packed with adsorbent material, used in fractional distillation

fractionation separation of a mixture into its components, esp. by distillation

fuel cell cell in which chemical energy of a fuel is converted directly into electrical energy

funnel hollow cone with open tube extending from smaller end, used to catch and direct downward flow of a liquid

g symbol used in chemical equations to indicate that a substance is in its gaseous state

galvanometer device used to detect and measure small electric currents

gas chromatography chromatographic technique for separating and analyzing mixtures of gases

gel filtration chromatographic technique in which substances with different size molecules move at different rates through a column containing a gel

glove box enclosed chamber with protective gloves sealed into its side, enabling someone to handle contents of box without incurring injury or causing contamination

graduated cylinder parallel-sided, closed-bottomed glass column with volume markings on its side, used for measuring

gravimetric analysis quantitative analysis involving measurements of weight

group any vertical column of the periodic table, containing elements with the same outer shell structure and hence similar properties

half-cell part of a cell, consisting of a single electrode in contact with an electrolyte, in which a half reaction takes place

hydrometer floating device used to determine the specific gravity of a liquid

indicator any substance, such as litmus paper, used to show the presence of a substance or ion by its color

ion-exchange chromatography chromatographic technique involving competition between different ions for ionic sites on the stationary phase

joule SI unit of energy, equal to the force of one newton acting through one meter, or 10^7 ergs

K symbol for Kelvin temperature scale

Kelvin K; temperature scale based on 0 degrees as absolute zero with units equal to Celsius scale, in which K = degrees C + 273.16

l symbol used in chemical equations to indicate that a substance is in its liquid state

Lewis structure model of covalent bonding using Lewis symbols

Lewis symbol symbol for an element, with one or more dots representing its valence electrons

Leyden jar glass jar lined inside and outside with tin foil, used to store electric charge

Liebig condenser distillation and condensation instrument consisting of two tubes, one inside the other, with space between for circulation of a coolant, usu. water

liter SI unit of volume, equal to one cubic decimeter or 1.056 quarts

litmus paper paper impregnated with acid-base indicator litmus, used to determine pH by color

manometer device for measuring gas pressure

mass number sum of protons and neutrons in an atomic nucleus, esp. of an isotope

mass spectroscopy technique for determining the masses of atoms or radicals by measuring their deflections in electric or magnetic fields

mobile phase portion of a chromatographic system that moves past the stationary phase and competes differentially with the stationary phase for different molecules in a sample mixture

molality unit of concentration by weight equal to number of moles of solute per kilogram of solvent

molarity unit of concentration by volume equal to number of moles of solute per liter of solution

molar mass mass of one mole of a substance; in grams, numerically equal to formula mass in atomic mass units

mole molecular weight of a substance expressed in grams, equal to its formula mass in atomic mass units, or 6.022×10^{23} molecules of a substance

molecular formula expression showing types and numbers of atoms present in a compound, using symbols for component elements and numerals for number of atoms of each element per molecule, such as H_2O for water; chemical formula

mole fraction unit of concentration designated x; ratio of the number of moles of one component of a mixture to the total number of moles of all components of the mixture

mortar round dish used with pestle for crushing and grinding solids

net ionic equation chemical equation in which only substances involved in a reaction, not spectator ions, are shown

newton N; SI unit of force required to accelerate a one-kilogram mass at a rate of one meter per second

normality number of equivalents of a substance per liter of solution

nuclear magnetic resonance spectroscopy technique for analyzing samples and determining structures based on the absorption of electromagnetic radiation by nuclei in a strong, external magnetic field

open system system that can exchange energy and mass with its surroundings

oxidation number number of electrons over which an element gains full or partial control when combined in a compound, a negative value indicating loss of control

packing adsorbent used in fractionating columns and in chromatography columns

paper chromatography chromatographic technique in which the stationary phase is paper

partition chromatography chromatographic technique in which substances are differentially dissolved in two immiscible liquids, one of which is absorbed by a stationary phase

pascal Pa; SI unit of pressure equal to one newton per square meter

percent yield actual yield of a chemical reaction, expressed as a percentage of the theoretical yield

percentage composition by mass percentage by mass of each element in a compound

period any horizontal row of the periodic table, containing elements with the same number of shells but increasing numbers of electrons in their outer shells as read from left to right

periodic table arrangement of the elements, in order of increasing atomic number, into horizontal periods determined by electron configurations, so that elements with the same outer shell structure and similar properties appear in vertical groups; currently consists of 107 elements

pestle club-shaped hand tool used with mortar for crushing and grinding solids

pipette narrow glass tube with volume markings, used to deliver specific small volumes of liquid accurately

polarimeter device for measuring rotation of the plane of polarized light

qualitative analysis determination of the nature of a substance or the compounds present in a mixture

quantitative analysis determination of the proportions of substances contained in a mixture

rate equation expression relating the rate of a reaction to concentrations of the reactants

recrystallization purification of a solid by separating the crystals formed upon cooling a saturated solution

resonance structures two or more formulas for a single molecule that cannot be described by a single structure

retort enclosed vessel or chamber with long tube open at one end, in which substances are distilled, sublimed, or decomposed by heat

s symbol used in chemical equations to indicate that a substance is in its solid state

scientific notation method of expressing very large and small numbers as powers of ten; exponential notation

separatory funnel funnel-shaped device for separating two immiscible liquids

SI units Système Internationale units; internationally accepted system of units of scientific measurement, expressed in modified metric system based on meter, kilogram, second, ampere, kelvin, mole, and candela

standard solution solution whose concentration is known with precision, used for comparison with solutions of unknown concentration

stationary phase portion of chromatographic system that remains stationary and competes differentially with the mobile phase for different molecules in a sample mixture

still apparatus used in distillation, consisting of chamber in which vaporization is carried out and cooling device in which vapor is condensed

structural formula expression that shows how atoms are bonded to each other in a molecule

surroundings everything in vicinity of a defined system used in an investigation

Syracuse watch glass round, flat-bottomed, shallow dish for staining and culturing

system defined substance, or set of substances, being studied

test tube plain or lipped tube of thin glass, closed at one end

thermochemical equation balanced chemical equation in which the value of change in enthalpy for molar amounts is specified

thermometer device for measuring temperature, esp. by the height of a column of mercury or by a thermocouple

thin-layer chromatography chromatographic technique in which substances are differentially absorbed by a thin layer of a solid

titration technique for determining concentration of a reagent by adding measured amounts of another reagent of known concentration until their reaction is complete

tracer isotope used to trace path of a specific substance through a chemical or physiological system

ultraviolet spectroscopy optical technique used to determine electronic structure of atoms and molecules

valency measure of combining power of an atom or radical, equal to the number of hydrogen atoms that the atom could combine with or displace in a compound

visible light spectroscopy optical technique used to study behavior of electrons in atoms

voltaic cell cell in which reactions between electrodes and electrolytes produce potential difference between the electrodes

volumetric analysis quantitative analysis using volume measurement

watt W; SI unit of power equal to one joule of work per second

Woulff bottle glass container with two or more necks, used for passing a gas through a liquid

X-ray crystallography technique for determining crystal structure, based on diffraction of X-rays projected through a crystal

zymoscope instrument that monitors amount of carbon dioxide produced by fermentation

MEDICINE

Disciplines and Specialties
Practitioners, Patients, and Facilities
Business and Practice of Medicine
Procedures
Tools and Equipment
Pharmacology
Dressings and Supports
Prefixes and Suffixes

See also: *Chap. 1: Anatomy; Medical Problems; Health, Fitness, and Enhancement; Chap. 2: Biology; Chap. 24: Drug Abuse and Alcoholism*

Disciplines and Specialties

acupressure manual application of pressure at points where acupuncture needles would be inserted

acupuncture Chinese practice that involves insertion of needles into body at specific points along meridians to treat disease and reduce pain

aerospace medicine prevention and treatment of disorders related to flight in Earth's atmosphere

allergy study and treatment of allergies

allopathy treatment by remedies that produce effects opposite those of disease, as in general practice of contemporary medicine

anesthesiology specialty concerned with pharmacological, physiological, and clinical bases of anesthesia, including resuscitation of patients and relief of pain

audiology evaluation and treatment of hearing disorder

Ayurveda ancient Hindu medicine that uses herbs, purgatives, and rubbing oils

bacteriology study of bacteria

behavioral medicine study and prevention of disorders that combines behavior modification with medical techniques

biomedicine medical studies derived from biological studies

cardiology study and treatment of the heart and its diseases

chiropody podiatry

chiropractic treatment method using manipulation of muscular and skeletal system, esp. the spine

chirurgical (*adj*) relating to surgery

clinical medicine direct observation and treatment of patients, as opposed to laboratory study

community medicine assessing health needs and trends of regional populations rather than individuals

cosmetic surgery plastic surgery performed to improve appearance only

dental surgery oral surgery

dentistry care and treatment of diseases of teeth, gums, and jaw

dermatology study and treatment of skin disorders

ear, nose, and throat ENT; treatment of diseases of these parts; otorhinolaryngology

embryology study of embryo development

emergency medicine specialization in rapid treatment of patients in crisis

endocrinology study of endocrine glands and hormones

endodontics dental specialty concerned with diseases of soft dental pulp in center of tooth

ENT ear, nose, and throat

environmental medicine study of effect of environment on human organism

epidemiology study of causes and control of epidemics

etiology science of causes and origins of diseases

family medicine general practice for entire family

folk medicine traditional, often regional, medical practices employed by common people, esp. use of herbs

forensic pathology investigation of causes of death or injury in unexpected circumstances, esp. crimes

gastroenterology treatment of digestive system disorders

general medicine prevention and treatment of wide range of diseases and disorders that appear in broad spectrum of population

geriatrics care of aged and treatment of disorders of old age

gerontology study of aging process and problems of the aged

gynecology study and treatment of diseases of women and girls, esp. in reproductive system

hematology study of blood and blood diseases

histology microscopic study of tissue structure

holistic medicine system based on treatment of whole body rather than of parts

homeopathy treatment of disease through small doses of drugs that normally produce symptoms of that disease

hygiene science of preserving health by cleanliness, disinfection

immunology study of phenomena connected with body's defense mechanisms

industrial medicine treatment of injuries and diseases sustained in workplace

internal medicine diagnosis and nonsurgical treatment of diseases

laboratory medicine experimentation and research on diseases without direct treatment of patients

medical science general study of medicine

medicine science and practice of diagnosing, treating, curing, and preventing disease, relieving pain, and improving health

mental hygiene treatment of psychological and emotional disorders

naturopathy treatment of disease that employs no surgery or synthetic drugs

neonatology study and treatment of children up to two months of age

nephrology study and treatment of kidney diseases

neurology study of functional processes and diseases of central nervous system and brain

neurosurgery surgical treatment of brain and spinal cord

nuclear medicine diagnosis and therapy using radioisotopes and radionuclides

nutrition study of proper diet to promote health

ob-gyn combined specialization in *ob*stetrics and *gyn*ecology

obstetrics care of women during pregnancy, childbirth, and first six weeks after birth; tocology

occupational medicine treatment of diseases associated with particular types of work

oncology study and treatment of tumors

ophthalmology study and treatment of eye diseases and disorders

optometry testing of eyes in order to prescribe corrective lenses

oral surgery surgery performed on mouth, esp. extraction of teeth and root canal; dental surgery

orthodontics treatment and correction of malocclusion of teeth

orthopedics correction of deformities or functional impairments of the skeletal system and associated structures

orthopedic surgery surgical correction of skeletal abnormalities or injury

osteopathy treatment of disease by manipulation and massage of musculoskeletal system

otolaryngology treatment of ear and throat diseases

otorhinolaryngology treatment of ear, nose, and throat diseases

parasitology study of parasites and treatment of diseases caused by parasites

pathology study of nature and causes of diseases, esp. through laboratory examination

pediatrics treatment and care of children

pedodontics care and treatment of children's teeth

perinatology practice concerned with phase surrounding birth, esp. obstetric care

periodontics branch of dentistry concerned with bones and tissue that support teeth

pharmacology study and practice of chemistry, preparation, use, and effect of drugs

physical medicine treatment of diseases and injuries by exercise, massage, heat, and light, but not drugs

plastic surgery reconstruction of damaged or deformed body parts after accident or burn or to improve appearance; reconstructive surgery

podiatry care of feet, esp. treatment of foot diseases; chiropody

preventive medicine study and practice of disease prevention, esp. through immunization and public health programs

proctology treatment of disorders of rectum, anus, and colon

prosthodontics dental surgery that replaces

missing teeth with artificial teeth to maintain oral function

psychiatry diagnosis, management, and prevention of mental disorders, as by medication

psychoanalysis school of psychology and method of treating mental disorders based on teachings of Sigmund Freud

psychology study of behavior and related mental processes and disorders

psychopharmacology study of behavioral effects of drugs and medication

public health study and maintenance of health of an entire community

radiology use of X-rays and radioactive substances in diagnosis and treatment of disease and injury

reconstructive surgery plastic surgery

rehabilitation medicine use of massage, exercise, and physical therapy to restore normal health and function or to prevent worsening of condition

rheumatology diagnosis and treatment of joint, muscle, tendon, and ligament diseases and injuries

serology study of blood serum and its ability to protect body from disease

space medicine prevention and treatment of diseases associated with flight outside Earth's atmosphere

sports medicine treatment of injuries incurred in athletic activities

surgery treatment of diseases, injuries, and deformities by operation, manipulation of internal organs, removal of body parts, and sometimes by replacement of parts

symptomatology study of the aggregate symptoms of a disease

teratology study of developmental malformations and their causes

tocology obstetrics

toxicology study of poisons, esp. their effects and antidotes

tropical medicine treatment of tropical diseases

urology study and treatment of diseases of urinary tract

veterinary medicine science of prevention and treatment of diseases and injuries of animals, esp. domestic animals

virology study of viruses

Practitioners, Patients, and Facilities

allergist practitioner concerned with allergy treatment

allopath practitioner of contemporary allopathic medicine

ambulatory (*adj*) designating patient able to move from bed

anesthesiologist practitioner of anesthesiology

anesthetist person who administers general anesthesia before surgery; gasser

apothecary pharmacist

asylum mental hospital

attendant hospital employee who assists doctors and nurses

attending physician member of hospital staff or private physician with hospital admitting privileges who is in charge of case

baby catcher *Slang.* practitioner in obstetrics

backup hospital second-choice hospital if primary choice is unavailable

base hospital hospital on military base

bleeder patient who suffers from hemophilia

blood bank facility in which whole blood, plasma, and other blood products are obtained, withdrawn, typed, and stored for later use

blood donor person who gives blood for storage in blood bank and future transfusion to another person

board certified physician doctor authorized to practice by local examining authority

bonesetter orthopedic surgeon

cadaver dead body, esp. one used for medical experiments; corpse

candy striper *Informal.* person who does volunteer work at hospital, often teenage girl or elderly person, usu. wearing red-striped uniform

case instance of disease with its attendant circumstances; patient

CDC Centers for Disease Control

Centers for Disease Control CDC, division of U.S. Public Health Service responsible for control of infectious diseases and epidemics and administration of quarantines

charge nurse nurse responsible for ward, unit, or floor

chemist *Chiefly Brit.* pharmacist

chief resident senior doctor or surgeon who oversees care of many patients and instructs interns

children's hospital facility that concentrates on treatment of childhood diseases

chiropractor practitioner who treats disease and injury by physical manipulation, esp. of spinal vertebrae, and alignment of bones

Christian Scientist patient whose religious faith prohibits medical treatment; practitioner who heals based on religious faith

clinic facility in which patients are treated by specialists in group practice

clinician practitioner of clinical medicine

community hospital public facility that serves specific local area

convalescent patient in period of recuperation and healing after disease or injury

convalescent hospital facility for care of recuperating patients, esp. the elderly

cooperative hospital facility operated for use by members of group practice

coroner public official who determines cause of death, esp. when not natural; medical examiner

corpse dead body; cadaver

county hospital local public hospital that provides service to all patients regardless of ability to pay

day hospital facility in which patients remain for day but not overnight, esp. for elderly and mentally ill

D.C. Doctor of Chiropractic degree

D.D.S. Doctor of Dental Science degree

dental hygienist licensed assistant to dentist who polishes teeth, takes X-rays

dental technician licensed assistant to dentist

dentist doctor who treats diseases of teeth, gums, and mouth

dietitian nutritionist

dispensary room in school or factory where medications and first aid are provided

D.M.D. *Latin.* Doctor Medicinae Dentalis; Doctor of Dental Medicine degree

doc *Informal.* physician

doc-box *Slang.* surgicenter

doctor physician

Doctor of Medicine M.D. degree; physician

donor person who provides blood, an organ, or other tissue for transfusion or transplant

Dr. standard abbreviation for doctor as title before name

druggist pharmacist

emergency medical service EMS; ambulance and emergency care unit on call in city

emergency medical technician EMT; person other than doctor or nurse who works in emergency room or ambulance

emergency room ER; area of hospital for treatment of patients in sudden crisis condition due to injury or disease, esp. those without admitting physician

EMS emergency medical service

EMT emergency medical technician

ER emergency room

examining room small private room in doctor's office or hospital in which patients are examined

faith healer practitioner who cures through patient's belief in prayer and divine intervention; healer

family doctor family practitioner

family practitioner physician who cares for all family members; family doctor

field hospital military hospital in combat area

FMG foreign medical graduate; doctor educated outside U.S.

gasser *Slang.* anesthetist

general practitioner G.P.; nonspecialist practicing internal medicine, usu. for entire family

gomer *Slang.* get out of *my* emergency room; derogatory term for debilitated patient in need of maintenance rather than care

G.P. general practitioner

handicapped (*adj*) denoting patient with physical disability

healer nonmedical practitioner; faith healer

health facility any hospital, clinic, group practice, or other place providing medical care by several practitioners

hit *Slang.* patient without admitting doctor, assigned randomly to resident

homeopath practitioner of homeopathic medicine

hospice institution that provides care and counseling for terminally ill patients and their families

hospital large institution that provides continuous, overnight medical treatment on inpatient basis

ICU intensive care unit

infirmary small hospital facility, usu. for school or factory

inpatient patient who stays in hospital overnight or longer

intensive care unit ICU; area within hospital for care of critically ill and postoperative patients

intern physician who receives first year of practical experience and instruction after graduation from medical school

internist doctor who specializes in internal medicine

invalid patient incapacitated by disease or injury

isolation ward area within hospital for treatment and lodging of patients with highly communicable diseases

laboratory technician trained assistant to doctors who evaluates laboratory tests

licensed practical nurse LPN; nurse with less training than registered nurse, state licensed for specific duties

LPN licensed practical nurse

maternity area within hospital for care of newborn babies and their mothers

maternity hospital hospital that deals exclusively with childbirth

M.D. Doctor of Medicine degree; physician

medic military noncommissioned officer who provides first aid in combat

medical examiner coroner

medicine man person deemed to have supernatural curative powers, esp. among American Indians; shaman

mental hospital hospital for care and treatment of patients with psychiatric disorders; sanitarium

midwife nonphysician who provides assistance to women during labor and childbirth, sometimes at home

naturopathic doctor ND; doctor who uses natural cures, esp. herbs, vitamins, and spinal manipulation, but no prescribed drugs

nurse person trained to care for sick, injured, or elderly patients and to assist doctors

nurse midwife trained nurse who serves as midwife

nurse practitioner registered nurse with extra specialized training

nurse's aide person who assists nurse with duties

nursing home facility for care of chronically ill, elderly, and disabled persons

nutritionist specialist in proper diet to maintain health; dietitian

oculist former term for ophthalmologist

operating room OR; specially equipped room in which surgery is performed

ophthalmologist specialist in treatment of eye disease

optician expert who grinds and fits prescription lenses for eyeglasses

optometrist person trained to give eye examinations and prescribe, make, and fit corrective lenses and eyeglasses

OR operating room

orderly male hospital attendant with rudimentary training

orthodontist dentist who corrects malocclusion

orthopedic surgeon doctor who performs surgery on bones, joints, and muscles

osteopath practitioner of osteopathic medicine

outpatient person treated at hospital or clinic without overnight stay

paramedic person professionally trained to give esp. emergency health care in absence of physician; military doctor who parachutes into combat zones

patient person examined by doctor for diagnosis or treatment of disease or injury

pharmacist person trained to mix and dispense drugs; apothecary; chemist; druggist

pharmacologist person trained in sources, chemistry, clinical use, and action of drugs

physical therapist practitioner of infrared, ultraviolet, hydro, and heat treatments as well as exercise and massage; physiotherapist

physician person licensed to practice medicine, esp. one other than a surgeon; doctor

physiotherapist physical therapist

plumber *Slang.* practitioner in urology

practical nurse nurse with less training than registered nurse, often licensed for specific duties

practitioner person trained in and practicing medicine or specialty; Christian Science healer

private duty nurse registered nurse who is employed by and works with one patient, often in patient's home

private hospital for-profit hospital, esp. one that limits admission to those in particular group or insurance plan

provider doctor, nurse, or other practitioner providing health services

psychiatrist doctor who specializes in treatment and medication of mental disorders

psychotherapist practitioner with or without medical degree who provides treatment for mental disorders

quack person who practices medicine without training or license

radiographer specialist who evaluates X-rays

radiologist practitioner of radiology

radiotherapist person who treats disease with X-rays or other radioactive emissions

recovery room postoperative holding room for close observation of patients immediately after surgery in which general anesthesia was used

registered nurse R.N.; person with training and state license to perform certain nursing services

resident medical school graduate who receives supervised postgraduate training, usu. in specialty, at hospital

rest home convalescent hospital; nursing home

R.N. registered nurse

sanitarium facility for care of invalids and convalescents or treatment of specific disease; mental hospital

sawbones *Slang.* surgeon

school nurse practical or registered nurse who dispenses first aid at school

scrub nurse operating room nurse able to handle sterilized instruments

shaman medicine man

sick bay hospital and medication dispensary, esp. on ship

sick bed bed occupied by patient

sick room room occupied by or assigned to patient

specialist doctor who concentrates on one particular area of medical practice

Surgeon General chief medical officer of U.S. Public Health Service

surgicenter outpatient surgery center; doc-box

teaching hospital hospital affiliated with medical school, used for instruction

terminal (*adj*) designating incurably ill and dying patient

therapist specialist in any form of therapy; psychotherapist

trauma center advanced emergency room staffed with trauma surgeons 24 hours a day

VA hospital Veterans Administration hospital administered by U.S. federal agency

veteran's hospital hospital for exclusive use of veterans of U.S. military service, esp. VA hospital

waiting room area adjacent to examining room in doctor's office or hospital in which patients await treatment

ward room or portion of hospital used for number of patients, often of specific type, such as a maternity ward

witch doctor person in primitive culture deemed to have power to cure disease through sorcery and incantation

X-ray technician assistant to radiologist who takes and develops radiographs

Business and Practice of Medicine

ABO system classification of human blood into four major groups, A, B, AB, and O, used in determining compatibility for transfusions

AMA American Medical Association

ambulatory care treatment provided patients not confined to hospital

American Medical Association AMA; professional organization of U.S. physicians

average length of stay figure used to set hospital fees and predict treatment

BAC blood alcohol concentration

bed occupancy percentage of hospital beds in use

bedside manner doctor's ability to put patient at ease during examination or treatment

bioethics concern for ethical implications in medical application of biological research

blood alcohol concentration BAC; measurement of amount of alcohol absorbed by body, used to determine intoxication

bloodmobile vehicle equipped and staffed to receive blood from donors

Blue Cross *Trademark.* national, private nonprofit health insurance organization used by individuals and many groups and institutions

Blue Shield *Trademark.* national, surgical expense insurance plan, usu. operated in conjunction with Blue Cross

capitation fee cost per person of care or insurance

case history compilation of medical information about patient's illness for use in diagnosis and treatment

catastrophic coverage medical insurance that covers lengthy or expensive hospitalization and care

census patient-occupancy level of hospital

charity patient hospital patient who cannot pay for health care and is without medical insurance

closed panel practice medical practice with patients restricted to one prepayment group, usu. an HMO

code call call to resuscitate dying patient in hospital

cognitive service any medical service which is not a procedure, such as consultation or patient advocacy

coinsurance medical insurance plan in which patients pay portion of cost of treatment, often 20 percent

comprehensive medical insurance coverage that extends to all areas from doctor visits to hospitalization, surgery, medications, therapy, and nursing care

copayment portion of fee paid by patient, not by insurance company, in coinsurance plan

cost effectiveness estimate of costs of different diagnostic and treatment plans against probable cost of disease, as public health strategy

death certificate government document that states cause of person's death, time of death, and demographic information on deceased

diagnosis-related group DRG; group of diagnoses with similar need for intensity of care and cost

DNR do not resuscitate; notation on chart of terminal patient who does not wish to be kept alive by extensive life-support efforts

DRG diagnosis-related group

dumping *Slang.* denial of care to patient without medical insurance and transportation to public hospital for treatment

fixed fee set prospective payment for care

follow-up return visit to health care provider to evaluate progress

for-profit (*adj*) designating any medical care facility or program owned by investors

gatekeeper primary care physician who screens incoming patients at health facility to determine which need specialized or hospital care

gray market illegal dispensing of unprescribed psychoactive drugs to friends, relatives, or associates

group insurance health insurance available at special rates to company employees or organization members

group practice association of two or more doctors who share facilities and divide income

HCFA Health Care Financing Administration

health administrator person responsible for supervising public health programs

Health Care Financing Administration HCFA; U.S. government umbrella organization that oversees Medicare and Medicaid

health insurance insured coverage for medical expenses

health maintenance organization HMO; prepaid group insurance plan that provides comprehensive care to defined portion of public in specific region

high-touch product service that requires physical contact with patients

Hippocratic oath ethical code of medical profession traditionally sworn to by doctors

HMO health maintenance organization

hospital administrator person responsible for nonmedical business of hospital

hospitalization placement of patient into hospital for treatment and care; coverage of hospital stays by health insurance plan; insurance plan that covers only hospital stays

house call visit by doctor to patient's home for examination or treatment

independent practice association IPA; form of PPO in which each doctor receives standard fee per group member per year

IPA independent practice association

living will document instructing physicians and relatives not to prolong one's life artificially under certain circumstances, esp. by naming proxy to discontinue use of life-support systems

major medical medical insurance that covers regular doctor visits as well as hospitalization

malpractice harm caused to patient by negligent or unprofessional care and treatment

malpractice insurance very expensive insurance that protects physician in malpractice suit

managed care health care under umbrella plan such as HMO

Medicaid health insurance for poor provided by U.S. government

Medicaid mill *Slang.* substandard clinic in which all patients are Medicaid recipients

medical insurance any of various forms of health insurance, including prepaid and group, hospitalization and major medical

medically indigent low income patients who do not qualify for Medicaid but cannot afford medical cost

Medicare health insurance for people over 65 provided by U.S. government

national health government sponsored, comprehensive health insurance, paid for by taxes

National Institutes of Health NIH; federally funded agencies for medical research

NIH National Institutes of Health

not-for-profit (*adj*) designating health facility or program owned by educational institution, foundation, or other nonprofit group

notifiable disease disease that must be reported to public health authorities, esp. endemic communicable disease or imported disease; reportable disease

ombudsman person who helps patient appeal improper treatment or discharge due to Medicare limitations and guidelines

on-call (*adj*) available for consultation in person or by telephone during off-duty hours

patient advocacy advice and assistance given to patients in order that they may better handle costs and complexity of medical care

PCN primary care network

peer review organization PRO; doctors and hospital administrators who review quality of all admissions and medical practices for Medicare and Medicaid

physician liability medical malpractice

PPO preferred-provider organization

practice professional pursuit of career in medicine

preexisting condition patient condition that predates time insurance plan or HMO was joined

preferred-provider organization PPO; group insurance that covers care performed by specific list of doctors and hospitals

primary care care rendered by first physician contacted by patient before referral to specialist

primary care network PCN, variation on HMO in which each patient has private doctor as case manager who refers the patient to specialists or hospitals

private insurance health insurance program open to all individuals, usu. provided by profit-making company

private practice operation of medical practice that charges fee for services

PRO peer review organization

procedure any medical service that requires patient to be cut, jabbed, injected, or tested

procedure capture doctors' referral of specialized cases to other doctors, which creates network for control of business

product line extension service arranged by hospital away from hospital site

prospective payment fixed fee for specific medical services, known in advance by patient, determined by average costs of a diagnosis-related group

Public Health Service U.S. federal agency that administers disease control, drug abuse, health, fitness, research, and public information programs

RDA recommended dietary allowance

recommended dietary allowance RDA; government guideline for nutritional requirements by age, weight, and sex

referral sending of patient to another physician, usu. a specialist

reimbursement amount of medical costs paid by insurance after patient has initially paid entire bill

reportable disease notifiable disease

retail customer patient who pays with private insurance

retrospective billing patient's bill as calculated after services are rendered

rounds regular circuit taken by doctor among hospitalized patients

secondary care treatment by specialist or hospital staff after referral from primary care doctor making diagnosis

shift work hours, esp. at hospital or clinic

socialized medicine system that provides complete medical care to all persons in nation through public funds and has some control over physicians' decisions and actions

tertiary care treatment at special hospitals or clinics or by specialist doctors for disorders that cannot be treated by secondary care physicians and hospitals

uncompensated care hospital care free of charge for patient who cannot pay

USRDA U.S. recommended daily allowance

U.S. recommended daily allowance USRDA; standard indication of nutritional value of food on label

utilization review committee hospital administrators' committee that reviews doctors' decisions for cost effectiveness

WHO World Health Organization

World Health Organization WHO; United Nations agency for improvement of physical and mental health of world's people

Procedures

abduct (*vb*) move limb or any part away from midline of body

ablation removal of tissue, usu. by cutting

abortion expulsion or removal of fetus before it is capable of independent survival, usu. prior to twelfth week of pregnancy

abscission removal of tissue by cutting

adduct (*vb*) move limb or any part toward midline of body

AIDS test evaluation of blood sample for presence of antibodies to HIV virus; ELISA; Western blot

alimentotherapy treatment of disease through diet and nutrition

allograft tissue or organ taken from one member of species and grafted to a genetically dissimilar member of same species

amniocentesis analysis of amniotic fluid extracted by needle puncture from uterus early in second trimester of pregnancy, usu. to detect fetal abnormalities or sex

amputation surgical removal of limb or part of limb

analgesia any procedure that induces absence of pain in fully conscious patient

anesthesia introduction of local or general anesthetic into body, usu. preparatory to surgery

angiocardiography X-ray examination of heart chamber after radiopaque medium has been introduced into blood

angiography X-ray examination of blood vessels that contain radiopaque medium

Apgar score clinical measurement used to assess cardiopulmonary function in baby immediately after birth

appendectomy surgical removal of vermiform appendix

arthroscopy insertion of fiber optic device into space, esp. joint cavity, for diagnosis or treatment

artificial insemination mechanical introduction of semen into vagina

artificial respiration maintaining airflow in and out of lungs of patient who has stopped breathing, by mouth-to-mouth resuscitation or respirator

aspiration withdrawal of fluid by suction

audiogram hearing test

auscultation act of listening through stethoscope to movement of liquid or gas inside body

autograft tissue or organ that is grafted into new position on body of individual from which it was removed

autopsy examination of corpse to determine cause of death

aversion therapy conditioning with unpleasant stimulus to reduce undesirable behavior

balloon angioplasty repair of damaged blood vessel by insertion of tiny inflatable balloon on catheter

ballottement technique that examines fluid-filled body part to detect floating object, esp. during pregnancy

barium meal ingestion of radiopaque barium sulfate as contrast medium for X-rays of digestive system

bed rest period of days spent in bed as part of treatment, esp. for cold or influenza

biofeedback self-training method in which electronic sensors are used to modify and control autonomic body functions

biopsy removal of small piece of tissue for microscopic examination and diagnosis, esp. for cancer

blood count determination of number of different blood cells in volume of blood

blood group classification of person's blood based on presence or absence of certain antigens in red blood cells

bloodletting phlebotomy

blood pressure measurement of pressure exerted by blood against walls of main arteries

blood test any of various laboratory analyses of blood sample to discover abnormalities or presence of foreign substances

blood typing determination of blood type and sorting of blood samples by type

bone graft transplant of piece of bone from one part of body to another, where it becomes permanently affixed

Breathalyzer *Trademark.* test to determine alcohol concentration in blood

bridge dental cementation of immovable metal prosthesis as base for dentures in gap left by missing teeth

bypass surgical procedure in which artificial channel or channels allow blood to pass around arterial blockage

cap (*vb*) place artificial crown of gold or porcelain on top of damaged tooth

cardiopulmonary resuscitation CPR; revival of patient whose respiration and heartbeat have ceased by compressing sternum and blowing air into mouth

catharsis cleansing or purging of bowels by administration of laxative

CAT scan computerized axial tomography; soft tissue radiology in which cross-sectional images of body are generated by computer from series of X-ray scans of area examined

cautery destruction of tissue by direct application of heated instrument, esp. to remove small growth

Cesarean section surgical delivery of baby through abdominal wall; C-section

checkup regular basic physical examination by primary care practitioner

chemical stimulation of brain introduction of drugs or other chemicals directly into brain to stimulate local region of brain cells

chemotherapy use of drugs and other chemicals to treat disease, esp. cancer

chest X-ray radiographic examination of chest

cholecystectomy surgical removal of gallbladder

circumcision surgical removal of foreskin of penis, usu. shortly after birth

cobalt therapy radiation cancer treatment using cobalt-60 radioisotope

colonic irrigation flushing of large bowel by repeated enemas

colostomy surgical drainage of large intestine in which part of colon is brought through abdominal wall

computerized axial tomography CAT scan

consultation discussion of condition or diagnosis, esp. when more than primary physician is involved

contact therapy radiotherapy in which needles or capsules of radioisotope are implanted in or around tumor

cordotomy surgical severing of nerve fibers of spinal cord to relieve chronic pain

corneal transplant replacement of diseased portions of cornea by clear corneal tissue grafted from donor; keratoplasty

coronary artery bypass bypass operation involving arteries of heart

corrective remedial treatment to fix condition

cosmetic surgery plastic surgery, usu. of face, to improve appearance

couching cataract operation in which lens is pushed out of pupil by small knife, rarely performed today

CPR **c**ardio**p**ulmonary **r**esuscitation

crown replacement of top of damaged tooth by porcelain, plastic, or gold crown

cryosurgery surgical use of extreme cold to destroy unwanted tissue, such as cataracts

C-section Cesarean section

culture examination made to identify population of microorganisms grown in laboratory from specimen taken from patient's body

cupping drawing blood to specific area by placement of heated cup over it, which is then allowed to cool, no longer performed

debridement cleansing of open wound by removal of foreign substances and dead cells

decompression surgical reduction of pressure on body part or organ, usu. by incision

dermabrasion surgical scraping off of top layers of epidermis, usu. to repair scars

desensitization process of decreasing subject's allergy to certain substance by exposure to gradually increasing dosages of the offending allergen

detoxification removal of toxic substances, esp. addictive drugs, from body and neutralization of their effects

dextran glucose polymer solution used to increase plasma volume in transfusions

diagnosis evaluation of signs and symptoms to determine nature of disease or condition

dialysis use of semipermeable membrane to sift different-size particles from liquid mixture in artificial kidney

diathermy heating body part by exposure to high frequency current between two electrodes on skin, used to increase blood flow to relieve deep pain

differential diagnosis diagnosis based on interpretation of signs and symptoms common to more than one disease

dilation and curettage D and C; scraping tissues of uterus walls by insertion of instrument through widened cervix for diagnosis or abortion

dilation and evacuation D and E; removal of contents of uterus by dilation and curettage

dosimetry calculation of required amount of radiation for cancer treatment

DPT immunization against **d**iphtheria, **p**ertussis, and **t**etanus, administered esp. to children

ECG **e**lectro**c**ardiogram

echocardiography use of ultrasound waves to examine action of heart

echography use of ultrasound waves to display and analyze body's internal structure

EEG **e**lectro**e**ncephalo**g**ram

EKG **e**lectro**k**ardiogram

electrical stimulation of brain application of very small electrical current to point in brain by ultrafine electrodes implanted in skull, usu. experimental technique to test response to stimulus

electrocardiogram EKG; interpretation of tracing of electrical activity produced by contractions of heart recorded by electrocardiograph

electrocardiophonogram phonocardiogram

electrocautery destruction of unwanted tissue, such as warts or polyps, by electrically heated needle

electroencephalogram EEG; interpretation of tracing of electrical activity in various parts of brain recorded by electroencephalograph

electromyogram EMG; interpretation of tracing of electrical activity in muscles recorded by electromyograph

electrophoresis process that separates particles by allowing them to migrate toward poles in electric field

electrosurgery use of electricity in surgery or cautery

electrotherapy passing electric currents through tissue to treat disease or stimulate nerves and muscles

ELISA **e**nzyme-**l**inked **i**mmuno**s**orbent **a**ssay; test used chiefly to safeguard blood supplies from contamination by virus that causes AIDS

EMG **e**lectro**m**yogram

enema infusion of fluid into rectum by tube passed through anus, usu. to evacuate and flush large intestine

enterostomy surgically constructed outlet from intestines to surface of abdominal wall

episiotomy incision of perineum to enlarge vaginal opening during childbirth

ergotherapy treatment by physical exercise

euthanasia act of causing or allowing painless death to end suffering of terminal patient, usu. when treatment is withheld or by active intervention; mercy killing

exchange transfusion exchange of patient's blood for newly transfused blood by use of large syringe with three-way tap

excision surgical removal of tissue or organ from body

exploratory surgery surgical investigation of patient to obtain correct diagnosis

extraction removal of broken or diseased tooth by dental surgery

face-lift cosmetic surgery in which facial folds are stretched taut

fenestration creation of artificial opening into labyrinth of inner ear to relieve deafness

filling substance placed by dentist in hole drilled in carious tooth

first aid simple emergency procedures used to help patient until doctor arrives

fluoroscopy direct examination of X-ray images projected onto fluorescent screen

fracture reduction restoration of fragments of broken bone to proper position by manipulation

gastrectomy surgical removal of part or all of stomach

gene therapy treatment of genetic disease by substitution of healthy genes for affected ones

graft transplantation of skin, bone, or other tissue from its original site to repair defect elsewhere, taken either from same individual or from donor

Heimlich maneuver emergency application of sudden sharp pressure to abdomen below rib cage to dislodge object stuck in trachea

hemodialysis removal of toxins from blood by dialysis

hepatectomy surgical removal of all or part of liver

hospitalization admission to hospital for treatment

hydrotherapy treatment of arthritis or partial paralysis by exercise and physiotherapy in swimming pool

hygiene sanitary practices used to maintain health and prevent disease

hyperbaric oxygenation therapy exposure to high pressure oxygen to treat carbon monoxide poisoning, severe burns, breathing difficulties, or gas gangrene

hypnosis artificially induced trance in which subject is susceptible to suggestion, used in psychotherapy and drug treatment

hysterectomy surgical removal of uterus

ileostomy construction of artificial opening from ileum through abdominal wall, used to drain small intestine

immune therapy administration of sera, vaccines, and other immune products to treat or prevent infectious diseases

immunization vaccination with treated antigens to stimulate antibody production that results in immunity

incision surgical cut into soft tissue with scalpel

injection introduction of drugs into body by hypodermic syringe and needle; shot

inoculation vaccination; introduction of vaccine into body

intravenous (adj) IV; designating blood transfusion, nutritional solution, or drugs fed directly into vein of patient

intubation insertion of tube into body part or cavity for diagnosis or treatment

irradiation use of electromagnetic radiation therapy

IV **i**ntra**v**enous

keratoplasty corneal transplant

knife Slang. surgery

laparoscopy abdominal examination by illuminated tube inserted through small incision in abdominal wall

laparotomy surgical opening of abdominal wall

laryngectomy removal of all or part of larynx

laser surgery use of very thin beams of focused light to operate on small areas without damage to neighboring tissue

laser therapy treatment with laser light, often to remove tattoos or birthmarks

lavage washing out of body cavity, such as colon or stomach

leeching use of sucking worm for bloodletting, no longer in practice

liposuction plastic surgery technique in which body fat is sucked out of tissues beneath epidermis

lithotripsy destruction of stone in body cavity with high frequency sound waves prior to its removal

lobotomy cutting into skull to sever nerve fibers connecting thalamus with frontal lobes of brain, formerly used to treat mental disorders

magnetic resonance imaging MRI; use of high-powered magnetic field to scan body interior

maintenance treatment and medication used to stabilize patient in present condition

major surgery surgical operation of significant scope, esp. on internal organ or system, usu. with general anesthesia

mammography X-ray or infrared photographic examination of breast

mastectomy surgical removal of all or part of breast

mercy killing euthanasia

microsurgery delicate operation performed under binocular microscope with miniature instruments

minor surgery brief or simple surgical operation on tissue or body part, usu. with local anesthesia

MRI magnetic resonance imaging

nephrectomy surgical removal of a kidney

nephrolithotomy surgical removal of a kidney stone

neurotomy surgical severing of a nerve, esp. to relieve neuralgia

noninvasive surgery surgical operation that does not require incision through soft tissue

open-heart surgery repair of exposed heart or coronary arteries while blood is circulated mechanically

operation any surgical procedure

oral surgery dental procedure that involves extraction of tooth, root canal, or other surgery of mouth

organ transplant surgical replacement of defective organ, such as heart or kidney, by implantation of healthy organ taken from donor

orthodontics dental procedures to correct malocclusion of teeth

ostectomy excision of part or all of a bone

osteoclasis surgical fracturing of a bone to correct deformity

palpation examination of body part by feeling and probing with hands and fingers

Pap test test that uses Papanicolaou stain to detect cancer of cervix or uterus by taking tissue specimen and studying it microscopically

patch test application of various allergens to scratches made on skin to determine patient's allergies

percussion striking or tapping of body part, either with fingers or plessor, during examination, thus producing sounds which are studied for diagnostic purposes

perfusion passage of fluid into tissue through blood vessels

periodontics dental treatment of gum disease

PET scan positron emission tomography; measurement by tomography of emissions from injected radioactive molecules to evaluate tissue, esp. in brain

phlebotomy surgical opening of vein to remove blood; bloodletting

phonocardiogram tracing of heart sounds picked up and amplified by microphone

phototherapy exposure of patient to high intensity ultraviolet light, used to treat newborn jaundice and skin conditions

physical physical examination

physical examination general medical examination of body

physical rehabilitation treatment and therapy to assist convalescence from injury or disease

physical therapy exercise, massage, heat, and light treatments; physiotherapy

physiotherapy physical therapy

plastic surgery reconstruction and repair of damaged or defective external body parts

polishing mechanical cleaning and shining of tooth enamel

positron emission tomography PET scan

postmortem autopsy

pregnancy test any of various methods for determining presence of embryo or fetus in uterus, esp. by detecting the hormone human chorionic gonadotropin in urine

pressure point technique stoppage of bleeding by manual application of pressure to key arteries

prognosis forecast of likely course of disease

prophylaxis prevention of disease

prosthesis design, manufacture, and implantation of artificial body parts to replace missing or defective body parts

prosthodontics replacement of missing teeth and other oral fixtures with artificial parts

psychosurgery surgical procedure practiced on brain or central nervous system in order to alter behavior

purge stimulation of intestinal activity and evacuation of bowel contents

pyelography X-ray examination of kidneys, usu. with aid of injected radiopaque substance

radial keratotomy incision into cornea of eye

radiation therapy treatment of disease, esp. cancer, with beams of X-rays, beta rays, or gamma rays, emitted by machine or radioactive isotopes, that penetrate body

radiotherapy radiation therapy

reconstructive surgery surgical rebuilding of damaged or defective external body part

regimen systematic combination of treatments used over time

rehabilitation restoration of normal functions after disease or injury

relief treatment to eliminate symptoms and relieve distress

replacement therapy rapid replacement of lost substance, such as transfusion of blood and plasma into shock patient

resection surgical removal of portion of body part

rhinoplasty reparative or cosmetic surgery on nose

rhizotomy surgical cutting of spinal nerve roots to eliminate pain

root canal dental surgery to repair infected base of tooth in gum

salpingectomy surgical excision of fallopian tubes, used esp. for sterilization

scan viewing inside of body without surgical incision, esp. by X-ray or CAT scan

scratch test test for allergies in which allergens are introduced into epidermis through scratches on it

section act of surgical cutting

self-treatment treatment administered without assistance of physician or nurse

serum-cholesterol measurement of cholesterol level in blood serum

serum transfusion massive injection of blood serum

sex change operation reconstructive creation of sex organs of opposite sex

shock therapy use of electric currents to stimulate nerves and muscles

shot injection

single photon emission computed tomography SPECT scan; measurement by tomography of radioactive emissions from injected photon

skin graft cutting piece of healthy skin from body and using it to replace damaged skin elsewhere

sonogram tracing that represents sound waves

SPECT scan single photon emission computed tomography

stat (adv) short for Latin statim; designating procedure to be performed immediately

stress test comparison of heart's performance at maximum stress, at rest, and as it recovers

surgery treatment by operation, usu. by incision and removal or repair of internal part

test electronic, laboratory, or manual examination of body part or function for diagnosis or prognosis

therapy any procedure or combination of procedures that heal, induce health, relieve symptoms, or cure disease

thoracotomy incision into chest cavity

tomography tracing produced by X-rays or ultrasound waves of image at specific depth inside body

tonsillectomy surgical removal of one or both palatine tonsils lying at base of tongue above pharynx

tracheotomy incision through skin of neck into trachea, or windpipe, to assist breathing

traction use of force that pulls on body parts, esp. to correct alignment of broken bone fragments or in physical therapy on spinal cord

transfusion injection of blood or blood products into circulation of patient

transplant organ transplant

treatment systematic course of medical care prescribed for specific condition

triage allocation of emergency treatment by priority of need

tubal ligation female sterilization procedure in which fallopian tubes are tied or surgically cut

tuberculin test injection beneath skin of protein extracted from culture of tubercle bacilli, which forms inflammation if patient has been exposed to tuberculosis

type and cross-match determine blood type and check its compatibility with blood of potential donor

ultrasonic therapy exposure of patient to concentrated sound at inaudibly high frequency over 20,000 Hz to treat deep tissue disorders

urinalysis physical, chemical, and microscopic tests to detect abnormalities in urine

uroscopy microscopic examination of urine

vaccination injection of antigenic material to produce immunity to disease; inoculation

Valsalva maneuver forced expiratory effort against blocked air passage, esp. to equalize middle ear pressure on ascent or descent, esp. in aircraft

vasectomy male sterilization procedure in which vas deferens that carries sperm from testes to urethra is surgically cut

venipuncture puncture of vein with hypodermic needle for IV injection or to withdraw blood

ventilation passage of air into and out of respiratory tract

Western blot test for confirming presence of full-blown AIDS virus in blood by detecting antibodies in blood serum samples spread on special paper

workup evaluation of patient, esp. while hospitalized or in preparation for surgery

X-ray penetration of body by short-wavelength electromagnetic radiation to produce images used in diagnosis

Tools and Equipment

antishock trousers tight leggings used to force blood to heart and brain in case of cardiac arrest or traumatic shock

armamentarium all equipment used in practice of medicine

arthroscope instrument inserted into joint cavity to inspect contents

artificial heart prosthetic mechanical heart used as alternative to donor-organ transplant

artificial kidney portable dialysis machine

artificial limb man-made arm or leg or section thereof, used to replace limb lost by amputation or injury

artificial lung respirator

aspirator hollow instrument used to withdraw fluid, esp. from cysts or joints

audiometer apparatus that measures ability to

hear sounds at different frequencies, used to diagnose deafness

autoclave device used to sterilize instruments by pressurized superheated steam

autoette three-wheeled vehicle used by disabled persons to move about

bedpan shallow receptacle used as toilet by bedridden patient

bistoury narrow-bladed surgical knife used to open abscesses and make small incisions

bitewing radiograph dental X-ray film in frame clamped between teeth

blood pressure cuff sphygmomanometer

bougie hollow or solid, flexible, cylindrical instrument used to dilate or calibrate tubular organs such as esophagus, rectum, or urethra

braces metal bands attached to teeth to correct malocclusion

bridge mounting base for dentures, either fixed or removable, inserted in gap in teeth

bronchoscope device used to examine trachea and bronchi, esp. flexible fiber optic instrument

bulb syringe syringe with pressure supplied by squeezing bulb rather than by plunger

cannula hollow tube with pointed interior core for insertion into body cavity, such as bladder, with tube left in place when core is removed

cardiograph electrocardiograph

catheter tube inserted into narrow opening for removal or introduction of fluids, esp. into urethra to drain urine and empty bladder

clamp surgical instrument used to compress blood vessel or close off end of intestine

clinical thermometer sealed glass tube with bulb ending that contains mercury, calibrated to register body temperatures between 95 and 110 degrees F

colostomy bag sack for collection of discharge from colon through artificial anal opening

cord clamp flexible band used to compress part or close off opening

crown porcelain or metal top fitted by dentist onto damaged tooth

curette spoon-shaped instrument used to scrape tissue from body cavities

cystoscope instrument used to view interior of bladder

defibrillator agent or device for arresting cardiac fibrillation

dental drill electrical drill with tiny bit that clears debris from carious tooth prior to filling

dental extraction forceps long forceps, with jaws at right angle to handle, for removal of teeth

dental floss thin, strong, waxed thread used to clean between teeth and on unexposed surfaces

dentures set of artificial teeth mounted on base that fits onto gums; false teeth

dermatome surgical instrument that cuts thin slices of skin, as for grafting

dialysis machine artificial blood filtration machine, used esp. for kidney malfunction

diathermy knife electrode-tipped blade used to coagulate tissue or small blood vessels

drain tube or wick used to draw fluid from body cavity to surface

drain tube tube used to drain fluid from inside body

duck *Slang.* portable urinal for bedridden hospital patients

electrocardiograph machine used to record electrocardiogram; cardiograph

electroencephalograph machine used to record electroencephalogram

electromyograph machine used to record electromyogram

endoscope slender, tubular instrument used for viewing and examining interior part of body

endotracheal tube tube inserted into trachea for examination or administration of anesthetic gas or oxygen

evacuator hollow rubber bulb attached to tube inserted into body cavity, with valve leading to discharge tube for withdrawal of fluids

false teeth dentures

fluoroscope fluorescent screen on which X-rays may be viewed, eliminating need to develop photographs

Foley catheter indwelling catheter with inflatable end at bladder for draining urine, kept in place for variable durations

forceps any of various instruments used by surgeons and dentists to grasp and pull objects

gastroscope flexible fiber optic instrument used to inspect and photograph stomach interior

gurney stretcher

heart-lung machine pumping apparatus that can temporarily assume functions of heart and lungs while heart surgery is performed

heating pad electric heating element encased in cloth pad, used to apply heat to external body parts

heat lamp focused heat source placed near body part, esp. in physical therapy

hemostat device used to stop or prevent hemorrhaging

hospital bed adjustable bed with criblike sides and optional positions for comfort and safety of patient

hyperbaric chamber sealed chamber in which high pressure is used to treat decompression sickness and infant heart defects and to retard bacterial growth

hypodermic needle and syringe used for subcutaneous injections

infusion pump small dispenser worn externally or implanted in patient's body for slow, steady administration of minute quantities of drugs such as insulin

inhalator device used to administer medicinal vapors; inspirator

inspirator inhalator

iron lung respirator

Ishihara test sheet containing dots in various sizes and colors, used to detect color blindness

isolation chamber dark, silent container, free of stimuli, in which patient lies, used in physical therapy and psychotherapy

ivy pole *Slang.* rack from which intravenous equipment hangs

kidney basin receptacle for excretions in dialysis machine

kymograph instrument for measuring and recording variations in pressure of pulse

lancet wide, two-edged, pointed surgical knife

laryngoscope device with small light and curved blunt blade to depress tongue, used to examine larynx

life-support system equipment that sustains life or substitutes for body functions in incapacitated patients

ligature nylon, wire, or catgut tied around structure to close or secure it to impede bleeding

lingual braces orthodontic braces bonded to interior side of teeth

lithotrite surgical instrument used to crush stone in organ

manometer U-shaped tube with graduated scale, used to measure gas pressure, esp. sphygmomanometer

microscope combination of lenses used to greatly magnify image of examined object

nebulizer device that applies a fine liquid mist

needle slender pointed instrument used to make surgical sutures; hollow needle attached to syringe for injections

ophthalmoscope instrument that directs fine beams of light into eye, used to examine inside eye

oral thermometer clinical thermometer inserted into mouth

orthodiagraph undistorted X-ray photograph used to make accurate measurements of body part

otoscope apparatus with light source, magnifying lens, and speculum, used to examine eardrum and passage to ear

oxygenator machine that oxygenates blood outside body, used with heart-lung machine in open-heart surgery

oxygen mask covering for mouth and nose connected by tube to oxygen supply

oxygen tank enclosed, pressurized container of oxygen that supplies mask or tent

oxygen tent transparent plastic enclosure around bed of patient into which oxygen is passed

pacemaker battery and insulated electrode used to stimulate normal heart rate

percussion hammer plessor

plessor small hammer used to check nervous reflexes; percussion hammer; plexor

plexor plessor

pneumograph instrument that records respiratory movements

probe thin, flexible, metal rod with blunt end, used to explore cavities and wounds

proctoscope hollow, tube-shaped instrument for inspection of rectum

radioisotope heavier form of an element that

emits alpha, beta, or gamma radiation as it decays, used as tracer and in radiotherapy

radio knife needlelike surgical instrument that uses high frequency oscillations to form electric arc at cutting edge, which simultaneously cuts tissue, sterilizes edges of cut, and seals blood vessels

radiopaque substance substance that absorbs X-rays, used as contrast medium in radiography

rectal thermometer clinical thermometer inserted into anus

respirator device used to maintain respiration by inflation of lungs with mixture of oxygen and air; airtight container that encloses paralyzed patient except for head, in which pressure is increased and decreased; iron lung

respirometer device used to measure extent of respiration

resuscitator artificial respiration device that forces oxygen into lungs

retainer dental instrument used to correct minor malocclusion or maintain alignment of teeth

retractor surgical instrument that draws aside edges of skin or tissue to expose operation site

scalpel small, pointed surgical knife with convex blade edge, used to cut tissue

scoop special stretcher in two parts that clip together, used to transport person with spinal injury

scope flexible fiber optic instrument for inspection of interior of body

scrubs *Slang.* scrub suit

scrub suit gown, often green, worn in surgery by doctors; surgical gown

Seeing Eye dog *Trademark.* dog trained to guide blind person in walking about

sigmoidoscope rigid or flexible tube for visual examination of rectum and sigmoid colon

snare wire noose for surgically removing tumors or polyps by the roots

sound rodlike surgical instrument with curved end, used to explore or dilate body structures

specimen bottle small glass container for collection of urine and other liquids

speculum instrument inserted into cavity, esp. vagina or ear, to hold it open during examination

sphygmograph instrument for measuring and recording arterial pulse

sphygmomanometer device that measures blood pressure when sensor cuff connected to manometer and wrapped around upper arm is inflated and then deflated

spirograph instrument used to record tracing of respiratory movements

spirometer device used to measure volume of air inhaled or exhaled

stethoscope diaphragm connected to earpieces, used to listen to sounds within body, esp. heart and lungs

stirrups apparatus in which women place feet for gynecological examination

stitches suture

straitjacket coat with arms that bind behind body, used to restrain violent persons

stretcher bedlike device on wheels, used to transport sick or injured person; gurney

stylet slender probe, esp. wire inside catheter, that provides rigidity during insertion

surgical gloves sheer, hygienic plastic gloves worn by surgeons

surgical gown sterile cotton gown worn over clothes by surgeon and operating room personnel; scrub suit

surgical instruments various sterilized tools, such as forceps or scalpels, used in surgery

surgical mask cotton mask worn over mouth and nose by surgeons

surgical needle suture needle

surgical sponge soft, sterile material that absorbs blood and other body liquids during surgery

surgical staple device used to close surgical opening without sutures

suture sterile thread, often of silk or catgut, used to stitch closed a wound or surgical opening; stitches

suture needle needle used to make suture; surgical needle

syringe piston in tube attached to hollow needle, used to give injections or remove material, esp. blood, from body

tenaculum small, sharply pointed hook, used for seizing and holding blood vessels and other body parts during surgery

thermometer clinical thermometer

tongue depressor flat piece of wood used to push tongue aside in throat examination

tonometer instrument used to measure pressure in eyeball

toothbrush rows of short bristles mounted at end of long handle, used to clean teeth

tracer often radioactive substance introduced into body whose circulation can be followed to assess body function

trephine small circular saw in form of hollow tube with interior cutting edge, used to remove circular section of bone or tissue, esp. from skull

trocar metal tube with pointed, three-cornered shaft, inserted into body cavity to draw off fluids

volsella surgical forceps with clawlike hooks on both jaws

walker lightweight, four-legged framework on which old or disabled persons can lean while walking

wheelchair chair mounted on wheels, sometimes equipped with motor, for use by disabled, ill, injured, or elderly persons who cannot walk

whirlpool bath bath with swirling jets of warm water used in hydrotherapy

wick thin, absorbent thread inserted in body cavity for drainage of fluids

X-ray machine device that emits radiation and takes photographs for radiographic diagnosis

xyster surgical instrument for scraping bones

PHARMACOLOGY

abortifacient drug that induces abortion or miscarriage

acetaminophen mild analgesic without anticoagulant activity

acetylsalicylic acid active ingredient in aspirin

addiction dependence

addictive drug that causes physical or psychological dependence with habitual consumption

adrenalin epinephrine

aerosol medication under pressure dispensed as spray through small valve

agar polysaccharide derived from seaweed, used as culture medium for microorganisms; gelatinous natural laxative

agglutinin substance, esp. antibody, that causes bacteria, blood cells, and antigens to clump together

Alka-Seltzer *Trademark.* OTC antacid with aspirin, taken dissolved in water

amitriptyline substance used to treat depression

amobarbital moderate hypnotic barbiturate

amoxicillin semisynthetic penicillin taken orally as broad-spectrum antibiotic

amphetamine central nervous system stimulant that alleviates fatigue and produces feeling of mental alertness

ampicillin broad-spectrum semisynthetic antibiotic

ampule sealed glass or plastic container that holds one dose of medicine

amyl nitrite rapidly absorbed inhalant that causes rapid drop in blood pressure, faintness, and flushing

anabolic steroid steroid

Anacin *Trademark.* OTC analgesic drug

analgesic drug that reduces or eliminates pain; painkiller

anesthetic agent that diminishes or abolishes sensation and can produce unconsciousness

anodyne substance that soothes or relieves pain

Antabuse *Trademark.* medicine that, when combined with any alcohol, causes nausea, vomiting, headache, palpitations, and breathing difficulties, used to treat alcoholism; disulfiram

antacid substance that neutralizes acid, esp. intestinal

antagonism nullification of effect of one drug by another

anthelmintic vermifuge

antibiotic substance, derived from microorganism or fungus, that destroys or inhibits growth of another microorganism, used to treat bacterial infections

antibody protein manufactured by lymphocytes that reacts with specific antigen to fight invasion as principal component of human immunity

anticoagulant agent that prevents blood from clotting

anticonvulsant drug used to prevent or stop epileptic seizures

antidepressant drug that alleviates symptoms of depression

antidiuretic substance that inhibits discharge of urine by increasing water retention of kidneys

antidote agent that counteracts effects of poison

antiemetic drug that prevents vomiting

antihistamine drug that counters effects of histamines in body, esp. in allergies

antipruritic agent that relieves itching

antipyretic drug that reduces fever

antiserum serum that contains antibodies against one or more particular antigens

antispasmodic drug that relieves smooth muscle spasms

antitoxin antibody, usu. obtained from animal, used to combat toxin, esp. from bacteria

antitussive substance that reduces coughing, esp. one that affects activity in the brain's cough center and depresses respiration

antivenin antiserum with antibodies against specific poison, esp. animal venom

aphrodisiac substance that increases sexual arousal

aspirin acetylsalicylic acid in tablet or pill form, used to relieve minor pain, reduce fever and inflammation, and reduce platelet aggregation in blood, available OTC

astringent substance that causes cell shrinkage, used to reduce secretions and slow or stop bleeding

Atabrine *Trademark.* antimalarial drug quinacrine

atropine belladonna extract that inhibits activity of autonomic nervous system and relaxes smooth muscle

attenuated virus virus with reduced disease-producing ability, used for immunization

Aureomycin *Trademark.* antibiotic in general use

AZT azidothymidine; drug that can eliminate symptoms of AIDS but may have deleterious side effects

bacitracin antibiotic for external use

bactericide substance that kills bacteria, esp. antibiotic or disinfectant

bacteriostat substance that retards growth of bacteria

baking soda sodium bicarbonate

barbiturate barbituric acid derivative that depresses central nervous system activity, induces sleep, and produces tolerance

barium sulfate opaque barium salt used as contrast medium in radiography

belladonna atropine

benzocaine topical anesthetic applied to skin or mucous membrane

beta blocker drug that decreases heart activity by affecting receptors of sympathetic nervous system

bicarbonate of soda sodium bicarbonate

birth-control pill oral contraceptive

bolus single, large mass of substance, esp. food or intravenous fluid, often injected into blood vessel as contrast medium or radioactive tracer

booster shot secondary inoculation that serves to maintain immunity

Brioschi *Trademark.* OTC antacid, taken dissolved in water

broad-spectrum (*adj*) describing a drug that is effective against wide variety of microorganisms

Bromo-Seltzer *Trademark.* OTC antacid, taken dissolved in water

bronchodilator drug that relaxes bronchial muscle to open air passages to lungs

cachet flat capsule used to enclose unpleasant-tasting drug

caffeine natural stimulant found in coffee, tea, and cola

camphor crystalline substance used in liniments and to treat flatulence

caplet tamper-resistant, solid tablet with capsulelike coating

capsule small, soluble gelatin container for single dose of medication

castor oil unpleasant-tasting, irritant laxative or cathartic

cathartic laxative

catholicon cure-all, panacea

chloral hydrate sedative hypnotic drug, used primarily by children and elderly in syrup form

chloramphenicol antibiotic used against various microorganisms

chloroform volatile liquid formerly used as general anesthetic

chloroquine synthetic antimalarial drug

clove oil oil of clove, used to relieve toothache

cocaine alkaloid derived from coca leaves, used as local anesthetic, that causes dependence when ingested as stimulant

codeine drug derived from morphine, used as analgesic and cough suppressant

cod-liver oil oil rich in vitamins A and D, used for nutritional purposes, esp. for children

collodion solution of nitrocellulose in alcohol or ether, applied to skin for protection of minor wounds

collyrium medicated solution used to bathe eyes

condom latex, rubber, plastic, or skin sheath for penis, used as contraceptive or to prevent disease

contraceptive medication or device to prevent conception

contraceptive foam frothy, spermicidal substance inserted in vagina to prevent conception

cortisone natural steroid hormone produced by adrenal cortex, used to treat various diseases

cough syrup cough suppressant in thick, sweetened solution

Coumadin *Trademark.* widely used anticoagulant warfarin

counterirritant agent that causes irritation when applied to skin in order to relieve more deep-seated pain

cresol strong antiseptic used in general disinfectants, occasionally applied to skin

curare bark extract that relaxes and paralyzes voluntary muscle

curative any substance that tends to relieve symptoms and treat disease; sanative

cure medicine or remedy for disease

cure-all universal remedy; panacea

cytotoxin substance that has toxic effect on certain cells, used against some tumors

Darvon *Trademark.* analgesic drug

decongestant substance used to reduce nasal mucus production and swelling

Demerol *Trademark.* synthetic morphine derivative used as painkiller; meperidine

dentifrice toothpaste or toothpowder

dependence physical and/or psychological compulsion to continue taking drug; addiction

depressant drug that lowers nervous or functional activity; sedative

DES diethylstilbestrol

dextran water-soluble polysaccharide used as blood plasma extender in treatment of shock

Diabinese *Trademark.* oral agent chlorpropamide, used to control diabetes

diaphragm hemispherical rubber disk fitted over cervix as contraceptive

diazepam tranquilizer, muscle-relaxer, and anticonvulsant used esp. to treat epilepsy and relieve tension; Valium

dicoumarin anticoagulant used to reduce and retard blood clots

diethylstilbestrol DES; synthetic compound that acts like estrogen, used in morning-after pill to prevent implantation of fertilized egg, dangerous during pregnancy

digitalis foxglove leaf extract used as heart stimulant

Dilantin *Trademark.* phenytoin, used to treat epileptic seizures

disinfectant cleansing agent that destroys bacteria and other microorganisms, used on surfaces and surgical tools

disulfiram Antabuse

diuretic agent that promotes excretion of salt and water by kidneys

dose prescribed, measured quantity of drug to be administered at one time

DPT single vaccine that contains antigens for diphtheria, pertussis, and tetanus, administered esp. to children

Dramamine *Trademark.* OTC drug dimenhydrinate, used to treat motion sickness, nausea, and vertigo

dressing medicated and/or antiseptic substance applied to soothe and protect external wound

drug substance that affects structure or functional processes of an organism, esp. to prevent or treat diseases or relieve symptoms

Elavil *Trademark.* mild stimulant

electuary medication mixed with honey

elixir substance that contains alcohol or glycerin, used as solution for bitter or nauseating drugs

emetic substance that induces vomiting

Empirin *Trademark.* analgesic drug

ephedrine widely used drug similar to epinephrine

epinephrine hormone secreted by adrenal medulla that stimulates circulation, muscles, and sugar metabolism; adrenalin

Equanil *Trademark.* minor tranquilizer

erythromycin genetic antibiotic used to treat staphylococci, streptococci, and pneumococci infections

estrogen hormone produced by ovary that stimulates breast and uterine growth, used to treat amenorrhea and menopausal disorders and to inhibit lactation

ether volatile liquid formerly used as anesthetic by inhalation

Excedrin *Trademark.* analgesic drug

expectorant drug that increases secretion of less viscous sputum by respiratory system, used in cough mixtures

febrifuge substance that relieves or reduces fever

fertility drug any hormonal substance used to induce ovulation and produce pregnancy

formaldehyde formic acid derivative, used to sterilize and disinfect

gamma globulin part of blood serum that contains antibodies, used in temporary prevention of infectious diseases

gargle antiseptic, often medicated, liquid used to rinse mouth and throat; mouthwash

general anesthetic agent that depresses central nervous system activity to induce unconsciousness, used in surgery

generic basic, nonproprietary form of medication without trade name, usu. priced lower than brand name drug

germicide any agent, such as an antibiotic or antiseptic, that destroys microorganisms

Glauber's salt colorless, crystalline, water-soluble substance used as laxative

glycerin clear, viscous liquid used externally as emollient or internally as laxative

half-life time required for body to reduce initial peak concentration of drug in blood by one half

hallucinogen drug that produces hallucinations

heparin natural anticoagulant produced by liver cells as a polysaccharide

heroin opiate produced when morphine is treated with acetic acid

hexachlorophene disinfectant used in soaps and skin treatments

hormone substance produced by endocrine gland that travels to another body site where it alters structure or function

hypnotic any sleep-inducing drug; sedative; sleeping pill; soporific

ibuprofen nonaspirin analgesic agent, esp. used to treat inflammation

immunosuppressant drug that reduces resistance to infection and foreign bodies by suppression of immune system, used in organ and tissue transplants

inhalant gas, vapor, or aerosol inhaled for treatment of respiratory conditions

insulin protein hormone secreted by pancreas that regulates blood sugar, injected to treat diabetes

interferon substance produced by infected cells that inhibits specific viral growth

intrauterine device IUD; small plastic contraceptive device inserted into uterus

isoniazid drug used in treatment of tuberculosis

IUD intrauterine device

killed-virus vaccine antigenic material composed of dead organisms, used to stimulate antibodies and create immunity to disease

laudanum morphine solution, formerly used as narcotic analgesic taken orally

laxative substance that stimulates bowel evacuation; cathartic; purgative

L-dopa synthetic substance used to control Parkinson's disease

Librium *Trademark.* tranquilizer chlordiazepoxide hydrochloride

lidocaine local or topical anesthetic, also injected into heart to correct abnormal rhythms, as after myocardial infarction

live-virus vaccine antigenic material composed of weakened organisms, used to stimulate antibodies and create immunity to disease

local anesthetic substance used to numb specific area without inducing loss of consciousness

lozenge medicated tablet with sugar that is dissolved in mouth to soothe throat

Maalox *Trademark.* liquid or tablet OTC antacid

major tranquilizer antipsychotic drug such as Thorazine, used to treat serious mental illness

medication substance taken orally, by injection, or applied externally to body to treat disease or injury or relieve symptoms

medicinal (*adj*) having curative or symptom-relieving properties

medicine drug or preparation used for treatment or prevention of disease

megadose dosage many times that normally required or prescribed, esp. of vitamins

meperidine Demerol

meprobamate substance used as tranquilizer for anxiety, tension, and muscle spasm; Miltown

mercurous chloride powerful antiseptic, poisonous if ingested

methadone powerful, synthetic narcotic used as painkiller or as heroin substitute in detoxification therapy

Methedrine *Trademark.* methamphetamine hydrochloride, a powerful stimulant amphetamine

microbicide substance that kills microorganisms

Milk of Magnesia *Trademark.* combination laxative and antacid available OTC

Miltown *Trademark.* minor tranquilizer used for nervous tension; meprobamate

mineral oil colorless, tasteless petroleum derivative used as laxative

minor tranquilizer drug prescribed to relieve minor tension and anxiety, such as Valium or Miltown

miracle drug substance supposed to cure all diseases or an incurable disease; panacea; wonder drug

MMR vaccine single vaccine that contains

antigens for measles, mumps, and rubella, administered esp. to children

morphine potent narcotic used as analgesic, derived from opium

mouthwash gargle

muscle-relaxer depressant or tranquilizer that acts to relieve tension in muscles

narcotic sleep-inducing and painkilling drug, esp. opiate, usu. addictive

Nembutal *Trademark.* powerful barbiturate depressant; pentobarbital

neomycin antibiotic, esp. for infections of eye or skin

nitroglycerin vasodilator used in crisis to prevent or treat angina

norepinephrine commercial form of neurotransmitter used for emergency treatment of lowered blood pressure

Novocaine *Trademark.* local anesthetic, used esp. by injection; procaine

Nupercaine *Trademark.* local OTC anesthetic

OD overdose

opiate derivative of opium that depresses central nervous system, relieves pain, and induces sleep

opium poppy extract that contains morphine and has a narcotic, analgesic effect

OPV oral polio vaccine; Sabin vaccine

oral contraceptive medication that contains synthetic female sex hormones and prevents conception when taken daily; birth-control pill

OTC over the counter; medication available without doctor's prescription

overdose OD; excessive amount of drug taken at one time, causing negative reaction and death in case of powerful hypnotics

painkiller agent that relieves or inhibits pain; analgesic

palliative medicine that relieves symptoms but does not cure disease

panacea cure-all believed to remedy all ailments

paregoric camphorated tincture of opium used to relieve diarrhea, formerly used as painkiller

patent medicine trademarked medication available without prescription

penicillin antibiotic, orig. derived from mold, used to treat bacterial infections

pentobarbital powerful barbiturate hypnotic and anticonvulsant; Nembutal

Pentothal *Trademark.* short-acting barbiturate, thiopental sodium, used as intravenous anesthetic

Pepto-Bismol *Trademark.* OTC liquid antacid

pessary vaginal appliance or medicated suppository

pharmaceutical drug or medication manufactured and sold by pharmacy

pharmacology study and practice of chemistry, preparation, use, and effect of drugs

pharmacopoeia official, authoritative reference book containing descriptions, formulas, uses, and tests for most drugs and medical preparations

pharmacy preparation and dispensing of drugs; place where this is done

phenacetin mild, nonaddictive painkiller and fever reducer, often combined with aspirin

phenelzine powerful inhibitor used to prevent certain kinds of depression

phenobarbital very slow-acting, barbiturate depressant

phenolphthalein phenol derivative used in laxatives

physic medicine or remedy, esp. laxative or cathartic

pill small ball or tablet of medicine to be swallowed whole; oral contraceptive

pitocin synthetic hormone administered to pregnant women to induce labor

placebo inactive substance taken by patient who believes that it is an effective drug, which often causes improvement in condition

plasma extender any of various substances that increase volume of plasma in body, used to restore blood flow in treating shock, thrombosis, and critical blood loss

polio vaccine Salk or Sabin vaccine against poliomyelitis

prednisone synthetic steroid, administered orally, used to treat leukemia and Hodgkin's disease

prescription medication that requires doctor's authorization for purchase and use; slip of paper with this authorization

preventive substance used to prevent disease

procaine synthetic local and spinal anesthetic; Novocaine

progesterone hormone that prepares uterus to receive and develop fertilized egg

prophylactic contraceptive device, esp. condom

psychedelic drug that induces altered consciousness, often hallucinogenic

psychoactive drug that affects central nervous system as depressant, stimulant, or hallucinogen

purgative laxative

purge purgative or cathartic medication

quinine alkaloid drug used to treat malaria

remedy medicine that cures, treats, or relieves symptoms of disease

reserpine derivative of the shrub rauwolfia, used to treat hypertension by acting as sedative, often also producing depressive side effect

reverse tolerance increased sensitivity to certain drugs the more they are taken, as with marijuana

Rolaids *Trademark.* mild OTC antacid in tablet form

rubber *Slang.* condom

Sabin vaccine polio vaccine that contains attenuated live viruses, administered orally; OPV

Salk vaccine polio vaccine that contains dead viruses, administered by injection

sanative curative

scopolamine belladonna derivative used to induce sleep or as sedative during labor in childbirth

secobarbital substance used as sedative and hypnotic; Seconal

Seconal *Trademark.* secobarbital

sedative drug that depresses central nervous system to induce calm or sleep; depressant; hypnotic

senna kind of laxative

serum blood serum that contains agents of immunity used as antitoxin

sleeping pill drug that sedates or induces drowsiness; hypnotic; soporific

smelling salts preparation, as of ammonia, used as stimulant or restorative

sodium amobarbital sedative and hypnotic, sometimes called truth serum, used to facilitate interrogation

sodium bicarbonate salt of sodium that neutralizes acid, used for mild intestinal disorders; baking soda; bicarbonate of soda

sodium hypochlorite strong disinfectant

soporific hypnotic drug; sleeping pill

spermicidal jelly contraceptive substance that kills spermatozoa

spermicide agent that kills spermatozoa

sterile saline solution solution of 0.9 percent sodium chloride, used to dilute drugs for injection and as plasma substitute

steroid any of large family of chemical compounds including hormones produced by adrenal glands, ovaries, and testes; medication used for immunosuppression and hormone replacement, often also used in physical therapy and to promote muscle building; anabolic steroid

stimulant substance that stimulates central nervous system, which prevents sleep and increases alertness and energy

streptomycin antibiotic used esp. to treat tuberculosis

sulfadiazine sulfa drug used to treat pneumococcal, streptococcal, and staphylococcal infections

sulfa drug sulfonamide

sulfonamide class of antibiotics, such as sulfadiazine and sulfapyridine, that stop bacterial growth and combat infection; sulfa drug

sympatholytic drug that affects sympathetic nervous system

synergism phenomenon in which each of two or more drugs is more active in combination than when used alone

syrup of ipecac solution prepared with dried root, used as emetic or purgative

tablet small disk, made from compressed powders of one or more drugs, that is swallowed whole

teratogen substance that can cause birth defects

Terramycin *Trademark.* antibiotic compound based on tetracycline derivative

testosterone principal male sex hormone produced by testes, used in replacement therapy and as anabolic steroid

tetanus toxoid tetanus bacteria treated to eliminate toxic qualities, used as antigenic vaccine

tetracycline antibiotic compound effective against wide variety of bacterial infections

thalidomide tranquilizer known to cause birth defects in children born to women who used it during pregnancy

Thorazine *Trademark.* major synthetic tranquilizer chlorpromazine

Tinactin *Trademark.* brand of tolnaftate, used as antifungal treatment

tolbutamide drug that stimulates release of insulin from pancreas, used to treat diabetes

tolerance decreased effectiveness of drug due to prolonged or repeated use, requiring larger dose for same effect

tolnaftate antifungal substance, used topically to treat superficial skin infections

tonic healing, soothing, or invigorating agent

toothpaste paste used to clean teeth, applied with brush; dentifrice

toothpowder powder used to clean teeth, applied with brush; dentifrice

topical (of a drug) applied directly to skin surface, not taken internally

toxin poisonous substance

toxoid vaccine made from poisonous waste products of disease-causing microorganisms

trank *Slang.* tranquilizer

tranquilizer drug that produces calming effect and relieves anxiety and muscle tension without inducing sleep

troche small, medicinal lozenge that soothes mouth and throat

Tuinal *Trademark.* barbiturate sedative or hypnotic of secobarbital and amobarbital

Tums *Trademark.* mild antacid available OTC in tablet form

Tylenol *Trademark.* OTC acetaminophen, an analgesic drug

universal antidote mixture of activated charcoal, magnesium oxide, and tannic acid in water, used as antidote to unidentified poisons

vaccine antigenic preparation that stimulates antibodies and confers immunity against specific disease

valerian drug made from root of valerian plant, formerly used as sedative and antispasmodic

Valium *Trademark.* minor tranquilizer; diazepam

vasoconstrictor drug that narrows blood vessels and decreases blood flow, used to raise blood pressure during shock or severe bleeding

vasodilator drug that widens and opens blood vessels and increases blood flow, used to lower blood pressure

vermicide chemical agent that kills parasitic worms in intestine

vermifuge chemical agent used to expel parasites from intestine; anthelmintic

vitamin any of various organic compounds, natural or synthetic, required for normal metabolic functions

warfarin preparation of water-insoluble anticoagulant, used to manage potential or existing blood-clotting disorders; Coumadin

withdrawal cessation of use of drug to which one is addicted; symptoms associated with such withdrawal

wonder drug miracle drug, panacea

Xantac *Trademark.* antacid anti-ulcer drug

Dressings and Supports

Ace bandage *Trademark.* elastic bandage

adhesive compress compress held in place by sticky tape

adhesive tape plastic strips with sticky substance on one side, used to hold bandages in position

alcohol solution of ethyl alcohol used as preservative or antiseptic

ammonia pungent, colorless, gaseous solution, used as counterirritant and smelling salts

antiseptic slightly toxic chemical that destroys bacteria and other microorganisms, used on skin and mucous membrane to cleanse wounds and prevent infection or internally for intestinal and bladder infections

application medication, remedy, or antiseptic placed externally on body part, as in compress

balm fragrant ointment or aromatic oil with medicinal value

balsam aromatic gum resin from various plants, used as balm

bandage absorbent pad or strip of material applied to wound or injury

Band-Aid *Trademark.* adhesive strip bandage

binder bandage or strip of material used to cover and compress wound or hold dressing in place

boric acid white, crystalline, mildly acidic compound used in mild antiseptic solution

brace device used to support weak, injured, or deformed body part

braces metal bands used by orthodontists to correct malocclusion of teeth

calamine lotion topical solution of pink zinc oxide powder used on skin irritations

camphor crystalline substance used in liniments to soothe irritations and relieve pain

carbolic acid phenol

cast rigid case made from bandage soaked in plaster of Paris, used to prevent movement of aligned bone ends in broken limb

compress moistened pad of folded cloth, often medicated, applied with heat, cold, or pressure to soothe body part

cotton ball fluffy clump of cotton for gentle application of medications or antiseptics

cotton swab small, flexible stick of cardboard or plastic with cotton tips, used for application in small or inaccessible places

counterirritant substance that impedes or reduces skin irritation

crutch tall support device with handgrip and padded crosspiece that fits under arm, used as walking aid

demulcent soothing, usu. oily substance used to relieve pain in irritated mucous surfaces

disinfectant cleaning agent that destroys bacteria and other microorganisms, esp. for use on tools and surfaces

dressing protective or healing material applied externally to wound or diseased body part

elastic bandage long strip of stretchable bandage wrapped tightly around injured extremity to hold it in position

emollient medical preparation that soothes and softens external tissue

Epsom salts white, crystalline magnesium salt used as cathartic in dilute solution, esp. bath

eyewash medicinal solution that soothes eyes

gauze thin, open material used in layers for dressing, swab, or bandage

gentian violet violet dye used as antiseptic

glycerin glycerol

glycerol syrupy liquid prepared by hydrolysis of fats and oils for use as skin lotion; glycerin

hydrogen peroxide colorless liquid used in dilute solution as disinfectant

ice pack rubber or plastic container filled with ice and applied to relieve pain and prevent swelling

iodine nonmetallic chemical element used in tincture as antiseptic

knee brace specially designed support for knee that restricts or prevents movement

lanolin fatty wool substance used as base for ointments

liniment soothing camphor and alcohol preparation rubbed into skin or applied on surgical dressing

lint scraped, softened linen, formerly used as dressing for wounds

lotion viscous liquid solution used to cleanse, soothe, or heal skin

lubricant greasy substance applied to reduce friction on body surface

Lysol *Trademark.* disinfectant used on nonbody surfaces

medicated dressing dressing that contains healing agents

menthol white, pungent, waxy alcohol crystal used in medications and emollients

Mentholatum *Trademark.* menthol preparation

merbromin water-soluble powder that forms red solution in water, used as antiseptic germicide; Mercurochrome

mercuric chloride poisonous white crystal used as powerful antiseptic or pesticide; mercurous chloride

Mercurochrome *Trademark.* organic compound that turns red in water solution, used as antiseptic germicide; merbromin

mercurous chloride mercuric chloride

Merthiolate *Trademark.* crystalline compound that turns red in water solution, used as antiseptic; thimerosal

mustard plaster powdered mustard paste that acts as rubefacient, applied on cloth to soothe skin

neck brace specially designed support for head and injured neck

ointment fatty substance used to soothe or heal skin; salve; unguent

pack folded, moistened, often medicated pad of

cotton or cloth applied to body or inserted in cavity

peroxide hydrogen peroxide

petrolatum colorless, greasy hydrocarbon mixture used as ointment base or salve; petroleum jelly

petroleum jelly petrolatum

phenol strong disinfectant used to clean wounds, treat mouth and throat irritations, and as preservative in injections; carbolic acid

plaster pasty medicinal dressing applied to body part on cloth as curative counterirritant

poultice thick, warm paste made from herbs and water, used in folk medicine

prosthesis artificial body part

rubefacient salve or plaster that causes skin to turn red

salve medicinal ointment used to soothe or heal skin irritations, burns, or wounds; ointment; unguent

sanitary napkin cotton pad worn to absorb menstrual discharge

sitz bath soothing bath, esp. with Epsom salts solution

sling loop of cloth that encircles neck, used to support injured arm

splint length of rigid material bandaged to injured limb to prevent movement

sponge soft pad of gauze or cotton used in surgery

stupe soft, moist, medicated cloth used as hot compress

support device used to relieve pressure on, or hold position of, injured part

surgical dressing medicated substance used as healing antiseptic during surgery

swab small cotton ball used to clear discharge or apply medicine; cotton swab

tampon plug of absorbent material used to absorb blood or secretions, esp. in vagina for menstrual discharge

tape strip of material, often adhesive, used to hold dressing, compress, or bandage in place

thimerosal water-soluble powder that forms red solution in water, used as antiseptic; Merthiolate

tincture alcohol solution of medication

tincture of iodine alcohol solution of iodine used as antiseptic

tourniquet strip of cloth or bandage wrapped tightly around body part, esp. extremity or digit, to control bleeding temporarily through applied pressure

traction splint device that pulls limb to hold it in position, used to set fractured or dislocated bone

unguent fatty substance used to soothe and heal skin; ointment; salve

vapors mentholated salve applied to chest and nose to relieve congestion

Vaseline *Trademark.* petrolatum

Vicks Vaporub *Trademark.* mentholated vaporous salve

witch hazel alcohol solution made with liquid extract from leaves and bark of this shrub, used as lotion

zinc oxide white powder that is active ingredient in calamine lotion and other ointments

Prefixes and Suffixes

NOTE: *When used before a word beginning with a vowel, most prefixes drop or change the final "o", "a", or "i".*

adeno- gland

-agra seizure of pain

-aholic one having addiction to something

algo- pain

arterio- artery

arthro- joint

bacill- rodlike

bacteri- bacteria

blepharo- eyelid

brady- slow

broncho- windpipe, throat

carcino- cancer

cardio- heart

-cele tumor

cephalo- head

cerebro- brain, esp. cerebrum

chilo- lip

chiro- hand

cholo- bile

chondrio- cartilage

-coccus spherical bacterium

colo- lower intestine

coro- pupil of eye

cortico- cortex

costo- rib

cysto- bladder, cyst

cyto- cell

dacryo- tears

denti- tooth

dermato- skin

dextro- right side

dys- ill, impaired

-ectomy surgical removal

-emia blood condition

encephalo- brain

entero- intestine

erythro- red

febri- fever

fibro- fibrous

gastro- stomach

-genic producing or causing, produced or caused by

geronto- old age

glosso- tongue

-gram record or image made by a device

-graph recording or tracing device

gyneco- woman

hema- blood

hemo- blood

hepato- liver

histo- tissue

hydro- water

hyper- extreme, excessive, beyond

hypno- sleep

hypo- insufficient, below, under

hystero- uterus, womb

-ia name of disease or condition

-iasis disease

-iatrics medical treatment

-iatrist physician or healer

iatro- medicine

-iatry specific area of healing or medical practice

ilio- flank, upper hipbone

immuno- immune

-itis inflammation or abnormal condition

kerato- hornlike

labio- lip

laparo- flank, abdominal wall

laryngo- windpipe, larynx

leuko- white

lipo- fat

litho- stone, calcification

-logy science or body of knowledge

-lysis breaking down, decomposing

masto- breast

melano- black, dark

musculo- muscle

myco- fungus, mold

myelo- marrow, spinal cord

myo- muscle

narco- stupor, drugged state

nephro- kidney

neuro- nerve

-odont having or relating to teeth

odonto- tooth

-odynia pain

-oid resembling or referring to form

-oma tumor

ophthalmo- eye

-opia eye, sight

-opsy medical examination

opto- eye

orchido- testes

ortho- erect, straight, normal

-osis diseased or abnormal condition or state

ossi- bone

osteo- bone

oto- ear

ovi- egg

patho- disease, sickness, suffering

-pathy suffering, disease, or treatment

pedi- foot

pedo- child

pharmaco- drug or medication

pharyngo- pharynx

-phasia speech disorder

phlebo- vein

-phrenia lack, deficiency, disorder

-plasia growth

-plast cell, living substance

-plasty surgical repair or molding formation

pleuro- rib, side of body

pneumo- lung, air

podo- foot

polio- gray matter
procto- anus, rectum
psycho- mind
pulmo- lung
pyelo- pelvis
reni- kidney
-rrhagia rupture, profuse flow or discharge
-rrhaphy suture
-rrhea flow, discharge
-rrhexis rupture
sangui- blood
sarco- flesh
schizo- split
-scope instrument for viewing
-sect cut
sero- serum, blood
somato- body
somni- sleep
stomato- mouth
-stomy surgical operation involving creation of artificial opening
tachy- rapid
thanato- death
thrombo- blood clot, coagulation
-tome cutting instrument
tomo- cut, section
-tomy surgical incision or excision
-tonia muscle or nerve tension
toxico- poison
toxo- poison
tracheo- windpipe, trachea
tricho- hair
-trophic having nutritional requirements
tropho- nourishment
urino- urine
uro- urine
utero- womb, uterus
vaso- vessel
veno- vein
ventro- abdomen
vermi- worm
zymo- fermentation

MEASURES AND WEIGHTS

Systems and Units
Measuring Devices
Measures and Standards of Time
U.S. System
Metric System
Special Measures
Foreign and Historical Measures
Combining Forms

See also: *Chap. 4: Physics; Mathematics; Chemistry; Chap. 5: Electricity and Electronics; Chap. 23: Time Perception; Spatial Positions and Relations*

Definitions for historical, foreign, and special measures generally provide both U.S. and metric system equivalents. Within the U.S. system, metric conversion is provided. Conversion from metric to U.S. system is given only for basic units, such as meter to foot or gram to ounce, since other conversion factors can be derived by moving the decimal point to the left or right.

Systems and Units

angular measure units used to measure angles and sections of circles
apothecaries' measure units of weight used chiefly for dispensing liquid drugs
apothecaries' weight system of weights used chiefly in compounding and dispensing drugs
avoirdupois weight U.S. and British units of weight used for articles other than drugs, gemstones, and precious metals
circular measure units used to measure circles: quadrants, degrees, minutes, and seconds
cubage cubic measure
cubic measure units used to measure volume filled in three dimensions; cubage
dry measure units of capacity used to measure dry commodities
land measure units of linear and square measure, used to measure land
linear measure units used to measure length
liquid measure units of capacity used to measure liquids
mariners' measure units of linear measure used in navigation
measures units of standard systems, used to express dimension, extent, mass, and volume
metrication establishment of metric system as standard system of measurement
metric system decimal system of weights and measures, used in science and in most nations other than the United States, with basic units of meter, gram, and liter
metrology science of weights and measures
square measure units used to measure area covered in two dimensions
surveyors' measure units of linear measure used in surveying
time measure units used to measure the passage of time
troy weight system of weights used for precious metals and gemstones
U.S. units system of weights and measures, used primarily in the United States, with basic units of foot, ounce, and quart
weights units used to measure mass or heaviness
wood measure units of cubic measure used for wood

Measuring Devices

analytical balance precision balance having sensitivity of 0.1 milligram
balance weighing instrument that opposes a known weight to the object being weighed across a lever supported exactly in its middle
bathroom scale small platform scale on which one stands to measure body weight
beam balance, esp. its crossbar

caliper tool with adjustable, usu. curved jaws on pivot, used to measure thickness or diameter
compass instrument for drawing or measuring circles, consisting of two movable, rigid legs hinged at one end
conversion table tabular arrangement of equivalent values of units of measure of different systems
counterweight weight used to counterbalance an opposing object that is to be weighed
cyclometer instrument that records the revolutions of a wheel to measure distance or speed
extensometer instrument for measuring minute degrees of expansion, contraction, and deformation
folding rule rule made of hinged sections, usu. of light wood, that fold out to increase length; zigzag rule
measure instrument with graduated markings for measuring
measuring cup cup with graduated markings, used to measure dry and liquid volume
measuring spoons set of spoons in graduated sizes, used esp. in cooking
micrometer device for measuring minute distances and angles, esp. in connection with a telescope or microscope
platform scale scale with platform for holding object being weighed
rule rigid strip of material having straight edge marked off with units of measure; ruler
ruler rule
scale balance, platform scale, or other device for measuring weight
sonic depth finder device that uses sonar echolocation to measure underwater depths
steelyard portable balance with two unequal arms, the shorter one having a hook or device for holding an object to be weighed and the longer one having a movable counterweight
tape measure length of flexible material with graduated markings that unreels to measure linear dimension
theodolite surveying instrument having telescopic sight for precise measurement of vertical and horizontal angles
ultramicrometer micrometer calibrated to and capable of measuring extremely small magnitudes
vernier small, movable, graduated scale running parallel to the fixed, graduated scale of a sextant or other measuring device
weighbridge large platform scale standing flush with roadway, used to weigh trucks or livestock
yardstick rule 36 inches in length
zigzag rule folding rule

Measures and Standards of Time

ab urbe condita *Latin.* lit. from the founding of the city; used in dating system based on founding of Rome in 753 B.C.; A.U.C

A.D. **a**nno **D**omini; *Latin.* lit. in the year of the Lord; used to designate years of Christian era

age measure of one's time alive

alarm clock small clock that sounds alarm at set time to awaken sleeper

a.m. **a**nte **m**eridiem; *Latin.* lit. before noon; morning

analemma scale shaped like figure 8 showing declination of sun and equation of time for each day

analog clock timepiece with hands revolving on face to indicate time

ante meridiem *Latin.* lit. before noon; a.m.

atomic clock extremely accurate timepiece whose operation is based on vibrations of certain atoms

A.U.C ab urbe condita

Aurora goddess of dawn (ancient Rome)

B.C. **b**efore **C**hrist; used to designate years before Christian era

B.C.E **b**efore **C**hristian (or **C**ommon) **e**ra; equivalent of B.C.

beat musical measure of time

bell device sounded on ship every half hour during each four-hour watch or segment of day

calendar system or device for marking time by days, weeks, months, and years

C.E. **C**hristian (or **C**ommon) **e**ra; equivalent of A.D.

Central time time zone in U.S. Middle West, one hour earlier than Eastern time

century measure of time equal to 100 years

chrono- Greek prefix meaning time

chronograph instrument that measures and records time

chronology science of computing and measuring time and sequentially ordering events

chronometer instrument for measuring time; timepiece

chronoscope instrument for measuring time

clock mechanical timepiece marking passage of minutes, hours, and sometimes seconds

date designation by number of each day of each month

day basic unit of time equal to 24 hours

daylight-saving time time attained by moving timepieces one hour ahead of standard time from spring to fall

decade measure of time equal to 10 years

dial face of clock, watch or sundial showing time of day

digital clock timepiece indicating time by regularly changing display of numerical digits

Eastern time time zone in U.S. Atlantic coast region, three hours later than Pacific time

embolism insertion of time period to regulate calendar, esp. day added for leap year

gnomon raised part of sundial that casts shadow to indicate time

Greenwich mean time worldwide standard time relative to time at meridian running through Greenwich, England

Gregorian calendar corrected Julian calendar incorporating leap year every fourth year

horography art of making timepieces

horologe timepiece, esp. sundial

horologist maker of clocks and timepieces

horology art or science of measuring time and making timepieces

horometry practice or science of measuring time

hour unit of time equal to 60 minutes

hourglass necked glass vessel containing sand or mercury, used to measure time, esp. period of one hour

intercalary (*adj*) inserted into calendar, as with leap year's added day

International Date Line imaginary line at 180 degrees longitude, exactly opposite Greenwich meridian, at which one day is added when passing westward across it

Julian calendar standard twelve-month, 365-day calendar introduced in ancient Rome

minute basic unit of time equal to 60 seconds, or 1/60 of an hour

month unit of time equal to 1/12 of a year, usu. 30 or 31 days, except February, which has 28 or 29 days

Mountain time time zone in U.S. Rocky Mountain area, one hour later than Pacific time

o'clock (*adv*) of the clock, used in telling time, as in one o'clock

Pacific time time zone along U.S. western seaboard, three hours earlier than Eastern time

pendulum suspended, swinging mechanism used in clockworks or as timepiece

p.m. **p**ost **m**eridiem; *Latin.* lit. after noon; afternoon and evening

post meridiem *Latin.* lit. after noon; p.m.

quartz clock timepiece whose mechanical operation is based on electrical frequencies and resulting regular vibrations of quartz crystal

real time actual elapsed time, esp. when editing film

second unit of time equal to 1/60 of a minute

sidereal time time measured by rotation of Earth relative to a star on celestial sphere other than the sun

solar time time determined by calculating time required for sun to cross same point in sky a second time

space-time four-dimensional continuum incorporating time with three physical dimensions as means of locating events

standard time worldwide time system based on Greenwich meridian; time attained when daylight-saving time is reversed and clocks are turned back one hour in fall; time officially adopted by a country or region

stopwatch watch with hand that can be stopped or started at any instant for precise timing

strike (*vb*) make known the time by sounding, esp. a bell

sundial instrument indicating time of day by casting shadow of sunlight on dial

tempo rate of movement, speed; time in which musical passage is written and/or played

time dimension of reality characterized by sequential flow of events and phenomena through irreversible procession of moments from past to present to future; systematized demarcation of the passage of such moments into units of seconds, minutes, hours, days, and years; period or point in time; fourth dimension in space-time continuum

time capsule container holding records or objects of current culture, deposited for discovery at future date

timecard paper on which hours worked by employee are recorded

time chart chart showing standard times in various parts of world

time clock clock with mechanism to record time on timecard that employee begins and ends workday

timekeeper one appointed to record and announce time at event, esp. athletic contest

time machine hypothetical device permitting travel forward or backward through time

timepiece clock, watch, or other device for measuring and indicating time

timer device used to keep time or measure brief periods

time sheet paper for recording arrival and departure times of workers

time signature fractional sign used in musical notation to show number of beats per measure and kind of note lasting one beat

timetable schedule of times for some event, esp. arrivals and departures of railroads, buses, or airplanes

time zone longitudinal region within which same standard time is used

watch small timepiece worn on wrist or carried in pocket

week measure of time equal to 7 days

year measure of time required for Earth to complete one revolution around the sun, equal to either 365 or 366 days, or 12 months

U.S. System

acre unit of square measure, usu. for land, equal to 43,560 square feet (4047 sq. m)

barrel unit of cubic measure equal to 5.8 cubic feet; unit of liquid measure equal to 31.5 U.S. gallons (119 l) or 42 U.S. gallons (159 l) for petroleum

board foot cubic measure used for lumber, equal to 144 cubic inches or 12 inches by 12 inches by 1 inch

bushel cubic measure equal to 2150 cubic inches

cental hundredweight

circle circular measure equal to 360 degrees

cloth yard unit of linear measure for cloth, formerly equal to 37 inches (0.93 m), now equal to 36 inches (0.91 m) or 1 standard yard

congius unit of liquid measure used in prescriptions, equal to 1 gallon (3.7853 l)

cord cubic measure of wood, equal to 128 cubic feet (3.6 cu. m)

cubic foot 1728 cubic inches; 1/27 cubic yard
cubic inch 1 inch by 1 inch by 1 inch
cubic yard 27 cubic feet
cup unit of liquid measure equal to 8 fluid ounces (237 ml) or 16 tablespoons
degree unit of angular or circular measure equal to 60 minutes or 1/360 of a circle
dram unit of apothecaries' weight equal to 60 minims or 1/8 fluid ounce (3.89 g); unit of avoirdupois weight equal to 1/16 ounce (1.77 g)
fathom unit of linear measure equal to 6 feet (1.8 m), used in nautical and mining measurements
fluid ounce unit of liquid measure equal to 2 tablespoons or 1/8 cup (29.573 ml)
foot basic unit of linear measure equal to 12 inches; equivalent to 30.48 centimeters
furlong unit of linear measure equal to 220 yards (201 m) or 1/8 mile (0.2 km)
gallon unit of liquid measure equal to 4 quarts (3.7853 l)
gill measure of liquid volume equal to 1/2 cup or 4 fluid ounces (118 ml); noggin
grain smallest measure of weight, being 437.5 grains per avoirdupois ounce
half-inch unit of linear measure equal to 1/24 foot (1.27 cm)
hogshead unit of liquid measure usu. equal to 63 gallons (238 l)
hundredweight unit of avoirdupois weight equal to 100 pounds (45.359 kg); cental; short hundredweight
inch unit of linear measure equal to 1/12 foot; equivalent to 2.54 centimeters
lb. abbreviation for pound
microinch unit of linear measure equal to one-millionth of an inch
mil unit of length equal to one-thousandth of an inch (0.0254 mm), used esp. to measure diameter of wire or thickness of plastic
mile unit of linear measure equal to 5280 feet (1.609 km); statute mile
minim smallest unit of liquid measure, equal to 1/60 of a fluid dram, or approximately one drop
minute sixty seconds in angular measure; 1/60 of a degree
nautical mile unit of linear measure equal to 6080.20 feet (1853.25 m), used in navigation
noggin gill
octant the eighth part of a circle, equal to 45 degrees
ounce unit of avoirdupois weight equal to 16 drams or 1/16 pound; equivalent to 28.35 grams
oz. abbreviation for ounce
peck unit of dry volume equal to 8 quarts or 1/4 bushel (8.81 l)
pennyweight unit of troy weight equal to 24 grains or 1/20 of an ounce (1.555 g)
pint unit of liquid measure equal to two cups (0.6 l); unit of dry measure equal to 35 cubic inches
pole unit of square measure equal to 1 square rod or 30 1/4 square yards (25.3 sq. m)

pound unit of avoirdupois weight equal to 16 ounces; equivalent to 0.45359 kilogram
quadrant unit of circular measure equal to 90 degrees, or one quarter of a circle
quart unit of liquid measure equal to 1/4 gallon, or 57.749 cubic inches (0.946 l); two pints; unit of dry measure equal to 1/8 peck, or 67.201 cubic inches (1.101 l)
road unit of square measure equal to 1/4 acre
rod unit of linear measure equal to 5.5 yards or 16.5 feet (5.029 m)
scruple unit of apothecaries' weight equal to 20 grains or 1/3 dram (1.295 g)
second unit of angular measure equal to 1/60 of a minute or 1/3600 of a degree
short hundredweight hundredweight
short ton measure of avoirdupois weight equal to 2000 pounds (0.907 metric ton)
square mile unit of square measure equal to 640 acres (2.59 sq. km)
statute mile mile
ton short ton; 2000 pounds
yard unit of linear measure equal to 3 feet or 36 inches (0.9144 m)

Metric System

are a; unit of land measure equal to 1/100 hectare or 100 square meters
centiare ca; one square meter
centigram cg; ten milligrams, 1/100 gram
centiliter cl; ten milliliters, 1/100 liter
centimeter cm; ten millimeters, 1/100 meter
centner fifty kilograms, or sometimes 100 kilograms
decigram dg; one hundred milligrams, 1/10 gram
deciliter dl; one hundred milliliters, 1/10 liter
decimeter dm; one hundred millimeters, 1/10 meter
dekagram dag; ten grams, 1/10 kilogram
dekaliter dal; ten liters, 1/10 kiloliter
dekameter dam; ten meters, 1/10 kilometer
gram g; basic metric measure of mass equivalent to 0.035 ounce or 15.432 grains
hectare ha; unit of surface or land measure equal to 100 ares, or 2.471 acres (10,000 sq. meters)
hectogram hg; one hundred grams, 1/10 kilogram
hectoliter hl; one hundred liters, 1/10 kiloliter
hectometer hm; one hundred meters, 1/10 kilometer
kilogram kg; one thousand grams; equivalent to 2.205 pounds
kiloliter kl; one thousand liters
kilometer km; one thousand meters; equivalent to 0.621 miles
liter l; basic metric unit of liquid volume equivalent to 1.057 quarts
long ton ton
meter m; basic metric unit of linear measure equivalent to 3.281 feet
metric hundredweight fifty kilograms

microgram ug; one-millionth part of gram, used primarily in chemistry
micrometer micron
micron u; one-millionth part of meter; micrometer
milligram mg; one-tenth centigram, one-thousandth gram
milliliter ml; one-tenth centiliter, one-thousandth liter
millimeter mm; one-tenth centimeter, one-thousandth meter
nanogram ng; one-billionth part of gram
nanometer nm; one-billionth part of meter
picogram pg; one-trillionth part of gram
quintal measure of weight equal to 100 kilograms or 1/10 ton
ton measure of weight equal to 1000 kilograms or 10 quintals; long ton

Special Measures

arpent unit of area equal to one acre, orig. French, still used in Quebec and Louisiana
assay ton measure of weight used in assaying ore, equal to 29.167 grams
baker's dozen group of thirteen units or things; long dozen
bale large bundle of dry goods, approximately 500 pounds (U.S.)
base box unit of square measure, representing 112 sheets of tin each 14 by 20 inches (35 by 50 cm), equal to 31,360 square inches (196,000 sq. cm)
bolt linear measure for cloth equal to 40 yards (36.576 m)
cable nautical unit of length equal to 720 feet (219 m) in U.S. Navy and 608 feet (185 m) in British navy
caliber diameter of a gun's bore measured in hundredths of an inch
capful amount that a cap will contain
carat measure of weight for gemstones, equal to 206 milligrams (3 grains); measure of amount of gold per twenty-four parts of gold alloy
case carton containing usu. four, twelve, or twenty-four units or things
centistere one-hundredth part of stere
chain unit of linear measure used in surveying, equal to 66 feet (20 m) and divided into 100 links
chiliad group of one thousand
cicero printer's measure approximately equivalent to one pica or 0.1776 inch (4.5 mm)
crate quantity, esp. of fruit, packed in crate, approximately 2 cu. ft. (0.05 cu. m)
dash a few drops or grains, used as cooking measure, esp. for liquids
double magnum jeroboam
dozen group of twelve units or things
em printer's measure designating square width of given type size
fifth unit of liquid measure equal to approximately one-fifth gallon (750 ml), esp. for spirits

frail quantity of raisins contained in frail basket, approximately 75 pounds (34 kg)

freight ton unit of volume for shipping equal to 40 cubic feet

gauge diameter of a gun's bore measured in millimeters

great gross group of twelve gross, or 1728, units or things

great pace unit of linear measure representing distance between places at which same foot touches ground in walking, approximately 5 feet (1.5 m)

gross group of twelve dozen, or 144, units or things

hand linear measure equal to 4 inches (10 cm), used esp. for horses

handbreadth unit of linear measure equal to 2.5 to 4 inches (6.4 to 10 cm)

hectostere one hundred stere, equal to 130.8 cubic yards, used to measure cordwood

jeroboam unit of liquid volume equal to two magnums or approximately 4/5 gallon (3 l), esp. for wine; double magnum

jerry can can used as measure of liquid volume equal to five gallons (19 l) in U.S. or 4.5 imperial gallons (20.4 l) in Britain

keel measure of coal equal to 21 long tons and 4 hundredweight (21.3 metric tons)

kip dead weight load equal to 1000 pounds (453.6 kg)

knot rate of speed equal to one nautical mile per hour

league any of various units of linear measure equal to 2.4 to 4.6 statute miles

light year unit of linear measure used in astronomy, equal to distance light travels in one year in a vacuum, or approximately 5.878 trillion miles (9.46 trillion km)

link unit of linear measure used in surveying, equal to one hundredth of a chain

long dozen baker's dozen

magnum unit of liquid volume equal to approximately two-fifths gallon (1.5 l), esp. for wine

megaton one million tons, esp. an explosive force equal to one million tons of TNT

military pace unit of linear measure equal to 2 1/2 feet

nail unit of cloth measure equal to 2 1/2 inches

nebuchadnezzar unit of liquid measure equal to 20 quarts (18.9 liter), used esp. for wine

pace unit of linear measure representing span covered by feet in taking one step, approximately 30 to 40 inches (75 cm to 1 m)

palm unit of linear measure equal to 3 inches (7.5 cm)

pica unit of measure in typography equal to one-sixth inch or 12 points

pinch a few grains, used as dry measure in cooking

pipe cask used as measure of liquid volume, equal to 4 barrels, 2 hogsheads, or half a tun, containing 126 gallons (477 l), esp. of wine

point unit of measure in typography equal to one seventy-second inch or one-twelfth pica

puncheon cask used as measure of liquid volume, equal to 80 gallons (304 l)

quire twenty-five sheets of paper

ream five hundred sheets of paper or 20 quires

rood unit of linear measure varying from 5 1/2 to 8 yards (5 to 7 m); unit of land measure equal to 40 square rods (0.101 ha); unit of 1 square rod (25.29 sq. m)

score group of 20 units or things

sextant unit of circular measure equal to 60 degrees or one sixth of a circle

span unit of linear measure representing distance between fully extended tips of thumb and little finger, usu. equal to 9 inches (23 cm)

stere one cubic meter, used to measure cordwood; equivalent to 1.3080 cubic yards

tablespoon unit of measure equal to 3 teaspoons (14.8 ml)

teaspoon unit of measure equivalent to 4.9 milliliters

township unit of territory used in surveying, approximately six miles square (93.2 sq. km)

troy ounce unit of weight for precious metals and gemstones, equal to 31.103 g, with 12 troy ounces equal to 1 pound

Foreign and Historical Measures

amphora vase holding 10.3 gallons (38.99 l) (ancient Greece)

ardeb unit of dry measure equal to 5.62 U.S. bushels (Egypt)

arroba unit of avoirdupois weight varying between 25.37 pounds (9.5 kg) and 32.38 pounds (12 kg) in Spain, Portugal, and Latin America; unit of liquid measure equal to 4.26 gallons (16 l liters) (Spain)

arshin unit of linear measure equal to 28 inches (71 cm) (Russia)

aune historical unit of measure for fabric equal to 47 inches (119 cm) (France)

barleycorn historical unit of length, equal to 1/3 inch (8.5 mm)

bath unit of liquid measure varying between 10 and 11 gallons (38 and 42 l) (Hebrew); 6.8 gallons (25.7 l) (ancient Rome)

bovate historical unit of land area varying between 7.5 and 20 acres, equal to one-eighth carucate (Britain)

braccio historical unit of length, usu. equal to 26 or 27 inches (66 or 68 cm) (Italy)

braza unit of length representing reach of outstretched arms, equal to 5.48 feet (1.67 m) (Spain, Latin America)

cab ancient liquid measure equal to 2 quarts (Hebrew)

carucate unit of land area varying between 60 and 160 acres (Britain)

catty measure of weight equal to about 1 1/2 pounds (680 g) (China, Southeast Asia)

chopin historical unit of liquid measure equal to one quart (Scotland)

congius unit of liquid measure equal to 0.8 gallons (3.2 liters) (ancient Rome)

crore total of ten million units, esp. rupees; 100 lacs (India)

cubit linear measure based on length of forearm, usu. equal to 17 or 18 inches (43 to 46 cm) (ancient Greece, ancient Rome)

denarius measure of weight equal to 4.6 grams (0.162 oz) (ancient Rome)

dessiatine unit of land measure equal to 2.7 acres (1.1 ha) (Russia)

drachma measure of weight equal to 4.36 grams (0.153 oz) (ancient Greece)

ell unit of linear measure for cloth equal to one thirty-second bolt or approximately 1 1/4 yards (114 cm) (Britain)

ephah unit of dry volume equal to 40 liters or approximately one bushel (Hebrew)

fanega unit of dry measure equal to 1.58 bushels (55.7 l) (Spain, Latin America)

fanegada unit of land measure equal to from 1.25 to 1.75 acres (0.5 to 0.7 ha) (Spain, Latin America)

feddan unit of area equal to 1.038 acres (0.42 ha) (Egypt)

firkin unit of liquid volume equal to 9 imperial gallons (41 l); one-half kilderkin (Britain)

haikwan tael customs unit equal to 1.20666 troy ounces of fine silver (China)

hekat unit of dry volume equal to 4.77 liters (4.33 qt) (Hebrew)

hide historical unit of land measure varying from 60 to 120 acres (24 to 49 ha) (Britain)

homer unit of volume equal to 10 baths liquid measure or 10 ephahs dry measure; kor (Hebrew)

imperial gallon 1.20095 U.S. gallons (Britain)

imperial quart 1.20095 U.S. quarts (Britain)

kantar measure of weight corresponding to hundredweight (Middle East)

kilderkin unit of liquid volume equal to 18 imperial gallons (82 liters), or 2 firkins (Britain)

koku unit of dry measure equal to 5.12 bushels (1.8 hl) (Japan)

kor homer

kos linear unit of land measure varying from 1 to 3 miles (1.6 to 4.8 km) (India)

lac total of 100,000 units, esp. rupees (India)

liang measure of weight equal to 1 1/3 ounce (37 g); tael (China)

livre measure of weight equal to 0.5 kilogram, equivalent to 1.1 pounds (France)

long hundredweight hundredweight equal to 112 pounds (50.8 kg) (Britain)

mark former measure of weight for precious metals equal to 8 ounces (249 g) (Europe)

maund measure of weight varying from 25 to 82.286 pounds (11 to 37.4 kg) (India)

mina ancient measure of weight and value equal to one-sixtieth part of a talent

mite measure of weight equal to 1/20 grain (3.24 mg) (Britain)

momme measure of weight equal to 3.75 grams (0.13 oz) (Japan)

morgen old Dutch unit of land measure equal to 2 acres (0.8 ha) (South Africa)

mutchkin unit of liquid measure equal to slightly less than one pint (Scotland)

obolus measure of weight equal to 1/10 gram (Greece)

oka measure of weight equal to 2 3/4 pounds (1.25 kg) (Turkey)

perch measure of volume for stone equal to 24 cubic feet (0.7 cu. m) (Britain)

pfund measure of weight equal to 0.5 kilogram or 1.1 pounds (Germany)

picul measure of weight equal to 100 catties, or about 133 to 143 pounds (60 to 64 kg) (China, Southeast Asia)

pocket measure of weight, esp. for hops, equal to 168 pounds (76.4 kg) (Britain)

pood measure of weight equal to about 36 pounds (16 kg) (Russia)

pottle former liquid measure equal to two quarts

quart unit of liquid measure comparable to U.S. quart, equal to 69.355 cubic inches (1.136 l) (Britain)

quartern one-fourth part of certain weights and measures (Britain)

reed ancient unit of linear measure equal to 6 cubits

Roman mile unit of linear measure equal to 1620 yards (1480 m) (ancient Rome)

rotl measure of weight and dry measure varying widely, but approximately one pound (Islamic countries)

rundlet former measure of volume equal to 15 imperial gallons (68 liters) (Britain)

ser measure of weight usu. equal to one fortieth of a maund, varying in value but officially 33 ounces (950 gm) (India)

shekel measure of weight equal to 1/2 ounce (Hebrew)

stack unit of cubic measure, esp. for coal and wood, equal to 108 cubic feet (3 cu. m) (Britain)

stadion unit of linear measure equal to 622 feet (189.6 m) (ancient Greece)

stadium unit of linear measure equal to about 607 feet (185 m) (ancient Rome)

stone measure of weight equal to 14 pounds (6.4 kg) (Britain)

tael liang

talent ancient measure of weight equal to 3000 shekels or 6000 drachmas

tierce former unit of liquid volume equal to one-third pipe or 42 gallons (159 l), esp. for wine

tod measure of weight, esp. for wool, equal to 28 pounds (12.7 kg) (Britain)

toise former unit of linear measure equal to 6.395 feet (1.949 m) (France)

tola measure of weight equal to 180 grains (11.7 g) (India)

tower pound measure of weight equal variously to 12 ounces (350 grams), 15 ounces (437 grams), or 16 ounces (467 grams) (Britain)

tun unit of liquid volume equal to 252 gallons (953.9 l), esp. used for wine cask (Britain)

vara unit of linear measure varying from 32 to 43 inches (81 to 109 cm) (Spain, Portugal, Latin America)

verst unit of linear measure equal to 3500 feet (1.067 km) (Russia)

virgate former measure of land area equal to about 30 acres (12 ha) (Britain)

Combining Forms

atto- one-quintillionth part of given base unit
centi- one-hundredth part of given base unit
deci- one-tenth part of given base unit
deka- ten of given base unit
exa- one quintillion of given base unit
femto- one-quadrillionth part of given base unit
giga- one billion of given base unit
hecto- one hundred of given base unit
kilo- one thousand of given base unit
mega- one million of given base unit
micro- one-millionth part of given base unit
milli- one-thousandth part of given base unit
myria- ten thousand of given base unit
nano- one-billionth part of given base unit
peta- one quadrillion of given base unit
pico- one-trillionth part of given base unit
tera- one trillion of given base unit

CHAPTER FIVE
TECHNOLOGY

Machinery and Mechanical Devices

absorbing dynamometer device that absorbs and dissipates the power it measures

aeolipile early steam engine consisting of round vessel rotated by exhaust jets; simple turbine

agitator apparatus in machine that shakes and stirs objects

air pump machine that removes, compresses, or forces air into something

alternator alternating current generator or dynamo

apparatus complex device or machine that has a specific use

appliance device for specific purpose; machine for household task, usu. electric

arc lamp unit that produces light by maintaining arc between two electrodes, esp. carbon rods

assembly group of machine parts put together to form independent unit

automatic machine machine that regulates its own operation

automaton mechanical contrivance that appears to act by its own motive power; robot

auxiliary device unit that assists or supplements primary device, but is subordinate to it

backhoe hydraulic excavating tractor with hinged boom operating jawed bucket

backup device unit that takes over in event primary device fails and performs same task

balance instrument that opposes objects of known weight and object being weighed on lever supported exactly in middle, in order to measure weight

balance crane two-armed apparatus in which one arm counters the load on the other

baler device that compresses and wraps loose material into standardized bundles

ball bearing low-friction bearing in which moving parts revolve or slide on freely rolling metal balls

ball cock valve connected to hollow floating ball which rises and falls in tank to open and shut valve, controlling water supply to tank

battery device that generates electricity by chemical reaction

bearing machine part in or on which another part revolves or slides

bellows device that produces stream of air through narrow opening when sides are pressed together

belt endless, flexible band passing about two or more pulleys, used to transmit motion between pulleys or to convey materials

bevel gear gear having teeth cut into conical surface, usu. meshing with similar gear set at right angle

blinker warning light that flashes steadily on and off

block and tackle combination of fixed and movable pulley blocks with rope or cable, used to hoist large weights

block gauge hardened steel with ground faces, used to check accuracy of other gauges

blower device for supplying air at moderate pressure

blowtorch small torch that produces hot flame from liquid fuel with pressurized air to melt metals

boiler closed tank in which water is heated and converted to steam in order to power engine or supply heat

brake device that connects moving part to frame, used to hold parts in position, control direction of motion, or absorb energy; any device that slows or halts motion, esp. by friction

buffer padding device or cushion used to lessen or absorb shock

burner part that produces flame or direct heat

business machine machine for doing office work, such as computer, photocopier, or calculator

butterfly valve disk-shaped valve on axis at its diameter, used esp. as damper in pipe or choke in carburetor

bypass engine turbine or jet engine in which compressed air is diverted to join exhaust gases to increase thrust

cableway cables connecting two towers, used to move skip for transporting materials

cam rotating wheel or projection on wheel that gives or receives uneven rotation or reciprocating motion to or from another wheel

camber slight arching, upward curvature or convexity of member, for specific purpose

capstan rotating drum with cable used to hoist heavy weights

carburetor device in which air and gasoline spray combine to form explosive mixture in internal combustion engine

carousel flat machine that revolves

caster swivel wheel that supports movable weight, esp. heavy furniture

centrifuge machine that rotates to generate centrifugal force, used to separate particles of varying density or shed moisture

clamp device with two parts that can be brought together to grip, fasten, or brace something

cogwheel wheel with toothed rim that meshes with another wheel to transmit or receive motion

combine machine used to harvest crops

compactor device that crushes and compresses loose material into compact bundles

compressed air machine device operated by expansion of air under pressure in enclosed container

compressor pump that places air or gas under pressure

computer electronic device that stores information and performs complex calculations very rapidly

contraption mechanical device

conveyor belt endless mechanical belt used to transport objects along its path

coupling linkage between machine shafts

crampon hooked device used to lift heavy weights

crane long-armed machine used to lift or lower objects at great height

crank arm bent at right angle and connected to shaft of machine, used to transmit or transfer circular motion to and from shaft

crankshaft shaft with cranks that transmits motion

cyclometer instrument that records revolutions of wheel to measure distance or speed

cylinder chamber in which piston moves in reciprocating engine

damper device that reduces shock, vibration, or air flow

deadbolt lock bolt that closes and opens by turning of knob or key

derrick hoisting beam with tackle rigged over it

device mechanical contrivance used for specific purpose

diaphragm dividing wall or partition between parts, usu. opening and closing to regulate entry or passage

die punch sheet metal cutter used to make exact duplicates of die shape in heavy machinery; permanent mold

diesel engine internal combustion engine that uses extremely high temperatures to burn fuel without spark

differential gear series of gears that permit two or more shafts to rotate at different speeds

differential motion movement in which speed of driven object equals difference in speeds of its connected parts

dog mechanical gripping or holding device

dredge apparatus used to scoop up mud and rocks from bottom of body of water

drill pointed instrument that makes holes in hard substances

drive belt endless loop that transmits power in engine

driver mechanism that imparts motion to another machine or part

dwell period in cycle of operation in which given machine part remains motionless

dynamo device that generates electric current by using coiled wire in magnetic field

electric motor motor that utilizes electric power to run machinery

electromechanical (*adj*) designating a device activated electrically, as by a solenoid, and also working mechanically

elevator platform or cage suspended on motor-operated cables to hoist or lower objects

engine machine or device that uses fuel or energy to develop mechanical power, often to transmit motion to another machine

epicyclic train series of gears or pulleys in which one or more axes revolve around central axis of sun gear

extractor rotating device that draws off water by centrifugal force

floodgate gate designed to control and regulate flow of water

fluid coupling mechanism in which fluid, usu. oil, transmits torque from one shaft to another

flywheel heavy, notched wheel used to regulate machine's speed and uniformity of motion

four-stroke engine internal combustion engine with power stroke occurring once every four piston strokes

fulcrum support point on which lever turns

funicular device, esp. carriage, worked by overhead cable from which it hangs

gantry frame on wheels that spans a distance, esp. used to carry cranes

gauge device used to measure dimensions or test degrees

gear device that transmits motion and power by contact between toothed wheels

generator machine that creates electrical power

Geneva wheel indexing device that provides period of motionlessness during operating cycle of machine

gimmick ingenious mechanical device

gin machine used to hoist heavy objects

gizmo *Informal.* device or gadget

go-devil flexible, jointed implement used to free pipes of obstruction

governor device for maintaining uniform speed of engine, as by regulating fuel supply

gyroscope wheel mounted in set of rings so that axis of rotation is free to turn in any direction

harrow toothed device used to pulverize materials

helical gear gear with teeth set at oblique angle to rotation of wheel

hoist device that lifts objects

hopper storage tank with discharge chute

hydraulic engine engine powered by liquid, esp. by pressure created when liquid is forced through an aperture

hydrostat instrument used to detect presence or monitor level of water

hypoid gear bevel gear designed to mesh with similar gear, with axes at right angle

idle gear gear placed between driving and driven gear to transmit motion between them

idle wheel wheel gear for transmitting motion between driving part and driven part

impeller rotating part of centrifugal pump

implement tool or other device required to perform given task

inclined plane simple machine: flat surface at angle to level ground

induction motor electric motor in which rotation is induced by interaction of magnetic fields

internal combustion engine fuel-burning reciprocating or rotary engine in which fuel/air mixture is converted into power in enclosed cylinder

jack support, brace; ratchet device used to lift heavy weight

jet engine engine that generates reaction force when compressed outside air and hot exhaust gases are forced through nozzle

laser beam cutting or welding tool that uses highly concentrated beam of light made up of particles in excited energy state

lathe machine that supports rotating object worked on by stationary cutting, boring, or drilling tool

lever simple machine: rigid bar that transmits or modifies lifting force applied at one point and is supported by fulcrum at a fixed point

linkage arrangement and coupling of simple machine elements into compound machines

loom frame for weaving horizontal and vertical elements

machine any device or instrument composed of interrelated functioning parts that aids in performing work by transmitting or modifying force or motion

machinery working parts of a machine; assemblage of mechanical devices or machines

machine tool heavy-duty power tool used to shape metal machine parts or wood, as on a lathe

mainspring principal spring in mechanism

mechanical advantage ratio of resistance or load to applied force of machine

mechanical device anything produced or operated by machinery or a mechanism, esp. used to produce, transmit, receive, or alter motion

mechanism any device for performing work or transmitting motion; piece of machinery; assembly of moving parts performing one function within larger machine

mill device or machine used to cut, grind, mix, shape, or process

mole powerful boring machine used in construction of tunnels through earth and rock

motor small engine; electric-driven machine that powers a mechanical device

muffler device that reduces noise

needle valve valve in which opening is controlled by fine point that fits into conical seat

nuclear reactor device that releases energy from nuclear reaction in controlled form, used for large-scale energy production

pallet platform used to move and store goods

parbuckle doubled rope with middle secured at specific height and ends passed around cylindrical object that is to be raised or lowered

pawl device with hinged tongue whose tip engages notches of cogwheel or ratchet to allow one-directional rotation

pendulum weight suspended from fixed point so as to swing freely back and forth due to gravity and momentum

permanent mold die punch

pile driver machine with heavy drop hammer used to sink large timbers into ground

pilot device that guides action of machine or part

pilot valve valve that controls action of another valve

plasma arc torch machine that uses very hot gas to cut metal

plow device used to cut up, turn, and lift soil

plug electrical connection that fits into jack; device that closes off flow of liquid or gas

pneumatic engine engine powered by compressed air

poppet rising and falling valve consisting of disk on stem

power tool usu. electric device used to perform specific mechanical task

power train sequence of gears and shafting that transmits power from engine to driven mechanism

press device that uses pressure to form or manufacture

pulley simple machine: small wheel with rope or chain in grooved rim around its circumference, used to increase applied force, lift, or change direction of object at end of rope or chain

pump device that draws or moves liquids

rack and pinion large-toothed bar, or rack, that meshes with small gear, or pinion, to receive or transmit motion

ratchet device that converts continuous motion into intermittent motion, esp. toothed wheel on handle that imparts one-directional motion to tool

reciprocating engine engine in which back-and-forth movement of pistons causes rotary motion of crankshaft, either two-stroke or four-stroke

reduction gear combination of gears that reduces input speed to lower output speed

retort container with long tube used to distill substances

robot automaton

rolamite flexible, S-shaped metal loop in which two rollers are suspended with loop fastened to two parallel guide rails

roller rotating cylinder used to press or shape some object

rotary engine engine in which rotary motion is produced directly by triangular rotor, not as reciprocating motion from pistons

rotor any mechanism that rotates, esp. in motor or dynamo

sander machine or device that smoothes and polishes with sandpaper or abrasive material

scale balance or other device used to determine weight

scope instrument used to observe

scraper device that smoothes or cleans surfaces

screw simple machine: inclined plane turned around a cylinder

screw conveyor device for moving loose material, consisting of shaft with broad, helically wound blade rotating in tube or trough; worm

self-regulating machine automated machine in which feedback input determines changes in future output

semaphore apparatus that conveys information by means of visual signals

servomechanism automatic control system that compares input and output to regulate differential

shunt electrical switch or diverter

simple machine basic mechanical device, such as inclined plane, lever, pulley, screw, wedge, or wheel and axle

siphon tube bent into legs of unequal length with shorter leg placed in upper of two containers to draw liquid through and down into lower container by atmospheric pressure

skidway usu. inclined platform or path for sliding heavy objects, esp. logs or planks

skip basket or bucket, usu. suspended from crane or cables, used to transport materials

solar cell photovoltaic cell used to convert radiant energy of sunlight into electric power

sonar device that transmits sound waves through water and registers reflected vibrations

spigot stopper plug, often with valve to regulate flow

spring elastic contrivance, esp. coiled length of wire, that regains its shape after being compressed, bent, or stretched, used to impart force

spring-loaded (adj) designating machine part held in specific position by spring

sprinkler device that disperses drops of liquid over wide area

spur gear gear having teeth cut on rim parallel to its axis of rotation

stator part of machine that remains fixed with respect to its rotating parts

steam engine engine that derives its power from steam under pressure in a cylinder

steam shovel excavating machine with bucket on arm, operated by boiler-driven engine

stopcock plug, spigot, or valve that controls fluid flow

subassembly structural or functional group of machine parts that forms part of larger assembly

sun gear central gear around whose axis other gears in epicyclic train revolve

switch device used to open, close, or divert, esp. electric current

synchronous motor electric motor whose speed is proportional to frequency of current driving it

tachometer instrument that measures rate of rotation

theodolite surveying instrument used to measure vertical and horizontal angles

thermometer device that registers temperature

thermosiphon series of siphon tubes that circulate water in heating unit by convection

thermostat instrument that regulates temperature

tool instrument, esp. handheld, that works, shapes, cuts, or joins

transformer device that converts one form of electricity into another

treadle lever or pedal that turns wheel

triple-expansion (adj) designating power source using same fluid to do work at three successive stages of expansion

truckle small wheel or pulley

turbine engine with curved blades or vanes on spindle that rotates to convert energy from fluid entering enclosed casing into rotary motion

two-stroke engine internal combustion engine having compression and power stages only, with power stroke occurring once every two piston strokes

universal joint flexible connection used to transmit rotary motion from one shaft to another shaft not in line with it

vacuum enclosed space out of which nearly all air or gas has been pumped

vacuum pump pump used to draw air or gas out of enclosure to form vacuum

valve device that regulates flow through pipe or tube, esp. one that permits flow in one direction only

vehicle means of conveyance or transport, sometimes motorized, that moves on wheels, runners, or tracks

ventilator device that regulates air flow, used to maintain fresh air

venturi tube with concave sides that controls flow of liquid by producing suction

vernier small device with secondary, graduated scale, used to make fine adjustments on precision instruments

waterwheel wheel on shaft moved by weight of water hitting floats or paddles, used to transmit motion

weapon instrument or device for use in attack or defense in combat

wedge simple machine: two inclined planes joined to form device with pointed end and thicker base

welding torch device used to fuse metal parts by heat

wheel solid disk or circular frame connected by spokes to central axis, used to transmit power or motion in machinery

wheel and axle simple machine: grooved wheel or pulley fixed to shaft or drum, used to increase mechanical advantage or speed

whorl flywheel on spindle, used to regulate its speed

widget small mechanical device or gadget, esp. one whose name cannot be recalled

winch device with crank on handle, used to transmit motion, esp. for hoisting

windlass rotating drum with cable wound around it, used for hoisting

windmill mill operated by large oblique vanes that radiate from shaft and rotate by force of wind

wind tunnel tunnellike chamber through which air is forced to test airplanes and motors

working part machine, mechanical device, or element thereof that performs some function for a specific purpose, esp. related to motion

worm screw conveyor

worm gear mechanism consisting of rotating shaft cut with helical threads that engages with and drives toothed gear whose axis is at right angle to shaft

Fabrication and Manufacturing Processes

automate (vb) use only machine power in construction, assembly, production, or operation

balance (vb) even out weight distribution

bale (vb) compress and bind into standard-size bundle

bevel (vb) cut intersection of two faces to form third face at oblique angles to both

blanch (vb) bleach, clean in acid; coat with tin

blast (vb) blow up or move with explosives; polish or cut with stream of small particles projected by steam or air

blend (vb) mix or combine

bond (vb) connect or fasten together two or more parts

bore (vb) drill out a hole or cavity to increase its size

braze (vb) solder with soft flux

broach (vb) remove metal from surface with toothed cutting edge

buff (vb) polish, shine, smooth

build (vb) construct from different elements to form unified whole

burn (vb) transform with fire or intense heat

burnish (vb) polish, rub until shiny

cannibalize (vb) build or repair machine with parts salvaged from similar machines

cant (vb) tilt, pitch at an angle

cantilever (vb) construct as or support with projecting beam

cast (vb) form in a mold

caulk (vb) fill seam or joint with waterproof material

check (vb) hold back, restrain

chill (vb) harden by sudden cooling

chop (vb) cut into small pieces

churn (vb) agitate vigorously

clarify (vb) separate suspended particles from liquid

cold-work (vb) work metal at temperature below level at which recrystallization occurs

collimate (vb) make parallel or level; adjust line of sight

compact (vb) compress, reduce under pressure

compress (vb) flatten, change shape by pressure

constrict (vb) make smaller, esp. at one place; squeeze or limit

construct (vb) build from different elements into unified whole

countersink (vb) set below surface into fitted hole

couple (vb) join together, link, connect

crate (*vb*) box into large containers for shipping

crush (*vb*) pulverize, reduce to small bits

crystallize (*vb*) form crystals by evaporation

cut (*vb*) pierce with sharp object

cybernate (*vb*) use computers to control and carry out manufacturing or other operations

dam (*vb*) form barrier to flow of liquid

distill (*vb*) purify by vaporization into separate components

dredge (*vb*) enlarge or clear bottom of body of water

drill (*vb*) form hole in object with pointed instrument

drop-forge (*vb*) hammer hot metal into shapes between two dies

elevate (*vb*) raise to higher position

extrude (*vb*) force fluid material through press to shape objects

fabricate (*vb*) construct, esp. from standardized parts

finish (*vb*) apply final touches and embellishments

fire (*vb*) bake in oven to harden or glaze object, esp. pottery

fit (*vb*) join elements that conform in shape; insert; adjust elements to conform in shape

forge (*vb*) shape molten or heated metal

form (*vb*) give shape to

found (*vb*) lay the base for, begin to build

frame (*vb*) construct framework, support, or skeletal structure

glaze (*vb*) coat with smooth, impermeable finish

grade (*vb*) level, make smooth; sort by size or quality

grind (*vb*) cut and smooth surface with abrasive material; pulverize

hoist (*vb*) lift heavy weight mechanically

hone (*vb*) grind to smoothly finished surface

install (*vb*) fit fixture into housing; place machinery in position to function

join (*vb*) fit; bond

knead (*vb*) work into pliable mass by folding over, squeezing, and pressing

knurl (*vb*) form beaded or ridged metal surface

lap (*vb*) machine to an extremely fine, smooth finish

lay (*vb*) establish and prepare groundwork for

machine (*vb*) make or shape by action of machines

manufacture (*vb*) produce items in quantity with standardized, technologically advanced equipment

mechanize (*vb*) make mechanical; operate or perform by machinery

mill (*vb*) grind, cut, or shape; process

mold (*vb*) form in frame, cavity, or matrix

plane (*vb*) cut away large, flat surface area

plaster (*vb*) coat with layer of plaster

press (*vb*) exert force upon, esp. form by stamping on die or template

produce (*vb*) make, manufacture

pump (*vb*) move up and down, esp. move liquids by suction or pressure

quarry (*vb*) excavate stone by cutting or blasting at surface

ream (*vb*) widen a hole or opening

refine (*vb*) remove impurities

regulate (*vb*) systematically control operations

retrofit (*vb*) equip with parts not available at time of original construction

salvage (*vb*) repair and save from destruction

sand (*vb*) rub smooth with abrasive

scrape (*vb*) rub surface with rough tool or abrasive

shape (*vb*) cut and mold material into definite structure or form according to specific plan

shear (*vb*) stamp or cut into forms

solder (*vb*) join or cement with hot, liquefied metal

splice (*vb*) join by interweaving

stamp (*vb*) press and cut with a die

strip (*vb*) remove paint or finish, esp. from wood

thread (*vb*) apply ridges to smooth surface, usu. metal

toenail (*vb*) join with nail driven at oblique angle

tool (*vb*) work or shape with instruments or tools

turn (*vb*) form on rotating device, tool, or machine

water-cool (*vb*) cool engine or other machine part by water circulating around it in pipes

weld (*vb*) fuse metal components by application of heat

Types of Construction

bricklaying art of building structures with fired clay blocks cemented together into walls

bridge construction process of building structures that span waterways or other geographical features

cabinetmaking construction of finished woodwork and furniture

component building construction from standardized, prefabricated parts

construction systematic devising, forming, and building of something with parts that fit together

dam building construction of barrier to water flow

earthmoving excavation of ground, esp. for highway or building

excavation formation of large hole or cavity in earth

fabrication making or constructing of something with parts that must be assembled

finishing applying outer layer and decorations to structure

foundation construction of base or support for structure

frame construction building a structural framework with wood, rather than masonry, steel, or concrete

framing process of using a wood frame for construction

general building construction of residential and commercial buildings without specialized features

grading moving earth to form smooth, even inclination, esp. for roadway

heavy construction building of large-scale structures with complex and powerful tools and machinery

highway construction building of paved roadways

home building construction of residential buildings

HVAC **h**eating, **v**entilation, and **a**ir **c**onditioning installation

insulating installation of insulating materials

landscaping development of land and foliage into decorative, useful arrangements

masonry building with stone, brick, or cemented elements: now also refers to plaster and concrete

modular construction design and building with units of standardized length and size

painting application of paint to finished surfaces

platform framing building process in which each story is framed and constructed independently

plumbing installation of water supply, drainage, and sewage system in buildings

post-and-beam construction wall construction of upright posts and crossbeams with planks laid crossways on beams

prefab building construction from standardized, prefabricated components

remodelling modification of existing structure to new needs or designs

roofing construction of protective top layer of building

steel-frame construction building a structure on a reinforced steel rod framework

tilt-up construction building method in which concrete walls are cast on site in horizontal frames, or wooden walls are preassembled, then lifted into final, vertical position

timber framing frame construction with heavy timbers as posts and beams, rarely done in 20th c.

tooling work done with one or more tools; arrangement of tools for particular manufacturing process

tunnel building excavation and surfacing of underground passageways

wattle and daub construction with upright rods or stakes interwoven with twigs or branches and plastered with clay and straw mixture

wiring installation of electrical facilities

wood-frame construction frame construction

Builders and Construction Workers

architect one who designs and supervises the construction of buildings

asbestos worker person who covers surfaces, esp. pipes, with insulation materials

boilermaker worker who makes, assembles, or fixes boilers

bricklayer worker who builds with bricks

builder worker who constructs buildings, esp. supervisor of large construction projects

building trades trades such as carpentry, masonry, and plastering that are primarily concerned with construction and finishing of buildings

cabinetmaker worker who builds fine wooden furniture

carpenter worker who builds and repairs wooden things, esp. buildings

cement mason worker who applies finish to concrete floors, slabs, and other low concrete structures; worker who makes low forms in concrete

construction worker general laborer on construction of buildings or large structures

contractor one who agrees to purchase materials for and construct buildings at arranged price and time period

designer one who conceives and draws plans for construction or decoration

drywaller worker who cuts and installs plasterboard

electrician worker who installs and repairs electric wiring in buildings

elevator constructor worker who installs elevators, dumbwaiters, and escalators

engineer one who applies scientific and mathematical principles to design and build machines or structures

equipment operator worker who runs and manages operation of mechanical devices used in construction

floor covering installer worker who puts carpeting, linoleum, and rubber or vinyl tile on floors

gardener one who cultivates and maintains gardens

glazier one who cuts and fits glass panes in windows

house painter worker who applies paint to exterior or interior of buildings

insulation worker worker who installs insulation in buildings

interior decorator one who plans and decorates the inside of buildings, esp. furniture arrangement, fittings, and color schemes

ironworker one who makes iron decorations, esp. gratings, usu. by bending and joining iron rods

laborer general worker

lathe operator worker who cuts and shapes objects, usu. of wood or metal, on a lathe

machine operator worker who runs usu. heavy equipment used in construction

marble setter worker who cuts and sets marble

mason worker who builds with stones or bricks bonded by cement or mortar

mechanical engineer one who applies mathematical and scientific principles, esp. kinetics, to design and build machines, usu. with parts that move

metalworker one who makes objects of metal

operating engineer one who runs and maintains heavy construction machinery, such as bulldozers or cranes

operator worker who runs heavy machinery, such as bulldozers or cranes

painter worker who paints walls and ceilings

paperhanger worker who cuts and affixes decorative wallpaper

pipe fitter worker who installs or repairs pipes

plasterer worker who applies stucco and other plaster finishes to walls and ceilings

plumber worker who installs and repairs pipes and fixtures for sewage and water systems

rigger one who supervises the transport and installation of large machinery, such as conveyors, pumps, and heaters

roofer worker who covers roofs with shingles, slate, tile, or other materials

sheet metal worker person who makes and installs sheet metal products, such as ducts and gutters

stonemason mason who builds with natural stone

subcontractor worker who contracts to general contractor for specialized work, such as an electrician or plumber

terrazzo worker person who sets terrazzo or small marble tiles

tilesetter worker who lays tiles on floor or walls

welder worker who joins pieces of metal by application of heat and sometimes pressure until separate pieces fuse together

woodworker person who builds custom wooden structures, such as cabinets, fixtures, trim, and molding

---

STRUCTURAL COMPONENTS
Building and Machine Parts
Carpentry

See also: *Chap. 5: Machinery and Fabrication; Building and Construction Materials; Tools and Hardware; Containers; Chap. 7: Exterior Structure; Interior Structure; Chap. 16: Architecture*

Building and Machine Parts

abutment plane or point designed to give support or withstand thrust, esp. on projecting part of structure

adapter connector that enables different parts or devices to fit or function together

anchor bolt threaded rod embedded in foundation for support and stabilization of wood sill

angle iron metal brace used to reinforce corners or angles

angle rafter rafter in sloping roof

aperture usu. narrow opening, slit, or crack

apron plate or covering for mechanical device that protects its operator; interior trim beneath window stool

arbor short spindle that supports rotating machine part

arm small extension attached horizontally at angle to large base

axle shaft or spindle that supports rotating wheel

backstay supporting or checking piece in mechanism, esp. anchored tension member that supports compression member

baffle obstructing member, esp. used to hold back or turn aside flow of gas or liquid

bail supporting half hoop; hinged bar that holds paper to platen in typewriter

ball-and-socket joint joint between rods or links in which ball-like termination fits into concave, spherical socket

baluster small vertical member connecting stair tread and handrail

band ring or encircling strip, used esp. to bind something

bar straight supporting rod

barb sharp, hooked projection

barb and shaft point and length of weapon, missile, or tool

base bottommost component on which structure rests

baseboard finished interior trim where wall meets floor

baseplate steel plate at bottom of steel column

baseshoe molding placed against baseboard at floor

batten narrow wood strip that covers seam between boards

batter boards horizontal crosspieces nailed to posts in ground at corners of excavation to locate corners and establish level

beam horizontal structural member of wood or steel, used to support load

beam pocket notch that holds supporting beam

bearing sliding or turning machine part; point of support

bearing pile column sunk into ground or foundation to support vertical load

bearing wall wall that supports a floor or roof and walls above it

becket looped rope with large hook and eye, used to secure loose ropes and spars

bed horizontal layer of masonry mortar that holds bricks

berm narrow dirt ledge that supports beams

bilge point of largest circumference of cask or barrel

bit cutting or drilling part of tool

block enclosure for pulley; mold; building unit

boom projecting beam, spar, or supporting arm

boss raised knob on flat surface

box beam hollow structural member that supports loads

brace connecting or reinforcing element, usu. of wood

bracket projecting support fixture

brake machine element used to stop motion

breather vent, as in machine covering or storage

tank, used to equalize pressure or permit entry or escape of vapor

bridging rows of small diagonal braces nailed between ceiling joists to support floor weight

bristle stiff hair, filament

building block component or part of structure

building material substance from which something is made or constructed

built-ins furniture and other nonstructural elements permanently incorporated in building

built-up beam support made of several smaller beams joined together

bulkhead partition; retaining wall

bulwark fortified wall or rampart

bumper shock-absorbing element

bung stopper in opening or spout of cask

butt thick end of something

button small, pressable control knob

buttress projecting support structure

bypass auxiliary pipe or channel connected to main passage, used to conduct gas or liquid around pipe or fixture

cable heavy-duty rope of wire strands, usu. wound together

cage openwork structure or frame, esp. of bars or wires

caisson underwater housing for structure or foundation

cantilever extension of structural member beyond point of support

cap tightfitting cover or top

capstone topmost stone in structure

carriage movable machine part designed to carry or convey something

casing trim or molding on doors or windows

caster small, swiveling wheel used to support or move furniture and heavy objects

casting part cast in mold

ceiling joist horizontal support piece for ceiling

chain rope or wire of connected metal links

chamfer beveled edge or channel on piece of wood

channel passageway, esp. for gas or liquid; three-sided, U-shaped element, usu. metal

chase vertical groove in masonry wall for pipes, ducts, or conduits; frame that holds paper in printing press

chassis framework or support for working parts

chimney vertical flue that draws off gases and heat from furnace or fireplace

chock wedge of hard material that prevents movement or fills gap

chord outside horizontal member of truss

chute inclined or vertical downward passageway

clack valve valve having hinged flap that permits flow in one direction only

clasp fastener, esp. clip

cleat wood brace

clevis U-shaped device with pin across opening

clew metal loop fastened to corner of hung canvas

cog tooth or radial support on wheel or gear

coil wire turned in loops

coil spring wire spring coiled helically into conical or cylindrical shape

collar ring or flange, esp. on pipe, to connect parts or prevent sideward motion

collar beam horizontal member placed between pair of opposing roof rafters to stiffen roof

column vertical structural support

common rafter rafter that extends from ridgepole to top plate

component part or element of structure

conduit tube, pipe, or channel, esp. for fluids or electric wiring

connecting rod reciprocating rod that connects two or more machine parts

corner point at which two or more surfaces meet, often a right angle

corner board exterior finish board at corner that abuts siding

corner brace diagonal structural support

cornice exterior trim at juncture of roof and wall, consisting of fascia, soffit, and molding

cotter split pin with spreadable ends

counterflashing metal surfacing, esp. for chimneys at roof line

coupling machine part that connects two rotating shafts at their ends to transmit torque between them

cove molding concave-faced molding, esp. between wall and ceiling

cover something placed over a part or structure, esp. to conceal or protect it

cowling removable metal housing or cover for engine

cradle supportive framework on which something rests

creel basketlike cage or rack

crest projecting ridge, top, or summit

crib framework of strips or planks, open at top

cripple short wall stud above or below door or window

crossbar connective bar placed in horizontal position

crossbeam transverse beam in structure, such as joist

cross bridging bridging of crisscross wood pieces; herringbone bridging

crosshead sliding member of reciprocating engine for maintaining straight motion between piston rod and connecting rod

crosspiece any element lying across another or connecting two or more parts

cross section side or end section of object

crosstie beam or rod placed crosswise for support

crown top point, part resting at top

crutch usu. forked support element on which another part rests

culvert drain or waterway under road or embankment

curb enclosing framework or border; element that restrains or checks

curtain wall exterior wall that protects interior wall from weather but bears no structural load

dam barrier to water flow

deck horizontal structure extending from exterior wall

door frame casing around door from which it is hinged or hung

doorjamb door frame cut into wall

dovetail joint projecting, wedge-shaped tenon that fits into mortise

dowel cylindrical length of wood used to fasten or hang

downspout vertical pipe that carries water from roof to ground

drain pipe or filter for removal of fluid

drip cap molding at exterior top side of doors and windows that sheds rain

duct pipe or channel for passage of gas or liquid

ductwork system of ducts used for heating, ventilation, or cooling

edge border; part farthest from middle

elbow L-shaped fastener or connective piece, esp. for pipes

expansion joint joint in masonry or concrete that accommodates expansion and contraction of materials without damaging structure

exterior structure elements and components of a structure that are visible from outside it

exterior wall flat, vertical surface that faces away from studs

facade exterior face on front of building

facet small cut face, as on precious stone

facing lining, finishing surface

fairing element that reduces wind drag

fascia flat, vertical member of cornice attached to outer edge of eave at end of rafter

fastener hardware device that holds separate parts together: bolt, nail, plug, screw, pin, toggle, clasp, or clamp

felloe rim or rim segment of spoked wheel that holds outer ends of spokes

fender guard, impact absorber

ferrule metal ring or cap at end of handle or tool

filler substance used to fill holes or smooth surface irregularities

filter device that separates particles from air or liquid

firestop fire-retardant element inside walls and floors, esp. horizontal wood member between studs to stop updrafts inside wall

fire wall partition made of fireproof material, used to prevent spread of fire within building

fitting small part or device, usu. of standardized size and shape

fixture plumbing or electrical unit

flange projecting rim or collar of wheel, pipe, rail, or beam, used to hold it in place or guide action

flashing sheet metal strip or wall for waterproofing or insulation, usu. by sealing joint

flitch bundle of veneer sheets; component of beam or girder

floorboard any of the strips of wood composing a floor

floor joist horizontal support piece for floor

flue enclosed passageway used to direct current of gas; chimney, channel for smoke or air

fluke pointed blade on anchor, barb

flume channel or inclined chute that carries water

foliated joint joint between overlapping, rabbeted edges of two boards, forming continuous surface

footing concrete pad that supports and distributes foundation weight

forelock cotter pin, split pin, or linchpin

forms panels joined as molds for concrete

foundation supporting part of structure beneath first floor joists, usu. concrete or masonry

frame open, supporting structure

frieze horizontal piece that connects siding to soffit, usu. decorative

furnishings usu. movable articles for use or decoration in structure

furring wood strips fastened to nonwood walls or ceiling to form straight surface for application of finished wall material

gable end end wall bearing a gable

gain notch, mortise, or groove, esp. to receive hardware

gasket flat sheet of material used to form gas-tight joint between engine parts

gibbet jib or projecting arm of crane

girder horizontal structural member that supports wall; floor joist between piers or columns; beam

girder pocket notch in foundation for base of girder

grate metal grid or frame of parallel bars, used for support, ventilation, and filtration

grid grate; metal openwork surface

groove long, narrow, hollow cut into surface

gusset plywood or metal plate that joins wooden members or reinforces joints

gutter trough to siphon fluid, esp. rainwater from roof

guy reinforcing wire, chain

haft handle, esp. of knife or ax

handle rod, knob, part to be grasped by hand

handlebar rod or bar with handle at each end

hanger iron strap used to suspend pipes and joists

hank coil, loop, or ring, esp. of rope

hardware metal fittings and utensils for building construction

harness assemblage of interconnected straps that restrain or fasten

H-beam long iron or steel I-beam with wide flanges

head top of door or window frame

header horizontal support that spans an opening in frame of wall or floor

headpost post at top of part

herringbone bridging cross bridging

hilt handle, esp. of knife or sword

hinge swiveling metal joint that fastens swinging element to stable support: butt, spring, strap, T-hinge

hip rafter diagonal rafter extending from ridgepole to corner intersection of top plates of two walls

hoop circular binding strip

housing frame or covering for part; recess in piece of wood for insertion of another piece

hub center part, esp. of wheel where it is fastened to axle

I-beam long iron or steel beam with cross section in form of I, used in heavy construction

insulation layer of material resistant to heat or sound conduction

interior structure elements and components of a structure that are visible from inside or functioning within it

interior wall flat, vertical surface facing inward from studs

jack brace, support

jack rafter shorter-than-common rafter

jamb side frame of door or window in wall

jib projecting crane arm

joggle joint formed between notch cut in one surface and projection made in another, usu. in wood or stone

joint point of contact between elements, usu. held by glue, nail, or screw

joist horizontal support beam for floor or ceiling

journal portion of shaft or axle contained by bearing

keystone central, uppermost stone of arch

keystone joist joist made of reinforced concrete with sloping sides and tip wider than bottom

keyway groove or slot cut in shaft or hub to hold key

king post vertical member between apex and base of triangular roof framework

knob round handle

knuckle joint joint permitting movement between parts in one plane only

L angled support beam, brace, or bracket

Lally column steel pipe with concrete-filled post used to support girders

landing floor area at top or bottom of stairs

lap joint joint between two members in which end or edge of one is partly cut away to be overlapped by end or edge of the other, resulting in a flush surface

latch fastener, esp. for door

lath narrow wood strips for lattice, trellis, and plastering base for wall; metal or gypsum panels nailed to studs on which plaster is applied

lattice wood strip framework

leader downspout connected to gutter

leaf sliding or hinged side or division, esp. of door or window

leaf spring long, multiple spring used in suspension systems of vehicles

ledger wood strip nailed to underside of wood beam or stud for support

lever bar used to lift heavy object or pry open something

ligature thread, wire, or small hoop that serves for binding or tying up

linchpin fastener that prevents slippage; linkage device

lining inner coating or layer

lintel horizontal, weight-bearing crosspiece above door or window

load-bearing wall wall that carries vertical load from above

lookout extending horizontal framing member that supports roof overhang, fascia, and soffit

lug and slot projection and hole into which it fits

lumber milled hardwood or softwood boards, used to build construction and cabinetry

moldboard flat or curved blade that pushes material aside as machine advances

molding wood strip with curved or decoratively cut surface

mortise notch or hole in wood that holds fitted tenon to form joint

mullion narrow bar that divides small windowpane glass or screen; vertical framing member that separates adjacent doors or windows

muntin wood member that separates glass panes in door or window

newel large post at foot of stairs

nog wooden peg, pin, or block, esp. one inserted into brickwork or between principal timbers of wall

nonbearing wall wall that supports no weight other than its own

nosing rounded edge of stair tread extending beyond riser

notch concave or V-shaped cut or indentation in edge or across surface

nozzle tube or vent used to expel fluid with force

panel flat piece of wood fitted into larger surface area

part component, one element of which something is made

partition interior wall

peg short, usu. tapered rod used to hold parts together or fill opening

pier vertical masonry column, usu. concrete, that supports beam or load from above

pilaster rectangular support or pier projecting from wall

pile concrete, steel, or wood column that supports building foundation

piloti column of iron, steel, or reinforced concrete that supports structure above open ground level

pin peg, post, or rod used to fasten objects

pinion small cogwheel, with teeth, that fits into large gearwheel or rack

pintle usu. upright pivot pin on which another part turns

pipe metal or plastic tubing used in plumbing and heating works

plancier underside of eave or cornice; soffit

plank long, flat, wood member 2-4 inches (5.1-10.2 cm) thick and 6 inches (15.2 cm) or more wide

plate horizontal structural member, usu. wood

platen flat plate in printing press, or roller in typewriter, on which paper rides

platform horizontal floor area, esp. midway up stairs

plenum box on furnace from which ducts run to outlets

pole shaft, narrow column

post vertical structural member, esp. timber set on end to support beam

projection part that juts out from surface

purlin horizontal roof support between rafters

pylon slender, towering structure flanking entrance or supporting wires

queen post either of a pair of vertical posts extending from tie beam in roof framework, one on each side of center

quoin block at corner of building; arch keystone

raceway narrow channel for water; tube used to protect electric wires

rack frame; toothed bar into which pinion fits

rafter horizontal wooden support member for roof

rail horizontal cross member of panel door or window sash

railing several connected rails or posts

rake flat, inclined edge on gable roof

ramp sloping, sometimes curved, surface that joins different levels

rampart barrier, bulwark

rebar steel reinforcing rod for concrete

register heating duct unit that directs airflow

reinforcing rod round, steel bar used to strengthen concrete

removable wood form framework used to form concrete slabs, removed once concrete hardens

reservoir receptacle, usu. at bottom of structure, used to collect fluid

revetment facing of stone or concrete to sustain embankment

rib crosswise reinforcing element

ribbon wood member joined to studs to support floor joists in balloon framing

ridge beam ridgepole

ridgepole highest horizontal timber in peaked roof to which rafters are nailed; ridge beam

riffle bars or slats across bottom of sluice that catch nuggets, as of gold

rigging system of ropes or chains used to support, suspend, or position equipment

rim edge or border, esp. of something circular, often raised

ring circular element used to bind, reinforce, or seal objects

riser vertical part of stair

rod straight, rigid piece of wood or metal

roof top surface of structure

roofing materials that form roof surface

roof plate top plate

rough opening gap in wall, floor, or ceiling formed by structural framing members

rounce handle that moves printing press bed under platen

rowel revolving disk with sharp points at end of spur

rung supporting piece or crossbar, esp. on ladder

rynd iron bar across upper millstone that supports it on spindle

sally rafter projection notched to fit over and extend beyond plate or horizontal beam

sandwich panel wall or other structural panel consisting of core of one material between two sheets of a different material

sash movable frame that contains glass windowpanes

scab wood piece nailed to two butting pieces of wood as splice

scantling beam or timber of small cross section, such as 2x4

scarf joint joint in which two timbers are fitted together with end laps and held together by bolts or straps

sconce cover, protective shell

scrap used metal parts reclaimed for other uses

screen frame covered with mesh, usu. of wire

scupper opening in building wall, used for drainage from flat roof

shackle U-shaped fastener with pin

shaft rotating cylinder; column that supports rotating machine elements

shank straight or central element of fitting or tool; loop or eye on back of solid button

sheathing material used to cover roof rafters or exterior wall studs

shell outer covering or framework

shim thin piece of material used to smooth, level, or finish area between two irregular surfaces

shiplap siding boards with overlapping joints along edges, applied over sheathing

shoring wood or metal braces used for temporary support during building construction

shunt switch used to deflect motion

shutter device that controls passage of light

shuttle device that controls back-and-forth movement

siding surface covering for exterior building walls

sill horizontal member at base of window or door

sill plate horizontal structure bolted to foundation beneath flooring

skid plank or low platform on which load is supported

slab strip of concrete, poured as single piece, esp. reinforced concrete floor

slat flat, narrow strip

sleeper wood member attached to concrete floor as base for wood floor

sleeve tube that surrounds another part

sluice gated or valved water channel

soffit undersurface of cornice from fascia to wall; plancier

soil pipe drainage system component that receives waste discharged from toilet and sometimes from other plumbing waste pipes

soil stack vertical soil pipe

soleplate horizontal member in subfloor below line of wall studs

sound insulation section of insulating material that damps sound waves

spar lengthwise support structure

spider machine part consisting of several radiating spokes or arms, usu. not connected at outer ends

spile peg or plug made of wood, often used as spigot

spindle pin or shaft that holds rotating bit or wheel

spit pointed, narrow rod

splice joint made by weaving together rope ends

spline thin wood strip fitted into grooves

splint flexible strip used for weaving and bracing

spoke radial reinforcement for wheel

spool cylindrical container used to wind and store rope and chain

spout chute used to move loose substances or liquids; projecting lip through which liquid is poured

spring flexible wire coil that provides resilience and absorbs shocks

sprocket one of series of teeth or points on wheel rim arranged to fit links of chain or another set of sprockets

spur projecting element

stack vertical shelves, pipes, or flues

staff shaft, rung

stanchion upright support bar or beam

standard upright support or support structure

stave strip of wood curved and bound with others to form vessel

stool framing structural frame made from stool members

stem shaft, support

stile vertical member, esp. of panel door

stilt pole that supports and elevates structure or load

stock main upright part of supporting structure

stool interior, horizontal molding on window sill between jambs

stop wood strip used to hold window in place or against which door closes

story pole pole cut to height between floor and ceiling and marked with minor dimensions for use in construction

strake single line of planking that extends the entire length of a structure, esp. ship

strap narrow, flexible band of leather or fabric that binds or secures objects

strike plate metal plate set in door frame to receive lock plunger

stringer side of stair cut to receive threads; long, horizontal timber connecting upright posts

strip long, thin section of material

structural component portion, element, or raw material used in something built or constructed

strut bar or piece that resists longitudinal pressure or stress along its length

stud vertical framing member for wall, usu. wood

subfloor boards nailed directly to floor joists, used as base for finished floorboards or carpets

sump pit, trap, or reservoir that collects liquid

support element that bears weight of another part or parts

suspended ceiling ceiling hung from floor or roof above it

switch device used to open or close flow, esp. electric current

tackle rigging; ropes and pulleys used to hoist objects

tail end of rafter that extends beyond exterior wall

tappet sliding rod struck by cam to move another part

T-bar iron or steel beam with flanges along one edge forming T-shaped cross section

tee T-shaped structural member

template horizontal member of wall that receives and distributes pressure of beam or girder

tenon projecting part cut in wood to insert in corresponding mortise as joint

thill vehicle shaft

threshold beveled strip, usu. wood or stone, fastened to doorsill directly below door

tie structural member that joins stress pieces in frame

tie beam horizontal beam that connects two structural members and keeps them in place

tierod steel rod that serves as structural brace

timber wood member, esp. one 5 inches (12.7 cm) or more in smallest dimension

tine slender, pointed projection of implement or weapon

toe part placed vertically in bearing, such as lower end of shaft

toggle pin or crosspiece placed across end of rope or chain to prevent slippage

tongue projecting piece of wood fitted into corresponding groove

tongue-and-groove joint joint between two boards, one of which is cut with a raised area on its edge that fits into corresponding groove in edge of other board to form flush surface

tooth regular projection on gear rim

top plate horizontal member at top of wall studs; roof plate

trace bar hinged to two parts of machine, for transferring motion between them

track belt or tread that guides line of motion

transom crosspiece in structure, esp. above window or door

trave crossbeam; section between crossbeams

traverse rod horizontal rod on which curtains open and close

tread horizontal part of stair on which one steps

trellis lath lattice support

trestle reinforced supporting framework

trim wood molding, strips for finish and decoration

trimmer beam or joist that forms rough opening in wall, floor, or roof into which header is framed

tripod three-legged support, usu. adjustable

trippet projection or cam that strikes another machine part at regular intervals

truckle small wheel or pulley

trundle small wheel or caster

truss rigid reinforcing framework; preassembled support unit used in roof construction, including rafters, joists, and bracing

truss beam beam that is part of truss

tube hollow cylinder, pipe

tumbler single cog or cam on rotating shaft that transmits motion to the part it engages

underlayment materials on top of subfloor that form smoother surface for finished flooring

unit single, distinct part with specific purpose; combination of elements into single part

valley V-shaped depression at intersection of two sloping roofs

valley jacks rafters that extend from ridgepole to valley rafter

valley rafter diagonal rafter that extends from ridgepole to top plate to form intersection of two sloping roofs

valve device that regulates flow of liquid or gas

vane flattened, curved piece on revolving wheel

vapor barrier section of material that resists passage of water vapor

vent opening, esp. in wall, serving as outlet for air, smoke, or fumes

vent stack top section of soil stack that extends out through roof

volute spring conical coil spring extending in direction of axis of coil

wale bracket horizontal timber or steel beam that braces vertical members

waler horizontal wood support used to cast concrete

wall vertical structure that forms interior or exterior side of room, attached to studs

wall section part of wall taken as structural or support unit

waste pipe horizontal pipe used to carry waste from bath and kitchen fixtures to soil pipe

wattle rod or stake interwoven with twigs or branches to form wall, fence, or roof

W-beam iron or steel beam with W-shaped cross section

weather stripping metal or fabric strips placed around edges of doors and windows to reduce heat loss

web internal, diagonal brace between chords in truss

weep hole water drainage opening in masonry wall

weir notch in dam or levee that regulates and directs flow of water

winder triangular tread on winding staircase

winding wire or thread coiled or wrapped around something, esp. single turn of such wire or thread

wing part extending laterally from main part

withe partition between flues of chimney

wood roof truss rigid framework of structural members to carry roof load

worm rotating shaft or cylinder cut with helical threads

yoke forklike end of rod or shaft within which another part is secured; viselike piece holding two parts firmly together

Z-bar steel bar with Z-shaped cross section

Carpentry

balloon framing building with continuous studs from sill to roof plate

benchmark reference mark on construction site for land measurements and elevations

bias angle between construction lines

blank piece of material to be cut or worked into finished item

blind nailing placing of nails where they will be hidden when unit is complete

blueprint architect's detailed drawings of construction plan in standardized form; working drawings

board foot measure equal to 144 cubic inches of wood

brick veneer construction in which wood-framed building has layer of bricks as exterior siding

building codes local regulations for design and construction of buildings

building permit document issued by local government that grants the right to build

built-up roof roof of alternate layers of building paper and asphalt with final gravel layer

carpenter worker who builds large structures, esp. of wood

carpentry work and trade of building structures with wood

catwalk narrow elevated bridge, esp. temporary walkway around building site

contractor person who agrees to supply materials and do construction work for set price and hires subcontractors and laborers

core central layer of plywood sheet

course continuous row of bricks or shingles

crossbands layers of veneer glued at right angles to form plywood

crosscutting cutting wood across the grain

cross section side view through construction, esp. on drawings

d symbol for penny, indicating nail size

dado groove cut perpendicular to wood grain

dead load permanent load, such as roof, on structure

dimension lumber surfaced softwood milled to standard sizes, used to frame buildings

dressed size size of lumber after drying and planing

elevation drawing that shows design of exterior walls; height of building part above established point

face nail nail driven through board so that it is visible

finish grade elevation of ground relative to building after landscaping

floor plan detailed drawing that shows layout

and dimensions of building interior as viewed from above

foundation plan detailed drawing of foundation that includes its dimensions and location of footings, piers, and walls

framing joining of wooden structural members as skeletal structure for building

frostline depth frost penetrates into earth

grade line level at which ground intersects foundation of building

growth ring layer of wood developed during annual period of growth

half-timbered construction exterior walls in which exposed heavy wood members are separated by masonry

haunch tapered end of tenon

heartwood hard, older wood at core of tree

horse support frame or stand with legs

identification index stamp on plywood that indicates its quality

impact insulation class material's ability to resist transmission of impact noise

kerf slot in wood formed by saw blade

knocked-down (*adj*) something delivered to job with parts cut to size but not assembled

live load load on building structure, such as furniture, that may be moved or removed

lumbermill place in which logs are milled and dressed as lumber

lumberyard place with open areas and structures in which lumber is stored for sale

matched lumber lumber with edges shaped as tongue-and-groove

mil measure of thickness equal to one thousandth of an inch (.0254 mm)

millwork cutting, sizing, shaping, and planing of lumber and wood parts

miter (*vb*) cut piece of wood on 45-degree angle

mockup model of structure, often full-size

on center measurement taken from center of one member to center of another

out-of-plumb (*adj*) not in proper vertical alignment

penny designation of nail length, shown as d

pitch ratio of rise to span of roof

platform framing framing in which studs extend for one floor only and rest upon subfloor of each story

plot plan drawing that shows size, slope, and location of structure on lot

plumb (*adj*) in true vertical position

quarter-sawed (*adj*) designating lumber cut at 90-degree angle to tree's growth rings

rabbet open groove cut into edge of board to form joint

ripping cutting wood in direction of grain

rise vertical height of stair

roughing-in installation of plumbing and electrical systems that will later be concealed by interior finishing

run total horizontal length, esp. of stairs

R-value measure of resistance of insulating material to heat flow

sapwood light-colored wood located between heartwood and bark in tree

sawhorse rack with two slanting legs at each end, used to support wood being sawed

scaffold movable platform supported by frame or suspended by ropes to support workers and materials above ground

scale proportion of drawings or blueprints to actual structure, represented by ratio

scribing marking material to be cut to fit irregular surface

shear force producing opposite but parallel sliding motion in each of the contacting planes in a structural member

slope rise of roof in inches per foot of run

sound-transmission class measure of material's resistance to passage of airborne sound

span distance between two supporting members, esp. between exterior walls

specifications architect's detailed instructions not shown on blueprints or working drawings

subcontractor person or company hired by contractor to do specialized tasks, such as plumbing or wiring

superstructure part of building above basement

toenail (*vb*) drive nails at slant

true (*adj*) precisely or accurately formed, fitted, placed, or calibrated, esp. to conform to pattern or form

warp variation in wood board from flat plane

weatherize (*vb*) secure structure against cold or wind by adding insulation, siding, strips, or storm windows

working drawings complete set of drawings that shows all details of structure to be built; blueprints

BUILDING AND CONSTRUCTION MATERIALS
Cuts, Sizes, Treatments, and Forms of Wood
Softwoods
Hardwoods
Paneling and Composite Boards
Stones, Bricks, Tiles, Glass, and Metals
Plastics, Paper, and Textiles
Adhesives and Binders
Surfaces and Finishing Materials

See also: *Chap. 2: Plants; Chap. 3: Minerals, Metals, and Rocks; Chap. 5: Structural Components; Tools and Hardware; Chap. 7: Exterior Structure; Interior Structure; Ornamental and Functional Articles; Chap. 10: Fashion and Garment Parts*

Cuts, Sizes, Treatments, and Forms of Wood

a/d air-dried

air-dried (*adj*) a/d; designating lumber stacked out of doors so that air circulates between boards to remove moisture

batten sawed strip of wood, esp. used as seam or fastener

beam long, thick piece of lumber, used esp. as support for roof

bevel siding siding cut with sloping surface at edge

board milled, sawed piece of wood up to 2 inches (5.1 cm) thick and 2 or more inches wide

board foot standard measure of lumber, equal to 1x12x12 inches or 144 cubic inches

caning slender, flexible wood stems split into narrow strands and woven together, esp. for chairs

ceiling board cut board used in ceilings

clapboard narrow board thicker at one edge, used for outside walls; weatherboard

close-grained (*adj*) designating wood having fine, compact grain

construction wood dimension lumber

cork light, thick, soft, elastic bark of cork oak tree

cut amount of wood; style in which wood is sawed

decking construction boards for exterior use

dimension lumber usu. softwood lumber used for framing or as sheathing

dowel solid, cylindrical rod of wood

dressed size dimensions of lumber after drying and planing

drop siding siding with tongue-and-groove, rabbeted, or shiplap joint; matched siding

edge-glued (*adj*) designating flat-edged lumber bonded by gluing

edge-matched (*adj*) designating lumber with tongue-and-groove edges

end-matched (*adj*) designating lumber with tongue-and-groove ends

excelsior fine, curled wood shavings that form resilient mass, used for packing

exterior plywood usu. rough-grade plywood sheets with exterior glue, used under finishing materials

fencing long, thin posts or rails used to make fences

finish lumber high-quality softwood lumber to be left natural or stained for appearance

flat-grained (*adj*) designating wood having smooth, consistent grain

flooring long strips of tongue-and-groove finishing lumber, used for flooring

framing softwood construction lumber used for skeletal frame of structure

furring strips narrow, unfinished wood strips attached to masonry or concrete as base for finishing material

grading standardized system of rating and marking wood to indicate quality

grape stakes thick, unfinished posts used to support vines

green lumber undried lumber

hardwood lumber made from the wood of deciduous trees, used primarily for trim, finishing, and built-ins

heartwood mature wood at center of tree

interior finish material used to cover interior walls and ceiling surfaces

jambs strips used as side frame of door or window

k/d kiln-dried

kiln-dried (*adj*) k/d; designating lumber dried in kiln using regulated steam and hot air

knotty (*adj*) designating lumber with cross-grained, rounded areas, or knots, formed by lump where branch grew out of tree trunk

lath thin, narrow strips nailed to two-by-fours and rafters as foundation for plaster, tiles, and finishing boards

lauan Philippine mahogany, in trade usage

log long section of tree trunk or thick branch of felled tree to be cut and milled into lumber

louver door door with overlapping, horizontal slats

lumber timber sawed and milled into standard size beams, planks, and boards

lumber sizing standard sizes of lumber, in inches: 1x2, 1x3, 1x4, 1x5, 1x6, 1x8, 1x10, 1x12, 2x2, 2x3, 2x4, 2x6, 2x8, 2x10, 2x12, 3x3, 4x4, 4x8, 4x12

matched siding drop siding

milling cutting, shaping, and shaving of lumber and wood products on large scale in manufacturing plant

mixed-grain (*adj*) designating wood with both closed and open grains

molding shaped strip of wood used to finish or decorate walls: astragal, base, batten, bead, casing saddle, chair rail, corner guard, cove, crown, full round, half round, handrail, lattice, mantel, nose and cove, ogee, oval, picture frame, pilaster, quarter round, round edge, scalloped, sprung cove, stop, threshold, and window stool

open-grained (*adj*) designating wood having irregularly patterned grain, usu. wide

paneling broad, flat sections of wood from which panels are cut

parquet flooring squares in which grains of adjacent squares run at right angles

partition large sheet of wood or other material used to divide interior areas

pinoleum fine wooden sticks, stitched together as blinds

plank long, broad, thick board

plywood thin sheet of wood made by gluing and pressing together layers, often with grains at right angles; grades: AB, ACX, AD

plywood circle round plywood sheet

plywood sizing standard sizes of plywood: 4x8 feet or 4x10 feet by 1/4, 3/8, 1/2, 5/8, 3/4, or 1 inch thick

pole long, slender piece of wood, usu. cylindrical

post thick square or cylindrical beam section used in upright position

pressure-treated (*adj*) designating wood with resin compressed under great heat to increase hardness and resistance to moisture and decay

puncheon short post, used upright in framing

rabbeted (*adj*) designating board or plank with groove cut in edge to accept another piece of wood to form joint

rattan slender, tough stem of palm tree, used in furniture

reed fencing thick grass stalks plaited into fence

roofing rafter beams or plywood sheets used in roof frame; exterior material, such as shingles or shake, used on roof

rush round, pliant stem of certain marsh grasses, used in thatch roofs, furniture, and baskets

sapwood light-colored, living wood layer between heartwood and bark

seasoning aging and drying process that matures lumber to improve its workability

sen Oriental ash, in trade usage

shake long shingle split directly from log

sheathing layer of boards that covers roof rafters or outside wall studs

sheeting broad pieces of wood used to cover a surface

shelving thin, flat section of board to be fixed at right angles to wall

shingle thin, wedge-shaped piece of wood to be laid in overlapping rows over roof or wall sheathing

shiplap boards or siding rabbeted along edge to overlap and form joint

shutter louvered window covering

siding materials applied over wall sheathing as finished surface: hardboard, lap, metal, plastic, plywood

siding shingle shingle used over wall sheathing

slat thin, narrow wood strip

softwood lumber made from the wood of evergreen trees, used primarily for framing, construction, and some finishing

split flexible strip of wood or wood stem used in baskets or furniture

stake thin length of wood pointed at one end

stock tree trunk

stud boards, esp. 2x4s, used in upright position as framing to which sheathing, panels, or siding are nailed

thatch rushes or palm leaves used as roofing

timber heavy, dressed beam, usu. 5 inches (12.7 cm) or more in least dimension

tongue-and-groove (*adj*) designating lumber, esp. paneling and flooring, in which boards interlock along edges

treatment aging, drying, or seasoning done to improve quality of wood

trim finished interior and exterior moldings

two-by-four most common board used in framing, being 2 inches by 4 inches

veneer thin sheets of wood assembled in layers into plywood

vertical-grained (*adj*) designating lumber with grain running lengthwise

walling sheathing for walls

weatherboard clapboard

weatherizing treatment of exterior finish wood to conserve heat and resist water

wicker pliant twigs or rods plaited together into chairs or baskets

windows boards framed into windows

wood hard, fibrous substance beneath tree bark, cut and prepared as timber or lumber

woodwork interior moldings, doors, windows, and stairs

Softwoods

softwood lumber made from the wood of evergreen trees, used primarily for framing, construction, and some finishing

appearance pine
balsam fir
cedar, clear pine, cypress
Douglas fir
Englemann spruce
fir
hemlock
incense cedar
jack pine, juniper
knotty pine
larch, loblolly pine, lodgepole pine
mountain hemlock
Pacific yew, pine, ponderosa pine
red cedar, redwood
shortleaf pine, sound cedar, spruce, sugar pine
tamarack
white cedar, white fir, white pine
yellow pine, yew

Hardwoods

hardwood lumber made from the wood of deciduous trees, used primarily for trim, finishing, and built-ins

acacia, alder, American ash, American beech, American elm, apple, ash, aspen
balsa, bamboo, banyan, basswood, beech, birch, black cherry, black walnut, black willow, brasswood, briarwood, burl birch, buttonwood
calamander, cherry, chestnut, Circassian walnut, concept oak, cork, cottonwood, crystal elm, cypress
dogwood
ebony, elite walnut, elm, eucalyptus
frontier birch
Garry oak, golden oak, gum, gumwood
harewood, hazel, heirloom cherry, hickory
ironwood
lauan, lemonwood, linden, locust, logwood
magnolia, mahogany, maple
Niagara ash
oak, olive, orangewood, Oriental ash
peach, pecan, Philippine mahogany, plane, poplar
red oak, rock elm, rosewood
sandalwood, satinwood, Savannah hickory, sen, shagbark hickory, spartan oak, sugar maple, sumac, sweet gum, sycamore
teak, tulipwood, tupelo
walnut, white ash, white oak, wicker, willow
yellow birch, yellow poplar
zebrawood

Paneling and Composite Boards

beaverboard compressed wood fiberboard for walls and partitions

buttonboard hard, stiff paperboard

ceiling tile usu. 2x4 foot acoustic tile sheet of composite board

Celotex *Trademark.* insulation board made from sugarcane residue

chipboard compressed wood pulp, sawdust, and wood chips with resin binder

Compoboard *Trademark.* composite board

composite board class of high-strength, lightweight sheet materials made by combining various elements with a binder

compreg wood impregnated with resin, then compressed under great heat to increase hardness and resistance to moisture and decay; impreg

corkboard sheet of porous, elastic cork

diffuser panel mounted at angle to wall to absorb or disperse sound or light

drywall gypsum or hardboard panels joined as interior wall finish; plasterboard

fiberboard compressed wood or vegetable fibers in sheets

gyp board gypsum board

gypsum board laminate with gypsum core and layers of fibrous paper; gyp board; plasterboard

hardboard wood fibers placed under heat and pressure and pressed into sheets

homosote soft construction wallboard with crumbly edges, used esp. for displays

impreg wood impregnated with resin, then compressed under great heat to increase hardness and resistance to moisture and decay; compreg

insulation board sheets of material that resist transfer of heat or sound

laminate very strong or stiff multilayered material, esp. of plastic

laminated board sheets of multilayered material

Masonite *Trademark.* hardboard of pressed wood fibers for construction and insulation

panelboard composite board or laminate used as paneling

paperboard composite board of varying thickness and rigidity composed of layers of paper with binding

particle board panel of wood fibers, flakes, and shavings bonded together with synthetic resin

pasteboard layers of paper pressed together or pressed and dried paper pulp formed into sheets

pegboard composite or particle board pierced with holes into which pegs are placed for hanging objects

perfboard hardboard with holes into which hooks or pegs can be inserted for hanging objects

pinboard cork or soft board that can be pierced with pins to hold papers

plasterboard plaster of Paris core covered with heavy sheets of paper, used for walls or partitions; drywall; gypsum board

plastic laminated wood plastic coating bonded to plywood or particle board, used as countertop

plastic plywood layers of plastic pressed together as plywood

plyboard layers of composite board or plasterboard pressed together

Pregboard *Trademark.* compreg or impreg

pressboard variety of pasteboard

pressed hardboard wood fiber hardboard

scagliola imitation marble of ground gypsum with glue, used on floors and interior finishing

Sheetrock *Trademark.* popular brand of plasterboard

Upson board *Trademark.* easy-cutting, lightweight wallboard with clean edges of varying thickness, used esp. for displays

wallboard fibrous material made with gypsum in sheets for covering walls or ceilings or for displays

weatherboard laminate clapboard for exterior use

Stones, Bricks, Tiles, Glass, and Metals

acoustical tile sound-absorbent ceiling tiles made with slotted insulation board, polystyrene, or fiberglass

adobe mixture of reddish clay, straw, and water, used for building walls

aggregate cement formulation made from sand, gravel, and rock fragments, used esp. for tiles and shingles

alloy metal that is a mixture of two or more metals or a metal and nonmetal

aluminum lightweight, noncorrosive metal used in various forms

aluminum screen fine mesh formed of aluminum wires

aluminum shavings tiny, curled shreds of aluminum

aluminum siding aluminum panels for exterior walls

asbestos tile insulating tiles made from fireproof fibrous mineral

ashlar thin, square-cut, dressed stone used for facing masonry walls

asphalt brown or black bituminous coal tar residue used for paving and to make roofing tiles

asphalt shingle asphalt sheet cut into flat shingles

asphalt tile asphalt squares used in roofing

barbed wire strands of twisted wire with sharp barbs projecting at regular intervals, used for fencing

bead small, round piece of glass, metal, or wood, usu. strung with others like it

bitumen natural asphalt; hard or semisolid, tarlike residue from distilled coal, wood tar, or petroleum

blacktop bituminous asphalt mixture, used for road surfaces

brass yellowish alloy of copper and zinc

brick molded clay baked into hard oblong blocks, esp. of reddish-brown color, used as building blocks

brickface flat material with appearance of red bricks, used for decoration, not structural support

brownstone reddish-brown sandstone used in large blocks for building

cable strands of heavy wire wound to form metal rope

capstone stone in top layer of masonry wall

castiron hard, molded iron alloy

cast stone block of concrete made to resemble natural stone

ceiling tile tile made from acoustical material or fiberboard, used in ceiling

cement powder of lime and clay mixed with water and sand into mortar that hardens when dry; concrete

ceramic clay pottery, earthenware

ceramic tile fired clay tiles with hard glaze

chain series of connected metal links

chain link galvanized steel links interwoven into fencing

chicken wire thin, flexible wire fencing with large, hexagonal mesh

chrome chromium alloy used in plating

chromium hard grayish-white metal, highly resistant to corrosion, used esp. in alloys

cinder aggregate mixture of concrete and small rock fragments

cinderblock concrete and cinder aggregate building block in any of various shapes, typically having a lateral hole through its center

clay brick brick molded from clay

cobble cobblestone

cobblestone rounded stone used in paving, cobble

common brick standard size, oblong, reddish-brown brick; red brick

concrete mixture of cement, sand, gravel, and water that dries to form hard surface

copestone stone used in top layer of masonry

copper reddish-brown, conductive, corrosion-resistant metal

cork tile square-cut piece of cork

corrugated steel thin sheet of galvanized steel shaped into parallel grooves and ridges for added strength

cullet glass scraps that can be remelted

curbing stones or bricks used to form raised edge

curbstone stone that makes up a section of curb

cut glass ornamental flint glass with patterns cut into its surface by abrasive wheel

cut stone flat stone cut to particular shape

damask steel with wavy damascene markings

face brick brick with specific color or surface treatment, used for building facades

ferroconcrete high-strength, reinforced concrete, usu. layered in thin sheets

firebrick highly heat-resistant brick, used esp. for fireplaces

flag flat slab of stone; flagstone

flagstone flat piece split from hard stone, used for paving

freestone stone, such as limestone or sandstone, that may be cut freely without splitting

glass hard, brittle, usu. transparent substance composed of fused and rapidly cooled silicates mixed with potash or soda and lime

glass block square or oblong, hollow glass structure, used as decorative building block; glass brick

glass brick glass block

glass tile flat, hard, shatterproof glass square

glass wool fine glass fibers woven into dense mass, used for insulation

glazing panes or sheets of glass to be set in frames such as windows or mirrors

gravel mixture of pebbles and rock fragments graded by size from coarse to fine, used for outdoor surfaces

hanging wire thin, strong wire used to suspend or hoist objects

iron common, strong, malleable metallic element that is basis of alloy steel

limestone white calcium oxide used to make cement and mortar

linoleum hard, smooth floor covering made of solidified linseed oil mixed with gum, cork dust, or wood flour set on a backing of burlap or canvas, often cut into kitchen tiles

macadam rock fragments mixed with tar or asphalt to form roadway

marble hard, crystalline limestone with white, streaked, or mottled surface that takes high polish

marl brick composed of loose, crumbling earth

masonry brick, cinderblock, stone, or tile bonded with mortar or concrete

masonry veneer surface layer with appearance of stonework

mirror glass coated on one side with reflective substance

nickel silver-white, malleable metallic element used for plating and in alloys

pane glass transparent glass sheets cut to size for windows

pantile roofing tile that is curved in its width so as to overlap flanking tiles laid alternately convex and concave side up

paving gravel, stone, concrete, or asphalt, used to surface outdoor area or roadway

pipe hollow metallic cylinder

piping section or system of pipes

pisé rammed earth

plate glass clear ground glass in large sheets, used for windows; sheet glass

prestressed concrete concrete reinforced with embedded cables or wires under tension to increase strength

quarry tiles durable fired tiles of unrefined clay, used as flooring

rammed earth mixture of sand, loam, and clay rammed into forms; pisé

rebar reinforcing steel bars

red brick common brick

reinforced concrete concrete masonry embedded with steel bars or mesh for greater tensile strength

reinforcing rod steel bar used to reinforce concrete

retarder mixture of concrete or plaster with another ingredient that retards its set

riprap broken stone chunks used for foundations

roofing any of various ceramics, tiles, asphalts, or stones used to make roofs

roof tile ceramic or asphalt square of roofing material

rough-cut stone rubble; irregular, rough-dressed rock fragments

rubble masonry made of rough, irregular rock fragments; rubblework

rubblework rubble

safety glass shatterproof glass made by placing layer of resin or transparent plastic between two panes of glass

scrap discarded fragment, esp. of metal, that can be reused, often in altered form

scrap iron fragments of iron which can be recast

screening fine, close mesh composed of metal wires, used esp. to allow ventilation through doors or windows while excluding insects

shake rock fragments scattered about and set in mortar as roofing

sheet glass plate glass

sheeting any material, esp. metal or glass, cut into large, thin, flat pieces

sheet metal metal cut into large, thin, flat pieces

slate hard, bluish-gray, fine-grained rock used for roof tiles

smoked glass glass colored or darkened by smoke

spun glass fine threads of liquid glass

stained glass glass colored by fusing of metallic oxides, enameling, or burning pigments into its surface, used for decorative windows

steel hard, tough, rust-resistant iron alloy, used extensively for many purposes

steel mesh fine, interwoven strands of steel

steel plate hard, smooth sheets of steel

stone hard, solid, nonmetallic mineral substance of which rocks consist

Syndecrete *Trademark.* synthetic concrete

terra cotta hard, reddish-brown clay earthenware, used for ornamental facing

tile thin, usu. square or rectangular piece of stone, concrete, or fired clay, used for roofing or flooring

tinfoil paper-thin sheet of tin, or alloy of tin and lead, used for insulation

wire long, very thin metal thread

wrought iron tough, malleable, soft commercial iron with 1 or 2 percent slag content, used for furniture and fixtures

Plastics, Paper, and Textiles

asbestos fibrous material of fireproof mineral, used for insulation and tiling

Bakelite *Trademark.* black plastic made of synthetic resin

batting cotton, wool, or synthetic fiber wadded and quilted into sheets

batt insulation insulation made of batting

buckram stiffened linen cloth

bunting thin, translucent cloth used for decorations

burlap coarse sacking; hessian

canvas coarse, dense hemp or cotton cloth

cardboard thick, stiff material made from paper pulp; paperboard

carpeting thick, heavy wool, cotton, or synthetic fiber woven with pile, used for floor covering

cellophane thin, transparent, moisture-proof material made from cellulose

cellulose chief substance in fibers of all plant tissue, used in making paper and textiles

chamois soft leather made from skin of goatlike, European antelope or sheep, used as polishing cloth

cheesecloth very loosely woven thin cotton cloth

crepe paper thin, stiff, crinkled paper

fiber slender, threadlike structure found in vegetable tissue or made synthetically

Fiberglas *Trademark.* brand of fiberglass

fiberglass finespun glass filaments woven into sheets, used with backing as thermal or acoustical insulation or pressed and molded with resin as plastic

fibrous pad thick, soft sheet composed of fibers

flax fibers of flax plant spun into thread

foam rubber rubber treated to form firm, spongy mass

Formica *Trademark.* laminated, heat-resistant plastic, used esp. for countertops

grass cloth soft fabric made from plant bark fibers

grass paper fine grass fibers plaited into paper

hessian coarsely woven cloth; burlap

insulation any of various, usu. fibrous, materials that do not conduct heat or sound

jute strong fiber used for rope, burlap, and mats

kraft paper strong, brown paper made from wood pulp prepared with sodium sulfate solution, used for wrapping

leather animal skin prepared by removing hair and tanning

Lucite *Trademark.* clear, synthetic resin that hardens when cooled, used for storefront windows instead of glass

millboard strong, heavy cardboard used for book covers or furniture panels

muslin cotton with plain weave, often heavyweight with coarse finish

Mylar *Trademark.* very thin sheets of reflective polyester with great tensile strength, used for insulation and fabrics

Naugahyde *Trademark.* imitation leather

paper very thin, flexible sheets made from wood pulp or other fibrous material

paperboard stiff, heavy material made from wood pulp, thicker than paper; cardboard

papier-mâché shredded paper mixed with glue to form highly plastic molding material

pasteboard stiff material made from pasted layers of paper or pressed and dried paper pulp

Perspex *Trademark.* hard, transparent, acrylic resin similar to Plexiglas

plastic laminate plastic glued to plywood or particle board, used for countertops

plastics various nonmetallic organic compounds produced synthetically by polymerization, which can be molded, hardened, or formed into pliable sheets, fibers, or foams

Plexiglas *Trademark.* lightweight, transparent, thermoplastic synthetic resin, used in place of glass

polyester polymeric synthetic resin used in making plastics and synthetic fibers

polymer natural or synthetic substance formed by chaining together many simple molecules to form giant molecules with different physical properties

polypropylene polymerized propylene, a very light, highly resistant thermoplastic resin, used for packaging and coating

polystyrene tough, clear, colorless plastic polymer of styrene, used esp. for containers and apparatus

polyurethane various synthetic polymers, used in elastic fibers, foam, insulation, molded products, and coatings

quilt fibrous material matted together between layers of heavy paper, used for heat insulation

raffia fiber obtained from Mediterranean palm, used for baskets or ropes

rice paper thin, translucent paper made from straw of rice grass

rubber hard, elastic substance obtained by coagulating and drying sap or latex of various tropical plants, or made synthetically

rubber floor tile hardened, flat rubber squares

strawboard coarse straw cardboard, used esp. for boxes

styrene easily polymerized aromatic liquid, used to make synthetic rubber and plastics

Styrofoam *Trademark.* rigid, lightweight polystyrene, used for insulation and commercial products

tagboard strong cardboard

tarpaper heavy paper impregnated with tar, used as base for roofing

Teflon *Trademark.* tough, insoluble polymer, used for nonstick coatings on cookware, in gaskets, and as insulation

textiles woven fabrics made of natural or synthetic fibers

vinyl compound derived from ethylene and polymerized into various resins and plastics

vinyl floor tile stiff, flat, vinyl plastic squares

Vinylite *Trademark.* any of various vinyl resins

wallpaper decorative strips of paper used to cover walls, usu. applied with glue

Adhesives and Binders

acrylic resin transparent, thermoplastic, polymeric resin, used in making molded plastics, paints, and textile fibers

adhesive any substance that binds or adheres

adhesive tape long, narrow, wound strip of tape with sticky substance on one side

astringent substance that causes binding by contraction

binder substance that holds things together

birdlime extremely sticky substance made from holly bark

caulking whitish tar or oakum putty used to stop crack or fill joint

cement soft substance that binds objects together when it hardens between them

compo composite mortar or plaster

court plaster adhesive plaster composed of silk coated with isinglass and glycerin

creosote brownish, oily liquid distilled from coal tar, used as wood preservative

daubing soft, sticky plaster or grease smeared on surface

double-stick tape tape with adhesive substance on both sides

duct tape wide, silver-gray, strong adhesive tape, used for Sheetrock work, household repairs, etc.

electrical tape strong, highly elastic, black adhesive tape

epoxy thermosetting, quick-drying chemical resin blended with other chemicals to form strong, hard, adhesive bond

gaffer's tape duct tape used esp. by TV and movie electricians

gesso white plaster of Paris or chalk mixed with glue, used as base for paint or gilding

glue sticky, viscous liquid made by boiling animal skins, bones, and hoofs to a jelly

glycerin syrupy alcohol used as a solvent or plasticizer

grout thin mortar or plaster, used to fill joints in masonry, tiles, or brick

gum adhesive substance made from sticky colloidal carbohydrate found in certain trees and plants

gutta-percha rubberlike gum latex, used for insulation and binding

gypsum naturally occurring hydrated sulfate of calcium, used in making plaster of Paris for binding plasterboard

isinglass semitransparent whitish gelatin derived from air bladders of fish, used as clarifier or glue

joint compound spackling compound

lime white calcium oxide obtained by heating limestone or shells, used in mortar and cement

linseed oil yellowish oil of flaxseed with unique drying qualities, used in paints, adhesives, and linoleum

lute clayey cement used as sealing agent

masking tape thin, weak, usu. beige adhesive tape

mastic yellowish tree resin used in adhesives and varnish

mortar mixture of lime or cement with sand and water, used to bind bricks or stones in building or as plaster

mucilage thick, sticky plant substance; watery gum or glue solution

mud *Slang.* joint or spackling compound

oakum loose, stringy hemp fiber treated with tar, used for caulking

parget plaster or mortar, used to coat masonry

paste mixture of flour or starch with water and alum or resin, used as adhesive on light materials

pitch dark, sticky substance distilled from coal, wood tar, or petroleum, used for waterproofing, roofing, or paving

plaster of Paris calcined gypsum in heavy, white powder form, mixed with water to form quick-setting paste

pointing mortar used for finishing brickwork

Portland cement cement that hardens underwater, made by burning mixture of lime and clay, used to bind aggregate

putty mixture of powdered chalk and linseed oil, used to secure glass panes and fill cracks; cement composed of quicklime, water, and plaster of Paris or sand, used as plastering coat

resin any of various viscous, usu. clear or translucent, substances exuded from trees or plants, used in varnish, lacquer, and in making synthetic plastics

sealant wax, plastic, or silicone substance used for making a joint airtight or watertight

sizing thin, pasty substance used as glaze or filler on porous paper, plaster, or cloth prior to finishing

solder metal alloy melted and used to join or patch metal parts when it hardens

Spackle *Trademark.* spackling compound

spackling compound gypsum plaster mixed with glue, silica flour, and water, used as putty or filler; joint compound

stucco plaster applied as finish to interior walls and exterior surfaces

tape any of various adhesive tapes

tar thick, sticky, dark brown to black, viscous, liquid hydrocarbon obtained from distillation of wood, coal, or peat, used esp. in roofing and paving

tarmac bituminous binder used for surfacing roadways

travertine plaster made with light-colored Italian limestone

viscin clear, viscous substance obtained from mistletoe or holly sap

viscum birdlime made from mistletoe berries

wax plastic, dull-yellow substance, insoluble in water, used as sealant or to protect surfaces

weather stripping thin length of metal, fabric, wood, or composite, used to cover joint and keep out wind or water

Surfaces and Finishing Materials

acrylic paint pigments in solution of acrylic resin, quick-drying and brilliant

alabaster translucent, whitish, fine-grained gypsum

blacking black polish or stain

bleaching chemical substance used to remove color

bluing blue liquid or powder that prevents yellowing of white fabrics

brecciation process of giving surface the appearance of sharp rock fragments cemented together

carnauba wax hard brittle wax obtained from palm leaves, used in polishes

cladding process of covering one material, esp. metal, with another by bonding

clinquant imitation gold leaf

cottage cheese lumping plaster, used esp. for finishing ceilings

damascene wavy patterns like watered silk on metal; inlays of precious metals on iron or steel

deck paint strong, dense, hard-wearing exterior paint

dye natural or synthetic substance, esp. in solution, used to produce color

enamel opaque, usu. glossy, vitreous coating for metal, glass, and earthenware; paint drying to such a glossy finish

faux bois artificial wood grain finish made by swirling paint or stain; graining

finish manner in which surface is painted, varnished, coated, smoothed, or polished; material applied to complete or perfect surface

gild (*vb*) overlay with very thin layer of gold

gold leaf very thin layer of gold overlaid on surface

grain pattern of fibers in wood

graining faux bois

high-gloss (*adj*) designating very bright, lustrous surface finish, esp. of enamel paint

lacquer durable, nonoily varnish, esp. of sumac, applied in layers to wood and polished to mirrorlike finish; comparable synthetic organic solution

lamina thin flake or scale of metal or animal tissue

latex waterbase paint made by suspending particles of synthetic rubber or plastic in water; milky, resinous liquid present in rubber trees

leaf very thin sheet of metal; lamina

marbling painting technique that gives veined, mottled, marblelike appearance to objects

matte flat finish without shine or luster, esp. in paints

moire watery, wavy design, as on silk

oil any of various greasy substances obtained from animal, vegetable, or mineral sources, used to treat absorbent surfaces

oil-base paint paint made by grinding pigment in drying oil, esp. linseed oil, not soluble in water

paint mixture of pigment with water, oil, or latex in liquid or paste form, applied to surfaces for protection and coloring

parging application of mortar to masonry surface to smooth and waterproof it

patina surface coating due to aging, esp. green coloration on copper

pewter alloy of tin with antimony, copper, or lead

planish (*vb*) toughen, smooth, or polish metal by hammering or rolling

plaster pasty mixture, made from lime or gypsum, sand, and water, that hardens on drying, used to coat walls and ceilings

plate thin, overlaid coating of metal, esp. gold, silver, or tin

polish wax, oil, or liquid plastic rubbed onto surface to provide bright, glossy finish

primer paint or sizing applied to raw surface prior to finishing coat

rag-rolling wiping wet painted surface with rag to create patterns in paint

roughcast coarse stucco used on exterior walls

rubber cement quick-evaporating, unvulcanized rubber in solvent, used to bind light materials

semigloss (*adj*) designating paint that dries to a finish more lustrous than matte and less lustrous than high-gloss

shellac thin, clear solution of refined lac resin in alcohol, used as wood filler and finish

stain liquid coating to darken or color wood and bring out grain

stencil design cut out of waxed paper or acetate and reproduced on surface below paper with paint or ink

swirling allowing undercoat of paint to show through top coat

thinner turpentine or other substance added to dilute paint or varnish

tortoise shell synthetic imitation of the hard, mottled, yellow-and-brown shell of certain turtles

turpentine colorless, volatile hydrocarbon used in paint and varnish

Varathane *Trademark.* oily wood varnish that dries to hard, clear, water-resistant surface

varnish resin dissolved in oil or thinner that dries to hard, lustrous, usu. transparent finish on wood

veneer thin overlay of finishing material, esp. wood, on base of another material

verdigris greenish-blue coating that forms naturally on brass, bronze, or copper

waterbase paint pigment mixed with water or latex, soluble in water

wax soft, resinous, water-resistant substance rubbed on surfaces, esp. wood and leather, to protect and shine

whiting powdered chalk used in paints and dyes; bleaching agent

---

TOOLS AND HARDWARE
Common Tools and Tool Types
Edged, Pointed, Carving, and Turning Tools
Saws
Shaving, Shaping, Sharpening, and Smoothing Tools
Shovels and Digging and Lifting Tools
Drills and Bits
Hammers
Wrenches
Gripping, Tightening, and Fastening Tools
Measuring and Marking Tools

Miscellaneous Tools, Objects, and Supplies
Hardware and Supplies

See also: *Chap. 5: Machinery and Fabrication; Structural Components; Building and Construction Materials; Containers; Electricity and Electronics; Chap. 6: Automobiles; Chap. 10: Fashion and Garment Parts; Chap. 16: Graphic Design and Printing; Chap. 17: Gardening*

Each subcategory lists and defines the major representatives of that tool type. These are followed by an undefined list of other tools of that type that are either less common or whose name is self-explanatory, such as "jeweler's saw."

Common Tools and Tool Types

bit detachable, usu. interchangeable cutting, drilling, or boring part of a drill or other tool, available in various sizes suited to hole desired or specific need

blade broad, thin, flat, sharpened edge of cutting tool

chisel any of various wedgelike tools with cutting edge at end of blade, used for shaping solid materials, esp. wood or stone

clamp device that holds two or more objects tightly together between parts that draw together

digging tool any shovel, hoe, spade, or rake used for moving earth or rocks

drill shafted device, usu. affixed to handle, with point and two or more cutting edges for piercing hard surfaces, usu. by rapid rotations

edged tool tool with cutting edge or blade

fastening tool any screwdriver, clamp, vise, or cord used to hold parts together

file steel hand tool with abrasive surface for shaping and smoothing objects

fixture usu. decorative piece of hardware

gauge any device for measuring, testing, or registering measurements

gripping tool tool with jaws or pincers, such as pliers

hammer any of various handheld or power tools with hard, metal head at end of handle, used for pounding and nailing

hardware metalware usu. forming functional or decorative component part

hook curved, pointed, often barbed device for clasping or moving objects

implement any article used to facilitate some activity, such as a tool or utensil

knife blade, either attached to a handle or part of a machine, used for cutting, slicing, or shaping

marking tool device for scratching surface or applying mark at specific spot

measuring tool any device such as scale, rule, level, or square, used to determine magnitude, dimension, precision, or trueness

plane tool with horizontally mounted, adjustable blade in handle, used for smoothing or paring wood surfaces and for forming moldings, chamfers, and grooves

pliers small pincer tool with long, grasping jaws and two handles

pointed tool tool tapering to sharp point at one end

power tool any tool driven by more than human energy, esp. electrical power

rule length of straight hard material marked in units for measuring

sander power tool for smoothing surfaces with abrasive material, usu. on belt or disk

saw toothed blade attached to handle or in machine, used for cutting wood and other hard materials

scraping tool file or rasp for roughly removing surface material, esp. from wood

screwdriver handle with long, narrow, metal extension that tapers and flattens so as to fit into screwheads to turn and drive them

shaping tool any plane, sander, router, or lathe that precisely trims surface material to predetermined design

sharpener device for honing blade of edged tool

shaving tool device for removing excess material from surface

shovel broad, slightly hollowed, blade-edged scoop on handle for digging, scooping, or lifting heavy, often loose material

smoothing tool sandpaper, hone, or plane for finishing surface of shaped object

square instrument with straight edges and at least one ninety-degree angle, used to plot right angles

tightening tool screwdriver, clamp, or vise for forcing parts together

tool any implement, instrument, or device held in hand or driven by machine power and used to facilitate some physical or mechanical task

trowel small hand tool with flat blade attached to handle, used to spread or smooth loose material

wrench any of various hand or power tools for holding or turning a bolt or nut in a set or adjustable mouth at end of handle

Edged, Pointed, Carving, and Turning Tools

adz thin, curved blade mounted at right angles to handle, used for trimming and shaping wood

awl small, pointed instrument for marking and piercing holes, esp. in leather

ax heavy blade head attached to handle, used esp. for chopping and splitting wood

ax head heavy blade attached to ax handle

bale breaker bladed device for cutting and opening bales

barb sharp point projecting in opposite direction from main point of tool

bill curved blade set on handle, used for pruning or cutting; billhook

billhook bill

blade broad, thin, flat, sharpened edge of cutting tool

bodkin slender, pointed instrument for piercing cloth or leather

bowl gouge deeply fluted gouge

bradawl awl for making small holes in wood for brads

burin engraving tool with steel blade and sharp point

caulking iron chisellike edged tool for applying caulk to seams

chisel any of various wedgelike tools with cutting edge at end of blade, used to shape solid materials, esp. wood or stone

church key small, flat implement with pointed triangular head for penetrating beverage can tops

cleaver heavy cutting tool with broad blade, usu. used by butcher

clipper tool for cutting or shearing, often with multiple blades

colter sharp blade or wheel attached at front of plow, used for cutting earth

cotter key puller steel hook on short handle, used to remove cotter pins

crampon spiked plate attached to boot for use in climbing; device for lifting or grasping loads, usu. consisting of two hooks suspended from a cable or chain

crotchet small hook or hooked tool

dagger pointed blade on handle

dibble small, handheld, pointed device for poking holes in earth for plants or seeds

drawknife blade mounted between and at right angles to two handles and drawn over surface to be cut; drawshave

edger revolving blades set on long handle, used to trim edge of lawn

frow cleaving tool with wedge-shaped blade at right angle to handle

gouge grooving chisel with concave blade, used esp. in turning

grapnel small anchor with several flukes or claws

grappling iron hook for anchoring boat to dock or to another boat

graver any of various bladed tools, such as burin or scauper, used for engraving

hardy blacksmith's chisel with square shank for insertion into anvil

hatchet short-handled ax, often with a hammerhead

hook curved, pointed, often barbed device for clasping or moving objects

inshave curved blade set between and at right angles to two handles, used for removing surface of round objects

knife blade, either attached to a handle or part of a machine, used for cutting, slicing, and shaping

machete large heavy knife, often with blade widening at end away from handle

nibbler edged device for cutting sheet metal

peavey lever with spike and pivoting hook at one end, used by lumberjacks in handling logs

pick tool with heavy metal head, pointed at one or both ends, attached to wooden handle

pickaroon pike or hook at end of pole, used by lumberjacks, esp. on rivers

pickax head having ax blade and pick point attached to long handle

pike pointed head on long shaft

pinking shears shears with serrated edges for cutting fabric

pipe cutter hand tool with three wheels, one for cutting and two for guiding, that are pressed inward to cut through pipe as tool is rotated

piton spike pounded into rock fissure or ice for support in climbing

punch small, metal spike, used for perforating and stamping materials, marking layout lines, and driving nails

puncheon pointed stamping tool for goldsmith work

razor very fine-edged cutting blade, usu. of steel

ripping bar steel bar with clawed hook at one end and ripping wedge at the other

round-nose scraper scraper with blunt end, used for turning

scissors two hinged blades that cut when edges move past each other as handles are squeezed together

scraper edged tool used in turning on lathe

scythe long, curving blade on handle, esp. for cutting grass

shears large, powerful scissors for gardening or metalwork

sickle curved, hooklike blade on short handle, used for cutting grain

skew chisel with blade having angular front edge

slick large chisel for jointing large timbers; foundry tool for smoothing core or surface of sand mold

spring shears scissorslike cutting tool with nonpivoting jaws that spring open when released

spur pointed, sometimes barbed hook or metal device

square-end chisel chisel with blade ending square to its length

stylus hard-pointed needle for cutting or marking

tang projecting point or prong on chisel, file, or knife

trier hollow tube narrowing to point, used to withdraw samples of bulk material from sacks or other containers

utility knife razor blade held in small handle

wedge metal rod tapering to blade end, used for raising weights or splitting hard objects

wire cutter plierslike tool with edged jaws, used to cut through wire

Other edged and pointed tools

alpenstock

belt punch, bistoury, bob punch, bolster chisel, bread knife, bricklayer's chisel, brick set, broadax, bushwhacker, butcher knife, butt chisel cant hook, carpet knife, carving chisel, carving knife, carving set, case knife, celt, chaser, chopping knife, clasp knife, claw hatchet, cold chisel, cold cutter, croze, cutting pliers

dogleg chisel, drawshave, drove chisel

eaves hook, electric razor

firmer chisel, fluted gouge, framing chisel, frowglass cutter

garnish awl, glazier's chisel, goosewing ax, groover, grub ax, grub hoe

hack, half hatchet, hedge trimmer, hook blade, hot cutter, hunting knife

iron

jackknife, jeweler's chisel

kranging hook

lance, lancet, letter-opener, linoleum knife

masonry chisel, mason's chisel, mat knife, mill knife, mortise chisel

nippers, nooker knife

palette knife, panga, paper cutter, paper knife, paring chisel, paring knife, penknife, plowshare, pocketknife, pole tree pruner, prick punch, pruner, pruning hook, pruning shears, putty knife

reed knife, rigger's knife, ripping chisel, roofing knife, roughing-out gouge

safety razor, saw knife, sax, scalpel, scauper, scoop, scorper, scraper, scuffle hoe, share, shearing hook, sheath knife, sheet metal punch, shingling hatchet, sidecutters, slotter, snips, spear, spindle gouge, surgical knife, swan neck chisel

table knife, taping knife, tin snips, turning chisel

wood chisel

Xacto knife

Saws

backsaw short saw with reinforced back

band saw saw consisting of endless, toothed steel band passing around two wheels

bayonet handsaw with long, deep-toothed, bayonetlike blade on small handle

bench saw circular saw mounted on workbench

bucksaw saw with blade mounted across upright frame, held in both hands for cutting wood on sawhorse

buzz saw stationary, power-operated, circular saw with teeth on large disk attached to shaft

chain saw usu. portable power saw with teeth set on endless, revolving chain

circular saw handheld electric saw with disk-shaped blade

compass saw small handsaw with narrow, tapering blade for cutting curves; keyhole saw

coping saw saw with thin, light blade in U-shaped frame with handle, used to cut small curves or do ornamental work in thin wood; fret saw

crosscut saw saw for cutting wood perpendicular to grain

crown saw rotary saw consisting of hollow cylinder with teeth at one end or edge; cylinder saw; hole saw

dial saw small blades mounted on circular plate whose diameter can be adjusted, used to cut holes

dozuki Japanese craftsman's saw with blade that widens away from handle and teeth that cut on the pull, not push, stroke

flush cut saw single-edged saw with extremely flexible, thin, unbacked blade that will bend to cut off pegs without marking adjacent surface

frame saw saw, often with multiple detachable blades that are attached to handle at both ends, used esp. for precision work

friction saw high-speed, usu. toothless, circular saw that cuts metals by melting them with frictional heat

hacksaw narrow, fine-toothed blade fixed in frame, used to cut metal

handsaw common saw with handle at one end for manual operation

jigsaw usu. stationary electric saw with narrow blade mounted vertically in frame, used to cut curves and other irregular lines

keyhole saw compass saw

log saw sturdy blade with large, deep teeth for cutting logs or timber

miter saw portable, electric, circular saw with adjustable guide for cutting miters

panel saw stationary power tool, either horizontal or vertical, used to cut large sheets of material accurately

power saw any of various electrical, gas-powered, pneumatic, or battery-driven saws

radial arm saw stationary, electrically powered saw with blade on overhead arm that moves across width of wood

ripsaw saw used for cutting wood with the grain

ryoba Japanese craftsman's saw with teeth on both sides of a blade that widens away from the handle and cuts on the pull, not push, stroke

saber saw portable, handheld electric jigsaw

saw toothed blade attached to handle or in machine, used for cutting wood and other hard materials

scroll saw narrow saw mounted vertically in frame and moved up and down in cutting curved ornamentation, usu. benchtop power saw

stationary circular saw power saw with disk-shaped blade, affixed to bench or in standing unit

table saw small, stationary power saw with benchlike table on which wood is placed for cutting

veneer saw small saw with a handle that is flat on one side and has a blade along its length, this blade having teeth facing in both directions, used for cutting veneer sheets

whipsaw saw operated between two persons, used to divide timbers lengthwise

Other saws

azibiki

belt saw, board saw, bow saw, builder's saw, butcher's saw

contractor's saw, cordwood saw, cutoff saw, cylinder saw

diamond saw, double-cut saw, dovetail saw, dry-wall saw

electric saw

flooring saw, fret saw

helicoidal saw, hikimawashi, hole saw

jeweler's saw

kerf saw, kitchen saw

lightning saw, logging saw, lumberman's saw

marquetry saw, meat saw, mill saw, mortise saw

pad saw, panther-head saw, pitsaw, plumber's saw, plywood saw, pocket saw, portable saw, portable sawmill, pruning saw

reciprocating saw

saw knife, saw machine, Sawzall, scribe saw, skewback saw, Skilsaw, splitsaw, surgeon's saw, sweepback saw

tenon saw, trim saw, trock saw, two-handed saw

utility saw

vertical saw

wallboard saw, wire saw, wood saw

Shaving, Shaping, Sharpening, and Smoothing Tools

abrader handheld scraping tool

anvil heavy iron block on which metals are placed for shaping by pounding

belt sander electric sander with abrasive surface on continuous belt

block plane small plane for cutting across grain

buffer any of various polishing devices, usu. with smoothing surface attached to handle or other mechanism

bullnose plane small, blunt-ended planing tool

butteris L-shaped shank with flat blade, used for paring horse hooves

chamfering plane plane with blade that shaves and smooths wood at 45-degree angle to adjacent face

circular file file with cylindrical abrasive surface, often tapering toward end away from handle; round file

darby two-handled, wooden plasterer's float

die any of various tools for forming material into a specific shape, esp. by pressure of cutting

disk sander electric sander with abrasive surface attached to rotating disk head

drum sander usu. stationary power tool with rotating cylinder, used to smooth curved surfaces

electric sander electrically powered, orbital or straight-line hand tool for smoothing surfaces

emery wheel grinding wheel

file steel hand tool with abrasive surface for shaping and smoothing objects

flatiron device with flat metal bottom that is heated and used to smooth materials, esp. cloth

flatter blacksmith's flat-faced tool, laid on forging and struck with hammer to smooth surface of forging

float trowellike tool with thick rubber face attached at each end to handle, used for smoothing grout or similar material

grinding wheel circular head of abrasive material for sanding and grinding; emery wheel

grindstone revolving wheel of abrasive material, usu. Carborundum, for grinding and shaping

half-round file file that is flat on one side and rounded on the other

hone abrasive whetstone for sharpening bladed cutting tools

honing guide handles that attach to a chisel or plane blade to guide it across sharpening stone

jack plane any plane for rough surfacing

jointer large plane for smoothing wood surfaces; stationary power tool used to achieve smooth, flat surface on wood

lapping kit grains of silicon carbide in several sizes, used for lapping stones and finishing plane blades and chisels

lathe stationary power tool with fixed tool mechanism and machine that rotates work around axis, used for shaping cylindrical objects

machine tool power-driven device used to shape or trim objects

multiplane versatile plane, with up to forty interchangeable cutting blades, for large variety of uses

oilstone block of fine-grained stone, usu. oiled, for sharpening certain cutting tools by abrasion

plane tool with horizontally mounted, adjustable blade in handle, used for smoothing or paring wood surfaces and for forming moldings, chamfers, and grooves

planer power tool for surfacing rough wood

power sander high-speed electrical sander, either rotary, orbital, or straight belt, with attachments from fine to coarse grain

punch press power tool used to cut and shape metal sheets with dies under pressure

putty knife broad, flexible blade on short handle for spreading putty

rabbet plane plane for cutting deep notch or rabbet at edge of board to make joint with another board

rasp metal file with coarse raised nubs

riffler small file with curved abrading surface

round file circular file

router machine with rotating, milling, or cutting bits mounted on vertical spindle, used for gouging wood surfaces

router plane plane for cutting interior angles, as at bottom of groove

sander power tool for smoothing surfaces with abrasive material, usu. on belt or disk

sandpaper paper with sand or other abrasive glued to one side, used for smoothing surfaces, esp. wood

scraper any of various hand tools with blades that are usu. pulled, rather than pushed, to shape wood surface

shaper any of various tools or machines for shaping and pressing sheet metal; stationary power tool with cutters, used to contour edge of wood

shavehook small tool with blade set at right angle at end of shank, pulled for scraping effect, rather than pushed like plane

slipstone sharpening stone with rounded and tapering edges, used on gouges and other carving tools

spokeshave blade set between two winglike handles, used for forming and dressing curved edges of wood

steel wool matted mass of steel shavings used by hand for shaving and smoothing surfaces

stone grindstone or whetstone

stroke sander stationary power tool with continuous overhead belt, used to sand large panels or surfaces

strop strip of leather for sharpening razors

swage heavy tool for shaping metalwork, which is hammered against swage surface

swage block iron block used for shaping objects not easily worked on anvil

tamper wide blade set perpendicular to handle, used for flattening and evening out soft or loose materials

thickness planer plane with strong blade and wide cut, used for shaving deeply into wood surfaces

trimming plane plane with L-shaped body that hooks over board, used for trimming edges

trowel small hand tool with flat blade attached to handle, used for spreading or smoothing loose material

trying plane very long, wide-bladed plane for making tight-edged glue joints and leveling large boards

waterstone sharpening block, made of stone, that is used while wet

whetstone stone block for sharpening blades

wood mill stationary or portable device with multiple blades for making moldings

Other shaving, shaping, sharpening, and smoothing tools

auger bit file
bastard file, beading plane, bench plane, bench stone, bending fork, brick trowel, buffing-and-polishing bonnet
cabinet scraper, cabinet rasp, capping plane, chuck, circle trowel, circular plane, combination plane, compass plane, contour sander, core box plane, corner trowel, cove trowel, curbing trowel
dado plane, dovetail plane
edge plane, electric plane
faceplate lathe, fillister plane, finger plane, finishing sander, flat file, fore plane
grinder, grooving plane, guttering trowel
hand plane, hand sander, hand scraper
jeweler's lathe
lute
match plane, mill file, molding plane, multiplane
needle rasp
orbital sander
pad sander, palm plane, perimeter sander, plasterer's float, plastering trowel, plough plane, plunge router, pointing trowel, portable handheld shaper, portable router, power plane
radius trowel, reed plane, rotary rasp, roughing plane, round bastard file
sanding belt, sash plane, scraper plane, scrub plane, seaming plane, shoe rasp, shoulder plane, slick, smoothing plane, surform plane
tamping bar, tamping pick, tamping stick, tape file, thumb plane, tonguing plane, toothing plane, trenching plane, trimmer, trimming block

violin plane
warding file, wood plane, wood rasp

Shovels and Digging and Lifting Tools

bail scoop for removing accumulated water, esp. from boat

bar long, straight, rigid piece of metal for lifting or prying

bull tongue wide plow blade for cultivating or marking soil

crowbar metal bar with flattened wedge at one end, used as a lever

cultivator implement with flat blade, drawn between rows of plants to loosen earth and remove weeds

fork pronged tool for lifting, throwing, or piercing

hoe flat blade at end of long handle, used for working earth around plants

lever rigid bar on axis or fulcrum, used to lift weight or exert pressure to dislodge something

loy long narrow spade, esp. one with broad chisel point for digging post holes

mattock pickaxlike tool with one broad end, used for loosening soil by digging

pinch bar crowbar with projection at one end that acts as fulcrum, used for removing spikes or wedged under heavy wheel to be rolled; wrecking bar

pitchfork large, two- or three-tined fork on long handle, used for lifting and tossing

plow implement with blade for cutting or lifting soil or clearing away debris

pry bar tool similar to crowbar, used for lifting or moving heavy objects

rake head with multiple, sometimes splayed prongs on long handle, used for gathering loose material or leveling ground

scoop deeply concave shovel or hollowed spoon for digging and carrying earth

scooper shovel, scoop, or ladle

shovel broad, slightly hollowed, blade-edged scoop on handle, used for digging, scooping, or lifting heavy, often loose material

spade small, flat blade at end of long handle, pushed into ground with foot for digging

spatula spreading or scooping tool with flat, thin blade on handle

spud spadelike tool with narrow blade, used esp. for digging up weeds

tire iron crowbar used to remove hubcaps and lug nuts

trowel small, scooplike hand shovel

wrecking bar pinch bar

Other shovels and digging and lifting tools

air shovel, air spade
bar spade
coal shovel
ditch spade, drain spade, draw hoe
entrenching tool
fire shovel
garden spade, garden trowel, gasoline shovel, grub hoe, gumming spade

irrigating shovel
peat spade, posthole digger, power shovel
salt shovel, scuffle hoe, split shovel, stump spud
trenching spade
wedge bar, Wonder bar

Drills and Bits

auger boring tool consisting of bit rotated by transverse handle

auger bit long bit with square tang at upper end, rotated by brace to bore through wood

bench drill large, stationary power drill

bit detachable, usu. interchangeable cutting, drilling, or boring part of drill or other tool, available in various sizes suited to hole desired or specific need

bore tool with bit, such as an auger, used for boring out holes

bow drill antique drill operated by cord wrapped around shank with ends attached to bowlike device

brace device for holding and turning a bit for boring or drilling

breast drill portable drill with plate at end of handle that is pressed against the chest to force drill against work

center bit bit with sharp, projecting point, easily centered in hole to be drilled

chamfer bit bit used to bevel edge of hole

chaser tool with multiple teeth for cutting screw threads

chuck threaded portion of drill that holds bit

cordless drill battery-operated power drill not requiring AC cord

corkscrew pointed, metal spiral on handle, inserted in corks to pull them from bottles

countersink drill bit or funnel-shaped metal piece used to enlarge upper part of hole, allowing a cone-shaped screwhead to lie flush with surface

drill shafted device, usu. affixed to handle, with point and two or more cutting edges for piercing hard surfaces, usu. by rapid rotations

drill press powerful, stationary drill with single vertical spindle and hand lever used to apply pressure in drilling accurate holes

eggbeater drill antique drill operated by rotary motion of handle similar to an eggbeater

electric drill any electrically powered hand tool for drilling holes

gimlet small boring tool with spiral point and cross handle

hand drill any small, hand-cranked drill

jackhammer powerful, portable drill operated by compressed air, used to break up rock or concrete

keyhole router bit bit that cuts keyhole-shaped hole in object to be hung over nail

mandrel metal rod or bar around which wood, metal, or glass is cast, molded, or shaped

nail set short steel rod used to drive nail below or flush with surface

plug cutter special bit that routs a circular groove

push drill hand drill operated by pressure of handle along line of shank

reamer rotary tool with helical or straight flutes, used for finishing or enlarging holes drilled in metal

screw starter threads on tapering point of short shank with bulb handle, used to make threaded holes for screws

snake device with head at end of flexible metal band, fed into curved pipes to remove obstruction

tap pluglike device with sharp ridges, inserted in opening and twisted to cut screw threads in it

wimble any of various boring devices, used esp. in mining to extract material from bored hole

woodborer boring tool for wood, operated by compressed air

Other drills and bits

accretion borer, air drill, angle drill, automatic drill
beading bit, bench grinder, bevel trim bit, bitstock, bore bit, brad point bit, breast auger, broach, burr
carbide bit, circle cutter, compressed-air bit, core box bit, cross bit
diamond drill, disk drill, dovetail bit, dowling jig, drill set, drill stand
expansive bit, extensive bit
flat drill, Forstner bit
gimlet bit, glass bit
hinge bit
keyway drill
lockset bit
masonry bit, mortising bit, multispur bit
ogee fillet bit
panel pilot bit
parallel hand reamer, portable drill, post drill, posthole auger, Powerbore bit, power drill, pump drill, punch drill
raised panel bit, ratchet drill, roman ogee bit, rose reamer, rotary drill, round over bit, router bit
shell drill, shell reamer, spade bit, spade-handle drill, spike bit, star drill, strap drill
taper drill, tapping drill, tile bit, trepan, trephine, twist bit, twist drill
vix bit

Hammers

ball-peen hammer machinist's hammer with one cylindrical and one hemispherical head

battering ram heavy beam or bar used to knock down walls and doors

beetle heavy, usu. wooden instrument for hammering, ramming, or driving wedges

brad pusher tool with long, narrow head on small bulb handle, used to drive brads while avoiding hammer marks on surface

brick hammer hammer having one broad flat head and one long, axlike head

claw hammer hammer with one head curved and forked into claw for pulling nails; rip hammer

club heavy, wooden rod, often narrowing at one end

double-claw hammer hammer with claws on both heads and no pounding surface

drop forge heavy object allowed to fall on piece of work placed on anvil; drop hammer

fuller hammer for grooving or spreading iron

hammer any of various handheld or power tools with hard, metal head at end of handle, used for pounding and nailing

hammerhead heavy, hard, usu. metal portion of hammer at end of handle, designed for striking

hatchet short-handled ax, usu. with one hammerhead

mallet hammer of wood, plastic, rubber, or metal, usu. with a barrel-shaped head, used esp. for driving a chisel

maul sledgehammer for driving piles, sometimes with wooden head, sometimes with one ax edge for splitting wood

peen hammer hammer with hemispherical or wedge-shaped head, used esp. for shaping material

pestle club-shaped device made of hard substance, used for grinding and pulverizing material in mortar

ram battering ram or other device for driving something by impact

rammer instrument for driving something by impact

rip hammer claw hammer

scutch hammer with elongated heads for shaping bricks

sledge sledgehammer

sledgehammer large, heavy hammerhead on long handle, swung with both hands

small anvil nonstanding, handheld anvil used to pound materials

tack hammer light hammer, often with magnetized head that holds tack

tamp tool for driving down an object or firmly patting down a filling

tilt hammer forging hammer with heavy head at one end of pivoted lever

triphammer heavy hammer raised and released by means of tripping device to fall on object being hammered

Warrington hammer light, balanced cabinetmaker's hammer with flat peen head and narrow tapering head

Other hammers

adz-eye hammer, air hammer
blacksmith's hammer, boilermaker's hammer, bushhammer
chipping hammer, cooper's hammer, cross peen hammer
demolition hammer, die hammer, drilling hammer, drop hammer, drywall hammer
electric hammer, engineer's hammer
framing hammer, goathead hammer
hand drilling hammer, hardie, high nailer
joiner's mallet
long-handled hammer
machinist's hammer
nail claw hammer
pile hammer

pneumatic hammer
raising hammer, ripping claw hammer, riveting hammer, rubber mallet
set hammer, shingler's hammer, shoemaker's hammer, soft-faced hammer, spalling hammer, steam hammer, stone hammer, stonemason's ax, stonemason's hammer, stud driver
tiler's hammer
upholsterer's hammer
veneer hammer
wooden mallet

Wrenches

adjustable wrench any wrench with adjustable jaws

Allen wrench hexagonal bar bent at right angle, used to turn Allen screw having axial hexagonal hole in its head

alligator wrench wrench with V-shaped, serrated jaws set at right angles to shank, used for turning cylindrical or irregularly shaped parts

box-end wrench wrench having closed ends that completely surround nut or bolthead

box/open-end wrench wrench having one closed box end and one open end

Crescent Wrench *Trademark.* hand wrench with parallel, adjustable jaws that have smooth surfaces

crowfoot wrench box or open-end wrench with opening set at right angle to shank

lug wrench wrench with hollow end, used to loosen or tighten lug nuts

monkey wrench wrench with adjustable jaws, used to grasp nuts or boltheads of different sizes

obstruction wrench wrench with bent shank for use in confined areas

open-end wrench wrench having partially open end that slips over nut or bolthead

pipe-gripping wrench any of various wrenches with differing jaw shapes, used to grip pipes

pipe wrench tool with two toothed jaws, one fixed and one free to grip pipes when wrench is turned in one direction only

ratcheting box-end wrench box-end wrench with teeth mounted in round openings and ratchet lever

socket set series of different-sized socket attachments for ratchet-style socket wrench

socket wrench wrench with hollow end, or socket, that fits nut or bolt, often ratchet-operated and equipped with socket set

spanner wrench having curved head with hook or pin at one end for engaging notches or holes in collars and certain nuts

spark plug wrench ratchet-style wrench with socket that fits over automobile spark plugs

speeder wrench socket wrench with long offset handle

Stillson wrench *Trademark.* monkey wrench with adjustable jaw that tightens as pressure is applied to its handle

torque wrench wrench having register that

shows amount of torque, or rotational force, being applied

wrench any of various hand or power tools for holding or turning a bolt or nut in a set or adjustable mouth at end of handle

Other wrenches

adjustable spanner
bicycle wrench
carriage wrench, chain wrench
end wrench
flare-nut wrench
gooseneck wrench
hexagonal wrench
lever wrench
Mack truck wrench
pin wrench,
ratcheting box
screw key, S-wrench
tappet wrench, tap wrench, tuning wrench
valve wrench

Gripping, Tightening, and Fastening Tools

anchor device that firmly binds one part of a structure to another, usu. by being implanted in one part

bar clamp clamp with two jaws attached to bar, one jaw fixed and one adjustable by means of a screw mechanism

bench dog device that fits in hole on workbench top and in moving face of bench vise, used to hold work in place

bench vise vise that clamps to bench or table

brace device that clasps or connects two pieces

C-clamp C-shaped clamp with a screw threaded through one end in the direction of other end

chuck device for centering and clamping work in a lathe

clamp device that holds two or more objects tightly together between parts that draw together

claw device with forked end for removing nails

clip gripping device using pinching action of two hinged arms

cordless screwdriver battery-operated power screwdriver not requiring AC wire

diagonal-cutting pliers pliers with clipping blades set at an angle in jaws

electric riveter power tool for fastening rivets

forceps hinged device for gripping small objects

grip pinching or grasping tool

hand screw clamp with two wooden jaws, tightened by two long screws passing through both jaws

impact driver screwdriver that turns when downward pressure is exerted on handle

lineman's pliers pliers with reinforced jaws and insulated handles, used with electrical cable and wire

locking pliers pliers whose jaws connect at sliding pivot that may be temporarily locked to aid in grasping and turning

nail puller plierslike device with strong, wide, curved jaws for removing nails from wood

needlenose pliers pliers with jaws tapering to point, used for grasping small objects

Phillips screwdriver screwdriver with cross-shaped, pointed tip

pincers two-handled gripping device with pivoting jaws

pinchcock clamp for compressing flexible pipe or tube to regulate flow of liquid

plate joiner electric doweling machine that fastens wooden members together using oval biscuits

pliers small pincer tool with long, grasping jaws and two handles

pneumatic stapler compressed-air powered staple gun

power nailer automatic nailer driven by compressed-air chamber

pucellas pointed gripping jaws on spring pivot, used for handling molten glass

puller device for gripping and removing spikes or nails

riveter device for pressing rivets together in order to fasten pieces of material together

screw clamp any clamp tightened by a screw mechanism

screwdriver handle with long, narrow, metal extension that tapers and flattens so as to fit into screwheads to turn and drive them

screw gun power screwdriver

slip-joint pliers pliers having sliding joint that permits adjustment of jaw span

snap ring pliers tool with short jaws for removing and replacing snap rings on power tools

spring clamp any clamp tightened by an elastic spring mechanism, rather than by a screw mechanism

staple gun pneumatic or electrically powered stapler

stapler small hand implement for affixing objects with thin wire staples

stubby screwdriver screwdriver with very short shank and thick handle

tongs two hinged arms used for grasping objects

tweezers small device with two jointed arms held between thumb and forefinger, used to grasp small objects

veneer press press frame for small veneering and assembly jobs

vise tool with two clamping jaws that are brought together or separated by means of a screw or lever, used to hold objects and work tight and steady

vise grip handheld vise that screws tight to hold work

Yankee screwdriver *Trademark.* handheld tool with spiral ratcheting action

Other gripping, tightening, and fastening tools

adjustable bar clamp, auger screwdriver
band clamp, bent-nose pliers
cabinet-pattern screwdriver, channel-lock pliers, clamp-on vise, clutch-head tip screwdriver, corner clamp, cutting pliers

edging clamp, electric screwdriver, electric staple gun
flat-head screwdriver
glue gun
hammer staple, handspike, hand vise, holddown clamp
joint fastener
long-nose pliers
machinist's vise, magnetic screwdriver, miter clamp
nippers
offset screwdriver
patternmaker's vise, piling clamp, pin vise, pipe clamp, plastic tape, punch pliers
ratcheting screwdriver, ring pliers
saw vise, slab-handle screwdriver, spiral ratchet screwdriver
tacker, toggle clamp, tongue-and-groove pliers
utility tweezers
web clamp, welding clamp, wood bar clamp, wood hand screw
Z-bar, Z-clip

Measuring and Marking Tools

bevel rule with adjustable arm that opens to form measured angles, used for drawing or shaping sloped edges

butt gauge gauge with three cutters for marking mortise outlines, as for door butts

caliper adjustable, often curved jaws on pivot, used for measuring thickness or diameter

center punch small device with conical point for marking shallow impressions, used to center drill bits for making holes

combination square adjustable device used as level, miter square, and try square

compass instrument consisting of two movable legs hinged at one end, used to draw arcs and circles

dividers pair of compasses used to measure lines or divide a large space into sections

feeler gauge device for measuring gaps by inserting one of several arms of different thicknesses

folding rule measuring device with multiple, pivoting lengths for compact storage

level any of various devices for determining true horizontal lines, esp. one that has a bubble suspended in liquid in a glass tube set in a long straight board

marking gauge any device for marking measurements with a sharp point, usu. having graduated scale on sliding arm

micrometer precision instrument with spindle moved by finely threaded screw, used for measuring thicknesses and, by machinists, for turning shafts and boring holes

miter box fixed or adjustable guide for saw angle, used in making a miter joint or crosscut

miter square two straightedges joined at a 45-degree angle

plumb bob weight hung on line, used to determine true vertical line; plummet

plumb rule narrow board with plumb line and bob suspended from upper edge, used to determine verticality

plummet plumb bob

protractor device for measuring and marking off angles, esp. on drawings and plans

rafter square roofer's square with premarked rafter tables for cutting hips and joists

rule length of straight, hard material marked in units for measuring; straightedge

ruler rule

scale any of various devices for determining weight of objects

scratch awl long blade tapering to sharp point for making fine marks

screed wooden strip that serves as guide for making a true level surface, esp. by dragging it across freshly poured concrete

scriber pointed tool for marking wood as guide for cutting or assembly

slide caliper pocket caliper with ruler along which one arm slides

square any instrument with straight edges and at least one ninety degree angle, used to plot right angles

straightedge length of straight, rigid material for measuring or marking; rule

tape measure narrow strip of flexible material, often in coil, marked off in measuring units

try square pair of straightedges fixed at right angles to one another, used to lay out right angles or test squareness

T square rule with perpendicular crosspiece at one end, used for marking parallel lines

turning caliper caliper into which a cutting or parting tool fits, used to make repetitive sizing cuts in turning

vernier caliper caliper in which two pieces slide across one another, one piece having a movable, graduated scale running parallel to the scale on the other piece

wing divider device consisting of adjustable arms and a graduated gauge for dividing lines and scribing circles

Other measuring and marking tools

adjustable bevel, adjustable square, automatic center punch
bevel square
carpenter's level, carpenter's square, chalk, chalk line, charcoal
depth gauge, dial caliper, diameter gauge, dovetail square
flex, flex tape, framing square
grease pencil, guide
height gauge
machinist's rule, machinist's square, mortise gauge
pencil, power miter box
right angle
sizing caliper, sliding bevel, spirit level, steel rule, studfinder
T-bevel, trammel
zigzag rule

Miscellaneous Tools, Objects, and Supplies

bench long table providing workspace and tool storage

blowtorch small, portable device blasting out intense gasoline flame, used in metalworking

broom stiff, bundled fibers attached to long handle, used for sweeping

brush close-set bristles on short handle, used for painting, sweeping, or cleaning

cant hook blunt-ended lumberjack's lever with hooked arm

carpenter's apron heavy, often canvas, protective covering for trunk and upper legs, having pouches, pockets, and loops to hold tools and supplies

carpenter's belt heavy leather belt with loops and other attachments for carrying tools

dolly wheeled platform, sometimes with handles, for moving heavy objects

dust mask small filter in frame that fits over mouth and nose, providing protection from dust and nontoxic fumes

earplug plug placed in ear to block out job noise

extension ladder adjustable ladder with two or more levels which may be extended and locked in place for greater height

face guard face shield

face shield protective visor covering entire face with transparent section for eyes; face guard

flail short, thick, wooden stick loosely attached to handle, for threshing

flashlight small, portable electric lamp, usu. battery-powered, that gives off a directed beam of light

funnel hollow cone narrowing to long tube for focusing downward flow of liquids

gaff barbed hook on handle, used esp. for lifting; spur attached to shoe for climbing

glue gun device that holds and fires stream of melted glue

gluepot double boiler in which glue is melted and stored

glue press large, stationary, multibeamed press for producing glue

grease gun handheld device for directing pressurized flow of thick lubricant

hammer holster leather loop attached to carpenter's belt, used to hold hammer

hard hat sturdy, framed, protective helmet made of metal or fiberglass

hawk small, square board on handle, used to hold mortar or plaster

hearing protectors earplugs or coverings for ears designed to reduce damage from exposure to noise of power tools

hose flexible tube through which fluids flow to a point

jack any of various portable devices for lifting or supporting weight

jackscrew jack operated by a screw that is steadied by a threaded support, having a plate to bear load

jack stand base with plate for supporting heavy object that has been lifted by a jack

ladder two long, rigid strips connected at intervals by crosspieces on which one steps to climb

mop absorbent cloth or fibers attached to handle, used for cleaning, esp. floors

mortar hard receptacle in which material is ground or pounded with pestle

nail pouch bag for carrying nails, as on carpenter's belt

oilcan metal container for oil, usu. with narrow spout

padlock detachable lock with pivoted or sliding shackle that can be passed through loop or ring

paintbrush closely bunched bristles on handle, used to apply paint

paint pot jar or other deep container for holding paint

paint roller cylinder of absorbent material set perpendicular at end of handle, used to apply wide swaths of paint

paint tray flat, wide receptacle for holding paint, esp. for use with roller

platform truck wheeled device with handles, used to move heavy objects

plumber's helper plunger

plunger rubber suction cup on handle, used to unblock obstructed pipes and traps by suction; plumber's helper

respirator protective mask used when spraying toxic finishes

safety goggles protective eyeglasses, sometimes tinted and ventilated at sides, encased in frames that rest on cheeks and brow

sawbuck sawhorse

sawhorse movable frame or trestle for supporting wood being sawed; sawbuck

scaffold elevated platform for supporting workers during building construction or repair

soldering iron often electrically powered device for melting and applying metal alloys used to fuse metal objects together

sponge chunk of porous skeletal matter from various marine animals, used to absorb liquid

sprinkler device for scattering liquid in fine drops

squeegee rubber blade on handle for spreading or wiping liquids over a surface

stepladder small, freestanding, portable ladder with hinged support stand

straight ladder usu. tall, single length of ladder that is leaned against a stationary surface for support

toolbox receptacle or case, often of metal, in which tools are stored

tool cabinet shelf with multiple compartments and hooks for storage and display of tools

tool kit small, portable tool container

welder gas-powered or electrical machine tool, used for cutting and joining metal parts by heating them to molten state

wood-burning kit electrical hand tool with multiple attachments, used to burn ornamental details and designs into woodwork

workbench sturdy table with broad surface at which work is performed

Hardware and Supplies

adapter any of various pieces of hardware that permit nonmatching parts to mesh, connect, or function together

Allen screw screw turned by insertion of Allen wrench into hexagonal hole cut into axis of screwhead

alligator clip clip with long, narrow, toothed jaws, used esp. for electrical connections

anchor bolt bolt inserted and fixed in masonry to hold timbers or shelves

arbor any spindle or bar that holds rotating cutting tools

ball bearing bearing composed of several hard balls running in grooves of two concentric rings, one of which is mounted on a rotating or oscillating shaft

beam anchor wall anchor

bearing supporting and guiding part of machine, in which another part moves smoothly

bibcock faucet with nozzle bent downward

bit detachable, usu. interchangeable cutting, drilling, or boring part of tool, available in various sizes suited to hole desired or specific need; drill bit

blade broad, thin, flat, sharpened edge of cutting tool

boat nail nail having convex head and chisel point

bolt metal fastening rod, threaded at one end, held in place by nut

box nail long nail with flat head

box nut nut with blind hole closed off at one end; cap nut

brace device that clasps or connects two pieces

bracket projecting support element, esp. for attaching a horizontally set piece to a vertical surface

brad thin wire nail with barrel head; thin nail, tapering in width, with lip at top of one side of head

buckle clasp consisting of rim with one or more movable tongues, fixed to one end of a strap and fastened to the other end

bushing removable lining or sleeve inserted in an opening to resist wear or serve as guide

butt hinge hinge secured to the butting surfaces of a door or the like

cable strong, heavy rope made of metal strands

cap fitted covering for end of something, esp. tube or pipe

cap nut box nut

caster small, swiveling wheel used to support and move heavy objects, esp. furniture

catch latch or other device for checking motion

chain length of connected metal links used for support or transmission of power

chevron L-shaped metal connector hammered into two pieces of wood to form strong miter joint, hidden beneath surface of wood and covered with putty; pair of pinch dogs connected at right angle

chuck clamplike device by which work to be turned is held; threaded portion of drill bit

clamp device holding two or more objects firmly together

clevis U-shaped yoke at end of chain or rod, through which hook or lever can be pinned or bolted

clip gripping device using pinching action of two hinged arms

collar protective or controlling ring or band at one end of a rod or shaft

common nail any of various size nails, distinguished from finishing nail by having wider head

corner brace L-shaped connecting piece

cotter pin, wedge, or key fitted or driven into opening to hold parts together

cotter pin split metal strip, whose arms are separated after insertion in hole to hold position

crank bent end of shaft by which circular motion is transmitted to or from shaft

cross-garnet T-shaped strap-hinge with stationary crosspiece

cut nail tapering, rectangular-shaped nail with blunt point

doornail large-headed nail formerly used for strengthening doors

driftbolt spike having round shank, used to fasten heavy timbers together; driftpin

drill bit bit

elbow pipe fitting or connection with right-angled bend

expansion bolt bolt inserted into hole in machinery and mechanically expanded to serve as anchor for something

eye loop through which hook slips to fasten something

eyebolt bolt with ring-shaped head

eyelet grommet

female adapter recessed element of connection that receives male adapter

finishing nail thin nail with very small, globular head, driven to point just beneath wood surface and concealed by filler or sawdust

flange strip along length or around end of object, such as pipe, for directing or strengthening it

gasket ring, esp. of rubber or tallowed rope, placed or packed around piston or joint to make it fluid-tight

gooseneck iron pipe joint bent like neck of goose

grommet metal ring for lining small opening in soft material to protect or strengthen it; eyelet

guide device that regulates or controls motion or direction of another piece

hanger bolt bolt with tapered lag-screw thread on one end and machine-bolt thread on the other, used in timber construction

hardware metalware usu. forming functional or decorative component part

hasp fastening device consisting of hinged, metal strap held in place over staple by pin

hinge jointed device on which a movable part turns or swings freely

hook bent piece of inflexible material for restricting movement of attached object

hook and eye latching device consisting of hook and loop or screw eye through which the hook slips

hoop circular band of stiff material, used esp. to hold something together

jam nut thin, supplementary nut screwed down on regular nut to prevent it from loosening

joint connection, often reinforced, between two pieces of similar material, esp. between two sections of pipe

knob usu. rounded projection, esp. used as handle

knuckle cylindrical projecting part of hinge, through which a pin passes

L elbow or L-shaped support piece, usu. metal

lag screw wood screw with flat, boltlike head, used esp. with expandable metal anchor in concrete or stone

latch bar sliding into a catch, groove, or hole, used to hold movable part in place

lock nut nut with extra friction between itself and screw to prevent it from loosening

lug nut capped nut used esp. to attach automobile tires

machine bolt large bolt with square or hexagonal head and threads on lower portion for use with nut; machine screw

machine screw machine bolt

male adapter extending element of connection that enters female adapter

nail thin, tapering, pointed fastening device, usu. of metal, with head that is pounded to drive point into object that is to be held in place, made in various lengths designated by penny number, usu. up to sixty penny or 6 inches (15 cm) long

nipple piece of pipe threaded on each end, used for joining valves

nut any open ring-shaped, hexagonal, or square piece of metal with internal threads for tightening over end of bolt

O-ring ring made of rubber or other flexible material, used as gasket

pad soft, cushioning, protective insert

Phillips head screw screw with cross-shaped notches in its head

pin slender piece of hard material inserted into hole to secure something

pinch dog metal connector with points at either end that are driven below surface of two pieces of wood and covered with putty

pipe length of hollow, cylindrical tubing for conducting gas or liquid

pipe fitting coupling, such as elbow or tee, for connecting pipe sections

plate flat sheet of metal of uniform thickness, used as base or covering

plug small stopper that fits securely into opening to prevent passage of gas or liquid; wooden filler produced by plug cutter

pull handle, knob, or other piece of hardware that is pulled

ring fitted round band used for hanging, securing, or sealing

ringbolt bolt with ring fitted in an eye at its head

rivet metal pin or bolt passed through two or more pieces and pressed down at both ends to fasten them

rod length of straight, thin metal or other hard material for securing or connecting objects

roofing nail short nail with broad head, used for nailing down asphalt roofing shingles

rubber washer washer made of rubber that compresses to form tight seal

screw thin fastening device with spiral groove threaded around its length, secured by rotating it into object that is to be held: lag, machine, set, or wood

screw eye screw having ring-shaped head

screw nail fastener with helical thread and point that can be driven into wood with hammer and removed with screwdriver; drive screw

setscrew machine screw that passes through threaded hole in one part and into another to prevent movement

shackle U-shaped fastening or coupling piece, esp. bar of a padlock

slide moving part on track, channel, or guide rails

snap ring ring that must be forced open for use and snaps shut to make snug fit

spike long, heavy, naillike fastener for heavy timbers or railroad ties

spring spiral elastic device for exerting pressure by compression or contraction, recovering original shape when released

square nut nut with square sides

staple U-shaped loop of metal attached to something and through which a hasp, bolt, wire, or rope is secured fast

stirrup U-shaped or W-shaped rod for supporting longitudinal reinforcing rods

strap-hinge hinge having one long flap attached to face of movable object such as door

stud projecting rivet or infixed rod used for fastening or as a support

switch electrical device for altering, closing off, or releasing flow of current

swivel connecting device that allows both connected objects to pivot freely

tack short, sharp nail with broad head

thumbscrew screw with head shaped so that it can be turned with thumb and forefinger

thumbtack tack with wide flat head that can be pushed into material with thumb

toggle bolt bolt consisting of screw and two hinged arms which open when inserted, used to hold heavy objects in soft material

trap U- or S-shaped section of pipe under sink that seals off sewer gases

treenail wooden pin that swells when moist, used to fasten timbers together

turnbuckle sleeve with swivel at one end and internal screw thread at other, or thread at each end, used for coupling or tightening two parts

U bolt U-shaped bolt with screw thread and nut on each arm

upholstery tack small tack used to attach material in upholstering furniture

valve device for controlling flow of gas or liquid, as through pipe, by opening and closing

volute spring conical coil spring extending in direction of axis of the coil

wall anchor heavy-duty device used to tie walls together; beam anchor

washer flat, thin ring used, esp. with bolt and nut, to increase tightness, prevent leakage, or distribute pressure

waste nut internally threaded floor flange for pipe

wing bolt bolt having flared head like wing nut

wing nut nut with two flat, flared sides for turning between thumb and forefinger

wire nail thin nail made of wire, designed for specific use such as finishing

wood screw screw tapering to sharp point for use in wood

wye Y-shaped connecting device, esp. for three-phase electrical circuit

Other hardware and supplies

angle brace, angle bracket, astragal

backflap hinge, ball catch, bar bracket, barrel bolt, bell, bend, B nut, brad nail, brass screw, bullet catch, bullet latch, bumper, butterfly hook, buttonhook

cabinet knob, cabinet pull, cad cut washer, castellated nut, chain bolt, channel, climbing iron, coated nail, coil spring, concealed hinge, Condulet, continuous pull, corrugated nail, coupler, coupling, cover plate, crook, cross, cutoff riser

deadlock, deep thread screw, door slide, dowel screw, drawer slide, driftpin, drive screw, drop-leaf hinge, drop ring pull, drywall screw

edge pull, ell, extension bolt

fence bracket, finger pull, finish washer, flat head screw, flat washer, flex connector, flipper slide, flush mount, flush pull

galvanized nail, gate, glide

hexagonal nut

jet rail bracket, joist hanger

kep nut, kick plate, knife bracket

lazy Susan, lead shield, leg bracket, leveler, lock washer

magnetic catch, masonry nail, mending plate, metal screw, Molly fastener

nut-driver, nut-runner

outlet, oval head screw

panhead screw, piano hinge, pipe strap, pivot hinge, plastic shield, plate strap, plug clip, P-trap, pushpin

Rawl plug, riser extension, rod coupling, rope clip, round head screw

safety plate, sash lock, screw shield, sheave, shelf rest, socket head screw, Soss hinge, speed nut, spiral spring, spud washer, square U bolt, stanchion, standard, stay, strip, studfinder

tapping screw, tee, T hinge, threaded insert, threaded rod, Tite-joint, T nut, Toggler, touch bar, touch latch, track

union

wall box, wet post anchor, wire nut

KNOTS

See also: *Chap. 6: Ships and Boats; Chap. 17: Hunting and Fishing*

anchor knot fisherman's bend

barrel knot fisherman's knot used esp. to fasten together two strands of leader; blood knot

becket bend sheet bend

bend any loop or knot for joining end of one rope to another rope or to some other object, esp. nautical

bight middle portion of rope, esp. when looped or bent, as distinct from ends

bitter end inboard end of nautical line

Blackwall hitch hitch for temporarily securing line to hook

blood knot barrel knot

bow knot comprised of two or more loops and two ends, used esp. to tie together ends of ribbon or string; bowknot

bowknot bow

bowline knot used to make nonslipping loop at end of rope

builder's knot clove hitch

carrick bend knot or bend for joining ends of two ropes

cat's-paw nautical hitch in middle of rope forming two eyes to hold hook

clinch knot in which eye is made by looping the rope and seizing one end to a standing part

clove hitch knot for fastening rope to spar or larger rope, consisting of two half hitches made in opposite directions; builder's knot

crown knot made by interweaving the strands at the end of a rope, usu. as first stage in tying knot

cuckold's neck nautical hitch for holding spar, consisting of single loop with overlapping parts of rope held together; ring seizing; throat seizing

diamond hitch knot for tying pack to an animal, in which interlacing ropes form a diamond atop the load

diamond knot diamond-shaped knot tied in strands of rope

double knot any knot formed by repeating the tying process

eye loop formed at end of rope

figure of eight knot resembling the numeral 8, formed by looping rope around itself twice, the second loop above the first

fisherman's bend knot for attaching rope to an object, made by passing end of rope around

object and the standing part and then under the round turn; anchor knot

flat knot reef knot

flat seizing seizing in which lines are parallel and a single binding layer is used

granny knot faulty square knot in which bights cross each other in the wrong direction; lubber's knot

half hitch knot made by forming loop and passing end of rope around the standing part and through the loop

half-knot common knot joining the ends of two ropes, used to make square and other knots

harness hitch hitch forming loop around rope, esp. at end of bowline

hawser bend nautical knot joining the ends of two lines

heaving-line bend nautical knot for attaching the end of a weighted heaving line to a hawser

hitch any of various knots used to attach rope to something so as to be easily loosened

inside clinch clinch knot with the seized end of line inside the noose

knot interlacing, looping, bending, hitching, or folding together of pliant, slender length of cord or rope so as to fasten, bind, or connect two such lengths together or one length to something else

lanyard knot stopper knot

lash binding or fastening with rope or cord

loop section of rope folded or doubled upon itself, leaving an opening between parts

loop knot knot made by doubling over line at its end and tying both parts into square knot so as to leave a loop; open hand knot

lubber's knot granny knot

Magnus hitch knot for fastening rope to spar or larger rope, consisting of clove hitch with one more turn around object to which rope is bent

manrope knot double wall knot with double crown, used to attach a manrope railing to its gangway or ladder

marlinespike hitch hitch into which pointed metal implement is inserted in order to draw the seizing taut

marling hitch one of a series of knots used to lash long rolls or bundles

Matthew Walker knot formed at end of rope by retying loosened strands

mesh knot sheet bend

midshipman's hitch nautical hitch made by tying a rolling hitch with end of line to the standing part

nail knot nooselike fisherman's knot that tightens when pulled and does not slip

netting knot sheet bend

noose loop with running knot that tightens as rope is pulled

open hand knot loop knot

outside clinch clinch knot with seized end of line outside noose

overhand knot simple, small knot that slips easily, used as part of another knot or to

prevent ends from fraying; single knot; thumb knot

prolonge knot knot made up of three overlapping loops formed by passing a single rope over and under itself at crossings; sailor's breastplate

reef knot nautical square knot used in tying down sails; flat knot

reeving-line bend nautical bend for joining two lines so that they will pass easily through a hole or ring

ring seizing cuckold's neck

rolling hitch nautical hitch on a spar, composed of two round turns and a half hitch, that tightens under stress applied parallel to the spar

rope-yarn knot knot made by splitting rope yarns apart and joining their ends in half-knots

round seizing seizing in which lines are parallel and a double binding layer is used

round turn complete turn of rope around object

running bowline slipnoose made by tying end of bowline around its own standing part

running knot knot made around and sliding along the standing part of the same rope, thus forming a noose

running part part of rope or tackle that is hauled upon, separate from the standing part

sailor's breastplate prolonge knot

seizing method of binding or fastening together two ropes or parts of same rope by a number of longitudinal and transverse turns

sheepshank knot, bend, or turn used to shorten rope, often temporarily

sheet bend bend or hitch used to fasten rope temporarily to the bight of another rope or to an eye; becket bend; mesh knot; netting knot; weaver's knot

single knot overhand knot

slide knot knot formed by two half hitches on the standing part, the second hitch being next to the loop, which can be tightened

slipknot any knot that rides easily along rope or cord around which it is made, esp. an overhand knot on the standing part

slipnoose noose whose knot slides along the rope, tightening as the rope is pulled

splice joining together of two ropes or rope strands by interweaving of strands

square knot common knot formed of two half-knots, used to join two rope ends that emerge alongside standing part

standing part length of rope that is in use and terminates in a knot or around which a knot is formed

stevedore's knot stopper knot

stopper knot knot forming a lump to prevent rope from passing through a hole or opening; lanyard knot; stevedore's knot

stunner hitch double Blackwall hitch

surgeon's knot knot similar to reef knot, used by surgeons to tie ligatures

tack bend bend or loop used for temporary fastening

throat seizing cuckold's neck

thumb knot overhand knot

timber hitch nautical knot or hitch formed by taking a turn on the spar, wrapping the end around the standing part, then several times around itself

truelove knot elaborate, ornamental double knot formed by two interlacing bows

Turk's-head turbanlike knot of small cords, formed around rope or spar

turle knot fisherman's knot used to attach artificial fly or eyed hook to leader

turn passing or twisting of rope or cord around itself, another rope or cord, or some object

wall knot overhand or double knot made by interweaving strands at end of rope, terminating in crown or double crown

weaver's knot sheet bend

Windsor knot wide, triangular knot used for tying four-in-hand necktie

---

CONTAINERS

Receptacles and Casks
Basins, Ladles, Cups, and Pots
Bottles
Cases, Boxes, and Bags
Baskets

See also: *Chap. 7: Furnishings; Ornamental and Functional Articles; Chap. 9: The Kitchen; Chap. 10: Ornaments and Accessories*

Receptacles and Casks

ashcan metal can for trash

ashtray small receptacle for tobacco ashes, cigarette and cigar butts

barrel bulging cylindrical vessel made of staves held together with hoops and having flat parallel ends the same size

billycan metal or enamel container with one open end, used for outdoor cooking or to carry food

breaker small water container in lifeboat

bucket pail

butt large cask for wine, beer, or water

caddy small box, can, or chest, used to store frequently used items

cage enclosure with wire or bars, used to confine people or animals

can cylindrical receptacle, usu. of metal, open at one end or closed off to seal in contents

canister cylindrical metal receptacle with removable, close-fitting top

cannikin wooden bucket; small can

cask barrel-shaped container for liquids

catchall container for miscellaneous articles

cistern large, underground reservoir for storing rainwater or other liquid

coal scuttle deep metal bucket with handle and lip, used to hold coal; hod

coaster small dish or mat placed under glass to protect furniture

container anything that holds other objects within itself

crock thick earthenware pot or jar

crucible vessel made of metal or refractory material, used to melt substances at high heat

dinner pail enclosed pail, carried by worker, that contains food

drum large, cylindrical receptacle, usu. for liquids

Dumpster *Trademark.* very large, metal trash container, usu. emptied directly into dump truck

dustbin *Chiefly Brit.* garbage can

firkin small, lidded, wood or metal cask

gallipot small ceramic vessel with small mouth, used by pharmacists for medicine

garbage can usu. metal container in variety of sizes, used to hold trash

harness cask tub on ship, used to soak and store salt meat prior to use

hod trough with pole handle, carried on shoulders for mortar or bricks; coal scuttle

hogshead large barrel or cask holding 63 to 140 gallons (238 to 530 l)

hopper funnel-shaped receptacle with opening at bottom, used for temporary storage and delivery of material; tank for liquids with mechanism that allows release of contents through pipe

jemcan container for liquids holding 5 gallons (18.9 l)

keg small cask or barrel holding 30 gallons (113.6 l) or less; rundlet

kibble iron bucket used in mines to hoist ore

kilderkin cask equal in size to half a barrel

magazine room or storage place for supplies, esp. ammunition

mess kit portable container used to cook and hold food, usu. by soldiers

milk pail receptacle into which cow's milk falls during milking

mortar small, bowllike porcelain vessel used to pound substances with pestle

mortarboard three-foot square board that holds mortar

oilcan can with long, slim spout, used to oil machinery

pail cylindrical vessel, usu. with handle, used to carry liquids or solids; bucket

palette thin oval or oblong board on which artist saves and mixes pigments

piggin wooden, pail-shaped vessel with one stave reaching above rim as handle

pipe cask, esp. for wine, holding two hogsheads, or 126 gallons (476 l)

pipkin small earthenware pot with horizontal handle

pitcher container that holds and dispenses liquids, made of glass, earthenware, or plastic, with wide mouth having lip on one side and handle on other

plate shallow, usu. round vessel of earthenware, glass, plastic, or metal that holds food

powder horn container for gunpowder made from horn of ox or cow

puncheon large cask in variety of sizes, usu. 80 gallons (304 l)

receptacle any open storage container

rundlet keg

salver tray used to serve food or drinks

saucer small plate, esp. with indentation at center for holding cup

slop pail bucket used for toilet or household wastes

tank large enclosed container, often cylindrical, used for storing or carrying gas or liquid

tin can can made of tin

trash can large metal container, esp. for dry refuse

tray flat receptacle with low rim, used to carry, hold, or exhibit objects

trencher wood tray used to serve food

tub wide, low receptacle with flat bottom

tun large cask that holds wine or beer

vat large tub or barrel, usu. for liquids

waiter tray on which tea service is carried

wastepaper basket small trash can, used for discarded papers

watering can metal can with long spout and narrow mouth, used to water plants by hand

---

Basins, Ladles, Cups, and Pots

ashpan pan under grate, used to collect ashes

bail container used to remove water from boat

basin shallow, round vessel with sloping sides, used to hold water, esp. for washing

beaker large, widemouthed drinking cup without handles

biggin percolator or pot with stand and lamp, used to warm coffee (19th c.)

blackjack large beer mug made of leather coated with tar

bowl deep, round dish with wide opening at top

calabash hard rind of inedible calabash fruit, used as dipper, bottle, or kettle; gourd

caldron large kettle

cannikin small can or cup

cistern large, silver vessel used to cool wine at dinner table

cup small, bowl-shaped drinking vessel with handle and base

cuspidor spittoon

cyathus long-handled ladle used to fill wine cups (ancient Greece)

dipper cup or ladle with handle, used to scoop up liquids

flowerpot usu. round container with small hole in bottom, used for growing plants

gourd hard rind from any of various fruits, used as dipper or kettle

horn hollowed animal horn used for drinking or for holding ink or gun powder

jardiniere large, round, decorative flowerpot

jorum large drinking vessel

kettle container for boiling liquids, cooking foods, etc.

ladle long-handled, cuplike spoon used for dipping or conveying liquids

macock horn in shape of animal's head, used for drinking (ancient Greece)

mug cylindrical drinking cup, usu. with handle

pan broad, shallow, open household container, usu. round

patella small pan or vase (ancient Rome)

patera metal or earthenware drinking saucer, once used for sacrificial libations (ancient Rome)

pipkin small metal or earthenware pot with horizontal handle

porringer small, shallow, one-handled bowl used to feed children; pottinger

pot deep, metal or earthenware container with handle, usu. round, used esp. for cooking

pottinger porringer

rhyton earthenware horn with base in shape of head of animal or mythological creature, used for drinking (ancient Greece)

scoop any of various open, hemispherical utensils used to remove liquid or loose materials

shovel large hand tool with broad scoop and handle, used for lifting or scooping

spade heavy digging tool with flat blade and long handle

spittoon low, round receptacle used for disposal of tobacco juice; cuspidor

trough long, shallow receptacle that holds animal's water or feed

trowel scoop-shaped hand tool used to dig in or plant gardens

urn vase on pedestal

vase tall, hollow vessel of porcelain, glass, metal, or earthenware, used to hold flowers or decoration

vessel hollow or deep container that holds objects, esp. liquid

washbasin bowl used for washing hands or face

washtub usu. round metal tub used to wash clothes

water butt receptacle for water, as in fountain or lavatory

Bottles

amphora tall jar with narrow neck and base and two handles (ancient Greece)

beaker deep, thin, glass laboratory vessel with lip, used for pouring

bottle usu. glass or plastic rigid container for liquids with narrow neck and no handle, sometimes with cap

canteen hip flask used by soldiers or campers to carry water

carafe ornamental glass vessel with narrow neck and wider mouth, used for holding water or wine

carboy large bottle encased in protective wooden crate, used to hold corrosive liquids

caster small glass container used to serve condiments; cruet

cruet caster

cruse small earthenware container for oil, honey, or water

decanter ornamental glass bottle used to serve wine

demijohn glass bottle with capacity of 1 to 10

gallons (3.79 to 37.9 l), encased in wicker, with one or two handles

ewer wide-mouthed jug or pitcher made of brass or ceramics

fifth bottle that holds 1/5 gallon (0.76 l) of liquid

flacon small flask with tight cap, used to hold perfume

flagon large vessel with handle, spout, and lid, used to hold wine or liquor

flask flat container with neck and stopper, used for holding liquid, usu. carried in jacket or pants pocket

flasket small flask

ginger jar ceramic jar with wide mouth, globular body, and domed cover (China)

jar usu. cylindrical glass or earthenware container with no spout and large opening on top, capable of being sealed at top

jeroboam oversize wine bottle that holds 3 liters (3.17 quarts)

jug large, deep glass or earthenware container for liquids, with handle and small opening at top

hip flask flask worn attached to belt

hot-water bottle soft rubber container with stopper, used to hold hot water

krater jar with broad body, wide neck, and two handles (ancient Greece)

lota brass or copper water vessel (India)

magnum wine bottle that holds 2/5 gallon (1.52 l)

olla large earthenware jug with wide mouth and looped handles, used as water container or stewpot (Spain)

phial small, sealed glass container, used esp. to hold medicine; vial

pocket flask small flask carried in pocket

potiche vase or jar made of porcelain with rounded body that narrows at top

rehoboam oversize champagne bottle holding 5 quarts (4.73 l)

stoup flagon or tankard

tankard tall, one-handled vessel, esp. of pewter, often with hinged cover, used for drinking

thermos vacuum bottle

vacuum bottle tall, cylindrical container, usu. of metal or plastic, with glass or stainless steel vacuum liner and tightfitting lid, used for maintaining liquids at original temperature for several hours; thermos

vial phial

Cases, Boxes, and Bags

ammunition box container used to store firearm ammunition

ark orig. covered basket or small chest

backpack lightweight canvas or nylon sack, often on frame, used to carry objects on back while walking

bag flexible, pouchlike container that may be closed, used to hold, store, or carry objects

bin box, frame, or enclosure used for storage

bindle bundle that contains clothes and cooking utensils

boot leather case used to carry rifle; *Chiefly Brit.* trunk of automobile

box rigid, usu. rectangular container used to store or carry nonliquid articles

bridget leather pouch or pack carried on back

bundle package, usu. bound

bunker large bin, esp. one used to store ship's coal or oil

caddie bag bag used to carry golf clubs

caisson ammunition box; watertight enclosure used for underwater construction

capsule small gelatin shell, used esp. to enclose medicine

card case small rectangular receptacle used to carry business cards

carton cardboard box

case usu. flat box or receptacle that closes, used to store, ship, or carry objects

casket small ornamental chest; coffin

cedar chest large box made of cedar, used for protective storage of woolen items

chest storage box with lid, often with lock

coffer strongbox

coffin long, heavy box used for burial of corpse; casket

cone hollow, conical-shaped, baked cookie that holds scoop of ice cream

crate large, wood-framed container used for shipping wares

crib framework enclosure, esp. for animal or baby

diplomatic pouch sealed mail pouch, used to carry communications between diplomatic offices

dispatch box oblong box or case with lock, used to carry written dispatches

envelope flat paper container with gummed sealing flap

file metal or wooden cabinet used to organize stored papers for easy reference

file folder light, cardboard, folded cover or large envelope, used to hold loose papers stored in a file

folio case or folder that holds loose papers, often tied with ribbon

footlocker small, flat trunk with lock, esp. one that stands at foot of bunk in army barracks

golf bag bag used to carry golf clubs and balls

gunny sack loose burlap bag

holdall soft traveling bag

holster leather pistol case, open at the top, worn on belt or under one arm

hope chest box used to store young woman's collection of clothing and linen in anticipation of marriage

housewife pocketsize bag or roll of cloth that holds thread, needles, and scissors

hussy *Slang.* housewife

kit round, wood or metal shipping container with tapered sides

kit bag rectangular leather traveling bag with straps and sides that open

letter file file or file folder used for correspondence

locker usu. metal storage case, often built into wall

mail pouch large reinforced envelope in which objects are sent through mails

matchbox small wood or cardboard box that holds matches

moneybag cloth sack used by banks to store and transport money

money box metal box with lock, used to store money

monstrance receptacle holding consecrated host for veneration by Catholics; ostensorium

nesting box one of a series of boxes in graduated sizes that may be stored within one another

net mesh of interwoven threads or ropes, used esp. to catch birds, fish, or insects

nose bag canvas bag that covers horse's muzzle and ties at top of head, used for feeding

ostensorium monstrance

pack bundle arranged for ease in carrying, esp. on back

package small or moderately sized bundle, usu. wrapped

packet small bundle, parcel, or thin package

packing case wooden shipping crate used for bulk goods

packsack leather or canvas backpack

parcel wrapped or tied bundle; package

pillbox small case that holds pills, usu. carried on person

pod protective pouch or removable housing

portfolio large flat case with handle, used to carry papers or drawings without folding them

pouch sack or satchel of moderate size, used to store or transport goods

powder box heavy case, usu. metal, used to store gunpowder

quiver long, thin, cylindrical case, open at one end, used to carry arrows

rack framework on which bulky loads are arranged for carrying

reliquary casket or container used to exhibit relics

sack soft, large, usu. oblong bag

sarcophagus stone coffin with sculpture, placed in a church, tomb, or vault

satchel small bag, often with shoulder strap

scabbard leather or metal sheath that encloses blade of sword or dagger when not in use

scrip small bag or wallet carried by pilgrim or shepherd

sheath tightfitting rigid case for sword or dagger

skippet small box that covers and preserves seal for documents

sleeping bag large, warmly padded bag in which to sleep outdoors

socket opening or hollow that forms receptacle for something

strongbox solid chest or case used to store money or valuables; coffer

tea chest square wooden case lined with lead or tin, used for shipping tea

till money drawer behind counter in store or bank

tinderbox metal box that holds tinder, flint, and steel used in striking spark

trunk luggage with rigid frame, usu. too large to carry by hand, used for transporting clothes and personal items; enclosed storage compartment of car

vanity bag small case or handbag used to hold or transport toilet articles

vanity case rigid vanity bag

vasculum metal, cylindrical, or flat box with lengthwise cover, used for collecting plants

wallet flat, folding leather case, used esp. for holding paper money

wineskin bag of animal skin, used to hold wine

Baskets

basket container made of interwoven cane, rushes, or strips of wood, open at top

bassinet small basketlike crib for infant, hooded at one end

breadbasket low basket, usu. of straw, used to hold and serve bread on table

bushelbasket round receptacle with capacity of 32 dry quarts (35.24 l)

clothesbasket oval basket used to hold and carry household laundry

clothes hamper wooden or plastic receptacle with lid, used to hold soiled laundry

corbeil sculptured basket of fruit or flowers, used as architectural ornament

creel wickerwork basket used to carry fish and fishing tackle

dosser pannier

flower basket wickerwork basket that holds or displays cut flowers

frail basket made of rushes, used for shipping figs or raisins

fruit basket basket that holds and displays fruit

hamper basket with lid, used for storage or to send food or other items; clothes hamper

mocock birch bark food basket (Algonquian Indian)

pannier wicker basket used to carry loads on back, often used in pairs when carried by pack animal or over rear wheel of bicycle; dosser

punnet *Chiefly Brit.* small fruit basket, often made of cardboard

reed basket basket woven of reeds

rush basket basket woven of rushes

scuttle shallow wood or wicker basket, used to carry or move loose substances

sewing basket small hamper used to store threads, needles, and thimbles

skep rough farm basket of twisted straw

splint basket rectangular basket of woven splints, with handle

stave basket basket formed of wood strips

trug coarse basket of wood strips, used to carry vegetables or flowers

wash basket often oval basket used to hold and carry household laundry

wastebasket small, open basket for discarded papers

wastepaper basket wastebasket

wicker basket basket of small flexible twigs

wooden basket basket of wood strips

WEAPONS AND ARMAMENTS
Blades, Clubs, and Projectiles
Guns and Firearms
Firearm Parts, Accessories, and Processes
Bombs, Mines, and Explosives

See also: *Chap. 5: Tools and Hardware; Chap. 11: War and Military; Chap. 17: Hunting and Fishing; Chap. 24: Crime; Chap. 24: Violence*

Blades, Clubs, and Projectiles

anlace tapering medieval dagger

arbalest crossbow

archery weaponry of bows and arrows

armguard band of leather or other material worn about wrist or forearm for protection and support, esp. while using bow

arrow pointed shaft, shot from bow

arrowhead wedge-shaped stone or metal striking end of arrow

assegai slender iron-tipped wood spear (southern Africa)

atlatl spear or throwing stick (ancient Mexico)

ax short, heavy blade affixed to long handle

axe ax

backsword single-edged sword

ballista crossbow; device used to hurl large missiles (ancient Rome)

banderilla decorated barbed dart, used in bullfights

barb sharp backward-extending projection on arrow

barlow sturdy inexpensive jackknife

barong broad-bladed knife or sword (Philippines)

bastinado cudgel

bat stout stick or club

baton cudgel, truncheon

battering ram heavy beam used to beat down fortifications

battle-ax ax with heavy curved blade

bayonet short dagger; blade fitted on end of rifle

bilbo sword

billy club bludgeon

blackjack leather-covered club with flexible handle; cosh

blade flat, pointed, usu. sharp-edged piercing or slashing part of sword or knife

blowgun tube or pipe through which air is blown to propel dart or other missile; blowpipe; blowtube

blowpipe any of various blowguns used throughout Southeast Asia, on Malay Peninsula, and Indonesia: balasan, kahuk, kina, pocot, pucuna, sumpitan, tulup, zarabatana

blowtube blowgun

bludgeon club with thick, heavy striking end

bola two or more stones or iron balls at ends of cord, hurled at target (Latin America)

bolo knife long heavy single-edged knife, used for hacking

bolt missile or shaft shot from catapult; crossbow arrow, shorter than longbow arrow

bombard late-medieval cannon that hurled large stones

boomerang club bent at angle, thrown in arc; throwing stick (Australia)

bow curved, flexible frame used to propel arrow

bow and arrow curved, flexible frame fitted with arrow that is launched by spring tension

bowie knife foot-long straight blade with slightly curved point

brass knuckles metal piece fitted over fingers at knuckles

brickbat hurled piece of brick

broad arrow arrow with flat barbed head

broadsword broad-bladed sword

butt shaft target arrow without barbs

catapult ancient tension-powered device that hurled stones or other missiles

clasp knife pocketknife with one large, folding blade held open by catch

claymore large, two-edged, two-hand sword (Scotland)

cleaver butcher's heavy chopping knife, often with wood handle

club heavy stick or staff

cosh *Brit. slang.* blackjack

crossbow bow set horizontally on rigid stock or brace, used to fire arrows or bolts

cudgel heavy short stick or club

curtalax cutlass

cutlass short curved sword; curtalax

dagger weapon with short, straight, pointed blade attached to handle

dart short slender pointed missile, often ejected from blowpipe

dirk dagger

dudgeon dagger with handle of dudgeon wood

elastic gun cross between rifle and crossbow, having riflelike body and crossbow firing mechanism

elephant ax heavy, sturdy ax hurled at big game, such as elephants

epee sharp-pointed sword with three-sided blade; fencing sword

falchion broad-bladed, slightly curved medieval sword

flail swinging bar attached to long handle, used in close combat

flick-knife *Chiefly Brit.* switchblade

foil blunt or button-pointed fencing sword with four-sided blade

gladius short double-edged sword (ancient Rome)

grip handle or clasp portion of sword or knife

halberd long-handled, broad-bladed sword; pikestaff with axlike blade and spike

handguard lateral, protective piece dividing grip from blade of sword or knife

hanger light saber, often used by sailors (17th-18th c.)

harpoon large spear with barbed head

harpoon gun small cannon used to fire harpoons

hatchet ax with heavy hammer-shaped head

hilt handle of sword or knife

hunting knife large knife with stout blade, used for skinning and cutting up game

hunting sword short, light saber with slightly curved blade (18th c.)

Irish confetti *Derogatory slang.* rocks used for stoning

jackknife small knife with folding blade

javelin light spear thrown long distances

kard knife with straight blade and no handguard (Southeast Asia)

katana samurai sword (Japan)

kirpan small dagger worn by orthodox Sikhs

knife any small sharp-edged blade attached to handle

knobkerrie short wooden club with heavy round knob at one end, used hand-to-hand or hurled (southern Africa)

kris dagger with two scalloped edges and serpentine blade (Indonesia)

kukri short curved sword of Gurkhas with broad blade that is sharp on its concave side (India, Nepal)

kuttar short dagger with handle consisting of two parallel bars joined by crosspiece (India)

lance long, spearlike, sharp-headed weapon

Lochaber ax pole with long ax head and hook attached (Scotland)

longbow large wooden bow, drawn by hand

mace spiked heavy club, usu. metal

machete large, broad-bladed knife

mangonel medieval device for hurling stones, darts, or other missiles

maul heavy club with metal-studded head

misericord thin-bladed dagger

nulla-nulla Aboriginal hunting club or cudgel (Australia)

nunchaku two hardwood sticks joined at ends by short length of cord or chain (Japan)

onager heavy catapult

panga large, broad-bladed knife used as a weapon or like a machete to cut jungle growth (Africa)

parang short sword, cleaver, or machete (Malaysia)

parazonium dagger (ancient Greece)

partisan shafted weapon having spear blade as head with pair of curved lobes at its base (16th-17th c.)

pikestaff long shaft with pointed metal head

pilum long, heavy spear (ancient Rome)

pocketknife small knife with folding blade

pogamoggan flat curved club with knobbed head or stone fastened at one end (American Indian)

point sharpened forepart of arrow, sword, knife, or spear

poleax battle-ax, esp. one with hook opposite blade

pommel knob on hilt of sword

poniard dagger with slender blade of triangular or square cross-section

projectile object fired or thrown through air, often long and pointed

punji stake sharp bamboo stake hidden in high grass to gash feet and legs of enemy, often coated with excrement so as to cause infection

puntilla small, sturdy dagger used to sever bull's spinal cord in bullfight

quarterstaff long stout staff wielded with two hands

quiver sheath or long container for arrows

rapier straight double-edged sword

saber long curved sword

sap small club cut from sapling tree

scabbard sheath for sword, knife, or bayonet

scimitar saber with sharply curved single-edged blade

scythe long curved blade fastened at angle to long handle

shaft long pole forming body of weapon, as spear

sheath protective case for blade

shillelagh cudgel

shiv *Slang.* knife or blade

skean dhu small knife tucked into top of stocking in full Scottish Highland dress

sling device for hurling stones, consisting of short strap with long cords at each end, operated by placing stone in strap, which is then whirled until one cord is released to project the stone

slingshot forked handheld bow used to launch stones or other projectiles

slung shot stone or chunk of metal fastened to strap or chain

smallsword light tapering sword for thrusting, formerly used in dueling and fencing

snickersnee large knife used in cut-and-thrust fighting

spatha blunt-pointed sword (ancient Rome)

spear sharply bladed head mounted on long shaft

spike sharp-pointed piece of metal set with its point outward or upward

spontoon spear with crossbar at base of pointed blade on shaft (17th-18th c.)

staff club, lance, or spear

stave club, cudgel, or staff

stick crude wooden club

stiletto short dagger with thick blade

Swiss army knife *Trademark.* pocketknife with multiple, folding attachments

switchblade knife with folding blade that springs open; flick-knife

sword any long, bladed, pointed weapon

throwing stick short, straight, or curved stick with hand grip, used for hunting in preliterate societies; *Australian.* boomerang

Toledo sword of fine-tempered steel (Spain)

tomahawk lightweight ax; combination pipe and ax (American Indian)

trebuchet medieval sling for hurling missiles

trench knife short knife for stabbing in close combat, sometimes equipped with brass knuckles as handguard

trident three-pronged spear, used for fishing

truncheon club, cudgel; spontoon

twibill double-edged battle-ax

two-handed sword heavy broad-bladed sword swung with both hands on hilt

waddy heavy, tapered wooden war club (Australian Aborigine)

war club crude club-shaped implement (American Indian)

woomera wooden rod with notched end, used to propel spear or projectile (Australian Aborigine)

yataghan long saber with doubly curved blade (Turkey)

Guns and Firearms

ack-ack *Brit. slang.* antiaircraft gun

air gun air rifle

air rifle firearm powered by compressed air; air gun; toy rifle

AK-47 automatic rifle

antiaircraft gun firearm used against attack by airplanes

arms weapons, esp. firearms

assault rifle usu. automatic rifle firing high-powered ammunition, often having pistol grip and long, detachable magazine

autoloader semiautomatic weapon, either gas-operated or recoil-operated

automatic rifle firearm that loads, fires, and ejects cartridges automatically while user depresses trigger

basilisk large, early cannon capable of firing a stone shot weighing 200 pounds (90.7 kg)

bazooka shoulder-fired rocket launcher

BB gun firearm that shoots small-sized shot, designated BB

Big Bertha *Informal.* large-bore cannon used by Germans (World War I)

blunderbuss short, old-fashioned, highly inaccurate firearm

Bofors gun usu. double-barreled, 40 mm automatic antiaircraft gun

bolt-action rifle firearm with hand-operated bolt as breechblock that unlocks to eject empty case and seals new cartridge in bolt assembly

bombard medieval cannon that threw stone balls

break-action basic single-shot shotgun

breechloader firearm loaded with cartridges at its rear or breech

Bren gun .303 caliber, gas-operated, clip-fed submachine gun

Browning automatic rifle .30 caliber, gas-operated, magazine-fed automatic rifle (World War II)

Browning machine gun .30 or .50 caliber, recoil-operated machine gun, fed by cartridge belt (World War II)

burp gun *Slang.* small submachine gun

cannon gun; large firearm mounted in place, firing explosive charges

cap gun toy pistol with paper holding very small explosive

carbine lightweight rifle of short overall length

carronade short, light iron cannon (Scotland, 18th c.)

chassepot bolt-action rifle that fires paper cartridges

chokebore shotgun with bore that narrows toward muzzle

Colt *Trademark.* brand of revolver

culverin early musket or long cannon (16th-17th c.)

derringer large caliber, very short-barreled pocket pistol

double-barreled shotgun double-action shotgun with two barrels, either side by side or over-and-under, often with two triggers

elephant gun very large caliber gun, .410 caliber or greater, used for hunting heavy, often dangerous game such as elephant, rhinoceros, lion, or Cape buffalo

Enfield rifle muzzle-loading .577 caliber rifle used by British in Crimean War; .30 caliber rifle used by U.S. troops (World War I)

falcon light cannon (15th-17th c.)

field gun gun mounted on wheels, used on field of war

firearm weapon that uses explosive charge to fire projectile at high speed

firelock gun having lock in which priming is ignited by sparks struck from flint and steel

flamethrower mounted or portable device that sprays ignited incendiary fuel at some distance

flintlock gun with old-fashioned firearm lock, esp. musket

forty-five .45 caliber pistol

forty-four .44 caliber pistol

fusil light flintlock musket

Gatling gun early, mounted machine gun with revolving cluster of barrels

gun any weapon consisting of metal tube (barrel) from which projectile (bullet or shell) is discharged by force of explosive

handgun small, handheld firearm; pistol; revolver

harpoon gun mechanism used to fire harpoon

harquebus primitive, heavy matchlock or wheel-lock firearm (15th c.)

heater *Slang.* pistol

Henry .44 caliber, lever-action repeating rifle holding 16 rounds (U.S., 1860's)

howitzer lightweight, short cannon that fires charges with curved trajectory

jingal large musket fired from support, often mounted on carriage, formerly used in India and China

lever-action rifle early repeating firearm in which ejection of shell case and recocking are accomplished by hand-operated lever arm near trigger

Long Tom large, long-range gun mounted on ship's deck; towed 155 mm cannon (World War II)

Luger *Trademark.* brand of automatic 9 mm caliber pistol

M-1 .30 caliber, gas-operated, clip-fed semiautomatic rifle (World War II)

M-14 7.62 mm gas-operated, magazine-fed automatic rifle

M-16 5.56 mm gas-operated, magazine-fed automatic rifle (1960's)

machine gun firearm that automatically loads and discharges cartridges for sustained periods

machine pistol fully automatic pistol; submachine gun

magazine gun repeater

magnum firearm using cartridges equipped with extra-large charge

matchlock firearm with old-fashioned slow-match mechanism as gunlock, esp. musket or handgun

mitrailleuse breechloading machine gun with several barrels

mortar short cannon

musket old-fashioned firearm with long barrel and smooth bore

muzzleloader firearm loaded through front end or muzzle by pouring powder in and stuffing rag patch down barrel

over-and-under double-action shotgun with barrels placed one above the other

pepperbox pistol with five or six revolving barrels (18th c.)

percussion gun firearm with percussion lock fired by detonation of cap that is struck by hammer

petronel large-caliber firearm that fired with butt resting against chest (15th-17th c.)

piece gun

pistol small handheld firearm; handgun

pompom automatic antiaircraft cannon of 20 mm to 40 mm, esp. mounted on ships in pairs

popgun toy gun

pump-action (*adj*) designating manually-operated repeating shotgun or rifle; slide-action

pump gun firearm operated by pumping action that advances new cartridges

recoilless rifle firearm without rebound motion from firing

recoil-operated rifle firearm that utilizes kickback movement of parts to operate action

repeater rapid-firing, small firearm; magazine gun

revolver small firearm with revolving chamber for cartridges; handgun; pistol

rifle firearm having long bore cut with spiral interior grooves that spin and thus stabilize bullet's flight, usu. fired from shoulder

rocket launcher tube used to fire rocket shells; bazooka

rod *Slang.* pistol, revolver

roscoe *Slang.* gun

Saturday night special *Informal.* cheap, easily obtained handgun

sawed-off shotgun smoothbore firearm with barrel cut off to scatter shot more widely

scattergun shotgun

self-loading firearm semiautomatic weapon

semiautomatic weapon firearm that automatically ejects cartridges and reloads after each firing, activated by successive squeezing of trigger; autoloader

serpentine cannon of various calibers (15th-17th c.)

Sharps single-shot, lever-action breechloader, used by U.S. military and buffalo hunters (mid-19th c.)

shotgun smoothbore firearm, often double-barreled

side arm handgun; pistol; revolver; weapon worn at side in holster or in belt

side-by-side double-action shotgun with barrels placed side by side

siege gun field gun

single-action (adj) designating firearm that requires cocking of hammer before firing each shot

six-gun six-shooter

six-shooter six-chambered revolver; six-gun

slide-action (adj) designating rifle or shotgun with mechanism that ejects shell case and cocks and reloads firearm when slid back and forth quickly; pump-action

small arm handheld firearm

Springfield rifle .30 caliber, bolt-action repeating rifle (World War I)

Sten gun light submachine gun (Britain)

stern chaser cannon mounted at stern of sailing ship, facing aft

Stinger shoulder-fired antiaircraft missile that uses infrared guidance

stun gun battery-powered, handheld firearm that discharges nonlethal cartridges, darts, or electric charges to immobilize its target

submachine gun portable automatic firearm, fired from shoulder or hip; machine pistol

submarine gun firearm designed to function underwater

swivel gun gun mounted on pedestal or on wall so that it can be turned vertically or horizontally

10-gauge shotgun using shells of 2 cm diameter

thirty-eight .38 caliber handgun

thirty-thirty .30 caliber rifle that fires cartridge with thirty-grain powder charge

thirty-two .32 caliber handgun

Thompson submachine gun .45 caliber submachine gun with magazine, pistol grip, and detachable buttstock; Tommy gun

Tommy gun Thompson submachine gun

trench gun portable cannon or mortar fired from trenches in warfare

twenty-two .22 caliber firearm

Uzi short, 9 mm submachine gun

Winchester rifle Trademark. any rifle made by Winchester Arms Company, esp. magazine rifle of 19th c.

zip gun crude, homemade gun that fires real bullets

Firearm Parts, Accessories, and Processes

accuracy measure of variation in group of shots or how close shot is to target

action mechanism by which firearm is operated

ammo Informal. ammunition

ammunition bullets, grenades, or bombs; explosive projectile fired from weapon; munitions

armaments weapons, military equipment

armory repository of arms

arsenal place of manufacture and storage of arms

artillery mounted missile-launching or projectile-firing weapons, esp. larger cannon, guns, and catapults

ball any of various spherical or conical projectiles or missiles

ballistics science and study of projectile motion; study and development of missile weapons

barrel tube of gun, through which bullet fires

bead careful aim

bird shot shot with diameter of less than 1/10 inch

black powder explosive powder containing saltpeter, sulfur, and charcoal, esp. for sporting guns

blank cartridge without projectile

blast explosive charge; explosion

bolt breech closure of gun that controls opening of bore

bore cylindrical, hollow part of gun barrel, usu. longer than it is wide; caliber measure

breech part of firearm at rear of bore

buckshot large-sized lead shot of .24 to .33 inches diameter, used in shotgun shells carrying nine to fifteen of such pellets

bullet small projectile discharged from firearm at great speed

bullet drop description of descending trajectory of bullet in flight, requiring that sightline be set above target depending on range

butt buttstock

buttstock shoulder end of firearm at rear of breech mechanism

caliber diameter of firearm bore; diameter of bullet

canister case of small projectiles to be fired at once from cannon; case shot

cannonball round, solid missile fired from cannon

cap explosive paper or metallic cap, used to ignite larger charge

cartridge cylindrical casing, usu. of brass, that holds primer, powder charge, and bullet

cartridge belt strap with loops that hold cartridges, worn around waist or over shoulder

cartridge case cylindrical, powder-holding element of cartridge

case shot canister

chamber firearm compartment that holds cartridge

chape metal mounting of scabbard or sheath of knife

charge (vb) load a weapon; (n) amount of powder or shot used to load weapon; load

choke narrowing of bore near muzzle of shotgun to concentrate shot pellets leaving muzzle; device that regulates muzzle constriction on shotgun

cleaning rod long rod, often with wire brush at one end, used to clean barrel of rifle

clip clasp that holds bullets to be fed into firearm chamber

cock hammer; (vb) pull back and set hammer prior to firing

conventional weapons nonnuclear weapons

cradle part of gun carriage on which recoiling gun slides

detonator device, esp. small amount of explosive, used to set off larger explosive

double-O buck common shotgun buckshot, used esp. for hunting deer

drop at heel term for measurement of shotgun length

elevation angle at which a weapon, esp. an artillery piece, points away from horizontal plane

engines of war military weapons

firing pin plunger in firing mechanism that strikes cartridge primer, thus igniting charge

flint gunflint

flintlock old-fashioned firearm lock that ignites powder charge when hammer holding a flint strikes spark from metal

front sight sight nearest muzzle of firearm

fuse flammable wick or tube made of combustible substance, used to ignite explosive

gas substance dispersed through atmosphere as poison, irritant, or asphyxiant

gas-operated (adj) using some of exhaust gases to operate action

gauge unit of measure of internal diameter, or bore, of shotgun barrel, 12 gauge being equal to approximately 3/4 inch (19 mm)

grapeshot cast-iron balls formerly used as cannon charge

grenade launcher device attached to muzzle of rifle that permits firing of rifle grenades

group series of shots on target, esp. pattern thus formed and span between centers of widest shots in group

gunflint small flint that produces spark, formerly used in firearm ignition

gunlock firearm mechanism that ignites charge: flintlock, matchlock, percussion lock, or wheel lock

gunpowder explosive chemical mixture used to propel firearm projectile

gunstock usu. wooden frame brace supporting firing mechanism and barrel of rifle or machine gun; stock

hair trigger sensitive firearm trigger

hammer firearm part that strikes firing mechanism of gunlock; cock

hasty sling method of inserting arm in sling to facilitate rapid firing of rifle

holster leather case for pistol, opening at top, usu. worn on belt

home (*vb*) proceed toward specified target, esp. under control of automatic guidance mechanism

jacket metal outer casing of bullet

load charge; single cartridge with bullet and powder; (*vb*) fill weapon with cartridges

loaded (*adj*) containing ammunition or explosive charge

lock gunlock

magazine sometimes removable or reloadable storage receptacle that holds extra cartridges in repeating rifles and shotguns; military storehouse for arms and ammunition

magnum (*adj*) designating a cartridge equipped with larger charge than other cartridges of comparable size; (*n*) firearm thus equipped

matchlock old form of gunlock in which priming is ignited by slow match

Minié ball bullet with cylindrical body, conical head, and hollow base (19th c.)

munitions ammunition; military equipment

mustard gas oily liquid used as chemical weapon

muzzle fore end of firearm barrel, point of departure for bullet

muzzle energy impact energy of bullet at muzzle velocity, expressed in foot-pounds

muzzle velocity speed of projectile as it leaves muzzle of gun, usu. expressed in feet or meters per second

open sight rear sight of firearm, consisting of notch in which gunner aligns front sight on target

ordnance large firearms; military supplies, esp. weapons, ammunition, and artillery

pan depressed part of lock that holds priming in older firearms

patch greased or moistened cloth formerly used as wadding for rifle ball; cloth used to clean bore of firearm

payload size of weapon's explosive charge

peep sight plate with small hole through which gunner makes sighting

pellet piece of shot

percussion lock lock of gun fired by percussive impact

pin metal peg that, when removed, activates fuse that detonates grenade

pistol grip handle, esp. of rifle, shaped like butt of pistol

plug single shot

powder gunpowder

primer cap or cylinder holding compound that may be exploded by percussion or other means, used for firing charge of powder

propellant explosive substance used to force projectile out of firearm barrel

range finder instrument used to determine distance to target

rear sight sight nearest breech of firearm

recoil distance through which a weapon moves backward after discharging

recoil pad cushion placed against shoulder to absorb jolt of recoil on high-powered rifles

reloading making one's own cartridge from shell casing, powder, primer, and bullet

rifling system of spiral grooves cut into gun barrel; process of cutting such grooves

round unit of ammunition equal to one shot

saddle scabbard sheath attached to horse saddle for storage of rifle

safety device on gun that prevents inadvertent firing

scope telescopic sight

set trigger trigger that can be adjusted to set pressure required to pull it; on some rifles with pair of triggers, the one set to very light touch

shell cylindrical casing that holds firearm charge; bullet, cartridge, or torpedo shell

shot lead pellets discharged from firearm: bird shot, buckshot, grapeshot

shrapnel cartridge filled with bursting charge; fragments from exploding charge

side lock method of discharging rifle in which hammer and percussion mechanism are on side of firearm rather than in line with barrel

sight mechanical or optical device used to guide aim of firearm; (*vb*) visually direct or aim firearm

sight in (*vb*) adjust sights to strike target at selected range

silencer attachment to muzzle of firearm that muffles noise

sling leather strap attached to fore and butt end of rifle, used to carry rifle on shoulder and esp. to steady aimed rifle when arm is placed through sling loop

slug bullet

smokeless powder any of various substitutes for ordinary gunpowder that emit little or no smoke, esp. one made of guncotton

smoothbore (*adj*) having a grooveless, unrifled bore

soft point bullet with point made of lead, not steel, which deforms as it enters object

spitzer pointed bullet

star shell shell that bursts in air and produces a bright light to illuminate enemy positions

stock gunstock

tampion protective plug placed in muzzle of firearm when not in use

target practice shooting at targets to test or improve accuracy in one's use of firearms

telescopic sight firearm aiming device equipped with magnifying lens; scope

tracer bullet that emits trail of smoke or luminous gas

trigger mechanism pulled by finger to fire gun

trunnion projection on either side of cannon, used to support it on its carriage

wad soft plug used to retain powder charge in muzzleloading gun

wheel lock obsolete gunlock in which revolving wheel strikes flint to make spark

windage degree to which gunsight must be adjusted to correct for deflection of projectile by wind

Bombs, Mines, and Explosives

ABM antiballistic missile

A-bomb atomic bomb

aerial bomb large explosive device dropped from airplane, esp. with parachute to slow descent

antiballistic missile ABM; missile designed to intercept and destroy ballistic missiles

antimissile missile ballistic missile designed to detect and destroy missiles in flight

antipersonnel bomb bomb that produces shrapnel designed to damage persons more than property

ashcan *Slang.* depth charge

atomic bomb immensely powerful bomb that utilizes nuclear fission reaction; A-bomb

ballistic missile unmanned military rocket with warhead

blockbuster aerial bomb that contains high explosives

bomb highly explosive charge thrown at or dropped on target

buzz bomb V-1 rocket

castrator mine explosive that detonates at crotch level

cherry bomb powerful, globular firecracker

claymore mine antipersonnel mine that produces fan-shaped fragment pattern

cluster numerous bombs dropped simultaneously over target and its immediate surroundings

cluster bomb canister that can be dropped from aircraft and opens to release large number of fragmentation explosives over wide area

demolition bomb bomb with powerfully destructive explosive charge

depth charge explosive charge detonated underwater against submarines

dynamite safe-handling, solid explosive that contains nitroglycerin, used esp. in mining, quarrying, and engineering

dynamite bomb explosive charge of dynamite or nitroglycerin embedded in stabilizing material

explosive substance that can blow up or detonate; weapon containing such a substance

fireball grenade, bomb

firebomb explosive device with incendiary effects

firecracker paper cylinder holding weak, noisy explosive and fuse, used in displays and celebrations, not as weapon

fission bomb bomb detonated by atomic fission reaction; atomic bomb

floating mine explosive charge used on water surface against ships

fragmentation bomb charge that detonates into many shrapnel fragments

fougasse mine attached to missile, stone, or launched object

fuel-air explosive explosive that achieves

powerful, concussive blast effect by releasing and detonating highly volatile fuels in the air, used on troops in bunkers or tunnels and to clear mine fields

fusion bomb bomb detonated by atomic fusion reaction; hydrogen bomb

gas bomb bomb that contains poison or chemical gas

grenade missile or container with charge of explosive or chemical gas, launched or hand-thrown

ground mine land mine

hand grenade explosive device hurled by hand

H-bomb hydrogen bomb

hydrogen bomb immensely powerful bomb that utilizes atomic fusion reaction; H-bomb

ICBM intercontinental ballistic missile; supersonic missile with range of at least 3500 nautical miles (6500 km), usu. with thermonuclear warhead

incendiary bomb bomb that sets target on fire

intercontinental ballistic missile ICBM

land mine explosive charge shallowly buried underground, detonated by pressure from person or vehicle; ground mine

mine explosive charge in container buried underground or placed in sea, detonated by contact

MIRV multiple independently targetable reentry vehicle; missile with two or more warheads aimed at separate targets

missile projectile with explosive charge, launched through air toward target

Molotov cocktail homemade bomb consisting of gasoline-filled bottle ignited by rag in bottle neck

napalm incendiary bomb consisting of aluminum soaps in jelling gas

neutron bomb nuclear bomb that kills by radiation, with detonation that is destructive to persons but not property

nitroglycerin oily, highly explosive liquid

nuclear bomb violently explosive bomb with power derived from splitting nuclei of heavy chemical elements such as uranium or plutonium

nuke *Informal.* nuclear or thermonuclear bomb

Patriot U.S. antiaircraft missile with range of 37 miles (60 km), launched from a tracked vehicle with computer guidance, also effective against low-flying missiles

petard encased explosive charge attached to wall or gate

pineapple *Slang.* hand grenade

pipe bomb homemade or primitive bomb made with explosive charge inserted into lead pipe

plastic explosive puttylike substance holding and concealing explosive charge, detonated by fuse or remote control

plutonium bomb atomic fission bomb in which plutonium is bombarded by neutrons to produce explosive chain reaction

pressure mine explosive charge detonated by pressure

report loud noise of explosion

robot bomb rocket-propelled, gyroscopically steered bomb equipped with wings and control surfaces

rocket explosive charge inside missile

rocket bomb small bomb on missile fired by rocket launcher

SAM surface-to-air missile

Scud medium-range Soviet tactical missile with 200 pound (90 kg) warhead for surface-to-surface attacks

Sidewinder short-range, air-to-air missile that homes in on heat of target aircraft's engine exhaust

smart bomb *Slang.* steerable air-to-surface bomb guided to its target by television or laser beam

smoke bomb explosive charge yielding large amount of smoke

sonic mine explosive charge used in water against ships, activated by sound waves

stink bomb chemical charge that detonates to produce foul odor

submarine mine underwater mine that floats at predetermined depth

surface-to-air missile SAM; rocket launched from ground or water surface, aimed at aerial target

tear gas bomb grenade filled with chemical that causes extreme eye irritation

thermonuclear bomb bomb that utilizes nuclear fusion reaction; hydrogen bomb

time bomb explosive charge set to detonate at prearranged moment

TNT trinitrotoluene; highly explosive chemical used as charge in bombs

torpedo explosive underwater projectile

TOW tube-launched optically-guided wire-tracked missile; short-range antitank missile that trails thin wire

V-1 rocket pilotless, jet-powered plane with explosive warhead, used by Germans in World War II; buzz bomb

V-2 rocket early rocket with explosive charge, used by Germans in World War II

warhead front section of torpedo, missile, shell, or bomb, containing explosive charge

ELECTRICITY AND ELECTRONICS

See also: *Chap. 4: Physics; Chap. 5: Machinery and Fabrication; Telecommunications; Computers; Chap. 7: Furnishings; Chap. 15: Popular Music; Television and Radio*

AC alternating current

accumulator storage cell or battery of storage cells

alternating current AC; current that periodically changes direction at certain levels, measured in volts; current from wall socket

alternator electrical generator that produces alternating current

ammeter instrument that measures electric current in amps

ammonium chloride white crystalline salt used in dry cells

amp ampere; *Informal.* amplifier

ampere unit of electric current produced by one volt acting through one ohm, equal to one coulomb per second; amp

Ampere's law electric current and changing electric field create a magnetic field

amplidyne direct-current generator that magnifies small power input to create large power output

amplifier device or circuit that increases voltage or current of an input signal

amplitude maximum deviation of AC current from its average value during its cycle; peak value of waveform

analog (*adj*) designating electronic process in which data is represented by physical quantities that correspond to the variables involved

anion negative ion drawn to anode in electrolyzed solution

anode positive terminal of electrolytic cell; negative terminal of storage battery

arc luminous bridge formed between electrodes or across gap in circuit

arc lamp light in which current passes between electrodes through pressurized gas

argon colorless, odorless, inactive gas used to fill electric bulbs and lamps

armature wound rotor in generator that transforms electric current in coil into mechanical motion

attenuator device that reduces amplitude of signal with minimal distortion

ballast device used to maintain current in circuit by varying resistance in response to changes in voltage

band specific range of wavelengths or frequencies

band-pass filter filter that amplifies frequencies in specific range and reduces all others

battery number of primary or secondary cells that work together to produce flow of electric charge

blackout period of darkness due to electric power failure

bombardment stream of particles against surface, such as electrons against TV screen

boost (*vb*) raise voltage through circuit

bridge network configuration in which no two elements are in series or parallel; two-branch instrument that measures unknown impedance by balancing ratio of voltages in each branch to a known ratio

brownout enforced reduction of electric power usage

bulb rounded glass housing for filament of incandescent lamp

bus common path for multiple connections

cable strands of electrical conductor insulated from each other and laid together, often twisted around central core

capacitance measure of capacitor's ability to store a charge

capacitor device that accumulates and holds a charge of electricity; condenser

carbon carbon rod used in arc lamp

cathode negative electrode that emits stream of electrons and attracts positive ions in electrolytic cell; positive terminal of storage battery

cathode-ray tube CRT; heated filament that emits electron beam that can be controlled by externally applied potentials to produce luminous effect when electrons hit screen, as in a television or computer

cation positively charged ion drawn to cathode in electrolysis

cell housing for electrodes and electrolyte, used to generate electricity or in electrolysis

cesium alkali metal used in photoelectric cells; most electropositive element known

charge basis of electric energy, manifested in current, voltage, and electric field as positive or negative element that attracts unlike and repels like charged bodies

chip tiny electronic integrated circuit; microchip

circuit continuous path along which current flows: generator, resistors, conductors, other elements

circuit breaker switch that automatically interrupts electric circuit under abnormal conditions to prevent harmful, excessive current

clip waveform distortion due to excess level in circuit; something that attaches a wire to another element

coaxial cable insulated cable with two conductors, central signal line, and outer shield, used to transmit telephone, telegraph, and television signals

coil copper wire wound around solid object, used to produce electromagnetic effect and conduct current; inductor

commutator device for changing frequency or direction of a current

condenser capacitor that accumulates and holds a charge

conductance reciprocal of resistance, measured in mho units

conductivity capacity of a substance to conduct electric current

conductor material, esp. metal, through which electrons can flow as electric current

contact connection of touching but not soldered electric conductors, usu. metal

controlled source voltage or current source controlled by another circuit property

converter mechanical device that changes the form of electric energy or converts the frequency of radio signals

copper wire good conductor used in coils and wiring

core middle part of coil or solenoid, often a metal rod

coulomb quantity of charge transferred by one ampere in one second between two points in circuit

coupling connection of two electric circuits by part common to both; interaction of circuit elements

CRT cathode-ray tube

cryotron device based on fact that changing magnetic field causes superconductive element to oscillate between low and high resistance

current rate of flow of electric charge through solid or liquid, measured in amperes

DC direct current

depolarizer substance added to electrolyte to prevent polarization and remove gas deposits at electrodes

diamagnetic (*adj*) designating materials in which induced current field opposes applied magnetic field

dielectric (*adj*) designating insulating material for opposing electrical fields, esp. between plates in capacitors

digital (*adj*) designating an electronic process that defines frequencies and other data as discrete, binary bits of information

diode solid-state device or tube with anode and cathode that rectifies AC and allows current to pass freely in one direction only

dipole two equal but opposite charges held a small distance apart

direct current DC; current that flows in one direction only and has virtually invariable magnitude; current produced by a battery

discharge conversion of stored energy into electric energy

discharge tube glass vessel in which current passes from anode to cathode through a high vacuum

doping process in which impurities are added to semiconductors to control conductivity

dry cell battery one or more cells that work together in an ammonium chloride paste instead of a solution

dynamo *Chiefly Brit.* small direct-current generator

electric (*adj*) describing any device that uses or produces a charge of electricity

electrician specialist in the installation, maintenance, and repair of electrical equipment

electricity physical agency caused by movement of electrons and other charged particles, manifested as attraction, repulsion, light, and heat

electrode wire, rod, or plate that conducts electric current into or out of any device

electrolysis passage of current through electrolyte with migration of charged ions to like-charged electrodes

electrolyte conducting medium in which flow of current leads to movement of charged ions

electrolytic cell housing in which electrolysis occurs

electromagnet coil with soft iron core that acts as magnet when current flows through it

electromagnetism interaction of electricity and magnetism, esp. magnetic effects produced by currents

electromotion mechanical motion produced by electricity

electromotive force EMF; potential difference, expressed in volts, between terminals of a source of electric energy

electron negatively charged particle in all atoms that is basis of electricity

electronics branch of physics dealing with the emission and flow of electrons and the application of the energy produced to various devices

electron tube vacuum tube that controls passage of current through it by variations in grid potential; thermionic valve

electrostatic (*adj*) describing effects caused by charges at rest, such as electric charge on object

EMF electromotive force

extension cord long electric cord fitted with plug at one end and receptacle at other

farad unit of capacitance equal to one coulomb per volt

faraday quantity of electricity transferred in electrolysis and electric flux

ferromagnetic (*adj*) designating materials that retain magnetism

field region of space containing lines of force with direction and strength

filament thin, conductive heating element, usu. wire in vacuum tube, that produces light in light bulb

filter device that selectively damps or suppresses certain oscillations and frequencies while not affecting others

flex wire that bends to any shape to make connections, covered with insulating material such as rubber

flux field lines of direction and strength

flux density number of field lines per unit area

frequency number of complete oscillations per unit time of an electromagnetic wave or alternating current

fuse safety device that breaks circuit if current is too great, usu. a piece of wire that melts

gain ratio of increase in output over input in amplifier

galvanometer instrument used for comparative measurement of small currents in units other than amperes

gamma ray shortest wavelength of electromagnetic radiation

gauss basic unit of flux density; magnetic induction equal to magnetic flux density necessary to move electromotive force along wire at specific speed

generator machine used to transform mechanical energy into electric energy through electromagnetism

gilbert unit of magnetomotive force equal to 0.7958 ampere-turns

grid element that controls electron flow between anode and cathode in tube

ground large conductor connected to electric circuit as general return point; connection to such a body; circuit reference point at which potential is zero

heating element low resistance wire that heats when current flows through it

henry unit of inductance in which a variation of one ampere per second produces an induced electromotive force of one volt

IC integrated circuit

impedance total resistance to AC flow in circuit, combining resistance, inductance, and capacitance

induced current current that flows in coil moved in magnetic field

inductance flux in magnetic field caused by changing current in electric circuit or device, inducing voltage in that circuit or a nearby circuit

induction process by which electrification, magnetization, or electromotive force is produced in bodies and circuits through proximity to charge or field

inductor loop or loops of conducting material that produces oriented magnetic field when current is passed through it; coil

infrared rays electromagnetic waves with wavelengths longer than those of red light in visible spectrum

input impedance total opposition to AC by circuit, measured in ohms

insulation material that prevents current from escaping or entering where it is not wanted, used esp. to separate conductors

insulator material that prevents flow of current, including most nonmetals and gases

integrated circuit IC; electronic circuit conducted on single semiconductor wafer or microchip

intensity rate at which a wave transports energy across a unit area

inverter device that converts direct current into alternating current

ion electrically charged atom or group of atoms that results from loss or gain of one or more electrons by neutral atom

ionization conversion of atoms into positively or negatively charged particles

jack connecting device in circuit into which plug is inserted

laser light amplification by stimulated emission of radiation; device that excites atoms to higher energy levels in order to generate intense, coherent beam of light from electromagnetic radiation

lead common electrical conductor, usu. insulated, used esp. to connect wires to test instrument

load object of power delivery in circuit

local action effect caused by impurities in zinc plate of primary cell, making it less efficient

loop continuous current path

magnetic field condition of space in vicinity of magnetic substance or current-carrying body, in which forces can be found

magnetomotive force force that gives rise to magnetic flux

maser microwave amplification by stimulated emission of radiation; laser that functions only in microwave region of spectrum

maxwell unit of magnetic flux per square centimeter in which magnetic induction is one gauss

microchip chip

microphone device that transforms sound waves into current by use of vibrating diaphragm

microwave electromagnetic radiation with wavelength between infrared and radio waves

modulation alteration in waveform frequency or amplitude due to superimposition of another wave or signal

motor device that transforms electric energy into mechanical energy, esp. one that produces motion by means of coil of wire around armature turning between poles of a magnet

moving coil instrument that uses motion of coil in magnetic field

mutual inductance interactive inductance between inductive circuit elements

node network or circuit junction

ohm unit of resistance in circuit when potential difference of one volt produces current of one amp between two points

Ohm's law the ratio of voltage to current in a circuit is equal to the resistance

open circuit discontinuous circuit in which current cannot flow

oscillator wave generator

oscilloscope instrument that uses cathode ray tube to display waveform images of periodic changes in voltage or current

outlet electric receptacle that leads to power source, into which electric devices are plugged

parallel circuit circuit in which positive and negative terminals connect to two distinct points, with voltage applied equally throughout

paramagnetic (adj) designating materials that have slight magnetic susceptibility

Paschen's law breakdown of voltage between electrodes in a gas is product of distance and pressure

patchbay patchboard

patchboard central jackfield that connects all elements in circuit configuration; patchbay

patchcord insulated connector in patchboard

period time required for one waveform cycle to be completed; inverse of frequency

phase shift time difference between waveforms

phasor diagram that illustrates phase and amplitude relations in AC circuits

photoelectric cell cell whose electrical properties are modified by illumination by light waves

piezoelectricity production of electric current in certain crystals through deformation by mechanical stress

pile several disks of two dissimilar metals stacked in alternating series and separated by pads of cloth or paper moistened with an electrolyte, used to produce current

plate positive anode toward which electrons are attracted in tube

plug fitting inserted into receptacle to establish contact connection in circuit

polarization effect produced when simple primary cell produces current; deposits of gas on plate that increase cell resistance during electrolysis

potential work needed to bring unit of positive charge from distance to given point

potential difference difference in electric force between any two points in circuit, with current flowing from high to low level

potentiometer variable resistor directly controlled by dial, knob, or lever

power time rate of electric energy in device or circuit, measured in watts

power cord insulated electric cord with specific current and material ratings, used as power supply line

power supply source of current and voltage

primary cell nonrechargeable device that produces flow of electric charge by means of chemical reaction of two different metals in acid

probe sensing device with lead tip, used for testing equipment

raceway tube used to protect electric wiring

radio use of electromagnetic waves to send message from microphone to receiver

radio wave longest wavelength of electromagnetic radiation

reactance impedance of AC circuit due to capacitance or inductance, expressed in ohms

receiver device that transforms electromagnetic radiation signals into electric current and voltage

rectifier device used to change AC to DC

regulator automatic device used to maintain current or voltage in circuit

relay device that uses small current to control greater current in another circuit by electromagnetic switching

resistance force that opposes flow of current through a conductor, measured in ohms; reciprocal of conductance

resistor passive circuit component that exhibits relatively constant resistance to current flow at all frequencies at same temperature

resonance peak frequency response characteristic of AC-driven circuit

resonator hollow enclosure of conductor resonated by certain frequencies of electromagnetic radiation

rheostat device that regulates current by means of adjustable resistors

rotor part of generator that turns

sawtooth wave serrated waveform with one slope steeper than the other

schematic standardized diagram of circuit

secondary cell device that produces current by chemical reaction, rechargeable by passing current in opposite direction from discharge; storage cell

semiconductor any of class of materials with

conductivity near that of conductor at high temperatures and nearly absent at low

series circuit circuit with all parts connected in sequence so that same current flows through each part

short circuit abnormal condition caused by direct connection between points of low resistance on circuit, usu. resulting in bypass or break due to excess flow of current

signal flow impulse transmitted through circuit or network

sine wave waveform that represents periodic oscillations with same representation as sine curve

socket receptacle for plug or screw-in devices

solenoid coil with length very much greater than its diameter that acts as magnet when current passes through it; simple polar magnet equally magnetized along its full length

solid-state (*adj*) designating electronic device that utilizes properties of semiconductor materials, not electron tubes

spark instantaneous appearance of light and sound in electrostatic discharge of very short duration

speaker transducer that changes electric energy into sound waves

spectrometer instrument used to measure spectral wavelengths

square wave waveform that changes direction at right angle

static disturbance of radio or television reception by natural, atmospheric, or electrical phenomena

stator stationary part of generator

steady state long-term continuous circuit condition

step-up/step-down process in transformers that increases or decreases voltage depending upon turn ratio

storage cell secondary cell

superconductivity ability of certain metals to conduct current without resistance at very low temperatures

surge control multiple outlet plug that provides transient protection from sudden increases in current in electronic devices

switch device used to join or break parts of circuit, thus permitting or preventing flow of current

target surface at which stream of particles is directed

terminal point of current entry or departure from circuit; metal nut on screw or other mechanical device that connects wire to another apparatus

tetrode vacuum tube with four electrodes, a plate, two grids, and a cathode

thermionic valve *Chiefly Brit.* electron tube

thermistor semiconductor device that exhibits negative coefficient of resistance with temperature

thermocouple electric circuit composed of two

dissimilar metals joined at different temperatures

thermoelectric (*adj*) describing production of electric current directly from heat

thermopile instrument with thermocouples connected in series behind cone, used to detect heat radiation and produce thermoelectric current

tracer device that follows current through circuit to locate trouble

transducer device that receives power from one system and supplies power in a different form to another system, usu. by converting physical quantity into electrical quantity

transformer two coils of wire on same core that induce AC transfer from one circuit to another at same frequency

transient (*adj*) designating an instantaneous peak

transistor small block of semiconductor with three terminals that acts like a vacuum tube in solid-state electronic devices

transmission emission of electromagnetic waves and their passage from one location to another

transmitter device that sends electromagnetic waves

triode three-electrode tube with negative grid between anode and cathode, used to increase voltage

tube device that controls passage of current through it by variation in grid potential, named for number of its electrodes: diode, triode, or tetrode

tuner device for receiving AM, FM, and shortwave radio signals

turn ratio ratio of number of turns of wire in primary and secondary windings of transformer

turns number of loops of wire in coil

tweeter small speaker that operates most efficiently at high frequencies

ultraviolet rays electromagnetic waves with wavelengths shorter than those of violet in visible spectrum

vacuum tube sealed glass bulb used to amplify, detect, or rectify AC to generate electrical oscillations, composed of plate, grid, and triode; electron tube; valve

valve *Chiefly Brit.* vacuum tube

variable resistor resistor whose resistance can be changed when contact slides around a length of wire

volt unit of potential difference between two points of conductor with constant one ampere current when one watt of power is dissipated between them

voltage measure of volts in a circuit, or energy per unit charge

voltaic cell two electrodes made from different metals in solution, used to produce electromotive force by chemical action

voltmeter instrument used to measure electromotive force or potential difference in volts

watt unit of power equal to one joule per second or one ampere flowing across potential difference of one volt

wave progressive disturbance or variation that propagates energy from point to point in a medium; undulating or jagged representation of this action

waveform repeating pattern of wave shape

wavelength distance along wave between points of same phase

weber practical unit of magnetic flux, equal to one volt second or 10^8 maxwells

Wheatstone bridge test instrument that joins two branches of circuit to measure resistance by comparing it with a known resistance

winding wire wound around armature to act as coil

woofer large speaker that operates most efficiently at low frequencies

X-ray electromagnetic radiation of extremely short wavelength that penetrates solid bodies, acts like light on photographic film and plates, and ionizes gases

TELECOMMUNICATIONS
Data Transmission
Voice Transmission and Telephony

See also: *Chap. 5: Electricity and Electronics; Computers; Chap. 15: Cinema; Television and Radio*

Data Transmission

AT command set the standard commands for controlling modems

bandwidth smallest range of frequencies within which certain signal can be transmitted

baud unit of measure of speed at which information is transmitted in number of signal impulses or bits per second

broadband type of data transmission in which a single medium carries several separate signals at once

bulletin board service accessed by modem, permitting users to leave, store, and retrieve messages

bus topology network architecture in which all devices are connected to a central cable

cable telegram; (*vb*) send a telegram

cablegram message transmitted by underwater cable

CCITT **C**omité **C**onsultatif **I**nternational **T**éléphonique et **T**élégraphique, organization that sets standards for international data communications via modem, fax, and e-mail

channel hardware device or path that transfers data between two elements of system

coaxial cable high-frequency telecommunications transmission line made up of insulated central conductor surrounded by conductive material that protects central conductor from interference

communications network interlocking system

of lines, circuits, and organizations for telecommunications

communications satellite artificial satellite used in radio, telephone, and television transmission by means of reflection or amplification and retransmission of signals between Earth stations

continental code international Morse code

converter device for changing electric energy or data from one form to another

cybernation automatic, computer control of a process or operation

cybernetics science of communication and information theory, esp. automatic control and regulation of communication between humans and machines; information theory

dash telegraph signal of longer duration than dot, used in combination to represent letters in Morse code

data transfer rate speed at which information moves between two devices, measured in bits per second or bauds

data transmission sending of information, usu. in digital form, by coded electrical impulses

day letter low-priority telegram to be delivered on following day

dedicated line phone or other communication line devoted to one device, such as a fax machine

demodulation conversion of alternating carrier wave or current into direct, pulsating current equivalent to transmitted data signal, esp. by modem; detection

detection demodulation

dish satellite dish

dot telegraph signal of shorter duration than dash, used in combination to represent letters in Morse code

duplex (*adj*) designating a telecommunications system capable of simultaneous transmission of messages in opposite directions on one channel

Earth station terminal equipped to receive from, and sometimes to transmit to, communications satellite

electronic communications telecommunications

electronic mail message system using telecommunications network lines between computers; E-mail

E-mail electronic mail

Ethernet standard protocol for local area networks, using bus topology

facsimile method or device for reproducing graphic material in permanent form and transmitting it over telephone line; fax; phototelegraphy

fax facsimile

fax modem device combining the functions of a fax and modem on one board or unit

fiber optics branch of optics that deals with thin, transparent, flexible glass or plastic fibers used for high-speed, clear transmission of signals carrying masses of data along their length

full duplex communication mode in which data can be transmitted and received simultaneously

half duplex communication mode in which data can be sent in only one direction at a time

hardware electronic systems and devices used in telecommunications

Hayes-compatible (*adj*) designating a modem that utilizes the control commands of Hayes modems, the industry standard

hub central connection base for distribution of data to networked computers

Kermit file-transfer protocol for data transmission over phone lines via modem

information theory mathematical theory concerned with statistical analysis of information and communications between humans and machines; cybernetics

Intelsat *International Telecommunications Satellite* organization; global communications satellite network

interface meeting place of systems and means by which communication occurs there

interference imperfect or distorted signal reception, esp. due to stray or unwanted signals

international Morse code form of Morse code used in international telegraphy; continental code

ISDN integrated services digital network; digital transmission of voice and data simultaneously over several channels on one line

jack electrical device into which plug fits to make connection

kilobaud one thousand bits per second

link one element of telecommunications system or network

log on (*vb*) enter code or password to access telecommunications network

modem *modulator/demodulator*; device for converting and transmitting or receiving digital computer signals over telephone lines linking computer to network or to another computer

modulate (*vb*) vary amplitude, frequency, phase, or intensity of carrier wave in accordance with signal wave of much lower frequency

Morse code code system of long and short sounds or dots and dashes used in transmitting telegraph signals

multiplex telecommunications system capable of simultaneous transmission of multiple signals over single channel

network service for electronic distribution of data to subscribers

night letter reduced-rate telegram sent in evening and delivered on following day

node one individual site on a network, as for a computer or printer

packet switching efficient data transmission system in which initial message is broken into relatively small units that are sent independently and subsequently reassembled

phototelegraphy facsimile

plug electrical device that fits into jack to make connection

radiophotograph graphic image transmitted by radio waves

radiotelegram message transmitted by radiotelegraphy

radiotelegraph telegraph in which messages or signals are sent by radio waves rather than through wires or cables

remote device that controls communications system without direct wire connection

ring topology network architecture in which each device is connected to two others, the entire network forming a closed loop

satellite dish transmitter or receiving antenna in wide, concave, often round shape

signal sound or data conveyed over telephone or telegraph line, radio link, or optical fiber

star topology network architecture in which all devices are connected to a central hub

stock ticker device for electronic transmission of stock prices from stock exchange receivers in brokerages and banks

switch device for establishing, breaking, or altering electrical connections in circuit

switching connecting, disconnecting, and redirecting of signals over network

technetronic (*adj*) pertaining to, shaped, or influenced by technological changes in society such as telecommunications and computers

telecommunications all forms of electromagnetic transmission and reception of data, sounds, and images; electronic communications

telecommuting working at home at computer terminal linked to another site, as by modem

telefacsimile facsimile

telefoto *Informal*. Telephoto

telegram message sent by telegraph

telegraph device that transmits messages by sending signals by electronic impulses through wire or by conversion to radio waves

telegraph cable insulated wires over which telegraph transmissions are sent

telegraph codes characters represented as groups of electrical pulses during telegraph transmission

telegraph line suspended wires carrying telegraph transmissions

telegraph operator person who types out coded messages in Morse code for telegraph transmission

telegraphy construction and operation of telegraph systems

Telephoto *Trademark*. apparatus for electronic transmittal of photographs

teleprinter device that types out material received as electrical impulses over communications system

teleshopping electronic shopping via videotex

Teletype *Trademark*. automatic printer connected to communications line

teletypewriter TTY; form of telegraph in which typewriter keys produce electrical impulses conveyed to receiving unit

telex *teleprinter exchange;* service using teletypewriter to send and receive information

terminal originating or receiving point for signals in telecommunications system

ticker telegraphic receiver that prints messages on paper tape

time-out (*vb*) disconnect automatically from a remote connection because of lack of input

token-ring network closed-loop computer network in which computers exchange data tagged with a special bit pattern (token)

topology the basic shape or architecture of a local-area network

TTY *teletypewriter*

twisted-pair cable type of network cable using two insulated copper wires, as in a phone cable

Unifax *Trademark.* UPI wire service

uplink transmission path from Earth station to communications satellite

upload transmit data from a computer to a network, bulletin board, etc.

videotex system for transmission of data over telephone lines for display on video terminals

WAN *wide-area network,* linking computers that are geographically distant from each other

Western Union *Trademark.* national telegraph service company

wire telegram; (*vb*) send a telegram

wireless telegraphy without use of wires

Wirephoto *Trademark.* photograph transmitted by Telephoto equipment, esp. for use in newspapers

wire service press association news wire that transmits news dispatches via Teletype to radio, TV, and newspapers, esp. Associated Press, United Press International, and Reuters

Voice Transmission and Telephony

access ability to connect to line, circuit, or exchange, usu. denoting long-distance company's connection to local telephone company

American Telephone & Telegraph *Trademark.* AT&T; largest U.S. phone service company

answering machine electronic device that answers unattended phone and tapes incoming message

answering service service in which calls are picked up and messages taken by attendant when called party is unable to answer phone

area code prefix to phone number, specifying region in U.S. or Canada to which call is being made

AT&T American Telephone & Telegraph

auto-dial service feature whereby call is made automatically in response to pressing of single, preprogrammed button

available line telephone number not in use and obtainable by new customer

Baby Bells *Slang.* regional telephone companies formed out of breakup of Ma Bell, or AT&T

bad connection telephone transmission with distortion or interference

beeper device carried to alert bearer that phone call has been received at home or office; pager

buried cable underground telephone lines, esp. in large city

business office central administrative office handling customer billing, complaints, and service calls

business phone multiextension telephone for use in offices

busy signal standard, repeating tone indicating that telephone line is engaged

busy verification operator check to determine that busy line is actually being used and not out of order

buzz (*vb*) *Informal.* place phone call to someone

cable insulated assembly of copper wire or fiberglass strands for transmission of telephone signals or data

call (*vb*) attempt to contact another by telephone; (*n*) message delivered or contact made by telephone

call box *Chiefly Brit.* outdoor phone for calling police or fire department; public telephone booth

caller ID telephone service that allows subscriber to identify caller, whose telephone number is displayed on a small screen, before answering call

call forwarding automatic transfer of incoming calls to another telephone line on which called party can be reached

calling card credit card with individualized customer number for billing calls to home or business phone when call is placed from another location

calling party person placing telephone call

call waiting system in which a tone alerts user that another incoming call is on line and allows user to switch from one call to another on a single line

car phone cellular or other radiotelephone installed in automobile

cellular phone mobile radiotelephone connected to computer-controlled communications system divided into small cells, each with its own transmitter; cell phone

central local telephone operator who had to be contacted to place call prior to introduction of direct dialing

channel frequency bandwidth suitable for two-way telephone communication

circuit two-way communications path

coin call call placed from public or pay phone by insertion of coin

coin-operated (*adj*) describing public telephone requiring insertion of coin to place call

collect call operator-assisted call in which charges are paid by receiving party

conference call multiparty call requiring simultaneous connection of three or more telephone lines; teleconference

cordless phone mobile phone connected without wiring to base station that is connected by wire to standard telephone outlet

cradle part of telephone instrument in which handset rests when not in use

crossed lines electronic failure in which calls overlap, connect improperly, or otherwise interfere with each other

cross talk interference due to unintentional linkage to another communications channel

custom calling phone company designation for special services, such as call waiting or call forwarding, available at extra cost

custom local-area signaling service highly sophisticated custom calling service, esp. for businesses

dead (*adj*) having no dial tone on the line; nonfunctioning

desk telephone standard telephone instrument designed to rest on flat surface

dial usu. disk-shaped device on face of telephone instrument used to indicate number being called, now usu. replaced by keypad on touch-tone phone; (*vb*) place a call by using such a device

dial-a- designation used as prefix by businesses offering service or product over the phone (as: dial-a-prayer)

Dial One service selection of long distance company to provide service automatically accessed by dialing 1 prior to number

dial tone buzz heard when functioning phone receiver is lifted

Dictograph *Trademark.* device with highly sensitive transmitter, used for secretly listening to or recording conversations

direct dialing placing call without operator assistance, esp. long distance call

direct line number with direct access to called party at one of several extensions on same line without first going through general line answered by receptionist

directory book listing all residential and business telephone numbers in region or district

directory assistance assistance obtained by contacting special operator, usu. by dialing 411, to provide number that cannot be found in directory

directory listing individual or business entry listing name, address, and telephone number

disconnect breaking off of call due to electronic problem or intentional action to halt telephone service, usu. for nonpayment of bill

disconnect notice official telephone company warning that service will be discontinued on specific date, usu. due to nonpayment of bill

800 number special area code for numbers that permit calls without charge to calling party

emergency number special, often three-digit, number for use in emergency or to summon help

exchange central telephone office where local lines are connected and area served by it

extension one of several extra telephones connected to a single incoming line, often with its own number

field telephone early cellular telephone for military and business use

flat-rate service untimed service

foreign exchange central receiving station for all international calls to specific foreign country or region; any exchange outside local calling area

411 standard three-digit code for local directory assistance

handset telephone mouthpiece transmitter and earpiece receiver mounted on handle

hang up (*vb*) replace telephone receiver in cradle, terminating call; do this abruptly while caller is speaking

headset earphone receiver and microphone transmitter for telephone mounted on attachment fitting onto head, used instead of handset

hold status on multiline phone in which call is removed from auditory circuit and caller waits without being disconnected

hold the line instruction to wait and not hang up

home wiring circuitry providing access from single residential phone to company line

hookup assembly and connection of parts linking single phone line to circuit or network

horn *Informal.* telephone

hot line direct line between two phones always kept open for instant access without dialing

information former term for directory assistance

installation process of activating single phone or phone system and connecting it to network

instrument single telephone with internal circuitry, bell, transmitter, mouthpiece, receiver, earpiece, and housing

intercom simple, two-way, short-range communication system with microphone and loudspeaker at each end

international call telephone call to location outside nation of origin

international country code routing code that directs call to correct nation without operator assistance

international dialing prefix three-digit code, usu. 011, giving caller access to international connection

interrupt service service that allows operator to cut in on call in emergency

key individual dialing button on touch-tone phone; switch that opens or closes communications circuit, moving from one line to another

keypad grid of numbered, lettered buttons used to indicate number being called on touch-tone phone

LATA local access and transport area; one of 161 local telephone calling areas established after breakup of AT&T; calls from one LATA to another are long distance

life line reduced rate telephone service for low-income customers in many states

line telephone wiring that connects individual, local, and national systems; single telephone connection

line charge cost of operating line to residence or business, usu. assessed monthly

lineman telephone repairman responsible for maintenance of aboveground lines strung between telephone poles

listing single entry of name, address, and telephone number in directory

local access and transport area LATA

local call call placed to phone within immediate area, usu. at no additional cost

local loop local line from business or residential phone to closest telephone company switch

local network telephone system handling calls in one city or region, usu. connected to larger network

long distance telephone service beyond local area, billed for timed toll

Ma Bell *Slang.* interlocking, national telephone company and system, formerly operated by AT&T

memory phone telephone instrument equipped with programmable memory that holds frequently dialed numbers accessed by punching a single key

message rate charge determined by time of day, distance, and duration of call

mobile call call placed from radiotelephone such as cellular phone

modular equipment standardized, interchangeable instruments, wiring, and jacks for easy removal and connection

mouthpiece end of handset containing microphone

network large, interconnected system of communications lines, central exchanges, and processing computers

network interface point at which network connects with individual line or system

900 number special area code for numbers that charge a fee to the caller, used in marketing, public opinion surveys, and sales

911 emergency number for police, fire, or ambulance

nonpublished listing telephone number not printed in directory at customer's request, also not revealed by directory assistance; unlisted number

not in service designating telephone line that has been disconnected or is not functioning properly

off-premises extension connection of telephone line and number to second location

operator person who controls routing, connection, and disconnection of calls through telephone switchboard

operator-assisted call call placed through operator rather than by direct dialing

pager beeper

party line shared telephone circuit that connects two or more customers to exchange

pay phone telephone in public place requiring coin deposit or credit card number for use

PBX private branch exchange; telephone system that functions within one business or building

PCS personal communications service

personal communications service PCS; any of a wide variety of proposed low-power, low-cost, mobile radiotelephones, representing an inexpensive alternative to cellular phones having fewer features

person-to-person (*adj*) designating operator-assisted call connected only to person designated by calling party

phone telephone instrument; (*vb*) place a telephone call

phone book directory of names, addresses, and phone numbers for specified area; telephone directory

phone booth small cubicle, generally with sliding door and often located outdoors, from which public may place coin-operated or credit card calls; telephone booth

Picturephone *Trademark.* device that combines telephone with television screen, enabling users to see each other, used briefly in 1960's

PIN personal identification number; computerized code used in placing credit card calls

prefix first three digits of seven-digit telephone number, often indicating location of line and exchange

private line telephone line intended for exclusive use of one person, family, or organization

public telephone telephone located in public place, operated by coin or credit card

push-button phone phone on which push-button keys bear numbers and letters used in placing a call

radiotelephone telephone in which communication is carried on through radio waves only

random noise unpredictable noise and interference in circuit

RBocs regional Bell operating companies; collective term for the Baby Bells (pronounced "ARE-BOX")

receiver portion of telephone equipment that converts incoming electrical signals into auditory sound waves

reverse charges charge toll for call to receiving party

right of privacy government-guaranteed right to freedom from interference with or eavesdropping on personal phone calls

ring bell-like tone generated by telephone to indicate incoming call; (*vb*) *Chiefly Brit.* place a phone call

ring off (*vb*) *Chiefly Brit.* hang up

ring up (*vb*) *Chiefly Brit.* place call

rotary phone traditional phone on which numbers and letters are arranged in circle beneath dial, which is rotated to indicate number being called

scramble (*vb*) alter signal to make it unintelligible without special unscrambling device

service installation, repair, maintenance, billing, and call-placing operations of telephone company

service call call to repairman to come to home or business to investigate and remedy problem with service

service charge basic monthly telephone company fee for use of system

service order request for service from phone company

service rep *Informal.* phone company employee who handles service orders, complaints, and installation and disconnect requests

signal sound conveyed over telephone or telegraph line

speakerphone telephone equipped with loudspeaker and microphone so that it can be operated without using handset or headset

speed calling service permitting memory storage of frequently called numbers and quick dialing with one or two digits

station-to-station (*adj*) designating operator-assisted call to anyone answering number dialed or any direct dial call

subscriber customer paying for use of telephone service

surcharge additional charge added to telephone fee

switchboard device for connecting, controlling, and disconnecting multiple phone lines, as in office

tap (*vb*) make secret connection into telephone circuit to eavesdrop on private conversations; wiretap

tariff schedule of rates charged by telephone company

telco *Informal.* local telephone company

teleconference conference call

telephone instrument for converting sound into electrical impulses to be transmitted over distances by wire; (*vb*) communicate by telephone

telephone booth phone booth

telephone box *Chiefly Brit.* phone booth

telephone directory phone book

telephone man one who repairs, installs, and maintains telephone service

telephone number basic seven-digit code by which calls are directed to each phone line

telephone pole tall wooden or metal pole from which telephone lines are suspended

telephone tag repeated unsuccessful attempts by two persons to reach each other by telephone

telephonics science of conveying sound over distances, as by telephone

telephony construction and operation of telephone systems; telecommunications system based on telephone equipment that transmits speech or other sounds between two points, with or without wires

three-way calling service that allows customer to call two other parties and speak to them simultaneously

tie-in linkage between different lines, exchanges, or systems

tie line direct line connecting extensions in two or more PBX systems

time and charges service in which duration and fee information are provided by operator at termination of call

toll fee for telephone call

toll call call requiring payment of fee beyond basic service charge

toll-free (*adj*) requiring no additional fee beyond basic service charge

touch-tone tone-dialing system equipped with push-button keys for indicating number called by transmission of electronic beeps

traffic aggregate of calls handled by telephone company in given time

transmitter device, esp. mouthpiece, for converting sound waves into electrical impulses to be sent by telephone wire

trunk line circuit between two central telephone exchanges for making multiple connections; line from central office to PBX

tympanum diaphragm of telephone

unlisted number nonpublished listing

unscramble (*vb*) make telephonic message comprehensible by tuning receiver to frequencies used in transmission

untimed service telephone service that permits unlimited duration of certain local calls without additional per minute charge; flat-rate service

videoconference teleconference conducted via television equipment

videophone telephone with both audio and video capabilities

voice mail electronic system for recording and storage of voice messages, often in digitized form, for later retrieval by intended recipient

wall phone telephone instrument mounted on wall

WATS Wide Area Telecommunications Service; special fixed-rate, long-distance service for companies making many toll calls, with cost unrelated to number of calls made

white pages alphabetical directory listing names and addresses with residential and business phone numbers in specific area

wiretap act or instance of tapping a telephone so as to eavesdrop on calls made or received; (*vb*) tap

wrong number undesired telephone connection due to dialing of incorrect digits

yellow pages directory listing business names, addresses, and telephone numbers in specific area, organized by category of business

COMPUTERS

General Technology
Hardware and Peripherals
Software, Languages, and Programming
Memory and Data Storage
Internet and World Wide Web

See also: *Chap. 5: Electricity and Electronics;*
Telecommunications; Chap. 11: Publishing and
The Press; Chap. 16: Graphic Design and Printing

General Technology

abort termination of program that returns control to operating system

access code password that allows entry into computer

access time interval required to retrieve information from memory or a disk

A/D conversion from analog signal to digital data

ADP automated data processing

AI artificial intelligence

algorithm predetermined instructions for step-by-step solution to specific problem

alphanumeric (*adj*) consisting of both alphabetic and numeric characters

Alt key used alone or in conjunction with control and/or shift key to change meaning of another key with which it is used

analog signal with continuous range of values, opp. of digital

applications areas or operations of business, art, and technology in which computers are useful

artificial intelligence AI; capacity of machines to exhibit intelligent behavior and perform operations similar to learning and decision making

automated data processing ADP; processing data using computer program or system that reduces human intervention to a minimum

automation science and technology concerned with making self-regulating machines in which electronic devices replace or enhance human control

backup duplicate copy of program or file made as insurance against loss or damage

bar code thin and thick lines alternating in a coded pattern readable by scanner, typically printed on packaging to represent price and other data

batch group of records or transactions that can be processed together

batch processing noninteractive computing mode in which input is gathered into groups or batches and additional input cannot be made once program is being executed

baud unit of measure of speed at which information is transmitted in number of signal impulses or bits per second

BBS bulletin board system

BCD binary coded decimal

bells and whistles *Informal.* unessential, but often attractive, features

binary system in which numbers are represented as sequences of zeros and ones, which is basis of digital computing

binary coded decimal BCD; method of encoding four bits of binary code to represent ten decimal digits

bit vector method of coding information as string of binary choices forming a vector

bomb error message on Macintosh computers indicating a general failure

Boolean (*adj*) describing systems in which variable values are restricted to true and false

boot (*vb*) start up computer by loading operating system

bootstrap set of instructions that begin operation of operating system

branch program statement to control transfer to nonsequential instruction

bug error, esp. in program

bulletin board service, accessed by modem, that permits users to leave, store, and retrieve messages, shareware, and public-domain software

bundling selling hardware and software or several software programs together at set price

burn act of leaving new computer system turned on for several days or more to test for failure of electronic components

bus series of communications channels in which signals are passed, usu. sockets into which components are plugged

CAD computer-aided design; system that uses graphics display to design products

CAI computer-aided instruction; interactive teaching software system

calculator simple computer for arithmetic calculations

capture (*vb*) record and enter data into computer for processing or storage

card printed circuit board or module; punch card used in keypunch encoding of data

CAT computer-assisted tomography; use of computer technology in assembling special X-ray

CCD charge coupled device; semiconductor sequential information storage technology

chad material punched out when holes are made along margins of perforated computer material; any wasted material

channel hardware device or path that transfers data between two elements

character letter, digit, or graphic symbol used to represent data

chip very small piece of silicon processed or burned to form integrated circuit; microchip

chunk conceptual unit of data or information

CISC complex instruction set computer; CPU able to recognize 100 or more instructions, slower and more common than RISC

clear (*vb*) erase stored or displayed data

clock electronic device that controls, measures, and monitors system functions

coaxial cable transmission wire composed of multiple layers of conductor and insulation

cold boot loading sequence in which entire operating system is loaded into computer at start-up or after reset

command coded instruction to computer

compatible (*adj*) able to use same programs or hardware, esp. matched to major brand but manufactured by smaller company

computer-aided design CAD

computer-aided instruction CAI

computer-assisted tomography CAT

computerese argot of computers, their users, and their designers

computer game usu. video game based on computer operations, often with joystick

computer graphics conversion of digital information into visual format for display on terminal or output on printer

computerize (*vb*) equip with or automate by computers

computer literacy nontechnical study and understanding of computers and basic familiarity with their uses in society

computer science study of design and use of computers and software

concatenate (*vb*) sequentially connect independent items

configuration computer and all devices connected to it; collection of set-up choices for software program

control Ctrl, command key that changes meaning of another key with which it is used

control character any keyboard character used as a command

conversational (*adj*) designating computer systems that engage user in two-way dialogue

crash system failure and shutdown due to software or hardware malfunction

cross talk interference between two signals

crunch (*vb*) perform many numerical calculations and manipulations of data

crystal piece of quartz whose piezoelectric vibrations are used to generate timing signals

cursor special character used to denote position on video display, usu. an underline, solid block, or highlight arrow

cyber- combining form connoting computers or virtual reality (cyberspace, cyberart)

cybernation automatic control of a process or operation by computers

cycle time time required by system to complete specific function

D/A conversion from digital data into analog signal such as voltage or sound

data bus set of communications channels that carry data between elements of computer

data entry inputting of information for processing by computer

data management system series of commands used to search and retrieve data and update or reference portions of database

data processing basic computer operations in general

data transfer rate speed at which information moves between two devices, measured in bits per second

debug (*vb*) locate and correct malfunction or error in program code

dedicated (*adj*) designed for specific application or function

delimiter blank space, comma, character, or symbol that indicates beginning or end of character string, word, or data item

desktop publishing DTP; use of personal computer with graphics and typographic layout programs, sometimes an image scanner, and usu. a laser printer to design and create publications

digital signal with two discrete values, zero and one, represented by presence or absence of electric pulse

digital imaging scanning and recording of visual images in digital form

digitizer device that converts images into numeric form comprehensible to computer

DIP dual inline package; standard method of switching integrated circuits, with pins carrying signals to and from circuit

directory table of contents that lists files

documentation written and graphic material describing and explaining use, operation, maintenance, or design of piece of hardware or software

down (*adj*) not operational; said of a computer, network, or system

download (*vb*) transfer programs or files from one computer to another device or computer

downtime interval when computer is inoperable due to malfunction

drag (*vb*) move cursor across screen by sliding mouse

DTP desktop publishing

dump (*vb*) print or display contents of internal storage on output medium, esp. during program failure

dynamic range levels of voltage or analog input signal needed to generate digital output

EDP electronic data processing; outmoded term for computer operations

electronic mail message system that uses telecommunications network links between computers; E-mail

E-mail electronic mail

enable button function on Macintosh screen that is lit up to indicate that it will work when double-clicked on by mouse, with gray indicating it is not enabled

end user person who uses specific hardware or software product

enter key command to perform operation

escape ESC; ASCII control key used in combination with others to provide added functionality, esp. to interrupt command or return to previous level of program

even parity scheme in which eighth bit in ASCII code is used to make sum of eight bits even so that it can be checked for errors

execute (*vb*) perform command or series of commands

execution time interval required to perform operation

exit (*vb*) leave specific context, often to return to system

expert system basis of artificial intelligence that captures information in particular domain through hierarchy of if/then questions

fetch (*vb*) read contents of specific memory location

field unit of data forming part of a record in structured database

FIFO first in, first out; processing of information in order received

fifth generation dawning new era of computer systems that use artificial intelligence and parallel processing by multiple CPUs capable of handling billions of calculations per second

floating point representation of numbers using scientific notation of decimal fraction times power of ten

flow chart symbolic, logical representation of program control

footprint area of desk or floor space occupied by piece of hardware

format (*vb*) prepare disk to receive information; (*n*) organization of data on disk into tracks and sectors

fractal geometrical structure that has regular or uneven shape repeated over all scales of measurement and a dimension that is greater than the spatial dimension of the structure

function key key designated to send specific command code

fuzzy (*adj*) approximate, not precise: used to describe search or operation that generates a set whose members lie across a spectrum of values approximating a central value

generation hardware developed at one period based on previous level of technology

GIGO **g**arbage **i**n, **g**arbage **o**ut; output quality is dependent on input quality

glitch *Slang.* sudden, inexplicable malfunction

graphics use of computer to generate and display images on screen

graphics tablet wire grid in solid base that, when drawn on by stylus, inputs line drawings and graphics to computer

hacker *Slang.* person extremely knowledgeable about computers, frequently an amateur programmer

handshaking synchronization technique used to expedite transfer of data between two devices

hang (*vb*) cause (a computer or application) to lock up

help level portion of menu displayed on screen for user

hexadecimal sixteen-base number system commonly used in computers, employing numerals 0 through 9 and letters A through F

hierarchical (*adj*) describing any vertical, pyramidal organization of information in related levels and sublevels

high resolution video display system or printer that depicts images in great detail with high degree of accuracy

hit useful or informative response to a query or online search

housekeeping administrative functions required for efficient system operation but not contributing to specific task execution

hypermedia combination of computer and hypertext system with CD audio, VCR, or laser disc capabilities

IC **i**ntegrated **c**ircuit

icon graphic representation, esp. of option on computer menu accessed by mouse

IDP **i**ntegrated **d**ata **p**rocessing

image scanner graphics device that brushes over image to enter it entirely on disk without key commands

index hole hole in floppy disk that indicates beginning of first sector of track, used to trigger drive

informatics computer science and the study of information processing

inheritance network hierarchical organization of data for artificial intelligence in which elements in each descending level have characteristics of those in levels above them

input data received by computer from external source

instruction command; single operation to be executed

integrated circuit IC; electronic circuit on single chip of material, usu. silicon; microchip

integrated data processing IDP; processing data by using language common to all machines in system and requiring minimal human intervention

integrated imaging combination of image scanning, graphic, and digital recording techniques

interactive (*adj*) designating any program or system that has a dialogue with human user and responds to input

interactive page layout bidirectional desktop publishing process that establishes page layout

interface hardware and/or software required to connect peripheral to computer system, one computer system to another, or for user's access to system; point at which any two parts of system connect

interrupt signal from I/O device or peripheral to CPU to stop current processing and start new operation

job program and data submitted to computer for execution

joystick mechanical lever used to control cursor movement on video display

jump programming instruction that stops sequential processing and transfers control to another point in program

jumper nonmechanical switch that provides options on circuit board

kerning capacity of certain programs, esp. when printing, to vary spacing between pair of letters, esp. reducing space to create balanced appearance

keypunch outmoded system with keyboard-controlled device that encodes data by punching holes in card

keypunch operator individual who enters data by encoding it on cards punched with holes

keystroke single depression of one key on keyboard

kilobaud one thousand bits per second

kludge *Slang.* inelegant or sloppy but workable solution to problem in software or hardware

label several characters that identify file or storage area

LAN **l**ocal **a**rea **n**etwork; system for linking terminals, PCs, or work stations with each other or with mainframe to share data, peripherals, and programs, usu. in one building

large scale integration LSI; placement of large number of integrated circuits on one silicon chip

leading spacing between lines of type in computer-generated typeset output

LED **l**ight-**e**mitting **d**iode; feedback device permitting current to flow in one direction only

LIFO **l**ast **i**n, **f**irst **o**ut; most recently received information is processed first

light pen photoelectric stylus that sends signals to computer by movement against CRT screen

line drawing two- or three-dimensional graphic representation of objects on video display screen, esp. done with outlines

line feed control key used as return or to advance to next line

line surge sharp fluctuation in AC voltage that can damage computer circuits and magnetic media

load (*vb*) move data or program instructions from storage medium into computer memory for execution

local area network LAN

lock up (*vb*) cease functioning or responding to input

log on (*vb*) enter personal identification data, such as name and/or password, into multiuser system so as to access it

loop set of instructions designed to be repeated

LSI **l**arge **s**cale **i**ntegration

management information system MIS

manual book containing operating instructions and sometimes design specifications for particular piece of hardware or software

massively parallel processing use of thousands of processors acting together to create supercomputer

microchip integrated circuit; chip

MIPS **m**illions of **i**nstructions **p**er **s**econd; measure of processing speed

MIS **m**anagement **i**nformation **s**ystem; software or department in corporation that supports management in keeping track of and running organizations or departments under it

mnemonic programming code or other shortened form that is easy to remember

MOS **m**etallic **o**xide **s**emiconductor; material used to create high-density integrated circuits

mouse small handheld device that is rolled across a surface to point at objects and control cursor movement on video display

multimedia combination of text, graphics, video, animation, voice, and music in computer system using optical disc, videocassette, and compact disc audio

multitasking ability of user to have multiple activities or programs in progress simultaneously

multiuser (*adj*) describing operating system that permits several users to share access to computer

nesting programming technique that employs hierarchical levels of instruction

network set of communications channels that connect computers

neural network basis for advanced artificial intelligence by which computer forms and recognizes patterns, enabling it to reach conclusions not laid out for it by binary architecture

noise random signals, interference, or nonmanaged data

null cycle time required to scroll through entire program without introducing new data

number crunching repetitive, arithmetic-intensive processing

OCR optical character recognition

octal (*adj*) of or pertaining to an eight-base number system, sometimes used to encode data, employing numerals 0 through 7

odd parity scheme in which eighth bit in ASCII code is used to make sum of eight bits odd so that it can be checked for errors

off-line (*adj*) designating equipment not directly linked to central computer or CPU

on-line (*adj*) designating equipment directly linked to central computer or CPU

on-screen (*adj*) designating data displayed on video terminal

opening menu initial set of options that appear when program is loaded

operand data unit or equipment item operated upon

operator user of computer system

optical character recognition OCR, process that optically scans printed text and converts it into machine-readable code

optical reader wand mechanical device that reads bar codes

output result of computer operation, usu. in form of hard copy or video display

override instruction that stops execution of previous command

palette complete range of colors available for display through computer graphics card

parallel processing data processing by multiple CPUs acting simultaneously

parameter definable characteristic or limit of system or program

parity error-detecting technique using eighth bit; odd parity or even parity

parity bit eighth bit in ASCII code that becomes zero or one to make sum of all eight bits even or odd as a data check

password code or sequence of characters used to protect system or specific file from unauthorized use

patch piece of program code inserted to debug or modify existing program

pico one thousandth of a billionth; one trillionth

pixel single dot and smallest element in visual display; square picture unit that is basis of computer graphics

plotter device used to make drawing on video display

poke program operation that loads specified value into specific memory location

power down orderly shutdown of computer and peripherals

power supply device that converts AC line voltage into DC voltage, used by computer

power surge sudden, dangerous fluctuation in AC voltage

power-up orderly start-up of computer and peripherals

procedure logical set of program commands called by single name

program counter CPU register storing address of next instruction to be fetched from memory for execution

prompt character displayed on terminal that indicates that computer is awaiting further instructions from user, often also identifying logged drive

protocol set of rules governing information exchange

pseudobus computer designed with all connective devices on single board and sockets for adding modules

quad density storage density of some disk media

queue FIFO-organized sequence of items awaiting processing or action by peripheral

QWERTY designation for traditional typewriter keyboard layout, named after six letters at upper left

read (*vb*) receive data into memory

readout manner in which computer presents processed information, such as visual display or line printer

real time actual time required for computer operations involving rapid analysis of data, esp. as it affects a physical process

reboot (*vb*) restart (a computer) by resetting or powering down and back up

record group of related fields forming unit of information in structured database

recursion repeated application of algorithm to define function or make calculation

refresh (*vb*) update a screen display to show current status

relational (*adj*) describing development of database as large matrix

response time interval between input of data and computer output or response

RISC reduced instruction set computer; computer designed with chip that eliminates all but minimum number of instructions needed to perform most common tasks, providing increased processing speed

robotics control by computer of machine programmed to perform industrial or other tasks

rollover keyboard ability that allows rapid typing yet codes characters in order struck

run single, continuous execution of program by computer

seek time time required to move disk read/write head to specific track

semiconductor material that can be manipulated to improve its conductivity for the passage of electrons, esp. silicon used for integrated circuits

sentinel tag

serial access obtaining data sequentially by searching through all preceding data on that file or program

serial processing computer operations in which programs are run sequentially, not simultaneously

Silicon Valley area in northern California, south of San Francisco in the Santa Clara valley region, with concentration of semiconductor and computer companies

silicon wafer thin silicon disk used to make chips

smoke test checkout of new equipment

solenoid device that converts electric current into linear motion by magnetizing hollow coil

spikes sharp, temporary fluctuations in signal or voltage

SPOOL simultaneous peripheral operations on-line; technique that allows I/O operation of peripheral device such as printer while simultaneously executing another program

stepper motor rotating motor used to move read/write heads on floppy disk drives

string ordered sequence of data elements, usu. characters, treated as a unit

stylus light pen; scanning device used for input on graphics tablet

support personnel, documentation, or programs that complement hardware or software technology

surge control device that protects system from AC power surges

sysop *Informal. system operator;* operator of bulletin board

systems analysis examination of operations in order to improve them or determine how to accomplish specific goals

tag indicator of beginning or end of unit of information; sentinel

technical support assistance offered by vendor of hardware or software to end user, usu. by telephone or through bulletin board

telecommuting working at home at computer terminal linked to another site, as by modem

terminate (*vb*) exit from program and usu. return to opening menu

throughput measure of system's execution efficiency in instructions per second

timesharing sharing of CPU by several users at once for different purposes through buffers and switching

toggle on/off switch with two positions that initiates or halts function

tree structure hierarchical organization of data for efficient search and retrieval

turnaround time interval needed to provide answer to question or execute task

tweak (*vb*) *Slang.* make fine adjustments to

unbundling pricing of system's hardware and software separately

universal product code UPC; machine-readable bar code used for labeling merchandise

up (*adj*) functioning properly

UPC **u**niversal **p**roduct **c**ode

user individual who accesses a computer system

user-friendly (*adj*) easy for user to understand and execute without extensive training

user group people who share information on systems and software through meetings and publications

variable named program entity capable of representing different values during program execution

very large scale integration VLSI; placement of from one hundred thousand to one million circuits on single chip

virtual reality creation of imaginary, animated, three-dimensional landscape that one may explore and change by means of sensors attached to one's body and connected to computer that generates scenes; cyberspace

VLSI **v**ery **l**arge **s**cale **i**ntegration

voice recognition ability of system to accept spoken words as input

voice synthesis system capable of generating audio output responses in simulated voice using specific vocabulary of electronic phonemes

wafer thin silicon disk used to make chips

warm boot function that reads directories and reloads portions of operating system into RAM

window individually controlled portion of screen on which information can be shown, esp. without exiting document file or program

work station powerful, single-user computer, esp. one used for CAD, often networked

WYSIWYG **w**hat **y**ou **s**ee **i**s **w**hat **y**ou **g**et; term designating video display that shows text as it will appear in printout

zap *Informal.* unintentional overwrite of file; intentional use of command found in many programs to clear screen

Hardware and Peripherals

accumulator special purpose register of CPU that stores numeric data for arithmetic or logical operations

acoustic coupler early type of modem, consisting of rubber cups that attached to earpiece and mouthpiece of telephone handset

ALU **a**rithmetic/**l**ogic **u**nit; portion of CPU that performs arithmetic calculations and other logical operations

arithmetic/logic unit ALU

backplane motherboard

bidirectional printing operation of printer from left to right and right to left for added speed; boustrophedon

boustrophedon bidirectional printing

buffer intermediate, temporary storage device for holding data until computer or peripheral such as printer is ready to process it

card printed circuit board or module

carriage moving portion of printer that carries paper

cathode-ray tube CRT; common computer display screen

CD drive disk drive that accepts compact disk storage medium

central processing unit CPU; main part of computer system

client single computer connected to a network file server

clock speed measurement, in megahertz, of the processing speed of a CPU

clone IBM-compatible computer

coder-decoder chip used in analog-digital translation

computer general purpose, digital, information processing device composed of a central processing unit, memory, input and output facilities, power supply, and housing

computer system information processing package that includes computer and peripherals

configure (*vb*) adjust printer, modem, or other peripheral to follow central processor; set up software with user-designated parameters

console part of computer, such as keyboard and monitor, that enables operator to communicate with system

continuous form unseparated sheets of paper with sprocket holes along margins, fed automatically into printer

converter device that accepts data in one form and changes it into another, as from analog to digital

CPS **c**haracters **p**er **s**econd; designation of dot-matrix or daisy wheel printer speed

CPU **c**entral **p**rocessing **u**nit; key component of computer that processes and executes program instructions

Cray *Trademark.* massive, parallel processing computer

CRT **c**athode-**r**ay **t**ube used as monitor to display characters or designs

daisy wheel rimless wheel with characters stored on ends of spokes, attached to moving carriage for use in letter-quality printing

daisy wheel printer impact printer using daisy wheel for letter-quality printing

digitizer device that converts information into numeric form comprehensible to digital computer

disk drive electromechanical device that spins magnetic disk and allows data to be written to or read from disk through read/write head

display video monitor, such as CRT or LCD, that temporarily shows information

dot-matrix printer printer that forms characters with dots organized in matrix, usu. by impact process

dot pitch measurement, in millimeters, of the vertical distance between pixels on a display screen

drive disk drive

dual-processor (*adj*) designating computer

system with two CPUs performing different operations simultaneously

Dynabook *Trademark.* prototype of palmtop computer with handwriting recognition

emulator hardware or software that allows one computer to simulate the behavior of another type of computer

ENIAC *Trademark.* **e**lectronic **n**umerical **i**ntegrator **a**nd **c**alculator; early mainframe computer that filled a large room

execute (*vb*) run (a program)

expansion slot connection to which new board can be added

external slot point at which additional peripherals and modules can be connected to motherboard

fanfold paper continuous form paper, folded on perforations and stacked in zigzag fashion

file server computer acting as file storage for other networked computers, allowing multiple users access to individual file

first generation earliest model of hardware in specific upgrade path

form feed printer default parameter that controls automatic paper supply to printer through tractor feed

486 computer using full 32-bit microprocessor chip

front end processor small computer interfacing large host computer and peripherals that reduces I/O interruptions to host

full-page display vertically elongated video monitor able to display entire page of text

graphics tablet wire grid embedded in screen, activated by stylus to record points traced by stylus

hard copy computer output printed on paper; printout

hard drive device, either external or internal, that spins and reads high-capacity storage hard disk

hardware physical components of system: computer, external memory system, terminal, printer, modem

hard-wired (*adj*) built into hardware, as through electronic circuits, rather than functioning through software

IBM-compatible (*adj*) designating computer system that can interface with IBM hardware or software designed for IBM machines

impact printer printer that generates characters by character striking ribbon against paper

ink-jet printer printer that generates characters by squirting ink droplets against paper, controlled by deflection magnets

input/output I/O; devices or communications channels that move information into and out of computer

I/O **i**nput/**o**utput

I/O port data channel that connects peripherals to computer

IRQ **i**nterrupt **r**equest **l**ine, a setting that controls communication of peripheral devices with the CPU

keyboard device for inputting data by depressing keys that generate all standard characters (letters, digits, punctuation marks) and other keys that have special functions, such as cursor arrow keys or programmable function keys

keypad special purpose numeric keyboard to which other commands or characters may be assigned; numeric pad

landscape printing in which image or text is turned sideways, using top and bottom of page as sides

laptop computer very small personal computer, designed to fit on lap

laser perf paper continuous, fanfold paper with very fine perforations on edges

laser printer high-quality printer that forms images by focusing laser beam on photosensitive drum

LCD liquid crystal display

letter-quality printer impact printer that produces hard copy of high quality, comparable to that of electric typewriter

line printer impact printer capable of producing full line of 80 to 132 characters at one time

liquid crystal display LCD; flat-panel video screen that uses solution of liquid crystal subjected to voltage to block rear light transmission and generate display

local network computers in close proximity sharing peripherals

logic board motherboard for Apple and Macintosh computers

Macintosh Trademark. line of Apple computers, mouse-operated, with extensive graphics capabilities, hypertext, and graphical user interface

mainframe giant institutional computer that requires conditioned environment and allows for multiple users at work stations

micro microcomputer

microcomputer small home or office desktop computer that uses a CPU on a single chip, with power supply and I/O interfaces; micro

microprocessor complete CPU in integrated circuit on single chip

mini minicomputer

minicomputer intermediate size, usu. multiuser computer frequently used as work station or connected to work stations

modem modulator/demodulator; device linking two computers by telephone lines

module computer circuit board with specific function, used as building block in system

monitor high-resolution display screen; low-level CPU control that operates program

motherboard circuit board with series of parallel bus sockets into which computer modules and circuitry are plugged; backplane

near-letter-quality printer correspondence quality printer, such as dot-matrix, thermal, or ink-jet printer

notebook computer small laptop or portable computer, usu. under seven pounds in weight

numeric pad keypad

open architecture system design that permits easy replacement and upgrading of circuit boards, even the use of those made by third parties

optical scanner device that scans light from surface of printed matter and converts analog signals into machine-readable input for storage in computer

overstrike multiple striking of each character by impact printer to give darker impression

page printer printer that determines character pattern for entire page at once, rather than printing line by line

palmtop very small portable computer that can be held in one hand

parallel configuration interface between computer and peripheral that transfers entire byte or word of data at once, with separate line for each bit

parallel port actual connection in parallel configuration

parallel printer printer designed for parallel interface with computer

PC personal computer

PC-compatible (adj) designating a device, application, etc., designed to run on a PC

PCMCIA Personal Computer Memory Card International Association, a consortium of companies that have promulgated standards for card-type peripheral devices

Pentium computer with microprocessor chip that succeeded the 486

peripheral device such as printer, modem, or hard drive, connected to and dependent on computer

personal computer PC; small, relatively low-cost microcomputer designed for home or business use

plug-and-play (adj) designating a peripheral device, etc., designed for easy, non-technical installation and use

PnP plug-and-play

port channel connecting I/O device to computer

portrait normal printing in which image or text runs from top to bottom of page

printout hard copy; printed version of document file

proportional spacing printing technique in which character width determines space allowed

PS/2 Trademark. IBM Personal System/2 computer that uses MS-DOS operating system

rack-mountable (adj) designating equipment designed for installation in standard nineteen-inch metal rack

radiation shield protective shield placed over video display to reduce eye strain and block radiation emissions

read/write head electromagnetic device used to read from or write to magnetic storage medium such as disk

reconfiguring resetting instructions that connect computer to peripheral such as printer

retrofit (vb) upgrade hardware, esp. with

components that were not available at time of original manufacture

reverse video video display with dark characters on light background

scanner device that digitally records images and text from paper

screen video display terminal; contents of what appears on monitor

SCSI small computer system interface; pronounced "scuzzy"; cable or other method of connecting peripheral to computer

serial configuration interface between computer and peripheral that passes information one bit or character at a time

serial port actual connection in serial configuration

serial printer printer designed for serial interface with computer

server file server

sheet feeder tray or other device that feeds paper into printer one sheet at a time

single-board computer computer with design placing CPU, main memory, and I/O controllers on single circuit board

smart terminal terminal with buffer to store certain amount of information and with microprocessor that allows for some processing capabilities

split screen screen divided into two or more windows that display independent or connected data

stepper motor rotating motor used to move read/write heads on floppy disk drives

supercomputer very fast, powerful mainframe, esp. for military and scientific research

supermini fastest and most powerful minicomputer, with capabilities nearly equal to those of a mainframe

surge protector device installed on a power supply line to protect against irregularities in electrical current

SVGA Super VGA, an improvement on the VGA graphics standard, allowing higher resolution and more colors

system computer and all its related components

terminal peripheral device through which user communicates with computer, including keyboard for input and video display for output

thermal printer low-speed, moderate quality, small format, nonimpact printer that forms characters by applying heat to specially sensitized paper

thimble printer variation on daisy wheel printer with spokes bent up at 75 degree angle and two characters on each thimble-shaped spoke

386 computer with 32-bit microprocessor chip

tractor feed device that moves continuous form, fanfold paper through printer

286 computer with 16-bit microprocessor chip

UNIVAC Trademark. universal automatic computer; first generation, vacuum tube, mainframe computer introduced in 1951

VAX Trademark. line of minicomputers manufactured by Digital Equipment Corp.

VDT **v**ideo **d**isplay **t**erminal; CRT monitor or other screen used to display computer output and communicate with computer; VDU

VDU **v**ideo **d**isplay **u**nit; VDT

VGA **v**ideo **g**raphics **a**rray, a widespread graphics standard for PCs

video card control device that runs color monitor

word processor dedicated computer used to write and process text documents

workstation computer with more processing power and graphics capabilities than a standard PC

XT *Trademark.* second-generation IBM personal computer

Software, Languages, and Programming

ALGOL **algo**rithmic **l**anguage; early, high-level mainframe language, esp. used for teaching; forerunner of Pascal

app particular software application, as a word processor, spreadsheet, etc.

AppleDOS disk operating system used in Apple computers

applet applications program that can be executed within another application

application software programs designed to handle particular types of information to achieve specific results, such as word processing or spreadsheet

ASCII **A**merican **S**tandard **C**ode for **I**nformation **I**nterchange; code most commonly used to represent characters, using seven bits to represent each of 128 characters, including control codes

assembler program that converts assembly language into binary machine language

assembly language machine-specific, low-level, mnemonic language used to write efficient programs

authoring system group of programming tools used to develop usu. multimedia product

background program multitask program executed when CPU is not busy with priority task

backslash oblique stroke slanted to left, used as delimiter in some computer operating systems

BASIC **B**eginner's **A**ll-purpose **S**ymbolic **I**nstruction **C**ode; simplified language for programmers on microcomputers

benchmark program standardized program used to compare speed of different computers

beta introductory version of new software program still being tested by outside users

beta test test of new or upgraded software conducted at select user sites just prior to release of product

BIOS communications medium between DOS and machine language

block operation task involving manipulation of information block

bridgeware software that serves as bridge

between one kind of system or platform and another

bundled software several software programs sold together or sold with piece of hardware

C high-level programming language

C++ widely used high-level programming language, incorporating object-oriented features

chaining breaking up of program that exceeds memory capacity into smaller units that are executed sequentially

click single, quick tap and release of a mouse button

COBOL *common business*oriented language; high-level business language used on mainframes

code programming language that tells machine what to do

command line line on a display where a command is expected to be entered

compatibility ability of software to run on specific computers

compiler program that translates high-level language into machine code that computer can execute

compression programming technique that compacts large amounts of data for storage on disks or inclusion in program

control character non-printing ASCII character used to control device functions

conversion translation of data from one operating system or program to another

courseware educational software designed esp. for classroom use

CP/M *Trademark.* **C**ontrol **P**rogram for **M**icrocomputers; early operating system for eight-bit microprocessors

DA **d**esk **a**ccessory

data bank database or number of databases

database systematically structured collection of information organized for easy input, access, retrieval, storage, and update

DBMS **d**ata**b**ase **m**anagement **s**ystem; program that creates, maintains, and accesses database

DDT **d**ynamic **d**ebugging **t**ool; program used to analyze and correct software problems

default option or value built into program or system in lieu of user input, but able to be overridden; default setting or parameter

delete word processing command to remove one or more characters

delimiter marker of the end of a tag, field, record, etc., in a data string

desk accessory DA; program built into Macintosh system so that it is always available regardless of current process in operation

diagnostic program used to find source of errors or malfunctions

directory in DOS, a top-level storage area for files and collections of files

disk operating system DOS; program managing operation of entire disk drive-based system

DOS **d**isk **o**perating **s**ystem

dot command printing and page formatting instruction in WordStar and some other

word-processing programs, distinguished by period placed before command letters

drag-and-drop (*adj*) allowing movement of icons, etc., to another area on the screen via mouse control

driver software that controls the basic operation of a device, as a printer, mouse, video display, etc.

EBCDIC **e**xtended **b**inary-**c**oded **d**ecimal **i**nterchange**c**ode; eight-bit character code for 256 characters, used by IBM mainframes instead of ASCII

edit (*vb*) make changes in document file

emacs a simple text-editing software program for UNIX systems

emulation real-time simulation program that allows one computer to mimic operations of another

EOF **e**nd **o**f **f**ile

.exe suffix in DOS designating an executable file, one that will launch an application

executable code machine-readable version of code that machine can actually run, all in bits

expert system application that can perform operations formerly done only by human experts, as diagnosing an illness

export (*vb*) format data for use in another application

extension secondary part of a file name; in DOS, the three characters following the dot, often specifying a file type

file management system program or programs that facilitate creation and management of files

Finder *Trademark.* portion of operating system for Macintosh computers that locates elements to be processed

firmware program stored in ROM and built into computer, usu. to implement function previously provided in software

folder in Macintosh operating systems, a storage area for individual file and other folders

FORTRAN **for**mula **tran**slator; early general-purpose, high-level compiled language, used primarily for mainframes and minis

front-end (*adj*) designating software that provides a user interface for access to an application

GIF **g**raphics **i**nterchange **f**ormat, a bit-mapped graphics file format for storing and compressing images

global search program or command that searches for and acts upon every occurrence of a character, word, or phrase within file

graphical user interface GUI; video-display environment based on icons, WYSIWYG screen, and mouse operations, used orig. on Macintosh computers

groupware business or office software designed for use by network of users at connected work stations

GUI **g**raphical **u**ser **i**nterface

hat circumflex character; ^

high-level language programming language,

such as C, COBOL, or Pascal, with form similar to English or mathematics

hit a successful result from a query or search of a database

hot key keyboard sequence to perform a command or open another application

hyperlink a built-in link from one word, icon, etc. to another related item, as a cross-reference, image, audio or video clip, etc.

hypertext file or database system with built-in links from text to other related texts, images, sounds, or video clips

icon small graphic representation of a file, folder, application, etc., ready for use

iconize (*vb*) reduce an open application, file, etc. to an icon

import (*vb*) read and display data from another application

init *init*ialization procedure; usu. shareware utility that loads itself into RAM on start-up of Macintosh computer

installed base entire number of users of particular program

intermediate compiler program that translates high-level computer language into object code and saves it, prior to conversion into executable machine language

interoperability capacity of software to run on more than one platform, such as MS-DOS or Macintosh

interpreter program that translates high-level language into machine language to allow immediate execution of program

JCL Job control language

job control language JCL; language that provides system with information needed to execute specific batch programs

JPEG Joint Photographic Experts Group, designating a compression technique for color images

justify (*vb*) align text against right and/or left margins

kluge makeshift or inelegant remedy or fix that circumvents a software or device problem

language arbitrarily designed and coded syntax and vocabulary that allows user to communicate with computer

LISP list processing language; high-level interpretive or compiled language used in artificial intelligence

LOGO powerful programming language for use by children

Lotus 1,2,3 *Trademark.* powerful and popular spreadsheet program

low-level language coding specification that is close to language understood by computer and therefore more difficult for people

machine language binary code language that can be directly executed by CPU; basic language understood by computer

machine-readable (*adj*) encoded in or translated into form suitable for processing, such as ASCII

macro single command that expands into series

of instructions temporarily or permanently saved as that command

memory resident designating program that remains in internal memory while other programs are being executed

menu list of program options displayed for user

menu-driven (*adj*) run by choosing from presented options rather than by entering commands

merge (*vb*) combine two files of ordered information into single file

MPEG Motion Picture Experts Group, a leading standard for data compression of full-motion video

MS-DOS *Trademark.* MicroSoft-Disk Operating System; dominant 16-bit disk operating system for IBM-compatible personal computers

multiprogramming process in which two or more programs are run simultaneously in same computer

multitasking ability of a computer to perform more than one task or run more than one application at a time

object code intermediate stage between source code and executable code

opening menu initial set of options available when program is loaded

operating system OS; software that organizes and manages resources of system, communicates with peripherals, interacts with users, handles files, and accesses software

operation code assembly language that tells machine what to do

OS operatingsystem

output information computer produces by executing program; means of displaying or extracting information from computer

parent directory the directory containing another directory

Pascal popular, high-level structured programming language

PC-DOS standard operating system for IBM PC, marketed for compatibles as MS-DOS

pipe(s) character consisting of a single vertical line, or two vertical lines, one above the other; |

platform major piece of software, such as an operating system, operating environment, or database, under which various smaller applications are designed to run

pop-up window window that can appear from background, remains hidden until needed, and goes away after use

PostScript *Trademark.* an object-oriented page description language developed by Adobe Systems, widely used in the printing and publishing industries

presentation software graphics program designed for use in live presentation to audience

print command to send file to printer to produce hard copy of file

productivity software business applications that directly aid work of an organization, such as

word-processing, spreadsheet, database, or desktop-publishing programs

program sequence of instructions to computer to perform specific work

programmer individual trained to design, write, and implement programs in any of various computer languages

programming study and practice of designing and building computer software programs; translation of problem from physical environment to a language computer can understand

QuickTime *Trademark.* a video and animation display system developed by Apple Computer

radio button selection among two or more options in a window or menu, only one of which may be selected at any time

readme file file supplied with an application that notes improvements, cautions, etc., not found in the product manual

relational database collection of data arranged logically into tables rather than hierarchically

reprogram (*vb*) rewrite or revise computer program

restore (*vb*) recover a file that has been lost, deleted, or corrupted

retrofit correction of one facet of program while program is in effect

return key that instructs computer to perform command just entered; key that produces hard-carriage return in word processing

root directory highest-level directory in a file system

RPG report program generator; business-oriented programming language used with databases

save command to write data or an update to a hard disk, floppy, etc.

screen saver application that automatically changes the screen display when there has been no input for a set time, to prevent burn-in of an unchanging image

scrolling using screen as window on a file while moving vertically or horizontally through the file

search and replace capacity of editing program to find any appearance of specified character, word, or phrase in file and replace it with another specified character, word, or phrase

SGML Standard Generalized Markup Language, a standard for marking and defining data descriptively to enable use on differing systems and platforms

shareware often simple programs available at no charge, but for which a token donation is requested

shell user inferface program enabling access to applications; large macro of saved keystrokes used as special commands

slash character slanting downward from right to left (/; also called virgule, or solidus)

SNOBOL string-oriented symbolic language; high-level programming language used to manipulate character strings

soft hyphen hyphen automatically inserted in

word at line break that will not appear if reformatted paragraph alters word placement

software instructions and programs that tell hardware what to do

software package computer program and documentation designed and marketed to fill a specific need, such as word processing

source code program in commonly understood, high-level language that must pass through compiler or interpreter to execute

speech synthesis recognition of text characters and conversion of these to audible speech

spell check program designed to find and/or correct spelling errors in document, usu. used with word-processing program

splat alternate term for asterisk character

spreadsheet program that simulates business or scientific worksheet and performs calculations when data is changed

SQL structured query language, a standard language used in database management software

stand-alone (adj) designating self-contained software program or computer system that operates independently

star alternate term for asterisk character

structured language high-level computer language such as Pascal or ALGOL that stresses logical flow of control and extensive self-documentation

subscript usu. small character printed below normal line of type

superscript usu. small character printed above normal line of type

System Trademark. operating system for Macintosh computers, working in conjunction with Finder

systems software collection of essential utilities programs for use with particular computer system

text editor program for revising stored documents and moving text

toolbar onscreen area with selection of most-used options

toy system experimental, small-scale application intended for display or demonstration

Trojan horse computer virus disguised as a useful application

TRS-DOS Trademark. family of disk operating systems designed for Radio Shack computers

Unicode standard for representing characters digitally, using 16 bits for each character

UNIX Trademark. multiuser operating system orig. developed at Bell Telephone Labs

unzip (vb) decompress a file that has been zipped

upgrade new, improved version of previously released software program

user assistance help instructions built into program

user interface part of program that provides interaction between person and rest of software through video display and input devices

utility operating system-specific software used

to perform routine tasks such as sorting, debugging, formatting, and copying

vaporware software that is promoted or marketed while still in development and may never be produced

virus self-replicating program intentionally designed to disrupt operations of one computer or computer network

vertical bar pipe(s)

wild card character that stands for any other possible keystroke, usually represented by an asterisk or question mark

Windows Trademark. operating environment featuring graphical user interface and mouse operation for MS-DOS computers

Windows 95 Trademark. upgrade of the Windows operating environment, released in 1995, supporting 32-bit applications

Word Trademark. popular word-processing program

word processing computer creation and manipulation of text by editing, formatting, storing, and printing

WordPerfect Trademark. popular word-processing program

WordStar Trademark. popular word-processing program

word wrap word-processing program's capacity to automatically place word on next line if it extends beyond margin

worm computer virus that spreads from one computer to another over a network, etc.

zip (vb) compress a file to save storage space

Memory and Data Storage

access time time required for a device, as a hard drive, to find requested data

address label designating numerical position of storage location in memory

address bus set of communications channels that determine amount of main memory computer can control

bad sector area on a hard disk or floppy disk that cannot be used for storage

bank logical unit of memory

batch group of records or programs considered as single unit for processing

Bernoulli drive Trademark. type of floppy disk drive allowing high storage capacity

bit one binary digit, whose value is either zero or one; basic unit of computer memory

block logical unit of stored data

bubble memory high-capacity semiconductor memory technology that stores information in tiny magnetic bubbles

buffer temporary storage area for input, as data to be printed

byte eight bits of information, usu. represents one character of data in memory

cache memory very high-speed, not addressable, semiconductor storage device for executing instructions

cartridge removable module holding secondary

storage medium, esp. magnetic tape; similar module holding program stored in ROM, such as computer game

cassette cartridgelike tape storage device using 1/8 inch (3.2 mm) tape

CD-ROM compact disc read-only memory; compact disc used for permanent storage of massive amounts of data

close operation in which file is stored on external memory device and rendered unreadable until reopened

copying duplicating files or programs from one magnetic storage medium to another

corrupted (adj) designating a file, etc., in which data is jumbled or has been lost

DAT digital audio tape, a storage medium using magnetic tape on removable cartridges

data information that may be organized and processed by programs

data file information stored in external memory and recalled under unique file name

direct access random access

directory table of contents for files on disk

diskette floppy disk

document file collection of data stored on disk

double density storage density of some disk media, greater than single density and less than high density

double-sided disk disk able to store data on both sides

DRAM dynamic random-access memory; fast-access, rewriteable, volatile memory chip

drum cylinder coated with magnetic material, used as high-speed external memory device in mainframe computers

dump (vb) copy or transfer contents of memory, esp. from one level to another

dupe (vb) duplicate information, esp. from one disk to another

EPROM erasable programmable read-only memory; read-only memory that can be erased under high intensity ultraviolet light and reprogrammed

Exabyte standard format for magnetic tape storage on removable cartridges, developed by Exabyte Corp.

external memory disk drive, cassette, or other storage device not directly addressed by CPU and not part of main memory

fetch (vb) read contents of specific memory location

field sector of memory designated for specific kind of information

file organized collection of data stored under single name

file directory organized collection of information stored under single name; list of file names and sizes on disk

flash memory type of ROM memory that can be updated within a PC

flippy double-sided floppy disk turned over and used in single-sided drive

floppy disk mylar disk storage medium in cardboard jacket

fragmentation condition in which files are stored in fragments on separate areas of a disk, lengthening access time

GB gigabyte

gigabyte GB; 1,024 x 1,024 x 1,024 bytes or approximately one billion bytes

gulp *Slang.* group of bytes or bits

hard disk high-speed, large capacity disk made of rigid substratum covered with magnetic oxide

head device that reads or writes information on magnetic media

high density storage density of some disk media, greater than double density

index hole hole in floppy disk indicating beginning of first sector of track, used to trigger drive

K kilobyte

KB kilobyte

kilobyte K or KB; 1,024 bytes

laser disc optical disc

load (*vb*) move data or program instructions from storage medium into computer memory for execution; move disk drive read/write head into operation

logged disk drive engaged drive in dual drive system

magnetic bubble tiny, mobile magnetized area that is basis of storage medium

magnetic card flexible, plastic 3x7 inch card with magnetic surface used for data storage

magnetic disk flat, round, magnetic-mechanical data storage medium coated with oxide that is selectively magnetized to record data and rotates on drive past read/write head which records data on concentric circles called tracks

magnetic media material used to store information on cards, tapes, floppy disks, hard disks, or drums by magnetizing particles

magneto-optical drive type of removable-disk drive using both magnetic and optical storage technologies

mailbox file for storing electronic mail

main memory internal memory of computer, generally RAM

mass storage external memory device such as a disk or cassette

MB megabyte

mechanical memory external memory device such as disk or drum

megabyte MB; 1,024 x 1,024 bytes or approximately one million bytes

memory internal or external storage area and capacity to store and retrieve binary data and programs; storage

memory management use of hardware and software to control and allocate memory resources

microfiche 4x6 inch film used to store miniaturized photographic images of data

microfloppy newer floppy disk, actually rigid, with 31/2-inch (8.9-cm) diameter

minifloppy original 51/84-inch (13.3-cm) diameter floppy disk

mirror (*vb*) copy on an ongoing basis for security

nibble four bits or half a byte

nonvolatile memory memory that retains contents on storage medium when power is shut off

optical disc grooveless disk on which digital data are stored as tiny pits in the surface and read by laser beam scanning the surface

park (*vb*) position the read-write head of a hard disk safely for transport

primary memory main storage area for data and programs

punch card standardized, stiff paper card that stores information via punched holes denoting numerical values

RAM random-access memory; volatile read/write memory that allows direct access to data and loses its data contents when power is turned off

random access technique for storing or retrieving data in location where access does not require sequential search; direct access

random-access memory RAM

read-only memory ROM

refresh (*vb*) maintain information stored in volatile memory

register high speed storage location in CPU that operates on small amounts of data

reset key button or key that clears computer's volatile memory back to cold boot

retrieval accessing of data in storage

ROM read-only memory; memory storage device that can be written to once and not changed, used for nonvolatile, machine-specific instructions

ROM chip integrated circuit with read-only memory implanted on it

save place data on nonvolatile magnetic media for storage

scratchpad small, fast, volatile storage in certain computers

sector one of contiguous portions of disk track, so divided for rapid and efficient data storage

sequential access storage method, such as on magnetic tape, that allows access to elements only in fixed order

single density storage density of some disk media, less than double density

single-sided disk disk that stores data on one side only

SRAM static random-access memory; volatile memory technology using RAM chip that holds its contents without being constantly refreshed from CPU, faster and more expensive than DRAM

storage memory

storage capacity amount of data that can be stored in computer memory

streaming mode magnetic tape system for copying data from hard disk as backup

swapping technique for transfer of program and data code from one storage medium to main memory and back, or between levels of main memory

Syquest *Trademark.* hard drive storage system with removable disks

tape memory data-storage medium that consists of electromagnetic tape

TB terabyte

terabyte TB; 1,024 x 1,024 x 1,024 x 1,024 bytes or approximately one trillion bytes

TPI tracks per inch; measure of disk storage density

track concentric circle on disk or drum surface for storage of data at designated address

virtual storage extension of addressable memory through secondary storage controlled by systems software that treats it as addressable main storage

volatile memory memory that does not retain data when power is turned off

Winchester disk drive former term for high-speed hard disk

WORM write-once, read many, a type of optical-storage disk that may be written to once only

write (*vb*) record data in memory

write-protect (*adj*) designating notch on 5 1/4-inch disk that, when covered, prevents inadvertent writing over of stored information; designating similarly functioning mechanical switch on 3 1/2-inch disk

Internet and World Wide Web

address string of identifying characters for directing e-mail, accessing a Web site, etc.

anonymous FTP most common use of FTP, allowing data transfer without need of a password

AOL *Trademark.* America Online, a commercial service providing Internet and Web access, etc.

archie software tool giving access to archives of the indexed contents of anonymous FTP sites

ARPA Advanced Research Projects Agency (later DARPA), the agency of the US Department of Defense that in the late 1960s developed ARPAnet, the precursor of the Internet

avatar Web graphic representing a person, as a portrait or facial image on that person's home page

backbone large network enabling connection to other subordinate networks

BITNET Because It's Time Network, university-based computer network later connected to the Internet

'bot program that sends multiple messages, etc., automatically (short for *robot*)

CERN acronym for the French name of the European Center for Nuclear Research (now the European Particle Physics Laboratory) in Geneva, Switzerland; scientists there developed the software that led to the World Wide Web

chat real-time communication between sites, as in a telephone conversation

.com domain designator (at the end of an Internet address) for a commercial enterprise

CompuServe *Trademark.* commercial service providing Internet and Web access, etc.

connect time time connected to an online service, often the basis for a fee charged by the service

cyberspace term (from William Gibson's novels) for the non-physical reality and culture of the Internet and the Web

DARPA **D**efense **A**dvanced **R**esearch **P**rojects **A**gency, later name for ARPA

dial-up (*adj*) pertaining to a service, account, etc., accessed via modem

discussion group people who communicate regularly on a specific topic or interest, as in a newsgroup or forum

domain final portion of an Internet address, following the final dot

dot character (in other contexts known as a period) used as a separator in addresses

.edu domain designator (at the end of an Internet address) for an educational institution

e-zine an *le*ctronically published, online ma*gazine*

emoticon combination of keyboard characters to express emotion, attitude, etc., such as a smiley

FAQ **f**requently **a**sked **q**uestion, usually collected into a list for newcomers to a newsgroup, FTP site, etc.

fetch (*vb*) copy a file from a remote site to a host computer

firewall security software limiting access to data at a particular site or local network

flame (*vb*) insulting, critical, or demeaning comment in e-mail or a posting to a newsgroup, etc.

forum discussion group on a BBS or online service

freenet a service providing free Internet access to members of a community

FTP **f**ile **t**ransfer **p**rotocol, the standard for file transfers on the Internet

gate computer enabling connection and communication between networks or systems with differing formats; gateway

gopher software tool enabling browsing of data available on the Internet or Web

.gov domain designator (at the end of an Internet address) for a government institution

home page starting point for a Web site, with links to other graphics, documents, data, sites, etc.

host name leftmost portion of an Internet address, designating a specific computer

HTML **h**ypertext **m**arkup **l**anguage; a variety of SGML specifying how to tag text for use on the Web

HTTP **h**ypertext **t**ransfer **p**rotocol, controlling how Web sites request data

Internet global network for communication of data among computers and smaller networks using the TCP/IP protocols

intranet local network utilizing Internet protocols for sharing of data, graphics, etc., as within a company's offices

IRC **I**nternet **r**elay **c**hat, a protocol enabling real time communication on the Internet

Java *Trademark.* language for programming for the Web developed by Sun Microsystems

Jughead index of high-level gopher menus

listserv type of automated mailing list software developed for mainframe computers

mailbox file or storage area used to hold transmissions until pickup

mailing list discussion group in which each address on the list receives a copy of all postings by any member of the group

meme self-propagating idea, phrase, or manner of thinking that circulates from person to person

.mil domain designator (at the end of an Internet address) for a military facility

Mosaic first graphical Web browsing software, developed by the National Center for Supercomputing Applications

Net the Internet

.net domain designator (at the end of an Internet address) for a network

netiquette unofficial code of acceptable behavior on the Internet

Netscape *Trademark.* widely-used brand of Web browser

newbie someone new to Internet or Web use

newsgroup discussion group on Usenet

.org domain designator (at the end of an Internet address) for a nonprofit organization

post message sent to a mailing list or newsgroup; (*vb*) send such a message

Prodigy *Trademark.* commercial service providing Internet and Web access, etc.

protocol agreed set of rules enabling communication between otherwise incompatible software, networks, etc.

put (*vb*) copy a file to a remote site

session single, continuous period of connection to the Internet, Web, or an online service

shouting typing E-mail in ALL CAPS, done for emphasis

sig block information appended to the end of E-mail messages, etc., identifying a particular user (name, address, favorite quote, etc.)

site Internet or Web location allowing remote access

smiley :-) emoticon made by typing colon, hyphen, and close parenthesis; viewed with head tilted left, looks like a smiling face

snail mail surface mail, delivered by postal or courier service

snarf (*vb*) fetch a set of files or a quantity of data

spam (*vb*) post huge amounts of data, or post a message to many users

spoiler part of a message that reveals an identity, solution to a puzzle, etc.

surf (*vb*) browse serendipitously from one Internet or Web site to another

TCP/IP *Transmission Control Protocol/Internet Protocol,* the standard protocols for Internet data exchange, developed by DARPA in the late 1970s

telnet protocol for terminal emulation, enabling remote login

thread related theme or topic running through a series of messages or posts

tunneling encapsulating data that uses one protocol within that of a different protocol to allow transport across a backbone that does not support the original protocol

URL **u**niform **r**esource **l**ocator; an address on the Web (begins "http://")

Usenet **Use**r **Net**work, that part of the Internet devoted to newsgroups

Veronica searchable index of gopher menus

WAIS **w**ide-**a**rea **i**nformation **s**erver, a program for finding information on the Internet

Web, the World Wide Web

Web browser software enabling use of hypertext documents on the Web, such as Mosaic or Netscape Navigator

Web page home page

Web site computer or server accessible via a Web address

World Wide Web global computer network for communication of documents that include graphics, sound, etc., and hypertext links

WWW **W**orld **W**ide **W**eb

CHAPTER SIX

TRANSPORTATION

Types of Aircraft

ACV air cushion vehicle

aerodyne early term for any heavier-than-air craft that derived lift from aerodynamic forces

aerostat balloon or other lighter-than-air craft lifted by container of gas

Airbus *Trademark.* large, short range aircraft for mass transportation of passengers

aircraft structure designed to travel through the air; aerodyne or aerostat

air cushion vehicle ACV; Hovercraft

airliner large passenger aircraft operated by airline

airplane fixed-wing, heavier-than-air craft kept aloft by aerodynamic forces and powered by screw propeller or jet propulsion; also, *esp. Brit.* aeroplane

airship steered lighter-than-air craft with engine, esp. dirigible or blimp

air taxi small commercial airliner carrying passengers and mail to places not regularly served

amphibian aircraft capable of takeoff and landing on water and land

autogiro aircraft with freely rotating rotor in place of fixed wing and propeller for propulsion, cannot take off vertically or hover

balloon lighter-than-air, engineless aircraft propelled by airflow and lifted by enclosed bag of gas

biplane airplane with two sets of wings mounted one above the other

blimp nonrigid or semirigid airship

Boeing 727 *Trademark.* most common midsize commercial jetliner, with three engines and capacity to hold 150 passengers

bomber air force plane designed to drop bombs

chopper *Informal.* helicopter

crop duster small aircraft that flies low over crops to spray pesticide

Cub *Trademark.* light, low-horsepower, high-wing Piper airplane

DC-3 *Trademark.* most common propeller-driven commercial airliner, still in use

dirigible airship with lifting cells; as zeppelin

dive bomber aircraft that releases bombs while diving at target

fighter small, fast, highly maneuverable craft used in aerial combat

gasbag *Slang.* hot-air balloon

gas balloon hot-air balloon

glider heavier-than-air craft supported in flight by action of air against lifting surfaces, not dependent on engine and usu. not having one; sailplane

grasshopper *Slang.* small, light, military scouting and liaison plane

gyrodyne rotorcraft with engine-driven rotors and independent conventional propellers for propulsion

gyroplane rotorcraft with rotors started by engine but rotated by action of air, with independent propellers for propulsion

heavier-than-air craft aircraft that is heavier than air it displaces and is lifted by application of propulsion to aerodynamic forces

heavy aircraft class of aircraft capable of takeoff weights over 325,000 pounds

helibus helicopter used for short-range mass transportation of passengers

helicopter rotary-winged aircraft having one or more power-driven rotors on vertical axes, dependent for horizontal motion on rotors

high-altitude reconnaissance plane military surveillance craft capable of flying at altitudes over 50,000 feet (15,240 m)

hot-air balloon aerostat lifted by enclosure filled with heated air; gas balloon

Hovercraft vehicle that travels across land or water on cushion of air formed by downward thrust of jet engines; air cushion vehicle

hydroplane seaplane

interceptor fast-climbing fighter jet used defensively against attack

jet aircraft powered by jet propulsion

jetliner jet-powered commercial airliner

jumbo jet very large commercial jet airliner, such as the Boeing 747, DC-10, or Tristar L-1011, that holds over 300 passengers

Lear jet *Trademark.* small, powerful, noncommercial jet aircraft

lighter-than-air craft aircraft that rises and remains suspended by use of contained gas weighing less than the air it displaces, esp. balloon

monoplane aircraft or glider with one pair of wings

ornithopter experimental aircraft propelled by flapping wings

pursuit plane pre-World War II air force fighter plane

rotorcraft heavier-than-air craft principally dependent for flight on lift generated by one or more rotors

sailplane glider

seaplane aircraft designed to land on and take off from water; hydroplane

747 jumbo jet manufactured by Boeing

short takeoff and landing STOL; aircraft capable of operating from short runway

spy plane high-altitude military reconnaissance plane

SST supersonic transport

STOL short takeoff and landing aircraft

supersonic transport SST; commercial airliner that flies faster than speed of sound

tandem airplane craft with two or more sets of wings with similar dimensions, placed one in front of the other on same level

tanker aircraft carrying fuel for in-air refueling of other aircraft

tilt-rotor amphibious military aircraft with rotors that stand vertically during takeoff and tilt to horizontal position to act as propellers in flight

transport large military aircraft used to convey troops or cargo

triphibian aircraft capable of takeoff or landing on land, water, or snow and ice

ultralight class of extremely low-weight, single-seat aircraft not requiring pilot's license for operation

vertical takeoff and landing VTOL; term applied to aircraft capable of taking off and landing vertically and flying horizontally, such as helicopter

VTOL vertical takeoff and landing aircraft

warplane military fighter or bomber

widebody jumbo jet with two aisles in passenger cabin, usu. able to carry over 300 passengers

zeppelin any rigid airship

Aviation and Aerodynamics

abort (*vb*) terminate preplanned maneuver, esp. takeoff

absolute altitude vertical distance between aircraft and Earth's surface

absolute ceiling altitude beyond which aircraft cannot climb in standard atmospheric conditions

aerial reconnaissance camera camera with extremely long-range focus for high-altitude surveillance

aero- prefix meaning aircraft or flying

aerobatics intentional, abrupt maneuvers that alter normal flight pattern, esp. done in performance

aerodonetics science of flying gliders

aerodynamics science of the motion of air and other gases and the forces they produce on bodies in relative motion

aeronaut pilot of balloon or airship

aeronautics science, art, and business of designing, building, and flying aircraft

aerophotography long-range photography from aircraft

afterburning process of fuel injection and combustion for increasing thrust in turbojet exhaust, used only in military aircraft and SST

airborne (*adj*) carried through air by aerodynamic forces

airflow stream of air in motion relative to a body

airframe icing formation of ice on parts, esp. airfoil, due to certain moisture and temperature conditions, causing instability and control problems

air lane route regularly used by aircraft; jet route, victor airway

airman aviator

airsickness nausea, dizziness, headache, and

cold sweat due to motion and altitude of air flight

air space space extending vertically above area of Earth's surface

airspeed speed of aircraft relative to air through which it is moving rather than Earth's surface

airstream airflow around aircraft in flight

airway specific route for air travel

airworthy (*adj*) safe and fit for flying

altitude height above Earth's surface or sea level

angle of attack angle between airfoil and relative flow of wind

angle of incidence angle between chord line of airfoil and thrust of aircraft

approach final period of descent prior to landing

asymmetric landing emergency landing in which engine on one side has failed

attitude position of aircraft expressed as inclination of its three axes (pitch, roll, and yaw) to frame of reference

augmentation increase of thrust by various methods

autorotation condition of flight achieved when lift is derived solely by effect of aerodynamic forces on unpowered rotor of autogyro or helicopter, or when power is lost

aviation art and science of flying aircraft; development of heavier-than-air aircraft

aviator flier; airplane pilot; airman

aviatrix female aviator

bank (*vb*) roll to attitude in which one wing tip is higher than the other; (*n*) condition of flight in which aircraft slopes laterally during turn

barnstorm (*vb*) tour country to give short demonstration airplane rides and stunt flying exhibitions

barrel roll complete roll by aircraft around longitudinal axis while simultaneously completing one spiral revolution in air

bearing horizontal direction to or from any point, measured in degrees clockwise from true north

belly landing emergency landing directly onto bottom of fuselage with landing gear retracted

blind landing instrument landing in zero visibility

brake horsepower actual horsepower of engine measured by brake attached to drive shaft

buffeting vibration of aircraft part caused by a burble

burble irregular flow of air around aircraft

buzz (*vb*) fly aircraft very low, esp. over structure

calibrated airspeed indicated airspeed corrected for installation error of cockpit gauge

calibration correction of airspeed

CAT clear air turbulence

ceiling height above Earth's surface of lowest significant cloud layer; altitude at which rate of climb of given aircraft falls to 100 feet (30 m) per minute

center of gravity point in body toward which every external particle of matter is attracted by gravity

chandelle abrupt, steep climb caused by aircraft's momentum

chord line imaginary line from leading to trailing edge of airfoil

circling flight pattern adopted by pilot while awaiting landing clearance or to position aircraft for landing

clear air turbulence CAT; unpredictable high-altitude turbulence with no clouds present, esp. wind shear due to jetstream

climb ascent, esp. to cruising altitude

climbout portion of flight between takeoff and initial cruising altitude

close formation flying in which several aircraft maintain relative positions near one another, often as exhibition

contrail white trail of condensed water vapor behind aircraft in flight; vapor trail

corridor flight route designated by international agreement

crabbing sideways motion of aircraft with respect to ground due to crosswind

crash landing forced landing in which aircraft is brought down without landing gear away from airport runway surface

critical altitude maximum altitude at which it is possible to maintain specified power and manifold pressure in standard atmosphere

crosswind wind not parallel to path of aircraft or runway

cruise (*vb*) maintain constant speed and altitude for period of time

cruising altitude constant altitude maintained for portion of flight

decision height point in ILS at which pilot sees runway and begins visual landing

decompression formation of nitrogen bubbles in blood or body tissues due to rapid ascent, causing pain in joints and convulsions

density altitude altitude corresponding to given air density in standard atmosphere; pressure altitude corrected for temperature

depressurization loss of cabin pressurization

direct stability propensity of aircraft to remain in stable flight attitude

ditch (*vb*) make crash landing in water and abandon aircraft

dive steep, sudden descent

drag sum of air resistance encountered in flight plus induced drag created by airfoil

drag ratio ratio of lift to drag as characteristic of wing; lift ratio

drift deviation from course, esp. due to crosswinds

egress route airway used for departure

engine failure loss of power in one or more engines, often necessitating emergency landing

envelope operating regime suited to particular aircraft

equivalent airspeed calibrated airspeed corrected for compressibility of air

external load cargo attached and carried outside fuselage

feather (*vb*) change pitch of propeller blades to reduce drag as engine is stopped

final approach period of final instrument approach from fixed point to landing, usu. last five to seven miles

flame-out failure of jet engine combustion in flight

flight distance covered by aircraft between takeoff and landing

flutter abnormal vibration in control surface due to aerodynamic force

flying blind flying by instruments only in low visibility

forced landing emergency landing on surface other than airport runway prior to completion of flight

formation flying flying in which several aircraft maintain positions relative to each other in simultaneous flight

goaround abandoning of approach just prior to landing in order to circle around airport

ground speed aircraft speed relative to ground it is passing over; airspeed corrected for headwind or tailwind

guidance direction of course of craft

gust sudden, brief change of wind speed or direction

heading compass reading expressing horizontal direction in which aircraft is facing

headwind wind blowing in direction opposite to course flown by aircraft

hedgehop (*vb*) fly very close to ground, esp. for crop dusting

hypersonic (*adj*) designating supersonic speeds of Mach 5 and above

icing accumulation of ice on exterior of aircraft during flight; airframe icing

IFR instrument flight rules

ILS instrument landing system

Immelmann maneuver in which aircraft makes a half loop followed by a half roll to regain level flight position

indicated airspeed speed as shown on cockpit gauge

induced drag portion of wing drag resulting from generation of lift

in-flight (*adj*) done or occurring while aircraft is airborne

instrument flight rules IFR; type of flight plan and rules governing procedures for instrument flight

instrument landing avionic approach and landing in which ILS, PAR, or VOR is used

instrument landing system ILS; precision instrument approach based on beams transmitted from glide slope on ground that give vertical and lateral guidance by localizer up to decision height for visual landing

JATO jet-assisted takeoff

jet-assisted takeoff JATO; use of jet propulsion in takeoff only

jet blast jet engine exhaust

jet propulsion momentum derived from ejection of exhaust stream or rapid flow of gas from within propelled body by mechanical, thermal, or chemical process: turbojet, fanjet, ramjet, pulsejet, rocket

jet route high-altitude air lane

jet stream migrating stream of high-speed winds at high altitudes

jettison (*vb*) lighten load by dropping objects from aircraft in flight, esp. fuel in emergency

jet wash slipstream

jump specific instance of parachuting from aircraft

lateral axis axis from side to side of aircraft, perpendicular to direction of flight; pitch axis

lateral stability minimal pitch rotation; tendency of aircraft to return to equilibrium following forces applied to pitch

lazy eight maneuver in which aircraft gradually climbs, banks, and turns, tracing an imaginary figure eight on its side

lift upward aerodynamic force exerted on wing

liftoff vertical takeoff, esp. of helicopter or rocket

lift ratio drag ratio

limit load factor maximum pull of gravity to which airframe may be subjected in flight without structural damage

load in-flight weight carried by aircraft, including cargo, fuel, passengers, crew, and weight of aircraft when empty

load factor pull of gravity in absence of acceleration (load factor of 4 equals 4G); amount of load an aircraft can carry

longitudinal axis axis from nose to tail of aircraft, parallel to direction of flight; roll axis

loop circular figure performed as flight maneuver, beginning with aerobatic pull-up through vertical plane and ending with return to horizontal flight in same direction

mach number ratio of airspeed of an object to the speed of sound at given altitude and atmosphere, being 762 mph at sea level

manifold pressure factor used to determine grade of fuel required by aircraft engine

mass ratio ratio between mass of aircraft with fuel and after fuel has been used up

Mayday international radiotelephone distress signal, repeated three times to indicate imminent, grave danger

missed approach approach aborted by pilot at decision height when instrument approach cannot be completed safely

moment measure of aircraft's tendency to produce motion about an axis

nose dive swift, steep downward plunge of aircraft with nose toward ground

octant 45-degree angle, being one-eighth of a circle, used to state heading

over-the-top (*adj*) indicating position of aircraft above cloud layer or other obscuring phenomena forming ceiling

Pan international radiotelephone distress signal

parachute umbrellalike cloth contrivance used to retard falling speed of person or object dropped from aircraft

payload commercial revenue-producing load;

expendable or deliverable load, such as bombs, used in military operations

pilot person who operates aircraft controls

pitch distance advanced by propeller in one revolution; movement of aircraft about lateral axis

polar (*adj*) having directional setting at north magnetic pole

power loading ratio of gross weight of airplane to its power

precision approach standard instrument approach in which electronic glide slope is provided by precision approach radar or instrument landing system

pressure altitude altitude relative to given pressure in standard atmosphere, uncorrected for temperature

pressurization regulation of cabin pressure for comfort of crew and passengers at high altitudes with low atmospheric pressure

probe and drogue method of in-air refueling in which tanker plane extends hose and funnel, or drogue, to which trailing plane extends intake pipe, or probe

propulsion driving force in engine that moves aircraft

prop wash slipstream

pull out (*vb*) exit from dive

pull-up maneuver in which nose of plane is lifted from level flight through vertical plane

quadrant quarter of circle centered on navigational aid, oriented clockwise from magnetic north

ram force of air being compressed into engine inlet by high velocity of aircraft

ram effect pressure resulting from ram

range distance aircraft is capable of flying without refueling or landing

reaction propulsion forward thrust due to engine expelling jet of fluid or particle stream

roll rotation of aircraft about longitudinal axis

service ceiling altitude at which rate of climb of given aircraft falls to 100 feet (30 m) per minute

skyway air lane, flight route

skywriting tracing words or figures in sky by trail of smoke released from small aircraft

slipstream current of air thrust backward by spinning propeller or jet; jet wash; prop wash

solo flight operation of aircraft by one person, esp. as part of pilot training

sonic (*adj*) designating speed of sound at given altitude

sonic barrier critical speed at which shock waves cause increased drag by exceeding speed of sound; sound barrier

sonic boom loud shock wave formed when speed of body exceeds speed of sound in same medium

sound barrier sonic barrier

spin nose-first descent along spiral path of large pitch and small radius; tailspin

spiral circling around longitudinal axis

stall loss of lift, sudden drop, and possible loss

of control due to exceeding critical angle of attack and disruption of airflow around airfoil

straight-in landing landing on runway aligned within 30 degrees of final approach course

stunt pilot expert flier who performs exhibitions of formation flying and stunt maneuvers

supersonic (*adj*) greater than speed of sound at given altitude

tailspin nose-first spiraling descent with tail up

tailwind wind blowing in same direction as course flown by aircraft

takeoff act or moment of lifting off from ground to begin flight

thrust force in direction of motion of aircraft produced by jet exhaust

torque force that tends to produce rotation

touchdown point at which aircraft makes contact with landing surface

transonic (*adj*) just below or just above speed of sound

true airspeed indicated airspeed on cockpit gauge corrected for installation error, compressibility of air, pressure, and temperature; equivalent airspeed corrected for pressure and temperature

turbulence irregular motion of air that disrupts smooth flight

vapor trail contrail

vector compass heading; course followed by aircraft, provided by air-traffic control

velocity rate of motion in particular direction

VFR visual flight rules

victor airway low-altitude air lane

visibility distance at which unlighted objects can be seen under existing atmospheric conditions on ground or in flight

visual flight rules VFR; flight plan or maneuvering and rules governing conduct of flight based on pilot's visual observations in acceptable weather conditions

volplane downward glide with engine turned off

wake turbulence turbulence caused by passage of aircraft through atmosphere

washin increase in angle of incidence from root to tip of wing

washout decrease in angle of incidence from root to tip of wing

wind shear change of wind speed or direction over short distance, esp. due to thunderstorm

wing flex design of wings to flex and not remain rigid, providing smoother flight by allowing apparent flapping

wing loading gross weight of aircraft expressed as weight per unit area of wing surface

wingover flight maneuver beginning with climbing turn to point of stall, after which nose falls as turn continues so that aircraft emerges flying in opposite direction

yaw rotation of aircraft about vertical axis; deviation from line of flight, controlled by rudder

zero-lift angle of attack angle of attack at which no lift is created

zero visibility weather condition in which pilot can see nothing and must rely on instrument flight and air-traffic control

zoom (*vb*) climb suddenly and sharply at greater than normal angle

Airframe and Engines

accessory drive drive shaft and gears for transmitting part of engine's power to generators, hydraulic pumps, and other accessories

actuator motor that moves elevators

aft (*adj*) toward the tail

afterburner device attached at exit of jet engine exhaust pipe to burn unburned fuel and exhaust gases, thus producing added thrust

aileron hinged or movable control surface, usu. on trailing edge of wing near tip, that regulates banking by causing movement about longitudinal axis

air brake airfoil that can be extended to produce additional drag for slowing aircraft

airfoil any surface, esp. wing, designed to produce a useful reaction when properly positioned in airstream

airframe any part of aircraft other than engine: fuselage, booms, nacelle, cowlings, fairings, airfoils, landing gear

airscrew propeller

antitorque rotor tail rotor on helicopter

articulated blade helicopter rotor blade hinged at hub

athodyd aerothermodynamic duct; continuous fuel-burning ramjet

baffle device for deflecting airflow

balance tab device that moves in opposite direction from control surface to which it is affixed

ballonet auxiliary air container on balloon or airship that can be inflated or deflated during flight to control altitude

bay compartment in fuselage

belly bottom of fuselage, esp. with landing gear retracted

block metal casting that houses engine cylinders

boom retractable metal tube for in-flight refueling

booster rocket engine that assists takeoff by supplementing main power supply

bubble transparent, hemispherical, seamless, unbraced cockpit canopy

bulkhead upright partition separating compartments and providing structural strength

bypass duct auxiliary channel through which compressed air is diverted around combustion chamber to join exhaust gases for added thrust

cabane struts used to support wing above fuselage

cabin enclosed portion of aircraft for passengers and crew

cabin air intake mechanism for drawing air into cabin

camber curvature of airfoil surface from leading to trailing edge

canard airframe with stabilizing and control surface ahead of main supporting surfaces and wings

canopy transparent, hinged cockpit cover

cantilever beam or member supported at one end only

cermet ceramic-metal alloy used to resist friction heat at supersonic speeds

cockpit compartment with controls for pilot and crew

contraprop pair of propellers mounted on coaxial shafts and geared to turn in opposite directions to reduce torque

controls devices that enable pilot to operate air control surfaces and various accessories in aircraft

control stick vertical lever used to operate elevator and ailerons in fighters and high performance aircraft; joy stick; stick

control surface movable surface used to control attitude or motion and guide aircraft: airfoil, aileron, elevator, or flap

control tab device that provides aerodynamic actuation of control surface

control yoke steering wheel with two arms used to operate elevator and ailerons in transports, bombers, and airliners

cowling metal cover, usu. faired, enclosing aircraft engine and portions of fuselage

deceleron aileron used to slow aircraft in flight

delta wing triangular wing with large sweepback and small thickness ratio

diffuser duct that converts high-speed gas flow to lower speed at increased pressure

dihedral up-and-down angle formed by aircraft wings relative to fuselage

dorsal fin long, narrow fin running aft on top of fuselage to leading edge of primary fin

drag wire wire in some wing structures running from forward inboard to aft outboard point to resist drag

drogue funnel-shaped device towed behind aircraft for in air refueling

effective span measure of span of airfoil less corrections for tip

ejection seat emergency escape device by which both pilot and seat are catapulted from plane

elevator movable airfoil in tail assembly, usu. hinged to stabilizer, that controls vertical movements and rotation of aircraft about lateral axis

elevon one of a pair of control surfaces that act together as an elevator or separately as ailerons

empennage tail assembly, usu. comprised of vertical fin, rudder, elevators, and horizontal stabilizers; tail section

engine pod unit containing engine isolated from rest of aircraft, detachable in emergency

envelope folded outer covering of material for aircraft wing or for rigid airship

fairing secondary structure added to streamline

aircraft part and reduce drag, usu. by covering nonstreamlined part

fanjet engine turbofan

fin fixed, vertical stabilizing surface on tail assembly; tail fin

firewall fire-resistant bulkhead separating engine from rest of aircraft

flame damper fitting on piston engine that hides exhaust flames, used to prevent detection of aircraft at night

flap hinged or pivoted airfoil on trailing edge of wing that increases lift by reshaping or fattening wing on takeoff and landing

flaperon airfoil surface hinged to wing and raised or lowered for lateral control

flapperette hinged rear half of flaperon, normally locked in line, but independently operative if flaperon fails

flapping hinge hinge that allows helicopter rotor blade to swing up and down within limits

flex wing nonrigid wing used on most aircraft

flight deck front compartment of aircraft housing crew; runway portion of aircraft carrier

fore (*adj*) toward the nose

fuselage elongated main body of airplane housing engines, crew, cargo, passengers, and equipment

gas turbine propulsion engine using hot, compressed gas as working fluid, consisting of compressor, combustion chamber, and turbine through which expanded gases are discharged to drive compressor and propel aircraft

gondola cabin suspended under airship or balloon for passengers and engine

gull wing wing that slants upward from fuselage for short distance, then levels out

hatch doorway in side or bottom of fuselage

heat barrier highest temperature at which skin can retain its strength

hold cargo storage area in belly of fuselage

honeycomb sandwich panel used for airplane skins: thin outer layers of metal, wood, or plastic with honeycomb core of metal, plastic, or paper for lightness and strength

horizontal stabilizer stabilizer mounted horizontally in tail assembly, to which elevators are attached for lateral stability

horn short lever fastened to control surface, to which operating cable or rod is attached

hull main body of airship

hydroplane attachment to bottom of fuselage of seaplane that allows it to glide across water

inboard (*adj*) close or closest to fuselage or body of aircraft

inboard flap flap closest to fuselage

inboard spoiler spoiler closest to fuselage

inlet throat

interplane strut strut between two wings or other surfaces

jet jet engine

jet engine any aircraft engine based on jet propulsion, always incorporating a gas turbine: turbojet, fanjet, ramjet, pulsejet, rocket

joy stick *Informal.* control stick, esp. one located between pilot's legs

JP fuels jet propulsion fuels, usu. petroleum derivatives

jury strut auxiliary strut bracing main strut

landing gear understructure, such as wheels and shock absorbers, capable of supporting weight of aircraft on ground; undercarriage

lap joint point at which sections of skin are connected

leading edge foremost edge of airfoil or propeller blade

longeron main longitudinal member of fuselage framing

mixture control control over fuel/air mixture in piston engine of light or older aircraft

monocoque fuselage relying on skin to carry most or all of load

nacelle wing housing for engine; enclosure other than fuselage for people, cargo, and engine; basket under balloon

navigation lights lights on ends of wings, red on left and green on right

negative dihedral airfoil displaced downward from level fuselage

nose foremost section of fuselage enclosing cockpit

nose assembly structural and mechanical parts comprising nose and cockpit enclosure

nose cone foremost portion of nose, usu. tapering to point and made of heat-resistant material

nose landing gear single, retractable wheel assembly beneath nose

nose turret observation or gun turret positioned at nose of military aircraft

nozzle portion of jet engine in which fuel is sprayed into burner can or tailpipe

onboard (*adj*) inside aircraft cabin, cockpit, or cargo hold

outboard (*adj*) far or farthest from fuselage or body of aircraft

outboard flap flap farthest from fuselage

outboard spoiler spoiler farthest from fuselage

plating heavy metal skin, esp. covering wings of large aircraft

propeller assembly with airfoil blades on hub of engine-driven shaft, used to propel aircraft; airscrew

propjet turboprop

pulsejet jet engine that burns fuel intermittently with air from outside that is compressed by ram effect due to forward motion

pusher propeller propeller mounted toward rear that pushes aircraft forward

pylon structure used to attach engine and fuel tank to aircraft, usu. under wing

radar dome radome

radial engine engine of older propeller-driven aircraft with cylinders arranged like spokes around crankshaft

radome housing for radar system on nose; radar dome

ramjet jet engine having no compressor and depending for operation on ram compression of air due to high forward velocity of aircraft

RATO rocket-assisted takeoff

retroengine engine capable of retrofiring to produce thrust in opposite direction of flight

retrofire (*vb*) reverse direction of thrust on engine or rocket

reversible propeller propeller with blades that may be reversed, usu. electrically, to aid braking

rib structural crosspiece attached to spar to strengthen wing

rocket jet engine carrying its own oxidizer along with fuel; missile propelled by rocket engine

rocket-assisted takeoff RATO; takeoff aided by auxiliary rocket device that provides extra thrust

rod thin strip of filler metal used to seal welded joint

root inboard end of wing where it joins fuselage

rotor one of rotating set of bladelike wings that provides lift for helicopter

rudder vertically hinged airfoil for yawing aircraft about vertical axis in flight

ruddevator control surface at wide dihedral angle that operates as both rudder and elevator; V-shaped tail

sandwich structural material with two skins stiffened by thick core; honeycomb

shock absorber device built into landing gear to absorb impact of landing

skin panels of metal riveted in place to cover fuselage

slat narrow auxiliary airfoil mounted ahead of wing or flap for better direction of airstream

sound suppressor equipment for reducing engine noise

span maximum distance from tip to tip of any airfoil

spar main lengthwise support member of wing or airfoil

spinner conical or parabolic fairing over propeller hub that spins with propeller

spoiler surface designed to be extended from wing under certain conditions to spoil airflow over it, decrease lift, or increase drag

stabilator horizontal structure serving as both stabilizer and elevator

stabilizer fixed or adjustable airfoil designed to give stability; vertical or horizontal stabilizer

standby auxiliary piece of equipment or system

stick control stick

stick control movement of elevator and ailerons by control stick

stinger sharp, pointed fairing at end of tail cone

stressed skin covering that contributes to strength of structure

strut supporting brace bearing compression and/or tension loads

supercharger engine-driven compressor that increases flow of air and fuel into cylinders to improve power in nonjet engines and maintains pressure in cabin and engine

sweep fore-and-aft angle of airfoil relative to fuselage

sweepback wing with leading edge at sharp angle to fuselage; swept-back wing

swept-back wing sweepback

tab small hinged surface on trailing edge of control surface, used to assist movement or to trim control surface

tail rear part of aircraft, providing stability

tail assembly empennage

tail fin fin; vertical stabilizer

tail rotor small rotor mounted on shaft at tail of helicopter to counteract torque of main rotor and provide directional control; antitorque rotor

tail section empennage

tail wheel small wheel that supports tail of aircraft with conventional landing gear on ground

throat most constricted part of jet exhaust nozzle; inlet

throttle hand-operated lever connected to valve that controls amount of fuel delivered to engine cylinders; fuel control for gas turbines in jet engines

thrust chamber chamber of jet engine, in which combustion of fuel and air, or oxidizer, takes place

thrust spoiler jet device used to reduce forward thrust without decreasing mass flow from engine

tip outboard end of wing farthest from fuselage

tractor propeller propeller mounted toward front that pulls aircraft

trailing edge rearmost edge of airfoil or propeller blade

trim tab attached to trailing edge of airfoil

truss assembly of structural members forming rigid framework for fuselage

turbine rotary engine with drive shaft powered by action of liquid or gas against curved vanes of wheel or escaping through nozzles located around wheel

turbofan turbojet engine that creates additional thrust by diverting secondary airflow around combustion chamber; fanjet engine

turbojet jet engine supplied with air from compressor driven by turbine that is activated by energy of jet exhaust gases

turboprop variation of turbojet in which gas turbine also drives conventional propeller to produce major portion of thrust; propjet

turret transparent dome for gunner on bomber or fighter

undercarriage landing gear

vane one of flat curved pieces rotating around axle in supercharger, used to compress air

variable-sweep wing sweepback whose angle can be changed during flight

vertical axis axis from top to bottom of aircraft, perpendicular to direction of level flight; yaw axis

vertical stabilizer section of airfoil on tail forward of rudder, providing longitudinal stability; fin

wing part of airplane that provides lift, esp. main lateral airfoil, usu. in pairs

wing flap flap

wing rib chordwise member that gives wing its shape and transmits load from skin to spars

wingspan lateral distance between tips of wings

wing spar principal spanwise structural member of wing

wing tip extreme outboard point of wing

yaw control equipment designed to reduce and control yaw: ailerons, elevators, rudder

yoke pilot's steering wheel with two upward-pointing arms

Avionics and Instrumentation

absolute altimeter radar altimeter

accelerometer instrument that measures acceleration or deceleration

ADF automatic direction finder

ADI attitude direction indicator

aerometer instrument for measuring weight and density of gases

aeroscope device for gathering bacteria and dust from air for examination

air log instrument that records distance traveled by aircraft relative to air through which it moves, used to calculate true airspeed

airspeed indicator dial or gauge showing airspeed

altigraph altimeter that automatically records altitude on chart

altimeter device for measuring altitude, usu. above sea level

anemograph instrument for recording wind direction and speed

anemometer gauge for determining wind speed

anemoscope instrument for displaying direction of wind

atmometer instrument for measuring evaporating capacity of air; evaporimeter

attitude direction indicator ADI; instrument showing attitude of aircraft in space

automatic direction finder ADF; aircraft navigation radio

automatic pilot self-regulating control mechanism for keeping aircraft in level flight and on set course, or for executing maneuvers; autopilot

autopilot automatic pilot

autosyn type of gauge construction

avionics development and use of electronic equipment and control systems for aircraft

avionics box black box that plugs into avionics rack

backup system auxiliary instrument or device used to control aircraft if primary system fails

bank indicator instrument that tells pilot rate at which airplane is turning

black box flight data recorder and cockpit voice recorder encased in fire- and shock-resistant container, used in accident investigations; any replaceable unit that plugs into avionics rack

bombsight instrument on bomber that determines when to drop bomb in order to strike target

Bourdon-tube gauge crescent-shaped tube with one closed end, used to measure pressure in high-pressure fluid systems

ceilometer automatic device for determining height of cloud ceiling by reflected light beam

chronometer device for precise measurement of time

climatometer instrument for measuring sensile temperature of atmosphere

cockpit voice recorder device in black box that records radio and direct conversations of crew

compass magnetic compass

compass card circular card on pivot to which magnetic compass is attached, marked in increments of 5 degrees

console cockpit instrument panel with controls, gauges, and meters; control panel

control panel console

deviation deflection of magnetic compass due to installation error

directional gyro gyro rotor mounted on pair of gimbals with horizontal spin axis, set to magnetic compass and used for directional reference

direction finder radio receiver with direction-sensing antenna, used in navigation and to take bearings

distance measuring equipment DME; instrument that measures nautical miles between aircraft and VOR station

drift meter instrument that shows drift of aircraft from left to right over ground

Earth inductor inclinometer

emergency locator transmitter ELT; automatic radio transmitter attached to aircraft structure and operating at set frequency on its own power source, used for locating downed aircraft

evaporimeter atmometer

flight data recorder device in black box that monitors flight data, used esp. in accident investigations; flight recorder

flight recorder flight data recorder

fuel flowmeter fuel pressure gauge marked in gallons per hour of usage or pounds per hour for gas turbines in jets

fuel quantity indicator gauge that indicates amount of fuel remaining

galvanometer device for detecting and measuring very small electric current

gimbals pair of rings pivoted on axes at right angles so that one swings freely within the other, used to support magnetic compass or gyro device

glide slope device that emits electronic signals to provide vertical guidance during approach or takeoff during ILS

gyrocompass motor-operated gyroscope whose rotating axis is kept parallel to axis of Earth's rotation and points to geographic, not magnetic, North Pole

Gyropilot *Trademark.* automatic pilot

gyroscope wheel mounted on spinning axis that is free to rotate around one or both of two axes perpendicular to each other and to the spinning

axis, used as directional reference for keeping aircraft level in flight

hub dynamometer instrument for measuring power of engine in shop

hygrograph meter for continuously recording atmospheric humidity

hygrometer device for measuring absolute or relative humidity in air

inclinometer instrument that shows inclination of longitudinal axis of aircraft to horizontal plane of flight; Earth inductor

inertial guidance self-contained, automatic guidance system composed of gyroscopes, accelerometers, and computers used to maintain course in automatic pilot; inertial navigation system; INS

inertial navigation system INS; inertial guidance

INS inertial navigation system; inertial guidance

instrument panel cockpit console

interference error avionic error caused by unwanted or distorted radio signals

intervalometer device that controls frequency of exposures in aerial photography

localizer landing instrument that provides course guidance to runway, esp. in ILS

LORAN long range navigation; electronic navigational system that measures difference in time of reception of synchronized pulse signals from two transmitters

machmeter instrument that gives ratio of aircraft speed to speed of sound under existing atmospheric conditions

magnetic compass instrument with needle that indicates direction of North Pole due to action of Earth's magnetic field; compass

manometer gauge for measuring pressure of gases or vapors

meteorograph instrument that automatically records various weather conditions simultaneously

NAVAID navigational aid; visual or electronic device, airborne or on Earth's surface, that provides guidance or position data

nephoscope instrument for determining direction and speed of cloud movement

ozonometer device capable of measuring ozone level in cabin, not in general use

PAR precision approach radar

pelorus device for taking bearings that fits over compass card or gyrocompass

photometer device for measuring relative intensity of light

Pitot-static system method of providing or measuring pressure to operate altimeter, airspeed indicator, or other instrumentation

pluviometer instrument for measuring rainfall

position indicator navigational instrument that displays horizontal situation of aircraft

power unit onboard device that converts battery voltage to voltages required by various instruments

precision approach radar PAR; radar equipment used in final approach course to airport to provide precision instrument approach

pressure altimeter aneroid instrument that measures differences in atmospheric pressure to determine altitude

pressure head Pitot-static tube used to actuate air-speed indicator

pyrometer instrument for measuring temperatures above range of normal thermometer

radar radio detecting and ranging; system for determining direction, distance, height, and speed of aircraft by reflection of radio waves, also used as weather sensor on aircraft

radar altimeter instrument that uses reflection time of radio waves to and from ground to determine altitude of aircraft; absolute altimeter

radio direction finder little-used direction finder employing radio waves

radiogoniometer radio direction finder

rate gyroscope device sensitive to rate of angular motion

rate-of-climb indicator instrument that indicates rate at which aircraft is ascending or descending in feet per minute

recording meter any instrument that records readings on chart or traces them on screen: recording altimeter, anemometer, hygrometer

sextant simple navigational instrument for measuring angular distance of celestial body from horizon, rarely used on aircraft

slip indicator instrument for measuring longitudinal deviation about vertical axis; yawmeter

sound ranging altimeter instrument that determines altitude by timing sounds received from specific points

squelch control device that helps eliminate undesired noise in radio

static tube Pitot-static tube carrying static pressure of outside air

synchroscope instrument for determining difference in phase between two engines

TACAN tactical air navigation; ultra-high frequency electronic navigation aid used primarily on military aircraft

tachometer instrument that measures rate of rotation of revolving engine shaft

telemetry electronic tracking system, esp. for missile or experimental aircraft

terrain clearance indicator instrument for maintaining altitude above terrain of highest obstruction

thermograph instrument for automatically recording variations in temperature

thermostat device for automatically regulating temperature

torquemeter meter for measuring torque in shaft of nonjet engine

transit instrument sight level used to determine level line on fuselage as reference for repair

transponder electronic device that receives radio signals and generates distinctive reply pattern on radar

turn-and-bank indicator instrument for showing rate of turn of aircraft

turnmeter instrument for measuring angular velocity of aircraft about predetermined axis

variometer instrument that measures and records small variations in pressure

venturi tube suction gauge in slipstream that indicates reduction in pressure

vertical-speed indicator instrument that registers rate of climb

very high frequency VHF; band for radio communication and navigation

very high frequency omni range VOR; basic radio navigation system that relies on communications between aircraft and transmitting stations on ground, used esp. by military aircraft

viscometer instrument for measuring viscosity, esp. of fuel

VOR very high frequency omni range

weather radar system using radio signals to analyze weather conditions

yawmeter instrument that measures yaw of aircraft

Commercial Airlines, Airports, and Air Force

aerodrome *Brit.* small airport

air base military facility for operation and maintenance of aircraft

air cargo air freight

air carrier person or company that undertakes transportation of cargo by air

aircraft carrier large warship that serves as floating air base

airfield landing area of airport, esp. military air base

air force aviation branch of armed forces

Air Force One jet aircraft used by U.S. president

air freight shipping of goods and cargo by air

airline company that moves freight and passengers on aircraft

airliner large passenger aircraft, usu. jet, operated by airline

airmail mail transported by air

airman enlisted person in Air Force or Naval Air Corps

air piracy skyjacking

airport area of land with control tower and runways for landing and takeoff of aircraft, facilities for storage and maintenance, and terminal for passengers

airstrip hard-surfaced area used as runway

air-to-air (*adj*) designating weapon launched from aircraft and directed at airborne object

air traffic aircraft in air near airport or on airport runways and approaches

air-traffic control ATC; radar facility with tower from which approaches and departures of air traffic in and around airports and along air routes are monitored and directed

air-traffic controller person trained and authorized by FAA to provide ATC services; controller

approach lights lights that indicate direction and termination of runway to approaching aircraft

apron area of land at airport used for loading and unloading of passengers and cargo, refueling, parking, and maintenance; ramp

ATC air-traffic control

blast fence barrier used to divert jet fuel blast

blue room *Slang.* lavatory on aircraft

boarding movement of passengers onto aircraft preparatory to flight

boarding pass ticket distributed at gate that permits passengers to enter aircraft

bombardier member of bomber crew who operates bombsight and releases bombs

bug smashers *Slang.* small private planes flying in congested traffic areas

bumped (*adj*) refused seating on flight for which one has reservation

CAB Civil Aeronautics Board

captain commanding officer of aircraft, esp. commercial airliner; air force commanding officer

carousel circular baggage conveyor from which passengers retrieve luggage at airport

carrier airliner; commercial airline

carry-on luggage small items of luggage taken on board by passenger and placed in overhead rack or under seat

centerline line marked down center of runway, imagined to extend beyond it onto clearway or stopway

charter flight flight on aircraft hired by group or organization for special trip not regularly scheduled

chock block or wedge set against wheel to keep it from turning

Civil Aeronautics Board CAB; federal agency that regulated airline industry activities until deregulation in 1978

clearance permission from air traffic control, esp. for approach, landing, takeoff, or routing

clearway area at least 500 feet wide around extended centerline of runway free of obstructions and under airport authority

combat pilot air force fighter pilot

commercial pilot pilot of commercial airliner who holds FAA commercial license

commuter flight frequently scheduled short flight between two nearby metropolitan areas; shuttle

computer reservation system CRS; computer linkup between all commercial airlines and travel agents for booking flight reservations

controlled airspace airspace within which aircraft may be subject to air-traffic control

controller air-traffic controller

copilot assistant pilot who relieves pilot; first officer

deregulation federal removal of certain restrictions on commercial airline practices, esp. ticket pricing and routes, in 1978

direct flight journey without change of aircraft but with one or more intermediate landings

egress route pathway out of aircraft in emergency evacuation

ETA estimated time of arrival; scheduled or anticipated time for completion of flight

evacuation slide inflatable chute used as emergency escape device from commercial airliner

FAA Federal Aviation Administration

Federal Aviation Administration FAA; federal government agency responsible for administering air-traffic control and investigating accidents

first officer copilot and second in command of commercial airliner

flight scheduled trip on airplane to fly specific route at certain time; such a scheduled route

flight attendant person on commercial airliner responsible for passengers' comfort and safety; stewardess or steward

flight crew pilot, copilot, flight engineer, and others who operate an aircraft during flight

flight plan information filed with air-traffic control that describes intended flight

flight simulator pilot training device that simulates flight conditions on ground

forward cabin first-class passenger compartment nearest cockpit

frequent-flyer program marketing incentive that rewards passengers with free flights for accumulated mileage

gate location where passengers board or disembark from airliner

gate hold air-traffic control instruction that requires loaded aircraft to remain at gate due to departure delay of over five minutes

gosport flexible tube formerly used for spoken communications between different compartments of aircraft, esp. in training

ground crew maintenance and repair workers

hangar large enclosure for storage, repair, and maintenance of aircraft

helipad landing and takeoff area used by helicopters

heliport small land or water area or structure used by helicopters for landing and takeoff

hijacking skyjacking

holding procedure maneuver by which aircraft remains in specified airspace while awaiting further ATC clearance

hop very short flight

hostess stewardess

hub and spoke system system of air transportation in which local flights are made to central hub airport from which connections are made to final local or long-distance destinations

hub carrier airline primarily serving specific hub airport

jetway tube-shaped bridge from terminal to aircraft for boarding passengers

landing slot airport runway space controlled by airline leasing slot from government

landing strip airstrip, often temporary runway surface

layover break partway through journey, esp. overnight away from home base

local traffic aircraft operating within sight of tower or under its control in IFR conditions

Mae West inflatable life jacket vest designed for use in water

major carrier large national or international commercial airline

marker beacon aural and visual signal transmitter that provides aircraft with its position on landing

milk run routine military mission, unlikely to be dangerous

mission flight by military aircraft, esp. bomber

naval pilot naval aircraft flier, esp. one based on aircraft carrier

navigator flight officer responsible for plotting course

nonstop service flight directly to final destination with no intermediate stops

no-show passenger with confirmed reservation who fails to arrive for flight

off-line (adj) designating travel on carrier other than one that sold ticket

offset parallel runways staggered runways with parallel centerlines

outer marker marker beacon located four to seven miles from runway threshold on extended centerline of runway

overbooking airline practice of selling more seats than are available based on statistical likelihood that some passengers will not show up

overhead rack compartment above seat for stowing carry-on luggage on airliner

overshoot (vb) fail to come to complete stop on runway; fly through final approach course

oxygen mask face mask connected to oxygen tank located above seat on commercial airliners, used in decompression emergency

paratrooper military parachutist

radar contact appearance of aircraft on radar display at air-traffic control

radar service services provided by air-traffic control to aircraft in radar contact

ramp apron

red-eye Informal. all-night, transcontinental flight arriving near dawn

run regularly scheduled flight between two points

runway defined rectangular area marked off on airport or aerodrome surface and prepared for landing and takeoff, usu. with centerline and marker lights on sides

seat belt protective restraining strap that buckles across passenger's lap

second officer member of flight crew with least seniority who monitors instruments and observes flight

security search physical search and X-ray examination of luggage and passengers prior to

boarding flight, esp. to detect explosives or firearms

shuttle frequently scheduled flight between two nearby metropolitan centers; commuter flight

skycap airport employee who helps passengers with luggage or assists disabled passengers

skyjacking taking control of aircraft by force and making it alter destination by holding crew and passengers hostage; air piracy; hijacking

standby status of passenger waiting for open place on flight for which he or she does not have confirmed reservation

stew Informal. stewardess

steward male flight attendant

stewardess female flight attendant; hostess; stew

stopover brief landing at intermediate airport en route to termination point of flight

stopway area beyond takeoff runway and centered on its extended centerline, used in aborted takeoff

stow (vb) pack away in safe, orderly manner, esp. luggage

taxi (vb) move slowly on ground, esp. on airport ramps and aprons to and from runways (said of aircraft)

terminal airport structure used by arriving and departing passengers and for cargo handling; connection point on flight

test flight monitored flight on which new aircraft or equipment is tested

test pilot specially trained operator of experimental or new aircraft and equipment

tower tall airport structure from which air traffic control services are provided

traffic routes and positions of aircraft in specific area

tray table small, flat surface that folds down from back of seat in front of passenger on commercial airliners

turnaround flight on which crew returns to home base on day of departure from it

undershoot (vb) miscalculate approach so that touchdown occurs before reaching runway

upgrade (vb) move to business or first-class seat from tourist or business class

Valsalva maneuver technique for relieving pressure in head due to imbalance of air pressure in ascending or descending aircraft by blowing hard with nose and mouth closed

white knuckler Slang. anxious passenger

widebody jumbo jet, usu. able to carry over 300 passengers

wind tunnel tunnellike structure used for testing aircraft parts or models by forcing wind past them at known velocity

AUTOMOBILES

Types of Automobiles
Trucks and Buses
Internal Combustion Engine
Working Parts
Body Parts and Accessories
Driving and Repair

See also: *Chap. 5: Machinery and Fabrication; Electricity and Electronics; Chap. 6: Other Vehicles; Chap. 11: The City; Chap. 12: Insurance*

Types of Automobiles

ambulance emergency conveyance to hospital

automobile four-wheel passenger vehicle, usu. having internal combustion engine; car

beach buggy dune buggy

cab taxicab

car automobile

cement mixer *Slang.* noisy old car

cherry (*adj*) *Slang.* describing older car in excellent condition

coach two-door enclosed sedan

compact small car

convertible automobile with retractable canvas roof

coupe small, enclosed, two-door, two-passenger automobile

deuce *Slang.* 1932 Ford coupe

dragster customized car modified for rapid acceleration racing

dune buggy roofless recreational car with oversize tires for sand traction; beach buggy

fastback car with slanting aerodynamic roof that sometimes opens at rear

flivver *Slang.* small, cheap, old automobile

go-kart miniature self-propelled chassis without body, esp. for racing

golf cart low-power, open vehicle with canvas roof

grand touring car sporty two-passenger coupe; orig. large, vintage, open sedan with side rails

gran turismo *Italian.* sporty grand touring car for two passengers; GT

GT gran turismo

gypsy cab cab licensed to pick up passengers on call, but that often illegally cruises in search of passengers

hack *Informal.* taxicab

hardtop car with permanent, rigid top covering frame

hatchback usu. two-door car with roof lifting open at rear in lieu of trunk

hearse long station wagon for carrying corpse at funeral

horseless carriage early term for automobile

hot rod modified or souped-up, customized car

jalopy dilapidated automobile

Jeep *Trademark.* sturdy, four-wheel-drive vehicle designed for rough terrain

junker *Slang.* old, dilapidated car

landaulet vintage convertible car with open driver's seat and folding top over rear seat

Land Rover *Trademark.* jeeplike vehicle designed for rough terrain

lemon *Informal.* bad car, esp. one that is new but has mechanical problems

limo limousine

limousine long, luxurious chauffeur-driven sedan; limo

lowrider customized car fitted with specialized

suspension that allows the chassis to ride just a few inches above pavement

microbus box-shaped station wagon similar to bus

midget racer tiny, open racing car

motorcar motorized automobile

off-road vehicle vehicle, such as a four-wheel drive Jeep, beach buggy, or snowmobile, designed for travel off public roads

patrol car squad car

pimpmobile *Slang.* large, ostentatious car, esp. limousine

prowl car squad car

race car specially-designed, high-speed car for racing; racing car

racing car race car

ragtop *Slang.* convertible

roadster open two-seater automobile with folding top and rear luggage compartment or rumble seat

sedan enclosed car seating four to seven persons, often four-door

shandrydan *Slang.* old, broken-down car or vehicle

snowmobile small motorized vehicle equipped with ski-like runners and revolving tread

sports car low, small, high-powered, agile two-seater automobile

squad car police vehicle; patrol car; prowl car

station wagon passenger car with roof extended to rear to increase cargo and passenger space, seating up to ten persons; wagon

stock car factory-built passenger car modified for racing

stretch extra-long limousine with bar, TV, and other amenities

subcompact smallest automobile used in U.S.

taxicab sedan that carries passengers for fare determined by mileage; cab; hack

touring car vintage auto with two seats, four doors, and folding top

town car four-door car with rear passenger compartment separated from driver by sliding glass partition

wagon *Informal.* station wagon

wheels *Slang.* automobile, esp. one's own

woodie *Slang.* wood-paneled station wagon

Trucks and Buses

amphibian flat-bottomed vehicle that moves over land or water on tracks with fins

armored car vehicle with bullet-resistant panels and doors, used by military or police

autobus bus

big rig *Slang.* multiunit or eighteen-wheeler truck

bulldozer tractor with broad, blunt blade for moving earth and debris, used in road building and construction

bus motorized, box-shaped vehicle used to transport numerous paying passengers, usu. on a fixed schedule; autobus

camper van with bed and kitchen

caravan large vehicle with living quarters

carryall passenger vehicle used as small bus

Caterpillar *Trademark.* tractor or construction vehicle propelled by two endless belts

club cab pickup truck with expanded cab that includes rear seat and/or storage area

coach *Chiefly Brit.* bus

crawler heavy construction vehicle that travels on Caterpillar treads

delivery truck enclosed freight-carrying truck

diesel large truck with diesel fuel engine

dray small truck for hauling goods

duck amphibious military truck with code designation DUKW (World War II)

dump truck heavy, open truck used to transport loose freight

eighteen-wheeler large tractor and semitrailer truck with eighteen wheels

fire engine heavy truck or tractor and trailer with firefighting equipment

flatbed truck with open platform or shallow box body

float trailer with platform for parade exhibit

forklift small work vehicle that hoists heavy loads on steel prongs

garbage truck municipal truck used for trash collection and removal

grader truck equipped with earth-leveling device

haulaway truck with two-level trailer, used to transport new automobiles

hook and ladder fire engine with ladders and other apparatus

jitney small passenger bus or van with flexible schedule over regular route

juggernaut *Chiefly Brit.* heavy truck

limousine van for transportation of passengers, esp. to airport

lorry *Chiefly Brit.* truck

microbus station wagon shaped like van

mobile home large van or trailer with living quarters; motor home

motor home mobile home

moving van large, enclosed truck used to haul household goods

omnibus public carrier for at least twelve passengers, usu. with door in rear

paddy wagon panel truck used to transport prisoners

panel truck enclosed, windowless van

pantechnicon *Chiefly Brit.* moving van

pickup small truck with cab, shallow box body, and tailgate

recreational vehicle RV; large van with living facilities

RV recreational vehicle

semi *Informal.* semitrailer truck

semitrailer freight trailer designed so that most of its weight rests on another vehicle, attached to tractor by fifth wheel or pivot

six-by-six six-wheeled truck with six driving wheels

skidder four-wheel tractor equipped with grapple, used to haul logs or timber over rough terrain

steamroller steam-powered tractor with heavy roller for roadwork

tank military armored tractor propelled by two endless metal belts

tow truck pickup equipped with winch for hauling other vehicles; wrecker

tractor powerful vehicle with large rear wheels or endless belt treads, used to haul equipment or do work; cab and engine section that hauls semitrailer

trailer engineless container drawn by tractor or other vehicle; auto-drawn highway vehicle with living facilities

transfer passenger or baggage carrier used between locations by transfer company

truck self-propelled motor vehicle designed for transportation of goods or special-purpose equipment, often with swivel for hauling trailer

van multipurpose, enclosed, box-shaped vehicle having side panels, with or without windows in panels

water wagon truck equipped with tank for hauling and sprinkling water

weasel tractorlike vehicle used in snow

wrecker tow truck

Internal Combustion Engine

afterburner auxiliary device that burns exhaust fumes from combustion

air-cooled engine engine in which heat of combustion is dissipated by air flow, usu. by movement of fan

automatic choke temperature- or time-controlled device that enriches air/fuel mixture for cold starts

block aluminum or iron casting housing cylinders and crankshaft

bore cylinder diameter

cam one of rotating pieces along camshaft

camshaft shaft that changes rotary motion into linear motion to operate valves

carburetor device that controls and monitors air/fuel mixture fed to cylinders

choke plate near top of carburetor that can be partially closed to restrict air entering carburetor and enrich fuel mixture

combustion chamber area within cylinder above piston where fuel/air mixture ignites

compression reduction in combustion chamber volume prior to power stroke on ignition

compression-ignition engine diesel engine

compression ratio ratio of maximum to minimum combustion chamber volume as piston strokes

connecting rod linkage between piston and crankshaft; rod

crankcase lower part of engine that contains lubricating oil

crankshaft main engine shaft that converts linear motion of pistons into rotary motion

cylinder hollow tube in engine block, containing piston

cylinder head combustion chamber area of cylinders atop engine block; head

dead center either of points at each end of stroke in reciprocating engine where crankshaft and connecting rod are in same line

diesel engine compression-ignition engine in which air is heated by compression and diesel fuel is injected directly into the combustion chamber, where it then self-ignites

displacement total volume swept by pistons in single stroke

dual carburetor engine equipped with two carburetors operating together

exhaust manifold metal casting that routes exhaust from each combustion chamber to common exhaust pipe

exhaust valve device that opens to allow burned gases to be expelled from combustion chamber

four-stroke cycle engine internal combustion engine working in four stages: intake, compression, power, and exhaust

fuel injection fuel delivery system in which a high-pressure pump meters and atomizes fuel directly into diesel engine cylinder or into intake manifold of spark ignition engine

glow plug element for each cylinder of diesel engine that heats incoming fuel and air to promote combustion when engine is cold

head cylinder head

head gasket packing element that seals cylinder head from engine block

intake manifold tube or casting with combination of passages that routes fuel/air mixture from carburetor to combustion chamber in spark ignition engine

intake port opening in cylinder wall of two-stroke cycle engine through which air or fuel/air mixture is forced into combustion chamber

intake valve device in four-stroke cycle engine that opens to allow air or fuel/air mixture to be drawn into combustion chamber

internal combustion engine reciprocating or rotary engine in which combustion of fuel is in direct contact with pistons or rotor

lifter element connecting camshaft to pushrod or valve

piston component moving up and down in cylinder, linked by connecting rod to crankshaft, and converting pressure of combustion into work

piston ring circular device fitted into groove in piston to keep oil out and seal gases in; ring

power stroke burning of fuel/air mixture in combustion chamber to force piston downward

pushrod mechanical device through which camshaft activates rocker arm to open valve

reciprocating engine two-stroke or four-stroke cycle engine

ring piston ring

rocker arm pivoting lever that pushes valve open

rod connecting rod

rotary engine internal combustion engine without pistons, in which triangular rotor moves orbitally and rotationally; Wankel engine

slant six six-cylinder engine with row of cylinders mounted at an angle

spark ignition engine engine in which spark or glow plug ignites an explosive air/fuel mixture

stroke one phase in piston cycle

supercharger engine-driven compressor that increases density of fuel/air mixture

throttle device that controls volume of mixture delivered to spark ignition engine or quantity of fuel injected into diesel engine

torque measure of twisting force generated by crankshaft

turbocharger compressor driven by exhaust heat to increase density of fuel/air mixture

two-stroke cycle engine internal combustion engine that works in two stages, compression and power, with blower or other means of delivering fresh air and fuel with piston at bottom dead center prior to compression stroke

V-6 six-cylinder engine with three cylinders in each of two banks set at ninety degree angle forming a V

V-8 eight-cylinder engine with four cylinders in each of two banks set at ninety degree angle forming a V

valve device used to close off and meter flow of intake and exhaust into and out of combustion chamber

valve clearance size of opening of valve necessary for proper engine operation

valve guide hole through which stem of valve passes

valve lifter cam extension that opens valves

Wankel engine rotary engine

water-cooled engine engine in which circulated coolant, or water and glycol mixture, extracts combustion heat

wrist pin steel pin that links piston to connecting rod

Working Parts

accelerator pedal operated by driver's right foot that varies amount of fuel fed to engine, thus controlling speed

air cleaner device containing air filter and protecting against backfire

air conditioner refrigeration and ventilation system for lowering temperature of passenger compartment

air filter device that keeps solid particles out of fuel/air mixture

alternator alternating current (AC) generator that supplies power to run car's electrical system

automatic transmission gearbox that changes gear ratios independently of driver based on speed and load

axle full shaft on which wheels revolve

battery electrochemical storage unit of 6 or 12 volts

bearing part, such as wheel bearing, on which another part revolves

blower fan

brake friction device used to slow or stop car

brake drum metal arc mounted on hub against which shoes rub to stop car

brake lining replaceable friction material attached to brake shoes and pressed by shoes against brake drums to stop car

brake shoes arc-shaped pieces that fit inside and press against drums

breaker points electrical switch in distributor used to control high voltage needed by spark plugs; points

capacitor device for storage of electrical energy

catalytic converter emission control device for converting pollutants to benign substances

clutch coupling mechanism by which rotating shafts of engine and transmission may be engaged and disengaged; pedal operated by driver's left foot in manual transmission cars

clutch plate flat coupling disc in clutch mechanism

coil pulse transformer that increases voltage to fire spark plug

condenser electrical device that prevents arcing

cruise control automatic setting for continuous, high-speed driving

CV joints constant velocity universal joints that keep input and output speed equal, contained in rubber boots into which grease is packed at each end of axle

damper *Chiefly Brit.* shock absorber

differential gear system that allows outer wheel to travel greater distance than inner wheel during turn

disc brakes brakes whose friction is generated by pads rubbing rotor mounted on wheel assembly

distributor device for directing high voltage from coil to appropriate spark plugs in turn

distributor cap top of distributor with wires to each spark plug

distributor rotor component that directs voltage to appropriate spark plug wire

driveline drive train

drive shaft shaft connecting transmission to rear axle in rear-wheel drive car

drive train universal joint and drive shaft connecting transmission to axles; driveline

drum brakes brakes with lined shoes that rub against inner circumference of metal, hub-mounted drums for friction

electronic ignition spark ignition system without breaker points

emergency brake manually operated brake that sets rear brakes in locked position, usu. while car is parked

expansion strut steel or alloy segment cast into piston to control its expansion under heat and maintain constant piston-to-cylinder wall clearance

fan belt engine-driven belt that operates fan

fifth wheel pivot with which trailer attaches to tractor

filter device that removes foreign substances from air, oil, gasoline, or water

fluid drive power coupling between engine and transmission, consisting of two vaned rotors in sealed, lubricated casing, permitting smooth start in any gear

flywheel heavy disk at rear of crankshaft that smooths separate power pulses from each cylinder

four-wheel drive system in which differential conveys power to all four wheels

front-wheel drive system in which differential conveys power only to front wheels, which steer and propel car

fuel pump device that supplies fuel from gas tank to carburetor or fuel injection system

fuse safety device that controls current flow to elements in electrical system

gear one of toothed wheels in transmission that determine direction and relative speed of travel and mechanical advantage of engine

gearbox transmission

gear ratio ratio of speeds between input and output shafts of transmission in each gear

generator direct current (DC) generating device

half-shaft one of pair of half-axles that serves left or right wheel

hand brake manually operated emergency brake

header exhaust manifold designed for free flow of exhaust gases

hydraulic brakes brake system operated by pressure of fluid in cylinders

hydraulic clutch clutch operated by hydraulic pressure from engine cooling system

ignition switch key switch in dashboard that sets ignition system in operation

ignition system electrical system designed to produce spark in cylinders and ignite fuel, consisting of battery, coil, condenser, breaker points, distributor, spark plugs, and wires

linkage series of metal rods or levers that transmit motion from one unit to another

manifold exhaust manifold and/or intake manifold

manual transmission gearbox in which selection of gear is controlled by driver through clutch and gearshift

master cylinder brake fluid sump and piston that powers slave cylinders in hydraulic brake system

muffler baffle exhaust device used to lessen noise of combustion

oil cooler auxiliary radiator used to lower oil temperature

oil filter engine-mounted device that removes contaminants from engine oil

oil pump device that forces lubricating oil through engine

overdrive device used to lower overall gear ratio and hence reduce rpms necessary to achieve given road speed, thus decreasing fuel consumption

PCV valve positive crankcase ventilation valve; device that prevents crankcase vapors from discharging directly into atmosphere

plug spark plug

points breaker points

power brakes hydraulically actuated brakes with vacuum assist mechanism that reduces brake pedal pressure needed

power steering hydraulically assisted steering linkage that reduces turning effort

rack-and-pinion steering system in which rotation of steering wheel is translated into linear motion by pinion gear mounted in toothed rack

radiator unit of pipes that dissipates heat in engine coolant

rear axle axle connecting wheels at back of car

rear-wheel drive conventional system in which differential conveys drive power to rear wheels only

reduction gear combination of gears that reduce input speed so as to lower output speed

regulator device that controls voltage sent by alternator to battery

seals permanently installed rubber or leather components that keep lubrication from leaking

shift driver-operated lever that controls transmission

shock absorber device fitted to each corner of suspension to damp spring oscillations and smoothen ride

slave cylinders hydraulic brake cylinders on each wheel that convert hydraulic pressure from master cylinder into mechanical force applied to brakes

solenoid magnetic device that exerts force when current flows through coil

spark ignition system ignition system in which high voltage current from coil is sent through distributor to appropriate spark plug at proper timing to ignite fuel/air mixture in combustion chamber

spark plug electrical component threaded into cylinder head whose spark initiates combustion; plug

spark plug gap opening across which spark jumps to ignite air/fuel mixture

springs main suspension units that absorb force of road shocks by twisting or flexing

starter high-torque electric motor used to start engine

steering system that transmits directional force from steering wheel to axle and wheels

steering column central pivoting unit of steering system

steering wheel wheel connected to steering column by which driver steers car

stick shift device by which driver controls gears in manual transmission

suspension springs, shock absorbers, and other components that connect wheels to car body

sway bar torsion coupling between right and left front-wheel suspensions to reduce roll and sway

thermostat device that regulates engine temperature by controlling flow of coolant through system

timing setting that initiates spark at appropriate point in piston's compression stroke

torsion bar flexible steel bar that twists to provide spring in suspension

tranny *Informal.* transmission

transaxle integrated transmission, differential, and drive unit on drive axle, front or rear

transmission assembly of gears and selector linkage that connects engine output shaft to rest of drive train by matching engine speed with desired road speed; gearbox; tranny

universal joint multidirectional joint in drive shaft that permits changes in angle while shaft is rotating

water pump device that circulates water coolant through engine

Body Parts and Accessories

aerial metal rod mounted on body for receiving radio signals

air bag bag that inflates during collision to prevent driver or passenger from being thrown forward

antifreeze glycol and water mixture used in water-cooled engine to lower freezing point of coolant

antiknock (*adj*) relating to any fuel additive that helps resist engine knocking

ashtray retractable metal receptacle in dash for extinguished cigarettes

backseat seat behind driver's seat in passenger compartment

backup light exterior light illuminated when car is in reverse gear

belt tread continuous band around sets of wheels on tanks and tractors

bias-ply tire tire with supporting cords embedded at angle to rotational direction

body external housing and structure of vehicle

bonnet *Chiefly Brit.* hood

boot *Chiefly Brit.* trunk

brake fluid viscous liquid used in hydraulic brake cylinders

brake lights rear lamps illuminated when brakes are in use

brake pedal foot control by which driver operates brakes

bucket seat low, individual, front seat for one passenger

bulb electric lamp

bumper protective member fitted over front and rear wheels; fender

cab enclosed passenger portion of truck

camber angle of wheel when viewed head-on

caster positioning that provides directional stability to front wheels

chains chain-link units attached to tires to increase traction on snow, ice, or mud

chassis substructure on which components of car are mounted

chrome shiny chromium alloy used to coat parts of body trim

compartment enclosed passenger seating area

convertible top retractable vinyl or fabric roof

coolant alcohol or glycol mixed with water to increase efficiency of cooling system

cove scooped-out area on side door or panel

dash dashboard

dashboard instrument panel facing driver in compartment; dash

defroster heating/ventilation system that directs air onto windshield to clear ice or condensation

diesel fuel fuel oil burned in diesel engine

directional signal turn signal

emergency light hazard light

exhaust pipe metal tube that routes exhaust fumes out of manifold

fairing custom part added to smooth contour of body and reduce drag

fender bumper

fuel gasoline or oil burned to supply power for engine

gas gasoline

gasket packing that seals joint, as between cylinder head and engine block

gasohol combination of gasoline and up to ten per cent alcohol, used as fuel

gasoline complex hydrocarbon blend used as fuel by internal combustion engines; gas

gas tank storage container for gasoline attached to chassis

gearshift mechanism by which gears are engaged and disengaged

glove box *Chiefly Brit.* glove compartment

glove compartment small storage area with door in dashboard; glove box

grill gridlike chrome covering placed over front of engine compartment to permit air to flow freely through engine

hatchback vehicle with rear hatch opening into passenger compartment

hazard light blinking front or rear light used when vehicle is stopped for mechanical trouble or in dangerous place; emergency light

headlights high-powered lamps that illuminate area in front of car for night driving

headrest unit attached to seat top as head support

heater unit using engine heat to warm passenger compartment

high beam second headlight for added illumination at distance

hood hinged cover over engine compartment

horn audible electric warning device controlled by driver

hose usu. rubber tube for carrying air or water from one unit to another

housing protective metal covering for engine part

hub wheel mounting on end of axle

hub cap often decorative chrome covering for lug nuts that attach wheel to axle

inner tube replaceable rubber lining that held air in old-fashioned tires

instrument panel dashboard with gauges and meters

jack device for lifting side of car to change tires

Jaws of Life *Trademark.* heavy-duty tool used to cut through and pry apart crumpled metal to free trapped accident victims

jumper cable insulated electrical cable for recharging battery or starting car with dead battery

jump seat removable or folding seat for extra passenger, esp. in limousine or taxicab

lamp electric filament bulb for illumination or signaling

license plate metal plate issued by state bearing car's identifying number

loaded (*adj*) having many optional features

lubricant engine oil or grease that reduces friction and heat on operating parts

lug nuts bolts that hold wheel on axle

mag wheel shiny magnesium wheel rim

mud flap splash guard

mud guard splash guard

odometer accumulated mileage gauge mounted on dashboard

oil gauge meter that indicates engine oil pressure

oil pan sump in which oil collects when not circulating through engine in operation

panel section of auto body

parking light small front or rear light

pedal foot control by which driver operates accelerator, brake, or clutch

petrol *Chiefly Brit.* gasoline

premium high-octane gasoline used in high-compression engines

radial tire tire with supporting cords embedded in line with direction of rotation

raked (*adj*) describing car, esp. hot rod, with lowered front end

rearview mirror small mirror affixed above windshield that allows driver to see what lies behind car

recap retread tire

retread used tire with new tread applied; recap

rim outer metal band on wheel to which tire is attached

roll bar protective bar over open driving compartment, esp. in racing cars

roof top of passenger compartment

rumble seat uncovered folding seat in back of car

running board footboard at base of door on side of car

seat belt safety device strapped across passenger to secure position in case of accident

seat cover vinyl, leather, or fabric placed over seat springs

shift knob end of gear shift handled by driver

side mirror rearview mirror mounted on side of car

side pipes chromed exhaust pipes mounted on side of exterior body of customized car

side window window on left or right side of car

snow tire special tire with deep tread or rubber cleats to provide traction on snow or ice

spare tire extra tire, usu. stored in trunk

speedometer road speed gauge mounted on dashboard

splash guard flap suspended behind rear wheel to prevent tire splash from muddying windows of following vehicles; mud flap; mud guard

stick shift upright gearshift protruding from floor, used to operate manual transmission

stud metal cleat inserted in snow tire to increase traction

sump part of oil pan containing oil

sunroof retractable section of roof

sun visor flap that may be lowered to shield passenger's eyes from sun

tachometer gauge mounted on dashboard that measures engine speed in revolutions per minute (rpms)

tailgate small gate at rear of vehicle that can be lowered to form horizontal surface

taillight rear light

tailpipe pipe that routes exhaust fumes from muffler to rear of car

tire pneumatic casing mounted on wheel forming interface between car and road: tubeless, tube, bias-ply, or radial

tow bar unit attached to rear bumper, used to haul another vehicle or trailer

transmission fluid viscous liquid used in hydraulic transmission

tread grooved portion of tire that touches road

trim decorations, chrome, and insignia attached to auto body

trunk enclosed storage compartment, usu. at rear

tubeless tire tire without inner tube

turn signal external, front and rear, driver-controlled lights used to indicate direction of turn; directional signal

unleaded fuel gasoline with low lead content, less polluting and forming fewer deposits than leaded fuel

vanity plate license plate customized with owner's initials, nickname, or other chosen letters or word

wheel circular frame at hub of axle to which tire attaches

whitewall tire with circular white strip on black

windscreen *Chiefly Brit.* windshield

windshield front window of passenger compartment; windscreen

windshield wiper motor-driven device with rubber blade for clearing water from windshield

wiper blade rubber attachment to windshield wiper

Driving and Repair

automotive (*adj*) self-propelled on land, sea, or air, usu. referring to land vehicles

backfire improperly timed explosion of fuel mixture, esp. occurring outside cylinder in exhaust system

balance (*vb*) adjust new tires for even rotation

bleed (*vb*) drain brake fluid to clear hydraulic brake lines of air

blindside (*vb*) strike another car without warning from rear or side

blow-by leakage of combustion gases between piston and cylinder wall into crankcase

blown engine *Slang.* general, extensive engine breakdown

blowout sudden, severe flat tire while driving

Blue Book *Trademark.* reference manual listing the standard, accepted values of used cars

body shop garage for repairs to body and repainting

bodywork nonmechanical repairs

bottleneck narrowing roadway that causes traffic congestion

Botts dots raised, reflective markers on roadway that alert driver when car drifts out of its lane

broadside (*vb*) strike another car full on side

bumper-to-bumper (*adj.*) describing long line of slow-moving traffic

burn rubber *Slang.* accelerate abruptly with tires squealing and leaving black marks on pavement

center divider barrier down center of two-way road

chicken game in which two drivers drive toward each other or toward obstacle, with first driver to turn away losing contest

cornering ability of driver or car to negotiate curves and turns

crank (*vb*) start engine

crosswalk lane marked off for pedestrian use while crossing street

cruising driving slowly back and forth along particular roadway in city

curb low bump at edge of roadway that separates it from sidewalk; also, *esp. Brit.*, kerb

customizing additions or alterations made by owner to standard body and engine

dead battery battery without stored voltage until recharged from external source

Denver boot device locked in place on wheel of illegally-parked car to prevent it from moving

detonation knocking or pinging sound when gasoline is inadequate for acceleration or ascending grade

dieseling abnormal self-ignition in which engine continues running after ignition is turned off

double clutch pump clutch pedal twice in shifting gear

double parking illegal parking on street side of another parked car

downshift (*vb*) change to lower gear when decelerating

driver's license permit to operate car issued by state; license

driveway narrow private roadway leading to garage or residence from public roadway

driving school training institution for drivers

drop the engine remove entire engine for repairs; pull the engine

drunk driving driving recklessly while intoxicated; DUI

DUI driving under the influence; drunk driving

emission control smog control

engine overhaul complete replacement of working parts in engine

EPA Environmental Protection Agency; government agency that sets smog standards and tests cars for gasoline mileage

feeler gauge tool with several blades, used to measure gap in spark plugs or valve clearance

fender bender *Informal.* minor car accident

flat tire punctured tire from which air has escaped

freeway divided highway with several lanes in each direction for fast driving

garage repair shop; place for storing car at one's home

gas guzzler *Informal.* car getting low mileage per gallon of gas

grade steep hill

green light signal to continue moving

gun the engine increase rpms

hang (*vb*) *Slang.* make a turn or U-turn

head-on (*adj*) describing direct collision with car moving in opposite direction

hit-and-run (*adj*) describing accident in which driver flees the scene

hitchhike (*vb*) stand by roadside with thumb extended seeking a ride

horsepower unit measuring power of engine, equal to 550 foot-pounds per second

hot-wire (*vb*) *Slang.* contact wiring around ignition switch to start car without key

hydroplane (*vb*) skid over very shallow water

idle running speed of engine with no load and closed throttle

jackknife accident in which tractor-trailer truck folds in half like knife blade closing

jump-start (*vb*) start car by using jumper cables to connect dead battery to good battery in another vehicle

knock noise from poorly controlled combustion in cylinder

leadfoot *Informal.* person who drives at high speed with foot pressed on accelerator

learner's permit state-issued permit to operate car only in presence of licensed driver

license driver's license

lube addition of lubricant and transaxle grease

lug the engine drive at rpm too low for engaged gear

mechanic person trained in auto repair

mileage miles traveled for each gallon of gasoline consumed

moving violation violation of driving laws cited by police; traffic violation

no-fault insurance insurance system in which liability is not dependent upon who is at fault in accident

no parking designation for roadway where parking is prohibited

octane measure of gasoline's ability to resist knock and detonation

oil change replacement of dirty crankcase oil

one-way street roadway with passage allowed in one direction only

overhaul engine overhaul

parallel parking parking in space parallel to direction of street

parking lot area reserved for parking of numerous cars

parking ticket citation issued by police for illegal parking

passing lane lane nearest center of roadway on two-way street, designed for cars traveling fastest

pedestrian person walking along or across roadway

peel out (*vb*) *Slang.* accelerate abruptly from a standstill

ping mild knock in detonation

pit stop *Informal.* stop for fuel and servicing, esp. on long drive or in race

pop the clutch *Informal.* disengage clutch abruptly, not smoothly

pull the engine drop the engine

rear-end (*vb*) strike another vehicle from behind

rebuild (*vb*) do complete engine overhaul

reckless driving dangerous, high-speed, drunk, or erratic driving

red light signal to stop and wait for green light

registration annual record of auto ownership filed with state

rental car automobile leased when no personal vehicle is available

rev (*vb*) increase engine rpms suddenly

ride shotgun *Informal.* ride in passenger seat located to driver's right

roadway usu. paved strip of land designated for use by automobiles

roll start roll standard-transmission car and pop clutch to achieve ignition when electrical system fails

rpm revolutions per minute; measure of engine speed

rubberneck (*vb*) strain to see accident scene from passing vehicle, causing slowing of traffic and danger

rush hour period of heavy traffic at beginning and end of workday

school zone area near school with special low speed limit

scope meter for measuring and monitoring operations of car's electrical system

servicing tune-up, oil change, lube, and other basic maintenance

shunpiking driving on back roads to avoid highways

sideswipe (*vb*) graze another car's side in minor accident

skid loss of control due to ice, water, or sudden stop

slipstreaming driving closely behind another vehicle to take advantage of reduced air resistance

smog check required monitoring of emission control system to ensure it meets certain standards

smog control system regulating automobile exhaust emissions; emission control

smog device emission control component

souped-up (*adj*) *Slang.* customized for increased power and speed; stroked

specifications precise measurements of proper settings for engine operations

speeding driving in excess of speed limit

speed limit maximum driving speed allowed by law on given roadway

spin-out rotating skid made by automobile, causing it to leave roadway

stall come to a halt though failure of enough fuel to pass through carburetor to engine, causing engine to cease operating

sticker price undiscounted price for car, usu. affixed to window as itemized list on sheet of paper

stock (*adj*) designating standard design, parts, and color of factory-manufactured automobile

stop sign usu. red, octagonal street sign reading "Stop"

stroked (*adj*) *Slang.* souped-up, esp. by lengthening piston stroke for greater power

test drive trial run to evaluate new car

toe-in slight forward convergence given to front wheels to improve steering alignment

tool (*vb*) drive, esp. down highway

total (*vb*) damage one's car beyond repair in accident

towaway zone no-parking area from which cars are removed to city or police garage, esp. at rush hour

towing pulling another vehicle or trailer with one's vehicle

traffic vehicles on roadway, esp. many vehicles

traffic court local court with jurisdiction over violators of traffic laws

traffic signal traffic control device usu. having red, yellow, and green lights

traffic violation violation of driving laws; moving violation

tune-up periodic adjustment of ignition, valve clearance, and fuel delivery system and replacement of electrical parts

upshift (*vb*) change to higher gear when accelerating

U-turn reversal of driving direction on same roadway

vapor lock boiling or vaporizing of fuel in lines due to excess heat, often causing stoppage of fuel flow

vehicle ID identification number stamped on engine block or dashboard

wheel alignment proper adjustment of wheel's caster, camber, and toe-in

whiplash neck strain due to sudden, violent accident involving rear-end impact

winterize (*vb*) prepare auto for cold weather by adding antifreeze, thinner oil, and insulation

wrecker one who hauls away and disposes of cars after accidents

yellow light signal to slow down before proceeding or as warning of imminent red light requiring stop

RAILROADS
Types of Trains, Cars, and Lines
Railroad Personnel
Parts, Practices, and Argot

See also: *Chap. 6: Other Vehicles*

Types of Trains, Cars, and Lines

air car freight car with air brakes

baggage car freight car that carries baggage

baggage train train that carries freight and passenger baggage

bar car passenger train car in which refreshments are served

booster extra engine used to assist on steep grade

boxcar roofed freight car with sliding doors on its sides; crate

branch side road leading off main line

buda car *Slang.* automobilelike inspection car with small engine

bullet train very fast express train

bunk car sleeping car for loggers or track workers

cable car car powered by loop of underground cable

caboose last car on freight train, occupied by conductor, rear brakeman, and crew, in which their meals are taken; *Slang.* ambulance, anchor, ape wagon, bazoo wagon, bed house, brain cage, buggy, cabin car, cage, chariot, cook shack, cracker box, crib, den, doghouse, doodlebug, glory wagon, go-cart, hack, hearse, kipps, monkey cage, parlor, pavilion, penthouse, perambulator, saloon, shack, shanty, strawberry patch, sun parlor, van, zoo

calliope *Slang.* steam locomotive

can *Slang.* tank car

cannonball express *Slang.* fast express train

car individual railway vehicle, carrying passengers or freight, coupled to other cars to form train

carriage *Chiefly Brit.* railway car

caterpillar *Slang.* streamlined passenger train

center dump ballast car gondola car with chute beneath center of gondola, used to spread ballast on tracks

chair car passenger car with pairs of adjustable seats down each side of aisle

choo-choo *Baby talk.* train

coach car with seats for passengers

coalburner coal-burning locomotive

coal car freight car for coal, usu. gondola

cog railway rail line on steep mountain with locomotive that uses a cogwheel to engage cogs on tracks to gain traction

crate *Slang.* boxcar

cut of cars cars coupled together and/or attached to engine but without caboose

day coach ordinary passenger car

diesel locomotive engine powered by internal combustion engine that uses diesel fuel fired by compressed air in cylinders

diner dining car

dinghy Slang. sleeping car for train workers

dining car car in which meals are served to passengers; diner

Donegan Slang. old railroad car without wheels, used as office or residence

doodlebug Slang. caboose

double-decked stock stock car with two floors, esp. for sheep

doubleheader train hauled by two locomotives

drawing room car sleeping car with lounge areas

drill switch engine

drop-bottom dump car gondola with bottom that opens to disperse its load

dummy switching locomotive with housed boiler and running gear

dump car gondola that tips sideways to empty its load

el elevated

electric car single-car electric railway, such as trolley

electric railway railroad car or cars powered by electricity from cables or generator

electric train electrically powered urban railway

elephant car Slang. head brakeman's car behind locomotive

elevated railway raised above ground on trestle

engine locomotive

express car railway express cargo car on passenger train

express train fast train that makes few or no stops

fantail Slang. switch engine with sloping tender

feeder line secondary rail line connecting to main line

flatcar platform freight car without roof or sides; platform car

flier very fast train, esp. passenger express

freight car any of various cars designed to haul freight, usu. enclosed with sliding doors on sides

freight train nonpassenger train

funicular cable railroad that travels up and down a slope, often suspended from cable

giraffe Slang. mining car with one end elevated for inclines

goat Slang. engine that pushes cars around yard

go-devil handcar

gondola freight car with sides but no roof

gravity car unpowered car that runs downhill only

handcar small, flat, four-wheeled railway car propelled by two-handled pump, used to carry section gangs to work

hand truck hand car built like flat truck

Hart convertible car flat gondola car with drop bottom

helper auxiliary engine in doubleheader to aid on grade

highline main track

high-sided gondola freight car with tall sides and no roof

hog Slang. large steam locomotive for hauling freight

hopper car steel-sided freight car with chutes that discharge freight such as gravel or coal

horse railway street railway car drawn by horses

house track section of track at station, used for loading or unloading

idler unloaded flatcar placed ahead of or behind oversize load projecting from next car

jimmy Slang. four-wheel coal car

jitney four-wheel electric baggage car in terminal

kettle Slang. small steam locomotive, esp. decrepit one

lay-by Chiefly Brit. sidetrack

limited top-service train with few cars making selected stops

line track and roadbed following specific route

liner luxurious passenger train

local passenger train that stops at every depot along line

local express passenger train that stops at most depots

locomotive steam-, electric-, or diesel-powered railroad engine that pulls or pushes other cars; engine

log car flatcar for carrying piles of long logs

lounge car passenger car with seats at windows, bar, and refreshment facilities

luggage van Chiefly Brit. baggage car

mail car car for carrying postal freight

main line primary track

metro metropolitan underground railway (France)

milk car tank car for hauling milk

milk train Informal. train that makes frequent stops

mill Slang. steam locomotive

mixed train train with both passenger and freight cars

model railroad miniature-scale railroad built and run as hobby

monorail train running along single track

Mother Hubbard Slang. engine with cab over middle of boiler

night owl Slang. late-night passenger train

observation car passenger car with large sightseeing windows or elevated split-level section

officers' car private passenger coach for railroad company officials

outfit car boxcar with bunks for section men

paddle wheel Slang. narrow gauge locomotive with driving boxes outside wheels

palace car luxurious sleeping car

parliamentary train required by Parliament to run daily each way over entire length of system, stopping at every station and providing low-cost service (Britain, 19th c.)

parlor car first-class lounge or day car with plush seats

passenger car coach

passenger train train that carries only passengers and their baggage

pike Slang. railroad line, esp. short one

platform car flatcar

plug run Slang. local train, esp. one serving small towns

postal car enclosed freight car for hauling mail bags

Prairie locomotive with 2-6-2 wheel arrangement

private car passenger or parlor car owned or hired by group or individual for exclusive use

produce car ventilated or refrigerated boxcar specially equipped to carry fresh fruit and produce

puller switch engine that hauls cars around yard

Pullman car comfortable, well-appointed passenger car that converts into sleeping car or is divided into roomettes

rack-and-pinion railway railway with rack between rails that meshes with gear wheel or pinion on locomotive to assist on steep grades

rack car freight car with racks that hold lumber or pulpwood

rail detector car car equipped with instruments used to locate defects in rails

railhead farthest point from terminus to which rails have been laid

rail line route followed by particular railroad

railroad roadway of parallel steel rails that serve as track for passenger or freight cars drawn by locomotive; system of such tracks; company operating trains on railroad

rails railroads, their lines and equipment

railway railroad, esp. lightweight line operating locally

rammer Slang. extra engine on train

reefer Slang. refrigerator car

refrigerator car freight car with refrigerated compartment for perishables; reefer

rocket sled sled propelled along tracks by rocket engine, used to test effects of rapid acceleration and deceleration

rolling stock railroad cars of all types, esp. those owned by one company

scoot Slang. shuttle

short line train operating over short distance

shuttle train that makes short, frequent, round-trip runs over same track; scoot

skeleton car car for hauling logs in which truck carriages are held together by center beam without deck

sleeper sleeping car

sleeping car car outfitted with sleeping berths, esp. Pullman car; sleeper

smoker smoking car

smoking car passenger car in which tobacco smoking is allowed; smoker

special train running on irregular schedule or carrying unique cargo or passengers

steam locomotive engine powered by steam from boiler

steam shovel large mechanical shovel connected to motor in small enclosure on flatcar (snow plow and pile driver can also be thus connected)

stemwinder brakeless trolley; locomotive with special gear system

stock car ventilated or slatted car for livestock, esp. cattle, often with feeding mangers on sides

streamliner fast train

streetcar passenger car on municipal railway

streetcar line system of rails that provides public transportation on city streets

street railway rail system on city streets

string line of coupled cars

stub *Slang.* train that takes over part of another's schedule

subway underground municipal railway, usu. electric; underground

supply train train that gathers scraps and delivers supplies to all points along division

switch engine engine used solely to switch cars in yard; drill

tangent track portion of track adjacent to curve

tank car freight car for hauling fluids or gases in large, enclosed tank; tanker

tanker tank car

tap line short feeder line, owned by industrial concern, leading from regular tracks to factory or warehouse

tender car fuel and water supply car coupled directly behind engine

trailer flatcar pushed ahead of engine to couple to other cars on section unfit for locomotive

train several railroad cars coupled together

tram *Chiefly Brit.* streetcar; open railway car used in mines

tramline *Chiefly Brit.* streetcar line

tramway *Chiefly Brit.* streetcar line; system in which cars are supported by overhead cables

trimmer engine used to shove errant cars clear in hump yard switching

trolley street railway car

truck carriage with one or more pairs of wheels that guide one end of car or locomotive on sharp curves

trunk line main line of railroad system

tube *Chiefly Brit.* underground railway

underground subway

varnish *Slang.* highly lacquered wooden passenger car

wagon *Chiefly Brit.* railroad car

wagon-lit sleeping car (Europe)

way car local-line freight car

work train boxcars converted into living quarters with bunks, kitchen, and office for repair and maintenance crews, sometimes with flatcars that carry tools and supplies

wrecking crane flatcar with enclosure at one end holding steam boiler, engine, and hoisting mechanism

wreck train train equipped to clear tracks of debris or damaged equipment following storm or accident

yard engine engine used to switch and move trains in yard

yard goat *Slang.* yard engine

Railroad Personnel

air jammer worker who connects air hoses and air signals between coupled cars

ash eater *Slang.* fireman

baggageman person who handles passenger luggage

baggage master person who supervises baggage room at terminal

bakehead *Slang.* fireman

boilermaker person who assembles and maintains boilers

boomer *Slang.* itinerant railroad worker

brakeman person who operates train brakes; roughneck

brotherhood railroad workers' union, esp. one of Big Four: engineers, firemen, conductors, trainmen

butch *Slang.* person who peddles snacks and newspapers to passengers

car inspector person who checks for defects in cars

chief clerk person who handles correspondence, accounts, and paperwork

conductor person who supervises train crew and collects passenger fares; person in charge of street railway

crew track workers and trainmen

dispatcher person who manages train movements, schedules, and track assignments

electric owl *Slang.* night operator

end man rear brakeman

engine driver *Chiefly Brit.* engineer

engineer person trained to operate locomotive and drive train

field man yard brakeman

fireman person who shovels coal into firebox and puts water in boiler to maintain steam level; apprentice to engineer who works with him in cab

flagman person who gives signals at designated sites

floater *Slang.* migratory railroad worker

gripman porter

guard *Chiefly Brit.* conductor; elevated or subway brakeman

head brakeman brakeman at front of train who opens and closes switches, takes on water, and acts as flagman

hoghead *Slang.* engineer

hop *Slang.* porter

hostler roundhouse or terminal engine maintenance worker

lineman track inspector who reports damage to section gang

news butch *Slang.* peddler on passenger trains who moves down aisle with candy, fruit, drinks, snacks, and newspapers

parlor brakeman rear brakeman in caboose on freight train

paymaster railroad employee who travels about paying salaries

pin lifter *Slang.* yard brakeman or switchman

pin puller *Slang.* yard switchman

porter passenger baggage carrier at terminal; sleeping car attendant; gripman; hop; redcap

railroader one who works on railroad

redcap porter

roughneck *Slang.* brakeman

roundhouse mechanic engine service and maintenance worker in yard roundhouse

section boss foreman of section gang; warden

section gang group of section men who weed right of way, replace ties, reballast, and repair tracks

section man worker who maintains certain section of track

signal maintainer person who operates and services signals located at distance from depot

signal man operator of railroad signals

smoke agent *Slang.* fireman

spiker worker who drives spikes when laying rails

stationmaster operations supervisor at depot or terminal

steel gang *Slang.* crew that lays rails

steward passenger train crewman who manages provisioning of food and serves passengers

stoker fireman

switchman operator of switches that run cars from one track to another, either manually or electrically

telegraph operator person who sends messages over telegraph lines from yard or depot to train

ticket agent person in station or railroad office who sells passenger tickets

train captain former term for conductor

trainman member of train crew supervised by conductor

trainmaster person who maintains schedules and operates switch yards

warden section boss

watchman safety inspector, esp. in shack at junction of two tracks

wrecking crew relief crew

yard clerk assistant at yard office

yardman yardmaster

yardmaster supervisor of operations in railroad yard; yardman

Parts, Practices, and Argot

adverse uphill road grade

air brake system of continuous brakes worked by compressed air and pistons

air pump machine that compresses air in cylinders to drive air brake

alley *Slang.* clear track in yard

alleyway passage beside compartments in sleeping and parlor cars

apron flat, metal platform separating locomotive and tender

atmospheric brake original compressed-air brake in 1869

automatic air brake standard air brake since 1871

baggage room terminal area in which incoming

and outgoing luggage is held for pickup or shipment

bail (*vb*) *Slang.* fire up a locomotive

ballast gravel or slag bed for railroad ties

ball the jack *Slang.* increase speed

barn locomotive roundhouse

berth bed or bunk built into sleeping car

blasting burst of steam exhaust

Blenkinsop rack toothed third rail engaged by gear on some locomotives for traction on grade

blizzard lights two emergency lights flanking locomotive headlight

block signal signal at block entrance that controls trains entering and leaving

block system organization of railroad line into three- or four-mile sections governed by signals which assure that one train leaves block before another enters

blue flag warning that workers are repairing crippled car

board conductor's cry of "all aboard" as passenger train prepares to leave station

boiler metal tank in which water is heated and converted to steam to drive locomotive

brake club hard, three-foot club used to tighten hand brake

broad gauge road with rails wider than 4 feet 8 1/2 inches (1.43 m) apart

bug *Slang.* telegraph instrument; *Slang.* switchman's light

bumper retaining post at end of spur track that absorbs shock in collision

bunk elevated bed built into wall of sleeper compartment

cab enclosed area of locomotive in which engineer and fireman operate controls

Casey Jones *Slang.* engineer on fast-moving locomotive, named after legendary engineer who died in wreck

cattle guard device with projecting triangular spikes or widely spaced bars placed at road crossings to prevent cattle from passing

catwalk rungs or plank running board on boxcar or locomotive platform, used by brakeman to clamber between cars

cinder partly burned piece of fuel coal

cinder pit area in which cinder pans are dumped before train enters roundhouse

clinker fused mass of hot coals

clinker hook device that moves and breaks fused masses of hot coals

commutation ticket reduced fare, multitrip, time-limited ticket good on one line only

consist conductor's report by which yardmaster at next stop plans switchings

couchette fold-out, shelflike bed in low-fare compartment of European passenger train

coupler device used to fasten together individual cars; drawbar; pin

cowcatcher outthrusting metal bumper on front of locomotive that pushes aside obstructions, esp. cattle; pilot

crossing intersection of railroad tracks and public roadway

crosstie tie

crown (*vb*) couple caboose to line of freight cars

cupola observation area atop caboose

dead freight bulky, nonperishable freight

deck front part of cab; catwalk atop boxcar

depot train station or terminal for loading passengers and freight

derailing accident in which one or more cars slip off tracks; intentional forcing of car off tracks

dirt track roadbed without ballast under ties

ditch area beside and below roadbed

division section of line between terminals, approx. one hundred miles

drawbar coupler

drop bottom door and chute at base of hopper car or gondola for emptying cargo such as coal or gravel

em one thousand pounds of tonnage

embankment pile of earth holding up roadway

engine cab enclosed cab on locomotive

extra train not listed on timetable

ferrophiliac amateur lover of railroading

flag colored cloth signal used in daylight

flange inside projecting rim on wheel that guides it down track

frog implement used to derail car wheels or permit them to cross intersecting tracks

full stroke at top speed

full throttle at top speed

gangway space between rear of steam locomotive cab and tender

gantlet section of track through narrow passage in which two track lines overlap, one rail of each line lying between rails of the other

gantry bridgelike framework over tracks that supports signals or is used for loading

gare *French.* station

gate switch that may be opened or closed to control movement of trains on tracks

gauge recognized standard measure of distance between two rails: narrow 3' 6" (1.07 m), standard 4' 8 1/2" (1.43 m), broad 5' 6" (1.68 m)

glory road *Slang.* railroad

go light *Slang.* run engine without cars

grab iron steel bar on car or engine, used as handhold

grade tracks running up steep hill

gravy train *Slang.* short, easy haul

green flag signal indicating permission to proceed, displayed at front of train

green light nighttime permission-to-proceed signal

highball signal in which hand or lantern sweeps in high, wide semicircle to indicate full speed ahead

hitch (*vb*) couple cars together

hobo tramp who hitches free ride on freight train

hump rise built at end of freight yard from which cars roll to separate tracks for coupling

hump yard yard built on incline to allow switching by natural, gravitational momentum

indicator illuminated designation of train's number on locomotive and caboose

ingersoll trainman's open-faced watch

iron *Informal.* railroad track

iron horse former term for railroad, esp. steam locomotive

jerkwater (*adj*) *Informal.* designating small town at which train draws water from track pan without stopping

jill pole *Slang.* thick pole used to shove cars out of siding when engine is on main line and cannot pick up cars

Johnson bar reverse lever on locomotive

joint length of rail, usu. 33 to 39 feet (10 to 12 m)

journal part of axle that turns in shaft

junction intersection of two tracks or lines

key telegraph transmitting instrument; (*vb*) send a message by telegraph

ladder central track in yard, from which other tracks lead off

lantern flagman's night signal lamp

layover time lost in delay connecting with another train

library *Slang.* cupola of caboose

marker signal on rear of train, flag by day, lantern by night; signal on main line

merry-go-round *Slang.* roundhouse turntable

Morse code standard telegraphic code by which most railroad messages were sent prior to electronic telecommunications

mudhole *Slang.* small town or station

mule cable-operated device used to lift coal cars up incline for dumping

narrow gauge road with rails less than 4 feet 8 1/2 inches (1.43 m) apart

off-peak (*adj*) designating noncommuting hours with reduced passenger fare

on the advertised *Slang.* on schedule

on the card *Slang.* on schedule

order instructions telegraphed from dispatcher to conductor

paddle *Slang.* semaphore signal

pass free entry to car for passenger

pick up (*vb*) add cars at station

pile tall support member sunk into earth as foundation for trestle

pilot cowcatcher

pin coupler

pod intentional derailing to prevent cars on siding from entering main line

point intersection of gauge lines in switch or frog

quill *Slang.* railway whistle

rack rail third rail used for traction when engaged by gear on locomotive

rail long metal bar laid upon ground parallel to another such bar and connected to it by crossties, serving as track for railroad cars; railroad as means of transport

rail anchor device sprung into rail base to hold it in place

railroading construction and operation of railroads; travel by railroad

railway bridge trestle or covered bridge

supporting tracks across land depression or water

ride the bumpers travel perched between freight cars

right of way land occupied by and immediately surrounding railroad main line

roadbed base upon which rails, ties, and ballast of railroad track rests

roadway railroad right of way with tracks, stations, and signals

rods underbracing of car

roomette individual compartment in Pullman car

roundhouse circular structure in yard housing idle locomotives for storage and repair

round trip journey to specific destination and back to starting point over same route

run regular route of train line

runaway train that is out of control and unstoppable by normal means, usu. due to mechanical failure

runaway unit individual car on runaway train

saddle first step of freight car under lowest grab iron

sand dome bin atop engine boiler filled with sand to be spread on tracks for traction

scoop fireman's shovel

semaphore apparatus giving signals to trains by position of movable arms

service application gradual reduction in speed

sidedoor sliding door on side of boxcar

sidetrack siding

siding short track connected by switch to main line and used for bypassing or unloading; sidetrack; turnout

signal marker, either flag or lantern

smokestack steel chimney for discharge of engine smoke and gases; stack

snowfence barrier placed along tracks to protect against snowslides

snowshed wooden shelter built over section of track, esp. in mountains, to protect against snowslides

span bridge or trestle

spar pole for clearing cars when switching; stake

spot (vb) place car in designated location, esp. for loading or unloading

spur short sidetrack connecting to main line, often dead end

stack smokestack

stake pole used to move cars in manual switching operation; spar

standard gauge railroad track and carwheel width of 4 feet 8 1/2 inches (1.43 m)

stateroom lavish, first-class suite of connected passenger compartments with separate sitting and sleeping areas

station regular stopping place for train line, with loading platform and usu. shelter for passengers

steam brake emergency braking procedure in which valve gear is reversed to slow engine

steam stop halting train by steam braking cars but not engine

stroke single movement of piston rod; measure of engine speed or drive

stub *Slang.* dead-end spur

switch device consisting of two movable rails that connect to tracks, used to direct cars from one siding to another or onto main line

switchback zigzag line over hill too steep for direct ascent

switching moving of cars or trains from one track to another

switch shanty small building in yard in which switchman rests and keeps lanterns

switch tower elevated lookout point in switch yard

switch yard yard in which cars are moved from one track to another to make up trains

tack coupling pin

take water draw water at overhead tank into storage container or boiler

tank town small town, often one in which only stop is to take water

telegraph traditional railroad communications system

telltale dangling ropes at approach to low bridge or tunnel entrance that warn of low overhead clearance

temporary track tracks laid for use while regular tracks are being repaired

terminal city or town at endpoint of line with station or depot; station at junction of lines; yard at end of division

terminus endpoint of line

third rail extra rail added on curves to prevent derailing

throat fan-shaped convergence of tracks at tunnel entrance

throttle equipment that determines amount of steam entering cylinders and thus controls speed of engine

ticket punch handheld device used by conductor to cancel tickets by perforation

tie wood plank supporting and connecting rails; crosstie

timetable folded sheet with schedule of arrivals and departures in both directions over one line

tonnage weight carried by entire train or individual car; amount of weight locomotive can pull

trackage lines of railroad tracks

track layer machine and vehicle used in laying tracks

track pan water dispenser hanging over tracks and attached to large tank

tracks pair of parallel metal rails, usu. with crossties, that guide car or engine wheels

transfer table flat, movable or rotating surface with single track that is turned to align with other tracks to transfer locomotive to new track

trap storage box that receives sand from sand dome and releases it onto rails below

trestle framework support on piles for tracks across river or depression; rudimentary railroad bridge

turnout siding

turntable platform with track used to rotate

locomotives in yard at end of track and outside roundhouse

undercarriage frame and running gear of locomotive

valve gear device that directs steam in or out of cylinders to run locomotive forward or backward

Wabash *Slang.* big fire in locomotive firebox; (vb) *Slang.* hit car entering adjacent switch; slow for stop without completely stopping

waiting room area in station where passengers await trains

walkway area for walking along side of locomotive

washout emergency stop signal, in which arms or lamp are swung in wide, downward arc across track

way bill document prepared by carrier with details of shipment, routing, and charges

way station small, often remote station at which train stops only on signal

Westinghouse *Trademark.* original air brake, invented by George Westinghouse in 1869

wheel base distance from first pair of locomotive wheels to last pair of tender wheels

whistle railroad sound used to signal departure, arrival, approach to station, or crossing; also used to send message or warning by coded series of blasts

whistle stop small town at which passenger train does not normally stop

Whyte classification system that classifies locomotives by wheel arrangement, such as 4-0-2, 4-4-2, 2-0-0-4, etc.

wigwag grade crossing signal

wye tracks off main line arranged in Y-formation, used to reverse cars and engines without turntable

X designation for empty car

yard open area at terminus of line with network of tracks for storage of cars and assembly of trains

zulu car *Slang.* freight car ridden by immigrant farmers

SHIPS AND BOATS

Types of Ships and Boats
Parts of Ships, Sails, and Equipment
Nautical Occupations
Seamanship and Port

See also: *Chap. 3: Landscapes and Seascapes; Weather and Natural Phenomena; Chap. 5: Structural Components; Chap. 11: War and Military; Chap. 17: Sports*

Types of Ships and Boats

airboat light, flat-bottomed, aluminum vessel driven by propeller revolving in air

aircraft carrier very large, flat-decked seagoing airbase; carrier

argosy large, richly laden merchant ship; fleet of ships

ark large, flat-bottomed riverboat

barge flat-bottomed cargo vessel without power

bark three- or four-masted square-rigger

bateau *French*. boat

bathyscaphe submarine-shaped float filled with fluid lighter than water, used for deep-sea diving

bathysphere enclosed globe for deep-sea observations

battleship large, armored naval ship heavily outfitted for war

bireme galley with two banks of oars

boat small vessel used at sea or on inland waterway

brigantine two-masted ship with square-rigged topsail on mainmast

bumboat small boat used in port or at anchor to sell goods to ships' crews

buss rugged, square-sailed boat formerly used by herring fishery

cabin cruiser motorboat with enclosed cabin and living facilities

caique light rowboat or sailboat (Bosporus, eastern Mediterranean)

canal boat flat boat that operates on inland canals

canoe light, narrow boat with sharp or pointed ends, powered by one or more paddles

caravel small, fast sailing ship with narrow, high poop and lateen sails (Portugal and Spain, 15th-16th c.)

cargo ship power vessel that carries supplies, not passengers

carrack galleon or merchant vessel used in Mediterranean (15th-16th c.)

carrier aircraft carrier

catamaran twin-hulled sailing vessel

clipper speedy, fully rigged sailing vessel with sharp bow (19th c.)

cockboat small, oar-propelled boat used as ship's tender

collier ship outfitted for or employed in transporting coal

container ship freighter outfitted to carry large cargo containers

coracle small, round or very broad boat made of interwoven laths or wicker covered with skin or tarred or oiled cloth (Ireland, Wales)

corsair pirate ship

corvette small, fast warship, esp. for convoy; formerly a sailing warship larger than a sloop, smaller than a frigate

craft boat or vessel, esp. small one

cruiser speedy, armored warship with six to eight guns; cabin cruiser

cutter single-masted vessel with fore-and-aft rigged sails; sloop

dahabeah large passenger boat, orig. with lateen sails, used on Nile River

destroyer speedy warship armed with guns, torpedoes, and depth charges

dhow coastal ship with lateen sail and raised deck at stern (Indian Ocean)

dinghy small rowboat; small boat carried on ship or used as tender

dink small boat, esp. for duck hunting

dogger two-masted fishing vessel with blunt bow (Holland)

dory small, flat-bottomed boat with sharp bow and tapering stern

dreadnought large armored battleship armed with heavy-caliber guns in turrets

dredge low workboat that scrapes bottom of waterway to make it navigable

drogher freight barge rigged as cutter or schooner (West Indies)

dromond large, fast medieval galley or cutter

dugout boat or canoe hollowed out of large log

escort vessel accompanying and protecting another

felucca small, narrow ship propelled by oars or lateen sails (Mediterranean)

ferry vessel used to convey passengers and cargo back and forth across bay or stream

fishing boat any boat from which fish are caught

fishing smack fore-and-aft rigged vessel equipped with well for holding live catch

flatboat boat with flat bottom, esp. for use in shallow waterway

fore-and-after sailing vessel with fore-and-aft rigging

freighter large cargo vessel

frigate light boat orig. propelled by oars, later by sails; intermediate, square-rigged war vessel (18th-19th c.); heavy, missile-firing warship (20th c.)

full-rigged (*adj*) designating sailing vessel with three or more square-rigged masts

galiot small, swift ship propelled by sails and oars, formerly used in Mediterranean

galleass lateen-rigged fighting galley used in Mediterranean (15th-18th c.)

galleon heavy square-rigger with several decks and elaborate poopdeck; Spanish treasure ship (15th-18th c.); carrack

galley large, low, ancient or medieval ship propelled by sails and oars

gig captain's boat; long lifeboat rowed with four to eight oars

gondola small, flat canal boat sculled with single oar or hand-propelled by pole

gufa round rowboat of wickerwork (ancient Mesopotamia)

hatch boat small fishing boat equipped with covered wells for holding fish

houseboat boat outfitted with living quarters, usu. moored permanently in one place

hoy heavy harbor barge; sloop-rigged fishing vessel (17th-18th c.)

hydrofoil small, high-speed racing boat equipped with hydrofoils

hydroplane light, high-speed motorboat that skims along water on hydrofoils or flat bottom rising toward stern

iceboat triangular frame with sail mounted on runners, used on frozen waterways

icebreaker sturdy, powerful vessel for cutting channels through heavy ice

ironclad wooden warship armored with steel plate (19th c.)

jangada fisherman's log raft with sail, seat, and steering oar (Brazil)

johnboat flat-bottomed, square-ended fishing boat, used on inland waterways

jolly boat small boat carried at stern of sailing vessel

junk flat-bottomed boat with high stern and lateen sails (China, Japan)

kayak canoe made of skins that entirely cover frame except for paddler's seat in middle (Eskimo); small boat resembling this

ketch small, two-masted vessel rigged fore-and-aft

knockabout small, single-masted sailboat with no bowsprit

launch largest off-boat on warship; open motorboat

lifeboat small boat carried on ship or kept ready ashore for emergency use

life raft small, inflatable or balsa raft carried on ship for emergency use

liner large, elaborately-outfitted passenger ship

longboat largest boat carried on merchant sailing ship

longliner commercial fishing vessel that uses long line with multiple hooks

lorcha three-masted sailing ship with lugsails (southeast Asia, Philippines)

lugger small ship rigged with lugsails on two or three masts

man-of-war warship

market boat vessel that transfers fish from fishing boats to market on shore

merchant ship commercial oceangoing vessel

minesweeper military vessel equipped to detect underwater explosive mines

moleta short-masted fishing boat with lateen sail and two outriggers (Portugal)

motorboat usu. small, open boat powered by internal combustion or electric engine; powerboat

New Orleans lugger broad-hulled fishing boat with single mast and large, dipping lugsail

nickey lug-sailed fishing boat (Isle of Man)

nobby small fishing boat (Isle of Man)

nuggar cargo boat with single square sail (Nile River)

ocean liner large, elaborately-outfitted passenger ship for ocean crossings

off-boat small boat carried on ship, esp. for emergency use as lifeboat

oiler tanker

paddle steamer river-going steamboat propelled by wheels with paddles set at right angles about their circumference; paddle wheeler

paddle wheeler paddle steamer

pinnace small sailing ship, esp. tender to larger ship

pirogue dugout canoe or canoe-shaped boat having two masts

polacre two- or three-masted sailing ship (Mediterranean)

pontoon wooden, flat-bottomed boat or float used in building bridges; type of barge

powerboat motorboat

pram small, flat-bottomed sailboat with square bow

proa swift sailing boat with flat lee side and balancing outrigger (Indonesia)

PT boat patrol torpedo boat; small, speedy torpedo boat

pulwar light, keelless vessel (India)

punt small, flat-bottomed riverboat with square ends

raft flat structure of logs or boards fastened together; small, flat-bottomed, inflatable rubber boat

riverboat steam-powered passenger boat used on inland waterways, esp. paddle wheeler

rowboat small, oar-powered boat

runabout light, open motorboat

sailboat boat with at least one mast, propelled by wind in sails secured to mast

sampan small boat with sail, steered with stern oar, often with small cabin of mats (China, Japan)

schooner fore-and-aft rigged vessel with two or more masts, mainmast at aft, and square sails

scow large, flat-bottomed boat with square ends, used to carry coal or sand, often towed by tug

scull light, narrow racing boat for four or fewer rowers

shallop small, open boat fitted with oars and/or sails

sharpie long, narrow, flat-bottomed fishing boat with one or two masts rigged with triangular sails (New England)

shell long, narrow, thin-hulled racing boat rowed by team of up to eight

ship large vessel navigating sea or other deep waterway, powered by sails or engine

ship of the line largest class of warship, usu. with guns along two or more decks; battleship

side-wheeler vessel with paddle wheels on sides

skeeter small iceboat

skiff small boat, usu. rowed

skipjack small sailboat with flat, V-shaped hull and vertical sides

slaver Informal. slave ship

slave ship freighter used to transport slaves from their native home to market; slaver

sloop fore-and-aft rigged, one-mast vessel; cutter

smack small sailboat, usu. rigged as sloop; fishing boat, esp. trawler, with well for keeping fish alive

speedboat very fast motorboat

sportfisherman inboard motorboat, usu. 36 to 42 feet (12 m) long, used for offshore fishing

square-rigger sailing ship rigged with square sails

steamer steam-powered vessel

steamship ship driven by steam-powered engine

sternwheeler vessel with paddle wheel at rear

sub Informal. submarine

submarine warship carrying torpedoes and missiles that can function underwater; sub

supertanker extremely large tanker, usu. for oil

tanker cargo ship with large tanks in hull for carrying oil or other liquid; oiler

tender auxiliary vessel used in the supply and repair of other ships

tern three-masted schooner

three-master sailing vessel with three masts

tin can Slang. naval destroyer; old, rundown vessel

torpedo boat small, fast, maneuverable warship that fires torpedoes

towboat tugboat; boat for pushing barges on inland waterway

tramp vessel that will go anywhere for profitable cargo

transport ship used to carry soldiers or freight over long distance

trawler fishing boat that uses net to drag bottom of sea or lake

trimaran catamaran with three parallel hulls

trireme galley outfitted with three rows of oars

tug small, powerful vessel that aids in docking or towing larger ships

twelve-meter internationally recognized racing yacht

U-boat German submarine

umiak large, open rowboat of skins stretched on wooden frame (Eskimo)

vaporetto large motorboat for public transport on Venetian canals

vedette small naval launch used for scouting

vessel ship or boat

warship ship armed for combat, esp. battleship; man-of-war

whaleboat small, oar-powered boat used in whaling industry; whaler

whaler craft used in whaling

wherry light rowboat for rivers; one-person racing scull

windjammer large sailing ship

xebec three-masted sailing ship with long, overhanging bow and stern (Mediterranean)

yacht pleasure boat, esp. narrow-hulled sailboat

yawl ship's small boat; two-masted vessel with small aftermast behind wheel

Parts of Ships, Sails, and Equipment

abeam (adj) directly outward from or at right angle to fore-and-aft line of ship

aft rear of ship; stern; (adj) toward the stern, behind

aftermast mast closest to stern

alleyway narrow passageway below decks

anchor large hook that grips bottom and holds ship in place

anchor chock casting through which anchor lines pass

athwartships (adv) running across ship from side to side

backstay line or cable running aft from masthead to side or stern

ballast heavy object used to maintain ship at proper draft

batten strip used to fasten canvas over hatchways or to stiffen sails

beam ship's breadth at widest point; side of ship; direction outward from fore-and-aft line

becket looped rope or grommet for securing lines, oars, and spars

belowdecks (adv) in area within hull beneath deck surface

berth bed or bunk mounted in wall of cabin belowdecks; dock space at wharf

bibb wooden support bracket fastened to ship's mast

bight any part within ends of line, esp. a bend

bilge low point of ship's hull

binnacle case, box, or stand for ship's compass and lamp

bitt one of twin deck posts to which cables or lines are secured

block heavy pulley used for rigging

bobstay rope, chain, or rod from outer end of bowsprit to cutwater

boiler room location of power-generating boilers belowdecks on steamship

booby hatch covering over small hatchway

boom long pole or spar that extends and holds bottom of sail

bow most forward part of ship

bower heavy anchor carried toward bow

bowsprit large spar projecting forward, used to carry headsail

brace any of various support pieces, esp. rope to sway yards on sailing vessels

bridge uppermost front cabin; platform for captain

brig place of confinement, ship's prison

broadside side of ship above waterline; volley fired simultaneously by all guns on one side of warship

bulkhead upright wall or partition separating compartments

bulwark rail around ship's deck

buntline rope used to haul square sail up to yard for furling

burgee swallow-tailed flag used for signals and identification

burton tackle made of single or double blocks, used to tighten rigging or hoisting

buttock convex, aftmost part of ship above waterline

cabin room used for passengers or officers

camel float between ship and pier that prevents chafing

capstan cylindrical spool revolving on shaft, used to wind cable

carlings fore-and-aft deck supports or frame for deck opening

chock metal casting on deck through which lines and hawsers pass

cleat small, metal or wood fitting with projecting ends, used to secure lines on deck

clew reinforced metal loop fastened to corner of sail

coaming raised steel frame around hatch or other opening on deck

companionway narrow stairway

compass navigational instrument with magnetized needle indicating north, used to determine heading

conning tower heavily armored pilothouse on warship

container very large receptacle of standard size for shipping

course sail on lower yard of square-rigger; direction to be steered

crossjack lowermost square sail set on mizzenmast of ship with four or more masts

crosstrees two short bars across masthead, used to spread rigging that supports mast

crow's nest lookout station atop mast on sailing vessel

cuddy small deck cabin; galley or pantry; platform on which fishing net is stored

cutwater forward edge of stem at and below waterline

davit crane projecting over side for hoisting lifeboats, anchors, or cargo on board

deadlight heavy plate glass window in portholes

deck flat, open surface of ship; floor

deck chair lightweight folding chair with arms, used on deck

depth charge underwater explosive directed against subs

depth sounder device for determining depth of water by measuring time required for sound wave to reach and return from bottom

derrick pivoting mast with tackle used to raise and lower boom

engine room room belowdecks housing engine works

fantail aft overhang of ship shaped like duck's bill

fidley framework or railing around hatch

fluke flat, triangular end of anchor that bites bottom

flying jib sail on extension outside jib

fore (adj) ahead, toward the bow

fore-and-aft sails rigged lengthwise from bow to stern; (adj) having no square sails; running lengthwise

foredeck deck area toward bow

foremast mast nearest bow

foresail sail rigged on mast toward bow

futtock curved timbers forming lower part of ship's ribs in wooden hull

gaff iron hook; spar rising aft from mast for sails

galley ship's kitchen

gangplank movable bridge used to board and leave ship; gangway

gangway gangplank

garboard lowest strake next to keel

gennaker oversized headsail behind mast on yacht, esp. for tacking in which wind crosses side of boat

genoa large jib overlapping mainsail on yacht; jenny

gimbal suspended setting for ship's compass that allows it to remain stable in rough seas

gooseneck curved member at foot of boom that pivots so that boom can be pointed in wide angle vertically or horizontally

grapnel light anchor with many hooks or prongs

grappling iron hooked iron used to pull another vessel alongside or for anchoring

ground tackle anchoring components

gunwale side rail where topsides and deck meet

halyard line or tackle for raising sails and flags

hatch door in deck or floor; covering over such a door

hatch cover closure that fits over hatch

hatchway covered opening in deck with stairs that lead belowdecks

hawser heavy line, esp. for towing or mooring ship to dock

head ship's toilet

headsail small sail rigged forward of mast

heaving line light line with weight on free end and other end attached to hawser, used to draw heavier line into position

helm lever or wheel for controlling rudder to steer ship; wheel

hold cargo area within hull belowdecks

hull frame or main body of ship that sits in water

hydrofoil winglike structure attached to hull that lifts boat to skim along water at high speed

Jacob's ladder portable ladder with wooden rungs and flexible rope or wire sides

jenny Slang. genoa

jib triangular sail forward of foremast, fastened to foredeck

jigger small hoisting tackle; small, aftmost sail of yawl

kedge light anchor used for getting off shoal

keel longitudinal structural member along center of ship's bottom, running from stem to stern

keelson beam or plates fastened longitudinally inside hull along keel to add structural strength

kite small sail set high on mast in light wind

lanyard line for fastening shrouds and stays or raising flags; cord around sailor's neck with knife hung on it

lateen triangular, fore-and-aft rigged sail on long yard suspended obliquely from short mast

launch ramp inclined chute for releasing launches into water

lee side of ship facing away from wind

life preserver buoyant, halterlike garment that keeps person afloat when overboard

line rope

lugsail four-sided sail with upper edge attached to yard, fastened obliquely to mast

mainmast principal mast of sailing vessel

mainsail primary sail rigged on mast

mainstay line extending forward from and stabilizing mainmast

marlinespike iron tool that tapers to point, used to separate strands of rope

mast long pole or spar rising from deck to support yards, booms, and rigging

masthead top part of mast

midship (adj) in or at middle of vessel

mine explosive charge in container placed in sea

mizzen fore-and-aft rigged sail on mizzenmast

mizzenmast mast nearest stern, esp. third mast from bow in ship with three or more masts

moonraker light, square sail rigged high on clipper ship mast in light winds

oakum strands of old tarred line used as caulking

oar long pole with flat blades for rowing boat; paddle

orlop deck lowest deck of ship with four or more decks

outboard (adv) in lateral direction from hull

outboard motor engine hung off stern of small, open boat

outrigger support, brace, or float extending from side of boat

paddle oar

paddle wheel wheel with paddles set at right angles about its circumference, used to propel steamboat

paravane pair of torpedo-shaped devices towed by cables from ship's bow, used to cut moorings of submerged mines

pelorus compasslike navigational instrument with two sighting vanes instead of magnetic needle

pennant small, triangular signal flag

periscope upright tube fitted with prisms and mirrors, extended upward from submarine for observation above sea level

pink stern sharp stern with narrow, overhanging transom

pole long slender piece of wood used to hand-propel raft, small boat, or gondola

poop raised deck at stern, usu. roofed

port left side of vessel when facing bow

porthole round window in ship's hull

propeller slanted blades turning on shaft extending from hull, used to propel ship

prow bow above the waterline

quarterdeck ceremonial open space on after deck

ratline small pieces of tarred rope or wood that join shrouds and serve as ladder rungs for climbing rigging

reefed sail sail reduced in size by rolling or tying

ribs framework of hull to which skin is attached

rigging cables, chains, lines, blocks, and tackle

royal sail small sail above topgallant sail

rudder pivoting vertical blade at vessel's stern, used for steering

sail large canvas or synthetic fiber sheet hung from mast to catch wind and propel ship forward: flying jib, foresail, gaff, gennaker, headsail, jib, lateen, mainsail, mizzen, moonraker, reefed sail, royal sail, skysail, spinnaker, square sail, staysail, studding sail, topsail

scull long oar mounted at stern and worked from side to side; one of a pair of light oars used on each side of boat

scupper drainage opening at deck level through ship's side

sea anchor large, canvas-covered frame let out as drag or float to reduce ship's speed

seabag sailor's large cylindrical bag for personal items

sextant optical instrument used to measure angular distances at sea to determine latitude

shank straight part of anchor above hooks or barbs

sheave grooved wheel inside pulley block

sheer upward curve of deck toward bow and stern

sheet line or chain at lower corner of sail that controls set

shrouds heavy lines bracing mast athwartships; stays

sick bay ship's infirmary

skeg after part of keel to which rudder is secured

skin outer surface of hull

skysail sail rigged above royal sail

spanker fore-and-aft sail on aftermost lower mast of ship with three or more masts

spar mast, gaff, or boom that supports sails

spinnaker baggy, triangular headsail on yacht, used to run before wind

spring line rope leading from bow or aft to dock to prevent movement ahead or astern while moored

sprit pole or spar reaching diagonally from mast to topmost corner of fore-and-aft sail to extend it

square-rigged (adj) having square sails as principal sails

square sail four-sided sail rigged on yard set athwart keel and horizontal to mast

staff post that supports flag or banner at stern or bow

stanchion upright bar or post that supports life line

starboard right side of vessel when facing bow

stateroom private cabin

stay heavy line or cable bracing mast

staysail fore-and-aft sail rigged on stay

stem front or bow of vessel, esp. upright piece at prow to which side timbers are attached

stern back or rear of vessel

stopwater canvas backed with lead or other material, fitted between metal parts for watertightness

strake plank extending length of ship from stem to stern

strakework lines of strakes

stringer longitudinal plank or plate for strengthening deck

strut outboard support piece between stern and propeller

studding sail light sail rigged outboard of major square sail

swivel freely rotating fastening device for lines and tackle

tackle blocks and rope lines used in rigging

taffrail upper, flat part of ship's stern with panels; rail around ship's stern

thole pin set vertically in gunwale as fulcrum for oar

tiller handle for turning rudder

timber wooden rib set lengthwise in hull

toerail extension of side planking above deck for safety

topgallant mast mast fixed to head of topmast on square-rigged vessel

topgallant sail sail set on yard of topgallant mast

topmast mast usu. formed as a separate spar above lower mast and used to support yards or rigging of topsails

topsail sail next above lowermost sail on mast of square-rigger

topsides deck and outer surface of hull above water

torpedo underwater projectile containing explosives

transom transverse part of squared stern

truce iron band around mast with gooseneck for securing yard

turret armored revolving platform for heavy guns on naval vessel

vane long streamer that indicates wind direction

vang steadying rope from peak of a gaff to ship's rail or mast

ventilator bell-mouthed tube on deck that provides fresh air belowdecks

wales strakes or heavy planks fastened to outside of hull

warp mooring line

water line one of several lines painted on side of hull that indicates submergence due to load

wheel helm

winch deck engine with drum for hoisting heavy objects

windlass crank driven spindle for hoisting lines or hauling

yard long, slender rod fastened horizontally across mast to support sail

yardarm either half of yard supporting square sail

Nautical Occupations

able-bodied seaman able seaman

able seaman experienced seaman qualified to perform routine duties, rating below boatswain's mate; able-bodied seaman

admiral top-ranking naval officer

Argonaut crew member sailing with Jason in search for Golden Fleece (Greek mythology)

bilge rat *Slang.* boiler worker or belowdecks sailor

boatswain foreman; warrant officer in charge of deck crew's work; bo's'n; pipes

bo's'n boatswain

bowman deck hand on yacht who sets spinnaker and works at bow

buccaneer pirate

cabin boy boy who serves officers and passengers on ship

captain officer who is master or commander of ship; skipper

CB construction battalion crewman in navy; Seabee

chief petty officer CPO; highest ranking naval enlisted man

commander captain of vessel

commodore naval captain commanding two or more vessels

coxswain naval petty officer in charge of steering small boat; person who steers racing shell and calls rhythm to rowers

CPO chief petty officer

crew personnel working on ship, usu. excluding officers

crewman individual member of ship's crew

crew member crewman

deck hand ship's lowest-ranking worker

dockhand longshoreman

ensign lowest-ranking naval commissioned officer

ferryman operator of ferryboat

first mate ranking crew member below captain

fisherman person who fishes from a boat for livelihood or recreation

Flying Dutchman legendary mariner condemned to sail seas until Judgment Day

gondolier operator of gondola

grinder crew member on yacht who turns handle on winch that hauls in lines and raises halyards

gunner naval warrant officer specializing in guns and torpedoes

helmsman person who holds helm and steers ship; pilot; steersman

jack *Slang.* seaman

longshoreman laborer who loads cargo from docks; dockhand; stevedore

marine member of military unit associated with navy, esp. Marine Corps

mariner person involved in navigation of ship; seaman or sailor

mate deck officer on merchant ship ranking below captain

merchant seaman crewman of merchant ship

middy *Informal.* midshipman

midshipman naval recruit, esp. student at Naval Academy

navigator person responsible for guiding ship's course

oarsman crew member who works oars to propel vessel

pilot harbor officer who boards and steers ship's entry into harbor; person who steers a ship into port; helmsman

pipes *Slang.* boatswain

pirate person who commits robbery on high seas; buccaneer; sea rover; rapparee

privateer crewman, esp. commander, of armed private ship or pirate ship cruising against commercial ships or warships of enemy

purser agent handling passengers' money and valuables

quartermaster steersman or signal and weather expert

radio operator communications officer or crewman

rapparee freebooter or pirate, esp. armed Irish plunderer of 17th c.

sailmaker person who designs, makes, and repairs sails, esp. for racing boats

sailor seaman; member of ship's crew; member of navy

salt *Informal.* crusty old mariner

Seabee CB; young sailor

sea dog seasoned sailor, mariner

seafarer mariner

seaman person who sails the seas; mariner

sea rover pirate

shipbuilder person who designs and constructs ships

ship chandler person dealing in ship's supplies

shipfitter welder who fits together structural parts of ships

shipmaster commander of vessel other than warship

shipmate fellow member of ship's crew

shipowner owner of ship or ships

shipwright carpenter skilled at shipbuilding and repair

skipper *Informal.* captain

steersman helmsman

stevedore longshoreman

steward waiter, porter, or kitchen help in crew

swabby *Slang.* deck hand

tar *Informal.* sailor

Viking Scandinavian sea rover or pirate (8th-11th c.)

warrant officer noncommissioned naval officer, usu. specialist such as electrician, pay clerk, machinist, or gunner

watch person responsible for observation duty on ship

whaler crewman on whaling ship

windjammer *Slang.* crewman on large sailing windjammer

yachtsman yacht owner; recreational sailor on yacht

yeoman naval petty officer with duties of clerk

Seamanship and Port

aboard (*adv*) on board a vessel

adrift (*adj*) floating freely without being steered; not at anchor

afloat (*adj*) floating on surface of water; flooded

aground (*adv*) snagged on shore or bottom of waterway

ahoy (*interj*) call of attention; hello

all hands entire ship's personnel

amphibious (*adj*) used on both land and sea

armada fleet of warships

ashore (*adv*) to or on land

avast (*vb*) command to stop, cease, or give attention

aweigh (*adj*) designating anchor coming up

backwater reverse rowing stroke employed to halt vessel or propel it in reverse

bail (*vb*) empty accumulated water with paddle or bucket

barnacles hard-shelled sea growth on pier or ship bottom

bear down (*vb*) approach from windward

bearing navigational term indicating direction of one point with reference to another

bear off (*vb*) prevent vessel from touching or rubbing against dock or another vessel

bear to (*vb*) head in given direction

belay (*vb*) fasten or secure with lines; stop

bells indication of time on ship

bend any loop or knot for joining end of one rope to another rope or to some other object

berth mooring place or slip in docks

bilge water water accumulating in bilge

bitter end inboard end of ship's line

Blackwall hitch hitch knot for temporarily securing line to hook

boat trailer frame that supports boat, usu. on two wheels, and is hauled by vehicle

bollard post on pier, used to secure hawsers

breakwater offshore barrier that protects shore or docks from waves

buoy floating marker anchored to bottom, used to indicate channel or underwater object

cabin class accommodations better than tourist class, inferior to first class

canal artificial waterway for navigation

cant (*vb*) pitch to one side

capsize (*vb*) overturn at sea

cast (*vb*) throw

cast off (*vb*) let go of line; set sail

cat's-paw hitch in middle of rope, forming two eyes to hold hook

celestial navigation charting course by position of stars and planets

change course alter direction

chart navigational map

circumnavigate (*vb*) sail around, esp. the Earth

clear the decks send all idle crew belowdecks

clove hitch knot for fastening rope to spar or large rope

colors flag or flags

come to (*vb*) bring ship's prow nearer the wind; stop moving, drop anchor

conn (*vb*) direct ship's steering

convoy merchant vessels under protection of warships

course direction taken, stated in degrees from north

crank (*adj*) unstable, liable to capsize

crest top of wave that curls over

cruise pleasure voyage; (*vb*) sail from port to port

current horizontal flow of water

dead ahead located directly before bow

dead reckoning calculation of position from course and distance sailed

debark (*vb*) disembark

disembark (*vb*) go ashore from ship

displacement weight of water displaced by ship

dock long, often wood structure, extending into water, to which ships are moored; pier

dockyard storage and repair facility for ships

downwind (*adv*) in same direction as wind

draft depth to which ship is submerged, measured from keel

draw (*vb*) require specific depth of water to float

dry dock artificial, drainable basin in which ships are repaired

embark (*vb*) go on board ship

even keel condition of floating properly upright in water

fag end frayed or untwisted end of line

fast (*adj*) secured, tied, fastened, or arranged, esp. of lines

fathom unit of nautical measurement equal to six feet (1.8 m)

fleet large group of ships of various sorts

flotsam floating wreckage

following sea waves running in same direction as course

founder (*vb*) take on water to point of capsizing and sinking; struggle in storm, going nowhere

free port port where goods may be unloaded, stored, and reshipped without paying customs or duty

furl (*vb*) roll up or take in sails

gale strong wind of 30-55 knots (32-63 mph)

go to sea begin life as mariner

harbor protected body of water deep enough for anchoring, usu. with docks constructed along shore; port

hawser bend knot joining ends of two lines

heading compass direction of vessel

heave (*vb*) throw; (*n*) vertical oscillation of vessel

heaving-line bend knot for attaching end of weighted heaving line to hawser

heel (*vb*) list to one side

high seas open ocean outside national territorial waters; international waters; open sea

hitch knot used to secure line to spar

hoist (*vb*) pull on line or halyard to raise something

horse latitudes area on each side of equator where westerlies change to trade winds and reverse direction

international waters high seas

jetsam cargo and equipment, cast overboard to lighten load in storm, that sinks or is washed ashore

jettison (*vb*) abandon or discard cargo overboard

knot unit of speed equal to 6076 feet (1851 m) per hour or one nautical mph

landfall sighting of land

landlubber land-bound person not familiar with sea

latitude distance measured in degrees north or south of equator

leeward (*adj*) at side of vessel away from wind

lie to (*vb*) remain stationary with bow to wind

lighthouse tall structure topped by powerful, revolving signal light that marks land's end or danger area

list (*vb*) tip to one side in water

lock section of canal filled with water to carry vessels through

log record of all events during voyage

longitude distance measured in degrees east or west of Greenwich, England

lubber's knot faulty square knot

luff (*vb*) turn bow toward wind; sail close or closer to wind, causing sails to flap

Magnus hitch knot for fastening rope to spar or larger rope

make sail (*vb*) raise or set sails or additional sail; set out on voyage

manifest itemized list of ship's cargo, esp. for customs

marlinespike hitch hitch into which pointed metal implement is inserted in order to draw seizing taut

Mayday international radiotelephone distress signal

merchant marine personnel and ships of one nation used in commerce

mole breakwater or stone barrier in harbor

moor (*vb*) attach lines or cables, usu. to dock, to hold vessel in place

mooring place where vessel is secured by lines or cables, esp. dock or slip; such securing lines or cables

mothball (*adj*) designating vessel not in current use or held in reserve, often older vessel

nautical (*adj*) of or pertaining to ships, sailors, or navigation

nautical mile international unit of measurement for sea navigation equal to 6076 feet (1851 m) or 1.15 statute miles (1.85 km)

navigable (*adj*) passable to vessels

navigation plan and direct course of ship at sea

open sea high seas

overboard (*adv*) over ship's side and into the water

passage travel on board ship, esp. from port to port

pay out (*vb*) let out line

pier dock

pile upright post driven into bottom that shows above water

pilot (*vb*) direct ship's course, esp. in and out of port or through difficult waters

pitch rocking, fore-and-aft motion at sea

plot (*vb*) plan course on map or chart

port harbor

prolonge knot knot made up of three overlapping loops formed by passing single rope over and under itself at crossings; sailor's breastplate

put about (*vb*) reverse direction

put out to sea begin voyage; join ship's crew

quay stone dock, often parallel to roadway along edge of water

range line determined by two or more objects on shore, used to plot safe course

reach tack in which wind crosses side of boat

reefed sail sail partly lowered and secured

reef knot square knot used in tying in sails

reeving-line bend knot for joining two lines so that they will pass easily through hole or ring

registry certificate showing nationality of merchant ship

ride at anchor float in position with anchor dropped

roll tipping, side-to-side motion at sea

rolling hitch hitch on spar that tightens under stress parallel to spar

row (*vb*) power vessel by hand with oars

run tack in which wind crosses stern of boat

run aground (*vb*) encounter waters too shallow for depth of keel

run before the wind sail swiftly in direction of wind

sail (*vb*) travel by water, esp. on vessel propelled by wind in sails; manage or steer a sailing vessel

sailing art and practice of navigation

sailor's breastplate prolonge knot

scrimshaw carved or engraved piece of ivory

scud (*vb*) run before a gale

sea biscuit hardtack biscuit eaten on long sea voyages

seagoing (*adj*) made for use in open sea

sea legs ability to walk on board ship, esp. in rough seas

seamanship skill in sailing, navigation, and handling ships

seasickness nausea and dizziness caused by roll and pitch

seaworthy (*adj*) fit to travel on the open sea

seizing means of binding together two objects or lengths of rope by number of longitudinal and transverse turns of thin line or wire

set manner and position in which sails are rigged

set sail begin voyage, depart from mooring

shakedown initial test cruise for ship

shipboard (*adj*) aboard ship

ship out (*vb*) go to sea, esp. join ship's crew

shipping commerce conducted by watergoing vessels

shipshape (*adj*) having everything in good order

ship's papers legally required papers carried on board, showing ship's registration and nature of cargo; registry

shipwreck destruction or loss of ship in accident

shipyard facility in which ships are built and repaired

slip mooring place or berth in dockyard

SOS save our ship; Morse code distress signal

soundings depth measurements

squall sudden, intense, localized storm at sea

steamer rug heavy woolen blanket used to cover lap and legs of passenger in deck chair

steerage space below forward deck, allotted to passengers paying lower fare

stem-to-stern (*adv*) from front to back of vessel

stowaway person concealed on board to secure free passage

strike (*vb*) shorten or take down sails

swab (*vb*) mop the deck

sway horizontal oscillation of ship's hull; (*vb*) heave object aloft

swell long, heavy undulation in sea's surface caused by distant disturbance

tack (*vb*) make course back and forth through wind by reversing after corner of sail; (*n*) direction of movement in relation to position of sails

take bearings determine one's position at sea relative to other objects

take in sail lower or remove sail from mast or yard

tender (*adj*) riding too high in water, therefore unstable; tending to heel excessively under sail

territorial waters area within three-mile (4.8-km) limit over which nation has jurisdiction

three-mile limit extent of territorial jurisdiction of any nation outward from its coastline

tides rise and fall of ocean level due to gravitational force of sun and moon

timber hitch knot formed on spar or other object by wrapping rope around object and itself

trade winds easterly winds prevailing at low latitudes and blowing toward equator

trim way in which boat floats in water; (*vb*) rig and put sails in order for sailing

tumble home inclination inward above waterline from greatest breadth

turn turtle capsize

under sail rigged and in motion

upwind (*adj*) sailing toward direction of wind; (*adv*) to windward

voyage journey by ship, esp. both outward and homeward

wake water disturbance pluming up behind moving vessel

watch observation of surrounding sea for storms, danger, or enemies, esp. four-hour period of such duty

water line line to which surface of water comes on hull

weigh (*vb*) hoist anchor

westerlies prevalent westerly winds of Temperate Zone

wigwag act of signaling by movement of two flags waved according to code

windward (*adj*) at side of vessel facing wind

yachting sport or recreation of sailing yachts

yaw (*vb*) deviate back and forth from course

Trolleys

autobus omnibus

cable car trolley operated by underground or overhead cable loop

el elevated trolley or railway

elevated railway urban passenger trolley suspended from overhead rail

funicular overhead cable railway up hill or mountain

gondola long, narrow boat serving as bus carrying passengers, esp. on canals of Venice

herdic small, horse-drawn omnibus with side seats and rear entrance (U.S., 19th c.)

jitney small passenger bus or van with flexible schedule over regular route

monorail trolley suspended from or balanced on single rail

omnibus public carrier for at least twelve passengers, usu. with door in rear

streetcar vehicle usu. on rails, esp. for city passengers

subway underground trolley or municipal railway, usu. electric

tram streetcar on overhead rail or cable

trolley wheeled carriage, usu. with overhead cable, often electric

trolley bus trackless electric bus with overhead cable

trolley car trackless electric streetcar with overhead cable

wagonette covered, four-wheel carriage bus with facing passenger seats for six or more

Carriages

araba cab or coach (Turkey)

barouche four-wheel carriage with facing double seats and folding top

berlin four-wheel carriage with suspended body (Germany, 18th c.)

brougham low, closed, four-wheel carriage for two passengers with driver's seat outside

buckboard four-wheel carriage with seat mounted on springlike board

buggy light, four-wheel, one-horse, two-passenger carriage

cab orig. cabriolet; light closed carriage for hire

cabriolet light, two-wheel, one-horse carriage with folding hood

calash caleche

caleche carriage with two small wheels in front and folding top; calash

cariole light, one-horse carriage

caroche luxurious, horse-drawn carriage

carriage any horse-drawn vehicle, esp. for private use

carromata light, two-wheel carriage with single pony (Philippines)

carryall light, covered carriage that seats four or more

cart heavy, horse-drawn, two-wheel carriage used for hauling freight

chaise small, usu. two-wheel carriage suspended on leather straps

charabanc large sightseeing coach

chariot ancient, two-wheel, seatless, horse-drawn battle car

chuckwagon large, closed supply wagon (U.S. West, 19th c.)

clarence closed, four-wheel, four-seat carriage with driver outside; growler

coach large, four-wheel, enclosed carriage with driver's seat outside

Concord buggy large, covered, four-wheel carriage with driver's seat outside and covered baggage compartment

Conestoga broad-wheeled covered wagon drawn by six horses

coupe enclosed, four-wheel carriage with driver's seat outside

covered wagon large, canvas-topped, four-wheel vehicle for moving families west (U.S., 19th c.)

curricle light, two-wheel carriage drawn by two horses abreast (18th-19th c.)

diligence four-wheel, four-horse public stagecoach (France, 18th c.)

dogcart light, usu. one-horse, two-wheel cart with two transverse seats back-to-back

dos-a-dos four-wheel dogcart with seats set back-to-back

Dougherty wagon passenger wagon on steel springs (U.S. West, 19th c.)

drag large, private, four-horse sporting coach with roof, rumble seats, and enclosed compartment

dray low, sturdy cargo cart with detachable sides

droshky low, open, four-wheel carriage with narrow bench (Russia)

fiacre small, four-wheel hackney coach

fly horse-drawn public coach or delivery wagon

four-in-hand carriage drawn by four horses

Germantown two- or three-seat carriage, esp. in Pennsylvania

gharry horse-drawn cab (India, Egypt)

gig light, two-wheel, one-horse carriage

growler *Brit. slang.* clarence

hack hackney

hackney four-wheel, two-horse, six-seat carriage kept for hire; hack

hansom two-wheel, two-horse, two-passenger, covered carriage with driver's seat elevated at rear; hansom cab

hansom cab hansom

herdic horse-drawn omnibus with side seats and rear entrance (U.S., 19th c.)

jaunting car light, two-wheel, open vehicle with lengthwise back-to-back seats

landau large, four-wheel carriage with top that folds into two parts (Germany)

mudwagon flat-sided, simple stagecoach, smaller than Concord

phaeton light, four-wheel carriage with seats front and rear, folding cover, and no coachman's seat

post chaise four-wheel coach, used to carry mail and passengers (18th-19th c.)

prairie schooner broad-wheeled covered wagon used in cross-country travel (U.S. West)

quadriga two-wheel chariot drawn by four horses (ancient Rome)

rig general term for carriage and horse

rockaway carriage with enclosed top (U.S., 19th c.)

runabout topless buggy

shandrydan hooded chaise; rickety carriage

spider phaeton very high, light carriage with covered seat and rear footman's seat

spring wagon light, versatile wagon with removable seats and canopy top

stagecoach public passenger and mail coach that ran on regular schedule (U.S. West, 19th c.)

stanhope light, open, one-seat, two-wheel carriage

sulky light, one-passenger, two-wheel carriage used in trotting races

surrey modest, four-wheel, two-seat carriage used for pleasure or to carry family, with or without top

tandem two-seat carriage drawn by team of horses harnessed one before the other

tilbury light, two-wheel gig

tonga two-wheel carriage (India)

trap light, one-horse carriage with springs

troika sleigh or carriage drawn by three horses abreast (Russia)

victoria large, luxurious, four-wheel, two-horse carriage

volante two-wheel carriage with axle behind body and driver riding horse (Cuba)

Wagons, Carts, and Sleds

baby carriage covered crib on four springy wheels

barrow two-wheel cart with shallow body and shaft handles

Bath chair hooded, glassed wheelchair pushed by attendant

bobsled large, metal racing sled on runners

caisson two-wheel wagon used to carry artillery ammunition

camion strongly built cart or wagon for transporting heavy loads; dray

cariole light covered cart; dog-drawn toboggan

carrier device used to contain and transport articles; baby's reclining plastic seat, carried by a person

cart heavy, horse-drawn, two-wheel vehicle used to carry freight

coaster small sliding sled or wagon

dogsled small sled hauled by dogs

dolly platform on rollers for moving heavy loads

dray strong, low, sideless cart for hauling goods; camion

fourgon baggage wagon (19th c.)

go-cart lightweight handcart; small framework on wheels for children

gurney flat, wheeled cot for transporting disabled or injured person

handcart hand truck

hand truck small, hand-propelled, two-wheel carrier; handcart

hay wagon large, open wagon for hay

jinrikisha small, two-wheel passenger cab drawn by one or two persons (Japan, China)

jumper sled for hauling goods over bare ground

kibitka covered vehicle on wheels or runners (Russia)

komatik sled on wooden runners, with crossbars lashed with rawhide (Eskimo)

laundry cart upright, mesh vehicle on wheels, used to carry laundry

luge small racing sled driven in supine position down chute

milk wagon large wagon used to deliver milk

oxcart ox-driven freight cart

perambulator *Chiefly Brit.* baby carriage

pram *Brit. informal.* baby carriage

pulka one-man sledge on runners (Lapland)

pung sleigh with box-shaped body, drawn by one horse (Algonquian Indian)

push cart cart or barrow on wheels, pushed by hand

ricksha jinrikisha

shopping cart mesh, four-wheel grocery cart

skid low platform on wheels for moving heavy objects

sled vehicle made of flat body on runners for use over snow and ice

sledge any of various carts on runners for carrying goods over ice, often drawn by draft animals

sleigh large passenger sled on runners, usu. open and horse-drawn, for use over snow and ice

spring wagon light farm or ranch wagon on springs

stroller seat on wheels for baby

tipcart cart whose body tips to empty contents

toboggan long, flat-bottomed sled with one end curved up and handrails

trundle low hauling cart on wheels

tumbrel farm tipcart, used to carry prisoners to execution (France, 18th c.)

wagon any of various four-wheel vehicles, motorized, animal-drawn, or human-propelled, ranging in use from child's toy to transportation of bulky goods

wain farm wagon or cart

wheelbarrow single-wheel cart with shallow body, held and pushed by handles, used to transport small loads

wheelchair chair on wheels for invalid or disabled person

Cycles

ATV all terrain vehicle; sturdy three-wheel motorcycle for cross-country driving

bicycle two-wheel cycle operated by foot pedals; bike

bicycle-built-for-two two-wheel, two-seat, pedal-driven cycle; tandem

bike *Informal.* bicycle

chopper *Slang.* motorcycle

cycle open, pedaled or engine powered, single-passenger vehicle, usu. having two wheels in tandem

dandy two-wheel velocipede

dirt bike small, motor-driven cycle with extra-heavy tires

hog *Slang.* large, heavy motorcycle

minibike small motorcycle with raised handlebars

monocycle unicycle

moped pedal-started motor scooter with small engine

motorbike low-power, lightweight motorcycle

motorcycle two wheel, motor-driven cycle; chopper

motor scooter small, lightweight motorcycle; bicycle propelled by attached motor

mountain bike rugged, fat-wheeled bicycle with deep tread for traction and stability on dirt trails

ordinary early bicycle with a very large front wheel and a very small rear wheel

pedicab tricycle with separate two-seat passenger compartment; trishaw

penny-farthing *Chiefly Brit.* bicycle with large front wheel and small rear wheel

quadricycle four-wheel cycle

scooter small motorbike; child's two-wheel, self-propelled vehicle with long, narrow footboard

sidewalk bike child's training bicycle with detachable set of extra rear wheels

skateboard short board with pair of wheels at each end, powered by free foot while standing on board

tandem bicycle-built-for-two

ten-speed powerful, lightweight bicycle with ten gears

trail bike small motorcycle designed for use on unpaved roads

tricycle small, three-wheel, pedal-driven bicycle, esp. for young children; trike

trike *Informal.* tricycle

trishaw pedicab

unicycle one-wheel bicycle with very tall seat, often used in circus; monocycle

velocipede early, lightweight wheeled vehicle, self-propelled by rider

Litters

brancard stretcher

camel litter seat fitted on camel's hump

dooly enclosed palanquin litter (India)

handbarrow light, flat, rectangular frame with handles at both ends

horse litter seat carried by horse

howdah covered seat carried by elephant or camel (India)

jampan sedan chair borne on two poles (India)

jinrikisha two-wheel passenger cab with fold-down top, pulled by one or two persons (Japan, China); ricksha

kajawah litter (India)

litter covered, often curtained couch on long shafts or poles, borne by animals or people

norimon litter (Japan)

palanquin enclosed litter (Asia)

ricksha jinrikisha

sedan chair portable, covered, single chair borne on poles

stokes litter wire basket for transporting ill or injured person

stretcher flat, open litter for carrying ill or injured person; brancard

tonjon open litter (India)

travois platform or net on two trailing poles drawn by animal (American Indian)

PART THREE
DOMESTIC LIFE

CHAPTER SEVEN
THE HOME

BUILDINGS
Living Places
Types of Buildings

See also: *Chap. 7: Exterior Structure; Chap. 11: The City*

Living Places

abode place where one lives

accommodations lodgings, sometimes including food

apartment single unit within multiunit residential building, rented by person who usu. occupies the space

building any enclosed structure with walls and roof

camp group of tents or cabins used as temporary shelter

caravan wagon or vehicle equipped with living quarters

casa *Spanish.* house

cave underground chamber opening at earth's surface, used as dwelling by prehistoric man

cliff dwelling cavelike dwelling built into rock face of cliff

condominium single unit within multiple-unit structure, owned by its individual deed holder, usu. its occupant

co-op unit within multiunit structure jointly owned by residents of all units

countryseat *Chiefly Brit.* usu. substantial rural house of urban dweller

den shabby dwelling or cave, esp. used as hiding place

digs *Brit. slang.* living quarters

dive *Informal.* disreputable establishment, esp. commercial

domicile customary, fixed, permanent dwelling; legal residence

dump *Informal.* run-down, sloppy dwelling

dwelling abode, living place

edifice usu. large, elaborate building

estate privately owned land with substantial residence on it

farmhouse residential structure on farmland

guesthouse small building separate from but near a main residence

habitat one's regular place of residence

habitation dwelling, residence

hacienda primary dwelling on large ranch or estate (Spain, Latin America)

haunt place regularly visited or inhabited

home place where one lives

homestead land and buildings in which a family dwells

house building used as dwelling place

household home and its occupants

housing shelter or living accommodations

lair hidden lodging place

lodging place for dwelling, often temporary

maison *French.* house

nest safe, often secluded living place

pad *Slang.* dwelling place

place home, dwelling

quarters lodging, dwelling place

ranch rural house and surrounding land used for raising stock animals

rancho ranch, hut for ranch workers (Spain, Latin America)

residence place in which one regularly lives

retreat hidden or secluded dwelling

roof over one's head basic housing, shelter

rooms portion of house used as living quarters

roost place for resting or lodging, often temporarily

shelter any protective structure used as temporary or permanent living place

squat public or unoccupied dwelling used without permission

structure building constructed for human use or occupation

unit portion of structure partitioned for occupation by single person or group of persons

Types of Buildings

acropolis fortified, columned structure (ancient Greece)

A-frame building constructed of a three-piece frame shaped like capital A

alcázar fortress, palace (Spain)

amphitheater roofless oval or circle with rising tiers of seats

apartment building with several separate dwelling units

arena large, open or enclosed building for contests, entertainments

auditorium large room or hall for public gathering

aviary place for confining birds, usu. screened

balok small, fabric-covered, mobile cabin (Eskimo)

barn large, open building for storing farm equipment, housing animals

barracks set of buildings, often resembling sheds or barns, housing soldiers in garrison

basilica oblong building with broad nave flanked by colonnaded aisles, ending in semicircular apse

bathhouse structure containing baths, often also pools, steam rooms, and whirlpools; structure housing changing rooms for bathers, as at beach

bi-level house having at least two levels of living space

blockhouse heavy timber military structure with projecting upper story

boardinghouse home converted to rooms for rent, with food sometimes included for tenants

booth small enclosure isolating occupant

bower rustic cottage

bungalow one-story residence with low, sweeping lines, often with veranda

cabana tentlike structure with projecting canopy

cabin small, simple, one-story, low-roofed dwelling

campanile tall, freestanding bell tower

Cape Cod cottage compact, rectangular, one-and-a-half-story dwelling with steep gable roof and central chimney

caravan *Chiefly Brit.* mobile home

caravansary hotel or inn, orig. where caravans rested

carriage house building for storage of carriages

castle large, fortified building or group of buildings, usu. stone, housing ruler or nobleman

chalet dwelling with unconcealed structural members emphasized by decorative carvings

château large country house, esp. in French wine regions

church Christian house of worship, often with spire, finial cross

condominium multiple-unit residence jointly owned by deed holders, who are usu. its occupants

conservatory glass-roofed house for plants

coop roofed cage or small enclosure for poultry

cottage small, detached dwelling, often rural

crib small, narrow dwelling; framework stall

dacha country cottage, summerhouse (Russia)

dormitory large residence hall with many bedrooms

duplex single residence divided into two units

earth lodge circular, dome-shaped dwelling made of posts and beams covered by branches, grass, and earth (American Indian)

flat apartment built on one floor of building

garage small, enclosed building for storing cars and equipment

gazebo freestanding, roofed summerhouse open on sides

greenhouse glassed enclosure for growing plants

hall large structure for public use; residence on country estate

hangar high-roofed, enclosed shed for repairing and storing aircraft

high-rise multistory apartment house or office building

hippodrome oval arena for equestrian events

hogan rough log and mud dwelling (Navajo)

hostel housing maintained by institution for specific group

hotel building of many rooms licensed to provide lodging

house building intended for human habitation

houseboat moored barge or low boat fitted for use as dwelling

hovel small, miserable shed or open-roofed structure

hut small, rudimentary structure for temporary habitation

hutch animal pen or coop; shack, shanty

igloo dome-shaped dwelling of ice blocks (Eskimo)

inn public house for lodging, usu. in countryside

izba traditional, rural log hut (Russia)

jacal thatched roof hut with walls of mud-plastered upright stakes (Mexico)

kennel shelter for dogs, with fenced yard

kiosk small structure with one or more open sides; open summerhouse or pavilion

laura monastery of Eastern orthodox church

lean-to rough shed, its roof having one slope

lighthouse tower with powerful light as signal of coastline to ships

lodge inn or resort hotel; house set aside from main house for hunting or other special use

loft upper floor of warehouse building converted to living area

log cabin rustic dwelling built of logs laid horizontally

long house long wooden communal dwelling (Iroquois)

maisonette *French.* small house or apartment

mall very large building housing stores, with adjacent parking lots

manor large hall on estate property

manse large, elegant residence

mansion grand, elaborate dwelling

market public building for wholesale trade

mobile home movable trailer with living facilities

mosque Islamic place of worship with rounded spires and minaret

motel hotel for automobile travelers, usu. long and low

Nissen hut prefabricated shelter, semicircular, with arching corrugated steel roof and concrete floor

obelisk upright, four-sided pillar tapering to pyramid top

outbuilding small structure, such as stable or woodshed, separate from main residence

outhouse small enclosed toilet set apart from main house, usu. without plumbing

pagoda structure resembling tower of several stories with projecting, concavely curved roofs (Asia)

palace large, stately house, usu. ruler's official residence

palazzo palace or large residence (Italy)

pavilion large, often sumptuous tent or canopy

pen small, open enclosure for animals

pension modest hotel or boardinghouse in Europe

penthouse dwelling unit built on roof of building

pied-à-terre temporary or second lodging; townhouse

pile large and lofty building or group of buildings

plant land, buildings, and equipment of factory

port-a-potty small, movable, enclosed booth used as toilet, esp. on construction sites

posada country inn (Spain, Latin America)

possum-trot plan house in two parts connected by breezeway

prefab structure built of interchangeable, prefabricated parts

pueblo communal dwelling, esp. contiguous flat-roofed adobe houses several stories high or arranged in terraces (Southwest American Indian)

pyramid massive stone structure, having square

base with four triangular walls that meet in point at top (ancient Egypt)

Quonset hut prefabricated structure with semicircular arched corrugated steel roof on bolted steel truss foundation

ranch house low, sprawling, one-story suburban residence

resort complex of structures for recreational use

rialto exchange, marketplace, or theater building

roadhouse inn or hotel, usu. beyond city limits

rotunda round, domed building

saltbox frame dwelling, two stories in front, one in rear, with double-sloping roof extending farther in back

semidetached (*adj*) designating pair of residences joined by common wall

shack small, roughly built, crudely furnished house; shebang

shanty small, crudely built, shabby dwelling, usu. of wood

shebang primitive dwelling; shack

shed small structure, usu. for storage

shop small retail establishment

skyscraper very tall urban office or apartment building

split-level residence with rooms built on floor levels differing by about half a story

stable shelter for horses or stock animals

stadium very large, unroofed structure with tiered seats, used for sporting events

stall small booth or stand for retail sales, open at one side

stand small, open-air structure for retail business

stupa dome-shaped mound, tower, or Buddhist shrine

supermarket large, one-story store, with adjacent parking lots, that sells food and other household goods

synagogue Jewish house of worship

tabernacle usu. large meeting house or assembly hall, used esp. as place of worship

tavern building used as bar or saloon

temple edifice for non-Christian religious observance

tenement multiunit apartment building, usu. a cheap dwelling for urban poor

tent small shelter of canvas supported or suspended on poles

tepee conical tent of skin drawn on poles, used as dwelling (American Plains Indian)

terminal central transport station serving multiple lines

theater edifice that is site of various kinds of performances on stage

tholos circular building (ancient Greece)

town house often luxurious house in the city, esp. distinguished from house in country owned by same person; one of group of two- or three-story houses of uniform design joined by common sidewalls

tract home one of many identical, prefab residences in suburban cluster

triplex single residence divided into three units

trailer movable structure with living facilities

tupik sealskin tent used as summer dwelling (Eskimo)

villa large country estate; *Chiefly Brit.* small suburban house

warehouse large storage or manufacturing structure, often windowless

washhouse building equipped for washing clothes

wickiup elliptical hut used as residence by nomads (American Indian)

wigwam domed structure of poles overlaid with bark, used as residence (Great Lakes American Indian)

woodshed crude shed for storing wood

yurt circular, domed tent of skin on collapsible lattice frame, used by Mongol nomads (Mongolia, Siberia)

ziggurat temple pyramid built in successive stepped-back stages with shrine at top (ancient Mesopotamia)

EXTERIOR STRUCTURE

Windows, Walls, and Facades
Roofs and Towers
Entryways and Lateral Extensions
Ornamental and Structural Parts
Outbuildings, Gardens, and Fences

See also: *Chap. 5: Structural Components; Building and Construction Materials; Chap. 7: Buildings; Interior Structure; Ornamental and Functional Articles; Chap. 16: Architecture; Chap. 17: Gardening*

Windows, Walls, and Facades

anta support pier formed by thickening end of wall

bailey outer wall or space between two outer walls of castle

bay window large window set in bay or recess in room and projecting from outside wall, often three-sided

bondstone stone used to bond facing masonry to masonry backing

bow window rounded bay window; compass window

bulkhead retaining wall

bull's-eye window œil-de-bœuf

casement hinged window frame with two windows opening outward from middle

Catherine wheel window small, round window with spokes extending outward from its center

clapboard narrow board, thicker at one side, used in covering outside of house, usu. painted white

clerestory outside wall carried above adjoining roof, pierced with windows

compass window bow window

coping finishing or protective cap to exterior masonry wall

cornerstone first stone laid where walls meet

curtain wall nonbearing exterior wall in framed building

dead wall wall without openings

Diocletian window Palladian window

dormer vertical window set in projection beneath sloping roof; entire projecting structure with such a window

double-hung window window with top and bottom sashes that move vertically

embrasure opening in wall for door or window, sloped or beveled to enlarge interior outline; reveal

facade outer surface of building, esp. front wall; face

face facade

fanlight semicircular window with radiating bars like ribs of fan, often above door or rectangular window

French window pair of casement windows reaching to floor and opening in middle

front building facade facing street

frontispiece highly ornamental, principle feature of a facade

grille grating forming barrier or screen over opening

horizontal sliding window window that opens sideways on tracks

Judas hole small window with sliding panel set in door, used as peephole

lancet window high, narrow, sharply pointed window set in lancet arch

louver opening in wall with overlapping slats that allow ventilation, prevent entry of rain, and provide privacy

mullioned window window with multiple panes divided by slender vertical strips

œil-de-bœuf small circular or oval window; bull's-eye window

oriel large projecting bay window supported by corbel or bracket

Palladian window central arched window with two small flanking compartments, usu. mullioned; Diocletian window

perpend wall wall built of bricks or large stones passing through entire thickness of wall and acting as binders

picture window large, undivided window usu. opening onto scenic view

porthole small, round window, esp. on ship

quarrel small, quadrangular or diamond-shaped glass set diagonally in latticed window

retaining wall wall that resists lateral pressure, esp. from earth

reveal side of opening between frame and wall; embrasure; jamb

revetment stone or concrete facing used to protect embankment

ribbon window long, divided window forming continuous horizontal band across face of building

rose window circular window decorated with tracery that is symmetrical about the center

roundel small, round window

scarp vertical side of ditch below parapet of fortification

sconcheon reveal of window from frame to inner face of wall

screen frame holding fine wire mesh over door or window to exclude insects but permit ventilation

shutter movable cover or screen for window or door, often of wood slats

siding weatherproof boards or facings that form outer wall or facade

skylight opening in roof and ceiling covered with transparent material, usu. overhead window of glass

storm window protective window set in jamb outside permanent window in winter to conserve heat

transom window above door or other window, usu. hinged to horizontal crosspiece; such a crosspiece separating windows or door and window

Trombe wall glass-fronted, exterior masonry wall that absorbs solar heat for radiation into building

wall continuous upright surface connecting floor and ceiling or foundation and roof, subdividing interior space, or supporting other parts of structure

window opening in wall for admission of air and light, set with frame holding transparent substance, usu. glass

windowpane individual section filling a window sash, usu. of glass

Roofs and Towers

awning rooflike covering extending outward from structure

barbican fortified tower at gate or bridge

barrack roof movable roof sliding on four posts, used to cover hay or straw brick

bartizan small, overhanging turret on wall or tower, esp. of castle

bastion projecting part of fortification

battlement parapet atop wall with alternating open spaces and merlons, used for defense or decoration

belfry tower, cupola, or turret in which bell is housed

bell tower tower in which bell is housed

butterfly roof roof with shallow valley and gently sloping sides

buttress projecting support structure providing stability for wall or building

campanile tall, straight, freestanding bell tower

castellated (*adj*) designating upward projection with battlements, like a castle

chimney vertical structure usu. of brick or stone, with flue for carrying off smoke from fireplace

chimney pot earthenware or metal pipe at top of chimney to increase draft and disperse smoke

corbie gable gable with corbie steps

corbiestep one of a series of steps terminating in upper part of gable wall

cowl hoodlike covering over chimney to improve draft

crenel opening in battlement between projecting merlons

crenelation series of open spaces and notches atop battlement

crest horizontal ridge of roof

cullis gutter in roof

cupola small dome on roof; rounded roof or ceiling

curb roof roof peaked at center with double slope on each side

dome hemispherical roof, usu. large

donjon massive central tower or stronghold in castle

dormer gabled extension off attic room, with sloping roof and vertical window

eave edge of roof projecting beyond side of building

fastness fortified, secure place, often elevated

flat roof roof without ridge, slope, or dome

flèche tall, thin church spire

gable extending, ridged roof section of triangular wall enclosed by sloping sides, usu. with window

gambrel roof roof having two slopes on each side, with lower slope steeper than upper

geodesic dome domed roof made of light, straight, structural elements forming polygons in tension

gutter metal drainage trough under roof eaves

helm roof four-faced, steeply pitched roof, rising to point from base of four gables

hip-and-valley roof shaped with hips and valleys

hipped roof roof with sloping ends and sloping sides

jerkinhead roof having hipped end over truncated gable

lantern decorative open structure admitting light at top of roof or dome; similar structure used for ventilation

lean-to roof having one slope, often projecting from wall

lean-to hipped roof single slope with hipped ends, usu. projecting from wall

lou wood-framed tower, forerunner of pagoda (China)

louver roof turret with slatted aperture for vent; slanted fins opening off attic to exclude rain and sun and admit light and air

mansard roof having two slopes on each of four sides, with lower slope steeper than upper

Martello tower circular stone fort with guns on top

merlon solid interval between battlement crenels

minaret tall, slender mosque tower with projecting balconies from which Moslems are called to prayer

monopitch roof single-slope lean-to atop freestanding structure

obelisk tapering, four-sided monolithic tower with pyramid at top

observation tower tall structure overlooking surroundings

pagoda tower with projecting, encircling roofs at each of several levels (Asia)

pantile roof roof of semicylindrical tiles laid with alternate concave and convex surfaces uppermost

pitched roof roof with sloping sides

platform raised, horizontal, flat surface

pyramid roof four triangular slopes rising to point from square base

rainbow roof gable roof with gentle convex slopes giving rounded appearance

rainspout pipe or duct that drains roof gutter

roof top covering of building

sawtooth roof two or more parallel roofs like teeth of a saw, with one slope steeper than the other

scupper water drainage opening in wall at floor or roof

shed roof roof forming single slope from peak to wall

shingle roof roof composed of overlapping strips of wood or other material

skirt roof small section of roofing between stories of building, usu. nonbearing and decorative

slate roof roof shingled with laminated rock material

spire tower or steeple tapering to point

steeple pointed tower, esp. atop church

stupa domed-shaped tower, esp. on Buddhist shrine

thatched roof roof made of thick layer of interwoven straw or reeds

tile roof roof composed of semicylindrical strips of fired clay or stone

tower tall, standing structure attached to larger structure or freestanding

turret short, projecting tower, usu. at corner of building

valley low point between two roof slopes

watchtower tall lookout tower

widow's walk railed lookout platform or walkway on roof

ziggurat pyramidal temple tower in successive stories with winding outside staircase and shrine at top (ancient Mesopotamia)

Entryways and Lateral Extensions

addition room or extension built onto already existing structure

ambulatory sheltered place for walking in cloister

archway entry or passageway beneath series of arches

areaway sunken space leading to cellar or basement entrance or window

atrium open court leading into building, often with a glassed side and roof

backdoor entryway at rear of building

balcony railed platform attached to upper story of building

bay three-sided projection from side of building

belvedere open, roofed, upstairs gallery, esp. overlooking pleasant scene

breezeway roofed passage between two buildings or sections of one building

bulkhead inclined door over stairway leading to cellar or shaft

cloister covered walkway along wall of monastery, usu. opening through columns onto inner court

deck broad, open balcony extending from house

door solid, swinging or sliding barrier for opening or closing entryway to room or building

doorway entryway to building in which door is set

drawbridge bridge which may be raised or lowered to prevent or allow passage

entrance point of entry

entryway passage for or point of entry

extension added portion of building attached to main structure

fire escape structure of metal platforms and ladders or stairways down outer wall of structure, used for escape in case of fire

French doors adjoining doors that open in middle, with rectangular glass panes

front door main entryway at front of building; primary doorway

frontispiece highly ornamented portico or principle entryway

gallery outdoor balcony; roofed promenade or colonnade

gate swinging, grated doorway in fence or exterior wall, usu. opening onto drive or grounds

gateway entrance that may be closed by gate

hatch small door or opening, esp. in airplane or ship; opening in ship's deck or in floor or roof of building

lanai porch, veranda (Hawaii)

lich gate roofed churchyard gate under which coffin rests while awaiting clergy during burial

moon gate circular opening through wall (China)

opening entryway or doorway

pai-loo elaborate, monumental archway in three compartments (China)

parvis enclosed court in front of building, esp. church court with row of columns

passageway opening or hallway allowing entry to room

perron outdoor platform with entrance door to building at top of stairway

porch covered approach or appendage to building

portal doorway or opening, esp. elaborate or imposing one

portcullis grating of iron bars or timbers suspended over gateway, lowered to prevent passage

porte-cochere arched entryway for carriages, leading from street to inner courtyard

portico roof supported by columns and attached to building as porch

revolving door two or more doors turning on common axis within cylindrical vestibule

scaffolding elevated platform, esp. movable one for workers

screen door doorway of fine mesh allowing ventilation but preventing entrance of pests

skybridge skywalk

skywalk enclosed elevated walkway connecting two buildings; skybridge

sliding door door mounted on runners that slides aside to open

storm door additional protective door placed outside regular door

sun deck unroofed top surface of building

torii post and lintel gateway of Shinto temple (Japan)

trapdoor lifting or sliding door flush with surface of roof, ceiling, or floor

turnstile four revolving arms pivoted atop post to permit single-file passage of people, usu. in one direction only

veranda large balcony or open porch along side of building, often roofed and railed

walkway open or covered passageway from area to area within or between structures

wicket small gate or door

wing section or room projecting from main structure

zaguán *Spanish.* passageway from entrance into central patio

Ornamental and Structural Parts

arch curved masonry support structure spanning an opening: basket handle, flat, horseshoe, lancet, ogee, parabolic, round, shouldered, trefoil, Tudor

bargeboard elaborately carved, ornamental wood that conceals projecting end of gable or sloped roof

bracket projecting support element

bridge elevated crossing between buildings

capital upper end of column atop shaft, bearing weight of entablature

caryatid sculptured, robed female figure used as column (ancient Greece)

cheval-de-frise row of projecting spikes atop wall for defense

colonnade series of columns at regular intervals

column tall, round support member on pedestal in one of three basic types: Corinthian, Doric, or Ionic; other styles include Byzantine, Gothic, Moorish, Romanesque, and Tuscan

corbel bracketlike member that supports weight, esp. one projecting upward and outward from wall surface

Corinthian column column of late classical period characterized by high base, slender fluted shaft with fillets, and ornate capital with acanthus leaves

cornerstone quoin

cornice prominent, projecting horizontal member surmounting a wall or dividing it horizontally

courtyard interior walled area surrounded by building

crawlspace shallow, unfinished area beneath first floor or under roof, usu. for plumbing and wiring; crawlway

crawlway crawlspace

dentils series of small, rectangular, toothlike blocks beneath corona of classical cornice

Doric column undecorated column of early classical period characterized by short fluted shaft and convex circular molding as capital, with no distinct base

engaged column column attached to wall, not freestanding

finial ornament atop spire or gable

footscraper edged plate or bar fixed on doorstep for removing mud from boots

gargoyle elaborately carved creature, often functioning as a waterspout, projecting from a building

gingerbread showy, elaborate trim on house

Ionic column column of middle classical period characterized by slender fluted shaft with molded base and volute or spiral capital

jamb upright structural member at side of door or window

lintel horizontal member carrying weight above opening or doorway

miter covering on top of chimney to keep rain out

mudsill lowest lip of structure, often embedded in mud

parapet low wall or railing on balcony, bridge, or roof to prevent falls and provide cover from below

pediment low, triangular gable with horizontal cornice set above colonnade or section of facade

peristyle row of columns around outside of temple (ancient Greece)

pier vertical, structural support

pilaster upright, rectangular pier projecting less than half its width from wall

pillar firm, upright support column or shaft

platform raised, horizontal, usu. unroofed surface

pylon massive structure flanking entry or towers by gate; tower or support post for bridge

quoin one of several large stones forming corner of masonry wall; cornerstone

sash frame in door or window in which panes of glass are set

shaft column, esp. main cylindrical central portion of column

skewback inclined surface of masonry against which stones of arch rest

stilt pile or post supporting raised structure

story any entire level or floor of a building

telamon sculptured male figure, similar to female caryatid, used as column or pilaster

trestle support brace with crossbar on two pairs of legs

trough gutter under eaves of building for rain drainage

vane movable device atop spire or tower that indicates wind direction; weather vane

weathercock vane in shape of rooster

weather vane vane

Outbuildings, Gardens, and Fences

apiary collection of beehives; shed where bees are kept

aqueduct elevated structure that supports water pipe or conduit

arbor plot of grass, lawn, or garden; lattice trellis or vine bower for shade

arboretum place where trees, shrubs, and herbs are grown for study or display

artesian well deep-bored well in which water rises under pressure like a fountain

backhouse outdoor toilet

backyard outdoor area at rear of house, often fenced

band pavilion open, roofed stage or gazebo on lawn

band shell band pavilion, usu. semicircular

barbed-wire fence fencing of twisted wires with sharp points

barn large building for storage of farm equipment and feed and for housing of livestock

barnyard usu. fenced area next to barn

bed plot of soil where plants are cultivated

belvedere small summerhouse

botanical garden outdoor garden and greenhouses for growth, study, and display of unusual plants

bower arbor or leafy shelter of twined boughs or vines

cabana small cabin or tent opening onto beach or pool

carport open-sided automobile shelter with roof, often extending from main building

cesspool underground cistern or pit for household sewage

chain-link fence fence of thin wire mesh

chicken coop small enclosure or cage for poultry

clothesline cord strung between two suspended points for hanging and drying laundry

conservatory glass-enclosed greenhouse for growing or displaying plants

corral pen or enclosure for livestock

court open space surrounded wholly or partly by building

curtilage enclosed area of land occupied by structure, gardens, and outbuildings

cyclone cellar underground shelter used during windstorms

Cyclone fence *Trademark.* type of chain-link fence

doghouse small roofed enclosure for pet dog

espalier trellis or lattice on which shrubs are trained to grow

exedra covered area open on one side; semicircular outdoor alcove with bench seat (ancient Greece and Rome)

flagstone large, flat slab of stone for paving garden or walk

flower bed cultivated area for planting flowers

fountain mechanical water spout, usu. in decorative, raised structure containing a pool

front yard open area between house and roadway

garage enclosed area for storage of automobiles and other equipment, usu. adjoining main building

garden plot of cultivated, manicured lawns, plants, and flowers

garden wall enclosure along one or more sides of garden

garth enclosed yard or garden, esp. within cloister of religious institution

gazebo open or screened pavilion or summerhouse set on lawn

greenhouse glass-enclosed building for growing plants

grotto cavelike summer structure or shrine

grounds land surrounding house, esp. lawns and garden

guesthouse small building separate from main structure, often with bathroom and kitchen, used to accommodate visitors

hedge dense shrubbery forming boundary or enclosure; hedgerow

hedgerow *Chiefly Brit.* hedge

hothouse artificially heated greenhouse for tropical plants

hutch animal pen

incinerator container for burning refuse

kennel series of cages or living quarters for dogs

kiosk small pavilion, open on one or more sides, used as newsstand, bandstand, or covered entryway

lathhouse structure with walls and roof of narrow lath strips

latrine outdoor pit used as toilet, often enclosed; outhouse

lattice openwork structure of crossed strips used as screen or support

lawn flat expanse of mowed grass

manger open food trough in stable, for horses or cattle

mew *Chiefly Brit.* stables built along courtyard or alley

moat wide trench around building or fortified place, usu. filled with water

nursery building in which plants are grown, esp. for transplanting

orchard field of cultivated fruit trees

outhouse latrine

paddock enclosed field for pasturing or exercising animals

paling fence picket fence

palisade stake or paling fence used for defense

parterre ornamental flower beds set among paths

path usu. unpaved walkway through grounds or garden

patio usu. paved area adjoining house, used esp. for outdoor dining and recreation

pavilion open tent, building, or shelter adjoining main body of building or separate from it

pergola openwork arch or covering for walkway with plants trained on it; arbor or trellis
picket fence fence of thin, white, vertical boards pointed at tops; paling fence
pigpen fenced area for swine
pool hole or large vessel lined with stones, concrete, or other material and filled with water, used for fish or swimming
privy outhouse, latrine
promenade public walk; gallery or balcony for walking
quad *Informal.* courtyard surrounded by buildings on four sides
rail fence barrier of crossed stakes connected by bars
railing fence or barrier of horizontal rails and widely spaced supports
rock garden ornamental garden laid out among rocks
septic tank sunken container in which solid organic sewage is decomposed by bacteria
snake fence zigzag fence of rails lying across one another at an angle; Virginia fence; worm fence
snow fence barrier on windward side of structure, serving as protection from drifting snow
stable building for housing livestock
stake-and-rider fence with top bar supported by cross stakes
stall compartment for domestic animal in barn; small booth or freestanding display stand
stile series of steps for passing over fence or wall
stoa usu. detached portico with colonnade, used for meetings or shelter (ancient Greece)
stockyard large holding area for livestock being transported, often to slaughter
stone wall barrier or boundary of piled rocks
sunken garden cultivated area lying in ground depression
sunk fence wall or fence set in ditch to create barrier without marring landscape
swimming pool large water-filled tank for swimming, usu. made of concrete, set above or sunk into ground adjacent to house
swing seat suspended freely at end of rope or chain
tack room stable room for storage of riding gear and display of trophies
tennis court measured area with net for playing tennis, adjacent to house and yard
terrace unroofed, paved area adjacent to building
toolshed small enclosure for storage of tools
topiary hedge of trees or shrubs trimmed into ornamental, often fantastic shapes
trellis open structure of thin crossed strips used to support vines or plants
vegetable garden bed of earth for growing vegetables for personal use
viaduct bridge of several short spans, supported on towers, that carries road or railroad across valley

vineyard field of cultivated grapevines
Virginia fence snake fence
walkway open or covered passageway through garden
weir stake fence or net enclosure in waterway for catching fish
well hole sunk into earth to tap water supply
woodshed small outbuilding for storing firewood
worm fence snake fence
yard open area adjacent to house, often walled and paved; lawns and unpaved grounds of building
xyst long, covered portico for exercise in winter (ancient Greece); garden walk lined with trees (ancient Rome)
zigzag fence fence running in series of sharp turns and bends

INTERIOR STRUCTURE
Rooms
Parts of Rooms
Doors, Partitions, and Walls
Structural and Decorative Elements
Plumbing, Heating, and the Bathroom

See also: *Chap. 5: Structural Components; Chap. 7: Exterior Structure; Ornamental and Functional Articles; Chap. 16: Architecture*

Rooms

antechamber outer room leading to another room, often used as waiting room
anteroom antechamber
atelier artist's studio or workshop
atrium central hall, often with open roof, off which other rooms open (ancient Rome)
attic room immediately below roof; cockloft; garret
auditorium large, open room used for public gatherings
ballroom large, open room for dancing
banquet room large room, esp. in hotel or restaurant, used to serve elaborate meals to numerous persons
basement room wholly or partly beneath ground level; cellar
bathroom room containing bathtub or shower, wash basin, and toilet
bedchamber bedroom
bedroom room containing bed, used for sleeping
ben inner room, esp. combined parlor and bedroom of two-room cottage (Scotland)
boudoir *French.* bedroom
buttery pantry; provision room off kitchen
calefactory warmed sitting room in monastery
catacomb burial vault beneath ground level
cave cellar; underground storage room, esp. for wine
cavern large underground chamber
cell small, single room for one person, esp. in prison or monastery

cellar storage room beneath ground level; basement; cave
chamber room
chancellery office of chancellor or secretary to high personage
chapel room for meditation, prayer, or religious services
checkroom place where baggage or clothing is left for safekeeping; cloakroom; coatroom
cloakroom checkroom; anteroom to legislative chamber
closet small, private room
coatroom checkroom
cockloft small garret; attic
conservatory glass-enclosed room for growing and displaying plants or flowers; greenhouse
corridor hall
cubiculum small family burial chamber in catacombs (ancient Rome)
cyclone cellar storm cellar
den small room for solitary work; study
dining room room for eating, usu. between kitchen and living room
drawing room formal reception room; living room; sitting room
dressing room small room adjoining bedroom, with mirror, dressing table, wardrobe; backstage area in theater where actors put on costumes
elevator enclosure with sliding door, suspended on pulley system for transporting passengers or freight from one floor to another of structure; lift
entertainment center TV room
exhibition hall salon
family room informal living room for leisure activities, often with television; playroom
foyer vestibule
garage storage area outside main house, esp. for automobiles
garret room just below roof, esp. with sloping roof; attic; cockloft
greenhouse conservatory
guest room bedroom reserved for use by guests
hall passageway between rooms; entrance room of building; hallway
hallway hall
hidden chamber room with concealed entrance
keep strongest, most secure part of castle
kitchen room where food is prepared, usu. equipped with oven, range, refrigerator, sink, and counters
landing level area at end of flight of stairs
larder small room or closet for food storage
laundry small utility room with washing machine and dryer for laundering clothes
library room where books are stored on shelves; study
lift *Chiefly Brit.* elevator
living room room for common social usage, often largest room in house; drawing room; sitting room
lobby corridor or hall serving as passageway or waiting room adjoining larger rooms; hotel or theater foyer

loft attic; room above floor level within larger room

master bedroom large bedroom used by primary adult occupants of house

multipurpose room family room or utility room

nursery baby's room

office study; room designed or used for work

pantry small room for storage, esp. of kitchen supplies; serving room between kitchen and dining room

parlor room for entertaining guests

pavilion detached or semidetached division of building, often for display of objects

playroom family room; children's rumpus room

porch roofed or enclosed projection from main portion of structure, serving as entrance or sunroom

powder room women's rest room, esp. in restaurant or nightclub

refectory dining hall, esp. in monastery or convent

repository storage room

rest room bathroom, esp. in public building

room partitioned section of inside of building, usu. for some specific purpose

rumpus room room for parties, games, or recreation, often in basement

sacristy room in church for storing sacred vessels and vestments

sala large reception hall or sitting room

salon elegant apartment or living room; exhibition hall

scullery room adjoining kitchen, used for cleaning and storage of cookware and other rough kitchen work

sitting room drawing room; living room

solarium glass-enclosed sunroom

stoop small porch at entrance of house, often enclosed

storeroom room for storage of supplies

storm cellar basement room or excavation secured for protection against windstorms; cyclone cellar

studio artist's workroom; place in which audio or video recordings are made

study office, library, or room for studying

sunroom solarium

throne room formal audience room containing sovereign's throne

tomb subterranean chamber or vault, esp. for burial of the dead

TV room recreation or family room with television set; entertainment center

utility room laundry room

veranda roofed, screened porch or gallery

vestibule small entrance hall or room; enclosed passageway leading into building; foyer

ward section of prison; hospital room for several patients

wine cellar cool subterranean storage room for wine

wing portion of building that projects from main part

workroom workshop

workshop room for performing manual labor or making handicrafts; workroom

Parts of Rooms

aisle passage for walking between sections of seating or tall shelves

alcove recessed portion of room, open at one end; niche

altar raised structure for religious rituals

ambry recess in church wall for storage of sacramental vessels

apse recessed, usu. vaulted, semicircular portion of room, esp. at end of choir in church

archway passage beneath arch; arch over passage

back stairs stairs at rear of house

balcony railed platform extending from wall of second or higher story

bandstand platform in ballroom on which musicians perform

bay angular, recessed section of room projecting outward from exterior wall, often with windows on several walls

bema part of Eastern church containing altar

built-in immovable part of room that is integral to larger construction

cabinet case with doors and shelves, sometimes attached to wall

ceiling overhead inside lining of room adjoining tops of walls

chancel enclosed space around altar of church, designed for use by clergy and officials

china closet closet for storing dining supplies

clavel *Chiefly Brit.* mantel over fireplace

closet cabinet, recess, or small room for storage

coffer recessed panel in ceiling or vault

corner point where two converging walls meet

counter flat, built-in work surface

cubbyhole small space open on one side

cubicle small space partitioned off from main room

cupboard attached cabinet with shelves for storing kitchenwares and supplies; *Chiefly Brit.* any small closet

dais platform raised above floor level in hall or large room

dumbwaiter small elevator for conveying food, dishes, etc. from one floor to another

entresol mezzanine

escalator power-driven stairs on endless belt continuously ascending or descending

fireplace framed opening of stone or brick in chimney that holds open fire; hearth

flight of stairs staircase

floor underfoot inside base of room adjoining wall bottoms

gallery balcony or covered walk along wall at second story

hearth fireplace

ingle *Chiefly Brit.* large open fireplace

ledge narrow flat surface projecting from wall

locker storage cupboard or compartment secured with lock

loft raised section of room with floor, often reached by ladder

loggia roofed or open gallery, esp. facing inner court, often extending several stories

mantel facing of stone, marble, wood, or brick above and around fireplace; shelf above fireplace

mezzanine mid level of room between floor and ceiling, extending partway over ground floor; entresol

mihrab prayer niche facing Mecca in wall of mosque

minbar pulpit of Islamic mosque

niche alcove

panel flat, rectangular, distinct section of wall

paneling wall area composed of panels

piano nobile *Italian.* principal story of large building or villa

platform section of flooring raised above room level

podium speaker's platform

pulpit podium in church for minister

riser series of long, narrow platforms that are combined like steps for group of spectators or performers

rostrum raised platform, esp. for public speaker

safe secure receptacle for storage of valuables, often hidden in wall

shelf long, flat piece of material fastened horizontally to wall, used for storage

shutter movable, attached window shade of inflexible material

split-level section of room raised above floor level, reached by stairs

stage large platform, usu. at end of room, for performances

staircase structure containing stairs; flight of stairs

stairs series of steps leading from one level to another

stairway one or more flights of stairs with connective landings

stairwell vertical shaft in building containing stairway

steps stairs

Tiepolo ceiling decorative Italian Renaissance ceiling

tokonoma niche or shallow recess for display (Japan)

trottoir escalatorlike moving ramp on level floor

walk-in closet very large closet

wardrobe large closet for clothing

window bench window seat

window seat shelf attached to wall beneath window for sitting; window bench

Doors, Partitions, and Walls

back door rear entrance to house

baffle screen or partition used to control passage of light or sound

bulkhead upright partition

door swinging or sliding barrier across entryway

doorway entrance into building, closed by door

double leaves two doors, hinged at sides, opening in middle

Dutch door door divided horizontally so that upper or lower half may be opened independently

folding door door with hinged sections that can be folded back, accordion style; one of pair of sliding doors between rooms

French doors two adjoining doors, hinged at sides, opening in middle, with glass panes throughout all or most of their length

hopper casement window frame with superimposed fanlights, used in hospitals

jalousie window shade or door made of adjustable slats to regulate flow of air or light

partition interior dividing wall, sometimes movable and not reaching to ceiling

pier wall between two openings; vertical structural support; section of wall between windows

pocket door usu. one of a pair of communicating doors that slides into and out of recess in wall

reredos back wall of fireplace or open hearth; ornamental wood or stone partition behind altar

screen movable partition used to conceal or protect area of room

sliding door unhinged door, frequently of glass, that slides open and shut, esp. between rooms

standing wall wall providing support to ceiling and floor above

transom small, hinged window directly over door

trapdoor lifting or sliding door covering opening in and flush with ceiling or floor

wall one side of room connecting floor and ceiling

Structural and Decorative Elements

arch curved structural support member spanning an opening: basket-handle, flat, horseshoe, lancet, ogee, parabolic, round, shouldered, trefoil, Tudor

architrave molded, decorated band of wood forming panel or opening for door or window; lowest part of entablature

archivolt ornamental molding around arch

arris sharp ridge formed at meeting of two surfaces

backsplash strip of water-resistant tile or formica above sink or beside bathtub

baldachin ornamental canopy over altar or important person

baluster upright, vase-shaped support for railing

balustrade row of balusters topped by railing

band narrow decorative or binding strip

banister handrail or balustrade

barrel roof ceiling having semicylindrical, vaulted form

baseboard molding covering juncture of wall and adjoining floor

bas relief raised ornamental molding, plasterwork, or sculpted stone on flat wall surface

beam principal horizontal support structure of building

border ornamental design along edge of wall or floor

brace structural element that transmits or supports weight

bracket projecting shelf support, often decorative

bridgeboard notched board acting as a string to support stair treads and risers

canopy rooflike covering of fabric on poles

casement hinged frame opening outward for French doors or double windows

casing enclosing frame around door or window

chink strip of wood used to cover gap between logs in log cabin

colonnade series of columns at regular intervals

colonnette small colonnade

column vertical supporting pillar; post

compluvium square opening in sloping roof over atrium through which rain falls into impluvium (ancient Rome)

console member projecting from wall to form bracket

corona crown-shaped projection above bed from which drapery is hung

course continuous horizontal layer of stone, bricks, or tiles in wall

cover strip decorative molding or length of material used to conceal structural parts

coving carved molding that connects ceiling and wall

cresting ornamental ridging on wall or ceiling

curtain rod horizontal suspension piece for curtain

dado lower part of wall separated from upper part by rail, molding, or border

embrasure side of window between frame and outer surface of wall; opening in wall sloped to large interior outline; reveal

engaged column column which is not freestanding but attached to wall

fillet flat molding separating other moldings

fluted column column with long, rounded, vertical grooves

frieze richly ornamented band; entablature between architrave and cornice

girder primary horizontal structural member supporting vertical load

handrail railing on staircase or gallery; banister

hob projection at back or side of fireplace on which pot is hung to be kept warm

jamb side post of doorway, window frame, or other opening

lacunar coffered vault, ceiling, or soffit

machicolation opening between corbels or in gallery floor for discharging missiles onto assailants below

molding ornamental strip of wood separating sections of wall or at juncture of wall and ceiling: bird's beak, cavetto, congé, cyma recta, cyma reversa, fillet and fascia, ovolo, plate rail, quarter round, reeding, scotia, torus

mullion slender, vertical dividing bar in window or screen

newel central upright pillar of winding staircase

newel post post supporting one end of handrail on flight of stairs

nosing usu. rounded edge of stair tread that projects over riser

ogive diagonal pointed arch or rib on Gothic vault

parapet protective low wall or railing

pargeting ornamental plasterwork on walls or ceiling

parquetry inlaid woodwork in geometric forms of different colors, esp. in floor

pegboard board perforated with holes for pegs on which objects are hung

pelmet valance

pillar firm, upright support or post; ornamental column or shaft

plate rail narrow shelf on upper wall for holding plates and ornaments

post upright piece, column

rafters angled crossbeams in roof, sometimes exposed

railing barrier, fence, or baluster of rails and supports; handgrip on baluster or gallery

reglet flat, narrow architectural molding

reveal embrasure

ridgepole highest horizontal member in roof

riser upright member between stair treads

scalloping continuous series of circle segments or angular projections forming border

scrolling spiral or convoluted ornamentation, esp. in wood

scupper opening in wall at roof or floor level for water drainage

slat thin, narrow, flat strip of wood or metal

soffit underside of structural member or part of building, such as overhang of staircase

squinch support at corner of room for superimposed mass such as arch, lintel, or corbel

template horizontal piece placed in wall under beam to distribute weight over door

tracery branching, interlacing ornamental work, esp. stonework in upper part of Gothic window or vault

trave division or bay in ceiling made by traverse beams

traverse rod horizontal metal rod on which curtains slide open and shut, controlled by lines and pulleys

tread upper horizontal part of stair

valance strip of fabric on frame that covers sides of bed or top of window frame; pelmet

vault arched, domed, usu. masonry structure forming ceiling

viga heavy rafter or log that supports roof in native Indian and Spanish architecture (Southwest U.S.)

wainscoting lower section of wall or story when distinct from top section, esp. when wood-paneled

window frame casement, jamb, and sill of window

window sill horizontal member at bottom of window frame

Plumbing, Heating, and the Bathroom

basin circular vessel with sloping sides and drain, used to hold water for washing
bath bathroom; bathtub
bathroom room containing bathtub and/or shower, plus wash basin and toilet; sometimes used to denote room with toilet and wash basin only
bathtub large, fixed tub for bathing
bidet chairlike fixture for bathing genitals and anus
calidarium hot-water room in public bath (ancient Rome)
can *Vulgar slang.* toilet bowl; bathroom
cloaca *Archaic.* sewer; toilet bowl
comfort station public bathroom
commode movable washstand with cupboard underneath; box holding chamber pot under open seat
crapper *Vulgar slang.* bathroom
faucet fixture through which water flows; tap
Franklin stove iron fireplace connected to chimney by funnel
furnace enclosed chamber, usu. in basement, where heat is produced to warm building
half bath bathroom with basin and toilet only
hammam communal bathhouse in Islamic countries, usu. with separate facilities for men and women
head toilet, esp. on ship
impluvium cistern, tank in floor of atrium that receives water from compluvium (ancient Rome)
jakes *Chiefly dial.* toilet
john *Slang.* toilet
lavatory toilet; bathroom
loo *Brit. informal.* bathroom
ofuro large Japanese-style bath, often of wood or stone, used by several people simultaneously
radiator nest of pipes for heating room by steam
rest room bathroom, esp. in public building
sauna hot, dry-air bath in enclosed wooden room, used to induce perspiration
shower enclosed stall with overhead water outlet for bathing
sink stationary basin connected to drain and water supply
steam room tiled room designed to expose user to steam in order to induce sweating
tank enclosed vessel holding water, esp. for toilet
tap *Chiefly Brit.* faucet
toilet bathroom fixture with seats over bowl through which water is flushed to dispose of human waste material; bathroom
tub bathtub
wash basin sink with running water used in bathing, esp. washing face and hands
water closet WC; toilet
WC water closet

wet bar counter for mixing drinks, with built-in sink and running water
whirlpool soothing bath in which jets agitate very hot water
wood-burning stove enclosed metal unit that burns wood for heat, with vent to dispense smoke out of house

FURNISHINGS

Chairs and Sofas
Beds
Tables and Desks
Cases, Cupboards, and Chests
Stools and Stands
Curtains, Draperies, and Screens
Carpets and Rugs
Lamps and Mirrors
Accessories and Appliances

See also: *Chap. 7: Interior Structure;
Ornamental and Functional Articles; Chap. 9: The
Kitchen; Chap. 10: Ornaments and Accessories*

Chairs and Sofas

Adirondack chair wooden outdoor chair with sloping back and seat declining to rear
armchair chair, often hardback, with sidepieces to support person's forearms or elbows
banquette long, upholstered bench, often built into wall; sofa with one rollover arm
barber chair heavy-duty, adjustable, swiveling chair with headrest and footrest
Barcelona chair armless, leather-covered chair with cushioned seat on X-shaped stainless steel frame
basket chair deep wicker chair with rounded back and adjoining arms
Bath chair hooded, often glassed invalid's wheelchair
bench long, backless seat for several persons
Brewster chair heavy colonial chair with upright spindles in two tiers on the back and below the seat
butterfly chair canvas or leather sling chair, with sling suspended from metal frame
camp chair light, folding chair, often with canvas seat and back
captain's chair chair with rounded back in which vertical spindles support rail that forms arms
Carver chair heavy, turned colonial chair with three vertical and three horizontal spindles in back
cathedra official chair or bishop's throne
chair seat for one person, usu. four-legged, with backrest and sometimes armrests
chaise couchlike lounging seat with leg and back supports
chaise longue couchlike seat lengthened to form leg rest and with raised back support at one end
channel back chair upholstered chair or sofa with deep vertical grooves in backrest

chesterfield large, heavily stuffed sofa with upholstered upright arms
Chippendale chair graceful, ornately ornamented chair in English style (18th c.)
club chair deep, low, heavily upholstered easy chair with low back, solid sides and arms
collapsible chair folding chair
comb back chair Windsor chair with comblike vertical spindles topped by a curved top rail
confidente sofa divided by armrests into large center section with triangular flanking seats (18th c.)
contour chair chair designed to fit form of human body
couch long, upholstered, stuffed seat for two or more persons, with back and armrests at one or both ends; sofa
courting chair love seat
curule chair folding, backless seat reserved for high dignitaries (ancient Rome)
Dante chair Savonarola chair
davenport large, upholstered sofa that converts to bed
daybed armless couch with long seat and sloping back, for reclining or sleeping (18th c.)
deck chair folding chair of metal or other durable material for outdoor use
Derbyshire chair armless oak chair with broad carved top rail between square uprights; Yorkshire chair (Britain, 17th c.)
desk chair upright chair designed for sitting at desk, often with armrests
dining chair small upright chair for sitting at dining table, usu. armless
director's chair folding armchair with canvas seat and back panel on wood frame
divan large couch or sofa, usu. without back or arms
dos-à-dos seat or sofa built so occupants sit back to back
duchesse *French.* daybed with rounded, covered head, often in two or three pieces
Eames chair armless chair with seat and back of molded plywood attached to tubular steel frame
easy chair stuffed, upholstered, comfortable chair
ergonomic chair work chair specially designed for comfort and support of back and neck
fanback chair Windsor chair having spindle back spread like fan from seat to upper rail
farthingale chair armless chair with high seat and low, straight back
fauteuil *French.* stuffed arm chair
folding chair usu. armless seat on legs that fold flat against it; collapsible chair
Glastonbury chair small, light, folding chair, with two crossed straight legs at each side and arms connected to front seat rail
highchair infant's chair on tall legs with attached shelf for food
inglenook bench in nook by open fireplace
lawn chair reclining chair, usu. of durable material, for outdoor use

lounge chair long seat with headrest, used for reclining

love seat small sofa with arms, suitable for two persons; courting chair

méridienne *French.* short sofa with one arm higher than the other

morris chair easy chair with adjustable back and removable cushions

ottoman stuffed, long, low cushioned seat without back or arms, sometimes circular, able to accommodate several people

overstuffed chair heavily padded, upholstered easy chair

page chair porter chair

parlor chair dining room chair with low back and no arms (18th c.)

pew long wooden bench with back for seating in church

platform rocker rocking chair with base set on curved rockers

porch swing bench seat freely suspended from ceiling on porch

porter chair straight-backed chair with enclosed side walls that form arch over seat; page chair (18th c.)

potty-chair infant's low seat with removable bowl, used for toilet training

pouf plumply cushioned, usu. circular, backless couch

prayer chair low, stiff-backed, armless chair

prie-dieu low bench fitted with shelf, used for kneeling during prayer

recliner chair with adjustable reclining back

rocker rocking chair

rocking chair chair on two curved members that connect its front and back feet, allowing it to rock back and forth; rocker

rout seat small, armless seat set along wall in ballroom

Savonarola chair Renaissance chair with several pairs of interlaced curved slats extending from their intersection beneath the seat to form sides and legs; Dante chair; scissors chair (Italy)

scissors chair Savonarola chair

seat any chair, bench, or stool on which people sit

sectional sofa composed of modular sections that can be arranged in various combinations

settee medium or small seat or bench with back and usu. arms

settle wooden bench with arms and straight back

sling chair canvas or leather back and seat loosely fitted onto wood or metal frame

slipper chair low, armless bedroom chair with skirt covering short legs

sociable S-shaped sofa with two seats partially facing each other

sofa upholstered seat for three or more persons with fixed back and arms at each end; couch

sofa bed sofa with removable cushions and fold-out mattress

spindle-back chair chair with woven seat and carved rods from seat to top rail

squab couch with removable, thickly stuffed, soft cushions

stall fixed, enclosed seat in church for priest or choir

stool low seat without back or arms on three or four legs

straight-backed chair seat with upright, usu. high back

studio couch small, armless, backless, upholstered couch, convertible to double bed

swing seat suspended from frame or ceiling, usu. by chains at each end, for recreational use

swivel chair chair that revolves on its base

tablet chair seat with one arm widened for use as writing surface, esp. in schools

tête-à-tête S-shaped sofa that allows two people to face each other when seated

throne royal chair of state, usu. large and ornate

triclinium couch or set of couches surrounding three sides of table

tub chair *Chiefly Brit.* semicircular, upholstered easy chair with arms and back in one unit

tuxedo sofa overstuffed sofa with slightly curved arms at same height as back

wagon seat pair of attached, slat-back post chairs

wicker chair chair of plaited or woven twigs, often with high, fan-shaped back

Windsor chair wooden chair with curved spindle back, legs slanting outward, and saddle seat (18th c.)

wing chair large, upholstered armchair having high, solid back and winged sides

Yorkshire chair Derbyshire chair

Beds

angel bed bed with suspended canopy extending partway over it (French); bed without posts

bassinet infant's portable bed with hood over one end

bed usu. stuffed mattress with springs, in various sizes, for sleeping upon, often with frame of wood or metal

bedroll portable bedding that rolls up

bedstead frame and headboard for bed that supports springs and mattress

berth sleeping accommodation on ship or vehicle, often folding out from wall

box spring mattress base of spiral springs enclosed in cloth-covered frame

bunk bed two beds on frame set one above the other

canopy ornamental rooflike structure over bed, esp. cloth

car bed portable bed for infant, used in automobile

charpoy bedstead or cot frame strung with light rope (India)

cot flat, folding bed without padding, often of canvas

cradle infant's bed on legs with rockers

crib infant's bed, usu. having slatted sides

davenport large, upholstered sofa that converts to bed

double bed mattress and box spring for two persons, smaller than queen-size bed, 54 inches (137 cm) wide; full-size bed

feather mattress soft mattress stuffed with feathers

foldaway bed bed designed to double over and slide aside or out of view when not in use; folding bed

folding bed foldaway bed

fourposter traditional bed with upright post at each corner to support canopy or curtains

French bed postless bedstead with head and foot rolled outward in scroll form

full-size bed double bed

futon folding, Japanese-style sleeping pad stuffed with cotton batting

gurney rolling cot or stretcher for carrying sick or injured persons

hammock hanging bed of netting or canvas suspended from supports by cords attached at each end

headboard upright board forming head of bed

hospital bed adjustable bed with movable, criblike protective sides and variable positions, designed for hospital patients

king-size bed extra large mattress and box spring, at least 76 inches (193 cm) wide

mattress fabric case filled with resilient material, used as bed or on bedstead or box spring

Murphy bed bed on metal frame that folds into wall or closet when not in use

paillasse straw mattress; pallet

pallet straw bed or hard mattress of poor quality; paillasse

poster bed bed with upright posts at two or four corners

queen-size bed mattress and box spring larger than double bed, smaller than king-size bed, 60 inches (152 cm) wide

rack *Slang.* bed

rollaway bed on folding frame with wheels for easy storage

single bed narrow mattress and box spring for one person, 39 inches (102 cm) wide

sofa bed sofa with removable cushions and fold-out mattress

tatami mat thick, woven, straw floor mat, usu. grouped together in sections, on which futon rests (Japan)

tester bed with frame for canopy

truckle bed low bed on casters, rolled under higher bed when not in use; trundle bed

trundle bed truckle bed

twin bed one of pair of single beds, 39 inches (102 cm) wide

waterbed bed having large rubber or plastic sack filled with water and set in rigid frame, able to conform to sleeper's body position for comfort

Tables and Desks

ambo raised reading desk in nave of early Christian church

banquet table large dining table; long, flat serving table

bar counter at which food and beverages are served

basin stand small table with round hole in top surface to hold wash basin (18th c.)

bed table nightstand

bench long, flat worktable

billiard table rectangular, felt-covered slate table of standardized dimensions for playing billiards

buffet counter or table for serving food

butterfly table small drop-leaf table with round or oval top, leaves supported by brackets shaped like butterfly wings

capstan table drum table

card table small, flat, square table with folding legs; folding table

carrel table or desk with three sides raised above surface to serve as partitions for private study, esp. in library

cocktail table coffee table

coffee table long, low table usu. set before sofa

computer table multilevel desk adapted to hold computer and printer

console table small table supported by ornamental brackets fixed to wall

counter level surface over which transactions are conducted or food served, usu. long and narrow

credence small sideboard or table for valuables, esp. bread and wine used in Eucharist; credenza

credenza credence

davenport *Chiefly Brit.* small writing desk

desk table with flat surface for writing, often with drawers or compartments

dinette small table for informal dining, usu. in kitchen

dining table large round, rectangular, or oblong table, often with leaves, at which meals are eaten

door desk desk or tabletop formed by setting door across supporting drawers or legs

drawing table flat surface adjustable to various heights and angles

drop-leaf table table with hinged ends or leaves that may be lowered and insertible sections to increase length, esp. for dining

drum table table having cylindrical top with drawers or shelves, rotating on a central post with three or four outwardly curving legs; capstan table

end table small table, usu. with one drawer, that stands at end of couch or beside chair

envelope table small table with triangular drop leaf or leaves

escritoire writing desk

extension table table with insertible leaf or leaves to increase length

folding table usu. small, flat table with legs that flatten against the underside of the top surface when stored; card table

gate-leg table table with movable paired legs on hinges that swing out to support drop leaves

kitchen table informal dining table in kitchen; dinette

kneehole desk flat-topped desk with space for knees between drawers

lamp table small table that holds reading lamp beside chair

leaf hinged or removable section of table that changes table's length

lectern chest-high, stand-up reading desk for school or church

nesting tables set of usu. three or four tables graduated in size so that they may be stacked together

nightstand small, low table standing at bedside, often with single drawer; bed table; night table

night table nightstand

Parsons table square, contemporary table whose straight legs are flush with the edges of the top so as to appear jointless

Pembroke table small table with two drop leaves and one drawer (18th c.)

piecrust table round table with raised decorative edge like piecrust

pier table table designed to stand against a wall between and below two windows

pool table billiard table with pockets at corners and on sides, used for playing pool

pouch table small worktable with fabric bag suspended under top to hold needlepoint, chess pieces, or other tools

refectory table long, heavy, narrow table with trestlelike legs connected by a single strip

rent table drum table with circular top and six drawers (18th c.)

roll-top desk writing desk with sliding, flexible cover that rolls up beneath top

salon table long, dining-height serving table

secretary upright writing desk with bookshelves on top and foldout writing space

sideboard dining room table with compartments and shelves for table service articles

side table small table without drawers, usu. placed beside dining table or against wall

step table small table topped by one or more progressively narrower shelves

table smooth, flat surface supported usu. by four legs

tambour rolling desk top of rounded wood strips glued to canvas

teapoy stand small, ornamental, three-legged table that supports tea chest or caddy for tea service

tray table small folding table with low rim around surface, often with crossed pairs of legs

tripod stool, table, or altar with three legs

trolley cart or stand on wheels used for conveying things

TV table usu. metal, lightweight, folding tray table, used for eating in front of television

typewriter table small, flat table, often on wheels, used to hold typewriter

vargueno decorative, fall-front writing desk or chest on low table (Spain, 17th c.)

workbench large, flat, sturdy table at which craftsman works

writing desk flat-topped table with drawers or pigeonholes; escritoire

writing table desk with retractable drawer used as writing surface and pigeonhole cupboard above, sometimes roll top

Cases, Cupboards, and Chests

armoire tall, movable cupboard or wardrobe

Biedermeier cabinet cabinet, usu. of fruitwood with matched veneers, incorporating architectural motifs (Germany, 19th c.)

bin enclosed box, frame, or crib for storage

bookcase set of bookshelves in freestanding unit

bookshelves open, multilevel storage area for books

breakfront large cabinet with center section standing out from flanks

buffet drawers and cupboards for storage of dishes and linen; sideboard

bunker storage bin or compartment, esp. on ship

bureau chest of drawers for storage, often with mirror standing on top

cabinet standing storage unit with shelves and drawers

caddy container or rack for storing objects when not in use

canterbury small stand with tray top and upright partitions to hold music, magazines, or papers

case box or receptacle for enclosing objects

cellarette sideboard for bottles of wine or liquor

chest large, solid wood piece with lid and often interior drawers for storage; chest of drawers

chest of drawers upright set of enclosed storage receptacles on frame with short legs; dresser

chiffonier ornamental cabinet with shelves, drawers, and sometimes with mirror; tall, narrow chest of drawers

chifforobe combination wardrobe and chest of drawers

china cabinet standing storage shelves for china that requires protection or deserves display

clothes chest enclosed, heavy-topped container for clothing

coffer chest or strongbox for valuables

commode low, ornate chest of drawers; movable washstand with cupboard underneath

console large cabinet that rests on floor, esp. housing radio and/or television

crate wood slat storage or shipping box, usu. open on top

credenza large buffet or sideboard, often without legs; closed cabinet for papers and office supplies, often of desk height

crib rack or framework storage enclosure
cupboard small closet with storage shelves
display case enclosed, glass-faced unit for storage and exhibition of objects
dresser chest of drawers for clothing with flat top, often with mirror
étagère cabinet of tiered shelves open on all sides
filing cabinet vertical storage unit for papers, with two or more sliding drawers, usu. metal
hamper large, covered basket for storage or transport
highboy tall chest of drawers with legs; tallboy
Hoosier cabinet tall oak kitchen cabinet with drawers, shelves, breadboard, and enameled work surface
hope chest trunk in which young woman collects linens and clothing in anticipation of marriage
hutch bin or chest for storage
kitchen cabinet enclosed unit containing storage shelves, usu. mounted on kitchen wall
locker small drawer or compartment for secure storage when closed with lock
lowboy three-foot-high dressing table with drawers on short legs
mantel shelf above fireplace
playpen small, often collapsible enclosure in which young child may play without close supervision
poudreuse small dressing table with mirror (18th c.)
press closet or cupboard, esp. large cupboard shelf with small cupboards behind it (16th c.)
rack framework of open shelves on which articles may be placed
safe sturdy, usu. cast-iron receptacle with strong lock, used for storing valuables
sarcophagus wooden, coffinlike wine cooler under sideboard
shelf thin, long strip of material, often wood, fastened horizontally on wall or in frame to support objects
shelves set of horizontal strips arranged vertically on wall
sideboard buffet or dining-room piece, used for storage of linen, silver, and china, or for serving food
strongbox sturdy receptacle with lock for storage of valuables
tallboy chest with seven or more drawers in two stacks and two small drawers on top; highboy
tea caddy small box, can, or chest for storing tea
tea wagon tea caddy on wheels for service
trunk large storage box of wood or metal
vanity lady's dressing table with small case for cosmetics; wide shelf around wash basin, often with shelves or drawers
vitrine glass showcase for memorabilia, valuables, and art objects
wardrobe freestanding closet fitted with hooks and bars for hanging clothes
wet bar small bar with sink and compartments, used for mixing and serving drinks

whatnot stand with open tier shelves on corner posts for books, papers, or ornaments
Yorkshire dresser dresser with clock

Stools and Stands

bar stool tall stool, sometimes with low back, for sitting at bar
bentwood hanger Victorian-style hanger of wood bent to form hooks
bier stand for coffin
campstool small, portable folding stool with crossed legs and canvas seat
cart small stand with two wheels and two legs, moved by hand
catafalque elaborate stand for coffin
clotheshorse frame on which to hang laundry for drying
clothes tree upright pole with hooks at top for hanging clothes
coatrack tall wood or metal stand with hooks for hanging coats
cricket low wooden footstool
cutty stool low stool, esp. seat in church where offenders against chastity received public rebuke (Scotland)
easel upright support frame, often with three legs joined at top, esp. for artist's canvas
foldstool small stool that folds into compact unit for storage
footrest low stool set before chair for feet
footstool surface on short legs, used for resting feet while seated
hall stand small, flat table in hall
hassock firmly stuffed mat or cushion used as footstool
hatrack tall spindle with hooks for hanging hats
lamp stand small lamp table
mora low wicker stool or footstool (India)
music stand display case for sheet music with adjustable, inclined surface
music stool round stool with adjustable seat that swivels up or down
pedestal flat-topped base or stand for display of ornamental object
prop supporting stand
sawhorse rack for holding wood with crosspiece linking two sets of legs that form inverted V's
smoking stand ashtray mounted on tall wood or metal stand, usu. on single upright
stand support frame on or in which articles may be placed
step stool stool with one or two steps which fold away beneath seat
stool low seat without back or arms on three or four legs
tabouret cylindrical seat or stool without arms or back; small portable stand for holding work supplies
tripod three-legged stand
truss tripod of logs or timbers for farm use
umbrella stand low, open, often cylindrical receptacle for umbrellas
work stand small, metal stand with several

movable leaves, covered with loops and hooks for holding supplies

Curtains, Draperies, and Screens

arras hanging screen or tapestry on wall
bamboo shade hanging bamboo strips used as shade
blind roll-up or retractable window shutter or shade
café curtains pair of curtains that cover only lower half of window
curtain fabric hung on hooks or rod to cover window or adorn wall
draperies heavy decorative material hung in long, loose folds on wall or opening and closing over window; drapes
drapes draperies
fire screen standing metal screen that keeps sparks from fireplace off rugs or floor
jalousie blind with adjustable horizontal slats that admit light and air while excluding rain and sun's rays
panel flat wall section used as partition to divide room
partition interior wall or barrier that divides room into sections
priscilla curtains pair of ruffled, tieback curtains
purdah screen or curtain used by Muslims and Hindus to seclude women from sight of men and strangers
rollup shade blind, often of cloth, that retracts onto spring roller
roman shade one-piece, pleated, fabric window shade
screen freestanding partition, often hinged, that shields or separates an area of a room
shade flexible screen or fabric mounted over window; window shade
shoji screen rice paper mounted on wood frame, used as sliding door or partition (Japan)
shutter solid, movable cover or screen for window or door
tapestry heavy woven cloth with designs, hung on wall or used as furniture covering
tieback curtain curtain held open by tie strip usu. of same material
valance drapery hung at top of window or along edge of bed, altar, table, or shelf to conceal another member
veil concealing curtain or cloth covering
venetian blind window shutter with overlapping, horizontal slats that may be opened, closed, raised, or lowered by pulling a cord
window shade flexible sheet covering for window; shade

Carpets and Rugs

area rug small rug covering only part of floor; scatter rug
Aubusson ornate rug woven to resemble figured scenic Aubusson tapestry, often in pastel colors

Axminster carpet machine-woven carpet with pile tufts in variety of textures and many colors

bearskin fur of bear used as rug

Belouch type of Persian rug

Bokhara rich Persian rug

broadloom carpet woven on wide loom, esp. in solid color

Brussels carpet carpet of colored worsted yarns drawn up in uncut loops to form pattern

carpet heavy woven or felted fabric used as floor covering, usu. attached to entire floor and nonmovable

Caucasian rug rug woven in Caucasus mountains

chenille deep pile fabric used for rugs

dhurrie type of Indian rug

drugget coarse cotton or jute rug from India

flokati handwoven, woolen Greek rug with thick, shaggy pile

flossa handwoven Scandinavian carpet

Heriz type of Persian rug

hooked (*adj*) designating rug made by drawing loops through coarse fabric with a hook

Indian rug rug from India; American Indian rug (as: Navaho, Hopi, Zuni)

Indo-Heriz type of Persian rug

Indo-Tabriz type of Persian rug

kilim pileless woven rug from Turkey, the Caucasus, or Iran

Kirman Persian rug with ornate, flowing designs in soft colors

Kurdistan Persian-style rug from Kurdistan

mat coarse woven fabric or plaited reeds used as floor covering

moquette French carpet with velvety pile

nap hairy surface of rug

Navaho rug Southwest American Indian rug, often in geometric design

nylon carpeting machine-made carpet of synthetic nylon yarn

Oriental rug rug or carpet from Far East or Asia

Persian carpet distinctive rug or carpet in rich colors and intricate designs, made in area of Iran: Afshar, Ardabil, Aubusson, Bijar, Belouch, Farahan, Hamedan, Heriz, Indo-Heriz, Indo-Tabriz, Isfahan, Joshegan, Kashan, Kirman, Ladik, Mashad, Moud, Nain, Pak Persian, Sarough, Serapi, Taba, Yalameh

pile velvety surface of rug made by cutting off upright loops of yarn; rug with such a surface

puma rug rug of cougar fur

rag American folk art rug of cotton or garment scraps in cheerful colors, usu. with rounded ends

rug thick, heavy fabric, usu. with nap or pile, used as movable floor covering

runner long, rectangular hall rug

rya handwoven Scandinavian rug with deep, resilient, flat pile

Savonnerie handmade, one-piece French pile carpet

Saxony carpet rug of fine, closely twisted yarn

scatter rug small rug that covers only part of floor; area rug

shag rug with long, coarse, loose pile

steamer rug warm covering for lap and feet, used esp. at sea

Tabriz Persian rug with cotton warp and wool pile, in medallion design

tapestry rug rug woven in intricate pattern, designed to hang on wall

throw rug small rug

Tientsin distinctive style of Chinese rug

Turkish rug made in Turkey

Turkoman rug made by peoples of eastern Turkey and Soviet Union

wall-to-wall carpeting that covers entire floor of room

Wilton carpet woven with loops and having velvet-cut pile

Lamps and Mirrors

arc lamp arc light

arc light electric light in which current passes in arc between two incandescent electrodes surrounded by gas; arc lamp

arm lamp lamp with light source at far end of shaft attached to base

bathing mirror small mirror, often attached to bathroom wall or above tub

bedlamp small, focused reading light placed beside or above bed

chandelier branched, ornate, multibulb lighting fixture suspended from ceiling

cheval glass full-length mirror that can be tilted in hinged frame

Chinese lantern light enclosed in translucent paper globe or shade

desk lamp standing lamp beside desk or arm lamp on desk top

floor lamp lamp that stands on floor; standing lamp

fluorescent lamp tubular electric lamp coated on inner surface by fluorescent material and containing mercury vapor

gaslight light fixture that burns illuminating gas

girandole mirror mirror set in ornamental, branched, showy frame

glass mirror

gooseneck lamp desk lamp with long, thin shaft, usu. curved or flexible

incandescent electric light lamp in which filament heated by electric current gives off light

lamp device holding electric bulb, gas, or burning wick, used for illumination

lampshade covering for lamp bulb, made of molded, translucent material; shade

lantern light enclosed in portable, protective case with transparent openings

light device for illumination by electricity

looking glass small mirror, handheld or attached to wall

mirror reflecting glass surface set in frame, usu. mounted on dresser, door, or wall; glass

neon lamp discharge bulb containing neon gas that glows when voltage is applied across two electrodes

night-light small light fixture that faces wall, providing dim light in dark room

phoebe lamp shallow, early American, fat-burning lamp of metal or pottery, with spout for wick and cup to catch drippings

pier glass tall mirror set in wall section between windows

reading light small light placed above bed or beside chair

searchlight light and reflector on rotating base, used to project beam to great distance

shade device partially covering lamp to reduce glare; lampshade

shaving mirror small mirror attached to bathroom wall

speculum optical reflector; ancient mirror of polished bronze or silver

spot spotlight

spotlight lamp that produces powerful, focused beam of light; spot

standing lamp floor lamp

student lamp adjustable desk lamp with one or two arms, esp. oil-burning (19th c.)

sunlamp electric lamp that emits ultraviolet radiations, used to tan skin indoors

table lamp small lamp that stands on table

task lighting lamp mounted to illuminate specific work area, such as kitchen counter or portion of desk

Tiffany lamp lamp with shade of Tiffany stained glass

toilet glass dressing table mirror, often with attached drawer

torchiere tall floor lamp that emits indirect light from source within reflecting bowl that is open at top

track lighting series of small, adjustable spotlights arranged along track, usu. mounted on ceiling

trouble light device that provides emergency illumination or lights hard to reach places, esp. screened bulb on long power cord

trumeau mirror with carved panel above or below glass set in same frame

uplight lamp that projects illumination upward

vanity lamp small, shaded lamp that stands on dressing table

Venetian lamp delicate lamp with shade of Venetian glass

wall mirror usu. tall reflecting glass mounted on wall

wall washer lamp that evenly illuminates large area of wall

Accessories and Appliances

AC **a**ir **c**onditioner

air conditioner AC; electrical device that reduces interior temperature and humidity of building or room

appliance any of various service units, usu. operated electrically, found in contemporary homes, esp. in the kitchen: refrigerator, freezer, stove, washing machine, dryer, dishwasher, vacuum cleaner, air conditioner, toaster, blender, food processor, can opener

basin shallow, circular vessel with sloping sides for holding water

bathtub large, usu. fixed vessel for bathing; tub

bidet chairlike fixture for bathing genitals and anus

ceiling fan large fan with circular blade motion, suspended from ceiling

dishwasher enclosed electrical appliance for automatically washing and rinsing dishes

dryer enclosed heater for drying washed clothing

fan electrical device for blowing air by movement of series of vanes or blades radiating from hub and revolving on its axis

Franklin stove iron, wood-burning stove with exhaust funnel running to chimney

freezer section of refrigerator or separate appliance with temperature low enough to freeze and preserve foods

fridge *Informal.* refrigerator

Frigidaire *Trademark.* type of refrigerator

furnace enclosed structure in which heat is produced by gas, oil, coal, or electricity to warm home

icebox insulated container with section for ice, used to cool foods

meat locker very large freezer, esp. for meat

oven fixed or freestanding chamber for baking, heating, roasting, or drying, using heat produced by gas or electricity

potbelly stove stove with rounded, bulging body, esp. wood-burning stove shaped thus

punkah ceiling fan (India)

range cooking stove with oven and flat top equipped with gas burners or electrical heating elements

refrigerator large, airtight cabinet or box for chilling foods by means of ice or electrical condensation

stove fixed or portable fuel-burning or electrical device for cooking food or heating room

toilet bathroom fixture with seat over bowl through which water is flushed to dispose of human waste material

tub bathtub

washing machine electrical apparatus with enclosed tub for cleaning clothing and linens

water heater apparatus with large storage tank where water is heated by gas or electricity for use in bathroom and kitchen

wood stove heavy metal heating and cooking apparatus, with heat supplied by wood burned in large chamber

---

**ORNAMENTAL AND FUNCTIONAL
ARTICLES**
*Decorations, Ornaments, and Symbolic Objects
Functional Household Articles and Appliances
Linens and Fabrics
Glass and Ceramics*

See also: *Chap. 5: Building and Construction Materials; Containers; Chap. 7: Interior Structure; Furnishings; Chap. 9: The Kitchen; Chap. 16: Architecture*

Decorations, Ornaments, and Symbolic Objects

accouterment accessory item; trappings

aigrette heron's plume, sometimes placed in vase

anthemion flat, floral ornament in bas relief

barber pole cylinder with red and white spirals, used to indicate barbershop

bas relief sculptural relief in slight projection from surrounding surface

beading beaded molding; openwork trimming with beads

bibelot small household ornament or trinket; elegant miniature book

bijou small, dainty ornament of delicate workmanship, usu. jewelry

birdbath small, ornamental basin set outside for birds to bathe in

bric-a-brac small objects placed about room for ornamentation; curios; knickknacks

cachepot ornamental receptacle used to conceal flowerpot

calabash large, hard-shell gourd, used as utensil

calami cup for wine, used in Eucharist

candelabrum large, branched candlestick

candleholder candlestick

candlestick holder with socket for candle or candles; candleholder

cartouche ornate frame; oval or oblong figure enclosing sovereign's name (ancient Egypt)

centerpiece decorative display at center of table

chalice large cup or goblet, often of gold or silver, esp. for Eucharist wine

chandelier branched, ornate, multibulb lighting fixture suspended from ceiling

chime set of bells

Chinese lantern light with large paper shade, often globular

ciborium goblet-shaped vessel for storing Eucharist wafers

cornucopia curved goat's horn overflowing with fruit and grain, representing abundance

crucifix symbolic representation of Christ on cross, or cross itself

cuckoo clock clock equipped with mechanical birds that appear and emit sounds to announce hours

curio knickknack, bric-a-brac, or objet d'art

cuspidation decoration with horn or crescent moon

decoration any object used for its ornamental value

diptych two-leaved hinged tablet with pictures painted or carved on it

epergne ornate, tiered centerpiece with wrought metal frame bearing dishes, vases, and candleholders

espagnolette decorative metal knob on French door or window

---

figurine small carved, molded figure; statuette

filigree precious metal ornamentation of fine wire, applied to surfaces or in openwork setting

font receptacle for liquids, esp. holy water

gaslight gas burner affixed to wall with flame for illumination

globe spherical model of Earth on stand

girandole ornamental, branched candlestick or mirror frame

grandfather clock tall pendulum clock standing on floor

jardiniere ornamental stand for plants, often a large ceramic flowerpot

knickknack small, often trivial, ornamental object; curio; objet d'art

lares and penates treasured household belongings; household gods (ancient Rome)

luster glass pendant ornamenting candlestick or chandelier; object hung with such pendants

menorah candelabrum, esp. one holding nine candles for use during Jewish festival of Hanukkah

modillion ornamental block or bracket under corona of cornice

monteith large, silver punch bowl with scalloped rim

napkin ring metal ring for holding napkin in dining service

niello decorative object of metal with incised designs filled with black niello alloy

objet d'art decorative object of artistic value; curio; knickknack

objet trouvé found object

ornament any object used to adorn or embellish

paten plate for wafers, used in Eucharist

plume decorative feather, cluster of feathers

pontypool decorative japanned metalware used esp. on trays

quatrefoil panellike ornament composed of four lobes radiating from common center

salver serving tray for food and drink; tray on which letters or calling cards are presented

samovar elaborate urn with spigot, used for heating water to brew tea

sconce bracket candlestick hung from wall; similar electric fixture

speculum ancient mirror of bronze or silver

spray ornamental cluster of flowers and greenery

statuary collection of statues

statue sculpted, modeled, or cast three-dimensional representation, usu. of person or animal

statuette small statue; figurine

swag suspended wreath or garland

taper squat, round candle used for religious observance

tazza ornamental cup or vase with large, flat bowl and pedestal or pillar, often with handles

torchère tall, ornamental candlestick on tripod base (18th c.)

trappings largely ornamental household articles

trefoil ornament in form of stylized trifoliate leaf

trim material used for decoration or embellishment along borders of larger piece

trinket small, inexpensive ornament

triptych picture or panel in three panels side by side

urn ornamental vase on pedestal, used for storage; closed vessel on stand with spigot for serving beverages

vermiculation decorative markings in irregular fine lines

wind-bell wind chimes

wind chimes cluster of small pieces of glass or metal that tinkle in wind; wind-bell

wreath ornamental circle of flowers and greenery

Functional Household Articles and Appliances

alarm clock small bedside clock equipped with bell or buzzer set to sound at particular time

ampule sealed vial used to hold liquids

andirons metal supports with horizontal bar on legs, used to hold firewood on hearth

appliance any of various service units, usu. operated electrically, found in contemporary homes, esp. in the kitchen

aquarium enclosed, glass-sided container filled with water, serving as home to fish and other underwater life

ashcan metal refuse receptacle

ashtray small, flat, lipped receptacle for tobacco ashes

basket receptacle of interwoven material or light wood for trash, storage, transport, or display

bed board board placed under mattress for greater firmness

bedpan shallow vessel or receptacle used as toilet by bedridden person

bed tray stand with short, retractable legs, used for holding dishes and other objects while person is sitting up in bed

bedwarmer covered pan containing hot coals to warm bed

bell hollow metallic device that vibrates with ringing sound when struck; electronic signal device that simulates this sound

bellows blower that draws air through valve and expels it through tube, esp. to fan open fire

bibcock faucet having bent-down nozzle

billet chunky piece of firewood

birdcage grated enclosure that houses birds

blotter soft, spongy, unsized paper used to absorb ink

bookends heavy supports that hold books in place on shelf

broom bundle of firm, stiff fibers or twigs bound together on long handle, used for sweeping floor

brush bristles set into handle, used for scrubbing, sweeping, or smoothing

bucket round vessel for catching, holding, or carrying liquids

bulletin board soft board attached to wall for posting notices; pegboard

caddy small box, can, or chest for storage

candle molded or dipped mass of wax containing wick that may be burned for illumination

candlelighter long device for lighting ceremonial candles

candlesnuffer long device having hollow cone at end of handle, used for extinguishing ceremonial candles

cantilever bracket-shaped support for balcony or cornice; projecting beam supported at one end only

carboy protective rectangular container housing bottle with capacity of 5 to 15 gallons (18.9 to 56.8 l)

carton cardboard or wooden box

censer cup-shaped vessel with holes, suspended on chains and used for burning incense

chamber pot bedroom receptacle for human waste material

circular file *Slang.* waste basket

clock device for keeping and telling time, usu. circular, with hours around perimeter and two hands, one to show hours, one to show minutes

coal scuttle metal carrying pail with sloped lip and bail

coaster shallow container, small mat, or plate used to hold glasses and protect surfaces, esp. from moisture

coat hanger slender, arched device of metal, plastic, or wood, shaped like person's shoulders and used for hanging garments; hanger

cresset iron vessel or basket for holding illuminant, mounted as torch or suspended as lantern

cuspidor spittoon

dry mop long-handled mop with cloth, rope, or feather head, used for dusting floors

dust mop dry mop

feather duster soft feathers attached to handle, for dusting surfaces

fixture item of movable property incorporated into structure, both ornamental and functional

flowerpot container for growing plant, usu. of clay or plastic

fly swatter flat piece of rubber, plastic, or wire mesh attached to long handle, used for killing insects

frog small metal, glass, or plastic holder with spikes or perforations for holding flowers in place in vase

garbage can large metal or plastic container for trash; trash can

grate frame of parallel or crossed bars, esp. of iron, used to contain stove or furnace fire

hanger coat hanger

hatrack set of pegs or hooks that holds hats

hose long, flexible tube for conveying liquids

iron usu. electrical device with flat, long, metal base, heated to press clothes

ironing board flat, padded, cloth-covered surface on which clothes are pressed with an iron

ladder two long sidepieces joined by series of short crosspieces, used for climbing or reaching high places

lampshade any of various translucent, often fabric devices used to shield direct glare of lighted bulb in lamp

lampstand base on which shade and illuminating device rest

lantern portable, protective light case with transparent openings or covering, usu. with handle

light fixture device attached to wall or ceiling that holds lamp or light bulb

mop absorbent material fastened to long handle, used to clean floors

nesting box one of a series of boxes in graduated sizes that may be stored within one another

oil lamp usu. metal illuminating device that burns oil

pail bucket, usu. with handle, for carrying liquids

pegboard flat section of porous material attached to wall for posting notices; bulletin board

planter wood, ceramic, or glass receptacle used to hold live plant and earth

plug small object used to close opening; stopper

plunger rubber suction cup on handle for clearing plumbing traps

pricket candlestick with protruding point on which candle is impaled

scuttle shallow, open basket for carrying something, esp. metal pail for carrying coal

shoe rack hanging or floor device for storing shoes

silent butler receptacle with hinged lid for collecting table crumbs or emptying ashtrays

sleeveboard small ironing board for pressing garment sleeves

spice rack narrow storage shelves with front strips, usu. attached to wall

spittoon receptacle for expectorate; cuspidor

steamer enclosed container in which something is subjected to steam

steam iron clothes iron with compartment for holding water that is converted to steam and emitted onto fabric being pressed

stopper plug

stoup beverage container; basin

stretcher bedlike device on wheels for transporting sick or injured person

terrarium small glass enclosure for keeping, raising, and observing plants or animals

tie rack hanging device with slots or bars for storing ties

torch burning stick carried in hand for illumination

towel rack horizontal bar for hanging towels

trash basket small receptacle for dry trash

trash can garbage can

tray open, flat-bottomed receptacle with rim for carrying or holding objects

vacuum cleaner electrical device that sucks dirt and dust through hose into chamber

valet rack or tray for holding clothing and personal effects

ventilation system or means of providing fresh air to room

wall bracket usu. angle-shaped support attached to wall

wastebasket small garbage receptacle, esp. for paper

whisk broom small broom with short handle

window box box holding soil for growing plants on windowsill

wine rack wood frame with slots for storing bottles of wine on their sides

wringer device for pressing liquid out of washed clothes, usu. between two rollers, operated with crank handle

zarf ornamental holder for coffee cup without handle

Linens and Fabrics

antimacassar delicate, often lace, protective covering on back or arms of chair

arras decorative wall hanging, screen, or tapestry

backrest pillow, bolster, or cushion placed behind back for support

banderole long, narrow, forked flag or streamer

banner strip of cloth on which sign is painted; flag, pennant

bath mat small, thick, fabric rug on bathroom floor

bath towel large towel for drying entire body

beach towel extra large towel for use at beach

bedding pillows, cases, sheets, blankets, and covers for bed

bed pillow stuffed fabric on which to support head while sleeping

bedsheet sheet

bedspread decorative fabric placed over blankets on bed

blanket large, usu. oblong woven fabric used as bed covering for warmth

bolster long, narrow cushion or pillow, sometimes with arm rests, used as prop on backless sofa or bed

bunting lightweight, loosely woven fabric for flags and patriotic decorations

comforter thick, often quilted, cloth blanket; duvet

cover blanket, quilt, bedspread, or sofa covering

coverlet bedspread, small cover

crazy quilt patchwork quilt without regular design

cushion small, often decorative, covered pillow on which people sit, lie, or recline

dish towel small cloth for drying dishes

doily small, protective and decorative napkin or linen, set on table or furniture

doormat flat piece of absorbent material on which people wipe their feet before entering house

duvet down- or fiber-filled quilt; comforter

eiderdown quilted blanket stuffed with duck feathers

facecloth very small towel, used wet to scrub face; washcloth

fitted sheet bedsheet that fits snugly over mattress

flag usu. rectangular piece of cloth with distinctive symbolic design; banner; pennant

hand towel medium-size towel for drying hands and face

hanging curtain, tapestry, or other suspended decoration

lap robe heavy fur or blanket used to cover legs, usu. when outdoors

linens general term for bedding, sheets, napkins, towels, and tablecloths

mattress pad usu. quilted, protective cloth covering for mattress

napkin usu. square piece of paper or cloth for wiping hands and lips, esp. after eating

pennant flag or banner, esp. one tapering to a point at one end

pillow fabric stuffed with feathers, foam, or fibers, used as soft resting place for head or back

pillowcase protective or decorative cloth covering for pillow

place mat decorative cloth, reed, or plastic sheet used by individual diner to protect table from plates and glasses

quilt bedcover consisting of two cloth layers filled with cotton or down and stitched together in crisscrossed lines or patterns

sampler decorative needlework with embroidered letters and verses

sham covering, esp. for pillow, that provides altered outward appearance

sheet oblong linen or cotton cloth placed between mattress and blanket on bed

slipcover removable protective covering for article of furniture

spread cover or cloth placed on top of bed or sofa; bedspread

standard long, narrow, tapering flag bearing heraldic devices or symbols

streamer banner or pennant; long, narrow, wavy cloth strip

tablecloth decorative fabric used to cover and protect entire tabletop

tapestry heavy, handwoven, highly decorative wall hanging

throw pillow small, decorative pillow

towel absorbent cloth of various sizes, used for wiping or drying the body

upholstery material used to make soft covering, esp. for seat or sofa

washcloth very small towel, used wet to scrub body; facecloth

white goods bedding and linens

Glass and Ceramics

amphora jar or vase with large oval body, narrow neck, and two handles rising near level of mouth (ancient Greece)

ampulla glass or earthenware wine flask with two handles and globular body (ancient Rome.)

bell jar bell-shaped glass vessel for covering objects

bottle usu. glass container for liquids with narrow neck and opening at top

carafe liter or half-liter glass bottle, esp. for holding wine

caster small glass bottle for serving condiments; cruet

china plates, cups, and serving platters of delicate, translucent ceramic porcelain

cistern large, usu. earthenware vessel for storing water

crock thick earthenware pot or jar

crockery earthenware plates, cups, and serving utensils

cruet caster

crystal objects, esp. bottles and drinking glasses, made of fine, cut glass

cut glass glass with ornamental patterns cut into its surface

decanter ornamental bottle for wine, port, or sherry, often made of cut glass

etched glass decorative cut-glass objects

ewer widemouthed jug or pitcher of brass or ceramics

faience decorative, enameled French Renaissance earthenware

jar widemouthed container, usu. of glass or earthenware

jeroboam oversized wine bottle with capacity of 3 liters (3.3 quarts)

jug large, deep, narrowmouthed container with handle, usu. of glass or earthenware

Limoges enamelware or porcelain made at Limoges, France

majolica glazed, richly colored, ornamental Italian earthenware

pitcher container with lip and spout, used for holding and pouring liquids, usu. made of glass or earthenware

porcelain hard, fine-grained, nonporous ceramicware, usu. translucent and white

Satsuma vase large pottery vase over five feet tall, often placed by fireplace (Japan)

Sèvres vase fine porcelain vase from Sèvres, France

stoneware decorative white earthenware crocks, jugs, plates, and cups

vase ornamental glass or earthenware vessel of greater depth than width, often used to hold flowers

Wedgwood *Trademark.* type of bone china ceramicware

CHAPTER EIGHT
THE FAMILY

KINSHIP AND FAMILY RELATIONS
Kinship and Ancestry
Relationships by Blood and Marriage
Family Affairs

See also: *Chap. 3: Geography; Chap. 8: Marriage and Divorce; Parents and Children; Chap. 13: Anthropology; Sociology*

Kinship and Ancestry

affinity kinship relationship by marriage

agnate paternal kinsman, esp. male relative on father's side

ancestor person from whom one is descended, usu. more remote than grandparent; forefather

ancestry line of descent or lineage

antecedents ancestors

blood relation by birth

bloodline sequence of direct ancestors; family

blood relation family member by birth

branch division of family descended from common ancestor

breed persons of the same stock

breeding lineage

clan extended family; tribe

collateral kin descended by different line from same stock, such as uncle and nephew

common descent blood relationship of two or more people with common ancestor; consanguinity

congenital (*adj*) existing at birth

consanguinity relationship by descent from common ancestor

crossbreed (*vb*) interbreed

descendant person born of same blood as ancestor in later generation; progeny

descent extraction; lineage, derivation from an ancestor

direct line descent by blood from parent to child

distaff female side or branch of family; spindle side

extended family ancestors and descendants by birth and marriage over several generations

extraction ancestry; descent or lineage

family persons of common ancestry or stock; persons related by birth or marriage; parents and their children by birth or adoption

family tree generational chart of ancestry

female line descent through mother

filopietism excessive veneration of one's ancestors

forefather ancestor

fruit descendants

full blood relationship between offspring of same parents

full-blooded (*adj*) of pure, unmixed ancestry

genealogy account of person or family's descent from first known ancestor

generation persons constituting single step in line of descent

gens clan, esp. one tracing patrilineal descent

heir one receiving endowment from parent or predecessor

heredity sum of qualities transmitted from ancestor to descendant

heritage property or trait descending to heir, transmitted by immediate ancestor

house family, including ancestors and descendants

hybrid one born of mixed breeds, races, or diverse cultural traditions

inbred (*adj*) born of closely related individuals; from the same stock

incest sexual relations or interbreeding between two closely related persons, esp. between siblings or parent and child

interbreed (*vb*) breed within closed population; crossbreed

kin one's relatives; persons of common ancestry

kindred group of one's relatives; kinship

kinfolk one's relatives

kinship state of being related

kinship group individuals composing one's kin

kinsman relative, esp. male

kinswoman female relative

kith close friends, neighbors, or relatives

kith and kin close friends and relations

line lineage; bloodline

lineage descent in direct line from common progenitor; ancestry or extraction

male line descent through father

matriarch female, esp. mother, who rules or dominates family

matriarchy family or group dominated by mother; state governed by woman

matrilineal (*adj*) tracing descent through mother's line

moiety one of two basic tribal or clan subdivisions based on unilineal descent

next of kin one's closest relative

nuclear family family unit composed of parents and children only

offspring children

origin ancestry; parentage

parentage descent from parents or ancestors; lineage

patriarch male, esp. father, who rules or dominates a family

patriarchy family or group dominated by father; state governed by man

patrilineal (*adj*) tracing descent through father's line

patrimony anything derived from one's father, esp. an estate; heritage

pedigree ancestral line, esp. of distinguished lineage

people one's family and relations; racial, national, or tribal group

philoprogenitive (*adj*) tending to produce offspring

posterity all future generations descended from one progenitor; descendants

progenitor forefather; ancestor in direct line

progeny descendants; children

pure blood one of unmixed ancestry, bred from members of recognized strain, group, or class

race family, tribe, or people of same stock

relation relative

relative person connected to another by blood; relation

seed ancestry or origin

sire father; male ancestor or progenitor

spear side male side or branch of family

spindle side female side or branch of family; distaff

stirp line descending from common ancestor; stock

stock descendants of one individual; family, lineage

strain group with common ancestry producing physiological distinctions

totem emblem of family or clan, symbolic of its ancestry

tree chart of family lineage

tribe people of common stock; clan

ultimogeniture system of inheritance favoring youngest son

unilineal (*adj*) tracing descent through maternal or paternal line only

Relationships by Blood and Marriage

aunt sister of one's father or mother; uncle's wife

auntie *Informal.* aunt

blood brother brother by birth

blood sister sister by birth

bro *Informal.* brother

brother male sibling with one or both parents in common

brother-in-law brother of one's spouse; husband of one's sister; husband of one's spouse's sister

cater-cousin intimate friend; one not related

child son or daughter by birth or adoption

cousin child of one's uncle or aunt; relative descended from one's grandparents or ancestors in different line

cousin-german first cousin

cousin once removed cousin by marriage or by descent from grandparents, not through parents' line

cousin twice removed relative descended from grandparents' line through marriage or from more remote ancestors

daughter female child

daughter-in-law wife of one's son

father male parent

father-in-law father of one's spouse

first cousin child of one's uncle or aunt; cousin-german

gaffer *Informal.* grandfather

gammer *Informal.* grandmother

grammy *Informal.* grandmother

grampa *Informal.* grandfather

gramps *Informal.* grandfather

grandaunt great-aunt

grandchild child of one's child

granddaughter female child of one's child

grandfather father of one's parent
grandma *Informal.* grandmother
grandmother mother of one's parent
grandnephew male child of one's sibling's child; great-nephew
grandniece female child of one's sibling's child; great-niece
grandparents grandmother and grandfather; parents of one's parents
grandson male child of one's child
granduncle great-uncle
granny *Informal.* grandmother
great-aunt sister of one's grandparent; grandaunt
great-nephew grandnephew
great-niece grandniece
great-uncle brother of one's grandparent; granduncle
half brother brother related through one parent only
half sister sister related through one parent only
husband male spouse
in-law any relation by marriage
kid brother younger brother
kid sister younger sister
maternal grandfather mother's father
maternal grandmother mother's mother
mother female parent
mother-in-law mother of one's spouse
nana *Informal.* grandmother
nephew son of one's sibling or sibling-in-law
niece daughter of one's sibling or sibling-in-law
novercal (*adj*) relating to one's stepmother
nuncle *Chiefly Brit.* uncle
parent mother or father; progenitor
paternal grandfather father's father
paternal grandmother father's mother
second cousin cousin descended from grandparent, not through parent's line
sibling brother or sister
sibling-in-law brother or sister of one's spouse; spouse of one's sibling; spouse of spouse's sibling
sis *Informal.* sister
sister female sibling with one or both parents in common
sister-in-law sister of one's spouse; wife of one's brother; wife of one's spouse's brother
son male child
son-in-law husband of one's daughter
spouse husband or wife; person to whom one is married
stepbrother son of one's stepparent by former marriage
stepchild child of one's spouse by former marriage
stepdaughter daughter of one's spouse by former marriage
stepfather husband of one's mother by subsequent marriage
stepmother wife of one's father by subsequent marriage

stepparent spouse of one's parent by subsequent marriage
stepsister daughter of one's stepparent by former marriage
stepson son of one's spouse by former marriage
unc *Informal.* uncle
uncle brother of one's father or mother; aunt's husband
wife female spouse

Family Affairs

adult one who has reached specified age of majority; grownup
baptism Christian sacrament of naming and admission to Christian community
bar mitzvah celebration of Jewish boy's coming of age
bat mitzvah celebration of Jewish girl's coming of age
big daddy representative of paternalistic authority
birthday date of one's birth; annual celebration of date of birth
blood feud multigenerational dispute between families
bonding formation of close personal relationship through constant association, esp. between mother and child
breadwinner one who earns money to support family
change of life climacteric; menopause
charge person, esp. child, committed to one's care
chastity abstention from sexual intercourse, esp. unlawful sexual intercourse
climacteric period in male of declining sexual activity; change of life
close-knit (*adj*) bound together by intimate social or familial ties
cognomen surname; last name
come out (*vb*) make one's debut
connate (*adj*) congenitally united, born together
creature comforts food, warmth, and shelter
crèche *Chiefly Brit.* foundling hospital; day nursery
debut formal entrance into society, usu. of teenage girl
demoiselle *French.* young lady
domestic science housekeeping
dowager widow holding property or title of deceased husband
elder respected, senior member of family or tribe
ephebe young man, esp. eighteen- to nineteen-year-old (ancient Greece)
etiquette social conduct prescribed by proper breeding
family clinic facility that provides counseling and medical care for family-related problems
family counseling therapy relating to family issues

family likeness physical appearance common to family members
family planning use of contraception to control number of children
folk people or tribes forming nation; group with common traditions and culture preserved over generations
folks *Informal.* persons of one's family; parents
fraternal (*adj*) brotherly
given name first name, chosen by parents
grownup adult
guardian adult who is legally responsible for another's child
houseguest overnight visitor in one's home
household those living together as a family in same dwelling
housekeeping management of home affairs; domestic science
house sitter person who occupies a home while tenant or owner is absent
junior child bearing same given name as parent
kissing cousin friend or relative known well enough to kiss upon meeting
last name surname
majority age at which child is legally an adult
matchmaker individual, esp. older woman, who arranges potential marriages
matron mature or distinguished married woman
menfolk males of a family or clan
menopause time of natural cessation of female menstruation and associated changes, usu. occurring between ages forty-five and fifty; change of life
middle age period of life from about ages forty to sixty
midlife period of emotional turmoil associated with aging; middle age
minor individual beneath age of legal majority, usu. eighteen to twenty-one years old
name day feast of saint for whom one is named
naming act of giving child a name
noblesse oblige obligation of honorable behavior associated with noble birth
parricide act of killing a member of one's family
patronymic name derived from father or paternal ancestor, usu. by addition of suffix or prefix
propagate (*vb*) breed or produce offspring
purse strings family finances or resources
retirement age at which one ceases working, usu. around sixty-five years old
reunion reconciliation or gathering of separated family members
rite of passage ceremony marking major transition in life, such as birth, puberty, marriage, or death
senior citizen elderly member of clan or society
seniors elders
sterility inability to conceive offspring
surname name borne in common by family members; cognomen; last name
ties associations or bonds between family members
womenfolk females of family or clan

MARRIAGE AND DIVORCE

See also: *Chap. 8: Kinship and Family Relations; Parents and Children; Chap. 11: Law; Chap. 22: Sex, Love, and Romance*

adultery sexual intercourse by married person with someone other than spouse

affair temporary, often secret romance outside marriage

affiance promise of marriage; betrothal

alimony legally required financial support paid to one marriage partner by the other as term of divorce

anniversary annual celebration on wedding date

annulment legal invalidation of marriage

bachelor unmarried man

bachelor party party given a bachelor by his male friends before his marriage, often a night of carousing prior to wedding day

banns public announcement of proposed marriage, esp. in church

bedmate spouse

benedict newly married man formerly a longtime bachelor

best man principal groomsman at wedding; paranymph

betrothal engagement to be married

better half one's spouse

bigamy illegal marriage to more than one person at a time

bluebeard man who marries and kills one wife after another

bouquet flowers carried by bride and tossed to single bridesmaids and guests after wedding

bridale usu. rustic wedding celebration

bridal wreath small, white, spring flowers used in bride's bouquet

bride woman just married or about to be married

bridegroom man just married or about to be married

bride price money or property given by prospective husband to bride's family

bridesmaid woman or girl attending bride at wedding; paranymph

bride-to-be woman engaged to be married; fiancée

broken home single-parent family in which child of divorced parents is raised

celestial marriage Mormon marriage held to be binding in present and future life

celibacy state of being unmarried

cestus bride's symbolic belt

child support payments made by one party following divorce for care and upbringing of children

chuppah *Hebrew.* canopy beneath which bride and groom stand during Jewish wedding ceremony

church marriage marriage performed by minister, priest, or rabbi

civil marriage marriage performed by magistrate

cohabitation living together, esp. while unmarried

commitment emotional and material trust that forms basis of marriage

common-law marriage marriage based on declaration, intent, or length of time living together without benefit of wedding

community property property acquired after marriage that is jointly owned by both partners and that by law must be divided equally upon divorce

companionate marriage form of marriage proposed in 1920's allowing birth control and uncontested divorce of childless couples, with no economic claims on partner

compatibility ability to live together in harmony

concubinage cohabitation of persons not legally married

condonation defense to prevent divorce; forgiveness for offense so it cannot be used as grounds for divorce action

confirmed bachelor never-married man; man living singly and not pursuing marriage

conflict-habituated marriage relationship dependent on conflict as part of its basic communication mechanism

conjugal (*adj*) pertaining to marriage or the relationship between husband and wife; connubial; marital; nuptial

conjugal rights rights of husband and wife to union and affection

connivance defense to prevent divorce

connubial (*adj*) conjugal; marital; nuptial

consanguineous marriage marriage between blood relatives

consort spouse of monarch

consummate (*vb*) complete or fulfill marriage bond by sexual intercourse

contested divorce legal proceeding for divorce that is challenged by party against whom proceedings are aimed

contract act of marriage; agreement to marry

couple married man and woman; (*vb*) join in wedlock

courtship social activities of potential mates culminating in engagement and marriage

coverture legal status of married woman

cuckold man with sexually unfaithful wife

curtesy right of husband, upon wife's death, to an interest in her property

custody immediate charge and care of children, usu. given to one partner in divorce

Darby and Joan very devoted elderly married couple

desertion abandonment of one's spouse and family

deuterogamy digamy

digamy second marriage after divorce or death of first spouse; deuterogamy

dissolution divorce

divorce legal termination of marriage; dissolution

divorcé divorced man

divorcée divorced woman

dotal (*adj*) pertaining to woman's marriage dowry

double-ring ceremony wedding in which both partners receive rings

dowager widow with title or property derived from dead husband

dower dowry; property woman brings to her marriage; right of widow to interest in husband's property

dowry money and real or personal property brought to marriage by woman

dual-career marriage marriage in which both spouses have full-time jobs or careers outside of household responsibilities

dutch *Slang.* wife

eligible (*adj*) single; available for marriage

elope (*vb*) run away to be married, esp. without parental consent

endogamy marriage traditionally within one's social, kinship, religious, or ethnic group

engaged (*adj*) describing one who has announced an intent to marry

engagement formal announcement of intention to marry; period or state of being pledged to marry

Enoch Arden divorce divorce based on disappearance of one partner for specified length of time

epithalamion song or poem in honor of wedding couple

espousal wedding; marriage ceremony

estrangement physical separation of married couple

exogamy marriage traditionally outside one's social, kinship, religious, or ethnic group

extramarital (*adj*) describing that which occurs outside the bonds of marriage

family man married man who is deeply involved in family life

father-in-law father of one's spouse

fiancé man to whom one is engaged to marry

fiancée woman to whom one is engaged to marry

fling extramarital affair

flower girl young girl who carries flowers before bride at wedding

gay marriage formalized, monogamous union between two persons of the same sex

golden anniversary fiftieth wedding anniversary

Gretna Green place where eloping couples are married

groom bridegroom

groomsman man attending groom at wedding

group marriage marriage between more than two persons, illegal in U.S.

hand bride's hand, given by her father, symbolizing his permission for her to marry; woman's agreement to marry

happy couple bride and groom at wedding

hausfrau housewife; married woman (Germany)

helpmate spouse

henpeck (*vb*) nag, esp. when done by wife

hitched (*adj*) *Slang*. married

holy matrimony state of being married

homemaker housewife

homogamy marriage among persons of similar age, social class, race, education, and religion

honeymoon vacation taken by newlyweds to begin their marriage

honeymoon period transitional time between single and married life; early, romantic period in marriage

househusband man who stays home to manage the household while his wife goes out to work

housemate spouse

housewife woman whose work is caring for home and children

hubby *Informal*. husband

husband married man; male spouse

hypergamy marriage into caste at least as high as one's own, esp. by Hindu woman

hypogamy marriage to person of lower socioeconomic status

incompatibility grounds for divorce based on mutual inability to live together with shared values, goals, and lifestyles

inconstancy fickleness in affections; infidelity

infare housewarming party for newly married couple

infidelity sexual unfaithfulness in marriage

in-laws relatives by marriage, esp. spouse's parents

intended one's future husband or wife

interlocutory preliminary divorce decree prior to final settlement

intermarry (*vb*) marry outside one's racial, religious, or ethnic group

legal separation legal arrangement to live apart made by estranged marriage partners

levirate ancient Hebrew marriage custom requiring brother of deceased man to marry his widow

little woman *Informal*. pejorative term for one's wife

Lucy Stoner married woman who keeps her maiden name

maiden name woman's surname prior to marriage

maid of honor principal unmarried woman attending bride at wedding ceremony

man and wife married couple

marital (*adj*) pertaining to marriage; conjugal; connubial; nuptial

marriage social and legal institution of formalized union between man and woman, typically foundation of family unit; matrimony; wedlock

marriage counseling therapy for partners in troubled marriage

marriage license document required for completion of legal establishment of marriage

marriage of convenience legal union based on circumstances other than love or affection, such as financial gain or naturalization

marriage squeeze demographic difference in number of eligible women and eligible men

married (*adj*) joined in marriage; conjugal

marry (*vb*) join in wedlock; unite man and woman in marriage; take another as one's spouse

mate spouse

matrimony marriage; rite, ceremony, or sacrament of marriage

matron long-married woman; wife; widow

matron of honor principal married woman attending bride at wedding ceremony

mental cruelty nonphysical abuse used as grounds for divorce

miscegenation marriage between persons of different races

mistress married man's regular female lover

mixed marriage marriage between persons of different races, religions, or ethnic groups

monandry practice and custom of having one husband at a time

monogamy practice of having only one spouse at a time

morganatic marriage union between person of high rank and person of lower rank in which children do not inherit higher-ranking parent's title or property

mother-in-law mother of one's spouse

nest (*vb*) settle into cozy, safe living place as couple or family; (*n*) family home

newlyweds recently married man and woman

no-fault divorce legal dissolution of marriage in which neither partner is blamed for its failure

nonsupport failure of one mate to provide financial support for spouse and family, as contracted in marriage agreement

nubile (*adj*) marriageable, esp. in reference to young girls

nuptial (*adj*) pertaining to marriage and the wedding ceremony

nuptials marriage ceremony; wedding

old lady *Informal*. wife

old maid *Derogatory slang*. elderly or confirmed spinster

old man *Informal*. husband

on the rocks *Slang*. failing, esp. in reference to a troubled marriage

on the side designating extramarital affair

open marriage arrangement whereby partners are free to have sexual relations outside marriage

palimony financial compensation paid to person previously lived with, but not married to, by more financially able partner

paranymph best man; bridesmaid

partner spouse

philander (*vb*) have sexual relations with no possibility of marriage

play around *Informal*. indulge in extramarital affairs

plight one's troth become engaged; take wedding vows

polyandry practice and custom of having more than one husband at a time

polygamy marriage to two or more spouses simultaneously

proposal offer of marriage

prothalamion song or poem that celebrates a marriage

provider spouse whose work generates income that pays family expenses

proxy marriage ceremony conducted with another person substituting for one of partners to be wed

reception party following wedding ceremony

reconciliation resolution of differences between estranged or separated couple

rib wife

run around play around; be unfaithful to one's spouse

sannup married man; husband (American Indian)

scarlet letter badge of an adulterer, esp. letter "A" worn as symbol of adultery

separation move to independent living quarters by couple with marriage problems, often prior to divorce action

serial monogamy series of monogamous relationships, none of which leads to marriage

set up housekeeping get married or cohabit

seven-year itch supposed temptation to have affair in seventh year of marriage

shivaree noisy mock serenade to newly married couple

shotgun wedding marriage compelled by bride's pregnancy

shower celebration with gifts for bride-to-be, given by her female friends

significant other mate or spouse

soul mate empathic, loving spouse

spinster unmarried woman past common age for marrying; old maid

spousals nuptials; wedding

spouse one's husband or wife

squaw *Derogatory slang*. wife

support payments money paid by one parent under terms of divorce settlement to care for children in custody of other parent

suttee custom in which widow is cremated on funeral pyre of her husband (India)

swap (*vb*) trade marriage partners with another couple for sexual activity; swing

swing (*vb*) swap

tie the knot *Informal*. get married

traditional marriage union in which husband is breadwinner and head of household while wife is child rearer and housekeeper

trial separation temporary break in cohabitation by married couple to determine whether they should separate permanently and initiate divorce proceedings

troth pledge of fidelity at engagement or wedding

trousseau bride's gown and accessories

uncontested divorce dissolution of marriage without legal dispute between partners

union joining in marriage; physical consummation of marriage

unmarried (*adj*) single; not married
uxorial (*adj*) wifely in behavior
uxoricide murder of wife by husband
uxorious (*adj*) inordinately submissive to one's wife
viduity widowhood
visiting privilege right of divorced person to visit children living in custody of other parent
vital marriage relationship with high morale, mutual interest, affection, and emotional investment
vows promise of fidelity; formal marriage pledge
war bride woman marrying in wartime, esp. one whose husband leaves for military service immediately after wedding
wear the pants display dominant behavior and control, esp. as exhibited by wife
wed (*vb*) marry
wedded (*adj*) married
wedding marriage ceremony and festivities; nuptials
wedding band wedding ring
wedding day date on which marriage occurs
wedding ring gold band presented at wedding and worn by one or both spouses to signify married status
wedlock marriage; matrimony
widow woman whose husband is dead
widower man whose wife is dead
widowhood state of being widowed
wife married woman; female spouse
wive (*vb*) take a wife; marry a woman
woo (*vb*) court
yoke (*vb*) join in marriage

PARENTS AND CHILDREN
Pregnancy and Birth
Infancy
Upbringing and Development
Names and Relationships

See also: *Chap. 1: Anatomy; Chap. 2: Biology; Chap. 8: Kinship and Family Relations; Marriage and Divorce; Chap. 13: Psychology; Chap. 22: Sex, Love, and Romance*

Pregnancy and Birth

abortion spontaneous or induced expulsion of fetus early in gestation period, usu. before twelfth week
accouchement act of giving birth
afterbirth placenta and fetal membranes expelled from uterus in parturition
artificial insemination introduction of semen into uterus by other than sexual means
barren (*adj*) unable to conceive or produce offspring
bar sinister proof, condition, or stigma of illegitimacy
bastard illegitimate child
beget (*vb*) conceive and bear child
biological clock woman's natural life cycle that controls ability to conceive and bear children

biological parent parent who has conceived or sired child, though not always legal parent or guardian
birth act or process of bringing forth child from mother's womb; parturition
birth certificate official hospital record of birth
birth control devices and methods used to prevent conception and reduce number of children born by woman
birthday date of birth, celebrated annually
birth defect physical defect present at birth that may be inherited or environmentally induced during pregnancy
birthing art and practice of giving birth
carry (*vb*) be pregnant
Cesarean section delivery of child by surgical incision through walls of abdomen into uterus; C-section
childbearing act of carrying and giving birth to children
childbirth parturition; birth
conception act of becoming pregnant, in which sperm fertilizes ovum and embryo begins growth in woman's uterus
confinement period of lying-in immediately preceding birth of child
congenital (*adj*) describing trait derived or inherited from parents through genes
contraception devices and methods used to prevent pregnancy
contraceptive device used to prevent pregnancy; (*adj*) tending to prevent conception
couvade practice among some peoples in which husband enacts birth experience in his bed immediately preceding birth of his child
C-section Cesarean section
delivery act of giving birth to a child; assistance given to mother during childbirth
embryo unborn child developing in mother's womb
expecting (*adj*) pregnant
false pregnancy signs of pregnancy, esp. absence of menstruation, without presence of embryo, due to psychological or glandular disturbance or tumor
family planning use of birth control to limit number of children in family
family way pregnant
fertile (*adj*) able to conceive children
fertility capability of reproducing; ability to conceive
fertility drug medication used to enhance ability to conceive
fetus embryo from three months after conception to birth
fraternal twins twins of either sex, developed from separately fertilized ova, therefore not identical
full term pregnancy lasting nine months
gestation period of embryonic growth from conception to birth
gravid (*adj*) heavy with child; pregnant
identical twins twins of same sex, developed

from single fertilized ovum, very similar in appearance
illegitimate (*adj*) born out of wedlock; misbegotten
inbreeding conception of children among closely related individuals
in utero conception in uterus of woman; unborn
in vitro fertilization and conception outside living body, in artificial environment
knock up (*vb*) *Slang.* make pregnant
labor painful physical activities and sensations involved in giving birth
Lamaze method system of special exercises and breathing used in childbirth
legitimate (*adj*) lawfully begotten and born in wedlock
love child illegitimate child
lying-in confinement; period immediately preceding childbirth
maternity motherhood; hospital ward for childbirth and care of newborn infants
midwife woman who assists mother during childbirth
midwifery practice of being a midwife
misbegotten (*adj*) illegitimate
miscarriage expulsion of underdeveloped fetus, usu. between twelfth and twenty-eighth weeks of pregnancy
miscarry (*vb*) have miscarriage
morning sickness nausea associated with first months of pregnancy
natal (*adj*) relating to or associated with birth
natal mother biological mother
nativity birth
natural childbirth birth in which mother does not use anaesthesia
out of wedlock illegitimate
ovum female germ cell that, when fertilized, develops into embryo
parturition process of giving birth
paternity fatherhood
paternity test test to determine biological father of child by comparison of genetic traits
placenta structure within uterus connected to umbilical cord through which fetus receives nourishment and eliminates feces
Planned Parenthood *Trademark.* family planning organization that disseminates information and offers advice on birth control and sexually transmitted diseases
preggers *Brit. informal.* pregnant
pregnancy state of being with child
pregnant (*adj*) having unborn child in one's body; expecting; gravid; with child
premature birth birth occurring after a gestation period of less than thirty-seven weeks
prenatal (*adj*) before birth
primipara woman bearing a first child
pro-choice (*adj*) advocating legalized abortion
procreation reproduction; act of begetting and bringing forth young
pro-life (*adj*) opposing legalized abortion
quadruplets birth of four children from one pregnancy

quintuplets birth of five children from one pregnancy

sextuplets birth of six children from one pregnancy

sire (*vb*) beget as father

spawn (*vb*) reproduce, esp. in large numbers

spermatozoon male germ cell in semen that fertilizes ovum to produce embryo

sperm bank supply of spermatozoon used for artificial insemination

sterile incapable of producing offspring; barren

stillborn (*adj*) describing infant dead at birth

stork bird that in legend brings babies to parents

term nine months of normal pregnancy

test-tube baby embryo produced by laboratory fertilization and surgical implantation in uterus

thalidomide baby child with birth defect caused by mother's use of drug thalidomide during pregnancy

trimester one of three three-month periods during pregnancy

triplets birth of three children from one pregnancy

twins birth of two children from one pregnancy

umbilical cord structure connecting navel of fetus with mother's placenta; emotional connection of mother and child

unfertile (*adj*) physiologically unable to conceive and reproduce

unwed mother woman bearing child out of wedlock

uterus womb

war baby child conceived during war, often born when father is absent

whelp (*vb*) give birth to or bring forth young, usu. said of animals

with child pregnant

womb female uterus where embryo develops

Infancy

babe infant

baby infant

baby food purée of easily digested food for toothless infant

baptism Christian sacrament involving ritual use of water and naming of child, who is thus received into faith; christening

bassinet infant's basketlike, hooded bed

bottle-feeding feeding of suckling child with sterilized, milklike formula from bottle

breast-feeding suckling of child on milk from mother's breast

bris Jewish circumcision ceremony performed on eighth day following birth as rite of inclusion into religious community

buggy baby carriage

burp (*vb*) help infant expel gas from stomach by patting on back

carriage light-wheeled seat, often with hooded cover, for transporting infant

change (*vb*) replace child's soiled diaper with clean one

chrisom child infant that dies in first month of life

christening baptism, esp. naming of child in Christian faith

circumcision removal of prepuce from tip of male infant's penis

cradle infant's bed, often with spoke walls; infancy

crib baby's small bed with high sides

crib death inexplicable sudden infant death syndrome

dandle (*vb*) bounce baby playfully on one's knee

diaper folded cloth or absorbent material worn between legs and around waist by infant to collect urine and feces

diaper rash irritation that develops under wet diapers

first step initial indication of child's ability to walk, usu. around one year of age

formula milklike mixture used for bottle-feeding infants

foundling infant discovered when abandoned by unknown parents

housebreak (*vb*) toilet train, usu. said of animals

infancy period of early childhood

infant child in first year or two of life

infanticide murder of a baby

lullaby song sung to lull child to sleep

mewling (*adj*) crying weakly, whimpering; (*n*) an infant

nap brief period of sleep during daylight hours

nappy *Chiefly Brit.* diaper

neonatal (*adj*) relating to infant in first month of life

newborn child in first month of life

nipper *Chiefly Brit.* infant, baby

nurse (*vb*) suckle or breast-feed an infant

nursery infant's room in house

pacifier rubber nipple or teething ring for infant

Pampers *Trademark.* disposable diapers of soft, absorbent paper covered with thin layer of plastic

perambulator *Chiefly Brit.* baby carriage

postnatal (*adj*) referring to period after birth

postpartum (*adj*) referring to period following birth, esp. mother's depression during this time

potty-chair small seat with bowl used in toilet training

potty training training of child to use toilet

preemie *Informal.* prematurely born infant

puling (*adj*) whining, whimpering, mewling

rocker child's cradle on curved base

stroller seat on wheels for transporting infant

suckle (*vb*) breast-feed an infant

suckling infant still feeding on mother's milk; act of breast-feeding

swaddling clothes strips of cloth wrapped around infant to restrict movements

teether object for baby to bite while teething, esp. ring

teething painful first growth of teeth through infant's gums

toddler child who is beginning to walk, usu. aged one or two; tot

toilet training process of teaching child to control bladder and bowel functions and use toilet

tot toddler

tyke small child

wean (*vb*) accustom child to take nourishment other than by nursing

wee tot child (Scotland)

wet nurse woman who suckles infant not her own

Upbringing and Development

adolescence period of growing up, from puberty to maturity

adoption legal taking of a child born to someone else as one's own

adult fully developed and mature person, esp. over age twenty-one

age of consent age at which child is legally allowed to give consent to sex or marriage, usu. eighteen years old

allowance weekly stipend given by parent to child as spending money, often earned by doing chores

apron strings state of being under dominance or control of one's parents at an advanced age

au pair foreign person, usu. young girl, living with family and serving as domestic and baby-sitter

baby-sitter person hired to care for children; sitter

baby-sitting act of caring for children during short absence by parents

bedtime story story told by parent to help child fall asleep

bedwetting inability of toilet-trained child to control urination in sleep

biparental (*adj*) relating to or derived from both parents

bobbysoxer preadolescent girl

brat spoiled, obnoxious, demanding child

bring up (*vb*) raise child to maturity

changeling child secretly substituted for another, usu. at birth

chaperone older person accompanying youngsters at social function to ensure proper behavior

child abuse physical mistreatment of children

childcare day care

chip off the old block child who closely takes after one parent

chores household tasks performed by child, often rewarded by payment

Christian name first name; name given by parents

coming of age reaching majority or age of consent

corporal punishment physical punishment, such as spanking

curfew time, set by parents, at which child must return home, esp. in evening

custody immediate charge and care of child;

right to be child's guardian as determined in divorce or separation

day care supervision of preschool children, esp. while parents work; childcare

day nursery day-care facility

development stages of growth and maturation of child

domestic household help during day; maid

duenna chaperone or governess, esp. elderly woman serving in this capacity (Spain, Portugal)

familial (*adj*) of or relating to the family

farm out (*vb*) place children under care of paid guardian

fatherhood state of being a father

favorite child preferred by one or both parents

filial (*adj*) befitting relationship of child to its parent

foster (*vb*) provide parental care for a child not one's own

foster home place in which child lives with foster parents

fosterling foster child

foster parents individuals caring for a child not theirs legally or by birth

gifted child child with superior intelligence or talents

godchild child sponsored by godparents at baptism

godparents individuals who sponsor a child at baptism, thereby assuming certain responsibilities

growing pains emotional adjustments encountered during stages of development

grownup adult

guardian individual other than biological parents taking responsibility for child's upbringing

infancy first year or two of childhood

JD juvenile delinquent

juvenile teenager

juvenile delinquent JD; incorrigibly ill-behaved adolescent

killcrop former term for child who ate so much that parents feared he or she was descended from fairies

latchkey child young child of working parents who spends part of day at home unsupervised

majority age at which full civil rights are accorded, usu. twenty-one years

maternal (*adj*) characteristic of, related to, or inherited from mother

matricide act of killing one's mother

maturity final stage of development in which child is fully grown and able to care for itself

minor child under age of consent, which is usu. eighteen or twenty-one years of age

minx saucy young girl

motherhood state or quality of being a mother; maternity

nanny child's nursemaid

nest security of the family group; home

nonage period of youth before majority; immaturity

nubile (*adj*) of marriageable age, esp. young girl

nursemaid person employed regularly to care for children

nymphet sexually precocious adolescent girl

only child child with no siblings

orphan child whose parents are both dead or unknown

paddle (*vb*) spank

parent person who has begotten a child or is legally responsible for its upbringing; mother or father

parentage state of being a parent

parenting act and practice of raising children

paternal (*adj*) characteristic of, related to, or inherited from father

patricide act of killing one's father

patrimony estate inherited from father; anything derived from one's father

phase behavior and problems associated with particular period in child's development

philoprogenitive (*adj*) producing offspring; having deep affection for one's children

playmate play companion, esp. another child

preadolescent child just below age of puberty, approximately ages nine to twelve; preteen

prepubescent (*adj*) designating child just before age of puberty, about twelve years old

preteen preadolescent

puberty period marked by sexual development, when child is first capable of reproducing, usu. age fourteen in boys, age twelve in girls

raise (*vb*) bring up, educate, and nurture a child

rear (*vb*) raise a child

restraint device such as car seat or leash that restricts child's movement

rite of passage ritual associated with development stage, such as puberty

runaway unhappy adolescent fugitive from home

sass *Informal.* impudent backtalk from child to parent

schoolboy preadolescent male child

schoolgirl preadolescent female child

scold (*vb*) admonish misbehaving child

sibling rivalry natural hostility and competition between siblings

single parent individual raising child without spouse

sitter baby-sitter

spanking punishment consisting of slaps across buttocks, esp. with open hand

spoiled (*adj*) designating child overindulged by parents and lacking restraint or responsibility

stripling youth

subadult adolescent youth

subdeb adolescent girl

subteen preadolescent child

talk back (*vb*) make rude or impertinent answer to parent

teenager child between ages of twelve and twenty; juvenile

teenybopper *Slang.* teenager, esp. young girl

terrible two's difficult phase in child's life that occurs around age two, when child is first able

to interact with environment and must learn limits

tomboy boyish preadolescent or adolescent girl

transitional object familiar object, esp. blanket or doll, carried by child in stage of early socialization

unfathered (*adj*) raised by mother only

unfilial (*adj*) not befitting child's relations with parents

upbringing manner in which parents supervise child's development

waif orphan; lost child

ward child under supervision of court or court-appointed guardian

wetting bedwetting

working parent parent who is unavailable to care for child while at job

younger generation those of same age as one's children

youngster member of younger generation

younker youngster (Holland)

youth young person, esp. child or adolescent but not infant

Names and Relationships

baby of the family youngest child in family

bairn child (Scotland)

bambino *Italian.* infant

big brother older male sibling

big sister older female sibling

boy male child

brat child, esp. spoiled, troublesome one

brood family; children

brother male sibling

bub *Informal.* male child

bubba *Informal.* male child

child offspring; son or daughter between infancy and adolescence

children more than one child; sons and daughters born to or living with one set of parents; brood; kids; progeny

chit small child

consanguinity relationship by descent from common ancestor

cub child

dad *Informal.* child's name for father

daddy *Informal.* child's name for father

daughter female child

daughter-in-law wife of one's son

dilling *Chiefly Brit.* youngest child in family

enfant *French.* child

father man who has begotten a child; male parent

father-in-law spouse's father

firstborn eldest child in family

flesh and blood one's biological family, consisting of siblings and parents

folks *Informal.* parents

forebear parent or ancestor

forefather parent or ancestor

girl female child

godchild someone else's biological child whom one sponsors at baptism

goddaughter female godchild
godfather male godparent
godmother female godparent
godparent person who sponsors another person's child at baptism
godson male godchild
half-blood person related to another by having one common parent
half-brother male sibling with one common parent
half-sister female sibling with one common parent
heirs children; descendants
issue children
junior child, esp. male, having same first name as father
kid *Informal.* child
kiddy *Informal.* child
kids children
lad boy
lass girl
little bugger *Informal.* small child
ma *Informal.* child's name for mother
mama *Informal.* child's name for mother
mammy *Informal.* child's name for mother
man-child son
man of the house provider; father
master form of address for male youth too young to be called mister
materfamilias female head of household
missy *Informal.* pet name for girl child
mom *Informal.* child's name for mother

momma *Informal.* child's name for mother
mommy *Informal.* child's name for mother
moppet young child
mother woman who has given birth to a child; female parent
mother-in-law spouse's mother
mum *Chiefly Brit.* child's name for mother
mummy *Chiefly Brit.* child's name for mother
mumsy *Chiefly Brit.* child's name for mother
namesake child with same name as older family member
nana *Informal.* child's term for grandmother
ne (*adj*) born, used to indicate former name under which one was born
nee (*adj*) female form of ne
nuclear family parents and their children
offspring child or children
old lady *Informal.* mother
old man *Informal.* father
pa *Informal.* child's name for father
papa *Informal.* child's name for father
papoose young child (American Indian)
pappy *Informal.* child's name for father
parent mother or father of child; forebear
paterfamilias male head of household
patronymic name derived from father or paternal ancestor, esp. by addition of affix, such as Johnson, son of John
peewee *Informal.* child
pop *Informal.* child's name for father
poppa *Informal.* child's name for father
poppy *Informal.* child's name for father

pops *Informal.* child's name for father
posterity all future generations of offspring from one progenitor
primogeniture state of being firstborn
progenitor ancestor in direct blood line
progeny children; descendants
punk *Slang.* child
scion child; descendant
sibling brother or sister; one of two or more individuals with at least one common parent
sire male ancestor
sister female sibling
small fry young children
son male child
son-in-law husband of one's daughter
sonny male child
stepbrother male sibling by either parent's prior or subsequent marriage
stepchild child of one's spouse by prior or subsequent marriage
stepdaughter female stepchild
stepfather male stepparent
stepmother female stepparent
stepparent spouse of one's parent by prior or subsequent marriage
stepsister female sibling by either parent's prior or subsequent marriage
stepson male stepchild
surname name common to all members of family; last name
venter legal term designating maternal parentage

253

CHAPTER NINE
EATING

bolt swallow food or drink hurriedly
break bread eat, esp. with another or others
breakfast eat morning meal
chew bite off and grind food between teeth; masticate
chomp chew or bite down hard and noisily
chow down *Informal.* eat, esp. main meal of day
consume eat or drink, esp. in large amounts
cram stuff with food
devour eat voraciously, often to excess
diet eat sparingly; restrict one's intake of food
digest alter food by action of body chemicals into form that can be absorbed by body
dig in *Informal.* begin eating
dine eat dinner or any substantial meal
dispatch eat up quickly
drain drink everything in (container)
drink consume a liquid
eat place food in mouth, chew if necessary, and swallow
eat out have meal in a restaurant
eat up consume all of
engorge eat greedily; gorge
fall to begin eating
feast eat rich, elaborate meal
feast on enjoy eating (some specific, usu. lavish, food)
feed eat, esp. out of hunger only, usu. said of animals
finish off consume all of
gobble eat hurriedly and sloppily
gorge stuff oneself with food
graze snack continuously or nibble small portions and samples of food
gulp swallow hastily and greedily in large amounts
guzzle drink greedily in large amounts
imbibe drink, esp. alcoholic beverage
ingest take food into body, usu. by swallowing
ingurgitate consume greedily in large amounts
inhale *Informal.* eat or drink very rapidly
lap consume liquid food by licking it up with the tongue like an animal
lap up eat or drink greedily with the tongue
lunch eat midday meal
masticate chew
munch chew steadily and slowly; eat with pleasure
nibble eat small amounts of something, esp. in quick bites
nosh *Informal.* munch or eat a snack
partake eat or drink one portion of a meal, esp. with others
peck at eat in small amounts
pick at eat sparingly and fussily
pig out *Slang.* overeat
polish off complete (a meal or dish)
pork out *Slang.* overeat; pig out
put away eat in large quantity

quaff drink deeply and thirstily
refect refresh with food or drink (archaic)
refresh revive with food or drink
relish eat with great pleasure
sample eat small portions of (several different foods), esp. to taste quality
savor enjoy the taste of one's food
scarf *Slang.* eat greedily and very quickly
set to begin eating
sip drink slowly and carefully in small amounts
slug down drink rapidly in large amounts
slurp drink or eat noisily
snack eat small portions of food, esp. between regular meals
stuff oneself eat until one can eat no more
sup dine; eat supper or evening meal
swallow pass food or drink from mouth through throat to stomach
swig drink in large mouthfuls or quantities
swill drink greedily in large quantities
take in consume; digest
taste sense flavor of one's food; test flavor of by placing a little in one's mouth; eat or drink a small amount of
toss down gulp or eat rapidly, almost without chewing
tuck in *Chiefly Brit.* eat heartily
wash down ease the swallowing of (food) by drinking liquid
wine and dine entertain (guests) with food and drink
wolf down eat ravenously and quickly

Food in General

aliment food as nourishment
alimentation nourishment or sustenance
board daily meals, esp. at table or provided for pay or with lodging
bread food in general
chow *Informal.* food
chuck *Slang.* food, esp. in old West
comestibles food; edibles
cuisine prepared food; specific style of food
daily bread basic sustenance
delicacy very rare, costly, or fine food
diet foods or cuisine one eats regularly, esp. when low in calories
drink liquid food
eats *Informal.* food
edibles anything that may be eaten
fare food, esp. specific kind of diet or cuisine
feed one meal; animal food or fodder
fodder food given to animals; feed
food anything eaten as nourishment for sustenance; solid food as distinguished from liquid
food and drink solid and liquid nourishment
foodstuffs edible substances
goodies *Informal.* foods one especially likes; treats
grub *Slang.* food, usu. simple and basic
leftovers food remaining after completion of meal, often saved
meals food consumed at specific times of day
mess food eaten by a group together, esp. soldiers
morsel small portion of food
nourishment food eaten for sustenance
nutriment food taken as nourishment
provisions supply of food
rations supply of food, esp. for soldiers
refection food eaten esp. after interval of hunger
refreshment food and drink, esp. taken to restore energy
scraps bits of food remaining after completion of meal, often discarded
slop unappealing food, esp. leftovers
sustenance any substance consumed to keep one alive
swill unappealing food, often table scraps
tidbit small morsel of food
treat any food one particularly likes, esp. a sweet
tucker food (Australia)
viand food, esp. choice dish
victuals food; provisions
vittles victuals (colloq. spelling)

Types of Food

additive often chemical substance added to improve some aspect of food, esp. as preservative or flavor enhancer
aromatic any of certain herbs, spices, or

vegetables, such as onions, garlic, or shallots, that give off a distinctive flavor and aroma

beverage liquid food

bread baked food, usu. made from flour or meal mixed with water and yeast

cake baked, sweetened dough, often frosted

candy flavored food sweetened with sugar or syrup, usu. in small chunks

cereal grain produced from grass

cheese solidified form of ripened curds of soured milk

condiment substance eaten with another food to add flavor

confection any sweet, esp. one prepared with fruit

cookie small, sweet cake

cracker thin, crisp, often unleavened bread

cut part of an animal's flesh cut as one piece

dairy food derived from milk, esp. cow's milk

dessert usu. sweet substance eaten at end of meal

dressing sauce or stuffing

fat greasy substance forming most of adipose tissue of animals

fish flesh of cold-blooded vertebrate animal living in water

flour fine powder of ground grain

fruit edible portion of mature, flowering plant

fungus edible, growing, parasitic organism

game flesh of wild birds or animals

grain small, hard seed of certain cereal grasses

herb seed plant used esp. as seasoning

leavening substance that causes baked goods to rise

legume pod or seed of certain herbs or shrubs

meat flesh of animals, esp. mammals and fowl

noodle flat strip of dough

nut edible kernel of certain one-seeded fruits

oil greasy liquid obtained from animal, mineral, or vegetable, used in cooking

pasta flour or semolina dough dried in various shapes

pastry fancy, sweetened baked goods

pâté paste of meat, animal organs, and seasonings

poultry flesh of fowl

pulse edible seeds of certain legumes, such as peas, beans, or lentils

roll small bread

salad combination of usu. raw, chopped vegetables

sauce liquid flavoring or dressing added to other foods

sausage chopped, seasoned meat, usu. stuffed into thin casing

seafood fish or shellfish and their parts

seasoning herb or spice, used to enhance flavor of food

seed edible, mature ovule of flowering plant

shellfish flesh of invertebrate, aquatic animal covered by hard shell

shortening butter, lard, or fat, used to make pastry or bread flaky and crumbly

soup liquid food, usu. with bits of solid food,
made by cooking meat, fish, vegetables, and seasonings in water

spice portion of plant, esp. seed or leaf, used to season food

stew mixture, esp. of meat and vegetables, cooked in liquid

sweetener sugar or syrup used to make food sweet

syrup thick, sweet liquid prepared from sugar, molasses, or glucose

vegetable edible plant

Meats and Cuts of Meat

meat flesh of mammals raised to be eaten, esp. cattle, pigs, and sheep

bacon, beef, beefburger, braciola, brains, breast, brisket, burger, butt, butterfly
Canadian bacon, center loin chop, charqui, Châteaubriand, chitterlings, chops, cold cuts, corned beef, cutlet
filet mignon, flanken, flitch
gizzards, goat
ham (Danish, picnic, prosciutto, Serrano, Smithfield, Virginia, Westphalian), **hamburger, hock**
jerky, joint
kid, kidney, knuckles
lamb, liver, loin chop
marrow, medallion, mountain oysters, mutton
noisette, numbles
oxtail
pastrami, pig's feet, pork, prairie oysters
rack, red meat, ribs, roast (blade, chuck, crown, eye of round, pot, rack, rib, rolled, round, rump, shoulder, sirloin tip, standing rib)
saddle, salt pork, short ribs, shoulder chop, slab bacon, spare ribs, steak (blade, club, cube, Delmonico, fillet, flank, hamburger, New York, porterhouse, rib, rib eye, round, rump, saddle, Salisbury, shank, shell, shoulder, sirloin, skirt, Spencer, strip, T-bone, tenderloin, top loin, top round), **sweetbreads**
tongue, tournedos, tripe
umbles
veal

Sausage and Pâté

pâté paste of meat, animal organs, and seasonings

sausage chopped, seasoned meat, usu. stuffed into thin casing

andouillettes
bangers, blood sausage, bologna, boudin blanc, boudin noir, Bratwurst, Braunschweiger
chicken liver pâté, chorizo
duck sausage
fish sausage, foie gras, forcemeat, frank, frankfurter
galantine, Genoa salami
head cheese, hot dog, hot link
Italian sausage
kielbasa, knockwurst, kosher salami
linguica, liver pâté, liverwurst
merguez, mortadella, mulliatelle
pâté de foie gras, pâté de campagne, pâté en croûte, pork sausage
salami, saucisse, saucisson, sausage, scrapple
terrine

Vienna sausage
weenie, wiener, wurst
zampone

Poultry and Game

game flesh of wild birds or animals

poultry flesh of fowl raised to be eaten

bear, boar
capon, chicken (broiler, free range, fryer, roaster, stewer), **Cornish hen**
deer, duck
fowl, frog legs
game, goose, grouse, guinea fowl
hare
partridge, pheasant, pigeon, pullet
quail
rabbit
squab
turkey
venison
wild turkey

Fish and Shellfish

fish flesh of cold-blooded vertebrate animals living in water

shellfish flesh of invertebrate, aquatic animals covered by hard shells

abalone, anchovy, angelfish
bacalao, bass, blackfish, bluefish, bonito, brisling, butterfish
calamari, catfish, caviar, clam, cod, codfish, conch, coral, crab, crawdad, crawfish, crayfish
eel, escargot
finnan haddie, flounder
gravlax, grunion
haddock, halibut, herring
John Dory
kipper
langoustine, lobster, lotte, lox
mackerel, mahimahi, milt, monk, mussel
octopus, orange roughy, oyster
perch, pompano, prawn
red snapper, roe
salmon, sand dab, sardine, scallop, scampi, scrod, scungilli, sea bass, sea urchin, shark, shrimp, skate, smelt, smoked salmon, snail, snapper, softshell crab, sole, sprat, squid, striped bass, sturgeon, surimi, swordfish
teal, terrapin, tile, tomalley, trout, tuna, turbot
weak, whitefish
yellowtail

Dairy Foods

dairy food food derived from milk, esp. cow's milk

bonnyclabber, butter
cheese, clabber, cream, crème fraîche, curds
eggs
goat's milk
half-and-half, heavy cream
ice cream
kefir
leben, light cream
milk (buttermilk, condensed, dry, evaporated, homogenized, lowfat, nonfat, pasteurized, raw, skim, whole)
sour cream, sweet butter
ultrapasteurized heavy cream

whey, whipping cream
yogurt

Cheese

cheese solidified form of ripened curds of soured milk

American
Banon, Bel Paese, blue, Boursin, brick, Brie
Caciocavallo, Caerphilly, Camembert, cheddar, Cheshire, chèvre, Chevret, clabber, coeur à la crème, colby, comte, coon cheese, cottage cheese, cream cheese, crema Danica
Danish blue, Derby, Dunlop
Edam, Edelpilzkäse, Emmenthaler, Epoisses
farmer's cheese, feta, fontina, fromage blanc
Gammelost, Gjetost, Gloucester, goat cheese, Gorgonzola, Gouda, Gruyère
Havarti, hoop cheese
jack cheese, Jarlsberg
Kumminost
Lancashire, Leicester, Liederkranz, Limburger, Liptauer, Livarot, long horn
Maroilles, Mimolette, Monterey Jack, Montrachet, mozzarella, muenster
Neufchâtel
Parmesan, Pecorino, Pont L'Évêque, Port-Salut, pot cheese, processed cheese, provolone
Quargel
rat cheese, red Windsor, ricotta, Romano, Roquefort
sapsago, smoked cheese, Stilton, St. Marcellin, string cheese, Swiss
Teleme, Tillamook, Tilsit
Vacherin, Velveeta
Wensleydale, white cheddar

Vegetables, Legumes, and Fungi

fungus edible, growing, parasitic organism
legume pod or seed of certain herbs or shrubs
vegetable edible plant, eaten raw or cooked

alfalfa sprout, artichoke, arugula, asparagus, aubergine
bamboo shoot, bean (aduki, black, broad, butter, chickpea, fava, garbanzo, green, haricot, kidney, lentil, lima, mung, navy, northern, pink, pinto, red, soya, string, wax, white), bean sprout, beet, Bermuda onion, black-eyed pea, bok choy, broccoli, Brussels sprout
cabbage, cactus, cardoon, carrot, cassava, cauliflower, celeriac, celery, chard, chayote, chicory, Chinese cabbage, chive, collard greens, corn, courgette, cowpea, cress, cucumber
daikon, dandelion greens
eggplant, endive, escarole
finocchio
green bean, green onion
Japanese eggplant, Jerusalem artichoke
kale, kohlrabi
leek, lettuce (Bibb, Boston, butter, corn salad, cos, curly, green leaf, iceberg, mache, red leaf, romaine), lovage
maize, manioc, mung sprout, mushroom (black, button, champignon, chanterelle, enoki, fungi, morel, oyster, porcini, shiitake, tree ear), mustard greens
nopal, nori
okra, onion, oyster plant

parsnip, pea (black-eyed, green, snow, split, sugar), pearl onion, pepper (bell, capsicum, chile, green, Italian, jalapeño, pimiento, red, serrano, wax, yellow), potato, pumpkin
radiccio, radish, rampion, ramson, red cabbage, red onion, rhubarb, rutabaga
salsify, scallion, seaweed, shallot, snap bean, sorrel, soybean, spinach, sprout, squash (acorn, butternut, crookneck, cymling, spaghetti, summer, winter, yellow, zucchini), string bean, succory, sugar pea, sweet potato, Swiss chard
taro root, tomatillo, tomato, truffle, turnip
water chestnut, watercress, wax bean
yam
zucchini

Fruits

fruit edible portion of mature flowering plant

ananas, apple (Baldwin, delicious, empire, golden, Granny Smith, gravenstein, Jonathan, Macintosh, macoun, pippin, Rome, winesap), apricot, atemoya, avocado
banana, berry (bilberry, bearberry, blackberry, black raspberry, blueberry, boysenberry, candleberry, checkerberry, cloudberry, cranberry, dewberry, elderberry, gooseberry, huckleberry, lingonberry, loganberry, mulberry, raspberry, strawberry, whortleberry), black currant, blood orange, breadfruit, bullace
calmyrna, canistel, carambola, cherimoya, cherry, citron, clementine, coconut, copra, crabapple, currant, custard apple
damson plum, date, durian
fig
granadilla, grape (Cabernet Sauvignon, cardinal Chardonnay, Chenin Blanc, Concord, Delaware, Italia, Merlot, Muscadet, muscat, Pinot Blanc, Pinot Noir, Riesling, seedless, Thompson seedless, Tokay, zinfandel), grapefruit, greengage, guava
jackfruit, jujube
kiwi, kumquat
lemon, lime, loquat
mandarin orange, mango, medlar, melon (cantaloupe, casaba, Crenshaw, honeydew, muskmelon, Persian, watermelon, winter melon)
naartje, navel orange, nectarine
olive, orange, ortanique
papaya, passion fruit, pawpaw, peach, pear (Anjou, Bosc, Bartlett, Comice, winter nellis), pepino, persimmon, pineapple, pitahaya, plantain, plum, pomegranate, pomelo, prickly pear, prune, pummelo
quince, quinoa
raisin, rambutan
sapodilla, sapote, satsuma, soursop, spanspek
tamarillo, tamarind, tangelo, tangerine
ugli fruit
Valencia orange

Nuts and Seeds

nut edible kernel of certain one-seeded fruits
seed fertilized, matured ovule of certain flowering plants, usu. eaten dried

acorn, almond
beechnut, ben, betel, black walnut, Brazil, butternut
candlenut, cashew, chestnut, chinquapin, cobnut, corozo
dika
filbert
grugru
hazelnut, hickory, horse chestnut
kola
litchi
macadamia
palm, peanut, pecan, physic nut, pignola, pine, pistachio, pumpkinseed
quinoa
sassafras, sesame seed, souari nut, sunflower seed
walnut

Herbs and Spices

herb seed plant used esp. as seasoning
spice portion of plant, esp. seed or leaf, used to season food

achiote, allspice, angelica, anise, asafetida
basil, bay leaf, benne seed, berbere, black pepper, borage, bouquet garni
cacao, calamint, capers, caraway seed, cardamom, carob, cayenne, celery seed, chervil, chicory, chili pepper, chili powder, Chinese parsley, chives, cilantro, cinnamon, cloves, coriander, cubeb, cumin, curly parsley, curry
dill
elephant garlic
fennel, fenugreek, fines herbes, finochio, flaxseed
garam masala, garlic, ginger, green peppercorn
iodized salt, Italian parsley
juniper berry
kosher salt
lemon basil, lemon grass, licorice, lovage
mace, marjoram, mint, mustard
nutmeg
oregano
paprika, parsley, pepper, pepper flakes, peppermint, pickling spice, poppy seed, pumpkin seed
red pepper, rock salt, rosemary
saffron, sage, salt, sea salt, sesame seed, shallots, sorrel, St. John's-bread, summer savory, sunflower seed, sweet basil
table salt, tarragon, thyme, turmeric
vanilla
white pepper

Grains and Flours

flour fine powder of ground grain, used esp. in baking
grain small, hard seed of certain cereal grasses

barley, blue cornmeal, bran, buckwheat, bulghur
corn, cornmeal, couscous
farina, flour (bleached, enriched, gluten, pastry, rice, rye, semolina, unbleached, wheat, white)
grits, groats
hominy
kasha
masa, millet
oat bran, oats
polenta

rice (basmati, brown, enriched, long-grain, minute, quick-cooking, short-grain, white), rye
semolina
wheat, wheat germ, wild rice

Pasta and Noodles

noodle flat strip of dough
pasta flour or semolina dough dried in various shapes
angel hair
bucatini
cannelloni, cappelletti, chow fun noodles, chow mein noodles, conchiglie
dumpling
egg noodles
farfel, fettuccine, fettucelle, fusilli
gelatin noodles, glass noodles, gnocchi
knodel, kreplach
lasagne, linguine, lo mein noodles
macaroni, mafalde, manicotti, mostaccioli
noodles
penne
quenelle
ravioli, rice, rigatoni, rotelli, rotini
soba, spaetzle, spaghetti, spaghettini
tagliatelle, tortellini
vermicelli
won ton
ziti

Cereals

cereal grain produced from grass, used esp. as breakfast food
Cheerios, Chex, corn flakes, Cream of Wheat
Frosted Flakes
granola, Grape Nuts, grits, gruel
mush
oatmeal, porridge, puffed rice
Raisin Bran, Rice Krispies, rolled oats
Shredded Wheat
Wheaties

Breads, Rolls, and Crackers

bread baked food, usu. made from flour or meal mixed with water and yeast
cracker thin, crisp, often unleavened bread
roll small bread
anadama bread
bagel, baguette, bialy, biscuit, black bread, bran muffin, breadcrumbs, breadstick, brioche, brown bread, bun
challah, chapati, cheese bread, cornbread, corn dodger, cracknel, crisp, croissant, crouton
egg bread, English muffin
French bread
garlic bread, graham cracker
hardtack, hush puppy
johnny cake
matzo, melba toast, muffin
nan, nut bread
oatcake
papadam, pita, poori, popover, pretzel, pumpernickel bread
raisin bread, roll (cinnamon, dinner, hard, Kaiser, onion, Parker House, sourdough), rusk, rye bread
saltine, seeded rye bread, semolina bread, ship

biscuit, sippet, soda biscuit, soda bread, sourdough bread
toast, tortilla
unleavened bread
wafer, water biscuit, whole-grain bread, whole-wheat bread
yeast cake
zwieback

Cakes

cake baked or pan-cooked, sweetened dough, often frosted
angel food cake
Banbury tart, Battenberg cake
cheesecake, chocolate cake, coffeecake, cupcake
devil's food cake
fruitcake
gâteau, genoise, gingerbread
honey cake
jelly roll
kuchen
layer cake, loaf cake
marble cake
pancake (battercake, blini, blintz, buckwheat, crêpe, flapjack, griddle cake, hotcake, johnnycake, latke, potato, waffle), pound cake
Sacher torte, sally lunn, savarin, shortcake, simnel cake, spice cake, sponge cake, stollen
tart, tartlet, teacake, torte
upside-down cake
waffle, wedding cake, white cake
yellow cake

Pastry

pastry fancy, sweetened baked good, often with filling
baba au rum, baklava, beignet, berry pie, Boston cream pie
cake, cornet, cream pie, cream puff, crescent, cruller, crumpet
Danish, doughnut
Eccles cake, éclair
feuilletée, frangipane, fritter, fruit pie
jelly doughnut
madeleine, meringue pie, mille-feuilles
napoleon
pain au chocolat, pâté à choux, petit four, phyllo, pie, profiterole, puff
quiche
schnecken, scone, shoo-fly pie, sopaipilla, strudel, sweet roll
tart, timbale, turnover
Washington pie

Cookies

cookie small, sweet cake
animal cracker
bar, biscuit, brandy snap, brownie, butter
chocolate chip cookie
fig bar, florentine, fortune cookie
garibaldi, gingersnap
hermit
jumble
lady finger
macaroon
oatmeal cookie, Oreo
palm leaf, panettone, peanut butter cookie

ratafia
shortbread, sugar cookie
tollhouse
wafer

Candy

candy flavored food sweetened with sugar or syrup, usu. in small chunks
bark, bonbon, brittle, butterscotch
candy bar, candy cane, caramel, chocolate, chocolate bar, confection, cotton candy
fondant, frosting, fudge
halvah
icing
jawbreaker, jellybean, jimmies, jujube
kiss
lemon drop, licorice, Lifesaver, lollipop
marchpane, marshmallow, marzipan, mint, M'n'M
nonpareil, nougat
peanut brittle, penuche, peppermint, praline
rock candy
saltwater taffy, sweets
taffy, toffee, Turkish delight, tutti-frutti

Desserts

dessert usu. sweet substance eaten at end of meal, often frozen or baked
apple pandowdy
baked Alaska, banana split, Bavarian cream, blocking pudding, blancmange, bombe, Boston cream pie, brown betty
cannoli, cassata, charlotte russe, clafoutis, cobbler, compote, coupe, crème brûlée, crème caramel, crêpe suzette, custard
deep dish pie, duff
Edinburgh fog, flan
floating island, flummery, frappé, frozen custard, frozen dessert, frozen yogurt, fruit cup, frumenty
gelato, glacé, granita
ice cream, ice cream bar, ice cream sandwich, Indian pudding, Italian ice
Jell-O
marrons glacés, meringue, moor-in-a-shirt, mousse, mud pie
parfait, pashka, peach Melba, pie, poached pear, pudding
rice pudding
Sacher torte, sherbet, snow cone, snow pudding, sorbet, soufflé, strawberry shortcake, streusel, sundae, syllabub
tiramisu, tortoni, trifle
vacherin
zabaglione, zuppa inglese

Dessert Sauces

dessert sauce sweet liquid used as flavoring or dressing over dessert
butterscotch
charlotte russe, chocolate, crème Anglais, crème Chantilly, crème pâtissière
frangipane
hard sauce, hot fudge
marshmallow
Nesselrode
pineapple
topping

Sweeteners

sweetener sugar or syrup used to make food sweet

  corn syrup
  fructose
  honey
  Karo syrup
  maple sugar, maple syrup, molasses
  sorghum, sugar (barley, brown, cane, caramel, castor, confectioner's, cube, granulated, icing, light brown, powdered, raw, spun, superfine), syrup
  treacle

Cooking Fats and Oils

fat greasy substance forming most of adipose tissue of animals

oil greasy liquid obtained from animal, mineral, or vegetable source, used in cooking

  almond oil, avocado oil
  bacon fat, butter
  canola, chicken fat, cocoa butter, coconut oil, corn oil, cottonseed oil, Crisco
  drippings
  extra virgin olive oil
  fat
  ghee, goose grease, grapeseed oil
  hazelnut oil
  lard
  margarine
  oleomargarine, olive oil
  partially hydrogenated vegetable oil, peanut oil
  rapeseed, rendered chicken fat
  safflower oil, schmaltz, sesame oil, shortening, solid vegetable shortening, soya oil, soybean oil, suet, sunflower oil
  vegetable oil, virgin olive oil
  walnut oil, wheat germ oil

Additives and Thickening and Leavening Agents

additive often chemical substance added to improve some aspect of food, esp. as preservative or to enhance flavor

leavening substance that causes baked goods to rise

  agar, alum, arrowroot
  baking powder, baking soda, brewer's yeast
  cornstarch, cream of tartar
  food coloring, flour
  gelatin
  hydrolyzed vegetable protein
  isinglass
  lecithin
  monosodium glutamate, MSG
  neat's-foot jelly
  potato flour
  rennet, roux
  sago, sodium benzoate, starter
  tapioca, tomato paste
  yeast

Salad Dressings

salad dressing usu. sharply flavored liquid mixture poured over raw vegetable salad

  aioli
  blue cheese
  creamy garlic, creamy Italian
  French
  honey Dijon
  Italian
  oil and vinegar
  ranch, Russian
  Thousand Island
  vinaigrette

Sauces

sauce liquid flavoring or dressing of mixed ingredients added to other foods

  aioli, allemande, A-1 sauce, applesauce
  barbecue, Béarnaise, béchamel, Bercy, Bordelaise, brown
  chasseur, chili, cranberry, cream, curry
  diable, duck
  espagnole
  giblet gravy, gravy
  hoisin, hollandaise sauce, hot sauce
  marinara, mayonnaise, mole, Mornay, mousseline, mushroom
  nantua
  oyster
  pan gravy, pesto, pistou
  ravigote, red-eye gravy, rémoulade
  satay, soubise, soy sauce, suprême, sweet-and-sour sauce
  Tabasco, tahini, tamari, tartar, tomato sauce
  velouté
  white, Worcestershire sauce

Condiments

condiment substance eaten with another food to add flavor

  anchovy, angostura bitters, aspic
  bread and butter pickle, brine
  caper, catsup, chutney, confiture, conserves, cornichon
  dill pickle
  gherkin
  horseradish
  jalapeño relish
  ketchup
  jam, jelly
  lemon curd, lemon peel
  marmalade, mustard
  picante sauce, piccalilli, pickle, pimiento, preserves
  relish, rosewater
  salsa, sambal, sweet pickle
  tahini
  vinegar (balsamic, cider, malt, red wine, rice wine, white wine)
  wasabi
  zest

Soups and Stews

soup liquid food, usu. with bits of solid food, made by cooking meat, fish, vegetables, and seasonings in water or milk

stew mixture, esp. of meat and vegetables, cooked in liquid

  alphabet soup, avgolemono
  beef broth, beef stew, bird's-nest soup, bisque, blanquette, borscht, bouillabaise, bouillon, broth, Brunswick stew, burgoo
  callaloo, caldo verde, chicken broth, chicken
  noodle soup, chicken soup, cholent, chowder, cioppino, civet, cock-a-leekie, consommé, cream soup, cullis
  daube
  egg drop soup
  fumet
  gazpacho, goulash, gumbo
  hasenpfeffer, hot and sour soup
  lobscouse
  madrilène, matelote, matzo ball soup, menudo, minestrone, miso soup, mulligan, mulligatawny, mushroom, navarin
  olla podrida, onion soup, oxtail soup
  pepper pot, potage
  ragout, ramen, rassolnik
  Scotch broth, shark's fin soup, slumgullion, split pea soup, stock
  tomato soup, turtle soup, tzimmes
  vegetable soup, vichyssoise
  won ton soup

Beverages

beverage liquid food

  ambrosia, apple juice
  barley water, beef tea, beer, birch beer, black tea, bouillon, buttermilk
  café au lait, café filtre, café noir, caffé latte, cappuccino, chocolate milk, cider, club soda, cocoa, coconut milk, coffee, cola, cordial, cranberry juice, cream soda
  Darjeeling tea, decaf(feinated coffee)
  Earl Grey tea, egg cream, eggnog, espresso
  float, frappe, fruit juice
  ginger ale, ginger beer, ginseng tea, grapefruit juice, grape juice, green tea
  herb tea, hot chocolate
  ice cream soda
  kava, kefir, kumiss
  lemonade, limeade, lime rickey, liqueur
  malted, maté, milk, milk shake, mineral water, mixer, mocha, mulled cider
  nectar
  orangeade, orange juice, orange pekoe tea
  phosphate, pineapple juice, punch
  root beer
  Sanka, sarsaparilla, seltzer, shrub, soda water, soybean milk, spice tea, spirits, syllabub
  tea, tisane, tomato juice, tonic water, Turkish coffee
  vegetable juice
  water (branch, distilled, mineral, seltzer, soda, sparkling, spring, tap, Vichy) whiskey, wine

COOKING AND CUISINE
Preparations and Presentations
Cooking Techniques
Cuisines, Meals, and Restaurants
Cooks and Servers
Prepared Dishes

See also: *Chap. 9: Foods; The Kitchen*

Preparations and Presentations

à la king (*adj*) served with cream sauce

à la mode (*adj*) in the style of; served with ice cream

al burro (*adj*) served with butter

al dente (*adj*) firm to the bite
amandine (*adj*) served with almonds
anglaise (*adj*) boiled
argenteuil (*adj*) with asparagus
aspic jellied stock or juice
au bleu (*adj*) poached instantly upon being killed
au fromage (*adj*) with cheese
au gratin (*adj*) covered with sauce and crumbs; toasted
au jus (*adj*) served with natural juices
au naturel (*adj*) uncooked or cooked simply
beurre blanc butter, shallots, and wine
beurre manie flour kneaded with fat for sauce base
beurre noir browned butter with vinegar and capers
bouquet garni herb mixture in cheesecloth, removed after cooking
broth liquid in which meat, fish, grains, or vegetables have been cooked; stock
brunoise diced vegetables, used as sauce or stock base
cacciatore (*adj*) hunter's style; containing tomatoes, mushrooms, herbs, and other seasonings
calzone folded pizza
canapé small, savory sandwich appetizer on toast, cracker, or crustless bread
chasseur (*adj*) brown sauce usu. containing tomatoes, mushrooms, shallots, and white wine
chiffonade mixture of minced herbs and vegetables, used in soups
clamart (*adj*) with peas
clean (*vb*) remove unwanted portions of raw food prior to cooking or serving
clotted cream cream thickened by cooking; Devonshire cream
consommé clear soup made from stock
cracklings crisp residue left after rendering hog or chicken fat
Crécy (*adj*) with carrots
creole (*adj*) spicy sauce or dish, usu. with rice
crêpes thin pancakes rolled with filling or jam
croustade baked or fried pastry shell, sometimes made of noodles, rice, or mashed potatoes, filled with ragout
dauphine (*adj*) with straw potatoes
Devonshire cream clotted cream
dough flour or meal combined with water or milk and shortening, to be shaped and baked
drawn butter melted, clarified butter, often seasoned
dress (*vb*) prepare for cooking or serving
drippings juices and fats from roast meat or poultry, used as base for gravy
drizzle (*vb*) sprinkle drops of liquid lightly over food
dunk (*vb*) dip a cake or bread into liquid before eating
dust (*vb*) sprinkle food with a dry ingredient
duxelles coarse hash of mushrooms and shallots sautéed
en brochette (*adj*) cut into chunks and broiled on a skewer

en croûte (*adj*) encased in pastry and baked
entremets vegetables or savories served with main course
espagnole (*adj*) with brown sauce
estragon (*adj*) with tarragon
étouffée (*adj*) smothered
farci (*adj*) stuffed
flambé (*adj*) served aflame after dousing with potable alcohol
florentine (*adj*) with spinach
flute (*vb*) form scalloped or undulating edge on pastry
fondue melted cheese with flavorings
forcemeat mixture of minced meat with egg white, used esp. as stuffing
forestière (*adj*) with mushrooms and bacon
fumet reduced stock, esp. fish
galantine boned, stuffed meat in aspic
garnish (*vb*) decorate with edible ornaments, such as parsley
grecque (*adj*) with olive oil and lemon
grind (*vb*) reduce solid food to small particles
hash fried, chopped meat and vegetables
hold (*vb*) serve dish without some usual ingredient or garnish, which is held back
hull (*vb*) remove leaves and stem of soft fruit
Indienne (*adj*) with curry
jardiniere (*adj*) with variety of fresh vegetables
julienne (*vb*) cut into matchstick-shaped pieces
kabob skewered, grilled cubes of meat and vegetables
lardon strip of fat drawn through meat with a needle
lyonnaise (*adj*) with onions
macédoine assortment of chopped fruits or vegetables
maître d'hôtel sauce of melted butter, minced parsley, and lemon juice or vinegar
marinière (*adj*) cooked in white wine, esp. fish
mask (*vb*) enhance appearance or taste of food by adding sauce or garnish
meatballs small spheres of ground meat cooked and served with sauce, soup, or pasta
meunière (*adj*) with browned butter, lemon, and parsley
mirepoix bed of cut vegetables on which to cook food
nesselrode (*adj*) with chestnuts
Newburg (*adj*) with cream, egg yolk, butter, and paprika sauce
niçoise (*adj*) with tomatoes, garlic, and olive oil
normande (*adj*) cooked with cider and cream
omelette sautéed eggs mixed with or folded around other ingredients
over easy (*adj*) describing fried egg that is flipped over and cooked briefly before serving
pancake egg and flour batter fried into circular cakes on griddle
papillote (*adj*) wrapped and cooked in greased paper or foil
parmentier (*adj*) with potatoes
patty thin, round, molded piece of ground or minced food; piece of food covered with batter and fried or baked

peel (*vb*) remove outer skin or layer of food, esp. of vegetable or fruit
périgord (*adj*) with truffles
piccata (*adj*) with lemon and parsley, also sometimes with capers
pipe (*vb*) squeeze soft mixture through pastry tube to form decorations or squeeze dough onto baking sheet
pizza circular, flat bread baked with cheese and tomato topping
plump (*vb*) soak dried fruits in liquid until they swell
Provençale (*adj*) with tomatoes, garlic, onions, and herbs
quiche savory egg custard tart with filling
rare (*adj*) cooked briefly, esp. meat
ripieno (*adj*) stuffed
roast meat, game, or poultry cooked over fire or in oven
roulade rolled, stuffed slice of meat or pastry
roux mixture of melted fat and flour, used as sauce base
salad fresh greens and other ingredients served cold and usu. raw: Caesar, chef's, coleslaw, composed, green, niçoise, pasta, potato, salmagundi, slaw, tabbouleh, tossed, Waldorf
sandwich assorted cold meats and fillings between bread slices: BLT, club, cold cuts, Cuban, Dagwood, double-decker, grinder, hero, hoagie, Italian sandwich, poor boy, Reuben, Sloppy Joe, submarine, torpedo, triple-decker, wedge
sashimi raw fish cut into very thin slices, arranged with ginger and wasabi horseradish
savory (*adj*) piquant and not sweet
scallopine thinly sliced, flour-dredged, sautéed meat
short (*adj*) crisp, flaky, and crumbling, esp. pastry
stack pile of pancakes
sticks food sliced or shaped into long pieces, often fried
stock meat, fish, or poultry broth, esp. when stored for use at later time
stroganoff (*adj*) with sour cream and mushrooms
subgum (*adj*) prepared with mixed vegetables in Chinese style
sunnyside up (*adj*) describing egg fried on one side only
tandoori (*adj*) baked in a clay tandoor oven
temper (*vb*) prepare egg for immersion in hot liquid
unmold (*vb*) remove from mold without losing shape
vacuum-packed (*adj*) sealed in a jar or can with nearly all air evacuated before sealing to preserve freshness
Véronique (*adj*) garnished with white grapes
vol-au-vent flaky pastry shell for filling with meat or vegetables and sauce
well done (*adj*) thoroughly cooked until all redness is gone, esp. meat
whitebait any small fish, esp. sprat, cooked whole without being cleaned

zest outer peel of citrus fruit, used for flavoring

Cooking Techniques

bake (*vb*) cook with dry oven heat

barbecue (*vb*) cook over hot coals on grill or spit; grill

bard (*vb*) wrap meat with thin sheets of fat before roasting to prevent drying out

baste (*vb*) spoon liquid over food to moisten it while cooking

batter (*vb*) coat with flour, eggs, and breadcrumbs before frying

beat (*vb*) blend ingredients with rapid, rotary motion

blacken (*vb*) cook meat or fish over high, direct heat

blanch (*vb*) rinse or cook briefly in boiling water

blend (*vb*) stir ingredients together

boil (*vb*) heat to boiling point

boil down (*vb*) boil until reduced in volume

braise (*vb*) brown in fat, then cover and cook in liquid

bread (*vb*) coat with breadcrumbs

broil (*vb*) cook with hot coals or direct flame

brown (*vb*) sear surface of meat in pan, broiler, or oven to seal juices

bruise (*vb*) crush partially to release flavor

butterfly (*vb*) cut open and flatten

can (*vb*) preserve by sealing in airtight can or jar

candy (*vb*) cook in heavy syrup until glazed; coat with sugar

caramelize (*vb*) cook sugar until it forms brown syrup

carbonado (*vb*) score and broil, usu. meat

casserole (*vb*) bake mixed ingredients in casserole dish

charbroil (*vb*) broil or grill until blackened on outside

chop (*vb*) cut loosely and rapidly into small pieces

churn (*vb*) agitate milk in a container to make butter

clarify (*vb*) purify solid matter from fats or stock

coddle (*vb*) cook in water just below boiling point

concentrate (*vb*) make less dilute

cream (*vb*) blend until creamy and soft

crisp (*vb*) make brittle, usu. by frying

crystallize (*vb*) coat with sugar

cube (*vb*) cut into cube-shaped pieces

curdle (*vb*) coagulate, esp. milk; turn sour

cure (*vb*) prepare meat or fish for preservation by smoking, drying, or salting

cut in (*vb*) incorporate shortening into flour using two knives, so that mixture resembles uneven, coarse crumbs

deep fry (*vb*) cook by entirely submerging in hot fat

deglaze (*vb*) dissolve browned particles with liquid in sauté pan

degrease (*vb*) remove accumulated fat from surface of hot liquid

dehydrate (*vb*) remove moisture from, esp. to preserve

desiccate (*vb*) preserve by drying or dehydrating

devein (*vb*) remove dark dorsal vein from shrimp

devil (*vb*) season with mustard, cayenne, and other hot spices

dice (*vb*) cut into small cubes

draw (*vb*) remove entrails

dredge (*vb*) coat with flour, sugar, or crumbs

dry (*vb*) remove moisture from

dry-roast (*vb*) roast without oil, esp. nuts

enrich (*vb*) restore nutrients that have been lost in processing

eviscerate (*vb*) remove entrails from

fillet (*vb*) remove bones, esp. backbone from fish

flake (*vb*) break apart along natural separations

flash-freeze (*vb*) quick-freeze

fold (*vb*) blend ingredients lightly and gently so as to retain air

force (*vb*) stuff

freeze-dry (*vb*) dry a heat-sensitive food by freezing it and converting the ice to vapor in a high vacuum

fricassee (*vb*) cut up, brown, then cook in liquid

frizzle (*vb*) form into small, crisp curls, esp. by frying

fry (*vb*) cook in hot fat, either in deep fat or by pan-frying

glaze (*vb*) cover with glossy coating of juices, aspic, syrup, or egg

grate (*vb*) shred into particles or strips

gratiné (*vb*) bake or broil with sauce and crumbs in au gratin style

grill (*vb*) cook on open grid over hot coals; barbecue

hard-boil (*vb*) boil an egg until white and yolk solidify

homogenize (*vb*) prepare emulsion of milk by reducing size of fat globules to distribute them equally throughout

knead (*vb*) mix and work dough with one's hands

lard (*vb*) stuff meat with slices of fat

macerate (*vb*) steep in liquid, esp. liqueur

marinate (*vb*) soak in seasoned broth, juices, or wine

mash (*vb*) reduce food, usu. boiled, to soft, pulpy mass by pressure

microwave (*vb*) cook in a microwave oven

mince (*vb*) chop finely

mix (*vb*) blend evenly

mold (*vb*) form into firm shape

nap (*vb*) cover with sauce that adheres to outline of food

pan-broil (*vb*) cook in uncovered frying pan over direct heat, using little or no fat

pan-fry (*vb*) fry in small amount of fat in skillet or shallow pan; sauté

parboil (*vb*) partially cook by boiling

pare (*vb*) remove skin or peel

pickle (*vb*) preserve in spiced brine

poach (*vb*) cook in liquid at or near boiling

preserve (*vb*) prepare fruit or vegetable by cooking with sugar, pickling, or canning, so as to resist spoilage

purée (*vb*) put solid food through sieve or blender or mash in mortar

quick-freeze (*vb*) freeze cooked or uncooked food very rapidly to facilitate lengthy storage; flash-freeze

raise (*vb*) make light by using yeast but not baking powder or soda

reconstitute (*vb*) return to liquid state by adding water

reduce (*vb*) cook liquid to decrease quantity and concentrate flavor

refresh (*vb*) plunge hot food into cold water to halt cooking

render (*vb*) remove animal fat

rice (*vb*) break soft food into small bits by forcing it through ricer

ripen (*vb*) advance or bring to maturity or best condition for use, esp. cheese

roast (*vb*) cook with dry oven heat, esp. meats

salt (*vb*) cure or preserve meat or fish by coating with salt

sauté (*vb*) brown quickly in small quantity of hot fat; pan-fry

scald (*vb*) heat food just to boiling point

scallop (*vb*) bake in layers topped with breadcrumbs

score (*vb*) cut surface of food

scramble (*vb*) stir vigorously and then cook in pan while stirring

sear (*vb*) brown surface quickly with high heat

shirr (*vb*) bake in shallow dish, esp. eggs

shred (*vb*) cut or grate into thin, irregular strips

sift (*vb*) remove lumps from dry ingredient by passing it through strainer or sieve

simmer (*vb*) cook in gently boiling water

slice (*vb*) cut lengthwise or crosswise into long or round pieces

smother (*vb*) steam slowly in heavy, closed vessel with minimal liquid

soft-boil (*vb*) boil an egg until white and yolk partially solidify, usu. for three to four minutes

souse (*vb*) pickle in vinegar or brine

steam (*vb*) cook over boiling water without allowing food to touch the water

steep (*vb*) pour boiling water over food and allow it to sit

stew (*vb*) simmer for a long time

stir (*vb*) mix with rotary motion

stir-fry (*vb*) cook quickly over high heat in wok or large fry pan

stuff (*vb*) fill cavity with seasonings, grains, or chopped vegetables; force

sweat (*vb*) cook vegetables or fruits slowly to release their juices

thread (*vb*) form a fine stream when poured boiling from a spoon

toast (*vb*) brown surface on grill, oven, or toaster, esp. bread

toss (*vb*) mix by flipping ingredients together

truss (*vb*) tie or sew legs and wings of poultry while roasting

whip (*vb*) beat lightly to incorporate air and increase volume

whisk (*vb*) beat vigorously until mixed or blended

Cuisines, Meals, and Restaurants

à la carte (*adj*) designating foods priced and chosen separately by dish

alfresco (*adj*) eaten outdoors

antipasto assorted Italian appetizers, esp. marinated vegetables and sliced meats

appetizers snacks; small items eaten before main course: antipasto, canapés, cold cuts, crudités, dim sum, dips, finger foods, hors d'oeuvres, kickshaw, rollmop, rumaki, spreads, starters, tapas, vorspeise

Bake-Off *Trademark.* contest in which baked goods are judged

banquet large, sumptuous spread of many dishes

barbecue outdoor meal consisting of meats cooked over charcoal; cookout

bistro small, unpretentious restaurant or tavern serving simple fare

bite small meal or snack

blue plate special restaurant main course at special low price

box lunch prepared lunch packaged in box

brasserie informal restaurant serving hearty food

breakfast morning meal

brown bag lunch carried in brown paper sack, esp. to office

brunch late morning meal, combining breakfast and lunch

buffet foods arranged for self-service

cafeteria self-service restaurant

carryout establishment that sells food to be eaten away from premises

carte du jour *French.* menu for the day

carvery roasted meats and poultry carved to diner's request in restaurant; restaurant providing such meats

catering food and service supplied at banquet

charcuterie delicatessen

chophouse restaurant that specializes in steaks and chops

chuck wagon provisions and cooking wagon used in American old west

clambake shellfish baked in sand on beach

cocktail party early evening gathering at which appetizers are served

coffee break snack taken on break from work, esp. midmorning

coffee shop simple, low-priced restaurant serving plain fare

convenience food fast food

cookery cooking

cooking art and practice of preparing food; cookery

cookoff contest in which competitors prepare their specialties

cookout barbecue

continental breakfast breakfast of breads and coffee or tea

course one element of a meal, served at one time

C ration prepared, packaged soldier's meal

crudités sliced raw vegetables

cuisine manner of preparing food; style of cooking

cuisine minceur *French.* light foods prepared with minimal fat

déjeuner *French.* lunch

deli delicatessen

delicatessen shop serving prepared cooked meats, salads, and cheeses at counter; deli

delivery food delivered by restaurant to one's home

dietetic (*adj*) designating low-calorie food eaten to lose weight

diner small restaurant serving simple American fare

dinner main meal of day, eaten midday or evening

dip creamy mixture, esp. of savory ingredients, that is scooped up on chips or crudités

dish particular type, serving, or preparation of food

doggie bag bag supplied by restaurant in which leftovers are taken home

drive-in restaurant in which patrons are served or place orders while sitting in their cars

early-bird special reduced-price meal at restaurant for those seated early

elevenses *Brit. slang.* late-morning coffee or tea break

entrée dish served as main course of meal

fast food cheap, mass-produced dishes served quickly at walk-in or drive-in outlets; convenience food

feast banquet

finger foods appetizers that can be eaten with one's fingers, usu. in bite-size chunks

first course opening element of multicourse meal, usu. in smaller portion than entrée

gourmet food for connoisseur with sophisticated tastes

greasy spoon cheap diner or coffee shop

haute cuisine classic French cooking with rich sauces

health food natural or organic food with high nutritive value and low sodium or fat content, believed to promote good health

high tea *Chiefly Brit.* substantial late-afternoon snack with tea

home cooking simple, hearty fare

hors d'oeuvres appetizers

junk food low-quality, low-nutrition, starchy, sugary food

kickshaw tidbit or delicacy served as appetizers

kosher (*adj*) prepared according to Jewish dietary laws

light meal insubstantial meal, not a full-course meal

lo-cal (*adj*) *Informal.* designating cuisine or dish that is low in calories

luau outdoor Hawaiian feast with entertainment

lunch midday meal, usu. simpler than dinner or supper

lunch counter restaurant that serves meals, esp. lunch, to patrons seated at counter

luncheon formal midday meal, usu. with guests

luncheonette small diner serving lunch only

macrobiotics dietary philosophy based on yin and yang principles of balancing foods

meal customary time for eating, such as breakfast, lunch, or dinner; foods eaten at such a time

meat and potatoes plain, substantial fare

mess military self-service dining

nouvelle cuisine modern style of cooking emphasizing fresh, local ingredients and imaginative presentation

on wheels *Slang.* takeout food or food to go

petit déjeuner *French.* breakfast

picnic outdoor meal

pit stop *Informal.* roadside restaurant where one stops to eat on long car trip

plat du jour *French.* featured entrée of the day at restaurant

pot luck meal to which each guest contributes one dish

power breakfast breakfast meeting for usu. high-level business discussions

prix fixe *French.* meal served at restaurant at set price

rabbit food *Slang.* raw vegetables

repast meal; food consumed at one time

restaurant establishment serving and selling meals

salad bar self-service selection of ingredients for salad in restaurant or takeout establishment

self-service (*adj*) designating restaurant in which one takes food from serving area to table

serving amount of some particular food sufficient for one person

servis compris *French.* service charge included in price

side dish secondary dish served with entrée

smorgasbord Swedish cold buffet

snack small meal taken between regular meals

soul food southern U.S. African-American home cooking

soup du jour featured soup of the day at restaurant

spread extravagant, multicourse meal or feast

square meal substantial, full-course meal

stay-on cocktail party at which certain guests are invited to remain for full dinner

supper evening meal, lighter than dinner

surf'n'turf meat and seafood, esp. steak and lobster, served on same plate

table d'hôte *French.* complete meal served at stated time and set price

takeout food bought at restaurant to eat at home

tapas snack or appetizer served at bar in Spain

tea *Chiefly Brit.* late-afternoon snack with tea

three-martini lunch *Slang.* long business lunch on expense account, often with alcoholic beverages

to go (*adj*) describing food bought at restaurant to eat at home

trattoria small, inexpensive Italian restaurant

TV dinner frozen, prepackaged meal

vegetarian (*adj*) describing meals or cuisine without meat, chicken, or fish

veggies *Informal.* vegetables; meal of vegetables only

Cooks and Servers

baker person who makes and sells breads and cakes

barkeeper person who owns bar or serves alcoholic drinks; bartender

barmaid female who serves drinks at bar

barman bartender

bartender preparer and server of alcoholic drinks; barman

busboy person who clears dishes and resets tables in restaurant

carhop waiter or waitress at drive-in restaurant

caterer person who supplies, prepares, or serves food at large or private gatherings

chef chief cook, esp. one who plans menus and supervises others in preparation of food

chef de cuisine *French.* chef

chief cook chef

confectioner person who makes or sells candy and sweets

cook person who prepares food

dishwasher person who cleans dishes that have been used for cooking, eating, or serving food

headwaiter person who supervises waiters and busboys in restaurant

host person who receives and assists patrons at restaurant

hostess female host

innkeeper person who owns or operates an inn

kitchen maid female servant who assists cook and cleans up in kitchen

maître d' maître d'hôtel

maître d'hôtel headwaiter; maître d'

pastry chef person who prepares pastries; pastry cook

pastry cook pastry chef

prep cook kitchen assistant responsible for preparing ingredients to be used by chef

publican *Chiefly Brit.* proprietor or manager of tavern or bar

restaurateur owner or manager of restaurant

scullery maid female servant who prepares food for cooking

server waiter

short-order cook cook who prepares foods quickly, esp. at lunch counter

soda jerk *Informal.* person who prepares and serves ice cream dishes at soda fountain

sommelier wine steward

sous-chef person ranking next after chef in kitchen

steward person who supervises tables, wine, and waiters in restaurant or club

waiter person, esp. male, who serves food to others at tables

waitperson waiter, either male or female

waitress female waiter

waitron waitperson

wine steward waiter responsible for serving wine in restaurant; sommelier

Prepared Dishes

adobo Philippine dish of marinated chicken or pork that is simmered and fried

angels on horseback appetizer of oysters wrapped in bacon

arroz con pollo Latin American dish of chicken and rice cooked with saffron

atole cornmeal eaten as mush or gruel

baba ghanouj Middle Eastern mashed eggplant salad with olive oil, garlic, and tahini

bacon and eggs fried bacon strips, usu. with fried or scrambled eggs

baked Alaska dessert of ice cream encased in sponge cake and meringue, lightly browned in an oven

bangers and mash British dish of sausage and mashed potatoes

barbecued spareribs pork ribs cooked over open fire and served with sauce usu. containing tomatoes, vinegar, and spices

beef Bourguignonne French beef dish with red wine, onions, and mushrooms

beef en daube French beef stew braised with vegetables, red wine, and herbs

beef pilau East African dish of beef, peanuts, coconut, tomatoes, and green beans

beef stroganoff beef dish with sour cream, onions, and mushrooms

beef Wellington beef fillet with pâté de foie gras, covered with pastry

bigos mixed meat dish with sauerkraut

bird's nest soup Chinese soup made from swallows' nests simmered in a rich stock

bitterballen Dutch fried spiced meatballs

blancmange white pudding dessert made with gelatin, milk or cream, almonds, and sugar

blanquette de veau veal stew served with egg sauce

blini Russian buckwheat pancake, often served with caviar and sour cream

blintze crêpe filled with cheese or fruit and sauteed

bobotie South African dish of ground beef or lamb, seasoned with curry and topped with baked custard

boiled dinner meal of boiled meat, potatoes, and vegetables

borscht Eastern European beet soup

Boston baked beans navy beans cooked with molasses and salt pork

bouillabaisse French stew of variety of fish and shellfish in seasoned vegetable broth

bubble and squeak British dish of fried cabbage and potato, sometimes with meat

buffalo wings spicy fried chicken wings, usu. served with hot sauce

burrito Mexican dish consisting of flour tortilla stuffed with meat, rice, beans, and cheese

cabbage rolls cabbage leaves stuffed with a filling of rice and ground meat and simmered in sauce

Caesar salad salad of romaine lettuce, grated Parmesan cheese, and croutons in dressing of raw egg, lemon juice, and oil, sometimes with anchovies

callaloo West Indian fish and crab soup

cannelloni stuffed tubular pasta baked with sauce

carbonara pasta sauce of minced pancetta, egg yolks, and grated cheese

cassoulet French casserole of beans baked with meat

cervelles au beurre noir brains cooked with darkened butter sauce

Charlotte russe dessert mold of ladyfingers and a cream filling

chateaubriand thick slice of rare beef tenderloin, served with bearnaise or other sauce

chicken Kiev boneless chicken breast stuffed with butter and chives, breaded and deep-fried

cheese soufflé light, puffed, baked dish made with cheese, white sauce, and beaten egg whites

chicken à la king diced cooked chicken and vegetables in a creamy sauce, usually served on toast or rice

chicken and dumplings chicken served with small pieces of steamed or boiled dough

chicken cacciatore Italian chicken dish with herbs, tomatoes, and white wine

chicken cordon bleu breaded, sautéed chicken stuffed with ham and cheese

chicken divan chicken and broccoli baked in a creamy wine sauce

chicken Kiev boneless chicken breast stuffed with butter and chives, breaded and deep-fried

chicken Marengo chicken casserole with tomatoes, wine, onions, and mushrooms

chicken paprika chicken simmered in paprika and sour cream

chicken Tetrazzini baked dish of diced chicken, noodles, mushrooms, and cream sauce

chili con carne highly spiced Texas dish of beef, chilies, and usu. beans

chili dog hot dog covered with chili con carne

chilies rellenos Mexican dish of stuffed jalapeño peppers

chimichanga crisp tortilla filled with meat and covered with salsa and sour cream

chipped beef dried, smoked beef sliced very thin

cholent Jewish stew of beef, beans, and potatoes, traditionally eaten on the Sabbath and cooked slowly for twenty-four hours

chop suey Chinese-American dish of bean

sprouts, meat, mushrooms, and bamboo shoots, served with rice

choucroute garnie Alsatian dish of sauerkraut cooked with meats

chow-chow pickled mixture of cucumbers, onions, tomatoes, green beans, cauliflower, celery, and red pepper

chowder soup usu. with milk, salt pork, vegetables, and often seafood

chow mein Chinese-American stew of meat and vegetables, served with fried noodles

churrasco beef grilled under flames or broiled over open fire

cioppino shellfish, fish, and vegetable stew

clams casino broiled clams on the half shell, topped with bacon, breadcrumbs, and butter

cobb salad salad of chopped greens and tomatoes, topped with diced chicken, bacon, avocado, and hard-boiled egg

cock-a-leekie soup Scottish chicken-and-leek soup

codfish balls fried cakes of cod, potatoes, and egg

colcannon Irish dish of boiled cabbage, potatoes, and kale mashed together

coleslaw salad of shredded cabbage, carrots, etc., in a mayonnaise or sour cream dressing

compote dessert of fruit stewed in syrup

confit duck or goose cooked in its own fat and preserved

coq au vin French dish of chicken cooked in red wine with mushrooms and onions

coquilles St. Jacques scallops cooked in cream sauce with mushrooms, white wine, and Parmesan cheese

corn dog hot dog impaled on a stick and baked or deep fried in corn bread coating

corned beef hash mixture of diced corned or salted beef, potatoes, white sauce, and seasoning

Cornish pasty British dish of meat and vegetables wrapped in pastry and baked

coulibiac traditional Russian fish pie

couscous North African dish of steamed, cracked wheat, usu. served with lamb or chicken and sauce with vegetables

crab Louis cold crab in a spicy mayonnaise dressing

creamed chipped beef chipped beef simmered in milk and seasoned

crème brulée dessert of egg custard topped with carmelized brown sugar

crêpe very thin French pancake, usually with a savory or sweet filling

crêpes Suzette dessert dish of crêpes in a butter and orange sauce, served flambe

croquettes small, rounded masses of cooked meat and vegetables coated with breadcrumbs and egg and deep-fried

curry Indian stew seasoned with combination of ground spices

daube stew of braised meat and vegetables

deviled eggs hard-boiled eggs with yolk mixed with mayonnaise or sour cream and paprika

deviled ham chopped, highly seasoned ham

dhal Indian sauce of puréed lentils and spices

dim sum Chinese-style steamed dumplings and other savory dishes, served in small portions

dirty rice rice with Cajun spices, beans, and usu. sausage

dolma vine leaves stuffed with mixture of meat, rice, and spices

duchess potatoes potatoes mashed with butter and eggs

duck à l'orange roast duck served with an orange sauce and sliced oranges

egg foo yong Chinese-American dish of beaten egg fried with meat and onions

eggplant parmigiana casserole of eggplant slices, tomato sauce, and cheese

egg roll Chinese appetizer of thin pastry with a filling of chopped meat and vegetables, deep-fried

eggs Benedict poached eggs and ham served on an English muffin and covered with hollandaise sauce

empañadas Central American sweet or savory turnovers

enchilada Mexican dish of rolled tortilla with meat or cheese filling, baked with chili-flavored tomato sauce

fajitas Mexican marinated beef or chicken cooked with variety of sauces and rolled in a tortilla

falafel Middle Eastern spicy, deep-fried patty of ground chickpeas or other vegetables

fettuccine Italian-style egg noodles in the form of flat, narrow strips

fettuccine alfredo fettuccine served with a rich cream and cheese sauce

fish and chips British dish of fried, batter-coated fish with French-fried potatoes

flambé (adj) designating a dish served in flaming brandy or other liquor

fondue dish consisting of small pieces of meat, fruit, or bread dipped into a hot liquid such as melted cheese or chocolate

French onion soup onion soup topped with toast and cheese, then baked

French toast bread dipped in egg-and-milk batter, then fried

fricassee chicken or turkey simmered with onions, carrots, celery, and rice

fried rice Oriental dish of rice fried with meat and vegetables

frijoles Mexican-style beans

frikadeller Danish meatballs

frittata chopped vegetables or meat cooked in egg mixture

fritter battered, deep-fried food mixture

gado-gado Indonesian vegetable salad with peanut sauce

gazpacho Spanish soup with tomatoes, cucumbers, peppers, and onions

gefilte fish Jewish dish consisting of cakes of seasoned, chopped fish, eggs, and matzo meal cooked in fish broth

German potato salad hot salad of potato chunks, bacon, and a vinegar dressing

gorp trail mix

goulash Hungarian stew with meat, vegetables, and paprika

groundnut stew West African stew of chicken, beef, vegetables, and peanut butter

guacamole Mexican dip or salad of mashed avocado, lemon juice, salsa, garlic, and sometimes cilantro

gumbo Creole soup with okra, including seafood, vegetables, and meat

haggis Scottish dish of lungs, heart, and liver of a sheep or calf, with suet, oatmeal, and seasoning, boiled in the animal's stomach

ham and eggs traditional breakfast dish of cooked eggs served with slice of ham

Hangtown Fry omelet with bacon, fried oysters, and sometimes onions

hasenpfeffer marinated rabbit stew, usu. garnished with sour cream

hash dish of chopped potatoes and meat, often corned beef, usually fried and served with eggs

hot dogs and beans baked beans cooked with sliced frankfurters

hot pot British dish of mutton or beef cooked in a pot with potatoes

howtowdie Scottish dish of roast chicken with spinach and poached eggs

hummus Middle Eastern dish of mashed chickpeas with olive oil, garlic, lemon juice, and tahini

hush puppy deep-fried cornmeal fritter

Irish stew stew of lamb or beef, vegetables, and spices

jambalaya Creole stew of rice, meat, vegetables, and spices

kedgeree Indian dish of rice, lentils, fish, seasonings, and sometimes egg

kidney pie British meat pie of kidney stew wrapped in dough

kishke animal intestine stuffed with flour, fat, onion, and seasoning; stuffed derma

knish dough stuffed with a filling, such as chopped meat and mashed potatoes, and baked

kugel baked pudding of potatoes or noodles

lasagne Italian baked dish consisting of layers of wide, flat pasta, tomato sauce, cheese, and usu. meat

linguine pasta in the form of very thin ribbons

liver and onions liver and onions sautéed together

lobscouse Scandinavian stew of meat, potatoes, onions, and ship biscuit

lobster Newburg dish of diced lobster cooked in cream sauce

lobster thermidor dish of lobster in cream sauce that is stuffed into lobster shell and browned

London broil flank or other steak marinated and broiled, sliced thin

macaroni and cheese usu. tubular pasta baked with cheese sauce

manicotti Italian pasta tubes usu. stuffed with a meat or cheese mixture and baked with a tomato sauce

mansaf Middle Eastern lamb and rice dish

marinara tomato sauce with garlic and spices served over pasta or seafood

matelote fish stew with seasoned wine sauce

meatballs small clumps of ground, seasoned meat, often served with gravy or sauce

meat loaf baked loaf of ground meat, egg, breadcrumbs, and seasoning

Melton Mowbray pie English pork pie with apples, raisins, and onions

minestrone Italian vegetable and macaroni soup

mole Mexican sauce made with chili peppers and unsweetened chocolate

Mongolian hot pot stewlike dish of sliced meat, seafood, and vegetables cooked in a simmering pot of broth and seasoned with hot sauce

Mornay (*adj*) designating a dish served with a white cheese sauce

moussaka Greek dish with layers of ground meat and sliced eggplant, baked with seasoned sauce and cheese

mulligatawny soup East Indian curried chicken or turkey soup

ossobuco Italian dish of veal shanks stewed in white wine and tomatoes

oysters Rockefeller oysters topped with mixture of spinach, bacon, and seasonings and broiled on the half shell

paella Spanish dish of saffron-seasoned rice baked in stock with meat, seafood, and vegetables

pakora Indian fritter of chickpea flour

pâté appetizer of seasoned liver, etc., chopped very fine into a paste, often molded

peach Melba chilled poached peaches served with vanilla ice cream and raspberry puree

Peking duck Chinese dish of roasted duck with crisp skin, served in thin crêpes

pemmican American Indian dish of powered dried meat mixed with hot fat and dried fruits and pressed into a loaf

peperonata Italian dish of peppers, tomatoes, onions, garlic, and olive oil

pepper steak strips of beef cooked with green peppers

pig-in-a-blanket hot dog or sausage wrapped in dough and cooked; also, *esp. Brit.*, toad-in-the-hole

pilaf dish of seasoned rice or wheat

piperade Spanish omelet with strips of cooked ham

piroshki small pastry turnovers stuffed with meat, cheese, or vegetables

pizza thinly rolled dough covered with spiced mixture of tomatoes, cheese, and meat or vegetables and baked

poi Hawaiian dish of taro root that is baked, pounded, moistened, and fermented

pork and beans baked beans cooked with salt pork

pork pie pork stew covered with dough and baked

potage thick French soup, esp. made with cream

potage St. Germain French green pea soup

potato chip thin slice of potato fried crisp and usu. salted

potatoes O'Brien potato cubes fried with green peppers and onions

potato salad cold salad of diced potatoes, mayonnaise, and seasonings, garnished with chopped hard-boiled eggs

pot-au-feu French dish of boiled meat and vegetables

potpie meat and vegetables covered with pastry and baked in a deep dish

pot roast cut of beef stewed in a pot, usu. with vegetables

pot stickers Chinese savory fried and steamed dumplings

profiterole pastry puff, served with savory or sweet filling

quennelle poached dumpling of minced fish or meat

quiche open egg-custard pie made with various fillings

ragout Eastern European stew of meat, potatoes, and spices

raita Indian dish of chopped cucumber or onion in yogurt

ratatouille seasoned vegetable stew of eggplant, tomatoes, zucchini, and peppers

ravioli square pockets of pasta stuffed with meat or cheese

rigatoni pasta in the form of small, ribbed tubes

risotto Italian dish of rice cooked in broth and seasonings

rollmop pickled herring, wrapped around an onion or pickle and skewed, served as an appetizer

rumaki chicken liver or water chestnut wrapped in bacon and broiled as appetizer

salsa Mexican-style seasoning dip made with tomatoes, onions, and jalapeño peppers

Salisbury steak seasoned ground beef formed into patties, broiled or fried

saltimbocca Italian dish of veal and ham wrapped together and sautéed in butter and sage

satay Southeast Asian dish of beef or pork, grilled on a skewer

sauerbraten beef marinated in vinegar, onions, and spices before cooking

sauerkraut cut cabbage fermented in brine of its own juice with salt

scallopine thin slices of meat, esp. veal, sautéed in herbs and wine

scampi large shrimp broiled in garlic flavored sauce

schnitzel fried, breaded cutlet of veal or chicken

Scotch egg British dish of hard-boiled egg encased in sausage, breaded and deep-fried

scrapple seasoned chopped pork and cornmeal mush, formed into loaves that are sliced and fried

seviche raw fish marinated in lime juice with tomatoes, peppers, and seasonings

shepherd's pie British meat pie baked with mashed potato crust

shish kabob Middle Eastern dish of meat marinated, skewered, and broiled

souvlaki Greek shish kabob consisting of small pieces of marinated meat and vegetables on a skewer

spaghetti pasta in the form of thin, long strings

spaghetti and clam sauce Italian dish consisting of spaghetti pasta served with white or red sauce containing clams and garlic

spaghetti and meatballs Italian dish consisting of spaghetti pasta served with tomato sauce and meatballs

Spanish rice rice cooked with tomatoes, green peppers, and onions

spoon bread baked side dish of cornmeal, milk, eggs, and shortening

steak and kidney pie British meat pie of steak and kidney stew wrapped in dough

steak tartare raw ground steak mixed with onions and seasonings

stuffed cabbage cabbage leaves wrapped around seasoned meat and rice mixture

stuffed derma Jewish dish consisting of animal intestine stuffed with matzo meal and onions, then roasted; kishke

stuffed grape leaves Greek dish of grape leaves wrapped around mixture of rice, herbs, and meat

stuffed peppers green peppers stuffed with rice, meat, or vegetables

succotash lima beans and corn kernels cooked together

sukiyaki Japanese dish of thinly sliced meat, vegetables, and bean curd, cooked with soy sauce, sugar, and sake

sushi Japanese dish consisting of cold cakes of rice flavored with vinegar and garnished with raw fish or vegetables

sweet-and-sour (*adj*) designating a Chinese-style dish of meat, seafood, etc., cooked in a sugar and vinegar sauce

Swiss steak steak pounded with flour and browned with vegetables and seasonings

tabbouleh Middle Eastern salad of cracked wheat, parsley, and tomatoes in olive oil and lemon juice

taco Mexican dish of fried tortilla that is folded and filled with mixture of meat, cheese, and salad

tahini Middle Eastern sauce of sesame-seed paste

tamale Mexican dish of ground meat and peppers rolled in cornmeal, wrapped in cornhusks, and steamed

tempeh fermented soybean cake

tempura Japanese dish of seafood or vegetables dipped in egg batter and deep-fried

teriyaki Japanese dish of meat or fish marinated in spicy soy sauce and grilled or broiled

terrine chopped meat or vegetable mixture cooked in earthenware dish

tofu curdled, thickened soybean milk

torte layered, filled cake usu. made with ground nuts instead of flour

tostada Mexican dish consisting of deep-fried, flat tortilla covered with meat, cheese, and salad

trail mix mixture of nuts, grains, seeds, and dried fruits, eaten as snack for energy; gorp

tzatziki Greek salad of yogurt and cucumber

veal parmigiana veal cutlets coated with breadcrumbs and fried, served with tomato sauce and Parmesan cheese

veal scallopine veal cutlet dredged in flour and sautéed in butter and wine sauce

vichyssoise French potato soup, usually served cold

vol-au-vent French puff pastry shells

Waldorf salad salad of chopped apple, celery, and walnut in mayonnaise

Welsh rabbit melted, seasoned cheese, often mixed with beer, served on toast

western omelette containing ham, green pepper, and onion

Wiener schnitzel breaded veal cutlet that is fried and sometimes garnished with lemon slice and anchovy

wonton Chinese fried dumpling, usu. filled with a meat mixture

yakitori Japanese dish of small cubes of marinated chicken skewered and grilled

Yorkshire pudding unsweetened batter of flour, salt, eggs, and milk, baked under roasting meat to catch drippings or baked alone with drippings from roast

zabaglione Italian dessert made with beaten egg yolks, sugar, and Marsala wine

ziti pasta in the form of small tubes

THE KITCHEN

Cookers
Pots and Pans
Utensils and Appliances
Dishes and Serving Containers
Glassware
Cutlery and Flatware
Linens and Accessories

See also: *Chap. 5: Containers; Chap. 7: Ornamental and Functional Articles; Chap. 9: Cooking and Cuisine; Chap. 17: Drinking and Alcoholic Beverages*

Cookers

autoclave pressure cooker

barbecue grill or rack over hot coals, often on movable stand

boiler vessel, esp. kettle, for boiling or heating

brazier simple cooker containing live coals covered by a grill

broiler oven compartment with overhead flame or heated coil

burner gas or electric stove-top unit for heating food in pots and pans

camp stove portable stove for outdoor cooking, usu. by gas

convection oven oven unit with fan that circulates and intensifies heat, decreasing normal heating time

cooker appliance or utensil for cooking food; *Chiefly Brit.* oven

cooktop cooking surface consisting of a flat sheet of glass and ceramic material over a heating element, usu. electric

corn popper enclosed vessel for popping corn kernels

deep fat fryer often electric-powered basin with hot oil in which to immerse food

espresso maker device that forces pressurized boiling water through finely ground coffee to make espresso, usu. with attachment for steaming milk

griddle flat, wide, rimless cooking surface

gridiron broiling grate in frame

grill metal grid rack over coals

hibachi small barbecue grid over hot coals (Japan)

immersion heater electric heating coil dipped in liquids

infrared broiler unit using infrared heat and having no flame

microwave oven electronic cooker in which short microwave penetrations of food produce heat to cook food rapidly

oven dry-heat cooker: electric, gas, pizza, tandoori

pressure cooker airtight, steam-pressure cooking pot, usu. of reinforced steel or aluminum; autoclave

rack grill

range appliance with oven, broiler, and burners

roaster oven or open fire for cooking with little liquid

rotisserie small oven with attached spit, operated electrically

salamander small browning or glazing broiler

slow cooker electric cooking pot with tight-fitting lid, used for cooking meats at low temperatures over several hours

smoker enclosure for flavoring or curing foods with smoke

spit pointed skewer to hold meat over fire or coals

steamer perforated rack fitted into pot containing boiling water

steam table warming table on which food is held over boiling water

stove cooking appliance with oven, broiler, and top burners; range

tandoor cylindrical clay oven (India)

toaster browning oven with electric heating coils, positioned vertically esp. for browning and crisping bread

toaster oven electric appliance that toasts, broils, or bakes on heating coils positioned horizontally

waffle iron two hinged metal griddles that close to cook batter

Pots and Pans

baba small mold

baking dish baking pan

baking pan metal or glass ovenproof pan; baking pan

baking sheet cookie sheet

bean pot deep, round earthenware pot with narrow opening at top

bread pan usu. rectangular pan for baking bread; loaf pan

Bundt pan *Trademark.* tube-shaped cake pan with ridged surface

cake pan round, square, or loaf-shaped ovenproof dish

casserole deep, heavy pot with lid, used for baking

cauldron very large pot or kettle

chafing dish dish for cooking and keeping dishes warm on stand over low flame

clay cooker large, round, tightly sealed earthenware casserole

cocotte small ovenproof dish

coffeepot electric or stovetop pot with internal mechanism for brewing coffee

cookie sheet flat metal baking sheet

cookware pots and pans

coquille shell-shaped ovenproof dish

cover flat fitted top for pot or pan

Crockpot *Trademark.* electric slow cooker

dariole small, cylindrical mold

double boiler pot fitted snugly atop another pot filled with boiling water

Dutch oven cast-iron pot with lid

electric frying pan frying pan with electrical heating unit

feenjon small metal pot with handle, used for boiling Turkish coffee

frier frying pan

frying pan shallow long-handled pan for use above flame; frier; fry-pan; skillet

fry-pan frying pan

jelly-roll pan cookie sheet with one-inch-high lip around edge

kettle metal pot for boiling water, often with narrow opening or spout at top

loaf pan bread pan

marmite large, steep-sided, metal or ceramic pot

mold pan used to form food into shapes: butter, charlotte, chocolate, pâté, ring

muffin pan baking pan with individual deep, round holders; muffin tin

muffin tin muffin pan

omelet pan slope-sided, long-handled frying pan for eggs

paella pan very wide, shallow pan, often with two handles, used for baking

pan broad, shallow, open, metal cooking container with handle

percolator coffeepot in which boiling water bubbles up through tube and filters down through ground coffee held in perforated container near top

pie pan shallow, round, ovenproof baking dish; pie tin

pie tin pie pan

pizza pan circular, flat, ovenproof metal plate

poacher poaching pan

poaching pan long, narrow pan with removable, porous tray; poacher

pot usu. round, deep, covered cooking container with handle

pudding mold round, heavy steaming dish with tight-fitting lid

quiche pan shallow, circular baking pan with pinched edge

ramekin small, shallow, ovenproof baking dish

ring mold circular form used to set food into ring shape

roasting pan cooking container for oven or open fire, usu. with rack or trivet inside

samovar urn with spigot and heating element for boiling water to make tea

saucepan medium-deep pot with handle

sauté pan thick-bottomed, straight-sided skillet

savarin ring mold

skillet frying pan

soufflé dish ovenproof, round, straight-sided baking dish

spider cast-iron frying pan, orig. with legs to stand on hearth or over coals

springform pan baking pan with detachable bottom

steamer pot fitted with perforated insert that sits above water

stew pan stewpot

stewpot heavyweight pot for slow cooking, esp. of meat; stew pan

stockpot large, tall, heavyweight pot

tart tin vary small pie tin

teakettle metal pot with small opening for boiling water

Teflon pan *Trademark.* frying pan or pot coated with nonstick substance

terrine earthenware baking dish, often rectangular

timbale small, cylindrical mold

tin metal baking pan

tube pan deep, doughnut-shaped cake pan

wok large, bowl-shaped frying pan (China)

Utensils and Appliances

apple corer pointed tube on handle for removing apple cores

appliance usu. electrical device used in food preparation

bain-marie warming dish using steam heat

banquet cloth long, protective tablecloth for banquet table

biscuit cutter deep, round device for cutting out dough

blender electric appliance with rotary blades that chop, purée, or liquefy foods

bottle opener metal lever for removing bottle caps

breadboard solid wood slab for cutting bread and other foods; cutting board

brochette spit or skewer

brush small bristle brush for basting meat or buttering pastry

bulb baster rubber tube and bulb for siphoning fats and liquids

butcher block slab of wood up to three inches thick for cutting food, esp. meat; chopping block

cake break wide-tined fork for slicing cake

cake rack low grid for cooling baked items

calabash large, hard-shell gourd used as scoop or ladle

canister wide-mouthed container with tight-fitting lid, used for storing dry goods

can opener manual or electrical device with rotary blade for cutting can lids

cherry pitter small plunger for extracting pits

china cap cone-shaped sieve; chinois

chinois china cap

chopping block butcher block

chopping board wooden cutting surface

chopsticks two small sticks for lifting food, operated in one hand

church key device for opening cans by punching V-shaped hole in top

churn container with paddle or agitating mechanism in which cream or milk is stirred to make butter

cleaver heavy knife with broad blade, used esp. to cut meat through bones or joints or into large chunks

coffee grinder closed container with rotary blades for grinding coffee, operated electrically or manually; coffee mill

coffee mill coffee grinder

colander perforated bowl for rinsing and draining

cookie cutter form used to shape and cut cookie dough

cookie press tube and plunger used to form cookie dough

cooking fork long-tined fork on handle, used to move cooking foods

cooler usu. insulated container for keeping foods cold

corkscrew spiral, lever, or pincer used to extract cork from wine bottle

Cuisinart *Trademark.* food processor

cutting board breadboard

dasher plunger with paddles at one end for mixing liquids in churn or ice cream freezer

drum sieve round frame with screen in bottom through which food is forced with a pestle

egg beater rotary beater also used for whipping cream and smoothing batter

egg slicer parallel wires on hinged frame, used for cutting eggs

food mill perforated pot with crank for puréeing

food processor electric appliance with set of blades revolving inside container, used for cutting, blending, grating, and puréeing solid foods

fork tined spearing utensil

frying basket perforated enclosure on handle, used for dipping foods into deep fat

funnel cone open at top and leading into thin tube opening at bottom

garlic press small perforated masher with handle

grapefruit spoon teaspoon with serrated tip

grater punched metal surface for shredding foods, sometimes rotated by handle or freestanding with different size holes on each side

grinder manual or electrically powered tool used to pulverize, shred, or powder foods, esp. meats, coffee beans, and nuts

hand beater handheld rotary beater powered electrically

ice cream maker electric or hand-cranked device packed with ice around container that holds ice cream ingredients

ice pick pointed metal stick for breaking ice cubes

jagging wheel jagged-edged wheel on handle, used for cutting pastry into ornamental shapes

jar opener pliers with wide jaws that clamp around jar lids to loosen them

juicer electric appliance for extracting juice from fruit and vegetables

kitchen shears scissors for cutting foods

knife bladed instrument with handle, used for cutting, slicing, chopping: boning, bread, butcher, carving, chef's, chopping, coring, filleting, grapefruit, paring, serrated, slicing, utility

ladle deep, large spoon for serving soups

mandolin grater and slicer with wooden frame and adjustable blade

masher stiff wire instrument for puréeing, esp. potatoes

measuring cup marked or sized container for determining amounts

measuring spoon any of various sized spoons for determining amounts

meat grinder blades that rotate on handle to reduce meat to pulp

meat pounder wooden mallet with smooth and rough surfaces, used for thinning or tenderizing meat

meat thermometer gauge on pointed stem that is inserted in meat to register internal temperature and determine when it is properly cooked

melon baller bowl-shaped spoon for scooping melon

mixer manual or electric beating instrument for blending ingredients

mixing bowl round container for blending

mortar and pestle heavy bowl and grinding stick for pulverizing

nutcracker pliers for breaking nutshells

nutpick slender, pointed implement for removing meat from nut shells

oven thermometer temperature gauge that hangs on rack in oven

oyster knife short, rigid knife with hand guard at base of handle

pastry bag cloth bag with nozzled tube for shaping dough

pastry blender mixing utensil of wire tines bound at their ends on handle

pastry brush soft, small bristles bound to handle

pastry jagger notched wheel for decorating dough

pastry scraper flat blade on handle, used for manipulating pastry dough

pastry tube conical tube with patterned opening at one end, fitted on cloth bag for shaping icings and soft foods as they are squeezed through the bag

pepper mill peppercorn grinder

peeler rotating blade used to skin fruits and vegetables

pitter clamping device with small punch for removing fruit or olive pits

pizza cutter circular blade that rotates on handle, used for cutting pastry or pizza

poultry shears strong scissors for disjointing chickens and other poultry

rack wide grate used to support roast in pan

reamer ridged cone for juicing citrus fruits

ricer utensil with small holes through which soft food is forced to produce rice-size particles

rolling pin long, narrow cylinder for flattening dough

rubber spatula spatula with flexible rubber blade, used esp. for scraping bowls

salad basket mesh container used to wash and drain lettuce

salad spinner enclosed salad basket operated by handle

scoop small shovel, esp. used to take up dry materials

scraper serrated utensil for removing skins; rubber spatula for scraping sauces out of bowls

sharpener sharpening steel

sharpening steel solid block or long tube of steel on handle, used for sharpening knives; sharpener

sieve dome-shaped strainer with mesh bottom, esp. for separating coarse from fine parts of loose matter

sifter strainer for flour or sugar

skewer long, slender, pointed utensil of metal or wood, inserted through meat or other food while cooking

skimmer flat, very fine mesh strainer on handle, used for removing scum or particles from surface of liquid

slotted spoon large spoon with perforations, for removing solid pieces from liquid

spatula flat, usu. flexible-bladed device of metal, wood, or rubber, used for scraping or turning

spoon small, shallow bowl on handle: ice-cream scoop, measuring, slotted, table, tea, wooden

spork combination spoon and fork, esp. for removing spaghetti from water

standing electric mixer round bowl and mixing blades that attach to electric motor

steamer basket perforated basket on feet that holds food and stands above boiling water in steaming pot

strainer device for retaining solid bits and passing liquids

tampon absorbent cloth roll for wiping and tidying serving dishes

tea ball perforated enclosure on chain for brewing tea

timer device that can be set to make sound after set interval of time

tongs pincers for lifting and holding food

trivet metal support or rack, decorative or protective

trussing needle metal pin used to fasten meats while roasting

utensil implement, instrument, or vessel used in cooking

vegetable parer pair of parallel blades on handle, joined at tip, used to peel fruits and vegetables

whip whisk

whisk beater consisting of several wire loops held together in handle; whip

wood spoon long-handled spoon made of wood, used for stirring foods, esp. batter

zester small knife with serrated lateral blade, used for cutting citrus rind

Dishes and Serving Containers

boat small, deep, usu. oblong serving dish

bowl deep, rounded, hemispherical container that is open at the top: cereal, chopping, compote, cream, finger, fruit, porringer, punch, revere, salad, soup

breadbasket often wickerwork container for serving bread, also made of wood or pottery

charger large, shallow dish or platter

coffee cup small cup, often with handle and matching saucer

coffeepot pitcher or enclosed pot for serving coffee

compote long-stemmed dish for serving fruit or sweets

cookie jar lidded container for storing cookies

creamer small pitcher with spout for serving cream or milk with coffee or tea

cruet small glass bottle with stopper, used esp. for holding oil and vinegar

cup small, open beverage container, often round and with handle: breakfast, coffee, custard, demitasse, egg, kylix, mug, noggin, tea

decanter decorative, quart-size, glass bottle with stopper for serving wine

demitasse small, delicate cup for serving strong black coffee

dessert plate plate smaller than salad plate

dinner plate large plate that holds individual portion of main course of meal

dish shallow, slightly concave, usu. round container made of glass or ceramics, on which food is served

eggcup small, deep-bowled cup for serving boiled egg

finger bowl small, low bowl that holds water in which to rinse fingers at table

gratin dish low, round baking and serving dish with two handles

gravy boat medium serving pitcher with handle, often on saucer

jar cylindrical container with large opening and no spout

jug large container for liquids with small opening or spout and handle

kylix shallow bowl with two handles, used as drinking cup (ancient Greece and Rome)

lazy Susan revolving serving platter, usu. placed in center of table

nappy small, shallow serving dish, often of glass, with flat bottom and sloping sides

noggin small mug or cup

pitcher large container with handle and lip or spout for pouring liquids

plate shallow dish, usu. round, from which food is eaten: bread and butter, dessert, dinner, luncheon, salad, saucer, service

platter large, flat serving dish, usu. with lip: charger, chop, fish, nappy, well-and-tree

porringer low dish with handle, from which soup or porridge is eaten

punch bowl large bowl from which punch is served, usu. with ladle

revere bowl round, silver serving bowl with stand

salad bowl large, deep bowl, often of wood, for tossing and serving salads

salad plate medium-sized plate intermediate between dessert plate and dinner plate, holding one serving of salad

salt cellar small container with perforated top for storing and shaking out salt

salver tray on which food is served

saucer small, round, shallow dish used under another container, esp. with indentation to hold cup

scallop shell wide, flat shell of a scallop, used as a serving dish

service plate large plate, often having lip, from which food is served to diners' plates

serving container any vessel used for storing and serving food or drink

soup bowl wide or deep bowl that holds one serving of soup

sugar bowl small, decorative bowl for serving sugar

teapot usu. round, ceramic or china container with top and spout for brewing and serving tea

tea service complete set of china or silver pots, pitchers, bowls, cups, and saucers for serving tea

thermos bottle with inner and outer walls enclosing vacuum to keep liquids at or near original temperature

tray flat, wide surface, often with slightly raised edges, for carrying and serving food

tureen large, deep serving dish with lid, esp. for soups

well-and-tree platter platter with depression in shape of tree whose trunk ends in deep well for accumulation of liquids

wine basket tall reed container for holding open wine bottle

Glassware

balloon large, round, stemmed red-wine glass

beer mug thick-walled glass cup, often with handle

brandy snifter balloon-shaped, stemmed glass

champagne coupe glass with shallow bowl, flared lip, and stem

champagne flute narrow, conical, stemmed glass

champagne saucer very wide, flat, stemmed glass

champagne tulip gently curved, stemmed glass

cocktail tall, narrow glass for mixed and iced drinks

collins tall, narrow, iced drink glass

cooler tall, narrow, iced drink glass

copita stemmed sherry glass

cordial small, stemmed glass

flagon large metal or pottery vessel with handle

footed pilsener tall, conical beer glass with wide base on stem

glass any drinking vessel made of hard, brittle, transparent, crystallized material

goblet large, round, stemmed wineglass

heavy goblet thick-walled goblet

highball tall, straight-sided cocktail glass

hock glass thick or knobby-stemmed wineglass

hourglass glass that narrows in middle to stemmed bottom

jigger small glass used to measure 1 1/2 fluid ounces

juice glass plain, cylindrical glass for fruit juice

mug heavy drinking cup with handle, esp. earthenware

mug stein large, glass beer mug

old-fashioned short, squat tumbler

parfait small, narrow, stemmed glass

Paris goblet glass with large, round bowl and tall stem

pilsner tall, conical beer glass with short stem

pony small beer glass; small liqueur glass

port glass small, narrow, conical, stemmed glass

punch cup small, bowl-shaped cup with handle

red-wine glass large, stemmed wineglass

rock glass short glass for liquor over ice

schooner large beer mug

seidel large beer mug, often with hinged lid

sham pilsner short, conical beer glass

sherbet small, slant-sided glass

sherry glass flared-lipped, wide, conical glass with short stem

shot very small, heavy-bottomed, narrow glass

snifter balloon-shaped, stemmed glass

sour glass small, slant-sided glass, often with stem

stein large, usu. earthenware beer mug

tankard tall, one-handled, lidded mug, often pewter or silver

Trier stemmed, cut-glass, white-wine glass

tulip goblet round bowl glass with flared rim and stem

tumbler medium-tall, cylindrical glass

whiskey sour glass tall, narrow, stemmed cocktail glass

white-wine glass medium-size, stemmed wineglass

wineglass tall, rounded glass on stem, often of crystal

zombie very tall cocktail glass

Cutlery and Flatware

butter knife small knife with dull blade, used for cutting and spreading butter

carving fork fork with two long tines and rim on which to rest thumb and forefinger at base of handle, used to hold meat being carved

carving knife large, sharp knife for slicing meat

cheese knife small knife, often with blunt end and wide blade

chopsticks two small sticks of wood or ivory held in one hand and used to lift food to mouth, esp. in Asia

cocktail fork small, three-tined fork

cutlery knives

dessert fork fork that is smaller than dinner fork

dessert spoon spoon intermediate in size between tablespoon and teaspoon

dinner fork large fork used for eating main course of meal

flatware eating tools, esp. forks, spoons, and knives

fork instrument with two or more prongs at end of handle, used to lift food to mouth: carving, cake break, cocktail, cold meat, dinner, fish, lemon, olive, oyster, pickle, salad

grapefruit spoon teaspoon with serrated tip, used to eat sections of grapefruit

knife small blade on handle, used for spreading and cutting: butter, carving, cheese, fish, jelly, oyster, pie, steak

oyster fork small, three-tined fork, used in eating shellfish

runcible spoon combination fork and spoon with concave body and pronglike tines

serving spoon large, often deep spoon with long handle, used for serving food

silverware cutlery and utensils of silver

soupspoon large spoon, usu. with rounded bowl, for eating soup

spoon device with small, shallow, concave bowl on handle, used for stirring or eating liquids: coffee, cream, dessertspoon, five o'clock, fruit, grapefruit, iced tea, nut, pierced, runcible, salt, serving, soupspoon, tablespoon, teaspoon, tomato

steak knife small knife with serrated cutting edge, used to slice meat

tablespoon spoon larger than teaspoon or dessertspoon, used in serving food and as standard measure

teaspoon small spoon, used esp. to stir coffee and tea or eat desserts

Linens and Accessories

aluminum foil paper-thin sheet of aluminum on roll, used to wrap foods, line cookers, and serve as lid

cheesecloth fine mesh cloth for straining broth or binding herbs

cookbook book containing recipes and cooking instructions

cozy padded covering used to retain warmth of liquid in container, esp. in teapot

dish drain open rack used to stack drying dishes

dish towel small cloth for washing and drying dishes

glove insulated hot pad in form of glove that encloses entire hand

hot pad potholder

linens objects made of cloth, esp. napkins

napkin paper or cloth square for wiping hands and lips; serviette

napkin ring metal ring for holding napkin at place setting

paper towels thin sheets of absorbent paper, usu. on roll, for drying and cleaning surfaces

parchment thick parchment paper used to wrap certain baked items

place mat decorative cloth, reed, or plastic sheet for place setting, used to protect table

place setting cutlery, glassware, dishes, and napkin, often arranged on place mat

plastic wrap very thin sheet of clear plastic on roll, used to wrap foods and seal moisture or flavor

potholder heavy, insulated, usu. square piece of material for lifting very hot objects; hot pad

serviette *Chiefly Brit.* napkin

silent butler receptacle with hinged lid, used for collecting table crumbs and emptying ashtrays

spice box rack or box for holding spices

tablecloth large, decorative cloth covering entire table

tidy porous plastic container for collecting garbage in sink

trivet support or rack used to protect surfaces from hot serving dishes

wax paper thin sheet of waxed paper on roll, used to cover surfaces or placed on standing sauces to prevent formation of skin

CHAPTER TEN
CLOTHING

OUTER GARMENTS

Overcoats and Cloaks
Coats and Jackets
Suits and Uniforms
Sweaters and Vests
Shirts and Tops
Dresses and Skirts
Trousers, Shorts, and Leggings
Sporting and Exercise Wear
Liturgical Vestments
Armor

See also: *Chap. 10: Ornaments and Accessories;*
Footwear; Hats, Headgear, and Hairpieces

Overcoats and Cloaks

academic gown long, flowing robe worn during college ceremonies, esp. graduation

anorak parka, often hooded (Eskimo)

Aquascutum *Trademark.* raincoat

balmacaan loose overcoat, single-breasted, with raglan sleeves

benjamin *Slang.* man's loose-fitting overcoat

bertha woman's loose, round-shouldered cape

boubou long, loose, often brightly colored outer garment worn by either sex (Africa)

Burberry *Trademark.* raincoat

burnoose man's hooded, cloaklike robe, worn by Arabs

caftan cotton, ankle-length, long-sleeved cloak (Middle East)

cagoule light, hooded raincoat

cape sleeveless garment with fitted neck that hangs loose over shoulders

capelet small shoulder cape

capote long, hooded overcoat

capuchin woman's hooded cloak

car coat hip-length overcoat or jacket

cardinal woman's short cloak with hood, orig. scarlet

chesterfield topcoat with fly front and velvet collar, often double-breasted

chiton rectangle of fabric, esp. gown or tunic, turned down at top and gathered at waist, knee- or full-length (ancient Greece)

chlamys man's thigh-length, oblong mantle (ancient Greece)

cloak long, sleeveless, capelike concealing robe

covert coat short topcoat

cowl monk's hooded cloak

djellabah loose-fitting, hooded gown or robe worn by men (North Africa)

domino loose, hooded cloak worn as costume with half-mask

dreadnought heavy woolen coat; fearnought

duffle hooded coat of heavy wool with toggle fasteners

duster lightweight protective driving coat

fearnought dreadnought

frock tunic, mantle, long coat, smock, or monk's robe

fur coat luxurious dress coat of animal fur

fur-lined coat overcoat lined with animal fur

gaberdine long, coarse coat or smock worn esp. by medieval Jews

greatcoat *Chiefly Brit.* heavy, full-length overcoat; long coat

haik long, loose, white cloth worn as outer garment (North Africa)

hauberk chain-mail tunic (12th-14th c.)

himation long, loose cloth draped over left shoulder (ancient Greece)

Inverness overcoat with detachable cape (Scotland)

joseph woman's long cloak (18th c.)

jubbah full-length outer garment with long sleeves (Middle East and North Africa)

kaross cloak of animal skins (southern Africa)

kibr hooded, sleeved robe (Middle East)

kimono long, wide-sleeved, sashed robe (Japan)

kirtle tunic; woman's long gown (medieval Europe)

loden coat of short-piled, waterproof, loden fabric

London Fog *Trademark.* brand of belted trench coat

long coat greatcoat

macfarlane heavy, caped overcoat with sides slit open for arms

mackintosh *Chiefly Brit.* lightweight raincoat

manta square blanket used as cloak (Latin America)

manteau loose coat, cloak, robe

mantelet very short cape or cloak

mantle loose, sleeveless cloak

mantua woman's loose-fitting cloak (17th-18th c.)

monk's robe long, usu. dark cloak worn in religious orders

Newmarket long, close-fitting coat worn as woman's overcoat or man's riding coat (19th c.)

oilskin raincoat of oiled, waterproof cloth; slicker

opera cape short, elegant evening cloak

paletot loose cloak with one or more capes (19th c.)

pallium man's draped rectangular cloth (ancient Greece and Rome)

parka fur, down, or nylon cold-weather jacket; hooded jacket

peacoat sailor's hip-length coat of dark blue wool; pea jacket

pelerine woman's narrow fur or fabric shoulder cape, with ends hanging down front (19th c.)

pelisse woman's long cloak with fur collar and trim

peplos woman's shawl (ancient Greece)

petersham man's bulky overcoat of petersham wool

poncho wool blanket with slit opening for head; similarly cut nylon or rubber raincoat

raglan topcoat with sleeves extending to collar, esp. for improved water resistance

raincoat waterproof overcoat

rebozo colorful wool shawl (Mexico)

redingote man's three-quarter-length,

double-breasted coat with wide flat cuffs (18th c.)

robe long, loose outer garment, often ceremonial

roquelaure knee-length cloak that buttoned in front (18th-19th c.)

ruana wool covering with slit for head, like poncho (Colombia)

serape man's wool shoulder shawl (Mexico)

shador garment that covers all of body and head, worn by Muslim women

shawl heavy oblong, triangular, or square cloth worn over head and shoulders, esp. by women

shearling coat of sheepskin from recently shorn sheep

shroud burial garment

slicker oilskin

smock loose, protective, often yoked outer shirt garment

sou'wester sailor's long oilskin coat with buckles

stole long scarf or shoulder wrap with hanging ends in front

surcoat tunic worn over medieval armor; any outer coat

surtout man's long, fitted frock coat; woman's hooded mantle

tabard knight's short, loose, and sleeveless tunic; herald's cape emblazoned with lord's arms (medieval Europe)

talma long, circular cape or shoulder cape and hood (19th c.)

tippet fur or cloth shoulder cape

toga crescent-shaped fabric that is wrapped and draped around the body (ancient Rome)

topcoat lightweight overcoat

topper woman's short, loose-fitting topcoat

topsider heavy-duty, capelike, rubber raincoat

trench coat double-breasted raincoat with deep pockets, wide belt, and epaulets

tunic loose, draped gown, gathered at hips (ancient Greece and Rome)

ulster long, loose, belted, heavy coat, esp. with hood or cape (Ireland)

watch coat sailor's heavy overcoat

wrap outer garment worn wrapped and overlapping around body

Coats and Jackets

basque woman's tight bodice jacket with attached skirt

bi-swing jacket with pleat or gusset at back of arms, allowing free movement

blazer single-breasted, informal coat with three patch pockets and metal buttons, in solid color or stripes

blouse loose, calf-length worker's garment

bolero very short, open jacket without lapels, often sleeveless

bomber jacket fitted leather jacket, orig. for bomber pilot; pilot jacket

box coat short, square-cut coat

bush jacket safari jacket

car coat protective coat for driving; coach coat

cardigan close-fitting, knitted jacket that opens down front

claw hammer *Informal.* swallow-tailed coat (18th c.)

coach coat car coat

combat jacket adaptation of close-fitting, waist-length woolen jacket with tight cuffs and waist, formerly worn by military personnel

cutaway single-breasted coat with knee-length skirts in back

denim jacket sturdy, fitted jacket of coarse blue twill fabric; jean jacket

dinner jacket short, dark coat with silk rolled collar and no tails; tuxedo jacket

dolman woman's coat with wide dolman sleeves tapering at the wrists

double-breasted jacket jacket having deep, overlapping front closure and two rows of buttons

doublet man's close-fitting jacket, sometimes sleeveless (16th c.)

Eton jacket short, black jacket with wide lapels and long sleeves

flyaway jacket loose, flowing jacket with fullness at back

formal man's evening jacket

frock coat close-fitting dress coat with no waist seam and long skirts front and back

guernsey man's heavy, close-fitting, knitted sporting jacket

hacking jacket riding jacket with tight waist and flared skirt having slit sides or back

jean jacket denim jacket

jerkin close-fitting, hip-length, sleeveless jacket

justaucorps fitted, knee-length coat with flaring and stiffened skirts (17th c.)

kirtle man's tunic (medieval Europe)

lounge coat single- or double-breasted informal coat with no waist seam; smoking jacket

mackinaw short, belted coat of heavy, nappy mackinaw wool, often in plaid

Mao jacket jacket with long, close-fitting cut and narrow, tight, stand-up mandarin collar, popular in China

maxicoat full-length coat

mess jacket fitted, waist-length uniform jacket; monkey jacket

monkey jacket mess jacket

morning coat coat with front cut away to tails at center-vented back

Nehru jacket lightweight, fitted jacket with band collar (India)

Norfolk jacket usu. tweed jacket with box pleats, patch pockets, and belt

pilot jacket bomber jacket

pourpoint padded, quilted doublet

Prince Albert long, double-breasted frock coat

reefer short, double-breasted jacket

sack coat man's straight-backed jacket of coarse black cloth

safari jacket long, belted cotton jacket with pairs of pleated pockets above and below belt; bush jacket

sanbenito Spanish sackcloth coat for penitents

shell jacket short, tight, front-buttoning military jacket

shooting jacket loose-fitting, durable hunting jacket

shrug woman's tight-fitting, one-button, waist-length jacket

single-breasted jacket jacket having single button row and no overlapping closure

ski jacket lightweight, waterproof jacket, insulated for protection from cold, usu. worn in snow

smoking jacket lounge coat

spencer waist-length jacket (19th c.)

spiketail coat tails

sport coat man's casual coat

sport jacket sport coat

swagger coat coat flaring from shoulder to hem

swallow-tailed coat tails

tails man's fitted dress jacket cut short in front, with two long, tapering skirts at back; spiketail coat; swallow-tailed coat

tuxedo jacket dinner jacket without tails

Windbreaker *Trademark.* thin jacket of wind-resistant material, esp. nylon

woolly wool jacket

Zouave jacket short, colorful military jacket, closed at neck only (French Algerian)

Suits and Uniforms

bib and tucker *Brit. slang.* entire outfit of clothing, esp. formal

black tie man's semiformal evening wear usu. tuxedo jacket worn with black bow tie

blues formal blue U.S. military uniform; dress blues

bodysuit close-fitting, one-piece torso garment, often with sleeves and snap crotch opening

business suit traditionally tailored, two- or three-piece suit

butternuts homespun overalls dyed brown with butternut extract

cap and gown ceremonial, full-length gown with sleeves and mortarboard cap, worn at commencement and other academic ceremonies

casual suit man's informal two-piece suit

civvies *Informal.* civilian clothes, as opposed to military uniform

coverall one-piece protective garment reaching from neck to ankles

double-breasted suit trousers and jacket with overlapping front closure and two rows of buttonholes

dress blues blues

dress suit man's formal or business suit

dress whites whites

fatigues heavy-duty military work uniform, often colored khaki or in camouflage design

full dress most formal military uniform

gi thick cotton jacket and loose trousers worn by martial arts practitioners (Japan)

gray flannel suit conservative gray wool business suit

jumper workman's jumpsuit

jumpsuit one-piece garment consisting of shirt with attached trousers; one-piece suit

layette newborn infant's complete outfit

leisure suit man's casual trousers and matching jacket styled like a shirt, often in pastel polyster (1970's)

livery identifying uniform of servants or workers

lounge suit suit with short-skirted jacket, slightly fitted; *Chiefly Brit.* man's suit for informal occasions

mod suit fitted suit in exaggerated fashion of 1960's, esp. with bell-bottom trousers and wide or no lapels

olive drab sturdy military field uniform

one-piece suit jumpsuit

pantsuit woman's suit with slacks instead of skirt matching jacket; slack suit

pinstripe suit dark suit with thin, white, vertical stripes

regimentals military uniform of particular regiment

riding habit fitted jacket and breeches worn while riding horseback

sack suit suit with short, loose-fitting sack coat

sailor suit traditional white or blue cotton naval uniform with wide collar and bell-bottomed trousers

scrub suit gown worn in surgery by doctors and assisting personnel

seersucker suit man's summer-weight suit in striped cotton

slack suit pantsuit

snow suit child's one- or two piece cold-weather garment consisting of heavily lined pants and jacket

sport suit outfit of casual cut and cloth; town-and-country suit

stripes prison garb, traditionally wide-striped shirt and pants

suit jacket and trousers or skirt in matching material, sometimes including vest

summer suit suit of lightweight fabric

tailor-made jacket and skirt or trousers made to measure

three-piece suit jacket, trousers, and vest

town-and-country suit sport suit

tropical suit suit of very lightweight fabric and pale color, designed for comfort in tropics

tuxedo man's semiformal outfit consisting of single- or double-breasted jacket with satin lapels and trousers with stripe down their sides

two-piece suit suit consisting of jacket and trousers only, without vest

undress informal military uniform, as opposed to full dress

whites formal white U.S. military uniform; dress whites

white tie man's formal evening jacket with tails, usu. worn with white vest and white bow tie

zoot suit flashy suit with extremely baggy trousers, padded shoulders, and high waist

Sweaters and Vests

bodice woman's laced vest worn over blouse or dress
bulky thickly knit, voluminous sweater
bulletproof vest protective vest of bulletproof mesh worn under shirt or jacket
cardigan close-fitting, casual sweater buttoning down front
cashmere sweater of soft cashmere wool
crew neck pullover with round, collarless neck
fisherman sweater heavy wool sweater knit in traditional patterns
gilet *Chiefly Brit.* woman's waistcoat
hand-knit sweater made by hand, not by machine
Irish knit hand-knit sweater of Irish wool, often white
liberty bodice sleeveless vest with buttons
pullover sweater with no fastenings, slipped on over head; slipover; *Chiefly Brit.* sweater
shoulderette woman's light, knit shawl, with ends formed into sleeves
ski sweater heavy wool sweater for cold weather
slipover pullover
Sloppy Joe girl's loose, baggy sweater
sweater knitted or crocheted jacket, usu. of wool, silk, acrylic, or cotton, in pullover or cardigan style
turtleneck close-fitting sweater with high, folded band collar
vest short, tight-fitting, sleeveless garment worn under jacket or coat, esp. by men
V-neck sweater with neck forming V open to sternum
waistcoat *Chiefly Brit.* vest

Shirts and Tops

aloha shirt brightly colored sport shirt, usu. short sleeved (Hawaii)
basque tight-fitting bodice
bib protective cloth or plastic tied around neck under chin
blouse woman's loose shirt extending from neck to waistline, with or without collar and sleeves
blouson voluminous shirt with close-fitted waistband
body shirt woman's close-fitting top with attached panties that snap at the crotch
bush shirt loose-fitting, cotton shirt with patch pockets
bustier woman's tight-fitting, sleeveless, strapless, waist-length top
button-down shirt shirt on which collar points button to shirt body
camise lightweight, loose-fitting, long-sleeved shirt
camp shirt short-sleeved shirt or blouse with notched collar, usu. having two breast pockets
dashiki voluminous, collarless pullover shirt, often in bright colors (Africa)

dickey detachable insert worn to fill neckline and simulate shirt front
dress shirt man's shirt to be worn in evening or with necktie
evening shirt formal white shirt
evzone palace guard's pleated, white, gauze shirt (ancient Greece)
flannel shirt durable work shirt of flannel cotton
garibaldi woman's loose, high-necked, full-sleeved blouse, orig. red
hair shirt rough shirt of animal hair, worn over skin as penance
halter woman's top that covers breasts and leaves shoulders bare, often with straps around neck
Hawaiian shirt loose-fitting, short-sleeved shirt of lightweight fabric printed in colorful, bold designs, usu. of nature scenes
hickory shirt sturdy, cotton work shirt with vertical stripes
jersey casual, close-fitting, stretchy-knit cotton or wool shirt
jumper *Chiefly Brit.* loose blouse or pullover
jupe man's shirt or woman's bodice (Scotland)
jupon tight-fitting, padded garment worn under armor (medieval Europe)
long-sleeved shirt shirt with sleeves ending at wrist
middy blouse woman's or child's loose-fitting, hip-length, pullover blouse with sailor collar
Pendleton *Trademark.* heavy, plaid wool shirt
plaid shirt shirt in tartan pattern
polo shirt close-fitting casual knit pullover with short sleeves and turned collar or banded neck
romper child's one-piece garment with short, loose trousers gathered at knees
rugby shirt knitted pullover sport shirt, usu. in broad, horizontal stripes with white collar
Russian blouse hip-length shirt with full sleeves, tall collar, and embroidery (19th c.)
sacque unfitted or semifitted bodice
sark shirt (medieval Britain)
shell woman's simple sleeveless blouse
shirt cloth garment for upper part of body, usu. with collar, sleeves, and open front
shirtwaist woman's blouse tailored like man's dress shirt
short-sleeved shirt shirt with sleeves ending above elbow
sport shirt casual, outdoor shirt
tank top sleeveless, scoop-necked shirt of thin fabric
top garment worn over chest and shoulders, sometimes with sleeves
T-shirt collarless, short-sleeved, cotton-knit casual shirt
tunic blouse extending to hips or knees and gathered at waist
turtleneck long-sleeved jersey with high, turned down, tubelike collar

Dresses and Skirts

apron protective cloth panel tied around waist at back
Beardsley gown formal gown (Britain, 19th c.)
bouffant skirt extremely full, puffed-up skirt
bridal gown elaborate white wedding dress
bustle framework that supported full skirt (19th c.)
cheongsam dress with slit skirt and high mandarin collar (Asia)
coat dress dress with buttons in front, from neck to hem
cocktail dress short-skirted party dress
cotehardie man's or woman's long-sleeved, thigh-length, belted, buttoned, or laced garment (medieval Europe)
crinoline petticoat of stiff netting and/or taffeta, worn under hoop skirt
culottes full skirt divided into knee-length pants
dirndl full skirt gathered at waist or dress with close-fitting bodice and full skirt
dress woman's garment with top and skirt in one piece
evening gown formal, full-length dress of high-quality fabric such as silk or satin
fillebeg kilt
float loose, flowing, sometimes fancy dress
flounce wide ruffle attached to skirt
formal full-length evening gown
gown loose-flowing, usu. full-length, often formal dress
granny dress old-fashioned, full-length, loose-fitting dress, esp. in black
grass skirt skirt of grass reeds hung from waistband; hula skirt (Oceania)
gymslip girl's knee-length school skirt
harem skirt skirt divided into two parts and gathered at ankles
hobble skirt narrow skirt tapering to ankles, with side slit
hoop skirt full skirt stiffened with hoops
housedress loose, casual cotton dress
hula skirt grass skirt
johnny hospital patient's gown that is open at back, collarless, and short-sleeved, usu. in white or green
jumper sleeveless, one-piece dress
jupe woman's skirt (Scotland)
kilt man's plaid, wool, wraparound skirt, hanging to knees; fillebeg (Scotland)
kirtle long gown or dress; man's tunic (medieval Europe)
lavalava colorful cloth wrapped around body as skirt (Polynesia)
maxiskirt ankle-length skirt
microminiskirt skirt ending at top of thighs
midiskirt midcalf-length skirt
miniskirt midthigh-length skirt
Mother Hubbard loose, shapeless dress
muumuu loose, full-length dress, usu. of bright print fabric (Hawaii)
pant dress dress with culotte-style skirt

peplum short, flared skirt with overskirt hanging in points

petticoat fancy underskirt, often with ruffled or lace hem

pinafore sleeveless dress with biblike bodice over blouse

pleated skirt girl's skirt with multiple pleats from waist to knees

pollera embroidered fiesta skirt with capelike top (Latin America)

princesse dress fitted one-piece dress without waist seam

robe de style long, formal gown with tight bodice and bouffant skirt

sari long, wrapped silk or cotton dress, worn with one end draped over head or shoulders (India)

sarong full-length, wrapped or draped skirt (Oceania and Malaysia)

sheath woman's close-fitting, unbelted dress

shift woman's loose-fitting dress that hangs straight and has no waistline

shirtdress dress tailored like shirt, with button-down front closure

skirt free-hanging outer garment that extends downward from waist

slit dress usu. close-fitting dress, cut open along one thigh at side

sundress sometimes strapless dress with bodice that exposes arms, shoulders, and back

tea gown semiformal, midcalf-length dress that has a yoke and full sleeves

tent dress loose-fitting dress without waistline that flares outward from shoulders to great fullness at hem

trousseau bridal gown and accessories

tube dress close-fitting, straight, full-length dress

Turkish skirt full skirt divided into loose trousers

tutu ballerina's very short, stiff, projecting skirt

wraparound skirt or dress that encircles body and overlaps at full-length opening

wrapskirt seamless piece of material worn wrapped around waist and legs as skirt

Trousers, Shorts, and Leggings

antigropelos waterproof leggings

baggies Slang. loose, knee-length swim trunks

bell-bottoms trousers widely flared at hem

Bermuda shorts knee-length shorts, often in bright plaids

bloomers woman's or child's full trousers, gathered at knee

blue jeans denims

breeches trousers, esp. knee-length

britches breeches; trousers

buckskins heavy leather trousers

Capri pants fitted casual pants to midcalf, with slit at bottom of sides

chaps cowboy's protective leather leggings, worn over pants and joined by belt or lacing

chinos casual trousers of polished chino cotton

clam diggers midcalf casual pants

cords corduroys

corduroys trousers of corduroy cotton with vertical wales; cords

culottes knee-length shorts, cut wide to resemble skirt

cutoffs full-length trousers cut off above knee to form shorts

denims pants of durable blue denim cotton; blue jeans; dungarees; jeans

dhoti man's long loin cloth (India)

ducks trousers of durable duck cotton

dungarees denims

gabardines dress trousers of gabardine wool

gaiters cloth or leather leggings buttoned over shoe tops and ankles

galligaskins loose, wide leggings (16th-17th c.)

gamashes horseback rider's leggings or gaiters (Scotland)

gambados horseman's leggings worn under jodhpurs

high-waters Slang. pants hemmed above ankles

hiphuggers woman's trousers that fit tight over hips and flare below knee

hot pants short shorts

jeans denims

jodhpurs riding breeches cut full at thigh, with stirrup foot strap; riding breeches

kerseys work pants of coarse, ribbed kersey wool

knee breeches pants fitted at knees like knickers

knickerbockers knickers

knickers short, loose pants, banded at knee, usu. for women and children; knickerbockers

lederhosen leather shorts with suspenders (Bavaria)

leggings protective covering for leg below knee, esp. of leather or canvas

Levi's Trademark. popular blue denim trousers

loincloth simple cloth wrapped around waist and groin

long pants pants hemmed at ankle

matador pants toreador pants

moleskins pants of durable cotton with thick nap on one side

overalls loose protective trousers with bib front and shoulder straps

Oxford bags extremely baggy trousers (1920's)

pantaloons short, loose-fitting trousers

pants outer garment covering each leg separately from waist to ankle; trousers

pedal pushers woman's tight-fitting, calf-length pants

pegleg trousers trousers cut full at hips and narrow at ankles

plus fours voluminous breeches hemmed four inches below knees

puttees cloth wrapped around lower leg; buckled leather leggings with straps; putts

putts puttees

riding breeches jodhpurs

rompers child's one-piece playsuit with bloomer pants

shorts casual trousers hemmed above knee

short shorts very brief shorts, barely covering buttocks; hot pants

slacks casual trousers

spandex pants skintight pants of spandex stretch fabric

spats cloth or leather gaiter over ankle and instep and attached to shoes

spatterdashes protective knee-high buckled leggings (18th c.)

stretch pants tight trousers of elasticized fabric

tights skintight, often sheer, knitted leggings extending from waist to toes or neck to toes

toreador pants fitted trousers banded at knee, patterned after bullfighter's trousers; matador pants

trews tight tartan shorts worn under kilt; full-length tartan trousers

trousers pants

trunk hose short, full breeches reaching to midthigh (16th-17th c.)

tweeds trousers of patterned tweed wool

waders waterproof trousers reaching from armpits to attached rubber boots, worn over regular trousers

Sporting and Exercise Wear

bathing suit man's or woman's swimming outfit: trunks, two-piece bikini, or one-piece leotard; swimsuit; swimwear

bikini woman's scanty two-piece bathing suit comprised of panties and brassiere

body stocking sometimes sheer, tight-fitting torso garment, often with sleeves and legs

bodywear leotard, tights, or body stocking

gym pants loose exercise pants

gym suit track suit or jogging suit

jams Trademark. long, baggy, brightly colored men's swim trunks

jogging suit usu. matching, loose-fitting top and pants, worn during athletic workout

leotard close-fitting torso garment, with or without sleeves, worn by dancers and acrobats

muscle shirt sleeveless T-shirt, usu. tight-fitting, worn typically by body builders

one-piece bathing suit sleeveless leotard for swimwear

ski pants pants of stretch fabric with foot stirrup

ski suit stretch pants and parka, worn for skiing and outdoor winter activities

string bikini skimpy two-piece bathing suit that barely covers crotch and nipples

sweatpants loose, fleece-lined, cotton athletic pants, gathered at waist with drawstring or elastic

sweats sweat suit

sweatshirt loose, long-sleeved, cotton-knit, fleece-lined shirt for athletic wear

sweat suit loose, cotton-knit exercise pants and pullover; sweats

swimsuit bathing suit

swimwear bathing suit

track suit loose-fitting sweat worn by athletes, esp. runners, before and after competition and during workouts

trunks shorts, esp. for swimming or boxing

two-piece bathing suit woman's bathing suit comprised of brassiere and panties; bikini

unitard close-fitting, clingy, full-body garment reaching from ankles to neck and wrists

wetsuit close-fitting rubber suit, sometimes worn in parts, that covers body from ankles to wrists and neck and retains body heat in cold water

Liturgical Vestments

alb priest's long, white, linen robe for Mass

amice priest's square cloth worn over shoulders

cassock priest's full-length garment with tight-fitting sleeves; soutane

chasuble priest's ornamented, knee-length outer garment without sleeves

cincture cord looped twice around waist to hold alb in place

clerical collar priest's narrow, stiff collar that buttons at back

cope bishop's long, open cloak

cotta altar boy or chorister's short, white, loose shirt

dalmatic deacon's tunic with wide sleeves and stripes descending from shoulders

Geneva gown loose, large-sleeved black gown worn by some Protestant clergy

maniple priest's long, silk band, worn looped over left arm

miter tall, pointed bishop's hat

mozzetta short shoulder cape with hood, worn by pope, cardinals, and bishops

pallium thin, ringlike band of wool across shoulders, with lappets in front and back, worn by pope and archbishops

rochet prelate's close-fitting, long-sleeved, winged, or sleeveless ceremonial garment

soutane priest's cassock or tunic

stole long, narrow scarf worn around neck, with ends hanging down or crossed over chest

surplice loose, white, knee-length outer garment with wide sleeves

tunicle sub-deacon's tunic worn over alb

vestment any garment worn by clergy or their assistants during religious service

Armor

ailette protective shoulder plate of forged steel worn over coat of mail

armor protective body covering of metal, leather, or chain mail (medieval Europe)

backplate piece of armor covering back from shoulders to waist

beaver visor

brassard upper arm covering of armor

breastplate cuirass

brigandine medieval body armor of scales or plates

chain mail lightweight, flexible armor of interlinked metal rings

coat of mail upper body chain mail

cubitiere rounded elbow covering of armor; elbow piece

cuirass fitted leather or cloth bodice armor that protects breast and back; breastplate

cuisse plate armor for thigh front

elbow piece cubitiere

epaulière shoulder covering of armor; pauldron

fauld armor piece below breastplate, comprised of thin, overlapping plates

footpiece attached covering of armor for top of foot; solleret

gauntlet reinforced protective glove

gorget neck-encircling collar of armor on which helmet sits

greave lower leg protector of armor; jambeau

hauberk knee-length tunic of chain mail

heaume armor helmet outside mail hood that rests on shoulders

helmet rigid covering for head and neck with visor front

jambeau greave

kneepiece circular armor joint at knee; poleyn

lame one of several thin, overlapping plates that form a piece of armor

pallette round armor plate above heart, upper chest, and shoulder

pauldron epaulière

placate piece of armor that reinforces breastplate over lower torso

plastron plate armor for front of upper torso

plate individual section of suit of armor

poleyn kneepiece

shoulder piece connective armor joint between trunk and arm piece; epaulière

skirt of tasses armor plates hung around hips to which tasses and sword attach

solleret footpiece

surcoat garment worn over medieval armor, often embroidered with heraldic arms

taces tasses

tasses overlapping armor plates forming skirt at hips; taces

tuille hinged armor plate above thigh

vambrace piece of plate armor for forearm

visor protective helmet plate that lowers over face; beaver

UNDERGARMENTS
Lingerie and Support Garments
Men's Underwear
Nightclothes and Dishabille
Hosiery

See also: *Chap. 10: Ornaments and Accessories; Chap. 22: Sex, Love, and Romance*

Lingerie and Support Garments

bandeau strapless, band-shaped brassiere

bikini very brief, high-cut underpants

bloomers full, loose underpants, gathered at knee

bodice tight-fitting torso covering

body stocking close-fitting, one-piece torso garment with sleeves and legs

bodywear leotard, tights, or body stocking

bra brassiere

brassiere garment supporting breasts in two cups; bra

bustle framework used to support full skirt (19th c.)

camisole light, loose bodice worn over corset or brassiere; sheer blouse with shoulder straps and low neck

chastity belt belt of leather or forged metal that covered crotch to prevent sexual intercourse (medieval Europe)

chemise loose, short slip; shimmy

chemisette detachable, lace neckline filler

combinations one-piece undergarment with sleeves and legs

corselet combination brassiere and girdle

corset boned, laced, elasticized foundation garment, used to firm waist and hips, often including garter belt and brassiere

crinoline coarse, stiff petticoat worn under hoop skirt

crotchless panties bikini underpants with opening at crotch

cutty sark woman's short undergarment (Scotland)

drawers woman's knee-length undershorts

dress shields absorbent pads worn in armpits

falsies *Informal.* shaped pads worn inside a brassiere; padded bra

farthingale hoop or padded roll worn beneath skirt to extend hipline (16th c.)

foundation garment woman's support garment, such as corset

garter belt belt with straps attached, used to hold up stockings; suspender belt

garters elastic bands or straps that hold up hosiery

girdle light corset extending from waist to thighs

G-string backless panties covering crotch only, held up by cord at waist

knickers loose underpants, banded at knee; *Chiefly Brit.* panties

leotard close-fitting, skintight torso garment consisting of briefs and often sleeveless top

lingerie woman's underwear, often lacy or decorative

merry widow *Slang.* corset

padded bra brassiere with foam padding in each cup to make breasts appear larger

pannier hoop worn to extend skirts (19th c.)

pantalets long drawers with attached ruffle visible below knee (19th c.)

panties underpants

panty girdle girdle with sewn-in crotch, often with garters

pasties small, round coverings for woman's nipples, chiefly worn by striptease dancers

peek-a-boo brassiere with openings at each nipple

petticoat underskirt with ruffled or lace hem

pettipants thigh or knee-length underpants, banded in lace

push-up bra brassiere with added support under cups to lift breasts; uplift brassiere

scanties abbreviated bikini panties

shimmy chemise

slip dress-length undergarment with shoulder straps

smock yoked undershirt; chemise

stays *Chiefly Brit.* bone-stiffened corset

step-ins short panties

support garment usu. elastic device that binds or bears up part of body

suspender belt garter belt

tap pants loose-fitting underpants, similar to pants worn for tap dancing

teddy loose-fitting, one piece underslip with crotch; combination chemise and panties

tournure bustle worn for hip extension

truss extremely binding girdle, used esp. for treatment of hernias

underall garment that covers torso and hips

underpants woman's or child's underwear that covers groin, buttocks, and crotch; panties; undies

underskirt loose waist-to-knee undergarment

undies woman's or child's underwear, esp. underpants

uplift brassiere push-up bra

wyliecoat warm, woolen or flannel undershirt; petticoat (Scotland)

Men's Underwear

athletic supporter tight-fitting support garment for genitals, esp. worn by dancer or athlete; cup; jockstrap

baggies *Informal.* loose, boxer-style underpants

boxer shorts loose-cut underpants reaching to midthigh

breechcloth loincloth

briefs abbreviated, jockey style underpants

BVD's *Trademark.* jockey shorts

codpiece bag or flap used to conceal opening of man's trousers; decorative external G-string (15th-16th c.)

cup athletic supporter

drawers underpants, esp. boxer style

flannels boxer shorts of flannel

G-string athletic supporter

jockey shorts brief, close-fitting underpants that end at top of thigh

jockstrap athletic supporter

linens linen underwear

loincloth cloth wrapped around waist and loins that covers genitals; breechcloth

long johns *Informal.* long underwear

long underwear full-length, usu. cotton-knit underwear that covers limbs, worn esp. in cold weather

shorts underpants

singlet *Chiefly Brit.* undershirt

skivvies *Informal.* man's underwear

tank top sleeveless, low-necked undershirt

thermals knitted cotton or wool long underwear, designed to retain body heat

T-shirt collarless, short-sleeved, cotton-knit undershirt

underclothes underwear

underdrawers undershorts

underpants undershorts

undershirt underwear for torso; undervest; union vest

undershorts underwear for groin, crotch, and buttocks; underdrawers; underpants

undervest *Chiefly Brit.* undershirt

underwear undergarments, shirt or shorts; underclothes

union suit *Chiefly Brit.* one-piece undergarment

union vest *Chiefly Brit.* undershirt

unmentionables undergarments

vest *Chiefly Brit.* undershirt

woolens heavy woolen long underwear

Nightclothes and Dishabille

at home casual wear; lounging clothes

baby doll woman's sheer, two-piece nightgown

bathrobe loose, absorbent robe worn before or after bath or as dressing gown

bed gown sleeping gown

bed jacket upper body sleepwear

boudoir dress loose dressing gown

brunch coat casual housecoat worn at late breakfast

camisole woman's short negligee

coverup woman's loose, sheer robe or lounging coat

creeper infant's one-piece garment

diaper absorbent cloth folded between baby's legs and fastened around waist

dishabille casual, informal dress worn inside one's home

dressing gown robe, esp. of silk, worn while dressing or resting; morning dress

dressing jacket coat worn while dressing or resting

gertrude infant's pajama top that buttons across shoulders

housecoat woman's long-skirted, informal coat

jammies *Baby talk.* pajamas

kimono long, sashed, wide-sleeved traditional robe (Japan)

lounging robe loose, comfortable dressing gown

morning dress dressing gown

negligee woman's loose, diaphanous, often lacy nightdress

nightclothes sleeping garments

nightdress woman's sleeping garment

nightgown loose, dresslike garment worn in bed

nightie *Informal.* woman's or child's nightgown

nightshirt short nightgown

pajamas loose, lightweight sleeping shirt and trousers; also, *esp. Brit.*, pyjamas

peignoir negligee or dressing gown, esp. with fur cuffs, lace, or other decoration

p.j.'s *Informal.* pajamas

robe loose, informal garment for dressing, bathing, or resting

robe de chambre *French.* dressing gown

sleeper child's pajamas with attached foot coverings

smoking jacket man's loose-fitting lounging jacket

wrapper jacket or clothing wrapped around body

yukata dressing gown or robe of lightweight cotton (Japan)

Hosiery

anklet woman's short sock that reaches just above ankle

argyles socks knitted in varicolored diamond pattern

athletic sock thick cotton sock, usu. white

bobbysocks girl's socks that fold above ankle

boothose long socks worn under boots

crew sock short, bulky, ribbed sock

dress sheer woman's finely knit stocking

fishnet stocking full length stocking woven in coarse mesh

footlet woman's thin, very low sock, worn as protective shoeliner instead of hosiery and not meant to be seen; Ped

garter stocking stocking extending to midthigh, held up by garter

halfhose elasticized stocking extending to just above knee

hose knitted coverings for foot and leg; hosiery

hosiery garments for foot and leg, esp. socks and stockings; hose

knee-high sock or stocking that reaches to knee

knee-hose stockings that reach to knee

knee-sock hose that reaches to knee

leg warmer footless knit legging for dancers or athletes

lisle hose hose of lisle cotton

maillot tights for dancers or acrobats

mesh stocking coarse-knit hose; fishnet stocking

nylons woman's stockings of synthetic material, esp. nylon

pantyhose woman's one-piece undergarment, combining panties and skintight, full-length hose

Peds *Trademark.* footlet

rayon stocking woman's stocking made from rayon

seamless stocking sheer stocking without seams

sheers *Informal.* sheer stockings

sheer stockings finely knit thin hose; sheers

silk stockings finely knit silk hose

slouch sock sock with long top that is bunched around ankle

sock knitted foot covering that extends above ankle

stocking close-fitting knitted covering for foot and leg

stretch sock hose of elastic material
support hose elasticized stocking that provides support for leg
sweat sock heavy wool or cotton sock
tights skintight sheer garment that extends from waist to toes
tube sock sock with unformed heel, knitted in cylindrical shape
varsity sock athletic sock banded with school colors
work sock sturdy wool or cotton sock
woolens hose made from wool

ORNAMENTS AND ACCESSORIES

Ornaments
Jewelry
Eyeglasses
Neckwear
Hand wear and Gloves
Waistbands and Belts
Functional Attire and Accessories
Symbolic and Emblematic Attire
Luggage and Cases

See also: *Chap. 3: Minerals, Metals, and Rocks; Chap. 5: Containers; Chap. 7: Ornamental and Functional Articles; Chap. 10: Outer Garments; Clothing Materials; Hats, Headgear, and Hairpieces; Fashion and Garment Parts*

Ornaments

agrafe ornamental clasp on armor or costume
armlet band around upper arm
band narrow, decorative strip worn on arm, neck, or waist
bodkin ornamental pin-shaped clasp for hair
bouquet bunch of flowers fastened together
boutonniere single flower worn in lapel buttonhole
bow ribbon doubled into two or more loops, usu. worn in hair
comb strip of hard material with teethlike projections, used to hold hair in place
cordon decorative cord or ribbon
corsage arrangement of flowers worn pinned to clothing, esp. by women
crest plume on helmet; heraldic emblem
epaulette often fringed shoulder ornament on military jacket
feather bird's feather worn in hair or on hat
festoon wreath or garland hanging in loop
garland ornamental wreath or festoon of flowers
netsuke small, finely carved toggle on kimono sash (Japan)
nosegay small bunch of flowers; bouquet; posy
panache tuft of feathers or tassel on helmet
plume cluster of feathers
pompom tuft or ball of fabric and fringe
posy bouquet of flowers; nosegay
shoulder knot ornamental knot or ribbon on shoulder of military uniform

sporran fur pouch hung off belt in front of kilt (Scotland)
tassel dangling fringed cords hanging from a roundish knob
whim-wham fanciful object or ornament on clothing
wreath braided, circular band of flowers worn in hair

Jewelry

aigrette spray of gemstones depicting plume of feathers, worn in hair or on hat
anklet band around ankle
armlet jeweled armband above elbow
band narrow ring encircling finger, usu. of precious metal
bangle rigid, ring-shaped, slip-on or clasped anklet or bracelet
bauble decorative trinket
beads rounded, pierced pieces of glass, metal, wood, or stone strung together in strands
bezel groove and flange holding gem in setting; slanting facets of exposed portion of cut gem in setting
bibelot small trinket of curiosity, beauty, or rarity
bijou small piece of delicate jewelry; trinket
bracelet ornamental chain or band encircling wrist
brooch large pin with clasp, worn at breast
cameo gem carved in relief, esp. portrait
carat unit of weight for gemstones equal to 200 milligrams
carcanet jeweled ornamental collar or necklace
chain series of small, connected, metal links, usu. worn around neck
chaplet garland for head; string of beads
charm representational item worn as protection from evil, token of luck, or to invoke magic powers
chatelaine woman's ornamental clasp at waist for keys or purse; decorative chain suspended between two points
coronet small crown
costume jewelry inexpensive jewelry made from nonprecious substances
crown jeweled royal headdress of precious metal
crown jewels crown, scepter, and other royal regalia
cuff links ornamental buttons joined by chain or shank for fastening French cuff
diadem royal headdress; crown
diamante synthetic diamond
earring ornamental object hung from earlobe either by clasp or through hole pierced in lobe
fob chain for pocket watch
gem precious stone or pearl cut and mounted as ornament
gemstone precious or semiprecious stone used as a gem
gewgaw showy bauble or trinket
gimcrack showy trinket of little value

girandole earring or brooch with large gemstone surrounded by smaller ones
glass *Informal.* precious stone; plain glass substituted for precious stone
intaglio ornament with engraving beneath surface of material
knickknack trivial ornament
labret gemstone or other small ornament worn in hole pierced in lip
locket small, lidded case of precious metal on chain necklace, inside of which a memento or photograph can be placed
money clip two-armed metal fastener for holding paper money
necklace ornamental string or chain worn around neck
nose ring ring worn through hole pierced in one nostril of nose
parure set of jewelry worn together, such as earrings, bracelet, and necklace
pearl smooth, hard, rounded, white nacreous growth found within shell of some oysters, mounted or strung and used as jewelry
pendant decorative object hanging on chain or from earring
pin ornamental fastener attached to clothing with pointed wire or shaft
pinkie ring ring worn on little finger, esp. by men
post straight bar that pierces ear, often with attached setting that holds single pearl or stone as earring
precious stone class of gemstones of great value, esp. diamond, emerald, ruby, sapphire
rhinestone colorless synthetic gem, often of glass
ring band of precious metal worn on finger, often set with gem
rivière necklace of precious stones, usu. in several strands
rondelle small round bead used as spacer in necklace
scrimshaw carved, engraved object of whalebone
semiprecious stone any of a class of gemstones of moderate value, such as amethyst, garnet, opal, or topaz
setting decorated metal base in which stone or stones are placed, esp. on ring
signet ring ring bearing seal or initials
solitaire single gem set alone, esp. on ring
stickpin ornamental pin, esp. worn on necktie
stone gemstone
stud solid button mounted on metal post and inserted in garment as ornamental fastener
tiara small, crownlike, jeweled headdress, often in semicircular shape
tie clip tiepin
tiepin tie clasp or stud with ornamental head, used to attach tie to shirt; tie clip
torque metal collar or neck chain used in ancient Germany and Gaul
trinket small, cheap, ornamental object

wampum polished shells strung as beads (American Indian)

wedding band plain gold ring worn to indicate married status

wristband bracelet or ornament encircling wrist

wristlet close-fitting, knitted wristband often attached to glove or sleeve

Eyeglasses

aviator glasses contoured, metal-framed goggles worn by fliers

bifocals eyeglasses with lenses that have separate sections, one for seeing close up and one for distance

blinkers opaque sidepieces that reduce peripheral vision

cheaters Slang. eyeglasses

contact lens thin lens that fits directly on cornea

dark glasses sunglasses

eyeglasses glass lenses that correct impaired vision, set in a frame with earpieces; spectacles

glasses eyeglasses

goggles protective glasses in flexible frame fitting snugly against face

granny glasses round lenses in thin metal frames

horn rims glasses with frames of variegated animal horn or similarly colored plastic

lens glass portion of eyeglasses that is ground to correct vision

lorgnette eyeglasses with attached handle; opera glasses

lorgnon monocle, pince-nez

monocle eyeglass for one eye, attached to cord; lorgnon

opera glasses lorgnette

peepers Slang. eyeglasses

pince-nez eyeglasses attached by spring or clamp to bridge of nose; lorgnon

Polaroids Trademark. popular sunglasses of glare-reduction polarized glass

quizzing glass small, single eyeglass on handle

reading glasses glasses used exclusively to aid in reading or close work

shades Slang. sunglasses

specs Informal. spectacles; eyeglasses

spectacles eyeglasses

sunglasses glasses with dark lenses that protect eyes from sunshine; dark glasses

Neckwear

ascot necktie or scarf knotted under chin, with broad ends hanging loose

bandanna large, colorful, patterned handkerchief tied around neck

bertha collar woman's wide, round shoulder cape and collar

boa long stole or scarf of fur or feathers

bolo tie thin cord with ornamental clasp; long string tie

bow tie small tie formed into bow at neck

chemisette lace filler for woman's shirt front

choker necklace that fits snugly around neck, often of velvet

clerical collar priest's narrow, stiff collar, buttoned at back; priest's collar; Roman collar

clip-on tie necktie that clips onto shirt collar instead of tying around neck

collar band, strip, or chain around neck

comforter heavy scarf, often of wool

cravat necktie or scarf worn around neck

dickey detachable collar and shirt front

dog collar chain with military identification tag

fichu woman's light, triangular scarf worn over shoulders and fastened in front, esp. to fill low neckline

foulard necktie or scarf of light foulard silk in small print design

four-in-hand long necktie or scarf tied in slipknot or Windsor knot with ends hanging

fur scarf, stole, or neckpiece of animal fur

Geneva bands two narrow strips of white cloth hanging from front collar of some Protestant clergy

golilla starched white linen collar standing out from neckline (Spain, 17th c.)

guimpe wide cloth covering nun's neck and shoulders

jabot lace cravat or frill on bodice front, often attached to neckband

kerchief square of cloth worn around neck or shoulders; neckerchief

lei necklace of flowers (Hawaii)

muffler wool or fur scarf

neckband cloth around neck

neckerchief kerchief

necktie narrow band of fabric looped around neck and fastened or tied in front

old school tie necktie with public school colors (Britain)

polo neck closed, round neckband of jumper or polo shirt

priest's collar clerical collar

rabato wide, stiff, lace-edged collar, standing at back on wire frame (17th c.)

Roman collar clerical collar

ruff stiff, wide neckpiece gathered in deep folds and radiating from neck

scapular band of cloth slitted for head opening and draped over shoulders by monks

scarf broad cloth or woven band worn over head or shoulders or around neck

school tie necktie with school colors or emblem

shawl rectangular or triangular piece of fabric worn over head and shoulders

stock clergyman's wide-banded scarf; long neckerchief worn with formal riding dress

stole woman's long, wide cloth worn around shoulders; priest's narrow scarf with ends crossed over chest

string tie narrow cord or cloth tie with ornamental clasp

tallith fringed prayer shawl worn by Jewish men

tie necktie

tippet long black prayer scarf of Anglican clergy;

scarf or stole worn with ends hanging down front

tucker lace or cloth worn in neckline of dress

vestee ornamental front worn beneath woman's blouse or jacket and visible at neckline

Windsor tie broad necktie knotted in loose bow or wide triangular knot

Hand wear and Gloves

baseball glove large leather glove for catching a baseball

batting gloves tight-fitting gloves worn when swinging a baseball bat

boxing glove heavily padded leather glove for boxing

brass knuckles set of connected metal rings worn as weapon on fist

cesta long, curved wicker basket worn on hand for jai alai

cestus boxer's leather hand covering reinforced with metal (ancient Rome)

driving gloves fitted leather gloves that end at knuckles, leaving fingertips uncovered

gauntlet high-cuffed glove; armored glove

glove hand covering with separate sheath for each finger and thumb

hockey gloves protective gloves for ice hockey

kid gloves soft kid leather gloves

long gloves woman's gloves that reach to elbow or upper arm

mitt fingerless glove; athletic glove, esp. baseball glove

mittens gloves with thumb sheath and single wide section for all fingers

mousquetaire woman's long glove with lengthwise buttoned opening at wrist

muff fur or wool cylinder open at both ends to insert hands for warmth

suede gloves gloves of napped leather

weight gloves tight-fitting leather gloves that terminate at knuckles, used for weightlifting

Waistbands and Belts

baldric ornamented belt worn over one shoulder, used to hold sword or bugle

bandolier ammunition belt worn over shoulder and across chest

bellyband band worn across stomach or around waist

belt waistband used esp. for holding up trousers or for decoration

breechcloth loincloth

cartridge belt belt holding ammunition, usu. worn around waist

ceinture belt or sash

cestus woman's symbolic belt, esp. for bride

cincture cord that holds priest's alb in place

cummerbund man's broad, tight-fitting waist sash, worn with formal attire

fascia broad, distinctly colored band worn at waist

garter belt undergarment belt with clips to hold up stockings

girdle close-fitting, elasticized support garment worn around waist and hips, usu. by women

hamaki wide, often elasticized belt worn for warmth (Japan)

loincloth cloth wrapped around loins and hips, often as only garment worn; breechcloth; waistcloth

obi broad sash for kimono (Japan)

rope belt belt of hemp or rope

sash ornamental band, ribbon, or scarf draped over shoulder and around waist

surcingle beltlike fastening for cassock or other garment

suspender belt garter belt with elastic straps for stockings

waistband strip of fabric attached to waistline of trousers or skirt, sometimes elasticized

waist belt strip of material worn around waist

waistcloth loincloth

Functional Attire and Accessories

accessory article or set of articles added to basic clothing for decoration, convenience, or completeness

apron protective, skirtlike piece of material tied around waist

atomizer sprayer for medicine or perfume

barrette clip or comb with toothlike projections for holding hair

bib protective covering for shirt front

blindfold covering for eyes, tied at back of head

brace frame providing support for injured neck or limb

braces *Chiefly Brit.* suspenders

bretelle suspenderlike shoulder straps that attach to waistband of garment

cane stick, usu. wood, for support in walking

crutches tall supports fitting under armpits to aid walking in case of debility

eyepatch protective patch covering one eye, held in place by cord around head

fan folded, collapsible silk or paper semicircle on rods splayed from pivot, moved back and forth to create cooling air current

handkerchief soft square of linen, cotton, or silk for grooming face or wiping nose; hanky

hanger any of various devices for hanging garment when not in use, esp. shoulder-shaped frame with hook at top

hanky *Informal.* handkerchief

hatpin long stickpin with ornamental top, used to fasten hat

holster leather case for pistol, open at top, worn on belt or under one arm

inro small lacquer box containing cosmetics and medicines, worn on waist sash of traditional costume (Japan)

money belt waistband with pouch to conceal money

parasol woman's lightweight umbrella, used to shield sun's rays

pomander aromatic mixture in bag used to scent stored clothes

sachet small bag or pad holding potpourri or perfumed powder, usu. placed in drawer or closet to scent clothes

scabbard leather or metal sheath for tool or sword

shield broad piece of protective material, esp. armor, carried on arm as defense against blows and projectiles

shoehorn metal, horn, or plastic implement with troughlike blade, placed at heel of shoe to aid in insertion of foot

shoe tree form inserted in shoe to stretch it or maintain its shape when not in use

sling cloth looped around neck to hold injured arm

spur U-shaped attachment for heel of shoe with blunt, pointed, or roweled projection, used by rider to urge on horse

suspenders straps attached to trousers in front and back and slung over shoulders; braces

swagger stick short, metal-tipped stick covered with leather and carried in hand

sweatband strip of absorbent material worn around head and across forehead, esp. when exercising

umbrella protective, water-resistant, collapsible cloth dome on frame

walking stick cane or stick used for support in walking

watch small timepiece on wrist strap or carried in pocket

watch fob vest pocket for watch; watch chain

wrist watch small timepiece strapped to wrist

Symbolic and Emblematic Attire

amulet good-luck charm, often a necklace

ankh cross with looped upper arm, viewed as symbol of life (ancient Egypt)

badge emblem, often metal, denoting membership or rank of wearer

blazon coat of arms

brassard cloth armband with insignia

caduceus herald's staff

chrisom white baptismal robe denoting innocence

cockade hat ornament worn as badge

cointise article of apparel worn as emblem, esp. lady's scarf on knight's helmet as token of favor

crepe black band of crinkled silk fabric, worn as token of mourning

fourragère braided, decorative, military cord worn on shoulder

mace ornamental staff carried as emblem of authority

menat amulet believed to bring divine protection (ancient Egypt)

orb sphere surmounted by cross, carried as symbol of royal power

orphrey ornamental band or border on ecclesiastical vestment

prayer shawl cloth worn around neck during prayer

phylactery either of two square leather boxes containing scripture, worn on left arm and head by Jewish men during prayer

rosary string of beads used for counting Catholic prayers

rosette fabric gathered to resemble rose, worn as badge of office

scarab stone or faience beetle, used as symbol of resurrection (ancient Egypt)

scepter ornamental rod or staff denoting authority

shoulder patch cloth with insignia worn on uniform sleeve

tallith fringed prayer shawl worn by Jewish men

zizith fringe of tassels on Jewish man's ceremonial garments

Luggage and Cases

alforja saddlebag

aparejo packsaddle of canvas or leather, used to hold load on pack animal

attaché case briefcase

backpack lightweight canvas or nylon sack, often on lightweight frame, carried on back while hiking

bag flexible sacklike container of paper, cloth, leather, or plastic, usu. capable of being closed at mouth

baggage luggage

bandbox cylindrical cardboard or wood box for lightweight items

barracks bag sturdy military cotton bag for personal items

belt bag small bag worn attached to belt

Bermuda bag round, cloth handbag with wooden handle

billfold leather case that folds flat, used to hold paper money

Boston bag traveling bag with two handles at top

botta bag leather wine sack carried over shoulder

bridget leather pouch or pack carried on back

briefcase flat, rectangular, usu. leather container for business papers and documents

caddie bag golf bag

cargo bag large, durable bag for freight

carpetbag small traveling bag made of carpeting

carryall large bag or case

carry-on bag small luggage taken on airplane

case small box or receptacle for storing items

cedar chest chest made of or lined with cedar, used for storage of clothing for protection against moths

cigarette case small, flat, often metal box for cigarettes

club bag rectangular leather traveling bag that narrows to zippered top closure

clutch woman's small, strapless handbag

compact small cosmetic case, esp. for pressed face powder

cosmetic bag small bag for holding cosmetics

disco bag small handbag on long strap or chain

ditty bag sailor's bag for small articles

Dorothy bag open-topped handbag with drawstring

duffel bag large, oblong, frameless, often canvas bag

etui small ornamental case

evening bag woman's elegant handbag of leather or fine fabric

fanny pack small zippered pouch suspended from belt around waist

flight bag small, lightweight travel bag, usu. with zippered outside pockets

footlocker small trunk, usu. placed at foot of bed

gamebag hunter's backpack with straps

garment bag long, soft, folding bag with hangers for clothing

Gladstone bag leather bag on rigid hinged frame that opens flat into two compartments

glasses case small protective case for eyeglasses

golf bag upright bag on frame, used for carrying golf clubs; caddie bag

grip hand luggage

gripsack traveling bag with handles

gym bag small, usu. nylon bag for athletic wear and equipment

handbag woman's small, leather bag for holding personal effects

hatbox cylindrical, rigid box for storing a hat

haversack knapsack with single strap worn over one shoulder

holdall all-purpose luggage container

housewife *Chiefly Brit.* pocket-size bag, esp. for carrying sewing implements

impedimenta baggage and other encumbrances

kit collection of matching bags used for travel

kit bag rectangular leather traveling bag with straps and sides that open

knapsack canvas or nylon bag strapped on back; rucksack

locker storage chest with lock

luggage suitcases or traveling bags; baggage

lunchpail child's or workman's metal food container with lid

musette bag small knapsack with one shoulder strap

overnight case small traveling bag for brief journeys

packsack *Chiefly Brit.* leather or canvas backpack

pocketbook woman's handbag; wallet or billfold

poke pouch, purse, or sack, esp. for gold dust and nuggets

portfolio large, flat leather case for holding photographs or drawings

portmanteau large leather trunk or suitcase that opens into two compartments

pouch small drawstring bag; lockable case for diplomatic papers

pullman case large suitcase

purse woman's handbag; small bag or case for coins

reticule woman's small handbag of beaded silk, brocade, or netting

rucksack knapsack

sack usu. rectangular pliable bag

saddlebag two bags on straps slung over horse

Saratoga trunk large traveling trunk with arched lid (19th c.)

satchel small bag, often with shoulder strap

schoolbag bag for schoolbooks and supplies

seabag sailor's soft, cylindrical duffel bag

shoulder bag bag with shoulder strap

snuffbox small, ornamental, lidded case for snuff

string bag mesh bag of heavy string or netting with two handles at top

suitcase rectangular or oblong traveling bag with rigid frame

tobacco pouch small folding bag for pipe and tobacco

toilet kit usu. zippered bag for toiletries

tote bag large handbag, esp. canvas

traveling bag hand-carried bag for traveler's clothes and personal items

traveling case small traveling bag

trunk large, sturdy, boxlike luggage or storage container

tucker bag food bag for outdoor use (Australia)

valise traveling bag or suitcase that can be carried by hand

vanity bag small case or handbag for toilet articles

wallet small, flat, folding pocketbook with compartments for personal papers, currency, and credit cards

wardrobe standing box or chest for clothes on hangers

wardrobe trunk upright trunk with clothes hangers and storage compartments

watchcase small, rigid box for storing watch

CLOTHING MATERIALS

Fabrics and Cloth
Synthetic Fibers and Textiles
Laces
Furs, Leathers, and Pelts

See also: *Chap. 10: Ornaments and Accessories;*
Chap. 10: Fashion and Garment Parts

Fabrics and Cloth

alpaca long, soft, silky fleece of Peruvian llama wool

Angora soft hair of Angora goat or rabbit, esp. for sweaters

astrakhan lustrous, closely curled wool of young Russian lamb

baize thick, soft, woolen cloth, usu. green, esp. for billiard table covers

balbriggan plain-knit cotton, esp. for underwear and hosiery

baldachin richly embroidered silk brocade, with gold and silver threads

barathea silk, worsted, or synthetic fabric with pebbly surface

barege sheer worsted cloth of silk or cotton, esp. for veils

batik fabric that is hand-dyed, using wax to repel dye in a marblelike pattern

batiste fine, sheer linen or muslin in plain or figured weave

bayadere fabric with horizontal colored stripes

beaver heavy cloth of felted wool similar to beaver fur, esp. for overcoats

bengaline lightweight fabric with crosswise cord woven from coarse yarn

bombazine twilled silk or rayon dyed black, having worsted filling

bouclé tufted, nubby cloth with loose yarn loops

brilliantine lightweight, lustrous cotton and mohair warp

broadcloth densely woven fabric with soft finish in plain or twill weave

brocade heavyweight silk cloth with elaborate raised design, often in gold or silver

brocatelle heavyweight silk or linen fabric with figures in high relief, esp. for upholstery

buckram stiff, sized cotton or linen, esp. for linings or bookbinding

bunting coarse, open-weave worsted or cotton fabric, esp. for flags

burlap coarse cloth of jute, flax, or hemp, esp. for sacking or wallpaper; hessian

byssus fine linen cloth used for wrapping mummies (ancient Egypt)

calico plain-woven cotton cloth with figured pattern

cambric fine white linen, esp. for linings or handkerchiefs

camel's hair soft, silky, felted camel wool or fabric resembling it, esp. for coats

camlet durable, waterproof cloth for outerwear

candlewick usu. cotton fabric of loosely twisted yarn bunched and tufted to form design

Canton crepe soft, heavyweight crepe with finely wrinkled surface

canvas stiff, closely woven, heavy fabric of hemp or cotton, esp. for shoes, sails, and tents

cashmere very soft, downy wool from hair roots of Kashmir goat

cassimere smooth, twilled worsted for suits, often in stripes

castor heavy wool, esp. for overcoats

cavalry twill sturdy double twill fabric of cotton, wool, or worsted; tricotine

cerecloth wax-treated cloth for wrapping corpses

challis soft, lightweight cotton or wool in plain weave, esp. for neckties

chambray lightweight cotton, silk, or linen with colored warp and white weft

charmeuse lightweight, drapable silk with semilustrous satin face and dull back

cheesecloth lightweight cotton gauze in open mesh

chenille tufted, velvety cord of silk or worsted, esp. for trim, embroidery, spreads, and nightgowns

cheviot heavy, coarse wool of Cheviot sheep, for suits and coats

chiffon sheer, fluffy silk or synthetic fabric, esp. for blouses and dresses

chiné fabric with variegated Chinese designs

dyed or printed on warp threads before weaving

chino durable, twilled khaki cotton

chintz often glazed, printed cotton, esp. for draperies and upholstery

cloque pique fabric with embossed or quilted design

cloth woven, knitted, felted, or pressed fabric of fibrous material, such as cotton, wool, silk, hair, or synthetic fibers

combing wool strong-fibered wool for manufacture of worsteds

cord corduroy

corduroy sturdy cotton with piled surface in lengthwise ridges; cord

cotton soft, white, absorbent fabric woven from fibrous hairs of cotton plant

covert durable cotton or woolen twill of mixed color yarns, sometimes waterproofed

crape crepe

crash rough, irregular fabric, esp. for draperies and toweling

crepe lightweight, crinkled fabric of silk, cotton, or rayon; crape

crepe de Chine soft, silky fabric with minute irregularities of surface

crepon heavy crepe fabric

cretonne heavyweight, unglazed cotton or linen in colorful prints, esp. for curtains or upholstery

crinoline coarse, stiffened horsehair or cotton, esp. for linings

damask fine, twilled, reversible silk, linen, or cotton in figured weave

denim heavyweight, durable twill cotton, esp. for blue jeans

dimity sheer, plain weave, usu. checked or striped cotton, esp. for curtains and bedspreads

Donegal tweed heavyweight, plain wool with colorful weft (Ireland)

drill durable twilled cotton; drilling

drilling drill

drugget coarse, durable wool (India)

duchesse highly lustrous satin

duck heavy, closely woven cotton, esp. for bags and outer garments

duffel rough, woolen, thickly napped cloth, esp. for coats and luggage

dungaree denim

duvetyn smooth, lustrous, napped fabric

ecru satin, unbleached linen, or raw silk of very pale brown color

etamine light, loosely-woven cotton or worsted fabric

fabric material made from fibers or threads by means of weaving, knitting, or felting

faconne fabric with small, elaborate pattern, esp. velvet

faille semilustrous ribbed fabric of silk, cotton, rayon, or lightweight taffeta

felt nonwoven fabric of wool, cotton, or hair pressed together with heat

fiber slender, filamentous substance formed into threads for making fabric

flannel soft, loosely woven, napped wool or wool blend

flannelette lightweight cotton flannel, napped on one side

fleece soft knit or woven fabric with silky pile

foulard lightweight silk or rayon with printed design, esp. for ties and scarves

frieze heavyweight wool with rough, uncut nap

fustian stout cotton or linen in twill weave with short pile

gabardine firm woolen cloth in twill weave

galatea durable cotton, usu. striped, esp. for children's clothing

gauze thin, transparent cotton or silk

Georgette sheer silk or rayon crepe with pebbly surface

gingham striped or checked cotton in plain weave, esp. for housedresses

gossamer very thin, delicate cloth, esp. gauze for veils

grenadine thin silk or synthetic in leno weave

grogram coarse, loosely woven fabric of silk, silk and mohair, or wool

grosgrain heavy, closely woven, corded silk or rayon, esp. for ribbons

gunny coarse, heavy jute or hemp, esp. for sacks

haircloth stiff, wiry horsehair woven with cotton, used for stiffening and lining

harrateen English linen or wool, esp. for curtains or bed canopies

Harris tweed *Trademark.* tweed of fine, heavy Scottish wool from the Outer Hebrides

herringbone twilled fabric in pattern resembling fish skeleton, with series of V's in vertical row

hessian burlap

homespun plain-weave wool or linen made from homespun yarn

hopsack coarse, loosely woven cotton or wool

horsehair sturdy, glossy fabric woven from horse's mane

huck huckaback

huckaback absorbent, durable cotton or linen, esp. for towels; huck

ikat woven fabric in which warp and/or weft yarn has been tie-dyed (India)

jaconet thin cotton, esp. for bandages

jacquard intricate, variegated woven fabric

jardiniere multicolored material in floral or fruit print

jean denim

jersey soft, often elastic knit cotton, esp. for shirts

Kendal green coarse woolen cloth, green in color

kersey heavy, coarse, ribbed wool, esp. for work clothes

khaddar handloomed cotton cloth (India)

khaki durable, twilled, dull yellow-brown cotton, esp. for military uniforms

knit any fabric made with interlocking loops of yarn

lace delicate, netlike, figured fabric of thread or yarn, esp. for trim

lamé fabric in which silver or gold threads are interwoven with silk, cotton, or rayon

lawn sheer linen or cotton in plain weave

leno firm, open-mesh weave in which warp yarns are paired and intertwined

linen cloth woven from flax yarns

linsey-woolsey coarse fabric of wool and linen

lisle twisted, hard cotton thread, esp. for hosiery and gloves

lisse lightly crinkled, gauzy silk, esp. for ruffles or trim

loden heavy, waterproof wool, esp. for coats

luster *Chiefly Brit.* cotton warp with wool or mohair filling

mackinaw heavy, napped wool in plaid design, esp. for coats

mackintosh lightweight, waterproof, rubberized cotton, esp. for raincoats

madras fine, hard cotton or durable silk, in colorful plaid or stripes

malines fine, stiff mesh of silk or rayon, esp. for veils

marocain heavy crepe of silk, wool, or rayon with strong rib effect, esp. for women's suits

marquisette sheer leno weave, esp. for curtains or netting

marseilles thick cotton that is figured or striped, esp. for coverings

mat tough, coarse, woven or plaited fabric

material any cloth or textile fabric

matte jersey jersey with a dull finish

melton heavy twilled wool with smooth face in solid colors

merino fine, soft wool of Spanish merino sheep, esp. for stockings

mesh woven, knit, or knotted material of open texture with evenly spaced strands

messaline soft, lightweight silk in satin weave

mohair long, silky wool made from fleece of Angora goat

moiré silky fabric with watered or wavy pattern; watered fabric

monk's cloth coarse, heavy cotton in a basket weave, orig. for monk's habit, now used esp. for draperies

moquette thick, velvety fabric, esp. for carpets and upholstery

moreen heavy wool or wool and cotton with moiré finish, for curtains or petticoats

motley varicolored cotton fabric, esp. for jester's costume

mousseline *French.* muslin; sheer rayon resembling muslin

mousseline de laine *French.* lightweight worsted wool or muslin with print

mousseline de soie *French.* gauzelike, stiff silk or rayon, esp. for blouses

mull soft, thin muslin

muslin plain-weave cotton with sheer to coarse finish, often printed or embroidered; mousseline

nainsook fine, lightweight cotton, often striped

nankeen durable, brownish-yellow Chinese cotton, esp. for trousers

net open-mesh fabric twisted or knotted at uniform intervals

ninon sturdy, sheer silk or rayon in plain or novelty weave

oilcloth cotton cloth waterproofed with oil and pigment, esp. for table or shelf covering

organdy very sheer, stiff, lightweight cotton with crisp finish, esp. for blouses

organza sheer silk, nylon, or rayon with crisp finish, stiffer than organdy, used for gowns and trim

organzine silk that has been additionally twisted in opposite directions, used warpwise in weaving silk fabrics

oxford cotton in plain, twill, or basket weave, esp. for shirts

paisley soft woolen fabric or silk printed with colorful, swirled designs

panne velvet or satin with lustrous, flattened pile

paramatta lightweight twilled dress fabric of wool, with cotton or silk warp

pedaline strawlike material of hemp core covered with cellulose, esp. for braids and ribbons

percale fine, closely woven cotton, esp. for bed sheets

petersham heavy wool for bulky outergarments

Pima fine broadcloth cotton, esp. for shirts

pique durable, ribbed cotton, rayon, or silk

plaid fabric in checkerboard, crossbarred pattern, esp. twilled wool

plush fabric with pile higher than 1/8 inch (3 mm), less dense than velvet

pointelle lacy, openwork fabric

pongee thin, soft, tan raw silk (China); similar cotton or rayon fabric in uneven weave

poplin sturdy, plain-weave cotton with fine ribs

poult-de-soie rich, shiny, ribbed silk and alpaca for dresses

prunella twilled, lightweight, worsted fabric

qiviut very soft, dense wool from undercoat of musk ox

ragg sturdy wool fiber blended with nylon to make flecked, grayish yarn

ratine loosely woven cotton or wool with nubby surface; ratteen

ratteen ratine

raw silk woven fabric of spun silk without sericin, a natural binder, removed

rep plain-weave fabric with prominent, rounded, crosswise cording

russet coarse, homespun, reddish-brown cloth

sackcloth coarse, rough cloth, orig. of goat's hair, now of hemp or jute, esp. for mourning clothes

sailcloth lightweight canvas, esp. for curtains and outer garments

samite rich medieval silk, interwoven with gold and silver

sarcenet soft, fine silk, esp. for veils and trim

sateen smooth, durable, lustrous cotton in satin weave

satin rich silk with glossy face and dull back; similar acetate, nylon, or rayon

saxony fine, closely knitted, soft wool for coats

scrim durable, open-weave cotton or linen, esp. for curtains

seersucker lightweight, crinkled linen or cotton, usu. striped

serge twilled worsted or wool, esp. for suits

shahtoosh very fine, brownish-gray wool from throat area of Indian goat

shalloon light, twilled wool or worsted, esp. for linings

Shantung medium coarse Oriental silk

sharkskin smooth wool or worsted with small woven design; similar fabric of acetate or rayon with dull appearance

Shetland wool soft, fine wool from undercoat of Shetland sheep

shirting cotton or other fabric, such as broadcloth or oxford, esp. for shirts

shoddy inferior fabric of reclaimed wool or shredded waste

sicilienne blend of silk and fine wool

silk soft, fine fabric of thread woven from fibers of silkworm cocoons

slipper satin sturdy satin for lightweight slippers

stammel coarse wool dyed red for penitents' undershirts

stockinette soft elastic cotton, esp. for bandages or infant wear

stuff Chiefly Brit. finished wool or worsted

surah soft, twilled, lustrous Indian silk or rayon, esp. for ties and dresses

swansdown heavy cotton flannel with thickly napped face, fine, soft, thick wool

tabby plain silk taffeta with watered moiré finish

taffeta finely woven, stiff silk, cotton, or rayon, with high sheen and fine crosswise ribs

tapa coarse cloth of pounded mulberry bark with geometric patterns (Pacific islands)

tarlatan thin, meshlike, stiffened cotton, sometimes glazed

tartan emblematic plaid-patterned, multicolored, twilled wool (Scotland)

tattersall fabric with colored crossbars on solid background

terry absorbent cotton fabric with uncut pile loops on both sides

textile fabric woven or knitted from natural or synthetic fiber

ticking durable linen or cotton, esp. for upholstery and covers

tiffany thin silk or cotton gauze

tissue fine, gauzy, sheer fabric

toile sheer, transparent linen or cotton

toweling narrow fabric of cotton or linen, in plain, twill, or huck weave, for towels

tricot plain, warp-knit fabric of wool, silk, or nylon, with fine ribs

tricotine cavalry twill

tulle thin, fine netting of silk, acetate, nylon, or rayon, esp. for veils and gowns

tussah tan, medium-coarse Oriental silk

tweed coarse woolen fabric in plain or herringbone weave

twill any fabric woven in parallel diagonal lines or ribs

veiling light, sheer netting for veils

velour cloth with velvetlike nap, esp. for upholstery and draperies

velvet richly woven fabric of silk, acetate, nylon, or rayon, with soft, thick pile

velveteen twilled, plain-weave cotton with short, velvety pile

Venetian cloth wool or worsted fabric in satin or twill weave, sometimes napped

vicuna very soft, light brown wool made from undercoat of South American llama

vigogne wool in twill weave and neutral color

voile sheer cotton, wool, silk, or rayon in plain weave, esp. for dresses or curtains

wadmal coarse, bulky, woolen fabric with heavy nap, esp. for protective clothing (Scandinavia)

watered fabric moiré

whipcord cotton, woolen, or worsted fabric with steep, diagonally ribbed surface

wool fabric woven from the soft, curly undercoat or fleece of mammals such as sheep, goats, and camels

worsted woolen fabric with smooth, hard surface and no nap

zibeline soft, lustrous fabric of wool mixed with alpaca or camel hair to form long, silky nap, esp. for coats, suits, and dresses

Synthetic Fibers and Textiles

acetate acetic ester of cellulose with satiny appearance

Acrilan Trademark. acrylic, wrinkle-resistant textile

acrylic quick-drying synthetic fiber made by polymerization of acrylonitrile

Banlon Trademark. synthetic textile

Celanese acetate Trademark. specially produced acetate textile

Dacron Trademark. resilient polyester fiber

double-knit polyester material

durable press permanent press

fiberfill resilient, lightweight, fluffy synthetic fiber, used esp. as filling for quilts or sleeping bags

Fortrel Trademark. bonded polyester fabric with acetate tricot backing

Gore-Tex Trademark. highly waterproof fabric laminated with thin membrane of stretched polytetrafluoroethylene (PTFE), which allows body to breath

Lastex Trademark. elastic material with latex rubber core covered by fabric strands

leatherette synthetic leather of paper and vinyl

Lurex Trademark. silver or gold synthetic textile

nylon strong, elastic, thermoplastic polyamide textile

Orlon Trademark. soft, lightweight, wrinkle- and sun-resistant acrylic fiber

permanent press textile treated with resin and heat to resist wrinkling; durable press

polyester synthetic, woollike knit material made from fibers formed by polymerization

polypropylene lightweight fiber that is a polymer of propylene, used in bonded fabrics

polyvinyl textile of polymerized vinyl compounds

rayon synthetic textile fiber of woven or knit cellulose that resembles wool, silk, or cotton fabric

ripstop nylon durable, tear-resistant nylon, esp. for parkas and tents

Sarelon *Trademark.* synthetic textile

spandex highly elastic, long-chain polymer fiber

synthetic fiber slender, threadlike structure derived from mineral or chemical components and used to make synthetic textile

Thinsulate *Trademark.* thin, versatile, spun-bonded fabric that is a good insulator

Ultrasuede *Trademark.* synthetic leather with suedelike texture

Vicara *Trademark.* wooly fiber for textile blends

vinyl polymer textile derived from vinyl

vinyon strong, easily molded, long-chain polymer vinyl textile fiber

wash-and-wear fabric permanent press fabric that can be washed and dries quickly

Laces

Alençon delicate, fine mesh needlepoint in solid floral pattern

bobbin lace handmade lace formed by intertwisting threads on bobbins over patterns marked by pins in pillow; pillow lace

bobbinet machine-made net in hexagonal mesh

Breton handmade lace from Brittany

Brussels lace needlepoint or bobbin lace with floral design, orig. made near Brussels

Carrickmacross guipure appliqué lace with floral designs, from Ireland

Chantilly delicate silk or linen bobbin lace in hexagonal mesh with scrolled or floral design, usu. black, handmade in France

Dieppe lace in design originated at Dieppe, France

duchesse fine Flemish bobbin lace in delicate floral designs

gros point Venetian point lace with large, raised designs

guipure heavy, large-patterned lace of linen or silk

illusion delicate, gauzy tulle, esp. for veils

lace delicate, netlike, figured fabric of thread or yarn

Mechlin delicate bobbin lace from Belgium

mignonette narrow bobbin lace with scattered small designs, of French and Flemish origin

Milan point needlepoint Italian lace in braided floral pattern

needlepoint lace handmade lace worked entirely with needle over paper pattern in buttonhole stitch; point lace

pillow lace bobbin lace

point lace needlepoint lace

raised point needlepoint lace with padded floral design in high relief, orig. from Venice, Italy

reticella old-fashioned needlepoint lace in geometric pattern

rose point needlepoint lace in rose designs, orig. from Venice, Italy

tambour lace made on a frame of two interlocking hoops with designs embroidered or darned onto machinemade net

tatting lace made by hand looping and knotting a single, heavy thread

Tenerife handmade lace with spiderweb designs, from the Canary Islands, used for edging

torchon durable bobbin lace of coarse linen or cotton in simple, open, geometric patterns with scalloped edges

Valenciennes flat bobbin lace in simple floral pattern of fine, diamond-shaped mesh, with same thread forming ground and motif

Venetian point needlepoint lace from Venice, Italy, esp. raised and rose point laces

Furs, Leathers, and Pelts

alligator skin of alligator with distinctive block pattern

badger short fur of badger

bearskin thick fur of bear, esp. for rugs

beaver soft, brown fur of beaver, esp. for hats

black marten soft, thick, very dark marten fur

broadtail fur of very young karakul lamb

buckskin pliable, suede-finished skin of deer

buff supple, oil-tanned cowhide

cabretta light, soft leather from skin of hairy sheep

calfskin young, domestic cowhide

capeskin flexible sheepskin with natural grain, esp. for gloves

chamois soft, pliant antelope or sheepskin

chevrette leather made from skin of young goat

chinchilla soft, pearly gray fur of chinchilla

cony rabbit fur

coonskin raccoon fur, esp. for hats

Cordovan fine-grained, dense, nonporous skin of horse, pig, or goat

cowhide sturdy hide of domestic cow

doeskin skin of female deer or sheep

deerskin skin of wild deer

ermine soft, white weasel fur, esp. for coats and trim

fox fox fur

frosted mink fur of mink with chemically lightened strands, giving it a streaked appearance

fur soft, thick mammal hair; skin bearing such hair, stripped and processed

goatskin skin of domestic or wild goat

golden sable golden fur of sable

horsehide dressed or raw skin of horse, esp. for baseballs

kid leather made from skin of young goat, esp. for gloves

krimmer dressed lambskin with loose soft curls of pale wool, from Crimea

lambskin soft skin of young sheep

leather animal skin prepared for use by removing all hair and tanning

leopard spotted fur of leopard

Levant morocco leather patterned with irregular creases

maribou thick fur of northern deer, esp. for capes

marmot coarse, woolly fur of marmot

marten soft, thick marten fur

miniver white fur of miniver, esp. for robes of state

mink brown, black, or white fur of cultivated mink

mocha pliable, suede-finished African sheepskin, esp. for gloves

moleskin furry, taupe-colored skin of mole

morocco fine, firm, flexible goatskin tanned with sumac, having pebbly grain and reddish color

muskrat glossy, dark brown fur of muskrat

nappa soft leather from sheepskin or lambskin, used for gloves and shoes

nutria beaverlike fur of coypu, used for coats, hats, and trim

otter dark brown fur of otter

patent leather stiff, shiny, varnished or lacquered leather, esp. for shoes

pelt skin of fur-bearing animal stripped from carcass, with hair removed

pigskin tough leather of swine skin, esp. for footballs

pig suede suede made from pigskin, used for jackets, shoes, and gloves

puma cougar fur

rabbit soft, light rabbit fur

raccoon long, coarse raccoon fur, esp. for coats

ranch mink fur of commercially raised, semiaquatic mink

rawhide untanned hide

red fox reddish-brown fox fur

Russia leather fine, smooth leather, esp. dyed dark red

sable rich, dark brown sable fur

sealskin slick, black fur of seal

shagreen untanned horsehide or sharkskin with granular surface

shearling tanned skin from recently shorn sheep or lamb

sheepskin hide of sheep, used esp. for parchment

silver fox silvery-white fox fur

skunk bushy, black-and-white skunk fur

suede tanned leather with flesh side buffed to a slight nap

swakara fur of karakul sheep, from Namibia

vair bluish-gray or white squirrel fur

white fox very pale or white fox fur

white leather animal hide bleached of natural color

wild mink brown fur of noncultivated mink

Parts of Shoes and Accessories

aglet tag that covers end of shoelace

arch midsection of shoe that supports arch of foot

breasting inside forepart of heel

bootjack yokelike instrument for removing boot by catching its heel

bootstrap strip of material, esp. leather, sewn at top rear or sides of boot and grasped to help pull boot on

buckle latch fastening for two loose straps

captoe forepart of shoe, set off by line of stitching from one side of foot to other

collar top of shoe that encircles foot, ankle, or leg

counter stiffener inserted between liner and outside leather to shape shoe around heel

creeper attachment with iron points that is strapped to shoe to prevent person from slipping on ice

cuff trimming or finishing strip sewed around outside top of shoe

eyelet small hole through which shoelace passes

facing ornamental or protective lining

French heel high, curved heel used on women's shoes, characterized by heel breast that curves into shank

heel rigid attachment to sole beneath rear of foot

hook curved piece of metal through which shoelace passes

insole thin support strip inside shoe

lace hook one of a series of hooks for lacing ankle portion of high-top shoe

lace stay part of oxford into which eyelets and laces are inserted

lift special arch support built into or inserted in footwear; one of the layers of leather forming heel

mudguard insert between sole and body of shoe

outsole sole

platform insert that adds height to heel

quarter rear part of shoe above heel

seam stitching where sections of shoe are attached

shank portion of sole of shoe beneath instep that provides support for arch section; metal or fiber piece that gives this part shape

shoehorn stiff, troughlike blade on handle, held at back of shoe to aid in inserting heel

shoelace cloth or leather string for binding shoe closed

shoetree form of wood or metal inserted in shoe to preserve its shape when not in use

sole thick bottom of shoe that rests on ground; outsole

strap cord of leather or cloth used to hold shoe on foot

tassel ornamental knob of loose, knotted strands of leather hanging over upper

thong upright piece between toes on certain sandals

tip front of toe

toe forepart of shoe over toes of foot

toe box piece of stiffened material placed between lining and toecap of shoe

toecap piece of leather or other material covering toe of shoe, sometimes of different color than upper

tongue attached piece across top of foot, esp. under laces

upper main part of shoe above sole

vamp upper covering forepart of foot, extending back

wedge heel heel on woman's shoe formed by triangular wedge that extends from front or middle to back of sole

welt strip of leather between insole and outsole through which they are stitched or stapled together

wingtip toecap perforated in wing-shaped design

Shoes and Footwear

aerobic shoe lightweight athletic shoe designed for high impact aerobic movement

anklet low woman's shoe with one or more ankle straps

arctic warm, waterproof overshoe

athletic shoe canvas or leather shoe with rubber sole

babouche ornamental heelless slipper (Middle East)

ballet slipper light, soft, close-fitting dance shoe

balmoral ankle-high laced boot or shoe

basketball shoe high-topped athletic shoe designed for playing basketball

blucher shoe with one-piece tongue and front vamp, overlapped by quarters that lace together

boot fitted leather upper reaching above ankle; waterproof rubber or plastic covering for shoe and ankle

bootee ankle-length boot; infant's knitted or crocheted sock worn as indoor shoe

bootie soft, sometimes disposable sock or bootlike covering for foot or shoe, for protection or informal wear

brogan heavy leather, ankle-high work shoe, stogy

brogue heavy shoe with punched design on uppers, such as wingtips or oxfords

buck light brown buckskin shoe

bulldog shoe shoe with deep, boxed toe

buskin thick-soled, laced, shin-high shoe

button shoe shoe with button closure and no laces

chopine woman's thick-soled shoe (16th-17th c.)

chukka ankle-high, laced, leather boot with two eyelets

cleat athletic shoe with metal or hard rubber grips on sole

clodhopper large, heavy, rustic shoe

clog shoe with thick wooden sole; klomp; wooden shoe (Holland and Scandinavia)

combat boot sturdy, high-laced military boot

corespondent shoe two-tone shoe, either tan or brown and white; buck

cothurni thick-soled elevator boots for dramatic costume (ancient Greece)

cowboy boot midcalf boot with high heels, pointed toe, and fancy stitching, traditionally for horseback riding

Cuban heel shoe with broad, medium high heel with curved back

dancing shoe flexible, light, low-cut shoe

decker flat, rubber-soled sandal; flip-flop; zori

desert boot soft leather boot for walking

docksider casual, rubber-soled leather moccasin

d'orsay woman's pump or slipper with circular vamp

dress shoe formal, shiny leather shoe

duck casual slip-on, water-resistant shoe with canvas upper and rubber sole

espadrille shoe with hemp or crepe sole, canvas upper, and flat or wedge heel; rope-sole shoe

everett low-backed man's lounging slipper

Faust slipper high-cut house shoe with V-shaped sides

flats woman's casual, low-heeled shoes

flip flop flat, loose, backless, rubber sandal held on with thong between first two toes; decker; zori

flippers broad, flat, fish rubber attachments to feet, with toe end expanded into paddle for swimming, diving, or body surfing

footwear shoes, sandals, and slippers intended as outer covering for feet

gaiter ankle-high shoe of cloth or leather with elastic inserts in sides

galoshes high rubber overshoes for protection from snow and rain; overshoes

geta wooden clog elevated by transverse supports on bottom of sole (Japan)

gillie low-cut shoe with decorative lacing through loops and around ankle

gumshoe rubber overshoe or boot

gym shoe comfortable, rubber-soled athletic shoe, often with canvas upper

half-boot boot ending just above ankle

heels woman's high-heeled dress shoes

Hessian boot tasseled military boot ending just below knee (19th c.)

high-button shoe shoe buttoning to ankle

high heels woman's dress shoes with elongated heels and low-cut upper

high-topped shoe shoe with ankle-high upper

high-topped sneakers athletic shoe extending over ankle for extra support

hiking boot sturdy, lightweight boot with nonslip sole

hip boot tall boot extending above knee to top of thigh

hobnail boot rustic boot with short nails on sole to prevent wear

huarache woven leather sandal with rubber sole (Mexico)

jackboot heavy, glossy, midthigh military boot (17th-18th c.)

jazz shoe close-fitting, low-heeled oxford of soft leather or fabric, having thin, flexible sole, worn for jazz dancing

kiltie shoe with long tongue in tassels or fringe folding over instep

klomp wooden shoe; clog

lace shoe shoe with lace and eyelet closure

larrigan oil-tanned moccasin that extends up legs, used by lumbermen

loafer low-cut, slip-on shoe

lounger casual shoe

military heel woman's shoe with heel lower and thicker than Cuban

moccasin soft leather, heelless shoe with sole stitched to upper

monk shoe low, plain shoe with buckle closure

mukluk heavy sealskin or reindeer boot (Eskimo)

mule woman's low-heeled house shoe or lounging slipper, with upper across open toes

overshoes galoshes

oxford shoe laced over instep, with facings sewn on front of vamp for laces

pac laced, heelless sheepskin or felt shoe worn inside boot in cold weather

pantofle bedroom slipper

paratrooper boot sturdy boot that laces to knee

patent leather shoe dress shoe of shiny patent leather

patten clog or sandal with thick wooden sole for walking in mud

penny loafer casual slip-on shoe with flap in vamp, sometimes used to hold coin

platform shoe shoe with very thick, elevated sole

plimsoll light, rubber-soled shoe with mudguard and canvas top

pump woman's low-cut, low-heeled, thin-soled, casual shoe

puttee leather legging secured by strap or catch

riding boot high, close-fitting boot for horseback riding

Roman sandal flat-soled shoe with long straps tied around foot, ankle, and calf

romeo man's shoe or slipper with U-shaped elastic inserts at sides

rope-sole shoe shoe with thatched rope sole; espadrille

rubber low rubber shoe worn over regular shoes for protection from rain

running shoe athletic shoe with sole and support designed for running

sabot wooden shoe with strap across instep

saddle oxford saddle shoe

saddle shoe oxford-style, two-tone shoe, esp. in brown and white; saddle oxford

sandal usu. leather sole attached to foot by straps

scuff flat-soled slipper with no quarter or heel strap

seaboot high, waterproof wading boot for fishing and sailing

shoe outer covering for foot, usu. with sturdy sole and attached rigid heel

ski boot heavy boot that clamps to ski

slip-on shoe shoe without lace, button, or buckle closure, such as loafer

slipper soft, low-cut, slip-on shoe, esp. for indoor wear

sneaker canvas or leather sport shoe with pliable rubber sole

snowshoe oval, light, wooden frame strung with thongs that attaches to shoe for walking over deep snow

soft-sole shoe infant's shoe with moccasin seam and soft leather bottom

spectator pump woman's medium-heeled shoe with contrasting colors at heel and toe of upper

spike athletic shoe with metal spikes in sole

spike heel woman's very tall, narrow-heeled shoe; stiletto heel

squaretoed boot boot with squared-off toe

steel-toed boot work boot with steel-reinforced toe

step-in pump with high vamp and concealed goring

stiletto heel spike heel

stogy brogan

tennis shoe canvas athletic shoe with rubber sole

thigh boot boot extending to midthigh, flexible at knee

thong sandal with strip of material fitted between toes, strapped across foot

toe shoe woman's ballet slipper with wood block inside toe for en pointe dancing

top boot high riding boot with leather bands around upper

track shoe light, heelless shoe with steel spikes for running outdoors or rubber sole for running on indoor track

veldschoen heavy rawhide shoe without insole, made without nails

wafflestomper ankle boot with ridged sole, esp. for hiking

wader knee-high or chest-high waterproof boot for fishing and hunting

Wallabee *Trademark.* comfortable, hard-soled moccasin with soft leather or suede upper, orig. from Ireland

wedgie shoe with wedge-shaped heel joined to half sole

Wellington boot leather boot loosely fitted above knee

white buck casual oxford of white buckskin

wingtip man's dress shoe with toecap perforated in wing-shaped design

wooden shoe clog or other wood-soled shoe

work shoe durable leather shoe or boot

zori lightweight, usu. rubber, thong sandal (Japan)

HATS, HEADGEAR, AND HAIRPIECES
Hats
Helmets, Headdresses, and Hairpieces

See also: *Chap. 1: Hair and Grooming; Chap. 10: Outer Garments; Ornaments and Accessories*

Hats

astrakhan hat of curly astrakhan wool (Russia)

Balmoral *Scot.* round, flat cap with projecting top all around

bangkok hat woven of fine palm fiber (Philippines)

baseball cap hat with close-fitted crown, front brim, and insignia

beanie small, close-fitting skullcap, formerly worn by college freshmen

bearskin large, military dress hat of bear fur

beret soft, round, flat, visorless, wool cap, banded to fit head

bicorne hat with brim turned up in two places

biggin child's cap; nightcap (16th-17th c.)

billed hat hat with visor

billycock *Chiefly Brit.* derby

biretta square cap with three corner points and tassel on top, worn by Catholic clergy

bluebonnet *Scot.* wide, flat, round cap of blue wool

boater flat-topped, stiff straw hat with round, flat brim

bonnet woman's brimless hat with chin ribbon

bowler felt hat with low, round crown and narrow brim

brass hat high-ranking officer's cap with gold braid

Breton round sailor hat with turned-up brim, for women

brimmed hat hat with projecting edge

busby tall, military dress hat of fur, with bag hanging on one side

calash woman's bonnet that folds back on top (18th c.)

calpac high-crowned cap (Turkey and Iran)

campaign hat broad-brimmed felt hat with four dents in crown, worn by members of U.S. Army and Marine Corps

cap usu. close-fitting hat, esp. with visor and no brim

capote stiff-brimmed hat with soft crown; bonnet

castor hat made of beaver or rabbit fur

caul woman's close-fitting net cap

chapeau *French.* hat

chapeau bras ceremonial, plumed bicorne carried under arm (18th c.)

chaperon round, stuffed hat with dangling cloth folds (15th c.)

chéchia cylindrical, brimless, tasseled Arab cap

cloche woman's bell-shaped, close-fitting hat worn well down on head

cocked hat tricorne with brim turned up in three places

coif nun's close-fitting skullcap worn under veil

commode woman's tall, ornate cap (17th–18th c.)

coolie hat conical, straw sunhat (Asia)

coonskin cap of raccoon skin, often with tail at back

cowboy hat wide-brimmed hat with large, soft crown

coxcomb jester's cap adorned with strip of red

crusher soft, felt, crushable hat; crush hat

crush hat crusher

deerstalker close-fitting woolen cap with visor in front and back and earflaps that are tied across top of crown when raised, orig. worn for hunting

derby man's stiff, felt hat with narrow brim and domed crown; billycock; pot hat

dink beanie with button on top

Dolly Varden woman's broad-brimmed, flower-trimmed costume hat (19th c.)

dress cap cap worn with military dress uniform

dunce cap tall, conical, brimless hat, formerly worn as punishment by poor students

Dutch cap woman's cap of triangular cloth rolled back at each side

fedora low, soft, felt hat with crown creased lengthwise

felt hat soft fedora or other hat made of felt

fez brimless, cone-shaped felt hat with tassel (Turkey)

flowerpot hat with turned-down brim like upturned flowerpot

fool's cap three-crowned or conical cap or hood with bells, worn by jesters; jester's cap

forage cap small, nondress military cap with visor and round, flat crown

fore-and-after cocked hat having visors front and back and earflaps

fur hat head covering made of animal fur

garrison cap overseas cap

gibus collapsible opera or top hat

glengarry woolen cap with straight sides, crease along top, and sometimes ribbon streamers at back (Scotland)

hard hat protective rigid hat of metal or fiberglass worn by construction workers

hat shaped head covering, usu. with brim (projecting edge) and crown (rounded or peaked top)

havelock cloth cap with flap hanging down back of neck as sun shield

helmet hat close-fitting hat with sides that extend over ears

homburg hard felt hat with indented crown and rolled-up brim with ribbon edge

jester's cap fool's cap

jipijapa Panama hat made from leaves of jipijapa plant

jockey cap lightweight cap with long visor worn by jockeys

juliet cap close-fitting beaded or jewel-embroidered cap

kamelaukion tall, brimless, flat-topped hat worn by Eastern Orthodox clergy

kelly man's stiff, flat-topped straw hat

kepi military cap with close-fitting band, round, flat top sloping toward front, and visor

kossuth hat large hat with flat-topped crown and rolled brim (Hungary)

leghorn hat or bonnet of fine leghorn straw

liberty cap limp, close-fitting, conical cap worn as symbol of freedom in French Revolution

lid *Slang.* hat

millinery women's hats in general

mobcap woman's indoor cap with full, high crown, tied with strap under chin

monkey cap small pillbox hat with chin strap

montero round hunter's cap with earflaps

mortarboard close-fitting academic cap with flat, square top and tassel

mutch *Scot.* woman's or child's close-fitting linen cap

nightcap soft, brimless cap worn in bed

opera hat silk top hat, often collapsible

overseas cap visorless wool or cotton cap without stiffening; garrison cap

Panama hat high-crowned, brimmed hat of pale, plaited jipijapa leaf fibers

peaked hat hat with tall, peaked crown

petasus broad-brimmed, low-crowned hat (ancient Greece and Rome)

Phrygian cap close-fitting, conical cap (ancient Greece)

picture hat woman's dressy, broad-brimmed day hat

pillbox woman's small, stiff, brimless, cylindrical cap

pinner woman's cap with long lappets (17th–18th c.)

pixie woman's skullcap with pointed crown

plug hat man's stiff bowler or top hat

poke bonnet woman's bonnet with projecting front bill

porkpie low-crowned felt hat with creased top and brim turned up in back, down in front; stingy brim

postilion woman's hat with high, narrow crown and narrow, rolled brim

pot hat derby

rain hat waterproof or water-repellent hat

sailor stiff straw hat with low, flat crown and circular brim; soft cotton sailor's hat with brim folded up

scraper *Slang.* cocked hat

service cap flat-topped military hat with visor

shako stiff, high-crowned, plumed military hat with metal plate in front

shovel hat clergyman's hat with shallow crown and wide brim curved up at side

silk hat top hat

skimmer flat-crowned straw hat with wide, straight brim

skullcap close-fitting, brimless cap that fits high on head

slouch hat soft felt hat with wide flexible brim

snap brim soft felt hat with brim pulled down in front

sombrero large, high-crowned, felt or straw hat with very wide, turned-up brim (Mexico)

sou'wester waterproof hat with brim that is wide and slanted at back

Stetson *Trademark.* broad-brimmed, high-crowned cowboy hat

stingy brim porkpie

stocking cap knitted conical cap with tassel or pompon on top, for winter wear

stovepipe hat *Slang.* man's tall, silk top hat

straw hat hat of woven straw, usu. flat and stiff, with straight brim

sugarloaf conical-shaped hat, usu. with flat brim (17th–18th c.)

sunbonnet ruffled cloth poke bonnet with protective neck cover

sundown woman's broad-brimmed hat

sun hat broad-brimmed hat with high crown for sun protection

tam *Informal.* tam-o'-shanter

tam-o'-shanter soft, flat, knitted wool hat with pompon on top; tam

tarboosh red, fezlike Muslim hat

ten-gallon hat large cowboy hat

terai double felt, subtropical sun hat with wide, turned brim

three-cornered hat tricorne

top hat tall, formal hat, often collapsible, esp. of silk; silk hat; topper

topper top hat

toque woman's small, close-fitting, brimless hat (16th c.)

tricorne hat with brim turned up in three places; three-cornered hat

trilby *Chiefly Brit.* soft felt hat with indented crown

tuque knitted stocking cap, often pointed at top (Canada)

Tyrolean hat wide-brimmed felt or straw hat with feather on side

watch cap knitted, close-fitting, navy blue, cold weather cap worn by sailors

Watteau hat straw hat with feather and ribbon trim

wide-awake soft felt hat with low crown and wide brim

yarmulke skullcap worn by Jewish men

zucchetto skullcap worn by Catholic ecclesiastics, with color indicating rank

Helmets, Headdresses, and Hairpieces

aigrette long white heron's plume headdress

anadem *Archaic.* garland or wreath

babushka kerchief or scarf worn as woman's headdress (Russia)

bagwig wig with back hair enclosed in small, silk bag (18th c.)

balaclava hoodlike, close-fitting, knitted pullover mask that reaches to shoulders

bandanna large, colored kerchief tied around head

bandeau band or ribbon worn around head to hold hair

basinet lightweight, pointed steel helmet

bathing cap tight-fitting elastic cap, usu. of rubber, worn to keep hair dry while swimming or bathing

burgonet peaked armor helmet (16th c.)

capuche Capuchin monk's hood

casque armor helmet with eye slits

chaplet garland or wreath

cornet woman's tall, cone-shaped headdress, usu. of delicate fabrics with lace lappets (14th-18th c.)

coronet small, crownlike, jeweled headdress

cowl monk's hood

crash helmet usu. round, rigid, protective helmet for drivers and fliers

crest feather plume worn on helmet

crown jeweled headdress for royalty

diadem bejeweled cloth headband for royalty; type of crown

earmuffs soft, warm ear coverings connected by band across skull

eyeshade visor attached to head to shield eyes from sun

fall long, false hairpiece

fanchon kerchief folded into triangle and worn as cap

fascinator crocheted or lace scarf, narrowing toward ends, worn as head covering by women

feathers bird's feathers worn as headdress, esp. by American Indians

fillet narrow strip of material worn as headband

football helmet rigid, round helmet with faceguard and chin strap

gas mask close-fitting face piece connected to air canister, worn for protection from poisonous air

garland wreath of flowers or foliage

hair net mesh cap of fine material that holds hair in place

hairpiece section of false hair

headband fabric, leather, or flower headpiece that encircles head across forehead

headcloth kerchief, bandanna, or other cloth worn on head

headdress any decorative covering for head

headgear head covering of any kind

heaume armor helmet that rested on shoulders (13th c.)

helmet protective head covering of hard material

hennin woman's tall, conical, veiled headdress (15th c.)

hood soft fabric covering for head and neck

kaffiyeh square cloth folded into triangle and held on head by agal cord (Middle East)

kerchief small square of cloth used as head covering

lambrequin protective woven covering worn over helmet

lappet headdress with many folds, streamers, or flaps; one of these hanging flaps

mantilla woman's veil covering head and shoulders

miter bishop's tall, peaked headdress

morion visorless, high-crested, Spanish soldier's helmet (17th c.)

panache feather plume, esp. on helmet

pelage hair or feather head covering

penna headdress of feathers

periwig long, formal wig, often white (17th c.)

peruke wig (17th-19th c.)

pith helmet round, broad-brimmed, protective jungle helmet

plumage plumes and feathers worn as headdress

plume long bird's feather used as headdress

postiche artificial hairpiece

pschent Pharaoh's headdress (ancient Egypt)

puggaree light scarf wrapped around sun helmet as hatband

ramillie wig with long plait at back, tied top and bottom with bows (18th c.)

ribbon strip of often colorful material tied around hair for decoration or to hold hair in place

riding hood loose, enveloping hood

rug Slang. wig

rumal man's checked cotton or silk kerchief worn as headdress (India)

sallet light helmet, with or without visor, with projection over neck (15th c.)

scarf cloth worn over head

ski mask pullover woolen hood with openings for eyes and mouth

snood fine material or net, pinned at back to contain hair

sun helmet topee

switch long, thick strand of usu. real hair, fastened together at one end and added to one's own, esp. by women

tiara crownlike headdress of jewels or flowers

tin hat metal helmet of tin

topee jungle helmet with cloth covering and cork insulation for protection from sun; sun helmet

toupee false hairpiece worn to cover baldness, usu. by men

turban long cloth wrapped around head or over cap by Muslims (Asia and Middle East)

veil length of cloth worn as woman's head covering, often covering face as well

war bonnet Native American headdress consisting of headband and tail of ornamental feathers

welder's helmet arc welder's helmet with tilting visor that covers face and a protective eye lens

wig synthetic hairpiece for entire skull

wiglet small wig used to supplement existing hair

wimple nun's headcovering of cloth that extends in folds over cheeks, chin, and neck

wreath braided foliage encircling head; anadem; chaplet; garland

yashmak Muslim woman's veil wrapped around upper and lower parts of face so that only eyes show

FASHION AND GARMENT PARTS
Clothing in General
Garment Parts
Fashion, Trim, and Sewing
Fasteners

See also: *Chap. 10: Ornaments and Accessories; Clothing Materials*

Clothing in General

accouterments personal clothes and effects

activewear sportswear designed for exercise, hiking, bicycling, and other sports activities

apparel clothing; garments; robes

array finery, fancy dress

attire clothing, esp. finery

beachwear bathing suits and other garments designed for use at beach or swimming pool

bib and tucker Brit. slang. entire outfit of clothing, esp. formal

caparison richly ornamental outfit of clothing

clothes clothing

clothing usu. cloth articles worn on body for covering and decoration; garments

costume complete outfit in specific style, esp. worn in some type of performance; robes

disguise outfit designed to conceal identity

drapery garments of cloth

dress clothing, esp. when suited to specific occasion

duds Informal. clothes

ensemble complete outfit, esp. when well-coordinated

evening dress complete outfit of formal clothing

fashion specific, esp. current, style of clothing

fig dress or apparel

finery fancy, decorative apparel

formals clothing suitable for ceremonies and elegant parties

frippery affected finery of low quality, considered to be in poor taste

full fig formal dress

garb attire, esp. in characteristic style

garments clothing, esp. outerwear

garmenture clothing; general attire (archaic)

gear clothing

getup Informal. outfit, often costume

glad rags Informal. showy or fancy clothing

guise style of dress

habiliment clothing, esp. for specific work or event

habit characteristic garb

hand-me-downs used clothing received from another

fashion current or specific style of dress

mufti ordinary clothes worn by person normally in uniform

outfit complete set of clothing

playclothes casual or functional clothing worn for leisure and recreational activities

rags old, tattered clothes

raiment clothing, general attire

regalia fancy or ceremonial attire

rig outfit, esp. unusual costume

robes apparel; costume

robing clothing

soup-and-fish *Slang.* man's formal evening clothes

sportswear activewear designed for exercise, hiking, bicycling, and sports; casually styled pieces of clothing that can be worn singly or in combination

style specific manner of dress, esp. current fashion

suit complete outfit of clothing, esp. formal

Sunday best one's finest outfit of clothing

tatters old, worn, ragged clothes

threads *Slang.* clothing in general

toggery *Informal.* clothing, esp. fancy dress; togs

togs clothing in general, esp. specific outfit; toggery

toilette formal outfit or specific costume

trappings articles of clothing, esp. decorative adornments

trim dress, esp. gear

uniform outfit of clothing characteristic of position or occupation

vestments official, esp. ecclesiastical, garments

vesture *Archaic.* clothing; garments

wardrobe one's complete supply of clothing

wear clothing, esp. of specific style or function

Garment Parts

accessory article or set of articles of dress that adds completeness, convenience, or decoration to basic outfit

arm tube of material from shoulder to wrist

armhole opening at shoulder for arm attachment

barrel cuff cuff formed from single band of material, usu. fastened by button

batwing collar man's high, flaring collar

batwing sleeve loose, long sleeve that fits into shoulder, ending at fitted wristband or cuff

bell-bottom leg trouser leg that widens at bottom

bertha woman's collar worn about shoulders, esp. over low-necked dress

bishop sleeve full sleeve gathered to fitted wristband

bodice blouse or upper part of dress

body torso covering

bosom front section across chest

breast pocket usu. outside pocket sewn on one or both sides of upper front of shirt or jacket

bretelle ornamental shoulder strap extending from front of dress to back

bustline portion of garment covering woman's breasts

button-down collar collar with points that button to shirt front

button stand strip of cloth on front edge of coat for buttons or buttonholes

cap sleeve short sleeve extending from bodice and covering top of shoulder

caul network at back of woman's cap

coattail rear skirts of dress, cutaway, or frock coat

collar piece of fabric surrounding neck opening of shirt or coat

cowl neckline loose, draped neckline

crew neck round neckline without collar

crotch point at which two pant legs meet

cuff wristband on shirtsleeve; turned-back hem of trouser leg

décolletage neckline, esp. woman's low-cut neckline

Directoire empire waist

dolman sleeve sleeve as an extension of bodice, with deep armhole tapering to fitted wrist

dropped waist waistline set below natural waist

drop seat rear section, as on children's pajamas, that may be opened and lowered independently

earflap either of a pair of flaps attached to cap or hat, for covering ears in cold weather

empire waist high, fitted waistline (France, 19th c.); Directoire; lifted waist

epaulette decorative tab across shoulder, often fringed, esp. on uniform

Eton collar broad, stiff collar worn folded outside of Eton jacket

fastener device for joining or attaching garments or garment parts, such as zipper, button, or hook

fly front cloth overlap concealing buttons or zipper, esp. from waist to crotch at front of pants

French cuff folded double shirt cuff fastened by cuff links

gigot sleeve sleeve with full shoulder and fitted wrist

godet fluted pleat for fullness on lower skirt or sleeve

gore tapering wedge of material that adds fullness to skirt or shoe

gusset triangular expansion insert in seam

high collar collar extending up to cover all or most of neck

kimono sleeves large, square sleeves with underarm seam open, cut in one piece with garment

lap loose, overhanging panel or flap

lapel turned-back fold on front of coat, jacket, or blouse, joined to collar

leg tube of material from hip to ankle

lifted waist waistline set above natural waist; empire waist

magyar sleeve very full sleeve cut in one piece with bodice

mandarin collar narrow collar that stands up from neckline, often open at front

Medici collar collar that stands high across back and low at front

neck opening at top of garment, across upper chest

neckline style of opening at top of garment

notched collar collar forming notch with lapels of garment at seam where collar and lapels meet

overskirt skirt worn over skirt of dress and draped or held up to reveal it

pagoda sleeve long, narrow arm widening at wrist to show undersleeve

patch pocket pocket made by sewing piece of material to outside of garment

peg leg trouser leg that tapers to tight hem at ankle

peplum short, flared flounce attached at waist of dress, blouse, or coat and extending over hips

Peter Pan collar flat, attached, close-fitting collar with rounded ends meeting at round neckline

placket faced slit at top of garment, esp. skirt, that facilitates putting it on and taking it off

plunging neckline neckline cut very low in front

pocket small, open-topped pouch sewn in or on garment

pocket flap covering over top of pocket

pouf fluffy, puffed part of garment

Prussian collar high collar with ends almost meeting in front

raglan sleeve sleeve cut in one piece with shoulder; set-in sleeve

revers usu. wide lapels on jacket, coat, or dress

rolled collar shirt collar that stands up slightly from neckline of garment and folds over on itself to lie flat

roll-neck collar collar that turns back on itself

saddle shoulder shoulder of raglan sleeve in which seam at neckline runs parallel to shoulder before angling down to armpit

sailor collar collar with neckline that is square at back, narrowing to point at front closure

seat material across buttocks

set-in sleeve sleeve joined to body of garment at shoulder by seam at that juncture; raglan sleeve

shawl collar attached collar and lapels in one piece, rolled back continuously along neckline to closure

shirt front front of shirt that is exposed beneath jacket or vest

shirttail part of shirt below waist, usu. worn inside trousers; tail

shoulder cloth across shoulders to which sleeves attach

shoulder pad cushion in shoulder providing protection or shape

shoulder strap narrow band over shoulders, for decoration or to hold up pants, dress, or skirt; similar strap used to carry handbag or carryall

skirt free-hanging material from waist down, either in single strip or encircling body

slash pocket pocket set into garment, esp. below waistline, opening with exterior vertical or diagonal slit

sleeve part of garment covering all or portion of arm between shoulder and wrist

spaghetti strap very narrow shoulder strap on dress or blouse, sometimes decorative

spread collar shirt collar with front points set widely apart

stay strip of stiffening material in corset or shirt collar

stiff collar starched or stiffened upright shirt collar

stomacher embroidered center front of bodice (15th16th c.)

strap flat strip of material for securing, binding, or supporting

tab collar shirt collar with small flap on one point that fastens to opposite point to hold both points in place

tail shirttail

tails divided skirts of man's formal jacket

train length of material attached to and trailing behind gown

turtleneck tall, close-fitting collar that rolls over on itself

Vandyke collar wide lace or linen collar with scalloped edge or deep points

vent small opening or section of permeable material allowing passage of air through garment

V neck neckline cut in deep V shape

waist torso covering that extends from neck to waistline

waistband belt or band of trousers or dress fitted around waist

waistline part of garment encircling natural waist at narrowest point of lower trunk

watch pocket small pocket just below front waistband of man's trousers or at front of vest

Watteau back loose, flowing back of woman's gown or robe, formed by box pleats falling from shoulder to hem

welt pocket pocket with reinforcing cord sewn to open edges

wing collar standing collar with high, stiff, turned-back corners

wristband lower sleeve covering wrist, esp. strip of fabric sewn to edge of sleeve

yoke fitted top of bodice, shirt, coat, or skirt to which lower part is sewn

Fashion, Trim, and Sewing

accordion pleats narrow pleats resembling accordion folds

acid washed (*adj*) describing denim processed with bleach to fade color

A-line shape of woman's skirt, dress, or coat that is narrow at top and flaring to bottom, like letter A

allover (*adj*) describing a fabric with single repeating design motif

applied casing strip of fabric or bias tape sewn as casing

appliqué flat, decorative material or trim sewn on garment

argyle fabric with diamond-shaped designs, esp. in socks

backstitch hand stitching, one backward on garment front, two forward on reverse, to form solid line of stitching

banded (*adj*) having narrow cloth strips for decoration and to prevent raveling

bargello straight stitch used to form variety of

zigzag and oblique designs in high and low relief; Florentine stitch

basket weave checkered weave resembling plaited basket

baste (*vb*) make long, loose, temporary stitches for fitting

batting layers of cotton or synthetic fiber for stuffing or lining

beadwork decorative beads stitched to fabric

beson pocket interior pocket with edging or stitching around opening

bias line at forty-five-degree angle to border in cutting for fit

bind off (*vb*) cast off knitting stitch to form an edge

bird's-eye textile pattern of small diamonds with center dot

blanket stitch embroidery or sewing stitch of variable size and width, often used to finish fabric edges decoratively

bobbin spool of thread or yarn on sewing machine

bolt measured roll of fabric of standard length

bonded (*adj*) made of two layers of the same fabric, or of a fabric and lining material, attached to each other by a chemical process or adhesive

box pleat parallel edges folded to face in opposite directions

braiding strips of interwoven yarn, fabric, or leather for binding or decoration

burl small knot of wool, thread, or yarn for imparting nubby texture

buttonhole stitch closely worked loop stitch making firm, finished edge; close stitch

cable-stitch series of knitting stitches used to produce cable appearance

caddis worsted ribbon or binding for garters and girdles

candlewicking series of knot stitches made in fabric with cotton embroidery thread

casing tunnel of stitched fabric holding elastic or drawstring

cast off (*vb*) make last row of stitches in knitting to prevent unraveling

chain stitch looped, ornamental stitch resembling chain links

check fabric woven or printed in checkerboard pattern

ciré highly glazed finish made by applying wax to fabric

cleavage revealing hollow between woman's breasts, esp. when revealed by low-cut neckline

clew ball of thread or yarn

clocks decorative embroidery on side of socks or stockings

close stitch buttonhole stitch

collection clothes produced by one designer, usu. for seasonal line

colorfast (*adj*) describing fabric with permanent color dyed into its yarn, so that it will not fade or run

color scheme selection of colors in outfit or garment to form some type of pattern

coordinate (*vb*) combine complementary elements and colors into outfit

cording ribbed surface of cord cloth

couching stitching with two threads, one of which stitches the other to the fabric

crease ridge or fold in garment

crewel embroidery loosely twisted wool yarn decoration

crimping act of pressing fabric into narrow, regular folds like pleats

crocheting needlework done with single strand of yarn or thread interlocked in loops to form fabric or garment

cross-stitch series of needlework stitches forming Xs

crystal pleats narrow, tightly pressed pleats, all facing in same direction

custom-tailored (*adj*) designed, manufactured, or fitted to individual specifications

cutwork openwork embroidery on linen, with pattern outlined in buttonhole stitch and ground fabric cut away

damassé (*adj*) woven in reversible, figured pattern like damask

darn (*vb*) mend with crossed or interwoven stitches; embroider with rows of running stitches

dart tapering tuck of fabric stitched down to improve fit

designer (*adj*) created by or carrying label of specific fashion designer, but often mass-produced

diaphanous (*adj*) transparent or translucent and gauzy

double-knit fabric made with double set of knitting needles that produce double-thick, ribbed fabric joined by interlocking stitches

double stitch two loops of single thread fastened in center of fold

dressmaker person who makes or alters women's dresses; (adj) having soft lines or elaborate detail

dry cleaning cleaning of garments with chemical rather than water

dye colorfast coloring agent for textiles

ease (*vb*) make seams narrower to allow fullness in garment or to permit free body movement

embroidery various types of decorative stitching with a needle

engageantes sleeve ruffles

facing plain or decorative lining at garment edge

fagoting openwork fabric decoration in which thread is drawn in crisscross stitches across open seam

fashion prevailing style or usage; design and manufacture of garments in this style

fashion plate person who wears latest fashions; drawing of specific style

featherstitch embroidered ornament in which succession of branches extends alternately on each side of central stem

fell seam with one raw edge folded under other, sewn flat on underside

felting nonwoven fabric of wool or hair, matted together by heat, moisture, and pressure

fiber slender, threadlike structure from which either natural or synthetic yarn is made

figured (*adj*) ornamented, marked, or formed into repeating pattern

filling yarn that interlaces the warp in fabric; yarn carried by shuttle

Florentine stitch bargello

flounce wide strip of material attached by one edge as trim, usu. at the bottom of skirt

flue soft, fluffy feathers, lint, or dusty debris

fluting long, round, ornamental grooves

frayed (*adj*) worn or ragged from use or age, esp. collars and cuffs

French seam seam in which raw edges of cloth are completely covered by sewing them together on both sides

fringe border or trim of loose or bunched threads

frog ornamental braided loop fastener with button

froufrou frilly ornamentation usu. on women's clothing

full (*adj*) having ample folds and abundant material

furbelow flounce on woman's clothing

galloon ornamental trim, esp. braid with gold or silver threads and scalloped edges

garter stitch knitting stitch that produces evenly pebbled texture on both sides of work

gathers soft folds in cloth formed by drawing fabric along a thread

gauging fullness gathered in parallel, stitched rows

goffering series of ornamental plaits, frills, and borders

gray goods unfinished fabric as it comes from loom

gros point large embroidery stitch

hand tactile quality of fabric

hangtag tag attached to garment providing information about its size, manufacturer, fabric, care, and sometimes price

hardanger openwork embroidery having elaborate symmetrical designs

harlequin variegated, often diamond-shaped color pattern on textiles

haute couture high fashion (France)

hem bottom of dress or pants folded back and stitched down

hemline height of skirt relative to leg and knee, changing with fashion

herringbone twilled wool weave in pattern resembling fish skeleton, with series of Vs in vertical rows

high fashion most up-to-date international styles

hound's tooth small, broken checks in cloth

inseam inner seam of trouser leg from crotch to bottom of leg

intarsia decorative pattern, as in knitted garments, resembling inlay

interfacing layer of fabric between facing and outer fabric

inverted pleat reverse of box pleat, with folds meeting on face

jetted pockets pockets piped and bound with same material

kick pleat inverted pleat extending as much as 10 inches (25 cm) upward from hemline at back of narrow skirt, to allow freedom in walking

knife pleat one-directional pleat folded so only one crease shows

knit (*vb*) make cloth by looping yarn or thread together with special needles

knit and purl make cloth by alternating knitted and purled stitches

leno weave in which paired warp yarns are intertwined in series of figure eights with filling yarn passed through each interstice to give fine, open mesh

line type of clothing available from one designer or during one season

lining inner garment, constructed separately and joined to outer garment at major seams

list band or strip of material

locker loop loop at back of garment near neck, orig. for hanging up garment

long-waisted (*adj*) having greater than average length between shoulders and waistline

low-necked (*adj*) having neckline cut low to leave neck and shoulders bare

machine-stitch (*vb*) sew on sewing machine

macramé decorative knots tied in geometrical patterns

mannequin model of human body used to design and display clothes; person who models clothes

menswear clothing designed for men

mercerizing treatment of cotton fiber with caustic alkali under tension to increase strength and luster

missy (*adj*) designating young girls' clothing sizes

modiste former term for female maker or seller of women's fashionable attire

motley (*adj*) of variegated material, like Renaissance fool's outfit

nap soft, hairy surface of fabric

needle slender, pointed, usu. steel instrument with eye in one end, used to draw thread through fabric in sewing

needlepoint embroidery worked on a gridlike formation of canvas

needlework process or result of stitching with a needle, esp. embroidery, needlepoint, and appliqué

neutral color white, black, tan, or gray, with no pigment added

nonwoven fabric material with fibers interlocked by heat, moisture, or adhesives, as in synthetics or felting

notch V-shaped juncture of collar and lapel

notions sundries or small articles, esp. trim, ribbon, and buttons

nubby (*adj*) having rough, knotted weave

off-the-rack (*adj*) readymade; not made to individual specifications

orphrey rich, usu. gold embroidery, esp. band or border

overcasting sewing along edges of material with long, spaced stitches to prevent raveling

outer garment piece of clothing worn as protection or decoration and usu. visible to others

overlock seam special stitch connecting fabric and finishing edge in one operation

paillette ornamental spangle for costume

passementerie ornamental trim combining braid, cord, beading, or metallic thread

pattern instructional plan of design for sewing garment

peekaboo (*adj*) made of sheer and revealing material

permanent press process in which fabric is treated with resin and heat to hold shape and resist wrinkling

petit point small embroidery stitch

pile upright yarn loops that produce velvety surface when cut

pincushion small, soft, stuffed article into which pins are stuck when not in use

pinstripes very thin, vertical stripes

piping narrow, bias-cut cloth strip folded as edging or seam

plaid checkerboard or crossbarred pattern

plain weave most common and tightest weave, in which filling threads pass over and under successive warp threads

platting weaving or braiding

pleat fold of material doubled over on itself and stitched or pressed in place

plissé puckered finish on fabric produced by caustic soda solution treatment that causes shrinkage

polka dots pattern of regularly distributed round, solid markings

preshrunk (*adj*) designating a cotton garment shrunk to fit before sale

prewashed (*adj*) designating garments washed before sale, usu. to produce faded or worn look or soft texture

primary color red, blue, or yellow

print fabric on which color or design is printed rather than woven or resist dyed

pucker crimp, wrinkle, or furrow in fabric finish

purl (*vb*) embroider or edge with twisted gold or silver thread; invert stitches in knitting for ribbed effect; finish a garment with looped edge

quilling band of material fluted into small ruffles resembling a row of feather quills

quill work quills stitched decoratively onto clothing

quilting two layers of fabric stitched together over soft filling material

rag trade *Slang.* fashion business

raveled (*adj*) unwoven, untwisted, or unwound

readymade any garment made in advance for sale, not custom tailored

ready-to-wear (*adj*) designating mass-produced apparel, esp. synthetics

resist dye fabric dye unaffected by water

reversible (*adj*) being a garment that may be worn with lining side out

ribbing vertical ridge on cloth, esp. on knit material

rickrack flat, zigzag braid or ribbon used for trim

ruching strips of lace, ribbon, muslin, or net frilled or pleated for trim

ruffle trim with ornamental pleats or gathers along one edge

run ravel in knit fabric, esp. hosiery

running stitch small, consistent stitching made by passing needle in and out of fabric

runway long platform down which models walk in fashion show

saddle stitch decorative running stitch near edge of fabric

sartorial (*adj*) relating to tailoring and tailored clothes

satin weave weave in which filling threads are interlaced with warp at wide intervals, giving effect of smooth surface

Savile Row cut elegant, expensive, upper-class British style of tailoring

scalloped edge waved pattern at border

seam stitched line where two pieces of fabric are joined

season spring or fall of single year when specific fashion styles appear

seconds manufactured garments with small imperfections, sold at discount

selvage narrow, woven border of heavy material finished so as to prevent raveling

sennit straw, grass braid, or cord for hats

sericeous (*adj*) downy or silky in finish or appearance

sequin small, shiny disk or spangle

sewing act of forming and fastening by thread stitches

shirring decorative gathering of fabric in parallel rows of short stitches to control fullness

short-waisted (*adj*) having less than average length between shoulders and waistline

shuttle device that holds thread in place or passes woof through warp

silkscreen printing dyeing method in which pattern is made by letting dye seep through unsealed areas of silkscreen

sizing glutinous solution used for covering or stiffening fabric

slip stitch concealed stitch for sewing hems; unworked knitting stitch

smocking honeycomb stitches dividing and holding together tiny pleats

soutache narrow, herringbone braid trim

spangles small, shiny, metal disks sewn on fabric

sprang weaving technique in which threads are intertwined and twisted to form mesh

standaway (*adj*) designed to stand upright or outward from the body

static cling tendency of clothing to adhere to surfaces due to accumulation of static electricity, esp. in synthetic fibers

step collar lapel joined to garment with V notch

stitching small loops of thread or yarn used to fasten garment parts

stonewashed (*adj*) washed prior to sale with pebbles or stones to give worn appearance

strapless (*adj*) designating dress or woman's top made without shoulder straps

stripes pattern of long, parallel bands, vertical or horizontal, on fabric

style current fashionable way of dressing; distinctive flair or elegance in one's attire

sunray pleats pleats radiating from one central point

swatch fabric sample

sweetheart neckline dress neck cut low in front and curved to resemble conventionalized heart shape

tack (*vb*) fasten together with temporary stitches

tailor (*vb*) make, style, fit, trim, mend, or adapt garments; (*n*) person who does this work

tambour round embroidery frame consisting of two hoops, one fitting within the other; embroidery done on such a frame

tanning processing of rawhides into soft leather by soaking in bath of tan bark

tassel tuft of ornamental thread hanging from knot

tatting cotton lace made by looping and knotting single heavy thread on hand shuttle

template pattern for making garment, usu. a thin plate of wood or metal

tent stitch short, slanting embroidery stitch

terry loop forming uncut pile

textile fabric woven or knitted from natural or synthetic fiber

thimble small, protective cap worn on fingertip, used for pushing needle through cloth

thread single strand of fibers used in making cloth or in sewing pieces of cloth together

threadbare (*adj*) designating fabric having nap worn so that threads show

tie-dyeing process of hand-tying portions of fabric or yarn to prevent absorption of dye and to produce pattern

tinsel glittery, sparkling thread or strip in fabric

topstitch line of stitches sewn on face side of garment along seam

torsade twisted cord, esp. for draperies

trademark logo or name of designer or manufacturer

tram double, twisted silk thread used as weft in silk and velvet

tuck fold of material stitched down partway or completely

tuft cluster of closely drawn threads fastened at base

turn-up edge or cuff of trouser (Britain)

twill fabric woven in parallel diagonal lines or ribs

two-ply (*adj*) designating fabric woven with two sets of warp thread and two of filling

undergarment usu. protective item of clothing hidden under outer garments

underlining fabric layer stitched to back of each piece of outer fabric

understitching row of stitches that prevents facing from rolling to outside of garment

unisex apparel clothing designed for men or women

unisize (*adj*) made to fit all sizes or types in normal range

vogue that which is currently in fashion; (*vb*) strike pose like a model

vulcanization hardening of substance, esp. rubber, by heat

wale even, lengthwise ridge in woven fabrics, esp. in corduroy

wardrobe collection of clothing, esp. for one season or in possession of one person; storage cabinet or space for clothing

warp yarns woven lengthwise in fabric and crossed by weft

warp knit knit made with several yarns

waterproof (*adj*) designating fabric treated so water will not penetrate it

water repellent (*adj*) designating fabric treated to resist water absorption

water resistant (*adj*) designating fabric sometimes slightly more absorbent than that which is water repellent

wearing ease amounts by which sewing pattern should exceed body measurements to ensure comfortable fit

weave any pattern of interlinking threads to form cloth; (*vb*) make cloth by interlacing strands of yarn or thread

weaving fabric formed by interlacing two sets of yarn or thread at right angles to each other

webbing sturdy, narrow, closely woven tape for straps and upholstery

weft yarns carried horizontally by weaving shuttle, crossing and interlaced with warp

welted pocket slit pocket with reinforcing cord sewn on open edge

welting reinforcing strip or double edge at garment seam

whipstitch stitch that passes over an edge for joining, finishing, or gathering

Winnies annual industry awards for excellence in fashion design

women's wear clothing designed for women

woof yarn carried by shuttle and crossing warp in weaving; texture of woven fabric

worsted smooth, hard, twisted thread used to make wool with smooth, hard surface

Fasteners

band thin, flat, encircling strip of material

barrette ornamental hair clip

belt encircling strip of flexible material, esp. at waist

bobby pin flat, metal or plastic hairpin with pinching arms

brace clasp, connector

braid cord or ribbon with three or more intertwined strips

buckle fastener for two loose ends, attached to one end and grasping the other by catch or prong

button small knob or disk attached to garment, passed through loop or buttonhole to connect two parts

catch fastener that holds something in place, usu. by clamping or hooking

chain series of connected metal links

cinch tightly gripping belt or girth

clamp fastener that presses two or more pieces together

clasp hook and loop that holds objects together; brace

clip clasping device, usu. with two pinching arms

clothespin two wood or plastic arms on spring, esp. for clamping clothes to line

connector device that connects one object to another; brace

cord long, slender, flexible strip of twisted strands used for binding

drawstring cord or thin rope that tightens to close an opening when its ends are pulled

D-ring D-shaped metal ring through which belt or strap passes to close or secure something

elastic fabric made of yarns containing rubber that stretches and returns to shape

frog ornamental braided button and loop through which it passes

hairpin long, open, U-shaped pin for holding hair in place

hook rigid, curved or bent device for catching and holding

lace cord or string used to draw together two flaps by passing through holes in opposite edges

loop ring, curved piece, or doubled-back length of line through which hook passes

peg short, pointed piece of wood or metal that holds parts together

pin small, solid piece of wood or metal that clamps or pierces object to hold it in place

ribbon narrow strip of material, usu. used for tying hair

ring circular band, usu. of rigid material, used to gather and hold fabric

rope cord of interwoven fiber strands

safety pin pin bent back on itself to form spring, with guard covering point when pin is fastened

stitch portion of thread left in material after in-and-out motion of needle

strap loop or strip of flexible material

string thin cord or rope

stud small, buttonlike device with smaller button or shank on back, inserted through shirt front to fasten two sides together

suspenders thin bands worn over shoulders, with clasps at end to hold up trousers or skirt

tack temporary stitch holding materials together while they are being sewn

thole pin or peg

tie line, ribbon, or cord used for binding items together

toggle ornamental, rod-shaped button passed through loop or frog

twine sturdy string or thin rope for typing

Velcro *Trademark.* nylon material with one surface of clinging pile so that matching strips can be pressed together

zipper two parallel rows of interlocking teeth, metal or plastic, on strips of material drawn together by sliding pull piece

PART FOUR
INSTITUTIONS

CHAPTER ELEVEN
SOCIAL ORDER

THE CITY
Cities, Towns, Villages, and Districts
Roadways and Driving
Urban Structures and Phenomena

See also: *Chap. 6: Automobiles; Chap. 7:
Buildings; Chap. 11: Government; Chap. 13:
Sociology*

Cities, Towns, Villages, and Districts

arrondissement administrative district of city (France)

banlieue *French.* suburb

bedroom community suburb

boom town town experiencing rapid unplanned growth due to economic activity

borough one of five political divisions of New York City; *Chiefly Brit.* incorporated, self-governing urban area, comparable to municipality

bourg town; market town (France)

Bowery district of cheap bars and homeless persons in New York City

burbs *Informal.* suburbs

burg city or town

burgh incorporated town with partial local jurisdiction (Scotland)

capital city serving as seat of government; city renowned for some activity

central city inner city

city densely inhabited place larger and more important than town or village, usu. incorporated as an administrative and judicial unit

ciudad *Spanish.* city

commercial district nonresidential business district

community group of individuals living together as a unit within larger population; area occupied by such people

conurbation connected series of urban communities

county seat city where county administrative offices are located

cow town small, unsophisticated town, esp. within cattle-raising area

crossroad town located at juncture of two or more roads

district quarter, ward, or section of city

dorp village

downtown main business or government district of city or town

dynapolis planned city consisting of several communities along central roadway

enceinte town encircled by fortifications

exurb area outside city and beyond suburbs, often inhabited by wealthy families

exurbia region of exurbs

faubourg suburb; outlying quarter of city (France)

ghetto district occupied primarily by one religious or ethnic group, usu. poor

ghost town once active town that is now

deserted, usu. due to depletion of a natural resource

greater (*adj*) designating metropolitan area surrounding city

hamlet small village

hick town small, often isolated, unsophisticated town

hometown city or town of one's birth or principal residence

inner city older, densely populated, often rundown central district; central city

kampong small native village (Southeast Asia)

kraal native village (South Africa)

market town city to which farmers and artisans from surrounding countryside bring goods to sell at market

megalopolis very large city; heavily populated region encompassing several cities

metropolis large or important city, often a capital or center of business or cultural activity

metropolitan area large city and its immediate suburbs

midtown central section of city or town, esp. main shopping district

mir *Russian.* village community collectively owned but cultivated by individual families

municipality incorporated, self-governing, urban political unit

neighborhood district with particular character or appearance, often covering very small area

one-horse town small, rural town

outskirts districts far from center of city

Podunk small, insignificant, or remote town

polis city-state (ancient Greece)

precinct electoral subdivision of town, city, or ward; section of city for police control

purlieu outlying district

quarter division or district of town or city

red-light district area with houses of prostitution

residential area nonbusiness district of private homes

satellite suburban community

settlement place newly settled; small village

shtetl *Yiddish.* formerly a small Jewish village in Eastern Europe

suburb residential community lying just outside or within commuting distance of city; bedroom community

suburbia outlying part of city or town

thorp village or hamlet

town any group of structures considered a distinct place with a distinguishing placename; closely populated area larger than a village but smaller than a city, having fixed boundaries that distinguish it from surrounding rural territory

township small incorporated city

trailer park area set up to accommodate house trailers on permanent basis

uptown fancier residential or commercial district of city or town

vicinity surrounding area or district; neighborhood

village often rural community larger than a

hamlet and smaller than a town; small incorporated municipality

ville *French.* city

ward administrative or electoral district of city

whistle stop small rural town, esp. on railroad line

zone division of city designated for specific purpose, esp. numbered postal delivery

Roadways and Driving

alley narrow street, often providing access to rear of buildings

alleyway narrow street or passageway

artery principal roadway in branching system of roads

asphalt black bituminous composition used for paving roads

autobahn high-speed multilane expressway (Germany and Austria)

autoroute high-speed multilane expressway (France and Canada)

autostrada divided expressway connecting major cities (Italy)

avenida *Spanish.* avenue

avenue moderate-sized roadway wider than a lane and narrower than a boulevard; *Chiefly Brit.* driveway to house off main road

back street small, remote, obscure, or inaccessible roadway

beltway highway encircling an urban area; ring road

blacktop bituminous material used for surfacing roads; surface paved with this material

blind alley narrow, dead-end roadway

boreen *Irish.* narrow country lane

bottleneck narrowing point of traffic congestion

boulevard broad landscaped thoroughfare

bumper-to-bumper (*adj*) marked by heavy traffic with long rows of slow-moving cars

bypass route around town

by-street side street

byway rarely traveled roadway

calastand taxi stand

camino *Spanish.* boulevard

carpool arrangement among automobile owners to take turns driving a group to some common activity

carrefour crossroads, square, plaza

carriageway *Chiefly Brit.* highway

car wash area with facilities for washing automobiles

cater-corner (*adj*) diagonally opposed at an intersection; kitty-corner

causeway highway

center strip divider down middle of large roadway

checkpoint designated inspection place for vehicles

chuckhole rough hole or rut in road

circle rotary

circus *Chiefly Brit.* circular area at intersection of several roadways

close *Scot.* narrow passage running from street

to court surrounded by houses; *Scot.* dead-end road

cloverleaf intersection of two highways where traffic is routed from one highway onto branches leading in a circle to another highway

cobblestone road paved with rounded stones larger than pebbles and smaller than boulders

concourse open space where roads or paths meet; junction

congestion excess traffic clogged or concentrated in too small a space

corner place or intersection of two streets or roads

corniche road built at top of a cliff running along a coast

court broad alley with single opening onto main street

crescent short roadway curved in a half-circle

crossing area designated for passage of pedestrians or vehicles across roadway; place where railroad track transects a roadway; crosswalk

crossroads intersection of two or more roads

crosswalk lane designated for pedestrians to cross road in safety

cul-de-sac street closed at one end; dead end

curb edging built along roadway forming lip of gutter; also, *esp. Brit.*, kerb

dead end street without exit at one end

deck roadway across multilevel bridge

detour roundabout route temporarily replacing section of roadway that is damaged or being repaired

dirt road unpaved roadway

double-park (*vb*) park vehicle on street side of vehicle already parked along curb

drive avenue, roadway

drive-in place of business laid out so that patrons can be served while remaining in vehicles

driveway road leading from public roadway to private building

expressway high-speed, divided, multilane highway for through traffic with limited access at intersections with other roadways; thruway

filling station service station

flyover *Chiefly Brit.* overpass

freeway toll-free highway

frontage road local road alongside expressway that provides access to property along it; service road

garage shelter or repair facility for automobiles, trucks, or buses

gassen *German.* lane or alley

gas station service station

grade sloping road; degree of inclination of sloping road

grade crossing crossing of rail or roadway or pedestrian walkway on one level

gravel road unpaved road covered with loose rock fragments

green light traffic signal indicating permission to proceed

gridlock traffic jam, esp. at intersection, in which all vehicles are blocked from moving

gutter recessed area at side of street to carry off surface water

hairpin turn extremely sharp U-shaped bend in road

high road *Chiefly Brit.* main street in village

high street *Chiefly Brit.* main or principal street

highway main direct roadway, usu. high speed and multilane

impasse dead end or cul-de-sac

interchange multilevel junction of two or more highways that makes it possible for traffic to change roadway without obstructing cross traffic

interstate multilane divided highway connecting major cities in several states

jaywalk (*vb*) cross roadway heedlessly or illegally so as to be endangered by traffic

jersey barrier strip of concrete at center of highway that divides oncoming traffic

junction intersection of roads, often where one terminates

kitty-corner (*adj*) cater-corner

lane narrow roadway, esp. between barriers or trees; strip of roadway designated for single row of vehicles

macadam roadway constructed by compacting a layer of small broken stone using bituminous binder

manhole opening in street that provides access to underground utilities

main drag *Slang.* principal roadway in town or city

main street principal business street, esp. in small town

median strip paved or planted area that divides highway into sections for traffic moving in opposite directions

mew back street, alley

motor pool several vehicles centrally based and dispatched for specific use

motorway *Chiefly Brit.* expressway

one-way (*adj*) designating roadway for movement in one direction only

overpass crossing of highways, or of highway and pedestrian crossing, at different levels, allowing traffic to pass on lower level; upper level of such a crossing

park (*vb*) temporarily leave vehicle at side of roadway or in parking lot or garage

parking lot open area or structure for parking vehicles

parking meter coin-operated register from which parking time is purchased for vehicle

parkway broad, usu. landscaped, thoroughfare

paseo *Spanish.* public walk or boulevard

pavement surface of roadway covered with asphalt or other hard substance; *Chiefly Brit.* sidewalk

pike turnpike

pileup serious collision involving several vehicles

place small, usu. residential, roadway

plaza point in toll road at which tollbooths are located

post road road used for mail conveyance

pothole large hole in road surface

red light traffic signal indicating that drivers or pedestrians must stop

ring road road encircling city; beltway

road long, open way with paved surface for traveling, esp. by vehicle

roadblock obstruction, usu. set up by police, to halt or impede passage on roadway

road hog aggressive driver of vehicle who invades others' traffic lanes

road test check of vehicle under normal operating conditions; test of driving ability required for obtaining license

roadway land over which road is built and on which vehicles travel

rotary circular roadway at multiple intersection around which all traffic moves counterclockwise; circle; traffic circle

roundabout *Chiefly Brit.* rotary

route course for travel from one point to another; highway

row *Chiefly Brit.* street

rue *French.* street

rumble strip one of a series of rough or raised strips of highway pavement, used to make drivers slow down speed of their vehicles

rush hour period at beginning or end of business day when traffic is at its peak

safety island portion of roadway from which vehicles are excluded

safety zone area of roadway for pedestrians or streetcar passengers only

secondary road feeder or artery to main roadway

service road frontage road

service station retail outlet for care of vehicles, esp. sale of gasoline; filling station; gas station

shoulder edge of roadway alongside driving area

side street small roadway; roadway leading off main street; by-street

sidewalk paved strip for pedestrians at side of street

signpost post with information or directions for drivers

skyway elevated highway

speed limit maximum legal driving speed permitted on given roadway

speed trap roadway patrolled by concealed police officers to catch drivers exceeding speed limit, esp. by radar

speedway public roadway for high-speed driving; expressway

square open area where two or more streets converge, usu. surrounded on all sides by buildings

stop-and-go slow driving in heavy traffic involving frequent stops

stoplight electric traffic signal

stop sign octagonal sign, usu. red, that requires drivers to come to full stop

strasse *German.* street
street roadway that is wider than alley or lane and usu. includes sidewalks; thoroughfare with abutting property
streetlight one of a series of lights mounted on poles spaced at intervals along public roadway
subway *Chiefly Brit.* underpass beneath street
superhighway wide highway designed for high-speed travel between major points
switchback zigzag road, esp. in hilly region
tailgate (*vb*) drive too closely behind another vehicle
tarmac roadway of tarmacadam
taxi stand place where taxis park while awaiting customers
thank-you-ma'am bump or hollow in roadway, esp. for runoff of surface water
thoroughfare main roadway
through street street that provides for continuous passage of traffic, with outlets at both ends
thruway expressway
ticket summons issued for traffic violation
tie-up stoppage of traffic due to congestion, construction, or accident
toll tax or fee paid for use of roadway
tollbooth enclosed stall on roadway where tolls are paid
toll bridge bridge at which toll is paid for crossing
tollgate barrier at which driver of vehicle must pay toll to pass
toll road roadway to which access requires payment of toll; tollway
tollway toll road
towaway zone no-parking area from which vehicles are removed by authorities
traffic vehicles or pedestrians moving between points or along roadway
traffic circle rotary
traffic cone conical, usu. rubber, brightly colored marker, placed in roadway as warning of danger to be avoided
traffic island paved or planted area in roadway that controls flow of traffic in opposite directions
traffic jam congestion and slow movement of traffic due to excess of cars on roadway, construction, or accident
traffic light traffic signal
traffic signal electrically-operated visual device for controlling traffic by use of colored signals; traffic light
trench long ditch, esp. at side of roadway
turnout place where one road branches off another; space along highway where vehicles may park or pull over to allow passing
turnpike toll road or road that previously charged toll; pike
two-way street roadway that allows passage in both directions
underpass lower level of overpass roadway interchange
U-turn 180-degree change in direction

van pool carpool using multipassenger van
via *Spanish.* way, street
way route; course for travel from point to point
white line stripe painted on road to guide traffic
wynd *Scot.* very narrow lane
zebra crossing pedestrian crosswalk marked by series of thick white stripes

Urban Structures and Phenomena

agora city marketplace (ancient Greece)
alameda public walkway lined by trees
aqueduct channel for large volume of flowing water
arcade long, arched gallery or passageway between shops
arch bridge span supported by series of arches and towers
asphalt jungle large, crowded urban area, esp. dangerous part where people must struggle to survive
Bailey bridge bridge constructed from interchangeable latticed steel panels joined by steel pins
barrio Spanish-speaking quarter in U.S. city
bascule bridge movable bridge in which rising section is counterbalanced by a weight
bidonville impoverished settlement of shanties on outskirts of city (France and North America)
block rectangular unit in city grid, enclosed by intersecting streets and occupied by buildings; length of one side of such a unit; row of houses between two streets
boardwalk raised promenade along beach
bridge structure carrying roadway for vehicles and/or pedestrians over depression, obstacle, or body of water: arch, bascule, cantilever, draw, flyover, foot, lift, pontoon, suspension, swing, toll, truss
canal man-made waterway for transportation or for draining and irrigating land
cantilever bridge span consisting of rigid construction elements that extend horizontally well beyond its vertical support members
Casbah native Arab section of North African city; Kasbah
city hall primary administrative building in city
city planning rational organization of urban growth
cluster group of buildings constructed close together on sizable tract to preserve open spaces
commute (*vb*) travel back and forth regularly between home in suburbs and work in city
commuter person who commutes regularly, esp. to work
complex large group of buildings or apartments
compound fenced or walled-in area containing group of buildings
court open space enclosed wholly or partly by buildings or surrounded by single building
courthouse building that houses law courts
covered bridge bridge with roofed or enclosed roadway

crosstown (*adj*) located at opposite points of town; (*adv*) from one side of town to the other
deck story or tier of building
depot storage place for cargo or motor vehicles; building for passengers and freight on public conveyances
dike bank of earth constructed to control or hold back water; ditch
drawbridge bridge built in sections that may be raised or lowered to permit or obstruct passage
elevated railroad urban or interurban railroad that runs along tracks raised above ground level
elevator enclosed box on pulley system for transporting passengers or freight in multistory building
embankment raised area along waterway or roadway
embarcadero landing place on bay or river
emporium commercial center; large retail establishment
escalator mechanical set of stairs arranged as endless belt that continuously ascends or descends
esplanade flat expanse of paved or grassy land along shore, esp. for driving or walking
factory large building with manufacturing facilities
fairground area where outdoor fairs, circuses, and exhibitions are held
footbridge bridge for use by pedestrians only
forum marketplace and central public area of city (ancient Rome)
greenbelt area of parkways or farmland encircling city
high rise multistory building with elevators
hôtel de ville *French.* city hall
housing development cluster of individual residences or apartment buildings of similar design under one ownership
housing estate *Chiefly Brit.* housing development
housing project publicly financed and administered housing development for low-income families
interurban (*adj*) between or connecting cities or towns
Kasbah Casbah
kiosk small, open, circular building used as newsstand or telephone booth
landfill low area of land that is built up from trash and garbage wastes embedded between layers of earth
lift bridge bridge having section that can be raised vertically to permit passage beneath it
mall large complex of shops and restaurants with attached passageways and parking space; public promenade lined with trees and closed off to motor vehicles; paved or planted divider in roadway; pedestrian passageway providing access to rows of stores
marina basin providing dockage for motorboats and yachts, with supply and repair facilities
market traditional urban center where goods are sold
metro subway system

metropolitan (*adj*) relating to or characteristic of a city

mew *Chiefly Brit.* houses built around a court

minimall group of small shops clustered around parking area, usu. on business street

municipal (*adj*) restricted to one self-governing locality

noise pollution environmental pollution consisting of bothersome or harmful noise; sound pollution

off-hour period of time other than rush hour or outside regular business hours

off-peak off-hour period with reduced public transportation fares

park tract of ground in or around city maintained in natural state or cultivated for recreational use

passageway path or narrow roadway that permits movement in, out, or through

pedestrian one who moves by foot

people mover movable sidewalk

piazza open square (Italy)

pissolr *French.* public urinal along street

place *French.* public square, plaza

playground outdoor area equipped with children's recreational facilities

plaza public square

pontoon bridge bridge supported by series of floats

pound depot for holding personal property until it is claimed by owner

projects *Informal.* housing project

promenade public walkway

public transportation buses, trolleys, and subways for use by general public for set fare, running on schedules over specific routes

quay paved bank or landing beside navigable waterway

rapid transit fast, modern, public transportation system

residential (*adj*) restricted to or occupied by private homes and apartments

rialto exchange or marketplace; theater district

right of way strip of land over which a public road is built; land used by a public utility

row area dominated by specific kind of structure or activity

sewer artificial underground channel to carry off sewage and surface water overflow

shopping center group of retail stores and service establishments with parking facilities, serving community or neighborhood

shopping mall shopping area with stores facing enclosed area restricted to pedestrians

skid row downtown district of cheap bars and hotels for transients

skyscraper very tall building

skywalk enclosed, elevated walkway that connects two buildings

slum densely-populated urban area marked by crowding, poor housing, poverty, and social disorder

slurb shabby, ill-planned suburban area

sound pollution noise pollution

span bridge or overpass

storefront side of store or building facing street

straphanger person who commutes on public transportation, esp. while standing up holding a strap for support

street railway system of streetcars or buses

strip long stretch of land, often used as highway divider; commercially-developed roadway

subway underground electric railway

superblock very large commercial or residential block, closed to through traffic and crossed by pedestrian walks and access roads, often with grassy malls

supermarket large, self-service retail outlet for food and household merchandise

suspension bridge bridge with roadway suspended from two or more cables that pass over towers and are anchored at ends

swing bridge bridge that opens by pivoting on central pier to permit passage

telephone booth enclosure on street within which one may sit or stand while making a telephone call

telephone box *Chiefly Brit.* public telephone booth

tenement house residential building that meets minimum standards of sanitation, safety, and comfort, occupied by poor families

terminal centrally-located freight or passenger station of public carrier that serves as junction for several lines

terrace row of houses or apartments on raised ground; strip of park in middle of street; small avenue or lane

town hall building that houses administrative offices of town

tram *Chiefly Brit.* streetcar, trolley, or vehicle running on rails

tramcar *Chiefly Brit.* streetcar

tramline *Chiefly Brit.* street railway

tramway *Chiefly Brit.* streetcar line; overhead cable or rails for trams

transfer ticket that entitles passenger on public conveyance to continue journey on another line

transfer point junction at which passenger changes public transportation lines

transit local transportation of passengers by public conveyance

truss bridge bridge supported by bracketlike framework

tube *Chiefly Brit.* subway

tunnel hollow conduit or recess for passage; covered passageway through obstruction or under ground

underground *Chiefly Brit.* subway system

urban (*adj*) of, relating to, characteristic of, or constituting a city

urban blight decay and poverty of old inner city

urban planning systematic development of new urban areas or renovation of existing areas to improve conditions there

urban renewal planned renovation of older city districts

urban sprawl spreading of urban phenomena onto undeveloped land near city

utility service such as water, gas, or electricity provided by public or private company

vacant lot undeveloped and unused plot of land

viaduct bridge made up of several short spans supported by reinforced concrete arches and towers, carrying road or railroad over obstruction or valley

walk-up multistory building without elevator

walkway pedestrian passage

warren densely populated tenement or district

waterfront land or district adjacent to body of water

water supply facilities for bringing water to a community through reservoirs, aqueducts, tunnels, and pipelines

wharf structure built along shore of navigable waters at which ships may lie to receive and discharge cargo or passengers

zoning partitioning by ordinance of city, borough, or township into sections reserved for specific purposes

GOVERNMENT
Forms, Systems, and Philosophies
Governmental Bodies and Institutions
Government Officials and Citizens
Acts, Powers, Conditions, and Procedures
Postal Service

See also: Chap. 11: Politics, Law, International Relations; Titles of Rank; Chap. 12: Business and Economics; Finance

Forms, Systems, and Philosophies

absolute monarchy kingdom in which monarch has complete power

absolutism theory and practice of government by single absolute ruler

anarchy absence of government; advocacy of this state

aristocracy government by wealthy, privileged minority or hereditary ruling class

autarchy absolute sovereignty; autocracy

autarky economic self-sufficiency of a state

authoritarianism principle of submission to authority; concentration of power in hands of autocratic leader or powerful elite not constitutionally bound or responsible to the people

autocracy government power placed in hands of one ruler; autarchy

autonomy self-government, esp. state and local

benevolent dictatorship nonrepressive absolute rule that works for good of citizens

bicameral (*adj*) having two legislative houses in government

caliphate government ruled by Islamic civil and religious leader

caretaker government temporary regime during lapse in normal government functions

centralism assignment of power to central leadership

centralization organization under single authority; shift of political authority from local to state government

checks and balances principle of interdependency of governmental branches through power of limitation

city-state self-governing state composed of independent city and adjacent territory controlled by it, esp. in ancient Greece and medieval Europe; polis

civil government government established by laws made by citizens or their representatives; nonmilitary, nonreligious authority

civil liberty freedom from arbitrary governmental interference, esp. as prescribed in U.S. Bill of Rights

coalition government temporary alliance of members of two or more parties to form governing majority

collective group or institution organized and run by all members equally

colonialism control by one state over dependent state or people

commission plan system of municipal government in which all powers lie in hands of elected commission

common law unwritten law developed over time and based on accepted notion of right and wrong

commonwealth government in which ultimate authority lies with people

concurrent powers rights exercised by both national and state governments

constitutionalism government based on written constitutional principles

constitutional monarchy government headed by monarch and regulated by constitution

council-manager plan form of city government in which strong elected council hires city manager to administer laws

crown monarch; government in constitutional monarchy

decentralization distribution of power among several groups

democracy government by the people, with majority rule exercised in periodic free election of representatives

democratism democratic government

despotism system of government in which ruler exercises absolute power

dictatorship government in which absolute power rests with one person or a few

direct democracy pure form of democracy in which people's will is expressed in mass meetings and becomes public policy

dirigisme *French.* theory that government should take part in direction of economic affairs

divine right of kings authority of sovereign considered to be granted by God, not people (16th-17th c.)

dominion sovereignty, authority over; self-governing member of British Commonwealth giving allegiance to British monarch

duarchy government by two equally powerful rulers; duumvirate

duumvirate government in which two persons rule jointly; duarchy

dyarchy dual responsibility shared by colonial government and native ministers

empire several territories, nations, or peoples governed by single sovereign authority

fascism government based on establishing oppressive, one-party, centralized national regime

federal government system in which political units surrender individual sovereignty to central authority but retain designated powers; such central authority

federalism principle of shared power between national and state governments

feudalism political system in Europe from 9th to 15th century in which lord owned all property worked by vassals

gerontocracy rule by elders

governance a method or system of government; exercise of government authority

government organized political institutions, laws, and customs by which state fulfills its authorized functions

gynecocracy government by women

hagiocracy government by group of persons believed to be holy

hierocracy rule by priest or clergy

home rule provision allowing local self-government while under state control

isocracy government in which all individuals have equal political power

kingdom monarchy ruled by a king

limited government constitutional principle that government may do only what people have empowered it to do

local government authority over town, city, county, or other small locale by citizens rather than state or federal government

martial law temporary suspension of law and use of military to maintain order during emergency

matriarchy government or monarchy in which power rests with females or descends through female line

mayor-council plan system of municipal government with elected mayor as executive and elected council as legislature

meritocracy government in which criterion for leadership is skill or intellectual achievement

militarism belief that war and its preparation are most important functions of state

mobocracy rule by mob

monarchism government by monarchy

monarchy government with absolute hereditary ruler who serves for life

municipal (*adj*) pertaining to local self-government

nationalism loyalty to interests of one's own nation

neocolonialism economic domination of one nation by a more powerful nation without imposition of colonial government

ochlocracy rule by multitude or mob

officialism rigid adherence to regulations and absence of creativity in government activities

oligarchy government by small group of privileged individuals

one-man rule despotism, dictatorship

one world philosophy and dream of a single world government

pantisocracy utopia in which all members rule equally

parliamentary government system in which executive (prime minister) is chosen by elected legislature (parliament) from among its members

participatory democracy democratic system permitting direct involvement of individuals

paternalism benevolent, fatherly control by authority of individuals' interactions with each other as well as with government

patriarchy government or monarchy in which power rests with males or descends through male line

pluralism governmental system that embraces cultural diversity and advocates general participation in decision making

plutocracy government by the wealthy

police state repressive system dominated by all-powerful police, esp. secret police, instead of elected officials

polis city-state (ancient Greece)

popular sovereignty principle that government exists only with consent of the governed, i.e., power lies with the people

presidential government system based on separation of powers between elected executive and legislative departments

principality state ruled by prince, often part of larger state or empire

provisional government temporary authority during lapse in normal government functions

regency reign of nonmonarch during youth or indisposition of monarch

regime system of administration and its practitioners

representative democracy indirect democracy in which people's will is expressed through elected representatives

republic government in which power is vested in elected representatives of citizenry

republicanism principles and advocacy of government by republic

self-government political power lying in hands of inhabitants of state or territory rather than outside authority; self-rule

self-rule self-government

separation of powers doctrine that division of responsibility among legislative, executive, and judicial branches is conducive to equitable government

social contract understanding between citizens and government on which government is based

sovereignty political autonomy and freedom of state from outside authority

state government authority over single state

statism highly centralized government control of economy

stratocracy government by the military

technocracy government run by experts and technicians

thearchy government based on divine sovereignty

theocracy government by church officials, who believe they have divine authority

timocracy government based on love of honor and military glory or on requisite ownership of property

totalitarianism authoritarian political system in which citizen is totally subject to will of state

town meeting oldest and most direct form of democracy, in which local citizens assemble to vote on issues

triarchy government ruled jointly by three persons; triumvirate

tricameral (*adj*) having three legislative houses or chambers in government

triumvirate triarchy

tyranny government by single absolute authority, esp. one exercising oppressive power

unicameral (*adj*) having a single legislative chamber in government

unitary government system in which power is held by single central source and local governments are merely administrative agents, the opposite of federalism

welfare state system in which ultimate responsibility of government is well-being of all citizens

world federalism principle of federal union of all nations with limited authority

world government principle of single governing authority for all nations

Governmental Bodies and Institutions

administration activity and actions of all branches of government; collective body managing government affairs

agency unit of executive branch that administers programs, sets rules, and settles disputes in specific policy area

Althing oldest European legislature, the Icelandic parliament

assembly lower legislative house

board group of elected or appointed functionaries

board of aldermen governing body of city

board of supervisors governing body of county

brain trust informal group of advisers

branches of government tripartite division of U.S. government: executive, legislative, judicial

Bundesrat upper house of German parliament

Bundestag lower house of German parliament

bureau independent government office

bureaucracy large body of appointive

government officials; complex structure of executive branch

cabal secret group seeking to exercise authority over government

cabinet chief advisory body to chief executive, president, or prime minister

camarilla secret group of advisers, often engaged in intrigue; cabal

canton small territorial division (France and Switzerland)

capital seat of government

capitol building where congress or state legislature meets

Capitol building in Washington D.C., in which Congress meets

Capitol Hill small hill on which U.S. Capitol stands; U.S. Congress, the Hill

chamber legislative house

chamber of deputies legislative body, usu. lower house

city large, usu. self-governing, municipality

city council legislative body of city

city hall building housing offices of city government

civil service nonmilitary governmental employees selected through merit system

commissariat major government division in Soviet Union prior to 1946

commission government agency with authority in one area; individuals appointed to investigate specific issues

committee body delegated to consider specific legislative matters

committee of the whole committee of all members of a legislative body, meeting under relaxed rules to expedite business

commonwealth federation of nations; official designation of four U.S. states: Kentucky, Massachusetts, Pennsylvania, and Virginia

commune smallest administrative district of some European nations; rural community based on collectivism

confederacy alliance for some specific purpose; eleven Southern states that seceded from United States in 1860; confederation

confederation confederacy

conference committee committee composed of members of both legislative houses

congress national legislative branch of government, esp. in republic; national or international representative assembly

Congress national legislative body of United States, consisting of Senate and House of Representatives

Congressional committee group of legislators chosen to consider details of legislation in one area and advise on Congressional action

council small governmental body, esp. for city

county political subdivision of state

county board governing body of county

county seat town that is site of county government

court judicial body; reigning sovereign with his or her family, retinue, and officers

courthouse building housing courts and local government offices

D.C. *District of Columbia*

department large administrative division of executive branch headed by cabinet member; regional division within nation comparable to state

Department of Agriculture U.S. executive department appointed to administer programs regarding farming

Department of Commerce U.S. executive department appointed to administer programs regarding domestic and foreign business

Department of Defense U.S. executive department appointed to administer programs regarding the military

Department of Education U.S. executive department appointed to administer programs regarding schools

Department of Energy U.S. executive department appointed to administer programs regarding sources and uses of energy

Department of Health and Human Services U.S. executive department appointed to administer programs regarding medicine and social welfare

Department of Housing and Urban Development U.S. executive department appointed to administer programs regarding city affairs and construction of dwellings

Department of Justice U.S. executive department appointed to administer programs regarding criminal and civil law

Department of Labor U.S. executive department appointed to administer programs regarding employer-employee relations

Department of State U.S. executive department appointed to administer programs regarding international relations

Department of the Interior U.S. executive department appointed to administer programs regarding land and natural resources

Department of the Treasury U.S. executive department appointed to administer programs regarding finance and money

Department of Transportation U.S. executive department appointed to administer programs regarding travel and shipping

Department of Veterans Affairs U.S. executive department appointed to administer programs regarding veterans of military service

diet national or provincial legislative body; assembly of princes

District of Columbia D.C.; seat of U.S. federal government

divan council of state or council chamber in Middle East

duma council or official assembly in pre-Soviet Russia

duumvirate coalition of two people in official capacity

emirate state or territory ruled by an Islamic emir or prince

exchequer national treasury and revenue department, as in Great Britain

executive branch law-enforcing and administrative branch of government, in United States headed by President

federation alliance of autonomous states

floor working area occupied by members of U.S. House or Senate

folkmoot general assembly of people of a town or shire in medieval England

government corporation public corporation that is government-owned but partially independent financially, organized to carry out a particular program

grand duchy territory ruled by grand duke or grand duchess

Hill *Informal.* short for Capitol Hill, where U.S. Congress is located

Home Office department responsible for administration of England but not the rest of United Kingdom

house one division of bicameral legislature

House U.S. House of Representatives

House of Commons elective lower house of British Parliament

House of Lords upper house of British Parliament, in which peers and church officials sit for lifetime appointments

House of Representatives lower house of U.S. Congress, with two-year elective term

inner circle group of advisers closest to leader

interest group private organization attempting to influence government policy; lobby on specific issue

interim committee committee of Congress active between sessions

joint committee legislative committee composed of members from both houses

judicial branch section of government that administers justice and tries cases involving governmental or constitutional issues, composed primarily of judges

judiciary combined system of federal and state courts

kitchen cabinet unofficial, sometimes secret, advisers to head of state

land office government office for transaction of business relating to public lands

legislative branch lawmaking branch of government, usu. composed of elected representatives

legislature body charged with enacting laws

lobby interest group

lower house one branch of a bicameral legislature, usu. containing more members than upper house; U.S. House of Representatives; British House of Commons

majlis legislative body in Southwest Asia and North Africa

ministry department of government

municipality city, town, or village incorporated for self-government

nation independent, politically organized territory and its citizens

national assembly legislative body of nation

office public position or job

Office of Management and Budget OMB; U.S. executive agency that prepares federal budget

OMB Office of Management and Budget

parish political subdivision of Louisiana

parliament usu. bicameral elected legislature, as in Britain

possession territory ruled by government of another state

privy council board of personal advisers to monarch

province administrative division of a nation

public anything pertaining to the state or its subdivisions

puppet government government whose policies are orchestrated by another state

regulatory commission small board within executive chosen to manage particular government function

Rules Committee House committee that sets procedures for debate on bills

rump fragment of political group acting on behalf of original body after departure or expulsion of large number of its members

secretariat administrative department of government organization

Secret Service unit responsible for protecting U.S. President and Vice President

select committee legislative committee established for specific task and limited time

senate lawmaking assembly; state council

Senate upper house of U.S. Congress, with two senators from each state elected to six-year terms

shadow cabinet leaders of minority or opposition party in parliamentary system

sinecure public office requiring little or no work

sovereignty self-governing territory or state

soviet government council and basic unit of political leadership of the former Soviet Union

special committee legislative committee established for specific task

standing committee permanent committee intended to consider specific subject

state politically organized community independent of other states; sovereign nation; major subdivision of United States

statehouse building housing offices of state government

steering committee committee of legislative or deliberative body that prepares agenda for session

subcommittee division of committee with limited purpose or authority

supreme court highest court in political unit with ultimate authority in judicial and constitutional matters

Supreme Court highest federal court in United States, consisting of nine judges

synod governing council or assembly of church

territory region over which government has authority

think tank institution conducting interdisciplinary research on issues of public policy

town municipal settlement larger than a village, smaller than a city

town hall location of mayoral and council offices; city hall

town meeting assembly of local citizens acting as legislative body

township New England territorial and political unit governed by town meetings

triumvirate group or association of three

troika administrative body of three

union combination of two or more autonomous political units

upper house one branch of bicameral legislature; U.S. Senate; British House of Lords

village smallest municipal corporation

watchdog agency commission responsible for protecting public by regulating an industry

Government Officials and Citizens

administrator one who manages and executes government programs

alderman city council member in some U.S. cities

appointee nonelective official, usu. chosen by executive branch

assemblyman member of legislative assembly, esp. male

assemblywoman female member of legislative assembly

attorney general chief law officer of nation or state; chief of U.S. Department of Justice

autocrat ruler possessing absolute authority

backbencher any member of British Parliament other than leaders of the party

bureaucrat member of bureaucracy

burgess former representative of borough or town in British Parliament

burgher inhabitant of borough or town

burgomaster mayor or chief magistrate of certain European cities

caudillo dictator, in Spanish-speaking countries

chairman official in seat of authority, esp. male

chairwoman female official in seat of authority

chancellor chief minister of state in certain parliamentary governments; prime minister; premier

chief executive principal administrative officer of government

chief justice ranking justice of court, esp. supreme court

chief of staff person responsible for supervising top executive's assistants and advisers

chief of state formal head of state, often not part of government process

citizen native or naturalized person owing allegiance to specific government

city father councilman or alderman

city manager official appointed by elected councilors to manage city administration

civilian person not in military or government service

civil servant member of civil service; elected or appointed government official serving the people

clerk record keeper

commander in chief supreme commander of armed forces; U.S. President

commissar supervisor of government department in Soviet Union before 1946

congressman member of House of Representatives, esp. male

congresswoman female member of House of Representatives

constituent resident of legislator's district

coroner county official responsible for investigating circumstances of deaths

councilman member of city council, esp. male

councilor member of city council

councilwoman female member of city council

crown office or person of monarch

czar absolute hereditary monarch of Russia until 1917; one having authority over major program

deputy member of lower legislative house; chief assistant to department head

designate (*adj*) used following title it modifies to indicate that person has been selected for office but not yet installed, as in ambassador-designate

despot absolute ruler

dictator absolute ruler, esp. oppressive tyrant

disenfranchised citizens denied right to vote

doorkeeper person in U.S. Congress who announces arrival of president and controls gallery passes

duce Italian fascist leader, esp. Mussolini

dynasty sequence of rulers from same family or group

emperor monarch governing an empire

enfranchised citizens granted right to vote

etharch ruler of a people or tribe

fed *Informal.* employee of federal government, esp. law enforcement officer

federal agent employee or representative of federal agency

freeholder one who has inherited and holds for life an estate of land

freshman newly elected member serving first term in U.S. Congress

Führer *German.* leader, esp. Hitler

government employee individual elected or appointed to work for any branch of federal, state, or local government

governor chief executive of U.S. state or imperial possession

head of state sovereign or chief executive, sometimes in ceremonial capacity only

jemadar any of various government officials in India

king male monarch

lawgiver member of legislature who draws up and enacts laws

lawmaker legislator

legislator member of legislature, usu. elected

lieutenant governor official next in line to state governor

macebearer official who carries ceremonial staff of office

magistrate public official entrusted with administration of law, often with judicial function

manager one who directs or supervises others

mayor highest executive official of city or town

minister high official managing government department or serving as diplomatic representative in foreign state

minister without portfolio government official with responsibilities in various areas

monarch hereditary ruler of kingdom, empire, or constitutional monarchy

MP **M**ember of **P**arliament (Britain)

official middle- or high-level government employee

ombudsman government official who serves as intermediary between public and government and investigates complaints of misconduct by public officials

page person who carries messages and runs errands for members of legislature

Pharaoh absolute hereditary sovereign in ancient Egypt

philosopher king one who rules based on wisdom, proposed in Plato's *Republic*

policymaker top-level government official involved in creating and directing policy

premier prime minister

president head of executive branch

President chief executive of United States

president pro tempore presiding officer of Senate when vice president is absent, usu. senior member of majority party

prime minister first minister; head of cabinet in parliamentary government; chancellor; premier

public servant government employee owing first allegiance to citizens of nation he or she serves

queen female monarch

recorder official who sets down or transcribes information

regent one who rules monarchy when sovereign is disabled or too young

representative one elected to legislative body to serve interests of specific constituency

secretary executive official supervising operations of one department

secretary-general primary administrative official of organization

selectman municipal official in New England

senator member of senate

Senator member of U.S. Senate

sergeant at arms officer of legislative or judicial body charged with preserving order

sky marshal armed federal marshal responsible for preventing airline hijackings

solon member of legislature, esp. wise lawgiver

sovereign one exercising absolute power; monarch

Speaker of the House presiding officer in U.S. House of Representatives

statesman one exercising leadership and conducting governmental business at a high level

strongman absolute ruler who rules by force; dictator

subject citizen governed by sovereign authority

supervisor member of county executive board

treasurer officer responsible for public funds

tyrant single absolute ruler, often oppressive or cruel and violent

under secretary second in command in executive department

usurper one who assumes and holds office without right

vice- prefix indicating official first in line to take place of immediate superior, as in vice-chancellor

vice president official next in line to president

viceroy governor of territory who represents monarch

warlord supreme military leader, often holding civil power by force

Acts, Powers, Conditions, and Procedures

abdicate (*vb*) give up throne or office

abstain (*vb*) withhold one's vote or participation

acclamation vote of legislature by voice only

act law passed by legislative body

ad hoc with specific or particular purpose

adjourn (*vb*) end legislative session

advice and consent constitutional power of Senate to approve all presidential appointments and treaties

affirmative action plan to rectify discrimination against minorities and women

agenda list of items to be brought before meeting

allegiance basic obligation of loyalty to state

amendment formal alteration of bill, law, or constitution

amnesty pardon by government authority, usu. head of state, to violators of federal law

annexation addition of territory into existing domain

appointment selection to fill nonelected office or function, usu. by president or executive

apportionment distribution and assignment of legislative seats

appropriations funds set aside by law for specific purpose

arbitration hearing or judgment of controversy by statutorily appointed body

archives collection of public documents

articles divisions of U.S. Constitution containing procedures for organization and implementation of government

assessment listing and evaluation of property for tax purposes

authority power to rule vested in government by people, constitution, or revolution

bill proposed piece of legislation

bill of attainder legislative act finding a person guilty of treason or felony without court trial

Bill of Rights first ten amendments to U.S. Constitution

bloc voting united voting of legislators or delegates to advance or obstruct action

bond certificate indicating government has borrowed money from individual or organization and will pay interest until bond is sold

boondoggle frivolous expenditure of public funds

bribe illegal payment to public official for favor

briefing act of providing information or instructions

budget financial plan for funding operations of government

bull decree of pope

calendar legislative schedule

carry (*vb*) secure passage or adoption; win majority of votes

casting vote deciding vote cast by presiding officer when other votes are equally divided

caucus closed meeting of legislative party members to decide status of forthcoming issues or select leaders

censure condemnation by vote of legislature

census official population count and informational survey taken every ten years

charter fundamental law or constitution granted cities by state legislature

citizenship full rights, duties, and privileges as a member of a nation, by birth or naturalization

civil disobedience refusal to obey government demands and laws, usu. passive resistance as matter of conscience

civil law laws pertaining to disputes between private parties or between private parties and government

classified (*adj*) secret

clause separate article of law or other formal document

clearance official authorization to know of or participate in classified activities

cloture procedure by which legislative body, esp. U.S. Senate, limits debate

coalition alliance of states or political parties

committee hearing publicly conducted information-gathering process by which committee reaches decision on issue

commonweal general welfare

concurrent powers powers held by both states and federal government

concurrent resolution congressional opinion requiring approval of both houses, but not a law

confirmation legislative approval of executive appointment

conflict of interest incompatibility between private interests and public responsibilities

Congressional Record official transcript of proceedings of both houses of Congress

consensus agreement by majority within group

consent willingness of people to submit to authority of civil government

constitution fundamental written law of state or nation

Constitution fundamental written law of United States

constitutionality accordance with constitution of a nation

convene (*vb*) come together as legislative body to commence session

cooperative federalism programs that feature joint effort of federal, state, and local governments to solve common problems

coronation act or ceremony of crowning a monarch

debriefing questioning and instruction of one privy to classified information

debt ceiling upper limit set for national debt

Declaration of Independence proclamation of liberty by American colonies in 1776

decree executive proclamation having force of law

dedication gift of private lands for public use

delegated powers constitutional powers of federal government

deregulation removal of established controls over business or industry

devolution transfer of power from central government to local government

discharge petition petition by half of House of Representatives to withdraw proposed bill from committee consideration

dissenting opinion written view on case by minority of U.S. Supreme Court

domestic (*adj*) pertaining to internal affairs of state

domestic tranquility state of peace within nation

draft compulsory selection of persons for military duty

edict official order or proclamation with force of law

eminent domain constitutional power of government to take private property for public use

enactment passage of bill into law

enumerated powers powers of federal government stated in U.S. Constitution

exclusive powers powers exclusive to federal or state government

executive agreement pact between U.S. President and head of foreign state not requiring senatorial approval

executive order rule issued by President, governor, or administrative authority that has force of law

executive privilege right of President to withhold certain information, usu. to protect national security

executive session hearing held by legislative body or committee that is closed to public

expenditures government spending of revenue

extradition return of criminal from one state or nation to another for trial

fiat authoritative government order or decree

filibuster delaying tactic to prevent legislative action

first reading initial submission of bill before legislature, often by number or name only

fiscal policy governmental use and manipulation of public revenues

foreign policy principles and goals determining one nation's relations with other nations

forum assembly for discussion of issues of public interest

franking privilege right to mail official papers without charge, enjoyed by members of Congress, President, and cabinet

gag rule any rule restricting open discussion or debate on a given issue in a deliberative body

gavel-to-gavel (*adj*) designating entire period from opening of legislative session to adjournment

grant-in-aid federal money given to state or local government for use in health, education, or public works

hopper box into which representatives drop bills to introduce them into the House

impeachment formal accusation brought to remove civil official from office; charges articulated in U.S. House of Representatives and tried in the Senate

implied powers authority of federal government based on indirect expression in U.S. Constitution

inauguration installation of President or other official into office

inherent powers authority of all national governments based on sovereignty as nation-states

initiative petition to place legislation or constitutional amendment on ballot for voters' direct approval

internal revenue money collected by government from citizens in form of taxes

interpellation procedure by which legislature asks government official to explain an act or policy

interposition doctrine that states may block enforcement of federal laws

interregnum temporary lapse in government functions, esp. during transition between two regimes or administrations

item veto executive veto of part of bill without rejection of entire measure

joint resolution formal expression of congressional opinion with force of law, esp. on unusual or temporary matter

judicial review power of courts to decide constitutionality of act of government

junket trip taken at public expense by government employee

jurisdiction authority over people or territory

kill (*vb*) prevent enactment of bill into legislation or veto enacted bill

law binding legislative act

legislative power constitutional authority allowing Congress to make laws

lobby (*vb*) attempt to influence government policy on specific issue, esp. by swaying legislative votes

measure legislative bill or enactment

merit system selection of civil servants on basis of demonstrated abilities rather than patronage

minutes written notes and record of meeting

motion formal proposal

move (*vb*) introduce a motion

municipal charter document creating city government and setting forth its powers and duties

national supremacy constitutional doctrine that national laws supersede state or local laws

omnibus bill all-inclusive or broad-ranging legislation

ordinance law, statute, or government regulation

override legislative vote to annul executive veto of legislative act

pardon legal forgiveness for crime granted by executive without judicial action

parliamentarianism study and practice of rules of conduct for legislative body

parliamentary procedure any of the rules and precedents governing proceedings of legislatures or meetings of other legislative bodies

pass (*vb*) approve

passage legislative enactment of bill into law

patronage awarding of government positions in return for support or other favors

petition formal written request, often signed by many citizens and submitted to government, esp. as means of placing referendum on ballot

pigeonhole (*vb*) set aside bill in committee and not bring it before legislature

pocket (*vb*) retain legislative bill without action to prevent it from becoming law

pocket veto process by which President prevents bill from becoming law by leaving it unsigned past end of legislative session

portfolio office and duties of minister of state

position paper detailed report on an issue, usu. advising specific action

prerogative exclusive special right or privilege inherent in position or office

prime the pump increase government funding to stimulate the economy

private bill bill dealing with individual concern

proclamation official public executive announcement

progressive tax tax rate that increases as taxable income increases

proportional representation allocation of legislative seats by party based on percent of popular or electoral vote received

proviso clause stating conditions of bill or document

public assistance government funds used to satisfy basic needs of poor citizens

public lands territory owned by federal government

public policy government programs approved by legislature or initiated by executive departments and agencies

public service actions that supply essential commodity or service for benefit or welfare of people

public works roads, dams, and other structures for public use that are paid for by government funds

quorum number of members of body required to transact official business, usu. a majority

railroad (*vb*) rush legislation through without considering opposition

ratify (*vb*) vote approval; sanction formally

reapportionment reorganization of electoral districts by new formula

recall procedure by which public official is removed from office by popular vote

recess suspension of legislative session or procedure

redistricting revision of legislative district boundaries

red tape excessive bureaucratic procedure that causes delay

regalia emblems of office

regulation executive actions to bring activities into conformity with law

repeal (*vb*) cancel or revoke legislative enactment

report (*vb*) send bill to full legislature with committee recommendation

rescind (*vb*) cancel, annul

reserved powers powers not delegated to federal government by U.S. Constitution and not denied to states

resolution formal expression of opinion or intent by governmental body

revenue government income, primarily from taxation

revenue sharing system by which state and local governments receive fixed amounts of federal tax revenues

revoke (*vb*) annul statute or recall official

rider provision that might not pass on its own but that is likely to pass when attached to important bill

roll call alphabetical recital of names of legislators on floor for vote on issue

secession formal separation from organized body or government

second (*vb*) endorse another's parliamentary motion

second reading legislative proceeding in which a bill is reported back from committee for full debate before vote

sedition verbal incitement of resistance to lawful authority

senatorial courtesy unwritten rule that U.S. Senate will approve an appointee only if acceptable to senators in President's party from state involved

seniority system assignment of most important posts and committee chairmanships to members of U.S. Congress with longest service

serfdom condition of being bound to land and subservient to feudal lord; thralldom

session period of time during which legislative body meets

sittings sessions of U.S. Supreme Court

slavery ownership of persons who are absolutely subject to slaveholder's will

special session legislative assembly at abnormal time

states' rights governmental authority exercised by states, not to be infringed upon by federal government

statute law; act of legislature

statutory law law enacted by legislative body such as congress, state legislature, or city council

strict construction interpretation of U.S. Constitution to mean that federal government has no powers or rights not expressly granted by Constitution, esp. limiting use of presidential power

subjugation conquest or domination of a people or territory

subsidy government funds paid to individual or group to enhance economic position

succession order in which officials move up to vacated higher position, esp. procedure for filling presidential vacancy

table (*vb*) remove bill from consideration, usu. indefinitely; *Chiefly Brit.* place bill or motion on agenda

tax monies collected by government from citizens to support government

taxation government imposition of taxes; revenue derived from taxes

term two-year session of House between elections; six-year incumbency in Senate before facing reelection

thralldom slavery, serfdom

top secret highly classified information requiring special clearance for access

town meeting assembly of local citizens to discuss and vote on issues

treason betrayal of one's government by making war on it or giving aid and comfort to its enemies

ukase edict issued by Russian czar

unconstitutional (*adj*) in violation of constitutional principles

undemocratic (*adj*) not in accord with democratic principles, esp. totalitarian

unincorporated area territory beyond any local jurisdiction

unseat (*vb*) remove from office, usu. by defeating in election

unwritten constitution informal constitution based on series of laws over time

vassalage condition of subordination to feudal lord as tenant

veto power of executive to reject legislation passed by Congress; (*vb*) exercise such power

veto power executive authority to reject legislation

voice vote vote by acclamation

vote exercise of political franchise in election of officials or expression of views on issues

vote of confidence formal expression of political support for governing ministry by legislative majority in parliamentary system

war powers extended presidential powers of commander in chief in time of war

ways and means manner of raising and allocating revenues for conduct of government business

white paper detailed government report on specific subject

yield (*vb*) allow another member of body to express views in debate

Postal Service

aerogram sheet of lightweight paper folded to form its own envelope and bearing postal stamp imprint, sent via airmail, usu. overseas

air express system for overnight delivery of letters and packages by air

air freight shipment of packages by air

airmail postal transportation by aircraft, formerly at higher rate than first-class mail, now at standard rate

APO **A**rmy and Air Force **P**ost **O**ffice; designation for overseas mail intended for military personnel

Army and Air Force Post Office APO

bulk mail low-cost, slowest class of postal service, esp. for large quantities of printed matter

carrier person who delivers mail

certified mail first-class mail for which proof of delivery is obtained and often returned to sender

envelope folded paper with sealing flap into which letters are placed for protection when sent by postal service

express mail guaranteed overnight delivery

first-class mail regular priority mail service, sent by air over long distances; priority mail

forwarding address new address given to post office when moving to guarantee mail forwarding

general delivery department at post office where mail is held for pickup at window

indicia postal markings or labels affixed to mail

key device that operator uses to send telegram

letter carrier mailman

mail nation's postal system; letters and other matter sent by mail; bags of postal matter; (*vb*) send a letter or package by post

mailbag canvas container used by postal service for gathering mail; letter carrier's shoulder bag

mailbox public receptacle for deposit of outgoing mail

mail drop receptacle for deposit of outgoing mail

mail forwarding postal service by which mail sent to person's old address is forwarded to new address

mailman one who delivers mail, esp. door-to-door on foot or by vehicle; letter carrier; postman

mail order business of selling of goods by mail; order for goods sent through mail

parcel post postal service and fees for handling packages

PO box *post-office* box

post national postal delivery system; single delivery of mail; (*vb*) send a letter or package

postage fee required for postal service; stamps

postage due additional fee required for delivery of letter with insufficient postage

postage meter device that prints postage on mail, records amount, and subtracts it from amount prepaid to postal service

postage stamp government-issued, adhesive-backed design on paper indicative of prepayment of specified postage fee; stamp

postal (*adj*) relating to or conducted by postal service

postal money order receipt issued by post office that is good for payment of cash at any post office

postal scale small scale for weighing letters and packages to determine required postal fee

postal service nation's institutions, regulations, and personnel for delivery of mail

post-bag *Chiefly Brit.* mailbag

postcard small card on which message is written and to which stamp is affixed for mailing without envelope

postcode *Brit.* code of numbers and letters for routing mail

poste restante direction written on envelope, esp. in Europe, that mail should be held at post office for addressee

postman mailman

postmark official mark showing date and place of mailing, printed over stamp as cancellation symbol

postmaster supervisor of post office

postmaster general director of national postal system

post office government department handling mail service; local branch of this department through which mail is processed; building housing local branch

post office box PO box; numbered box at post office used as address for receipt of mail

postpaid (*adj*) having postage prepaid by sender

post road route over which mail is transported

priority mail first-class mail

railway express system for shipment of packages by railroad

registered mail mail recorded in originating post office and at successive points of transmission for guarantee of special handling and safe delivery

return to sender postal designation indicating recipient is no longer at address and no forwarding address is known

RFD **r**ural **f**ree **d**elivery

RR **r**ural **r**oute

rural free delivery RFD; designation for postal service to rural location

rural route RR; postal delivery route in rural area

special delivery mail delivery for extra fee by messenger immediately upon arrival at destination post office

stamp postage stamp

star route route in rural area serviced by private carrier under contract with postal service

stationery writing paper and envelopes used for letters and other mail

surcharge overprint on stamp that alters denomination

zip code five- or nine-digit postal code that indicates local post office through which mail should be routed to recipient

---

POLITICS

Philosophies, Principles, and Parties
Party Functions and Political Practices
Politicians and Activists
Elections and Campaigns
Revolution and Antigovernment Activity

See also: *Chap. 11: Government; Law; Chap. 13: Sociology*

Philosophies, Principles, and Parties

anarchism belief that all government authority is harmful; advocacy of government by voluntary personal cooperation

anarcho-syndicalism syndicalism

art of the possible politics based on practical expediency rather than theoretical visions

Bill of Rights basic human rights and privileges guaranteed in first ten amendments to U.S. Constitution

Bolshevism doctrine of wing of Russian Communist party advocating violent revolution, which seized power in 1917

capitalism political and economic system in which capital goods are privately or corporately owned and managed

center principles midway between liberal and conservative views

centrist (*adj*) being party of moderate views; positioned at middle of one's own party

chauvinism extreme, dogmatic patriotism

civics study of government, politics, and the duties and rights of citizenship

civil rights fundamental protections and nonpolitical rights, esp. individual freedoms, enjoyed by all citizens under Constitution

collective group or institution organized and run by all members equally

collectivism socialist system in which centralized group controls production and distribution of goods and services

commons third estate

commune usu. rural community organized on collective basis

communism political system based on elimination of private property and state ownership and control of means of production and distribution of goods and services

Communist party political party advocating

principles of communism, esp. Marxism-Leninism

conservatism political posture based on preservation of traditional, established values and systems

Democratic party more liberal of two major U.S. parties

domestic (*adj*) relating to political affairs carried on within one's own country

domination exercise of authority or supremacy over another political entity

egalitarianism advocacy of removal of inequalities among people based on belief in human equality

emancipation granting of freedom, esp. from slavery

enfranchisement right to vote

establishment ruling class and institutions by which it maintains existing order in society

evolutionary socialism belief that transition from capitalism to socialism can be made through voting, without revolution

extremism political views of far right or far left

Fabianism gradual, nonrevolutionary change to socialism advocated by English Fabian Society (late 19th c.)

Fourierism social system based on small cooperative communities (mid-19th c.)

fourth estate the press, esp. as it wields political power and influence

franchise suffrage, right to vote

freedom individual option to make choices without coercion

freedom of speech right of citizens to express their opinions publicly without government interference, subject to laws against libel and incitement to violence

freedom of the press right to publish information or opinions without government restriction, subject only to laws of libel, obscenity, and sedition

free enterprise freedom of business activity from government interference or control

free thought unorthodox, independently formed, sometimes revolutionary notions

geopolitics influence of and concern with geography and demographics in nation's politics and foreign policy

GOP **G**rand **O**ld **P**arty; U.S. Republican Party

Green party liberal political party focusing on environmental issues, esp. in Germany

guild socialism socialism in which government contracts workers through national guilds and controls means of production (Britain)

hard line uncompromising or unyielding position or policy

ideological party minor party based on particular political, economic, and social views

ideology systematic body of sociopolitical theories and programs based on particular vision

independence freedom from political control or domination by others

iron hand often cruel authoritarian rule, esp. by military

John Birch Society ultraconservative, white supremacist, anticommunist political group

Know-Nothing party excessively patriotic group hostile to subversive foreign influence (U.S., mid-19th c.)

laissez faire opposition to government interference with personal freedom, esp. in economic affairs

left wing those supporting progressive reform and greater welfare of common man

Leninism principles and practice of communism developed by V. I. Lenin

liberalism belief in personal liberty and autonomy, progress, and government aid to those in need

liberation freeing of group or state from domination

libertarian advocate of absolute free will and freedom of thought

liberty freedom to exercise various rights, esp. choice of one's government and individual freedoms

loyal opposition minority party in legislature that maintains allegiance to government

Magna Carta charter of fundamental liberties granted to English barons by King John in 1215

mainstream predominant political views or trends

majority rule principle empowering that part of group with over fifty percent of vote to make decisions binding on all

major party party with sufficient electoral strength to win control of government with regularity; one of two major U.S. parties: Democratic or Republican

Maoism theory and practice of communism developed in China by Mao Zedong (mid-20th c.)

Marxism system of socioeconomic and political thought developed by Karl Marx that is basis of communism, esp. doctrine that class struggle will be main agency of change from exploitative capitalist system to classless society under socialist order

middle-of-the-road (*adj*) moderate

minority party loyal opposition; that major party with fewer members in legislature

minor party party with limited platform and following, unable to control government; any third party in United States

moderatism support for views midway between liberal and conservative

multiparty system sharing of political power among more than two parties

national socialism Nazism

Nazism totalitarian system of Third German Reich, based on racial supremacy; national socialism

neofascism fascist movement or principles promoted after defeat of fascist states in World War II

New Left movement advocating radical political and social change, begun by U.S. students in 1960's

New Right movement advocating conservative social values and nationalistic foreign policy, orig. 1960's United States

nihilism belief in nothing; advocacy of destruction of government without creation of something new

nonpartisan (*adj*) holding views and policies without regard to party

Old Left pro-Soviet socialist movement of 1930's in United States

oppression unfair, harsh exercise of authority

partisan (*adj*) advocating or based on views of one party

party group of like-minded individuals organized to direct and control government policy by winning elections

party line official, often standardized, policies and principles of one political party

patriotism love for one's country and loyalty to its government

pinko *Derogatory slang.* person with left-wing, often communistic, political views

planned economy socialist system advocating centralized government control of all economic functions

political (*adj*) of or relating to elections and government functions

political economy science dealing with interrelationship of political and economic processes

political science study of politics

politics art or science of guiding and controlling government, esp. in conjunction with attaining political office; principles and doctrines on which such activity is based

polity specific form of any political organization or unit

populism egalitarian political philosophy or movement that promotes interests of common people

power elite ruling class, esp. small group wielding inordinate political power

proportional representation system in which each party is represented in legislature in proportion to its percentage of electorate

radicalism advocacy of doctrines and policies for extreme change in political system

reaction resistance to change and clinging to old or outmoded social and political forms

reactionary (*adj*) holding ultraconservative political views that firmly support status quo and advocate suppression of those favoring change

realpolitik politics based on practical considerations, not theoretical objectives

red communist

reform party group advocating correction of abuses in government

reign of terror maintenance of power through violence and terrorism

repression prevention of unpopular or antigovernment views

Republican party GOP; more conservative of two major U.S. parties

right wing those supporting conservative positions, established order, and traditional values

royalist advocate of monarchy

ruling class privileged, wealthy individuals who collectively hold political and economic power

self-determination freedom of citizens to determine form of government of their home region

social democracy socialist state marked by gradual, peaceful, nonrevolutionary transition from capitalism to socialism

socialism various political and economic theories based on government ownership of all or most of means of production and distribution of goods, with control over aspects of social welfare and planning

soft line moderate or flexible position or policy

splinter party minor party that has split from major party

state socialism partial socialism introduced by moderate political action

stewardship obligation of ruling class to manage state with regard for welfare of all

suffrage right to vote

suppression prohibition or restraint of views unfavorable to government authority

syndicalism communism based on direct seizure of government control by workers; anarcho-syndicalism

Tammany Hall organized group exercising political control of a city through corruption, orig. 19th-century New York

third estate third class in threefold political division of kingdom; commons

third party independent party, often organized around one issue, that temporarily challenges major U.S. parties

thought control manipulation and suppression of public opinion and political perceptions

Tory political conservative, esp. 17th-19th c. British supporters of royal authority

Trotskyism branch of communism advocating worldwide revolution

two-party system American political system in which two major parties compete for control of government

ultraconservative (*adj*) reactionary, right wing, extremely conservative

ultraliberal (*adj*) radical, left wing, extremely liberal

undemocratic (*adj*) lacking in adherence to democratic principles

universal suffrage right of all members of society to vote

utopian socialism belief in transition to socialism by voluntary transfer of property from owners to state

war party legislative supporters of military action

Whig parliamentarian, esp. advocate of limited royal authority (Britain, 17th-19th c.)

wing opposing faction within legislature or party

Party Functions and Political Practices

abdicate (*vb*) give up office or throne

acclamation voice vote

adapt (*vb*) vote to pass or accept

affiliation association of like-minded individuals, esp. with specific party

apparat political organization or existing power structure

appointment nonelective office

ascendancy assuming position of increased power and dominance

back room meeting place for small inner circle to plan and manipulate political moves, often in secret

beadledom pointless, stupid, rigid bureaucracy

bipartisan (*adj*) pertaining to both major parties

boodle bribe money

bossism control of political organization by local boss

cloakroom anteroom to legislative chamber for informal conversations among legislators

clout political influence

coalition alliance among members of different parties for specific vote or cause

corruption use of political influence for personal gain

cronyism practice of granting political favors to friends

deal coherent series of programs set forth by one party, as in New Deal or Fair Deal

declaration statement of policy

doctrine basic political policy of party

filibuster delaying tactic, esp. lengthy speech to prevent passage of legislation

front coalition of divergent elements for common goals

frying the fat securing substantial political contributions

fusion coalition of political parties or factions

gerrymandering arranging legislative voting districts to favor one party

graft use of political influence or position to acquire personal gain

issue subject of dispute or debate

jawboning use of influence and office to affect behavior

jobbery corruption in public office

junket personal trip financed by public funds

Komsomol communist youth organization (Soviet Union)

logrolling trading of legislator's vote for reciprocal support on future votes

machine disciplined influential political organization, esp. under control of boss or clique

movement group pursuing organized actions to attain specific end

national committee group of leaders that controls party business between conventions

nepotism granting of political favors to relatives

party line official, established policies of one party

patronage system executive appointments reflecting partisan bias

policy overall plan embracing government goals

pork barrel legislation manipulated for political advantage to one's constituency or district, usu. public works projects

power base source of political power, usu. support of organized bloc of voters or ethnic minority

pressure group individuals with specific common interest organized to influence public policy

program plan of action

propaganda techniques used to influence or control the opinions of groups or individuals, esp. to promote one's views or damage an opponent's by dissemination of rumors and allegations

proposition idea set forth for debate

prorogue (*vb*) suspend or terminate legislative session, esp. of British Parliament, by royal prerogative

public interest group individuals organized to influence government policy for benefit of general citizenry

public opinion poll questions asked of random sampling of potential voters to determine views and preferences

pull influence

purge elimination of unfit or unfaithful party members

roorback libel for political effect

seniority legislative system by which members with longest continuous service achieve positions of privilege and power

smoke-filled room private gathering place where inner circle of politicians plan and scheme

smoking gun evidence of indisputable guilt

special interest group political group organized to further its specific common concerns; lobby

spoils system practice of appointing party loyalists to public office

statecraft skill at conducting political affairs

statesmanship skill and vision in governing; political acumen

turn (*vb*) to defect from one's party or professed view

union political unit formed by combination of two or more previously independent entities

vest (*vb*) imbue with authority

vested interest special interest in existing economic or political system for personal advantage

war chest campaign funds held in reserve by incumbent to defeat future challengers

watchdog function role of political party out of power in monitoring conduct of party in power

Politicians and Activists

activist individual engaged in direct action for political change or to influence specific issue; party worker

agent provocateur one who infiltrates suspect organization and incites its members into incriminating actions

alternate one who acts as substitute, esp. for convention delegate

apparatchik member of political organization, esp. Communist

baby kisser politician who endears himself or herself to voters by displays of personal warmth, as by kissing babies

bedfellow close political ally

boss powerful politician who controls votes or party, often by corrupt practices

cabal secret union of conspirators or advisers

cacique local political boss (Spain and Latin American)

cadre inner group of dedicated leaders who advocate particular views

camp follower politician who supports party solely for personal gain

candidate one who aspires to public elected office

chairman leader of party organization, esp. male

chairperson male or female leader of party organization

chairwoman female leader of party organization

committeeman member of party committee, esp. male

committeewoman female member of party committee

conservative adherent to political conservatism

constituent voter in defined electoral district represented by specific official

dark horse relative unknown; underdog in election

delegate representative

demagogue one who appeals to and manipulates mass prejudice

Democrat member of more liberal of two major U.S. political parties

district leader party leader within single district

Dixiecrat conservative southern Democrat who opposes civil-rights programs and advocates states' rights

dove opponent of military action as political solution

elector one entitled to vote in election

éminence grise individual with unofficial, secret powers

extremist advocate of extreme political positions

fat cat *Slang.* wealthy individual from whom large financial contribution is expected

favorite son state's candidate for presidential nomination and leader of delegation to party convention

floater person voting in more than one polling place

floor leader party member in charge of strategy during legislative sessions

hack experienced but unprincipled politician

handler one who manages political campaign, esp. media exposure

hanger-on one who associates himself or herself with politician for personal gain

hatchet man one employed to engage secretly in unscrupulous activities that would tarnish elected official

hawk supporter of military action as political solution

heeler local party worker or henchman for boss

henchman political supporter seeking personal gain or performing unsavory tasks

holdover one continuing in same office

ideologue political theorist rather than practitioner; zealous advocate of an ideology

incumbent officeholder

independent one not affiliated with any party

jack-in-office small-minded, disrespectful individual in position of authority

jackleg unprincipled, dishonest, or amateurish politician

Jacobin radical extremist, orig. terrorist supporter of democracy in French Revolution

keynoter one delivering keynote address

kingmaker person wielding sufficient political power to influence choice of candidates for office

lame duck officeholder who has been defeated in bid for reelection, during interval before inauguration of successor

leadership those who set party policies and strategy

liberal advocate of progressive reform

lobbyist person who works for special interest group

machine politician one owing allegiance to political machine

majority leader ranking member of party holding majority in legislature

minority leader ranking member of party in minority in legislature

moderate one supporting views midway between right and left

mouthpiece spokesperson, esp. for political leader

mugwump political independent, orig. one who left Republican party in 1884

national chairman head of national committee of major party

new broom individual new to power and zealous in duties

nominee one selected by party to oppose other party's candidates in election

noncandidate potential candidate for office who has officially announced that he or she will not run

old guard veteran political figures, usu. resistant to new ideas

old-line (*adj*) conservative, established, having seniority

party boss powerful individual who controls party operations, often by corrupt means

party chairman one chosen by party members to lead party

party faithful veteran, dependable, active party loyalists

party hack one blindly loyal to party and prepared to carry out orders

placeman *Chiefly Brit.* person appointed to office as reward for political support

polemicist one skilled in debate

politician person engaged in party politics or government, esp. one seeking or holding elected office; politico

politico politician

pollster one who polls public to determine preferences and advises candidates based on findings

poll watcher person who ensures legal voting process at poll

powerbroker influential individual who controls bloc of votes

precinct captain one responsible for overseeing party activities in one precinct

precinct leader chief member of party in precinct

president-elect one who has been elected president but not yet inaugurated into office

progressive one supporting political change and social improvement by moderate government policies

radical advocate of extreme, sometimes violent, measures to improve society or alter established form of government

reactionary advocate of ultraconservative political views, esp. suppression of those favoring change

reformer one seeking to change and improve political institutions and government policies

regular party member who can be depended on for votes or support

Republican member of more conservative of two major U.S. political parties

running mate candidate for lower office linked with candidate for higher office, usu. of same party, esp. vice president

sachem *Slang.* political party leader or boss

seatwarmer legislator appointed to fill vacancy with understanding that he or she will not run in next election

stalking-horse candidate put forth to draw votes from rival or to conceal candidacy of another person

standard-bearer head of party's slate in election

state chairman leader of party for single U.S. state

statesman skilled practitioner in art of governing

suffragette female activist advocating voting rights for women

superdelegate party leader or official chosen as uncommitted delegate to national political convention

troubleshooter one skilled at mediating political disputes

ward heeler worker in local political machine

war-horse *Informal.* experienced, dependable political veteran

whip party leader in legislature appointed to enforce party discipline and voting solidarity

Young Turk insurgent within group

Elections and Campaigns

absentee ballot vote cast by mail when voter is not at designated polling place on election day

absolute majority more than half of eligible voters

acceptance speech candidate's address to nominating convention

at large designating legislator, esp. member of British Parliament, elected by all voters rather than by voters of single district

backlash negative reaction to events among voters that causes swing to opposite view

ballot printed list of candidates and measures; voting

ballot box receptacle where ballots are placed after voting

bandwagon party, cause, or movement that readily attracts followers or supporters because of its mass appeal or apparent strength

barnstorm (*vb*) conduct campaign by making brief stops in many small towns

big fix citywide graft system for controlling votes

blanket primary open primary in which voter chooses between two or more parties

bloc group of voters

body politic people who compose a politically organized unit under a single government authority

borough *Chiefly Brit.* urban parliamentary constituency

bunkum insincere oratory by politician, designed to please constituents

by-election special parliamentary election between general elections (Britain)

campaign process undertaken to secure public office; (*vb*) actively run for office

campaign button small badge imprinted with candidate's name or slogan

campaign trail series of public appearances made by office seeker prior to election day

canvass count or sample of public opinion; soliciting of votes

carry (*vb*) win majority of votes or gain passage

caucus party meeting to choose candidates and plan strategy

charisma candidate's personal magnetism and charm

closed primary election to select party candidates limited to registered party members

coattail effect tendency of strong candidate for higher office to increase votes for weaker candidates of same party

congressional district territorial division of state whose residents elect member of House of Representatives

constituency defined electoral district

convention assembly of delegates to nominate candidates for office and draft platform, usu. for one party

cross-file (*vb*) register as candidate for more than one party or in primaries of more than one party

crossover vote vote of person registered in one party cast for another party's candidate

declaration formal announcement of candidacy

delegation representatives at convention from one state

direct primary preliminary election in which voters of one party select candidates for final bipartisan election

dirty politics corruption, bribery, deception, and covert activity on behalf of candidate

district electoral unit composed of precincts

elect (*vb*) choose public official through voting

election selection of public officials or expression of views on issue by poll of voters

election day day on which votes are cast

electioneer (*vb*) work for candidate or party; (*n*) one who does so

electoral college pledged presidential electors from each U.S. state, determined by popular vote in that state, assembled to elect president and vice president

electoral votes votes of each state in electoral college, equal to total of its Senate and House members

electorate total number of people qualified to vote

ethnic vote bloc of voters of specific racial or ethnic background who frequently vote alike

fund-raiser event held to raise money for candidate or cause

general election regularly scheduled election for state, local, or national officials

glad-hand (*vb*) greet voters with excessive cordiality to gain votes for one's candidacy

grass roots local organization or opinion, esp. as symbolized by constituents at district level

hat in the ring indication of candidacy

hustings any place from which campaign speeches are made; campaign trail in general

initiative procedure whereby voters sign petition to place issue or proposed law on ballot before electorate

keynote address opening speech that sets tone and outlines primary issues for convention

landslide overwhelming majority of votes

local election election for candidates and on issues governing small political unit such as town or city

mandate desires of constituents as expressed through votes and interpreted by politicians

media campaign extensive use of newspapers, radio, and television to reach voters

minority less than half of votes cast

mudslinging malicious personal attacks and invective directed against political opponent

multiple voting casting of ballots by one voter in different places in same election

national convention assembly meeting every four years of major party's representatives to select presidential candidate and articulate a party platform

national election voting for candidates to govern entire nation, often with simultaneous voting for officials from many states

nomination selection of candidate to run in election

nonpartisan election election in which candidates are not identified by party

off year year without major, esp. presidential, election

open primary election to select party candidates in which any qualified voter may participate, regardless of party

PAC **p**olitical **a**ction **c**ommittee

plank party policy on specific issue stated in platform

platform principles and policies supported by party or candidate in election

plebiscite vote in which district or nation expresses yes or no opinion, esp. choice of government or ruler

plurality largest number of votes, esp. when no one candidate receives a majority

political action committee PAC; organization that collects contributions and distributes funds to candidates and causes

politicking engaging in political activity, campaigning

poll survey of a scientifically selected sample of voters prior to election to determine preferences; expression of opinion by voting; (*vb*) process or count votes

polling place location where voters cast votes

polling station *Chiefly Brit.* location where voters cast votes

poll tax tax levied on every voter for right to vote

popular (*adj*) representative of majority of people

precinct smallest voting subdivision of city or ward

preferential voting system of voting in which voter indicates order of preference for candidates listed on ballot

primary preliminary election to determine party candidates in general election

projected winner election night estimate of eventual winner based on early returns and projection of trends

proposition statement of issue or suggested plan placed on ballot for direct popular vote on whether it will become law

proxy authority, esp. of deputy, to act for another

public opinion views on issues and candidates held by enough of electorate to be politically significant

rally meeting to arouse group enthusiasm or support for candidate

recall removal of unpopular elected official by special election

recount counting of votes a second time in case of possible mistakes or illegalities

referendum popular vote on measure proposed by legislature or by popular initiative

registration enrollment of individuals on voter lists, esp. during designated time period

registration drive movement to enroll those previously denied or not exercising voting rights

returns election results, voting totals

run (*vb*) place oneself before voters as candidate for office

runoff election held when primary is not conclusive

safe seat incumbency that faces only token opposition in election

sample ballot ballot distributed to voters before election to familiarize them with candidates and issues

secret ballot process by which voters' privacy is ensured

slate list of candidates, usu. all from one party; ticket

slush fund party campaign fund, the size and purposes of which are not necessarily legal

smear campaign crude, unsubstantiated attacks against opposing candidate

special election preliminary election held when issue must be decided by voters before primary or general election is held

split ticket votes cast for candidates of more than one party on same ballot

stand (*vb*) *Chiefly Brit.* run for office

stand down (*vb*) *Chiefly Brit.* step aside or withdraw from election, nomination, or office

stepwinder *Slang.* stirring political address

straight ticket vote for all candidates of single party

straw poll unofficial, random sample vote taken as measure of public opinion

stump (*vb*) move from town to town making speeches on behalf of issues or candidates

swing vote determining vote in close election, often one that changes at last moment

ticket list of candidates; slate

turnout percentage or number of eligible voters who cast ballots

undecided voter voter indicating no definite choice in political poll and therefore sought by all candidates

vote formal expression of opinion at ballot box

voting booth place where voter marks ballot

voting machine machine that registers and tallies votes

ward political subdivision of city, esp. as basis for election of city council members

whistle stop political stop in small community

winner-take-all system electoral college system in which candidate receiving majority of popular vote in state receives all of its electoral votes

write-in handwritten vote for candidate not listed on ballot

write-in candidate individual not on ballot but campaigning for office

Revolution and Antigovernment Activity

activism direct, often intense, engagement in actions for political change

anarchist one who opposes all forms of authority and advocates violence to overthrow existing order

antiestablishment (*adj*) working against existing power structure

assassination murder of political officeholder

blacklist list of people or organizations considered undesirable, used to exclude them from jobs or organizations

card-carrying (*adj*) firmly identified with one party or group, esp. Communist party

cell smallest group within party organization, esp. Communist party

civil disobedience nonviolent refusal to obey authorities as means of political pressure

civil disorder riot or disruption of normal activities as means to political change

counterrevolution movement to overthrow government created by earlier revolution

coup coup d'état

coup d'état sudden exercise of political force, esp. violent overthrow of government by small group; coup

demonstration mass public meeting and display of opinion

destructionist person who advocates destruction of existing political institution

direct action action such as strike or boycott that seeks an immediate response from established authority

dissent opposition to established political order

dissident person expressing opposition to established government

fellow traveler Communist party sympathizer

fifth column group undermining a cause from within

foco small, rural, often secret group engaged in local revolutionary actions

foquismo Che Guevara's theory that revolution can be engendered from activities of many focos

freedom fighter person who battles against established forces of tyranny and oppression

guerrilla one conducting irregular warfare, sabotage, and terrorism to foment revolution

incendiary one who inflames or excites public to revolutionary acts

insurgency minor, often disorganized revolt against government

insurrection organized revolt against established government authority

internal exile banishment of person, esp. political dissident, to remote place within same country

Jacobin radical extremist, orig. terrorist supporter of democracy in French Revolution

junta small group controlling government after seizing power

march organized mass walk as demonstration of opinion or protest

movement coalition of groups and individuals seeking political change

outside agitator one who infiltrates group or situation to create greater disturbance

popular front coalition of leftist and sometimes centrist political factions to oppose common opponent, usu. reactionary government

peacenik *Slang.* antiwar demonstrator or activist

proletariat workers who will control government after Communist revolution

protest declaration, usu. accompanied by some action, of disapproval for politician or policy

putsch sudden surprise revolt against government

radical advocate of extreme, sometimes violent, measures to improve society or alter established form of government

rally mass gathering to express protest or opinion

rebellion direct defiance of established government, often armed and violent

resistance underground organization opposing government, esp. occupying force, through sabotage

revolt movement of dissent, esp. armed uprising against government

revolution activities intended to overthrow and replace existing government with preferred system

ringleader leader of small group, often engaged in illegal or rebellious act

sabotage destruction or obstruction aimed at disrupting government authority

safe house refuge for political fugitive

sit-in obstruction of public place through refusal to leave as nonviolent protest of government policy

terrorism systematic use of terror as political tool

underground secret, usu. antigovernment, terrorist group

unrest unhappiness with existing government that results in minor disturbances against it

uprising often localized or spontaneous act of violence against government

---

LAW

Courts, Legal Bodies, and the Law
Judges, Lawyers, and Others in the Court System
Laws, Procedures, and Court Proceedings
Decisions, Judgments, and Conditions
Customs, Formalities, and Practices
Crimes, Criminals, and Civil Offenders

See also: *Chap. 8: Marriage and Divorce; Chap. 11: Government; Chap. 12: Business and Economics; Finance; Real Estate; Chap. 24: Crime*

Courts, Legal Bodies, and the Law

adjective law branch of law dealing with rules of procedure

administrative law statutes governing procedures before government agencies

admiralty law maritime law

appellate court higher court that reviews decision of lower court

appellate jurisdiction authority of appellate court to reverse lower court decision

assizes former periodic sessions of English superior courts

bar entire body of lawyers and counselors-at-law

bar association local or state organization of lawyers voluntarily or mandatorily registered in that jurisdiction

bench entire body of judges; where judge sits in court

canon law codified law governing church

case law precedent-setting judicial opinions

chambers judge's private office in courthouse

chancery separate judicial system that administers natural right or golden rule in courts of equity without jury, used esp. for obtaining relief other than financial

circuit court court sitting at two or more places

civil law codes, statutes, and case law governing civil actions; Roman law set forth in Justinian Code

code systematic statement of body of law

commercial law body of laws governing all business transactions not covered by maritime law

common law precedents set by court decisions, distinguished from statute law; body of English law forming foundation of legal system

constabulary body organized by government to preserve public order

constitutional law body of decisions and precedents that results from interpreting a constitution

court official assembly for transaction of judicial business; session of such an assembly; chamber for such an assembly

courthouse building in which court of law convenes

court of appeals court hearing appeals of lower court decisions

court of claims court with jurisdiction over claims, esp. against government

court of common pleas former English civil superior court; intermediate court in some U.S. states with civil and criminal jurisdiction

court of inquiry military court that investigates military matters

court of law court hearing and deciding cases based on statutes and common law

court of record court whose acts and proceedings are kept on permanent record and that has power to impose penalties for contempt

court of sessions state criminal court of record

courtroom chamber in which court proceedings are held

criminal court court with jurisdiction to try and punish violators of criminal law

criminal justice administration and enforcement of criminal law

criminal law statutes and common law of crimes and their punishment

customs court federal court having jurisdiction over tariff law cases

district court trial court with jurisdiction in specific judicial district

divorce court court handling dissolution of marriages

equity natural right or justice; flexible body of law and nonjury court system, esp. for gaining relief other than financial

federal court court established under U.S. Constitution, esp. to deal with violations of federal statutes

firm partnership or association of two or more lawyers

forum tribunal, court of law

grand jury body of usu. twelve to twenty-three citizens who investigate facts to determine whether a crime has been committed and return indictment

Hammurabi Code ancient Babylonian code of criminal and civil law written in cuneiform characters (18th c. B.C.)

Inns of Court four legal societies that admit persons to the practice of law in Britain: Inner Temple, Middle Temple, Lincoln's Inn, Gray's Inn

international law body of rules recognized as binding between national states, based on treaties, agreements, and customs; jus gentium

judiciary court system; governmental branch charged with administration of justice

jurisdiction scope of authority of specific court to hear particular cases

jurisprudence system, body, or philosophy of law

jury body of citizens sworn to weigh evidence and decide facts of case; petit jury as opposed to grand jury

jus gentium *Latin.* lit. law of nations; international law based on customs of all nations in Roman law

justice establishment and administration of rights based on rules of law and equity

Justinian Code Byzantine revision and codification of Roman law with addition of Corpus of Civil Law (6th c.)

juvenile court court with jurisdiction over children under age of legal responsibility regarding matters of delinquency or dependency

kangaroo court unauthorized, irregular court operating with disregard for normal legal procedures

law body of recognized rules of conduct and order established and enforced by government

law office place of business of lawyer or law firm

law school institution of graduate studies for instruction in law

legal aid legal assistance to those who cannot afford lawyers' fees

lex talionis *Latin.* law of retaliation; principle of correspondence between punishment and crime, as an eye for an eye

maritime law branch of commercial law relating to commerce and navigation; admiralty law

military law system of rules governing military personnel, including establishment of tribunals

moot court pretend student trial

municipal court city or town court with jurisdiction over local criminal and civil cases

Napoleonic Code civil code of France and basis of civil law (early 19th c.)

patent law legal system for issuance and court jurisdiction over patents that protect rights of invention

petit jury trial jury made up usu. of twelve citizens, as distinct from grand jury

probate court surrogate court

pro bono lit. for the good (Latin); legal work undertaken on behalf of public for little or no fee

procedural law prescribed steps and methods of enforcing one's rights in court, opposite of substantive law

Roman law legal system of ancient Rome that is basis of modern civil law and English common law

small-claims court special court handling disputes over minor debts

special court court created for exceptional and temporary purpose

substantive law law that describes what one's legal rights are, opposite of procedural law

superior court court of general jurisdiction in many states

Supreme Court usu. highest judicial tribunal of a political entity

surrogate court court with jurisdiction to prove wills and administer estates and guardianships; probate court

tax court court that decides tax cases

tort law form of law settling rights of monetary damages for injuries in civil and private cases

trial court court in which trials are conducted

tribunal court of justice; seat of particular judge

unwritten law law based on custom rather than legislative statute

United States District Court USDC; court with jurisdiction in specific region

USDC United States District Court

venue court's geographic jurisdiction; place where significant elements of cause of action took place or where case is tried

Judges, Lawyers, and Others in the Court System

accused one charged with an offense; defendant in criminal case

adversary opposite party in litigation

advocate lawyer, esp. one pleading client's cause in court

agent person authorized to act for principal in case

alleged one accused of crime before proven guilty

alternate juror jury member chosen to fill in should regular juror be unable to continue

amicus curiae *Latin.* lit. friend of the court; counselor assisting and seeking to persuade court on case to which he or she is not a party

arbitrator private, disinterested person chosen to conduct arbitration

associate subordinate member of law firm

attorney one who acts for another, esp. in legal proceedings

attorney-at-law lawyer admitted to bar and qualified to litigate in court

attorney general chief law officer of state or nation

attorney-in-fact one given power of attorney to act for another but not necessarily an attorney-at-law

bailiff court attendant charged with keeping order and escorting prisoners in court

barrister counsel admitted to plead at bar and in public superior court trials (Britain)

bencher *Chiefly Brit.* senior member of an Inn of Court

bondsman one who assumes responsibility of paying bond if defendant fails to appear in court

character witness one who verifies another's reputation as honest and law-abiding

chief justice presiding judge of court, esp. Supreme Court

circuit judge judge presiding over circuit court

claimant one asserting claim, esp. in civil case

clerk one who keeps records, has power to issue specific writs, and files documents

client person hiring attorney as representative

competent party individual who is legally able to enter into binding contracts

condemned criminal sentenced to death

conservator person designated to protect interests of an incompetent

convict one found guilty of a crime

counsel lawyer managing court trial; lawyer advising and representing an individual, corporation, or public body on legal matters

counselor lawyer; counsel

counselor-at-law lawyer

court judge as embodiment of a particular court

court attendant low-level functionary at legal proceeding

court officer bailiff or other official of court

court reporter stenographer who records and transcribes court proceedings verbatim

DA district attorney

defendant party sued by plaintiff or accused by state

defense attorney lawyer representing a defendant

district attorney DA; public officer acting as lawyer for government in prosecuting criminal cases; prosecutor

executor one responsible for administration of decedent's estate and for carrying out terms of a will

executrix female executor

eyewitness person who actually saw crime committed

fiduciary one entrusted to care for another's property

garnishee one in possession of another's property pending settlement of debts

guardian one legally empowered to manage affairs of a minor or incompetent person

heir one who would be entitled to inherit property of deceased by intestate succession under terms of will

hostile witness witness unfriendly to side calling him, subject to cross-examination by that side

judge presiding court officer, elected or appointed

judiciary judges of court system

junior partner lawyer with lesser status and seniority among partners in firm

jurist judge or lawyer

juror member of jury

justice judge; member of Supreme Court

justice of the peace local magistrate empowered to administer oaths, perform marriages, and handle minor cases

law clerk law student working for lawyer or judge, usu. at low pay to learn from experience

lawgiver legislator; one who enacts laws

lawmaker legislator; one who enacts laws

lawman police officer; one empowered to enforce laws

lawyer one licensed to represent people in court and advise on legal matters; attorney or counselor-at-law

legal secretary specially trained secretary for lawyer

litigant party to a lawsuit

litigator lawyer who participates in court trials; trial lawyer

magistrate public officer, esp. judge of lower criminal court

maker party executing a promissory note

marshal officer of judicial district who executes court processes, performing duties similar to those of sheriff

master court representative appointed to do specific act

material witness witness whose testimony is essential to case

mediator person who settles disputes and serves as intermediary between parties

mouthpiece *Slang.* lawyer, esp. criminal lawyer

notary officer of state authorized to administer oaths and acknowledge signing of documents; notary public

ombudsman government official who investigates complaints against public officials

paralegal specially trained aid to lawyer

partner member of law firm who shares ownership of firm

party one who sues or is sued in court

petitioner one seeking court remedies or making formal complaint or statement of cause of action in civil suit

pettifogger unethical lawyer who engages in petty arguments and obstruction of justice

plaintiff one who complains of another by bringing court action to obtain remedy

presiding (*adj*) designating judge who directs

court proceedings, including assigning cases to be heard by other judges

principal one on whose behalf an agent acts; party to contract

process server person who hands over process to person sought by court

prosecutor lawyer hired by government to conduct criminal proceeding; district attorney

public defender lawyer hired by government to defend accused who cannot afford lawyer's fees

receiver person appointed to hold property to be disposed of by court order; one who receives goods knowing they are stolen

referee court officer appointed to hear argument on matter whose decision is final or is reported back to court

respondent defendant in certain proceedings; one required to answer appeal from judgment; party replying to petition

security person bound to pay debt if another fails

senior partner ranking partner in law firm

sheriff elected chief law enforcement officer of county

solicitor personal lawyer; lower court trial lawyer who prepares cases for barristers in higher courts (Britain)

special prosecutor individual appointed to investigate and indict in single, exceptional case

surety person promising to make good another's obligation

surrogate judge in court that administers estates and guardianships

talesman bystander summoned as juror when too few are called

tenant one who temporarily possesses another's real property

trial examiner person appointed to hold hearings, investigate, and make recommendations to court

trial lawyer lawyer who participates in trials; litigator

trustee one who holds property in trust for another as a fiduciary

ward minor child or incompetent person in care of guardian or conservator

witness one who testifies under oath in judicial proceeding as to what he or she has seen or observed; one present at some event, such as the signing of a document

Laws, Procedures, and Court Proceedings

accusation charge of wrongdoing

acknowledgment formal declaration that one has executed a particular legal document

action lawsuit or court proceeding

adjourn (*vb*) suspend court proceedings until later stated time

admission voluntary declaration of facts made by one party in suit, esp. acknowledgment of guilt

affidavit written statement sworn under oath before authorized officer or notary

allegation contention or accusation; statement by party to legal action as to what will be proved

amended complaint written pleading that contains additional information, allegations, or causes of action in case

amendment legislative modification or addition to statute or constitution

appeal procedure by which case is brought from lower to higher court for revised ruling or rehearing

arbitration investigation and resolution of dispute by persons named by involved parties, usu. agreed on in contract as way to settle dispute without formal court trial

argument attorney's statements in support of client's case

arraignment calling of accused before court to hear charges and enter plea

arrest restraint or detention of person by legal authority

assignment transfer of rights from one person to another

assize legislative enactment, statute; judicial inquest

assumpsit action to recover damages for breach of contract or verbal or implied promise

bail payment of bond that is forfeited if one fails to appear in court

bench warrant arrest order issued by judge, usu. for failure to appear in court

bill of attainder unconstitutional legislative act that finds person guilty of high crime and imposes sentence

bill of particulars statement filed in court that gives details of claim or counterclaim

binding arbitration arbitration stipulated in contract as obligatory to all parties

bind over (vb) put under bond to appear in court for trial; shift case to grand jury or superior court from lower court

case court action, cause, suit, or controversy

cause case, claim, or lawsuit seeking recovery from another

certiorari Latin. lit. to be made more certain; higher court's review procedure on actions of lower court or government agency

cessation temporary adjournment of case

challenge objection to prospective juror during pretrial jury selection

charge judge's instructions to jury at close of trial regarding what to consider in reaching verdict

charter state grant allowing corporation to exist

citation writ issued by court commanding person to appear in court and perform some duty or show cause why not

cite (vb) issue citation; call upon to appear; hold someone responsible for objectionable conduct, such as contempt

citizen's arrest arrest made by private citizen rather than law officer

civil action lawsuit between private parties, usu.

to recover money, property, or remedies, or to enforce rights

civil case lawsuit between private parties, as distinguished from criminal case

claim demand for something rightfully due but possessed by another

class action suit brought on behalf of many persons with similar interest in alleged wrong

closing final exchange of title and monies in real estate transaction

codicil amendment or addition to will

commital Chiefly Brit. commitment

commitment court order to take person into custody in penal or mental institution

community property property recognized in some states as owned in common by spouses

confession voluntary admission of guilt or responsibility

constitution fundamental law by which state governs

contest (vb) dispute or challenge by litigation

continuance deferral of court proceedings to future date

contract voluntary, lawful, mutual agreement to do or not do something in return for consideration

cop a plea Informal. plead guilty to lesser offense to avoid standing trial for more serious one

copyright law law protecting exclusive ownership of and rights to artistic and intellectual properties

counterclaim case brought against plaintiff by defendant

counterplea plaintiff's reply to defendant's plea or counterclaim

court hearing preliminary examination of arguments by judge

court-martial judicial court proceeding in armed forces

court trial trial by judge without jury

criminal case charge by state against individual, brought to punish violation of criminal laws

cross-claim claim made by defendant against plaintiff

cross-complaint complaint arising from original complaint, made by defendant against codefendant or third party

cross-examination questioning of witness by lawyer for other party in case

cross-question (vb) Chiefly Brit. cross-examine

deed document transferring ownership of real property

defense reasons of law put forth as to why adversary or claim should be denied

deliberations jury's consideration of case to reach verdict

depose (vb) elicit testimony outside court under oath or by affidavit; take witness's deposition

deposition sworn testimony of witness taken outside court proceedings

direct examination questioning of witness by lawyer who called him or her to stand

direct testimony statements of witness in

answer to questions posed by attorney who called him or her to stand

discovery pretrial fact-finding through interrogatories, depositions, and other investigative procedures

double jeopardy repeat prosecution for same criminal offense, prohibited by U.S. Constitution

enter plea place plea in court record in proper form

ex delicto Latin. lit. out of wrong; cause of action arising from crime or tort

ex post facto Latin. lit. after the fact; fixing or changing punishment for act after it was committed, now forbidden by U.S. Constitution

fair hearing special administrative procedure required by court when person might otherwise be denied rights without due process

file (vb) perform first act of lawsuit; place among official records, return to office of court clerk

gag rule court order banning all parties involved in case from publicly disclosing anything about it or reporting on it in the media

go to trial determine that dispute warrants trial and commence proceedings

habeas corpus Latin. lit. have the body; court order requiring that detained prisoner be produced in court to inquire into legality of detention

hearing preliminary court examination of contested issues in criminal or civil proceeding

impanel (vb) select jury from official list of names

impeachment of witness providing evidence or engaging in questioning that attacks credibility of witness

in camera Latin. lit. in chambers; judicial proceeding from which public is excluded

indictment criminal charge made by grand jury

information criminal accusation made by prosecutor rather than by grand jury indictment

in personam Latin. lit. against the person; action directed against individual or owner of property

inquest official inquiry or examination before jury; coroner's investigation of cause of death

in rem Latin. lit. against the thing; action directed against specific piece of property

instructions judge's explanation of applicable law to jury

interrogatories written questions answered under oath by witness before trial

intervention third-party protection of alleged interest in legal proceeding begun by others

jurat notarized certification that affidavit has been sworn to

jury is out jury is deliberating while it reaches verdict

jury trial consideration of case by jury as opposed to by judge or arbitrator

law rule of conduct or action formally recognized as binding and enforced by controlling authority

lawsuit case in court instituted by one party to achieve justice from another

legal age minimum age at which person has capacity to enforce legal rights and fulfill obligations

legality quality of being legal; obligation imposed by law

litigation legal case contested in court before judge

majority age at which person is legally responsible for his or her actions

minutes official records and notes of proceedings

motion formal oral or written request to court, seeking judge's ruling

nolle prosequi *Latin.* lit. not wishing to prosecute; choice by district attorney or plaintiff not to proceed with action

nolo contendere *Latin.* lit. I do not wish to contest; essential admission of guilt by defendant, appealing to mercy of court

novation substitution of new contract or obligation for an old one

objection lawyer's protest to judge over statement or question by opposition

offer of proof lawyer's explanation to judge, away from jury, of intentions on some point

open court proceedings that are accessible to public

own recognizance condition of release of accused person without payment of bail

patent government grant of exclusive intellectual property rights for an invention

peremptory challenge veto challenge by lawyer to prospective juror that precludes any debate

personal injury physical damage to body, usu. as a result of accident or negligence, forming grounds for suit

plea legal suit or action; defendant's answer to plaintiff's declaration; accused's answer to criminal charge

plea bargaining agreement whereby defendant pleads guilty to reduced charge

plead (*vb*) argue case in court of law; make allegation or answer previous pleading

post bail pay bond to guarantee appearance in court

power of attorney written authority allowing one person to act for another in specific situations

preliminary hearing hearing before magistrate to determine whether sufficient evidence exists to justify trial

presentment accusation by grand jury, based on its own investigations

press charges pursue accusations into court action

pretrial hearing meeting in which lawyers and judge plan procedures for upcoming trial

preventive detention holding of prisoner without bail or on very high bail

prior restraint court order prohibiting publication or broadcast of certain material, generally not used in society committed to free speech and freedom of the press

probate proof that will is valid and genuine

proceeding legal action, esp. in court

process summons, subpoena, or warrant used to compel witness or party to appear in court

process service service

prosecution government proceeding in court against person accused of crime

rebuttal reply; evidence counter to that of opponent

recess brief break in court proceedings

reconvene (*vb*) continue court proceedings after recess

recording public filing of documents to give notice to interested parties

reference proceeding in which matter is heard by referee

replevin action to recover actual item of personal property rather than its value in damages

restraining order court order barring one party in suit from contacting, harassing, or acting against another

RICO **R**acketeer **I**nfluenced and **C**orrupt **O**rganization; statute detailing laws relating to organized crime

search warrant court order authorizing search of certain premises or persons for stolen or illegal property

sequester (*vb*) isolate jury in private place for purposes of discussion and reaching a verdict

service physical act of handing warrant or subpoena to person who is required to appear in court; process service

stand trial defend oneself in court of law, usu. against criminal charges

statute legislative act with power of law

statute of limitations legislative act limiting time in which plaintiff may bring civil suit or state may bring criminal action and also limiting period of liability

statutory (*adj*) designating crime or law enacted by legislature

stipulation arrangement agreed upon between parties

subpoena (*vb*) *Latin.* lit. under penalty; command to appear in court and testify

substituted service process service by mail, newspaper publication, or to third party when person named cannot be found

sue (*vb*) bring suit against another, usu. to collect damages

suit court action or proceeding to recover rights or make claim

summons court paper announcing suit and stating time for court appearance

tender (*vb*) offer money or property to fulfill an obligation

testimony oral evidence given by witness under oath

tort civil wrong or injury, other than breach of contract, that is grounds for suit

transcript written record of court proceedings; copy of document

trial court examination of facts to decide issue in dispute

trial by jury usu. criminal trial decided by jury of citizens

true bill grand jury endorsement of indictment as warranting trial

venire facias *Latin.* lit. make come; writ summoning jurors to court

voir dire *French.* lit. to speak truly; preliminary examination of qualifications of juror or witness

waiver intentional abandonment of right

warrant court order authorizing action by public officer, usu. arrest or search and seizure

writ written court order issued to serve administration of justice, usu. stipulating that something be done or not be done

writ of certiorari request by higher court for case records for review

Decisions, Judgments, and Conditions

abandonment relinquishing of possession of property without intent to recover it

abatement termination, esp. of nuisance; reduction from full amount, esp. of tax

abeyance temporary suspension or inactivity

abolition act of annulling or completely destroying

accountable (*adj*) answerable, responsible for some action

acquittal not-guilty verdict absolving accused party from guilt

adjudication judicial determination, decision, or sentence

advisory opinion nonbinding court opinion on legal question submitted by government official but not on specific case

alimony court-ordered payment to be made by one spouse to former spouse in divorce case

amerce (*vb*) punish by fine in amount fixed by court

annul (*vb*) cancel or make void, esp. marriage deemed void from beginning

arrogate (*vb*) claim, seize, or assume without justification

assessment determination of amount of damages, fine, or tax

attachment taking another's property by legal process, esp. as payment of debt

award final judgment; decision of arbitrators on case; document containing arbitrators' decision

bailment condition in which one person has possession of another's personal property, with responsibility for its protection

bankruptcy procedure used when person's total assets are insufficient to cover debts

beat the rap *Slang.* evade penalties connected with charge; receive not-guilty verdict

bequest gift by will of personal property

binder preliminary real estate or insurance agreement

capital punishment execution as criminal sentence

cease and desist order prohibiting a specific activity; mandatory injunction

clear of charges acquit; find not guilty

clemency reduction of sentence, usu. by executive branch

community service punishment requiring convicted person to perform unpaid work for community instead of serving term of imprisonment

commutation reduction of sentence after conviction

compensatory damages damages measured by harm suffered or loss incurred

compurgation clearing of accused by oaths of persons swearing to his or her innocence

condemnation unfavorable judgment, conviction; judgment by which authority confiscates private property

conditions terms of agreement or settlement

condonation forgiveness, esp. in spousal adultery

consent decree consent judgment

consent judgment judicial decree sanctioning voluntary agreement between parties in dispute to cease activity and drop action; consent decree

consignment delivery of property for sale by another with proceeds, less commission, returned to consignor

conveyance transfer of ownership title in real property

conviction guilty verdict in criminal trial

costs expenses other than attorney's fees incurred in litigation, sometimes awarded to prevailing party to be paid by losing party

countermand (*vb*) revoke an order or decree

court order decree issued by court, usu. requiring party to do or not do something

cure (*vb*) make acceptable any defective evidence or charges by admission of certain other evidence

custody care and keeping of something, esp. parent's right to raise child in divorce case

damages compensation sought by or awarded to litigant for loss or injury

decision verdict or determination in case

declaratory judgment determination stating legal rights or duties or interpretation

decree final decision and judgment of court

default judgment judicial decision rendered without trial proceedings, usu. due to default by one party, esp. failure to appear in court

devise gift of real property by will

dictum portion of opinion contained in court decision that is not essential for deciding narrowest construction of the facts

directed verdict judge's decision in civil case so one-sided that reasonable minds could not conclude otherwise and jury need not hear it

disbarment expulsion of attorney from legal profession; revocation of right to practice law

disclaimer act of declining to accept gift by will or trust, thereby allowing it to pass to next beneficiary entitled to it

disculpate (*vb*) acquit of charges

dismiss (*vb*) throw case out of court, drop charges; relieve hung jury of duties

dissent minority opposition to majority judgment

dissenting opinion written minority opinion in opposition to majority

distrain (*vb*) seize and hold goods as compensation due or to obtain satisfaction of claim

divorce legal dissolution of valid marriage

drop charges dismiss case; cease prosecution

enforcement effective carrying out of laws

entail rule of descent for estate beyond one generation, so that individual heir may not dispose of it

entry of judgment official statement and recording of decision

escheat turning of decedent's property over to state when no heirs are found

execution of judgment collection of award or enactment of sentence

extradition transfer of accused fugitive from state where arrested to state where charged

finding basis in fact or law for judgement

fine money payment required by decision

foreclosure procedure forcing sale of property to meet unpaid obligation

garnishment collection of judgment debt by interception of money owed to debtor

grant transfer of real property or interest therein

guilty (*adj*) found justly responsible for offense and liable to punishment

hung jury trial jury unable to reach minimum consensus needed for verdict

immunity protection of potentially incriminated witness or informer from prosecution based on information given

indemnify (*vb*) secure against loss or damage

indemnity exemption from penalties or liabilities; reimbursement for loss sustained

injunction court order directing someone to do or not do something

instrument formal legal document, such as deed, bond, or contract

interdict prohibitory act or decree of court

interlocutory decree temporary court decision that becomes final after certain time period

intestate (*adj*) having died without a will

joint custody sharing of child's upbringing by divorced parents

judgment court's final decision on matter in favor of plaintiff or defendant

lease agreement by which tenant rents property from landlord

legacy gift of property or bequest by will

levy seizure of property to satisfy judgment

liability legal obligation, duty, or accountability

license permissive right to do something granted by authority or by owner

lien claim on property for debt

living trust trust that takes effect during life of its creator

mandamus *Latin*. lit. we command; superior court writ ordering specific act or duty

mandatory injunction cease and desist order

martial law suspension of judicial procedures

and imposition of military rule by executive branch of government in emergency circumstance

mistrial trial without legal effect due to error or prejudicial misconduct in proceedings

mitigation of damages steps taken by victim of wrongdoer to reduce monetary harm in civil case

moratorium legally authorized period of delay for performance of some obligation

naturalization granting of citizenship to one born in another country

nominal damages token award to party when court or jury finds in his or her favor but feels no serious damage has been sustained

not guilty designating defendant's plea or jury's verdict that law was not violated

notice formal indication between parties of intention to exercise right or terminate agreement at specific time; notification to person whose interests may be affected by upcoming proceeding

nullity state of being legally invalid

obligation duty or payment owed to another

on the merits judgment based on facts of case, not legal technicality

opinion formal court decision with factual determinations and legal reasons supporting it

order judgment or formal direction of court to do or not do something; request for silence in courtroom

out-of-court settlement agreement reached between parties in civil suit before or outside court proceedings

pardon executive act releasing convict from court sentence of punishment

parole release of prisoner after serving sentence, with assurance that he or she will abide by law

per curiam *Latin*. lit. by the court; unanimous decision of all judges on court

precedent former decision based on same or similar facts used as guide for judicial reasoning in current action

probation relief from all or part of prison sentence on promise of proper conduct

promissory note written promise to pay money to another

property execution enforcement of judgment involving property

proprietary (*adj*) having exclusive legal right to use, make, or market

public policy court's right to refuse to honor contract that undermines public good

punitive damages damages in excess of actual loss awarded to wronged plaintiff to punish defendant

quash (*vb*) set aside for insufficient grounds

quit claim deed releasing all claims against real property

ratification agreement that confirms previous action

recovery gaining by legal process

redress (*vb*) remove or make right a cause of complaint

release discharging or giving up of claim or rights in settlement

remand (*vb*) return to custody pending further trial or detention; return case from appellate to lower court for further proceedings

remedy legal means to recover right or obtain redress for wrong; relief given by court for wrong

remittitur *Latin.* lit. it is sent back; reduction of damages awarded at trial that are deemed to be excessive

reprieve delay in execution of sentence

rescission cancellation, annulment, or vacating of law, judgment, or contract, as by restoration to opposite party of what one has received from that party

restitution restoration to rightful owner; making good or providing equivalent for some harm

reversal judicial decision to overturn lower court ruling

reversion return of title to real estate to former owner or owner's heirs at termination of temporary grant

review judicial reexamination, esp. of lower court proceedings

revoke (*vb*) annul or rescind a document, decision, or offer

satisfaction discharge of legal obligation, esp. compensation for loss or injury

sentence court judgment stating punishment in criminal case

set aside (*vb*) annul or override jury's verdict, done by judge

settlement resolution of civil case, usu. without trial

specific performance obligation to carry out contractually promised performance when breach cannot be compensated by award of money

stay delay or suspension of legal proceedings, esp. execution of sentence

stay of execution limited suspension of judgment, usu. to allow appeal

sub judice *Latin.* lit. under a judge; awaiting judicial determination, therefore not open to public discussion

summary judgment judicial decision in civil case, usu. pretrial, deciding particular issues or entire matter

supplementary proceedings court action to collect judgment

surcharge award of damages imposed on one owing fiduciary duties to trust or estate

suspended sentence deferment of punishment, usu. over period of probation

temporary restraining order court order barring one party from action that might harm another, esp. through physical contact, until hearing on specific date

testament will, usu. restricted to personal property

testamentary trust trust created by will that comes into existence when probate court orders deceased's estate assets distributed to trustee

trust arrangement in which person or institution holds legal title to property with obligation to care for it for the benefit of another

unanimous verdict agreement of all jurors, required for criminal conviction

verdict decision of jury

void (*adj*) having no effect; without legal force to bind

will declaration on disposition of property and guardianship of minor children, taking effect upon death

without prejudice (*adv*) final and binding in accordance with res judicata

Customs, Formalities, and Practices

abstract of title compiled history of land ownership

actus reus *Latin.* wrongful act, as distinct from intent behind it

admissible (*adj*) allowable in court, being pertinent to case, esp. with regard to evidence

alibi proof that accused was not physically present at scene of crime; excuse

ambit sphere or limit of action or complaint

amicus brief statement or report by friend of court

ancillary (*adj*) supplementary, subordinate, esp. such evidence

attest (*vb*) witness a document in writing

bail bond obligation to pay bail if defendant fails to appear in court

bar exam lengthy test prospective lawyer must pass before being authorized to practice law in specific jurisdiction

base fee estate held from lord on condition of performing some service in feudal Britain

bond written, sealed obligation to pay sum of money

bounty payment promised for capture of fugitive outlaw

brief lawyer's written presentation of statutory and case law to support client's case

burden of proof duty to produce evidence to prove disputed facts, which lies with prosecutor in criminal case and with plaintiff in civil case

calendar schedule of cases coming to trial

capacity ability to understand facts and implications of one's behavior

caseload number of cases handled by court or lawyer in particular period

causes of action facts or specific complaints giving one party right to bring civil case against another

caveat *Latin.* lit. let him beware; warning

charge judge's instructions to jury; criminal accusation

chattel item of personal property other than real property and land

circumstantial evidence indirect evidence not based on direct observation that tends to prove other facts

civil liability legal obligations under civil law

civil rights personal liberties guaranteed by U.S. Constitution, its amendments, and acts of Congress

closing statement lawyer's summation of case to judge or jury

collateral (*adj*) incidental or additional to matter being discussed

comity courtesy rule by which courts recognize decisions of other courts and other states

competency minimum requirements to qualify as witness or party to contract or to serve in some capacity

complaint plaintiff's written claim in court proceedings

compliance conformity in fulfilling legal obligations

confidential communications exchanges, esp. between client and lawyer, protected from disclosure to others by legal privilege

consensual (*adj*) existing or made by mutual consent but usu. unwritten

consideration thing or act of value that one party provides another when entering into contract

constitutional (*adj*) in accordance with or authorized by constitution

corpus delicti *Latin.* lit. body of the crime; proof that crime has been committed and that charges should be brought

corroboration evidence from two or more witnesses that is identical or supports the other's word

courtesy rules of appropriate conduct in legal proceedings; favors and allowances granted by one lawyer to another

covenant written promise, esp. owner's obligations in deed on property

cui bono *Latin.* lit. to whose advantage; principle that probable responsibility for an act lies with one having something to gain by it

de facto *Latin.* lit. actual, in reality; how matters are by custom, though not required by law to be thus

de jure *Latin.* lit. by right, by law; how the law requires that matters be

demonstrative evidence evidence that is conclusive in proving something

direct evidence proof given by those who saw acts or heard words in question

disclosure descriptive information and revelations, esp. in patent application

docket court's official record of proceedings and calendar of upcoming cases

document (*vb*) provide written evidence as proof of something

domicile person's sole permanent legal residence

due process orderly administration of justice by proper court according to established rules and laws, entitling one to proper notice and fair opportunity to be heard

earnest money deposit or token sum paid as binder or to indicate intention to consummate deal

eminent domain government right to take

private property for public use with just compensation

encumbrance right in real property held by third party that diminishes its value

estate grouping of all property of person, esp. deceased, in legal category

estoppel doctrine precluding change of one's previous position to detriment of others

evidence everything considered by court or jury to settle question of what truly is fact

exclusionary rule prohibition from use at criminal trial of evidence obtained by unreasonable search and seizure

exhibit physical object or paper used as evidence

ex parte *Latin.* lit. from or on one side; partisan communications with one party to dispute absent, as between one lawyer and judge

extraterritoriality immunity and exemption from arrest enjoyed by diplomats

fair use conditions under which copyright material may be used by another

fee lawyer's charge for his or her services

fee simple unencumbered ownership of real property without limitation to particular class of heirs

fiduciary position of high trust and confidence required of one entrusted with care of another's property

flagrante delicto *Latin.* lit. while the crime is burning; caught in the act of committing a crime

forensics relation of principles and facts from another profession, such as medicine, to legal proceedings

freedom of the seas principle of international law that holds that no state has sovereignty beyond its territorial waters

gavel wooden mallet used by judge to call court to order

grandfather clause legal provision that exempts a business or class of persons from new regulations that would affect prior rights and privileges

gravamen most significant part of grievance or complaint

hearsay evidence inadmissible secondhand evidence, usu. told to witness by another

holograph will or document in handwriting of its maker

hornbook general treatise or primer on some aspect of law

immaterial evidence facts of no consequence or relevance in deciding issues before court

inadmissible evidence facts not legally allowable as part of a case

insanity plea not-guilty plea based on accused's inability to comprehend wrongful conduct

intellectual property individual's creative or artistic work, protectable under copyright or patent law

intent design or resolve with which one acts; external manifestation of an inward will

intestate succession passage of ownership

interests in property from decedent without will to successors determined by state law

irrelevant evidence evidence unrelated to issue before court

J.D. *Latin. Juris Doctor;* Doctor of Laws degree; Doctor of Jurisprudence

J.D.S. Doctor of Juridical Science degree

jeopardy defendant's risk of conviction and punishment when brought to trial

judicial notice court's acceptance of well-known facts as true without evidence

judicial review doctrine that court system may annul legislative or executive acts deemed unconstitutional

jury duty obligation of citizen to serve on jury

laches unreasonable delay that bars party from pursuing legal claim

law-abiding *(adj)* obedient to the law

lawful *(adj)* in accordance with established law

law journal publication of and for legal profession

lawless *(adj)* not regulated or restrained by law

law review law school publication with authoritative articles on legal trends or developments, written and edited by top students

lawyering practice of law; functions of an attorney

leading question question by lawyer that suggests answer desired from person being questioned

legal *(adj)* conforming to rules of law; related to practice of law

legalese jargon and argot of lawyers and court system

legalism legal term or expression; strict conformity to law

lis pendens *Latin.* lawsuit pending and listed on court docket; document announcing pending litigation

litigious *(adj)* prone to engage in lawsuits

LL.B. *Latin. Legum Baccalaureus;* Bachelor of Laws degree

LL.D. *Latin. Legum Doctor;* Doctor of Laws degree

LL.M. *Latin. Legum Magister;* Master of Laws degree

malice aforethought premeditated evil or antisocial intent

material evidence facts with significant bearing on case

mens rea *Latin.* lit. guilty mind; criminal intent required for conviction of particular crime

merits intrinsic nature of case apart from procedural matters

mitigating circumstances conditions under which crime was committed that reduce punishment due

motive implied reason for action, as distinct from intent

non compos mentis *Latin.* lit. of unsound mind; used to indicate insanity, temporary or permanent, and lesser forms of mental

incompetence that make person unfit to stand trial

oath affirmation or solemn pledge binding one to tell the truth according to the law, after which false statements are punishable as perjury

opening statement outline of position and proposed proof by lawyer near start of trial

overrule *(vb)* refuse to honor lawyer's objection, esp. judicial refusal to do so

personal property all tangibles and intangibles in which one may hold interests of ownership other than real property

physical evidence objects presented to court that have bearing on trial

pleadings court papers in which parties assert allegations or contentions in support of positions

polling the jury asking each juror in open court to confirm concurrence with verdict

practice scope, priority, and manner in which one conducts legal suits, esp. the business of being a lawyer

premeditation prior intent or design to commit crime

preponderance of proof evidence that outweighs that of opposition

presumption of law rule binding judges or juries to draw certain inferences from facts

prima facie *Latin.* lit. at first sight; sufficient evidence to prove case unless contradicted

privileged communications statements and confidences that cannot be inquired into by others or made basis for suit, esp. between lawyer and client, husband and wife, or doctor and patient

probable cause having good reason to believe a crime has occurred and sufficient basis for arrest and accusation but not conviction

pro forma *Latin.* lit. as a matter of form; carried out with proper formality

proof establishment of fact in court by presentation of evidence

property something owned, esp. a piece of land or real estate; ownership or right of possession

proxy authority to act for another; document granting such authority

public domain unprotected status of intellectual property whose copyright has expired or that never had copyright

quantum meruit *Latin.* lit. according to what he deserves; reasonable value of services rendered

read rights state legal rights to person at time of arrest, required of arresting officer

real property real estate; land or buildings on it

reasonable doubt principle of law establishing criteria jury must apply to prosecution's case in order to return guilty verdict

relevant *(adj)* logically connected to case, esp. evidence

represent *(vb)* act as lawyer for client

res ipsa loquitur *Latin.* lit. the thing speaks for itself; rule of negligence based on occurrence itself though defendant was absent

res judicata *Latin.* lit. the matter has been

decided; rule that case decided in court may not be pressed again by same parties and that decision is therefore final

respondeat superior *Latin.* lit. let superior give answer; doctrine transferring liability for agent's negligence to principal

retainer advance fee paid on hiring lawyer's services

rights proprietary interest in intangible thing; something one may claim as justly due; protections guaranteed by law and constitution

scilicet (*adv*) *Latin.* lit. to wit; used in affidavits at place of swearing

seal imprint on document certifying authenticity

security pledge of money or property as means of assuring payment of debt or performance of some act

self-defense act of repelling physical assault by force, used as plea to justify otherwise criminal act

self-incrimination statement that implicates oneself in a crime

show cause provide good reason why something should or should not be done in case, usu. ordered of litigant

sovereign immunity rule that government may not be sued without its consent

speculation expression of opinion for which one has no direct evidence; mere conjecture, esp. by witness

ss scilicet

stand witness stand

stare decisis *Latin.* lit. to stand by decided matters; doctrine of following rules and principles from previous judicial decisions unless they contravene general principles of justice

strike (*vb*) eliminate from official record of court proceedings

subrogation assumption of obligations of another party

substantive (*adj*) having a bearing on fundamental rights and merits as opposed to procedural aspects of case

summation lawyer's final argument and closing statement to jury

suppress (*vb*) keep secret by failure to disclose, esp. evidence

sustain (*vb*) grant lawyer's objection, esp. judicial decision to do so

tangible property physical objects taken as property, as distinguished from real and intellectual properties

title evidence or right of property ownership

trademark distinguishing design, symbol, or words used by manufacturer or dealer to identify product or service from competitors, registered by its owner and designated ™

trial date day set for commencing trial

ultra vires (*adj*) *Latin.* lit. beyond strength; designating acts beyond scope of corporate charter

under advisement with careful deliberation or consultation, esp. by judge

unjust enrichment doctrine that prevents profit at another's expense

usufruct legal right to use or enjoy profits of another's property

vital statistics public records of births, deaths, and marriages

warranty promise related to contract

witness box witness stand

witness stand space in courtroom occupied by witness while testifying; stand; witness box

wrongful death condition giving survivors right to sue for damages in death caused by some person or persons

your honor proper form of address to judge

Crimes, Criminals, and Civil Offenders

abduction kidnapping, esp. of underage female for sex or prostitution

accessory one who unlawfully aids a criminal

accessory after the fact one who helps criminal elude arrest

accessory before the fact one who induces or counsels another to commit a crime

accessory during the fact one who witnesses a crime but does nothing to prevent it

accomplice criminal's active partner in crime

adultery voluntary sexual intercourse between married person and nonspouse

aggravated assault common assault combined with intent to commit another crime or with use of deadly weapon

arson willful and malicious burning of another's property

assault threat or attempt to inflict physical harm on another

battery unlawful act of touching, beating, or inflicting physical violence on another person, assault

bigamy state of having two or more living spouses

blackmail extortion by threat

breach violation of law, failure to meet obligation

breach of contract violation by one party having contractual duty or obligation

breaking and entering entry into another's property, forcibly or with criminal intent

bribery payment offered for favors, esp. to public officer

brutality unlawful ruthlessness or harshness, esp. by legal authorities

burglary unlawful presence in a building to commit crime, esp. theft

capital crime offense punishable by death

civil offense violation of civil statutes

coercion force or compulsion used to make person act against his or her will

collusion cooperation between persons to commit crime

compounding a crime offense of agreeing not to prosecute in return for a consideration

concealment fraudulent hiding of material facts

condemned (*adj*) sentenced to death for crime

connivance aiding in another's illegal act, thereby consenting to it

conspiracy agreement between two or more persons to commit illegal act or use unlawful means to carry out legal act

contempt of court willful disobedience or disdain for court rules

contravention opposition to or violation of a law

contributory negligence plaintiff's conduct held partly responsible for injury in negligence case

convict one found guilty of a crime

crime violation of public law punishable by state

criminal one found guilty of violating the law

criminal liability responsibility, with punishments due, for violation of criminal laws

defamation harm to another's reputation by libel or slander

default failure to fulfill legal obligation, esp. failure to appear in court when case is called

delict wrongful act, usu. misdemeanor, for which injured party is entitled to compensation

disorderly conduct any of various activities that disturb public peace

duress force, compulsion, threat, or pressure that deprives another person of free will

embezzlement appropriation of property by one to whom it has been entrusted

extortion act of taking another's money or property by threat or duress, esp. under pretext of authority

false pretense taking another's property by trickery or fraud

felon one convicted of serious crime or felony

felony serious crime, punishable by imprisonment in penitentiary and loss of some rights

forgery act of making, altering, or counterfeiting a document or signature with intent to deceive

frame (*vb*) *Informal.* contrive false evidence to make innocent party appear guilty

fraud perversion of truth with intent to deceive

graft bribery, esp. of public official

grand larceny theft of personal property exceeding specified value

homicide unlawful taking of human life

infraction violation of law, usu. a misdemeanor

infringement unauthorized use of patented or copyrighted invention or intellectual property

injury violation of person's rights so as to cause damage

involuntary manslaughter taking of human life through criminal negligence

jury tampering contact with jury member by lawyer to exert illegal influence

kidnapping willful abduction or detention of another against his or her will

larceny wrongful possession or use of another's property

lawbreaker one who violates the law

lawless (*adj*) not regulated or restrained by law

libel written statement defaming another's reputation

malfeasance act wrongful in itself or which

perpetrator had no right to do, esp. performed by public official

malicious mischief willful or reckless damage to another person's property

malpractice wrongful conduct by a professional, through neglect or lack of ethics

manslaughter taking of human life without malicious intent

mayhem willful damage or violence to another person

misdemeanor lesser offense than felony, punishable by fine or imprisonment in jail but not penitentiary

misfeasance wrongful performance of lawful act

moral turpitude depraved, immoral, antisocial behavior

murder taking of another's life, esp. by deliberate and premeditated design

negligence failure to act in a reasonably prudent manner to protect interests of others, often encompassing recklessness

nonfeasance failure to do something one is duty-bound to do

nuisance wrongful use of one's property, causing damage or inconvenience to another

obscenity purveying of something having indecent, offensive content without redeeming value

obstruction of justice hindrance to or prevention of completion of the legal process

offense breach of criminal or civil law

peculation embezzlement of public funds

perjury false statement made under oath

petty larceny theft of personal property of less than legally specified value

principal chief wrongdoer in crime

racketeering operation of business characterized by systematically dishonest practices

rape sexual intercourse forced on another person, usu. a woman

receiver one who accepts goods knowing they are stolen

reckless endangerment action that could result in injury to another though it may not have

resisting arrest attempting to evade or physically prevent one's arrest

robbery theft aggravated by force or threat of assault

skip bail fail to appear in court after posting bail bond, which is then forfeited

slander defamation of another's reputation by spoken falsehoods

smuggling import or export of goods that are outlawed or in avoidance of customs duty

sodomy unnatural sexual intercourse, esp. anal or oral

statutory rape sexual activity with person under the age of consent

subornation inducement to commit illegal act, esp. perjury

trespass illegal entry of another's property or injurious encroachment on another's rights

undue influence threat or improper persuasion that overcomes one's free will to govern actions

usury practice of charging higher interest rate than allowed by law

vandalism wanton and malicious damage to another's property

voluntary manslaughter taking of human life with mitigating circumstances

PUBLISHING AND THE PRESS

Publishing
Publications
Journalism
Newspaper Names

See also: *Chap. 5: Telecommunications; Chap. 12: Advertising; Chap. 14: Literature; Chap. 15: Television and Radio; Chap. 16: Graphic Design and Printing; Photography; Chap. 18: Grammar, Phonetics, and Linguistics*

Publishing

aa designation for author's alterations on galley proofs, for which compositor must be paid

ABA American Booksellers Association; its annual spring trade convention for the publishing industry

abridge (*vb*) shorten or condense a text

academic press publishing house usu. specializing in scholarly works, often owned by university; university press

acknowledgments author's credit and thanks to family, colleagues, assistants, contributors, editors, and researchers, usu. in front matter

acquisitions editor publishing house editor who reviews and secures new writers and projects

ad card list of author's books, usu. facing title page; card page

addendum supplementary information published after book's initial publication

advance publisher's payment to author that is earned back from a percentage of book's income from sales and subsidiary rights

advance copy copy of book available before publication date

appendix supplementary information or material at back of book

author writer, esp. of books

author's tour promotional trip by author to publicize book's publication

backlist list of publisher's previous publications still in print

back matter information following main body of book text, including appendix, index, bibliography, and/or glossary

bestseller book that sells extremely well, usu. for a short period of time

bibliography list of source materials and related readings

binding spine, cover, and end papers of bound volume

blockbuster enormous bestseller

blueline contact print from offset negative that is final proof before press run; blues

blue-pencil (*vb*) make editor's corrections, usu. in blue pencil

blues *Informal.* blueline

blurb comment, usu. from well-known person or authority, praising book, used in promotion and advertising; puff

boards rigid covers for book, attached at spine

bodice ripper *Informal.* cheap, sensationalist, often hackneyed romantic or thriller novel

BOM proof cut and bound proof of uncorrected galleys, orig. made for submission to Book-of-the-Month Club

bookbinding process of fitting printed pages into protective covers to form book

book club membership organization offering books for sale through mail

book jacket often decorative, removable paper cover that protects book binding and usu. gives information about book and author

bookman one who sells books for a publisher; sales rep

bookplate label identifying book's owner

bookseller person in retail business of selling books

bookstall stand where books are sold, esp. outdoors

bookstore retail business establishment that stocks and sells books

bound galleys uncorrected galleys cut and bound in booklike form for final corrections and revisions

buckram binding coarse cotton or linen stiffened with glue or sizing for binding books

bulk thickness of book, based on weight of paper and number of pages

caption description under illustration or photograph

card page ad card

caret proofreader's mark indicating place where material is to be inserted

case book cover ready to be fitted with pages

cast off (*vb*) estimate number of pages a manuscript will make in book form

censorship practice of removing or restricting material published

chain national network of bookstores owned by one company

chapter opening first page of new chapter

chapter title heading for book chapter

children's books juvenile books

clothbound (*adj*) designating hardbound book with cloth-covered boards

colophon publisher's logo or identifying mark

contents list of book parts, including chapters, bibliography, index, and illustrations

copy material to be printed and published

copyediting correction and revision of grammatical, stylistic, and factual elements of book

copyeditor person who corrects and revises grammatical, stylistic, and factual elements of book

copyreader person who checks proofs or copy for errors

copyright exclusive legal right to publish and sell a written work, designated ©

crane cut and bound uncorrected galley proof

crime novel fiction genre that focuses on criminal acts and characters

dedication inscription of book to person or cause

desktop publishing publication of materials using personal computers and printers with graphic capabilities and various type fonts

detective novel fiction genre emphasizing crime detection

dime novel melodramatic or sensational novel of late 19th and early 20th century, sold in paperback for ten cents

dust cover protective paper jacket around hardbound book; dust jacket; jacket

dust jacket dust cover

edit (*vb*) work on written material, esp. with writers, to prepare it for publication

edition particular imprint or publishing run of book

editor person who works with writers and prepares written material for publication

editorial director supervisor of editorial staff and policies of publishing house; editor in chief

editor in chief policymaking executive and principal editor, esp. of magazine or journal; editorial director

educational publishing publication of textbooks

end papers decorative binding papers inside book cover

epilogue additional commentary at end of book

errata slip list of errors in a publication with their corrections, inserted on a separate sheet of paper slipped into book

excerpt passage of book reproduced, esp. for review

ex libris *Latin.* lit. from the library; owner's bookplate

faction blend of actual events and people into fictional story

f and g's printed, folded, gathered sheets ready for binding into book form

fascicle one section of book published in separate parts

fiction imaginative work involving invented prose narrative

first edition book printed in first print run of publication

flyleaf blank leaf in front or back of book

folio book page size; one-half sheet of foolscap

footnote note at page bottom with additional information or commentary on text

foreword introductory statement

format physical dimensions of publication

frontispiece illustrated page preceding title page of book

front matter material preceding book's main text, esp. acknowledgments, dedication, foreword, and introduction

galley proof first printed correction proof, orig. pulled from type in galley tray

gathering section in book, usu. a sheet cut into various leaves

genre distinct literary category such as poetry, thriller, detective novel, or gothic novel

ghost writer person who writes for another person, under that person's name, without receiving credit as author

glossary list of defined vocabulary terms used in text

gothic novel fiction genre using melodramatic, dark, romantic, and often frightening elements

government press state-operated publishing house

hack writer aiming at commercial success who produces banal and mediocre work; writer able to produce assigned work competently and quickly

half title title set on first page of book and before beginning of text

hard copy printout of text stored on computer

hardcover book bound in stiff boards rather than paper

holiday reading diverting books intended for readers on vacation

house publishing house

house style editorial style of particular publishing company

imprint publisher's name printed on book's title page; division within publishing house

index list of names, terms, ideas, and facts in book arranged alphabetically with page numbers for location in text

in-print (*adj*) designating book currently available for sale

International Standard Book Number ISBN; unique number code imprinted on book

introduction formal statement of intention or scope of book

ISBN International Standard Book Number

jacket dust cover

juvenile books books of fiction or nonfiction for children, often illustrated

Kirkus Reviews *Trademark.* book review service

launch promotional sales campaign at time of publication

leader book expected to sell best during particular season and receiving greatest attention and promotion from publisher, esp. paperback

leaf single sheet or page

lexicon listing of words in one language

line editing working line by line through manuscript to improve and clarify tone, text, sequence, phrasing, and style

list publisher's catalog of new titles to be published in particular season, esp. spring or fall

literary agent author's representative, esp. in sale and contract negotiations with publisher

literary publishing publication of literature, as opposed to purely commercial fiction and nonfiction

literary work written work of literary merit, esp. of imaginative or critical nature

long discount forty or fifty percent discount given by publisher when selling books in multiple quantities, usu. to wholesalers and retailers

mail-order publishing book publication or distribution by mail, esp. through book clubs

manuscript book in author's original form, usu. typewritten or word-processed

mass market (*adj*) designating small, rack-size paperback book, esp. for distribution on newsstands

ms manuscript

mystery fiction genre emphasizing suspense

nonfiction writing based on fact, not invention

np no pagination; designation for published work without page numbers

option right to develop published literary work for other media; publisher's right of first refusal on author's next work

oral history oral recollections of people representative of certain historic period, usu. tape-recorded

out-of-print (*adj*) designating book no longer available from publisher

overrun copies of book printed beyond actual orders received

overstock excess copies of specific book that publisher cannot sell

over-the-transom manuscripts submitted to magazine, publisher, or agent without prior arrangement

packager independent contractor who conceives idea for book, finds authors, illustrators, and designers, and makes business arrangement with publisher for publication and, sometimes, production

page proofs printed sheets in page form

paperback book bound in flexible, paper cover

paperbound (*adj*) designating paperback book

part title page showing title of major portion or part of book

permissions right to exploit published matter in some form

piracy illegal publishing of copyrighted material

plagiarism appropriation and publication of another's writing without consent

pocket book rack-size paperback book

potboiler fast-paced, heavily plotted popular fiction produced for financial gain only

preface introductory matter at front of book

prepack marketing package for store display containing several copies of book

presales planning session of sales force and management on development of sales campaign for books

presentation copy book copy to be formally presented by author as gift, often with special binding

printer's error error introduced into typeset copy by compositor, who cannot charge to correct it

printing mass production of printed material into book or periodical form

proof trial impression of type, for correction and revision

proofreader person who checks printed copy for errors

proofreading marks standardized symbols used to indicate corrections and revisions in text sent to printer

proof sheet trial printing of single page for correction and revision

pub date *Informal.* publication date

publication printing and distribution of book or periodical; something that is published

publication date date on which published book is first available for sale; pub date

public domain material that is not copyrighted and can be published without permission or payment

publicist person responsible for informing media and public of book's publication

publicity exposure and promotion of new book in media

publisher person or company engaged in publication of books and periodicals; chief executive of publishing house

Publishers Weekly *Trademark.* PW; news magazine of publishing industry

publishing business and practice of reproducing and issuing for sale books or periodicals

publishing house company engaged in soliciting, editing, publishing, and selling of books; house

puff blurb

puff piece uncritical article written to publicize book

pulp cheap, hackneyed fiction

PW Publishers Weekly

rack-size (*adj*) describing typical format of paperback for mass market

reader person who reviews manuscripts for publisher

recto right-hand page of book

redact (*vb*) edit or revise, adapt for publication

reissue newly printed edition of previously published book; reprint

rejection slip notice of publisher's rejection of manuscript

release date or act of publication; sheet sent out to media to publicize book, author, or event

remainder (*vb*) sell book at lowered price, usu. from overstock; (*n*) book that has been remaindered

replacement newly released book that replaces old book on store shelves

reprint reissue

reserves royalty payments withheld from author until it is certain that bookstores will not return distributed copies of book

returns unsold books returned by bookseller for credit from publisher

review published critical assessment of new book

review copy advance complimentary copy of book for reviewer

revision change in manuscript or edition

rights and permissions right to reprint, excerpt, condense, or otherwise exploit published matter in some form, negotiated by department of publishing company; permissions

romance fiction genre that presents melodramatic love story

royalty author's percentage of profits from book sale

running foot material printed at bottom of each page, usu. title, author's name, chapter title, or subject of page or section

running head material printed at top of each page, usu. title, author's name, chapter title, or subject of page or section

sales conference marketing meeting where new books are presented to publisher's salespeople, who then solicit orders

sales force publishing house employees involved with selling books to bookstores, wholesalers, and others

scholarly publishing publication of books and periodicals on academic, research, or scholarly topics

science fiction fiction genre focusing on speculation about future, other worlds, or highly advanced alien technologies

self-publishing books financed and published by author

serial rights commercial rights to publication of parts of work in magazine or newspaper, either before or after book publication

shelf life duration for which books are stocked by bookstores before being returned to publisher

short discount discount given by publishers to libraries, colleges, and other institutions who will not resell the books

signature folded, printed sheets to be bound into book pages

sinkage distance from page top to first line of type or illustration

slush pile *Informal.* unsolicited manuscripts submitted to publishing company, rarely published

small press publishing house with limited output, sometimes in specialized field

special sales sales of book other than through normal wholesale and retail channels, as in special outlets or to particular market

spine binding that connects book's covers along one edge

spiral binding binding with coiled wire through holed paper

submission manuscript offered to publisher, usu. by agent

subsidiary rights allied rights related to a book, including paperback, serialization, television and motion picture, electronic, and foreign publication rights

synopsis abstract of written work, as by reader in publishing house

technical publishing publication of research, educational, review, or report material in scientific and technological fields

text written body of book

textbook publishing publication and distribution to schools and universities of teaching manuals and textbooks

thriller fiction genre incorporating fantastic, suspenseful, or exciting situations

title name of publication; published book

title page book page with title, author's name, and publisher's imprint

trade book book for general market, distributed largely through bookstores and libraries

trade paperback large-size paperbound book for general market, distributed largely through bookstores

trade publishing publication of hardcover and paperback books of interest to general public distributed largely through bookstores and libraries

translation text rendered in language other than original language in which it was written and published

trim size page size after final cutting; dimensions of cover

typescript typewritten manuscript copy

unabridged (*adj*) designating complete text of book, story, or article; uncut

uncut (*adj*) unabridged

unedited (*adj*) not modified by editorial changes

university press academic press

unpaginated (*adj*) denoting book, usu. brief or for children, with no page numbers; np

unsolicited manuscript book or article submitted to publisher without prior arrangement

vanity press company that charges authors a fee to publish their work

verso left-hand page of book

vetting legal and expert checking of book's contents, esp. facts

western fiction genre featuring cowboy, Indian, and outlaw stories from U.S. West of 19th century

young adult books category of books for teenagers

Publications

almanac book published annually, with seasonal information; yearly reference book with general information about countries of the world

annals written account of year's events in chronological order

annual yearbook, esp. of school or organization

anthology selection of poems, stories, or essays published together; compilation; treasury

article report, story, or essay complete in itself and forming part of a publication

atlas book of maps and charts

audio book book on cassette

autobiography story of one's own life

bimonthly periodical published once every two months or twice a month

biography story of another person's life

biweekly periodical published once every two weeks

book large number of sheets of printed material bound together along one edge between protective covers and published; text and graphic material printed on such pages

booklet small book, esp. paperbound

book on cassette audio recording of reading of a book; audio book

boxed set multivolume book packaged and sold as one unit

broadside large sheet of paper printed on one or both sides with advertisement or political message, usu. folded

brochure pamphlet, usu. promotional or descriptive

bulletin regular publication for members of organization or community group

catalog comprehensive descriptive listing, esp. of articles for sale or college courses

circular letter or advertisement printed for mass distribution

codex manuscript volume, esp. of classic text or scripture

comic book paperbound booklet of extended cartoons in series, usu. humorous or adventurous

communiqué official bulletin or correspondence

compendium brief treatment or account, usu. of extensive subject

compilation anthology

concordance alphabetical listing of significant words used in text or by particular writer, citing where they occur, used esp. with Bible

cookbook book of recipes

daily newspaper published each day

diary daily record of one's thoughts and experiences

dictionary alphabetical listing of words with definitions and etymological information

digest condensation or abridgment of material

directory listing of names, addresses, and other information about a specific group of people

encyclopedia book or set of books with information on many branches of knowledge, usu. arranged alphabetically

gazette newspaper; official publication with announcements

gazetteer dictionary of geographical terms

guidebook listing of directions and information for particular place, esp. for tourists

handbook manual of information on particular subject

hornbook book or primer providing basic information on particular subject

house organ in-house publication

how-to book manual or instruction book on particular subject

incunabula extant copies of earliest printed books, pre-1500

index extensive alphabetical listing of items, esp. in collection, with information on each

in-house publication bulletin or other regular publication of an organization, intended for employees or members; house organ

irregular serial serial not published at set intervals

journal any periodical or newspaper, esp. daily newspaper; regular publication of specific profession

lexicon dictionary or other vocabulary book

magazine periodic publication, usu. bound in paper, containing articles by various writers, often with photographs and illustrations, frequently focusing on some unifying theme or subject

manifesto public statement of policies and reasoning, esp. by government or political group

manual book of facts and instruction on particular subject

monograph scholarly book or long article on specific subject

monthly periodical published once a month

newsletter regular informational bulletin for subscribers, employees, or organization members

newspaper regular publication, esp. daily, containing news, opinion, general interest features, photographs, illustrations, and advertisements

notice formal announcement, esp. printed warning, rules, or information

pamphlet thin, simply bound or stapled collection of sheets, usu. on topic of current interest

periodical any publication appearing at regular intervals

position paper formal, detailed statement of policy

primer elementary handbook on particular subject or used to teach reading

quarterly periodical published every three months

reference book authoritative book used for research and information gathering on one or many subjects

regional magazine with coverage directed at readership in specific geographic area

report formal or official presentation of facts or record of proceedings

self-help book guidebook for personal development or improvement

semimonthly periodical published twice a month

semiweekly periodical published twice a week

serial something published in series of continuous segments at regular intervals

slick magazine printed on glossy paper; such a magazine regarded as possessing sophistication

textbook book giving detailed instruction in principles of some subject for students

thesaurus extensive listing of words and their synonyms, arranged alphabetically or topically

tome large, scholarly book

tract treatise, esp. proselytizing on politics or religion

treasury anthology

volume one of two or more separate books constituting a complete set; any single book

weekly periodical published once a week

white paper detailed authoritative report, esp. official government report

who's who listing of well-known people, in one specific field or many, with biographical information

yearbook periodical published once a year, esp. with information on previous year; annual publication of graduating class of school or college

yellow pages telephone directory of businesses, arranged topically

Journalism

add new copy added to already written article

advance copy story prepared before event it describes has occurred and held until release date

advertorial copy that is paid for by advertisers but laid out and written in style of regular copy

agony column newspaper advice column

alternative press journalism devoted to counterculture or antiestablishment interests

angle point of view taken in news story or feature

AP Associated Press

article complete written piece in newspaper or magazine

assignment news story or feature that a reporter or photographer is asked to cover

Associated Press AP; major American news cooperative that supplies news, photos, and soft features to newspapers and broadcasters by wire service

attribution credit given to source of news story

banner large, front-page headline extending width of page

beat reporter's regular, assigned geographical or topical territory

bio Informal. background material, often prepared by publicist, used in profile or feature on an individual

blackout absence of news coverage due to power failure, labor dispute, or strike, or at news subject's insistence

blind lead beginning of news story that does not identify its subject directly or by name

blowup enlarged photograph

boilerplate syndicated, standardized periodical material

book complete magazine or periodical

book review description and critique of recently published book

box straight lines of type formed into box to enclose copy or illustration

break division of word onto two lines

broadcast journalism news programming on radio and television

bulldog edition earliest daily edition of a newspaper

bulletin brief announcement of latest news, usu. coming directly from news source

bureau news department covering geographical or topical area

bureau chief supervising editor of newspaper office in foreign city or on specific news desk

byline author's printed name appearing with story

canned copy copy supplied by news agency, public relations firm, or other outside source

caption description under illustration or photograph

carry (*vb*) include or run a story

cartoon illustration, esp. for political commentary, amusement, or as space filler, in newspaper or periodical

cause célèbre news incident, often a legal case, that excites widespread public interest

censorship deletion of material deemed objectionable from publication

centerfold foldout double page at center of magazine, usu. containing illustration, sometimes featuring nude photographs

center spread pair of pages facing each other in center of publication that make up single unit

circulation publication's readership and subscribers

city editor newspaper editor in charge of local news and distribution of assignments

city room office of city editor and staff, where assembly of local news takes place

classified advertisement newspaper advertisement listed according to type of goods or services offered or desired; want ad

clipping article cut from journal

clips collection of journalist's published writings, used as résumé or portfolio in soliciting future work

clipsheet newspaper sheet reissued by another organization

cold type type set by a method that does not use the casting of molten lead

column feature in newspaper by regular writer, often including personal views; printed block of type, usu. justified between vertical lines

column inch one vertical inch of copy in one column

columnist writer of regularly featured article in periodical

comics part of newspaper devoted to comic strips

comic strip humorous series of illustrations with text, regularly featured in newspaper or magazine

COMSAT *com*munications *sat*ellite that relays news stories around the world

contributing editor frequent contributor to magazine who is not on staff

contributor writer whose name is not listed on masthead but who has article appearing in periodical

copy written text of article

copyboy errand person at newspaper, esp. one who carries copy for processing

copy desk newspaper room in which copyreaders edit copy and write headlines

copyediting correction, revision, and refinement of copy before publication

copyeditor person who corrects and revises grammatical, factual, and stylistic aspects of written news story

correspondent reporter covering stories in location distant from newspaper offices

cover (*vb*) report news or take pictures of event; (*n*) front outside binding of magazine

coverage extent to which news event is included in periodical

cover copy text for cover of periodical

cover girl attractive young woman photographed for magazine cover illustration

cover story magazine article featured on cover illustration

critic person who reviews artistic and literary works for newspaper or magazine

cub reporter beginning reporter

cut deletion of copy

daily newspaper published at least once each day

dateline line at beginning of news story indicating place and time of origin of story

deadline time at which prepared story must be submitted for editing and publication

deep throat *Slang.* highly-placed, reliable, unattributable source

diophead headline beneath banner

dispatch news item filed by correspondent

distribution system of marketing newspapers and periodicals to points of sale

double truck photographs spread over two pages, as in centerfold

edition updated version of daily newspaper published at certain hour, such as morning, early, late, or final edition

editorial column by editor expressing newspaper policy or view on current issue

editor in chief supervisor of editorial policy of publication

essay often first-person column expressing writer's point of view on one subject

exposé news story revealing scandal or hidden corruption

extra special edition of newspaper, published between regular editions to cover news of unusual importance

fanzine usu. nonprofessional magazine produced by and for enthusiasts of specific field or person, esp. in pop music

feature general interest story, often of human interest or providing background on news, as distinguished from hard news

feeding frenzy ruthless attack on or exploitation of someone, esp. by media

feuilleton newspaper section, esp. in Europe, covering general features and serialized fiction

filler general-interest material plugged into empty newspaper space

final last edition of daily newspaper

First Amendment amendment to U.S. Constitution that guarantees freedom of the press

first-time rights sale of publication rights based on assumption that article or photograph has not been previously published

flack sometimes disparaging term for press agent

flag masthead

follow-up continuing coverage of ongoing news story

fourth estate the press

freelancer worker, esp. writer, not on staff of periodical

free press uncensored publication of newspapers and periodicals

front page first page of newspaper, devoted to major news stories of national, international, and local importance

gossip columnist writer who reports on real and rumored activities of celebrities

graph *Informal.* paragraph of copy

graveyard shift lobster shift

hard news current-events stories of importance

headline large-type descriptive heading over printed news story

investigative journalism in-depth coverage of news story and related background material, often requiring extensive interviewing and research

issue single edition of a periodical

item piece of news; single article

journal any periodical or newspaper, esp. daily newspaper

journalism factual writing, esp. news coverage, and photographs in support of such writing

journalist person who researches, photographs, or writes news, current events, or feature stories

jump continuation of article on another page or column

kicker brief head in small type above headline to indicate subject or draw reader's interest

kill (*vb*) abandon intention to publish story or article

kill fee reduced payment to writer or photographer for work that has been assigned but will not be used

Kyodo international news agency and wire service based in Japan

layout page design

lead introduction of news story, esp. its first sentence; most important news story of day; information or clue that draws reporter to story

lead-in introductory or transitional sentence in article

leading spacing inserted between lines by printer

lead story most important news story of the day

legend list of map or chart symbols

libel publication of false or defamatory statements

lobster shift *Informal.* night shift in newspaper office; graveyard shift

makeup layout of pages

managing editor person below editor in chief who oversees output of senior editors and regular production of periodical

mass media newspaper, radio, television, and movie media capable of reaching general public

masthead statement of staff, address, and other vital statistics of publication; flag

media all means of communication providing information to public

media event public event staged to gain publicity and media attention

muckraking search for and exposure of scandal, corruption, hidden crime, or abuse

nameplate newspaper name on top of front page

news important current events; reporting of current events

news agency organization for gathering and distributing news, features, and photos to subscribers

newsdealer person who sells newspapers and magazines

news flash news bulletin issued immediately after occurrence of event

newsmagazine periodical, esp. weekly, covering major news stories and features

newsroom office and information center for gathering news and housing writers and reporters

newsworthy (adj.) interesting or important enough to warrant media attention

obit Informal. obituary

obituary announcement of person's death with information on his or her life; obit

Op-Ed page special features and commentary page *opposite* editorial page in newspaper

pan (vb) give highly negative review of event; (n) such a review

paparazzi photographers who pursue celebrities without regard for their willingness to be photographed

personals classified advertisements for those seeking personal relationships

photo editor person responsible for assigning and selecting photographs for publication

photo essay group of photographs, often with supplementary text, that conveys a unified story

photojournalism news coverage emphasizing photographic images that depict current-events stories; pictorial journalism

pictorial journalism photojournalism

pipeline channel for passing information to journalist

play (vb) determine angle of news story or amount of coverage

plug Informal. favorable publicity in news media

political cartoon newspaper illustration, usu. humorous, with political message

press newspaper publishing; news media; newspaper

press agent person who writes and circulates news items about organization or important person; publicist

press association organization of journalists and newspaper publishers

press box area set aside for members of press, esp. at sports events

press card newspaper reporter's credentials, used to cross police or security lines

press conference prearranged interview with reporters to provide requested information or generate publicity

press corps group of journalists from various publications and media who regularly cover the same beat

press release information on event, organization, or person written by publicist and circulated for use by news media

press secretary person responsible for handling press and public relations for prominent figure or organization

profile in-depth article focusing on one individual

propaganda persuasive, esp. biased, dissemination of information

publicist press agent

puff piece Informal. coverage of subject that is exaggerated in praise and totally uncritical

put to bed complete all editorial work on newspaper and send it to printer

query inquiry from writer to editor regarding acceptability of story, usu. presented in letter outlining or describing piece

rave (vb) give extremely positive review to event; (n) such a review

report (vb) cover and write a news story

reportage stories based on research or detailed coverage of documented observation of news events, including photo essays

reporter person who investigates news event and writes story for media

retraction printed statement reversing previously held position or relinquishing previously made claim

Reuters major international news agency and wire service based in Britain

review critique of current event, esp. in arts

rewrite editorial revision of copy; (vb) revise copy

rewrite man person whose job is to condense and revise articles written by other writers

run (vb) carry a news story

running head headline repeated on continuous pages

runover story material exceeding allotted publication space and carried over to an extra line, column, or page

scandal sheet cheap newspaper featuring tawdry stories about celebrities

scoop Informal. major news story published ahead of one's competitors

screamer newspaper headline with extremely sensational slant

second-time rights rights to previously published article or photograph

section part of newspaper covering sports, news, features, advertisements, or finance

senior editor magazine or newspaper editor responsible for specific region, beat, or field

sensationalism extreme reportorial style intended to arouse readership interest based on emotional appeal, often with questionable accuracy

sensationalize (vb) publish news story with undue attention to sensational elements

service piece article offering consumer information for specific industry

sidebar additional material presented alongside major story

silly season late summer news slump that inspires far-fetched news stories

slant angle or approach to coverage of news story

slipsheet paper fitted between freshly printed pages to prevent offsetting

slug one- or two-word label for news story

soft news background or feature stories of general interest

source person supplying information to journalist

sportswriter person who covers sports events for newspaper or magazine

spread article or illustration covering large amount of space, esp. two facing pages

squib filler or short news item

staffer full-time reporter on newspaper

stet Latin. lit. let it stand; proofreader's mark indicating that material marked for deletion should remain

story single article appearing in periodical

stringer part-time reporter for newspaper, often paid by the column-inch

subhead small heading within text of story

Sunday supplement feature magazine insert in Sunday newspaper

syndication service company selling newspaper columns and features to many newspapers

tabloid newspaper characterized by sensationalism; newspaper or journal with small page size, usu. half of regular size

tag attention-grabbing item at end of story

Tass state-owned news agency and wire service of former Soviet Union

tear sheet sheet of newsprint or magazine copy retained for reference

teaser headline that arouses curiosity

thirty mark "30," used to indicate end of story

thumbnail Informal. capsule news story or summary

trade journal magazine catering to specific business, industry, or field

underground press journalism devoted to counterculture and/or radical interests

United Press International UPI; major U.S. news organization that supplies news, photos, and soft features to newspapers and broadcasters by wire service

update follow-up article that brings news story up to date

UPI United Press International

volume year's issues of periodical, esp. bound into single volume

want ad classified advertisement

weekly newspaper or magazine published once a week

Wirephoto *Trademark.* news photograph transmitted by special device over long distances by wire

wire service news agency supplying news stories to newspapers

write-up description of news event; story

yellow journalism newspaper coverage in sensationalized, often irresponsible, style

Newspaper Names (usu. capitalized)

banner bulletin
call, capital, chronicle, clarion, courier
daily, diario, diary, dispatch
enquirer, examiner, exponent
free press
gazette, globe
herald
independent, inquirer, intelligencer
journal
leader, ledger, light,
mail, mercury, messenger, mirror, monitor
news
patriot, post, press
review
sentinel, star, sun
telegraph, times, tribune
union
weekly, world

WAR AND MILITARY

Types and Techniques of Warfare
Soldiers and Military Life
War Machinery and War Zones
Military Ranks
Army, Air Force, and Marines
Navy and Coast Guard

See also: *Chap. 5: Weapons and Armaments;*
Chap. 11: International Relations; Titles of Rank;
Chap. 24: Violence

Types and Techniques of Warfare

abort (*vb*) cancel mission before completion

action military encounter or battle

act of war provocation by one nation of sufficient seriousness to start war

advance attack; forward movement of troops

aggression use of armed force to accomplish goals

air cover use of aircraft to protect ground or naval operations

air raid air strike

air strike attack using airplanes, esp. bombers; air raid

air support bombing used esp. to support ground forces

alert warning of impending attack; readiness for attack

ally army of another nation fighting one's common enemy

amphibious operation military maneuver using troops and vehicles able to travel on land and water

armistice general truce; cessation of war

array battle order; deployment of troops for battle

assault attack

attack sudden, violent armed aggression; assault

balance of terror mutual deterrence from engaging in hostilities based on both sides having relatively equal and devastating destructive capabilities

barrage wave of continuous artillery fire, often protective

barricade obstacle across roadway to prevent enemy advance

battle armed conflict between armies or forces

besiege (*vb*) surround with forces and attack continuously

biological warfare use of toxic organisms to kill and incapacitate enemy; germ warfare

blitzkrieg *German.* lit. lightning war; intense infantry attack spearheaded by tanks and supported by aircraft

bloc group of nations acting together for military and political purposes

blockade action aimed at restricting movement of enemy troops and supplies

bloodbath massacre, slaughter

bombardment attacks by artillery, bombs, or missiles

broken-back war continuing conflict between nations after use of devastating nuclear force

brush-fire war local, quickly escalating war

camouflage colors and materials such as nets, foliage, and special clothing used to make equipment or personnel blend in with natural setting

campaign specific stage or area of war

cannonade bombardment, heavy artillery fire

capability ability to implement military strategies and tactics

capitulation surrender

capture (*vb*) gain control of an area by force

carpet bombing massive bombing of specific area

cease-fire truce; temporary stoppage of attacks

charge sudden, rapid advance on enemy

chemical warfare use of weapons composed of toxic chemicals, generally recognized as illegal

civil defense organized system for protection of lives of noncombatants during wartime

civil war war between factions within one nation

cold war state of international tension with conflict expressed not in armed hostilities but in economic, ideological, and political measures

collateral damage civilian casualties and damage to nonmilitary targets, esp. due to bombing raids

column long, narrow formation deploying troops in lengthwise direction

conflict armed hostilities, including undeclared war

containment policy and actions to prevent expansion of hostile forces or ideology

controlled war warfare conducted according to continuous flow of information to commanders of troops

conventional war war using no nuclear, chemical, or biological weapons

convoy ships or vehicles traveling together for mutual protection

counterattack attack in response to aggressor's attack

counterinsurgency organized activity in opposition to rebels

counterintelligence information gathering and processing to thwart or distort enemy's intelligence efforts

counteroffensive attack in response to enemy aggression

crusade military expedition undertaken with zeal for specific cause

cryptanalysis translation of enemy's secret encoded communications by breaking codes and ciphers

decisive action final battle of war; turning point in campaign

deep interdiction attacks on enemy communication and supply lines far behind battle zone

defeat state of being overcome by superior enemy force

deployment positioning of troops into place in readiness for battle or maneuvers

deterrence steps taken to prevent armed actions

disarmament reduction, by mutual agreement, of armed forces and weapons

dogfight engagement between two or more airplanes

economic warfare offensive or defensive use of trade and financial transactions to gain advantage against hostile forces or nations

electronic warfare use of electronic technology to thwart enemy weapons and disrupt communications

enemy adversary or opponent in military action

engagement battle or encounter with enemy

escalation increase in violence, arsenal, or area of conflict

fail-safe safety plan aimed at deterrence of accidental nuclear attack whereby bomber pilot must receive confirmation of attack plan at preordained stations before proceeding with attack orders

firefight intense, usu. brief, encounter with heavy gunfire between small tactical units

first strike use of one's nuclear weapons before enemy, esp. surprise attack

flying column troops equipped and deployed to move independently of principal unit

formation position of troops for battle or maneuvers

friendly fire artillery or other fire that causes damage or casualties to one's own forces

general warfare large-scale armed conflict between major powers, with national survival at stake

germ warfare biological warfare

give ground retreat

global thermonuclear war general warfare using nuclear weapons resulting in mass destruction and annihilation

ground war attack or operation by infantry and artillery only

guerrilla warfare small-scale military operations conducted inside hostile territory by irregular units

gunboat diplomacy policy employing threat of armed aggression

holding attack aggressive tactic to restrict enemy movement

hostilities instances of armed conflict

hot-line agreement arrangement between United States and former Soviet Union to maintain instant communication line to deal with crisis or accident that might lead to war

house-to-house battle extremely close, hard ground fighting for a city or town that is strongly defended

infiltration passage of troops through gaps in enemy lines

insurgency insurrection

insurrection revolt against existing political structure and power; insurgency

intelligence collection and evaluation of military information regarding enemy

interdiction preventive action that blocks enemy's access to routes, areas, or supplies

international conflict armed hostilities between nations

intervention interference in affairs of another state, esp. insertion of military presence

invasion large-scale assault to take over enemy territory

katabasis retreat or backward march

land power military capability of forces mobilized on land

launch-on-warning policy of firing ballistic missiles immediately on detection of enemy missile attack without waiting for missiles to reach targets before retaliating

laws of war universal ethical guidelines governing basic conduct of forces toward enemies in wartime

limited conventional warfare general warfare without use of nuclear or biological weapons and with observance of voluntary restrictions on both sides; limited strategic warfare

limited strategic warfare limited conventional warfare

local warfare geographically confined conflict

logistics science of planning and executing troop movements, procurement and supply, provision, and related support services

low-intensity conflict isolated acts of violence, esp. hostage taking, terrorism, and counterinsurgency

MAD **M**utually **A**ssured **D**estruction

maneuver movement to place military supplies or personnel in advantageous position

massacre slaughter of many people

mass destruction widespread devastation, loss of life, and sometimes irrecoverable damage caused by conflict

military intervention introduction of armed force into state of tension or disagreement

military posture strength, capability, and readiness of armed forces

military science study of causative factors and tactical principles or warfare

mobilization preparations for war

mutually assured destruction MAD; deterrence based on capacity for total reciprocal annihilation

national security protection of state from external aggression and subversion

neutrality attitude of impartiality during period of tension or armed conflict

nonalignment policy of neutrality in situations of international armed conflict, esp. with respect to United States and other world powers

nuclear club *Informal.* nations possessing nuclear armaments

nuclear nonproliferation policy aimed at control and restriction of acquisition of nuclear weapons by nations that do not have them

nuclear proliferation process of additional nations acquiring nuclear weapons

nuclear stalemate deterrence from use of nuclear weapons based on mutual possession of them

nuclear winter global darkness and extreme cold over prolonged period due to dust cloud blocking sunlight following nuclear holocaust

occupation seizure of and continued presence in another state's territory by military force

offensive aggressive action

operation military action; combat, attack, defense, or maneuver

order of battle orderly disposition of military force in response to identification and assessment of enemy strength

orders military commands

outgoing mail *Slang.* friendly artillery fire

overkill excessive destructive capability beyond what could be required for victory; use of such capability

peaceful coexistence avoidance of armed conflict by adversaries

penetration aggressive advance into enemy territory

phalanx body of troops in close ranks and files

pincers movement maneuver using two-sided attack formation to enclose enemy

pitched battle intense conflict

privateering use of armed vessel by private person against hostile nation

preemptive strike nuclear attack in anticipation of enemy's nuclear attack; preventive strike

preventive strike preemptive strike

proxy war limited war between allies of actual enemies

psychological warfare use of propaganda and pressure to weaken and confuse enemy

Pyrrhic victory military supremacy won at debilitating cost

raid sudden attack on enemy by air on small land force

rear guard unit protecting rear of larger force

reconnaissance movement to gather information about enemy

red alert final stage of readiness when enemy attack appears imminent

regroup (*vb*) change military formation, esp. reorganize after defeat or retreat

retreat forced withdrawal of troops in face of enemy attack

revolutionary war military action aimed at seizing political power, esp. from existing government

rout decisive, overwhelming victory

saber-rattling show or threat of military force, used to intimidate other nations

sabotage destruction or injury to national defense, security, or resources through covert operations

sally rushing forward of troops from defensive position to attack enemy

salvo volley

scorched-earth policy devastation of property and agriculture in a region before abandoning it to enemy

screen protective arrangement of military vehicles and equipment

sea power military capability of naval forces mobilized at sea

second strike retaliatory nuclear attack in wake of first strike

shock tactics use of forceful, sudden assault on enemy

show of force intentional display of military strength to deter enemy action

siege blockade of enemy city or fort to force depletion of resources and ultimate surrender

skirmish brief, inconclusive battle

sortie sudden attack from defensive position; combat air mission

spasm warfare brief, cataclysmic conflict that uses all forces and resources without regard to consequences

strafe (*vb*) attack from the air with gunfire

stratagem tactical maneuver to surprise or deceive enemy

strategic (*adj*) pertaining to overall military power and goals

strategy long-term deployment and use of military forces and national resources with intent to achieve position of advantage

strike attack, esp. preemptive, preventive, first, or second thermonuclear attack; aircraft attack on surface target

subversion action from within to undermine military strength and national security

surge capability ability to generate and maintain greatly amplified military strength

surgical strike precisely planned and executed military attack on specific target area

surprise attack aggressive action that takes enemy by surprise

surrender formal declaration and acceptance of defeat; capitulation

surveillance observation for intelligence purposes, esp. from air or concealed position

sweep rapid movement of forces through area to assume control and eliminate enemy

symbolic attack show of force

tactical (*adj*) pertaining to battlefield operations or any immediate military objective

tactical maneuver purposeful operation involving deployment of forces and weapons in combat

tactics detailed plans and methods used to accomplish specific military objectives

talionic attack equal give-and-take exchange

terrorism employment of unethical tactics and violence in civilian settings, esp. hostage taking and assassination, for political or military advantage

threat declaration of intention and capacity to inflict injury

thrust advance rapidly against opposition

tooth-to-tail ratio proportion of combat forces to administrative or logistical support

total war complete involvement in war effort of nation's military, civilian, economic, and political resources

treason betrayal of one's country, esp. in wartime

trench warfare fighting from makeshift battlefield defenses over prolonged period

triage process of dividing war wounded into groups requiring immediate treatment, delayed treatment, and those beyond treatment

truce temporary cessation of hostilities

unconventional warfare military operations in enemy-held territory; clandestine hostilities and espionage; undeclared warfare; chemical, biological, or nuclear warfare

underground organized resistance to occupying army

vanguard troops at forefront of advancing army, sent to prepare main attack or maneuver

victory military supremacy in wartime or in specific battle

volley simultaneous discharge of numerous weapons; salvo

war sustained, often widespread, armed conflict, esp. between nations

war crimes unethical, criminal behavior and actions contrary to laws of war

warfare armed conflict between nations

war games simulations of battle or military operations that depict possible actual situations, used to test strategy and tactics

war of independence insurrection against colonial or oppressive powers; revolution

wedge troops arrayed in formation that tapers to a point at the front

white flag symbol of surrender

withdrawal retreat; backward movement of troops

wolf pack group of submarines or fighter planes making coordinated attack

world war extensive combat involving many nations around the world

Soldiers and Military Life

active duty full-time military service

adjutant administrative assistant to commanding officer

admiral highest ranking naval officer

aide-de-camp assistant to commanding officer

airborne (*adj*) designating ground forces carried in aircraft

air force military branch of airborne forces

Air Force air force of the United States

airman enlisted member of Air Force or aircrew member in another service branch

all hands alert call in navy

armada fleet of warships

armed forces military personnel and resources used in protection of national interests against enemies and aggressive action against foreign powers

armored division military unit with tanks and other armored vehicles

army major national defense force; military branch of land forces; largest military unit, commanded by general

Army army of the United States

attention erect soldier's posture with heels together, arms at sides, eyes to front

AWOL absent without leave; unauthorized desertion of post or duty

barracks building used to lodge soldiers

basic training initial period of military training for molding recruits into soldiers

battalion tactical unit larger than company and smaller than regiment, commanded by lieutenant colonel

battle fatigue combat fatigue

bells designation for time or hour of day in navy

billet lodging for soldiers; official order to provide such lodging

blockhouse fortified structure; corner of stockade

bluebonnet soldier wearing a blue cap (Scotland)

body count count of enemy dead in battle, often used as morale booster to troops

bombardier member of bomber crew who releases bombs; noncommissioned officer in British artillery

boot camp training facility for recruits

brass *Informal.* officers of rank

break ranks move out of formation

brevet commission providing officer with higher nominal rank than that for which he or she is paid

brig jail on warship or naval base

brigade tactical unit larger than regiment and smaller than division, commanded by colonel

brownshirt Nazi storm trooper before World War II

buck private lowest grade of private

cadet student at military academy

call-up conscription of eligible civilians into military service

camp follower individual who profits off military camp, esp. as prostitute

cannon fodder foot soldiers who are subjected to greatest risk from enemy fire

carabiniere cavalry soldier armed with carbine, esp. in British 6th Dragoon Guards

casern military barracks in garrison town

casualty military person wounded or killed in battle

cavalry troops mounted on horseback

centurion commander of company of one hundred soldiers (ancient Rome)

chaplain military minister

chesseur cavalry or infantry soldier equipped for rapid movement (France)

chevron one of one or more inverted V-shaped stripes, worn on arm by noncommissioned officers

Chief of Naval Operations highest office of U.S. Navy

chief of staff ranking officer serving as commander's chief adviser; highest ranking officer of U.S. Army or Air Force

chief petty officer top-ranking naval noncommissioned officer

chief warrant officer top-ranking noncommissioned officer, below second lieutenant or ensign

close order exact arrangement of troops for drills or march

coast guard military forces that guard coastal waters and maritime traffic

colonel highest field grade rank in army

color guard honor guard that carries flags

column vertical array of troops into line

combat fatigue posttraumatic stress disorder among soldiers engaged in combat; battle fatigue; shell shock

command and control centralized decision-making, intelligence-gathering, and communications system of a military force

commandant senior officer and head of U.S. Marine Corps

commander ranking officer; commissioned naval officer below captain

commander in chief top-ranking leader of armed forces

commanding officer officer in charge of tactical unit

commando soldier specially trained for close combat, raids, and dangerous missions

command post headquarters of commander of military unit

commissary military supermarket and provisions store

commissioned officer military officer holding by commission a rank of second lieutenant or higher

commodore naval rank equivalent to that of brigadier general

company basic army unit, larger than a platoon and smaller than a battalion, commanded by captain and first sergeant

condottiere leader of band of mercenary soldiers (Italy, 14th-15th c.)

conscientious objector person who refuses to serve in armed forces on religious or moral grounds

conscription compulsory registration of selected individuals for military service; draft

corps any unit of soldiers; esp. tactical unit larger than a division and smaller than an army, commanded by lieutenant general

court-martial trial for military crimes presided over by military personnel; (*vb*) try by court-martial

court of inquiry court that inquires into and reports on alleged misconduct but does not pass judgment or impose sentence

C ration combat ration, usu. canned or powdered food

deferment temporary exemption from induction into military service

Delta force U.S. Army elite force trained in antiterrorist tactics

deserter soldier who intentionally abandons his or her post, disappearing from military authority without intention of returning

detail specific assigned task

digger Australian or New Zealand soldier of World War II

Distinguished Service Cross bronze medal awarded by United States for distinguished service in combat

division tactical unit larger than a brigade and smaller than a corps, commanded by major general

dog biscuit *Informal*. hard, dry biscuit, used as emergency ration

dogtag identification piece worn on chain around neck

doolie *Slang*. Air Force Academy cadet

doughboy *Informal*. U.S. infantryman, esp. in World War I

dove person opposed to war

draft conscription

draftee person conscripted into military service

dragoon orig. an infantryman mounted on horse; European cavalryman

drill exercise repeated in training

drill sergeant noncom who trains recruits in basic soldiering

echelon level of military command; military formation in parallel lines

enlist (*vb*) join military of one's own free will

enlisted man nonofficer in U.S. military

enlisted woman female nonofficer in U.S. military

ensign lowest-ranking commissioned officer in U.S. Navy

escadrille squadron on divisional unit of aircraft

evzone member of elite infantry corps (Greece)

executive officer second in command of unit or organization

fall in (*vb*) form up and come to attention as unit

fall out (*vb*) break ranks

fatigues drab uniform worn on fatigue duty, while laboring in camp, or in training

fedayee member of Arab commando unit operating esp. against Israel

field grade officer any mid-level officer, such as a major or colonel

field marshal highest-ranking military officer (Britain); officer of second-highest rank (France)

five-star general highest-ranking general of the U.S. Army

flak bursting shells fired from antiaircraft guns

flank extreme left or right side of array of troops

FLASH precedence code for urgent messages about combat or enemy contact

fleet group of ships under single command

flight basic Air Force unit, consisting of two or more aircraft

flight pay supplementary pay for minimum flight time per month for member of Air Force

flyboy *Informal*. airman

foot soldier infantryman

frag (*vb*) do violence against one's superior officer, esp. with fragmentation grenade

frogman underwater operative equipped with air tanks and wet suit, esp. for salvage, demolition, and reconnaissance

fusilier member of unit formerly armed with flintlock muskets (Britain)

garrison permanent military post or installation

general top-ranking army or air force officer

generalissimo supreme commander of armed forces (Italy, Spain, and Latin America)

ghazi Muslim soldier, esp. one fighting against non-Muslims

GI government issue; common soldier

gob *Slang*. sailor in U.S. Navy

Green Berets Special Forces

ground forces infantry and artillery, excluding naval and air forces

group administrative and tactical unit consisting of two or more battalions or squadrons and their headquarters

grunt *Slang*. low-ranking military man, esp. marine

guard duty duty as sentry

guerrilla member of unofficial or independent fighting unit operating in hostile territory

guidon soldier carrying small flag or streamer for signaling

gunner occupational title in artillery; Marine warrant officer

hawk person supporting war as national policy

high command highest headquarters of military force

hitch *Slang*. period of military service

honor guard ceremonial escort for important person or casket

hoplite heavily armed foot soldier (ancient Greece)

hussar European cavalry soldier, orig. Hungarian light cavalryman (15th c.)

induction act of drafting someone into military service

infantry armed foot soldiers

inspection formal, official scrutiny of assembled troops

insubordination disrespect and disobedience toward any person of higher rank

irregular member of unofficial or independent military unit

janissary soldier in Turkish army

jarhead *Slang*. member of U.S. Marine Corps.

Joint Chiefs of Staff principal military advisory board of U.S. president, including Chiefs of Staff of Army and Air Force, Marine Corps Commandant, and Chief of Naval Operations

kamikaze Japanese pilot who suicidally crashed airplane into target during World War II

kern soldier in Ireland and Scottish Highlands

kitchen police KP; soldiers assigned to assist cooks

KP kitchen police

K ration emergency field ration

lance corporal U.S. Marine enlisted rank between private first class and corporal; *Chiefly Brit*. corporal

leatherneck *Slang*. member of U.S. Marine Corps

legionnaire member of national association of former servicemen; Roman soldier

letter of marque government license to private person to outfit armed ship for warfare

lieutenant lowest-ranking commissioned officer in U.S. Army or Air Force

lifer soldier remaining in military for entire adult life

lines combatant forces on front lines, as distinguished from officers

Luftwaffe *German*. air force, esp. during World War II

marine member of elite branch of military serving in association with navy

Marine Corps branch of U.S. armed forces specially trained for land, sea, and air combat in conjunction with troops of other branches

master sergeant next-to-highest noncommissioned officer in Army, Air Force, and Marine Corps

Medal of Honor highest decoration awarded by United States for bravery in combat at risk of life above and beyond the call of duty

medic *Informal*. medical officer or member of military medical unit

mercenary soldier for hire, not fighting for his or her own nation; soldier of fortune

mess place where meals are prepared and eaten by military personnel; mess hall

mess hall mess

mess kit soldier's personal plate and utensils

MIA missing in action; military person lost in action whose fate is unknown

middie *Informal*. midshipman

midshipman cadet at U.S. Naval Academy; middie

military entire armed forces, its personnel and resources

military police MP; Army unit that fulfills police functions

militia military troops liable for call only during emergency, usu. civilians on nonactive duty

Minuteman member of group of American militia before and during Revolutionary War

mission operational task ordered by command to be completed before reporting back to headquarters

MP military police

muster (*vb*) assemble troops, esp. for inspection or discharge

national guard peacetime military force commanded by governor of each U.S. state, used for police work

navy military branch consisting of sea forces

Navy navy of the United States

Navy Cross decoration for outstanding heroism in U.S. naval operations

NCO noncommissioned officer

noncom *Informal.* noncommissioned officer

noncombatant soldier serving outside combat zone

noncommissioned officer NCO; enlisted person above rank of private, esp. corporal or sergeant; noncom

oak leaf cluster decoration in form of bronze twig with leaves and acorns, signifying second award of same medal to one person

obstacle course rigorous training field in boot camp consisting of various obstacles that must be overcome

officer commissioned military person

olive drab military uniform made of woolen cloth in deep olive color

pandour brutal, marauding soldier, orig. from Croatia

panzer *German.* armored unit with tanks

parade rest position with feet one foot apart, hands clasped behind back, and head forward

paratrooper soldier trained to parachute from airplane

patrol small group of soldiers on reconnaissance

petty officer noncommissioned naval officer

pilot airplane flier

platoon tactical unit larger than a squad and smaller than a company, commanded by lieutenant and sergeants

plebe freshman at military or naval academy

point man soldier who leads a patrol

post exchange PX; department store on base for sales to military personnel and families only

POW prisoner of war

present arms salute position in which rifle in held vertically before chest with muzzle upward

presidio garrison; military post

prisoner of war POW; military person captured and held by enemy forces during war

private soldier of the lowest rank

pull rank exercise the power of one's rank over others

Purple Heart medal awarded by United States for wounds received in action

PX post exchange

quartermaster officer who provides clothes and provisions for troops; petty officer who attends to ship's helm and signals

R and R rest and recreation

ranger soldier specially trained for raids, reconnaissance, and irregular warfare

rank position in military hierarchy

rear echelon troops removed from combat zone who are responsible for administration and matériel

recruit person who recently joined armed forces

recruitment campaign to generate enlistment in armed forces

reenlist (*vb*) rejoin military at end of tour of duty

regiment tactical unit larger than a battalion and smaller than a brigade, commanded by colonel

regular member of standing army

Reserve Officers Training Corps ROTC; body of students being trained at college or university to become officers in armed forces

reserves soldiers not on active duty but subject to call in emergency

reservist member of the reserves

resistance organized opposition to occupying enemy forces

re-up (*vb*) reenlist for another tour of duty

reveille wake-up call, esp. played on bugle or drum

revolutionary person who fights for violent overthrow of existing government

rotate (*vb*) return to home country after period of service overseas

ROTC Reserve Officers Training Corps

sailor enlisted person in naval military service

salute formal gesture of respect, esp. by raising right hand to side of headgear

sapper soldier who builds trenches or tunnels to undermine enemy positions

sarge *Informal.* sergeant

sawbones *Slang.* military surgeon

SEALS sea-air-land forces; special forces of U.S. Navy

section eight dishonorable discharge for physical or emotional incapacity

selective service compulsory military service

sentry soldier standing guard and preventing passage of unauthorized persons

sepoy native infantryman formerly in service of British (India)

sergeant noncommissioned officer in U.S. Army, Air Force, or Marines

serial number identification number given to all military personnel

service period as member of armed forces; military forces, collectively

serviceman member of armed forces

service stripe stripe worn on left sleeve indicating period of time on active duty

shavetail *Slang.* second lieutenant

shell shock combat fatigue

shock troops elite corps trained to lead attack

shore leave permission to leave ship and go ashore in port

shore patrol U.S. Navy personnel having police duties similar to those of military police

situation room area at headquarters through which latest reports are channeled

soldier military fighting person; member of armed forces, esp. army

soldier of fortune mercenary

spahi member of native cavalry in service of French (Algeria)

special forces specially trained elite fighting troops

Special Forces U.S. Army personnel trained to work with indigenous forces engaged in guerrilla warfare and counterinsurgency operations and to conduct unconventional warfare; Green Berets

specialist enlisted person with technical or administrative duties but no command, ranked in four grades comparable to corporal through sergeant first class

Spetznaz special forces (U.S.S.R.)

squad smallest tactical unit, consisting of ten or more people, commanded by staff sergeant

squadron naval or airborne unit, esp. subdivision of fleet; armored cavalry unit; Air Force unit smaller than group, composed of two or more flights

staff officer officer attached to commander's staff

standard any of various military or naval flags

standard-bearer soldier who carries flag

star rank brigadier general or higher, having one or more stars

stockade fortification; military jail

storm trooper member of private Nazi army known for brutality; soldier resembling such Nazis

stripes chevron or strip of cloth on sleeve indicating rank

sutler civilian selling provisions on army post (18th-19th c.)

swabby *Slang.* sailor or deckhand in U.S. Navy or Coast Guard

tactical units subdivision of military; for U.S. Army, from smallest to largest, with commanding officer: squad (staff sergeant), platoon (lieutenant), company or battery (captain), battalion (lieutenant colonel), regiment (colonel), brigade (colonel), division (major general), corps (lieutenant general), army (general)

taps bugle sounded at end of day or at funeral

terrorist military or paramilitary person who employs extreme, unethical, often fanatical methods, esp. hostage taking, assassination, and murder of civilians, to gain political and military advantage

tiger stripes *Slang.* camouflaged uniform worn esp. in tropics

top-secret (*adj*) pertaining to security

classification for information vital to national defense

tour of duty period of time on active military duty; period enlisted for

troops soldiers

uhlan lancer in light-cavalry unit

unit any of various subdivisions of military; tactical unit

Unknown Soldier unidentified soldier killed in combat whose tomb is a memorial to all unidentified dead service personnel

veteran former member of armed forces

vexillary one of a class of veteran soldiers (ancient Rome)

volunteer person who joins the military of his or her own free will

war college military training institution for teaching tactics and strategy of war

war-horse Informal. veteran soldier

warison bugle call to attack

warpath state of preparing for war or hostilities

warrant officer officer ranking above noncommissioned and below commissioned officer, holding rank by certificate

weekend warrior reservist who fulfills military obligation by attending weekend meetings of unit

WIA wounded in action; military person injured in action

wing administrative and tactical unit of U.S. Air Force consisting of two or more groups, headquarters, and support services

wounded soldiers who have been injured in combat

yardbird Slang. untrained soldier assigned to menial task or restricted to limited area for disciplinary reasons

yeoman naval petty officer who performs clerical duties

Zouave member of cavalry formerly in French army, orig. composed of Algerians, known for their dash and Oriental uniforms

War Machinery and War Zones

AAM air-to-air missile

ABC weapons atomic, biological, and chemical weapons

ABM antiballistic missile

air base installation that services air force planes

airburst bomb explosion above ground surface

aircraft carrier large, flat-topped ship used as mobile airstrip

air power collective military strength of a nation in airplanes, bombers, jet fighters, pilots, and airborne technology

all-terrain vehicle vehicle with treads and/or wheels designed to traverse uneven terrain

ammo Informal. ammunition

ammunition projectiles fired from guns, including fuse, charge, and cartridge; any military explosive; ammo

antiaircraft artillery fired from ground or ships against enemy planes

antiballistic missile ABM; missile for interception and destruction of incoming ballistic missiles

antimissile missile ballistic missile used to detect and destroy enemy missiles in flight

antipersonnel (adj) designating weapons intended to maim or kill human beings rather than to damage property and equipment

antitank (adj) designating missile or artillery designed for use against armored vehicles

area of war geographical region involved in armed conflict

armada fleet of warships

armaments military equipment, esp. weapons

armored personnel carrier tracked vehicle with armored hull and light armament, for transporting troops in combat

armory place for storage of arms and equipment, esp. for training of reserves

arms race competitive development and proliferation of weapons, both conventional and nuclear

arsenal storage facility for weapons, sometimes also government manufacturing site for weapons; weapons stored there

artillery projectile-firing weapons

ashcan Slang. depth charge

ASM air-to-surface missile

assault boat portable boat for landing troops on beaches

AWACS Airborne Warning And Control System; sophisticated aircraft with powerful radar and computer, used to track other aircraft

ballistic missile self-propelled missile guided in trajectory ascent and falling freely in descent

barrage balloon one of several balloons anchored around military area to protect it from low-flying aircraft

base permanent center of military operations

battery tactical unit of artillery composed of six guns; two or more artillery pieces; guns on battleship

battlefield area of active armed conflict; battleground

battlefront front

battleground battlefield

battle line line of contact between opposing forces

battleship heavily armed and armored ship designed to shell other ships and shore targets

beachhead shore area in occupied territory seized as landing point for invading troops

beaten zone ground area that is receiving direct fire

bivouac temporary encampment, often with little or no shelter

bomber airplane designed principally to drop bombs

bunker fortified underground chamber of reinforced concrete with slant-sided openings

caisson two-wheeled vehicle for artillery ammunition

cannon large-caliber mounted gun

cheval-de-frise timber or iron barrel topped with spikes and barbed wire, used for defense

clean weapon nuclear bomb producing relatively little fallout

combat drone pilotless aircraft equipped with surveillance cameras, used to monitor battle areas; drone aircraft

combat zone area in which battle is occurring

conventional weapons traditional weapons and warheads, excluding nuclear, biological, and chemical weapons

cross fire gunfire from two or more points located so that lines of fire transect

cruise missile winged, jet-powered guided missile designed to fly low and carry a warhead

D-day day of planned military operation; June 6, 1944, day of Allied invasion of western Europe in World War II

decoy device that misleads soldier or weapon as to its target

defensive weapons armaments used for protection from attack

defoliating agent chemical that causes foliage to die, thus exposing hidden enemy

delivery system device, such as a missile, for transporting warhead to target

demilitarized zone DMZ; area forbidden to military installations and operations, often between opposing lines

depth charge powerful explosive dropped from ship or airplane that explodes underwater

destroyer speedy warship with guns, torpedoes, and depth charges

direct fire line-of-sight gunfire, esp. from close range

dirty bomb nuclear weapon producing large amount of fallout

DMZ demilitarized zone

drone aircraft combat drone

field area of active operations or combat, usu. away from command headquarters

field artillery mobile artillery that accompanies troops in combat

fighter plane small, maneuverable military plane equipped with automatic guns to attack other planes

fire-and-forget weapons electronically programmed weapons that require no human intervention to find targets and detonate

firepower amount of gunfire or explosives deliverable by weapon or armed forces unit

flank left or right section of army; wing

fleet organized unit of ships, aircraft, and marine troops under one administrative command

fort fortified structure occupied by troops, often surrounded by ditch, moat, rampart, or parapet

foxhole hastily dug pit for protection from enemy gunfire

fratricide nuclear warhead explosion that causes disturbance large enough to prematurely detonate other incoming warheads

front point of contact between two enemy forces; battlefront; battle line

ground zero area directly beneath a nuclear explosion

gunnery design, construction, and firing of heavy guns

half-track armored vehicle with rear driving wheels on caterpillar treads

hard base launching base protected against nuclear attack

H-hour specific hour of D-day when operation begins

hunter-killer operation offensive antisubmarine action

ICBM intercontinental ballistic missile

interceptor fighter plane utilized to divert or shoot down attacking enemy planes; missile used to explode incoming enemy missiles

intercontinental ballistic missile ICBM; rocket-propelled missile carrying warhead at long ranges

jump jet jet aircraft capable of nearly vertical takeoff that requires little or no airstrip

laager German. military camp or defensive position protected by circle or armored vehicles

land-based missile missile fired from site on land rather than air or sea

landing force amphibious assault unit

line military formation with several elements abreast of one another, esp. in closest contact with enemy

Maginot line line of fortifications built along French eastern frontier prior to World War II; any elaborate line of defense

matériel arms, ammunition, and other equipment

medevac helicopter used to evacuate wounded from battlefield

minefield area filled with hidden explosive charges

Minuteman ICBM with nuclear warhead

missile pilot, jet- or rocket-powered vehicle for delivering nuclear or conventional warhead

mobile missile launcher large truck and trailer used to launch missiles, allowing launch site to change rapidly

MRV multiple reentry vehicle

multiple reentry vehicle MRV; ballistic missile with two or more warheads

mustard gas oily liquid used as chemical weapon that causes blisters, blindness, and often death

MX ICBM with multiple nuclear warheads, capable of attack against bases, often concealed in underground silo

nerve gas often odorless and colorless, poisonous, easily absorbed liquid that interferes with nervous system and inhibits respiration

nonnuclear weapons tactical weapons

nuclear weapons bombs using atomic fission or fusion to create massive radiation doses and often irrecoverable damage to environment and property

occupied territory area under control of hostile armed forces

ordnance explosives, bombs, and ammunition

paramilitary forces troops similar to but separate from regular armed forces

paravane toothed, torpedo-shaped, protective device used by ship to cut moorings of underwater mines

payload warhead

poison gas nerve gas or other chemical weapon

position arrangement and disposition of troops at given time

redoubt secure, defended position; small, temporary, defensive enclosure

round cartridge or shell for single shot

SADARM sense-and-destroy armor

SAM surface-to-air missile

SDI Strategic Defense Initiative

sense-and-destroy armor SADARM; sensor-fused smart weapon

silo underground installation of concrete and steel that houses ballistic missile and mechanism for launching it

situation map map showing military plans and operations

SLBM submarine-launched ballistic missile

smart weapons steerable bombs and missiles electronically programmed to find target, esp. by heat detection

soft base target or launching base not protected against nuclear attack

spoils goods or property of defeated party claimed by victor

Star Wars program to use earth- and space-based weapons and technology to detect, intercept, and destroy enemy missiles; Strategic Defense Initiative

stealth technology use of special design and materials to enable aircraft to evade detection, esp. by radar

sternutator respiratory irritant used as chemical weapon

stinkpot jar of combustibles that generate noxious odors, formerly used as weapon

Strategic Defense Initiative SDI; Star Wars

strategic weapons weapons intended to attack enemy's military and industrial facilities

strike configured weapons delivery system arranged to carry out strike mission

stronghold fortified position secure from enemy attack

tactical aircraft planes providing air attack in support of ground forces

tactical weapons armaments designed for limited or specific purposes, usu. nonnuclear weapons

tank heavily armed, turreted, armored vehicle that moves on two continuous steel belts

target area, object, or installation destined to be destroyed by bomb or missile

theater geographical area of warfare

trench long cut in ground with excavated earth thrown up in front to protect troops

triphibian (adj) designed or equipped to operate on land, water, or in air

turret low, armored, revolving structure for guns on fortress, warship, airplane, or tank

vesicant burning and blistering agent used in chemical warfare

warhead part of missile or rocket that contains explosive charge of nuclear, toxic, or detonating substance; payload

war machine military hierarchy, infrastructure, weapons, technology, equipment, and personnel working together to wage war

war zone combat area

weapons of mass destruction nuclear, chemical, biological, and radiological weapons of massive lethal strength

weapons system general type of weapon, esp. related series of weapons

wing left or right section of army or fleet; flank

wooden bomb Informal. reliable, stable, easily stored bomb

yield force of nuclear explosion, measured in equivalent tons of TNT

Military Ranks (in descending order)

ARMY, AIR FORCE, AND MARINES

general of the army (5-star)
marshal (Europe)
general (4-star)
lieutenant general (3-star)
major general (2-star)
brigadier general (1-star)
colonel
lieutenant colonel
major
captain
first lieutenant
second lieutenant
chief warrant officer (W-4)
chief warrant officer (W-3)
chief warrant officer (W-2)
warrant officer (W-1)
sergeant major
first sergeant
chief master sergeant
master sergeant
sergeant first class
specialist 7
gunnery sergeant
technical sergeant
staff sergeant
specialist 6
sergeant
specialist 5
corporal
specialist 4
lance corporal
private first class (PFC)
airman first class
private
airman
recruit
cadet

NAVY AND COAST GUARD

fleet admiral
admiral
vice admiral
rear admiral

commodore
captain
commander
lieutenant commander
lieutenant
lieutenant junior grade
ensign
chief warrant officer (W-4)
chief warrant officer (W-3)
chief warrant officer (W-2)
master chief petty officer
senior chief petty officer
chief petty officer
petty officer 1st class
petty officer 2nd class
petty officer 3rd class
seaman
seaman apprentice
seaman recruit
midshipman

INTERNATIONAL RELATIONS
Diplomacy and Diplomats
World Relations and Conditions
Security and Defense
Espionage and Intelligence

See also: *Chap. 11: Government; Law; War and Military; Chap. 12: Business and Economics; Finance*

Diplomacy and Diplomats

accord formal agreement; treaty

agent-general respective of a British dominion to England; chief representative

alliance agreement of mutual support between independent states

ally state or ruler associated with another by treaty

ambassador highest-ranking diplomatic officer

ambassador-at-large high-ranking diplomat not assigned to one particular foreign state

amnesty pardon granted to individual or group by government

annexation acquisition of another state or territory by a sovereign state

Anschluss political or economic union between nations, esp. Austria and Germany in 1938

asylum protection, esp. from extradition, given political refugees by state or agency with diplomatic immunity

attaché official of nondiplomatic government department attached to diplomatic post

bilateralism agreement between two nations to pursue common interests of mutual benefit

bloc group of aligned nations

cahier report of proceedings of any body

cartel international group joined together for common political or economic purpose; agreement between belligerents

chancellery office and personnel of embassy or consulate

chargé d'affaires envoy sent to state to which higher level diplomat is not sent; diplomat of lowest class who takes charge of business

during temporary absence of ambassador or minister

communiqué official statement issued by parties at meeting

compact agreement between two or more states

compromise accord reached by mutual concession

concession yielding on some point so as to reach agreement

concord harmonious agreement among nations

concordat official agreement or compact; agreement to which pope is one party

confederation alliance or league of nations

consul official sent by one state to another to protect and assist its nationals in commercial relations

consular agent consular officer of lowest rank

consulate office or position of consul; premises occupied by consul

consul general top-ranking consul in key station or having authority over several consulates

convention general agreement among states regarding matters of common concern, less binding than treaty

courier diplomat bearing confidential documents

covenant formal, binding agreement between two or more nations

delegate representative of nation at conference or meeting

deputy substitute or assistant who assumes authority in absence of diplomatic superior

detainee person held for questioning, esp. civilian in wartime or political deserter

détente lessening of world tension

diplomacy art and practice of conducting international relations

diplomat political representative of one national government to another, appointed to conduct official negotiations and maintain relations between the two governments

diplomatic corps diplomatic personnel in residence in another state

diplomatic immunity special exemption from foreign laws afforded to diplomatic corps

diplomatic mission term served at foreign mission by diplomat; diplomat and his or her staff

diplomatic pouch case or package in which messages and information are transported

diplomatic privilege diplomatic mission's exemption from local jurisdiction

diplomatic recognition official acknowledgment of nation's sovereignty and legitimacy of its government

diplomatic service body of professional diplomats

dispatch message sent by diplomat from foreign post to home government

doctrine proclamation of basic governmental policy in international affairs

dollar diplomacy diplomatic activities to

increase economic power of nation in foreign states

embassy ambassador's mission, entourage, and official residence in foreign nation

emissary representative, sometimes secret agent

entente international agreement of friendship or alliance, usu. stipulating common course of action; parties to such an agreement

envoy diplomatic agent of any rank

exequatur written recognition and empowerment of consul by government of nation in which he or she is stationed

extradition return of criminal to officers of state in which crime was committed

foreign office government ministry managing foreign affairs

foreign policy system of methods and objectives for maintaining relations with other states

foreign service diplomatic and consular staffs of one nation serving abroad

General Assembly highest deliberative body of United Nations, with representatives from all member nations

Geneva Convention internationally recognized rules for treatment of dead, wounded, and prisoners of war

head of state president, prime minister, sovereign, or other titular ruler of nation

high seas oceans and connecting waters not within territorial jurisdiction of any state

international affairs conduct and course of relations between two or more sovereign states

International Court of Justice judicial agency of United Nations that arbitrates disputes between nations; World Court

international law set of rules governing interactions of nations

international relations branch of political science concerned with military, economic, and diplomatic affairs between states

internuncio papal legate ranking below nuncio

interpreter person who provides oral translation between speakers of different languages such as diplomats from different nations

league association of nations with common purpose

League of Nations post-World War I organization of nations dedicated to promoting peace

legate emissary from one nation to another

legation diplomatic mission sent to foreign state; offices of diplomatic staff

minister diplomatic agent of second rank

minister plenipotentiary diplomat ranking below ambassador but wielding full powers

mission party sent overseas to conduct specific negotiations; permanent legation in foreign state

nuncio top-ranking papal legate to civil government

pact international agreement or treaty

passport official certificate issued to citizen by a government affirming his or her nationality and allowing foreign travel

power politics nationalistic policy based on military and economic coercion

protocol preliminary diplomatic agreement or records of diplomatic conference that form basis for final treaty

secretary-general principal officer of United Nations; principal officer of a secretariat

secretary of state appointed official who supervises department conducting U.S. foreign affairs

Security Council permanent peacekeeping council of United Nations, composed of five permanent and ten rotating two-year members

shuttle diplomacy negotiations between two hostile states conducted by intermediary traveling back-and-forth between them

sovereign immunity autonomy and independence of each sovereign state under international law

sovereign state self-governing, autonomous nation

sovereignty independence from external control by another nation

State Department U.S. executive department responsible for conduct of foreign affairs

statesman national leader with international respect

statesmanship exercise of astute national leadership based on world vision

summit conference of highest level officials from two or more states

three-mile limit ocean waters within three miles of coast considered part of national territory

trade mission delegates to foreign state seeking economic cooperation

treaty international agreement

trust territory nonself-governing region under authority of United Nations prior to becoming independent

United Nations post-World War II organization of nearly all nations dedicated to peace, economic development, and social welfare

vice-consul diplomatic officer subordinate to consul

vice-legate diplomatic officer subordinate to legate

visa license issued by nation permitting entry by foreigner, usu. in form of endorsement stamped in passport

World Court International Court of Justice

World Relations and Conditions

alien resident of a state who is not a citizen or national of that state

amity international friendship or accord

appeasement unilateral concessions as means of pacifying hostile nation

balance of power world equilibrium in which no single power predominates

Balkanize (vb) divide a territorial entity into smaller, often hostile, units

bamboo curtain symbol of Chinese Communist ideological and political barrier to West

banana republic small Latin American state, dependent on foreign investment, often governed by despot

banishment expulsion from or relegation to a country or region by authoritative decree; exile

border national territorial demarcation

carnet customs document allowing automobile to be driven across international border at no cost

client state nation that is dependent on richer, more powerful nation for its political, economic, or military welfare

colonialism control of one state over other dependent territories or states

colonization acquisition and maintenance of dependent colonies

colony territory and citizens of state dependent on another state

Common Market European Economic Community

compatriot fellow countryman

country nation; fatherland; state

crown colony British colony without constitution or representative government, controlled directly by crown

customs duty tax on goods imported into country

decolonize (vb) allow a colony to become self-governing

dependency subject territory that is not an integral part of ruling country

deport (vb) expel, esp. an alien, from one country

destabilize (vb) take actions that render a government unable to function

developed nation industrialized state with well-developed economy and high standard of living

developing nation poor state in process of industrializing, with low standard of living

domain territory governed by single ruler or government; realm

dominion territory over which single government rules; sovereign authority over such territory

domino theory belief that unsuccessful containment, esp. of communism, in one state will be repeated in neighboring states

dual citizenship status of person who is legal citizen of two or more countries

EEC European Economic Community

embargo governmental prohibition on export of goods to specific foreign state

emigrant one who emigrates from native state

emigration departure of citizen of one state so as to become citizen of another

enclave territory completely enclosed by another state

European Economic Community EEC; cooperative economic partnership among states of western Europe, esp. for trade and finance; Common Market

exile compulsory or voluntary departure from

homeland due to differences with government; banishment

expatriation citizen's voluntary renunciation of national allegiance

extraterritoriality right of state to extend its jurisdiction over its nationals into territory of another state

fatherland one's native country or that of one's ancestors; motherland

foreign affairs relations of one nation with others

foreign aid assistance, esp. economic, given to poorer nation by richer one

free trade international commerce without restrictive tariffs

frontier national boundary

geopolitics study of connections between geography and relations among nations

glasnost *Russian.* Soviet policy of openness about internal affairs and receptivity to Western influence during 1980's

global (adj) pertaining to entire world

global economy interrelated trade and development factors that affect all nations

global interdependence impact of each nation's foreign policy on all other states

globalism involvement of a country in international affairs and alliances, opposite of isolationism

Good Neighbor Policy U.S. policy toward Latin American states that pledges friendship and unified hemispheric defense

Great Power a nation that is predominant in international affairs

hegemony influence or authority of one nation over others

human rights basic freedoms and welfare of all world citizens, with which governments have no rights to interfere

IMF International Monetary Fund

immigrant one who immigrates into foreign state

immigration movement into country by noncitizens with intent to settle

imperialism policy of extending rule over other states

imperium area of dominion or empire; sphere of control

incident seemingly minor occurrence between nations that can lead to serious consequences

international (adj) that which involves two or more sovereign states

International Bank for Reconstruction and Development World Bank

internationalism principle of cooperation among nations to promote the common good

International Monetary Fund IMF; agency that promotes trade and development through contributions from member nations

iron curtain symbol of Soviet ideological and political isolation from West after World War II

irredenta territory historically or culturally related to one state but presently subjected to another

isolationism policy that peace and economic growth are best achieved by abstaining from alliances with and commitments to other nations

Manifest Destiny doctrine that it is U.S. destiny to expand territory in North America (19th c.)

ministate small, independent nation

Monroe Doctrine early 19th-century U.S. policy that opposed outside interference in Americas

most-favored-nation (*adj*) pertaining to treaty signatory that is accorded most favorable commercial benefits by another nation

motherland one's native country or that of one's ancestors; fatherland

nation people who share specific territory, have common customs, history, language, and culture, and are organized under a single government; country; sovereign state

national noncitizen who owes allegiance to a nation and enjoys its protection

nationalism allegiance to one's sovereign state

nationality status of citizenship in particular nation by birth or naturalization; people sharing common culture, organized to constitute sovereign state

national supremacy absolute military and economic power of one nation

nation-state sovereign state inhabited by fairly homogeneous group of people who share feeling of common nationality

naturalization process, other than by birth, through which citizenship is attained

nonaligned nation country not siding with one of the Great Powers

OAS Organization of American States

OPEC Organization of Petroleum Exporting Countries

open door policy of equal and impartial trade opportunities for all foreign nations

Organization of American States OAS; group that promotes cooperation and trade among nations of Latin America

Organization of Petroleum Exporting Countries OPEC; policy and price-setting cartel of oil-producing nations

patriotism love for or devotion to one's country

power politics nationalistic policy based on military and economic coercion

protectionism policy of restrictions on imported foreign goods to support domestic business

realm sphere of dominance, esp. royal domain over which monarch rules

reciprocity trade policy based on mutual benefit to both nations through exchange of special privileges

refugee one who has fled or been driven from his or her country to avoid persecution or danger

refusenik Soviet citizen refused permission to emigrate

sanction coercive economic or military action taken by one or several nations against another

sovereign state nation having supreme and independent power or authority in government

sphere of influence influence exerted by a Great Power over nearby states

state independent, sovereign nation

superpower extremely powerful nation with worldwide influence

suzerain nation controlling another state's foreign affairs

tariff government duty on imported goods

territorial waters waters, traditionally within 3 miles (4.8 km) of its shore, that are regarded as under jurisdiction of a state

territory geographical area under authority of single national government; area under U.S. authority that is not actually a state

thalassocracy dominion over the seas, esp. in trade

Third World underdeveloped nations of Asia, Africa, and South America

trade balance equilibrium of imports and exports between nations

World Bank international bank that makes loans to developing nations; International Bank for Reconstruction and Development

world power nation whose actions affect entire world

Security and Defense

Allies nations united against central European powers in World War I, or against Axis powers in World War II

angary international law permitting state at war to seize or destroy property of neutrals

antiterrorism strategy and actions to offset terrorism

Arab League confederation of Arab states formed in 1945 to promote unity and cooperation

armistice suspension of military operations between belligerents

arms control international agreements and diplomacy designed to regulate or stabilize use of weapons and armed forces

arms race competition between nations in building and stockpiling weapons to attain military superiority

atomic age period in history initiated by first use of atomic bomb and characterized by various uses of atomic energy

atomic power status of any nation that possesses nuclear weapons

Axis Germany, Italy, and Japan, opponents of Allies in World War II

belligerent nation at war that has been granted status in international law subjecting it to obligations and laws of war

big stick intimidation of smaller nations by threat of military intervention

brinkmanship tactic of maneuvering a dangerous situation to the limits of safety

buffer state small, neutral state separating two belligerents

capitulation act or terms of surrender

chauvinism excessive patriotism or nationalism

coexistence avoidance of warfare among hostile states

Cold War post-World War II ideological conflict between the United States and Soviet Union, conducted without direct military action

collective security multinational system in which members of alliance pledge mutual support against aggressors

containment policy that seeks to restrict influence of nation by confining it geographically

détente lessening of world tension

deterrence maintenance of large military arsenal to discourage belligerents from attacking

disarmament abolition, reduction, or limitation of arms

dove advocate of compromise and negotiation; supporter of peace and disarmament

enemy opposing state in war

escalation dynamic increase in tension, hostility, and conflict

first strike preemptive nuclear attack

hawk supporter of warlike defense posture

insurgency status in international law given to revolutionaries who possess insufficient organization to be granted the status of belligerency

irenic (*adj*) conducive to peaceful relations

jingoism aggressive, militaristic national policy

limited war hostilities conducted without resorting to use of nuclear weapons

massive retaliation use of nation's nuclear arsenal in response to attack

militarism belligerent international posture of intervention and intimidation

mutual-defense treaty agreement among nations to provide military assistance to any member coming under attack

national security nation's system of protection from foreign infiltration or attack

National Security Council NSC; U.S. executive agency that deals with defense, intelligence, and foreign affairs

NATO North Atlantic Treaty Organization; post-World War II organization formed among Western nations for mutual defense against Soviet aggression

neutrality state of impartiality and abstention from hostility in time of war

nonaggression pact pledge to refrain from acts of war

nonaligned state country not allied with one of prime belligerents

North Atlantic Treaty Organization NATO

NSC National Security Council

peaceful coexistence willingness or intention of belligerent nations to avoid armed conflict

peace offensive intensive diplomatic effort to achieve peace

piracy act of violence or theft committed at sea

police action localized military action undertaken without formal declaration of war, esp. against violators of international law

preparedness state of adequate advance planning for potential war

rapprochement reestablishment of friendly relations between hostile nations

reprisal retaliatory force short of war

revanche policy of regaining areas that have been lost to other states as result of war

sabotage action intended to disrupt or destroy nation's military or economic capabilities

SEATO Southeast Asia Treaty Organization; post-World War II alliance between United States and small Asian nations to protect those nations from Communist influence or attack

security measures taken to ensure national freedom from espionage, sabotage, and military attack

Southeast Asia Treaty Organization SEATO

state of war condition or period marked by armed conflict between nations, which are subject to international laws of war

strategic nuclear weapons long-range nuclear weapons capable of destroying enemy's civilian and military targets

tactical nuclear weapons nuclear weapons intended for specific, limited purpose

terrorism covert violent acts used to influence national policies

treason acts intended to overthrow government of one's own nation

truce temporary suspension of hostilities

war armed conflict between sovereign states

Warsaw Pact post-World War II organization formed by Soviet Union and eastern European nations for mutual protection from the United States and NATO states

West non-Communist countries of Europe and the Americas

Espionage and Intelligence

agent one engaged in intelligence operations

Central Intelligence Agency CIA; covert intelligence gathering agency of U.S. government since World War II

CIA Central Intelligence Agency

cipher secret code used in diplomatic communications

collaboration cooperation with enemy of one's state, esp. an occupying force

collaborator traitor who works with enemy state

Company *Informal.* Central Intelligence Agency

counterespionage spying intended to offset enemy espionage

counterintelligence actions intended to deceive or misinform enemy intelligence service and halt sabotage

counterspy one engaged in counterespionage

courier spy bearing secret documents

covert (*adj*) secret, hidden

disinformation deliberately false information, esp. about one's military strength or plans, released to confuse enemy government

double agent spy working for two opposed states

espionage spying to obtain information about plans and activities of foreign government

Football *Slang.* briefcase containing codes and options for use by U.S. President in launching nuclear attack

infiltration subtle or covert subversive involvement in another nation's affairs

intelligence political, military, economic, or other information about another state

intelligence agency government department engaged in obtaining secret information about other states

Interpol *Inter*national Criminal *Police* Organization; international criminal investigative organization

joe *Slang.* espionage operative, usu. recruited from outside service

laundered money illicit funds given the appearance of legitimacy by passing through hands of third party

listening post location used for obtaining secret information about an enemy

mole undercover agent, esp. one who infiltrates another nation's intelligence agency

quisling traitor, collaborator with enemy

reconnaissance covert intelligence gathering, esp. regarding enemy military capabilities

safe house secret location where individuals may hide or plot sabotage and terrorism

secret agent spy, undercover operative

spy one who acts in a clandestine manner to obtain secret information about other states

spying secret intelligence-gathering activities against another nation

traitor person disloyal to his or her own nation

TITLES OF RANK

See also: *Chap. 11: Government; Politics; War and Military; International Relations; Chap. 12: Occupations; Chap. 13: Education; Chap. 20: Terms of Endearment and Respect; Chap. 25: Religion*

abbé French secular clergyman

abbot superior of men's monastery

admiral highest-ranking commissioned naval officer; naval commander in chief

aga general or leader in Ottoman Empire

alcalde chief administrative and judicial officer of Spanish town

alderman member of municipal council; magistrate ranking below mayor in English or Irish city

ambassador highest diplomatic representative of government serving as resident agent to foreign government or sovereign; special, temporary diplomatic representative

amir emir

archbishop bishop at head of ecclesiastical province

archduchess wife or widow of archduke; woman holding rank of archduke in her own right

archduke sovereign prince of imperial family in Austria

archimandrite dignitary of Eastern Orthodox Church ranking below bishop; superior of monastery or group of monasteries

archon chief magistrate in ancient Greece; presiding officer

armiger squire entitled to bear heraldic arms

ataman elected chief of Cossack village in Russia; hetman

atheling Anglo-Saxon prince or nobleman; heir apparent

ayatollah religious leader among Shiite Muslims, esp. one who is not an imam

banneret knight leading vassals into battle under his own banner, ranking above knight bachelor

baron lowest grade of peerage in Great Britain; continental European nobleman; lowest order of nobility in Japan

baroness wife or widow of baron; woman holding rank of baron in her own right

baronet peerage rank below baron and above knight

bashaw pasha

beefeater yeoman of the guard of English monarch

bey provincial governor of Ottoman Empire; title of respect in Turkey and Egypt

bishop high-ranking Anglican, Eastern Orthodox, or Roman Catholic clergyman having authority over other clergy and usu. governing a diocese

boyar Russian aristocrat ranking below ruling prince

brigadier general commissioned military officer with one star, ranking above colonel

brother male member of religious organization having a priesthood

burgomaster chief magistrate of certain European towns

burgrave hereditary governor of castle or town (Germany)

cacique native Indian chief in areas dominated primarily by Spanish culture; local political boss in Spain and Latin America

caliph spiritual head of Islam

capo chief of branch of Mafia family

captain commissioned army officer ranking above lieutenant and below major; naval officer with command of ship, ranking above commander and below commodore or admiral

cardinal highest official of Roman Catholic Church below pope

castellan governor or warden of castle or fort

catholicos primate of Eastern Orthodox Church, esp. Armenian

caudillo head of state in Spanish-speaking country, esp. military dictator

centurion commanding officer of century unit in ancient Rome

chamberlain chief officer in household of king or nobleman

chancellor secretary of nobleman, prince, or king; chief secretary of embassy

chaplain clergyman in charge of chapel or

attached to branch of military, institution such as a college, important family, or royal court

chatelaine wife of castellan

chevalier lowest rank of French nobility, comparable to knight

chief justice presiding judge of court having several members, esp. Supreme Court

colonel commissioned military officer ranking above lieutenant colonel and below brigadier general

commander in chief supreme commander of nation's military forces

commissar Communist party official assigned to military unit to teach and ensure party loyalty

commodore former commissioned officer in navy ranking above captain and below rear admiral

constable warden or governor of royal castle or fortified town; police officer

consul either of two annually elected chief magistrates in ancient Rome

consul general highest-ranking consular officer

corporal noncommissioned military officer ranking above private first class and below sergeant

count European nobleman corresponding to British earl; former name for British earl

countess wife or widow of earl or count; woman holding title of earl or count in her own right

crown prince heir apparent to crown or throne

crown princess wife of crown prince; female heir apparent or presumptive to crown or throne

czar emperor of Russia until 1917 revolution; tsar

czarevitch son and heir of czar

czarevna daughter of czar or wife of czar's son

czarina empress of Russia, wife of czar

daimyo Japanese feudal baron

Dalai Lama former ruler and chief monk of Tibet, believed to be reincarnation of Buddhist saint

dame wife or daughter of lord; female member of order of knighthood

dauphin eldest son of king of France

deacon Roman Catholic cleric ranking below priest; layman elected by church to fulfill pastoral or administrative duties

dean Roman Catholic priest supervising one district or diocese

dewan prime minister of East Indian state

dey ruling official of Ottoman Empire in northern Africa

doge chief magistrate in republics of Venice and Genoa

Don Spanish title equivalent to Mr. or Sir, prefixed to man's given name; Spanish nobleman or gentleman

Dona Portuguese title equivalent to Madam or Lady, prefixed to woman's given name

Doña Spanish title equivalent to Madam or Lady, prefixed to woman's given name

dowager widow holding property and title from deceased husband

duce *Italian.* leader; title of Benito Mussolini

duchess wife or widow of duke; woman holding ducal title in her own right

duke European nobleman of highest hereditary rank; member of highest rank of British peerage, ranking above marquis

earl British peer ranking below marquis and above viscount, formerly called count

effendi member of aristocracy or government official in Turkey

Elector one of German princes entitled to elect emperor of Holy Roman Empire

emeritus (*adj*) honorary title held after retirement and corresponding to that held during active service

eminence person of high rank or attainment, esp. Roman Catholic cardinal

emir native ruler in parts of Asia and Africa; amir

emperor sovereign or supreme monarch of an empire

empress wife or widow of emperor; woman who holds imperial title in her own right

ensign commissioned naval officer ranking below lieutenant

equerry officer of prince or noble charged with care of horses; attendant to British monarch

esquire member of English gentry ranking below knight

eupatrid hereditary aristocrat of ancient Greece

exarch Byzantine viceroy; Eastern Orthodox bishop ranking below patriarch and above metropolitan

excellency title for certain high dignitaries of state and church

Führer *German.* leader; used chiefly in reference to Adolf Hitler

general highest commissioned military officer, ranking above lieutenant general

generalissimo chief commander of army

gentry condition or rank of being a gentleman

governor official elected or appointed to act as ruler, chief executive, or nominal head of political unit

governor general one who governs large territory or has deputy governors under him

Graf *German.* count; title of nobility equivalent to British earl

grand duchess wife or widow of grand duke; woman who holds rank of grand duke in her own right

grand duke sovereign duke of certain European states

grandee man of eminence and social status, esp. Spanish or Portuguese nobleman

gunnery sergeant Marine Corps noncommissioned officer equivalent to first sergeant

hakim Muslim ruler, governor, or judge

headmaster man heading staff of private school

headmistress woman heading staff of private school

heir apparent next in line to title whose right to inheritance is indefeasible in law if he survives legal ancestor

heir presumptive next in line to title whose right to inheritance may be eliminated by birth of nearer relative

herald official of tournament of arms; ambassador acting as messenger between leaders during war

hetman Cossack leader; ataman

hidalgo member of Spanish lower nobility

high commissioner principal or high-ranking commissioner; ambassadorial representative of government of one nation stationed in another

highness title of address for person of exalted rank

high priest chief priest of Jewish Levitical priesthood; priest of Melchizedek priesthood in Mormon Church

high priestess chief female priest, esp. of ancient orders

imam Islamic ruler claiming descent from Muhammad and exercising spiritual and temporal leadership over region

incumbent holder of office or ecclesiastical benefice

infanta daughter of Spanish or Portuguese monarch

inspector general officer of military or naval corps of inspectors that investigates organizational matters

jarl Scandinavian noble ranking just below king

judge magistrate charged with administration of justice in court of law

junker member of Prussian landed aristocracy

justice judge or magistrate

kaiser emperor; ruler of Germany from 1871 to 1918

khan local chieftain or man of rank in countries of central Asia

khedive title of ruler of Egypt from 1867 to 1914, governing as viceroy of Turkish sultan

king male monarch of major territorial unit, usu. holding hereditary title and ruling for life

knight man honored by sovereign for merit, ranking in Great Britain below baronet

lady woman having proprietary rights or authority as feudal superior

ladyship title of address for woman having rank of lady

laird landed proprietor (Scotland)

lama Tibetan Buddist priest or monk

lance corporal enlisted man in Marine Corps ranking above private first class

landgrave count having jurisdiction over large territory; title of certain German princes

legate deputy or emissary

lieutenant official empowered to act for higher official; lowest ranking commissioned military officer

lieutenant colonel military officer ranking below colonel

lieutenant commander naval officer ranking below commander

lieutenant general commissioned military officer with three stars, ranking above major general

lieutenant governor deputy or subordinate governor

lord ruler by hereditary right or preeminence to whom service and obedience are due; holder of feudal tenure

madame title for woman of rank or office; French prefix for married woman

mademoiselle French prefix for unmarried woman

magistrate official entrusted with administration of laws; principal official exercising governmental powers over major political unit

magnifico Venetian nobleman

maharajah Hindu prince ranking above raja; also maharaja

maharani wife of maharajah; Hindu princess ranking above rani; also maharanee

maître d' maître d'hotel; majordomo; headwaiter

majesty form of address for reigning sovereign power, authority, or dignitary

major commissioned officer in military ranking above captain and below lieutenant colonel

majordomo man having charge of a large household; head steward; maître d'

major general commissioned military officer holding two stars, ranking above brigadier general

malik *Arabic.* king, leader

manciple steward or purveyor for college or monastery

mandarin public official of Chinese Empire

marchesa Italian woman holding rank of marchese

marchese Italian nobleman next in rank above count

marchioness wife or widow of marquis or marchese; woman holding title of marchesa in her own right; marquise

margrave military governor of German border province; German nobleman corresponding to British marquis

marquess marquis

marquis British peer ranking below duke and above earl; hereditary European or Japanese nobleman; marquess

marquise marchioness

marshal general officer of highest military rank; municipal or federal law enforcement officer; administrative head of police or fire department

master-at-arms petty officer charged with maintaining discipline aboard ship

master sergeant highest noncommissioned army officer, ranking above staff sergeant or sergeant major

mayor official elected or appointed to act as chief executive or nominal head of city or borough

metropolitan primate of ecclesiastical province

mikado emperor of Japan

milady term of address for Englishwoman of noble or gentle birth

milord term of address for Englishman of noble or gentle birth

minister Christian Protestant clergyman; diplomatic representative below ambassador; cabinet-level officer administering specific ministry in government

minister plenipotentiary plenipotentiary

miss conventional title for young unmarried woman

mister Mr.; conventional title for man not entitled to rank, honorific, or professional title

Mogul sovereign of 16th-century empire founded in India by conquering groups of Mongol, Turkish, and Persian origin

monarch hereditary sovereign or constitutional ruler of kingdom or empire

monseigneur French dignitary

monsieur French term of address for man, equivalent to mister; Frenchman of high rank or station

monsignor Roman Catholic prelate having dignity or titular distinction conferred by pope

Most Reverend term of address for archbishop or Roman Catholic bishop

Mr. conventional title before name of man not holding title of rank, honorific, or professional title; mister

Mrs. conventional title before name of married woman not holding title of rank, honorific, or professional title

Ms. title used instead of Miss or Mrs. when marital status of woman is unknown or irrelevant

mullah Muslim religious teacher of quasi-clerical class

nabob provincial governor of Mogul empire in India; man of great wealth or prominence

nawab viceroy or deputy governor in India

negus king or sovereign of Ethiopia

Nizam title of ruler of Indian state of Hyderabad until 1950

nobleman man of noble rank or birth

noblewoman woman of noble rank or birth

nuncio papal legate of highest rank, permanently accredited to civil government

overlord lord over other lords; lord paramount; absolute or supreme ruler

padishah chief ruler, sovereign, or shah of Iran

padre Christian clergyman; military chaplain

palatine feudal lord having sovereign power within domain; high officer in palace of Holy Roman Emperor

pandit wise or learned man of India

parson Protestant pastor

pasha Turkish or North African man of high rank or office; bashaw

pastor clergyman of local church or parish

patriarch Roman Catholic bishop ranking immediately below pope; bishop of Eastern Orthodox sees of Alexandria, Antioch, Constantinople, or Jerusalem, or of Western see of Rome; jurisdictional head of various Eastern churches

patrician person of high birth; orig. member of one of citizen families of ancient Rome

peer member of one of five ranks of British peerage: duke, marquis, earl, viscount, baron

petty officer subordinate officer in navy or coast guard appointed from among enlisted men

pharaoh sovereign ruler of ancient Egypt

plenipotentiary person, esp. diplomatic agent, invested with full power or authority to transact business; minister plenipotentiary

podesta medieval magistrate in Italian town or republic; mayor of Italian city under Fascist regime

pontifex member of council of priests in ancient Rome

pontiff Roman Catholic pope; pontifex

pope prelate who, as bishop of Rome, is head of Roman Catholic Church

potentate individual wielding great power; sovereign

praetor ancient Roman magistrate ranking below consul, having chiefly judicial functions

prefect any of various officials or magistrates of ancient Rome; chief officer or chief magistrate; student monitor in private school

prelate high-ranking ecclesiastic, such as bishop

premier prime minister; one who is first in position or rank

president chief executive of an organization; presiding officer of government body; elected chief of state and chief executive in most republics; ceremonial chief of state in republic with parliamentary government

prexy *Slang.* president, esp. of college or university

priest Anglican, Eastern Orthodox, or Roman Catholic clergyman ranking below bishop and authorized to perform certain rites

priestess female priest

prime minister chief minister of ruler or state; head of cabinet or ministry; chief executive in parliamentary government

prince male member of royal family, esp. sovereign's son or grandson; monarch or ruler of principality or state

prince consort husband of reigning female sovereign

princeling young, subordinate, or minor prince

princess female member of royal family, esp. daughter or granddaughter of sovereign; consort of prince; woman holding sovereign power

principal chief administrator of educational institution

prior officer ranking below abbot in monastery

private enlisted man of lowest military rank

private first class enlisted man ranking above private and below corporal

proconsul governor or military commander of ancient Roman province

proctor person appointed to supervise students, esp. during examinations

professor faculty member of highest academic rank at college or university

provost chief dignitary of collegiate or cathedral chapter; chief magistrate of Scottish burgh;

keeper of prison; high-ranking university administrative officer

purser official on ship or aircraft responsible for papers, accounts, and comfort and welfare of passengers

queen wife or widow of king or tribal chief; female monarch

queen consort wife of reigning monarch

queen mother queen dowager who is mother of reigning monarch

rabbi Jewish master or teacher; Jew trained and ordained for professional religious leadership; leader of Jewish congregation; reb

rajah Indian or Malay prince or chief; Hindu title of nobility; also raja

rani Hindu queen; rajah's wife; also ranee

rear admiral commissioned officer in U.S. Navy or Coast Guard with two stars, ranking above captain

reb rabbi

recording secretary officer of organization charged with keeping minutes of meetings and other records

rector Episcopal clergyman in charge of parish; Roman Catholic priest directing seminary or college

reeve chief town officer of Anglo-Saxon king; medieval English manor overseer; head of council in some Canadian provinces

regent one who governs kingdom in minority, absence, or disability of sovereign; member of governing board of state university

registrar officer of educational institution responsible for registering students and keeping academic records; admitting officer of hospital, university, or other institution

representative elected member of legislative body, esp. U.S. House of Representatives

reverend member of clergy; clergyman's title preceded by "the" and followed by name

sachem North American Indian chief, esp. Algonquian; Tammany Hall political boss

sacristan sexton; person in charge of sacristy and ceremonial equipment of church

sagamore subordinate chief of Algonquian Indians

sahib word meaning sir or master among Hindus and Muslims in colonial India, used when addressing European of social status

samurai military retainer of Japanese daimyo practicing chivalric code of Bushido; aristocratic warrior of Japan

satrap governor of province in ancient Persia

sayyid title given to Islamic teacher or royal personage said to be descended from Muhammad

scoutmaster adult leader of band of boy or girl scouts

secretary officer of business or organization who keeps records of meetings; cabinet-level officer of state directing government administrative department

secretary-general principal administrative officer

seigneur seignior

seignior man of rank or authority; feudal lord of manor; seigneur

senator member of legislative body, usu. upper house, esp. member of U.S. Senate

señor Spanish equivalent of Mr.

señora Spanish equivalent of Mrs.

señorita Spanish equivalent of Miss

signor Italian equivalent of Mr.

signora Italian equivalent of Mrs.

signorina Italian equivalent of Miss

sergeant police officer ranking below captain or lieutenant in United States and below inspector in England; noncommissioned army officer ranking above corporal and below staff sergeant

sergeant major noncommissioned military officer serving as chief administrative assistant in headquarters, ranking above first sergeant

sexton church officer who cares for church property, rings bell, and digs graves

shah sovereign of Iran

shammes sexton of Jewish synagogue

sharif descendant of prophet Muhammad through his daughter Fatima; one of noble ancestry or political preeminence in Islamic countries

sheik Arab chief or ruler

sheriff important official of shire or county charged primarily with judicial duties; police officer for county

shogun military governor ruling Japan until revolution of 1867-1868

sir man of rank or position, esp. title before given name of knight or baronet

sire man of rank or authority; lord; sovereign

sister female member of religious community that observes vows

sovereign one exercising supreme power in specific sphere; monarch, ruler, or king

squire shield- or armor-bearer of knight; male attendant; member of British gentry ranking below knight and above gentleman

sri conventional title of respect for distinguished Hindu Indian

stadtholder viceroy in a province of the Netherlands; chief executive officer of the Netherlands

staff sergeant noncommissioned military officer ranking above sergeant and below first sergeant or gunnery sergeant

steward one employed on estate to manage domestic affairs; employee on ship, aircraft, or train who buys and obtains provisions and is responsible for comfort of passengers

stewardess woman performing duties of steward

subahdar governor of province in India; chief native officer of native company in British Indian army

subaltern person holding subordinate position

subdeacon cleric ranking below deacon; person ranked lowest in major orders of Roman Catholic and Eastern Orthodox churches

suffragan Anglican or Episcopal bishop assisting diocesan bishop but not having right of succession

sultan king or sovereign of Muslim state

sultana female member of sultan's family, esp. wife

superintendent top executive for jurisdiction or organization

superior one who is above another in rank, esp. head of religious house or order

supervisor administrative officer in charge of business, government, or school

suzerain superior feudal lord to whom fealty is due

swami Hindu ascetic or religious teacher

taipan foreigner living in China and wielding economic power there

tetrarch ruler of fourth part of a province in ancient Roman Empire

thane free retainer of Anglo-Saxon lord; feudal Scottish lord

title of rank descriptive or distinctive appellation accorded to a person by right of office, position, status, birth, or achievement

trustee one of a body of persons appointed to administer affairs of a company or institution

tsar czar

tuchun Chinese warlord; provincial military governor in early 20th-century China

'ulama member of body of Islamic mullahs

vavasor feudal tenant ranking below baron; also vavasour

veep *Informal.* vice president

verger church official who keeps order during services and serves as usher or sacristan

vicar Episcopal clergyman having charge of mission or chapel; clergyman exercising broad responsibility as representative of prelate

vicar of Christ Roman Catholic pope

vice- prefix in title of official, such as vice-consul, who takes place of or succeeds a superior

vice-admiral commissioned U.S. naval officer with three stars, ranking above rear admiral

vice president person ranking below president and succeeding president in his or her absence

vicereine wife of viceroy

viceroy governor of country or province ruling as representative of king or sovereign

viscount member of British peerage ranking below earl and above baron

viscountess wife or widow of viscount; woman holding rank of viscount in her own right

vizier high executive officer of various Muslim countries, esp. Ottoman Empire

warden chief operating officer of prison; British governor or officer in charge of administrative department; chief administrator of college or governing officer of certain guilds in Britain

warlord supreme military leader; military commander exercising civil power by force in limited area

worship respectful term of address to British person of importance

zamindar collector of land revenue for government in Muslim India; landlord in British India paying fixed revenue

CHAPTER TWELVE
THE ECONOMY

BUSINESS AND ECONOMICS
Economics and Economic Theory
Commerce and Trade
Corporations and Business Practices
Labor
Employers, Employees, and Business People

See also: *Chap. 11: Government; Chap.12: Finance; Advertising; Occupations; Chap. 13: Sociology*

Economics and Economic Theory

accumulation addition to capital investment or capital stock from profits

affluence substantial wealth and economic power

aggregate total of some measured element of economy

aggregate demand total spending on goods and services by all sectors, including consumers, business, government, and foreign

aggregate equilibrium macroeconomic situation in which national demand for goods and services equals national supply of goods and services

agribusiness growing, processing, and marketing of crops by large corporations instead of individual farmers

agriculture growing crops and raising livestock, esp. as basis of economic structure

antitrust (*adj*) pertaining to policies or laws designed to curb monopolies

assumed debt others' liabilities taken on, as in a merger

austerity tightened economy characterized by shortages

autarky national policy of self-sufficiency, including elimination of imports

automation replacement of human laborers with machines, esp. self-regulating machines and computers

balanced budget spending equal to revenue, esp. in government

balance of payments periodic summary of difference between a nation's total payments to foreign countries and its receipts from them

balance of trade difference in value between nation's imports and its exports

bankruptcy inability to pay one's debts; legal insolvency

belt-tightening measures to reduce expenditures, cut costs, and eliminate deficits

bonanza source of great wealth or profits

boom high level of economic activity; period of business expansion

boondoggle wasteful or pointless business venture or government program

bottom out (*vb*) level out at low point of business cycle

bourgeoisie middle class or class of owners

boycott refusal to trade with a business, person, or nation as punishment or means of persuasion

bread line line of destitute people awaiting free food

break even achieve minimum sales needed to cover expenses and costs of production

broke (*adj*) bankrupt; having little or no available cash

budget plan of expenditures based on anticipated revenues, as for a nation or company

budget deficit state in which government expenditures exceed revenues

business cycle periodic rise and fall in economic activity

bust *Informal.* financial or economic collapse; state of bankruptcy

buyer's market market in which supply exceeds demand, giving buyers leverage

buying power purchasing power

cap upper limit to spending

capital money, assets, or property used as means of production or for investment

capital-intensive (*adj*) designating production using more capital than labor

capitalism economic system based on private ownership and profit incentive

cartel group of producers acting cooperatively to control production and prices

chattel movable item of personal property; slave

cheap (*adj*) low-priced; reluctant to spend money

circular flow diagram schematic representation of relationship between major economic sectors

class social rank or caste as determined by income or economic status

class struggle Marxist view of conflict between labor and capital, personified by workers and owners

clean up (*vb*) *Informal.* reap large profits

collectivism political/economic system based on public ownership of production

command economy system, such as communism, in which government controls factors of production and policy

commercialism practice and spirit of commerce or business, esp. high regard for profits

common market association of countries seeking economic cooperation, esp. through tariff concessions

Common Market European Economic Community

communism economic system based on collective ownership of means of production and control of distribution of goods and services

company town town whose inhabitants are largely dependent on a single company for jobs and services

compensation payment for services or labor, esp. wages

competition rivalry between similar businesses for customers or clients

conspicuous consumption acquisition and use of goods and services beyond one's needs as a display of wealth

consumer goods products purchased by individuals for personal use

consumerism consumption of goods and services; protection of consumers from poor products or misleading claims

consumer price index measure of fluctuation in prices of common consumer goods and services over fixed time period

containerization packaging and shipping large amounts of merchandise in single container

convergence theory theory that capitalist and socialist societies are becoming more alike

cost-benefit analysis ratio of dollar cost of project to dollar benefit it will produce, used to compare worthiness of various proposed projects

cost of living average cost for basic necessities of life

creeping inflation barely noticeable but persistent increase in prices

cut corners trim inessential budget items

dear (*adj*) expensive

decline period of reduced business activity

deficit budget imbalance in which expenditures exceed revenues

deficit financing financing of budget deficit by borrowing

deficit spending government spending in excess of revenues, esp. to stimulate national economy

deflation decrease in money supply, causing sharp fall in prices

demand capability and desire of consumer to purchase goods and services

demand curve graph showing amounts purchased at different prices

demand elasticity measure of change in quantity demanded caused by change in price

demand-side economics Keynesian economic theory emphasizing stimulation of aggregate demand

democratic socialism economic system based on socialist government regulated by democratic electoral process

depression severe, prolonged decline in business activity

deregulation planned, usu. gradual, removal of governmental control over business

destitution extreme poverty

devaluation official lessening of value of currency relative to other currencies

developed nation industrial and/or technological society with high standard of living

developing nation agricultural society with low standard of living and little technological development

diminishing returns any additional unit of one factor of production that yields a smaller increase in production while other factors remain constant; law of diminishing returns

disadvantaged (*adj*) deprived of decent standard of living by poverty or lack of opportunity

discomfort index statistic combining rate of inflation with unemployment rate

discretionary income money available for luxuries after basic needs have been met

disposable income income remaining after paying all taxes

distribution marketing of merchandise; process by which products reach ultimate consumers; portions or shares of total income received by different groups

diversify (*vb*) expand business or economy by increasing number of goods produced or operations undertaken

down-and-out (*adj*) poor, destitute

downside downward trend, esp. loss on investment such as securities

dumping selling goods below cost to other nations to eliminate surpluses or offset competition

duopoly market controlled by two sellers only

earning power potential for earning wages, income, or profits, esp. over a lifetime

easy money policy loose money policy intended to expand money supply and lower interest rates

econometrics statistically oriented economic theory and models used in forecasting changes

economic model simplified representation of a real-world phenomena based on likely reactions to economic changes

economics study of wealth and its creation, dissemination, and consumption

economic system manner in which a nation uses its resources and manages production and distribution

economist student and practitioner of economic theory; someone so trained serving as policy adviser, esp. in business or government

economy organization of social and political institutions and businesses for production, distribution, and use of goods and services; frugality or careful spending

elasticity amount of change in purchases or production caused by small change in price or another variable

embargo ban on import or export of specific item to or from particular nation

entitlement government transfer payment guaranteed to all members of a group

European Economic Community economic association established to abolish barriers to free trade among member nations

expansion period of recovery and growth in business cycle

expensive (*adj*) high in cost or price

extravagance excessive spending beyond one's means, esp. on unnecessary items

false economy seemingly effective but misguided efforts to save or cut back on costs

farm economy national economy based on agriculture

feudalism primarily medieval economic and political system based on relationship of lord to vassal living and working on lord's land

fiefdom in feudal system, heritable land held from lord in return for work and loyalty

Five-Year Plan economic plan specifying goals to be reached in five years, esp. in China and Soviet Union

food stamps coupons for food at reduced prices, issued monthly by government to qualifying poor persons

forecast analysis and prediction of market trends

foreign aid monetary and other assistance given by one nation to another

Fourth World nations without wealth or valuable resources and showing little economic growth

free enterprise system economic system based on private individual ownership of production with decision making based on profit motive in competitive market; capitalism

freehold land held for life with right to pass it on through inheritance

free trade area nations that have agreed to reduce or eliminate trade barriers and tariffs among themselves while external tariffs vary

freeze fixing of some economic factor, such as prices, employment, expenditures, or taxes, at a given level

full employment economic condition in which unemployment is deemed minimal and acceptable, usu. under six percent

gainful employment work for which one is paid wages

galloping inflation sudden, rapid, or extreme and uncontrollable increase in prices

GNP gross national product

goods things produced and purchased

goods and services end results of production: things people buy and activities performed for others

Gresham's law statement of tendency of inferior currency to circulate more freely than superior currency, which is hoarded

gross national product GNP; combined annual monetary value of all goods, services, and products sold on markets of national economy

guaranteed annual income proposed program in which family income is supplemented by government to reach base level

hand-to-mouth (*adj*) relating to bare existence with nothing to spare

hard up (*adj*) *Informal.* lacking resources

have-nots persons or nations with relatively little wealth

haves persons or nations with relatively great wealth

heir person who will inherit or does inherit another's property upon his or her death

hunting and gathering society primitive, preagricultural civilization or people that subsists through hunting and collecting wild plants

hyperinflation extremely rapid inflation and major shortages due to panic buying

index number showing percentage variation over time of economic factors from an arbitrary standard, usu. 100

index of leading indicators statistical measure

capable of predicting economic conditions in near future, based on several factors

indigence poverty

industrialization replacement of hand tools by machine and power tools and development of large-scale production, beginning in late 18th c.

inelasticity change in price that causes little change in purchases or production

inflation sustained rise in price of goods and services

inflationary spiral continuous increase in prices, costs, and wages

inheritance property, wealth, or business acquired at death of another

input-output model matrix in which rows and columns represent input or output of goods from various sectors of economy

insolvency inability to pay bills and debts

Keynesian economics theory emphasizing stimulation of aggregate demand over supply

labor-intensive (*adj*) designating production using more labor than capital

Laffer curve economic model relating lower tax rates to higher tax collections

laissez faire economic system with minimal government regulation of business, trade, and competition

landed class members of society who own property

latifundium great estate operated on feudal basis (Latin America)

law of diminishing returns diminishing returns

loose money policy stimulation of economy by making credit inexpensive and abundantly available

Lorenz curve graph showing variance between equal and actual distribution of income

lottery game of chance in which people buy numbered tickets and prizes are awarded by lot, used to raise funds by some states

lower class people occupying bottom rung of socioeconomic ladder

lumpenproletariat lowest level of society, comprised of unskilled workers, tramps, beggars, and criminals who lack solidarity with proletariat

macroeconomics economic branch dealing with broad aspects of the economy, esp. aggregates on national level

make ends meet keep one's expenditures equal to or less than one's income

Malthusian (*adj*) pertaining to the theories of T.R. Malthus regarding dichotomy between geometric population growth and arithmetic increase in means of subsistence, causing shortages unless war or famine intervenes to eliminate the imbalance

mammon wealth and material gain as an object of worship and evil

manufacturing production of commodities for sale

market activity of buying and selling; trade; potential customers for a product

market economy economic system ruled by

opportunity of consumers to buy and producers to sell

market equilibrium condition of equal supply and demand with stable prices

market mechanism interaction of supply and demand that determines market price and output level

market share percentage of total sales in specific market accounted for by one company

market socialism public ownership of means of production and use of market mechanism for distribution

Marxism socioeconomic theories of Karl Marx, esp. as basis of communism

mass production manufacture of large quantities of goods using standardized parts and assembly lines

material assets wealth, property, or businesses owned

materialism belief that accumulation of wealth and material objects is of primary importance in life

measure of value function of money as standard unit measure for value of commodities

mechanization substitution of machinery for human labor in production process

mercantilism preindustrial economic system emphasizing controlled balance of exports and imports (16th-18th c.)

microeconomics branch of economics dealing with single units of production and consumption

middle class heterogeneous socioeconomic group with common values, comprised of business and professional people, bureaucrats, farmers, and skilled laborers

mixed economy system combining elements of market and command economies

monetarism theory that level of economic activity depends primarily on quantity and growth rate of money supply

money medium of exchange and measure of value in economy

money supply amount of money in circulation at a given time

monopoly domination of market by single company

national debt total amount owed by federal government at given time to other nations, businesses, and individuals

nationalization government assumption of control over privately owned industry

natural resources industrial materials and capacities found in nature

needy those living in poverty

negative income tax guaranteed minimum income provided by government for all families existing below set income level

nest egg reserve fund of money

oligopoly market condition in which there are few sellers, enabling them to influence price and other factors

open market competitive market free from price control and not restricted to any individual or group

ophelimity economic satisfaction

out-of-pocket (*adj*) owed or paid out in cash

ownership lawful title or possession; proprietorship

panic public fear that economic entity, market, or system is failing, and consequent rush to liquidate assets

paper profit unrealized profit due to appreciation in value of something owned but not yet sold

pauperism condition of extreme poverty

pay wages or salary given for services

peak highest point in business cycle; boom

penury extreme poverty

per capita income total national income or GNP divided by total population

petite bourgeoisie lower middle class, such as small shopkeepers and artisans

Phillips curve statistical measure of increasing rate of inflation as unemployment decreases

physiocrats political economists who held that an inherent natural order governs society and advocated a laissez-faire system (France, 18th c.)

planned economy socialist or other economic system with centralized government control of production and distribution

plutocracy system of government controlled by wealthy

political economy social science that deals with economics in connection with politics and society

poor that portion of society with little wealth, low standard of living, and few opportunities

possession ownership of property or wealth

poverty lack of socially acceptable amount of money and material possessions; indigence

poverty level poverty line

poverty line government standard for personal or family income used for measuring portion of population living in poverty; poverty level

PPI producer price index

price controls government ceiling set on prices of basic goods and services to fight inflation

price index measure of fluctuation in prices from arbitrary standard over period of time

price supports government payments, esp. to farmers, to maintain minimum prices by buying up surpluses

prime cost that part of cost of commodity derived from labor and materials directly used in its manufacture

private enterprise capitalist economic system with minimal government interference, allowing individual ownership of property and encouraging competition and profit incentive

private property property owned by individuals, corporations, or organizations privately, without government intervention; right to own property that is basis of capitalism

private sector part of economy that is composed of individuals and privately owned businesses

privileged class property-owning, landed, wealthy members of society

producer price index PPI; scale that compares cost of producing goods now with cost in past year

production process of creating or making goods and services

productivity measure of ability to produce more output from given input

profit net amount earned after deducting costs in business enterprise

proletariat working class

propertied class members of society who own land or businesses

property land or other items of value owned by business or individual

property rights government guarantees of individual freedom to own, buy, and sell private property

proprietary rights right to ownership of a tangible or intangible thing or idea

proprietorship ownership, esp. of one's own business

prosperity high point of business cycle; state of wealth

public sector part of economy composed of federal, state, and local governments

public utility industry providing essential public service, such as electrical, water, or telephone service, in which single firm is granted local monopoly

purchasing power value of currency in terms of what it can buy compared with buying power at time established as base period; ability to purchase goods and services; buying power

purse strings control over funds

quotation current price of commodity or security

rationing limited distribution of a product so that everyone receives a fixed amount

raw goods materials gathered in original state from nature for use in production

Reaganomics supply-side economics espoused by former U.S. President Ronald Reagan

real dollars value of money in terms of what it can purchase

real property land and buildings and structures on it

real wages amount that can be purchased at given time with one's income, computed by dividing money wages by consumer price index

recession period of no growth in national economy for at least six months; stage in business cycle with decreased demand for goods, increased unemployment, and decline in GNP

recovery increase in business activity following recession or depression; upturn in business cycle

reflation restoration of economic health and higher levels of activity, usu. by changes in monetary policy

regulation government control and supervision of certain economic activities

remuneration payment in cash for goods or services

renewable resources natural resources that are not exhausted by use

reparation compensation paid to make up for something, esp. payments by defeated nation in war for economic losses suffered by victor

restitution making good for a loss; giving back something to rightful owner

restrictive practices trade agreements deemed to be unfair to competitors or against public interest

revaluation government increase in exchange rate to increase value of currency relative to other currencies

revenue total income of business, government, or individual before expenses

ruin total economic collapse; bankruptcy

sanctions coercive economic restrictions placed on one nation by another

scarcity lack of resources or funds; absence of a certain commodity in demand

seasonal fluctuations regular, predictable changes in business activity at certain times of year

sector any of the elements that interact in process of supply and demand, namely consumers, businesses, governments, and foreign countries

secular trend long-term economic direction

service work performed for another for payment

service economy economy emphasizing services over industrial production, esp. automated, cybernetic services

shakeout drop in economic activity that eliminates marginal or unprofitable businesses and products

shortage situation in which demand for goods exceeds supply, esp. at given price

shortfall shortage or deficiency

slavery former economic system based on ownership of workers by masters

sliding scale variable scale, as for wages or prices charged, based on changes in other factors or ability to pay

slump decline in business activity; slow portion of business cycle

smokestack industry heavy manufacturing, such as steel or automobile manufacturing

socialism state ownership of all or most of means of production and distribution, with control over aspects of social welfare and planning

social security federal government payments to elderly, unemployed, and disabled persons, financed by contributions from employers and employees

socioeconomic (*adj*) involving interrelation of social and economic factors

splurge (*vb*) indulge in excessive spending

squander (*vb*) spend resources extravagantly or foolishly

stagflation inflation and stagnation or high unemployment occurring together

standardization of parts use of interchangeable parts in mass production

standard of living quality of life measured by general level of consumption of material goods

stipend regular payment

storming practice of accelerating production to fill quotas (Soviet Union)

subsidy government payment to business or individual to improve economic condition

subsistence level level of production and consumption barely adequate for survival

subvention government or foundation grant for public benefit

supply quantity of goods or services available

supply and demand basic economic law stating that as price of a good increases, suppliers will be willing to produce more but consumers will demand less, so that price and quantity are both directly and inversely related

supply curve graph showing amount producers will supply at different prices

supply elasticity measure of change in supply caused by change in price

supply-side economics macroeconomic theory emphasizing stimulation of production as basic factor in growth

surplus situation in which supply of goods exceeds demand, esp. at given price

surplus value in Marxist theory, difference between value of work done or commodities produced and value of labor and other inputs, generally equal to profit under capitalism

technological monopoly exclusive rights held by developer company to patented product or process

tenancy possession of land or property by right

tight money policy slowing down of economy by making credit expensive and limiting money supply

title right of ownership, esp. document stating such right

trade barriers tariffs, quotas, and customs regulations used by one country to discourage importation of certain goods

trade deficit imbalance in which nation's imports exceed its exports

trade imbalance condition in which nation's exports and imports are not equal

transfer payment disbursement, such as social security or unemployment payment, for which no goods or services are received

trickle-down theory theory that government financial incentives to big business will eventually benefit smaller businesses and general public

trough lowest portion of business cycle before recovery

trust several companies acting together to control production, pricing, and distribution of a product

underdeveloped nation nation having weak economy and low standard of living

underprivileged persons at social disadvantage, esp. due to poverty

unemployment rate percentage of measured civilian labor force without jobs but actively seeking work

upper class social class at top of society, possessing wealth and owning means of production

urban economy economy in which most wealth and economic activity is centered in cities

value market price; worth of something in money at specific time; purchasing power of unit of currency; Marxist expression of labor embodied in commodity

wage-price controls laws intended to stabilize economy by limiting increase in wages or prices

waste reckless or excessive spending, esp. on unnecessary things

ways and means methods of raising money and obtaining resources for use by company or nation

wealth money, real property, or human resources; assets

welfare government assistance to poor; state or degree of well-being

welfare capitalism modified capitalism that incorporates government-funded social welfare programs

welfare state social system based on political responsibility for improvement in condition of all citizens

wholesale price index measure of changes in commodity prices at all stages of production; producer price index

work ethic belief system emphasizing social and personal value of work

working class those who work for a living with little control over working conditions, esp. unskilled manual and factory laborers; proletariat

working poor employed persons earning below poverty level wages

worth material value expressed in terms of money

worthless (*adj*) lacking monetary value

Commerce and Trade

ad valorem tax tax levied on certain goods as percentage of their value

army-navy store retail store that sells surplus military apparel and supplies at discount prices

asking price amount initially sought for goods or services

auction public sale at which items are sold one by one to highest bidder

automat restaurant with food in small compartments opened by inserting coins

bait and switch scam in which inexpensive merchandise is advertised but customer is then pressured to buy more expensive items

bar code set of vertical bars printed on consumer product with coded information to be read by computerized scanner

bargain something sold at price favorable to

buyer; (vb) negotiate terms of sale to one's advantage

bargain basement basement floor of department store, where goods are sold at reduced prices

barter (vb) exchange commodities, goods, or services without use of money

bazaar shop selling various goods; outdoor market or street of stalls, esp. in Middle East; sale of miscellaneous articles to benefit a charity

bid price amount initially offered in payment for goods

bill itemized statement of charges for goods or services; check; tab

bill of lading document issued to shipper by carrier describing goods shipped and terms of carriage

bill of sale written certification of transfer of ownership

black market illegal trade to avoid government regulation or taxation

blister pack display package in which clear plastic seals product against cardboard sheet

blue law law forbidding business transactions on Sunday

board of trade association of business people

bodega Spanish. grocery store, usu. small neighborhood shop

boiler room Slang. place where illicit brokers engage in high-pressure selling by telephone, esp. of securities

booth enclosed stall for display and sale of goods, esp. at outdoor market or fair

boycott organized effort to deter customers from patronizing a business or industry

brand name identifiable product label, esp. of a widely advertised and distributed item

buyer's market market in which supply is plentiful and prices are favorable to consumers

buyer's remorse regret or anxiety experienced immediately after making a purchase

cabotage trade in coastal waters or air space between two points within one country

callback recall of defective product by manufacturer

carriage trade wealthy patrons or elite clientele

cartage act or cost of delivering goods, esp. by truck

case goods products shipped and sold in multiple units in cardboard box

case sale sale of cased goods in large quantities at reduced prices

cash-and-carry (adj) sold for cash payment with no delivery included

cash down portion of total cost paid to hold goods or as first installment on credit sale

cash on delivery COD; payment due when shipped goods are received

cash register business machine with money drawer and tapes that display and tabulate amount of each sale

catalog published booklet containing list of items for sale and prices, often with pictures

catalog sales distribution of merchandise by mail with orders placed from catalogs

caveat emptor Latin. lit. let the buyer beware; principle that one buys at one's own risk

chaffer (vb) bargain; haggle over price

chain business with many retail locations

chain store individual outlet of retail chain

chamber of commerce organization of business people promoting economic development in particular area

charge account credit account in which merchant allows customer to pay for purchases over time

charm price price set just below even dollar amount, such as $9.99

check itemized statement of charges for goods or services; bill; tab

CIF cost, insurance, and freight; seller's designation that quoted price includes packing, shipping, and insurance charges

classified ads compact advertisements in newspaper columns arranged by subject

clearance sale to get rid of old goods and make room for new ones

clientele all of one's customers

closeout sale to dispose of all goods, esp. when ending business venture

COD cash on delivery

cold call telephone sales call to stranger who is unfamiliar with product or service

come-on Slang. incentive to buy

come to terms settle on price

commerce organized exchange of commodities on large scale, usu. involving transport from place to place; trade

commissary food and supply store, esp. in army camp

commission percentage of sales price paid to broker by owner of merchandise sold

commodity good traded in marketplace, esp. one that is transportable

common carrier company in business of transporting goods at uniform rates

comp Informal. free service or good, esp. admission ticket to event; (adj) complimentary

company store retail outlet operated by company for convenience of its employees, who often must shop there

comparison shopping collecting information on prices and quality of similar products from different outlets

competitive pricing practice, esp. by large companies, of setting prices slightly higher than competition while offering other advantages, usu. on brand name products

concession right granted to engage in activity for profit on grantor's premises

concessionaire person exercising a concession

consignment shipment of items to be sold; sale of personal items through a merchant on commission

consumer individual or group purchasing goods or services in marketplace

consumer goods products made for and sold directly to individuals to be used as sold

consumerism movement to educate consumers to obtain better, safer products from manufacturers

contraband unlawful or prohibited goods; trade in such goods

convenience store store open very long hours, carrying limited selection of goods, usu. at inflated prices

co-op cooperative store owned by and operated for benefit of members

corner the market attain a monopoly or predominant share of sales of a particular commodity

cost amount paid for goods or services, esp. wholesale price paid by retailers

counter long table in store for display of goods

coupon certificate or ticket entitling holder to reduced purchase price or redemption for cash

cover charge cost of admission to bar or club

cover the territory solicit orders from all potential customers in one area

cross sell (vb) attract customer by offering one product or service while selling another

curb service service for customers who remain in their cars, esp. at drive-in restaurant

customer person who buys, esp. regularly at same place

customs government duty on imported goods

cut-rate (adj) at reduced price

deal bargain, favorable price; (vb) trade, do business; bargain so as to reach favorable price

dealer buyer and seller of goods; franchise holder

department store large retail store with departments selling many kinds of goods

dicker (vb) haggle over price

discount price below standard retail or list price

discount house store that sells merchandise at less than standard price

door-to-door (adj) selling by calling at each house or apartment in an area; shipped directly from point of pickup to point of delivery

drive-in service establishment in which customers remain in cars

dry goods cloth or clothing products

dumping below-cost sale of goods, esp. to kill competition

durable goods consumer items with long-term market life, esp. cars or furniture; hard goods

ego goods expensive luxury items

emporium marketplace, trading center; large store selling variety of products

exchange place of trade; barter, trade; (vb) return one purchased item and replace it with another

excise tax tax on manufacture, sale, or consumption of goods and services

expense any of various costs of operating a business

export product sold outside country of origin; (vb) sell goods outside one's own country

factory outlet warehouse serving as point of sale for discount goods

fair gathering for exchange and sale of goods among individuals

fair market value price something can be expected to bring on open market at given time

fire sale sale of commodities actually or supposedly damaged in fire at greatly reduced prices

five-and-dime low-priced general merchandise store

flagship central or largest store in chain

flea market usu. outdoor market with numerous stalls selling used or handmade new articles

flood the market greatly increase available supply of some good to force price down

fly-by-night *Slang.* unreliable business

FOB free on board; assumption of responsibility by shipper for all costs until goods are placed on carrier

franchise contract or license permitting regional distributor to use name and sell products of another company or manufacturer

free (*adj*) available at no cost

freebie *Informal.* something available at no cost

frequency marketing rewarding consumer loyalty by offering an incentive or discount for frequent use of product or service

full-service (*adj*) offering broad range of services in one basic line of business

functional goods utilitarian articles such as tools or clothing

futures purchases or sales of commodities at speculative prices for future delivery or receipt

garage sale sale of used household and personal articles held at seller's home, usu. in yard or garage

general store usu. small store selling different kinds of goods

generic product lower-priced version of brand name product with plain label indicating kind of product only

give-and-take exchange on an even basis

giveaway product offered for free, usu. to attract potential customers for other goods

glut large oversupply of goods

good buy product whose value equals or surpasses its price

gouge (*vb*) grossly overcharge

gratis (*adj*) at no cost, free

gray market discount market that operates somewhere between legitimacy and the black market

guarantee seller's assurance that product is as represented and will be repaired or replaced if defective

haggle (*vb*) argue over price

half-price (*adj*) reduced to half of original price

handout *Informal.* something given at no cost

hard goods durable goods

hard sell high-pressure salesmanship

hawk (*vb*) sell goods in public, esp. by shouting advertisements

hedonic goods pleasure-oriented consumer items such as art, musical recordings, or toys

high-pressure (*adj*) pertaining to sales effort involving insistent arguments, forceful persuasion, or refusal to take no for an answer

import product bought from another country; (*vb*) buy products made in other countries

impulse buying sudden purchase of goods without prior intent, usu. stimulated by display or advertising

installment purchase purchase made on credit and paid off in series of payments over time

in stock (*adj*) available for sale at the present time

interstate commerce trade among and between states, regulated by federal government

inventory all items of merchandise in stock at given time

invoice itemized list of goods or services to be paid for

IOU informal written memorandum of indebtedness

job lot random assortment of goods for sale as one unit

juice *Slang.* exorbitant interest or commission

keystone (*vb*) price goods at twice their cost as standard practice

kiosk small structure open on one side for street sales

lading load of freight, shipment of goods

license legal right to use or sell another's patented or copyrighted material

line stock of goods of particular type carried by store

liquidation disposal of all remaining merchandise at reduced prices

list price official retail price; nondiscounted price

loss leader popular item sold at a loss or negligible profit to attract customers to retail outlet

low-pressure (*adj*) pertaining to sales effort involving subtle persuasion and soft-spoken arguments

low-price (*adj*) available at little cost

mail order technique of selling items and taking orders through the mail

mall large, usu. completely enclosed shopping complex comprised of many different shops and restaurants

manufacturing production of commodities

markdown reduction in price to promote sales

market place where people gather to sell and trade goods; store or shop for sale of provisions; (*vb*) offer for sale

marketable (*adj*) fit for sale

marketing activities involved in moving goods and services from producer to consumer: market research, advertising, promotion, distribution, and sales

marketplace world of trade and business; site where goods are offered for sale

market research collection and analysis of information to determine goods and services preferred by certain groups

markup amount added to cost by retailer to set price for customer

mart market, trading center

merchandise consumer goods for sale

merchandising advertising, display, promotion, and direct selling methods

mom-and-pop (*adj*) designating small, family-owned business, usu. retail

money's worth good value obtained for cost

monopsony existence of only one buyer for goods or services

nominal price stated price when bargaining or reduction is possible

nondurable goods items that will be consumed in a relatively short time, such as clothing or food

nonrefundable (*adj*) final and not subject to return or refund

notions small, useful items sold in store, esp. for sewing

OEM outside equipment manufacturer; company that exploits or develops another company's product as part of its own

oligopsony existence of only a few consumers for a product

on the block for sale

on the house offered gratis or free, with compliments of selling establishment

on time (*adj*) purchased on credit with payments to be made over fixed period of time

outbid (*vb*) offer better price than others seeking to purchase the same item

outlet store selling goods for specific manufacturer or distributor

outlet store retailer selling defective, damaged, or surplus goods at reduced price

overcharge (*vb*) set price higher than value of goods; charge more than stated price

overprice (*vb*) set price too high to sell

package store retail store selling alcoholic beverages for consumption off premises

packaging container or wrapping in which product is sold; design of such wrapping, often intended to attract customers

packing slip form listing items included in shipment

patent right granted by government that prevents others from using idea or invention or making same product as originator for seventeen years

patron person who is customer or client, esp. regular one, of store or other establishment

patronage clientele; business or trade

patronize (*vb*) be a regular customer

peddle (*vb*) sell, esp. travel about selling small items

penetration pricing pricing of new product at low level to lure customers away from established product

pennyworth bargain, value for price paid

peril point lowest possible import duty short of damaging domestic industry

pitch salesperson's discourse intended to persuade customers to buy

planned obsolescence design of consumer goods for limited use, necessitating frequent replacement or repair

plaza public marketplace in town

point-of-purchase (*adj*) relating to place where sales are made or purchases paid for

popular prices pricing designed to attract general sales

premium something offered free or at low price as inducement to buy something else

price quantity of money demanded in exchange for goods or services

price-cutting selling an article at a price reduced from prior or advertised level

price discrimination selling of same product to two different buyers at different prices

price fixing setting of prices by government or among competing businesses contrary to free market dictates

price tag label attached to commodity indicating its price

price war business competitors' repeated lowering of prices

product differentiation any of various devices that enable consumers to distinguish one firm's product from others in the same industry

product manager person who oversees all aspects of marketing of specific product

profit amount of sales revenues left for business after paying cost, overhead, taxes, and operating expenses

profit margin excess of income over expenses and costs

promotion something devised to advance a product or service in order to persuade consumers to buy or use it

prospect potential customer

protectionism policy of strict trade regulations to support domestic industry

purchase anything obtained by buying; act of buying; (*vb*) obtain by paying price

purchase order itemization of items being bought

purchase price amount paid for commodity

quality control maintenance of standards in production by checking product at stages during manufacture

quota fixed limit, esp. government limit on imports and exports

racket easy, profitable source of income, often illegal

rebate discount made by refunding percentage of purchase price

recall removal of defective product from market for correction

receipt written acknowledgment that payment has been received

reduced (*adj*) at less than original price

refund return of money previously paid for commodity

repo *Informal.* repossession

repossession taking back of commodity

from buyer who has failed to make payments when due

retail sale of goods directly to consumers

retailer business or individual that offers retail sales directly to consumers

rock bottom at the lowest possible price

rollback action that returns prices to earlier, lower level, as by government order

rummage sale sale of contributed items, used or new, to raise money, esp. for charitable organization

sale exchange of goods or services for agreed sum of money; special offering of goods at reduced prices

sales force employees engaged in selling

salesman person engaged in selling, esp. male; salesperson

salesmanship ability, skill, or technique of selling

salesperson person engaged in selling; salesman

sales slip receipt or form listing details of sale

sales tax tax levied by city or state on retail sales of merchandise

self-service practice of serving oneself without assistance of salesperson

seller's market market in which demand exceeds supply, with prices rising

selling act, practice, or technique of making sales

sell short (*vb*) underestimate value in setting price

service center authorized establishment for repair and purchase of replacement parts, esp. for cars and appliances

service charge amount added to price of goods to pay for service

service mark trademark applied to service offered, designated ^{SM}

shop usu. small outlet for retail sales; (*vb*) purchase goods

shop around (*vb*) search for bargains or special items in several places

shopping visiting one or more stores to look at, price, and buy items

shopping center outdoor complex of stores, restaurants, and movie theaters usu. grouped around common parking lot

shopping spree outing during which multiple purchases are made

shortage condition in which demand for goods exceeds available supply

showroom place where merchandise is displayed for sale

show window large store window in which merchandise is displayed

shrink wrap clear, flexible, plastic film that shrinks when exposed to heat, used to wrap and seal products

slash (*vb*) drastically reduce prices

smuggling importing of prohibited or outlawed goods

soft goods items lasting a relatively short time, esp. clothing

soft sell low-pressure sales technique

stall booth, table, or counter in market

staple chief commodity of region; item regularly stocked due to constant demand

steal *Informal.* product obtained at very low price, often less than its value

steep (*adj*) expensively priced

stock finished goods on hand or in storage and available for sale

stock in trade resources, abilities, or goods on hand required for carrying on specific business

store retail outlet selling consumer goods, such as chain, convenience, department, discount, specialty, or surplus store

storefront ground-level room with display windows, usu. used as retail store

storewide (*adj*) throughout all departments of store, used esp. of a sale

sublicensing granting of licenses to other companies to exploit, develop, or market one's product

supermarket large, self-service retail food store, often part of a chain

surcharge additional amount added to price

surplus store retail outlet selling extra or leftover goods at discount prices

swap (*vb*) barter, exchange

swap meet flea market, esp. one based on barter system

tab *Informal.* price, total cost; bill; check

territory area in which traveling salesman solicits orders

test marketing offering new product for limited time in small area to assess national sales potential

thrift shop retail store selling used items at low prices, often to support charitable organization

ticket slip of paper serving as evidence that holder has paid fare or admission and is entitled to some service

tickler file special file used to remind salesperson of customers requiring attention at certain dates in future

tie-in sale at which two or more items, only one of which is in demand, must be bought together as a unit

till money drawer at shop counter

trade commerce; exchange of goods for money

trademark symbol, design, or name used to distinguish product from its competitors, designated ^{TM}

trader person who engages in commerce or sells goods

trade show convention at which related companies in single industry show and compare new products and ideas

trading post store in remote region or settlement

trading stamp stamp given as premium by retailer, having specific value when redeemed for articles

traffic exchange of goods

transaction business deal; sale or exchange of items

transfer ticket entitling bearer to change from

one public vehicle to another at no additional charge

traveling salesman business representative soliciting orders in assigned territory

truck (*vb*) exchange or barter

twofer *Informal.* card or ticket entitling bearer to two items for price of one

underbid (*vb*) offer less than competition for commodity

undercharge (*vb*) ask less than normal or accepted price

undersell (*vb*) set price for a product that is lower that one's competition

unit pricing standard measurement for pricing different brands of same product

Universal Product Code UPC; computer code of bars and numerals printed on merchandise to identify it and confirm price

unload (*vb*) sell off unwanted merchandise, usu. at reduced price or in large quantities

UPC UniversalProduct Code

upset price minimum permissible bid at auction

used property commodity resold after period of use

variety store retail outlet selling many different commodities, esp. small, nondurable goods

vend (*vb*) sell

vending machine coin-operated machine selling merchandise, esp. candy or cigarettes

vendor one who sells

vendue public auction

voucher written document showing expenditure or receipt of money

warehouse building where merchandise is stored before shipment to retailers

wares commodities

warranty guarantee on product for limited time after purchase

waybill list of goods sent by common carrier with shipping directions

wholesale sale of goods in large quantity to retail businesses at cost substantially below retail price

wholesaler business or person purchasing goods from producers for resale to other businesses

will-call department in a store where merchandise is held for payment and pickup by customer

window shopping looking at merchandise without purchasing

yard sale garage sale held outdoors, esp. in yard

Corporations and Business Practices

advance partial payment of amount due on signing of contract

affairs matters of business

alien corporation company operating under foreign nation's charter

amalgamation combining of corporations into a new business entity

annual report corporate management's financial report to shareholders at end of fiscal year

annual review supervisor's regular assessment of job performance of subordinates

ante stake to be paid to begin participation in business

application business activity suitable for computerization

articles of incorporation formal document establishing corporation, describing its business, directors, finances, and stock issued

assembly line manufacturing process in which each worker performs specialized task in assembling product that passes by on moving belt or track

assignment transfer to another of one's claim or right, esp. to income

bailout instance of government coming to assistance of failing business

bankroll (*vb*) finance, supply with money

bankruptcy legal insolvency; inability to pay debts; procedure to dissolve company and be released from certain debts

belly up *Slang.* collapse or failure of a business

big business major corporations with political interests

board of directors group of top managers setting corporate policies and direction

bonus payment over and above salary given to employee, esp. executive, as incentive or reward

bottom line last line of financial statement, indicating net profit

bubble company fraudulent cover operation posing as legitimate business

budget schedule of expenses adjusted to estimated revenue for set period

budgeting curtailing expenses so as not to exceed income

business commercial, mercantile, or industrial enterprise conducted to make a profit

buyout outright purchase of business, esp. by management or employees with borrowed money

capital-intensive (*adj*) requiring large capital investment or expenditure relative to need for labor

capitalization total funds of corporation, including stocks, bonds, undivided profits, and surplus

cash cow *Informal.* business with dependable source of income

cash flow measure of liquidity equal to excess or deficiency of net income relative to cash expenses

ceiling upper limit set for spending

channels formalized hierarchical lines of communication of responsibility between managers and subordinates

Chapter 11 bankruptcy code section that applies to a corporation going out of business which may require restructuring

charter legal form establishing corporation and defining its purpose

close (*vb*) officially conclude business transaction

closed corporation company whose stock is held by a small group, usu. persons also involved in management

collapsible corporation company set up to be dissolved before realizing profits, thus avoiding taxes

collection division department responsible for obtaining payments due to company

collusion agreement between competitive companies, esp. to fix prices or limit production output

commission fee paid to broker or agent for services in business transaction

compagnie *French.* company

company organization formed for doing business

concern company, business firm

concession entitlement to operate business granted by government or other business

conglomerate corporation composed of smaller corporations in diverse business fields

consideration something of value given or done in return for comparable action by another as part of contract

consolidation organization combining two or more companies, each of which retains partial autonomy

consortium business alliance of companies

contract legally binding agreement between parties

controlling interest ownership of enough stock in company to set policies and make decisions

co-op membership-owned business

corner monopoly ownership of commodity, stock, or security

corporate veil protection of corporate owners from personal liability

corporation business organization existing and treated as legal entity independent of its individual owners

cost-effective (*adj*) producing good results for amount invested; efficient in use of funds

cost overrun amount by which project exceeds estimated cost

cottage industry small or home-based business

crapshoot *Informal.* speculation on business enterprise

cut a check *Slang.* write a check on business funds

cutback reduction in production, personnel, or budget

dba *doing business as*; fictitious business name

deal business transaction or agreement

dealings business affairs or relations

diminishing returns additional investments resulting in smaller proportion of profits

dissolution dismantling of business, contract, or partnership

diversification broadening of large corporate holdings into wide variety of investments

divestiture sale or dissolution of subsidiary business or investment

dividend portion of corporation profits distributed regularly to stockholders

economize (*vb*) cut costs to increase profits; reduce spending

endowment money placed in tax-exempt foundation by corporation

enterprise quality of risk-taking or initiative in business; company, venture, or firm

escalator clause contract provision requiring increases in payments based on economic fluctuations

establishment business or company, esp. its physical plant

fee amount charged for professional services

firm business or company

Fortune 500 list of 500 largest American corporations published annually by *Fortune* magazine

foundation tax-exempt institution, funded by corporate profits, that contributes to charities, arts, and education as means of avoiding corporate tax and generating goodwill

franchise government permission for company to carry on particular business in certain place, often involving partial monopoly

funding money available for use by company

golden parachute substantial compensation given to top executive as severance bonus when dismissed due to corporate merger or takeover

goodwill intangibles belonging to business, esp. its trade reputation

go public (*vb*) offer stock of privately owned company for sale to public

ground floor *Informal.* advantageous position or opportunity based on early involvement in new venture

growth area section of firm's business experiencing expansion and providing revenue base for operations

growth company company growing faster than economy in general and reinvesting most of profits into business

grubstake money provided by investors to individual starting a business

hardball *Slang.* highly competitive or ruthless business activities

headhunting search by professional recruiters for executives to fill high-level positions

holding company corporation whose business is buying and selling stock in other companies

home office headquarters of business with branches

honorarium payment in lieu of professional fee, usu. token amount

horizontal merger merger involving competitive companies that perform or produce the same or similar functions or products

house business establishment

incentives financial or other benefits offered for labor or services

industry large-scale business activity; particular branch of manufacturing

institution established corporation, esp. one serving public needs

interlocking directorates boards of directors of different corporations having common members

investment business expenditure made for eventual profit

labor-intensive (*adj*) requiring large supply of labor relative to need for capital investment

license government permission to operate business

liquidation sale of business in which all assets are converted to cash

lose one's shirt *Slang.* make a bad investment; fail at business

management organizational and administrative aspect and personnel of business

market research collection and analysis of data on consumer habits, trends, and preferences

market share percentage of sales controlled by one company in specific industry or segment of an industry

memorandum written communication within company relating to business operation, goal, or project

memo to the file written record on decisions for file of author only

merger assimilation of one business or corporation into another

mommy track career path in which woman forgoes rapid advancement in order to spend time with family

moneymaker business enterprise that generates profits

multinational corporation large company based in one country with interests, investments, and operations in others

nonprofit corporation business operating for reasons other than profit making, and paying no taxes

number-cruncher *Informal.* person or thing that performs numerous numerical calculations, such as an accountant or computer

operating expenses ongoing, recurring costs of conducting business, not including costs of production

operations research systematic analysis, usu. mathematical, of problems in business operations

organization administrative personnel and executive structure

overbudget (*adj*) describing venture in which costs exceed estimated costs

overhead total direct expenses in operating a business

Pac-Man defense attempt to prevent hostile takeover in which targeted company bids to take over hostile firm

Parkinson's law statement that work expands so as to fill the time available for its completion

parlay (*vb*) successfully exploit asset or position

partnership association of two or more individuals or business entities joined as part owners in business

patent right granted by government to exclusive rights to invention for certain number of years

pension fund fund created and maintained by corporation or government to provide benefits

under pension plan, with assets usu. invested in securities

perk *Informal.* perquisite

perquisite nonmonetary benefit for employee, such as free trip or company car; perk

personnel employees; department responsible for hiring new employees

Peter Principle statement that every employee in a hierarchy tends to rise to the level of his or her incompetence

petty cash cash fund on hand for small daily expenses

philanthropy gifts and endowments of foundations or charitable organizations

plant machinery, buildings, and grounds of factory or business

poison pill *Slang.* mechanism, such as issuing a new class of stock, by which company averts hostile takeover

positioning placement of company within industry or product within company

privately held corporation corporation not offering stock for sale to public, usu. family owned

profit motive impetus to engage in business activity for financial gain

prospectus description of company, its property, and its operations, circulated to prospective investors

proxy fight contest between factions of stockholders for control of company, in which each group solicits signed proxy statements for votes needed to gain control

public corporation corporation whose stock is traded on stock exchange

public relations activities intended to create favorable public opinion about company or product

public-service corporation private corporation chartered to provide essential commodity or service to the public

quality assurance quality control guarantees

quality control maintenance of production standards by checking product at stages during manufacturing process

realize (*vb*) convert into money; bring in profit

receivership status of bankrupt business placed in hands of receiver appointed to settle its debts

reinvest (*vb*) use profits to build company rather than disburse them to shareholders

retainer fee paid to lawyer or other professional adviser as advance on services

royalty payment for rights to property based on percentage of revenue generated by it

seed money funds for starting business venture

sole proprietorship unincorporated business with one owner

speculation engagement in transaction or venture involving risk in hopes of large gains

spin-off new company created by distribution to stockholders of stock of another company

staff regular, full-time, permanent employees

start-up company newly established company

start-up expenses costs involved in establishing a business

stock equipment, materials, and supplies of a business; shares of a company sold to public with value based on company assets and income

subcontract (*vb*) hire secondary company or individual to do part of contracted job

subsidiary business owned by parent company

sunrise industry industry with high growth potential, such as electronics industry

sunset industry industry, such as heavy manufacturing, with declining market due to social or technological changes

syndicate association of corporations formed to carry out costly financial project

syndication sale or licensing of commodity to network of similar businesses

take a bath *Slang.* lose everything on a business venture

takeover merger forced on one business by another

tender offer of money made to satisfy obligation

trade association organization with representatives from companies in same industry or business

trade convention gathering of representatives from many companies in same business, esp. to introduce new products

undercapitalized (*adj*) lacking sufficient operating funds

undertaking venture, enterprise

underwrite (*vb*) guarantee financial support for business

up-front (*adj*) invested or paid before service is rendered or product is delivered

upside measure of financial gain on investment

venture business enterprise, esp. one with high degree of risk but potential for large profits

venture capitalism financing of new businesses for eventual share in profits

vertical merger purchase by one company of a supplier or distributor

wheel and deal *Informal.* arrange business deals in aggressive, flamboyant manner

white knight *Informal.* business that prevents hostile takeover of another company by offering better terms

windfall profit unexpected return on investment

working capital portion of company's capital readily convertible into cash for paying expenses and wages

working vacation businessperson's vacation in which mail, phone calls, and office problems intrude

Labor

affirmative action government-regulated program ensuring that employers hire women and minorities

AFL-CIO American Federation of Labor and Congress of Industrial Organizations

agency shop work situation in which worker need not be union member but must pay union an amount equal to its dues

American Federation of Labor and Congress of Industrial Organizations AFL-CIO; umbrella organization for most American labor unions

arbitration negotiation between management and labor mediated and decided by neutral third party

backsheesh tip or gratuity, esp. bribe

base pay basic rate of pay before overtime, bonuses, or raises

benefits payments under annuity, pension plan, insurance, unemployment, or disability

blacklist roster of workers excluded or persecuted by management for pro-union views

blue-collar (*adj*) pertaining to factory or manual labor

bonus amount above regular salary given as reward or for motivation

Boulwareism "take it or leave it" collective bargaining technique of management

ca'canny *Brit. slang.* deliberate work slowdown to express discontent

calling profession or trade, esp. one's natural vocation

casual labor temporary or part-time work, often unskilled

closed shop business prohibited from employing nonunion members, outlawed by right-to-work laws

codetermination mutual setting of policy by labor and management

collective bargaining negotiations between employer and union representatives, esp. over wages or benefits

common labor manual or unskilled work

common situs picketing picketing of entire construction site by union in dispute with only one subcontractor

company town city or town whose economy is dominated by a single business enterprise or factory

company union workers in union in single company, not affiliated with group of unions, often under employer's control

compulsory arbitration negotiations requiring union and management to accept binding decision of outside mediator

contract labor-management agreement renegotiated regularly to determine wages, benefits, and working conditions

cost-of-living allowance guaranteed annual pay raise based on increase in cost of living

craft occupation requiring special training or skill

craft union union of skilled workers in specific trade or industry

crew small group of workers under direction of foreman

day job temporary or part-time position, esp. in field other than one's primary vocation

day shift regular hours of employment, usu. 8 or 9 A.M. to 5 or 6 P.M.

disability insurance guarantee of continued income for worker seriously or permanently disabled on the job

double time pay scale at twice the normal rate for work done on holidays, weekends, or after hours

earning power lifetime potential for earning wages, income, and profits

earnings total amount of wages during pay period

employable (*adj*) physically or mentally fit for work; meeting minimum job requirements

employment job or occupation at which one works; number or percent of persons holding jobs

farm labor unskilled agricultural work

featherbedding practice of forcing an employer to create unnecessary jobs

fringe benefit benefit in addition to wages, esp. health insurance, profit sharing, or paid vacation

gang work crew directed by foreman

general strike work stoppage by entire labor force of city or nation

giveback union agreement to relinquish benefits previously granted as part of new contract

gratuity amount given freely by customer above cost of service rendered, esp. to waiter or driver

graveyard shift hours of night employment, usu. midnight to 8 A.M.; lobster shift; night shift

guild union of people in same craft or trade

independent union union not affiliated with AFL-CIO or other association

injunction court or executive order, usu. requiring strikers to return to work

job position and duties of employment

labor work force, work performed by laborers

laborer worker, esp. semiskilled or unskilled

labor force total number of persons over age sixteen who hold or are looking for jobs

labor union organization of workers for protection, representation, and benefits in dealings with employers

layoff dismissal of workers, esp. temporarily

line of work vocation, trade, or profession

lobster shift graveyard shift

lockout shutdown of business by management to pressure workers and union into agreement

malingering pretending to be ill to avoid work

manual labor unskilled, physical work

mechanization use of machines in combination with semiskilled workers to replace unskilled workers

mediation arbitration of union-management dispute by neutral third party

minimum wage legally fixed lowest hourly rate payable to certain types of workers

moonlighting working at a second job, often at night

National Labor Relations Board NLRB; federal agency regulating and investigating unfair labor practices

night shift graveyard shift

NLRB National Labor Relations Board

occupation job, trade, or profession

occupational hazard danger inherent in particular job, esp. unsafe working conditions

on spec (*adj*) performed or made without guarantee of payment for work or service

overtime payments at higher than normal rate for extra hours worked during day or week

paycheck regular payment of wages or salary

payday day on which paycheck is received

pay period regular interval between paydays

payroll roster of employees and record of their wages

pension regular payments made to employee upon retirement

pension plan systematic plan by which corporation or government makes regular payments to retired or disabled employees, sometimes partially funded by employee contributions

picket (*vb*) stand or march with signs in front of workplace as display of dissatisfaction during strike; (*n*) striking worker who does this

piecework work done and paid for by unit produced instead of at hourly rate

pink-collar (*adj*) pertaining to low-paid work usu. done by women, esp. secretarial work

pink slip notice of dismissal from one's job

post specific position or duty on job

preferential shop shop in which management hires only union members as long as they are available

premium additional wages paid for overtime or dangerous work

profit sharing division of portion of company profits among employees

proletariat Marxist term for workers with no capital or means of production

raise increase in wages

rank and file all regular union members

retirement permanent termination of employment; pension benefits paid to former employee

right-to-work law state law allowing workers to work whether or not they join a union and outlawing a closed shop

salary money earned for regular work, paid periodically

scab strikebreaker who works for company being struck

seasonal unemployment annual, temporary loss of jobs due to seasonal conditions, esp. absence of farm work in winter

semiskilled labor usu. manual work requiring some training

seniority status obtained from length of time worker has been on job, usu. rewarded with higher pay and other benefits

serf person of feudal class bound to land and subject to will of lord

severance pay payment made to employee at time of termination of employment

shape-up method of selecting longshoremen from assembled group of available workers

shift regularly scheduled hours of work

sit-down strike strike in which workers remain idle in workplace until settlement is reached

skilled labor work, such as craft or trade, that requires training

slowdown intentional reduction in output by workers to force employer concessions without a strike

social security number nine-digit number issued when person registers for social security system, required to gain employment and used as identification number for taxation and banking

specialization of labor condition in which workers learn and perform very specific tasks

specialty skill or specific job performed by worker

split shift workday divided into two periods, with intervening break longer than meal or rest period

starvation wages wages barely sufficient to provide subsistence

steel-collar worker robot

stoop labor poorly paid farm labor, esp. immigrants harvesting crops

straight time standard work hours without overtime

strike organized and deliberate work stoppage used to attain benefits, esp. changes in working conditions or wages

strikebreaker worker hired to replace striking employee

sweatshop exploitative workplace characterized by long hours, low pay, and substandard conditions, esp. employing immigrants

sweetheart agreement agreement between employer and union on terms favorable to employer, often without approval of union members

swing shift work period between day and graveyard shifts, usu. 3 or 4 P.M. to midnight

sympathy strike work stoppage by laborers in support of striking workers elsewhere

syndicalism worker ownership and management of industries achieved by revolutionary movement and general strike

Taft-Hartley Act federal law protecting public welfare during labor disputes by allowing president power of injunction to halt certain strikes

take-home pay gross wages less deductions for taxes, insurance, union dues, retirement, or savings

time and a half pay scale at one and half times normal rate, for hours worked beyond normal workday; overtime

timecard card on which hours worked by each employee are recorded by time clock

time clock clock with mechanism for recording hours of arrival and departure of employees

tip gratuity received for service

trade occupation, esp. craft of skilled work

trade union organization of workers within craft, trade, or industry

Trade Unions Congress TUC; British umbrella organization for most trade unions

TUC TradeUnions Congress

turnover number of employees leaving jobs in given time period

underemployed overqualified or part-time workers

unemployable (*adj*) designating person unable to find work because of age, lack of skills, or disability

unemployed those who are out of work

unemployment lack of work; number or percent of persons not holding jobs

unemployment compensation regular payments, usu. from state funds into which employers have paid, to qualified unemployed persons

unfair labor practices union and employer activities banned by legislation to promote peaceful industrial relations

union workers' mutual benefit and protection organization

union card card identifying person as member of specific union

unionism principle of trade unions as protectors of workers' rights

union scale minimum wage for particular category of worker as fixed by union contract

union shop business employing union members and requiring nonmembers to join within stated time, often three months

unskilled labor manual or factory work requiring little or no training

vocation trade, profession, or occupation, esp. one for which one feels a calling

wage payment for labor on hourly or piecework basis

walk of life trade, profession, or occupation

walkout spontaneous strike

white-collar (*adj*) pertaining to office, sales, or professional work, usu. involving people, information, and ideas

wildcat strike work stoppage not authorized by labor union

work occupation, profession, trade, or business

workday regular hours during which work is performed

worker person employed to perform physical or mental activity in return for wages

workers labor force

workers' compensation protection provided by state governments for workers injured on job

working class proletariat, esp. unskilled manual and factory laborers

workingman industrial or manual laborer

workplace person's place of employment; any or all places where people are employed

work stoppage cessation of work by employees to protest working conditions; strike

workweek total number of hours worked at regular salary each week

yellow-dog contract illegal requirement that worker not join union

Employers, Employees, and Business People

administrator business executive; manager

agent one authorized to represent another; traveling salesman

apprentice person in process of learning trade

arbitrator third party called in to settle dispute

artisan craftsman in skilled trade

assistant helper serving in subordinate position

associate fellow worker of equal or slightly subordinate position

auctioneer person who conducts public sales at auction

backer supporter, sponsor, or provider of funds

bagman *Chiefly Brit.* traveling salesman

baron person with great or absolute power in one particular field

blue-collar worker crafts, manufacturing, or common laborer

boss person in authority; foreman, manager, or owner

breadwinner worker whose earnings support family

broker businessperson connecting buyers and sellers for fee or commission

bureaucrat official in large organization, esp. one following inflexible routine

businessman owner, manager, or business executive, esp. male

businessperson person in business of either sex

businesswoman female owner, manager, or business executive

CAO chief administrative officer

capitalist owner of business, esp. supporter of free enterprise system

captain of industry major figure in one particular industry and business leader

CEO chief executive officer

CFO chief financial officer

chairman of the board top corporate officer, appointed by board of directors, charged with supervision of high-level affairs of company

chief boss, top person in business hierarchy

chief administrative officer CAO; corporate executive responsible for day-to-day operations of business

chief executive officer CEO; corporate executive responsible for overseeing administration and setting policy

chief financial officer CFO; corporate executive responsible for financial operations

clerk low-level office worker; person who sells in store

common laborer unskilled manual worker

comprador native Chinese agent of foreign business serving as liaison to native employees

comptroller controller

controller chief accountant of business; comptroller

counsel adviser to business management, esp. attorney

craftsman skilled worker or artisan

dealer person who sells or trades some product

director member of board of directors; top corporate executive

distributor agent for business responsible for getting goods from producer to consumers

domestic person employed in another's home

employee worker hired for wages

employer person who hires workers and pays their wages, often owner of business

entrepreneur financial backer, often manager, of business enterprise

executive upper-level business administrator or manager

exporter person who sells goods in foreign countries

fat cat *Slang.* wealthy, powerful business executive

field rep *Informal.* outside salesman, usu. with some management responsibility

financier person engaged in large-scale financial operations

foreman person in charge of small group of workers

freelancer self-employed person contracting his or her services

fund-raiser person who solicits money for new or established business

hand manual worker, laborer

headhunter personnel agent who recruits executives, esp. from other companies

help casual workers in subordinate positions

high roller *Informal.* person or institution spending money freely or extravagantly

hired help part-time or temporary laborers

hireling person available for any work; mercenary

importer person who sells goods made in foreign countries

industrialist owner or manager of industrial enterprise

intrapreneur corporate employee given free rein to develop new products and services within company without observing normal protocols

Jaycee member of Junior Chamber of Commerce, a civic group for young business leaders

jobber middleman between manufacturer and retailer; distributor

journeyman skilled, experienced worker

laborer person doing manual, unskilled, or semiskilled work

lackey person in subordinate position, esp. servant

magnate powerful, successful businessperson

management employees hired to administer company policy

manager director or administrator of business operations; person responsible for running single retail outlet

mediator outsider brought in to settle dispute

mercenary person who works merely for money or reward

merchant seller of merchandise; retailer; trader

middleman dealer buying from manufacturer and selling to retailer

middle management middle echelon of business administrators

migrant worker farm laborer who travels about harvesting seasonal crops

mogul powerful businessperson

moneychanger person in business of exchanging currencies of different nations

monger dealer or trader

movers and shakers people who initiate actions and get things done

nabob rich, powerful person

officer person in position of authority in business, usu. with title

office worker clerical or subordinate white-collar worker

official executive, manager, or corporate officer

operator worker trained to run specific machinery

organization man person who identifies strongly with ideas and ethics of his or her employer

overseer manager; foreman

owner person with legal and financial rights of proprietorship over company

part-time worker person employed temporarily or less than full-time

patron wealthy person who finances or supports business or institution

paymaster person authorized to pay wages or salaries

peddler person who carries articles from place to place to sell them

player *Informal.* active and influential participant in business dealings

plutocrat powerful, wealthy member of ruling class

president top executive officer of company

professional person trained and engaged in highly skilled occupation

profiteer person who sells a product or service at excessive prices

prole *Informal.* proletarian; laborer

proletarian worker or laborer

proprietor owner of business

rainmaker *Slang.* executive with extraordinary ability to attract clients and use connections to increase profits

rep *Informal.* representative

representative salesperson or authorized agent for business

retailer person who sells directly to consumers

retainer person serving another

robber baron ruthless, exploitative capitalist (late 19th c.)

salesman person employed as sales clerk or sales representative, esp. male salesperson

salesperson male or female who sells goods or services

sales rep *Informal.* sales representative

sales representative person employed as sales agent for company in particular area

saleswoman female salesperson

secretary clerical office worker, esp. one subordinate to a single superior

self-employed (*adj*) designating person owning a business or working freelance

servant person employed to perform personal and household services

service worker person who provides services directly to consumers or clients

shopkeeper owner or manager of small retail business

silent partner partner investing capital in business but not taking part in decision making or operations

slave worker who is owned by master

small businessman owner of modest or personally run company

sponsor person who helps finance business or business activity

staff full-time, permanent company employees

subordinate person under authority or direction of another

superintendent person in charge of department or institution

superior person with authority over another

supervisor superintendent, manager, or director of unit within business

taskmaster person responsible for assigning and supervising rigorous tasks performed by others

team player person who respects organizational hierarchy and works well with others

temp *Informal.* temporary worker hired for specific job and excluded from union or fringe benefits

trader merchant, salesman; broker, agent

tradesman *Chiefly Brit.* shopkeeper

traveling salesman business representative who solicits orders by traveling through assigned territory

treasurer chief financial officer of company

tycoon powerful, successful businessperson

underling person working in subordinate capacity

unskilled laborer manual or factory worker with no training

vassal feudal serf; subordinate or servant

vendor one who sells

venture capitalist financier investing in high-risk and start-up companies in hopes of reaping large profits

wage earner salaried employee

wage slave person utterly dependent on current, often inadequate, salary

white-collar worker office, sales, or professional worker

wholesaler person who sells products to other businesses

wildcatter person who promotes risky or unsound business venture

workaholic compulsively hard worker to the exclusion of other interests

worker person employed to perform labor for wages

working girl sometimes disparaging term for female office or clerical worker

workingman laborer, esp. industrial or manual worker

working mother woman serving as both parent and employee

working stiff *Slang.* hardworking common laborer or factory worker

workingwoman female who is regularly employed

FINANCE

Banking and Financial Services
Securities
Taxation
    Types of Taxes
    Income Tax
Accounting
Spending, Receiving, and Possessing Wealth
Money, Currency, and Denominations
World Currencies

See also: *Chap. 11: Government; Chap. 12: Business and Economics; Insurance; Real Estate*

Banking and Financial Services

ABA number American Banking Association number

acceptance short-term credit arrangement used in financing trade in which banks substitute their credit for the customer's

account record of all financial transactions for specific person or entity

accrued interest interest owed but not yet paid

acquittance document or receipt held as evidence of discharge of debt

adjustable rate interest rate, esp. on mortgage, that varies with predetermined factors

agio fee paid to exchange one currency for another

American Banking Association number ABA number; bank's identification number in upper right corner of check

amortization paying off of debt in installments over time, with each payment covering current interest and part of principal

annuity investment plan providing guaranteed retirement income

appraisal estimate of property's true value, esp. by expert

arrears overdue debts

ATM automated-teller machine

automated-teller machine ATM; computerized electronic device for depositing and withdrawing funds from account; cash machine

bad debt uncollectable bill or loan

balance amount standing as credit in checking or savings account

balance due amount standing as debit on charge account

balloon payment large final loan payment after many smaller payments

bank institution receiving money on deposit, lending money on interest, and simplifying fund exchanges by use of checks and notes

bankbook small booklet in which account transactions are recorded

bank card personalized, magnetically imprinted plastic card used in combination with secret code for ATM transactions

bank check check drawn by bank on itself and signed by authorized bank officer; cashier's check

bank clerk *Chiefly Brit.* teller

bank draft check drawn by bank against funds deposited to its account in another bank

banker owner or manager of bank

banker's acceptance draft or bill of exchange drawn on bank and accepted by it

banking business and practice of operating a bank

banking house company in business of banking

bank note paper note issued by bank for use as money; currency

bank paper bank notes collectively

bank rate standard discount interest rate set by central bank, esp. in Britain

bank run series of large withdrawals made by bank depositors fearful of bank failure

bankrupt (*adj*) designating person or entity whose total property and assets are insufficient to pay debts

bank statement list of transactions and charges on customer's account during regular period, usu. issued monthly

bearer holder of note or other financial instrument

beneficiary person for whom funds are placed in trust, in whose favor letter of credit is issued, or who receives income from estate, insurance policy, or annuity

blind trust trust in which public official, to avoid conflict of interest, places assets under control of independent trustee who manages them without owner's oversight

borrow (*vb*) take out a loan with understanding that it will be repaid in specified time, usu. with interest

bounced check check returned by bank due to insufficient funds

branch bank bank office operating at distance from main bank

building and loan association savings and loan association

bursar treasurer, esp. of college

call loan loan repayable on demand

call money funds loaned by bank to stockbrokers that may be demanded at any time

capital money, assets, and property used as means of production; owner's equity in business plus creditors' advances

capital funds total capital accounts of bank, including par value of capital stock, surpluses, undivided profits, and capital reserves

cash (*vb*) turn in check at bank and receive currency

cashier bank officer responsible for receipts and disbursements

cashier's check bank check

cash machine automated-teller machine

CD certificate of deposit

central bank banker's bank, such as Federal Reserve

certificate of deposit CD; receipt for funds deposited, usu. for specified amount of time at fixed interest rate

certified check check with bank guarantee that sufficient funds are on deposit to cover it, usu. indicated by special stamp

charge purchase made on credit to be paid in cash over specified time, often with interest

charge account account, usu. with retail store, that allows customer to buy merchandise on credit

check written order for bank to pay funds held for depositor; also, *esp.Brit.*, cheque

checkbook book containing detachable forms for writing checks on bank account

checking account account at bank against which checks may be drawn

chit voucher for small sum of money owed

Christmas club savings account from which funds are withdrawn at Christmas to pay for shopping

clearinghouse central bank in which representatives of local banks meet daily to exchange checks and settle balances

collateral assets pledged by borrower to guarantee repayment of loan

collection recovery of loans in default of regular payments; department or agency responsible for this

collection items drafts or notes subject to collection before proceeds are credited to depositor's account

co-maker person signing another's note to strengthen credit

commercial bank bank primarily involved in taking demand deposits for checking accounts and offering short-term loans

commercial paper short-term negotiable debt instrument arising out of corporate commercial transactions

commute (*vb*) substitute single payment for series of smaller payments

compound interest interest calculated on total of principal plus accrued interest

consumer credit credit offered to individuals rather than institutional borrowers

correspondent bank bank that carries deposit balance for bank in another locality and exchanges services with that bank

cosigner person signing loan contract and promising to repay loan if borrower defaults

counter check check available at counter for use of depositors in making withdrawals

counterfoil *Chiefly Brit.* check or receipt stub

countersign (*vb*) sign another person's document in order to verify authenticity

courtesy card personalized card entitling bearer to special banking privileges

creative financing financing that combines different instruments, such as bonds and mortgages

credit arrangement for future payment, usu. with interest, on goods or money obtained immediately; funds available to borrower

credit bureau agency providing information to lenders on credit rating of individuals or companies

credit card plastic card certifying bearer's entitlement to charge purchases to credit account

credit limit largest amount that can be borrowed on credit card or account

credit line line of credit

creditor person or business to whom amount is owed

credit rating measure of past credit reliability, used to gauge degree of risk involved in loan or extension of credit to individual or business

credit union cooperative association for pooling savings of members or employees and making loans to them at low interest

debt amount owed to lender by borrower

debt service total interest on loan over full term of payments

default failure to make timely loan payments

deferred payment money withheld until certain date

delinquency failure to meet agreed-upon time for debt repayment

demand deposit bank deposit that may be withdrawn without notice

deposit money stored in bank or financial institution; partial payment for goods, services, or property

depository place where funds and valuables are placed for safekeeping

deposit slip written record of amount placed in bank on specific date

depreciation gradual devaluation or drop in price

deregulation elimination of government regulatory controls on deposits and loans, allowing freer banking activities

discount interest paid at beginning of loan period, deducted from principal in advance

discount rate interest charged by Federal Reserve Bank on loans to member banks

dishonor (*vb*) refuse check presented as payment; refuse to make due payment on debt

down payment initial payment required on credit purchase

draft written order for payment

Dun & Bradstreet agency furnishing information to subscribers on financial standing and credit rating of businesses

dunning harassment of debtor for payment

duty tax on imports or exports

early withdrawal withdrawal of funds from timed deposit before maturity, usu. involving interest forfeiture

earnest money funds given as partial payment and binding pledge in agreement

EFT electronic funds transfer

electronic funds transfer EFT; banking transaction via telecommunications network

embezzlement illegal appropriation of property or funds entrusted to one's care

encashment act of cashing a check

endorsement signature on back of item, usu. check, authorizing payment or transferring rights to someone else

equity money invested in property or business entity with mortgages, debts, and liens deducted

escrow written agreement deposited with third party, usu. bank, as custodian, to be delivered upon fulfillment of some condition

exchanges items presented for collection through clearinghouse or exchanged directly by local banks

exchequer treasury, esp. funds in British treasury

extortion obtaining money illegally, esp. by misuse of authority

FDIC Federal Deposit Insurance Corporation

Fed *Informal.* Federal Reserve System, esp. its Board of Governors

Federal Deposit Insurance Corporation FDIC; government agency guaranteeing funds placed in banks

Federal Reserve System federal banking system that regulates flow of money and acts as central clearinghouse for banks

fiduciary trustee administering estate, executing will, or serving as guardian of minor's assets

finance dealings concerning money in the business world, including circulation of currency, granting of credit, banking, and investment

finance charge monthly interest on revolving credit account

finance company institution specializing in consumer loans and lines of credit to businesses

financial services services provided by banking and investment banking institutions, savings and loan associations, mortgage companies, and brokerage houses

financial statement report summarizing impact of business transactions during fiscal period

financier person trained and engaged in large-scale financial operations

float uncollected amount of check cashed by one bank on another bank's account; brief interim before collection when bank on which check is drawn has use of depositor's money for free

floating debt short-term debt arising from current operations and having no specific time of repayment

foreclose (*vb*) deprive mortgagor of right to redeem property mortgaged for failure to fulfill conditions

frozen assets funds made unavailable to their owner

guaranty written promise to creditor by guarantor to be liable for debt should principal debtor fail in his or her obligations

high finance practices and institutions involved in banking and investment

honor (*vb*) accept and pay an obligation when called for

IMF International Monetary Fund

insolvency lack of resources to pay one's debts

installment loan note repaid in equal periodic payments, each including interest and part of principal

instrument formal legal document, such as deed, bond, note, or draft

insufficient funds deposits that are inadequate to cover check or withdrawal

interest fee charged for use of capital or extension of credit; sum paid as percentage of money on deposit

interest forfeiture loss of interest accrued on account, esp. due to early withdrawal of time deposits

internal revenue taxes collected on wages and business profits by government

international banking large-scale financial operations, esp. involving debt and credit to nations

International Monetary Fund IMF; international agency established to promote trade and economic cooperation and to stabilize balance of payments by making loans to member nations

investment outlay of money for income or profit

investment banking activities of financial institutions whose primary business is issuing and trading securities of other companies

IOU informal promissory note; written acknowledgment of indebtedness

joint account bank account held by more than one person

juice *Slang.* money loaned at exorbitant interest, esp. by bookmaker

kiting writing check against insufficient funds or moving funds from bank to bank to create temporarily expanded credit

land bank bank financing real estate transactions, esp. federal bank providing long-term loans to farmers

laundering concealing source of large sums of money, usu. by moving it through several accounts

layaway plan method of making installment purchase on revolving credit account

lending institution savings and loan association, mortgage company, or bank specializing in business and consumer loans

letter of credit document from one bank to correspondent bank requesting that letter bearer be given credit

line of credit credit limit set by lending institution; credit line

liquidity ease with which asset can be converted to cash

loan amount of money borrowed or lent on interest

loan office place where loans are made

loan officer bank employee responsible for interviewing loan applicants and approving and setting terms of loans

loan shark *Informal.* lender charging excessive interest

Lombard banker or moneylender

long-term loan loan with maturity date many years in the future

M-1 money held by public for use in current spending, including coins, paper currency, demand deposits, and traveler's checks

M-2 M-1 plus savings and time deposits, money market funds, overnight repurchases, and Eurodollars

M-3 M-2 plus large time deposits, institutional money market funds, and term repurchases

magnetic ink character recognition number MICR number; electronically coded number printed at bottom of check

maker person who signs and executes note or promise to pay

maturity due date of mortgage, note, draft, acceptance, or bond

MICR number magnetic ink character recognition number

MO money order

moneychanger person who exchanges national currencies at established rates

money market high-interest, unregulated, nonbanking investment entity that originated in 1970's

money market mutual fund entity that pools assets of investors and puts funds into short-term, high-interest bank CDs, treasury bills, and commercial paper

money order MO; order for payment or draft sold by bank for fee

mortgage method of pledging property as guaranty of payment of debt with interest

mortgage company lending institution specializing in large, long-term loans on real estate

mortgage holder institution or person holding mortgage on property

national bank federally chartered bank

near money assets with high degree of liquidity, such as savings deposits

negotiable instrument note or other instrument legally transferable to another by proper endorsement

negotiable order of withdrawal account NOW account; checking account in which unused money earns interest

never-never *Brit. slang.* installment plan

nonpar (*adj*) describing items on which payer bank deducts exchange charge before paying them to collecting bank

note promissory note issued to creditor (note payable) or accepted from customer owing money (note receivable)

noteholder one to whom loan payments and interest are due

NOW account negotiable order of withdrawal account

numbered account bank account identified by number only, to conceal identity of depositor, esp. in Swiss bank

obligation debt security, such as mortgage or corporate bond

on-demand (*adj*) pertaining to note payable immediately upon receipt

outstanding check check that has been written but not yet paid by bank on which it was drawn

overdraft bank withdrawal in excess of funds available

overdraw (*vb*) draw on an account in excess of available funds

par (*adj*) describing items that payer bank remits without charge

par value amount agreed to be repaid, exclusive of interest, on bond, note, or other obligation

passbook bankbook recording deposits, withdrawals, interest, and service charges on account

pawn something deposited with another as security for a loan; (*vb*) make such a deposit

pawnbroker person licensed to lend money at specified rates on items of personal property deposited as collateral

pawnshop place of business of pawnbroker

payback return on investment; period of time required to recoup investment

periodic payments regular, usu. monthly, payments of interest and principal required by terms of loan

PIN personal identification number; secret code used to access ATM

plastic credit card

points small percentage of loan, esp. mortgage, prepaid as origination fee and deemed interest

postdated check check dated in future and not payable until that date

premium amount paid for loan in addition to interest

prepayment penalty additional fee charged for paying off loan before it is due

price rate of interest charged on loan

primary deposit cash deposited in the bank

prime rate rate of interest charged by banks on loans to major borrowers, esp. businesses

principal face amount of loan, excluding interest

promissory note written contract to pay specified amount at set future date

protest notarized document giving notice that note or draft was presented for payment and refused

quittance discharge from debt

rate percentage of money returned as interest

receivership process by which assets of company in bankruptcy are held and administered by bank or other appointed trustee

recoup (*vb*) recover original investment

recourse debt negotiable instrument for which maker or endorser is liable

rediscount commercial paper discounted a second time

redlining discriminatory refusal or limitation of loans based on geography, esp. within inner-city neighborhoods

regulation control of U.S. banking operations by government

reimburse (*vb*) pay back, esp. for money already spent

remit (*vb*) make payment

remittance money paid, esp. sent as payment

repossession taking back of article by creditor when debtor fails to make payments

repurchase agreement contract between bank and investor in which bank agrees to buy back security it has sold to investor at fixed price on designated date

reserve bank bank holding money reserves of other banks

reserve requirement percentage of their deposits that member banks must keep as cash or on deposit with district Federal Reserve Bank

reserves funds set aside by bank to enable it to pay depositors in cash on demand

return item item returned unpaid by payer bank

return on capital profit or yield achieved on investments

revolving credit charge account in which portion of total is due each month and interest is added monthly

rubricated account special bank account, esp. one with special designation or title

run sudden large number of bank withdrawals

safe-deposit box rented space in bank vaults to which only renter has access, used for secure storage of valuable property

S and L savings and loan association

savings assets set aside for future use

savings account interest-bearing bank account

savings and loan association S and L, institution owned by depositors and making long-term real estate and other loans; building and loan association

savings bank institution specializing in small, timed deposits

secondary reserves bank assets, such as government securities or commercial paper, that can quickly be converted into cash

secured loan cash loan based on collateral that ensures repayment of borrowed money

security item standing as means of assuring payment of debt; person bound to pay debt if another fails

service charge fee charged by bank on depositor's account statements for services rendered, usu. in connection with checking account

share draft interest-bearing checking account in a credit union

shave (*vb*) purchase a note at rate discounted to illegal level

short-term loan loan with maturity date usu. under one year

Shylock person charging exorbitant interest on loans

signature card card containing signatures of individuals authorized to write checks on bank account

simple interest interest computed by multiplying principal by rate and by number of years

smart card plastic credit card with memory chip for financial transactions

smart money investments made with advantage of inside information

solvency ability to pay one's debts and meet one's financial responsibilities

speculation high-risk investment in hopes of rapid high return

spendthrift trust trust account in which principal is made inaccessible to one who might spend it recklessly

stale check check invalidated by lapse of time between writing and cashing

state bank bank chartered by nation or state, regulated by its laws

statement regular, usu. monthly, description of all transactions, deposits, and running balance in account

stop payment request by depositor that his or her bank refuse payment of check written on account

subordinated (*adj*) designating debt obligation whose holder is placed in precedence below preexisting creditors

surety person liable for another's debts

surety company institution that insures against various types of losses and executes bonds

survivorship account account in name of two persons that belongs to either survivor on death of other

Swiss account numbered account, esp. in Swiss bank

teller bank clerk who pays out and receives money directly from public

term length of time over which promissory note must be paid

terms conditions of promissory note, obligation, or contract

thrifts thrift institutions, savings and loan banks, or credit unions

till place for keeping cash; ready cash

time deposit savings account deposit that may not be withdrawn without penalty until specified time

time payments payments on installment

transit items cash items payable outside city of bank receiving them and transmitted to payer bank

transit number number printed on check identifying bank, its location, and proper routing

traveler's check replaceable check sold by banks, to be countersigned and used as money by those traveling away from home bank

treasurer person in charge of funds or finances of business or institution

treasury place where funds are kept; funds of corporation or state; agency administering treasury

treasury house building housing treasury offices

trust obligation on person (trustee) to hold and use property according to terms of special grant, esp. for benefit of others

trust account money deposited by one person and held in trust for another

trust company bank that handles trusts and all banking operations except issuance of notes

trustee person legally empowered to administer on behalf of beneficiary

trust fund trust account, esp. held for use by children after depositor's death

trust officer bank employee responsible for operations of trust department

unsecured (*adj*) not guaranteed by collateral

usury charging of excessive interest on loans

variable-rate mortgage mortgage with adjustable rate, often linked to prime rate

venture capital funds used for investment in high-risk enterprises, usu. for start-up companies

void (*vb*) invalidate check, as by writing "void" across it

voucher written statement attesting to expenditure or receipt of money and accuracy of account

welsh (*vb*) *Informal.* fail to pay one's debts

withdrawal removal of funds from account

World Bank U.N. agency established to make loans to underdeveloped member nations

yield percentage of money returned on investment

Securities

acquisition purchase of one company by another, including gaining control of its stock

actionnaire *French.* stockholder

agiotage *French.* speculation, esp. dealing in foreign exchange and stockjobbing

American Stock Exchange AMEX; exchange for stocks not listed on New York Stock Exchange

AMEX American Stock Exchange

arbitrage selling of assets in one market after purchase in another to profit by price differential; purchase and sale of large block of securities in company in expectation of profit, esp. when engaged in discussions of merger or takeover

arbitrageur one who engages in arbitrage

baby bond bond with value of less than $1,000

bearish (*adj*) pessimistic about security prices; causing or describing a fall in stock prices

bear market market in which stocks are declining

bid-and-asked price highest price offered and lowest price accepted for security at specific time

bid price amount initially offered for block of stock

Big Board *Informal.* New York Stock Exchange

block very large number of shares in one company sold as unit to one buyer

blue chip high-quality, generally nonspeculative stock or security

blue-sky law law designed to prevent sale and promotion of fraudulent securities

bond security certificate of loan, with principal to be repaid by issuing body, usu. government or corporation, at specified maturity date, with interest usu. paid at intervals

bond issue offering of bonds for sale with set interest rates and maturity dates

book value theoretical value of security based on company balance sheet

bourse stock exchange in European city

broker one who buys and sells stocks as agent for others, receiving a commission for this service

brokerage business that buys and sells stocks as agent for others

bullish (*adj*) optimistic about security prices; causing or expecting a rise in stock prices

bull market upward trend indicating stock market vigor

buy back purchase by corporate management of stock in its own company to reduce number of outstanding shares

buy-out purchase and retirement of outstanding securities of a company, which is thus taken private

call option to buy given quantity of stock at stated price within a specified time, purchased in anticipation of increase in price

capital gain profit on sale of a security: sales price less commissions less cost or basis

capital gain distribution regular payments to stockholders by corporation, similar to dividends

capital stock total value of corporate capital divided into negotiable shares of stock

Chicago Board of Trade major exchange that deals in futures, esp. of grains and metals

churn excessively fast turnover of securities for purpose of generating broker's commission, often for little gain

closely held describing securities not available for trading

commission broker's fee on stock sale or purchase

commodities broker individual licensed to trade on commodities exchange

commodities exchange place where trading in contracts on staple products is conducted

common stock share of ownership in company, providing eligibility for dividends and vote on company decisions

convertible security security that can be exchanged for another kind of security

correction brief movement of market in opposite direction from general trend, esp. to offset sharp advance or decline

coupon detachable printed statement specifying interest due on bond at given time

crash abrupt, sharp decrease in asset prices, esp. stocks

cross trade simultaneous, offsetting buy and sell orders taken by single broker without recording trade, often depriving investor of chance to trade at more favorable rate

curb market dealing in securities not listed on exchange

debenture unsecured bond

discount difference between issuing price and selling price of security

discretionary account account that empowers broker to make transactions on own discretion, without consulting client

diversify (*vb*) place investments in several different companies and forms to guard against collapse of one

dividend regular return on investment paid to stockholders from business profits

Dow Jones Average *Trademark.* index of relative price of securities based on daily price of selected industrial, transportation, and utility stocks traded on New York Stock Exchange

employee stock ownership plan ESOP; system by which employees acquire stock in company for which they work and receive distribution at retirement

ESOP **e**mployee **s**tock **o**wnership **p**lan

exchange place where trading of securities or commodities is conducted by brokers; commodities exchange; mercantile exchange; stock exchange

ex dividend recently declared dividend that is not paid to recent purchaser of security

Fannie Mae FNMA; any of various publicly traded securities backed by a pool of mortgages held by federal agency

financial district area where banks, investment houses, brokerages, and exchange are located, esp. Wall Street in New York City

fixing scheduled time for stock market status report

float (*vb*) place securities, esp. bond issue, on market; (*n*) amount of common stock not closely held and available for trading

floor area of stock exchange occupied by brokers and traders

FNMA **F**ederal **N**ational **M**ortgage **A**ssociation; Fannie Mae

futures contracts to buy specific commodity at set price, to be delivered at future date

futures exchange exchange that sells futures contracts on indexes for future value

gilt-edged (*adj*) designating highest quality securities and bonds

Ginnie Mae GNMA; bond or certificate issued by federal agency based on mortgages purchased from lenders

glamour stock popular, usu. blue-chip stock that rises quickly or steadily in price

GNMA **G**overnment **N**ational **M**ortgage **A**ssociation; Ginnie Mae

go private (*vb*) take company private by buying back all public-issue securities

go public (*vb*) offer stock of privately owned company on market

government bond bond issued by municipal, state, or federal government as means of obtaining capital

greenmail practice of purchasing large block of company's stock at special rate, either to force rise in stock prices or as offer to buy back stock at premium, often to thwart possible takeover

growth stock common stock in company with significant sales and earnings, having some degree of instability but opportunity for substantial increase in price

high yield strong return on investment, usu. anything over ten percent

high-yield security security that pays interest at significantly higher rate than government or corporate bonds, often carrying lower credit rating

holding company corporation whose sole business is to acquire, hold, and sell stock ownership in other companies

holdings securities one owns

hostile takeover assumption of control of company against wishes of management by appealing directly to shareholders, often for purpose of reselling stock at significant gain

income fund mutual fund providing current income

income stock stock in relatively stable company that produces regular return on investment with small chance of rapid price increase

indenture document detailing terms of bond issue

index arbitrage form of program trading based on manipulation of fleeting differentials between share price and futures price contracts

industrials stocks of industrial corporations, esp. those listed on New York Stock Exchange

insider information information that is not publicly available, used to obtain large, often illegal, profits on stock transactions

institutional trading buying and selling of large blocks of securities by banks, pension and mutual funds, and other financial intermediaries

investment outlay of money for income or profit

issue circulation or offering of securities for sale

junk bond high-yield, speculative bond often issued by lower credit-rated company, sometimes to finance corporate takeover

LBO **l**everaged **b**uy**o**ut

leverage use of credit in business activity, esp. to enhance speculative capacity; borrowed capital used in business

leveraged buyout LBO; change of company ownership through purchase of large block of stock financed by debt to be paid off out of future revenue

listed (*adj*) designating a security traded on one of the exchanges

margin cash or collateral required to be deposited with broker to protect broker and allow client to purchase securities on credit

margin account brokerage account in which trading on margin can occur

market institution of and place where trading of securities occurs; stock market

market index number showing percentage variation from arbitrary standard, used to measure rise and fall of market

market order instructions to buy or sell at current market price

market price prevailing price for security or commodity in given market

mercantile exchange place where trading in securities occurs, as distinguished from commodities exchange

merger combining of two or more companies by issuing stock of controlling corporation to replace most of stock of other companies

mergers and acquisitions department of investment banking firm or brokerage handling corporate mergers and acquisitions

municipal bond bond sold by local or state government

mutual fund investment company owned by shareholders and using funds to purchase stocks and bonds of other corporations

NASDAQ National Association of Securities Dealers Automated Quotations; system for quoting and trading over-the-counter securities

New York Stock Exchange primary security trading exchange, located on Wall Street in New York City

obligation debt security with required fixed payment, such as mortgage or corporate bond

odd lot quantity of stock purchased in units other than 10 or 100 shares

offering security made available for purchase at specific price for set period of time

option right to buy or sell security at fixed price within specified time

OTC (*adj*) over-the-counter

outstanding (*adj*) of securities, publicly issued and in circulation

overpriced (*adj*) designating securities priced above true value with potential to decline in price

over-the-counter (*adj*) OTC; designating stocks not listed on any exchange, sold directly to buyers

paid-in-kind security PIK security

panic sudden, widespread fear of financial collapse that results in attempts to sell off securities at any price

par issue security offered at face value

par value face value of share of stock or bond

penny stock highly speculative common stock, usu. selling for less than one dollar per share

PIK security paid-in-kind security; usu. high-yield security on which interest accrues as additional securities, not as interest, dividends, or cash

pit area of commodities exchange where brokers and traders work

point unit of variation in security market prices

portfolio investor's sum total of stocks, bonds, and securities

preferred stock share of ownership in business that provides first claim on assets after creditors, priority in receipt of dividends, but not necessarily a voice in company management

premium amount over par value for which preferred stock is sold

price-earnings ratio current price of a share of common stock divided by earnings per share over one-year period

proceeds earnings from security sale less commissions

profit taking selling of securities to take advantage of temporarily inflated price

program trading large, computerized security transactions, usu. made by institutional investors, that occur automatically at predetermined prices

public issue offer of securities for sale to public on exchange

publicly traded designating stock available for sale on exchange or over-the-counter

put option to sell given quantity of securities at specific price and within specified time, purchased in anticipation of decline in price

quotation current price of stock or commodity; record of opening and closing prices and number of shares traded on particular day

raider financier who uses greenmail, leveraged buyout, and arbitrage in attempt to purchase publicly owned entity against the wishes of its management

rally period of rising stock market prices

risk arbitrage investment in securities or commodities subject to takeover or other speculation

Sallie Mae SLMA; student loans issued by federal agency based on mortgages purchased from lenders

SEC Securities and Exchange Commission

securities government-regulated class of investments, including bonds, notes, stock certificates, and mortgages

Securities and Exchange Commission SEC; federal agency that regulates stock and commodity market transactions and conduct of market participants

sell-off decline in prices of certain securities due to pressure to sell

sell short (*vb*) sell securities that seller does not yet own but expects to cover later at lower price

Series E bond widely held bond issue of U.S. Treasury

Series H bond widely held bond issue of U.S. Treasury

shakeout rapid decrease in value of certain securities, often forcing speculators to sell holdings

share single unit of stock or other security

shareholder owner of share or shares in company

shares *Chiefly Brit.* stocks

SLMA Student Loan Marketing Association; Sallie Mae

slump general decrease in stock prices over period of time

soft market weak, declining market

speculation buying or selling of securities at high risk in anticipation of rise or fall in price

speculator one who speculates in securities

split dividing of securities by substituting multiple of original shares with equal par value but proportionately lower value per share

spot market market in which cash is exchanged for actual delivery of commodities

spots *Informal.* commodities

stock unit of ownership of corporation; outstanding capital of a company

stock bonus payment in company stock in addition to wages, esp. to corporate executive

stockbroker agent buying and selling shares of ownership in corporations for clients who pay sales commission

stock certificate written evidence of ownership of shares of stock

stock exchange market for trading in stocks; association of brokers who meet daily to buy and sell securities; stock market

stockholder owner of share or shares in capital of corporation

stockjobbing sales and promotion of often worthless securities

stock market market for stocks throughout a nation; stock exchange

stock option put or call

stock parking concealing one's ownership of securities

stocks and bonds securities in general

straddle option in which a put and a call are combined at same market price for same set period

street name broker's as opposed to owner's name on security, usu. for convenience

subscription agreement to pay certain amount for fixed number of securities

surety company company that insures against various types of losses and executes bonds

takeover assumption of management or ownership of company through acquisition of its stock

tax-exempt bond government obligation on which interest is exempt from federal and/or state income tax

T-bill U.S. Treasury bill or note

technical correction brief movement of market counter to general trend due to mechanics of pricing

tender offer offer at stated price for stock purchase from shareholders in takeover, often with promise of better management

ticker computer recording and displaying current stock prices

trader person whose business is buying and selling of commodities or securities

trading exchange, purchase, and sale of stocks and bonds

trading pit area of intense activity where trading occurs at exchange

Treasury bill short-term, interest-bearing obligation of U.S. Treasury, maturing in one year or less; T-bill

Treasury bond any of various series of bonds issued by U.S. Treasury, maturing over long periods of time

Treasury note interest-bearing obligation of U.S. Treasury, maturing in one to ten years

triple witching hour last hour of trading on any of four Fridays each year when options and futures expire, regarded as highly volatile time

underpriced (*adj*) priced below true value with potential to increase in price

underwrite (*vb*) agree to buy or guarantee purchase of securities issue on given date at fixed price

utilities stocks issued by corporations that provide power, water, or telephone services, forming a separate market index

voting stock shares of stock that give owner right to vote on certain corporate decisions

Wall Street street at center of New York City financial district serving as location of New York Stock Exchange; U.S. financial interests and business in general

war bond government bond issued to obtain revenue to support war effort

warrant call option with much longer maturity period than option, usu. up to two years or more

wash sale sale of stock at a loss and repurchase within thirty days for tax purposes; simultaneous purchase and sale of same stock or commodity to give impression of activity

water (*vb*) increase par value of shares without having assets to support this increase

watered stock stock illegally issued at above face value without corresponding increase in corporate assets

yield ratio of annual dividends or earnings per share to market price

zero-coupon bond bond sold at discount from face value and paying no regular interest, which is paid in full at time of maturity

Taxation

TYPES OF TAXES

ad valorem tax tax applied to value of what is being taxed, esp. imports

alcohol tax tax on sale of alcoholic beverages

alternative minimum tax special income tax on certain tax preference items

amusement tax tax on movies, plays, and other performances, included in admission price

capital gains tax tax on disposition of securities, business assets, or real property

capitation tax poll tax

customs duty tax on goods imported from another country

death tax inheritance or estate tax

direct tax tax levied directly on person by whom it is to be paid, as income or estate tax

douane *French.* customs duty; customs house

duty tax on imported, exported, or manufactured goods

estate tax tax on assets of deceased person

estimated tax income tax paid quarterly by

persons not subject to withholding, esp. self-employed people

excess-profits tax special tax on profits over fixed amount

excise tax tax on the manufacture, use, or sale of certain goods, esp. alcohol, tobacco, or firearms

federal tax tax levied by national government

franchise tax tax levied on corporations for right to do business in state or locality

gas tax tax on sale of gasoline as fuel

gift tax tax on very large gifts, paid by giver

graduated tax income tax with rates increasing at higher levels of income

hidden tax tax paid by manufacturer, supplier, or seller and passed on to consumer in market price; indirect tax

income tax federal, state, and local government tax on individual and business earnings, providing most of government revenues

indirect tax hidden tax

inheritance tax state tax on assets of deceased person, usu. paid by beneficiary

land tax tax on real property

levy imposition and collection of tax; amount of tax

local tax tax levied by city or county government

luxury tax excise tax on certain luxury items, such as boats

maximum tax tax computation that limits rate of taxation on net capital gains

minimum tax special minimum income tax

municipal tax tax levied by city government

personal property tax tax paid on movable items such as automobiles, furniture, or machinery used in business

poll tax tax sometimes levied for right to vote; capitation tax

progressive tax variable income tax rate that increases as amount to be taxed increases

property tax tax paid by owner of real property based on assessed value; real estate tax

proportional tax income tax that takes same percentage of income at all income levels

protective tariff tax on imports, intended to give domestic producers advantage in competitive pricing

real estate tax property tax

regressive tax tax rates that tax lower incomes at higher rates than higher incomes; tax rates equal at all levels of income, effectively taxing lower incomes more heavily

revenue stamp government stamp indicating payment of tax on commodity such as alcohol or tobacco

revenue tax tax usu. imposed on alcohol or tobacco

sales tax tax levied by city, county, or state on retail sales of merchandise

school tax local tax, usu. on property, with revenues used for support of schools

self-employment tax Social Security tax paid as percent of net income by usu. self-employed

persons not subject to FICA withholding by employers

severance tax tax on lump-sum distribution at termination of employment

single tax tax on land ownership that constitutes sole source of revenue (19th c.)

sin tax *Informal.* tax on alcohol, tobacco, gambling, or other activities considered to be neither luxuries nor necessities

Social Security tax tax withheld from wages by FICA or paid as self-employment tax by sole proprietors

state tax tax levied by state government

surtax extra tax or charge; tax levied on income exceeding specified amount

tariff schedule of taxes on imports

tax compulsory federal, state, or local charge levied on income, imports, or retail purchases and used to finance government expenditures

taxation act of taxing; revenues derived from tax

toll tax or fee paid for privilege such as crossing bridge or driving on highway

unemployment tax amount paid by employer, and sometimes by employee, to be used as unemployment compensation to workers who lose their jobs

value-added tax sales tax on producer based on value of contribution to final product

windfall profits tax federal excise tax on profits from domestically produced crude oil

withholding tax tax deducted by employer from wages as income and Social Security tax

INCOME TAX

ability to pay basis of principle that highest tax burden should fall on those with greatest ability to pay

abusive tax shelter investment scheme involving transactions that generate artificial losses in excess of actual investment for purpose of creating tax credits

accelerated cost recovery system ACRS; method of calculating depreciation, giving larger deductions in earlier years and smaller ones in later years

ACRS **a**ccelerated **c**ost **r**ecovery **s**ystem

active participation income-producing entity in which individual is directly involved

adjusted basis cost of asset less certain expenses and salvage value and/or plus improvements

adjusted gross income AGI; total taxable income before deductions and exemptions but after certain adjustments

adjustments reductions to gross income in determining AGI

AGI **a**djusted **g**ross **i**ncome

amended return corrected version of return previously filed based on new or corrected information

amortization method of deducting intangible

expenses by prorating them over fixed period, similar to depreciation

assessment amount of tax liability as determined by taxing authority

at-risk loss net loss on business for which taxpayer is ultimately liable

audit examination of books and records by taxing authority to determine validity of return

backup withholding federal tax withheld at source on nonwage income such as interest, dividends, or pensions

bad debt loan determined to be uncollectable, deductible as an expense

basis cost or value when placed in service of depreciable asset plus or minus certain adjustments

boot nonlike-kind property included in like-kind exchange to balance value

Bureau of Customs and Excise tax-collecting authority in Great Britain

capital gain profit on sale of business assets, securities, real property, personal property, or intangible property

capitalization transferring cost of certain assets to balance sheet rather than taking full expense in year of purchase

capital loss loss on sale of business assets, securities, real property, personal property, or intangible property

carryback application of tax benefit or credit to previous year's tax return

carryforward application of unused tax benefit, credit, or capital loss to following year's tax return; carryover

carryover carryforward

casualty loss loss not reimbursed by insurance due to act of God or criminal act, partially accepted as an itemized deduction

charitable contribution itemized deduction allowed for cash or goods donated to nonprofit organization

collection formal process of requiring payment of overdue tax to revenue service

contract labor business expense for payments to individuals subcontracting on job but not regular employees of taxpayer

corporation business entity that is organized under incorporation laws of one state and usu. pays taxes on net profits

cost of goods sold initial amount, either cost of merchandise and warehousing or direct labor and materials, by which gross income is reduced in determining gross profit before expenses

credit any of various amounts by which tax liability is reduced

decedent for tax purposes, a person who died in previous tax year

declare (*vb*) report received income on return

declining balance depreciation depreciation figured as percent of remaining undepreciated basis, which declines each year

deductible (*adj*) designating an amount or type of expense that may be used to reduce adjusted gross income before calculating tax

deduction standardized or itemized amount by which adjusted gross income is reduced in determining taxable income

dependent person half of whose support is paid by taxpayer, who claims an exemption for this person

depletion depreciation of certain intangible assets, esp. oil and natural gas

depreciation allowance made for decrease in value of capital assets over time; various means of prorating the cost of such assets as an expense over fixed number of years

distribution amount paid out by pension, IRA, profit-sharing plan, trust, estate, or corporation to shareholders

dividend annual taxable payment to shareholders on earnings of securities

earned income credit amount added to withholding and estimated payments in determining overpayment or tax due, for low-income persons with dependents

EID employer **id**entification number

employee business expense unreimbursed expenses incurred in course of work by salaried employee, an itemized deduction; such expenses reimbursed in W-2 as an adjustment

employer identification number EID; government-issued number that identifies corporation, partnership, trust, or individual who employs others

enrolled agent person who has passed IRS examination and is officially recognized as a tax preparer

estimated tax quarterly payment of income tax in lieu of withholding, made esp. by self-employed persons

exciseman *Brit.* government excise tax collector

exemption set amount allowed as deduction from income or credit on taxes for taxpayer, spouse, dependents, and those over sixty-five or blind

expense any of various costs associated with income production or a business, deductible from income

expensing taking entire cost of depreciable asset as expense in year of purchase

extension application for or permission granted to file return after due date

Federal Insurance Contributions Act FICA; legislation under which taxes are levied for support of Social Security

FICA **F**ederal **I**nsurance **C**ontributions **A**ct

fiduciary return tax return filed by trustee of an estate or trust

filing act of filling out and submitting tax return to taxing authority

filing date date on which return must be mailed in

foreign earned income exclusion amount of foreign earned income not liable to U.S. tax but subject to foreign tax

foreign tax credit reduction of U.S. tax liability based on taxes paid to foreign country on income from that country

gain profit on sale or exchange of asset

garnishment deduction of person's unpaid taxes or other debts directly from paycheck or bank account by order of court

gross income total income received before deductions

head of household unmarried person who pays over half the cost of maintaining home for child or other dependent

holding period period of time between acquisition and disposition of capital asset, used to determine whether asset is short or long term

income various forms of taxable and nontaxable revenue received by taxpayer

income property commercial or residential real property on which rent is paid to taxpayer

independent contractor self-employed person responsible for payment of own taxes

individual retirement account IRA; tax-free savings account into which annual contributions are made that allows deferment of tax payments until retirement

informational return tax return showing income and expenses but no tax liability, such as partnership or fiduciary return

in-kind contribution value and cost of services rendered to charitable organization, an itemized deduction

Inland Revenue federal taxing authority in Great Britain

interest income income derived as percentage of return on bank or savings deposits, bonds, or mortgages

internal revenue money collected by government from sources within country

internal revenue agent employee of IRS who audits, examines tax returns, and determines assessments

Internal Revenue Service IRS; tax-collecting agency of U.S. government

investment expense deductible amount, such as margin interest, incurred in production of investment income

involuntary exchange/conversion casualty, theft, or condemnation resulting in loss or decreased value of capital asset

IRA **i**ndividual **r**etirement **a**ccount

IRS **I**nternal **R**evenue **S**ervice

itemized deduction personal expense, such as medical or charitable outlay or mortgage interest paid, allowed as deduction from adjusted gross income in determining taxable income

joint return tax return reporting income for both members of married couple

Keogh plan personal retirement plan for self-employed individual, with contribution based on net income

K-1 form issued by partnership, trust, fiduciary, or subchapter S corporation showing individual's share of net profit or loss and certain other income, distributions, and deductions

like-kind exchange nontaxable exchange of the same type of property

limitation standardized amount or amount based on individual return that credit or deduction may not exceed

limited partnership partnership with at least one general partner who has unlimited liability and at least one limited partner who is liable only for his or her investment

long-term capital gain profit on sale of assets held over one year

loophole means of reducing taxes by careful use of laws; law written to benefit one class or group of taxpayers

lump-sum distribution single payment from pension or profit-sharing program to which employee contributed, usu. received at time of separation from job

MACRS modified accelerated cost recovery system

modified accelerated cost recovery system MACRS; method of calculating depreciation that allows smaller deductions in early years than ACRS

moving expense expense allowed as itemized deduction for cost of moving personal belongings and family when employee moves over 35 miles to take new job

net operating loss NOL; condition in which business expenses exceed total income for year, resulting in loss applicable to previous or later year's tax return

net profit gross income less all expenses

NOL net operating loss

nonemployee compensation amounts paid to self-employed person, subject to self-employment tax

nonprofit organization tax-exempt corporation filing informational return

nonresident taxpayer who is part-year resident or not a resident of taxing authority

nontaxable (*adj*) not liable to taxation

office-in-home portion of residence used for business, with percentage of housing costs taken as expense

ordinary income noncapital gains income that is taxable in full

out-of-state return tax return filed for income received from state of which one is not a resident

overpayment tax payment in excess of amount owed, generating refund or credit

partner active or passive member of partnership reporting portion of partnership's income on individual return

partnership return informational return filed by general or limited partnership, showing profit or loss, portions of which are transferred to each partner's individual return

part-year resident person who moved into and/or out of state during tax year

passive activity any source of income, esp. a limited partnership with real estate investment

or a trust, in which taxpayer has no active involvement

penalty additional assessment for failure to file on time, underpayment, or underestimation of tax liability

personal interest interest and finance charges paid on credit cards, charge accounts, and other personal loans, no longer deductible

points percent of face value of mortgage paid at closing and fully deductible as itemized deduction when paid on principal residence

portfolio income income derived from investments and securities, considered unearned income

preenactment (*adj*) designating property acquired or activities begun prior to tax reform act of October 23, 1986

premature distribution taxable distribution from retirement plan or IRA prior to designated age of collection

preparer professional trained and usu. licensed to fill out tax returns for others

preparer penalty IRS assessment against preparer for sloppiness, negligence, or fraud

recapture adding back of investment tax credit or depreciation taken on asset that has been disposed of before end of useful life

refund amount of overpayment returned to taxpayer after filing of return

reimbursement payment received for out-of-pocket expense that reduces deduction

rental income income derived from rental of business or residential real property

retirement credit credit for low-income, elderly, retired and totally disabled persons

return forms, schedules, and statements used to report income and expenses and determine tax liability

rollover reinvestment of distribution, esp. from pension or IRA, to postpone payment of tax

salvage value estimated remaining value of asset once it is fully depreciated

schedule tax form listing itemized expenses or showing income from various sources

self-employment tax Social Security tax paid as percentage of net income by those not subject to FICA withholding by employers

SEP simplified employee pension

short form simplified tax form for those with wages and unearned income but no enumerated deductions or credits

short tax year tax year of less than twelve months for tax entity existing less than full year or one changing from calendar-year to fiscal-year accounting

short-term capital gain profit on sale of securities, business assets, or real property held less than one year

simplified employee pension SEP; tax-deferred pension identical for all employees and distributable from outset of employment

sole proprietorship unincorporated business operated by one person with net income after

expenses taxed on individual return and subject to self-employment tax

special agent experienced IRS agent responsible for investigating cases involving possible fraud or tax evasion

standard deduction specified amount allowed to all taxpayers as deduction from AGI when not itemizing

straight-line depreciation traditional depreciation in which basis is divided equally by number of years over life of asset

subchapter S corporation corporation with less than thirty-five shareholders that elects not to be taxed at corporate level but to have each shareholder's portion of net income taxed individually, as in a partnership

taxable income income subject to taxation after subtracting deductions, adjustments, and exemptions

tax base taxpayer's regular residence

tax bracket income range with set tax rate

tax break legal means of reducing one's tax liability by taking advantage of specific regulation

tax code complete listing of all laws and regulations relating to income taxes

tax collector agency or individual responsible for calling for and receiving tax payments

tax court body that reviews and decides on serious tax issues and audits

tax dodge illegal or apparently illicit means of avoiding tax liability

tax evasion any attempt to illegally avoid paying taxes

tax-exempt (*adj*) not liable to taxation

tax-exempt status condition or requirement by which entity, usu. nonprofit organization, makes its income not liable to taxation

tax farmer one who collects taxes for taxing authority and receives commission or fee

tax-free exchange usu. like-kind exchange of business assets or real property in which transaction is nontaxable

tax haven nation or state with very low or no income tax

taxing authority federal, state, or municipal government empowered to collect taxes

tax liability amount of tax due

tax lien claim on or confiscation of wages, bank deposits, or other property by taxing authority for payment of overdue tax

taxman *Informal.* tax assessor or collector

taxpayer individual required to pay tax or file return

tax rate specified percentage of commodity, income, or service that is taxed

tax rate schedule list of variable taxes at different levels of income or assessed value

tax return annual report on earnings and calculation of tax due federal and state governments

tax shelter investment designed to postpone or avoid payment of taxes rather than generate taxable income

tax structure laws, codes, and regulations determining basic method of taxation for specific taxing authority

tax year twelve-month period taken as annual taxing period, not necessarily beginning January 1

TIN taxpayer identification number; either social security number or employer identification number

triple tax-exempt bond government bond whose interest is exempt from federal, state, and local taxes

trust taxable entity controlling assets for benefit of individual beneficiaries, with trust distributions being deductions to trust and usu. taxable to beneficiaries

unemployment compensation payment received by individual from unemployment insurance, often taxable in full or part

useful life period over which capital asset may be depreciated

wages salary paid to employee by employer, subject to withholding tax

wash sale transaction in which cost basis and proceeds are equal

W-4 form filed by employee indicating number of exemptions, used by employer to determine withholding

windfall profit profit on domestically produced crude oil, subject to special tax

withholding payroll deduction for taxes and other items made by employer for direct payment to government

withholding tax income tax deducted by employer from wages

write-off expense allowable as tax deduction

write off (*vb*) take expense as tax deduction

W-2 form prepared at year's end by employer, and filed with government, showing employee's compensation and taxes withheld

Accounting

account subdivision of basic accounting system used to record assets, liabilities, equity, sales, or expenses

accountancy keeping or inspecting of business accounts; work of an accountant

accountant person trained in accounting methods, general bookkeeping, and tax preparation

accounting system of recording and summarizing business and financial transactions

accounting clerk entry-level bookkeeping position in company

accounts payable amounts owed to creditors

accounts receivable amounts to be received from customers for credit purchases

accrual entering in books items of income or expense that have been earned or incurred but not yet received or paid; such an item of income or expense

accrual method accounting system that matches accruals to period in which they were earned or

incurred rather than period in which they were received or paid

adjusted trial balance statement of debt and credit balances and all transactions on all ledger accounts, used to complete balance sheet at end of fiscal period

adjustment amount added to or subtracted from account to bring balance up to date

allowance amount set aside for specific purpose, actual or budgeted

annualize (*vb*) project income or expenses for full year based on results for part of year

appreciation increase in value of asset over time

assessment determination of income or value of property for purpose of fixing tax

assets articles or property of value; property, materials, and economic resources owned by business or individual

at risk (*adj*) denoting the amount an owner or investor stands to lose should business go bankrupt

audit examination of business financial accounts

auditor person trained to examine accounts

balance amount standing as debit or credit on account

balance sheet report of total assets, liabilities, and owner's equity accounts at specific time

bank reconciliation tracing of all discrepancies until account books match bank statements

bar graph graph of differences between items at one point in time or the change at different times

basis cost adjusted by certain expenses, salvage value, and excess depreciation, used in calculating gain or depreciation

beginning inventory value of merchandise on hand at opening of fiscal period

black (*adj*) showing a profit; in the black

bookkeeper person responsible for keeping financial records

bookkeeping systematic recording of financial business transactions and records

books general accounts or records of business transactions

books and records general accounts, posting of transactions and balances, and substantiating evidence

book value value of asset at specific point in time, equal to initial cost less accumulated depreciation

bottom line net profit or loss after expenses, shown at bottom of profit and loss statement

business entity organization existing independent of its owner's personal holdings

calendar year accounting year running from January 1 to December 31

capital account total amount of investment in business entity by each owner or all owners

capital contribution investment of capital or value of goods invested in business entity

cash basis method accounting system in which income and expenses are entered in books only when paid and no accruals are made

cashbook book in which record of all receipts and disbursements of money are kept

cash disbursements journal special journal with record of all transactions involving cash payments

certified public accountant CPA; accountant who has passed state licensing examination

circle graph graph showing percentages of revenue or expenses in different areas of activity

clerk bookkeeper or record keeper for business

close an account reduce account to zero balance when no further transactions are anticipated

close the books balance out all income and expense accounts at end of period

closing entries net income or loss transferred to capital account as necessary to close books

compound entry journal entry having two or more debits and/or two or more credits

comptroller controller

constructive receipt condition in which funds not yet collected, such as an uncashed check, are deemed to have been received because they are controlled by recipient

continuous budget rolling budget

controller chief accounting officer of business or government, esp. responsible for internal auditing of books; comptroller

cook the books *Slang.* manipulate financial records to conceal profits, avoid taxes, or give false impression in audit

cost amount of money paid for goods or services

cost accounting system of recording, analyzing, and allocating production and distribution costs for internal use by business; managerial accounting

costing out *Informal.* applying cost accounting methods

CPA certified public accountant

credit amount of liability, equity, or revenue recorded as entry into account books on right side of T account

current assets liquid and semiliquid assets, such as cash, accounts receivable, and inventory

current liabilities business debts coming due for payment within next accounting period

current ratio relationship between current assets and current liabilities

daybook chronological record of each day's transactions

debit amount of asset or expense recorded as entry into account books on left side of T account

deficit net loss

disbursement payment of funds

double-entry accounting financial recordkeeping in which there must be an equal credit for each debit

draw withdrawal of capital from unincorporated business entity by owner or partner

ending inventory value of merchandise on hand at close of fiscal period

entry recording of single item in account book or ledger

equity owner's financial claim to or investment in assets or property of business

expense cost of goods or services that reduces owner's equity or profits for accounting period

face value principal amount of promissory note

factor entity that buys accounts receivable at discount from firm unable to carry them

financial accounting system of accounting used for reporting to investors, banks, and taxing authorities

financial statement report summarizing changes due to transactions during accounting period

fiscal year annual accounting period for business, either calendar year or sometimes July 1 to June 30 or October 1 to September 30

fixed costs expenses that are not variable during an accounting period, many of which are paid regularly

general ledger journal in which all business transactions are recorded and accounts balanced

gross total revenue before deduction of costs and expenses

gross profit difference between total sales revenue and cost of merchandise sold before deduction of other expenses

horizontal analysis comparison of changes in accounting statements from one period to next

income money received in sales, wages, or profits

independent contractor one who does work for another without being a regular employee, usu. setting own hours and conditions and hiring own workers

intangible asset property, such as patent, that represents value but has no physical form

in the black (*adj*) operating at a profit; black

in the red (*adj*) operating at a loss; red

inventory value of items of merchandise in stock at given time

invoice itemized list and billing statement of goods shipped or services rendered

journal entry book for recording daily transactions and indicating to which accounts they apply

journal entry orderly, usu. chronological, record of business transactions

journalize (*vb*) record transactions as journal entries

ledger book containing each business account on separate page, to which all journal entries are transferred

liabilities amounts owed to creditors; accounts payable

limited liability risk of loss fixed at some maximum amount, such as total investment

liquidation closing of business by collecting assets and settling debts

liquidity ease with which assets can be converted to cash

log (*vb*) enter transaction in journal or daybook

managerial accounting cost accounting

multicolumn journal journal using standard system of keeping books for several accounts

negative amortization increase of principal of loan by amount by which periodic loan payments fall short of interest due, usu. because of interest rate increase

negative cash flow excess of expenses over income

net money free from all charges, costs, and expenses

net income total revenue less costs and expenses

net loss amount by which expenses exceed revenue; deficit

net profit amount by which revenues exceed expenses

net sales total sales for period less returns, allowances, and discounts

net worth total assets minus liabilities of individual or business

notes payable promissory notes on loans issued to creditors

notes receivable promissory notes received by business from those who owe it money

number-cruncher *Informal.* accountant or clerk involved in bookkeeping and computer or statistical operations, but not management or decision making

outstanding account balance of unpaid debt, amount owing on loan

owner's equity owner's capital account in business

P and L **p**rofit and **l**oss statement showing gross income, expenses, and net profit

payment schedule agreement between debtor and creditor for repayment of loan in installments over specified time

payroll list of employees and payments made to each for specific pay period

payroll deduction amount subtracted from gross earnings before payment of salary

payroll register form summarizing employee's earnings for each pay period

pencil footing *Informal.* column total written in small penciled figures, to be carried forward

positive cash flow excess of income over expenses

posting transference of transactions from journal entry to ledger account

post up (*vb*) transfer journal transaction into general ledger

proceeds amount of cash received from transaction after commissions, costs of sale, and interest deductions

profit revenue earned less expenses incurred

public accounting accounting services provided to clients for fee by licensed practitioners

quarterly tax return regular payment of sales, unemployment, and other business taxes

ratio analysis numerical comparison of items on financial statement to evaluate their relationships

realize (*vb*) convert into money; gain as net result of transaction

reconciling process of determining and accounting for discrepancies between accounts, balances, or statements

red (*adj*) showing a loss; in the red

retained earnings corporate earnings not paid out as stockholders' dividends

revenue money earned from sales of goods, services, or other business transactions

rolling budget budget prepared month by month instead of annually; continuous budget

ruling horizontal line beneath column of figures to indicate that entries above line are complete

sales allowance price reduction on damaged goods

sales return merchandise returned to vendor for credit or refund

selling expenses costs incurred in selling or marketing goods

sole proprietorship noncorporate business with one owner

spreadsheet worksheet on which financial information is presented in two-dimensional matrix; computer program for maintaining such a record

statement regular, usu. monthly, record of all transactions, deposits, and balances of account

stockholders' equity value of stockholders' claims to corporate assets

subsidiary ledger separate ledger containing detailed accounts for each creditor, debtor, customer, or vendor

suspense account account into which items are temporarily placed until their disposition is determined

T account account record shaped like a T, used in analyzing transactions, with left side showing debits and right side showing credits

tangible assets items having material form and intrinsic value

temporary capital accounts records of contributions, draws, and other changes during fiscal period, to be transferred to permanent capital account at end of period

trial balance statement of debit and credit balance on all open accounts, used to check their equality and make adjustments in double-entry accounting

uncollectable account account receivable that cannot be collected and that may be written off as bad debt

valuation assessment of value

value worth in financial terms

vertical analysis restating of dollar amounts on financial statement as percentage of base amount

weighted average cost method method of calculating inventory by adding purchases to beginning inventory and dividing by total units to obtain average cost per unit

withdrawal return of cash or other business assets to owner

worth value of assets and securities

worthless (*adj*) lacking all value, bankrupt

write-down reduction of asset's value, as with damaged but not worthless inventory

write-off uncollectable debt; worthless asset

zero base accounting method in which each item is justified on basis of cost and need

Spending, Receiving, and Possessing Wealth

acquisition accumulation and retention of wealth

acquisitiveness eagerness for and skill at attaining and holding wealth

advance payment made or received before due

affluence abundance of wealth or riches

aid financial help, esp. institutional assistance to poor

alimony regular payments made by one spouse to the other as required by divorce decree

allotment one's portion; amount due to one

allowance amount of money given regularly, esp. to child

alms money or supplies given to the poor

angel *Informal.* financial supporter for a particular enterprise

annuity payment of fixed sum at regular intervals, usu. yearly

appanage person's rightful gain, perquisite; amount added to endowment

appropriation money given over or set aside for specific use; amount taken for one's own use, often improperly

assets all that one owns, all wealth possessed

assignee person to whom rights have been transferred and payments are due

assignment transfer of claim on certain rights or funds to another

avarice excessive desire for wealth; greed

award amount given by court decision, as result of judgment in competition, or for merit

backing financial support for some enterprise

banausic (*adj*) mundanely concerned with making money

barter direct exchange of goods and services without use of currency

benefactor person giving financial help to another

beneficiary person named to receive income, inheritance, or proceeds of trust or insurance policy

benefit public event or performance held to raise funds for specific group, person, or cause

bequest legacy

bestowal gift made to another

billionaire person whose net worth exceeds one billion dollars

blackmail extortion of payment by threat, esp. to reveal embarrassing information

bonanza source of great wealth

bounty generous gift given freely; substantial riches

brass ring *Informal.* wealth and success as a goal or prize

bribery giving of money to another to induce illegal act

capitalist person who has extensive capital, esp. invested in business enterprises

charity money given voluntarily to help those in need

cheap (*adj*) stingy

closefisted (*adj*) stingy, miserly

come into (*vb*) receive one's inheritance; unexpectedly obtain wealth

commission percentage of proceeds from sale or transaction paid in addition to or in lieu of wages

compensation wage, salary, fee, commission, or other payment received for services or product

consideration money given as part of business transaction, esp. for services rendered

Croesus very rich man

cumshaw gratuity or tip, sometimes obtained illegally

cut off (*vb*) disinherit

deep pockets abundance of wealth

disinherit (*vb*) exclude from inheritance

dole allotment of money or aid to those in need

donation contribution or gift, esp. to charity

donor one who gives money, esp. to an organization

double-dipping practice of receiving more than one form of compensation from same employer or organization

dowry wealth and property brought by bride to husband at time of marriage

economy careful management of wealth; restraint in spending

endowment gift or bequest used to provide income for institution or person

estate one's fortune or property, esp. when deceased

expenditure outlay of money for particular purpose

fat cat *Slang.* wealthy person, usu. politically influential

fee payment given, esp. for professional service or license

fellowship sum paid for support of graduate student

fixed income uniform rate or amount of income received over period of time

flush (*adj*) abundantly supplied with money

fortune large quantity of wealth

frugality thrift, economy, and care in spending

generosity willingness to give to others; giving in abundance

gift something freely handed over to another

giving act of making a gift, often associated with charity

Golconda rich mine or other source of great wealth

graft illicit profits gained by taking advantage of privileged position

grant formal gift, usu. by institution or government

grant-in-aid funds given, usu. by government or foundation, to support work of scholar, scientist, artist, or institution

gratuity money given for service provided in excess of regular price; tip

gravy *Slang.* money obtained easily, sometimes illegally

greed avarice

heir person who receives property, esp. great wealth, of dead person by will or law

heiress female heir

hemorrhage rapid loss of assets in large amounts

honorarium payment for acts or services for which custom or propriety forbids a price to be set

inheritance wealth and property received upon another's death

investment use of one's existing capital to generate income or profit and thus increase wealth

kickback reimbursement of funds based on secret collusion, often illegal or unethical

largess generous gifts

lavish (*adj*) generous, often extravagant, in giving or spending

legacy money or property left to another by will; bequest

liberality generosity in giving or spending

loaded (*adj*) *Slang.* very wealthy

lot one's due portion or fortune

lucrative (*adj*) profitable; tending to or likely to make money

man of means wealthy individual

means available wealth, resources

Midas one whose touch seems to turn everything to gold

millionaire person whose net worth exceeds one million dollars

millions great wealth

miser stingy person who hoards money, even at expense of own comfort

moneybags very wealthy person

moneyed (*adj*) wealthy, well-to-do

munificence generosity in giving

nabob very rich and influential person

net worth total value of one's possessions, property, and wealth

niggardly (*adj*) stingy, miserly

opulence great wealth, characterized by lavish spending

parsimony great caution in spending, stinginess

patron wealthy person who provides financial support for an activity, person, or institution

pay money handed over for work done or services performed

penny-pinching extreme frugality

penny-wise (*adj*) thrifty and careful over small sums or matters

pension regular payment given to one who has fulfilled certain conditions, esp. worked at a particular job until a certain age

penury extreme poverty

per diem *Latin.* lit. by the day; daily expense allowance received while traveling or being employed at some distance away from one's home

philanthropy charitable donations or gifts to needy individuals or nonprofit institutions

plutocracy group of wealthy, politically influential persons; rule by the wealthy

pop (*vb*) *Slang*. pay for something, esp. another's share

portion one's proper due or lot

possession ownership; condition of holding wealth

possessions wealth, property

pourboire *French*. tip, gratuity

premium additional amount paid for something

pretty penny *Informal*. large amount of money

prodigality free spending

prosperity accumulation or possession of wealth

public assistance government aid to the needy

purse sum of money offered or collected as prize, reward, or gift

purse-proud (*adj*) proud of one's wealth, esp. in a showy manner

quota one's proportional share of wealth or pay

ransom money paid for release of confiscated property or kidnap victim

rebate portion of payment returned at time of purchase

recipient person who receives money

relief public assistance or welfare payments

remuneration payment or reward for work, service, or trouble

resources available wealth, capital

retirement benefits money paid regularly at termination of one's employment by former employer or government

riches wealth, money in one's possession

salary payment received regularly for work performed

save (*vb*) avoid expense so as to put money aside for future use

savings funds set aside for future use

scholarship gift of money to assist needy student in paying for education

scotch (*adj*) *Informal*. (sometimes offensive) frugal; cheap

scrimp (*vb*) economize, try to save when little is available; skimp

skimp (*vb*) keep expenses low; scrimp

skinflint miser, niggardly person

slush fund money set aside for illicit or corrupt purposes

sparing (*adj*) frugal, cautious in spending

spending paying out of money

spendthrift person who spends money wastefully or carelessly

sponsor person responsible for providing financial support for an individual, activity, or institution

spring (*vb*) *Informal*. pay another's cost or expenses

squander (*vb*) spend money wastefully or extravagantly

stingy (*adj*) frugal, miserly, spending money grudgingly

stipend regular payment for service; allowance

subsidy grant of money, esp. from government for public benefit

testament will

thrift frugality, care in spending

tight-fisted (*adj*) stingy, reluctant to spend

tightwad *Informal*. miser, stingy person

tip gratuity

treasury accumulated and stored wealth

treat (*vb*) pay another's share

tribute regular, often forced, payment as show of subjugation

underwrite (*vb*) agree to pay costs and cover losses of undertaking or institution

ungenerous (*adj*) stingy, reluctant to spend money on others

usance income and other benefits derived from ownership of wealth

wages regular payments by employer for work performed

wastrel person who squanders money or spends extravagantly

wealth large amount of money and property

welfare government aid granted to those in need

well-to-do (*adj*) prosperous, wealthy

will legal statement of person's wishes for disposition of money and property following death; testament

worth value of one's assets, property, and money

Money, Currency, and Denominations

agio fee paid to exchange one currency for another

almighty dollar characterization of money as source of power

arm and a leg great sum of money

bale of hay *Slang*. large amount of money

bank note promissory note issued by bank, used as form of paper money

bankroll conspicuous wad of bills

bean *Slang*. one dollar

bill one piece of paper money

bill of exchange written order to pay specific sum of money to particular person

bob *Brit. informal*. shilling

boodle *Slang*. money, esp. taken in robbery or given as bribe

bouncing paper *Slang*. bad check

bread *Slang*. money

buck *Slang*. one U.S. dollar

bucks *Slang*. large amount of money

bullion gold or silver ingots or bars, held as standard for currency

cambio *Spanish*. foreign exchange bank

cambist dealer in foreign currencies

capital accumulated wealth, esp. used to increase wealth

cash paper currency and metal coins; actual money

cash in hand money available at given moment

cent basic fractional unit or coin in most countries, usu. one-hundredth of primary unit of currency; one-hundredth of a U.S. dollar

centavo cent in various Spanish-speaking countries

centime cent in various French-speaking countries

centimo cent in various Spanish-speaking countries

change coins

chicken feed *Slang*. insignificant amount of money

circulation paper currency and coins passed from person to person

clam *Slang*. dollar

C-note *Slang*. hundred-dollar bill

coin small, flat metal disk used as money

coinage metal currency; making of coins

coin collection accumulation of old, rare, or foreign coins as a hobby

coin of the realm legal tender

cold cash money paid in full at time of business transaction

Confederate note paper money produced by Confederate states during U.S. Civil War

copper a coin made of copper, bronze, or the like, esp. U.S. cent or British penny

counterfeit forged money not printed and issued by government

crown former coin of Great Britain, equal to twenty-five new pence

currency money circulated as medium of exchange in any country, esp. paper money

demonetization stoppage of use of gold or silver as currency standard

denarius silver coin and monetary unit of ancient Rome

devaluation reduction of currency's value relative to international monetary values

dime ten-cent U.S. coin

dinero *Slang*. money

dollar basic unit of U.S. currency; one hundred cents; smallest value of single bill

dollars money in one's possession

do-re-mi *Slang*. money

double eagle twenty-dollar U.S. gold piece

doubloon obsolete gold coin of Spain and Spanish America

dough *Slang*. money

drachma principal silver coin of ancient Greece; monetary unit of modern Greece

ducats *Slang*. money, esp. cash; gold or silver coins formerly used in Europe

eagle ten-dollar U.S. gold piece

Eurodollar U.S. dollar deposited in or credited to European bank

exchange conversion of one nation's currency into another's

exchange rate value of one nation's currency in relation to that of another; cost of exchanging one currency for another

farthing one-quarter penny, formerly used in Great Britain

Federal Reserve note paper currency issued by individual Federal Reserve Bank in denominations from one to ten thousand dollars; prevailing form of currency in circulation in United States

fen basic fractional unit or coin of China

fiat money currency without gold or silver backing, issued by government decree

fido coin with minting error

fin *Slang.* five-dollar bill

fiver *Slang.* five-dollar bill; five-pound note

five-spot *Slang.* five-dollar bill

floating exchange rates uncontrolled exchange rates in which currencies of various nations rise and fall based on supply and demand for each currency

florin former coin of Great Britain equal to two shillings, former gold coin of Florence

Fort Knox site of U.S. gold bullion depository

four bits *Slang.* fifty U.S. cents

funds money resources available; capital

gelt *Slang.* money

G-note *Slang.* thousand-dollar bill

gold yellow precious metal formerly used for coins, often held by nation as standard for issued currency

gold certificate former U.S. paper currency redeemable for gold

gold dust tiny bits of gold as it is normally found in placer mining

gold piece single gold coin

gold standard monetary system in which value of nation's currency is based on and backed by gold

grand *Informal.* one thousand U.S. dollars

green *Slang.* money, esp. paper currency

greenback U.S. legal-tender note, printed in green on the back

green stuff *Slang.* paper currency

groat former coin of Great Britain, equal to four pennies

guinea former coin of Great Britain, equal to twenty-one shillings

half C-note *Slang.* fifty-dollar bill

half crown former coin of Great Britain, equal to two shillings and sixpence

half dollar fifty-cent coin (U.S.)

ha'penny *Brit. informal.* half penny

hard cash actual coins and paper currency, as opposed to credit or other notes

hard currency paper money in circulation

K one thousand U.S. dollars

kale *Slang.* money

kitty small, informal savings fund; money pooled for specific purpose

kopeck basic fractional unit or coin of Soviet Union

legal tender official form of money, recognized as national medium of exchange in payment for purchases or debts; coin of the realm

lettuce *Slang.* paper currency, greenbacks

long green *Slang.* paper currency

lucre monetary gain or riches, often used in derogatory sense

mad money *Informal.* extra spending money for emergencies or impulse buying

mammon personification of riches as deity or evil spirit

mark former money of account in medieval England, equal to thirteen shillings, fourpence; monetary unit of Germany

medium of exchange currency used as measure of value in exchange for goods and services

megabucks *Informal.* very large amount of money

mill one-tenth U.S. cent

minor coin coin of nonprecious metal, neither gold nor silver

mint manufacturing site, depository, and government agency responsible for authorized coinage from metal

mintage process of making coins from metal; money produced at mint

monetary system coinage and circulation of currency

money medium of commerce, exchange, and banking that serves as recognized measure of value; paper currency and coins

money order order for payment of specified sum issued by bank or post office, serving as cash in exchange

moola *Slang.* money

mopus *Slang.* cash, ready money

napoleon former French coin with picture of Napoleon, equal to twenty francs

nest egg savings

new pence monetary unit of Great Britain, equal to one-hundredth of a pound since 1971

nickel five-cent U.S. coin

noble former coin of Great Britain, equal to half a mark

note single piece of paper currency issued by bank or government

numismatics science and study of coins and coinage

obol silver coin of ancient Greece, equal to one-sixth of a drachma

paper money authorized currency printed on paper

pecuniary (*adj*) pertaining to money

pelf money, esp. ill-gotten

pence *Brit.* plural of penny

penny one-cent coin, equal to one-hundredth of a dollar in United States or of a pound in Great Britain

petrodollars accumulation of surplus dollars by petroleum-exporting nations

petty cash small fund of money kept on hand for incidental expenses

pfennig one-hundredth of a German mark

piaster former Spanish dollar; *Informal.* money

piggy bank coin bank in shape of pig; any small bank of coins

pin money extra money; small savings

pocket money small amount of spending money kept on person

pot *Slang.* large sum of money; amount of money wagered at one time

pound basic monetary unit of United Kingdom, equal to one hundred new pence; prior to 1971, equal to twenty shillings or 240 pence

purse financial resources, money

quarter twenty-five cent U.S. coin

queer *Slang.* counterfeit money

quid *Brit. informal.* pound

ready money cash available for spending

real former silver coin of Spain and Spanish America

red cent *Informal.* penny

revaluation increase in currency's value relative to international monetary values

roll *Informal.* large number of paper bills, esp. rolled into bundle

rubber check bad check

sawbuck *Slang.* ten-dollar bill

scrip temporary paper to be exchanged for money; paper money in amounts less than one dollar, formerly issued in United States

shekel half-ounce gold or silver coin of ancient Hebrews; basic monetary unit of Israel

shekels *Slang.* money

shilling former monetary unit of United Kingdom, equal to one-twentieth of a pound or twelve pence

shoestring very small amount of available cash

silver white precious metal used in manufacture of coins and as monetary standard

silver certificate former U.S. paper currency redeemable for silver

simoleon *Slang.* dollar

sixpence former British coin equal to six pennies or one-half shilling

smacker *Slang.* dollar

small change coins of low denomination

solidus gold coin of ancient Rome and the Byzantine Empire

sou former coin of France, equal to five or ten centimes; *Slang.* small amount of money

sovereign former British gold coin valued at twenty shillings or one pound

specie coined money, as opposed to paper notes

spending money cash available for immediate use

sterling standard of British coinage in silver; British money

subsidiary coin U.S. coin with value under one dollar

tanner *Brit. slang.* sixpenny piece

tenner *Informal.* ten-dollar bill; ten-pound note (Britain)

ten-spot *Slang.* ten-dollar bill

token money coins with lower actual value as metal than their face value

treasury place for deposit and disbursement of funds, esp. government agency holding public tax funds

tuppence *Brit. informal.* twopence

two bits *Slang.* twenty-five U.S. cents

two-spot *Informal.* two-dollar bill

wad *Informal.* large amount of cash on hand

wampum *Informal.* money; beads used as medium of exchange by American Indians

wherewithal money for specific purpose

xenocurrency currency circulated and traded outside its country of issue

World Currencies

afghani currency of Afghanistan
austral currency of Argentina
baht currency of Thailand
balboa currency of Panama
birr currency of Ethiopia
bolivar currency of Venezuela
cedi currency of Ghana
colon currency of Costa Rica, El Salvador
cordoba currency of Nicaragua
cruzeiro real currency of Brazil
dalasi currency of Gambia
denar currency of Macedonia
deutsche mark currency of Germany
dinar currency of Algeria, Bahrain, Bosnia and Herzegovina, Iraq, Jordan, Kuwait, Libya, Serbia and Montenegro, Tunisia
dirham currency of Morocco, United Arab Emirates
dobra currency of São Tomé and Principe
dollar currency of Antigua and Barbuda, Australia, Bahamas, Barbados, Belize, Bermuda, Brunei, Canada, Dominica, Fiji, Grenada, Guyana, Hong Kong, Jamaica, Kiribati, Liberia, Micronesia, Nauru, New Zealand, Singapore, Solomon Islands, St. Kitts-Nevis, St. Lucia, St. Vincent and the Grenadines, Taiwan, Trinidad and Tobago, Tuvalu, United States, Zimbabwe
dong currency of Vietnam
drachma currency of Greece
dram currency of Armenia
emu proposed common currency of the European Union
escudo currency of Cape Verde, Portugal
forint currency of Hungary
franc currency of Andorra, Belgium, Benin, Burkina Faso, Burundi, Cameroon, Central African Republic, Chad, Comoros, Congo, Djibouti, Equatorial Guinea, France, Gabon, Guinea, Ivory Coast, Lichtenstein, Luxembourg, Madagascar, Mali, Martinique, Monaco, Niger, Rwanda, Senegal, Switzerland, Togo
gourde currency of Haiti
guarani currency of Paraguay
guilder currency of the Netherlands, Netherlands Antilles, Suriname
inti currency of Peru
karbovanets currency of Ukraine
kina currency of Papua New Guinea
kip currency of Laos
koruna currency of Czech Republic, Slovakia
krona currency of Iceland, Sweden
krone currency of Denmark, Greenland, Norway
kuna currency of Croatia
kwacha currency of Malawi, Zambia
kwanza currency of Angola
kyat currency of Burma (Myanmar)
lat currency of Latvia
lek currency of Albania
lempira currency of Honduras
leone currency of Sierra Leone
leu currency of Moldova, Romania
lev currency of Bulgaria
lilangeni currency of Swaziland
lira currency of Italy, Malta, San Marino, Turkey, Vatican City
lit currency of Lithuania
loti currency of Lesotho
manat currency of Azerbaijan, Turkmenistan
mark currency of Germany (also deutsche mark)
markka currency of Finland

metical currency of Mozambique
naira currency of Nigeria
ngultrum currency of Bhutan
ouguiya currency of Mauritania
pa'anga currency of Tonga
pataca currency of Macao
peseta currency of Andorra, Spain
peso currency of Bolivia, Chile, Colombia, Cuba, Dominican Republic, Guinea-Bissau, Mexico, the Philippines, Uruguay
pound currency of Cyprus, Egypt, Ireland, Lebanon, Sudan, Syria, United Kingdom
pula currency of Botswana
quetzal currency of Guatemala
rand currency of South Africa
rial currency of Iran, Oman, Yemen
riel currency of Cambodia
ringgit currency of Malaysia
riyal currency of Qatar, Saudi Arabia
ruble currency of Belarus, Russian Republic, and former Soviet Union
rufiyaa currency of the Maldives
rupee currency of India, Mauritius, Nepal, Pakistan, Seychelles, Sri Lanka
rupiah currency of Indonesia
schilling currency of Austria
shekel currency of Israel
shilling currency of Kenya, Somalia, Tanzania, Uganda
som currency of Kyrgyzstan, Uzbekistan
sucre currency of Ecuador
taka currency of Bangladesh
tala currency of Western Samoa
tenge currency of Kazakhstan
tolar currency of Slovenia
tugrik currency of Mongolia
vatu currency of Vanuatu
won currency of North Korea, South Korea
yen currency of Japan
yuan currency of China
zaire currency of Zaire
zloty currency of Poland

AGRICULTURE

Farming and Crops
Ranching and Animal Husbandry
Soils and Soil Management
Tools, Machinery, and Structures
Business and Science of Agriculture

See also: *Chap. 2: Biology; Animals; Plants;*
Chap. 3: Geology; Geography; Landscapes and
Seascapes; Chap. 9: Foods; Chap. 17: Gardening

Farming and Crops

agrarian (*adj*) pertaining to the land or farmers
agrichemical fertilizer, pesticide, or feeding supplement
alfalfa deep-rooted perennial of pea family used for fodder and as cover crop
annual plant that lives for only one year or one season
barley cultivated cereal grass, one of man's first grains
berry crops small, juicy, fleshy fruits
bone meal fertilizer made of fine bone, a natural source of phosphorus

bracero seasonally contracted Mexican migrant agricultural worker
bushel unit of dry measure for grain or fruit equal to 4 pecks or 32 quarts
campesino *Spanish.* farmer or farm laborer in Latin America
cereal any grain produced from grass and used as food
chaff useless husks of wheat or other grains, separated in threshing
citrus thorny trees and shrubs that grow in warm climates and produce pulpy edible fruit
clear-cutting removing all trees in a stand of timber
cocoa beans of small evergreen cacao tree, used primarily in making chocolate
coffee beans of coffee tree, grown in tropical highland regions, used to make beverage
complete fertilizer fertilizer containing three primary plant nutrients: nitrogen, phosphorus, and potassium
corn tall cereal plant whose kernels are used extensively for fodder and human food; maize
cotton most important textile fiber, produced from seed pods of shrubby tropical plant
cover crop grass or legume that improves soil by adding organic matter and discouraging erosion
crop plant or agricultural product grown and harvested for profit or subsistence; yield in a single season or place
crop rotation rotation of crops
cultivate (*vb*) prepare and till soil for planting of crops
cultivation growing of plants or crops from seeds, bulbs, or shoots
cutover land cleared of vegetation, esp. trees
cutting plant section from leaf, stem, or root capable of developing into new plant
DDT dichlorodiphenyltrichloroethane; hazardous pesticide in widespread use on crops
Demeter goddess of agriculture and fertility (ancient Greece)
dirt farmer owner of small farm who works his or her own land
disseminate (*vb*) sow or scatter seed
dry farming agriculture without irrigation, relying on drought-resistant crops and moisture-conserving soil cultivation techniques
dust (*vb*) sprinkle crops with insecticides, esp. from a low-flying airplane
everbearing (*adj*) continuously producing or bringing forth fruit
extensive cultivation farming system in which limited work is put into relatively large area of land
fallow (*adj*) designating cultivated land left unsown for one season or more
farm tract of land devoted to any agricultural purpose; (*vb*) engage in raising crops or animals
farmer person who cultivates land or raises crops or livestock, esp. one who owns farmland; grower
farm hand hired farm worker

farmhouse residence on farm for farmer and family

farming business of agriculture and farm operation

farmland land under cultivation

farmstead farmland and the buildings on it

farmyard enclosure within or connected to farm buildings

fertile (*adj*) rich in resources, fruitful; able to reproduce by seeds or spores

fertility gods supernatural beings to whom ancient primitive farmers turned for aid with crops

fertilizer organic or chemical soil additive that increases or accelerates growth

field cleared area of land used for pasture or growing

field crops crops grown on large tracts of land

first fruits earliest fruit of the season

fish meal dried, ground fish used as fertilizer or feed

flax annual plant grown for its fiber and seed

force (*vb*) cause plants to grow faster by artificial means

fruit edible plant structure of mature ovary of flowering plant or tree, usu. sweet and pulpy

fruit grower farmer who raises fruit trees or berries

furrow narrow groove in ground made by plow

Future Farmers of America community organization for young people in rural districts

garden plot of land where vegetables, fruits, flowers, or herbs are grown, esp. small plot for personal use

gardener person who tends plants in garden

germination sprouting of spore, seed, or bud as growth begins

glean (*vb*) collect grain after reaping

grain seed or fruit of some plants, including cereal grasses

grain farming cultivation of grain crops, usu. requiring large tracts of land

granary repository for grain storage

grow (*vb*) develop a plant from germination through maturity

grower farmer

growing season period in year during which crops can be raised in given region

hacienda large landed estate or plantation in Latin America

harvest crop gathering season; process of reaping and gathering crops; season's yield of crops

harvest moon full moon nearest to autumnal equinox

headland strip of unplowed land at ends of furrows

herbage nonwoody vegetation, esp. grasses upon which animals graze

hull outer covering of seed or fruit; (*vb*) remove this covering

husk dry outer covering of various crops, such as corn; (*vb*) remove this covering

insecticide pesticide that kills insects living on plants

inseminate (*vb*) sow seeds in earth

intensive cultivation farming system in which significant and continuous work is lavished on relatively small area to maximize yield

intercrop (*vb*) grow one crop between rows of another

irrigation any of various systems of bringing water to plants, including flood, border, furrow, sprinkler, drip, or surface irrigation systems

legumes plants with fruits or seeds in dry pods with two sutures, such as beans or peas, used for food or forage

lumber milled strips of wood cut from trees, used for building

lumbering work and business of tree farming or felling trees to make lumber

maize corn

manure fertilizer of livestock excrement

migrant worker seasonal farm laborer who moves from place to place to get work

monoculture growing only one type of crop on a piece of land

mowing cutting down of grass or grain

muck farmyard dung and decaying vegetable matter; manure

nitrogen one of three essential plant nutrients

no-tillage direct seeding without plowing of soil

nut dry fruit or seed with kernel inside separable rind, shell, or hull

open-field cultivation system in which farmer owns and cultivates strips of land, unfenced and scattered over several large fields

orchard area planted with trees that bear fruit or nuts

organic farming farming that relies on natural materials to control pests and for use as fertilizers

paddy plot of continuous wetland, esp. where rice is grown

pastoral (*adj*) characteristic of the rural life of farmers and shepherds, esp. in idealized state

patch small plot of ground for growing

peck unit of dry measure equal to 8 quarts or one-quarter bushel

pest insect, small animal, fungus, or weed that damages or kills crops

pesticide any of various pest killers, including fungicides (kill fungi), insecticides (kill insects), miticides (kill mites), molluskicides (kill snails and slugs), and ovicides (kill eggs), esp. chlorinated hydrocarbons (organochlorines), organic phosphates (organophosphates), and carbamate compounds

phosphate any substance containing salt and phosphoric acid, used as fertilizer

plant tree, shrub, or herb put into soil and grown to maturity, esp. an herb in context of farming; (*vb*) begin growing process by putting seed or seedling into ground

plantation large farm or estate on which cultivated crops are grown by resident workers, usu. in tropical or semitropical region

planter owner of plantation or large farm

planting one season's crop

plot small planted area of land

plow (*vb*) work the soil; till or furrow

plowboy boy leading team of animals pulling a plow

produce fresh agricultural products, esp. fruits and vegetables

pruning pinching, heading, thinning, or shearing plants to direct growth or improve health or appearance

raise (*vb*) cause to grow

reap (*vb*) gather a crop, esp. grain, by cutting

rear (*vb*) grow or breed

rest (*vb*) lie fallow

rice starchy seeds or grain of marsh grass, requiring much moisture and warm temperatures, used to feed more people than any other cereal

rotation of crops cultivation system in which crops are systematically changed on each plot to prevent nutrient loss in soil and to discourage weeds, pests, and diseases; crop rotation

rye main bread grain in parts of northern Europe, where wheat cannot be cultivated due to cold weather

seed (*vb*) sow; plant with seeds from which plants grow

seedbed plot of ground prepared for seeding

seeding scattering of seeds

seedling plant grown from seed, esp. young tree

semination propagation or dissemination by seed

sharecrop (*vb*) farm as a sharecropper

sharecropper farmer who exchanges works for share of crop's value less credited expenses

sheaf bound bundle of reaped grain, esp. wheat

shifting cultivation primitive system in which crops are grown in one area until it is exhausted and growers move on

side dressing plant nutrients used to fertilize at crop roots

slash-and-burn (*adj*) of a cultivation technique in which land is made usable by burning trees and undergrowth, thereby clearing as well as nourishing the land

slit planting tillage method in which seeds are dropped into narrow openings cut into soil

smudge smoky fire used to protect fruit trees from frost

soil surface of earth capable of supporting plant life

sow (*vb*) scatter or plant seed for growing

spading digging in earth with a spade

spring wheat wheat grain sown in spring to avoid harsh winter weather

stand group of trees growing together

stone fruit any fruit, such as a plum, having a hard, stonelike seed

strip farming planting of strips of closely growing plants, such as grasses or clover, between crops to hold up rainwater, thereby reducing erosion

stubble stumps of cut grain left in ground

subsistence crops crops grown for farmer's own food needs

subsistence farming cultivation of crops for one's own use only

sugar product of crystallization of juice of crops, esp. sugar beets and sugarcane

swath strip of space from which grain plants have been cut down

swidden tract of land cleared for planting by burning vegetation on it

tea white-flowered evergreen plant, grown throughout Asia, whose dried leaves are used to make a beverage

team two or more horses or oxen harnessed together to pull plow or other vehicle

terrace cultivation system of cultivating mountains and hills by carving out and reinforcing small fields with low embankments

thin (vb) remove weaker plants to maximize growth of remaining crop

threshing separating grains or cereals into usable and nonusable parts

till (vb) plow, cultivate, and fertilize land for the purpose of raising crops

tilth cultivation of land; land that is tilled

timber forest trees used for lumber

top dressing plant nutrients applied to surface of land

tract large area of land used for cultivation

transplant (vb) dig up growing plant or tree and place it in ground elsewhere

tree farming business and practice of growing trees, esp. for lumber

vegetable any herbaceous edible plant

vernalize (vb) shorten plant's growth period, usu. by chilling it or its seeds or bulbs

vine woody climbing plant, esp. grapevine

vineyard land used for cultivating grapevines, esp. for winemaking

weed undesirable plant that harms or inhibits growth of crop plants; (vb) remove such plants from soil

wheat cereal grass with dense, erect spikes that produces grain used as staple food throughout temperate regions

windrow row of hay or sheaves of grain raked together to dry

winnow (vb) blow off undesirable chaff from grain by current of air

winter wheat wheat grain sown in fall in regions where it can survive winter weather

work (vb) cultivate, plow, and till earth for planting

yield amount of crop produced in specific area by cultivation

Ranching and Animal Husbandry

animal husbandry care and raising of domesticated animals, esp. cattle, horses, and sheep

barn raising gathering of local people to help their neighbor build a barn

beast of burden domesticated animal used to carry loads or pull tools or wagons

beef full-grown ox, cow, bull, or steer bred and fattened for meat; flesh of this animal as food

beekeeper one who raises bees and gathers honey

branding iron long-handled metal rod with distinctive design at one end, used for marking livestock

break (vb) tame and train a horse

breed (vb) supervise the sexual propagation of animals; (n) group of animals of one species differentiated by common characteristics and descent

browsing grazing

cattle domesticated ruminant bovines raised for their meat or milk

cattle drive herding of large number of cattle from one place to another

coop small cage or pen housing poultry

cornfed (adj) designating beef cattle raised on diet of corn, believed to improve health and flavor

corral enclosure for domesticated animals, esp. horses

cote pen or enclosure for livestock

cowboy ranch worker on horseback who herds and tends cattle; cowpoke; rancher

cowhand ranch worker

cowpoke cowboy or cowgirl

cowpuncher cowboy or cowgirl

creamery dairy

cud mouthful of swallowed food regurgitated by cattle for second chewing

dairy farm or ranch for raising dairy cattle, producing milk and milk products; creamery

domestic animal animal tamed or bred for human purposes

dovecote cage or pen housing pigeons

eggs shelled ovum laid by hens, collected and sold for food

ensilage green fodder preserved in a silo

feed food or fodder for livestock

feedlot place where animals are fattened for slaughter

fodder domestic animal food

forage food eaten by browsing or grazing animal; fodder

free-range (adj) designating livestock and poultry permitted to graze or forage freely outside a small confinement

gaucho cowboy of the South American pampas

grass herbaceous vegetation upon which animals graze

grassland tracts of land covered with grass for grazing

grazing feeding of animals on growing grass or herbage; browsing

hatch (vb) bring forth young from an egg

hatchery place for hatching eggs

hay grass, alfalfa, or clover cut and dried for fodder

haycock conical stack of hay drying in field

hayrick Chiefly Brit. haystack

haystack large heap of hay piled outdoors; hayrick

herd group of cattle, sheep, or other animals living together under human supervision; (vb) control movement of livestock, esp. from horseback

herdsman one who tends or supervises a herd

hog large domestic swine

horse large domesticated mammal used for transportation and work

hutch animal pen, esp. for rabbits

incubation sitting on or keeping eggs in warm environment favorable for hatching

keep (vb) raise, as livestock

livestock domestic animals kept for work, by-products, or sale, esp. cattle, sheep, hogs, and horses

meadow expanse of grassland used as pasture or hayfield

milk dairy product secreted by lactating mammals, esp. cows and goats

oats cereal grass, used esp. for fodder

pack animal animal bred for strength and used to carry loads, esp. mule, donkey, or horse; sumpter

pasturage practice of grazing livestock on a pasture

pasture land on which livestock graze

pen small yard or enclosure for domestic animals

poultry birds raised for their meat or eggs

predator animal that feeds on other animals

raise (vb) cause to breed

ranch large farm, esp. in U.S. West, for raising cattle, horses, or sheep; (vb) operate or work on a ranch, esp. raise livestock

rancher owner or manager of ranch; cowboy

ranchero rancher in Latin America or U.S. West

ranch hand employee on ranch

rancho farm or ranch

range large open area over which livestock can roam and graze

rangeland tract of land suitable for livestock grazing

ruminant (adj) cud-chewing, esp. cattle and sheep

shearing cutting or clipping of animal hair, esp. for use as wool

sheep ruminant animals domesticated for wool and meat

sheepshearing clipping wool from sheep

sheepwalk Brit. sheep pasture

shepherd herdsman, esp. for grazing sheep

silage succulent feed made from fermented fodder in silo

silo usu. cylindrical, airtight tower for making and storing silage

sire male parent of four-legged animal, esp. horse; (vb) father a horse

slaughterhouse structure in which livestock are butchered

stall compartment in stable for one animal

stock strain or related group of animals; livestock

stock horse horse used in herding cattle

stockman person who raises livestock

stockyard enclosure for livestock, esp. where cattle, sheep, hogs, or horses are held before slaughter or shipment

straw mass of grain stalks, dried and used as fodder

stud male animal, esp. horse, used for breeding

sumpter pack animal

swine domesticated pig or hog

transhumance seasonal movement of livestock from valley to mountain pastures and back again

winterfeed feed given to livestock in winter when pasturage is impossible

wool soft, curly hair shorn from sheep; cloth made of this hair

workhorse horse used for plowing and hauling, not for riding

Soils and Soil Management

adobe soil heavy clay soil

aeration supplying abundant oxygen to soil through cultivation

alluvial soil sand or clay deposited at shore of waterway

amendment soil-conditioning substance that promotes plant growth by addition of vitamins, fertilizer, or other additive

arable (*adj*) fit for cultivation

available moisture water in soil that may be absorbed by plant roots

available nutrient nutrient in soil that may be absorbed by plant roots

backfill soil soil, sometimes amended, used to refill planting hole

bog wet, spongy soil with decaying mosses and peat

bole easily pulverized, reddish clay

chernozem fertile soil, rich in humus, covering large areas of temperate regions

clay firm, fine-grained soil, plastic when wet

clunch hardened clay

contour plowing erosion-prevention technique in which land is plowed around rather than up and down a slope, creating rain-catching furrows

cropland land suitable for cultivation of crops

decalcified soil soil deprived of lime or calcium compounds

deflocculated soil soil lacking well-aggregated structure, caused by soft water

desertification spread of desertlike conditions on previously arable land

diatomaceous earth soil amendment formed by skeletal remains of microscopic organisms

dispersed soil soil in which clumped aggregates are separated into individual components

drought prolonged period without rain that causes soil failure and crop death

dust bowl region that endures long droughts and intense dust storms

erosion gradual eating or wearing away of soil by water, wind, snow, or ice

fertile soil earth capable of sustaining growth

friable (*adj*) describing easily crumbled soil

ground water water stored within porous rock in earth, esp. near surface

horizon layer of soil with distinct characteristics

humus organic matter in soil resulting from decomposition of plants and animals

illuviation accumulation in one layer of soil of materials leached from another layer

land Earth's surface and its resources

laterite red, residual soil in well-drained tropical rain forest

leaching washing away of soluble plant foods from topsoil by rain

leaf mold rich soil composed largely of decayed leaves

loam fertile soil consisting of humus, clay, and sand

loess particles of soft, porous rock, carried by wind, that mix with humus to form loam

marl soft, friable mixture of clay and limestone, used as fertilizer in lime-deficient soil

mold loose, soft, easily worked soil rich with decayed animal or vegetable matter

mulch leaves, straw, or peat moss spread on ground around plants to prevent evaporation of water from soil and to protect roots

peat brownish, fibrous substance resulting from vegetative decay

pedology soil science

plow sole compressed layer at bottom of furrow resulting from repeated plowing

podsol grayish, relatively infertile soil in coniferous forest

reclamation making dry or useless land capable of cultivation

regosol soil composed of unconsolidated material without stones and without distinct horizons

rill erosion formation of numerous small channels that occurs on recently cultivated soil

sand soil composed of loose, gritty particles of worn or disintegrated rock

scarify (*vb*) loosen soil with a cultivator

sheet erosion type of soil erosion, esp. on sloping farmland, in which rain washes away thin layer of topsoil

silt soil composed largely of sediment carried by moving water, with particles larger than clay but smaller than sand

soil source of food and moisture for plants, consisting of small particles of rock together with humus

soil bank government program subsidizing farmers to stop growing surplus crops and enrich idle land

soil conservation protection of fertile topsoil from erosion and replacement of its nutrients

soil erosion wearing away of soil, esp. by wind and water

soil management organized soil conservation and care programs

spodosol acidic forest soil of low fertility, found in cool, humid areas of Northern Hemisphere

subsoil layer of harder soil beneath topsoil

terracing forming of hillside into series of flat, raised mounds to reduce erosion in growing areas

tillage land that is tilled

tilth land that is tilled; cultivation of land

topsoil upper layer of soil, usu. darker and richer than subsoil

wind erosion type of soil erosion in which powdered topsoil, due to cultivation, is carried away by wind

Tools, Machinery, and Structures

aqueduct large pipe or conduit for bringing water from distant source

backhoe excavating vehicle with hinged bucket on arm for digging

baler machine for compressing, binding, and wrapping grasses and hay in standardized bundles

barn storage building for feed, equipment, and other farm products; structure housing farm animals

barnyard usu. fenced area adjoining barn

billhook curved blade set on handle, used for pruning or cutting

binder attachment to harvester or reaper that binds cut grain

canal artificial waterway for drainage or irrigation

cannery factory for processing food and sealing it in metal containers

chisel plow plow that exposes minimal soil, aiding moisture retention and reducing soil runoff and wind erosion

colter sharp blade or wheel used to cut ground ahead of plowshare

combine multiprocess, in-field grain harvesting machine

crop duster device for spreading chemical dust over crops, often from low-flying airplane

cultivator tool drawn between rows of plants to loosen earth and uproot weeds

dibble pointed tool for making holes in soil for seeds, bulbs, or small plants

flail short, thick wooden stick loosely attached to handle, used for threshing

glasshouse greenhouse

grader machine that levels a slope, roadway, or plot of ground

grain elevator tall, cylindrical warehouse for grain

grange farmhouse and its outbuildings

greenhouse glass building with controlled temperature and humidity for cultivating plants out of season, sprouting seeds, or forcing plants; glasshouse

grub hoe heavy hoe used for digging up roots and stumps

harness assemblage of leather straps and metal pieces by which horse or mule is fastened to plow or other vehicle

harrow horse or tractor-drawn frame with

spikes or sharp-edged disks for breaking up and leveling plowed ground

harvester machine for cutting and gathering crops or grain

hayfork mechanical device for moving hay; pitchfork

hayloft elevated area in barn for storage of hay

hayrack frame from which livestock eat hay

hay rake tool used to rake hay from swath into windrow

hoe thin, flat-bladed, long-handled cultivation tool

hovel open shed, esp. for cattle or tools

incubator enclosed, warm environment for keeping and hatching eggs

lathhouse structure of thin narrow wood strips for support or protection of plants

manger trough in stable holding feed for livestock

mattock pickaxlike tool with one broad end, used for loosening soil by digging

mill building and machinery for grinding grain into flour or meal

moldboard curved metal plate attached to plow for turning soil

pick heavy tool with pointed iron or steel head on long handle, used to loosen and break up soil

pitchfork long-handled tool with sharp prongs for lifting and tossing hay or straw; hayfork

plow implement used to cut, turn up, and break soil

plowshare furrow-cutting blade of moldboard plow

reaper machine for cutting standing grain, often with mechanism for bundling and tossing out bundles of cut grain

rick stack of hay or straw in field, usu. covered for protection from rain

rotary plow implement with spinning blades set on power-driven shaft, used to break up unplowed soil prior to planting

rototiller electrically powered device with spinning blades for cultivating soil

scuffle hoe spadelike hoe that is pushed instead of pulled

scythe long, single-edged blade set at right angle to long curved handle, for hand-cutting grass or grain

self-feeder hopper and trough that automatically dispenses feed for livestock

shadoof long, suspended rod with bucket at one end, used for raising water for irrigation (Egypt)

shears device with multiple sharp edges for cutting wool, esp. from sheep

shelterbelt protective barrier of trees or shrubs; windbreak

sickle crescent-shaped blade on short handle for cutting tall grass or weeds

spade flat blade on long handle for digging or turning soil by pressing blade into ground with foot

spike-tooth harrow harrow with straight teeth set horizontally, used to smooth soil for planting or sowing

thresher machine for beating out grain from husks

tiller machine used to plow and cultivate soil

tractor vehicle with powerful engine and large rear wheels or endless treads, for pulling farm machinery

trough low, narrow receptacle for food for animals

windbreak hedge, row of trees, or fence for protection from wind

windmill machine for grinding grain powered by wind's rotation of large oblique vanes radiating from shaft

Business and Science of Agriculture

aeroculture practice of growing plants without soil by suspending them above spraying outlets that constantly moisten their roots; aeroponics

aeroponics aeroculture

aggie *Informal.* agricultural school or college; student at such a school

agribusiness business associated with processing, manufacturing, producing, and distributing of agricultural products

agricultural engineering design of farm machinery, mechanization of farming, and soil management

agricultural extension service government organization providing information and consultation services, often at state's land-grant university

agricultural sciences disciplines related to agricultural production, including mineralogy, virology, plant physiology, animal nutrition, microclimatology, and watershed management

agriculture science and practice of cultivating soil, raising crops, and raising livestock; farming

agrobiology science of plant growth and nutrition as applied to improvement of crops and soil management

agrology study of agricultural production

agronomy science and economics of soil management and crop production

agrostology branch of botany dealing with grasses and grains

angiosperm part of seed-producing plant that produces seeds in enclosed ovary within flower; any flowering plant

animal nutrition science and practice of feeding livestock, esp. to accelerate growth and improve quality of meat

aquaculture cultivation and regulation of water plants and water animals for human consumption

arboriculture cultivation of trees and shrubs, esp. for ornamentation

asexual propagation reproduction without union with another member of species

biomass living material

biomass conversion use of organic matter to create energy

botany science of plant life, structure, growth, and classification

breadbasket region that supplies most of nation's grain

canning preserving food in airtight containers of metal or glass

cash crops crops grown for income rather than subsistence

citriculture cultivation of citrus fruits

collective farm cooperative

commodity agricultural product seen as economic unit

Commodity Credit Corporation Department of Agriculture-sponsored market price-support organization that makes loans to farmers

cone conical-shaped, pollen-bearing fruit of tree, characterized by scales or bracts; seed-bearing fruit

conservation management of natural resources for their protection and preservation

conservation tillage erosion-reducing techniques, including plowless farming, reduced-tillage, no-till, eco-till, and slit planting

cooperative farm with several owners or group of farms organized by and operated for benefit of owners or members; collective farm

Corn Belt region in midwestern United States between Iowa and Indiana that is ideal for raising corn

croft *Chiefly Brit.* tenant farm

cross-pollination exchange of pollen between two plants, naturally or artificially

deforestation clearing of trees from tract of land

dehydration process of removing water from soil or products

demesne land legally held in one's possession

ecology science concerned with the interrelationship of organisms and their environment

enclosure transitional step in land use that replaces unfenced strips of land held in common with individually owned property with defined boundaries

environmental protection programs and techniques of assuring continued balance and abundance of Earth's resources

famine acute, widespread lack of food, esp. due to crop failure or drought

farm management techniques by which large, modern farms are run

fishery place where fish are bred

food basic human nourishment, usu. satisfied by agricultural products

food processing post-harvest handling of agricultural products, including milling, fermenting, freezing, drying, canning, dehydrating, pasteurizing, and radiating

forestry science of planting and caring for trees, esp. systematic management of timber production with regard for conservation

Four-H Club Department of Agriculture youth program providing training in agriculture, conservation, and home economics

Future Farmers of America community organization for young people studying vocational agriculture

gathering primitive system of collecting nuts and crops that are growing wild

genetic engineering technique of producing new, improved hybrid species by cutting and splicing of genetic units of DNA from different organisms

geoponic (*adj*) having to do with agriculture

grain reserve grain storage to offset crop failure

grange farmers' association

granger member of grange

green revolution introduction of high-yield crops and use of improved agricultural techniques, esp. in underdeveloped nations, to increase food production

gymnosperm part of seed-producing plants that produces seeds on open scales, usu. in cones

herbicide plant-killing agent

horticulture cultivation of fruits, vegetables, shrubs, and herbaceous and ornamental trees and plants

husbandry cultivation of plants and animals

hybrid offspring of two plants with different genetic material

hydrology science dealing with properties, distribution, and circulation of water on Earth's surface

hydroponics growing of plants in nutrient-rich solutions without soil

integrated pest management ecological pest control based on preventive measures and minimal use of pesticides

kibbutz collective farm (Israel)

land-grant school college or university given federal government aid, esp. in form of land, to offer agricultural studies

logging cutting trees for lumber

market garden farm on which vegetables are grown for market in local industrial areas; truck farm (Britain)

microclimatology study of weather and its impact on a small region

milling grinding of grain into flour; cutting of timber into lumber

mineralogy science of minerals found in soil and rocks

mixed farming farming of both crops and livestock

nitrogen fixation transformation of nitrogen from air into nitrates by certain plants; self-fertilization

nursery place where young plants are raised

nutrients nourishing substances

olericulture production, storage, and marketing of vegetables for home market

pasteurization method of destroying bacteria in milk by heating

peasant small farmer, tenant farmer, or farm laborer

pedology soil science

pisciculture artificial breeding and transplantation of fish

plant physiology study and experimentation on functions and growth of plants

pollution harmful waste material discharged into air, water, or soil

pomology fruit-growing science

precipitation rain, hail, snow, or mist; amount of water thus deposited

production limits voluntarily accepted limits established as eligibility for commodity loans

ranger warden of forest or park

reforestation planting of forests on denuded land

rubber product obtained as liquid latex by tapping trees, which is then treated to produce solid rubber

rural (*adj*) designating farming and ranching regions with small towns, away from large urban centers

serf person bound to feudal master's land

sharecropper tenant farmer paying rent in form of crops

silviculture cultivation of forest trees

stoop labor physical labor associated with picking of fruit and vegetables from low-growing plants

subsidy government payment to farmers to support prices, esp. on surplus products

tapping making hole in tree to draw off liquid, esp. sap or syrup

target prices income supplements, set higher than loan rates, calculated to reflect national average cost of producing crop

tariff government tax on imported or exported product

tenant farmer person farming land owned by another and paying rent in cash or share of crops

truck farming growing of vegetables or fruit to be marketed locally

vegetative propagation asexual plant reproduction

vermiculture raising and production of earthworms and their by-products

viniculture cultivation of wine grapes

virology study of viral diseases, esp. as they affect livestock

viticulture science and cultivation of grapes

water ubiquitous natural liquid essential to plant growth

watershed ridge dividing areas drained by different river systems; area drained by river system

weather atmospheric conditions at given time and place

zoology science of animal life, structure, growth, and classification

---

ADVERTISING

See also: *Chap. 5: Telecommunications; Computers; Chap. 11: Publishing and the Press; Chap. 12: Business and Economics; Chap. 15: Television and Radio; Chap. 16: Graphic Design and Printing; Photography*

A-board display in which two sloping boards are joined at top, used for outdoor signs

accordion hinged display structure that folds like an accordion and expands or contracts to fill space

account client or person employing agency to create ads

account coordinator person responsible for maintaining good relations between client and media

account executive advertising agency employee who oversees marketing and administrative efforts for one or more clients' campaigns and deals directly with client

account supervisor person who oversees account executives

action cards mail-order device in which set of postcards with order forms and return addresses for a variety of products and companies is sent to potential customers

ad advertisement

AD art director

admass *Chiefly Brit.* high-pressure marketing using mass media advertising to reach large numbers of people

advertisement paid public announcement describing something for sale

advertising calling public attention to a particular product by paid announcements so as to arouse desire to buy it; any public notice

advertising manager client representative responsible for overseeing marketing efforts related to product, including budgeting, creative activities, and liaison with agency

advertising sales representative media planner who contacts publications

advertorial advertisement that resembles newspaper editorial but promotes advertiser's product, service, or point of view

agate line measure of advertising space, 1 1/4 of an inch by one column wide

age group target audience based on age

agency company in business of creating advertisements, packaging, and product names for clients' products and services

airplane banner flag or banner bearing advertisement, trailing behind low-flying airplane

appeal approach used to promote sales

art direction general approach to and look of an advertisement

art director AD; person responsible for creative positioning and graphic design of advertisement

audiovisual (*adj*) A/V; pertaining to simultaneous use of tape recordings, slides, and video to support pitch, presentation, or display

A/V audio visual

billboard very large outdoor printed sign

billings gross income to agency from one account or several accounts

blister pack display package in which clear plastic seals product against cardboard sheet

book talent agency listing, with pictures, of actors and models

booking scheduling of talent and staff offered work on shoot or photo session

brainstorming meeting to generate creative ideas

broadside sheet printed on one or both sides with advertising message

brochure folded leaflet with advertising message, usu. illustrated

bumper sticker advertising strip attached to automobile bumper

bus card advertising poster attached to side or back of bus, esp. in city public bus system

business-to-business (*adj*) designating communications or dealings by agencies or between companies

buzzword word or phrase that takes on added significance or new meaning through repetition or special usage

calling card small card with person's name, business name, telephone number, and address; any identifying symbol, trademark, or object

campaign total planned sales effort on behalf of specific client, usu. multimedia and over period of time

catalog illustrated booklet listing available products

classified ad brief listing in periodical of items for sale and services offered, arranged by category; want ad

client company, or its representative, that employs agency to create advertisements

Clio annual award given for excellence in radio and television advertising

color separation photographic process using separate plates for each color

commercial advertising announcement on television or radio or in movie theater; (*adj*) designating product or service suitable for wide, popular market

competitive bid anticipated charges requested by agency from suppliers for preparing materials for advertising, compared with bids of other suppliers

concept general idea behind slogan, pitch, or campaign

consumer private individual at whom advertisements are aimed

consumer market defined group of consumers

cooperative advertising sharing of cost of advertisement between manufacturer and retailer

copy written part of advertisement

copywriter person responsible for writing advertising copy and creating concept with art director

corporate identity words and graphics that project image that corporate client wishes to convey to public

cost per thousand CPM; cost of advertising per thousand potential customers reached through publication, broadcast, or outdoor advertisement

CPM cost per thousand (roman numeral **M**)

creative director person responsible in agency

for developing concepts, coordinating production of art and copy, and executing campaign

creative team art director, copywriter, and creative director involved in initial development of advertisement

cycle schedule of periodic, often quarterly, residual payments to actors, models, and singers

dealer spot spot advertisement placed by retail dealer of product rather than manufacturer

decal specially prepared paper from which graphics can be transferred to another surface

direct mail direct marketing exclusively by mail

direct marketing marketing via leaflets, brochures, letters, catalogs, or print ads mailed or distributed directly to potential consumers; any medium used to elicit responses directly from consumers

display any of various structures used to describe or show product being advertised

display ad illustrated advertisement in newspaper or magazine

dog and pony show *Informal.* elaborate pitch, presentation, or campaign

drive time *Slang.* ads directed at commuters in cars, esp. during morning and late afternoon

dummy rough layout of assembled work for print advertisement

dump-bin floor display holding an assortment of loose items

electronic billboard electronic sign that displays animated, full-color messages in a public place

estimate proposed or expected budget of campaign

exclusivity prohibition on performing in commercial for product that is competitive with one for which actor has commercial currently on hold or running; right to use specific talent, art, music, etc., in advertising

exhibition public show or display

exposure number of potential consumers reached through specific medium

flack press agent or publicist, sometimes considered disparaging

flier fly sheet

flip chart chart with series of illustrated pages bound at top so that pages can be lifted vertically and dropped behind other pages, used in presentation

fly sheet handbill, loose sheet with printed advertisement; flier

focus group group of potential consumers used in market research to determine likely effectiveness of advertising

freelance copywriter, graphic artist, or creative person employed by agency or client on intermittent basis

giveaway promotion involving free novelties or gifts

graphic design any form of visual artistic representation of product or layout of advertisement

graphic designer person responsible for

implementing art direction of print advertisement

grinder *Slang.* actor impersonating doctor or other professional authority on television commercial

halftone printed image formed by close-set dots of varying sizes

handbill small, printed advertising sheet distributed by hand

hard sell aggressive advertising technique

head shot glossy 8 x 10-inch picture of actor's or model's face

hidden persuaders subtle or subliminal advertising messages and techniques

hold period during which commercial is held by agency prior to release

hook clever phrase or melody used to capture consumer's attention; peg; slant

huckster *Informal.* person who works in advertising industry

hymn *Slang.* hidden or subliminal message

hype *Informal.* extravagant promotion of person, idea, or product

IBM *Slang.* advertisement with corporate look

impact degree of success of campaign; reaching of consumers

impulse buying buying for momentary pleasure rather than out of genuine need, sometimes encouraged by advertising

independent agency functioning alone, without control by larger corporation

ink *Slang.* print publicity; press coverage

insert printed sheet or sheets inserted into publication or enclosed with mailing

jiffy hanger metal hook attached by grommet to piece of buckram coated with adhesive that is applied to wall or display surface

jingle catchy, repetitious musical refrain used in radio or TV advertising

junk mail unsolicited advertising material sent by post

kickapoo *Slang.* client's product

knockdown display or exhibit that can be disassembled easily for shipping

launch introduction of new product or service

layout design for graphic advertising production, roughly depicting look of advertisement

linage total lines of advertising placed in publication in one issue over period of time

live tag voice-over at end of prerecorded commercial that provides current or local information

logo recognizable trademarked design and lettering for trade, product, or organization; logotype

logotype logo

Madison Avenue advertising in general; New York City street that is location of many large agencies

magalog *Informal.* mail-order catalog that carries editorial matter and advertisements for other companies

mailer advertisement sent by mail

mailing list list of prospective customers

organized by location, income, or other aspect of consumer profile

mail order retail sales conducted by mail

mall-fixture advertisement poster advertisement mounted in glassed frame in kiosk or other public place in mall or transportation depot

market prospective customers for given product

marketing strategy and specific techniques used in reaching consumers

market profile characteristics of group or area targeted for campaign

market research study of consumer groups and business competition used to define projected market

market share percentage of specific market reached or sold by given product, advertisement, or agency

marquee billboard advertising theater performance

media forms of mass communication that carry advertising, esp. newspapers, magazines, television, and radio

media buying service company that specializes in buying print and television or radio time for advertisements

media planner employee of advertiser or advertising agency who coordinates media aspects of campaign and selects which media to use

media research study of radio, television, and magazines for purpose of reaching optimal consumer audience

mention brief item in press or on broadcast referring to person, product, or service

merger combining of two or more agencies to pool accounts and staff; takeover of one agency by another

Merry Andrew *Slang.* actor impersonating victim of headache or indigestion in commercial

message underlying theme or idea in advertisement

Middle America conservative, middle-class segment of U.S. population that makes up largest consumer group

mockup scale-dimensional display model used in planning

model actor employed by agency to appear in advertisement

mom-and-pop (*adj*) having a traditional, rural look in advertisements; designating a small advertising agency

MOS supposedly from Germanism m**it-o**ut **s**prache; commercial filmed without recording sound and without speaking actors

multimedia (*adj*) involving use of several media simultaneously in single advertisement or campaign

national advertising spot running throughout the country

novelties free items, such as matches, calendars, or buttons, bearing advertiser's logo

outdoor *Informal.* billboard, bus card, mall-fixture, or other outdoor advertisement

P and G *Slang.* lit. **P**roctor & **G**amble; advertisement with Middle American appeal, style, and art direction

paste-up formation of graphic design or layout by pasting objects to stiff board; mechanical

payback return on investment; success of advertisement

payoff results of advertising campaign

peg *Informal.* strong, appealing, notable element of press release or campaign; hook; slant

penalty payment required payment, usu. to actors, models, and singers, for violation of standard booking practices

photo opportunity sometimes staged event having visual appeal or interest to photographers, used to generate publicity and free advertising

piggyback (*vb*) run group of commercials back to back, usu. for same client, in time frame such as four fifteen-second spots for price of one sixty-second spot

piggy spot *Slang.* pain is good spot; radio or television commercial for painkiller featuring actor impersonating pain sufferer

pitch presentation of advertising message

planned obsolescence method of stimulating consumer demand by designing products to become outdated or broken after limited use

plug *Informal.* favorable mention or picture of product in nonadvertising portion of media presentation

point-of-purchase advertising signs, displays, and other techniques of attracting attention and promoting products at their point of sale, such as at the counter of a retail store

point-of-purchase display arrangement of goods in retail store with conspicuous advertising copy

POP **p**oint-**o**f-**p**urchase

pop-up display or mailer, part of which automatically moves or lifts from surface as it is opened

portfolio large, bound volume containing pictures from ads, used by agency or talent to generate new jobs

poster graphic advertisement attached to flat surface or standing up with clip backing

PR **p**ublic **r**elations

premium something offered free or at reduced price as inducement to buy something else

presentation pitch, description of advertising campaign

press agent publicist

press kit collection of editorial and promotional materials distributed to press

principal performer in commercial who can be recognized or identified, including but not limited to speaking parts

print advertising in newspapers, magazines, catalogs, or mailers, usu. photographs or other graphic material

production manager person responsible for overseeing details in making of video or print advertisement

promotion method of increasing sales of merchandise through advertising; any activity aimed at increasing sales

propaganda promotion of specific ideas or views, esp. political

publicist person hired to promote cause, individual, or product by generating free advertising; flack; press agent

publicity dissemination of promotional material to draw interest or generate sales

public relations PR; business of inducing goodwill and acceptance in public toward individual, cause, company, or product

puffery undue or exaggerated praise or claims used in advertising and publicity

rates cost per inch of print advertising; cost per minute of radio and TV advertising

rating measure of audience for television show, used to establish rates

refusal right of first actor or model selected for advertisement to refuse or accept assignment

regional advertisement appearing in one region only

release signed permission given by person to use his or her photo, voice, name, or testimonial statement commercially

remnant space unsold print advertising space sold at a discount

residual payment to model, actor, or singer each time advertisement is played, shown, or run

rollout *Informal.* geographic expansion of campaign from test market, as to regional or national market

sale offering of retail goods at reduced prices to induce increased consumption

sandwich board two hinged boards with advertising messages on them, worn hung over shoulders

SAU **s**tandard **a**dvertising **u**nit

scatter package arrangement to air television commercials at various times or intervals

sell (*vb*) promote an idea, product, or concept

session recording session for radio or TV commercial; photograph-taking session

session fee amount paid to talent or artist for day's work on single session

shill person planted in audience to lure onlookers into buying product or participating in activity

shoot taping or filming of commercial in studio or on location

show bill advertising poster

sizzle *Slang.* image rather than substance

skywriting writing across sky with chemically produced smoke emitted from airplane, usu. for purposes of advertising

slant emphasis of a campaign or advertisement; hook; peg

slice-of-life (*adj*) denoting advertisement that depicts naturalistic, everyday activities

slogan short, memorable advertising phrase

sniping pasting up outdoor posters over billboards or on empty structures, walls, and traffic poles, often without permission

soft sell subtle advertising technique

space page or section of page bought for advertisement in newspaper, magazine, or catalog

spokesperson well-known person serving as regular advocate of specific product or cause

spot spot announcement

spot advertising advertising in selected locales rather than nationally

spot announcement radio or television commercial of fifteen, thirty, or sixty seconds; spot

stabile display that is suspended or that rises from pedestal at different levels and on different planes, none of which move

staff permanent, full-time agency employees

standard advertising unit SAU; system of standard dimensions for print advertising based on six columns, each 2 1/16 inches wide

static ad photographic or print advertisement

storewide sale sale in all departments of large store

storyboard series of panels roughly depicting scenes, copy, and shots in television commercial

streamer long, narrow sign with message in bold type hung across open area, window, or doorway

stylist hair and makeup artist on television shoot

subliminal advertising concealed appeal to consumers' unconscious to buy product

subway card advertising poster attached to interior or exterior side of subway car

sweepstakes lottery in which winners are randomly selected, often used to induce purchase of product as means of entering contest

tabletop type of shoot in which product is photographed on a table, either life-size or in miniature

table topper exhibit arranged on table rather than floor

talent actors, models, and singers employed in advertisements

talent agency organization that represents actors and models appearing in advertisements

target audience consumer group most likely to buy product, identified by region, age, demographics, or economic status; target market

target market target audience

teaser advertisement or publicity that arouses interest or curiosity about forthcoming product or event, sometimes without naming it

telemarketing selling, advertising, or market research done by telephone

tent display card folded and set up with two sloping sides, like inverted V, esp. for small displays on tables

testimonial statement, often by celebrity or prominent person, affirming truth, fact, character, or value of a product, event, or service

test market consumer group interviewed to determine target audience

test market spot spot used exclusively on test market and monitored for its effectiveness

throwaway handbill or other printed matter that is distributed free to residences and contains local advertising; novelty item used to entice consumers into buying more costly item

tie-in campaign to link products, media, or markets

time slot specific time bought for airing of commercial on radio or television

trade name name used by company to describe and distinguish its brand of a generic product, usu. trademarked

trade-out barter arrangement for exchange of commercial time, advertising space, products, or services

trade show convention at which advertising agencies or related companies show and compare products and ideas

triptych three-sided display with central element and two wings

turntable revolving mechanical display platform

upscale (adj.) Informal. having a look aimed at the well-to-do urban market

VO voice-over

voice-over VO; recorded offscreen voice heard on television or radio commercial

volume dollar amount of billings or revenue

want ad classified ad

wild spot spot appearing in various slots and locales, neither regional nor national, or on non-network station

window display merchandise and/or advertising attractively arranged in store window

INSURANCE

See also: *Chap. 12: Finance*

accident unplanned event causing injury, death, or damage

accident insurance coverage for loss due to accidental bodily injury

act of God usu. catastrophic event arising from natural causes

actuarial tables tables showing life expectancies

actuary statistical specialist who computes insurance rates

adjustment estimate of loss; settlement of claim

adjustor insurance company representative trained to make accurate estimates of loss or liability

advertiser's liability protection for risk inherent in advertising claims

agent representative selling policies for insurance company

annuity periodic payments of specific amount made by insurer, often for life

assigned risk high-risk client assigned to insurance company by lottery-style method

assurance *Chiefly Brit.* insurance, esp. life insurance

automobile insurance coverage for drivers of automobiles

aviation insurance insurance against loss of life on air flight

beneficiary person eligible to receive insurance payments

benefits payments to insured person or his or her beneficiary

bond guarantee against financial loss caused by default of third party or by circumstance over which guarantor has no control

bordereau computerized billing statement used in international insurance claims

carrier insurance company, insurer

catastrophe sudden, violent loss

claim insured's application to receive benefits

cleanup fund life insurance policy covering expenses after insured's death

coinsurance jointly held insurance policy; policy in which insured pays portion of costs or losses

collision insurance protection against damage to one's own property in case of accident

comprehensive auto or health insurance policy covering all risk contingencies

coverage inclusion within scope of policy; insurance

damages amount paid to cover loss

deductible that part of loss to be paid by insured party, deductible from insurer's payment

dental insurance health insurance coverage for dental work

disability insurance government payments to cover loss of employment due to injury or sickness

disaster insurance coverage for damage due to act of nature, such as flood, hailstorm, or earthquake

double indemnity clause in policy providing for payment of twice the basic benefit

draft order issued by insurer for payment of benefits

dramshop law liquor liability law making server of alcohol liable for possible loss caused by intoxicated person

dramshop liability insurance coverage for sellers of alcoholic beverages

endorsement provision added to insurance policy altering its scope or application

endowment insurance life insurance policy that matures on set date or at death of insured, whichever occurs first

errors and omissions coverage for mistakes made in documents, esp. instances of libel and copyright infringement

estimate appraisal of loss for claim

excess carrier company that insures insurance company for losses in excess of policy liability limit

exclusion contingency not covered by policy

exposure maximum amount company may have to pay on claim

fair market value estimated value of lost property at time of loss, used for determining cost of replacement

fault liability under coverage

fine print often overlooked small type on policy outlining exclusions or limitations

fire insurance coverage for loss due to fire

gravamen essential part of claim

group insurance coverage for all members of organization or employees of company

hazard situation that increases possibility of loss

health insurance coverage for medical expenses

health maintenance organization HMO; health coverage in specific region in which doctors hired by HMO provide services for prepaid subscribers

HMO health maintenance organization

homeowner's policy coverage for fire, theft, or other damage to one's home

indemnification protection from loss or damage and promise to pay for what has been lost or damaged, usu. seen as basic premise of insurance

indemnity payment, repair, or replacement of insured loss

inland marine insurance coverage for freight on inland waterways

insurance system or business of insuring property or persons against loss or harm due to specific contingencies; contract providing for indemnification against loss

insurance policy printed contract between insured and insurer stating terms and limits of agreement

insured person paying premiums and receiving guarantee of indemnities

insurer insurance company or entity providing indemnities

jumping juvenile life insurance for child in which cost increases sharply when child reaches majority

lapsed policy policy that has expired due to nonpayment of premiums

liability insurance coverage for loss arising from insured's actions; insured's responsibility for damage or loss

lien charge or claim on policy by third party

life insurance coverage guaranteeing payment of specified sum to beneficiary on death of insured

limitations areas excluded from or not covered by policy

line particular type of insurance offered by company

loading extra charge above premium to cover special risks

major medical coverage of all medical and hospital expenses resulting from illness or injury

malpractice insurance coverage for professionals, esp. doctors, for damage caused by neglect or poor treatment, usu. at very high premium

marine insurance coverage for shipping and freight by sea

maturity date at which policy becomes payable

Medicaid government-subsidized medical insurance

Medicare government-subsidized medical insurance for aged

midnight clause clause setting expiration of policy at midnight on certain date

moral hazard insurance company's risk as to insured's honesty or trustworthiness

mortality table graph of selected population's death to age ratio, used to calculate risk

mortgage insurance government coverage for institutions making loans for purchase of property

multiple employer trust collection of insurance programs managed by intermediary organization under contract to actual insurance companies

natural death death other than from accident, homicide, or suicide

newspaper policy limited health insurance policy sold by newspapers to boost circulation

no-fault insurance covering loss regardless of responsibility for accident

nuisance value amount paid by insurer to dispose of claim

occurrence event or events, sometimes ongoing, constituting single loss

overage excess coverage

overinsured (*adj*) having coverage beyond value of insured objects

payable indemnity due on claim

peril cause of possible loss, such as fire or flood

personal injury condition that is basis for claim against carrier for damages or suffering resulting from accident

policy contract stipulating terms of insurance coverage

policyholder insured person

premium periodic payment made by insured to maintain coverage

primary insurer company issuing policy to insured

property damage insurance protection against liability for damage to another's property

redlining discriminating in issuing property insurance based on location

reinsurance insurance taken by insurance company with another insurer to deflect excess costs in case of catastrophic loss

renter's insurance coverage for furnishings and other property kept in rented premises

reparation compensation paid on claim

reserves cash amounts held by insurance company to pay potential and pending claims

rider attachment or amendment to policy

risk uncertainty of outcome of situation; likelihood of loss

schedule list in claim of losses; items covered by policy with corresponding values

self-insurance insurance of one's property or interest by creating special fund instead of seeking coverage with underwriter

settlement payment by insurer on claim for loss

shock loss immense loss that causes adverse effect on insurer's assets

Social Security government program of economic benefits to qualifying retired, elderly, surviving, or disabled persons

spendthrift clause clause preventing beneficiary's creditors from attaching life insurance benefits paid to beneficiary

statement breakdown of premium costs provided by insurer

subrogation assumption by third party of insured's right to seek reimbursement on policy

surety guarantor, usu. insurance company

surety bond bond guaranteeing performance of contract

surrender voluntary termination of policy by insured for cash payment from company

term time during which policy is in effect

term insurance policy that provides coverage for limited period

term life insurance policy with premiums paid until death of insured

theft insurance coverage for loss of property stolen from house or automobile

tontine life insurance in which chief beneficiaries are those whose policies are in force at end of specified term

uncovered (*adj*) unprotected under insurance policy

underinsured (*adj*) having insufficient insurance

underwrite (*vb*) determine rates and assign coverage of policy

underwriter expert in evaluating risks and assigning rates and coverage

unemployment insurance periodic payments, usu. by state government from payroll contributions, to qualified unemployed person

uninsured (*adj*) having no insurance

uninsured motorist coverage automobile insurance protection against losses incurred in accident caused by driver without insurance

vis major *Latin.* lit. greater force; act of God; accident without human cause

workman's compensation government disability insurance for workers

Real Estate Practice

abatement decrease in property tax due; improvement

absentee owner owner living away from site of property

abutment bordering of two pieces of property

abutting owner one whose land touches another's

acreage land measured in units equal to 43,560 square feet

acreage zoning zoning that permits development at low-density locations only

addition expansion of building to include new rooms or outbuildings

ad valorem *Latin.* lit. according to value; usual manner in which taxes are assessed on real property

agent person legally empowered to represent owner, buyer, or landlord in sale or rental of real estate

alligator *Slang.* investment property producing less income than expenses

apartment building structure with three or more rental units

apartments *Chiefly Brit.* set of rooms used as dwelling by one person or one family

appraisal authorized valuation of property based on market value, cost of replacement, or multiplying income derived from it by chosen constant

appreciation increase in property value over time

as is (*adj*) designating property to be purchased in its present condition with no guarantee of its future state

assessed value value placed on property by government for purpose of taxation

assessment valuation of property; appraisal, esp. for taxation

bachelor one-room rental unit in apartment building

Baltimore method appraisal of corner lot to equal total of all surrounding lots

beachfront property building with one side facing directly onto beach

bedsit *Chiefly Brit.* one-room studio apartment without kitchen

birdbath *Slang.* low, paved area that collects water

bird dog *Informal.* person finding new listings for real estate broker

blockbusting illegal scheme to induce property sale by owners fearing decreased value due to minority encroachment

boardinghouse building in which rooms are rented and meals served

board of realty local agency or council supervising real estate transactions

bottom fisher *Slang.* person seeking bargain prices on real property, usu. from distressed sellers

broker agent licensed to sell, rent, or manage property on commission

building codes local ordinances regulating standards of building construction

building inspector licensed official who checks construction sites to guarantee compliance with building codes

capital gain taxed portion of profit on property sale

caretaker one who cares for property of absentee owner

chartulary register of estate titles and deeds

commission fee paid to agent or broker on sale or rental

condo condominium

condominium individually owned property, usu. apartment that is part of larger, multiple-unit structure having other owners and often having common elements; condo

conversion change of building's use and status, as from rental to condominium

co-op cooperative

cooperative multiple-unit property collectively owned by owners of individual units, who hold proprietary leases on their apartments; co-op

Department of Housing and Urban Development HUD; federal agency responsible for providing low-cost housing

depreciation decrease in value of property over time

develop (*vb*) purchase real property with intention of increasing its value, usu. by subdivision, improvement, and construction

developer owner who improves and subdivides land into building lots

development tract of land subdivided into building lots

dockominium boat marina operated like a condominium, with each member owning his or her own slip

duplex single building divided into two residences

estate agent *Chiefly Brit.* real estate agent

exclusive listing listing given to one broker only while reserving right to sell property oneself

exclusive right to sell listing in which broker receives commission no matter who sells property

fair market value highest attainable asking price for property at a given time

finder's fee reward paid to third party for locating buyer or seller of property

first-and-last payment of two month's rent on commencement of rental

fixer-upper *Informal.* run-down property in need of substantial remodeling and repair, purchased at bargain price; handyman's special

fixing-up expenses final costs of minor improvements by owner prior to sale, deductible from taxable profit

fixture any article permanently attached to building or property

flat *Chiefly Brit.* apartment on one floor of building

flip immediate resale of property, usu. at a profit, sometimes before closing

frontage property line abutting public street or waterway

garden apartment apartment on ground floor of multiple-unit dwelling with private landscaped area; low-level apartment building surrounded by landscaped areas

greenbelt land zoned to prohibit construction

ground cover landscaped foliage planted to prevent erosion

habitable (*adj*) capable of being inhabited, usu. according to law

handyman's special fixer-upper

hectare measurement of land equal to 2 1/2 acres

high rise multistory building with elevators

home owner's insurance guarantee against property loss made by company to which owner pays regular premiums

homestead tract of federally owned land awarded to claimant meeting statutory requirements

housekeeping care and management of property

HUD Department of Housing and Urban Development

hundred percent location business area with greatest land value and highest rents

improved land property offered with necessities such as lights, sewers, sidewalks, and water lines

improvements facilities or amenities added to property to increase its value

income property property held primarily or exclusively for production of revenue

industrial park industrial complex, usu. in suburban or rural area, dominated by manufacturing plants, warehouses, and offices

inside lot parcel between corner lots

key lot parcel with increasing worth due to location

key money lump sum paid on moving into rental unit

land value worth of land as distinct from structures on it

leasehold improvements permanent, depreciable improvements made to leased or rented property, usu. for business

let (*vb*) offer for rental or lease

listing property offered for sale by one or more real estate brokers

loft floor of warehouse transformed into residence, usu. above ground level

low-cost housing moderately priced housing made available to poor families, esp. in urban areas

management company company owning and renting more than one building

manager landlord's representative living on premises and overseeing rental units

market value amount a piece of property is likely to bring when offered for sale on open market

model home decorated, vacant residential structure shown to prospective buyers of similar units

neighborhood small district with homogeneous income level, land value, and ethnic profile

occupancy use to which property is put; possession of land taken to acquire ownership

open house house or apartment open during specified hours for inspection by prospective buyers or tenants

open listing listing given to brokers on nonexclusive basis

option right but not obligation to purchase or lease property

outbuilding independent structure considered part of real property along with primary building

parcel tract or plot of land with set boundaries

penthouse dwelling unit on top floor of building

pied-à-terre residence used only part-time

project group of houses or apartments built and arranged in defined area, often low-cost housing

property tax tax levied on real property

rack-rent (*vb*) exact the highest possible rent

railroad flat long, narrow apartment in which one room follows another

raw land vacant, unimproved, unused land

real estate property in form of land and buildings; practice and business of selling, renting, and developing real property

Realtor *Trademark.* person who works in real estate and is a member of the National Association of Real Estate Boards

realty real estate; practice and procedures involved in disposition of real estate

record of title title to piece of real estate shown in public record

rent monthly payment by tenant to landlord for occupation or use of property

rental amount paid on rented property; act of renting; property rented

rental property property occupied by tenant for regular payment of set amount to landlord

rent control government regulation of rental charges

rent stabilization rent increases regulated by law

residence building in which people live

row house one of a series of uniformly built homes connected by common sidewalls

security deposit or pledge made to guarantee contractual obligation

security deposit amount deposited on rental as guarantee against damage to property

showplace building or estate shown as example of available properties

single one-room studio apartment

site parcel of land

slum area of substandard, overcrowded, decaying housing

slumlord absentee landlord who profits by charging exorbitant rents for neglected properties

snob zoning exclusionary residential zoning requiring large lots or prohibitively costly design standards

starter home relatively inexpensive, low-end home that is buyer's first owned property, purchased with the intent to sell it for a profit and acquire a better property in future

steering illegal direction of potential buyers toward or away from minority neighborhoods

studio one-room apartment with kitchen and no separate bedroom

subdivision tract of land divided into several lots for construction of individual residences

super superintendent

superintendent person living in building, managing rentals, and making repairs for absentee owner; super

tax break tax benefit allowed for property ownership

tax shelter property that generates negative income, held for purpose of obtaining tax deduction

tenement apartment house barely meeting minimum standards of sanitation, safety, and comfort

time-share unit single property, esp. vacation home, with multiple owners, each allocated specific amount of time for occupancy

title search examination of public records for liens prior to granting title to new owner

townhouse single-family, multistory urban dwelling, usu. attached to adjacent dwelling by common wall

tract house dwelling on defined area of land, usu. in development, built on similar model to that of adjacent dwellings

triplex single residence divided into three living units

vacation property dwelling used only for vacation, often rented as income property

valuation assessment of value of land and buildings

variance exception permitting noncompliance with normal building codes

walk-up apartment above ground floor in building without elevator

zero lot property in which edge of structure is edge of property lot

zoning dividing city or town into areas by specifying uses, such as commercial or residential, to be made of property in each zone

Deeds, Leases, and Real Property Law

abstract of title official records giving history of title to piece of property

accession addition to property by growth or improvement

access right to enter and leave property

accretion increase in property by gradual natural addition, esp. due to water, as by river silt

adverse possession legal acquisition of someone else's real property through prolonged, open, exclusive, unauthorized occupation

air rights legal right to use air space above building

alienation transfer of title of ownership to property from one person to another

assurance act and instrument of conveying real property

attorn (*vb*) agree to remain as tenant under new owner at same property

boilerplate *Informal.* standard legal language for deeds, contracts, or leases

cadastre official register of size, ownership, and value of property, used in determining taxes

certificate of occupancy municipal issuance stating that property meets minimum requirements for intended use

chain of title documentary history of ownerships of real estate parcel

clear title ownership free of all limits or conditions

cloud on title outside encumbrance or condition that impairs title of ownership

common element area or element of condominium in which each owner has an undivided interest

condemnation legal process by which government purchases private property for public use

conveyance instrument by which property title is transferred

cotenancy ownership or rights to property shared by two or more persons

curtilage enclosed, fenced space immediately surrounding dwelling

deed legal document transferring or establishing ownership of property

deed restriction provision in deed permanently restricting use and development of property

devise (*vb*) assign or transfer real property by will

easement privilege allowing use of or access to another's property for specific purpose

encroachment unauthorized occupancy or trespass upon another's property, esp. by structure or improvement

encumbrance hindrance that delays clearing of title

escalator clause provision in lease that increases or decreases rent under stated conditions

escheat reversion of property to state when no heir or legal claimant can be found

estate all property, real and personal, owned by a person

estate at will leasehold that can be terminated at will by either party

eviction legal dispossession of tenant by landlord

fee simple estate real estate with absolute ownership and no binding restrictions

foreclosure legal procedure depriving mortgagor of right to sell mortgaged property other than to pay debt

free and clear title property ownership with no claims against it

freehold estate in land, inherited or held for life

future estate right to property contingent on some future event

grant transfer of property

grantee person receiving deed to property

grantor person conveying deed to property

ground lease lease on land only, whether or not there are or will be structures on it

holdover tenant tenant whose lease has expired and against whom eviction action may be brought

index lease lease with rate escalation provision

joint tenancy property or lease held by two or more parties with right of survivorship
landlady female landlord
landlord owner of rented or leased property
lease terminating agreement covering possession, use, or occupancy of property
leasehold property acquired under a lease; rights in such property
lessee tenant to whom lease is granted
lessor landlord, grantor of rights to property through lease
lien claim on property to satisfy outstanding debt or duty
life tenancy right to use property that terminates with death of user or holder of right
lot legally identified parcel of land
marketable title title to property that is free of encumbrances and can be readily sold or mortgaged
mechanic's lien lien secured on property by contractor who has repaired or built it in order to ensure payment for labor and materials
metes and bounds system for describing boundaries and orientation of a piece of land
month-to-month tenancy rental agreement without set term of lease, terminated at any time, usu. with one month's notice
mortmain ownership of land by perpetual corporation, esp. religious organization
notice to quit landlord's notification that tenant must vacate premises
owner legal holder of property
property single piece of real estate owned or possessed
proprietary lease lease granted to shareholders of a cooperative for use and occupancy of their individual space
quiet enjoyment covenant in lease stating that tenant will peaceably enjoy possession of property
quitclaim transfer of all one's interests in property without warranty of title
real property land and permanent structures on it
recording act of entering a document into abstract of title of property
reliction increase in land area due to withdrawal of water
retaliatory eviction illegal eviction action by landlord in response to tenant's complaint
reversion return of property to original owner or heirs at expiration of temporary grant
right of survivorship right of one joint tenant to inherit real estate interest of a deceased joint tenant
riparian rights rights of owners of land adjoining a body of water
sandwich lease three-party rental agreement between landlord, original tenant, and subtenant
sky lease agreement to use air space above property
squatter person occupying public or private land or residence without benefit of legal title

squatter's right legal right to occupy property based on long-term tenancy
sublease lease by tenant to third party on already leased premises
subtenant person occupying subleased property; undertenant
survey legal description of land based on observations of licensed professional surveyor
tenancy occupation of building or land by rental or lease
tenancy in common ownership of undivided shares of real property by two or more persons without right of survivorship
tenant person with temporary, conditional use of property owned by another
tenants' rights legal rights of tenants
title all elements and written documents constituting legal ownership of property
title deed document constituting evidence of legal ownership
trust property interest held by one party for benefit of another
trust deed document that conveys interest to a trust as security for loan
undertenant subtenant
undivided share part ownership applied to entire property, rather than ownership of part of property

Mortgages and Financing

acceleration clause provision of mortgage that advances date for payment of balance under certain circumstances
adjustable-rate mortgage variable-rate mortgage
assumable mortgage mortgage taken over from seller by buyer
balloon payment single, large, final payment on loan
binder preliminary, temporary agreement to make down payment and purchase property pending formal contract
bonus amount above interest charged for loan on transfer of property
buy-down arrangement in which mortgage carries below-market interest rate for first few years
chattel mortgage loan secured by personal property
clear escrow receive approval of application for mortgage loan, required to gain title to property
closing final approval of escrow in property purchase; gathering of all parties to consummate real estate transaction; settlement
deposit amount paid to hold property until escrow clears
down payment initial cash sum paid at time of real estate purchase; front money
earnest money good-faith sum of cash used as binder
equity value of property in excess of claims and loans against it
equity of redemption right of mortgagor to

regain property lost through failure to make timely payments
escrow deed held by neutral party, such as bank, for delivery upon fulfillment of certain conditions, usu. making of payments
financing arranging purchase of property through down payment and mortgage loan
first mortgage mortgage having priority over other mortgages on property
Freddie Mac Federal Home Loan Mortgage Corporation, which buys mortgages from lenders
front money down payment
Ginnie Mae GNMA; Government National Mortgage Association; agency of federal government that buys pools of mortgages from lender institutions and sells interest in them to the public
home loan mortgage given for purchase of home
indexing method of adjusting interest rate on loan based on agreed-upon index or indicator
installment purchase loan paid off in multiple payments at set intervals over time
interest charge made at set rate on money borrowed to purchase property, added to principal amount borrowed
kicker loan surcharge
law day due date on mortgage after which debt is in default
loan-to-value ratio fraction of appraised value that lender will loan on property
Maggie Mae Mortgage Guarantee Insurance Corporation; federal agency that insures institutions making mortgage loans
mortgage transfer or conveyance of real property as security for debt; written instrument for such transfer
mortgagee person to whom property is mortgaged
mortgage insurance guarantee of mortgage payment to mortgagor by third party
mortgage tax local tax on face value of mortgage
mortgagor person who mortgages property
origination fee points charged on face value of mortgage at time of purchase
points percentage of loan principal added to cost of purchase, one point equaling one percent
principal amount of money borrowed from mortgagor, on which interest is computed; authorized party to sale, lease, or rental agreement
refinance (*vb*) borrow additional funds against equity in property
satisfaction of mortgage recordable document stating that loan has been repaid
second mortgage mortgage taken by third party on property already mortgaged
settlement closing
variable-rate mortgage loan on which interest rate changes with predetermined factors, such as prime rate; adjustable-rate mortgage
workout process by which a borrower, esp. one

near bankruptcy, fulfills a debt commitment by modifying the terms of repayment

wraparound mortgage mortgage that contains obligation to repay a smaller, previously existing mortgage; second mortgage

OCCUPATIONS

General Titles, Positions, and Status
Trades and Crafts
Occupations and Job Titles

See also: *Chap. 11: Titles of Rank; Chap. 12: Business and Economics*

General Titles, Positions, and Status

agent one who represents the interests of another

amateur one who is not paid for work

analyst one skilled in the examination of specific problems

apprentice one learning trade under experienced worker

artisan craftsman or skilled tradesman

assembler one who fits parts together

assistant one who helps or aids another; one subordinate to another in rank or function

associate partner or fellow worker

attendant one who serves customers

blue-collar worker laborer, nonoffice worker

boss supervisor, owner, or person with authority over others

broker agent or intermediary in sale

businessman man engaged in commerce, esp. owner or executive

businesswoman woman engaged in commerce, esp. owner or executive

chairman presiding officer or top executive of company

chairwoman female presiding officer

cleaner one whose work is cleaning

clerk low-ranking official responsible for recordkeeping; one engaged in retail selling

coach one who instructs others in how to perform duties, esp. in sports

common laborer unskilled, blue-collar worker

counselor one who advises others

craftsman one working in skilled trade or craft

director one entrusted with overall supervision

employee one who works for an individual or institution

employer one who has others working for him or her

engineer one who builds or manages machinery or complex systems

executive one with administrative or managerial responsibility

fabricator one who builds or puts things together

fitter one who installs or adjusts machinery

foreman chief worker leading crew or production workers

forger one who works with metal

freelancer one who is self-employed or works for various employers

functionary minor official who performs specific tasks

hand helper, esp. at unskilled jobs

helper general assistant

installer one who puts machinery into operation

instructor one who teaches another a skill

jack common worker, esp. one with more than one trade

journeyman one experienced in a trade

laborer unskilled worker

layman one outside some skilled profession

machinist one who makes or repairs machines; one who uses machine tools

maker one who manufactures or creates something

manager one who directs others

master highly skilled worker; manager or director

mover one who transports things from place to place

office worker white-collar worker

official one with rank and specific responsibilities

operator one who handles functioning machinery

overseer supervisor

partner one of two or more owners of business

performer one who entertains others

practitioner one skilled in and engaged in trade or profession

producer one who makes something; one who finances the making of something

professional one who is paid for work; one engaged in work requiring advanced education

proletarian worker, esp. blue-collar worker

public servant government employee

repairman one who maintains and fixes equipment

representative one who acts as agent for another

researcher one who undertakes careful investigation

salesperson one who sells some product to public, usu. retail

secretary clerical assistant

skilled laborer one who works at job requiring special training

slave one who is forced to work for no pay

smith forger or fabricator, esp. in metals

sole proprietor self-employed owner of business having no partners

steward one who manages provisions or affairs

superintendent one in charge and having executive overview

supervisor administrative officer; one who oversees other's work; overseer

technician specialist in technical details of job

tender one who provides support

tester one who examines and evaluates a product

tradesman one skilled in a trade or craft

trainer one who instructs and prepares others for a job

unskilled worker laborer at job requiring no training

vendor one who sells; salesperson

white-collar worker office worker

worker one engaged in manual or industrial labor

wright skilled worker, esp. in wood and other materials

yeoman one attending or assisting another

Trades and Crafts

armorer maker and repairer of armor and arms

arrowsmith maker of arrows

artisan skilled craftsman

baker maker of breads, biscuits, and cakes

barber beardcutter and hairdresser

blacksmith maker of forged iron objects

boatwright maker of seagoing vessels

boilermaker maker of boilers, esp. for engines

bookbinder maker of bindings for book pages

bookwright maker of books

brazier brass worker

brewer maker of malt liquors

bricklayer setter of bricks

butler house servant in charge of wines and table service

cabinetmaker maker of fine, finished woodwork, esp. furniture

candlewright maker of candles

carpenter cutter and framer of wooden structures

cartwright maker of carts and wagons

carver cutter of meat at table

chandler candle maker; dealer in provisions and small wares

cobbler shoemaker

collier coal miner

cooper maker of barrels and casks

die maker maker of dies or cutting and shaping tools

doll maker maker of dolls

draper maker and seller of cloth

farrier *Chiefly Brit.* blacksmith

fletcher maker of arrows

founder caster of metal objects

fuller maker of gathers in cloth garments

gatewright maker of gates

glassblower maker of glass vessels or sheet glass through blowing process

glazier maker and installer of glass

goldsmith gold worker

haberdasher retail dealer in men's furnishings

joiner one who does finishing woodwork, esp. construction by joining pieces of wood

lather worker on a lathe

luthier maker of stringed instruments

mason builder using stone or brick

mercer dealer in expensive fabrics

miller keeper or operator of mill or processing plant for grain, wood, coffee, or cotton

millwright builder of mills; one tending workshop fixtures

monger trader or dealer

pitwright carpenter working in or about a mine

playwright writer of dramatic pieces

plowright maker and repairer of plows

potter maker of fired earthenware vessels

puttier cementer; glazier

rigger scaffolder; person tending to rigging, esp. of ships or aircraft

saddler maker of horse saddles

shipwright builder of ships

silversmith forger or shaper of silver objects

smith worker who shapes or forges, esp. in metals, including: anvilsmith, blacksmith, bladesmith, boilersmith, clocksmith, coppersmith, goldsmith, gunsmith, hammersmith, ironsmith, jobsmith, knifesmith, locksmith, sawsmith, scissors smith, silversmith, stonesmith, swordsmith, tinsmith, toolsmith

steeplejack repairer of steeples and chimneys

stonecutter cutter, carver, and dresser of stone

stonemason cutter of stone or builder in stone

tanner maker of prepared animal hides

tilewright maker of tiles

tinker mender of metal objects

turner maker of articles turned on a lathe

vintner maker and seller of wines

wainwright maker of carts and wagons

weaver maker of textiles by loom or by mechanical or manual interlacing of threads

welder joiner of metals by use of heat

wheelwright maker and repairer of wheels

woodcutter chopper or engraver of wood

wright workman in construction; mechanic

Occupations and Job Titles

accountant, account executive, acrobat, actor, actress, actuary, adjustor, adman, administrator, adviser, aeronautical engineer, aerospace engineer, agricultural engineer, agronomist, air traffic controller, ambassador, anthropologist, apartment manager, apparel salesperson, appraiser, archaeologist, architect, architectural engineer, archivist, arc welder, army engineer, artisan, artist, asbestos worker, astrologer, astronaut, astronomer, astrophysicist, athlete, attorney, auctioneer, auditor, au pair, author, automotive engineer, auto repairman, auto worker

babysitter, baggage handler, bailiff, baker, ballerina, banker, bank teller, barber, bartender, bath attendant, beautician, beekeeper, bellboy, bellhop, bench carpenter, billing clerk, biochemist, biologist, biophysicist, blacksmith, boarding housekeeper, body worker, boilermaker, boniface, bookbinder, bookie, bookkeeper, bootblack, botanist, bouncer, bounty hunter, brakeman, braze welder, brewer, bricklayer, brickmaker, bridge operator, broadcaster, broker, budget analyst, builder, bus driver, businessman, butcher, butler

cabdriver, cabinetmaker, calligrapher, candy maker, carny worker, carpenter, cartographer, carver, cashier, caster, caterer, cement mixer, ceramic engineer, ceramicist, chairman, chauffeur, checkout clerk, chef, chemical engineer, chemical worker, chemist, chief administrative officer, chief executive officer, chief operating officer, chimney sweep, chiropractor, choreographer, cinematographer, city manager, civil engineer, civil service employee, clergyman, clerk, clockmaker, clothier, clown, cobbler, commercial artist, commodities broker, common laborer, communications engineer, communications specialist, composer, comptroller, computer programmer, computer technician, concessionaire, conductor, confectioner, con man, construction engineer, construction worker, consul, contractor, cook, cooper, coppersmith, copyeditor, copywriter, coremaker, coroner, correctional officer, cosmetologist, costermonger, counselor, courier, couturier, cowboy, crier, critic, cryptographer, curator, custodian

dancer, data processor, dealer, decorator, defender, dental hygienist, dental supply salesman, dental technician, dentist, designer, detective, die maker, dietitian, diplomat, director, disc jockey, dishwasher, distiller, distributor, docent, doctor, doll maker, domestic, doorman, door-to-door salesman, drafter, drainage worker, dramatist, dramaturge, driver, dustman

ecologist, economist, editor, educator, electrical engineer, electrician, electronics engineer, electroplater, elevator operator, embalmer, embroiderer, employment agent, engine driver, engraver, ensign, entertainer, entrepreneur, etcher, evangelist, excavator, extra

farmer, farm hand, fashion designer, federal employee, field hand, fieldworker, file clerk, filmmaker, filtration worker, financier, firefighter, fireman, fire-protection engineer, firer, fisherman, fishery worker, fitter, flier, floor layer, food processor, forester, forest ranger, forger, forklift operator, founder, foundryman, freight operator, fuel engineer, furnace engineer, furniture maker

gamekeeper, game maker, garbageman, gardener, garment worker, gas fitter, gas welder, gate clerk, gem cutter, gem dealer, geneticist, geographer, geological engineer, geologist, glassblower, glazier, goldsmith, governess, government worker, grammarian, graphic artist, gravedigger, groundskeeper, guard, guide, guru, gynecologist

haircutter, hairdresser, hand sewer, handyman, hardware salesman, harvester, hatcheck person, hat maker, heat-treater, high school teacher, highway engineer, highwayman, historian, hod carrier, home economist, homemaker, horologist, hostess, hostler, houseboy, housecleaner, housekeeper, housewife, hunter, hydraulic engineer

illuminating engineer, illustrator, indexer, industrial engineer, industrialist, information clerk, inspector, installer, instrumentalist, insulation worker, insurance salesman, interior designer, intern, interpreter, interview clerk, investigator, investor, irrigation engineer

jailor, janitor, jester, jeweler, jewelry maker, journalist, judge, juggler, jurist, juror, justice

keypunch operator, kitchen worker, knitter

labor leader, lab technician, laundress, lawyer, layout artist, leatherworker, legal secretary, legislator, lexicographer, librarian, lighting technician, linguist, liquor salesman, lithographer, locker room attendant, locksmith, logger, logician, longshoreman, lumberjack

machine operator, machinist, magician, maid, mailroom worker, maintenance man, maître d'hôtel, manicurist, manufacturer, marine, marine biologist, marine engineer, marine mechanic, marshal, mason, masseur, master, mate, mathematician, meat cutter, mechanic, mechanical engineer, melter, mental health worker, mercer, mercerizer, merchandise displayer, messenger, metallurgical engineer, metallurgist, metal processor, metalworker, meteorologist, meter maid, midwife, migrant worker, military engineer, miller, miner, mining engineer, minister, model, model maker, molder, mold maker, mortician, municipal employee, municipal engineer, musician

nanny, naval engineer, navigator, net fisherman, newscaster, night watchman, novelist, nuclear engineer, nuclear physicist, nurse, nursemaid, nutritionist

obstetrician, occupational therapist, oceanographer, ombudsman, opera singer, ophthalmologist, optician, optometrist, orderly, ordnance engineer, ore refiner, orthopedist, osteopath

page, painter, paleontologist, paperhanger, park ranger, patternmaker, paver, payroll clerk, personnel officer, pest control worker, petroleum engineer, petroleum worker, pharmacist, philosopher, photoengraver, photographer, physical therapist, physician, physicist, physiologist, pickler, pilot, pimp, plasterer, plastics worker, playwright, plumber, poet, policeman, political scientist, politician, pornographer, porter, potter, power engineer, power plant operator, power supply engineer, practical nurse, president, press agent, press secretary, priest, printer, private investigator, producer, product engineer, production clerk, professor, projectionist, proofreader, proprietor, prosecutor, prostitute, psychiatrist, psychoanalyst, psychologist, public administrator, publicist, public relations man, public servant, publisher, puddler, purchasing agent

quality control officer

rabbi, rack jobber, radar engineer, radio commentator, radio engineer, radio operator, railroad conductor, railroad engineer, rancher, real estate broker, receptionist, refrigerator engineer, registered nurse, rehab counselor, repairman, research assistant, research engineer, researcher, retail clerk, rigger, riveter, road worker, rocket engineer, rocket scientist, roofer, rubber worker

sailor, sanitary engineer, screenwriter, scribe, sculptor, seamstress, seaweed gatherer, secretary, securities analyst, security guard, semanticist, semiotician, serf, servant, service station attendant, sheet metal worker, shipper, ship's captain, ship's mate, shoemaker, shopkeeper, silversmith, slave, smuggler, social worker, sociologist, solderer, soldier, sole proprietor, solicitor, sound engineer, sound man, speech pathologist, spinner, sponge gatherer, sporting goods salesman, spotter, stainer, stand-in, state employee, statistician, steam engineer, steam fitter, steeplejack, stenographer, stevedore, stewardess, stockbroker, stock clerk, stonecutter, stonemason, stoneworker, street sweeper, structural engineer, stunt man, stylist, subcontractor, surgeon, surveyor, swami, systems analyst

tactician, tailor, talent agent, talent scout, tax collector, tax preparer, teacher, teamster, telegraph operator, telephone engineer, telephone operator, telephone repairman, teller, textile engineer, textile worker, therapist, thermal cutter, thief, ticket agent, ticket taker, tile setter, tinner, tinsmith, tobacconist, tobacco worker, toll taker, tool engineer, tour guide, tractor driver, trader, tradesman, trade unionist, traffic officer, translator, transportation engineer, transport worker, trapper, travel agent, traveling salesman, treasurer, tree farmer, truck driver, trucker, tutor, type-caster, type composer, typesetter, typist

undertaker, unskilled laborer, upholsterer, urban planner, usher, utility worker

valet, vending machine operator, vendor, ventilation engineer, venture capitalist, veterinarian, vice president, videotape engineer, vintner, vocalist, vocational therapist

waiter, waitress, wallpaperer, warden, warder, wardrobe attendant, warehouseman, waterproofer, water-supply engineer, waxer, weatherman, weaver, welder, welding engineer, wet nurse, wholesaler, winemaker, woodworker, wrecker, writer

yeoman

zookeeper, zoologist

CHAPTER THIRTEEN
SOCIAL SCIENCES

ANTHROPOLOGY

Branches and Disciplines
Ages, Species, and Races of Humankind
Kinship, Marriage, and Other Customs
Practice, Techniques, Artifacts, and Tools

See also: *Chap. 2: Biology; Chap. 3: Geology;*
Chap. 5: Weapons and Armaments; Chap. 8:
Kinship and Family Relations; Marriage and
Divorce; Chap. 13: Sociology; Psychology; Chap.
25: Mythology and Folklore

Branches and Disciplines

anthropogeography study of geographical
distribution of humankind and relationship of
peoples to their environment

anthropological linguistics study of
relationship between language and culture, esp.
in preliterate societies

anthropology study of physical and sociocultural
aspects of humankind, including human origins,
evolution, biological characteristics, customs, and
belief systems

applied anthropology purposive study of
specific, often primitive society, esp. by
authorities making practical decisions about it

archaeology scientific study of early historic and
prehistoric cultures by excavation and analysis
of their artifacts, monuments, and other remains

business anthropology study of group
behavior, workplace design, and other human
problems derived from corporate environments

cultural anthropology study of characteristics,
similarities, and differences among various
human cultures, based esp. on fieldwork and
empirical data

dendrochronology method of dating past
events by analysis of annual rings of trees

epigraphy study of ancient inscriptions

ethnoarchaeology study of contemporary
primitive cultures, esp. as means of
understanding prehistoric cultures

ethnobiology study of how different human
cultures use plants and animals

ethnobotany study of agricultural customs and
plant lore of a culture

ethnography systematic description of
individual cultures

ethnohistory study of development of cultures,
esp. through analysis of archaeological findings

ethnolinguistics study of interplay between
language and culture

ethnology analysis of cultures, esp. with regard
to their historical development, similarities, and
dissimilarities

ethnomethodology study of rules and rituals on
which most social interactions are based

ethnomusicology study of relationship between
primitive or folk music and culture to which it
belongs

ethnoscience study of systems and concepts of
knowledge and classification of objects and
concepts among primitive peoples

paleontology study of life forms existing in
earlier geologic periods, based on their fossil
remains

philosophical anthropology study of basic
nature and essence of humankind

physical anthropology branch of anthropology
concerned with fossil origins of man, evolution,
and human behavior

praxeology study of human conduct

social anthropology branch of anthropology
concerned with social relationships, esp. those
institutionalized into fixed behavior patterns
such as ritual, religion, kinship, marriage, and
political and economic structures

structural anthropology branch of
anthropology based on principles of structural
linguistics

Ages, Species, and Races of Humankind

anthropoid member of primate suborder
Anthropoidea, including monkeys, apes, and
human beings

Australopithecus extinct genus of
small-brained, large-toothed, bipedal hominid
near-men whose fossil remains date back to
four million years in Africa and who had the
ability to stand fully erect

Australopithecus afarensis earliest species of
Australopithecus that lived four million years ago
in East Africa

Australopithecus africanus species of
Australopithecus, characterized by small stature
and use of simple weapons, that lived three
million years ago

Australopithecus boisei species of rugged
Australopithecus, characterized by large teeth, that
lived one to two million years ago

Australopithecus robustus species of
Australopithecus, larger in stature but probably
less intelligent than *Australopithecus africanus*, that
lived two million years ago

bipedalism locomotion on two feet,
characteristic of hominids

Bronze Age period beginning around 4000 B.C.
characterized by use of bronze tools, the wheel,
and ox-drawn plows, and by growth of first
civilizations in Egypt and Sumeria

Caucasian race one of three traditional human
racial groupings, characterized by light skin
pigmentation, straight to curly hair, and light to
dark eyes, inhabiting Northern Hemisphere, esp.
Europe

cave man cave dweller, esp. of Stone Age

Copper Age cultural period between Neolithic
and Bronze ages, characterized by ability to
extract copper for use in making tools

Cro-Magnon man tall, erect Upper Paleolithic
prototype of modern *Homo sapiens* in Europe
between 40,000 and 30,000 years ago, that
used stone tools and produced cave paintings

Eolithic Age Dawn Stone Age, between 2.5 and
two million years ago, in which hominid
near-men used primitive, fractured stone tools

Folsom culture early North American
hunting-gathering culture that flourished about
9000 B.C., characterized by use of fluted stone
spearheads

Heidelberg man species of primitive hominid
contemporary with *Pithecanthropus* around
500,000 years ago, having massive teeth but
undeveloped chin

hominid any of modern or extinct bipedal
primates of family Hominidae, including genera
Homo and *Australopithecus*

hominoid member of superfamily Hominoidea,
including modern great apes, humans, and their
extinct ancestors

Homo genus of bipedal primates in family
Hominidae, including modern *Homo sapiens* and
several extinct species

Homo erectus extinct species of hominid,
formerly known as *Pithecanthropus erectus*,
known from Peking and Java man discoveries,
having erect stature and postcranial skull but
smallish brain, low forehead, and protruding
face, characterized by use of crude stone tools
and possibly simple speech, that lived from
500,000 to 250,000 years ago

Homo habilis extinct species of upright hominid
in East Africa that existed two to 1.5 million
years ago

Homo sapiens species of bipedal primate to
which modern human beings belong, beginning
250,000 years ago during Stone Age with *Homo
sapiens neanderthalensis*, characterized by use of
tools and language

humankind all members of human race

Iron Age period following Bronze Age, in which
humankind learned to smelt iron for tools and
weapons, beginning around 2000 B.C. in Near
East

Java man extinct race of early hominid,
Pithecanthropus erectus, with apelike skull and
human limb structure, whose skeletal remains
were found in Java

Lower Paleolithic period earliest portion of
Old Stone Age, between two million and
200,000 years ago

Mesolithic period Middle Stone Age following
Paleolithic age, from 10,000 to 8000 B.C. in
Europe, characterized by first food-producers,
development of boats and sleds, and use of
microliths

Middle Paleolithic period middle portion of
Old Stone Age, between 200,000 and 40,000
years ago

missing link hypothetical species assumed to
bridge evolutionary gap between anthropoid
apes and human beings, sometimes identified as
Australopithecus

Mongoloid race one of three traditional human
racial groupings, characterized by yellowish
complexion, straight black hair, and epicanthic
folds about eyes, esp. inhabiting Asia

Neanderthal man extinct race of Middle
Paleolithic man, powerful and physically robust
with brain capacity comparable to modern man,

that inhabited Europe and western Asia between 100,000 and 40,000 years ago

Negroid race one of three traditional human racial groupings, characterized by dark skin pigmentations, curly hair, and wide features, primarily inhabiting Southern Hemisphere, esp. Africa

Neolithic period New Stone Age preceding Bronze Age, between 8000 and 4000 B.C. in Near East, characterized by settlement into villages, domestication of animals, grain cultivation, pottery, textile weaving, cave painting, and flint-mining

Olmec (*adj*) of or pertaining to an early prehistoric New World civilization, from 1500 to 500 B.C. in Mexico, characterized by extensive agriculture, dating system, pyramids, trade, and fine artwork

Paleolithic period Old Stone Age period from two million years ago through 10,000 B.C., characterized by hunting-gathering society and use of increasingly sophisticated stone tools, divided into Lower, Middle, and Upper Paleolithic periods

Peking man extinct, early *Homo erectus* whose fossil remains were discovered in China, characterized by hunting and use of fire and stone tools

Piltdown man hypothetical early modern human being whose existence was based on skull fragments found in England, believed to be missing link between apes and man but later exposed as fake

Pithecanthropus former genus of extinct hominids now assigned to proposed species *Homo erectus*

prehistoric man certain hominid species of genus *Homo* that lived before recorded history

prehistory period of human development prior to recorded events, known through archaeological discoveries

Proconsul extinct hominoid subgenus that lived 17 to 20 million years ago and may have been ancestral to modern chimpanzees and apes

protohistory period of transition between prehistory and earliest recorded history

pygmy term denoting groups whose typical male averages less than 59 inches (150 cm) in height, generally hunter-gatherers with few crafts, found esp. in central Africa and Philippines

race one of the three major human groupings whose members tend to breed among themselves and share inherited physical characteristics: Caucasian, Mongoloid, Negroid

Ramapithecus extinct genus of late Miocene hominoid, formerly believed to have been ancestral to hominids, that lived about twelve million years ago

recorded history written record of history made by culture having formal language

Stone Age period beginning around two million years ago, characterized by use of increasingly sophisticated stone tools and weapons and, in latter ages, by development of food cultivation,

villages, and crafts, usu. divided into Paleolithic, Mesolithic, and Neolithic periods and ending with dawn of civilization in Bronze Age around 4000 B.C.

subrace division within one of the three major human racial groupings, usu. inhabiting specific region

Sumer ancient region in Near East in which city-states and written language first developed in late Neolithic period, after 4000 B.C.

troglodyte prehistoric cave dweller

Upper Paleolithic period latter portion of Old Stone Age, between 40,000 and 10,000 B.C.

Kinship, Marriage, and Other Customs

affinity kinship relationship based on marriage

ancestor worship veneration of spirits of dead ancestors believed to influence affairs of the living

animism belief in spiritual beings and esp. that natural objects and phenomena possess souls

anthropophagy cannibalism

bigamy accepted practice of marriage to more than one person at a time among certain cultures

bride price money or goods given by bridegroom or his family to bride's family

cannibal person who eats human flesh, esp. as part of tribal religious or magical ceremony

cargo cult any messianic native religious system found in southwestern Pacific islands, formed in response to white civilization, and characterized by belief that ancestors will return with cargoes of modern goods

caste system any endogamous, hereditary social grouping based on status, economic position, and mores

clan unilineal kinship descent group, either through male (patrilineal) or female (matrilineal) line

collateral kin descended by different line from same stock

conventionalized art art based on accepted manner of depicting subject matter; stylized art

death rites ceremonies, burial, and mourning that accompany passage of person from world of the living to the dead

decorative art ornamental designs applied to enhance beauty of objects having practical uses

dietary laws secular or religious rules for what foods may be consumed under certain conditions, used to maintain group's unique social identity

dominance relationships status systems within social groups based on power, possessions, and prestige

dowry money or goods given by bride's family to bridegroom at marriage

endogamy rules defining boundaries of marriage within specific tribe or social group; marriage within such tribe or group

exogamy rules defining social unit within which

marriage is forbidden; marriage outside specific tribe or social group

extended family kinship group including nuclear family and relatives, esp. when living in one household

family group of persons related by blood, esp. parents and children, forming basic biosocial unit

head deformation changing of head shape in infancy by binding infant's soft head, practiced esp. in Pacific Northwest and Borneo

headhunting taking and preserving the heads of one's enemies, practiced by certain primitive peoples

henotheism worship of particular god by family or tribe without precluding belief in other deities

hetaerism social system in which women are considered common property

incest taboo prohibition and accompanying horror of sexual relations within defined exogamous kinship group

kinship family relationships and system of social rules governing descent, inheritance, marriage, residence, and sexual relations within kinship groups

marriage state in which two persons are bonded together under socially prescribed rules, esp. for procreation and child-rearing

marriage rites religious, civil, and cultural traditions surrounding marriage ceremony

matriarchy social organization in which mother is head of family and descent is traced through female line

matrilineal (*adj*) having descent traced through female line

matrilocal (*adj*) designating extended family in which husband joins household of wife's parents; uxorilocal

moiety one of two divisions of tribe based on unilineal descent through either mother's or father's line

monogamy social practice of marriage with only one person at a time

naturalistic art realistic art

neolocal (*adj*) living away from both husband's and wife's relatives

nuclear family basic family unit restricted to parents and their offspring

patriarchy social organization in which father is head of family and descent is traced through male line

patrilineal (*adj*) having descent traced through male line

patrilocal (*adj*) designating extended family in which wife joins household of husband's parents; virilocal

pecking order hierarchical social organization based on dominance relationships and submission of those lower in status

polyandry practice of having more than one husband at a time

polygamy socially approved practice of having more than one spouse at a time

polygyny practice of having more than one wife at a time

realistic art art that strives to represent objects with exact likenesses; naturalistic art

representative art art that portrays nature and life in recognizable manner

rite formal or ceremonial act or procedure prescribed in solemn and religious occasions

rites of intensification ceremonies or rituals associated with periodic and seasonal events of crisis or special significance to a people

rites of passage ceremonies or rituals that accompany individual's passage from one social status to another, such as puberty, initiation, marriage, and burial

ritual established procedure or ceremony prescribed by custom for solemn occasions, such as rite of passage

stylized art conventionalized art

symbolic art art that employs symbols to signify objects and convey meaning

taboo culture-specific prohibition of certain behavior, word, or object

totem animal, plant, or object with which clan, tribe, or people identifies in its rituals, often believing it to be an ancestor

tribe group of persons, usu. of common descent, occupying one community and sharing common language, customs, and traditions

unilineal (*adj*) having descent traced through either male or female line

uxorilocal (*adj*) matrilocal

vendetta private, multigenerational family feud in which kin are obliged to avenge wrongs done their relatives

virilocal (*adj*) patrilocal

Practice, Techniques, Artifacts, and Tools

aborigine one of original inhabitants of a region

acculturation process of cultural change due to friendly or hostile interchange between two societies

anthropometry measurement of size and proportions of human body using calibrated instrument

artifact object made or used by human beings, esp. one found at archaeological excavation, providing evidence of an earlier culture's existence

band group of wandering people, usu. from one tribe and comparable in size to village

barrow tumulus

bladelet small, blade-shaped, sometimes reworked piece of stone used as cutting edge of tool or weapon in late Stone Age

cave dwellings Stone Age dwellings, located in caves during Upper Paleolithic period

cave paintings art form characteristic of Upper Paleolithic period, practiced in European caves from around 30,000 B.C.

cephalic index measurement of head used in physical anthropology, consisting of ratio of maximum width to maximum length, with results classified as dolichocephalic (long-headed), mesocephalic, or brachycephalic (short-headed)

cist prehistoric tomb or casket with stone walls

civilization stage of cultural development marked by written records, development of cities, and advanced levels of science, government, and art; one culture or people of a specific place and time

cliff dwellings shelters in caves or on cliff ledges built by members of prehistoric people in southwestern United States

convergent evolution tendency of different lines of descent to develop similar characteristics in adapting to specific environmental conditions

core tool stone tool made by chipping flakes from stone core until it has assumed desired size and shape

crannog lake dwelling built on artificial island

cromlech megalithic chamber tomb

cross dating method of determining age for archaeological site of unknown age by comparing its distinguishing traits to those of another site of known age

cultural relativism concept that cultural traits and values derive from social context peculiar to specific culture

culture shared knowledge, beliefs, and ways of living built up by members of group and transmitted from one generation to next; specific group sharing such knowledge, beliefs, and ways of living over defined period of time

culture area geographical region in which neighboring groups share distinct patterns of culture

culture complex number of interrelated culture traits dominated by one essential trait

culture diffusion spread of culture traits or cultural patterns from central point and borrowing from one culture by another

culture hero mythical or idealized historical figure embodying goals and ideals of a people

culture trait any single characteristic of human activity acquired through social life and communicated across generations

cuneiform triangular or wedge-shaped pictographic writing system characteristic of cultures of ancient Near East from around 3500 B.C.

Darwinism theory of origin and evolution of species which postulates survival of the fittest individuals or species through natural selection, based on works of Charles Darwin

dig excavation

dolmen megalithic tomb consisting of stone slab laid across two or more large, upright stones

enculturation process of learning the culture of one's group or society, through observation, experience, and instruction

ethnic group people distinguished by common racial or cultural background

ethnocentrism belief in inherent superiority of one's own ethnic group or culture; tendency to view alien groups or cultures through prism of one's culture

evolution theory of development of species from simpler forms, based on work of Charles Darwin

excavation archaeological site at which layers of earth have been systematically exposed by digging to uncover human artifacts or remains of earlier cultures; dig

flint piece of hard stone used as primitive tool or to strike spark for making fire

folklore traditional beliefs, customs, and legends of a people, esp. those expressed orally through memory and practice

folkways patterns of behavior and belief common to particular group of people, learned from other members of group

genealogy study and record of family origins and history of descent

geographical race people or peoples isolated from other groups by major geographical barrier such as ocean or mountain range

graffito drawing or writing scratched on wall or other surface

hand ax large, bifacial stone tool of Lower Paleolithic period.

henge Neolithic monument consisting of circular area enclosed by ditch and containing circles of upright stone or wood pillars, used for ritual purposes or astronomical observations

hieroglyphics pictographic script of ancient Egyptians, in which the symbols used are conventionalized, recognizable pictures of the things represented

hunting-gathering society any of the small-scale societies, primarily located in Southern Hemisphere, that subsist through hunting and collecting plants rather than by cultivation

indigenous native to or characteristic of a particular region

kitchen midden shell mound

kiva large, underground chamber used in Pueblo Indian religious ceremonies

lake dwellings remains of prehistoric settlements built on piles at shores of lakes in central Europe from Neolithic period into Iron Age

Lascaux Cave paintings fine Paleolithic wall paintings dating from 13,000 to 8500 B.C., found in cave in southwestern France

megalithic monuments large stone tombs and dolmens of undressed stone, such as Stonehenge, built in Europe during Neolithic period and early Bronze Age

menhir upright monumental stone standing alone or in arrangement with others

microlith tiny flint scraping tool for dressing skins, characteristic of Mesolithic cultures

migration movement of peoples from one geographical area to another

monolith monument such as obelisk constructed of a single, huge stone block, typical of Neolithic period

nomadism pastoral lifestyle in which group with no fixed residence moves from place to place on seasonal circuit

nonliterate (*adj*) preliterate

pastoralism often nomadic mode of subsistence, usu. among small groups, based on herding of domesticated livestock

people entire body of human beings forming one community, tribe, clan, nation, or other grouping

petroglyph prehistoric drawing or carving on stone

potsherd pottery fragment used in dating excavation sites or tracing cultural contacts, esp. in Neolithic period

preliterate (*adj*) designating culture or people who lack any writing system; nonliterate

primitive (*adj*) pertaining to preliterate or tribal people with strong cultural and physical similarities to their early ancestors

primitive communism way of life practiced among preliterate groups who shared possessions and cooperated closely to survive

racial characteristics physical traits such as skin pigmentation, hair quality, facial shape, or eye shape and coloring that distinguish one race

Rosetta stone stone slab, discovered in Egypt, bearing parallel inscriptions in Greek, Egyptian hieroglyphs, and demotic characters, facilitating decipherment of hieroglyphs

seminomadism pastoral lifestyle, esp. among Middle Eastern camel and goat herders, in which groups have settled abodes for part of year

shell mound prehistoric refuse heap containing remains of shellfish and human artifacts; kitchen midden

site exact location of single unit of territory studied by archaeologists

society autonomous community of persons sharing common customs, beliefs, goals, and attitudes, organized together under accepted rules

sociocultural (*adj*) of or pertaining to interaction of social and cultural elements

stele monumental, upright stone slab or pillar bearing an inscription or design

Stonehenge prehistoric, megalithic monument erected by a Bronze Age culture in England around 1500 B.C.

tablets flat rock slabs bearing hieroglyphs or cuneiform characters, used to reconstruct Bronze Age and Iron Age history

Tepe Gawra major excavation site in northern Iraq with twenty-six levels of cities dating to before 4000 B.C.

trilithon prehistoric structure consisting of two upright stones supporting a horizontal stone

tumulus artificial mound, esp. over grave; barrow

village small, settled community of several hundred people living together

woodhenge Neolithic henge monument constructed of upright timbers

SOCIOLOGY

Attitudes and Behavior
Cultural Movements, Events, and Institutions
Social Types, Norms, and Symbols
Social Structure and Conditions
Schools and Doctrines
Tools and Techniques

See also: *Chap. 11: The City; Government; Politics; Chap. 12: Business and Economics; Chap. 13: Psychology; Education*

Attitudes and Behavior

ableism discrimination against people having some physical or mental disability

adaptation ability to learn behavior that helps in adjusting to individuals, groups, and technology

ageism discrimination based on age

agnosticism belief that human beings cannot know whether there is a God or understand things beyond the material world

American dream popular belief that perseverance and hard work will bring forth America's bounty in the form of material well-being

anthropocentric (*adj*) regarding human beings as center of the universe

anthropomorphism attribution of human shape and character to animals, deities, or inanimate objects

anti-Semitism prejudice against and persecution of Jews

antisocial (*adj*) holding beliefs or taking actions harmful to well-being of society

apartheid policy of strict racial segregation and discrimination in South Africa

apolitical (*adj*) having no interest in politics

atheism conviction that there is no God

bias prejudice

bigotry intolerance of those different than oneself

blackball (*vb*) exclude socially

brave new world grand vision of benevolent, technological future in novel by Aldous Huxley, now considered ironic

chauvinism unreasoning devotion to one's race, sex, or country

chic (*adj*) pertaining to elegance and up-to-date style; (*n*) elegance and style

civility politeness, esp. as mere formality

class consciousness awareness of belonging to one class in the social order

classism discrimination based on class

collective behavior responses and reactions of groups, esp. crowds, to same stimuli

color bar barrier preventing nonwhites from living and working with whites

conformity living according to social expectations and norms

convention customary social practice or rule

conventional (*adj*) conforming to accepted social standards

craze latest passing popular fashion or idea

crime against humanity crime or crimes, such as genocide, directed against particular group that has committed no criminal act

crusade actions pursued zealously and vigorously to further some cause

custom traditional social convention enforced by general disapproval of its violation

decorum propriety and good taste; polite behavior

dehumanize (*vb*) make inhuman or machinelike

deviance marked divergence from society's accepted norms

discrimination different treatment for certain racial, ethnic, religious, or sexual groups

double standard moral code applying more stringent standards to one group than to another, esp. between sexes

doxy accepted belief, esp. religious

ethnocentrism belief that one's nation, culture, or ethnic group is superior

ethos characteristic and distinguishing attitudes and habits of group

etiquette established conventions of polite social intercourse

fad passing popular fashion

fashion current style, mode, or custom

fellowship companionship, generosity toward others

flag-waving display of zealous patriotism

folklore traditional beliefs, legends, and customs of one culture

folkways beliefs, preferences, and customs of social unit or group

formality propriety in observing prescribed customs

general will collective desire of a community

groupthink conformity to group values and ethics

hard-line (*adj*) uncompromising or unyielding in adherence to a dogma or plan, esp. in politics

hero worship idolizing of an individual, esp. a sports star or entertainer

honor system system that trusts people, esp. students or prisoners, to work honestly, without supervision

horse-and-buggy (*adj*) old-fashioned

iconoclasm opposition to accepted ideas and beliefs

ideology body of beliefs and ideas of one person, group, or culture

individualism view that society's primary goal is promotion of the individual over group welfare

indoctrination training others in one's beliefs

internalization incorporation of cultural values and attitudes within oneself, consciously or unconsciously

ism distinctive cause, doctrine, school, or principle

isolationism opposition to involvement in affairs external to one's community or nation

Jim Crow discrimination against blacks

jingoism excessive, often warlike, national chauvinism

latest thing fad or current fashion

left political liberalism; radical end of political spectrum

lifestyle consistent pattern of one's life, attitudes, customs, values, and economic standing

manners prevailing customs of polite, conventional behavior

martyrdom willingness to die rather than renounce one's beliefs or principles

mass hysteria irrational behavior on a wide scale caused by unfounded belief or fear

master race race that is supposedly biologically equipped to rule all others

middle-of-the-road (*adj*) favoring a point of view midway between extremes

mode current fashion or style

mores essential folkways and binding customs of a society

nationalism patriotism, belief in one's country

networking developing and maintaining a system of professional contacts aimed at furthering one's career

nihilism belief that there is no purpose to existence; rejection of established laws and institutions

nonviolence abstention from use of violence on moral grounds

particularism exclusive adherence to one doctrine, system, or interest

passive resistance opposition to established government by nonviolent acts of noncooperation

Peter Principle tendency in large organizations for people to rise to their level of incompetence

politically correct (*adj*) marked by or conforming to typically progressive, orthodox views such as environmentalism, pacifism, and social equality for those outside the white male power structure and Western, Judeo-Christian tradition

preferential treatment treatment of one person or group better than others based on social status

prejudice predisposition toward baseless intolerance and hatred for particular group; bias

pro-choice (*adj*) supporting the right to legal abortion

pro-life (*adj*) opposing the right to legal abortion

propriety socially acceptable conduct

provincialism narrow concern with one's own locale or people

public service work in the public interest, often for government

purge elimination of those regarded as undesirables, esp. from government without due process

race riot riot motivated by racial fear or hatred

racism segregation and persecution based on doctrine of superiority of one race over others

rage extremely popular fashion, usu. short-lived

redbait (*vb*) accuse an individual or group of being communist

regionalism devotion to culture of one's native area

religious tolerance acceptance of those practicing faith different from one's own

reverse discrimination bias against majority as a result of efforts to improve lot of minority

right political conservatism; reactionary end of political spectrum

right-to-life (*adj*) pertaining to opposition to right to legal abortion based on belief that fetus is a person

right-to-work (*adj*) pertaining to right of workers to employment regardless of labor union status

ritualistic (*adj*) performed according to a rigidly prescribed order

role pattern of expected behavior for individual in given situation in relation to social status

role conflict problems that occur when a person's roles conflict with each other or with his or her values

scapegoating blaming members of minority group for social or economic problems

sectionalism devotion to interests of one's native region

segregation social separation, esp. of races

separatism policy of racial, cultural, or national autonomy

sexism discrimination and denial of opportunity on basis of sex, esp. against women

sexual harassment unwanted advances and persistent pestering for sexual favors, esp. by person in position of authority such as employer

social perception manner in which people's perceptions of others are shaped by previous experience, attitudes, and expectations

states' rights rights belonging to each state rather than to federal government, esp. in connection with social policies

style current fashionable way of dressing, speaking, or acting

suppression forceful quelling of an idea or movement

taboo prohibition or superstition established through accepted social custom

taste attitude or style reflecting group preference at particular time

territoriality powerful attachment to physical area perceived as one's own property

terrorism use of wanton violence for political goals

Titanism open revolt against established social standards

tokenism practice of making a token gesture by hiring or admitting a small number of minority group members

tolerance liberal attitude toward differing lifestyles, cultures, and beliefs

tradition long-established custom or practice of a society

trendy (*adj*) following the latest fashion

tribalism intense loyalty to one's own group

un-American (*adj*) opposed to or inconsistent with the accepted notion of American ideals and institutions

unfashionable (*adj*) out of date

universal (*adj*) held by everyone

up-to-date (*adj*) conforming to latest styles and beliefs

upward mobility ascension of the socioeconomic ladder

values principles, standards, and goals given high intrinsic worth by society

vogue latest fashion

Cultural Movements, Events, and Institutions

affirmative action program to increase presence of women and minorities in public and private sectors

antinuke (*adj*) *Informal.* opposed to development and use of nuclear weapons or energy

asphalt jungle the city, esp. crowded, urban neighborhoods regarded as dangerous

baby boom burst of population in generation born just after World War II

backlash reaction opposite to that intended by a particular social movement

Bible Belt area of United States, particularly in South and Midwest, noted for religious fundamentalism

Big Brother officials of authoritarian state that erodes privacy of the individual to exercise control

blacklist privately circulated list of those to be denied employment because of allegedly subversive views

Black Muslims militant Islamic sect of black Americans who advocate racial separation, asceticism, and formation of a black state

black nationalism advocacy of establishment of separate black nation in United States

Black Panthers radical black power organization of 1960's

black power political and economic power sought by black Americans

boom swift and vigorous economic growth with accompanying societal euphoria

boycott group refusal to patronize a business or another person or group for economic or political reasons

brain drain ebbing of nation's intellectual and professional resources through emigration

busing transferring schoolchildren out of their neighborhoods to achieve racial balance in schools

Camelot the White House under John F. Kennedy from 1961 to 1963

cause principle or movement vigorously upheld and supported

childcare care for preschool children of employed parents, esp. at day-care center

civil disobedience nonviolent refusal to comply with laws or official policy on moral grounds

civil rights rights guaranteeing equal opportunity to all citizens, regardless of race, religion, sex, or national origin

consciousness-raising increasing awareness, esp. among women, of their secondary status and particular group needs and goals through interaction with other women

conspicuous consumption extravagant spending to enhance social status

cooptation winning over of an adversary to one's own belief

counterculture culture and lifestyle of late 1960's, esp. among young, characterized by opposition to war and society's prevailing values

credibility gap difference between official pronouncements and what is believable

crisis intervention intervention by group offering immediate help to potential suicides, addicts, and other troubled persons

Cultural Revolution radical sociopolitical movement in China during 1960's in which Mao Zedong attempted to restructure society and reinvigorate his revolution

culture of poverty values, attitudes, and behavior believed to be common to the poor

culture shock trauma resulting from movement from one culture or society to another

current affairs events, movements, institutions, and trends in political and social life at present time

deracination uprooting from one's social or cultural environment

designer (*adj*) originally designed by and carrying label of fashion designer, now used to describe various products considered unique or superior

environmentalism active concern for state of Earth's natural resources

equal opportunity employment hiring of employees without regard to race, sex, or national origin

establishment society's ruling class, representing all vested interests

ethnic group minority group linked by language, origin, culture, or religion within larger society

fallout radioactive residue that falls to Earth after nuclear explosion; repercussions of any event

feminism doctrine and programs promoting rights and interests of women, esp. in male-dominated society

food stamps government-provided food coupons for low-income families

freedom rides bus trips made by activists traveling south to work for racial integration, esp. in 1960's

free university institution for study of nontraditional subjects, usu. in unstructured curriculum

free world non-Communist world

future shock disorientation and anxiety due to inability to cope with continual, rapid, technological change and breakdown of old values

gay liberation sociopolitical movement to combat legal and social discrimination against homosexuals

gay power organized political influence exerted by homosexuals as a group, esp. to achieve equal rights and social justice

genetic engineering biological creation of improved species through recombining of spliced DNA from different species

genocide organized attempt to destroy an entire people or race

gentrification restoration of run-down urban neighborhoods by upper- or middle-income families

global village the world as one single community, esp. owing to mass media, communications, and rapid transportation

Götterdämmerung collapse of society linked with catastrophic violence and disorder, orig. from German mythology

green revolution increased food production for underdeveloped nations through improved agricultural methods

grievance committee group chosen to represent employer and employees to resolve workers' problems

groundswell rapidly growing wave of popular sentiment or opinion, often lacking overt leadership

halfway house place for societal readjustment after institutional confinement

haut monde high society

hip-hop *Slang*. popular subculture of urban youth, esp. African Americans, based in part on rap music, break dancing, and graffiti art

hippies youth culture of 1960's, alienated from society and interested in mysticism, psychedelic drugs, nature, pacifism, and sexual freedom

holocaust large-scale destruction of human life

Holocaust systematic murder of European Jews by the Nazis during World War II

hotline direct telephone line to assistance, for use in personal crisis

hunger strike refusal to eat, usu. by prisoners or demonstrators, until certain demands are met

information explosion computer-generated rapid increase in data available in all fields

inner city blighted, poor section of metropolitan area

iron curtain former military and ideological barrier isolating Soviet-controlled Eastern Europe

Kremlinology study of government and policies of Soviet Union

Ku Klux Klan anti-black, anti-Semitic, anti-Catholic, white supremacist secret organization advocating violence

land reform redistribution of agricultural land to peasants and small farmers

legal aid free representation by attorney for those unable to pay fees

lib *Informal*. liberation, usu. used after group name, as in women's lib

life-care (*adj*) designed to provide for basic needs of elderly residents, usu. in return for a regular fee

love-in gathering of people for purpose of

demonstrating mutual love or protesting inhumane policies

lunatic fringe extreme minority on periphery of any larger movement

Main Street provincial, conservative small-town life

mammon material wealth seen as evil

McCarthyism use of sensationalism and accusations to uncover supposed Communists in government in 1950's

Me Decade decade of 1970's, supposedly reflecting self-indulgence, narcissism, and lack of social concerns in youth, esp. as reaction to 1960's

movement organized actions taken by group working together to achieve specific goal

nativism policy of reviving or maintaining a native culture

New Left political movement of young people, esp. in 1960's and 1970's, seeking social change

old-world (*adj*) pertaining to traditional European customs and values

peaceful coexistence policy of cooperation and noninterference between United States and Soviet Union

Planned Parenthood *Trademark*. organization that disseminates information on birth control and sexually transmitted diseases

pop culture contemporary style, art, and media

population explosion rapid rise and continued increase of population

pronuclear (*adj*) supporting the development and use of nuclear energy

radical chic patronage of extremists and left-wing radicals by the rich and famous, sometimes without genuine conviction

rally mass demonstration in support of specific cause

recycling reprocessing of used paper, metals, and other waste materials to conserve national resources

redevelopment renovation of urban slum area

rent strike tenant refusal to pay rent until housing is improved

resistance organized underground movement opposing foreign occupation or government repression

revolution violent overthrow of government resulting in change in social order

riot violent, large-scale public disturbance, often for purposes of protest

samizdat clandestine circulation of banned manuscripts in former Soviet Union

Satyagraha Gandhian way to social reform through tolerance and nonviolent passive resistance (India)

sect faction of larger group or movement

sexual revolution era of promiscuity and open sexuality beginning in 1960's

shelter place where homeless people can sleep; underground refuge for use in event of nuclear attack

sit-in occupation of an institution to protest its policies

soup kitchen place set up in run-down neighborhood to feed poor and homeless

special interest group group seeking to advance specific cause by gaining government favors

storefront group self-help community action group housed in storefront

Sunbelt southern and southwestern United States, characterized by political conservatism since 1960's

teach-in lectures and debates at university or college to protest school's policy

technetronic (*adj*) influenced or characterized by advances in technology and electronics applied to social problems

test ban multinational agreement to stop nuclear testing

think tank government- or business-sponsored group organized for problem solving and intensive research

Third World underdeveloped countries of world

ticky-tacky (*adj*) *Informal.* relating to dull uniformity of style, esp. in housing development

tobacco road poor southern rural area, characterized by hopelessness and despair

underground secret resistance organization, esp. in totalitarian country

urbanization transformation of rural or suburban areas to urban ones

urban renewal redevelopment of run-down parts of city

women's liberation movement to combat sexual discrimination and achieve full rights and opportunities for women equal to men, orig. late 1960's

women's movement broad-ranging activities and beliefs involving legal, social, economic, vocational, educational, and personal rights of women in male-dominated society

Social Types, Norms, and Symbols

African-American preferred term for black Americans of African descent and for their culture

apologist one who justifies a questionable cause or doctrine

Asian American preferred term for Americans of Asian descent and for their culture

baby boomer person born just after World War II

bag lady poor, homeless, usu. old woman living in streets and carrying belongings in shopping bag; shopping bag lady

battered child child physically abused by his or her parents

battered wife woman physically abused by her husband

beatnik member of Beat Generation of 1950's, who were nonconformist in dress, attitude, and artistic expression

beautiful people wealthy or famous trendsetters

Bircher member or follower of John Birch

Society, an extremely conservative political group

bitch goddess stereotype of dominating, complaining, beautiful woman

black preferred term from 1960's to 1980's for Americans of African descent, formerly called Negroes

blue blood member of aristocratic or socially prominent family

blue book directory of socially prominent persons

blue-collar (*adj*) pertaining to class of workers who perform manual and unskilled labor or factory work

boat people refugees who fled Southeast Asia in boats, and to whom few countries granted asylum

bohemian person living unconventionally, esp. an artist

brother term denoting comradeship, esp. among blacks

café society fashionable high society

canaille riffraff

colored former term for American blacks, now considered pejorative

conscientious objector person who refuses to serve in armed forces on religious or moral grounds

cracker *Derogatory slang.* poor southern white person

DINK **d**ual **i**ncome, **n**o **k**ids; married couple without children, both of whom work

dissenter person who rejects established doctrines

dissident person who rejects establishment and often attempts to sway others into opposition

dominant group those in society setting norms, values, and standards

dropout person who leaves a program, esp. school, before completion; one who lives by norms alien to society

empty nester parent whose child or children have moved away from home

everyman typical or common man

expatriate person who has rejected allegiance to native land and lives elsewhere

fellow traveler Communist party sympathizer

flapper young woman of 1920's who behaved and dressed boldly and unconventionally

flower child hippie

folk common people

football widow woman whose husband ignores her on weekends or certain weekday nights to watch football on television

fugitive person who has run away from danger or justice

gaybasher heterosexual, often homophobic male, who physically assaults or defames gays

glitterati chic, wealthy, famous people

golf widow woman whose husband ignores her to play golf

good old boy *Informal.* stereotypical white male of U.S. South who drinks beer, hunts, jokes, and socializes with his friends

gray eminence one who exercises great power unofficially

Grundy personification of conventional social disapproval and narrow-mindedness

hard-hat *Informal.* working-class person, often holding politically conservative ideas

high society those who are fashionable, wealthy, and famous

hillbilly person from backwoods or remote rural area, esp. in U.S. South

hippie member of 1960's youth culture, alienated from society and interested in mysticism, pacifism, nature, psychedelic drugs, and sexual freedom; flower child

hoi polloi common people

homeland mother country

homeless those who have no permanent place to live and frequently sleep in streets

honky *Derogatory slang.* white person, esp. as referred to by nonwhites

in-crowd group with common interests and feelings of solidarity and exclusivity; in-group

indigenous (*adj*) native

in-group in-crowd

intelligentsia intellectual and academic leaders

jet set rich, fashionable group frequently traveling in pursuit of pleasure

John Doe anonymous average man

John Q. Public average person

junta military group that takes power after coup

Latino person of Latin-American or Spanish-speaking descent; preferred term for such Americans and for their culture

leading edge forefront of movement; new ideology or theory

leftist radical of political Left

liberal one who favors progressive, democratic political reform

life of Riley *Informal.* comfortable, carefree lifestyle

literati persons of letters

lonely-hearts (*adj*) pertaining to persons seeking companionship or love

loose cannon person whose reckless behavior endangers efforts or welfare of others

lumpenproletariat segment of underclass degraded by nonproductivity and shiftlessness, including tramps, beggars, and criminals

lynch mob mob that murders an accused person, esp. by hanging

man about town worldly man who is a member of fashionable society

man in the street average person

mass society impersonal modern society

Middle American middle-class Americans, esp. living in Midwest

minority group group within larger society with different language, culture, or religion, often subject to discrimination

mob disorderly or riotous crowd of people, often bent on or engaged in lawless violence

moral majority largely fundamentalist, conservative Christians of Middle America

mother country one's native land or that of one's ancestors

needy poor, destitute persons

Negro member of the peoples traditionally classified as the Negro race and usu. of sub-Saharan African descent, now called black or African American

out-group all those not part of the in-crowd or in-group

pecking order hierarchy of social dominance within group

people all citizens of one state or nation or of the world

power elite those in control of nation's government, economy, and resources

pressure group collection of like-minded people seeking to influence policies

public people of one community or nation as a whole

rabble disorderly crowd

rank and file ordinary people constituting major part of an organization, esp. a labor union

reference group social group that an individual views as the standard against which to judge his or her own actions

refugee person who flees his or her home or country to seek safety from war or persecution

refusenik _Informal._ Soviet citizen, esp. a Jew, who was denied permission to emigrate

role model person whom others copy when developing attitudes, values, and behavior patterns

sacred cow individual or institution deemed exempt from criticism or questioning

scab worker who refuses to honor strike or join a labor union

semiskilled worker manual laborer with some training

senior citizen person who is elderly or aged, esp. one living on a pension

shopping bag lady bag lady

significant other live-in lover, mate, or spouse

silent majority large, conservative group of Middle America whose views are supposedly unheard due to vocal protests on left and right

silk-stocking member of wealthy or aristocratic class

single parent one person, usu. divorced or never married, supporting and caring for a child or children

slumlord owner of substandard housing

smart set fashionable high society

social outcast person outside of or excluded from normal society

squatter unlawful settler on land or in abandoned housing

stereotype oversimplified, often unfavorable, commonly held picture of all members of certain group

storm trooper member of violent, brutal army corps, orig. a Nazi

stowaway one who hides on a vehicle to get free passage

straw boss member of work crew who supervises his or her colleagues

street person homeless person living on city streets

strikebreaker worker who returns to work during strike

suffragette militant female advocate of women's right to vote

teenybopper _Slang._ female teenager, esp. one following adolescent fashions and trends

temp _Informal._ temporary worker

Tom, Dick, and Harry common man; people generally

transient homeless person looking for work or place to live

troglodyte individual with reclusive habits or outmoded behavior; outcast from society

turnover number of employees replaced in given time period

Ugly American American visitor or diplomat abroad who behaves in an offensive manner and is insensitive to foreign customs

Uncle Sam personification of U.S. government as bearded man in red, white, and blue top hat

Uncle Tom black whose behavior is regarded as servile

underage (_adj_) below legal age, usu. for drinking or sex

underdog victim of social injustice; one attempting to overcome adversity

underprivileged (_adj_) socially and economically deprived

unperson someone treated as if he or she does not exist

unskilled (_adj_) having no job training or vocation

untouchable person outside and below the Hindu caste system

upper crust aristocratic, wealthy high society

urban guerrilla member of violent, terrorist, underground political group in urban area, esp. in 1970's

vanguard leaders or advance position of political or artistic movement

wannabe person who idealizes successful individuals and imagines being like them

WASP **w**hite **a**nglo-**s**axon **p**rotestant; member of dominant group setting standards and values of American society

Woodstock nation generation of baby boomers who came of age in 1960's, esp. those subscribing to counterculture epitomized by Woodstock music festival

working mother employed mother of young child

working poor employed persons living at subsistence level

Yuppie **y**oung **u**rban **p**rofessional characterized as ambitious, materialistic, and faddish

Social Structure and Conditions

acculturation adaptation to the customs of a culture

age groups divisions of society based on custom and age of members

anomie condition in which social norms have weakened or disappeared

assimilation integration of customs and values from previously distinct cultures into dominant culture

atomism society composed of clearly distinct elements and factions

biculturalism presence of two distinct cultures in one society

biracial (_adj_) involving or including two races

birthrate number of births per thousand in given population

bondage servitude or subjugation

bracket division of society based on age, income, or other demographic factor

bureaucracy authority concentrated in complicated structure of administrative bodies

caste station in life defined by birth, more rigid than class and allowing no chance for change

centralization power and authority in hands of one central agency

circle group bound together by common interests and activities

clan group with interest in common, often related persons

class social rank according to status, economic interest, and way of life

classless (_adj_) free from social class distinctions

clique small, exclusive circle of people; coterie

collective behavior common, spontaneous reaction of a group of people to the same event

colony community of those with similar interests, often isolated or concentrated in particular place

commonweal general welfare

communalism system of collective groups devoted to their own interests rather than to those of society as a whole

commune small group living together, usu. sharing work, earnings, and specific value system

community any group with shared interests, feelings, values, or geographic location

community center meeting place offering recreational and educational activities for community

coterie clique

counterculture segment of society with values and lifestyle opposed to those of prevailing culture

crosscurrents conflicting tendency or movement that may impede functioning of an institution

cross-fertilization exchange of values, customs, and ideas between different societies or groups within a society

culture values, beliefs, customs, and art of a specific society; civilization

disempowerment loss of influence, significance, or rights by individual or group

dominant group group setting society's norms, values, and standards

dynamic culture society undergoing rapid change

enculturation socialization into cultural mainstream

endogamy mating within one's social group

environment social conditions and surroundings as they affect behavior and attitudes

ethnic group societal subgroup with common cultural, religious, national, or racial heritage

etiquette established conventions of polite social intercourse

extended family relatives of different generations living together or in close proximity

favela shantytown or slum in or near a Brazilian city

ghetto section of city to which minority group is confined or lives by choice

ghost town permanently abandoned town, esp. in U.S. Old West

group dynamics intersection of individuals within group

guild association for promotion of common aims

heterogeneous (*adj*) composed of varied elements

homeostasis tendency of society to maintain social stability

homogeneous (*adj*) composed of similar elements

humanity entire human race; humankind;

humankind all members of the human race; humanity; mankind

indigenous (*adj*) native to a specific society or region

individuation loss of class identity by individuals

industrial (*adj*) related to industry; nonagricultural

inequality lack of fairness or justice in society

infrastructure basic facilities and systems serving country, region, or city, including transportation, communications, power, and schools

institution established pattern of norms and values; organization that meets important group or social needs

institutional family family in which propagation of race and care of children take precedence over happiness and personal freedom of parents

institutionalization making permanent certain patterns of behavior and values

institutionalized racism racial discrimination not based on individual attitudes but inherent in social structures and institutions

interaction coming together of individuals with mutual influence

kibbutz collective farm in Israel

kinship group extended family

kolkhoz collective farm in Soviet Union

labefaction decline in public morality and social order

lily-white (*adj*) exclusive of all nonwhites

living standard level of comfort, economic security, and stability

lower class working class, characterized by low standard of living

macrocosm model that is a large-scale and complex representation, often of one of its components

mankind humanity; humankind

matriarchy society in which mother is family or tribal head and descent is traced through female line

melting pot society that incorporates diverse social and cultural groups

microcosm group believed to be representative of a much larger entity

middle class socioeconomic group with comfortable standard of living and conventional beliefs and lifestyle

mythos underlying and enduring attitudes and beliefs characteristic of a society, esp. in connection with supernatural forces

neighborhood community of people living near one another

norms customary standards of behavior in a society, reflecting its values

nuclear family usu. married couple and their children

paternalism firm, fatherly control of government or employees

patriarchy society in which father is family or tribal head and descent is traced through male line

peer group those of same age and social position

petite bourgeoisie lower middle class

phenotype appearance of an organism resulting from interaction of heredity and environment

pluralism existence of diverse cultural groups within one society

polarization concentration of group interests around opposite extremes rather than along a continuum

police state country in which police suppress activities that conflict with government policy

poverty line economic level beneath which people are considered to be living in poverty

power structure those established in ruling positions in government or other institutions

primary group those with close, intimate relationships, such as family groups

Procrustean bed pattern into which one is arbitrarily forced

psychosocial (*adj*) relating psychological development to social environment

public the people as a whole; the community at large

public assistance government-funded social welfare programs for the needy; relief

race group of people with traits transmitted by descent sufficient to distinguish distinct human type

rat race *Informal.* intense, exhausting, usu. competitive urban business life that leaves little time for leisure life

relief public assistance

reservation public land on which American Indians are resettled

rite traditional, customary, often ceremonial or formal observance or procedure

ritual established practice or procedure performed regularly as a rite

royalty hereditary social class that rules certain countries

rural (*adj*) lying outside developed cities, in the countryside

scarcity period or condition of inadequate supply of food or other raw material

secondary group people relating on an impersonal, formal level, such as business colleagues

secret police undercover police used by totalitarian governments to observe and apprehend dissenters

sect faction of larger group

servitude subjection to a master or mistress

shantytown section of city with substandard housing, esp. rickety little huts

skid row area of city frequented by alcoholics and vagrants

slavery involuntary servitude

slum densely populated urban area marked by crowding, poverty, poor housing, and social disorder

social codes accepted, often unwritten, rules of behavior and value systems

social contract theoretical agreement between people to establish government and abide by its laws

social convention norm of behavior or belief

social intercourse exchange of thoughts or feelings

socialization process by which a child acquires and internalizes society's beliefs, values, and habits, so as to become functioning member of group

Social Register *Trademark.* book that lists members of high society

social structure framework of society's institutions governing interpersonal and group relations

social welfare system of services for improving condition of the disadvantaged

society institutions and value systems of people with similar traditions and customs who inhabit same geographical area over several generations; autonomous structure based on such institutions and value systems that provides group identity and basis for community living

squalor poverty, filth, and moral degradation

standard of living level of subsistence, esp. with regard to basic economic necessities

starvation wages wages too low to provide subsistence

status relative position within group or society

status quo existing state of affairs

stock race or ethnic group

strain subdivision within general race or ethnic group

strata specific socioeconomic level of society

subculture group within society whose social status, ethnic background, religion, or shared values and interests distinguish it from others in that society or culture

subsistence basic means required to support life

substandard (adj) beneath legal or acceptable levels

suburbia social and cultural aspects of life in residential communities lying just outside a city

system unity formed of diverse parts arranged according to a common plan

technology application of science to practical affairs

telesis planned progress through use of natural and social forces

trend prevailing direction in which society is moving at a given time

underclass lowest level of society, consisting of impoverished persons with low social status, often self-perpetuating from generation to generation

underdeveloped (adj) designating poor countries of Third World

upper class highest level of society, made up of those with wealth, power, and prestige

urban (adj) relating to cities

vacuum isolation from society

victimless crime illegal act, such as prostitution, to which all parties have consented

zero population growth condition in which birthrate and death rate are equal and population remains constant, esp. due to family planning

Schools and Doctrines

anomie state or condition marked by breakdown or absence of social norms and values

behavioral science study of human activity in attempt to discover recurrent patterns and postulate rules

behaviorism theory that all human behavior is learned or based on conditioning and that observed behavior forms only valid data

biosociology study of interactions between human biological characteristics and social behavior

conflict theory view of society as groups in conflict

criminology scientific study of crime, criminal nature, and its impact on society

cultural diffusion spread of cultural characteristics from one society to another

determinism theory that choice of action is determined by causes other than human will

ekistics scientific study of human settlements and communities

environmental determinism theory that social environment rather than hereditary factors determines personality

ergonomics study of adjustment to environment, esp. in workplace

eugenics science dealing with improvement of hereditary factors through social control of reproduction

euthenics science dealing with improvement of hereditary factors for human welfare through environmental control

evolutionary theory belief in gradual, sequential development of society

functionalism social theory of Emile Durkheim emphasizing integration of institutions, their interaction with society, and consensus of values that is external to individual and influences his or her actions

human ecology study of how human beings relate to their political, economic, and social environment

humanism nontheistic, rationalist belief that people are capable of self-fulfillment and ethical conduct without recourse to the supernatural

industrial sociology study of social relationships and institutions as influenced by industry

interactionist doctrine belief that social processes and institutions derive from one person reacting to action of another

labeling theory view that society creates deviance by prematurely labeling a person as inadequate or undesirable

linguistics study of structure, development, social impact, and interrelationship of languages

looking-glass theory theory that people develop their sense of self in response to how they think others see them

metalinguistics study of relationship of language to other culturally determined behavior

mutualism social dependence for general welfare

occupational sociology study of working roles on a broader scale than in industrial sociology

penology branch of criminology that evaluates programs and institutions dealing with criminals

Protestant ethic theory of Max Weber that the hard work and frugal life conducive to capitalism developed from the Calvinist doctrine of predestination

rising expectations theory that revolutions are more likely to occur as social and economic conditions begin to improve, causing increased expectations and frustration

Social Darwinism view that individuals will advance in society based on their ability to adapt to living conditions

social pathology study of social factors, such as poverty or crime, that tend to increase social disorganization and inhibit personal adjustment

social science scientific study of different aspects of society, including disciplines of political science, anthropology, sociology, criminology, and economics

sociocultural approach propaganda theory based on defining cultural norms that guide people's social behavior

sociology application of specific doctrines and

techniques to systematic study of social institutions, collective behavior, and human relationships

sociology of knowledge study of relationships between social and political structures and intellectual life

sociology of leisure study of social impact of increased leisure as by-product of technology and modernization

structural functionalism analysis of social phenomena within narrowly defined concepts of observable structures and functional consequences

structuralism theory based on study of social status systems and interdisciplinary analysis of social behavior, used to define the patterns of interaction between diverse modes of behavior that form society's underlying structure

urban sociology study of the relationship between urban environment and social structures within it

Tools and Techniques

case study study and research that analyzes a single group, person, or institution

casework social work that deals directly with individuals' specific needs and problems

census official population count and collection of demographic information on general population

cohort group having one demographic factor in common

content analysis study of document to learn about culture, esp. to determine number of times one term or value appears in given context

control group group of participants used as basis of comparison in controlled experiment

controlled observation research technique in which situation is set up and resulting phenomena observed

cultural base total number of cultural traits in given culture at one time

cultural relativity evaluation of culture's customs and their functions in context of entire culture

culture trait specific tool, act, or belief related to particular situation or need in one culture

demography study of relationship between human populations and vital and social statistics, esp. marital status, age, sex, and employment, usu. by statistical and quantitative methods

historical analysis study of historical records and writings to support or disprove a cultural hypothesis

participant observation research method in which researcher actively takes part in daily activities of group under study

population all people, things, ideas, or traits that possess those characteristics being measured or studied

population base total number of persons in society at a given time

random sample portion of population chosen at random to ensure impartiality in a study

real-life laboratory observation of people in arranged settings or natural environments without their awareness of being observed

sampling technique of drawing random and representative sample from a population

scientific method application of empirical, objective, and systematic data collection and analysis to study of culture and society

secondary document document written by someone not actually present at described event

secondary research research based on previously generated or collected data

social engineering application of findings of social science to solution of social problems

social service actions by professionals to improve social circumstances of people and communities

sociogram sociometric diagram representing pattern of relationships between group members

sociography use of statistical data to describe social phenomena

sociometry measurement of attitudes of social acceptance or rejection as expressed by group preferences

statistical analysis research technique using statistical data to formulate and test hypotheses

stratified random sampling method of selecting sample for survey that reflects proportions of different groups in population being studied

survey research method of obtaining information about population through interviews and questionnaires filled out by random sample

universe distinct field of thought or reality forming a closed system; all-inclusive group or population from which sample can be drawn for analysis

---

PSYCHOLOGY

Schools and Doctrines
Syndromes, Disorders, and Conditions
Phobias
Manias
Tools, Techniques, Principles, and Practitioners
Mental States, Processes, and Behavior

See also: Chap. 1: Medical Problems; Chap. 2: Biology; Chap. 4: Medicine; Chap. 8: Parents and Children; Chap. 13: Sociology; Education; Chap. 22: Sex, Love, and Romance; Chap. 24: Mental Disturbances; Chap. 25: Truth, Wisdom, and Spiritual Attainment

---

Schools and Doctrines

abnormal psychology branch of psychology concerned with basic theory, but not treatment, of psychotic and personality disorders

Adlerian psychotherapy theory of psychotherapy developed by Alfred Adler emphasizing overcompensation in denial of feelings of personal weakness or inferiority

analytic psychology school of psychoanalysis developed by Carl Jung

applied psychology use of psychological knowledge and skills to solve problems

associationism theory that holds that development proceeds from association of simple ideas gained from sensory data

behaviorism doctrine that emphasizes observable data, esp. from stimulus and response studies, as foundation for theories of behavior

bioenergetics school of therapy that employs breathing exercises, physical movement, and free expression to relieve stress and muscle tension

blank-slate hypothesis theory that human thought and behavior are based on experience, not innate components

child development child psychology focusing on weaning, feeding, and toilet training and acknowledging both environmental and hereditary factors

client-centered psychotherapy treatment in which client talks without direction or interpretation from therapist, whose attitude is characterized by unconditional empathy

clinical psychology branch of psychology that focuses on human development and interaction and supports therapeutic intervention to aid the problem solving of individuals, couples, families, and groups

cognitive psychology branch of psychology that bases research and treatment on analysis of mental processes in all aspects of human thought or cognition

community psychology subdivision of clinical psychology concerned with individuals' adaptation to their community

comparative psychology study of comparative behavior of different animal species to enhance understanding of human behavior

constitutional psychology psychological doctrine that attributes behavior patterns to body type

consulting psychology study and relief of individual problems in business, school, and government settings

cultural relativism belief that no absolutely correct standards of behavior exist against which varying cultural and personal behavior patterns can be measured

demonology superstitious belief in demons and evil spirits as cause of abnormal behavior

depth psychology study of unconscious mental processes

developmental psychology specialty that focuses on the course of social, emotional, moral, and intellectual growth over a lifetime

eclectic psychology branch of psychology drawing information, theories, and intervention techniques from different schools of thought

engineering psychology design of man-machine systems to fit human physiological and psychological needs

ethology scientific study of animal behavior

existential psychotherapy therapy emphasizing patient's subjective experience of existence, based on philosophical systems associated with Sartre, Heidegger, Jaspers, and Kierkegaard

experimental psychology research aimed at better knowledge of learning, memory, perception, and other basic mental processes

Freudian psychoanalysis psychoanalytic theories developed by Sigmund Freud, emphasizing importance of early stages of development, the dynamic unconscious, and the interplay of id, ego, and superego

functionalism psychological approach stressing mental functioning rather than mental structure

gestalt school of psychology that asserts that perceptual experience is a configuration or pattern in which the whole is more than the sum of its parts

hedonism theory that pleasure is the primary principle motivating human behavior

holistic approach approach emphasizing person as a whole, not isolated functions or disorders

humanistic psychology branch of psychology emphasizing individual and collective human behavior and its improvement

individual psychology branch of psychology emphasizing uniqueness of human personality and psychological struggle

industrial psychology specialty that focuses on issues and problems specific to organizations and deals with questions of management and power distribution within such groups

Jungian psychology psychological doctrines of Carl Jung regarding mythological, cultural, and racial inheritance and the collective unconscious

metapsychology high-level speculation on the origin, structure, and function of the mind

nativism theory that personality and behavior are primarily inherited, not learned

neoanalytic psychology psychoanalytic theory based on Freud and incorporating modern science

parapsychology study of phenomena beyond range of normally observable psychological events

personality theory integrated set of principles that explains the development of those characteristics that make each person unique

phenomenological approach psychological approach that focuses on individual's way of perceiving and interpreting the world

phrenology method of studying personality by measurement of skull shape and its irregularities (19th c.)

physiognomy outmoded theory of personality based on belief that outward appearance indicates inner character

psychoanalysis study and long-term treatment of personality disorders using free association, interpretation of dreams, transference, and empathic neutrality; Freudian psychoanalysis

psychobiology study of anatomy and biochemical processes as they affect behavior

psychodrama psychotherapy using role-playing

psychology scientific study of the mind, mental states and processes, and human behavior

psychopathology science of causes and development of mental disorders

psychophysics study and measurement of relationship between intensity of stimuli and of sensations they produce

psychophysiology study of interaction between physiological and psychological processes

psychotherapy treatment of mental disorders and difficulties by psychological methods

sleep and dreams psychological discipline concerned with interrelated phenomena of sleep and dreams

social psychology study of effects of social interaction on group behavior, individuals, and mental processes

somatopsychology study of effects of physical problems and disfigurement on behavior and methods of treating related adjustment problems

structuralism psychological school that emphasizes definition and structure of consciousness in formation of human behavior

Sullivanian theory theoretical approach that focuses on interactions between patient and therapist

theoretical psychology branch of psychology that emphasizes formulation of a general integrated set of principles rather than treatment of patients

transactional analysis psychotherapy emphasizing interpersonal exchanges, psychological games, and roles played over a lifetime

Syndromes, Disorders, and Conditions

abnormal behavior unhealthy, disturbed, or disintegrated behavior that interferes with normal, positive functioning

abulia loss of will or ability to act

acting out unconscious expression of previously repressed feelings through specific behavior

addiction physical dependence on chemical substance

affective disorder neurotic disorder involving disturbances in mood

aggression hostile, destructive behavior toward others

agita condition of general anxiety or agitation

alienation psychological isolation from interaction or identification with society and its values; withdrawal

amentia mental deficiency, esp. low intellectual capacity

amnesia partial or complete memory loss

animality expression of animal instincts in human behavior

anomie feeling of isolation or disconnectedness from social norms; cultural alienation

anorexia nervosa pathological fear of obesity, esp. in young women, leading to inability to retain food, loss of appetite, malnutrition, and sometimes death

antisocial personality disorder characterized by chronic violation of rules and customs of social group

anxiety state of general fear or dread, not necessarily connected to particular object or idea

anxiety neurosis neurositic disorder typified by feelings of pervasive anxiety

asthenic reaction fatigue as response to anxiety

autism condition marked by infantile onset of pervasive lack of responsiveness to others, with gross deficiency in language development

battle fatigue posttraumatic stress disorder affecting soldiers engaged in combat

bedwetting urination in bed at night by children who have been toilet trained, usu. due to repressed anxiety or resentment

belle indifference anxiety-free state of certain hysterical neurotics; calm, inappropriate attitude toward some physical symptom

bestiality act or fantasy of engaging in sexual relations with animals

bipolar disorder disorder involving alternation or intermixture of manic and depressive episodes

block psychological obstacle to doing what one has set out to do and is capable of doing; sudden interruption of speech or thought processes

borderline personality disorder characterized by impulsiveness, intense and unstable relations with others, identity disturbance, marked mood shifts, and chronic feelings of emptiness or boredom

bruxism unconscious grinding and gnashing of teeth, usu. during sleep

bulimia bouts of excessive eating followed by self-induced vomiting, accompanied by preoccupation with weight

catatonia syndrome, usu. in schizophrenia, marked by stupor with musculature rigidity or agitated overactivity

character disorder deeply ingrained, habitual, rigid reaction pattern that is maladaptive and limits optimal functioning in society

combat fatigue trauma following acutely stressful conditions of warfare

compensation defense mechanism in which sense of weakness or lack is offset by emphasizing positive traits

complex specific constellation of psychological symptoms arising from powerful emotions buried in unconscious mind and affecting behavior

compulsion repetitive behavior serving no rational purpose; need to act without understanding motives

compulsive personality disorder marked by rigid, inhibited, excessively orderly, and often unemotional character and inability to relax

condition state of one's mental health, esp. abnormal or unhealthy state

conversion disorder neurosis characterized by the conversion of psychological disturbances into physical symptoms

cretinism mental deficiency caused by thyroid disorder

cultural alienation anomie

cyclothymic personality disorder in which normally extroverted person suffers fluctuations in mood between sadness and elation

defense mechanism any of various mental processes, including compensation, denial, displacement, negation, procrastination, projection, rationalization, reaction formation, regression, repression, and substitution, used by the ego for protection against instinctual demands and to reduce anxiety

delusion false or distorted belief firmly maintained though contradicted by reality

dementia praecox schizophrenia

denial defense mechanism in which one refuses to acknowledge the existence of an unpleasant reality, esp. the significance of one's behavior

depersonalization disorder involving the experience of self as unreal or strange

depression depressive neurosis or psychosis

depressive neurosis disorder involving chronic feelings of sadness, lethargy, and hopelessness; depression

depressive psychosis major depressive episode involving feelings of self-hate and negativity, sometimes marked by hallucinations, delusions, or mutism; depression

deviance extreme or marked difference from the norm

disorder abnormality, unhealthy condition, or dysfunction of mental health

disorientation disturbance in understanding one's position in time or place or one's identity

displaced aggression transference of hostility from true object to another object

displacement defense mechanism in which repressed emotion or idea is transferred to more acceptable object

dissociative disorder separation or disunity among aspects of single personality

dysfunction abnormality or failure of mental process

Electra complex psychological consequences of girl's sexual attraction to her father and feelings of competition with mother

escapism behavior and fanciful thought processes induced to escape from reality

euphoria unstable feeling of well-being; in manic depression, elevated end of cycle

exhibitionism need to shock others, esp. those of opposite sex, by exposing one's genitals or engaging in overt sexual behavior when inappropriate

existential neurosis disorder involving sense of meaninglessness and isolation

fetishism sexual dysfunction in which object or body part is essential to sexual arousal

fixation extreme attachment to objects or ideas associated with earlier stage of psychic development; halting of stage of personality development

flattened affect general impoverishment of emotional reaction in which victim appears distant and removed

flight of ideas disorder involving inability to keep to point of narrative; constant digression and lack of continuity

frigidity inability of woman to achieve orgasm through coitus

fugue combination of temporary amnesia with apparent rational behavior

functional disorder mental disturbance without known organic brain disorder or disease

guilt recurrent feeling of self-reproach or self-blame for something wrong, often something beyond one's control

hallucination sense impression for which there is no real external stimuli, either visual, auditory, or olfactory

hebephrenia form of schizophrenia involving disintegration of personality, giggling and grinning, and childish behavior

hyperactive child syndrome syndrome involving inability of child to pay attention, sit still, or be calm or quiet

hypochondria neurotic preoccupation with one's own health; formation of imaginary symptoms and exaggeration of minor discomforts

hypomanic personality disturbance pattern in which person displays mixture of elevated mood and restless agitation

hysteria anxiety reaction involving dissociation and conversion, characterized by excitability, high anxiety, and sensory and motor disturbances

infantilism abnormal regression to childish behavior in adulthood

inferiority complex feelings of inadequacy, negative self-perception

insanity legal definition of personality disturbance that causes an inability to bear responsibility for one's actions

insomnia chronic or extreme sleeplessness

involutional psychosis severe disturbance, often of middle age, involving depression, guilt, and insomnia

koro syndrome found chiefly in China and Southeast Asia, characterized by anxiety over retraction of penis or breast and labia into body

learning disability any condition that interferes with the learning process or ability to learn specific skills

malaise persistent, vague feelings of unease and listlessness

mania extreme, chronic obsession with something; excessive excitability; manic or excited phase of manic depression

manic depression psychosis affecting moods, alternating between extremes of elation and dejection

martyrdom tendency to take blame or burdens upon oneself, esp. to elicit sympathy or guilt in others; self-victimization

masochism condition in which pleasure, esp. sexual, is derived from pain inflicted by another on oneself

melancholia deep sadness

minimal brain dysfunction nervous system impairment that may cause hyperactivity in children

multiple personality extreme dissociation resulting in belief that two or more distinct personalities reside within oneself, each taking conscious control at different times; split personality

narcissism immature self-love manifested by grandiose sense of importance, need for constant attention and admiration, hidden sense of shame, and difficulty in relating to or having true feelings for others

narcolepsy frequent, uncontrollable desire for sleep

nervous breakdown lay term for temporary, abrupt impairment of normal functioning due to psychotic or neurotic disorder

neurosis emotional disorder involving basic repression of primary instinctual urge and reliance on defense mechanisms that results in symptoms or personality disturbance; psychoneurosis

neurotic depression common disorder involving inability to recover speedily from depression

noctambulism somnambulism

nymphomania compulsive desire for sex in females

obsession persistent, pervasive, disturbing fixation on an emotion, idea, object, or person

obsessive-compulsive neurosis disorder involving fixation on disturbing ideas and impulsive repetition of certain acts

Oedipus complex psychological consequences of boy's sexual attraction to his mother and feelings of competition with father

overcompensation extreme, unbalanced effort to overcome feelings of inadequacy or guilt

paranoia persistent delusions of persecution or suspicion of others

paranoid schizophrenia disintegration of perception of reality combined with delusions of grandeur or persecution

paraphilia disorder characterized by preference for unusual sexual practices and perversions

passive aggressive personality personality marked by extreme passivity combined with hostility, stubbornness, lack of cooperation, and uncommunicativeness

pathology any abnormal condition or mental disease

pedophilia desire for sexual activity with children

persecution complex tendency to feel that one is being unfairly and constantly harassed

personality disorder fixed, rigid, and ingrained patterns of relating to others that limit effective functioning and impair relationships and are usu. at odds with basic values of one's culture or community

phobia unfounded, persistent fear of something based on externalization of anxiety

postpartum depression depressive symptoms in mothers associated with period immediately following childbirth; similar feelings experienced after completing some task

posttraumatic stress syndrome pattern of reactions and disorders that appears some time after a traumatic experience, esp. in soldiers after combat; battle fatigue

procrastination defense mechanism involving postponement or avoidance of stressful task or situation

projection defense mechanism involving attribution of one's own unacceptable and unwanted qualities and motives to others

psychological dependency dependency characterized by attachment to person or thing that results in severe distress if object is removed

psychoneurosis neurosis

psychopathic personality individual with personality disorder involving stunted or nonexistent moral values, antisocial or violent behavior, and inability to identify with others

psychosexual disorder sexual disorder in which psychological rather than organic factors are of major importance

psychosis severe mental illness, such as manic depression, paranoia, or schizophrenia, involving loss of contact with reality and breakdown of comprehensible behavior, speech, and thought

psychosomatic disorder physical illness or perception of illness arising from psychological disturbances

rationalization defense mechanism involving substitution of rational motive for genuine, but irrational, motive as excuse for one's behavior

reaction formation defense mechanism involving denial of unacceptable unconscious urges by behavior contrary to one's own feelings

reactive disorder abnormality or dysfunction appearing suddenly, as if in response to specific situation

real anxiety anxiety produced by situations of actual danger in the external world

reality anxiety disorder involving fear of punishment for behavior judged wrong only by oneself

regression defense mechanism involving return to behavior expressive of earlier developmental stage, usu. due to trauma, fixation, anxiety, or frustration

repression defense mechanism in which threatening or unacceptable ideas or urges are forgotten

resentment feeling of displeasure toward source of supposed injury or offense

retardation congenital subnormality of

intelligence or lack of normal mental capacity or development

reversion return to former or regressed condition

SAD **s**easonal **a**ffective **d**isorder

sadism condition in which pleasure, esp. sexual, is derived from inflicting pain on others

sadomasochism condition in which pleasure, esp. sexual, is derived from inflicting pain on others and from pain inflicted on oneself

satyriasis compulsive desire for sex in males

schizokinesis disorder involving lack of coordination between body's perception of stimulus and appropriate reaction

schizophrenia psychosis involving break with reality and disintegration of rational thought and communication; dementia praecox

seasonal affective disorder SAD; phenomenon in which mood changes are alleged to correspond to the seasons, esp. depression in winter

self-victimization tendency to view oneself as a victim of unfair treatment; martyrdom

senile psychosis disorder in elderly involving memory loss, irritation, and regressive behavior

sleepwalking somnambulism

sociopath psychopathic personality who exhibits extreme asocial and antisocial behavior

somatic delusion individual's false perception of his body

somatoform disorder neurosis involving physical symptoms without physical cause

somnambulism walking in one's sleep; noctambulism; sleepwalking

speech dysfunction speech abnormality or incapacity

split personality multiple personality

sublimation defense mechanism involving substitution of socialized behavior for unacceptable acting out of primary urge

substance use disorder chronic abuse of chemical stimulants or alcohol

substitution defense mechanism involving replacement of unacceptable behavior with acceptable behavior

suicidal (*adj*) having intense, uncontrollable, self-destructive impulses, often due to depression

superiority complex condition in which one considers oneself better than others, often due to lack of genuine self-esteem

syndrome group of symptoms characterizing ongoing disease or disorder

tic involuntary muscle twitch, esp. of face, usu. indicating unreleased tension

transient situational disorder temporary disruption of personality due to external stress or overwhelming circumstances

traumatic anxiety disturbance based on present situation instead of memories of trauma or unhappiness

vertigo dizziness and loss of balance

victimization tendency to view oneself as victim of unfair treatment; martyrdom

voyeurism practice of deriving sexual gratification from watching others naked or engaged in sexual acts

waxy flexibility symptom of catatonic schizophrenia in which person permits limbs to be positioned by others, then retains that posture for long periods of time

withdrawal detachment from meaningful relationships with others and retreat into inner world; cessation of consumption of addictive substance and attendant unpleasant symptoms

word salad disturbed and incomprehensible speech of schizophrenics

Phobias

acrophobia fear of heights
aerophobia fear of drafts of fresh air
agoraphobia fear of crowds or open places
agyrophobia fear of crossing the street
ailurophobia fear of cats
algophobia fear of pain
amathophobia fear of dust
androphobia fear of men
Anglophobia fear or dislike of England or anything English
anthophobia fear of flowers
apiphobia fear of bees
arachnaphobia fear of spiders
astraphobia fear of lightning and thunder
autophobia fear of loneliness
bathophobia fear of deep places
brontophobia fear of thunder
chromatophobia fear of money
claustrophobia fear of enclosed places
clinophobia fear of going to bed
coitophobia fear of coitus
coprophobia fear of feces
cremnophobia fear of precipices
cryophobia fear of cold
cynophobia fear of dogs
dipsophobia fear of drunkenness
doraphobia fear of fur
dromophobia fear of crossing streets
eisoptrophobia fear of mirrors
eleutherophobia fear of freedom
emetophobia fear of vomiting
entomophobia fear of insects
eremiophobia fear of being alone
ergophobia fear of work
erythrophobia fear of blushing and the color red
galeophobia fear of sharks
gametophobia fear of marriage
gephyrophobia fear of crossing bridges
gerascophobia fear of old age
gymnophobia fear of nudity
gynephobia fear of women
hedonophobia fear of pleasure
helminthophobia fear of worms
hematophobia fear of blood
hippophobia fear of horses
hodophobia fear of travel
homophobia fear or dislike of homosexuals
hydrophobia fear of water

hypegiaphobia fear of responsibility
hypnophobia fear of sleep
ichthyophobia fear of fish
ideophobia fear of ideas or reason
lalophobia fear of speaking, esp. in public
logophobia fear of words
lyssophobia fear of madness
maieusiophobia fear of pregnancy
microphobia fear of germs
musophobia fear of mice
mysophobia fear of dirt or contamination
necrophobia fear of death
neophobia fear of novelty
nyctophobia fear of night or darkness
ochlophobia fear of crowds
onomatophobia fear of a name or particular word
ophiciophobia fear of snakes
ornithophobia fear of birds
pathophobia fear of disease
pedophobia fear of children
peniaphobia fear of poverty
phasmophobia fear of ghosts
phobophobia fear of fear
phonophobia fear of noise
photophobia fear of light
pneumatophobia fear of spirits
pnigophobia fear of choking
pyrophobia fear of fire
scotophobia fear of dark
siderodromophobia fear of trains
tachophobia fear of speed
taphophobia fear of being buried alive
teratophobia fear of monsters
thalassophobia fear of the sea
thanatophobia fear of death
thermophobia fear of heat
tocophobia fear of childbirth
tomophobia fear of surgery
topophobia fear of a particular place
toxiphobia fear of being poisoned
traumatophobia fear of injury
triskaidekaphobia fear of the number thirteen
xenophobia fear or dislike of foreigners
xerophobia fear of dry places, esp. deserts
zoophobia fear of animals

Manias

ablutomania chronic obsession with bathing
ailuromania intense enthusiasm for cats
anthomania inordinate interest in flowers
arithmomania craze for counting and numbers
automania compulsion toward solitude
bibliomania inordinate interest in acquiring books
cacodemonomania inordinate obsession with demonic possession
cheromania compulsion toward gaiety
choreomania craze for dancing
chrematomania obsessive desire for money
coprolalomania obsession with foul speech
cynomania intense enthusiasm for dogs

dipsomania irresistible craving for alcoholic beverages

dromomania intense enthusiasm for traveling

egomania inordinate obsession with oneself

eleutheromania irresistible craving for freedom

entheomania obsessive zeal for religion

entomomania inordinate fascination with insects

eremiomania irresistible craving for stillness

ergomania obsessive zeal for work

erotomania uncontrollable obsession with sexual desire

florimania intense interest in plants

gephyromania irresistible fascination with bridges

glazomania inordinate fascination with listmaking

gymnomania compulsion toward nakedness

gynecomania obsessive and uncontrollable desire for sex in males; satyromania

hedonomania irresistible craving for pleasure

heliomania uncontrollable craving for the sun

hippomania fascination with and enthusiasm for horses

homicidomania irresistible impulse to commit murder

hydromania uncontrollable fascination with water

hypnomania uncontrollable desire for sleep

ichthyomania excessive fascination with fish

kathisomania uncontrollable compulsion to sit

kleptomania irresistible impulse to steal

letheomania obsessive fascination with narcotics

logomania obsession with talking

megalomania uncontrollable obsession with grandiose self-importance and extravagant acts

melomania excessive fascination with music

monomania obsessive zeal for one topic or interest in one idea

mythomania irresistible impulse toward exaggeration and lying

necromania excessive interest in the dead

nesomania intense obsession with islands

noctimania intense fascination with night

nymphomania obsessive and uncontrollable desire for sex in females

ochlomania intense obsession with crowds

oikomania irresistible craving for home

oinomania inordinate fascination with wine

oniomania uncontrollable compulsion to buy

ophidiomania excessive interest in reptiles

ornithomania inordinate fascination with birds

paramania irresistible impulse to derive joy from complaints

parousiamania obsessive zeal for the second coming of Christ

phagomania irresistible craving for food and interest in eating

phaneromania uncontrollable impulse to pick at a spot or growth on one's body

pharmacomania chronic fascination with medicines

phonomania obsession with noise or sound

photomania irresistible craving for light

plutomania uncontrollable craving for great wealth

pyromania compulsion to set things on fire

satyromania obsessive and uncontrollable desire for sex in males

scribomania obsessive zeal for writing

siderodromomania intense fascination with railroad travel

sitomania abnormal craving for food

sophomania inordinate estimation of one's own wisdom

thalassomania intense fascination with the sea

thanatomania inordinate obsession with death

timbromania inordinate enthusiasm for postage stamps

tomomania inordinate interest in surgery

trichomania intense fascination with hair

xenomania obsessive interest in foreigners

zoomania craze for animals

Tools, Techniques, Principles, and Practitioners

achievement test structured series of questions measuring progress or knowledge in specific field

analysand person treated by psychoanalysis

analysis method in which therapist treats subject through long-term series of regular psychoanalytic sessions

analyst psychotherapist or psychiatrist whose training qualifies him or her through analysis, courses, and supervision to analyze others

anima in Jungian theory, female aspect of a male's personality

animus in Jungian theory, male aspect of a female's personality

aptitude test structured measurement of capabilities, esp. through a series of questions

archetype in Jungian theory, primal character and predisposition to behavior within collective unconscious of individuals

aromatherapy use of scented oil to influence mood and treat stress

atomism theory that reduces all psychological phenomena to simple elements

autohypnosis practice of hypnotizing oneself

autosuggestion idea arising within oneself and affecting one's thinking and behavior

aversion therapy technique of linking deeply felt revulsion with a behavior to be reduced or eliminated

bataca stuffed pillow with handles used for pummeling to release aggression without causing damage

battery combination of various tests and measurements

behavior checklist list of personality traits used in psychological testing

behavior modification altering of behavior through conditioning and behavior therapy

behavior therapy treatment aimed at eliminating unacceptable symptoms or behavior rather than exposing underlying causes

Bender-Gestalt test test for neurological disorders in which subject must copy nine geometrical designs

bibliotherapy use of reading materials as aid in therapy

biofeedback behavior therapy technique involving control of health and personality problems by sensitization of individual to internal body mechanisms to reduce stress

birth trauma theory that explains neuroses in terms of shock experienced by infant during birth

brainwashing extreme psychological conditioning used to change ideological attitudes

case study detailed psychoanalytic history of an individual used for teaching or reporting purposes

catharsis therapy that allows pent-up, socially unacceptable emotions to be expressed

choice point area of maze requiring test subject to choose between alternative directions

classical conditioning process linking a conditioned stimulus with a conditioned response; Pavlovian conditioning

client-centered therapy therapy that emphasizes nonjudgmental support of client's point of view and encouragement of expression of feelings and growth needs

clinical judgment professional's trained personal judgment in evaluating case and recommending treatment

clinical psychologist professional in field of counseling individuals with psychological problems

conditioned response acquired response to stimulus not originally capable of causing it; Pavlovian conditioning

conditioned stimulus stimulus at first incapable of arousing response but later capable of eliciting one

conditioning form of learning that produces automatic response to stimulus

confederate assistant in experiment posing as subject

control group experimental group equal in all respects to other groups being tested but not subjected to experimental conditions

couch bedlike furnishing on which patient lies during psychoanalytic session

counseling therapeutic psychological treatment program involving professional testing, interviews, and guidance

counselor therapist specializing in providing advice on patient's specific problems

countertransference transference on part of analyst of repressed emotions aroused by patient during course of treatment

couple counseling treatment that focuses on problems in the relationship between two people, usu. romantically involved or married

culture fair test or measurement whose content has been scrutinized to eliminate cultural or ethnic bias

desensitization therapy therapy emphasizing reduction of unwanted behavior by gradual pairing of another response with original stimulus

diagnosis clinical identification of disorder affecting patient

dream interpretation psychoanalytical technique involving symbolic explanation of dream content

ECT electroconvulsive therapy

educational therapy treatment aimed at improving patient's learning skills

electric shock therapy therapy that uses passage of electric current through patient's brain; electroconvulsive therapy

electroconvulsive therapy ECT; electric shock therapy

encounter group small group that meets, usu. with professional leader, for collective therapy through open exchange of intimate thoughts and feelings

extinction elimination of learned response when reinforcement is no longer given

family therapy treatment of family members as a group

feedback information on results of behavior used to influence future behavior

figure-ground perceptual tendency for portion of field to stand out more clearly than less distinct background

free association technique requiring patient to speak freely about anything coming to mind so as to explore the unconscious

goal box box at end of experimental maze in which animal being tested finds food or reward

group leader therapist trained in and leading group therapy sessions

group therapy treatment of several patients at one time by therapist, with emphasis on group interaction

halfway house residence offering supportive environment and counseling in which patients live following release from mental institution to ease reentry into society

headshrinker *Slang.* psychotherapist; shrink

Holtzman technique projective technique for personality evaluation based on interpretation of ninety ambiguous inkblots

horizontal study study of individual's current status, not history

hypnotherapist psychotherapist specializing in hypnotherapy

hypnotherapy therapy employing hypnosis to treat symptoms and make suggestions for improvement of future behavior

idiographic (*adj*) involving study or explication of individual cases or events

implosion therapy technique of reliving frightening event in therapeutic setting until original trauma has lessened or disappeared

inkblot test Rorschach test; Holtzman technique

intelligence quotient IQ; ratio of mental age to chronological age, multiplied by 100

intelligence test measurement of intellectual abilities

intermittent reinforcement in operant conditioning, a sporadic pattern of administering reinforcement after a particular response occurs

IQ intelligence quotient

learning theory comprehensive theory of factors affecting learning, memory, and forgetting, drawing elements from Pavlov to the behaviorists and cognitive psychology

longitudinal study long-term study of individual development

manual arts therapy treatment involving use of industrial arts skills

maze device consisting of box with many pathways, one leading to goal or reward, used to study learning behavior

medication administration of any of various depressants, tranquilizers, stimulants, or other substances to alter behavior, ease symptoms, or enhance treatment

memory drum mechanical device used to display items to be memorized in psychological study

mental age average level of mental ability for specific age group

mental hospital facility for treatment of severely disturbed patients, many of whom are committed for duration of treatment

mental hygiene development and maintenance of a wholesome, integrated personality

Minnesota Multiphasic Personality Inventory MMPI; elaborate true/false test showing personal and social adjustment

MMPI Minnesota Multiphasic Personality Inventory

naturalistic observation behavioral observation in natural, not experimental, setting

negative reinforcement reinforcement obtained by stopping of punishment after a response, thus increasing appearance of that response

noise box small device emitting low-level white noise to drown out external sound during therapy session

nomothetic (*adj*) involving study or formulation of general or universal laws

nonschedule-standardized interview interviewing technique based on standard questions interpreted or phrased for each interviewee's maximum comprehension

nonstandardized test test not meeting all requirements of standardized test due to absence of dependable norms

norm average performance or score on psychological test

occupational therapy treatment using crafts, sports, and skills development to restore confidence and build social skills

operant conditioning form of learning based on immediate reward for response

organic therapy physical treatment of disorder

organismic theory belief that all behavior stems

from a whole, integrated personality guided by the drive for self-actualization

paired-associate learning learning task in which one of a pair of items previously presented is shown to subject who must try to give its associated match

paradoxical effect effect opposite the normal effect, as with certain stimulant drugs given to calm hyperactive children

patient person undergoing treatment or therapy

Pavlovian conditioning conditioning that creates reflex in which response is occasioned by secondary stimulus that has been repeatedly associated with primary stimulus

peer person regarded as equal to another or to others in group

performance test measure of nonverbal abilities, such as hand-eye coordination

personality inventory standardized questionnaire providing information about attitudes and behavior, evaluated with reference to norms

personality test measure of development of personality in areas of insight, goal definition and attainment, and interpersonal relationships

phallic symbol any long or tall narrow object that may resemble or represent the penis, esp. as symbol of power

phone therapy therapy session conducted by telephone

pigeonhole error tendency to slot people into invalid behavioral categories

placebo treatment that has no effect except in patient's own mind

play therapy treatment based on self-expression using dolls and puppets, esp. for children

pleasure principle id-motivated drive or instinct seeking immediate satisfaction of all needs and desires

positive reinforcement rewarding stimulus that strengthens learned behavior

posthypnotic suggestion instruction given during hypnosis in regard to behavior or experience to take place after hypnosis has terminated

prefrontal lobotomy surgical severing of neural connections in brain to control extremely violent patients

primal scream therapy treatment in which patient reenacts disturbing past experiences, esp. of infancy, and expresses repressed anger through screams, hysteria, or violence

profile diagram showing results of individual's psychological testing and evaluation

projective technique unstructured testing method using ambiguous material to elicit projected responses

proxemics study of human spatial requirements and effects of population density

psychiatrist medical doctor specializing in treatment of mental disturbances, including by prescription of medications

psychoanalyst professional therapist practicing

psychoanalysis as originated by Freud and later developed and modified by others

psychological test measurement and assessment of various aspects of personality

psychologist professional who has completed graduate training in any branch of psychology and fulfilled state requirements for licensing

psychologize (*vb*) reason or theorize psychologically, esp. in a naive way

psychometric test standardized, structured test measuring mental functioning in precise, uniform way

psychosurgery brain surgery used to treat chronic mental disorder

psychotherapist professional therapist who treats psychological disorders through verbal methods; therapist

reality principle mechanism by which child realizes postponement of immediate gratification is sometimes required in exchange for greater rewards

reciprocal inhibition behavior therapy technique using mutual exclusivity of certain responses to overcome behavioral problems

recreation therapy treatment emphasizing relaxation, games, outdoor activities, or lectures to promote free and expressive activity

reductionism explanation of complex phenomenon by analyzing its simplest basic mechanisms and components

rehab counselor therapist providing counseling on problems of rehabilitation

rehabilitation restoration of normal health and functioning following period of impairment due to mental or physical disorder

reinforcement reward that increases likelihood of appearance of a particular response

reinforcing stimulus in operant conditioning, reward for a particular behavior

rhesus monkey macaque monkey of India used extensively in medical and psychological research

role-playing assumption and acting out of role to resolve conflicts and practice appropriate behavior, usu. in group therapy

Rorschach test personality evaluation involving patient interpretation of inkblot images; inkblot test

sample selected members of population whom researchers wish to observe or study so as to formulate generalizations about that population

scapegoat substitute object for aggression

schedule-standardized interview printed, questionnaire-style interview with established reliability and validity that is presented to all subjects in invariable form

security blanket child's blanket used as transitional object

self-examination intense scrutiny of one's personality and behavior; self-review; self-criticism

selfness state of possessing a distinct, developed, individual personality

sensitivity training group therapy in which patients seek deeper understanding of

themselves and others by exchange of intimate thoughts and feelings, sometimes through physical contact

sensory deprivation experimental technique in which subject is confined in soundproof chamber and deprived of variation in sensory stimuli

sex surrogate person provided by therapist for sexual activity with patient in unorthodox treatment of sexual disorders

shaping procedure in operant conditioning in which abnormal behavior is encouraged by rewards

shock therapy use of electric shock in cases of severe disorder, catatonia, or depression; electric shock therapy

shrink *Slang.* psychotherapist

Skinner box laboratory device for study of operant conditioning in which animal learns to press lever for reinforcement such as food

speech therapist person who specializes in treatment of speech dysfunctions

standardized test psychological measure whose administration, scoring, and interpretation are identical for all who take it, providing a reliable and valid norm for comparison

stimulus signal received by sense organ

straitjacket coatlike device that binds arms against body, used to restrain violent patients

stress psychological or physiological pressures that threaten health, stability, or functioning of personality

structured test measurement designed to evoke specific responses

subject person or animal in psychological test or experiment

subliminal (*adj*) involving stimuli intended to take effect below level of consciousness

suggestion induction of an idea that is accepted and readily acted on, esp. under hypnosis; idea so induced

support group group of people who meet regularly to discuss problems affecting them in common, such as alcoholism or bereavement

systematic desensitization technique for reduction or elimination of oversensitivity, esp. fear

TAT **t**hematic **a**pperception **t**est

team group of professionals working toward common goal with patient, often including persons from different disciplines

T-group group engaged in sensitivity training

thematic apperception test TAT; measurement of personality and motivation based on subject's construction of a story based on a series of standardized pictures

therapeutic community treatment and rehabilitation center providing supportive environment for drug detoxification and recovery from mental disorders

therapist psychotherapist

therapy treatment intended to improve psychological condition and assist in understanding and resolving emotional problems

time-binding process of relating past and future to present behavior and increasing understanding of consequences

touchy-feely *Slang.* pertaining to sensitivity training

transference patient's identification of therapist with pivotal person in his or her life and subsequent transferral of feelings about that person to therapist

transitional object familiar object to which child clings during early socialization and that substitutes for mother's care

trial each attempt made to learn in learning study

twelve-step program method of recovery from addictive and obsessive-compulsive conditions through group reinforcement and spiritual awareness

unconditioned response response occurring naturally, without training or reinforcement

unconditioned stimulus stimulus eliciting innate response

unstructured test test designed with ambiguous stimuli that evoke individualized responses

verbal learning experimental psychology concerned with how humans learn and remember through language

verbal test measurement of ability to retain and use knowledge and express ideas verbally

visualization technique of encouraging subject to imagine or picture self in altered and improved condition, having achieved desired goal

vocational interest test measure of job or career aptitude and interest

vocational rehab therapy and counseling intended to assist person in resuming former work activities

word association technique involving subject's pairing of given word with whatever word comes to mind

Mental States, Processes, and Behavior

abandonment feeling of having been forsaken or neglected, esp. by one's parents

abreaction release of repressed feeling by mentally reliving experience causing that feeling

adaptation capacity to alter one's behavior to conform to social norms

addictive personality person who has a tendency toward compulsive behavior associated with one specific activity or object

affect emotion attached to ideas, objects, or mental representations

aggression drive characterized by anger, hostility, or territoriality

anal phase second stage of psychophysical development during which child, usu. at age 2, becomes preoccupied with defecation, dealing with issues of control and autonomy

angst anxiety

anticipatory grief experience of grief or mourning in period leading up to expected tragic event, which is often experienced as a relief when it occurs

apperception conscious perception

aptitude ability and natural skills in certain areas

archetype Jungian characterization of fundamental personality trait held in collective unconscious

attitude learned tendency toward pattern of response in accordance with deep feelings

automatic writing symptom of disturbed functioning in which subject writes things without being aware of the act or of what is written

avoidance behavior characterized by evasion and/or withdrawal

basic anxiety feelings of loneliness or helplessness toward a potentially hostile environment

behavior actions and activities of humans and animals

body language body movements, positions, and gestures that communicate an attitude

bonding development of close and powerful relationships with family or friends based on initial attachment of infant and mother

brutalization physical and mental abuse, esp. when inflicted by family or mate

castration complex unconscious male fear of castration or emasculation, esp. as punishment for oedipal feelings

cathexis concentration or buildup of mental energy and emotional significance in connection with an idea, activity, or object

civilian catastrophe reaction extreme stress suffered by victims of natural disasters

codependency any of various problems or disorders based on one person's close association with another's habits or addictions, resulting in blurred individuation

cognition perception

cognitive development stages of growth in thinking and perception from childhood concern with objects to adult use of symbols and logic

cognitive dissonance psychological discomfort resulting from individual's conflicting beliefs or desires

cognitive learning learning by understanding rather than by conditioning

collective unconscious Jungian characterization of major part of unconscious mind, containing ancestral memories and images from humanity's history

compensation effort to replace feelings of inadequacy with feelings of adequacy

concept learning ability to form an abstraction from some aspect of a group of objects or common events, which increases from childhood to maturity

conflict state of tension arising from opposing desires or tendencies

conscience moral sense of right and wrong and accompanying desire to do right

coping ability to function in society despite any of various conditions or disorders

creativity ability to perceive new combinations of information for problem solving or invention

death instinct destructive, aggressive compulsion to achieve nonexistence; thanatos

defense ego mechanism used to channel energy to middle area between id's wishes and ego's reality

disengagement shift from active to passive mode

disturbance departure from normal emotional state, esp. state of anxiety

dream images and thoughts in mind of sleeping person

drive condition of urgent basic need that causes motivation to satisfy need

dysfunctional family family in which emotional and physical support needed for individuation and healthy development are missing and family members are sacrificed to the family group itself

ego reality-oriented, structured component of personality that enables individual to function autonomously in the world; one of three divisions of psyche in psychoanalytic theory

eidetic imagery photographic memory in which vivid mental images can be described in detail

emasculation deprivation or reduction of male's sense of power, esp. by mate

emotion strong psychophysical response of individual

episode specific instance of behavior or condition

externalization perception of one's own difficulties as being caused by external forces, not innate characteristics

extrasensory perception phenomenon of perception or communication occurring independent of powers of sense organs

extroversion tendency to direct one's interest toward things outside the self

facade surface behavior

fantasize (vb) create mental world through one's imagination, esp. to fulfill a psychological need

Freudian slip statement or action that inadvertently reveals unconscious motive or desire

frustration disturbed state occurring when individual cannot attain goal or relieve tension

functional fixedness inability to perceive and use objects in innovative ways or engage in alternative thinking processes

genital phase final stage of psychophysical development, occurring at puberty, in which affectionate relationship with sexual partner can be achieved; childhood stage between ages 2 1/2 and 7, marked by increased sexual and genital interest

gestalt unified whole, esp. the psyche, having properties that cannot be derived from the sum of its parts

gratification basic, often sensual, satisfaction

group dynamics ways in which group members interact, esp. to achieve group goals

hang-up *Slang.* fixation or psychological block

homeostatic drive motivation to maintain constant or stable internal environment

hormone any of various chemicals secreted by glands that affect behavior

hyperactive (adj) abnormally animated or active, esp. in relation to children

id unconscious, unsocialized component of personality, containing unexpressed desires and motivations and driven by pleasure principle; one of three divisions of psyche in psychoanalytic theory

identification unconscious process of adopting attributes of another

identity crisis period or episode of psychological distress during which questions of self-definition become paramount

imagination ability to apply creative thought to real situations, forming unique mental images

imago idealized mental picture of another, esp. one's parent

imprinting early learning that occurs quickly and thoroughly

impulse wave of psychic energy that is either discharged, inhibited, directed, or sublimated

individuation development of a distinct personality, separate from one's mother's, and a sense of boundary between self and others

inhibition process of stopping an impulse

inner child part of a person's self that remains as it was in childhood and influences the way that person sees and relates to the world as an adult

instinct inborn, universal, biological drive

intelligence range of attributes centering around reasoning skills, knowledge of one's culture, and problem-solving abilities

internalization adoption of values through identification

introjection replacement of relationship with external object with relationship with internal, imagined object

introversion tendency to withdraw from others and turn inward upon the self

intuition ability to understand quickly through feeling, not analysis

kinesthesis sensory ability to feel body positioning

learning adaptive change in behavior caused by training, experience, or observation

leveling forgetting; failing to perceive adequate detail

libido in Freudian terms, sexual energy; in Jungian terms, psychic energy

looking-glass self self-image based on perceived view of other's, esp. child's perception of parent

merging loss of one's individual identity through intense and overly close association with another

midlife crisis feelings of anxiety and uncertainty about one's identity, relationships, and values, usu. experienced between ages 35 and 55

mind-set fixed point of view, attitude, or mood

mneme retentive basis in the mind accounting for memory

mood ongoing or passing emotional state

morale condition of confidence, enthusiasm, and good cheer, esp. in face of hardship

motivation desires and needs that inspire behavior

nesting forming strong relationships and creating secure home environment, esp. for rearing family

networking developing personal contacts for exchange of information or furthering of one's career

nightmare vivid, unpleasant, terrifying dream, often recurring

nocturnal emission ejaculation, esp. among boys undergoing puberty, usu. after erotic dream; wet dream

nurturing care and warmth that promote healthy development

nurturing environment conditions that encourage sense of security

nympholepsy frenzy of emotion, esp. for something unattainable

onychophagia habitual nail-biting, usu. as sign of anxiety neurosis or other suppressed feeling

oral phase first stage of psychophysical development after birth, in which mouth is main source of pleasure and stimulation

paramnesia distortion of memory in which fact and fantasy are confused

peak experience point of great joy, wonder, or surrender

penis envy in Freudian theory, female feelings of inadequacy and jealousy because of repressed wish to have a penis

perception process of conscious sensory input; cognition

persona in Jungian view, individual's facade or mask of socialized behavior

personality totality of traits, feelings, values, and expressions that characterize an individual

personal unconscious in Jungian view, unconscious mental contents unique to individual and not part of collective unconscious

phallic phase stage of development, usu. ages three to five, in which focus of pleasure shifts to genitals

preconscious (*adj*) referring to mental activity that is not immediately conscious but can easily be recalled

primal (*adj*) having to do with basic, primitive urges and emotions

process course of action or form of behavior

psychasthenia neurosis characterized by phobias and obsessions

psyche mental or psychological structure of an individual, esp. in connection with motivation

psychic energy in Jungian theory, general life force

psychodynamics in Freudian view, interplay of unconscious mental processes that determine human thought, feelings, and behavior

psychogenic (*adj*) caused by mental conflict

psychosexual stages of development in

Freudian theory, sexual development in oral, anal, and genital phases

psychotropic (*adj*) altering one's mental functions, used esp. of tranquilizers and hallucinogenic drugs

reflex inborn natural response

REM sleep rapid eye movement sleep; cyclical sleep state characterized by increased brain activity, dreams, and rapid eye movements

response activity resulting from stimulus

schema belief system or experience that produces specific mode of perception and behavior

self-abuse accusation and blame of oneself; masturbation

self-actualization fulfillment of individual's potential as independent, functioning, healthy, adjusted person

self-conscious (*adj*) awkward and embarrassed in presence of others due to excessive concern with others' opinions

self-control ability to curtail or sublimate one's natural desires and behavior

self-denial sacrifice of one's own desires or needs

self-examination deep study of one's personality, behavior, thoughts, and feelings

self-fulfilling prophecy unconscious tendency to make behavior and events conform to anticipated outcomes

self-love regard for oneself and one's feelings

self-pity excessive and self-indulgent sorrow for oneself

self-worth healthy sense of oneself as a valuable individual

sensation sense impression of sight, sound, smell, taste, or touch and resultant feelings

sentiment positive or negative feeling about idea, object, or person

set attitude or readiness to perceive in certain way

sex identity feelings of comfort with and adjustment to one's maleness or femaleness

shadow in Jungian theory, unsocialized, primitive, idlike aspect of self

sibling rivalry competition among brothers or sisters within family structure

sleep deprivation reduced sleep over prolonged period, causing personality disorganization, diminished cognitive abilities, and sometimes psychotic delusions and hallucinations

slough of despond hopeless dejection and depression

soma body or physical self

somatotype body type, classified as endomorphic (heavy), ectomorphic (frail), or mesomorphic (muscular), each associated with a type of temperament or personality

soul-searching deep, often painful, introspection and self-examination

state specific mental or emotional condition

stream of consciousness personal conscious experience regarded as an uninterrupted series of events

stress bodily reaction to danger, difficulty, or threat

strung-out (*adj*) *Slang.* debilitated from addiction to drug or alcohol; extremely anxious

subconscious mental activity and impulses occurring below threshold of active awareness; (*adj*) existing in mind beyond conscious level

superego aspect of personality involving conscience, guilt, imposition of moral standards, and introjected authoritative and ethical images; one of three divisions of psyche in psychoanalytic theory

suppression conscious attempt to forget unpleasant idea or object or inhibit an impulse

symbiosis intense mutual interdependence

synesthesia experiencing a sensation in one sense organ from stimulus to another organ, such as hearing colors or seeing music

tantrum violent, uncontrollable outburst of rage, esp. in children

temperament characteristic mental, physical, and emotional aspects of an individual

thanatos death instinct, esp. as expressed in violent aggression

trance state of altered and diminished consciousness, esp. under hypnosis, in which voluntary movement is lost

unbalanced (*adj*) having disturbed or uneven mental functions

unconscious aspect of mind and personality that holds thoughts, desires, images, and urges of which individual is not aware; (*adj*) not actively aware of oneself

unstable (*adj*) emotionally unsettled or unpredictable

verbal intelligence grasp of ideas, language, information, and numbers

Weltschmerz *German.* sentimental melancholy over state of world

wet dream nocturnal emission

wish fulfillment attainment in dreams or fantasies of often unconscious or unattainable desire or impulse

---

PHILOSOPHY
Schools, Doctrines, and Movements
Notions, Ideas, and Methods
Logic

See also: *Chap. 11: Government; Chap. 13: Sociology; Psychology; Chap. 23: Reasoning and Intuition; Chap. 25: Religion; Mythology and Folklore; Eschatology; Truth, Wisdom, and Spiritual Attainment*

Schools, Doctrines, and Movements

aesthetics branch of philosophy concerned with beauty and values in the judging of beauty, esp. in art; esthetics

Age of Reason Enlightenment

analytic philosophy highly structured approach

to philosophical problems through modern logic, developed by Ludwig Wittgenstein (20th c.)

animism belief in the conscious life, or soul, of inanimate objects as well as living beings

anthroposophy doctrine that cultivating spiritual development is humankind's most important task

antinomianism doctrine that rejects conventional moral law and maintains that salvation derives from faith and grace alone

Aristotelianism practical, empirical philosophy of Aristotle, highly influential throughout course of Western history (Greece, 4th c. B.C.)

atomism theory that reality consists of minute, independent material units or atoms (Greece, 5th c. B.C.)

axiology science of and inquiry into values, as in aesthetics and ethics

bioethics study of ethical issues arising from medical and biological research (late 20th c.)

Cartesianism doctrine of René Descartes that all knowledge can be firmly established based on certain truths (France, 17th c.)

conceptualism theory that universal ideas exist as mental objects available to all minds

Confucianism quasireligious ethical system of China, based on sayings of Confucius (6th c. B.C.)

cosmology study of origin and totality of universal realities as basis for metaphysical speculation

critical philosophy doctrine of Immanuel Kant that the world is understood only insofar as it conforms to the mind's structure

Cynicism school originating with Diogenes, professing moderation and virtue as sole good, later based on protest and opposition to prevailing philosophical ideas (Greece, 5th c. B.C.)

Cyrenaics hedonistic philosophy of bodily pleasure, precursor to Epicureanism (Greece, 4th c. B.C.)

deontology ethical doctrine of duty as basis of moral obligation

determinism theory that reality and events unfold according to a predetermined, inevitable course

dialectical materialism Marxist form of materialism based on Hegelian dialectic applied to philosophy of social history

dualism theory that two basic, irreducible opposites, such as light and dark, good and evil, or mind and matter, constitute reality

Eleaticism Presocratic doctrine of Parmenides that absolute reality is undifferentiated and immutable while change is merely apparent (Greece, 6th c. B.C.)

empiricism view that sense perception and experience are sole foundations of knowledge, esp. held by John Locke (Britain, 17th c.)

Encyclopedism rationalist, humanistic movement to compile an encyclopedic compendium of knowledge, edited by Denis Diderot (France, 18th c.)

Enlightenment Age of Reason; intellectual movement toward tolerance, positive social action, and humanism, based on belief in perfectibility of people through reason (18th c.)

Epicureanism ethical doctrine of Epicurus, holding pleasure to be highest good, with pleasure deriving from moral conduct (Greece, 3rd c. B.C.)

epistemology theory of knowledge; critical study of nature, limits, and validity of knowledge

esthetics aesthetics

ethics science and study of morality and human conduct

eudaemonism ethical system defining moral behavior in terms of happiness and well-being

existentialism philosophy emphasizing free will in coming to terms with subjective meaning and meaninglessness in one's existence, based on teachings of Sören Kierkegaard (20th c.)

fatalism doctrine that all events and occurrences are predetermined and inevitable

formal logic branch of logic that emphasizes form and principles of deductive reasoning rather than content of propositions

hard determinism theory that there is no free will or nonpredetermined action

hedonism ethical doctrine of pleasure as highest or only good

historical materialism historicism

historicism deterministic explanation of phenomena in terms of their origins and development, associated with Hegel and Marx (19th c.); historical materialism

humanism any philosophical doctrine emphasizing human concerns, motives, and aspirations rather than other natural or spiritual forces, holding human reason to be the source of its authority

hylozoism doctrine that life is inherent in all matter, whether animal, vegetable, or mineral

idealism theory that reality is a creation of mind, and that mental and spiritual values, rather than matter, constitute reality; immaterialism

ideology scope of ideas within a particular theory or belief system

immaterialism idealism

individualism political philosophical theory emphasizing personal freedom and autonomy

instrumentalism school of pragmatism that maintains that the value of ideas lies in their practical application to human problems

logic philosophical inquiry into principles and methods of validity and proof

logical empiricism logical positivism

logical positivism school rejecting metaphysics and emphasizing methods of criticism and analysis of science, with reliance on principle of verifiability in experience or language (20th c.); logical empiricism

materialism theory that reality consists solely of matter, without separate reality of mind or spirit

metaphysics branch of philosophy concerned with ultimate nature and categories of reality; study of being, existence, and essence; ontology and cosmology

monism doctrine that reality of mind and body are fundamentally one and undifferentiated and can be reduced to one fundamental force, advocated by Spinoza in 17th c.

mysticism doctrine of direct, inexplicable knowledge and experience of truth and reality without rational processes or reliance on creed, orthodoxy, or belief system

naturalism theory that reality consists solely of the natural, observable world, with no supernatural or spiritual realm

Neoplatonism school synthesizing Platonic, Aristotelian, Christian, Jewish, and mystical traditions (3rd-5th c. A.D.)

nihilism doctrine that social and economic order is inherently corrupt and morality cannot be justified (Russia, 19th c.)

nominalism theory emphasizing that ideas and objects exist only in particular, not in abstract or general forms, influenced by William of Occam (14th c.)

objectivism theory emphasizing external, objective, rather than internal, subjective, aspect of reality; ethical theory that good is of value independent of human feelings but based on universally valid moral truths

optimism doctrine holding that reality is fundamentally good and the world is governed by benign forces

ordinary-language school movement advocating use of everyday language to resolve philosophical problems (20th c.)

perspectivism doctrine that reality and truth are known only from perspective of individual or group viewing them at particular moment

pessimism doctrine holding that reality is fundamentally evil and the world is governed by malevolent forces

phenomenalism empirical theory that knowledge exists solely in the appearance of phenomena, or sense data, rather than in the ultimate reality of objects themselves

phenomenology science of describing and analyzing classes of phenomena and consciousness (20th c.)

philosophes leading thinkers of the Enlightenment (France, 18th c.)

philosophy study and pursuit of fundamental principles underlying knowledge, conduct, and universal reality, esp. disciplines of aesthetics, epistemology, ethics, logic, and metaphysics

Platonism idealistic philosophy of Plato, derived from teaching of Socrates; classic idealism and belief that the human mind can attain absolute truth (Greece, 4th c. B.C.)

pluralism theory that reality consists of several distinct, fundamental realities

political philosophy study of people as political animals and relationship between government and citizens

positivism theory that truth or knowledge is based solely on what is scientifically verifiable by direct experience, based on teachings of Auguste Comte (19th c.)

pragmatics branch of semiotics concerned with causal relationships between symbols and words and their users

pragmatism philosophical view emphasizing consequences and practical results of one's conduct rather than principles and categories of reality (19th c.)

pre-Socratics those Greek philosophers of nature who lived before Socrates, esp. the Pythagoreans

Pythagoreanism doctrines of Pythagoras, esp. that universe is manifestation of various combinations of mathematical ratios (Greece, 6th c. B.C.)

Ramism opposition to Aristotelianism and advocacy of new logic in doctrines of Ramus

rationalism theory emphasizing reasoned, not empirical, foundations of knowledge; truth apprehended by deductive reasoning independent of experience or observation (17th c.)

realism theory that universal concepts and reality exist independently of perception

relativism theory that truth and ethical values are relative, not absolute and independent, and are contingent on nature of mind

scholasticism medieval, Christian philosophical school based on empiricism of Aristotle and teachings of Thomas Aquinas (11th-13th c.)

scientific method empirical, experimental approach to proof and the analysis of phenomena

semantics branch of semiotics concerned with signs and things they signify

semiotics theory of signs and symbols used in communication

skepticism theory that man can never attain certain knowledge and that all knowledge should be questioned

soft determinism theory that although events are determined by cause and effect, free will is possible

Sophists wandering teachers who emphasized rhetoric over truth and taught whatever their students wanted to learn (Greece, 5th-4th c. B.C.)

Stoicism pantheistic philosophy founded by Zeno of Citium encompassing doctrine of submission to divine will and freedom from passions (Greece, 3rd c. B.C.)

subjectivism doctrine limiting knowledge of reality to that which is consciously apprehended, with moral values dependent on personal and subjective tastes; truth seen as relative to human nature and ability to comprehend

syntactics branch of semiotics concerned with formal properties of language or symbolic systems

Thomism theological philosophy of Thomas Aquinas; rational system teaching that at some point reason fails and faith provides revelation (13th c.)

transcendentalism philosophy emphasizing thought processes in discovery of reality;

philosophy emphasizing intuitive and spiritual rather than empirical basis of knowledge, developed by Ralph Waldo Emerson and Henry David Thoreau (U.S., 19th c.)

utilitarianism theory of moral conduct based on attainment of maximum good for greatest number of people (19th c.)

utopianism often impractical belief in and advocacy of ideal state

vitalism theory that living beings are governed by a vital force and by laws separate from those governing inanimate objects

Notions, Ideas, and Methods

absolute single, eternal explanation for all reality

abstraction that which is theoretical, dissociated from specific instances or phenomena

academicism purely speculative thoughts and opinions

a fortiori (*adj*) *Latin*. lit. from a stronger; even more certain, for an even stronger reason

agnosticism belief that we cannot know whether God exists

altruism principle or practice of unselfish concern for the good of others, esp. as a moral act

analytic (*adj*) being of a type of proposition or statement inherently true by virtue of its terms' meanings

antithesis second stage of dialectical process, being a proposition directly opposite and apparently contradictory to the thesis

a posteriori (*adj*) *Latin*. lit. from what comes later; derived from experience, based on empirical data; from a particular instance to a general law

appearance sensory aspect of existence to an observer

a priori (*adj*) *Latin*. lit. from what precedes; independent of and prior to experience; based on reason or inherent logic, independent of empirical data; from a general law to a particular instance

archetype original model from which all others follow, esp. perfect example of type

association of ideas basic principle explaining all mental activity in terms of combining and recombining of certain component elements

atheism rejection of all belief in God

automatism view of body as a machine and consciousness as noncontrolling element of body

becoming that which exists only temporarily or changes from one form to another

being that which has unchanging actuality or substance or is logically conceivable

casuistry skill in science and application of moral decisions and judgments; employment of specious reasoning in moral questions

categorical imperative unconditional moral rule of conduct, not dependent on personal preferences

category basic form or mode of existence

cause that which is responsible for an effect in

deterministic thinking; in Aristotelian thinking, that which is based on something's substance, design, maker, and purpose or function

chain of being hierarchical notion of universe as ordered structure of diminishing complexity from God on down

cogito ergo sum *Latin*. lit. I think, therefore I am; fundamental argument for idealism, attributed to René Descartes

concept idea capable of being defined and recognized; general idea or class

concretion that which is founded in fact; hard evidence, specific instances, or phenomena

connotation implication of a term, as distinguished from its denotation

consciousness awareness, sentience

contingence condition of being not necessary or of essence

corporeal (*adj*) relating to the body or physical matter

debate formal argument, esp. between those taking opposite views on single proposition

deduction mode of reasoning leading from general observation to particular conclusion

denotation specific meaning of a term, as distinguished from its connotation

dialectic orig. Socratic philosophic discourse or style of inquiry based on critical examination, later developed by Hegel as dynamic process of thesis, antithesis, and synthesis; Hegelian dialectic

dichotomy division into two classes; distinction based on a basic dissimilarity

ding an sich *German*. lit. the thing itself; essential being, prior to secondary qualities

discourse orderly, systematic communication, esp. in philosophic discussion

discursive (*adj*) characterized by analysis

dysteleology assumed absence of purpose and design in nature and phenomena

eclecticism combining of elements from different philosophical systems without resolving their conflicts

effect that which results from a cause in deterministic thinking

emotivism idea that ethical behavior is an expression of feelings and emotions

empirical (*adj*) pertaining to the senses; dependent on experience and direct observation

entelechy motive force for realization, completion, and perfection

epiphenomenalism idea that body can alter mind, but mind cannot alter body

essence inherent nature of an object, inseparable from its identity and contingent on nothing

ethical pluralism notion that more than one basic moral system can exist

evil moral wrongdoing; malevolence or ethical perversion

exegesis critical explanation

existence being; all that has being and continues to be

experience totality of what is perceived and thought

Forms absolute, eternal, immutable, and perfected Platonic models of which all earthly things are imperfect copies

four elements basic constituents of physical world: earth, air, fire, and water

free will option and power of moral choice in determining one's behavior

golden mean Aristotelian ethical doctrine of moderation as way to virtuous action

good character or behavior that is a model of moral order of the universe; that which promotes or inspires actions and attitudes supporting happiness and well-being

Gordian knot intricate and difficult problem or circumstance best resolved by cutting through it boldly and imaginatively

Hegelian dialectic dialectic

hermeneutics science of interpretation and explanation

heuristic (*adj*) characterized by ability to persuade or reveal rather than to convince logically

Hobson's choice choice between unacceptable alternatives; absence of real alternatives

holism notion that fundamental entities have existence beyond sum of their parts

hypothesis assumption, theory, or proposition made to account for some phenomena

hypothetical imperative conditional rule of conduct: if certain results are desired, certain actions must be taken

idea something present in consciousness; in Platonic terms, an archetype or essential concept

ideal world world of permanent truth

immanent (*adj*) existing within the mind only

indeterminism notion that some events do not have any cause

induction mode of reasoning leading from particular observations to general conclusions

inference mode of reasoning in which conclusion is derived from premises accepted as true

infinite regress endless series of arguments connected by interdependent premises and conclusions

innate ideas inborn ideas not based on experience

intellect ability to think

intuition direct apprehension of knowledge, without application of reason

knowledge understanding based on experience, intuition, and reason

li ultimate embodiment of good in Confucianism

Logos universal rational principle that orders the universe

maieutic (*adj*) pertaining to the Socratic method for clarifying ideas

methodology study of the nature of inquiry

mind-body duality idea that mind and body are distinct

model ideal form of image, object, or argument

monad *Greek*. lit. unit; ultimate, indivisible force center that is unit of all existence

moral skepticism notion that ethical principles have no objective basis

natural law naturally occurring moral rules that form universal law higher than man-made law

natural rights innate rights of humanity, such as life, liberty, equality, and the pursuit of happiness, that cannot be denied by society

noetics science of the intellect or of pure thought

noncontradiction principle that statement cannot be both true and false and object cannot both have and not have some quality

noumenon *Greek*. lit. that which is conceived; reality that cannot be experienced, as opposed to appearance or phenomena

nous *Greek*. lit. mind; universal principle of reason, embodied in God

Occam's razor principle that simplest explanation or theory is correct and should not be needlessly multiplied

ontological argument attempt to prove existence of God by analysis of definition of God

ontology metaphysical study of the essence of being and reality

organon system of rules or principles for demonstration or examination

pantheism belief that God and universe are identical

particular individual, specific instance, object, or term for a universal or general class

percept sense perception rather than idea of an object

perceptual error false or distorted sense perception

perceptual judgment judgment based on sense perception

Peripatetic follower of Aristotle, so called from practice of walking while teaching

petitio principii *Latin*. lit. postulation of the beginning; assumption of a premise identical with the conclusion

phenomena objects and events known through sensory experience

phenomenal world world of appearances

philosopher king Platonic ideal of philosopher ruling and leading society

physicalism theory that all factual statements can be reduced to observations of phenomena

poetic (*adj*) apprehended by the emotions

praxis action and practice rather than theory

primary quality characteristic inherent in an object, such as its shape, size, or mass

quintessence essence of a substance, substance other than four elements believed to compose celestial bodies

reality that which exists independently of ideas about it and independently of all other things, but from which all else derives

reason intellectual faculty, ability to comprehend by rational powers; systematic thinking, judgment of truth of propositions

secondary quality characteristic in object capable of stimulating sense perception, such as color or sound

sensationalism empiricist view that sensations

are both source and verification of all knowledge

sentience ability to sense or feel

situation ethics moral evaluation of any action in relation to specific circumstance

social contract concept that society is based on agreement among people to be governed

Socratic method dialectic technique of inquiry developed by Plato's teacher Socrates (Greece, 5th c. B.C.)

solipsism theory that one can be aware of nothing outside the self and one's personal perceptions and feelings

sophistry use of persuasive but misleading or unsound argument

spiritualism view that the spirit is ultimate reality in universe

state of nature concept in political philosophy describing condition of humankind without government

substance that which exists by itself or is the essential part of something

sufficient reason principle that there is a reason for every phenomenon being as it is and not otherwise

summum bonum *Latin*. lit. highest good; moral principle of action based on effecting the greatest good

superman ideal, superior being described in work of Friedrich Nietzsche

synthesis dialectical combining of thesis and antithesis into higher stage of truth

synthetic type of proposition or statement in which predicate adds, or synthesizes, knowledge

tabula rasa *Latin*. lit. blank tablet; empiricist description of human mind at birth, with no innate ideas, awaiting experience to develop ideas

teleology belief in purpose and design in nature and phenomena

theorem principle, rule

theory hypothesis or speculation rather than action

thesis proposition held for proof by argument

transeunt (*adj*) producing an effect outside the mind

truth accord between internal and external realities; established and accepted principles of observation, action, or behavior; reality itself

unexamined life existence apart from philosophical inquiry, deemed not worth living by Plato

universal general concept having unrestricted application; proposition true for all members of its class

values moral standards and social goals held worthy for their own sake

verifiability ability of statement to be confirmed as true or refuted as false

vice moral corruption or evil

virtue moral integrity or excellence

will ability to make choices

will to power Friedrich Nietzsche's view that

power is the prime motivating force in human nature

zetetic (*adj*) seeking; (*n*) seeker

Logic

ambiguity possibility of having more than one meaning

amphiboly argument in which statement's meaning can be interpreted in more than one way

analogy relation based on similarity; inference based on shared qualities

antecedent conditional element in proposition

antinomy contradiction or opposition of one law to another

argument set of reasoned statements leading from assumptions and premises to conclusion

assumption statement taken to be true without proof

axiom assumption accepted as basis for deductive reasoning

biconditional (*adj*) designating a proposition that asserts the mutual interdependence of two things or events

circular (*adj*) describing reasoning in which apparently proved conclusion has been assumed as premise

compound proposition combination of at least two simple propositions using conditional word such as "if," "or," or "then"

conclusion reasoned deduction drawn from argument's premises

conditional "if-then" proposition in which existence or occurrence of one phenomenon or event depends on existence or occurrence of another phenomenon or event

constant term with invariable meaning

contradiction logically false statement

converse statement with elements expressed in reverse order of original proposition; reverse

counterexample fact that refutes a generalization

deduce (*vb*) draw conclusion by reasoning process

deductive logic formal logic; study of relationship between premises and conclusions of arguments; reasoning in which premises necessarily lead to particular conclusions

demonstration proof of an argument

dilemma syllogism in which major premise contains two or more conditional propositions and minor premise is a disjunction

disjunction compound proposition, either inclusive or exclusive, produced by joining two simple propositions by the word "or"

enthymeme incomplete argument, missing premise or conclusion

Euler diagram overlapping circles representing classes of objects, used to illustrate syllogisms

fallacy incorrect reasoning; invalid argument; instance of false conclusion drawn from premises

generalization proposition applying to all

members of certain class of things or indefinite portion of that class

ignoratio elenchi *Latin*. lit. ignorance of the refutation; fallacy of offering irrelevant proof

implication relation between two propositions whereby one may be logically deduced from the other

indisputable (*adj*) incontestable, self-evidently true

induce (*vb*) conclude by induction

inductive logic study of relationship between premises and conclusions of inconclusive arguments

invalid (*adj*) incorrectly argued; not logically based on premises

inverse statement reversed in order, directly opposite form of original

irrefragable (*adj*) irrefutable, undeniable

irrefutable (*adj*) not capable of being refuted or disproved

lemma subsidiary proposition that helps prove another proposition

logic study and use of formal reasoning process for analyzing relationship between premises and conclusions of arguments

Lull diagram concentric circles and overlapping triangles used to illustrate circle of interconnected syllogisms

major premise premise in syllogism containing predicate of conclusion

metamathematics study of general properties of logical systems

minor premise premise in syllogism containing subject of conclusion

modal logic logic that classifies propositions according to their necessity and probability

obverse proposition inferred from another by denying the opposite of that which given proposition affirms

ordered pair set of two objects in definite order of first and second

paradox self-contradictory statement

postulate statement or proposition assumed to be true without proof

predicate that which is affirmed or denied concerning subject of proposition

premise general statement used as basis for argument and to support conclusion

proof series of statements used to show validity of argument

proposition point to be discussed, proved, disproved, or maintained in argument

QED **q**uod **e**rat **d**emonstrandum; *Latin*. lit. that which was to be demonstrated; designation for conclusion, equivalent to "therefore" or "thus"

quantifier term, such as "all" or "some," that establishes or restricts the quantity of a proposition

rational (*adj*) having reason; capable of reasoning

rationale explanation of principles or opinion

reciprocal terms terms with same signification

reductio ad absurdum *Latin*. lit. reduction to

absurdity; refutation of proposition by arguing to false conclusion from its premise

relationship connection by means of conditionals and/or quantifiers between two or more propositions

reverse converse

set group of things

sorites series of related syllogisms forming closed circle of premises leading to conclusion that connects back to original premise

sound (*adj*) having premises that are true and a conclusion that is valid

statement true or false sentence existing as part of argument

subject term of proposition concerning which predicate is affirmed or denied

syllogism form of deductive argument based on two premises or assumptions and conclusion drawn from them

symbolic logic mathematical logic using symbols to express propositions, quantifiers, and relationships; propositional calculus and functional calculus

tautology proposition necessarily true by virtue of its components; redundant proposition adding no new knowledge

truth-functional logic form of logic using connective terms "and" and "or"

truth table diagram or list of truth-value of each component of compound statement

truth-value truth or falsity of a statement

universe of discourse all objects possibly referred to in establishing and proving argument

valid (*adj*) correctly argued as a conclusion based on premises

variable term with different meanings depending on context

vice versa (*adj*) expressed as contrary of original statement

vicious circle two propositions that establish each other or two terms that define each other

---

EDUCATION

Colleges and Universities
Schools and Classes
Teachers and Students
Curricula, Studies, Learning, and Tests
Extracurricular Activities and Concerns

See also: *Chap. 8: Parents and Children; Chap. 13: Sociology; Psychology*

Colleges and Universities

A and M **A**gricultural and **M**echanical college

academe academia

academia community life or environment of a university; academe

academic (*adj*) relating to an institution of higher education

accredited (*adj*) issuing degrees recognized as valid

advanced degree degree beyond baccalaureate

advanced standing credit given to students for classes completed elsewhere

alma mater college or school from which one received a degree

art school college providing instruction in fine arts

B.A. Bachelor of Arts degree

baccalaureate bachelor's degree

bachelor's degree degree given at completion of studies at four-year college; baccalaureate; undergraduate degree

B.S. Bachelor of Science degree

B school *Informal.* business school

bursar financial officer at college

business school school for professional training in business theory and methods

certificate special degree, lower than bachelor's, awarded by junior college or training institution

chancellor university president; chief executive of state educational system

cluster college small college that specializes in one field of study and is affiliated with a university

college institution of higher education that provides general course of studies leading to bachelor's degree; part of university offering specific course of study

college try *Informal.* all-out effort

collegiate (*adj*) of or relating to college

colloquium conference or informal meeting at which specialists speak and answer questions on designated topic

commencement ceremonies surrounding awarding of degrees and graduation

community college junior college serving local residents

convocation ceremonial gathering of members of college

cow college *Informal.* agricultural college; small, rural college

credential degree awarded in professional field, such as teaching, after or separate from bachelor's degree

cum laude (*adv*) *Latin.* lit. with praise; designation on diploma indicating graduation with honors

dean official in charge of division, faculty, or school within a college

degree title conferred by college for completion of course of study or in honorary recognition

department division of college offering instruction in specific field

diploma official document bearing seal and recording receipt of degree

divinity school division within college providing training for ministerial candidates

D. Litt. *Latin.* Doctor Litterarum; Doctor of Letters degree

doctoral program studies leading to Ph.D. degree

doctorate highest university degree, esp. Ph.D.; doctor's degree

doctor's degree doctorate

D.Th. Doctor of Theology degree

fellowship stipend given to support advanced study

free university unaccredited institution established by students for discussion of nonacademic and often controversial subjects

graduate (*vb*) complete course of study; confer or receive degree; (*n*) student who has completed studies and received degree

graduate school university division in specific field attended after receipt of bachelor's degree

graduation ceremony of conferring degree at completion of studies

groves of academe academic environment

higher education college and university studies

honorary degree degree awarded in recognition of achievement, not for completion of studies

institute educational establishment usu. devoted to technical field

interdisciplinary major course of study involving two or more academic disciplines

intersession period between academic terms

ivory tower place remote from worldly things, esp. institution of higher education

ivy halls *Informal.* educational institution, esp. old university on East Coast

junior college two-year community college issuing certificates or associate degrees, often a vocational or technical school

land-grant college government financed college providing low-cost higher educations, esp. in agriculture and mechanical arts

law school graduate school for training to be lawyer

lecture hall large room or auditorium for addressing groups of students

liberal arts college studies emphasizing general knowledge rather than professional or vocational training

LL.D. *Latin.* Legum Doctor; Doctor of Laws degree

lower division first two years of college

M.A. Master of Arts degree, achieved after B.A.

magna cum laude (*adv*) *Latin.* lit. with great praise; designation on diploma indicating graduation with great honors

major student's primary field of study; (*vb*) select one's primary field of study

master's degree university graduate degree received after bachelor's and before doctorate

matriculation enrollment as student in college or university as degree candidate

M.D. Doctor of Medicine; doctoral degree awarded at completion of medical school

medical school four-year graduate program of studies and work experience for training as a doctor

minor student's secondary field of study; (*vb*) select secondary field of study

M.S. Master of Science degree, received after B.S.

multiversity large university composed of many schools, colleges, or divisions

normal school formerly, a teachers college

Oxbridge *Brit.* Oxford and Cambridge, the two most prestigious British universities

Ph.D. Doctor of Philosophy; highest university postgraduate degree

Phi Beta Kappa national university honor society for scholars

postdoctoral (*adj*) designating work and study undertaken after receipt of doctorate

postgraduate student who takes advanced work after graduation; (*adj*) designating study leading to postgraduate degree

postgraduate degree master's degree or doctorate, received after bachelor's degree

predoctoral (*adj*) designating student or course of study leading toward doctoral degree

premed program of undergraduate studies preparatory to medical school admission; student enrolled in such a program

professional school postgraduate division of university for training in profession such as medicine, law, or business

provost high-ranking university administrator

regent member of governing board of some state universities

registration enrollment in specific classes at beginning of term

research institute postgraduate academic institution devoted primarily to research, not instruction

sabbatical leave of absence for professor, originally granted every seventh year

Sc.D. *Latin.* Scientiae Doctor; Doctor of Science degree

scholarship funding granted to student, esp. on basis of need or merit

semester either of two, usu. eighteen-week, divisions of academic year, September to January or February to June

seminary institution that trains candidates for ministry or priesthood; theological seminary

Siwash small college with provincial outlook

S.J.D. *Latin.* Scientiae Juridicae Doctor; Doctor of Juridical Science degree

state college government-funded college, esp. for students of one state

summa cum laude (*adv*) *Latin.* lit. with highest praise; designation on diploma indicating graduation with highest honor

symposium formal meeting at which specialists deliver papers on given topic

teachers college college for training elementary and secondary school teachers, usu. in two-year program

tenure permanent employment granted to college or university professor after trial period

term division of academic year during which courses begin and end

theological seminary seminary

trimester segment of academic year divided into three quarters or semesters, usu. September to December, January to March, and April to June

tuition fee required for registration at educational institution

undergraduate degree bachelor's degree

university public or private educational institution operating at highest level, with facilities for teaching and research, undergraduate colleges granting bachelor's degrees, and graduate programs and professional schools granting master's degrees and doctorates

upper division third and fourth years of college

war college institution that provides training in military theory and practice

Schools and Classes

academic year period of school sessions, usu. September through June

academy high school or college emphasizing specific subjects; private high school

adult school institution providing education for adults, usu. without college credit

alternative school nontraditional elementary or secondary school

Bible school parochial school, esp. one run by fundamentalist religious order

boarding school school at which students reside during school year

board of education local government agency that supervises activities of public schools

church school educational institution run by church

class specific course of study, group of students, or period of instruction

classroom place where instruction takes place; schoolroom

common school public school usu. including both primary and secondary grades

conservatory school or academy offering training in one of the fine arts, esp. music

consolidated school public school created by merging students and faculty from several discounted schools, usu. in rural area

continuation school school for students who have been excluded from regular school for academic or disciplinary reasons

convent girls' school run by community of nuns

country day school private, nonboarding elementary or secondary school outside city limits

course lectures, assignments, class meetings, and tests on particular subject over set period of time

day care daytime supervision of preschool children

day nursery day school

day school place where day care is provided; nursery school; nonboarding private school; day nursery

école *French.* school

elementary school grades one through six or eight, often including kindergarten; grade school; grammar school; primary school

finishing school exclusive girls' private school emphasizing social and cultural activities, not academics

form grade in secondary school (Britain)

free school loosely structured alternative school, often allowing students decision-making power

grade one year's stage in elementary or secondary education

grade school elementary school

grammar school elementary school, grades one to six

gymnasium secondary school for students planning to go to university (Germany)

Hebrew school school for instruction in Jewish traditions and Hebrew language, usu. holding weekly sessions for Jewish children

high school secondary school, usu. grades nine through twelve, sometimes grades ten through twelve

homeroom classroom where students begin and sometimes end day

institution established, generally public, organization and facilities providing education

intermediate school elementary school, grades four through six; junior high school

junior high school seventh and eighth grades

kindergarten first year of school, for five-year-olds, before first grade

language institute school providing intensive training in foreign language

Latin school secondary school emphasizing instruction in Latin and Greek

lycée public secondary school, esp. in France

magnet school public school with specialized curriculum that draws students from broad region

middle school school between elementary and high school, usu. grades six through eight

military academy institution providing training in war and soldiering as well as academic disciplines

Montessori school institution following system of training young children developed by Maria Montessori, stressing free-form physical activity, individual instruction, and early literacy

night school school offering evening classes in continuing education, generally for older students employed during day

nursery school prekindergarten facility providing day care and some training for children from about three to five years of age

palestra sports school (ancient Greece)

parish school school run by local church

parochial school private elementary or secondary school supported and administered by religious body, esp. Catholic Church

playgroup informal preschool with adult supervision but no instruction

preparatory school usu. private secondary school aimed at preparing students for college; prep school

prep school preparatory school

preschool day-care or nursery school instruction for children prior to entering kindergarten

primary school elementary school

private school school maintained by nongovernment funds, including students' tuition fees

public school government-supported, usu. tuition-free, school (U.S.); privately-endowed secondary school offering classical curriculum (Britain)

scholarship money granted to student to help pay tuition

school institution providing instruction, esp. for children in grades one to twelve and kindergarten

school board local public school administrative body

school district administrative unit of public school system

schoolhouse building used to house school, esp. elementary school

schoolroom classroom

secondary school institution after elementary school and before college, particularly grades nine to twelve, public or private

seminary parochial, usu. Roman Catholic, secondary school, esp. for girls

senior high school four-year secondary school, grades nine through twelve

session hours in day or months in year when classes are given

storefront school urban school meeting in store fronting on street

summer school classes held between June and August, when school is normally not in session

Sunday school class held on Sunday for religious instruction, esp. Christian

trade school secondary school teaching vocational skills

training school school that prepares students for specific occupation

ulpan school school for intensive study of Hebrew, esp. by immigrants to Israel

upper school division of secondary school, usu. final two years

vocational school school providing instruction in industrial or commercial skills needed for particular trade or profession

yeshiva school for Talmudic study; Orthodox Jewish school for religious and secular studies

Teachers and Students

adviser teacher or school administrator who counsels students on academic or personal difficulties

alumna female graduate of institution; *pl.* **alumnae**

alumni collective term for all graduates of institution

alumnus male graduate of institution; *pl.* **alumni**

apprentice individual receiving training in specific profession through work experience

assistant professor lowest level of university professor

associate professor intermediate level of professor, below full professor

autodidact self-taught person

bookworm extremely serious student with few other interests

cadet undergraduate at military academy

chairperson head of university department, formerly and sometimes still chairman

class group of students graduating in same year

classmate member of one's own class

clock watcher student eager for class to end

coach tutor or trainer providing special instruction to individual student or help with specific problem

coed female college student

collegian student at college or university

docent college or university teacher or lecturer

doctoral candidate student participating in doctoral studies leading toward a degree

don college or university professor; tutor or fellow of Oxford or Cambridge (Britain)

donnish (*adj*) professorial in manner or disposition

educable (*adj*) capable of learning, though sometimes mildly retarded

educator teacher or school administrator

emeritus (*adj*) designating retired college professor holding honorary title

exchange student high-school or college student studying at foreign institution, usu. for one year, as part of reciprocal program between two schools or countries

faculty teaching staff of educational institution

faculty meeting closed-door gathering of teaching staff

fellow individual appointed to position and receiving allowance to pursue research or advanced study

freshman first-year student at high school or college; frosh

frosh *Informal.* freshman

Fulbright *Informal.* grant awarded to postgraduate scholar to study abroad; recipient of such a grant

full professor tenured professor of highest rank

gifted child child with exceptional intelligence and aptitude for learning

graduate student student in graduate program or school

greasy grind *Slang.* obsessively hardworking student with no interests other than academics

grind *Informal.* industrious, serious student

hall monitor student assigned to control student activities in elementary or secondary school hallways

handicapped child child who is limited by physical, intellectual, or emotional problems, causing difficulty in learning

headmaster man heading staff of private school

headmistress woman heading staff of private school

instructor teacher

intern advanced or graduate student in professional field, esp. medicine, receiving supervised work experience in addition to academic training

junior third-year student at high school or college

lector college lecturer

lecturer teacher who instructs class through long, formal discourses; university teacher below rank of assistant professor

licentiate person who has received license to practice an art or profession; holder of intermediate degree between baccalaureate and doctorate

master *Chiefly Brit.* male teacher, esp. in preparatory school

mentor teacher or older student who provides guidance and support for less experienced student

monitor student appointed to assist teacher

novice beginning student, esp. in specific field

opsimath person who begins to learn late in life

overachiever individual performing above expected capacity

pedagogue teacher

philomath lover of learning

plebe freshman at military academy

practice teacher student teacher

praepostor senior student at public school who has authority over other students (Britain)

preceptor headmaster or principal of school; teacher

prefect student monitor in private school

preppy student at preparatory school

preschooler child under five attending nursery school

principal chief executive officer of school

privatdocent university teacher who is receiving no salary, being compensated instead by fees

proctor individual chosen to monitor or supervise students, esp. at examination

prodigy extraordinarily talented child; wunderkind

professor highest-ranking university faculty member

professoriate body of professors at college; faculty

protégé student receiving special attention and encouragement from teacher or elder

pundit teacher; learned individual

pupil student

reader one who lectures to students (Britain)

rector chief administrator of school or university, esp. parochial school

Rhodes scholar holder of prestigious scholarship awarded to candidates from United States and British Commonwealth for postgraduate study at Oxford

salutatorian student ranking second in graduating class behind valedictorian

scholar student, esp. one doing advanced study in some subject; learned, erudite person

school-age (*adj*) old enough to begin school, generally six years old

schoolboy male schoolchild

schoolchild elementary and sometimes secondary school student

schoolgirl female schoolchild

schoolmarm female schoolteacher, esp. in small town school

schoolmaster man who teaches school

schoolmistress woman who teaches school

schoolteacher teacher, esp. at elementary level

seminarian student in seminary, esp. Roman Catholic

senior final-year student at high school or college

sophomore second-year student at high school or college

staff faculty and other school employees

student individual who attends school; one who studies so as to learn; pupil

student body all students at school or college

student teacher assistant teacher still studying to receive teaching credential or degree; practice teacher

substitute teacher elementary or secondary school teacher hired as interim replacement for absent teacher

swot *Brit. slang.* (*vb*) study hard; (*n*) very industrious student; grind

TA teaching assistant

teacher one trained to be and employed as an instructor of students; instructor; pedagogue

teacher's aide noncredentialed assistant to teacher

teacher's pet teacher's favorite student

teaching act, practice, and profession of instructing students

teaching assistant TA; graduate student aiding professor in instruction of undergraduate class

teaching fellow graduate student granted free tuition in return for assisting professors in class or laboratory

tenured (*adj*) designating college professor holding permanent employment

trainee student learning skills in specific field

transfer student who has changed from one school to another; (*vb*) change schools

truant student inexcusably or habitually late or absent from school

truant officer official charged with identifying and apprehending truant students

tutor private teacher for one individual; individual providing personalized instruction in British university

tyro novice or beginner in some field

underachiever individual performing at less than expected level

underclassman first- or second-year college student

undergraduate student in four-year college program

upperclassman third- or fourth-year college student

valedictorian student with highest grade ranking in class, selected to present valedictory address

wunderkind precociously bright child or prodigy

Curricula, Studies, Learning, and Tests

ABC's the alphabet; basic primary education

abecedarian (*adj*) relating to the alphabet; (*n*) person learning the alphabet

achievement test test that measures learning in a specific area

adult education courses offered to adults who have completed or discontinued formal education; continuing education

A level second of two standardized secondary school examinations required for university admission (Britain)

alphabet ordered letters used to form words of language

aptitude innate ability, capacity for learning

aptitude test measure of various abilities, esp. verbal and mathematical

assignment work to be completed in designated time

associative learning process by which discrete ideas become linked to each other

audiovisual aids educational materials and teaching devices, such as films and recordings, that appeal to both sense of hearing and sense of sight

audit (*vb*) attend class as an observer, without receiving credit

basal (*adj*) fundamental, esp. of a reading book

bilingual education classes given in two languages

blackboard hard, dark surface in classroom for writing and drawing on with chalk; chalkboard

black studies college curriculum on history and culture of African-Americans

blue book small notebook with blue cover, often used for taking college examinations

bone up (*vb*) *Informal.* study diligently for test, esp. at last minute

brushup course refresher course in subject previously studied

busywork effort expended on useless, irrelevant study

CAI computer-assisted instruction

career education vocational education

CEEB College Entrance Examination Board

chalkboard blackboard

civics study of government and politics, esp. in high school

classical education traditional academic course of study, sometimes including study of Greek and Latin; classicism

classicism classical education and study

cloze reading comprehension test in which test taker supplies words deleted from text

College Boards *Trademark.* aptitude and achievement tests used in determining college admission; SAT

College Entrance Examination Board CEEB; organization that administers SAT and achievement tests used to judge applicants for college admission

colloquy serious conversation or discourse

communications skills ability in language arts

compensatory education programs designed to make up for experiences missed by disadvantaged children

computer-assisted instruction CAI; instruction in which computer leads student through programmed lesson

continuing education adult education

core study basic curriculum of subjects related to central theme

correspondence course class conducted by mail

course series of lectures, assignments, class meetings, and tests on particular subject over set period of time

course of study curriculum

cram (*vb*) *Informal.* prepare for test at last minute

crash program intensive course for rapid learning of material

credit acknowledgment that student has completed a class requirement leading to a degree; unit of such acknowledgment, accumulated toward graduation requirement

crib (*vb*) *Informal.* plagiarize, copy, or cheat

criterion-referenced scoring scoring of test against predetermined specific set of scores by unique group

Cuisenaire rod *Trademark.* one of a set of colored rods used in teaching arithmetic

curriculum all courses offered by an institution; set of courses in area of specialization; course of study

curve grading system based on relative position of student within class, not raw score

dean's list honor roll of students with high grades

dialectic formal debate, esp. Hegelian or Platonic

didactic (*adj*) designed to instruct

discipline field of study or special knowledge

dissertation extended written treatment on subject, usu. involving research, esp. by degree candidate

drill repetitive practice in particular subject

dyslexia condition characterized by impairment of reading ability

early childhood education instruction at preschool and early elementary school level

education act and process of acquiring learning; knowledge and growth produced by schooling

Education Testing Service division of CEEB that administers SAT and achievement tests

educational television ETV; noncommercial television channels reserved by Federal Communications Commission for educational programs

elective course outside student's major field of study

ESL English as a second language; course of study in English for nonnative speakers

essay written examination or paper

ETV educational television

exam examination

examination scheduled classroom test of students' knowledge and progress; exam

exceptional children's education special programs for gifted, retarded, or other children with abnormal or unusual abilities

exercise something performed, studied, and repeated to develop skill

extension program that makes courses available to those without normal access to them, as by correspondence

fail (*vb*) receive grade indicating failure to pass a course

fescue long stick for pointing to letters to aid children learning to read

field area of study or specialty

field trip visit by students to site away from classroom to gain firsthand knowledge of subject

fill in the blanks designating an examination that requires student to add appropriate word or phrase omitted from sentence

final exam examination given at conclusion of course, covering all material studied

finals final examinations in all subjects at end of term

flashcard small card with words, numbers, or pictures on it, used in learning drills

flunk (*vb*) receive failing grade

4.0 perfect, straight-A grade point average

functional illiterate person with reading ability less than that needed to function in modern society

grade measure of knowledge gained in class, given on tests and written work and at end of course

grade-equivalent score measurement of test score by decimal representation of year and month of student's grade level, such as 7.3 for third month of seventh grade

grade point average average of total earned grade points on scale from zero to four divided by total class credits

gut *Slang.* easily passed course

home ec home economics; theory and practice of cooking and homemaking

homework assignments to be completed outside class

honor roll list of students with high grades

honors class accelerated class for advanced students

hornbook children's primer, orig. 16th century

humanities branch of learning concerned with human activities and institutions

illiteracy inability to read and write

independent study course of study designed by student outside normal curricula or requirements of major

indoctrination instruction in fundamentals of partisan point of view

industrial arts training in use of tools and machinery

Initial Teaching Alphabet expanded phonemic alphabet of forty-three characters, used to teach reading

innumeracy difficulty or inability in using mathematics

instruction teaching, lectures

intelligence quotient IQ; person's mental age, based on standardized intelligence test, multiplied by 100 and divided by chronological age

intelligence testing tests designed to identify exceptional children, measure intelligence levels, and diagnose disturbed children

IQ intelligence quotient

lab laboratory

laboratory period set aside for scientific experiments and instruction in use of equipment; lab

language arts reading, writing, spelling, and speech skills

language laboratory facility in which taped, question-and-answer material is used to aid learning of foreign language

learning acquisition of knowledge and understanding, esp. by study

learning disability physiological or emotional impairment of capacity for learning

lecture instructive discourse given to class

lesson one day's class instruction

lesson plan teacher's outline of class session and assigned work

lessons studies and homework

lexicon book containing alphabetical arrangement of words and definitions

literacy ability to read and write

makeup test examination given at later date for those unable to take it initially

master class advanced seminar, esp. in music or performing arts

memorization learning by rote

mick Slang. from Mickey Mouse; an easy class

midterm exam given halfway through course; midyear

midyear midterm

mnemonic device trick or technique used to assist memory

multiculturalism attempt to avoid racism, sexism, ageism, and ethnocentrism and to encompass various cultures and value systems, esp. in college curriculum

multiple-choice test examination offering several possible answers to each question, one of which is correct

multiplication tables chart used in elementary school to teach multiplication of numbers one through twelve

new math theory of mathematics instruction based on set and number theory leading to principles of arithmetic

norm-referenced scoring scoring of test against set of scores compiled by typical group of students

O level first of two standardized secondary school examinations required to continue education (Britain)

open classroom spacious teaching area shared by groups of students in elementary school, permitting movement from activity to activity and individualized instruction

orals oral examination by panel of professors as final test in doctoral program

paper written homework assignment

pass (vb) receive satisfactory grade on examination or for class

pass-fail grading system of grading in which students either pass or fail a course and do not receive a letter or number grade

pedagogy art, science, and profession of teaching

phonics rote memorization of syllable and letter sounds to learn reading

placement test entrance examination used to assign students to appropriate class level

polytechnic (adj) relating to instruction in technical arts and applied sciences

practice drills or homework assignments used to achieve proficiency in subject

practicum curriculum that includes supervised practical experience and training, esp. for teachers

précis brief written summary

Preliminary Scholastic Aptitude Test PSAT; SAT-type test taken by high school students in years prior to year of college application

primer brief introductory book on some subject, esp. reading

programmed learning instruction in which student proceeds through a series of highly structured materials at his or her own pace, receiving immediate feedback and testing from materials

progressive education instruction that rejects rote learning and strict discipline in favor of individual stimulation, group discussion, and more diverse curriculum

propaganda ideas and information intended to promote or degrade some group or viewpoint

proseminar graduate seminar open to advanced undergraduates

PSAT Preliminary Scholastic Aptitude Test

quadrivium upper division studies in medieval university, comprising arithmetic, music, geometry, and astronomy

question-and-answer (adj) designating a test given in the form of interrogation of student by teacher

quiz brief, often unannounced, test on material recently studied

raw score actual score on test unadjusted for student's relative position in group tested; number of correct answers on test

read (vb) study a specific field, esp. in Britain

reading disability learning problem that impairs person's reading skill

reading period period prior to final examinations during which classes are suspended, usu. for intensive study

realia objects used by teacher to illustrate everyday life

refresher brief course in subject previously studied

remedial (adj) designating courses intended to correct poor study habits or improve skills in specific field

report card periodic record of student's grades issued by school to parents

research systematic study of some topic, often involving accumulation of information and reference materials

responsions examination required for enrollment as undergraduate at Oxford

review study of all material covered during course, usu. in preparation for examination

rote learning mechanically by memory without really understanding

SAT Scholastic Aptitude Test

scholarship learning, knowledge, study in general

scholastic (adj) relating to schools or students

Scholastic Aptitude Test Trademark. SAT; standardized test used by colleges in evaluating reading and mathematics skills of applicants for admission

schoolbook textbook for specific class

schooling education

school without walls nontraditional educational program that uses community facilities as learning resources

schoolwork lessons, homework, and tests; general studies

score measure of test results, determined by one of various methods

self-paced (adj) designed so that student can learn at his or her own rate

self-taught (adj) having acquired learning or skills without formal education

semiliterate (adj) barely able to read and write

seminar small group of students pursuing advanced studies with professor

shop high school class providing vocational training, esp. in automobile mechanics, metalwork, or carpentry

skip (vb) pass over next grade in school and advance to higher level

slate small, handheld blackboard

social studies study of government, history, and culture; civics

special education course of study aimed at group of students with particular needs, problems, or goals

specialty primary field of study or interest

speed-reading technique for rapid reading by skimming without appreciable comprehension loss

speller manual used to teach spelling

spelling bee elimination contest to determine best speller

spoon-feed (vb) present information so thoroughly that independent thought is curbed and initiative destroyed

standardized test achievement test that measures knowledge in specific skill or subject without taking into account other factors

Stanford-Binet test intelligence test and scale for evaluating children

straight A's perfect report card; 4.0 grade point average

study use of one's mind for the gaining of knowledge; such activity in a particular field

study group several students studying together regularly, exchanging notes and information

study hall schoolroom set aside for individual study, not class discussion

subject department or field of knowledge and skills

Summerhill famous English school specializing in progressive education

syllabus outline or summary of course of study

tardy (*adj*) late for beginning of class

teach (*vb*) give instruction, guide studies, and offer knowledge or information to others

team teaching program in which two teachers incorporate their subjects into one course which they teach together

term paper lengthy written assignment in high school or college that displays student's progress and knowledge at end of course

test examination, measurement, and evaluation of student's knowledge and progress in course

text textbook

textbook book containing principles of subject, used in its study; text

theme written assignment, essay

thesis lengthy essay based on original research written by candidate for degree, esp. doctorate

Three R's reading, writing, and arithmetic; basic primary education

tracking assignment of students to specific curriculum based on aptitude level

tripos final honors examination (Britain)

trivium lower division studies in medieval university, comprising grammar, rhetoric, and logic

true-false test examination in which student must indicate whether answer is correct or incorrect

tutorial class conducted for one student or small number of students

valedictory farewell address at commencement ceremonies

visual aid instructional device, such as a map, chart, or model, that depicts the visual aspect of subject being studied

viva oral examination at university in Britain or Europe

vocational education vocational training; career education

vocational training instruction in industrial or commercial skills needed for particular trade or profession; vocational education

Wechsler Scales intelligence tests for adults, children, and preschoolers, used to show subject's strengths and weaknesses

whole language basis for method of teaching reading, used as alternative to phonics, in which students read interesting books, write stories before they can spell, and learn correct usage through correction of their work

workbook notebook used for homework, notes, or lab work

Extracurricular Activities and Concerns

academic freedom education without government or other external interference

beanie skullcap formerly worn by freshmen at some colleges

busing transportation of students from one area to another to achieve racial balance in schools

cafeteria school lunchroom

campus grounds and facilities of school or university

cap and gown mortarboard and full-length gown worn at commencement

coeducational (*adj*) being an institution for male and female students

common room lounge for use by faculty or residents of dormitory

commons plot of land on campus for general use by students

corporal punishment physical punishment of students

counseling professional advice for students on career planning and personal problem solving

custodian janitor

debate contest involving discussion of topic by teams presenting opposing arguments

detention keeping students at school after school hours as punishment

dorm dormitory

dormitory residence building for students at college, university, or boarding school; dorm

extracurricular (*adj*) designating student activities not receiving academic credit or engaged in outside classroom

extramural (*adj*) relating to extension courses (Britain)

ferule lit. flat strip of wood used to punish children; school discipline

fraternity selective men's social organization, usu. with its own residence, at college

Greek person who belongs to Greek-letter fraternity or sorority

gym physical education classes; building for indoor sports

hazing cruel pranks and harassment, esp. as fraternity initiation rite

homecoming annual weekend during which alumni return to college, usu. highlighted by athletic contest

hooky nonattendance at school

intercollegiate (*adj*) designating contests or activities conducted among or between colleges

interscholastic (*adj*) designating contests or activities conducted among or between schools

intramural (*adj*) designating contests or activities conducted within a single university or school

janitor person who cleans and maintains school grounds; custodian

jayvee junior varsity athletic team

locker student's personal storage compartment at school

mortarboard cap with flat top and tassel, worn at commencement

open enrollment voluntary enrollment in public school other than one indicated by residence; college acceptance of students regardless of qualifications

Parent-Teacher Association PTA; national society that brings parents in contact with their children's teachers

parietals rules regulating visiting hours for members of opposite sex in college dormitories

phys ed *Informal.* physical education classes

playing fields open areas for athletic contests

pledge person who has promised to join a fraternity or sorority; (*vb*) make such a promise

Pledge of Allegiance oath of loyalty to U.S. flag, repeated by class at beginning of day in some elementary and secondary schools

Project Head Start government program to help disadvantaged children

prom formal dance, esp. at high school

PTA **P**arent-**T**eacher **A**ssociation

recess brief suspension of studies for exercise and recreation

reunion gathering of alumni to commemorate graduation

roommate person sharing one's dormitory room

rush recruiting drive by fraternity or sorority

schoolbag case for carrying books and supplies

school bus vehicle that picks up and delivers children to and from school

school prayer brief prayer recited at beginning of day in some schools, but banned in others

show and tell period in elementary school during which students describe or display things of interest to class

sorority selective women's social organization at college, usu. with its own residence

student government organization of students elected as decision-making body on student affairs

student newspaper student-run journal of campus affairs

student union college building devoted to extracurricular student activities; center of student affairs; union

teach-in lengthy meeting on college campus for debate of controversial issues

union student union

varsity athletic team representing school or college in contests against other schools

work-study program program that offers high school or college students work experience and income in addition to schooling

yearbook annual publication that reviews year's activities and lists all students or all graduating students in high school or college

PART FIVE
ARTS AND LEISURE

CHAPTER FOURTEEN
FINE ARTS AND LITERATURE

Schools and Styles of Fine Art

abstract art nonrepresentational and nonfigurative style emphasizing formal values over representation of subject matter

abstract expressionism nonrepresentational style emphasizing emotion, strong color, and giving primacy to the act of painting (mid-20th c.)

academic art officially sanctioned art; traditional art, emphasizing grand themes and a rational approach to form and content

action painting active, aggressive methods of applying paint; tachism (U.S., mid-20th c.)

aestheticism movement characterized by eclectic search for beauty and interest in Japanese and classical art (U.S. and Britain, late 19th c.)

analytical cubism fragmented, multifaceted, and simultaneous depiction of a subject in several planes (early 20th c.)

antiart self-conscious, nihilistic break with traditional art forms and content (late 20th c.)

archaism use of old styles in contemporary art

art brut direct, primitive style, as found in the art of children or the mentally disturbed (France, 20th c.)

art deco style characterized by repetitive, ornamental, and highly finished curvilinear and geometric designs, esp. in synthetic materials such as plastics (1920's-1930's)

art nouveau decorative style emphasizing fluid, biomorphic lines and swirling motifs (late 19th c.)

ashcan school antiacademic, realistic depiction of the grimmer aspects of everyday life (U.S., early 20th c.)

avant-garde innovative art in advance of popular ideas and images, characterized by unorthodox and experimental methods

Barbizon School style emphasizing idyllic landscapes and nature (France, 19th c.)

baroque emotional, dramatic style, anticlassical in form and spirit (late 16th-18th c.)

Bauhaus school emphasizing the functional and geometric by incorporating craft elements in design (early 20th c.)

Blaue Reiter *German.* expressionist group; Blue Rider School (early 20th c.)

Brucke expressionist group (Germany, early 20th c.)

Byzantine (*adj*) designating a style with Oriental and Occidental elements and strong religious content (2nd-13th c.)

cave art prehistoric paintings and engravings on Paleolithic-era cave walls

classical style with emphasis on symmetry, proportion, and harmony of line and form (ancient Greece and Rome)

cloissonism style with flat colors, black-outlined forms, and a lack of modeling; synthetism (France, 19th c.)

colorfield (*adj*) characteristic of abstract, minimal styles without representation, line, form, or modeling, in which color is the sole element (mid-20th c.)

computer art electronically produced images displayed on video screens (late 20th c.)

conceptual art avant-garde, idea-oriented style with emphasis on performance, theory and criticism, and attitude (late 20th c.)

concrete art realism, opposed to abstract art (early 20th c.)

constructivism style with geometric abstraction and emphasis on three-dimensionality (Russia, early 20th c.)

cubism departure from traditional, naturalistic view of reality, emphasizing multifaceted, simultaneous views of subject and distorted perspectives (early 20th c.)

dada style with antirational approach and nihilistic, absurdist, and incongruous themes (1915-1925)

decadent art style with artificial, neurotic, sometimes bizarre themes (late 19th c.)

de Stijl school of art characterized by minimalism, geometric abstraction, and use of primary colors; neoplasticism (Netherlands, early 20th c.)

distressed art style utilizing materials, often found materials, that are abused or battered by the artist (late 1980's)

divisionism neo-impressionism

earthwork artistic work consisting of large-scale alteration or modification of area of land or artist's installation of soil and rock in display space; aboriginal, nonpermanent paintings done in dirt

expressionism style emphasizing emotional expression, strong color and composition, and a distorted, theatrical treatment of image (early 20th c.)

fantastic realism highly imaginative, magical subject matter rendered with academic, realistic technique (Austria, mid-20th c.)

Fauvism style with brilliant, unrestrained color and offhand approach to composition (France, early 20th c.)

fin de siècle *French.* sophisticated stylization (late 19th c.)

folk art any untrained, nonacademic, or unschooled style

Fontainebleau School style emphasizing the elegant and decorative (France, 16th c.)

funk art combination of painting and sculpture, deliberately messy and rough, often humorously depicting provocative or kitsch subjects (U.S., mid-20th c.)

futurism style glorifying modern technology, speed, and the machine age (Italy, early 20th c.)

Gothic style emphasizing Christian imagery, brilliant color, and strong verticality in composition (12th-16th c.)

grand manner academic painting style with adherence to traditional, often noble themes and reliance on formal rules of depiction

hard-edge (*adj*) characteristic of a style with geometric abstraction, a flat picture plane, perfection of surface, and graphic precision (U.S., mid-20th c.)

Hellenic (*adj*) of the classical style of Greek antiquity (8th-4th c. B.C.)

Hellenistic (*adj*) of the post-classical Greek style before the Roman conquest (4th-2nd c. B.C.)

Hudson River school group of American painters whose style was characterized by idyllic landscapes, esp. of the Hudson River area (19th c.)

hyperrealism extension of photorealism in which depiction of subject is indistinguishable from reality (late 20th c.)

Impressionism style emphasizing the depiction of light and its effects, with the act of seeing as its primary subject (France, 19th c.)

international style style with detailed depiction of Christian subjects and Gothic verticality in composition (14th c.)

intisme style with intimate interior scenes of domestic life (France, late 19th c.)

Italianate (*adj*) conforming to the style of the Italian Renaissance masters

Jugendstil art nouveau (Germany, early 20th c.)

Kamakura (*adj*) denoting high classical period (Japan, 13th-15th c.)

kinetic art art marked by incorporation of painted and sculpted mechanical parts into art piece that moves or creates the impression of movement (mid-20th c.)

light art art characterized by incorporation of steadily beaming or blinking electrical and neon lights (mid-20th c.)

lyrical abstraction nonfigurative, expressionistic, poetic style, lighter than abstract art in tone and theme (mid-20th c.)

Mannerism anticlassical style characterized by dramatic gestures and poses of figures, intense color, and complex perspective (16th c.)

merz collage style using junk or found objects (early 20th c.)

metaphysical painting pittura metafisica

Ming (*adj*) characteristic of a highly academic classicism, esp. in porcelains (China, 14th-17th c.)

minimal art abstract, simple, reductionist style with absence of all but basic formal elements and primary colors (U.S., mid-20th c.)

modernism style that breaks with traditional art forms and searches for new modes of expression (early 20th c.)

Mogul school Islamic art style (India, 16th-19th c.)

Nabis style with emphasis on painter's personal vision (France, late 19th c.)

naturalism style emphasizing the depiction of the actual appearance of nature and the visible world

neoclassicism style modeled after proportion and restraint of Greek and Roman classical antiquity (late 18th-early 19th c.)

neo-expressionism style using expressionistic emotionalism in post-expressionist era (mid-20th c.)

neo-impressionism style with emphasis on the scientific application of the optical effects of light and color (France, late 19th c.); divisionism

neoplasticism de Stijl

neue wilde new wave (Germany, late 20th c.)

new objectivity style with detailed, realistic depictions emphasized over expressionist values (Germany, early 20th c.)

new secession style modeled on the Post-Impressionist sensibility of form, content, and color (Germany, early 20th c.)

new wave combination of cartoon, graffiti, and performance art in a minimalist, unsophisticated style (late 20th c.)

New York school abstract expressionism practiced by artists in New York City that emphasized the emotional, dramatic, and heroic in scale and theme (mid-20th c.)

nonobjective (*adj*) characteristic of a style in which emotional, formal values are emphasized over representation of objects (20th c.)

nouveau realisme style characterized by a return to realistic forms in an abstract era (France, mid-20th c.)

op art style with graphic abstraction and pattern-oriented optical effects (mid-20th c.)

Orphism geometric, cubist-derived style using a broad color spectrum (early 20th c.); synchromism

performance art use of paintings, sculpture, and video in live theatrical performance by artist (late 20th c.)

photorealism style emphasizing the meticulously realistic depiction of banal contemporary subjects, esp. suburban, snapshotlike scenes (mid-20th c.)

pittura metafisica style with mysterious, symbolic, metaphysical subject matter; metaphysical painting (Italy, early 20th c.)

plein-air (*adj*) pertaining to a style of painting that represents luminous effects of natural light and open-air atmosphere as contrasted with artificial light and the atmosphere of work produced in a studio (France, 19th c.)

pointillism neo-impressionism employing tiny, closely spaced points of color that blend to produce a luminous quality (France late 19th c.)

pop art style-making use of images from popular culture and commerce, often reproduced exactly (mid-20th c.)

Post-Impressionism emotionally expressive, formally modern style with nontraditional approach to color and composition (late 19th-early 20th c.)

postmodernism style reflecting the exhaustion of modernist experimentation and a partial return to more traditional forms (late 20th c.)

postpainterly abstraction nongestural, nonrepresentational style with emphasis on clean, perfect surface (mid-20th c.)

pre-Columbian (*adj*) of or pertaining to native American art before the arrival of Columbus (pre-16th c.)

prehistoric (*adj*) pertaining to cave painting and other forms of Paleolithic art

pre-Raphaelite (*adj*) designating a style modeled on romanticized vision of medieval, pre-Renaissance styles (19th c.)

primitivism style with unsophisticated, pretechnological, simple approach to form and content

proletarian art social realism depicting working class life (early 20th c.)

Quattrocento art of Indian Renaissance (15th c.)

realism depiction of reality as it appears, without idealization or stylistic, imaginative distortion

Renaissance (*adj*) pertaining to humanistic art that is classical in form and content; (*n*) revival of aesthetics of classical antiquity (14th-17th c.)

representational (*adj*) designating art concerned with accurate, naturalistic depictions of reality

rococo style with ornamental, poetic, curvilinear forms and lyrical themes (18th c.)

Romanticism style characterized by an emotional, intuitive exaltation of nature over culture and imagination over realism (late 18th-early 19th c.)

seicento classical high Renaissance art (Italy, 17th c.)

social realism depiction of ordinary life as emblematic of social and political truths (20th c.)

suprematism style emphasizing geometric abstraction (Russia, early 20th c.)

surrealism style using subconscious mental activity as its subject matter, characterized by dreamlike, hallucinatory imagery (early 20th c.)

Symbolism movement that rejected realism and expressed subjective visions through evocative images (France, late 19th c.)

synchromism Orphism

synthetic cubism late cubism emphasizing surfaces, altered perspective, and often strong colors

synthetism cloissonism

tachism action painting

T'ang classical period (China, 7th-9th c.)

Tantra art mystical, diagrammatic, and symbolic art (Buddhist, Hindu)

tenebrism chiaroscuro style that depicted dramatic imagery in dark tones (17th c.)

verism fantastic, often disturbing subjects rendered with photographically accurate realism (Germany, early 20th c.)

video art use of filmed or videotaped material displayed alone or with other media (late 20th c.)

vorticism style characterized by abstract, geometric designs and energetic, machine-age themes (Britain, early 20th c.)

Yamato-e narrative painting style characterized by continuous illustrations executed on long scrolls (Japan, 12th-14th c.)

Painting Tools and Techniques

abstract (*adj*) designating reliance on pure form rather than representation of subject matter for effect

acetate color opaque, waterproof pigment

acrylic paint synthetic, fast-drying pigment

advancing color warm colors at red end of spectrum

aerial perspective type of perspective involving subject perceived from above by viewer

airbrush nozzled tube used to apply paint in spray form

alla prima completing oil painting in one sitting

aniline dye coal-tar dye used as paint pigment

appliqué application of foreign material to surface of painting for ornamentation

aquarelle transparent watercolor

aquatint etching of spaces rather than lines, producing tonal effect like wash or watercolor

architectonic (*adj*) controlled, linear, geometric in rendering

atelier artist's studio

base inert pigment used in manufacture of lakes

batik painting on wax-treated cloth

binder substance combining pigment particles into pliable, fluid medium

black glass small, convex black mirror for reducing landscape views, dulling color as compositional aid; Claude glass

brilliance radiance or intensity of color

brush bristles fixed on handle for applying paint or varnish: angular liner, bamboo, blender, bright, bulletin cutter, camel's hair, cutter, dabber, dagger striper, easel, fan blender, filbert, fitch, flat, highliner, lettering, limp, liner, mop, oval, poster, quill, red sable, round, script, shader, varnish, wash

brushwork artist's distinctive way of applying paint with brush

canvas woven fabric of linen, cotton, or hemp stretched on frame and used as painting surface; completed painting

cartoon full-size, preliminary painting or sketch for completed work

cerography painting using wax as pigment binder

chalk soft, white limestone, sometimes with color added, used in drawing

charcoal pencil made from chunk of soft, porous, black carbon

chiaroscuro technique of depicting light and dark tones to create an illusion of depth and modeling

chih-hua finger painting technique (China)

chinoiserie work patterned after Chinese art

chroma strength or purity of a color, measured by its departure from neutral color

chromolithograph colored picture printed from impressions made by a series of stone or metal plates, each in a different color

Claude glass black glass

coat single application of paint on surface

collage pasting together bits of found objects, newspaper, and cloth over other materials on a single surface

color paint, pigment, or dye that reflects light waves of a particular length

coloration color arrangement or manner in which colors are used in painting

complementary colors two colors at opposite points on color scale, such as red and green

composition aesthetically pleasing, harmonious, and effective arrangement of parts to form whole

construction paper heavy colored paper, esp. for cutouts

contrast use of striking differences, esp. in color or tone, between adjacent parts of painting

cool colors blue-green portion of spectrum

craquelure network of small cracks in painted or varnished surface of old painting

crayon small stick of chalk, colored wax, or charcoal used for drawing

crepe paper thin, crinkled paper

crosshatching shading technique that uses many parallel strokes

dab (*vb*) apply paint in light, quick strokes or dots

decoupage cutting out designs from paper or other material, mounting them on surface, and applying varnish or lacquer

designer's colors opaque watercolors

distemper water-base paint with glue binder; mix of powdered pigment and size

drawing picture, design, or sketch done with lines in pen or pencil; skill at using lines to depict something

drying oil oil painting medium that dries to form solid surface for pigment

easel vertical frame for supporting painting in progress

eclectic (*adj*) composed from disparate elements in many styles

emulsion liquid suspended in another liquid, esp. oil and varnish

enamel pigment mixed with varnish that dries to a hard, glossy finish

encaustic (*adj*) designating painting done with

pigment mixed with beeswax and blended with heat

ferrule metal tube clamping brush hairs to handle

figurative (*adj*) designating identifiable representation of human figure or object

finger paint water-soluble, nontoxic, creamy paint applied with fingers, esp. for children and crafts

finish fetish emphasis on high-gloss, perfectly and smoothly rendered surface

foreshortening technique of creating the illusion of a painted object projecting through the picture plane; use of linear perspective to depict three-dimensionality

forgery copy of an artwork, intended to pass as an original

framing designing and fashioning borders for paintings, usu. of wood, often ornamental

fresco technique of painting directly on a wet, plaster surface

fugitive color pigment with tendency to fade

gesso plaster of Paris used as white primer for painting surface, esp. canvas

gilding application of gold leaf to picture surface

glaze thin, translucent layer of color

golden section aesthetic formula expressed as ratio between two portions of a line, or two dimensions of a plane figure, in which lesser is to greater as greater is to sum of both

gold watercolor water-soluble gold in tablet form, for watercolor, illumination, or lettering

gouache opaque watercolor bound with gum

graphic art art and technique by which copies of an original design are printed, as from a plate or block

grisaille monochrome in primarily gray tints, esp. on glass, having appearance of relief

ground prepared painting surface

hachure hatching

hatching shading technique that uses parallel lines; hachure

highlight bright, light area emphasizing modeling

historiated (*adj*) having human or animal figure ornament

hue distinct qualities of a color that position it in the spectrum

iconography representation by images; study of such images

illumination decorative, esp. miniature, painting in books

impasto thick application of paint that forms an opaque relief surface

imprimatura painting surface prepared with a thin glaze of color

japan varnish mixed with pigment

lacquer protective, transparent, resinous liquid that dries to a glossy surface

lake pigment prepared with metallic compounds

limn (*vb*) represent in painting or drawing

line contour or shape of drawing

linear perspective type of perspective involving view perceived from in front of subject by viewer in arbitrarily fixed position

line drawing drawing done in lines only, showing gradations of tone through variations in width and density of lines

liver oil paint that has thickened into an insoluble, rubbery mass inside tube

long paint thin, watery paint

madder redroot used as pigment

mahlstick support piece for steadying painter's hand and brush while at work

malerisch (*adj*) *German.* painterly; emphasizing form over outline

mandorla halo of light on holy figure (Buddhist, Christian)

medium liquid in which pigment is mixed to form paint; type of paint or coloring matter used in painting

model person who poses for a drawing, painting, or sculpture

modeling technique of depicting three-dimensional objects on two-dimensional surface

monochromatic (*adj*) having a one-hued color scheme

monumental (*adj*) indicating scale, grandeur, and nobility of form or content

muller tool for grinding pigments

oeuvre *French.* entire body of an artist's work

oil paint pigment mixed with drying oil, esp. linseed oil

opalesce (*vb*) exhibit a play of colors

oxgall wetting agent used to improve pliability of water paints

paint pigment ground to a powder, then mixed with a liquid binding medium

painterly (*adj*) having qualities distinctive of painting, esp. rendering images in terms of color or tone rather than contour or line

painting art and technique of applying colored pigments and other materials to a flat surface, esp. stretched canvas, to depict an image or represent a feeling with consideration for composition, form, and color

palette handheld board for mixing paints

palette cup small container that clips onto palette to hold oil or water

palette knife thin, flexible blade for mixing and applying paint

pastel crayon made of color ground with chalk and compounded with gum water into paste, often of pale color

pastiche jumble of different styles

pentimento emergence of traces of oil paint underlayer as overlay dries to transparency

perspective system of realistically depicting three-dimensional objects or views onto two-dimensional, flat surfaces through convergent lines and planes; portrayal of objects in space

picture plane surface behind which a painting's subject is situated in space

pigment coloring matter mixed with binder to form paint

planes successive stages of depth within a painted image, foreground to background

polychromatic (*adj*) painted in many colors

poster paint opaque, water-base paint with gum or glue-size binder, sold in large jars, typically in bright colors

primary colors red, yellow, and blue, from which all other colors in spectrum can be mixed

proportion aesthetic relation of parts to whole

receding color cool color at blue end of spectrum

reducing glass double concave lens that reduces image seen through it

representational (*adj*) depicting recognizable objects, figures, or scenes

restoration repair of damaged or worn painting

rosin hard resin used as varnish ingredient

sand painting painting composed of colored sands spread on the ground

saturation degree of purity of a color; intensity of hue

scumbling brush technique that softens a painted surface by overlaying it with a light, irregular, textured, semiopaque color

secco painting on dry plaster on wall or ceiling

secondary colors orange, green, and purple, being those colors produced by mixing two of the primary colors

section d'or ideal proportion between the side of a square and a diagonal drawn inside the same square, giving a sense of design and harmony, based on golden section ratio

sfumato technique used to depict hazy, smoky shadows or outlines

sgraffito technique in which surface layer of paint is scratched through to reveal color beneath

shellac thin, clear varnish made from lac resin and alcohol

short paint thick paint

sinopis reddish brown pigment, esp. for drawings

size glue and water preparation for canvas

sizing process of applying a surface with size

sketch quick, preliminary drawing used as basis for painting

solvent liquid component of paint that evaporates to leave dried pigment on surface painted

spectrum series of colored bands arranged in order of respective wavelength from infrared to ultraviolet

stretcher backing frame for canvas

study detailed drawing or painting of a section of the planned work

taboret artist's chest with shelves and tabletop palette

tempera pigment mixed with water and an albuminous or gelatinous material, esp. egg yolk

tessera small tile or stone for mosaic illustration

texture characteristic visual and tactile quality of surface of work of art, resulting from manner in which materials are used

texture paint paint of heavy consistency and coarse grain consisting of gypsum and sand with binder, used for creating rough surfaces

thinner solvent used to dilute paint

tinctorial (*adj*) relating to colors, dyes, and stains

tint gradation of a color relative to the amount of white mixed into it

tone general coloration or balance of dark and light in a painting, creating harmony

tracing copy made by following lines as seen through transparent paper superimposed on original

traction cracking or fissuring of dry paint surface

trompe l'oeil extremely deft illusion in which a painted object appears real through depiction in fine detail

turpentine colorless, volatile oil used in paints and for cleaning brushes

underpainting preliminary coat of paint

value degree of lightness or darkness in a color

varnish protective film composed of resin dissolved in drying oil

wash thin coat of water-base paint

water-base paint pigment soluble in water; watercolor

watercolor pigment in binder of gum arabic, water, and glycerin; translucent stain of color on paper

Kinds of Paintings

altarpiece devotional image or shrine in church or temple

anastasis depiction of Christ harrowing hell

cabinet picture small easel painting

calathus bowl of fruits, in art symbolizing abundance; kalathos

capriccio depiction of fantastic architecture (18th c.)

cherub representation of a winged angel, or chubby child clothed in red, who supports the heavenly throne

cityscape depiction of an urban scene

contrapposto depiction of a strongly twisted human torso

deiesis depiction of Christ enthroned between Mary and St. John

diablerie depiction of hell and its inhabitants

diptych two-paneled altarpiece

dreamscape depiction of a fantasy world or figments of dreams

easel painting canvas painted at an easel, then framed and hung

ecce homo *Latin*. lit. behold the man; depiction of Christ in judgment before Pontius Pilate

ex-voto *Latin*. lit. out of a vow; image or painting giving thanks or left as offering to God

figure drawing of a human body and face

fusuma painting on a sliding screen (Japan)

genre realistic depiction of scenes from everyday domestic life

grotesque work combining animal, human, plant, and fantastical forms

hieratic (*adj*) designating a style characterized by prescribed religious content

history painting usu. academic depiction of scenes from mythology, history, or the Bible

icon image, esp. portrait

illuminated manuscript miniature painting used as decoration in a handwritten text; psalter

kakemono vertical scroll painting (Japan)

kalathos calathus

kwacho depiction of birds and flowers (Japan)

landscape depiction of natural landforms, sometimes allegorical

life drawing drawing of human figure, often nude

maesta depiction of Madonna and Child (Italy)

makemono horizontal scroll painting (Japan)

mandala schematized representation of the cosmos, usu. in form of concentric geometric shapes, in Oriental art

memento mori depiction of objects that are reminders of mortality

miniature very small painting

mosaic illustration composed of small, colored stones or tiles set into cement

mural large-scale painting, usu. on a wall or ceiling

namban portrait of foreigners, esp. Europeans (Japan)

nature morte *French*. lit. dead nature; still life

nocturne night scene

nude undraped human figure, sometimes allegorical

panel painting painting supported on freestanding framework, as distinct from a mural or fresco

pantocrator depiction of Christ as universal ruler (Byzantine)

pastoral (*adj*) designating painting that depicts rural life, often in idealized manner

pictograph picture symbolizing an idea or object, used as early form of writing

Pietà depiction of the Virgin Mary mourning over the dead Christ

polyptych altarpiece with more than three panels

portrait depiction of a person, esp. the face

psalter illuminated manuscript

putto stylized, decorative depiction of nude male child, often winged

rotulus illuminated manuscript in scroll form

seascape depiction of scene at sea

self-portrait depiction of artist's own face

silhouette side view of subject, esp. figure or head, filled in with black

stick figure depiction of human figure as single lines with circle for head

still life realistic depiction of inanimate objects, esp. flowers, fruit, or domestic items; nature morte

tanka scroll painting of a deity (Tibetan Buddhism)

tondo circular picture

triptych three-paneled altarpiece

triskelion figure composed of three curved or bent arms, legs, or branches radiating from the center

uchiwa-ye fan-shaped picture (Japan)

ukiyo-e depiction of scenes from everyday life (Japan)

vanitas still life representing mortality

vignette small, decorative painting used at intervals in a book

wall painting mural painted directly on wall

wen-jen-hua scholarly, literary painting (China)

Display of Art

artist's rep person responsible for selling artist's work on commission or arranging shows

auction showing of valuable artwork offered for sale to highest bidder

collector person who owns and displays artwork in his or her home

cooperative gallery noncommercial gallery run by artists

curator person in charge of a museum and the objects in it

docent tour guide at museum

gallery building devoted to exhibition and sale of artworks

group show showing of works by more than one artist

hanging aesthetic placement of paintings on wall, using considerations of light, shadow, and height

juried show show for which works are selected by panel of judges

museum large institution devoted to the acquisition, study, care, and permanent exhibition of works of art

opening first day of show

patron individual who supports the arts and artists

portfolio large, flat case for carrying drawings or paintings

private collection large number of valuable artworks owned by individual, sometimes lent out for public showing

retrospective show covering several phases in artist's career

show display of artworks in gallery or museum for specific length of time

studio artist's workroom, also used for casual display of works

vernissage varnishing day; the day before an opening, used for last-minute touch-up of paintings

---

SCULPTURE

Types of Sculpture
Sculpture Tools and Techniques

See also: *Chap. 5: Tools and Hardware; Chap. 14: Painting; Chap. 16: Architecture; Crafts*

Types of Sculpture

akrolith statue made of two materials, esp. with wooden body and stone head

anaglyph ornament sculptured or embossed in low relief

assemblage sculptural collage of unrelated parts, materials, or objects

bas-relief sculpture projecting less than half its depth from matrix; low relief

bust sculpture of upper part of body, esp. head and shoulders

collage composition of seemingly unrelated parts, materials, or objects

colossal extremely large-scale sculpture, larger than heroic

discobolus statue of athlete about to toss discus (ancient Greece)

heroic sculptural scale larger than life-size

high relief sculpture projecting more than halfway out from matrix

ice sculpture carving made from ice block in freezing environment

installation placing of sculptures and other objects in physical environment or room, which becomes part of piece

low relief bas-relief

mezzo-relievo sculpture projecting half its depth from matrix

mobile freely moving, three-dimensional sculpture made of several counterbalanced objects suspended at different levels and moving in the air

relief sculpture attached to a matrix or flat background, not freestanding

sculpture in the round freestanding piece with no supporting backing or matrix

stabile abstract sculpture constructed of stationary parts attached to fixed supports

statuary groups of statues; art of making statues

statue three-dimensional sculpture of human or animal form

statuette small statue

totem carved emblem, esp. animal or plant form

video sculpture three-dimensional piece incorporating prerecorded videotape

wax sculpture carving in wax

wood sculpture carving and assembling in wood

Sculpture Tools and Techniques

acrylic resin thermoplastic polymer used in making molded plastic

alabaster translucent, marblelike stone for carving

alloy mixture of two or more metals or a metal and nonmetal, such as bronze or brass

---

annealing softening of hammer-hardened metal by heating and gradual cooling

anodize (*vb*) coat metal with protective oxide film by electrolysis

armature framework used to support sculpture in modeling process

banker sculptor's workbench for dressing stones

base lowest part of sculpture, often separate part on which it rests

boss projecting volume to be carved or cut

boucharde toothed, metal, stone-carving hammer

brazing method of joining metals; coating with brass or giving brasslike appearance

bronze alloy of copper and tin for casting statuary

bronzing process of coloring a plaster cast to make it appear like bronze

burnishing rubbing or polishing to a high gloss

bush chisel toothed, stone-carving hand tool

carving cutting away of wood or stone to create three-dimensional forms, as opposed to modeling

casing plaster reinforcing shell used to hold flexible, negative mass

casting reproduction technique using a mold

casting plaster white plaster of Paris

cavo-relievo relief carving within recessed surface, in which highest point is flush with background stone

charge (*vb*) fill negative mold with positive material

chase (*vb*) finish metal surface

chisel sharp, metal carving tool: bush, claw, oval, pointed, or T-shape

chryselephantine (*adj*) covered with ivory and gold, esp. antique Greek statuary

cire perdue lost-wax process

coil method technique of construction with clay coils

core solid, internal portion of mold in metal casting

damascene decorative inlay of one metal on another

dead stone stone ruined by exposure to weather

drill tool for boring holes in wood, metal, or stone

electrum alloy of gold and silver for fine sculptural details

emboss (*vb*) decorate with low relief design

fabricate (*vb*) assemble parts into sculptural whole

file abrasive metal tool for smoothing and shaping

filler inert ingredients used to add bulk to mixture

foundry process of melting, casting, or molding metals

galvanize (*vb*) add zinc plating to metal

ganosis application of colored wax to stone sculpture to dull glare during carving

goggles transparent, protective eye coverings, esp. used when welding metal

gouge curved chisel

gradine toothed chisel

grounding finely polished marble

hammer malletlike tool for applying force to chisel

lathe device for shaping a piece by holding it against an abrading or cutting tool

lost-wax process technique for casting metal, in which modeled wax form is melted away and space between core and outer mold is filled with molten metal such as bronze

mallet cylindrical wooden block on handle

mantle clay mold around a wax model

maquette small, preliminary model of finished work

marble very hard limestone rock used as classic carving material

marmoreal (*adj*) resembling marble or marble statue

matrix base material to be carved

modeling building up of three-dimensional form, as opposed to carving

mold form for making cast of sculptural form

moulage process of making a mold, esp. with plaster of Paris

negative shell-like mold or impression into which casting material is poured or pressed

niello deep-black alloy of sulfur and lead or copper for decorative inlays on metal

origami art of folding paper to depict objects (Japan)

papier-mâché shredded paper soaked in water and glue to form pulpy medium

paraffin colorless, odorless, waxy hydrocarbon used for casting

patina usu. green film on surface of old bronze, caused by exposure to atmosphere or chemicals

pedestal base or stand for sculpture, esp. bust

peen wedgelike or spherical striking surface of hammerhead, used to shape material

pick pointed, metal hammer for removing large areas of stone

piece mold negative made in several parts to preserve original and permit many positive castings

plaster of Paris mixture of calcined gypsum with water to form quick-setting paste used for casts, moldings, and statuary

plastic (*adj*) capable of being shaped, molded, cast, or pressed into different shapes; (*n*) synthetic material with malleable quality

Plasticine *Trademark.* oil-base modeling paste used instead of clay or wax

plasticity flexible or shapable quality of a material

pointing system of copying from three-dimensional model by drilling holes to required depths

pointing device apparatus that marks or drills into a sculpture to set proportionate volumes in order to make copies on any scale

polychromy use of many colors, esp. on statuary

positive cast formed by filling negative mold with casting material

quarry excavation site for marble or stone

quenching quick-cooling of heated metal by immersion in brine, oil, or water

rasp sharply toothed carving and finishing tool

repoussé process of hammering metal into decorative forms in relief

sandblasting etching glass, or cleaning and grinding metal or stone surface, by application of sand carried at high speed by air or steam

sander hand or power tool for smoothing surfaces

sand molding coating the inside of a mold with sand to prevent material from sticking

sculpture art and technique of carving, molding, or welding plastic or hard materials into three-dimensional works of art

site-specific (*adj*) designating a sculpture which is created, designed, or selected for a specific location

slush casting casting of hollow, metal shape by pouring metal into mold and immediately pouring it out, leaving thin layer that hardens on walls of mold

soapstone soft, easily carved stone

spall chip or splinter broken from stone in carving

stainless steel rust-resistant steel alloy with high luster

stereotomy technique of cutting solids to form geometric shapes

stone mass of rock broken off from its matrix rock bed

stone carving cutting away of stone from a block to form three-dimensional shape

temper (*vb*) achieve desired consistency or hardness by mixing or treating, esp. by suddenly cooling heated metal

term pedestal supporting a bust or merging into a biomorphic shape

torch welding and heating tool

turn (*vb*) work on a lathe

vent passage in mold through which gases escape during casting

waste mold negative mold that must be destroyed to free positive cast

welding process of uniting metals by fusing them when molten or pressing them together when soft

LITERATURE
Schools, Styles, and Forms
Devices, Techniques, and Elements
Books and Pages
Literary Characters and Practitioners

See also: *Chap. 11: Publishing and the Press; Chap. 15: Theater; Chap. 18: Grammar, Phonetics, and Linguistics; Rhetoric and Figures of Speech*

Schools, Styles, and Forms

abstract poetry poetry emphasizing use of sound rather than the meaning of words to convey emotional tone

accentual verse poetry based on number of accents rather than duration of sounds or syllabic recurrence

aestheticism literary movement emphasizing aesthetic values over social and moral values (19th c.)

Amerind written and oral literary tradition of native American Indians

angry young man one of a group of writers whose works were characterized by an iconoclastic style reflecting bitter dissatisfaction with traditional society (Britain, mid-20th c.)

animal epic medieval narrative form using animal characters

antinovel piece of prose fiction lacking some elements of novel structure, such as plot or character development

Apollonian (*adj*) emphasizing formal elements and rationality

apologue allegorical fable typically containing a moral

Attic (*adj*) emphasizing clear, lucid, elegant prose

autobiography account of author's own life; memoirs

avant-garde innovative style that challenges traditional and established forms

ballad poem that tells a story, often meant to be performed out loud

ballad stanza four-line stanza of iambic tetrameter with second and fourth lines rhymed

baroque style emphasizing dramatic or distorted elements presented in classical ordered form (17th–18th c.)

Beat Generation rebellious style emphasizing colloquial language and nonconformist values (U.S., 1950's)

belles-lettres literature, esp. with creative and artistic style and content; letters

Bildungsroman novel narrating story of young person's coming of age and development

biography narrative of another person's life

Bloomsbury group group of writers and intellectuals, including Virginia Woolf and John Maynard Keynes, associated with Bloomsbury district in London (1920's)

Byronic (*adj*) characterized by romantic melancholy and melodrama, as in the works of Lord Byron

Celtic Renaissance revival of Gaelic language and literature (late 19th–early 20th c.)

chanson song; poem to be sung

chanson de geste song of great deeds; epic poem

chronicle medieval and Renaissance historical writing

classical (*adj*) pertaining to a style with great scope, depth, clarity, and elegance; pertaining to Greek and Roman classics

classicism adherence to classical principles, esp. in contrast with Romanticism (19th c.)

comedy literary and dramatic form emphasizing humor, treating events lightly or satirically, and having a happy ending

comedy of intrigue comic style emphasizing plot and situation more than characterization

comedy of manners comic style emphasizing use of manners and conventions of sophisticated society

comedy of morals comic style emphasizing ridicule of bad moral practices, aiming to instruct in moral improvement

comic relief humorous episode or scene intended as contrast in serious drama or literary work, often to emphasize primary action

concrete poetry unconventional, graphic arrangement of letters, words, and symbols to convey meaning

confession autobiography addressing very private topics

courtly love stylized code of conduct between lovers, esp. as described in medieval literature

criticism analysis and evaluation of literary works

cyberpunk science fiction characterized by violence, computer technology, and nihilism (1980's)

cycle collection of poems or narratives related by common subject matter, usu. a central character

dada literary and dramatic artistic movement emphasizing nihilism, irrationality, absurdism, and sometimes violent opposition to conventional values (Europe, 1915-25)

decadent member of literary and artistic movement emphasizing aesthetic values of art over nature and freedom from moral restraints (late 19th c.)

deconstruction literary analysis based on rejection of notion of hierarchy and belief that nature of language and usage prevents any text from having a fixed, coherent meaning that represents reality (mid-20th c.)

detective story literary form with crime and the apprehension of criminals as its subject

diary daily journal of personal activities and reflections

dime novel cheap paperback fiction, esp. detective story or melodrama; penny dreadful

drama composition in verse or prose, usu. for theatrical performance, that portrays character through story involving conflicts in which emotions are expressed through dialogue and action

eclogue pastoral poem

elegy song, poem, or speech lamenting one who is dead; poem in elegiac couplets

Elizabethan (*adj*) of or pertaining to drama and literature of the reign of Elizabeth I of England, including the works of Shakespeare (late 16th c.)

epic literary work recounting deeds of legendary hero

epic poem traditional form of long narrative poem recounting deeds of legendary hero

epigram terse, witty, often paradoxical saying, often in form of concise poem with ingenious ending

epistle letter, esp. formal or elegant one

epistolary novel novel written in the form of letters

epithalamium song or poem honoring bride and groom

epos epic poetry; group of poems, transmitted orally, concerned with facets of a common epic theme

erotica literary works devoted to sexual themes

essay brief, analytic, interpretive prose composition dealing, often formally, with a single subject from a subjective viewpoint

exemplum anecdote or short narrative with moral point, esp. used to sustain argument

Expressionism depiction by nonnaturalistic means of subconscious thoughts, subjective realities of characters, and the struggle of abstract forces (20th c.)

fable narration demonstrating a useful truth, esp. in which animals speak as humans; legendary, supernatural tale

fabulism writing of fables

faction *Informal.* novel or other writing that treats real events and people as if fictional; roman à clef

fairy tale story about fairies or other magical creatures, usu. for children

fantasy fiction with strange or otherworldly settings or grotesque characters

farce light, dramatic composition with improbable plot, broad satirical comedy

festschrift collection of learned essays by students and colleagues honoring a scholar on a special occasion

fiction invented or imagined story

fin de siècle *French.* style characteristic of the end of the 19th century, esp. fashionably sophisticated despair

Gongorism style characterized by ornate language and artificial diction

Gothic fiction with emphasis on horror and macabre, mysterious, or violent events, often in desolate, remote settings

graveyard school melancholy, romantically gloomy style (18th c.)

grotesque fanciful, fantastic, and bizarre representations of human life and events (19th-20th c.)

Grub Street literary hacks collectively (18th c.)

haiku unrhymed verse form with 17 syllables, usu. in three lines (Japan)

heroic (*adj*) dealing with or describing the deeds and attributes of heroes

high comedy comedy that employs subtle characterizations and witty language, often to satirize upper class lifestyles

historical novel fictional account of historical events or story of fictional characters and events in historical setting

idyll short lyrical poem or prose composition describing pastoral scenes or any charming episode of everyday life

Jacobean (*adj*) of or pertaining to the literary style characteristic of the age of James I of England (early 17th c.)

jeremiad prolonged lamentation or complaint

journal daily record of experiences and reflections, esp. for private use

juvenilia writings produced in an author's youth

kaleyard school school of writers who described homely life in Scotland (late 19th c.)

lampoon harsh satire usu. directed against an individual

letter personal, written message directed to a person or organization

letters literature; belles-lettres

limerick humorous verse rhymed aabba, usu. with a's of three anapestic feet and b's of two anapestic feet

literature writings in which ideas of permanent or universal interest are expressed through artistic use of forms such as novels, poetry, plays, histories, biographies, or essays

Lost Generation American writers living in post-World War I Europe

low comedy often farcical comedy of action with simple characters, burlesque, and horseplay

lyric poetry poems expressing intense personal emotion

masque short, allegorical drama performed by masked actors (16th-17th c.)

melic (*adj*) pertaining to an elaborate form of lyric poetry (ancient Greece)

melodrama work of extravagant theatricality, unlikely plot, and overwrought and simplistic characterizations

memoir record of events written by person having intimate knowledge of them; biography or biographical sketch

memoirs autobiography; recounting of one's life and experiences

minimalism style characterized by spare, simple, often impersonal and repetitive tone (mid-20th c.)

miracle play medieval drama based on the life of a saint or martyr

missive letter, usu. formal or official

mock-heroic (*adj*) of or pertaining to a form of satire in which trivial subjects, characters, and events are treated in the heroic style

modernism self-conscious break with past and search for new forms of expression (early 20th c.)

monograph scholarly work on some specific subject

mystery fiction dealing with the solution of a crime or the unraveling of secrets

mystery play medieval drama based on Scriptural incidents

myth legend or traditional narrative, often based in part on historical events, that reveals human behavior and natural phenomena by its symbolism

naturalism literature based on scientific observation of life, without idealization

New Criticism style of literary criticism emphasizing close textual analysis (mid-20th c.)

New Humanism works that reflect a belief in moderation, dignity, permanent values, and dualistic existence (20th c.)

nonfiction prose composition dealing with noninvented, nonimagined subject

novel extended fictional prose narrative, usu. involving a central character: novel of character, of incident, of manners, of sensibility, of the soil, or psychological novel

novelette brief novel or long short story

novella brief novel with compact plot

nursery rhyme short, simple, traditional rhymed poem or song for very young children

occasional verse poetry created for particular occasion

ode lyric poem marked by exalted feeling, varying line length, and complexity of form

Parnassian (*adj*) denoting school of poets who emphasized form over emotion (France, late 19th c.)

parody composition that imitates the style of another author or work for comic effect

pasquinade publicly posted lampoon or satire

pastel short, light prose sketch

pastiche literary work that borrows from or mimics the style of one or more sources

penny dreadful *Chiefly Brit.* dime novel

Petrarchan sonnet sonnet consisting of an octave with the rhymed scheme abbaabba and a sestet in one of several rhyme schemes, such as cdecde or cdcdcd

picaresque novel episodic adventures of usu. roguish protagonist

poem verse composition

poetry sometimes rhymed, usu. rhythmic writing with concentrated imagery in language selected to create an emotional response to its sound and sense; metrical writing; verse

polemic art of disputation; an argument

polyphonic prose rhythmic prose containing many poetic devices

postmodernism any of various reactions to modernist explorations and austere forms, often entailing some return to past forms, minimalism, fantasy, complexity, and pessimism

poststructuralism any of various theories of literary criticism, such as deconstruction, that hold that there is no single true reading of a text

potboiler usu. inferior work written for profit, esp. fiction

prose unrhymed, nonmetrical writing

prosody system or style of versification and metrical structure; science and art of versification

prothalamion song or poem written to celebrate a marriage

psychobiography biography that stresses childhood trauma or other bases for the unconscious motives of its subject

psychological novel novel delving deeply into characters' feelings and motivations

quantitative verse poetry based on temporal quantity or duration of sounds

Rabelaisian (*adj*) characterized by coarse, broad humor, suggestive of the work of François Rabelais

realism nonidealized fidelity to accurate literary representation of real or everyday life

Renaissance (*adj*) designating literature marked by the humanistic revival of classical influence in Europe (14th-17th c.)

Restoration comedy farcical comedies of manners written in the period following the Restoration of Charles II to the English throne (17th c.)

rhyme verse composition that rhymes

roman *French.* novel

roman à clef *French.* novel depicting real persons and actual events under fictional names

roman-fleuve *French.* saga

Romanticism period and style emphasizing emotional and imaginative intensity (19th c.)

rondeau verse based on two rhyme sounds, composed of ten or thirteen lines in three stanzas, in which the opening words of the first stanza are used as a refrain after the second and third stanzas

rondel short poem, usu. of fourteen lines on two rhymes, of which four are made up of the initial couplet repeated in the middle and at the end

saga heroic narrative about historic or legendary figures; lengthy, multigenerational, fictional narrative; roman-fleuve

satire work holding up human vices and follies to ridicule; ironic, witty work exposing or discrediting vice or folly

science fiction stories based on impact of actual, imagined, or potential science, usu. set in future or on other planets

semiotics study and analysis of the relationship of signs and symbols, esp. in language

serial work appearing in installments

Shakespearean sonnet sonnet having the rhyme scheme abab, cbcd, efef, gg, and consisting of three quatrains and one couplet

short short story highly condensed work of prose fiction

short story compact, fictional narrative with few characters, unified effect, and often more mood than plot

sirvente medieval poem or song, either heroic or satirical, composed by a troubadour

sketch short, usu. descriptive composition, intentionally slight, discursive in style, and familiar in tone

soap opera serialized melodrama for TV or radio

socialist realism state-approved literary style that glorifies worker's life in socialist country

song short musical composition with lyrics

sonnet fixed verse form of fourteen lines, usu. in iambic pentameter with set rhyming pattern, often ending in rhymed couplet

speech public address or discourse

Sturm und Drang German literature characterized by rousing action and high emotionalism, often featuring individual revolt against society (18th c.)

surrealism style emphasizing production of fantastic, incongruous imagery through unnatural juxtapositions (1920's)

Symbolism French reaction to realism, exalting symbolic representation over actuality (late 19th c.)

tanka five-line poem consisting of 31 syllables (Japan)

technothriller action-suspense novel featuring use of sophisticated technology, esp. weapons systems

tetralogy literary composition in four connected parts

textual criticism close analysis of a literary work, often aiming to determine author's original text

thriller gripping work with intrigue, adventure, and suspense

tongue twister amusing phrase, line, or verse that is difficult to pronounce due to a succession of similar consonantal sounds

tragedy serious narrative or drama having a sad or disastrous ending; in ancient drama, downfall of a great person due to a tragic flaw or fate

tragicomedy drama blending tragedy and comedy

translation rendering of literary work from one language into another

trilogy literary work in three connected parts

true life realistic narrative or drama, esp. of everyday life

verse poetry; metrical writing in general

versification act of composing verses; particular metrical structure or style; prosody

Victorian (*adj*) denoting writing often associated with strict moral standards and conduct in Britain during reign of Queen Victoria (late 19th c.)

vita brief, autobiographical sketch

western simple, action-packed narrative set in old American West, usu. involving cowboys

whodunit *Informal.* mystery story

Devices, Techniques, and Elements

agon dispute or debate between chorus and characters in classic Greek tragedy

Alexandrine verse with six iambic feet; iambic hexameter

allegory extended metaphor using objects, characters, and events to represent larger meanings

alliteration repetition of initial sound in two or more consecutive words

allusion figure of speech employing reference to famous or identifiable person, place, event, or literary passage

ambiguity expression of an idea in words that may be interpreted in more than one way

amphigory nonsense verse or composition

amplification figure of speech using restatement for emphasis

ana anecdotes, sayings, or literary curiosities about a particular subject

analects literary fragments or passages

analogy comparison of apparently or largely dissimilar objects to reveal similarities

anapest metrical verse foot with two short or unstressed syllables followed by one long or stressed syllable

anecdote brief narrative describing a particular interesting event or person

anticlimax narrative moment involving a small or trivial resolution in place of the expected larger and more significant resolution

antiphrasis irony; use of word or description to convey the opposite of its normal or literal meaning

antithesis figure of speech using emphatically contrasting images or words

arsis lighter, shorter part of poetic foot in quantitative verse; accented, longer part of poetic foot in accentual verse

assonance juxtaposition of similar sounds without actually rhyming, esp. vowels

atmosphere dominant mood or tone of a work

bathos unsuccessful attempt at profundity, resulting in ridiculous or humorous effect

bibliotics analysis of handwriting to authenticate a document or determine its authorship

blank verse unrhymed verse; unrhymed iambic pentameter, often with each second line accented

bombast inflated, extravagant expression

bowdlerize (*vb*) censor or abridge by cutting offensive sections

bucolic (*adj*) pertaining to descriptions of an idyllic, rural life

cacophony harsh, discordant sounds in recited poetry

cadence measured, rhythmic emphasis of language

caesura break in poetic rhythm

canto one of the main divisions of a long poem

caricature description employing extreme and comic exaggeration

carmen figuraturum poem printed to form the physical shape of its subject matter

character convincing, imaginary personality developed and realized in fiction

characterization creation, presentation, and exposition of personalities in literature

character sketch brief essay or story that describes a person

clerihew light verse quatrain rhyming aabb, usu. dealing with person named in first line

cliche timeworn and commonplace expression; trite description

climax culmination of dramatic narrative, often turning point in story

coda concluding or summary part of literary work

cognomen distinguishing name or epithet

collate (*vb*) compare two texts or editions

colloquialism informal usage of word or phrase, usu. not acceptable in formal use

common meter four-line stanza with lines one and three in iambic tetrameter, lines two and four in iambic trimeter

complaint lyric poem on subject of unrequited love or sadness

conceit dramatic, witty, ingenious metaphor or analogy

conflict struggle or contrast of opposing forces in plot

controlling image image or idea forming basic nature or structure of work

couplet two rhyming lines of verse

dactyl metrical foot with one long or stressed syllable followed by two short or unstressed syllables

dead metaphor overused figure of speech drained of its original power to evoke analogy

denouement final unfolding of plot; resolution or outcome

device word pattern, figure of speech, or dramatic convention used to evoke desired effect in literary work

diatribe bitter argument, accusation, or harangue

digression insertion of material unrelated to main body of work

dipody prosodic measure or unit of two feet

dithyramb short poem or chant in wild, irregular strain

ditty short, simple, or whimsical lyric

doggerel trivial or bad poetry

double rhyme rhyme consisting of two syllables of which the second is unstressed

effect language designed to produce distinctive, desired impression

elegiac couplet of dactylic hexameters with second lacking arsis in third and sixth feet

elision omission of unstressed vowel or syllable to achieve metrical uniformity

encomium expression of enthusiastic praise

epilogue concluding section after main body of work

epithet characterizing word or phrase used with or in place of name, esp. a disparaging or abusive term

euphony pleasantness of sounds in recited poetry

euphuism elegant Elizabethan style characterized by the frequent use of antithesis, alliteration, and mythological simile

exegesis critical interpretation of text

explication de texte *French.* close analysis of a literary text with focus on language, style, content, and textual interrelationships

exposition dialogue or descriptive material intended to convey information or background or to explain something

eye dialect use of misspellings to convey

character's poor education or humorous dialectal pronunciations

falling rhythm stress occurring on first syllable of each foot

fantasy fanciful design or imaginative creation

feminine rhyme rhyme of two or three syllables of which only the first syllable is stressed

figurative language metaphorical expression abounding in figures of speech

flashback narrative device by which an event that takes place outside the narrative framework is brought into the chronology of the story

flash-forward narrative device by which a future event or scene is inserted into the chronology of a story

flyting dispute or exchange of personal abuse in verse form

foil one character serving as contrast to another

foot basic unit of verse meter, consisting of any of various fixed combinations of stressed and unstressed, long and short syllables

footnote explanatory comment or reference to documentation at bottom of page

free verse unrhymed verse of irregular meter and nonmetrical rhythm

fustian pretentious or banal writing

genre category of composition with particular style, form, and content

georgic poem with agricultural theme

gloss brief marginal explanation of difficult or obscure passage; continuous commentary accompanying text; interlinear translation

hamartia tragic flaw that causes hero's misfortune in Greek tragedy

hapax legomenon word or phrase occurring one time only in a text or works of an author

heading title or caption of page or chapter

heroic couplet rhyming couplet in iambic pentameter

hexameter line of verse with six metrical feet

hiatus two vowel sounds that come together without pause or intervening consonantal sound

Hudibrastic verse mock-heroic verse in humorous octosyllabic couplets

hyperbole extravagant exaggeration for effect

iamb metrical foot of one short or unstressed syllable followed by one long or stressed syllable

iambic pentameter poetry consisting of five metrical feet per line, each foot having one short or unstressed syllable followed by one long or stressed syllable

imagery figurative language used to evoke mental picture or create atmosphere

interactive fiction adventure or mystery story in which reader is given choices as to how story line will develop

interior monologue extended representation in monologue form of a fictional character's thoughts and feelings; stream of consciousness

internal rhyme correspondence of sounds within units of composition

introduction opening section of work containing essential matter

irony literary form in which words express something other than, or opposite to, their literal meaning

kenning metaphorical compound word used in place of the usual name of a person or thing, esp. in Old English or Norse poetry

lampoon harsh satire directed against an individual

leitmotif dominant recurring theme

locale scene or setting of story or composition

macaronic (*adj*) composed of Latin words mixed with vernacular words or non-Latin words given Latin endings

metaphor word or phrase used in place of another to suggest likeness or analogy between them

meter rhythm in verse with continuously repeating basic pattern

metonymy figure of speech in which the name of one thing is used in place of something else with which it is associated

metrics study or theory of verse meter

mimesis imitation or mimicry of another's style or language

monologue long speech by one individual; dramatic soliloquy

motif recurring thematic element, esp. one dominant idea

narrative story or account of events, either fictional or true, usu. in chronological or linear order

obscurantism intentional obscurity and vagueness in writing

octavo verse stanza of eight lines

octet first eight lines of Petrarchan sonnet

onomatopoeia formation of a word that names a thing or action by imitation of a sound associated with it; use of words whose sounds suggest or imitate their meaning

pandect treatise on an entire subject

parable short story illustrating moral attitude or principle

paraenesis written piece containing advice

passim (*adv*) *Latin.* lit. here and there; used to indicate repetition of phrase or idea throughout book or article

passus section or division of story or poem

pathetic fallacy ascription of human traits and feelings to inanimate objects or nature

pathos evocation of sympathetic pity

pentameter verse line with five metrical feet

personification representation of an object or abstraction in human form or as an imaginary being

plagiarism literary theft; stealing another's work without giving credit, passing it off as one's own

plot plan or main story of work; story line

poeticism poetic expression that is trite or artificial

poetic license deviation from fact, rule, or convention for effect

point of view perspective of character from whose standpoint narrative events are seen

polymythy inclusion of many diverse subplots in literary work

preface introduction to larger work

proem preface or introduction

prolegomenon formal essay or critique introducing extended work

prologue preface or introduction; speech addressed to audience at beginning of play

purple prose excessively affected or sentimental writing intended to manipulate reader's feelings

pyrrhic metrical foot of two short or unstressed syllables

quatrain four lines of verse

recension critical revision of a text, esp. based on a study of its sources

refrain regularly recurring phrase or verse, esp. at end of each stanza in poem

rhyme correspondence in sounds of units of composition, esp. terminal sounds

rhythm ordered, recurrent alternation of strong and weak elements in flow of language

rising action narrative building to a climax

rising rhythm stress occurring on last syllable of each foot

roundelay poem with regularly repeated refrain

sarcasm caustic, ironic language directed esp. against an individual as a taunt

satire wit and irony used to expose and discredit a vice or folly

scansion metrical analysis of verse

scene subdivision of play, representing continuous action in one locale; place in which action occurs

sestina lyrical form of six six-line, unrhymed stanzas, in which endwords of first stanza recur in each following stanza in successively rotating order

simile figure of speech comparing two unlike things

soliloquy dramatic monologue expressing unspoken thoughts

spondee metrical foot of two long or stressed syllables

sprung rhythm poetic rhythm approximating natural speech

stanza division of poem; series of lines arranged together in recurring pattern

story fictional narrative or dramatic plot

story line plot

stream of consciousness continuous, unedited flow of conscious experience and thoughts; interior monologue

strophe two or more lines of verse constituting rhythmic unit; stanza; movement of the classical Greek chorus, characterized by turning from side to side of orchestra

style distinctive manner of expression, tone, or use of language, esp. characteristic of one author or genre

stylized (*adj*) conforming to established, conventional pattern or style rather than natural style

subplot subordinate story line in fiction or drama

subtext implicit, unstated, metaphorical meaning behind literary text, esp. dialogue

suspense use of uncertainty and anxiety as to outcome to heighten excitement

symbol something that stands for or suggests something else by association or convention

tetrameter verse line of four dipodies or metrical feet

text original words of written composition; main body of written work

theme unifying subject or topic of composition

tragic flaw defect in tragic hero's character that causes downfall

trimeter verse line of three dipodies or metrical feet

triple rhyme rhyme consisting of three syllables of which the second and third are unstressed; feminine rhyme

trochee metrical foot of one long or stressed syllable followed by one short or unstressed syllable

tropology use of figurative language in speech or writing

tushery affected writing characterized by archaic language

verisimilitude depiction of characters and setting, giving them the appearance of truth; realism

vignette brief incident, scene, or story

villanelle short poem of fixed form, usu. five groups of three rhyming lines followed by a quatrain

voice author's distinguishing style, tone, point of view, and use of language

wordplay use of rhetorical figures of speech and verbal wit to enhance literary work

writer's block psychological inhibition that prevents writer from continuing or completing work

Books and Pages

abridgment shortened version of work

adaptation rewriting an original work to fit another form

almagest any of various medieval works of a like kind, as on astrology or alchemy

almanac book with calendar, tables, information, and forecasts on various fields

anonymous (*adj*) published with no author's name; written by unknown author

anthology collection of writings by different authors

atlas book of maps and geographical charts

bestiary medieval collection of moralized fables about real and mythical animals

bibelot miniature book of elegant design

bible publication accepted as the preeminent authority in any given field

bibliography list of resources used in compiling a text, or works relating to a subject

binding manner and material in which printed book is covered and held together

canon works ascribed to author and accepted as genuine

chapbook small book or pamphlet, esp. of popular poetry or ballads

chrestomathy collection of selected literary passages, often by one author, and esp. from a foreign language

classic work of universally recognized and enduring excellence, great authority, and importance

codex manuscript book, esp. Biblical writing or other classic text

commonplace book reference book with organized collection of quotations, statements, essays, or treatises

compendium concise but comprehensive treatise or abstract

concordance alphabetical index of principal words in book, esp. the Bible; alphabetical index of subjects or topics

dictionary alphabetical list of words in one language with their definitions; list of defined terms in a given field

draft unfinished, preliminary version of manuscript

duodecimo book page size, equal to one-twelfth sheet of foolscap

edition particular form or version in which text is published; redaction

encyclopedia book or set of books containing information on many branches of knowledge in alphabetically arranged articles

fascicle one section of a book being published in separate parts

folio book page size, equal to one-half sheet of foolscap

foolscap large sheet of paper folded to form book pages

forgery fraudulently made or altered document

glossary alphabetical list of difficult, technical, or occupational terms with definitions, esp. for one field

Gutenberg Bible generally accepted as first book printed with movable type (15th c.)

hornbook rudimentary treatise on some subject; child's primer

incunabula copies of work of early art or industry, esp. book printed before 1501

inedita unpublished literary works

lexicon any wordbook or dictionary, esp. of an ancient language; the vocabulary of a particular field, subject, social class, or person

little magazine usu. noncommercial literary magazine featuring works of little-known authors

magnum opus one author's classic masterpiece

manuscript written or typewritten work, as distinguished from printed copy

marginalia marginal notes in book

masterpiece supreme intellectual or artistic achievement

minor classic extraordinary work of less significance or notoriety than a classic

octavo book page size, equal to one-eighth sheet of foolscap

octodecimo book page size, equal to one-eighteenth sheet of foolscap

omnibus volume containing collection of previously published works by single author or on single theme

onymous (*adj*) bearing the author's name

opus literary work

palimpsest parchment or tablet used more than once, from which the earlier writing has been erased

passage paragraph, verse, or brief section of written work

primer small introductory book on one subject, esp. for children

quartet tetralogy

quarto book page size, equal to one-quarter sheet of foolscap; book printed on quarto pages

redaction something put in writing; edition; version

reference authorative work containing many useful facts of organized information

reprint reissue of book previously published

signature sheet of foolscap folded into leaves of book pages

tetralogy set of four works connected by theme, subject, character, or setting

thesaurus extensive listing of words and their synonyms

tome very large or scholarly work

tour de force work of great skill, ingenuity, and brilliance

treatise systematic exposition of arguments, principles involved, and conclusions reached

trilogy three connected works

variorum edition of a text containing notes or different versions of the text by various editors or scholars

version edited, annotated, abridged, expanded, or revised form of previously published work; redaction

Literary Characters and Practitioners

amanuensis one employed to take dictation or copy manuscripts

anonymous ascription on work of unknown authorship

antagonist character opposed to protagonist; rival

antihero modern protagonist without traditional heroic qualities

archetype character embodying basic, universal human qualities

author writer who has composed a literary work

bard composer, singer, or declaimer of epic verse

belletrist author of amusing, sophisticated works

bibliognost person with comprehensive knowledge of books

bibliophile lover of books and literature

biographer one who writes history of another's life

bluestocking woman with bookish or learned tendencies (18th c.)

Boswell devoted biographer and caretaker of another's literary legend

bouquiniste person who buys and sells used books

character literary depiction of a fictional person, esp. one having some recognizable human trait or symbolizing an archetype or universal personality

chorus character or group of characters commenting on the action of a drama

confidant character emotionally close to protagonist, but relatively uninvolved in story's action

confidante female confidant

copywriter writer of advertising or magazine copy

critic person who assesses the value or merit of literary works

deuteragonist character second in importance to protagonist in classic Greek drama

dramatis personae list of characters in a literary or dramatic work

dramatist playwright

editor person who revises and corrects manuscripts and advises authors on their work

essayist writer of essays

fabulist person who writes or relates fables

farceur writer of broad, satirical comedy

fictioneer prolific writer of generally mediocre works of fiction

ghost writer one who writes for another without receiving credit

goliard one of a class of wandering scholar-poets noted for composing satiric Latin verses (Europe, 12th-13th c.)

hack writer working for hire, usu. producing material of little merit

hagiographer biographer of the saints

hero usu. male protagonist, esp. of epic, tragedy, or adventure

heroine female protagonist, esp. of epic, tragedy, or adventure

journalist writer for magazines or newspapers

literati persons concerned with, and knowledgeable about, literature

man of letters author, often in more than one form or genre; literary scholar

metaphrast person who translates or changes a literary work from one form to another, as prose into verse

nom de guerre *French.* lit. war name; pseudonym

nom de plume *French.* lit. pen name; pseudonym

novelist author of book-length fictional narratives

pen name pseudonym

persona character in a play, novel, or poem

playwright writer of dramas for theatrical performance; dramatist

poet writer of poems and verse

poetaster inferior poet

poet laureate most eminent poet of one nation

during a specific time, often having official standing

protagonist main character in narrative; hero or heroine

pseudonym fictitious name used for writing; nom de guerre; nom de plume; pen name

screenwriter author of scripts for movies or television

scribe official clerk and copier of manuscripts before invention of printing; author, esp. journalist; scrivener

scrivener professional or public copyist or writer; scribe

secretary general assistant to writer, esp. one who takes dictation and types manuscripts

skald bard, esp. ancient Scandinavian poet

speechwriter author of public speeches for another

stock character standard character in many literary works, easily recognized and classified by the reader or audience, who requires little or no development by the author

storyteller one gifted at reciting or writing tales and anecdotes

troubadour lyric poet and musician who told of courtly love in France and Italy (11th-13th c.)

wordsmith author, esp. one skilled at the use of language; writer

writer person engaged in composing books, articles, and other literary works as an occupation or profession; author; journalist

CHAPTER FIFTEEN
PERFORMING ARTS

Types of Music and Composition

accompaniment vocal or instrumental part that complements melody

adaptation piece based on existing melody or composition

air simple tune, melody, or song

allemande composition in moderate duple or quadruple time, basis for German court dance (17th-18th c.)

arabesque short, highly ornamented composition, esp. for piano

aubade sunrise music, esp. love song

bagatelle short, simple piece, usu. for piano

ballade piano composition in romantic mood suggesting epic ballad

ballet music written to accompany balletic dance

baroque (*adj*) designating music of period 1600-1750

berceuse lullaby

bourrée composition in quick duple time, basis of French dance (17th c.)

cantata vocal work in several movements, based on religious or dramatic subject

capriccio instrumental composition in free, unusual form

cavatina simple song or melody, usu. without second part or repeat

chaconne musical form characterized by continuous variation in a progression of chords which form the harmonic basis for each variation, usu. in triple time

chamber music instrumental music for small group in which each performer has a different part

classical (*adj*) denoting music of the European tradition marked by sophistication of structural elements and embracing vocal, symphonic, chamber, and solo music, esp. as distinguished from popular and folk music and jazz; designating typically homophonic music of the period 1750-1830

composition any written piece of music, esp. one of scope and complexity

concertino short concerto

concerto composition for one or more solo instruments with orchestral accompaniment, usu. in three movements

concerto grosso baroque composition contrasting small group of solo instruments with full orchestra

dirge slow, mournful piece, esp. accompanying funeral

divertimento instrumental form similar to suite

and symphony, containing dances and short movements

divertissement short ballet used as interlude between acts of opera

duet composition for two instruments or voices; duo

duo duet

écossaise Scottish country dance in 2/4 time

étude piece intended to aid student in learning instrument

evensong evening prayer, vespers music

fantasia composition in fanciful improvisational form

fugue contrapuntal composition with melodic themes announced or imitated by each voice entering in succession

gavotte French dance music used in suites (18th c.)

gigue early Italian dance in various triple times

humoresque whimsical or playful composition

incidental music music performed during play to project mood or accompany action

interlude brief musical passage played between parts of longer piece, drama, or religious service

intermezzo movement between main sections of longer work, such as an opera

invention short keyboard composition that develops single motif in counterpoint

march music for marching, usu. in 4/4 time

minuet early French dance in 3/4 time

modern (*adj*) designating music composed in classical forms during the 20th century

music art and science of combining tones or sounds in single line (melody), in combination (harmony), and in time relationships (rhythm) to express ideas and emotions in a structurally complete and unified work having an appealing sound when produced by one or more voices or instruments, or both

musique concrète *French*. recorded montage of electronically manipulated and transformed natural sounds presented as a composition

nocturne dreamy, romantic piece, esp. for piano (19th c.)

nonet composition for nine instruments or voices

octet composition for eight instruments or voices

opus composition, usu. numbered to indicate order in which composer's work was published

overture musical introduction to ballet, opera, or oratorio that foreshadows themes that appear later

partita suite or series of variations

pastorale piece of music, esp. opera or cantata, suggestive of simple, rural life

pavane music written to accompany a stately European court dance (16th c.)

piece composition

polonaise music for stately Polish dance in triple time

prelude orig. a musical introduction, later an independent piece

quadrille French dance alternating between 6/8 and 2/4 time (early 19th c.)

quartet composition for four instruments, usu. two violins, viola, and cello, or voices

quintet composition for five instruments or voices

raga music following traditional formula for melody, rhythm, and ornamentation (Indian)

requiem composition written for funeral mass

rhapsody composition in free, irregular form

romantic (*adj*) designating music of the late 19th century marked by free expression of imagination and emotion, virtuosic display, and some experimentation with form

rondo piece that alternates main and contrasting themes, usu. gay, playful, and fast

roundelay song in which phrase or line is continually repeated

sacred music compositions for religious services

saraband stately dance music in triple time (17th-18th c.)

scherzo playful piece in rapid triple time

semiclassical (*adj*) designating composition combining classical and contemporary, popular elements

septet composition for seven instruments or voices

serenade romantic song; instrumental piece for small group of string and wind instruments

serial composition nonmodal music using any or all of twelve chromatic tones in an arbitrarily set pattern (20th c.)

sextet composition for six instruments or voices

sinfonia concertante concerto for two or more solo instruments

sinfonietta symphony for small orchestra, esp. strings only, or of less than normal length

solo piece for single instrument or voice

sonata composition for one or two instruments, esp. piano, usu. in three or four movements in contrasting forms and keys

sonatina short, simplified sonata

string quartet composition for two violins, viola, and cello

suite instrumental music in several movements, each in a different dance form, all in the same key

symphonic poem large narrative orchestral work in one movement; tone poem

symphony composition for orchestra, usu. in four movements in contrasting tempos, moods, and keys

toccata keyboard piece with bold, rapid passages in contrapuntal style

tone poem composition for symphony orchestra, usu. in one movement, based on literary or historical subject; symphonic poem

transcription arrangement of composition for voice or instrument other than that for which it was written

trio composition for three instruments or voices

twelve-tone (*adj*) pertaining to serial

composition using all twelve chromatic tones
(early 20th c.)

villanella instrumental piece in style of rustic
Italian dance (16th c.)

voluntary musical piece, sometimes improvised,
performed by organist as prelude to larger work
or church service

waltz music for German dance in triple time
(19th c.)

Harmony, Melody, and Structure

accent recurring stress or emphasis

accidental sharp or flat not found in key
signature

affettuoso (*adv*) with tenderness and affection

agitato (*adj*) restless or hurried in manner

alto clef clef placing middle C on third line of
staff

amoroso (*adv*) with love

anacrusis upbeat; note or notes preceding
downbeat of musical phrase

animato (*adj*) with spirit, lively

appassionato (*adj*) with emotion or passion

appoggiatura grace note or brief, ornamental
tone sounded before another

arpeggio playing notes of chord in succession
rather than simultaneously

arrangement orchestration and structure of
composition

attack approach or manner of approach in
beginning to play a musical phrase

atonal (*adj*) without reference to key or mode,
using all twelve tones of chromatic scale at
random

augmentation modification of theme by
increasing time value of all its notes

augmented triad with fifth tone raised one-half
step

bar measure of set number of beats

bass clef clef placing F below middle C on
fourth line of staff

basso continuo continuo

beat metrical or rhythmic accent

cadence chords at end of phrase or piece that
suggest harmonic resolution

cadenza brilliant virtuoso passage at end of solo

cantabile (*adv*) in a songlike manner

canto melody in choral or instrumental music

cantus firmus fixed melody to which other
voices are added

chord two or more notes sounded together

chromatic (*adj*) containing all twelve half steps
in octave

clef sign at beginning of musical staff that
indicates pitch of notes

coda passage added to final section of piece

coloratura florid ornamentation in vocal music,
esp. runs, trills, and arpeggios

composition art and practice of writing pieces
of music

con amore (*adv*) in a tender manner

con anima (*adv*) in a spirited manner

con bravura (*adv*) with boldness

con brio (*adv*) in a vigorous manner

con dolore (*adv*) sadly, sorrowfully

con espressione (*adv*) with feeling

con moto (*adv*) with animation and spirit

consonance interval or chord that provides a
feeling of satisfaction and resolution: third,
fourth, fifth, sixth, octave

con sordino (*adv*) in a muted manner

con spirito (*adv*) with spirit or animation

continuo figured bass part for keyboard or
strings, esp. in baroque ensemble; basso
continuo

contrapuntal (*adj*) based on counterpoint

countermelody secondary melody sounded
simultaneously with primary melody

counterpoint several independent but related
melodies played simultaneously

crescendo gradual, steady increase in volume;
(*adj*) gradually increasing in volume

da capo (*adv*) repeated from the beginning

decrescendo gradual decrease in volume; (*adj*)
growing softer

degree tone or step of the scale

development elaboration of theme through
counterpoint, modulation, rhythm, and tempo
changes

diatonic (*adj*) designating major and minor
scales; designating eight-tone scale without
chromatic deviation

diminished triad with fifth tone reduced
one-half step

diminuendo (*adj*) decreasing in volume

dissonance interval or chord that is restless and
discordant

dolce (*adj*) soft and sweet

dominant fifth step of diatonic scale

double flat lowering of note's pitch two
chromatic half steps from natural

double sharp raising of note's pitch two
chromatic half-steps from natural

downbeat first beat of measure

enharmonic (*adj*) designating tones that have
same pitch but different notation, such as
C-sharp and D-flat

exposition statement of material on which
movement or piece is based

fanfare trumpet flourish, esp. at dramatic
entrance

fifth tone on the fifth degree from a given tone;
interval from tonic to dominant

figure shortest musical idea or motif in
composition

final bar heavy, vertical double line indicating
end of piece

finale closing part or movement of composition

flat lowering of note's pitch one chromatic half
step from natural

forte (*adj*) loud, forceful

fortissimo (*adj*) very loud

fourth tone on the fourth degree from a given
tone; interval from tonic to subdominant

fundamental root note of a chord

glissando gliding effect, esp. series of adjacent
tones sounded in rapid succession on keyboard

grace note brief, ornamental tone sounded
before another; appoggiatura

grazioso (*adj*) graceful, flowing

Greek modes ascending musical scale consisting
of two disjunct tetrachords: Dorian, hypodorian,
Phrygian, hypophrygian, Lydian, hypolydian,
mixolydian

harmonic overtone

harmony chord or combination of tones
sounded together; structure of music that deals
with the arrangement, voicing, and modulation
of chords

homophony music in which one melody and set
of chords predominates

ictus recurring stress or beat

interval difference in pitch between two tones

intonation production of a tone with a voice or
instrument

inversion chord with tones in other than
standard order

key major or minor scale with set flats and
sharps, used as basis for composition

key signature flats and sharps on staff that
indicate key of composition

leading tone major seventh

legato (*adv*) in a smooth, even style, with no
breaks between notes

ligature slur

maestoso (*adj*) majestic

major scale diatonic scale composed of five
whole steps and two half steps

major seventh note in diatonic scale one-half
step below tonic

marcato (*adj*) accented, stressed, marked

martellato (*adj*) detached, strongly accented, or
hammered with stroke of bow on stringed
instrument

measure notes and rests contained between
two bar lines

mediant third step of diatonic scale

melody tune, air, or theme composed of tones
arranged in a pleasing succession

meno mosso (*adv*) less rapidly, slower

microtone any interval less than a semitone, esp.
a quarter tone

middle C C note nearest middle of standard
piano keyboard

minor scale diatonic scale starting on sixth note
of relative major scale and composed of the
same notes

minor seventh note in diatonic scale one full
step below tonic

modal (*adj*) of or relating to a diatonic
eight-tone scale other than major or minor;
pertaining to mode, as distinguished from key

mode any of various arrangements of the
diatonic tones of an octave, differing from one
another in the order of whole and half steps;
one of the Greek modes; scale

modulation change from one key to another
within a single composition

molto (*adv*) very

monophony music consisting of unaccompanied
melody

mordent trill made by rapid alternation of a principal tone and another tone a half step below it

motif recurring subject, theme, or idea; motive

motive motif

movement section of sonata, symphony, suite, or concerto

musicology scholarly study of music history, theory, and acoustics

natural return of a sharp or flat tone to its original pitch; original or normal pitch of note

non troppo (*adv*) without excess

notation standardized system of characters and symbols used to represent musical composition

note written character indicating duration and pitch of tone with value that is relative and dependent on time signature of piece; a single tone

obbligato subordinate solo instrument or melody line above or behind main melody

octave interval of eight diatonic tones

orchestration arrangement of composition for instrumental ensemble, esp. full orchestra

ornament embellishing note not part of basic melody or harmony

ostinato musical figure regularly repeated at the same pitch

overtone acoustical frequency higher in frequency than the fundamental; harmonic

parlando (*adj*) sung or played as though speaking or reciting

part notes performed by one instrument or voice as solo or in combination with other parts

partial overtone or harmonic

passage section of composition

pedal prolonged or continuously repeated tone

pentatonic (*adj*) designating five-tone scale, esp. one arranged like a major scale with the fourth and seventh deleted

phrase complete musical figure

pianissimo (*adj*) very soft

piano (*adj*) soft, subdued

pitch frequency of tonal vibrations per second

pizzicato (*adj*) played with plucked strings

poco (*adv*) somewhat, rather

polyphony music consisting of two or more independent melodic lines sounding together

polyrhythm simultaneous use of contrasting rhythmic patterns

portamento continuous gliding from note to note, sounding all intervening tones, usu. by voice or stringed instrument

progression series of chords

quarter tone interval equivalent to half a semitone

rallentando (*adj*) gradually slowing

range limits of pitch encompassed by a melody; full extent of tones falling within capacity of a voice or instrument

refrain regularly recurring musical figure

register different parts in the range of a voice or instrument

relative keys major and minor keys composed

of the same notes and having the same key signature

repeat vertical arrangement of two dots on staff, indicating that preceding passage is to be repeated

reprise repetition of musical phrase

resolution progression from dissonance to consonance, esp. to the tonic note

rest interval of silence between tones; sign indicating duration of such silence, with value relative and dependent on time signature of piece

rhythm temporal relationship of successive notes; regular tempo, grouping, and accenting of tones that impel music forward

ritardando (*adj*) with gradual slowing of tempo

root tone on which a chord is built; fundamental

roulade series of rapid notes inserted in composition as ornamentation, esp. vocal coloratura

rubato (*adj*) having variation in speed within musical phrase, esp. juxtaposed against steady rhythm

scale series of notes arranged in steps at fixed intervals; mode

scherzando (*adj*) lively, brisk, playful

second tone on the next degree from a given tone; interval between such tones

segue seamless transition between sounds, themes, or pieces

semitone interval equal to one half of major second; half of a whole tone

semplice (*adj*) simple, straightforward

sempre (*adv*) always

seventh tone on the seventh degree from a given tone; interval from tonic to subtonic

sforzando (*adv*) with force

sharp raising of note's pitch one chromatic half step from natural

signature arrangement of sharps and flats on staff to indicate key; numerical indication of beats per measure

sixth tone on the sixth degree from a given tone; interval from tonic to superdominant

skip melodic interval greater than a second

slur curved line indicating that notes be sounded without pause; ligature

sostenuto (*adj*) sustained in time value of tones

spiccato (*adj*) performed with short, rapid bow stroke that allows bow to rebound between notes, giving detached effect to tones

staccato (*adj*) with abrupt, distinct breaks between notes

staff five horizontal lines and four spaces on which music is written; stave

stanza division in a vocal composition, formed by a recurring pattern of words

stave staff

step one degree of a scale; interval between two adjacent scale degrees, as a second

strain passage of composition; melody

stretto overlapping of response and call parts in fugue

subdominant fourth step of diatonic scale

subito (*adv*) suddenly

submediant sixth step of diatonic scale; superdominant

subtonic seventh step of diatonic scale, one degree below tonic

superdominant submediant

supertonic second step of diatonic scale, one degree above tonic

swell gradual increase followed by gradual decrease in loudness

syncopation accenting of normally unaccented beats to create rhythmic displacement

tablature notation indicating string, fret, key, or finger to be used rather than note to be played

tacet be silent

tenuto (*adj*) designating note or chord held to full extent of its time value

tessitura register including most notes of melody or vocal part or range of instrument where most tones lie

tetrachord diatonic series of four tones with perfect interval between first and fourth

theme complete musical idea; basis of musical variations

third tone on the third degree from a given tone; interval from tonic to mediant

tie slur connecting two held notes of same pitch

timbre characteristic quality of sound produced by an instrument; degree of resonance

tone cluster group of notes played simultaneously on keyboard with forearm, elbow, or fist

tone row set but arbitrary sequence of notes in serial composition

tonic first note of a scale

transition modulation; passage that connects one part of a piece to the next

transpose (*vb*) write or perform a piece in a key other than the original

treble upper register of vocal or instrumental range; highest part in harmonic music

treble clef clef with G above middle C on second line of staff

tremolo rapid reiteration of tone or alternating tones to produce a tremulous effect

triad chord made up of three tones, usu. first, third, and fifth

trill ornament consisting of rapid alternation between note and another note one half step above

triplet three notes played in amount of time normally required for two notes of same duration

tune melody

turn melodic embellishment or grace note consisting of principal tone with auxiliary tones above and below it

tutti (*adj*) all; performed by all voices or instruments together

unison simultaneous performance of identical parts by several instruments or voices

upbeat unaccented beat, often last beat of

measure, sometimes beginning phrase or composition

variation change in key, meter, rhythm, harmony, speed, or mood of basic theme

vibrato slight, rapid alternation in pitch that produces a pulsating effect less pronounced than tremolo

vigoroso (*adj*) vigorous or spirited in manner

vivace (*adv*) lively

voicing arrangement of notes in chord or parts in composition

volante (*adv*) moving with light rapidity

whole tone interval of a major second, equal to two semitones

whole-tone scale scale progressing entirely by whole tones

Time and Tempo

accelerando (*adj*) gradually faster

adagio (*adv*) slowly, in a leisurely manner, (*adj*) slow; slower than andante, faster than lento

alla breve 2/2 time with one breve per measure

allegretto (*adj*) light and moderately fast; faster than moderato, slower than allegro

allegro (*adj*) brisk or rapid; faster than allegretto, slower than presto

andante (*adj*) moderately slow and flowing; faster than adagio, slower than moderato

andantino (*adj*) slightly faster than andante

assai (*adv*) very, as applied to tempo directions

breve note equal to two whole notes

common time 4/4 time

compound time time in which each beat of bar is divisible into three

courante music in quick triple time; mixture of 3/2 and 6/4 time

crotchet *Chiefly Brit.* quarter note

demiquaver *Chiefly Brit.* sixteenth note; semiquaver

demisemiquaver *Chiefly Brit.* thirty-second note

dotted note note with dot after it, indicating it is to be prolonged by one-half its length

duple time two, or multiple of two, beats per measure, such as 2/4 or 4/4

eighth note note having duration equal to one eighth of whole note; quaver

eighth rest rest equal in duration to eighth note

4/4 time time signature indicating four beats per measure with quarter note lasting one beat; common time

grave (*adj*) serious; slower than lento, faster than largo

half note note having duration equal to one half of whole note; minim

half rest rest equal in duration to half note

hemidemisemiquaver *Chiefly Brit.* sixty-fourth note

larghetto (*adj*) slow; faster than largo, slower than grave

largo (*adj*) very slow; slower than grave

lento (*adj*) somewhat slow; faster than larghetto, slower than adagio

meter regular, recurrent grouping of beats and

accents, indicated by time signatures such as 4/4 and 6/8

minim half note

moderato (*adj*) at moderate speed; faster than andante, slower than allegretto

presto (*adj*) very fast; faster than allegro

quarter note note having duration equal to one quarter of whole note; one quarter of entire measure in common time; crotchet

quarter rest rest equal in duration to quarter note

quaver *Chiefly Brit.* eighth note

semibreve *Chiefly Brit.* whole note; one half of breve

semiquaver *Chiefly Brit.* sixteenth note; demiquaver

sixteenth note note having duration equal to one sixteenth of whole note; demiquaver; semiquaver

sixteenth rest rest equal in duration to sixteenth note

sixty-fourth note note having duration equal to one sixty-fourth of whole note; hemidemisemiquaver

sixty-fourth rest rest equal in duration to sixty-fourth note

tempo pace or rate of speed of piece, from slowest to fastest: largo, larghetto, grave, lento, adagio, andante, andantino, moderato, allegretto, allegro, presto

thirty-second note note having duration equal to one thirty-second of whole note; demisemiquaver

thirty-second rest rest equal in duration to thirty-second note

time time signature or rhythm of piece

time signature numerical fraction, such as 3/4 or 9/8, that shows number of beats per measure and kind of note that lasts one beat

triple time three, or multiple of three, beats per measure, such as 3/4 or 6/8

whole note note equal in duration to four quarter notes, lasting entire measure in common time; semibreve

whole rest rest equal in duration to whole note, lasting entire measure in common time

Opera and Vocal Music

a cappella (*adj*) without instrumental accompaniment

alto female voice or voice part lower than soprano; male countertenor voice or voice part

anthem sacred vocal composition with words from the Scriptures; song of praise

antiphony alternate or responsive singing or chanting of psalm or verse by two sections of choir

aria solo song in opera, cantata, or oratorio

aria da capo operatic aria in three sections with first and third matching and middle part contrasting

art song song usu. set to poem and performed

in recital with interdependent vocal and piano parts

ballad vocal song telling story, usu. of love

barcarole song of Venetian gondoliers

baritone male voice or voice part lower than tenor and higher than bass

bass lowest normal male voice or voice part; basso

basso bass

basso profundo exceptionally deep bass voice

bel canto agile, operatic vocal technique that stresses even tone

bravura florid, virtuoso composition or performance

buffo male opera singer who specializes in comic parts

canon strict form of composition in which each voice has same melody starting at different times

cantata vocal composition with instrumental accompaniment in several movements, based on religious or dramatic subject

canticle liturgical song based on Biblical text

canto part of choral work that carries melody

canzonet light song, less elaborate than madrigal

carol traditional song of faith, esp. heard at Christmas

cavatina operatic solo less elaborate than aria

chanson song (France)

chant sacred song and oldest form of choral music

chanteuse singer, vocalist (France)

choir group of singers, esp. one employed in church service; chorale

choirboy boy who sings in choir, esp. church choir

choral vocal music performed by chorus or choir; (*adj*) relating to or composed for a chorus or choir

chorale hymn or psalm sung to traditional melody in religious service; choir

chorister member of choir, esp. its leader

chorus organized group of singers, esp. singing in unison; such a group singing in connection with soloists in opera or oratorio; piece of music to be sung in unison

coloratura florid ornamentation, esp. runs, trills, and arpeggios, in vocal music; one who sings such music

comic opera light, humorous, often sentimental opera

contralto lowest female voice or voice part

countertenor adult male able to sing in alto range

descant counterpoint sung above main melody

falsetto artificial method of singing used by males to obtain notes above their normal vocal range

fioritura melodic ornamentation, often extemporized in Italian opera

glee simple part song, usu. for male voices

glee club choral group, usu. large

Gregorian chant unharmonized liturgical chant

with free rhythm, used in ritual of Roman Catholic Church

hymn religious or sacred song

Kyrie musical setting for brief liturgical prayer that opens mass

leitmotif short, recurring phrase associated with single character or situation in opera

libretto words and text of opera or oratorio

lieder stylized German song

light opera operetta

madrigal unaccompanied choral music in counterpoint, based on nonsacred text

Magnificat musical setting for the canticle of the Virgin Mary in Luke 1:46-55

Mass music for solemn Roman Catholic service in sequence of established parts

melisma ornamental phrase of several notes sung to one syllable of lyric, esp. in plainsong

mezzo-soprano female voice between alto and soprano

monody elegy or dirge sung by one person

motet vocal composition in contrapuntal style without accompaniment, based on sacred text

opera drama in which the text is entirely sung and acted to orchestral accompaniment, usu. with elaborate scenery and costumes

opera buffa farcical comic opera (Italy, 18th c.)

opera seria dramatic, classical opera (Italy, 18th c.)

operetta light, romantic, comic opera with songs and spoken dialogue

oratorio fairly long, usu. religious work for solo voices, chorus, and orchestra, performed without action, costume, or scenery

part song contrapuntal composition for three or more unaccompanied voices

pasticcio medley or opera made up of portions taken from other operas

plainsong liturgical chant, esp. Gregorian

precentor choir leader

presa cue marking the entry point for each voice in a canon

processional hymn or organ solo performed in church during entry procession of choir and clergy

recessional hymn sung at conclusion of religious service

recitative speechlike vocal composition without fixed rhythm, used for dialogue in opera

requiem funeral mass

round canon in which voices enter at regular intervals repeating the same melody

Sanctus ancient Christian hymn of adoration

singer vocalist

sol-fa syllables tones of scale sung as syllables: do, re, mi, fa, sol, la, ti

solfège solfeggio

solfeggio vocal exercise using the sol-fa syllables; solfège

song short, simple composition with words and music

soprano highest female vocal range or voice part

tenor male voice or voice part above baritone and below alto or countertenor

threne threnody

threnody dirge, song of lamentation at funeral; threne

tremolo prominent vocal vibrato

vocal portion of composition written for voice

vocalist person who has received formal voice training to perform lieder, opera, or choral music; singer

zarzuela comic Spanish operetta

Musicians and Performance

absolute pitch ability to sing or name a single isolated note out of context

accompanist single instrumentalist, usu. pianist, who plays for dancer or singer

baton conductor's light rod, used to keep time

beat tempo indicated by conductor to musicians and singers

bowing act or art of playing notes on stringed instrument with down or up motion of bow

chamber orchestra small ensemble for performing chamber music

choirmaster director of choral group

collegium musicum group of usu. amateur musicians who meet to perform old or obscure music, often at a university

coloration subtle variation in intensity or tone by performers

composer person who creates and writes down musical compositions

concert live performance of music before audience

concertmaster assistant to orchestra conductor; first violinist of orchestra

conductor leader of orchestra

consort ensemble of singers and instrumentalists

ensemble several musicians who perform together

improvisation composition of music while performing

instrumentalist performer on specific instrument

maestro respected conductor, orchestra leader, or composer

musicality sensitivity to and aptitude for music

music director creative director of a group of performers

musician composer, conductor, or instrumental performer

orchestra large group of musicians performing on many instruments of all sorts, usu. over 100 members

philharmonic symphony orchestra

pit sunken area in front of stage in which orchestra sits during opera or ballet performance

pitch pipe small reed pipe used to tune instruments or establish pitch for singer

player instrumental performer

program printed information about compositions and performers, handed out to audience; sequence of compositions to be performed

quartet ensemble of four instruments or singers, esp. string quartet

recital concert given by individual performer

score written copy of composition with all parts arranged on staves, used during performance

sheet music printed copy of composition

sight-read (*vb*) play or sing written music on sight without rehearsal

sinfonietta small orchestra, often composed solely of stringed instruments

string quartet ensemble of two violins, viola, and cello

symphony full orchestra

touch musician's innate feel for instrument

tuning adjusting pitch of instrument

virtuoso performer with great technical skill and artistry

POPULAR MUSIC

Styles and Genres
Performance, Airplay, and the Recording Industry
Sound Reproduction Technology
Rock Era Dances
 1950's
 1960's
 1970's
 1980's
 1990's

See also: *Chap. 5: Electricity and Electronics; Chap. 15: Classical Music; Musical Instruments; Television and Radio*

Styles and Genres

a cappella singing without instrumental backing

acid house intense, urban, black-influenced dance music of late 1980's, often with portions of different songs mixed together

acid rock free-form, psychedelic music of 1960's

acoustic rock rock-'n'-roll played on nonelectric instruments, esp. acoustic guitar

aleatory music music of indeterminate composition that incorporates random noises

alternative rock style of hard rock music popular in the 1990's, characterized by angst-filled lyrics, raw vocalization, and use of distortion

ambient music background music; music used as an environmental element

anthem highly emotional and dramatic song, often patriotic or devotional

ballad slow, sentimental, romantic song; song that tells a narrative story in short, repetitive verses

barrelhouse jazz piano style with lively beat, orig. 1920's

bebop jazz style emphasizing aggressive, energetic playing, esp. rapid and difficult chord changes, orig. 1940's; bop

big band style associated with large jazz orchestras, orig. popular in 1920's and 1930's

bluebeat 1950's precursor of reggae and ska

bluegrass traditional acoustic country style

blues spiritual and melancholy folk music song form originated by blacks in rural southern United States, derived in part from field hollers; major source of jazz, urban blues

boogie blues rock style popular in 1960's

boogie-woogie frenetic blues style, usu. on piano

bop bebop

bossa nova Brazilian jazz interpolations on samba dance music

bubblegum *Slang.* light, trendy, innocuous pop music

cabaret song style typical of nightclub entertainment

Cajun country music style of Cajun or French-Canadian residents of southern Louisiana

calypso popular Caribbean dance music, sometimes with improvised lyrics

chantey sailor's work song; shantey

country popular style derived from traditional English folk music, blues, and rock-'n'-roll, orig. a regional style

country-and-western recording industry designation for country music

cradlesong lullaby

disco dance-oriented pop music emphasizing heavy backbeat, simplistic lyrics, and polished production techniques, orig. late 1970's

ditty brief, simple, often humorous, song

Dixieland upbeat, brass-oriented jazz, orig. 1920's

doo-wop a capella, harmony-oriented rock-'n'-roll vocal style, orig. 1950's

electronic music music performed on electronic instruments such as synthesizers, orig. 1970's

elevator music Muzak

folk music traditional and ethnic songs usu. performed on acoustic instruments

folk rock modern or traditional folk songs played on electrified instruments

funk dance-oriented, predominantly black soul music, usu. with horns and irregularly accented beat

fusion combination of jazz and electric rock, orig. 1970's

gangsta rap rap music featuring themes of violence and criminal behavior

glitter rock highly theatrical rock with showy costumes, spectacular staging, and decadent themes, orig. early 1970's (U.S. and Britain)

Goa trance Hindi-influenced rave music

gospel popular Christian church music, esp. influenced by black spirituals from American rural south

hard rock rock with a simple, driving, repetitive dance beat and usu. accessible lyric themes

heavy metal highly dramatic, guitar-based rock noted for lyrics about adolescence and rebellion

high life urban West African mixture of jazz and indigenous musical forms

hip-hop rock and dance style emphasizing spoken lyrics, contemporary urban themes, and acrobatic steps; rap

honky-tonk white, country-inflected rhythm-and-blues

house music dance-oriented club music of late 1980's with derivative elements and intense, discolike backbeat

jazz major modern popular music form originating in New Orleans around 1900, derived from blues, ragtime, and gospel roots, characterized by free improvisation, virtuoso solo performances, syncopated rhythm, and a variety of original vocal and instrumental styles of varying complexity: bebop, big band, cool, Dixieland, fusion, hot, modern, New Orleans, progressive, ragtime, and swing

jug band blues and jazz style using primitive instruments such as washboards or jugs, orig. 1920's

juju guitar-driven West African dance music

jungle British hip-hop music

klezmer Yiddish folk music of Ashkenazi Jews performed by small band featuring clarinet and accordion

lullaby song sung to lull a child to sleep; cradlesong

mbaqanga rhythmic pop music of South Africa, derived from Zulu music and jazz, played on electric instruments and drums; township music

Motown upbeat, pop-influenced rhythm-and-blues originally produced by group of black artists recording in Detroit, esp. in 1960's 70's

Muzak *Trademark.* string-based adaptation of classical, show, and pop tunes, recorded as unobtrusive, environmental background music; elevator music

New Age repetitive, ambient acoustic jazz and serene background music, orig. 1980's

new wave punk-derived, dance-oriented pop, emphasizing uninhibited performance and antiauthority lyrics, orig. late 1970's

patriotic marches and other dramatic songs with lyrics zealously supporting one's country

polka Bohemian dance and folk music in distinctive duple rhythm

pop pop music

pop music popular music; contemporary music aimed at a mass audience and receiving wide exposure while evolving rapidly; pop

power pop strong, rhythmic, infectiously melodic, usu. guitar-driven pop music

protest music folk-derived, political reform songs of 1960's

psychedelic music hallucinogenic, drug-influenced 1960's rock

punk rock fast, loud, anarchic rock popular in late 1970's and early 1980's

ragtime syncopated jazz piano style of 1890's to 1920's

R&B rhythm-and-blues

rap dance-oriented pop style with insistent beat and rhyming, spoken lyrics, often couplets, that treat modern urban themes, esp. social protest and commentary, orig. 1980's among young blacks in inner cities; hip-hop

rave electronic dance music with a strong beat, often accompanied by lighting effects

reggae liltingly syncopated, Rastafarian-influenced popular music of Jamaica

rhythm-and-blues R&B: urban, dance-oriented form derived from blues and rock-'n'-roll, orig. late 1940's

rock rock-'n'-roll

rockabilly country-influenced, white rhythm-and-blues style of rock, orig. 1950's

rock-and-roll rock-'n'-roll

rock and soul rock-'n'-roll with strong rhythm-and-blues roots

rock-'n'-roll blues-influenced, popular, youth-oriented, usu. electric dance music emphasizing strong beat and repetitive phrasing, orig. 1950's; rock; rock-and-roll

roots music indigenous popular music of a specific region

salsa modern Latin-American dance music

scat jazz vocal style in which singer imitates the sound and style of a horn playing without using words

scratch urban, black dance music similar to rap but using rhythmic sound made by manually moving a record back-and-forth under a turntable needle, orig. 1980's

shantey chantey

shockabilly rock style influenced by punk and rockabilly

show tunes popular songs from Broadway musical shows

ska Jamaican dance pop of 1950's, precursor of reggae

skiffle unsophisticated, acoustic folk music using washboard, jug, and other homemade instruments

soca Trinidadian roots music with blues and Brazilian influences

soft rock melodic pop rock without driving beat, not emphasizing electric guitars, and often having soothing or romantic lyrics

soukous popular dance music of the Congo and Zaire, using electric instruments

soul pop music derived from rhythm-and-blues, orig. 1960's

soundtrack musical score for film

spirituals gospel music

stadium rock widely popular commercial rock, esp. performed in large sports arenas

steel band rhythmic Caribbean music played on tuned steel drums

stride piano jazz and blues piano style with energetic, syncopated beat

surf music rock-'n'-roll, esp. from California during 1960's, featuring close treble harmonies and exuberant lyrics about beach life

swing big band jazz of 1930's-1940's, esp. for dancing

synthpop glossy, elegant pop emphasizing electronic synthesizer sound, orig. early 1980's

thrash frenetic, loud, aggressive punk rock

torch song steamy love song or ballad

township music popular dance music originating in townships of South Africa, played on electric instruments and drums; mbaqanga

urban contemporary slick, blues-based, romantic pop of 1980's

washboard lively blues style using primitive instruments; jug band music

work song folk song sung by workers to the rhythm of their work

world beat indigenous, usu. third-world musical forms, such as reggae and African popular music, sometimes influenced by another culture's music, esp. Western rock and pop styles and electric instrumentation

zouk popular dance music from French Antilles, based on Caribbean rhythms and played on electric instruments

zydeco blues-influenced Cajun dance music popular with French-speaking black people in Louisiana and Texas

Performance, Airplay, and the Recording Industry

A&R artist and repertory; record company employee responsible for signing and developing acts, matching songs to artists

air guitar imaginary guitar played by singer or dancer, usu. with wild, highly expressive mannerisms

airplay exposure of record on radio program

album group of six to fifteen songs released together on compact disc, cassette, and/or a 33-rpm, long-playing record in a cardboard jacket

American Bandstand *Trademark.* television program featuring teenagers dancing to records

AM radio amplitude modulation radio broadcasting, generally associated with popular music programming

AOR album oriented rock; easy listening, light pop or soft rock radio programming

arranger person responsible for orchestrating a song for performance or recording

artist and repertory A&R

A-side primary hit side of 45-rpm single record

ax *Slang.* musical instrument, esp. guitar

backbeat danceable beat characteristic of rock-'n'-roll

backup singer harmony or background singer who complements featured vocalist

band group of musicians performing together

beat accent in rhythm; backbeat

belt (*vb*) *Informal.* sing a song loudly and energetically

Billboard *Trademark.* weekly trade magazine of the recording industry, including news, features, and charts

boogie (*vb*) become animated by dance music; play with soulful feeling

bootleg recording pirated record

bottleneck glass or metal cylinder, orig. the neck

of a bottle, used to create sliding guitar notes; guitar-playing style using bottleneck

bottom *Slang.* bass part of pop song

break dancing very acrobatic, urban, black dance style, orig. late 1970's

bridge segment of pop song that connects verses and chorus

B-side secondary song released with a single, not the hit; flip side

cartage transport of musical equipment to performance or recording session

cassingle prerecorded cassette sold to promote a single song

cassignle prerecorded cassette sold to promote a single song

casual informal performance at party or wedding

CD compact disc

CD single smaller compact disc

charts written musical arrangements; record industry tabulations on sales of popular records

chops *Slang.* level of musical skill and virtuosity; solo passage

chorus recurring segment of song, usu. after each verse, often containing the song's title or hook

clam *Slang.* musician's mistake, bad note

club small bar in which musicians perform

combo group of musicians playing together

compact disc disc on which music is recorded digitally and reproduced by laser light reflection; CD

concept album long-playing record with songs united by theme, narrative, and style

cook (*vb*) *Slang.* play an instrument with fire and inspiration

cover version new rendition of an older, familiar song; white version of black song in the 1950's

crooner easy, smooth-styled, romantic singer

crossover hit song belonging to a particular genre that achieves commercial success in another genre

cut individual song on an album; (*vb*) record a song

DAT digital audio tape

date recording session, esp. for jazz

deejay disc jockey

def jam *Slang.* excellent sound or record, esp. hip-hop

demo demonstration recording submitted by musicians seeking recording contract; rough version of a song, to be polished for finished recording

dinosaur rock performer or band emphasizing thunderous, formulaic rock, esp. with out-of-date style

disc compact disc or phonograph record

disc jockey DJ; announcer who hosts a radio music program or dance; deejay

Discman *Trademark.* compact, portable CD-player used with earphones

discography descriptive listing of recordings by category, artist, composer, label, or date

discotheque dance club with recorded music

DJ disc jockey

dub technique of mixing record or performance for very heavy bass line; mix without lead vocals; copy tape to tape

ear candy *Slang.* light, syrupy, easy-listening music

ears *Slang.* ability to recognize potential hit song based on keen appreciation of pop sensibility

easy rock light pop or soft rock

eight-track tape former enclosed-cartridge medium for prerecorded tape with four stereo channels

EP extended play

extended play EP; four-song, 45-rpm single

fan club organization devoted to following a particular group or performer

fanzine rock or pop music fan magazine

festival outdoor pop music event featuring many performers, often taking place over a period of several days

festival seating nonreserved seating, usu. on floor or ground

flip side B-side

folkie *Informal.* enthusiast or performer of folk music

format radio programming style and content

45 seven-inch, 45-rpm record, usu. with one song on each side; single

funky (*adj*) dirty, down-home, bluesy, or unsophisticated

fuzz electronic sound distortion, popular in 1960's

garage band rough, amateur pop group

ghetto blaster *Slang.* powerful yet portable stereo unit, usu. carried on street

gig *Slang.* musicians' job, usu. a performance date

go-go (*adj*) describing style of pop music fashion, orig. 1960's

golden oldie *Informal.* hit pop song from earlier years, esp. rock-'n'-roll; oldie

Grammys annual awards given by music industry for excellence and achievement in various categories of popular and classical music

groove *Slang.* period of inspired, easy collaboration and performance among musicians; coherent rhythmic sense

groupie *Informal.* pop music fan, esp. female, who follows the fortunes of a particular band, hoping to become intimate with its members

headbanger *Slang.* fan or performer of heavy metal; metalhead

hip (*adj*) knowledgeable about current trends in pop culture, esp. music; (*n*) up-to-date, latest sounds

hit song achieving large commercial success

hit parade current crop of hit songs, esp. used in the 1950's

honky-tonk rural or western-style bar

hook immediately memorable and appealing musical catch phrase

hootenanny folk song festival or sing-along

horn section trumpets, trombones, and saxophones backing a combo on recordings or performances

jam jam session; (*vb*) improvise with other musicians

jam session impromptu musical performance; jam

jewel box hinged plastic case for a compact disc

jingle brief, catchy song advertising a product

jukebox mechanical record-playing machine, esp. in bars and dance halls

juke joint roadhouse, esp. in rural South, in which blues and rhythm-and-blues music is performed

karaoke equipment that provides recorded instrumental music so that a person can sing lyrics to the music, either for a recording or broadcast by speakers as entertainment

label company producing recordings, identified by a distinctive label or logo featuring its trade name on its releases

lead short, instrumental passage over rhythm parts

lick *Slang*. musical phrase; riff

liner notes text sold with a recording offering background on musical content of record

lip-sync (*vb*) mouth lyrics in sync with recording during performance

live recording recording made at live performance

LP long-playing record, usu. 33 1/3 rpm with a 12-inch diameter

lyricist person who writes words that are set to another person's music to form song

metalhead headbanger

monster hit pop recording with very great commercial and popular success

MOR middle-of-the-road; radio programming style; precursor of easy rock or AOR

MTV *Trademark*. Music Television; twenty-four-hour-a-day cable network featuring music videos

music video commercial or promotional videotape featuring a performance of a song, often incorporating dancing, a narrative line, action, or animation, orig. 1980's; video

novelty record humorous pop song, often capitalizing on a topical subject

oldie pop song from earlier years; golden oldie

open tuning tuning guitar strings so that chords may be played without fretting individual strings

original song composed by its performer

part arrangement for each instrument used in a song

payola *Informal*. bribe taken by disc jockey from record company to promote a recording on radio

pickup electric amplification device on an instrument, esp. a guitar

pirate (*vb*) illegally record, manufacture, or sell records and tapes

platter *Slang*. a phonograph record

playlist specified songs to be aired on radio show

producer individual responsible for overseeing recording sessions by handling budget, hiring

musicians and singers, choosing and arranging songs, and shaping the final sound

product record or tape to be sold; music in general

race record recording by black musicians in 1920's-1930's, esp. in southern United States

record grooved disc on which music has been imprinted; (*vb*) register music on a medium from which copies can be made

record club mail order membership club for the purchase of compact discs, cassettes, and records

release distribution of a recording; date such distribution begins

reverb echo effect popular on many rock-'n'-roll recordings

riff short melodic passage played on an instrument; lick

rim shot *Informal*. comic punctuation played by drummer after punch line of joke

roadie *Slang*. equipment handler for touring band

scratch (*vb*) make rhythmic sound by moving record back-and-forth under a turntable needle

section group of horn or string players backing up band

session musical recording period, esp. one day

set complete performance for audience, including selection of songs played

set list order of songs to be performed during set

sideman musician employed on recordings or performances, usu. not member of band

single featured song promoted from an album to boost sales or performance tour

slam dance punk music dance in which dancers bump into and strike one another

sleeve envelope covering record inside album jacket

solo single instrument lead played over rhythm section, usu. in absence of vocals

songwriter composer of music and sometimes lyrics for short musical pieces usu. made up of verses, chorus, and bridge

soul ability to convey depth of feeling in musical performance

soundalike recording that imitates successful artist, attempting to pass as the original upon casual listening

standard familiar, often-played popular song with widely known lyrics

swing (*vb*) perform freely, with feeling, and in tempo

sync (*vb*) *Informal*. synchronize

talent performers, singers, musicians

Tin Pan Alley popular music, esp. of the recent past, named after New York site that housed many songwriters and music publishers

top 40 AM radio format emphasizing the forty most-popular pop songs; list of these songs calculated and distributed weekly

topical song narrative song that comments on a current event

tour extensive series of performances in different cities

track one song on album; single recording; each element of instrumental music behind vocals

unplugged (*adj*) performed without electronic amplification or effects

verse basic unit of a song, providing narrative and setting up chorus

video music video

video jockey VJ; host on music video program

VJ video jockey

vocal singer's part of popular song

wah-wah pedal pedal that distorts guitar sound, orig. 1960's

Walkman *Trademark*. compact portable cassette player used with earphones

wall of sound full, lush sound quality in pop record production, originated by Phil Spector in 1960's

wax (*vb*) *Informal*. record

Sound Reproduction Technology

amp *Informal*. amplifier

amplifier device that increases voltage of sound waves

analog recording storage of sound waves directly on tape in form of electromagnetic energy; recording made this way

cartridge small, closed container for cassette tape; case on phonograph holding needle and apparatus for converting stylus motion into electrical voltage

cassette small, enclosed tape cartridge

CD compact disc

channel recording track on tape recorder

compact disc CD; means of sound reproduction that uses laser to read digitally encoded disc

compressor device that controls dynamic range of frequencies

console mixing console

deck tape recorder

digital delay conversion of analog signal into digital information, which is stored briefly on a memory chip then released in analog form

digital recording sound recording in which a frequency or waveform is sampled at regular intervals, then assigned numerical value, usu. a binary notation; record or tape made this way

direct box device that converts high impedance level instrument output into lower microphone level input

Dolby *Trademark*. noise reduction system that reduces tape hiss

drum machine digital synthesizer with stored samples of drum sounds that can be reproduced in any sequence

dub (*vb*) copy mix onto cassette; (*n*) such a copy

echo chamber empty chamber in recording studio for live creation of echo effects

emulator digital computer synthesizing sounds from voice or other source

EQ equalizer

equalizer EQ; tone control that divides the

audio range into intervals and accentuates its parts

fade (*v*) decrease volume; control varying volume between two set of speakers

feedback electronic sound made by reflux of speaker output to a microphone

filter device for suppressing or minimizing certain frequencies

flanging slight slowing of tape machine produced by touching flange of reel with thumb; phase shifter

half-track tape recorder with two tracks, both in same direction, covering entire width of tape, used for final mix to stereo

headphones small speakers in frame that fits over ears

hi-fi *Informal.* high fidelity

high fidelity reproduction of sound with high degree of faithfulness to original; system doing this; hi-fi

horn *Slang.* loudspeaker

isolation booth chamber in studio for recording vocals or single instruments

limiter compressor with high ratio of gain reduction

loop endlessly repeating section of tape

master (*vb*) transfer taped recordings onto lacquer mold, disk, or tape from which other copies will be pressed or duplicated; (*n*) such a disk or tape; matrix

matrix master

mic *Informal.* microphone

microphone transducer that changes sound waves into electric current measured in voltage: condenser, crystal, dynamic, or ribbon; mic; mike

MIDI **m**usical **i**nstrument **d**igital **i**nterface; language used by keyboard instruments to talk to each other and to computers or sequencers

midrange medium frequencies; speaker that is most efficient at these frequencies

mike *Informal.* microphone

mix blending of tracks to produce completed recording; mixdown; (*vb*) execute such a blending

mixdown mix

mixing console master board that controls the mixing of all specialized functions on all recording tracks; console

monophonic (*adj*) designating sound recording having single transmission path

multitrack recorder tape machine used in recording: 2-track, 4-track, 8-track, 16-track, or 24-track

noise gate dynamic range control that permits shutting off of signal when too low

oscillator tone generator, either sine or square wave

overdub track added in sync with already existing tracks

PA **p**ublic-**a**ddress system

pan *Informal.* panoramic; variation of volume sent to two or more speakers, so that sound seems to move between speakers when played together

patchbay central field of jacks connecting all elements of recording system

phase shifting electronic flanging achieved by shifting waves slightly out of sync, creating whooshing effect

playback act of reproducing a newly made recording to check it

playback head part of tape recorder that is used to pick up magnetic pattern on tape in order to play back recorded material

pot *Informal.* potentiometer

potentiometer variable resistor directly controlled by dial, knob, or lever on recording console; pot

power supply source of alternating current voltage

preamp *Informal.* preamplifier

preamplifier device that increases signal strength for detection and further amplification; preamp

public-address system PA; combination of microphones and speakers that makes sound audible to many people

quadraphonic (*adj*) designating sound reproduction system using four speakers, usu. set in four corners of room

receiver radio tuner with built-in amp and preamp

record head part of tape recorder that is used to imprint a magnetic pattern based on sound waves onto tape

reel-to-reel (*adj*) of or pertaining to a system using large, open spools of tape: quarter-inch, half-inch, or three-quarter inch

reverb electronically produced echo effect

sampler device that allows digital encoding of any signal picked up with microphone or direct recording box

sequencer digital keyboard computer that records sequences of notes and tells other keyboards when to play them

speaker transducer that changes voltage into sound waves

stereophonic (*adj*) designating sound recording having two transmission paths

tape magnetic tape impregnated with metal oxide, used to record sound waves in form of voltage

tape recorder means of storing sound in form of voltage on magnetic tape; deck

track one channel on multitrack recorder

transducer device, such as microphone or speaker, that is activated by power from one system to supply power in either the same or a different form to another system

tuner device that receives AM and FM radio signals

turntable revolving platform carrying phonograph record

tweeter speaker that is most efficient at high frequencies

twenty-four track state-of-the-art multitrack recording studio console, sometimes used in

tandem with another machine to create forty-eight tracks

vibrato device that electronically produces slight, rapid variations in pitch to impart a tremulous effect to sound

volume degree of loudness or intensity of sound

woofer speaker that is most efficient at low frequencies

Rock Era Dances

1950's (birdland, continental walk, handjive, hucklebuck, hully gully, Madison, shake, slop, stroll)

1960's (alligator, bird, boogaloo, Boston monkey, camel walk, dear lady twist, dog, fly, frug, freddie, funky chicken, funky pigeon, hitchhike, jerk, loco-motion, mashed potato, monkey, Philly dog, pony, skate, slauson, swim, temptation walk, twine, twist, Watusi)

1970's (bump, disco, hustle, L.A. hustle, Latin hustle, line dance, New York hustle, night fever, popcorn, rocking chair, roller coaster, roller disco, shuffle, special K, sway)

1980's (acid house, bedrock, break dancing, dirty dancing, Egyptian, ET, file dance, guess, le freak, moonwalk, nasty, neutron dance, pogo, salsa, slam dance, snake, vogue, walk)

1990's (achy-breaky, boot scoot and boogie, cabbage patch, dive, electric slide, happy hitchhiker, hop, macarena, moshing, NY slide, running man, smurf, tush push, watermelon crawl)

MUSICAL INSTRUMENTS

Instrument Types and Groupings
Drums
Percussion
Mirlitons
Keyboards
Stringed Instruments
Wind Instruments
Accessories

See also: *Chap. 15: Classical Music; Popular Music*

Instrument Types and Groupings

band group of musicians playing together

big band brass, winds, piano, and drums

brass any wind instrument made of metal with a metal mouthpiece

chamber orchestra small orchestra of less than twenty-five players, largely strings and woodwinds

combo small jazz or dance band

dance band up to twenty musicians, primarily winds

drum membranes stretched on a frame, esp. a hollow cylinder, that are struck with hand or stick

electronic any instrument producing sounds by electronic synthesis

gagaku ensemble shawms, flutes, gongs, drums, koto, and biwa, used to perform classical music (Japan)

gamelan orchestra tuned percussion, fiddle, and drums (Indonesia)

instrument any contrivance or apparatus that produces musical sounds

jazz band horns, drums, woodwinds, guitars, and keyboards

jug band band with strings, rudimentary percussion, and jug, playing folk music

keyboard any instrument composed of strings of varying lengths held taut and struck or plucked mechanically

marching band horns, drums, woodwinds, and percussion instruments played while marching before crowd or in parade

mariachi guitars, percussion, and brass (Mexico)

mirliton any instrument composed of membranes stretched and vibrated by air, not struck

orchestra large musical ensemble, with woodwind, brass, percussion, and string instruments, that performs symphonic music

palm court orchestra small string group and piano

percussion any instrument that is a solid or hollow object struck, shaken, or scraped

piano trio piano and violin with either viola or cello; piano, drums, and bass

rock band electric guitars, bass, drums, and keyboards

string any instrument composed of strings, usu. of uniform length, stretched on a frame and bowed or plucked by hand

string quartet two violins, viola, and cello

wind any instrument composed of a hollow tube made of wood or metal, with small holes and a mouthpiece that is blown into while fingers cover the holes

wind quintet flute, oboe, clarinet, bassoon, and horn

woodwind any wind instrument made of wood with a reed mouthpiece

Drums

banana drum long, narrow, tubular drum (Congo)

barrel drum drum with convex sides

bass drum large, double-headed, cylindrical drum used in modern orchestra

bata one of a set of long, conical drums (Cuba)

bendir skin drum (Morocco)

bhaya left-hand drum of tabla set

bodhran drum with shallow frame, used in folk music (Ireland)

bongo one of a set of small, cylindrical, single-headed drums played with the hands (South America)

changko double-headed drum made of lacquered wood (Korea)

conga long conical drum played with the hands

conical drum drum that tapers to a point or small head

cylindrical drum hollow frame drum with same diameter top to bottom

da-daiko very large frame drum used in gagaku ensemble (Japan)

daibyoshi Shinto temple drum (Japan)

darabukke small, goblet-shaped drum (Middle East)

dauli cylindrical, double-headed drum (Greece)

dhola barrel drum played horizontally (India)

double drum two drums bound together

dugdugi double-headed pottery drum (India)

footed drum drum that stands on legs, often with carved bases in form of human feet

frame drum any drum with membrane stretched on a rigid frame

friction drum drum in which cord or stick pierces drum membrane and vibrates to form sound

gong drum single-headed cylindrical drum used in modern orchestra

human skull drum two skulls mounted top to top (Tibet)

ingungu friction drum made from gourd (South Africa)

isigubu cylindrical drum made from a hollow log (South Africa)

kakko barrel drum, mounted on stand, used in gagaku ensemble (Japan)

kalungu wooden talking drum (West Africa)

kelontong small frame drum, equipped with long handle, that forms sounds when pellets on strings strike its surface (Indonesia)

kettledrum single membrane stretched over large pot or container

kit set of drums and percussion instruments used by pop or jazz bands: snare drum, tom-toms, side drum, bass drum, suspended cymbals, and hi-hat cymbals

koboro conical church drum (Ethiopia)

mridanga ancient, elongated barrel drum with tuned heads, used for performing formal, traditional music (India)

murumbu pot-shaped drum (South Africa)

nakers small kettledrum of Arabic origin (medieval Europe)

naqara small pair of kettledrums (Arabia)

ngoma wooden kettledrum usu. played by women (South Africa)

ntenga conical drum (Uganda)

o-daiko Shinto barrel drum (Japan)

okedo Kabuki theater drum (Japan)

peyote drum iron pot drum, filled with water (Native American)

rommelpot friction drum made from household pot (Europe)

side drum small cylindrical drum equipped with snares, used in modern orchestra

snare drum small, double-headed drum with wires across bottom for amplified reverberation

steel drum metal barrel cut to form drum: ping-pong, guitar pan, bass pan, rhythm pan, cello pan

tabla pair of drums with variable pitch, played with hands (India)

tabor small cylindrical drum hung around neck (Europe)

taiko folk music drum (Japan)

talamba small, metal kettledrum (Yugoslavia)

talking drum any of various, usu. hollow, percussion instruments used to play rhythms and tones that have specific meanings (Africa)

tambour circular drum

tambourine shallow frame drum with metal disks attached for added percussion (Spain and Portugal)

tenor drum high-toned cylindrical drum used in modern orchestra

terbang shallow frame drum (Java)

timbale one of a set of single-headed cylindrical drums mounted on stand (South America)

timpanum tuned, orchestral kettledrum, mounted on footed base; pl. timpani

tom-tom hand-beaten drum (Native American), medium-pitched drum in trap set

trap set pop or jazz drum and percussion kit: snare drum, tom-toms, side drum, bass drum, cymbals, high-hat

tsuri daiko barrel drum decorated and suspended on frame, used in gagaku ensemble (Japan)

tsuzumi small, hourglass-shaped, double-headed drum, used in Nō drama (Japan)

uchiwa daiko frame drum with handle (Japan)

Percussion

bell metal, cup-shaped resonator with clapper or pellet inside that strikes wall to produce tone: cowbell, camel bell, temple bell, handbell, wind-bell, church bell

bell-lyra portable glockenspiel mounted on lyre-shaped frame, used by marching bands

bones pair of small bones that make a clicking sound when struck together

bonnang set of gong chimes in box frame (Java)

bull-roarer wood disk or blade spun on cord

buzz disk disk spun on twisted cord

carillon set of tuned bells

castanets hand-held wood or bone clappers, clicked together

chimes set of bells on pole or frame

clappers pair of sticks or blocks, held and struck together

clave one of a pair of wood sticks or blocks, struck together

cowbell large, metal bell struck with stick

cymbals conical or dished metal disks, struck together or with stick

electric xylophone vibraharp

gambang kayu xylophone (Java)

gamelan gong xylophone (Bali and Java)

gansa gambang metallophone (Bali)

glass harmonica water-filled wineglasses in box or set, resonated by rubbing rims

glockenspiel metallophone on stand, carried in marching band

gong metal disk struck by stick

high-hat two cymbals on stand, crashed together by foot pedal

humming top hollow vessel with holes, spun to produce sound

Jew's harp small frame with flexible metal tongue, plucked by finger while instrument is held to mouth

jingle small bell or rattle, often worn as ornament

kalimba marimba, zanza (Africa)

kenong bowl-shaped gong over resonating box (Java)

lithophone set of graduated stones in box frame

maraca gourd filled with beans or seeds that rattle when shaken (South America)

marimba xylophone with wood resonators under bars (Latin America)

mbira gourd resonator with tuned metal or wood strips, plucked with fingers (Africa)

metallophone set of graduated metal bars over resonating box, struck with mallet

rattle hollow form with seeds or stones inside, shaken to produce raspy sound

rhythm stick small wood stick struck against any surface; child's rudimentary percussion instrument

sansa thumb piano; zanza (Africa)

slit drum log or pole hollowed through slit, beaten with sticks

suspended cymbal single cymbal loosely attached to stand

tam-tam large bronze gong

thumb piano hollow resonating box with tongues of various lengths to be plucked; sansa

triangle metal rod bent into triangle, struck with stick

vibraharp percussion instrument that resembles a marimba, played with mallets and having metal rather than wooden bars and electrically powered resonators that create vibrato effect; electric xylophone; vibraphone

vibraphone vibraharp

washboard washing board scraped with rod or stick

woodblock resonant, hollow block of wood, struck with wooden sticks

xylophone set of tuned bars in box frame, struck with sticks or mallet

zanza wood box with graduated wood or metal tongues, plucked with fingers and thumbs; kalimba; sansa (Africa)

Mirlitons

comb and paper hair comb with paper folded around it

eunuch flute tube with membrane-covered aperture; onion flute (Europe)

kazoo toy horn with membrane-covered blowhole

onion flute eunuch flute

zobo kazoo-like toy horn in shape of conventional horn

Keyboards

accordion keyboard that controls vibrating reeds set in motion by bellows-forced air; piano accordion

baby grand small grand piano

barrel organ mechanical organ with revolving cylinder turned by hand

calliope steam-powered organ

celesta set of graduated steel plates struck with hammers that are activated by a keyboard

cembalo harpsichord or keyed dulcimer

chord organ simplified organ on which each key sounds a full chord

clavichord early keyboard, smaller than piano, having strings struck by brass pins attached to key ends

clavicytherium early, upright spinet

clavier any of various keyboard instruments, including piano and harpsichord

concert grand largest, highest-quality grand piano with richest tone

concertina small accordion

geigenwerk mechanical harpsichord (Germany)

grand piano large piano with horizontal frame and strings, supported on three legs

Hammond organ *Trademark.* electronic organ with double keyboard that produces sound of a pipe organ

harmonium small reed organ powered by bellows

harpsichord early wire-stringed double keyboard with seven stops, having strings plucked by quills; cembalo (17th-18th c.)

hurdy-gurdy mechanical violin with strings activated by keyboard

melodeon small reed organ; accordion

Moog *Trademark.* one of the earliest electronic synthesizers

ondes martenot electronically vibrated strings controlled by keyboard

organ set of pipes resonated by air: barrel, electric, mouth, pipe, portative, reed

orphica small portable piano (Europe, 19th c.)

piano steel strings struck by felt hammers operated from keyboard: grand, baby grand, upright, spinet, player, table, electric; pianoforte

piano accordion accordion

pianoforte piano

Pianola *Trademark.* brand of player piano

pipe organ large organ in which tones are produced by passage of air through sets of variable-length pipes operated by keyboard

player piano upright piano operated by moving scroll perforated with notations

reed organ organ in which tones are produced by set of free metal reeds

regal small, portable organ (16th-17th c.)

spinet compactly built, upright piano; early harpsichord with one keyboard

square piano piano with rectangular, horizontal body

squeezebox *Informal.* accordion or concertina

Stringed Instruments

synthesizer electronic console that produces sounds using keyboard-controlled oscillators, filters, mixers, and amplifiers, and sometimes by digital computer

theremin electronic tone generator controlled by distance between player's hands and two metal antennas

Tippoo's tiger mechanical organ in the shape of a tiger attacking an Englishman (Britain)

upright piano with vertical frame and strings

virginal small spinet with no legs, one wire per note (16th-17th c.)

vocoder electronic instrument that resolves human voice signals and transmits tones of same pitch by keyboard

Stringed Instruments

aeolian harp rectangular zither on which strings are not plucked but rather sounded by air currents

archlute lute with two pegboxes, one for bass strings

Autoharp *Trademark.* zither with dampers on strings controlled by buttons

bagana box-shaped, ritual lyre (Ethiopia)

balalaika flat, triangularly shaped lute with two to four strings (Russia)

bandore ancient lute, cittern, or pandora

bandoura large lute with many strings that produces continuous, low tones (Russia)

banjo shallow, circular body with parchment belly, long neck, and one short and four long strings

baryton bass viol

bass fiddle double bass

bass viol viola da gamba; double bass

biwa four-stringed lute (Japan)

bolon three-stringed harp lute with spherical gourd resonator and belly of animal skin with hair (Sierra Leone)

bouzouki lute with strings in double courses (Greece)

bow string attached to flexible stick

bull fiddle double bass

bumbass long, single string that is bowed or plucked (Europe, 17th c.)

cello large, bass violin with floor stand; violoncello

ch'in long, classical zither (China)

chitarra battente early, deep-bodied guitar (Italy)

chitarrone long-necked lute with two pegboxes

cittern flat-bodied, long-necked, pear-shaped instrument, similar to guitar (Europe, 15th-18th c.)

clarsach ancient harp (Ireland and Scotland)

cobza lute with strings in two groups around sound holes (Romania)

colascione very long-necked lute with three strings (Italy)

contrabass double bass

crowd crwth

crwth ancient lyre with shallow body, either plucked or bowed; crowd (Ireland)

cymbalom dulcimer in table frame (Hungary)

Dobro *Trademark.* lap guitar with metal resonator plate on body

double bass largest, deepest-pitched member of violin family; bass fiddle; bass viol; bull fiddle; contrabass; string bass

dulcimer zither struck with mallets or sticks

fiddle any stringed instrument bowed rather than plucked, esp. violin

fidla bowed zither (Iceland)

gittern early four-stringed guitar made from single piece of wood; cittern (Britain)

guitar flat-backed, long-necked, stringed instrument, usu. with waisted shape to soundbox that produces sounds when plucked: acoustic, electric, double-neck, electric bass, pedal steel, Hawaiian

guittaron very large bass guitar (Mexico)

gutbucket crude bass made of gut string attached to bucket, used in folk and some jazz music

hammer dulcimer set of tuned strings in frame, struck with hammer

harp angled strings set in frame attached to soundbox: bow, angle, frame, double, orchestral

harp lute any of various instruments in which plane of strings is at right angles to belly of instrument (West Africa)

Irish harp bow-shaped medieval harp (Ireland)

kantele traditional, five-stringed lute (Finland)

kerar bowl shaped folk lyre (Ethiopia)

kit very small, narrow violin

kithara large, box-shaped lyre (ancient Greece)

ko-kiu shallow, square-bodied, long-necked fiddle (Japan)

kora harp lute with sixteen to twenty-one strings and skin belly (West Africa)

koto long zither with thirteen silk strings (Japan)

lira three-stringed, pear-shaped folk fiddle (Greece)

lirica small, pear-shaped fiddle (Yugoslavia)

lute pear-shaped resonating box with long, often bent neck holding strings stretched over bridge, plucked to produce sound

lyre resonating box with attached strings on two curved arms joined by a yoke, struck with plectrum (ancient Greece and Egypt); solid wooden box with strings stretched over bridge (Europe)

machete fish-shaped guitar (Portugal)

mandola small lute with curved pegbox (Italy)

mandolin classical lute with usu. four pairs of strings (Italy)

mandolone bass mandolin

monochord ancient, single-stringed instrument with oblong sounding box, used esp. to determine intervals

moon guitar flat-backed, short-necked, silk-stringed lute (Asia)

obukano large, bowl-shaped lyre (East Africa)

orpharion ancient cittern with six to nine paired metal strings

oud short-necked lute (Middle East and North Africa)

pandora large, bass cittern; bandore

pedal steel guitar box-shaped guitar on legs, having ten strings altered in pitch by foot pedal and plucked while being pressed by movable steel bar

pipa shallow, silk-stringed, fretted lute (China)

psaltery medieval board zither that was plucked (Europe)

ramkie simple folk guitar (South Africa)

rebab medieval bowed fiddle with one to three strings (Middle East)

rebec pear-shaped fiddle with bowed strings (medieval Europe)

ruan long-necked, flat-backed lute (China)

samisen long-necked, shallow-bodied, three-stringed lute (Japan)

santir dulcimer with trapezoidal box and strings struck by curved beaters (Middle East)

sarod bowed lute (Northern India)

sintir dulcimer of santir family (Egypt)

sitar large lute made from a gourd, having arched metal frets on a long neck (India)

string bass double bass

tambura fretted, long-necked lute (Yugoslavia, India)

tamburitza plucked, guitar-shaped mandolinlike instrument (Yugoslavia)

theorbo bass lute with bass strings on second pegbox (Renaissance Europe)

ukulele very small, four-stringed guitar (Hawaii)

uti short-necked lute (Yugoslavia)

valiha tube zither (Malagasy)

vina stick-shaped zither with two gourd resonators (India)

viol predecessor to violin with flat back, broader bow, and fretted fingerboard (Europe, 17th c.)

viola four-stringed member of violin family, slightly larger than violin and with deeper pitch

viola da gamba cello; bass viol (17th c.)

viola d'amore fretless tenor viol with seven gut strings and seven wire sympathetic strings (Europe, 18th c.)

violin small, finely shaped, curved, resonating body with four strings that are bowed or occasionally plucked

violoncello cello

yang chin zither with movable bridges (China)

zither long resonator body with many strings attached over its entire length: raft, stick-shaped, trough, tube

Wind Instruments

alpenhorn long, powerful horn of wood with curved bell that produces single notes

arghool oboe with two pipes, one a drone (Arabia)

aulos double pipe with double reed (ancient Greece)

bagpipe air-filled bag with reeded mouth pipe, drone pipe, and melody pipe

basset horn bent or curved, reeded horn (Bavaria)

bassoon double-tubed bass horn with double reed mouthpiece

bombardon E-flat bass tuba

bosun's pipe whistle with variable pitch

bugle simple metal horn with reedless mouthpiece

chalumeau progenitor of orchestral clarinet (Europe)

clarinet horn or tube with reed inserted in mouthpiece that vibrates when blown

clarion ancient, curved trumpet

contrabass largest orchestral clarinet

contrabassoon double bassoon that reaches very low octaves

cor anglais English horn; curved, belled alto oboe (Europe, 17th c.)

cornet trumpet-shaped, flared metal horn played with valves

cornett wood horn with finger holes

cornu long trumpet curved into circle (ancient Rome)

crumhorn narrow, curved, double-reed horn (Renaissance Europe)

cuckoo whistle simple whistle flute

didgeridoo large, aboriginal bamboo pipe (Australia)

doodlesack goatskin bagpipe (Germany)

English horn large, deep-pitched oboe having pear-shaped bell; cor anglais

euphonium large, valved tenor tuba

fife small, side-blown flute

fipple flute any instrument with tubular body, finger holes, and whistle mouthpiece

flageolet six-holed whistle flute with bone or ivory mouthpiece (Europe)

flugelhorn valved, flared brass horn, esp. for military bands

flute tube producing tones by air blown through or across mouthpiece hole, with or without keys

French horn valved brass horn with coiled tube ending in flared bell

fujara very long, wood whistle flute (Slovakia)

glass flute tube made of glass

harmonica set of reeded tubes in box-shaped, metal shell; mouth organ

hautboy early oboe

helicon coiled tuba carried over shoulder in marching bands

horn curved, conical animal horn with reedless mouthpiece; any flared metal tube with reedless mouthpiece

hornpipe folk clarinet, often of animal horn

hunting horn earliest form of modern horn, consisting of coiled conical tube with flaring bell

jug large, deep, glass container with small opening at top, across which player blows

lituus curved military trumpet (ancient Rome)

lyricon wind synthesizer fingered like clarinet that controls analog synthesizer

megaphone cone-shaped device for intensifying or directing voice

mellophone valved, flared metal horn

mouth organ harmonica

musette early bagpipe with air supplied by bellows (France, 17th-18th c.)

nose flute tube played with breath from nostril instead of mouth

oboe keyed wood pipe with double-reed mouthpiece and conical tube

oboe d'amore oboe pitched a minor third below the conventional oboe, much used in music of baroque period

ocarina simple, oval-shaped flute with finger holes and mouthpiece

ophicleide conical metal tube bent double

panpipe set of small flutes of graduated sizes joined together in one unit; syrinx

piccolo small flute that reaches high octaves

pipe small whistle flute held in one hand

post horn straight or coiled metal horn with no valves or slide

recorder wood whistle flute in one of various pitches (Europe)

sackbut trombone (medieval Europe)

salpinx narrow ivory trumpet (ancient Greece)

sarrusophone brass horn with double-reed mouthpiece

saxhorn any of a family of brass instruments similar to cornet and tuba

saxophone metal horn with reed mouthpiece: sopranino, soprano, alto, tenor, baritone, bass, contrabass, subcontrabass

saxtuba large, bass saxhorn

serpent intricately curved wood horn with finger holes (18th c.)

shakuhachi bamboo flute (Japan)

shawm folk pipe with double-reed mouthpiece (Eastern Europe and Asia)

shiwaya vessel flute made from hollow fruit shell (South Africa)

shofar curved ram's horn that produces tones one-fifth apart, used to signal Jewish High Holidays

sousaphone large bass tuba

syrinx panpipe

talinka medieval, one-hole flute (eastern Europe)

ti-tzu bamboo flute (China)

tonette small, end-blown flute

trombone brass tube with a reedless mouthpiece and a slide for varying tube length

trumpet flared brass tube with reedless mouthpiece, usu. with three valves

tuba large, valved, deep-pitched brass horn with flared bell

urua very long double folk clarinet (Brazil)

whistle flute flute in which air is blown into mouthpiece rather than across it

Accessories

bell large end of tube of wind instrument, usu. with edge turned out and enlarged

bocal curved metal piece holding reed and connected to body of bassoon

bottleneck glass tube slid along guitar strings for glissando effect

bow horsehairs stretched on wood rod for playing stringed instrument

box soundbox

bridge thin, arched support over which strings are stretched at belly of stringed instrument

brush metal bristles on handle for playing drums

capo movable bar attached to fingerboard of fretted, stringed instrument to raise pitch

chanter melody pipe of bagpipe

damper device that deadens sound, esp. by halting vibration of string

drumhead stretched membrane struck by drumsticks

drumstick wood stick for striking drumheads

f-hole either of two f-shaped slits in body of stringed instrument, esp. of violin family

fingerboard fretboard of guitar or lute

finger hole opening in tube or body of wind instrument, covered by finger to regulate pitch

fret lateral ridge on fingerboard of stringed instrument, used to regulate pitch and finger placement

fretboard fingerboard of guitar with lateral ridges that regulate pitch

key elements depressed by fingers and connected to strings in keyboard

ligature metal binding that holds reed on wind instrument

mallet drumstick with padded, rounded head

membrane thin, pliable sheet of animal or vegetable tissue stretched to form drumhead

metronome device for exactly measuring tempo through regular, repeated clicking sounds

mouthpiece detachable end of wind or brass instrument that goes into player's mouth

mute device used to muffle tone, esp. inserted in bell of brass instrument

neck narrow extension from body to peghead of string instrument

nut ledge at upper end of fingerboard of stringed instrument over which strings pass

peg device that controls tension of strings

peghead base for arrangement of pegs that control tension on strings

pick plectrum

pipe tube forming essential part of wind instrument; tube from which tones of organ are produced

pitch pipe small reed pipe used to tune instruments or establish pitch for singer by producing specific tone; tuning pipe

plectrum thin piece of ivory, wood, metal, horn, quill, or plastic, used to pluck strings of stringed instrument; pick

purfling ornamental, inlaid border on back of violin and other stringed instruments

reed thin, elastic tongue of wood fastened over mouthpiece in wind instrument and set vibrating by air current

soundbox hollow, bell-shaped, resonating body of stringed instrument; box

spit valve valve that opens to release saliva, as from trumpet

string thin cord of nylon, gut, or metal stretched and plucked or bowed

tube long, hollow body of wind instrument, usu. with finger holes or valves

tuning fork two-pronged metal device that produces specific tone when struck, usu. 440 frequency A

tuning pipe pitch pipe

valve hole in body of brass instrument closed off by depression of key

yoke crosspiece that connects or binds other parts

DANCE

Dances of the World
Ballet
Events, Steps, and Dancers

See also: *Chap. 15: Classical Music; Popular Music; Theater*

Dances of the World

abstract dance modern dance form in which pure movements have no implied narrative or symbolic meaning beyond themselves

alegrias oldest and purest form of flamenco (Spain)

allemande court dance performed with interwound arms, developed from German folk dance (17th-18th c.)

ballet classical dance form based on conventional steps and positions with precise, graceful movements; a theatrical entertainment that conveys story or atmosphere through such dance and music

ballo standard popular dance and its music (Italy, 15th-16th c.)

barn dance rural American social dance, variation on schottische in triple time, sometimes held in barn

basse danse court dance that preceded minuet (16th-17th c.)

beguine vigorous, popular ballroom dance in bolero rhythm, similar to rumba (Caribbean)

belly dance solo dance performed by woman that emphasizes undulations of stomach (Middle East)

bergamasca fast, rustic dance in duple time, similar to tarantella (Italy)

Bharat Natya ancient, classical Vedic cult dance for women (India)

bocane sedate dance for couple in duple time

bolero lively dance in triple time, performed with sharp turns, stamping feet, and sudden stops (Spain)

bop shufflelike dance to modern bebop jazz

bossa nova dance similar to samba, with jazz influence (Brazil)

bourrée dance in quick duple time (France, 17th c.)

breakdown lively folk or jazz dance

bugaku classical dance for men, performed in the imperial palace to gagaku music (Japan)

bunny hug ragtime dance that is variation on Charleston

cachucha lively solo dance resembling the bolero, performed with castanets in triple time (Andalusia)

cakewalk African-American stage dance with eccentric strutting followed by solemn processional walk (19th c.)

canary lively European court dance (16th c.)

cancan high-kicking stage dance performed by women while holding up skirt front (France, 19th c.)

carioca variation on samba (Brazil)

carmagnole meandering street dance performed to lively song of French Revolution

cha-cha fast, rhythmic, ballroom dance, based on three quick steps and a shuffle (Latin America)

Charleston vigorous 1920's ballroom dance in which knees are swung in and out and heels turned outward on each step

clog dance in which performer beats out rhythm on floor with heavy wood shoes

conga ballroom dance for group in single line doing three steps forward and a kick (Cuba)

contredanse folk dance in which couples face each other in two lines

cooch hootchy-kootchy

cotillion lively social dance similar to quadrille with frequent changing of partners under leadership of one couple (France, 18th c.)

country dance traditional dance in which dancers form facing lines (Britian)

courante dance in quick triple time with running or gliding step (Italy, 17th c.)

czardas dance in duple time with slow first movement and fast, whirling second movement (Hungary)

djanger vigorous, dramatic children's dance in which dancers cry out (Bali)

écossaise country dance in quick duple time (Scotland)

erotic dance striptease

fan dance solo dance performed by nude or seminude woman using one or more large fans to cover her body

fandango dance in lively triple time performed by one couple with castanets to guitar accompaniment (Spain, Latin America)

farandole dance in lively sextuple time, in which couples join hands and follow leader in various figures (Provence)

flamenco vigorous, rhythmic gypsy dance performed with stamping of feet and clapping of hands (Spanish Andalusia)

fling Highland fling

foxtrot two-step ballroom dance in quadruple time

galliard spirited, five-step dance for two dancers, performed in triple time (Europe, 16th-17th c.)

galop lively round dance in duple time (France and Germany, 19th c.)

gavotte dance of peasant origin performed in quick quadruple time (France, 18th c.)

ghost dance ritual native dance that calls on ancestors to assist in revival of power of a people

gigue jig; suite dance in triple time (Italy)

gopak folk dance performed with stomping of heels (Ukraine)

habanera dance in slow duple time (Cuba)

haka traditional Maori dance (New Zealand)

Highland fling lively folk dance characterized by tossing of arms and legs; fling (Scotland)

hoedown square dance

hootchy-kootchy pseudo-Oriental carnival dance that involves suggestive torso movements performed by woman dancer; cooch

hora traditional round dance (Israel and Romania)

hula dance with sinuous hip movements and mimetic hand gestures that tell story to drumming and chanting accompaniment (Hawaii)

Interpretive dance highly personal form of modern dance

jazz dance modern dance form performed to jazz music, esp. in quadruple time, based on standardized movements

jig lively, springy folk dance in triple time; gigue

jitterbug American jazz two-step, performed by couples in the 1940's, consisting of standardized patterns with acrobatic swings, twirls, splits, and somersaults

joropo ballroom dance in rapid triple time (Venezuela)

jota folk dance performed by a couple in triple time with complex rhythms made with castanets and heels (Spain)

juba American southern plantation slave dance, accompanied by rhythmic clapping and slapping of knees and thighs

kathak classical dance form of Mongol era (India)

kathakali dance for men wearing facial makeup and using intricate hand gestures and expressions (India)

kazatsky lively Slavic folk dance for single male dancer

kebiyar popular children's fan dance (Bali)

khon dramatic dance for men performed to orchestral music (Thailand)

kolo folk dance in which a circle of dancers moves around a soloist who performs elaborate steps (Serbia)

lambada ballroom dance that combines elements of merengue, samba, and salsa, in which partners' bodies interlock closely to strong, sensual rhythm (Brazil)

Lambeth walk spirited 1930's ballroom dance combining jaunty strut with square dance figures

ländler folk dance in moderate triple time, antecedent of waltz (Austria and Germany)

legong elegant, traditional dance-pantomime, performed by girls in elaborate colorful costumes and accompanied by gamelan orchestra (Bali)

limbo competitive, acrobatic dance in which dancer bends backward from knees and moves under horizontal pole at progressively lower heights (West Indies)

lindy energetic jitterbug (1930's)

malaguena lively dance similar to fandango (Spain)

mambo ballroom dance similar to rumba and cha-cha with more complex steps (Cuba)

manipuri traditional folk dance (northern India)

maxixe syncopated ballroom dance in duple time (Brazil)

mazurka lively folk dance in triple time (Poland)

merengue ballroom dance performed with one stiff leg dragged on every step (Haiti)

Mexican hat dance lively courtship dance for solo male performed around brim of sombrero placed on ground (Mexico)

minuet slow, stately dance in triple time, performed with bowing and toe pointing (18th c.)

modern dance expressionistic, theatrical dance, developed after 1915 as alternative to ballet, with no formal conventions and unorthodox movements, done to eclectic music and based on one of various specialized techniques for using the entire body

morris dance vigorous rural dance for men wearing Robin Hood costumes, performed esp. on May Day (Britain, 16th c.)

nautch dance sinuous dance for female performer (India)

nihon buyo blend of ancient dance forms performed in Kabuki theater (Japan)

one-step ballroom round dance in duple time, performed to ragtime with quick walking steps backward and forward

ox dance comic men's folk dance like mock duel (Sweden)

pas de deux ballet dance for couple

passacaglia moderately slow dance in triple time (Italy, Spain, 17th c.)

pavane stately court dance in slow duple time (Europe, 16th c.)

peabody lively ballroom dance

polka lively dance for couples, performed in duple time using hop-step-close-step pattern (Bohemia)

polonaise stately promenade or march in slow triple time (Poland, 19th c.)

quadrille square dance with five complete parts, performed by four couples in duple and sextuple time

rain dance ritual native dance invoking rain

reel lively traditional Highland folk dance (Scotland)

rigadoon lively popular dance for one couple, performed in quick duple time (17th-18th c.)

round dance folk or ballroom dance in which couples move in circular motion around room

rumba ballroom dance performed in duple or quadruple time with step-close-step pattern and complex shifting of weight (Cuba)

salsa popular dance performed to rhythmic, big-band jazz (Latin America)

saltarello lively dance for soloist or couple, in which a hop step begins each measure (Italy, 17th c.)

samba dance of African origin, consisting of a step-close-step-close pattern with dips and leaps on the beat, performed to relaxed jazz music (Brazil)

saraband stately court dance, similar to minuet, in slow triple time (Spain, 17th-18th c.)

schottische round dance resembling a slow polka (Scotland)

seguidilla folk dance in triple time, performed to guitar and castanet accompaniment (Spain)

shag dance performed with vigorous hopping on each foot in turn (1930's-1940's)

shimmy ragtime dance characterized by shaking of shoulders and hips (1920's)

shuffle dance characterized by scraping feet across floor

siciliano folk dance in which partners are joined by a handkerchief (Sicily)

Sir Roger de Coverley country dance for two rows of dancers facing each other (Britain)

skirt dance folk dance performed in full, flowing skirts

slow dance contemporary popular dance in which couples embrace and sway gently to slow ballads

snake dance ritual dance performed with snakes, or in which their images are invoked or imitated by sinuous movements

soft-shoe tap dance steps in soft-soled shoes without metal taps

square dance set folk dance for four couples arranged in a square; hoedown

stomp dance to jazz music with driving rhythm, usu. marked by stamping of feet

strathspey slow folk dance in quadruple time, similar to reel (Scotland)

striptease burlesque dance in which performer suggestively removes clothing piece by piece; erotic dance

swing jazz dance performed in moderate, lilting syncopation to big band music

sword dance native male ceremonial dance performed around swords or in circle with flourished swords

tambourin dance in duple time accompanied by drone bass or steady drumbeat (Provence)

tango ballroom dance performed by couple in quadruple time with long pauses, varied steps, and stylized poses (Latin America)

tap dance rhythmic variations tapped out audibly by dancer usu. wearing shoes with metal taps or special hard soles

tarantella rapid, whirling folk dance in sextuple time (Italy, 18th c.)

Texas two-step variation on two-step done to country-and-western swing music

toe dance women's ballet executed on tips of toes while wearing pointe shoes with reinforced toes

trepak vigorous men's folk dance featuring leg flings and kicks (Ukraine)

turkey trot ragtime round dance having springy steps with straightened knees, body swings, and up-and-down shoulder movements

two-step ballroom dance performed in duple time with sliding step-close-step pattern

valse à deux temps *French.* bright, gliding ballroom dance similar to galop (19th c.)

villanella rustic, free-form dance performed to unaccompanied song (Italy, 16th-17th c.)

Virginia reel dance in which two facing lines of couples execute a series of figures in turn (19th c.)

waltz classical ballroom dance performed in moderate triple time with accent on first beat of step-step-close pattern and dancers revolving in circles (19th c.)

war dance native ritual dance performed prior to battle or in celebration of victory

Washington Post ballroom dance in sextuple time (19th c.)

zapateado solo dance performed with rhythmic foot tapping (Spain and Latin America)

Ballet

adagio slow, sustained movement stressing grace, balance; ballerina's lyrical performance in second part of grand pas de deux

allegro rapid movements accompanied by jumps, turns, and batteries

allongé extension of arms in arabesque

arabesque standing on one leg with raised leg extended in straight line to rear and foot pointed

assemblé rising off floor, straightening both legs in air, and returning to fifth position

assoluta (*adj*) extraordinary

attitude standing on one leg with raised leg behind body and knee bent; same position with raised leg in front of body

balance light, rocking waltz step in which weight is shifted from side to side

ballerina female dancer, esp. company's principal ballerina

ballet d'action ballet that tells a story, often tragic

ballet master ballet company's principal instructor, often also choreographer

balletomane enthusiastic and knowledgeable follower of ballet

ballon dancer's spring and lightness in leaps

ballonné broad leap with battement kick

barre horizontal bar opposite mirrors and along wall in studio for class exercises

battement high or low kick: grand battement or petit battement

batterie beating together of feet or legs, esp. in midair

bourrée traveling movement with feet moving in tiny steps from tight fifth position

brisé jump in which one leg beats against the other in midair

cabriole man's batterie with one leg kicked high and the other leg rising to beat against it one or more times

cambré bending back or to one side

Cecchetti method classic Italian style of ballet, as distinguished from French and Russian schools

chaîné series of short, usu. rapid turns made while moving across the floor

changement de pied jump begun in fifth position, ending in fifth position with opposite foot forward

character dance comic, semiserious dance, often a folk dance step or part performed with classical technique

chassé traveling movement in which one foot follows and displaces the other

choreographer creator of steps and patterns for ballet set to specific piece of music

choreography art of devising form, sequence, and purpose of ballet movements

ciseaux scissorslike leap with legs wide apart in midair

closed positions first, third, and fifth positions, in which feet are in contact with each other

coda final section of classical grand pas de deux

combination several movements in succession

contretemps step taken in counter time

corps de ballet ensemble or chorus of company dancers who perform together, not solo, usu. the junior members of a company

coryphée performer dancing in small group instead of solo or in corps de ballet

count measure of beats on which movements take place

coupé linking movement between steps, in which one foot replaces the other on a spot

couru (*adj*) running

croisé movement with body at oblique angle to audience and working leg crossing behind or in front of body

danseur male ballet dancer

danseur noble principal male dancer, equal to prima ballerina

dégagé freeing of foot prior to taking step, with working leg brushed out so that toes rise a few inches off the floor

demi-plié movement in which knee or knees are half-bent with heels on floor

demi-pointe dancing with weight of body on toes and ball of foot

developpé slowly bending and then straightening knee as leg is raised in extension from floor

divertissement dance or series of short dances without plot

écarté separated body position; position with perfectly square head and body leaning away from raised leg turned out to extreme

échappé jump with feet moving from a closed fifth to an open second position

effacé position with torso and hips at oblique angle to audience, working leg extended to front or back, and opposite arm raised above head

elevation apparent ability to remain suspended in midair while performing movements

emboîtés little hopping steps from leg to leg with working leg lifted in low front attitude

en arrière (*adj*) to the back; backward

en avant (*adj*) to the front; forward

enchaînement linking together of two or more movements to fit phrase of music; combination

en dedans (*adj*) moving arms or legs inward, toward body

en dehors (*adj*) moving arms or legs outward, away from body

en face (*adj*) facing body directly forward

en l'air (*adj*) performed off the ground

en seconde (*adj*) performed in second position

entr'acte interlude between main parts of a ballet

entrechat directly upward jump with body straight and feet reversing position several times in midair, named by number of reversals, as in entrechat quatre or entrechat six

épaulement bringing one shoulder forward in presenting step to audience with head turned over forward shoulder

extension dancer's ability to lift leg above head in nearly straight line from hip

failli linking movement between steps in which dancer jumps into quarter-turn

fifth position closed position with feet fully turned out and crossed one in front of the other, so that the heel of each touches the big toe of the other

figure step, leap, small combination

first position closed position in which feet form straight line perpendicular to body with heels touching

fish dive forward dive in which ballerina is caught by partner with her head and shoulders just above the floor

fondu lowering of body by slowly bending the knee of supporting leg with working foot pointing frontward

fouetté spin on one leg in which body is propelled by whipping motion of raised leg, performed by ballerina, usu. in series

fourth position open position with feet turned out from hip and placed horizontally, one in front of the other, a foot apart

frappé movement beginning with small beat with foot extended out strongly from knee

glissade gliding step from fifth to second to fifth position, performed on floor in low leap or prior to leap

grand battement high kick in any direction

grand jeté high leap covering a long distance in air

grand pas de deux formal, five-part pas de deux: entrée, ballerina's partnered adagio, male solo, female solo, coda

grand plié knees bending as deeply as possible with heels rising off floor

jeté leap made by pushing off on one leg and landing on the other

Labanotation standard choreographic notation technique, devised by Rudolf von Laban

open positions second and fourth positions, in which feet are placed apart

par terre (*adj*) performed on the ground

partnering strength, grace, rhythm, and certainty with which danseur assists and supports ballerina

pas formalized step; designation for type of dance

pas de basque linking movement between steps

pas de bourrée traveling step in any direction on pointe or demi-pointe

pas de chat leap from plié in fifth position

pas de cheval movement from fourth position that resembles a horse pawing the ground

pas de deux dance for two dancers, esp. grand pas de deux

pas de quatre dance for four dancers

pas de trois dance for three dancers

passé movement with working leg raised to side and knee bent, in which foot is pointed downward and brushed against standing leg

pas seul solo dance

penché (*adj*) leaning forward

petits battements small, quick movements with foot beating from front to back of ankle

petit tours short, fast turns made while progressing in straight line or circle

piqué stepping out onto pointe; little hop preparatory to traveling movement

pirouette turn of body while standing on one leg with raised leg held in position, performed on pointe for female, demi-pointe for male

placement good posture, turnout, and proper leg alignment

plié bending of knees while back is held straight with hips, legs, and feet turned out

pointe dancing on tips of toes; ballerina's dancing while maintaining continuous straight line from tips of toes to hip

pointe shoes ballerina's slippers with hard block in toes, used for standing on pointe

port de bras carriage and movement of arms

posé tours series of turns executed diagonally, around, or straight across floor

positions five basic positions of feet and arms

premier danseur principal male dancer

première danseuse principal ballerina

prima ballerina ballet company's principal ballerina

principals prima ballerinas and premier danseurs of ballet company

promenade slow turn of body on planted foot in adagio

régisseur stage manager who supervises performances

relevé rising onto pointe or demi-pointe

répétiteur rehearsal coach

révérence deep bow or curtsy

rond de jamb rotary movement of leg on floor or in air

rosin translucent, brittle turpentine resin used on shoes to prevent slipping on floor

royale changement de pied in which calves are beaten together before feet change position

saut de basque jump straight up, made with one leg bent at knee

saut de chat jump similar to grande jeté but with front leg passing through attitude

second position open position in which feet form straight line perpendicular to body while a foot apart

sissonne jump with legs straight and one leg extended to side

soloist dancer who performs occasional solos, ranked above corps de ballet and below principals in company hierarchy

soubresant leap from both feet to landing on both feet in fifth position

sous-sous rising from fifth position on flat feet to fifth position on pointe

soutenu (*adj*) sustained, esp. of battement rising into fifth position demi-pointe with equal weight on both legs

stulchak move in which male dancer holds ballerina above his head on one straight arm

sur le coup de pied position of pointed foot lightly wrapped around front of ankle or touching back of calf near floor

temps step in which weight is not transferred from foot to foot

temps de flèche sharp, hitch-kick jump in which legs pass in the air

temps levé hop taken from one foot starting in any of various positions

temps lié connected movement that combines leg and arm movements on second, fourth, and fifth positions of feet

tendu (*adj*) stretched and extended straight, esp. a leg

third position closed position with feet placed horizontally, one in front of the other, each heel at midpoint of the other foot

tour turn

tour à la seconde turn in second position

tour en l'air complete turn or turns executed in the air, begun and ended in fifth position

tour jeté high jump combining fast turn in the air and whiplike change of leg positions, ending in arabesque demi-plié

turnout outward rotation of legs at as close to 180-degree angle from hips as possible

tutu ballerina's short, flaring, fluffy skirt

variation solo dance, esp. third and fourth solo parts of classical grand pas de deux

vole traveling movements

Events, Steps, and Dancers

agitando heel work used in Spanish dances

balance balancing step in place, usu. in triple time

ball large, formal party featuring social dancing

ballroom dance any social or recreational dance, such as the foxtrot, tango, or waltz, performed by couples often in a ballroom

bump abrupt, suggestive forward hip thrust

bunny hop short leap forward to toe of one foot, followed by quick step onto other foot

chassé sliding dance step

chorus line group of background dancers who perform in unison in musical theater

country dance informal social dance in rural area

cut in (*vb*) tap another person's shoulder and take their dancing partner

dance succession of rhythmic steps and bodily movements in set patterns performed to music

dancercise aerobic exercises and calisthenics performed to intensely rhythmic music

discotheque nightclub featuring highly amplified, recorded popular dance music and lighting effects

do-si-do square dance figure in which woman passes around her partner and then the man on her right

figure dance step, position, or combination of steps

folk dance indigenous dance common to one region or people

formal ball; large social gathering with ballroom dancing

go-go dancer dancer who performs on platform raised above patrons of disco or nightclub

heel-and-toe (*adj*) pertaining to locked knee step in which heel of one foot touches ground before toe of other foot leaves it

hoofer *Slang.* dancer

hop informal dance, esp. 1950's teenage rock-'n'-roll dance held to live or recorded music

masked ball ball at which participants wear disguises, esp. face masks

mixer informal dance and social gathering

paso doble Latin march step associated with bullfighting

percussive movement modern dance movement whose original staccato force is not carried through

poussette figure in which couples dance in circle with hands joined

prom formal dance or ball for high school students

record hop hop held to recorded music

sashay square dance figure in which partners sidestep in circle around each other, man moving behind woman

set basic formation in country or square dance

splits move in which dancer sinks to floor with legs extending straight out at right angles to body

spotting fixing of dancer's eyes on single spot by moving head during series of rapid turns

square dance stylized form of country dance in which four couples respond to steps announced by caller

stag dance gathering to which men and women come separately, not as couples

step specific dance movement or figure

swing dance figure in which partners revolve with arms or hands joined

taxi dancer woman employed to dance with patrons, as of cabaret or club, who pay her a fee

tea dance dance held in late afternoon

Terpsichore Greek muse of dance

terpsichore choreography; the art of dancing

terpsichorean dancer; (*adj*) pertaining to dance

variation combination of dance steps or figures

THEATER

Theatrical Forms and Venues
Stagecraft, Production, and Dramatic Structure
Actors, Characters, and Theater People

See also: Chap. 14: Literature; Chap. 15:
Classical Music; Dance; Cinema; Television and
Radio; Chap. 17: Entertainments and Spectacles

Theatrical Forms and Venues

Actors Equity Association AEA; union for theatrical actors and stage managers

agitprop informal drama supporting radical leftist ideology

amphitheater large, esp. round, outdoor space with raised tiers of seats around a stage; originally a natural dip

arena theater central stage surrounded by seats without proscenium; performed in the round

auditorium room, hall, or building used for performances

avant-garde experimental or new drama

ballet theatrical form that uses dance and music to convey a story without words

benefit performance given to raise money for some charity, cause, organization, or person

big time *Informal.* Broadway and legitimate theater, esp. successful

black comedy comedy emphasizing morbid, gloomy, grotesque, or calamitous themes and events

borscht belt resorts in New York's Catskills region known for distinctive Jewish comedy and cabaret entertainment

Broadway professional, legitimate, mainstream theater; the street in New York City where such theater occurs

bunraku puppet theater (Japan)

burlesque satire; variety entertainment featuring comic skits, striptease, and magic

cabaret dancing, singing, and skits performed in a bar or café

chronicle play play based on loosely connected chronological episodes that depicts historical theme or events

circus traveling troupe of acrobats, clowns, and trained animals, usu. performing in oval arena

classical theater Greek tragedies, Shakespearean plays, or other long-established dramas or comedies

closet drama play intended to be read, not performed

comedy dramatic form using wit, humor, and satire; narrative with happy ending

comedy of manners dramatic form depicting and satirizing fashionable society

commedia dell'arte popular, folk-based comedic tradition of masked carnival mimes and acrobats, based on stock characters and situations (Italy, 16th-18th c.)

community theater little theater

dinner theater theater in which production is performed for audience that has been served dinner

drama theatrical form based on exposition of conflict through dialogue and actions of performers

experimental theater avant-garde; new and nontraditional dramatic form and narrative

farce low comedy, based on horseplay and absurd situations

floor show cabaret or nightclub theater; entertainment staged in conjunction with drinking and revelry in audience

fringe theater politically provocative or experimental theater in Britain, similar to U.S. off off Broadway

Globe Theatre traditional, round, open-air theater in London where Shakespearean drama was performed (early 17th c.)

Grand Guignol style of dramatic production that emphasizes grisly, frightening, violent, or morbid themes

Great White Way Broadway theater district in New York City

guerrilla theater performance, sometimes in streets, used esp. for social protest or propaganda; street theater

happening improvised, spontaneous theatrical performance, popular in 1960's

high comedy dramatic form characterized by witty, satiric depictions of upper class life

improv *Informal.* improvisation

improvisation unrehearsed, impromptu performance, usu. within larger dramatic structure or in rehearsal; type of entertainment featuring spontaneous, unrehearsed skits by a troupe of actors; improv

Kabuki highly choreographed, stylized, all-male theater (Japan)

legitimate stage professionally produced, traditional theater, as opposed to burlesque, vaudeville, and nonprofessional stagings

little theater amateur, neighborhood theater; community theater

low comedy dramatic form that employs burlesque, farce, and slapstick, usu. involving common folk, without clever or witty dialogue

masque elaborate costume play, orig. traditional folk theater and dance spectacles

melodrama dramatic form that exaggerates emotions and emphasizes plot over characterization

minstrel show theatrical entertainment

featuring white performers in blackface who sing, dance, and tell stories, based on stereotypes of African-American culture (U.S., late 19th c.)

miracle play medieval drama based on the Bible or the life of a saint or martyr

morality play medieval, allegorical dramatic form that provided instruction in Christian orthodoxy

musical light dramatic entertainment featuring musical interludes, story told largely through song and dance

nusical comedy comic musical play

mucic hall theater or room for variety shows; In Britain, form of popular entertainment consisting of variety acts

mystery play medieval drama based on Scriptural events, often illustrating points of religious doctrine and faith

national theater repertory company drawing on nation's best actors, technicians, and writers, often government-funded

neighborhood playhouse small, often semiprofessional local theater

No classical, all-male theater, elegant and serious in tone and form (Japan)

odeum small theater or concert hall

off Broadway low-budget, theatrical productions performed in modest venues, esp. in New York, sometimes as a pre-Broadway venture

off off Broadway highly experimental, sometimes nonprofessional theatrical productions performed in small venues far outside realms of legitimate theater

olio program consisting of musical numbers and skits; backdrop or curtain with advertisements; revue

one-acter Informal. play consisting of one, usu. uninterrupted, act

open-air theater performance in unenclosed auditorium or amphitheater, esp. Globe-type theater

opera musical drama composed of vocal pieces sung to orchestral accompaniment, esp. with tragic themes on grand scale

operetta romantic, light opera with songs and dance

pageant elaborately staged, open-air dramatic production, often with historical theme

pantomime performance without spoken words

passion play medieval religious drama dealing with Christ's passion

performance art often experimental, dramatic form combining theatrical performance, visual art, music, dance, cinema, or video in non-narrative, multimedia piece, originated in 1970's

performance space often bare, open area designed for performances, sometimes without seats for audience

play dramatic work performed by actors before an audience, usu. on stage and usu. from a written script

playhouse modest local theater used for live performances

playlet short play

puppet theater dramatic production using puppets instead of human actors

repertory company company that presents several works regularly or alternately using same performers

revue series of unrelated, often comic, skits, songs, dances, and monologues; olio

road show theatrical performance that travels from city to city

send-up mocking parody or spoof of another work

shadow play theater in which the shadows of puppets are cast on a screen between puppets and audience

showboat floating riverboat used as theater (U.S., 19th c.)

showcase small production used to expose actors to talent agents, producers, and directors; equity waiver

sketch brief, comic play or skit

skit short, informal, comic piece, esp. in imitation of longer, serious work; sketch

slapstick low comedy dependent on physical humor or horseplay

stand-up (adj) designating comedy in form of monologue delivered while standing alone before audience

strawhat (adj) pertaining to summer theater

street theater theatrical form using public areas or streets as a stage, often politically radical in theme; guerrilla theater

summer stock acting company that produces plays during summer

theater building in which plays are performed, usu. having stage and audience seating area

theater-in-the-round theatrical presentation in which the audience sits on all sides of an open stage; arena theater

theater of cruelty theatrical form using violence, sadism, and suffering to explore the cruelty of human existence and similar themes

theater of fact documentary theater

theater of the absurd theatrical form that dispenses with linear narrative and realistic dialogue and explores existential dimensions of life, esp. popular since 1950's

tragedy dramatic form dealing with a flaw, moral weakness, or maladjustment of the central character, resulting in downfall or catastrophe

tragicomedy dramatic form mixing elements of tragedy and comedy

variety show entertainment consisting of a series of different acts, orig. performed in music halls

vaudeville theatrical entertainment that featured a variety of performances by different singers, dancers, comedians, and other specialty acts (early 20th c.)

Yiddish theater traditional plays of eastern European Jews, performed in Yiddish

Stagecraft, Production, and Dramatic Structure

act major division of play; (vb) perform in dramatic stage production

action what a character does in order to reach his or her objective

ad lib spontaneous line or lines not part of script

anagnorisis critical moment of recognition leading to denouement in Greek tragedy

applause expression of audience approval by clapping hands

apron section of stage floor closest to audience, usu. in front of proscenium; forestage

aside actor's lines spoken to audience, not other actors

audience spectators viewing a performance

audition brief trial performance held to appraise actor's talent and suitability for role

backdrop curtain painted as scenery, hung at rear of stage

backlight lighting of stage from upstage area behind actors used to create visual depth

backstage wings, dressing rooms, and other areas behind proscenium out of audience view

balcony elevated seating area in auditorium, usu. jutting out over orchestra floor

barnstorm (vb) travel about country performing plays

beat small segment of a scene in which character has one specific objective

bill performance or piece being shown in theater

bit short theatrical routine

blackface black facial makeup, orig. burnt cork, worn by performers esp. in minstrel shows

blackout abrupt switching off of all stage lights at end of scene

blocking director's charting of actor's stage movements

boards stage floor; the theater in general

bomb play meeting with critical and/or commercial failure; (vb) fail badly

book words of a musical or opera

border narrow curtain or strip of canvas hung above stage to mask flies

born in a trunk Slang. born into a theatrical family

bow actor's acknowledgment of applause, usu. by bending head and body forward

box private seating compartment in theater, esp. an elevated one

box office small room near theater entrance in which tickets are sold; number and value of tickets sold for show

bravo audience shout of approval

break a leg actor's traditional expression of good luck

business minor piece of stage action, such as gesture or movement, used to create effect or portray character

callback actor's second audition for same part

cast actors chosen to perform parts in a play; (vb) select actors to play parts

cast party celebration of opening or closing night

catharsis purging of emotions through viewing play

cattle call *Slang.* publicly announced audition open to all comers

character person portrayed in play

circuit locations at which touring company gives dramatic performances

close (*vb*) end play's performance run

cold reading audition or rehearsal of previously unseen script

comic relief brief, humorous interlude in serious drama

costume actor's outfit, worn to create appearance of the character being played

cothurnus grave and elevated style of tragic acting; one of a pair of thick-soled boots worn in ancient Greek tragedy

coulisse side flat; space between two side flats

counterweight system a vertically tracked weight arbor corresponding to pulleys and pipe (baton) for hoisting scenery

cue word, phrase, or action signaling actor's line, entrance, or exit, or change in lighting or sound

curtain drapery separating audience from stage; descent of stage curtain at end of play or act

curtain call return of actors to stage to take bows in response to applause at play's end

curtain raiser short play or other selection presented before main play in a program

curtain warmer curtain raiser

cut drop drop scene that has been cut to reveal part of upstage area

cyclorama curved backdrop used to create the illusion of sky, space, or distance

dark (*adj*) description of theater on night without performance

debut actor's first performance, as in the professional theater or in a particular role

decor scenery, sets, or backdrops

denouement resolution of plot; outcome or dramatic unraveling of story complications and conflicts

deus ex machina *Latin.* lit. god from a machine; character or device introduced from outside the story to resolve plot

dialogue words spoken by characters in play

dimmer device by which the intensity of a lighting unit may be varied

dimmer board a panel of dimmers

downstage area of stage nearest audience

drama literary works written for the theater; theatrical presentation involving the creation, exploration, and resolution of conflict

dramatic structure traditional, formal composition of dramatic piece, based on resolution of conflict

dramaturgy art of dramatic composition

dress circle first balcony seating area above boxes

dress rehearsal rehearsal in full costume just prior to opening night

drop curtain curtain that is lowered from flies into position as rear wall of stage area

drop scene drop curtain used as background for scene played downstage while upstage set is being changed behind it

engagement run of scheduled performances

ensemble piece play or performance in which all actors share equal billing and size of part

entr'acte short performance, as music or dance, between acts of a play; interval between acts of a play or other production

epilogue brief section at conclusion of play

epitasis portion of Greek tragedy in which main action moves toward climax

finale final scene or musical number of performance

flat theatrical unit covered in muslin or lawn used as walls

flies area above stage with weights and ropes for manipulating scenery down and up

flop unsuccessful play or performance

footlights row of lights set along front edge of stage floor; acting profession in general

forestage apron

fourth wall imaginary wall at front of stage separating actors from audience

French scene division of a scene according to character entrances and exits

fright wig wig with spikey hair standing out in all directions, worn for comic effect

front of house audience area of theater

gallery top balcony, usu. containing the cheapest seats

gel colored plastic sheeting used to tint stage lights

gobo pattern inserted into lighting instrument and projected at stage

grease paint theatrical makeup

green room backstage room in which performers relax before, between, or after appearances on stage

ground plan overhead scale view of set that includes all scenery and set pieces

hall auditorium, stage, theater, music hall, or performance space

hamartia tragic flaw that causes hero's misfortune in Greek tragedy

histrionics acting in highly theatrical or exaggerated, dramatic style

hit extremely popular play or performance

hit one's mark stop movement in precisely designated spot marked on stage

house auditorium in which audience sits during performances

houselights theater lights in auditorium, not those on stage

house seat theater seat reserved by management for special guest or professional

instrument Method term for actor's body or theatrical light

intermezzo short, light interlude between acts

intermission interval between acts

jack stage brace for scenery

knee play *Slang.* intermission

leg drop narrow scenery flat or drop, often used in pairs to form inverted U

light bridge platform or elevated room from which lights are positioned

lighting board control panel for lighting stage and auditorium

limelight brilliant stage light that illuminates major characters; center of attention

lines words spoken during performance of play, esp. by one character

lobsterscope punched metal disk rotating in front of spotlight for lighting effects

loge balcony seating area of theater

makeup cosmetics and other materials applied to face, hands, and areas of body not covered by costume

marks tape or chalk marks on stage indicating actor positioning

marquee canopy on front of outside theater advertising play

mask face-covering of molded material or cloth, often used to indicate character

matinée afternoon performance

Method naturalistic acting technique, developed by Konstantin Stanislavski, that emphasizes actor's personal exploration of and identification with character

mezzanine lowest balcony in theater, esp. first few rows in this balcony

mise en scène *French.* props and scenery used in a performance; setting of play

monologue speech delivered at length by one actor

motley multicolored garment traditionally worn by jester

mug (*vb*) make exaggerated, often comic, facial expressions while acting

Muse mythological spirit believed to inspire poetry and drama (ancient Greece)

no-show person holding reservation who does not claim ticket

number song performed in theatrical production

objective what a character wants in scene or play

obstacle whatever prevents a character from reaching an objective, thereby forwarding the action of the play

off book (*adj*) designating rehearsal for which actors must have lines memorized

one-night stand single performance in one locale by touring company

one sheet paper work recorded and used by light and sound board operators to run show

open (*vb*) begin series of performances

opening night first performance of play, often a gala occasion

orchestra audience seats on ground floor of theater

overact (*vb*) perform in exaggerated, unconvincing manner

paper the house increase audience size by distributing free tickets

parados passageway between sets and wings

paraskenae projecting wings of stage building (ancient Greece)

parquet circle parterre

part role in play for which actor is cast

parterre seats on main floor of theater behind orchestra; parquet circle

patch manual or computer assignment of dimmers to channels on control board

peanut gallery *Informal.* rear balcony seating in theater; cheaper seats, from which rabble traditionally threw peanuts

perform (*vb*) act, sing, or dance before an audience

performance any entertainment presented before an audience; act of performing a theatrical piece; particular instance of presenting a theatrical piece

periactoid three side scenic unit conveying different scenes, usually used in a series

peripeteia sudden and unexpected turn of events or plot twist

pit sunken area directly in front of stage in which orchestra musicians sit

platform 3/4" plywood covered frame used for flooring or levels on a set

playbill theatrical program; handbill identifying cast and production members for audience

plot arrangement of narrative events in play or plan of lighting design

premiere first performance of play

preparation technique an actor uses to create an emotional state of being before entering a scene

preview performance of play given before official opening

production all elements involved in one particular staging of a play

program brochure or sheet describing play and listing performers and production staff, handed out before performance begins

project (*vb*) speak so that voice carries to entire audience

prologue introduction to play or performance

prompt (*vb*) supply (an actor) with forgotten line or missed cue from offstage

prompt script master script with all acting and technical cues, used by stage manager to supervise show during performance

prop property

property any article used to dress the stage for scenes, or any object carried by an actor; prop

proscenium arched part of stage, located in front of curtain, that separates stage from auditorium

protasis opening portion of ancient drama in which characters and plot are introduced

rake slope of stage floor from apron to rear wall

rave extremely favorable review

rehearsal practice performance; preparation of production by cast, crew, and director

rehearsal studio large room or hall for rehearsing

repertoire stock of plays performed by actor or company

repertory presentation of a stock of plays by a theater company over a regular season; company or troupe that presents plays this way

review critical description of performance, usu. by a member of the media

revolving stage stage set on circulating platform which turns 120 or 180 degrees, providing fast, smooth scene changes

ring down the curtain lower the curtain

ring up the curtain raise the curtain

riser stairlike theater seating or stage area

role actor's part; character in play

routine theatrical skit; dance combination; comedian's material

run total number of consecutive performances of a play at one theater or on tour

run-through rehearsal of entire piece

scenario outline of play's action, including notes on scenery and special effects; skeleton plot

scene uninterrupted action within play; division of an act

scenery backdrops or structures on stage that represent the play's locale

scene shop area in which scenery is constructed and painted

scrim open-weave cotton fabric, opaque when front lit and translucent when back lit

script working version of play's text

sensory technique used by actors in Method training in which specific sensory input is re-created by imagination

set scenery, flats, and properties composing play's environment

show play; production of play

show business entertainment industry, including the theater

show-stopper dramatic or musical moment during performance that draws prolonged applause, halting action

shtick *Slang.* comedian's or actor's unique style or material

sides pages of a script with lines and cues for one role only, commonly used at auditions

sight gag funny bit without dialogue

sightline line of vision from audience to extreme corners of stage

slapstick comedy stressing farce, horseplay, or sight gags

smash successful, long-running play

soliloquy monologue expressing character's inner thoughts, addressed to no one

sotto voce (*adv*) in a low, soft voice

spike marks taped marks for furniture, prop, or set placement

spirit gum solution of gum arabic in ether, used to attach false hair or beards

spotlight powerful light used to illuminate individual actor, manually operated on a rotating axis

SRO standing room only; designating a sold-out performance

stage area on which plays are performed before an audience

stagecraft skill in theatrical performance; art and practice of staging plays; art of set construction

stage direction instruction in script of play

indicating production requirements or performer's action or appearance

stage door actors' and production crew's entrance, located away from audience's street entrance to theater

stage fright extreme fear and anxiety at prospect of performing before audience

stage left stage area on actor's left when facing audience

stage right stage area on actor's right when facing audience

stagestruck (*adj*) infatuated with performing and the theater

stage whisper loud, easily overheard, mock whisper

stall theater seat with back and sides; *Chiefly Brit.* orchestra seat

standing room area at rear of orchestra in which audience may stand during sold-out performance; SRO

steal the show perform so brilliantly as to draw most of the audience's attention to oneself

stock scenery scenery of a standard size that is stored for reuse

strike (*vb*) take apart and remove (scenery or set) from stage

striplights encased set of lights on 3 or 4 separate circuits, used for color washes of cyclorama

subtext meaning and motivations underlying spoken text

supertitle translation of text or brief plot summary projected on screen above stage during performance

swan song actor's final performance

tableau stage picture created by actors posing motionless

tableau curtain curtain that opens in center, with sections drawing up and to side, creating draped effect

teaser drapery or flat member across top of proscenium arch that frames stage opening and conceals flies

tech rehearsal internal rehearsal held to check sound and lighting

theater art and practice of writing, producing, staging, and performing plays; building in which plays are staged; also, *esp.Brit.*, theatre

theatricality sense of what will work on stage

throwaway line unimportant line of dialogue lost in action

thrust stage stage extending beyond the proscenium, usu. surrounded by audience on three sides

Tony awards theatrical awards given annually by American Theatre Wing for best Broadway shows, performances, etc.; Antoinette Perry awards

top billing first or most prominent spot in a list of actors on a program or marquee

tormentor fixed curtain or flat on each side of stage that prevents audience from seeing into wings

touring company group of performers moving

453

from city to city to present a play or musical, esp. one already successful on Broadway

trap removable section of stage floor through which actors can enter or exit or scenery be brought in or removed

tryout actor's audition; test performance of play before official opening

turkey *Slang.* disastrous production or performance

turn brief performance

twofers *Informal.* two tickets for the price of one

typecasting assigning role to actor based on actor's appearance, personal style, or previous experience

upstage rear portion of stage; (*vb*) to move upstage from another actor, forcing him or her to turn away from audience; to draw audience's attention from another actor by distracting behavior

vehicle theatrical work with role designed or well-suited to display or exploit the talents of particular performer

venue type of performance space

vomitory large opening through banks of seats in auditorium that permits large members of people to enter or leave theater

walk-through early or casual rehearsal

whiteface white pancake makeup, used esp. by mimes

wings sides of stage beyond view of audience

workshop exchange of ideas and application of skill among director, writer, actors, and others involved in development of new play or work in progress

Actors, Characters, and Theater People

acrobat expert performer of physical tricks or feats

actor stage performer, esp. male, but may also apply to female; player; Thespian

actress female stage performer

alazon swaggering braggart, stock character in classic Greek comedy

angel *Informal.* financial backer, as of play production

antagonist adversary of leading character or hero

backer investor in production

bard epic poet, national minstrel

Bard William Shakespeare

barker person who stands at entrance to show, esp. carnival, attracting passersby

barnstormer traveling actor; actor in road production

bit player actor who performs a small role, usu. with few lines of dialogue

booking agent person who arranges venues for performances

buffoon fool

busker street performer

cameo small role played by a famous actor; brief appearance in play

cast actors who portray all the roles in play

character specific role in play, portrayed by actor

character actor player who specializes in roles depicting strong or memorable personalities, but not hero

child actor preadolescent who works as an actor

choragus leader of chorus; coryphaeus (ancient Greece)

chorus group of actors in ancient Greek drama speaking lines in unison, commenting on action of play but not interacting with characters; group of dancers and singers performing together in musical

chorus line chorus dancing in line across stage, esp. in musical comedy

coach acting teacher hired to help with specific part

comedian comic actor

comedienne female comic actor

comic comedian or comedienne

company group of actors, esp. stock company

comprere master of ceremonies

contortionist circus acrobat capable of assuming unnatural positions

coryphaeus leader of chorus; choragus (ancient Greece)

costume designer person responsible for costuming the actors

crew all nonperformers; stagehands and technicians involved in a production

dancer performer who specializes in graceful movements done to music, often without speaking or while singing

director person responsible for blocking stage movements, motivating actors, and providing unity to production

diseuse actress skilled at dramatic monologues

diva leading woman singer in grand opera

dossenus sharp-witted hunchback character in classical Roman comedy

dramatis personae cast of characters in a dramatic work

dramaturge composer of dramas; company's script analyst

dresser personal assistant responsible for helping actor into costume at time of performance

emcee master of ceremonies

ensemble group of actors performing together; full company

entertainer performer, esp. one skilled in singing and dancing

extra actor in minor, nonspeaking role

flyman member of set crew who works in the flies

foil role that provides contrast or opposition to hero

fool comic role in folk or morality play; buffoon; jester

gypsy *Slang.* singer/dancer who works in chorus line; experienced background player

ham actor with contrived, overworked, or insincere style

harlequin masked, comic character, usu. dressed

in multicolored, diamond-patterned tights and carrying a sword or magic wand, in commedia dell'arte

heavy villain

hero principal male character in drama

heroine principal female character in drama

impresario manager, director, or fund-raiser for theater company

ingénue role of innocent, naive young woman in drama

jester fool

juggler performer skilled at tossing several objects in the air in rapid rotation and catching them

juvenile young actor or one who plays young parts

lead principal character in drama

leading lady actress playing heroine or principal female character in drama

leading man actor playing hero or principal male character in drama

librettist writer of song lyrics for a musical

lighting designer person responsible for technical and aesthetic arrangement of lights used in production

magician entertainer who performs feats of sleight of hand

makeup artist person who applies makeup to actors

master electrician person responsible for hanging, focus, and integrity of designer's plot

master of ceremonies MC; person who presides over revue or variety show, esp. introducing acts and filling breaks with patter; comprere; emcee

matinée idol handsome actor popular with female audiences

MC master of ceremonies

merry-andrew clown or fool

mime actor who uses gestures and bodily movements to silently portray a character or communicate moods and ideas

minstrel medieval entertainer who traveled from place to place singing and reciting stories

monologist actor who performs a monologue

mummer masked, traveling performer of northern European folk plays (18th-19th c.)

pantomime actor in dumb show or silent performance

patron person who provides the major portion of funding for a company

Pierrot stock male character in French pantomime who wears loose white costume and whiteface

player actor

playwright author of plays

prima donna orig. principal woman singer; vain performer who wants all of the audience's attention

producer person responsible for financial and administrative aspects of production, esp. fund-raising

prompter person hidden from audience who

supplies next line of dialogue or other cue when actor forgets

protagonist main character in drama; hero or heroine

puppet doll or figure manipulated by hand on small stage

repertory company in which actors share leading roles in several different plays performed in rotation; stock company

saltimbanque street performer, esp. juggler or contortionist

Scaramouch cowardly braggart who is easily vanquished in farce and commedia dell'arte

scene-stealer performer who draws audience attention away from other actors on stage; prima donna

set designer person responsible for design and creation of stage sets and scenery

singer performer who specializes in rhythmic, melodic speech set to music

song-and-dance man entertainer who specializes in musicals

soubrette role of lady's maid, esp. flirtatious intriguer

sound designer person responsible for acoustic setup of speakers and special sound effects

spear carrier extra

stagehand person who sets up and changes scenery before and during performance

stage manager theater staff person responsible for functional details of production during rehearsal and performance

stand-by actor prepared to substitute for regular performer in part as needed but usually not a member of cast

stand-up comic entertainer who performs comic routine while standing alone onstage

star very popular, successful, and well-known actor who performs leading roles

stock stock company

stock company troupe of actors, each specializing in certain types of roles and sharing others, who perform a series of plays, usu. at one theater; repertory company

stooge *Slang.* comic foil, esp. one who feeds lines to other actors

straight man actor whose lines set up jokes for comedian

stripper burlesque performer who removes garments one at a time during elaborate dance set to music

supernumerary actor in walk-on part; extra

supporting actor person in role supporting, or secondary to, leading man or lady

talent scout person employed to find new performers

technical director person responsible for coordinating technical aspects of show including set, lights, and sound effects

Thespian actor

tragedian actor who specializes in tragic roles; writer of tragedies

tragedienne female actor who specializes in playing tragic roles

troubadour wandering medieval minstrel who wrote and performed poetry and songs

troupe company of actors

trouper dedicated, selfless, and versatile performer

tummler combined comedian, activities director, and master of ceremonies at borscht belt resorts

understudy actor versed in another's part, ready to step in if needed, usu. a member of the cast

usher theater attendant who guides audience members to their seats

vaudevillian performer of usu. comic vaudeville routines

villain character who opposes hero; bad guy; heavy

walk-on small, nonspeaking part; actor playing such a part

CINEMA

Genres and Types of Pictures
Cinematography Tools and Techniques
Movie People and Show Business

See also: *Chap. 15: Theater; Television and Radio*

Genres and Types of Pictures

action adventure fast-paced, exciting narrative of some dangerous or bold undertaking

animation series of drawings that depict action by means of slightly progressive changes, each photographed separately to create movie; cartoon

A picture high-budget, high-quality feature film, usu. with stars

art film low-budget, nonstudio, often nonnarrative film utilizing experimental techniques

biographical film film based on life story of actual person

blaxploitation film exploiting blacks

blue movie pornographic film

B picture low-budget studio film, often in genre and without major stars, formerly shown as added feature on bill with A picture

buddy picture narrative about adventures shared by two friends, usu. male

cartoon animated film

chiller *Informal.* horror film

cinéma vérité documentary filmed with handheld camera without added effects, authentic and candid in action and style

costume film period piece

cowboy picture western

crash and burn film *Slang.* violent action film featuring a series of spectacular vehicular explosions .

detective picture story involving criminal investigation

disaster picture narrative about effects on characters of natural or man-made catastrophe

documentary nonfiction narrative about actual event or characters in journalistic vein

epic long, episodic, large-scale story with heroic characters

experimental film avant-garde, unconventional, or abstract film

exploitation film film with highly commercial appeal to specific audience, esp. particular sex, race, or age group

fantasy fanciful departure from known realities

film noir 1940's American black-and-white style of film, esp. with a private detective as hero, that emphasized dark, sinister moods and bleak viewpoints

gangster film melodramatic narrative film about a violent, criminal antihero, esp. popular in the Depression era

genre film using a specific technique, style, story, or setting, such as western, gangster, or science fiction film

hard-core (*adj*) pruriently explicit, as in pornography that vividly depicts sex acts

horror films with strange, frightening events that threaten characters, esp. those emphasizing bloodshed or supernatural forces

horse opera western

independent film usu. low-budget film not produced by major studio

industrial promotional film for product or company

law-and-order film action-adventure story in which criminals are brought to justice by law officials

melodrama sensational story emphasizing emotional content over characterization

musical story told in large part through musical productions, esp. song-and-dance numbers

newsreel short documentary account of current events

new wave movement characterized by abstraction, subjective symbolism, improvisation, and experimental techniques, orig. France, late 1950's, early 1960's; nouvelle vague

nouvelle vague *French.* new wave

oater *Slang.* western

period piece narrative occurring in another era, with appropriate historical sets and costumes; costume film

porn *Informal.* pornography

pornographic film low-budget picture designed for sexual titillation; blue film; porn; skin flick

prequel sequel that depicts events preceding those of the original work

remake new version of old film

romantic comedy light comedy involving love interest

science fiction film depicting effect of science on society, esp. future society or other planets; sci-fi; space opera

sci-fi *Informal.* science fiction

screwball comedy light, imaginative, fast-paced film with witty dialogue and improbable plot line

sequel continuation of story or characters depicted in an earlier film

serial episodic motion picture, usu. seen in installments

sexploitation *Informal.* film that exploits sex

shocker horror, thriller, or monster film

shoot-'em up *Informal.* film that emphasizes gunplay and violent action

short subject short motion picture, usu. of less than 3000 feet of 35 mm film (or half an hour), often a documentary

silent film motion picture without sound, either from pre-1930 era or for effect

skin flick *Slang.* pornographic film

slapstick comedy humorous film that features boisterous, physical jokes and mugging

slasher movie film depicting violent killer who runs amok maiming or dismembering other characters, esp. young females

snuff film *Slang.* pornographic film that shows actual murder of performers

soft-core (*adj*) sexually stimulating, as in pornography that features nudity but not explicit sex acts

space opera science fiction involving space travel

spaghetti western *Informal.* Italian-made, low-budget cowboy film

stag movie pornographic film intended for male audience

student film production directed by film-school students

talkie early film produced with sound (1920's-1930's)

tearjerker *Informal.* sentimental melodrama

teen picture film depicting teenage characters and lifestyles, aimed at teen audience

thriller suspense drama

travelogue documentary motion picture showing and describing travels

western narrative set in lawless, 19th century American frontier; cowboy picture; horse opera; oater

whodunit *Informal.* detective or thriller film

Cinematography Tools and Techniques

academy leader countdown from 9 to 2 that appears on screen before film begins

acetate base plastic strip supporting emulsion in film

action director's command to actors to begin playing scene

ADR automatic dialogue replacement; looping and dubbing process

anamorphic lens type of lens that compresses wide camera angles into standard frame widths, used in CinemaScope

angle on shot of specific person, place, or thing

animation process of creating moving graphic images on film by small progressive changes between each drawing cel

answer print first acceptable, color-balanced print made from original negative

aperture camera shutter opening that admits light to expose film

arc light high-powered light for set illumination

aspect ratio ratio of width of a projected image to its height

assembly editing and splicing for rough cut

automatic dialogue replacement ADR

backlighting illumination from behind subject

back projection projection from rear of previously photographed material on translucent screen, used as background for shot

BCU big closeup

beep tone beep lasting 1/24 of a second that occurs at number 2 in academy leader countdown

big closeup BCU; shot of face filling screen

blackout abrupt fade to black at end of scene

blimp soundproof cover over motion-picture camera

blow-up enlargement

boom mic overhead microphone on extendible crane

bridging shot film shot connecting discontinuous images

camera angle angle of view: high, low, or wide

camera car vehicle equipped with camera mounts for filming while moving at traffic speed

camera mount any of various bases for a camera: crane, dolly, specialty mount, sticks

camera track camera's path of motion in following a scene

cel transparent celluloid sheet used for animation drawing, constituting one frame of an animated film

celluloid film; plastic formerly used for photographic film

century stand equipment used to support camera

changeover marks white circles that appear twice for a split second in upper right corner of frame just before reel ends

CinemaScope *Trademark.* wide-screen process using anamorphic lenses in photographing and projecting a film

cinematography art and science of motion-picture photography

Cinerama *Trademark.* wide-screen film photography and projection process using three synchronized cameras and three projectors

Claymation *Trademark.* animated film made by taking series of photographs of clay figures set in different positions

clip film clip

close medium shot photo of person from head to knees

close shot closeup

closeup CU; full screen shot of subject, esp. a person's head

composite print married print

continuity editing technique yielding smooth, coherent narrative from scenes shot out of sequence

crane mobile, counterweighted camera mount allowing camera great height and vertical movement

creeping titles titles or credits scrolled over film image

crosscutting jumping back and forth between two scenes happening simultaneously

cross-fade merging of images from end of one scene into beginning of next

cut quick transition from one shot to another

cut director's command to actors to cease playing scene

cutaway quick movement of camera away from shot; shot focusing on something other than main action

cut-in still shot inserted in film and interrupting the action or continuity; insert

cyclorama studio or stage background creating illusion of open scenery

dailies hastily printed footage from previous day's shooting, assembled for daily viewing by director and producer before editing or sound synchronization; rushes

day for night simulation of night scenes actually shot during daylight with filters

dialogue track recorded dialogue to be run in sync with picture

diffuser light-softening screen of silk, gelatin, or frosted glass

dissolve one shot gradually fading into another

dolly movable camera mount, usu. a small wheeled platform

dolly in shot in which dolly approaches subject

dolly shot shot taken from a moving dolly

dupes inexpensive black-and-white copies made from work print for use by various postproduction specialists

ECU extreme closeup

edge code code imprinted after filming at one-foot intervals on picture and sound to facilitate editing in sync

editing arrangement, splicing, and assemblage of film footage into desired sequences and synchronization of film with soundtrack

emulsion sensitive chemical solution that forms coating on film

establishing shot shot setting time and place of scene; master shot

exterior scene shot outside in natural or artificial light

extreme closeup ECU; closeup showing only subject's face or part of face

fade-in gradual emergence of image from black ground

fade-out gradual disappearance of image into black ground

fast motion effect of speeded-up action achieved by undercranking camera, then replaying film at normal speed

favoring shot shot focusing on specific person or object

file footage stock film footage, such as scenes of crowds and natural backgrounds, kept on file for use

film strip of cellulose acetate coated with sensitive emulsion for recording images when exposed to light, usu. 35 mm wide

film clip brief section extracted from film; clip

film gate device that holds film flat and steady as it passes through camera

final cut edited version of film that is approved and nearly ready for distribution

Foley *Trademark.* technique for adding special effects to soundtrack

footage section of film

frame single picture on strip of film, usu. 16 frames per foot of film; (*vb*) compose a single shot

freeze frame optical effect in which single frame is held as persistent, still image in film; stop motion

full frame shot of entire subject filling frame

FX *Slang.* special effects

gauge width of film in millimeters

glass shot part of scene painted on glass and inserted into scene

gobo black wooden screen used to block unwanted light; sound-absorbent screen used to shield microphone from external sounds

ground background or foundation behind or under focus of shot

head shot closeup of person's face and head

hold sustained shot on specific person or object

inky dink *Slang.* small lamp used to light limited area

insert close shot of an object, such as a newspaper headline or clock; cut-in

intercut (*vb*) move back and forth between two shots

interior shot scene shot inside, usu. on a sound stage, with artificial light

iris-in gradual appearance of on-screen image through an expanding circle, esp. in silent films

iris-out gradual disappearance of on-screen image through a contracting circle, esp. in silent films

jump cut sudden transition out of scene to speed narrative

key light main light on photographed subject

kinetoscope old-fashioned film loop viewer

klieg light carbon arc lamp producing intense light

library shot stock shot taken from film library

lighting cinematographer's art and skill of illuminating scenes for filming

locked cut final edited version of film, ready for postproduction work

long shot scene filmed from considerable distance, usu. wide angle

looping editing process in which speech and sound effects are synchronized to film already shot

magazine lightproof film container

M and E music and effects on soundtrack

married print image, sound, and dialogue tracks synchronized for projection or reproduction; composite print

master shot establishing shot

matte device that blocks part of film, to be exposed later

medium close shot showing subject from head to chest or waist

montage fast-moving sequence of superimposed images

Movieola *Trademark.* film editing machine

moving shot shot in which camera focus moves, as in dolly or pan shots

offscreen (*adj*) OS; taking place away from the screen, as a character's voice

optical effect special visual effect: dissolve, fade, wipe, freeze

original negative film that was actually loaded into camera, after it is developed, from which all copies are generated other than dupes

OS (*adj*) off screen

outtake footage deleted from final edit of film

overcranking photographing more than 24 frames per second of film, for slow motion effect

pan panoramic shot of wide, horizontal view; movement of camera eye across wide area as camera moves horizontally on mount

parallax slight difference between image in camera viewfinder and actual image seen through lens

pixilation technique using stop-action camera to move subjects between takes and shots, in order to achieve comic effect of jerky motion

point of view POV; camera angle on subject that places the viewer in the desired relationship to the character

POV point of view

print reproduction of original film

process cinematography special effects illusion in which foreground action or scene is superimposed on separately shot background

projection display of film images on screen

rack (*vb*) adjust film through projector gate

rack focus pulling of focus plane from one area to another on same frame

raw stock unused film

reaction shot shot showing subject reacting to action of preceding shot

rear projection special effect using prefilmed background against which scene is set and photographed; rear-screen projection

rear-screen projection rear projection

reel flanged spool for film; one section of feature film consisting of more than one reel

release print clean film print released for projection to audience

reshoot retake

retake shot or scene that needs to be taken more than once; reshoot

reverse shot change in point of view from previous shot

rolling (*adj*) indication that cameras are shooting scene

rollover written text scrolling over scene, often offering historical exposition

rotoscope device used to transfer live-action shot to animation

rough cut preliminary edit; first version of motion picture following initial cutting and editing

rushes dailies, esp. East Coast usage

safety film nonflammable film

sequence series of scenes or shots tied together by single idea, concept, or event

set design creation and construction of scenery

70 mm film size twice as large as standard 35 mm

shoot period of filming; (*vb*) film a scene

shooting filming of scenes

shooting script final version of screenplay with all camera angles, shots, and scene numbers included

shot continuous shooting of scene without stopping camera

skip frames technique in which every other or every third frame is omitted, giving film a faster, jagged look

skypan big, bowl-shaped light used to illuminate wide area

slo-mo *Informal.* slow motion

slow motion effect of very slow action achieved by overcranking camera, then replaying film at normal speed; slo-mo

smash cut jarring visual transition to next shot, often accompanied by loud sound

special effects visual and sound effects added to film by various laboratory techniques; FX

splice joining of two film sections; an edit

split screen process shot showing two different scenes at same time

squeezed print anamorphic process print

stereoscope optical instrument used to create a three-dimensional projection effect

sticks *Slang.* camera mounts

stock film used to make a motion picture, usu. 35 mm

stock shot prefilmed shot taken from newsreels or travelogues to insert into film as establishing shot

stop-action photography special effect technique in which performers stop moving and camera is stopped while something or someone is added to or removed from set, creating illusion of sudden appearance or disappearance

stop motion freeze frame

sweetening enhancing soundtrack quality electronically after filming and recording are complete

synchronize (*vb*) align picture and soundtrack

take shot filmed without stopping camera or action

Technicolor *Trademark.* color motion-picture process

telecine projector device for transferring 35-mm motion-picture film to television videotape format

3-D processing of film to give illusion of three-dimensional action when viewed through special lenses

three-point lighting basic lighting setup that includes front, back, and side lights

tilt vertical movement of camera on stationary mount

time code series of marks along edge of film used to synchronize sound and other effects

time-lapse photography technique in which slow, continuous process is photographed by exposing one frame at a time, creating speeded-up effect when projected at normal speed

titles written text on screen often superimposed over filmed images, usu. stating time and place of action or credits

tracking shot shot in which camera and action both move in parallel direction; dolly shot

traveling matte special-effect photography combining two separate film sequences into single shot

trucking shot image filmed with mounted camera on moving truck; movement of camera mount while filming

two-shot image of two people in frame

undercranking photographing fewer than 24 frames per second of film, thus creating fast-motion effect

wide-screen (*adj*) denoting panoramic dimension in film projection

wipe technique in which one image pushes another offscreen

workprint first, unmarried print made from original negative that editor splices together

zoom effect created by camera action or use of lens with variable focal length, not by moving camera or camera mount

Movie People and Show Business

above-the-line designating those on film budget not considered part of crew, such as the director, producer, and actors

Academy Awards Oscars

AD assistant director

adaptation screenplay with story taken from another medium

agent actor's, writer's, or director's representative for finding work, making deals, and creating packages

art direction direction that results in overall look of a film

art director person responsible for designing the look of a film

art house theater that shows primarily art films, foreign films, and classics

assistant cameraman person in charge of operating camera, usu. behind viewfinder

assistant director AD; person on set responsible for implementing the director's orders and overseeing the actors; first or second assistant director

associate director first AD for video production

associate producer person attached to project but not functioning as producer; line producer

auteur film director with strong personal style

backdrop flat scenery set up behind actors

back-end deal arrangement by which all or some of one's compensation for work on a film comes from final profits after all expenses have been met

background part of a scene or set situated behind the actors; extras

background music incidental music on soundtrack

backlot outdoor area, usu. adjoining studio, for shooting exterior scenes that depict locations

bankable star actor whose presence in film guarantees production and likely financial success

below-the-line designating crew, equipment, and production costs of film

best boy *Slang*. gaffer's assistant

billing order in which actors' names appear in credits, on marquee, and in advertising for film

bit small part for actor, sometimes with a few lines

boffo (*adj*) *Slang*. highly successful, esp. as designating a box office hit

boom operator technician who controls crane equipped with boom mike

breakdowns regular listing of upcoming parts to be cast, circulated to agents

buzz *Slang*. advance word on film in industry; heat

call arrival time at shoot

cameo small part played by actor who is usu. featured

cameraman chief operator of camera

cast actors, bit players, and extras

casting director person responsible for preauditioning and selecting right actor for each role

chase scene action sequence involving pursuit

cheat to camera turn one's face so that more of it can be seen on camera

cineaste devotee of films; person professionally involved in making films

cinema art, technique, and business of making motion pictures; movies

cinematheque small movie house showing avant-garde films

cinematic (*adj*) characteristic of films or the art of filmmaking

cinematographer person responsible for photographing film; director of photography

clapboard boards hinged at one end and banged together to mark filmed sequences with scene numbers for synching; clapperboard

clapperboard clapboard

clapper loader *Chiefly Brit.* third assistant cameraman

closing credits long list of all actors and technicians involved in production, shown at end of film

colorization addition of color to films originally shot in black and white

coming attractions trailers previewing upcoming films

commissary dining room or cafeteria on motion-picture studio lot

continuity *Chiefly Brit.* script supervisor

coproduction arrangement to cofinance picture between two or more producers or companies

cover (*vb*) read and synopsize script, story, or novel

credits lists of actors, artists, and technicians involved in making film, shown at beginning and/or end of movie

crew technicians, artists, and other workers involved in production

development stage after purchase of script or idea by studio leading toward production

dialogue words spoken by characters on soundtrack

director creative overseer of motion picture who guides actors, determines narrative style, and selects camera angles

director of photography head cameraman who determines ways to achieve director's desired effects; cinematographer

director's chair canvas on wood frame chair typically used on set

distribution placement of released film in theaters, usu. by studio acting as distributor

dolly grip crew member who helps move dolly

double bill double feature

double feature two films shown in theater for the price of one; double bill

dresser actor's wardrobe assistant on set

drive-in outdoor theater where audience remains inside cars

dubbing replacing part or all of an existing soundtrack, esp. with a translation into another language, or adding background music or special effects

editor creative organizer of film footage into assembled sequences of scenes

executive producer person responsible for raising money and initiating project, but not for daily administrative tasks

extra actor without speaking part, usu. hired by the day as part of a crowd scene; background

featured (*adj*) designating an actor with a significant part, often named in opening credits

feature film motion picture at least 3000 feet long in 35 mm film

film motion picture

filmmaker individual who creates movies, esp. director

first run film recently released for first time, esp. in wide distribution

flashback narrative device in which action taking place in the past is inserted into the chronological structure of the story

flash forward narrative device in which future scenes are inserted into a film's present time structure

flick *Slang*. motion picture

flying rig operator of special effects device used in stunts to create the illusion of falling

focus puller second assistant cameraman, who adjusts camera focus

Foley artist person who integrates special sound effects into soundtrack

front-end deal arrangement by which one's compensation for work on a film comes out of money that is available before or during production

gaffer electrician who operates and rigs lights

genre group of films defined by style or theme

green light go-ahead to commence production, given by studio head

greensman crew member who tends trees and plants

grip member of film crew who moves equipment, esp. lighting

hammer *Slang.* handyman on movie set

head of production top studio executive responsible for coordinating all projects in development and production

heat *Slang.* good word of mouth about a new movie; buzz

heavy male villain

high concept story idea for popular film that can be summarized in one catchy line or phrase

in-between assistant artist responsible for animation frames inserted between main frames drawn by chief animator

indie *Informal.* independent motion picture production company outside major studio system; film made by such a company

Industry, the the motion picture business in Hollywood

ingénue young, attractive female character; actress who plays such a part

in production (of a film) in the shooting stage, after development

in the can (of a film) completed but not yet ready for distribution

key grip head of grip crew

lead primary male or female part in film

leading lady actress playing only lead roles

leading man actor playing only lead roles

legs *Slang.* strength and longevity at the box office

lighting director person responsible for placement of lights to achieve director's desired effects

line producer studio executive responsible for day-to-day coordination of production and staying within budget

location place for filming scene outside studio or sound stage

location scout person who finds and arranges for use of shooting locations

log line one sentence description of story

lot motion-picture studio and its surrounding property

love interest provision for romance in narrative; star's romantic opposite

low-budget film usu. nonstudio production with minimal financing

majors large Hollywood studios

marquee rigid canopy of movie theater advertising film currently showing there

matinée screening of a film during daytime, usu. afternoon

McGuffin *Slang.* plot device for setting story into motion, esp. missing object or person

merchandising development and sale of products related to particular film and its characters

method actor student or practitioner of the naturalistic Stanislavski method of acting, which emphasizes a personal exploration of the character being played

motion picture series of photographic images projected in rapid succession on a screen to give the illusion of continuous action; film; flick; movie; moving picture; picture; picture show

motion pictures motion-picture industry; silver screen

movie motion picture

movies cinema

movie theater building in which films are displayed for public viewing; picture palace; picture show

moving picture motion picture

multiplex movie theater with several screens in different rooms showing different films

nickelodeon early movie theater, in which films were viewed individually through a small machine operated by a nickel

on location filming at a site away from studio or sound stage

opening credits names of primary actors, technicians, director, and producer shown at beginning of film

option purchase by individual, company, or studio of exclusive right to develop film project during designated time

Oscars annual awards for excellence in acting and filmmaking given by Academy of Motion Picture Arts and Sciences; Academy Awards

PA production assistant

package proposed combination of script, actors, and director, presented to studio, esp. by agent

pass free ticket to a screening; studio decision not to develop project or not to produce project already in development

persistence of vision short-term retention of image on retina, producing illusion that a series of rapidly changing images are in motion

picture motion picture

picture palace movie theater

picture show motion picture, movie theater

pitch meeting meeting at which screenwriter and/or producer proposes film idea to potential financier or studio

player actor

postproduction editing, dubbing, and addition of special effects after conclusion of filming

post punch supervisor person who supervises photocopying of cels and drawings used in animation

premiere opening night screening of new film

preproduction work done prior to filming and production, such as casting, selecting locations, designing production, and rewriting script

preview advance screening of new film before general release

principal leading actor in specific film

producer executive and financial overseer of film production; packager of film idea for sale and distribution

product film idea, script, novel, or completed film

production creation and shooting of film from script

production assistant PA; person responsible for carrying out day-to-day assignments given by line producer

production company company that develops projects for sale to studios or networks or for independent financing

production manager person who oversees daily activities during filming

production values quality of set, costumes, lighting, sound, and atmosphere of film

projection booth room in movie theater from which film reels are projected onto screen

projectionist technician who operates film projector in theater

property story idea, concept, novel, or script, the rights to which are owned by potential producer or studio

ratings system of motion picture grading based on age of admissible audience: G (general); PG (parental guidance suggested); PG-13 (no one under 13), R (restricted admission if under 17); NC-17 (no one under 17)

release distribution of completed film to theaters

revival house movie theater showing old films only

rewrite thorough revision of screenplay

rigger crew member who hangs suspended equipment, esp. lights

scale minimum pay approved by union for a specific job

scene division of film in which continuous action takes place in a single location

scenery painted screens, backdrops, hangings, and props

score musical background for film; (*vb*) compose background music for film

screen flat, reflective white surface on which films are projected; (*vb*) show a film to an audience

screening showing of a film before an audience

screenplay written form of film containing dialogue, description of scenes, characters, and action; script

screen test audition in which actor is filmed to check appearance on film and suitability for role

screenwriter person who conceives, writes, and rewrites screenplays

script screenplay

script doctor writer who makes usu. minor revisions of someone else's script

script girl director's assistant who holds shooting script

script reader person hired to read and synopsize new scripts submitted to producer, studio, or agent

script supervisor person who takes notes on arrangement of set for continuity and editing
second-assistant cameraman person who pulls focus while camera is operating
second unit crew filming minor scenes or extras, often without director present
set sound stage or location where filming takes place
sex goddess female star whose fame is based on sex appeal
shooting script final version of screenplay indicating all details of camera shots
show single projection of film from beginning to end, esp. at designated time
show business *Informal.* art, practice, and business of making films; entertainment industry in general
sides pages of scene given to actor at casting audition
silent bit small part without lines, distinct from extra
silver screen motion pictures
sneak preview unadvertised screening of new film before release
sound editor person who builds reels of sound effects and dialogue for mixing
sound effects sounds other than dialogue and music added to film soundtrack, usu. artificially produced
sound mix electronic blending of elements on soundtrack
sound stage cavernous, soundproof building or room on studio lot for shooting films
soundtrack band on edge of film carrying music, dialogue, and sound effects synchronized with picture
spin-off project developing as adjunct to existing film
stage manager second assistant director for video production
stand-in actor who substitutes for another during setup of scene for camera and lighting
star celebrated actor commanding major roles and high salary
starlet ingénue; young, up-and-coming actress being promoted as future star
star system practice of casting and promoting stars because of their ability to attract audiences
star vehicle film project developed specifically to exploit popularity of one star
still photography publicity photographs of actors taken on set
storyboard graphic representation of each scene in film sequence, serving as guide for production
story editor person responsible for development of story from initial concept to shooting script
studio buildings and grounds where films are made; company owning such, engaged in financing and distributing films
stunt dangerous or difficult feat required by scene; *Informal.* person who performs such feats
stunt man stand-in trained to perform stunts, esp. for male actors

stunt woman stand-in trained to perform stunts for female actors
stylist hairdresser and wardrobe assistant on set
subtitles text at bottom of screen providing continuous translation of foreign language film
superstar major star who enjoys wide recognition
supporting actor actor with featured nonleading role
supporting actress actress with featured nonleading role
take a meeting *Slang.* attend a meeting
talent actors and other performers
talent scout casting director or studio employee who looks for new talent
teamsters union truckdrivers employed on all studio productions
theater movie theater
third-assistant cameraman person who loads film in magazine, operates clapper, and cleans filter; clapper loader
tie-in project related to existing film
Tinseltown *Informal.* Hollywood, as center of the movie industry
Titan crane large, movable crane with seat for director
toon *Informal.* character in animated cartoon
trades movie industry journals, esp. *Variety* and *Hollywood Reporter*
trailer film clip used as in-theater advertisement; preview of upcoming release
treatment detailed outline of script not in screenplay form
turnaround status of projects which studio no longer wishes to produce but still owns
typecasting selecting actor based on physical appearance or previous parts rather than acting skills
unions representatives of actors and technicians in film industry that set wage scales and working conditions
unit production crew on location or in sound stage
unit publicist press and media liaison responsible for publicizing specific film during production and release
usher person who escorts audience to seats in theater
VO voice-over
voice-over VO; narration heard over film sequence, not spoken as dialogue by actors on screen
wardrobe actors' costumes; department responsible for them
world premiere first public screening of film
wrangler crew member responsible for horses and any other animals used on set
wrap conclusion of filming day and esp. of entire production
X-rated *(adj)* rating designating sexually explicit film not to be viewed by persons under seventeen, now replaced by NC-17; still used in reference to pornography

TELEVISION AND RADIO
Television Programming and Institutions
Broadcast Journalism
Television Technology
Radio Programming
Radios and Radio Technology

See also: *Chap. 5: Electricity and Electronics; Telecommunications; Chap. 11: Publishing and the Press; Chap. 12: Advertising; Chap. 15: Popular Music; Theater; Cinema; Chap. 17: Sports*

Television Programming and Institutions

ABC *Trademark.* American Broadcasting Company; one of the three major national U.S. television networks
across-the-board scheduled daily at same time
action line phone-in service for television viewers with consumer problems
affiliates local stations across nation associated with a major network and receiving its feed
AFTRA American Federation of Television and Radio Artists; primary union for broadcasting performers
air *(vb)* broadcast
air date scheduled broadcast date
airtime hour at which broadcast is scheduled to begin; duration of program; total broadcast time devoted to programming of one type or from one source
announcement commercial or promotional spot
announcer person who introduces programs, identifies station, or reads news reports
anthology show nonepisodic series connected by genre or theme instead of characters
audience participation program in which audience members take active role
BBC British Broadcasting Corporation; major British network that produces programming seen on educational and public television in United States
blackout mandated interruption or restriction on broadcast, esp. local sporting event
bleep sound covering censored material on soundtrack or tape
blooper *Informal.* embarrassing gaffe made on the air
boob tube *Informal.* television set
break program interruption, esp. for a commercial or station identification
broadcast presentation of a program; *(vb)* transmit by radio or television waves
broadcasting transmission of programs by television or radio over wide area
broadcast journalism news reporting by television or radio
bumper *Slang.* ID of show displayed briefly before commercial or next segment; brief news announcement so displayed
cable television station or network broadcasting programs receivable only by paying subscription fee for hookup

candid camera program showing unwitting or unrehearsed subjects reacting to situations, filmed with small, hidden camera

canned laughter prerecorded laugh soundtrack for comedy program

casting director individual responsible for auditioning and selecting performers for shows

CBS Columbia Broadcasting System; one of the three major national U.S. television networks

clip specific section of film or tape

close end of program; wrap-up

cold open unnarrated piece of film or video used to begin documentary or news segment

commercial paid advertisement broadcast during breaks in programming

commercial television station or network in business for profit by selling advertising time to sponsors

Corporation for Public Broadcasting federally chartered organization that promotes development of public radio and television, esp. by serving as a conduit for Congressional appropriations and a buffer between the government and Public Broadcasting System

couch potato Slang. chronic television viewer

counterprogramming offering a different type of program from others in given time slot in order to attract specific audience

credits graphics at beginning or ending of program that list names of performers, crew, and staff

daytime drama soap opera

dead air unintentional period of silence or a blank screen

dedicated channel cable channel for local government, educational, or public use

docudrama narrative, fictionalized treatment of actual event, person, or topic

documentary nonfiction program covering current events, issues, or personalities

docutainment documentaries that sacrifice information for sensationalism and entertainment values

dramatic series noncomic, recurring weekly program

dramedy dramatic comedy, as opposed to situation comedy

educational access channel small, local, noncommercial channel offering the public an opportunity to transmit educational programs

emcee MC

Emmys annual awards given by National Academy of Television Arts and Sciences for excellence in programming and performing

episode regular installment of ongoing program

episodic role actor's appearance in single episode of ongoing show

fairness doctrine policy mandated by FCC, requiring that stations grant equal time to political views and candidates in opposition to these already aired

FCC Federal Communications Commission; government agency that licenses and regulates operations of radio and television stations

font on-screen graphic or super; typeface used for on-screen graphics

footage shots of an actual event or scene

format specific type of programming provided by station or shown at particular time of day or week

Fox Network Trademark. major commercial network competing with ABC, CBS, and NBC

game show program in which contestants compete for prizes by playing a game

giveaway type of game show with prizes given to contestants or audience members

graphics mixture of designs and words used esp. to introduce and close shows, also during shows and in commercials, often computer-generated

guest star well-known actor playing episodic role

idiot box Slang. television set

infomercial program-length commercial cast in standard format, as a documentary or talk show, to disguise that it is an advertisement

infotainment programming that is both informative or educational and entertaining

instant replay immediate video rerun of section of broadcast event, esp. live sport

in-the-can (adj) designating a completed program or material that has been shot

kidvid Slang. television programs intended for children

laugh track canned laughter, esp. for sitcom

live (adj) broadcast as event or performance occurs, as opposed to prerecorded

local station affiliate of network in specific region, or small, independent broadcasting entity

magazine documentary show covering several topics in single broadcast; newsmagazine

makeover thorough course of beauty, hair, and cosmetic treatments for performer

mass communications activities of mass media

mass media means of communication, such as television and radio, that reach and influence large numbers of people

MC master of ceremonies; host of variety, talk, or game show; emcee

media means of public communication, such as television and radio, providing public with news, entertainment, and advertisements

medium television or radio as media

miniseries specially programmed, serialized drama or documentary broadcast over two or more days

MTV Trademark. MusicTelevision; first and most popular cable channel exclusively broadcasting music videos

music video short, colorful, often narrative videotaped accompaniment to pop song

NAB National Association of Broadcasters

NABET National Association of Broadcast Employees and Technicians

narration voice-over description of events on screen or gaps in visual story

narrowcast (vb) aim a program at specific, limited audience or market

National Association of Broadcast Employees and Technicians NABET; primary nonperformers' union

National Association of Broadcasters NAB; voluntary broadcasting group promoting self-regulatory codes

National Association of Television and Radio Announcers NATRA; organization of broadcast announcers

NATRA National Association of Television and Radio Announcers

NBC Trademark. National Broadcasting Company; one of the three major national U.S. television networks

network association of stations affiliated with one of the major broadcasting companies; ABC, CBS, CNN, Fox, or NBC

network executive representative of network charged esp. with monitoring or directing creative work on programs

newsmagazine magazine show

Nielsen rating widely accepted estimate of relative audience share for particular program, based on monitoring of preselected sample of viewers by A.C. Nielsen Company

noncommercial broadcasting publicly funded programs

OC (adj) on-camera

open beginning of program

outro wrap-up of program comparable to tag but for longer programs

paid political announcement advertisement for political candidate or cause

pay-per-view ppv; special cable hookup requiring single payment for one broadcast

pay television commercial service that broadcasts programs to viewers who pay monthly charge or per-program fee; subscription television

PBS Public Broadcasting Service; network of publicly funded, noncommercial stations

people meter device for recording in-home response to programming

personality actor famous for particular role or work as host or MC

phonathon prolonged, on-air fund-raiser soliciting phone-in participation by viewers

pilot introductory test episode of proposed new program

plug Informal. advertisement, esp. mention of product within context of program, not in paid commercial spot

ppv pay-per-view

preempt (vb) replace with another program

prerecorded (adj) taped or filmed prior to broadcast

prime time midevening hours of broadcast time, when largest audience is watching; 8 p.m. to 11 p.m.

producer person responsible for preparing, supervising production of, and editing program or news spot

production company company that develops pilots for networks and creates and produces programs

program single scheduled television broadcast

program analysis dissection of program content, success, and viewership, aimed at increasing ratings

programming determination or nature of broadcast content and balance of news, talk shows, sitcoms, dramas, documentaries, variety shows, movies, or sports programs

public access television local cable television station providing free time for low-budget, often nonprofessional programs; system of such stations

public service announcement advertisement or announcement done for public good with time donated by station

public television nonprofit television station or broadcast network emphasizing educational and cultural programming

quiz show program in which contestants compete for prizes by answering questions

rating measure of relative audience size for competing programs at same hour, used esp. to set price for commercials

reality show entertaining coverage of real-life events, including those staged for show

recurring (*adj*) occurring regularly, esp. of characters on program

renewal FCC approval of extended broadcast license

repeat reshowing of program in same season

rerun repeat broadcast of program, usu. in later year

season annual run of new shows, usu. beginning in September or January

segue seamless transition from program to program or segment to segment

serial program appearing in regular installments

share percentage of viewers watching particular show

shoot-'em-up *Informal.* western

sign off (*vb*) make closing announcement and show station identification at end of broadcast day

simulcast program broadcast over cooperating radio and television stations at same time to provide improved audio, esp. for televised music program

sitcom *Informal.* situation comedy

situation comedy usu. half-hour, comedic show with recurring characters in simplistic situations

skitcom *Informal.* comedy format in which star or stars perform in series of unrelated skits

slot time slot for regularly scheduled program

soap soap opera

soap opera melodrama series, usu. showing five days a week during daytime hours; daytime drama; soap

sound bite brief segment of audio and video transmission, esp. on talking-head show

space opera futuristic, melodramatic fantasy involving space travel and extraterrestrials

special program that appears one time only or is not part of regular schedule

specialty station station with single-format programming

spin-off series or program derived from a previously popular show or its characters

spokesperson popular or compelling individual who speaks on behalf of product or cause

sponsor advertiser buying time on particular show to promote product

sportscast broadcast of sporting event

sportscaster person who delivers sports news or describes sports event

spot spot announcement

spot announcement brief advertisement or promotional blurb on upcoming program, newsbrief, or station break; spot

standards and practices network department responsible for insuring that program content meets specific moral standards

stand by instruction to hold for further information or continuation of broadcast

station facility for producing and broadcasting programs

station break interruption of network program for local station identification and information on upcoming programs

station identification brief spot giving call letters and channel number of station or name of network, usu. before and after program or on the hour and half-hour

strip show program scheduled five days a week in same time slot

studio offices, engineering rooms, and originating site of live programs and news broadcasts

studio program broadcast recorded or transmitted live from stage in studio

STV subscription television

subscription television STV; pay television

subtitle written translation of foreign language program appearing on-screen simultaneously with audio

summer repeat rerun aired during summer months

super on-screen image superimposed on original video image

superstation independent, local television station that is distributed and broadcast nationally via satellite to cable systems

sweeps thrice-yearly rating surveys that coincide with highly competitive programming weeks for networks

syndication reissue of series for broadcast after show has ceased production of new episodes; marketing of show on station-by-station basis and not to networks

tag identification of producer or syndicator at end of program

talent actors, performers

talking head *Slang.* closeup shot of someone talking or being interviewed; programming based on such shots

talk show program with host interviewing unusual guests and celebrities

talk-show host engaging person who serves as regular moderator of talk show

taped show program prerecorded for later broadcast

target (*vb*) aim program at particular audience

telecast single television broadcast or program

teleplay script for a television program

telethon lengthy, uninterrupted program raising money for charitable cause

televangelist religious minister preaching over television and frequently soliciting donations for a church

television station facility for producing and broadcasting programs

television time-out time-out taken in sports event to accommodate television commercials

telly *Brit. informal.* television or a television set

tie-in program with content that relates to another program

time slot hour of day and day of week when weekly program is scheduled

TV television

under-five *Informal.* actor's part with less than five speaking lines

variety show program with host presenting several different entertainers and acts, such as music, dance, comedy, and magic

vast wasteland *Slang.* pejorative term for television programming

video game computer-controlled game attached to and played on television set

video jockey VJ; announcer for music-video program

viewer person who watches television

viewing public those who watch television and are potential consumers for advertised products

VJ video jockey

VO voice-over

voice-over VO; voice of offscreen narrator heard while other visuals are on screen

western dramatic program set in 19th-century American West

whodunit *Informal.* mystery program

Broadcast Journalism

add news story added to broadcast, esp. at last minute

advance news story circulated ahead of scheduled release date

air personality engaging announcer who attracts viewers to newscast

all-news station exclusively airing news programs

anchor principal journalist on news program

anchorman male anchor

anchorwoman female anchor

A roll interviews and stand-up portion of news broadcast

ARTNA **A**ssociation of **R**adio and **T**elevision **N**ews **A**nalysts

Association of Radio and Television News Analysts ARTNA; organization of broadcast journalists

BAN Black Audio Network

Black Audio Network BAN; news service for black radio stations

blind interview interview with unnamed source

blurb brief news release

bridge transition within story, esp. use of stand-up or walk and talk to relate portion of report

broadcast journalism reporting of news events on radio or television

B roll footage used to illustrate reports during news broadcast

bulletin report of news development important enough to warrant interruption of regular programming

CNN *Trademark.* Cable News Network; network of all-news cable channels

coanchor one of two anchorpersons on same news show

color commentary interpretation and background during sports play-by-play

commentary editorial analysis and interpretation of news

commentator news analyst

copy written text of news story

correspondent person supplying news and broadcasting from remote location

cover (*vb*) gather and report news

coverage pictures and accounts of an event broadcast live

depth interview interview characterized by intensive questioning of one individual on specific subject or subjects

electronic news gathering ENG; use of video equipment instead of film to expedite news gathering and eliminate delays in processing

ENG electronic news gathering

equal access broadcasters' desire for equality with newspapers in access to courtrooms and other news sources

equal time legal requirement that stations grant equal airtime to qualified political candidates and others with opposing viewpoints

eyewitness news news format stressing casual responses by news anchors

flash brief news report on something extraordinary that has just occurred; bulletin

follow-up news story providing additional or new information on previously broadcast item

group interview interview of individual by several journalists simultaneously

hard news serious events of immediate, general interest and value

hold for release agree not to air news story until specified date

human-interest story report designed to engage attention and sympathy of audience members who identify readily with people and situations described

interpretive reporting in-depth analysis of news events

interview questioning of individual by one or more reporters, esp. on personal views or activities

kicker cheery final story on newscast

kill (*vb*) decide not to air story

lead newscast's opening and most important or attention-grabbing story

lead-in introduction to news story

local news news broadcast based at local station, covering regional news and human-interest stories

meat essence of a news story

media coverage degree of attention given certain event by media

media event public appearance or event staged deliberately to gain attention from media

national news news of national and international significance broadcast by network from central studio

news reports of recent events of general interest or importance that are collected and broadcast on news programs

newsbreak station break typically consisting of two or three brief news items

newsbrief very short news item, often interrupting regular programming

newscast regularly scheduled news broadcast

newscaster person who reads news on broadcast

news hour time, usu. in early evening, when day's primary news broadcast occurs

news program regular newscast or special public-affairs broadcast

newsreel short film of recent news events, formerly shown as part of program in theaters

newsroom room in which news is written and edited prior to broadcast

news team anchorperson, weatherperson, sportscaster, and reporters who appear on news show

nonevent media-induced or -conceived news story

open-ended question broadly framed question allowing for freely formulated answer

panel show news show in which several journalists interview knowledgeable person on given issue

parachute journalism practice in which reporter arrives on location after producer has prepared story, tapes segment for on-screen appearance, and departs immediately

personal interview one-on-one, in-depth conversation between reporter and public personality

play-by-play live description of sporting event

press conference appearance of person, esp. government official, for questioning by group of reporters

public affairs program news or news analysis broadcast, esp. dealing with timely subjects related to general public welfare

public forum program providing opportunity for discussion of current events

recap news summary, esp. at end of broadcast

release copy advance copy or announcement of impending news story

reporter newsperson covering individual stories from field

rip and read tear news item from wire service teletypewriter and broadcast it immediately

segment relatively brief but complete treatment of specific news story, comprising portion of news broadcast

segment producer person responsible for single segment

sidebar brief item dealing with secondary aspect of news story

slant (*vb*) distort information to express a particular bias or viewpoint

soft news local human-interest stories of passing interest

spin control *Slang.* attempt to give bias to coverage of political candidate, esp. by casting potentially damaging information in a more favorable light

stand-up portion of news broadcast in which standing reporter faces camera and delivers report

straight news serious stories relating esp. to politics, business, and international affairs

structured interview interview in which reporter allows person being interviewed to set parameters for questions

tag newscaster's final on-screen words added to taped news story

update news story rewritten to include latest developments

use television appearance by legally qualified political candidate

vérité action portions of report, without narration or talking head

walk and talk stand-up in which reporter walks along while delivering report with camera following

weatherperson member of news team who describes and forecasts weather

wrap-up summary of day's news, esp. in final few minutes of broadcast

Television Technology

across the mike speaking from side of microphone to muffle plosive and sibilant sounds

aerial antenna

airwaves pathways of broadcast frequencies

antenna metallic rod or wire for receiving radio or television waves, often placed on top of building; aerial

audio electronically reproduced sound

audio frequency wavelength of sound

band group of communication frequencies, such as VHF or UHF

beam stream of radio waves sent continuously in one direction

Beta *Trademark.* secondary videocassette recorder format, now largely abandoned

big-screen television television with screen over 23 inches across

black-and-white (*adj*) displaying monochrome reproduction of television images

blip interruption of sound reception; spot of light on the screen

boom device from which microphones are suspended above performers out of camera view

booster radio-frequency amplifier for television set

brightness control knob on television set used to regulate amount of light emitted from tube

broadcast television signal sent via airwaves, as distinguished from cable or closed circuit

cable alternate way of transmitting television signals by cable lines rather than through air, requiring hookup to cable for reception

cable system local company that supplies cable channels to its subscribers

camcorder small, portable videotape recorder and camera

cameraman operator of video camera

cathode-ray tube CRT; electronic tube used as television screen

CC (*adj*) **c**losed-**c**aptioned

channel band of broadcasting frequencies used by station

character generator small computer producing letters and graphic images directly on screen, without use of camera

chroma key electronic special effects system that permits insertion of image onto another image already present on screen

chrominance signal color-coded video signal

closed-captioned (*adj*) CC; designating programs having subtitles for hearing-impaired viewers, with captions appearing only on specially equipped television sets

closed circuit broadcasting signal sent only to televisions connected by cable to transmitter

coaxial cable electronic cable used to transmit television signals to cable subscribers

color polychrome reproduction of television images

color bars series of strips representing colors in spectrum, used for adjusting color on set; horizontal bars

colorcast television program broadcast in color

color control knob on color television set regulating mixture of red, blue, and green

contrast degree of difference between black and white or colors of picture

control room room adjacent to studio from which production is directed and engineered

crew technical staff working on broadcast

CRT **c**athode-**r**ay **t**ube

cue off-camera signal to performer; signal from control booth to cameraman

cue card large card with dialogue held near camera to prompt performers

dead mike microphone that is not working; period of silence

definition clearness with which televised images are reproduced

detail degree of sharpness of visual image

distortion image deformity caused by lens imperfection

dot pattern image formed by closely placed, tiny dots of shaded or colored light

dub duplicate tape of broadcast

engineer operator of technical broadcasting equipment

fade gradual reduction in picture from brightness to black

feed program transmitted by network to affiliates for broadcast, usu. sent out before airtime; recording of event or live report transmitted to studio

fidelity accuracy and clarity of image and sound reproduction

film (*vb*) record program on film rather than videotape

flagging diagonal shift of top portion of picture, which seems to bend left or right

flicker fluctuations in picture

footage section of film or tape

frame one picture in series; complete image being transmitted by television

frequency number of oscillations of wave per second

generation number of duplications separating tape or film from original

ghost secondary image that repeats main picture image, caused by signal interference

glitch *Slang*. broadcast interference or malfunction

grain size of silver particles on film image

HDTV **h**igh-**d**efinition **t**ele**v**ision

headphones device worn over head with tiny speakers positioned over ears to receive audio transmission

headset device with headphones and attached microphone

high-definition television HDTV; receiver with high number of scanning lines per frame, producing extremely sharp image and resolution

hookup connection to assemblage of circuits used for radio or television transmission

horizontal bars color bars

horizontal hold control that regulates back-and-forth image

image picture on television screen

intensity strength of screen image

interference static or unwanted signals that distort image or audio

key light primary light focused on subject

lapel mike tiny microphone attached to clothing on chest; lavaliere microphone

lavaliere microphone small microphone clipped to person's clothing or placed around neck; lapel mike

lighting illumination of set

line recording recording both picture and sound at the same time

luminance signal black-and-white video signal

microphone electronic device for picking up,

magnifying, and converting sound waves to electric signals

minicam small, portable videotape camera

mix electronic blending, esp. of audio signals

mobile camera small, portable videotape camera

mobile unit truck equipped with videotape recording and transmission equipment for on-the-spot coverage of events

monitor television set with no audio output, used on stage to show performers and technicians what is being shot and/or broadcast

off-camera (*adj*) designating activity unseen by viewers

on the air designation that studio is in taping or broadcast mode

outtake section of tape not used on broadcast

pickup reception of network transmissions by individual station or affiliate

picture visual element of television program

picture tube electronic device that transforms broadcast signals into patterns of light on screen; cathode-ray tube

playback reproduction and rebroadcast of videotaped pictures

portapak lightweight, portable video camera system

projection television television with very large screen

pulse very short burst of electromagnetic waves

rabbit ears dipole receiving antenna on television set

rain vertical marks interfering with clarity of image

range full extent of area covered by transmission

rear-screen projection television in which image is projected onto screen from behind

receiver television set with cathode-ray tube

reception process by which radio or television waves are transformed into images on screen; clarity of these images

relay links devices activated by signal and operating other devices that connect elements in transmission path

remote control device for tuning television set from short distance away

resolution measurement of picture sharpness

satellite artificial station orbiting Earth and relaying television signals from one point on Earth to another

satellite dish large, shallow hemisphere used to receive transmissions relayed by satellite

scan lines electronic beam pattern of parallel lines translated by television set into screen image

scramble (*vb*) encode audio or visual signal so that only certain subscribers can receive it

screen television monitor displaying image

separation distinction of shades or colors in image

set television set

sharpness control device that regulates clarity of image

shoot (*vb*) to film or tape something

signal generation origination and production of radio or television waves to be transmitted

small screen television in general, as distinguished from cinema, which is big screen

snow fluctuating white spots that partially obscure image on screen due to weak signal

splice (*vb*) join together two pieces of film or tape

static atmospheric electrical discharges that interfere with television waves

steadycam portable video or film camera attached to operator by harness and frame to eliminate wavering of tracked image

subscriber terminal set receiving cable broadcasts

super (*vb*) superimpose one image on another

sweetening improvement of sound and image quality after original recording

swell gradual increase in sound volume

sync *Informal.* synchronization

synchronization exact alignment of audio and picture; sync

tape videotape; (*vb*) to record program on videotape

taped (*adj*) prerecorded, not live

technician television engineer

telecine device that converts film or slides into television signal

telecommunications electromagnetic transmission and reception of data to produce sound and images

TelePrompTer *Trademark.* device displaying cue cards to aid performers in remembering lines

teletext broadcast information services, esp. for news, stock market, and consumer goods; videotext

televise (*vb*) broadcast pictures and sound via television

television TV; electronic system for transmitting images and sound over wires or through space by conversion of light and sound into electrical waves and reconversion at receiving set into visible light projected by CRT and audible sound; receiving set in such a system

television channel specific broadcast frequency

television receiver TV set

test pattern fixed picture, often color bars, broadcast by station to assist viewers in adjusting reception

transmission passage of radio or television waves through space between transmitter and receiver

transmitter tower sending wave transmissions from source to viewers

tube *Informal.* cathode-ray tube used for projecting television images; television set; television in general

tuning control device for determining which channel or frequency is received by set

TV television set or receiver

TV set receiver for television transmissions, with cathode- ray tube for generating images

UHF ultra high frequency; frequency range between 300 and 3000 megahertz

VCP videocassette player; device that plays but does not record cartridge tapes

VCR videocassette recorder; device that plays and records cartridge tapes

vertical hold control of up-and-down image

VHF very high frequency; frequency range between 30 and 300 kilohertz

VHS *Trademark.* Video Home System; primary videocassette format

video television production in general, outside major commercial and subscription systems; film process used in television production

videocassette plastic tape cartridge on which VCR records

videodisk flat disk storing and playing back recorded image and sound

videotape (*vb*) record visual images and sound as electronic impulses on magnetic tape for television broadcasting; (*n*) magnetic tape used for such recordings

videotext teletext

VTR video tape recorder; device used for recording noncassette tapes

wavelength measurement of sound or light wave; frequency

wild (*adj*) designating recording of sound separately from picture

Radio Programming

all-news radio format airing news programs only

all-talk talk radio

alternative radio avant-garde, noncommercial programming

announcer person employed to speak on radio broadcasts

AOR radio format emphasizing album-oriented rock music

black radio programming aimed at black listeners

call-in show in which listeners telephone host to discuss issues live on the air

call letters initials identifying radio station

countdown playing of top pop hits in reverse order up to number one

country-and-western station broadcasting country-and-western and bluegrass music

disc jockey DJ; radio announcer for music program

DJ disc jockey

drive time periods in morning or evening when commuters typically are in their cars and listening to radio broadcasts

easy listening programming consisting of relaxing, bland music; middle-of-the-road

Emergency Broadcast System radio frequencies reserved for use by government and police agencies in an emergency

format emphasis and content of broadcasting, such as all-news, country music, talk show, Top 40 call-in, AOR, or classical

handle *Slang.* citizens band operator's nickname

listener-sponsored radio local noncommercial radio station funded by voluntary donations from listeners

middle-of-the-road MOR; easy listening

MOR middle-of-the-road

Muzak *Trademark.* environmental background music, usu. adaptations of classical, show, and pop songs, available to subscribers

National Public Radio NPR; noncommercial, publicly funded, educational and cultural radio network

newscaster announcer for news program

NPR National Public Radio

pirate radio unlicensed radio station

program director person responsible for establishing format and determining programming of station

radio drama dramatic show broadcast over radio

Radio Free Europe federally funded U.S. network that broadcasts news and entertainment to eastern Europe from European locations

radio wire news wire supplying up-to-date news to stations

segue seamless transition, esp. from one song to the next

sigalert traffic advisory warning broadcast

signature station identification, jingle, or slogan

soap opera old-fashioned radio melodrama, orig. sponsored by soap manufacturer

studio offices, engineering rooms, and originating site of broadcasts over radio station

talk radio broadcasting format featuring phone-in audience participation and guest interviews by radio personality; all-talk

talk show discussion-style program where host and guests converse

10-4 *Slang.* Citizens Band designation for okay

top 40 programming format featuring current popular-music hits and issuing weekly list of forty most popular songs

topless radio talk show specializing in sexual topics

underground radio unconventional, politically progressive, and musically avant-garde programming format

USIA United States Information Agency, operator of Voice of America overseas

Voice of America politically oriented U.S. station, broadcast overseas by USIA

Radios and Radio Technology

aerial arrangement of wires or metal rods for receiving radio transmissions

airwaves radio waves transmitted at various frequencies

AM amplitude modulation broadcasting band

amplifier radio component that strengthens signal received

band group of broadcasting frequencies, such as AM or FM

beacon radio transmitter; signal transmitted by radio transmitter

boom box *Informal.* very large but portable radio/cassette player

bug *Informal.* hidden radio transmitter

capsule radio tiny radio transmitter, swallowed for medical diagnosis; radio pill

car radio radio receiver in automobile with external antenna

CB Citizens Band

channel radio wave frequency of sufficient width for one- or two-way communication, used by broadcasting station

circuit means of transmitting interactive communications signals, usu. comprising two channels

Citizens Band CB; short-range, two-way radio frequency

clear channel strong signal on frequency with no interference; frequency cleared for long-distance transmission

clock radio alarm clock that turns on radio at designated hour

console often decorative enclosure for radio receiver, tuner, and amplifier

continuous wave CW; electromagnetic wave of constant amplitude and frequency, used to carry information by being modulated

crystal radio nonelectric receiver sensitive to radio waves

CW transmitter continuous-wave transmitter

descrambler device that makes radio signals intelligible by systematically tuning receiver to transmitted frequencies

detector device that rectifies alternating current in radio receiver

engineer person responsible for off-air activities that permit announcer to keep program running smoothly

equalization electronic amplification or reduction of particular ranges of audio frequencies

FM frequency modulation broadcasting band

frequency number of oscillations of wave per second

ghetto blaster *Slang.* portable radio with large speakers

ham amateur two-way radio operator

hertz measurement of frequency in vibrations per second

hi-fi high fidelity

high fidelity radio with excellent sound reproduction; hi-fi

kilohertz one thousand hertz

link radio relay station serving as connection in communications system

megahertz one million hertz

multiplex (*vb*) transmit two signals of sound over one channel, esp. for stereophonic radio reception

pocket radio small, battery-operated or transistor radio

power pack source of direct current to operate radio

power plug device that connects wire from radio to source of AC current

power transformer device for transferring AC current from one winding to another at constant frequency

quadcast four-channel FM broadcast

quadraphonic (*adj*) designating transmission of FM signals using four channels

radio conversion of sound signals into electromagnetic waves and transmission of these waves through space to receiving set, which then converts them back into sound; such a receiving set

radiophone equipment, such as a walky-talky or CB, for carrying on two-way communication by radio waves

radio signal particular frequency of transmitted radio wave

radiotelegraphy transmission of messages by radio waves rather than through wires or cables

radio wave electromagnetic wave moving at radio frequency, between 10 kilohertz and one million megahertz

receiver device for transforming radio waves into sound

recording engineer technician who operates equipment in recording studio

recording studio soundproofed, acoustically controlled room for radio broadcasting or recording of audio

shortwave radio radio that transmits or receives radio waves shorter than used in AM broadcasting, corresponding to frequencies over 1600 kilohertz

signal power of sound transmitted by station

speaker device for changing electrical signals into sound waves

station specific frequency or band assigned to a broadcaster; individuals and offices responsible for originating broadcasts; studio or building from which broadcasts originate

stereophonic (*adj*) designating transmission of FM radio signals using two channels

tower very tall structure transmitting station's programs as radio waves

transceiver combination radio transmitter and receiver

transistor tiny electronic device that controls flow of electricity in radio equipment

transmitter radio wave broadcasting device

tuner device sensitive to different radio wave frequencies, which permits selection of specific radio station by receiver

tuning adjustment of radio dial to specific frequency of given station

Walkman *Trademark.* small, portable, speakerless radio---cassette player utilizing earphones for listening

walky-talky portable, two-way radio receiver and transmitter, often battery-operated

wireless *Chiefly Brit.* radio; transmission of sound waves through air without wires or cables

CHAPTER SIXTEEN
APPLIED ARTS

ARCHITECTURE
Schools and Styles
Classical Elements and Design
Building Construction and Design

See also: *Chap. 5: Structural Components;*
Building and Construction Materials; Chap. 7:
Exterior Structure; Interior Structure;
Ornamental and Functional Articles; Chap. 11:
The City

Schools and Styles

architecture art and science of designing and building habitable structures, esp. with aesthetically pleasing, coherent forms

arcology fusion of architecture with ecology

art deco architectural style using stylized, repetitive geometric designs, esp. zigzags and lozenges, with emphasis on facades in tile and relief (early 20th c.)

art nouveau architectural style using decorative, biomorphic forms with curved, irregular lines (late 19th c.)

baroque architectural style using strong, dramatic design with imaginative use of theatrical, chiaroscuro effects (Europe, 17th-18th c.)

Bauhaus architectural school characterized by clean geometry and functionalism (Germany, 1920's)

brutalism use of exaggeration and distortion in architecture to create effect of massiveness and power (mid-20th c.)

Byzantine synthesis of Oriental and Occidental architectural styles, marked by domes and minarets (eastern Europe, 4th-13th c.)

churrigueresque (*adj*) of a baroque architectural style with elaborate surface decoration (Spain, 18th c.)

classical (*adj*) of the architectural style of ancient Hellenic Greece and imperial Rome, emphasizing columniation

Colonial variation of Georgian architectural style prevalent in colonial America (18th c.)

Directoire (*adj*) noting or pertaining to a style of architecture and decoration in France similar to Regency style in Britain (late 18th c.)

Egyptian (*adj*) of an architectural style prevalent from the third millennium B.C. through the Roman era, characterized by the use of massive, pillared stonework with emphasis on religious monuments

Egyptian Revival architectural style using monolithic, columnar forms, flat roofs, and ancient Egyptian decorative motifs (19th-early 20th c.)

flamboyant (*adj*) of a highly decorative Gothic style (France, 15th-16th c.)

Georgian (*adj*) of a style incorporating classical, Renaissance, and baroque elements of architecture, emphasizing formal, symmetrical design (U.S. and Britain, 18th c.)

Gothic architectural style with emphasis on verticality and intricate, decorative, pointed arches (Europe, 12th-16th c.)

Gothic Revival architectural style marked by a resurgence of Gothic verticality and sharply pitched roof forms (U.S. and Britain, late 18th-19th c.)

Greek Revival architectural style marked by a resurgence of classical Greek and Roman forms, with columns supporting pedimented roofs (U.S. and Britain, early 19th c.)

Hellenic (*adj*) of a monumental style of religious architecture, characterized by columnar supports of pediment-roofed temples (Greece, 8th-4th c. B.C.)

Hellenistic (*adj*) of a classical style that influenced imperial Roman architecture (Greece, 4th-2nd c. B.C.)

International Style modern architectural style and construction, emphasizing horizontal bands of windows, undecorated glass, curtain-wall facades, and skyscrapers (20th c.)

Moorish (*adj*) of an architectural style emphasizing overall decoration, carving, arabesque design, and intricate stuccowork (Spain, 11th-14th c.)

neoclassical (*adj*) marked by a return to classical architecture in response to romantic themes (Europe, 18th-19th c.)

Norman (*adj*) of an architectural style using massive stonework and rounded arches (Britain, 11th c.)

Palladian (*adj*) of an architectural style patterned after northern Italian Renaissance (Britain, 18th c.)

postmodern (*adj*) of an architectural style with eclectic, sometimes whimsical use of a variety of styles, esp. classical elements, often large-scale for corporate or institutional use (late 20th c.)

Prairie School group of American architects who emphasized a style using low-pitched roof and long horizontal lines (early 20th c.)

Queen Anne (*adj*) of a style of architecture and furnishing characterized by simplicity and restraint, esp. using red brick (Britain, 18th c.)

Regency (*adj*) of a style of architecture, furnishing, and decoration characterized by simple lines and increasing use of Greco-Roman forms (Britain, early 19th c.)

Renaissance resurgence and reinterpretation of classic forms of architecture with focus on symmetry, balance, and elegance (Europe, 15th-16th c.)

rococo architectural style using fanciful, carved spatial forms and excessively elaborate ornamentation (Europe, 18th c.)

Romanesque architectural style using massive forms and geometrical patterns (Europe, 11th-12th c.)

Tudor (*adj*) characteristic of a transitional style between Gothic and Palladian, with emphasis on privacy and interior design (Britain, 16th c.)

Victorian (*adj*) characteristic of a highly decorative architectural style with Gothic elements (U.S. and Britain, late 19th c.)

Classical Elements and Design

abacus flat slab forming uppermost member of capital of column

acanthus decorative scrolled leaf form

amphistylar (*adj*) having columns at both ends

annulet ring-shaped molding or ridge

anthemion decorative palmlike leaf form

apse vaulted, semidomed end of aisle or building

arabesque abstract, curled, or plantlike decorative forms

arcade series of arches bounded by columns

arch curved structural member spanning an opening and serving as support, esp. of stone blocks: barrel, basket-handle, bell, blunt, cinquefoil, cusped, elliptical, equal, flat, horseshoe, inflected, keel, lancet, ogee, parabolic, pointed, primitive, rampant, relieving, round, rowlock, scalloped, segmental, shouldered, trefoil, Tudor

architrave beam across tops of columns, forming base of the entablature

archivolt molding along curve or underside of arch

arcuate (*adj*) structurally dependent on arches

arris sharp edge or angle where two surfaces meet

atrium open courtyard bordered by walkways

attic part of the entablature above cornice that hides the roof

baldacchino canopy supported by columns

ballflower ornament consisting of ball placed in flower-shaped hollow of circular molding

barrel vault continuous, semicircular, arched vault

base bottom of column taken as architectural unit, consisting of torus, scotia, plinth, and fillets

basilica church with aisles and elevated nave

bas-relief sculptured relief on wall or pediment

bay area between columns; deeply recessed window

bezant flat discus used as ornament

boss ornamental projecting stud; raised block

buttress masonry supporting arch or vault

campanile freestanding bell tower

canopy decorative, rooflike covering over altar, tomb, or doorway

cantilever extension of beam, floor, or roof beyond its vertical support

capital decorative cap atop column, supporting entablature

capstone keystone of arch

caryatid column sculpted in form of standing female figure

chapiter capital of column

chigi finials on Shinto temple roof (Japan)

cloister courtyard bounded by walkways

colonnade series of columns at regular intervals

column round, vertical, supporting pillar with pedestal, shaft, and capital: Byzantine, Composite, Corinthian, Doric, Gothic, Ionic, Moorish, Romanesque, Tuscan

Composite column Roman order combining Corinthian acanthus with Ionic volutes

console member extending from wall to form bracket

corbeil ornamental, sculptured basket of fruit or flowers

corbel short, decorative cantilever projecting from wall

Corinthian column late-style column having high base, slender, fluted shaft with fillets, ornate capital, and acanthus

corona projecting part of cornice

cornice projecting top level of building or entablature

course single, continuous row of bricks, stones, or masonry

crenellation repeated indentations in molding or ornament

crossette projection at corner of architrave of door or window

crown uppermost part of column

cupola small, rounded structure atop roof

cusp pointed projection at intersection of two arcs or foils

cyma uppermost projecting molding with partly concave and partly convex profile

cymatium uppermost member of classical cornice, usu. a cyma recta molding

dado section of pedestal below shaft base and above ground base

dentil small, rectangular, toothlike blocks projecting under corona of cornice

Doric column earliest known style of column, undecorated, without base, and having short, fluted shaft

dosseret clearly defined block resting on capital of Byzantine or Romanesque column

echinus rounded molding forming bell of Doric capital

egg and dart closely set, alternating series of oval and pointed forms, used to enrich echinus

engaged column column attached to wall, not freestanding

entablature horizontal element above columns, including architrave, frieze, and cornice

entasis slightly convex curve in column, giving it the appearance of perfect verticality

extrados exterior curve or surface of arch

facade exterior face of building

fan vault vault composed of concave conoidal surfaces intersecting or touching at top and usu. decorated with curved ribs

filigree ornamental work of delicate, intricate design

fillet flat molding that separates others; space between two flutings in column shaft

finial ornament atop spire or gable

fluting vertical grooves in column shaft

flying buttress arch or arch segment projecting from wall and transmitting the thrust of a roof or vault outward and downward to a solid buttress or pier

foliation decorative member resembling leaves or flowers

folly fake ruin; structure built as functionless whimsy

frieze horizontal band in entablature between architrave and cornice, usu. ornamented

gable triangular area of wall at end of pitched roof

gargoyle waterspout in form of elaborately carved creature projecting from gutter

gopuram massive gateway to Hindu temple (India)

groin curved line or edge formed by intersection of two vaults

grotesque decorative design of human or animal figures and fanciful motifs

imbrication ornament with overlapping edges, such as tiles

impost post from which arch springs from pier, column, or wall

intrados interior curve or surface of arch or vault

Ionic column middle period column with an elegant base, tall, slender, fluted shaft, and a volute or spiral capital

keystone center stone of arch

lintel horizontal beam over door or window

loggia gallery or balcony open on at least one side

lunette round window; rounded niche for sculpture

masonry construction with stones or bricks

metope Doric frieze panel between triglyphs

minaret tall tower attached to mosque

molding decorative recessed or contoured strip used for finishing, usu. at juncture of wall and ceiling: beak, cavetto, congé, cyma recta, cyma reversa, echinus, facia, fillet, ovolo, plate rail, quarter round, reeding, scotia, torus

narthex porch at church main entrance of church

nave main axis of church or cathedral

niche recessed area in wall

oculus circular wall opening

order one of the classical styles of base, column, and entablature: Corinthian, Doric, or Ionic

pantheon classic domed temple form in ancient Greece and Rome

parquetry geometrically patterned, inlaid wood, esp. for floors

pedestal support at foot of column

pediment triangular shape at end of pitched roof

pendentive curved support in form of spherical triangle between dome and its supporting masonry

peristyle colonnaded courtyard behind entrance

pier isolated masonry support

pilaster flat, columnar form against wall

pillar upright support column or shaft

plinth projecting block at base of building or column

portico covered entryway or porch with columns

pylon monumental temple gateway (ancient Egypt)

quoin corner of building; stone forming building corner

relief moldings and ornamentation that stand out from a surface

reticulation ornamental design resembling a net

sarcophagus ornamental stone coffin

scotia concave molding in column base

shaft cylindrical pillar between capital and base of column

skewback course of masonry with a sloping surface against which stones of arch abut

soffit undersurface of arch

spandrel wall area above curved sides of arch

spire tall, tapering Gothic tower

springer first stone of arch above impost

squinch arch placed diagonally between two walls

steeple tall, narrow, conical tower

stellate (adj) star-shaped

stereobate foundation or base upon which building, esp. classical temple, is erected

stringcourse decorative, horizontal band, as of stone, projecting beyond or flush with face of building, often molded

stupa domed, Buddhist shrine

stylobate course of masonry forming foundation for a colonnade, esp. outermost colonnade of building

summer stone laid upon top of pier, column, or wall, from which arch springs

supercilium fillet above cyma of a cornice

tabernacle highly decorated niche

telamon male figure, similar to caryatid, used as column or pilaster

tholos circular building (ancient Greece)

tomb structure over or housing a grave

torii monumental post-and-lintel gateway to Shinto shrine (Japan)

torus large convex molding used as lowest molding in column base

trabeated (adj) dependent on upright-and-horizontal or post-and-lintel construction, not on arches

tracery ornamental pattern in Gothic architecture

transept transverse arms of cross-shaped church, usu. perpendicular to nave

trefoil decorative, three-lobed design

triglyph grooved projecting panels in Doric frieze

triumphal arch monumental gateway

tumulus earth or stone mound over grave

Tuscan column Roman order of column, similar to Doric with fluted shaft

tympanum area above doorway or arch, esp. triangular face of pediment

vault arched, domed, usu. masonry ceiling or roof: barrel, dome, fan, groin, ribbed

viga wooden beam that supports roof of adobe structure

vomitory aislelike entrance through bank of stadium or theater seats

voussoir one of the wedge-shaped stone blocks used to form arch

westwork monumental, Romanesque church front formed of porches and towers and containing an entrance with vestibule below and a chapel above

ziggurat mound built with stepped sides

Building Construction and Design

attic space between ceiling joists and roof rafters

backfill replacing earth around foundation

balloon frame one-piece studs extending from foundation to roof of two-story structure

baseboard wooden finish strip where interior wall meets floor

bearing wall wall that supports a vertical load, esp. the floors and walls above; load-bearing wall

blocking placement of wooden framing members between other members to add strength and provide nailing surface

blueprint detailed architectural design diagram

board measure system for measuring lumber, in which each board foot is equal to one inch by twelve inches by twelve inches

breast wall retaining wall

building codes ordinances regulating construction standards

casement window window hinged on one side, swinging outward

center to center distance from center of one member to center of next as shown on drawings

central heating single heat source supplying several ducts

compressive strength ability of material to withstand forces tending to shorten it

contractor builder responsible for implementing architectural designs and drawings, purchasing materials, and hiring labor

crawlspace area between floor joists and earth beneath building

curtain wall exterior wall that protects an interior wall from weather, but bears no structural load

dead load weight of materials used to build structure

deflection vertical distance that beam moves under load stress

double glazing door or window made of two panes of glass sealed together with a dead air space between them to provide insulation

double-hung window window with two sashes that move vertically

drafting mechanical drawing

dry wall interior wall composed of gypsum board panels

elevation building face; front drawing of structure projected geometrically on vertical plane parallel to one of its sides

ell wing of building at right angle to main structure

excavation pit dug in earth for foundation

fascia vertical boards at end of rafter forming face of cornice and attached to overhanging outer edge of roof

fixture plumbing or electrical equipment

floor plan drawing that shows the top view of one floor of a house

foundation masonry or concrete substructure of building beneath first-floor joists

grade elevation above sea level of building site; slope of ground for building site

half-timbered (*adj*) relating to exterior walls with exposed, heavy, wooden members separated by masonry

house drain large horizontal sewer beneath house that receives wastes from soil pipes

house sewer sewer line that connects house drain to city sewer or septic tank

interior trim molding, casing, and bargeboard used to finish walls, doors, or windows

kip deadweight load equal to 1000 pounds (453.6 kg)

knee wall short wall used in constructing top floor of one-and-one-half-story structure

landing platform at top, bottom, or between flights of stairs

live load weight of variable, movable loads placed on a building

load-bearing wall bearing wall

maquette small, preliminary model of designed structure

mechanical drawing stylized, precise drawing of plans and blueprints done with aid of rulers, scales, and compasses; drafting

mockup scale model of structure with full detail

modular construction construction of buildings from standardized units

modular unit factory-built finished section of building, room-size or larger, for modular construction

module standardized unit of measurement for determining building proportions

monolithic (*adj*) constructed of concrete, with all members cast at the same time as a single unit

nonbearing wall wall that bears only its own weight

orientation positioning of building with regard to sun, wind, or view

outlet electrical unit providing source of AC

overhang horizontal distance between fascia and exterior wall

perspective drawing of building to give same appearance as in three-dimensional space

plat drawing showing layout of housing development or mall

platform frame building in which each story is built on the story below but framed independently

plot piece of land with specific dimensions for construction

post-and-beam construction wall construction in which beams rather than studs support heavy posts

prefabricated (*adj*) assembled into complete, standardized, structural units at factory

radiant heating heating by direct heat rays, without blowers

retaining wall wall built to resist lateral pressure, esp. to hold back soil; breast wall

rise vertical height of roof from ground

sandwich wall masonry wall with two panels separated by insulation

scale use of proportional measurements in drawings

schedule list of parts for construction

section vertical cross-section diagram of building

service entrance access point for electric lines leading from power company pole to building

setback zoning regulation that limits how near to a street a building can be

shear force that produces opposite but parallel sliding motion on contacting planes in a structural member

slab flat concrete block laid as foundation or reinforced concrete floor

soil pipe part of drainage system that receives waste flow from all fixtures, esp. toilet, leading to house drain

solar heat heat generated by collected rays of sun

sound transmission class means of specifying ability of material to resist sound transmission

specifications record of design and construction details not shown on drawings

stress force acting upon a structural member

subfloor floor material nailed directly to floor joists and covered by finished wood or carpet

sump pit in basement that collects water

tensile strength ability of structural member to withstand forces tending to lengthen it

thermostat self-regulating device controlling heat and air conditioning

tilt-up (*adj*) designating concrete walls cast in horizontal frames, then lifted into vertical position

veneer facing one material with another finishing surface

waste pipe horizontal pipe that carries waste from fixtures to soil pipe

water table level of underground water beneath structure

weather stripping metal or fabric strips placed at edges of doors and windows to reduce heat loss

weep hole small opening at bottom of wall that permits moisture to drain out

working drawings drawings with design details, from which construction is done

zoning (*adj*) of or pertaining to ordinances regulating type, size, and uses of buildings which may be constructed in specific area

Graphic Design

acetate flexible plastic film used to protect artwork

air white space

airbrush handheld tool for spraying paint and touching up artwork

artwork any graphic image prepared for reproduction

asymmetry dynamic compositional principle that states that design not be identical on both sides of central line

binding adhesive or other means of keeping pages and cover of published work together

bleed extension of image up to or beyond edge of page

burnishing transfer of color overlay or dry transfer letters by rubbing with hard, smooth edge

calendered paper paper glazed and pressed to glossy finish

calligraphy beautiful, stylized, highly decorative handwriting, often with many flourishes

camera lucida prismatic device used to project image for tracing; lucie

camera-ready (*adj*) designating project that is ready to be photographed for reproduction

caricature exaggerated drawing, esp. of human subject, portraying humorous or grotesque qualities

cartoon preliminary drawing; humorous sketch or drawing, as in comic strip

center spread copy and illustration that spread across facing pages at the center of a publication

chart any organizational or quantitative diagram containing information and revealing relationships in visual arrangement of elements

china marker colored wax pencil for marking glazed or coated surfaces

Chinese ink India ink

close crop (*vb*) silhouette

collage compositional technique using various materials not normally associated with one another

Color Key *Trademark.* color acetate proofs of line negatives

color overlay transparent sheet of color film transferred by burnishing

color separation composite negative used to reproduce separate plates or layers for primary colors and black

column vertical unit of grid for type and images, separated by gutters

comp comprehensive; detailed mock-up of a layout for presentation purposes

compass instrument for drawing arcs and circles

comprehensive comp

copy textual matter; artwork to be photographed for reproduction

crop (*vb*) trim edges of illustration or photograph

crop marks indicators used to establish parameters of area to be reproduced

Day-Glo *Trademark.* fluorescent paint or ink

desktop publishing creation and printing of graphic presentations and designs using a computer

diagram graphic visualization of abstract data designed to reveal relationships

die steel rule with edge for cutting out paper or cardboard shapes very precisely; metal stamp for impressing or embossing a design

drafting mechanical drawing

drawing board work surface that can be secured by user at angles from horizontal to vertical

drop cap bold or stylized initial letter of chapter or paragraph set into body of text

dry-transfer letters sheet imprinted with letters of alphabet in various styles for transfer to surface by rubbing

dummy prototype layout of assembled graphic work

duotone reproduction of image in two colors, one for darker shade with greater detail, one for lighter flat tint

electrostatic printing process such as xerography in which images are produced by attraction between electrostatic charge and particles of toner

emboss (*vb*) raise printed design in relief by pressure of plate on which image is engraved below surface

eraser mildly abrasive material or tool used to remove marks on paper

felt-tip pen pen with absorbent cloth nib, filled with ink that dries instantly

figure-ground principle of perception in which parts of a visual field tend to appear as solid and well-defined against a less-distinct background

final art camera-ready version of project

fixative aerosol varnish

flop (*vb*) reverse an image by turning original back to front

flow chart plan that forecasts appearance and process of design job

folio page number

foundry establishment in which typefaces originate through casting or technical encryption prior to distribution

four-color process reproduction of a wide range of colors by printing superimposed sequence of cyan, magenta, yellow, and black in varying intensities

French curve drafting instrument for tracing curved lines

gestalt entire configuration of visual elements, having properties not ascribable to its component parts

glitter shiny, decorative flakes of light-reflecting material

graph any diagram representing interrelations among two or more things

graphic (*adj*) represented visually, esp. by drawing or printing; (*n*) visual representation or design

graphic design art, discipline, and profession of visual communication that combines images, words, and ideas to purposefully convey information to an audience, esp. to produce specific effect or achieve desired goal

graphite soft, black, shiny form of carbon used for marking, esp. as pencil lead

grid horizontal and vertical divisions of page surface, used as organizational system for type and illustrations

gutter empty space between and around columns of type and images on page

hairline thinnest of printing rules

halftone simulation of solid or continuous tone image by breaking it into pattern of dots of varying sizes

halftone screen field of tiny dots used to produce halftone print

hand composition setting of a galley of lead type by hand

ichnography drawing with compass and rule

illumination detailed hand-decoration of manuscript books

illustration graphic image, esp. used for explanation or clarification of a text

India ink permanent dye composed of lampblack and glue or size; Chinese ink

ink viscous fluid or powdered substance used for writing, printing, and graphic reproductions

justification spacing of letters and words within text lines so that all full lines in type column have even margins on both right and left sides

kerning fine adjustment of spacing between letter forms to attain uniform appearance

laid finish paper with watermarks in close parallel stripes or which shows wire marks of mold used in its manufacture

layout design of text and images for reproduction

lead thin strip of graphite used as marking part of pencil

lead holder mechanical pencil

letterspacing insertion of additional space between letters of words for balance or emphasis

light box display unit for viewing color transparency, consisting of frosted glass with diffuse light from incandescent bulb beneath it

line art high-contrast rendering for reproduction without screening, consisting of lines or areas of solid black and solid white

line copy graphic design consisting of two tones without intermediate gradations

logo distinctive design, emblem, and trademark of product or organization; logotype

logotype logo, esp. one made of letter forms

loupe small, freestanding magnifying lens used to inspect transparent and reflective surfaces

lucie camera lucida

markup instructions for typesetting or color treatment

mat stiff cardboard frame for photo or artwork

mat knife blade on handle for cutting paper or art boards

mechanical artwork and type pasted into position on boards, ready for photo-transfer to printing plate or silkscreen; paste-up

mechanical drawing precise drawing done with aid of rulers, scales, and compasses; drafting

mechanical pencil tube holding thin pencil lead; lead holder

moiré interference pattern of dots arising from overlaying regular patterns while printing four-color process

montage image made of composite graphic elements that are overlaid and superimposed

negative film on which values of a recorded image are the reverse of the original, used for duplication

negative space air; white space

pantograph device for enlarging or reducing drawing size

Pantone Matching System Trademark. PMS; color organization and numbering specification system that dictates quantity and type of inks needed to make specific colors

paper thin, felted sheet of wood, vegetable, or synthetic fiber in varying weights and qualities

parallel rule hinged straightedges for drawing parallel lines at varying widths

paste-up mechanical

pen drawing implement composed of ink-bearing tube and point or nib: ballpoint, dip, felt-tip, fountain, metal nib, quill, reed, reservoir

pencil drawing tool with marking substance made of graphite, lead, or colored wax encased in paper or wooden tube

Perspec Trademark. colored, acrylic sheets

photo collage technique in which photographs and portions of photographs are pieced together and overlayed to form single piece

Photostat Trademark. process using special graphic camera to produce paper positives

photostat copy made using Photostat process and camera

picture visual representation or image of something

pixel picture element; single dot, or smallest element in visual display; square picture unit that is basis of computer graphics

planography art or technique of printing from flat surface directly or by offset

PMS Pantone Matching System

portfolio flat case use to carry samples of work for presentation, usu. made of leather

positive film or paper print made from photographic negative

printing reproduction of image using inked surface to make copies: intaglio, lithography, offset, planography, relief

proof printing impression made for examination, correction, or approval

protractor instrument for measuring and drawing exact angles

pull (vb) take impression or proof from block, plate, or type

Rapidograph Trademark. technical pen used for precise renderings of line art, esp. rules and stipples

relief printing or design in which image stands out from surface

repro image or type proof ready for paste-up

reproduction exact copy of visual image

retouch (vb) change details of negative or photographic print with pencil, brush, airbrush, or computer

rivers combination of spaces in consecutive lines of type that creates vertical streaks of white space

rough preliminary sketch of concept, layout, or job

rubber cement bonding agent that permits removal of mounted work and rubbing away of excess cement

rubilith usu. red acetate transparency that photographs black and occupies place in mechanicals that will ultimately be filled by art to be reproduced

rules metal strips of various widths, used to draw straight lines; the lines themselves

saddle stitch binding method in which pages are stitched through their middle folds

scale proportion that the representation of something bears to the object itself

Scotchlite Trademark. chemical coating that gives signs their highly reflective properties

screen creation of tonal value in artwork by regular pattern, usu. measured as dots per square inch

seal embossed design or symbol, often impressed on wax by stamp or medallion engraved with such design

set square flat, triangular tool used to ensure correct alignment of paste-up

signage environmental graphics created to assist identification and way-finding

silhouette (vb) outline an image so that it is separated from its background; close crop

sketch rough, preparatory drawing, usu. done quickly

specifications specs

specs Informal. complete description of job, esp. for printing; specifications

stamp die or block for impressing or imprinting

stat Informal. paper positive produced by Photostat process

stationery writing paper and materials in general; family of letterhead, envelopes, notepaper, and business cards

stencil waxed cardboard or thin metal or plastic with letters or designs cut out, so that ink may be applied to surface through cut-out area

stipple gradation of light and shade produced by separate touches of small points, larger dots, and longer strokes

stock specified quality or kind of paper for printing

straightedge blade guide for drawing or cutting very straight lines

surprint overprinting of one image on top of another

swatch sample of paper or ink color

symmetry classical principle that states that design be identical on both sides of center line

template drawing guide for shapes, symbols, or lettering

tracing paper thin, semitransparent paper laid over earlier artwork to compare or relate parts of design

transparency image recorded on color film, viewed by projection of light shining through it, as on light box

T square drawing guide for parallel and perpendicular lines

vellum translucent paper used for tracing; thin, treated calfskin used for writing or printing

Velox Trademark. brand of photographic print, prepared from line negative, that has been screened for reproduction

washed-out (adj) having poor color reproduction; faded

wax (vb) apply heated beeswax as adhesive to repro for paste-up

weight degree of boldness of typeface

white space empty space or white area that gives contrast to layout; air; negative space

X-acto knife Trademark. thin blade or razor in knife handle, used for cutting stencils and mats

xerography electrostatic printing technique in which areas on paper are sensitized with static electrical charge so that they attract oppositely charged dry-ink particles from toner, which are then fused onto the copy paper

Xerox Trademark. brand name for copying machine using xerography; commonly used synonym for all photocopying by xerography

Graphic Arts

abbozzo sketch, first draft

aquatint engraved printing process in which tones resemble watercolor

block print design printed by means of one or more wood or metal blocks

bow pen drafting pencil

brayer small rubber roller for inking printing blocks or plates by hand, usu. for making proofs

burin pointed engraving tool

cartouche oval or rounded decorative border around frame

cerography process of engraving design or text by incision into wax surface

chalcography art of copper engraving

chalk calcium carbonate powder formed into drawing stick

chamois soft leather cloth used to blend charcoal lines

crayon powdered pigment in waxy binder molded into drawing stick

decal design or picture printed on special paper for transfer to another surface

decalcomania art or process of transferring images from paper to other surfaces

Ditto machine *Trademark.* machine that copies text and drawings by ink-transfer process

drypoint engraving technique using a sharply scratched, inked copperplate

enchase (*vb*) decorate with inlay, embossing, or engraving

engrave (*vb*) produce image or design on printing plate by scratching it with a sharp tool

engraving graphic reproduction technique in which lines are cut into a metal or wooden surface, which is then inked and printed; design so produced

etch (*vb*) form image or design on a metal plate or glass by corrosive action of acid

etching process of making graphic design on a metal plate or glass by corrosive action of acid instead of with a pointed tool as in engraving; design so produced; impression made from such an etched plate

etching tools points, scrapers, and burnishers

fitch lettering brush, made of bristle, with straight chiseled edges

frottage technique of obtaining textural effects or images by rubbing pigment on paper stretched over an irregular surface

glyptography art and process of engraving on gems

gold point drawing on slightly abrasive surface with gold point or wire

graphic arts arts and techniques by which copies of an original are printed, as from blocks or plates; printmaking

gravure intaglio process of photomechanical printing

hachure series of parallel lines for shading or modeling; hatching

hatching hachure

hyalography technique of etching or engraving on glass

incision cutting into, as linoleum or wood block

inlay design or decoration made by inserting or applying fine materials in surface of object

intaglio engraving process in which ink-retaining lines are cut into metal surface

linocut linoleum cut

linoleum block piece of thick, soft, cork linoleum mounted on block of wood, incised or carved in relief with design, and used to make prints

linoleum cut image carved into surface of linoleum, often mounted on wood block, then inked and printed; linecut

lithography printing and reproduction process using stone slab marked with greasy ink; similar process using another substance, such as aluminum or zinc

mezzotint engraving process using coarse, random-dot screen burred by chisel on a metal plate, which is then inked and printed

monotype single print made from engraving process

overlay decoration or layer of some material applied onto another surface

pastel chalk or crayon stick of ground pigment and nonoily binder

photogravure process by which intaglio engraving is formed on metal plate, from which ink reproductions are made

pounce cleaning powder for drafting paper; copying technique using fine powder and perforated paper

print picture or design printed from engraved or otherwise prepared block or plate

printmaking art and technique of making prints, esp. by engraving, etching, drypoint, woodcut, or serigraphy

rag paper high-quality paper made from cotton and linen mixed with wood pulp

repoussé relief design on paper

reproduction copy or duplication made from an original work

resist protective layer applied to parts of printing plate

restrike new print made from old engraving, woodcut, or lithographic stone

sanguine reddish chalk or pastel for drawing

serigraph silkscreen print

serigraphy printing technique using silkscreen process

silkscreen printing technique that uses inked silk cloth, mounted on frame, to which stencil film is affixed; serigraphy

silverpoint drawing made with sharp, pointed silver tool on coated paper

spline flexible guide for drawing long curves

steel engraving graphic reproduction made by incising design on steel plates, then imprinting on paper

stump rolled chamois for blending chalk or pencil on paper

sumi *Japanese.* black ink used by calligraphers

tooth abrasive quality of paper that helps it to hold pigment, charcoal, or chalk

tortillon small stump made of paper, used in drawing

tusche greasy liquid used as medium receptive to lithographic ink

wash drawing broad areas of color used in conjunction with line forms, as in watercolor painting

woodblock image carved into surface of wood, then inked and printed

woodcut technique of printmaking from woodblock; print or impression formed this way

zincography process of producing printing surface using zinc plate etched by acid

Printing and Typefaces

ascender part of lowercase letter that rises above x-height, as in b, d, f, or h

beard sloping part of type that connects face with shoulder of body

bed surface on which printing form holding type is locked on flat-bed press

bleed (*vb*) print so that material runs off edge of page after trimming

blueline (*vb*) check for and mark typos on first run of laid-out page with blue pencil; (*n*) proof of final negatives made on light-sensitive paper, used for checking specifications before making plates

boldface thick, heavy typeface, used for emphasis

bond paper superior quality paper, usu. with high cotton fiber content

capitals uppercase letters

card out (*vb*) add extra space between lines of text to fill out column or page exactly

chase rectangular metal frame in which composed type is secured for printing

chromolithography printing in color by lithography using a series of plates or stones

cold type type set by any method other than casting of molten lead, esp. handset composition

composing stick small, handheld, adjustable tray in which compositor places type before fitting it in galley

composition typesetting

computer typesetting high-speed phototypesetting, eliminating need for mechanical setting of type

condensed (*adj*) designating type that is narrow and elongate in proportion to its height

copy any issue of a given publication printed from the same plate or plates

cursive style of typeface simulating handwriting

cylinder press flat-bed press

descender part of lowercase letter that goes below main body of letter, as in g, j, p, or y

dingbat typographic symbol or ornament such as fist, arrow, or heart

dummy prototype layout that shows length and placement of items indicated for sizing

elite letter size measuring twelve characters per inch, widely used in typewriters

em unit of measure of column width in terms of type size

en unit of measure equal to one half the width of an em

engraving graphic reproduction technique in which lines are cut into a hard surface such as metal or stone, which is then inked and printed

expanded (*adj*) designating type that is wider in proportion to its height, having a flattened, oblong appearance

f and g's folded and gathered, unbound printed sheets in proper sequence for binding

flat-bed press printing device in which horizontal printing surface, or bed, moves against rotating cylinder that carries paper; cylinder press

flexography relief printing technique using soft plastic or rubber plates and fast-drying ink

font full assortment of letters and symbols in one size and family of type

form type assembled and secured in chase for printing; any made-up sequence of pages ready for printing

four-color process reproduction of range of colors by printing a superimposed sequence of cyan, magenta, black, and yellow in varying intensities

frame device that holds type, esp. galley

furniture pieces of wood or metal, less than type high, used to fill spaces on bed not occupied by type

galley sheets of final type proofs; with hot type, shallow tray holding typeset pages

gatefold spread that opens from center to reveal additional pages

grain direction of long fibers in sheet of paper

graphics photographs or illustrations to be printed

gravure process of intaglio printing, in which plate is inked only beneath its surface

hot metal type cast from molten lead; hot type

hot type hot metal

imposition arrangement of page plates in proper order on press to ensure correct sequence when folding and gathering at bindery

impression all copies of publication printed in one operation

indent (*vb*) set type in or back from margin

italics scriptlike style of letters or type

justify (*vb*) line up margins evenly in type column

kern portion of typeface projecting beyond body or shank; (*vb*) adjust space between specified letter pairs for printing

laser printing high-speed computer printing technique using laser to form dot-matrix patterns and electrostatic process to fuse metallic particles to paper

leading insertion of thin strips of type metal for spacing between lines of text; space so created

letterpress method of printing from raised type

ligature character or type combining two or more letters, such as æ

line-casting casting of entire line of type in a slug

Linotype *Trademark.* typesetting machine that sets each line of type in single slug

lowercase small letters in font of type

mackle blur in printing, as from double impression

majuscule uppercase letter

matrix mold for casting typefaces

mimeo *Informal.* mimeograph

mimeograph printing machine using waxed stencil wrapped around rotating, ink-fed drum, past which sheets of paper are fed; mimeo

minuscule lowercase letter

mold framed page of cast type from which plate is made

Monotype *Trademark.* brand of machine for setting and casting type, based on paper tape containing holes in coded pattern

Multigraph *Trademark.* rotary typesetting and printing machine, used esp. for duplicating written matter

newsprint cheaply produced, disposable wood pulp paper, used chiefly for printing newspapers

offset lithography printing process in which stone or metal or paper plate makes inked impression on a rubber blanket, that in turn transfers it to the paper being printed, instead of taking direct impression of plate on paper; photo-offset

offset printing printing method in which image is photographically engraved on metal sheet and then offset onto paper

orphan poor line break that dangles first line of new paragraph at end of column or bottom of page

overrun copies in excess of specified pressrun; overs

overs *Informal.* overrun

pallet typeholder

photocomposition method of composition in which type is set photographically

photoengraving reproduction technique using light-sensitive, emulsion-coated metal plates

photo-offset offset lithography

phototypography any of various techniques for making printing surfaces by light or photography

pi typefaces mixed together at random

pica letter size measuring ten characters per inch; unit of measure equal to twelve points or 1/6 of an inch

plate cast to be printed from, made from mold of set type or photo-offset negative

point standard unit of type measurement, approximately equal to 1/72 of an inch

press printing press

pressroom room in publishing establishment in which printing presses are located

pressrun operation of printing press for specific job; number of copies so printed

print (*vb*) produce impressions of inked type or plates on paper; publish large numbers of book or periodical in printed form

printer person who runs printing operations

printer's devil young worker below level of apprentice in print shop

printer's mark individual printer's identifying mark, usu. on copyright page

printing technique, process, and business of reproducing written or graphic material, esp. by impression from movable types or plates

printing press any of various machines for printing in mass form from inked type, plates, or rollers; press

print shop facility in which type is set, plates or rollers are made, and printing is done

proof sheet inked page made from galley or plate, used to check for errors before printing

quoin wedge of wood or metal for securing type in chase

reglet thin wood strip less than type-high, used to produce blank space around page of type

reprography duplication of documents or designs by any process using light rays and photography, such as offset printing or xerography

roller cylinder in rotary press to which plate is attached for printing

roman (*adj*) designating common, upright style of typeface

rotary press printing press with plates mounted on cylinders that pass over paper fed from continuous roll

rotogravure intaglio printing process using rotary presses

run quantity printed in pressrun

sans serif style of letters or type without serifs, or typefaces without serifs, such as Helvetica and Franklin Gothic

score (*vb*) make furrows in paper to facilitate folding

serif fine cross-stroke that terminates main stroke at top and bottom of letters; style of typefaces having serifs, such as Bodoni, Garamond, and Times Roman

shank body or stem of piece of type

signature letter or symbol placed at foot of first page of every sheet to guide binder in folding and gathering; printed sheet folded to page size for binding

slug line of type cast in single piece by Linotype machine

small capitals capital letters that are smaller than standard size for that font, designed to align visually with ordinary type line

swash extending ornamental flourish on letters of certain fonts of italic or cursive type

thermography technique for imitating embossed appearance by dusting printed areas with powder that adheres to wet ink, then fusing ink and powder to paper by heat

toner cartridge containing dry ink particles, used in xerography and laser printing

type piece of metal with raised letter or symbol in reverse on one end and used collectively, inked, and pressed against paper to leave impressions

typeface any of various distinctive styles of letters to be reproduced by printing or photography; alphabet designed with specific attributes that unify the character set

typefaces common text and display faces include:

Baskerville, Bembo, Bodoni
Caledonia, Caslon, Century, Cheltenham, Clarendon
Electra, English
Fraktur, Franklin Gothic, Futura
Garamond, Goudy
Helvetica

Janson
Melior
Old English, Optima
Palatino, Plantin
Renaissance
Times Roman
Univers

type family grouping of printing types with common design but different weights and styles, such as roman, italic, bold, condensed, or expanded

typeholder small device that holds a few lines of type, used esp. to stamp titles on covers; pallet

typesetting arrangement of type for printing, usu. by computer or machine; composition

typography art and process of setting and arranging type for printing; creation of typefaces

underlay sheets of paper placed under type to bring it to required height for printing

uppercase letters in font of type that differ from corresponding lowercase letters in form and height; capitals

watermark paper mark indicating maker or trademark of stock

web press printing press using continuous roll of paper

widow poor line break in which a single word or short line ends a paragraph; last line of paragraph when it is carried over to next column or page

x-height height of letters having no ascender or descender, typified by lowercase *x* in given typeface

---

PHOTOGRAPHY
Types of Photography
Cameras
Lenses
Tools and Techniques

See also: *Chap. 11: Publishing and the Press; Chap. 15: Cinema; Television and Radio; Chap. 16: Graphic Design and Printing*

Types of Photography

aerial photography pictures taken from airplane or satellite

animation graphic images sequenced for motion effect

architectural photography pictures displaying building design

black and white pictures using monochrome black-and-white film, without color; b/w

b/w black and white

calotype paper-negative photography, now obsolete

cinematography motion-picture photography

collodion wet-plate photography, now obsolete

color prints, slides, and film utilizing the full color spectrum

composite several shots of model or actor in different poses, printed together with head shot on reverse side

daguerreotype silver-plate photography, now obsolete

electron micrography image seen and photographed through electron microscope

fashion photography pictures of clothing and accessories on models for advertising

ferrotype iron-plate photography, now obsolete; tintype

fine-art photography work emphasizing aesthetic composition and emotional substance rather than some specific purpose

holography three-dimensional photography, using split laser beam

infrared photography exposures using infrared light, often at night

laser photography holography and other photography using lightwave amplification by stimulated emission of radiation

macrophotograph extreme closeup

microphotograph extremely small-scale photograph requiring optical enlargement

photocopy photographic reproduction of graphic material or document

photogram silhouette produced by direct exposure of paper, without lens or negative

photography reproduction of images of objects on sensitized film by exposure to light and chemical processing

photojournalism form of journalism in which pictures associated with news events, specific editorial content, or documentary features dominate the written material

portraiture photographs of posed individuals, done in selected environment or studio

print photography fashion and commercial photography for publications

product photography stylized, precise photographs of an object for advertising

radiography x-ray photography

reportage photojournalism, esp. photo essays based on research or detailed coverage of documented observation

scenic photography pictures of landscapes or seascapes

stereophotography simulation of binocular vision that produces two images

still life pictures of inanimate objects for product, tabletop, or fine-art photography

still photography still shots taken on the set of a movie or television show, or a single frame of film used like a still shot; unit photography

stroboscopic photography photography of moving subjects, using pulsing light source to apparently freeze movements

tabletop photography still life, product, or food photographed on tabletop

tintype ferrotype

travel photography photographs displaying beautiful locales around world

underwater photography photographs of underwater environment and fish, taken with special enclosed camera

unit photography still photography

xerography photocopying directly onto paper

Cameras

aerial-reconnaissance camera long-range camera designed for military and defense use

animation camera camera designed to expose one frame at a time, used for animated sequences

autofocus camera camera that automatically sets aperture and shutter speed for operator, sometimes also equipped with automatic flash

box camera simple, low-cost camera

camera lucida instrument using prism and mirrors to project image of object on plane surface for tracing

camera obscura primitive camera in which light aperture projects image on surface

8x10 camera format using eight-inch by ten-inch sheet film to produce same-size negatives

5x7 camera format using five-inch by seven-inch sheet film to produce same-size negatives

flash camera using high-powered burst of illumination

folding camera camera in which bellows collapses into fold when camera is not in use

4x5 camera format using four-inch by five-inch sheet film to produce same-size negatives

minicam portable, handheld video camera

panoramic camera camera equipped with motor that swivels it to take panoramic view in one exposure on 35 mm negative

pinhole camera rudimentary camera having tiny aperture and no lens

Polaroid *Trademark.* camera that develops film immediately within itself

portrait camera camera fitted with portrait lens

single-lens reflex camera camera in which image appears on ground-glass viewer after being reflected by mirror or passing through prism or semitransparent glass

6x9 camera format using 120 mm film to produce 6 mm by 9 mm negatives

6x7 camera format using 120 mm film to produce 6 mm by 7 mm negatives

6x6 camera format using 120 mm film to produce 6 mm by 6 mm negatives

stop-action camera that stops at intervals to allow for manipulation of photographed subject

35 mm camera any camera that uses standard 35 mm film

twin-lens reflex camera camera with two lenses in single focusing mount, using 2 1/4-inch format

underwater camera camera mounted in waterproof container or self-contained, using O-rings for waterproofing

video camera camera for electronically processed videotape that requires no developing

viewfinder camera viewing lens system that separates image from shutter lens system

Lenses

achromatic lens finely made, expensive lens with no chromatic aberration

anamorphic lens lens for wide screen effects

anastigmatic lens lens with vertical, horizontal lines focused in same plane

aplanatic lens lens free from spherical aberration

apochromatic lens lens in which all colors are focused at a common point

convertible lens lens for different focal lengths

fisheye lens short focal-length, wide-angle lens of over 180 degrees, used to create distorted image

fixed-focus lens usu. wide-angle lens with nonvariable focus

long-focus lens lens with narrow angle of view for greater magnification

normal lens lens with angle of view approximately equal to human vision, or 50 to 55 degrees

portrait lens moderately soft-definition, medium-long focal- length lens

process lens lens with precise color-separation capacity for reproduction and engraving work

standard lens normal lens usu. provided with camera at time of purchase, such as 50 mm lens with 35 mm camera

telephoto lens lens that reduces depth of field for distant objects: with 35 mm camera, telephotos are 80 mm, 105 mm, 135 mm, 180 mm, 200 mm, and 300 mm

wide-angle lens lens with wide field of view

zoom lens lens with focal length continuously variable to close in on small or distant objects or open up for wide view

Tools and Techniques

actinic light part of light spectrum that exposes photographic film and paper

albumen paper printing paper coated with egg white, salt, and critic acid, and sensitized with silver nitrate

ambrotype positive picture made from photo negative on glass backed by dark surface

angle of view degree of camera lens' width of vision

aperture opening that controls amount of light admitted into camera through lens

aperture-priority (*adj*) designating semiautomatic exposure system in which aperture is preset and camera selects shutter speed

ASA **A**merican **S**tandards **A**ssociation; organization that rates light sensitivity for film exposure

barn door *Slang.* adjustable blinder attached around light to prevent spillage

bellows accordion-pleated cloth that insulates camera body and lens from light

black back film holder

blimp soundproof plastic covering over camera being used to take stills on movie set

blow-up photo enlargement

book photographer's portfolio containing clippings and samples of work

boom projecting arm used to support lights over a subject while remaining out of the camera's view

bulb camera setting that keeps shutter open while release is pressed

burn in (*vb*) allow more light on certain photo areas while printing

buy out selling of all photos and future rights of photo shoot to one buyer

cable release wire that activates the shutter from a distance

camera lightproof box that records the image of an object viewed through the aperture of a lens onto light-sensitive film

candid snapshot taken without staging, lighting, or special effects, often of unsuspecting subject

century stand light stand with wide base composed of legs that fold together

cibachrome positive-to-positive color printing method

circle of confusion area outside focal point that is not in focus

click stop turnable control on diaphragm that engages with distinct click at setting positions

closeup photograph taken at very close range

collotype process for making prints directly from hardened colloid film with ink-repellent and ink-receptive parts

color separation separate negative containing portion of picture to be printed in one color

color transparency color positive on transparent film or glass, viewed by projected light

contact sheet print consisting of all frames of a developed roll of film on one sheet of paper, with prints the same size as actual negatives; proof sheet

contrast variance of light and dark tones in photo

coppertoning (*adj*) designating chemical additives that give warm brownish tinge to black-and-white photo

cove curved inset used to create illusion of infinite depth

crop (*vb*) remove outer portion of print

C-type color print made from negative by color-producing organic substance, or chromogen

cyan greenish blue color used in color printing

darkroom lightproof processing laboratory for film and prints

definition clarity of detail, image sharpness

depth of field zone between focal point and unfocused area in which image is reasonably sharp

develop (*vb*) chemically process latent image on exposed film or print paper

developer chemical solution producing images on exposed film or paper

diaphragm variable opening that allows light onto film in camera

dip and dunk method used in most color and some black-and-white film processing in which film is draped or dipped into chemical and rinsing baths

dodge (*vb*) shade area of photo from light to reduce density of dark areas during printing

emulsion light-sensitive chemical coating on film and paper

enlargement print made larger than original negative

enlarger magnifying device used in printing

exposure opening of shutter to allow light onto film, producing latent image; allowing light onto paper, producing print

exposure meter light meter

film light-sensitive chemical coating on flexible, plastic ribbon: black and white, color, microfilm, negative, nonchromatic, panchromatic, sheet, sound

film holder black receptacle for sheet film used in 4x5 or 8x10 camera; black back

filter glass or plastic gel or disc that screens certain light frequencies or colors from film exposure, also used in printing to alter contrast

finder camera indicator of focus or light

fixative chemical solution that makes negative or print exposure permanent by removing light-sensitive silver halides; fixer

fixer fixative

flag unit composed of metal frame with stretched black cloth, used to direct light

flash any device providing high-powered bursts of illumination

flashbulb single electric lamp that flashes when metal filament burns

flashcube four flashbulbs attached to camera

flashgun device that holds and repeatedly ignites flashbulb for taking continuous pictures without changing bulbs

focal length distance between lens and corresponding plane, where its subject is focused

focus point at which image is seen distinctly

format negative size, such as 35 mm

f-stop ratio of aperture opening to lens focal length

glossy shiny photographic print

glycerin sandwich badly scratched negative between glycerin-coated glass plates that obscure scratches for printing

grain size of silver particles in photographic film or paper, determines fineness of image

grease pencil marker for contact sheets, prints, and negatives

grid spot honeycomb grid placed over light to focus it in one direction

ground glass textured, flat pane of glass in camera, used to focus image

halation glow on photo resulting from overexposure

head shot close-up of face, esp. for actors or models; mug shot

hypo chemical solution used as fixative for film and prints

hypo clearing agent solution used to remove excess fixative from film or paper

iris diaphragm shutter shutter having group of overlapping blades that open and close at center when exposing film

leader black or transparent strip at end of film roll

lens curved-glass device that directs light rays from object onto camera plate to create image

lens cap protective cover for lens

lens shade hood to keep direct light off lens

light box container for color-corrected lights with one translucent side, used to view negatives or slides

light meter device that indicates light intensity; exposure meter

light stand usu. three-legged, adjustable support for strobe or tungsten light

loupe small magnifying lens worn directly on eye to inspect photos

magazine unit loaded with film that can be removed from camera and replaced by another unit in order to change film in use in middle of roll

matte photographic print lacking gloss and luster

microfilm film containing miniaturized copy of graphic material, esp. newspapers for archives

monopod light, compact, one-legged camera stand that must be held, designed for use when shooting in confined space

mug shot Slang. identification photo, esp. for police use

negative exposed film image with light and shade tones opposite original image

Newton's rings colored rings on photo caused by sun's glare

nonchromatic (adj) designating film that is not sensitive to colors

orthochromatic (adj) designating film that is sensitive to all colors except red

overexposure film or photographic paper exposed to too much light or radiation

panchromatic (adj) designating film that is sensitive to all colors

panning shot technique of moving camera at same speed as subject to blur background while subject remains in focus

paparazzo freelance photographer who pursues celebrities for candid photos

paper light-sensitive paper used for making photographic prints

parallax slight difference in fields of view between lens and viewfinder

passport photo small head shot in standard size for use on passport

photograph image produced on sensitized surface by action of radiant energy, esp. light; shot

plate glass or plastic sheet coated with light-sensitive emulsion to be exposed, developed, and printed as photograph

platinum process contact printing process that gives photo a very beautiful, silver hue with long tonal ranges, used for long-lasting archival pictures for museums

positive film that records light and shade tones similar to original image

power pack portable DC power supply, esp. for flash

print exposed, developed image on photographic paper; (vb) project image onto light-sensitive paper or contact sheet

projection display of slides or transparencies on screen by shining light through them

proof sheet contact sheet

range distance from camera to subject

range finder focusing system that measures distance from camera to subject, sometimes coupled to camera lens so that both work together

reel revolvable cylinder around which film is wound for development

reflector any substance used as background to reflect light

resolution sharpness of photographic image; ability of camera to record distinct detail

reversal any positive to positive, rather than negative-to-positive, printing process

safelight darkroom light that has no effect on film and paper

seamless Informal. backdrop consisting of no-seam paper

semigloss (adj) designating most common surface of paper for color prints

sepia print or photograph made in a brownish hue that resembles sepia

sheet film film that comes in single sheets, each of which produces one negative, as for 4x5 or 8x10 camera format

shoot (vb) take a photograph; (n) photographic session

shot photograph

shutter mechanical system that controls the length of time that light acts on sensitive emulsion by opening and closing aperture

shutterbug Slang. photography enthusiast

shutter-priority (adj) designating semiautomatic exposure system in which shutter speed is selected and camera sets aperture, used esp. to convey motion

slave unit mechanism that simultaneously fires a flash source when a photoelectric cell is activated by illumination from the camera linked to the flash

slide developed, mounted color-film exposure

snapshot informal, nonstudio photograph

snoot cone-shaped shield on strobe or spotlight that directs light over smaller, controlled area

soft box process process in which flash or spot is thrown through box, instead of using umbrella as light diffuser

soft focus photograph with indistinct outlines of images

solarization full or partial reversal of image by extreme overexposure

speed length of time shutter remains open to record image; sensitivity of film, expressed numerically as ASA rating

spotlight intense light directed on specific area

still photographic print of motion picture scene

stock house photo agency that sells photographer's stock photos to periodicals but does not make assignments

stop bath chemical solution that halts development of film or print

strobe electronic flash, balanced like blue daylight at 5200° K

studio professional photographer's specially equipped room for shooting photographs

tank cylinder or box containing developing solution

tear sheet proof sheet of single or multiple images torn from printed matter

time exposure exposure of film for more than one-half second, usu. to take photograph without sufficient light

toner solution used to impart color or hue to silver photographic image, such as in cyanotype, gold tone, palladium, platinum, or selenium process

transparency film negative viewed by projection of light shining through it

tripod three-legged support used to hold camera steady

tungsten light orange, halogen-quartz light source at 3200° K, used esp. for motion pictures and portraits

umbrella color-corrected white, silver, or gold concave material used to bounce light onto subject

underexposure film exposed to insufficient light or radiation

viewfinder finder indicating focus

vignette photograph gradually lightened or darkened at its edges to leave no definite line at border

---

CRAFTS
Ceramics and Glassmaking
Other Crafts

See also: *Chap. 10: Fashion and Garment Parts;*
Chap. 14: Painting; Chap. 16: Graphic Design
and Printing; Chap. 17: Hobbies

Ceramics and Glassmaking

agateware pottery variegated to resemble agate

argil potter's clay

ash glaze semitransparent glaze containing wood ashes

aventurine opaque brown glass with fine golden particles

banding wheel hand-operated turntable for coiling or decorating pots

basaltware unglazed Wedgwood stoneware, usu. black with dull gloss

bat removable disk atop potter's wheel

batch raw materials mixed in proper proportions for making glass

bat wash flint wash used on kiln shelf to prevent sticking during glost firing

Belleek ware fragile, Irish porcelain with bright luster

biscuit once-fired clay object, before glazing; bisque

bisque biscuit

blister glaze fault caused by impurities

bloat ceramic fault caused by impurities in clay

blow (*vb*) shape glass with steady current of air

blow mold hinged mold for shaping molten glass

blowpipe long metal tube used to gather and blow molten glass

blunger tank with mechanical arms for blending clay and water

bone china fine, naturally white china made with bone ash

celadon greenish, iron-containing glaze used in Oriental porcelain and stoneware

ceramics manufacture of works of art by firing of earthenware, porcelain, or brick at high temperature; works so produced

china delicate porcelain ceramic ware

clay potter's clay

cone pyrometric cone

crackle cracking of glaze after firing; craze

crackleware ceramic ware with finely cracked glaze

crank kiln shelf

craze crackle

crockery earthenware

cullet glass scraps that can be remelted

dead clay overly wet clay

delft glazed earthenware, usu. blue and white

dod box device for forming pottery handles

Dresden china porcelain ware produced near Dresden, Germany, characterized by dainty design

dunt (*vb*) crack because of sudden cooling, said of ceramic ware

earthenware coarse wares of kiln-baked clay; crockery

elephant ear sponge fine-grained surfacing tool for working clay

enamelware metalware or pottery covered with a glassy, opaque enamel surface

engobe coating of white slip

faience glazed earthenware for blocks or tiles

fat clay plastic, easily workable clay

fettling knife sharp, pointed blade for finishing surfaces

fictile (*adj*) made of earth or clay by a potter

firing baking ceramic objects in hot oven

flux material used to lower melting point of glaze

frit flux and silica compound for strengthening porcelain

gaffer master glassblower who shapes glassware

glacure thin glaze for fine pottery

glass hard, transparent substance formed by melting silica and soda ash

glassblowing art and practice of shaping a mass of molten glass by blowing air into it through a tube

glassmaking art and technique of making glass, usu. by fusing silicates containing soda and lime

glaze glossy, vitreous, waterproof coating fused by heat to pottery; glost; (*vb*) apply such a surface to a ceramic

glost clay ware with glaze applied but not yet fired

graffito technique of scratching design through glaze

graniteware pottery with speckled, granitelike appearance

greenware unfired ceramics

grog fired and crushed clay, added to fresh clay to reduce plasticity and shrinkage or give texture

hard (*adj*) fired at high temperature

hollowware deep ceramic dishes

impasto enamel or slip forming low-relief decoration on ceramic object

ironstone hard, white ceramic ware

jasperware fine, hard Wedgwood stoneware, stained in various colors by metallic oxides, with raised designs in white

jigger machine for forming ceramic objects in a plaster mold rotating beneath a template

kaolin pure, fine-grained white clay

kiln oven for firing pottery

lead glass glass containing lead oxide

lean clay unpliable clay; short clay

limekiln kiln in which limestone and shells are burned

luster metallic, iridescent sheen of glaze

majolica enameled, richly colored Italian pottery

Ming (*adj*) designating fine porcelains in brilliant colors made during Ming dynasty (China, 15th-17th c.)

mishima decoration of pottery by carving raw clay and filling the cuts with different-colored clay

muffle protective box around kiln flames

nankeen Chinese porcelain having blue ornament on white background

overglaze additional glaze or color applied to an existing glaze

oxidation firing with oxygen-rich flame

paddling beating clay with stick to shape or decorate it

pallet flat board or metal plate used to support ceramic objects during drying

Parian (*adj*) denoting fine, unglazed, marblelike porcelain

porcelain hard, white, nonporous ceramic ware composed of kaolin, feldspar, and quartz

pot usu. round earthenware vessel of any size

potsherd broken pottery fragment

potter's clay finely textured, pliable earth that is free of impurities and suitable for making ceramic objects: argil, ball, china, fire clay, kaolin, petuntse, porcelain, refractory, terra cotta

potter's wheel revolving disk for throwing pottery forms, usu. foot-operated; wheel

pottery clay objects, either glazed or unglazed, shaped and hardened by heat: Albin ware, basalt, biscuit, blackware, bone china, china,

crackleware, delft, Dresden china, earthenware, eggshell porcelain, faience, Imari ware, ironstone, Leeds pottery, Limoges, lusterware, majolica, Meissen, porcelain, saltglaze, Satsuma ware, Sèvres ware, Spode, spongeware, stoneware, terra cotta, Wedgwood

pressed glass molded glass shaped while molten by thrusting plunger into mold

primary clay clay found at natural site

prunt small lump of glass fused to larger glass piece

pug mill machine used to mix clay

punty iron rod used in handling hot glass in glassmaking

pyrometer device used to measure kiln temperature

pyrometric cone ceramic cone calibrated to melt at exact temperature, giving visual indication of kiln temperature; cone; Seger cone

raku open-air, high-firing technique that produces rough, dark, lead-glazed earthenware (Japan)

raw (*adj*) unfired

reduction high-temperature firing

refractory (*adj*) having high heat resistance

relief decoration raised above surface of piece

resist decoration by treating selected areas so that they reject slip or glaze

sagger box of clay for packing ceramic ware in kiln

salt glaze process in which salt is vaporized in kiln to leave pebbly texture on piece

Seger cone pyrometric cone

semiporcelain vitreous ceramic ware similar to but less hard and translucent than true porcelain

short clay lean clay

sieve sifter for removing clay lumps

slip watery, liquid clay for decorating and cementing biscuit

slip glaze glaze containing plastic clay, applied to raw earthenware

slob lumpy waste clay

slurry watery clay

smalt blue coloring agent for vitreous materials

soft (*adj*) fired at low temperature

Spode *Trademark.* fine porcelain or china

spun glass blown glass in which fine threads form surface texture

stoneware high-fired clay pottery, often glazed with salt

terra cotta hard, brown-red, unglazed earthenware

terre verte glazing clay

throw (*vb*) form pottery on wheel

underglaze color or decoration applied to piece before glazing

vitreous (*adj*) resembling glass in transparency, brittleness, hardness, or glossiness

vitrification fusing of clay body to state of glasslike imperviousness

ware ceramic objects

wash thin coating of glaze

wedge (*vb*) pound clay to remove air bubbles and improve workability

Wedgwood *Trademark.* brand of ceramic ware orig. made in 18th century by Josiah Wedgwood, typically basaltware and jasperware in blue-gray color

wheel potter's wheel

willowware china using decorative design of willow tree, bridge, and two birds (Britain, 18th c.)

zaffer cobalt oxide mixture that produces blue color in glass and ceramic glazes

Other Crafts

amber craft making jewelry from brownish-yellow fossil resin

appliqué decoration, as a cutout design, sewn on to a piece of material

assemblage arrangement of a collection of objects in aesthetic relationships or curious juxtapositions

basketry crafting of functional or decorative containers by interweaving strips of grass, reed, or other flexible material

batik technique of hand dyeing patterns on fabric by using wax to resist dyes

beadworking decorative working or weaving of beads onto surface of clothing, accessories, or household objects; stringing of beads, as to produce a necklace

block printing printing with ink from engraved blocks of wood or other hard material

boneworking making of jewelry and other decorative objects from animal bones

bookbinding craft of encasing books, esp. in fine leather or buckram

bookcraft making of books with particular attention to paper, printing techniques, folding of pages, and binding

burlap crafting making of objects, such as lampshades or wall hangings, out of burlap, which is often painted or decorated with other materials

cabinetmaking process or craft of making fine furniture and other woodwork

calligraphy art of highly decorative handwriting, as with many flourishes

candlemaking forming of candles by dripping, pouring, rolling, or casting wax, paraffin, or tallow around a cotton wick

caning making of articles by interweaving slender, flexible stems of certain plants

carving making of articles by cutting, shaping, or chipping a hard substance, as a block of wood

casting process or craft of making forms in plaster or resin from a mold

ceramics craft of making fired earthenware, porcelain, or brick pottery; pottery

chenille work making of small figures from a wire core covered with soft chenille fabric

cloisonné enamelwork in which the enamel surface is set in hollows between wires soldered on metal

copper enameling process in which heat is used to fuse enamel powder colored with copper oxide to surface of articles; etui

coralworking making jewelry from the pinkish, hard skeletal deposit of certain marine polyps

cork pictures making decorative objects by burning holes in a cork surface with a hot wire or bradawl, then inserting other substances, such as moss or bark, into the holes

corrugated cardboard crafting cutting and shaping three-dimensional decorative objects out of corrugated cardboard

craft any art, trade, or occupation requiring the skilled working of materials to form decorative or useful objects, often practiced as a recreational activity; handicraft

crewelwork decorative embroidery done with crewel yarn on cotton or linen, employing simple stitches worked in floral patterns

crocheting knitting with a hooked needle that draws thread or yarn through intertwined loops

cut-paper collage decoupage

damascening craft of making gold inlays

decalcomania process of transferring designs from specially prepared paper to wood, metal, or glass

dóohiroge making of collages with torn paper, esp. Japanese paper

decoupage technique of decorating a surface with paper cutouts; cut-paper collage

discharge printing bleaching designs onto dyed fabric

doll making making of small figures shaped like humans, usu. as toys, esp. out of paper, fabric, rag, or wood

dyeing process of tinting fabric or other absorbent material with colorants derived from plant extracts or synthetic chemicals

egg decorating painting on the shells of eggs whose contents have been blown out through a tiny hole

embossing decorating surfaces with raised ornamentation

embroidery working of raised and ornamental designs with a needle on woven fabric using contrasting or brightly colored thread

enameling fusing of clear, glassy flux of silica and potash, colored with metal oxides, to surface of metal or pottery as ornamentation

engraving cutting or corroding of designs into hard surfaces, such as metal or wood, which are usually inked for making impressions

etching technique of making designs on a metal plate or glass by the corrosive action of acid

etui copper enameling

fabric making weaving

fabric painting process of painting designs on fabric

featherwork making of decorative objects out of feathers

felt crafting cutting of designs and decorative objects out of felt, which is sometimes painted on

fiber arts design and crafting of objects from natural fibers or fibrous materials

flower making art or technique of making artificial flowers out of cut, folded, and mounted crêpe, tissue paper, or other stiff fabric

fraktur stylized and highly decorative watercolor painting, often bearing elaborate calligraphy

frottage technique in which textural effects or images are obtained by rubbing lead, chalk, crayon, or charcoal over paper laid on a granular or relief surface; rubbing

gem cutting craft of cutting and engraving gemstones; lapidary

glassblowing shaping of molten glass by blowing air into it through a tube

glass etching etching of designs onto glass with acid

glass painting painting of images and designs on plate glass

handicraft craft

ikat method of printing woven fabrics by tie dyeing warp yarns, weft yarns, or both before weaving, used esp. in Malaysia and Africa

ikebana Japanese art of arranging flowers in highly aesthetic designs, based on one of four traditional styles: Moribana, Nageire, Rikka, or Seika

inlay design or decoration made by inserting or applying layers of fine materials, such as gold or silver, in surface of object

intaglio process by which a design is incised or engraved into surface of plate or other object

ivoryworking carving of decorative objects out of elephant tusks

jetworking craft of making beads, jewelry, buttons, or other items from polished, dense, black coal

jewelry making design and production of ornamental objects, such as rings, earrings, or necklaces, worn for adornment, using materials such as precious and semiprecious stones and metals, glass, bones, feathers, shells, beads, and wood

jewelsmithing making of jewelry, esp. with cut stones

kitemaking design and construction of kites that are both aesthetically pleasing and aerodynamically sound

knitting interlacing loops of yarn to form decorative or functional garments and accessories

lacemaking crafting of fine, openwork fabrics in ornamental designs

lacquerwork process of coating wood with resinous varnish obtained as sap from Japanese tree

lapidary gem cutting

leathercrafting methods or techniques of making clothing and accessories, esp. for decorative or functional use, from animal hides that have been stripped of hair or wool

lithography printing process using stone slab, or zinc or aluminum plate, marked with greasy ink

macramé technique of making elaborately patterned knotwork with hand-knotted twine or rope, used esp. for wall decorations and hangings

marbling process of coloring or staining in imitation of marble by swirling ink or oil colors on water, then lowering paper onto its surface to pick up the design

maskmaking craft of forming coverings for the face from papier-mâché, wood, plaster of Paris, or other materials

metalworking process of shaping articles out of metal

mizuhiki Japanese craft in which bundles of wire are covered tightly in gold or silver paper and interwoven into delicate, symmetrical shapes

mobile making arranging of delicately balanced metal, paper, or plastic shapes that are suspended in midair from wire so as to move freely in air currents

mosaic making of designs by inlaying small pieces of colored stone, tile, or glass in mortar

needlecrafts handicrafts involving sewing with cloth or threads: crocheting, knitting, embroidery, crewel, needlepoint, quilting, rug hooking, trapunto

needlepoint embroidery using woolen yarn, esp. on canvas, usu. with uniform spacing of stitches

needlework art and process of working with a needle, esp. in embroidery, needlepoint, tapestry, quilting, and appliqué

niello ornamental work produced by inlaying metal with a black metallic substance consisting of silver, copper, lead, and sulfur

origami Japanese decorative art of folding paper to form recognizable shapes, esp. animals

papercraft making of decorative objects by cutting and folding paper; making of fine paper products

paper flower making craft or technique of forming artificial flowers from paper

papermaking handmaking of fine paper from pulp and size that is mixed with rag, linen, leaves, or other materials

paper sculpture making of decorative objects by cutting and folding paper into shapes

papier-mâché forming decorative objects from substance made of pulped paper or of rags or paper soaked in glue, formed into shapes when moist and becoming hard when dried

patchwork sewing together of pieces of cloth of various colors and shapes

pebble-and-stone polishing burnishing the surfaces of pebbles or small stones to produce smooth sheens and bring out their colors

perfumery art of blending natural and synthetic scents to make perfume

pin and thread process in which many pins are pushed into a soft base, such as cork or padded fabric, and thread is stretched back-and-forth around the pins to create intricate geometric patterns

plaiting and braiding interlacing of three or more lengths of yarn to create strong, decorative strips

plastics making of objects from molded plastic

pokerwork pyrography

poonah work painting or stenciling on velvet; theorem painting

potato printing cutting of relief designs in raw potato and using it to make prints

pottery making or collecting of decorative and functional vessels of fired clay; ceramics

printmaking art or technique of impressing designs on cloth or other material

puppetry making of and performing with small, painted, clothed figures operated by finger, hand, rod, sticks, or strings

pyrography process of burning designs on leather, wood, acrylics, or foam with heated tool such as electric pen; pokerwork

quillwork craft in which stiff paper is cut in strips, rolled tightly, and glued on surface such as small box to form patterns

quilting creation and collection of needlework or patchwork bedcovers, often antique

raffia fiber obtained from raffia palm, used to make baskets, hats, and mats

repoussage embossing by hammering designs on metal

resist printing process of printing designs on cloth with paste of flour and water that acts like wax in batik to resist dyes

rubbing frottage

rug hooking creating patterned rugs with a hooked tool

rugmaking weaving of rugs

rushwork weaving of rush stems into chair bottoms or mats

scrapcraft cutting and assembling of discarded and found objects, such as egg cartons, bottle caps, corks, ice cream sticks, paper clips, nut shells, pine cones, or leaves, into decorative objects

scrimshaw carving or engraving of ivory, bone, or shell

seed collage sorting and arranging colored seeds into mosaic pattern on some surface

serigraphy silkscreening

sewing process of creating or repairing garments by stitches

shell carving forming of decorative objects from shells

shellwork coloring, assembly, and arranging of shells to form decorative designs and shapes

silhouetting making of cutout profiles of figures in black paper

silkscreen printing process using inked silk cloth, mounted on frame, to which stencil film is affixed, esp. used for posters and clothing; serigraphy

spinning making of yarn or threads from fibers or filaments

stained glass work design and creation of objects, esp. windows and lampshades, from colored glass pieces, usu. joined by leaded strips

stenciling printing process in which ink or paint is applied to sheets perforated with designs or letters

stitchery decorative needlework, including embroidery or crewelwork

straw working practice of weaving, cutting, and assembling dried straw to form baskets and other objects

string pictures technique of gluing various types of string, thread, and yarn on surface to form design

textiles making cloth by weaving or knitting

theorem painting poonah work

tie-dyeing creating of designs on textiles by tying parts of the cloth so they will not absorb dye or forming barrier to dye with a clip or rubber band

tincrafting making of objects out of tin, sometimes using tin cans, often with patterns cut or punched into the metal

toymaking handcrafting of children's playthings

trapunto quilting done in high relief through two or more layers of cloth, produced by padding a stitched pattern with yarn or cotton

tritik form of tie-dying in which strong thread is stitched along line through fabric and pulled tight to exclude dye

watermark design making designs on paper by laying wire in the sieve on which paper pulp is poured, so that where wire touches pulp it dries to a more compact surface than surrounding paper, resulting in a design that shows up in light

weaving design and creation of fabrics, rugs, or textiles on a loom by interlacing threads or yarns; fabric making

whittling carving of decorative or functional objects by trimming and shaping a stick of wood

wickerworking making objects consisting of interlaced willow, twigs, or rods

wood engraving cutting of designs in end-grained block of wood

woodworking carving and shaping of articles in wood

yarn making spinning of natural fibers to make yarn

CHAPTER SEVENTEEN
LEISURE AND RECREATION

Annual National and Religious Holidays

Admission Day U.S.: date on which state entered Union, which varies by state

Advent Christian: beginning fourth Sunday before Christmas, period of fasting and prayer through Christmas celebrating Jesus' birth and anticipating his second coming

Allhallows All Saints' Day

All Saints' Day Christian: November 1, feast day to honor martyrs and saints; Allhallows

All Souls' Day Christian: November 2, day to pray for and honor departed souls

American Indian Day U.S.: fourth Friday in September, honoring Native Americans

Anzac Day Australia and New Zealand: April 25, commemorating landing of troops on Gallipoli, Turkey, in World War I

April Fools' Day April 1, traditional day for playing jokes

Arab League Day March 22, observed by most Arab nations

Arbor Day U.S.: last Friday in April, set aside for preserving trees, often by planting, and encouraging environmental awareness

Armed Forces Day U.S.: third Saturday in May, honoring the members of armed forces

Armistice Day Veterans Day

Ascension Day Christian: tenth day before Pentecost, forty days after Easter, feast day commemorating Christ's departure from Earth to heaven

Ash Wednesday Christian: first day of Lent, forty days before Easter

Assumption Day Christian: August 15, feast day commemorating Virgin Mary's ascension to heaven

Australia Day Australia: January 29, national holiday commemorating arrival of British

autumnal equinox U.S.: September 22, first day of fall

Bairam Id al-Adha Islamic, festival following Ramadan

Bastille Day France: July 14, celebrating beginning of French Revolution

Bon Japan: July, feast of lanterns honoring ancestral spirits

Boxing Day Great Britain: December 26, day after Christmas, originally celebrated by giving Christmas boxes or gifts to service workers and domestics

Canada Day Canada: July 1, commemorating union of provinces into a nation; Dominion Day

Candlemas Christian: February 2, celebrating presentation of Christ child and purification of Virgin Mary

Carnival Mardi Gras

Chinese New Year first new moon after sun enters Aquarius, in late January or early February, festive celebration of new year in Chinese calendar

Christmas Christian: December 25, holiday honoring the birth of Christ; Noel

Christmas Christian: January 6 on Eastern Orthodox Julian calendar

Christmas Eve Christian: December 24, day or evening before Christmas

Cinco de Mayo Mexico: May 5, holiday commemorating the defeat of Napoleon III's forces in 1867

Columbus Day U.S.: second Monday in October, orig. October 12, commemorating Columbus's landing in America in 1492

Commonwealth Day British Commonwealth: May 24, anniversary of Queen Victoria's birthday

Confucius's birthday China: around September 28, commemorating birth of Confucius

Constitution Day formerly in Soviet Union: December 5

Corpus Christi Christian: eleventh day after Pentecost, festival celebrated by Catholics honoring the Eucharist

Decoration Day Memorial Day

Diwali Hindu: late October, festival of lights celebrated in India

Dominion Day Canada Day

Easter Christian: first Sunday after full moon, occurring on or after March 21, celebrating resurrection of Christ

Election Day U.S.: first Tuesday after first Monday in November, reserved for electing public officials

Emperor's birthday Japan: April 29, day honoring birth of emperor

Epiphany Christian: January 6, twelfth day after Christmas, celebrating the Magi's visit to Jesus

Father's Day U.S.: third Sunday in June, honoring fathers

Flag Day U.S.: June 14, anniversary of adoption of American flag in 1777

Flower Festival Japan: April 8, Hana Matsuri, the spring flower festival

Fourth of July U.S. Independence Day

Gandhi's birthday India: October 2, honoring India's independence leader Mahatma Gandhi

Good Friday Christian: Friday before Easter, commemorating Christ's crucifixion

Groundhog Day U.S.: February 2, traditional day for predicting spring's arrival by observing a groundhog's shadow, indicating six more weeks of winter, or lack of shadow, indicating spring is imminent

Guy Fawkes Day Great Britain: November 5,

celebrating capture of Guy Fawkes, who blew up Parliament in 1605

Halloween U.S. and Canada: October 31, festive tradition including dressing in costume, trick-or-treating, and playing pranks

Hanukkah Jewish: eight days beginning twenty-fifth day of Kislev (December), festival of lights marking rededication of Temple of Jerusalem and miracle of oil lamp that burned for eight days on a one-day supply of oil

High Holy Day Jewish: Rosh Hashanah or Yom Kippur

Holi Hindu: spring festival celebrated in India by lighting of fires on Holi eve and throwing of water and colored powders during day

Human Rights Day December 10, observed by member states of United Nations

Immaculate Conception Roman Catholic: December 8, honoring Virgin Mary's freedom from original sin in conception

'Id al-Adha Islamic: major four-day festival beginning on tenth day of last month of calendar; Bairam

Inauguration Day U.S.: January 20 following presidential election, day of inauguration of newly elected president

Independence Day Israel: celebrated in April or May

Independence Day Mexico: September 16, celebrating revolution of 1810

Independence Day U.S.: July 4, honoring adoption of Declaration of Independence by American colonies in 1776; Fourth of July

Islamic New Year's Day vernal equinox, around March 21, celebrating first day of Islamic calendar

Jefferson Davis's birthday southern U.S.: June 3, celebrating birth of president of the Confederacy

Kenyatta Day Kenya: October 20, honoring Jomo Kenyatta

Kwanza African: December 26 to January 1, harvest festival

Labor Day U.S. and Canada: first Monday in September, honoring workers

Lammas Christian: August 1, in memory of St. Peter's imprisonment and deliverance; English harvest festival

Lenin Memorial Day formerly in Soviet Union: April 22, honoring Vladimir Ilyich Lenin, leader of socialist revolution of 1917 in Russia

Lent Christian: forty days from Ash Wednesday to Easter Sunday, period of penitence and fasting in preparation for Easter

Lincoln's birthday U.S.: February 12, celebrating birth in 1809 of U.S. President Abraham Lincoln, now celebrated on Presidents' Day

Mardi Gras Christian: Tuesday immediately before beginning of Lent, celebrated by feasting, carnivals, and parades; Carnival

Martin Luther King Day U.S.: third Monday in January, orig. January 15, celebrating birth of civil rights leader Dr. Martin Luther King, Jr.

Martinmas Christian: November 11, celebrating feast of St. Martin

Maundy Thursday Christian: Thursday before Easter, commemorating Christ's Last Supper

May Day May 1, traditional spring festival, also international holiday honoring workers

Memorial Day U.S.: May 30, honoring soldiers who died in battle; Decoration Day

Michaelmas Christian: September 29, feast of the archangel St. Michael

Midsummer Day Great Britain: June 24, feast of St. John the Baptist; traditional night when spirits are believed to wander

Moharram Islamic: first month of Islamic calendar, festival held during first ten days of new year

Mother's Day U.S.: second Sunday in May, honoring mothers

Muhammad's birthday Islamic: June 8, celebrating birth of prophet Muhammad

National Day People's Republic of China: October 1

National Day Spain: July 18

National Unity Day Italy: November 4

New Year's Day January 1, first day of new year on Gregorian calendar

New Year's Eve December 31, celebrating last day and night of year on Gregorian calendar

Noel Christmas

October Revolution Day formerly in Soviet Union: November 7, celebrating socialist revolution of 1917, when Bolsheviks seized power in Russia

Omisoka Japan: December 31, Grand Last Day celebration, equivalent to New Year's Eve

Palm Sunday Christian: Sunday before Easter, commemorating Christ's triumphal entry into Jerusalem

Pan American Day U.S. and Latin America: April 14, honoring understanding and cooperation among the Americas

Passover Jewish: eight days beginning fourteenth day of Nisan (March or April), commemorating Hebrews' deliverance by Moses from slavery in Egypt; Pesach

Peach Festival Japan: March 3, day when young girls decorate ceremonial dolls with peach blossoms to symbolize peacefulness

Pentecost Christian: seventh Sunday after Easter, commemorating arrival of Holy Spirit to the apostles; Whitsunday

Pesach Passover

Posadas Christian, esp. Mexico: December 16 to 24, commemorating Joseph and Mary's search for shelter

Presidents' Day U.S.: third Monday in February, interim date celebrating birthdays of Washington (February 22) and Lincoln (February 12)

Purim Jewish: fourteenth day of Adar (March), celebrating Persian Jews' deliverance by Esther from massacre by Haman

Queen's birthday Great Britain: April 21, but celebrated in June, honoring birthday of queen

Ramadan Islamic: ninth month of Islamic calendar, period of fasting commemorating revelation of the Koran to Mohammed

Reformation Sunday Protestant: Sunday nearest October 31, commemorating day Martin Luther began the Reformation

Republic Day India: January 26, commemorating founding of Republic of India

Respect for the Aged Day Japan: September 15, honoring the elderly

Robert E. Lee's birthday southern U.S.: January 19, celebrating birth of Confederate commander in chief

Rosh Hashanah Jewish: New Year, first two days of Tishri (September or October)

Sadie Hawkins Day U.S.: first Saturday after November 11, when women invite men to dance or celebrate

Saint Patrick's Day March 17, honoring Saint Patrick, patron saint of Ireland

Saint Stephen's Day Christian: December 26, honoring patron saint of bricklayers in Europe

Saint Valentine's Day Valentine Day

Shavuot Jewish: sixth and seventh days of Sivan (June), commemorating revelation of Ten Commandments to Moses at Mount Sinai

Shrovetide Christian: three days before Ash Wednesday, time of feasting in preparation for Lent

Shrove Tuesday Christian: last day of Shrovetide

Simon Bolivar's birthday Latin America, esp. Ecuador and Venezuela: July 24, honoring leader of South American revolt against Spain in early 19th century

Spring Bank Holiday Great Britain: last Monday in May, official public holiday in spring originating from Christian holiday Whitsuntide

Sukkoth Jewish: beginning fifteenth day of Tishri (October or November), Feast of Tabernacles, celebrating fall harvest and commemorating period when Hebrews wandered in wilderness after Exodus, marked by building of shelters

summer solstice June 21 in Northern Hemisphere, first day of summer

Tet Vietnam: New Year, occurring first new moon after sun enters Aquarius, late January or early February

Thanksgiving Day U.S.: fourth Thursday in November, day of giving thanks, commemorating Pilgrims' harvest festival

Trinity Sunday Christian: seventh day after Pentecost, honoring the Holy Trinity

Twelfth Night Christian: January 5 or 6, eve of Epiphany

United Nation's Day October 24, celebrating ratification of U.N. Charter in 1945

Valentine Day February 14, day for sending messages or gifts of love; Saint Valentine's Day

V-E Day May 8, anniversary of Allied victory in Europe at end of World War II

vernal equinox March 21 or 22, first day of spring

Veterans Day U.S.: November 11, honoring veterans of armed forces and commemorating end of World War I; Armistice Day

V-J Day August 14, anniversary of Allied victory in Japan at end of World War II

Walpurgis Night eve of May Day, April 30, believed in medieval times to be night when witches celebrate their sabbath

Washington's birthday U.S.: February 22, celebrating birth in 1732 of George Washington, first U.S. president, now celebrated on Presidents' Day

Whitsunday Pentecost

Whitsuntide Christian: week beginning with Whitsunday or Pentecost, esp. first three days of that week

winter solstice December 21 in Northern Hemisphere, first day of winter

Women's Day March 8, honoring work of women, esp. in socialist states

World Health Day April 7, observed by member states of the United Nations

Xmas Christmas

Yom Kippur Jewish: tenth day of Tishri (September or October), day of atonement marked by fasting and prayer

Celebrations, Observances, Rites, and Gatherings

affair social gathering or event

anniversary annual recurrence of special date, esp. wedding day

assemblage gathering of persons for specific purpose

at home reception at one's residence; open house

ball large, lavish, usu. formal dance

bank holiday legal holiday on which banks close (Britain)

banquet lavish meal for many people, esp. ceremonial or honorific

baptism sacrament of admission into Christian church, enacted by sprinkling of water on child

bar mitzvah initiation ceremony marking coming of age of thirteen-year-old Jewish boy

barn dance American social dance, orig. held in barn

bas mitzvah bat mitzvah

bat mitzvah initiation ceremony marking coming of age of thirteen-year-old Jewish girl; bas mitzvah

beanfeast *Chiefly Brit. slang.* formerly, annual dinner given by employer for employees

bee gathering for specific purpose, often for a competition; such as a spelling bee

benefit public performance, dinner, or gathering, proceeds of which go to certain person, group, or cause

birthday annual observance of day one was born

black-tie (*adj*) designating formal affair to which tuxedo is worn

bonfire large, open-air fire, usu. at night, around which people gather

box social fund-raiser auction with box lunches

bris Jewish rite of circumcision

call social visit paid to another's home

callithump noisy parade

carnival period, usu. several days, of feasting and merrymaking, esp. before Lent

cavalcade formal procession of vehicles

celebration instance or observation of holiday, religious ceremony, or festivity

ceremony formal act in observance of ritual or holiday

church feast festive observance of religious holiday, esp. saint's day

clambake outdoor social gathering, esp. at beach with food baked on hot rocks

cocktail party informal gathering, usu. in early evening, where refreshments are served but not a complete meal

coffee klatsch informal gathering for conversation at which coffee is served; kaffee klatsch

coming out debut in formal society

commemoration celebration in memory of someone or something

commencement ceremony at which school or college degrees are conferred

communion Christian sacrament commem-orating Christ's death by taking bread and wine

confirmation generally nonsacramental Christian rite of admission to full church membership

corroboree nocturnal festivity with song and ceremonial dance (Australian aborigine)

cotillion formal dance, esp. honoring debut

dance social gathering for purpose of dancing to music

date appointment for social engagement, esp. with member of opposite sex; such an engagement

debut party and dance honoring young woman's entrance into formal society; coming out

dinner gathering to eat evening meal, esp. feast or banquet

event noteworthy social occasion

extravaganza extremely elaborate or lavish social event

fair gathering, often over several days at one place, for feasting and amusements, usu. with exhibition of goods for sale

feast elaborate meal or banquet, often ceremonial

feria *Spanish.* market fair or festival, often on church holiday

-fest suffix added to indicate festival or celebration, as in sunfest or lovefest

festival period of celebration, feasting, and special observances

festive occasion joyous celebration that usu. includes feasting

festivity festival or festive gathering

fête *French.* festival; elaborate party or outdoor gathering, often commemorative

fête champêtre *French.* outdoor entertainment

fiesta processions, festivities, and dances on saint's day (Spain, Latin America)

formal dance to which men wear tuxedos and women wear gowns

function formal ceremony or large social gathering

funeral ceremony of burial or cremation of the dead; procession accompanying corpse to final resting place

gala celebration marking special occasion, esp. opening of public entertainment

gathering any assemblage of several persons for a specific, often social or ceremonial, purpose

gaudy joyous celebration, esp. reunion (Britain)

get-together informal social gathering

harvest home feast at end of harvest season

high tea substantial late afternoon snack at which tea is served, esp. in Britain

holiday day commemorating an event, usu. by suspension of work and other regular activities; *Chiefly Brit.* vacation

holiday season last two months of the year in United States, including Thanksgiving, Christmas and Hanukkah, and New Year's Eve

homecoming occasion marking return of group of people to their home, esp. annual celebration of university alumni

honeymoon vacation taken by newlyweds immediately after wedding

hootenanny informal folk or country song performance, often with audience sing-along

hop informal dance, often to recorded music

house party gathering at one's residence, often over more than one night

housewarming party celebrating one's move to a new home

jamboree large, festive gathering, often with mixed entertainment

jubilee special anniversary, esp. twenty-fifth, fiftieth, or sixtieth

kaffee klatsch coffee klatsch

kermis outdoor festival or charitable fair (Netherlands)

klatch small, informal gathering, esp. for idle chitchat

last rites Roman Catholic sacrament administered to person near death

legal holiday nationally established holiday on which banks and government offices are closed

luau feast or banquet (Hawaii)

luncheon formal midday meal, esp. as part of meeting

masked ball large dance to which guests wear masks

masquerade social gathering, esp. dance, at which guests wear masks and costumes

Mass celebration of Catholic church service and the Eucharist

matinée performance or gathering in the afternoon

meet assembly of persons, groups, or teams for competition or organized activity

memorial gathering to commemorate something or someone, esp. after death

mixer friendly, informal get-together

movable feast religious feast that occurs on a different date in different years

name day church feast honoring saint after whom one is named

national holiday legally established government holiday

observance standardized ceremony or rite honoring something

Oktoberfest fall beer-drinking festival (Germany)

open house informal, daylong hospitality offered at one's home to invited and uninvited guests

opening night celebration of first performance of public entertainment

pageant extravagant display, esp. procession with floats

parade formal public procession, usu. with floats and other displays, esp. on holiday

party informal social gathering for amusement or celebration, often with refreshments and entertainment

picnic excursion on which meal is eaten outdoors

potlatch ceremonial feast of Pacific Northwest Native Americans in which gifts are given by host and guests attempt to exceed them

powwow Native American ceremony with feasting and dancing, usu. in expectation of some beneficial result

procession orderly, often ceremonial or decorative movement of group of people

prom formal dance at school or college

promenade procession of guests beginning formal ball; leisurely walk, esp. in public square

receiving announced time when one welcomes visitors at one's home

reception social gathering of welcome, esp. for guests after formal event such as wedding

red-letter day special day

religious holiday holiday commemorating event observed by church

reunion gathering of persons after period of separation

revel uproarious, wild festivity

rite standardized, ceremonial act or occasion

rite of passage ceremony performed to mark person's change of status, such as at puberty or time of marriage

ritual observation of ceremony or event prescribed by custom for solemn occasions and rites of passage

roast gathering to humorously honor or kiddingly defame someone

Sabbath day of rest and religious observance; Saturday for Jews, Sunday for Christians

Sadie Hawkins party or dance to which females invite males

salute ceremonial honor and praise for someone

saturnalia wild, orgiastic, excessive celebration

séance gathering to communicate with spirits

seder Jewish dinner service on first evening of Passover

Shabbat *Hebrew.* Jewish Sabbath, observed from sunset Friday to sunset Saturday

shindig *Informal.* lavish social gathering, usu. with dancing; shindy

shindy *Informal.* shindig

show performance, entertainment, or public spectacle

shower party at which gifts are given to guest of honor, esp. bride-to-be or mother-to-be

sing-along gathering at which group of people sing songs informally, often under direction of leader; songfest

sit-down dinner formal dinner at which one is served while seated at table

soiree social gathering in evening

songfest sing-along

square dance lively folk dance in which couples perform designated steps and figures

stay-on cocktail party at which certain guests are invited to remain for full dinner

sun dance summer solstice ceremony of Plains Indians

tea light, late afternoon meal at which tea is served, esp. in Britain

tea ceremony traditional, formal, highly stylized Japanese green tea service for guests

tea party late afternoon gathering at which tea is served

testimonial formal expression of admiration

tribute formal expression or show of support and respect

vacation period of rest from normal activities, often spent away from home

wake often festive vigil over corpse prior to burial; *Chiefly Brit.* annual holiday or vacation

walkabout brief respite from regular work and period of roaming the bush among Australian aborigines

wayzgoose printers' annual celebration

wedding ceremony and festivities marking marriage

welcome warm reception of newly arrived person or persons

white-tie (*adj*) designating extremely formal affair to which men wear swallow-tailed coats and white bow ties

whoop-de-do *Informal.* uproarious festivity or revel

yuletide feast of Christmas

Parties and Partying

after-hours (*adj*) occurring or operating in early morning hours after regular bars close, when only a few, sometimes private, social clubs are open

bacchanalia drunken feast, orig. honoring Roman god Bacchus

bachelor party gathering of men honoring friend about to be married

bash *Informal.* wild party

birthday cake cake given to person on his or her birthday, usu. with one burning candle for each year in age

blast *Slang.* exciting event or party

blowout *Slang.* uninhibited, often lengthy party

bon vivant highly sociable person with well-developed tastes, esp. in food and drink

boogie (*vb*) dance to rock music; *Informal.* have a raucous good time

bridge party gathering at which groups of four people play bridge

BYOB bring your own bottle/booze/beer; designation that host will not supply drinks at party

card party social gathering at which card games are played, usu. with refreshments

carouse (*vb*) take part in noisy, merry, drinking party

carrying-on *Informal.* foolish, excited behavior

casual informal, sometimes spontaneous, social gathering

catering act or business of supplying and serving food and drink at parties

celebrate (*vb*) mark happy occasion by festivity and pleasurable activity

chaperon one delegated to insure proper behavior, esp. in young people

cheers greeting or toast indicative of hospitality and good times

chic (*adj*) stylish, elegant; following the latest trends

circulate (*vb*) move from person to person at party

clubhouse building or enclosed area used as regular gathering place by group

co-host one of two persons hosting party

company group of people gathered for social event, esp. guests in one's home

confetti bits of colored paper scattered about as form of decoration at celebration

costume party party at which guests wear clothes different from their normal attire

crash (*vb*) *Informal.* attend a party uninvited

cut in (*vb*) take another's place, esp. as a dance partner

cutup *Informal.* person who clowns and plays practical jokes, esp. to gain attention in a group

debauch orgy

dinner party social gathering featuring evening meal

Dionysian (*adj*) frenzied and orgiastic

dissipation excessive indulgence in pleasure

diversion amusing activity that distracts one's attention

do *Chiefly Brit.* affair, party

dress-up (*adj*) designating a gathering to which one dresses formally or in costume

engagement arrangement to attend social function

epicure person who enjoys and has discriminating taste in food and drink

fast lane *Informal.* social life marked by attendance at many parties and social functions, esp. the trendiest and most boisterous affairs

favor small gift or trinket given to guests at party

fling brief period of unrestrained pleasure and dissipation

frat party *Informal.* party at college fraternity house

fun and games good times, party activities, and merrymaking

gaiety good cheer, merriment, and festivity

garden party outdoor gathering in garden or backyard

gate-crasher *Informal.* person attending party uninvited, often forcing way into gathering

get down (*vb*) *Informal.* have a good time, esp. boisterously

get together (*vb*) assemble for social event

good cheer merrymaking and revelry; feasting

good times pleasurable social activities and entertainments

guest of honor person in whose honor party is thrown

hedonism dedication to self-indulgent pursuit of pleasure

hen party *Informal.* gathering for women only

high jinks *Informal.* boisterous fun, esp. lively pranks

high time *Informal.* good time, esp. while intoxicated

hobnob (*vb*) associate on very friendly terms

hoedown rollicking dance party, esp. one featuring square dancing

hoopla *Informal.* gay and excited commotion or celebration; whoopla

hospitality friendship and kindness extended to guests

host man who entertains others, esp. at his home

hostess woman who entertains others, esp. at her home

jollity gaiety, good times; *Chiefly Brit.* party, jolly occasion

key club private club where each member has key to premises

la dolce vita *Italian.* the sweet life; hedonism, good times, and dissipation

lark playful merrymaking, sometimes involving pranks

lawn party outdoor gathering on grass field, often under tents

life of the party gregarious, charming, entertaining individual at social affairs

lion prominent person or celebrity in demand socially

live it up *Informal.* enjoy oneself, have a boisterous good time

maffick (*vb*) *Chiefly Brit.* celebrate with boisterous public display

man about town worldly man who frequents fashionable clubs and parties

merriment gaiety, fun, amusement

merrymaking convivial festivity, fun

no-host bar bar at which party guests must pay for drinks

noisemaker horn or cowbell sounded or rung at celebration

orgy unrestrained merrymaking and dissipation in group, esp. with free sexual activity; debauch

pajama party slumber party

party informal social gathering for amusement or celebration; (*vb*) *Informal.* engage in social activities in boisterous, unrestrained manner

party down (*vb*) *Informal.* participate uninhibitedly at a party

party hearty *Informal.* participate boisterously at a party

partying *Informal.* indulging in and enjoying parties

party planner person hired to organize, orchestrate, and stage parties

pay a visit make social call at another's home

place card small card with guest's name indicating where guest is to sit at dining table

playboy often rich man given to pleasure-seeking, sexual promiscuity, and dissipation

pranks mischievous party games and practical jokes

regale (*vb*) entertain others with splendid feast or amusing stories

revel wild party or celebration

revelry noisy party or merrymaking

ripsnorter *Informal.* wild, boisterous party

roister (*vb*) engage in noisy revelry and carousing

rollick (*vb*) behave in lively, carefree manner, esp. with others

Roman holiday time of debauchery and licentiousness

RSVP *French.* répondez s'il vous plaît; request on invitation that one indicate whether he or she will attend

salon regular gathering of distinguished guests in private drawing room, esp. in celebrity's home

slumber party overnight house party, esp. for teenage girls; pajama party

smoker informal social gathering for men only

sociable (*adj*) friendly, enjoying the company of others; (*n*) informal social gathering

social informal gathering, esp. for group or organization

social call informal visit to another's home

social club group organized for recreation and entertainment

social intercourse conversation and interaction with others

stag party party for men only; bachelor party for bridegroom, often with pornographic movies

step out (*vb*) leave one's home seeking a good time

supper club expensive nightclub serving fine food and drink

surprise party party kept secret from guest of honor until last moment

table-hopping *Informal.* act of moving quickly from table to table at large party or club

taxi dancer girl employed by dance hall to dance with patrons for a fee

tea party social gathering in late afternoon at which tea is served

tear *Informal.* spree of carousing and dissipation

tête-à-tête *French.* intimate conversation between two people

TGIF thank God it's Friday; expression of relief at end of work week

treat meal or drinks paid for by another; (*vb*) to pay for another's meal or drinks

trendy (*adj*) fashionable in the latest social mode; faddish

Tupperware party gathering in home at which salesperson distributes samples and tries to sell Tupperware products to other women

vanity fair place or group characterized by pursuit of idle pleasures, decadence, and ostentation

wallflower shy or unpopular person who remains at periphery of social gathering

whirl series of parties in rapid succession

whoopee *Informal.* boisterous revelry and fun

whoop it up *Informal.* have a rollicking, boisterous good time

whoopla hoopla

wing-ding *Slang.* festive, lively party or event

work the room *Informal.* move from person to person at party, esp. seeking advantage or influence

Vacations and Interludes

absenteeism deliberate or habitual absence from work or school

AWOL absent without leave; unauthorized absence from military service

break cessation of normal activities, esp. work

breather pause for rest, esp. from difficult task

busman's holiday vacation spent pursuing one's regular activities

cocktail hour early evening, at end of workday

coffee break brief pause in workday for rest and refreshment

cut (*vb*) stay away without excuse, esp. from school

day off single day's paid vacation from work

day of rest day off, esp. Sunday

downtime period of worker inactivity or equipment repair, esp. on machinery such as computer or communications system

entr'acte *French.* intermission

escape getaway from regular activities, esp. to exotic place for relaxation

excursion brief, often one-day pleasure trip, esp. at bargain rates

expedition journey with specific purpose

field trip excursion, esp. to place under study for observation

free time period without normal duties or responsibilities

furlough leave of absence from duty, esp. for soldier

getaway departure from home for vacation

great escape long-anticipated vacation, esp. to exotic locale

halftime midpoint intermission during sports event

happy hour early evening, at end of workday, when bars reduce price of drinks

hiatus interruption or break in normal activities

holiday *Chiefly Brit.* vacation away from home

hooky unexcused absence from school

idyll romantic or bucolic interlude

interim period of time between two events

interlude brief respite from normal activities

intermission brief, scheduled interval between two events, esp. between acts of a performance; entr'acte

jaunt usu. short pleasure trip

journey trip taken away from home

junket trip or journey, esp. one taken by politician at public expense

knock off (*vb*)*Informal.* leave work at end of day

leave authorized absence from work or military duty, esp. for extended period; leave of absence

leave of absence leave

leisure time period free from normal duties, when one may rest, play, or travel

liberty brief, authorized absence, esp. from naval duty

Lord's day for Christians, Sunday, traditionally a day off from work

lull short period of calm or lessened activity

outing brief pleasure trip, usu. to outdoor location

paid vacation scheduled, authorized absence from work without loss of salary

pause temporary break or cessation of activity

playtime free or leisure time for recreation

R and R rest and recreation

recess temporary break in work or school day

respite temporary interval of relief from duties

rest refreshing period of inactivity after work or travel

rest and recreation R and R; regular vacation period from military duty

retreat act of withdrawing into seclusion or retirement; place of refuge or seclusion

sabbatical leave from regular work, esp. for extended period with pay

safari journey or hunting expedition, esp. in eastern Africa

shore leave authorized permission for sailor to go ashore briefly

sick leave authorized absence from work, with full or partial pay, due to illness or injury

sojourn temporary stay away from home

spare time unoccupied time available for leisure activities and recreation

take five (*vb*) *Informal.* stop activity briefly for rest

tea break brief pause in workday for tea, esp. in Britain

time off authorized break from regular duties

tour journey through several places, often led by guide, ending at starting point

travels journeys, often to places far from home

trip journey away from home for pleasure or business

truancy unexcused absence, esp. from school

vacation period of rest from normal activities, often spent traveling away from home

visit journey and stay at place away from home

voyage journey or period of travel, esp. by sea

weekend days between end of one work week and beginning of next, Saturday and Sunday in United States and Europe

Travel and Tourism

accommodations lodgings, sometimes including meals

Baedeker guidebook to foreign country, orig. published by Karl Baedeker in Germany during 19th century

bed-and-breakfast overnight accommodation, esp. in private home, that includes breakfast

bellboy man or boy employed to carry luggage and run errands at hotel; bellhop

bellhop bellboy

bon voyage French. lit. pleasant journey; expression of farewell to traveler

booking advance reservation for lodging or travel

business class travel at level between first class and coach class

cabin class accommodations on passenger ship superior to tourist class but inferior to first class

caravan company of persons traveling together, esp. in series of vehicles following one another

charter hire or lease of ship, bus, or airplane to transport large group at reduced fare

check in (vb) register at hotel, announce arrival for journey by public conveyance

check luggage turn over baggage for transport in cargo area

check out (vb) settle one's bill and leave hotel

Club Med Trademark. organization offering group vacation at relaxing tropical location

coach class standard travel facilities

Cook's tour guided, often cursory sightseeing tour

cruise ocean trip on comfortable passenger ship

double occupancy travel accommodation designed for two persons

emigrate (vb) leave one's country and settle in another

excursion fare low fare with special requirements

expatriate (vb) leave one's native country and take up permanent residence abroad

expedition journey or voyage for some definite purpose

exploration traveling in unknown region for educational purposes

first class finest accommodations in hotel or on public conveyance

gadabout person who wanders restlessly in search of pleasure

globetrotter person who travels widely and frequently

grand tour journey through continental Europe, usu. at completion of education

guide person hired to lead tourists or travelers

through unknown area, usu. providing information about it

hike vigorous walk of some distance, often for observation, recreation, and health

hostler person who cares for horses at an inn

hotel commercial establishment providing lodging and often meals for travelers

immigrate (vb) arrive in new country and settle there

inn establishment providing lodging and often food and drink for travelers, usu. smaller than hotel

itinerary detailed plan or record of journey

jet set wealthy people who travel frequently to fashionable, exclusive places

joyride automobile ride merely for pleasure, usu. at high speed, often in stolen vehicle

leg one stage of journey

lionize (vb) Chiefly Brit. visit interesting sights

lodging facility for temporary, overnight stay

motel hotel for automobile travelers at which car can be parked close to one's room

motoring vacation or travel by automobile

no-show person who makes reservation but does not appear

odyssey extended, often wandering journey

one-way ticket ticket valid for travel from one place to another without return

on the road engaged in ceaseless travel

open return round-trip ticket with unspecified return date

overbook (vb) accept more reservations than places available in expectation of no-shows

package tour group travel in which all accommodations and activities are organized and paid for in advance

passage journey from place to place, esp. by water

pension modest European hotel or boardinghouse, esp. one serving meals

peregrination travel, esp. on foot

peripatetic (adj) moving from place to place, itinerant

pilgrimage long journey to religious shrine or place of historical interest

pleasure trip journey taken for amusement only

porter person employed to carry one's baggage, esp. at hotel or depot

progress forward movement, esp. on official journey

remigrate (vb) return to country of one's birth after prolonged absence

reservation arrangement by which hotel room or seat on public conveyance is set aside and held

resort place where people go for vacations, esp. to rest and relax

return ticket Chiefly Brit. round trip ticket

round-the-world (adj) designating ticket for passage or trip around the world

round trip travel from starting point to destination and back again; fare or ticket providing for such a journey

route course followed on travels

rubbernecking sightseeing by twisting one's head to gaze about

safe passage successful journey through dangerous region

Sherpa member of Tibetan people who serve as porters and guides on mountain-climbing expeditions

sightseeing visiting places of interest for pleasure and education

slumming visiting poor urban slums, esp. out of curiosity

spa resort with mineral spring or health facilities and sauna, esp. fashionable spot

spin usu. brief pleasure trip in motor vehicle

steerage portion of ship occupied by passengers paying lowest fare

Sunday drive pleasure trip by auto on Sunday, esp. to view the countryside

tour journey or trip of some duration, usu. for sightseeing, esp. in organized group

tour bus vehicle carrying group of tourists

tour guide person leading others to points of interest, usu. providing relevant information

tourism travel of foreign visitors to another nation and income derived therefrom; similar travel within one's own country

tourist person who visits another country or region for pleasure and sightseeing

tourist class lowest-priced accommodations on ship or train

touristy (adj) typical of or intended for tourists, therefore often tasteless or banal

travel agency company that arranges itineraries, lodging, and transportation for tourists and other travelers

traveler person who journeys away from home

traveler's check replaceable bank draft issued to traveler, signed at issuance and again at time of cashing

travelogue lecture, accompanied by slides or film, about travel to foreign or out-of-the-way place

travels journeys, often to faraway places

trek slow, laborious travel, often by foot over long distance

turista Informal. acute intestinal infection and diarrhea, usu. caused by bacteria in food or water of foreign country

walk period or course of walking for pleasure or exercise

wayfarer person who travels from place to place, esp. on foot

world traveler person who journeys to many lands

year abroad year spent living in foreign country, esp. by college student

---

ENTERTAINMENTS AND SPECTACLES

See also: *Chap. 15: Dance; Theater; Chap. 17: Holidays, Celebrations, and Vacations; Sports; Hobbies; Games, Activities, and Toys*

acrobatics art and performance of gymnastics and tumbling

aerialism performance of feats in the air, esp. on a trapeze

aerobatics spectacular flying stunts and maneuvers such as rolls and dives by an airplane

amateur night entertainment featuring nonprofessional performers, often in competition for prizes

amusement any pleasurable or entertaining diversion

amusement park outdoor facility providing rides, shows, exhibitions, and other amusements

animal act circus act involving tricks by wild and domestic animals

aquacade swimming and diving to musical accompaniment

aquarium building in which live aquatic organisms are exhibited

aquatics water sports and performances

arm wrestling contest in which opponents face each other gripping hands and attempt to force each other's arm down

beauty contest staged show, usu. made up of women, in which panel selects most beautiful contestant

belly dancing solo performance, usu. given by woman, involving gyrations of abdomen and hips

big top circus; main tent of circus

botanical garden outdoor garden and greenhouses for study and exhibition of plants

buffoonery clown show

bullfight public spectacle in which men excite, fight with, and ceremonially kill bulls

bumper cars amusement park ride in which padded electric cars purposely collide with each other

burlesque broadly comic theatrical entertainment of short skits and sometimes striptease acts

callithump noisy, boisterous parade

card section large group seated in bloc at outdoor public event, turning multicolored cards in unison to form patterns when viewed from afar

carnival traveling program of amusements, exhibitions, and sideshows

carousel merry-go-round

casino facility for gambling, sometimes featuring floor show

cavalcade parade; procession of riders or carriages

chute the chute amusement park ride similar to roller coaster, often ending in water

circus public performance, often in tent, of feats of skill, acrobatics, animal acts, and clown shows

cirque *French.* circus

clown show performance by buffoons, jesters, and comics

concours *French.* public competition or contest

conjuring practicing magic

contest activity in which teams or individuals compete for victory

contortionism acrobatics in which performer twists body into unusual postures

convention annual gathering of members of an industry or trade to exhibit new products

county fair annual exhibition at county fairgrounds featuring displays of livestock, stage shows, and rides

crafts fair gathering for display and sale of handmade crafts

cyclorama large pictorial representation encircling viewer, often with real objects as foreground; panorama

demolition derby exhibition in which old automobiles are intentionally rammed until just one is left running

diorama scenic representation blending sculpted figures and details, often in miniature, with painted background

display exhibition

diversion pastime or amusement that agreeably distracts attention from daily routine

drum corps marching band, esp. of drummers, under direction of drum major and majorettes, who often twirl batons

entertainment diverting, amusing, and engaging public performance

equestrian show exhibition of horsemanship, esp. jumping

escape artist person who breaks free of seemingly impossible confinement

exhibit public display of objects

exhibition public showing of performance skills or objects of interest; display

expo exposition

exposition public exhibition or show, esp. of commodities; expo

extravaganza lavish or spectacular show

fair exhibition designed to acquaint buyers or public with products; gathering for exchange and display of articles

fantoccini puppet show using string-operated or mechanical puppets

fashion show display of stylish clothing on models

Ferris wheel amusement park ride consisting of a tall, rotating, upright wheel with attached cars for riders

figure skating dance performance on ice skates

fireworks pyrotechnics; explosive devices with loud discharge and spectacular appearance

float low, flat, decorated vehicle that carries exhibits or tableaux in a parade

floor show variety performance on stage, esp. dancing

freak show public exhibition of oddities or freaks of nature

funambulism tightrope walking

fun house building in amusement park containing devices designed to startle, amuse, or frighten visitors

gala public entertainment marking special occasion

girlie show *Informal.* striptease acts

gladiators slaves who fought other slaves or wild animals in arena (ancient Rome)

gymkhana automotive meet with several events that test driving skills

harlequinade pantomime or farce featuring Harlequin character in multicolored, diamond-patterned tights

high-diving diving from very high platform into small pool

high jinks boisterous, unstructured carrying-on

high-wire act tightrope walking and acrobatics

Icecapades *Trademark.* figure skating show performed by company of ice skaters to musical accompaniment

jamboree noisy, festive gathering; assembly of Boy Scouts or Girl Scouts

jongleur itinerant, medieval acrobat, juggler, and minstrel (France)

jousting tilting

jugglery juggling

juggling keeping several objects in motion in the air by alternately catching and tossing them; jugglery

legerdemain magic, esp. sleight of hand

light show kaleidoscopic display of colored lights and film loops

lists medieval tournament enclosed by high stake fence

loop-the-loop airplane ride that makes vertical loop; ride simulating this

magic producing illusions by sleight of hand or conjuring

marching band band composed of brass, woodwind, and percussion that performs while marching before crowd in parade or at athletic event

marine park public display of marine animals and fish in outdoor tanks

masquerade performance or party with guests in disguise

medicine show former traveling variety show that used entertainers to attract crowd to whom remedies were then sold

merry-go-round amusement park ride with seats, often in form of animals, on revolving platform; carousel

mime show pantomime

mummery comic or ridiculous pantomime performance

music hall vaudeville or variety theater

pageant elaborate exhibition or spectacle with music, dramatic tableaux, and a procession of floats

panorama cyclorama

pantomime act conveying a story or idea without words through facial gestures, hand movements, and dance; mime show

parade public procession of marching bands, performers, motorized displays, and floats

peep show often pornographic film or other object viewed through a small opening; raree show

planetarium facility housing a large model of

the solar system, which is projected onto its ceiling or dome for view from seats below

prestidigitation sleight of hand

prom promenade

promenade strolling or walking through a public square; formal dance or ball; prom

psychedelic show light show imitating visual effect of psychedelic drugs, often to rock music

public contest competitive event or events staged before spectators

public spectacle unusual, notable, and entertaining acts performed in public or before audience

Punch-and-Judy show traditional puppet show depicting battling couple

puppetry puppet show

puppet show manipulation of small, handheld, string-operated or mechanical jointed figures in staged show; puppetry

pyrotechnics spectacular display, esp. of fireworks

raree show peep show; unusual carnival or street show

regatta series of rowing, sailing, or speedboat races

revue stage performance consisting of a series of skits, songs, and dances; variety show

ride any of various mechanical devices at amusement park or carnival that provide frightening or amusing rides for patrons

rodeo public performance by cowboys, featuring broncobusting, Brahma bull riding, calf roping, and steer wrestling

roller coaster elevated railway constructed in curves and inclines as frightening amusement park ride

roller derby staged contest between two roller-skating teams on oval track

rope dancing acrobatics performed on suspended rope

roundabout *Chiefly Brit.* merry-go-round

saltimbanque show European street performance by clowns, acrobats, and contortionists

scavenger hunt party contest with time limit for locating several difficult-to-obtain articles

scenic railway brief, elevated railway for viewing scenery

shadow play show in which shadows of puppets or performers are cast on screen

show any public performance

sideshow incidental diversion offered with main show

sketch brief, often comic, theatrical piece

skit brief burlesque or comic sketch included as part of revue, sometimes in imitation of a serious work

sleight of hand magic and conjuring tricks requiring deception through manual dexterity and skill; prestidigitation

snake charming entertainment involving professed power to charm and control venomous snakes

son et lumière *French.* sound-and-light show

sound-and-light show outdoor spectacle at historic sight using recorded narration with sound and light effects

spectacle public exhibit or performance of something unusual, striking, notable, or entertaining, often on a large scale

spectacular spectacle or astonishing performance

spectator sport athletic contest performed before audience

sports organized, competitive athletic activities engaged in by trained athletes for the diversion of spectators

squib small firecracker

stage show performance, esp. song and dance, on stage, usu. inside a facility designed for such performances

street show performance staged in public street, esp. clown show or acrobatics

striptease act in which usu. female performer removes clothing piece-by-piece to musical accompaniment; girlie show

stunt act of daring, dexterity, and skill

synchronized swimming water ballet

tableau striking staged scene, usu. involving persons who remain in fixed positions

talent show amateur revue aimed at discovering talented new performers

thaumaturgy magic, performance of miracles

theme park amusement park in which structures and displays focus on central theme or motif

three-ring circus large circus with three acts performing simultaneously

tightrope walking balancing act performed on wire or rope suspended at some height; funambulism

tilting medieval contest in which two riders attempt to knock each other off horses with lances; jousting

tournament medieval contest between mounted knights armed with lances; series of contests leading to a championship in various sports and competitive fields

trapeze act acrobatic circus performance on horizontal bar suspended at some height from two parallel ropes

tumbling acrobatics involving somersaulting, rolling on floor, and handsprings

variety show revue

vaudeville traditional form of broad, comic revue

ventriloquism performance in which voice seems to come not from speaker but from dummy or other source

water ballet synchronized movement to music by performers in a pool of water; synchronized swimming

water park amusement park in which most or all of rides involve passing through water

wax museum exhibit of life-size wax effigies of famous people; waxworks

waxworks wax museum

Wild West show performance depicting scenes

of U.S. Old West and displaying feats such as horsemanship, marksmanship, and rope twirling

wrestling staged athletic contest involving physical combat

zoo parklike facility for public display of living animals; zoological garden

zoological garden zoo

SPORTS

Team Sports
Individual Sports and Competitive Events
General Sports Terminology
Auto Racing
Baseball
Basketball
Bowling
Boxing and Wrestling
Football
Golf
Gymnastics and Calisthenics
Hockey
Horse and Dog Racing
Ice Skating
Skiing
Soccer
Surfing
Swimming and Diving
Tennis
Track and Field

See also: *Chap. 15: Television and Radio; Chap. 17: Entertainments and Spectacles; Games, Activities, and Toys*

Basic definitions are provided for the names of twenty major competitive sports and games. The extensive lists of specialized technical and slang terms that follow these generic definitions are intended as a prompt or memory jog for users already familiar with the games they describe.

Team Sports

Australian Rules football
bandy, baseball, basketball, bobsledding
Canadian football, crew, cricket, curling
doubles tennis
field hockey, flag football, football
handball, hardball, hockey, hooverball, hurling
ice hockey
kickball
lacrosse
polo, pushball
relay race, Roller Derby, rounders, rugby
shinny, slow pitch softball, soccer, softball,
    speedball, stickball, stoolball, stoop ball
tag football, team handball, touch football
volleyball
water polo, whiffleball
yachting

Individual Sports and Competitive Events

acrobatics, Alpine skiing, archery, arm wrestling
balance beam, bareknuckle boxing, barrel racing,
    baton twirling, biathlon, biathlon relay,

bicycling, bobsledding, boloball, bowling, boxing, Brahma bull riding, broad jump, broncobusting, bullfighting, bull riding
calf roping, candlepins, canoeing, court tennis, cross-country, cross-country skiing, cycling
decathlon, deck tennis, discus, distance running, diving, downhill skiing, draw, dressage, duckpins
enduro biking, equestrian
fencing, field events, figure skating, fives, foot racing, freestyle wrestling
giant stride, golf, Greco-Roman wrestling, gymnastics
hammer throw, handball, high jump, hurdling
ice dancing, ice skating, Indian wrestling
jai alai, javelin, judo
kayaking, korfball
lawn bowling, lawn tennis, long jump, luge
marathon, martial arts, medley relay, miniature golf, modern pentathlon, motocross
ninepins, Nordic skiing
paddle tennis, pancratium, parallel bars, pelota, pentathlon, ping-pong, platform diving, platform tennis, pole bending, pole vault, pugilism
racquetball, relay race, rings, road racing, rowing, running
sambo wrestling, shooting, shot put, side horse, skiing, ski jumping, slalom, sled-dog racing, speed skating, springboard diving, sprint, squash, stall bar, steeplechase, steer-wrestling, sumo wrestling, surfing, swimming
table tennis, tennis, tenpins, track, track and field, triathlon, triple jump
ultramarathon
vaulting
walking, water skiing, weightlifting, wrestling, wrist wrestling

General Sports Terminology

AAU, all-American, All-Pro, all-star, all-star team, amateur, Amateur Athletic Union, America's Cup, anchorman, arena, athlete, athletic scholarship, at large, attackman (lacrosse, rugby), average
backup, ball, ballpark, barnburner, batsman (cricket), bench, bench press (weightlifting), bench warmer, best-of-five series, best-of-seven series, big game, bird cage, black belt (karate), blackout, blank, bleachers, bluff, body English, bonus, boo, boobirds, book, booster, box seat, breeze, Bronx cheer, brown belt, bulk up, bull's-eye (archery), burn, bush, bye
call, cape work (bullfighting), captain, carom, cash in, cellar, champion, championship, chaw, cheap shot, cheat, cheerleader, chukker (polo), chula (jai alai), circuit, clean and jerk (weightlifting), cleats, clock, club, clubhouse, clutch, clutch play, coach, cocaptain, colors, comeback, competition, conference, consolation prize, coxswain (crew), crosse (lacrosse), cuadrilla (bullfighting), cup
dark horse, deadlock, defender, dog it
eligibility, epée (fencing)
fan, field, field house, finesse, first division, first string, fix, forfeit, formation, free agent, fronton (jai alai), front runner
game ball, gamer, goal, good hands, go the distance, grandstanding, groundskeeper, guile, gym, gymkhana, gymnasium
halftime, Hall of Fame, homecoming, home field, home stand, host, hot dog
innings (cricket), in play, instant replay, iron man

jackpot, jam (roller derby), jammer (roller derby), jayvee, jib (yachting), jock, juice, junior varsity
keel (yachting), kill shot, kill the clock
laugher, light tower, lock, locker room, longshot
mainsail (yachting), manager, matador (bullfighting), match, match play, miscue, misplay, muff
NAIA, National Association of Intercollegiate Athletics, National Collegiate Athletic Association, NCAA
odds, odds-on favorite, official, officiate, off-season, Olympics, on a roll, out-of-play, overmatched, overtime
Pan American Games, parry (fencing), pase (bullfighting), phenom, phys ed, physical education, picador (bullfighting), pickup game, play, play-by-play, play catch-up, playing field, play-off, point, position, prelims, press box, pro, professional, promoter, prospect, psyched, psych-out, psych-up, push
quarter, quarterfinal, quickness
razzle-dazzle, recruiting, redshirt, ref, referee, regatta (yachting), rematch, repechage (crew, cycling), replay, reserve, ringer, roll, rookie, roster, round robin, rover (archery), rugger (rugby), runner-up, run out the clock
saber (fencing), score, scoreboard, scorecard, scrub, scrum (rugby), scull (crew), season, season ticket, second division, second effort, second string, second wind, seed, seesaw, semifinal, semipro, semiprofessional, series, set a record, shave points, shirts'n'skins, shoo-in, shuttlecock (badminton), side, sleeper, slump, snatch (weightlifting), spark plug, spectator, spoiler, spot points, spotter, spread, squad, stadium, standings, standoff, stiff, streak, stroke (crew), sub, substitution, sudden death, suit up, Summer Games, Summer Olympics, sweep
tailgate party, tally, taw (marbles), team, team play, teamwork, television time-out, test match (cricket), the wave, throw (rodeo), throw-in, thrust (rodeo), tie, timekeeper, time-out, to play, tossup, tote board, touché (fencing), tournament, tourney, trade, trading deadline, trainer, training, try (rugby), tryout, tune-up
underbird, underdog, upset
varsity, versus, vigorish
wager, waivers, walk-on, warmup, water boy, white belt, wicket (cricket), wild card, wind sprint, Winter Olympics, world champion, world championship, world class
yell leader
zip

Auto Racing

auto racing racing of stock or specialized automobiles by drivers competing over racing course or on closed public roadways
    apron, autocross
    black flag
    checkered flag, cyclocross
    demolition derby, draft, drag race, dragster
    formula one, funny car
    go-carting, Grand Prix, green flag, groove
    Indianapolis 500, infield
    kick
    lap, lap money, LeMans
    midget racer, motocross
    NASCAR, nitro-fueled
    off-road race

    pace car, pace lap, pit, pit crew, pit stop, pole position
    qualifying
    rally
    spin-out, stock car racing
    winner's circle
    yellow flag

Baseball

baseball game of ball between two nine-player teams played for nine innings on field built around a diamond, with home plate and three other bases at its points, around which a runner must pass after successfully hitting a pitched ball with a wooden or metal bat in order to score one run, the object being to score more runs in nine innings than one's opponent
    ace, AL, alley, all-star, All-Star Game, American League, apple, artificial turf, assist, Astroturf, at bat, average, away
    Babe Ruth league, backstop, backup, balk, ball, ball boy, ball club, ball game, ball girl, ball hawk, ballpark, ballplayer, Baltimore chop, barehanded, base, baseball, baseball bat, baseball cap, baseball card, baseballer, baseball game, baseball glove, baseball player, base hit, baseline, base on balls, base path, baserunner, basket catch, bat boy, batter, batter's box, batter up, battery, batting average, batting cage, bean, bean ball, beat out, big league, blank, bleachers, bloop, blooper, bobble, book, boot, bottom, bottom of the ninth, box, boxscore, box seat, broken bat, brush, brushback, bull pen, bunt, bush league, bushleaguer
    cage, called strike, catch, catcher, catcher's mask, caught looking, center field, center fielder, chance, change-of-pace, change-up, chase, check swing, chin music, choke up, chopper, classic, cleanup, cleanup hitter, clear the bases, closed stance, closer, clothesline, clout, club, clutch hit, coach, comebacker, commissioner, complete game, concessions, connect, control, Cooperstown, count, cover a base, curve, curve ball, cut, cut fastball, cutoff, cutoff man, Cy Young Award
    day game, dead ball, deck, deep, designated hitter, DH, diamond, dinger, dish, doctor the ball, double, doubleheader, double play, double play depth, double steal, double switch, drag bunt, drive, ducks on the pond, dugout, dying quail
    earned run, earned run average, ERA, error, extra-base hit
    fadeaway, fadeaway slide, fair ball, fall classic, fan, farm, farm club, farm system, farm team, fastball, field, fielder, fielder's choice, fielding average, fireman, first base, first base coach, first baseman, fly, fly ball, fly out, follow through, force, force out, force play, forkball, foul, foul ball, foul line, foul out, foul pole, foul territory, foul tip, fourbagger, frame, free agent, free pass, free trip, fungo
    game-winning hit, gapper, glove, glove man, go-ahead run, gold glove, good eyes, gopher ball, grand slam, ground ball, grounder, groundout, ground rule double, ground rules, gun
    Hall of Fame, handle, hang, hardball, head-first slide, heat, heater, heavy hitter, hickory,

hidden-ball trick, high, high-and-inside, high-and-tight, high hard one, high heat, hill, hit, hit-and-run, hit batsman, hit by pitch, hit for the cycle, hitter, hit the corner, hold, hold the runner, home plate, homer, home run, home stand, hook, horsehide, hot corner, hot-stove league, hummer, hurler

infield, infield back, infielder, infield fly rule, infield hit, infield in, infield out, inning, inside, inside pitch, inside-the-park home run, insurance run, intentional walk, in the hole

junior circuit, junk, junkball pitcher

K, keystone, knock, knuckle ball, knuckleballer, knuckler

LCS, lead, lead off, leadoff hitter, league, league lead, League Championship Series, leather, leatherman, left field, left fielder, left-handed batter, left-hander, leg out a hit, line drive, line out, liner, line score, lineup, little league, load the bases, long relief, low, low-and-away, low-and-outside

major league, major leaguer, manager, middle relief, minor league, minor leaguer, mitt, most valuable player, mound, move, MVP

nail the runner, National League, night game, nine, NL, no hits, no runs, no errors, no-hitter

official at bat, on, on base, on base percentage, on deck, one-bagger, one-base hit, one-hitter, open stance, opposite field, out, outfield, outfielder, outside, outside pitch, overthrow

pass, passed ball, payoff pitch, peg, pennant, pennant race, pepper, perfect game, pick-off, pick-off move, pill, pinch-hit, pinch hitter, pine tar, pitch, pitcher, pitcher's mound, pitchout, pivot, plate, play ball, pocket, Pony League, pop, pop fly, pop-up, power hitter, prospect, pull, pull hitter, pull the string, punch, put-out

rain check, rain delay, rainout, rally, rbi, reached on error, relay, relief pitcher, reliever, retire the batter, rhubarb, ribby, rife, right field, right fielder, right-handed batter, righthander, rip, road trip, rocket, rookie, Rookie-of-the-Year, rosin bag, rotation, Rotisserie League, rounders, round-tripper, rubber, rube, run, run batted in, rundown, runless, runner, runners at the corners, running catch, run through the sign

sack, sacrifice, sacrifice bunt, sacrifice fly, safe, safety squeeze, sandlot, save, score, scorecard, scorekeeper, scoring position, scout, scratch hit, screwball, scuff, season, second base, second baseman, senior circuit, series, shag, shell the pitcher, shift, shinguard, shoestring catch, short relief, shortstop, show, shutout, side, sidearm, single, sinker, slam, slice, slide, slider, slow pitch softball, slug, slugfest, slugger, slugging percentage, slurve, smash, smoke, softball, southpaw, speed gun, spitball, spitter, split-fingered fastball, spring training, squeeze bunt, squeeze play, stadium, stand, starter, steal, stickball, stolen base, stoopball, stopper, straightaway, stretch, stretch drive, strike, strikeout, strike zone, stroke, stuff, suicide squeeze, swat, swing, swinging strike, swipe, switch hit, switch-hitter

tag, tag up, take, take an extra base, take the pitch, tee off, Texas leaguer, third base, third base coach, third baseman, three-bagger, three-base hit, three up, three down, throw, throw behind the runner, throw out, tip, top,

top of the inning, toss, total bases, trap, trip, trip to the mound, trip to the plate, triple, triple-A, Triple Crown, triple-header, triple play, turn a double play, tweener, twin bill, twi-night, twirler, two-bagger, two-base hit

ump, umpire, uncork, underarm, underhand, unearned run, up, up-and-in, uppercut, upper deck, upswing, utilityman

waivers, walk, warmup, warning track, webbing, wheel, wheels, whiff, wide, wild pitch, win, windup, winning percentage, World Series

yield

Basketball

basketball game played between two teams of five players each on a rectangular court with a raised basket at each end, points being scored by shooting a round, inflated ball through the opponent's basket

air ball, alley-oop, assist, at the buzzer

backboard, backcourt, backcourt foul, backcourt violation, bank, bank shot, baseline, basket, basketball, bench, block, blocked shot, blocking, boards, bonus situation, bounce pass, boxing out, break, breakaway foul, brick, bucket

carom, carrying-over, center, charge, charging, charity stripe, cherry pick, chest pass, coast-to-coast, cold, continuation, conversion, cords, court, courtside, crosscourt pass

dead ball foul, defensive rebound, delay of game, deliberate foul, dish, disqualification, double dribble, double pump, double-team, downtown, draw iron, dribble, drive, dunk, dunk shot

ejection, elbow, endline

fadeaway, fadeaway jumper, fast break, field, field goal, field goal percentage, fill the lanes, Final Four, finger roll, five second violation, flagrant foul, follow shot, forty-five second clock, forward, foul, foul line, foul out, foul shot, free throw, free throw attempt, free throw lane, free throw line, front, front court, full-court press

give-and-go, glass, goaltending, guard, gun

hack, half-court game, hand check, hanging on the rim, hang time, high post, hit, holding, home court, home court advantage, hook shot, hoop

illegal defense, in and out, inbounds, inbounds pass, inside, in your face, iron

jam, jump ball, jump circle, jumper, jump shot

key

lane, lane violation, lay-up, line, loose ball foul, low post

man-to-man defense

National Basketball Association, National Invitation Tournament, NBA, net, NIT, no-look pass

offensive foul, offensive rebound, off guard, off the dribble, one-on-one, outlet pass, outside, over the limit, over the top

paint, palming, pass, penetration, perimeter, perimeter shooting, personal foul, pick, pick-and-roll, pivot, platoon, playmaker, point, point guard, post, post position, post up, power forward, press

quarter

reaching in, rebound, rejection, reverse dunk, rim, rotation, run-and-gun

screen, set a pick, set a screen, set shot, shoot, shooter, shot, shot clock, shot selection, sixth man, skyhook, slam dunk, small forward, spot up, steal, stuff, swingman, swish, switch

tap-in, team foul, team rebound, technical foul, ten-second rule, three-point line, three-point play, three-point shot, three-second violation, tip-in, tipoff, top of the key, touch, transition, transition game, trap, trap defense, traveling, triple double, turnaround jumper, turnover, twenty-four second clock, twenty second timeout

uptempo game

walking

yo-yo

zone defense

Bowling

bowling game in which a heavy ball is rolled down an alley toward ten pins standing in a triangular pattern, the object being to knock down all the pins at once

alley

bedposts, boccie, break

candlepins

duckpins

foul line, frame

guide marks, gutter

hook

kingpin

lane, lawn bowling, league bowling

open

perfect game, pin, pinsetter, pocket, poodle

scratch, seven-ten split, skip, spare, split, strike

tenpin, triple, turkey

Boxing and Wrestling

boxing contest between two fighters who punch each other with gloved fists over the designated number of rounds or until one has been knocked out

wrestling contest between two opponents who struggle hand to hand in order to pin each other's shoulders to a mat, held under varying styles and rules

airplane spin, apron, arm wrestling

back-pedal, bantamweight, bareknuckle, bicycle, body slam, bout, boxer, break, bum, butt

canvas, card, cauliflower ear, clinch, club fighter, combination, contender, corner, count, counterpunch, cross, crown, cut man

dance, decision, dive, draw, duck

fall, featherweight, fight, fighter, fisticuffs, flyweight, footwork, freestyle wrestling, full nelson

glass chin, glass jaw, glove, Golden Gloves, gouge, Greco-Roman wrestling, guard

half nelson, hammerlock, handler, hand lock, haymaker, headlock, heavyweight, hook

Indian wrestling

jab, judge, junior weight

kayo, kick boxing, kidney punch, knockdown, knockout, KO

lace finger, left, light heavyweight, lightweight, lock, low blow

Marquis of Queensberry rules, mat, match, middleweight
nelson, neutral corner
one-two, on the ropes
pin, point, prefight instructions, preliminary, press, prizefight, prizefighter, promoter, pug, pugilism, pugilist, puncher, punching bag, punchy
rabbit punch, rassling, referee, reversal, right, ring, ringside, roadwork, rope-a-dope, ropes, round, roundhouse
scissors, scissors hold, second, semifinal, shadowbox, sleeper hold, slugfest, spar, sparring partner, speed bag, speed work, split decision, stop, stranglehold, sumo wrestling
tag team, takedown, tandem, technical knockout, ten point must system, throw, thumb, title fight, titleholder, titlist, TKO, toehold, trainer, trunks
undercard, unranked, uppercut
weigh-in, welterweight, white hope, windmill, wrestler, wristlock

Football

football game in which two opposing teams of eleven players each defend goals at opposite ends of a 100-yard rectangular field, points being scored by carrying an inflated oval ball across the opponent's goal line or by kicking this ball over the crossbar between the posts of the opponent's goal

AFC, American Football Conference, armchair quarterback, audible, automatic
back, backfield, backfield in motion, back judge, ball-carrier, batting the ball, blindside, blitz, block, blocker, blocking back, bomb, bootleg, bowl, bowl game, breakaway, bring a load, broken field, bump and run, buttonhook
Canadian Football League, carry, catch, center, CFL, chair pattern, cheap shot, chip shot, clip, clipping, clothesline tackle, coffin corner, completion, conversion, convert, cornerback, corner pattern, Cotton Bowl, counterplay, coverage, crackback, crawling, crossbar, cut, cutback, cutoff block
deep, defense, defensive back, defensive coordinator, defensive end, defensive tackle, delay, dive play, double-team, down, down-and-out, downfield, down lineman, draft, draft pick, draw, draw play, drive, drive block, drop back, drop kick
eat the ball, encroachment, end, end around, end line, end run, end zone
face mask, fade, fair catch, fake, field goal, field judge, first-and-goal, first down, flanker, flanker back, flare pass, flare pattern, flat pass, flats, fleaflicker, flex, flex defense, flow, fly pattern, football, footballer, football player, formation, forward pass, fourth down, free kick, free safety, fullback, fumble
gain, game plan, gap, goal line, goal line stand, goalpost, goal-to-go, grass drills, Grey Cup, gridder, gridiron, guard
Hail Mary pass, halfback, halftime, hand-off, hash mark, head linesman, Heisman Trophy, helmet, hit, holding, hook pattern, huddle
I formation, illegal motion, inbounds, ineligible receiver, in motion, in play, inside, inside linebacker, instant replay, intentional grounding, interception, interference

juke, jump pass
keeper, kick, kicker, kickoff, kickoff return, kick return specialist
lateral, left side, line, linebacker, line judge, lineman, line of scrimmage, linesman, look-in pass
man-to-man defense, middle linebacker, misdirection, Monday morning quarterback, motion, muff
National Football Conference, National Football League, neutral zone, NFC, NFL, nickel defense, no-huddle offense, nose guard, nose tackle
offensive coordinator, offensive lineman, official, offside, off tackle, onside kick, open field, option, Orange Bowl, outlet pass, out-of-bounds, out-of-play, outside linebacker
pass, PAT, pay dirt, penalty, personal foul, physical, pigskin, pileup, pitchout, pits, place kick, placekicker, placement, platoon, play-action pass, playbook, pluggers, pocket, point after touchdown, post pattern, power play, power sweep, prevent defense, Pro Bowl, pulling guard, punt, punter, punt formation, punt return
quarter, quarterback, quarterback sneak, quick kick, quick read, quick release
read, receiver, reception, red-dog, red zone, ref, referee, release, replay official, return, reverse, right side, ring his bell, roll, rollout, Rose Bowl, run, run-and-shoot, runback, runner, running back, running play, rush, rushing
sack, safety, safety blitz, sandwich, scatback, scramble, screen pass, scrimmage, seam, secondary, second down, set position, shift, short, short yardage, shotgun, shovel pass, side judge, sideline, single wing, slant, snap, sneak, soccer-style kicker, special teams, spike, spiral, split backs, split end, spread formation, sprint-out, squib kick, Statue of Liberty play, stick-um, stiff-arm, straight-arm, strong left, strong right, strong safety, strong side, stunt, stutter step, sudden death, Sugar Bowl, suicide squad, Super Bowl, sweep, swing pass, swivel hips
tackle, tailback, taxi squad, TD, T formation, third down, throw, tight end, touchback, touchdown, touch football, touch-tackle, trap, trap block, trenches, triple option, triple threat, try for point, turf, turnover, two-minute warning
umpire, unnecessary roughness, unsportsmanlike conduct, upfield, upright, up the middle
veer offense
weak safety, weak side, wedge, wide receiver, wig-wag, wind field, wingback, wishbone
yardage, yard line, yards gained, yards per carry
zebra, zone, zone defense

Golf

golf game in which a small, white ball is struck with wooden or metal-headed clubs over a course of usu. eighteen holes placed at some distance from one another around natural or artificial obstacles, the object being to sink the ball into each successive hole in as few strokes as possible

address the ball, approach shot, apron
back nine, backspin, backswing, bag, best-ball foursome, best-ball match, birdie, bisque, bogey, brassie, bunker
caddie, carry, chip, chip shot, club, clubhouse, country club, course, cup, cut shot
divot, dogleg, dormie, double bogey, double eagle, downswing, drive, driver, driving range, drop, dub, duffer
eagle, eighteen holes
fade, fairway, fairway trap, fairway wood, flag, flagstick, follow-through, foozle, fore, foursome, fringe, front nine
gallery, gimme, golden ferret, golf ball, golf club, golf course, golf widow, Grand Slam, green, greens fee, grip
hacker, handicap, hazard, heel, hit up, hole, hole in one, hole out, hook
iron
leader board, lie, links, lip, loft
mashie, Masters, match play, medal play, mulligan
nassau, niblick, nineteenth hole
out-of-bounds, overplay, overshoot
par, pass-through, penalty stroke, pill, pin, pin high, pitch shot, play through, plus fours, press, pro-am, pull, putt, putter, putting green, putt out
rim, rough, round, run
sand trap, sclaff, shaft, shag, shank, shoot, skull shot, slice, slope, snap hook, spoon, stableford, stance, stroke, stroke play, stymie, swipe
tee, tee off, tee shot, three-ball match, threesome, toe, top, topspin, trap, triple bogey, twosome
unplayable lie
waggle, water hazard, wave up, wedge, wiff, wood
yips

Gymnastics and Calisthenics

calisthenics conditioning exercises usu. performed with little or no special apparatus
gymnastics performance of physical exercises that require strength, balance, and agility, esp. on special apparatus, usu. in judged competition
ariel
backflip, balance beam
chin-up, crossbar, crunch
dismount
flip, floor exercise, freestyle
gymnast
handspring, handstand, high bar, horizontal bar, horse
Indian club, iron cross
jumping jack
parallel bars, pommel horse, pull-up, push-up
rings, roadwork
scissors, setting-up exercises, sit-up, somersault, springboard, straddle
tilt board, trapeze, tuck, twist
uneven bars
vault, vaulting horse
walkover

Hockey

hockey game played on round-ended rectangle of ice between two teams of six skaters each, object being to shoot a hard rubber puck past defenders and goalkeeper into opponent's net using bent wooden stick

assist
back-check, blades, blue line, board check, boards, body check, break, breakaway goal
Campbell Conference, center, change-on-the-fly, charging, check, chippy, crease, cross-check, cross-ice
defenseman, draw, dribble, drop pass
empty net goal, end
face, face mask, face-off, fore-check, forward
glove save, goal, goalie, goalkeeper, goaltender, goon
hat trick, high-sticking, hip-check, holding, hooking
icing, interference
left wing, line, line change, linesman
major penalty, minor penalty
National Hockey League, net, neutral zone, NHL
offside
pass, penalty, penalty box, penalty killer, penalty shot, period, playmaker, point, power play, puck
rebound shot, red light, red line, right wing, rink, roughing
save, shorthanded, shot on goal, skate, slap shot, slashing, spearing, Stanley Cup, stick, sticked, stickhandler, stickhandling, stick save
tripping, T-stop
Wales Conference, white line, wing
Zamboni machine, zone

Horse and Dog Racing

dog racing contest of speed over track between dogs, usu. chasing a mechanical rabbit
horse racing contest of speed over oval track between horses either ridden by jockeys or pulling sulkies and their drivers

allowance race, also-ran
backstretch, Belmont Stakes, blind bet, blinders, blinkers, box bet, boxed-out, break, break away, break-from-the-gate, break stride, Breeder's Cup, buggy
chicane, claiming race, closer, colors, course
daily double, derby, distance, double play
exacta
fast track, favorite, feature race, filly, finish line, furlong, futurity
gelding, grandstand, grass, greyhound
handicapping, handle, head
jock, jockey, juvenile
Kentucky Derby
length, long shot
maiden race, mudder
neck, neck and neck, nose
odds-on favorite, off and running, offtrack betting, OTB
pacer, paddock, parimutuel, parlay, perfecta, photo finish, place, post, post race, post time, Preakness, prohibitive favorite
quarter horse, quinella
rabbit, race, racecourse, racehorse, racetrack, racing form, railbird
saddle, saddling barn, scramble, short odds, show, silks, simulcast, sire, speed horse, stable, stake horse, stake race, starting gate, starting price, steeplechase, steward, stretch, stretch run, stretch runner, string, stud, sulky
thoroughbred, tote, trainer, trial horse, trifecta,

Triple Crown, trotter, turf, turfman, turn, twin double
walking ring, walkover, water jump, weigh-in, wheel bet, whip, win, winner's circle, wire, wire-to-wire
yearling

Ice Skating

artistic impression aesthetics of a skating program, especially the judges' opinion of a skater's ability to keep time with the music, interpret the music, etc.
axel jump made from the front outer edge of one skate, followed by 1 1/2 turns, landing on the back outer edge of the other skate [for Axel Paulsen, Norwegian skater who popularized it]
broken leg spin sit spin in which the skater's extended leg is bent at the knee and held off to the side
butterfly movement in which the skater jumps into the air and arches the back while extending both the arms and legs and throwing back the head
camel spin spin made with the skater's body bent forward at the waist so that the upper body, with one leg extended behind the skater, is parallel to the ice
choctaw turn in which the skater changes from the outside edge of one skate to the inside edge of the other, or from the inside edge of one skate to the outside edge of the other
crossing straight straightaway area opposite the starting line in speed skating, where skaters must change lanes
compulsory (school) figures patterns made on the ice by the skate blade, as circles, figure eights, etc., required of competitive skaters
death spiral pair-skating movement in which the man pivots while holding the hand of the woman, who lowers her body to a horizontal position while skating a circle around her partner
double jump jump in which the skater makes two complete revolutions in the air
free dance ice dancing program that combines elements of set dances with free skating movements and usually features intricate footwork
free skating (program) skating that includes a variety of figures, movements, steps, and jumps, choreographed to express the mood of the accompanying music
freestyle informal name for free skating
Hamill camel spin that starts as a back camel spin and finishes as a back sit spin [for US skater Dorothy Hamill]
ice dancing skating by a man and woman together who execute certain steps in tempo with the music, usually traditional ballroom dance music
layback spin spin in which the skater bends backward at the waist
lift pair skating movement in which the woman is held above the ice by her partner

long program informal name for the free skating program
Lutz jump made from the back outer edge of one skate with an assist from the toe pick of the other skate, followed by one full rotation in the air and a landing on the back outer edge of the opposite skate [for Austrian skater Alois Lutz]
mohawk turn in which the skater goes from one skate's inside edge to the inside edge of the other skate, or from the outside edge of one skate to the outside edge of the other
pair skating skating by a man and woman together with the partners assisting one another in lifts and spins
precision skating skating performed by a group of skaters who interweave complex patterns
quadruple jump jump in which a skater completes four rotations in the air
Salchow jump in which the skater takes off from a back inside edge, swinging the other leg in front to assist the rotation [for Swedish skater Ulrich Salchow]
school figures compulsory figures
score (marks) in competitive skating, skaters are given two sets of marks—one for technical merit and one for artistic impression—with 6.0 as the highest possible mark
scratch spin fast upright spin in which the toe pick slightly scratches the ice
set pattern dance ice dance following a prescribed pattern for a particular type of dance (waltz, tango, rumba, etc.)
shadow skating skating by a pair who perform the same movements but do not touch
short program skating program of seven skating movements chosen by the officials, lasting no more than two minutes, in which the skater chooses the order of the movements and the music
sit spin spin in which the skater spins on one skate while in a squatting position, usually with the other leg extended straight in front of the body; also called the Haines spin [for US skater Jackson Haines]
spiral skating movement in which one leg is held extended behind the skater higher than the hip level
spread eagle skating position in which the skater's feet are turned outward, with the toes pointing in opposite directions
technical merit composition of a skating program, especially the judges' opinion on the difficulty and execution of the program
three jump jump in which the skater takes off on the right skate, makes half a turn in the air, and lands on the left skate; also called a waltz jump
three turn semicircular turn with a slight dip in the middle done on one skate, resembling a figure three
(toe) loop jump made from the back outer edge of the skate with a jab of the other toe pick into the ice, after which the skater makes one or

more complete turns in the air before landing on the back outer edge of the same skate
toe picks (or rakes) sharp serrated edges on the front of the blades of skates
triple jump jump in which the skater's body turns three revolutions while in the air
Walley jump in which the skater takes off from one skate's back inside edge, makes one turn in the air, and lands on the same skate's back outside edge; also called the low [for US skater Nate Walley]

Skiing

skiing racing over snow on a pair of long, narrow runners of wood, plastic, or steel; maneuvering between obstacles or jumping for distance on such runners over snow

Alpine skiing, au alement
bathtub, bunny
cement, chairlift, christie, cover, cross-country skiing
downhill
fall line
gate, giant slalom
hot dog
jumping
kick turn
langlauf
mogul
Nordic skiing
off-piste
piste, powder
rope tow
schuss, ski, ski bob, ski boots, skijoring, ski jump, ski lift, ski mask, ski pants, ski pole, ski run, ski suit, ski tow, slalom, snowplow, stem, stem turn, super giant slalom, swing
telemark, traverse, tuck
unweight
Vorlage
wedeln, wedge

Soccer

soccer game played between two teams of eleven players each on a long rectangular field in which a round inflated ball is advanced by kicking or bouncing it off any part of the anatomy except the hands and arms, the object being to put the ball in the opponent's net, which is defended by a goalkeeper who may use his hands to stop shots

association football
center, corner kick, crossbar
defenseman, dribble
football, footballer, forward, free kick, fullback
goal, goalie, goalkeeper, goal kick, goal kicker, goalmouth, goaltender
halfback, hat trick, header
kickoff
left wing, linesman
midfield, midfielder
NASL, North American Soccer League, nutmeg
offside
pass, penalty, penalty kick
red card, right wing, roughing
tiebreaker, touchline
volley

winger, World Cup
yellow card
zone

Surfing

surfing riding shoreline ocean waves while standing on a long, shaped board of wood or foam and fiberglass coated with resin, sometimes in judged competition

aggro
baggies, barney, beach break, bellyboard, board, body surf, body whomping, boogie board
choppy, close out, come up, crank a turn, crash and burn, curl
ding, drop, drop in
flat
glass-off, glassy, gnarly, goofy-foot, gremmie, gun
hang five, hang ten, ho-dad, hot curl, hot dog
jams
kick-out
leash, left, lineup, locked in, long board
noseride, noserider
offshore wind, onshore wind, outside, overhead
paddleboard, pearl
quasimodo
radical turn, rail, reef break, right, rip
set, shaper, shoot the curl, shoot the pier, shoot the tube, shore break, short board, stoked, surfboard, surfer, surfriding, swell
thruster, tube, tubed, turn
wahine, walk the nose, wall, wet suit, wipeout

Swimming and Diving

diving judged competition in which contestants plunge headfirst into water after leaping from an elevated platform and performing specified maneuvers in the air
swimming racing contest in which swimmers propel themselves across surface of water over designated distance, usu. in one of four strokes

back dive, backstroke, bathing cap, belly flop, breaststroke, butterfly
cannonball, crawl
diver, diving board, dolphin kick
flip turn, flutterboard, flutter kick, freestyle, frog kick, full gainer
gainer
half gainer, heat
individual medley
jackknife
kick lap, kick turn
medley relay
overarm
paddleboard, pike position, platform diving, pool, poolside
scissors kick, scull stroke, sidestroke, splits, springboard diving, starting block, stroke, swan dive, swimming pool, synchronized swimming
triathlon, tuck, twist
whip kick

Tennis

tennis game played on a rectangular court between two players or pairs of players who

use strung rackets to bat a small, hollow ball back and forth across a low net that divides the court in half, the object being to place an unreturnable shot within the opponent's half of court

ace, advantage, approach
backcourt, backhand, backspin, backstroke, ball boy, baseline, bisque, break, break point, break service
charge the net, clay court, country club, courtside, crosscourt
deuce, dink, double fault, doubles, drop shot
fault, fifteen, follow-through, footwork, forecourt, forehand, forty
game point, good, Grand Slam, grass court, ground stroke
hack, hard court
lawn tennis, let, line judge, linesman, lob, long, love
match, match point, mishit, mixed doubles
net, netball, net judge, netman
on serve, overhand, overhead smash
paddle, passing shot, placement, placement shot
racket, racquet, rally, retrieve, return
seed, serve, server, service, service break, service court, set, set point, sideline, singles, skein, slice, stop volley, stroke
tennis ball, tennis elbow, tennis shoe, thirty, tiebreaker, topspin
undercut, unforced error
volley
webbing, Wimbledon

Track and Field

track and field indoor or outdoor contest made up of several competitive events, including running races, hurdling, vaulting, jumping, and tossing objects

anchor, anchor lap
baton, break, broad jump
cinder track, cross-country
dash, decathlon, discus, distance medley, distance runner, distance work
fast start, field event, finish line, flying start, Fosbury flop
get set, go, gun lap
hammer throw, heat, heptathlon, high hurdles, high jump, homestretch, hop, step, and jump, hurdles
individual medley, infield, intermediate hurdles
javelin
kick
lap, long jump, low hurdles
marathon, medley relay, metric mile, middle distance, miler
neck and neck
on your mark
pacesetter, pentathlon, pole vault, prelim, pull up, put
qualifying race
relay, run, running start
shakedowns, shot put, speed work, splits, sprint, start, starter, starting block, steeplechase, stopwatch, straddle, straightaway
thin clads, time trial, track meet, track shoe, track suit, triple jump
walk, water jump, weightman, wind sprint

Hunting Practice and Techniques

airplane hunting hunting with shotgun and usu. .00 buck from airborne craft, illegal except for game control officers

archery hunting with bow and arrow

bag (*vb*) *Informal.* kill or capture game; (*n*) amount of game taken during one hunting trip

battue *Chiefly Brit.* beating ground to drive game from cover

bay position of stag or any cornered animal that has turned to face pursuers

beagling hunting with beagle hounds, esp. for cottontail or rabbit

beater person who flushes game birds or hoofed game to guns

big game any large game that is hunted, esp. deer, elk, bear, moose, bison, caribou, antelope, sheep, mountain goat, mountain lion, jaguar, peccary, or wild hog

blooding *Chiefly Brit.* smearing of initiate's face with blood of first fox or stag he or she has seen killed

blood sport any sport in which animals are killed, esp. hunting

boat hunting shooting game from a boat

bow hunting hunting with bow and arrow

canoe hunting hunting in areas reached by canoe on inland waterway but inaccessible overland

chase act of searching out and pursuing game and wild animals for purpose of killing them; *Chiefly Brit.* private game preserve, sometimes stocked with animals and birds to be hunted

chasse gardée *French.* private hunting preserve

chevy *Chiefly Brit.* hunting cry; a hunt

closed (*adj*) restricted as to permissible time, place, and game that may be hunted

closed season time of year when hunting for particular game is prohibited

cold scent scent left by quarry some length of time before hounds pick it up

competition shooting skeet, trap, or target shooting as competitive event

coon hunting hunting for racoons with hounds, usu. at night

course (*vb*) hunt game with dogs by sight rather than scent

covert hiding place of fox or upland game, esp. shrubs or thicket

curing preparing of animal flesh for preservation, usu. by drying or salting

dead set stiff posture of hunting dog indicating presence and location of game

drag scent left by fox or other animal

dress (*vb*) cut up, trim, and remove skin, feathers, and viscera from game prior to storage or transportation

drive portion of hunt in which beaters drive birds over hunters or in which deer are driven toward concealed standers

earth (*vb*) chase an animal into its burrow or den

falconer person who practices falconry

falconry hunting with falcons, hawks, or eagles; training hawks to hunt

fault loss of scent; break in line of scent

ferreting using ferrets to drive rabbits and other rodents from underground

fetch (*vb*) of hunting dogs, retrieve game

field dressing rough dressing of game, often hung from tree, immediately after killing

flush (*vb*) cause game, esp. birds, to break cover or take flight

foil (*vb*) *Chiefly Brit.* obscure scent with another scent

fowl hunting hunting of waterfowl

fox hunting traditional sport in which mounted hunters follow hounds in pursuit of fox

game wild animals and birds that are hunted and killed for sport and/or meat

game birds hunted land birds, esp. blackcock, capercaillie, dove, grouse, partridge, pheasant, pigeon, ptarmigan, quail, snipe, turkey, wild turkey, and woodcock

gamekeeper person employed to maintain game preserve, prevent poaching, and nurture animal life

game preserve area set aside for propagation of game

gillie *Scottish.* hunting or fishing guide

give tongue of hounds, bay while following a scent

gunning hunting of game with shotgun, not rifle

hounds pack of hounds used for hunting; huntsman's call to hounds

hunt (*vb*) pursue or search for game for purpose of catching or killing it; (*n*) act or practice of hunting game or other wild animals

hunter person who hunts game or other wild animals, esp. for sport

hunter's moon first full moon after harvest moon, in late September or early October

hunting practice and techniques associated with the pursuit and search for game for purpose of killing them

hunting ground region set aside for hunting game

huntress woman who hunts

huntsman hunter; manager of hounds during hunt

hunt's-up call formerly played on hunting horn to rouse participants in hunt

incomer duck or pheasant that flies directly toward shooter

kill end of run in which quarry, esp. fox, is caught and killed; any dead game

limit maximum number of game that may legally be taken in designated time or locale

open season time of year when hunting for certain game is permitted

plinking shooting at tine cans or other stationary targets with handgun

poach (*vb*) hunt or kill game illegally on another's property or preserve

poacher one who poaches game

point (*vb*) of hunting dog, stand rigid, facing in direction of located game to indicate its position; (*n*) *Chiefly Brit.* distance between two extreme ends of hunt in straight line

predator any animal that exists by hunting other animals for food, esp. bobcat, coyote, crow, fox, lynx, skunk, or wolf

preserve area designated for maintenance of game for hunting

prey hunted animal

pursuit act of following game so as to overtake and kill it

quarry game hunted, esp. by hounds or falconry

quartering cutting up of carcass of killed game into four pieces prior to transporting it

quest (*vb*) of hunting dogs, bay or give tongue in pursuit of game, search for game

reloading making of one's own bullets from shell casings, powder, and primer

retrieve (*vb*) of hunting dogs, fetch killed or wounded game

riot (*vb*) pursue animal other than intended quarry

safari hunting expedition for big game in Africa

scent distinctive odor left by animal that has passed, used by dogs in tracking prey

season legally designated time of year when specific game may be hunted in given region

set (*vb*) of hunting dogs, indicate position of game by standing stiffly and pointing muzzle

shikari person who hunts big game, esp. professional guide or hunter (India)

shoot trap or skeet shoot; *Chiefly Brit.* hunting expedition, esp. for game

shooting hunting with a gun for sport

shorebirds hunted birds that live by water, esp. curlew, plover, snipe, rail, gallinule, and yellowlegs

skeet shooting trapshooting in which clay targets are propelled singly or in pairs from several different positions at varying heights and speeds to simulate flight of game birds

small game any small, wild animal that is hunted, such as hare, rabbit, racoon, squirrel, woodchuck, groundhog, opossum, or prairie dog

snap (*vb*) fire shot without raising gun to eyes to aim; fire gun on an empty chamber

sporting (*adj*) engaging in or related to open-air sports such as hunting and fishing

sportsman person who engages in open-air sports such as hunting and fishing, esp. with sense of fairness and courtesy

spring (*vb*) *Chiefly Brit.* flush game bird from cover

stalking following prey or quarry closely with intent to kill or capture, esp. hunting game in open, broken country with little or no cover, as in stag hunting

stander hunter with gun over whom beater drives birds or toward whom deer hunter pushes deer

still-hunt (*vb*) hunt game alone, usu. in heavy, wooded cover and as silently as possible, esp. without a dog

surround hunting method in which prey is chased into location where it is encircled and cannot escape

tanning process of converting hides into leather

track (*vb*) follow scent left by animal

tracking pursuing prey by following readable track or physical markings, or by using hounds to follow scent

trapper one who engages in trapping

trapping capturing game and wildfowl by setting mechanical contrivance that springs shut when triggered

trapshooting shooting at clay pigeons hurled into air from mechanical trap

upland game birds hunted game birds such as grouse, pheasant, pigeon, quail, and wild turkey

venatic (*adj*) of or pertaining to hunting

venery *Archaic.* sport of hunting

waders hunted wildfowl, such as coots, curlews, and plovers, found in shallow waters

warrantable (*adj*) of legal age for being hunted, esp. deer

waterfowl hunted birds that live on water, such as brant, bufflehead, canvasback, coot, duck, eider, gadwall, goose, mallard, scoter, shoveler, teal

white hunter person who guides big game hunters in Africa

wildfowl hunted game birds such as wild ducks, geese, swans, or waders

wild fowling hunting wildfowl such as ducks, geese, or waders

wildlife management organized protection, preservation, and propagation of game and other wild animals

winged predators birds that live by feeding on other animals, such as crow, eagle, hawk, jaeger, or owl

woodsman person skilled at hunting and trapping

Fox Hunting

all on cry of whipper-in indicating that all hounds are accounted for

bait (*vb*) set dogs on prey

bolt (*vb*) force fox out of hiding place into open

call sound made on horn to encourage hounds

capping fee fee paid to hunter's association by nonmember for one day's hunting rights

carry (*vb*) hold or catch scent

challenge cry of hound on picking up scent

chop (*vb*) attack and kill fox that has not begun to run; mob

course (*vb*) run fox into full view

crop whip

cry (*vb*) of hounds, bay continuously while following scent

entered hound foxhound that has hunted in prior seasons

find discovery of prey, esp. fox

foxhound hound

fox hunting traditional sport in which mounted hunters follow hounds in pursuit of fox

gone away huntsman's cry indicating hounds are in pursuit and hunt is on

groom person who cares for horses used in fox hunting

halloa huntsman's cry used to incite hounds

hound breed of dog trained to pursue game by scent, used esp. in fox hunting; foxhound

hounds pack of hounds used for hunting; huntsman's call to hounds

hunting with hounds fox hunting

line trail of scent left by fox

mob (*vb*) chop

mort note played on hunting horn signifying that hunted animal has been killed

mute (*adj*) of a hound, following scent of fox without crying out

pink coat usu. scarlet coat worn by members of fox hunt

ratcatcher *Chiefly Brit.* informal costume, usu. tweed jacket and tan riding breeches, worn while fox hunting

run chase of fox from find to kill

run at hounds engage in fox hunting with hounds

tally ho cry of huntsman indicating that fox or other prey has been sighted

tantivy cry of huntsman when chase is at full tilt

thruster rider who remains at front of field in fox hunt

view halloa cry of huntsman on seeing fox break cover

whip whipper-in

whipper-in member of hunt responsible for hounds; whip

worry action of hounds in tearing fox carcass apart

yoicks huntsman's cry used to encourage hounds

Hunting Equipment

action mechanism by which firearm is operated

blind hiding place for hunting ducks or geese

block *Slang.* set of decoys

bow and arrow curved, flexible frame bent by string stretched between its ends to fire pointed shafts

bow net clam-shaped net that springs shut to trap hawks, usu. baited with pigeon

buckshot lead shot, larger than BB, used in shotgun shells for hunting deer, boar, and similar game

butt stand concealed by thicket or sunk in ground and used for shooting driven birds

camouflage clothing or other gear made of material with mottled design in brown and green that simulates forest environment

coursing hound hound used to run game into view, such as greyhound, whippet, or Afghan

cover underbrush or woods that conceal wild animal

deadfall trap in which disturbance of bait triggers fall of heavy weight onto prey

decoy lifelike dummy or model of hunted species, esp. game bird or wildfowl, set out to attract others of species; trained bird or animal used for same purpose, now illegal

double-O buck common buckshot, used esp. for hunting deer

float flat-bottomed, wide boat such as johnboat, used for hunting shorebirds and waterfowl

floating blind boatlike concealment used for hunting ducks or geese

gamebag bag with shoulder strap, usu. of canvas or leather, used to carry dead game birds

goose block set of decoys used to attract geese

hakapik iron or steel hook on long wooden pole, used in seal hunting

hide *Chiefly Brit.* small place of concealment for gun, built esp. of straw or camouflage netting

hip boots waterproof boots reaching to midthigh or hips, used for wading through water

hood cover for a hawk's head, used in falconry when bird is not pursuing game

hound breed of dog trained to pursue game by scent, used esp. in fox hunting

hunting box *Chiefly Brit.* house in hunting area used during hunting season

hunting dogs any dog used for hunting game, such as pointers, retrievers, setters, hounds, spaniels, beagles, bassets, and weimaraners

hunting horn small copper horn carried by huntsman during fox hunt

hunting knife large, sturdy knife with blade curved toward tip, used to skin and dress game

hunting scope telescopic sight on hunting rifle

jacklight portable lantern or electric light used to spot game at night and transfix it while hunter shoots, generally illegal

license formal permission authorizing bearer to hunt in specified place or time or for specific game

lure feathered decoy swung at end of line, sometimes baited with raw meat, used in falconry

natural blind natural growth or formation used as concealment while hunting ducks and geese

packhorse horse used for carrying equipment and supplies, esp. into remote hunting areas in mountains

pointer any of certain breeds of dog used for pointing birds

pointing dog any of various breeds of dog, including setters and Brittany spaniels, used for pointing game

profile decoy depicting bird in profile

purse net net with drawstring that fits over rabbit hole

rail boat low, flat-bottomed boat with protective rails, used in hunting waterfowl

recurve bow bow that is bent backward from its primary curvature at the tips

retriever dog used for retrieving game

rifle firearm with spiral grooves cut inside long bore, imparting more precise trajectory to bullet, usu. fired from shoulder

setter dog used to set game, including breeds such as longhaired pointing bird dogs

shooting stick devise resembling walking stick, with folding seat on one end and pointed tip, which is imbedded into ground

shotgun smoothbore firearm, often double-barreled, firing either single slug or multiple-pellet loads

silhouette two-dimensional representation of game animal or bird, used as target

snare nooselike trap used esp. for rabbits

spring trap trap that springs shut on prey when triggered

stool *Slang.* decoy, esp. set of decoys

straight bow bow that curves in one direction only

trap mechanical contrivance that springs shut or open when triggered by prey

trophy antlers, hide, or body part kept to memorialize successful hunt

tumbler dog similar to small greyhound, formerly used in rabbit hunting

waders waterproof boots reaching to mid-chest, used esp. by duck hunters for wading through water

Fishing Practice and Techniques

amadou absorbent fungus used to dry waterlogged dry flies

angle (*vb*) fish with hook and line

angler fisherman who is skilled in the art and practice of angling

angling art and practice of fishing with hook and line

backcast in fly casting, action of lifting line off the water through an upward and backward flip of fly rod's tip prior to forward cast of line that presents fly to quarry

backhand cast fly-fisherman's cast made across own body

backing between 100 and 250 yards of lighter, usu. braided line tied in behind heavier fly line as margin of safety against long run by big fish

backlash overrun of reel spool resulting in snarled line

bait casting casting of artificial lure or plug, as well as bait, with revolving-spool reel on fiberglass rod 4 to 7 feet long

beach (*vb*) bring fish in without net or gaff

beginner's luck initial success supposed to come to inexperienced and unskilled fishermen

bite action of fish taking hook and bait

boat (*vb*) bring fish into boat with net, gaff, or tailer

bottom-fishing fishing with live or dead bait for fish that are bottom feeders, such as ocean fish like flounder and sole or freshwater fish like catfish and carp

bowfishing shooting fish in shallow water with bow and arrow, esp. freshwater carp or bottom fish such as stingrays, skates, and sharks

casting act of projecting and placing artificial lure, fly, or bait within intended area and distance

catch all fish landed by an angler in one day

charter lease of boat by party for fishing expedition; any boat so leased

clamming digging for clams in mud flats and shallows with rake

closed season time of year when fishing for particular species is prohibited

coarse fishing *Chiefly Brit.* fishing for any freshwater fish other than salmon, trout, or grayling

cock (*vb*) of a float, turn up at one side; (*n*) male salmon or trout

crabbing fishing for crabs by dropping baited metal cage to bottom of water

dap (*vb*) allow fly to bounce lightly over surface of water using long rod up to 17 feet (5 m) in length

deep-sea fishing fishing from boat in ocean waters at some distance from shore

double haul fly casting technique used to achieve distance

drag unnatural movement of fly across water due to pull of current on line, often exceeding speed of current

drag adjustment device in reel mechanism that slows the pull of running fish

dress (*vb*) prepare a fly or bait a hook for use

drift-fishing fishing in which the fly's action is due entirely to current; still fishing with bait from a moving boat

electric fishing catching fish by submerging positive and negative electrodes, causing fish to swim toward positive electrode and become unconscious, illegal for sportfishing but used to move fish to other waters

false cast cast in which line and fly are prevented from hitting water by switching line forcefully back and forth

fillet (*vb*) remove flesh of fish from backbone in two strips for cooking

fingerling small trout

fish plural usage of fish except in scientific and technical context or to refer to several species, not individuals, where "fishes" is preferred

fish culture artificial breeding and propagation of fish to provide stock for angling or commercial sale

fisherman person who fishes, either for profit or pleasure

fishery fish hatchery

fish hatchery place where fish culture is carried out; fishery

fishing technique, practice, and diversion of catching fish for sport, usu. with line, hook, and rod

fishing banks shallow area of sea with abundant fish

fishing ground body of water designated, set aside, or preferred for commercial fishing

fish story *Informal.* exaggerated tale of fishing exploits

float-fishing river fishing in which boat continuously drifts while angler casts

fly-fishing method of fishing with artificial flies, in which weight of line, not lure, is propelled through air by switching it back and forth from a long rod to achieve velocity, with reel mounted below rod grip and used primarily to store line

freshwater fish most popular fish for freshwater fishing: esp. trout (brook, brown, golden, rainbow) also bass, bluegill, bullhead, carp, catfish, char, crappie, gar, grayling, perch, pike, salmon, sauger, shad, walleye, whitefish

game fish any species of fish that may legally be taken for sport and tends to resist capture

gentle craft sport of fishing or angling

greased line method fishing for salmon in stream with fly that sinks just beneath surface and plastic-coated line that floats with no drag; formerly, this line was greased to make it float

gut (*vb*) remove entrails from fish

hand line line that is pulled in by hand rather than reeled in, used esp. to extricate fish from weeds

harl (*vb*)*Chiefly Brit.* troll with flies, spoons, or prawn on a long line in boat or estuary or inland seaway, used. for salmon and sea trout

haul commercial catch, esp. all fish caught by seine in one day

hit strike

hole still, deep place in stream where fish feed; pool

hook (*vb*) catch fish when hook is planted in its mouth

horizontal cast method of casting line beneath overhanging branch or rock by swinging rod parallel to surface of water

ice fishing tecnique of fishing through a hole cut in ice, usu. in frozen lake in winter

jag (*vb*)*Informal.* touch fish with hook, but not hook it

jigging imparting up and down motion to lure or bait, esp. in ice fishing

keeper fish that is legally big enough to keep

kite fishing method of offshore fishing in which airborne kite trolls skipping bait or holds live bait at surface of water

lake fishing fishing in freshwater lake, from shore or by trolling from boat

land (*vb*) bring hooked fish in to shore or net

laying on *Chiefly Brit.* fishing in nearly still water by resting baited hook on bottom with half-cocked float

ledgering *Chiefly Brit.* type of fishing in which a ledger is used to hold bait on bottom

margin fishing technique of fishing under bank on side of lake toward which wind is blowing food by placing rod on rests and floating bait, which is blown back under bank

neck upstream end of pool

nibble response of fish preparing to take bait on line

nymph fishing most difficult form of wet-fly fishing, usu. for trout using nymphs cast upstream

permit official license granting an individual permission to fish

piscary place for fishing

piscatory (*adj*) relating to fishing or fishermen

play amount of slack in a line, allowing it to move freely in response to fish

playing fish maintaining proper tension on line to tire out and bring in fish without breaking line

plug casting bait casting using plug as lure

pool still, deep place in stream where fish feed; hole

present (*vb*) offer fly to fish by casting it

reef-fishing fishing on or from shallow ridge of rocks or sand in ocean

retrieve (*vb*) reel in or pull back fishing line by hand

rise act of fish coming to fly; circular ripples on water's surface indicating fish coming up to feed

roll cast fly-casting technique in which line does not go behind angler, used on streams with close overhangs

run (*vb*) of fish, take hook or bait and swim quickly away from fisherman

saltwater fish most popular fish, for saltwater fishing: esp. tuna, cod, salmon, and striped bass; also albacore, barracuda, blackfish, bluefish, croaker, dolphin, flounder, mackerel, marlin, pollock, pompano, red snapper, sailfish, shark, whiting

seiner commercial fisherman using seine

shoot line in fly casting, act of allowing forward cast of fly line to pull out extra loops of line held by noncasting hand, used to lengthen cast

sidearm cast cast performed by swinging rod parallel to ground at side of body, esp. to avoid overhang

sink-and-draw fishing with dead bait that is alternately allowed to sink, then drawn up to surface

skipper captain of boat

snag (*vb*) catch fly or lure in underwater obstruction or overhang when casting

snatch (*vb*) *Chiefly Brit.* use weighted triangle on hand line to poach fish

spin casting fishing with lure or bait and closed-face reel with fixed spool from which line peels off at end of long spinning rod, different from spinning

spin fishing spinning

spinning method of casting light lure with fixed-spool reel, mounted on underside of rod, in which line uncoils but spool remains stationary; spin fishing; thread-line fishing

sportfishing fishing for sport with rod and reel, usu. from motorboat for saltwater fish

squidding surf casting for squid

still fishing fishing with stationary bait from shore or boat

stock supply (stream or lake) with fish for fishing

stream fishing fishing in fresh waterway, either from shore or by standing in boots in water

strike moment when fish attacks and takes fly, lure, or bait and must be hooked; hit

surf casting technique and practice of using 8- to 12-foot spinning or bait-casting rod to cast heavy-duty line into sea while standing at shoreline

switch (*vb*) move fishing line with swift, lashing motion

tail downstream end of pool

take (*vb*) of fish, strike bait, lure, or fly and become hooked

taking fish fish rising to take bait, or one whose actions indicate it to be likely to strike

test designation for weight of line

thread-line fishing *Chiefly Brit.* spinning

tie (*vb*) design and make artificial fly

trawl (*vb*) fish by dragging net along bottom of sea, or with buoyed trawl line having numerous baited hooks spaced at intervals along it

troll (*vb*) tow baited hook or lure, either submerged or on surface, behind slow-moving boat, usu. in lake or sea

trolling fishing from slow-moving boat with lure or bait trailing behind at varying depths and speeds in lakes or saltwater

trotting angling in fast-moving water, using float and line that holds bait near bottom

tying art and practice of designing and making flies

underhand lob casting technique in which rod tip is raised vertically to propel bait or lure outward from fisherman

warp (*vb*) move boat about by pulling anchored rope

whaling hunting for and capturing whales with harpoons at sea

X designation for leader diameter in gut or monofilament, expressed in multiples of X

Fishing Equipment and Tackle

angleworm earthworm commonly used as live bait

antenna float float with long tip on top that shows above water surface

archer tackle spinning tackle used with dead bait

arlesey bomb streamlined ledger weight with swivel that slips through weeds

artificial bait object made to resemble fly, worm, fish, or animal and placed on hook

artificial fly imitation of fly, insect, or larva made from feathers, fur, silk, thread, and/or tinsel, with hook attached; fly

backlash snarled line on reel due to improper casting; bird's nest

bait living creatures such as minnows, earthworms, grubs, or grasshoppers attached to hook and used to entice fish into striking

bait-casting rod fiberglass rod for bait casting, usu. 5 to 6 feet (1.5 to 1.8 m) long

baitfish small fish such as minnow or shiner used as bait for larger fish

bait kettle *Chiefly Brit.* can used for carrying live bait

balanced tackle tackle used esp. in fly-fishing, in which relationship between rod action and reel-and-line weight is essential to effective casting

barb point projecting off hook in opposite direction from point, used to prevent fish from spitting out hook

barbless hook hook without barb, easier to remove from fish than barbed hook

barrel knot knot used esp. for fastening together two strands of leader gut or monofilament; blood knot

barrel swivel swivel consisting of two connected eyes, used to absorb twisting of line

bass bug large fly-rod lure with cork or deer-hair body that imitates bass food such as frog, bee, dragonfly, or mouse

bend crook in fishhook, often ending at barb

bird's nest backlash

black gnat artificial fly used for trout or salmon

blood knot barrel knot

boat rod rod for casting or trolling with lure or bait from boat, usu. 5 to 6 1/2 feet (1.5 to 2 meters) long

bob bobber

bobber float usu. made of cork and quills, used in still fishing to suspend bait at set depth and indicate strike; bob

boulter long, heavyweight line with several hooks attached

bubble float transparent, spherical float partly weighted with water

bucktail artificial fly with long wing, often of hair from deer's tail, that imitates minnow or other small baitfish

bucktail jig lure with weighted head and bucktail wings

bung *Brit. slang.* cork float

bunt bagging portion of fishing net

cast *Chiefly Brit.* leader

casting rod fishing rod, usu. 4 to 8 feet (1.2 to 2.4 m) long, for casting bait or spinning lure, usu. fitted with revolving reel that allows angler to control line with thumb during cast

check adjustable ratchet system on reel that prevents line from running freely when fish takes it

chugger plug that rests on water's surface and makes popping sound when retrieved; popper; popping plug

chum ground bits of bait or food discarded into water to attract game fish

clinch knot knot in which eye is formed by looping rope and seizing end to standing part, used as hook eye line knot

close-faced reel reel enclosed in housing with hole at center or edge of cover through which line passes

cloudbait finely minced bait discarded into water to attract fish

corkball float float made of ball of cork

cork bug fly with solid cork body that floats and imitates action of frog, mouse, or grasshopper, used in bass fishing

courge *Chiefly Brit.* perforated box hung over side of boat to keep bait alive

crawlers rubber cleats that attach to boots to prevent slipping on rocks

creel basket, esp. of wicker, for holding fish, often carried by strap over shoulder

cut bait bait-sized chunks of fish that are too large to be used whole as bait

cuttyhunk twisted linen fishline, esp. one laid by hand

Darter *Trademark.* plug that floats horizontally when at rest and submerges up to three feet (1 m) when wobbling slowly

dead bait any dead fish or insect used as bait

deep diver plug for bass and walleye that sinks upon hitting water; sinking plug

devon spinner with vanes at head and triangle at tail

diamond sinker long, slender sinker, tapering at each end, used for trolling

dipsey sinker small, teardrop-shaped, lead sinker

disgorger rodlike device with forked end, used to remove hook from fish's throat

diving plug plug that darts at surface of water, then plunges

dobber float or bob

doctor type of artificial fly, often silver

double-taper line leader line that tapers at both ends so that it can be reversed when wear requires it

drifter fishing boat using drift net

drift net fishing net held upright in water by floats at upper edge and sinkers at bottom edge, so as to be carried by current or tide

drop net circular net lowered by weighted cords at four points into water to catch fish and small crustaceans for bait

dry fly fly that imitates appearance and action of floating insect, with hackles projecting at right angles from hook to keep fly on surface

dusty miller artificial fly used esp. for trout and salmon

eye loop at end of fishhook shank through which line or leader passes

farm waters devoted to propagation of fish

ferrule any of several fitted, usu. metal joints, composed of socket and plug, that are spaced along length of rod so that it can be dismantled and reassembled

fiberglass rod basic material used for fishing rods, replacing bamboo after 1948

fighting chair seat attached to deck at stern of fishing boat, used by angler in landing very large fish

fish box covered box sunk into floor of boat to hold catch

fish eggs roe

fishfinder surf fishing device with pyramid sinker and barrel swivel that allows bait to cover broad area

fishhook slender, recurved, usu. barbed piece of metal wire at end of lure or on which fly is tied or bait placed for catching fish; hook

fishing line line of braided or twisted silk, cotton, or monofilament, used to connect hook to rod and reel; fishline

fishing pole rudimentary gear consisting of long, thin rod with line and hook fastened to one end for catching fish

fishing rod long, thin, flexible rod of bamboo, fiberglass, or graphite with reel attached, used with line and hooks for catching fish; rod

fishing smack large, usu. commercial fishing vessel containing well to keep catch alive

fishing vest armless jacket, usu. waterproof, with several pockets and places where fishing tackle may be stored or attached

fishline fishing line

fish stringer length of rope or line run through mouths and gills of catch and draped in water, esp. over side of boat or from shore

fixed-reel seat frame by which fixed spinning reel is attached to rod

fixed-spool reel spinning reel with open top

float cork, hollow plastic, or bobber used to buoy up baited line in water

floating-diving plug lure that dives beneath water's surface when retrieved

fly artificial fly

fly book folding case for storing flies, often containing several waterproof envelopes or lining of lamb's wool

fly box container in which artificial flies are stored in compartments with clear lids or on snap catches or cloth

fly leader monofilament between a hook or fly and a heavier line, used to reduce alarm in fish

fly line heavy test line, used in fly-fishing, whose weight propels the cast

fly reel reel used to store backing and fly line

fly rod long, light, flexible rod of bamboo or fiberglass, used in fly-fishing

gaff large, barbless steel hook on handle, used for landing or boating fish

gang hook hook with several points

gear tools, apparatus, and other equipment used in fishing; rig; tackle

gill net mesh wall held vertically in water by corks on top and lead weights on bottom, capturing anything too large to slip through it

golden shiner freshwater minnow used as live bait

grasshopper artificial fly resembling grasshopper

grip portion of end of rod below casting reel or above fly reel that angler holds while fishing, usu. having nonslip surface

gut embryo silk in varying thickness used for

leader or tippets, now largely replaced by monofilament nylon

hackle legs and feet of artificial fly made by wrapping long neck or saddle feathers, usu. from a cock or hen, around hook shank

hackle fly artificial fly made with hackles, usu. without wings

hand line hook at end of line dropped into water by hand, without rod or reel

harpoon barbed, spearlike missile attached to rope, fired or thrown at whales or large fish

hatch boat *Chiefly Brit.* small fishing vessel with covered wells for holding fish

hip boots waterproof boots reaching to hips

hook fishhook

ice auger device used to cut hole in ice for ice fishing

ice skimmer slotted, ladlelike device used to clear ice chips from hole and surrounding area in ice fishing

ice spud device with chisel-like blade on heavy handle, used to punch hole in ice for ice fishing

ice sounder device consisting of lead weight with spring clip on line, used to determine depth of water beneath ice in ice fishing

jig lure with weighted head, fixed hook, and tail made of feathers or nylon, often attached by wire leader; jigging lure

jig and eel narrow-bodied metal squid lure up to 12 inches (30.5 cm) long with eel rigged onto it, used for striped bass and sea trout

jigging lure jig

jigging rod spinning rod used with jigs

Jock Scot artificial fly with yellow and scarlet coloring in body and tail, and hackle of guinea fowl and grouse feathers, esp. for salmon

keeper ring small wire ring positioned at rod butt just above grip, used to attach hook when not fishing

keep net long, cylindrical net used to keep catch alive

Kendal sneck bent fishing hook with wide, square bend

landing net any baglike net on handle large enough to lift exhausted fish from water and land or boat it

leader length of wire or monofilament that protects line from fish or forms invisible link between main line and lure, bait, or fly; *Chiefly Brit.* cast

ledger *Chiefly Brit.* sinker designed to hold bait at bottom and allow line to run freely through it, usu. ball of lead with hole bored through it

ledger line *Chiefly Brit.* line set so that bait and sinker rest on bottom

line part of tackle that connects cast lure or baited hook to rod in fisherman's hand, usu. monofilament, also: braided nylon, copper, cotton, cuttyhunk, Dacron, linen, nylon, silk, or wire

live bait any natural organism placed on a hook and used to catch fish: angleworm, caterpillar, crayfish, cricket, darter, dragonfly, fish egg, frog, grasshopper, grub, hellgrammite, mayfly, minnow, night crawler, worm

lobster pot baited box trap dropped to seafloor for catching lobsters

lock-snap swivel swivel composed of wire, the end of which hooks onto itself

loop knot knot made by doubling over line at its end and forming square knot with loop from both thicknesses

lure any artificial bait used to attract fish, usu. distinguished from artificial flies

mayfly widely found insect used as bait and as prototype for artificial dry flies

midge mosquitolike insect whose larvae are used as bait for trout in streams and mountain lakes

monofilament single strand of extruded nylon used for fishing line

multiplier very free-running reel used for bait casting and spinning

muskie rod heavy bait-casting rod with offset handle

nail knot nooselike knot that tightens when pulled and does not slip, sometimes tied around nail for attaching sections of leader or attaching leader to fly line

net any of various mesh devices with handles, used to snare fish in water for landing or boating

nymph artificial fly modeled after any subaqueous insect and its larva, having no wings, soft hackle at head, tapered body, and sparse tail

palmer artificial fly with bushy body made entirely from wound hackle feathers

pencil float long, hollow, often plastic float

phantom spinning lure similar to devon

pillars cross bars from one plate to the other in reel frame

pirn *Brit. dial.* fishing reel

plastic ball float round, hollow float made of plastic

plastic lure lure made of plastic, as distinguished from metal or wooden lures

plug lure made of wood, plastic, or metal that darts through water imitating a small fish, fitted with one of more gang hooks

plummet *Chiefly Brit.* cork-bottomed lead weight used to plumb deep water such as in lakes

plunker casting lure that makes plunking sound as it hits water

point last section of tapered leader in fly fishing; tippet

popper chugger

popping plug plug that floats on surface and creates bubbles and popping sounds when it is jerked by moving rod tip; chugger

popping rod bait-casting rod with straight handle

pork rind strips of hog's skin preserved in liquid, used with lure or alone when shaped into lure that makes fishlike wiggle when retrieved

pounds test weight that a fishing line can lift without breaking

priest *Brit. slang.* cudgel for dispatching fish that have been landed or boated

purse line line used to close bottom of purse seine

purse seine large seine drawn by two boats around school of fish and closed at the bottom by means of a line passing through rings

pyramid sinker medium-sized lead sinker in form of pyramid

quill hollow stem of bird's feather, used for floats

reel device with rotating or fixed spool attached to butt of fishing rod, used to let out or bring in line

reel crank handle used to turn spool of line on reel

revolving-spool reel standard bait-casting reel in which spool drum revolves when casting or reeling in line

rig gear or tackle

rod fishing rod

rod butt end of rod behind grip and furthest from tip

rod guide one of several metal rings attached along length of rod so that line follows action of rod and can be controlled from reel to hook

rod rest *Chiefly Brit.* device used to support rod, often in tandem with other rod rests, esp. when ledgering

rod ring *Chiefly Brit.* ring at end of rod through which line runs; tip-top

rod tip attachment to end of rod farthest from butt with guide through which line runs

roe eggs of fish used as bait

saltwater bait live bait used for deep-sea fishing and surf casting: baitfish, crab, cut bait, herring, mullet, shrimp, squid

seaboot tall, waterproof wading boot

seine vertical fishing net suspended in water between floats at surface and submerged sinkers

shank straight body of fishhook, leading from eye to bend

single-action fly reel fly reel whose spool makes one turn with each turn of the reel handle

sinker metal weight, usu. made of lead, molded in various shapes and sizes, used to lower, troll, or anchor bait or lure at desired depth

sinking plug deep diver

sliding-clamp reel seat pair of clamps on butt of spinning rod that hold reel in place

sliding float float that is free to run along line between topmost weight and rubber stop, used in deepwater fishing

snap swivel swivel in shape of safety pin that snaps shut

spear long staff with sharply pointed metal head, used for stabbing fish

spent wing fly dry fly with extended wings

spider fly wet or dry fly with no tail or wings, an overlong hackle body, and long legs resembling spider

spinner lure with oval metal blade mounted on shaft that revolves when drawn through water

spinning reel fixed-spool reel with adjustable drag and antireverse lock, mounted on underside of rod

spinning rod lightweight bamboo, fiberglass, or graphite rod for spinning with small lure, lure-fly combination, or bait

split shot small lead shot partially split for easy placement on leader or line as weight

split-shot sinker sinker made of partially split lead shot

spool revolving apparatus in reel, around which line winds and unwinds

spoon brightly colored, spoon-shaped lure with one or more hooks that swivels and flashes to imitate small baitfish, used in casting or trolling

sproat fishhook having circular bend

stink bait sponge or dough impregnated with slime from decomposed matter, cheese, or small dead fish, used for catfish and carp

streamer fly artificial fly having long hackle wings extending beyond bend of fishhook, representing minnow or small baitfish

surface disturber type of floating plug shaped to splash on retrieval

surface plug nonspinning lure that darts along surface of water

surf rod long, sturdy rod used in surf casting

swivel two metal eyes joined by pin so that entire swivel unit revolves freely and absorbs torsion of lure or bait to minimize twist on line

tackle equipment and apparatus used in fishing; gear; rig

tackle box sturdy, waterproof, metal or plastic box in which fishing tackle is stored, usu. having several compartments

tag small piece of shiny material wound on hook shank at rear end of body of fly

tailer flexible noose on handle, slipped over fish's tail to land or boat it without net or gaff

tapered leader leader that is thinner at tippet end

terrestrial wet or dry fly representing a land insect such as an ant, beetle, or grasshopper in water

tilt ice-fishing device with crosspieces that span hole in ice, used to hold baited line leading from underwater revolving-spool reel and attached to cocked arm that releases when fish strikes; tip-up

tip guide metal ring at end of rod through which line runs and is controlled by movement of rod; tip-top

tippet finest end of tapered leader; tail or wing of artificial fly made from shaft of certain cock feather; point

tip-top tip guide

tip-up tilt

trace *Chiefly Brit.* section of spinning line between reel line and hook

trammel net three-layered net with a fine-meshed middle layer between two coarser

outer layers, so that fish become entangled in one or more of the nets

trawler fishing boat used to haul trawl net

trawl line buoyed fishing line with baited hooks attached at intervals

trawl net net dragged along sea bottom to catch fish

treblehook hook terminating in three bends and three barbed points

trident fishing spear having three-pronged point

trolling reel sturdy, open-spool reel for trolling from boat

trotline sturdy fishing line suspended across or submerged in stream with individual hooks attached at intervals by separate lines

tube fly artificial fly with tubular body that resembles a lure, used for salmon or trout fishing

turle knot knot used to attach artificial fly to leader

ultralight spinning tackle specialized spinning tackle orig. from France, no heavier than a 3-ounce rod and 3-pound test line, used for small game fish

waders thigh-high rubber boots, often with studded soles to provide traction over rocks; chest-high, waterproof boot trousers with suspenders

wading staff rod used to test bottom firmness while wading through water

waist boots waterproof boots reaching to waist

wet fly sparsely dressed, usu. flat fly that imitates action and appearance of submerged insect

worm fly *Chiefly Brit.* artificial fly with two bodies and two hooks but only one eye, used esp. beneath overhanging foliage

GARDENING
Gardens and Gardening Systems
Practice, Tools, and Techniques
Plants and Plant Parts

See also: *Chap. 2: Biology; Plants; Chap. 12: Agriculture*

Gardens and Gardening Systems

alpine garden garden of plants native to high altitudes

arboretum garden in which trees and shrubs are grown and displayed

bonsai garden of dwarf trees artfully cultivated in pots (Japan)

botanical garden collection of plants and trees kept for exhibition and scientific study

conservatory elaborate greenhouse where plants are grown and displayed

dry garden garden of cactus and other plants requiring little water for cultivation

flower bed small area of ground planted with flowers, often part of larger garden

flower garden garden of decorative, blossoming plants

formal garden elaborate, manicured, and carefully pruned decorative garden

garden plot of ground where plants are cultivated

Garden of Eden Biblical paradise, home of Adam and Eve

glasshouse *Chiefly Brit.* greenhouse

greenhouse translucent structure in which environment is controlled to allow delicate plants to develop and thrive

hanging garden garden with plants suspended in pots rather than growing from ground

hedge dense row of shrubs used to form boundary

herbarium collection of dried plants, esp. for botanical study

hortorium museum for collection, preservation, and study of plant specimens

Japanese garden manicured garden with bonsai, teahouse, and still water

jardin *French.* garden

kitchen garden small vegetable garden for personal use

landscape viewable portion of terrain and its features; (vb) manipulate a natural environment for aesthetic purposes

lawn ground covered with closely mowed grass

orchard cultivated fruit or nut trees

ornamental garden garden of flowers and decorative shrubs

park area of public land, esp. in or near city, with lawns, gardens, trees, paths, and recreational facilities

patch small garden; flower bed

rock garden artificial landscape containing natural-looking rock outcrops and soil surfaces

roof garden potted plants growing on roof of building, esp. in urban area with no open land surrounding buildings

rose garden ornamental garden of carefully pruned rose bushes

sunken garden garden built below level of surrounding land

tea garden Japanese garden with teahouse

terrarium miniature garden enclosed in glass container

truck garden garden in which vegetables are grown to be marketed

vegetable garden garden of cultivated, edible plants

victory garden home vegetable garden grown during wartime to supplement crop production

vineyard plantation of cultivated grapevines

xeriscape garden for drought-tolerant plants

yard cultivated area beside residence

Practice, Tools, and Techniques

acidity state of having excessive acid, or a relatively low concentration of hydrogen atoms in soil, esp. in areas of heavy rainfall and abundant organic matter

agronomy science and management of crop production

air layering propagation method by which roots develop on stems while attached to mother plant

alkalinity state of having high concentration of calcium and other minerals in soil, esp. in areas of light rainfall

arbor latticework bower on which vines are trained

arboriculture cultivation of trees and shrubs for ornament

arborist tree specialist

backfill soil returned after being dug up to cover positioned roots, often mixed with additives to improve its condition

balanced crotch two tree branches growing equally, rendering each branch weak

balled and burlapped designating soil-covered roots bundled and wrapped for protection until planting

bare root condition of dormant plant whose root is devoid of soil

bed area of ground prepared for plants

blanch (vb) shield plant, esp. vegetable, from sunlight to promote paler color in stems or leaves

blower power sweeper, esp. for leaves

bolt (vb) produce flowers or seeds prematurely

bone meal fertilizer of crushed bone

botany science of plant life, including structure, growth, and classification; characteristics of a plant or plant group

broadcast (vb) toss out seed by hand

brush cutter pruner

budding putting forth of buds; asexual propagation technique

chlorosis iron deficiency in plant

cloche transparent protective covering for delicate plants

cold frame low, transparent, unheated greenhouse box

compost nutrient-rich decomposed organic matter

cordon tree pruned to have only one main stem

crown soil level just below ground where stem and root join

cultivate (vb) prepare soil for plants and care for them to foster growth

cutting portion of plant removed and induced to propagate

damping-off condition caused by fungal disease in which stems of small seedlings wilt and rot

deadhead (vb) pinch off dead flower heads from stems to promote blooming

defoliation unnatural and often unhealthy loss of leaves

Demeter goddess of agriculture and fertility (ancient Greece)

dibber dibble

dibble pointed tool used to make holes in soil for insertion of plants or seeds; dibber

dieback death of plant stems, starting at tips

drainage movement of water through soil in plant's root area

drill straight furrow for sowing seeds in rows

drip line imaginary circle drawn around plant under its outermost branches, where rainwater is likely to fall

edger revolving blade on long handle, used for trimming lawn or flower bed

espalier lattice or trellis on which tree or shrub branches are trained to grow in flat pattern

etiolation bleaching of plant due to light deprivation

evapotranspiration process of transferring moisture from earth to atmosphere by evaporation of water and transpiration from plants

fertilize (*vb*) apply nutrient-rich materials to soil

fertilizer material containing one or more plant nutrients

flat rooting box for cuttings or seeds

floriculture cultivation of ornamental and flowering plants

florist person who grows and sells flowers

floristry growing and selling of flowers and ornamentals

flower pot plant container, usu. plastic, wood, or ceramic

force (*vb*) artificially induce rapid growth or blooming of plant

forestry science of planting and cultivating trees

friable soil easily crumbled soil

fruition bearing of fruit

furrow planting trench made by plow

gardener person who enjoys or is skilled at tending gardens

gardening process of making, caring for, and working in gardens

germination sprouting of seeds for planting

girdling act of cutting around plant through bark and cambium in order to kill it

graft union of one plant to another so that two will grow as one

greenhouse hothouse

green thumb exceptional facility for gardening and growing plants successfully

ground cover low, dense-growing plants used to cover ground where grass will not grow

groundskeeping care of gardens, playing fields, and lawns

grow light artificial indoor light for growing plants

harden-off (*vb*) gradually expose greenhouse seedlings to outdoor weather

harrow tool with spikes or sharp-edged disks for cultivating soil

heading back pruning to shorten branches

herbaceous (*adj*) designating nonwoody plant

hoe hand tool with thin, flat blade on handle for loosening soil and weeding

honeydew sticky, sweet substance produced by aphids and other insects

horticulture science and art of growing plants

hose flexible tube used to convey water to garden

hotbed plot of earth covered with glass and heated to accelerate plant growth

hothouse glass building artificially heated for growing plants; greenhouse

humus organic part of soil resulting from decomposition of plant or animal matter

hydroponics growing of plants without soil in nutrient-rich solutions of moist, inert material

inarching grafting while plants are still rooted

intercropping space-saving method of planting fast-growing crop between rows of slower-growing crop

irrigation bringing of water to plant beds, esp. by ditches or channels

landscape gardening practice of arranging lawns, flower beds, and bushes in attractive manner for human use, esp. as a profession

lath house overhead structure of narrow wood strips providing protection from sunlight or frost

lawn mower manual or power machine for cutting grass

leaching loss of soluble matter from soil due to filtering through of water

leaf mold rich soil composed largely of decayed leaves

lime calcium compound used as soil amendment to enhance crop growth

loam friable mixture of sand and clay

loppers long-handled pruning shears

manure fertilizer of animal excrement

mulch protective ground cover of leaves, straw, and peat moss

nozzle spout at end of hose for directing flow of water

n-p-k initials for ingredients in complete fertilizer: nitrogen (n), phosphorus (p), and potassium (chemical symbol k)

nursery place where young trees or plants are raised

offset small new plant at end of stem sent out from base of mature perennial

organic (*adj*) designating plants grown with animal or vegetable fertilizers only

peat moss mulch of slightly decomposed plant remains

perlite light, porous soil additive composed of volcanic material

pest destructive or troublesome insect, small animal, or weed

photosynthesis production of organic substances from carbon dioxide and water in green plant cells, which chemically transform radiant energy of sunlight

pinching removal of tips of twigs and branches to force bushy growth

plant classification standard botanical classification system: family, genus, species, variety (subspecies), strain, hybrid

planter decorative container for growing plants

plant food nitrogen-rich chemical mixture used to fortify plants and accelerate growth

pleaching training of plant growth so that plaited branches form hedge or arbor

plug small wedge or segment cut from plant for testing

pollard tree pruned to produce dense, leafy dome

pollination transfer of pollen from stamens to pistils

potted plant any plant grown in soil enclosed in a container, esp. indoors

propagation multiplication of an organism by natural reproduction

prune (*vb*) control growth of plant by trimming at top to increase quality and yield of flowers or fruit

pruner bladed device for cutting back plant growth; brush cutter

rake long-handled, toothed tool for gathering loose material or smoothing surface

root-bound (*adj*) designating potted plant whose roots have no room to grow

rootstock portion of grafted or budded plant containing root

salinity excess salt, measure of salt content

scree rocky debris, sometimes re-created as rock garden habitat

shade shelter or protection from light or sun

shearing pruning of outer foliage

shovel handled tool with broad scoop or hollowed-out blade for digging in earth

shredder compost maker

silt soil composed primarily of sediment that accumulates on bottoms of rivers and bays, with particles smaller than sand but larger than clay

sod carpet of grass; turf

soil upper layer of earth that may be cultivated, and that can support plant growth; this material collected and placed in gardens or pots, consisting of small particles of rock together with humus

soil amendments substances added to improve soil texture and fertility, such as compost, manure, peat moss, bark, perlite, lime, or chemicals

spade digging instrument with blade that is pushed into ground with foot

spading fork spade with forklike tines

species naturally existing population of organisms that interbreed; botanical classification between genus and variety

sphagnum long-fibered, highly absorbent peat moss

sprinkler device for distributing water evenly over large area of garden

staking providing support for plants with thin strips of wood stuck upright in ground

standard plant trained to form treelike shape with single trunk and crown of foliage

terrace raised, flat mound of earth with sloping sides, often in series of descending levels

thinning pruning by removing whole branches to create less density; removal of some seedlings to foster growth of others

tillage land that has been tilled

tiller machine designed for digging, cultivating, aerating, and mixing soil

tilth cultivation of land

top-dress (*vb*) apply mulch to protect seeds

topiary pruning of hedges into unique or formal shapes; hedge so pruned

topsoil rich, relatively fertile top layer of soil

transpiration loss of water from plant leaves into air

transplant (*vb*) transfer plant from one home to another

trellis structure of thin strips on which climbing plants are trained

trowel small tool with curved, scooplike blade on handle, used in turning earth and digging

turf sod

weed (*vb*) remove unwanted growth from garden

weed trimmer tool for cutting back weeds

wheelbarrow shallow, open container on single wheel with handles, used for moving soil and plants

wilting limpness in plant due to lack of water, poor root function, or disease

windbreak plants used as barrier to wind

window pot planter placed on or outside window sill

Plants and Plant Parts

annual plant with life cycle of one year or season

anther part of stamen that produces and releases pollen

bark outside covering of stems and roots of trees and woody plants

bedding plant plant adapted for open-air bed

biennial plant with two year life cycle, in which vegetative first-year growth is followed by fruiting and drying during second year

bloom flower

blossom flower, esp. of fruit-bearing plant

bole tree trunk

bolt (*vb*) prematurely produce flowers and seeds, esp. in hot weather

bonsai potted tree or shrub that has been dwarfed, usu. by pruning roots and pinching

bract leaflike structure growing below or encircling flower cluster or flower

broad-leaved (*adj*) describing a plant having leaves that are not needles

bromeliad plant with stiff, leathery leaves and spikes of bright flowers

bud small swelling on plant from which shoot, leaf cluster, or flower develops

bulb dormant underground bud stage of some plants

bush shrub

cactus fleshy-stemmed plant with reduced or spinelike leaves, living in dry places and requiring little water

calyx outer whorl of protective leaves of flower

cambium layer of formative cells beneath bark of tree

carpel ovule-bearing leaf or leaflike structure that is primary segment of pistil

climber vine or climbing plant with tendrils

conifer cone-bearing evergreen, usu. with narrow, needlelike or small, scalelike leaves

corm underground stem base that acts as reproductive structure

cormel small corm

corolla petals of a flower

cosmopolite plant living throughout world

cotyledon first leaf or two of seedling

crab grass weedy annual grass that roots and spreads rapidly in lawns and gardens

creeper plant whose stem puts out tendrils or rootlets and that moves along surface as it grows

crown topmost portions of tree's leafy canopy

cultivar plant variety originating in cultivation and persisting as species

deciduous (*adj*) designating any plant that sheds all its leaves once each year

dendroid (*adj*) treelike in form

double flower flower with petals that are numerous and clustered to cover center

epiphyte nonparasitic plant that lives on another plant

everbearing (*adj*) producing fruit throughout growing season

evergreen plant that maintains functional green foliage throughout year

exotic plant that is not native to growing area

eye bud of root or tuber

fern nonflowering plant having fronds instead of leaves and reproducing by spores instead of seeds

filament stalk of stamen bearing the anther

flora plants of specific region or time

flower (*n*) seed-producing plant with stem that bears leaflike sepals, colorful petals, and pollen-bearing stamens; plant cultivated for its blossoms; reproductive organ of some plants; bloom; blossom; (*vb*) produce blossoms

flower bud bud that produces a flower only, no fruit

flowering plant plant that produces flowers, fruit, and seeds

foliage groups of leaves, flowers, or branches; greenery

foliage plant plant cultivated for decorative foliage

frond fern or palm foliage

fruit mature ovary of flowering plant, usu. edible

fruit tree tree bearing fruit

go to seed pass to stage of producing seeds at end of growth cycle, used esp. of seasonal crops

grass member of family of flowering plants with long, narrow leaves, used for food and fodder or as lawns

greenery green vegetation; foliage

hardy (*adj*) designating a plant with high resistance or tolerance to cold or freezing temperatures

herb seed-producing plant with little or no woody tissue, valued for its medicinal, aromatic, or savory qualities

houseplants ornamental plants that can live indoors in small pots

kernel grain or seed, esp. inside fruit

latent bud dormant bud in stem or beneath bark

lateral bud bud growing on side of stem

leaf flat, thin structure growing from stem or twig of plant, used in photosynthesis and transpiration

leaflet small or young leaf

moss any of various small, green plants without true stems, reproducing by spores and growing in velvety clusters in moist areas on rocks, trees, or the ground

native plant indigenous to region

orchid perennial epiphyte cultivated for its brightly colored flowers

ornamental plant or shrub grown for its decorative effect

perennial plant that lives two years or more; herbaceous plant that lives beyond its flowering stage

petal one of the circle of flower parts inside the sepals

petiole stem connecting branch to leaf blade

pistil central, seed-bearing part of flower, comprised of one or more carpels, each with style and stigma

plant member of kingdom of living things capable of carrying on photosynthesis in cells, primarily adapted for terrestrial life

pollen fine, dustlike grains containing male sexual cells, produced in anthers or similar structures of seed plants

rhizome creeping horizontal stem lying at or just beneath soil surface, bearing leaves at its tip and roots from its underside

root underground part of plant that functions in absorption, aeration, food storage, and as support system

runner long, slender stem growing from base of some perennials; runner

seed fertilized plant ovule containing embryo and capable of germinating to produce new plant

seedling plant grown from seed rather than cutting; young plant or tree

sepal usu. green, leaflike outer circle of calyx

shoot new growth, sprout, or twig on plant

shrub woody perennial plant with several low-branching stems; bush

shrubbery cluster of shrubs

spike stem with flowers directly attached to its upper portion

spore reproductive cell in mosses and ferns, capable of producing new adult individual

sprout young growth on plant; new growth from bud, rootstock, or germinating seed

spur projection from rear of flower, arising from sepal or petal

stalk stem or main axis of plant; any slender, supporting or connecting part of plant

stamen pollen-producing part of central flower, comprised of filament and anther

stem main upward-growing axis of plant

stigma free upper tip of flower style on which pollen falls and develops

stolon stem that takes root at intervals along ground, forming new plants; runner

style slender, stalklike part of carpel between stigma and ovary

succulent plant with thick, fleshy tissues that store water

sucker strong offshoot from roots or lower stem of plant

taproot deep, main root from which lateral roots develop

tendril threadlike, often spiral part of climbing plant that clings to or coils around objects

terminal bud bud growing at end of stem

thorn sharp-pointed, leafless branch of plant

tree tall, woody perennial with single stem or trunk and branches usu. beginning at some height above ground

tropical plant plant that occurs naturally in tropical climate

trunk thick, primary stem of tree

truss compact flower cluster at tip of stem

tuber fat, underground stem from which certain plants grow, similar to but shorter and thicker than rhizome

tuberous root thickened underground food storage structure

twining stem tendrillike stem of certain climbing plants

variegated (*adj*) designating plant with patterned or bicolored leaves and petals

vegetable any herbaceous plant all or part of which may be used as food

vine plant that grows along the ground or clings to vertical support by means of twining stems, tendrils, and rootlets

water sprout nonflowering shoot springing from bud of main plant branch

weed undesired, uncultivated plant for which no purpose has been found, often growing in profusion and interfering with growth of desired plants

xerophyte plant adapted to growth in arid conditions

HOBBIES

See also: *Chap. 1: Health, Fitness, and Enhancement; Chap. 9: Cooking and Cuisine; Chap. 12: Occupations; Chap. 16: Crafts; Chap. 17: Holidays, Celebrations, and Vacations; Entertainments and Spectacles; Sports; Gardening; Games, Activities, and Toys; Chap. 25: Magic and the Occult*

Many of these hobbies are also practiced as crafts.

angling fishing with hook and line

antique collecting accumulating old and valuable items, esp. furniture, pottery and porcelain, silver, glass, and art

antique refinishing restoring old, finely crafted furniture to its original condition

aquarium building design, creation, and maintenance of small, glass-enclosed aquatic environments for fish and plants

audiophile one who studies and collects state-of-the-art electronic audio equipment

avocation hobby

backpacking rural or wilderness hiking, with equipment and tents carried in rucksack on back

ballooning riding aloft in observation basket borne upward by large, spherical bag filled with gas or hot air

bingo board game of chance played socially

bird-watching observing wild birds in their natural habitat

board games competitive, amusing diversion involving manipulation of objects on a board

bridge card game played by two sets of partners

camping excursion, with provisions, into rural or wilderness area

cards games of chance and skill played with ordered deck of playing cards

carpentry cutting, joining, and framing of wood to form cabinetry or buildings

ceramics craft of making fired earthenware pottery

climbing mountaineering

coin collecting accumulating valuable or historical metal currency; numismatics

collecting act of accumulating of specimens of antiques, autographs, bottles, buttons, china, coins, dolls, glass, matchbooks, postcards, rocks and minerals, stamps, wine labels, or other articles

cooking preparation of food dishes for entertainment as well as nourishment

crafts skilled working of materials to form decorative or useful objects; handicrafts

crewel embroidery needlework employing twisted stitch

crocheting needlework done with hooked needle

crossword puzzle written word game in grid format, solution to which is based on definition clues

customizing process of modifying mass-produced item to specific requirements for performance or finish

decoupage technique of decorative surfacing with paper cutouts

do-it-yourself (*adj*) pertaining to practice of building or repairing items oneself, esp. household objects

drying flowers hanging and preserving dead flowers as decorative objects

embroidery decorative needlework using threads of high gloss, bright color, or hues contrasting with cloth

fabric painting applying designs to fabric in paint

fiber arts design and crafting of objects from natural fibers or fiber materials

fishing sport of catching fish with rod and line, hook, spear, or net

fly fishing sport of catching fish with line attached to floating hook dressed with feathers to resemble an insect

folk dancing traditional ethnic dances performed socially

gambling playing at any game of chance for money or other stakes; wagering on the predicted outcome of any event; gaming

games structured, often competitive activities for amusement: games of chance, games of skill, athletic, board, card, and indoor and outdoor games

gaming gambling

gardening creation, design, and maintenance of decorative and edible plants, esp. for domestic use and enjoyment

glass painting painting of images and designs on plate glass

handicrafts crafts

hang gliding riding aloft in harness attached to large kite, esp. leaping off elevated place and floating down to flat ground

hobby leisure activity, skill, or sport engaged in for enjoyment and enrichment; avocation

home decorating practice of designing and furnishing domestic interiors

hunting pursuit, capture, and killing of game animals for sport rather than subsistence

ice-skating sport of gliding over ice wearing metal-bladed shoes

ikebana Japanese art of flower arranging

in-line skating roller-blading

jewelry making design and production of ornamental objects, such as rings or necklaces, worn for adornment

jogging running for health purposes

kite flying hoisting aloft and sailing of frame covered by light material attached to long string

knitting interlacing of yarn to form decorative or functional garments and accessories

landscaping design and maintenance of outdoor areas adjacent to buildings, esp. for use and enjoyment

macramé elaborate, mesh knotwork done with twine or rope

manège training and skilled riding of horses

mask making craft of forming masks from papier-mâché, wood, plaster of Paris, or other materials

mobile making making arrangements of wire and metal, paper, or plastic shapes that are suspended to move in air currents

model airplanes miniature replicas of aircraft that are handmade and collected as a hobby

model cars miniature replicas of automobiles, often historical, that are handmade and collected as a hobby

model trains working miniature replicas of railroad cars and trains that are collected and displayed as a hobby

mountain climbing mountaineering

mountaineering ascent of difficult mountain slopes with aid of equipment; mountain climbing

needlecrafts handicrafts involving sewing or

weaving with cloth or threads: crocheting, knitting, embroidery, needlepoint, quilting, rug hooking, trapunto, weaving

needlepoint embroidery with yarn, esp. on canvas

numismatics coin collecting

orchid growing cultivation of tropical orchids in hothouse environment

origami Japanese art of decorative paper folding

paper flower making craft of forming artificial flowers from paper

paperworking making of decorative objects by cutting and folding paper; making of fine paper products

papier-mâché craft of forming decorative masks or objects from rags or paper soaked in glue, formed into shapes, and dried

pastime activity pursued for pleasure and enrichment during leisure hours

pets care and feeding of household and domestic animals kept for pleasure

philately stamp collecting

phillumenism collecting matchbooks and matchbook covers

photography process of creating or collecting photographic images, esp. of nature, travel, and family

pottery making or collecting of decorative and functional vessels of fired clay

pressing flowers placing fresh flowers or leaves between sheets of blotting paper or absorbent tissue and flattening them between pages of a heavy book

puppetry making, collecting, and performing with hand-operated dolls

puzzles collection and use of toys, objects, and games designed to amuse and test ingenuity

quilting creation and collection of needleworked or patchworked bedcovers, often antique

recreation leisure activity pursued for pleasure, relaxation, or enrichment

riding using of horses for recreational touring of the countryside

rock climbing ascending rock faces and cliffs, usu. with equipment such as rope, pick, and petons

roller-blading skating on Rollerblades, a brand of in-line skates with a single row of wheels, like an ice skate blade

roller-skating skating on wheeled shoes for recreational exercise

scouting organized group recreation and education, esp. for development of social and out-of-doors skills in young people

scrimshaw decorative engraving of ivory, bone, or shell

scuba diving ocean diving with oxygen tank and breathing apparatus for extended underwater exploration

sewing design and creation of garments by needlework

shell carving forming decorative objects from shells

skateboarding use of small, wooden board on wheels for recreation and locomotion

skeet shooting firing of guns at clay targets thrown to represent birds in flight

skin diving underwater diving without aid of special breathing apparatus or oxygen tanks

skydiving jumping out of flying airplane to coast freely and perform maneuvers before opening parachute

sledding riding on vehicle with runners over snow and ice

snorkeling exploring coastal underwater areas using a breathing tube extending above surface of water

spelunking exploring caves

stained glass objects, esp. windows and lampshades, crafted of colored glass pieces, usu. joined by leaded strips

stamp collecting selection and accumulation of postage stamps, esp. historical, rare examples, or first printings; philately

stenciling printing by applying ink or paint to sheets perforated with designs or letters

stitchery decorative needlework, including embroidery or crewelwork

surf fishing fishing along shoreline of ocean

surfing sport of riding shoreline ocean waves on wooden or foam and fiberglass surfboard, or using body to ride such waves without board

taxidermy art of preserving stuffed, dead animals in lifelike form

terrarium building design, creation, and collection of small, glass-enclosed garden environment

tie-dyeing creating designs on textiles by tying parts of the cloth so they will not absorb dye

toymaking making of children's playthings

trapshooting sport of shooting at clay pigeons or pigeons released from cages

trapunto quilting done in high relief through two or more layers of cloth, produced by padding a stitched pattern with yarn or cotton

weaving design and creation of fabric, rugs, or textiles on loom

whittling carving of decorative or functional objects by trimming and shaping a stick of wood

windsurfing riding of wind-propelled, oceangoing apparatus resembling surfboard with attached sail

woodworking shaping of articles in wood

yachting recreational sailing of pleasure boat

Athletic Events and Activities

acrobatics, aerobics, aikido, aquaplaning
backpacking, ballooning, bareback riding, bellyboard riding, body-surfing
caber, calisthenics, canoeing, cartwheels, climbing
fishing, fly-fishing
gliding, gym, gymnasitics
handball, handsprings, hang gliding
iceboating, Indian wrestling
judo, jujitsu
karate, kendo, kung fu
martial arts, mountaineering
ninjutsu
racquetball, riding, rock climbing
sailing, sailplaning, sculling, shooting, skateboarding, skating, skeet shooting, skiing, skin diving, skydiving, sledding, snorkeling, snowboarding, somersaulting, squash, surf casting
tae kwon do, tobogganing, trapshooting, tumbling
waterskiing, whitewater rafting, windsurfing, wrestling

Public Contests and Performances

acrobatics, aquacade, aquatics
beauty contest, bullfighting
carousel, cavalletti, cockfighting, contortionism
demolition derby, dog racing, dog show, dressage
equestrian events
funny cars
Grand Prix racing
harness racing
Ice Capades, Ice Follies
jousting
lists
Maypole celebrations
quarterhorse racing, quintain
rodeo, rope walking
Soap Box Derby, stock-car racing, synchronized swimming
thoroughbred racing, tightrope walking, trampoline jumping, trapeze performing, trot racing

Outdoor Games

badminton, bandy, boccie, broomball, bumper cars, bungee jumping
capture the flag, catch, croquet, curling
dodge ball, Dodgem
Frisbee
gliding
hare and hounds, hide-and-seek, hopscotch, horseshoes
jacks, jump rope
keepaway
leapfrog
marbles, merry-go-round, miniature golf, muss
obstacle race

paddleball, paddle tennis, pall-mall, pepper, punchball, pushball
quoits
racquets, ring-a-lievio, ring-around-the-rosey, ring taw, ringtoss, roller-skating
sack racing, shuffleboard
tag, teetertotter, tetherball, three-legged race, tipcat, trapshooting, tug of war

Indoor Games

acrostics, anagrams
bagatelle, billiards, bingo, blindman's buff, bluff, board games, bo-peep
cards, cat's cradle, charades, consequences, crambo, craps, crossword puzzle
darts, dice, dominoes
fan-tan
games of chance, games of skill, ghosts
hazard
jacks, jackstraws
keno
lotto
mumbletypeg, musical chairs
nine ball, Nintendo
pachinko, parlor games, peekaboo, pick-up-sticks, pinball machines, pin the tail on the donkey, pocket billiards, pool, post office, put-and-take, puzzles, pyramids
raffle, reversi, roulette
skittle, slot machine, snooker, spillikins, spin the bottle
tic-tack-toe
video games

POOL AND BILLIARDS

billiards game played with hard ivorylike balls that are driven with a cue stick on cloth-covered, rimmed table without pockets
pool game played with fifteen numbered balls and white cue ball that is driven with a cue stick into other balls, the object being to sink balls into pockets at the perimeter of a cloth-covered, rimmed table
  backspin, balkline, bank shot, break, bumper
  carom, chalk, combination shot, crutch, cue, cue ball, cushion
  eight ball, English
  massé
  nine ball
  object ball
  pocket
  rack, rotation, run
  scratch, shot
  table scratch, topspin

Card Games

cards any game played with a set of marked pieces of cardboard, usu. in a deck of fifty-two divided into four suits (clubs, diamonds, hearts, and spades), each suit numbered one (ace) through ten plus a jack, queen, and king
  all fours
  baccarat, beggar-my-neighbor, bezique, blackjack, blind poker, Boston, brag, bridge
  canasta, casino, chemin de fer, clubs, concentration, conquian, contract bridge,
  cooncan, crazy eights, cribbage, cutthroat contract
  draw poker, duplicate bridge
  Earl of Coventry, euchre
  fan-tan, faro, fish, five-card stud, frog
  gin, gin rummy, go fish
  hearts, high-low
  loo, lowball
  Michigan, monte
  nap
  old maid, ombre
  pairs, patience, penny ante, pinochle, piquet, poker, Pope Joan, primero
  quadrille
  rouge et noir, rubber bridge, rummy, Russian bank
  seven-up, skat, slapjack, snap, snipsnapsnorum, solitaire, speculation, straight poker, strip poker, stud poker
  tarak, three-card monte, twenty-one
  vingt-et-un
  war, whist

CARD TERMS

ace, ante
bank, banker, bid, bluff, bug, bullet
call, check, contract, cowboy, crossruff, croupier, cut
deal, dealer, dealing box, deuce, deuces wild, discard, double, draw, draw poker
face card, fill up, flop, flush, four of a kind, full house
hand, hole card, house, hoyle
inside straight, in the hole
joker
lead, limit
major suit, manille, mechanic, meld, misdeal, moriah
nob, no trump
odd trick, one-eyed, overtrick, overtrump
pair, pam, pan, pass, penny ante, picture card, playing card, pot, pot limit, preemptive bid
raise, royal flush, rubber, ruff
singleton, shoe, shoot the moon, shuffle, slough, spadille, straight, straight flush, strong suit, stud poker, suit
three of a kind, trey, trump, two pair
underbid, undertrick
wild card
Yarborough

Board Games

board game game played on flat sheet of wood or cardboard with markings, usu. requiring moving of pieces about the board
  acey-deucy
  backgammon, Balderdash, Battleship
  Candyland, checkers, chess, Chinese checkers, Chutes and Ladders, Clue, Connect Four
  draughts
  fox-and-geese
  go
  Life
  mah-jongg, merels, Monopoly, morris, Mousetrap
  Operation, Othello
  Parcheesi, Pictionary
  Risk
  Scattergories, Scrabble, Scruples, shogi, Sorry! tiddlywinks, tivoli, trick-track, Trivial Pursuit, Trouble
  Uno, Yahtzee

CHESS

chess game played by two persons, each having sixteen pieces that are moved about a board having sixty-four squares
  advance
  bishop, black
  capture, castle, check, checkmate, chessman
  develop, draw
  end game, en passant, en prise
  fianchetto, fork
  gambit, grandmaster
  horse
  jeopardy
  king, knight, kriegspiel
  master, mate
  opening
  passed pawn, pawn, perpetual check, piece
  queen
  rook
  stalemate
  white

Electronic and Computer Games

GAME SYSTEMS

Atari
Game Boy
Nintendo
Sega, Sega Genesis, Sega Saturn Sony PlayStation

GAMES

Asteroids
Carmen Sandiego, Centipede
Dark Forces, Donkey Kong, Doom, Double Dragon
Flight Simulator
King's Quest
Legend of Zelda, Lemmings
Missile Command, Mortal Kombat, Myst
Oregon Trail
Pac Man
Rebel Assault
7th Guest, SimCity, Sonic the Hedgehog, Street Fighter, Super Mario Brothers
Tank Commander, Tetris
Virtua Fighter
Wing Commander, Wolfenstein

Types of Toys

balls, board games
cards
dolls
mechanical toys, models
novelties
playthings, pull toys, puzzles
soldiers, stuffed animals
windup toys

Toys and Playthings

toy usu. small object, often representing something familiar, for children to play with

action figure, air rifle, alphabet blocks, arrows
Barbie doll, Barney, battledore, beachball, beanbag, bell ringers, bells, bicycle, Big Wheels, blocks, bobblehead doll, boomerang, building blocks
Cabbage Patch doll, cap gun, carriage, chemistry set, Chia pet, Chinese puzzle, clockwork toy, cockhorse, coloring book, comic book, counters, crayons
darts, dice, doll carriage, doll clothes, doll furniture, dollhouse, dreidel
Erector set, Etch-a-Sketch, expression blocks
Gumby, gyroscope
hand puppet, historiscope, hobbyhorse, hoop, hula hoop
Irish mail
jack-in-the-box, jack-o'-lantern, Jenga, jigsaw puzzle, jolly jumper, jungle gym
kaleidoscope, Ken doll, kewpie doll, kite
Lego, Linkin' Logs
magic lantern, Magna Doodle, marionette, marbles, Matchbox car, maze, mechanical bank, Mr. Potato Head, model airplane, model railroad, music box, myriopticon
Nerf ball, Nerf gum, nested blocks, ninepins, Noah's ark
pail and shovel, paints, paper doll, pet rock, picture car, Pik-up-Stix, piggy bank, pinball, pinwheel, Play-doh, pogo stick, pop gun, Power Rangers, puppet, puzzle
rag doll, Raggedy Ann doll, rattle, rocking horse, roller skates, rubber ball
scooter, See 'n' Say, seesaw, shoufly, shuttloooak, Oilly Pully, skateboard, skatemobile, Sky Dancer, sled, sleigh, slide, slingshot, Slinky, slot car, Smurf, soapbox, space toys, squirt gun, stilts, swing
tanagram, teddy bear, teetertotter, tiddlywinks, Tinkertoys, tin rattle, tin soldier, top, toy animal, toy book, toy car, toy drum, toy soldier, toy train, toy truck, trading cards, Transformers, tree house, tricycle Troll
velocipede
wading pool, wagon, walky-talky, water pistol, wheels, whirligig, whistle, windmill
yo-yo
zoetrope

SMOKING AND TOBACCO

See also: *Chap. 24: Drug Abuse and Alcoholism*

ambeer tobacco juice
ash powdery burned tobacco, esp. burned portion of a cigar or cigarette
ashtray small receptacle for collecting ash and extinguishing smoking materials
baccy *Informal.* tobacco
black tobacco dark, strong-tasting cigarette tobacco
bong water pipe
boogie *Slang.* thin-bodied, air-cured tobacco from Kentucky
book pile or package of tobacco leaves
briar pipe carved from root burl of evergreen brier shrub
Burley light-colored tobacco with low nicotine content, grown esp. in Kentucky
butt portion remaining after cigarette or cigar

has been smoked and stubbed out; *Slang.* cigarette
calean Persian water pipe
calumet ornamental, ceremonial pipe of American Indians; peace pipe
canaster coarse pipe tobacco
cancer stick *Slang.* cigarette
carton box containing ten standard packets of cigarettes
cavendish pressed cake of tobacco that has been sweetened, esp. with molasses
chain-smoke (*vb*) smoke cigarettes compulsively
chaw *Informal.* plug of chewing tobacco
cheroot cigar cut square at both ends
chew plug of chewing tobacco
chewing tobacco tobacco leaf treated and pressed into small cakes, portions of which are broken off and chewed
chibouk pipe with long stem and clay bowl (Turkey)
chillum part of water pipe containing tobacco
cigar cylindrical roll of cured tobacco encased in tobacco leaf wrapper
cigar cutter device with blade and point for clipping and piercing cigars before smoking
cigarette thin tube of finely chopped, cured tobacco encased in thin paper, often with filter at one end
cigarette case small, flat container for holding cigarettes
cigarette girl (formerly) young woman selling cigarettes from tray carried around restaurant dining room or cabaret
cigarette holder long, thin, hollow device, often with built-in filter, used to smoke cigarette that is inserted in one end
cigarette machine vending machine that dispenses packages of cigarettes
cigarette paper rolling paper
cigarillo small, thin cigar
cigarro *Spanish.* cigar
cigar-store Indian wooden likeness of Native American, usu. standing outside tobacco shop
cinder portion of burned tobacco not yet reduced to ashes
claro light-colored, mild cigar
clay pipe pipe with bowl made of clay
coffin nail *Slang.* cigarette
colorado cigar of moderate strength and color
corncob pipe pipe made from dried cob of corn
corona cigar with long, straight sides and roundly blunted, unsealed end
cubeb dried tropical berry crushed and smoked in cigarettes
cud individual portion of chewing tobacco
curing process of treating and aging raw tobacco to improve its burn and flavor as smoke
cuspidor open receptacle for expectoration of tobacco juice; spittoon
dip (*vb*) place snuff against one's gums
dottle unburned or partially burned tobacco caked in bowl of pipe
drag single draw on cigarette

dudeen short, clay tobacco pipe
fag *Slang.* cigarette
filter porous substance used to remove impurities from smoke
filter tip cigarette with one end of cellulose or charcoal for filtering smoke
Flip-Top *Trademark.* cardboard cigarette box with hinged cover
gasper *Brit. slang.* cigarette
hand rolling making one's own cigarettes from loose tobacco and rolling papers
hard pack cigarette box made of thin cardboard
Havana high-quality Cuban cigar
hookah water pipe, usu. with long, flexible tube for inhaling smoke (Middle East)
humidor jar or receptacle for storing tobacco and cigars and maintaining their moistness
inhale (*vb*) breathe tobacco smoke into one's lungs, esp. from cigarette
kinnikinnick mixture of dried leaves, bark, and tobacco smoked by Native Americans
Latakia highly aromatic Turkish tobacco
lighter device, usu. with flint, wick, and flammable fuel, used to ignite smoking material
light up (*vb*) ignite and begin smoking, esp. a cigarette
low tar (*adj*) containing less tar than usual or standard, therefore less unhealthy
maccaboy high quality, usu. rose-scented snuff formerly, aromatic tobacco from Martinique
maduro cigar with dark brown leaf wrapper
meerschaum pipe with bowl made of the white, claylike mineral meerschaum
menthol cigarette containing menthol, which has cooling effect on mucous membranes
mundungus tobacco with unpleasant smell
nargileh water pipe of Near Eastern origin
navy plug compressed cake of strong, dark tobacco
nicotiana tobacco grown for its ornamental flowers
nicotine chief active ingredient of tobacco
nicotine addiction physical and psychological dependence on nicotine due to regular smoke inhalation
nicotinism addiction and other effects of regular, prolonged use of nicotine
nonsmoking section area of public space, esp. restaurant, where smoking is prohibited
no smoking admonition that smoking is prohibited
pack rectangular, paper or soft cardboard container usu. containing twenty cigarettes
packet cigarette pack
panatela long, slender, flat-sided cigar
passive smoking inhalation of cigarette, cigar, or pipe smoke of others, esp. by nonsmoker in enclosed area
peace pipe calumet
perfecto cigar tapering nearly to a point at each end
pigtail twisted strand of tobacco
pinch small amount of chewing tobacco or snuff
pipe smoking device consisting of hollow stem

with bowl-shaped receptacle for tobacco at one end and mouthpiece at other

pipe bowl rounded portion of pipe, open at top and connected to one end of pipestem at bottom, into which smoking tobacco is placed

pipe cleaner flexible wire coated with cotton and inserted through pipe stem to remove tar

pipe rack usu. wood device for storage and display of pipes

pipestem long, hollow portion of pipe with bowl at one end and mouthpiece at the other

pipe tobacco tobacco leaves cut in shreds suitable for smoking in a pipe

plug flat, compressed cake of tobacco

puff single drag on cigar, cigarette, or pipe; (vb) smoke, esp. cigar or pipe

quid plug of chewing tobacco

rappee snuff made of dark, pungent tobacco

rolling paper thin slip of paper, usu. gummed at one edge, for hand rolling cigarettes; cigarette paper

roll-your-own cigarette that has been hand rolled

secondhand smoke smoke from someone else's cigarette to which one is exposed secondhand through proximity, as in office or restaurant

seegar Informal spelling. cigar

shag strong, coarse pipe tobacco cut in fine shreds

smoke (vb) inhale and exhale fumes of burning tobacco, esp. do so habitually; (n) cigarette or other smoking material

smoke-free zone area in public place in which smoking is prohibited

smokeless ashtray receptacle for extinguished smoking material with lid to contain smoke

smokeout day during which smokers are encouraged to abstain from smoking as part of widespread campaign

smoker railroad car designated for smoking; smoking car; person who smokes regularly

smoke room room designated for smoking, usu. in public place or club

smoker's cough cough typical of cigarette smokers, due to habitual inhalation of smoke

smokes Informal. cigarettes

smoke shop retail store selling tobacco, pipes, and smoking supplies

smoking act of inhaling and exhaling fumes of burning tobacco

smoking car smoker

smoking jacket man's casual lounging jacket

smoking lamp ship's lamp, illuminated when smoking is permitted

smoking room room in public building or club designated for smoking

smoking section area of public place, esp. restaurant, designated for smoking

smoking stand ashtray set on top of wood or metal support

smoking zone area in public place designated for smoking

snipe Slang. cigar or cigarette butt

snort single inhalation of snuff

snuff tobacco preparation to be inhaled, chewed, or placed against gums

snuffbox small, lidded container for holding snuff

soft pack cigarette packet made of folded paper

spittoon cuspidor

stogy cigar, esp. roughly made, inexpensive one

stub out extinguish cigarette or cigar by crushing its burning portion against a surface

Surgeon General's Report published findings of U.S. government study regarding health dangers of cigarette smoking

tabac French. tobacco

tar dark, viscous, bituminous residue present in smoke and containing poisonous by-products

tobacco leaves of cultivated plant of the nightshade family, cured for smoking, chewing, or use as snuff

tobacco barn tobacco shed

tobacco juice discolored, brown saliva from chewing tobacco or snuff

tobacconist dealer in tobacco and smoking supplies

tobacco pouch soft, folding receptacle for pipe tobacco

tobacco shed long structure in which tobacco is hung for aging, drying, and curing; tobacco barn

tobaccosis nicotine addiction

tobaccoey (adj) like tobacco; filled with tobacco smoke

toke Slang. single drag of a marijuana cigarette

Turkish tobacco dark, aromatic cigarette tobacco, grown esp. in Turkey

twist hand-rolled cigarette

Virginia tobacco tobacco cultivated in eastern United States and cured by heat or dry air, stronger and darker than Burley

water pipe any of various devices in which smoke is cooled by passing through water before being inhaled

weed Informal. tobacco smoking material

DRINKING AND ALCOHOLIC BEVERAGES

Drinking Terms
Bars, Bar Tools, and Habitués
Toasts
Beers
Wines
Spirits
Liqueurs and Cordials
Mixed Drinks

See also: *Chap. 9: Foods; The Kitchen; Chap. 17: Holidays, Celebrations, and Vacations; Chap. 24: Drug Abuse and Alcoholism*

Drinking Terms

abstinence total restraint from consumption of alcohol

after-dinner drink liqueur taken after a meal; digestif

aging process of maturing liquor by long-term storage

alcohol colorless, inflammable liquid intoxicant in wine, beer, and spirits

ale liquor infusion of malt by fermentation, flavored with hops, and stronger than beer

apéritif drink taken as appetizer before meal

bacchanalia drunken revel, esp. honoring Roman god Bacchus

banger Slang. shot of straight spirits, such as vodka, on ice

bathtub gin homemade spirit made from raw alcohol and essential oils

beer alcoholic beverage brewed by slow fermentation from malt and hops; brew; suds

bitters alcoholic liquor flavored with astringent, aromatic, strong-tasting herbs

blue law law restricting alcoholic use, sale, or consumption

bock beer strong dark beer, aged very short time, drunk esp. in spring

bond designation for government-supervised distilled spirits, aged at least four years, and 100 proof

bootlegger one who smuggles or illegally sells liquor

booze Informal. liquor; (vb) drink alcohol

bracer drink taken as stimulant or refresher

brew Informal. beer

brewer one who makes beer

brewsky Informal. beer

brut (adj) designating very dry champagne

bubbly Informal. champagne

BYOB bring your own booze; designation on party invitation that drinks will not be supplied by host

carding Informal. requiring proof of age from customer before selling him or her alcoholic beverage

cask wooden container for aging and storage of alcoholic beverages

cellar stock of wines, usu. stored in cool basement

chaser drink taken immediately after another kind of drink, esp. beer after whiskey

chug-a-lug (vb) drink entire contents of container in one gulp

cocktail mixed alcoholic drink

cocktail party early evening gathering at which drinks and snacks are served

compotation rousing drinking party

cordial liquor sweetened with fruit

cork stopper for wine bottle made from tough outer tissue of cork oak

corkage charge by restaurant for opening bottle of wine purchased elsewhere

corn whiskey mash made from eighty percent corn

corpse reviver Slang. alcoholic drink

digestif after-dinner drink, esp. liqueur, that aids digestion

distillation purification of alcoholic liquor by heating, separation, and condensation

distiller one who makes alcoholic liquor by distillation, vaporizing and extracting its essence

distillery place where whiskey and other liquors are made

doctor (vb) alter or dilute composition of drink

double two shots of liquor in one drink

draft amount drunk in one swallow

dram small drink of liquor

drink alcohol in general; single serving or glassful of liquor; (vb) consume alcoholic beverage

drinking consumption of alcoholic beverages, usu. for pleasure; such consumption to excess

dry (adj) designating locale or time in which sale and consumption of alcohol is forbidden; describing wine that is opposite of sweet

eighty-six common measure of alcoholic content or proof in hard liquor

eyeopener drink taken on awakening or early in the day, esp. when suffering a hangover

fifth one-fifth gallon, standard U.S. bottle size for spirits

finger measure indicating drink filled to width of one finger

firewater Native American slang for alcoholic liquor

forbearance abstinence; temperance

gill measure equal to four fluid ounces

gulp single large swallow of drink

hangover unpleasant aftereffects of too much drink, esp. headache and nausea, experienced following day

hard liquor liquor with alcoholic content higher than that of wine and beer

highball liquor, esp. whiskey, mixed with soda in a tall glass

hogshead large cask, holding from 63 to 140 gallons (238 to 530 l)

home brew homemade alcoholic drink

hooch Slang. alcoholic liquor, esp. of inferior quality

imbibe (vb) drink, esp. to excess

jeroboam oversized wine bottle holding approximately 3 liters (3.3 quarts)

John Barleycorn personification of alcoholic liquor

jug large, narrow-mouthed, earthenware container, esp. for liquor; contents of jug or alcoholic liquor

juice Slang. alcoholic liquor

keg small barrel, esp. for beer on draught

keg party Informal. gathering at which beer is served from keg

knock back (vb) Slang. take a drink, esp. aggressively

lace (vb) fortify drink with alcohol

libation alcoholic drink, esp. wine, poured as offering to god

likker Informal spelling. liquor

liqueur usu. flavored, sweet, thick alcoholic liquor

liquor alcoholic drink, usu. distilled rather than fermented; booze

little brown jug Slang. alcoholic drink

long neck (adj) Informal. designating beer bottle with long neck

magnum large wine or champagne bottle holding 2/5 gallon (1.5 l)

malt liquor strong beer made by fermenting malt

maraschino cherry cherry preserved in sweet liqueur distilled from juice of bitter wild cherry, served in certain cocktails

mash crushed malt or meal mixed with hot water and fermented to form beer or whiskey

Mickey Slang. alcoholic drink doctored with knockout drug; Mickey Finn

mixer nonalcoholic beverage, often carbonated, combined with spirits in cocktail

moonshine Informal. low-quality, illegally distilled or smuggled whiskey, esp. corn liquor

must pulp and skins of crushed grapes before or during fermentation into wine

near beer malt liquor with very low alcohol content

neat (adj) straight up

nectar alcoholic drink

nightcap drink taken just before going to bed

nip small drink, sip of liquor

nog strong English ale

noggin small quantity of drink, esp. one-fourth pint

nondrinker one who practices temperance

off the wagon Slang. having drunk an alcoholic beverage after a period of abstinence

one for the road final drink before leaving bar or party

on the rocks poured over ice

on the wagon Slang. denying oneself alcoholic drink; designating a period of abstinence

package store outlet selling alcoholic beverages for consumption elsewhere

pick-me-up Informal. drink taken to restore one's energy, esp. at end of workday

potable something fit to drink

potation alcoholic drink or brew

potion mixture of liquors

prohibition legal forbidding of manufacture and sale of alcoholic drinks

proof arbitrary standard measure of alcoholic strength of beverage, often twice percent of alcohol content

pull swig or sip of drink

punch mixture of juice, soda, and liquor

punt hollow in exterior bottom of wine bottle

quaff (vb) drink copiously

redeye Slang. cheap, strong whiskey

refraining (adj) practicing temperance

refresher refill of empty drink

rocks Informal. ice cubes

rotgut Slang. inferior, cheap liquor

sauce Slang. alcoholic drink

sec (adj) dry, designating wine, usu. white

shandygaff Chiefly Brit. beer diluted with nonalcoholic drink such as ginger beer

shooter shot of spirits to be drunk in one gulp

sip small taste of drink

six-pack standard unit in which beer is sold

snort Slang. drink taken in one shot

sober (adj) not drunk, esp. habitually temperate in use of alcohol

sobriety quality of being sober

social drinking moderate drinking at gatherings

soft (adj) designating wine and beer, as opposed to hard liquor

soft drink nonalcoholic beverage or mixer

sparkling wine champagne and other effervescent wines

spike (vb) Informal. add alcohol to drink or increase amount of alcohol contained therein

spirits alcoholic beverages; liquor

splash tiny amount of one spirit or water or soda added to a mixed drink

split small bottle, esp. of champagne, usu. 6 ounces (177 l)

stiff (adj) strong, in describing drink; high in alcoholic content

stone cold sober Informal. absolutely unintoxicated

straight up (adj) designating an alcoholic drink without mixer or chilled drink without ice, such as a martini; neat

strong drink alcoholic beverage

suds Slang. beer

swear off (vb) cease drinking for period of time

sweet (adj) describing fruity wines, opposite of dry

swig large swallow of drink

swill (vb) drink in great gulps or guzzle, esp. beer

teetotaler one who does not drink alcohol

temperance moderation or abstinence from alcoholic drink

toast drink taken in honor of person or event, accompanied by words of praise or good wishes, often a standardized phrase

uncork (vb) remove cork stopper from wine bottle

unintoxicated (adj) abstinent, free of alcohol

vintage year in which wine grapes were grown

vintner winemaker

wassail riotous drinking and revelry

wet (adj) designating locale or time in which consumption of alcoholic drinks is permitted

whiskey distilled liquor made from fermented mash of cereal grain, such as barley, rye, or corn

white lightning Informal. moonshine; illegal, low-quality liquor

wine fermented grape juice

Bars, Bar Tools, and Habitués

after-hours (adj) designating establishment serving alcohol after normal bar hours

alehouse place where beer and ale are sold

back (adj) designating nonalcoholic drink served on the side with a shot of spirits

backbar shelves and counter space along wall behind bar, used for storing bottles and glasses

bar place where drinks are served across a long counter; such a counter

bar back busboy who brings supplies and cleans up for bartender

barfly *Slang.* person who frequents bars

barhop (*vb*) *Informal.* visit and drink at series of bars over course of evening

barkeep barkeeper

barkeeper person who owns or tends bar; barkeep

barmaid female serving drinks at bar

bar rag cloth for wiping surface of bar counter

barrelhouse cheap drinking and dancing establishment

barspoon long spoon for stirring drinks, often with spiral handle

barstool tall seat at bar counter, usu. without back or arms

bartender preparer and server of alcoholic drinks at bar counter

beer garden outdoor bar serving beer

beer hall large bar primarily or solely serving beer, esp. German

bistro small bar or tavern, esp. European

bottle club often private club serving drinks after normal legal closing hours

bouncer person employed to maintain order in bar, as by removing unruly customers

buvette *French.* small bar

buy back (*vb*) provide free drink to customer

cabaret club serving food and drink and providing entertainbment

café small, informal barroom or cabaret

call drink brand-label spirits requested by customer

cantina small barroom or saloon, esp. in southwest U.S. or Mexico

cash bar bar at special, often private function that sells drinks to those in attendance

champagne saucer very wide stemmed glass for champagne

cocktail lounge public room where drinks are served, esp. in hotel or restaurant

cocktail napkin small, square napkin served with drink

cocktail shaker glass or metal container for shaking certain chilled, mixed drinks

cocktail stirrer tall spoon or straw used to mix drink

cocktail strainer device to retain ice in shaker from which chilled drink is poured

cocktail waitress female serving drinks in bar

corkscrew spiral device with handle for removing cork stopper from wine bottle

cover charge entry charge, usu. for entertainment, in club or bar

crushed ice granulated bits of ice used in certain drinks

dive *Informal.* cheap, tawdry bar

dramshop bar or saloon

draught drawing of beer from large container or keg; beer so drawn

flight *Slang.* samples of three different wines offered for a set price

glass container for single drink

happy hour early evening hours, usu. between

four and seven p.m., when bar serves drinks at reduced price or with free snacks

honky-tonk cheap, often disreputable bar or club

ice tongs hinged device for lifting ice cubes

jigger small glass used to measure one and a half ounces of spirits

last call final chance to order drinks before bar closing

meat rack *Slang.* singles bar where primary objective is to find sexual partner

no-host bar bar, usu. at private party, requiring payment for drinks

on tap designating beer stored in keg or barrel and drawn off through tap

on the house designating drink purchased for customer at bar's expense

pitcher usu. glass container holding several servings of beer or other drink

pony glass short, narrow, stemmed glass for cordials and straight up cocktails

pourer spigot attachment for bottles allowing one serving to pour each time bottle is upended

pouring whiskey house brand kept on speed rack

pub public house; tavern or bar , esp. in Britain

pub-crawler one who drinks at one bar after another

publican *Chiefly Brit.* proprietor or manager of pub or tavern

rathskeller restaurant patterned after German beer hall, usu. in basement

roadhouse tavern or nightclub located on main thoroughfare outside city limits

rock glass short, stout glass for straight liquor on ice

round single serving of drinks for all present

rumshop *Informal.* cheap bar

run a tab accumulate bill for drinks, to be paid at end of evening or later time

saloon public room for sale and consumption of alcoholic drinks

service bar bar area where only waitresses pick up drinks

shaker container in which certain drinks are mixed

shot small measure of undiluted liquor, usu. one and a half ounces

shot glass small glass used to measure one shot

singles bar bar or tavern catering primarily to single men and women, esp. those seeking sexual partner or lover

snifter balloon-shaped, stemmed goblet that narrows at top, esp. for brandy

soda gun bar device with hose and selector for adding nonalcoholic beverages to drinks

sour mix lemon juice and sugar used in mixed drinks

speakeasy saloon or club selling alcohol illegally, esp. during Prohibition

speed rack bartender's device, on runners, with slots that hold bottles of house brands most frequently used

stand drinks (*vb*) *Informal.* buy a round of drinks for all present

steward supervisor of storage and service of wine in restaurant or large household

strainer flexible mesh device on handle for straining drink into glass

swizzle stick long rod, often in spiral shape, used to mix drinks

tab unpaid portion of bill accumulating at bar

tap (*vb*) draw off liquid, esp. beer, from keg or barrel; (*n*) device that does this

taproom bar serving beer on tap

tapster bartender, esp. in taproom

tavern place where liquor is sold and consumed; formerly an inn

tip cup container placed on bar for bartender's gratuities

top shelf name brands of spirits displayed above bar

twist slice of lemon peel curled over and served in certain drinks

water back glass of water served on side with shot of spirits

watering hole *Informal.* bar or tavern

well drink inexpensive, generic house brand of spirits

Toasts

toast drink taken in honor of person or event, accompanied by words of praise or good wishes, often a standardized phrase
  à votre santé
  bottoms up
  cheerio, cheers, chin chin
  down the hatch
  gesondheid, gun-bei
  health, here's looking at you, here's mud in your eye, here's to you
  kam pai
  l'chaim
  many happy returns
  na zdorovye
  prosit, prost
  salud, sante, skal, skoal
  to your health
  wassail

Beers

beer alcoholic beverage brewed by slow fermentation from malt and hops
  ale
  beer, bitter, bock beer
  craft-brewed beer
  dark beer, dortmunder
  ice beer
  kumis, kvass
  lager, light beer
  malt liquor, mead
  near beer
  pale ale, Pilsner, porter, pulque
  stout
  weiss, wheat beer

Wines

wine fermented grape juice
  Alsace, amontillado, amoroso, apple wine, Asti Spumante

Barbera, Bardolino, Barolo, Beaujolais, Bergerac, blanc de blancs, blanc de noirs, blush, Bordeaux, Burgundy
Cabernet Sauvignon, Catawba, Chablis, Champagne, Chardonnay, Châteauneuf-du-Pape, Chenin blanc, Chianti, Cinzano, claret, cold duck, concord, Côtes de Nuits, Côtes du Rhone
dandelion wine, dessert wine, Do, Dolcetto, Dom Perignon (trade name), Dubonnet (trade name)
fortified wine, Frascati, Fumé Blanc
Gamay, Gewürztraminer, Graves, Grenache
hard cider, hock
Johannisberg Riesling, jug wine
Lachryma Christi, Lambrusco, Liebfraumilch
Macon, Madeira, Malaga, Margaux, Marsala, Mateus Rose, Médoc, Merlot, Moselle, Muscadet, Muscat
Napa Valley, Navarra
oloroso, oporto, Orvieto
Pauillac, Petite Sirah, Pinot Blanc, Pinot Noir, Pomerol, Pommard, port, Pouilly-Fuissé, Pouilly-Fumé
red wine, Riesling, retsina, Rhine, Rhone, Rioja, rose, ruby port
sack, St. Estephe, St. Julien, sake, Sancerre, Sauterne, Sauvignon Blanc, sherry, Shiraz, soave, Sonoma, sparkling wine, Sylvaner
table wine, tawny port, Tokay
Valdepeas, Valpolicella, vermouth, vinho verde, Vouvray
white cabernet, white wine, white zinfandel
zinfandel

Spirits

spirits alcoholic beverages, liquor
advocaat, American whiskey, applejack, aquavit, Armagnac
bathtub gin, blended whiskey, bourbon, brandy
Campari, Canadian whiskey, Cognac, corn liquor, Courvoisier
Dutch gin
gin, grain alcohol, grappa, grog
Irish whiskey
mao-tai, marc, mash, mescal, Metaxa, moonshine
negra
ouzo
pulque
raki, Rémy Martin, rum, rye
Scotch whisky, single-malt Scotch, slivovitz
tequila
vodka
whiskey

Liqueurs and Cordials

cordial liquor sweetened with fruit
liqueur usu. flavored, sweet, thick, alcoholic liquor
absinthe, alcool blanc, amaretto, anisette, apricot brandy, Asiago
Baily's Irish Cream, B and B, Benedictine, bitters
Calvados, cassis, Chamborel, Chartreuse, Cointreau, crème de bananas, crème de cacao, crème de cassis, crème de fraise, crème de framboise, crème de menthe, crème de violette, curaçao
Drambuie
Frangelico

Galliano, Goldschalger, Grand Marnier
Irish Mist
Kahlua, Kir, kirsch(wasser), kummel
Marachino, Midori, mocha liqueur
pastis, Pernod, Pimm's, poire William
ratafia
Sabra, sambuca, schapps, sloe gin, Southern Comfort, Strega
Tia Maria, triple sec
Vandermint
Yukon Jack

Mixed Drinks

Alabama slammer amaretto, Southern Comfort, sloe gin, and lemon juice
alexander gin, crème de cacao, and light cream
angel's kiss crème de cacao, sloe gin, brandy, and light cream
Bacardi cocktail Bacardi rum, juice of lime, and grenadine
B & B Benedictine and brandy
Bahama mama rum, coconut liqueur, coffee liqueur, pineapple juice, and lemon juice
banshee crème de banana, crème de cacao, light cream
bay breeze vodka, pineapple juice, and cranberry juice
Bellini champagne, peach nectar, lemon juice, and grenadine
between the sheets brandy, triple sec, rum, and a squeeze of lemon
B-52 Kahlua, Irish Mist, Grand Marnier
Black Russian vodka and coffee liqueur
black velvet Guinness stout and champagne
bloody Caesar littleneck clam, vodka, tomato juice, Worcestershire sauce, Tabasco sauce, horseradish, and dash of salt
Bloody Mary vodka, tomato juice, lemon juice, Worcestershire sauce, Tabasco, and salt and pepper
blue lagoon vodka, blue curaçao, and lemonade
blue margarita tequila, blue curaçao, and lime juice
blue whale vodka, blue curaçao, orange juice, and lemon juice
bocce ball amaretto, orange juice, and soda
brandy alexander crème de cacao, brandy, and heavy cream
Bronx cocktail gin, dry vermouth, sweet vermouth, and orange juice
bullshot vodka, beef bouillon, and salt and pepper
buttered rum hot buttered rum
Cape Codder vodka or rum, cranberry juice, and squeeze of lime
cement mixer Irish cream liqueur and lemon or lime juice, mixed in the mouth
champagne cocktail champagne, sugar, and bitters
champagne cooler brandy, Cointreau, and champagne
chi-chi vodka, pineapple juice, and cream of coconut

clamato cocktail vodka, clam juice, and tomato juice
cobbler wine or liquor, fruit, and shaved ice
cocktail any mixed drink containing liquor
collins liquor, squeeze of lemon or lime, soda water, and powdered sugar
cooler wine or other spirits, fruit juice, and carbonated water
Cuba libre rum, cola, and a squeeze of lime
daiquiri rum, squeeze of lemon or lime, and sugar
a day at the beach coconut rum, amaretto, orange juice, and grenadine
depth charge shot of schnapps in a glass of beer
dirty banana Kahlua, banana liqueur, rum, and pincapple juice
eggnog liquor, milk, beaten egg or crème, and sugar
Fifth Avenue crème de cacao, apricot brandy, and light cream
firefly light crème de cacao, cream, and rosemint
fizz liquor, carbonated beverage, citrus juice, and sugar
flip liquor or wine, egg, and sugar
foxy lady amaretto, crème de cacao, and heavy cream
frappé liqueur poured over shaved ice
French connection Cognac and amaretto
fuzzy navel peach schnapps and orange juice
Gibson gin, dry vermouth, and a pearl onion
gimlet gin or vodka, lemon or lime juice, and sugar
gin and tonic gin and quinine water
gin fizz gin, squeeze of lemon, sugar and soda
gin rickey gin, lime juice, and soda
godfather scotch and amaretto
godmother vodka and amaretto
golden Cadillac crème de cacao, Galliano, and light cream
grasshopper crème de cacao, crème de menthe, and light cream
greyhound vodka and grapefruit juice
grog rum and water, served hot with lemon and sugar
Harvey Wallbanger vodka, Galliano, and orange juice
highball liquor and water or carbonated beverage
Hollywood vodka, Chambord, and pineapple juice
hot buttered rum rum, sugar, butter, and hot water; buttered rum
hot toddy toddy
Indian summer apple schnapps and hot apple cider
Irish coffee whiskey, hot coffee, sugar, and whipped cream
Jack Rose apple brandy, lime juice, and grenadine
kamikaze vodka, triple sec, and lime juice
King Alphonse dark crème de cacao and cream
Kir white wine and crème de cassis
Kir royale champagne and crème de cassis

Long Island iced tea rum, gin, vodka, triple sec, lemon juice, and cola

madras vodka, orange juice, and cranberry juice

mai tai rum, curaao, grenadine, lemon and pineapple juice, almond syrup, and sugar

Manhattan whiskey and sweet vermouth

Margarita tequila, triple sec, and lemon or lime juice

martini gin and dry vermouth

melon ball melon liqueur, vodka, and pineapple juice

Mexican coffee coffee liqueur, tequila, coffee, and whipped cream

mimosa champagne and orange juice

mind eraser Kahlua and vodka on ice, topped with club soda

mint julep bourbon, crushed ice, sugar, sprigs of mint, and water

Moscow mule vodka, ginger ale, and a squeeze of lime

mudslide Kahlua, Irish cream liqueur, and vodka, with cream and/or ice cream

negus wine, hot water, sugar, nutmeg, and lemon

nutcracker amaretto, hazelnut cream, and coconut

nutty professor Grand Marnier, hazelnut liqueur, and Irish cream liqueur

old fashioned whiskey, sugar, bitters, and water

orange blossom gin, orange juice, and sugar

passion mimosa champagne and passionfruit juice

peppermint pattie white crème de cacao and white crème de menthe

Pimm's cup Pimm's No. 1 Cup and lemonade or ginger ale

piña colada rum, coconut milk, and crushed pineapple

pink lady gin, grenadine, and egg white

pink squirrel crème de noyeaux, crème de cacao, and light cream

planter's punch rum, squeeze of lime, sugar, and carbonated water

platinum blonde rum, Cointreau, and cream

posset hot milk curdled with ale or wine, sweetened and spiced

pousse café grenadine, yellow chartreuse, crème de cassis, white crème de menthe, green chartreuse, and brandy, served in layers

prairie oyster cognac, vinegar, Worcestershire sauce, catsup, and angostura

presbyterian rye or bourbon, soda, and ginger ale

punch any combination of alcoholic beverages, fruit juices, and other beverages, usu. in a large bowl

quaalude vodka, hazelnut liqueur, coffee liqueur, and milk

Ramos gin fizz gin, egg white, cream, lemon juice, and sugar

red death amaretto, Southern Comfort, sloe gin, Yukon Jack, lemon juice, and lime juice

rickey gin or vodka, soda, and a squeeze of lime

Rob Roy Scotch and sweet vermouth

rum and coke rum and cola

rusty nail Scotch and Drambuie

salty dog gin or vodka, grapefruit juice, and salt

sangre tequila, tomato juice, lemon juice, Worcestershire sause, tobasco, and salt and pepper

sangria red wine, fruit juice, fruit chunks

San Juan cooler rum, lemon juice, and pineapple juice

Scarlett O'Hara Southern Comfort, cranberry juice, and lime juice

Scotch and Soda Scotch whiskey and Soda

screwdriver vodka and orange juice

sea breeze vodka, grapefruit juice and cranberry juice

Seven and Seven Seagram's Seven Canadian Whiskey and 7-UP

sex on the beach vodka, peach-flavored schnapps, orange juice, cranberry juice, and pineapple juice

shandy *Chiefly Brit.* beer and lemonade

sidecar brandy, cointreau, and lemon juice

Singapore sling gin, cherry-flavored brandy, sugar, and carbonated water

slam dunk Southern Comfort, orange juice, and cranberry juice

sling liquor, sugar, lemon or lime juice, and water

slippery nipple sambuca and Bailey's Irish Mist

sloe gin fizz sloe gin, squeeze of lemon, and powdered sugar

smash liquor, sugar, sprigs of mint, water, and ice

snake bite Yukon Jack and lime juice

sombrero coffee flavored brandy and milk or light cream

sour liquor, squeeze of lemon or lime, sugar, and sometimes soda water

spritzer white wine and carbonated water

stinger brandy and crème de menthe

syllabub sweetened milk or cream mixed with wine or cider

Tang orange-flavored vodka, orange juice, grapefruit juice, and 7-UP

tequila sunrise tequila, grenadine, and orange juice

toddy rum or other liquor, boiling water, and sugar; hot toddy

Tom and Jerry rum, spices, milk, egg, and sugar

Tom Collins gin, squeeze of lemon or lime, sugar, and carbonated water

velvet hammer vodka, crème de cacao, and light cream

virgin Mary tomato juice, Worcestershire sauce, Tabasco sauce, lemon juice, salt and pepper

vodka and tonic vodka and tonic water

vodka martini vodka and dry vermouth

Wassail spiced ale or wine, sometimes with baked apple

whiskey sour whiskey, squeeze of lemon, and powdered sugar

white lady gin, cream, egg white, and powered sugar

White Russian vodka, coffee liqueur, and milk or cream

white spider vodka and white crème de menthe

wild thing tequila, cranberry juice, club soda, and lime juice

wine cooler wine and carbonated beverage

wu-wu vodka, peach schnapps, cranberry juice, and grapefruit juice

zombie rum, apricot-flavored brandy, pineapple juice, squeeze of lime, squeeze of orange, and powered sugar

PART SIX
LANGUAGE

CHAPTER EIGHTEEN
STRUCTURE AND USAGE

Grammar and Usage

ablative case indicating noun is starting point, means, instrument, or agent

abstract noun noun describing something general or not perceivable by sense

accidence study of grammatical inflection

accusative case indicating noun is direct object of verb

active voice verb form indicating that subject is performing action expressed by verb

agreement parallelism, as between subject and verb, in person, number, gender, or case

antecedent substantive that is replaced by pronoun, usu. later in same or subsequent sentence

aorist verb tense, as in Classical Greek, expressing past action without reference to its completion or duration

apodosis clause expressing result in conditional sentence

apposition placing of word or phrase after a substantive to explain or identify it

article modifier "a," "an," or "the" used to signal presence and definiteness or indefiniteness of following noun

aspect verb form indicating nature of action expressed by verb with regard to duration, repetition, beginning, or completion

attributive adjective or noun placed adjacent to noun it modifies

auxiliary verb verb used with main verb to indicate tense, mood, or voice

case role of noun, pronoun, or adjective in relation to rest of sentence, usu. shown by inflection

causative word noting causation

clause group of words containing subject and predicate

collective noun noun that is singular in form but denotes a group

comma fault use of comma between related main clauses in absence of conjunction, usu. considered incorrect in formal usage; comma splice

comma splice comma fault

common gender class of words that may refer to either a male or female

common noun noun that refers to any or all members of a class of beings or things rather than a particular individual

comparative second degree of comparison of adjectives or adverbs, indicated by ending "-er" or the word "more"

comparison inflection of adverbs and adjectives to show degrees: positive, comparative, superlative

complement word or phrase that completes a grammatical construction in the predicate and describes or is identified with the subject or object

complex sentence sentence containing one independent clause and one or more dependent clauses

compound-complex sentence sentence containing more than one independent clause and one or more dependent clauses

compound sentence sentence composed of two or more simple sentences joined by coordinating conjunctions

compound word word formed by combining two or more existing words

concrete noun noun describing something that can be perceived by sense

conditional (*adj*) designating clause, word, mood, or sentence that expresses a condition or hypothetical state

conjugation inflection of a verb

connective word that joins words, phrases, clauses, and sentences

construction arrangement of two or more words or morphemes in grammatical unit

contraction shortened form of word or phrase, with omitted letters replaced by apostrophe

coordinating conjunction conjunction that connects two words, phrases, or clauses of equal grammatical rank

copula verb that links subject and predicate; linking verb

copulative (*adj*) designating a verb functioning as a copula; designating a conjunction that connects words or clauses of equal rank or function

correlative word used regularly in association with another word, such as the conjunctions "either" and "or"

count noun noun that refers to countable thing and can be used in the singular or plural, such as "bus"

dangling participle participle that appears from its position to modify a word other than the one intended

dative noun case for indirect object in inflected languages

declarative sentence sentence that makes a statement

declension inflection of nouns, pronouns, and adjectives for gender, number, and case; class of nouns or adjectives having similar inflected forms

definite article article "the" that classes modified noun as identified or specific

demonstrative pronoun or adjective that points out the person or thing referred to

dependent clause clause unable to function as

complete sentence on its own; subordinate clause

determiner word that modifies or restricts a noun and is placed before any other adjectives

diagram grammatical analysis of sentence in graphic form

direct address form of noun used to address person or object directly in a sentence

direct object word or phrase representing person or thing that receives action denoted by transitive verb

dual form in some languages that indicates reference to two persons or things

dvandva compound word composed of comparable, nonsubordinate elements, such as "bittersweet"

emphatic (*adj*) designating a form used to add emphasis, such as "do" in "I do like it"

epicene (*adj*) designating a noun or pronoun capable of referring to either sex

exclamatory sentence sentence expressing surprise or strong feeling

exophora use of word or phrase that refers to something outside its linguistic environment, such as "that" in "Look at that"

expletive word used to introduce a subject, esp. "there" or "it" used as introductory word

factitive (*adj*) pertaining to verb expressing process of making or rendering in a certain way

feminine grammatical gender that includes most nouns referring to females, as well as other nouns

first person form of pronoun or verb indicating speaker or group including speaker, as "I" or "am"

form class group of words or forms in specific language that have one or more grammatical features in common

function word word that expresses grammatical relationships and has little semantic content

future verb tense indicating action or state in the future

future perfect verb tense indicating action to be completed by or to extend up to specified time in the future

gender grammatical distinction applied to nouns and pronouns, often correlated with sex, but sometimes based on arbitrary assignment

genitive noun case indicating possession or origin

gerund verb form ending in English in "-ing" and functioning as verbal noun

govern (*vb*) require the use of a particular form of another word

grammar study of the way sentences of a language are constructed; these features or constructions themselves; set of rules accounting for these constructions

grammarian expert in grammar

grammatical (*adj*) relating to grammar; conforming to standard usage

head chief member of grammatical construction, which determines grammatical role of entire construction or upon which other members depend

helping verb auxiliary verb

heteroclite (*adj*) irregular in inflection

historical present present tense used in narrating past event

hypotaxis dependent or subordinate relation or construction

imperative verb mood indicating command or request

imperfect verb tense indicating habitual or incomplete action continuing at some temporal point of reference in past

impersonal (*adj*) being a verb with only third person singular forms and having an unspecified subject

inceptive verb form or aspect expressing beginning of an action; inchoative

inchoative inceptive

indefinite article article "a" or "an" that classes modified noun as singular but unidentified

indefinite pronoun pronoun such as "some" or "any" that does not specify the identity of its referent

independent clause main clause

indicative verb mood indicating statement or question

indirect object word or phrase representing person or thing with reference to which the action of verb is performed

infinitive basic verb form that does not show person, number, or tense and is often preceded by "to"

inflection change in grammatical function of word, as in case, number, or person, esp. by adding affix

intensifier intensive

intensive linguistic element, esp. an adverb, indicating increased emphasis or force; intensifier

interrogative word or construction used in asking a question

intransitive verb verb having no direct object of its action, which is complete

inversion change in usual word order, as in placement of auxiliary verb before subject

irregular (*adj*) not conforming to the usual pattern of inflection in a language

linking verb copula

locative noun case indicating place or position

loose sentence sentence in which subordinate clause or modifiers follow completion of main clause

main clause clause that could stand alone as complete sentence

marker element indicating grammatical class or function of construction

masculine grammatical gender that includes most nouns referring to males, as well as other nouns

mass noun noun that refers to indefinitely divisible substance or abstract notion, such as "electricity" or "truth"

middle voice verb form, as in Greek, indicating that the subject is acting on or for itself

misplaced modifier word, phrase, or clause erroneously placed in sentence so that it modifies a different noun from that intended

modal auxiliary auxiliary verb used with another verb to express mood, such as "can" or "must"

modifier word or phrase qualifying or describing meaning of another word, esp. adjective and adverb or prepositional phrase

mood indication of condition or manner of verb's action: indicative, imperative, subjunctive, optative

neuter grammatical gender for nouns not classed as masculine or feminine

nominative case usu. indicating that noun is subject of verb

nonrestrictive clause relative clause that describes or supplements modified element but is not essential to its basic meaning

noun phrase grammatical construction that functions as a noun, consisting of a noun and any modifiers or a noun substitute, such as a pronoun

number indication whether noun, verb, etc., refers to one or more than one: singular, plural, dual

object noun or noun substitute that receives or is affected by action of verb; noun or pronoun representing goal of preposition

objective grammatical case used for object of transitive verb or preposition

optative verb mood expressing a wish or desire

paradigm set of all inflected forms of a word

parataxis joining together of clauses or phrases without conjunctions

parse (*vb*) analyze, describe, and grammatically label the parts of a sentence

participle verb form that can be used as adjective or with auxiliary verb to form certain tenses

particle small, usually uninflected word that has grammatical use rather than lexical meaning, esp. a word that does not fit into part of speech categories

part of speech basic class of words in given language to which any word can be assigned based on meaning, form, or function in a sentence

passive voice verb form indicating that subject is receiver of action expressed by verb

past verb tense referring to events or states in times gone by

past participle verb form usu. ending in "-ed" or "-en," used as adjective or in forming passive voice or perfect tenses

past perfect verb tense indicating action or state completed before specific time in past

perfect verb tense noting action or state terminated prior to some temporal point of reference

perfect participle past participle

periodic sentence sentence in which

completion of main clause is suspended until end

periphrastic (*adj*) using two or more words instead of an inflected word to express a grammatical function

person indication of person speaking, spoken to, or spoken about: first (I, we); second (you); third (he, she, it, they)

personal pronoun any pronoun that distinguishes speaker or one spoken to or about: I, we, you, he, she, it, they

phrasal verb unit consisting of verb and one or more adverbs or prepositions, often having idiomatic meaning

phrase sequence of grammatically related words lacking subject and predicate

pluperfect past perfect

plural form designating more than one

positive first degree of comparison of adjectives or adverbs, being the basic form

possessive form or case indicating ownership or possession

postposition placing of word, particle, or affix after another word to modify it or relate it to other elements of sentence

predicate that which is said about subject of sentence

predicate nominative noun or pronoun that has same referent as subject and is used in predicate with copula

prepositional phrase phrase made up of preposition and its noun or pronoun object with any modifiers

present verb tense indicating action or state occurring or existing now

present participle verb form ending in "-ing" used as modifier or in forming the progressive

present perfect verb tense indicating action completed at present time or continuing from past into present

preterit verb tense indicating action or state, esp. completed action or state, in past

principal parts verb forms from which all other inflected forms can be derived, consisting of infinitive, past tense, and past participle

privative affix indicating negation or absence, such as "a-" in "apolitical"

progressive verb form indicating continuing action

proper noun name of specific person, place, or thing, usu. indicated by capitalization

qualifier adjective or adverb used to qualify or limit meaning of word modified

quantifier modifier that establishes amount or extent of word modified

reduplication doubling of syllable or other element, sometimes in modified form, to generate derivative or inflected form

reflexive verb taking subject and object with same referents; pronoun used as object to refer to subject of verb

regular (*adj*) conforming to usual pattern of inflection in a language

relative clause subordinate clause that modifies antecedent noun or pronoun

relative pronoun pronoun used to introduce relative clause

restrictive clause relative clause that identifies or limits meaning of word modified and is essential to meaning of sentence

run-on sentence sequence of two or more main clauses not separated by semicolon, conjunction, or period

second person form of pronoun or verb used in referring to one or ones addressed, as "you"

sentence grammatically independent unit expressing a statement, question, command, or exclamation, usu. consisting of subject and predicate

sentence fragment phrase or clause written as sentence but lacking subject or verb

serial comma comma used after next to last item and before conjunction in series of three or more items

simple sentence sentence consisting of only one main clause and no dependent clauses

singular form designating just one

split infinitive placing of word or phrase, usu. adverb, between "to" and its verb in infinitive form

strong verb verb that forms past tense and past participle by internal vowel change

subject word or phrase about which something is stated in sentence

subjunctive verb mood indicating doubt, wish, or hypothetical state

subordinate clause dependent clause

subordinating conjunction conjunction joining independent clause and dependent clause

substantive word or group of words functioning as a noun

superlative highest degree of comparison, of adjectives or adverbs, indicated by ending "-est" or the word "most"

suppletive (*adj*) describing inflected form of word entirely different from stem, such as past tense of "go"

tense verb form indicating time of action or state denoted by verb

third person form of pronoun or verb indicating person or thing spoken of, as "he" or "goes"

transitive verb verb indicating action upon direct object and able to form passive voice

verbal word derived from verb and used as noun or adjective: gerund, infinitive, or participle

verb phrase verb and its modifiers, objects, or complements functioning together in a sentence; main verb and auxiliary verbs functioning together as a verb

vocative noun case indicating direct address

voice verb form indicating whether subject acts or is acted upon

volitive (*adj*) pertaining to verb expressing a wish or permission

weak verb verb that forms past tense and past participle by adding suffix

word order sequence in which words are arranged in sentence or construction

Parts of Speech

adjective word modifying a noun usu. by describing, delimiting, or specifying quantity

adverb word modifying a verb, adjective, other adverb, or clause, usu. by indicating where, when, how, or to what degree

conjunction word connecting words or word groups

interjection word used by itself to express emphatic feeling, such as "hurrah" or "yikes"

noun word naming a person, animal, object, idea, quality, act, or place

preposition word expressing relation between its object and another word or phrase in sentence

pronoun word taking place of a noun or noun phrase

verb word expressing action, state of being, or a relation between things

Punctuation and Diacritics

accent mark mark used to show emphasis on a particular syllable or how a letter is to be pronounced

acute accent ´ short line slanting up to right placed over vowel to show that it has a certain sound quality or has the main stress

ampersand & standing for the word "and"

angle brackets < > used to set off what is enclosed

apostrophe ' used in contractions and possessives

asterisk * placed in printed matter as reference or to indicate omission of material found elsewhere; star

bang *Slang*. exclamation point (Printing and Computers)

braces { } used to connect words or items to be considered together

brackets [ ] used to enclose and set off matter within text, to indicate aggregation, or as parentheses within parentheses

breve ˘ small, open, U-shaped symbol placed over letter to indicate short vowel or short or unstressed syllable

bullet • large, solid, vertically centered dot placed in printed matter to call attention to particular passage, or used for syllable divisions in dictionaries

caret ^ used to indicate where something is to be inserted

cedilla ¸ hooklike mark placed under consonant, usu. "c," to indicate modification of usual phonetic value, as in French "façade"

circumflex ^ placed over vowel to show that it is long, pronounced with rise or fall in pitch, or pronounced with particular sound quality

colon : used to direct attention to matter that follows, esp. list, quotation, or explanation, and indicating a nearly full stop

comma , used to set off word, phrase, or clause or to separate items in list, and indicating slight pause

dagger † vertical cross widening at top of upright used as reference mark or to indicate person has died

dash — used to indicate break or shift in thought or sentence, around a parenthetical element, or prior to attribution of quote

diacritic mark placed over, under, or through a letter to indicate pronunciation or stress, or to distinguish words with identical spellings

diacritical mark diacritic

diagonal virgule

dieresis ¨ placed over second of two vowels to show that it is pronounced separately, as in "naïve"

diesis double dagger

ditto mark " placed on next line under word or phrase to indicate repetition

double dagger ‡ vertical cross with two horizontals used as reference mark; diesis

ellipsis ... used to indicate omission of letters or words

exclamation mark exclamation point

exclamation point ! used to replace period for emphasis at end of sentence; exclamation mark

fistnote index

full stop *Chiefly Brit.* period

grave accent ` short line slanting up to left placed over vowel to show that it has certain sound quality, has secondary stress, or is pronounced rather than silent

haček ˇ small V-shaped symbol over consonant, usu. indicating palatalized sound

hamza ʾ indicating glottal stop in Arabic

hyphen - used to divide or join compound words, to break word between two lines, and in writing out compound numbers

index ☞ stylized hand with one finger extended horizontally and other fingers curled, used to point out important note or paragraph in text

interrobang ‽ question mark overlaid on exclamation point used at end of exclamatory rhetorical question

interrogation mark question mark

leaders series of spaced dots or hyphens used to lead eye horizontally

macron ¯ horizontal line placed over vowel to indicate it is long or over syllable to indicate long or stressed syllable

obelisk dagger

paragraph mark ¶ used to indicate beginning of new paragraph

parallels ‖ used as reference mark in printing

parentheses ( ) used to enclose amplifying or explanatory word or phrase or alternative term

period . indicating end of sentence, also used after abbreviations and initials

pilcrow paragraph mark

prime ′ placed after letter or character to distinguish from another of the same kind, as A, A′, or to show primary stress

punctuation system of standardized graphic

symbols inserted in written matter to clarify meaning and separate structural units

question mark ? used to replace period at end of interrogative sentence

quotation marks " " used to set off and surround spoken or quoted material, some titles, and special or borrowed words; ' ' used to set off and surround a quotation within a quotation

quotes quotation marks

section mark § pair of S's stacked vertically and interlocking, used to indicate beginning of text subdivision or as reference mark

semicolon ; used to separate major elements of sentence, such as independent clauses, and to separate elements of series which themselves contain commas

slash virgule

solidus virgule

square brackets brackets

star asterisk

stress mark mark placed before, over, or after syllable to indicate stress in pronunciation

subscript any symbol written below normal line of letters

superscript any symbol written above normal line of letters

swung dash ~ used in place of word or part of word previously spelled out

tilde ~ placed over letter "n" in Spanish to indicate palatal sound (ny) or over vowel in Portuguese to indicate nasalization

umlaut ¨ two dots placed above vowel, esp. in German, to indicate modification of its sound, as in "Lübeck"

virgule / placed between words to separate alternatives, indicate "or," "and or," or "per"; diagonal, slash, or solidus

vowel point dot, line, or other mark placed above or below consonant symbol to indicate vowel sound, as in Hebrew

Phonetics

accent variation in pronunciation of words due to regional, class, or cultural factors; emphasis on particular syllable of word or word within phrase

affricate consonant sound involving complete closure in vocal tract gradually released with audible friction

allophone one of the alternate phonetic forms of a phoneme, depending on its environment

alveolar consonant sound made by tongue against bony ridge behind upper front teeth

apheresis loss of one or more sounds or letters at beginning of word

apocope omission of last letter, syllable, or part of word

aspirate sound characterized by audible breath accompanying sound's articulation

assimilation process by which speech sound becomes more like neighboring sound

bilabial consonant sound formed by coming together of both lips

breath expiration of air through open glottis, without vibration of vocal cords

brogue Irish accent in English pronunciation; any strong regional accent

buccal (*adj*) pertaining to sounds made in cavity of cheeks

cardinal vowel any of eight primary, sustained vowel sounds used as reference points for describing vowel sounds of a language

click sound formed by suction of air into mouth and sudden plosive or affricate release

close (*adj*) designating vowel produced with tongue close to roof of mouth

closed (*adj*) designating syllable ending with consonant

cluster succession of two or more consonants in a syllable

complementary distribution relationship between speech sounds that do not occur in the same environment

consonant one of two basic categories of speech sounds, based on closure or near-closure in vocal tract to produce blockage of air or audible friction

continuant consonant sound that may be prolonged without change in quality

coronal (*adj*) articulated with blade, or front, of tongue raised

dental consonant sound made by pressure of tongue against teeth

devoice (*vb*) pronounce a normally voiced sound as voiceless or with reduced vibration of vocal cords

digraph pair of letters representing single speech sound, such as "sh" in "show"

diphthong complex vowel sound characterized by gliding change in tone during articulation of single syllable

dissimilation process by which speech sound becomes different from neighboring sound or disappears because of identical sound nearby

distinctive feature phonetic property serving to characterize and distinguish between phonemes in a language

disyllable word consisting of two syllables

dorsal speech sound made by pressure of back of tongue on roof of mouth

egressive (*adj*) generated with exhalation of breath from lungs

ejective voiceless stop or fricative produced with air compressed above closed glottis

elision omission of sounds in connected speech

enclitic unstressed word or form closely connected in pronunciation with preceding word and not normally used on its own

epenthesis insertion of extra sound in middle of word

excrescent (*adj*) designating sound inserted in word due to articulation but without grammatical or etymological justification

flap consonant sound produced by rapid flip of tongue against roof of mouth or upper teeth

fortis (*adj*) designating consonant sound

characterized by relatively strong, forceful breath or effort

free variation relationship between speech sounds such that one may occur in place of the other with no change in meaning

fricative consonant sound characterized by audible friction of moving air forced between vocal organs; spirant

geminate doubled consonant sound

glottal (*adj*) articulated in opening at upper part of larynx, between vocal cords

glottal stop consonant sound made in larynx by closing glottis or vocal cords

guttural (*adj*) articulated in back of mouth or with tongue against soft palate

haplology omission of one of two similar sounds or syllables in a word

implosive consonant sound formed by inward-moving air, closure of mouth, and vocal cord vibration

inflection quality or variation of tone or pitch of voice

ingressive (*adj*) produced with air taken into mouth

interdental consonant sound made with tip of tongue between upper and lower teeth

International Phonetic Alphabet IPA; symbols used as universal system for transcribing speech sounds of any language

intonation pattern or form of pitch in articulation of words

intrusive (*adj*) designating speech sound inserted in connected speech where it is not present in the spelling

IPA International Phonetic Alphabet

labial speech sound formed by active use of lip or lips

labiodental speech sound formed by lower lip in contact with upper teeth

lallation lambdacism

lambdacism substitution of "l" for "r" or mispronunciation of "l"; lallation

laminal speech sound formed using blade of tongue

laryngeal (*adj*) articulated in the larynx

lax (*adj*) designating vowel pronounced with muscles relatively relaxed

lenis (*adj*) designating consonant sound characterized by relatively weak muscular tension and breath pressure

liaison linking of words, esp. in French, in which otherwise silent final consonant is pronounced as initial sound of following word that begins with vowel

liquid speech sound, such as "l", pronounced without friction and capable of being prolonged like a vowel

long vowel vowel sound relatively long in duration

metathesis transposition of letters, syllables, or sounds in a word

modulation variation in pitch and loudness of the voice

monophthong vowel retaining same quality throughout its duration

monosyllable word consisting of only one syllable

mouillé (*adj*) pronounced as a palatal or palatized sound, as the sounds spelled "ll" and "ñ" in Spanish

mutation phonetic change in initial consonant of a word under certain conditions, as observed in the Celtic languages; umlaut

nasal speech sound formed by audible passage of air through nose

obstruent speech sound characterized by stoppage or obstruction of exhalation: stop, fricative, or affricate

occlusion brief complete closure in vocal tract, resulting in stoppage of exhalation and ensuing pressure

open (*adj*) designating vowel produced with relatively large opening above the tongue; designating syllable ending with vowel

orthoepy study of pronunciation; standard pronunciation of a language

palatal speech sound formed with tongue close to or touching hard palate

paragoge addition of letter or syllable to end of word without changing meaning

pharyngeal speech sound produced in the pharynx

phone single speech sound

phoneme smallest unit of sound in a language that can distinguish one word from another

phonemics study of phonemes and phonemic systems of languages

phonetic alphabet alphabet having separate symbol for each distinguishable speech sound

phonetician specialist in phonetics

phonetics study of speech sounds and their production, transmission, reception, and transcription

phonology study of distribution and patterns of speech sounds in a language or languages

phonotactics patterns in which sounds of a language may combine to form sequences

pitch acoustic character of speech based on high or low quality of sound frequency

plosive consonant sound characterized by sudden release of complete closure in vocal tract, with audible expulsion of compressed air

polysyllable word consisting of two or more syllables

primary accent primary stress

primary stress strongest, principle stress of a word; primary accent

proclitic unstressed word or form closely connected in pronunciation with a following word and not normally used on its own

pronunciation act or manner of producing speech sounds; accepted way in which a word, syllable, or letter is sounded in a given language; phonetic transcription of word

prothesis addition of sound or syllable at beginning of word

quality characteristic timbre of a vowel sound

quantity relative duration, or length, of a sound or syllable

Received Pronunciation RP; prestigious, regionally neutral pronunciation of British English derived from educated speech of S England, widely used in British broadcasting

resonance amplification of speech sound by vibrations of air in vocal tract

retroflex (*adj*) designating speech sound made with tip of tongue curled up and back toward hard palate

rhotacism excessive use or misarticulation of the sound "r"

rounded (*adj*) designating speech sound pronounced with rounded lips

RP **R**eceived **P**ronunciation

sandhi modification of phonological entity determined by phonetic environment

schwa neutral, unstressed vowel sound made in center of mouth; symbol (ə) for this sound

secondary accent secondary stress

secondary stress stress in word weaker than primary stress but not unstressed; secondary accent

short vowel vowel sound relatively short in duration

sibilant speech sound characterized by "s" or hissing sound

sonant speech sound that is voiced; speech sound that forms syllable by itself

sonorant voiced speech sound made with relatively free passage of air, such as vowel or nasal

sound spectrogram graphic representation made by sound spectrograph

sound spectrograph electronic device that produces graphic representation of component frequencies and other acoustic features of a sound

spirant fricative

stop consonant sound made with complete closure at some part of vocal tract; plosive

stress degree of force applied in pronouncing sound, syllable, or word, producing relative loudness

suction stop click or implosive

surd (*adj*) voiceless; unvoiced

syllable basic uninterrupted unit of pronunciation consisting of vowel sound, vowel sound with one or more consonant sounds, or consonant pronounced alone

synaloepha blending of vowel at end of one word with vowel at beginning of next

syncope dropping of sounds or letters from middle of word

syneresis contraction of two syllables or vowels into one, esp. to form diphthong

synizesis combination of two vowels that do not form diphthong

tense (*adj*) designating vowel pronounced with muscles relatively tense

tonic syllable in an utterance having principal stress, usu. accompanied by change in pitch

transcription writing of speech sounds using phonetic symbols

trigraph three letters representing single speech sound

trill speech sound formed by rapid rolling or tapping motion of tongue or uvula

triphthong monosyllabic speech sound composed of three different vowel qualities

umlaut change in vowel sound in a Germanic language under influence of vowel originally occurring in following syllable

unstressed (*adj*) pronounced without stress or emphasis

unvoiced (*adj*) voiceless; surd

uvular speech sound made by placing back of tongue against fleshy process on soft palate

velar speech sound formed by placing back of tongue against soft palate

vocalic (*adj*) relating to or containing a vowel or vowels

voiced (*adj*) produced with vibration of vocal cords

voiceless (*adj*) produced without vibration of vocal cords; unvoiced; surd

voiceprint graphic representation of acoustic features of person's voice; sound spectrogram

vowel one of two basic categories of speech sounds, based on free passage of air through vocal tract

Linguistics and Writing Systems

abbreviation shortened or contracted form used to represent entire word or phrase

ablaut regular alternation of internal vowel, reflecting change in grammatical function; apophony

acrolect variety of creole that approximates most closely the standard language

acronym word formed from initial letters of set series of words

affix morpheme added before, after, or within base word to create new word; prefix, suffix, or infix

Afroasiatic family of languages including Semitic, Egyptian, Berber, Cushitic, and Chadic

agglutination word formation in which distinct morphemes are combined without fusion or change, esp. addition of affixes to base word

allomorph alternate phonological shape of morpheme, such as plural form "-en" in "oxen" and "-s" in "goats"

alphabet letters of a language, arranged in set order; system of symbols or characters representing individual speech sounds of language

alphabetize (*vb*) arrange words in order of letters of alphabet, either letter-by-letter or by word

alternation variation in form of linguistic unit as it occurs in different environments or under different conditions

amelioration melioration

American Sign Language language consisting

of manual signs and gestures, used by deaf people in the U.S. and parts of Canada

analogy process by which words or phrases are created or altered on model of existing language patterns

analytic (*adj*) designating a language that uses function words and changes in word order, rather than inflected forms, to express grammatical relations

Anglo-Saxon Old English

antepenult third syllable from the end in a word

anthropological linguistics study of relationship between language and culture, esp. in preliterate societies

antonym word opposite in meaning to another

apophony ablaut

applied linguistics use of linguistic theory in teaching, psychology, lexicography, and data processing

Aramaic ancient Semitic language from whose script were derived Hebrew, Arabic, and many other scripts

archaism word, form, or usage no longer in common use

argot special, often secret vocabulary and idiom of one group

artificial language language invented for specialized use, esp. for international communication or computer programming

Austronesian family of languages spoken in Malay Peninsula, Indonesia, Philippines, Vietnam, Madagascar, and Oceania; Malayo-Polynesian

baby talk style of speech addressed to children, characterized by eccentric pronunciations and simplified sentence structure

Baltic branch of Indo-European languages including Latvian, Lithuanian, and Old Prussian

Bantu subbranch of Niger-Congo family of languages spoken in central and southern Africa, comprising over two hundred languages including Kikuyu and Swahili

base root or stem

basilect variety of creole that is most distinct from acrolect or standard language

bilingual (*adj*) fluent in two languages

blend word formed from parts of other words, such as "brunch" or "motel"

bound form linguistic form that occurs only in combination with other forms, such as most affixes

boustrophedon ancient form of writing in which lines alternate running right to left and left to right

Braille system of writing using combination of raised dots that are read by touch, for use by the blind

Briticism word or usage characteristic of British English, esp. when employed in American English

calque loan translation

cant special language used by underworld group or by members of a profession

Celtic branch of Indo-European languages

including Irish, Scottish Gaelic, Welsh, and Breton

citation quotation or excerpt showing particular word or phrase in context

code-switching alternate use of two or more languages or varieties of a language within same conversation or passage

cognate language related to another by descent from same language; word related to another by descent from same root word

coinage newly invented word

collocation regular occurrence of lexical items together, such as "commit crime"

colloquial (*adj*) designating language characteristic of or suitable to familiar, casual conversation

combining form linguistic form that occurs only in combination with other forms

comment rheme

comparative linguistics study of patterns of similarities and differences between languages

competence unconscious internalized knowledge of the rules of a language enabling speaker to produce and understand the language

computational linguistics study of the applications of computers in processing and analyzing language, as in automatic machine translation

connotation associated or secondary meaning of word in addition to its explicit or primary meaning

contamination alteration in linguistic form due to influence of related form

corpus collection of spoken or written utterances taken as representative sample of a given language and used for linguistic analysis

creole pidgin that has developed in complexity over time and has become the native language of a group of speakers

cuneiform system of writing using wedge-shaped characters, used by the ancient Assyrians, Babylonians, and others

cursive (*adj*) designating handwriting or printing in which letters are joined together in flowing style

Cyrillic Greek-based alphabet used in Russian and other Slavic languages

dead language language no longer in use as sole means of oral communication in a community

deep structure (in transformational grammar) underlying semantic or syntactic representation of sentence from which surface structure may be derived

definiendum term to be defined at head of dictionary entry

definiens defining part of dictionary entry

demotic current, everyday form of a language, esp. the Modern Greek vernacular; simplified form of ancient Egyptian hieroglyphic writing

denotation explicit or direct meaning of word

derivation formation of new words by adding affixes or changing shape of base word

descriptive grammar approach to grammar concerned with actual usage of speakers rather than with norms of correctness

descriptive linguistics study of structure of one language without reference to its history or comparison with other languages

Devanagari alphabetic script with some syllabic features, used for writing Hindi and other languages of India

diachronic (*adj*) relating to study of a language as it changes over time

dialect regionally or socially distinct variety of a language

dialect atlas linguistic atlas

dialectology study of dialects

dictionary book containing alphabetical listing of words in a language with their meanings and other information

diglossia use in a society of widely differing formal and informal varieties of a language

direct discourse exact quotation of speaker's words

discourse analysis study of patterns and rules governing units of connected speech or writing longer than one sentence

doublet either of two different words ultimately deriving from the same source

Dravidian language family of South Asia, spoken mainly in S India

eponym person or mythological figure after whom something is named

Esperanto invented language intended for international use, based on words common to major European languages

etymology study of history and development of form and meaning of words; derivation of a word

etymon linguistic form from which another is historically derived

expression unit of speech composed of several elements

eye dialect use of spellings that are intended to convey speaker's dialectal or uneducated pronunciations but are actually respellings of standard pronunciations

fingerspelling communication in sign language by means of manual alphabet

fluency ease and proficiency of expression in specific language

folk etymology modification of word based on false assumption about its origin or irrelevant analogy with familiar word

formal (*adj*) referring to language use typical of impersonal and official situations, characterized by complex vocabulary and sentences, careful grammar, and avoidance of colloquial expressions

franglais French spoken with large admixture of English words

free form linguistic form that can be used by itself as an independent word

generative grammar formalized set of rules that can generate all acceptable grammatical sentences of a language to explain tacit understanding native speaker has of that language

Germanic branch of Indo-European languages including German, English, Dutch, and Scandinavian languages

ghost word word that has come into existence through error, as through a misprint

glossary alphabetical listing of specialized terms and their meanings, usu. for one particular field

grapheme smallest distinctive unit of a writing system, esp. one representing a single phoneme

graphology study of writing systems

Grimm's law pattern of consonant correspondence between Germanic and other Indo-European languages demonstrated by Jakob Grimm in 1822, establishing regular process of change in language as basis for future linguistic analysis

Hangul alphabet used in writing Korean

hapax legomenon word that appears only once in a text, the works of an author, or the written record of a language

headword word or phrase used as heading of chapter or as dictionary or encyclopedia entry

Hellenic branch of Indo-European languages including ancient and modern Greek

heteronym word spelled the same as another but having different sound and meaning, such as "lead" the metal and the verb

hieratic (adj) designating simplified form of hieroglyphics used by priests in ancient Egypt

hieroglyphic pictorial symbol used in ancient writing to represent word or sound

hieroglyphics system of writing, as that of ancient Egypt, that uses pictorial symbols

historical linguistics study of language as it changes over a period of time

Hobson-Jobson alteration of word borrowed from foreign language to fit patterns of borrowing language

holophrase single word functioning as phrase or sentence

homograph word with same spelling but different meaning from another word

homonym word with same pronunciation and spelling but different meaning from another word; homophone

homophone word with same pronunciation but different meaning from another word

honorific title or grammatical form showing respect

hypercorrection use of an inappropriate pronunciation, form, or construction to avoid using a seemingly incorrect form

ideogram written symbol representing idea or thing directly; ideograph

ideograph ideogram

idiolect individual person's distinct manner of speaking

idiom expression having a meaning not predictable from usual meanings of its constituent words; language or style of speech peculiar to a people

illiteracy inability to read and write one's native language

Indic Indo-Aryan

indirect discourse inclusion of speaker's words in altered form in longer sentence

Indo-Aryan subgroup of Indo-Iranian branch of Indo-European languages including Sanskrit, Hindi, and Urdu

Indo-European widespread family of languages spoken primarily in Northern Hemisphere, including Italic, Germanic, Slavic, Baltic, Hellenic, Celtic, and Indo-Iranian branches

Indo-Iranian branch of Indo-European languages including Indic and Iranian subgroups

infix affix added within base word

informal (adj) referring to language use suitable to or typical of casual or familiar speech or writing

informant native speaker of language who supplies utterances or other data for someone analyzing or learning the language

interlingual (adj) using two or more languages, as some dictionaries

Iranian subgroup of Indo-Iranian branch of Indo-European languages including Persian, Pashto, Avestan, and Kurdish

isogloss line on map marking limits within which particular feature of speech occurs

Italic branch of Indo-European languages including Latin and modern Romance languages such as French, Spanish, and Italian

Japlish Japanese spoken or written with large admixture of English words

jargon technical or specialized terminology of group or profession; obscure or unintelligible language

jive special slang jargon, often flippant or misleading

kana Japanese writing system using syllabic characters, having two varieties

kanji Japanese writing system based on Chinese characters

king's (or **queen's**) **English** correct, standard speech and usage of educated persons in England

Kufic early form of Arabic alphabet used in writing Koran

language system using combinations of vocal sounds, written symbols, or gestures with accepted meanings to express thoughts and feelings common to one people of specific region or culture; communication using such a system

language family group of related languages descended from common parent language

language universal property or feature common to all languages

Latin Italic language of ancient Rome that is primary source of Romance languages

Latin alphabet twenty-three letter alphabet of ancient Rome that is basis for English and other European alphabets

lemma form of word or phrase that represents its entire inflectional range, such as the form glossed in a dictionary

letter written symbol representing speech sound in particular alphabet

lexeme smallest distinct lexical unit in language system; item of vocabulary

lexical (adj) pertaining to the words or vocabulary of a language

lexicographer writer or editor of dictionaries

lexicography art and practice of making dictionaries

lexicology study of formation and use of words

lexicon vocabulary; listing of words in a language; total stock of words in a language

lingo language, esp. jargon or slang, of a particular field, group, or individual

lingua franca language used for communication between persons who ordinarily speak different languages

linguist specialist in linguistics; polyglot

linguistic atlas set of maps showing distribution of linguistic features in the speech of an area; dialect atlas

linguistics study of sound, structure, meaning, vocabulary, and development of language, including fields of phonetics, phonology, morphology, syntax, semantics, pragmatics, comparative, and historical linguistics

lipreading understanding of spoken words from movement of speaker's lips without hearing sounds made

literacy ability to read and write

literatim (adv) letter for letter; literally

loan translation compound word or phrase formed by translation of each of the elements of a compound from another language

loanword word borrowed from another language

logogram character or symbol that represents entire word

longhand normal handwriting in which words are spelled out in full

macaronic (adj) made up of Latin words mixed with vernacular words often given Latin endings

Malayo-Polynesian Austronesian

manual alphabet set of finger signals representing letters of alphabet, used in sign language

melioration semantic change in a word over the course of time to a more approved or respectable meaning

metalanguage language used to describe or analyze language

metalinguistics study of relation of language to other culturally determined behavior

Middle English English language of period c1150-1475

Modern English English language since c1475

morpheme smallest distinctive grammatical unit of a language that is meaningful in itself and indivisible

morphology branch of linguistics involving forms and structure of words and patterns of word formation in particular language; these patterns of word formation themselves

morphophoneme abstract phonological entity representing corresponding allomorphs of one morpheme

morphophonemics study of relationship between morphemes and their phonological form

mother tongue language first learned by a person

multilingual (*adj*) able to speak several languages

native speaker person speaking particular language learned naturally during childhood

natural language language that is the native language of a group of speakers

neologism new word or existing word with new meaning introduced into language

Niger-Congo large family of African languages

nonce word word invented or formed for particular occasion

nonstandard (*adj*) designating grammar, word choice, etc., used and considered acceptable by most educated native speakers

nonverbal communication communication without words, as by gestures, postures, and facial expressions

Old English English language before c1150; Anglo-Saxon

onomastics study of origin and use of proper names

orismology science of defining technical terms of a field of study

orthography representation of language sounds by written symbols or letters; study of letters and spelling; correct or standard spelling

paradigmatic (*adj*) referring to a relationship among linguistic elements that can substitute for each other in a given context

paragraph subdivision of written composition set in block, usu. beginning on indented line, and having some coherence

paralanguage vocal qualities, gestures, and facial expressions that accompany speech and contribute to communication but are not part of actual language system

parlance specified style of speaking, esp. involving choice of words

paronym word derived from same root as another; cognate

patois provincial dialect differing from standard form of the language; jargon

patronymic name derived from name of one's father or ancestor, esp. by addition of affix

pejoration semantic change in a word over the course of time to a less favorable or less respectable meaning

penult next to the last syllable in a word

performance person's actual use of language in speaking or writing

philology study of written texts to determine meaning and authenticity; older term for linguistics, esp. historical and comparative linguistics

phonogram symbol representing word, sound, or syllable

phraseogram written symbol that represents phrase, as in shorthand

pictograph pictorial symbol representing idea or thing, as in picture writing

picture writing system using pictures or pictorial symbols to record events or express ideas

pidgin auxiliary language with simplified grammatical structure and vocabulary drawn mostly from one language, used by speakers of two different languages for communication

pinyin system for romanizing Chinese into Latin alphabet

pochismo English word borrowed into Spanish use

polyglot (*adj*) multilingual; composed of numerous linguistic groups; (*n*) person who knows several languages

polysemous (*adj*) having many meanings

polysynthetic (*adj*) designating language that uses long words with many affixes to express grammatical relations and meanings

portmanteau word blend

pragmatics branch of linguistics concerned with language in context, including speaker's intent and relation to listener; branch of semiotics concerned with relations between symbols and their users

prefix affix added before base word

prescriptive grammar approach to grammar concerned with establishing norms of correct and incorrect usage or rules based on these norms

protolanguage assumed parent form of language

provincialism word, phrase, or sound distinct to particular region or dialect; regionalism

proxemics study of varying patterns of physical proximity in interpersonal communication

psycholinguistics study of relationship between language and psychological processes of its users

queen's English king's English

reconstruction determination of hypothetical earlier form of a language by comparison of data from a later stage of the language

reflex element in a language that has developed from corresponding element in earlier form of the language

reformed spelling simplified spelling that eliminates unpronounced letters, such as "thru" for "through"

regionalism provincialism

rheme portion of sentence providing new information about topic; comment

rhotacism change of speech sound to "r" as language evolves

romaji system of writing Japanese using letters of Latin alphabet

Roman alphabet Latin alphabet

Romance language one of the group of Indo-European languages descended from Latin, including French, Spanish, Italian, Portuguese, and Romanian

romanization use of Latin alphabet to write a language usu. written in a different alphabet

root morpheme that is the basic element of a word, underlying inflected or derived forms

rune character of ancient Germanic alphabet

Sapir-Whorf hypothesis theory that language shapes behavior and thinking of those who speak it

script distinctive formation of letters by hand; handwriting; any system of writing

semantics branch of linguistics concerned with nature, structure, and development of meaning in language; branch of semiotics concerned with relationship between signs or symbols and what they denote

semiotics study or theory of signs and symbols in language and other communicative behavior

Semitic subfamily of Afroasiatic languages including Akkadian, Aramaic, Arabic, and Hebrew

shorthand rapid writing system using simple strokes and symbols to represent letters, words, and phrases

sign meaningful gestural unit belonging to a sign language; sign language

signed English form of communication using the signs of American Sign Language but using English grammar

signing communication by sign language

sign language system of hand motions and finger configurations representing letters, ideas, and things, used in communication among deaf

Sino-Tibetan family of Asian languages including Mandarin and other Chinese dialects, Burmese, and Tibetan

slang informal, often nonstandard language consisting of newly coined words and extended meanings; specialized vocabulary, jargon, or vernacular

Slavic branch of Indo-European languages including Russian, Polish, Czech, Bulgarian, Serbo-Croatian, and Slovene

sociolect dialect used by particular social group

sociolinguistics study of interactions of language and society

sound symbolism nonarbitrary connection between phonetic features of words and their meanings

source language original language of text to be translated

speech community all people using one language or dialect

spelling standardized arrangement of letters to form specific words

Sprachgefühl sense of established usage and what is linguistically effective or appropriate

standard (*adj*) designating relatively unified, institutionalized form of language accepted as norm to be spoken and taught

stem part of inflected word which remains unchanged, to which inflections are added

structuralism structural linguistics

structural linguistics study of nature and structure of language as network of coherent systems of formal units

substandard (*adj*) designating colloquial usage differing from standard dialect and deemed incorrect

substratum set of features of a language traceable to influence of earlier language that it has replaced

suffix affix added after base word

Sumerian language of ancient Mesopotamia, attested in pictographic and cuneiform writing

superstratum set of features of a language traceable to influence of a language formerly spoken in the society by a dominant group

surface structure representation of final syntactic form of sentence derived from deep structure in transformational grammar

syllabary system of written symbols each representing a syllable

synaesthesia direct relation or association between word's meaning and its form or sound

synchronic (*adj*) relating to study of a language as it exists at one point in time

syncretism merging of two or more different inflected forms into one

synonym word with same or essentially similar meaning as another word

syntactics branch of semiotics dealing with formal properties of symbol systems and relationship of signs to each other

syntagmatic (*adj*) referring to relationship among linguistic elements that occur sequentially

syntax rules for arranging words to form phrases, clauses, and sentences; study of this

synthetic (*adj*) designating language that uses affixes, rather than separate words, to express grammatical relationships

tagmeme grammatical unit based on relationship between a grammatical function and the class of items than can fill that function

tagmemics school of linguistics using tagmeme as basic unit of grammatical analysis

target language language into which text is to be translated; language that one is learning

taxeme feature of arrangement of elements in construction, such as selection, order, or phonetic modification

theme first major element in a sentence, about which the rest of the sentence communicates information; topic

thesaurus book listing words and their synonyms and antonyms

tone language language in which otherwise phonologically identical words are distinguished by different pitches, such as Chinese

toneme phoneme consisting of contrasting tone in tone language

tongue language or dialect

topic portion of sentence containing item about which information will be provided by rest of sentence

transformational grammar system of grammatical analysis, esp. a form of generative grammar, concerned with process by which surface structure is derived from deep structure

translation rendering of passage from one language into another

transliteration representation of letters or words from one language in characters or letters of another language

ultima last syllable of a word

uncial style of writing using large, rounded letters, esp. in Greek and Latin manuscripts of the 3rd to 9th centuries A.D.

usage actual or customary manner in which language is used in a community; way in which particular word or phrase is used, esp. when choice of words is involved

variant one of two or more different spellings, pronunciations, or forms of the same word

verbatim (*adv*) word for word

vernacular language or dialect indigenous to place; common spoken language, distinct from formal written language

vocabulary words of a language; body of words known or used by an individual or group; list of words, usu. arranged in alphabetical order and defined or translated

vulgar (*adj*) designating the popular or informal variety of a language, esp. Latin

vulgarism commonly used word or phrase regarded as substandard, coarse, or obscene

Wade-Giles system system for the romanization of Chinese, widely used esp. before the adoption of pinyin

word basic, discrete unit of meaning in language, composed of one or more speech sounds or their written representation

word-hoard individual's vocabulary

zoosemiotics study of communication systems used by animals

RHETORIC AND FIGURES OF SPEECH

See also: *Chap. 13: Philosophy; Chap. 14: Literature; Chap. 18: Grammar, Phonetics, and Linguistics*

accismus insincere refusal

adage proverb; traditional wise saying

agnomination echoing of word's sound or repetition of word in different sense for emphasis or as pun

allegory extended metaphor; representation of idea with concrete, structured image

alliteration succession of words or stressed syllables of word group beginning with same consonant sound or with same letter

allocution address; formal speech

allusion reference to famous, historical, or literary person or event

ambages roundabout form of speaking the truth in misleading manner

ambiguity expression of idea in words that may be interpreted more than one way

amplification figure of speech that emphasizes ideas through reiteration, embellishment, or elaboration

ana miscellaneous sayings or bits of information on some topic

anacoluthon deliberate failure to complete sentence, followed by shift to another thought or construction

anadiplosis repetition of last word in phrase or sentence, to constitute first word in following phrase or sentence

anagram rearrangement of letters in one word to form another

analogy comparison of things alike in certain respects to establish basis for exposition or argument

anaphora repetition of same word or phrase to begin consecutive sentences or clauses

anastrophe deliberate reversal of usual, logical order of sentence parts for emphasis

anathema formal denunciation

anecdote short narrative or description revealing point of interest about person or event

anonym pseudonym formed by backward spelling of real name

antiphrasis ironical description meant to convey impression opposite that normally conveyed by words used

antithesis use of strongly contrasting words and images

antonomasia substitution of epithet or appellative for proper name, or proper name for common noun or general class of words

aphorism succinct, memorable statement of a truth; maxim

apophasis statement of assertion while denying intention of mentioning that subject

aposiopesis abrupt interruption that leaves thought incomplete

apostrophe direct form of address aimed at someone or something not present

apothegm tersely worded maxim

appellative descriptive name, designation, or epithet

ara long, formally worded curse

archaism old, obsolete diction or vocabulary, esp. when used for effect

argumentation form of discourse emphasizing persuasion

assonance juxtaposition of similar word sounds, esp. vowels

asyndeton condensed expression characterized by omission of conjunctions

atticism concise and elegant expression

aureate (*adj*) distinguished by flowery rhetoric

axiom self-evident truth, succinctly stated

banality expression devoid of originality or wit; cliché

bathos unsuccessful attempt at lofty, dignified style, resulting in triteness, triviality, or unintentional humor

bombast inflated, grandiloquent language

bon mot clever remark or comment; witticism

brachylogy concise expression or diction

brief summary of ideas or points of argument

brocard short, proverbial rule

bromide commonplace saying or turn of phrase

buzzword slogan or catchword conjuring popular idea or image

byword proverb; word or phrase associated with a person or thing

cacology poor diction or pronunciation

cadence rhythm and measure of written or spoken language

cant insincere language intended to convey impression of genuine feeling

catachresis wrong use of one word for another that sounds similar to it or has similar meaning

catchword commonly repeated word or phrase; slogan

chestnut old and familiar anecdote or joke

chiasmus reversal of word order in two otherwise parallel constructions

circumambages instance of indirect or evasive speech or writing

circumlocution roundabout mode of expression; use of unnecessary verbiage

cliché stereotyped expression; trite description; banality; platitude; truism

cognomen distinguishing name or epithet

conceit ingenious idea expressed as elaborate, fanciful metaphor or analogy

concinnity harmony of tone and logic in discourse

connotation shades and variety of meanings attached to word or phrase in addition to specific denotation; implication

conundrum question or riddle whose answer involves a pun

curse invocation of evil upon someone; imprecation; malediction

dead metaphor figure of speech drained of its power of analogy; metaphor grown colorless with overuse

debate formal argumentation

declamation recitation as exercise in oratory or elocution

denotation specific, literal meaning

description form of discourse emphasizing portrayal

diatribe abusive, bitter style of speech

diction selection and use of words to convey meaning; quality, style, and sound of an individual's speech relative to prevailing standards

digression departure from subject at hand to another, unrelated one

discourse speech; lengthy, formal discussion of subject

dithyramb wildly enthusiastic speech or writing, usu. of irregular form, esp. impassioned poem or chant

double entendre intentionally ambiguous statement, esp. with one possibly indecent meaning

double-talk intentional ambiguity; mixture of sense and nonsense

dysphemism harsh or unpleasant language used as substitute for more direct or neutral expression, opposite of euphemism

echoism onomatopoeia

effect distinctive impact or impression that language produces

elaboration development of theme or image

ellipsis omission of words essential to meaning and structure, but easily filled in by reader or listener

elliptical (*adj*) tending to be ambiguous, unclear, or roundabout

elocution practice of oral delivery or public speaking

eloquence artful, persuasive, elegant, or vivid language

emphasis rhetorical weight given to ideas by placement, repetition, elaboration, or contrast in words used

enallage intentional replacement of one grammatical form with another

endearment affectionate form of address

epigram concise, vivid saying

epilogue concluding remark or statement; last of seven parts of oration in classical rhetoric

epistrophe repetition of word or phrase at end of consecutive sentences or clauses

epithet descriptive, often disparaging phrase characteristically applied to a person or thing because of its accuracy and color

equivocation use of ambiguity in order to deceive or evade

equivoque amusing usage of word that suggests several other similar meanings; pun

eulogy formal, extended statement of praise, esp. to honor deceased person; panegyric

euphemism indirect, mild language used as substitute for direct, possibly offensive description; opposite of dysphemism

euphuism florid, affected, artificial style of speech

exclamation sharp, sudden utterance; vehement protest or complaint

excursus long, formal digression

exordium introduction to oration; first of seven parts of oration in classical rhetoric

expatiation speaking or writing at great length

expletive emphatic interjection

exposition form of discourse emphasizing explanation

expression particular word or phrase used to represent something verbally

figurative language metaphorical language used outside its usual forms of construction and meaning for purposes of description, persuasion, or originality of expression

figure of speech expressive language construction in which word meaning differs from literal sense of words

flourish fine language used merely for effect

flowery (*adj*) ornate, excessive, or showy in expression

forensics art, study, and use of argumentation and debate

glossolalia unintelligible, ecstatic speech; speaking in tongues

grandiloquence pompous, bombastic language

harangue bombastic ranting; extended attack or complaint; Philippic

hendiadys separation of an idea into two parts, which are then joined by a conjunction

homily morally instructive speech

hypallage reversal of expected syntactic relation between two words

hyperbaton transposition of normal sentence order

hyperbole extravagant exaggeration for comic or colorful effect or emphasis

hypocorism pet name; diminutive form imitating baby talk

hypothesis tentative assumption to be tested in argument

hysteron proteron reversal of logical order of two-part statement

illeism excessive use of pronoun "he" or "she" in reference to oneself

implication connotation

imprecation curse

innuendo insinuation; words with an unpleasant connotation

invective abusive language

inversion change in normal word order for effect

invocation address to God or higher power

Irish bull apparently sensible but actually incongruous expression

irony figure of speech conveying intent or reality different from, or opposite to, literal meaning of words used; speech employing elements of restraint, humor, sarcasm

lingo strange, obscure language or jargon peculiar to one group

litany prayer or supplication

litotes understatement, such as "not bad," in which affirmative is expressed by negating contrary statement

locution style of expression

logodaedaly arbitrary and capricious coinage of words

malapropism incorrect use of word similar to appropriate word

malediction curse

maxim aphorism, proverb

meiosis understatement, esp. for humorous effect

metaphor identification of one thing by another; trope, or turn of phrase, describing one idea in terms of another idea or image analogous to it

metonymy substitution of name of an object associated with a word for the word itself

mot brief, witty saying

motto word or phrase used regularly to characterize something or some group

mouthful very long word or phrase; statement rich in meaning, full of impact

narration form of discourse emphasizing recounting of event

nonsense expression lacking meaning, logic, or clarity of thought

nutshell brief statement reducing something to its essence

oath any profane expression, esp. one irreverent toward God

obiter dictum *Latin.* lit. saying by the way; incidental, uncalculated remarks

onomatomania obsession with words, their sounds, and meanings

onomatopoeia use of words whose sounds imitate or suggest their meaning; echoism

oration formal speech intended to persuade; in classical rhetoric, a speech divided into seven parts: exordium, narration, exposition, proposition, confirmation, confutation, and epilogue

ornate (*adj*) florid, overly embellished, or high-flown

oxymoron combination of two contradictory terms

palindrome word, phrase, or sentence reading the same backward or forward

panegyric eulogy

pangram sentence or verse containing all letters of the alphabet

parable short story that illustrates a moral attitude or principle

paradox apparently contradictory statement that is actually true

paralipsis concise treatment of subject suggesting that much is being omitted; preterition

paraphrase restatement of thought to retain meaning while changing form of expression

parenthesis remark made as explanation

paronomasia pun or play on words

password secret word or phrase used to gain admission to restricted area; shibboleth

pathetic fallacy assigning of human traits and feelings to natural or inanimate objects

pedantry style of expression emphasizing allusions, quotations, and ostentatious or inappropriate displays of erudition

periphrasis indirect, wordy style of expression

peroration summation of major points and persuasive concluding remarks occurring at end of speech

persiflage banter; light chatter

personification act of verbally endowing animals, objects, or abstractions with human attributes

phatic (*adj*) designating speech used to express goodwill or sociability rather than to impart information

Philippic harangue

phraseology style of expression

platitude trite or commonplace remark; cliché

play on words pun

pleonasm redundancy

polemic argument set forth, esp. on controversial subject

polysyndeton use of number of conjunctions in close succession

preterition paralipsis

profanity common or vulgar language, esp. characterized by irreverence toward God or sacred things

prolepsis anticipation and response to opponent's argument before it is actually stated

prologue introductory remark or statement

prosopopoeia personification of absent or dead person as present and speaking

proverb brief popular saying, usu. of unknown origin, expressing a commonplace truth; wise saying succinctly stated; adage; maxim; saw

pun wordplay based on similarity of sound but difference in meaning between words; paranomasia; play on words

punch line concluding phrase or line of joke, pun, or riddle

quibble pun or device used for evasion of argument

quip witty retort

rebuttal reply to argument

redundancy use of more words than needed to express idea; pleonasm

repartee conversation characterized by wit; clever reply

repetition reiteration of word, phrase, or idea for emphasis

retort sharp, incisive, often retaliatory reply; reply in kind

rhetoric theory and use of clear, persuasive, vivid language in presentation of argument or point of view; principles of oratory; undue use of exaggeration or bombast

rhetorical figure nonstandard usage that does not alter meaning of words

rhetorical question question asked solely for effect, and not to elicit a reply

riposte quick, sharp reply

sarcasm caustic, ironical language intended to wound or belittle another

saw sententious saying; maxim

saying formulation grown familiar through repetition; adage; saw

scheme rearrangement of words for effect of changed sound

sesquipedalianism use of very long words

shibboleth phrase characteristic of particular group; password

shop talk jargon or lingo of particular occupation

simile expression showing similarity between two unlike things, generally begun with comparison word "like" or "as"

slogan catchword

slur disparaging remark or characterization

Socratic method question and answer format of discourse; assumption of ignorance in debate for ironical effect

solecism ungrammatical combination of words; error in diction

speaking in tongues utterance of incomprehensible sounds while in ecstatic state, usu. believed to be words of deity

speech theory and practice of oral communication, esp. before an audience

spoonerism intentional or accidental transposition of initial sounds of two or more words; confusion resulting from such transposition

syllepsis construction placing one word in relationship to two other words, effecting two different senses

symploce simultaneous use of anaphora and epistrophe

synecdoche metaphoric form in which a part signifies the whole and less general stands for more general, or vice versa

synthesis dialectic combination of thesis and antithesis to deduce solution or truth

thesis position set forth for argument by speaker or writer

threnody dirge, lamentation

trope figure of speech; turn or twist on ordinary, literal sense of word or words

truism commonplace statement of truth; cliché

understatement form of irony in which something is represented as less than it really is

verbigeration continual repetition of words and phrases

vitriol extremely caustic speech or writing

watchword motto used as sign of recognition within group or as guiding principle for action

wellerism well-known quotation followed by facetious sequel

wordplay verbal wit; use of rhetorical figures of speech

zeugma syllepsis in which modifier is inappropriate in relation to one term or appropriate to each term in a different way

QUALIFIERS AND CONNECTIVES

Conjunctions
Prepositions
Limitations and Conditions
Reflections and References
Comparisons
Approximations and Generalizations
Emphasizers
Maximizers and Superlatives
Absolutes and Guarantees

See also: *Chap. 18: Prefixes and Suffixes; Chap. 23: Time Perception; Spatial Positions and Relations*

Qualifiers are those familiar words, phrases, and idioms that we use, often without thinking, to alter the intensity of another word or phrase, to modulate the language, and to provide subtle gradations and shadings of meaning. Connectives are words, such as conjunctions and prepositions, that express a relation or connection between two things, especially a relation involving place or time. This list includes all the conjunctions and prepositions and nearly a thousand other words and phrases, primarily adverbs and adjectives, that function to qualify and connect other words. Subcategory titles describe the impact on a sentence of the words in that particular list.

Conjunctions

according as, afore, after, against, albeit, also, altho, although, an, and, and also, and/or, as, as far as, as how, as if, as long as, as though, as well as
because, before, being, both, but
considering
directly
either, ere, ergo, except, excepting
for, forasmuch as, fore
gin
how, howbeit, howe'er, however
if, immediately, inasmuch as, insofar as, insomuch as, instantly
lest, like
much as
neither, nor, notwithstanding, now
once, only, or, otherwise
plus, provided, providing
save, saving, seeing, since, sith, so, sobeit, so long as, still, supposing, syne
than, that, then, tho, though, till
unless, unlike, until
well, what, when, whence, whencesoever, whene'er, whenever, whensoever, where, whereabout, whereabouts, whereas, whereat, whereby, where'er, wherefore, wherefrom, wherein, whereinto, whereof, whereon, whereso, wheresoe'er, wheresoever, wherethrough, whereto, whereunder, whereunto, whereupon, wherever, wherewith, whether, while, whiles, whilst, whither, whithersoever, why, without
yet

Prepositions

a, abaft, aboard, about, above, absent, according to, across, adown, afore, after, against, agin, à la, aloft, along, alongside, amid, amidst, among, amongst, an, anent, après, around, as, aside, aslant, as of, as to, astraddle, astride, at, athwart
bar, barring, bating, because, before, behind, below, ben, beneath, beside, besides, between, betwixt, beyond, but, by
chez, circa, concerning, considering, contra, cum
despite, down, during
ere, ex, except, excepting, excluding
failing, for, forby, fore, forth, frae, from
in, including, inside, instead of, into
less, like
maugre, mid, midst, minus, mongst
near, neath, next, next to, nigh, notwithstanding
o', o'er, of, off, on, onto, opposite, or, out, outside, over
pace, past, pending, per, plus
re, regarding, respecting, round
sans, save, saving, since, sith, syne
than, thorough, thro, throughout, thru, thwart, till, times, to, touching, toward
under, underneath, unless, unlike, until, unto, up, upon
versus, via, vice, vis-à-vis
wanting, while, with, withal, within, without, worth

Limitations and Conditions

a bit, a breath, a couple, additionally, admitting, a few, albeit, a little, all but, all the same, all things considered, alone, although, a mite, as far as, as good as, aside from, as is, as it is, as long as, as soon as, as the case may be, as well, at all, at best, at least, at most, a trifle, at worst, au contraire
barely, barring, below, besides, be that as it may, bit by bit, briefly, but, by any chance, by any means, by chance, by degrees, by hook or by crook, by no means, by the same token
catch, circumstantially, conceivably, conditionally, considering, contingent on, cursory
decreasingly, demi-, depending, discounting
else, even, even so, even still, even though, even with, ever less, everything being equal, except, except for, excepting, except that, excluding, exclusive of, exempting, expressly
faintly, few, for all one knows, for all that, for aught one knows, formerly, for my part, for the most part
God willing, gradually, grain of salt, granting
half, halfway, handful, hardly, hardly ever, hedged, hemi-, hen's teeth, hereby, how, howbeit, however, howsoever
if, if and only if, if and when, if at all, if it so happens, if not, if only, if possible, if then, ill, in, in addition, in any case, in any way, in a way, in brief, in case, infrequently, in no way, in part, insofar as, in some measure, in spite of, in that case, iota, irregardless
just, just in case, just so, just the same
kicker, kind of
latter, least, leastways, leastwise, leaving aside, less, less and less, less than, let alone, like, little by little
maybe, mayhap, mere, merely, midway, might, mildly, mini-, minimus, minus, minutely, mite, moderately, modestly, modicum, momentary, mostly
namely, nary, nay rather, needless, negligible, neither, never, nevertheless, nohow, no less than, nominal, no more than, nonetheless, nor, not hardly, not in the least, not much, not often, notwithstanding, nowhere near, null
occasionally, off, on balance, once, on condition that, only, only if, on the whole, otherwise, overly, overmuch
part by part, partial, partially, partly, partway, passing, pending, pennyworth, perchance, perhaps, personally, picayune, piddling, piecemeal, pittance, possibly, pretty, pretty much, provided, providing, provisionally, purely
qualifying, quasi, quite the contrary
rarely, rather, regardless, relatively, remote, restricting, restrictive
sans, satisfactory, save, saving, scarcely, seldom, semi-, several, short of, slightly, sliver, smattering, smidgen, so as, sobeit, so far, so long as, so many, some, somehow, somehow or other, someway, somewhat, soon, sort of, soupçon, sparely, sparsely, speck, sporadically, spot, step by step, still, still and all, stipulated, strings, subject to, submarginal
tad, temporary, that being said, that being so, that is to say, though, thumbnail, tittle, to, to a certain point, to a degree, token, to some degree, to some extent, trace
under, under par, under the circumstances, unless, upon my word, up to

verge, videlicet, viz
waiving, waning, wee, well, were it not, when, whereof, whichever, whit, with a catch, withal, without, with reservations, with strings, with the proviso, with the stipulation, worse
yet

Reflections and References

according, accordingly, according to, aforementioned, again, against, allowing for, all the same, all things considered, along, along with, amid, amidst, among, amongst, and so, and so forth, and so on, anent, apart, apparently, arguably, around, as, as a result, as being, as far as, as if, as they say, as though, as to, asunder, as well as, attended by, at the same time
because, because of, between, betwixt, by, by and by, by dint of, by the way, by virtue of, by way of
concerning, conjointly, consequently, considering, contrary to, counter to, coupled with
ditto, due to
either, else, elsewise, ergo, etcetera, evidently
finally, for each, for example, for instance, for that reason, for this reason
given
hence, henceforth, henceforward, hereat, hereby, herein, hereinafter, hereinbefore, hereinbelow, hereon, heretofore, hereunder, hereunto, hereupon, herewith, hither, hitherto, how come
ibid, imprimis, in addition to, inasmuch as, incidentally, incidental to, including, in conjunction, indeed, in keeping with, in lieu of, in line with, in other respects, in other words, in passing, in re, in relation to, in return, insofar as, insomuch as, instead, instead of, in the matter of, intro-, in turn, in twain, in two, in view of, irrespective
jointly
loc cit
midst, mongst, much as, much less, mutually
natch, naturally, naturellement
of, of course, on account of, only, on that account, on the other hand, op cit, or, or else, other than, otherwise, outwardly
penultimate, per, peripheral
qua
re, readily, regarding, respecting, respectively
secondary, seeing that, selectively, self-styled, separately, severally, side, since, snap, so, so as, soever, sofar as, so forth, so much, so on, specified, spotty, square, stated, subsidiary, such, supposed, supra, surfeit
tacit, that is to say, then again, thence, there, thereat, thereby, therefore, thereinafter, thereof, thereon, thereto, theretofore, thereunder, thereupon, thus, thus and so, thusly, together with
uncommon, undue, unduly, unusual, unusually, upon
variable, various, variously, veritable, vice, virtual
what for, what if, whence, where, whereat, wherefor, wherefrom, whereinto, whereon, wheresoever, whereupon, whichever, while, why, with, with regard to, with relation to, with respect to
yet

Comparisons

about, above, à la, alike, all get-out, all that, almost, and then some, another, as, as much as, as well as
beside, better
close to, comparably, comparatively, compared to, complementary
different
either, either-or, enough, equally
farther, further
in comparison, increasingly, in kind, in like manner
just about
like, like so, like that, likewise
mainly, middling, mixed, moiety, more
nearly, near miss, next to, nigh, no less than, nor
opposite, or, over, over against, over and above
premium
rather, relatively
same, second best, second class, second fiddle, second rate, similar, so, somewhat, so-so, sufficient, super, surpassing
tantamount, than, third rate, to-and-fro, to wit
unlike, unparalleled, unprecedented
vice versa, vis-à-vis
well-nigh, what, whereas, whether, while, worse

Approximations and Generalizations

about, a few, after all, again, a little, all in all, a lot, any, anyhow, anyway, apparently, approximately, around, as a rule, as a whole, as it were, as much as, at all events, at any rate, at large, aught
ballpark, before long, belike, be that as it may, borderline, broadly, by and large
circa, close, close to, collectively, commonly, comparatively
en masse, essentially, ever
fairly, for all that, for that matter, for the most part
generally
here and there
in all, in any case, in any event, in a way, in general, in short
just about, just the same
kind of
lately, latterly, like, long and short of it
mainly, mas o menos, mezzo-mezzo, more or less, much
near, neither here nor there, now and then
often, only just, on the whole, overall
possibly, primarily, probably, proportionately
relatively, reputedly, roughly, roundly
say, seeming, seemingly, simply, some, sometimes, somewhat, somewhere, somewhere near, soon, sooner or later, sort of, so-so, so to speak, such and such, sundry
then again, thereabouts, to a degree, to an extent, to the tune of, truth of the matter
virtually
whatever, what have you, whatnot, wherever

Emphasizers

above, after all, again, all, all-around, all of, all told, a lot, also, altogether, and how, as well, awfully
beside, besides, big deal, by far
decidedly
either, especially, even, evermore so, ever so, exceedingly, expressly
far and away, fine, further, furthermore

increasingly, indeed, in detail, in particular, in the main
just, just so
lastly
mainly, mighty, moreover, more than ever, mostly
namely, no matter, notably, not to mention
obviously, on top of, over, over and above
particular, particularly, plus, primarily, pronounced
quite
real, really, resounding, respective, right
simply, singularly, so, specially, specifically, still, strong, such
tall order, telling, terribly, to boot, too, to say nothing of, to say the least
up
very
well, whopper

Maximizers and Superlatives

all, all along, all-embracing, all get-out, all-inclusive, all over, a lot, always, aplenty, a sight, at length
best, bevy
chiefly, chock-full, commonly, considerable, copious
decidedly, doozie
ever, evermore, every, exceedingly, extremely
far, far and away, farthest, first water, foremost
galore
head and shoulders, head over heels, hook, line, and sinker, hyper
ideally
jillion
lickety-split, likely, lots
major, many, maxi-, mighty, more and more, most, much, multiplicity, myriad
nth, numerous
oft, often, oftentimes, oodles
part and parcel, plenteous, plentiful, premium
radically, rattling, real, rife, right, rip-roaring, roaring
scads, slew, smashing, socko, spanking, spate, staggering, stiff, strong, super, super-duper, supreme, surpassing, sweeping
thumping, thundering, tiptop, top
ultra-, unbounded, unbridled, unmitigated, unremitting, unrivaled, untold, up
vast, vaulting, very
walloping, waxing, way, whacking, whopping, wide-ranging, widespread, withering
zillion

Absolutes and Guarantees

above all, absolutely, actually, after all, all, all along, all out, all over, all the while, altogether, always, as a matter of course, as a matter of fact, at any cost, at first, at last, at long last, at that
bar none, by all means
cap-a-pie, certainly, clean, clearly, complete, completely, conclusively
dead on, decidedly, definitely
entirely, even, eventually, exactly, expressly
fare-thee-well, finally, first, first and foremost, firstly, first of all, first things, forever, forever and ever, forevermore, for good, for keeps, forsooth, for sure, full-out, fully
granting
hands down, head to toe
identically, immeasurably, in all respects, in a

word, in conclusion, indeed, indubitably, inevitably, in fact, infinitely, in full, in no way, in particular, in point of fact, in reality, in the first place, in the long run, in toto, invariably, irrespective of
just, just so
lastly, literally, literatim, lock, stock, and barrel
minimus
nada, naught, necessarily, needless to say, never, nil, nix, nohow, no ifs, ands, or buts, no more, none, not a bit, not at all, not a whit, now and forever, no way, nowise, null, null and void
of course, once, once for all, one and all, only, out-and-out, outright
paramount, par excellence, perfectly, plain, plenary, plumb, precisely, premier, prime, primo, principal, proper, purely
quite
really, right
same, selfsame, sheer, simply, smack-dab, solely, solid, so much as, squarely, stark, stock-still, stone, supreme, sure, sure enough, surely
thoroughly, through and through, to a tee, top flight, topnotch, total, totally, to the limit, to the utmost, truly
ultimately, unadulterated, unconditional, unconditionally, undeniably, under no circumstances, unlimited, unmistakably, unqualified, unreservedly, uppermost, utmost, utter, utterly, uttermost
verbatim, verily, veritably, versal, void
well, whatever, whatsoever, wherever, whole, whole hog, wholly, wide, without exception, word-for-word, world, worst
zero, zilch

PREFIXES AND SUFFIXES

Prefixes
Suffixes

See also: *Chap. 4: Medicine; Chap. 18: Abbreviations*

NOTE: *When used before a vowel in combining form, most prefixes drop or change the final o, i, a, or y. Only the full combining form, with the final vowel, is listed here. Where a prefix or suffix has two or more distinct meanings, examples are given that reflect each usage.*

Prefixes

a- not (*asocial*)
ab- away from (*absent*)
acantho- spine, thorn (*acanthus*)
aceto- vinegar, acetic acid (*acetometer*)
acro- top, tip (*acrophobia*)
actino- ray, beam (*actinometer*)
adeno- gland (*adenovirus*)
aero- air, gas (*aerodynamic*)
agri- farming (*agribusiness*)
agro- field, soil, crop production (*agronomy*)
algo- pain (*algolagnia*)
allo- other (*allotrope*)
alti- high (*altitude*)
ambi- both (*ambidextrous*)
amphi- both, around (*amphibious*)
amylo- starch (*amyloplast*)

an- not, lacking (*anarchy*)
ana- up, against, back (*anabasis*)
andro- male (*androgenous*)
anemo- wind (*anemometer*)
angio- container (*angiosperm*)
aniso- unequal (*anisotropic*)
ante- before (*antebellum*)
antho- flower (*anthophore*)
anthropo- human (*anthropology*)
anti- against (*antibody*)
apo- away, apart (*apogee*)
aqui- water (*aquifer*)
arbori- tree (*arboriculture*)
archeo- ancient, old (*archeology*)
archi- first, most basic (*architrave*)
arterio- artery (*arteriosclerosis*)
arthro- joint (*arthropod*)
asco- sac (*ascomycete*)
astro- star (*astronomy*)
atmo- vapor, gas (*atmosphere*)
audio- hearing, sound reproduction (*audiophile*)
auri- gold (*auriferous*); ear (*auriform*)
auto- self, same (*automatic*)
avi- bird (*aviculture*)
bacterio- bacteria (*bacteriophage*)
baro- weight, pressure (*barometer*)
batho- deep (*bathosphere*)
bene- good (*benevolent*)
biblio- book (*bibliography*)
bio- life (*biography*)
blasto- bud, embryo (*blastosphere*)
brachio- arm (*brachiopod*)
brachy- short (*brachylogy*)
brady- slow (*bradycardia*)
branchio- gills (*branchiopod*)
broncho- throat (*bronchoscope*)
caco- bad (*cacology*)
calci- calcium (*calcify*)
calli- beautiful (*calligraphy*)
cardio- heart (*cardiology*)
carpo- fruit (*carpophore*)
cata- down, against, back (*cataclysm*)
ceno- common (*cenobite*)
centi- hundred (*centigram*)
centri- center (*centrifuge*)
cephalo- head (*cephalothorax*)
cerebro- brain (*cerebrospinal*)
cero- wax (*ceroplastic*)
chalco- copper (*chalcocite*)
cheli- claws (*cheliped*)
chilo- lip (*chiloplasty*)
chiro- hand (*chiropractor*)
chloro- green (*chlorophyll*)
choreo- dance (*choreography*)
chromo- color (*chromolithography*)
chrono- time (*chronometer*)
chryso- gold (*chrysolite*)
circum- around (*circumference*)
cis- near to, on near side of (*cisalpine*)
clado- branch (*cladogenesis*)
clino- slope (*clinometer*)
co- variation of com-, used esp. to form new words (*coworker*)
coel- cavity (*coelenteron*)

com- with, together with (*combine*)
contra- against (*contravene*)
copro- excrement (*coprophilia*)
cortico- cortex (*corticosteroid*)
cosmo- universe (*cosmology*)
costo- rib (*costotomy*)
cranio- skull (*craniotomy*)
cruci- cross (*cruciform*)
cryo- cold (*cryogenics*)
crypto- hidden (*cryptography*)
cteno- rake, comb (*ctenophore*)
cupri- copper (*cupriferous*)
cysto- bladder (*cystoscope*)
cyto- cell (*cytoplasm*)
dactylo- finger, toe (*dactylomegaly*)
de- negation (*dehumidify*)
deca- ten (*decagon*)
deci- tenth (*decimeter*)
demi- half, lesser (*demitasse*)
demono- devil, demon (*demonolatry*)
dendro- tree (*dendrology*)
denti- tooth (*dentifrice*)
dermato- skin (*dermatology*)
deutero- second (*deuteropathy*)
di- two, double (*dicotyledon*)
dia- thorough, opposed, completely (*diagnosis*)
dicho- in two parts (*dichotomy*)
dino- terrifying (*dinosaur*)
diplo- double (*diplopod*)
dis- apart, asunder, away, or having a general negative or reversing force (*disability, discontent, dislike*)
dodeca- twelve (*dodecahedron*)
dorsi- back of body (*dorsiflexion*)
duo- two (*duologue*)
dyna- force, power (*dynamotor*)
dys- evil, bad, impaired (*dysfunction*)
eco- ecology (*ecosystem*)
ecto- outside, external (*ectoderm*)
electro- electric (*electromagnetic*)
enantio- opposite (*enantiomorph*)
encephalo- brain (*encephalogram*)
endo- within (*endogenous*)
ennea- nine (*enneahedron*)
entero- intestine (*enterology*)
entomo- insect (*entomophagous*)
eo- early, dawn (*eolith*)
epi- on, over, near (*epidermis*)
equi- equal (*equilateral*)
ergo- work (*ergonomic*)
eroto- sexual desire (*erotogenesis*)
erythro- red (*erythrocyte*)
ethno- race, nation (*ethnography*)
eu- good (*eugenics*)
eury- broad, wide (*euryphagous*)
ex- former (*ex-president*); out of, thoroughly (*extract, exhaust*)
exo- outside, external (*exogamous*)
extra- outside, external (*extraterrestrial*)
febri- fever (*febrifuge*)
ferro- iron (*ferromagnet*)
fibro- fiber (*fibroblast*)
fissi- split, cleft (*fissiped*)
flori- flower (*floriculture*)

fluoro- fluoride (*fluorocarbon*)
fructi- fruit (*fructiferous*)
galacto- milk (*galactophorous*)
gameto- mature reproductive cell (*gametogenesis*)
gamo- joined, united (*gamopetalous*)
gastro- stomach (*gastronomy*)
geo- land, earth (*geology*)
geronto- old age (*gerontocracy*)
glosso- tongue (*glossolalia*)
glotto- tongue (*glottochronolgy*)
glyco- sugar, sweet (*glycogen*)
gono- sexual, reproductive (*gonophore*)
grapho- writing (*graphomotor*)
gymno- naked, nude (*gymnogynous*)
gyneco- woman (*gynecology*)
hagio- holy (*hagiography*)
halo- salt (*halogen*)
haplo- single, simple (*haplology*)
hecto- hundred (*hectoliter*)
helico- spiral (*helicospore*)
helio- sun (*heliotherapy*)
hema- blood (*hemagglutination*)
hemato- blood (*hematocyst*)
hemi- half (*hemisphere*)
hemo- blood (*hemoglobin*)
hendeca- eleven (*hendecagon*)
hepato- liver (*hepatotoxin*)
hepta- seven (*heptagon*)
hetero- different (*heterogeneous*)
hexa- six (*hexagon*)
hiero- sacred (*hierogram*)
histo- tissue (*histology*)
holo- complete, whole (*hologram*)
homeo- similar, like (*homeostasis*)
homo- same (*homogeneous*)
homoio- similar, like (*homoiothermal*)
hyalo- glass (*hyaloplasm*)
hydro- water (*hydrodynamic*)
hyeto- rain (*hyetograph*)
hygro- wet (*hygrometer*)
hylo- matter (*hylotheism*)
hyper- above (*hyperactive*)
hypno- sleep, hypnosis (*hypnotherapy*)
hypo- under (*hypothermia*)
hystero- womb (*hysterectomy*)
iatro- medicine (*iatrogenic*)
ichythyo- fish (*ichthyology*)
icono- image, likeness (*iconology*)
ideo- idea (*ideology*)
idio- peculiar (*idiosyncrasy*)
il- not (*illogical*)
ileo- intestinal ileum (*ileocolitis*)
ilio- ilium portion of hipbone (*iliofemoral*)
im- not (*impartial*)
immuno- immune (*immunology*)
in- not, used to give negative or privative force, esp. to adjectives (*inexpensive*)
inter- between (*interscholastic*)
intra- inside, within, interior (*intracellular*)
ir- not, against (*irreducible*)
irido- rainbow, iris of eye (*iridotomy*)
iso- equal (*isometric*)

jejuno- jejunum portion of intestine (*jejunostomy*)
juxta- close, near, beside (*juxtaposition*)
karyo- cell nucleus (*karyolysis*)
kerato- horn (*keratogenous*)
kineto- movement (*kinetoscope*)
labio- lip (*labiovelar*)
lacto- milk (*lactogenic*)
lamelli- plate, scale (*lamelliform*)
laparo- abdominal wall (*laparoscope*)
laryngo- larynx (*laryngoscope*)
lepido- scale (*lepidopteron*)
lepto- thin, fine (*leptodactylous*)
leuko- white (*leukocyte*)
levo- left (*levorotatory*)
ligni- wood (*ligniform*)
litho- stone (*lithography*)
logo- word, spoken (*logomachy*)
longi- long, length (*longicorn*)
luni- moon (*lunitidal*)
lympho- lymph (*lymphocyte*)
lyso- decomposition, dissolving (*lysosome*)
macro- large (*macrocosm*)
magni- great, large (*magnify*)
male- evil, bad (*malevolent*)
masto- breast (*mastopathy*)
matri- female (*matriarchy*)
mechano- machine (*mechanoreceptor*)
mega- great (*megalopolis*)
megalo- great (*megalomania*)
melano- black (*melanocyte*)
mero- part (*merogony*)
meso- middle (*mesopause*)
meta- after, beyond, changed (*metaphysics*)
metro- measure (*metronome*)
micro- small (*microorganism*)
milli- one thousandth (*millimeter*)
mis- wrong, ill, incorrect (*misprint, mistrust*)
miso- hatred (*misogyny*)
mono- single, one (*monotone*)
morpho- shape (*morphology*)
muco- mucus (*mucopurulent*)
multi- many (*multifaceted*)
musculo- muscle (*musculoskeletal*)
myco- fungus, mold, mushroom (*mycotoxicosis*)
myelo- marrow, spinal cord (*myelocyte*)
myo- muscle (*myocardium*)
myria- ten thousand (*myriagram*)
mytho- myth (*mythology*)
myxo- mucus, slime (*myxovirus*)
nano- one billionth (*nanosecond*)
narco- stupor, drugged state (*narcoanalysis*)
naso- nose (*nasolacrimal*)
necro- dead body (*necrophilia*)
nemato- thread (*nematocyst*)
neo- new (*neologism*)
nepho- cloud (*nephometer*)
nephro- kidney (*nephrology*)
neuro- nerve (*neurology*)
neutro- neutral (*neutrosphere*)
nocti- night (*noctilucent*)
nomo- custom, law (*nomology*)
non- not, freely implying negation or absence of something (*nonprofessional, nonpayment*)

noso- disease (*nosogeography*)
noto- back of body (*notochord*)
nucleo- nucleus (*nucleotide*)
nycto- night (*nyctophobia*)
ob- against (*obverse*)
octa- eight (*octagon*)
oculo- eye (*oculomotor*)
odonto- tooth (*odontogeny*)
oleo- oil (*oleomargarine*)
oligo- few (*oligopoly*)
omni- all (*omnipotent*)
oneiro- dream (*oneiromancy*)
onto- being, existence (*ontology*)
oo- egg (*oocyte*)
ophio- snake (*ophiolatry*)
ophthalmo- eye (*ophthalmology*)
opistho- back, behind (*opisthograph*)
opto- eye (*optometry*)
organo- body organ (*organoleptic*)
ornitho- bird (*ornithology*)
oro- mountain (*orography*); mouth (*oropharynx*)
ortho- straight (*orthopedic*)
ossi- bone (*ossiferous*)
osteo- bone (*osteopath*)
oto- ear (*otolaryngology*)
out- beyond, to an end point, abnormal (*outdoors, outlast, outmoded*)
over- too much, to excess (*overweight*)
ovi- egg (*oviparous*)
oxy- sharp, acute (*oxymoron*)
pachy- thick (*pachyderm*)
paleo- ancient, old (*paleolithic*)
pan- all (*pantheism*)
para- beside, beyond; guard against (*parallel, parachute*)
pari- equal (*paripinnate*)
partheno- without fertilization (*parthenogenesis*)
patho- disease, suffering (*pathological*)
patri- male (*patriarchy*)
pedi- foot (*pedicab*)
pedo- child (*pedophilia*)
penta- five (*pentagon*)
per- through, very (*pervade*)
peri- around, very (*perimeter*)
petro- stone (*petrology*)
phago- eating (*phagocyte*)
pharmaco- drug (*pharmocology*)
pharyngo- pharynx (*pharyngoscope*)
pheno- shining, appearing (*phenotype*)
philo- loving (*philosophy*)
phlebo- vein (*phlebotomy*)
phono- sound (*phonograph*)
photo- light (*photography*)
phreno- brain (*phrenology*)
phyco- seaweed, algae (*phycology*)
phyllo- leaf (*phyllotaxy*)
phylo- race, tribe, species (*phylogeny*)
physio- nature (*physiology*)
phyto- plant (*phytogenesis*)
piezo- pressure (*piezoelectric*)
pinni- web, fin (*pinniped*)
pisci- fish (*pisciculture*)
plagio- oblique (*plagiotropic*)
plano- flat (*planogamete*)

pleo- more (*pleomorphism*)
pleuro- side, lateral (*pleurocarpous*)
pluto- riches, wealth (*plutocracy*)
pluvio- rain (*pluviometer*)
pneumato- air, breath (*pneumatophore*)
pneumo- air, breath (*pneumococcus*)
pod- foot (*podiatry*)
polio- gray matter (*poliomyelitis*)
poly- many (*polygon*)
post- after (*postmortem*)
pre- before (*preproduction*)
preter- beyond (*preternatural*)
primi- first (*primipara*)
pro- before, forward (*prologue*); for, favoring (*proslavery*)
proprio- one's own (*proprioceptive*)
proto- first (*prototype*)
pseudo- false (*pseudonym*)
psycho- mind, spirit, soul (*psychosomatic*)
pterido- fern (*pteridology*)
ptero- wing (*pterodactyl*)
pyelo- pelvis (*pyelonephritis*)
pyo- pus (*pyorrhea*)
pyro- fire (*pyromania*)
quadri- four (*quadrilateral*)
quinque- five (*quinquevalent*)
re- again (*revitalize*)
recti- straight (*rectilinear*)
reni- kidney (*reniform*)
retro- backward (*retroactive*)
rhabdo- rod, wand (*rhabdovirus*)
rheo- flow, current (*rheostat*)
rhino- nose (*rhinoplasty*)
rhizo- root (*rhizogenic*)
rhodo- rose (*rhodolite*)
sacchar- sweet, sugar (*saccharide*)
sangui- blood (*sanguiferous*)
sapro- rotten, decomposed (*saprogenic*)
sarco- flesh (*sarcophagous*)
scato- excrement (*scatology*)
schizo- split (*schizophrenia*)
sclero- hard (*scleroderma*)
seleno- moon (*selenography*)
self- of or by oneself (*self-analysis*); to, with, or toward oneself (*self-abnegating*); independent or automatic (*self-governing, self-operating*)
semi- half, partially, somewhat (*semiweekly, semidetached*)
septi- seven (*septilateral*)
sero- serum (*serology*)
sesqui- one and a half (*sesquicentennial*)
sex- six (*sexpartite*)
shm- used to form jocular variations as replacement for initial consonant in standard form of word (*fancy shmancy*)
sidero- iron (*siderolite*)
siphono- tube (*siphonostele*)
socio- society (*sociology*)
somato- body (*somatotype*)
somni- sleep (*somnifacient*)
spermato- seed (*spermatozoon*)
spermo- seed, germ (*spermophyte*)
spheno- wedge (*sphenography*)
sphygmo- pulse (*sphygmometer*)

spiro- respiration (*spirograph*); coil, spiral (*spirochete*)
sporo- spore (*sporophyte*)
steato- fat, tallow (*steatopygia*)
stego- cover (*stegosaur*)
stelli- star (*stelliform*)
steno- close, narrow (*stenography*)
stereo- solid (*stereoscope*)
stomato- mouth (*stomatoplasty*)
strati- stratum (*stratification*)
strepto- twisted (*streptococcus*)
stylo- column, pillar (*stylolite*)
sub- below, under (*subarctic*); secondary (*subplot*)
super- above (*supernatural*)
supra- above, beyond (*supraorbital*)
sus- under, beneath, secondary (*suspend*)
syl- with (*syllepsis*)
sym- with (*symmetry*)
syn- with (*synoptic*)
synchro- occurring together (*synchrotron*)
tacho- speed (*tachometer*)
tachy- rapid (*tachycardia*)
tauto- same (*tautology*)
techno- technique, skill (*technology*)
tele- distant (*telekinesis*)
teleo- final (*teleology*)
telo- end (*telophase*)
teno- tendon (*tenotomy*)
tera- trillion (*terabyte*)
terato- monster (*teratology*)
terri- land, earth (*terricolous*)
tetra- four (*tetralogy*)
thanato- death (*thanatology*)
thaumato- miracle, wonder (*thaumatology*)
theo- god (*theology*)
thermo- heat (*thermoplastic*)
thrombo- blood clot, coagulation (*thrombocyte*)
toco- birth, child (*tocopherol*)
tomo- cut, section (*tomography*)
tono- stretching, tension (*tonometer*)
topo- place, local (*topology*)
totl- entire (*totipalmation*)
toxico- poison (*toxicology*)
toxo- poison (*toxoplasmosis*)
tracheo- trachea (*tracheotomy*)
trachy- rough (*trachycarpous*)
trans- across, through, on far side of (*transverse*)
tri- three (*trilateral*)
tribo- friction (*triboluminescence*)
tricho- hair (*trichocyst*)
tropho- nourishment (*trophosome*)
tropo- turn, response, change (*troposphere*)
ultra- beyond (*ultrasonics*)
un- not, freely used to give negative or opposite force to adjectives (*unhappy*); used to reverse action or state of verb (*unfasten*)
under- beneath, below, or lesser in place, grade, or extent (*undersized*)
uni- single, one (*unicycle*)
urino- urine (*urinoscopy*)
uro- urine (*urology*)
vaso- vessel (*vasoconstrictor*)
veno- vein (*venostasis*)
ventro- abdomen (*ventrodorsal*)

vermi- worm (*vermiform*)
vini- wine (*viniculture*)
vitri- glass (*vitriform*)
vivi- living, alive (*vivisection*)
xantho- yellow (*xanthophyll*)
xeno- foreign (*xenophobia*)
xero- dry (*xeroderma*)
xylo- wood (*xylophone*)
zoo- animal (*zoology*)
zygo- yoke, double (*zygomorphic*)

Suffixes

-ability combination of -able and -ity for nouns corresponding to adjectives ending in -able (*capability*)
-able capable of, fit for, tending or given to (*laudable, singable*)
-ably combination of -able and -ly for adverbs corresponding to adjectives ending in -able (*tolerably*)
-acea used in formation of names of zoological classes and orders (*Crustacea*)
-aceae used in formation of names of botanical families (*Rosaceae*)
-aceous resembling, made of (*herbaceous*)
-acious used in formation of adjectives corresponding to nouns ending in -acy or -acity (*fallacious, audacious*)
-acity quality of, having characteristics of (*tenacity*)
-acy ending for nouns of quality, state, or office (*delicacy, papacy*)
-adelphous having stamens growing together in bundles (*monadelphous*)
-agogue leader, bringer of, practitioner (*demagogue*)
-aholic one who has addiction to or obsession with something (*workaholic*)
-al having form or character of, pertaining to (*autumnal, natural*); used to form nouns from verbs (*refusal*)
-ales used in formation of names of botanical orders (*Cycadales*)
-algia pain (*neuralgia*)
-amine variation of amino- in chemical compounds (*chloramine*)
-an used to form adjectives, esp. of place and membership (*American, Elizabethan*)
-ana collection of items (*Americana*)
-ance used to form nouns corresponding to verbs or to adjectives ending in -ant (*brilliance*)
-ancy combination of -ance and -y denoting state or quality (*brilliancy*)
-androus male (*polyandrous*)
-andry used in nouns corresponding to adjectives ending in -androus (*polyandry*)
-ane used in names of hydrocarbons of methane or paraffin series (*propane*)
-anthous having flowers of specified type or number (*monanthous*)
-arama variation of -orama (*foodarama*)
-arch chief, leader, ruler (*matriarch*)
-archy rule, government (*monarchy*)

-arian used to form personal nouns from adjectives or nouns ending in -ary (*librarian*)
-aroo variation of -eroo (*buckaroo*)
-arooni variation of -aroo, diminutive or additionally jocular (*sockarooni*)
-asis used in scientific and medical words from Greek (*psoriasis*)
-ast one connected with or given to (*enthusiast*)
-ate use to form nouns that denote office or function or a person who exercises function (*consulate, magistrate*); used in chemistry to indicate salt of acid ending in -ic (*nitrate*)
-athon used in compound words to indicate event drawn out to unusual length (*danceathon*)
-ation combination of -ate and -ion used to form nouns corresponding to verbs with stem -ate (*separation*)
-ative combination of -ate and -ive to form adjectives corresponding to verbs with stem -ate (*regulative*) or from other stem words (*normative*)
-biosis mode of life (*aerobiosis*)
-blast bud, sprout (*ectoblast*)
-carp part of fruit or fruiting body (*endocarp*)
-carpic used in formation of adjectives from stems ending in -carp (*endocarpic*)
-carpous having fruit (*apocarpous*)
-cele tumor (*variocele*)
-cene variation of -ceno (*Pleistocene*)
-ceno new, recent (*cenogenesis*)
-cephalic variation of -cephalous (*brachycephalic*)
-cephalous having a specific kind of head (*brachycephalous*)
-chroic variation of -chroous (*monochroic*)
-chrome color (*polychrome*)
-chroous having a specific kind of color (*isochroous*)
-cide killer, act of killing (*suicide*)
-clase used in formation of compound words for minerals with specified cleavage (*plagioclase*)
-clasis breaking (*thromboclasis*)
-cle used to form diminutive nouns (*particle*); used to form nouns that denote place appropriate to action of verb from which they are formed (*receptacle*)
-coccus spherical bacterium (*streptococcus*)
-coele cavity (*enterocoele*)
-colous inhabiting specified place or thing (*nidicolous*)
-cracy rule, government (*democracy*)
-crat ruler, supporter of particular form of government (*autocrat*)
-cule variation of -cle (*molecule, ridicule*)
-cyst cyst sac (*statocyst*)
-cyte cell (*leucocyte*)
-dactyl used to form nouns corresponding to adjectives ending in -dactylous (*pterodactyl*)
-dactylous having toes or fingers (*tridactylous*)
-dendron tree (*rhododendron*)
-derm skin (*pachyderm*)
-drome running; racecourse or other large structure (*hippodrome, airdrome*)

-ectomy excision or removal of particular part (*appendectomy*)

-elle used to form diminutive or derivative nouns (*bagatelle, organelle*)

-emia blood condition (*anemia*)

-ence used to form nouns from verbs or from adjectives ending in -ent (*abstinence, difference*)

-ensis pertaining to or originating in, usu. in scientific terms (*carolinensis*)

-eous composed of, resembling (*igneous*); used to form adjectives from nouns, esp. those ending in -ty (*beauteous*)

-er used to form comparative degree of adjectives or adverbs (*smaller, faster*); used in formation of nouns of person from object of occupation, place of origin, or specific characteristic (*hatter, villager, teetotaler*); used to form agent nouns from verbs (*employer*); used to form occupation names (*butcher*)

-ergic activated by, sensitive to, releasing (*allergic*)

-ern used to form adjectives from directions (*northern*)

-eroo used to form familiar, usu. jocular nouns (*switcheroo*)

-ers *Chiefly Brit.* informal variation of noun or adjective (*preggers*)

-ery used to form nouns denoting occupation, condition, place, products, things collectively, actions, or qualities (*archery, bakery, cutlery, trickery*)

-esce used to express beginning of action of verb (*convalesce*)

-escence used to denote nouns of action or process, change, or condition corresponding to verbs ending in -esce or adjectives ending in -escent (*convalescence*)

-escent used in formation of adjectives expressing beginning of action (*convalescent*)

-ese used to form adjectival derivatives of place names, esp. for inhabitants or language of place (*Japanese, Viennese*); used to characterize jargon (*computerese*)

-esis used in nouns of action or process (*genesis*)

-esque indicating style, manner, or distinctive character of adjective or individual (*picturesque, Kafkaesque*)

-ess used to form feminine nouns (*countess*)

-est used to form superlative degree of adjectives or adverbs (*smallest, fastest*); formerly used to form second person singular indicative of verbs (*knowest*)

-eur used to form agent nouns or occasionally adjectives from verbs (*masseur, provocateur*)

-euse used to form feminine nouns corresponding to nouns ending in -eur (*masseuse*)

-ey variation of -y, esp. after words end in "y" (*clayey*); used informally or to denote little one (*Charley*)

-fest assembly of people for common purpose (*songfest*)

-fex maker (*spinifex*)

-fic making, producing, causing (*honorific*)

-fication used to form nouns of action or state corresponding to verbs ending in -fy (*specification*)

-fid split, divided (*bifid*)

-florous having flowers (*uniflorous*)

-fuge that which repels or drives away something specified (*vermifuge*)

-fy make, cause to be, render (*beautify*)

-gamy marriage (*monogamy*)

-gen that which produces (*hydrogen*)

-genesis origin, beginning (*parthenogenesis*)

-genetic used to form adjectives from nouns ending in -genesis (*parthenogenetic*)

-genic producing or causing, produced or caused by, used to form adjectives corresponding to nouns ending in -gen or -geny (*hallucinogenic, cosmogenic*)

-genous giving rise to the thing specified (*androgenous*)

-geny origin (*phylogeny*)

-glot having a tongue or speaking, writing, or written in a language (*polyglot*)

-gnathous having a jaw (*prognathous*)

-gnomy knowledge (*physiognomy*)

-gnosis knowledge (*prognosis*)

-gnostic used to form adjectives from nouns ending in -gnosis (*diagnostic*)

-gon angled (*polygon*)

-gony production, origination (*cosmogony*)

-grade walking or moving in specified manner (*retrograde*)

-gram something written or drawn (*epigram, diagram*); message, bulletin (*telegram*)

-graph drawn or written, esp. instrument used to produce writing (*telegraph*)

-graphy process, science, or art of drawing, writing, recording, or representing (*biography, photography, choreography*)

-gynous taking an attitude toward women (*misogynous*)

-gyny used to form nouns corresponding to adjectives ending in -gynous (*misogyny*)

-hedral used to form adjectives from nouns ending in -hedron (*polyhedral*)

-hedron figure with faces or sides of specified number (*octahedron*)

-holic variation of -aholic (*chocoholic*)

-ia used in names of diseases, places, Roman feasts, and Latin plurals (*malaria, Romania, Saturnalia, Reptilia*)

-ial variation of -al (*editorial*)

-ian variation of -an, esp. denoting type, engagement in, or practice of (*reptilian, Episcopalian, electrician*)

-iasis disease (*psoriasis*)

-iatrics medicine, treatment (*pediatrics*)

-iatry specific area of healing or medical practice (*psychiatry*)

-ibility variation of -ability when base adjective ends in -ible (*responsibility*)

-ible variation of -able (*horrible*)

-ibly combination of -ible and -ly for adverbs corresponding to adjectives ending in -ible (*visibly*)

-ic used to form adjectives from other parts of speech (*poetic*); having some attribute of, in the style of (*sophomoric, Byronic*); used in chemistry to show higher valence in opposition to -ous (*ferric chloride*)

-ical combination of -ic and -al to form adjectives corresponding to nouns or adjectives ending in -ic (*economical*)

-ician used to form personal nouns denoting occupation (*beautician*)

-ics field of study, body of knowledge or principles, usu. corresponding to adjectives ending in -ic or -ical (*ethics, physics*)

-id descendant of, esp. for names of dynasties (*Abbasid*); name of zoological family or class or adjective pertaining to taxonomic division (*arachnid*); used to form adjectives corresponding to nouns ending in -or (*pallid*)

-idae denoting names of zoological families (*Candiae*)

-ide indicator of chemical compounds (*chloride*)

-idine denoting names of chemical compounds derived from other chemical compounds (*guanidine*)

-idion variation of diminutive -idium (*enchiridion*)

-idium diminutive for scientific terms (*peridium*)

-ie variation of -y or -ey, esp. denoting little one (*birdie*)

-iensis variation of -ensis (*mississippiensis*)

-ier indicating person engaged in trade or occupation (*cashier*); used on loanwords from French, often with loss of final "r" sound (*dossier*)

-iform shaped like (*cruciform*)

-iformes taxonomic names of animals (*Passeriformes*)

-ify variation of -fy used to form verbs from adjectives (*intensify*)

-il variation of -ile (*civil*)

-ile used to form adjectives expressing capability, susceptibility, liability, or aptitude (*agile, docile, fragile, prehensile*)

-ility used to form abstract nouns corresponding to adjectives ending in -le, -ile, or -il (*ability, agility, civility*)

-illion indicating numerals of specified exponential degree (*trillion*)

-ine like, pertaining to, made of (*marine, crystalline*); names of chemical substances (*chlorine*)

-ing used to form nouns that express action, result, or product of verb (*building*) or participial adjective form of verb (*thinking man*); belonging to, descended from (*farthing*)

-ious used to form adjectives corresponding to nouns ending in -ity (*atrocious*)

-isation *Brit.* variation of -ization (*organisation*)

-ise *Brit.* variation of -ize (*specialise*)

-ish used to form adjectives from nouns denoting belonging to, having characteristics of, or inclined to (*British, childish, bookish*); used to form adjectives from adjectives meaning somewhat or rather (*sweetish*)

-ism used to form nouns denoting action,

condition, doctrine, or usage (*criticism, barbarism, Darwinism, realism, witticism*)

-ist used to form personal nouns corresponding to verbs ending in -ize or nouns ending in -ism (*apologist, socialist*)

-istic used to form adjectives from nouns ending in -ist or -ism (*socialistic, altruistic*)

-istical combination of -istic and -al to create additional adjectival form (*linguistical*)

-istics combination of -ist and -ics to form collective noun (*linguistics*)

-ite denoting person associated with place, group, belief, or system (*Israelite, laborite*); mineral and fossil names (*anthracite, ammonite*); names of chemical compounds (*sulfite*); used to form adjectives and nouns from adjectives and some verbs (*opposite*)

-itious used to form adjectives from nouns ending in -ition (*ambitious*)

-itis inflammation (*arthritis*); abnormality or excess (*computeritis*)

-itive used in substantives of Latin origin (*transitive*)

-ity used to form abstract nouns expressing state or condition, esp. from adjectives (*insincerity*)

-ium used on nouns borrowed from Latin (*tedium*), certain compound words (*equilibrium*), and associative derivatives of personal nouns (*collegium*)

-ization combination of -ize and -ation (*civilization*)

-ize added to adjectives and nouns to form transitive verbs meaning make, give form to, or subject to some process (*fossilize, dramatize, terrorize*), or to form intransitive verbs denoting change of state, kind of behavior, or activity (*crystallize, apologize, philosophize*)

-kinesis movement (*telekinesis*)

-lalia abnormal or disordered speech (*glossolalia*)

-latry worship of (*idolatry*)

-lepsy seizure, fit (*epilepsy*)

-less without (*childless*)

-like used to form adjectives denoting similarity, preceded by hyphen if base word ends in double "l" (*childlike, bell-like*)

-ling denoting one concerned with, often pejoratively or diminutively (*hireling, duckling*); used with adverbs to express direction, position, or state (*underling, darkling*)

-lith stone (*paleolith*)

-lithic used in names of archaeological ages (*Neolithic*)

-logue used in names of kinds of discourses or writing (*monologue, travelogue*)

-logy science of, body of knowledge (*biology, theology*)

-ly used to form adverbs from adjectives (*slowly*); added to nouns denoting every time (*hourly*); used to form adjectives meaning like (*cowardly*)

-lysis dissolving, breaking down, decomposing (*electrolysis, analysis, paralysis*)

-lyte something subjected to a process, often where process ends in -lysis (*electrolyte*)

-lyze used in verbs corresponding to nouns ending in -ysis (*analyze*)

-machy battle, fighting (*logomachy*)

-mancy divination (*oneiromancy*)

-mania obsession with, craving for (*pyromania*)

-megalia variation of -megaly (*hepatosplenomegalia*)

-megaly abnormal enlargement of specified part (*cardiomegaly*)

-ment used in nouns denoting action, product, or means (*refinement, fragment, ornament*)

-mer member of particular chemical group (*polymer*)

-merous having parts of specified kind or number (*pentamerous*)

-metric used to form adjectives based on nouns ending in -metry (*geometric*)

-metry process of measurement (*chronometry*)

-morph form or structure (*allomorph*)

-morphic variation of -morphous (*anthropomorphic*)

-morphism used to form nouns corresponding to adjectives ending in -morphous or -morphic (*isomorphism*)

-morphous having specified shape, form, or structure (*polymorphous*)

-mycete fungus, mushroom (*ascomycete*)

-mycetes taxonomic names of fungi, esp. classes (*Myxomycetes*)

-ness used to form abstract nouns denoting quality and state from adjectives and participles (*darkness, preparedness*)

-nomy distribution or arrangement (*economy, taxonomy*)

-oate denoting names of chemical compounds (*benzoate*)

-ock used to form descriptive and diminutive names (*bullock, hillock*)

-odont having or relating to teeth, esp. used as base in combination with -ia or -ics (*orthodontia*)

-odus variation of -odont, used for names of zoological genera (*ceratodus*)

-odynia pain (*pododynia*)

-oid similar to, like (*ovoid*)

-oidea used for names of zoological classes (*Echinoidea*)

-ola used in various commercial coinages and jocular variations of other words (*granola, crapola*)

-oma tumor (*melanoma*)

-onym word, name (*synonym, pseudonym*)

-oon used in formation of nouns from Romance languages (*bassoon*)

-opia eye, sight (*myopia*)

-opic used to form adjectives corresponding to nouns ending in -opia (*myopic*)

-opsia variation of -opia (*hemianopsia*)

-opsis likeness, esp. to named thing (*coreopsis*)

-opsy medical examination (*biopsy*)

-opy variation of -opia (*amblyopy*)

-or denoting condition or property, sometimes in noun form corresponding to adjective ending in -id (*squalor*); used to form animate or inanimate agent nouns, often as variation of -er (*traitor, projector*)

-orama used in compound words, esp. in advertising and journalism (*scoutorama*)

-orial used to form adjectives based on nouns ending in -tor or -tory (*editorial, valedictorial*)

-ory used to form adjectives that imitate words ending in -tory or -sory (*excretory, sensory*); used in nouns denoting place or receptacle (*crematory*)

-ose full of, given to (*verbose*); used in chemical names of sugars and carbohydrates (*fructose, lactose*)

-osis denoting action, condition, or state, esp. abnormal one (*hypnosis, tuberculosis*)

-ota used in plural form of taxonomic names, esp. phyla (*Eukaryota*)

-ote used to form singular nouns from taxonomic names ending in -ota (*eukaryote*)

-otic used to form adjectives denoting relationship to indicated action, process, state, or condition, often based on nouns ending in -osis (*hypnotic*)

-our *Brit.* variation of -or (*honour*)

-ous used to form Anglicized adjectives, generally meaning possessing or full of (*nervous, tremendous*); used in chemistry to show lower valence in opposition to -ic (*ferrous chloride*)

-pagus used in names of malformed conjoined twins (*thoracopagus*)

-parous bearing, producing (*oviparous*)

-pathic used to form adjectives from nouns ending in -pathy (*homeopathic*)

-pathy suffering, feeling, disease, or treatment (*antipathy, sympathy, psychopathy, homeopathy*)

-ped having specified feet (*biped*)

-pede variation of -ped (*centipede*)

-penia lack, deficiency (*leukopenia*)

-phage thing that devours (*bacteriophage*)

-phagia variation of -phage (*hemophagia*)

-phagous eating, feeding on, devouring (*creophagous*)

-phagy eating, devouring (*anthropophagy*)

-phany appearance, manifestation (*epiphany*)

-phasia denoting names of speech disorders (*aphasia*)

-phil variation of -phile (*eosinophil*)

-phile lover of (*bibliophile*)

-philia affinity for or tendency toward, also unnatural attraction (*hemophilia, necrophilia*)

-philiac used to form adjectives from nouns ending in -philia (*hemophiliac*)

-philic used to form adjectives from nouns ending in -phile (*bibliophilic*); affinity for, among class of substances (*acidophilic*)

-philism used to form abstract nouns based on nouns ending in -phile (*bibliophilism*)

-philous liking, having affinity for (*dendrophilous*)

-phily variation of -philia (*hydrophily*)

-phobia fear (*acrophobia*)

-phone speech sound or instrument of sound transmission (*homophone, microphone*)

-phony used to form abstract nouns

corresponding to nouns ending in -phone (*telephony*)

-phore bearer of (*gonophore*)

-phorous used to form adjectives corresponding to nouns ending in -phore (*gonophorous*)

-phrenia indicating names of mental disorders (*schizophrenia*)

-phyllous having leaves (*monophyllous*)

-phyte plant (*lithophyte*)

-plasia growth (*hypoplasia*)

-plasm living tissue, cell substance (*ectoplasm*)

-plast cell, living substance (*chloroplast*)

-plasty molding formation or surgical repair (*rhinoplasty*)

-plasy variation of -plasia (*homoplasy*)

-plegia paralysis (*paraplegia*)

-ploid having chromosome sets (*hexaploid*)

-pnea breath (*dyspnea*)

-pod having specified kind or number of feet (*cephalopod*)

-poda having specified feet, used in names of zoological classes (*Cephalopoda*)

-pode variation of -podium (*pseudopode*)

-podium footlike part (*monopodium*)

-podous used to form adjectives from nouns ending in -pod (*cephalopodous*)

-poiesis making, formation (*hematopoiesis*)

-poietic used to form adjectives from nouns ending in -poiesis (*hematopoietic*)

-pterous having wings (*dipterous*)

-rel used in diminutive or pejorative noun (*scoundrel*)

-rhiza variation of -rrhiza (*coleorhiza*)

-rrhagia rupture, profuse flow or discharge (*bronchorrhagia*)

-rrhaphy suture (*herniorrhaphy*)

-rrhea flow, discharge (*diarrhea*)

-rrhexis rupture (*enterorrhexis*)

-rrhiza root (*mycorrhiza*)

-rrhoea variation of -rrhea (*melanorrhoea*)

-saur used in names of extinct reptiles (*dinosaur*)

-saurus variation of -saur (*tyrannosaurus*)

-scope instrument for viewing (*microscope*)

-sepalous having specified sepals (*polysepalous*)

-ski jocular or informal addition derived from Slavic names (*Russki*)

-sky variation of -ski (*buttinsky*)

-some used to form adjectives from verbs and nouns (*burdensome*); meaning body in compounds (*chromosome*); collective used with numerals (*threesome*)

-sophy science of, wisdom (*philosophy*)

-sperm one having specified seeds (*angiosperm*)

-spermal used to form adjectives from nouns ending in -sperm (*gymnospermal*)

-sporous having specified spores (*helicosporous*)

-stichous having specified rows (*distichous*)

-stome organism having a mouth (*cyclostome*)

-stomous having specified mouth (*monostomous*)

-stomy surgical operation involving creation of artificial opening (*colostomy*)

-taxis arrangement or order (*heterotaxis*)

-taxy variation of -taxis (*epitaxy*)

-teen used to form cardinal numerals from 13 to 19 (*fifteen*)

-therm heat (*isotherm*)

-thermy heat, heat generation (*diathermy*)

-tion used to form abstract nouns, esp. from verbs, expressing action, state, or associated meanings (*revolution, relation*)

-tious added to various stems to form adjectives (*facetious, bumptious*)

-tome cutting instrument (*osteotome*)

-tomous cut, divided (*dichotomous*)

-tomy cutting, incision, surgical excision (*appendectomy*)

-ton used to form nouns from adjectives (*simpleton*)

-tonia muscle or nerve tension or personality disorder (*hypertonia, catatonia*)

-tonic used to form adjectives from nouns ending in -tonia (*catatonic*)

-trix used to form feminine, esp. of nouns ending in -tor (*executrix*)

-trope one turned toward (*heliotrope*)

-troph nutrient matter or organism with specified nutritional requirements (*embryotroph, heterotroph*)

-trophic having nutritional requirements, maintaining an activity (*autotrophic, gonadotrophic*)

-trophy used to form nouns meaning feeding or growth (*mycotrophy, hypertrophy*)

-tropic turned toward, having an affinity for (*geotropic, psychotropic*)

-tropism variation of -tropy (*heliotropism*)

-tropous turned, curved (*anatropous*)

-tropy used to form abstract nouns corresponding to adjectives ending in -tropic or -tropous (*psychotropy*)

-tude used in abstract nouns and formation of new nouns (*platitude*)

-ty used in nouns denoting quality or state (*unity*); added to numerals to denote multiples of ten (*twenty*)

-type having a particular characteristic, regarded as a group or class (*prototype, phenotype*)

-urgy technique or art of dealing or working with something (*chemurgy*)

-vore one that eats (*carnivore*)

-vorous eating (*omnivorous*)

-ward used to denote spatial or temporal direction (*backward, afterward*)

-wards variation of -ward (*towards*)

-xion *Brit.* variation of -tion (*connexion*)

-y characterized by, inclined to (*juicy, dreamy*); added to usu. monosyllabic bases to create informal nouns (*granny, cabby*); used to denote little one (*Billy*)

-yer variation of -er in formation of occupational names (*lawyer*)

-zoa used in names of zoological classes (*Protozoa*)

-zoon animal or organism, esp. single member of zoological class name ending in -zoa (*protozoon*)

ABBREVIATIONS

See also: *Chap. 3: Geography; Chap. 4: Physics; Chemistry; Medicine; Chap. 5: Weapons and Armaments; Computers; Chap. 11: Government; War and Military; Titles of Rank; Chap. 12: Finance; Chap. 13: Education; Chap. 15: Popular Music; Television and Radio; Chap. 17: Sports; Chap. 24: Crime; Chap. 25: Religion*

This section does not include acronyms and initials for organizations, entities, and trademarked products such as AMA, FCC, MS-DOS, NATO, and SDI, which appear in their appropriate categories. Most of the abbreviations listed here have been normalized to one form, without periods, except where the period is required, as in certain titles, academic degrees, or A.D. and B.C., or to distinguish the abbreviation from a word, as a.m. or mach. In practice, there is great variety in the use of periods and capitalization for abbreviations.

A.B. *Latin.* artium baccalaureus; Bachelor of Arts

abbrev abbreviation

abr abridged

AC alternating current; air conditioning

ack acknowledge, acknowledgment

A.D. *Latin.* anno Domini; in the year of the Lord

adj adjective

admin administration

adv adverb

aeron aeronautics

agcy agency

agric agriculture, agricultural

aka also known as

alt alternate; alternation; altitude

a.m. *Latin.* ante meridiem; morning

AM amplitude modulation

amb ambassador

ammo ammunition

amp ampere; amplifier

anat anatomy

anon anonymous

approx approximate

Apr April

apt. apartment

arch. architecture

arith arithmetic

art. article

ASAP as soon as possible

assoc associated, association

asst assistant

astron astronomy

att attached; attorney

aug augmented

Aug August

aux auxiliary

ave avenue

avg average

AWOL absent without leave

B.A. Bachelor of Arts

bal balance
b and w black and white
bbl barrel
B.C. before Christ
B.C.E. before Christian (common) era
bd board
bet between
bf boldface
bibliog bibliography
biog biography
biol biology
blvd boulevard
bot bottom; botany
bro brother
B.S. Bachelor of Science
bskt basket
BTU British thermal unit
bu bushel
bull. bulletin
bur bureau
BYOB bring your own booze/beer/bottle
C Celsius, centigrade
c cent; century; copyright
ca circa
cal calorie
calc calculate
cap. capitalize
capt captain
cat. catalog
CB Citizens Band
cc cubic centimeter
Cdr Commander
C.E. common era, same as A.D.
cent. century
CEO chief executive officer
cert certificate, certified
cf *Latin.* confer; compare
cg centigram
chap. chapter
chem chemistry
chm chairman
chron chronology
cie *French.* compagnie; company
circ circular
cl centiliter
class. classified, classification
cm centimeter
CNS central nervous system
co company
c/o care of
COD cash on delivery
Col. Colonel
col colony; column
collab collaboration
colloq colloquial
comb. combination, combining
comm commander; commerce; committee
conc concentrated
cond condition
conf conference
confed confederate
Cong Congress
conj conjunction
const construction; constitution

contd continued
contemp contemporary
contr contraction
contrib contributor, contribution
coroll corollary
corp corporation
corr correct; correspondence
CPA certified public accountant
CPI consumer price index
cpl corporal
CPR cardiopulmonary resuscitation
cr credit; crown
crim criminal
crit critical, criticism
CRT cathode-ray tube
ct court
ctr center
cu cubic
cum cumulative
CYA cover your ass
d *Latin.* denarii; penny (Britain); diameter; dime; dollar
DA district attorney
dba doing business as
dbl double; decibel
DC direct current
D.D. Doctor of Divinity
D.D.S. Doctor of Dental Science
Dec December
dec deceased
def definition
deg degree
Dem Democrat
dcnom denomination
dept department
deriv derivative, derived
dial. dialect
diam diameter
dict dictionary
dim. diminished; dimension
DINK dual income, no kids
dip. diploma
dir director
dist district; distance
div division; divorced
do. ditto
DOA dead on arrival
doc. document
dol dollar
doz dozen
Dr. Doctor
DST daylight-saving time
dt's delirium tremens
dup duplicate
E east, eastern
ea each
eccl ecclesiastical
ecol ecology
econ economics
ed editor
educ education
EEG electroencephalogram
e.g. *Latin.* exempli gratia; for example
EKG electrocardiogram

el elevation
elec electric
elem elementary
elev elevation
enc enclosure, enclosed
encyc encyclopedia
env envelope
eq equal, equalization
equiv equivalent
ERA earned run average
esp. especially
ESP extrasensory perception
Esq. Esquire
est estimated
et al *Latin.* et alia; and others
etc. *Latin.* etcetera; and so forth
et seq *Latin.* et sequens; and the following one
etym etymology
ex. example
exam examination
exc except
exec executive
ex lib *Latin.* ex libris; from the books of
exp expense; express
ext extension; exterior
F Fahrenheit
f feminine; father; feet
fac facsimile
fath fathom
Feb February
fec *Latin.* fecit; he made it
fed federal; federation
fem feminine
ff and following
fid fiduciary
fig figurative
fin. finance; finish
fka formerly known as
FM frequency modulation
fn footnote
f.o.b. freight on board
fol folio; following
foll and the following entry
for. foreign
freq frequent
Fri Friday
frt freight
frwy freeway
Ft. fort
ft foot, feet
fur. furlong
furn furnished
fut future
fwd forward; foreword
fx special effects
FYI for your information
g gram
gal. gallon
gaz gazette
gds goods
gen general
geneal genealogy
geog geography
geol geology

geom geometry
GIGO garbage in, garbage out
gloss. glossary
gm gram
GOP Grand Old Party
Gov. governor
Govt government
gp group
GQ General Quarters
gr gram; gross; grade
grad graduate
gram. grammar
gtd guaranteed
guar guarantee
ha. hectare
hdqrs headquarters
hf half
HMS His (or Her) Majesty's Ship
Hon. Honorable
hor horizontal
hosp hospital
hq headquarters
hr hour
HRH His (or Her) Royal Highness
ht height
hwy highway
ibid *Latin.* ibidem; in the same place
id. *Latin.* idem; the same
i.e. *Latin.* id est; that is
illus illustrated
imper imperative
in. inch
inc incorporated
incl including
incorp incorporated
ind independent; index
indic indicative
inf infinitive
init initially
in loc cit *Latin.* in loco citato; in the place cited
insp inspector
inst institute
instr instructor
int interior; interim
interj interjection
interrog interrogative, interrogation
inv invoice
I/O input/output
IOU I owe you
IQ intelligence quotient
irreg irregular
ISBN International Standard Book Number
isl island
ital italics
Jan January
jct junction
J.D. *Latin.* Jurum Doctor; doctor of law
Jly July
Jn June
jour journal
JP justice of the peace
jr junior
juv juvenile
k kilogram; thousand; karat; kilobyte

kg kilogram
kHz kilohertz
kilo. kilogram
km kilometer
kn knot
KO knockout
Kt knight
kW kilowatt
L *Latin.* libra; pound (Britain)
l liter
lab laboratory
lang language
lat latitude
lb. *Latin.* libra; pound
l.c. lower case
lect lecturer
lex lexicon
lf lightface; left field
lg large
lic license
Lieut lieutenant
ling linguistics
liq liquid
lit. literally
Litt. D. *Latin.* litterarum doctor; doctor of letters
LL.B. *Latin.* legum baccalaureus; bachelor of law
LL.D. *Latin.* legum doctor; doctor of laws
ln lane
loc cit *Latin.* loco citato; in the place cited
long. longitude
LPN licensed practical nurse
Lt. lieutenant
lt light
Ltd limited
m meter; masculine; million
M.A. Master of Arts
mach. machine
mag magazine
Maj. Major
Mar March
masc masculine
math mathematics
max maximum
MC master of ceremonies
M.D. Doctor of Medicine
mdse merchandise
meas measure
mech mechanical, mechanics
med medicine
memo memorandum
met. metropolitan
M.F.A. Master of Fine Arts
mfd manufactured
mfr manufacturer
mg milligram
mgr manager
mi mile
mid middle
milit military
min minimum; minister; minute
misc miscellaneous
ml milliliter
mm millimeter

MO *Latin.* modus operandi, method of operation; money order; mail order
mo. month
mod. moderate
Mon Monday
MP Military Police; Member of Parliament
mph miles per hour
Mr. mister
Mrs. title of respect for a married woman
Ms. title of respect for a woman regardless of marital status
M.S. Master of Science
ms manuscript
MSG monosodium glutamate
Msgr Monsignor
M.S.W. Master of Social Work
Mt. Mount; mountain
mtge mortgage
mtn mountain
muni municipal
N north, northern
n noun; neuter; noon
N/A not applicable
nat national; natural
naut nautical
NB *Latin.* nota bene; note well
NE northeast; northeastern
neg negative
neut neuter
no. *Latin.* numero; number
nom nominative
Nov November
np no pagination
nr near
num numeral
NW northwest; northwestern
OBE Order of the British Empire
obit obituary
obj object; objective
obs obsolete
occas occasional, occasionally
Oct October
off. officer; official
op opus
op cit *Latin.* opere citato; in the work cited
opp. opposite
orch orchestra
org organization
orig. originally, origin
ot overtime
oz. ounce
p page
PA public address (system)
P and L profit and loss
par. paragraph
paren parentheses
Parl Parliament
part. participle
pat. patent
PC personal computer; politically correct
pc parsec
pd paid
PE physical education
per. period; person

perh perhaps
perm permanent
pers personal
pfd preferred
ph phase; phone
pharm pharmacy
Ph.D. Doctor of Philosophy
philos philosophy
photo photograph
phr phrase
phys ed physical education
pk peck
pkg package
pl plural; place
p.m. *Latin.* post meridiem; afternoon
PO post office
poss possessive
POV point of view
pp pages
ppd postpaid; prepaid
pref preface; preferred
prelim preliminary
prep. preposition
pres president
priv private
prod. product
pron pronoun; pronunciation
pronun pronunciation
pro tem *Latin.* pro tempore; for the time being
prov province
P.S. postscript
Ps Psalms
pseud pseudonym
psych psychology
Pt. Point
pt part; pint
p/t part time
pub. publication
pvt private
pwr power
PX post exchange
q quart
QED *Latin.* quod erat demonstrandum; which was to be demonstrated
qt quart
qty quantity
qv *Latin.* quad vide; which see, in reference to
R *Latin.* Rex, Regina; king, queen
R and R rest and recreation/recuperation
rbi run batted in
rd road
rec recipe; receipt
ref reference
refrig refrigerator
reg registered; regulation
rel relative
REM rapid eye movement (sleep)
Rep Republican
res reserve; residence
ret. retired
rev reverse; review; revised

Rev. Reverend
RFD Rural Free Delivery (postal route)
rh relative humidity
rhet rhetoric
RIP rest in peace
riv river
R.N. registered nurse
rnd round
rpm revolutions per minute
RR railroad
RSVP *French.* répondez s'il vous plait; please answer
rt right
rte route
Rx pharmaceutical prescription
S south, southern
s second
SASE self-addressed stamped envelope
Sat Saturday
S.B. *Latin.* scientiae baccalaureus; bachelor of science
sci science
sd sound
SE southeast; southeastern
secy secretary
Sept September
seq *Latin.* sequens; the following
sgd signed
sing. singular
sm small
S.M. *Latin.* scientiae magister; master of science
soc society; sociology
sol. solution
SOP standard operating procedure
soph sophomore
SOS save our ship, international distress signal
spec special; specification
specif specifically
SPQR *Latin.* senatus populusque romanus; the senate and Roman people
sq square
SS steamship
St. Saint; street
st state
std standard
Ste. Saint (female)
stet *Latin.* it stands; let the original stand
sub. subject; subtract
subj subject; subjunctive
Sun Sunday
supp supplement
supr supreme
supt superintendent
sur surface
surv survey
SW southwest; southwestern
sym symbol
syn synonym
t ton
tba to be announced
tbs tablespoon

TCB take care of business
TD touchdown
tech technical
tel telephone; telegraph; telegram
temp temporary
terr territory
Test. Testament
TGIF thank God it's Friday
theol theology
therm thermometer
Thurs Thursday
tit. title
TKO technical knockout
tkt ticket
TNT trinitrotoluene (explosive)
tot. total
Tpke turnpike
tr translation; transpose
treas treasury
trib tributary
tsp teaspoon
Tues Tuesday
u.c. upper case
UFO unidentified flying object
ult ultimately
unan unanimous
uncert uncertain
univ universal
u.s. *Latin.* ut supra; as above
usu. usually
util utility
v verb; versus
val value
var variable, variety
vb verb
ver verse
vet veteran
vi intransitive verb
VIP very important person
viz *Latin.* videlicet; that is to say, namely
voc vocative
vocab vocabulary
vol volume; volunteer
VP vice president
vs versus
vt transitive verb
vv verses; *Latin.* vice versa, conversely
W west, western
w week; wide; watt
Wed Wednesday
whsle wholesale
wk week
wt weight
X extra
x cross
Xmas Christmas
yd yard
yr year
z zero; zone
zool zoology

CHAPTER NINETEEN
ACTION AND SENSE WORDS

See also: *Chap. 23: Spatial Positions and Relations*

VERBS OF MOTION

Gaits
Mood and Intent
Directions

See also: *Chap. 23: Spatial Positions and Relations*

Gaits

amble walk at an easy pace or in a leisurely manner

barrel move along rapidly and heavily; roll along

bounce move in a lively manner, as if by sudden leaps

bound move by leaping forward

bustle hurry with a great show of energy and purpose

canter move with a three-beat gait, easier than a gallop, used esp. of horses

caper skip along gaily

clamber climb using both hands and feet

clomp clump

clump walk clumsily and noisily

crawl move slowly or laboriously; move in a prone position without the use of hands or feet

curvet prance or canter, used esp. of horses

dander saunter; stroll at a leisurely pace

dart move suddenly and rapidly

dash move with a sudden burst of speed; flash

dogtrot move at a quick, easy gait, like a dog

drift float smoothly or effortlessly; move in an aimless or casual way

flash dash

flit move swiftly and lightly in irregular motion; skim along

flitter move lightly, like a bird; flutter

flow glide smoothly, as though in fluid

flutter move with quick, irregular, or flapping motions; flitter

fly move very quickly

foot it *Informal.* walk, run, or dance

footslog tramp or march heavily, esp. through mud

frogmarch force a person to walk forward with arms grasped behind the back

gallop bound quickly in a three-beat gait, like a horse

gallumph tromp heavily in clumsy gait

glide move smoothly and effortlessly

goose-step move in high-kicking soldier's march with stiff knees

hobble proceed unevenly or haltingly; walk lamely, with a limp

hoof *Slang.* walk; move on one's feet

hop move in short, bounding leaps, like a rabbit

hotfoot it *Informal.* hurry

hurdle bound over (obstacles)

hurry go quickly

hurtle rush forward recklessly

inch move slowly, bit by bit

jog run at a moderate pace

jounce move joltingly in an up-and-down manner; bounce

jump spring; leap; bound

leap spring forward through the air

limp walk lamely or jerkily, favoring one leg

lope move in a long, easy, bounding gait

lumber move slowly with heavy feet and drooping shoulders

march move with a regular, measured gait, in step with others; proceed with purpose

maunder move in a dreamy, aimless way

mince walk with short steps in a dainty, affected manner

mosey stroll, amble, or saunter; leave quickly

pace walk with a slow, measured tread, often back and forth

pad walk with dull, muffled footsteps

patter move as though on little feet, making a light noise

plod walk heavily, slowly, or tediously; trudge

prance move by springing forward; strut about in a spirited manner

prowl move about stealthily; pace nervously

ramble roll along in a leisurely, aimless manner

reel walk unsteadily

run spring forward quickly so that both feet are off the ground between each step

sashay glide or move in a nonchalant way

saunter strut or stroll in a leisurely manner

scamper run or dash quickly, lightly, or playfully; scurry; skelter

scrabble scratch and claw; grope and clamber for a foothold

scramble move or climb quickly, using hands and feet

scuff walk without lifting one's feet

scuffle shuffle; scrape one's feet

scurry scamper

scuttle run or move with hasty steps, esp. away from danger

shamble walk in a lazy, awkward manner, dragging one's feet

shlep *Slang.* drag or haul oneself along in an awkward, heavy manner

shuffle drag one's feet; move along rhythmically; scuffle

skelter scamper

skip spring or leap lightly in bounding gait

skitter move quickly and lightly over a surface; skip

slide move easily and smoothly over a surface

slither slip or glide over a surface; slide along smoothly

slog plod heavily; tramp over a difficult path

slosh flounder and splash about in mud, water, or slush

spring leap forward through the air

sprint run at top speed, esp. for a short distance

stagger reel, sway, or totter along unsteadily

stamp proceed by bringing one's feet down firmly with each step

step move by lifting each foot and setting it down in a new position

step lively move lightly, with springy step

stomp stamp; step down hard

straddle walk with legs spread apart

stride move vigorously with long, measured steps

stroll proceed idly, at a leisurely pace

strut walk with vain, pompous, or affected air

stumble walk unsteadily or clumsily; trip over one's own feet

stump walk heavily and clumsily

swagger walk with an arrogant strut

tiptoe walk quietly or cautiously, with weight on one's toes

tittup *Chiefly Brit.* prance or caper like a spirited horse

toddle walk with short, uncertain steps

totter proceed weakly, wobbling with faltering steps

tramp walk, tread, or step heavily; tromp

trample tread heavily and noisily, esp. while crushing things under one's feet

tread step or walk on, along, or over something

trip stumble and fall

tromp tramp

trot move in a quick, steady, bouncy gait between a walk and a run

trudge walk wearily or laboriously; plod

waddle move with slow, short steps, rocking from side to side like a duck

wade walk through water or mud

walk advance at a moderate pace in steady steps; move along by foot

waltz move in a breezy, conspicuous manner; dance along

wamble move in unsteady, shaky, or staggering gait

whisk move lightly and rapidly

wobble proceed with an unsteady rocking motion, esp. clumsily, from side to side

zip move with great speed and vigor

zoom move quickly, esp. with loud hum or buzz

Mood and Intent

accelerate move more rapidly; quicken one's step

ambulate walk easily from place to place

balk hold back or hesitate

barge move forward heedlessly or clumsily, often colliding with things

bestride stand, ride, or walk across

blunder move unsteadily, in confusion

bob move up and down with a short, jerky motion

bop shuffle along as if to music; go quickly

brush touch lightly in passing

buck charge against; spring into the air

budge move slightly; begin to move

buzz off *Slang.* move rapidly; depart unceremoniously

caper leap or skip about playfully

careen swerve from side to side while moving forward

career go at full speed

catapult move quickly or forcefully through the air

cavort frolic playfully; romp

charge rush to attack; bear down on

chase pursue hastily

chug move laboriously and noisily

clip move swiftly

coast move forward under acquired momentum

convoy escort for protection

course move swiftly through or along designated path

cover ground move quickly across distance

cower crouch and pull away in fear

creak along move slowly, unsteadily, and squeakily

creep go timidly or cautiously so as to escape notice

cringe shrink in fear or deference

crouch bend low to the ground

crowd press forward; advance by pushing

cruise move at controlled speed; wander about with little purpose

crumple collapse in a heap

dally tarry

dance move lightly in time to music

dawdle loiter; waste time; piddle

decelerate slow down

dillydally loiter

dither move in a trembling, agitated manner

dive plunge headfirst

dodder proceed feebly and unsteadily

dodge move to and fro on irregular course

drag dawdle; proceed laboriously

drift float smoothly or effortlessly; move in aimless or casual way

duck bend over to avoid some object

ease maneuver carefully; move against slight resistance

elude evade skillfully

escape get away from danger or restraint; evade

escort accompany as protection

evade avoid deftly; escape

falter stumble; walk unsteadily

fiddle about putter aimlessly; dally

fidget move nervously or restlessly

flail move or toss about freely, often to no effect

flap flutter; toss about ineffectually

flee run away in haste

flick go or pass abruptly and swiftly

flip leap up and turn over in air

float move gently and lightly, as though suspended in fluid

flock assemble and move together in a group

flounce move with jerky motions or angry impatience

flounder struggle with stumbling movements

flump fall suddenly and heavily

flurry move in an excited, confused manner

frisk jump, skip, or frolic in a playful manner

frolic romp about in a frisky, merry way

gad move about restlessly and to no purpose

gallivant roam frivolously

gambol frolic, jump, or skip playfully

glissade glide down slope in standing or squatting position

grovel crawl in a submissive, facedown position

gush issue forth suddenly, forcibly, or copiously

halt come to a stop

hasten move rapidly; hie

herd assemble and move together in a group

hie hasten

hike walk a great distance for exercise or pleasure

hover hang suspended in place above something

hulk move heavily and clumsily

hunch push forward in bent posture

hustle proceed in aggressive, hurried manner

idle saunter aimlessly; loiter

intrude enter a place uninvited, often by force

jaunt make short journey for fun

jet move very rapidly, in a rush

jostle push or shove one's way forward roughly, esp. through a crowd

journey travel to a set destination; voyage

knife move through something swiftly and easily, like a knife

leapfrog vault over the backs of others

linger remain in place longer than expected

loaf lounge lazily or idly

loiter remain in place for no apparent reason; move slowly and idly; dillydally; idle; loll

loll loiter; lounge; sprawl

lollop bound or leap forward

lounge move idly or lazily; loll

lunge thrust oneself forward suddenly

lurk move furtively to avoid notice; slink; sneak

make way allow another to pass or enter

maneuver change direction or position adroitly for specific purpose

maunder move in a dreamy, aimless way

meander wander aimlessly, without direction; ramble or drift along a winding course

mooch wander about without purpose in a slow, lazy manner

moonwalk *Slang.* slide backward, apparently without lifting one's feet

motor *Informal.* move in haste

muddle through work one's way clear of obstacles without planning or direction

muscle *Informal.* force one's way by strenuous effort

nip up spring to one's feet from supine position

obtrude force oneself in where one is not welcome

paddle move through water by flailing one's hands and feet

parade march as if in procession, esp. to show off

patrol move about to observe an area or maintain security

piddle dawdle

plane glide across a surface; fly along effortlessly

play move in a lively, cheerful manner

plow proceed steadily or laboriously; push through

plug away keep moving against one or more obstacles

poke along move slowly, without direction

post move rapidly

potter wander vaguely; putter

promenade take a leisurely public walk, esp. to show off

prowl roam stealthily; pace restlessly

pursue follow intently so as to overtake

pussyfoot tread cautiously or stealthily

putter move aimlessly or idly among objects; potter

quicken one's step accelerate

quickstep make energetic march

ramp rear up and advance menacingly, used esp. of four-legged animals

rampage rush about wildly

range pass across large area

rip rush headlong

ripple flow in small undulations

roam wander without purpose; rove

rock move oneself rhythmically to and fro

romp run in a lively, effortless, energetic manner; cavort

rove roam

rumble move heavily, esp. with a deep, muffled sound

rush move in great haste; dash forward in attack

rush headlong move rapidly and out of control

sail skim across a surface as through propelled by wind

scoot move hastily; dart lightly

scrieve *Scot.* move rapidly and smoothly

seep flow or pass slowly through something

settle become fixed in one place

shadow follow someone secretly, at a distance, for the purpose of observation

shilly-shally dawdle; go indecisively

shimmy shake, vibrate, or wobble with a dancelike motion

shoot move rapidly; pass rapidly over

shoulder push one's way roughly through a crowd

shunt force or turn someone aside or out of the way

skate glide along smoothly, as if crossing ice

ski glide over a surface as if wearing skis on snow

skid slide out of control sideways

skim glide lightly across a surface

skulk sneak or lurk about in a stealthy or cowardly manner; slink

sled slide across a surface as though on runners

slink move stealthily or furtively; lurk

slouch move idly, drooping with hunched back

slump fall or sink suddenly; assume drooping posture

snake make one's way quietly along a winding course

sneak slink; lurk

souse plunge into liquid

speed move rapidly

splash flail or move about noisily in water

sprawl lie back carelessly with limbs outspread

spurt gush forth; rush forward

squirm wriggle or twist about

stalk pursue a quarry or prey; walk stiffly and proudly

stampede flee headlong in panic as a group

steal come or go secretly, unexpectedly, and unobserved
stir begin to move from position of rest
straggle hang back; fall farther behind
streak rush past rapidly
stream issue forth or flow from someplace
surge rise and fall in waves
swarm move in great numbers, hovering like bees
swim propel oneself smoothly as through water
swoop rush down upon suddenly, esp. in attack
swoosh move swiftly with a rustling sound
tail *Informal.* follow
tarry remain in place; wait for something; dally
tear move with great haste
toodle *Slang.* move along in an easygoing manner
tool cruise or drive along
toss move restlessly; jerk about
tour range over an area for pleasure or inspection
track follow the footprints or path of
trail follow; come after
traipse tramp about; wander aimlessly without reaching one's destination; proceed haphazardly
trek make slow, difficult progress over long route
trespass enter upon another's property uninvited
trickle move slowly, bit by bit
troop gather together and move in a group
truck *Slang.* roll along in an easy, untroubled manner
trundle roll along
twinkle flutter lightly about
twitch move erratically or jerkily; fidget
undulate move with a sinuous, wavelike motion
upspring bound up from place
usher lead the way to help others find their place
vamp move in a bewitching manner
visit come or go to see someone or someplace
voyage journey
waft move or float lightly as though through air
wag move jerkily from side to side or up and down
wallow move slowly and with difficulty, as though through mud
wash flow along; run up against
welter toss or heave about
wheel roll along easily and swiftly
whid *Scot.* move deftly and quietly
whiz move swiftly and effortlessly
whoosh rush past with a sudden hissing noise
wiggle move from side to side with quick, jerky motions
wince shrink back from a blow, recoil
wing fly as if on wings; move swiftly
worm creep along in a devious, stealthy manner
wrench move aside with a violent twist
wrestle move by force
wriggle writhe; squirm from side to side
writhe move in twists and bends
zap *Informal.* move with great speed or force

Directions

about-face turn in the opposite direction
absquatulate *Slang.* depart or flee
advance move forward
angle move indirectly toward or away from a person or object; turn sharply in a new direction
approach draw near
arise move upward from lower position
arrive reach one's destination
ascend move or climb upward
attain arrive at
back off step away from
back-pedal step back rapidly
backtrack return over course already covered
back up move backward
bear down on catch up with; approach rapidly
beat it *Informal.* leave hastily
begone depart
betake oneself cause oneself to go
blast off *Slang.* depart abruptly
blow in *Slang.* arrive from somewhere, esp. unexpectedly
bolt make sudden, hasty departure or escape
bounce strike a surface and rebound
bowl along move along smoothly and quickly
burst forth issue forth suddenly from spot
bypass circumvent (an obstacle)
carom strike and rebound
cast veer
catch overtake
check out *Informal.* depart quickly or abruptly
circle revolve around
circumambulate circle on foot, esp. ceremonially
clear out depart permanently or abruptly
climb ascend; make steady upward progress
close in on begin to overtake
come move toward something; approach; arrive at
come about reverse direction; tack
come along *Informal.* arrive
come back return
come down move from higher to lower position
come forth emerge
come in enter
come out emerge
come up move from lower to higher position
commute travel back and forth regularly between two points
continue keep on same course as before
converge tend or incline toward a single point
crab move sideways, diagonally, or obliquely, esp. with short bursts of speed
crisscross move in many intersecting lines across a given space
cross move or traverse from one side or place to another
cruise be on one's way; travel
cut move abruptly at a sharp angle
debouch march out into open ground from confined place, used esp. of troops
decamp depart from resting place, often quickly or secretly

decline slope downward from straight course
deflect turn from true course or straight line
depart begin a journey; go away; leave; set out
descend move downward
desert depart from someplace, often permanently
deviate turn aside from normal course
diddle move rapidly back and forth or up and down
divagate stray from course
double back return over same course
draw away increase distance from given place
draw near reduce distance from given place; approach
ebb recede, like the tide
eddy move against current; move in a circle
edge advance gradually; move sideways
egress depart
embark set out from a place, esp. on a voyage
emerge rise; appear; come forth from concealment; come out
emigrate leave one's native country and settle elsewhere
enter arrive at; come in
evacuate depart rapidly from an endangered place
exit leave; go out
fade drift away from focus of activity
fall descend freely under force of gravity
fall back lag
fall down collapse to ground
fishtail swerve or slide from side to side out of control while moving forward
flinch pull back in abrupt movement
follow come behind or after, moving in same direction
ford wade across body of water
gain arrive at; follow more closely
gain ground lessen distance between oneself and another so as to follow more closely
get along depart
get going move faster; depart
go move along; proceed; move on a set course, esp. depart from someplace
go away depart
gravitate move toward; tend toward
gyrate revolve around fixed point or on axis
hang back remain at some distance behind
head move forward toward set point; go in certain direction
head out *Informal.* depart
hightail it *Informal.* depart hastily
hit the road *Informal.* begin a journey; depart
hunker down squat or stoop on one's haunches
immigrate enter and settle in a foreign country
issue forth pass or come out from enclosed place
jag change direction repeatedly in irregular pattern
jerk move with abrupt, erratic motion
jibe shift suddenly from one side to the other, used esp. of ships
jiggle move with short jerks up and down or back and forth

jink move unexpectedly with abrupt turns and shifts

juke move evasively through obstacles; fake another out of position, esp. in football

lag fail to keep up; fall back

land attain one's destination, esp. from above

lap overtake another in race, increasing lead by one full circuit of course

lead go before others

leave depart

light arrive at and come to rest

light out *Slang.* depart hurriedly

list veer to one side

loop move in curves or arcs

lose ground follow less closely; fall farther behind

lunge rush forward with sudden thrust

make tracks *Informal.* run away; go in a hurry

migrate move from one country to another

mizzle *Brit.* depart suddenly

mount ascend; climb on top of

move go or pass from one place to another; progress

move along proceed in one direction

move it *Slang.* depart hastily and under pressure

navigate set one's course at sea

negotiate maneuver through, around, or over

nip away *Chiefly Brit. slang.* sneak away; leave stealthily

outpace exceed in speed and pass

outstrip get ahead of; leave behind

overhaul overtake

overtake catch up with and pass; overhaul

pass move; proceed; depart; move past another going in the same direction, come up to, then move beyond

peel off veer sharply aside from group moving in one direction

peel out *Informal.* depart quickly

perambulate travel or walk over or through

peregrinate wander; traverse; travel over on foot

piss off *Slang.* depart hastily and unceremoniously

pitch plunge forward, often rising up abruptly afterward

pivot turn in place as if on a shaft

plummet descend rapidly

plunge rush or fall violently, with headlong haste

pounce swoop down upon suddenly

press on move forward despite obstacles

proceed continue forward in same direction

progress move forward, upward, or onward

pull back move away from

put about turn in new direction

quit leave someplace

radiate proceed from or toward a center

rappel descend steep incline by sliding down rope passed around one's body

rear rise up on one's hind legs like a horse

rebound reverse direction; bounce back

recede pull back; withdraw

recoil draw back, esp. in alarm or disgust

reel fall back from a blow; recoil

reenter come in again

regress move backward

repair go; betake oneself

retire withdraw; fall back

retract draw back

retreat draw back from a dangerous situation; flee; turn tail

return come back to a place formerly visited

reverse change direction of one's movement, usu. to opposite direction

revolve turn in a complete circle on an axis in place

ricochet bounce back or off

rise get up or move upward

roll move by turning over and over

rotate turn in circles on central axis in place

run away retreat; move off rapidly

sally forth set out; depart

scale climb over

scat *Informal.* go away quickly, often under compulsion

scatter disperse in all directions

schuss make straight, high-speed downhill run on skis

scram *Informal.* depart unceremoniously and in haste

scrooch crouch down on one's haunches, leaning forward

scrunch crouch; hunker down

scud move or run swiftly, like a ship driven by a gale

seesaw move up and down or back and forth

separate move away from

set foot in enter (new region or place)

set forth begin a journey; leave someplace

set off start moving

set out depart; begin journey

sheer deviate from one's course

shift change place or position

shin draw oneself up by holding fast with hands and legs

show up arrive

shunt travel back and forth

shuttle move or transport to and fro

sidestep step around so as to avoid

sidle move sideways

sink descend slowly toward the bottom

skedaddle *Informal.* depart hastily and unceremoniously

skiddoo *Informal.* depart hastily; skedaddle

skirt pass around; move along the border of

slalom zigzag between and around obstacles

slant move at an angle

slip away retreat; depart quietly

soar rise up to great height

somersault tumble head over heels

spin revolve rapidly in place

spiral move in circles around axis

split *Slang.* leave; depart abruptly

squat crouch near ground without sitting

stand forth move forward

start out begin progress; set out

steer direct one's course

steer clear of stay away from; avoid

step out depart at energetic pace

stray wander from set course; roam about

stretch extend over distance in particular direction

strike out set out; depart

sway swing slowly and rhythmically to and fro

sweep move steadily in wide circuit or curve

swerve alter one's course abruptly; turn aside

swing move freely in wide curve; move back and forth

swivel turn as if on pivot

tack change direction, used esp. of ships

tag along come after someone; follow another closely

take a powder *Slang.* depart hurriedly, esp. without taking leave

take off begin to move; depart; rise up into the air

teeter move back and forth, esp. near an edge

topple fall down

travel move or go from one place to another; depart from current location

traverse move along or across, from one side to the other

tumble turn end over end, esp. in flight

turn reverse or alter direction; veer from course; rotate on axis

turn about veer from course

turn back reverse direction; retrace one's steps

turn tail *Informal.* retreat

twine wind about in twisting course

twirl revolve rapidly in place

twist follow winding course; change direction sharply

up *Informal.* start out abruptly

vamoose *Slang.* depart in haste

vault leap over, esp. with aid of hands or pole

veer change direction; turn to one side; cast

verge move or incline in some direction

waggle move from side to side shakily

walk *Informal.* depart, split

wander move without direction or purpose; roam about in irregular course

wave waver

waver sway in place; move to and fro; wave

weave follow zigzag or side-to-side course

wend proceed over long, winding course

whirl spin in a circle; turn rapidly in place; move or be carried along quickly

wind proceed by twists and turns, changing direction constantly

windmill move like a windmill, esp. by rotating one's arms in wide arcs

withdraw pull back; retreat

wobble proceed with unsteady, rocking motion; go clumsily in side-to-side motion

wreathe turn in circles or spirals

yaw deviate from a straight course, used esp. of ships

yo-yo *Informal.* move back and forth or up and down between two points

zag execute sharp turn

zig alter direction sharply

zigzag proceed in zigs and zags, making sharp turns first to one side, then to the other

VERBS OF SIGHT

See also: *Chap. 23: Verbs of Thought; Judgment and Criticism*

admire regard with respect or wonder

assay examine and evaluate

avert one's eyes look away to avoid another's glance or some unpleasant sight

bat an eye blink with surprise or emotion

behold gaze upon; see

bird-dog *Informal.* watch carefully

blear make one's eyes dim or watery

blink look glancingly; close and open one's eyes quickly

browse look over in a casual, leisurely manner

canvass examine carefully; survey entire area

cast about seek by looking around

cast a glance direct one's gaze at something

catch sight of become aware of; distinguish; manage to see

check examine carefully

check out examine and evaluate

command a view of overlook, esp. from strategic position

compare examine two or more items to determine differences or similarities

contemplate view thoughtfully and with steady attention

descry catch sight of; discover

detect note; discover the true nature of; spot

discern come to recognize; perceive by sight

distinguish single out; perceive clearly; recognize differences; spot

draw a bead on focus one's aim at

drop one's eyes lower one's eyes before another person's gaze

envisage visualize in a specific way

envision picture in one's mind

espy catch sight of

examine look over closely; inspect

eye view; gaze at

eyeball *Informal.* observe closely

face look at directly

fix one's eyes on gaze at intently

focus adjust one's eyes to produce a clear image at a particular range

follow watch the movements of

gape gaze dumbly, esp. with mouth open

gawk stare stupidly

gaze look at intently, eagerly, or steadily

get a load of *Slang.* take notice of

give the evil eye stare at with malicious intent

give the once-over scrutinize rapidly in detail, from top to bottom

glance look quickly

glare stare angrily or relentlessly

glaze get a blurred, glassy look in one's eyes

glimpse take or get a brief look at; identify quickly

glint glance briefly; have bright emotion in one's eyes

gloat observe with unpleasant, superior satisfaction

glower stare with brooding, sullen anger

goggle stare with wide, protuberant eyes

identify observe to establish the identity or nature of a person or thing

inspect examine carefully and thoroughly

keep tabs on watch closely or maintain surveillance on

leer cast a lascivious, wanton look; ogle suggestively; make eyes

look use one's power of vision so as to see something

look askance at take a sidelong glance at

look away avert one's eyes; turn one's eyes from object

look daggers glare or glower sullenly and with hostility

look for search

look on observe passively

look out be watchful

look over examine or inspect, usu. briefly

look sideways at glance sidelong at, usu. implying disapproval

look up lift one's eyes toward the sky

look upon view; regard; scrutinize

make eyes at ogle or leer at

make out see and identify, esp. with difficulty

mark take note of

marvel gaze with amazement or curiosity

mind notice; heed attentively

monitor observe over time; check for specific reason

moon gaze at dreamily or longingly

note observe with attention

notice mark with attention; take note of

observe regard with attention, esp. to form judgment

ogle eye amorously or lewdly; make eyes at

overlook gaze down on from above; look past; fail to see

oversee survey, inspect, or supervise (some activity)

overview survey generally

peek look quickly or furtively from a concealed place

peep look cautiously or stealthily, esp. through a small opening

peer gaze searchingly, with difficulty or curiosity

perceive observe so as to understand; become aware of the presence of

pick out distinguish one among many

pick up catch sight of

pore over gaze at or study intently

preview view in advance

pry look at carefully or inquiringly, esp. against another's will

read observe so as to discern the true nature of; scan; study

recognize see to be that which is already known

reconnoiter appraise and examine so as to gain information

regard heed with attention; look attentively

register perceive; take note of

remark observe with attention

review view or examine again, esp. to form judgment

rivet fix the eyes in a steady, intent gaze

roll one's eyes shift gaze continuously; turn eyes up in sockets as sign of disapproval

rubberneck *Informal.* stare with exaggerated curiosity by craning one's neck

scan examine or search hastily from point to point

scope *Slang.* check out; observe closely

scour pass eyes over in search of something

scout observe to acquire information

scowl contract one's brow and glower in disapproval

screen examine in detail to differentiate

scrutinize inspect closely; look upon

search look over carefully for purpose of discovery; look for

see perceive with one's eyes; examine; recognize; watch

seek search out

set eyes on catch sight of, esp. for first time; look at

sift pass one's eyes over so as to differentiate

sight look carefully in one direction; catch sight of; aim at

size up examine closely to evaluate

skim pass one's eyes over swiftly; give a cursory glance to

skirr search about; glance over rapidly; skim

snoop look into or pry in a sly or intrusive manner

spectate observe passively

spot distinguish; take note of; detect

spy catch sight of; observe in secret, esp. with hostile intent

squint look with one's eyes partly shut

stare gaze fixedly or intently, often with wide eyes

stare down gaze at with fixed stare to force another back down

study consider and examine carefully or in detail

supervise oversee

survey examine overall; inspect and evaluate

take a gander *Slang.* take a look

take note of observe with particular attention; spot; take notice of

take notice of take note of

take stock of examine and appraise

tend pay close attention to; observe closely

trace follow or examine carefully, in step-by-step detail

view watch attentively; regard in a special light; survey or inspect

visualize see and form a mental image of

watch observe closely; look at; see

watch out be vigilant and watchful

wink close and open one eye quickly, esp. as a signal or hint

witness see by personal presence or perception

Modes and Manners of Expression

add speak further; go on to say
affect feign; make a pretense to
air express publicly or aloud; ventilate
announce proclaim, esp. publicly; foretell; give notice of; annunciate
annunciate announce
assert declare forcefully as true; postulate
babble talk foolishly, excessively, and unintelligibly
banter address in a playful, joking, or teasing manner
beckon call to; attract attention of
bicker argue incessantly over petty issues
bid command another's action; greet; make an offer
blab reveal indiscreetly; chatter thoughtlessly
blabber blab; speak foolishly
blather talk foolishly
blatter talk noisily and rapidly
blither talk foolishly
blurt utter suddenly and inadvertently
break begin uttering a sound or series of sounds
broach mention for first time
bubble gurgle; speak excitedly
bullshit *Vulgar slang.* talk nonsense, esp. intended to deceive; talk foolishly, boastfully, idly, or vulgarly; shovel shit; sling shit; wank
burble babble excitedly; prattle
call command or order; summon or invite
chat talk informally, lightly, and familiarly
chatter talk incessantly and rapidly
chew the fat *Informal.* make friendly, familiar conversation; chew the rag
chew the rag *Informal.* chew the fat
chime in insert remark into others' conversation
chitchat chat idly; gossip
chorus speak in unison with others
clam up cease speaking and remain silent
command give an order; direct with authority
comment utter brief opinion or explanation
confab confabulate
confabulate speak at an informal, impromptu conference; confab
confide tell a secret; entrust information
continue add to; resume after interruption
converse hold a dialogue; speak with others
couch phrase in specific language
coze converse informally or familiarly
declaim speak impressively or dramatically

declare state firmly; announce formally and openly
deliver bring forth in words; utter; enunciate
demand request as if by right; insist on
deny say something is untrue or does not exist; refuse to acknowledge; disown
dictate order with force of authority; speak aloud for another to write down
echo repeat another's words exactly
embellish add entertaining details
evoke call up or inspire a particular response
exaggerate overstate; make unfounded claims; speak of something as greater than it is
excuse pardon; justify a fault or error; release from obligation
express put into words; make known; state
falter stammer; speak hesitantly
fib speak dishonestly; lie on unimportant issue
footle *Informal.* gab foolishly
gab *Informal.* chatter
go *Informal.* say
greet receive another in specified way, usu. upon meeting
harangue make lengthy, often pompous and bombastic, speech
harp speak repeatedly and tiresomely about something
hem and haw speak hesitantly and evasively
herald proclaim the approach of
hesitate speak slowly and uncertainly, esp. with pauses
indite put into words; compose
ingeminate repeat
insist declare or demand emphatically
interject interrupt; throw in a remark
interrupt stop a person in the midst of something, esp. by inserting a remark; speak while another is speaking
introduce announce (a speaker); present to another to make acquainted; acquaint with a subject
invoke call upon God in prayer; summon up a spirit by incantation
issue send out; put forth, usu. officially; state
iterate repeat
jabber talk rapidly and unintelligibly
jaw *Slang.* talk; scold
jive *Slang.* attempt to deceive through fast talk; talk foolishly and unintelligibly; use hip jargon, esp. of jazz
kibitz *Informal.* offer unsought advice; make unsolicited comments
lie tell an untruth; deceive another
maintain assert as true; affirm in agreement
maunder ramble; mumble incoherently
mention speak of briefly; refer to by name
mimic imitate another's speech; repeat words exactly
muster summon; call
narrate give an account of; recount events; tell a story
natter chatter
note remark upon; speak of attentively
observe remark; take note of

orate speak pompously; make a formal speech
order command; ask for
outspeak speak frankly or boldly; excel in speaking
overstate exaggerate
page summon by calling name
palaver chatter idly; talk aimlessly and profusely
parody mimic humorously
parrot mimic or imitate; repeat words mechanically
pass change the subject of conversation
patter speak rapidly and mechanically; employ the glib, rapid speech of salesman or comedian
perorate deliver lengthy, rhetorical speech
persist continue to repeat or press an opinion
phrase express in words or in appropriate terms
piffle *Informal.* talk nonsense
pipe up begin talking
pontificate speak pompously, pretentiously, and dogmatically
portray describe in words; represent verbally
prattle chatter childishly
predict forecast or prophesy
present introduce one to another; bring before the public; bring formal charge in court
prevaricate speak evasively; lie
proclaim declare loudly; announce officially
profess claim; pretend
promise declare that one will or will not do something
prompt incite to action; assist with words
prophesy predict with assurance based on mystical knowledge; speak as if divinely inspired; vaticinate
put it state something in particular way
quip utter witty or sarcastic remark
quote repeat exact words of
ramble talk disconnectedly at length; wander from the subject
rap *Slang.* talk, esp. freely and openly
rattle ramble quickly and obliviously; chatter incessantly
recount narrate story; tell in detail
rede *Chiefly Brit.* give counsel, advise; interpret, explain
reel off list rapidly
refer allude to; call attention to
regale entertain with stories
rehash express old material in new form with little change
reiterate say again or repeatedly
relate narrate; tell in detail
remark say; comment on
repeat say again; say something said by another; say over; ingeminate; iterate
require order or oblige to do something; claim by right or authority
say express in words; state opinion or belief; utter or pronounce
schmooze *Slang.* gossip and chat familiarly, esp. to endear oneself
sermonize give long, moralizing talk
shoot off one's mouth talk too freely or indiscreetly

shoot the breeze chat casually

shovel shit *Vulgar slang.* talk nonsense, esp. to deceive; bullshit

simper say with a weak, silly smile

sling shit *Vulgar slang.* bullshit

slobber fawn over; speak with spittle running from one's mouth

smatter speak words of a language with little or no knowledge of the language

sneer speak with upper lip curled, usu. contemptuously

soft-pedal *Informal.* de-emphasize or avoid stressing

soliloquize utter one's thoughts without addressing anyone, esp. in stage performance

sound utter or pronounce

speak utter words to express something; make a public speech; converse politely; use one particular language to communicate

speak out speak loudly, freely, and frankly

spell out name letters of word aloud in order; explain methodically

spiel *Informal.* talk glibly and at length, esp. to persuade

spit it out say what is on one's mind without delay

squib utter in an offhand manner; speak in brief, satiric bits

state express in words; declare; report particulars of

stretch exaggerate or extend beyond the truth

stumble make blunders in speech; speak haltingly and awkwardly

summon send for; call together; call upon

swear promise on an oath; state emphatically; curse

talk convey or exchange ideas or information with spoken words; express, utter, or discuss in words; have the power of speech; use one particular language to communicate

talk down silence another by speaking loudly and persistently

tell inform; reveal

title provide a name for

touch on mention briefly

trifle talk frivolously; toy with; treat casually

turn a phrase speak gracefully and precisely

twaddle talk nonsense

twitter talk rapidly, in an anxious manner

utter make a sound with the mouth, esp. a word

vaticinate prophesy

ventilate air

venture dare to utter; suggest

verbalize put into words

vocalize express aloud in words; use one's voice in speech or song

voice express in words; utter aloud; pronounce

vouchsafe grant in gracious or condescending manner

vow promise solemnly

waffle talk vaguely, indecisively, and evasively

wank *Vulgar slang.* speak foolishly and boastfully; bullshit

warn inform of danger; advise of action to avert danger

warrant guarantee or assure

wrangle argue, quarrel noisily or angrily

yabber *Australian.* talk foolishly; jabber

yak *Slang.* chatter persistently and foolishly

yammer *Informal.* persist in talking loudly; wail; grumble

yarn tell tales, esp. invented and grandiose ones

Intonation and Inflection

accent stress (a particular sound or syllable)

articulate utter distinctly; give clear expression to

bawl cry loudly

bellow roar; speak in a loud, deep voice

belt *Informal.* sing out loudly

blare utter raucously and noisily

blubber weep noisily

bray cry harshly, like a donkey

breathe whisper; speak softly

buzz hum, like a bee; murmur or whisper; speak dully and continuously

cachinnate laugh loudly or excessively

cackle laugh shrilly, with sound like a hen's

call speak loudly and distinctly, so as to be heard at a distance

cant talk or beg in whining singsong

catcall express disapproval loudly

caterwaul cry out harshly; quarrel noisily

chant recite in monotonous, repetitive tones

cheer encourage or applaud with shouts

chuff make noisy explanations or grunts

chunter *Brit. informal.* talk in a low, inarticulate way; mutter

clatter talk noisily

croon sing sweetly and softly

cry shout shrilly; call out like an animal

devoice pronounce a formerly voiced sound without vibration of vocal cords

drawl speak slowly, usu. prolonging vowels

drone make sustained murmur or humming sound; utter at length in monotonous tone

enounce pronounce distinctly; articulate

enunciate pronounce words clearly and distinctly

gabble talk quickly and indistinctly

groan make long, deep sound of pain, grief, or disapproval

growl make low, threatening, animal-like sound

grumble make low, unintelligible sounds in throat

hammer make point emphatically and repeatedly

holler shout

hoot cry out in scorn or disapproval with long "o" sound, like an owl

howl utter long, wailing cry, like a dog's, in amusement, pain, or scorn; weep loudly; yowl

incant utter magical words or sounds

inflect alter tone or pitch of speaking voice

intone recite as a chant, esp. in monotone

jabber chatter, like a monkey

keen utter high, wailing tones

lilt speak in light, pleasant rhythm

mince speak affectedly, esp. to appear refined

mispronounce utter word sounds incorrectly

moan emit or speak with low, mournful, inarticulate sound of pain or suffering

modulate vary pitch or tone of voice, esp. to softer level

mouth form words with lips only; declaim with exaggerated distinction

mumble speak indistinctly

murmur speak in low voice with continuous sound

mutter utter subdued grumbles, often in low, unclear tones

nasalize speak with a twang, as though pushing voice through one's nose

proclaim declare loudly

pronounce utter distinctly, correctly, or in a particular way

pule whimper softly and plaintively

raise one's voice speak loudly; shout

rasp speak in rough, grating voice

rhyme speak in words with identical sounds, esp. at end of lines of speech

roar utter long, deep, loud sound, like a lion's; laugh loudly

roll off one's tongue be uttered eloquently, smoothly, and glibly

rumble utter with heavy, deep, rolling sound

scream utter a sudden, sharp, loud cry

screech utter a high, shrill, piercing cry, esp. in terror or pain

shout speak loudly, esp. to attract attention or to express strong emotion; holler; yell

shriek utter a shrill cry or scream

shrill utter in high, thin, piercing tone

sigh utter a long, audible exhalation expressing grief, exhaustion, or relief

sing speak in musical sounds and rhythm, esp. to set melody

slur pronounce indistinctly, running sounds together

snarl growl angrily, esp. with bared teeth, like a beast

sob utter through uneven breaths caused by heavy weeping

speak up speak more loudly

splutter speak rapidly and indistinctly, esp. with rapid series of spitting sounds; sputter

sputter speak in series of quick, explosive sounds; splutter

squeak speak in a high-pitched cry

squeal speak with a long, shrill crying sound, like a pig

stammer speak with a series of involuntary pauses or rapid repetitions of one syllable

stress place accent on particular syllable

stutter suffer involuntary disruption of speech, esp. repeating first consonant sound of words

sustain prolong sound of word

susurrate whisper

tongue produce speech effects with one's tongue; sound certain words

trill speak with vibrating sound in one's voice, like a bird's song
troll sing in carefree, jovial way
trumpet proclaim in bright, rising tone
twang speak with nasal intonation
ululate howl or wail; hoot
wail utter a long, sad cry
warble sing with a gentle trilling sound, like bird's song
whimper make feeble frightened or complaining sounds; whine softly
whine make a long, high, complaining cry
whisper speak softly, using breath but not vocal cords
whoop utter a loud, excited cry; holler
yammer persist in talking loudly; wail; grumble
yell shout
yowl howl

Speech Sounds and Noises

bark cry out sharply and gruffly, like a dog
bay howl; make a prolonged barking noise
bell speak in ringing tones, resembling a bell's
blat make sharp, loud noise
bleat cry pathetically, like a sheep
boo utter a long exclamation of disapproval by sounding the syllable "boo"
boom make prolonged, deep, resonant sound
caw utter harsh, raucous call, like a crow's
cheep utter faint, shrill sound, like a bird's
chirp emit short, sharp sound, like a bird's
chitter twitter
clack chatter; prattle; make abrupt, sharp sound
cluck utter throaty cry or laugh, like a hen's
coo make soft, murmuring sound
cough emit sharp, rasping sound from the chest
crack emit sharp, sudden, explosive sound
croak make deep, hoarse sound, like a frog's
crow make loud, shrill cry, like a crow
gargle make sound like liquid bubbling in throat
gasp speak with sudden, short intakes of breath, esp. out of fear or shock
gibber make meaningless, unintelligible sounds, esp. in fear
giggle laugh in silly, nervous way, often shrilly
gobble speak with guttural sound, like a turkey
grunt make gruff, snorting sound, like a pig
gulp suppress words by swallowing hard; choke or gasp for air; swallow hard in shock or fear
gurgle make low, bubbling sound in throat
hawk clear throat noisily
hem make sound of clearing throat, esp. while searching for words
hiss speak, esp. expressing disapproval, with prolonged "s" sound, like a snake
huff blow or bluster, esp. in annoyance; breathe heavily
hum utter prolonged "m" sound; drone like an insect
lisp speak defectively, with "s" and "z" sounds pronounced as "th"
mew speak weakly, with a cry like a cat's
mewl cry weakly; whimper

moo emit low, deep sound, like a cow
neigh make long, high-pitched cry, like a horse
oink make grunting sound, like a pig
peep make high, weak, chirping sound, like a bird
puff emit short, light exhalations; breathe hard
purr make low, soothing, vibrating sound, like a cat
quack utter harsh cry, like a duck
roll emit deep, prolonged sound, like a drum's
scat improvise nonsense syllables, esp. to jazz
snap make sharp cracking sound
sniffle speak while repeatedly drawing air up into nose
snuffle speak with noisy sniffs through partly blocked nose
squall utter harsh cry or scream, esp. like a baby
squawk utter loud, harsh cry, like a bird
titter giggle with high-pitched sound
twitter make a rapid series of light, chirping sounds, like a bird's; chitter
wheeze speak with audible hoarse whistling sound from the chest
whinny speak with low, gentle neighing sound, like a horse would make
yap bark shrilly, like a dog
yelp utter sharp, shrill cry or bark, like a dog's; yip
yip yelp
yodel utter prolonged musical call, with voice alternating between falsetto and normal pitch
zing utter high-pitched, shrill sound

Expressions of Feeling

avow declare openly or assuredly
bait tease; torment maliciously
bellyache Informal. complain or find fault peevishly
bemoan complain; express regret
bewail express sorrow over; cry about
bitch Slang. complain noisily and incessantly; rag
blarney flatter, wheedle, or con
bluster boast; talk loudly or boisterously
boast exaggerate oneself; speak with unwarranted pride; vaunt
brabble squabble; argue noisily
burst out express suddenly with feeling
chaff tease good-naturedly; banter
cheer encourage or applaud with shouts
chortle laugh loudly and gleefully
chuckle laugh quietly, half suppressing the laughter
clamor protest or demand loudly
complain express dissatisfaction or pain; find fault; protest wrongs; gripe; grouse; squawk
confess admit to sins, errors, or weaknesses; state one's attitude reluctantly
crack make a joke; wisecrack
crow express gleeful triumph
cry call out in pain or grief; emit a loud, wordless expression of grief
curse exclaim violently in anger; call evil upon another; utter oath or obscenity; cuss

cuss Informal. curse
dish Slang. gossip nastily
enthuse express with enthusiasm
exclaim cry out suddenly from pain, pleasure, or surprise
exhort urge on energetically
exult rejoice greatly
fume seethe and splutter angrily
gam engage in friendly conversation
gibe jeer or ridicule
giggle laugh in silly, nervous way
greet speak in a friendly or respectful manner, esp. upon meeting
gripe complain
groan make long, deep sound of pain, grief, or disapproval
grouse complain
grumble complain with ill temper; grump
grump grumble
gush talk with extravagant enthusiasm or flattery, esp. in an affected manner
harass attack or annoy repeatedly
heckle interrupt and harass a public speaker
howl utter long, wailing cry in amusement, pain, or scorn; weep loudly
hurl utter vehemently, esp. abuse or curses
hype exaggerate merits of; mislead by sensationalizing
imprecate utter curses; invoke evil
insult speak ill so as to hurt another's feelings or arouse anger; treat with insolence or contempt
jape joke
jeer shout at rudely or scornfully
jest joke, esp. lightly
joke make humorous remarks; poke fun at; make light of; jape; jest
jolly keep another in good humor to win cooperation
josh joke, tease, or kid
kid tease; deceive in fun
lament express great sorrow or regret
lash out attack violently; hurl insults
laugh utter sound of mirth with a smile and expulsion of air
moan emit or speak with low, mournful, inarticulate sound in pain or suffering
needle annoy; provoke intentionally
obsess speak of continuously and at undue length
paint describe in vivid detail
pledge promise solemnly
pop off Informal. speak loudly or indiscreetly; express anger
pour out express freely
preach deliver a public religious address; urge people to adopt certain moral ways, esp. in an obtrusive manner
profess declare openly or affirm, esp. one's belief
promise vow or pledge to do or not do something; declare emphatically
protest express disagreement or disapproval; declare firmly

psych *Informal.* arouse to action, urge on, or inspire, esp. oneself

quip utter clever or witty remark

rag *Informal.* complain incessantly; bitch

rage talk angrily or wildly; rave

rail speak loudly or insistently; scold harshly; complain bitterly

rally rouse; urge on

rant speak loudly, violently, and theatrically

rave talk wildly, furiously, and nonsensically; speak about with great admiration; rage

razz tease or ridicule good-naturedly

reassure restore confidence; remove fears of

refuse express unwillingness to do something

regret express sorrow over loss; state disappointment, repentance, or annoyance

renounce reject; refuse to abide by; formally give up claim

repent express regret over one's actions

repine fret; express discontent or longing

repudiate deny; disown utterly; reject

rhapsodize speak of ecstatically

rib tease

ridicule make fun of; laugh at another's weaknesses or faults, esp. in malicious, scornful way

rip tear apart verbally; utter violently; spit out

rouse urge on, awaken, or excite

sass speak rudely or impertinently

scoff express scorn, derision, or contempt

scorn reject as unworthy or contemptible; express contempt

scream utter a sudden, sharp, loud cry; express intense hysteria

share describe something so that others may experience it

sigh utter a long, audible exhalation expressing grief, exhaustion, or relief

simper utter weakly or sadly

slash speak of cuttingly or harshly

slight insult by discourtesy or lack of respect

snap speak with sudden irritation

snarl speak in a bad-tempered manner

sneer express scorn or contempt, esp. with curled upper lip

snicker giggle slyly; laugh at covertly, in a suppressed manner; snigger

snigger snicker

snivel cry miserably; complain with a whine

snub speak unkindly or scornfully to reject or humiliate another

sob utter through uneven breaths caused by heavy weeping

spit utter violently, often while saliva is ejected from mouth

spout gush forth; speak at length

spur urge on, arouse, or incite

squawk complain

squeal protest sharply, esp. in long, loud, high cry

swear promise on an oath; state emphatically; curse; use profanity

sweet-talk *Informal.* flatter

talk back reply defiantly

talk down speak condescendingly

taunt try to provoke with scorn or criticism; jeer at

tease try to provoke playfully by jokes, questions, or sarcasm

threaten express intention to punish or harm another

unburden oneself confess to relieve one's conscience

unleash make (unrestrained verbal assault); let loose (a torrent of words)

unload release one's emotions through words

urge encourage; try hard to persuade; recommend strongly

vaunt boast

vent give verbal outlet to, esp. one's feelings

wail utter long, sad cry; lament or complain persistently

weep express sadness or sorrow by shedding tears; cry at length

welcome greet with pleasure or ceremony

whimper make feeble, frightened, complaining sounds; whine softly

whine complain in petty, feeble way

wisecrack make witty, clever remarks

wish express one's desire, aim, or hope

yawn express boredom by inhaling deeply with mouth wide open

yawp squawk noisily; clamor; complain

yowl utter loud, wailing cry; howl

Reasoning and Informing

accent stress or emphasize

advise counsel; warn; recommend

allege assert without proof; give as reason or excuse

allude refer to indirectly

apprise inform; give notice

attest affirm to be true; bear witness or testify

attribute assign cause, characteristic, or origin to

bandy exchange comments, esp. argumentatively

beat around the bush speak evasively; wander from subject to subject

belabor make a point to absurd lengths

break the news make something known

cajole persuade by flattery

cant speak hypocritically

chaffer bargain for; haggle over

chew over discuss at length

clarify explain or make understandable

clear the air speak openly to remove hostility, tension, or confusion

coax persuade gently

collogue confer privately

communicate succeed in conveying information or feelings; transmit; make known

con *Informal.* persuade after gaining confidence

confer discuss with others

confide tell a secret; entrust information

constate assert positively

contend assert or argue a point

contrast compare or appraise differences

convey impart information; communicate

convince persuade by argument; overcome doubts

counsel advise, esp. professionally

decree order based on lawful authority

define state or explain precisely, esp. meaning of word or thing

delineate describe clearly in accurate detail

depict describe

describe set forth the nature of something; depict

disclose reveal or make known

discourse speak extensively on same subject; lecture

discuss talk about with others; examine by means of argument

divulge reveal something unknown

elucidate clarify; explain

emphasize stress the importance of

enounce state as a proposition

equivocate speak ambiguously to conceal truth or avoid commitment

explain show meaning of, make clear; state reasons for

expound explain in detail

fill in inform more fully; provide additional information

get across make one's point clear

get over get across; convince another

gloss over cover up, esp. a mistake

gossip reveal personal or sensational facts; spread rumors

hash over discuss further, esp. when already settled

hint suggest; refer to indirectly

hold forth speak at length; lecture about

illustrate explain by giving examples

imply suggest indirectly, hint at

import imply; indicate

impute attribute or ascribe

induce persuade

inform provide information

insinuate imply or hint, esp. artfully or unpleasantly

instruct inform; teach another; direct or command

interpret explain meaning of; analyze; translate speech to another language

itemize state in list form

lay down assert, allege; set down, impose

lecture discuss formally and at length, often before a group

limn describe, portray

list state as a series of names or items

name mention specifically; provide the word that designates something

narrate give an account of; tell a story

notify inform; report on; make known

offer propose or suggest; declare oneself ready

open broach subject; declare ceremoniously

outtalk surpass verbally; get the better of in talking

parley discuss or confer, esp. with enemies or to settle dispute

persuade convince by reasoning; induce

philosophize speak thoughtfully on moral issues
pitch attempt to sell by persuasion
plead make an appeal or entreaty; address court as an advocate
postulate state as true as the basis for reasoning
powwow *Informal.* discuss in group or at conference
preface introduce; lead up to
prelect discourse formally and publicly; lecture
prescribe lay down a course to follow
proffer propose; offer
propagate transmit or spread widely; publicize
propose offer for consideration; declare as one's plan
proselytize try intensely to convert others to one's point of view
psychologize analyze motives and feelings of oneself or others
read utter written words aloud; interpret
reason discuss calmly and thoughtfully
rebut refute; disprove
recant formally withdraw one's former statement
recap recapitulate
recapitulate state again, esp. main points of discussion; recap
recite state in order, esp. facts; repeat aloud from memory
recount tell in detail; narrate
refute prove a statement wrong
relate narrate; tell in detail
relay pass on a message or information
repeat tell another what one has heard or learned
report give an account of; describe as news
represent describe as; declare to be
resolve settle an issue
restate say again, often in altered form
retell inform of again; narrate again
retract withdraw statement or opinion; unsay
reveal make known; uncover
snitch *Informal.* give incriminating information against; inform on
specify mention or state in detail
spell out explain explicitly; detail unmistakably
spill *Informal.* divulge or reveal
spill one's guts *Informal.* reveal one's inner emotions or deepest secrets
spill the beans *Informal.* disclose a secret, either accidentally or imprudently, esp. so as to ruin a surprise or plan
squeal *Slang.* inform on
stipulate insist on as part of agreement
stress emphasize a point
submit offer or propose for consideration; contend
suggest propose for consideration
summarize list key points of; sum up; synopsize
sum up summarize; state essentials of
sustain confirm; uphold validity of
sway influence
synopsize summarize
take back withdraw or deny earlier statement
talk into persuade to do or think something

talk out of discourage from doing or thinking something
talk over discuss; review
talk sense speak reasonably
talk turkey *Informal.* speak frankly
tattle reveal another's secrets, esp. misbehavior; gossip
tell inform; reveal
tell all reveal everything, including secret information
testify express personal conviction; attest to; bear witness, esp. in court
transmit convey to another, esp. information
treat deal with some subject; discuss
typify represent in essentials common to a group
understate describe in restrained terms; represent something as less than it is
unsay retract
unswear retract; recant on an oath
unveil disclose or make known publicly
validate confirm truth of
verify check or confirm truth of
voice express a given position or point of view
vouch guarantee certainty or accuracy of
wheedle persuade or obtain by coaxing and flattery
withdraw take back an earlier statement
witness testify or attest to, esp. in court
word phrase carefully; select words that best express something
work in find place for something in conversation

Judgments Pro and Con

acknowledge recognize as valid
affirm validate or confirm; state positively
agree accept; concede as true; assent
animadvert make critical remarks
argue dispute or contend; give reasons pro or con; discuss; give evidence for or against
assent agree
attack criticize with great vigor; denounce
aver assert in pleading; verify
avouch declare as a matter of fact; confirm; acknowledge; confess
backbite say mean or spiteful things
bad-mouth *Slang.* criticize severely
barrage subject to repeated verbal attacks
belittle speak slightingly of; disparage; decry
berate scold vigorously and repeatedly
carp complain about; find fault with
castigate criticize severely, esp. as punishment
comminate denounce
complain express dissatisfaction or disapproval
concur approve; express agreement
confront face boldly; take opposing position
contradict disagree or state opposition, esp. in an arbitrary, impatient manner
criticize comment unfavorably; express judgment on; discuss critically
decry belittle
demur object mildly
denigrate sneer at; blacken the reputation of

denounce speak against; accuse; proclaim publicly to be guilty or evil; comminate
deplore regret deeply; express shock or distaste over
discredit damage reputation of; cause to be disbelieved
disparage belittle
dispute argue, debate; quarrel; question truth of
dissuade persuade against; alter another's opinion
espouse support position or cause
execrate declare to be evil
flatter compliment excessively, esp. to gain favor
fulminate utter with denunciation; issue censure or invective
fuss complain vigorously or pettily
hector intimidate with bullying attacks; bluster
judge state one's considered opinion on, esp. critical opinion
laud praise
lecture address another reprovingly, esp. to correct faults
make fun of ridicule, esp. jokingly
malign say unpleasant and untrue things about; castigate
mock scoff or jeer contemptuously; ridicule by mimicry of speech
moralize speak of right and wrong conduct
nag complain or find fault incessantly
niggle find fault in petty way; fuss over details
object express disfavor; protest or disagree
opine express judgment
poke fun at ridicule or tease
praise speak highly of and express approval; laud
profane speak of irreverently and disrespectfully
promote publicize; speak well of
put down *Informal.* criticize harshly; ridicule
question express doubt about
quibble raise petty objections
rate scold angrily
rebuke scold sharply; reprove
recommend advise an action; endorse; praise one to another
remonstrate protest; complain
reprehend rebuke; blame
reprimand rebuke, esp. formally
reproach express disapproval of another's fault
reprove condemn for a fault or offense
revile criticize angrily and abusively
ridicule make fun of another's faults, esp. in scorn
salute express respect or admiration for
scandalize slander, defame, or speak maliciously of
scold rebuke or censure severely; find fault with noisily
score berate; denounce
slander utter false statements damaging to another's reputation
slash criticize cuttingly and harshly
slur speak ill of
smirch discredit another's reputation

sound off *Informal.* express opinions loudly and freely
speak one's mind express opinions frankly; speak one's piece
speak one's piece speak one's mind
speculate express an opinion without knowledge
support state one's approval of; corroborate
talk up discuss favorably; promote
tout praise highly
trash *Informal.* subject to invective or harsh criticism; attack
upbraid reproach; criticize
vilify speak evil about
vindicate clear of blame or suspicion; prove to be valid
vote give formal expression of one's opinion or choice
wig *Brit. informal.* rebuke
zing *Slang.* criticize harshly

Questions and Answers

acknowledge admit agreement with
admit concede as true; acknowledge; allow
allow *Informal.* suppose to be; admit
answer respond to question or accusation; reply
appeal request earnestly; ask for corroboration or vindication
ask call for an answer; put a question to; request; invite
ask about pose question on
badger question persistently
beg ask for earnestly and humbly; evade; sidestep
beseech beg for earnestly; implore
come back respond; answer quickly
concede admit truth of something; admit defeat
confess admit to sins, errors, or weaknesses
consult seek advice or opinion of
cross-examine pose a series of questions, esp. to court witness
cross-question *Chiefly Brit.* cross-examine
demand request as if by right; insist on
deny refuse to acknowledge
divulge reveal something unknown
entreat beg, implore
examine inquire into; ask questions of
explain elaborate on a brief answer
grant admit that something is true
grill question intensely at length
impetrate ask for; entreat
implore request earnestly, beg for
importune request persistently
inquire ask, question; investigate; also, *esp. Brit,* enquire
interrogate question, esp. formally and at length
investigate inquire systematically in close examination
invite ask another for comments or to do something
offer propose or suggest an answer
pester annoy with frequent requests or questions

petition request earnestly and formally
plead make an appeal or entreaty
pose state a question
pray entreat someone, esp. God
press demand insistently; urge or pressure; beseech
proffer offer, esp. in answer
pry inquire into, often furtively or impertinently
pump question persistently for information
put a question to ask; inquire
query ask a question; express doubt
question ask for information; seek or demand an answer
quiz question or examine briefly or rapidly
react respond to a question
rebut prove false or oppose by evidence or argument
refuse deny request or demand; answer "no'
rejoin reply sharply or critically
reply answer
request ask for something
respond answer, esp. a specific question
retort answer, esp. with quick, witty, or angry reply; riposte
retract change or withdraw statement or opinion; unsay
riddle pose question that is both amusing and puzzling
riposte retort
supplicate ask for humbly; beseech
talk back answer or respond defiantly
temporize evade direct answer, esp. to gain time
testify bear witness, esp. in court
unsay retract, esp. a previous statement

SOUNDS AND NOISES
Sound, Hearing, and Deafness
Actual Sounds
Descriptions of Sounds
Speech Sounds
Comic Sound Effects

See also: *Chap. 1: Anatomy; Medical Problems; Chap. 4: Physics; Chap. 15: Classical Music; Chap. 18: Grammar, Phonetics, and Linguistics; Chap. 19: Verbs of Speech; Chap. 20: Exclamations; Nonsense, Confusion, and Trouble;*

Sound, Hearing, and Deafness

acoustic (*adj*) pertaining to the sense or organs of hearing or to sound
acoustics branch of physics that deals with sound and sound waves
attend (*vb*) listen to
audio (*adj*) pertaining to transmission, reception, or reproduction of sound
audiology study of hearing disorders and rehabilitation of those with hearing impairments
audiometer instrument for recording acuity of hearing
audition act, sense, or power of hearing
auditory (*adj*) pertaining to hearing, sense of

hearing, or organs of hearing; perceived through the sense of hearing
aural (*adj*) pertaining to the ear or sense of hearing; auricular
auricular (*adj*) perceived by the ear; aural
babel confused mixture of sounds or noises
be all ears listen with all one's attention
bend an ear listen attentively; give ear
bug hidden, electronic listening device
cacophony harsh discordance of sound; dissonance
clamor loud and continuous noise
closed-captioned (*adj*) designating television program broadcast with captions visible with use of a decoder, intended for the hearing-impaired
consonance harmony of sounds
deaf (*adj*) partially or wholly deprived of sense of hearing
deaf-mute person who is unable to hear or speak
decibel unit of measure used to express differences in power in acoustics, designating degree of loudness
din loud, confused, continuous noise
discord inharmonious or confused combination of sounds; harsh noise; dissonance
dissonance inharmonious or harsh sound; cacophony; discord
dumb (*adj*) mute
ear organ of hearing in human beings and other vertebrates; sense of hearing
earshot distance within which a sound or voice can be heard
eavesdrop (*vb*) listen secretly to a private conversation
euphony agreeableness of sound, esp. harmonious or pleasant-sounding combinations of tones
faint (*adj*) lacking loudness
frequency number of cycles per unit time of a sound wave, determining its pitch
give ear listen carefully; bend an ear
hard-of-hearing (*adj*) hearing-impaired
hark (*vb*) listen attentively
harmony pleasing combination of tones
hear (*vb*) perceive sounds by the ear; listen to; have the faculty of perceiving sound vibrations
hearing sense by which sounds are perceived; act of perceiving sound
hearing aid compact electronic amplifier, usu. placed behind one's ear to improve hearing
hearing-impaired (*adj*) having reduced or deficient hearing ability; hard-of-hearing
hertz unit of frequency equal to one cycle per second
hush silence or quiet, esp. after noise; (*vb*) make silent
inaudible (*adj*) incapable of being heard
lend an ear listen carefully
listen (*vb*) give attention with the ear for purpose of hearing; wait attentively in expectation of perceiving a sound
listen in (*vb*) overhear; eavesdrop

loud (*adj*) designating a sound or tone having exceptional volume; noisy or clamorous
loudness measure of a sound's intensity, independent of its pitch and timbre
lull temporary quiet or stillness; soothing sound
muffle (*vb*) deaden sound, esp. by wrapping that which is producing it
mum (*adj*) silent
mute (*adj*) silent, esp. refraining from speech; not emitting sound; incapable of speech, dumb
noise sound, esp. loud, harsh, or confused one; clamor
noisy (*adj*) making much noise; loud
otology study and treatment of diseases of the ear
overhear (*vb*) hear, esp. speech, without speaker's intention or knowledge; eavesdrop; listen in
pitch degree of height or depth of a tone or sound, depending on the relative rapidity of its frequency
prick up one's ears listen attentively
quiet (*adj*) making little or no sound or noise; silent
racket loud, disturbing noise or uproar; clamor; din
register tonal range of a voice, instrument, or sound-producing device
resonance prolongation of sound by reflection or reverberation; characteristic quality of a particular voiced sound
resonant (*adj*) deep and full of resonance; sonorous
resonate (*vb*) resound
resound (*vb*) echo or ring with sound; sound loudly; resonate
reverberate (*vb*) reecho; resound; be reflected repeatedly, as sound waves from walls of a confined space
ring (*vb*) give forth a clear, resonant sound; resound or reverberate
sibilation hissing sound
silence absence of sound; stillness
soft (*adj*) designating sound or tone having very little volume; low or subdued in noise level
sonant (*adj*) sounding; having sound
sonic (*adj*) pertaining to sound
sonority condition of being resonant or sonorous
sonorous resonating with sound; loud and deep-toned; rich and full in sound
sound sensation produced by stimulation of organs of hearing by vibrations transmitted through air or other medium; mechanical vibrations transmitted through an elastic medium that produce stimulation of organs of hearing; particular auditory effect thus produced; any noise, vocal utterance, or musical tone; (*vb*) make or emit a sound
soundproof (*adj*) impervious to sound
still (*adj*) free from sound or noise; silent; subdued or hushed in sound
stone-deaf (*adj*) totally deaf
stridor harsh, grating, or creaking sound

timbre characteristic quality of a sound, independent of its pitch and loudness
tone any sound considered with reference to its pitch, strength, timbre, and source; quality of a sound
tone-deaf (*adj*) unable to distinguish differences in pitch in musical tones
turn a deaf ear to refuse to listen to
ultrasound sound with frequency greater than 20,000 hertz, approximately the upper limit of human hearing
voice sounds uttered through mouth of living creature, esp. human being; such sounds as distinctive to an individual
volume degree of sound intensity or loudness

Actual Sounds

ahh, arf, arp
baa, beep, birr, blap, blat, boing, boo, bowwow, burp, buzz
caw, cheep, chink, chirp, chirr, chirrup, churr, clang, clank, clap, click, cling, clink, clinkety-clank, clip, clip-clop, clomp, clonk, clop, clop-clop, clunk, coo, cuckoo
ding, ding-a-ling, ding-dong, dong, drivit
eek
fizz
gong, goo
haw, hom, hiccup, hiss, honk, hoo, hum, hurrah
ick
meow, mew, mewl, moo
oink
pat, ping, pit-a-pat, pitter-patter, plink, plonk, plunk, pop, pow, purr
quack
rat-a-tat, ring, ring-a-ling, riprap
splat, splish, squish, swish, swoosh
tantara, tap, tat, tick, ticktock, ting, ting-a-ling, toot, tweet
varoom
whap, whirr, whish, whizz, whomp, whoop, whoopee, whoosh, woof, wow
yahoo, yikes, yip, yo, yoo-hoo, yow
zap, zing

Descriptions of Sounds

baffle, bang, bawl, bay, belch, bell, blare, blast, bleat, bleep, bong, boom, boop, bray, bruit, buffet, bugle, bump, burble
cacophony, catcall, caterwaul, cheer, chime, chip, chuff, chug, chunk, clack, clamor, clangor, clash, clatter, cluck, clump, conk, crack, crackle, crash, creak, crinkle, croak, cronk, crool, croon, crow, crump, crunch
drill, drone, drum
fart, flick, flump, flutter
gag, gaggle, gargle, glop, gnash, gobble, grate, grind, gulp, gurgle, guzzle
hammer, hawk, hoot, howl, huff, hush
jangle, jingle
keck, keen, knell, knock
lap, lisp, low
mash, mizzle
neigh, nip
pad, paradiddle, patter, peal, pestle, pip, pipe, pitter, plash, plop, pound, pule, pummel
racket, rap, rasp, rattle, report, roar, rollick, rumble, rustle

scrape, scratch, screak, scream, screech, shake, shatter, shriek, shrill, shush, sizzle, skirl, slam, slap, slur, slurp, smack, snap, snarl, sneeze, sniff, sniffle, snivel, snore, snort, snuffle, sob, splash, splatter, squall, squawk, squeak, squeal, squib, stertor, stomp, strum, swat
tamp, thill, throstle, thrum, thud, thump, thunder, thunk, thwack, ticktack, tinkle, tintinnabulate, tirl, toll, tootle, tramp, tread, trill, tromp, trumpet, twang
ululate
warble, whack, wham, whang, wheeze, whinny, whistle, whiz, whop, whump, winnow, wolf
yak, yakety-yak, yawp, yelp, yodel
zip, zoom

Speech Sounds

babble, bark, bellow, blab, blabber, blather, blatter, bleat, blither, blubber, blurt, bluster, brattle, bray, bubble, bumble, burble
cackle, caw, chat, chatter, chitter, chuff, cry
gab, gabble, gibber, giggle, groan, growl, grumble, grunt, guffaw
holler, hoot
jabber
murmur, mutter
natter, nicker, noodle
patter, prattle, pribble
quibble
shout, simper, sing, snicker, splutter, sputter, squeal, stammer, stutter, susurrate
tattle, titter, trill, twaddle, twitter
wail, warble, whimper, whine, whisper
yabber, yammer, yap, yell, yelp, yowl

Comic Sound Effects

aaaa, aaargh, aaarrgh, ack, ahchoo, ak
babrom, bada, ba-da-bam, badow, baff, balump, bam, bammm, bang, bash, ba-wrooo, bawww, bdlm, bdlmp, bdmp, beep, bep, bida-bom, biff, bing, blaff, blam, blamma, blang, bl-eech, bleed, bleeed, bllam, bllom, blm, blodom, blog, blom, bloo, blop, blouw, blrashh, blug, bof, boing, bom, bong, bonk, boom, boom-ba-doom, bop, bounce, boyng, bradada, brat, brrrrram, brrt, burble
chomp, chonk, chop, chsh, chugalug, clang, clank, clash, clik, clikety, clrrash, coff, crack, crackle, crak, crash, creak, crunch, cut
dang-a-lang, danglang, dig, ding, dingdong, dinggg, dong, doof, drinnggg, dzzzz, dzzzzz
ech, eeeeeeeee, eeeeek, eep, ert
feh, flink, floom, floosh, foomf, fooosh, foosh, froosh, fsst, fwadoom, tweet
gag, gah, gasp, ge-boom, gha, ghaaa, gleh, glig, glk, glook, glub, glug, go, gong, gonng, goo, gop, gring, grinngg, grrr
hack, ha-ho, hf, hmf, hnf, honk, hrf, huf, huh, humph
inng
jab
kaf, kchow, kchunk, klak, klaket, klakkety, klek, klik, klink, klomp, klop, kneek, kortch, kpow, krak, kree, kreet, krk, krr-oomf, kr-rumf, krumf, kruuungg, ktak, kweeg
mf, mff, mhf, nf, nfs, nggg, ngs, nok, nyaaoooo
oof, oop, ooze, oww
paf, piu, plip, ploosh, pok, poof, poom, poot, pop, pow, ptung, ptweeeeng, punt

rap, rat, rat-tat, rattle, ring, room, rowf, rrinngg, r-rip, rrip, rrowr, rrrooaar, runch

schplivartz, scree, screeech, screeee, shmek, skeee, skloorgle, skntch, skramm, skreech, skrotch, skwee, skweee, slam, slap, slap-ap-ap, slash, slep, slosh, smak, smash, smashh, smeeeeeeer, smek, smesh, smooch, snap, snf, snick, snif, snuf, sob, spa-bam, spla-poom, splash, splat, splinter, sploog, sploosh, splow, splush, spong, sponggg, spung, sput, squeee, sreiikk, stomp, swish, swok, swop

tap, tat, thud, thunk, tick, tilt, tinkle, toot, treee, tromp, trompitty, tsk, tsss, tsssboom, twang, twee, tweep, twerp

ugh, ung

vaaaagglum, vash, va-va-voom, voof, voom, vroooom, vrrumm

waa, waaah, waf, wak, wee, weoooeeeoooee, wham, whap, whirr, whom, whomp, whoom, whoosh, whuf, wok, woop, wrraaammmm, wurf

yap, yappa, yatata, yayter, yeaaaaa, yeeeaaaakk, yhaaa, yitti, yoop, yotter, youch, yyp

z, zaaaaa, zap, zetz, zing, zip, zok, zop, zot, zzap, zzip, zzz, zzzzz

SMELLS AND TASTES
Smells
Tastes

See also: *Chap. 1: Anatomy; Chap. 9: Foods; Chap. 17: Smoking and Tobacco*

Smells

air (*vb*) ventilate by exposure to open air

ambrosia something appealing to smell or taste, orig. food of the gods

anosmic (*adj*) having complete or partial loss of sense of smell

aroma usu. agreeable odor, often arising from spices or plants; bouquet of wine

aromatic (*adj*) having a pleasing scent or odor

attar perfume or essential oil obtained from flowers

bad breath halitosis

balm aromatic fragrance or sweet odor, esp. in resinous, oily substance exuding from certain plants

balsam fragrant or aromatic substance exuding from certain trees

BO **b**ody **o**dor

body odor BO; natural smell of human body, esp. unpleasant odor of perspiration

bouquet distinctive aroma of wines and liqueurs

breath hint or mere suggestion of scent, esp. carried on a light current of air

cologne mildly perfumed toilet water

corky (*adj*) having a spoiled scent, esp. from tainted cork

deodorant any agent used for eliminating odors

deodorize (*vb*) eliminate unpleasant odor

eau de toilette perfumed toilet water; cologne

effluvium slight trace or invisible exhalation of vapor, usu. noxious or disagreeable

emanation breath or issuing forth of vapor

essence perfume or scent; basic or intrinsic smell of something

ester fragrant volatile liquid found in essential oils and synthesized for use as scent

exhalation vapor or emanation

fetid (*adj*) having a strong, unpleasant smell; olid

fetor strong, offensive smell; stench

foul (*adj*) unpleasant smelling

fragrance sweet or pleasing odor

fragrant (*adj*) having a sweet or pleasing odor

fresh (*adj*) well-ventilated and airy

fulsome (*adj*) sickening or disgusting to the senses

fume usu. vaporous smokelike exhalation, esp. of odorous or harmful nature

fumigation exposure to smoke or vapors, usu. in disinfectingprocess

funk strong, offensive smell

fust strong, musty, or moldy smell

gamy (*adj*) having the tangy, slightly tainted odor of uncooked game

graveolent (*adj*) having a rank smell

halitosis condition of having foul-smelling breath

heady (*adj*) intoxicating and exhilarating to the sense of smell

incense aromatic substance that produces sweet odor when burned; any fragrant scent or perfume

malodorous (*adj*) foul-smelling

mephitic (*adj*) noxious and stinking

mephitis any poisonous stench, esp. noxious exhalation from the earth

miasma noxious exhalation, esp. from decomposing organic matter

musk strong odor of substance secreted in gland of male musk deer, or synthesized, used in making perfume; must

must musk, esp. powdered form

nares nostrils or nasal passages

nasal (*adj*) pertaining to the nose or nostrils

nidor strong smell, esp. of burning meat or fat

nidorous (*adj*) rank-smelling, esp. like burning or decaying animal matter

nose organ of smell

nostril one of two external openings of nose; one of nares

odor sensation perceived by sense of smell, either agreeable or disagreeable

odoriferous (*adj*) yielding or diffusing an odor

olfaction sense of smell; act of smelling

olfactory (*adj*) pertaining to sense of smell

olid (*adj*) fetid

perfume agreeable scent, odor, or volatile particles emitted by a substance; (*vb*) impart a pleasant fragrance

pomander ball-shaped mixture of aromatic substance

pong *Brit. informal.* disagreeable smell, stink

potpourri fragrant mixture of dried flower petals and spices

putrefy (*vb*) cause to rot or decay with offensive odor

putrescent (*adj*) becoming putrid, undergoing putrefaction

putrid (*adj*) in state of foul decay and decomposition with accompanying odor of rot

rancid (*adj*) having an unpleasant, stale smell

rank (*adj*) having an offensive, foul smell or taste

redolent (*adj*) fragrant, having a pleasant odor; smelling of

reek strong, unpleasant smell, esp. vaporous stink; (*vb*) give off strong, unpleasant odor

rose (*adj*) sweetly scented like a rose

rot state of putrefaction and decay and its attendant unpleasant odor

rotten eggs distinctive smell of decaying, uncooked eggs, used to indicate particular foul smell

sachet small bag or case of perfumed powder, used for scenting clothes or linens

savor quality of a substance that affects sense of smell; particular smell

savory (*adj*) agreeable in smell, esp. fragrant

scent distinctive, usu. agreeable odor; perfume; sense of smell; (*vb*) imbue with odor or perfume

skunk animal that emits noxious scent when endangered, used to represent any powerfully unpleasant stink

smell odor or scent that may be perceived through the nose by the olfactory nerves; (*vb*) perceive by sense of smell or inhale odor of

smelly (*adj*) having or emitting a strong, unpleasant odor

sniff scent or odor perceived; (*vb*) smell something by short inhalations through the nose

snuff (*vb*) perceive by smelling; sniff

snuffle (*vb*) draw air into nose so as to smell something

spoor scent left by a wild animal, used in tracking

stench foul or offensive smell

stink (*vb*) emit a strong, offensive smell; (*n*) a strong, offensive smell

stinking (*adj*) foul-smelling

stink to high heaven smell extremely unpleasant or foul

stinky (*adj*) foul-smelling

stuffy (*adj*) poorly ventilated, stale, lacking fresh air

sweet (*adj*) fragrant, perfumed, or fresh to the smell

trace hint or suggestion of a particular scent; whiff

unscented (*adj*) having no smell; without scent or odor added

vapor visible exhalation of gaseous particles into the air

ventilate (*vb*) provide fresh air to enclosed place

waft faintly perceived odor; trace of scent in the air

whiff slight trace of odor or smell of something

Tastes

acerbic (*adj*) sour or astringent in taste

acidic (*adj*) sharp and biting in flavor

acrid (*adj*) sharp, biting, or bitterly pungent

aftertaste sensation of taste remaining after substance causing it is no longer in mouth

appetizing (*adj*) appealing to the taste

astringent (*adj*) harshly biting, esp. constrictive to taste buds

biting (*adj*) sharp, somewhat acidic, producing harsh taste

bitter (*adj*) having a harsh, disagreeably acrid taste; being one of the four basic taste sensations

brackish (*adj*) having a slightly salty or briny flavor

briny (*adj*) salty in flavor

caustic (*adj*) sharp and acidic

delectable (*adj*) delicious or appetizing

delicious (*adj*) very pleasing to taste

dry (*adj*) of wines, not sweet or fruity

dulcet (*adj*) *Archaic.* sweet to the taste

dulcify (*vb*) sweeten

flavor distinctive taste; additive imparting specific taste

flavorful (*adj*) possessing strong flavor; tasty

flavoring something that imparts a particular taste

four basic tastes elemental taste sensations that are mediated by sense organs and form basis of most other tastes: bitter, salt, sour, sweet

fruity (*adj*) tasting of fruit; of wines, sweet

full-bodied (*adj*) at full strength or flavor, esp. of wines

gamy (*adj*) having the tangy, tainted flavor of uncooked game

goût *French.* taste, relish

gustation act of or faculty for tasting

gustatory (*adj*) pertaining to taste or tasting

honey (*adj*) sweet

hot (*adj*) sharply pungent or peppery

juicy (*adj*) succulent, mouth-watering

mouth-watering (*adj*) appetizing

nip biting or tangy taste

palatable (*adj*) good-tasting

palate sense of taste

peppery (*adj*) hot and pungent, tasting of pepper

pickled (*adj*) preserved in and tasting of brine

piquant (*adj*) pleasingly sharp, biting, or tart

pungent (*adj*) biting or acrid; having a sharp affect on taste organ

rancid (*adj*) having an unpleasant, stale taste

rank (*adj*) having an offensive, foul taste

relish pleasing or appetizing flavor; enjoyment of the taste of something

saccharine (*adj*) very sweet; artificially sweet

saline (*adj*) salty

salt (*adj*) producing that one of the four basic taste sensations that is not sweet, sour, or bitter

salty (*adj*) tasting of salt

sapor flavor; quality of substance affecting sense of taste; savor

saporific (*adj*) imparting or producing flavor

savor quality of substance affecting sense of taste; sapor

savory (*adj*) agreeable to the taste, sometimes piquant

scrumptious (*adj*) delicious

seasoning salt, herbs, or spices that enhance flavor of food

sec (*adj*) of wines, dry, not sweet

sharp (*adj*) strongly pungent or biting

smack taste or flavor, esp. hint of flavor

sour (*adj*) tart, acidic, lemony; being one of the four basic taste sensations

spicy (*adj*) piquant or pungent; seasoned with spices

strong (*adj*) having a powerful, dominant, specific flavor

succulent (*adj*) juicy and full of good flavor

sugary (*adj*) sweet like sugar

sweet (*adj*) tasting of sugar or honey; being one of the four basic taste sensations

sweet-and-sour (*adj*) combining the tastes of sugar or honey and vinegar or lemon juice

syrupy (*adj*) very sweet, esp. of viscous liquids

tang strong, distinctive taste or flavor

tart (*adj*) sour or acidic, sharp to the taste

taste sense by which flavor or savor of things is perceived and appreciated; (*vb*) perceive or try the flavor of something

taste buds small bodies, primarily on tongue, that are perception organs for sense of taste

tasteless (*adj*) having no distinct flavor

tasting act of perceiving or testing the flavor of something

tasty (*adj*) good-tasting, delicious, savory

tongue movable organ on floor of mouth used in eating and containing taste buds that perceive flavors

toothsome (*adj*) agreeable to the taste, palatable

treacly (*adj*) extremely, sometimes sickly, sweet

whet one's appetite stimulate one's appetite through pleasing taste or smell

yummy *Informal.* very tasty

zest agreeable or piquant flavor imparted to something

zesty (*adj*) agreeably piquant

CHAPTER TWENTY
COMMON EXPRESSIONS

EXCLAMATIONS
Grunts, Calls, and Sounds
Interjections
Curses and Oaths

See also: *Chap. 19: Sounds and Noises; Chap. 20: Nonsense, Confusion, and Trouble*

Grunts, Calls, and Sounds

aah, achoo, ack, ah, aha, ahem, ah-ha, aw
baa, bah, blah, boo, bowwow, brrr
cheep
eek, eh
guffaw
hah, ha-ha, harrumph, haw, heehaw, heigh-ho, hem, hi-ho, hmmm, ho, ho-hum, hoo, hoy, huh, humph, hunh, hup, hut
ick
la-di-da, lo
nah
o, oh, oink, oof, ooh, ooh-la-la, oompah, oomph, ooo, ow
peugh, pip-pip, poof, pshaw
rah
shh
ta-da, tut, tut-tut
ugh, uh-huh, uh-oh, umph, unh-unh
varoom
wahoo, wha, whee, wo, wow, wowee
yah, yahoo, yay, yech, yikes, yo, yoikes, yoo-hoo, yow, yuck, yum, yummy, yum-yum
zap

Interjections

alack, alas, alleluia, amen, and how, avast, aw-shucks, aye
banzai, boy, bravo, by jingo
cheerio, cheers, chop-chop
dear, dear me, ditto
egads, eh, what, eureka
fiddlesticks, fore, forsooth
gadzooks, gee, gee whillikers, gee whiz, gesundheit, giddyap, golly, golly gee, golly whillikers, good golly, good gracious, goody, gracious, gracious me
hallelujah, hark, heads up, hear ye, hear ye, heave-ho, heavens, heavens to Betsy, here here, hey, hip-hip, holy cow, holy mackerel, holy moly, holy toledo, hooray, hosanna, hurrah, huzzah
jeepers
lackaday, lo and behold
mama, marry, my gracious, my my, my stars, my word
nah, nay, nerts, nope, nuts
oh boy, oh dear, oh my, okay, okey-doke, okey-dokey, ole, oops, oopsy-daisy, ouch, oy, oyez
peekaboo, phew, pooh, prithee, prosit
rah, rah-rah, roger, rot
salud, scram, shaddup, shucks, shush, skoal
tallyho, ten-four, there, there, timber, touché, tsk tsk, tush, tut-tut
viva, voila
whatever, well, whew, whoa, whoop-de-do, whoopee, whoops, why, woe is me, wowie, wowie-zowie
yea, yeah, yep, yippee, yo mama, yup
zooks, zounds, zut

Curses and Oaths

arse, ass, asshole
bastard, bejesus, blame, blast, bleep, blimey, bosh, brother, bull, bullroar, bullshit, by cracky, by Jove
Christ, cockadoodie, cocksucker, cottonpickin', crap, crapola, crikey, criminy, cunt
dad-blamed, dadburn it, dad-gummed, dammit, damn, damnation, damn it, dang, darn, dash, dod, doggone, doodie, drat, durn
faugh, feh, fie, for Christ's sake, frig, frigging, fuck, fuckin', fuckin'-A, fucking, fuckin'-hell, fuck it
God, goddamn, goddamnit, gol blame, gol darn, good God, good Lord, gramercy
heck, heckuva, hell, hellacious, hell's bells, helluva, holy gosh
jeez, jeez Louise, Jesus, Jesus Christ, Jesus H. Christ
merde, motherfucker, mother of God, my ass
noogie
Od
phooey, pish, piss, piss off, poop, pox
sacre bleu, Sam Hill, sheesh, shit, shoo, shoot, son of a bitch, son of a gun, sumbitch
tarnation
what the dickens, what the hell, what the Sam Hill

GREETINGS AND FAREWELLS
Greetings
Farewells
Interchangeables

See also: *Chap. 20: Exclamations*

Greetings

ahoy, all hail
bonjour
glad to see you, good to see you, greetings
hail, halloa, have a good one, hello, hello there, hey, hey-ho, hi, hi, there, hi ya, hola, how are you?, how do?, how do you do?, howdy, howdy-do, howdy-doody, how d'ye do?, how goes it?, how's by you?, how's everything?, how's it going?, how's the world treating you?, how's things?, how you be?, how you been?, how you doing?, hullo
many happy returns
que pasa?
salud, salutations, shake
welcome, what it is?, what's happening?, wie gehts?
yo

Farewells

à bientôt, à demain, adieu, adios, arrivederci, à toute à l'heure, Auf Wiedersehen, au revoir
be good, be seeing you, bless you, bonne nuit, bon voyage, buenas noches, buona notte, bye, bye-bye
catch you later, come again
das vedanya
enjoy
fare thee well, farewell
God be with you, God bless, Godspeed, good-bye, good luck, good night, gute Nacht
happy trails, hasta la vista, hasta luego, hasta mañana, have a good one, have a nice day

later, later on
mañana
over, over and out
peace
regards, roger
sayonara, see ya, see you later, see you later alligator
take care, take it easy, ten-four, toodleoo

Interchangeables

all hail, aloha, ave
bonjour, bon matin, bon soir, buenas tardes, buenos dias, buona sera, buon giorno
check, cheerio, cheers, ciao
good afternoon, good day, good evening, good morning, good to see you, guten Abend, guten Morgen, guten Tag
hail
konbanwa, konichiwa
pip-pip
regards
salaam, shalom

INSULTS, SLURS, AND EPITHETS
Appearance or Style
Intelligence or Aptitude
Behavior or Personality
Morality or Character
Sexuality or Gender
Ethnic Origin, Race, or Religion

See also: *Chap. 1: Physical Appearance; Chap. 20: Terms of Endearment and Respect; Chap. 22: Personality and Behavior; Sex, Love, and Romance; Strategy, Intrigue, and Deception; Chap. 23: Judgment and Criticism; Mental Disturbances; Crime; Violence*

Insults, Slurs, and Epithets are grouped into six lists of virtual synonyms, each representing insults to a specific characteristic. Thus, all the definitions under Appearance or Style essentially mean "unattractive," while all the insults under Intelligence or Aptitude essentially mean "ignorant" or "stupid." Definitions would tend to be repetitive. Vulgar and derogatory labels apply to virtually all the insults under Sexuality or Gender and Ethnic Origin, Race, or Religion, and thus have been omitted.

Appearance or Style

Amazon, ape, armpit
baboon, bag, bag lady, bear, beggar, behemoth, beldam, biddy, blastie, blimp, blob, bohunk, booger, bruiser, brute, bug, bumpkin, bunny, burrhead, butterball, buzzard
chit, city slicker, clotheshorse, codger, Colonel Blimp, conehead, coot, cootie, cornpone, cow, cripple
dandy, dinosaur, dirt bag, dog, dotard, dwarf eyesore
fancyass, fatso, fatty, feeb, ferret face, fleabag, fogy, fop, fossil, four-eyes, Frankenstein, freak, frump
geek, geezer, ghost, ghoul, gimp, golem,

golliwogg, goon, gorgon, gorilla, grease monkey, greaser, guttersnipe

hag, have-not, hayseed, heifer, hick, hillbilly, hobbledehoy, hobo, ho-dad, hog, homunculus, hoyden

invalid

jarhead

lard, lardass, Little Lord Fauntleroy, longhair, lummox, lump, lunger

malkin, mannequin, measle, meatball, Medusa, monkey, monstrosity, moose, mossback, mug, mutant, mutt

Neanderthal

old bag, ox

peacock, peewee, picklepuss, pig, pilgarlic, pimple, pimpleface, pinhead, pipsqueak, pizzaface, plain Jane, plugugly, porker, preppy, prune, pus bucket, pustule, pygmy

ragabond, ragamuffin, ragtag, relic, reptile, ronyon, rooster, rube, runt

sad sack, scarecrow, scrag, shlump, shorty, shrimp, shriv, skinhead, slattern, slicker, slob, slouch, sloven, small fry, sow, spas, spastic, specter, spud, squirt, stick, string bean, stumblebum, sweat hog, swell

tank, tawpie, Teddy boy, toad, toff, tomboy, troglodyte, troll, tub

ugly duckling

waif, wallflower, wart, weenie, whale, whiffet, white bread, wombat, wraith

yokel

zit

Intelligence or Aptitude

addlebrain, addlehead, addlepate, airhead, ament, April fool, automaton

bananahead, basket case, beefhead, beetlehead, bimbo, birdbrain, blatherskite, blockhead, blubberhead, blunderhead, bonehead, boob, bozo, brain, bubblehead, bufflehead, buffoon, butthead

cabbagehead, chawbacon, chickenbrain, chowderhead, chucklehead, chump, clod, clodhead, clodpate, clodpoll, clot, cluck, conehead, crackbrain, cretin, criticaster, cuckoo

deadhead, dimwit, ding-a-ling, dingbat, dingdong, ditz, dodo, dodo brain, dolt, dolthead, donkey, doofus, dope, dork, dullard, dullhead, dumbbell, dumb bunny, dumb cluck, dumbhead, dumbo, dumdum, dummkopf, dummy, dunce, dunderhead, dunderpate, dupe

easy mark, egghead

fathead, fatwit, featherbrain, featherhead, feeb, flathead, flibbertigibbet, fool

gaby, gawk, gudgeon

half-wit, hammerhead, harebrain, highbrow

idiot, ignoramus, imbecile

jackass, jiggin, jobbernowl, jolterhead, jughead, klutz, know-nothing, knucklehead

lackwit, lamebrain, lightweight, loggerhead, loon, lowbrow, lumpkin, lunkhead

meatball, meathead, mental midget, mongoloid, moron, muddlehead, mumpsimus, musclehead, mushhead, muttonhead

nincompoop, ninny, ninnyhammer, nitwit, no-brainer, noddy, noodlehead, nudnik, numskull

patzer, peabrain, peahead, pinbrain, pinhead, pointyhead, potatohead, puddinghead, puttyhead

rattlebrain, rattlehead, retard, rockhead

sap, saphead, scatterbrain, sciolist, shit for brains, silly fool, simp, simpleton, slobbering idiot,

slowpoke, softhead, stupe, submoronic twit, sucker

techie, thickhead, thickwit

vegetable, void

witling, woodenhead

yoyo

ziphead

Behavior or Personality

acidhead, agent provocateur, agitator, airy-fairy, alky, alien, also-ran, amateur, android, animal, annoyance, appendage, apple polisher, archenemy, artiste, artsy-fartsy, ass, asshole, ass-kisser

backbreaker, badass, baggage, bag lady, banana, banshee, barbarian, barfly, bastard, bear, beast, beggar, bellyacher, bête noir, bighead, bigmouth, big shot, bindle stiff, bitch, blabbermouth, black sheep, blatherskite, blellum, blow-hard, Boeotian, boaster, bookworm, boor, bore, botcher, brat, brawler, bruiser, brute, bugbear, bugger, bullshit artist, bullshitter, bully, bullyboy, bungler, buster, busybody, butt, butterfingers, buttinsky, buzzard

carper, chatterbox, chauvinist, cheapo, cheapskate, chicken, chimp, chiseler, chowhound, chuff, chump, churl, cipher, clam, clochard, clod, clodhopper, clown, clunk, clunker, cold fish, Comstocker, copycat, cornball, couch potato, cousin, crab, crackpot, crank, crazy, cream puff, creaturo, crumb, crybaby, cube, cur, curmudgeon, cuss, cutup

dabbler, deadwood, dick, dickhead, dilettante, dinosaur, dip, dipshit, ditz, dog breath, dog meat, do-gooder, dogsbody, donkey, do-nothing, doofus, doormat, dork, dotard, doubting Thomas, drag, draggle-tail, dreamer, drifter, drip, drone, dropout, drudge, druggle, drunk, dud, duffer, dweeb

earbender, eightball, enfant terrible, extremist

fart, fat cat, fathead, fawner, featherweight, finagler, firebrand, fish, flake, flamer, flâneur, flash in the pan, flibbertigibbet, floater, flop, flubber, flunky, fogy, fox, fraidy-cat, freak, freebooter, freeloader, fucker, fuckface, fuckhead, fuckup, fuddy-duddy, fumbler, fungus, fussbudget, fusspot

gadfly, galoot, gasbag, gawk, geep, geezer, glutton, goat, goldbrick, golem, goody-goody, goody two shoes, goof, goofball, goof-off, goon, goose, gossipmonger, gourmand, gowk, grease monkey, greenhorn, griper, grobian, grouch, groupie, grump, gull

hack, ham, hambone, hamburger, hangdog, hanger-on, hard case, hardhead, hard-nose, harridan, has-been, head, heathen, hedonist, hellion, hellhound, hell-raiser, high-muck-a-muck, hippie, homebody, horse's ass, hot dog, hothead, hotshot, hoyden, hypochondriac, hypocrite

iceberg, icicle, idler, incendiary, incubus, inebriate

jackal, jackanapes, jackass, jack-off, jailbird, jay, jerk, jerk-off, jester, Johnny-come-lately, joker, juicehead, juicer, junkie

kibitzer, killjoy, klutz, knave, knight-errant, know-it-all, know-nothing, kook

lackey, laggard, lamb, lame, lame duck, landlubber, larrikin, layabout, lazybones, lemming, lemon, leper, lightweight, litterbug, loafer, loggerhead, lollygagger, looby, loon,

loser, lotus-eater, loudmouth, lounge lizard, lout, lowbrow, lubber, lug, lunatic, lurdan, lush

madman, madwoman, maenad, malcontent, mama's boy, maniac, marshmallow, Martian, martinet, masher, meanie, meatball, meddler, megalomaniac, mercenary, merry-andrew, meshugene, milksop, milquetoast, mimic, misanthrope, mischief-maker, miscreant, miser, misfit, misogynist, mobster, mole, mollycoddle, Momus, moneybags, monger, mongrel, mooch, mooncalf, mother, motherfucker, motor-mouth, mouse, muck-a-muck, muckraker, mugwump, mule, mutt

nag, namby-pamby, name-dropper, narc, nebbich, nemesis, nerd, nervous Nellie, nibs, niggard, ninny, nit, nitpicker, nobody, nomad, nonentity, nonperson, noodle, no one, Nosy Parker, nothing, nouveau riche, novice, nut, nutter

oaf, oddball, odd man out, old fart, old fogy, outcast, outsider, oyster

pack rat, pain, pain in the ass, pain in the neck, palooka, panhandler, pantywaist, pariah, patch, patsy, pauper, pawn, peasant, peckerwood, pedant, penny pincher, peon, pepper pot, pest, petticoat, pettifogger, pharisee, philistine, pigeon, piker, pill, pinchbeck, pip, pipsqueak, pisher, pisser, playboy, playgirl, plebe, plunderer, poetaster, polecat, Pollyanna, pollywog, poltroon, poop, poseur, prankster, pretender, prima donna, princess, procrastinator, profiteer, provocateur, pseudo, psycho, pub-crawler, puckfist, pug, punching bag, punk, pussy, putty, putz

quicksilver, quidnunc

rabble-rouser, rake, rapscallion, reb, rebel, recluse, redneck, reject, renegade, revisionist, reynard, riffraff, roach, roadhog, robot, roughneck, roundheel, roustabout, rover, rowdy, rube, ruffian, rummy, rumormonger, runabout, runagate

sad sack, sap, sawney, scapegoat, scaramouch, scaredy-cat, scavenger, scofflaw, scrapper, screwball, scrooge, scrounger, scut, seadog, second banana, second fiddle, sheep, shit, shithead, shlemiel, shlep, shlimazel, shlub, shlump, shmegege, shmo, shmuck, shmutz, shnook, showboat, show-off, shrink, shrinking violet, silly ass, sissy, sitting duck, skinflint, skunk, slacker, slasher, slave, slave driver, slowpoke, slug, slugabed, sluggard, slut, sly boots, smart aleck, smarty-pants, smellfungus, snail, snip, snitch, sniveler, snob, snoop, so-and-so, SOB, sob sister, social climber, sod, sodbuster, soft touch, softy, son of a bitch, sop, sorehead, sot, sourball, sourpuss, souse, speedfreak, spendthrift, spider, spoilsport, sprat, spud, spy, square, squealer, squirt, stick, stick-in-the-mud, stickler, stiff, stinkard, stinker, stockjobber, stooge, straight arrow, stranger, stray, street arab, street person, strutter, stuffed shirt, succubus, sucker, swab, swagman, swellhead, swine, sycophant

tagalong, taskmaster, tattletale, tease, tenderfoot, termagant, terror, tightwad, tinhorn, tinker, toad, toady, tomboy, tomfool, tool, toper, tosspot, touch, toughie, tourist, tout, townie, tramp, tramper, transient, trickster, tripe, troublemaker, truant, tumbleweed, turd, turkey, twerp, twit, Typhoid Mary, tyro

ulcer, underling, unperson, upstart

vagabond, vagrant, vandal, varlet, vassal, Venusian, vulture wacko, waffler, wag, wage slave, Walter Mitty, wangler, wanker, war-horse, washout, weakling, weenie, weirdo, wench, wet blanket, wethead, wheedler, wheeler-dealer, whiffler, whippersnapper, whipping boy, white trash, wildcatter, wild man, wimp, windbag, wino, wiseacre, wise guy, wise-ass, wisenheimer, witch, wolf, workaholic, worm, worrywart, wowser, wreck, wretch, wuss

Xanthippe

yahoo, yardbird, yenta, yes-man, yobbo

zany, zealot, zero, zombie, zonker

Morality or Character

adulterer, Ananias, Antichrist, archfiend, arriviste

Babbitt, backbiter, backstabber, bamboozler, bandit, betrayer, bigamist, bigot, bilker, blackguard, blank, bloodsucker, Bluebeard, bogeyman, bounder, brigand, brown-noser, buccaneer, bum, burglar, butcher

cad, caitiff, cancer, cannibal, cardsharp, carline, cateran, charlatan, cheat, chintz, chiseler, churl, commie, comsymp, con artist, con man, counterfeiter, coward, creep, crook, crud, culprit

dastard, deadbeat, debauchee, deceiver, delator, demagogue, demon, desperado, despot, devil, dictator, dissembler, dodger, dog, double-crosser, double-dealer, dregs, dreck, dross

failure, faitour, faker, fascist, felon, fibber, fiend, finagler, fink, flimflam man, fly-by-night, forger, fraud, freeloader

ganef, goldbrick, gold digger, good-for-nothing, gouger, grafter

heel, heretic, highwayman, hilding, hoaxer, hoodlum, hooligan, huckster, humbug, hypocrite

idolator, impostor, Indian giver, indulger, infidel, informer, ingrate, insurgent, interloper, intruder

jackal, jailbird, jellyfish, JD, judas, juvenile delinquent

kaffir, killer, kleptomaniac, knave

leech, liar, libertine, lily-liver, louse, lout, lowlife

mafioso, malingerer, mammon, miscreant, miser, monster, monstrosity, mountebank

ne'er-do-well, no-account, no-goodnik

ogre, operator, opportunist, outlaw

pagan, pariah, parasite, Peeping Tom, perjurer, pervert, philanderer, philistine, phony, picaro, pickpocket, pimp, pinko, piranha, pirate, pissant, plagiarist, plague, poacher, poltroon, ponce, prevaricator, profligate, psychopath, puke, pusher

quack, quisling, quitter

racketeer, rake, rapist, rat, ratfink, recreant, recusant, red, reprobate, ringleader, robber, robber baron, rodent, rogue, rotter, roué, rustler

saboteur, sadist, saltimbanco, savage, scab, scalawag, scandalmonger, scoundrel, scourge, scum, scumbag, scumsucker, scuzz, scuzzball, serpent, sham, shark, sharp, shill, shirker, Shylock, shyster, sickie, sicko, Simon Legree, sinner, slanderer, slave driver, sleaze, sleazebag, sleazeball, slime, slimebag, slimeball, slime bucket, slumlord, slyboots, snake, snake in the grass, sneak, snipe, snitch, snollygoster, sociopath, sponge, stoolie, stool pigeon, swindler, swine

thief, thug, traitor, transgressor, trash, trickster, troublemaker, turncoat, two-timer, tyrant

usurer, usurper

vampire, vermin, vicemonger, villain, viper, vulture

warmonger, waster, wastrel, weasel, whoreson, witch, worm, wrongdoer

yellowbelly

Sexuality or Gender

Amazon

bawd, bearded clam, bitch, brazen hussy, bugger, bull dyke, butch

castrato, cat, chicken, chicken hawk, chippy, closet queen, cock, cocksucker, concubine, coquette, courtesan, cow, cream puff, cuckold, cunt, cyprian

deviate, dick, diesel dyke, dildo, dingleberry, dink, dong, douche bag, drag queen, dyke

fag, faggot, fag hag, fairy, fetishist, flit, floozy, fox, fruit, fruitcake, fucker

gigolo, gunsel

hag, harlot, harpy, harridan, heifer, hen, homo, hooker, hussy

jade, john

lech, lecher, les, lesbo, libertine, lily, Little Lord Fauntleroy

mama's boy, masher, meat, minx, mo, motherfucker

nance, nancy, nympho

old maid

pansy, pantywaist, pecker, pederast, pedophile, Peeping Tom, pervert, philanderer, piece, pimp, playboy, playgirl, ponce, poof, poofter, prick, prig, procurer, prong, prostitute, prude, punk, pussy, puta

queen, queer, quim

rosy piglet, rut hostess

satyr, shmuck, shrew, sissy, slattern, slit, slut, snatch, sodomist, spinster, stag, streetwalker, stripper, strumpet, stud, swinger, swish, switch hitter

tail, tart, tomboy, tramp, transvestite, trick, trollop, twat

vamp, virago, vixen, voyeur

wanker, wanton, weenie, wench, whore, wiener, wienie, wolf, woman of the street

Ethnic Origin, Race, or Religion

abo, alien, arkie, Aunt Jemima, Auslander

babu, blackie, bohunk, Brit, buck, burrhead

Charlie Chan, Chinaman, Chink, cockney, coolie, coon, cracker

dago, darky, dink

foreigner, Frenchy, frog

ginzo, gook, goomba, goy, gringo, Guinea

half-breed, Hebe, heinie, high yeller, honky, howley, hun, hymie

immigrant, Injun

Jap, JAP, Jew boy, jig, jigaboo, jungle bunny

kike, kraut

limey

Mick, moke, Mr. Charlie

nigger, niggra, Nip

ofay, okie

pachuco, paddy, paleface, picaroon, Polack

redskin

Russki

sheeny, shegatz, shikse, slant, slant-eye, slope, spade, spic, squaw

Ubangi, Uncle Tom

WASP, wetback, whitey, wog, wop

yid

Zulu

Pet Names

acushla, angel, angel baby

babe, baby, baby doll, baby face, beau, boo-boo, bubaloo, bubbles, bubehleh, buttercup

calf, candy, cara mia, cherry, chickabiddy, chickadee, cookie, corazon, cupcake, cutie, cutie pie

daddy, daisy, darling, dear, dearest, dear heart, dearie, dimples, doll, dollface, dove, dreamboat, duck, duckie, duckling, ducks, dumpling

goose

hon, honey, honeybunch, honey child

kitten

lamb, lambchop, lambkin, liebschen, loosker, love, lover, luv

mi amore, monkey, monkey face, muffin, my dear, my love, my pet, my sweet

noodles

pet, pigeon, pooch, pooh, poppet, precious, puddin' head, pumpkin, punkin, puss, pussy willow

snooks, snookums, sugar, sugarpie, sugarpie honeybunch, sweetheart, sweetie, sweetie pie, sweetkins, sweetness, sweet patootie, sweet pea, sweet potato, sweets, sweet thing, sweetums

tomato, toots, tootsie, turtledove

valentine

Friendly or Familiar Address

ace, amigo, auntie

big fella

big guy, binky, boyo, brat, bro, brother, bub, bubba, bud, buddy

cap, captain, champ, chap, chief, chuck, chum, cock, cousin, cove, coz, curly

dad, daddy, deadeye, doc, dude

fella, friend

gaffer, gal, gill, girl, girlie, girlie-girl, goofus, gov, governor, gramma, grammy, grampa, gramps, granny, guy

hombre, home, homeboy, homes, hotshot

jack

kid, kiddo

lad, laddie, lady, lass, lassie, little one

ma, ma'am, mac, maestro, mama, master, mate, mio, missy, mom, momileh, mommy, monkey, moose, muchacho, munchkin, my main man, my man

neighbor, nuncle

old bean, old boy, old chap, old fellow, old man, old scout, old thing, old timer, old top padre

pa, pal, pal o' mine, papa, pard, pardner, peewee, pooh-bah, pop, poppa, pops

rascal

sarge, shrimp, sis, sister, scout, skip, skipper,

skippy, sleepyhead, slick, slim, slugger, son, sonny, sonny boy, soul brother, speedy, sport, sprout, squirt, stretch

tot

unc, uncle

whippersnapper, whiz, whizzer

youngster

Titles and Honorifics

babu, Brother, bwana

Dame, dean, diva, Dom, don, dona

Eminence, Esquire, Excellency

Father, Frau

grace

Herr, Highness, Holiness, Holy Father, Holy Mother, Honor, Honorable

Imperial Highness, Imperial Majesty

lady, ladyship, liege, lieutenant, lord, lordship

ma'am, madam, madame, mademoiselle, maharishi, majesty, massa, master, memsahib, milady, miss, mister, mistress, monsieur, monsignor, most honorable, most reverend, Mother, Mr., Mrs., Ms., my lady, my liege, my lord

officer

padre

rabbi, reverence, reverend, right honorable, right reverend, rinpoche, Royal Highness, Royal Majesty

sahib, sergeant, señor, señora, señorita, Serene Highness, Serene Majesty, signora, signore, signorina, sir, sire, sirrah, Sister, sister, sri, swami

taipan

worship

yogi, Your Eminence, Your Excellency, Your Grace, Your Highness, Your Holiness, Your Honor, Your Majesty, Your Reverence, Your Worship

Affectionate Reference

alter ego, apple of my eye

beauty, belle, beloved, best friend, best girl, blood brother, boy, boyfriend, brat, brother

calf, candy, card, Casanova, chap, character, charmer, cherub, chick, chit, choice, chum, cohort, colleen, colt, companion, comrade, confidant, confrere, cowpoke, crackerjack, crème de la crème, critter, crony, cub, Cub Scout

damsel, darb, diamond in the rough, dilly, dish, Don Juan, doozer, dream, dreamboat, dulcinea, dynamo

eager beaver, eagle, elf, enchantress, enchilada

familiar, fatso, favorite, fellow, filly, fireball, firecracker, flash, fox

gal, gamine, geezer, gem, girl, girlfriend, go-getter, goose, green thumb, guy

handyman, heartthrob, hepcat, highroller, hombre, honcho, hotshot, humdinger, hunk

idol, imp, inamorata, ingenue

jewel, jim-dandy, junior

kingpin

lad, lady love, lamb, lass, lefty, light, live wire, looker, love, lovebird, lucky devil, lucky stiff, lulu

main squeeze, mensch, minikin, minx, monkey, moose, moppet

neighbor, number one, numero uno, nymph

old duffer, old geezer, old lady, old man

partner, peach, pearl, pigeon, pip, pippin, pixie, playmate, plum, pollyanna, pooch, pooh-bah, posy, powerhouse, prince, protégé, puck, pud, pup, puppy

raconteur, rascal, Romeo, rose

scamp, sensation, sharpy, showman, sidekick, slim Jim, smoothie, sophisticate, soul brother, spring chicken, sprite, spud, steady, sugar daddy, swan, sylph

teammate, top banana, top dog, tops, tot, treasure, trouper, trump

urchin, vamp, Venus

water nymph, whippersnapper, whiz, whizbang, whiz kid, whizzer, wiz, wonder, wrangler

Yankee Doodle dandy, youngster, yours truly

Respectful or Admiring Reference

ace, adept, aficionado, agha, all-American, all-around girl, all-around guy, all-star, altar boy, Atlas, avatar

bahadur, ball of fire, bellwether, big name, big timer, blockbuster, blood brother, blue blood, blue ribbon, boy wonder, Brahman, brownie, buck

captain, celeb, chief, classic, colleague, colonel, connoisseur, crackerjack

deadeye, diva, doyen, dynamo

eagle scout, elder, elder statesman, expert

fashion plate

genius, gentleman, gentlewoman, gourmet, governor, grand dame, gray beard, guru

handyman, Hercules, hero, heroine, homecoming queen, honcho, humanitarian

impresario, individual, insider, intellectual, iron man

jack-of-all-trades, jack rabbit, journeyman, judge

keeper, king, knockout

lady, laureate, leader, leading lady, leading man, leatherneck, liege, lifesaver, lion, luminary

Madonna, maestro, maiden, man about town, man of God, man of letters, martyr, marvel, master, mastermind, matinée idol, matron, maven, maverick, mentor, millionaire, muse

natural, nonesuch

old hand

padrone, paladin, paragon, past master, patriot, patron, phenom, phrasemaker, pick, pilot, pioneer, poet laureate, pres, president, pro, prodigy, pundit

queen

rara avis, reformer, Robin Goodfellow, Robin Hood, role model

sage, saint, samaritan, Samson, savant, savior, seer, select, self-starter, senator, sensei, sharpshooter, sleuth, smart cookie, socialite, soldier, solon, somebody, sovereign, spark plug, specimen, spitfire, sponsor, standard bearer, star, statesman, strongman, stud, superman, superstar, superwoman, supremo, swami, swashbuckler

teacher, thoroughbred, titan, torchbearer, trailblazer, trendsetter, troubleshooter, tutor, tycoon

up-and-comer

veteran, VIP, virgin, virtuoso, visionary, volunteer

warrior, watchdog, winner, wise man, wit, wizard, wonder, wonder-worker, workhorse, worldbeater, worthy, wunderkind

yeoman, yogi

zaddik

NONSENSE, CONFUSION, AND
TROUBLE
Foolishness, Bunkum, and Trifles
Drivel and Silly Talk
Fusses and Troubles
Confusion
Nonsense Words and Cutesies

See also: *Chap. 19: Verbs of Speech; Chap. 19: Sounds and Noises; Chap. 20: Exclamations; Chap. 20: Insults, Slurs, and Epithets; Chap. 21: Yiddish Borrowings; Chap. 24: Violence*

Foolishness, Bunkum, and Trifles

airy-fairy

bagatelle, balderdash, ballyhoo, baloney, bauble, bilge, blah, blahs, blatherskite, bluff, blunder, bluster, bogus, bollocks, bosh, braggadocio, bravado, brummagem, buffoonery, bull, bullshit, bunkum, bunk, burlesque

caacaa, cheek, claptrap, cock, cockalorum, cockamamie, codswallop, corn, cow pat, crambo, crap, crock, crud, curliewurly

diddlyshit, diddly-squat, doodad, doodle, doo-doo, doohickey, dreck, dregs, drool, dung

fancy, fanfaronade, farce, fiddlededee, fiddle-faddle, fiddlesticks, fig, flapdoodle, flimflam, flotsam, flubdub, fluff, flumadiddle, flummery, flummox, folderol, foofaraw, foolishness, footle, foozle, fribble, frills, frippery, froth, fudge

gadget, gammon, gas, gewgaw, gibberish, gimcrack, glob, goop, guff, gunk

hambone, hanky-panky, hem and haw, hogwash, hokum, hooey, hoot, horseshit, hot air, humbug, humdinger, humdrum

idiocy, inanity

jabberwocky, jazz, jetsam, jiggery-pokery, jingle, jive, joke, jot, junk

kitsch, kludge, knavery

lampoonery, lip

malarkey, meshuge, mickey mouse, mishegaas, mockery, monkeyshine, muck, mush

nonsense, non sequitur

oddment

pap, piddle, poop, poppycock, puffery, pulp, put-on

quackery

raffle, raillery, rattletrap, razzmatazz, refuse, ribbing, rigmarole, rodomontade, roguery, rot, rubbish, Rube Goldberg

sap, sass, scat, scum, scuttlebutt, send-up, sham, shit, shlock, shtick, skullduggery, slag heap, slapdash, slobber, slop, slurry, slush, sob story, spoof, sport, stuff, swagger, swill

taradiddle, tittle, tomfoolery, tommyrot, tongue-in-cheek, tosh, trangam, trash, trickery, trifle, trinket, tripe, trivia, trumpery

vapors

waggery, wank, waste, whatnot, whigmaleerie, whim, whimsy, white elephant, whoopla, whopper, widget, wind, wisecrack

yuck

Drivel and Silly Talk

babble, badinage, bibble-babble, blabber, blather, blatter, blither

chatter, chitchat, chitter, chitter-chatter, claptrap, cliché

ditty, doggerel, drivel
footle, fribble, fustian
gab, gabble, gibber, gibber-gabber, gibberish, gibble-gabble, gobbledegook, gossip
jabber, japery
logorrhea
natter, nitpicking
palaver, persiflage, piffle, pleasantries, prattle, prittle-prattle
scribblings, silliness, small talk, squiggles, stultiloquence
tittle-tattle, twaddle, twiddle-twaddle, twitter
verbiage
yabber, yak, yakety-yak, yikety-yak

Fusses and Troubles

ado
bear, bickering, billingsgate, blooey, bobbery, boo-boo, boondoggle, bother, brannigan, brawl, broil, brouhaha, bug, bugaboo, bugbear, bummer
callithump, cattawumpus, collywobbles, commotion, conniption, crash
delirium, derring-do, disturbance, dither, donnybrook, doozie
feud, fit, fix, flap, flurry, fluster, foible, foul-up, fracas, fray, free-for-all, frenzy, furor, fuss
glitch
haggle, hash, hassle, hell, helter-skelter, high jinks, hoopla, hubble-bubble, hubbub, hullabaloo, hysteria
imbroglio
jam, jumble
katzenjammer, kibitzing, kink
lather, loggerheads, logjam

madhouse, maelstrom, megillah, melee, mess, mishmash, mix-up, moil, muss
no-no
peeve, pickle, pother, pratfall
quarrel
racket, rage, raise Cain, raise hell, rat's nest, rattrap, rhubarb, roughhouse, row, rowdydow, ruckus, ruffle, rumble, rumpus
scramble, scrap, scrape, screwup, seizure, set-to, shambles, shenanigan, shindig, shindy, short circuit, slam-bang, snafu, snarl, snit, spasm, spat, squabble, stew, stink
tamasha, tiff, tizzy, to-do, trouble, tsimmes, tsores, tumult, tussle, twitter
unrest, uproar
vendetta
whoop-de-do, whoopee, whoopla, wingding, wormwood, wrangle, wreckage

Confusion

absurdity, addlement, agitation, anarchy, ataxia
bafflement, bewilderment, blooper, bollix, boner, boo-boo, botch, bungle
cacophony, catawumpus, chaos, churn, clinker, cloud, cloudland, clutter, confusion
daze, disorder
embranglement, entropy
farblondjet, farmisht, farrago, fartumlt, flutter, fog, folly, fret
gaffe, gallimaufry, goof
haze, higgledy-piggledy, hocus-pocus, hodgepodge, hokey-pokey, hotchpotch
jumble, jungle
ludicrousness

maze, medley, mishmash, mist, mix-up, motley, muddle, mumbo jumbo
olio, olla podrida
pandemonium, pastiche, patchwork
ridiculousness, rummage
scattershot, shambles, slaphappy, swirl, switcheroo
tintamarre, tohubohu, topsy-turvy, Tweedledum and Tweedledee
unset
voodoo, vortex
waffling, whirligig, whirlpool, whirlwind

Nonsense Words and Cutesies

artsy-craftsy
bleep
caboodle, chichi, comfy, coo, cuckoo, cutesy
dingus, doodad, doodle, doohickey
gaga, gizmo, gussy up
harum-scarum, heebie-jeebies, ho-hum, hoity-toity, hugger-mugger, hunky-dory, hurly-burly, hurry-scurry
itsy-bitsy, itty-bitty
kit'n'caboodle, knickknack
lardy-dardy
mollycoddle
namby-pamby, newfangled, niminy-piminy
okey-dokey, oodles
palsy-walsy, peekaboo, pell-mell, p's and q's
raggle-taggle, razzle-dazzle, rinky-dink
screaming-meemies, shilly-shally, skimble-scamble
teensy, teensy-weensy, thingamabob, thingamajig, thingummy, tidbit, tutti-frutti
whatchamacallit, whatsis, whim-wham, whoosis, willies, willy-nilly, wishy-washy

CHAPTER TWENTY-ONE
FOREIGN EXPRESSIONS

LATIN WORDS AND PHRASES

See also: *Chap. 4: Medicine; Chap. 8: Kinship and Family Relations; Chap. 11: Law; Chap. 13: Philosophy; Chap. 14: Literature; Chap. 15: Theater; Chap. 18: Qualifiers and Connectives; Chap. 23: Time Perception; Chap. 25: Mythology and Folklore*

ab initio from the beginning
ab intra from within, from inside
ab origine from the origin or source
ab urbe condita lit. from the foundation of the city; Roman dating system; AUC
ad astra per aspera to the stars through difficulties
ad extremum to the extreme; at last
ad hoc lit. for this; for this purpose
ad hominem lit. to the man; argument directed at man's character, not his position
ad infinitum to infinity; endlessly
ad interim temporarily
ad libitum at one's pleasure, without restriction; ad lib.
ad nauseam to the point of nausea; repeatedly; endlessly
ad patres lit. to his fathers; deceased
adsum I am here, used in response to a roll call
ad valorem according to value, esp. tax thus imposed
ad verbum lit. to the word; worded exactly as the original
Agnus Dei lamb of God, i.e., Christ
alma mater lit. nourishing mother; one's academic institution
alter ego other self; best friend
alumna female graduate of academic institution
alumnus male graduate of academic institution
amor vincit omnia love conquers all
anno Domini in the year of the Lord
annuit coeptis God favored our undertaking
annus mirabilis notable, remarkable year or event
ante bellum before the war
ante meridiem a.m.; before midday
a posteriori from what comes after; cause deduced from effect
a priori from what comes before; deduced from what is known
ars gratia artis art for art's sake
ars longa, vita brevis art is long, life is short
ave be well; farewell
bona fide in good faith
carpe diem seize the day
caveat emptor let the buyer beware
caveat lector let the reader beware
cave canem beware of the dog
ceteris paribus other things being equal
circa ca; around or about, esp. of time
cogito, ergo sum I think, therefore I am
compos mentis of sound mind
con against, opposite of pro
cornucopia horn of plenty

corpus delicti body of the crime; evidence of crime
cui bono to whose advantage?; legal principle that responsibility for act lies with one gaining by it
cum with
cum grano salis with a grain of salt
cum laude with praise or honors
curriculum vitae lit. course of life; resumé
de facto from fact; in reality
Dei gratia by the grace of God
de jure by right
delirium tremens dt's; advanced, trembling alcoholic delirium
Deo volente God willing
de profundis from depths of despair
desideratum something much wanted or needed
deus ex machina lit. god from a machine; divine intervention
Dominus vobiscum the Lord be with you
dramatis personae cast of a drama
ecce homo lit. behold the man; Christ crowned with thorns
ecce signum lit. behold the sign; behold the proof
editio princeps first edition
emerita female who has served with honor
emeritus one who has served with honor
eo nomine by or under that name
e pluribus unum one out of many, inscribed on U.S. coins
ergo therefore
errare humanum est to err is human
erratum error
et alia and others
et cetera etc.; and the rest; and so on
et sequens and the following
et tu, Brute lit. and you, Brutus; even you are guilty of betrayal
ex cathedra lit. from the chair; with authority
excelsior higher; ever upward
exeunt they go out, esp. leave stage
exit he or she goes out, esp. leaves stage
ex libris from the books or library of
ex nihilo nihil fit from nothing comes nothing
ex officio by virtue of office
ex parte lit. from one side, used esp. of partisan legal communications
ex post facto derived from what was done after
ex tempore lit. out of time; spontaneously, without preparation
factotum person, esp. servant, who does various chores
fiat lux let there be light
gaudeamus igitur therefore let us rejoice
habeas corpus lit. you may have the body; esp. a writ used by defense lawyer to require formal pressing of charges against accused
hic jacet here lies, used on tombstones
homo sapiens lit. rational man; species of modern human beings
homunculus miniature man, thought to reside within humans or in spermatozoon by 16th-century scientists

horribile dictu horrible to relate
humanum est errare to err is human
ibidem ibid.; in the same place, used in bibliographies and footnotes
idem the same; something previously mentioned
id est i.e.; that is
ignoramus lit. we ignore; extremely ignorant person, know-nothing
illuminati persons possessing enlightenment
imprimatur lit. let it be printed; license to print; sanction or approval in general
in absentia in one's absence
incunabula lit. swaddling clothes; origin or earliest stages, esp. of printed books
in excelsis in the highest degree
in extremis at the moment of death
in flagrante delicto while the crime or act is occurring
infra dignitatem beneath one's dignity
in loco citato in loc. cit.; in the place cited, used in bibliographies and footnotes
in loco parentis in place of the parent
in medias res in the middle of things
in memoriam in memory of
in omnia paratus prepared for all things
in re in the matter of; regarding
in situ in place; in its natural or original position
in statu quo in the former or current state
inter alia among other things
inter nos between ourselves
inter se among themselves
in toto in all; entirely
in utero in the womb
in vino veritas in wine lies the truth
in vitro in glass, esp. a test tube
in vivo in that which is living
ipse dixit lit. he himself said it; statement made but not proved
ipso facto by or based on the fact itself
jacta alea est the die is cast
lapsus linguae slip of the tongue
lex talionis law of corresponding retaliation, as an eye for an eye
literati highly educated, literate persons
locus place
lusus naturae freak of nature
magna cum laude with great praise or honors
magnum opus one's great work
mala fide in bad faith
mandamus lit. we demand; writ commanding specific act or duty
margaritas ante porcos pearls before swine
materfamilias female head of household
mea culpa my fault
memento mori lit. remember you must die; reminder of death
mens rea lit. guilty mind; criminal intent
meum et tuum mine and thine
mirabile dictu wonderful to relate
mirabile visu wonderful to behold
mittimus lit. we send; warrant of commitment to prison
modus operandi method of operating

modus vivendi way of living

mons veneris lit. mound of Venus; round protuberance beneath female pubic hair

mutatis mutandis after changing what had to be changed

ne plus ultra lit. not more beyond; highest level of perfection

nolens volens whether unwilling or willing

noli me tangere touch me not

nolo contendere lit. I do not wish to contend; legal plea of no contest to charges

non compos mentis not of sound mind

non possumus lit. we cannot; statement of inability to do something

non sequitur it does not follow

nota bene note well; pay attention

obiter dictum passing remark without legal weight

omnia vincit amor love conquers all

opere citato op. cit.; in the work cited, used in bibliographies and footnotes

opus work, esp. musical composition

passim lit. here and there; repeated in many places

paterfamilias male head of household

paternoster our father

pax peace

pax vobiscum peace be with you

per annum per year; annually

per capita lit. per head; per person

per diem daily

per se in itself; inherently

persona non grata unwelcome person

post meridiem p.m.; after midday

post mortem after death, esp. an examination

postscriptum lit. written after; used to tag addition to a letter

prima facie at first view

primus inter pares first among equals

pro in favor of

pro bono publico for the public benefit

pro et contra for and against

pro forma lit. for form; done perfunctorily, as a formality

pro patria for one's country

pro rata proportionately according to an exact formula

pro tempore for the time being; temporarily

qua lit. who; in the capacity of; as

quid nunc what now?

quid pro quo something given for something; an exchange

quod erat demonstrandum Q.E.D.; which was to be demonstrated

quod erat faciendum which was to be done

quodlibet lit. whom it pleases; philosophical point for disputation

quod vide q.v.; which see, referring to something

quorum lit. of whom; minimum attendance at assembly or meeting

quo vadis where are you going?

rara avis lit. rare bird; anything unusual or rare

re regarding, short for in re

reductio ad absurdum leading logically to an absurd conclusion

redux brought back

regina queen

requiescat in pace rest in peace

res thing; matter; fact

res ipsa loquitur the thing speaks for itself

res publica popular affairs; commonwealth

rex king

rigor mortis stiffness of death

sanctum sanctorum lit. holy of holies; sacred place

saturnalia revelry or uproarious festivities

semper fidelis always faithful

sequitur it follows

sic thus, esp. to note a textual mistake

sic passim thus throughout, used of word or idea found throughout text

sic semper tyrannis thus always to tyrants

sic transit gloria mundi so passes the glory of the world

sine die indefinitely, with no set date in the future

sine qua non lit. not without which; indispensable thing or condition

status quo conditions as they are now

stet lit. it stands; let the original stand, used in proofreading

stupor mundi wonder of the world

subito immediately; suddenly, esp. as a musical direction

sub rosa lit. under the rose; in secret, covertly

sui generis of its own kind; one of a kind

summa cum laude with the highest praise or honors

summum bonum the highest or chief good

tabula rasa clean slate

tempus fugit time flies

terra firma solid ground; dry land

terra incognita unknown ground, uncharted territory

ultra vires exceeding legal authority

ut infra as below

ut supra as above

uxor wife

vade mecum lit. go with me; pocketbook carried for ready reference

veni, vidi, vici I came, I saw, I conquered

verbatim word for word

verbum sap enough said, inferring something left unsaid

versus lit. toward opposite; against or in competition with

via media middle way

vice versa conversely; the opposite way

vide see, used to direct or refer a reader elsewhere

videlicet lit. it is permitted to see; namely

viva voce lit. with the living voice; by word of mouth

vox populi lit. the voice of the people; popular opinion

vox populi, vox Dei the voice of the people is the voice of God

See also: Chap. 9: Foods; Cooking and Cuisine; Chap. 11: Titles of Rank; Chap. 15: Classical Music; Musical Instruments; Chap. 20: Greetings and Farewells; Chap. 21: Latin Words and Phrases; Yiddish Borrowings

FOREIGN WORDS AND PHRASES

French
Other Romance Languages
German, Greek, and Other Languages

Many foreign words have been naturalized in the English language to such a degree that they no longer have the feel or sound of a foreign expression. Such words as "debutante" and "séance" are not included in this section. Words like "voilà" and "déclassé," which sound French when used in English speech, and foreign phrases used as English idioms (such as "bon voyage"), form the bulk of this list.

French

à bas down with

à bientôt see you soon

adieu good-bye, farewell

affaire d'amour love affair

agent provocateur outside agitator who incites others to criminal acts or riot

aide de camp senior military officer or confidential adviser

à la carte lit. on the card; priced separately on the menu

à la mode in the fashion

amour love

ancien régime the old or former regime

à propos relative or pertaining to; fitting; to the purpose

au contraire on the contrary

au courant up to date

au fait well-versed, expert

au naturel in its natural state, esp. nude

au revoir good-bye, until we meet again

avant-garde the vanguard, esp. in the arts

à votre santé to your health

beau geste fine gesture, often for effect

beau idéal model or conception of excellence

beau monde fashionable society

beaux arts fine arts

belles lettres serious literature

bête noire pet peeve

billet-doux love note

bon appétit good appetite; enjoy your meal

bonhomie good nature

bonjour hello, good day

bon marché inexpensive

bon mot witty turn of phrase

bonne chance good luck

bon vivant person who lives well and enjoys socializing

bon voyage have a good journey

bric-à-brac trinkets, baubles

cachet sign or expression of approval; superior status

canaille common people, rabble

canard insult or hoax

ça ne fait rien no matter, it is not important

carte blanche unrestricted authority or access

cause célèbre notorious incident

c'est la guerre that's the way of war, used to express resignation

c'est la vie that's life

chacun à son goût each to his own taste

chef-d'oeuvre masterpiece

chez la famille at home with one's family

chez moi at my home

comme ci, comme ça so-so, neither one way nor the other

comme il faut proper, appropriate

contretemps unfortunate mishap or inconvenience

coup d'état usu. violent overthrow of government

coup de grâce final blow

crème de la crème very best or top level, usu. used of people

cul de sac dead end

danse macabre dance of death

déclassé reduced to or having low status

décolletage low-cut neckline on dress

déjà vu lit. already seen; illusory sense of having previously experienced something

demimonde group whose activities are ethically or legally questionable, esp. prostitutes

dénouement resolution or outcome, esp. of story

de rigueur strictly according to the rules

dernier cri the last word

déshabillé state of being poorly or carelessly dressed

désolé heartbroken, disconsolate

double entendre word or expression having two meanings in context

éclat flair, dash

élan vital creative force

embarras de richesses embarrassment of riches

éminence grise person wielding power in the background

en famille just among the family

enfant terrible irresponsible person, esp. incorrigible child

en garde on guard

en masse as a group

en passant in passing

entr'acte intermission

entrée main course of meal

entre nous just between us

esprit de corps spirit of and loyalty to one's group

fait accompli accomplished fact

faute de mieux for lack of something better

faux pas social error

femme fatale dangerous, enticing woman

fin de siècle end of the century, usu. decadent

gaucherie vulgarity, awkwardness

grande dame aristocratic elderly lady

habitué one who frequents some establishment

haute couture high fashion

haute cuisine elegant, often rich food

hauteur snobbish, aloof manner

haut monde high society

hors d'oeuvre appetizer

idée fixe obsession

je ne sais quoi lit. I do not know what; that indescribable something

joie de vivre exuberant high spirits

laissez faire policy of government in which affairs are allowed to run their own course

lèse majesté attack on ruler or established authority

l'état c'est moi I am the state

longueur tedious, dreary passages of language

ma chère my dear, said of females

madame married woman

mademoiselle unmarried woman

maison house

maître d'hôtel chief waiter

manqué having failed

Mardi Gras lit. fat Tuesday; pre-Lenten festival on Shrove Tuesday

mélange mixture

ménage à trois three-way relationship, usu. sexual

merci thank you

merci beaucoup thank you very much

métier vocation or calling

mon cher my dear, said of males

monsieur mister, sir

mot juste word that conveys precise meaning

n'est-ce pas? isn't it so? don't you agree?

noblesse oblige obligations of noble birth

nom de guerre lit. war name; pseudonym, stage name

nom de plume pen name

nouveau riche person who is newly rich

objet d'art work of art

objet trouvé found object, usu. of artistic value

papier-mâché paper and glue mixture used to form sculptures

par example for example

par excellence superior, preeminent

parti pris point of view determined in advance; prejudice

parvenu newcomer, upstart

passé out of date, no longer in fashion

petit bourgeois person who belongs to lower middle class, usu. made up of shopkeepers and clerks

pièce de résistance principal or showpiece object or event

pied-à-terre temporary or part-time residence

plat du jour featured dish of the day

plus ça change, plus c'est la même chose the more things change, the more they remain the same

potpourri medley, usu. of scented herbs and spices

prix fixe set price

protégé person under's one care or tutelage

provocateur one who challenges or agitates others

raconteur storyteller

raison d'être reason for being

recherché esoteric, rare; mannered, affected

répondez s'il vous plaît please respond

risqué indelicate or suggestive

roman à clef novel depicting historical figures under fictional names

sacré bleu exclamation meaning good God

sang-froid composure, self-possession

sans souci without concern or worry

savoir-faire knowledge of what to do or say, esp. in social situation

s'il vous plaît please

soi-disant so-called

son et lumière sound and light show

succès d'estime critical success, esp. for work of art

table d'hôte set meal served at fixed time and place

tant mieux so much the better

tant pis so much the worse

tête-à-tête intimate, private conversation

touché lit. touched; signifying strike in fencing or comment that is on the mark

tour de force display of power, skill, or virtuosity

tout de suite immediately

tout le monde everyone

trompe l'oeil fooling the eye, esp. illusion of perspective in painting

vis-à-vis regarding, relating to

voilà there it is, look at that, it is so

volte-face reversal, turnabout

Other Romance Languages

a cappella *Italian.* sung without instrumental accompaniment

adios *Spanish.* good-bye

aficionado *Spanish.* fan, enthusiast

al dente *Italian.* lit. to the tooth; firm to the bite, said esp. of food

alfresco *Italian.* in the open air

amigo *Spanish.* friend

arrivederci *Italian.* good-bye, until we meet again

auto-da-fé *Portuguese.* lit. act of faith; execution of condemned heretics after public declaration of judgment

bambino *Italian.* baby, child

basta *Italian.* enough! stop it!

bodega *Spanish.* wineshop; small market

buenas dias *Spanish.* hello, good day

caballero *Spanish.* horseman, gentleman, cavalier

campesino *Spanish.* farmer, peasant

cantina *Spanish.* bar, café

caramba *Spanish.* exclamation of amazement, anger, or dismay

che sarà sarà *Italian.* what will be, will be

ciao *Italian.* good-bye, see you later

cognoscenti *Italian.* those in the know, esp. intellectuals

compañero *Spanish.* male companion or partner
con mucho gusto *Spanish.* with great pleasure
conquistador *Spanish.* conqueror
desperado *Spanish.* bold, reckless bandit or outlaw
diva *Italian.* exalted female singer
dolce far niente *Italian.* sweet inactivity
dolce vita *Italian.* the good life
gaucho *Spanish.* cowboy, mounted herdsman
gracias *Spanish.* thank you
hacienda *Spanish.* ranch
hombre *Spanish.* man, fellow
inamorata *Italian.* female sweetheart or lover
incognito *Italian.* anonymously or in disguise
incommunicado *Spanish.* isolated from any contact with others
junta *Spanish.* usu. military council serving as government
machismo *Spanish.* strong sense of masculinity and virility
maestro *Italian.* master, esp. of music
magnifico *Italian.* great man
mañana *Spanish.* tomorrow
mas o menos *Spanish.* more or less
mucho *Spanish.* much
olé *Spanish.* shout of approval or encouragement
padre *Spanish.* father, esp. clergyman
peccadillo *Spanish.* minor offense, venial sin
pentimento *Italian.* appearance of earlier stages or images, esp. in painting
per favore *Italian.* please
por favor *Spanish.* please
posada *Spanish.* inn
prego *Italian.* please
presto *Italian.* quickly, right away
prima donna *Italian.* principal female, leading lady
pronto *Spanish.* quickly, right away
que pasa? *Spanish.* what's happening?
que será será *Spanish.* whatever will be will be
quién sabe? *Spanish.* who knows?
salud *Spanish.* to your health
señor *Spanish.* sir, mister
señora *Spanish.* married woman
señorita *Spanish.* unmarried woman
siesta *Spanish.* afternoon nap or rest
sotto voce *Italian.* softly, under one's voice
toro *Spanish.* bull
vamos *Spanish.* let's go
vaya con Dios *Spanish.* God be with you
vertù *Italian.* love of arts and fine things
virtuoso *Italian.* person skilled in one field, esp. a performer
viva *Spanish.* exclamation of approval

German, Greek, and Other Languages

acedia *Greek.* listlessness, sloth
Achtung *German.* attention
agape *Greek.* non-erotic love
ahimsa *Hindi.* doctrine of nonviolence
aloha *Hawaiian.* hello or good-bye
Angst *German.* anxiety

anomie *Greek.* lawlessness and loss of purpose leading to despair
apocrypha *Greek.* secret, hidden things, esp. in texts
ataxia *Greek.* lack of control or order
auf Wiedersehen *German.* good-bye, until we meet again
babushka *Russian.* grandmother, old woman; head scarf
banzai *Japanese.* lit. 10,000 years; cry of victory or salute
Blitzkrieg *German.* sudden, violent attack
bwana *Swahili.* sir, master, father
catharsis *Greek.* cleansing or purification, esp. from guilt through drama or art
charisma *Greek.* capacity to inspire and lead others
cosmos *Greek.* orderly universe
danke schön *German.* thank you very much
ding hao *Chinese.* very good, excellent
Doppelgänger *German.* phantom double
do svidaniya *Russian.* good-bye, until we meet again
Dummkopf *German.* dummy, blockhead
ersatz *German.* fake, imitation
eureka *Greek.* I've found it; it is real or true
Frau *German.* married woman
Fräulein *German.* unmarried woman
geisha *Japanese.* young woman trained as companion for men
Gemütlichkeit *German.* good-natured, friendly cordiality
Gestalt *German.* unified whole that cannot be inferred from its component parts
Gesundheit *German.* good health to you, used esp. after someone sneezes
glasnost *Russian.* openness, esp. social and political
gnothi seauton *Greek.* know thyself
gulag *Russian.* forced-labor camp
guru *Hindi.* venerable teacher
halcyon *Greek.* lit. kingfisher; calm, peaceful
hara-kiri *Japanese.* ritual suicide by disembowelment
Hausfrau *German.* housewife
hoi polloi *Greek.* common people
hubris *Greek.* excessive pride and arrogance
iota *Greek.* atom; small amount
jawohl *German.* yes, definitely
kamikaze *Japanese.* person on a suicide mission, orig. a pilot; any reckless person
kaputt *German.* finished, ruined, broken
kismet *Turkish.* fate
Kitsch *German.* vulgar, trashy, valueless work
kowtow *Chinese.* fawn, bow low
kudos *Greek.* fame, glory, adulation
l'chaim *Hebrew.* to your health
Lebensraum *German.* additional room needed for expansion
logos *Greek.* rational principle that governs the universe
Lumpenproletariat *German.* vagrants, criminals, and rabble without class consciousness

mazel tov *Hebrew.* congratulations
nabob *Hindi.* man of wealth and power
nirvana *Sanskrit.* extinction of desire and achievement of perfect holiness
pariah *Hindi.* outcast
perestroika *Russian.* policy of Soviet economic and political reform
pogrom *Russian.* massacre or persecution
pundit *Hindi.* authoritative, scholarly commentator
Putsch *German.* insurrection
Rathskeller *German.* basement tavern
sahib *Arabic.* master
salaam *Arabic.* peace
samurai *Japanese.* member of feudal warrior caste
sayonara *Japanese.* good-bye, farewell
Schadenfreude *German.* pleasure derived from another's misfortune
shalom *Hebrew.* peace
skoal *Swedish.* to your health
stasis *Greek.* cessation of movement or circulation
Sturm und Drang *German.* storm and stress
swami *Sanskrit.* master, esp. religious teacher
taboo *Polynesian.* prohibited act
tovarishch *Russian.* comrade
Übermensch *German.* superman
uhuru *Swahili.* freedom
ukase *Russian.* command or edict
verboten *German.* forbidden
Wanderjahr *German.* year of travel
Wanderlust *German.* desire to travel
Weltanschauung *German.* comprehensive world view or outlook
Weltgeist *German.* spirit of the times
Weltschmerz *German.* world-weary sorrow
Wunderkind *German.* prodigy
yogi *Sanskrit.* practitioner of yoga
Zeitgeist *German.* spirit of the time

YIDDISH BORROWINGS

See also: *Chap. 8: Kinship and Family Relations; Chap. 20: Insults, Slurs, and Epithets; Terms of Endearment and Respect; Nonsense, Confusion, and Trouble; Chap. 22: Sex, Love, and Romance*

baleboste efficient, competent housewife or hostess
beheyme cow, or big dummy, used esp. of women
bube grandmother
bubele little bube; dear, sweetie
bubkes lit. beans; nothing
chazerei lit. pig food; junk, unpalatable stuff
chutzpah gall, nerve, or brashness
drek *Vulgar.* shit, literally or figuratively
farblondzhet (*adj*) wandering aimlessly; confused or out of it
farmisht (*adj*) confused, mixed up
farshtunkener stinking, nasty one
fartumlt (*adj*) disoriented, confused
feigel lit. bird; *Slang.* homosexual male

futz (*vb*) *Vulgar.* screw around; mess with

gelt money

gevalt lit. violence, force; outcry of alarm, as in "oy gevalt"

golem robot, lifelike creature; clay icon

goy gentile, non-Jew

goyim gentiles, non-Jews

goyish (*adj*) non-Jewlike

haimish (*adj*) homey, cozy

kibitz (*vb*) meddle, offer gratuitous advice

kishke intestine, gut; stuffed derma

kish meyn tokhes *Vulgar.* kiss my ass

klutz dullard; clumsy person

knish lit. stuffed dumpling; *Vulgar slang.* vagina

kosher (*adj*) fit to eat under Jewish dietary laws; proper, legitimate

kreplach lit. triangular dumplings; *Slang.* nothing

kvell be delighted

kvetch (*vb*) complain, whine, nag; (*n*) crotchety person

luftmensch person whose head is in the clouds, dreamer

macher wheeler-dealer, big shot

mamzer lit. illegitimate child; despicable individual; *Slang.* con man

maven expert, connoisseur

megillah long story, rigmarole

mensch admirable human being, person of dignity and integrity

meshugas insanity, nonsense

meshuge (*adj*) crazy, mad, or nuts

meshugene crazy person

mishpoche family, clan

nakhes good feeling, pride and joy; pleasure

nebbish nobody, loser, drip, or hapless one

nogoodnik bum to be avoided at all cost

noodge (*vb*) nag, pick at; (*n*) nagger, badgerer

nosh (*vb*) snack, nibble, or eat a bit; (*n*) tidbit or snack

nosher one who nibbles constantly

nu (*interj*) well? so? so what?

nudnik talkative bore; dummy

ongeblozn (*adj*) puffed up, conceited, or arrogant

oy (*interj*) oh!

parnose livelihood

patsh slap

patshke (*vb*) fiddle about lazily

pisher little squirt; someone of no consequence

plotz (*vb*) burst, explode

punim face

pupik bellybutton

putz *Vulgar.* lit. penis; jerk

schmooze (*vb*) have a heart-to-heart talk; chitchat or gab with one's associates

shadchen marriage broker, matchmaker

shegetz non-Jewish boy or young man; Jewish boy who fails to observe religious practices

shiksa non-Jewish woman, esp. girl or young woman

shlemazel born loser, someone always unlucky

shlemiel fool, social misfit, or failure; awkward person

shlep (*vb*) drag, haul around; trudge; (*n*) slob, bum

shlock shoddy, poorly crafted items

shlong *Vulgar.* penis

shlump slob, drip

shmaltz lit. rendered chicken fat; mawkish oversentimentality, maudlin mush

shmate rag, cheap dress; shoddy garment or object

shmeer (*vb*) bribe, grease the palm of; (*n*) complete array of things

shmegege buffoon, idiot

shmendrik weak, ineffectual person

shmo boob, dummy

shmuck *Vulgar.* lit. penis; bad person, idiot, fool, or bastard

shmutz garbage, dirt

shnook pathetic but lovable fool, easy mark, or sucker

shnorrer beggar, panhandler; miser, wheedler, or cheapskate

shnoz nose, esp. large one

shpritz (*vb*) lit. spray; inject life into, poke fun at

shtick verbal bit, esp. comic routine; one's special interest or talent

shtunk something that smells unpleasant; louse

shtup (*vb*) stuff, push; *Vulgar.* have sex with

shvitzer someone who sweats a lot; braggart

tchatchkes knickknacks, trinkets

tokhes rear end, buttocks; tush

tsimes fuss, big to-do, or brouhaha

tsores worries, woes, or afflictions

tush toches

vey pain, as in "oy vey"

vitz joke, wisecrack

yenta gossipy person, busybody

yid derogatory term for a Jew

zaftig (*adj*) juicy, plump; voluptuous, sexy

zhlub someone insensitive and boorish

PART SEVEN

THE HUMAN CONDITION

CHAPTER TWENTY-TWO
CHARACTER AND BEHAVIOR

PERSONALITY AND BEHAVIOR

Appealing/Unappealing
  Appealing, Elegant, Neat, Rich, or Fancy
  Unappealing, Shabby, Messy, Poor, or Clumsy
Warm/Cold
  Warm, Friendly, Sensitive, or Loving
  Cold, Unfriendly, Irritable, or Cruel
Extroverted/Introverted
  Extroverted, Outgoing, Outspoken, or
    Dramatic
  Introverted, Reserved, Isolated, or Mysterious
Dominant/Submissive
  Dominant, Stubborn, Proud, or Confident
  Submissive, Uncertain, or Tentative
Strong/Weak
  Strong, Bold, or Tough
  Weak, Fearful, or Anxious
Active/Inert
  Active, Lively, Awake, or Limber
  Inert, Lazy, Tired, or Insensate
Happy/Sad
  Happy, Playful, Optimistic, or Elated
  Sad, Serious, Pessimistic, or Discontented
Calm/Angry
  Calm, Gentle, or Easygoing
  Angry, Emotional, Aggressive, or Passionate
Moderate/Excessive
  Moderate, Sane, Conservative, or
    Old-Fashioned
  Excessive, Mad, Insane, or Radical
Proper/Vulgar
  Proper, Courteous, Refined, or Puritanical
  Vulgar, Rude, Degenerate, or Wild
Intelligent/Stupid
  Intelligent, Informed, Clever, or Articulate
  Stupid, Ignorant, or Confused
Special/Ordinary
  Special, Bright, Skillful, or Unusual
  Ordinary, Dull, Plain, or Banal
Wise/Foolish
  Wise, Mature, or Experienced
  Foolish, Immature, Bigoted, or Trivial
Good/Bad
  Good, Sincere, Honest, or Just
  Bad, False, Evil, Insincere, or Dishonest
Giving/Demanding
  Giving, Trusting, Innocent, or Generous
  Demanding, Critical, Calculating, or Selfish
Helpful/Troublesome
  Helpful, Positive, Responsible, or Nice
  Troublesome, Negative, Irresponsible, or
    Unpleasant

See also: Chap. 1: Physical Appearance

Nearly 4000 adjectives describing human personality and behavior have been grouped into sixteen pairs of opposites, such as Happy/Sad. Each pair is broken down into two undefined lists of virtual synonyms and words with casually related meanings. The parameters for these lists are defined by the four or five adjectives forming the section title. While the meanings of the terms in each list vary, the category is intended to serve as a reminder of similar but slightly different and familiar words and to help provide variety in the adjectives one might use in describing a person. While this system of categorizing adjectives is by no means scientific, and is not based on accepted psychological standards, it is hoped that the associations and divisions of these words will prove stimulating and useful to readers and writers, especially those engaged in creative writing.

Appealing/Unappealing

APPEALING, ELEGANT, NEAT, RICH, OR FANCY

adorable, affluent, alluring, appealing, aristocratic, arresting, attractive
beautiful, becoming, beguiling, bewitching, breathtaking
caparisoned, captivating, charismatic, charming, chic, Circean, classy, clean, clubby, couth, crisp, cuddly
dandy, dapper, dashing, dazzling, dear, debonair, decorous, desirable, devastating, dignified
elegant, enchanting, engaging, enthralling, enticing, entrancing, exquisite
fancy, fashionable, fetching, finished, flowery, flush
galluptious, glamorous, glorious, graceful, gracious
handsome, healthy, highborn, hygienic
immaculate, impeccable, imperial, ingratiating, intoxicating, inviting, irresistible
kempt, kingly
lardy-dardy, lavish, lush, luxuriant, luxurious
magnetic, mellifluous, mod, modish
natty, neat, nifty, nobby, nubile
opulent, ornate
patrician, photogenic, picturesque, plush, plushy, polished, posh, prepossessing, pretty, princely, privileged, prosperous
redolent, refined, regal, resplendent, rich, ritzy, royal
sanitary, sartorial, scrumptious, seductive, select, sexy, silk-stocking, sleek, slick, smart, smooth, snazzy, soigné, sophisticated, spanking, spellbinding, spiffy, splashy, splendid, spotless, spruce, stainless, stately, sterling, striking, stunning, stylish, suave, sumptuous, surefooted, sure-handed, svelte, swank, swanky, swell, swish
tantalizing, tasty, tidy, trendy, trig, trim
ultrachic, ultramodern, ultrarich
voguish
wealthy, well, well-groomed, well-heeled, well-off, winning, winsome
yummy

UNAPPEALING, SHABBY, MESSY, POOR, OR CLUMSY

abysmal, accident-prone, all thumbs, angular, askew, awkward, awry
blowsy
cadaverous, chunderous, clumsy, contaminated, crumpled
déclassé, decrepit, derelict, destitute, dingy, disfigured, disgusting, dowdy, down-and-out, drippy, dumpy
fiddle-footed, filthy, frightful, frowzy, funky
gaudy, gawky, geeky, ghastly, gnarly, graceless, grisly, grotesque, gruesome
hard-up, heavy-footed, hideous, homely, horrid, horrific
icky, imperfect, impoverished, impure, incondite, incongruous, indecorous, indigent, inelegant, infelicitous, insolvent
lowborn, lowly
macabre, malodorous, meretricious, messy, monstrous
odious, oily, oleaginous, overdressed
penniless, penurious, plain, poor, putrescent, putrid
ragged, ragtag, rancid, ratty, repellent, repugnant, repulsive, revolting, rough, rugged
scabrous, scandalous, scraggly, scummy, scuzzy, seedy, shabby, shaggy, shocking, shoddy, sickening, simian, slatternly, slavering, sleazy, slimy, slobbery, sloppy, slovenly, slummy, sordid, squalid, stinky, subhuman
tacky, tatty, tawdry, tenth-rate, tousled
ugly, ulcerous, unappealing, unbecoming, unclean, uncoordinated, uncouth, underprivileged, undesirable, undignified, unfashionable, unfit, unhandy, unhealthy, unkempt, unpolished, unsanitary, unsavory, unsightly, untidy, unvarnished, unwashed
weather-beaten, woolly
yucky

Warm/Cold

WARM, FRIENDLY, SENSITIVE, OR LOVING

adoring, affable, affectionate, agreeable, amatory, amenable, amiable, amicable, amorous, appreciative, approachable, ardent, avuncular
chummy, companionable, compassionate, congenial, convivial, cordial
devoted, disarming
earthy, empathic
familiar, favorable, fond, forgiving, friendly
genial, good-humored, good-natured, gracious, gregarious
heartwarming, hearty, hospitable
ingratiating, intimate
kind, kindhearted, kindly, kindred
largehearted, likable, lovable, loving
merciful
neighborly
open, open-hearted
pally, palsy-walsy, personable
reverent, romantic
sensitive, sensual, sentimental, sociable, soft, soft-hearted, summery, sympathetic
tender, tender-hearted, touching
warm, warm-hearted, well-disposed, worshipful

COLD, UNFRIENDLY, IRRITABLE, OR CRUEL

abrupt, alien, aloof, arctic, arid, asexual, ashen, astringent, atrabilious, austere
bad-tempered, bilious, bitter, bleak, bloody, blunt, brusque, brutal
callous, cantankerous, catty, cheap, chilly, chintzy, chippy, churlish, closed, cold, cold-blooded, cold-hearted, contemptuous, crabby, cranky, cross, crotchety, cruel, crusty, cryptic, curmudgeonly, cursed, curt, cussed, cutthroat, cynical

dispassionate, distant, domineering, dour, Draconian, dry, dyspeptic
egocentric, empty, envious
forbidding, formidable, freezing, frigid, frosty
gelid, glacial, glowering, gray, greedy, grouchy, grudging, gruff, grumpy
hardened, hardhearted, hateful, haughty, heartless, hollow, huffish, humiliating
icy, ignoble, ill-humored, ill-natured, ill-tempered, impersonal, inconsiderate, indifferent, inhospitable, insensitive, insulting, insusceptible, intolerant, inured, irreconcilable, irritable
jealous
liverish
matter-of-fact, mean, mechanical, merciless, misanthropic, miserly
nasty, niggardly, nippy
ornery
parched, parsimonious, peckish, peevish, penurious, persnickety, petty, piercing, pinchbeck, pitiless, Procrustean, psychopathic
raw, reactionary, remorseless, remote, ruthless
sadistic, salty, self-serving, sere, sexless, sharp-tongued, shrewish, snappish, snarly, snippety, snippy, snitty, snotty, sour, spiteful, spleenful, splenetic, stark, steely, stern, stiff, stingy, stoical, stony, strict, surly, suspicious
tasty, tetchy, thick-skinned, tight, tight-fisted, touchy, troglodytic, truculent, tyrannical
uncharitable, uncommunicative, uncongenial, unfeeling, unforgiving, unfriendly, ungrateful, unkind, unkindly, unmerciful, unmoved, unsympathetic
vengeful, venomous, vexatious, vicious, vitriolic
waspish, wintry, withholding, wizened, wooden, wrongheaded

Extroverted/Introverted

EXTROVERTED, OUTGOING, OUTSPOKEN, OR DRAMATIC

ambitious, assertive, atwitter
blatant, bloviating, blustering, boisterous, bold, bombastic, brash, brazen, breathy
chatty, choleric
defiant, dramatic
emphatic, evangelical, excited, exhibitionistic, expansive, expressive, extemporaneous, extroverted, exuberant
flagrant, flamboyant, flashy, flirtatious, forward, freewheeling
garrulous, grandiloquent, gregarious, gushy
high-profile, histrionic
immodest, indiscreet, intrusive
jabbering
lippy, logorrheic, loquacious, loud, loudmouthed
madcap, malapert, meteoric, militant, multiloquious
noisy
obstreperous, obtrusive, orotund, outgoing, outspoken, overbearing, overt, overweening
pert, petulant, presumptuous, prolix, protrusive, protuberant, public, pugnacious, pushy
rah-rah, raucous, red-hot, rousing
shrill, sonorous, spectacular, splashy, stagestruck, stagy, stentorian, strident, stridulous, swinging, switched-on
talkative, theatrical, throaty, turgid
uninhibited, unreserved, unselfconscious, uproarious

verbose, visible, vitriolic, vocal, vociferous, voluble
wordy

INTROVERTED, RESERVED, ISOLATED, OR MYSTERIOUS

abashed, alien, alienated, alone, aloof, anonymous, antisocial, ascetic, asocial, austere, autonomous, awkward
bashful
chary, clannish, claustral, cloistered, cloistral, concealed, confidential, covert, coy, crafty
delitescent, detached, discreet, distant
elliptical, elusive, enigmatic, eremitic, estranged, evasive
ghostly, guarded
hermitic,
incommunicado, indirect, inhibited, inner-directed, inscrutable, insular, introspective, introverted, invisible, inward, isolated
laconic, latent, lone, lonely, low-profile
misty, misunderstood, modest, monastic, monkish, mum, mute, mysterious
nebulous, nonverbal
oblique, obscure, occult
paradoxical, passive, phantom, private
quiescent, quiet
reclusive, reluctant, remote, repressed, reserved, restrained, reticent, retiring
secluded, secretive, self-absorbed, self-conscious, self-effacing, sensitive, sequestered, shadowy, shamefaced, sheepish, short-spoken, shy, silent, smoky, sneaky, soft-spoken, solitary, solo, spectral, sphinxlike, spooky, standoffish, stay-at-home, stealthy, still, stolid, strange, sub rosa, subterranean, surreptitious, suspicious
taciturn, tactful, tight-lipped, tiptoe
ultracool, unapproachable, unassertive, unassuming, unclear, uncommunicative, undemonstrative, understated, unexpressive, unfathomable, unobtrusive, unsociable
vanishing, veiled, voiceless
wary, watchful, wistful, withdrawn, wordless, wraithlike
xenophobic

Dominant/Submissive

DOMINANT, STUBBORN, PROUD, OR CONFIDENT

abusive, adamant, ascendant, assuming, assured, authoritative, autocratic
bossy, bullheaded, bumptious
certain, cock-a-hoop, cocksure, cocky, commanding, compelling, conclusive, confident, controlling, contumacious
decisive, determined, direct, directed, dogged, dogmatic, dominant, domineering, do-or-die
egoistic, egotistic, emphatic, enduring, entitled, entrenched
firm, fixed, focused, forceful, formidable
grandiose
hard-ass, hard-bitten, hard-boiled, hard-edged, hardened, hardheaded, headstrong, hellbent, high and mighty, high-flown, high-handed, high-powered
immovable, impenetrable, imperative, imperious, impervious, implacable, impregnable, independent, indestructible, indomitable, inexorable, inflated, inflexible, insistent, insuperable, intent, intimidating, intractable,

intransigent, invincible, invulnerable, ironbound, ironclad, irresistible
lordly
macho, magisterial, magistral, messianic, mighty, militaristic, mulish
obdurate, obstinate, omnipotent, one-sided, opinionated, orgulous, orotund, ossified, overweening, overwhelming
persistent, persuasive, pertinacious, pervicacious, pigheaded, poised, portentous, possessive, predominant, preponderant, presumptuous, prideful, prodigious, proprietary, proud, purposeful, pushy
ramrod, recalcitrant, redoubtable, refractory, relentless, renitent, resolute, rigid
secure, self-assured, self-confident, self-important, self-involved, self-possessed, self-righteous, self-satisfied, self-seeking, single-minded, smug, stiff, strident, strong-minded, strong-willed, stubborn, sure, swaggering, swashbuckling, swellheaded
take-charge, tenacious, territorial, thick-skinned, turgid
unassailable, unbending, undaunted, unfaltering, unflagging, unflinching, unreceptive, unregenerate, unrelenting, unstinting, unstoppable, unswerving, unwary, unwieldy, unwilling, unyielding
vain, vainglorious, vehement, volitive
whole hog, willful

SUBMISSIVE, UNCERTAIN, OR TENTATIVE

accommodating, acquiescent, adaptable, ambivalent, apologetic, apprehensive, assailable, awkward
balky
caducous, chameleonic, changeable, chary, chivvied, compliant, concessive, conciliatory, culpable, cursory
dainty, deferential, dependent, diffident, doubtful, downtrodden, dubious, ductile
effeminate, equivocal, exposed
fatalistic, fawning, flexible, flimsy
halfhearted, halting, haphazard, harmless, hesitant, humiliated
ill at ease, impalpable, inconclusive, inconstant, incredulous, indecisive, indirect, inoffensive, insecure, irresolute
labile, lambent, loath, lost
malleable, masochistic, mealy-mouthed, meek, mousy, mutable
noncommittal, nude
obedient, obeisant, obsequious
penitent, phlegmatic, plastic, pliable, pliant, prostrate, protean
qualmish, queasy, questioning, quizzical
receptive, reconciled, reluctant, repentant, reserved, resigned, respectful
self-abnegating, self-denying, sequacious, serviceable, servile, shackled, slavish, solicitous, squishy, subdued, submissive, subservient, suggestible, supple, suppliant, susceptible, sycophantic
tentative, tenuous, thin-skinned, timid, tongue-tied, tractable, tremulous
unresisting
vacillating, vague, vulnerable
wavering, wishy-washy
yielding

Strong/Weak

STRONG, BOLD, OR TOUGH

able-bodied, adventuresome, adventurous,
    all-powerful, audacious
ballsy, belligerent, bluff, blunt, bold, brash, brave,
    brawny, burly
clutch, courageous
daring, dauntless, decisive, doughty, durable
effective
fearless, firm, flinty, forbidding, formidable,
    full-blooded
gritty, gutsy, gutty
hale, hard-ass, hardball, hard-nosed, hardy,
    heavy, hell-for-leather, hoydenish
indestructible, inexhaustible, intrepid
lionhearted, lusty
manly, massive, mettlesome, mighty, militant,
    motivated, muscular
nervy
oppressive
physical, plucky, potent, powerful
ready, red-blooded, reliant, resilient, robust,
    rocky, rough, rugged, ruthless
scrappy, self-made, self-reliant, self-sufficient,
    self-supporting, self-sustaining, skookum, solid,
    spartan, spirited, spunky, stalwart, staunch,
    steadfast, steely, stout, stout-hearted, strapping,
    street-smart, streetwise, strong, sturdy,
    substantial
thriving, tough, truculent
unblinking
valiant, valorous, venturesome
warlike
yeomanly

WEAK, FEARFUL, OR ANXIOUS

abashed, afraid, ailing, alarmed, anemic, anxious,
    apprehensive, ashamed, asthmatic
bedridden, bloodless, brittle
candy-ass, clinging, consumptive, cowardly,
    craven, creaky, cringing
debilitated, decrepit, delicate, desperate, dilute,
    disconcerted, doddering
effete
faint, fainthearted, faltering, fearful, feckless,
    feeble, fidgety, fitful, flimsy, fragile, frail,
    frangible, frightened, futile
gimpy, gutless
hagridden, helpless, horrified, horror-struck,
    humbled, humiliated, hung-up
ill, impotent, impoverished, impuissant,
    incapacitated, ineffective, inept, infirm,
    insecure, insufficient
jittery
lame, lily-livered, limp, limp-wristed
mawkish, meager, milk-livered, mortified
namby-pamby, needy, nervous, neurotic
oversensitive, overwhelmed
pale, pallid, paltry, panicked, panic-stricken,
    paranoid, pathetic, pavid, petrified, phthisic,
    pitiful, plaintive, poor-spirited, punchless, puny,
    pusillanimous
recreant
scared, shaky, sheepish, short-winded, shrinking,
    sickly, simpering, skimpy, skittish, slight,
    sniveling, snuffling, spasmodic, spineless,
    spooked, squeamish, stressed, stressed-out,
    sulky

terrified, timid, timorous, toothless, tottering,
    trapped, trembling, tremulous
uncomfortable, undernourished, uneasy, unnerved,
    unwell, uptight
vertiginous
wan, wary, washed-out, washy, watery, weak,
    weakhearted, weak-kneed, wet, whining, whiny,
    white, white-livered, wimpy, wispy, wormy
yellow

Active/Inert

ACTIVE, LIVELY, AWAKE, OR LIMBER

acrobatic, active, adroit, agile, alert, alive,
    ambulatory, athletic, attentive, avid, awake
bouncy, breezy, bright-eyed, brisk, bubbly,
    bustling, busy, buxom
catalytic, chipper, crisp, curious
deft, diligent, dynamic
eager, effervescent, elusive, energetic, energized,
    enterprising, errant, exhilarated, exuberant
fecund, feisty, fervent, fleet, fleet-footed, fluent,
    fluid, footloose, free, fresh, frisky, frolicsome
galvanic, go-go, gymnastic
hale, high-spirited, high-strung, hurried
industrious, interested, intrigued, irrepressible,
    itinerant
jaunty, jingly
kinetic
lambent, liberated, light, limber, lissome, lithe,
    lively, lyric
mercurial, mobile, motile
nimble, nomadic
operose, outdoorsy
peppy, peripatetic, perky, productive, prolific,
    prompt
quick, quicksilver
rambunctious, rapid, raring to go, ready, reborn,
    renascent
saltatory, sassy, saucy, sentient, sinuous, skittish,
    snappy, speedy, spirited, sprightly, springy,
    spruce, spry, strenuous, supple, swift,
    switched-on, sylphlike
tireless
unencumbered, up-and-coming
vibrant, vigilant, vigorous, vital, vivacious, volant,
    volatile
wakeful, whippy, wide-awake, wide-eyed, willowy
zappy, zestful, zesty, zingy, zippy

INERT, LAZY, TIRED, OR INSENSATE

abstracted, aged, apathetic, asleep, atrophied
barren, beat, benumbed, blank, blasé, bored,
    bovine, bushed
cadaverous, comatose, complacent
dazed, dead, delitescent, dilatory, disinterested,
    docile, doltish, dopey, dormant, draggy,
    dreamy, drooping, droopy, drowsy, drugged,
    dull, dulled
emotionless, empty, enervated, exhausted
fallow, fatigued, flat, floppy
glassy, glassy-eyed, groggy
haggard, hazy, hoary, hypnotic, hypnotized
idle, immobile, impassive, impervious, inactive,
    inanimate, inattentive, incapacitated,
    indifferent, indolent, inert, insensate, insipid
jaded
kaput
lackadaisical, languid, languorous, late, latent,

lazy, leaden, lethargic, lifeless, listless, logy,
    lymphatic
malingering, moribund, mute
numb
otiose, overripe
paralyzed, passive, phlegmatic, placid,
    pococurante, poky, porcine, punch-drunk, punchy
rusty
sagging, sapped, satiated, sedentary,
    semicomatose, semiconscious, senseless,
    shiftless, shot, slack, sleepy, slothful, slow,
    sluggish, sodden, somnolent, spaced-out, spent,
    spiritless, stagnant, static, stiff, stuporous,
    supine
tardy, tepid, tired, torpid, truant
uninterested, unmindful, unmotivated,
    unresponsive
vacant, vacuous
weary, wizened, world-weary, worn-out
yawning
zomboid, zonked

Happy/Sad

HAPPY, PLAYFUL, OPTIMISTIC, OR ELATED

agrin, airy, amazed, amused, amusing, astonished
beatific, bemused, blissful, blithe, bonhomous,
    buoyant
carefree, cavalier, cheerful, cheery, chipper,
    content, contented, convivial
delighted, devil-may-care, droll
ebullient, ecstatic, elated, enchanted, enraptured,
    enthusiastic, espiègle, euphoric, expectant,
    exuberant, exultant
fanciful, fancy-free, festive, flying, frolicsome,
    fulfilled, fun-loving, funny
gamesome, gay, gemütlich, giddy, giggly, glad,
    gleeful, glowing
happy, happy-go-lucky, harmonious, hilarious,
    hopeful, humorous
impish, infectious
jaunty, jocose, jocular, jocund, jolly, jovial, joyful,
    joyous, jubilant
laughing, lighthearted, lilting, ludic
merry, mirthful, mischievous
optimistic, overjoyed
perky, playful, pleased, psyched, puckish
radiant, rapturous, ravished, relieved, rhapsodic,
    riant, risible, roguish, roseate, rosy
sanguine, sated, satisfied, silly, sky-high, spirited,
    sportive, starry-eyed, stoked, sunny
thankful, triumphant
up
waggish, whimsical, wishful

SAD, SERIOUS, PESSIMISTIC, OR DISCONTENTED

abject, absorbed, abysmal, achy, afflicted,
    aggrieved, agonizing, anguished
beleaguered, bereaved, bereft, bleak, blue,
    brokenhearted, brooding, bummed, bummed out
chagrined, cheerless, contrite, crestfallen, crushed
dark, dejected, demure, depressed, deprived,
    desolate, despondent, disconsolate,
    discontented, discouraged, disenchanted,
    disgusted, disillusioned, dismal, dissatisfied,
    distraught, distressed, disturbed, doleful,
    dolorous, doomed, dour, down, down-at-heel,
    downbeat, downcast
elegiac, embittered

fatalistic, forlorn, fretful, funereal
gloomy, glum, grave, grief-stricken, grieving, grim, grouchy, grum, grumpy, guilt-ridden, guilty
hapless, harried, heartbroken, heavy-hearted, homesick, hopeless, humorless, hurt
inconsolable, indisposed, injured
joyless
lachrymose, languishing, lonely, lonesome, lovesick, lugubrious
maudlin, melancholy, miserable, misty-eyed, moody, mopey, morbid, morose, mournful
nostalgic
oppressed, out-of-sorts, owlish
pained, pathetic, pensive, perturbed, pessimistic, pining, pitiable, pitiful, plaintive, plangent, poignant, pouty, pungent
regretful, remorseful, repentant, rueful, ruthful
sad, saturnine, serious, severe, sighing, sober, solemn, somber, soppy, sorrowful, sorry, stern, stricken, Stygian, subdued, suffering, suicidal, sulky, sullen, surly
teary, teary-eyed, tortured, tragic, tristful, troubled
unfortunate, unfulfilled, unhappy, unlucky
wailful, weepy, wistful, woebegone, woeful, wounded, wrecked, wretched, wronged

Calm/Angry

CALM, GENTLE, OR EASYGOING

apollonian
calm, casual, composed, constrained, cool, cool-headed
dégagé, demure, dewy, dispassionate, dry-eyed
easygoing, emollient, even-tempered
gentle
imperturbable
laconic, laid-back, lenient, levelheaded, low-key, low-pressure
matutinal, meditative, mellow, mild, muted
neutral, nonchalant, nonviolent
objective
pacific, pacifistic, passive, patient, peaceful, poised
quiet
relaxed, restrained, reticent
sedate, self-disciplined, self-possessed, serene, soft, steady, stoical, subdued
taciturn, tame, temperate, tempered, tranquil
unbothered, unemotional, unflappable, unforced, unhassled, unhurried, unruffled, unstirred, untroubled

ANGRY, EMOTIONAL, AGGRESSIVE, OR PASSIONATE

aggravated, aggressive, aghast, agitated, amorous, angered, angry, animated, annoyed, antsy, appetent, argumentative, avid
bellicose, belligerent, blooming, brash, breathless
choleric, combative, competitive, contentious
dedicated, defiant, dramatic
edgy, effusive, emotional, engagé, enthusiastic, excitable, excited, explosive
ferocious, feverish, fierce, fiery, fire-eating, flighty, flustered, frazzled, free-swinging, frenzied, fuming, furious
harried, hassled, henpecked, hepped-up, het up, high-keyed, high-pressure, high-strung, hostile, hot, hot-blooded, hotheaded, huffy, hungry, hyper, hysterical

impassioned, impetuous, impulsive, incensed, indignant, inflammatory, intemperate, intensive, intent, irascible, irate, irrepressible
jealous
livid, lusty
mad, manic, miffed, militant, militaristic
overwrought, overzealous
passionate, peeved, peppery, perfervid, piqued, pissed, pissed off, pugnacious, pushy
quarrelsome
rabid, raddled, raging, rambunctious, rash, resentful, restive, restless, ruffled, rumbustious
scrappy, seething, self-indulgent, sensuous, short, short-tempered, sick and tired, snappish, sore, soulful, spontaneous, steaming, stewing, sthenic, stir-crazy, stirred up, stormy, strained, subjective, sulfurous, sultry
temperamental, tempestuous, tense, testy, ticked, ticked-off, ticklish, torrid, touchy, trigger-happy, troubled, truculent, tumultuous, turbulent, turned-on
unglued, unreasonable, unreconciled, unremitting, unrestrained, unsettled, unstable, upset
vehement, Vesuvian, vexed, violent, visceral, volcanic
warm-blooded, white-hot, worked-up, wound-up, wrathful, wrought-up, wroth
zealous

Moderate/Excessive

MODERATE, SANE, CONSERVATIVE, OR OLD-FASHIONED

abstemious, abstinent, adjusted, assiduous
balanced, businesslike, buttoned-down
careful, cautious, celibate, chary, circumspect, clocklike, closemouthed, collected, composed, concise, concrete, conscientious, conservative, consistent, constant, controlled, conventional, cool-headed
diplomatic, down-to-earth
equitable
factual, frugal
gingerly, gradual
inveterate
laconic, levelheaded
matter-of-fact, middle-of-the-road, mild, moderate, modest
no-nonsense
objective, obsolete, old-fashioned, orderly, orthodox, ossified, outdated, outmoded
passé, penny-wise, pious, practical, pragmatic, prudent
rational, reasonable, regimented, regular
safe, sane, sensible, sober, sound, sparing, square, stable, standardized, standpat, steady, stick-in-the-mud, sticky, stodgy, strait-laced, stringent, studied, superannuated
tactful, temperate, thrifty, tough-minded
ultraconservative, utilitarian
workmanlike

EXCESSIVE, MAD, INSANE, OR RADICAL

aberrant, abnormal, addictive, alcoholic, amok, anarchic, anarchistic, apoplectic, avaricious
berserk, brash
chaotic, crazed, crazy
daffy, daft, delirious, demoniacal, deranged, deviant, dizzy, dotty, dysfunctional

eldritch, epicurean, erratic, esurient, excessive, extravagant, extreme
fanatic, fanatical, febrile, fey, flagrant, flaky, florid, frantic, freakish, frenetic, frenzied
gonzo, greedy
headlong, hedonistic, heedless, hog-wild, homicidal, hyper, hysterical
immodest, incendiary, inordinate, insane, insatiable, irrational
kamikaze, kooky
loco, lunatic
mad, madcap, maniacal, monomaniacal
nihilistic
obsessive, odd, off, off-the-wall, overwrought
perfervid, phrenetic, pinko, pixilated, potty, prodigal, profuse, psycho, psychotic, punk
quirky
rabid, radical, raging, rakish, rapacious, rash, ravening, raving, reckless
screwy, spasmodic, strange, streaky, surreal, sybaritic
temerarious
ultra, ultraist, unbalanced, unbridled, unconventional, uncurbed, unfettered, unhinged, unrestrained
voracious
wacky, warped, wasteful, way-out, weird, wiggy, wild-eyed, wired
zany, zooey

Proper/Vulgar

PROPER, COURTEOUS, REFINED, OR PURITANICAL

aesthetic, appropriate, auspicious
ceremonious, chaste, citified, civil, civilized, classical, clubby, conforming, conventional, correct, courteous, courtly, couth, cultivated, cultured
decent, decorous, delicate, demure, dignified, diplomatic, discreet
effete, elitist, established, esthetic, ethical
fastidious, felicitous, finicky, formal, fussy
gallant, genteel, gentlemanly, gracious
hoity-toity, holier-than-thou, honorable
ingratiating, irreproachable, Ivy League
kosher
law-abiding, legitimate
maidenly, mannered, matronly, modern, modest, moral, moralistic
obedient, official, orthodox
pietistic, polite, pompous, precious, presentable, priggish, prim, prissy, pristine, professional, proper, prudent, prudish, pudibund, punctilious, punctual, puritanical
refined, religious, reputable, respectable, respectful, rhetorical, righteous, right-thinking, rigid
safe, sanctimonious, seemly, self-righteous, smooth, smug, snobbish, snooty, soapy, sporting, sportsmanlike, squeamish, stable, staid, starchy, stiff, stilted, straight, straight-arrow, strict, stuffy, suave, suitable
tactful, tasteful, taut, tight-assed, too-too, traditional, tweedy
U, unflappable, upright, uptight, urbane
Victorian
well-behaved, well-bred, well-mannered, white, white-bread

VULGAR, RUDE, DEGENERATE, OR WILD

abandoned, aberrant, abnormal, abominable, aboriginal, abusive, animalistic, anomalous, atavistic
barbaric, base, bawdy, beastly, bibulous, bizarre, blasphemous, blooey, blunt, boorish, brash, brazen, brutish
caddish, cannibalistic, carnal, cheap, cheeky, coarse, common, concupiscent, coquettish, crass, crude
debauched, decadent, degenerate, depraved, deviant, dirty, dirty-minded, discourteous, disobedient, disorderly, disreputable, dissipated, dissolute
egregious, erotic
farouche, feral, flatulent, flip, flippant, flooey, foul, fresh
garish, gauche, gross
heathenish, heteroclite, heterodox, hoggish, hokey
ill-bred, illicit, ill-mannered, immoderate, immoral, impertinent, impolite, impolitic, improper, impudent, inappropriate, incestuous, incongruous, indecent, indecorous, indelicate, inexcusable, informal, insolent, intoxicated, irregular, irreverent
kinky, knockabout
lascivious, lawless, lecherous, lewd, libertine, libidinous, licentious, loose, loud, low, lowbrow, lubricious, lustful
mannerless, meretricious
native, naughty, non-U
obscene, obstreperous, offbeat, offhand, opprobrious, outlandish, outrageous, outré, overdressed
perverted, plebeian, pornographic, primitive, profane, profligate, promiscuous, prurient, prying, purple
queer
Rabelaisian, racy, raffish, rakish, rambunctious, randy, rank, raucous, raunchy, raw, rebellious, recherché, refractory, revolutionary, ribald, riotous, ripped, rip-roaring, risqué, roily, rough, rough-and-tumble, rough-hewn, rowdy, rowdydowdy, rude, rumbustious, rustic, ruttish
salacious, sassy, savage, scabrous, scandalous, scurrilous, self-abandoned, shameless, showy, slutty, smutty, steamy, swinish
tactless, tasteless, tawdry, tipsy, trashy
unbecoming, unblushing, uncivil, uncivilized, uncontrollable, unconventional, uncool, uncouth, uncultured, undiplomatic, ungracious, unmanageable, unmannered, unmannerly, unnatural, unrefined, unruly, unseemly, unsportsmanlike, untamed, untoward
vulgar
wanton, weird, whorish, wild

Intelligent/Stupid

INTELLIGENT, INFORMED, CLEVER, OR ARTICULATE

abreast, accurate, acute, analytical, apt, argute, articulate, astute, au fait, authoritative
bookish, bright, brilliant, broad ranging
canny, cerebral, clear, clearheaded, clear-sighted, clever, cogent, cognizant, coherent, comprehensive, concise, conscious, conversant, cunning
discerning, donnish, droll
educated, erudite, expert
facile, fluent

glib, heads-up, heady, highbrow, high-minded, hip
imaginative, incisive, informed, ingenious, innovative, inquiring, inquisitive, insightful, intellectual, intelligent, interpretive, inventive
keen, knowing, knowledgeable
learned, limpid, literate, logical, lucid, luminous
mental
observant, omnilegent, omniscient, organized
pawky, pedagogic, penetrating, perceptive, percipient, perspicacious, piercing, pithy, precocious, prescient, proficient, profound
quick-witted
rational, recondite, reflective, retentive, right, ruminant
savvy, serious-minded, sharp, sharp-witted, shrewd, silver-tongued, smart, smooth-tongued, subtle, succinct
terse, trenchant, tuned-in
ultrasmart, uncanny, understanding, unerring, urbane
versed
well-advised, well-informed, well-read, well-rounded, well-spoken, with-it, witty, worldly, worldly-wise

STUPID, IGNORANT, OR CONFUSED

absent-minded, abstracted, addlebrained, addled, agog, amnesiac
backward, baffled, befogged, befuddled, benighted, besotted, bewildered, blithering, bovine
confounded, confused, cretinous
dense, dim, dimwitted, disorganized, disoriented, doltish, dull, dumb, dumbfounded, duncical
empty-headed, erroneous
fallible, fatuous, fat-witted, feeble-minded, foggy, fuzzy
hazy
idiotic, ignorant, illiterate, imbecilic, inarticulate, incognizant, incoherent, incompetent, inconscient
lumpish
maundering, mindless, mixed-up, moronic, muddled, muddleheaded, myopic, mystified
nescient, numb
oblivious, obtuse, opaque
perplexed, preoccupied, purblind, puzzled
rambling, rattled, retarded
scatterbrained, senile, simple, simpleminded, slaphappy, slow, slow-witted, sophomoric, spaced, spaced-out, spacey, speechless, stunned, stunted, stupefied, stupid, stuporous, subliterate, subnormal
thick, thickheaded, thick-witted, turbid
unclear, unconscious, undiscerning, unfocused, uninformed, unknowing, unlearned, unlettered, unorganized, unread, unschooled, unskilled, untutored, unversed
vacant, vacuous
witless, woodenheaded, woozy, wrong
zoned out, zonked out

Special/Ordinary

SPECIAL, BRIGHT, SKILLFUL, OR UNUSUAL

ablaze, able, acclaimed, accomplished, adept, adequate, admirable, admired, ageless, aglow, all-around, amazing, ambidextrous, anointed,

artful, artistic, arty, atypical, auspicious, avant-garde
bedazzling, blessed, bodacious, breathtaking, bright, brilliant
capable, celebrated, charismatic, colorful, competent, conspicuous, consummate, controversial, coordinated, corking, creative, creditable
dazzling, different, distinct, distinctive, distinguished, divine
eccentric, efficient, effulgent, eminent, esteemed, estimable, excellent, exceptional, exclusive, exemplary, exotic, extraordinary
famous, fascinating, favored, fine, first-class, first-rate, flashing, foremost, fortunate
glimmering, glittering, glorious, glossy, glowing, grand, great
handy, heavenly, hip, honored
iconoclastic, idiosyncratic, illuminated, illustrious, imaginative, imperial, important, imposing, impressive, incandescent, incomparable, incredible, individual, indubitable, inimitable, inspiring, invaluable, inviolate, iridescent
jazzy
light, lucky, luminous, lustrous
magical, magnificent, majestic, major, marquee, marvelous, masterful, matchless
nonpareil, notable, noted, noteworthy, novel
original, otherworldly, outstanding
peculiar, peerless, perfect, phenomenal, praiseworthy, preeminent, prepared, prestigious, priceless, primary, Promethean, prominent, protean, proverbial
quaint, qualified, quality
radiant, rare, refulgent, remarkable, renowned, resourceful, respected, resplendent, reverential, ripe
sacred, saintly, scintillating, select, sensational, serendipitous, sexy, shining, signal, significant, singular, skillful, sole, sovereign, sparkling, special, spicy, splendid, startling, stellar, storied, stupendous, sublime, successful, super, superb, superhuman, superior, superlative, supernatural, supreme, surefooted, sure-handed
talented, terrific, tiptop, titled, together, top, topflight, topnotch, top-of-the-line, tops, towering, transfigured
uncommon, unconventional, unequaled, unexcelled, unique, unmatched, unorthodox, unprecedented, unusual, unwonted, utopian
valuable, valued, varied, vast, versatile, victorious, vintage, vivid
well-known, well-spoken, well-thought-of, whiz-bang, wonderful, wondrous, worthwhile, worthy

ORDINARY, DULL, PLAIN, OR BANAL

automatic, average
banal, bland, blank, boring, bourgeois
characterless, colorless, common, commonplace, conventional, cursory, customary
dated, derivative, dim, dingy, dismal, down-to-earth, drab, dreary, dull
empty, everyday, expressionless
faded, fair, fallible, familiar, faulty, flat
garden-variety, glib, gratuitous
habitual, hackneyed, homespun, humble, humdrum
imitative, inartistic, inconclusive, inconspicuous,

indifferent, inefficient, inept, inferior, inglorious, innocuous, insignificant, insipid
jejune
lackluster, lifeless, low-class, lowly, low-quality, lukewarm, lusterless
matter-of-fact, mediocre, menial, middling, mild, minor, modest, mortal, mundane, musty
negligible, nondescript, normal
obvious, okay, one-dimensional, ordinary
passable, pedestrian, perfunctory, petit bourgeois, plain, plain-spoken, plastic, plebeian, proletarian, prosaic, prototypical
regular, repetitive, rinky-dink, run-of-the-mill
secondary, second-class, second-rate, shoddy, simple, small time, soggy, soporific, spare, stagnant, stale, standard, stereotypical, sterile, stock, stripped-down, subordinate, superficial, superfluous
tarnished, tasteless, tedious, tepid, terrestrial, timeworn, tiresome, tolerable, trite, typical
unadorned, unassuming, undistinctive, undistinguished, unexceptional, unexciting, unhip, unimaginative, uninspiring, uninteresting, unprepared, unpretentious, unqualified, unsung, untalented, untitled, useless, usual
vapid
workaday, working-class, would-be

Wise/Foolish

WISE, MATURE, OR EXPERIENCED

actualized, adult, all-knowing, all-seeing, august, aware, awesome
balanced, broad, broad-minded
centered, clear, clear-sighted, cogent, coherent, complex, contemplative
deep, discriminating, disinterested, dispassionate
eloquent, enlightened, ethereal, exalted, experienced
farseeing, farsighted, focused
grand, grown-up
immortal, impartial, infallible, infinite, influential, integrated
judicious, just
large-minded, levelheaded, lofty, lucid
magisterial, majestic, mantic, masterful, masterly, mature, metaphysical, mystical
noble
old, Olympian, omnipresent, omniscient, open-minded, orbicular, oriented
patriarchal, perfect, philosophical, practiced, prescient, profound, prophetic, psychic
realized, resonant
sacred, sacrosanct, sagacious, sage, sapient, serene, sophisticated, spiritual, sublime, supernal, supreme, sybilline
telepathic
unassailable, unbiased, understanding, universal
vatic, venerable, veteran, visionary
weathered, weighty, wise, wizardly

FOOLISH, IMMATURE, BIGOTED, OR TRIVIAL

abstract, absurd, adolescent, affected, amateurish, anthropocentric, anti-intellectual, artless, artsy, asinine, awe-struck
balmy, barmy, bathetic, bedazzled, biased, bigoted, blind, bumbling

callow, capricious, careless, childish, chumpish, clownish, comical, corny, cretinous, cute, cutesy
daffy, daft, distracted, dopey
ethnocentric
farcical, flabbergasted, flatulent, flighty, foolhardy, foolish, foppish, frivolous, frothy
garrulous, gibbering, giddy, goofy
half-assed, half-baked, half-cocked, harebrained, harum-scarum, hasty, highfalutin, homophobic
idiotic, ill-advised, imbecilic, immature, impetuous, impractical, imprudent, inane, indiscreet, inexperienced, infantile, injudicious, in the clouds, irrational
juvenile
kooky
la-di-da, laughable, lightheaded, long-winded, loquacious, ludicrous
melodramatic, mincing, minor, misanthropic, misogynous, moronic, mushyheaded, muzzy
naif, naive, narrow, narrow-minded, nattering, nerdy, nonplussed, nutty
parochial, pedantic, petty, picayune, piddling, pinchbeck, prejudiced, preposterous, pretentious, prolix, provincial, pubescent, puerile
quixotic, quizzical
rash, rattlebrained, redundant, repetitious, ridiculous
sappy, sectarian, sententious, shallow, shortsighted, sightless, silly, singsong, skin-deep, small-minded, small-time, soft-headed, sophistic, speechless, spoony, superficial, superstitious
trifling, trivial
unfledged, ungrounded, unrealistic, unwise, unworldly
verdant
waggish, wide-eyed, windy, woolly-headed
yeasty, youthful
zany

Good/Bad

GOOD, SINCERE, HONEST, OR JUST

aboveboard, angelic, authentic
benevolent, bona fide
candid, capital, choice, conscientious, constant
dear, decent, deserving, devout, direct
earnest, ethical
fair, fair-minded, fine, first-rate, forthcoming, forthright, foursquare, frank, free
genuine, God-fearing, good, guileless
harmonious, high-minded, holy, honest, honorable, humane
idealistic, impartial, incorruptible, irreproachable
judicious, just
loving, loyal
magnanimous, moral
natural, noble
organic
prelapsarian, principled, pure
real, reliable, reverent, righteous, right-minded
scrupulous, selfless, seraphic, simon-pure, sincere, straightforward, sublime
true, true-blue, truthful
unimpeachable, up-and-up, up-front, upright, upstanding
veracious, veridical, vestal, virtuous
wholehearted, wholesome, worthy

BAD, FALSE, EVIL, INSINCERE, OR DISHONEST

accursed, adulterous, affected, amoral, apocryphal, apostate, arch, artificial, awful
backhanded, bad, baleful, baneful, barefaced, base, bent, bloodthirsty, bogus
calumnious, canting, casuistic, contemptible, corrupt, counterfeit, crafty, crooked, cunning, cursed
damned, debased, deceitful, deceptive, delusive, demoniacal, despicable, detestable, devilish, devious, diabolical, disgraced, dishonest, disingenuous, disloyal, dissembling, duplicitous
egregious, ersatz, evasive, evil, execrable
fake, fallen, false, fatuous, feigned, fell, fiendish, flagitious, flagrant, foul, foxy, fraudulent, fulsome, furtive
guileful
hangdog, heinous, heretical, hexed, high-sounding, hollow, horrid, hypocritical
ignoble, ignominious, infamous, infernal, insidious, insincere, irredeemable
Janus-faced, jive
loathsome, lowdown
malefic, malevolent, malignant, mealy-mouthed, mendacious, miscreant, misleading, mock, monstrous, moralistic, murderous
nefarious
odious, ostentatious
perfidious, pernicious, perverse, pharisaic, phony, piacular, predatory, pretentious, pseudo, purulent
recreant, reprobate, rotten
sanctimonious, scurvy, selfish, serpentine, shady, sham, shameful, shifty, sinful, sinister, slanderous, slippery, sly, smarmy, sneaky, sophistic, sorcerous, specious, spurious, stealthy, synthetic
tainted, terrible, traitorous, treacherous, two-faced
unashamed, unconscionable, unctuous, underhanded, unfair, ungodly, unholy, unjust, unpardonable, unprincipled, unscrupulous, untruthful, unworthy
vain, venal, venomous, vile, villainous, viperous, virtueless, vulpine
wicked, wily, worthless

Giving/Demanding

GIVING, TRUSTING, INNOCENT, OR GENEROUS

accessible, accommodating, adaptable, approving, artless
beatific, believing
candid, careless, childlike, complaisant, compliant, credulous
democratic, dewy-eyed, doting, dulcet
easy
faithful, frank, free
game, generous, giving, good-natured, gracious, grateful, guileless, gullible
hopeful, humble
impressionable, inconsistent, indiscriminate, indulgent, ingenuous, innocent, insouciant, instinctive, intuitive
lax, liberal
naive, natural
obliging, open
permissive
rapt, reciprocating
saccharine, selfless, simple, sugary, sweet, syrupy
tender, tolerant, transparent, trustful, trusting

ultraliberal, unabashed, uncritical, understanding, undesigning, unguarded, unquestioning, unsophisticated, unsparing, unsullied, unsuspecting, unwitting
virginal
young

Demanding, critical, calculating, or selfish

abrasive, accusatory, acerbic, acidic, acquisitive, admonishing, agnostic, anal, aporetic, arbitrary, arrogant, assiduous, assumptive, atheistic, attentive
biting, blameful, bumptious
cagey, calculating, captious, carping, categorical, caustic, caviling, censorious, challenging, cheap, chiding, choosy, clinical, compulsive, conceited, condescending, constipated, contemptuous, contradictory, contrary, costive, covetous, crafty, critical, cryptic, cutting
definite, deliberate, demanding, deprecatory, derogatory, dictatorial, didactic, disabused, disapproving, disbelieving, disciplined, discriminating, disdainful, disparaging, distrustful, doctrinaire, dogmatic
edacious, egocentric, exacting, exigent
facetious, fastidious, fault-finding, fussy
gluttonous, grabby, greedy, guarded
hard, harsh, high-and-mighty, hubristic, huffy, hypercritical
impatient, incisive, insistent, ironic
judgmental
logical
materialistic, measured, methodical, meticulous, mocking, mordacious, mordant
narcissistic, niggling
obsessive, omnivorous, opinionated, opportunistic
painstaking, particular, patronizing, pejorative, peremptory, perseverant, persistent, pertinacious, picky, pointed, political, precise, procacious
querulous
ravenous, rebuking, reproving, Rhadamanthine, rigorous
sanctimonious, sarcastic, sardonic, satiric, satirical, scolding, scornful, scrimping, scrupulous, sedulous, selective, self-centered, selfish, self-serving, self-willed, set, sharp, sharp-edged, skeptical, slashing, specific, supercilious, superior, systematic
tactical, tendentious, thorough, tireless, trenchant
ultracritical, unbelieving, ungenerous, unrelenting, unstinting, uppish, uppity, usurious
vain, vituperative, voracious
withholding, wolfish, wry

Helpful/Troublesome

Helpful, positive, responsible, or nice

accessory, accommodating, aggrandizing, altruistic, amenable, amicable, attached, avuncular
beneficent, benevolent, benign, big-hearted, brotherly
caring, charitable, chivalrous, civic-minded, clement, compassionate, concerned, conciliatory, conscientious, considerate, constructive, cooperative
dutiful
eager, equable, equitable

faithful, fatherly, felicitous, fortunate, fraternal
good-hearted
helpful, heroic, humane, humanitarian, hunky-dory
indulgent, instructive, intimate
large, lenient, loving, loyal
magnanimous, maternal, merciful, motherly, munificent
neighborly, nice
obliging
paternal, patriotic, philanthropic, pleasant, positive, progressive, propitiatory, propitious, protective, provident
reliable, responsible, responsive
selfless, self-sacrificing, sensitive, sharing, sisterly, social, social-minded, solicitous, soothing, sunny, supportive, sympathetic
tender, thoughtful, tonic, tried-and-true, trustworthy, trusty
unfailing, unselfish, upbeat, useful
valuable, voluntary
well-intentioned, well-meaning, wholesome, worthwhile

Troublesome, negative, irresponsible, or unpleasant

abrasive, abusive, acrid, acrimonious, annoying, antagonistic, arch, argumentative, avaricious, averse
balky, baneful, bilious, bitter, bothersome, bullying
cagey, capricious, carking, cloying, comminatory, complaining, covetous, crafty, crappy, creepy, crotchety, crummy, cutthroat
dangerous, designing, destructive, difficult, discontented, disquieting, disturbing, divisive, dour, downbeat
envious
fearsome, feral, fickle, fierce, foxy, fractious
harsh, horrendous, horrible, horrid, horrific
importunate, incompatible, infamous, inhumane, invidious, irksome, irreconcilable, irresponsible
jackleg, jangly, jaundiced
libelous, lousy, lupine
maddening, maladjusted, manipulative, mean, meddlesome, menacing, minatory
nagging, nauseating, negative, negligent, nerve-racking, nettlesome, nihilistic, nosy, notorious, noxious
objectionable, obnoxious, odious, offensive, officious, ominous, onerous, oppressive
parlous, pernicious, pesky, pestilent, pesty, petulant, polypragmatic, pompous, prankish, preachy, prickly, provocative, pugnacious
querulous
rancid, rancorous, rapacious, rascally, remorseless, renitent, reprehensible, restrictive, rivalrous, roguish
sacrilegious, savage, scary, scathing, scurrilous, seditious, self-destructive, severe, sharp, sick, slanderous, slashing, slinking, sly, small, smirking, snide, sniffish, sniffy, snobbish, snoopy, snotty, sordid, sour, spiteful, spleenful, sticky, stroppy, stuck-up, subversive
terrifying, thorny, thoughtless, toxic, treacly, tricky, troublesome, truculent, trying
unconcerned, undependable, unfaithful, ungrateful, unpleasant, unsympathetic, useless
venomous, vicious, vindictive, virulent, vitriolic, vituperative, vulpine
wayward, wearisome, wily, worrisome, wrongheaded

Love and Romance

adoration great love and devotion; worship
affection warmth, liking
amative (*adj*) inclined to love and lust
amatory (*adj*) pertaining to love and lovemaking
amorist lover, devotee of love
amorous (*adj*) full of love; feeling sexually aroused
amour love affair, esp. illicit one
Aphrodite ancient Greek goddess of love and beauty
ardor enthusiasm in love
Astarte ancient Semitic goddess of fertility and sexual love
beloved greatly loved person
break a heart reject or wound one's lover
brokenhearted (*adj*) rejected in love
caring concern and esteem for loved one
carry a torch endure unrequited love
Casanova man engaging in many love affairs
celibacy state of being unmarried; abstention from sexual love
cheat (*vb*) deceive one's lover with another; secret lover
chemistry animal attraction; sympathetic understanding; rapport
cherish (*vb*) love devotedly
chivalry courageous, honorable, supportive attitude toward women
cohabit (*vb*) live together
commitment bond of love and responsibility
compatibility harmonious coexistence
concubine mistress, kept woman; secondary wife of polygamous male, usu. of inferior rank
conjugal love affection and relations between married couple
constancy faithfulness in love
corazón *Spanish.* heart; love and affection; lover
cotton to (*vb*) *Informal.* take a liking to
couple two people who are in love with each other or relating erotically
courtly love polite, formal, old-fashioned love
crush *Informal.* infatuation
cuckold husband of woman who is having sex with another man
Cupid ancient Roman god of love

Dear John *Informal.* letter from woman telling her lover she is ending the relationship

devotion faithful, enduring love

Don Juan seducer of women

dote on (*vb*) care for excessively or foolishly

ecstasy sexual bliss

enamor (*vb*) charm, fill with love or desire

enchant (*vb*) delight with love

enthrall (*vb*) enslave with love

Eros ancient Greek god of love

fair sex women collectively, sometimes considered offensive

fall for (*vb*) *Slang.* fall in love with; take a shine to

fancy (*vb*) be attracted to or fond of

fascination state of being spellbound by love

favor token of love

fondness tender affection

forbidden love any prohibited form of love

game of love typical give-and-take in developing romantic relationship

go for (*vb*) be attracted to

goo-goo eyes *Slang.* foolishly amorous glances

have eyes for *Slang.* be attracted to

head over heels in love extravagantly in love

heartache pain caused by being in love

heartbreaker person causing pain to lover

heartsick (*adj*) extremely unhappy in love

heartthrob person attracting much romantic attention

honor and keep love vow taken at wedding ceremony by couple

illicit love prohibited acts or forms of love

inamorata woman who loves or is loved

inamorato man who loves or is loved

infatuation temporary, intense feeling of love

intimacy special, deep closeness growing from mutual love

item *Slang.* couple known to be together

jealousy resentment caused by real or imagined rival

keep company be involved in love relationship with another

knight courtly male lover

lady courtly female lover

Lolita extremely seductive young girl

longing desire for love or beloved person

lose one's heart fall in love

Lothario seducer and deceiver of women

love strong emotional attachment to another person; sexual passion or desire based on such feelings; intense affection or caring for another

love at first sight instantaneous attraction on meeting

lovebirds loving couple

lovelorn (*adj*) heartsick, rejected, or unhappy in love

lover person who is in love with another, esp. one having a sexual or romantic relationship with another; person with whom one is having an extramarital affair

lovers' quarrel stormy and emotional fight between lovers

lovesick (*adj*) anxious or emotionally unbalanced from love

main squeeze *Slang.* primary lover or mate

make up (*vb*) patch up a lovers' quarrel; reconcile

mate spouse; lover

mistress lover of man married to another

moonstruck (*adj*) dreamily romantic; in love

mush overly sentimental affection

obsession overriding preoccupation with beloved

other woman love interest of married or attached man

paramour married person's lover

passion strong emotional response to lover

philander (*vb*) engage in love affair without willingness to marry

pine (*vb*) long for one's lover

platonic love nonsexual love

puppy love youthful, immature love

rapture ecstasy of love

reconciliation settlement of differences with one's lover and resumption of romantic relationship, as after a separation

rejection lack of acceptance by or of lover; failure to elicit love from an object of one's love

relationship involvement of two persons in love

romance close emotional and physical relationship; love affair

romantic (*adj*) pertaining to sexual love; inspiring emotions of romance; (*n*) romantic person

Romeo male lover, esp. man preoccupied with or noted for amatory success

run after (*vb*) pursue lover or would-be lover

seduction enticement of another into having sex

seductress woman who entices men into having sex

shack up (*vb*) *Slang.* live together as a couple without marriage

smitten (*adj*) infatuated, in love

soul mate cherished lover, true love

stardust naively romantic quality

sugar daddy *Informal.* man using his wealth to attract young woman as his lover

swept off one's feet fallen madly in love

swoon (*vb*) faint with love

take a shine to fall under the spell of another's attraction; fall for

take up with (*vb*) *Informal.* begin romantic relationship with

toy with (*vb*) play at love with no commitment

triangle situation involving two people who are both in love with a third person

true (*adj*) faithful

true love deep, abiding love

turtledoves sweethearts, lovers

two-timer *Informal.* person who is unfaithful to lover or spouse

under one's thumb (*adj*) dominated by one's lover

unfaithful (*adj*) betraying a lover or spouse by taking another

unrequited love love for someone who does not love in return

Venus ancient Roman goddess of love

womanizer man pursuing women for sexual purposes

worship intense love and adoration

yearn (*vb*) long for love or lover

yen craving for someone or for love

Flirtation, Dating, and Courting

admirer person making obvious show of affection

advances overtures made in hopes of starting a relationship or sexual encounter

affair temporary romantic relationship

assignation lovers' arrangement to meet

attraction sexual and romantic interest

babe *Derogatory.* girl or woman

beau male suitor; boyfriend

belle beautiful, charming lady

bewitch (*vb*) charm or delight with feelings of love

billet-doux love letter

bird *Brit. slang.* attractive young woman

bird-dog (*vb*) *Slang.* steal or attempt to steal another person's date

bitch *Slang.* aggressive, difficult, critical, or aloof and disdainful woman

blade dashing, jaunty young man

blind date arranged meeting between previously unacquainted people

boyfriend frequent or favorite male companion; beau

boy toy *Derogatory slang.* young man who serves as sexual plaything, esp. to a famous or wealthy person

bunny *Derogatory slang.* pretty, alluring young woman

buss (*vb*) kiss

caress (*vb*) fondle gently

chaperon older escort of dating couple

charm (*vb*) attract and please another

chase pursuit of loved one

chick *Slang.* girl, young woman

cockteaser *Vulgar slang.* female who purposely arouses males sexually but refuses to have intercourse; male homosexual who acts similarly

come-hither (*adj*) beckoning in a flirtatious manner

come-on *Slang.* flirtatious advance

computer dating service that matches couples based on personal information put into computer

coo (*vb*) speak gently, lovingly

coquetry flirtation

coquette coy, teasing, flirtatious girl

cosset (*vb*) fondle as one would a pet

court (*vb*) woo, be suitor to

courtship act and process of seeking to become another's lover; wooing of one person by another

cruise (*vb*) *Informal.* travel about in search of sexual companionship

cuddle (*vb*) lie close together affectionately

dalliance flirtation; fondling, amorous foreplay

darling sweetheart, lover

date arrangement to meet for pleasant or romantic activity; romantic partner; (*vb*) see a romantic partner on regular basis

dear sweetheart, lover

double date *Informal.* social engagement involving two couples

Dutch treat date on which each person pays his or her own costs

embrace (*vb*) hold another in one's arms

endearment word or term of affection; pet name

femme fatale irresistibly attractive woman

filly *Informal.* girl or young woman

fling inconsequential love affair

flirt (*vb*) court playfully; (*n*) person who tempts others through playful courting

flirtation frivolous or playful love affair

fondle (*vb*) caress, stroke gently

forbidden fruit attractive but unavailable love interest

French kiss deep kiss with tongue inserted in partner's mouth

gallivant (*vb*) run around in search of sexual companionship

girlfriend frequent or favorite female companion; sweetheart

going steady (*adj*) regularly dating one person

hanky-panky *Informal.* questionable sexual conduct

hit it off *Informal.* find each other attractive or compatible as lovers

hit on (*vb*) *Slang.* make persistent sexual advances to

holding hands gently gripping each other's hands as a gesture of affection

honey *Informal.* sweetheart, lover

hug enthusiastic, affectionate embrace

indiscretion coy or ill-advised reference to sexual encounter

jilt (*vb*) abandon one's sweetheart

kiss (*vb*) press mouths together as sign of love, affection, or desire; (*n*) such an act

ladies' man extremely flirtatious, sexually interested male

lady-killer *Informal.* devastatingly attractive man who fascinates women

liaison sexual encounter or affair

liberties impertinent or unwarranted sexual actions

love letter affectionate, passionate correspondence to one's beloved

make out (*vb*) *Slang.* kiss and fondle passionately for extended time

meat rack *Derogatory slang.* singles bar

minx pert young girl

Mr. Right man who is viewed as ideal romantic partner or potential spouse (sometimes used with Miss, Mrs., or Ms. when referring to a female)

necking prolonged kissing and fondling

nuzzling lying close and snuggling affectionately, esp. with heads

oeillade *French.* amorous glance

ogling closely eyeing the object of one's affection

one-night stand *Informal.* casual, unrepeated sexual encounter

on the make searching for a sexual partner; on the prowl

on the prowl on the make

osculation kiss

parietal (*adj*) having to do with rules governing contact between sexes and dating hours, esp. at institution

pass *Informal.* approach to another with intimated offer of sex

paw (*vb*) *Informal.* handle roughly with sexual intent

peck small kiss

personals classified advertisements for sexual partners

pet sweetheart, lover

pet name affectionate term of address

petting fondling, foreplay

pickup *Informal.* casual sexual partner, esp. one met in public place

pick up (*vb*) *Informal.* become acquainted with informally, usu. in expectation of sexual encounter

pin (*vb*) formalize steady dating arrangement with girl by giving her one's fraternity pin

play the field *Informal.* have numerous sexual partners or romantic attachments

pucker up (*vb*) *Slang.* prepare to kiss

put the make on aggressively court with intention of having sex

reconcile (*vb*) resolve differences and renew affection

rendezvous meeting between lovers, sometimes in secret

roving eye interest in having many sexual encounters

run around (*vb*) pursue sexual partners, esp. in addition to primary partner

seduce (*vb*) entice or persuade doubtful or unwilling person into sexual intimacy

serenade courting song

singles unmarried persons interested in dating

singles bar drinking establishment designed for meeting of singles

skirt *Disparaging slang.* woman or girl

smack loud kiss

smooch (*vb*) *Informal.* kiss; pet

smoothie *Informal.* person who is seductive in manner and speech

snow job *Slang.* extreme, often manipulative, persuasion to have sex

snuggle (*vb*) cuddle affectionately

soul kiss passionate, open-mouthed kiss with tongue of one partner in mouth of the other; French kiss

spark (*vb*) *Informal.* court or woo

spoon (*vb*) *Informal.* court by caressing and kissing, esp. in a sentimental manner

squire (*vb*) escort woman to social gathering, esp. in a proper manner

stand up (*vb*) *Slang.* fail to appear for a date with

steady regular date or lover

step out (*vb*) go on date

string along (*vb*) *Informal.* encourage suitor with no intention of responding

suitor man courting a woman; swain

swain suitor

sweetheart darling, lover

sweet nothings *Slang.* sweet talk, esp. whispered in lover's ear

sweet talk *Informal.* endearments spoken to one's lover

swinger *Slang.* extremely sexually active person

tease (*vb*) engage in coy, playful flirtation; (*n*) flirt, coquette

temptress female who entices or allures

tête-à-tête intimate talk

tomato *Slang.* attractive young woman

tongue wrestling *Slang.* French kissing

tryst romantic meeting, rendezvous

valentine sweetheart; greeting card or note sent to one's lover or object of one's affection on February 14

vamp seductive woman

walking out *Brit. slang.* going steady

wolf *Informal.* sexually aggressive male

wolf whistle man's whistle of appreciation for woman's appearance

woo (*vb*) attempt to win affection or favor; court

Sexuality and Libido

age of consent age when one may legally engage in sex

animal person with abundant sexual energy

animal magnetism erotic attraction

aphrodisiac substance that increases sexual desire and performance

asexual (*adj*) having no sexual orientation

birds and bees euphemism for basic information about sexuality and reproduction

bisexual (*adj*) attracted to both males and females

carnal (*adj*) relating to physical desire

chastity virginity, sexual innocence

Circean (*adj*) dangerously or fatally attractive

cold (*adj*) sexually unresponsive

concupiscence strong sexual desire

conjugal rights sexual rights of husband and wife

continence total abstinence from sexual activity

craving desire for sex

dark meat *Vulgar slang.* African-American considered as sexual partner

desire intense sexual urge

dirty old man mature or elderly man with lewd or obscene preoccupations

easy (*adj*) available for indiscriminate sex

emasculate (*vb*) deprive male of his power and sexuality, literally by castration or figuratively

epicene (*adj*) with characteristics of both sexes; sexless, neither male nor female

erotic (*adj*) pertaining to sexual love; strongly sexual

erotica art and literature with erotic content

eroticism sexual quality or character

estrus period of sexual heat or rutting

facts of life basic information about sexuality and reproduction

fast (*adj*) easily available for sex

female woman; (*adj*) characteristic of women

feminine (*adj*) characteristic of women; female

fox *Slang*. extremely sexually attractive young female or male

free love uninhibited sexual behavior, generally without expectation of conventional social contracts such as marriage

frigid (*adj*) sexually unresponsive, said esp. of women

gender sexual identity, both biological and learned

heat period of sexual arousal and interest in mating; estrus

he-man *Informal*. virile, macho male

heterosexual one attracted to opposite sex

homosexual one attracted to same sex

horny (*adj*) *Vulgar slang*. craving sex; sexually aroused

hot (*adj*) *Slang*. sexy; aroused, stimulated

hot number *Slang*. sexy, attractive woman

hots *Slang* usu. **the hots**; intense sexual desire or attraction

hunk *Slang*. attractive man with well-developed physique

impotent (*adj*) unable to achieve erection for sexual intercourse

itch *Slang*. sexual urge

ithyphallic (*adj*) lewd, obscene; displaying an erect penis

jade wanton woman

keep one's honor resist sexual temptation, remain chaste

Kinsey scale sevenfold numerical scale of sexual orientation, devised by Alfred Kinsey, in which zero is exclusive heterosexuality and six is exclusive homosexuality

lascivious (*adj*) lustful, lewd

lechery lewdness, lustfulness

letch *Slang*. lecherous individual

lewd (*adj*) lustful, lecherous, obscene in desires

liberated (*adj*) without sexual inhibition

libertine one who indulges freely in sex

libido sexual desire and energy

Lord Fauntleroy effeminate man

love potion magic substance that creates desire; aphrodisiac

lubricity wanton lechery

lust strong sexual desire, esp. without deep affection

lusty (*adj*) filled with sexual desire

machismo exaggerated, showy claims of virility

macho (*adj*) overly assertive, virile, and domineering

magnetism fundamental sexual attractiveness

maiden virgin

male man; (*adj*) characteristic of men

manly (*adj*) virile, macho

masculine (*adj*) characteristic of men; male

masher *Slang*. man who makes passes at women

misogyny hatred of women

musth sexual excitement or frenzy, esp. in rutting season among certain animals

neuter (*adj*) having no sex

nubile (*adj*) ready for marriage, said esp. of young women

nymphet sexually precocious girl in early teens

oversexed (*adj*) having excessive sexual interest and energy

pantywaist *Informal*. weak, effeminate man

passion intense emotion and sexual desire

philter magic substance that arouses passion; love potion

piece *Vulgar slang*. person regarded as sex object, esp. a female; piece of ass

piece of ass *Vulgar slang*. piece

piece of meat *Derogatory slang*. man or woman regarded as sex object

potency virility, sexual ability

prig person tending to see pornographic content where it does not exist

promiscuity indiscriminate, casual, frequent sexual activity

prudery extreme modesty, sexual restraint

prurience lewd, lascivious desire or thought

pudibund (*adj*) prudish

pure (*adj*) chaste

racy (*adj*) spirited, sexually zestful

randy craving sex; sexually aroused; horny

raunchy (*adj*) coarse, earthy

rutting mating urge; estrus; heat

ruttish (*adj*) salacious; lustful

salacious (*adj*) lewd, lascivious

satyr lecherous man

scabrous (*adj*) risqué; obscene

sensual (*adj*) carnal; devoted to sensory pleasure

sensuality fondness for and indulgence in sensory pleasure; lasciviousness

sex appeal sexual attractiveness

sex fiend person excessively intent on having sex

sex goddess woman revered as ultimate sex object

sex kitten *Informal*. sensuous, seductive young woman

sex object person, esp. woman, valued only for sex

sexpot *Informal*. person with sex appeal

sex surrogate professional who has sex with clients for therapeutic purposes

sex symbol celebrity known for sex appeal

sexuality state of being or feeling sexual

sexually active regularly engaging in sex

sexual orientation gender preference in sexual partners

sissy weak or effeminate man

slut loose, promiscuous woman

Spanish fly preparation used as aphrodisiac

stag (*adj*) designating all-male event, esp. with lewd entertainment

steamy (*adj*) sexually arousing

straight (*adj*) *Informal*. heterosexual

stud *Slang*. exceptionally virile sexually active male

sultry (*adj*) characterized by or arousing passion

supermacho (*adj*) given to extreme displays of virility

superstud *Slang*. extremely sexually active male

sybarite sensualist, voluptuary

tail *Vulgar slang*. woman viewed as a sex object; piece

thigh *Derogatory slang*. female as sex object

throbbing (*adj*) pulsing with sexual arousal

tramp loose, promiscuous woman

transsexual (*adj*) sexually oriented as if one's body were of the opposite sex

trollop promiscuous woman

undersexed (*adj*) having inadequate sexual interest and energy

unisexual (*adj*) of one sex

unsexual (*adj*) not sexual

urge sexual desire

urge to merge *Informal*. sexual desire

vamp wily, seductive woman

vanilla sex *Slang*. ordinary, nonkinky sexual activities

vestal virgin chaste woman

virgin person who has not experienced sexual intercourse, used esp. of women

virginity state of being chaste and without sexual experience

virile (*adj*) manly, masculine

virility manly strength and sexual potency

virtue traditional chastity, esp. in female

voluptuary person given over to sensual gratification

voluptuous (*adj*) devoted to sensual gratification

wanton (*adj*) loose, lewd, promiscuous, immoral

wench lewd woman

wimp *Informal*. weak, effeminate man

Homosexuality

AC/DC (*adj*) *Slang*. bisexual

age-differentiated (*adj*) designating homosexuality involving usu. bisexual adult male and sexually passive young boy prized for his androgynous qualities, predominant in Islamic world, ancient Greece, and pre-industrial Europe

androphilia homosexuality involving two adults, both of whom self-identify as males, predominant in 20th-century United States and Europe

auntie *Slang*. older male homosexual

baby butch *Slang*. young, boyish lesbian

bear *Slang*. hirsute, often husky gay male

beefcake *Informal*. photographs of nude or nearly nude young men in magazines, posed to display their muscles or genitals

bent (*adj*) *Chiefly Brit. slang*. homosexual

bisexual (*adj*) attracted to and sexually active with both males and females; (*n*) such a person

bugger (*vb*) *Vulgar slang*. have anal intercourse with

bull dyke *Derogatory slang.* masculine-appearing lesbian

butch (*adj*) *Slang.* designating a masculine-appearing or -behaving female; designating a masculine-behaving male homosexual; (*n*) lesbian

camp something involving self-conscious and extravagant humor, irony, or amusement, often with playful inversion of values; (*vb*) behave in an extravagantly theatrical and stereotypically effeminate manner

catamite boy or youth in homosexual relationship with man; gunsel

chicken *Slang.* young male homosexual, esp. one sought by older men

chicken hawk *Slang.* older homosexual male who prefers young men

clone homosexual male who adopts stereotypical appearance featuring short hair, clipped mustache, flannel shirt, and denim trousers, often with leather accessories

closet queen *Disparaging slang.* man who keeps his homosexuality a secret

cock ring *Vulgar slang.* ring worn at base of penis, used to prolong erection

cocksucker *Vulgar slang.* person who performs fellatio, esp. male homosexual

come out (*vb*) declare one's homosexuality to family and friends or publicly; enter gay subculture

daisy chain *Slang.* line of males joined penis-in-anus or sometimes penis-in-mouth

diesel dyke *Derogatory slang.* masculine-appearing lesbian

drag clothing worn by one sex that is characteristic of the other sex

drag queen male transvestite

dyke *Derogatory slang.* lesbian

effeminate (*adj*) not masculine in appearance or behavior, said esp. of homosexuals

ephebophobia male homosexuality involving age-differentiated attraction

fag *Derogatory slang.* faggot

faggot *Derogatory slang.* male homosexual; fag

faggotry *Derogatory slang.* state, condition, and acts of homosexual males

faggy (*adj*) *Derogatory slang.* of or resembling male homosexuals; effeminate

fag hag *Derogatory slang.* heterosexual woman who cultivates friendships with gay males

fairy *Derogatory slang.* male homosexual

feigele *Yiddish derogatory slang.* male homosexual

fem *Slang.* very feminine lesbian, in contrast to butch

fish *Derogatory slang.* usu. heterosexual woman

fist fuck *Vulgar slang.* insert one's closed fist into another's anus

flaming (*adj*) *Slang.* blatantly or outlandishly gay

flit *Derogatory slang.* male homosexual

fruit *Derogatory slang.* male homosexual

gay (*adj*) homosexual, either male or female, sometimes restricted to males only

gay liberation sociopolitical movement to combat legal and social discrimination against homosexuals, begun in late 1960's

gay power organized political influence exerted by homosexuals as a group, esp. to achieve equal rights and social justice

gay pride communally nurtured sense of self-esteem and self-assertion among homosexuals

gay subculture social environment of self-identified homosexuals, comprising neighborhoods, events, organizations, and other formal and informal institutions that promote a sense of community and identity

gender-differentiated (*adj*) designating homosexuality involving fixed sexual roles in which one partner is passive and the other active-penetrative or one butch and the other fem

glory hole *Vulgar slang.* hole in men's room wall used to perform fellatio

go both ways *Slang.* engage in bisexual acts

granola dyke *Slang.* New Age lesbian who rejects cosmetics and feminine beauty accessories

gunsel *Slang.* catamite

heterosexism prejudicial discrimination against nonheterosexual practices based on tacit belief in universality of heterosexual norms

homo *Derogatory slang.* homosexual, usu. male

homoeroticism sexual arousal caused by member of same sex

homophile one who is homosexual; (*adj*) supportive of gay rights and interests

homophobia irrational fear of or aversion to homosexuals

homosexual person sexually attracted to and usu. sexually active with members of the same sex

homosociality male bonding without implication of sexual contact

in the closet secretly homosexual

lace *Vulgar slang.* foreskin on penis

latent (*adj*) in popular usage, designating one who appears heterosexual while repressing unconscious homosexual tendencies

leather scene sub-subculture involving suggestion of sadomasochistic activities and wearing of leather accessories

lesbian female homosexual

lesbian separatism extreme lesbian movement advocating complete separation from males

lesbo *Derogatory slang.* lesbian

lez *Derogatory slang.* lesbian

licorice stick *Vulgar slang.* black man's penis

limp wrist *Derogatory slang.* male homosexual

lip service *Vulgar slang.* fellatio

mary *Derogatory slang.* homosexual male

mo *Derogatory slang.* homosexual, usu. male

nance *Derogatory slang.* effeminate male; homosexual male

nellie (*adj*) *Slang.* designating an effeminate male; *Derogatory slang.* designating a homosexual male

outing public exposure of another's homosexuality against his or her will

out of the closet having revealed one's homosexuality

pansy *Derogatory slang.* male homosexual; effeminate male

pederasty sexual relations between a man and an boy, usu. under sixteen

poof *Brit. slang.* male homosexual; effeminate male

Princeton style *Vulgar slang.* ejaculation achieved by friction between another male's thighs

punk *Slang.* young male coerced into passive sexual role by older, often heterosexual, male prison inmate; any young, passive male partner of older homosexual

queen *Derogatory slang.* effeminate male homosexual, esp. one who dresses in woman's clothing

queer *Derogatory slang.* homosexual, esp. male

queer bashing physical and verbal assault on gays, usu. by young homophobic males who self-identify as heterosexual

rim (*vb*) *Vulgar slang.* lick or suck anus

salt-and-pepper (*adj*) designating interracial couple

sapphist lesbian

seafood *Slang.* sailors with reputed fondness for oral sex

service (*vb*) *Slang.* perform fellatio on nonreciprocal basis

situational (*adj*) designating homosexuality that occurs in sex-segregated situations, such as prisons, ships, or boarding schools, where heterosexuals are deprived of contact with the opposite sex, usu. temporary and without homosexual self-identity

stud *Slang.* very sexually active male homosexual or butch lesbian

sucked dry (*adj*) *Vulgar slang.* fellated with great passion

swish *Derogatory slang.* effeminate male homosexual; (*vb*) employ effeminate body language

switch-hitter *Slang.* one who is bisexual

tearoom *Slang.* men's bathroom in public place

trade *Slang.* usu. self-identified heterosexual or bisexual male who restricts himself to penetrative role in sex with passive homosexual

transvestite person who dresses in clothing of opposite sex, esp. drag queen

tribade lesbian

tribadism sexual practices of lesbians

tubs gay bathhouse

twinky *Slang.* handsome, young, gay male

vegetable *Derogatory slang.* rare term for lesbian, as distinguished from male "fruit"

well-hung (*adj*) *Vulgar slang.* having a large penis

Anatomy and Physiology of Sex

AIDS **a**cquired **i**mmune **d**eficiency **s**yndrome; fatal disease characterized by inability of body to fight various infections due to HIV virus, which attacks immune system, transmitted by direct contact of body fluids

androgen male hormone

androgynous (*adj*) having both male and female characteristics

ARC **A**IDS-**r**elated **c**omplex; various diseases and infections to which AIDS sufferers are susceptible

areola pigmented area around nipple

arousal condition in which there are physiological signs of sexual stimulation, such as erection

ballocks *Vulgar slang*. testicles

balls *Vulgar slang*. testicles

basket *Vulgar slang*. man's genital area

bazongas *Vulgar slang*. woman's breasts

bearded clam *Vulgar slang*. female genitals

beaver *Vulgar slang*. woman's pubic area

beget (*vb*) generate (offspring)

bone *Vulgar slang*. penis, esp. in erection

boner *Vulgar slang*. erection

boob *Vulgar slang*. woman's breast, esp. large

booby *Vulgar slang*. woman's breast

bosom woman's breast

box *Vulgar slang*. woman's pubic area, esp. vagina

breast woman's mammary gland

brick house *Slang*. well-built woman

brown eye *Vulgar slang*. anus

bum *Chiefly Brit. slang*. buttocks

bunghole *Vulgar slang*. anus

buns *Slang*. buttocks

bush *Vulgar slang*. woman's pubic hair

bust woman's breasts

buxom (*adj*) describing woman having large breasts and full body

callipygian (*adj*) having shapely buttocks

castration removal of man's testicles

cervix neck of uterus

cheeks *Slang*. buttocks

cheese *Vulgar slang*. smegma

cherry *Vulgar slang*. hymen; (*adj*) virginal

chlamydia gonorrhealike venereal disease caused by parasite

clap *Vulgar slang*. gonorrhea

cleavage area between woman's breasts

climax orgasm

clit *Vulgar slang*. clitoris

clitoral orgasm woman's climax, centered in clitoral tissue

clitoris small, sensitive, erectile protuberance at upper end of female vulva

cock *Vulgar slang*. penis

cojones *Spanish vulgar slang*. testicles

come *Vulgar slang*. ejaculation; (*vb*) *Informal*. have orgasm

conception fertilization of egg by sperm

cooze *Vulgar slang*. vagina

crabs pubic lice

crack *Vulgar slang*. vagina

cramps pain caused by menstrual period

crotch genital area

cryptorchidism undescended testicles

cum *Vulgar slang*. semen

cumstain mark left by semen, esp. on bedding

cunt *Vulgar slang*. vulva

dental dam device placed in mouth to prevent

entrance of body fluids during oral sex, used as an AIDS preventative

dick *Vulgar slang*. penis

dink *Vulgar slang*. penis, esp. small one

dong *Vulgar slang*. penis

dork *Vulgar slang*. penis

ejaculation male orgasm with emission of sperm

erection stiffening of blood-filled penis due to sexual arousal

erogenous (*adj*) designating areas of body that are sensitive to sexual stimulation; erotogenic

erotogenic (*adj*) erogenous

estrogen female hormone

estrous cycle period of increased sexual interest and activity

eunuch castrated male

fallopian tube female internal tube that carries eggs from ovaries to uterus

family jewels *Slang*. man's genitals

fern *Vulgar slang*. female genitals

foreskin fleshy covering of head of penis

fur *Vulgar slang*. woman's pubic hair

gash *Vulgar slang*. vagina

genitalia genitals

genitals external sexual organs, male or female; genitalia

get (*vb*) beget

gonad organ producing eggs or sperm

gonorrhea infectious venereal disease characterized by inflammation of and discharge from mucous membrane

goose bumps raised body hairs due to intense sexual excitement

G spot extremely sensitive and erogenous spot in front wall of vagina, instrumental in orgasm

gynandrous (*adj*) having physical characteristics of both sexes

hard-on *Vulgar slang*. erection

heinie *Slang*. buttocks

hermaphrodite person with physical characteristics of both male and female

herpes simplex recurrent, incurable venereal disease affecting mouth or genitals with sores

hickey *Slang*. love bite; purplish bruise made by vigorous sucking of skin

honeypot *Vulgar slang*. vagina

hung (*adj*) *Vulgar slang*. having a large penis

hymen membrane that partly closes vagina of virgin; maidenhead

jelly roll *Vulgar slang*. vagina

jewels *Vulgar slang*. man's genitals

jissom *Vulgar slang*. semen

Johnnie *Vulgar slang*. penis

joint *Vulgar slang*. penis

jugs *Vulgar slang*. woman's breasts, esp. large ones

knockers *Vulgar slang*. woman's breasts

labia majora outer folds at vaginal opening

labia minora inner folds at vaginal opening

lingam *Sanskrit. lit.* male gender; penis, phallus

load *Vulgar slang*. sperm in one ejaculation; wad

love drop *Slang*. small quantity of semen emitted prior to full ejaculation; preorgasmic ejaculation

love juice *Slang*. semen

maidenhead hymen

mammary (*adj*) pertaining to woman's breasts

meat *Vulgar slang*. penis

member penis

merkin false hair for female pudenda

mons veneris female pubic mound

muff *Vulgar slang*. female pubic area

multiply (*vb*) have sexual intercourse, conceive, and bear children

nipple dark, sensitive, protuberant opening of breast through which milk flows

nooky *Vulgar slang*. vulva

nuts *Vulgar slang*. testicles

organ penis

orgasm convulsive climax of intercourse

ovary egg-producing organ of female

ovulation monthly dropping of egg from ovary to uterus

ovum egg produced by female

pecker *Vulgar slang*. penis

pelt *Vulgar slang*. woman's pubic hair

penis male erectile organ of copulation and bonding, used esp. by heterosexuals for insertion of sperm into uterus

period monthly menstruation

peter *Vulgar slang*. penis

phallic (*adj*) pertaining to the penis

phallus penis; object that represents or symbolizes penis

pizzle animal penis

PMS premenstrual syndrome

pole *Vulgar slang*. penis

premenstrual syndrome PMS; physical and emotional changes associated with hormonal fluctuations prior to menstruation

preorgasmic ejaculation small quantity of semen emitted prior to full ejaculation

prepuce foreskin

priapic (*adj*) pertaining to the penis

priapism abnormal, persistent erection without accompanying sexual desire

Priapus god of male sexuality (ancient Greece and Rome)

prick *Vulgar slang*. penis

primary sex characteristic feature differentiating male from female in relation to reproduction

private parts external sexual organs; genitals

procreate (*vb*) have sexual intercourse resulting in childbirth

prong *Vulgar slang*. penis

prostate gland gland at base of urethra in males

prunes *Vulgar slang*. testicles

puberty onset of sexual maturity

pubes pubic hair

pubescence arrival at puberty

pubic (*adj*) pertaining to or situated in area of pubis

pubic hair hair appearing at puberty around lower abdomen and genitals

pubic lice small parasitic insects living in pubic hair and transmitted by sexual contact

pubis lower abdomen, covered with hair and forming bony protuberance above genitals

pudenda external female genitals

pussy *Vulgar slang.* female genitals

putz *Vulgar slang.* penis

quim *Vulgar slang.* female genitals

racks *Vulgar slang.* female breasts

reproduction sexual process of conception, pregnancy, and birth of young

rim *Vulgar slang.* anus

rocks *Vulgar slang.* male genitals

rod *Vulgar slang.* penis

root *Vulgar slang.* penis

safe sex use of condom during intercourse as protection against disease; practice of oral sex or mutual masturbation for same purpose

scrotum sack holding testicles

secondary sex characteristic feature, such as body hair or breasts, that differentiates males and females but is not directly connected to production of egg or sperm

semen male ejaculate containing sperm

sex basic division of a species into male and female, for purpose of reproduction; sexual activity; instinct or attraction drawing one sex toward another; sexual intercourse; genitals

sex change operation surgical reconstruction of one's sexual organs as those of the opposite sex

sexually transmitted disease any of various infections acquired through contact of sexual organs, including AIDS, ARC, chlamydia, crabs, gonorrhea, herpes simplex, pubic lice, syphilis, trichomoniasis, venereal disease, and yeast infection; venereal disease

short hairs *Slang.* pubic hair

slit *Vulgar slang.* vagina

smegma sebaceous matter secreted around penis or clitoris; cheese

snatch *Vulgar slang.* female genitals

social disease venereal disease

spado castrated man

sperm spermatozoon, male seed in semen

spotting menstrual discharge occurring between periods

stacked *(adj) Slang.* having voluptuous, sexually appealing body, esp. large breasts

sterile *(adj)* barren, incapable of procreating

syphilis infectious degenerative venereal disease acquired through sexual contact or congenitally

T and A tits and ass

testicle sperm-producing gland at base of penis; testis

testis testicle; *pl.* **testes**

testosterone male hormone

tit *Vulgar slang.* breast

tool *Vulgar slang.* penis

trichomoniasis parasitic infestation of vagina causing heavy discharge

tumescence stiffening and engorging of penis

tush *Slang.* buttocks

twat *Vulgar slang.* female genitals

uterus organ of conception and nurturance of fetus; womb

vagina canal from vulva to uterus

vaginal orgasm orgasm occurring in vagina

vas deferens tube carrying sperm from testicle to penis

venereal disease disease transmitted by sexual contact with infected person; sexually transmitted disease; social disease

Venus mound *Slang.* female genitalia; mons veneris

vulva external female genitals

wad *Vulgar slang.* unejaculated sperm; sperm in single ejaculation

wet dream ejaculation during sleep

wet spot semen-soaked mark on sheets after sex, or on man's underpants

whang *Vulgar slang.* penis

wiener *Vulgar slang.* penis

wieny *Vulgar slang.* penis

willy *Vulgar slang.* penis

wing-wang *Vulgar slang.* penis

womb uterus

wong *Vulgar slang.* penis

yeast infection fungus living in vagina

yoni *Sanskrit.* vulva

Contraception and Fertility

abortion induced expulsion of fetus from mother's womb

artificial insemination insemination of woman for purposes of conception through medical procedure rather than intercourse

barren *(adj)* infertile; unable to conceive

bilateral tubal ligation BTL; surgical sterilization of female

birth control prevention of conception by chemical or mechanical means; contraception

birth-control pill contraceptive hormone, usu. estrogen and progesterone, taken daily in tablet form by women, that causes temporary infertility

BTL bilateral tubal ligation

catcher's mitt *Slang.* diaphragm

cervical cap diaphragmlike device used with spermicidal jelly to prevent sperm from entering uterus

climacteric period of major physiological change, such as menopause

coil intrauterine contraceptive device

coitus interruptus contraception through withdrawal of penis before ejaculation

condom usu. rubber sheath worn on penis to capture semen during intercourse and thus prevent conception

contraception prevention of pregnancy

contraceptive sponge absorbent material containing spermicide placed on cervix for contraception

curse *Slang.* monthly menstrual period

diaphragm rubber disk worn on cervix during intercourse for contraception by preventing sperm from entering uterus

douche water or cleansing agent used for washing semen from vagina after intercourse, considered ineffective contraceptive method

emmenagogue substance or practice that promotes menstruation

false pregnancy symptoms of pregnancy without having actual embryo in womb

fertility ability to conceive or impregnate

fertility drug hormonal substance used to induce ovulation and produce pregnancy

flying Baker *Slang.* menstrual period

foam spermicidal substance placed in vagina for contraceptive purposes

French tickler *Slang.* condom

geld *(vb)* castrate, usu. in reference to animals

glove *Slang.* condom

gravid *(adj)* pregnant

hysterectomy surgical removal of uterus

impregnate *(vb)* make (a female) pregnant; cause (an egg) to be fertilized

infertility inability to conceive or impregnate; barrenness; sterility

intrauterine device IUD; contraceptive device worn continuously for up to several years inside uterus to prevent fertilization or implantation

in trouble *Slang.* pregnant and unmarried

in utero *(adj)* in the womb or uterus

in vitro *(adj) Latin.* lit. in glass; artificially inseminated and maintained, as in a test tube

IUD intrauterine device

knock up *(vb) Slang.* impregnate

loop type of IUD

menarche first menstruation, at beginning of fertility

menopause end of menstruation and fertility

menses monthly menstruation

menstruation monthly discharge of blood from uterus when conception has not occurred

morning-after pill contraceptive chemical taken after intercourse to prevent implantation of embryo

Norplant *Trademark.* contraceptive device implanted under woman's skin, where it slowly releases hormone progestin for five years

pessary contraceptive device worn in vagina

pill birth-control pill

pregnant *(adj)* carrying fetus inside womb; with child

prophylactic device something that prevents conception and venereal disease, esp. a condom

rag *Vulgar slang.* menstrual period

rhythm method contraceptive method that gauges likelihood of fertility during woman's menstrual cycle

rubber *Slang.* condom

salpingectomy surgical severing of fallopian tubes to sterilize a woman

skin *Slang.* condom

spermicidal jelly sperm-killing, jellylike substance placed in vagina during intercourse

spermicide substance that kills sperm

sterility inability to produce living offspring

sterilization surgical procedure that prevents conception

Trojan *Trademark.* condom

tubal ligation sterilization of female by sealing

off of fallopian tubes to prevent ovum from reaching uterus

tying one's tubes *Slang.* tubal ligation

vasectomy surgical procedure for sterilizing men by cutting vas deferens

with child pregnant

Sex Acts

action *Slang.* sexual activity

act of love intercourse

adultery sex act by married person with someone other than spouse

anal intercourse penetration of anus by penis

anilingus oral anal sex

ass *Slang.* sexual intercourse

astride (*adj*) taking a dominant position during penetration

autoeroticism self-stimulation, masturbation

ball (*vb*) *Vulgar slang.* have sexual intercourse

bang (*vb*) *Vulgar slang.* have sexual intercourse

beat off (*vb*) *Vulgar slang.* masturbate

bed (*vb*) take to bed for sexual activity

blow (*vb*) *Vulgar slang.* perform fellatio on

blow job oral penile sex, fellatio

boff (*vb*) *Vulgar slang.* have sexual intercourse

bundling cuddling in bed without undressing

circle jerk *Vulgar slang.* mutual masturbation among three or more persons

coition coitus

coitus sexual intercourse; coition

come (*vb*) *Informal.* reach orgasm

congress sexual intercourse

consummation sexual intercourse, esp. on wedding night

cop a feel touch another's body sexually, often in quick and surreptitious way

copulation sexual intercourse

cornhole (*vb*) *Slang.* perform anal intercourse

couple (*vb*) have sexual intercourse

cream (*vb*) *Vulgar slang.* come, reach orgasm

cream one's jeans *Vulgar slang.* reach orgasm

cunnilingus oral vaginal sex

deflower (*vb*) have sexual intercourse with a virgin

diddle (*vb*) *Slang.* have sexual intercourse

do it (*vb*) *Slang.* have sexual intercourse

eat (*vb*) *Vulgar slang.* perform fellatio or cunnilingus on

ejaculate (*vb*) emit sperm at orgasm

feel act of touching another sexually

feel up (*vb*) *Vulgar slang.* fondle someone in a sexual manner, esp. touch a woman's breasts

fellatio oral penile sex

fingerfuck (*vb*) *Vulgar slang.* manually stimulate female's genitals

foreplay fondling and caressing before actual intercourse

fornication sexual intercourse, esp. between unmarried persons

frig (*vb*) *Vulgar slang.* have sexual intercourse

fuck (*vb*) *Vulgar slang.* have sexual intercourse

fucking *Vulgar slang.* sexual intercourse

get down (*vb*) *Slang.* have sexual relations

get it on *Vulgar slang.* have sexual relations

get it up *Vulgar slang.* achieve erection of penis

get off (*vb*) *Vulgar slang.* reach orgasm

give head *Vulgar slang.* perform oral sex

go all the way *Slang.* have sexual intercourse

go down on *Vulgar slang.* have oral-genital sex with

hand job *Vulgar slang.* stimulation by hand of another's genitals; masturbation

have sex (*vb*) engage in sexual intercourse

hide the salami *Vulgar slang.* have sexual intercourse

hump (*vb*) *Vulgar slang.* have sexual intercourse

inseminate (*vb*) ejaculate into (vagina); impregnate (a female)

intercourse copulation between male and female

in the saddle having mounted one's usu. female partner

irrumation oral penile sex, esp. involving active thrusting of penis; fellatio

jack off (*vb*) *Vulgar slang.* masturbate

jerk off (*vb*) *Vulgar slang.* masturbate

jump (*vb*) *Vulgar slang.* engage in sexual intercourse with

know (*vb*) have sexual intercourse with (biblical)

lay (*vb*) *Vulgar slang.* have sexual intercourse with

lie with (*vb*) have sexual intercourse with

lovemaking sexual relations

make (*vb*) *Slang.* have sexual relations with

make it *Slang.* have sexual intercourse

make love have sexual intercourse

masturbation self-stimulation of one's sexual organs

mate (*vb*) have sexual relations

ménage à trois sex act among three people

missionary position sexual intercourse with man on top and woman underneath lying face to face

mount (*vb*) position oneself atop female

muff diver *Vulgar slang.* cunnilingus enthusiast

mustache ride *Vulgar slang.* oral sex

nooky *Vulgar slang.* sexual intercourse

onanism masturbation; uncompleted intercourse

peel (*vb*) *Slang.* undress prior to having sex

penetration entry of male into female

play with oneself masturbate

pork (*vb*) *Vulgar slang.* have sexual intercourse

pound off (*vb*) *Vulgar slang.* masturbate

premarital sex sexual relations before marriage

pull a train *Vulgar slang.* have uninterrupted sex with a series of male partners, esp. bikers

pump (*vb*) thrust with pelvis during intercourse

quickie *Informal.* brief, often secretive sex act

ravish (*vb*) force someone to have sexual relations

ream (*vb*) *Vulgar slang.* have sexual intercourse with a woman

relations sexual intercourse

rim job *Vulgar slang.* anilingus

rocks off *Vulgar slang.* ejaculation

romp (*vb*) have playful sexual relations

rut (*vb*) *Vulgar slang.* have sexual intercourse

safe sex sexual relations using condoms or other devices as precautionary measure against disease, esp. AIDS

score (*vb*) *Slang.* entice another into having sexual intercourse

screw (*vb*) *Vulgar slang.* have sexual intercourse

seduce (*vb*) entice unwilling or doubtful person into sex

service (*vb*) *Vulgar slang.* have sexual intercourse to satisfy another's needs

sexual intercourse copulation between male and female

sexual relations intercourse and related sexual activities

shoot one's wad *Vulgar slang.* ejaculate

shtup (*vb*) *Vulgar slang.* have sexual intercourse

sixty-nine *Vulgar slang.* simultaneous, mutual oral genital sex

slam (*vb*) *Vulgar slang.* have sexual intercourse with

slam bang *Vulgar slang.* quickie

sleep around (*vb*) *Informal.* have casual sex with numerous partners

sleep with (*vb*) have sexual intercourse with, make love to

statutory rape sex with person under legal age of consent

suck (*vb*) pull gently with mouth, esp. on partner's genitals

swive (*vb*) *Archaic.* have sexual intercourse

take (*vb*) have sexual intercourse with

take a lover find or accept sex partner

twiddle (*vb*) *Vulgar slang.* have sexual relations

union sexual intercourse

venery gratification of sexual desire

wank off (*vb*) *Vulgar slang.* masturbate

whack off (*vb*) *Vulgar slang.* masturbate

Perversions, Fetishes, and Titillations

algolagnia pleasure and gratification derived from inflicting or suffering pain; sadism

bestiality sexual activity with animals

bondage sex involving forcible restraint or tying up of partner

breather person excited by telephoning someone, often unknown, and breathing heavily over phone

bugger (*vb*) *Vulgar slang.* sodomize

buggery *Vulgar slang.* anal intercourse

child abuse sexual molestation of child by adult

clitoridectomy excision of clitoris to curb female sexual desire

coprophilia sexual stimulation from feces

crime against nature sexual perversion

date rape rape inflicted by person with whom victim is socializing voluntarily

defile (*vb*) humiliate or brutalize sexually

delicate self-cutting usu. female perversion in which normal cosmetic tweezings and pluckings are extended to self-infliction of small cuts

deviance behavior that is socially disapproved of and considered unnatural or abnormal

deviant (*adj*) departing from the norm,

considered perverse or unnatural; (*n*) one who acts thus

dildo *Slang*. artificial penis, used as sexual aid

dominance sex in which one partner humiliates, degrades, or intimidates the other for sexual stimulation

exhibitionism exposing oneself to others for sexual stimulation

exploitation degradation, victimization, or profit making from sexual activity

fetish sexual obsession with a specific object or usu. nonerogenous body part

fig leaf coy covering of genitals on nude body or statue

flagellation sexual stimulation by whipping or beating

flashing sudden public exposure of one's nudity for sexual stimulation

frottage practice of deriving stimulation by rubbing up against another person, as in a crowded place

gangbang *Vulgar slang*. sexual intercourse, usu. forcible, engaged in by several persons successively with one partner

golden shower urination that causes sexual stimulation

group grope *Slang*. orgy

homeovestism dressing oneself as a sexual object, esp. among women, to derive sexual excitement

incest sexual relations among family members

incubus evil male spirit who has sex with women in their sleep

indecent exposure public nudity

infibulation sewing shut of vagina

jailbait *Slang*. person under legal age of consent taken as sexual partner

kinky (*adj*) perverse, decadent, or unusual in one's sexual habits

masochism derivation of sexual pleasure from undergoing pain, abuse, or cruelty

molestation sexual assault, esp. of defenseless person or child

mooning *Slang*. exposing one's bare buttocks in public

necrophilia sexual stimulation from corpses

nymphomania insatiable sexual craving in women

off-color (*adj*) somewhat offensive, indecent

orgy group sexual relations

panty raid college prank involving males' theft of females' underwear

paraphilia mental disorder characterized by preference for unusual sexual practices and perversions

pedophilia sexual desire in an adult for children

Peeping Tom voyeur

perversion deviance or sexual maladjustment; such an act; paraphilia

pervert person who is sexually maladjusted, with abnormal tastes and habits

rape forcible sexual relations

renifleur person sexually aroused by odors

sadism derivation of sexual pleasure from inflicting pain on others

sadomasochism derivation of sexual pleasure from inflicting and undergoing pain or cruelty; S and M

S and M **s**ado **m**asochism

satyriasis insatiable sexual craving in men

scopophilia sexual pleasure derived by looking at nude bodies or erotic photographs

sex crime immoral, illegal sex act; sexual outrage against another

sexual assault rape or molestation

short eyes *Slang*. pedophile

sodomy anal intercourse; intercourse with animals

stimulator electric dildo; vibrator

streaking running naked through public place as form of exhibitionism

submission allowing oneself to be dominated to derive sexual stimulation

succubus female demon who has sex with men in their sleep

swinging *Slang*. exchanging partners with another couple

taboo (*adj*) forbidden due to indecency or bad taste

telephone sex stimulation through verbal sexual fantasies heard over telephone

titillate (*vb*) excite sexually

titillation erotic stimulation

transsexuality predisposition to identify with opposite sex, often accompanied by sex change operation

transvestism practice of dressing in attire of opposite sex, esp. among men

unnatural act sexual practice considered abnormal

urolagnia deriving sexual stimulation from urination, esp. drinking of urine

vibrator electric dildo

vice immoral or illegal sexual practice

voyeurism watching others disrobe or engage in sex for purposes of sexual stimulation

vulgarity coarse sexual behavior and language

water sports *Slang*. erotic urination; urolagnia

zoophilia sexual excitement derived from animals

Pornography and Prostitution

bagnio brothel

bawd female procurer, madam

beefcake *Informal*. photographs of nude or nearly nude young men in magazines, posed to display their muscles or genitals

bordello brothel, whorehouse

brothel whorehouse; bagnio

call girl *Slang*. often high-class prostitute who arranges appointments for sex by phone

camp follower prostitute on military base

cat *Slang*. prostitute

cathouse *Slang*. whorehouse

centerfold photo of nude woman or man featured in magazine

cheesecake *Informal*. photographs of nude or scantily clad women posed suggestively

chicken *Slang*. young prostitute, esp. homosexual

chicken hawk *Slang*. older male customer for young male prostitute

chippy *Slang*. prostitute

concubine woman serving as mistress or member of harem

courtesan prostitute for upper classes of society

demimondaine female prostitute

demimonde society of female prostitutes

easy woman prostitute

escort service service providing call girls under guise of being public dates

fallen woman prostitute

floozy *Slang*. disreputable woman, usu. prostitute

geisha professional hostess for men's parties, often mistakenly thought to be prostitute (Japan)

gigolo man supported by women in return for sex

groupie *Informal*. female who pursues celebrities, esp. rock musicians, for sex

hard-core (*adj*) graphic and explicit in pornographic content

harem group of wives or concubines belonging to polygamous male

harlot prostitute

hetaera highly-cultured courtesan or concubine (ancient Greece)

hooker *Slang*. prostitute

hustler *Slang*. prostitute

john *Slang*. person paying prostitute for sex

knocking shop *Chiefly Brit*. house of prostitution

lady of the night *Slang*. prostitute

madam woman managing whorehouse

massage parlor business usu. providing sexual services for sale in addition to nonsexual massage

obscenity indecent, offensive sexual behavior or content

odalisque female slave, harem concubine

pander (*vb*) solicit customers for prostitutes

peep show lewd entertainment featuring nude women

pimp procurer

pinup girl usu. naked or scantily clad woman posing seductively for photographs

ponce *Brit. slang*. pimp

pornography writing or pictures portraying sexual activity and intending to arouse

procurer man who solicits customers for prostitute; pimp

prostitute person who sells sexual acts to strangers

prostitution sexual intercourse or acts for payment

red-light district area of city with whorehouses and prostitutes

seraglio Muslim harem; whorehouse

skin flick *Slang*. film that features nudity and explicit sexual activity

smut pornography

snuff film *Slang.* pornographic film involving real, not staged, killing of performers

soft-core (*adj*) having borderline pornographic content

solicit (*vb*) offer sexual services for hire

streetwalker prostitute doing business on public streets, usu. cheaper than call girl

stripper person doing striptease dance

striptease lewd entertainment featuring woman or man removing clothes in time to music

strumpet prostitute

tart prostitute

tramp prostitute

trick *Slang.* prostitute's customer

trollop prostitute

turn a trick perform sex act with customer

wench former term for prostitute

white slavery prostitution ring using young, often rural girls kidnapped into bondage

whore prostitute

whorehouse building where prostitutes are available for hire

X-rated (*adj*) pornographic, used esp. of a book or film

zenana harem, seraglio

STRATEGY, INTRIGUE, AND DECEPTION

Strategy and Tactics
Intrigues, Plots, and Corruption
Secrecy and Concealment
Pranks and Tricks
Falsehood, Pretense, and Exaggeration
Fraud, Treachery, and Deception

See also: *Chap. 11: War and Military; Chap. 20: Insults, Slurs, and Epithets; Chap. 23: Judgment and Criticism; Chap. 24: Crime*

Strategy and Tactics

about-face sudden reversal of position

aggrandizement actions intended to increase power or wealth

angle secret motive; (*vb*) attempt to gain advantage, often by improper or illicit means

approach preliminary steps taken in setting about task or problem

arm-twisting application of direct, personal pressure to achieve desired result

arrangement informal, often secret agreement or plan

artfulness skill and cunning in adapting means to ends

artifice clever, artful stratagem

baffle (*vb*) confuse, perplex

bait (*vb*) tease or torment with persistent, malicious attacks to generate desired response

bedevil (*vb*) utterly confuse and harass so as to take advantage of

befuddle (*vb*) confuse, perplex

bewilder (*vb*) utterly confuse or puzzle by number or complexity of considerations

bind situation in which one is obstructed or held in check; predicament

blow hot and cold change from favorable to opposing view and back again

blueprint detailed plan

brain-picking *Informal.* act of gaining information from another by careful questioning

brinkmanship pushing a risky situation to the limit of safety

buttonhole (*vb*) detain in conversation as if by physical restraint

buy off (*vb*) persuade to action or restraint by payment or other inducement

cage trap or ensnaring device

cagey (*adj*) shrewd, esp. cautious not to be entrapped

calculated (*adj*) carefully thought out to accomplish an end

call one's bluff confront and expose another's empty threat or pretense

canny (*adj*) clever, calculating, or shrewd

capitulation act or condition of surrender and submission

captious (*adj*) designed to confuse or ensnare, esp. in argument

capture (*vb*) take or attain domination of by stratagem or guile

carrot something used as a lure or incentive

cash in on (*vb*) obtain advantage or profit from

cat and mouse act of teasing and playing with something before destroying it

catch concealed drawback, complication, or means of entrapment

Catch-22 paradoxical problem whose solution is made impossible by circumstances inherent in it; senseless and self-contradictory policy or bureaucratic regulation

change of heart reversal of opinion or point of view

chart (*vb*) carefully plan out (a course of action)

chink *Informal.* small opening permitting evasion or escape

circuitous (*adj*) indirect or evasive in deeds or language

clout predominant influence within particular circle

coax (*vb*) persuade or influence by flattery; manipulate to desired end by prolonged effort and adroit handling

coercion use of force or intimidation to obtain compliance

competition rivalry between two or more parties to secure the favor of a third party

complicate (*vb*) make more difficult or complex than necessary

compromise (*vb*) make mutual concessions to achieve overall end or reach agreement

concession act of yielding on or acknowledgement of disputed point

concoction scheme or plan that has been devised; fabrication

conduit person who serves as means of transmitting or distributing information or goods

confound (*vb*) perplex, baffle, or throw into confusion

confrontation face-to-face encounter with adversary

confuse (*vb*) make unclear or blurred; perplex or bewilder

contrivance artificial arrangement or scheme

convoluted (*adj*) tortuously involved, complex, or confusing

cook up (*vb*) *Informal.* concoct, devise, or improvise

corner (*vb*) drive into a position without escape; entrap

countermine (*vb*) devise stratagem or counterplot, esp. for halting enemy attack

coup swift, cunning, and successful action

craft skill or cunning in achieving ends or deceiving others

create (*vb*) devise, fabricate, or make up

cross (*vb*) oppose, contradict, or thwart

cunning ingenuity, craftiness, and subtle skill, often used for deception

curve deceptive or misleading maneuver

dare (*vb*) meet boldly or defiantly; challenge another to prove himself or herself

deploy (*vb*) spread out, place, use, or arrange strategically

design specific purpose; plans and schemes formed to achieve some purpose

device stratagem or trick, esp. method of deception

devise (*vb*) contrive or plan to bring about

diagram detailed plan or outline in graphic form

disown (*vb*) refuse to acknowledge as pertaining to oneself; deny responsibility for

distraction something intended to divert attention away from something else

diversion pretense or feint that draws attention away from one's true purpose or primary action

dodge clever expedient or contrivance, used to evade or gain advantage

double duplicate; counterpart of another

edge advantage over an adversary

embarrass (*vb*) involve in public shame or difficulty; place in doubt; impede by obstacles or difficulties

encroach (*vb*) advance gradually or stealthily beyond proper limits; trespass into another's territory

engineer (*vb*) manage by skillful contrivance

enticement temptation that leads on or excites false hopes

entrap (*vb*) place in position from which there is no escape; corner

evasion elusion or escape by trickery or clever stratagem; avoidance of one's obligations

expediency adherence to what is advantageous in achieving a specific end, often without regard for what is ethical or just

expedient means to an end

fabrication concoction

feather one's nest take advantage of opportunities for gain, esp. at another's expense

feint attack aimed at one point as a distraction from the real point of attack

fence (*vb*) parry arguments by avoiding direct answers

finesse (*vb*) handle situation with skill and adroitness

flip-flop *Informal.* abrupt, often repeated, change of position

foil (*vb*) keep from succeeding; thwart

foment (*vb*) promote or incite, esp. to create discontent or rebellion

forestall (*vb*) obstruct or thwart by prior action

fox (*vb*) trick or outwit by cunning

frame (*vb*) contrive or devise, as a plan

freeload (*vb*) *Informal.* take advantage of another's generosity

gag (*vb*) restrain from speaking freely

gambit maneuver calculated to gain an advantage, esp. at the outset

gamble venture of uncertain outcome or involving risk

game stratagem, often tricky or illegal

game plan carefully thought out, long-range strategy or course of action toward a specific end

gamesmanship use of ethically dubious or improper but not strictly illegal means and expedients to achieve an objective

gimmick ingenious scheme or device; hidden feature

guideline general indicator for future course of action

haggle (*vb*) bargain or wrangle, esp. in petty or quarrelsome way

hatch (*vb*) invent, fabricate, or initiate

hedge intentionally evasive, vague statement; line of retreat left open in order to avoid commitment

hogtie (*vb*) make helpless so as to hamper or thwart

hook something that entices or attracts others

horse trading crafty negotiating or self-serving compromise

house of cards scheme or plan that is delicately balanced and vulnerable to imminent collapse

hucksterism use of aggressive or flashy methods to influence others, esp. to make a sale

hunch strong premonition; guess

impede (*vb*) hinder or retard in progress by means of obstacles

incite (*vb*) urge on to action

infringe (*vb*) encroach upon and violate, esp. the rights of others

instigate (*vb*) incite or provoke to action

interlope (*vb*) intrude upon another's rights or territory

inveigle (*vb*) obtain, persuade, or entice by flattery and artful talk

invention original idea, concept, or plan

jockey (*vb*) maneuver cleverly for position of advantage

juggling act process of skillfully managing several elements at once

jury-rig (*vb*) construct or arrange temporarily in haphazard manner

knack clever method or stratagem

labyrinth complex, sometimes devious arrangement or maze

lead on (*vb*) induce to follow unwise course; draw into trap

live by one's wits achieve one's goals through cunning, guile, and mental quickness

loophole means of escape, esp. through an ambiguity or omission in a document permitting an evasion or misconstruction of its intent

low blow unscrupulous or unfair attack

lull (*vb*) cause to feel a false sense of security, esp. prior to attack

lure (*vb*) attract or entice into danger by false promise or decoy

Machiavellian (*adj*) devious, cunning, or unscrupulous

machination scheme or crafty design with evil purpose

maneuver (*vb*) employ clever stratagems or schemes to achieve an end; skillfully manipulate a person or situation to one's advantage

manipulate (*vb*) manage skillfully, esp. control by cunning or insidious means to one's advantage

map out (*vb*) envision and plan beforehand

mastermind (*vb*) provide skillful direction and supervision for (an important activity)

meddle (*vb*) interfere with or involve oneself in another's activity without right or invitation

method system, technique, or specific plan of action

nepotism favoritism shown toward one's relations

nickel-and-dime (*vb*) defeat by small, gradual incursions

obstruction something that impedes another's course

obviate (*vb*) eliminate (a difficulty) before it arises

on the make seeking to improve one's position by any means necessary

operate (*vb*) exert a force or influence, often by following an irregular course of action

opportunism unscrupulous or unprincipled exploitation of opportunities

orchestrate (*vb*) arrange so as to achieve best result

outflank (*vb*) bypass (one's adversary)

outfox (*vb*) outwit

outguess (*vb*) outwit by anticipating others' actions

outline general or preliminary plan indicating only its essential features

outmaneuver (*vb*) outdo or defeat by skillful planning

outreach (*vb*) take advantage of through deception

outsmart (*vb*) outwit

outwit (*vb*) use superior cunning or ingenuity to get the better of; outfox; outsmart

parlay (*vb*) use (one's assets) to achieve greater success or wealth

parry (*vb*) evade or adroitly ward off

pass the buck shift one's responsibility to another

pawn person used or manipulated to further another's purposes

perpetrate (*vb*) execute or commit (an act, esp. a crime)

perplex (*vb*) hamper with complications or confusion

pitch *Informal.* persuasive line of reasoning

pitfall trap or hidden danger

placebo inert substance substituted for active one in experiment as trick or test control

plain dealing direct and honest conduct in one's transactions with others

plan procedure, design, or method of action with specific objective

play both ends against the middle maneuver opposing groups against each other to one's own advantage

play possum gain advantage of someone by feigning sleep or death

ploy maneuver or stratagem, esp. used to frustrate adversary

ply (*vb*) supply or offer something so as to gain advantage

political (*adj*) adept at influencing and manipulating allies and adversaries

posture viewpoint or attitude regarding specific condition

program detailed, long-range plan for achieving an end

projection visualization of a plan to its anticipated end; scenario

prospectus initial description and projection of a venture

provoke (*vb*) stir up intentionally

pull strings exercise covert influence or control

put up to (*vb*) incite or instigate

raid surprise attack; daring escapade, esp. against adversary; sudden incursion by legal authorities

ransack (*vb*) search thoroughly, esp. during a robbery

rejigger (*vb*) *Informal.* change or rearrange in a new or different way, esp. by using techniques not always considered ethical

retaliate (*vb*) exact revenge upon an adversary

retraction disavowal of previous view or statement

retreat tactical withdrawal from difficulty or danger

retrench (*vb*) reduce, diminish, or curtail to economize or shift emphasis of plans

revenge (*vb*) inflict injury in return for

sandbag (*vb*) *Informal.* coerce by threat or force; treat harshly; thwart

scenario description of possible outcome based on projected actions

scheme cunning, usu. secret plan of action

scuttle (*vb*) abandon, withdraw from, or eliminate (prior plans or resources)

shrewd (*adj*) astute, keen, clever

skull session meeting held to plan strategy

sly fox crafty, cunning, often devious individual

smooth operator one who maneuvers and manipulates with deft cunning

snaffle (*vb*) *Brit. informal.* acquire by devious or odd means

song and dance long, misleading or irrelevant statement, often used as distraction

stratagem clever trick or device for outwitting or gaining advantage over adversary or attaining objective

strategy careful, cleverly devised plan or series of maneuvers for attaining a specific goal or result

string along (*vb*) *Informal.* draw into a circumstance and keep in an unresolved state

subtlety astute perception in handling others

system highly organized method or procedure for attaining an end or maintaining a position

tactic plan, procedure, or expedient for promoting a desired end or result

tactics system or method for achieving success or advantage by use of one's means and resources

tantalize (*vb*) torment by tempting with something unattainable

tap (*vb*) draw on (one's resources)

tease (*vb*) tempt, tantalize, or taunt, esp. with persistently petty annoyances

temptation something that entices another to do wrong

throw off (*vb*) mislead or distract

thwart (*vb*) successfully frustrate (another's purpose)

linker (*vb*) adjust or arrange in an unskilled manner

toy with (*vb*) amuse oneself at another's expense

trimmer one who alters his or her view to achieve ends

trip up (*vb*) detect in a fault or mistake; expose

trump card *Informal.* final, conclusive factor that gives advantage to one group or person

turn (*vb*) change or cause to change allegiance

twist clever and unexpected device or development

undermine (*vb*) subvert and weaken in degrees by insidious, often secret actions

use (*vb*) manipulate; take advantage of

vacillate (*vb*) alter one's opinion or position frequently; hesitate in one's decisions

vantage position of advantage or superiority

venture speculative undertaking

vex (*vb*) puzzle or confound

volte-face *French.* about-face; reversal of position

vulpine (*adj*) foxy, cunning or sly

waiting game delaying of an action in hopes of a better opportunity to come

weave (*vb*) contrive by an elaborate combination of elements

wheel and deal *Informal.* pursue one's goals without restraint by using personal power

wheeler-dealer *Informal.* shrewd, unrestrained operator

wild card unpredictable person or element with determining impact

window of opportunity most advantageous moment for doing something or implementing a plan

work (*vb*) exploit; make use of

wrangle (*vb*) obtain by petty, persistent argument

wrinkle innovative device, trick, strategy, or aspect

Intrigues, Plots, and Corruption

agent provocateur one who associates with and incites suspected persons to incriminating acts

agitator one who stirs up public feeling, esp. inciting unlawful acts

baksheesh tip or bribe

bane curse; source of harm

barratry purchase or sale of preferment or office in church or state

Black Hand any of various secret criminal societies, orig. Italian

blood feud persistent conflict between families or clans

boiler room *Slang.* central location for telephone salesmen using high-pressure techniques to sell things of dubious value

boodle *Slang.* bribe money

bookmaking determining odds and accepting illegal bets

brew (*vb*) contrive, plot, or scheme

bribe something given secretly to influence opinion, esp. money; payoff

Byzantine (*adj*) characterized by devious, surreptitious, intentionally convoluted operation

cabal plot, esp. persons secretly united against their government

camarilla *Spanish.* group of secret, scheming advisors

camorra secret society with dishonorable ends, orig. 19th-century Italy

catch up (*vb*) cause to be apprehended for illicit activities

cell small group acting as a unit within larger organization, often in secret

Chinese puzzle something complicated, obscure, and perplexing

choplogic convoluted, often sophistic reasoning

cloak-and-dagger (*adj*) pertaining to melodrama, intrigue, and espionage

close call narrow escape

close shave *Informal.* near miss; narrow escape

coalition temporary alliance of distinct parties for specific purpose

cobweb network of confusion, deception, or complexity

co-conspirator one who joins another in a conspiracy

cohort companion or colleague, esp. in some scheme

collaborator one who cooperates and assists in a scheme

collogue (*vb*) conspire; confer privately

collusion secret agreement to cooperate for deceitful purpose

complicity taking part in or having knowledge of another's illicit activity

conclave private meeting or secret assembly of a group

confederacy conspiracy or agreement among persons, often for unlawful purpose

connivance knowledge of, consent to, or cooperation in illegal or deceitful act

consort (*vb*) associate with someone, esp. in criminal or illicit activities

conspiracy secret agreement or scheme among several parties to perform wrongful act

conspirator one taking part in a conspiracy

conspire (*vb*) form a conspiracy with one or more people

contract secret arrangement for hired assassin to commit murder

conventicle unauthorized assembly, esp. for unsanctioned worship

corruption inducement to or engagement in improper or wrongful acts

counterplot scheme devised to thwart opponent's plot

coup d'état secret plot by small group to overthrow existing government in sudden, decisive action

covin conspiracy to defraud or harm others

cult secret organization intensely devoted to promotion of specific goals, individuals, or beliefs

deal private arrangement with another for mutual advantage

defection desertion, esp. betrayal of one's national allegiance

depose (*vb*) remove from office

dethrone (*vb*) remove from power, esp. from royal throne

dive faking of knockout in boxing match that has been prearranged for benefit of wagerers

double agent one pretending to serve one government while secretly serving its enemy

éminence grise *French. lit.* gray eminence; confidential agent wielding unofficial power

escape (*vb*) avoid evil, danger, or threat; find a way out of confinement before release date

espionage intelligence gathering by agents of one government or company about plans and actions of another

feud bitter, prolonged opposition

fix (*vb*) illegally predetermine or prearrange outcome of something, usu. for profit

fixer *Informal.* one who arranges the outcome of an event through bribery or influence

gang group secretly organized to perform illegal acts; ring

gerrymandering inequitable division of political territory

grease someone's palm give a bribe to someone

grudge prolonged and deep-seated feeling of ill will

guerrilla one engaged in sabotage, terrorism, and irregular warfare

heeler ward heeler

henchman unscrupulous, often violent, subordinate

in cahoots *Informal.* in league; having a partnership, esp. to deceive

infiltrate (*vb*) enter unobtrusively and establish oneself for purpose of subversion

inside information details or plans known only to select individuals and held in confidence

insurgency often disorganized and sporadic revolt against a government

insurrection organized, open rebellion against a government

intrigant one who engages in intrigues and schemes

intrigue secret scheme or plot; underhanded or deceitful stratagem, often very intricate

jimmy (*vb*) force open with a crowbar, esp. for purpose of robbery

jobbery unscrupulous conduct by public officials for private gain

kickback reimbursement of funds based on secret collusion, usu. to defraud another

load (*vb*) alter balance of dice to make them predictable

maze intricate, confusing, often misleading sequence of actions or purposes

mole double agent whose cover is established before spying begins

morass something that entraps or obstructs

mutiny organized opposition to authority, esp. on ship

net entrapping device or circumstance

network interconnected group of individuals with common goal

on the take *Slang.* accepting bribes or payments for favors granted

outbreak initiation of uprising or insurrection

pack (*vb*) influence makeup of (an institution or body) to secure one's purpose

patronage awarding of official jobs to gain political advantage

payoff *Informal.* bribe

payola *Informal.* secret payments for promotion or service, esp. to radio disc jockeys by record companies

perquisite bonus or fringe benefit in excess of regular salary

plant something or someone secretly put in place for later discovery to create a desired effect

plot secret plan, usu. for evil or unlawful end; intrigue

powerbroker person whose influence is based on control of votes or individuals

power play maneuver or strategy in which concentrated power is used to control a situation or rival

propaganda information and ideas spread deliberately to further one's goals or hinder those of one's adversary

provocateur one who incites or arouses others to illegal acts

push (*vb*) urge support for (specific position or cause); engage in sale of (illicit substance, esp. drugs)

putsch secret plot to overthrow a government, usu. relying on a sudden and swift uprising

rebellion defiance of or resistance to established authority

revolt organized uprising against a government

rig (*vb*) manipulate in advance to one's advantage

ring group organized, often in secret, for unethical or illicit purposes; gang

ringleader chief member or leader of a gang or ring

sabotage destruction of property or interference with the operation of a business or government so as to undermine it

saboteur one who engages in sabotage

salt (*vb*) enrich appearance of (a mine) by secretly introducing minerals to be found there

scandal disgraceful or discreditable action or circumstance; public slander

sedition incitement of public disorder or insurrection against legal authority

simony sale of church office or preferment

sinecure office providing income for little or no work

slush fund money used for buying influence and corrupt political favors

smoke-filled room back room in which small group of politicians make secret deals

snitch (*vb*) *Informal.* inform; (*n*) informer

spy (*vb*) observe others or act in secret to obtain information about one's adversaries

stack (*vb*) prearrange secretly for purpose of cheating, esp. a deck of cards

subversion systematic efforts to undermine an organization by working secretly within it

terrorism coercion by use of systematic, random violence and intimidation

thick (*adj*) in an intimate, often secret, association with someone

tokenism practice of making only insignificant, symbolic actions to satisfy demands

tong secret Chinese fraternal organization engaged in gang warfare and racketeering

treason violation of allegiance to one's government, esp. an attempt to overthrow it or kill its leader

Trojan Horse something with a deceptive appearance, intended to undermine an adversary from within

underground secret organization plotting disruptions of civil order and concealing fugitives

unwholesome (*adj*) corrupt

uprising popular, often regional acts of opposition to authority

usurpation taking of another's office without right

venal (*adj*) open to corruption and bribery

vendetta prolonged, bitter feud involving revenge killings

vice corruption, esp. habitual moral failing

villainy state of depravity, corruption, and vice

ward heeler henchman working for local politician or party machine; heeler

web intricate network; snare

whitewash (*vb*) gloss over or excuse the wrongdoings of

wirepulling using one's influence with superiors to gain objective or manipulate others

Secrecy and Concealment

abscond (*vb*) depart secretly

alias assumed name

alphanumeric (*adj*) utilizing both numbers and letters, esp. designating such a code or cipher

ambuscade ambush

ambush trap in which persons lie concealed and attack by surprise

arcanum secret mystery unknowable without initiation

backdoor (*adj*) indirect, concealed, or devious

background less obvious or somewhat obscured information

backstage (*adj*) secretly or in private

backstairs (*adj*) secret or furtive; scandalous

beard decoy or disguise in social situation

befog (*vb*) confuse or render obscure that which is clear or true

behind-the-scenes (*adj*) working in secret

between you and me in confidence

black market illicit trade in regulated goods

blind activity or organization used to conceal another, often illicit, purpose

blow one's cover reveal one's true identity, esp. inadvertently

blow the whistle on inform on, reveal secrets of

blur (*vb*) obscure (the truth); make dim or unclear

booby trap bomb or mine concealed from the unwary in an apparently harmless object; any hidden trap set for an unsuspecting person

bug concealed device for eavesdropping

burke (*vb*) suppress quietly or indirectly; keep quiet

bury (*vb*) conceal by covering from view

bushwhack ambush, esp. by those hiding out in the woods

buzz (*vb*) speak softly, as if concealing secrets; gossip

cache hiding place, esp. for concealed provisions; something hidden or stashed away

camisado ambush, esp. a night attack

camouflage deception or concealment by disguise and artifice

carapace disguising, often ornamental shell

cipher message in code; method of altering a text to conceal its meaning

clandestine (*adj*) done in secret; surreptitious

classified (*adj*) designating information not to be revealed publicly, esp. for reasons of national security

cloak (*vb*) disguise; conceal completely

cloud (*vb*) hide or conceal; confuse, make unclear or dim

code system of arbitrary symbols with assigned meanings, used to communicate in secret

code name name assigned to conceal person's true identity, or to conceal true purpose of a plan

code word secret password, esp. allowing entry into code

conceal (*vb*) hide; prevent disclosure of the truth

concealment means, place, state, or act of concealing or being concealed

confidence secret communication

contraband smuggling or illegal trafficking in prohibited goods

cover disguise; something that conceals or obscures the truth

cover one's tracks hide traces of oneself to evade detection or pursuit

covert (*adj*) secret or veiled; undercover

coverup stratagem for concealing, esp. conspiracy to prevent public disclosure of illegal or unethical act

cryptic (*adj*) intentionally obscure; used to conceal

cryptography writing and analyzing of messages written in secret code or cipher

decipher (*vb*) decode; determine the meaning of (anything obscure or difficult to understand)

decode (*vb*) translate (encoded message) into intelligible form

decoy something used to entice unsuspecting victim into trap

disguise clothing and makeup used to conceal one's identity; misrepresentation of how something really is; masquerade

dissemble (*vb*) conceal facts or true motives by some pretense; give or put on a false appearance; dissimulate

dissimulate (*vb*) dissemble

divulge (*vb*) reveal; leak (secrets)

doggo (*adj*) *Informal.* lying in hiding, esp. concealed at a distance

eavesdrop (*vb*) listen in secret to what others are saying in private; listen in

exposé public revelation of damaging information

expose (*vb*) reveal or display to public view; deprive of protection

fine print something deliberately obscure, esp. limitations of agreement

foxhole hiding place

fugitive one who runs away, hides, or assumes a disguise to evade capture

furtive (*adj*) sly or shifty; obtained by stealth

get away with (*vb*) evade apprehension or punishment for (wrongdoing)

get out (*vb*) become publicly known, esp. leaked secrets

grapevine secret source of news; informal channel of gossip

hide (*vb*) screen from view, keep secret; conceal; obscure

hideaway hideout

hideout place where one is safe or concealed, esp. from the law; hideaway

hole up (*vb*) take refuge, as from pursuers; hide

hugger-mugger (*adj*) secret; muddled or confused

hush-hush (*adj*) highly secret

hush-up intentional suppression of information to avoid consequences

imposture practice of deception under an assumed name or character

incognito (*adj*) having one's identity concealed

indiscretion failure to maintain secrecy or propriety

informant informer

informer one who provides incriminating information against others or reveals group secrets; informant

innuendo vague hint or insinuation; indirect intimation about another's reputation

inside information true or essential facts about something, often not widely known

insinuation indirect, subtle derogation; stealthy introduction of oneself into a situation

intelligence information gathered covertly about enemy activities

in the dark in secrecy; lacking knowledge of something

in the know possessing inside information

leak (*vb*) surreptitiously reveal (secret information); (*n*) something or someone that allows secret information to become public

lie low (*vb*) remain in hiding or out of sight for a period of time

listen in (*vb*) eavesdrop

low-profile (*adj*) in a deliberately inconspicuous or anonymous manner; without attracting attention

lurk (*vb*) sneak about; conceal oneself and wait for chance to do evil or harm another

mask part of a disguise; something that conceals the truth

masquerade false or misleading appearance; disguise

mum (*adj*) silent; kept secret

nose out (*vb*) discover by investigation, esp. through prying into others' secrets

obfuscate (*vb*) confuse or cause to become obscure

oblique (*adj*) indirect, devious, or underhanded; obscure

obscurantism deliberate withholding of knowledge to gain advantage

obscure (*vb*) conceal or hide by making dim and unclear; (*adj*) dim, concealed from view, or unclear; oblique

on the lam escaping or hiding from authorities, esp. as a fugitive

palimpsest writing material erased and written over

password secret word or phrase, usu. used to gain entry to something

pig in a poke something offered with its true value concealed

private (*adj*) not to be generally disseminated; out of public view or knowledge

pry (*vb*) inquire into others' business

pussyfoot (*vb*) move stealthily and with great care

recess partly concealed area

reconnaissance covert information-gathering, esp. preliminary observation of enemy territory

reveal (*vb*) make known (that which was secret)

rifle (*vb*) search through with intent to steal or take something away

rumor statement or opinion in general circulation but of unknown source and dubious authenticity

rumormonger one who spreads rumors

safe house haven where one may hide or safely engage in secret activities

score (*vb*) *Slang.* acquire, esp. illicit drugs

screen something that shelters, protects, or conceals

second-story man burglar skilled at entering through upstairs window

secrecy state or condition of being secret or concealed; ability to keep secrets; habit of being secretive

secret (*adj*) hidden, obscure, or covert

secretive (*adj*) given to keeping things concealed

shadow (*vb*) observe another over time from a distance without being noticed; (*n*) one who does this

shirk (*vb*) evade (one's obligations)

sing (*vb*) *Slang.* provide information or evidence against others; act as an informant

skulk (*vb*) move in stealthy, furtive manner

slyboots one who engages in stealthy trickery and mischief

smell a rat detect tricky or dishonest behavior

smoke screen something intended to obscure or mislead

sneak (*vb*) move or act in a stealthy, furtive manner; (*n*) one who moves or acts in this fashion

sneak thief one who steals what is available without violence and by entering open buildings

snoop (*vb*) meddle or pry into another's affairs; (*n*) one who does this

spill (*vb*) divulge a secret

spill the beans *Informal.* indiscreetly disclose all known information

spy (*vb*) observe secretly with hostile intent; (*n*) one who does this

squeal (*vb*) turn informer

Star Chamber secret, arbitrary, unfair tribunal

stash (*vb*) keep concealed for future use; (*n*) something so concealed

steal (*vb*) take (another's property); come and go in secret

stealth furtive or secret movements or procedures

stonewall (*vb*) *Informal.* act in an evasive,

obstructive manner; refuse to cooperate, esp. with official inquiry

stool pigeon *Slang.* person acting as a decoy or informer

stowaway someone concealed on a vehicle so as to obtain transport

sub rosa (*adv*) covertly or secretly

subterfuge deceptive artifice or stratagem, esp. to conceal or evade

subterranean (*adj*) operating secretly outside normal society

suppress (*vb*) keep hidden or withhold from the public

surreptitious (*adj*) stealthy and underhanded; clandestine

surveillance concealed observation, esp. of an adversary

tail (*vb*) secretly observe or follow; (*n*) one who does this

tap (*vb*) cut in on (electric circuit or telephone line), usu. to eavesdrop

tattle (*vb*) disclose someone's secrets

tittle-tattle gossip

top-secret (*adj*) designating secret information, the revelation of which would pose grave danger to authority or security

track (*vb*) follow traces of and observe secretly; trail

trail (*vb*) track

ulterior (*adj*) beyond what is shown or avowed; intentionally kept concealed

undercover (*adj*) acting in secret; engaged in spying; covert

underhanded (*adj*) secretive or deceptive; sly; dishonest

under-the-counter (*adj*) clandestine, usu. involving illicit transaction or merchandise

under-the-table (*adj*) secret, underhanded; as a bribe

under wraps *Informal.* hidden away; kept concealed

unearth (*vb*) discover and bring to public attention

unmask (*vb*) recognize and disclose the true character of (a person or action)

up one's sleeve kept hidden, esp. for last-minute use, as a trick

veil something that serves to conceal or obscure

vizard disguise or mask

watch surveillance or close observation, esp. at night

waylay (*vb*) ambush; attack by surprise

weasel *Slang.* informer or stool pigeon

whistle-blower one who informs on another or publicly reveals wrongdoing and corruption

wind (*vb*) entangle, insinuate, or introduce by stealth

wiretap device attached to telephone line in order to eavesdrop

wise (*adj*) *Slang.* possessing inside information

wriggle out (*vb*) escape from difficult situation by shifts or expedients

Pranks and Tricks

antic attention-grabbing, playful prank

caper frivolous prank; illegal or questionable act

caprice impulsive, unpredictable change or action

chicanery deception by cunning artifice or trickery

culprit one guilty of wrongdoing or mischief

deviltry mischief or wicked behavior

dido mischievous antic; prank

elf mischievous, often magical troublemaker

escapade unconventional and reckless adventure

fourberie trickery, esp. underhanded maneuvers

frolic (*vb*) act in a playful manner; (*n*) playful, carefree behavior

hocus-pocus nonsense, sleight of hand, or trickery used to conceal deception

imp small, mischievous person

joke (*vb*) toy playfully with someone

knavery mischief or rascality

lark carefree adventure, escapade, or frolic

legerdemain sleight of hand; trickery

mischief conduct causing minor harm or trouble; knavery; naughtiness; rascality; waggery

monkeyshine prank

naughtiness mischief or minor rascality

playfulness sense of fun, mischief, and caprice

practical joke prank intended to cause minor harm or embarrassment

prank mildly mischievous act or playful trick; dido; monkeyshine

prankster one given to pranks, practical jokes, and playful mischief

prestidigitation sleight of hand

Puck mischievous scamp in English folklore

pull a fast one perpetrate a trick or fraud

rapscallion mischievous trickster; rogue

rascality mischievous character or conduct; knavery

rogue playful mischief-maker or scamp

roguery playful mischief

ruse trick or subterfuge

scamp impish prankster; rogue

shenanigan *Informal.* mischievous trick or nonsense

skulduggery unscrupulous activity; devious tricks

sleight of hand cleverly executed, deceptive tricks or conjuring, usu. requiring manual dexterity; legerdemain; prestidigitation

slippery (*adj*) untrustworthy, devious, or tricky

spoof good-natured hoax, often a parody

sportive (*adj*) playful or mischievous

sprite elf, imp, or prankster

trick clever and deceptive maneuver; mischievous prank; delusive appearance

trickery deception by crafty ingenuity and artifice; legerdemain

trickster one who deceives others by using tricks

trouble difficulty or annoying circumstance that causes disturbance or worry

waggery mischief; inclination to play practical jokes

wild-goose chase futile pursuit, esp. one intentionally induced by someone

wile trickery, guile, or ensnaring stratagem

witchcraft use of sorcery or magical influence

Falsehood, Pretense, and Exaggeration

adulterate (*vb*) alter so as to make less pure or less valuable

affected (*adj*) not genuine in manner

apocrypha writings or statements of doubtful authenticity

apostasy total departure from one's beliefs

audacity bold, arrogant disregard for conventional thought or restrictions

backhanded (*adj*) indirect and devious

baloney *Slang.* trivial lies and exaggeration

belie (*vb*) give false impression of

bend (*vb*) distort to one's own ends

big lie major distortion of truth, esp. for propaganda use

bill of goods *Informal.* something intentionally misrepresented

bogus (*adj*) not genuine; counterfeit

brown-nose (*vb*) *Slang.* ingratiate oneself; seek favor

bull *Slang.* vain, empty talk intended to mislead

bum rap *Slang.* false accusation; frame-up

bum steer *Informal.* intentionally bad advice or misdirection

butter up (*vb*) *Informal.* gain favor of through lavish flattery

by hook or by crook by any available means

cajole (*vb*) persuade by flattery or false promises

calumny misrepresentations that injure another's reputation

canard false, fabricated, or exaggerated story or report

cant insincere statements; private language of some group, esp. the underworld

careerism devotion to advancement in one's profession at the expense of integrity and one's personal life

castle in the air idealized condition or unrealizable dream

charade deceptive act; pretense

chimerical (*adj*) wildly improbable and imaginative

cock-and-bull story outrageous fabrication related as truth

contrive (*vb*) fabricate or invent, esp. in crafty manner

cook the books manipulate financial records to give a false impression

cop out (*vb*) *Informal.* back down on agreement or back out of unwanted responsibility

coquetry flirtatiousness; coy, insincere attempts to gain favor, usu. by female

counterfeit (*vb*) make imitation of with intent to deceive; feign; (*adj*) bogus; fake; imitation; phony

cozen (*vb*) win over or influence by shrewd trickery and artful persuasion

cozy up (*vb*) ingratiate oneself or try to become familiar for personal advantage

crocodile tears hypocritical sorrow; false tears

crooked (*adj*) insincere, indirect, or dishonest

cry wolf (*vb*) give false or needless alarm

defamation injury to another's reputation by libel or slander

delude (*vb*) deceive or trick, esp. mislead the mind or judgment of

dirt *Informal.* malicious gossip

dirty pool *Informal.* underhanded behavior; misconduct

dishonesty inclination or willingness to defraud or deceive; falsehood; mendacity; untruth

disloyalty absence of devotion or faithfulness; failure to fulfill one's obligations to another

distortion lacking, or altered from, a true sense or proportion

doctor (*vb*) tamper with or falsify, as a document

double-talk deliberately ambiguous or contradictory language with the appearance of sense, intended to deceive or confound

duplicity dishonesty about one's true motives or meaning

elusion skillful evasion of an adversary or difficulty

embellish (*vb*) add to or adorn for effect; exaggerate

equivocation use of ambiguous statements in order to mislead others or evade the truth

evasion means or instance of escape

exaggeration enlarging on truth or reality; overemphasis; baloney; fish story; hokum; tall talk

exorbitant (*adj*) exceeding the bounds of what is proper or customary

extravagance excessive, unrestrained behavior or notion

fabricate (*vb*) invent, esp. concoct so as to deceive

facade false appearance; false front

facsimile exact copy or forgery

fairy tale exaggerated, implausible story

fake impostor, charlatan; worthless imitation of something; (*adj*) counterfeit

fallacy deceptive or delusive appearance; mistaken idea

false (*adj*) intentionally untrue; treacherous or disloyal; counterfeit

false front facade

falsehood dishonesty, lies; extreme exaggeration; untruth

falsify (*vb*) misrepresent; make false by alteration; fudge

fast and loose (*adv*) in a cunning and deceptive manner

fast-talk (*vb*) influence or deceive by glib, deceitful speech

Fata Morgana mirage or illusion

feign (*vb*) give false appearance of; pretend

fib trivial lie; (*vb*) tell a trivial lie

fictitious (*adj*) false, assumed, or imaginary

fish story *Informal.* tall tale; exaggeration of true facts

fishy (*adj*) questionable or suspicious

flannelmouthed (*adj*) speaking in a shifty, ingratiating way

fob off (*vb*) pass off (inferior substitute) as genuine

foist (*vb*) assert surreptitiously, by stealth or deceit; pass off as genuine

fool's paradise condition of imaginary satisfaction

forgery fabricating or altering of a document for purpose of fraud; document so produced

frame (*vb*) incriminate (an innocent person) by prearranged trick

fudge (*vb*) fail to meet responsibilities or commitments; welsh; exaggerate or falsify

funny money *Slang.* counterfeit or artificially inflated currency

gammon *Brit. informal.* deceptive talk; humbug

gilding making things appear better than they are

gin trap

glad hand *Informal.* insincere, ingratiating greeting

gloss deceptively appealing appearance

goldbrick one who malingers or shirks duties

gossip false or misleading statements made covertly to defame another's reputation

guise false appearance; pretext

half-truth statement that mixes truth with falsehoods in order to deceive

hokum silly, nonsensical exaggeration and lies

hook something intended to attract and entrap

huckster one who employs showy methods or extravagant claims to promote and peddle merchandise or ideas

humbug something intended to deceive or mislead; someone pretending to be what he or she is not; gammon

hype (*vb*) promote by extravagant, often misleading propaganda; (*n*) such propaganda and exaggerated claims

hyperbole extreme exaggeration for effect

hypocrisy false appearance or pretense of virtues and beliefs one does not hold

illusion state of being intellectually deceived; misleading image

illusory (*adj*) deceptive; producing illusion

imitation (*adj*) counterfeit

impersonation disguising oneself or pretending to be another

impostor someone assuming false character or name for purpose of deception; fake

indirect (*adj*) tending to evade or misrepresent what really is; backhanded

inflation increase out of proportion to normal

jive false, misleading, or insincere and deceptive talk

lay it on (*vb*) exaggerate in order to impress or persuade

levant (*vb*) *Brit. slang.* evade one's debts

libel written or published defamation of another's reputation

lie (*vb*) make dishonest, misleading statement, esp. with intent to deceive; (*n*) dishonest statement

line *Informal.* dishonest, evasive, or misleading statement

lip service insincere statement of devotion or support

lowball (*vb*) state deceptively low price or estimate

magnify (*vb*) make seem greater; overstate

make believe (*vb*) pretend or feign

malinger (*vb*) pretend illness in order to avoid duties

mealy-mouthed (*adj*) inclined to use indirect or devious language

mendacity deception; dishonesty

mirage something that appears other than it is or seems to exist when it does not

mislead (*vb*) deceive; give false impression or advice to

misrepresent (*vb*) provide false information about or mistaken impression of

overdo (*vb*) exaggerate in the extreme

overreach (*vb*) take advantage of by cunning or unscrupulous methods

overstate (*vb*) exaggerate

pass off (*vb*) offer or sell with intent to deceive; misrepresent

perjury dishonest statement under oath in court of law

phantom (*adj*) fictitious or illusory

phony (*adj*) false; counterfeit; (*n*) insincere or deceitful person

pipe dream unrealizable aspiration

piracy unauthorized appropriation or use of another's property, esp. in copyright infringement

plagiarize (*vb*) represent (another's work) as one's own

playact (*vb*) pretend to be other than one is

pose attitude or appearance assumed for effect

pretend (*vb*) give false appearance; feign; make believe

pretender one who claims position of authority that is not his or her right

pretense false, professed, or make-believe act or intent; charade

pretext assumed appearance or purpose used to conceal true intent

prevaricate (*vb*) equivocate; veer from truth

prodigal (*adj*) reckless, extravagant, or excessive

pseudo (*adj*) false or spurious

pull someone's leg trick or deceive another playfully

put on (*vb*) mislead deliberately; feign

put something over on deceive

quasi (*adj*) resembling or seeming

questionable (*adj*) doubtful or suspicious; likely to be false

razzmatazz *Informal.* misleading or ambiguous speech or actions; double-talk

591

recant (*vb*) go back on one's beliefs or renounce former position

recreant one who deserts friends or betrays beliefs

red herring distraction or false clue

ringer impostor, esp. one entering competition under false pretense

roorback defamatory, published political lies

scalp (*vb*) *Informal.* buy and resell at greatly increased price

seduction something that attracts irresistibly; temptation or enticement into unwise act

shadowy (*adj*) unreliable, doubtful, or illicit

shady deal arrangement of dubious merit and authenticity

shifty (*adj*) given to deception, evasion, and fraud

shuck and jive *Slang.* insincere, deceptive talk that gives false impression

shuffle (*vb*) act in shifty, evasive manner

simulation act or object that is counterfeit or feigned

slander false oral statements that defame another's reputation

snare something deceptively appealing; trap

so-called (*adj*) misrepresented as such

soi-disant (*adj*) *French.* so-called

sophistry false though apparently valid argument used to deceive

spoof good-natured hoax, esp. parody

spurious (*adj*) superficially similar but innately false

story fabricated excuse, explanation, or evasion

stretch (*vb*) amplify or exaggerate beyond the norm for one's own advantage

suborn (*vb*) induce another to lie or commit perjury

subreption intentional misrepresentation or concealment of truth and the resulting inferences

sweet talk *Informal.* insincere flattery

synthetic (*adj*) contrived as a substitute for the real thing

tale intentionally untrue or exaggerated report

tall tale extremely fanciful or highly exaggerated story; yarn

tall talk exaggeration

tampering altering of something so as to falsify it; engaging in secret improprieties

tergiversation equivocation or evasion

tortuous (*adj*) characterized by indirect tactics; tricky, crooked, or devious

traduce (*vb*) betray with falsehoods and thus defame

trap (*vb*) entrap, snare; (*n*) something devised to trick or capture unsuspecting persons

trifle (*vb*) deal lightly or in a mocking manner

trump up (*vb*) concoct or invent for purpose of deception

two-time (*vb*) *Informal.* jilt or betray, esp. one's lover

untruth lie or falsehood

veneer superficial, deceptively pleasing appearance

warp (*vb*) falsify or distort

wheedle (*vb*) influence or persuade by smooth or artful flattery

whiffle (*vb*) vacillate or change position easily

whole cloth total and utter fabrication

whopper extravagant lie or deception

window dressing misrepresentation intended to give favorable impression of something

yarn highly embellished story; tall tale

Fraud, Treachery, and Deception

abuse corrupt or improper practice or custom

alibi excuse used to avert blame

arrogate (*vb*) claim or appropriate for oneself without right

backslide (*vb*) fail to live up to one's beliefs or moral values

bamboozle (*vb*) dupe or deceive by trickery or flattery; hoodwink

banditry activities and practices of bandits, such as plunder and robbery

barefaced (*adj*) unscrupulous; not concealing one's vices

baseness lack of noble qualities of mind or spirit; villainy

beat (*vb*) *Slang.* swindle; cheat

befool (*vb*) delude or deceive

beguile (*vb*) influence by deception; cheat out of by cunning

betrayal disloyalty in time of need, esp. treacherous exposure to an enemy

bewitch (*vb*) influence or charm as if by witchcraft

bilk (*vb*) cheat by evading payment due

blackmail extortion through intimidation or by threat of public revelation or exposure

blind subterfuge intended to mislead; agent acting as decoy or distraction for another person

bluff (*vb*) deceive or frighten by pretense of strength

bounce (*vb*) draw (check) on insufficient funds

bucket shop *Slang.* gambling house or brokerage that does not execute orders, profiting at customer's expense by fluctuations in price

bunko *Informal.* swindle or scheme that takes advantage of another's ignorance

burn (*vb*) *Slang.* deceive or cheat in transaction, esp. by overpricing or failing to deliver goods

capper *Slang.* shill

cardsharp one who habitually and successfully cheats at cards

catchy (*adj*) clever and beguiling, often tricky

cat's-paw person used to serve the purposes of another; dupe; tool

caught napping duped by trickery, usu. due to lack of vigilance

charlatan person making extravagant pretense of knowledge or skill; fraud; mountebank; quack

cheat (*vb*) practice fraud and trickery; influence or deprive of something expected by using deceit

chiaus *Slang.* swindler

chisel (*vb*) get by cunning or trickery; cheat, esp. out of funds

chump *Informal.* dupe; easy mark

clip (*vb*) *Slang.* profit unfairly from, esp. by overcharging

clip joint *Slang.* place of business that overcharges customers

con *Informal.* confidence game; swindle

con artist *Informal.* one who cheats others in confidence games; con man; swindler

confidence game appropriation of funds by making false promises of quick profits, usu. from unethical investment; con; sting; swindle

confiscation appropriation of another's property

con man *Slang.* con artist

cop (*vb*) *Informal.* purchase or obtain (illicit goods); steal or swipe

crib (*vb*) *Informal.* plagiarize, steal, or cheat on examination by use of concealed notes

cully *Archaic.* (*vb*) cheat or deceive; (*n*) one so deceived; dupe

deceit act of deception; trick; state of falseness

deceive (*vb*) mislead by false appearance or statement that is passed off as true, usu. to gain advantage or as a trick; befool

deception act of deceiving; that which deceives

decoy someone or something used to lure an unsuspecting victim into danger or distract attention from some other action

defraud (*vb*) cheat out of something by deception

desertion abandonment of proper post or responsibilities

devious (*adj*) scheming, cunning, or deceptive

diddle (*vb*) *Informal.* cheat, swindle, or fool; toy with

dirty trick *Informal.* fraudulent or unscrupulous secret act

discredit (*vb*) injure the reputation of; cast aspersions on the authenticity of

do a job on cheat, swindle, or take advantage of

do a number on confound thoroughly so as to swindle

dodge clever expedient or contrivance used to evade, trick, or deceive

double-cross (*vb*) *Informal.* betray by treachery; cheat by acting contrary to expectations

double-dealing (*adj*) marked by duplicity; deceitful

dupe one easily deceived or fooled; object of a swindle; cat's-paw; chump; easy mark; fool; gull; mark; patsy; pigeon; pushover; sap; sucker; tool

easy mark one highly susceptible to fraud or swindle; dupe

embezzle (*vb*) steal or appropriate to one's own use, as funds entrusted to one's care; peculate

extort (*vb*) obtain from another by intimidation, misused power, or ingenuity

fair-weather (*adj*) loyal only during good times

faithless (*adj*) disloyal; deceitful

fall guy *Slang.* one who takes the blame for another's misconduct

filch (*vb*) steal casually or furtively

finagle (*vb*) get by using trickery or deception; swindle, cheat, or trick

fink (*vb*) *Slang.* betray or inform on someone; (*n*) one who does this; ratfink

fink out (*vb*) *Slang.* cop out or renege

fleece (*vb*) defraud or extort money from; gaff; overcharge

flimflam *Informal.* deception or fraud, esp. one involving misleading talk

fool (*vb*) deceive or trick; (*n*) dupe

foul play any treacherous, deceitful, our unfair dealing

fraud deception and trickery, esp. a breach of confidence to gain an advantage, or an inducement to part with something of value; impostor; one who practices trickery and deception

fraudulence deceit by falseness and trickery

front one who serves as a cover for illegal activity, or induces victims to engage in scheme perpetrated by another

fuck over (*vb*) *Vulgar slang.* misuse; take advantage of deceitfully

gaff (*vb*) *Slang.* cheat or fleece

go back on (*vb*) betray; renege on

gouge (*vb*) extort from or overcharge

graft use of dishonest or illegal means for gain or profit

greenhorn naive person who may easily be swindled or tricked

grift methods used to obtain illicit profits, esp. from confidence game

guile craft, duplicity, or cunning

gull dupe; (*vb*) take advantage of or deceive

gyp (*vb*) cheat or swindle by some sharp practice

highway robbery *Informal.* exorbitant profit or gain derived from business transaction

hoax act intended to deceive or trick, esp. into accepting as real that which is not; mischievous deception

hocus (*vb*) perpetrate a hoax on someone

hoodwink (*vb*) deceive by false appearance

hornswoggle (*vb*) *Slang.* swindle, cheat, or perpetrate a hoax on

ill-gotten (*adj*) acquired by improper or evil means

illicit (*adj*) prohibited by law or custom; not permitted or authorized

Indian giver *Informal (offensive).* person who gives something away and then takes it back

infidelity lack of faith; betrayal, esp. of one's spouse

insidious (*adj*) designed to draw another into a trap or fraud

jerk around (*vb*) *Slang.* mislead; take advantage of

jilt (*vb*) abruptly abandon, esp. one's lover

Judas one who betrays another while acting as a friend

juggle (*vb*) manipulate to achieve desired end or give false appearance

kangaroo court court that disregards legal principles and justice, esp. so as to make fair trial impossible

lame *Slang.* one not in the know; unsophisticated person

launder (*vb*) *Informal.* disguise source of (illicit funds) so that they appear legitimate

lift (*vb*) *Informal.* steal; plagiarize

loan shark *Informal.* person charging excessive interest on loans

mark *Slang.* target or victim of swindle; dupe; easy mark

milk (*vb*) exploit illicitly or excessively for advantage; drain someone or something of resources

monte gambling card game, usu. a swindle

mooch (*vb*) *Slang.* scrounge, steal, or sponge

mountebank unscrupulous trickster; charlatan

nemesis formidable, persistent, and vengeful adversary who cannot be defeated

nick *Brit. slang.* steal or cheat

nobble *Brit. slang.* swindle, cheat, or steal

operator *Informal.* person who accomplishes his or her purposes by devious means, esp. by evading difficulties or regulations

palm off (*vb*) dispose of (something valueless) by deception

palter (*vb*) haggle, equivocate, or act deceitfully

parlous (*adj*) dangerously shrewd and cunning

patsy *Slang.* dupe

pawky (*adj*) *Chiefly Brit.* cunning or crafty

peculate (*vb*) embezzle

perfidy treachery, esp. disloyalty or betrayal

pervert (*vb*) turn or lead astray; put to improper use; corrupt

pettifogger shyster, esp. disreputable lawyer

pigeon *Slang.* dupe

pilfer (*vb*) steal

pinch (*vb*) *Slang.* steal

plunder (*vb*) loot; take by theft or fraud

Ponzi investment swindle in which early investors receive return from money of later ones, who never see return

predatory (*adj*) preying upon or living off others

prey (*vb*) attack for booty; exert harmful influence upon; (*n*) victim unable to resist attacks

profiteering making exorbitant profit, esp. on scarce or rationed articles

pull a fast one enact a trick or fraud

pull the wool over someone's eyes prevent another from seeing true circumstances; hoodwink

purloin (*vb*) take dishonestly, by breach of trust

pushover *Informal.* dupe; easy mark

pyramid (*vb*) speculate in securities by using paper profits as margin for additional trading

quack fraudulent or ignorant pretender to medical skills; charlatan

quisling traitor who betrays his or her country to an invading enemy

racket organized illegal scheme or activity; swindle

racketeer one engaged in organized illegal activities, esp. extortion through intimidation

rat (*vb*) *Slang.* inform on or betray one's associates

ratfink *Slang.* informer; fink

renege (*vb*) deny or renounce; fail to fulfill one's obligations

rip off (*vb*) *Slang.* steal, cheat, or defraud

robber baron businessman profiting by exploitation of unscrupulous but legal activity

rook (*vb*) cheat or defraud by swindle

runner smuggler or distributor of illicit goods

sap *Slang.* dupe

scam fraudulent operation or swindle

scoundrel deceitful, unscrupulous person

sell (*vb*) gain acceptance for; betray; cheat

sell out (*vb*) betray

setup arrangement that draws unsuspecting party into swindle

shaft (*vb*) *Informal.* treat poorly by taking advantage of or betraying

shake down (*vb*) extort money from

sham deceptive trick or hoax; spurious imitation or counterfeit object; impostor

shark shrewd individual preying upon others through extortion and trickery

shell game fraud involving sleight-of-hand substitution of valueless item for one of value; thimblerig, using walnut shells instead of balls

shill *Slang.* decoy for pitchman, gambler, or con game; capper

shlemiel *Yiddish slang.* awkward, unlucky person, often taken advantage of by swindler or con artist

shortchange (*vb*) cheat by returning less than correct change

short con *Slang.* simple confidence game perpetrated by single operator, involving small amount of money

shyster *Informal.* one unscrupulous in professional duties, esp. a lawyer

sitting duck helpless or easy target or victim of swindle

skim (*vb*) *Slang.* fraudulently conceal or underestimate (profits, as from gambling), esp. to avoid paying taxes

skin game swindle or con game

slicker *Informal.* cunning swindler

snooker (*vb*) *Slang.* deceive, cheat, or dupe

sponge (*vb*) acquire without paying for or by taking advantage of another's generosity

squeeze (*vb*) pressure so as to obtain or extort something

steal (*vb*) vengefully take (something that belongs to another), esp. in secret or by force; pilfer; pinch; swipe; walk off with

sting *Slang.* apparent swindle used by authorities in investigation of fraud or racket; confidence game

string along (*vb*) *Informal.* perpetrate hoax upon; fool by misleading

sucker dupe

Svengali one using physical force and mind control to dominate another

swindle (*vb*) obtain (another's assets or money) by fraud or deceit; (*n*) action or scheme intended to defraud or deceive; con; confidence game; racket; skin game

swipe (*vb*) *Informal.* steal

take (*vb*) *Informal.* cheat, swindle, or victimize

take advantage of exploit; get the better of; impose swindle on

thimblerig sleight-of-hand swindle involving small ball that must be found under one of three cups, similar to three-card monte

three-card monte sleight-of-hand swindle in which mark must identify one of three cards that have been moved around facedown by dealer

tool one used by another; cat's-paw; dupe

traitor one who betrays his or her country or another person or reneges on responsibilities

treachery failure of faith or trust; act of perfidy or treason

turncoat one who betrays a cause or supports an enemy

two-faced (*adj*) double-dealing; inconstant in allegiance; hypocritical

unconscionable (*adj*) unscrupulous; done without conscience

unscrupulous (*adj*) lacking principles; willing to do anything to achieve one's goal

victimize (*vb*) defraud, cheat, or take advantage of

walk off with (*vb*) steal

wangle (*vb*) obtain by underhanded methods; manipulate for fraudulent ends

water (*vb*) artificially increase value of without necessary assets as basis

weasel (*vb*) evade one's obligations; manipulate situation to one's advantage; (*n*) *Slang.* informer

welsh (*vb*) *Informal.* renege on one's obligation or debt, esp. a bet

wildcat (*adj*) financially reckless and conducted in violation of normal business practices

wrong (*vb*) do harm to; defraud or discredit

CHAPTER TWENTY-THREE
COGNITION

TIME PERCEPTION

Fixed Times
Periods of Time
Relative Time

See also: *Chap. 3: Weather and Natural
Phenomena; Chap. 4: Physics; Chap. 18:
Qualifiers and Connectives*

Fixed Times

anniversary commemoration of each full year's passage since original event

annual (*adj*) yearly, once a year

appointment meeting at designated time

autumnal equinox September 22 in Northern Hemisphere

bedtime hour of going to sleep for night

biannual (*adj*) occurring twice a year; occurring every two years; semiannual

bicentennial (*adj*) occurring every 200 years; (*n*) 200th anniversary

biennial (*adj*) occurring every two years; (*n*) two-year anniversary; event that occurs once in two years

bimensal (*adj*) bimonthly

bimonthly (*adj*) occurring every two months; twice a month; bimensal; semimonthly

birthday annual commemoration of day of one's birth

bissextile day February 29, occurring every fourth year

biweekly (*adj*) occurring every two weeks; twice a week; semiweekly

calends first day of a month (ancient Rome)

canonical hour any of certain times of the day set apart for prayer and devotion

centenary observation of hundred-year anniversary

centennial hundredth anniversary; (*adj*) occurring every hundred years

Christmastide holiday season from Christmas until after New Year's Day; period from Christmas Eve to Epiphany, esp. in Britain

Christmastime holiday season in December commemorating Christ's birth

cockcrow dawn

cockshut *Chiefly Brit.* dusk

curfew time designated by authority to retire or stay indoors for the night

daily (*adj*) occurring each day

dawn sunrise

deadline final moment at which something must be done

decennial (*adj*) occurring every ten years

dinnertime time for main meal of day, in afternoon or evening

diurnal (*adj*) daily

dog days hottest part of summer

duodecennial (*adj*) occurring every twelve years

dusk twilight, darkening hour during and after sunset

eleventh hour last possible moment for some action

equinoctial (*adj*) pertaining to equinoxes

equinox moment in year when center of sun is in line with equator and day and night are of equal length: about March 21 and September 22

estival (*adj*) pertaining to summer

eve evening

evening period of time from sunset to end of twilight; eve; eventide

eventide evening

first light sunrise

gloaming twilight, dusk

halcyon days peaceful, happy, or prosperous times

harvest moon full moon nearest autumnal equinox

hebdomadal (*adj*) weekly, every seven days

heyday time of greatest flourishing

high noon exactly twelve o'clock noon

high tea *Chiefly Brit.* time of late afternoon snack or light supper, usu. five o'clock

horary (*adj*) pertaining to hours; hourly

hourly (*adj*) occurring every hour

ides fifteenth or thirteenth day of each month in ancient Roman calendar

inception beginning

in the nick of time just at the last minute

last-ditch (*adj*) done in final moment out of desperation

last-minute (*adj*) done when time is running out

latter Lammas day that will never come

lunchtime hour for eating light midday meal

mañana *Spanish.* tomorrow

matinal (*adj*) pertaining to morning

matutinal (*adj*) early, pertaining to morning

midday noon, middle of day, when a.m. turns to p.m.

midnight middle of night; twelve o'clock at night, when p.m. turns to a.m.

midweek middle day or time of week, esp. Wednesday

millennial thousandth anniversary; (*adj*) occurring every thousand years

monthly (*adj*) occurring every month

morn morning, dawn

morrow tomorrow

nocturnal (*adj*) pertaining to night; nightly

nonce present occasion

noon twelve o'clock midday, when a.m. turns to p.m.; noontime

noontime noon

now (*adv*) at the present moment

once (*adv*) one time only; at one time in past

on time (*adj*) punctual, at the specified time

perennial occurring year after year

post time time of day's first horse race at track

premiere first occurrence of event

present-day (*adj*) contemporary, modern

punctual (*adj*) prompt, on time

quadrennial (*adj*) occurring every four years; lasting four years

quadricentennial 400th anniversary; (*adj*) occurring every 400 years

quarterly (*adj*) occurring four times per year

quincentennial 500th anniversary; (*adj*) occurring every 500 years

quinquennial (*adj*) occurring every five years

quotidian (*adj*) daily, everyday

salad days time of youth, exuberance, or innocence

semiannual (*adj*) occurring every half year or twice a year; semiyearly

semicentennial (*adj*) occurring every fifty years

semidiurnal (*adj*) occurring every half day or twice a day

semimonthly (*adj*) occurring every half month or twice a month

semiweekly (*adj*) occurring every half week or twice a week

semiyearly (*adj*) semiannual

septennial (*adj*) occurring every seven years

small hours extremely late at night; hours after midnight and before dawn

solstice time in year when sun is farthest north or south of celestial equator, in Northern Hemisphere about June 21 or December 21, respectively; longest or shortest period of sunshine during year

stitch in time timely or punctual act or repair

summer solstice June 21 in Northern Hemisphere

sundown sunset

sunrise time in morning when sun appears over eastern horizon; dawn; first light; sun up

sunset hour in early evening when sun disappears over western horizon; sundown

sun up *Informal.* sunrise

suppertime time designated for evening meal

teatime time for light late-afternoon repast of tea and cakes, generally four o'clock

time dimension of reality characterized by flow of events and phenomena through irreversible procession of moments; systematized demarcation of the passage of such moments into units of seconds, minutes, hours, days, and years; period or point in time; fourth dimension in space-time continuum

today this present day

tomorrow day after today; morrow

tonight present or coming night

tricennial (*adj*) occurring every thirty years

tricentennial 300th anniversary; (*adj*) occurring every 300 years

triennial (*adj*) occurring every three years; continuing or persisting for three years

trimonthly (*adj*) occurring every three months

triweekly (*adj*) occurring every three weeks; occurring three times a week

twilight period of dimming light just after sunset

under the wire at last possible moment

vernal equinox March 21 in Northern Hemisphere

vespers prayer said at evening; sixth canonical hour

vicennial twentieth anniversary; (*adj*) occurring every twenty years

vintage one season's harvest of wine grapes

vintage year year in which something outstanding is made or done, esp. wine harvest

weekly (*adj*) occurring once a week

winter solstice December 21 in Northern Hemisphere

yearly (*adj*) occurring once a year

yesterday day before today

zero hour moment for commencement of plan; beginning of ordeal or crisis

Periods of Time

aeon eon

afternoon period from noon to evening

age period of time corresponding to life of object or individual; period in Earth's history

all-day (*adj*) lasting from morning to evening

all-night (*adj*) lasting from evening to morning

always (*adv*) forever, all the time

annus mirabilis *Latin.* notable or remarkable year

April fourth month of year, containing 30 days, following March, preceding May

around-the-clock (*adj*) at all times of day and night

August eighth month of year, containing 31 days, following July, preceding September

autumn season of shortening days ending in winter solstice, extending from September 22 to December 20; fall

awhile (*adv*) for a short time

bicentenary *Chiefly Brit.* bicentennial

bicentennial (*adj*) lasting 200 years

bimillenary (*adj*) lasting 2000 years

bimillennium 2000 years

blue moon long period of time

calendar year 365 days, beginning January 1 and ending December 31; 366 days in leap years

centenary 100 years; one century

century 100 years

chiliad 1000 years

circadian (*adj*) occurring in twenty-four-hour cycles

coffee break period of short rest in morning or afternoon, usu. at place of work

coon's age *Informal.* long time

cycle regular, recurring interval of time; set period of days or years

day period of twenty-four hours; sunrise to sunset

daytime time in which there is sunlight

decade period of ten years

December twelfth and last month of year, containing 31 days, following November, preceding January, including first day of winter

donkey's years *Informal.* long period of time

duration extent of time during which something takes place

elapse (*vb*) pass away, said of period of time

elapsed time time measured from beginning to end of event

eon extremely long period of time; aeon

epoch significant time period marked by

historical events; geologic time division smaller than period

era significant period of time marked by historical events; major geologic time division including periods

eternal (*adj*) lasting forever

eternity forever, time without end; immeasurable time

everlasting (*adj*) endless, unceasing, eternal

fall autumn

February second month of year, containing 28 days or 29 days every fourth year, following January, preceding March

fiscal year twelve-month-period, used in business and accounting, usu. beginning July 1 or October 1

forever (*adv*) always, eternally, in perpetuity

for good permanently

for keeps forever

fortnight period of two weeks

Friday sixth day of week, following Thursday, preceding Saturday; last day of regular workweek in United States

future time yet to come

hiatus break or gap in continuity

historical year year beginning with January 1

hitch *Slang.* period of time served in military

hour one twenty-fourth of one day; sixty minutes

immemorial (*adj*) extending beyond memory

indiction repeating cycle of fifteen years, used in Roman Empire

infinity boundless, limitless time

instant moment, time period of extremely short duration

interim interval of time

interlude short time intervening between events or dramatic acts

intermittent (*adj*) periodic, interrupted in time, recurrent

interregnum period of vacancy of throne or royal office; period of time when there is lapse in normal government functions

interval pause, break, recess

January first month of year, containing 31 days, following December, preceding February

jiffy *Informal.* brief amount of time

July seventh month of year, containing 31 days, following June, preceding August

June sixth month of year, containing 30 days, following May, preceding July, including first day of summer

lasting (*adj*) enduring, unending

lead time time period allotted between start-up time of task and emergence of results

leap year 366-day year, occurring every fourth year, in which February has 29 days

lifelong (*adj*) for the duration of one's life

life span period of life from birth to death

lifetime period of time that life of someone or something lasts

long-drawn-out (*adj*) lasting or seeming to last a very long time

longevity length of a life span

long haul extended period of time

long-run (*adj*) extended over a long period of time

longstanding (*adj*) of great duration or age

long-term (*adj*) of extensive duration

lustrum period of five years

March third month of year, containing 31 days, following February, preceding April, including first day of spring

May fifth month of year, containing 31 days, following April, preceding June

Metonic cycle period of nearly 19 years, after which phases of moon return to some calendar date, used in Gregorian calendar

microsecond one millionth of a second

millenary (*adj*) lasting 1000 years

millennium 1000 years

millisecond one thousandth of a second

minute sixty seconds; one sixtieth of an hour

moment brief span of time; second, instant

Monday second day of week, following Sunday, preceding Tuesday; first day of regular workweek in United States

month period of approximately thirty days, based on time required for one complete revolution of the moon; one of twelve divisions of year

moratorium period of delay

morning period of day from dawn to midday

nanosecond one billionth of a second

Neolithic (*adj*) designating period of cultural development from about 10,000 to 3000 B.C.

night and day (*adj*) all the time, at all hours

nine-to-five (*adj*) *Informal.* pertaining to standard working day in forty-hour week

November eleventh month of year, containing 30 days, following October, preceding December

October tenth month of year, containing 31 days, following September, preceding November

olympiad period of four years

overnight period of time from night until next morning

past period of time already gone by

period duration or division of time; geologic division within era including epochs

perpetual (*adj*) eternal, everlasting

perpetual day period at North and South poles when sun does not set

perpetual night period at North and South poles when sun does not rise

perpetuity endless time; state of lasting forever

picosecond one trillionth of a second

playtime leisure time, free time

posterity the future; subsequent generations

prehistoric (*adj*) pertaining to period before written history

present period of time occurring now

protracted (*adj*) extended over time, drawn out

quarter-hour one quarter of an hour; fifteen minutes

round-the-clock (*adj*) at all hours of the day or night

Saturday seventh and last day of week,

following Friday, preceding Sunday; first day of weekend; Jewish Sabbath

season period of time characterized by particular weather, events, and holidays; one of four major divisions of year

second one sixtieth of a minute; fundamental unit of time equal to 9,192,631,770 emission cycles of cesium-133

sempiternal (*adj*) eternal, perpetual

September ninth month of year, containing 30 days, following August, preceding October, including first day of autumn

short-run (*adj*) occurring over a short span of time

sidereal day time taken for one complete rotation of Earth

since (*adv*) from a time in the past until the present

sojourn temporary period spent in one place

split second very short time; fraction of a second

spring season of lengthening days ending in summer solstice, extending from March 21 to June 20

stint limited period of time, esp. for accomplishment of some task

stretch duration of time; *Slang.* term of incarceration

summer season of shortening days ending in autumnal equinox, extending from June 21 to September 21

Sunday first day of week, following Saturday, preceding Monday; last day of weekend; Christian Sabbath

take five *Informal.* stop working for a few minutes' rest

term fixed period of time in which an activity, office, tenure, or agreement is valid and ongoing

Thursday fifth day of week, following Wednesday, preceding Friday

time frame period of time designated for completion of something; timespan

time immemorial time before recorded history or beyond memory; time out of mind

time-lag interval between two related events or phenomena

time-lapse (*adj*) designating photography in which very slow process is made to appear rapid by taking multiple exposures over time

time limit maximum duration allowed for something

time-out cessation of activity for specified duration, esp. in athletic contest

time out of mind time immemorial

timespan period of time; time frame

trice very brief time; moment

Tuesday third day of week, following Monday, preceding Wednesday

twelvemonth *Chiefly Brit.* one year

twinkling very short time

Wednesday fourth day of week, following Tuesday, preceding Thursday; midweek

week period of seven days

weekday working day; any day of week except Saturday or Sunday

weekend end of week; Saturday and Sunday; nonwork days

while period or interval of time; (*conj*) during or throughout the time that

window period of time considered highly favorable for beginning or accomplishing something

wink brief period of time

winter season of lengthening days ending in vernal equinox, extending from December 21 to March 20

workday weekday; Monday through Friday and sometimes Saturday

year period of 365 days, during which Earth makes one full revolution around sun; twelve months

Relative Time

after (*prep*) later in time than; (*adv*) later in time

aftertime future time

afterward (*adv*) subsequently

again (*adv*) once more

ago (*adj*) time past

ahead of time (*adj*) early

already (*adv*) before a specific time

anachronism misplacement or incongruity in time

ancient (*adj*) of very great age

anew (*adv*) again, repeated

anon (*adv*) at once; soon

ante- prefix meaning before or prior to

antiquated (*adj*) of great age, obsolete

antique (*adj*) very old, belonging to bygone age

anymore (*adv*) any longer; nowadays

anytime (*adv*) without restriction or regard to time

aperiodic (*adj*) not periodic, with no regular recurrence

après (*prep*) *French.* after

archaic (*adj*) old-fashioned, of an earlier time

asynchronous (*adj*) not concurrent

atemporal (*adj*) outside of time

at once (*adv*) immediately; at the same time

at the drop of a hat promptly, as soon as the slightest opportunity is given

at times (*adv*) occasionally

auld lang syne *Scottish.* good old days

before (*prep*) prior to, at a previous time

belated (*adj*) delayed, too late

betimes (*adv*) in a short or good time; occasionally; early

betweentimes (*adv*) during intervals

borrowed time time that is overextended or overdue

brief (*adj*) of very short duration

by-and-by future

by turns (*adj*) alternately

chronic (*adj*) constant, continuing over time

chronological (*adj*) arranged in order of time

circa (*prep*) about

coeval (*adj*) of the same age

conclusion ending

concurrent (*adj*) at the same time

constant (*adj*) perpetual, occurring continually

contemporaneous (*adj*) existing at the same time

contemporary (*adj*) at the same time; belonging to the same or current time period

continual (*adj*) chronic, constant, unceasing, uninterrupted

continuous (*adj*) without break or interruption

current (*adj*) at present, now

dated (*adj*) antiquated, old enough to be out of fashion

delay (*vb*) postpone, cause to wait, slow down; (*n*) instance of such postponement or slowing

directly (*adv*) at once, immediately

during (*prep*) at the same time as, in the time of

early (*adv*) at or near the beginning; before or ahead of time; (*adj*) occurring in the first part of a period of time

ephemeral (*adj*) lasting for one day; short-lived

ere (*prep*) before

erelong (*adv*) soon, before long

erenow (*adv*) before now

erewhile (*adv*) some time ago

erst (*adv*) previously, earlier

erstwhile (*adj*) former, of times past

eve evening or day before

eventually (*adv*) finally, in the end

ever (*adv*) always, at any time

first (*adv*) earliest, preceding others; (*adj*) before all others

fore (*adj*) coming first, prior to

forenoon morning, before noon

former (*adj*) prior, earlier, preceding in time

formerly (*adv*) in a previous time

for the time being temporarily

frequent (*adj*) often

from time to time occasionally, not often

fugitive (*adj*) not durable, transient

henceforth (*adv*) from the present time forward

hereafter (*adv*) in the future, after the present

heretofore (*adv*) previously, up to the present time

immediate (*adj*) without delay or interval, next

imminent (*adj*) about to happen immediately

impermanent (*adj*) temporary, lasting for a limited time

impromptu (*adv*) extemporaneously; (*adj*) done without previous preparation

in a flash instantaneously, extremely quickly

in a moment very soon, right away

in a trice at once, in a moment

in a twinkling at once, immediately, quickly

in a wink at once, in an instant

infrequent (*adj*) seldom, not often

in good time on time; early, in advance

in no time almost at once

instantaneous (*adj*) happening and concluding in an instant; without duration

interim (*adj*) temporary; (*n*) intervening time

intermediate (*adj*) in an intervening time

in the meantime temporarily

in the offing occurring in the near future; soon

in time sooner or later; early enough

in turn eventually; in due order of succession

isochronal (*adj*) occurring at regular intervals

last (*adj*) final; time immediately prior to the present

late (*adj*) after the appointed or usual time, tardy

lickety-split (*adv*) very quickly, right away

long ago far in the past

long since long ago

meantime (*adv*) meanwhile

meanwhile (*adv*) in the intervening time; at the same time; meantime

meta- prefix meaning after or beyond

ne'er (*adv*) never, at no time

never (*adv*) not ever, at no time

never again (*adv*) not to occur anymore

nevermore (*adv*) never again, no more

new (*adj*) not existing prior to this moment; of recent origin

nonce present or immediate occasion or purpose

nowadays (*adv*) in the present, currently

now and then occasionally

occasional (*adj*) occurring infrequently or irregularly

occasionally (*adv*) now and then; sometimes

off and on intermittently

off-peak (*adj*) pertaining to time period of less than maximum use, frequency, or duration

off-season less busy season

often (*adv*) frequently, many times

ofttimes (*adv*) frequently, often

old (*adj*) having lived or existed for a long period of time

on again, off again intermittently

ongoing (*adj*) enduring or continuing

parachronism chronological error, usu. placing event later than correct time

part-time (*adj*) lasting fewer hours than full-time, usu. said of employment

permanent (*adj*) continuing without change, not temporary

post- prefix meaning after or behind

postdate (*vb*) date after time of transaction or occurrence, esp. a check

posthaste (*adv*) speedily, with haste

pre- prefix meaning before or prior

precedence act or state of going before; right to priority

preceding (*adj*) going before

precursor person or thing that goes before

predate (*vb*) date or affix before actual time of transaction or occurrence

preliminary (*adj*) preceding, before

preprandial (*adj*) relating to time just before dinner

presently (*adv*) soon

presto (*adv*) in rapid tempo; immediately

previous (*adj*) before, preceding, former

primeval (*adj*) from original time, ancient, primal

prior (*adj*) before, preceding, previous to

procrastination habit of delaying or postponing

prolong (*vb*) lengthen, extend, continue

promptly (*adv*) without delay, quickly

pronto (*adv*) *Informal.* quickly, right away

proximo (*adv*) in the next month after this month

rare (*adj*) not frequent

rarely (*adv*) not often, infrequently

recent (*adj*) pertaining to the near past, lately; new

recurrent (*adj*) returning periodically

remote (*adj*) distant

repeatedly (*adv*) at intervals, again and again

respite postponement, delay, pause

retrospective (*adj*) directed toward looking backward

right away immediately, without delay

seldom (*adv*) not often, rarely

semipermanent (*adj*) lasting, but not permanent; durable

simultaneous (*adj*) occurring at same moment

someday (*adv*) at some future time

sometime (*adv*) at an unknown or unspecified point of time; (*adj*) having been formerly

sometimes (*adv*) now and then, on occasion

soon (*adv*) promptly, immediately; earlier than usual

sooner or later eventually

sporadic (*adj*) happening in scattered instances

spur-of-the-moment (*adj*) impromptu; occuring without planning or rehearsal

straightaway (*adv*) immediately, without delay; straight off

straight off straightaway

subsequent (*adj*) following, later

successive (*adj*) following in order

sudden (*adj*) abrupt, happening unexpectedly; quick

summary (*adj*) quickly done, without delay

tardy (*adj*) late; slow

temp *Informal.* temporary employee

temporal (*adj*) pertaining to, defined, or limited by time; transitory

temporary (*adj*) of certain limited duration, not permanent

tempus fugit *Latin.* time flies

terminal (*adj*) final, occurring at the end

then (*adv*) at that time; following, next

thence (*adv*) from that time; thereafter

thenceforth (*adv*) from that time forward

thereafter (*adv*) subsequently; after that

theretofore (*adv*) before or until then

thereupon (*adv*) immediately following that

therewith (*adv*) thereupon

time after time repeatedly

time and again repeatedly

time-consuming (*adj*) requiring or taking up a great deal of time

time-honored (*adj*) esteemed due to age or longstanding use

timeless (*adj*) outside limits of time; unrestricted by time period or era; undated; eternal, with no beginning or end

timely (*adj*) early, seasonal, opportune, or executed on time

time of life one's age

timesaver something intended to expedite an action

time-tested (*adj*) having effectiveness proved over a long period of time

time warp hypothetical peculiarity in progression of time that would allow movement back and forth in time

transience state of being limited by time; impermanence

transitory (*adj*) temporary, fleeting

unceasing (*adj*) continuous, without interruption

until (*conj*) up to the time of; at any time before

untimely (*adj*) premature, unseasonable; occurring at improper time

upcoming (*adj*) about to occur; coming to pass

upon (*prep*) without interval or delay

up-to-the-minute (*adj*) extending to the present moment; new, modern

urgent (*adj*) requiring immediate attention

vestigial (*adj*) relating to or indicating something formerly present

vintage (*adj*) old, antique

well-timed (*adj*) propitious

when (*adv*) at a particular time; at which time

whenever (*adv*) at any time; as soon as

whensoever (*adv*) at whatsoever time

while (*conj*) during the time that

yesteryear year past; recent past

yestreen *Scottish.* last evening or night

yet (*adv*) present time; any time until the present; at some future time; in the time remaining

yore time past; (*adv*) long ago

SPATIAL POSITIONS AND RELATIONS
Fixed Positions and Points
Dimensions and Directions
Relative Positions

See also: *Chap. 4: Mathematics; Chap. 18: Qualifiers and Connectives; Chap. 23: Shapes*

Fixed Positions and Points

acme highest point

aloft (*adv*) high in the air

angle point at which two lines converge

antinode area of maximum amplitude between adjacent nodes

apex highest point

apical (*adj*) at the highest point

apogee highest or most distant point

attitude position in space determined by relationship of object's axis and a reference point

balanced (*adj*) in equilibrium due to even distribution of weight on all sides

base bottom point or position

beginning origin; point at which something starts

benchmark point of reference for making measurements

blind spot area that cannot be seen
capsheaf highest point, acme
center middle, esp. point around which circle is drawn
chink narrow opening or division
circumcenter center of circumscribed circle
cleft split; depression between ridges
corner point where converging lines, edges, or sides meet
crest highest point
crisscross (*adj*) intersecting; having a number of crossing lines or paths
crossed (*adj*) intersecting at a specific point
crown highest point
depth farthest or innermost part or point
dorsal (*adj*) near or on the back
dorsolateral (*adj*) on both the back and sides
edge line at which area begins or ends; border
end point marking most extreme extent; part lying at limit
endpoint either of two points at ends of line segment
epicenter exact center, esp. Earth's surface beneath focus of earthquake
erect (*adj*) in upright or vertical position
extremity farthest point
farthest (*adj*) at the greatest possible distance
first (*adj*) situated at the beginning or in front
fissure narrow break in surface produced by separation of parts
fix charted position or bearings
focal point focus
focus point at which lines or rays come together, cross, or diverge; focal point; hub
fork point of branching
gap break in space; empty space in continuity
grade position on scale or hierarchy
hanging (*adj*) suspended from a point
here (*adv*) in or at this place
hereat (*adv*) at this place
hindmost (*adj*) nearest the rear position
hub focus
innermost (*adj*) farthest inward
in the way located so as to be an obstacle in one's course
inverted (*adj*) with top and bottom parts reversed
last (*adj*) situated farthest to the rear, after all others
low (*adj*) lying close to or at the bottom point
metacenter intersection of lines through centers of buoyancy of a floating body at rest and when tipped to one side
midpoint point at or near the center or middle
nadir lowest point, esp. opposite zenith in celestial sphere
navel central point, middle
node point at which parts begin or focus; point at which curve crosses itself at different tangents
omphalos center or navel
outmost (*adj*) farthest from the center
outrance *French*. ultimate extremity
pendent (*adj*) suspended, hanging

perigee point in orbit of heavenly body at which it is nearest to Earth
perihelion point in orbit of celestial body at which it is nearest to sun
plumb (*adj*) perpendicular; exactly vertical
point definite, unique position on scale; geometric element positioned by ordered set of coordinates
polycentric (*adj*) having more than one center
position space occupied by an object at a given moment
prone (*adj*) having front surface facing downward
prostrate (*adj*) lying facedown on the ground
quadrant one of four parts into which an area is divided by two perpendicular lines
quincunx arrangement of five items around a square or rectangle with one at each corner and one in the center
reclining (*adj*) leaning backward from vertical position
recumbent (*adj*) lying down, reclining; leaning
ridge line where two slopes meet at their highest points
ringside (*adj*) located around a ring
rolled (*adj*) turned around itself
section distinct part of something, esp. solid cut by plane
sector portion of circle bounded by two radii
segment portion of larger figure, esp. circle, cut off by one or more lines or planes
site specific location
situated (*adj*) having or designating a specific location
slit long, narrow opening
somewhere (*adv*) to or at an unspecified place
square (*adj*) exactly aligned; straight, level
stationary (*adj*) fixed in position
stone's throw *Informal*. short distance
summit highest point
supine (*adj*) on back with front surface facing upward
suspended (*adj*) hanging freely from a point
terminus end of a line
there (*adv*) in, to, or at that place
thereat (*adv*) at that place
tip top, summit, or apex
top highest point
transverse (*adj*) reaching across, esp. at right angles to front-back axis of object
ultimate (*adj*) farthest, esp. most remote; last in series
ultima Thule *Latin*. lit. ultimate Thule; farthest point or limit of a journey, esp. point farthest north
underside surface on bottom, usu. hidden from view
up (*adv*) in or toward a higher position; facing upward; in vertical position
uppermost (*adj*) located at the highest position
ventral (*adj*) situated on the front side of a body
verge something that limits, borders, or bounds something else; edge
vertex highest point; point opposite and farthest

from base; termination of line; intersection of two or more lines
whereabouts general place where something is
whereat (*conj*) at or toward which point
zenith highest point, esp. point in celestial sphere opposite nadir
zonal (*adj*) pertaining to or having the shape of a zone
zone specifically defined and bounded area of a surface

Dimensions and Directions

aligned (*adj*) arranged in a straight line; set in order
allover (*adj*) extending over an entire surface
altitude distance upward from surface
anyplace (*adv*) anywhere
anywhere (*adv*) at or to any place or point
approach (*vb*) come near or closer to
area extent of space or surface bounded by fixed lines
ascending (*adj*) moving upward from lower to higher level
askew (*adv*) to one side
aslant (*adv*) obliquely, at a slant
aslope (*adv*) in a slanting position
asymmetrical (*adj*) lacking symmetry, irregular; unsymmetrical
atilt (*adv*) in an inclined position
axis straight line about which a body rotates or around which parts of body are symmetrical
azimuth arc of horizon measured clockwise from fixed point at north or south
back-and-forth (*adj*) backward and forward, from side to side; to-and-fro
backward (*adv*) in reverse of normal direction; with back foremost; toward the rear
bearing horizontal direction of one point measured in degrees from another point
beeline direct course, straight line
bidirectional (*adj*) capable of moving in two, usu. opposite, directions
bilateral (*adj*) having or concerning two sides
bilevel (*adj*) divided horizontally into two usu. equal parts
bisect (*vb*) divide into two usu. equal parts
border outer edge or boundary of a space
boundary indicator that sets limit or extent; edge
breadth dimension from side to side; width
brink edge, esp. of steep place
broad (*adj*) extending to a great range or width
bulk three-dimensional magnitude
cavity hollowed space
centrifugal (*adj*) moving away from center or axis
centripetal (*adj*) moving toward center or axis
chasm wide, deep gap
chockablock (*adj*) crowded together; extremely full
circuit circular line bounding an area
circuitous (*adj*) following an indirect path
circumambient (*adj*) lying on all sides

circumference outer boundary, esp. perimeter of circle

clockwise (*adj*) in direction in which clock hands rotate

coast-to-coast (*adj*) extending across an entire nation or continent

compass enclosing limits of any space; space within such limits

contour general outline of a shape

counterclockwise (*adj*) in direction opposite that in which clock hands rotate; backward

country mile *Informal*. long distance

cross-country (*adj*) extending across an entire country

dangling (*adj*) hanging loosely

decline gradual downward movement

depth dimension downward from top, horizontally inward, or from back to front

descending (*adj*) moving downward from higher to lower position

dextral (*adj*) on or leaning to the right

diagonal (*adj*) running in an oblique direction from a reference line

diameter straight line from one side of circle to the other through center point

dimension magnitude measured in one direction, esp. width, length, or thickness that determines a position in space

direct (*adj*) from point to point by shortest course; straight

direction line along which something is pointing, facing, or moving

directional (*adj*) designating direction in space

distance extent of space between two points, lines, surfaces, or objects, usu. along shortest path

drop distance from one level to some lower level

east direction of sunrise; direction to one's right when facing north

edgewise (*adj*) sideways

elevation distance upward from fixed surface

elongation condition of being stretched or lengthened

encircling (*adj*) running completely around in a circle

equiangular (*adj*) having all angles equal

equilateral (*adj*) having all sides equal

everywhere (*adv*) in all places or parts

extension stretching or enlargement in scope

extensive (*adj*) covering a great area or scope

extent maximum space across or through which something stretches out or reaches

facedown (*adv*) with the front side down

faceup (*adv*) with the front side up

falling (*adj*) descending freely, usu. straight downward

far and wide (*adv*) covering great distances in all directions

far cry great distance

field region covered by a feature or through which a force acts

forward (*adv*) moving toward a point in front

fourth dimension time dimension used as coordinate with length, depth, and breadth in space-time continuum

frontal (*adj*) located at or moving against the front

frontward (*adv*) moving forward

geocentric (*adj*) having Earth as center

geodesic (*adj*) pertaining to the geometry of curved surfaces

grade degree of inclination of slope

heading specific direction, esp. compass point toward which something is moving

height distance from bottom to top; extent upward above surface; highest part or point

high (*adj*) reaching upward, esp. to great extent; elevated from a surface

high and low (*adv*) everywhere possible

horizontal (*adj*) parallel to the horizon or level ground; level; at right angles to vertical

inch (*vb*) move by small degrees

incline grade, slant, or deviation from vertical or horizontal position

inclined (*adj*) at an angle with another surface

indirect (*adj*) deviating from straight line or path

infinite (*adj*) boundless in all directions; immeasurable

infinity immeasurable extent of space

involute (*adj*) curled or curved inward

inward (*adv*) toward or at the inside or center

isometric (*adj*) having equality of measure

isosceles (*adj*) having two sides equal and nonparallel

latitudinal (*adj*) having side-to-side extent, esp. as measure of distance from Earth's equator

left (*adj*) located toward the west when facing north

length longest linear extent or dimension of object

lengthways (*adv*) lengthwise

lengthwise (*adv*) longitudinally, in direction of length; lengthways

level (*adj*) flat; horizontal; having all parts at equal height

light-year distance light travels in one year, used in astronomical measurements

limit greatest extent

linear (*adj*) consisting of or moving in a straight line; having a single dimension

long (*adj*) of a considerable extent; extending to greater length than breadth; far, distant

long-distance (*adj*) situated at or extending a great distance

longitudinal (*adj*) placed or moving lengthwise; having top-to-bottom extent

mile unit of linear distance equal to 5280 feet or 1760 yards (1.609 km)

multilateral (*adj*) having many sides

nationwide (*adj*) extending across an entire country

north cardinal point of a compass in direction of north terrestrial pole, to the left of a person facing the rising sun and directly opposite south

nowhere (*adv*) not at any place; (*n*) unknown or distant place

oblique (*adj*) neither perpendicular nor parallel to another surface; slanting or sloping

obtuse (*adj*) designating an angle greater than 90 but less than 180 degrees

off (*adv*) away from a course or path

on (*prep*) used to indicate location or immediate proximity; (*adv*) toward a place; forward or along a given course

out (*adv*) in a direction away from the center or normal position

outline general shape or boundaries of something

out-of-bounds (*adj*) outside designated limits or boundaries

outreach length or extent of reach

outward (*adj*) directed away from the center; situated on the outside

outwardly (*adv*) toward or on the outside

parallax apparent displacement of moving object as viewed from two different points

parsec 3.26 light-years

patulous (*adj*) spreading widely from the center

perimeter boundary of closed plane figure

pervasive (*adj*) spread throughout every part

plane flat or level surface; two-dimensional body

prolate (*adj*) extended in line joining the poles

protracted (*adj*) extended in space, esp. forward or outward

radial (*adj*) extending from a center; moving along a radius

radiating (*adj*) extending in a direct line away from or toward a center

radius line extending from center of circle to its boundary

range maximum extent outward

ray line extending from point or center

rearward (*adv*) toward the back

rectilinear (*adj*) moving in or forming a straight line

retroflex (*adj*) turned sharply backward

retrograde (*adj*) directed or moving backward, against the general direction

reverse (*adj*) moving opposite to the regular direction; having backside forward

revolution movement around center or axis and return to original position

right (*adj*) located toward the east when facing north

ringed (*adj*) encircled; formed of rings

rising (*adj*) moving to a higher position

rotary (*adj*) turning on an axis

rotation turning of body on an axis; single complete turn around axis

seesaw (*vb*) move back and forth or up and down

shouting distance relatively short distance

sideways (*adv*) facing to the side; toward or from one side; edgewise

sinistral (*adj*) on or leaning to the left

skew lines nonintersecting straight lines in different planes

slant slope or incline away from level

slope slant, oblique course; measure of upward or downward inclination

south cardinal point of a compass in direction of south terrestrial pole and directly opposite north

space particular extent in one, two, or three dimensions; distance between two or more objects

space-time four-dimensional continuum having three spatial coordinates with which to locate an event or object

span distance between two points, esp. endpoints

statewide (*adj*) extending throughout an entire state

straight (*adj*) moving or extending continuously in one direction without turning

straightforward (*adj*) moving in a direct line

stratified (*adj*) forming layers in a graded series

stretch considerable extent, length, or area

sweep continuous, entire range; curving course of line

symmetrical (*adj*) corresponding in size, form, and relative position on opposite sides of line, plane, point, or axis

tabular (*adj*) arranged in vertical and horizontal rows

tangential (*adj*) digressing suddenly from one course and turning to another

three-dimensional (*adj*) having height, width, and depth

throughout (*prep*) in or to every part

tilt surface slanting from level position

to-and-fro (*adj*) back-and-forth

trajectory curve followed by body projected through space

triangulation technique for determining location through bearings from two fixed points at a given distance

two-dimensional (*adj*) having height and width only

ubiquitous (*adj*) existing everywhere

uniaxial (*adj*) having one axis

unidirectional (*adj*) moving in one direction only

unilateral (*adj*) arranged on one side

universal (*adj*) existing everywhere; distributed throughout space without limit or exception

unsymmetrical (*adj*) asymmetrical

up-and-down (*adj*) moving alternately upward, then downward

upright (*adj*) having main axis perpendicular or vertical

vector line segment with both magnitude and direction in space

vertical (*adj*) perpendicular to horizon or level surface; upright; designating an extent to the highest point; at right angles to horizontal

void empty space

-ward suffix meaning moving or located in a direction, as in homeward or upward

way path from one place to another; length of such a course

-ways suffix meaning in or toward a direction or position, as in sideways

west direction of sunset; direction to one's left when facing north

wherever (*conj*) toward or in any place at all

wide (*adj*) of specific extent from side to side; covering a large area

width extent from side to side, at right angles to length

worldwide (*adj*) extending throughout the world

Relative Positions

abeam (*adv*) at right angles to, esp. a ship's keel

about (*adv*) near to; on every side

above (*adv*) in a higher place, over

abutting (*adj*) touching at border, esp. ending at contact point

across (*prep*) from side to side; on the other side

adaxial (*adj*) on the same side as or facing the axis

adjacent (*adj*) nearby; just before or facing; adjoining

adjoining (*adj*) connected at point or along line

advance (*adj*) located before others

afar (*adv*) at a great distance

afield (*adv*) away from a base

after (*prep*) following behind

against (*prep*) directly opposite; close beside or in front of; in contact with; in an opposite direction to

ahead (*adv*) in front of

alongside (*adv*) at or by the side of

ambit boundary or limit of a place

amid (*prep*) in the middle of, among; amidst

amidst (*prep*) amid

among (*prep*) surrounded by, in the midst of; amid

anent (*prep*) *Chiefly Brit.* alongside; in line with

anterior (*adj*) located toward the front; before

antipodal (*adj*) at the opposite side of the globe

apart (*adv*) separately, at some distance

apposed (*adj*) placed side by side or in proximity

around (*adv*) on all sides; nearby; here and there

aside (*adv*) toward or on one side

astraddle (*adv*) with one extension or leg on each side; astride

astride (*prep*) on both sides of from above; with a leg on each side of

at (*prep*) situated in, on, or near

at hand (*adj*) in close proximity

athwart (*prep*) across; from side to side

atop (*adv*) above, on, or at the top

away (*adv*) at a distance, far off; aside

axial (*adj*) forming, situated on, or in the direction of an axis

back (*adv*) toward or at the rear

back-to-back (*adj*) facing in opposite directions from a common point

before (*adv*) in front, ahead

behind (*adv*) in or toward the back or rear; in the place already passed

below (*adv*) in or toward a lower place; underneath

beneath (*adv*) in a lower position; directly below

beside (*prep*) by the side of, usu. nearby

between (*prep*) occupying the intermediate space or interval that separates; 'tween

betwixt (*prep*) between, in a middle position; 'twixt

beyond (*prep*) on or to the farther side; more distant than; outside the reach of

bordering (*adj*) located or in contact at the edge

bottom under or lower side; lowest point or place

by (*prep*) near, close to; in the direction of; aside, away

cater-corner (*adj*) located diagonally opposite; kitty-corner

caudal (*adj*) at or toward the tail or posterior end

central (*adj*) at or near the center, in the middle

centric (*adj*) in or at the center; central; focused on a center

close (*adj*) being near; having little space between elements

coaxial (*adj*) having a common axis

coextensive (*adj*) having identical spatial extent or boundaries

coincident (*adj*) filling the same space

colinear (*adj*) having corresponding parts arranged along the same straight line

collateral (*adj*) parallel or conforming in position or order; running side by side

collinear (*adj*) lying in or sharing the same straight line

concentric (*adj*) having a common center

configuration arrangement of parts relative to one another

confocal (*adj*) having a common focus

consecutive (*adj*) following one another in unbroken order

conterminous (*adj*) having a common boundary; lying within one common boundary

contiguous (*adj*) touching along one side or at some point; adjacent

convenient (*adj*) close at hand, accessible

converse (*adj*) reversed

coplanar (*adj*) occupying the same plane

coterminous (*adj*) having the same boundary

covering (*adj*) entirely enclosing or overlaying

decussate (*adj*) crossed or intersected

deep (*adj*) extending far from surface or edge, esp. downward

detached (*adj*) not connected, separate

discontinuous (*adj*) not continued, discrete; out of or without sequence

discrete (*adj*) consisting of separate, unattached elements; constituting a distinct individual or entity

distal (*adj*) farthest from the point of attachment or origin; terminal

distant (*adj*) far away, separated by a wide space

distinct (*adj*) separate, clearly differentiated from others

down (*adv*) in or to a lower position; toward or at the bottom

elsewhere (*adv*) some place other than here

encircling (*adj*) forming a circle around
enclosed (*adj*) surrounded on all sides
enclosing (*adj*) surrounding on all sides, encircling
encompassing (*adj*) enclosing, forming a border around
enveloping (*adj*) completely enclosing
equidistant (*adj*) equally spaced from a fixed point
even (*adj*) at the same level or point
exterior (*adj*) situated on or outside a surface, beyond the bounds of
external (*adj*) outside, beyond the surface of
face-to-face (*adj*) in direct contact, with front sides directed toward each other
facing (*adj*) with front surface directed toward
far (*adj*) at a great distance
far and away by a significant margin
farther (*adj*) more distant, more remote
flanking (*adj*) lying beside, often on both sides
flush (*adj*) even with the edge of, directly in contact
foot bottom
fore (*adj*) toward the front, forward
fore and aft in or at both front and rear
forth (*adv*) forward, from one place
forward (*adj*) situated at or toward the front
fringe (*adj*) at the edge
from (*prep*) indicating a starting point, esp. beginning at; indicating separation from a starting point
front part or surface facing forward
fronting (*adj*) lying before; facing
further (*adv*) to a greater extent; farther
halfway (*adj*) at the midpoint
hard by near, in close proximity to
hence (*adv*) from this place, away
hereabout (*adv*) nearby, in close proximity
here and there (*adv*) in a number of places
hither (*adv*) to or toward this place; (*adj*) being on the closer or adjacent side
hithermost (*adj*) nearest on a specific side
immediate (*adj*) present, near at hand; without intervening space
indoors (*adj*) situated or occurring within a roofed structure
inferior (*adj*) lower
infra- prefix meaning below
inner (*adj*) situated farther within; being closer to the center
inside (*adv*) in the inner part; within
interior (*adj*) located within fixed boundaries
intermediate (*adj*) in the middle; between two points
interposed (*adj*) placed between, intervening
intersecting (*adj*) crossing at a point
interspersed (*adj*) scattered at intervals among
interstice space situated between things, esp. a narrow interval
intervening (*adj*) lying or placed between
kitty-corner (*adj*) cater-corner
lateral (*adj*) situated at or directed to the side
leeward (*adj*) facing away from the source of wind

levitated (*adj*) elevated into the air in apparent defiance of gravity
long-distance (*adj*) located at a great distance
lower (*adj*) situated below; in a lesser position than another
maximum upper limit, greatest value attained
mean position midway between extremes
medial (*adj*) in the middle
median (*adj*) being in the middle or in an intermediate position
mid (*adj*) situated in a middle position; amid, amidst
midair any point in the air that is more than just above the ground
middle (*adj*) halfway between extremes; intermediate
midline median line or median plane
midst central or interior position
midway (*adj*) halfway, in the middle of a distance
near (*adv*) within or at a short distance
nearby (*adj*) close at hand
next (*adj*) immediately before or following; nearest
next to directly beside, sometimes bordering at the edge
nigh (*adv*) near
nip and tuck so close that advantage alters rapidly between competitors
not far relatively near or close
obverse (*adj*) facing the observer, often in opposition
off (*adv*) at a distance, away from
on (*adv*) in contact with or in close proximity to a surface
onward (*adv*) forward, moving ahead
opposite (*adj*) situated across from or at the other side of an intervening space
out (*adv*) away from, at a distance
outdoors (*adj*) situated or occurring outside any enclosure or beneath open air
outer (*adj*) situated relatively farther out or distant from center
outside (*adj*) located beyond a boundary or outer surface; external; outdoors
over (*prep*) higher than or above another; (*adj*) beyond the upper surface or edge
overlying (*adj*) situated directly above and entirely covering
parallel (*adj*) extending in the same direction, at all points equidistant, and not converging
peripheral (*adj*) situated at the external boundary or surface
perpendicular (*adj*) exactly at right angles to a flat surface or plane
point-blank (*adj*) direct, at very close range
port (*adj*) located on the left side, esp. of a vessel
position location relative to other places at any given moment
posterior (*adj*) located toward the rear; behind
propinquity nearness, proximity
proximal (*adj*) near, esp. close to the center
proximate (*adj*) next to; very near
proximity nearness

rear (*adj*) toward or at the back
remote (*adj*) far or distant
retral (*adj*) located at or toward the back; posterior
retro- prefix meaning backward or behind
separate (*adj*) disconnected in space, distinct from others
side by side next to each other, esp. facing in same direction
spatial relation connection or relative position in space of one point or object with reference to one or more other points or objects
starboard (*adj*) located on the right side, esp. of a vessel
sub- prefix meaning below, beneath, or under
successive (*adj*) following one after another
super- prefix meaning over, above, or on top
superior (*adj*) located higher up or above
superjacent (*adj*) overlying
supra- prefix meaning above or over
surrounding (*adj*) enclosing or overlaying on all sides
thence (*adv*) from that place
thenceforth (*adv*) onward from a given place
thereabout (*adv*) somewhere close or near to a given place
therefrom (*adv*) away from that place
therein (*adv*) in or into that place
thither (*adv*) to or toward that place; there; (*adj*) on the farther side
through (*prep*) in one side and out the other; from one edge to another
toward (*prep*) in the direction of; in the vicinity of; turned to, facing
trans- prefix meaning across, beyond, or through
traverse (*adj*) extending across
'tween (*prep*) between
'twixt (*prep*) betwixt
ulterior (*adj*) lying on the far side; more remote
under (*prep*) below or beneath something, esp. so as to be covered, enveloped, or hidden
underneath (*prep*) directly below the surface or level of, esp. so as to be hidden
up (*adv*) in or toward a higher position; relatively higher than
upside down having upper and lower parts reversed from normal position
upward (*adv*) in or toward a higher position
via (*prep*) by way of
vicinity area in proximity; state of nearness
whence (*adv*) from what place? (*conj*) from what place
where (*adv*) at, in, or to what place? (*conj*) in or at what place
whereto (*conj*) to which place
whither (*adv*) to what place? where? (*conj*) to which place
windward (*adj*) facing toward the source of wind
within (*adv*) in the interior, inside; enclosed
within an inch very close but not quite touching
without (*adv*) on the exterior, outside; external to
yon (*adv*) yonder
yonder (*adv*) over there, at some distance; yon

SHALES

See also: *Chap. 4: Mathematics; Chap. 23: Spatial Positions and Relations*

In addition to adjectives that describe the shapes of physical and natural objects, and mathematically defined forms, this section includes certain concrete nouns, such as "anchor," "bell," and "doughnut," that have distinctive and distinguishing shapes.

acicular (*adj*) needle-shaped
acuminate (*adj*) tapering to a slender point
acute (*adj*) of an angle of less than ninety degrees
amygdaloid (*adj*) almond-shaped
anchor object that has a broad, hooklike arm
angular (*adj*) sharp-cornered; having points from which two lines diverge
annular (*adj*) ring-shaped
apical (*adj*) narrowing to a pointed tip
arc unbroken segment of a curved line
arcuate (*adj*) curved like a bow
asymmetrical (*adj*) lacking balance; not the same on both sides of central axis
attenuated (*adj*) tapering to long, slender point
awry (*adj*) turned or twisted from a central axis
bacillary (*adj*) rod-shaped
ball round or spherical shape
bell hollow, curved shape with open, circular base and surface curving to a central apex
biconcave (*adj*) concave on both sides
biconvex (*adj*) convex on both sides
bifurcate (*adj*) divided into two branches
bilateral (*adj*) two-sided; symmetrical on both sides of an axis
biradial (*adj*) having both bilateral and radial symmetry
block cube
bolus lumpy, rounded mass
botryoidal (*adj*) formed like a bunch of grapes
bowl concave hemisphere opening upward
box rectangle with upright sides; cube
branching (*adj*) forming subdivisions like a tree
brick rectangular solid longer than it is wide
bulbous (*adj*) round like a bulb
bump swelling or lump in flat surface
bursiform (*adj*) pouch-shaped
campanulate (*adj*) bell-shaped
capitate (*adj*) enlarged at the head and spherical; forming a head
catenary curve formed by flexible, nonelastic cord hanging freely between two points
catenulate (*adj*) chainlike in shape
chevron V or inverted V
circinate (*adj*) rolled up on the axis at the apex; ring-shaped
circle curved line every point of which is equidistant from a fixed center
circular (*adj*) circle-shaped
clavate (*adj*) club-shaped and thicker at one end; claviform

claviform (*adj*) club-shaped; clavate
clothoid (*adj*) tear-shaped loop
cloverleaf figure formed by four leaves on one stem
club stylized cloverleaf figure on playing cards
coil series of loops, spiral
columnar (*adj*) arranged in vertical rows
compass (*adj*) curved; forming a curve or an arc
concave (*adj*) hollowed, rounded, or curved inward
concavo-convex (*adj*) concave on one side and convex on the other, esp. with greater curvature on concave side; convexo-concave
cone solid with circular base and vertical surface of line segments that join every point of base circumference to common vertex
conical (*adj*) cone-shaped
conoid (*adj*) conelike or nearly conelike
contour outline of curving, irregular figure
convex (*adj*) curved or rounded outward, as with exterior of sphere or circle
convexo-concave (*adj*) concavo-convex, esp. with greater curvature on convex side
convoluted (*adj*) twisted; coiled
cordate (*adj*) heart-shaped; cordiform
cordiform (*adj*) heart-shaped; cordate
crenate (*adj*) having margin or surface cut into scallops or notches
crenulate (*adj*) having irregularly wavy or serrate outline
crescent shape bounded by convex and concave edges of less than half a hemisphere
crook bent or hooked form
cross two lines intersecting, esp. at right angles; X-shaped figure
cruciform (*adj*) cross-shaped; (*n*) cross
cube regular solid of six equal square sides
cubical (*adj*) cube-shaped
cucullate (*adj*) hooded; hood-shaped
cuneal (*adj*) wedge-shaped
cuneate (*adj*) triangular at base and tapering toward a point; cuneal
curlicue figure with multiple, nonduplicating curves and spirals
curvature amount or state of being curved
curve path of a point not moving in a straight line
cusp point or apex; tip of crescent
cuspidate (*adj*) terminating in a point
cycle circular or spiral arrangement
cycloid curve generated by point on circumference of circle as it rolls along a straight line
cylinder straight tube joining two equal, parallel, circular bases
cylindrical (*adj*) cylinder-shaped
decagon ten-sided polygon
decahedron ten-faced polyhedron
decurved (*adj*) curved or bent downward
decussate (*adj*) X-shaped
deltoid (*adj*) triangular
dendriform (*adj*) resembling a tree; dendroid
dendroid (*adj*) tree-shaped; dendriform
dentiform (*adj*) tooth-shaped

diamond four-sided figure with long diagonal vertical; lozenge
discoid (*adj*) disk-shaped
disk flattened, circular object, sometimes thicker at center than at edge
dodecagon twelve-sided polygon
dodecahedron twelve-faced polyhedron
dogleg course that takes a sharp bend or abrupt turn
dome convex hemisphere, usu. opening downward and attached at base
donut doughnut
double helix pair of intertwined helixes
doughnut ring-shaped solid; donut
egg oval
elbow otherwise straight shape that is bent, esp. at ninety-degree angle near its center
ellipse elongated closed circle, oval
elliptic (*adj*) ellipse-shaped; elliptical
elliptical (*adj*) elliptic
elongate (*adj*) stretched out
ensiform (*adj*) sword-shaped
falcate (*adj*) hooked or curved like a sickle; falciform
falciform (*adj*) sickle-shaped; falcate
fastigiate (*adj*) narrowing toward the top; having upright clustered branches
foliate (*adj*) branching, esp. into leaves
frustum part of solid cone or pyramid left by cutting off top portion by plane parallel to base
fungiform (*adj*) mushroom-shaped
fungoid (*adj*) funguslike in form
funnel hollow cone with tube extending from base
globe sphere, esp. the Earth
globose (*adj*) globular
globular (*adj*) globe-shaped, spherical; globose
gurge spiral, whirlpool
hastate (*adj*) triangular or arrow-shaped with two spreading lobes at base
heart standardized representation of heart as matching curves joined at vertical axis and tilted upward to form V-notch at top
helical (*adj*) spiral, helix-shaped
helicoid (*adj*) forming or arranged in a flat coil or flattened spiral
helix spiral; curve traced on cylinder or cone by point moving at constant oblique angle across right sections
hemihedral (*adj*) having half the number of planes required by symmetry
hemisphere half a sphere
heptagon seven-sided polygon
heptagonal (*adj*) having seven angles and seven sides
hexagon six-sided polygon
hexagonal (*adj*) having six angles and six sides
hexagram figure formed by completing externally an equilateral triangle on each side of a regular hexagon
horn curved ends of a crescent
hump rounded, protruding, often irregular lump
hyperbola plane curve generated by a point

moving so that the difference of its distances from two fixed points is constant

icosahedron twenty-faced polyhedron

infundibuliform (*adj*) funnel- or cone-shaped

involute (*adj*) curled or spiraling inward

knot interlacing or tying of strands

lanceolate (*adj*) narrow and tapering at one end, like the head of a lance

ligulate (*adj*) strap-shaped

linear (*adj*) narrow and elongated

lobate (*adj*) having roundish projections or divisions

loop curving or doubling of line to form closed or partly open curve within itself

lozenge diamond

lump often irregular bump, hump, or knob

lunette crescent or half-moon shape

meniscus crescent; concave or convex upper surface of column of liquid

moline (*adj*) having the end of each arm forked and recurved

moniliform (*adj*) resembling a string of beads

napiform (*adj*) globular at top and tapering off gradually; parsnip- or carrot-shaped

nodular (*adj*) in shape of rounded or irregular mass

nodule small, rounded lump or irregular mass

nonagon nine-sided polygon

notched (*adj*) having V-shaped or rounded indentation, esp. at edge

obcordate (*adj*) heart-shaped with notch at apex

oblate (*adj*) flattened or depressed at poles

oblique (*adj*) inclined; neither parallel nor perpendicular; having no right angle

oblong square, circle, or sphere elongated in one dimension

obovate (*adj*) ovate with narrower end at base

obovoid (*adj*) ovoid with broad end toward apex

obtuse (*adj*) being an angle of more than 90 but less than 180 degrees

obverse (*adj*) having base narrower than top

octagon eight-sided polygon

octagonal (*adj*) having eight angles and eight sides

octahedron eight-faced polyhedron

ogee pointed arch with reversed curve near each side of apex

ogival (*adj*) ogee or ogive-shaped

ogive pointed arch

ophidiform (*adj*) resembling snakes

orb circle; spherical body

orbicular (*adj*) spherical, circular

oval (*adj*) broadly elliptical; egg-shaped

ovate (*adj*) shaped like longitudinal section of an egg with basal end broader

ovoid (*adj*) egg-shaped; ovate

palmate (*adj*) resembling a hand with fingers spread

parabola plane curve that is the path of a moving point whose distance from a fixed point remains equal to its distance from a fixed line

parabolic (*adj*) parabola-shaped; bowl-shaped

parallelepiped prism with six faces that are parallelograms

parallelogram quadrilateral with opposite sides parallel and equal

parted (*adj*) divided into distinct portions by deep, lengthwise cuts

peaked (*adj*) coming to a point at top

peltate (*adj*) shield-shaped

pentacle pentagram

pentagon five-sided polygon

pentagonal (*adj*) having five angles and five sides

pentagram five-pointed star with alternate points connected by a continuous line; pentacle

pentahedron five-faced polyhedron

pentangle pentagram

pinnate (*adj*) resembling a feather, with similar parts arranged on opposite sides of an axis

plane flat, two-dimensional surface; (*adj*) two-dimensional

plano-concave (*adj*) flat on one side, concave on the other

plano-convex (*adj*) flat on one side, convex on the other

polygon closed plane figure bounded by three or more straight lines

polygonal (*adj*) shaped like a plane bounded by three or more straight lines

polyhedral (*adj*) having the shape of a polyhedron

polyhedron solid figure having many faces

pretzel shape that resembles a loosely tied knot

prism polyhedron with two polygonal faces lying in parallel planes and other faces being parallelograms

prismatoid (*adj*) polyhedral with all vertices in two parallel planes

prismoid (*adj*) prismatoid with parallel bases having the same number of sides

prolate (*adj*) elongated in direction of a line joining poles

pyramid polyhedron with polygonal base and triangular sides with common vertex

pyriform (*adj*) pear-shaped

quadrangle quadrilateral

quadrangular (*adj*) quadrilateral-shaped

quadrilateral four-sided polygon; quadrangle

rectangle parallelogram all of whose angles are right angles, usu. with adjacent sides of unequal length

rectangular (*adj*) rectangle-shaped

rectilinear (*adj*) forming a straight line

reniform (*adj*) kidney-shaped

retroflex (*adj*) turned or bent abruptly inward

retuse (*adj*) having apex that is rounded or obtuse with a slight notch

rhomboid (*adj*) rhombus-shaped

rhombus equilateral parallelogram having oblique angles

right angle angle bounded by two lines perpendicular to each other

right triangle three-sided polygon with two sides meeting at right angle

ring circular shape

rondure circle or sphere; graceful curving roundness

round (*adj*) circular; ring- or ball-shaped

sagittate (*adj*) shaped like an arrowhead

scalloped (*adj*) having a border formed by a continuous series of circle segments or angular projections

scroll spiral, rolled, or convoluted form

scutate (*adj*) shield-shaped

semicircle half a circle

serrate (*adj*) notched or toothed along edge

shape specific external surface or outline of an object having a distinct form

shell upright concave shape, usu. hemispherical, often open horizontally

sickle curve in a half circle

sigmoid (*adj*) curved like the letter C; curved in two directions like the letter S

solid three-dimensional shape; (*adj*) three-dimensional

spade stylized spearhead shape used on playing cards

spatulate (*adj*) thin and flat like a spatula

sphere solid bounded by a surface on which all points are equidistant from a fixed central point; ball

spherical (*adj*) sphere-shaped

spicate (*adj*) arranged in the form of a spike

spiral three-dimensional curve generated by a point moving in one or more turns about an axis; (*adj*) winding around a fixed line in a series of planes; coiling around a center while receding from or approaching it; helical

square parallelogram with four equal sides and four right angles; (*adj*) having four equal sides and four right angles in plane figure

star figure with five or more points formed by overlapping triangles with common center

stellate (*adj*) star-shaped

straight line series of points arranged without angles; direct line between two points

styliform (*adj*) bristle-shaped

switchback zigzag arrangement

tapering (*adj*) becoming narrower at one end than the other

terete (*adj*) cylindrical or slightly tapering

ternate (*adj*) arranged in threes

tetartohedral (*adj*) having one-fourth the number of planes needed for symmetry

tetrahedron four-faced polyhedron

toothed (*adj*) having series of notches resembling teeth

toroid surface generated by a closed plane curve rotated about a line lying in the same plane as the curve but not crossing it

toroidal (*adj*) torus-shaped

torus doughnut-shaped surface

trapezium four-sided plane having no two sides parallel

trapezoid four-sided plane having two parallel sides

trapezoidal (*adj*) having the form of a trapezoid

triangle three-sided plane figure with three angles

triangular (*adj*) three-sided and plane

trifoliate (*adj*) having three lobes

trifurcate (*adj*) branching into three
trihedral (*adj*) having three faces
trilateral (*adj*) having three sides
trochoid curve generated by a point on the radius of a circle as the circle rolls on a fixed straight line
truncated (*adj*) having the end square or even
tube hollow, elongated cylinder, often flexible
tubular (*adj*) tube-shaped
turtleback raised, convexly arched surface
unciform (*adj*) hook-shaped
uncinate (*adj*) bent at the tip like a hook
V two equal line segments diverging upward at an acute angle from a point
vermiculate (*adj*) having irregular, thin, wavy lines like the trail of a worm
villiform (*adj*) closely set and resembling bristles or velvet pile
virgate (*adj*) shaped like a rod or wand
volute (*adj*) spiral- or scroll-shaped
wheel round, circular form
whorl something that whirls, coils, or spirals
winding (*adj*) describing a line that is curved, sinuous, or irregular
worm irregular spiral or tube; vermiculate; zigzag
X two crossed line segments, usu. of equal length
zigzag series of sharp, angular turns; switchback

COLORS

White
Gray
Black
Brown
Reddish Brown
Red
Pink
Orange
Yellow
Green
Blue
Purple

See also: *Chap. 4: Physics; Chap. 14: Painting; Chap. 16: Graphic Design and Printing*

The names of colors are often evocative or refer to an object in nature distinguished by a particular color or shade. While elaborate numbering systems based on hue and chroma exist to differentiate colors, actual definitions tend to be circular and self-referential (such as a greenish blue darker than teal and greener than aquamarine).

White

alabaster, argent
blond, bone
chalk, Chinese white, columbine
dove
eggshell
flake white
gauze
ivory
milk-white

nacre
off-white, oyster
pearl, platinum, pure white, putty
silver, snow
white
zinc white

Gray

ash
battleship
charcoal, cinder, cinereous, cloud
dark gray, dove
flint
granite, gray, greige
iron
lead, light gray
merle, moleskin, mouse, mushroom
neutral
obsidian
pale gray, pelican, plumbago
salt-and-pepper, silver gray, slate, smoke, steel
taupe

Black

black, blue-black, Brunswick black
carbon
ebony
ink
jet
lampblack
pitch, pure black
raven
sable, soot

Brown

acorn, amber, anthracene, autumn leaf
beige, biscuit, bistre, brindle, bronze, brown, brunet, brunette, buff, burnt almond, burnt umber, butternut
café au lait, camel, Cologne brown
dark brown, doeskin, Dresden, dun
earth, ecru
fallow, fawn, fox
hazel
khaki
leather, light brown
manila, maple sugar, Mars brown, mink, mocha
negro, nougat, nutria
otter
peppercorn, pongee, putty
raffia, raw sienna, raw umber
sandalwood, seal
tan, tanaura, tawny, toast, topaz
umber
Vandyke brown
walnut

Reddish Brown

auburn
baize, bay, brick, burgundy, burnt ocher, burnt sienna
caramel, Castilian brown, chestnut, chocolate, cinnamon, cocoa, cordovan
fulvous
ginger
henna
light red-brown, liver
mahogany

nutmeg
ocher, oxblood
piccolopasso
reddish brown, roan, russet
sand, sedge, sepia, sienna, sorrel
terra cotta, titian
Venetian red

Red

alizarin crimson, alpenglow, annatto
blood-red, bois de rose, bougainvillea, Bourdeaux, brick red, brownish red
cadmium red, cardinal, carioca, carmine, carnelian, Castilian red, cerise, cherry, Chinese red, cinnabar, claret, cochineal, cranberry, crimson, crimson lake
damask, dark red
faded rose, fire-engine red
garnet, geranium, grenadine, gules
Indian red, iron red
jockey
light red, lobster
madder lake, maroon, Mars red, murrey
orange-red
paprika, peach, Persian red, pinkish red, ponceau, poppy, Prussian red, puce
red, rhodamine, rose madder, ruby, rust
scarlet, stammel, strawberry
tile red
Venetian red, vermilion
wild cherry, wine

Pink

begonia, blush
cameo, carnation, casino pink, coral
deep pink
fiesta, flamingo
hot pink
incarnadine
livid pink
mallow pink, melon, moonlight
nymph
ombre, orchid rose
pale pink, peach, petal pink, pink
reddish pink, rose, royal pink
salmon, shell pink, shocking pink
tea rose

Orange

apricot, aurora
burnt Roman ocher
cadmium orange, carotene, carrot, chrome orange, copper
dark orange
helianthin, hyacinth
mandarin, marigold, mikado
ocher, orange
pale orange, pumpkin
realgar, red-orange, Rubens' madder
Spanish ocher
tangerine, terra cotta
yellow-orange

Yellow

amber, auramine, aureolin, azo yellow
barium yellow, blond, brass, brazen, brazilin, buff, butter
cadmium yellow, calendula, canary, Cassel yellow,

chalcedony, chamois, champagne, chrome
  yellow, citron, corn, cream, crocus
dandelion
flax
gamboge, gold, goldenrod, green-yellow
honey
Indian yellow
jonquil
lemon, linen
maize, mustard
Naples yellow
orange-yellow, orpiment
pale yellow, palomino, pear, primrose, purree
quince
reed
saffron, safranine, sallow, sand, snapdragon,
  straw, sulphur, sunflower
wheaten
yellow, yellow ocher, yolk

Green

absinthe, aqua, avocado
bay, beryl, bice, blue-green, brewster, Brunswick
  green
cadmium green, celadon, chartreuse, chrome
  green, clair de lune, corbeau, cucumber, cypress
dark green, drake
emerald
fir green, flagstone, forest green
grass, gray-green, green, gunpowder
holly
jade
kelly green, Kendal green
leaf, light green, lime, Lincoln green, lizard,
  loden, lotus
malachite, marine, mint, moss, myrtle
Niagara green, Nile green
olive
pale green, parrot, patina, pea green, pistachio
  green
reseda
sea green, serpentine, shamrock, spruce
teal, terre verte, tourmaline, turquoise
verdigris, viridian
willow green
yellow green, yew

Blue

aquamarine, azure
baby blue, blue, blueberry, bluebonnet
calamine blue, cerulean, cobalt blue, Copenhagen
  blue, cornflower, cyan
Delft blue, Dresden blue
flag blue
gentian, greenish blue
Havana lake, Helvetia blue, huckleberry, hydrangea
ice blue, Indanthrene, indigo
jouvence
lapis lazuli, light blue, lucerne, lupine
marine, midnight blue, milori
Napoleon blue, navy blue
pale blue, peacock blue, powder blue, Prussian
  blue, purple-blue
reddish blue, royal blue
saxe blue, sea blue, sky blue, smalt, steel blue
teal blue
ultramarine
Venetian blue
water blue, Wedgwood blue, wisteria, woad
zaffer

Purple

amaranth, amethyst, Argyle, aubergine
blue-violet, bluish purple, bokhara
campanula, clematis
dahlia, damson, deep purple
fuchsia
grape, gridelin
heliotrope, hyacinth
Imperial purple
lavender, light purple, lilac
magenta, mauve, monsignor, mulberry
orchid
pale purple, pansy, periwinkle, phlox, plum, prune,
  purple
raisin, raspberry, reddish purple, royal purple,
  rubine
solferino
tulip, Tyrian purple
violet, violetta

VERBS OF THOUGHT
Thinking, Judgment, and Consideration
Reasoning and Examination
Learning and Memory
Knowledge and Understanding
Belief and Conception

See also: *Chap. 23: Reasoning and Intuition;*
Judgment and Criticism

Thinking, Judgment, and Consideration

appraise estimate the nature or merit of
assess appraise, judge
assume suppose to be true
attend consider, give heed to
attitudinize form opinion
brainstorm (*n*) sudden idea; exchange ideas with
  others to stimulate creative thinking
brood meditate quietly; ponder moodily, think
  persistently about
browse consider casually
chew over mull, think over at length
cogitate meditate, ponder hard
concentrate focus one's thoughts
conceptualize think about, interpret
conjecture conclude or suppose from scant
  evidence; surmise, guess
consider think about carefully
contemplate meditate on, consider thoroughly
  with deep attention
count consider
decide arrive at conclusion or solution
dope out *Slang.* figure out
dwell on linger over in thought
engross occupy the mind or attention
  completely
entertain take into consideration
esteem consider or believe to be of a certain
  value; regard highly
estimate guess extent of, conjecture about
figure regard, consider
fret worry, brood
gather conclude from observation or hints
gauge estimate, judge

grope search for answer or comprehension
guess arrive at a conclusion by intuition and
  without sufficient evidence; surmise; conjecture
  about accurately
hazard guess, estimate
heed pay attention to, mind
interpret construe in a certain way, conceive;
  explain the meaning of
judge form an opinion of, esp. by weighing
  evidence
look into consider, explore
meditate think contemplatively; center one's
  thoughts; muse, reflect
mind heed closely
mull ponder at length
muse reflect on something from all sides, often
  inconclusively
note give careful attention to
occupy one's thoughts totally engage one's
  mind
occur come to mind
opine form an opinion about
outfox outsmart
outguess anticipate another's plans or motives
outsmart get the better of by thinking; outfox;
  outthink; outwit
outthink excel in thinking; get the better of by
  thinking
outwit get the better of by superior ingenuity
  and clever thinking; outsmart
percolate penetrate; brood over
perpend reflect on carefully
ponder meditate on; consider quietly, deeply,
  and thoroughly
predetermine decide on beforehand
prejudge form an opinion prematurely
premeditate consider or plan out before acting
preoccupy engross to the exclusion of all else
psych *Informal.* intimidate psychologically
rack one's brain strain for solution
read make out the significance of
reappraise evaluate again
reckon estimate; figure, assume
reconsider consider again with a view toward
  change of decision or action
reevaluate reconsider; appraise again
reflect consider quietly
regard take into account or consideration
rethink consider again
revise reconsider, change one's opinion
revolve in one's mind mull over, consider at
  length
ruminate ponder, muse; go over in one's mind
  repeatedly and slowly
second-guess use hindsight to criticize or
  correct; predict
select choose one over another
simmer be in initial stages of consideration
sink become deeply absorbed, as in thought
size up appraise, evaluate, judge
sleep on consider overnight
speculate reflect or meditate on some subject;
  indulge in idle conjecture; guess, surmise
stew *Informal.* brood over

surmise guess; infer without strong evidence
tackle think seriously about some problem
take into account consider
theorize speculate
think employ one's powers of judgment or reason; consider; remember; ponder; occupy one's mind in reflection on
think about consider
turn over consider; revolve in one's mind
view examine, survey, consider
weigh consider carefully, evaluate
wonder think or speculate curiously or doubtfully; ponder over
worry fret; experience concern over
wrestle with occupy oneself in serious thought about; consider all sides of; debate internally

Reasoning and Examination

abstract determine and summarize essentials; consider as general instance apart from specific examples
adduce offer as evidence
analyze subject to careful scrutiny
arrive at conclude by reasoning
attribute regard as based on or having specific meaning
belabor apply unreasonable scrunity
calculate consider logically and dispassionately
canvass examine carefully in detail
cast about contrive, plan
cerebrate use reason, think about
check test validity by examining closely
check out examine and approve; consider carefully
clarify make intelligible; free from confusion
clear up explain so as to eliminate confusion; clarify
compare examine for differences or similarities
conclude determine or decide by reasoning
construe analyze and explain
contrast compare with something else
convince prove by argument
correlate determine and establish an orderly connection between two or more things
crack puzzle out and resolve
debate consider from all sides
deduce infer or conclude by reasoning from something known or assumed
deliberate consider carefully and thoroughly
derive infer, deduce
diagnose analyze to determine the cause of
dig into *Informal.* study, examine thoroughly
dissect examine minutely in all component parts; analyze
educe deduce from something undeveloped
establish determine, prove
evaluate study and determine value or amount of
examine inspect or investigate carefully
explore analyze, study, investigate
figure calculate; conclude
figure out solve, determine

find out discover truth of by study or observation
follow keep one's mind on, attend to
hypothesize make an assumption as premise in an argument
infer derive a logical conclusion from premise or evidence; guess, surmise
inspect examine critically
integrate bring together and unite information and thoughts into a coherent whole
intellectualize consider the rational content or form of
interpolate estimate unknown from known
interpret explain the meaning of; construe or conceive in a specific way
investigate examine closely and systematically
metagrobolize tackle a difficult or puzzling problem
observe examine carefully; consider from all sides
penetrate discover the true nature of by careful examination
place estimate the nature of; determine proper order or position of
plumb examine deeply, closely, and critically
pore over study attentively; meditate on intently
probe investigate thoroughly
prove establish the truth or accuracy of
puzzle exercise one's mind to understand something mysterious; attempt a solution by guesswork
question analyze, examine; doubt, dispute
rationalize consider logically; invent plausible reasons for
reason think logically so as to reach a conclusion
redefine clarify meaning; reexamine
reduce comprehend something complex by analyzing its component parts
research investigate thoroughly
review evaluate critically; examine or study again
scrutinize examine very closely
search look into carefully in an effort to find something hidden; examine
sift through separate and examine various possibilities
solve determine the answer to a problem
sort out examine and place in order
strategize plan carefully toward a specific end
study investigate carefully and in detail; think deeply, reflect on
surmise imagine; infer from scant information
survey inspect or consider comprehensively
syllogize reason by means of premises that support a logical conclusion; deduce
synthesize combine elements to reach a conclusion
think over evaluate from all sides for possible action
think through consider thoroughly and reach a conclusion
trace follow logically from beginning to end
work out devise or arrange by careful calculation
work over consider at length; examine thoroughly

Learning and Memory

absorb take in, learn
acquaint oneself with become familiar with, furnish oneself with knowledge about
ascertain discover, learn with assurance
assimilate absorb and comprehend
bear in mind remember, consider
bethink oneself think, consider; remind oneself; remember
bone up *Informal.* refresh one's memory; study intensely to assimilate quickly
call to mind remember
catch on grasp mentally, understand
commit to memory memorize
digest assimilate information; arrange methodically in the mind
discover gain knowledge of for the first time; realize
evoke call up or produce memories
fix in one's mind remember; settle on
get wise *Slang.* become informed
glean gather information slowly and patiently
inquire into investigate, seek information about
learn acquire information, knowledge, or understanding
master become adept through understanding and study
memorize learn exactly by rote; commit to memory
pick up learn; acquire understanding of through light study
recall remember
recollect remember
remember call back to the level of consciousness; think of again; retain in one's memory; recall; recollect
reminisce think about past experiences, often wistfully
retain hold in one's mind or memory
sink in have something penetrate one's mind
soak up absorb and fill one's mind with
study apply one's mental faculties so as to acquire knowledge
summon up recall, evoke
take in grasp the meaning of, comprehend; absorb
wise up *Slang.* learn or become aware of or knowledgeable about, esp. something unknown or known to others

Knowledge and Understanding

appreciate be fully aware of nature or value of
apprehend understand, perceive
collect one's thoughts organize one's thinking
comprehend understand
crystallize give one's thoughts a definite form
dawn on begin to be perceived
determine resolve conclusively
dig *Slang.* understand; recognize
discern recognize or understand, esp. as distinct or different
distill determine the essence of

distinguish separate mentally; recognize as different

familiarize make known to oneself

fathom penetrate and understand thoroughly

get at penetrate, determine the truth of

get it *Informal.* understand

grasp comprehend

grok *Slang.* understand, comprehend

identify determine the particular nature or identity of; recognize

ken *Scottish.* recognize, know

know perceive clearly with certainty; recognize, be acquainted with; understand the nature of; be convinced of

make out decipher meaning of, comprehend

perceive become aware of; gain understanding of

pierce see into and understand against resistance

prehend apprehend

realize understand clearly or fully, apprehend

recognize perceive clearly, realize to be real or true; identify from past experience

resolve reach conclusion or solution

savvy *Informal.* understand, catch on to

see perceive, comprehend

see through recognize the true nature of

sense become aware of; comprehend, grasp

suss out *Chiefly Brit. slang.* reach an understanding of; figure out

understand grasp the idea or meaning of; comprehend

Belief and Conception

believe have confidence in the truth of without proof; hold an opinion

buy *Informal.* believe or accept

conceive originate, imagine

concoct originate, fabricate, conceive

conjure up imagine or contrive as if by magic

contrive fabricate, invent

create conceive, originate; imagine

daresay believe or assume to be probable

deem believe; hold as an opinion

divine discover or perceive intuitively, not by reason

dream fantasize or imagine; consider as a remote possibility

dream up conceive or devise an idea or plan

envisage have a mental picture of

envision imagine, picture to oneself

evoke re-create from memory or imagination; conjure up

expect imagine; suppose

fabricate conceive, create, concoct

fancy form a conception of; believe without assurance

fantasize imagine; dream

feel believe, think

find feel; discover

foresee know beforehand, esp. by intuition

harbor maintain a thought or feeling about

hatch conceive or concoct an idea or plan

have a hunch guess, intuit

hold believe, have an opinion

ideate form an idea or thought; conceive

imagine form mental image or notion of; guess or conjecture; create

incline lean toward one view or plan of action

incubate hatch; give form to an idea

intuit understand or know without rational thought; feel

invent imagine, contrive

make up conceive, imagine, devise

moon indulge in dreams over

opine hold an opinion on; suppose

originate conceive, create

picture envision in one's mind, imagine

preconceive form an opinion in advance without real knowledge

prefigure picture or imagine beforehand

presume assume or suppose to be true as a matter of fact

realize become fully aware of; conceive of

reify ascribe concrete qualities to an abstraction

rely on believe, trust

suppose assume, often for the sake of argument

suspect believe to be true or likely

take it assume, imagine

tend pay heed to; exhibit disposition toward

think up imagine, contrive, devise

trust believe

visualize envision or form a mental image of

weave form by elaborate combining of elements into a connected whole

REASONING AND INTUITION
Reason and Rationale
Order, Hierarchy, and Systems
Intuition and Imagination

See also: *Chap. 13: Philosophy; Chap. 13: Education; Chap. 22: Strategy, Intrigue, and Deception; Chap. 23: Verbs of Thought; Chap. 23: Judgment and Criticism; Chap. 25: Truth, Wisdom, and Spiritual Attainment*

Reason and Rationale

adduce (*vb*) bring forward, cite, allege

analogy inference derived from likeness between two or more things

analysis systematic separation and examination of parts

antithesis contrast or opposition, esp. of ideas or argument in dialectic process

apologia reasoned defense or justification

apprehension understanding

argument chain or sequence of reasons leading to conclusion

assumption statement accepted as true before being proved

axiom generally accepted truth or principle

biconditional (*adj*) pertaining to the relation between two statements that is valid only when both are true or false

brainstorm (*vb*) engage in a session of energetic thinking, often in a group; (*n*) sudden valuable idea

circumscribe (*vb*) define clearly

clarification something that reduces confusion or makes an issue understandable

clincher final, irrefutable statement that wins an argument

cogent (*adj*) compelling, persuasive; relevant

cogitation deep thinking

cognition process of knowing or gaining knowledge, esp. intellectual process

cognitive (*adj*) involving the acquisition of knowledge

coherent (*adj*) logically clear and consistent

comprehension intellectual understanding, mental grasp

conception ability and process of forming ideas

confutation refutation of an argument

conjecture inference, guess

construe (*vb*) explain, interpret; understand

contend (*vb*) argue, contest

contest (*vb*) challenge, attempt to refute

contradiction assertion of contrary statement; opposition

contradistinction distinction by contrast or opposition

contraposition antithesis, opposition

controvert (*vb*) dispute, deny, contradict, contest

convention general agreement in principle

convince (*vb*) prevail in argument, persuade

correct (*vb*) remove errors, rectify; (*adj*) factual, true

counterexample example that refutes another statement

counterproposal alternative proposal made after rejecting initial proposal

criterion measure or standard of judgment

crux central or decisive point in argument

cumulative (*adj*) increasing by successive additions; tending to lead to the same conclusion

cut-and-dried (*adj*) done according to routine, formula, or set plan

data facts or information; material providing grounds for discussion

datum given fact on which argument or premise is based or from which conclusion may be drawn

debate (*vb*) dispute, deliberate; examine question or issue verbally; (*n*) formal argument or discussion of opposing views

deduction reasoning process that proceeds from general to particular

define (*vb*) determine or describe in specific terms

definition formal statement or explanation of meaning

definitive (*adj*) conclusive; most reliable or complete

delimit (*vb*) set boundaries or limits

demystify (*vb*) explain clearly so as to remove confusion

determine (*vb*) define, settle, fix, ascertain, limit

dialectic art or practice of logical discussion, esp. in investigating truth of a theory or opinion

didactic (*adj*) instructive, pertaining to teaching

differentiate (*vb*) distinguish; mark or perceive differences

discursive reasoning reasoning that draws inferences from logical thought patterns

disjunction separation into elements

disprove (*vb*) refute

dispute (*vb*) contend, argue

disquisition formal inquiry or discourse

dissect (*vb*) analyze

dissertation disquisition, discussion; essay

egghead *Informal.* intellectual person, often with pretentious manner

epistemic (*adj*) concerning knowledge

esemplastic (*adj*) capable of shaping diverse elements into a unified whole

examination thorough, detailed investigation or study

excogitate (*vb*) think out, contrive

explicate (*vb*) interpret, explain

expostulate (*vb*) reason earnestly, usu. against something

extrapolate (*vb*) infer an unknown from something that is known

fact something known to be true or real

facultative (*adj*) relating to mental activity or capacity

fallacy false idea, error in reasoning

forensic (*adj*) pertaining to argumentation

forethought premeditation

generalization general inference derived from particular

gist essential point of argument or story

grasp comprehension

hypothesis unproved assumption for debate or discussion; proposition

idea concept, mental impression, or notion

ideation process of forming ideas or images

ignoratio elenchi *Latin.* lit. ignorance of proof; type of fallacy using irrelevant proof

implausible (*adj*) not particularly believable

implication something implied or suggested as naturally inferred or understood

induction reasoning process that proceeds from particular to general

inference logical conclusion drawn from premise

information knowledge, data

intellect mental faculty for knowing, judging, perceiving, and reasoning

intellection intellectual activity

intellectualize (*vb*) seek or consider rational content or form of; apply reason and ignore emotional or psychological significance of

interpretation explanation of meaning

irrelevant (*adj*) not pertinent, immaterial

ken (*vb*) *Scottish.* know, discern

last word conclusive point in discussion

logic method of sound reasoning that relates sequence of facts, events, or notions

lucid (*adj*) clearly expressed

middle ground reasonable position between extremes

moot (*adj*) open to discussion or debate; irrelevant to an issue in debate

notion idea, proposition, theory

nub point, gist

perception capacity for comprehension; keen mental faculty or observation

perspicacious (*adj*) endowed with keen mental perception

perspicuous (*adj*) presented in clear and precise manner

pertinence relevance to the matter at hand

polemic controversial argument; person who argues in opposition to another

position point of view; statement of proposition or thesis

postulate hypothesis assumed as basis for line of reasoning

prehension mental understanding

premise something assumed as basis for argument or position

proposition anything stated for consideration or discussion or to be proved

proviso conditional stipulation

ratiocination process of careful, precise reasoning

ratio cognoscendi *Latin.* lit. grounds of knowledge; grounds by which something is known

rational (*adj*) conforming to reason

rationale fundamental reason, basis, or explanation

reason power to form logical conclusions and sound judgments

reasoning orderly use of mental faculties to reach conclusions and draw inferences

reductionism simplification of a complex concept, phenomenon, or issue, esp. oversimplification or distortion

reflection careful consideration of something

refutation use of evidence to prove something false

relation connection between things that belong or function together

riddle cleverly puzzling or confounding question

rumination extended meditation; going over of something in one's mind

sophistry deceptive or fallacious reasoning

sound reasoning valid thinking

specious (*adj*) unsound though appearing to be true

speculation assumption of truth based on insufficient evidence

standard criterion for judgment; established rule or measure

statement proposition, presentation of point

sticky wicket *Chiefly Brit.* difficult problem requiring sound reasoning for solution

stipulation specific, essential condition or accepted point

syncretism reconciliation of conflicting beliefs or forms

synthesis combining of disparate elements into a whole

tangent sudden change or digression in reasoning process

tenable (*adj*) defensible; reasonable

theorem proposition that can be drawn from premises or is part of general theory

theory coherent series of plausible propositions that serve as explanation for something

thesis position or proposition set forth for proof or argument

thought act or process of thinking; cogitation; reasoning power

thought-out (*adj*) derived by careful mental consideration

thrust essential element or principal goal of argument

treatise systematic exposition of essentials of argument and its conclusion

unilateral (*adj*) one-sided, imbalanced

viable (*adj*) having likely chance of working

watertight (*adj*) flawless; having no possibility of evasion or misunderstanding

well-founded (*adj*) based on sound or valid reasoning

well-grounded (*adj*) having a sound basis or foundation

well-taken (*adj*) justified, based in truth or fact

wit mental soundness or ability, esp. facility for making unusual connections and brief, clever expressions

Order, Hierarchy, and Systems

agenda outline or list of things to be considered

antecedent conditional element in proposition

antinomy contradiction or opposition between two apparently true statements

aperçu *French.* brief outline or summary

aspect particular phase or light in which something is viewed

basis principal component of something; essential condition

breakdown classification into categories

canon system of rules or laws; body of criteria and standards

case set of circumstances or conditions

case history recorded details and past, used for analysis

catalog list, register of items arranged systematically

category specific division within classification system

catena chain or sequence of linked things, events

chain sequence of connected things, events

check criterion used for testing or evaluation

circular reasoning reasoning involving unproved conclusion of argument as proof

class large, inclusive set sharing common characteristics

classification systematic arrangement into classes, groups, or categories with specific characteristics

clause particular section

codify (*vb*) organize systematically

coherence logical or natural consistency

cohesion unity, coherence

collate (*vb*) place in order; compare critically

collateral (*adj*) corresponding, esp. in parallel sequence; secondary

colligation bringing together of separate facts under unifying principle, idea, or theme

columniation organization of material into rows and columns

comparison examination of two or more items to determine similarities and differences

compartmentalize (*vb*) separate into distinct categories

compendium collection of information; brief summary of larger work

component element or facet

comprise (*vb*) constitute; include within scope; be made up of

concatenation connected series or chain

concinnity harmony or elegance of structure

condition something that defines, limits, or changes a more general case or set

connection causal or logical relation between objects or ideas

consecutive (*adj*) in order

consequence inference or logical conclusion; result

construct something organized or structured by mental activity

content analysis classification and evaluation of material to determine its meaning or likely effect

continuity unbroken connection or succession

continuum consistent series or whole, esp. sequence progressing by small gradations

convention standard rule or practice

corollary one proposition that is proved incidentally by another

correlative (*adj*) related as reciprocal proofs

correspondence relation by similarity or congruence

course usual procedure; progression in steps

delineate (*vb*) outline; set forth in precise detail

design arrangement of elements or details

dichotomy division into two mutually exclusive or contradictory parts

division distinct group forming portion of larger group

doctrine basic principle in branch of knowledge or belief system

domino effect cumulative effect that results when one action initiates a series of events

element basic constituent part

example single instance that shows character of larger set

explicit (*adj*) fully demonstrated, expressed, or explained

extrinsic (*adj*) external; inessential, not part of

facet element, aspect, component

feedback automatic furnishing of data from the output of a system or process and evaluation of such information by a control device to shape future output

flow chart diagram using symbols to display step-by-step procedure or system

form distinguishing shape or component; established method of proceeding; formula

formula standard statement; general fact or rule

framework basic underlying structure or plan

full circle series of developments that return to source, original position, or opposite position

fundamental minimum determining aspect or part of something

go/no-go (*adj*) requiring a decision to continue or halt

gradation arrangement in levels or stages; single level within such a series

grade level within hierarchy

gradient measure of rate of change

grid network of evenly spaced horizontals and perpendiculars; any system so organized

hierarchy organization into a branching or ranked structure

hyponym term used to denote subcategory of a more general class

increment something added, esp. very small amount or series of regular successive additions

index list of specific data or items, usu. arranged alphabetically

infrastructure basic, underlying framework or feature of an organizational system

instance example, case; one stage viewed as part of process

interconnectedness cohesive relation between elements

interface point at which independent systems meet and interact

interlocking (*adj*) connected, interrelated

interpenetration mutual penetration between two things

intrinsic (*adj*) essential to nature of system or object

jigsaw complex, intricate puzzle

juxtapose (*vb*) place side by side

key guide providing explanation to system and its symbols

knot cluster of things together

labyrinth something extremely complex in structure; maze

lattice network of elements or design organized in crossed pattern like a matrix

level grade or rank within structure

limit point or number that may not be exceeded

linear (*adj*) proceeding logically or sequentially in a straight line

list meaningful sequence of items

logistics detailed planning, implementation, and coordination of an operation, esp. military

matrix arrangement of elements into rows and columns

maze confusing, intricate network; labyrinth

method systematic procedure or mode of inquiry in a field or discipline

model structural design for system or object

moiré irregular, wavy pattern

morphology science of structure, form, and patterns

network interlocking or interconnected system

nexus connection; connected group or series

nomenclature system of terms and symbols for describing something

non sequitur *Latin.* lit. it does not follow; inference or conclusion that does not follow logically from premises or evidence

norm average, standard

offshoot collateral branch; secondary element

order arrangement or sequence of things or events; category, class, rank, or level

ordonnance arrangement or disposition of parts, esp. of artistic creation

organization act or process of arranging systematically into logical or consistent form

outline hierarchical organization of material; summary; plan

paradigm model, example

paradox statement, belief, or idea apparently contrary to truth, reality or itself, but actually possible or true

parameter limit or boundary; characteristic defining element

partition division into constituent elements

patchwork organization into an interconnected network

pattern coherent design or arrangement of parts

pertinent (*adj*) essential, basic, or relevant

plan design; detailed program; orderly arrangement of parts

point most important element of argument, story, or line of reasoning

position order or place within structure or hierarchy

position paper detailed report advising plan of action on given issue

precedent established standard or rule

précis concise summary of essential points or facts

premise proposition previously proved or assumed; basis for argument

prerequisite something required before proceeding to the next level

principium *Latin.* lit. that which is first; fundamental principle

principle comprehensive, fundamental law or assumption

probability chance or likelihood that given event or result will occur

qualitative (*adj*) pertaining to the essence or inherent nature or character

quantitative (*adj*) measuring an exact or specified amount or quantity

random (*adj*) without order or sequence

rank (*vb*) organize into hierarchy of relative positions; (*n*) position in such a hierarchy

reciprocal (*adj*) shared by or affecting both sides equally

reference definitive source of information relating to something

relative (*adj*) associated, relevant; referring or connected to another thing

relevant (*adj*) having importance to the matter at hand; providing conclusive evidence

reticulate (*vb*) divide, arrange, or mark into network

rudiment basic principle or element

salient (*adj*) prominent, conspicuous

section separate part or portion

sector distinctive portion of larger system, esp. one bounded by specific lines

sequence continuous, connected series

sequitur *Latin.* lit. it follows; conclusion, consequence

set number of things with common characteristics classed together

side effect secondary response, often adverse

sift (*vb*) separate out or sort

skeleton structural framework

solution explanation or answer; process of finding answer or resolving problem

spectrum continuous sequence or range

spider web complex network of interconnected elements

step one stage in process; grade or rank in scale

step-by-step (*adj*) taken in proper sequence, one at a time

stratagem cleverly contrived scheme or plan, esp. to surprise, deceive, or gain advantage over an adversary

strategy detailed plan or method for obtaining specific goal

structure defined organizational pattern or arrangement

structuring act of forming something according to a structure

subcategory division of category within structure

subdivision smaller set within larger set forming division of whole

subset set each of whose components is part of a larger, inclusive set

subsidiary secondary part ranked lower in hierarchy

succession sequence; process of following in order

sui generis *Latin.* lit. of his, her, or its own kind; constituting a class unto itself

summary concise, general description of larger argument or system

superstructure overlying framework or extension built on top of or added to basic structure

switchery network

syndetic (*adj*) connective; interconnected

synoptic (*adj*) characterized by general overview; pertaining to a brief or condensed statement

syntax connected, organized system; harmonious placement of parts, esp. linguistic

system interacting or interdependent combination of things forming unified whole

systemic (*adj*) relating to or common to a particular system

tactics strategy, esp. careful or devious planning and maneuvering to gain advantage

template model or pattern for duplicating existing object or system

test critical evaluation to prove or disprove; criterion for such evaluation

thread of an argument course or outline of ideas expressed

track course or sequence of argument or discussion

train of thought course of argument, discussion, or reasoning

tree branching hierarchical structure

trusswork latticelike network of interconnected elements

unity state of being complete in itself or combining with others to form a whole

vicious circle chain of events in which each response generates a new problem

warp and woof foundation composed of interlocking elements

web complex network; spider web

well-ordered (*adj*) organized into logical and coherent form

workable (*adj*) capable of functioning properly

wrinkle change in traditional or routine procedure or method

Intuition and Imagination

air castle castle in the air

aperçu *French.* sudden intuitive insight

caprice sudden, unpredictable, apparently unmotivated idea

castle in the air daydream; impractical idea; air castle

chimerical (*adj*) imaginary; visionary; wildly fanciful

clairvoyance ability to perceive matters beyond one's senses; precognition; second sight

collective unconscious genetically determined part of unconscious common to all members of one race or people

common sense sound practical judgment not based on reasoning or special knowledge

conation impulse or tendency to act with resolution

conceit fanciful idea or thought

conception inception and understanding of ideas and abstractions

concoction fabrication, fanciful creation

conjecture guess; speculation

conjuring imagining or contriving ideas

creation act of making, imagining, or inventing something new

creativity ability to imagine and make new or original forms, ideas, or things, esp. by transcending traditional thinking

daydream wishful product of one's imagination

delirium hallucinatory, visionary mental disturbance

dream visionary product of one's unconscious imagination

eidolon ideal; phantom of imagination

enchantment state of imaginative rapture

ESP extrasensory perception

extrasensory perception ESP; ability to perceive another's thoughts or things beyond one's normal senses

fabrication creation, invention, or construction

fabulous (*adj*) being the product of imagination

fancy whim, notion

fantastical (*adj*) conceived by unrestrained imagination

fantasy creation of unrealistic images and dreams; caprice

feeling intuitive sense separate from rational process

fiction creation or invention of the imagination

figment something invented or contrived

flash sudden intuitive perception

flight of fancy extravagant indulgence in whim and imagination

guess opinion not based on specific evidence

hallucination fantastic, unrealistic vision or impression

haptic (*adj*) denoting one who draws primarily on cutaneous sense data and tactile experience

humor sudden, inexplicable whim or notion

hunch strong intuitive feeling about future

idea newly formulated or original thought or notion

idealization overestimation of something in its ultimate, perfected form

illusion misapprehension, hallucination, or misleading image

image mental representation of something not present

imagination creative faculty to produce mental images of things not present, previously unknown, or suggestive of something stored in memory

implicit (*adj*) unexpressed but essential to nature of something

impression distinct image of something; reaction

impulse sudden, spontaneous inclination or idea

ingenuity skill and cleverness in conception or design

innovation new way of doing or viewing something

insight clear, deep perception

inspiration power of arousing intellect or emotions, esp. to receive or conceive new insights or ideas; such a new insight or idea

instinct perceptions or impulses coming from below the conscious mental level; natural aptitude or faculty

intimation indirect or subtle communication of idea

intuition direct knowledge or insight independent of any reasoning process

invention creation, fabrication, contrivance

juice essence, strength, or vitality

make-believe fancy, daydream, illusion

mind's eye inner eye that provides the ability to conceive of or remember imaginary scenes

myth fanciful, usu. traditional, imaginary tale serving as basis for commonly held belief

mythopoeia creation of myths

notion one's opinion or view of something, often fanciful or vague; personal theory, whim, or inclination

novelty innovation, fresh idea

passing fancy notion or whim held briefly

perception awareness of one's environment, esp. recognition by intuition or senses

phantasm fantasy, illusion, figment of imagination

phantasmagoria constantly shifting, hallucinatory succession of images

precognition clairvoyance

premonition intuitive anticipation of an event without reason; presentiment

presentiment premonition

pretend (*adj*) make-believe or imagined

psychic sense sensitivity to immaterial or supernatural powers and influences

quixotism capricious, impractical devotion to ideals and dreams

rapture powerful experience involving heightened perception and sensations, as of another sphere of existence

reverie daydream; state of being lost in thought

second sight clairvoyance

sixth sense extraordinary intuitive power of perception beyond the five senses; intuition

spark something that ignites one's imagination or thoughts

speculation conjectural consideration of a matter; guess; surmise

surmise conjecture; speculation

telepathy extrasensory communication from one mind to another, as by ESP

theory imaginative but unverifiable speculation serving as explanation for something

vagary erratic or unpredictable action or idea

visile (*adj*) denoting one who draws primarily on visual data and input

vision perception with one's imagination; extraordinary or vivid discernment or insight; supernatural appearance that provides insight

visualization ability to imagine or conceive

whim sudden, unusual, or capricious notion or thought

whimsy imaginative, playful, and fantastic creation; whim or caprice

wishful thinking unrealistic dream; ascribing reality to one's hopes and wishes

---

JUDGMENT AND CRITICISM

Judgments and Critiques
Approval, Respect, and Recognition
Support, Encouragement, and Agreement
Praise, Exaltation, Flattery, and Applause
Disapproval, Disrespect, and Denial
Opposition, Disagreement, and Attack
Blame, Censure, Ridicule, and Contempt

See also: *Chap. 11: Law; Chap. 19: Verbs of Speech; Chap. 20: Insults, Slurs, and Epithets; Terms of Endearment and Respect; Chap. 23: Verbs of Thought*

Judgments and Critiques

adjudge (*vb*) deem; decide, rule upon, sentence

analysis critical evaluation of whole or parts

appraise (*vb*) estimate value, worth, or significance

arbitration act of hearing and determining the outcome of a controversy by a mediator

argue (*vb*) give reasons pro and con

assess (*vb*) form opinion of, appraise

attitude mental position, feeling toward something

auto-da-fé pronouncement of judgment

candor forthrightness; lack of prejudice

censor supervisor of morals and conduct; official who passes judgment on material

chord individual feeling or reaction

commentary explanation and evaluation, usu. written

conclusion reasoned determination or inference

consensus general or unanimous agreement; majority of opinion

contention point put forth in argument or debate

criticism act of passing judgment as to the merits of anything; faultfinding; analysis and evaluation of a literary or artistic work or performance; critique

criticize (*vb*) consider and assess merits of, find fault with

critique critical evaluation; usu. written; review

decide (*vb*) reach choice or pass judgment

decision resolution reached after consideration; conclusion, judgment

deem (*vb*) judge; hold an opinion of

designate (*vb*) indicate or choose for specific purpose

discretion personal choice or judgment; ability to form free and responsible decisions

discriminate (*vb*) distinguish between, exercise selective judgment

disposed (*adj*) inclined, tending toward or against

distinguish (*vb*) discern a difference; separate from others

editorial expression of opinion on some subject, esp. in newspaper

estimation opinion, judgment

evaluate (*vb*) assess, form opinion on

forejudge (*vb*) prejudge

frame of reference point of view, basis for judgment

free will exercise of free or voluntary choice or decision

gauge (*vb*) estimate, judge

guess (*vb*) estimate; reach opinion with little evidence

hairsplitting making overly fine distinctions; quibbling

inclination disposition, esp. favorable; slant

intercede (*vb*) intervene to reconcile conflict

judge (*vb*) form an opinion through careful deliberation

judgment pronouncement of one's opinion; process or capacity for forming opinions

judicious (*adj*) having or exercising sound judgment

misjudge (*vb*) form an unjust or mistaken opinion

misread (*vb*) misinterpret, judge incorrectly

notice critical review

opine (*vb*) form, hold, or express opinion

opinion point of view, appraisal of particular matter

option power or freedom to choose or make independent judgment

outlook point of view, opinion

overlook (*vb*) inspect and examine so as to reach judgment on

partiality bias, predisposition

parti pris *French.* preconceived prejudice or bias

partisan adherent to cause, supporter of point of view

pass (*vb*) render favorable judgment or verdict

pass judgment express firm, irrevocable opinion

peremptory (*adj*) allowing no contradiction, precluding all debate

point of view opinion; position from or manner in which something is considered or appraised; viewpoint

position firm point of view or opinion on something

preconception opinion formed without knowledge or experience

predisposed (*adj*) inclined in advance, pro or con

prejudge (*vb*) form opinion in advance; forejudge

prepossession prejudice or opinion formed beforehand, esp. favorable one

rank (*vb*) determine relative value or position of

rate (*vb*) set value of; assign rank to

reconsider (*vb*) assess previous judgment and form new opinion

referee (*vb*) arbitrate as judge; (n) one who so arbitrates

regard (*vb*) consider and appraise from one point of view

reservation exception; act of withholding

reserve judgment defer opinion until later time

review (*vb*) provide critical analysis, esp. written or broadcast

second thoughts reservations about previous position or judgment

sentence formal judgment arrived at by deliberation, esp. in court of law and specifying punishment

sentiment judgment based on feeling; opinion

settle (*vb*) decide, resolve conclusively

slant personal opinion, point of view

snap (*adj*) designating judgment reached hastily and without deliberation

sound judgment reasonable opinions free of error

speculate (*vb*) form or express opinion without knowledge of subject

suppose (*vb*) hold as one's opinion; think likely to be true

surmise (*vb*) infer on scant grounds; conjecture

tendency leaning in one direction

think better of reconsider

turn the tables reverse relative positions of opposing parties

two cents worth opinion offered on topic being discussed

umpire (*vb*) wield authority to resolve disputes; (*n*) one who has such authority

unbiased (*adj*) fair, free from prejudice

undercurrent concealed viewpoint or feeling, esp. opposite of that expressed

vacillate (*vb*) hesitate or waver in opinions

value judgment opinion as to worth of something

vantage point point of view, position

verdict opinion based on evidence

vet (*vb*) appraise, verify, or check

view opinion or judgment on something

viewpoint position from which or basis on which judgment is made; point of view

vote (*vb*) state one's opinion, esp. express formal opinion in political process

will disposition, inclination

winnow (*vb*) separate useful from useless elements

Approval, Respect, and Recognition

accept (*vb*) approve of, admit to; recognize as true

acknowledge (*vb*) recognize as rightful or genuine; state agreement with

admire (*vb*) regard with approval and respect

appreciate (*vb*) recognize value of; hold in high esteem

approbation approval, esp. formal approval

approval ratification; favorable opinion

approve (*vb*) express favorable opinion; give formal consent

begrudge (*vb*) view with reluctant approval

bow (*vb*) incline head or body in respect

carte blanche full discretionary power; unconditional authority

choose (*vb*) select freely; have preference for

cite (*vb*) give credit to

coddle (*vb*) treat with extreme care

command respect deserve and receive respect as one's due

commemorate (*vb*) honor memory by ceremony or observance

compassion sympathetic awareness and concern for others' distress

condone (*vb*) pardon, excuse

consideration esteem, regard; opinion based on matters taken into account

coopt (*vb*) assimilate as one's own

cotton to (*vb*) *Informal.* take a liking to

countenance (*vb*) extend approval, sanction

credence mental acceptance as true

credibility capacity for belief; ability to instill or evoke belief

credit (*vb*) consider favorably as source of action or possessor of trait

cup of tea something one likes or is well-suited to

curtsy slight dip of body and bending of knees as show of respect by women

deference respect for another's wishes

deserving (*adj*) deemed worthy

dignify (*vb*) give distinction to, show respect for

elect (*vb*) choose or select, esp. by formal vote

esteem high regard

estimation esteem, honor

exemplary (*adj*) commendable, deserving imitation

fancy (*vb*) take a liking to, often capriciously

favor (*vb*) support, view positively, prefer; (*n*) partiality, warm regard

favorable (*adj*) expressing approval or partiality

favoritism partiality, showing of special favor

genuflect (*vb*) touch knee to floor as show of respect or reverence

grant (*vb*) accord another his or her due

gratuity something given freely as show of recognition for service or favor

high opinion esteem, respect or regard for

honor (*vb*) hold in high regard, show recognition of

idealize (*vb*) hold in excessively high regard, esp. as model for imitation

imprimatur formal approval, sanction

inclination liking, disposition toward

indulge (*vb*) take pleasure in; treat with excessive consideration

kowtow (*vb*) show servile deference; touch forehead to ground as sign of deep respect

laurels honors

like (*vb*) approve, feel inclined toward, prefer

love (*vb*) feel strong or active affection, admiration, and respect for; enjoy greatly

obeisance gesture of respect

oblige (*vb*) perform a favor; put another in one's debt by doing favors

opt (*vb*) decide in favor of

pardon (*vb*) forgive; excuse; tolerate another's fault

partiality favorable bias or predisposition

pass muster obtain approval or acceptance

pay respects express esteem and regard for

pet one favored with great kindness or consideration

pick (*vb*) select one out of many

pick over (*vb*) select the best and discard the unwanted

play up (*vb*) exaggerate merits of

popular (*adj*) widely approved of or preferred

pourboire *French.* gratuity

predilection favorable opinion or bias

prefer (*vb*) like better, promote over others

preference special choice; favorable view

presume (*vb*) assume to be true without proof

prize (*vb*) value highly, hold in esteem

proclivity inclination, predisposition toward

propensity strong inclination or tendency

prostrate (*vb*) lie facedown on ground as show of submission and respect

ratify (*vb*) formally approve, usu. by vote

recognition acknowledgment; special attention

red carpet show of exceptional courtesy

regard esteem, respect

relish (*vb*) appreciate, be pleased by

reputation one's place in public esteem, overall character as judged by others

repute condition of being known, esp. in positive light

respect (*vb*) consider worthy of high regard and esteem

reward something given in return for service or merit

rubber-stamp (*vb*) approve routinely or automatically

salaam ceremonial salutation and show of respect made by bowing with right palm on forehead

salute (*vb*) express respect and admiration; make any of various gestures of respect; (*n*) gesture of respect, esp. with right palm at forehead

sanction authoritative approval or permission

satisfaction state of contentment or gratification; confident acceptance of something as good or true

save face maintain dignity, prestige, or reputation

say-so authoritative approval

seal of approval official indication or mark of approval

select (*vb*) choose, express preference, discriminate

self-pride sense of satisfaction at one's own character and achievements

self-regard consideration for oneself

self-respect proper regard for oneself and one's dignity and value as a person

smile on (*vb*) look favorably on

submit (*vb*) yield, abide by another's judgment or authority

superiority quality or state of having higher status or worth

take kindly to develop a partiality toward

take to respond favorably to

testimonial expression of appreciation; recommendation

think better of improve one's opinion of

thumbs-up *Informal.* act or gesture of approval or assent

tribute show of respect, gratitude, or affection

untouchable (*adj*) above criticism

valuation assessment of worth

value (*vb*) place high relative worth on

vote of confidence expression of support or approval

vouchsafe (*vb*) grant as privilege or special favor, esp. in condescending manner

warm (*vb*) grow to like, view favorably

well-disposed (*adj*) favorably inclined

wow (*vb*) elicit enthusiastic approval or delight from

Support, Encouragement, and Agreement

adopt (*vb*) accept formally
advocate (*vb*) plead a cause; (*n*) one who pleads a cause
aegis support, esp. formal guidance and protection
affirm (*vb*) declare as valid or confirmed
agree (*vb*) settle by mutual consent; concur
appoint (*vb*) select officially
assent (*vb*) agree
assist (*vb*) help, support
aver (*vb*) assert; verify
avouch (*vb*) guarantee as factual or provable; affirm
beau geste *French.* fine but often empty gesture
beneficent (*adj*) resulting in good; kindly or charitable
beneficial (*adj*) conducive to well-being, producing an advantage
benefit (*vb*) produce well-being or an advantage
bonhomie geniality
boon timely benefit, blessing
boost (*vb*) assist, promote
booster enthusiastic supporter
buck up (*vb*) raise morale of; become more cheerful
buoy (*vb*) support or sustain; raise spirits of
champion (*vb*) actively support or defend
choice act of selecting; best part; one selected
cold comfort limited sympathy or encouragement
comfort consolation in time of affliction; feeling of encouragement
commiserate (*vb*) express sympathy or condolences
concur (*vb*) agree
condolence expression of sympathy
confirm (*vb*) ratify, sanction; establish the validity of
congratulate (*vb*) salute another's success or good fortune
console (*vb*) comfort another in distress or sorrow
corroborate (*vb*) support with evidence; confirm
embrace (*vb*) accept readily, gladly
encourage (*vb*) inspire with courage or confidence; give assistance to
encouragement support, inspiration, aid
endorse (*vb*) express definite, public approval
espouse (*vb*) embrace or adopt a cause
exculpate (*vb*) clear of alleged fault
exhort (*vb*) urge strongly
exonerate (*vb*) relieve of obligation or duty; free from blame
find for (*vb*) decide in favor of
hold up (*vb*) bring to notice for support
hold with (*vb*) agree, concur with
hortatory (*adj*) giving encouragement, urging on
humor (*vb*) accommodate another by indulgence
indulgence act of great consideration
ingratiate (*vb*) gain favor or acceptance by a deliberate act
mollify (*vb*) appease, soften in temper or feeling

name (*vb*) decide on, choose
nod indication of one's support or assent
nominate (*vb*) designate, propose for honor or office
nurture (*vb*) further the development of through kind support
OK informal expression of support or approval; (*adj*) all right; (*vb*) express or give one's support or approval to
okay OK
okey-doke (*adj*) OK
on behalf of on the side of, in support of
palliate (*vb*) excuse; mitigate gravity of
partisan adherent to a cause; supporter of point of view
pass (*vb*) approve formally, as by a legislative body
pep talk brief, emotional talk calculated to arouse support or foster determination
persuade (*vb*) prevail on by argument or entreaty
placate (*vb*) appease, calm by concessions
please (*vb*) give pleasure or satisfaction to
prelation promotion to higher status, grade, or rank
preselect (*vb*) choose in advance
pro (*adv*) favoring or supporting; (*n*) argument in affirmation; proponent of an issue
promo *Informal.* something devised to advertise or promote
promote (*vb*) encourage or advance a person or thing through one's support
prop up (*vb*) support or sustain
proponent supporter, advocate
proselytize (*vb*) attempt to convert others to one's opinion
protestation solemn declaration or affirmation
pump up (*vb*) fill with enthusiasm and excitement
recommend (*vb*) support or represent as worthy
reinforce (*vb*) strengthen by support or assistance
relent (*vb*) become less severe, give in
second (*vb*) give support or encouragement; endorse a motion
see eye to eye agree in all ways
side with agree with, support
single out (*vb*) select, distinguish from group
soothe (*vb*) appease by attention or concern
suit (*vb*) be agreeable, satisfactory, or appropriate to
support (*vb*) uphold, advocate; aid, help; corroborate
swallow (*vb*) accept without opposition
unanimous (*adj*) having the agreement and consent of all
uphold (*vb*) support
validate (*vb*) give official approval or confirmation of; support, corroborate
vindicate (*vb*) relieve of blame; justify; defend, support
vouch for (*vb*) attest, guarantee; supply supporting evidence for

whitewash (*vb*) cover up the faults of, protect from blame
win over (*vb*) convince of one's opinion
witness (*vb*) affirm, support
yea (*interj*) expression of affirmative response or vote
yea-say (*vb*) agree, affirm something
yes-man one who always agrees with a superior

Praise, Exaltation, Flattery, and Applause

acclaim shouted approval or praise
acclamation approval loudly expressed, esp. by applause, cheers, or shouts
accolade expression of praise; award or honor
adore (*vb*) esteem, worship, or honor
adulate (*vb*) flatter or admire excessively or servilely
aggrandize (*vb*) make great or greater in power, wealth, or honor
apotheosize (*vb*) elevate to divine status, deify
applause display of public approval, esp. hand clapping
awe fearful reverence, admiration, or submission
belaud (*vb*) praise excessively
bepraise (*vb*) praise
blandish (*vb*) cajole with gentle flattery
blarney clever, often coaxing flattery; cajolery
bless (*vb*) speak kindly of; wish well; extol
boast (*vb*) brag, praise oneself
bow and scrape submit oneself before a superior
brag (*vb*) boast, indulge in self-glorifying talk
bravo (*interj*) shout of praise
butter up (*vb*) *Informal.* charm with flattery or praise to gain favor
cajole (*vb*) persuade with clever flattery
canonize (*vb*) sanction by authority, esp. ecclesiastical
celebrate (*vb*) honor; present for widespread public notice and praise
cheer (*vb*) comfort, restore hope to; encourage or salute with shouts; (*n*) shout of encouragement or praise
commend (*vb*) praise; present as worthy of confidence
compliment (*vb*) express respect, affection, or admiration for; flatter; praise
court (*vb*) seek to attract or win over by flattery and attention
crown (*vb*) bestow favor on as a mark of honor
curry favor seek advancement through flattery and fawning attention
dote (*vb*) bestow lavish, excessive fondness
elevate (*vb*) exalt in rank or status
encomium glowing, enthusiastic praise
encore demand, as by audience, for reappearance or additional performance as expression of approval for performer
eulogize (*vb*) speak or write high praise for
eulogy formal commendation or high praise, esp. for deceased person
exalt (*vb*) glorify or elevate by praise
extol (*vb*) praise highly, glorify

fawn (*vb*) show excessive affection, esp. by servile flattery

flatter (*vb*) praise excessively or insincerely

flattery insincere or excessive praise

glorify (*vb*) extol, elevate

grace (*vb*) confer favor or honor on

hail (*vb*) acclaim, greet with approval

hallow (*vb*) respect highly, venerate

hand outburst or round of applause

here-here (*interj*) *Chiefly Brit.* expression of support or encouragement

hip-hip hooray (*interj*) signal for applause or intensifier of cheers

homage reverential regard, respect, or tribute

hooray (*interj*) expression of appreciation or encouragement; hurrah

hosanna (*interj*) shout of praise or acclamation

hurrah (*interj*) hooray

huzzah (*interj*) hurrah

hype extravagant promotion; excessive praise

idolatry excessive or blind devotion or reverence

idolize (*vb*) admire to excess; worship

immortalize (*vb*) confer undying fame on

inflate (*vb*) expand or puff up, esp. unjustifiably

kudos honor, praise

laud (*vb*) praise, acclaim

lionize (*vb*) treat as person of importance

make much of treat with great affection or special consideration

merit (*vb*) possess praiseworthy qualities and virtues

olé (*interj*) shout of approval; bravo

ovation prolonged, enthusiastic applause

paean song of praise or tribute

panegyric formal, elaborate written or oral praise

pay a compliment express favorable opinion, praise

plaudits enthusiastic expression of approval; round of applause

plug (*vb*) *Informal.* promote insistently; praise highly

praise (*vb*) express approval; commend

praiseworthy (*adj*) deserving of praise

put on a pedestal elevate, exalt

rave extravagantly enthusiastic appraisal or review

resound (*vb*) be celebrated

revere (*vb*) regard with high esteem or awe

root for (*vb*) wish success; applaud noisily

salvo round of cheers or applause

self-congratulation uncritical satisfaction with one's own accomplishments

self-flattery exaggeration of one's strengths along with denial of one's weaknesses

self-glorification boastful exaggeration of one's strengths

set up (*vb*) extol as model

stroke (*vb*) *Informal.* flatter, promote feelings of self-approval in

sweet-talk (*vb*) *Informal.* coax or persuade by flattery and cajolery

talk up (*vb*) praise, extol

tout (*vb*) flatter loudly or extravagantly

venerate (*vb*) regard with reverence and deference

viva (*interj*) *Spanish, Italian.* exclamation of approval

worship (*vb*) regard with high honor and reverence

Disapproval, Disrespect, and Denial

adverse (*adj*) unfavorable; opposed to one's interest

animosity feeling of strong dislike or enmity, esp. when displayed in action

animus strong dislike, often prejudiced and hostile; animosity

antipathy aversion, dislike

askance (*adv*) with disapproval, suspicion, or mistrust

aversion repugnance coupled with a strong desire to avoid; dislike

avoid (*vb*) shun or keep away from as indication of distaste

bias prejudice

brush-off *Informal.* curt, rude dismissal

censorious (*adj*) given to censure

chasten (*vb*) discipline by inflicting suffering on so as to improve or purify

cold shoulder intentionally unsympathetic and disrespectful treatment

confound (*vb*) refute or contradict

contradict (*vb*) assert the contrary, imply the opposite; deny directly

correct (*vb*) point out another's errors; punish with a view to improving

correction rectification of errors

critical (*adj*) inclined to find fault

criticism unfavorable observations or comments

cross out (*vb*) eliminate from consideration; x out

debase (*vb*) lower another in status or esteem

decry (*vb*) express strong disapproval of

deflate (*vb*) reduce in size or importance

denial refusal to recognize or acknowledge something; disavowal or disowning of

deny (*vb*) refuse to recognize or acknowledge; disavow, disown

deprecate (*vb*) express earnest disapproval of; belittle

detest (*vb*) dislike intensely, loathe

detract from (*vb*) take away a part from

dim view skeptical or unfavorable attitude

disapproval unfavorable judgment or condemnation

disapprove (*vb*) express unfavorable judgment on

disavow (*vb*) deny knowledge of

discard (*vb*) reject as useless

disclaim (*vb*) deny interest in or connection with; disavow

discommend (*vb*) cause to be viewed unfavorably; disapprove of

discontent dissatisfaction with

discount (*vb*) view with doubt; underestimate importance of

discountenance (*vb*) treat or view with disfavor

discredit (*vb*) deprive of good repute; destroy confidence in accuracy of

discriminate (*vb*) treat unfavorably without justification

disenchantment state of freedom from illusion, esp. from overoptimism

disesteem disfavor, low regard

disfavor disapproval, dislike

disgruntled (*adj*) discontented; having ill humor

dishonor (*vb*) bring shame on, deprive of honor or prestige; treat in degrading manner

disillusionment condition of being free of illusions

dislike (*vb*) regard with displeasure

dismiss (*vb*) put aside from serious consideration, make light of

disown (*vb*) repudiate, refuse to acknowledge

displease (*vb*) incur disapproval or dislike

disqualify (*vb*) deprive of right or privilege; render unfit

disregard (*vb*) treat as worthless by ignoring

disrepute state of being held in low regard

disrespect lack of consideration; low regard

dissatisfaction condition of displeasure or discontent

distaste dislike, aversion

downgrade (*vb*) minimize or depreciate in quality or importance

embarrass (*vb*) place in state of confusion or self-conscious discomfort

enmity feeling of ill will or extreme dislike and animosity

eschew (*vb*) abstain from or avoid on moral or practical grounds

fair game deserving of or susceptible to criticism

frown on (*vb*) express disapproval of or displeasure toward

harp on (*vb*) dwell on persistently, esp. by voicing criticisms

hate (*vb*) dislike intensely

hiss sibilant sound made as expression of disapproval

hoot cry or shout of derision or objection

hypercritical (*adj*) excessively critical, censorious

ignore (*vb*) refuse to notice; deem unworthy of consideration

inconsequential (*adj*) unimportant, insignificant

inexcusable (*adj*) incapable of being justified

inferiority sense or state of having low status or worth

in the dog house *Slang.* in a state of disfavor

judgmental (*adj*) tending to pass moral judgment and view others as inferior to oneself; quick to judge

knock (*vb*) *Informal.* find fault with, esp. with trivial criticisms

libel unjustly damaging or unfavorable opinion expressed in written or printed form; anything defamatory

lose face be deprived of one's dignity, prestige, or reputation

low opinion lack of regard or respect for

make light of (*vb*) treat as object of little importance

muckrake (*vb*) search for and expose misconduct, esp. of officials

nay (*interj*) expression of negative reply or vote; denial or dissent

naysay (*vb*) deny; reject; express negative opinion

neglect (*vb*) disregard, ignore

one-upmanchip art or practice of maintaining an advantageous position over others

ostracize (*vb*) exclude from group by common consent

pass up (*vb*) neglect to take advantage of; decline, reject

pejorative (*adj*) tending to disparage or devalue

pet peeve frequent subject of complaint

pharisaism hypocritical and judgmental self-righteousness

pick apart (*vb*) find fault with all aspects of

pick at (*vb*) criticize repeatedly, esp. for minor faults

pick on (*vb*) single out for undeserved criticism and harassment

play down (*vb*) understate merits or significance of

pooh-pooh (*vb*) express disdain for; dismiss lightly

potshot random or aimless critical remark

prejudice preconceived judgment or opinion, esp. unfavorable

question (*vb*) express doubt about

reduce (*vb*) downgrade, demote

reject (*vb*) refuse to accept or consider; rebuff; turn down

reprehend (*vb*) voice disapproval or censure

reproach (*vb*) express disappointment or displeasure

reproof expression of censure or criticism

reprove (*vb*) scold or correct gently; express disapproval of

repudiate (*vb*) disown, refuse to accept, reject with denial or condemnation

riot act firm reprimand or warning

segregate (*vb*) distinguish and separate from others

serve one right treat as one deserves, esp. criticize or punish justly

shun (*vb*) deliberately avoid or look down on

skepticism attitude of doubt

slight (*vb*) treat with disdain or indifference

slough over (*vb*) treat as slight or unimportant

snobbishness air of superiority coupled with rebuffing of those deemed inferior to oneself

snooty (*adj*) showing disdain and snobbishness

snub (*vb*) slight, disregard, or insult

spank (*vb*) strike on buttocks with open hand as expression of disapproval

stereotype oversimplified characterization; unjustified generalization

stigma mark of shame or discredit; stain or reproach

stigmatize (*vb*) bring disgrace or infamy on

stricture adverse criticism

stuck-up (*adj*) *Informal.* self-important, snobbish

stultify (*vb*) cause to appear stupid, foolish, or irresponsible

supercilious (*adj*) patronizing and haughtily disdainful of others

take to task criticize for shortcomings

talk down (*vb*) deprecate, criticize

target (*vb*) set as object, esp. for criticism

tease (*vb*) disturb or provoke by persistent irritating remarks and distractions

thumbs-down gesture of disapproval

toy (*vb*) act with indifference; trifle

turn down (*vb*) reject, show disfavor toward

uncomplimentary (*adj*) unfavorable, derogatory

underrated (*adj*) valued at less than true worth

undervalue (*vb*) depreciate, treat as though of little worth

undeserving (*adj*) not worthy of consideration, respect, or assistance

unfavorable (*adj*) adverse, contrary; not propitious

unflattering (*adj*) unfavorable, derogatory

unpopular (*adj*) disapproved of or disliked in general or by a particular group

unpromising (*adj*) appearing unlikely to succeed

unsatisfactory (*adj*) inadequate; worthy of disapproval or rebuke

unsung (*adj*) insufficiently praised

unworthy (*adj*) lacking in value, undeserving

veto (*vb*) refuse to approve, reject or prohibit emphatically

vitiate (*vb*) debase or corrupt; make ineffective or weak

write off (*vb*) depreciate; regard as lost or worthless

wrong (*vb*) treat unfairly or disrespectfully

x out (*vb*) cross out

Opposition, Disagreement, and Attack

abjure (*vb*) repudiate or renounce firmly and solemnly

admonish (*vb*) express warning or disapproval, esp. gently

adversary person or group that opposes or attacks; opponent

afflict (*vb*) assault or attack repeatedly

argue (*vb*) dispute, contend

assail (*vb*) attack violently with ridicule or abuse

assault (*vb*) attack violently

at odds (*adj*) of opposing viewpoints

attack (*vb*) direct unfriendly words or unfavorable criticism against; set upon in hostile manner

ban censure, condemnation

banish (*vb*) remove by authority or force; exile

blackball (*vb*) vote against; ostracize or exclude socially

blast (*vb*) attack vigorously with vehement words

boo (*interj*) sound exclaimed as disapproving shout

brand (*vb*) stigmatize, mark with disapproval

bring to terms compel to agree or submit

buck (*vb*) *Informal.* oppose, resist

carp (*vb*) find fault, complain unreasonably

cavil (*vb*) raise trivial objections

challenge (*vb*) dispute, call in question

chuck (*vb*) discard or set aside as unwanted

combat (*vb*) oppose

complain (*vb*) express displeasure

con (*adv*) in opposition, against

confront (*vb*) oppose or challenge directly

contest (*vb*) dispute, challenge

contumacious (*adj*) obstinately disobedient or rebellious

counter (*vb*) act in opposition

cow (*vb*) intimidate with threats

cross (*vb*) oppose, run counter to, contradict

damage (*vb*) do harm or injury to

daunt (*vb*) lessen the courage of

debunk (*vb*) expose and strip of falseness

decline (*vb*) withhold consent

demur (*vb*) object or hesitate based on one's scruples

differ (*vb*) disagree in opinion or belief; be at variance

disagree (*vb*) differ in opinion; fail to agree; dissent

discourage (*vb*) hinder by disfavoring

dispute (*vb*) argue, debate, quarrel with

dissent (*vb*) speak out against; differ in opinion, esp. with the majority (n) expression of disagreement

dissidence disagreement

dissuade (*vb*) deter through advice or persuasion

division separation by disagreement or difference of opinion

exclude (*vb*) bar from consideration or inclusion

excommunicate (*vb*) exclude from membership, esp. from church group

exile expulsion from one's native land

fight (*vb*) oppose

find against (*vb*) decide for opposite view or side

flak annoying criticism or opposition

forbid (*vb*) prohibit, rule against

gainsay (*vb*) deny, dispute; contradict, oppose

harass (*vb*) annoy, attack, or impede repeatedly

heckle (*vb*) harass with questions or gibes

hostile (*adj*) critical, antagonistic toward, opposed

hostility enmity or antagonism; opposition or resistance to an idea or project

hound (*vb*) harass or attack without respite

impeach (*vb*) accuse of misconduct in office; challenge the credibility of

impugn (*vb*) oppose or assail as false or without integrity

lash out (*vb*) make severe verbal attack, esp. reproach

niggle (*vb*) find fault constantly in petty way
nitpick (*vb*) engage in petty, unjustified criticism
object (*vb*) oppose firmly; express distaste for
obstruct (*vb*) hinder, impede by blocking
offend (*vb*) cause dislike, anger, or resentment
offense assault, attack; something that insults, displeases, or outrages
onslaught furious attack or assault
opponent person who is on the opposing side; adversary
oppose (*vb*) take contrary view; resist, combat
opposed (*adj*) contrary; set in contrast to†
oppugn (*vb*) assail by criticism; dispute
plaint lamentation, protest, complaint
polemic controversial refutation of another's opinion; person who makes such a refutation
press (*vb*) assail, harass, afflict
protest complaint, objection, expression of dissent
quibble (*vb*) equivocate, hedge; cavil, carp
rebut (*vb*) contradict or oppose by argument
recriminate (*vb*) retort bitterly, make retaliatory accusation
redbait (*vb*) attack as communistic
renounce (*vb*) withdraw or abandon one's previous support; repudiate
reprobation condemnation or rejection as unworthy or evil
repudiate (*vb*) reject as untrue
resist (*vb*) exert force against
resistance opposition by one to another
run counter to oppose, be contrary to
squelch (*vb*) put down with crushing force
stymie (*vb*) hinder or block
taboo (*adj*) forbidden; banned as evil; (n) prohibition
take issue with oppose, form contrary opinion
take on (*vb*) contend against
take sides state opinion in opposition to another
tear into (*vb*) attack without restraint
tee off (*vb*) *Slang.* make angry denunciation
torment (*vb*) afflict, cause severe distress
variance disagreement, dispute, or quarrel
verboten (*adj*) forbidden; prohibited by law
withstand (*vb*) resist or oppose with determination, esp. successfully
write down (*vb*) depreciate or disparage in writing
wrong (*adj*) incorrect, judged to be false

Blame, Censure, Ridicule, and Contempt

abuse (*vb*) attack verbally, revile; maltreat
accursed (*adj*) under a curse, damned
accuse (*vb*) find fault with, blame
affront (*vb*) insult
allegation assertion, esp. of culpability, made with little or no proof
anathema something detested; ban or curse, esp. by ecclesiastical authority
animadversion unfavorable or censorious comment or criticism

arrogance feeling of superiority over others, esp. offensive display of superiority
aspersion derogatory remark or malicious charge
backbite (*vb*) slander, speak ill of
backstab (*vb*) attempt to discredit by underhanded means
bad-mouth (*vb*) *Slang.* criticize severely; speak disloyally of
barb pointed or biting and openly unpleasant remark
baste (*vb*) scold soundly; denounce vigorously
bawl out (*vb*) *Informal.* reprimand severely
belittle (*vb*) portray as little or less than might seem; mock; disparage
beneath contempt at the lowest possible level of respect; utterly degraded
berate (*vb*) condemn vehemently at length
besmirch (*vb*) tarnish or detract from another's honor
blacken (*vb*) defame, sully, ruin the reputation of
blame (*vb*) find fault with; hold responsible
blasphemy insult to, contempt for, or irreverence toward something sacred
blot mark of reproach, stain of infamy
booby prize prize given in good-natured acknowledgment of poor performance or achievement
brickbat uncomplimentary or unkind comment
bring to account reprimand
Bronx cheer raspberry
burlesque (*vb*) imitate derisively or mock, esp. by caricature
butt victim of abuse or ridicule
calumniate (*vb*) malign with false statements or misrepresentations
calumny false and malicious statements damaging to another's reputation
caricature distortion or exaggeration to make someone or something appear ludicrous
castigate (*vb*) punish or criticize severely; chastise
censure (*vb*) find fault with in a harsh or vehement manner; (n) vehement expression of condemnation
chaff (*vb*) ridicule in a good-natured, teasing manner
charge (*vb*) accuse of wrongdoing; blame
chastise (*vb*) criticize severely
chew out (*vb*) *Slang.* reprimand, scold harshly
chide (*vb*) voice disapproval; reproach, rebuke
comeuppance *Informal.* deserved rebuke or penalty
commination denunciation
condemn (*vb*) express strong disapproval or adverse judgment; pronounce guilty; declare to be wrong
contemn (*vb*) scorn, treat with contempt
contempt disdain, lack of respect; disgrace
contumely insulting or humiliating behavior based on contempt
correction punishment, rebuke
criticize (*vb*) find fault with; censure

crucify (*vb*) persecute or treat cruelly with gross injustice
culpable (*adj*) deserving condemnation or blame
curse (*vb*) invoke evil or harm upon; revile profanely
cuss (*vb*) *Informal.* curse
damn (*vb*) condemn harshly as a failure
debase (*vb*) reduce in status or value
defamation calumny, disgrace, or harm done to another's reputation
defame (*vb*) use malicious statements to disgrace or harm another's reputation
degrade (*vb*) bring into contempt or low esteem
demean (*vb*) degrade; lower in status or dignity
denigrate (*vb*) defame, cast aspersions on
denounce (*vb*) condemn publicly as evil or blameworthy
depreciate (*vb*) disparage, represent as of little value
derision bitter, contemptuous ridicule
derogate (*vb*) express low opinion of
desecrate (*vb*) treat irreverently or contemptuously; profane that which is sacred
despise (*vb*) look down upon with contempt; regard as worthless
detest (*vb*) dislike intensely
diatribe bitter, abusive, sarcastic criticism
disdain (*vb*) view scornfully, treat with contempt
disgrace (*vb*) humiliate; cause to lose favor; bring shame upon
disgust marked aversion, total repugnance
disparage (*vb*) degrade, speak slightingly of
dress down (*vb*) censure severely
dump on (*vb*) *Informal.* belittle; bad-mouth
effigy crude figure representing and ridiculing a hated person
epithet descriptive word or phrase, esp. one that is disparaging or abusive
excoriate (*vb*) censure severely; scathe
execrate (*vb*) detest utterly; denounce as evil
fault (*vb*) criticize, blame
find fault criticize
flay (*vb*) criticize harshly
fleer (*vb*) sneer or laugh at derisively; mock
flout (*vb*) scorn, treat with contemptuous disregard
fulminate (*vb*) utter denunciations and invective
fustigate (*vb*) criticize harshly
gibe (*vb*) deride, taunt; (n) mocking, sarcastic remark
gloat (*vb*) view with triumphant and often malicious satisfaction, esp. another's misfortune
goat one who takes blame for something, often undeservedly; victim
going-over severe scolding
grill (*vb*) question intensely; torment
harangue passionate, critical, or scalding speech; tirade or vehement attack
hatchet job forceful, malicious critique
high horse contemptuous, superior attitude or manner
humble (*vb*) destroy another's prestige, spirit, dignity, or power

humble pie embarrassing humiliation and submission under pressure

humiliate (*vb*) cause another a painful loss of dignity or self-respect

implicate (*vb*) show incriminating connection; blame

imprecate (*vb*) curse, invoke evil upon

impute (*vb*) lay blame on; discredit

incriminate (*vb*) charge with or show evidence of involvement in wrongdoing

indict (*vb*) formally charge with wrongdoing; criticize, accuse

infamy bad public reputation or reproach received for evil ways

insolence insulting and contemptuous behavior or attitude

insult (*vb*) treat or speak of with contempt or indignity; affront

irreverence lack of proper or accustomed respect

irrision derision

jape (*vb*) make mocking fun of

jeer (*vb*) taunt, mock, or speak of with derision

lambaste (*vb*) *Informal.* berate harshly; censure

lampoon (*vb*) ridicule harshly with satire

laugh at (*vb*) express scorn or derision for by laughter; make fun of

laughingstock object of ridicule

loathe (*vb*) feel intense contempt and aversion for; abhor

make fun of ridicule, mock; make sport of

make sport of make fun of

malediction curse

malign (*vb*) speak evil of; utter injurious, often false, statement; defame, slander

mock (*vb*) treat with contempt or ridicule

Momus god of censure and mockery (ancient Greece); carping critic

moralize (*vb*) express opinion on right and wrong conduct; chastise others for misconduct

mortify (*vb*) subject to severe embarrassment and shame

mud *Informal.* abusive, malicious remarks

mudslinging using offensive epithets and false attacks to discredit one's opponent

name-calling using offensive terms to humiliate and induce condemnation of another

needle (*vb*) *Informal.* tease, torment, or goad repeatedly

objurgate (*vb*) denounce or berate harshly; castigate

obloquy abusive, condemnatory language, esp. by numerous persons

odium intense loathing and contempt

onus disagreeable burden or blame

opprobrium disgrace or reproach due to shameful conduct; cause or object of infamy

pan (*vb*) *Informal.* criticize severely, esp. in review of a performance

Philippic speech full of bitter condemnation

piece of one's mind *Informal.* severe scolding or rebuke

pillory (*vb*) expose to public ridicule

pink (*vb*) wound by piercing criticism or ridicule

poison-pen (*adj*) written with malice, usu. anonymously

poke fun at ridicule

pollute (*vb*) debase, defile, make impure

pox curse, evil; expression of distaste or aversion

profane (*vb*) desecrate or defile with abuse or irreverence

put down (*vb*) *Informal.* disparage, belittle; criticize, esp. contemptuously

put to shame expose faults of, censure, or humiliate

rag (*vb*) *Informal.* scold; subject to prolonged torment; tease

rail (*vb*) revile; denounce vehemently and bitterly

rap (*vb*) *Slang.* rebuke, criticize sharply

raspberry *Informal.* expression of disapproval, esp. contemptuous sound made through compressed lips; Bronx cheer

razz (*vb*) *Slang.* heckle, deride, tease

rebuff (*vb*) snub or reject peremptorily

rebuke (*vb*) reprimand; express strong disapproval to

reprimand (*vb*) reprove or censure sharply, esp. from position of authority

revile (*vb*) subject to verbal abuse

revulsion strong sense of distaste and repugnance

ridicule (*vb*) make fun of, mock, deride

roast (*vb*) *Informal.* criticize mercilessly, often in public

roorback defamatory falsehood published for political effect

rub it in *Informal.* emphasize something unpleasant to tease or annoy

sacrilege gross irreverence toward sacred person or thing

sarcasm sharply ironical utterance or cutting remark

satirize (*vb*) censure or ridicule by ironic description of human vices and follies

scald (*vb*) subject to heated criticism or censure

scapegoat one who bears blame for others

scathe (*vb*) assail with severe denunciation

scoff (*vb*) mock; express scorn or derision

scold (*vb*) censure severely or find fault with, esp. from position of authority

scorch (*vb*) censure, attack harshly

score (*vb*) berate, censure, denounce

scorn (*vb*) reject or dismiss disdainfully as unworthy; deride

self-criticism harsh assessment of oneself

self-flagellation extreme criticism of oneself

self-incrimination act of incriminating oneself, esp. by giving evidence

shame (*vb*) cause to feel guilt or humiliation

shoot down (*vb*) *Informal.* deflate, ridicule, discredit

show up (*vb*) embarrass, discredit, expose faults of

silent treatment aloof expression of disapproval made by completely ignoring another

slam (*vb*) *Informal.* criticize harshly

slander (*vb*) damage another's reputation by uttering falsehoods

slap down (*vb*) assault verbally, insult

slash (*vb*) criticize viciously

slur (*vb*) insult, disparage

smear (*vb*) maliciously attack another's reputation; vilify

smirch (*vb*) discredit, disgrace

sneer at (*vb*) laugh at scornfully; jeer and mock

soil (*vb*) damage or disgrace another's reputation

spurn (*vb*) scorn, reject disdainfully

stain (*vb*) bring dishonor or blame on; blemish

sully (*vb*) defile, tarnish

supercilious (*adj*) patronizing; haughtily disdainful

swipe *Informal.* sharp, critical remark

taint (*vb*) contaminate morally, corrupt; tarnish

talking-to reprimand, scolding

tarnish (*vb*) bring disgrace on; sully

taunt (*vb*) reproach or challenge in a mocking or insulting manner

tear down (*vb*) vilify, denigrate

tell off (*vb*) *Informal.* reprimand, scold

thumb one's nose *Informal.* express contempt, esp. through rejection

thunderbolt sudden, severe attack

tick off (*vb*) *Chiefly Brit.* scold severely; rebuke

tirade prolonged outburst of verbal abuse

tongue-lashing harsh verbal criticism or scolding

traduce (*vb*) speak maliciously or falsely of, slander

trash (*vb*) *Informal.* censure, revile; utterly destroy by criticism; dismiss as worthless

travesty grotesque or debased imitation

twit (*vb*) subject to light ridicule or reproach

umbrage vague feeling of resentment over perceived insult

upbraid (*vb*) find fault with; criticize harshly, scold vehemently

vilify (*vb*) defame or slander with abusive statements

vilipend (*vb*) regard with low opinion; disparage, depreciate

vituperate (*vb*) censure severely, revile harshly

walk all over treat contemptuously and without regard

whispering campaign systematic dissemination of derogatory rumors

wig (*vb*) *Brit. informal.* scold severely, rebuke

wipe one's boots on treat contemptuously with no regard

CHAPTER TWENTY-FOUR
THE DARK SIDE

Drug Names and Forms

Abbott *Slang.* hypnotic Nembutal manufactured by Abbott Laboratories

A-bomb *Slang.* heroin and marijuana cigarette

Acapulco gold *Slang.* powerful Mexican marijuana; gold

ace *Slang.* barbiturate or amphetamine capsule or pill

acid *Slang.* LSD

addictive drug substance inducing physical or psychological dependence

Amanita muscaria hallucinogenic mushroom; death's-head; fly agaric

amphetamine central nervous system stimulant; amphetamine sulphate

amphetamine sulphate amphetamine

amyl nitrite pharmaceutical drug that dilates blood vessels, producing brief exhilaration

Amytal *Trademark.* barbiturate depressant amobarbital sodium

anabolic steroid muscle-building hormonal substance with dangerous side effects

analgesic painkilling drug

angel dust *Slang.* PCP

antidepressant pharmaceutical treatment for depression or apathy

aphrodisiac drug that increases sexual arousal

ataraxic drug tranquilizer

atropine antispasmodic drug

Aunt Emma *Slang.* morphine

bag *Slang.* small measure of a drug, esp. heroin

bale *Slang.* pound of marijuana

balloon small measure of heroin stored in toy balloon

bam *Slang.* barbiturate and amphetamine combination

bang *Slang.* drug injection or sniff of cocaine

banji *Slang.* marijuana

bar *Slang.* block of pressed marijuana

barbital addictive hypnotic sedative taken as white powder

barbiturate pharmaceutical central nervous system depressant and muscle relaxer

B-bomb *Slang.* benzedrine inhaler

belladonna psychoactive depressant derived from deadly nightshade

benny *Slang.* benzedrine

Benzedrine *Trademark.* pharmaceutical amphetamine

Bernice *Slang.* cocaine

bhang *Slang.* mild preparation of marijuana leaves, drunk with milk or water

bindle paper in which drugs are wrapped

Biphetamine *Trademark.* pharmaceutical stimulant combining two amphetamines

bird's eye *Slang.* tiny package of narcotics

black *Slang.* opium

black beauty *Slang.* Biphetamine in black capsule

blackstuff *Slang.* opium

blank *Slang.* nonnarcotic substance sold in place of real drug

blow *Slang.* cocaine

blowzeen *Slang.* cocaine

body drug physically addictive substance

bomber *Slang.* thick marijuana cigarette

boo *Slang.* marijuana

bouncing powder *Slang.* cocaine

boy *Slang.* heroin

brick *Slang.* block of pressed marijuana, usu. one kilo

brown *Slang.* Mexican heroin

bud marijuana, esp. the resinous flower of the female plant

bullet *Slang.* line or snort of cocaine

bundle *Slang.* package of small, preweighed bags of heroin

bush *Slang.* marijuana

button *Slang.* peyote or mescal top

caffeine mild stimulant in coffee and tea

California sunshine *Slang.* form of LSD

Cam red *Slang.* Cambodian marijuana

can *Slang.* ounce of marijuana

candy *Slang.* cocaine

Cannabis indica powerful hybrid of cannabis sativa; indica

Cannabis sativa hemp plant from which marijuana is derived

cantharides supposed aphrodisiac Spanish fly

cap *Informal.* capsule of any drug

cargo load of drugs

cartwheel *Slang.* amphetamine tablet

Cecil *Slang.* cocaine

cephalotropic drug drug that changes physiological functions of the brain

Chinese molasses *Slang.* opium

chloral hydrate crystalline compound used as sedative

Christmas tree *Slang.* hypnotic sedative Tuinal

clear light *Slang.* very pure, powerful LSD

coca plant with stimulant alkaloids from which cocaine is derived

cocaine addictive central nervous system stimulant derived from coca leaf; *Slang:* Bernice, blow, blowzeen, bouncing powder, candy, Cecil, coke, crack, flake, girl, lady snow, nose candy, Peruvian perfume, snow, toot, white girl

codeine painkilling depressant

coke *Slang.* cocaine

cola caffeine-containing seeds or nuts of African tree

Colombian gold *Slang.* potent marijuana grown in South America

controlled substance any behavior-altering or addictive drug whose possession and use are restricted by law

crack extremely powerful and addictive form of smokable cocaine

crank *Slang.* methamphetamine

crystal meth *Slang.* methamphetamine in crystalline form

cube *Slang.* LSD-dosed sugar cube

dagga *Slang.* marijuana from Africa

datura plant with strong hallucinogenic and intoxicant effects; jimson weed; locoweed

death's-head *Slang.* hallucinogenic mushroom *Amanita muscaria*

deck *Slang.* small, folded packet of heroin

Demerol *Trademark.* highly addictive pharmaceutical painkiller, or synthetic opiate

desoxyn pharmaceutical amphetamine

DET diethyltryptamine

Dexamyl *Trademark.* pharmaceutical amphetamine with added barbiturate sedative; purple heart

Dexedrine *Trademark.* pharmaceutical amphetamine; dexie

dexie *Slang.* Dexedrine

diet pill drug taken to reduce appetite, esp. amphetamine

diethyltryptamine DET; synthetic derivative of tryptamine hallucinogenic effects

Dilaudid *Trademark.* morphine-derived painkiller

dime bag *Slang.* small container of heroin or other drug sold for $10

dimethyltryptamine DMT; intensely hallucinogenic synthetic drug

DMT dimethyltryptamine

doll *Slang.* amphetamine or barbiturate

doobie *Slang.* marijuana cigarette

dope *Slang.* any drug or narcotic, esp. heroin or marijuana

dose amount of drug to be taken by one person at one time

dot *Slang.* microdot

downer *Informal.* any depressant or sedative-hypnotic drug

drug any habit-forming, behavior-altering, or damaging illicit substance, esp. narcotic

dust *Slang.* PCP

ecstasy *Slang.* mild hallucinogen

eighth *Slang.* one-eighth ounce of heroin

fireplug *Slang.* large pellet of opium

flake *Slang.* cocaine

flea powder *Slang.* extensively cut heroin

fly agaric *Amanita muscaria*

freebase *Slang.* ether-purified cocaine

gage *Slang.* marijuana

gangster *Slang.* marijuana

ganja *Slang.* marijuana

girl *Slang.* cocaine

gold *Slang.* Acapulco gold

goofball *Slang.* barbiturate

gow *Slang.* opium or heroin

grass *Slang.* marijuana

H *Slang.* heroin

hallucinogen any drug producing intense visual and sensory distortion

hard drugs physically addictive substances, esp. heroin, morphine, and cocaine

hash *Informal.* hashish

hashish concentrated form of marijuana resin; hash; resin

hash oil oil derived from hashish

hay *Slang.* marijuana

head drug *Informal.* psychologically addictive substance, esp. hallucinogen

heart *Slang.* amphetamine

hemp *Cannabis sativa* plant, source of marijuana

herb *Slang.* marijuana

heroin addictive narcotic opium derivative produced by treating morphine with acetic acid; *Slang:* boy, dope, gow, H, horse, junk, noise, poison, scag, skag, smack, tecata

homegrown (*adj*) locally grown or nonimported, as of marijuana

hooch *Slang.* marijuana

hop *Slang.* opium

horse *Slang.* heroin

hotshot *Slang.* lethal mixture of heroin and poison, or overdose of pure heroin injected to kill user

hypnotic sleep-inducing drug

ibogaine plant-derived stimulant

ice *Slang.* smokable methamphetamine with prolonged effect

indica *Cannabis indica*

jay *Slang.* marijuana cigarette

jelly bean *Slang.* stimulant pill

jimson weed datura

joint *Slang.* hand-rolled marijuana cigarette

jolt *Slang.* heroin injection

junk *Slang.* heroin

K *Slang.* kilo, esp. of marijuana

kef marijuana

key *Slang.* kilo of marijuana

killer weed *Slang.* marijuana

kilo *Slang.* pressed bundle of marijuana weighing one kilogram; one kilogram of any drug

lady snow *Slang.* cocaine

laudanum opium in solution

laughing gas nitrous oxide

leaper *Slang.* amphetamine pill

Librium *Trademark.* pharmaceutical tranquilizer

lid *Slang.* ounce of marijuana

line *Slang.* small amount of chopped cocaine, arranged in a strip for inhalation

locoweed datura

L-pill lethal potassium cyanide pill

LSD lysergic acid diethylamide; powerful, psychedelic, synthetic hallucinogen

'lude *Informal.* Quaalude

Luminal *Trademark.* barbiturate pill

lysergic acid LSD

M *Slang.* marijuana; morphine

magic mushroom *Slang.* mushroom containing the hallucinogen psilocybin

majoon *Slang.* hallucinogenic drug in candy form

mandrake narcotic herb

mannite milk sugar for cutting heroin

marahoochie *Informal.* marijuana

marijuana dried *Cannabis sativa* or *Cannabis indica* leaves and flowers, smoked or eaten as mild hallucinogen; *Slang:* banji, bhang, boo, bush,

dagga, gage, gangster, ganja, grass, hay, herb, hooch, kif, killer weed, M, marahoochie, Mary Jane, mezz, mota, muggle, pot, reefer, shit, smoke, tea, 13-m, viper's weed, weed, yerba

Mary Jane *Slang.* marijuana

matchbox *Informal.* small container of marijuana, esp. empty kitchen matchbox

Maui wowie *Slang.* extremely potent marijuana from Hawaii

MDA methyldiamphetamine, a stimulant

meperidine crystalline narcotic used as sedative and painkiller

meprobamate nonbarbiturate sedative; Miltown

mescal small succulent with hallucinogenic, buttonlike tops

mescaline hallucinogen derived from succulent mescal plant or peyote cactus

meth *Informal.* methamphetamine

methadone synthetic opiate used to replace heroin in treatment of addicts

methamphetamine amphetamine, esp. street drug in powder form; crank

methaqualone nonbarbiturate sedative-hypnotic substance used to induce sleep; Quaalude

Methedrine *Trademark.* pharmaceutical amphetamine

mezz *Slang.* marijuana

michoacán *Slang.* potent green marijuana from Mexican state of Michoacán

microdot *Slang.* tiny LSD tablet; dot

mike *Informal.* one microgram, esp. of LSD

milk sugar white lactose crystals for cutting cocaine or heroin

Miltown *Trademark.* pharmaceutical minor tranquilizer meprobamate

MMDA amphetamine with hallucinogenic properties

morning glory seeds mildly hallucinogenic plant seeds

morphine painkilling opium alkaloid narcotic; *Slang:* Aunt Emma, M, unkie, white nurse

mota *Slang.* marijuana

mother's helper *Slang.* Valium

muggle marijuana

narcotic painkilling or sleep-inducing substance, esp. opiate or pharmaceutical hypnotic, usu. addictive

Nembutal *Trademark.* pharmaceutical barbiturate

neuroleptic drug antipsychotic drug that reduces anxiety and tension; tranquilizer

nickel bag *Slang.* small container of heroin or other drug sold for $5

nicotine poisonous alkaloid present in tobacco leaves

nitrous oxide inhaled anesthetic with hallucinogenic properties; laughing gas

Nixon *Slang.* poor-quality drug passed off as high quality

noise *Slang.* heroin

nonbarbiturate sedative pharmaceutical depressant that affects the central nervous system

nose candy *Slang.* cocaine

number *Slang.* marijuana cigarette

nutmeg mildly hallucinogenic plant seed

opiate narcotic derived from or containing opium

opium narcotic derived from poppy plant; *Slang:* black, blackstuff, Chinese molasses, gow, hop, poppy

orange wedge *Slang.* LSD in tall orange tablet

Owsley *Slang.* high-quality LSD of 1960's, named for its chemist

o-z *Informal.* ounce of drugs, esp. marijuana

Panama red *Slang.* reddish marijuana from Panama

paper *Informal.* folded paper containing dose of drugs

paregoric soothing opium extract

PCP phencyclidine; addictive drug orig. used as animal tranquilizer, acting as depressant, anesthetic, stimulant, convulsant, and hallucinogen; angel dust

peace pill *Slang.* LSD or sometimes PCP

pep pill stimulant

Percodan *Trademark.* morphine-derived narcotic painkiller

Peruvian perfume *Slang.* cocaine

peyote hallucinogenic cactus, chewed or used as source of mescaline; top

pharmaceutical drug manufactured legally by company but acquired without prescription

phencyclidine PCP

pill *Slang.* pellet of opium

pinks *Slang.* barbiturates

pink wedge *Slang.* powerful LSD in tall pink tablet

pinner *Slang.* very thin marijuana cigarette

poison *Slang.* heroin

popper vial of amyl nitrite

poppy opium

pot *Slang.* marijuana

psilocin substance produced after ingesting psilocybin

psilocybin hallucinogen derived from *Psilocybe mexicana* mushroom

psychedelic intensely mind-altering substance that produces heightened awareness and hallucinations, esp. LSD, psilocybin, and mescaline

psychoactive drug depressant, stimulant, or hallucinogen that affects central nervous system

psychotropic drug substance affecting mood or behavior, without central nervous system stimulation or depression, esp. tranquilizers, antidepressants, marijuana, and hashish

pure *Slang.* unadulterated heroin

purple haze *Slang.* LSD in purple tablet

purple heart *Slang.* Dexamyl

Quaalude *Trademark.* pharmaceutical sedative methaqualone; 'lude; soaper

quack *Slang.* Quaalude

quinine substance used in cutting heroin

rainbow *Slang.* red and blue Tuinal capsule

rainy-day woman *Slang.* marijuana cigarette

red *Slang.* Seconal capsule

red chicken *Slang.* Chinese heroin

reefer *Slang.* marijuana cigarette; marijuana
resin *Slang.* hashish
roach *Slang.* small butt end of marijuana cigarette
rock *Slang.* crack cocaine
roller coaster *Slang.* combination of stimulant and tranquilizer in one pill
rope *Slang.* marijuana cigarette
San Francisco bomb *Slang.* cocaine, heroin, and LSD mixture
scag *Slang.* heroin
Seconal *Trademark.* pharmaceutical depressant-hypnotic secobarbital sodium
sedative-hypnotic drug that depresses central nervous system
shake *Slang.* loose, mildly intoxicating leaves of dried marijuana that have fallen from flowering stems
shit *Slang.* drugs; marijuana
shot hypodermic injection of a drug
sins *Slang.* sinsimilla
sinsimilla seedless, unpollinated, female marijuana with high THC content; sins
skag *Slang.* heroin
sleeping pill pill or capsule containing a barbiturate for inducing sleep
smack *Slang.* heroin
smoke *Informal.* marijuana
snop *Slang.* marijuana cigarette
snow *Slang.* cocaine
soaper *Slang.* Quaalude
soft drug nonaddictive or psychologically addictive substance
soma legendary hallucinogen made from intoxicating plant
soporific hypnotic or sleep-inducing drug
Spanish fly preparation of powdered blister beetles, used as an aphrodisiac; cantharides
speed *Slang.* any central nervous system stimulant, esp. amphetamine
speedball *Slang.* injected mixture of cocaine or amphetamine and heroin
spliff *Slang.* large marijuana cigarette, esp. of Jamaican ganja
spoon *Slang.* tiny heroin dose, usu. one-sixteenth ounce
stick *Slang.* marijuana cigarette
stimulant any drug that increases central nervous system activity; upper
STP *Slang.* legendary, powerful hallucinogen used esp. in 1960's that causes three-day trips, often with permanent bad side effects, orig. 2.5 dimethoxy-4-methylamphetamine
stuff *Slang.* drugs, esp. illicit ones
sugar cube *Slang.* form of liquid LSD dropped on cube of sugar
synthetics narcotics produced in laboratory
tab single drug dose in form of compressed powder
taste minute quantity of a drug, often offered to entice buyer
tea *Slang.* marijuana
tecata *Slang.* heroin
ten-cent pistol *Slang.* bag of poisoned heroin

tetrahydrocannabinol THC; active substance in marijuana and hashish
Thai stick *Slang.* powerful marijuana in stick form from Thailand
THC tetrahydrocannabinol
13-m *Slang.* marijuana
toot *Slang.* cocaine
topi *Slang.* peyote
toye *Slang.* small container of opium
trank *Informal.* tranquilizer
tranquilizer pharmaceutical drug that alleviates anxiety; trank
Tuinal *Trademark.* hypnotic barbiturate combining amobarbital and secobarbital
twist *Slang.* marijuana cigarette
unkie *Slang.* morphine
upper *Informal.* stimulant
Valium *Trademark.* pharmaceutical minor tranquilizer diazepam
viper's weed *Slang.* marijuana
weed *Slang.* marijuana
white girl *Slang.* cocaine
white lightning *Slang.* LSD in small, white tablet form
white nurse *Slang.* morphine
whites *Slang.* amphetamine pills
windowpane *Slang.* form of LSD
yellow *Slang.* yellow jacket
yellow jacket *Slang.* yellow capsule of Nembutal
yenshee *Slang.* opium residue
yerba *Slang.* marijuana
z *Slang.* ounce of any drug
Zacatecas purple *Slang.* purple marijuana from Zacatecas, Mexico

Drunkenness, Drunkards, and Alcoholism

AA Alcoholics Anonymous
addled (*adj*) drunk; confused by drink
alcoholic one suffering from alcoholism; beverage containing alcohol; boozer; chronic drunk; drunkard
Alcoholics Anonymous AA; organization that helps alcoholics to stop drinking by following twelve-step program
alcoholism condition of uncontrollable continual or sporadic heavy drinking of alcohol
Antabuse *Trademark.* pharmaceutical treatment for alcoholism
bender prolonged period of drunkenness
besotted (*adj*) stupefied by drink
bibber one addicted to drink
bibulous (*adj*) inclined or addicted to drink
binge drinking spree
blasted (*adj*) *Slang.* very drunk
blind drunk (*adj*) extremely inebriated
blotto (*adj*) *Slang.* very drunk
bombed (*adj*) *Slang.* drunk
boozer *Informal.* one who drinks to excess; alcoholic
brannigan drinking spree
canned (*adj*) *Slang.* drunk
cheap drunk one who becomes intoxicated on one or two drinks

chronic drunk alcoholic
cockeyed (*adj*) *Slang.* drunk
crapulence drunkenness to point of sickness
crapulous (*adj*) sick from overindulgence in liquor
crash (*vb*) *Slang.* experience aftereffects of intoxication
crispy (*adj*) *Slang.* hung over
crocked (*adj*) *Slang.* drunk
debauchery indulgence in excessive drinking or other immoral pleasures
delirium tremens dt's; violent hallucinations and seizures induced by prolonged alcohol abuse
Dionysian (*adj*) drunken and orgiastic, after Greek god Dionysus
dipsomania uncontrollable craving for alcohol
dissipation excessive consumption of alcohol
drunk (*adj*) intoxicated by alcoholic drink; temporarily impaired, excited, or stupefied by alcoholic drink; *Slang:* blasted, blotto, bombed, canned, cockeyed, crocked, fried, high, in one's cups, lit up, loaded, oiled, pickled, pie-eyed, pissed, plastered, polluted, potted, ripped, shitfaced, shnockered, skunk drunk, sloshed, smashed, sotted, sozzled, squiffed, stewed, stinko, stoned, swacked, tanked, tiddly, tight, tipsy, wasted, wiped out, woozy, wrecked, zonked
drunkard person often or habitually drunk
dt's delirium tremens
ebriosity habitual intoxication
enabler one who permits and encourages an alcoholic to drink
fantods jitters; delirium tremens
fried (*adj*) *Slang.* very drunk
fuddle (*vb*) stupefy with alcoholic drink
giddy (*adj*) somewhat inebriated
grog blossom alcoholism
hair of the dog *Informal.* drink of liquor supposed to relieve a hangover
hangover severe headache, nausea, or other unpleasant aftereffects of too much drink
high (*adj*) *Informal.* intoxicated
hit the bottle *Slang.* drink heavily
hit the sauce *Slang.* drink heavily
hooch hound *Slang.* drunkard
hung over (*adj*) feeling unpleasant aftereffects of too much drink
immoderation excessive drinking
indulgence act of drinking, esp. to excess
inebriated (*adj*) drunk
in one's cups *Slang.* drunk
intemperance excessive drinking of alcohol
intoxication loss of control, excitement, or stupefaction due to consumption of alcohol
jake leg *Slang.* paralysis from drinking strong liquor
jimjams *Slang.* delirium tremens
juicer *Slang.* drunkard
katzenjammer severe headache due to hangover
liquor up (*vb*) *Informal.* make drunk; drink to excess
lit up (*adj*) *Slang.* drunk

loaded (*adj*) *Slang*. drunk
lush one who drinks to excess; alcoholic
morning after period upon awakening when aftereffects of night of drinking are felt
muzzy (*adj*) *Informal*. muddled or confused, esp. by drink
oenophile one who loves or is a connoisseur of wine
off the wagon *Slang*. having returned to drinking after period of temperance
oiled (*adj*) *Slang*. drunk
one too many extra drink that pushes one over edge into drunkenness
pass out (*vb*) become unconscious from drunkenness
pickled (*adj*) *Slang*. drunk
pie-eyed (*adj*) *Slang*. very drunk
pissed (*adj*) *Vulgar slang*. very drunk
plastered (*adj*) *Slang*. very drunk
polluted (*adj*) *Slang*. drunk, intoxicated
potted (*adj*) *Slang*. drunk
problem drinker alcoholic, one who cannot control drinking
ripped (*adj*) *Slang*. very intoxicated, drunk
rummy *Slang*. alcoholic, esp. one intoxicated on cheap liquor
shiker *Yiddish*. drunkard
shitfaced (*adj*) *Vulgar slang*. very drunk
shnockered (*adj*) *Slang*. drunk
skunk drunk (*adj*) *Slang*. extremely inebriated
sleep it off overcome aftereffects of drink by sleep
sloshed (*adj*) *Slang*. very drunk
smashed (*adj*) *Slang*. very drunk
soak (*vb*) *Informal*. become drunk
sober up (*vb*) take action or pass time to end a state of drunkenness
sot chronic drunkard
sotted (*adj*) drunk
soused (*adj*) *Slang*. drunk
sozzled (*adj*) *Slang*. very drunk
spree prolonged period of drunkenness
squiffed (*adj*) *Slang*. very intoxicated, drunk
stewed (*adj*) *Slang*. drunk
stinking (*adj*) *Slang*. very inebriated
stinko (*adj*) *Slang*. drunk
stoned (*adj*) *Slang*. intoxicated
swacked (*adj*) *Slang*. very drunk
swizzle (*vb*) drink to excess
tanked (*adj*) *Slang*. drunk
tank up (*vb*) take drink; become inebriated
tiddly (*adj*) *Brit. slang*. slightly drunk
tie one on *Slang*. drink until inebriated
tight (*adj*) *Slang*. drunk
tipple (*vb*) drink liquor habitually or excessively
tippler one habitually drunk
tipsy (*adj*) slightly intoxicated
toot *Slang*. drinking spree
tope (*vb*) drink to excess
toper one who drinks to excess
tosspot drunkard, sot
twelve steps step-by-step program for recovery from addiction, originated by Alcoholics Anonymous

under the influence inebriated, esp. while driving a car
under the table so intoxicated as to be lying on floor; outdrunk by another
wasted (*adj*) *Slang*. intoxicated
wino *Informal*. one chronically addicted to drink, esp. cheap wine
wiped-out (*adj*) *Slang*. drunk to the point of unconsciousness
woozy (*adj*) intoxicated; slightly dizzy
wrecked (*adj*) *Slang*. drunk
zonked (*adj*) *Slang*. extremely intoxicated, drunk

Paraphernalia and Behavior

abuse (*vb*) use any drug to excess; (*n*) excessive use of drug
acid trip *Slang*. experience of taking LSD
addiction physical or psychological dependence on drug
army disease *Slang*. morphine addiction, esp. among military personnel who first received drug to alleviate pain
bad trip *Slang*. negative response, including panic, fear, and psychosis, due to hallucinogenic drug; bummer
bang (*vb*) *Slang*. inject drugs
bang a gong *Slang*. sniff cocaine
black market covert, illegal sale of drugs
blow (*vb*) *Slang*. inhale drugs; smoke marijuana
bogue *Slang*. withdrawal symptoms
bong *Slang*. water pipe for smoking marijuana
boot technique of injecting heroin gradually to prolong euphoric sensation
bummer *Slang*. bad trip
burn (*vb*) *Slang*. cheat someone on drug deal; (*n*) drug swindle
bust *Slang*. arrest for possession or sale of drugs
buzz *Slang*. initial mild effect of drug
cap gelatin capsule for holding drug dose; (*vb*) insert drug into capsules
carry (*vb*) have drugs on one's person
charge *Slang*. sudden, exhilarating effect of drugs
chillum short clay marijuana pipe
chipping *Slang*. occasional or recreational use of hard drugs
clean (*adj*) *Slang*. not in possession of drugs; (*vb*) remove stems and seeds from marijuana
cold turkey *Informal*. sudden withdrawal from addictive drug use
come down (*vb*) feel drug high depart, return to normal state
connect (*vb*) *Slang*. buy or find source for drugs
contact high mildly altered state caused by proximity to marijuana smoke or smokers
cook (*vb*) dissolve heroin powder in water over heat prior to injection
cop (*vb*) *Slang*. buy drugs; score
cotton cotton filter for straining cooked heroin prior to injection
cotton mouth *Slang*. dryness in mouth due to inhibited salivation caused by marijuana smoking

crack house building used as crack distribution center, usu. in poor urban area
crack pipe small glass pipe used for smoking crack cocaine
crash (*vb*) *Slang*. fall asleep or come down from effect of drug
cross-tolerance tolerance to effects of one drug because of tolerance to a similar substance
crutch device for holding butt of marijuana cigarette
cut (*vb*) dilute a drug, esp. heroin or cocaine, with adulterating inactive substance
deal (*vb*) *Slang*. sell drugs
dependency physical or psychological addiction to drugs
detox *Informal*. detoxification
detoxification period of treatment and counseling during which addict overcomes drug dependency
do dope (*vb*) use or take drugs
drop (*vb*) *Slang*. swallow a pill or drugs; take LSD
dropper medicine dropper used as homemade drug injection equipment
drug abuse excessive use of any drug or narcotic
drug testing examination and analysis, usu. of blood or urine, to determine presence of drugs, usu. conducted by government or employer
dusted (*adj*) under the influence of PCP, or angel dust
dusting *Slang*. addition of heroin to marijuana cigarette
fix (*vb*) *Slang*. inject oneself with narcotic; (*n*) single injection of a drug
flash *Slang*. rush
flip out (*vb*) *Slang*. experience psychotic state, or extreme mental or physical reaction, as a result of taking a drug
fly (*vb*) *Slang*. experience intoxication due to drugs
freak (*vb*) *Slang*. freak out
freak out (*vb*) *Slang*. hallucinate uncontrollably; experience dramatic, frightening, drug-induced distortion of perception and feeling; freak
freebase (*vb*) *Slang*. process cocaine with ether and heat to intensify its effects; smoke freebased cocaine
geeze (*vb*) *Slang*. inject drugs, esp. heroin
get high (*vb*) *Slang*. achieve euphoria or other drug-induced state
get off (*vb*) experience effects of drugs, esp. by injection
glue sniffing breathing glue fumes for hallucinogenic or euphoric drug effect
goof (*vb*) *Slang*. be under the influence of narcotics or barbiturates; nod out
habit physical dependence on addictive drug; amount required each day to satisfy dependency
hassle (*vb*) *Informal*. buy drugs, bargain for drugs
high (*adj*) euphorically under the influence of drugs; (*n*) *Slang*. such a state
hit *Slang*. (*vb*) inject drugs; (*n*) single drug injection; one drag on a marijuana cigarette

holding (*adj*) *Slang*. carrying drugs on one's person

hookah water-cooled pipe for smoking marijuana or hashish

hooked (*adj*) *Informal*. physically dependent on drug

hustle (*vb*) *Slang*. get money for drugs, esp. by prostitution or other illegal means

hypo *Informal*. hypodermic syringe

hypodermic syringe small glass syringe used to inject drugs; hypo

ice-cream habit *Slang*. moderate social use of hard drugs

jag state of intense, protracted drug stimulation

jones *Slang*. drug addiction, esp. to heroin

joypop (*vb*) *Slang*. inject heroin occasionally, esp. subcutaneously instead of into vein

kick (*vb*) *Slang*. give up or break drug habit or dependency

kick the gong around *Slang*. sniff cocaine

kick the habit *Slang*. give up drug use; kick

kit *Slang*. hypodermic needle and equipment for injecting drugs

kitchen *Slang*. drug laboratory

life *Slang*. **the life;** syndrome of drug addiction and attendant patterns of behavior and activity

loaded (*adj*) *Slang*. high on drugs

mainline (*vb*) *Slang*. inject drug into vein

methadone maintenance program of legally administered methadone provided to prevent recidivism of former heroin addicts

miss drug injection that misses vein

monkey on one's back *Slang*. drug addiction or dependency

munchies *Slang*. intense craving for food, esp. sugar, experienced after smoking marijuana

nail *Slang*. hypodermic needle for drug injections

narcoterrorism terrorist tactics employed by drug dealers against government agents

narghile type of water pipe

needle hypodermic needle used for drug injections

needle park *Slang*. meeting place in which heroin addicts inject drugs

nod out (*vb*) *Slang*. be under the influence of narcotics; doze off into drug stupor

OD overdose

outfit equipment for injecting drugs

overdose OD; intake of quantity of drugs above one's tolerance, producing debilitation or death

panic bad reaction to drug; heroin shortage

paraphernalia implements and objects used in preparing and ingesting drugs

physical dependence physiological addiction to drug

pinned (*adj*) *Slang*. having constricted eye pupils due to narcotics use

pipe device for smoking marijuana, hashish, or crack cocaine; *Slang*. easy-to-inject vein

plant (*vb*) place drugs on premises or on person set up to be arrested for drug possession

pop (*vb*) *Slang*. inject heroin under skin, not into vein

possession having drugs on one's person or property

potentiate (*vb*) cause drug to act more powerfully by action or use of another drug

psychological dependence drug craving based on desire for pleasure, not physical addiction

reverse tolerance increased sensitivity to smaller doses of drug the more it is taken, as with marijuana

rig equipment for injecting drugs

roach clip *Slang*. gripping device for holding end of burning marijuana cigarette; roach holder

roach holder *Slang*. roach clip

run *Slang*. period of intense drug use

rush *Slang*. sudden sensation of drug's effects, esp. from injection; flash

score *Slang*. (*vb*) buy or obtain illicit drugs; (*n*) any drugs so purchased; any illicit drug transaction

scrip *Informal*. prescription for drugs, esp. narcotics

setting environment and mental state of person preparing for hallucinogenic drug experience

shoot (*vb*) *Slang*. shoot up

shooting gallery *Slang*. location where addicts inject drugs

shooting gravy *Slang*. reinjection of blood backed up into needle during drug injection

shoot up (*vb*) *Slang*. inject drugs into vein

sick (*adj*) suffering from drug withdrawal

skin-pop (*vb*) *Slang*. inject drugs subcutaneously, not into vein

snort (*vb*) *Slang*. inhale powdered drug through nose

spaced-out (*adj*) *Slang*. feeling floating sensation or numbing effects of drug use

spike *Slang*. hypodermic needle

spoon *Slang*. small measure of heroin

stash hiding place for drugs; hidden supply of drugs

stem *Slang*. glass pipe for smoking crack or ice

stoned (*adj*) *Slang*. intoxicated by drugs

straight (*adj*) *Informal*. not using illicit drugs

straw thin tube used for sniffing drugs in powdered form, esp. cut-off straw

street *Slang*. usu. **the street;** world of drug use, abuse, and hustling required to acquire money for drugs

strung-out (*adj*) *Slang*. severely addicted to drugs

substance abuse long-term addiction to or excessive use of narcotics or controlled substances

tea pad *Slang*. room or other location for smoking marijuana

tie off (*vb*) wrap cord or strap around upper arm to force veins into prominence for injection

toke *Slang*. single puff on marijuana cigarette

tolerance resistance to the effects of a drug, resulting in the need to use increasingly large doses of that drug for the same effect

toot *Slang*. a snort of a drug, esp. cocaine

tracks *Slang*. needle marks from repeated drug injections

trip *Slang*. (*n*) hallucinogenic drug experience; (*vb*) take a hallucinogen, esp. LSD

turn on (*vb*) *Slang*. take drugs; become intoxicated from drug use

using (*adj*) *Slang*. taking drugs; addicted to drugs

wasted (*adj*) *Slang*. intoxicated; very high

water pipe device in which marijuana smoke is cooled by passing through water before entering hose leading to smoker's mouth

white light *Slang*. sensation of intense light produced by hallucinogenic drugs

wig out (*vb*) *Slang*. experience dramatic mental effects from drug use

wings *Slang*. first drug injection

wired (*adj*) *Slang*. very high on drugs, esp. stimulants

withdrawal cessation of use of addictive drug with painful or unpleasant symptoms

works *Slang*. equipment for drug injection

yen-shee *Slang*. painful opium-induced constipation

Zig-Zag *Trademark*. brand of cigarette rolling papers

zoned out (*adj*) *Slang*. very intoxicated, nearly senseless from drug use

zonked out (*adj*) *Slang*. very intoxicated, nearly senseless from drug use

Users and Abusers

acid freak *Slang*. LSD user

acid-head *Slang*. habitual user of LSD

addict person who is physically or psychologically dependent on some drug; junkie

A-head *Slang*. habitual user of amphetamines

bagman *Slang*. drug seller

burnout person who is apathetic and disoriented from prolonged drug use, esp. from marijuana smoking

candy man *Slang*. drug seller

chef *Slang*. chemist, esp. in illicit amphetamine laboratory

connection *Slang*. drug seller; supplier of drugs

cook *Slang*. chemist in illicit drug laboratory; chef

copilot *Slang*. guide

croaker *Slang*. doctor supplying narcotics to addicts

dealer *Slang*. drug seller

dope fiend *Slang*. drug addict

dopehead *Slang*. drug addict

dope peddler *Slang*. drug seller

dope pusher *Slang*. drug seller

doper *Slang*. regular drug user, esp. marijuana smoker

drug seller person who buys and sells drugs illegally; *Slang*: bagman, candy man, connection, dealer, man, pusher, source

explorers' club *Slang*. group of LSD users

flower children youthful psychedelic drug users in the 1960's, esp. in San Francisco's Haight-Ashbury district

freak *Slang*. person using particular kind of drug on frequent basis, such as a speed freak

gee head *Slang*. paregoric user

ground control *Slang.* guide

guide person experienced in LSD use who guides another's LSD trip; copilot; ground control

head *Slang.* drug user or addict, esp. one using a particular drug, such as a pothead

hustler *Slang.* drug addict forced into stealing or prostitution to support habit

junkie *Informal.* heroin addict; drug addict

man *Slang.* **the man;** one's drug supplier; the police

mother *Slang.* one's regular drug supplier

narc *Slang.* police officer on narcotics detail

pillhead *Slang.* habitual amphetamine or barbiturate user

poison people *Slang.* heroin addicts

pothead *Slang.* regular marijuana user

pusher *Slang.* drug seller

shmecker *Slang.* heroin user

source one's drug supplier; dealer

speed freak *Slang.* regular user of amphetamines

square *Slang.* user's term for person not using drugs

straight *Slang.* person not using drugs

take-off artist *Slang.* heroin addict who supports habit by robbing other addicts

tea head *Slang.* marijuana user

trafficker large-scale drug seller or importer

travel agent *Slang.* LSD seller

vice squad narcotics division of police

viper *Slang.* marijuana smoker

MENTAL DISTURBANCES
Insanity
Mental Institutions
Agitation, Abnormality, and Instability

See also: *Chap. 1: Medical Problems; Chap. 13: Psychology; Chap. 20: Insults, Slurs, and Epithets*

Insanity

amok (*adj*) in a murderous frenzy; raging violently

ape (*adj*) *Slang.* crazed, nuts, or wildly overactive; apeshit

apeshit (*adj*) *Vulgar slang.* ape

around the bend *Slang.* crazy

balmy (*adj*) *Informal.* crazy

bananas (*adj*) *Slang.* crazy, deranged

barmy (*adj*) *Brit. slang.* balmy

batty (*adj*) crazy; demented

bent (*adj*) abnormal, esp. somewhat crazed or perverse

berserk (*adj*) frenzied; crazed

bonkers (*adj*) *Slang.* crazy; mentally unbalanced

cracked (*adj*) *Slang.* insane

crackpot *Informal.* one given to eccentric or lunatic notions

crazed (*adj*) distracted, overexcited, slightly nuts

crazy (*adj*) mentally deranged or demented; insane; (*n*) *Slang.* one who acts or is insane

criminally insane prone to criminal acts or threats; dangerous

cuckoo (*adj*) *Slang.* crazy

daffy (*adj*) *Slang.* nutty, screwy

demented (*adj*) perversely insane; mad

dementia insanity, esp. severe mental impairment due to brain damage

demoniac (*adj*) behaving as though possessed by the devil

deranged (*adj*) insane

feeble-minded (*adj*) mentally deficient; moronic

flip (*vb*) *Slang.* lose one's mind

flip out (*vb*) *Slang.* go crazy or become frenzied

flipped (*adj*) *Slang.* deranged; crazy

frenzied (*adj*) marked by violent agitation; berserk

frenzy temporary madness; intense agitation and compulsive activity

fruitcake *Slang.* crazy or eccentric person; nut

go ape *Slang.* become violently emotional

go mad become insane; suffer a breakdown

gone (*adj*) *Informal.* lost in madness, outside reality

goofy (*adj*) *Slang.* nutty, silly

go to pieces break down, suffer an emotional collapse

have a screw loose be crazy

haywire (*adj*) *Slang.* out of control; disordered

homicidal (*adj*) having murderous intent or making threats

idiot one who is severely mentally deficient

insane (*adj*) mentally disordered or deranged; suffering from insanity; *Slang:* around the bend, balmy, bananas, barmy, batty, bonkers, cracked, crazy, deranged, loco, loony, nuts, off one's rocker, out of one's tree, psycho, wacko

insanity various deranged states of mind, mental disorders, conditions, and incapacity; dementia; lunacy; madness

kook *Slang.* one who is odd, eccentric, or unbalanced

kooky (*adj*) *Slang.* eccentric or peculiar

lather *Informal.* agitated or overwrought state

loco (*adj*) *Slang.* crazy

loony *Informal.* (*n*) lunatic; (*adj*) crazy; insane

lose one's mind go insane

lunacy insanity

lunatic insane person

mad (*adj*) mentally disturbed or deranged; insane; completely senseless or disordered

madman insane person; lunatic

madness insanity

maniac one who is totally, often dangerously, insane

mental (*adj*) affected with a disorder of the mind

moonstruck (*adj*) mentally deranged

moron one of very low mental capacity

moronic (*adj*) feeble-minded

nut mildly crazy or eccentric person, usu. harmless; fruitcake

nuts (*adj*) *Slang.* crazy; insane

nutter *Brit. slang.* mildly crazy person

nutty (*adj*) *Slang.* eccentric, mildly crazy; daffy

oddball *Informal.* eccentric or abnormal individual

off (*adj*) *Slang.* slightly crazy; abnormal

off one's head crazy

off one's rocker *Slang.* crazy

out of one's head crazy

out of one's mind crazy

out of one's tree *Slang.* crazy

overdrawn (*adj*) *Slang.* oddball, nuts

over the edge gone crazy

possessed (*adj*) behaving as though controlled by supernatural power or powerful subconscious impulse

potty (*adj*) *Brit. slang.* slightly insane or eccentric

psycho (*adj*) psychopathic; insane; (*n*) psychopathic person

psychopath *Slang.* one who is mentally ill, esp. exhibiting amoral and antisocial behavior

psychopathic (*adj*) exhibiting amoral and antisocial behavior, including the inability to tell right from wrong

psychosis major, severe form of mental disorder

psychotic one afflicted with severe mental disorder; insane person

rabid (*adj*) frenzied, raging uncontrollably

raving (*adj*) speaking wildly, deliriously

schizoid (*adj*) suffering from schizophrenia or multiple personality; schizy

schizy (*adj*) *Informal.* schizoid

screaming-meemies *Informal.* extreme terror or nervous hysteria

screwy (*adj*) *Slang.* slightly insane; daffy

sick (*adj*) mentally ill

sicko *Slang.* perverse, deranged person

sociopath psychopathic personality with extremely asocial or antisocial behavior

stark raving mad *Slang.* completely insane

touched (*adj*) unbalanced or slightly crazy

twisted (*adj*) *Slang.* perverse, diabolical

unbalanced (*adj*) mentally disordered, deranged

unglued (*adj*) *Slang.* mentally unstable or upset

unhinged highly distraught or unsettled

wacko *Slang.* (*adj*) insane, crazy (*n*) one who is insane

wacky (*adj*) *Slang.* slightly crazy or eccentric

weirdo *Informal.* extraordinarily strange individual

whacked-out (*adj*) *Slang.* strung out, agitated, or slightly insane

wigged out (*adj*) *Slang.* agitated, anxious, or slightly insane

zany (*adj*) eccentric or mildly abnormal in behavior

Mental Institutions

asylum institution for the relief and care of the mentally ill

bedlam *Archaic.* lunatic asylum

booby hatch *Slang.* insane asylum

bughouse *Slang.* insane asylum

commit (*vb*) place someone in mental hospital

committed (*adj*) required to enter and remain in mental hospital

funny farm *Slang.* mental hospital

halfway house residence for formerly

institutionalized patients that helps to facilitate their readjustment to normal life

home mental hospital

insane asylum institution for the care and treatment of the mentally ill; booby hatch; bughouse

institution mental hospital

loony bin *Slang.* mental hospital

lunatic asylum mental hospital

madhouse mental hospital

mental home low-security mental hospital

mental hospital institution for the care and treatment of the mentally ill; funny farm; home; institution; loony bin; lunatic asylum; madhouse; nut house; snake pit

mental ward section of hospital reserved for mentally ill

nut house *Slang.* mental hospital

padded cell heavily padded, individual holding room for confinement of psychotic patient

psychiatric ward section of regular hospital reserved for the mentally ill; psycho ward

psycho ward *Slang.* psychiatric ward

sanatorium sanitarium

sanitarium hospital for the treatment of the mentally ill; sanatorium

snake pit *Informal.* mental hospital

Agitation, Abnormality, and Instability

abandon freedom from normal restraints in behavior

aberrant (*adj*) departing substantially from standard behavior

abnormality deviation from normal, accepted behavior

agita *Informal.* anxiety; agitation

agitated (*adj*) overly excited or anxious

agitation mental excitement or disquiet; perturbation

agony intense mental pain or tortured state of mind

amentia mental deficiency, esp. low intellectual capacity

analgesia insensibility to pain while conscious

angst feeling of anxiety, apprehension, and insecurity

anguish extreme mental distress

anomaly any abnormality or deviation from the norm

anxiety distress, uneasiness, apprehension, and psychic tension caused by fear of impending or imagined danger or misfortune

at loose ends distracted, unsettled, uncertain

at sea confused, dazed, or disoriented

attack fit of disorder; active episode of recurrent illness

at wit's end perplexed, esp. having exhausted one's mental resources

baffled (*adj*) confused; confounded

bewildered (*adj*) extremely confused and disoriented

bizarre (*adj*) odd, extravagant, or eccentric in behavior

black out (*vb*) undergo temporary loss of consciousness, vision, or memory

blow one's mind *Slang.* become overwhelmed with wonder or bafflement, esp. when drug-induced

brainsick (*adj*) mentally disordered

breakdown physical, mental, or nervous collapse; nervous breakdown

breaking point point at which one succumbs to stress

broken (*adj*) completely crushed in mind and spirit

brooding (*adj*) depressed, moody

bugaboo imaginary object of fear, causing disproportionate anxiety

bundle of nerves extremely anxious individual

butterflies *Informal.* queasy feeling due to nervousness or agitation

cabin fever restless irritability from isolation or prolonged confinement

catatonic (*adj*) marked by stupor, rigidity, muteness, and bizarre or purposeless activity; (*n*) one suffering from catatonia

cold sweat concurrent chills and perspiration from fear or shock

collapse nervous breakdown or extreme depression

comatose (*adj*) in a state of prolonged unconsciousness

come to (*vb*) awaken from unconsciousness

compulsive (*adj*) unable to control an irrational impulse to do something

confounded (*adj*) baffled or confused

confused (*adj*) unable to differentiate reality; disturbed in mind or purpose; muddled

conniption fit of hysteria, rage, or alarm

consternation amazement or dismay causing confusion

crack up (*vb*) *Informal.* suffer a breakdown; go insane

crisis turning point in mental disorder

crumble (*vb*) suffer emotional collapse; go to pieces

death wish conscious or unconscious desire to die

delirious (*adj*) suffering from delirium

delirium state of confusion, disordered speech, hallucination, and frenzy

delusion persistent false belief regarding self or others

depression condition of general despondency, dejection, and withdrawel

despair utter loss of hope and confidence

deviant (*adj*) straying from normal behavior; (*n*) one who so strays

diabolical (*adj*) perverse, as though possessed by devil

disorientation displacement from a normal sense of time, place, and identity

distracted (*adj*) confused, unfocused, at loose ends

distraught (*adj*) extremely agitated

distress mental pain or suffering

disturbed (*adj*) showing symptoms of emotional illness and distress

dither nervous, disoriented, or indecisive state

dizzy (*adj*) mentally confused

doldrums spell of inactivity or depression

dotty *Informal.* mentally unbalanced; amiably eccentric

eccentric one who behaves abnormally; oddball

eccentricity bizarre or abnormal, but harmless, activity

erratic (*adj*) peculiar, inconsistent, or unpredictable in behavior

euphoria feeling of extreme elation

fanatic (*adj*) marked by excessive behavior

fantasy delusive view or idea

fantods emotional outburst or fit

fazed (*adj*) disturbed or disconcerted

fit sudden, violent emotional reaction or outburst

flustered (*adj*) confused, anxious, or agitated

frantic (*adj*) mentally deranged, out of control, or very nervous

frazzled (*adj*) in state of extreme nervous fatigue

freak *Slang.* abnormal individual

freak out (*vb*) *Slang.* behave irrationally, withdraw from reality, or experience nightmarish hallucinations, esp. when drug-induced

hallucination perception of objects not really there

heebie-jeebies *Slang.* condition of extreme anxiety and nervousness; jitters; willies

hysteria uncontrollable, irrational outburst of emotion or intense anxiety

hysterics fit of hysteria

imbalanced (*adj*) mentally disturbed or abnormal

instability tendency to behave in an unpredictable or erratic manner

insufficiency lack of mental fitness

jangled (*adj*) tense, irritated, nervous

Jekyll and Hyde person marked by dual personality, one good and one evil

jimjams *Slang.* jitters

jitters extreme sense of panic and nervousness; heebie-jeebies; screaming-meemies; willies

kamikaze (*adj*) recklessly self-destructive

lobotomized (*adj*) sluggish, dull-witted, or calmed due to lobotomy

maladjusted (*adj*) poorly adapted to normal society; eccentric

malcontent one rebelliously opposed to societal norms

manic (*adj*) hyperactive; excessively excited or agitated

mental (*adj*) *Informal.* affected with a disorder of the mind

mental illness disorder of the mind

mixed-up (*adj*) completely confused or emotionally unstable

muddled (*adj*) confused

nervous breakdown breakdown

neurotic (*adj*) excessively anxious or indecisive

non compos mentis *Latin*. lit. not of sound mind; mentally incompetent or unsound

obsessive (*adj*) unable to escape some persistent idea or need

off-the-wall (*adj*) *Informal*. extreme terror or nervous hysteria; jitters

on pins and needles experiencing nervous anxiety or anticipation

on tenterhooks in a state of uneasy suspense or anxiety

overwrought (*adj*) extremely anxious or agitated

paroxysm sudden emotional outburst

peculiar (*adj*) odd or eccentric in behavior

perturbation agitation

perverse (*adj*) obstinately unreasonable, willful, or evil

phobic (*adj*) suffering from exaggerated, illogical fears

pixilated (*adj*) slightly unbalanced

prostration state of overwhelming exhaustion or helplessness

queer (*adj*) peculiar or eccentric in behavior

rage uncontrollable anger directed at any available target

rattled (*adj*) confused, disconcerted, and anxious

retarded (*adj*) severely mentally deficient

rocky (*adj*) *Informal*. unstable, upset, or unsteady

screaming-meemies *Informal*. extreme terror or nervous hysteria; jitters

shaken-up (*adj*) disoriented or confused

shattered (*adj*) in a state of mental, emotional, or nervous collapse or disintegration

shock sudden, violent emotional disturbance, usu. caused by traumatic event or injury

slough of despond state of extreme depression

spell period of mental distress

spooked (*adj*) *Slang*. fearful over imagined threats

state abnormal condition of mind

stressed-out (*adj*) *Informal*. exhausted or extremely anxious

strung-out (*adj*) *Slang*. addicted to a drug; in an extreme state of nervous exhaustion

stupor state of extreme apathy or torpor from stress or shock

swivet state of extreme agitation

tangled (*adj*) disoriented or bewildered

tantrum uncontrollable fit of rage or hysteria

tizzy *Slang*. state of disorientation, anxiety, or upset

trance sleeplike state of suspended animation

trauma disordered psychic state due to emotional stress or physical injury

turmoil state of extreme agitation and confusion

turn *Informal*. nervous shock, as from fright

twitter state of anxiety, agitation, or extreme upset

unsound (*adj*) abnormal or disordered, as in the mind

unstable (*adj*) unable to control one's emotions or behave within accepted norms

up the wall extremely anxious or agitated

willies *Slang*. extreme state of anxiety and jitters; heebie-jeebies

worked-up (*adj*) agitated, unable to contain emotions

zoned (*adj*) *Slang*. dazed, disoriented, or confused

CRIME

Crimes
Criminals
Police Procedures and Detection
Legal Procedures and Trials
Prison and Punishment

See also: *Chap. 11: Law; Chap. 22: Strategy, Intrigue, and Deception; Chap. 24: Drug Abuse and Alcoholism; Violence; Death*

Crimes

abduction carrying off of person by force, esp. for sex or prostitution or as hostage

adultery engaging in extramarital sex

aggravated assault severe physical attack

air piracy skyjacking

arson intentionally setting fire to property

assassination murder of public figure

assault personal physical attack or threat of violence

assault and battery assault with actual physical contact or violence upon other person

battery physical violence upon another person, esp. beating

bigamy marrying while already legally married

blackmail demand for payment based on threat of embarrassment, exposure, or harm; extortion

bootlegging illegal production, distribution, or sale of something already owned or copyrighted, or something unregistered or outlawed; piracy

break-in illegal entry of another's property

breaking and entering entry into another's property, forcibly or with criminal intent

bribery offering payment for favors or corrupt behavior, esp. involving a public official

bunko confidence game or swindle that takes advantage of victim's ignorance

burglary breaking into and entering private property for purpose of crime, usu. theft

capital crime crime punishable by death

chop shop *Informal*. garage where stolen cars are dismantled so that their parts can be sold separately

collusion action by two or more persons to commit crime, esp. fraud

confidence game fraud or swindle involving misleading trickery; bunko

conspiracy secret plan among two or more persons to commit unlawful act

contempt of court willful disrespect for rules and orders of a court

counterfeiting manufacture of fake money

crime illegal act against person or property for which offender is liable to punishment

crime against humanity sinful act of monstrous proportions, such as genocide, directed against a group because of race, religion, or national origin

crime of commission illegal act involving specific violation of law

crime of omission illegal act involving failure to perform specific requirement of law

crime of passion illegal act committed in heat of anger or jealousy

defalcation failure to meet promise; act of embezzlement

defamation injury to person's character; spoken slander or written libel

disorderly conduct any of various activities that disturb public peace

drive-by shooting usu. gang-related shooting by unseen assailant in passing car

embezzlement theft of money or appropriation of property entrusted to one's care

extortion demand for payment based on threat of embarrassment, exposure, or harm; blackmail

felony serious crime, punishable by imprisonment

forgery fraudulent imitation of documents or signatures

frame (*vb*) falsely accuse or incriminate an innocent party

fraud deception or trickery for illegal gain

graft bribery, esp. of public officials

grand larceny theft of personal property exceeding specified value

gunrunning smuggling of firearms

hijacking takeover of public vehicle by violent means

hit-and-run (*adj*) guilty of leaving the scene of an auto accident to avoid responsibility for injuries and damage caused

holdup armed robbery

homicide taking of human life, usu. intentionally

hot (*adj*) *Slang*. stolen

infraction violation of a law

involuntary manslaughter taking of human life through criminal negligence

job *Slang*. crime

justifiable homicide killing person for defensible reason

kidnapping holding person, esp. child, captive in exchange for ransom

killing taking of human life

larceny theft of personal property

libel publication of statement damaging to another's reputation

lift (*vb*) *Informal*. steal

looting stealing from locations left unprotected after violent event or natural catastrophe

malfeasance wrongdoing or misconduct, esp. an act in violation of public trust committed by a public official

malicious mischief intentional or reckless harm or damage to property of another

manslaughter taking of human life by accident or negligence

mayhem willfully inflicting bodily injury on another person; deliberate violence or damage; state of rowdy disorder

misconduct intentionally improper behavior by a public official, esp. malfeasance

misdemeanor illegal act less serious than a felony, usu. punishable by fine or probation

mugging robbery, esp. in public place

murder taking of human life for no defensible reason

mutiny rebellion against authority, esp. military

nuisance use of one's property to damage or inconvenience another

numbers racket illegal lottery run by organized crime syndicate

obstruction of justice act that hinders or prevents completion of legal process

offense breach of criminal laws

organized crime network of criminals acting systematically in illegal activities; syndicate

payola *Informal.* bribery to promote commercial product, esp. music

peculation embezzlement of public funds

perjury lying while under oath, esp. giving false testimony in court

petty larceny theft of personal property of less than a specified value

pickpocketing theft from unsuspecting victim's person, esp. from a pocket

pilferage theft of small amounts of goods done over time to avoid detection

piracy bootlegging

plunder robbery by force, esp. in wartime; taking of property by force or fraud

poaching taking of fish or game from private property or protected reserve

premeditated crime crime planned and committed with malice aforethought

prostitution sexual intercourse for payment

purse snatching forceful theft of woman's handbag from her arm

pyramid scheme confidence game in which first investors are paid off with investment of later ones, who never see a return

racketeering operation of a business characterized by systematically dishonest practices

rackets *Informal.* often **the rackets**; businesses controlled by racketeering

rape forcible sexual intercourse without consent, esp. committed by a man against a woman

reckless endangerment action that could result in injury to another though it may not have

resisting arrest attempt to evade or physically prevent arrest

robbery theft aggravated by force or threat of assault

roll (*vb*) *Slang.* rob a helpless person, esp. an insensible drunk

rumrunning smuggling of liquor

rustling *Informal.* stealing, usu. cattle or horses (U.S. Old West)

safecracking forcible entry into locked safe to steal its contents

sedition incitement to rebellion against government

shanghaiing kidnapping a person into service aboard ship, esp. by drugging

shoplifting theft from store by person posing as customer

skyjacking forcible, violent seizure of aircraft; air piracy

slander making of false and malicious verbal statements damaging to another's reputation

smuggling import or export of goods that are outlawed or in avoidance of customs duty

sodomy performance of unnatural sex acts, usu. anal sex or sex with an animal

soliciting seeking clients for prostitute

stealing wrongfully taking another's property; theft

subornation inducing another to commit an illegal act, esp. perjury

swindling performing fraudulent business transactions

syndicate organized crime

terrorism use of intimidation and random violence, esp. as a political weapon

theft stealing

tong war violence between Chinese secret societies seeking to control organized crime

treason betrayal of one's country or government

trespass illegal use or occupation of another's property, esp. entry upon another's land

vagrancy wandering idly in a public place without home or money

vandalism defacing or damaging of another's property, often random and purposeless

voluntary manslaughter taking of human life with mitigating circumstances

white-collar crime illegal acts by professionals or office workers against institutions, government, or businesses

white-slave trade organized recruitment or abduction of victims, usu. women, into prostitution

wilding *Slang.* wanton, random assault and vandalism

Criminals

accessory person who, though absent, assists another to commit a crime or evade capture

accomplice criminal's active partner in crime

arsonist person who intentionally sets a fire

bandit robber, esp. one who attacks victims in public places

bluebeard any man who allegedly murders a series of women he has married

bookie person accepting illegal bets

bootlegger seller of illegal items; smuggler

brigand bandit, esp. member of gang operating in forest or mountains

burglar thief

call girl high-class prostitute reached by telephone

cannon *Slang.* pickpocket

career criminal one who habitually engages in crime

cat burglar one skilled at breaking into

buildings, even those secured against theft, by climbing through upstairs windows or across roofs

cateran member of gang of roving brigands

con artist confidence man

confidence man swindler or instigator of fraudulent business schemes; con artist; con man

con man confidence man

Cosa Nostra *Italian.* lit. our affair; Mafia

criminal person engaging in illegal acts; crook

crook criminal

dacoit robber and murderer in organized gang (India)

delinquent person who violates the law

Fagin fence; trainer of pickpockets

family *Slang.* Mafia

felon person guilty of a felony

fence receiver of stolen property

first offender person guilty of crime for first time

fugitive person fleeing arrest or imprisonment

gang organization of street criminals, usu. young

gangster person working in criminal organization; highbinder

gun moll *Slang.* gangster's girlfriend; female criminal

gunslinger *Informal.* violent criminal who wore gun on hip (U.S. Old West)

hardened criminal habitual criminal committed to life of crime

highbinder gangster

highwayman person who stops travelers to rob them

hit man *Slang.* hired assassin

hoodlum violent young ruffian; member of organized crime syndicate

hook *Slang.* pickpocket; (*v*) work as a prostitute

hooker *Slang.* prostitute

hooligan violent young ruffian; street gang member

horse thief stealer of horses

juvenile delinquent criminal under age of legal majority; youthful offender

killer murderer

kleptomaniac person unable to stop stealing

loan shark *Informal.* lender charging illegally high interest rates

Mafia organized crime syndicate, orig. Sicilian; Cosa Nostra

mafioso member of Mafia

mass murderer killer of many people

mob gang of criminals; organized crime syndicate

mugger person attacking and robbing others on street

murderer person who willfully takes another's life; killer

Peeping Tom person who spies on sexual or private activities of others

peterman *Slang.* safecracker

pickpocket person who steals money or valuables from victim's pocket, esp. in crowded place; cannon; hook

pimp person soliciting for prostitutes

poacher person who steals fish or game from another's land or protected reserve

point *Informal.* person who occupies lookout position during illegal activity or crime

prostitute person engaging in sex for pay

prowler person entering another's home for purpose of robbery or violence

public enemy dangerous criminal widely sought by law enforcement agencies

racketeer person involved in rackets, organized crime, or illegal business operations

safecracker robber specializing in forcing open safes; peterman

scofflaw person who violates the law with contempt, esp. one who fails to pay fines owed

second-story man burglar specializing in entering buildings through upstairs windows

serial killer mentally unbalanced person who kills one victim after another

smuggler transporter of illegal goods, esp. across borders; bootlegger

squatter person illegally occupying another's vacant property

streetwalker prostitute who solicits on the streets

thief one who steals; burglar

thug brutal, petty criminal; professional strangler

tong member of secret Chinese gang

underworld segment of society engaged in crime as profession

vandal person engaged in wanton violence to property, usu. not motivated by theft

youthful offender defendant who may be sentenced with special consideration due to age; juvenile delinquent

Police Procedures and Detection

AKA also known as; prefix before alias

alias false name used by criminal

all-points bulletin APB; description of wanted criminal issued to all police in area

APB all-points bulletin

apprehend (*vb*) catch suspect or criminal

arrest (*vb*) lawfully detain suspect; (*n*) act of apprehending and detaining suspect; bust

arrestee person arrested on suspicion of crime

at large describing a criminal who is free, having evaded arrest

badge *Informal.* policeman

ballistics study of firearms and bullets, used in detection and identification of weapons used in crimes

beat police officer's assigned area of duty

Bertillon system fingerprinting and identification system

billy club policeman's heavy wooden stick or baton; night stick

blotter book in station house in which arrests are recorded as they occur

bobby *Brit. informal.* policeman

book (*vb*) register arrestee at jail or place of detention

bounty payment offered for capture of criminal at large

break piece of luck that helps to solve a crime

bust *Slang.* arrest

canary *Slang.* person confessing a crime or offering information to police

case unsolved crime or one being tried

citizen's arrest arrest made not by police but by person whose authority rests on fact of citizenship

clamp down (*vb*) increase police activity, usu. on specific problem

clue piece of information leading toward arrest of criminal

collar (*vb*) *Informal.* arrest

comb (*vb*) thoroughly inspect scene of crime; search intensely for clues

confession admission of guilt

cop *Informal.* policeman

copper *Informal.* policeman

coroner public officer investigating deaths likely to be due to criminal acts

crack (*vb*) solve a case

crackdown intensification of police efforts to control crime

crime lab laboratory in which evidence is examined scientifically to aid in apprehension of suspects

criminology study of crime, its causes, detection, correction, and prevention

custody arrest and detention of suspect or criminal

dactyloscopy method of studying fingerprints to establish identification

delator professional informer

detection art and practice of finding solutions to crimes

detective police officer or private individual skilled at acquiring information about crimes and tracking down suspected criminals; dick; hawkshaw; shamus

detention holding of suspect or criminal in custody to await charges, trial, or sentencing

deterrence prevention of crime

dick *Slang.* detective

DNA fingerprinting identification of criminal suspect by matching genes in known segment of labeled DNA with those in forensic sample, as blood or hair, obtained from suspect

dragnet systematic police search for criminal

evidence facts or objects leading to apprehension of suspect or solution of crime

facial identification system FIS; computerized method of identifying suspects

false arrest improper arrest without legal cause or due process

FBI Federal Bureau of Investigation

Federal Bureau of Investigation FBI; U.S. national police and investigative agency

finger (*vb*) *Slang.* identify someone as a suspect; inform on someone

fingerprints inked impression of lines on tips of fingers, used in identification of suspect

fink *Slang.* informer

first degree designation for police procedure involving initial arrest of suspect

FIS facial identification system

forensics investigative procedures used in deciding legal matters; scientific examination of evidence for use in criminal case

frisk police search of person believed to be carrying concealed weapon or stolen or illegal goods, usu. by patting suspect's clothing

fuzz *Slang.* police

gendarme police officer, esp. in France

get small *Slang.* evade arrest and flee

G-man government man; law enforcement officer

handcuffs metal bands that lock around wrists, used to restrain hands of prisoner or suspect

hawkshaw detective

heat *Slang.* police

informer person giving information on crime to police; fink; stool pigeon

K-9 corps dogs used in law enforcement

lead clue aiding in apprehension of suspect

lie detector polygraph

lineup technique in which victim or witness is asked to identify suspect from several people standing in line

Mace *Trademark.* nonlethal chemical spray used to temporarily incapacitate or subdue a person

manhunt intense police search for suspect or fugitive

marshal federal judicial officer who performs duties of sheriff; police officer

Miranda rule law requiring that police inform persons being detained or interrogated of their constitutional rights

MO modus operandi

modus operandi *Latin.* mode of operating; characteristic procedure followed by habitual criminal, useful in detection; MO

most wanted list FBI's roster of criminals with highest priority for arrest

moulage taking of plaster impression as evidence in criminal investigation

MP military police

mug shot *Slang.* photo taken of suspect in custody and filed for future reference

nab *Informal.* catch and arrest suspect

narc *Slang.* narcotics law enforcement officer

night stick policeman's billy club

paddy wagon *Informal.* police van for transporting arrestees

pinch (*vb*) *Slang.* arrest

police governmental organization concerned with maintaining public order and safety, enforcing laws, and apprehending criminal suspects

policeman member of a police force, esp. male; *Slang* or *Informal:* badge, bobby, cop, fuzz, heat, the man

police officer member of a police force

polygraph machine registering biological stress signals when subject is questioned about suspected activities; lie detector

posse group empowered by law to pursue and apprehend criminal suspect

precinct police headquarters for section of city

private detective investigator for hire, with no legal authority to make arrests; private eye

private eye *Slang.* private detective

rap *Slang.* criminal charge; (*vb*) arrest, detain

rap sheet *Slang.* record kept by law-enforcement officials of a person's arrests and convictions

roll over on (*vb*) inform on one's accomplice to help police make arrest

run in (*vb*) *Slang.* arrest suspect and bring to jail

Scotland Yard metropolitan London police

search and seizure search of person or premises by police with probable cause warrant

search warrant legal document empowering police to search premises for evidence of illegal activity

second degree designation for police procedure involving transport of suspect to jail or detention

shamus *Slang.* detective

sheriff law-enforcement officer of county or other civil subdivision of state

snitch *Informal.* informer

stakeout waiting in hiding for suspect to appear or illegal act to occur

stool pigeon *Slang.* informer; person acting as decoy to trap suspect

suspect person suspected of committing crime but not yet convicted by legal due process

sweep movement of large number of police across area where suspected crimes are occurring or criminals hiding

third degree designation for police procedure involving interrogation of suspect; brutal or unethical methods of police questioning

vice squad police unit enforcing laws against immoral acts, esp. prostitution and drugs

vigilante individual or group attempting to enforce law and punish offenders without legal authority

voiceprint method of coding human voice into electronic pattern, used for identification of suspects

warrant legal document authorizing police action

wired (*adj*) carrying a concealed microphone or recording device in order to collect evidence

Legal Procedures and Trials

acquittal act of relieving accused from charge of alleged crime; not-guilty verdict

alibi excuse intended to avert blame, esp. one in which accused person claims to have been elsewhere at time crime was committed

arraignment appearance in court for indictment on charges

attorney practitioner in court of law, trained and qualified to prosecute or defend accused persons

bail money or security deposit paid to court for release of person awaiting trial, guaranteeing

defendant will appear for trial or forfeit bail money

bail bondsman person in the business of posting for suspects bail in return for a fee, usu. ten percent of posted amount

bailiff court officer serving as messenger or usher

bar-and-grill *Slang.* criminal legal system, esp. the handing down of harsh sentences

chambers judge's private office adjoining courtroom

charges crimes of which suspect is accused

circumstantial evidence evidence that implies one fact by proving other events or circumstances suggesting it

complicity association or participation in crime

confession suspect's admission of guilt

conviction legal establishment of guilt in committing crime, usu. after trial

cop a plea *Informal.* plead guilty to lesser crime than the one that is charged

courtroom chamber in which trial takes place

custody charge and control over suspect, exercised by court and esp. by police

defendant suspect on trial in court of law

detainer writ or order for further detention of a person already in custody, sometimes from another jurisdiction

entrapment illegal method of enticing suspect into committing or revealing crime

evidence legally admissible facts or objects that help to establish guilt or innocence of defendant

exonerate (*vb*) clear of all charges or guilt

extradition transfer of criminal suspect from place of apprehension to location of legal jurisdiction

eyewitness person who actually saw a crime committed

finger (*vb*) *Slang.* identify to authorities as having committed a crime

frame (*vb*) set up innocent person to appear guilty of crime

grand jury jury with power to indict only

guilty (*adj*) justly charged with and convicted of the commission of a crime

hearsay evidence testimony given as secondhand information rather than by eyewitness

incrimination showing evidence or proof of involvement in crime

indictment formal charging with commission of crime

insanity plea seeking exoneration on basis of temporary insanity or lack of responsibility for actions

judge official overseeing courtroom proceedings and sentencing individuals convicted by jury

jump bail fail to appear in court after bail bond has been posted

jury panel of citizens sworn to pass judgment on accused

misconduct improper behavior by attorney or judge

penal code body of law dealing with punishment of crime

plaintiff filer of legal complaint against defendant

plea formal declaration of guilt or innocence by defendant

plea bargaining reduction of criminal charges in exchange for guilty plea to lesser offense

preventive detention holding a prisoner without bail or on very high bail

probable cause reasonable grounds for assuming validity of criminal charge

probation suspension of sentence, allowing convicted offender freedom based on accountability to authorities

prosecutor government official responsible for presenting case against accused

protective custody detention of person solely for his or her safety

public defender government official appointed by court to defend accused person unable to afford attorney

remand (*vb*) return accused to custody pending further action

self-defense defense of criminal act by claiming danger to accused existed at time of commission

sentence punishment handed down by judge on convicted offender

sequester (*vb*) isolate jury in private place for discussion or to pass judgment

state's evidence testimony of accomplice in crime, who becomes voluntary witness for the prosecution in return for reduced sentence

subpoena writ commanding a person to appear in court or face penalty

substantiate (*vb*) verify another's testimony; give proof

summation attorney's concluding remarks to jury

summons written notice requiring appearance in court

suspended sentence court's permission for convicted offender not to serve prison sentence

testify (*vb*) provide sworn statement in court

testimony statements by witness under oath during trial

trial legal procedure for hearing testimony, weighing evidence, deciding guilt or innocence of criminal suspect, and setting sentence

verdict decision of jury as to suspect's guilt or innocence

warrant writ issued by court, esp. to make arrest

witness person giving evidence at trial

Witness Protection Program program of U.S. government designed to insure safety or anonymity of witnesses, esp. informers

writ formal legal document or instrument

Prison and Punishment

administrative segregation placement in solitary confinement of prisoner not accused of any disciplinary infraction

amnesty pardon handed down to group or class of offenders

bastinado punishment by beating soles of feet with stick

behind bars *Informal.* imprisoned or in jail

big house *Slang.* penitentiary or prison

bilboes shackles attached to long iron bar for prisoner's feet

black hole any wretched place of imprisonment or confinement

break escape from jail or prison

brig naval prison, esp. on ship

cage prison cell

calaboose *Slang.* jail

can *Slang.* jail or prison

cangue large wooden yoke formerly fastened about neck as punishment (China)

capital punishment sentence of death; death penalty

captive prisoner

cat-o'-nine-tails whip of nine knotted cords attached to handle, used for flogging

cell small room in which prisoner is held or lives

cellblock prison unit consisting of a number of cells

chain gang group of convicts chained together, esp. when doing manual labor outside

chair *Informal.* electric chair

city hotel *Slang.* jail

clemency mercy shown to prisoner by authorities

clink *Slang.* jail or prison

commitment sentencing of criminal to prison term

commute (*vb*) reduce sentence

con *Informal.* convict

concentration camp enforced labor and execution center, esp. one run by Nazis in World War II

condemned (*adj*) sentenced, esp. to death

confinement imprisonment

conjugal visit private visitation privilege extended to prisoner for exercise of conjugal rights with his or her spouse

convict person found guilty of crime serving time in prison; con

cooler *Slang.* jail

coop *Slang.* prison

correctional institution prison or penal colony for long-term incarceration

count census of prisoner, during which all other prison activity halts

county jail local center for short-term incarceration of persons awaiting trial or sentencing or convicted of minor offenses

death penalty capital punishment

death row area in prison housing convicts sentenced to death

debtor's prison prison in which debtors were formerly held until able to pay debts

detention facility jail, camp, or hall for inmates awaiting trial or sentencing and for aliens awaiting deportation

dime *Slang.* ten-year prison sentence

do time *Slang.* serve a sentence

drunk tank *Informal.* city jail cell in which persons arrested for public drunkenness, and other arrestees, are held overnight

dungeon prison, esp. dark and forbidding one

electric chair seat in which condemned prisoner is strapped for electrocution

electrocution execution by electric charge

ex-con *Informal.* former convict, now released from prison

execution putting to death of person convicted of crime, usu. by electrocution, gas chamber, firing squad, hanging, injection, or guillotine

executioner prison officer charged with carrying out execution

false imprisonment illegal confinement of someone against his or her will and without cause

firing squad group of soldiers who execute prisoners by simultaneously shooting them

fish *Slang.* new prisoner

flogging whipping as punishment

gas chamber airtight prison room in which execution by poison gas takes place

gibbet upright post with projecting arm at top for hanging bodies of executed criminals as warning

guillotine instrument for execution by beheading, in which a heavy blade is dropped between two grooved uprights

hack *Slang.* prison guard

hanging execution by strangulation or breaking of neck, usu. by suspending prisoner from rope tied around his or her neck

hangman public executioner who administers hangings

hitch prison term

holding cell prisoners' temporary place of confinement

hole solitary confinement

house arrest confinement under guard in one's normal living quarters instead of prison

house of correction place of confinement and reform for criminals convicted of minor offenses

house of detention place of confinement for alleged criminals awaiting trial, and sometimes for witnesses

incarceration imprisonment

injection execution by injection of toxic substance

inmate prisoner

inside (*adv*) *Slang.* in prison

jacket *Slang.* prisoner's file or arrest record; prisoner's reputation

Jack Ketch *Brit. slang.* official hangman

jail building for short-term confinement of prisoners and those accused of crimes; county jail; *Slang.* calaboose, can, city hotel, clink, cooler, jug, poky; also, *esp. Brit.,* gaol

jailbird inmate, esp. longtime or repeat inmate

jailer official overseeing jail operations and guarding prisoners; turnkey; warder

jailhouse lawyer prisoner who does legal

research and writing for others while serving time

joint *Slang.* usu. **the joint**; prison

jug *Slang.* jail

keeper jailer, prison guard

kite *Slang.* note passed from one cell to another

knout (*vb*) flog

lam *Slang.* escape from prison or flight to evade authorities

lifer *Slang.* prisoner sentenced to life term

life sentence prison term lasting for entire life span

lockdown confinement of all prisoners to their cells

lynching illegal execution of suspect, usu. hanging by mob

man *Slang.* usu **the Man**; police officer or prison guard

maximum-security prison heavily guarded prison housing prisoners with long sentences and dangerous or hardened criminals

medium-security prison prison with moderate security, less than maximum and more than minimum

minimum-security prison moderately guarded or unguarded prison, such as a work farm, housing white-collar and less serious offenders and those serving short sentences or nearing release

mittimus warrant of commitment to prison

mule *Slang.* person who smuggles contraband, esp. into jail or prison

nickel *Slang.* five-year prison sentence

on ice *Slang.* imprisoned, esp. in solitary confinement

oubliette concealed dungeon with trapdoor in its ceiling

pardon official cancellation of sentence or punishment for crime

parole release from prison before full sentence has been served

parolee prisoner who has been set free but must maintain contact with authorities

pen *Informal.* penitentiary

penal (*adj*) pertaining to or constituting legal punishment

penal colony prison, esp. one in isolated area

penal institution jail, reformatory, or prison

penitentiary maximum-security prison, esp. one maintained by a state or the U.S. government for serious offenders

pillory wood frame used to restrain head and hands as punishment

poky *Slang.* jail

political prisoner person deemed politically dangerous by state and falsely imprisoned for supposed crimes

population prisoners who are not in segregation and are allowed to mix with others

POW prisoner of war

prison state or federal institution for long-term confinement of convicts, usu. felons; *Slang.* big house, can, clink, coop, joint, slammer, stir

prisoner person accused or convicted of crime and held in jail or prison; captive; inmate
prisoner of war POW; person held captive by enemy during wartime
prison riot violent outburst by prisoners against prison conditions
probation suspension of prison sentence on guarantee of good behavior and regular reporting to authorities
protective custody administrative segregation of prisoner deemed in danger if allowed to mix with other prisoners
punishment penalty imposed by legal system on convicted offender
punk Slang. male prisoner coerced into sexually passive or submissive homosexual role
quarter Slang. twenty-five-year prison sentence
rack torture device in which victim's body is bound to frame and stretched
rat Slang. (n) informer; (vb) inform on
recidivism repetition of, or chronic engagement in, criminal acts; return to confinement for any reason, including technical parole violations
reformatory penal institution for reform and rehabilitation of young offenders, esp. minors; reform school
reform school reformatory
rehabilitation preparation of prisoners for reentry into society by eliminating criminal impulses
reprieve delay in execution of sentence
segregation locked-down housing apart from other prisoners, usu. in solitary, either disciplinary or administrative
sentence punishment determined by law
serve time pass time of sentence in prison
shakedown search of prisoner or prison cell, undertaken by guards, esp. for contraband or weapons
short time Informal. period of sentence just prior to prisoner's release; brief sentence
slammer Slang. prison
solitary confinement holding of prisoner alone in isolated cell for extended period
stir Slang. prison
stockade military prison
stocks heavy wooden frame with holes for confining ankles and wrists, formerly used for punishment
street Slang. usu. **the street**; world outside confinement
tank Slang. prison or jail cell for more than one prisoner, usu. temporary holding cell
tar and feather cover offender's body with hot tar and feathers as punishment, usu. by mob action
time prison sentence
torture cruel and unusual punishment, esp. infliction of extreme pain
trusty well-behaved and trustworthy prisoner given special privileges and responsibilities, often having power over other prisoners
turnkey jailer
up the river Slang. serving time in prison

violate (vb) Slang. return to incarceration as a parole violator
warden prison administrator
warder jailer
ward of the state minor or incompetent person under protection or custody of court
water torture punishment in which water is dripped slowly onto victim's forehead
whipping punishment by flogging with whip
work camp work farm
work farm minimum-security prison in which inmates are allowed out of their cells to work, esp. outdoors; work camp
yard enclosed outdoor area for exercise of inmates, where prisoners can mingle
yardbird Slang. convict or prisoner
yard hack Slang. guard in prison yard

VIOLENCE

Violent Events
Fights
Attacks
Violent Actions
Violent Persons

See also: Chap. 5: Weapons and Armaments; Chap. 11: War and Military; Chap. 22: Strategy, Intrigue, and Deception; Chap. 24: Mental Disturbances; Crime; Chap. 25: Magic and the Occult

---

Violent Events

annihilation total destruction; extinction
atrocity cruel, inhumane act
barbarity brutal or inhuman conduct; cruelty
bastinado beating with stick or cudgel
bedlam place or occasion of uproar and commotion
bloodbath violently gory conflict
bloodshed slaughter; taking of life, as in war or murder
brouhaha uproar
brutality savagery; cruel or harsh treatment
butchery brutal, heartless killing
carnage large-scale destruction of life
collision violent meeting of opposites; striking or crashing together
commotion agitated or disturbed activity; fray; tumult
conflagration extensive, extremely destructive fire
contest conflict, fight, or struggle for victory over opponent; altercation
coup de grâce French. lit. blow of mercy; deathblow; final, decisive stroke
deathblow coup de grâce
decimation large-scale destruction
demolition act of destruction
despoilment forceful, violent deprivation or destruction of goods or property
destruction tearing down or totally eliminating something
devastation total destruction; laying waste

disturbance outbreak of public disorder; disruption of the peace
explosion sudden, violent expansion or outburst, esp. involving combustion and loud noise, as with explosive material
extinction annihilation
fight physical conflict between opponents
furor rage or frenzy of activity or feeling
fury anger, rage, or wrath
fuss tumult, or small disturbance; a quarrel over something trivial
havoc ruinous destruction or devastation; chaos
holocaust destruction or sacrifice, esp. of human life on grand scale
inferno hellishly violent conflagration
internecine (adj) mutually destructive, esp. due to conflict within a group
massacre indiscriminate mass killing; widespread butchery
mass murder large-scale killing; slaughter
mayhem maiming or disfiguring of another person; random or deliberate violence
monstrosity very large-scale, severe, shocking event
outbreak sudden instance of violence
outburst sudden expression of violent emotion or action
outrage instance of violent brutality
paroxysm convulsive and uncontrollable seizure; fit of violent action or emotion
rage intense, uncontrollable anger
reign of terror period of violence and fear; situation of ruthless oppression
revolt violent attempt to overthrow established authority
rhubarb Slang. argument or conflict
riot violent disruption of public order or peace; uproar
ruin destruction by defeat or decay
savagery barbarity or cruelty
shambles place of slaughter or wreckage
slaughter ruthless killing, esp. in large numbers
spoliation robbery and plunder, esp. during war
Sunday punch knockout punch; one's most powerful blow
tumult violent and noisy disturbance; commotion
upheaval widespread social unrest or agitation
uproar disturbance or tumult; outbreak of chaos; brouhaha
violence exertion of rough physical force to injure or abuse
war organized, armed conflict between nations
wrack and ruin state of destruction or wreckage
wreckage remains of something after a violent event resulting in extensive damage to it

Fights

altercation dispute; contest
argument dispute between proponents of opposing views
battle conflict between soldiers or armies

Violence

battle royal battle distinguished by great valor and bloodshed
brawl noisy fight or quarrel
broil quarrel, dispute, noisy argument or fight
clash hostile meeting of opponents; conflict
combat fight, esp. armed military encounter; fray
conflict fight or struggle between enemies
contention struggling or striving together in a contest; rivalry
contest conflict, fight; struggle for victory over an opponent; altercation
contretemps inopportune occurrence; dispute
dispute combat or controversy over a difference of opinion; altercation; contretemps; quarrel
dogfight rough physical fight
donnybrook riotous event with uncontrolled fighting
duel fight between two persons, esp. with witnesses and rules of conduct
duke it out fight, esp. with fists; do battle
feud protracted hostility between two parties, with alternate strikes against each other
fight physical conflict between opponents
fisticuffs striking with the fists
flap noisy argument
fracas noisy fight or brawl
fray combat, fight; commotion; contest
free-for-all wild and uncontrolled fight with many participants
go to the mat engage in physical struggle, as in wrestling
gunfight fight between opponents armed with pistols or rifles; shootout
hammer and tongs vigorously, with great violence or force
horseplay playful fighting
infighting battle at close quarters
joust contest between knights mounted on horseback and armed with lances
knock-down-drag-out (*adj*) describing esp. violent and prolonged fight
melee confusing crush of battling opponents
mix-up fight or brawl
quarrel angry disagreement; dispute
roughhouse (*vb*) engage in playful, boisterous fighting
row noisy quarrel; abusive, quarrelsome dispute
ruckus noisy commotion; fracas; rumpus
rumble *Slang.* battle between two groups or gangs
rumpus noisy disturbance; ruckus
run-in unexpected, violent encounter
scrap *Informal.* fight, usu. casual or brief
scrape fight or quarrel
scuffle confused, disordered fight; tussle
set-to brief, sharp fight or argument
shootout gunfight
shoving match fight conducted by rough pushing
skirmish light, brief conflict
spat petty quarrel
squabble noisy dispute or brawl
strife contest; fight

struggle difficult, exhausting fight, often prolonged
tiff small, angry outburst; petty quarrel; spat
tussle physical contest between opponents
vendetta prolonged feud involving killing for revenge
war sustained, widespread conflict, esp. between nations or peoples, with heavily armed and equipped soldiers

Attacks

accost (*vb*) approach in challenging manner
aggravated assault severe attack
ambush surprise attack by concealed force
assail (*vb*) attack vigorously or violently; assault
assault sudden attack or invasion; physical attack on a person; (*vb*) assail; attack
attack (*vb*) set upon in a forceful, aggressive, violent manner; begin hostilities against; (*n*) hostile and aggressive action; assault
battery physical beating of a person
blitz lightning quick, all-out attack
blow sudden, hard stroke with hand or weapon
bombard (*vb*) attack with projectiles or bombs
breathe down someone's neck chase menacingly and begin to overtake
charge (*vb*) rush at or advance aggressively
cheap shot attack from blind side or at weakest point
close in on (*vb*) surround; gain ground on
crowd (*vb*) close in on or press against
foray raid, esp. for booty in war
go at (*vb*) advance aggressively on an opponent
harass (*vb*) badger or persecute repeatedly
harry (*vb*) raid, invade, harass, or torment
have at (*vb*) make hostile advance upon
intrusion entry without permission or invitation; invasion
inundate (*vb*) overcome by superior force
invasion forceful or hostile intrusion, infringement, or entry, esp. by an army
lash out (*vb*) strike or kick suddenly and aggressively
light into (*vb*) *Informal.* attack suddenly and vigorously
lunge (*vb*) thrust or plunge forward
noogie *Slang.* light, often playful blow, esp. to the head, struck with extended knuckle of curled-up second or third finger
onrush strong forward rush or movement
onslaught vigorous, powerful attack
pay back (*vb*) retaliate against or punish
pillage robbery or plunder, usu. in war; rapine
raid sudden invasion, esp. by surprise
rapine pillage
sneak attack surprise attack, esp. by hidden forces
start something *Informal.* pick a fight
storm (*vb*) attack with overwhelming force
strafe (*vb*) attack with machine-gun fire from the air
strike (*vb*) hit with force; (*n*) sudden attack
swing at (*vb*) aim blow at an opponent

thrust at (*vb*) move aggressively toward an opponent
tilt (*vb*) charge at an opponent

Violent Actions

abuse do wrongful harm to someone; maltreat
accost approach forcibly
act up behave uncontrollably and unpleasantly
afflict inflict injury or distress
annihilate destroy completely, make extinct
annoy harass repeatedly in quick attacks
antagonize provoke; act in hostile manner
avenge exact satisfaction for a wrong
batter beat repeatedly
beat up strike forcefully with hands or weapon
belt hit, often with a belt or strap
blast ruin, destroy; afflict with blight
blight ruin; cause to wither or decay
blow off steam *Informal.* forcefully vent strong feelings
blow one's top *Informal.* explode with anger
blow up *Informal.* lose one's temper
bludgeon hit with a clublike weapon
boil over lose one's temper
bomb drop bombs on; bombard; shell
bombard bomb
bop *Slang.* hit over the head
bother purposefully annoy or irritate
brain *Slang.* hit over the head, dash out opponent's brains
brandish wave a weapon menacingly
brawl argue noisily
break smash or split violently into pieces
broadside hit from side
browbeat intimidate
brutalize treat cruelly
buffet hit with hand or fist; cuff repeatedly
bug *Slang.* bother, annoy
bulldoze overpower with intimidating force
bully intimidate
burn set fire to; incinerate
burst break apart with sudden violence
bust *Informal.* hit or break
butcher chop up or kill brutally
butt strike with head
cane strike with thin stick
chafe rub against so as to wear away
choke strangle by applying pressure around neck
chop cut up with knife
churn shake violently, stir up
clap hit across back
claw strike or tear with something sharp or pointed, esp. fingernails
clobber strike hard blow
clout strike
club hit with heavy weapon
coerce compel by force
collar seize by neck
come to blows engage in physical fight
commandeer seize arbitrarily, often for military or public use
confront face an enemy; provoke hostile encounter

conquer take by force, defeat opponent
consume destroy completely, esp. by fire
countervail exert equal force against
crack strike so as to break open
crash collide violently, shatter or break in pieces
cream *Slang.* defeat decisively in a fight
crucify execute by crucifixion; defeat utterly
crunch grind or press with crunching sound; step on
crush squeeze or press until damaged or destroyed; oppress
cudgel beat with heavy stick
cuff strike with one's hand; slap
cut penetrate, divide, or detach with a sharp-edged instrument
cut up damage or injure, esp. by lacerations; slice into pieces
damage cause injury to; impair
dash hurl or throw forcefully
decimate destroy a significant portion of, orig. every tenth person
deck *Informal.* strike forcefully to the ground
defeat overcome, esp. in battle
defile pollute
demolish destroy, ruin, or take apart
dent make a depression or hollow in something
depopulate destroy or reduce the number of inhabitants of
deracinate uproot from home or native culture
desecrate treat without respect
despoil plunder or ravage
destroy ruin, demolish, or exterminate; reduce to fragments or useless form
devastate lay waste; destroy utterly
devour destroy by consuming
disembowel eviscerate
dismantle take apart
dismember cut limb from limb
do mischief commit intentional harm
drill bore a hole in; hit dead on
drub cudgel; defeat soundly in battle
drum hit repeatedly
embroil engage in battle
eradicate wipe out
erupt burst out, break into rage or anger
eviscerate remove innards of; disembowel; gut
explode burst violently
expunge obliterate
exterminate destroy completely, annihilate
extirpate root out, eradicate, or expel
fell cause to fall, knock down; kill
fire cause to burn; shoot a gun
flail beat, esp. with free-swinging stick attached to handle
flay skin, strip off surface
flog whip
fly at rush, attack
force coerce, impose, or take violently
fracture break, crack
fragment break into parts
gash cut deeply
gnash grind
gouge force or scoop out, esp. an eye

grapple fight closely; seize and hold opponent in physical contest
graze strike glancing blow upon
grind wear down to powder or fragments; gnash
gut eviscerate
hack chop up, mangle
hammer strike or beat heavily
have it out engage in a fight
hew cut or strike forcibly with ax
hit strike, knock, or deliver blow to
horsewhip flog with whip
hurt wound, cause pain or injury
impair damage, harm, or injure
impale pierce with sharp stick or rod
impinge collide with or strike
implode burst inward
incinerate burn
infect contaminate or pollute with disease
injure harm or damage
intimidate frighten with threats of harm; browbeat; bully
invade make an assault on; enter forcefully and with hostility
irritate provoke, annoy; attack sore spot
irrupt violently burst or break in
jab poke, punch
jar conflict or clash; shake
jolt shake roughly, knock
jump on leap upon in attack
kayo *Slang.* knock out
kick strike with foot
kick ass *Vulgar slang.* defeat opponent soundly and forcefully to gain desired result
kick butt *Vulgar slang.* kick ass
kill take another's life by violence
knee jab with knee
knife strike or attack with blade
knock hit; make a striking blow
knock out KO; strike hard to render unconscious; kayo
knuckle press or strike with knuckles or fists
KO knock out
lacerate tear or cut
lash strike suddenly, esp. with a whip
lather *Informal.* beat or whip severely
lay low knock down, beat
level demolish completely, raze to the ground
lick hit repeatedly, defeat in fight
liquidate eliminate opponents, esp. by killing
loot rob, plunder
lop off cut off
maim disfigure, mutilate
maltreat abuse
mangle mutilate, injure
manhandle treat roughly
mar injure, damage
maraud plunder, raid
mash smash, reduce to pulp
maul beat up, injure
mess up dishevel, disarrange
mistreat abuse
mob attack in group
molest bother, intrude on, or interfere with; attack sexually

mug attack and rob in public place
mutilate damage, esp. by cutting off a body part
nab *Informal.* seize
nail *Slang.* hit; *Informal.* seize
nettle irritate, sting, or provoke
nip sever, bite off, or snap at
nuke *Informal.* obliterate with or as if by nuclear weapon
obliterate destroy completely, erase; expunge
off *Slang.* kill
oppress master by superior force; control through intimidation or by force
oust forcibly eject, drive out
overpower overcome by superior force
overrun trample, run over, or overwhelm
overwhelm oppress or overpower
paste *Slang.* hit or smack hard, esp. on the face
paw *Informal.* handle roughly
pelt strike repeatedly
pepper assault or hit repeatedly with small blows
persecute harass, oppress
pestle grind or pulverize
pick a fight incite another into conflict
pierce penetrate sharply, as if by stabbing
pillage plunder or rob
pinch squeeze or compress tightly and painfully
pistol-whip strike repeatedly with gun
plague torment; infest
plaster *Informal.* strike hard; defeat decisively
plow under force out of existence; overpower
plunk *Informal.* strike; hit with a ball or other object
poison harm or kill with poisonous substance
poke thrust, intrude
pollute poison, taint, or make foul
pound batter or hammer
powder beat into small pieces; pulverize
prod jab or poke, with or as if with pointed object
pulverize reduce to fragments
pummel beat or pound
pump strike rapidly and repeatedly
punch strike with fist; sock
punch out *Slang.* beat up or knock out with one's fists
puncture pierce with pointed object
punish injure in retaliation; do severe harm to
push thrust or press forcefully
push around shove from place; bully
quash suppress, subdue
rabbit punch (*n*) quick, sharp blow to neck or base of skull
rack torture or torment; stretch body of another on rack
rage show or proceed with violent anger
raid invade or attack suddenly
ram batter; strike with great force
rampage act wildly and recklessly
ransack plunder, search for booty
rap hit with sharp blow
rape seize or plunder; assault sexually
ravage devastate, plunder
raven seize violently; devour

raze tear down or demolish

ream *Informal.* batter, esp. by stretching apart

rend tear apart, split; rive

retaliate injure someone in return for injury inflicted

riddle attack repeatedly, esp. with bullets

riot disturb the peace or public order

rip tear, cut

rive rend

rock knock backwards with a blow

rough up abuse; handle harshly

rout set to flight, drive from place

rub abrade

ruin destroy, wreck

run amok behave wildly, with uncontrollable violence

rupture tear apart, break open

rush assault

sack plunder or loot

sail into *Informal.* assault vigorously

savage attack in a ferocious, barbarous way

scald burn, esp. with boiling liquid

scalp cut or pull skin from skull of

scar cut and disfigure; wound permanently

scathe damage or harm as if by scorching

scorch parch or shrivel with heat

screw twist into strained position; abuse

sear burn or char surface of

seize grasp forcefully, confiscate; nab; nail

set upon attack suddenly

shatter break into fragments; destroy violently

shed blood engage in savage, bloody fighting

shell bomb

shellac *Slang.* beat soundly

shoot hit with a bullet or arrow

shove push roughly

shred tear into strips

sic attack (used esp. to incite dog upon victim)

sideswipe strike along side with glancing blow

sink destroy by submerging

skewer pierce with sharp object

slam strike or shove forcefully

slap strike with open hand; cuff

slash cut or gash, esp. with sharp blade

slay destroy, esp. kill by violence

slice cut

slit cut to strips; make long, narrow slice in

slug *Informal.* hit hard with fist

smack strike with loud sound

smash crush, shatter, or break up

smite strike hard with hand or weapon; strike down or slay

smother stifle; suffocate

snip cut to bits, clip

snipe shoot at from a distance

sock *Slang.* punch

spank beat on buttocks

spike pierce with pointed object

spill blood fight so as to cause bleeding

splinter break or split into long, narrow pieces

split tear apart, divide forcefully

squash mash or crush; suppress

squeeze apply pressure to

squelch crush down; suppress or stamp out

squish squash or squeeze

stab puncture with knife or sharp object

stamp beat upon with foot; crush or pound

stave break a hole in; splinter or smash

steamroller flatten in a fight; roll over an opponent with superior force

stick pierce with pointed object

sting pierce or wound with poison

stomp stamp or step on heavily

stone hit repeatedly with rocks, esp. to kill

storm attack suddenly with superior force

strafe attack with machine-gun fire from the air

strangle suffocate or choke by squeezing around neck

strike hit with one's fist or an object; clout

strong-arm use violence or intimidation to persuade

stun daze or deaden with blow

subdue beat into submission

subject bring under domination, force to submit

suffocate (n) choke; smother

sunder rend, split, or break apart

swamp overwhelm by submerging; sink

swat strike or hit

take on oppose (another); entice (someone) to fight

tap hit lightly

tear rip, split, or pull apart

thrash beat or flog

thresh thrash, beat, or cut up

throttle choke or strangle

thump beat or pound; *Informal.* thrash severely

thwack strike or hit with something flat

tilt cause to fall over; upset the balance of

torment torture

torture cause extreme pain to, inflict suffering on; torment

trample crush under one's feet

trash *Informal.* lay waste, ruin, or vandalize

trim *Informal.* administer beating to

trounce beat soundly

tussle scuffle; struggle at close range

tweak pinch and pull with a twist or jerk

twist wrench and turn with rotary motion

tyrannize oppress, intimidate

vandalize destroy or desecrate property with malicious intent

vanquish conquer or defeat in battle

violate ravish, rape; mistreat

wallop beat soundly; *Informal.* hit hard

waste devastate or totally demolish; *Slang.* murder

whack strike with solid blow

whale strike soundly; beat on repeatedly

wham hit hard

whip strike with a lash, flog; defeat decisively

whomp *Informal.* inflict loud, heavy blow or slap

whop *Informal.* strike forcibly

whump thump

whup regional variation of *whip*; beat or defeat decisively

work evil cause damage or injury, esp. by immoral or wicked means

work over *Informal.* beat up; hit repeatedly

wrack wreck, destroy

wreak inflict or exact punishment, injury, or vengeance

wreak havoc cause destruction or chaos

wreck ruin, destroy

wrench twist or pull sharply

wrest wrench or seize violently

wring twist (another's neck) with the hands

yank pull sharply

zap *Informal.* strike or stun with sharp blow

zonk *Slang.* knock out; strike soundly

Violent Persons

aggressor initiator of unprovoked attack

agitator one who incites others to violence; firebrand

anarchist one who resists all authority, esp. by terrorism

animal brutish person

annihilator one who utterly destroys

arsonist one who sets things on fire; incendiary

assailant attacker

assassin murderer, esp. the fanatical or hired killer of a politically prominent person

attacker one who uses force to harm others or start a fight; assailant

barbarian cruel, uncivilized brute, Goth

beast brutal, animallike person

berserker frenzied and ferocious warrior of Norse legend

bomber one who sets off explosions

brute savage, cruel, unfeeling person

bully blustering, overbearing person who terrorizes weaker people

butcher brutal or indiscriminate killer

cannibal person who eats human flesh

cutthroat merciless murderer, esp. one who cuts throats

destroyer one who crushes, kills, and totally wipes out opponents; exterminator

devil cruel, evil, remorseless person

dynamitard political terrorist who uses dynamite

exterminator destroyer

fiend cunningly evil person; hellhound

firebrand agitator

fire-eater angry person always ready to attack others

fury raging, vengeful person

goon *Informal.* hoodlum or thug, esp. one hired to attack others

gorilla *Slang.* large, brutish, animallike person

Goth barbarian

hard-nose *Slang.* tough, obstinate person

hellcat evil, vengeful woman

hellhound fiend

hellion *Informal.* mischievous troublemaker
hell-raiser *Informal.* one who stirs up trouble
henchman person hired to perform violent acts for another
hijacker terrorist who commandeers planes and other vehicles
holy terror *Informal.* uncontrollable troublemaker
hood *Slang.* hoodlum
hoodlum tough, young street ruffian, esp. member of lawless gang; hooligan
hooligan hoodlum
hothead person easily aroused to anger or attack; hotspur
hotspur hothead
Hun savage barbarian
incendiary arsonist
invader one who attacks another's territory
killer murderer
knave unprincipled, untrustworthy, or dishonest person; rascal
mad dog *Slang.* vicious, uncontrollable person
maniac wildly insane person
monster cruel, vicious person
mugger one who assaults others with intent to rob
murderer one who takes another's life; killer
predator one who lives by plunder and robbery
raider one who suddenly attacks or invades
rapist one who forces another to have sexual intercourse
rascal mischievous troublemaker; knave; rogue
rogue rascal; scoundrel
rough *Chiefly Brit.* ruffian
roughneck crude, rowdy person
rowdy rough, disorderly, quarrelsome person
ruffian brutal, lawless person, esp. hoodlum; rough; tough
savage ferocious, brutal, beastly person; rogue
scoundrel wicked, disreputable person; rogue
she-wolf evil, vicious, predatory woman
slasher one who attacks with knife or blade
spitfire easily-angered person, esp. woman
terminator cold-blooded killer, esp. one for hire
terror *Informal.* wildly uncontrollable person
terrorist one who uses force, often random, to intimidate or gain political ends
thug brutal hoodlum, thief, or murderer, esp. gang member
tiger fiercely belligerent person
tigress ferocious woman
tinderbox highly excitable or inflammable person who is potential source of widespread violence
tough ruffian
troublemaker one who agitates or incites others to quarrel
vandal malicious, destructive person
villain wicked person, criminal
virago quarrelsome, foul-tempered woman
vixen ill-tempered, evil woman
warrior person with fighting spirit
witch evil, devilish person, esp. a woman, who professes to have supernatural powers
wolf fierce, cruel person

DEATH

Dead or Dying
Unnatural Deaths
Murder and Suicide
Dead Bodies
Burial and Funerals
Beyond the Grave
Language of Death

See also: *Chap. 1: Medical Problems; Chap. 24: Crime; Chap. 25: Magic and the Occult; Eschatology*

Dead or Dying

asleep *(adj)* dead; into the state of death
at peace *(adj)* dead
bite the dust die
buy the farm *Slang.* die or be killed
cash in one's chips *Slang.* die
casualty person killed in war or accident
croak *(vb) Slang.* die
dead *(adj)* no longer living; *(n)* **the dead**; dead persons collectively
death act of dying; total and permanent cessation of life
deceased *(adj)* dead
demise death
departed *(adj)* dead
die *(vb)* experience death; cease living
DOA dead on arrival; term used to indicate person was dead on arrival at hospital
done for *Informal.* dead or close to death
done in *Informal.* dead, esp. from unnatural causes
drop dead *Informal.* die suddenly
dying *(adj)* about to die; approaching death
eclipsed *(adj)* having died
eighty-sixed *(adj) Slang.* dead, esp. killed
elapsed *(adj)* having died
end death
expire *(vb)* die, esp. after prolonged disease
extinct *(adj)* no longer living, esp. of a species
fatality person who has died, esp. in accident, war, or crime
final rest death
final sleep death
goner *Informal.* one who is dead or about to die
gone to Davy Jones's locker *Slang.* dead, esp. at sea
have one foot in the grave be dying
iced *(adj) Slang.* dead, esp. from unnatural causes
in extremis *(adj)* at the point of death
kick in *(vb) Slang.* die
kick off *(vb) Slang.* die
kick the bucket *Slang.* die
late *(adj)* recently deceased, used as reference with person's name
lost *(adj)* dead
meet one's Maker die
moribund *(adj)* dying, about to die
mortal living being who must eventually die; *(adj)* causing or liable to cause death
on ice *Slang.* dead
pass away *(vb)* die

---

pass on *(vb)* die
perish *(vb)* die, esp. in violent or untimely manner
pop off *(vb) Informal.* die, esp. suddenly
rest state of death
six feet under *Slang.* dead and buried
sleep state of death
succumb *(vb)* die, esp. from disease
terminal *(adj)* dying, esp. from fatal illness
waste away *(vb)* die slowly from disease
wither and die degenerate from disease until death

Unnatural Deaths

asphyxiation death by lack of oxygen or from breathing obstruction; smothering; suffocation
beheading executive by decapitation
Black Death bubonic plague
brain death cessation of brain activity, indicated by flat EEG reading
buried alive asphyxiated beneath the ground
burn *(vb) Slang.* die in the electric chair
choking windpipe obstruction by physical pressure or due to breathing of poisoned air
crucifixion nailing of hands and feet to cross
decapitation removal of head from neck
disease fatal wasting or impairment of body function
electrocution death by electric shock
evisceration death by disembowelment
execution putting to death as legal punishment for crime
fatal illness disease that results in death
firing squad execution by several rifles fired at once
gallows structure for hanging by the neck
guillotine structure with large blade for decapitation
hanging execution by strangulation or breaking of neck in suspended noose wrapped around neck
immolation death by fire
murder unlawful taking of another's life with malicious intent
natural causes old age, infirmity, or general debility
noose loop of rope for hanging
OD overdose
old age general infirmity resulting from aging
overdose OD; ingestion of toxic amount of drug
pestilence devastating epidemic of contagious disease
poisoning ingestion of a toxic substance
sacrifice being offered to deity as victim
smothering being deprived of air or overcome by smoke or fumes; asphyxiation
stake wood post to which person is tied and burned
starvation total deprivation of food
stoning being beaten by thrown stones
strangulation stoppage of breath by compression of throat

suffocation being deprived of oxygen or prevented from breathing; asphyxiation
suicide taking of one's own life
vaporization dissipation into small particles due to pressure or molecular disturbance
widdy *Scottish.* hangman's noose

Murder and Suicide

assassination murder of a public figure
bloodshed taking of life; slaughter
blow away (*vb*) *Slang.* murder
bump off (*vb*) *Slang.* murder
butcher (*vb*) slaughter or kill in a barbarous or indiscriminate manner
carnage bloody slaughter of large numbers of people; massacre
chill (*vb*) *Slang.* murder
-cide suffix meaning killer or killing of
contract *Slang.* agreement to commit murder for payment
disembowelment evisceration; removal of the bowels or entrails
dispatch (*vb*) murder deftly; eliminate quickly
dispose of (*vb*) murder or eliminate
do away with (*vb*) murder
do in (*vb*) *Informal.* murder
dust (*vb*) *Slang.* murder
euthanasia merciful, painless killing of hopelessly sick person; mercy killing
extermination complete and immediate elimination by killing
felo-de-se one who kills himself or herself or dies as a result of committing an unlawful malicious act
fratricide killing one's brother
garrote method of strangulation in which iron collar is tightened around neck
genocide killing of entire race or nation
grease (*vb*) *Slang.* murder
hara-kiri ritual suicide by disembowelment; seppuku (Japan)
hecatomb sacrifice or slaughter of numerous victims
hit *Slang.* murder by hire, esp. by organized crime
hit list *Slang.* list of those contracted to be murdered
hit man *Slang.* hired murderer, esp. by organized crime
holocaust genocide, esp. of Jews by Nazis in World War II
homicide taking another's life with malicious intent; murder
ice (*vb*) *Slang.* murder
infanticide killing a baby
kill (*vb*) take another person's life by violence
knock off *Slang.* murder
liquidate (*vb*) eliminate by killing
lynching execution, usu. hanging, by mob without legal sanction
manslaughter accidental murder without malicious intent
martyrdom self-sacrifice for the sake of some principle or cause

massacre indiscriminate, ruthless killing of numerous, often helpless persons
mass murder murder of numerous individuals, usu. by one person
matricide killing one's mother
mercy killing euthanasia
murder unlawful taking of another's life with malicious intent; (*vb*) commit an act of murder; *Slang.* blow away, bump off, chill, dispatch, dispose of, do away with, do in, dust, grease, knock off, off, rub out, snuff out, stretch out, whack, waste, wax, zap
off (*vb*) *Slang.* murder
parricide killing one's parent or close relative
patricide killing one's father
pogrom organized massacre of a minority people, esp. Jews
poisoning secret administering of toxic substance to cause another's death
purge elimination of undesirable elements in group or society
regicide killing one's king or queen
ritual murder killing by group in ceremonial rite
ritual suicide killing oneself in a prescribed manner
rub out (*vb*) *Slang.* murder, often by organized crime
sacrifice taking victim's life as religious offering
self-immolation burning oneself to death
self-slaughter suicide
seppuku hara-kiri
serial killing murder of one victim after another over time by same killer
shooting killing by gunshot
slaughter brutal or violent killing of single person or large numbers of people
slay (*vb*) murder
snuff out (*vb*) *Informal.* murder
strangulation killing by choking or cutting off air supply
stretch out (*vb*) *Slang.* murder
suffocation killing by smothering or strangulation
suicide taking one's own life; self-slaughter
suicide pact agreement between two people to commit suicide simultaneously
waste (*vb*) *Slang.* murder
wax (*vb*) *Slang.* murder
whack (*vb*) *Slang.* murder
wrist-slitting killing oneself by cutting arteries in wrists
zap (*vb*) *Slang.* murder

Dead Bodies

bones dead body, esp. one decomposed
cadaver dead body, esp. one prepared for dissection
carcass *Slang.* human body, esp. when dead
carrion dead body left out for animals and birds to eat
clay *Slang.* dead and buried body
corpse dead body
crowbait *Slang.* dead body left unburied

dead body remains of a person who has died
dead man corpse
deceased polite or formal term for one who is dead
decomposition natural decay of dead body
dust one who is dead and decomposed into dust
dust and ashes one who is dead and decomposed into dust
loved one overly polite euphemism for dead person
mortal remains corpse
remains corpse
rigor mortis temporary stiffening of body shortly after death
skeleton bones of body after decomposition of flesh
stiff *Slang.* corpse

Burial and Funerals

autopsy examination and dissection of corpse to determine cause of death; necropsy; postmortem
barrow mound of earth and stones over grave
bereaved family and friends of deceased
bier stand or pedestal for a coffin or the coffin itself
body snatcher graverobber
boneyard *Slang.* cemetery
burial interment of dead body in grave
burial ground cemetery, esp. tract of land set aside for primitive cemetery
burial mound mound built over burial ground or grave
cairn heap of stones set up as memorial to the deceased
canopic jar vessel containing deceased's entrails for burial with mummy (ancient Egypt)
casket elaborate coffin
catacomb underground cemetery consisting of tunnels with recesses for tombs
catafalque ornamental bier on which body lies in state
cemetery area set aside for burying the dead in graves or tombs; boneyard; burial ground; graveyard; necropolis
cenotaph honorary tomb for person buried elsewhere
cerecloth waxed cloth for wrapping corpse
cerement waxed shroud or graveclothes
charnel house repository for bodies and bones of the dead
cinerarium vessel, esp. urn, used to receive ashes of the cremated dead
cist neolithic burial chamber with stone walls
coffin box or case for burying corpse; pall
columbarium vaulted structure with recesses for cinerary urns
coronach funeral dirge played on bagpipes (Scotland)
coroner public official who investigates deaths not due to natural causes
cortege funeral procession
cremains ashes of cremated body

cremation reduction of body to ashes for interment

crematorium crematory

crematory place, such as funeral establishment, at which cremation is done; furnace for cremation; crematorium

cromlech circle of stone monoliths on burial mound

crypt underground vault or burial chamber

death march funeral procession

death watch vigil kept over dead or dying person

deep six burial at sea

dirge song of lamentation at funeral

dolmen prehistoric tomb, usu. consisting of two upright stone slabs supporting one horizontal slab (Britain and France)

elegy funeral song or poem of lamentation for the dead

embalming treatment of corpse to prevent decay

entomb (vb) place corpse in burial tomb

epitaph memorial inscription on tomb or grave

eulogy praise for the deceased at funeral service

exequies funeral rites or ceremonies

exequy funeral procession

exhumation digging up of corpse from grave

extreme unction anointment of dying person with oil and prayer for recovery, administered by priest; final Catholic sacrament before death; last rites

funeral observance held for dead person before interment

funeral director manager of funeral home

funeral home establishment for embalming and preparation of dead for burial or cremation

funerary (adj) associated with burial

grave excavation in ground for burial of body

gravedigger person who digs graves

graverobber person who steals corpses after burial, as for medical dissection or profit; body snatcher

gravestone monument marking burial site

graveyard cemetery

hearse large automobile used to convey corpse to burial place

in dust and ashes mourning

inhume (vb) bury, inter

in memoriam in memory of, written in epitaph

inter (vb) perform interment; bury

interment disposition of dead body in earth or tomb, or by cremation

inurn (vb) place ashes in a burial urn

Kaddish Jewish prayer of mourning

keen loud, wailing lamentation for the dead

knell bell tolled to signal death or funeral

kurgan burial mound (Eastern Europe and Siberia)

lamentation mourning aloud for the dead

last rites extreme unction

lay out (vb) prepare corpse for viewing prior to interment

lay to rest bury corpse

lich gate roofed gateway at entrance to churchyard under which coffin rests at beginning of burial service

lie in state be laid out on public display in official recognition of one's stature in life

mausoleum large building for aboveground entombment

memorial service in honor of the deceased after burial or interment

monument tombstone or other grave marker

morgue storage place for dead bodies pending identification and burial

mortician undertaker

mortuary building for storing dead bodies and preparing them for burial

mourning customary show of grief for deceased person

mummy body embalmed and wrapped in cloth for burial (ancient Egypt)

necropolis cemetery

necropsy autopsy

obsequy funeral rite or ceremony

pall coffin; cloth draped over coffin, bier, or tomb

pallbearer one of several persons carrying coffin to grave

plot individual burial site in cemetery

postmortem autopsy

pyre combustible heap for burning dead body as part of funeral rite

Requiem Mass Catholic Mass and liturgy celebrated for the repose of the dead

requiescat prayer for the repose of the dead

rest in peace RIP; standard acknowledgment of death; wish or prayer for the deceased

RIP rest in peace

sarcophagus coffin, esp. one of stone

sepulcher tomb or other place of burial

shrine tomb or other receptacle for the dead

shroud cloth or sheet in which corpse is wrapped for burial; cerecloth; cerement; winding sheet

taps bugle call at military funerals

threnody elegy or song of lamentation, esp. for the dead

tomb place of interment; excavation for a grave; burial vault or chamber

tombstone stone marker placed on or over burial site

tumulus ancient grave; artificial mound over burial site

undertaker one who prepares the dead for burial and manages funerals; mortician

urn ornamental vessel containing ashes of cremated dead person

vault underground burial chamber or tomb

vigil long, prayerful watch over dead or dying person

wake often festive vigil held over body of dead person prior to burial

winding sheet shroud

Beyond the Grave

abyss bottomless pit, gulf of nonexistence after death

afterlife existence of the soul in heaven; great beyond

below (adv) in hell

damnation condemnation of soul to hell

dark void beyond life, esp. hell

devil, the ruling spirit of hell; Satan

Erebus mythological place of darkness on the way to Hades (ancient Greece)

Final Judgment determination of soul's fate by God

ghost soul of deceased returning in bodily likeness; specter; wraith

ghoul evil being that robs graves and feeds on corpses

great beyond afterlife

Grim Reaper personification of death as cloaked skeleton holding scythe

Hades mythological underworld (ancient Greece)

heaven dwelling place of God and joyful abode of the souls of the dead

hell dwelling place of the devil and abode of the condemned souls of the dead

hellfire fire in hell

hereafter life after death or beyond mortal existence

infernal (adj) relating to or inhabiting the eternal inferno of hell

manes venerated, appeased spirit of dead person (ancient Rome)

nether world hell

purgatory in Roman Catholic belief, intermediate state after death in which the souls of sinners become fit for heaven

resurrection act of rising from the dead, esp. for Final Judgment

revenant one who returns from death

rise from the dead achieve resurrection; return as a ghost

saint one of the dead entered into heaven, esp. the canonized or holy dead

Satan the devil

soul nonbodily spirit of deceased that exists after death

specter visible yet incorporeal spirit or ghost; wraith

spirit soul of deceased, esp. malevolent being or ghost

Styx principal underworld river in myth (ancient Greece)

transmigration passage of soul at death from body of one being to another

underworld hell

upstairs Informal. heaven

vampire reanimated corpse that returns at night to drink blood of living people

void unknown darkness beyond life

wraith apparition of living person in exact likeness, seen just before death; ghost, specter

Language of Death

amort (*adj*) *Archaic.* at the point of death

antemortem (*adj*) preceding death

black humor morbid comedy, esp. relating to death

body bag large receptacle made of heavy material, used to transport corpse from battlefield or death scene

capital punishment legal execution for certain crimes

condemned (*adj*) sentenced to death for crimes committed

coup de grâce *French.* lit. blow of mercy; deathblow

cryonics freezing of recently deceased people in hopes of resuscitation when cure exists for their fatal disease

dead duck person or thing about to fail or die

deathbed bed on which someone dies

deathblow destructive stroke or event; coup de grâce

death camp concentration camp to which prisoners are sent for execution

death instinct self destructive impulse based on desire to achieve state of harmonious nonexistence in death; Thanatos

death mask cast taken from face of dead person

death rate number of deaths per thousand in specific group or at given place and time

death rattle gurgle of air passing through mucus in throat of dying person

death's-head human skull as symbol of mortality

death toll number of casualties from particular incident

dying breath last breath at moment of death

dying day end of life; last day of life

Enoch Arden missing person who is presumed dead but is later found alive

fey (*adj*) *Scottish.* fated to die

intestate (*adj*) without a valid will at time of death

kiss of death action or relationship ultimately causing one's ruin

lethal (*adj*) deadly

memento mori object, esp. skull, serving as reminder of mortality

morbidity dwelling on gloomy thoughts of death

mortality being subject to death; death in large numbers; proportion of deaths in population due to specific cause

necrology list of those who have died within a given period; obituary

necrophilia achieving erotic stimulation from corpses

obit *Informal.* obituary

obituary biographical notice of person's death published in newspaper; necrology

on one's deathbed in the last few hours before death

posthumous (*adj*) occurring after one's death

post-obit (*adj*) effective after particular person's death

predecease (*vb*) die first; die before another person or event

quietus removal from activity, as in death

skull and crossbones emblem of death depicting skull and two crossed skeleton bones, esp. on pirate flag or as warning sign for poisons

stillbirth birth of dead child

stillborn (*adj*) dead at birth

swan song farewell appearance or last act, sometimes before death

testament will or act relating disposition of one's property after death

testate (*adj*) having made and left a valid will

thanatology study of death and its circumstances

Thanatos primal, instinctual desire for death; personification of death (ancient Greece)

vanishing point point at which one ceases to exist

vital signs index of essential body functions, including pulse, breathing, and body temperature, that indicate life

widow surviving wife of dead husband

widower surviving husband of dead wife

will legal directions for disposition of one's property after death

CHAPTER TWENTY-FIVE
FAITH

World Religions

Baha'i modern religion developed in Iran in 1863 by Baha'Allah, emphasizing universal brotherhood, social equality, and the unification of all religions

Brahmanism pantheistic religious system of highest Hindu caste, based on the Brahmanas and Upanishads text commentaries on the Vedas, source of pre-Hindu religion introduced in 2nd millennium B.C.

Buddhism religion and philosophic system founded in India in 6th c. B.C. by Siddhartha Gautama, the Buddha, teaching that meditation and the Eightfold Path enable one to escape suffering and achieve Nirvana

Byzantine Church Orthodox Eastern Church

Catholicism Roman Catholicism

Christianity doctrine, faith, and monotheistic religious practice based on belief in Jesus Christ as Messiah and Son of God and on Old and New Testaments of Bible

Christian Science Christian religious movement and system of healing through prayer founded in 19th c. America by Mary Baker Eddy

Church of Jesus Christ of the Latter-day Saints Mormon Church

Church of Rome Roman Catholicism

Confucianism ethical and social teachings based on sayings of Confucius in China in 6th c. B.C., later incorporated into Taoist and Buddhist religions

Druze independent religious sect founded in 11th c. and containing elements of Islam, Christianity, and Judaism, believing in transmigration of souls, now practiced chiefly in Syria, Lebanon, and Israel

Eastern Orthodox Church Orthodox Eastern Church

Gnosticism esoteric salvational system from 2nd c., based on secret knowledge combining elements of mythology, ancient religions, and Christianity

Hinduism religion and social system of Hindus of Indian subcontinent, recognizing authority of Vedas and other sacred texts, emphasizing karma and reincarnation and worship of various deities, based on four goals and four stages in human life and socially rooted in four castes

Islam doctrine, faith, and practice of monotheistic Muslim religion in which Allah is supreme deity and Koran is sacred revelation, devoted to worship of Allah through Five Pillars, founded by prophet Muhammad in 7th c. Arabia; Muhammadanism

Jainism ancient monastic religion of India, influential on Hinduism, founded by Mahavira in 6th c. B.C., emphasizing asceticism, reverence for all living things, and cycles of rebirth

Judaism doctrine, faith, and practice of ancient monotheistic Israelite religion based on written Torah (first five books of Hebrew Bible or Old Testament) and teachings of the Talmud, which view religion as part of everyday family life, founded around 2000 B.C.

Lamaism form of Mahayana Buddhism and Tibetan Bonism, with elaborate ritual and strong hierarchy under Dalai Lama, practiced in Tibet, Nepal, and Mongolia

Latter-day Saints Mormon Church

Mazdaism Zoroastrianism

Mormon Church Christian religion founded in United States in 1830 by Joseph Smith and now centered in Utah, based on Book of Mormon accounts of ancient American peoples who were to found Zion, emphasizing revelation and proselytizing; Church of Jesus Christ of the Latter-day Saints

Muhammadanism Islam

Orthodox Eastern Church Christian church comprising local and national churches in southwest Asia and eastern Europe that split from Western church in 5th c. because of its rejection of the Roman pope and communion with patriarch of Constantinople, marked by elaborate ritual and iconography: includes Albanian, Bulgarian, Greek, Rumanian, Russian, Serbian, Syrian, and Ukrainian Orthodox churches; Byzantine Church; Eastern Orthodox Church

Protestantism any of various Christian denominations established during or following the Reformation against papal authority and Roman Catholicism in 16th c.

Roman Catholicism highly ritualistic, dogmatic Christian doctrine and faith based on Scripture and tradition, with hierarchy of celibate clergy under an infallible pope claiming direct historical line from apostle Peter, formal sacraments and Mass, and veneration of saints and Virgin Mary; Catholicism; Church of Rome

Shinto polytheistic, highly ceremonial, native religion of Japan, influenced by Confucianism and Buddhism, emphasizing worship of nature and ancestors and formerly divinity of emperor

Sikhism institutional mixture of Hinduism and Islam, founded by Nanak in northern India in 16th c., that rejects caste system

Taoism Chinese religion and philosophy based on 6th c. B.C. teachings of Lao-tzu, advocating simplicity and selflessness in following the Tao or path to enlightenment through balance of yin and yang

Theosophical Society eclectic belief system founded by Madame Blavatsky in 1875, based largely on Brahmanic and Buddhist teachings

Vedanta Society nondualistic Hindu philosophical system in fulfillment of the sacred Vedas and Upanishads

Zen variety of Mahayana Buddhism seeking intuitive illumination of satori through simplicity, meditation, and instruction from masters, practiced esp. in Japan and Korea

Zoroastrianism religious system of Persia prior to founding of Islam, established by Zoroaster in 6th c. B.C. and based on Avesta as holy scripture, emphasizing continuous apocalyptic struggle between good and evil; Mazdaism

Christian Denominations and Sects

Amish strict Mennonite community distinguished by self-sufficient living style that rejects technology, inspired by 18th c. Swiss bishop Jacob Amman

Anabaptist Protestant sect important in 16th c. advocating adult baptism and separation of church and state, precursor to Mennonites and Baptists

Anglican Church Protestant denomination developed after Henry VIII of England separated from Roman Catholic Church in 1534 and consolidated in reign of Elizabeth I, retaining many theological and hierarchical elements of Catholicism; Church of England

Armenian Apostolic Church Monophysite Christian church organized in United States in 1899

Assemblies of God largest of Pentecostal churches founded in early 20th c., practicing faith healing, speaking in tongues in enthusiastic services, and believing in second coming of Christ

Baptist Church Christian Protestant denomination whose evangelical beliefs include religious liberty with no creeds or hierarchy, priesthood of all believers, and adult baptism by total immersion, founded by John Smyth in 1609

Calvinism religious doctrine, based on beliefs of 16th c. Reformation leader John Calvin, advocating austere morality, predestination and election, and piety

Christian Science Christian religious sect and system of healing founded in 19th c. by Mary Baker Eddy; Church of Christ, Scientist

Church of Christ offshoot of Presbyterian Church founded in 1804, emphasizing literal interpretation of New Testament

Church of Christ, Scientist Christian Science

Church of England Anglican Church

Church of God any of various Christian denominations that emphasize personal conversion, imminent return of Christ, and sometimes speaking in tongues

Church of the Brethren Dunkers

Church of the New Jerusalem Swedenborgians

Congregational Church Christian church organization, developed from 16th c. separatist revolt in England, in which each local congregation is independent in governance and recognizes only Christ as its head

Coptic Church Christian Egyptian and Ethiopian Monophysite Church recognizing St. Mark the Evangelist as its founder and using Arabic in its services, known as Coptic Orthodox since 19th c.

Dunkers Christian denomination founded in 1708 in Germany that practices trine immersion and opposes taking of oaths and military service; Church of the Brethren

Episcopal Church Christian denomination that evolved from Church of England within Anglican communion, developed in United States in 1784, with worship based on Book of Common Prayer

Friends Quakers

Greek Orthodox Church autonomous branch of Eastern Orthodox Church that consists of Church of Greece, patriarchate of Constantinople, and churches using Greek in the liturgy and Byzantine rite

Huguenots French Protestant denomination of 16th and 17th c. comprised of followers of John Calvin

Jehovah's Witnesses evangelical Christian sect, founded in United States in 19th c. by Charles Russell, that refuses to participate with the government, actively proselytizes, and believes in imminent second coming of Christ

Lutheran Church conservative Protestant denomination based on teachings of Martin Luther, 16th c. German leader of Reformation, emphasizing authority of Scripture with justification and salvation by faith alone

Mennonites evangelical Protestant denomination, descended from Anabaptists, named after 16th c. Dutch religious reformer Menno Simons, that emphasizes simplicity and separation from worldly things, including military service, and adult baptism

Methodist Church Christian Protestant denomination, founded as 18th c. evangelical movement by Anglican John Wesley, emphasizing God's grace, individual responsibility, and study of the Bible as interpreted by reason and tradition

Metropolitan Community Church Christian congregation of gay men and lesbians

Millenial Church Shakers

Moravians Christian denomination descended from Bohemian Brethren, holding Scriptures to be only rule of faith and practice

Presbyterian Church Christian Protestant denomination founded by John Knox in Scotland in 1557 as British form of Calvinism, governed by its ministry and congregationally elected elders

Puritans Protestant group in England and American colonies in 16th and 17th c. that wanted to reduce Roman Catholic elements of Church of England, characterized by strict religious and moral discipline, influenced by John Calvin

Quakers Christian religion founded in 17th c. England by George Fox, emphasizing individual's spiritual inner light and rejecting sacraments and ordained ministry, associated with pacifism and social activism; Friends; Religious Society of Friends

Reformed Church Christian Protestant denomination governed by its ministry and congregationally elected elders and serving as continental European form of Calvinism

Rosicrucians occult group founded in 1868 by R.W. Little, claiming descent from ancient brotherhood said to be founded by 15th c. Christian Rosenkruez

Russian Orthodox Church autocephalous branch of Eastern Orthodox Church whose liturgy is in Old Church Slavonic, headed by patriarch of Moscow in communion with patriarch of Constantinople

Seventh Day Adventists Christian denomination whose evangelical doctrine anticipates the imminent return of Christ to Earth and observes Saturday as Sabbath, founded in United States in 1863

Shakers religion founded in England in 1747, led by Ann Lee, advocating celibacy, communal property, and simple way of life; Millenial Church; United Society of Believers in Christ's Second Appearing

Swedenborgians religious sect founded in 18th c., influenced by Emanuel Swedenborg, a Swedish mystic who claimed to receive divine revelations; Church of the New Jerusalem

Uniates Eastern Orthodox church that is in union with Roman Catholic Church, acknowledges the Roman pope, but maintains its own liturgy, discipline, and rites

Unitarianism Christian denomination that arose during the Reformation that rejects doctrine of the Trinity, posits universal salvation, emphasizes religious tolerance and congregational autonomy, and incorporates humanism and nontheistic thought

Unitarian-Universalism American liberal religious denomination in Christian tradition, formed by merger of Unitarians and Universalists in 1961

United Church of Christ American Protestant denomination formed by merger of Evangelical and Reformed churches and Congregational Christian Church in 1957, with simple services and governing synod

United Society of Believers in Christ's Second Appearing Shakers

Universalism liberal Christian denomination founded in 1779, emphasizing universal fatherhood of God and final salvation of all souls

Zwinglianism religious system following doctrines of Ulrich Zwingli, 16th c. Swiss Protestant reformer, maintaining that Eucharist is merely symbolic and not literally the body of Christ and that church should model itself on ancient Christianity

Christianity

Abel second son of Adam and Eve, killed by his brother Cain

Adam first human, father by Eve of Cain and Abel

Advent period of prayer and fasting beginning four Sundays before Christmas

agape divine love of God or Christ for humankind

Agnus Dei liturgical prayer to Christ the Savior

Agony Christ's suffering in garden of Gethsemane

agrapha sayings of Jesus other than those in Gospels

Annunciation announcement of Christ's coming birth, made by archangel Gabriel to Mary

Antiohriot principal opponent of Christ, Satan

apostolic succession unbroken chain of succession from apostles, perpetuated through pope and other bishops by laying on of hands in ordination of clergy in Catholic, Orthodox, and Anglican churches

Ascension Christ's bodily ascent into heaven following Resurrection

Assumption the bodily taking up of the Virgin Mary to heaven

aureole halo

Ave Maria Roman Catholic prayer to the Virgin Mary; Hail Mary

beatification official papal recognition of dead person as blessed, often prior to canonization

beatitudes blessings spoken by Jesus in Sermon on the Mount

Beelzebub chief devil, Satan

bull edict from pope in form of sealed letter

Cain eldest son of Adam and Eve, murderer of his brother Abel

Calvary place where Christ was crucified

canonical hours periods of day designated for prayer and devotion: matins and lauds, prime, tierce, sext, nones, vespers, and compline

canonization official recognition by Roman Catholic Church of dead person as a saint

canticle liturgical song based on Biblical text

catechism formal religious instruction in form of questions and answers

christen (vb) bring into the church by baptism

Christendom Christian church and its congregation throughout world

Christmas celebration of birth of Christ on December 25 among Western Christians and on January 6 in Eastern Orthodox Church

Christology study of nature of and deeds of Jesus Christ

church lit. members of the body of Christ, used to designate Christian house of worship

communion Holy Communion

compline final canonical hour, following vespers

confession Catholic sacrament received on admitting one's sins to priest and receiving absolution and doing penance

confirmation Catholic sacrament received at and Protestant rite performed at ceremony of acceptance of membership into church at time of adolescence

consubstantiation actual presence of Christ, embodied in bread and wine of the sacrament of the Eucharist

Counter Reformation movement in Catholic Church in response to Protestant Reformation

credo statement of beliefs recited in unison at Mass

cross symbol of Christianity, Christ's Crucifixion and death, and the redemption of humankind

crown of thorns wreath placed on Christ's head before Crucifixion

crucifix representation of Christ crucified on cross

Crucifixion Christ's death on the cross

Crusades Christian wars of Middle Ages to reclaim Jerusalem from Islam

denomination religious body with particular name and practices, esp. one of various Protestant sects

Doxology words of praise for God beginning "Praise God from whom all blessings flow"

Easter celebration of Resurrection of Christ

ecumenism Christian movement toward unity that transcends denominational distinctions

Eden paradise in which Adam and Eve resided before the Fall

encyclical letter from pope to all bishops on religious or civil matters

Epiphany commemoration of manifestation of Christ to the Magi

eschatology doctrine of last things; second coming of Christ and Judgment Day

Eucharist sacrament of Holy Communion; sacrifice of the Mass; Lord's Supper

evangelical counsels vows taken by members of religious order, including poverty, chastity, and obedience

Eve first woman, wife of Adam, mother of Cain and Abel

ex cathedra *Latin* lit. from the chair; from seat of authority, applied to infallible pronouncements of pope

excommunication expulsion from Catholic Church

Fall, the lapse of humans into state of sinfulness through sins of Adam and Eve

Father one of three-part aspect of God

fundamentalism beliefs and practices based on literal interpretation of Bible, esp. among Protestants

genuflection bending of knee and crossing of oneself in reverence

Gloria in Excelsis Deo liturgical hymn based on Psalms

golden rule Christ's maxim that we should do unto others as we would have them do unto us

gospel good news message of salvation and kingdom of God, esp. as announced to world by Christ; story of Christ's life and teachings

Great Schism rift in Roman Catholic Church from 1378 to 1417, characterized by two and sometimes three claimants to papacy

Hail Mary Catholic prayer repeated as atonement for sins; Ave Maria;

halo radiant light surrounding head of Jesus, Mary, or any saint

heaven dwelling place of God and resting place of souls of the faithful dead

hell dwelling place of Satan and place of eternal torture for souls of the damned

High Mass Catholic Mass in which celebrant and choir sing specified parts

Holy Communion sacrament in which one eats body and drinks blood of Jesus Christ; communion; Eucharist

Holy Grail cup or platter used by Christ at Last Supper

Holy Mother Virgin Mary

holy rood cross or crucifix symbolizing cross on which Christ died; rood

Holy Spirit one of three-part aspect of God

holy water water blessed by Catholic priest

Homoiousian believer in 4th c. creed that essence of Son is similar to, but not same as, that of Father

Homoousian believer in 4th c. creed that Son and Father are made of same substance

host wafer representing flesh of Christ in communion

Immaculate Conception Catholic dogma that Mary was conceived without sin and that Christ was born to Virgin Mary through miraculous agency of God

indulgence removal of punishment for sin based on penance or on certain prayer practices; writ of forgiveness sold at one time by Catholic Church, protested by Martin Luther in 95 Theses

indult privilege given by Catholic ecclesiastical authority

infallibility principle of papal immunity from liability to error and pontiff's unfailingly correct judgment in matters of faith

Inquisition medieval tribunal of Catholic Church intent on persecution of nonbelievers and those seen as heretics

Jansenism movement in Holland and France during 17th c. that advocated reform of Catholic Church rather than abandonment of it

Jesuits largest Roman Catholic order of men, founded by Ignatius Loyola in 1540, which played a role in Counter Reformation and later in missionary work; Society of Jesus

Jesus 1st century Jewish prophet from Nazareth and founder of Christianity

John the Baptist Nazarite prophet who baptized Jesus, later executed by Herod Antipas

Judas Iscariot one of Christ's twelve apostles, who betrayed him to Romans

Judeo-Christian tradition Western religion, culture, and heritage based on both Judaism and Christianity

Kyrie eleison short Greek liturgical prayer used in Mass

Last Supper Passover meal eaten by Jesus and his disciples on the eve of his Crucifixion

Latin language of Roman Catholic liturgy and Mass

lauds canonical hour in early morning, accompanied by psalms of praise, usu. recited with matins

Lent forty-day period of penitence prior to Easter

logos word of God; actively expressed, revelatory, creative wisdom and will of God through Christ

Lord's Prayer prayer beginning "Our Father" that Jesus taught his disciples; Paternoster

Lord's Supper Eucharist; Holy Communion

Lucifer angelic form of Satan

Madonna Virgin Mary

Manicheanism Gnostic Christian movement of 3rd c. based on teachings of Persian sage Mani that universe is characterized by struggle between good and evil, influenced by Zoroastrianism

Mary Virgin Mary

Mary Magdalene follower of Christ who witnessed his Crucifixion and was first to see him resurrected

Mass central religious rite of Roman Catholic Church, which reenacts Christ's Last Supper in celebration of Eucharist

matins first canonical hour of day, designated for morning prayer and psalms of praise

Melchite Christian in Egypt and Syria who accepts definition of faith adopted by Council of Chalcedon in 451 A.D.

miracle event deviating from laws of nature and being sign of God's power or presence

Mithraism Persian mystery cult centered on benevolent god Mithra, supplanted by Christianity in 4th c.

Mother of God Virgin Mary

Nativity birth of Christ, esp. as depicted in art

Nicene Creed statement of Christian faith in 325 A.D. stipulating that Jesus is only begotten Son of God and of one substance with the Father

Ninety-Five Theses document written by Martin Luther in 1517, protesting sale of indulgences, which began Protestant Reformation

nones fifth canonical hour, orig. midafternoon

novena Roman Catholic devotion consisting of nine separate days of prayer or services

obsecration prayer of supplication

Our Lady Virgin Mary

passion sufferings of Christ between night of the Last Supper and his death

Paternoster Lord's Prayer

patristics study of writings of church fathers

Pentecost festival celebrating descent of Holy Spirit on apostles

Peter chief among Christ's twelve apostles, founder of church in Rome and first pope

Pietism Lutheran movement of 17th c. Germany that emphasized personal devotion

prelapsarian (*adj*) before the Fall

Prince of Darkness Satan

proof text Biblical text used as evidence for assertion

Protestant any of various Christian churches outside Roman Catholic Church

Protestant Reformation Christian schism within Catholic Church in 16th c. that resulted in Protestantism; Reformation

Providence divine guidance and care of God over earthly creatures

purgatory place where penitent souls are purified for ascent to heaven

Rastafarianism religious sect, orig. Jamaican, holding Haile Selassie to be the Messiah and Ethiopia to be Eden, and anticipating eventual return of blacks to Africa

Reformation Protestant Reformation

Requiem Mass Catholic funeral Mass

requiescat prayer for repose of the dead

Resurrection rising of Jesus from the dead after his Crucifixion and burial, an essential event in Christian belief

Roman Catholicism Christian church headed by pope as bishop of Rome

rood holy rood

rule document on which religious order bases its practice

Sabbath holy day consecrated to worship of God, Sunday for Christians

Salvation Army evangelical and social service organization founded in England in 1865 by William Booth

Satan supreme evil spirit residing in hell

Second Coming Christ's promised return after Ascension

Society of Jesus Jesuits

Son Jesus Christ, Son of God

stations of the cross images representing fourteen stages of Christ's passion

stigmata bodily marks resembling wounds of crucified Christ that appear supernaturally on bodies of certain inspired persons

strict interpretation literal interpretation of events described in Bible

synod ecclesiastical council

Te Deum hymn of praise to God in form of psalm beginning "Te Deum laudamus"

transcendentalism liberal Protestant movement of 19th c. that sought direct contact with deity outside institutional church

transubstantiation change during consecration of bread and wine of Eucharist into Christ's body and blood

Trinity three aspects of God, as Father, Son, and Holy Spirit

Vatican see of bishop of Rome; city-state serving as headquarters of Roman Catholic Church

vespers evening religious service

virgin birth conception of Jesus by Virgin Mary through miraculous agency of God

Virgin Mary Mary, mother of Jesus by virgin birth; Holy Mother; Madonna; Our Lady

wafer thin piece of unleavened bread used in Eucharist; host

Judaism

Abraham patriarch and founder of ancient Hebrew nation

Aggadah nonlegal, narrative material in Talmud and Midrash containing parables and illustrative anecdotes

ark sacred gilded wood chest containing stone tablets bearing the Covenant; enclosure for Torah in synagogue

Ashkenazim German and Eastern European Jewry

bar mitzvah ceremony marking boy's reaching age of religious responsibility and maturity

bas mitzvah bat mitzvah

bat mitzvah ceremony marking girl's reaching age of religious responsibility and maturity, bas mitzvah

bris brith milah

brith milah rite of circumcision for male infant performed on eighth day after birth; bris

cabala mystical interpretation of Scriptures, with emphasis on secret meanings in text, by medieval Jews; kabala

Canaan ancient land promised by God to Abraham, occupying region that is now Israel; Holy Land

Chanukah Hanukkah

Chasidim Hasidim

Chosen People the Israelites, according to the Old Testament

Conservative form of the practice of Judaism, adapting ritual and traditional forms to modern life, less strict than Orthodox practice in adherence to rituals

covenant God's agreement to protect the faithful of Israel, as revealed in the Torah

daven (*vb*) recite Jewish prayers, esp. with nodding motion of upper body

David second king of Israel, who unified Jewish tribes and established capital at Jerusalem circa 1000 B.C.

Decalogue Ten Commandments

Diaspora historical exile of Jews from Israel to Babylonia in 6th c. B.C., when Judaism became distinguishable in modern form

Essenes Palestinian sect of Roman period characterized by ascetic practices and apocalyptic theology

Exodus flight of Israelites from Egypt led by Moses, forming second book of Pentateuch

First Temple Solomon's Temple at Jerusalem, destroyed by the Babylonians in 6th c. B.C.

Flood great deluge that covered Earth, described in Genesis

Gabriel archangel of Hebrew tradition, serving as divine messenger

Haggadah book containing liturgy and songs for Seder service at Passover

Halakhah body of Jewish law contained in the Bible, Talmud, and oral tradition

Hanukkah festival of lights celebrating victory of the Maccabees over the Syrians, observed for eight days to commemorate miracle of oil lamp in temple at Jerusalem; Chanukah

Hasidim followers of form of Jewish mysticism that emphasizes strict rituals and religious zeal, originating in Eastern Europe in 18th c.; Chasidim

Hebrew classical language of Judaism; in modern form, an official language of Israel

Hebrews Semitic people of Palestine traditionally descended from Jacob and considered ancestors of modern Jewry; Israelites

Herod king of Judea from 37 to 4 B.C., builder of Second Temple at Jerusalem

High Holy Day Rosh Hashanah (New Year) and Yom Kippur (Day of Atonement)

Holy Land Canaan; Palestine

holy of holies innermost part of tabernacle

Israel northern kingdom of the Hebrews traditionally descended from Jacob, including ten of the Twelve Tribes; modern Jewish state founded in 1948; chosen people of God; name given to Jacob

Israelites Hebrews descended from Jacob and inhabiting ancient kingdom of Israel

Jacob second son of Isaac and father of patriarchs of twelve tribes, forefather of Hebrew people

Jewish calendar lunisolar calendar reckoned from 3761 B.C., containing twelve months and 353 to 355 days, adjusted every nineteen years to match solar cycle, used to determine religious holidays

Jewry Jewish people

Judah southern kingdoms of the Hebrews, including the tribes of Judah and Benjamin; fourth son of Jacob or the tribe descended from him

Judeo-Christian tradition Western religion, culture, and heritage based on both Judaism and Christianity

kabalah cabala

Kaddish Hebrew prayer for the dead

Kol Nidre opening prayer of Yom Kippur

kosher (*adj*) following dietary and ceremonial laws governing what is fit to eat by Jews

Maccabees Jewish family led by Judas Maccabeus, who regained Jerusalem from the Syrians in 164 B.C., as commemorated by Hanukkah, and lost it to Rome in 63 B.C.

Magen David Star of David

manna miraculous food supplied to Israelites during their journey through the wilderness

Masada mountaintop fortress overlooking Dead Sea that was site of Zealots' last stand against Romans circa 70 A.D.

Midrash rabbinic explanation and exegesis of Jewish Scripture focusing on nonliteral meaning of text

mikvah *Hebrew.* ritual bath of purification

minyan *Hebrew.* quorum of ten men needed for Jewish worship

Mishnah formal code of Jewish law, finalized in 3rd c.

mitzvah act that fulfills a commandment or injunction; in modern usage, any kindness

Moses prophet who led Israelites out of slavery and received God's law on Sinai

Noah tenth descendant of Adam, chosen by God to survive the Flood with sons and animals in ark

Orthodox form of Judaism strictly conforming to rituals and traditions of Torah and Talmud

Passover commemoration of deliverance of Israelites from slavery; Pesach

Pesach *Hebrew.* Passover

Pharisee member of ancient Jewish sect who strictly adhered to oral laws and traditions, distinguished from the Sadducees

Purim festival in which costumes and masks are worn in celebration of Jews' deliverance by Esther from massacre in Persia

Rabbinical Judaism form of Jewish practice founded after destruction of Second Temple in 70 A.D.

Reform modern practice of Judaism that does not require observance of rituals and emphasizes ethical aspects and rational thought

Rosh Hashanah Jewish New Year

Sabbath holy day consecrated to worship of God, Saturday for Jews

Sadducee member of ancient Jewish sect, composed chiefly of priests and aristocrats, who opposed the Pharisees

Sarah wife of Abraham

Saul first king of Israel

Second Temple Herod's temple at Jerusalem, destroyed by Romans in 70 A.D. except for Western Wall

Seder Passover service that recounts story of Exodus from Egypt through Haggadah

Sephardim medieval Spanish and Portuguese Jews who emigrated to North Africa, Turkey, and Palestine to escape the Inquisition; their descendants

shalom *Hebrew.* peace, used as a greeting or farewell

Shavuoth holiday commemorating revelation of Ten Commandments to Moses on Mount Sinai

Shema liturgical prayer recited daily expressing love of God

shtetl *Yiddish.* Jewish village or community in Eastern Europe

shul *Yiddish.* synagogue

Star of David six-pointed star that is symbol of Judaism, formed from two equilateral triangles; Magen David

Sukkoth Jewish holiday celebrating the fall harvest and commemorating shelters of Hebrews during Exodus

synagogue Jewish house of worship; shul

Ten Commandments fundamental rules for life, given by God to Moses; Decalogue

Twelve Tribes original groups of Hebrews descended from Jacob, who settled kingdoms of Israel and Judah

Wailing Wall Western Wall

Western Wall holy stone wall remaining from Second Temple, destroyed in 70 A.D., used as site of Jewish prayer in Jerusalem; Wailing Wall

yeshiva all-day school of religious and secular learning

Yiddish Germanic language with mixture of Hebrew words, written in Hebrew letters, used primarily by Ashkenazim of Eastern Europe

Yom Kippur day of atonement and repentance following Rosh Hashanah, observed by fasting and prayer

Zealots Jewish sect of Roman period, characterized by revolutionary political ideology, that violently resisted Roman rule

Zion Palestine as Jewish homeland and symbol of Judaism, orig. hill in Jerusalem on which temples were built

Zionism worldwide Jewish movement, begun in late 19th century, that resulted in establishment of state of Israel

Islam

adhan call to prayer five times daily

Allah God; Supreme Being

Allah akbar God is great; rallying cry and call to faith of Islam

Ash-Shaytān Satan; the devil

ayatollah teacher, judge, and leader of Shi'ite sect

azan call to prayer made five times a day by the muezzin

baqa in Sufism, the pure spiritual state remaining after extinction of the self

Black Muslims Nation of Islam

caliph spiritual leader claiming succession from Muhammad

dervish mystic, esp. Sufi, engaging in ecstatic whirling and dancing

fana in Sufism, annihilation of the self and union with the Divine

Fatiha first chapter of the Koran, recited at beginning of each of the five daily prayers

fatwa authoritative opinion or judgment in Islamic law

Five Pillars of Faith five requirements of faith in Islam: profession, worship, alms-giving, pilgrimage to Mecca, and fasting during Ramadan

giaour person outside Islamic faith, esp. an infidel

hadith tradition, esp. relating to sayings and deeds of Muhammad and his followers

hafiz title of respect for a Muslim who knows the Koran by heart

hajj pilgrimage to Mecca

hajji Muslim who has made pilgrimage to Mecca

Hegira Muhammad's exodus from Mecca to Medina in 622 A.D.

'Id al-Adha major four-day festival in last month of calendar

ihram white robes worn by male Muslims on their pilgrimage to Mecca

imam Muslim religious leader

iman act of faith in God

jihad holy war or crusade undertaken as Islamic duty

Ka'ba shrine in Great Mosque at Mecca that is objective of Muslim pilgrimage, regarded as House of God

kafir infidel or unbeliever

kamal perfection of Allah

kashf revelation

Koran Allah's revelation to Muhammad, arranged in written form as sacred Islamic text; Qur'an

Mahdi Muslim messiah who will establish reign of righteousness throughout world

Mahomet Muhammad

marabout hermit or holy man, esp. in North Africa

maulvi term of respect for expert in Islamic law in India

Mawlid celebration of birthday of Muhammad

Mecca holy city of Islam and birthplace of Muhammad, in what is now Saudi Arabia, toward which Muslims bow in prayer

Mohammed Muhammad

Moharram Islamic new year festival, in first month of lunar calendar

mosque Islamic house of worship

muezzin caller of faithful to prayer

mufti jurist who explains Islamic law

Muhajirun people who accompanied Muhammad on the Hegira

Muhammad 6th-7th c. A.D. Arab prophet and founder of Islam; Mahomet; Mohammed

mujtahid Shi'ite teacher with authority to interpret Islamic law and religion

mullah teacher of religious law; 'ulama

Muslim follow of Islam

nabi prophet

namaz ritual prayer

Nation of Islam organization of African-Americans advocating teaching of Islam and racial separatism

qadi Islamic scholar and judge in primarily religious court with civil authority

Qiyama last judgment

Qur'an Koran

Ramadan sacred month of fasting from sunrise to sunset during ninth month of lunar calendar

sayyid title of teacher descended from prophet Muhammad

shari'ah religious law and practical ordinances based on the Koran

sherif governor of Mecca, claiming descent from Muhammad

Shi'ah Shi'ite

Shi'ite member of the smaller of two major Islamic sects, given to fundamentalism, led by succession of imams; Shi'ah

Sufi follower of Sufism

Sufism mystical Islamic sect and system that seeks union with God through ecstatic trance, associated esp. with Iran

Sunni member of the larger of two major Islamic sects, based on orthodox law and theology of Koran and other works

sura any one of the 114 chapters of the Koran

tariqah spiritual path of Sufism

'ulama teacher and doctor of Muslim law and religion; mullah; Muslim religious teachers collectively

ummah people of the Muslim world

Wahhabi member of conservative Muslim group, found mainly in Saudi Arabia, practicing strict interpretation of Koran

wali saint

zahid ascetic

zuhd asceticism

Eastern Religions

ahimsa principle of nonviolence to living things (Hinduism, Jainism)

amrita beverage of immortality (Hinduism)

ananda perfect bliss (Hinduism)

anatta doctrine of nonexistence of personal soul (Buddhism)

anekantavada seeing issues from more than one side (Jainism)

anicca doctrine of impermanence through cycle of birth, growth, decay, and death (Buddhism)

atman individual self; principle of life (Hinduism)

Atman World Soul, from which individual souls derive

bardo plane of intermediate existence between death and rebirth, basis of Tibetan *Book of the Dead* (Vajrayana Buddhism)

bhakti devotional acts (Hinduism)

Bhakti religious movement centered around worship of gods (Hinduism)

bhikshu monk, esp. disciple of Buddha (Buddhism)

bodhi supreme knowledge and Enlightenment (Buddhism)

Bodhisattva enlightened person who postpones Nirvana in order to help others attain enlightenment (Buddhism)

bo tree sacred fig tree, under which the Buddha is believed to have attained enlightenment

Brahman ultimate reality, characterized as pure being, consciousness, and bliss (Hinduism)

Buddha 6th c. B.C. Indian, Siddhartha Gautama, whose teachings are basis of Buddhism; first of three Tisarana, or sources of refuge

bushido spiritual path of samurai class (Japan)

caste one of many subdivisions of the four religious and social classes of Hinduism: Brahman or priest, warrior, merchant/farmer, artist; varna

chakra one of seven sources of spiritual energy within body, tapped by yoga, lying at the intersection of cosmic order and human order (Hinduism)

cit pure consciousness (Hinduism)

Confucius Chinese philosopher of 6th-5th c. B.C. whose *Analects* and sayings form basis of Confucianism

dagoba shrine housing sacred relics

Dhamma teachings of the Buddha; truth; second of three Tisarana, or sources of refuge (Buddhism)

dharma cosmic law; everyday duty; spiritual doctrine (Hinduism)

dhyana meditation (Hinduism, Buddhism)

Diwali festival of lights in October (Hinduism)

dukkha first noble truth of Buddhism, that life is suffering caused by craving and attachment (Hinduism)

Eightfold Path eight pursuits leading to Enlightenment: understanding, motives, speech, action, livelihood, effort, intellectual activity, and contemplation (Buddhism)

Enlightenment spiritual awakening; awareness that releases one from cycle of dependent origination (Buddhism)

Ganges sacred river in northern India in which Hindus bathe

Golden Temple principal site of Sikh worship in India

guna three aspects of nature: passion, inertia, and purity (Hinduism)

Hare Krishna Vedic sect whose members engage in group chanting of Krishna's name, founded in United States in 1966

hatha yoga physical discipline using postures and breathing to effect changes in awareness (Hinduism)

Hinayana Theravada

jiva individual soul or ego self taken as manifestation of Atman (Hinduism)

jnana wisdom acquired through meditation and study (Hinduism)

karma action and results of action; moral cause and effect (Hinduism, Buddhism, Jainism, Sikhism)

karma yoga yoga of action (Hinduism)

koan baffling aphorism that inspires awakened mental state or disrupts discursive thought (Zen Buddhism)

lama monk or priest (Mahayana Buddhism)

Lao-tzu Chinese teacher of 6th c. whose *Tao Te Ching* forms basis of Taoism

Lingayat sect of southern India that does not recognize caste distinctions (Hinduism)

lotus symbolic water lily (Buddhism)

Mahavira last of Tirthankara and consolidator of Jainism in 5th c. B.C.

Mahayana later of Buddhism's two main

branches, predominant in China, Japan, Korea, Tibet, and Vietnam, encompassing Vajrayana

mandala complex design of circle surrounding square, with symbolic and ritual power, used in temple design and as art form (Hinduism, Buddhism)

mantra holy word or sound used in meditation (Hinduism)

maya illusion; phenomenal world seen without awareness (Buddhism, Hinduism)

Middle Path middle way of life, between asceticism and luxury (Buddhism)

moksha liberation, release from cycle of ordinary experience and reincarnation of samsara (Buddhism, Hinduism, Jainism)

mudra sacred hand gesture (Hinduism, Buddhism)

Nanak founder of Sikhism in 16th c. India, who combined elements of Islam and Hinduism

naos ancient temple or shrine

neti neti *Sanskrit.* lit. neither this nor that; ineffable and undifferentiated nature of Brahman (Hinduism)

Nirvana release from endless cycle of rebirth into state of cosmic bliss (Buddhism)

Om mantric sound that is complete expression of Brahman (Hinduism); also used in Vajrayana Buddhism

panth community of Sikhs

parinirvana Nirvana achieved at death of physical body

prajna knowledge, wisdom, spiritual insight, and enlightenment (Hinduism, Buddhism)

prana breath, sacred life force (Hinduism)

rahit ritual and ethical code enumerating five signs of faith: uncut hair, dagger, breeches, comb, and bracelet (Sikhism)

raja yoga yoga of kingly discipline and spirituality (Hinduism)

samadhi union of meditator with object of meditation; transcendence (Hinduism, Buddhism)

samsara cycle of rebirth and transmigration of souls (Hinduism); rebecoming and reexistence (Buddhism)

Sangha greater community of Buddhist practitioners; monastic order founded by the Buddha; third of three Tisarana, or sources of refuge

Sankhya yoga one of six leading systems of Hindu philosophy, stressing duality and reality of spirit and matter

sat realm of existence or being (Hinduism)

Satcitananda reality, combining sat (being), cit (consciousness), and ananda (bliss), seen through qualities of Brahman (Hinduism)

satori enlightenment, awakening (Zen Buddhism)

stupa memorial mound that may contain relics of saint (Buddhism)

Sunyata that which exists absolutely and without predication (Buddhism)

t'ai chi ch'uan neo-Confucian concept of single, ultimate principle and source of all things;

stylized meditation exercise based on this concept (China)

Tantra tradition incorporating secret ritual with mystical practices rooted in harmony of masculine and feminine aspects of cosmos, often expressed in sexual ritual (Hinduism, Buddhism)

tantrayana Vajrayana (Hinduism)

Tao the way or path to self-realization and enlightenment (Taoism)

tapas yoga techniques of breath control and bodily conditioning for greatest creative power (Hinduism)

Theravada earlier of Buddhism's two main branches, predominant in Sri Lanka, Burma, and Southeast Asia; Hinayana

Tirthankara twenty-four chronologically sequential Jain sages, last of whom is Mahavira, consolidator of Jainism

Tisarana three levels or sources of refuge: Buddha, Dhamma, and Sangha (Buddhism)

tope shrine or stupa (Buddhism)

Trimurti divinity in three aspects of Brahma, Vishnu, and Shiva (Hinduism)

upaya instructional device such as koan (Buddhism)

Vaishnava Bhakti sect devoted to worship of Vishnu (Hinduism)

Vajrayana tantric Buddhism, with mystical aspects, emphasizing male and female symbolism and deities, predominant in northern India, Tibet, and Nepal; tantrayana

varna caste (Hinduism)

Vedanta classical philosophy in fulfillment of Vedas, dealing with nature of Brahman in dualistic (Dvaita) and nondualistic (Advaita) doctrines (Hinduism)

vinaya monastic code of discipline (Buddhism)

Way, the Tao (Taoism)

yang cosmic force of masculine, active, light, warm, contracting, creative energy of heaven (Taoism)

yantra diagram for meditation (Hinduism)

yin cosmic force of feminine, passive, dark, cold, expansive, material energy of earth (Taoism)

yin and yang two modes of cosmic energy that form dynamic Tao, or way of the universe, and combine in various proportions in all things

yoga spiritual discipline and practice involving meditation, physical postures, breathing exercises, and devotional acts: hatha (physical), jnana (wisdom and intellect), karma (action), raja (kingly spirituality), and sankhya (philosophic) (Hinduism)

zazen cross-legged meditation practice (Zen Buddhism)

zendo retreat for meditation; monastery (Zen Buddhism)

God and Divinity

Adonai *Hebrew.* the Lord, God

Agnus Dei figure of a lamb as representation of Jesus Christ

Ahura Mazda Supreme Being, representing forces of good and evil (Zoroastrianism)

Allah God, Supreme Being (Islam)

All-Knowing God the omniscient (Christianity)

Almighty God the omnipotent (Christianity)

anima mundi *Latin.* world soul

Atman soul, self (Hinduism)

Brahma god of creation, mediating between Vishnu and Shiva (Hinduism)

Buddha enlightened being (Buddhism)

Christ anointed Jesus Christ, Savior and Son of God, second element of Trinity (Christianity)

Creator Supreme Being, God

dea *Latin.* goddess

deity supreme being, god, divine being

demigod half divine being, born of union of god and mortal

deus *Latin.* god

deva a god or divinity (Buddhism, Hinduism); one of an order of evil spirits (Zoroastrianism)

Divine Mind Supreme Being (Christian Science)

divinity deity, god, divine being

Dominus *Latin.* God, the Lord

earth mother great mother, goddess

Elohim *Hebrew.* God

Father God, first element of the Trinity (Christianity)

First Cause Supreme Being as creator of universe

god immortal being or personification of natural or psychic force

God Supreme Being (Christianity)

God Almighty God

goddess female god or deity

godhead divine being

Godhead essence of God, Supreme Being; Holy Trinity

godhood state of being a god

God the Father Christian God in aspect of creator of universe and humankind

God the Son Jesus Christ

Good Lord usu. **the Good Lord**; God (Christianity)

Good Shepherd Jesus Christ

Great Mother ancient nature goddess (pre-Hellenic Europe, Near East)

Holy Ghost Holy Spirit

Holy Spirit spirit of God, third element of the Trinity; Holy Ghost; Spirit

Holy Trinity tripartite nature of God: Father, Son, and Holy Spirit; Godhead (Christianity)

idol image or representation of deity, or object made into god

Immanuel *Hebrew.* lit. God is with us; name attributed to Christ by Christians

immortal being with eternal life

incorporeal (*adj*) pertaining to nonbodily attribute of God

Indra sky, storm god (Hinduism)

Jahweh Yahweh

Jehovah Yahweh, God (Judaism)

Jesu Jesus

Jesus Christ Son of God and Savior of humankind, both fully human and fully divine

kami gods, spirits of the divine (Shinto)

King of Heaven God (Christianity)

King of kings Jesus Christ

Krishna avatar of Vishnu (Hinduism)

Lamb of God Jesus Christ

living Christ Christ as present through the Eucharist

Lord Supreme Being, God; Christ

Lord of hosts Jehovah, God

Lord of lords Jesus Christ

Mahdi expected restorer of Islam

Maker God

Messiah Jesus Christ; expected deliverer of Jewish people

Nazarene Jesus Christ

numen divine spirit

Omnipotent (*adj*) all-powerful: attribute of God (Christianity)

Omnipresent (*adj*) all-present: attribute of God (Christianity)

Omniscient (*adj*) all-knowing: attribute of God (Christianity)

pantheon group of gods

Paraclete Holy Spirit

Prince of Peace Jesus Christ

Rama incarnation of Vishnu (Hinduism)

Redeemer Jesus Christ

Sat Guru God (Sikhism)

Savior Jesus Christ

Shaddai *Hebrew.* God

Shiva god of destruction (Hinduism); Siva

Siva Shiva

Son of God Jesus Christ

Son of Man Jesus Christ

Spirit Holy Spirit

Supreme Being God; deity responsible for creation

Tathagata Buddha's name for himself

theos *Greek.* god

Trimurti triad of gods Brahma, Vishnu, and Siva (Hinduism)

Trinity god in three aspects: Father, Son, and Holy Spirit (Christianity); creator/mediator, preserver, and destroyer (Hinduism); Holy Trinity

unmoved mover God; supreme being as creator

Vishnu god the preserver (Hinduism)

Yahweh *Hebrew.* God in Old Testament; Jahweh

Yama god of the dead (Hinduism)

Practice and Doctrine

ablution ritual bathing of body or washing of object or person

absolution forgiveness for sins

agnosticism belief that God's existence is unknowable; nescience

amen solemn ratification of faith used at end of prayer by Christians and Jews

anathema curse, ban, or excommunication pronounced by religious authority; offering consecrated to deity

animism belief that natural objects and phenomena have souls

anthropomorphism investing God or divinity with human attributes

antinomianism belief in Christian faith alone as necessary for salvation, without necessity of moral law

apotheosis deification, esp. by elevating mortal to god

asceticism religious practice of strict discipline and self-denial

atheism nonbelief in God

atonement reconciliation with God through forgiveness of sins; suffering and death of Jesus for human sins Christ

autocephalous (*adj*) having its own chief bishop but in communion with other Orthodox churches

baptism Christian sacrament of admission into church shortly after birth; immersion in water to symbolize such admission

belief itemized codification of religious assertions or affirmations of faith

benediction blessing

benison benediction or blessing

blasphemy sacrilege; intentional offense to God

blessing act of consecrating or wishing God's favor upon; benediction; benison

camp meeting religious gathering, often evangelical, held in tent or outdoors; tent meeting

canon religious code or doctrine; canon law, authoritative texts

catechism elementary guidebook for Christian religious instruction

celibacy abstention from marriage and sexual relations, as by priest

charismatics followers of Christian movement who believe in ecstatic religious experience, sometimes manifested by speaking in tongues and instantaneous healing

chastity abstention from sexual activity

collegial (*adj*) marked by sharing of authority among Roman Catholic bishops

commandment one of Biblical Ten Commandments

communion Holy Communion

conclave meeting of Roman Catholic cardinals to select pope

concordat ecclesiastical agreement between pope and sovereign

confession disclosure of sins to achieve absolution

consecration dedication of person or object to sacred use

conventicle assembly for worship, esp. secret or unsanctioned one

conversion formal change from one religion to another

Creation formation of Earth and beginnings of humanity as told of in sacred texts, esp. fundamentalist view that God created world in seven days as in Genesis

creationism doctrine that matter and all its forms were created by an omnipotent God, esp. literal belief in story of Creation in Genesis

creed formal statement or system of religious beliefs, esp. for specific denomination

cult particular system of religious practice or religious group, usu. unorthodox or deviating from major faith and practicing in an absolute, oppressive, or obsessive way, often under the direction of a charismatic leader

deadly sins seven sins held to be fatal to spiritual progress: pride, covetousness, lust, anger, gluttony, envy, and sloth

deism belief in transcendent God as creator without further intervention in human affairs

devotions religious practices, esp. prayers

dispensation God's ordering of affairs of the world; exemption from practices authorized by religious authority

ditheism belief in two equally powerful gods; belief in existence of antagonistic forces for good and evil, as in Zoroastrianism

doctrine religious teaching

dogma religious teaching formally stated as creed or article of faith

dualism doctrine of two independent eternal principles; distinction between conventional and ultimate reality in Hinduism

ecclesiastical (*adj*) relating to church as formal and established institution

ecumenical (*adj*) pertaining to whole Christian church, esp. promoting its unity

ethics fundamental moral principles that guide one's behavior toward others and world at large

Eucharist sacrament of Holy Communion; sacrifice of the Mass; Lord's Supper

evangelize (*vb*) spread the gospel

Evensong evening prayer

exegesis analysis and interpretation of Scripture

expiation atonement for one's sins

extreme unction Christian sacrament of anointing one who is near death; sacrament of the sick

faith emotional belief in divine order as ultimate reality, usu. involving existence of God and practice of specific religious doctrine, not requiring proof

faith healing miraculous healing by power of God

fast abstention from food, usu. as religious discipline

fideism exclusive reliance on faith and exclusion of science and philosophy in religious matters

grace undeserved love and mercy of God toward humankind; sanctifying energy mediated by God's word in Protestantism and through sacraments in Catholicism

hagiography writings and critical studies of saints

hagiology literature or biography dealing with lives of saints

hajj pilgrimage to Mecca (Islam)

hallelujah expression of praise for God

healing curing of physical affliction through faith and prayer

henotheism allegiance to one god while

allowing worship of any of several other gods by family or tribe

heresy unorthodox or dissenting religious belief

hermeneutics science of theological interpretation

heterodoxy unorthodox theological views

Holy Communion sacrament in which one eats body and drinks blood of Jesus Christ; Eucharist; communion

holy orders Christian sacrament of ordination as priest or deacon

hosanna cry of love for God

hymn sacred song in praise of God

idolatry worship of physical image of deity

indigenous religion religion limited to a particular region

insufflation rite of breathing on person to symbolize spiritual inspiration

interdenominational (*adj*) common to or involving different religious denominations

invocation act of calling upon deity, usu. in prayer

isagogics branch of theology introductory to Bible study and exegesis

kenosis doctrine that Christ gave up His divine attributes to experience human suffering

laying on of hands rite in which cleric places hands on head of person being confirmed or ordained, also used in faith healing

libation pouring out of wine to honor deity

libertinism indulgence of flesh as religious expression

litany prayer in form of call and response, usu. between minister and congregation

literalism literal interpretation of Bible

liturgy rites of religious worship

love feast meal of fellowship and charity taken as rite

lustration ritually purifying bath

mantra holy word or sound used in meditation (Hinduism)

matrimony Christian sacrament of marriage before God

meditation spiritual and mental discipline or exercise involving contemplation and awakened state of awareness

monasticism system and way of life of monks

monotheism belief in a single God

morals specific attitudes and behaviors derived from broad ethical principles and beliefs

mortal sin serious, willful transgression against law of God that deprives soul of divine grace until absolution and possibly results in eternal damnation

native religion any of various religions indigenous to a particular region, particularly one inhabited by preliterate people; primitive religion

nescience agnosticism

nondualism lack of distinction between conventional and ultimate realities (Hinduism)

oblation offering to God of bread and wine in Eucharist

observance recognition and celebration of religious rite

offertory offering of bread and wine before consecration at Eucharist service; period for collection during worship service

ordination Christian sacrament received upon joining priesthood

original sin sin or evil innate in humankind, stemming from Adam's sin

orthodoxy correct religious belief according to specific doctrine

orthopraxy correct religious behavior and rituals according to specific doctrine

paganism belief in god other than Christian, Jewish, or Muslim God

pantheism belief that God is manifested by and throughout the universe; worship of eclectic body of deities

path spiritual process of discipline and manner of conduct

penance specific act of repentance for sins; Catholic sacrament

Pentecostalism belief in and practice of revivalism, baptism, speaking in tongues, and faith healing, with emphasis on activity of Holy Spirit (Christianity)

piacular (*adj*) making atonement

pilgrimage journey to sacred place to reaffirm religious faith

polytheism belief in and worship of more than one god

prayer address, petition, or offering to God or deity

prayer meeting gathering for communal prayer, often in evangelical, high-spirited religious service

preach (*vb*) deliver a sermon proclaiming the gospel or stating religious and moral truths

predestination notion that salvation of human soul is preordained by God

preterition Calvinist doctrine that God passes over those not elected to salvation

primitive religion native religion

proselytize (*vb*) attempt to convert others to one's beliefs or religion

psalm any sacred song or hymn from Bible's Book of Psalms used in worship

purification ceremonial cleansing of spiritual pollution

redemption salvation and deliverance from evil, esp. through Christ's act of mercy toward humankind

reincarnation rebirth of soul in another body (Hinduism)

religion system of beliefs and practices involving worship of a supreme being or principle and explaining the origin, nature, and meaning of the universe

repentance contrition for sins

retreat period of seclusion for religious exercises and meditation

revival evangelistic rekindling of religious fervor

rite solemn ceremonial practice following specific form

ritual specified form, manner, and language of religious ceremony

sacrament religious act or practice symbolizing conferment of divine grace; Catholic sacraments are baptism, confirmation, Eucharist, penance, extreme unction, holy orders, and matrimony; Protestants include only baptism and communion

sacrament of the sick extreme unction

sacrifice religious offering made to deity

sacrilege act or statement that degrades the sacred

salvation deliverance from damnation, liberation from sin and its punishment; redemption and reconciliation to God

schism split or division over orthodoxy in religious group, esp. Great Schism, as between Roman and Eastern churches in 9th c. and during period of rival popes in 14th to 15th c.

scholasticism philosophical system of 11th to 15th c. that attempted intellectual analysis of religious doctrine, based on teachings of St. Thomas Aquinas and St. Augustine

scripturalism detailed, often literal, analysis of the Bible

sect religious group deviating from orthodox faith, usu. having specific practices prescribed by its leader

secularism system or philosophy that rejects religious necessity or interpretation

sermon religious discourse delivered by clergyman as part of service

service form followed at religious meeting

sign of the cross cross formed in the air by moving hand rapidly from head to chest and shoulder to shoulder as sign of prayer

simony buying or selling of church office or indulgence

solemn vow irrevocable public vow taken by clergy and members of religious orders in Catholic Church committing them to observe rule of an order, often against ownership of property and marriage

soteriology doctrine of salvation through Christ

supplication earnest prayer of petition

syncretism attempted reconciliation of elements from two or more religions to create new religion

tent meeting camp meeting

theism belief in God; belief in gods

theology systematic study of God and religious faith and practices

theonomy state of individual or society that regards its own nature as being in accord with divine nature

theurgy working of divine or supernatural agency in human affairs

tithing paying one-tenth of one's income to support church

total immersion baptism in which candidate's entire body is immersed in water

tradition source of authority, doctrines, practices, and institutions of religion, such as Mosaic law

in Judaism, teachings of Christ in Christianity, and Koranic revelation in Islam

trine immersion baptism in which candidate is immersed three times, once for each part of Trinity

unction anointing with oil as consecration

unfrock (*vb*) deprive priest of right to exercise office

venial sin sin that does not deprive soul of sanctifying grace, unlike mortal sin

viaticum Eucharist given to person near death

virtues seven natural and cardinal virtues: faith, hope, charity, prudence, justice, temperance, and fortitude

worship showing honor and devotion to a deity

Individuals and Titles

abbé member of secular clergy, esp. in France

abbot superior of monastery

acolyte altar server; member of highest-ranking of four minor orders in Catholic Church

agnostic one who does not know whether God exists

altar boy boy assisting celebrant in liturgical service but not formally inducted as acolyte

altar girl girl who performs functions of altar boy

anchorite religious hermit or extreme ascetic

angel divine being, esp. messenger of God

apostate deserter of religious faith

apostle messenger or preacher of religious principles, esp. one of twelve original followers of Jesus

archangel chief angel; one of seven chief angels in Bible

archbishop chief bishop (Christianity)

archdeacon chief deacon, ranking below bishop (Christianity)

archpriest chief priest

Arhat one who has attained Nirvana through ascetic practices (Buddhism)

atheist nonbeliever in God

avatar deity in physical form on Earth (Hinduism)

ayatollah teacher, judge, or leader of Shi'ite sect, with superior training in theology and law (Islam)

believer person with faith, esp. in specific religion.

bhikshu monk observing rules of his order, such as vows of poverty (Buddhism)

bishop high-ranking ecclesiastical officer with authority over diocese and its clergy (Christianity)

Bodhisattva enlightened person who postpones Nirvana in order to help others attain Enlightenment (Buddhism)

bonze monk (Buddhism)

brother fellow member of religious order (Christianity)

buddha enlightened being with fully realized awareness of true nature of existence; statue of the Buddha used as symbol in Buddhism

caliph spiritual leader claiming succession from Muhammad

cantor singer or leader of choir (Judaism)

cardinal ecclesiastical officer ranking above bishop, usu. an archbishop; member of Roman Catholic Church's College of Cardinals

celebrant person performing rite, esp. priest officiating at Eucharist

cenobite member of religious order living in convent or monastery

chaplain person conducting religious services and performing sacraments in place other than church, as in military field or hospital, or for an organization

chela disciple of a guru (Hinduism)

cherub one of second order of angels, represented as winged child

choir group of singers in church

church whole body of Christian believers; building in which Christian worship services are held

clergy ordained priests, ministers, and rabbis, as distinct from laity; clerics

clergyman or **-woman** ordained priest, minister, or rabbi; curate

cleric member of the clergy

college clergy living together for specific purpose

colporteur person who travels about to sell Bibles

communicant church member entitled to receive the Eucharist

congregation gathering of people as religious community, esp. for specific services in church

convert person adopting or changing religion

convocation consultative assembly of Christian clergy

council assembly of bishops

crucifer carrier of cross at head of procession

crusader participant in medieval expeditions to Holy Land to reclaim it from Muslims

curate clergyman

curé parish priest in France

damned those souls predestined for condemnation

Dalai Lama chief lama of Tibetan Buddhism

deacon minister or layman assisting priest (Christianity)

dean Roman Catholic priest supervising one district of diocese; head of chapter of cathedral church

defrocked (adj) describing minister or priest who has been removed from office or excommunicated

dervish Islamic mystic, esp. Sufi, engaging in ecstatic whirling and dancing

devil evil spirit

devil's advocate official of Catholic Church who examines evidence given in demand for canonization

devotee person dedicated to spiritual master, teaching, or practice

dewal priest (Hinduism)

disciple follower of religious teacher or leader

ecclesiastic member of clergy or religious order

elder minister or esteemed congregation member

elect those souls predestined for salvation

Eminence title of honor applied to cardinals of Catholic Church

eparch bishop or metropolitan of administrative subdivision of Orthodox Eastern Church

eremite member of religious order living as hermit or recluse

evangelist itinerant or special preacher of Protestant denomination

Evangelist any of the writers of the four Gospels

exarch bishop of Orthodox Eastern Church, ranking below patriarch and above metropolitan

faithful those subscribing to a particular faith

fakir monk or wandering mendicant believed to possess magical powers (Hinduism, Islam)

father form of address for priest

father confessor priest who administers sacrament of confession

freethinker person of liberal religious views, usu. skeptical of dogma and doctrine

friar member of mendicant order

gentile person who is not Jewish

giaour person outside Islamic faith, esp. infidel

glebe Chiefly Brit. cultivable land belonging to parish church or benefice

guru spiritual master, esp. Hindu

hajji Muslim who has made pilgrimage to Mecca

heathen pagan, esp. nonbeliever in Christian, Hebrew, or Muslim God

heavenly host angels and others dwelling with God in heaven

hegumen head of Orthodox Eastern monastery

heretic person rejecting orthodox or accepted religious beliefs

hermit religious recluse

high priest chief priest; primary priest of ancient Jewish Levitical priesthood

Holy Roller derogatory description of member of Pentecostal sect, based on frenetic quality of services

illuminati person claiming spiritual grace or enlightenment

imam leader (Islam)

infidel disbeliever in specific religious doctrine, esp. that of Islam

Jesus freak Informal. member of fundamentalist group, usu. comprised of young people, that emphasizes intense personal devotion to Jesus Christ

kaffir infidel or nonbeliever in Islamic faith

laity congregation of people ministered to by clergy

lama priest (Tibetan Buddhism, Lamaism)

latitudinarian person having liberal religious views

magi priests (ancient Persia)

maharishi great teacher or wise man (Hinduism)

mahatma great soul, sage (Hinduism)

maniple steward of a monastery

man of the cloth member of clergy

martyr person put to death for defending religious principles

master religious sage or teacher

mendicant member of religious order living by alms or charity

Messiah expected deliverer of Jewish people; Jesus Christ

metropolitan bishop of diocese of Orthodox Eastern Church, ranking below exarch

minister clergyman or -woman, esp. Protestant one

ministry all ministers of a specific religion

missionary Christian proselytizer in non-Christian region

mohel Hebrew. person who performs brith milah, or rite of circumcision

monk man living in religious order, either Christian or Buddhist

Monophysite person who believes that Christ has one nature, partly divine and partly human

Monsignor title conferred on certain Catholic prelates

Mother Superior head nun of convent

muezzin caller of faithful to prayer (Islam)

mufti jurist who explains Islamic law

mullah teacher of religious law (Islam)

neophyte recent convert to a faith

novice person undergoing probationary period before taking vows of religious order

nullifidian person without religious faith, esp. skeptic

nun woman living in cloistered religious order, either Christian or Buddhist

padre father or priest; chaplain in military service

pagan heathen, nonbeliever in Christian, Hebrew, or Muslim God; formerly, follower of ancient Roman religion

palmer pilgrim returning from Holy Land carrying a palm branch, esp. in Middle Ages

Pariah member of lowest caste in India or Burma (Hinduism)

parishioner member or inhabitant of parish

parson rector; Protestant clergyman

pastor priest, minister, or spiritual shepherd of congregation; shepherd

patriarch bishop of Eastern Orthodox Church; Roman Catholic bishop next in rank to pope; church father

penitent person who confesses sin and seeks repentance

pilgrim person traveling to sacred place as affirmation of devotion, usu. Christian to Holy Land or Muslim to Mecca

pillar saint stylite

pontiff pope

pope bishop of Rome and head of Roman Catholic Church

preacher member of clergy, esp. Christian one; predicant

precentor person, sometimes of the clergy, who leads church choir or conducts choral service

precisian strict adherent to moral or religious standards, esp. Puritan of 16th or 17th c.

predicant preacher

prelate ecclesiastic of high order, such as bishop or archbishop

preterite those passed over by God; those not elected for salvation

priest ordained member of clergy, official minister

priesthood office and institution of being a priest; all priests collectively

primate archbishop or bishop ranking first among the bishops of a province or country

prior superior ranking next to abbot in monastery

prophet messenger of God, esp. one revealing judgment of God

proselyte new convert to a religion

provost chief dignitary of a cathedral

pundit learned, religious man (Hinduism)

qadi Islamic judge, scholar, and religious teacher

rabbi leader of a Jewish congregation; title of respect for Jewish scholar or teacher

rabbinate office of a rabbi; all rabbis collectively

Reb *Yiddish.* form of address or title for rabbi

recreant one who renounces faith

rector member or clergy in charge of parish

reprobate one who is damned

Reverend form of address for member of clergy

rishi religious sage (Hinduism)

sadhu holy man (Hinduism)

sage wise, pious person

saint holy person consecrated by religious body

sannyasi wandering beggar and ascetic (Hinduism)

sayyid title given to teacher descended from prophet Muhammad (Islam)

seeker person pursuing religious knowledge

seer person with spiritual insight

seminarian person studying to become member of the clergy

sensei spiritual teacher (Japan)

seraph one of the highest order of angels, usu. pictured as six-winged

sexton person who watches over church property and usu. rings bells for services

shaman person with spiritual insight and authority, empowered to conduct religious rites in nativist religions

shepherd pastor

sister member of woman's religious order; form of address for nun

starets religious teacher or counselor

stylite ascetic saint living atop pillar; pillar saint

subdeacon cleric ranking below deacon

swami religious teacher, holy man (Hinduism)

televangelist evangelist who preaches over television

tertiary lay member of religious order, usu. living in its community

theologian person who has studied religious faith and practices

true believer faithful follower of specific religious doctrine

tulku reincarnation of holy man (Tibetan Buddhism)

twice-born (*adj*) pertaining to a person of Brahman caste; pertaining to a person who has undergone reincarnation (Hinduism)

verger *Chiefly Brit.* church attendant, esp. to bishop

vicar member of Episcopal clergy in charge of mission chapel; representative of Anglican prelate with broad pastoral duties

votary person bound by religious vows

wali saint (Islam)

wise man religious sage

yogi practitioner of yoga philosophy and discipline (Hinduism)

zahid ascetic (Islam)

Zealot member of militant Jewish sect that flourished between 100 B.C. and 100 A.D.

Structures and Institutions

abbey monastery

altar raised platform where sacrifices and offerings are made to God

apse recessed, vaulted niche at end of choir in church

archdiocese area of jurisdiction of archbishop

basilica early Catholic church

bema sanctuary of Orthodox Eastern Church; altar in Jewish synagogue

benefice ecclesiastical office guaranteeing fixed income

bethel church for seamen

cathedral church that is diocesan seat of bishop or archbishop, often large and elaborately decorated

chancel area near altar reserved for clergy and choir

chancery office of diocese

chapel small house of worship associated with larger church

church place of worship, esp. structure in which Christian services are held

cloister monastery, esp. area within monastery restricted to its members

College of Cardinals chief ecclesiastical body of Roman Catholic Church, advisory to pope and including all cardinals

confessional stall in which Catholics make confession of their sins to unseen priest

convent residence for nuns or sisters of religious order; nunnery

curia the papal court

dagoba shrine housing sacred relics of Buddha

diocese territorial jurisdiction of bishop

divinity school Protestant seminary

Holy See See of Rome; Vatican

house of worship church, synagogue, or temple

jube screen separating chancel from nave, often supporting a rood

mandira Hindu temple

meeting house church or house of worship

mihrab prayer niche in Islamic mosque

misericord room in monastery set aside for monks permitted relaxation of monastic rules

mission local church or parish supported by larger religious organization, usu. in effort to convert nonbelievers

monastery home for persons of particular religious order, esp. monks; abbey

mosque Islamic house of worship

naos ancient temple or shrine

nave main axis of church or cathedral

nunnery convent

order community of monks or nuns following specific rules; major Catholic orders include Benedictine, Dominican, Franciscan, Jesuit, Marist, Paulist, and Trappist

pagoda Buddhist or Shinto temple

pantheon temple dedicated to all gods

papacy institution and office of the pope

parish local church or ecclesiastical district

parsonage house provided by church for Protestant clergyman, such as parson

pew bench or seat on which several persons sit in church

priory religious house governed by prior or prioress, usu. part of an abbey

pulpit lectern from which preacher conducts religious service, esp. interpreting the Bible as God's word

rectory residence of rector or parish priest

sacristy room in church for storage of sacred vessels and for clergy's preparation for services

sanctuary sacred portion of church surrounding altar

sanctum any sacred or hallowed place

see seat of bishop's office and authority

See of Rome seat of power of the pope, who has jurisdiction over Catholic churches throughout world; Holy See; Vatican

seminary institution providing training for ministry or esp. for priesthood

shrine place of devotion to saint or deity

shul *Yiddish.* synagogue

stupa memorial mound that may contain relics of saint (Buddhism)

Sunday school place of religious instruction on Sundays for children, esp. Christian

synagogue Jewish house of worship; shul; temple

synod church council

tabernacle house of worship, esp. large tent for evangelical services; portable sanctuary in which Ark of the Covenant was carried by Israelites after the Exodus

temple edifice for religious services; Jewish synagogue; shrine to specific deity or saint; primary locus for a religion

tope dome-shaped Buddhist monument for relics

Vatican Holy See of the pope; city-state serving as headquarters of Roman Catholic Church

vestry room in church for storage of vestments

Sacred Texts and Objects

Abhidhamma Pitaka third section of Pali Canon, consisting of abstract philosophical treatises (Buddhism)

Acts book in New Testament describing the inception of Christianity

Adigranth Granth (Sikhism)

American Standard Version American version of Bible, published in 1901

Analects text of teachings of Confucius

Angas sacred texts of Jainism

Apocrypha writings originally within the Bible, but judged unsuitable for inclusion by rabbinical or church authorities

aspergillum brush or small perforated container for sprinkling holy water (Catholicism)

aspersorium vessel for holding holy water (Catholicism)

Atharva-Veda one of ancient Aryan Vedic sacred texts (Hinduism)

Avesta book of sacred writings of Zoroastrianism

Bhagavad-Gita part of Indian epic poem the Mahabharata, written between 200 B.C. and 200 A.D., in form of dialogue between hero and avatar Krishna (Hinduism)

Bible sacred texts of Old and New Testaments, source of teachings and religious authority for Judaism and Christianity; Christian Bible

Book of Books Bible

Book of Common Prayer official book of services and prayers for Anglican communion

Book of Mormon sacred book of Mormon church, revealed by Joseph Smith

Book of the Dead book of prayers and charms for use of soul in afterworld (ancient Egypt)

Brahmana ritual text of Vedic period (Hinduism)

breviary book of prayers, hymns, and psalms used by priests in daily office

butsu representation or figure of the Buddha

canon church law, authoritative sacred texts

censer ornamental container in which incense is burned; thurible

chalice Eucharistic cup

chrism consecrated oil used in baptism and other sacraments

chrisom white cloth or robe worn by person during baptism

ciborium vessel containing Eucharistic bread or host

cloth attire worn by clergy

crosier bishop's or abbot's staff

Dead Sea Scrolls scrolls dating from Essene period, containing partial texts of Hebrew Bible or Old Testament and some non-Biblical scrolls, in Hebrew and Aramaic

Dhammapada text containing essential teachings of the Buddha

Epistle extract from Epistles of New Testament, usu. attributed to Paul, used in Eucharistic service

Five Classics basic ethical texts of Confucianism, attributed to Confucius, including I Ching, Book of Rites, Book of History, Book of Songs, and Spring and Autumn Annals

font vessel for holy water, often of stone

Genesis first book of Bible, describing Creation and history of patriarchs

Good Book Bible

Gospels story of life and teachings of Christ in first four books of New Testament

Granth sacred scripture of Sikhism; Adigranth

habit attire worn by clergy and members of religious orders

Hagiographa third part of Hebrew Bible containing the Psalms, Proverbs, Job, Ruth, Esther, and other books besides the Pentateuch and Prophets; Ketuvim; the Writings

Hebrew Bible Old Testament: Torah, Prophets, and Hagiographa

Holy Bible Bible

Holy Scriptures sacred writings of Old or New Testament or both together

Holy Writ Bible

hymnal book of Christian hymns

I Ching Book of Changes, one of Five Classics of Chinese Confucian canon, dealing esp. with divination through trigrams that reflect yin and yang

icon powerful image of sacred personage, usu. painted on wooden panel (Orthodox Eastern Church)

Jataka stories and fables concerning previous lives of the Buddha

Kama Sutra teachings of Hindu god of erotic love Kama

Ketuvim *Hebrew.* Hagiographa

King James Bible edition of Christian Bible published during reign of King James I of England circa 1610

Koran Islamic holy book, composed of 114 chapters or suras, believed to have been revealed to Muhammad by Allah; Qur'an

Law, the Pentateuch; Torah

lectionary book listing selections of sacred texts to be read in divine service

Mahabharata epic containing Hindu religious text Bhagavad-Gita

megillah *Hebrew.* scroll of Biblical books, esp. Book of Esther, read on Purim

menorah candelabrum, esp. one with nine branches, used at Hanukkah (Judaism)

mezuzah scroll with words from Deuteronomy, placed in small container affixed to doorjamb (Judaism)

missal large book of prayers and authorized readings for celebration of Catholic Mass

Nevi'im *Hebrew.* Prophets

New Testament portion of Bible that describes life and teachings of Christ and his followers, through Gospels and Epistles, written circa 100 A.D.

Old Testament portion of Bible that describes God's covenant with the Israelites, made up of the Torah or Pentateuch, Prophets, and Hagiographa, compiled between 1000 B.C. and 100 B.C.; Christian name for Hebrew Bible

Oral Law Talmud

Pali Canon ancient Buddhist sacred texts, orig. recorded from oral traditions in 1st C. B.C., consisting of sermons, rules of monastic order, and philosophical treatises; Tripitaka

Pentateuch first five books of Hebrew Bible; Torah

phylactery either of two small leather containers holding scriptural passages, worn on left arm and forehead during prayers by Jewish men; both phylacteries comprise the tefillin

Pitaka any of the three divisions of the Pali Canon: Abhidhamma Pitaka (philosophy), Sutta Pitaka (sermons), and Vinaya Pitaka (rules of monastic order) (Buddhism)

prayer book formal book of prayers, esp. Book of Common Prayer

Prophets second part of Hebrew Bible, containing books by prophets such as Isaiah, Jeremiah, and Ezekiel; Nevi'im

Proverbs book of Old Testament representing earliest example of Hebrew wisdom dealing with practical piety

Psalter book of Psalms

pseudepigrapha Christian and Jewish sacred texts not recognized in the canon and considered possibly spurious

Qur'an Koran

Ramayana second great Hindu epic, containing story of Prince Rama

relic part or piece of saint's physical remains

reliquary container or shrine for sacred relics

Revelation book of New Testament describing Apocalypse

Rig Veda oldest of ancient Aryan Vedic sacred texts (Hinduism)

rosary string of beads used by Roman Catholics, Hindus, and Buddhists for counting prayers or mantras

rubric directions for conducting religious service

sacred text writings that are source of authority and legitimacy for a religion

Sama-Veda one of ancient Aryan Vedic sacred texts (Hinduism)

Scripture sacred text

Septuagint oldest Greek version of Old Testament

shofar ram's horn sounded on Rosh Hashanah (Judaism)

stoup basin for holy water, usu. located near entrance of church (Christianity)

sutra religious text, esp. collection of aphorisms on any of various aspects of life (Hinduism, Jainism); any of the Buddha's sermons (Buddhism)

Sutta Pitaka second section of Pali Canon, consisting of sermons of the Buddha and stories about him (Buddhism)

Synoptic Gospels first three gospels in New Testament: Matthew, Mark, and Luke

tallith fringed prayer shawl (Judaism)

Talmud text of canon and civil law and rabbinical teachings, incorporating the non-Scriptural oral law, compiled in 6th c., codified in Jerusalem and Babylon; Oral Law (Judaism)

Tantra any of several books of esoteric doctrine regarding rituals and meditation (Hinduism)

Tao Te Ching teachings of Lao-tzu, basic text of Taoism, composed of eighty-one brief chapters describing the way of the Tao

tefillin both phylacteries (Judaism)

thurible censer

Torah first five books of Hebrew Bible, containing entire written body of Jewish law and wisdom sealed for all time in the form of holy scrolls; the Law; Pentateuch

Tripitaka Pali Canon (Buddhism)

Upanishads philosophical commentaries forming final portion of Vedic texts, written beginning circa 900 B.C.

Vedas ancient, sacred Hindu scriptures composed of Atharva-Veda, Rig-Veda, Sama-Veda, and Yajur-Veda, compiled between 1000 B.C. and 500 B.C.

vestment ceremonial garment worn by clergy during religious rite

Vinaya Pitaka first section of Pali Canon, consisting of the rules of the monastic order (Buddhism)

Vulgate Latin version of Christian Scriptures

Word usu. **the Word**; the Word of God; the Bible

Writings, the Hagiographa

Yajur-Veda one of ancient Aryan Vedic sacred texts (Hinduism)

yarmulke skullcap worn by Jewish males, esp. during prayer and religious study

Zend-Avesta Zoroastrian sacred texts

Zohar definitive text of the cabala, consisting chiefly of interpretations of the Pentateuch (Judaism)

Books of the Bible

Old testament

Genesis, Exodus, Leviticus, Numbers, Deuteronomy, Joshua, Judges, Ruth, I Samuel, II Samuel, I Kings, II Kings, I Chronicles, II Chronicles, Ezra, Nehemiah, Esther, Job, Psalms, Proverbs, Ecclesiastes, Song of Solomon (also Song of Songs, Canticle of Canticles), Isaiah, Jeremiah, Lamentations, Ezekiel, Daniel, Hosea, Joel, Amos, Obadiah, Jonah, Micah, Nabum, Habakkuk, Zephaniah, Haggai, Zechariah, Malachi

Apocrypha

I Esdras, II Esdras, Tobit, Judith, (additional parts of Esther), Wisdom of Solomon, Ecclesiasticus, Baruch, (additional parts of Daniel), Prayer of Manasses, I Maccabees, II Maccabees

New testament

Matthew, Mark, Luke, John, The Acts (of the Apostles), Romans, I Corinthians, II Corinthians, Galatians, Ephesians, Philippians, Colossians, I Thessalonians, II Thessalonians, I Timothy, II Timothy, Titus, Philemon, Hebrews, James, I Peter, II Peter, I John, II John, III John, Jude, Revelation (also Apocalypse)

Religious States and Experiences

acroamatic (adj) esoteric and revealed only to chosen disciples orally

adoration worship of a divine being

afflatus inspiration, divine bestowing of knowledge

afterlife state of existence following physical death

antediluvian (adj) before the Flood

apostasy abandonment of one's faith

astral plane subtle dimension more refined than physical reality

beatitude blessedness, bliss

blessed (adj) consecrated, holy, enjoying bliss; state prior to sainthood

bliss perfect, heavenly joy

born-again (adj) designating person who has experienced spiritual awakening and new religious commitment to Christ as personal savior; reborn; saved

calling in ancient use, God's selection of individual; now spiritual impulse toward religious vocation

canonization elevation to sainthood

charity love for one's fellow man and acts conveying such goodwill

damnation condemnation to eternity of suffering in hell

devotion piety, worshipful ardor

divinity state of being godlike

ecstasy state of absorption in the divine, with loss of awareness of body or outside world

enlightenment state of spiritual awakening

enthusiasm extreme religious devotion, usu. associated with intense emotionalism

epiphany direct manifestation of God or deity to a person

exaltation state of heightened spiritual awareness

faith state of trust in divinity

get religion (vb) have sudden, inspirational experience inducing faith

glossolalia speaking in tongues while in state of religious ecstasy

God-fearing (adj) deeply fearful or respectful of God

godliness piety, devotion to one's faith

grace state of being in divine favor; effect of God's mercy

hallowed (adj) blessed, made or kept holy

holy (adj) sacred, saintly, pure, whole

immanence inherent presence of God or divinity in Creation and daily life

immortality unending life without death

impiety lack of reverence for God

inspiration sudden spiritual awakening resulting from divine influence

irreverence disrespect for and discounting of divinity, Creation, and religion

joy bliss, beatitude

manna divinely supplied spiritual nourishment

martyrdom self-sacrifice to point of death in service of others or for maintenance of one's faith

metanoia profound transformation or conversion

metempsychosis rebirth, reincarnation

Molinism quietism

mystical (adj) involving direct communion with God or the divine

numinous (adj) inspiring awe and fascination, pertaining to mysterious aspect of divine power and religious experience

piety devotion to religious duty and practice; piousness

piousness piety

profane (adj) irreverent, unholy; defiling what is sacred

quietism type of religious mysticism marked by attainment of perfection through systematic contemplation; Molinism

rebirth reincarnation; transmigration of soul

reborn (adj) born-again

receive Christ (vb) be reborn, accept Christ as one's personal savior

recreant (adj) failing to keep faith

redemption salvation, deliverance from sin or evil

reprobation rejection by God and exclusion from salvation

revelation disclosure of God's will to humankind

reverence respect and awe for divinity, Creation, and religion

righteousness freedom from sin, sanctity

sacred (adj) consecrated, holy

sacrosanct (adj) extremely sacred or holy

saintliness charity, piety, holiness of spirit and action

salvation deliverance from sin, evil, and punishment; redemption

sanctity state of being sacred or holy

saved (adj) having accepted Christ as one's personal savior; born-again

spirituality conviction in one's experience of the mysterious aspect of divine power

transcendence state of God's nature or highest principle as above and apart from immanent Creation

transformation experience in which adherent to religion moves from one state to another, as by conversion, leap of faith, or following a path

transmigration of soul rebirth, reincarnation

unholy (adj) lacking in purity

venerable (adj) blessed, honorable; state prior to sainthood

veneration reverential love and adoration

zeal intensely passionate religious fervor

Mythological and Folkloric Beings

Abominable Snowman legendary creature living in high Himalayas; yeti

Achilles greatest Greek hero of Trojan War, invulnerable to weapons except for one heel

Adapa heroic fisherman son of Ea who preferred great knowledge to offer of immortality (Babylon)

Adonis beautiful young man loved by Aphrodite, who symbolized the death of nature in fall and rebirth the following spring (Greece)

Aeneas son of Aphrodite who led survivors of Troy west to found Rome

Aeon personification of time (Greece)

Aesculapius son of Apollo and the nymph Coronis, the first physician (Greece)

afreet powerful evil demon or monster (Arabia)

Agamemnon leader of the Greeks during siege of Troy

Aladdin poor boy in *Arabian Nights' Entertainments* who possessed magic lamp with jinn that would do his bidding

Ali Baba poor woodcutter and hero of *Arabian Nights' Entertainments* who opened a door by saying "open sesame" and found hidden treasure of the Forty Thieves

Amazons single-breasted Scythian women warriors

amphisbaena serpent having head at each end (Greece)

Antaeus giant son of Poseidon and Gaea, ultimately crushed by Herakles (Greece)

Argus hundred-eyed being who guarded Io, and whose eyes were transferred to peacock's tail after death (Rome)

Arthur semilegendary British king of Camelot during 6th century

Atlas Titan bearing Earth and firmament on his shoulders (Greece and Rome)

Atropos one of the Fates (Greece)

Azazel *Hebrew.* evil spirit of wilderness to which scapegoat was released

Baba Yaga female monster who feeds on children (Russia)

Babe the Blue Ox legendary blue ox belonging to Paul Bunyan (United States)

banshee female spirit who warns of death by wailing (Ireland and Scotland)

barghest legendary doglike goblin that portends death or misfortune

basilisk serpent with deadly breath and glance; cockatrice

behemoth any creature of monstrous size and power

Beowulf hero of medieval epic poem (Britain, 8th c.)

bogeyman frightening, demonic figure of popular folklore

brownie tiny, fanciful brown elf who does household chores at night

bugbear goblin that devours disobedient children

bunyip creature inhabiting swamps and lagoons in Aboriginal legend (Australia)

Calliope chief muse; muse of epic heroic poetry (Greece)

Callisto nymph loved by Zeus, changed into she-bear by Hera and then into Great Bear constellation (Greece)

Calypso daughter of Atlas who held Odysseus captive on her island (Greece)

Cassandra priestess daughter of King Priam of Troy whose prophecies were never believed (Greece)

Castor and Pollux twin brothers of Helen who protect seagoers (Greece)

Cecrops founder of Athens who had a snake's tail (Greece)

centaur half-horse, half-human monster

Cerberus three-headed dog who guards entrance to underworld (Greece)

Chaos representative of the void prior to creation of Earth (Greece)

Charybdis woman turned into whirlpool by Zeus; companion to Scylla (Greece)

Chimera flame-belching monster, part goat, part lion, and part dragon

Cinderella fairytale heroine who escapes mistreatment by stepmother and stepsisters to marry prince (Europe)

Circe evil woman who turned humans into swine (Greece)

Clio muse of history (Greece)

Clotho one of the Fates (Greece)

cockatrice basilisk

colossus giant human statue (Greece)

Cyclops member of a family of one-eyed cannibal giants (Greece)

daemon supernatural force, spirit for good or evil, in popular folklore

Daphne nymph loved by Apollo and turned into laurel tree, whose branch Apollo wore on his head (Greece)

Delphic oracle oracle of Apollo whose answers were enigmatic and ambiguous (Greece)

demigod half divine, half human minor deity; deified mortal

demon evil spirit, devil

deus otiosus distant or retiring deity; authority or father figure

Don Juan legendary, dissolute Spanish nobleman famous for his many seductions

dragon reptilian monster, often with breath of fire

Dryad forest nymph who protects trees (Greece)

dwarf small, usu. misshapen and ugly creature with magic powers

dybbuk dead person's evil spirit that invades living person (Jewish folklore)

dying god autumnal figure symbolizing harvest and decline of cosmic cycle of time

earth mother female deity symbolizing life or fertility

Echo mountain nymph who could only repeat others' last words, spurned in love by Narcissus (Greece)

Eight Immortals holy men who have attained immortality (Taoism)

elf mountain fairy, seen by moonlight

Enkidu quasihuman creature aiding Gilgamesh in quest (Babylonia)

Erato muse of love poetry (Greece)

Eumenides the Furies (Greece)

Euterpe muse of music (Greece)

Fafnir dragon slain by Sigurd (Scandinavia)

fairy small, supernatural being with magic powers; fay

familiar spirit supernatural servant of priest or magician, often represented as an animal

Fates three sisters who spin, weave, and cut the thread of life: Atropos, Clotho, and Lachesis (Greece and Rome)

faun sylvan demigod (Rome)

Faust character in medieval legend who sold his soul to the devil for knowledge and power

fay fairy

fiend evil spirit

Furies three snake-haired female torturers of the damned (Greece and Rome)

Galahad noblest and purest of knights of the Round Table, who gained the Holy Grail

Ganymede cupbearer of Zeus (Greece)

genie spirit in human form summoned to carry out one's wishes

genius tutelary spirit attending a person throughout life; *(pl.)* **genii**

genius loci *Latin.* guardian spirit of a single location

ghost spirit of dead person

ghoul evil being that feeds on corpses

giant huge and monstrously formed creature, enemy of gods and people (Scandinavia and Greece)

Gigantes huge monsters, children of Gaea, who were defeated by Olympian gods (Greece)

Gilgamesh hero of Sumerian and Babylonian epics

gnome dwarfish creature who lives underground

goblin demon of popular folklore in the form of a grotesque, often malicious sprite

golem figure artificially constructed in human form and endowed with life (Jewish folklore)

Gorgons three hideous monsters in the form of winged sisters with power to turn person viewing them to stone (Greece)

Graces three daughters of Zeus attendant on Aphrodite, embodying beauty and charm (Greece)

gremlin type of elf, usu. mischievous

troublemaker said to be responsible for minor malfunctions

Grendel half-human monster slain by Beowulf

griffin monster that is half eagle and half lion

Guinevere King Arthur's wife

hamadryad nymph who is spirit of a particular tree

Harpy winged, ravenous, half-woman monster that robs its victims of food (Greece)

Hecatoncheires hundred-armed, fifty-headed sons of Uranus and Gaea (Greece)

Helen Greek queen whose abduction instigated the Trojan War

hellhound watchdog of the underworld

Herakles Hercules (Greece)

Hercules son of Jupiter and greatest hero, who performed twelve labors (Rome)

Hermaphroditus son of Hermes and Aphrodite, united with a nymph to form one body with sexual characteristics of both genders (Greece)

hero mythic person whose story is told in epic tale of adventure or struggle

hippocampus creature who is half horse and half dolphin

hippogriff griffin with horse's body

hobbit small, furry creature who lives in burrow in the earth

hobgoblin mischievous goblin or sprite, esp. Puck

Houyhnhnm one of a race of horses endowed with reason in Jonathan Swift's *Gulliver's Travels*

Hydra nine-headed serpent whose heads grew back as they were cut off, slain by Hercules (Greece)

Hyperion one of the Titans, son of Uranus and father of Helios, Selene, and Eos

Icarus son of Daedalus who flew too near the sun, melting his wax and feather wings and causing him to fall into the sea (Greece)

incubus evil demon that has sex with women while they sleep

Iris messenger of God in multihued robe representing rainbow (Greece)

Izanagi and Izanami creators of Japanese islands who emerged from chaos and were progenitors of later gods (Japan)

Jack Frost personification of cold and frost (U.S.)

Jason leader of the Argonauts who retrieved the Golden Fleece (Greece)

jinn spirit capable of appearing in human or animal form (Arabia)

John Henry legendary black railroad worker who outdrove steam drill (U.S., 19th c.)

Jotun any of a race of giants often in conflict with the gods (Scandinavia)

kelpie horse-shaped water spirit (Scotland)

kobold mischievous underground gnome (German folklore)

Kraken legendary monster of northern seas (Scandinavia)

Kriss Kringle Santa Claus

Lachesis one of the Fates (Greece)

lamia monster with head and breast of a

woman and body of a serpent that allured children to suck their blood

Lancelot greatest knight of King Arthur's round table and lover of Queen Guinevere

Lares household gods who are spirits of ancestors (Rome)

lemures spirits of the dead (Rome)

leprechaun dwarf or sprite; fairy and beneficent spirit (Ireland)

Leviathan huge Biblical sea monster, either reptile or whale

Lilith woman or phantom said to be former wife of Adam in Jewish folklore

little people leprechauns, fairies, elves

Loch Ness monster dinosaurlike creature reportedly seen emerging from waters of Loch Ness (Scotland)

Lorelei siren or river spirit with fatal charm (Teutonic folkore)

loup-garou *French.* werewolf

maenads frenzied female followers of Bacchus or Dionysus (Greece and Rome)

manes spirits of dead (Rome)

manitou spirit that controls nature and is source of natural and supernatural power (Algonquian Indians)

manticore monster with man's head, lion's body, and scorpion's tail

Manu primal ancestor (India)

Medusa snake-haired woman monster beheaded by Perseus; one of the Gorgons (Greece)

Melpomene muse of tragic drama (Greece)

Merlin magician and seer of Arthurian legend

mermaid creature with fatal charm who is half woman and half fish

Metis first wife of Zeus, mother of Athena, and personification of prudence (Greece)

Midas legendary Phrygian king whose touch turned objects to gold (Greece)

Midgard serpent monster that grew to surround the entire world (Scandinavia)

Minotaur bull-headed, human-torsoed, flesh-eating monster slain by Theseus (Greece)

Mnemosyne mother of the muses and goddess of memory

Moirai Fates (Greece)

monster any of various legendary, mythical creatures, usu. hybrid of animal forms

Muses nine daughters of Zeus and Mnemosyne who inspire artists: Calliope (heroic poetry), Clio (history), Erato (love poetry), Euterpe (music and lyric poetry), Melpomene (tragedy), Polyhymnia (eloquence and sacred poetry), Terpsichore (dance), Thalia (comedy), Urania (astronomy)

naiad freshwater nymph (Greece)

Narcissus youth who loved his own reflection and was turned into a flower (Rome)

Nereid sea nymph; Oceanid (Greece)

Nibelungs race of dwarfs who possessed a treasure of Rhine gold that was captured by Siegfried (Teutonic)

Niobe bereaved daughter of Tantalus who wept

for her slain children even after being turned to stone (Greece)

nix water spirit that lures its victims into its underwater home (German folklore)

nymph semidivine spirit of natural region such as water, forest, mountains, or valleys (Greece)

Oceanid Nereid

Oedipus king who unwittingly killed his father and married his mother after solving Sphinx's riddle (Greece)

ogre hideous giant cannibal

oracle intermediary between gods and man who answered questions at shrine (Greece)

orc monster similar to an ogre

oread mountain nymph (Greece)

Orpheus lyre-playing musician who tried unsuccessfully to rescue his wife from Hades (Greece)

Pandora original woman who opened forbidden box, bringing woes and evils to humanity (Greece)

Parsifal knight who sought Holy Grail (Teutonic)

Paul Bunyan giant lumberjack with a pet blue ox named Babe, reputed to have shaped the Rocky Mountains (U.S., 19th c.)

Pecos Bill legendary cowboy who dug the Rio Grande River (U.S., 19th c.)

Pegasus winged horse born of Medusa's blood (Greece)

Penates gods who serve as family household guardians (Rome)

Perseus hero who slew Medusa (Greece)

Peter Pan boy who never grew up in Sir James Barrie's play

phantom specter or apparition

phoenix immortal bird that cremates itself every 500 years, then emerges reborn from ashes (Greece)

Pied Piper legendary folk hero who led people by entrancing them by playing his flute (Germany)

pixie fairy, said to be spirit of dead child

poltergeist noisy ghost

Polyhymnia muse of eloquence (Greece)

preta wandering or disturbed ghost (India)

Prometheus hero who stole fire from gods for mankind and was punished by Zeus (Greece)

Proteus sea god who assumed different shapes (Greece)

Psyche beautiful mortal loved by Eros (Greece)

Puck mischievous sprite of English folklore; Robin Goodfellow

Python dragon who guarded chasm at Delphi, slain by Apollo (Greece)

Queen Mab playful fairy of English folklore who controlled dreams

Rama hero of the epic tale Ramayana and perfect, devoted Hindu (India)

Ravana giant ten-faced demon (India)

Remus twin brother of Romulus (Rome)

Rip Van Winkle man who slept twenty years and awakened to a changed world, from story by Washington Irving (U.S., 19th c.)

Robin Goodfellow Puck

Robin Hood legendary, benevolent folk hero outlaw (Britain)

roc bird of enormous size and strength (Arabia)

Romulus one of twin brothers raised by a wolf, founder of Rome

Rudra father of storm gods who controls powers of nature (Vedic)

Rumpelstiltskin dwarf who spins flax into gold in German folktale

salamander mythical creature, esp. a reptile, thought to be able to live in fire

sandman folkloric character who puts sand in the eyes of children to make them sleepy

Santa Claus benevolent purveyor or gifts to children on Christmas Eve; Kriss Kringle

satyr goat-footed demigod of forest and field, noted for lasciviousness

scapegoat goat let loose on Yom Kippur after sins are laid on its head

Scheherezade in *Arabian Nights' Entertainments*, wife of sultan of India, who spared her life because she told such wondrous tales each night

Scylla sea nymph who was transformed into sea monster, companion of Charybdis (Greece)

sea horse creature who is half horse with fish tail

sea serpent large marine animal resembling snake

sibyl any woman who served as mouth piece of the gods in delivering prophecies and oracles

Siegfried hero of the *Nibelungenlied* (Teutonic)

Sigurd hero of the *Volsunga Saga*, counterpart of Siegfried in the *Nibelungenlied* (Scandinavia)

Silenus forest spirit, sometimes called oldest of satyrs (Greece)

Sinbad sea-voyaging adventurer of *Arabian Nights' Entertainments*

Siren singing sea nymph who charms sailors to their deaths (Greece)

Sisyphus crafty murderer and thief condemned by Zeus to roll a stone up a slope so that each time he approached the top the stone escaped him and rolled down again (Greece)

Sleeping Beauty fairy tale princess awakened from a prolonged, charmed sleep by the kiss of her true love

Sphinx human-headed, winged lion and poser of enigmatic riddles (Greece)

spirit supernatural being

sprite spirit, esp. mischievous elf

stork bird that is symbolic deliverer of new babies

succubus female demon who has sex with men while they sleep

sylph air spirit

Syrinx mountain nymph who was transformed into the reed from which Pan made his panpipe

Tannhäuser German lyric poet and hero of legend set in 13th c.

Tantalus son of Zeus condemned in Tartarus to forever reach for unattainable fruit and water

Termagant mythical deity in form of violent, dominating personage, believed by Medieval Christians to be worshipped by Muslims

Terpsichore muse of dance (Greece)

Thalia muse of comic and lyric poetry (Greece)

Theseus hero who slew Minotaur (Greece)

Tiki first man of Maori legend (Polynesia)

Titan one of a race of giant deities, children of Uranus who held power under Cronus and were overthrown by the Olympian gods (Greece)

Tom Thumb tiny hero of folk tales

tooth fairy fairy who exchanges gift for baby tooth placed under pillow of child

trickster god, hero, or personage who creates trouble and plays practical jokes in myth and legend

Triton half fish, half man and son of Poseidon with power over waves (Greece)

troll misshapen, woodland-dwelling dwarf or giant of limited intelligence (Scandinavia)

Typhon hundred-headed giant who caused violent wind, killed by Zeus (Greece)

undine female water spirit

unicorn creature with horse's body, lion's tail, and single horn, representing purity and supernatural powers

Urania muse of astronomy (Greece)

Valkyries maidens who escort warriors to Valhalla (Teutonic and Norse folklore)

vampire reanimated corpse who exists on blood of sleeping victims

vestal virgin one of the virgins tending sacred fire of Vesta (Rome)

water nymph semidivine marine creature

werewolf man capable of transmogrifying into shape of a wolf who preys on human victims; wolfman

William Tell rebellious hero of Swiss legend forced to shoot arrow through apple on his son's head

windigo evil spirit, cannibal demon (Native American folklore)

wolfman werewolf

wood nymph semidivine forest creature

world parents cosmic couple who symbolize creation of human race, such as Adam and Eve

wyvern two-legged, winged creature resembling dragon

xiphopagus Siamese twin monster

yeti Abominable Snowman

Ymir first living creature and progenitor of giants, whose corpse formed earth, water, and heavens (Scandinavia)

zombie reanimated corpse under spell of demon or deity

Gods and Divinities

Aeolus god of winds (Greece)

Agni god of fire (India)

Amphitrite goddess of the sea, wife of Poseidon (Greece)

Amun-Ra supreme national god (Egypt, 18th dynasty)

Anshar father of Anu, Ea, and Enlil (Mesopotamia)

Anu supreme sky god (Mesopotamia)

Anubis jackel-headed god of the underworld, death, and judgment of soul (Egypt)

Aphrodite goddess of love and beauty (Greece)

Apollo god of arts, intellect, and prophecy (Rome)

Apollon god of arts, sciences, reason, and inspiration (Greece)

Ares god of war (Greece)

Artemis goddess of hunting (Greece)

Ashur winged national god of battle (Assyria)

Astarte goddess of fertility and love (Phoenicia)

Athena goddess of wisdom and crafts (Greece)

Aurora goddess of dawn (Rome)

Baal god of fertility (Phoenicia)

Bacchus god of wine; Liber (Rome)

Balder god of sunlight personifying goodness, son of Frigg (Scandinavia)

Bel goddess and wife of Anu (Mesopotamia)

Benten goddess of love and the arts (Japan)

Brahma creator god in Trimurti (India)

Ceres goddess of fertility and agriculture (Rome)

Chloris goddess of flowers (Greece)

Comus god of revelry and feasting (Greece and Rome)

Cronos leader of the Titans and son of Uranus who castrated his father and fathered Zeus and other Olympian gods by his sister Rhea; Kronos (Greece)

Cupid god of love (Rome)

Cybele great mother goddess (Phrygia)

Daikoku god of wealth (Japan)

Demeter goddess of agriculture and fertility (Greece)

Diana goddess of the moon and forest (Rome)

Dionysus god of ecstasy and wine (Greece)

Dis god of the underworld and the dead (Rome)

Ea god of freshwater and wisdom (Mesopotamia)

Emma-O ruler of hell (Japan)

Enlil god of air and king of the gods (Mesopotamia)

Eos goddess of dawn (Greece)

Eris goddess of strife and discord (Greece)

Eros god of love (Greece)

Faunus god of fields and shepherds (Rome)

Flora goddess of flowers (Rome)

Frey fertility god (Scandinavia)

Freya goddess of beauty and love (Scandinavia)

Frigg mother goddess, consort of Odin (Scandinavia)

Fu-hsing god of happiness (China)

Gaea goddess of earth, mother and wife of Uranus (Greece)

Ganesha god of wisdom (India)

Geb earth god, father of Osiris (Egypt)

Gula goddess of healing (Mesopotamia)

Hades god of the dead and underworld (Greece)

Hanuman monkey god (India)

Hathor goddess of love and joy (Egypt)

Hebe goddess of youth (Greece)

Hecate goddess of magic and dark powers (Greece)

Helios sun god (Greece)

Hephaestus god of the forge and crafts (Greece)

Hera goddess of women and childbirth, consort of Zeus (Greece)

Hermes messenger of gods (Greece)

Hestia goddess of hearth and home (Greece)

Horus solar god, son of Isis and Osiris who ruled earth after avenging his father's murder (Egypt)

Huitzilopochtli god of war and the sun (Aztec)

Hygeia goddess of health (Greece)

Hymen god of marriage (Greece)

Hypnus god of sleep (Greece)

Indra rain god (India)

Inti personification of the sun (Inca)

Ishtar mother goddess of fertility and love, daughter of Anu (Mesopotamia)

Isis goddess of maternity, wife of Osiris (Egypt)

Janus god of beginnings and doorways (Rome)

Jove Jupiter (Rome)

Juno goddess of women and maternity, consort of Jupiter (Rome)

Jupiter sky god and chief god; Jove (Rome)

Juventas goddess of youth (Rome)

Kali goddess of motherhood and death, consort of Shiva (India)

Kore Persephone

Krishna god of love (India)

Kronos Cronus

Kuan Yin goddess of compassion (Chinese Buddhism)

Kubera god of riches (India)

Lakshmi lotus goddess of prosperity, wife of Vishnu (India)

Liber god of ecstasy and wine; Bacchus (Rome)

Loki trickster god of evil (Scandinavia)

Lug sun god (Celtic)

Luna moon goddess (Rome)

Mahakala god of wealth (India)

Marduk chief god (Babylonia)

Mars god of war (Rome)

Maui trickster god (Oceania)

Mercury messenger of the gods; god of communication (Rome)

Minerva goddess of wisdom and the arts (Rome)

Mnemosyne goddess of memory, mother of Muses (Greece)

Morpheus god of dreams (Greece)

Mors god of death (Rome)

Mot god of sterility (Phoenicia)

Nemesis goddess of punishment and reward (Greece)

Neptune sea god (Rome)

Nike goddess of victory (Greece)

Njord god of winds and prosperity (Scandinavia)

Nox goddess of night (Rome)

Nut sky goddess, wife of Geb (Egypt)

Nyx goddess of night (Greece)

Odin god of wisdom, magic, and death; chief god (Scandinavia)

Orcus god of the underworld, identified with Pluto (Rome)

Osiris god of the Nile, vegetation, and the dead (Egypt)

Pallas Athena bright Athena (Greece)

Pan shepherd god (Greece)

Pauguk personification of death (North American Indians)

Persephone daughter of Demeter, wife of Hades; Kore (Greece)

Phoebus Apollo shining Apollo (Greece)

Picus god of divination (Rome)

Pluto god of the underworld (Rome)

Plutus god of wealth (Greece)

Pomona goddess of orchards and gardens (Rome)

Poseidon sea god (Greece)

Priapus god of fertility (Greece)

Proserpina daughter of Ceres, wife of Pluto (Rome)

Psyche goddess of the soul, unified with Cupid (Rome)

Ptah creator of the universe, depicted as upright mummified man (Egypt)

Quetzalcoatl feathered serpent god of creation (Aztec and Toltec)

Ra sun god (Egypt)

Rahu mischievous, four-armed deity of natural disasters (India)

Rhea great mother goddess, wife and sister of Cronus and mother of Zeus (Greece)

Rhiannon goddess associated with horses (Wales)

Salacia goddess of oceans (Rome)

Sarasvati goddess of learning and wisdom (India)

Saturn agriculture god, father of Jupiter (Rome)

Selene moon goddess (Greece)

Seth brother and enemy of Osiris and god of evil (Egypt)

Shiva destroyer god in Trimurti (India)

Sin moon god (Mesopotamia)

Sol one of two sun gods (Rome)

Somnus god of sleep (Rome)

Surya sun god (India)

Svetovid god of fertility and war (Eastern Europe)

Tammuz vegetation god (Mesopotamia)

Thanatos god of death (Greece)

Themis goddess of law and justice (Greece)

Thor god of thunder and war (Scandinavia)

Thoth god of wisdom, arts and sciences, and magic; scribe of the gods (Egypt)

Thunderbird culture god (North American Indians)

Tlaloc rain god (Aztec)

Tuatha Dé Danann ancient gods (Ireland)

Tyche goddess of fate (Greece)

Uranus original god of heaven and father of the Titans, including Cronus (Greece)

Venus goddess of love and beauty (Rome)

Vesta goddess of the hearth (Rome)

Victoria goddess of victory (Rome)

Vishnu preserver god in Trimurti (India)

Vulcan god of the forge and fire (Rome)

Wotan chief god (Germany)

Xipe god of vegetation (Aztec)

Xochipilli god of flowers and pleasure (Aztec)

Yama ruler of hell and lord of the dead (India)

Zephyrus god of the west wind (Greece)

Zeus chief god and ruler of heaven; god of thunder and lightning (Greece)

Myths, Legends, and Fables

Aegis shield of Zeus with head of Medusa at its center, borne by Athena on missions (Greece)

Aesir pantheon of the gods (Scandinavia)

Aesop's Fables collected animal fables attributed to Phrygian slave Aesop

ages of humankind major, significant eras in mythological history of humankind: golden age, silver age, bronze age, iron age

allegory narrative with characters and actions having symbolic dimension

amaranth purple flower that never fades or dies

ambrosia food of the gods, conferring immortality

amrita elixir of immortality (India)

animal fable tale with animals personifying human characteristics to illustrate moral point

anthropomorphism practice of endowing natural world with human attributes

Arabian Nights ancient Oriental tales told by Scheherazade

archetype original or ancestral idea or type

Argonauts fifty Greek heroes who sailed with Jason to retrieve the Golden Fleece

Asgard city of the gods (Scandinavia)

Atlantis legendary continental island that disappeared into Atlantic Ocean during ancient or prehistoric times

Bifrost rainbow bridge between heaven and Earth (Scandinavia)

Book of the Dead texts placed as protection in tombs of the dead (Egypt)

caduceus winged staff of Mercury

Camelot site of King Arthur's palace and court (Britain)

cautionary tale traditional story with moral lesson

charm amulet or object that brings luck or wards off evil

chthonic (*adj*) pertaining to the underworld

cosmic egg mythic image of creation

cosmogony creation myth

creation myth mythic explanation of formation of universe; cosmogonic myth

culture hero mythical or folk hero who personifies cultural development and ideals

Deluge, the great flood of various legends

Edda collection of traditional poems on mythological and religious subjects (Iceland)

epic traditional tale of hero's adventures or creation

etiological myth myth explaining creation of the universe

Excaliber King Arthur's sword

fable story with fantastic events and creatures having allegorical meaning; legend

fairyland home of fairies; enchanted place

fairy tales universal stories about fairies or other imaginary and magical creatures, esp. for children, usu. based on oral tradition

Flood universal deluge that is subject of myth and legend in many cultures, including Mesopotamian and Judeo-Christian

folklore traditional beliefs, narratives, and superstitions of a culture

folkway pattern common to cultural group, expressed in traditional stories, beliefs, and customs

fountain of youth legendary spring whose waters restore health and youth to anyone who drinks them

gest traditional romantic tale of adventure

Gilgamesh major epic text of Mesopotamia

Gladsheim great hall in Odin's palace (Scandinavia)

golden age mythical earlier, happier, idealized era

golden apples treasure of Garden of the Hesperides, retrieved by Herakles (Greece)

Golden Fleece magical treasure retrieved from Colchis by Jason (Greece)

Gordian knot intricate knot whose untier would rule Asia, supposedly cut by Alexander the Great with sword

Great Turtle upholder of world (Native American)

Grimm's fairy tales folklore collection compiled by the Grimm brothers, including Snow White, Rumpelstiltskin, Tom Thumb, and Hansel and Gretel

Hesperides legendary garden at western extremity of world, where golden apples grow (Greece)

Holy Grail cup that was object of mystical quest by Arthurian knights

Iliad epic poem of Homer describing siege of Troy by Greeks

land of Nod mythical land of sleep

legend traditional story or narration

lore folk knowledge, body of information

lotus legendary fruit that induces state of dreamy forgetfulness (Greece)

Mother Goose fictitious author of a compendium of traditional nursery rhymes written down by Charles Perrault

motif recurrent theme in myth or legend

myth tale or traditional narrative that describes adventures of gods and legendary heroes, and reveals human behavior and natural phenomena through its symbolism

mythology collected body of myths of one people or culture

mythopoeia mythmaking

nature myth myth concerning natural phenomena

nectar wine conferring immortality (Greece)

Nibelungenlied medieval German epic relating the life and heroic acts of Siegfried

nursery rhyme simple, traditional, rhymed song or poem for very young children

nursery tale traditional story for very young children

Odyssey epic poem of Homer describing return of Odysseus from Trojan War

Olympus mountain home of the gods, ruled by Zeus (Greece)

Oz magical or otherworldly land described in Oz books of L. Frank Baum

Palladium statue of Pallas Athena, believed to provide protection for city of Troy (Greece)

parable short allegorical story with a moral

pathetic fallacy attribution of human feeling or motive to natural world or inanimate object

personification embodiment of human character in inanimate object or abstract idea

proverb pithy, epigrammatic saying, usu. a kernel of condensed folk wisdom

Ragnarok end of the world and destruction of the gods and humankind in a final battle with evil powers (Scandinavia)

Ramayana Hindu epic concerned with the life of Ramachandra

romance imaginative fiction, esp. describing adventure of a hero

sacrifice ritual offering of valuable object, human being, or animal to divine powers

saga legendary narrative about heroic adventures

scarab representation of a beetle, esp. as symbol of sun or cyclical cosmic pattern (Egypt)

soteriological myth myth describing hero as bringer of salvation

spell charm cast over person; bewitchment

sun disk symbolic representation of sun or sun god, as in Egyptian, Babylonia, and Aztec mythology

tale legendary, fictitious, traditional story told dramatically

theogony account of the origin of the gods and their genealogy

theriomorphic (*adj*) having form of an animal

Trojan Horse horse filled with Greek soldiers, used to trick Trojans into opening their city gates, thus losing their war

underworld regions of the dead; realm of afterlife, esp. for punishment

Valhalla great hall where Odin received souls of heroes fallen in battle (Scandinavia)

Vanir race of fertility gods originally in conflict with the Aesir (Scandinavia)

Volsunga Saga Icelandic saga of late 13th c. concerning the Volsungs, the theft of the treasure of Andvari, and the adventures of the hero Sigurd; basis of the *Nibelungenlied*

Yggdrasil giant tree that supported the world (Norse)

Utopia

Agapemone communistic, free love establishment founded in 1849 at Spaxton, England

Arcadia region of innocence and simplicity

asylum place of refuge and protection

Atlantis legendary island in Atlantic Ocean with highly developed, utopian society, said to have sunk beneath the sea

Avalon island home of Morgan Le Fay, represented as earthly paradise, to which King Arthur was taken after his death

Big Rock Candy Mountain place of refuge in children's song

brave new world futuristic society described in novel by Aldous Huxley

Brook Farm egalitarian utopian farming community founded in 1841 in Massachusetts

bucolic (*adj*) pastoral, rural

cloudland dreamland

cloud nine *Informal.* state of perfect happiness

Cockaigne imaginary land of idleness and luxury

dreamland place where one's dreams come true; cloudland; fantasyland

dystopia opposite of utopia, where everything is wretched and people are miserable; kakotopia

El Dorado place of fabulous wealth and abundance sought by 16th-century explorers

Erewhon utopia in Samuel Butler's novel of same name

fairyland place of great beauty and magical charm

fantasia artistic work of free imagination and fancy

fantasyland dreamland

Fountain of Youth magical fountain providing eternal youth, held by Spanish explorers to lie somewhere in Americas

Goshen land of plenty, esp. land assigned to Israelites in Egypt

Happy Valley utopia in writings of Samuel Johnson

haven place of asylum, refuge, and peace

heaven on earth earthly dwelling place as peaceful and perfect as heaven

Hesperides garden at western extremity of world that produces golden apples (Greek mythology)

idyll time and place of peaceful, pastoral life

kakotopia dystopia

kingdom come heaven on earth

land of milk and honey land of plenty; Canaan, as envisioned by the ancient Hebrews

land of plenty earthly dwelling place that provides for all of humanity's physical and spiritual needs

Laputa utopia in writings of Jonathan Swift

lotus land legendary Greek land of dreamy idleness

lubberland imaginary land of idleness and leisure amid plenty

Modern Utopia utopia as described in book by H.G. Wells

Nephelococcygia utopia in plays of Aristophanes

never-never land illusory, ideal land or condition

New Atlantis utopia in writings of Sir Francis Bacon

New Harmony socialistic colony, founded in

Indiana in 1825, that established first kindergarten, free public school, and free library in United States

oasis isolated, often unexpected, place of refuge and refreshment, esp. in desert

Oneida Community utopian settlement in New York State, founded on theory that sin can be eliminated by social reform

pastoral (*adj*) pertaining to idealized, peaceful, simple, and natural life of farmers and shepherds

pie in the sky state of perfect happiness or utopia, esp. when illusory

pipe dream illusory or fantastic plan or way of life

Prester John figure in story of utopian land

Quivira utopian tale

refuge haven, place of safety and peace

safe harbor refuge or haven

sanctuary asylum; place of refuge, protection, or immunity from law

Seven Cities of Cibola utopian legend

Shangri-la remote, imaginary paradise on earth and land of eternal youth, after fictional Himalayan land described by James Hilton in *The Lost Horizon*

utopia any ideal place or state, esp. in its laws and social conditions; any visionary, sometimes impractical scheme for social improvement

Utopia imaginary island with ideal government, from 16th-century book by Sir Thomas More

wonderland place of wonders or marvels

Xanadu legendary city of opulence and pleasure, home of Kublai Khan

MAGIC AND THE OCCULT

Belief Systems and Theories
Rites, Practices, Spells, and Symbols
Occult States and Experiences
Individuals and Objects

See also: *Chap. 4: Astronomy and Space Science;*
Chap. 22: Strategy, Intrigue, and Deception;
Chap. 25: Religion; Mythology and Folklore;
Truth, Wisdom, and Spiritual Attainment

Belief Systems and Theories

alchemy medieval chemistry and speculative philosophy aimed at transforming base metals into gold and prolonging life

ancestor worship adoration of ancestors, whose spirits are believed to have power to intervene in affairs of the living

animal magnetism mysterious natural force used by Franz Mesmer to hypnotize and cure patients; mesmerism (France, 18th c.)

animism belief in existence of spirits separate from bodies; attribution of conscious life to objects in nature

astrology divination according to positions of stars and planets

black magic magic used for evil or diabolical purposes

cabalism belief in the esoteric, the occult, or mysticism

Chaldean (*adj*) belonging to ancient Semitic sect of Babylonia, versed in occult arts and astrology

chiromancy palmistry

diabolism devil worship

Gnosticism early Christian heresies stressing esoteric knowledge of spiritual truth, practiced by secret, self-styled elite sect

hermetics Gnostic teachings of Hermes Trismegistus, characterized by abstruse occultism

macumba Brazilian voodoo

mesmerism animal magnetism

Mithraism men's Persian mystery cult of late Roman Empire

mysticism belief in acquisition of spiritual truth, power, and communion with ultimate reality through intuition, insight, or application of specific secret rites, sometimes expressed in romantic love of the divine

numerology divination through numbers and study of their occult significance and interrelationships

obeah sorcery and magic among blacks of the Caribbean, Africa, and southeastern United States

oneiromancy divination through dreams

palmistry divination by analysis of creases in palm of hand; chiromancy

panpsychism belief that every physical event has a psychic aspect

parapsychology branch of psychology concerned with investigation of paranormal phenomena such as clairvoyance and telepathy

phrenology analysis of character based on size and shape of skull

santeria Afro-Caribbean belief system that includes animal sacrifices and uses Catholic saints as representations of the spirit world

Satanism devil worship

shamanism animistic belief in unseen world of gods, demons, and ancestral spirits responsive only to shamans (northern Asia)

sorcery use of evil power for divination or manipulation of the natural world for specific ends

tarot any of a set of twenty-two specially marked cards that symbolize archetypal personalities and situations, used for fortunetelling

telepathy communication between minds by paranormal means

voodoo West Indian religion derived from African ancestor worship, characterized by rites, trances, animistic deities, spells, and hexes

white magic magic practiced with intent to do good or benefit others

wicca witch theology based on empowerment of women who care for Earth and cosmos

witchcraft sorcery and magic acquired through communication with devil

zombiism belief in voodoo cult of the zombie

Rites, Practices, Spells, and Symbols

abracadabra magical incantation, often rapid and nonsensical

aleuromancy use of flour for divination

apotropaic (*adj*) intended to guard against evil

arcanum mystery or rite known only to initiates

ascendant zodiacal sign rising at eastern horizon at moment of one's birth

aspect relative position of planets and stars having astrological influence on human affairs

astral house position of planets in connection with influence on specific aspects of life

astral traveling leaving one's body and venturing forth as a spirit

augury divination by omens and signs

auspice prophetic sign

bewitch (*vb*) cast spell over through witchcraft or magic

black art magic practiced by witches, conjurers, and diabolists

Black Mass perversion of Catholic Mass by worshiping Satan

blessing invocation of a good or benefit upon another person

cabala esoteric, occult, or secret doctrine; orig. medieval Jewish mystical theosophy and thaumaturgy

call up spirits summon mystical forces by incantation

cargo cult Pacific Islands religious cult believing in acquisition of material goods through intervention of spirits

cast a chart calculate, diagram, and analyze all zodiacal positions at time of person's birth

cast a spell impose magic power over; conjure

conjure (*vb*) summon by incantation; affect by magic

conundrum riddle whose answer involves a pun; mystery

coven assembly of witches or diabolists, esp. thirteen such

crystal gazing divining by looking into a crystal ball

cult secret or restricted society characterized by rituals and initiations, demanding absolute loyalty or suppression of ego; sect

curse invocation of harm on another; (vb) wish or invoke calamity or injury upon

cusp period of transition from one zodiacal sign to next

deicide killing of a god

divination foretelling future through analysis of omens by prescribed methods

dowsing art of finding water, oil, or metals by means of magic rod

effluvium vapor; offensive-smelling emanation

enigma obscure occurrence; riddle or mystery

ephemeris table of positions of celestial bodies at stated times, used in divination

esotericism doctrine and practice of arcane or secret rites

ESP extrasensory perception

ether rarefied element; medium in which spirits appear; intoxicating gas

evil eye glance or stare believed to cause harm; silent curse; malocchio

exorcism rite or spell that casts out evil spirit from possessed person or object

extrasensory perception ESP; ability to perceive phenomena beyond normal physical dimensions and senses

faith healing miraculous curing of disease or injury through belief in God and his servants

Fata Morgana mirage consisting of multiple images that resemble castles

fetish superstitious belief in object's magical or supernatural powers; object of such belief

folk medicine primitive healing based on nature or ritual, not medical technology and science

foreordain (vb) predetermine the future

fortunetelling divining and predicting future events, esp. concerning an individual's life

grigri African amulet or fetish; gris-gris

gris-gris grigri

haoma intoxicating, sacramental plant drink used in Zoroastrian ritual; soma

haruspication divination by examination of entrails or liver of slaughtered animal

haunting habitual reappearance of ghost or specter

hex curse, jinx, evil spell

hocus-pocus nonsense and sleight of hand used to cloak deception in magic rites

hoodoo voodoo, bad luck

horoscope prediction based on astrological chart

house one of twelve equal sectors of celestial sphere in astrology

hypnosis sleeplike state induced by repetitious speech or movement, marked by heightened suggestibility

idolatry worship of physical object or living person

incantation verbal spell or charm used in magical rites and sorcery

initiation ceremony admitting new member to secret cult, brotherhood, or belief system

jinx spell bringing bad luck; curse

levitation phenomenon of floating on air in apparent defiance of laws of gravity

lifeline long crease in hand consulted for divination in palmistry

lycanthropy delusion that one has become a wolf

magic use of illusion, sleight of hand, ritual, and incantations for divination, enchantment, or to invoke a curse

malison curse, invocation of harm

malocchio evil eye

medicine show show offering supposed cures through sale of patent medicines

mental telepathy reception or transmission of thoughts without words

mind reading ability to perceive another's thoughts through preternatural power

mirage illusion or appearance of something that does not really exist

mumbo jumbo verbal nonsense and sleight of hand associated with rites, spells, or magic

mysteries secrets on which cult or belief system are based

necromancy conjuring spirits of the dead for magic or divination

nympholepsy demoniac frenzy induced by nymphs

occult (adj) pertaining to magic or any system claiming use or knowledge of secret or supernatural powers or agencies

oddity inexplicable, magical occurrence

omen event or phenomenon said to portend future

open sesame magical incantation that causes desired result

Ouija Trademark. board with alphabet and signs for reception of telepathic messages

patent medicine packaged nonprescription drug with incompletely described ingredients; quack remedy; harmless potion sold as cure-all

phase particular stage in regular cycle of moon, used in astrology

portent omen of future event, usu. an unfortunate one

potion usu. secret mixture of liquids with magic powers

precognition clairvoyance relating to future events

prediction foretelling of future events

prophecy prediction of the future

psychokinesis movement of objects through mental processes, without use of physical means; telekinesis

rainmaking rites, esp. dances, intended to bring rain

riddle mystifying or misleading question posed as problem to be solved

rite prescribed ceremony or liturgy for specific purpose

rune character of medieval Germanic alphabet; aphorism, poem, or saying with mystical meaning

Sabbat midnight assembly of diabolists to renew allegiance to devil through rites and orgies (14th-16th c.)

scrying crystal gazing; divination by crystals

seance session or meeting to receive spirit communications

secret society cult or brotherhood with oath of silence and secret rites and disciplines

sect often extreme or heretical group dissenting from established belief system or religion; any small branch of a larger movement; cult

shadow phantom; faint representation of spirit

shamrock trifoliate plant considered symbol of good luck, esp. by Irish

sigil sign, word, or device of occult power

sign one of twelve divisions of zodiac

signification suggestion, symbolic representation

sodality brotherhood with common purposes, beliefs, and rites

soma haoma

soothsaying prophecy, divination

sortilege divination by lots

spell words with magic powers; state of enchantment

spellbind (vb) bind or hold by spells

spirit rapping communicating with spirits of dead by rapping on table

spirit writing writing of medium under supposed influence of spirits

stargazing practicing divination through astrology

summons spiritual calling

sun dance ceremony consisting of dancing, symbolic rites, and often self-torture (North American Indians of the Plains)

superstition belief or practice resulting from fear of unknown, trust in magic, or false concept of causation

taboo often ritualized fear or prohibition of specific object or practice

telekinesis psychokinesis

telepathy extrasensory communication between minds

thaumaturgy working of magic or miracles

time machine theoretical device for traveling forward or backward in time

touch contact by spirit world

transubstantiation change of one substance into another, esp. Eucharistic transformation of bread and wine

vapor something insubstantial or transitory

vaticination prediction, prophecy

voodoo sorcerer's charm or curse; hoodoo

vortex gateway into another dimension

Walpurgis Night eve of May Day, when witches congregate and ride

wanga voodoo charm or spell

whammy Informal. magic curse or spell that brings bad luck

wish invocation of good or evil on someone or something

wizardry practice of sorcery; magical power of transformation

Zener card one of twenty-five cards marked with five different objects, used in extrasensory perception research

zodiac imaginary belt in heavens encompassing paths of planets, divided into twelve astrological signs

Occult States and Experiences

adumbrative (adj) vaguely foreshadowed, with sketchy sense of future

apocalyptic (adj) forecasting or suggesting end of world

aura luminous radiation surrounding object or individual

aureole radiant light around head of sacred person; halo

bliss serenity, inner peace, complete happiness

blissed-out (*adj*) *Slang.* experiencing a continual, trancelike state of bliss or euphoria

chimerical (*adj*) visionary and improbable; existing only in fantastic imagination

clairaudience power of hearing something not audible to the ordinary ear

clairvoyance ability to discern objects not present to the senses; perception beyond normal range; precognition

creeps *Informal.* sense of foreboding

deep (*adj*) possessed of heightened consciousness; perceptive beyond the norm

déjà vu uncomfortable sense of familiarity with new experience; sense of having been in a situation before; paramnesia

devoid (*adj*) empty, blank, lacking sensibility

disbelief incredulity or difficulty in accepting reality of what has been experienced

disembodiment separation of spirit or mind from physical body

dread heightened fear, esp. of the unknown

ecstasy complete, rapturous delight; trancelike, often prophetic state beyond self-control

eerie (*adj*) spooky, filling one with dread of the unknown

entrancement supersensible, nonrational, trancelike state

extrasensory (*adj*) beyond realm of senses

extraterrestrial something or someone from outer space

fatidic (*adj*) prophetic

foresight ability to see and predict future; vision

foretell (*vb*) predict future events

fourth dimension something outside range of ordinary experience as measured in length, breadth, and depth, usu. time

glossolalia pseudolanguage of ecstasy or possession; speaking in tongues

hallucination visual or auditory perception of objects without reality, often experienced in trancelike state

halo aureole

hermetic (*adj*) recondite, characterized by occultism or Gnosticism

hypnotic (*adj*) suggesting hypnosis, trance, or detachment from consciousness

imaginary (*adj*) inexplicable by reason; distinct from three-dimensional reality of senses

in the dark ignorant, unknowing, or unaware

kef dreamy tranquility produced by use of a narcotic (Middle East)

manifestation physical evidence of phenomena

mantic (*adj*) prophetic, divinatory

materialization physical manifestation of nonmaterial phenomenon or spirit

nepenthe forgetfulness of sorrow, orig. a potion used to induce such forgetfulness

obsession persistent, usu. disturbing, preoccupation with one idea, feeling, person, place, or thing

occult (*adj*) beyond ordinary knowledge or understanding; mysterious or supernatural

oneiric (*adj*) of or relating to dreams

orphic (*adj*) mystic, oracular

Orphic (*adj*) relating to rites and doctrines ascribed to Orpheus and the cult of Dionysus

out-of-body experience sensation of perceiving oneself from external viewpoint as though mind or soul had left body

paramnesia déjà vu

paranormal (*adj*) supernatural, scientifically inexplicable

phantasmagoria rapidly fluctuating, dreamlike scene or imagery

possession domination by evil spirit or passion; replacement of one's normal personality by another's

precognition clairvoyance

prescience foreknowledge of events; divine omniscience

preternatural (*adj*) extraordinary, existing outside nature

psi extrasensory perception; psychic phenomena in general

psychedelic (*adj*) describing abnormal psychic state of heightened awareness, often produced by drugs and accompanied by hallucinations

psychic (*adj*) sensitive to nonphysical, supernatural forces

Pythian (*adj*) relating to the oracle at Delphi, noted for giving ambiguous answers

second sight clairvoyance, precognition

sixth sense keen, intuitive power of perception beyond that of the five senses

somnambulism sleepwalking

speaking in tongues incomprehensible, nonhuman or mystical language while in a state of ecstasy or possession; glossolalia

spellbound (*adj*) in state of enchantment

supernatural extraordinary phenomena inexplicable by science or senses

supersensible (*adj*) spiritual; beyond realm of senses

surrealistic (*adj*) having bizarre, dreamlike quality

touched (*adj*) having received divine revelation, inspiration, or supersensible powers

trance state of profound abstraction, deep hypnosis, or suspended animation

transcendental (*adj*) beyond limits of ordinary experience, reality, and comprehension; supernatural

unbelievable (*adj*) impossible to explain by reason or senses

uncanny (*adj*) eerie, mysterious, of supernatural origin or power

unfamiliar (*adj*) strange, difficult to explain

unimaginable (*adj*) beyond powers of imagination and intellect

unreal (*adj*) fantastic; beyond normal senses and dimensions

vatic (*adj*) prophetic, oracular

vibration characteristic aura or spiritual emanation that infuses individual or body, sensed intuitively

vision supernatural, often revelatory appearance in dream, trance, or ecstasy

xenoglossia magical knowledge of a language one has never learned

Individuals and Objects

acolyte follower

adept trained practitioner

alkahest universal solvent in alchemy

anchorite one living in seclusion for religious reasons

ankh cross with loop at top, used as symbol of enduring life (ancient Egypt)

apparition unusual phenomenon or vision, esp. ghostly figure

archimage great wizard or magician

astrologer practitioner of astrology and stargazing

azoth mercury, regarded as first principle of all metals by alchemists

banshee female spirit

barsom bundle of sacred twigs

bogy evil spirit, goblin

botanica store in which plants and other materials are purchased for use in rituals, esp. in santeria

channel individual through whom spirits make contact

charm amulet worn to ward off evil and bring good fortune

chiromancer palm reader

conjurer magician, wizard

crystal ball glass orb used for divination

daemon demon

demiurge supernatural being that possesses an autonomous creative power in subordination to the Supreme Being

demon evil spirit; daemon

dervish member of Muslim order known for frenzied, whirling devotional practice

devil Satan, master of all evil spirits and demons

disciple devoted follower

djinn jinn

doomsayer soothsayer who predicts apocalypse

Doppelgänger ghostly double of living person

Dracula deranged, possessed individual, orig. a Transylvanian count, who draws strength by drinking blood of others; vampire

Druid ancient Celtic priest, magician, or wizard

effigy crude physical representation or image, esp. of hated person

fakir Hindu or Muslim ascetic or wonder-worker; dervish

familiar spirit spirit of dead person who attends or serves another

flying saucer unidentified moving object in air reputed to be from another planet or solar system; UFO

fortune cookie folded Chinese dessert cookie with written prophetic message or advice enclosed on slip of paper

fortuneteller individual claiming ability to prophesize future

genie jinn

ghost spirit of dead person that reappears in bodily likeness to haunt or roam in earthly realm

ghoul evil being that robs graves and feeds on corpses

glyph symbolic figure carved in relief

gnome ageless, often deformed dwarf who guards precious ores and has secret knowledge

gnosis essential esoteric and spiritual knowledge held to be achieved through faith by Gnostics

goblin grotesque, often malicious sprite or demon

gremlin small, mischievous being said to be responsible for minor malfunctions

hag ugly female demon or witch

haruspex minor priest who practiced divination, esp. from entrails of animal killed in sacrifice (ancient Rome)

hei-tiki Maori charm worn around neck

hobgoblin mischievous goblin; bogy

icon idol, symbol, or object of devotion

illuminati persons claiming superior religious enlightenment

incubus evil spirit that has sexual intercourse with sleeping women

initiate new convert to belief system

jinn supernatural spirit that assumes human and other forms and serves its summoner; djinn; genie

joss Chinese idol; cult image

juju African magical fetish or charm

kachina doll representing deified ancestral spirit of Hopi Indians

leprechaun mischievous old elf with knowledge of hidden treasures (Irish folklore)

loup-garou *French.* werewolf

magician practitioner of illusion, sleight of hand, and incantation for prophecy

magus wise man, sorcerer, or magician

marabout Muslim hermit

mascot person, animal, or object adopted by group as symbolic good luck figure

medicine man shaman, sorcerer, or priest healer, esp. among American Indians; witch doctor

medium individual serving as channel for communications with spirits

megalith very large, rough stone, esp. used for primitive religious monuments

menat amulet used to secure divine protection (ancient Egypt)

mind reader person who can discern thoughts of others through supernatural means

moly mythical herb with magical powers

monolith single great stone, obelisk, or column, often built as symbolic religious monument

Moonie devoted cult follower of Sun Myung Moon or Unification Church; often considered derogatory

mystagogue one who initiates another into mystery cult

neophyte novice, recent convert

nightrider member of secret society who rides masked at night to perform acts of terrorism, esp. member of Ku Klux Klan

omen occurrence or phenomenon portending future event

oracle person or shrine through which deity reveals secret or divine purpose

palm reader one who divines by examining creases in person's palm; chiromancer

panpsychist advocate of belief that every physical event has psychic aspect

phantasm ghost, specter, figment of imagination

phantom specter or apparition, esp. one inspiring dread

philosophers' stone stone believed to have power to convert base metals to gold, sought by alchemists

philter potion, charm, or drug with power to cause person to fall in love

planchette small, triangular or heart-shaped board on casters with suspended pointer, used to produce automatic writing, esp. on Ouija board

poltergeist noisy, mischievous ghost

precursor incident or phenomenon that portends future event

premie recent initiate to cult

prophet person who predicts future events

psychic individual sensitive to supernatural and spiritual forces; medium

puck mischievous sprite or hobgoblin

pythoness female practitioner of divination, esp. priestess of Apollo

querent person who asks questions or seeks information, esp. through medium

rabbit's foot foot of rabbit carried for good luck

revenant person who returns as ghost or specter

scarab stone beetle used as talisman and symbol of destruction (ancient Egypt)

seer person with power to foretell events

sensitive medium, psychic

serpent demon, treacherous creature

shadow phantom, ghost

shaman priest who uses magic for cures, divination, and sorcery, esp. among tribal peoples; witch doctor

sibyl female fortuneteller

sign omen; one of twelve divisions of zodiac

soothsayer person who practices divination

sorcerer wizard, shaman, practitioner of sorcery

specter ghost, phantasm, visible disembodied spirit

spellbinder person who casts spells

spirit often malevolent disembodied but visible being

spook *Informal.* ghost or specter

sprite fairy or elf, esp. mischievous one

succubus demon who assumes female form to have sexual intercourse with sleeping men

swastika mystic symbol in form of cross with arms of equal length, with all arms extended at right angles in same direction, also used as symbol of Nazis

talisman charm or object held to bring good luck and avert evil

tea leaves leaves from emptied cup of tea

whose arrangement is used in divination and prophecy

teleplasm emanation from body of medium that serves as means for telekinesis

thaumaturge magician, performer of miracles

third eye spot in forehead receptive to occult or mystical knowledge or perception; intuition

tiki Polynesian wood or stone image of supernatural power

totem pole carved, painted pillar with series of American Indian symbolic images

UFO unidentified flying object believed to be from outer space; flying saucer

vampire reanimated corpse that rises from grave at night to suck blood of living; Dracula

visionary mystic, prophet, or psychic

wand slender rod used by conjurers and magicians

warlock sorcerer; man who practices black magic

werewolf person transformed into wolf or who assumes shape of wolf; wolfman

wicca witch in wicca doctrine

witch woman practicing white or black magic or sorcery, said by Christians to be possessed by the devil

witch doctor medicine man; shaman

wizard male sorcerer or magician

wolfman werewolf

wraith apparition of living person seen just before death; ghost, specter

zombie supernatural voodoo power that reanimates dead body; speechless, will-less human embodiment of such power

---

ESCHATOLOGY

Fate
Heaven and Paradise
Hell

See also: *Chap. 24: Death; Chap. 25: Religion; Mythology and Folklore; Magic and the Occult*

Fate

apocalypse prophetic revelation of cataclysm that results in forces of good defeating forces of evil

apocalyptic number 666, number of the beast in Revelations

appointed lot one's predetermined worldly fate or fortune

Armageddon final battle between forces of good and evil

balance determination of one's fate

bane source of ruin or destruction

bounty reward or good fortune

break *Informal.* stroke of luck

cataclysm violent upheaval, usu. at end of the world

certainty inevitability; that which is fixed, settled, or destined to be

chance luck, contingency

chaos state of utter confusion or lack of organization

contingency that which is possible but uncertain or subject to chance

coup de grâce *French.* decisive act or event; deathblow

crack of doom signal that indicates moment at which one's fate is decided; doomsday

crapshoot *Informal.* unpredictable situation involving risk

cup one's lot in life

curse ill fate or misfortune, esp. due to external intervention

curtains *Slang.* doom; end of one's life

damnation condemnation to hell or ill fate

deserts one's deserved reward or punishment

destiny inevitable and predetermined course of one's life

doom unhappy destiny; ruin or death

doomsday day of Last Judgment at end of the world

end fate or destiny

eschatology study of or religious doctrine concerning the end of time, judgment day, death, resurrection, and immortality

fatality something established by fate; disaster that results in death

fate inevitable outcome of one's life; prescribed order of things or predetermined cause of events

Fates three sisters who determine man's fate; weird sisters (Greek mythology)

finality irrevocable end toward which life moves

Final Judgment final determination of mankind's ultimate fate at end of the world

fluke unexpected stroke of luck

fortune destiny or fate, esp. favorable; hypothetical force that unpredictably determines events

future that which is going to occur in time; that which exists after death

Götterdämmerung destruction of the gods; Twilight of the Gods (German mythology)

immortality eternal life

inevitable that which is predetermined and cannot be avoided

infinity doomsday, day of Final Judgment

judgment Last Judgment

Judgment Day day of God's judgment at end of the world, determining fate of mankind

karma force generated by a person's actions, determining his or her destiny in future existence (Eastern religions)

kismet fate

Last Judgment final judgment of mankind

Last Things end of history and final fate of individuals and humankind

lot one's worldly fate or fortune; that which comes one's way in life

luck force, circumstances, or events that bring good or evil

millennium period of Christ's Second Coming and His reign of holiness on Earth

mischance mishap or misfortune

misfortune ill fate

moira individual destiny or fate (ancient Greece)

Moirai Greek Fates

oblivion finality or death; condition of being unknown or lost

odds likelihood or chance of particular event or fate

omen portent or indication of one's fortune

oubliette oblivion, finality, or death

Pandora's box source of extensive troubles and curses

payoff reward, retribution, or resolution

portion one's lot, fate, or fortune

predestination God's foreordination of all events; fate or destiny; predetermination

predetermination predestination

Ragnarok destruction of the gods and the world in a final battle (Scandinavian mythology)

random (*adj*) determined by chance or luck

redemption deliverance from a state of sin

reincarnation rebirth of soul in another body (Hinduism)

retribution reward or punishment, esp. in hereafter

Revelations last book of Bible, in which apocalypse is described

salvation soul's redemption from eternal punishment for sin

samsara indefinitely repeated karmic cycle of birth, misery, death, and rebirth or rebecoming (Hinduism and Buddhism)

serendipity propensity for achieving unsought good fortune

stars celestial bodies said in astrology to determine one's destiny; luck

stygian (*adj*) extremely gloomy and foreboding

sword of Damocles situation that threatens impending disaster or ill luck

terra incognita unknown or unexplored region

Twilight of the Gods Götterdämmerung

twist of fate unexpected development, reversal of one's fortune; wild card

uncertainty chance or contingency

ups and downs variations in one's affairs and fortunes

vagary unpredictable, erratic, or uncertain action or event

vicissitude favorable or unfavorable event or change that occurs by chance

weird sisters Fates; Moirai

wheel of fortune imaginary revolving wheel symbolizing inconstancy of fortune

wild card twist of fate

world beyond hereafter, afterlife

writing on the wall portent of one's fate or destiny

zero hour time at which Final Judgment occurs or one's fate is determined

Heaven and Paradise

above heaven

Abraham's bosom heaven

afterlife life after death; great beyond

afterworld place of life after death

Alfardaws Muslim paradise

Assama Muslim paradise

bliss heaven

Canaan promised land of rest and refuge (Judaism)

Celestial City heavenly Jerusalem in Bunyan's *Pilgrim's Progress*

City of God heaven, paradise

Civitas Dei *Latin.* city of God, esp. in Catholicism

Eden original paradise recorded in Book of Genesis in Old Testament; Garden of Eden; paradise

Elysian fields Elysium

Elysium heaven of Greek and Roman mythology

empyrean highest paradise; visible heavens

eternal life immortal life of soul after death of body

eternal reward eternal life of the soul in heaven as reward for living a good life

eternity timeless state into which soul passes after death

everlasting afterlife, eternity

Fiddler's Green heaven reserved for sailors and soldiers

Garden of Eden Eden

Garden of Irem fabled Islamic garden of paradise

glory heaven

great beyond usu. **the great beyond;** afterlife

happy hunting ground paradise of hunting and feasting for warriors after death (Native American)

heaven realm of bliss and eternal happiness after death; abode for souls of the dead at God's side

heaven's throne heaven, esp. God's seat in heaven

hereafter afterlife, eternity

Kingdom of God heaven (Christianity)

Kingdom of Heaven heaven (Christianity)

Land of Beulah quiet paradise for those waiting to enter Celestial City in Bunyan's *Pilgrim's Progress*

Land of the Leal heaven (Scotland)

New Jerusalem heaven

Nirvana freedom from rebirth (Buddhism)

Olympus heavenly dwelling place of ancient Greek gods

on high in heaven

paradise realm of eternal goodness and happiness after death; Eden; reward

Pearly Gates entrance to heaven

Promised Land heaven

purgatory place of temporary suffering and punishment where souls are purified of sin prior to entry into heaven (Christianity)

reward paradise

salvation redemption or deliverance from sin

seventh heaven highest heavenly realm (Islam)

upstairs heaven

Valhalla heavenly hall and dwelling place of Norse gods and deceased heroes

welkin vault of heaven

Zion heaven as gathering place of true believers

Hell

abyss hell, bottomless infernal regions

Amenti region of the dead (ancient Egyptian mythology)

Arallu region of the dead (ancient Babylonian mythology)

Avernus hell

below (adv) in hell

bottomless pit hell; pit

brimstone fire and sulfur of hell

damnation eternity in hell

dark void beyond life in hell

down below in hell

Erebus place in underworld that dead pass through to reach Hades (Greek mythology)

eternal punishment banishment of soul into hell for infinity

Gehenna place of suffering and torture; hell where dead are punished after death (Judaism)

Hades realm of the dead (Greek mythology); hell

hell region or condition of punishment for wicked persons after death; abode of evil spirits, esp. the devil

hellfire fire of hell

inferno hell in form of fiery region of torture

limbo region adjacent to hell for souls forbidden from heaven

Naraka region of punishment after death (Hinduism)

Nastrond dark, noxious hall of punishment (Norse mythology)

nether world hell

Nifleheim place of eternal cold, darkness, and fog that is abode of those who die of illness or old age (Scandinavian mythology)

Pandemonium hell, demonic region; capital of hell in Milton's *Paradise Lost*

perdition hell; place of utter damnation

pit bottomless pit

Sheol abode of the dead; hell (Judaism)

Styx principal river of the underworld (Greek mythology)

Tartarus infernal regions below Hades (Greek mythology)

Tophet hellish place of punishment after death in the Bible

underground underworld

underworld underground region for the dead; hell

void abyss; dark, unknown regions beyond life

TRUTH, WISDOM, AND SPIRITUAL ATTAINMENT

Mystical States and Experiences
Practice, Discipline, and Belief
New Age
Enlightenment, Truth, and the Unknowable

See also: *Chap. 1: Health, Fitness, and Enhancement; Chap. 13: Philosophy; Chap. 23: Reasoning and Intuition; Chap. 25: Religion; Magic and the Occult; Eschatology*

Mystical States and Experiences

accord harmony, balance, proportion

acme highest stage or point; perfected form of something; zenith

actualization realization, esp. achievement of potential

afflatus divine inspiration or communication of wisdom and power

ardor zealous intensity of feeling

attuned (adj) in harmony with or responsive to spiritual life

awakening becoming aware of spiritual life and one's true self

awe sense of enormous wonder, delight, reverence, or fear

balance harmony, proportion, or emotional equanimity

beatific (adj) marked by sheer bliss; saintly, angelic

beatitude consummate bliss, transcendent happiness; state of being blessed

blessed (adj) enjoying spiritual contentment; hallowed, consecrated; highly favored

bliss serenity, inner peace, or complete happiness

celestial (adj) heavenly, suggesting divine inspiration

concord harmony; agreement between persons

consciousness awareness, esp. of spiritual life

dark night of the soul negativity and dissatisfaction that precede spiritual enlightenment

delight joy; extreme satisfaction or gratification

deliverance liberation, state of being freed, esp. from darkness or bondage

disembodied (adj) lacking substance or reality normally present; having spirit separated from corporeal substance

divine (adj) proceeding from God, devoted to God; supremely good or admirable

divine revelation enlightenment or perception of truth through act or intervention of God

divinity nature and essence of God; state of man so endowed

ecstasy complete, rapturous delight; trancelike state of receptivity to enlightenment

elevated (adj) exalted in mood or feeling; with a sublime nobility, moral rectitude, or higher consciousness

enchantment state of delight and rapture; influence by charms and incantation

enrapture (vb) fill with delight, gratification, and enchantment

epiphany revelation or manifestation of God or the divine; sudden intuitive perception of something's essential meaning

equilibrium balance and harmony with nature, other men, or oneself

ethereal (adj) celestial, heavenly; airy, nonmaterial

euphoria feeling of supreme well-being or elation

evanescent (adj) tending to vanish like vapor; fragile, airy, imperceptible

exalted (adj) marked by purity or nobility of thought and manner

existential (adj) relating to, grounded in, or based on human existence, as distinguished from essence

extrasensory (adj) beyond one's normal sense perceptions

fervor intensity of feeling, passion; earnest belief

fulfillment realization of one's full potential; sense of completion

glory aureole, nimbus; splendor; spiritual ecstasy; beatific happiness of heaven

godhead quality or state of being divine

harmony integration into consistent whole with balance, internal tranquility, and peace with one's surroundings

high *Slang.* state of euphoria and spiritual exaltation; (adj) lofty, elevated

holy (adj) spiritually whole, sound, or perfect; infinitely good, righteous, or selfless; godlike; sacred

inner joy bliss, inner light

inner light divine presence in soul that provides spiritual enlightenment and moral guidance

inner space spiritual universe within a person as opposed to physical universe of outer space

inspiration divine influence, sacred revelation, or spiritual awakening

integrated (adj) characterized by united and harmonious coordination of parts into whole

irradiate (vb) illuminate, enlighten spiritually, make clear

joy state of bliss, delight, and satisfaction

love Godlike benevolence; people's adoration of the divine in God, others, and themselves

mystical (adj) possessing spiritual reality separate from senses and intellect; involving direct communion with God or spirits

nirvana highest state of enlightenment, salvation, harmony, and transcendence

numinous (adj) inspiring awe or religious feelings

oneness harmony, integrity, and wholeness of spirit

pacific (adj) peaceful, harmonious, tranquil

peace serenity of spirit; tranquility, concord

perfection condition of fullness or completion; attainment of highest state; flawless state or condition

plenty fullness, abundance of spiritual satisfaction

positive (adj) marked by acceptance, approval, hope, and honesty

presence something nontangible felt or believed to be present; person's manner, bearing, or aura

purity perfection of spirit; absence of flaws or disharmony

quietism passive, withdrawn posture toward worldly matters

radiance spiritual brightness, glory

rapture spiritual ecstasy and exaltation due to knowledge of divine things

realized (*adj*) spiritually enlightened, in harmony with oneself
repose rest, inner peace, tranquility
revelation divine or supernatural communication of spiritual truth
reverie trancelike thought, contemplation, or dream
sacred (*adj*) hallowed, consecrated, worthy of veneration, holy
saint one distinguished by piety, virtue, and benevolence, without regard for self; spirit of departed person canonized by church to serve as guide for spiritual growth
salvation deliverance from spiritual estrangement and attachment to material world into state of religious fulfillment and recognition of ultimate reality
sanctity holiness, saintliness of life and character
selfdom essence of one's individuality
selfhood one's own character or personality
sensitive (*adj*) aware of spiritual and mystical matters beyond information offered by senses; (*n*) one in tune with spiritual life
serenity calm, peaceful condition of repose and harmony
spirituality sensitivity to or concern with nonmaterial values, as distinguished from body and mind concerns
splendor radiant glory, esp. of spiritual fulfillment
sublime (*adj*) spiritually exalted and noble
supernal (*adj*) having spiritual character; coming from above
supersensible (*adj*) beyond the realm of the senses; spiritual
supreme (*adj*) loftiest, ultimate, highest
totality state of being complete, comprehensive, and unified
touched (*adj*) having received divine revelation, inspiration, or supersensible powers
tranquility peace, repose, serenity, harmony of spirit
transcendence state of being beyond limits of everyday experience, reality, or comprehension; supernatural, unified, or spiritual realm
tuned-in (*adj*) *Informal.* spiritually aware or enlightened
unity condition of concord and harmony
virtue correct attitude and conduct according to moral values
vision supernatural, revelatory appearance in dream, trance, or meditative state
within spiritual, interior life; inner space
wonder state of delight, marvel, mystery, or surprise coupled with admiration
yes indicator of positive, hopeful outlook on life
zenith ultimate point or greatest height; acme

Practice, Discipline, and Belief

anagogic (*adj*) having spiritual meaning or sense; arising from or striving toward lofty ideals
anthroposophy mystical religious system similar to that of theosophy

antinomian one who holds that divine grace is sufficient for salvation and moral law is unnecessary
ark place that provides protection and security through divine presence
asceticism strict self-denial and austerity as measure and means of spiritual discipline
ashram religious retreat for sage and disciples
astral (*adj*) relating to the stars; denoting a supersensible substance held in theosophy to pervade all space and survive the individual after death
astral traveler spiritual guide; one who makes spiritual, out-of-body journey
augur (*vb*) predict future by omens
blessing something conducive to spiritual attainment; consecration by divine care or intervention
chakra in yoga, any of seven body points that are sources of psychic energy and spiritual power
channel (*vb*) convey information from spiritual world
communion contact and communication with God or spirits
contemplation deep thought; silent meditation on spiritual matters
cornerstone that which is essential, basic, or indispensable to all that follows or is built upon it
devotion profound dedication and religious fervor, esp. acts evincing this; ardor, zeal
discipline self-control, self-restraint, self-denial; proper conduct in accordance with self-imposed rules
élan vital life force, vital principle of life
embodiment physical incarnation of noncorporeal thing
empyrean true and ultimate heavenly sphere; transcendentally exalted source of noble ideas or feelings
eudemonics art or method of attaining happiness
fasting prolonged abstention from food for purification and spiritual insight
forgiveness act or state of ceasing to feel resentment or seek retribution over wrong committed by another
grace beneficence or generosity, esp. of God toward humankind; disposition to kindness and compassion
guru master, teacher, spiritual guide
healing removal of negative energy, making one sound and whole; restoring spiritual integrity
higher law guiding principles of divine or moral law
hylozoism doctrine that all matter is inseparable from life
indwell (*vb*) exist within as guiding spirit or motivating force
key something serving to reveal or solve a mystery or provide an entrance to spiritual enlightenment

keystone part or force on which related things depend
leap attainment of enlightenment through sudden awareness or revelation
life, the occupation with and devotion to spiritual matters, esp. to the exclusion of material concerns; the way
lotus position erect sitting posture in yoga, with each foot resting on thigh of the opposite leg with sole upturned
mandala graphic, mystic representation of universe used as meditation aid, esp. concentric geometric shape such as square within a circle
manifestation perceptible outward expression of something, esp. form or guise of spirit or divinity
manna divine or spiritual nourishment
mantra ritualistic incantation used in meditation
master wise individual, learned in spiritual discipline and inspiring devotion among disciples
material (*adj*) corporeal or bodily, the opposite of spiritual
meditation private devotion; spiritual exercise of deep contemplation or sustained introspection, esp. silent repetition of mantra
medium individual believed to be capable of channeling information from spirit world
meridian flow lines of energy movement through body
miracle inexplicable, extraordinary event suggesting divine intervention or spiritual guidance
moral (*adj*) ethically good, principled; conforming to or acting on inner conviction of what is right
music of the spheres ethereal harmony supposed to be produced by movements of spheres of heavenly bodies
mysteries secret initiation rites for supposed betterment of worshipers
nimbus shining cloud around divine being
numen divine spirit inhabiting natural object or phenomenon; dynamic, creative force; human need for and capacity to have spiritual life
odyssey long, adventurous journey, esp. in search of enlightenment
omni- prefix meaning all
one divinity
one way life devoted to spiritual attainment
panacea universal remedy for all ills
past life previous physical existence of spirit, esp. as basis of one's karma
path spiritual direction, one way; attainment of enlightenment through systematic spiritual discipline
perseverance steadfast persistence in pursuit of spiritual grace, esp. until succeeded by state of glory
pietism intensity of devotional experience and practice
pundit learned wise man
purging self-purification by expulsion of harmful substances

purification cleansing of sin; moral or spiritual purgation

querent one who consults a spiritual guide

quest search for enlightenment and harmony

realization act or process of becoming real, taking form, or achieving potential

rebirth spiritual regeneration or revival

reflection meditation; consideration of something with view to understanding

reflexology massage of foot or hand to promote generalized healing and relieve stress

regimen strict practice

rejuvenation regeneration of youthful vigor

renunciation ascetic self-denial; rejection of one's previous values or lifestyle

rhythm harmonious, orderly movement or flow

rigor strict discipline, austerity

sacrifice self-denial, loss, or abstinence from something to promote spiritual growth

seeker one who devotes life to search for enlightenment and salvation

self entire individual: mind, body, and spirit

self-denial restraint of one's impulses to facilitate spiritual goals

self-discipline regulation and training of oneself for improvement

self-purification spiritual cleansing, esp. through self-denial and discipline

silence peaceful, meditative tranquility conducive to spiritual attainment

soul noncorporeal essence and spiritual principle of one's life

source point of origin; generative force

spirit essence of deity serving as invisible activating power; soul; noncorporeal essence and animating principle of life

sustenance spiritual nourishment or support; source of strength

swami master, teacher, wise man

theosophy religious beliefs held to be based on special mystical insight into divine nature

TM transcendental meditation

transcendence quality of being beyond what is experienced and perceived in material world

transcendental meditation TM; simple Hindu technique of two daily twenty-minute meditations with chanted mantra, now popular in the West

transfiguration act or process of undergoing ennobling spiritual change

trust faith and confidence in spiritual truth

visionary one who sees beyond common experience or perception

visitation special administration of divine favor, affliction, or revelation

votary devotee living by vows

way, the path to spiritual attainment and harmony; the life

Word usu. **the Word**; divine guidance and inspiration

zazen meditation practice in cross-legged position

Zen practice of self-discipline and meditation to achieve direct spiritual enlightenment

New Age

affirmation positive thought consciously used to create a desired result

akashic records universal memory of nature and all souls; the book of life

All That Is God; Creative Forces; Divine Mind

altered state of consciousness any shift of primary focus to levels of reality other than the physical plane; trance or hypnotic state

ambient sound soothing, environmental background music; New Age music

amulet bag small protective pouch for carrying items of personal sacred significance, such as crystals

Aquarian Age two-thousand year astrological World Age beginning around 2000 A.D., in which humanity is expected to evolve towards peace, spiritual enlightenment, global community, and renewal of the Earth

aromatherapy use of essential oils for relaxation and healing, usu. in conjunction with massage and acupuncture

astral body inner body composed of electromagnetic energy that links the soul with the physical body; energy body

Atlantis lost, legendary island civilization in Atlantic Ocean between Europe and North America, said to have sunk beneath the sea in ancient times

aura magnetic energy field, luminous quality radiating from a person

belief system primary ideas or attitudes about life that shape one's relationship to reality

biomagnetics study of magnetic energy as it effects human health

bodywork any of various psycho-physical, hands-on healing techniques utilizing massage, movement, and seeking to balance the energy and emotional bodies

catalyst guide or teacher who functions as facilitator to speed one's psychic or spiritual growth

chakra system major channels through which life force flows into physical body; mediating channels between astral and physical bodies associated with major glands and acupuncture points

channeling receiving energy and information from other levels of reality ranging from discarnate beings to the Divine Mind or collective unconscious

core belief idea or attitude ingrained in one's mental patterns as truth

core tone vibrational essence of the individual soul carried within each incarnation

Creative Forces God; All That Is; Divine Mind; life force

creative visualization technique using mental imagery and affirmations to produce positive energy and conditions conducive to harmony and positive changes in life

crystal transparent, usu. quartz crystalline structure that vibrates at high frequency, used in conjunction with gemstones for healing and meditation

discarnate being incorporeal being or spirit

Divine Mind God; All That Is; Creative Forces

Earth plane physical world of external reality

emotional body octave or level of body that vibrates with all unresolved emotions from any incarnation

energy body astral body; level of body containing chakra system

feeling tone vibration of being, emanating from emotional body, that resonates from core tone

Great Year in astrology, cosmic cycle of twelve World Ages, occurring once every 26,000 years; Aquarian Age marks beginning of next Great Year

guiding spirit source of channeled information, usu. spirit of deceased person

hands-on healing channeling life-force energy through hands to remove negative energy, make oneself whole, and restore spiritual integrity

Harmonic Convergence shift point at end of Mayan Great Cycle, occurring in August, 1987, when a synchronized global meditation coincided with passage of a galactic beam through Earth and the sun in expectation of 5000 years of peace and harmony

harmonizing bringing something or someone into accord and balance

healer person who is a channel for the life force with intent to be of service to others

healing circle group of healers who gather together to combine and multiply their healing power

higher mind level of mind fueled by soul rather than ego and capable of accessing broader perspective

higher self one's essence or eternal nature; soul

holistic (adj) emphasizing organic or functional relation between parts and whole

incarnate (adj) in a physical form; within a body

inner child part of emotional body that holds unfinished childhood business as well as the capacity to be eternally childlike

inner guide spiritual guide; inner voice; part of greater being that is not presently incarnate

karmic bond deep connection of two souls from past incarnations that is carried into present lifetimes

karmic debt good deeds owed in present life to balance or complete a past incarnation

Lemuria legendary pre-Atlantean civilization located on lost subcontinent in Pacific Ocean whose people were known as the Mu

light positive energy; the source

light being spirit guide; discarnate being; saint

magnet body that produces magnetic field capable of attracting iron, influencing personal vibrations, and healing

mindfulness meditation technique in which full awareness is focused on the present moment

negative energy energy that is toxic or draining to the life force and counter to affirmation of life

New Age evolution of human consciousness and spiritual movement toward the light of the Aquarian Age; spiritual healing based on various techniques and methods such as astrology and crystal interpretation

New Age music ambient or environmental acoustic jazz that is spiritually soothing or uplifting, often using a blend of ancient and modern instruments

octave harmonic interval or level of consciousness

organic (*adj*) forming an inherent vital part; composed of, using, or grown only with animal or vegetable matter

oversoul supreme reality or mind; spiritual unity of all being

past-life therapy technique of releasing karmic blocks through a regression process in order to access one's full potential

peak experience glimpse of enlightenment

pendulum suspended body swinging freely from fixed point, used as simple means of receiving channeled information

personal power ability to access one's creative energy, tune it with the core tone, and use it to take action in the physical world

primal body level of the body that contains the cellular memory of humanity's animal heritage and the dark side of nature from one's past lives

psychic person who can access energy and information from nonphysical realms; sensitive, medium, or channel

psychic therapy spiritually based therapy that utilizes altered states to experience and integrate the soul level of consciousness

pyramid structure in the form of a square base with triangular walls meeting at apex that concentrates and transmits energy for meditation and regeneration

regeneration spiritual renewal or rebirth, esp. a radical transformation of one's life

self-actualization fulfillment of one's potential; attainment of peace of mind and harmony

soul eternal being; energy essence; higher self

soul consciousness eternal perspective and link between the ego/mind and the Divine Mind

soul mates two or more souls originally split off from the same or larger oversoul

soul purpose spiritual task a soul is working on mastering or learning in any particular incarnation

third eye sixth chakra at center of forehead, connected with pineal gland, through which soul sees into physical plane; energy center through which psychic sense of vision operates

vibes *Informal.* vibrations

vibration velocity of movement of energy or life force through a body; characteristic aura, derived from this movement of energy, that one senses intuitively from an individual or body

vibratory tone essential spiritual feeling one senses emanating from another individual or body

Enlightenment, Truth, and the Unknowable

attainment accomplishment or acquisition of enlightenment

clear (*adj*) free of mundane, worldly matters, enabling one to see the spiritual essence of things as they are; at the highest state of enlightenment

compassion consciousness of other people's suffering and selfless tenderness toward it

empathy capacity for vicarious experiencing of another's thoughts or feelings and understanding based on it

enlightenment state of being in harmony with laws of the universe; realization of ultimate universal truth and absence of desire

entelechy realization or actuality, as opposed to potential

essence basic underlying nature; most significant element or quality of something

farseeing (*adj*) visionary, prophetic

humility freedom from pride and arrogance; modesty of spirit and ability to view others and oneself realistically

illumination spiritual enlightenment

imponderable (*adj*) beyond exact measurement or evaluation

incomprehensible (*adj*) lying beyond reach of human mind; unfathomable

indescribable (*adj*) too vague, extreme, or far beyond experience to be accurately described

ineffable that which is unspeakable or indescribable

inexplicable (*adj*) incapable of being explained or accounted for

infinity boundless space, energy, knowledge, or capacity

inherent (*adj*) essential or intrinsic to something

innate (*adj*) belonging to essential character of something; originating in the mind rather than experience

innominate (*adj*) unnamed or of unknown name; unnamable

insight apprehension of inner nature of things; intuitive understanding of others and oneself

integral (*adj*) inherent, essential to completeness

intuition revelation by insight or innate knowledge, without reasoning

knowledge awareness or understanding

light, the spiritual illumination, enlightenment, ultimate truth

mastery great skill or knowledge in some discipline

matrix point of origin

meaning intent and significance of something; reason for being

mercy compassion, pity

nobility superiority and righteousness of character or mind

omniscience infinite knowledge and understanding

perspective capacity to view things in their true relationships

profundity depth of insight; spiritual awareness

quietude tranquility, peace, inner harmony

quintessence purest, most concentrated form or part, esp. of immaterial thing

realized (*adj*) spiritually enlightened, in harmony with oneself

recognition discovery of true nature of something or someone

revealed (*adj*) pertaining to truths based on intuition or divine inspiration

sagacity wisdom, keenness of discernment, understanding

sage wise, learned, venerable one

seeing enlightenment

self-discovery process of attaining self-knowledge

self-exploration study of one's potential for sake of understanding and improvement

self-knowledge understanding one's own true character and feelings

self-realization acknowledgment and understanding of oneself so as to fulfill one's potential

self-revelation recognition and statement of one's own thoughts and feelings, esp. unintentionally

sense of self understanding and acceptance of one's true nature

Tao eternal order of the universe and source of reality; right way of life, virtuous conduct

timeless (*adj*) eternal, everlasting; beyond measurement in time

true self one's innate nature and essence

truth fundamental, spiritual reality that lies beyond perceived reality and experience

uncharted territory mysterious regions beyond what has been explored, observed, or experienced

understanding recognition of spiritual truth or essence of something

universal (*adj*) present in all spheres of human life; (*n*) an ultimate truth

unknowable ultimate reality lying beyond human perception and experience, understood only through spirituality

unknown that which has yet to be discovered, identified, revealed, understood, or explained

unseen reality beyond human perception

unspeakable (*adj*) beyond verbal description; that may not or cannot be uttered

unspoken (*adj*) tacit, silent but understood

unwritten (*adj*) of truths known and passed on orally

verity state of being eternally and fundamentally true or necessary; something that is true, as a principle, belief, or idea

window revelation of truth, esp. moment or point of such revelation

wisdom understanding of spiritual truth; enlightenment; capacity to discern the essence of the ways of human beings and the universe

INDEX

This index provides an alphabetical list of all entries in the book that have definitions. Entries in boldface type show the major categories of words along with the range of pages on which they appear.

anacrusis, 435
anadem, 287
anadiplosis, 524
anaerobe, 45
anaerobic, 38
anaglyph, 424
anagnorisis, 451
anagogic, 668
anagram, 524
analects, 428, 655
analemma, 143
analgesia, 132, 628
analgesic, 137, 622
anal intercourse, 583
analog, 179, 186
analog clock, 143
analog recording, 441
analogy, 36, 410, 428, 521, 524, 609
anal phase, 404
analysand, 402
analysis, 114, 125, 402, 609, 613
analyst, 383, 402
analytic, 408, 521
analytical balance, 142
analytical chemistry, 119
analytic cubism, 420
analytic geometry, 114
analytic philosophy, 406
analytic psychology, 398
analyze, 608
anamorphic lens, 456, 476
ananda, 649
anapest, 428
anaphase, 36
anaphora, 524
anaphylaxis, 16
anarchism, 308
anarchist, 313, 637
anarcho-syndicalism, 308
anarchy, 301
anastasis, 423
anastigmatic lens, 476
anastrophe, 524
anat, 534
anathema, 524, 618, 650
Anatomy, 6–12
anatomy, 36
Anatomy and Physiology of Sex, 580–582
anatta, 649
-ance, 531
ancestor, 246
ancestor worship, 389, 662
ancestry, 246
anchor, 167, 217, 462, 604
anchor bolt, 152, 169
anchor chock, 217
anchorite, 652, 664
anchor knot, 171
anchorman, 462
anchorwoman, 462
ancien régime, 563
ancient, 598
ancillary, 319
-ancy, 531
andante, 437
andantino, 437
andirons, 242
Andorra, 76
andro-, 529
androgen, 40, 47, 581
androgynous, 581
Andromeda Galaxy, 106
androphilia, 579
androphobia, 401
-androus, 531
-andry, 531
-ane, 531
anecdote, 428, 524
anechoic, 105
anekantavada, 649
anemia, 16
anemo-, 529
anemograph, 203
anemometer, 87, 89, 203
anemoscope, 203

anencephaly, 18
anent, 602
aneroid barometer, 89, 103
anesthesia, 20, 132
anesthesiologist, 129
anesthesiology, 128
anesthetic, 137
anesthetist, 129
aneurysm, 20
anew, 598
angary, 337
Angas, 655
angel, 367, 454, 652
angel bed, 237
angel dust, 622
angel's kiss, 511
angels on horseback, 264
angina, 20
angina pectoris, 20
angio-, 529
angiocardiography, 132
angiography, 132
angiosperm, 58, 374
anglaise, 261
angle, 117, 325, 497, 542, 585, 599
angle brackets, 518
angle iron, 152
angle of attack, 199
angle of declination, 72
angle of depression, 72
angle of elevation, 72
angle of incidence, 104, 199
angle of reflection, 104
angle of refraction, 104
angle of view, 476
angle on, 456
angler, 497
angle rafter, 152
angleworm, 498
Anglican Church, 644
angling, 497, 504
Anglophobia, 401
Anglo-Saxon, 521
Angola, 76
Angora, 281
angry macrophage, 38
angry young man, 425
angst, 404, 565, 628
angstrom, 99
anguish, 628
angular, 604
angular displacement, 96
angular impulse, 96
angular measure, 142
angular momentum, 96
angular velocity, 96
anhydrous, 124
anicca, 649
aniline dye, 421
anilingus, 583
anima, 402
animadversion, 618
animadvert, 549
animal, 45, 51, 578, 637
animal act, 89
animal epic, 425
animal fable, 660
Animal Groups, 52–53
animal husbandry, 372
Animalia, 50
animality, 399
animal magnetism, 578, 662
animal nutrition, 374
Animals, 50–58
Animal Types and Parts, 51–52
anima mundi, 650
animation, 455, 456, 475
animation camera, 475
animato, 435
animism, 389, 407, 650, 662
animosity, 616
animus, 402, 616
anion, 119, 179
aniso-, 529
anisogamy, 47
Ankara, 80
ankh, 280, 664

ankle, 8
anklet, 277, 278, 285
ankle weights, 26
ankylosis, 20
anlace, 174
annals, 324
annealing, 424
Annelida, 50
annexation, 305, 335
annihilate, 635
annihilation, 634
annihilator, 637
anniversary, 248, 483, 596
anno Domini, 562
announce, 545
announcement, 460
announcer, 460, 465
annoy, 635
annual, 58, 324, 370, 503, 596
annualize, 365
Annual National and Religious Holidays, 482–483
annual report, 351
annual review, 351
annuit coeptis, 562
annuity, 356, 367, 378
annul, 317
annular, 604
annular eclipse, 107
annulary, 8
annulet, 468
annulment, 248
annulus, 58
annunciate, 545
Annunciation, 645
annus mirabilis, 562, 597
anode, 99, 125, 179
anodize, 424
anodyne, 137
anodynia, 23
anomaly, 628
anomie, 395, 397, 399, 565
anon, 534, 598
anonym, 524
anonymous, 429, 430
anonymous FTP, 195
anorak, 272
anorexia nervosa, 16, 399
anosmic, 552
anoxia, 17
Anschluss, 335
Anshar, 659
answer, 550
answering machine, 184
answering service, 184
answer print, 456
anta, 229
Antabuse, 137, 624
antacid, 137
Antaeus, 657
antagonism, 137
antagonist, 38, 430, 454
antagonize, 635
antapex, 107
Antarctic, 89
Antarctica, 72
Antarctic Circle, 72
ante, 351, 329, 598
ante bellum, 562
antecedent, 410, 516, 610
antecedents, 246
antechamber, 233
antediluvian, 656
ante meridiem, 143, 562
antemortem, 641
antenna, 463
antenna float, 498
antepenult, 521
anterior, 602
anteroom, 233
anthelion, 107
anthelmintic, 137
anthem, 437, 438
anthemion, 241, 468
anther, 58, 503
antho-, 529
anthology, 324, 429

anthology show, 460
anthomania, 401
anthophobia, 401
Anthophyta, 50
-anthous, 531
anthracite, 66
anthrax, 12
anthropic principle, 102
anthropo-, 529
anthropocentric, 391
anthropogeography, 388
anthropoid, 388
anthropological linguistics, 388, 521
Anthropology, 388–391
anthropology, 388
anthropometry, 390
anthropomorphic soil, 74
anthropomorphism, 391, 651, 660
anthropophagy, 389
anthroposophy, 407, 668
anti-, 529
antiaircraft, 333
antiaircraft gun, 176
antiart, 420
antiballistic missile, 178, 333
antibiotic, 23, 137
antibody, 23, 40, 137
antic, 590
Antichrist, 645
anticipatory grief, 404
anticlimax, 428
anticline, 66
anticoagulant, 137
anticodon, 36
anticonvulsant, 137
anticyclone, 87
antidepressant, 137, 622
antidiuretic, 137
antidiuretic hormone, 40
antidote, 137
antiemetic, 137
antiestablishment, 313
antifreeze, 209
antigen, 23
antigravity, 102
antigropelos, 275
anti-G suit, 112
Antigua and Barbuda, 76
antihero, 430
antihistamine, 41, 137
antiknock, 209
antilogarithm, 115
antimacassar, 243
antimatter, 100
antimissile missile, 178, 333
antinodal line, 96
antinode, 599
antinomian, 668
antinomianism, 407, 651
antinomy, 410, 610
antinovel, 425
antinuke, 392
antiparticle, 100
antipasto, 263
antipathy, 616
antipersonnel, 333
antipersonnel bomb, 178
antiperspirant, 30
antiphony, 437
antiphrasis, 428, 524
antipodal, 602
antipodes, 69
antipruritic, 137
antipyretic, 137
antiquark, 100
antiquated, 598
antique, 598
antique collecting, 504
antique refinishing, 504
anti-Semitism, 391
antiseptic, 140
antiserum, 137
antishock trousers, 135
antisocial, 391
antisocial personality, 399
antispasmodic, 137
antitank, 333

antiterrorism, 337
antithesis, 408, 428, 524, 609
antitorque rotor, 201
antitoxin, 137
antitrust, 344
antitussive, 137
antivenin, 41, 137
antler, 51
antonomasia, 524
antonym, 521
Anu, 659
Anubis, 659
anus, 9
anvil, 164
anxiety, 20, 399, 628
anxiety disorder, 17
anxiety neurosis, 399
anymore, 598
anyplace, 600
anytime, 598
anywhere, 600
Anzac Day, 482
A-OK, 112
AOL, 195
AOR, 440, 465
aorist, 516
aorta, 9
aortic-body chemoreceptor, 41
AP, 325
aparejo, 280
apart, 602
apartheid, 391
apartment, 228
apartment building, 380
apartments, 380
APB, 631
ape, 627
apéritif, 508
aperçu, 610, 612
aperiodic, 598
aperture, 152, 456, 476
aperture-priority, 476
apeshit, 627
apex, 107, 599
Apgar score, 132
aphasia, 18
aphelion, 107
apheresis, 519
aphorism, 524
aphrodisiac, 137, 578, 622
Aphrodite, 576, 659
apiary, 232
apical, 599, 604
apiphobia, 401
aplanatic lens, 476
aplastic anemia, 12
apnea, 20
APO, 308, 529
apocalypse, 665
apocalyptic, 663
apocalyptic number, 665
apocenter, 107
apochromatic lens, 476
apocope, 519
apocrine, 10
apocrine secretion, 41
apocrypha, 565, 590, 655
apodosis, 516
apogee, 107, 599
apolitical, 391
Apollo, 112, 659
Apollon, 659
Apollonian, 425
apologia, 609
apologist, 394
apologue, 425
apophasis, 524
apophony, 521
apoplexy, 12
aposiopesis, 524
apostasy, 590, 656
apostate, 652
a posteriori, 408, 562
apostle, 652
apostolic succession, 645
apostrophe, 518, 524

bondage, 395, 583
bond angle, 119
bond axis, 119
bond character, 119
bonded, 290
bond energy, 119
bond issue, 360
bond paper, 473
bondsman, 315
bondstone, 229
bone, 11, 581
bone china, 478
bone graft, 132
bone meal, 370, 501
boner, 581
bones, 443, 639
bonesetter, 129
bone up, 414, 608
boneworking, 479
boneyard, 639
bonfire, 483
bong, 507, 625
bongo, 443
bonhomie, 563, 615
bonjour, 563
bonkers, 627
bon marché, 563
bon mot, 524, 563
bonnang, 443
bonne chance, 563
bonnet, 209, 286
bonsai, 501, 503
bonus, 351, 353, 382
bon vivant, 485, 563
bon voyage, 487, 563
bony orbit, 6
bonze, 652
boo, 547, 617, 622
boob, 581
boob tube, 460
booby, 581
booby hatch, 217, 627
booby prize, 618
booby trap, 588
boodle, 310, 368, 587
boogie, 439, 440, 485, 507
boogie-woogie, 439
book, 325, 375, 451, 476, 507, 631
bookbinder, 383
bookbinding, 322, 479
bookcase, 238
book club, 322
bookcraft, 479
bookends, 242
bookie, 630
booking, 376, 487
booking agent, 454
book jacket, 322
bookkeeper, 365
bookkeeping, 365
booklet, 325
bookmaking, 587
bookman, 322
Book of Books, 655
Book of Common Prayer, 655
book of man, 36
Book of Mormon, 655
Book of the Dead, 655, 660
book on cassette, 325
bookplate, 322
book review, 325
books, 365
Books and Pages, 429–430
books and records, 365
bookseller, 322
bookshelves, 238
Books of the Bible, 656
bookstall, 322
bookstore, 322
book value, 360, 365
bookworm, 413
bookwright, 383
Boolean, 186
Boolean algebra, 114
boom, 152, 201, 217, 344, 392, 464, 476, 547

boom box, 466
boomer, 213
boomerang, 175
boom mic, 456
boom operator, 458
boom town, 298
boon, 615
boondoggle, 306, 344
boost, 179, 615
booster, 201, 211, 464, 615
booster rocket, 112
booster shot, 137
boot, 173, 187, 209, 285, 363, 625
boot camp, 330
bootee, 285
booth, 228, 348
boothose, 277
bootie, 285
bootjack, 285
bootlegger, 508, 630
bootlegging, 629
bootleg recording, 440
bootstrap, 187, 285
booze, 508
boozer, 624
bop, 439, 446, 540, 635
bora, 87
bordello, 584
border, 72, 235, 336, 451, 600
bordereau, 378
bordering, 602
borderline personality, 399
bore, 71, 88, 150, 166, 177, 207
boreal, 07
boreal forest, 45
boreen, 298
borehole, 71
boric acid, 140
born-again, 656
born in a trunk, 451
borough, 298, 312
borrow, 356
borrow pit, 71
borscht, 264
borscht belt, 450
bosc, 85
boscage, 85
bo's'n, 219
Bosnia and Herzegovina, 76
bosom, 7, 289, 581
boson, 100
boss, 11, 152, 311, 355, 383, 424, 468
bossa nova, 439, 446
bossism, 310
Boston bag, 280
Boston baked beans, 264
bosun's pipe, 445
Boswell, 437
'bot, 195, 535
botanica, 664
botanical garden, 232, 488, 501
botany, 36, 58, 374, 501
Botany and Plant Parts, 58–60
bother, 635
bo tree, 649
botryoidal, 604
Botswana, 76
botta bag, 280
bottle, 173, 243
bottle club, 510
bottle-feeding, 251
bottleneck, 210, 298, 440, 446
bottle opener, 268
Bottles, 173
bottom, 440, 602
bottom fisher, 380
bottom-fishing, 497
bottomless pit, 667
bottom line, 351, 365
bottom out, 344
bottoms, 84
Botts dots, 210
botulism, 12
boubou, 272
boucharde, 424

bouclé, 281
boudoir, 233
boudoir dress, 277
bouffant, 29
bouffant skirt, 274
bougie, 135
bouillabaisse, 264
boulder, 66
boulevard, 298
boulter, 498
Boulwareism, 353
bounce, 540, 542, 592
bounced check, 356
bouncer, 510
bouncing paper, 368
bouncing powder, 622
bound, 540
boundary, 600
bound form, 521
bound galleys, 322
bounty, 319, 367, 631, 665
bouquet, 52, 248, 278, 552
bouquet garni, 261
bouquiniste, 430
Bourdon-tube gauge, 203
bourg, 298
bourgeoisie, 344
bourrée, 434, 446, 448
bourse, 360
boustrophedon, 190, 521
boutonniere, 278
bouzouki, 444
bovate, 145
bovine, 51
bow, 171, 175, 217, 278, 444, 446, 451, 614
bow and arrow, 175, 496
bow and scrape, 615
bowdlerize, 428
bow drill, 166
bowel, 9
bower, 217, 228, 232
Bowery, 298
bowfishing, 497
bow hunting, 495
bowie knife, 175
bowing, 438
bowknot, 171
bowl, 83, 172, 269, 604
bowl along, 542
bowleg, 18
bowler, 286
bowl gouge, 163
bowline, 171
Bowling, 491
bowling, 491
bowman, 219
bow net, 496
bow pen, 472
bowsprit, 217
bow tie, 279
bow window, 229
box/open-end wrench, 167
box, 173, 325, 446, 451, 581, 604
box beam, 152
box camera, 475
box canyon, 83
boxcar, 211
box coat, 272
boxed set, 325
box-end wrench, 167
boxer shorts, 277
boxing, 491
Boxing and Wrestling, 491–492
Boxing Day, 482
boxing glove, 279
box lunch, 263
box nail, 169
box nut, 169
box office, 451
box pleat, 290
box social, 484
box spring, 237
boy, 252, 622
boyar, 338
boycott, 344, 348, 392
boyfriend, 577

Boyle's law, 103, 124
boy toy, 577
B picture, 455
bra, 276
brabble, 547
braccio, 145
brace, 140, 152, 166, 167, 169, 217, 235, 280, 293
bracelet, 278
bracer, 30, 508
bracero, 370
braces, 135, 140, 280, 518
brachio-, 529
brachy-, 529
brachylogy, 524
bracken, 85
bracket, 152, 169, 231, 235, 395
brackets, 518
brackish, 553
bract, 58, 503
brad, 169
bradawl, 163
brad pusher, 166
brady-, 141, 529
bradycardia, 20
bradykinin, 41
brae, 83
brag, 615
Brahma, 650, 659
Brahman, 649
Brahmana, 655
Brahmanism, 644
braid, 29, 293
braiding, 290
Braille, 521
brain, 8, 635
Brain and Central Nervous System, 8–9
brain damage, 20
brain death, 638
brain drain, 392
brain-picking, 585
brainsick, 628
brainstorm, 607, 609
brainstorming, 376
brain trust, 303
brainwashing, 402
braise, 262
brake, 85, 148, 152, 208
brake club, 214
brake drum, 208
brake fluid, 209
brake horsepower, 199
brake lights, 209
brake lining, 208
brakeman, 213
brake pedal, 209
brake shoes, 208
brancard, 223
branch, 85, 187, 211, 246
branch bank, 356
Branches and Computational Systems, 114–115
Branches and Disciplines,
    Anthropology, 388
    Biology, 36
    Chemistry, 119
    Geography, 72
    Geology, 66
    Physics, 96
Branches, Laws, Theories, and Techniques, 109–111
branches of government, 303
branching, 604
branchio-, 529
brand, 617
branding iron, 372
brandish, 635
brand name, 348
brandy alexander, 511
brandy snifter, 270
brannigan, 624
brass, 159, 330, 442
brassard, 276, 280
brasserie, 263
brass hat, 286
brassiere, 276

brass knuckles, 175, 279
brass ring, 367
brat, 251, 252
brattice, 71
brave new world, 391, 661
bravo, 451, 615
bravura, 437
brawl, 635
bray, 546
brayer, 472
braza, 145
braze, 150
brazier, 267, 383
Brazil, 76
brazing, 424
Brazzaville, 80
breach, 321
breach of contract, 321
bread, 256, 257, 259, 262, 368
breadbasket, 7, 174, 269, 374
breadboard, 268
bread line, 344
bread pan, 267
Breads, Rolls, and Crackers, 259
breadth, 600
breadwinner, 247, 355
break, 20, 325, 372, 460, 486, 545, 631, 633, 635, 665
break-action, 176
break a heart, 576
break a leg, 451
break bread, 256
break dancing, 440
breakdown, 124, 446, 610, 628
breakdowns, 458
breaker, 172
breaker points, 208
break even, 344
breakfast, 256, 263
breakfront, 238
break-in, 629
breaking and entering, 321, 629
breaking point, 628
break ranks, 330
break the news, 548
breakwater, 220
break wind, 21
breast, 7, 71, 581
breast augmentation, 25
breastbone, 7
breast drill, 166
breast-feeding, 251
breasting, 285
breastplate, 276
breast pocket, 289
breast reduction, 25
breast wall, 470
breath, 87, 519, 552
Breathalyzer, 132
breathe, 546
breathe down someone's neck, 635
breather, 152, 486, 583
breathing, 41
breathing exercises, 25
breathlessness, 21
breccia, 66
brecciation, 162
breech, 177
breechcloth, 277, 279
breeches, 275
breechloader, 176
breech presentation, 23
breed, 246, 372
breeder reactor, 100
breeding, 246
breeze, 87
breezeway, 231
Bren gun, 176
Brennschluss, 112
bretelle, 280, 289
Breton, 284, 286
breve, 437, 518
brevet, 330
breviary, 655
brew, 508, 587
brewer, 383, 508
brewsky, 508

cañon, 83, 430, 437, 610, 651, 655
canonical hour, 596
canonical hours, 645
canonization, 645, 656
canonize, 615
canon law, 314
can opener, 268
canopic jar, 639
Canopus, 106
canopy, 45, 201, 235, 237, 468
cant, 150, 220, 521, 525, 546, 548, 590
cantabile, 435
cantata, 434, 437
canteen, 173
canter, 540
canterbury, 238
cantharides, 622
cant hook, 168
canticle, 437, 645
cantilever, 150, 153, 201, 242, 468
cantilever bridge, 300
cantina, 510, 564
canto, 428, 435, 437
Canton, 81, 303
Canton crepe, 281
cantor, 653
cantus firmus, 435
canvas, 160, 281, 421
canvass, 312, 544, 608
canyon, 83
canzonet, 437
CAO, 355
cap, 25, 58, 132, 153, 169, 177, 286, 344, 535, 622, 625
capability, 328
capacitance, 179
capacitor, 180, 208
capacity, 319
cap and gown, 273, 416
caparison, 288
cape, 86, 272
Cape Cod cottage, 228
Cape Codder, 511
capelet, 272
caper, 540, 590
capeskin, 284
Capetown, 81
Cape Verde, 76
capful, 144
cap gun, 176
capillary, 9
capillary attraction, 96, 122
capillary network, 9
capillary repulsion, 122
capillary tube, 126
capital, 231, 298, 303, 344, 356, 368, 468
capital account, 365
capital contribution, 365
capital crime, 321, 629
capital funds, 356
capital gain, 360, 363, 380
capital gain distribution, 360
capital gains tax, 362
capital-intensive, 344, 351
capitalism, 308, 344
capitalist, 355, 367
capitalization, 351, 363
capital loss, 363
capital punishment, 317, 633, 641
capitals, 473
capital stock, 360
capitate, 604
capitation fee, 131
capitation tax, 362
Capitol, 303
Capitol Hill, 303
capitulation, 328, 337, 585
caplet, 137
cap nut, 169
capo, 338, 446
capon, 51
capote, 272, 286
capper, 592
capping fee, 496
capriccio, 423, 434

caprice, 590, 612
Capricorn, 111
Capri pants, 275
capsheaf, 600
capsid, 36
capsize, 220
cap sleeve, 289
capstan, 148, 217
capstan table, 238
capstone, 153, 159, 468
capsule, 112, 137, 173
capsule radio, 466
capt, 535
captain, 204, 219, 338
captain of industry, 355
captain's chair, 236
caption, 322, 326
captious, 585
captive, 633
captoe, 285
capture, 187, 328, 585
capuche, 288
capuchin, 272
car, 206, 211
carabiniere, 330
Caracas, 81
carafe, 173, 243
caramba, 564
caramelize, 262
carapace, 588
carat, 69, 144, 278
caravan, 206, 228, 487
caravansary, 228
caravel, 216
car bed, 237
carbine, 176
carbohydrate, 28, 41
carbolic acid, 140
carboloading, 28
carbon-14 dating, 69
carbon, 119, 180
carbonaceous chondrites, 108
carbonado, 262
carbonara, 264
carbon cycle, 45
carbonic anhydrase, 41
carboniferous, 69
Carboniferous period, 70
carbon 14, 100
carboy, 173, 242
carbuncle, 13
carburetor, 148, 207
carcanet, 278
carcass, 639
carcino-, 141
carcinogen, 23
carcinoma, 13
car coat, 272
card, 187, 190
cardboard, 160
card-carrying, 313
card case, 173
Card Games, 506
cardiac arrest, 13, 21
cardiac muscle, 9
cardiac output, 41
cardiac stenosis, 13
cardigan, 273, 274
cardinal, 272, 338, 653
cardinal number, 115
cardinal points, 72
cardinal vowel, 519
carding, 508
cardio-, 141, 529
cardiograph, 135
cardiology, 128
cardiomyopathy, 13
cardiopulmonary resuscitation, 25, 132
cardiorespiratory endurance, 25
carditis, 13
card out, 473
card page, 322
card party, 485
cards, 504, 506
card section, 488
cardsharp, 592

carryout, 263
carryover, 363
carsickness, 17
cart, 222, 239
cartage, 348, 440
carte blanche, 564, 614
carte du jour, 263
cartel, 335, 344
Cartesian coordinate, 115
Cartesian geometry, 114
Cartesianism, 407
cartilage, 11, 12
cartogram, 72
cartography, 72
carton, 173, 242, 507
cartoon, 326, 421, 455, 471
cartouche, 241, 472
cartridge, 177, 194, 441
cartridge belt, 177, 279
cartridge case, 177
cartwheel, 622
cartwright, 383
carucate, 145
carver, 383
Carver chair, 236
carvery, 263
carving, 424, 479
carving fork, 270
carving knife, 270
car wash, 298
caryatid, 231, 468
casa, 228
Casablanca, 81
Casanova, 576
Casbah, 300
cascade, 85
cascade particle, 100
case, 129, 144, 173, 238, 280, 316, 322, 516, 610, 631
case goods, 348
case history, 131, 610
case law, 314
caseload, 319
casement, 229, 235
casement window, 470
casern, 330
case sale, 348
Cases, Boxes, and Bags, 173–174
Cases, Cupboards, and Chests, 238–239
case shot, 177
case study, 397, 402
casework, 397
Casey Jones, 214
cash, 356, 368
cash-and-carry, 348
cash bar, 510
cash basis method, 365
cashbook, 365
cash cow, 351
cash crops, 374
cash disbursements journal, 365
cash down, 348
cash flow, 351
cashier, 356
cashier's check, 356
cash in hand, 368
cash in on, 585
cash in one's chips, 638
cash machine, 356
cashmere, 274, 281
cash on delivery, 348
cash register, 348
casing, 153, 235, 290, 424
casino, 488
cask, 172, 508
casket, 173, 639
casque, 288
Cassandra, 657
Cassegrain reflector, 110
casserole, 262, 267
cassette, 194, 441
cassignle, 440
cassimere, 281
cassingle, 440
cassock, 276

cassoulet, 264
cast, 23, 49, 66, 140, 150, 220, 451, 454, 458, 498, 542
cast about, 544, 608
cast a chart, 662
cast a glance, 544
castanets, 443
cast a spell, 662
caste, 75, 395, 649
castellan, 338
castellated, 230
caster, 148, 153, 169, 173, 209, 243
caste system, 389
castigate, 549, 618
castile soap, 30
casting, 153, 424, 479, 497
casting director, 458, 461
casting plaster, 424
casting rod, 498
casting vote, 306
castiron, 159
castle, 228
castle in the air, 590, 612
cast off, 220, 290, 322
castor, 281, 286
Castor and Pollux, 657
castor oil, 137
cast party, 451
castration, 581
castration complex, 405
castrator mine, 178
cast stone, 159
casual, 440, 485
casual labor, 353
casual suit, 273
casualty, 330, 638
casualty loss, 363
casuistry, 408
CAT, 187, 199, 535, 584
cata-, 529
catabolism, 39, 41
catachresis, 525
cataclysm, 69, 665
catacomb, 233, 639
catafalque, 239, 639
catalepsy, 17
catalog, 325, 348, 376, 610
catalog sales, 348
catalysis, 124
catalyst, 119, 669
catalytic converter, 208
catamaran, 216
catamite, 580
cat and mouse, 585
cataplexy, 17
catapult, 175, 540
cataract, 17
catarrh, 21
catastrophe, 378
catastrophic coverage, 131
catatonia, 17, 399
catatonic, 628
cat burglar, 630
catcall, 546
catch, 169, 293, 497, 542, 585
catchall, 172
catcher's mitt, 582
catchment area, 74
catchment basin, 66
catch on, 608
catch sight of, 544
catch up, 587
catchword, 525
catchy, 592
Catch-22, 585
catechism, 645, 651
catecholamines, 41
categorical imperative, 408
category, 408, 610
catena, 610
catenary, 604
catenulate, 604
cateran, 630
cater-corner, 298, 602
cater-cousin, 246
caterer, 264
catering, 263, 485

charge nurse, 129
charger, 51, 269
charges, 632
chariot, 222
charisma, 312, 565
charismatics, 651
charitable contribution, 363
charity, 367, 656
charity patient, 131
charlatan, 592
Charles' law, 103, 124
Charleston, 447
charley horse, 20
Charlotte russe, 264
charm, 52, 100, 278, 577, 660, 664
charmeuse, 281
charm price, 348
charnel house, 639
Charon, 106
charpoy, 237
chart, 72, 220, 471, 585
charter, 306, 316, 351, 487, 497
charter flight, 204
charts, 440
chartulary, 380
Charybdis, 657
chase, 153, 424, 473, 495, 541, 577
chaser, 166, 508
chase scene, 458
Chasidim, 647
chasm, 83, 600
chassé, 448, 450
chasse gardée, 495
chassepot, 176
chasseur, 261
chassis, 153, 209
chasten, 616
chastise, 618
chastity, 247, 578, 651
chastity belt, 276
chasuble, 276
chat, 195, 545
chateaubriand, 264
chatelaine, 278, 339
chattel, 319, 344
chattel mortgage, 382
chatter, 545
chatter mark, 66
chauvinism, 308, 337, 391
chaw, 507
chazerei, 565
cheap, 344, 367
cheap drunk, 624
cheap shot, 635
cheat, 576, 592
cheaters, 279
cheat to camera, 458
chêchia, 286
check, 150, 290, 348, 357, 498, 544, 608, 610
checkbook, 357
check in, 487
checking account, 357
check luggage, 487
check out, 487, 542, 544, 608
checkpoint, 298
checkroom, 233
checks and balances, 302
checkup, 132
cheek, 6
cheekbone, 6
cheeks, 581
cheep, 547
cheer, 546, 547, 615
cheers, 485
cheese, 257
Cheese, 258
cheese, 258, 581
cheesecake, 584
cheesecloth, 160, 270, 281
cheese knife, 270
cheese soufflé, 264
chef, 264, 626
chef de cuisine, 264
chef-d'oeuvre, 564
chela, 653
chelate, 119

cheli-, 529
chem, 535
chemical, 119
chemical engineering, 119
chemical equation, 126
chemical formula, 126
chemical peel, 25
**Chemical Properties and
   Reactions**, 123–124
chemical property, 124
chemical specificity, 41
chemical stimulation of brain, 132
chemical warfare, 328
chemical weathering, 69
chemiluminescence, 124
chemise, 276
chemisette, 276, 279
chemist, 129
Chemistry, 119–127
chemistry, 119, 576
chemoreceptors, 41
chemosurgery, 119
chemosynthesis, 39
chemotaxis, 41
chemotherapy, 119, 132
chemurgy, 119
Chengdu, 81
chenille, 240, 281
chenille work, 479
cheongsam, 274
cherish, 576
chernozem, 74, 373
cheromania, 401
cheroot, 507
cherry, 206, 581
cherry bomb, 178
cherry pitter, 268
cherub, 423, 653
che sarà sarà, 564
chess, 506
chesseur, 330
chest, 7, 173, 238
chesterfield, 236, 272
chestnut, 525
chest of drawers, 238
chest X-ray, 132
cheval-de-frise, 333
cheval-de-frises, 231
cheval glass, 240
chevalier, 339
cheviot, 281
chevrette, 284
chevron, 169, 330, 604
chevy, 495
chew, 256, 507
chewing tobacco, 507
chew out, 618
chew over, 548, 607
chew the fat, 545
chew the rag, 545
Cheyne-Stokes respiration, 21
chez la famille, 564
chez moi, 564
chiaroscuro, 422
chiasmus, 525
chiaus, 592
chibouk, 507
chic, 391, 485
Chicago, 81
Chicago Board of Trade, 360
chicanery, 590
chi-chi, 511
chick, 51, 577
chicken, 210, 580, 584
chicken à la king, 264
chicken and dumplings, 264
chicken cacciatore, 264
chicken coop, 232
chicken cordon bleu, 264
chicken divan, 264
chicken feed, 368
chicken hawk, 580, 584
chicken Kiev, 264
chicken Marengo, 264
chicken paprika, 264
chickenpox, 13
chicken Tetrazzini, 264

chicken wire, 159
chide, 618
chief, 355
chief administrative officer, 355
chief cells, 39
chief clerk, 213
chief cook, 264
chief executive, 304
chief executive officer, 355
chief financial officer, 355
chief justice, 304, 315, 339
Chief of Naval Operations, 330
chief of staff, 304, 330
chief of state, 304
chief petty officer, 219, 330
chief resident, 129
chief warrant officer, 330
chiffon, 281
chiffonade, 261
chiffonier, 238
chifforobe, 238
chigi, 468
chignon, 29
chih-hua, 422
chilblain, 20
child, 246, 252
child abuse, 251, 583
child actor, 454
childbearing, 250
childbed fever, 13
childbirth, 250
childcare, 251, 392
child development, 398
Children. See **Parents and
   Children**
children, 252
children's books, 322
children's hospital, 129
child support, 248
Chile, 76
chiliad, 144, 597
chili con carne, 264
chili dog, 264
chilies rellenos, 264
chill, 150, 639
chiller, 455
chill factor, 90
chills, 21
chillum, 507, 625
chilo-, 141, 529
chime, 241
chime in, 545
Chimera, 657
chimerical, 590, 612, 664
chimes, 443
chimichanga, 264
chimney, 153, 230
chimney pot, 230
chin, 6, 444
China, 76, 243, 478
china cabinet, 238
china cap, 268
china closet, 234
china marker, 471
chinchilla, 284
chine, 83, 281
Chinese ink, 471
Chinese lantern, 240, 241
Chinese molasses, 622
Chinese New Year, 482
Chinese puzzle, 587
chink, 83, 235, 585, 600
chino, 282
chinois, 268
chinoiserie, 422
chinook, 87
chinos, 275
chintz, 282
chin whiskers, 30
chip, 20, 83, 180, 187
chipboard, 159
chipped beef, 264
Chippendale chair, 236
chipping, 625
chippy, 584
chiro-, 141, 529

chiromancer, 664
chiromancy, 662
chiropody, 128
chiropractic, 128
chiropractic adjustment, 25
chiropractor, 129
chiropteran, 53
chirp, 547
chirurgical, 128
chisel, 162, 163, 424, 592
chisel plow, 373
chi-square distribution, 115
chit, 252, 357
chitarra battente, 444
chitarrone, 444
chitchat, 545
chitin, 41
chiton, 272
chitter, 547
chivalry, 576
chlamydia, 13, 581
chlamys, 272
chloral hydrate, 137, 622
chloramphenicol, 137
Chloris, 659
chloro-, 529
chloroform, 137
chlorophyll, 58
chloroplast, 39, 58
chloroquine, 137
chlorosis, 501
chm, 535
chock, 153, 204, 218
chockablock, 600
choctaw, 493
choice, 615
choice point, 402
choir, 437, 653
choirboy, 437
choirmaster, 438
choke, 177, 207, 635
chokebore, 176
chokedamp, 71
choker, 279
choking, 21, 638
cholecystectomy, 132
cholecystokinin, 41
cholelithiasis, 17
cholent, 264
cholera, 13
cholesterol, 28, 41
cholinergic, 41
cholo-, 141
chomp, 256
Chondrichthyes, 50
chondrio-, 141
chondrite, 108
Chongqing, 81
choo-choo, 211
choose, 614
chop, 150, 262, 496, 635
chophouse, 263
chopin, 145
chopine, 285
choplogic, 587
chopper, 198, 223
choppers, 7
chopping block, 268
chopping board, 268
chops, 440
chop shop, 629
chopsticks, 268, 270
chop suey, 264
choragus, 454
choral, 437
chorale, 437
chord, 153, 435, 613
Chordata, 50
chordate, 51
chord line, 199
chord organ, 444
chorea, 13
choreo-, 529
choreographer, 448
choreography, 448
choreomania, 401
chores, 251

chorionic gonadotropin, 48
chorister, 437
chorograph, 72
chorography, 72
choroid coat, 6
chortle, 547
chorus, 430, 437, 440, 454, 545
chorus line, 450, 454
Chosen People, 647
chott, 84
choucroute garnie, 265
chow, 256
chow-chow, 265
chowder, 265
chow down, 256
chow mein, 265
chrematomania, 401
chrestomathy, 430
chrism, 655
chrisom, 280, 655
chrisom child, 251
Christ, 650
christen, 645
Christendom, 645
christening, 251
**Christian Denominations and
   Sects**, 644–645
Christianity, 644
Christianity, 645–647
Christian name, 251
Christian Science, 644
Christian Scientist, 129
Christmas, 482, 645
Christmas club, 357
Christmas Eve, 482
Christmastide, 596
Christmastime, 596
Christmas tree, 622
Christology, 646
-chroic, 531
chroma, 422
chroma key, 464
chromatic, 435
chromatic aberration, 104
chromatics, 104
chromatid, 36
chromatin, 36
chromatography, 49, 126
chrome, 159, 209, 531
chrometophobia, 401
chrominance signal, 464
chromium, 159
chromo-, 529
chromolithograph, 422
chromolithography, 473
chromosome, 36
chromosome map, 37
chromosphere, 108
chron, 535
chronic, 23, 598
chronic drunk, 624
chronic fatigue syndrome, 13
chronicle, 425
chronicle play, 450
chrono-, 143, 529
chronograph, 143
chronological, 598
chronology, 143
chronometer, 143, 203
chronoscope, 143
chronostratigraphy, 66
-chroous, 531
chryselephantine, 424
chryso-, 529
chthonic, 660
chuck, 166, 167, 169, 256, 617
chuckhole, 298
chuckle, 547
chuckwagon, 222, 263
chudan, 27
chuff, 546
chug, 541
chug-a-lug, 508
chugger, 498
chui, 27
chukka, 285
chum, 498

dendroid, 503, 604
dendrology, 36
-dendron, 531
dengue, 13
denial, 399, 616
denigrate, 549, 618
denim, 282
denim jacket, 273
denims, 275
Denmark, 77
denom, 535
denomination, 646
denominator, 115
denotation, 408, 521, 525
denouement, 428, 452, 564
denounce, 549, 618
density, 96, 122
density altitude, 199
dent, 636
dental, 519
dental dam, 581
dental drill, 135
dental extraction forceps, 135
dental floss, 30, 135
dental hygienist, 129
dental insurance, 378
dental surgery, 128
dental technician, 129
denti-, 141, 529
dentiform, 604
dentifrice, 30, 138
dentil, 469
dentils, 232
dentine, 7
dentist, 129
dentistry, 128
dentures, 135
Denver boot, 210
deny, 545, 550, 616
deodorant, 30, 552
deodorize, 552
deontology, 407
Deo volente, 562
deoxyhemoglobin, 42
deoxyribonucleic acid, 37
depart, 542
departed, 638
department, 303, 411
Department of Agriculture, 303
Department of Commerce, 303
Department of Defense, 303
Department of Education, 303
Department of Energy, 303
Department of Health and Human
    Services, 303
Department of Housing and Urban
    Development, 303, 380
Department of Justice, 303
Department of Labor, 303
Department of State, 303
Department of the Interior, 303
Department of the Treasury, 303
Department of Transportation, 303
Department of Veterans Affairs,
    303
department store, 348
dependence, 17, 138
dependency, 336, 625
dependent, 363
dependent clause, 516
dependent variable, 115
depersonalization, 399
depict, 548
depilatory, 30
depletion, 363
deplore, 549
deploy, 585
deployment, 328
depolarization, 39
depolarizer, 180
depopulate, 636
deport, 336
deportment, 31
depose, 316, 587
deposit, 67, 71, 357, 382
deposition, 316
depository, 357

deposit slip, 357
depot, 214, 300
deprecate, 616
depreciate, 618
depreciation, 357, 363, 380
depressant, 138
depression, 84, 90, 344, 399, 628
depressive neurosis, 399
depressive psychosis, 399
depressurization, 199
de profundis, 562
dept, 535
depth, 600, 601
depth charge, 178, 218, 333, 511
depth interview, 463
depth of field, 476
depth psychology, 398
depth sounder, 218
deputy, 305, 335
deracinate, 636
deracination, 393
derailing, 214
deranged, 627
derby, 287
Derbyshire chair, 236
deregulation, 204, 306, 344, 357
de rigueur, 564
derision, 618
deriv, 535
derivation, 521
derivative, 115
derive, 608
derived unit, 96
-derm, 531
dermabrasion, 25, 133
dermatitis, 13
dermato-, 141, 529
dermatology, 128
dermatome, 135
dermestid, 49
dermis, 12
dermopteran, 53
dernier cri, 564
derogate, 618
derrick, 148, 218
derringer, 170
dervish, 648, 653, 664
DES, 138
descant, 437
descend, 542
descendant, 246
descender, 473
descending, 601
descending colon, 9
descent, 112, 246
descrambler, 466
describe, 548
description, 525
Descriptions of Sounds, 551
descriptive geometry, 114
descriptive grammar, 521
descriptive linguistics, 521
descry, 544
desecrate, 618, 636
desensitization, 133
desensitization therapy, 403
desert, 46, 84, 542
desert boot, 285
deserter, 331
desertification, 373
desertion, 248, 592
deserts, 74, 666
deserving, 614
déshabillé, 564
desiccant, 120
desiccate, 262
desiccator, 126
desideratum, 562
design, 585, 611
designate, 305, 613
designer, 152, 290, 393
designer's colors, 422
desire, 578
desk, 238
desk accessory, 192
desk chair, 236
desk lamp, 240

desk telephone, 184
desktop publishing, 187, 323, 471
desmosome, 39
désolé, 564
desoxyn, 622
despair, 628
desperado, 565
despise, 618
despoil, 636
despoilment, 634
despot, 305
despotism, 302
dessert, 257, 259
dessert fork, 270
dessert plate, 269
Desserts, 259
dessert sauce, 259
Dessert Sauces, 259
dessert spoon, 270
dessiatine, 145
destabilize, 336
de Stijl, 420
destiny, 666
destitution, 344
destrier, 51
destroy, 636
destroyer, 216, 333, 637
destruction, 634
destructionist, 313
DET, 622
detached, 602
detached retina, 20
detail, 331, 464
detainee, 335
detainer, 632
detect, 544
detection, 183, 631
detective, 631
detective novel, 323
detective picture, 455
detective story, 426
detector, 166
détente, 335, 337
detention, 416, 631
detention facility, 633
deterioration, 23
determine, 608, 609
determiner, 516
determinism, 103, 397, 407
deterrence, 328, 337, 631
detest, 616, 618
dethrone, 587
detonation, 210
detonator, 177
detour, 299
detox, 625
detoxification, 25, 133, 625
detract from, 616
detritus, 46, 67
Detroit, 81
detumescence, 21
deuce, 206
deus, 650
deus ex machina, 452, 562
deus otiosus, 657
deuteragonist, 430
deuterium, 101
deutero-, 529
deuterogamy, 248
deuteromycota, 63
deuteron, 101
deuterostome, 48
deva, 650
devaluation, 344, 368
Devanagari, 521
devastate, 636
devastation, 634
devein, 262
develop, 380, 476
developed nation, 336, 344
developer, 380, 476
developing nation, 336, 344
development, 48, 252, 380, 435,
    458
developmental biology, 36
developmental psychology, 398
développé, 448

deviance, 391, 399, 583
deviant, 583, 628
deviate, 542
deviated septum, 19
deviation, 21, 115, 203
device, 148, 428, 585
**Devices, Techniques, and
    Elements**, 427–429
devil, 262, 637, 653, 664
deviled eggs, 265
deviled ham, 265
devil's advocate, 653
devil, the, 640
deviltry, 590
devious, 592
devise, 318, 381, 585
devoice, 519, 546
devoid, 664
devolution, 306
devon, 499
Devonian period, 70
Devonshire cream, 261
devotee, 653
devotion, 577, 656, 668
devotions, 651
devour, 256, 636
dew, 88
dewal, 653
dewan, 339
dewfall, 88
dew point, 88, 103
Dexamyl, 622
Dexedrine, 622
dexie, 622
dextral, 601
dextran, 133, 138
dextro-, 141
dcy, 339
Dhaka, 81
dhal, 265
Dhamma, 649
Dhammapada, 655
dharma, 649
dhola, 443
dhoti, 275
dhow, 216
dhurrie, 240
dhyana, 649
di-, 529
dia-, 529
diabetes, 13
diabetes insipidus, 13
diabetes mellitus, 13
Diabinese, 138
diablerie, 423
diabolical, 628
diabolism, 662
diachronic, 521
diacritic, 518
diacritical mark, 518
diadem, 278, 288
diagenesis, 69
diagnose, 608
diagnosis, 23, 133, 403
diagnosis-related group, 131
diagnostic, 192
Diagnostic Terminology, 23–25
diagonal, 518, 601
diagonal-cutting pliers, 167
diagonal relationship, 122, 124
diagram, 471, 516, 585
dial, 143, 184, 535
dial-a-, 184
dialect, 521
dialect atlas, 521
dialectic, 408, 414, 610
dialectical materialism, 407
dialectology, 521
dialogue, 452, 458
dialogue track, 456
Dial One service, 184
dial saw, 164
dial tone, 184
dial-up, 196
dialysis, 133
dialysis machine, 135
diam, 535

diamagnetic, 122, 180
diamagnetism, 99
diamante, 278
diameter, 115, 601
diamond, 67, 604
diamond hitch, 171
diamond knot, 171
diamond sinker, 499
Diana, 659
diapause, 48
diaper, 251, 277
diaper rash, 17, 251
diaphanous, 290
diaphoresis, 21
diaphragm, 10, 138, 148, 476, 582
diarrhea, 21
diary, 325, 426
Diaspora, 647
diastole, 9, 42
diastolic pressure, 42
diastrophism, 74
diathermy, 133
diathermy knife, 135
diatomaceous earth, 373
diatonic, 435
diatribe, 428, 525, 618
diazepam, 138
dibber, 501
dibble, 163, 373, 501
dice, 262
dicho-, 529
dichotomy, 408, 611
dick, 581, 631
dicker, 348
dickey, 274, 279
dicot, 59
dicotyledon, 59
dicoumarin, 138
dict, 535
dictate, 545
dictator, 305
dictatorship, 302
diction, 525
dictionary, 325, 430, 521
Dictograph, 184
dictum, 318
didactic, 414, 610
diddle, 542, 583, 592
didgeridoo, 445
dido, 590
die, 164, 471, 638
dieback, 501
dielectric, 99, 180
die maker, 383
Dieppe, 284
die punch, 148
dieresis, 518
diesel, 206
diesel dyke, 580
diesel engine, 148, 207
diesel fuel, 209
dieseling, 210
diesel locomotive, 211
diesis, 518
diet, 25, 28, 256, 303
dietary laws, 389
dietetic, 263
diethylstilbestrol, 138
diethyltryptamine, 622
dietitian, 129
diet pill, 622
differ, 617
difference, 115
differential, 115, 208
differential calculus, 114
differential diagnosis, 133
differential equation, 116
differential gear, 148
differential microwave radiometer,
    103
differential motion, 148
differentiate, 610
differentiation, 48
diffraction, 104
diffraction angle, 104
diffraction grating, 104
diffuse nebula, 106

edgewise, 601
edibles, 256
edict, 306
edifice, 228
Edison effect, 103
edit, 192, 323
editing, 456
edition, 323, 326, 430
editio princeps, 562
editor, 323, 430, 458
editorial, 326, 613
editorial director, 323
editor in chief, 323, 326
EDP, 187
.edu, 196
educ, 535
educable, 413
Education, 410–416
education, 414
educational access channel, 461
educational publishing, 323
educational television, 414
educational therapy, 403
Education Testing Service, 414
educator, 413
educe, 608
EDV, 42
EEC, 336
EEG, 133, 535
EEG arousal, 42
eerie, 664
efface, 449
effect, 408, 428, 525
effective resistance, 99
effective span, 201
effector, 42
effeminate, 580
effendi, 339
efferent neuron, 42
efficiency, 97
effigy, 618, 664
efflorescence, 21
effluent, 46
effluvium, 552, 662
effusion, 122
EFT, 357
e.g., 535
egalitarianism, 309
egg, 48, 604
egg and dart, 469
egg beater, 268
eggbeater drill, 166
eggcup, 269
egg decorating, 479
egg foo yong, 265
egghead, 610
eggnog, 511
eggplant parmigiana, 265
egg roll, 265
eggs, 372
eggs Benedict, 265
egg slicer, 268
ego, 405
ego goods, 348
egomania, 402
egress, 542
egressive, 519
egress route, 199, 205
Egypt, 77
Egyptian, 468
Egyptian Revival, 468
EID, 363
eiderdown, 243
eidetic imagery, 405
eidolon, 612
8x10, 475
eighteen-wheeler, 206
Eightfold Path, 649
eighth, 622
eighth note, 437
eighth rest, 437
800 number, 184
Eight Immortals, 657
eight-track tape, 440
eighty-six, 509
eighty-sixed, 638
eisoptrophobia, 401

ejaculate, 583
ejaculation, 581
ejection seat, 201
ejective, 519
EKG, 133, 535
ekistics, 397
el, 212, 222, 535
elaboration, 525
élan vital, 564
elapse, 597
elapsed, 638
elapsed time, 597
elastic, 293
elastic bandage, 140
elastic collision, 97
elastic gun, 175
elasticity, 69, 97, 345
Elavil, 138
elbow, 8, 153, 169, 604
elbow piece, 276
elder, 247, 653
El Dorado, 661
Eleaticism, 407
elec, 535
elect, 312, 614, 653
election, 312
election day, 312, 482
electioneer, 312
Elections and Campaigns, 312–
   313
elective, 414
elector, 311, 339
electoral college, 312
electoral votes, 312
electorate, 312
Electra complex, 399
electric, 180
electrical stimulation of brain, 133
electrical storm, 87
electrical tape, 161
electric car, 212
electric chair, 633
electric charge, 99
electric circuit, 99
electric current, 99
electric drill, 166
electric field, 99
electric field intensity, 99
electric field lines, 99
electric fishing, 497
electric force, 99
electric frying pan, 267
electrician, 152, 180
electricity, 96, 99, 180
Electricity and Electronics, 179–
   182
Electricity and Magnetism, 99–
   100
electric motor, 148
electric owl, 213
electric railway, 212
electric razor, 30
electric riveter, 167
electric sander, 164
electric shock therapy, 403
electric train, 212
electric xylophone, 443
electro-, 529
electrocardiogram, 133
electrocardiograph, 135
electrocardiophonogram, 133
electrocautery, 133
electrochemistry, 119
electroconvulsive therapy, 403
electrocution, 633, 638
electrode, 99, 180
electroencephalogram, 133
electroencephalograph, 135
electrolysis, 124, 180
electrolyte, 42, 99, 120, 180
electrolytes, 28
electrolytic cell, 126, 180
electromagnet, 99, 180
electromagnetic force, 99
electromagnetic induction, 99
electromagnetic interaction, 99
electromagnetic spectrum, 108

electromagnetic wave, 99
electromagnetism, 99, 180
electromechanical, 148
electromotion, 180
electromotive force, 99, 180
electromyogram, 133
electromyograph, 135
electron, 99, 120, 180
electron affinity, 122
electron cloud, 101
electron collision excitation, 99
electron configuration, 120
electron-deficient compound, 120
electronegative, 122
electron gas, 120
electronic, 442
Electronic and Computer Games,
   506
electronic billboard, 376
electronic communications, 183
electronic funds transfer, 357
electronic ignition, 200
electronic mail, 183, 187
electronic music, 439
electronic news gathering, 463
electronics, 96, 99
Electronics. See **Electricity and
   Electronics**
electronics, 180
electronic warfare, 328
electron micrography, 475
electron microscope, 49
electron spin, 120
electron tube, 180
electrophoresis, 49, 126, 133
electropositive, 122
electroscope, 99
electrostatic, 180
electrostatic charge, 99
electrostatic printing, 471
electrosurgery, 133
electrotherapy, 133
electrum, 424
electuary, 138
elegiac, 428
elegy, 426, 640
elem, 535
element, 120, 611
elementary arithmetic, 114
elementary colors, 104
elementary particle, 101
elementary school, 412
Elements, 121–122
elephant ax, 175
elephant car, 212
elephant ear sponge, 478
elephant gun, 176
elephantiasis, 13
elephant man's disease, 19
eleutheromania, 402
eleutherophobia, 401
elev, 535
elevate, 151, 615
elevated, 212, 667
elevated railroad, 300
elevated railway, 222
elevation, 69, 73, 84, 156, 177, 449,
   470, 601
elevator, 149, 201, 233, 300
elevator constructor, 152
elevator music, 439
elevenses, 263
eleventh hour, 596
elevon, 201
elf, 590, 657
eligible, 248
elimination reaction, 124
ELISA, 133
elision, 428, 519
elite, 473
elixir, 138
Elizabethan, 426
ell, 145, 470
-elle, 532
ellipse, 118, 604
ellipsis, 518, 525
ellipsoid, 118

elliptic, 604
elliptical, 525, 604
elliptical galaxy, 106
El Niño, 88
elocution, 525
Elohim, 650
elongate, 604
elongation, 601
elope, 248
eloquence, 525
El Salvador, 77
elsewhere, 602
elucidate, 548
elude, 541
elusion, 591
eluvium, 67
Elysian fields, 666
Elysium, 666
em, 144, 214, 473
emaciation, 21
emacs, 192
E-mail, 183, 187
emanation, 552
emancipation, 309
emasculate, 578
emasculation, 405
embalming, 640
embankment, 214, 300
embarcadero, 300
embargo, 336, 345
embark, 220, 542
embarras de richesses, 564
embarrass, 585, 616
embassy, 339
embellish, 545, 591
embezzle, 592
embezzlement, 321, 357, 629
embodiment, 668
emboîtés, 449
emblem, 20, 143
embolism, 23, 42
embolus, 23, 42
emboss, 424, 471
embossing, 479
embrace, 578, 615
embrasure, 230, 235
embroidery, 290, 479, 504
embroil, 636
embryo, 11, 48, 250
embryology, 36, 128
emcee, 454, 461
emerge, 542
emergency brake, 208
Emergency Broadcast System, 465
emergency light, 209
emergency locator transmitter, 203
emergency medical service, 129
emergency medical technician, 129
emergency medicine, 128
emergency number, 184
emergency room, 129
emergent coast, 69
emerita, 562
emeritus, 339, 413, 562
emery board, 30
emery wheel, 164
emesis, 21
emetic, 138
emetophobia, 401
EMF, 99, 180
EMG, 133
-emia, 141, 532
emigrant, 336
emigrate, 487, 542
emigration, 46, 336
eminence, 339, 653
éminence grise, 311, 564, 587
eminent domain, 306, 319
emir, 339
emirate, 303
emissary, 335
emission control, 210
emission lines, 108
emission spectrum, 104
Emma-O, 659
emmenagogue, 582
Emmys, 461
emollient, 140

emoticon, 196
emotion, 405
emotional body, 669
emotivism, 408
empanadas, 265
empathy, 670
empennage, 201
emperor, 305, 339
Emperor's birthday, 482
emphasis, 525
emphasize, 548
Emphasizers, 528
emphatic, 516
emphysema, 13
empi, 27
empire, 302
empire waist, 289
empirical, 408
empirical formula, 126
empiricism, 407
Empirin, 138
employable, 353
employee, 355, 383
employee business expense, 363
employee stock ownership plan,
   360
employer, 355, 383
employer identification number,
   363
**Employers, Employees, and
   Business People**, 355–356
employment, 353
emporium, 300, 348
empress, 339
empty calories, 28
empty nester, 394
empyema, 21
empyrean, 666, 668
EMS, 129
EMT, 129
emulation, 192
emulator, 190, 441
emulsification, 42
emulsion, 422, 456, 476
en, 473
enable button, 187
enabler, 624
enactment, 306
enallage, 525
enamel, 7, 162, 422
enameling, 479
enamelware, 478
enamor, 577
enantio-, 529
en arrière, 449
en avant, 449
en brochette, 261
enc, 535
encashment, 357
encaustic, 422
-ence, 532
enceinte, 298
encephalitis, 13
encephalo-, 141, 529
enchaînement, 449
enchant, 577
enchantment, 612, 667
enchase, 473
enchilada, 265
encho-sen, 27
encircling, 601, 603
enclave, 336
enclitic, 519
enclosed, 603
enclosing, 603
enclosure, 374
encomium, 428, 615
encompassing, 603
encore, 615
encounter group, 403
encourage, 615
encouragement, 615
encroach, 585
encroachment, 381
en croûte, 261
enculturation, 390, 396
encumbrance, 320, 381

joseph, 272
josh, 547
joss, 665
jostle, 541
jota, 447
Jotun, 658
joule, 97, 126
Joule's law, 99
Joule-Thomson effect, 125
jounce, 540
jour, 536
journal, 154, 214, 325, 326, 366, 426
journal entry, 366
Journalism, 325–328
journalism, 326
journalist, 326, 430
journalize, 366
journey, 486, 541
journeyman, 355, 383
joust, 635
jousting, 488
Jove, 660
Jovian satellites, 106
joy, 656, 667
joypop, 626
joyride, 487
joystick, 188, 202
JP, 536
JPEG, 193
JP fuels, 202
JPL, 112
jr, 536
juba, 447
jubbah, 272
jubc, 654
jubilee, 484
Judah, 647
Judaism, 644
Judaism, 647–648
Judas, 593
Judas hole, 230
Judas Iscariot, 646
Judeo-Christian tradition, 646, 647
judge, 315, 339, 549, 607, 613, 632
Judges, Lawyers, and Others in the Court System, 314–315
judgment, 318, 613, 666
judgmental, 616
Judgment and Criticism, 613–619
Judgment Day, 666
Judgments and Critiques, 613–614
Judgments Pro and Con, 549–550
judicial branch, 304
judicial notice, 320
judicial review, 306, 320
judiciary, 304, 314, 315
judicious, 613
judo, 27
judoka, 27
jug, 173, 243, 269, 445, 509, 633
jug band, 439, 443
Jugendstil, 420
juggernaut, 206
juggle, 593
juggler, 454
jugglery, 488
juggling, 488
juggling act, 586
Jughead, 196
jugs, 581
juice, 349, 358, 509, 612
juice glass, 270
juicer, 268, 624
juicy, 553
jujitsu, 25
juju, 439, 665
juke, 543
jukebox, 441
juke joint, 441
Julian calendar, 143
julienne, 261
juliet cap, 287
July, 597

jumbo jet, 198
jumbuck, 52
jump, 188, 200, 326, 540, 583
jump bail, 632
jump cut, 457
jumper, 188, 223, 273, 274
jumper cable, 209
jumping jack, 25
jumping juvenile, 379
jump jet, 334
jump on, 636
jump rope, 26
jump seat, 209
jump-start, 210
jumpsuit, 273
junction, 214, 299
June, 597
Jungian psychology, 398
jungle, 46, 85, 439
junior, 247, 253, 413
junior college, 411
junior high school, 412
junior partner, 315
junk, 216, 623
junk bond, 360
junker, 206, 339
junket, 306, 310, 486
junk food, 28, 263
junkie, 627
junk mail, 376
Juno, 660
junta, 313, 394, 565
jupc, 274
Jupiter, 106, 112, 660
jupon, 274
Jurassic period, 70
jurat, 316
juried show, 424
jurisdiction, 306, 314
jurisprudence, 314
jurist, 315
juror, 315
jury, 314, 632
jury duty, 320
jury is out, 316
jury-rig, 586
jury strut, 202
jury tampering, 321
jury trial, 316
jus gentium, 314
justaucorps, 273
justice, 314, 315, 339
justice of the peace, 315
justifiable homicide, 629
justification, 471
justify, 193, 474
Justinian Code, 314
jute, 160
juv, 536
juvenile, 252, 454
juvenile books, 323
juvenile court, 314
juvenile delinquent, 252, 630
juvenilia, 426
Juventas, 660
juxta-, 530
juxtapose, 611

k/d, 158
k, 125, 126, 195, 369, 536, 623
Ka'ba, 648
kabalah, 647
kabob, 261
Kabuki, 450
Kabul, 81
kachina, 665
Kaddish, 640, 647
kaffee klatsch, 484
kaffir, 653
kaffiyeh, 288
kafir, 648
kaiser, 339
kajawah, 223
kakato, 27
kakemono, 423
kakko, 443
kakotopia, 661

Kalaallit Nunaat, 77
kala-azar, 14
kalathos, 423
kale, 369
kaleyard school, 426
Kali, 660
kalimba, 444
kalungu, 443
kama, 27
kamae, 27
Kamakura, 420
kamal, 648
Kama Sutra, 655
kame, 67
kamelaukion, 287
kami, 650
kamikaze, 331, 511, 565, 628
kampong, 298
Kampuchea, 77
kana, 522
kangaroo court, 314, 593
kanji, 522
Kanpur, 81
Kansas, 80
kansetsu, 27
kantar, 145
kantele, 445
kaolin, 478
kaon, 101
Kaposi's sarcoma, 14
kaputt, 565
Karachi, 81
karaoke, 441
karate, 25, 27
kareta-ka, 27
karma, 649, 666
karma yoga, 649
karmic bond, 669
karmic debt, 669
kaross, 272
karst topography, 69
karyo-, 530
karyotype, 37
Kasbah, 300
kashf, 648
kata, 27
katabasis, 329
katabatic wind, 87
katame, 27
katamewaza, 27
katana, 27, 175
kathak, 447
kathakali, 447
kathisomania, 402
katzenjammer, 624
kayak, 216
kayo, 636
kazatsky, 447
kazoo, 444
KB, 195
kebiyar, 447
kedge, 218
kedgeree, 265
keel, 145, 218
keelson, 218
keen, 546, 640
keep, 233, 372
keep company, 577
keeper, 497, 633
keeper ring, 499
keep net, 499
keep one's honor, 579
keep tabs on, 544
keet, 52
kef, 623, 664
keg, 172, 509
keg party, 509
keikogi, 27
keikoku, 27
kekomi, 27
kelly, 287
kelontong, 443
kelpie, 658
Kelvin, 103, 126
ken, 609, 610
Kendal green, 282

Kendal sneck bent, 499
kendo, 27
Kennedy Space Center, 112
kennel, 53, 228, 232
kenning, 429
kenong, 444
kenosis, 651
kentsui, 27
Kentucky, 80
Kenya, 77
Kenyatta Day, 482
Keogh plan, 363
kepi, 287
Kepler's laws, 110
kerar, 445
keratitis, 14
kerato-, 141, 530
keratoplasty, 133
kerchief, 279, 288
kerf, 71, 157
keri (or geri), 27
keri waza, 27
kermis, 484
Kermit, 183
kern, 331, 474
kernel, 59, 503
kerning, 188, 471
kersey, 282
kerseys, 275
ketch, 216
ketone, 43
kettle, 172, 212, 267
kettledrum, 443
kettle lake, 67
Ketuvim, 655
key, 73, 86, 185, 214, 308, 435, 446, 611, 623, 668
keyboard, 191, 443
Keyboards, 444
key club, 485
key grip, 459
keyhole router bit, 166
keyhole saw, 164
key light, 457, 464
key lot, 380
key money, 380
Keynesian economics, 345
keynote address, 312
keynoter, 311
keypad, 185, 191
keypunch, 188
keypunch operator, 188
key signature, 435
keystone, 154, 349, 469, 668
keystone joist, 154
keystroke, 188
keyway, 154
kg, 536
khaddar, 282
khaki, 282
khamsin, 87
khan, 339
Khartoum, 81
khedive, 339
khon, 447
kHz, 536
ki, 27
kiai, 27
kibble, 172
kibbutz, 375, 396
kibitka, 223
kibitz, 545, 566
kibr, 272
kick, 326, 636
kickapoo, 376
kick ass, 636
kickback, 367, 588
kick boxing, 27
kick butt, 636
kicker, 326, 382, 463
kick in, 638
kick off, 638
kick pleat, 291
kickshaw, 263
kick the bucket, 638
kick the gong around, 626
kick the habit, 626

kid, 52, 253, 284, 547
kid brother, 247
kiddy, 253
kid gloves, 279
kidnapping, 321, 629
kidney, 10
kidney basin, 136
kidney pie, 265
kidney stone, 17
kids, 253
kid sister, 247
kidvid, 461
Kiev, 81
kihon, 27
kilderkin, 145, 172
kilim, 240
kill, 85, 306, 326, 463, 495, 636, 639
killcrop, 252
killed-virus vaccine, 138
killer, 630, 638
killer weed, 623
kill fee, 326
killing, 629
killing frost, 88
kiln, 478
kiln-dried, 158
kilo-, 146, 536, 623
kilobaud, 183, 188
kilobyte, 195
kilogram, 144
kilohertz, 466
kiloliter, 144
kilometer, 144
kilt, 274
kiltie, 286
kime, 27
kimono, 272, 277
kimono sleeves, 289
kin, 246
kindergarten, 412
kindred, 246
Kinds of Paintings, 423–424
kine, 52
kinesiology, 25
-kinesis, 533
kinesthesia, 43
kinesthesis, 405
kinetic art, 420
kinetic energy, 97, 123
kinetics, 96, 119
kinetic theory, 125
kinetic theory of heat, 103
kinetic theory of matter, 97
kineto-, 530
kinetoscope, 457
kinfolk, 246
king, 305, 339
King Alphonse, 511
kingdom, 49, 302
kingdom come, 661
Kingdom of God, 666
Kingdom of Heaven, 666
King James Bible, 655
kingmaker, 311
King of Heaven, 650
King of kings, 650
king post, 154
king's (or queen's) English, 522
king-size bed, 237
kinin, 43
kinky, 584
kinnikinnick, 507
Kinsey scale, 579
Kinshasa, 81
kinship, 246, 389
Kinship and Ancestry, 246
Kinship and Family Relations, 245–247
kinship group, 246, 396
Kinship, Marriage, and Other Customs, 389–390
kinsman, 246
kinswoman, 246
kiosk, 228, 232, 300, 349
kio tsuke, 27
kip, 145, 470

717

London, 81
London broil, 265
London Fog, 272
lonely-hearts, 394
lone pair, 120
long., 536, 601
long ago, 599
longboat, 216
longbow, 175
long coat, 272
long discount, 323
long distance, 185, 601, 603
long dozen, 145
long-drawn-out, 597
longeron, 202
longeur, 564
longevity, 597
long-focus lens, 476
long gloves, 279
long green, 369
longhand, 522
long haul, 597
long house, 229
long hundredweight, 145
longi-, 530
longing, 577
Long Island iced tea, 512
longitude, 73, 221
longitudinal, 601
longitudinal axis, 200
longitudinal study, 403
longitudinal wave, 97
long johns, 277
longliner, 216
long neck, 509
long paint, 422
long pants, 275
long program, 493
long-run, 597
longshoreman, 219
long shot, 457
long since, 599
long-sleeved shirt, 274
longstanding, 597
long-term, 597
long-term capital gain, 364
long-term loan, 358
Long Tom, 176
long ton, 144
long underwear, 277
long vowel, 519
long-waisted, 291
longwall, 71
loo, 236
look, 544
look askance at, 544
look away, 544
look daggers, 544
look for, 544
looking glass, 240
looking-glass self, 405
looking-glass theory, 397
look into, 607
look on, 544
lookout, 154, 544
look over, 544
looks, 32
look sideways at, 544
look up, 544
look upon, 544
loom, 149
loony, 627
loony bin, 628
loop, 171, 181, 188, 200, 293, 442, 543, 582, 605
loophole, 364, 586
looping, 457
loop knot, 171, 500
loop-the-loop, 488
loose cannon, 394
loose money policy, 345
loose sentence, 517
loot, 636
looting, 629
lope, 540
lop off, 636
lopolith, 67

loppers, 502
LORAN, 203
lorcha, 216
lord, 340, 650
Lord Fauntleroy, 579
Lord of hosts, 650
Lord of lords, 650
lordosis, 19, 48
Lord's day, 486
Lord's Prayer, 646
Lord's Supper, 646
lore, 661
Lorelei, 658
Lorenz curve, 345
lorgnette, 279
lorgnon, 279
lorry, 206
Los Angeles, 81
lose face, 617
lose ground, 543
lose one's heart, 577
lose one's mind, 627
lose one's shirt, 352
loss leader, 349
lost, 638
Lost Generation, 426
lost-wax process, 425
lot, 367, 382, 459, 666
lota, 173
Lothario, 577
lotion, 140
lottery, 345
lotus, 649, 661
lotus land, 661
lotus position, 668
Lotus 1,2,3, 193
lou, 230
loud, 551
loudness, 551
Lou Gehrig's disease, 14
lough, 85
Louisiana, 80
lounge, 541
lounge car, 212
lounge chair, 237
lounge coat, 273
lounger, 286
lounge suit, 273
lounging robe, 277
loupe, 472, 477
loup-garou, 658, 665
louse, 14
louver, 230
louver door, 158
Love. See **Sex, Love, and Romance**
love, 577, 614, 667
Love and Romance, 576–577
love at first sight, 577
lovebirds, 577
love child, 250
loved one, 639
love drop, 581
love feast, 651
love handles, 7
love-in, 393
love interest, 459
love juice, 581
love letter, 578
lovelock, 29
lovelorn, 577
lovemaking, 583
love potion, 579
lover, 577
lovers' quarrel, 577
love seat, 237
lovesick, 577
low, 90, 600
lowball, 591
low blood pressure, 22
low blow, 586
lowboy, 239
low-budget film, 459
low comedy, 426, 450
low-cost housing, 380
low-density lipoprotein, 43
lower, 603

lowercase, 474
lower class, 345, 396
lower division, 411
lower house, 304
Lower Paleolithic period, 388
lowest common denominator, 116
low-grade fever, 22
low-impact aerobics, 25
low-intensity conflict, 329
low latitudes, 73
low-level language, 193
low-necked, 291
low opinion, 617
low-pressure, 90, 349
low-price, 349
low-profile, 589
low relief, 424
lowrider, 206
low tar, 507
low tide, 91
LOX, 113
loxodromic, 73
loy, 165
loyal opposition, 309
lozenge, 138, 605
LP, 441
L-pill, 623
LPN, 130, 536
LSD, 623
LSI, 188
lt, 536
Ltd, 536
luau, 263, 484
lubberland, 661
lubber's knot, 171, 221
lube, 210
lubricant, 140, 209
lubricity, 579
lucid, 610
lucie, 472
Lucifer, 646
Lucite, 160
luck, 666
lucrative, 367
lucre, 369
Lucy Stoner, 249
'lude, 623
luff, 221
luftmensch, 566
Luftwaffe, 331
Lug, 660
lug and slot, 154
luge, 223
Luger, 176
luggage, 281
Luggage and Cases, 280–281
luggage van, 212
lugger, 216
lug nut, 170
lug nuts, 209
lugsail, 218
lug the engine, 210
lug wrench, 167
lull, 486, 551, 586
lullaby, 251, 439
Lull diagram, 410
lumbago, 22
lumber, 154, 158, 371, 540
lumbering, 371
lumbermill, 157
lumberyard, 157
lumen, 43, 104
Luminal, 623
luminance signal, 464
luminescence, 105, 123
luminosity, 108
luminous body, 105
luminous flux, 105
luminous intensity, 105
lump, 605
lumpenproletariat, 345, 394, 565
lump-sum distribution, 364
Luna, 660
lunacy, 627
lunar, 108
lunar eclipse, 88, 108

lunar excursion module, 113
lunar module, 113
lunar occultation, 108
lunar orbiter, 113
lunar rock, 113
lunatic, 627
lunatic asylum, 628
lunatic fringe, 393
lunch, 256, 263
lunch counter, 263
luncheon, 263, 484
luncheonette, 263
lunchpail, 281
lunchtime, 596
lunette, 469, 605
lung, 10
lung cancer, 14
lunge, 541, 543, 635
luni-, 530
lupine, 52
lupus, 14
lupus erythematosus, 14
lupus vulgaris, 14
lure, 496, 500, 586
Lurex, 283
lurk, 541, 589
lush, 625
lust, 579
luster, 69, 241, 282, 478
lustration, 651
lustrum, 597
lusty, 579
lusus naturae, 562
lute, 161, 445
luteinizing hormone, 48
Lutheran Church, 645
luthier, 383
Lutz, 493
Luxembourg, 78
luxury tax, 362
-ly, 533
lycanthropy, 665
lycée, 412
lycopod, 59
lying-in, 250
Lyme disease, 14
lymph, 9, 43
lymphatic system, 9
lymph node, 9
lympho-, 530
lymphocyte, 9, 39
lymphoid tissue, 43
lymphokine, 43
lymphoma, 14
lynching, 633, 639
lynch mob, 394
lyonnaise, 261
lyre, 445
lyrical abstraction, 420
lyricist, 441
lyricon, 445
lyric poetry, 426
lysergic acid, 623
-lysis, 141, 533
lyso-, 530
Lysol, 140
lysosome, 39
lyssophobia, 401
-lyte, 533
-lyze, 533

m, 536, 623
maitre d', 340
maitre d'hôtel, 564
ma, 253, 411, 536
Maalox, 138
Ma Bell, 185
macadam, 160, 299
Macao, 78
macaroni and cheese, 265
macaronic, 429, 522
Maccabees, 647
maccaboy, 507
mace, 175, 280, 631
macédoine, 261
macebearer, 305
Macedonia, 78

macerate, 262
macfarlane, 272
Mach, 113, 536
macher, 566
ma chère, 564
machete, 163, 175, 445
Machiavellian, 586
machicolation, 235
machination, 586
machine, 149, 151, 310
machine bolt, 170
machine gun, 176
machine language, 193
machine operator, 152
machine pistol, 176
machine politician, 311
machine-readable, 193
machinery, 149
Machinery and Mechanical Devices, 148–150
Machinery and Fabrication, 148–152
machine screw, 170
machine-stitch, 291
machine tool, 149, 165
machinist, 383
machismo, 565, 579
machmeter, 203
mach number, 200
macho, 579
-machy, 533
Macintosh, 191
mackinaw, 273, 282
mackintosh, 272, 282
mackle, 474
macle, 67
macock, 172
macramé, 291, 480
macramé, 504
macro, 193, 530
macrobiotics, 28, 263
macrocosm, 396
macroeconomics, 345
macroevolution, 37
macron, 518
macronutrients, 28
macrophage, 39
macrophotograph, 475
MACRS, 364
macule, 22
macumba, 662
MAD, 329, 627
Madagascar, 78
madam, 584
madame, 340, 564
madder, 422
mad dog, 638
mademoiselle, 340, 564
madhouse, 628
Madison Avenue, 376
madman, 627
mad money, 369
madness, 627
Madonna, 646
Madras, 81, 282, 512
Madrid, 81
madrigal, 438
maduro, 507
mae, 27
maelstrom, 87
maenads, 658
maesta, 423
maestoso, 435
maestro, 438, 565
Mae West, 26, 205
maffick, 485
Mafia, 630
mafic magma, 67
mafioso, 630
mag, 536
magalog, 376
magazine, 172, 178, 325, 457, 461, 477
magazine gun, 176
Magellan, 113
Magellanic clouds, 106
Magen David, 647

numinous, 656, 667
numismatics, 369, 505
nun, 653
nunatak, 84
nunchaku, 27, 175
nuncio, 335, 340
nuncle, 247
nunnery, 654
Nupercaine, 139
nuptial, 249
nuptial plumage, 52
nuptials, 249
nurse, 130, 251
nursemaid, 252
nurse midwife, 130
nurse practitioner, 130
nursery, 232, 234, 251, 375, 502
nursery rhyme, 427, 661
nursery school, 412
nursery tale, 661
nurse's aide, 130
nursing home, 130
nurture, 615
nurturing, 406
nurturing environment, 406
nut, 59, 170, 257, 258, 371, 446, 627, 660
nutation, 59, 108
nutcracker, 268, 512
nut house, 628
nutmeg, 623
nutpick, 268
nutria, 284
nutrient, 28
nutrients, 375
nutriment, 256
nutrition, 28, 36, 128
Nutrition For Fitness, 28
nutritionist, 130
nuts, 581, 627
Nuts and Seeds, 258
nutshell, 526
nutter, 627
nutty, 627
nutty professor, 512
nuzzling, 578
NW, 536
nyanza, 85
nycto-, 530
nyctophobia, 401
nylon, 283
nylon carpeting, 240
nylons, 277
nymph, 500, 658
nymphet, 252, 579
nymph fishing, 498
nympholepsy, 406, 663
nymphomania, 400, 402, 584
nystagmus, 19
Nyx, 660

oak leaf cluster, 332
oakum, 161, 218
oar, 218
oarsman, 219
OAS, 337
oasis, 70, 74, 85, 662
-oate, 533
oater, 455
oath, 320, 526
oats, 372
ob-, 530
obbligato, 436
obcordate, 605
OBE, 536
obeah, 662
obeisance, 614
obelisk, 229, 230, 518
Oberon, 107
obesity, 18, 22, 28
obfuscate, 589
ob-gyn, 128
obi, 27, 280
obit, 327, 536, 641
obiter dictum, 526, 563
obituary, 327, 641
obj, 536

object, 517, 549, 618
object code, 193
objection, 317
objective, 110, 452, 517
objective lens, 105
objectivism, 407
objet d'art, 241, 564
objet trouvé, 241, 564
objurgate, 619
oblate, 605
oblation, 651
obligation, 318, 358, 361
oblige, 614
oblique, 118, 589, 601, 605
obliquity, 599
obliterate, 636
oblivion, 666
oblong, 118, 605
obloquy, 619
oboe, 446
oboe d'amore, 446
obol, 369
obolus, 146
obovate, 605
obovoid, 605
obs, 536
obscenity, 322, 584
obscurantism, 429, 589
obscure, 589
obsecration, 646
obsequy, 640
observable universe, 110
observance, 484, 652
observation car, 212
observation tower, 230
observatory, 110
observe, 544, 545, 608
obsess, 547
obsession, 400, 577, 664
obsessive, 629
obsessive-compulsive neurosis, 400
obstacle, 452
obstacle course, 332
obstetrics, 128
obstruct, 618
obstruction, 586
obstruction of justice, 322, 630
obstruction wrench, 167
obstruent, 520
obtrude, 541
obtuse, 601, 605
obtuse angle, 118
obukano, 445
obverse, 410, 603, 605
obviate, 586
OC, 461
ocarina, 446
Occam's razor, 409
occas, 536
occasional, 599
occasionally, 599
occasional verse, 427
occipital lobe, 9
occiput, 6
occluded front, 90
occlusion, 7, 24, 90, 520
occult, 663, 664
occultation, 109
Occult States and Experiences, 663–664
occupancy, 380
occupation, 329, 353
occupational hazard, 354
occupational medicine, 128
occupational sociology, 397
occupational therapy, 403
Occupations and Job Titles, 384–385
occupied territory, 334
occupy one's thoughts, 607
occur, 607
occurrence, 379
ocean, 47, 74, 86
ocean basin, 74
oceanfront, 86
Oceania, 73
Oceanid, 658
ocean liner, 216

oceanography, 66
ochlocracy, 302
ochlomania, 402
ochlophobia, 401
-ock, 533
o'clock, 143
OCR, 189
Oct, 536
octa-, 118, 530
octagon, 605
octagonal, 605
octahedron, 605
octal, 189
octane, 210
octant, 144, 200
octave, 105, 429, 436, 670
octavo, 430
octet, 429, 434
octet rule, 125
October, 597
October Revolution Day, 483
octodecimo, 430
oculist, 130
oculo-, 530
oculus, 469
OD, 139, 626, 638
o-daiko, 443
odalisque, 584
oddball, 627
oddity, 663
odd lot, 361
odd number, 116
odd parity, 189
odds, 666
ode, 427
odeum, 451
Odin, 660
odium, 619
odometer, 209
-odont, 141, 533
odonto-, 141, 530
odor, 552
odoriferous, 552
-odus, 533
odynia, 141, 533
Odyssey, 661
odyssey, 487, 668
Oedipus, 658
Oedipus complex, 400
œil-de-bœuf, 230
œillade, 578
OEM, 349
oenophile, 625
oeuvre, 422
off., 536, 601, 603, 627, 636, 639
off and on, 599
off-boat, 216
off book, 452
off Broadway, 451
off-camera, 464
off-color, 584
offend, 618
offense, 322, 618, 630
offensive, 329
offer, 548, 550
offering, 361
offer of proof, 317
offertory, 652
off-hour, 301
office, 234, 304
office-in-home, 364
Office of Management and Budget, 304
officer, 332, 355
officers' car, 212
office worker, 355, 383
official, 305, 355, 383
officialism, 302
off-line, 189, 205
off off Broadway, 451
off one's head, 627
off one's rocker, 627
off-peak, 214, 301, 599
off-premises extension, 185
off-road vehicle, 206
offscreen, 457
off-season, 599

offset, 502
offset lithography, 474
offset parallel runways, 205
offset printing, 474
offshoot, 611
offshore, 86, 87
offshore drilling, 71
offspring, 246, 253
off-the rack, 291
off the wagon, 509, 625
off-the-wall, 629
off year, 312
often, 599
ofttimes, 599
ofuro, 236
ogee, 605
ogival, 605
ogive, 235, 605
ogle, 544
ogling, 578
ogre, 650
Ohio, 80
ohm, 100, 181
Ohm's law, 100, 181
-oid, 141, 533
-oidea, 533
oikomania, 402
oil, 162, 257, 260
oil-base paint, 162
oilcan, 169, 172
oil change, 210
oilcloth, 283
oil cooler, 208
oiled, 625
oiler, 216
oil filter, 208
oil gauge, 209
oil lamp, 242
oil paint, 422
oil pan, 209
oil pump, 208
oilskin, 272
oilstone, 165
oil well, 71
oink, 547
oinomania, 402
ointment, 140
OK, 615
oka, 146
okay, 615
okedo, 443
okey-doke, 615
Oklahoma, 80
Oktoberfest, 484
-ola, 533
old, 599
old age, 638
Old English, 523
old-fashioned, 270, 512
old guard, 311
oldie, 441
old lady, 249, 253
Old Left, 309
old-line, 311
old maid, 249
old man, 249, 253
old school tie, 279
Old Testament, 655
old-world, 393
olé, 565, 616
oleo-, 530
olericulture, 375
olestra, 28
O level, 415
olfaction, 552
olfactory, 59, 552
olfactory lobe, 9
olid, 552
oligarchy, 302
oligo-, 530
Oligocene epoch, 71
oligopoly, 346
oligopsony, 349
olio, 451
olive drab, 273, 332
olla, 173
Olmec, 389

olympiad, 597
Olympus, 661, 666
Olympus Mons, 109
Om, 649
-oma, 141, 533
Oman, 78
OMB, 304
ombudsman, 131, 305, 315
omega particle, 101
omega-3 fatty acid, 28
omelet pan, 267
omelette, 261
omen, 663, 665, 666
Omisoka, 483
omni-, 530, 668
omnia vincit amor, 563
omnibus, 206, 222, 430
omnibus bill, 307
Omnipotent, 650
Omnipresent, 650
omniscience, 670
Omniscient, 650
omnivore, 47, 52
omphalos, 600
on, 601, 603
on again, off again, 599
onager, 175
onanism, 583
on behalf of, 615
onboard, 202
on-call, 131
once, 596
on center, 157
oncology, 128
on-demand, 358
ondes martenot, 444
one, 668
one-acter, 451
one for the road, 509
one-horse town, 298
Oneida Community, 662
oneiric, 664
oneiro-, 530
oneiromancy, 662
one-man rule, 302
oneness, 667
one-night stand, 452, 578
one-piece bathing suit, 275
one-piece suit, 273
one sheet, 452
one-step, 447
one too many, 625
one-to-one function, 116
one-upmanship, 617
one-way, 299, 668
one-way street, 210
one-way ticket, 487
one world, 302
ongeblozn, 566
ongoing, 599
on high, 666
on ice, 633, 638
oniomania, 402
onion flute, 444
on-line, 189
on location, 459
only child, 252
onomastics, 523
onomatomania, 526
onomatophobia, 401
onomatopoeia, 429, 526
on one's deathbed, 641
on pins and needles, 629
onrush, 635
on-screen, 189
onshore, 87
onslaught, 618, 635
on spec, 354
on tap, 510
on tenterhooks, 629
on the advertised, 214
on the air, 464
on the block, 349
on the card, 214
on the house, 349, 510
on the lam, 589
on the make, 578, 586

on the merits, 318
on the prowl, 578
on the road, 487
on the rocks, 249, 509
on the side, 249
on the take, 588
on the wagon, 509
on time, 349, 596
onto-, 530
ontogeny, 48
ontological argument, 409
ontology, 409
onus, 619
onward, 603
on wheels, 263
onychophagia, 406
-onym, 533
onymous, 430
oo-, 530
oocyte, 48
oogamy, 48
oogenesis, 48
oolite, 68
-oon, 533
ooze, 74
op, 536
opalesce, 422
opaque material, 105
op art, 421
op cit, 536
OPEC, 337
Op-Ed page, 327
open, 452, 461, 520, 548
open-air theater, 451
open architecture, 191
open circuit, 181
open classroom, 415
open cluster, 107
open court, 317
open cut, 71
open door, 337
open-ended question, 463
open-end wrench, 167
open enrollment, 416
open-field cultivation, 371
open-grained, 158
open hand knot, 171
open-heart surgery, 134
open house, 380, 484
opening, 231, 424
opening credits, 459
opening menu, 189, 193
opening night, 452, 484
opening statement, 320
open listing, 380
open market, 346
open marriage, 249
open positions, 449
open primary, 312
open return, 487
open sea, 221
open season, 495
open sesame, 663
open sight, 178
open system, 127
open tuning, 441
opera, 438, 451
Opera and Vocal Music, 437
opera buffa, 438
opera cape, 272
opera glasses, 279
opera hat, 287
operand, 189
operant conditioning, 403
opera seria, 438
operate, 586
operating engineer, 152
operating expenses, 352
operating room, 130
operating system, 193
operation, 134, 329
operation code, 193
operations research, 352
operator, 152, 185, 189, 355, 383, 593
operator-assisted call, 185
operator gene, 38

opere citato, 563
operetta, 438, 451
operon, 38
ophelimity, 346
ophiciophobia, 401
ophicleide, 446
ophidiform, 605
ophidiomania, 402
ophio-, 530
ophthalmo-, 141, 530
ophthalmologist, 130
ophthalmology, 128
ophthalmoscope, 136
-opia, 141, 533
opiate, 139, 623
-opic, 533
opine, 549, 607, 609, 613
opinion, 318, 613
opistho-, 530
opium, 139, 623
opp., 536
opponent, 618
opportunism, 586
opportunistic, 24
oppose, 618
opposed, 618
opposite, 603
Opposition, Disagreement, and Attack, 617–618
oppress, 636
oppression, 309
opprobrium, 619
oppugn, 618
-opsia, 533
opsimath, 413
-opsis, 533
-opsy, 141, 533
opt, 614
optative, 517
optical activity, 123
optical character recognition, 189
optical density, 105
optical disc, 195
optical double, 109
optical effect, 457
optical fiber, 105
optical isomer, 121
optical reader wand, 189
optical scanner, 191
optician, 130
optic nerve, 6
optics, 96
Optics, 104–105
optics, 105
optimal length, 43
optimism, 407
option, 323, 361, 381, 459, 613
opto-, 141, 530
optometrist, 130
optometry, 128
opulence, 367
opus, 430, 434, 563
OPV, 139
-opy, 533
OR, 130, 533
oracle, 658, 665
oral contraceptive, 139
oral history, 323
Oral Law, 655
oral phase, 406
orals, 415
oral surgery, 128, 134
oral thermometer, 136
-orama, 533
Orange, 606
orange blossom, 512
orange stick, 31
orange wedge, 623
orate, 545
oration, 526
oratorio, 438
orb, 280, 605
orbicular, 605
orbit, 109, 113
orbital, 121
orbital angular momentum, 98
orbital cavity, 6

orc, 658
orch, 536
orchard, 85, 232, 371, 501
orchestra, 438, 443, 452
orchestrate, 586
orchestration, 436
orchid, 503
orchid growing, 505
orchido-, 141
orchitis, 15
Orcus, 660
order, 49, 214, 318, 469, 545, 611, 654
ordered pair, 410
Order, Hierarchy, and Systems, 610–612
orderly, 130
order of battle, 329
orders, 329
ordinal number, 116
ordinance, 307
ordinary, 223
ordinary income, 364
ordinary-language school, 407
ordinate, 116
ordination, 652
ordnance, 178, 334
ordonnance, 611
Ordovician period, 70
ore, 71
oread, 658
orebody, 71
Oregon, 80
.org, 196, 536
organ, 12, 43, 444, 581
organdy, 283
organelles, 40
organic, 502, 670
organic chemistry, 119
organic compound, 121
organic disorder, 15
organic farming, 371
organic food, 28
organic material, 68
organic therapy, 403
organism, 38
organismic theory, 403
organization, 352, 611
organization man, 355
Organization of American States, 337
Organization of Petroleum Exporting Countries, 337
organized crime, 630
organo-, 530
organ of Corti, 7
organon, 409
organ system, 43
organ transplant, 134
organza, 283
organzine, 283
orgasm, 581
orgy, 486, 584
-orial, 533
oriel, 230
Orientale basin, 109
Oriental rug, 240
orientation, 470
orig., 536
origami, 425, 480, 505
origin, 116, 246
original, 441
original negative, 457
original sin, 652
originate, 609
origination fee, 382
O-ring, 113, 170
Orion Nebula, 107
orismology, 523
Orlon, 283
orlop deck, 218
ornament, 241, 436
Ornamental and Functional Articles, 241–243
Ornamental and Structural Parts, 231–232

ornamental garden, 501
Ornaments, 278
Ornaments and Accessories, 278–281
ornate, 526
ornitho-, 530
ornithology, 36
ornithomania, 402
ornithophobia, 401
ornithopter, 198
oro-, 530
orogeny, 70
orography, 66, 72
orphan, 252, 474
orpharion, 445
Orpheus, 658
Orphic, 664
orphica, 444
Orphism, 421
orphrey, 280, 291
orrery, 110
ortho-, 141, 530
orthochromatic, 477
orthodiagraph, 136
orthodontics, 128, 134
orthodontist, 130
Orthodox, 648
Orthodox Eastern Church, 644
orthodoxy, 652
orthoepy, 520
orthography, 523
orthopedics, 128
orthopedic surgeon, 130
orthopedic surgery, 128
orthopraxy, 652
-ory, 533
OS, 193, 457
osaekomi, 27
Osaka, 81
Oscars, 459
oscillator, 181, 442
oscilloscope, 49, 100, 181
oscine, 55
osculation, 578
-ose, 533
Osiris, 660
-osis, 141, 533
Oslo, 81
osmolarity, 40
osmoreceptor, 43
osmosis, 40, 123
osmotic pressure, 40
ossi-, 141, 530
ossicle, 7
ossification, 11
ossobuco, 266
ostectomy, 134
Osteichthyes, 50
ostensorium, 174
osteo-, 141, 530
osteoarthritis, 15
osteoblast, 40
osteoclasis, 134
osteomyelitis, 15
osteopath, 130
osteopathy, 128
osteoporosis, 15
ostinato, 436
ostracize, 617
ot, 536
-ota, 533
otalgia, 22
OTC, 139, 361
-ote, 533
Other Crafts, 479–480
Other Romance Languages, 564–565
Other Vehicles, 222–223
other woman, 577
-otic, 533
otitis, 15
oto-, 141, 530
otolaryngology, 128
otology, 551
otorhinolaryngology, 128
otoscope, 136

Ottawa, 81
otter, 284
ottoman, 237
oubliette, 633, 666
oud, 445
Ouija, 663
ounce, 144
-our, 533
Our Lady, 647
-ous, 533
ouse, 27
oust, 636
out-, 530, 601, 603
outbid, 349
outboard, 202, 218
outboard flap, 202
outboard motor, 218
outboard spoiler, 202
outbreak, 588, 634
outbuilding, 229, 381
Outbuildings, Gardens, and Fences, 232–233
outburst, 634
outcropping, 68
outdoor, 377
Outdoor Games, 505–506
outdoors, 603
outer, 603
outer core, 68
outer ear, 7
outer garment, 291
Outer Garments, 271–276
outer marker, 205
outer space, 109
outfit, 288, 626
outfit car, 212
outflank, 586
outfox, 586, 607
outgassing, 109
outgoing mail, 329
out-group, 395
outguess, 586, 607
outhouse, 229, 232
outing, 486, 580
outlet, 85, 181, 349, 470
outlet store, 349
outline, 586, 601, 611
outlook, 613
outmaneuver, 586
outmost, 600
out-of-body experience, 664
out-of-bounds, 601
out-of-court settlement, 318
out of one's head, 627
out of one's mind, 627
out of one's tree, 627
out-of-plumb, 157
out-of-pocket, 346
out-of-print, 323
out-of-state return, 364
out of the closet, 580
out of wedlock, 250
outpace, 543
outpatient, 130
output, 189, 193
outrage, 634
outrance, 600
outreach, 586, 601
outrigger, 218
outro, 461
outside, 603
outside agitator, 313
outside clinch, 171
outskirts, 298
outsmart, 586, 607
outsole, 285
outspeak, 545
outstanding, 361
outstanding account, 366
outstanding check, 358
outstrip, 543
outtake, 457, 464
outtalk, 548
outthink, 607
outward, 601
outwardly, 601
outwash, 68

outwash plain, 70
outwit, 586, 607
oval, 118, 605
oval window, 7
ovarian follicle, 48
ovary, 10, 11, 48, 59, 581
ovate, 605
ovation, 616
oven, 241, 267
oven thermometer, 268
over-, 530, 603
overachiever, 413
overact, 452
overage, 379
overalls, 275
over-and-under, 176
overbite, 7
overboard, 221
overbook, 487
overbooking, 205
overbudget, 352
overcasting, 291
overcharge, 349
Overcoats and Cloaks, 272
overcompensation, 400
overcranking, 457
overdo, 591
overdose, 139, 626, 638
overdraft, 358
overdraw, 358
overdrawn, 627
overdrive, 208
overdub, 442
over easy, 261
overexposure, 477
overglaze, 478
overhand knot, 171
overhang, 470
overhaul, 211, 543
overhead, 352
overhead rack, 205
overhear, 551
overinsured, 379
overkill, 329
overlay, 473
overlock seam, 291
overlook, 84, 544, 613
overlord, 340
overlying, 603
overnight, 597
overnight case, 281
overpass, 299
overpayment, 364
overpower, 636
overprice, 349
overpriced, 361
overreach, 591
override, 189, 307
overrule, 320
overrun, 323, 474, 636
overs, 474
overseas cap, 287
oversee, 544
overseer, 355, 383
oversexed, 579
overshoes, 286
overshoot, 205
overskirt, 289
oversoul, 670
overstate, 545, 591
overstock, 323
overstretching, 25
overstrike, 191
overstuffed chair, 237
overtake, 543
over-the-counter, 361
over the edge, 627
over-the-top, 200
over-the-transom, 323
overtime, 354
overtone, 436
overtones, 105
overture, 434
overview, 544
overwhelm, 636
overwrought, 629
ovi-, 141, 530

oviduct, 48
oviparous, 48
ovoid, 605
ovoviviparous, 48
ovulation, 581
ovule, 59
ovum, 11, 48, 250, 581
owner, 355, 382
owner's equity, 366
ownership, 346
own recognizance, 317
Owsley, 623
oxbow, 85
oxbow lake, 86
Oxbridge, 411
oxcart, 223
ox dance, 447
oxford, 283, 286
Oxford bags, 275
oxgall, 422
oxidation, 124, 478
oxidation number, 124, 127
oxidative, 44
oxidative fast fibers, 44
oxidative phosphorylation, 40
oxidative slow fibers, 44
oxide, 121
oxidizing agent, 121
oxy-, 530
oxygenator, 136
oxygen cycle, 47
oxygen mask, 26, 136, 205
oxygen tank, 136
oxygen tent, 136
oxyhemoglobin, 44
oxymoron, 526
oxyntic cells, 40
oxytocin, 48
oy, 566
oyster fork, 270
oyster knife, 268
oysters Rockefeller, 266
oz., 144, 536, 623, 661
ozone depletion, 89
ozone hole, 74
ozone layer, 74
ozonometer, 203

p, 536
pa, 253, 442, 459, 536
pâté, 257, 266
pac, 286, 312
pace, 53, 145, 540
pacemaker, 44, 136
pachy-, 530
pacific, 667
Pacific time, 143
pacifier, 251
pacinian corpuscle, 44
pack, 53, 140, 174, 507, 588
package, 174, 459
packager, 323
package store, 349, 509
package tour, 487
packaging, 349
pack animal, 372
packet, 174, 507
packet switching, 183
packhorse, 496
packing, 127
packing case, 174
packing slip, 349
packsack, 174, 281
Pac-Man defense, 352
pact, 335
pad, 170, 228, 540
padded bra, 276
padded cell, 628
paddle, 214, 218, 252, 541
paddle steamer, 216
paddle wheel, 212, 218
paddle wheeler, 216
paddling, 478
paddock, 232
paddy, 371
paddy wagon, 206, 631
padishah, 340

padlock, 169
padre, 653
padre, 340, 565
paean, 616
paella, 266
paella pan, 267
pagan, 653
paganism, 652
page, 305, 545
pageant, 451, 484, 488
pageboy, 29
page chair, 237
page printer, 191
page proofs, 323
pager, 185
pagoda, 229, 231, 654
pagoda sleeve, 289
-pagus, 530
paid-in-kind security, 361
paid political announcement, 461
paid vacation, 486
pail, 172, 242
paillase, 237
paillette, 291
pai-loo, 231
pain, 22
painkiller, 139
paint, 162, 422, 547
paintbrush, 169
painter, 152
painterly, 422
painting, 151
Painting, 420–424
painting, 422
Painting Tools and Techniques, 421–423
paint pot, 169
paint roller, 169
paint tray, 169
pair-bonding, 47
paired-associate learning, 403
pair production, 101
pair skating, 493
paisley, 283
pajama party, 486
pajamas, 277
Pakistan, 78
pakora, 266
palace, 229
palace car, 212
palanquin, 223
palatable, 553
palatal, 520
palate, 7, 553
palatine, 340
Palau, 78
palaver, 545
palazzo, 229
paleo-, 530
Paleocene epoch, 71
paleogeography, 66
Paleolithic period, 389
paleontology, 36, 66, 388
Paleozoic era, 70
palestra, 412
paletot, 272
palette, 172, 189, 422
palette cup, 422
palette knife, 422
palfrey, 52
Pali Canon, 655
palimony, 249
palimpsest, 430, 589
palindrome, 526
palingenesis, 38
paling fence, 232
palisade, 84, 232
palisade cell, 59
pall, 640
Palladian, 468
Palladian window, 230
palladium, 661
Pallas Athena, 660
pallbearer, 640
pallet, 149, 237, 474, 478
pallette, 276
palliate, 615

palliative, 139
pallium, 9, 272, 276
palm, 145
palmate, 605
palm court orchestra, 443
palmer, 500, 653
palmistry, 662
palm off, 593
palm reader, 665
Palm Sunday, 483
palmtop, 191
palpation, 134
palpitation, 22, 44
palsy, 19
palter, 593
paludal, 84
palynology, 59
pampas, 84
pampero, 87
Pampers, 251
pamphlet, 325
pan, 173, 178, 200, 267, 327, 442, 457, 530, 619, 660
panacea, 139, 668
panache, 278, 288
Panama, 78
Panama City, 81
Panama hat, 287
Panama red, 623
Pan American Day, 483
panatela, 507
pan-broil, 262
pancake, 31, 261
panchromatic, 477
pancreas, 10
pancreatic juice, 10
pancreatitis, 15
pancreozymin, 44
pandect, 429
pandemic, 24
Pandemonium, 667
pander, 504
P and G, 377
pandit, 340
P and L, 366, 536
pandora, 445, 658
Pandora's box, 666
pandour, 332
pane glass, 160
panegyric, 526, 616
panel, 154, 209, 234, 239
panelboard, 159
paneling, 158, 234
Paneling and Composite Boards, 158–159
panel painting, 423
panel saw, 164
panel show, 463
panel truck, 206
pan-fry, 262
panga, 175
Pangaea, 68
pangolin, 55
pangram, 526
panic, 346, 361, 626
panicle, 59
panne, 283
pannier, 174, 276
panning, 71
panning shot, 477
panorama, 488
panoramic camera, 475
panpipe, 446
panpsychism, 662
panpsychist, 665
pansy, 580
pantalets, 276
pantaloons, 275
pant dress, 274
pantechnicon, 206
panth, 649
pantheism, 409, 652
pantheon, 469, 650, 654
panties, 276
pantile, 160
pantile roof, 231
pantisocracy, 302

pantocrator, 423
pantofle, 286
pantograph, 472
pantomime, 451, 454, 488
Pantone Matching System, 472
pantry, 234
pants, 275
pantsuit, 273
panty girdle, 276
pantyhose, 277
panty raid, 584
pantywaist, 579
panzer, 332
papa, 253
papacy, 654
paparazzi, 327
paparazzo, 477
paper, 160, 415, 472, 477, 623
paperback, 323
paperboard, 159, 160
paperbound, 323
paper chromatography, 49, 127
papercraft, 480
paper flower making, 480, 505
paperhanger, 152
papermaking, 480
paper money, 369
paper profit, 346
paper sculpture, 480
paper the house, 452
paper towels, 270
paperworking, 505
papier-mâché, 425, 480, 564
papier-mâché, 160, 505
papillote, 261
papoose, 253
pappy, 253
Pap test, 134
Papua New Guinea, 78
papule, 22
PAR, 203, 358, 536
para-, 118, 530
parable, 429, 526, 661
parabola, 118, 605
parabolic, 605
parabolic relationship, 98
parachronism, 599
parachute, 200
parachute journalism, 463
Paraclete, 650
parade, 484, 488, 541
parade rest, 332
paradigm, 517, 611
paradigmatic, 523
paradise, 666
parados, 452
paradox, 410, 526, 611
paradoxical effect, 403
paradoxical sleep, 44
paraenesis, 429
paraffin, 425
paragoge, 520
paragraph, 523
paragraph mark, 518
Paraguay, 78
parahormone, 44
paralanguage, 523
paralegal, 315
paralipsis, 526
parallax, 98, 110, 457, 477, 601
parallel, 73, 118, 603
parallel circuit, 181
parallel configuration, 191
parallelepiped, 118, 605
parallelogram, 118, 605
parallel parking, 211
parallel port, 191
parallel printer, 191
parallel processing, 189
parallel rule, 472
parallels, 518
paralysis, 19
paramagnetic, 123, 181
paramagnetism, 100
paramania, 402
paramatta, 283
paramedic, 130

roundhouse mechanic, 213
round-nose scraper, 163
rounds, 132
round seizing, 171
round-the-clock, 597
round-the-world, 487
round trip, 215, 487
round turn, 171
rouse, 548
rout, 329, 637
route, 299, 487
router, 165
router plane, 165
routine, 453
rout seat, 237
roux, 261
rove, 541
Rover, 113
roving eye, 578
row, 221, 299, 301, 635
rowboat, 217
rowdy, 638
rowel, 155
row house, 381
rowing machine, 26
royale, 449
royalist, 310
royal sail, 218
royalty, 324, 352, 396
RP, 520
RPG, 193
rpm, 211, 537
RQ, 44
RR, 308, 537
-rrhagia, 142, 534
-rrhaphy, 142, 534
-rrhea, 142, 534
-rrhexis, 142, 534
-rrhiza, 534
-rrhoea, 534
R selection, 47
RSVP, 486, 537
rt, 537
rte, 537
ruan, 445
ruana, 272
rub, 637
rubato, 436
rubber, 139, 161, 286, 375, 582
rubber cement, 162, 472
rubber check, 369
rubber floor tile, 161
rubberneck, 211, 544
rubbernecking, 487
rubber spatula, 269
rubber-stamp, 614
rubber washer, 170
rubbing, 480
rubble, 68, 160
rubblework, 160
rubdown, 26
rubefacient, 141
rubella, 15
rubeola, 15
rubilith, 472
rub it in, 619
rub out, 639
rubric, 655
rubricated account, 359
ruching, 292
rucksack, 281
ruckus, 635
rudder, 202, 218
ruddevator, 202
rudiment, 612
Rudra, 659
rue, 299
ruff, 279
ruffian, 638
ruffle, 292
rug, 240, 288
rugby shirt, 274
rug hooking, 480
rugmaking, 480
ruin, 347, 634, 637
rule, 142, 163, 168, 647
ruler, 119, 142, 168

rules, 472
Rules Committee, 304
ruling, 366
ruling class, 310
rumaki, 266
rumal, 288
rum and coke, 512
rumba, 448
rumble, 541, 546, 635
rumble seat, 209
rumble strip, 299
ruminant, 52, 372
ruminate, 607
rumination, 610
rummage sale, 350
rummy, 625
rumor, 589
rumormonger, 589
rump, 304
Rumpelstiltskin, 659
rumpus, 635
rumpus room, 234
rumrunning, 630
rumshop, 510
run, 86, 157, 189, 205, 215, 221,
  292, 313, 327, 359, 453, 474,
  496, 498, 540, 626
runabout, 217, 222
run after, 577
run aground, 221
run amok, 637
run around, 249, 578
run a tab, 510
run at hounds, 496
runaway, 215, 252, 543
runaway unit, 215
run before the wind, 221
runcible spoon, 270
run counter to, 618
rundlet, 146, 172
rune, 523, 663
rung, 155
run in, 632, 635
runnel, 86
runner, 60, 240, 503, 593
running, 26
running board, 209
running bowline, 171
running foot, 324
running head, 324, 327
running knot, 171
running mate, 311
running part, 171
running shoe, 286
running shoes, 26
running stitch, 292
runny nose, 22
runoff, 74, 86, 89, 313
run-on sentence, 518
runover, 327
runs, 22
runt, 52
run-through, 453
runway, 205, 292
rupture, 20, 637
rural, 375, 396
rural free delivery, 308
rural route, 308
ruse, 590
rush, 85, 158, 416, 541, 626, 637
rush basket, 174
rushes, 457
rush headlong, 541
rush hour, 211, 299
rushwork, 480
russet, 283
Russia, 78
Russia leather, 284
Russian blouse, 274
Russian Orthodox Church, 645
rustling, 630
rusty nail, 512
rut, 84, 583
Rutherford atom, 102
rutting, 579
ruttish, 579
RV, 206

R-value, 157
Rwanda, 78
Rx, 537
rya, 240
rye, 371
rynd, 155
ryoba, 164
ryu, 27

s, 127, 537
Sabbat, 663
Sabbath, 484, 647, 648
sabbatical, 411, 486
saber, 175
saber-rattling, 329
saber saw, 164
Sabin vaccine, 139
sable, 284
sabot, 286
sabotage, 313, 329, 338, 588
saboteur, 588
sacchar-, 530
saccharine, 553
saccule, 7
sachem, 311, 341
sachet, 280, 552
sack, 174, 281, 637
sackbut, 446
sackcloth, 283
sack coat, 273
sack suit, 273
sacque, 274
sacrament, 652
sacrament of the sick, 652
sacré bleu, 564
sacred, 656, 668
sacred cow, 395
sacred music, 434
sacred text, 655
Sacred Texts and Objects, 655–
  656
sacrifice, 638, 639, 652, 661, 669
sacrilege, 619, 652
sacristan, 341
sacristy, 234, 654
sacrosanct, 656
sacrum, 8
SAD, 401
SADARM, 334
saddle, 84, 215
saddlebag, 281
saddle oxford, 286
saddler, 384
saddle scabbard, 178
saddle shoe, 286
saddle shoulder, 289
saddle stitch, 292, 472
Sadducee, 648
sadhu, 654
Sadie Hawkins, 484
Sadie Hawkins Day, 483
sadism, 401, 584
sadomasochism, 401, 584
safari, 486, 495
safari jacket, 273
safe, 234, 239
safecracker, 631
safecracking, 630
safe-deposit box, 359
safe harbor, 662
safe house, 313, 338, 589
safelight, 477
safe passage, 487
safe seat, 313
safe sex, 582, 583
safety, 17
safety film, 457
safety glass, 160
safety goggles, 169
safety island, 299
safety lamp, 71
safety pin, 293
safety razor, 31
safety zone, 299
saga, 427, 664
sagacity, 670
sagamore, 341

sage, 654, 670
sagger, 478
Sagittarius, 111
sagittate, 605
sahib, 341, 565
sai, 27
Saigon, 82
sail, 218, 221, 541
sailboat, 217
sailcloth, 283
sailing, 221
sail into, 637
sailmaker, 220
sailor, 220, 287, 332
sailor collar, 289
sailor's breastplate, 171, 221
sailor suit, 273
sailplane, 198
saint, 640, 654, 668
Saint Elmo's fire, 89
saintliness, 656
Saint Patrick's Day, 483
Saint Stephen's Day, 483
Saint Valentine's Day, 483
sala, 234
salaam, 565, 614
Salacia, 660
salacious, 579
salad, 257, 261
salad bar, 263
salad basket, 269
salad bowl, 269
salad days, 596
salad dressing, 260
Salad Dressings, 260
salad plate, 269
salad spinner, 269
salamander, 267, 659
salary, 354, 368
Salchow, 493
sale, 350, 377
sales allowance, 366
sales conference, 324
sales force, 324, 350
salesman, 350, 355
salesmanship, 350
salesperson, 350, 355, 383
sales rep, 355
sales representative, 355
sales return, 366
sales slip, 350
sales tax, 350, 362
saleswoman, 355
salient, 612
salina, 85
saline, 553
salinity, 74, 502
Salisbury steak, 266
saliva, 7, 44
salivary glands, 10
Salk vaccine, 139
sallet, 288
Sallie Mae, 361
sally, 155, 329
sally forth, 543
salmonella poisoning, 15
salon, 234, 486
salon table, 238
saloon, 510
salpingectomy, 134, 582
salpinx, 446
salsa, 266, 439, 448
salt, 71, 121, 220, 262, 553, 588
salt-and-pepper, 580
saltarello, 448
saltbox, 229
salt cellar, 269
salt flat, 85
salt glaze, 478
saltimbanque, 455
saltimbanque show, 489
saltimbocca, 266
salt lake, 86
salt marsh, 85
salt pan, 85
saltwater bait, 500
saltwater fish, 498

salty, 553
salty dog, 512
salud, 565
salutatorian, 413
salute, 332, 484, 549, 614
salvage, 151
salvage value, 364
salvation, 652, 656, 666, 668
Salvation Army, 647
salve, 141
salver, 172, 241, 269
salvo, 329, 616
SAM, 179, 334
samadhi, 649
Sama-Veda, 655
samba, 448
samiel, 87
samisen, 445
samite, 283
samizdat, 393
samovar, 241, 268
sampan, 217
sample, 256, 404
sample ballot, 313
sampler, 243, 442
sampling, 398
samsara, 649, 666
samurai, 341, 565
sanative, 139
sanatorium, 628
sanbenito, 273
sanbon, 27
sanction, 337, 614
sanctions, 347
sanctity, 656, 668
sanctuary, 654, 662
sanctum, 654
sanctum sanctorum, 563
Sanctus, 438
sand, 68, 150, 373
sandal, 286
sandalwood oil, 31
sandbag, 586
sandbank, 86
sand bar, 86
sandblasting, 425
sand dome, 215
sand dune, 86
sander, 149, 163, 165, 425
sandfly fever, 15
sandhi, 520
San Diego, 82
S and L, 359
S and M, 584
sandman, 659
sand molding, 425
sand painting, 423
sandpaper, 165
sandstone, 68
sandwich, 202, 261
sandwich board, 377
sandwich lease, 382
sandwich panel, 155
sandwich wall, 470
San Francisco, 82
San Francisco bomb, 624
sang-froid, 564
Sangha, 649
sangre, 512
sangria, 512
sangui-, 142, 530
sanguine, 473
sanitarium, 130, 628
sanitary napkin, 141
San Juan cooler, 512
Sankhya yoga, 649
San Marino, 78
sannup, 249
sannyasi, 654
sansa, 444
sans serif, 474
sans souci, 564
Santa Ana, 87
Santa Claus, 659
santeria, 662
Santiago, 82
santir, 445

shoehorn, 280, 285
shoelace, 285
shoe rack, 242
Shoes and Footwear, 285–286
shoestring, 369
shoe tree, 280, 285
shofar, 446, 655
shogun, 341
shoji screen, 239
shoot, 71, 377, 457, 465, 477, 495, 503, 541, 626, 637
shoot down, 619
shoot-'em up, 456, 462
shooter, 509
shooting, 457, 495, 639
shooting gallery, 626
shooting gravy, 626
shooting jacket, 273
shooting script, 457, 460
shooting star, 107
shooting stick, 497
shoot line, 498
shoot off one's mouth, 545
shoot one's wad, 583
shootout, 635
shoot the breeze, 546
shoot up, 626
shop, 229, 350, 415
shop around, 350
shopkeeper, 356
shoplifting, 630
shopping, 350
shopping bag lady, 395
shopping cart, 223
shopping center, 301, 350
shopping mall, 301
shopping spree, 350
shop talk, 526
shore, 86
shorebird, 56
shorebirds, 495
shore leave, 332, 486
shoreline, 86
shore patrol, 332
shoring, 155
shorn, 29
short, 261
shortage, 347, 350
shortchange, 593
short circuit, 182
short clay, 478
short con, 593
short discount, 324
shortening, 257
short eyes, 584
shortfall, 347
short form, 364
short hairs, 582
shorthand, 523
short hundredweight, 144
short line, 212
short-order cook, 264
short paint, 423
short program, 493
short-run, 598
shorts, 275, 277
short shorts, 275
short short story, 427
short-sleeved shirt, 274
short story, 427
short subject, 456
short takeoff and landing, 198
short tax year, 364
short-term capital gain, 364
short-term loan, 359
short time, 634
short ton, 144
short vowel, 520
short-waisted, 292
shortwall, 71
shortwave radio, 466
shot, 113, 134, 178, 270, 457, 477, 510, 624
shot glass, 510
shotgun, 177, 497
shotgun wedding, 249
shoulder, 8, 289, 299, 541

shoulder bag, 281
shoulder blade, 8
shoulderette, 274
shoulder knot, 278
shoulder pad, 289
shoulder patch, 280
shoulder piece, 276
shoulder strap, 289
shout, 546
shouting, 196
shouting distance, 601
shove, 637
shovel, 163, 165, 173, 502
shovel hat, 287
Shovels and Digging and Lifting Tools, 165–166
shovel shit, 546
shoving match, 635
show, 424, 453, 460, 485, 489
show and tell, 416
show bill, 377
showboat, 451
show business, 453, 460
showcase, 451
show cause, 321
shower, 87, 236, 249, 485
showplace, 381
showroom, 350
show-stopper, 453
show tunes, 439
show up, 543, 619
show window, 350
shpritz, 566
shrapnel, 178
shred, 262, 637
shredder, 502
shrewd, 586
shrewdness, 53
shriek, 546
shrill, 546
shrine, 640, 654
shrink, 404
shrink wrap, 350
shroud, 272, 640
shrouds, 219
Shrovetide, 483
Shrove Tuesday, 483
shrub, 60, 61, 503
shrubbery, 85, 503
Shrubs, 61
shrubs, 85
shrug, 273
shtetl, 298, 648
shtick, 453, 566
shtunk, 566
shtup, 566, 583
shuck and jive, 592
shuffle, 448, 540, 592
shul, 648, 654
shun, 617
shunpiking, 211
shunt, 150, 155, 541, 543
shuto, 28
shutter, 155, 158, 230, 234, 239, 477
shutterbug, 477
shutter-priority, 477
shuttle, 113, 155, 205, 212, 292, 543
shuttle diplomacy, 336
shvitzer, 566
Shylock, 359
shyster, 593
SI, 98
sialic magma, 68
sial layer, 68
Siamese twins, 19
sibilant, 520
sibilation, 551
sibling, 247, 253
sibling-in-law, 247
sibling rivalry, 252, 406
sibyl, 659, 665
sic, 563, 637
siciliano, 448
sicilienne, 283

sick, 626, 627
sick bay, 130, 219
sick bed, 130
sickle, 163, 374, 605
sick leave, 486
sickle cell anemia, 16
sickness, 16
sicko, 627
sic passim, 563
sic semper tyrannis, 563
sic transit gloria mundi, 563
SIDA, 16
side arm, 177
sidearm cast, 498
sidebar, 327, 463
sideboard, 238, 239
sideboards, 30
sideburns, 30
side-by-side, 177, 603
sidecar, 512
side dish, 263
sidedoor, 215
side dressing, 371
side drum, 443
side effect, 22, 612
side lock, 178
sidelocks, 30
sideman, 441
side mirror, 209
side pipes, 209
sidereal, 111
sidereal day, 598
sidereal period, 111
sidereal time, 111, 143
sidero-, 530
siderodromomania, 402
siderodromophobia, 401
sides, 453, 460
sideshow, 489
sidestep, 543
side street, 299
sideswipe, 211, 637
side table, 238
sidetrack, 215
sidewalk, 299
sidewalk bike, 223
sideways, 601
side-wheeler, 217
side whiskers, 30
Sidewinder, 179
side window, 209
side with, 615
siding, 155, 158, 215, 230
siding shingle, 158
sidle, 543
SIDS, 16
siege, 329
siege gun, 177
Siegfried, 659
siemens, 100
sierra, 84
Sierra Leone, 79
siesta, 565
sieve, 269, 478
sieve tube, 60
sift, 262, 544, 612
sifter, 269
sift through, 608
sigalert, 465
sig block, 196
sigh, 546, 548
sight, 178, 544
sight gag, 453
sight in, 178
sightline, 453
sight-read, 438
sightseeing, 487
sigil, 663
sigma particle, 102
sigmoid, 605
sigmoid flexure, 10
sigmoidoscope, 136
sign, 22, 523, 663, 665
signage, 472
signal, 183, 186, 215, 466
signal flow, 182

signal generation, 465
signal maintainer, 213
signal man, 213
signal-to-noise ratio, 111
signature, 324, 430, 436, 465, 474
signature card, 359
signed English, 523
signet ring, 278
significant digits, 117
significant other, 249, 395
signification, 663
signing, 523
sign language, 523
sign off, 462
sign of the cross, 652
signor, 341
signora, 341
signorina, 341
signpost, 299
Signs and Symptoms, 20–23
Signs of the Zodiac, 111
Sigurd, 659
sike, 86
Sikhism, 644
silage, 372
silence, 551, 669
silencer, 178
silent bit, 460
silent butler, 242, 270
silent film, 456
silent majority, 395
silent partner, 356
silent treatment, 619
Silenus, 659
silhouette, 423, 472, 497
silhouetting, 480
silica, 68
silicon dioxide, 68
silicone implant, 26
Silicon Valley, 189
silicon wafer, 189
silicosis, 16
silk, 283
silk hat, 287
silkscreen, 473, 480
silkscreen printing, 292
silk-stocking, 395
silk stockings, 277
sill, 68, 155
sill plate, 155
silly season, 327
silo, 113, 334, 372
silt, 68, 373, 502
Silurian period, 70
silver, 369
silver certificate, 369
silver fox, 284
silverpoint, 473
silver screen, 460
silversmith, 384
silverware, 270
silviculture, 375
s'il vous plaît, 564
sima layer, 68
simile, 429, 526
simmer, 262, 607
simoleon, 369
Simon Bolivar's birthday, 483
simony, 588, 652
simoom, 87
simper, 546, 548
simple fracture, 20
simple harmonic motion, 98
simple interest, 359
simple machine, 98, 150
Simpler Life Forms, 63–64
simple sentence, 518
Simplesse, 28
simplex, 118
simplified employee pension, 364
simulation, 592
simulcast, 462
simultaneous, 599
simultaneous equations, 117
Sin, 660
Sinbad, 659
since, 598

sine, 117
sinecure, 304, 588
sine die, 563
sine qua non, 563
sine wave, 182
sinfonia concertante, 434
sinfonietta, 434, 438
sing., 537, 546, 589
sing-along, 485
Singapore, 79, 82
Singapore sling, 512
singer, 438, 455
single, 381, 441
single-action, 177
single-action fly reel, 500
single bed, 237
single-board computer, 191
single-breasted jacket, 273
single density, 195
single knot, 171
single-lens reflex camera, 475
single out, 615
single parallel postulate, 117
single parent, 252, 395
single photon emission computed tomography, 134
singles, 578
singles bar, 510, 578
single-sided disk, 195
singlet, 277
single tax, 362
singular, 518
singularity, 103, 111
singularity theory, 103
sinistral, 601
sink, 84, 86, 236, 543, 607, 637
sinkage, 324
sink-and-draw, 498
sinker, 500
sinkhole, 84
sink in, 608
sinking plug, 500
sinoatrial node, 44
sinopis, 423
Sino-Tibetan, 523
sins, 624
sinsimilla, 624
sin tax, 362
sintir, 445
sinus, 6
sinusitis, 16
sinusoidal projection, 73
sip, 256, 509
siphon, 150
siphono-, 530
sir, 341
sire, 52, 246, 251, 253, 341, 372
Siren, 659
sirenian, 54
Sirius, 107
sirocco, 87
Sir Roger de Coverley, 448
sirvente, 427
sis, 247
sissonne, 449
sissy, 579
sister, 247, 253, 341, 654
sister-in-law, 247
Sisyphus, 659
sitar, 445
sitcom, 462
sit-down dinner, 485
sit-down strike, 354
site, 196, 381, 391, 600
site-specific, 425
sit-in, 313, 393
sitology, 28
sitomania, 402
sit spin, 493
sitter, 252
sitting duck, 593
sitting room, 234
sittings, 307
situated, 600
situational, 580
situation comedy, 462
situation ethics, 409

spacewalk, 113
Spackle, 161
spackling compound, 161
spade, 165, 173, 374, 502, 605
spading, 371
spading fork, 502
spado, 582
spaghetti, 266
spaghetti and clam sauce, 266
spaghetti and meatballs, 266
spaghetti strap, 289
spaghetti suit, 114
spaghetti western, 456
spahi, 332
Spain, 79
spall, 425
spam, 196
span, 145, 157, 202, 215, 301, 602
spandex, 284
spandex pants, 275
spandrel, 469
spangles, 292
Spanish fly, 579, 624
Spanish rice, 266
spank, 617, 637
spanker, 219
spanking, 252
spanner, 167
spar, 155, 202, 215, 219
spare time, 486
spare tire, 8, 210
sparing, 368
spark, 182, 578, 613
spark chamber, 102
spark ignition engine, 207
spark ignition system, 208
sparkling wine, 509
spark plug, 208
spark plug gap, 208
spark plug wrench, 167
spasm, 22
spasm warfare, 329
spastic colon, 10
spasticity, 22
spat, 635
spatha, 175
spatial dimension, 103

Spatial Positions and Relations,
  599–603
spatial relation, 603
spatial summation, 44
spats, 275
spatter cone, 68
spatterdashes, 275
spatula, 165, 269
spatulate, 605
spawn, 251
spay, 52
speak, 546
speakeasy, 510
speaker, 182, 442, 466
Speaker of the House, 305
speakerphone, 186
speaking in tongues, 526, 664
speak one's mind, 550
speak one's piece, 550
speak out, 546
speak up, 546
spear, 175, 500
spear carrier, 455
spear side, 246
spec, 537
special, 212, 462
special agent, 364
special committee, 304
special court, 314
special delivery, 308
special education, 415
special effects, 457
special election, 313
Special Forces, 332
special interest group, 310, 394
specialist, 130, 332
specialization of labor, 354
Special Measures, 144–145
Special/Ordinary, 574–575
special prosecutor, 315

special-purpose map, 73
special sales, 324
special session, 307
special theory of relativity, 98
specialty, 354, 415
specialty station, 462
speciation, 38
specie, 369
species, 50, 502
species diversity, 47
specif, 537
specific, 125
specifications, 157, 211, 470, 472
specific dynamic action, 44
specific heat, 104
specific heat capacity, 123
specificity, 44
specific performance, 319
specify, 549
specimen, 49
specimen bottle, 136
specious, 610
specs, 279, 472
spectacle, 489
spectacles, 279
Spectacles. See **Entertainments
  and Spectacles**
spectacular, 489
spectate, 544
spectator ion, 121
spectator pump, 286
spectator sport, 489
specter, 640, 665
spectral type, 111
spectrograph, 111
spectroheliograph, 111
spectrometer, 182
spectroscope, 105
spectroscopic binary, 107
spectroscopic parallax, 111
spectroscopy, 111, 119
spectrum, 105, 109, 423, 612
spectrum-luminosity diagram, 111
SPECT scan, 134
speculate, 550, 607, 613
speculation, 321, 352, 359, 361,
  610, 613
speculator, 361
speculum, 136, 240, 241
speech, 427, 526
speech community, 523
speech disorders, 19
speech dysfunction, 401
Speech Sounds, 551
Speech Sounds and Noises, 547
speech synthesis, 194
speech therapist, 404
speechwriter, 431
speed, 477, 541, 624
speedball, 624
speedboat, 217
speed calling, 186
speeder wrench, 167
speed freak, 627
speeding, 211
speed limit, 211, 299
speed of light, 105
speed of sound, 106
speedometer, 210
speed rack, 510
speed-reading, 415
speed trap, 299
speedwalking, 26
speedway, 299
spell, 629, 661, 663
spellbind, 663
spellbinder, 665
spellbound, 664
spell check, 194
speller, 415
spelling, 523
spelling bee, 415
spell out, 546, 549
spelunking, 505
spencer, 273
spending, 368
spending money, 369

spirillum, 24
spirit, 640, 650, 659, 665, 669
spirit gum, 453
spirit rapping, 663
spirits, 509
Spirits, 511
spirits, 511
Spiritual Attainment. See **Truth,
  Wisdom, and Spiritual
  Attainment**
spiritualism, 409
spirituality, 656, 668
spirit writing, 663
spiro-, 531
spirochete, 24
spirograph, 136
spirometer, 136
spit, 70, 86, 155, 267, 548
spit curl, 29
spitfire, 638
spit it out, 546
spittoon, 173, 242, 508
spit valve, 446
spitzer, 178
splash, 509, 541
splashdown, 114
splash guard, 210
splat, 194
spleen, 9
splendor, 668
splice, 151, 155, 171, 457, 465
splicing, 38
spliff, 624
spline, 155, 473
splint, 141, 155
splint basket, 174
splinter, 637
splinter party, 310
split, 158, 361, 509, 543, 637
split brain, 44
split ends, 29
split infinitive, 518
split-level, 229, 234
split personality, 401
splits, 450
split screen, 191, 457
split second, 598
split shift, 354
split shot, 500
split-shot sinker, 500
split ticket, 313
splurge, 347
splutter, 546
Spode, 478
spodosol, 373
spoil, 71
spoiled, 252
spoiler, 196, 202
spoils, 334
spoils system, 310
spoke, 155
spokeshave, 165
spokesperson, 378, 462
spoliation, 634
spondee, 429
spondylosis, 18
sponge, 58, 141, 169, 593
sponsor, 356, 368, 462
spontaneous, 123, 124
spontaneous abortion, 20
spontoon, 175
spoof, 590, 592
spook, 665
spooked, 629
spool, 155, 189, 500
spoon, 269, 270, 500, 578, 624,
  626
spoon bread, 266
spoondrift, 89
spoonerism, 526
spoon-feed, 415
spoor, 552
sporadic, 599
sporangium, 60
spore, 24, 60, 503
spork, 269
sporo-, 531

sporophyte, 60
-sporous, 534
sporran, 278
sport coat, 273
sportfisherman, 217
sportfishing, 498
sporting, 495
Sporting and Exercise Wear,
  275–276
sportive, 590
sport jacket, 273
sports, 489
sports bra, 27
sports car, 206
sportscast, 462
sportscaster, 462
sport shirt, 274
sportsman, 495
sports medicine, 129
sport suit, 273
sportswear, 289
sportswriter, 327
spot, 215, 240, 378, 462, 544
spot advertising, 378
spot announcement, 378, 462
spotlight, 240, 453, 477
spot market, 361
spots, 361
spotted fever, 16
spotting, 450, 582
spousals, 249
spouse, 247, 249
spout, 86, 155, 548
SPQR, 537
Sprachgefühl, 523
sprain, 20
sprang, 292
sprawl, 541
spray, 241
spread, 243, 263, 327
spread collar, 289
spread eagle, 493
spreadsheet, 194, 366
spree, 625
spring, 86, 91, 150, 155, 170, 368,
  496, 540, 598
Spring Bank Holiday, 483
spring clamp, 167
springer, 469
Springfield rifle, 177
springform pan, 268
spring line, 219
spring-loaded, 150
springs, 208
spring shears, 163
spring trap, 497
spring wagon, 222, 223
spring wheat, 371
sprinkler, 150, 169, 502
sprint, 540
sprit, 219
sprite, 590, 659, 665
spirituals, 439
spritzer, 512
sproat, 500
sprocket, 155
sprout, 503
sprue, 18
sprung rhythm, 429
spud, 165
spun glass, 160, 478
spur, 84, 155, 163, 215, 280, 503,
  548
spur gear, 150
spurious, 592
spurn, 619
spur-of-the-moment, 599
spurt, 541
Sputnik, 114
sputter, 546
sputum, 10, 22
spy, 338, 544, 588, 589
spying, 338
spy plane, 198
sq, 537
SQL, 194